Praise for Barbara Ann Kipfer's *The Order of Things: How Everything in the World is Organized Into Hierarchies, Structures & Pecking Order*

"Start with Kipfer, who understands the unbearable frustration of unanswered questions."

—*The Dallas Morning News*

"A browser's delight and a definite reference 'must'. . ."

—Ralph Hollenbeck, *King Features Syndicate*

Praise for Barbara Ann Kipfer's *Roget's 21st Century Thesaurus in Dictionary Form: The Essential Reference for Home, School, or Office*

Named "One of the best reference books of the year" by *Entertainment Weekly*

"Exceptional . . . unique words and grouping . . . this source is a gem!"

—*Booklist*

"Outstanding!"

—*American Bookseller*

"Innovative . . . clean, thorough . . . a perfect adjunct to the dictionary . . . It's a treasure."

—*San Diego Writers' Monthly*

Flip Dictionary

Barbara Ann Kipfer, Ph.D.

Author of *The Order of Things* and *Roget's 21st Century Thesaurus*

WRITER'S DIGEST BOOKS
Cincinnati, Ohio
www.writersdigest.com

Visit our Web site at www.writersdigest.com for information on more resources for writers.

To receive a free weekly e-mail newsletter delivering tips and updates about writing and about Writer's Digest products, send an e-mail with "Subscribe Newsletter" in the body of the message to newsletter-request@writersdigest.com, or register directly at our Web site at www.writersdigest.com.

06   05   04   03   5   4   3   2

Library of Congress has catalogued hardcover edition as follows:

Kipfer, Barbara Ann
    The writer's digest flip dictionary / by Barbara Ann Kipfer
        p.   cm.
    ISBN 0-89879-976-7 (hardcover)
        1. English language—Terms and phrases. 2. English language—Synonyms and antonyms. I. Kipfer, Barbara Ann. II. Title
    ISBN 1-58297-140-4 (pbk. : alk. paper)   00-057225
                                                                          CIP

Edited by David Borcherding
Interior designed by Angela Wilcox
Cover designed by Brian Roeth
Cover photography by Robert M. Hale/Hale Photography
Production coordinated by Kristen Heller

ABOUT THE AUTHOR

D r. Barbara Ann Kipfer is a Research and Dictionary Specialist with Ask Jeeves, the Internet question-answering service. She is the author of twenty-one books, including *Roget's 21st Century Thesaurus*, *21st Century Spelling Dictionary*, *21st Century Manual of Style* (Dell/Laurel), *The Order of Things* (Random House), *Dictionary of American Slang* (with R. Chapman; HarperCollins), *Sisson's Word and Expression Locater* (Prentice-Hall), *The Encyclopedic Dictionary of Archaeology* (Kluwer Plenum), *the wish list* and *1,400 things for kids to be happy about* (both Workman) and the best-selling *14,000 things to be happy about* (also Workman). She is also the editor of *Roget's International Thesaurus*, Sixth Edition (HarperResource). Her web pages are *www.lexicalcontent.com* and *www.thingstobehappyabout.com*.

Barbara holds a Ph.D. in linguistics (University of Exeter), a Ph.D. in archaeology (Greenwich University), a Master's in linguistics (Exeter) and a Bachelor's in physical education (Valparaiso University). She has worked for such companies as idealab!, Mindmaker, General Electric Research, IBM Research, Wang, Bellcore and Knowledge Adventure. ❦

ACKNOWLEDGMENTS

Keir Magoulas and Kyle Kipfer: the people who helped me think onomasiologically during this project.

Paul Magoulas: the person who helped me compile everything but the kitchen sink for this and spurred me on.

Mark Dinan: the person who helped me computationally organize the data.

Jack Heffron, David Borcherding, and Meg Leder: my supportive editors at Writer's Digest.

Thank you: what each of these people deserves! ❦

How to Use This Book

There *is* a word for your idea. We all know the frustration of trying to find the word for what we mean, locating the precise word for what we want to say. For people who have an idea, concept or definition but who do not know, cannot remember or are uncertain of the word, there is help in the form of *Flip Dictionary*. Why "flip"? Because this reference resource offers a reversed method for finding the right word for thousands of words and phrases describing people, places and things. On top of that, it is combined with thesaurus entries.

Flip Dictionary takes you from a "meaning" you are aware of to the "word" you need. In conventional, alphabetically arranged dictionaries, you have to know the word to read about its meanings. If you don't know the word, you cannot look it up in an alphabetical dictionary! An example of this is trying to find the adjectives used for the words "glove" (gauntlet, mitt) or "goat" (caprine, hircine, hircinous). Think of it: How would you find these in a standard alphabetical dictionary? But in *Flip Dictionary*, look under *goat* and you will find *goat, like a*: caprine, hircine, hircinous.

Flip Dictionary contains thousands of definitions plus numerous tables covering major subjects such as architecture, art, dance, the human body, language, minerals, music, sports and more. It is a helpful book and fun to browse, too.

How do you find what you want in *Flip Dictionary*? Cue or clue words are the words you have in your mind (or on the tip of your tongue) that lead you to the target words. The compiler has selected the same familiar words that you, the user, would think of when trying to find the target words. The cue/clue words are carefully framed in ways that make the target words readily findable.

For example, you may want to know:

bread, crescent-shaped: croissant

doctor specializing in heart health and disease: cardiologist

go off or explode: detonate

goat, female: nanny goat

shedding of feathers or skin: molt

shovel used by pizzamakers: peel

solve a puzzle: decipher

Though it would be impractical to provide every possible cue/clue to a target word, *Flip Dictionary* includes the most probable and generative choices. The A-to-Z listings include components, concepts, ideas and parts. Even if you have never used a reverse dictionary, you'll come to understand what constitutes useful and unuseful cue/clue words. It is really easy to get the hang of it. Good bets are the more concrete cues/clues like *ear, church, office, clear, emotion* and *soften*. Less useful or unuseful cues/clues might generate too many entries. Examples like *tiny, first* and *fat* are cues/clues which could be used to describe hundreds of target words which would make it much harder to find the target word that you need.

Words may have several cue/clue words to help ensure the users will find the word they need. For example:

design using initial letters: monogram
initials, in design: monogram
letters as design, initial: monogram

The tables of terms by subject cover prolific lists which do not require much definition. Subjects such as flowers and flowering plants, types of boats, church terms and Olympic sports are surveyed via this format of presentation. The subject charts can be found in the A-to-Z text as close as possible to the main word's location (for example: flower, boat).

One important thing to remember is that this book should be used in conjunction with a good dictionary, preferably a college-sized or unabridged dictionary. By looking up definitions in a traditional dictionary, you can be sure that you have found the right term for the idea you had in mind.

Based on research in the author's Ph.D. dissertation, *Flip Dictionary* is compiled by well-known lexicographer Barbara Ann Kipfer, who holds a Master's and Ph.D. in Linguistics from the University of Exeter. Her doctoral thesis was entitled *Towards the Onomasiological Dictionary: The Use of the Computer in Providing Diversified Access*, and she has spent nearly twenty years in computational lexicography developing hierarchies of ideas and concepts for the natural language systems of IBM, Bellcore, Ask Jeeves and General Electric. ❦

A-line or shirtwaist: dress

aardvark: antbear, anteater, earth pig, edentate, farrow

aback: behind, sudden, suddenly, unaware, unawares, unexpectedly

abacus: calculator, swan pan

Abaddon: Apollyon, Hades, Hell, Sheol

abaft: after, arear, astern, back, behind, rearward

abalone: ear shell, mollusk, ormer, sea ear, shell

abandon: abjure, chuck, depart, desert, discard, ditch, drop, flee, forsake, forswear, freedom, give up, junk, leave, leave in the lurch, liberty, license, maroon, neglect, quit, rashness, reject, remit, renounce, repudiate, resign, scrap, scuttle, stop, surrender, turpitude, vacate, waive, yield

abandon (enthusiasm): élan, exuberance, spontaneity, wantonness

abandon idea, habit, friendship: renounce, repudiate

abandon position: abdicate, resign

abandon something once held dear: forsake, reject

abandon something valued for something else: forgo

abandon to someone else: relinquish

abandon totally: abscond, apostatize, defect, desert

abandon under compulsion: surrender

abandon undertaking: scuttle

abandon, give up: relinquish

abandoned: corrupt, denigrate, derelict, deserted, desolate, destitute, dissipated, dissolute, flagrant, forlorn, forsaken, humiliated, immoral, incorrigible, left, lewd, lost, put down, shameless, sinful, stranded, wanton

abandoned child: foundling, orphan

abandoned ship: hulk

abandoned, deserted: forlorn

abandoning of claim or right: waiver

abandonment of principles or faith: apostasy

abase: cower, demean, downgrade, humble, lower, malign, sink

abash: bewilder, chagrin, confound, confuse, discomfit, disconcert, discourage, dismay, humble, mortify, put out, shame, upset

abate: allay, alleviate, annul, assuage, deduct, die down, diminish, ease, ebb, end, eradicate, fall, invalidate, lessen, let up, lower, lull, mitigate, moderate, nullify, omit, quash, recede, reduce, relax, remit, slacken, slake, slow, subside, taper, vitiate, void, wane, weaken

abatement: allowance, decrease, deduction, lessening, lull, myosis, rebate, reduction, relaxation, subsidence

aberration: delusion, deviation, eccentricity, error, fault, hallucination, insanity, lapse, mania, quirk

abbess's assistant: prioress

abbey: church, cloister, convent, friary, hermitage, nunnery, priory, seminary

abbey, head of: abbess, abbot

abbot's assistant: prior

abbreviate: abridge, clip, condense, contract, curtail, cut back, digest, epitomize, prune, shorten, simplify, truncate

abbreviation or sign representing a word (e.g., $): logogram, logograph

abbreviation pronounced as a word: acronym

abbreviation pronounced letter by letter: initialism

abdicate: abandon, demit, forgo, leave, quit, relinquish, renounce, resign, retire, step down, surrender, vacate, withdraw

abdomen: bay window, belly, middle, midriff, paunch, pot, pot belly, stomach

abdomen cavity membrane lining: peritoneum

abdomen network of nerves: solar plexus

abdomen upper area below ribs: hypochondrium

abdomen, concerning: gastric, ventral, visceral

abdominal: ventral

abdominal examination or surgery using a tubular endoscope: laparoscopy

abdominal pain from muscle spasms: colic

abdominal protrusion: hernia

abduct: kidnap, shanghai, snatch, steal

abecedarian: amateur, beginner, dabbler, fledgling, learner, neophyte, novice, tenderfoot

abele or aspen: poplar

aberrant: abnormal, anomalous, atypical, deviant, devious, different, disparate, peculiar, strange, unusual

aberration: madness, oddity, psychopathic

abet: advocate, aid, assist, back, countenance, egg, egg on, encourage, endorse, espouse, foment, further, goad, help, incite, instigate, second, support, sustain

abettor: accessory, accomplice, auxiliary, coconspirator, confederate, conspirator, promoter, supporter

abeyance: break, intermission, latency, letup, pause, respite, suspension

abhor: abominate, despise, detest, disdain, dislike, eschew, execrate, hate, loathe, shun

abhorrence: antipathy, aversion, disgust, loathing, odium, repugnance, repulsion, revulsion

abhorrent: hateful, odious, vile

abide: await, delay, dwell, exist, last, live, pause, stand, stay, stomach, tarry, visit

abide, go on unchanged: subsist

abiding affection: love

ability: aptitude, caliber, capacity, competence, dexterity, efficiency, energy, expertise, faculty, force, gift, ingenuity, knack, know-how, potential, power, proficiency, skill, strength, talent

ability equal to demand: competence

ability in certain direction: aptitude

ability or character: caliber

ability or expertise: acumen

ability to carry out specific task: dexterity, skill

ability to do quickly and well: efficiency

ability to feel: sentience

ability to instigate activity: initiative

ability, exceptional: talent

ability, great: knack, prowess

ability, inborn: endowment, faculty, gift

ability, unproven: potential

abject: base, contrite, cringing, degraded, humble, ignorable, mean, miserable, paltry, poor, servile, slavish, submissive, wretched

abjure: abandon, avoid, desert, disavow, disclaim, eschew, forswear, give up, recall, recant, reject, renounce, repudiate, retract, revoke, spurn, withdraw

ablaze: afire, aflame, ardent, blazing, burning, fiery, glowing, ignited, inflamed, radiant

able: adept, apt, au fait, capable, clever, competent, dexterous, efficient, fit, good, learned, masterful, proficient, qualified, skillful, smart, strong, suitable, suited, talented, versatile, vigorous

able and suitably qualified: competent, proficient

able to read: literate

able, extremely: adept, adroit

ablution: bath, purification, wash

abnegate: abjure, disclaim, eschew, forgo, forswear, refuse, reject, relinquish, renounce, waive

abnormal: aberrant, anomalous, deviant, eccentric, erratic, exceptional, extraordinary, irregular, offbeat, queer, rare, unnatural, unusual, weird

abnormal and inconsistent: anomalous, incongruous

abnormal breathing: rale

abnormal from usual or natural: preternatural

abnormal in sexual behavior: deviant, deviate, perverted

abnormal or unconventional: aberrant, bizarre, divergent, eccentric, heretical, heteroclite, heterodox, idiosyncratic

abnormal plant swelling: gallnut

abnormal position of a body part: ectopia

abnormal, irregular: anomalous

abnormal, outside ordinary: preternatural

abnormality as a state or disease: pathology

aboard: across, alongside, astride, athwart, on deck, present

abode: address, apartment, cottage, domicile, dwelling, estate, flat, habitat, home, house, manor, residence, tenement

abode of dead: Aalu, Aaru, Aralu, Hades, Heaven, Hell, Orcus, Perdition, Purgatory, Sheol, Valhalla

abolish: abate, abrogate, annihilate, annul, cancel, discontinue, do away with, eradicate, erase, exterminate, kill, nullify, quash, repeal, rescind, revoke, vacate, wipe out

abominable: atrocious, damnable, disagreeable, execrable, heinous, horrid, loathsome, odious, revolting, vile

abominable snowman: yeti

abominate: abhor, despise, detest, execrate, hate, loathe, scorn

abomination: anathema, antipathy, bête noire, crime, disgrace, disgust, horror, infamy, odiousness, outrage, plague, repugnance

aboriginal: endemic, indigenous, primeval, primitive, primordial

aboriginal Japanese: Ainu

aborigine: autochthon, indigene, native, savage

abortion: misbirth, miscarriage, termination

abortion, bring on: induce, terminate

abortion-inducing thing: abortifacient

abortive: fruitless, futile, ineffective, unproductive, useless, vain

abound: crawl, flourish, overflow, swarm, teem

abounding: abundant, alive, flush, jammed, packed, plentiful, replete, rich, rife

abounding in shrubs: broomy

abounding in small waves: choppy

abounding with cattails: rush

abounding with invective: epithetic

about: active, almost, anent, approximately, apropos, around, as regards, astir, circa, concerning, in re, near, nearly, respecting, some, surrounding, throughout

about to happen: imminent, impending

about-face: flip-flop, reversal, switch, turnabout, volte-face

above: aloft, atop, beyond, exceeding, extra, higher, north, on top, over, overhead, past, superior, supra, transcendent, upon

above all: chiefly, especially, indeed, mostly, primarily

above comparison: par excellence

above everything in importance: paramount

above in quality: par excellence

above or on top of: surmounting

above or previous: supra

aboveboard: blunt, bona fide, candid, ethical, frank, honest, open, overt, truthful

abracadabra: hocus-pocus, incantation, jargon, magic, mumbo jumbo, sorcery, spell

abrade: annoy, chafe, corrode, erode, excoriate, file, fray, fret, gall, graze, grind, irritate, rasp, rub, ruffle, scrape

abrading instrument: file

abrasive: annoying, coarse, harsh, irritating, provoking

abrasive material: emery, quartz, sandpaper

abrasive mineral: corundum

abreast: abeam, aligned, alongside, au courant, au fait, beside, contemporary, informed, modern, popular, side by side

abridge: abbreviate, capsule, condense, curtail, diminish, lessen, limit, minimize, reduce, retrench, shorten, shrink, trim

abridgment: compendium, decrease, digest, epitome, lessening, outline, precis, reduction, sketch, summary

abroad: astir, astray, away, distant, forth, out, overseas

abrogate: annul, cancel, dissolve, negate, nullify, overrule, quash, remit, repeal, repudiate, rescind, revoke, void

abrupt: blunt, brief, brisk, brusque, fast, gruff, hasty, headlong, impetuous, impolite, precipitous, quick, rude, sharp, snippy, steep, sudden, swift, terse, unceremonious

abrupt and sharp emphasis: staccato

abrupt change: flip-flop

abrupt in manner: curt

abrupt tide rise: eagre

abrupt withdrawal: cold turkey

abrupt, brief: cursory

abruptly cause: precipitate

abruptly in music: subito

abscess: botch, fistula, lesion, sore, ulcer

abscond: absquatulate, bolt, decamp, elope, escape, flee, run, scram, skip, split, vanish

absconded: escaped, fled

absence: AWOL, deficiency, lack, leave, omission, truancy, vacuum, void, want, withdrawal

absence of laws or rules: anarchy

absence of life: abiosis

absence or opposite of positive: negation

absence without permission or notification: AWOL, French leave

absent: away, empty, gone, lacking, missing, out, truant

absent, while: in absentia

absentee: truant

absentminded: abstracted, daydreaming, distracted, distrait, dreaming, faraway, inattentive, oblivious, preoccupied, unseeing

absentminded and idealistic: quixotic

absentmindedness: woolgathering

absolute: actual; arbitrary; autocratic; categorical; complete; definite; despotic; downright; explicit; imperious; implicit; in black and white; no ifs, ands or buts; perfect; positive; real; sheer; simple; stark; sure; total; true; unconditional; undoubted; utter; whole

absolute and complete: rank, unadulterated, unequivocal

absolute bottom: lowest

absolute control by the government: totalitarianism

absolute power: autarchy, autocracy

absolute refusal: never

absolute ruler who is kind: benevolent despot

absolute smallest: teeniest

absolute, complete: categorical, plenary, unmitigated

absolute, unquestioned: implicit, peremptory

absolutely: amen, certainly, definitely, indeed, no way, positively, quite, really, thoroughly, truly, unequivocally, wholly, yes

absolutely certain: cocksure

absolutely necessary: vital

absolutely not: no way

absolution: amnesty, cleansing, disculpate, exculpation, forgiveness, pardon, release, remission

absolution granted: shrift

absolution, obtain or give: shrive

absolve: acquit, clear, discharge, exculpate, excuse, exempt, exonerate, forgive, liberate, overlook, pardon, release, remit, vindicate

absolved: forgiven

absorb: assimilate, blot, combine, consume, digest, engage, enwrap, imbibe, immerse, incorporate, ingest, occlude, permeate, soak up, swallow, unite

absorb as part or participant: assimilate, incorporate, integrate

absorb by swallowing: ingest

absorb completely: engross

absorb gradually: osmosis

absorb moisture: soak

absorbed: engrossed, immersed, intent, involved, preoccupied, rapt, riveted

absorbed by: into

absorbed completely: rapt

absorbed liquid: soakage

absorbing gas or liquid: porous

absorbs: digests, immerses, sops

absorption: uptake

absorption in thoughts: brown study

absorption, opposite, where thin film accumulates on surface of solid, liquid: adsorption

absquatulated: fled

abstain: avoid, cease, deny, desist, eschew, fast, forbear, forgo, pass up, refrain, reject, spurn, teetotal, waive

abstain from eating: fast

abstainer: nonuser

abstainer from alcohol: teetotaler

abstaining from sex: celibate

abstemious: abstinent, ascetic, austere, moderate, sober, sparing, straitlaced, temperate

abstinence: abstention, fast, renunciation, restraint, self-denial

abstract: abstruse, brief, compendium, deduct, deed, detached, divert, elude, epitomize, esoteric, excerpt, expressionism, ideal, imaginary, obscure, pure, purloin, recondite, remove, separate, summarize, summary, theoretical, unreal, withdraw

abstract and excessively complex: metaphysical

abstract and imaginary: notional

abstract and simplified: conventionalized

abstract and symbolic: figurative

abstract philosophy: metaphysics

abstract sculpture: construction

abstract, purely intellectual: noetic

abstract, summary: precis

abstracted: absentminded, absorbed, bemused, engrossed, oblivious, pensive, preoccupied

abstracted essence: distillation

abstraction treated as concrete thing: reify

abstruse: abstract, complex, deep, esoteric, ideal, mysterious, obscure, perplexing, profound, recondite, remote, subtle

absurd: asinine, crazy, foolish, inane, inept, irrational, kooky, loony, ludicrous, meaningless, nonsensical, preposterous, ridiculous, senseless, silly, stupid, wacky

absurd appearance: stultified

absurd or self-contradictory statement: paradox

absurd pursuit of idea or principle: reductio ad absurdum

absurd, ridiculous: ludicrous

absurd, senseless: irrational

absurdity: charade, travesty

absurdity of logical consequence: reductio ad absurdum

abundance: affluence, amplitude, fullness, mass, oodles, plenitude, plentitude, plenty, profusion, prosperity, riches, store, surplus, wealth

abundant: abounding, ample, brimming, copious, fertile, fruitful, galore, generous, lavish, lush, numerous, opulent, overflowing, plenteous, plentiful, profuse, prolific, rich, rife, teeming

abundant source: lode

abundant stream: river

abundant, numerous: galore

abundant, plentiful: profuse, rife

abuse: affront, bedevil, belittle, blaspheme, castigate, cruelty, curse, defame, defile, derogate, desecrate, disparage, exploit, fault, flay, give the works, harm, hurt, injure, insult, invective, manipulate, maul, misapply, mistreat, misuse, obloquy, opprobrium, pervert, punish, scold, scurrility, slander, tax, violate, vituperation, wrong

abuse by satire: lampoon

abuse via words: invective

abuse, manhandle: maul

abuse, vilify: opprobrious, revile

abusive: blasphemous, calumnious, corrupt, harsh, insolent, insulting, libelous, offensive, profane, rough, savage, scurrilous, vile

abusive criticism: diatribe

abusive in language: scurrilous

abusive speech, addicted to: maledicent

abusive words: diatribe, harangue, obloquy, vituperation

abut: adjoin, border, flank, touch

abutting: next to, adjacent

abysmal: bottomless, boundless, dreary, endless, infinite, profound, unending

abyss: bottom, cavity, chasm, crevasse, deep, deepness, depths, gulf, Hades, hell, inferno, pit, void

acacia: babul, catechu, gum arabic, legume, locust, mimosa, myall, thorn, wattle

acacia tree: koa

academic: bookish, classic, collegiate, educated, erudite, formal, learned, pedantic, scholarly, theoretical

academic conference: colloquium, seminar

academic course without credit, attend: audit

academic disciplines, general: liberal arts

academic institution's approval: accreditation

academic robes' white cloth strips: Geneva bands

academic subjects, relating to two or more: interdisciplinary

academic thesis for higher degree: dissertation

academic year division: quarter, semester

academy: academia, college, institute, institution, school, seminary, society, university

Academy Award: Oscar

acaudal: tailless

accede: acknowledge, acquiesce, admit,

agree, allow, approve, assent, attain, comply, consent, enter, grant, permit, yield

accelerate: advance, dispatch, expedite, forward, hasten, hurry, increase, precipitate, quicken, race, rev, rush, speed, speed up, stimulate

accelerate, briefly: rev

accelerated: increased, picked up, quick

accelerator: activator, cyclotron, throttle

accent: brogue, burr, cadence, dialect, drawl, emphasis, emphasize, ictus, inflection, intonation, mark, pitch, pulse, rhythm, sound, stress, throb, tonality, tone

accent and vocabulary of regional or social group: dialect

accent indicating stress of a spoken sound: acute accent

accent on last syllable, word with: oxytone

accent that is throaty: guttural

accent, Irish: brogue

accented and stressed: tonic

accented in music: sforzando

accentuate: bring out, emphasize, feature, intensify, sharpen, stress

accentuate the negative: caricature

accept: acknowledge, acquiesce, admit, adopt, agree, allow, approve, bear, believe, continue, endure, espouse, honor, ratify, receive, remain, reside, sojourn, submit, suffer, sustain, take, tolerate, understand, withstand

accept a challenge: take a dare

accept as a charge: take upon oneself

accept as true: allow

accept as valid: honor

accept blame: take the rap

accept decision: accede to, acquiesce in, comply with

accept joyfully: adopt

accept the consequences: face the music

accept unconditionally: take as read

accept, take for granted: postulate

acceptability, meet standards of: pass muster

acceptability, standard of: norm

acceptable: adequate, all right, average, decent, palatable, pleasant, satisfactory, sufficient, suitable, viable

acceptable and legal: valid

acceptable to one's taste or mind: palatable

acceptance as true: credence

acceptance of agreement: accession

acceptance of decision: endorsement, sanction

accepted: approved, believed, canonical, chosen, conventional, correct, customary, normal, popular, prevalent, proper, routine, sanctioned, standard, taken

accepted everyday speech: vulgate

accepted maxim: axiom

accepted practice: praxis

accepted widely: received

accepting, passively: acquiescent, resigned

accepts blindly: takes on faith

accepts willingly: takes kindly to

access: admittance, approach, attack, door, entrance, entree, entry, gate, increase, onset, paroxysm, passage, path, portal, ramp, right of way, road, route, spell, street, tunnel

accessible: approachable, available, convenient, handy, nearby, obtainable, open, patent, pervious, procurable, public, reachable, unrestricted

accession: acquisition, addition, agreement, approach, arrival, inaugural, increment, induction, installation

accessories and adornment: trappings

accessory: abettor, accompaniment, accoutrement, add on, additional, additive, adjunct, ally, appurtenance, assistant, attachment, auxiliary, component, concomitant, contributor, contributory, extra, helper, incidental, plus, secondary, subordinate, subservient, subsidiary, supplement, tool

accessory for roasting: spit

accident: calamity, case, catastrophe, chance, collision, contretemps, disaster, event, fate, fluke, hazard, incident, luck, misadventure, misfortune, mishap, wreck

accident causing death: fatality

accident from bad luck: mishap

accident marker: flare

accident, lucky discoveries by: serendipity

accident, minor: fender bender

accidental: adventitious, casual, chance, conditional, extraneous, extrinsic, fortuitous, haphazard, incidental, random, secondary, serendipitous, subordinate, unexpected, unintended, unintentional, unplanned

accidental crack: leak

accidental developments: vicissitudes

ACADEMIC DEGREES

Name/Abbreviation:

Adjunct in Arts/Adj.A.
Associate in Applied Science/A.A.S.
Associate in Arts/A.A.
Associate in Nursing/A.N.
Associate of Science/A.S.
Bachelor of Arts/A.B. or B.A.
Bachelor of Arts in Education/B.A.Ed. or B.A.E.
Bachelor of Arts in Library Science/B.A.L.S.
Bachelor of Arts in Nursing/B.A.N.
Bachelor of Business Administration/B.B.A.
Bachelor of Chemical Engineering/B.C.E. or B.Ch.E.
Bachelor of Civil Law/B.C.L.
Bachelor of Divinity/B.D.
Bachelor of Education/B.Ed. or Ed.B.
Bachelor of Engineering/B.E. or B.Engr.
Bachelor of Fine Arts/B.F.A.
Bachelor of Laws/LL.B., B.L.
Bachelor of Literature/B.Litt. or B.Lit. or Lit.B. or Litt.B.
Bachelor of Medicine/B.M. or M.B.
Bachelor of Music Education/B.M.E. or B.M.Ed.
Bachelor of Music/B.Mus.
Bachelor of Naval Science/B.N.S.
Bachelor of Philosophy/B.Ph. or B.Phil. or Ph.B.
Bachelor of Sacred Theology/S.T.B.
Bachelor of Science/B.S.
Bachelor of Science in Architecture/B.S.Arch.
Bachelor of Science in Nursing/B.S.N.
Bachelor of Theology/Th.B.
Doctor of Arts/Arts.D. or D.A.
Doctor of Business Administration/D.B.A.
Doctor of Canon Law/J.C.D.
Doctor of Chemistry/Ch.D.
Doctor of Chiropractic/D.C.
Doctor of Civil Law/D.C.L.
Doctor of Dental Medicine/D.M.D.
Doctor of Dental Surgery/D.D.S.
Doctor of Divinity/D.D.
Doctor of Education/D.Ed. or Ed.D.
Doctor of Fine Arts/D.F.A.
Doctor of Humane Letters/L.H.D.
Doctor of Humanities/D.H. or H.H.D.
Doctor of Juridical Science/S.J.D. or J.S.D. or D.J.S. or D.Jur.Sc.
Doctor of Jurisprudence/J.D. or D.J. or D.Jur.
Doctor of Laws/LL.D. or Dr.LL.
Doctor of Letters/Litt.D. or D.Lit. or D.Litt.
Doctor of Medicine/M.D.
Doctor of Ministry/D.Min.
Doctor of Music/D.Mus. or Mus.D.
Doctor of Musical Arts/A.Mus.D.
Doctor of Natural Philosophy/Ph.N.D.
Doctor of Optometry/O.D.
Doctor of Osteopathy/D.O.
Doctor of Pharmacy/Phar.D. or Pharm.D.
Doctor of Philosophy/Ph.D. or D.Ph. or D.Phil.

Doctor of Psychology/Psy.D.
Doctor of Public Administration/D.P.A.
Doctor of Public Health/D.P.H.
Doctor of Sacred Theology/S.T.D.
Doctor of Science/D.S. or Sc.D. or D.Sc. or S.D.
Doctor of Social Work/D.S.W.
Doctor of Surgical Chiropody/D.S.C.
Doctor of Theology/Th.D.
Doctor of Veterinary Medicine/D.V.M.
Education Specialist/Ed.S.
Executive Master of Business Administration/E.M.B.A.
Master of Applied Mechanics/M.A.M.
Master of Architecture/M.Arch.
Master of Arts in Education/M.A.E. or M.A.Ed.
Master of Arts in Library Science/M.A.L.S.
Master of Arts in Teaching/M.A.T.
Master of Arts/A.M. or M.A.
Master of Business Administration/M.B.A.
Master of Divinity/M.Div.
Master of Education/M.Ed. or Ed.M.
Master of Fine Arts/M.F.A.
Master of Laws/LL.M. or M.L.
Master of Letters/M.Litt.
Master of Library Science/M.L.S.
Master of Literature/M.Litt.
Master of Materials Science/M.M.S.
Master of Philosophy/M.Phil.
Master of Planning/M.P.
Master of Public Administration/M.P.A.
Master of Religious Education/M.R.E.
Master of Science for Teachers/M.S.T.
Master of Science in Education/M.S.Ed.
Master of Science in Nursing/M.S.N.
Master of Science/S.M. or M.S. or M.Sc. or Sc.M.
Master of Social Work/M.S.W.
Master of Teaching/M.T.
Master of Theology/M.Th. or Th.M.

Abbreviation/Name:

A.A./Associate of Arts
A.A.S./Associate in Applied Science
A.B./Bachelor of Arts
A.M./Master of Arts
A.Mus.D./Doctor of Musical Arts
A.N./Associate in Nursing
A.S./Associate of Science
Adj.A./Adjunct in Arts
Arts.D./Doctor of Arts
B.A./Bachelor of Arts
B.A.E./Bachelor of Arts in Education
B.A.Ed./Bachelor of Arts in Education
B.A.L.S./Bachelor of Arts in Library Science
B.A.N./Bachelor of Arts in Nursing
B.B.A./Bachelor of Business Administration
B.C.E./Bachelor of Chemical Engineering
B.C.L./Bachelor of Civil Law

B.Ch.E./Bachelor of Chemical Engineering
B.D./Bachelor of Divinity
B.E./Bachelor of Engineering
B.Ed./Bachelor of Education
B.Engr./Bachelor of Engineering
B.F.A./Bachelor of Fine Arts
B.L./Bachelor of Laws
B.Lit./Bachelor of Literature
B.Litt./Bachelor of Literature
B.M./Bachelor of Medicine
B.M.E./Bachelor of Music Education
B.M.Ed./Bachelor of Music Education
B.Mus./Bachelor of Music
B.N.S./Bachelor of Naval Science
B.Ph./Bachelor of Philosophy
B.Phil./Bachelor of Philosophy
B.S./Bachelor of Science
B.S.Arch./Bachelor of Science in Architecture
B.S.N./Bachelor of Science in Nursing
Ch.D./Doctor of Chemistry
D.A./Doctor of Arts
D.B.A./Doctor of Business Administration
D.C./Doctor of Chiropractic
D.C.L./Doctor of Civil Law
D.D./Doctor of Divinity
D.D.S./Doctor of Dental Surgery
D.Ed./Doctor of Education
D.F.A./Doctor of Fine Arts
D.H./Doctor of Humanities
D.J./Doctor of Jurisprudence
D.J.S./Doctor of Juridical Science
D.Jur./Doctor of Jurisprudence
D.Jur.Sc./Doctor of Juridical Science
D.Lit./Doctor of Letters
D.Litt./Doctor of Letters
D.M.D./Doctor of Dental Medicine
D.Min./Doctor of Ministry
D.Mus./Doctor of Music
D.O./Doctor of Osteopathy
D.P.A./Doctor of Public Administration
D.P.H./Doctor of Public Health
D.Ph./Doctor of Philosophy
D.Phil./Doctor of Philosophy
D.S./Doctor of Science
D.S.C./Doctor of Surgical Chiropody
D.S.W./Doctor of Social Work
D.Sc./Doctor of Science
Dr.LL./Doctor of Laws
D.V.M./Doctor of Veterinary Medicine
E.M.B.A./Executive Master of Business Administration
Ed.B./Bachelor of Education
Ed.D./Doctor of Education
Ed.M./Master of Education
Ed.S./Education Specialist
H.H.D./Doctor of Humanities
J.C.D./Doctor of Canon Law

J.D./Doctor of Jurisprudence
J.S.D./Doctor of Juridical Science
L.H.D./Doctor of Humane Letters
Lit.B./Bachelor of Literature
Litt.B./Bachelor of Literature
Litt.D./Doctor of Letters
LL.B./Bachelor of Laws
LL.D./Doctor of Laws
LL.M./Master of Laws
M.A./Master of Arts
M.A.E./Master of Arts in Education
M.A.Ed./Master of Arts in Education
M.A.L.S./Master of Arts in Library Science
M.A.M./Master of Applied Mechanics
M.A.T./Master of Arts in Teaching
M.Arch./Master of Architecture
M.B./Bachelor of Medicine
M.B.A./Master of Business Administration
M.D./Doctor of Medicine
M.Div./Master of Divinity
M.Ed./Master of Education
M.F.A./Master of Fine Arts
M.L./Master of Laws
M.L.S./Master of Library Science
M.Litt./Master of Letters or Master of Literature
M.M.S./Master of Materials Science
M.P./Master of Planning
M.P.A./Master of Public Administration
M.Phil./Master of Philosophy
M.R.E./Master of Religious Education
M.S./Master of Science
M.S.Ed./Master of Science in Education
M.S.N./Master of Science in Nursing
M.S.T./Master of Science for Teachers
M.S.W./Master of Social Work
M.Sc./Master of Science
M.T./Master of Teaching
M.Th./Master of Theology
Mus.D./Doctor of Music
O.D./Doctor of Optometry
Ph.B./Bachelor of Philosophy
Ph.D./Doctor of Philosophy
Ph.N.D./Doctor of Natural Philosophy
Phar.D./Doctor of Pharmacy
Pharm.D./Doctor of Pharmacy
Psy.D./Doctor of Psychology
S.D./Doctor of Science
S.J.D./Doctor of Juridical Science
S.M./Master of Science
S.T.B./Bachelor of Sacred Theology
S.T.D./Doctor of Sacred Theology
Sc.D./Doctor of Science
Sc.M./Master of Science
Th.B./Bachelor of Theology
Th.D./Doctor of Theology
Th.M./Master of Theology ❧

accidental homicide: chance-medley, manslaughter

accidental occurrence: happenstance

accidental or random: aleatory, contingent, haphazard

accidental or unintended: impulsive, unpremeditated

accidental transposition of initial sounds: spoonerism

accidentally: inadvertently, unintentionally, unwittingly

accidentally pours: spills

acclaim: applaud, approbation, approve, bravos, cheer, commend, compliment, éclat, extol, fame, glorify, hail, homage, honor, kudos, laud, ovation, plaudits, repute, salute

acclaimed: hailed

acclimate: accommodate, accustom, climatize, condition, habituate, harden, inure, season, toughen

acclivity: elevation, hill, incline, rise, upgrade

accolade: award, ceremony, compliment, decoration, encomium, eulogy, honor, hosanna, kudo, laudation, laurels, medal, praise, recognition, salutation, salute, tribute

accommodate: adapt, adjust, board, change, comply, conform, contain, defer, give, help, hold, house, lend, modify, oblige, reconcile, serve, suit, tailor, yield

accommodation for military: billet, canton, quarter

accompany: assist, associate, attend, chaperon, conduct, convey, convoy, escort, follow, lead, supplement, usher

accompany someone for propriety, protection: chaperon

accompany troops, etc., for protection: convoy

accompanying: concomitant, with

accompanying thing: concomitant

accomplice: abettor, accessory, associate, cohort, colleague, confederate, crony, flunky, helper, henchman, pal, partner

accomplice in crime: abettor

accomplice (poser) in con game: shill

accomplish: achieve, attain, carry out, complete, consummate, effect, end, engineer, finish, fulfill, furnish, gain, implement, manage, perform, produce, put into effect, reach, realize, succeed, transact, win

accomplished: able, adept, brilliant, did, done, ended, expert, gifted, polished, proficient, proven, qualified, skilled, talented

accomplished fact: fait accompli

accomplished nicely: well done

accomplisher: doer

accomplishment: act, craft, culmination, deed, feat, learning, performance, realization, skill, success, triumph

accomplishment, impressive: tour de force

accomplishment, irreversible: fait accompli

accomplishment, realization: fruition

accord: accede, adjust, affinity, agree, allot, award, compliance, concede, concert, concur, conformity, consent, correspond, give, grant, merge, rapport, reconcile, tally, treaty, unison, volition

accord in relationship: rapport

accordant: assenting, attuned, coherent, congruous, consistent, consonant, corresponding, harmonious, parallel, suitable

according to: à la

according to one view: in a sense

according to the rules: by the book

according to the value (in Latin): ad valorem

accordingly: consequently, ergo, hence, then, therefore, thereupon, thus, whence, wherefore

accordion-like instrument: concertina

accost: approach, bother, confront, encounter, greet, hail, hound, meet, salute, solicit, speak, waylay

account: advantage, basis, bill, bookkeeping, chronicle, client, commentary, count, customer, description, detail, discourse, esteem, estimate, explanation, history, inventory, invoice, item, ledger, narrative, rank, rate, recital, recitation, record, report, repute, story, tale, use, value, view, worth

account book: ledger

account detailing goods, services provided: invoice, statement

account entry: item

account of accident, described vividly: graphic

account or record: tally

account, alter to deceive: falsify

account, settling of: reckoning

accountable: amenable, answerable, culpable, explicable, responsible

accountant: actuary, adder, auditor, bookkeeper, clerk, controller, CPA, reckoner

accounted: reported

accounts, examine or adjust: audit

accouter: array, attire, clothe, costume, decorate, dress, embellish, equip, furnish, gear, outfit, rig

accredit: approve, assign, attribute, authorize, certify, charge, commission, confirm, empower, endorse, license, notarize, ratify, sanction, validate

accredited: licensed

accretion: accumulation, addition, coherence, enlargement, expansion, growth, increase, increment, rise

accrue: acquire, amass, collect, earn, gain, grow, increase, multiply, redound, snowball, swell

accumulate: aggregation, amass, backlog, fund, heap, interest, inventory, mass, pile, stack, stock, store, treasure

accumulated beliefs: lore

accumulated, as tears: welled up

accumulates: piles up

accumulating: hoarding

accumulation: buildup, collecting, gathering

accuracy or adherence to truth: veracity

accuracy, demander of: stickler

accurate: authentic, certain, correct, errorless, exact, meticulous, precise, reliable, right, true

accurate and certain: unerring

accurate and verbatim spelling or quote: sic

accurate reproduction: fidelity

accurate statement, etc.: verity

accursed: abhorrent, abominable, damned, detestable, doomed, hellish, infamous, loathsome, odious, repugnant

accusation: smear

accusation against public official: impeachment

accusation and blame: imputation

accusation and persecution: witch-hunt

accusation, acknowledgment of: touché

accusation, bitter and mutual: recrimination

accusation, false: aspersion, calumny

accusation, reject or deny: repudiate

accusation, stop and confront with: accost

accusation, virulent: invective

accuse: allege, arraign, attack, blame,

calumniate, charge, defame, denounce, finger, incriminate, inculpate, indict, recriminate, reproach

accuse and charge with crime: indict

accuse and imply guilt: incriminate

accuse falsely: calumniate

accuse mutually: recriminate

accuse of crime, esp. treason: impeach

accuse or criticize: tax

accuse or inform against: denounce

accuse with crime in court of law: arraign, indict

accuser: complainant, incriminator, plaintiff, prosecutor

accustom: acclimate, adapt, condition, drill, enure, familiarize, habituate, harden, inure, orient, toughen, want

accustom to hardship: inure

accustom, harden: condition

accustomed to: acclimatized, attuned, habituated, inured, wont

ace: adept, crackerjack, expert, flyer, hero, star, tip-top, topnotch, tops

acerbate: embitter, envenom, exasperate, infuriate, irritate

acerbic: acid, acrid, astringent, bitter, corrosive, harsh, sarcastic, sharp, sour, tart

aces, double: ambsace

acetic acid: corrosive, vesicant, vinegar

ache: agonize, anguish, desire, grieve, hunger, long, mourn, pain, pang, smart, soreness, suffer, throb, yearn

ache for: crave

achieve: accomplish, actualize, attain, complete, earn, effect, fulfill, gain, get, obtain, reach, realize, succeed, triumph

achieve or obtain: compass, encompass

achievement: accomplishment, attainment, coup, deed, effort, feat, mastery, realization

achievement with skill or strength: tour de force

achievement, great: éclat

achievement, highest: meridian, pinnacle, summit, zenith

achieves, as an agreement: hammers out

aching: sore

achromatic: achromous, colorless, diatonic, neutral

acicula: spine

acid: acerb, acetic, acetose, acetous, acetyl, acrid, acyl, alkali, amino, base, benzoic, benzyl, biting, bitter, boric, carbolic, corrosive, cyanic, fo-

lic, formic, iodic, lactic, malic, malonyl, oleate, oleic, pungent, sharp, sour, stannate, tart, tartaric

acid-alkali indicator: litmus paper, pH test, phenolphthalein

acid and base, reacting like: amphiprotic, amphoteric

acid chemical: corrosive

acid for etching on printing plate: mordant

acid in apples: malic

acid in lime: citric

acid in protein: amino

acid neutralizer (soluble base): alkali

acid plus chemical compound which forms salt: base

acid salt: ester, oleate, stannate

acid used for bleaching: oxalic

acidic: astringent, sour

acidlike substance, theoretical: alkahest

acids, bottle for: carboy

acidulous: tart

acknowledge: accept, admit, affirm, allow, answer, assent, avow, concede, confess, declare, disclose, divulge, own, proclaim, profess, recognize, reveal, tell, thank

acknowledge gracefully: take a bow

acknowledgment of appreciation: acme, top, tribute

acme: apex, apogee, climax, crest, crown, culmination, height, heyday, maximum, peak, pinnacle, top, zenith

acolyte: aide, altar boy, assistant, attendant, devotee, follower, helper, novice

aconite: monkshood, wolfsbane

acorn: balanoid, camata, camatina, mast, oak, seed

acorn producer: oak

acorn-shaped: balanoid

acorn, cuplike base: cupule

acorns as pig food: mast

acquaint: advise, apprise, disclose, enlighten, familiarize, inform, introduce, notify, orient, present, teach, tell

acquaintance: associate, cognizance, companion, comrade, conversance, conversancy, familiarity, friend, friendship, mate

acquaintance, close: intimacy

acquaintances: kith

acquainted: conversant, familiar, informed, versed

ACIDS

acetic acid
amino acid
ascorbic acid
bile acid
carbolic acid
carboxylic acid
citric acid
conjugate acid
deoxyribonucleic acid
essential fatty acid
fatty acid
folic acid
formic acid
free fatty acid
hydrochloric acid
lactic acid
linoleic acid
malic acid
metenoic acid
mineral acid
monobasic acid
nitric acid
nitrohydrochloric acid
organic acid
pangamic acid
para-aminobenzoic acid
polyunsaturated fatty acid
protonic acid
prussic acid/hydrocyanic acid
ribonucleic acid
salicylic acid
sulfuric acid
tannic acid
tartaric acid
tribasic acid
uric acid 🐦

acquiesce: abide, accede, accept, agree, allow, assent, concede, concur, conform, grant, submit, succumb, yield

acquire: amass, attain, collect, contract, earn, gain, garner, gather, get, grab, have, learn, make, obtain, procure, reap, secure

acquire a patina: age

acquire by labor: earn

acquire dishonestly: steal

acquire fresh vigor: rally

acquire knowledge: learn

acquire sight unseen: buy a pig in a poke

acquired relative: in-law, stepdaughter, stepson

acquisition: gain

acquisitive: covetous, greedy, prehensile, selfish

acquit: absolve, amnesty, clear, discharge, excuse, exonerate, free, liberate, pardon, parole, release, reprieve, vindicate

acrid: acidulous, astringent, biting, bitter, corrosive, harsh, irritating, pungent, reeking, sharp, stinging

acrimonious: acerbic, acid, angry, belligerent, bitter, caustic, contentious, cross, harsh, irate, nasty, quarrelsome, rancorous, resentful, sharp, spiteful, stinging, surly, testy

acrobat bar: trapeze

acrobat who does somersaults, cartwheels: tumbler

acrobat who twists limbs and body: contortionist

acrobatic feats: splits

acrobat's apparatus: trampoline, trapeze

acronym for a social class: WASP

across: altogether, athwart, beyond, opposite, over, sweeping, total, transverse, wholly

across or crossways: athwart, transversely

acrostic: acronym, cipher, composition, phrase, puzzle, wordplay

acrostic with final letters of lines forming word: telestich

acrostic with middle letters of lines forming word: mesostich

acrylic: Orlon

act: behave, bestir, decide, deed, emote, exploit, fake, feign, have an effect, impersonate, perform, portray, pretend, represent, serve, simulate

act amorously: coo

act as middleman: broker

act in entertainment: feat, function, gig, move, performance, play, skit, stunt, theatrical, turn, work

act in law: decree, edict, ordinance, bill, statute

acting as: qua

acting award: Emmy, Oscar, Tony

acting game: charade

acting hastily: brash

acting or provisional: interim, surrogate

acting part: role

acting profession: footlights, the boards, the stage

acting ruler: regent

acting technique emphasizing identifying with and individualizing character: Method

acting, dramatic: histrionics

action: adventure, affair, animation, arena, battle, behavior, case, conduct, conflict, deed, enterprise, excitement, function, litigation, maneuver, means, motion, movement, proceeding, process, stadium, stage, step, suit, transaction, work

action before firing: aiming

action expressed by the verb: active

action-film caper: stunt

action resisting change or defeat: rearguard action

action to avoid problems: evasive action

action to minimize opposition, course of: tack

action word: verb

action, automatic or involuntary: automatism

action, mental processes directed toward: conation

action, receiving or being subjected to: passive

action, spur to: incentive, inducement, motivation

actions of pompous officials: bumbledom

actions, devious: shenanigans

activate: arouse, bestir, charge, energize, impel, prompt, raise, rouse, spark, start, vitalize

activate mechanism with trigger or switch: actuate, trip

activator, inspiration: spark plug

active: alert, alive, animated, assiduous, awake, brisk, doer, dynamic, energetic, industrious, kinetic, lively, moving, nimble, peppy, quick, spirited, sprightly, spry, vigorous, vivacious, working, zippy

active and energetic: indefatigable

active and hardworking: diligent, industrious

active and ready: alert, vigilant

active and skillful: agile

active and swift: nimble

active and vigorous in old age: sprightly, spry

active Washington group: lobby

active, excessively: frenetic, hectic, hyperactive, manic

active, no longer: extinct

active, potentially: dormant, latent

actively promoting cause: engage

activity: action, ado, business, bustle, flurry, function, life, movement, occupation, pursuit, stir, tumult, undertaking, work

activity or hobby: avocation, distraction, diversion

activity outside spacecraft: extravehicular activity

actor: artiste, barnstormer, cast, comedian, company, diva, emoter, entertainer, extra, ham, hero, heroine, histrio, ingenue, lead, mime, mimic, mummer, performer, player, portrayer, prompt, role, stand-in, starlet, thespian, tragedian, trouper

RELATED TERMS

actor or cast reappearance to acknowledge applause: curtain call

actor using only gesture and expression: mime

actor who gives comedian lines: straight man

actor who knows and can replace another in emergency: understudy

actor who overacts: ham

actor with much experience: trouper

actor with nonspeaking role: supernumerary

actor's adage: the show must go on

actor's arena: stage

actor's comment: aside

actor's cue to speak, enter: catchword, line

actors' entrances: stage doors

actor's first appearance: debut

actor's help: cue

actor's remark to the audience: aside

actor's singular speech: monologue, soliloquy

actor's union: SAG

actors, group of: condescension ❦

acts: behaves, deeds, does, emotes

acts of kindness: favors

acts snobbish: puts on airs

actual: authentic, bona fide, certain, concrete, extant, factual, genuine, indisputable, material, positive, prevailing, real, substantial, tangible, true, veritable

actual, important: substantive

actual, realized existence: entelechy

actuality: being, existence, fact, reality, truth, verity

actually: de facto

actually existing: real

actuate: agitate, animate, arouse, cause, drive, enact, enliven, impel, incite, inspire, instigate, motivate, propel, provoke, spark, start, stimulate, stir, trigger, urge

acuity: keenness

acumen: acuteness, astuteness, discernment, insight, keenness, perception, percipience, perspicacity, sagacity, wisdom, wit

acupuncture, gentle cauterizing: byssocausis, moxibustion

acute: astute, canny, clever, crucial, discerning, extreme, incisive, ingenious, intelligent, intense, intuitive, keen, knifelike, penetrating, piercing, piked, pointed, quick, sensitive, sharp, shrewd, smart, subtle, urgent

acute, keen: incisive

acutely pleasing: exquisite

ad lib: extemporaneous, extempore, impromptu, improvisational, off-the-cuff

ad-libbed: improvised

ad rem: applicable, pertinent, straightforward

adage: aphorism, apothegm, axiom, cliché, dictum, homily, maxim, motto, precept, proverb, quip, saw, saying, truism

adagio: lento

adagio and allegro: tempi

adamant: firm, hard, immovable, inflexible, relentless, rigid, stony, stubborn, unbendable, unyielding

adapt: acclimate, accommodate, adjust, alter, arrange, assimilate, change, conform, convert, harmonize, inure, modify, qualify, reshape, shape, suit, tailor

adapt and become absorbed: assimilate

adapt or arrange music: transcribe

adapt to hardship: inure

adapt to new circumstance: orientate

adaptable: adjustable, alterable, amenable, changeable, conformable, flexible, malleable, pliable, pliant, reconcilable, supple, tractable, versatile

add: affix, amplify, annex, append, attach, augment, calculate, combine, compound, compute, connect, expand, figure, fuse, increase, join, plus, reckon, strengthen, subjoin, supplement, tally, tot, total

add at end: append, subjoin, suffix

add element: incorporate

add on: affix, annex

add-on: option

add one's two cents: opine

add something to reinvigorate: infuse

add spice to life: vary

add sugar to champagne: dose

add territory: annex

add to: enrich

add to complete: complement

add to problem: compound

add to the pot: ante

add up: tot, total

added a room: remodeled

added and not essential: adscititious, adventitious, extraneous, extrinsic, superfluous

added by steps: cumulative, incremental

added clause on legislative bill: rider

added clause or qualification: codicil

added feature, not essential: adjunct

added material at end of book: addendum, afterthought, annex, appendix, postscript, supplement

added more news to: updated

added more spirits: relaced

added repetitious words: tautology

added syllable at end of word: suffix

added syllable at start of word: prefix

added unnecessary words: pleonasm

added wing: ell

addenda: riders

adder: asp

addict: acidhead, aficionado, buff, druggie, enthusiast, fanatic, fiend, head, hophead, hound, junkie, mainliner, pothead, slave, user

addicted or unchanging: chronic, compulsive, habitual, confirmed, inveterate

addiction: compulsion, enslavement, fetish, fixation, obsession, surrender

addiction to substance: dependence

adding device with beads: abacus

addition: accession, accretion, adjunct, amendment, annex, appendage, calculation, codicil, extension, extra, increase, joining, more, rider, suffix, summation, totaling

addition and insertion: interpolation

addition of syllable to end of word: suffix

addition of syllable to front of word: prefix

addition of syllable within word: infix

addition or amendment to will: codicil

addition to a document: rider

addition to collection: accession

addition to milk: sop

addition, gradual: accretion

addition, increase: increment

addition, total reached in: summation

additional: another, auxiliary, else, extra, more, other, supplemental, supplementary

additional comment: footnote

additional item: accessory, fitment, fittings

additional meanings: overtones

additional money or bonus paid: premium

additional part, unnecessary: appurtenance

additional passage in book, music for formal close: coda

additional proposition with little or no proof required: corollary

additionally: also, and, plus

addled: befuddled, bewildered, confused, flustered, foolish, giddy, muddled, silly

address: abode, home, location, residence

address in speech: accost, allocution, appeal, approach, call, converse, direct, discourse, dispatch, greet, hail, harangue, lecture, oration, petition, speak to, statement, talk

address of absent or imaginary person: apostrophe

address of post office for pickup: general delivery, poste restante

address to graduating class: baccalaureate

address, authoritative: allocution

address, closing: valedictory address

address, welcoming: salutatory address

addressing dead or absent thing: apostrophe

adds liquor to: laces

adds quickly: slaps on

adds to the pot: antes

adds vitamins: enriches

adduce: advance, allege, cite, document, mention, name, offer, present, produce, quote, submit, suggest, tender

adduced: cited

adept: acceptable, adroit, apt, artist, capable, consummate, dexterous, expert, handy, master, masterful, maven, professional, proficient, sharp, skilled, tolerable

adept at many things: versatile

adequate: ample, answerable, commensurate, competent, decent, effective, okay, plenty, possible, satisfactory, sufficient, suitable, tolerable

adhere: cleave, cling, cohere, fasten, glue, stick

adhered: clung, held, hewed

adherence: attachment, cohesion, constancy, devotion, faithfulness, fidelity, loyalty, obedience

adherent: acolyte, ally, believer, disciple, follower, henchman, partisan, pupil, supporter, upholder, votary

adhesive: bond, cement, clinging, epoxy, glue, gooey, mastic, mucilage, paste, stickum, sticky, tape, tenacious

adhesive and sticky: viscid

adhesive friction: traction

adieu: adios, aloha, au revoir, cheerio, exit, farewell, good-bye, leave-taking, so long, ta-ta, valediction

adipose: fat

adiposity: corpulence

adit: access, admission, approach, channel, entrance, entry, opening, passageway, stulm, tunnel

adjacent: abutting, adjoining, against, beside, close, conterminous, juxtaposed, limitrophe, meeting, nearby, neighboring, next, tangent, touching

adjective: dependent, gerundive, qualifier

adjective and adverb degrees of comparison: comparative, superlative

adjective denoting a maiden name: née

adjective describing noun just following it: attributive

adjective mismatched with noun: hypallage, transferred epithet

adjective or adverb: modifier, qualifier

adjective separate from noun by linking verb: predicative

adjective that is disparaging: epithet

adjective used as noun: adnoun

adjective, word limiting noun and placed just before: determiner

adjoin: abut, append, attach, border, connect, contact, juxtapose, meet, neighbor, touch, unite, verge

adjoins: abuts, meets, touches

adjourn: close, defer, delay, disband, discontinue, dismiss, dissolve, postpone, recess, shelve, terminate

adjudge: adjudicate, arbitrate, award, consider, decide, decree, determine, rate, referee, rule, settle

adjudicated: ruled

adjunct: accessory, addition, affix, annex, appendage, appendix, appurtenance, associate, colleague, complement, quality, subordinate, supplement

adjure: appeal, beg, beseech, charge, entreat, exhort, implore, petition, plead

adjust: accommodate, accustom, adapt, address, align, alter, arrange, attune, balance, bend, change, conform, coordinate, correct, harmonize, modulate, move, rectify, regulate, reset, rig, set, straighten, suit, tailor, temper, trim, true, tune

adjust and correct: rectify, redress, remedy

adjust and temper: modulate

adjust one's wheels: align

adjust oneself: adapt

adjust or adapt: modify, regulate

adjust piano: tune

adjust to new circumstance: orientate

adjust to new environment: acculturate, assimilate

adjust tone: modulate

adjust wind instrument, organ pipes: voice

adjust, as in sewing: ease

adjust, as sails: trim

adjusted: tuned

adjusted again: reset

adjusted and resigned to situation: reconciled

adjuster: tuner

adjustment: adaptation, orientation

adjustment to cultural norms: acculturation, enculturation

adjustment to environmental demands: reality principle

adjutant: aide, assistant, auxiliary, helper, officer, stork

administer: apply, boss, control, direct, dispense, distribute, dose, execute, furnish, govern, issue, manage, oversee, rule, superintend, supervise, treat

administer extreme unction: anele

administered medicine: dose

administrative bureau: agency

administrator: director, executor, executrix, officer, official, provost, trustee

admirable: deserving, excellent, laudable, praiseworthy, splendid, venerable, worthy

admirable, great: exquisite

admiration and high regard: approbation, veneration

admiration, deserving: commendable, estimable, laudable

admiration, excessive: idolatry

admire: adore, approve, dig, esteem, idolize, look up to, praise, prize, regard, respect, revere, treasure, value, venerate

admire greatly: think the world of

admired person or thing: cynosure, idol

admirer: backer, booster, buff, devotee, fancier, follower, lover, votary

admirers: beaux

admirers, group of: claque

admiring one: adorer

admission: access, charge, concession, confession, disclosure, entrance, entrée, entry, gate, testimony, ticket

admission ceremony or ritual: initiation

admission of guilt: mea culpa, peccavi

admission qualifications or ceremony: matriculation

admission ticket: ducat

admit: accept, acknowledge, agree, allow, avouch, avow, concede, confess, declare, enroll, enter, grant, include, let in, own, permit, profess, receive, welcome

admit defeat in election: concede

admit frankly: avow

admit to the ministry: ordain

admittance: access, entry

admitting or permitting something: susceptible

admixture: alloy

admonish: advise, alert, caution, chide, criticize, enjoin, lecture, rebuke, remind, reprehend, reprimand, reproach, reprove, scold, upbraid, warn

admonish strongly, appeal: exhort

admonitory contraction: don't

ado: bother, bustle, commotion, confusion, excitement, flurry, fuss, hassle, hubbub, hullabaloo, racket, ruckus, stir, tizzy, turmoil

adobe: brick, clay, house, mudcap, tile

adolescence: nonage, teens, youth, youthfulness

adolescence, beginning of maturing in: puberty

adolescent: callow, girl, green, immature, juvenile, lad, lass, minor, pubescent, teen, teenager, youthful

adolescent, awkward: hobbledehoy

adopt: accept, advocate, appropriate, approve, assume, borrow, choose, employ, enact, espouse, naturalize, pass, practice, receive, select, support, take

adorable: charming, cuddlesome, cute, delightful, divine, irresistible, lovable, lovely, precious, sweet, winsome

adoration: devotion, idolatry, veneration, worship

adore: admire, cherish, enshrine, esteem, exalt, glorify, honor, idolize, love, praise, revere, venerate, worship

adorn: array, beautify, bedeck, bedizen, begem, decorate, dignify, dress, embellish, enhance, enrich, furbish, garnish, glamorize, grace, ornament, primp, prink, trim

adorn magnificently: emblazon

adorn with raised figures: emboss

adorned: arrayed, clad, graced, ornate, plumed

adornment for Miss America: tiara

adrift: afloat, aimless, astray, aweigh, derelict, insecure, loose, straying, wandering

adroit: able, adept, artful, brainy, canny, clever, cunning, deft, dexterous, facile, handy, ingenious, intelligent, proficient, quick, resourceful, sharp, skillful, slick, smart

adult: developed, elder, grown, mature, nubile, ripe, seasoned, tempered

adult chicken: roaster

adult elver: eel

adult insect: imago

adulterate: alter, counterfeit, debase, denature, dilute, doctor, falsify, mix, spike, spurious, taint, thin, water, weaken

adulterous: extramarital

adultery: criminal conversation, infidelity

adultery partner cited in divorce case: corespondent

adultery, encouragement of: connivance

adultery, legal name: criminal conversation

adultery, man who tolerates wife's: wittol

adultery, man whose wife has committed: cuckold

adumbrate: augur, bode, cloud, darken, foreshadow, foretell, indicate, intimate, mist, obfuscate, obscure, outline, portend, sketch, suggest

advance: accelerate, aggrandize, allege, assign, better, boost, charge, cite, creep, elevate, encourage, forward, further, gain, hasten, help, improvement, inch, increase, lend, loan, overture, preferment, prepay, proceed, progress, promote, propose, raise, serve, upgrade, uplift

advance arrival or announcer: bellwether, forerunner, harbinger, herald, precursor, predecessor

advance by foot: stride

advance explorer: outrider, scout

advance into territory of another: encroachment, incursion, infringement, inroad, trespass

advance notice giver for doom, disaster: Cassandra

advance of a sea: onlap

advance payment: ante

advance showing: preview

advance steadily: march

advance to higher level: graduate

advance, sudden and dramatic: quantum leap

advanced: ahead, along, elderly, farthest, foremost, lent, liberal, precious, premature, progressive, tolerant

advanced academic degree: doctorate

advanced and experimental: avant garde

advanced beyond years: precocious

advancement: step

advancing by degrees: gradation

advantage: account, asset, avail, behalf, benefit, boot, edge, favor, gain, handicap, interest, lead, leverage, odds, opportunity, start, stead, superiority, use

advantage held in reserve: ace in the hole

advantage of an opportunity, person who takes: opportunist

advantage of an opportunity, take: capitalize on, utilize

advantage of another's generosity, person who takes: leech, parasite, spooner

advantage of, person who is taken: cat's-paw, dupe, mark, patsy, stooge

advantage of, unfairly take: exploit

advantage or benefit: boon

advantage over, gain: outflank

advantage taken in mean way: cheap shot

advantage, be of: avail

advantage, have an effect to one's: redound

advantage, something that can be turned to an: grist

advantage, temporary: toehold

advantage, use to greatest: exploit

advantageous: auspicious, beneficial, benign, benignant, conducive, encouraging, expedient, favorable, gainful, profitable, valuable

advantageous move, chance: gambit

advantageous position: catbird seat

advent: approach, arrival, beginning, coming, commencement, incarnation

adventitious: accidental, casual, extrinsic, foreign, fortuitous, nonessential

adventure: chance, danger, enterprise, event, experience, exploit, feat, gest, hazard, quest, risk, saga, stunt, undertaking

adventure story: conte, gest, saga

adventure, heroic: exploit

adventure, mischievous: caper, escapade

adventurer: daredevil, gambler, mercenary, picard, picaroon, sportsman, swashbuckler

adventurous: audacious, brash, brave, courageous, daredevil, daring, errant, hazardous, perilous, rash, reckless

adventurous expedition: safari

adverb ambiguously modifying two words: squinting modifier

adverb of negation: not

adversary: antagonist, anti, assailant, competitor, enemy, foe, opponent, rival, Satan

adverse: against, conflicting, contrary, counter, critical, detrimental, difficult, disinclined, harmful, inauspicious, inimical, negative, opposed, opposite

adverse, perverse: untoward

adversity: affliction, calamity, catastrophe, hardship, misery, misfortune, setback, sorrow, tragedy, trial, trouble

advert: attend, consider, notice, observe, refer

advertise: announce, ballyhoo, blazon, boast, broadcast, declare, exploit, inform, notify, plug, proclaim, promote, publicize, publish, push, report, show

advertise a product by public statement: endorse, pitch

advertisement: banner, bill, blurb, broadside, circular, commercial, dodger, flyer, handbill, handout, insert, leaflet, notice, placard, promo, release, sign, skywriting, spot, stuffer, teaser

RELATED TERMS

advertisement and editorial: advertorial

advertisement catchphrase: slogan

advertisement catchy tune: jingle

advertisement distributed widely: circular, flyer, handbill, handout, notice

advertisements, person who writes: copywriter

advertising and publicity campaign: promotion

advertising and publicity language: hype

advertising display, large: billboard

advertising measurement: agate line

advertising medium: billboards, direct mail, magazine, press, radio, skywriting, television

advertising offer for one item to lure to higher-priced item: bait and switch

advertising promotion: buildup

advertising sign: neon

advertising symbol: logo

advertising with quickly flashed images: subliminal advertising

advertising, aggressive: hard sell

advertising, sensational: ballyhoo ❦

advice: admonition, caution, consult, counsel, direction, guidance, information, instruction, intelligence, news, notice, opinion, pointer, rede, suggestion, tip, word

advice or warning: monition

advice, observer offering unwanted: kibitzer

advice, seeking someone out for: consultation

advisable: desirable, expedient, fitting, judicious, politic, proper, prudent, sensible, sound

advise: acquaint, advocate, apprise, counsel, encourage, guide, inform, instruct, notify, post, recommend, rede, suggest, tell, urge, warn

advise earnestly, recommend: admonish, exhort

advise in Brit.: rede

adviser: aide, coach, confidant, consultant, counselor, instructor, mentor, nestor, right-hand person, tipster, tout

adviser and critic, harsh: Dutch uncle

adviser on suitability of academic article: referee

adviser or teacher: mentor

advisers, unofficial, of ruler or businessperson: kitchen cabinet

advising group: brain trust

advising group, secret: camarilla

advisory: cabinet, committee, council, instructive, ministry, notice, panel, report, warning

advocacy of cause: espousal

advocate: advise, back, defend, espouse, favor, plead, promote, recommend, uphold, urge

advocate as person: backer, barrister, champion, counselor, defender, intercessor, lawyer, paraclete, partisan, proponent, supporter

advocate of an ideology: ideologue

advocate of preservation: conservationist

advocate unwisely: oversell

advocates of the new: neos

adz, adze: axe, hatchet, pickax

aegis: armor, athena, auspices, backing, control, defense, guidance, protection, shield, sponsorship

Aeneas mother: Aphrodite

Aeneid author: Virgil

Aeolian harp: lyre

aeon: eternity

aerate: aerify, charge, freshen, inflate, oxygenate, ventilate

aerial: airy, atmospheric, dreamy, ethereal, imaginary, lofty, soaring, unreal, unsubstantial

aerial conveyance: helicopter

aerial for radio, TV: antenna

aerial maneuvers: barrel roll, chandelle, snap roll, wingover

aerial parade: flyby

aerial railroad: el

aerialist: tightrope walker

aerialist's perch: trapeze

aerie: brood, nest, penthouse

aerie builder: eagle, eglet, erne, hawk

aerie site: treetop

aerobatic maneuver: zoom

aerobics wear: leotards

aeronaut: aviator, balloonist, pilot

aerosol for substances: dispersant, propellant

aerosol propellant, formerly: freon

aerosol spray: mist

Aesop's fables: morality tales

aesthete: connoisseur, dilettante

aesthetic: beautiful, esthetic, pleasing, tasteful

aesthetic discernment: taste

affable: accessible, agreeable, amiable, benign, charming, civil, complaisant, cordial, courteous, easygoing, genial, gracious, likable, pleasant, polite, social

affair: action, activity, business, cele-

bration, concern, endeavor, engagement, event, gala, gathering, issue, occasion, party, proceeding, shindig, transaction

affair of honor: duel

affair outside marriage: adulterous, extramarital

affair, romantic: amour, liaison, love, relationship, romance, tryst

affairs: matters

affect: actuate, alter, assume, bluff, change, concern, counterfeit, cultivate, embrace, fancy, feign, frequent, hit, influence, move, operate, pretend, profess, simulate, stir, strike, sway, touch

affect or influence: militate, redound

affectation: airs, artifice, facade, fakery, hypocrisy, mannerism, pose, pretense, pretension, sham

affected: afflicted, artificial, camp, changed, effete, genteel, impaired, influenced, involved, la-di-da, mincing, moved, overblown, precious, pretentious, recherché, stilted, touched, unnatural, upset

affected by fungi: mildewed

affected display of modesty: prudery

affected manner: air

affected readily: susceptible

affected smile: smirk

affected with tedium: bored

affectedly coy: cutesy

affectedly prim, dainty: mincing

affectedly refined in manner, language: precious

affecter of attitude to impress: poseur

affecting or touching: pathetic, poignant

affecting superiority: pretentious

affecting the body generally: systemic

affecting the mouth: oral

affection: ailment, devotion, esteem, fancy, feeling, fondness, friendship, liking, love, malady, passion, propensity, regard, sickness, tenderness, virtue, warmth, weakness

affection, excessive: dotage

affection of, alienate the: estrange

affectionate: adoring, amorous, ardent, caring, devoted, fond, loving, romantic, sentimental, tender, warm

affectionate appellation: dearie

affectionate touch: caress

afferent: sensory

affianced: betrothed, engagement, intended, plighted, promised

afficionado: fan

affiction: heartache

affidavit: attestation, deposition, document, jurat, statement

affiliate: ally, associate, attach, branch, chapter, colleague, fraternize, group, join, merge, relate, subsidiary, unite

affinity: accord, analogy, attraction, bias, connection, fancy, fellowship, fondness, liking, preference, propensity, rapport, relation, resemblance, similarity

affirm: allege, assert, asseverate, attest, aver, avouch, avow, claim, contend, declare, depose, maintain, predicate, profess, state, swear, testify, uphold, validate

affirmation: yes

affirmations of witnesses: testimony

affirmative: amen, assertive, aye, categorical, conclusive, dogmatic, emphatic, ere, hopeful, nod, positive, predicative, yea, yeah, yes

affirmative expressed by negating its opposite: litotes

affirmative vote: aye, yea

affix: anchor, annex, append, apply, attach, connect, fasten, glue, join, nail, paste, rivet, seal, staple, subjoin, unite

affix attached before a word: prefix

affix attached to the end of a word: suffix

affix firmly: rivet

affix name: sign

afflict: annoy, beset, bother, burden, distress, gripe, hurt, oppress, pain, pester, plague, smite, torment, trouble, try, wound

afflicted: ailed, cursed, depressed, distressed, doleful, dolent, grieved, impaired, stricken, suffering

afflicted with mal de mer: seasick

affliction: adversity, anguish, calamity, cross, distress, evil, grief, hardship, illness, malady, misery, misfortune, ordeal, pain, scourge, sickness, sorrow, trial, tribulation

affliction caused by drudgery: housemaid's knee

affluence: abundance, fortune, money, opulence, plentitude, prosperity, riches, wealth

affluent: copious, flush, in the money, loaded, pecunious, rich, river, stream, tributary

affluent gent: sugar daddy

affluent one: have, nawab

afford: furnish, give, grant, incur, invest, manage, provide, risk, spare, supply, sustain, yield

affording redress: remedial

affray: altercation, assault, attack, battle, brawl, clash, disturbance, donnybrook, encounter, fight, fracas, melee, quarrel, riot, ruckus, scuffle, skirmish

affright: alarm, daunt, fright, intimidate, panic, scare, spook, startle, terrify

affront: abuse, anger, defamation, defy, disgrace, dishonor, humiliate, indignity, injury, insult, irritate, meet, nettle, outrage, provoke, slap, slight, slur, snub

afghan: blanket, covering, coverlet, crochet, dog, throw

aficionado: admirer, adorer, buff, devotee, enthusiast, fan, follower, hound, pupil, student

afield: amiss, astray, beyond

afire: ablaze, aflame, ardent, burning, flaming, flaring, ignited

AFL partner: CIO

aflame: on fire

afloat: adrift, asea, buoyed, circulating, natant, operating, rumored, sailing

afoot: abroad, astir, brewing, happening, walking

afore: ere

aforesaid: ditto

afraid: aghast, alarmed, apprehensive, chicken, concerned, cowardly, craven, fainthearted, hesitant, loath, petrified, reluctant, scared, sorry, terrified, timid, timorous

afreet: genie

afresh: again, anew, de novo, encore, lately, newly, over, repeated

aft: astern, behind, past, posterior, rear

after: anon, back, behind, beyond, concerning, ex post facto, following, later, next, past, post, posterior, postscript, rearward, since, soon, subsequent

after a bit: anon

after a delay: at last

after a loss: sad

after-bath item: talc

after death: posthumous

after-dinner treats: mints

after-event perception: hindsight, retrospect

after taxes: net

after the fact: ex post facto

after the finish: postscript

AFRICAN TERMS

African antelope: addax, eland, gnu, impala, kudu, nagor, oribi, oryx, topi

African cattle disease: nagana

African fly: tsetse

amulet or fetish: juju

arrow poison: inee

baboon: chacma

butter tree: shea

buttonless shirt: dashiki

cat: civet

cobra: asp

dark skin pigment: melanin

hartebeest: tora

lily: agapanthus, aloe

lute: oud

magic: juju

monkey: guenon, mona

native village: stad

nut tree: kola

oasis: wadi

oil-yielding tree: owala

ravine: wadi

snake: asp

soldier: askari

witchcraft: obeah ❦

---

after the manner of: à la

afterbirth: placenta, secundines

afterdinner: postprandial

aftereffect and reverberation: repercussion

aftereffects: sequela

afterlife region for unbaptized babies and innocent souls: limbo

afterlife region where sinners can atone: purgatory

aftermath: consequence, impact, offshoot, outcome, payoff, remainder, result, sequel, upshot, wake

aftermath of an earthquake: rubble

aftermath, unfortunate: afterclap

afternoon affair: tea

afternoon nap: siesta

afternoon show: matinee

afternoon snacks, in London: afters

afternoon, relating to: post-meridian

afterthought: epilogue, postscript, reconsideration, sequel

afterwards: eventually, following, later, subsequently, then, thereupon

aga, agha: authority, chief, commander, leader, officer, official

again: additionally, afresh, anew, besides, bis, de novo, encore, further, more, moreover, over, recur

again and again: ad nauseam

again, from the beginning: de novo

again, musical direction to perform: da capo

again, poetically: anon

against: anti, beside, concerning, facing, from, into, near, opposed, opposite, respecting, touching, upon, versus

against change: conservative, reactionary

against one's interests, welfare: adverse

against the law: illegal, illegitimate, illicit

against, argument: con

against, strive: militate

agape: ajar, amazed, astonished, awestruck, confounded, open, overwhelmed, shocked, staring, yawning

agar source: kelp

agate: achate, brazil, chalcedony, ider, landscape, marble, mib, quartz, ruby

agatized mecca: petrified forest

agave: alde, aloe, amole

agave fiber: istle, pita, sisal

age: aeon, century, cycle, duration, eon, epoch, era, generation, interim, lifetime, majority, millennium, period, span, time, years

age, to: date, develop, grow, mature, mellow, ripen, wane, wither

age according to years lived: chronological age

age and length of life: longevity

age as another, person of around same: coeval, contemporary

age for study: era

age for whiskey: seven years old

age of girl who can agree to sex: age of consent

age or era: epoch

age, being legally under: minority, nonage

age, reaching advanced: longevity

age, retired due to: superannuated

age, the spirit of the: zeitgeist

aged: anile, antiquated, antique, dated, elderly, feeble, hoary, infirm, passe, ripe, seasoned, senile, shot, timeworn, venerable

aged and infirm: senile

aged and respectable: venerable

aged artificially: distressed

aged beer: lager

aged, discrimination against the: ageism

ageless: dateless, enduring, eternal, timeless

agency: bureau, cause, channel, charge, influence, means, medium, news, office, operation, vehicle

agency for cartoons, columns, serials: syndicate

agenda: calendar, docket, lineup, list, plan, plans, program, rota, schedule, slate, timetable

agenda component: item

agent: 10-percenter, advocate, assignee, ator, bailiff, broker, cause, channel, commissary, deputy, doer, emissary, envoy, executor, facient, facilitator, force, instrument, means, medium, middleperson, nark, operator, organ, proxy, seller, spy, steward, surrogate, underwriter

agent assisting ruler, as king: vice-regent

agent for another: assignee, minister, proxy, vicar

agent for buying and selling securities: broker

agent in business matters: broker, factor, syndic

agent-in-place: mole

agent in sexual relationship: maquereau, panderer, pimp, procurer

agent legally controlling property of another: trustee

agent mediating matter: intermediary, ombudsman

agent of illegal activity: agent provocateur

agent or representative at conference: delegate

agent or substitute: vicar

agent running estate for someone: bailiff, steward

agent secretly representing someone: dummy, front

agent sent on mission: ambassador, emissary

agent that changes others: catalyst

agent, appoint as one's: depute

agent, intermediary in espionage: cutout

agent, powerful and advice-giving: eminence grise

agent's fee or percentage: commission

aggitated state: swivet

agglomerate: aggregate, bunch, cluster, collection, lump, mass, mobilize, pile

agglomeration: clot, coherence

aggrandize: augment, boost, broaden, dignify, dilate, elevate, extend, glorify, increase, magnify, multiply, parlay, promote, widen

AGES, DECADES, ERAS

Age of Anxiety
Age of Aquarius
Age of Enlightenment
Age of Man
Age of Reason
Ages of Humankind
Air Age
American Revolution
Atomic Age
Automobile Age
Bronze Age
Christian Era
Classical Age
Cold War
Computer Age
Copper Age
Crusades
Dark Age
Depression Era
Early Middle Ages
Electronic Age
Elizabethan Age
Eolithic Age
Era of Good Feeling
Flapper Era
Gay Nineties
Gilded Age
Golden Age
Ice Age
Industrial Revolution
Iron Age
Jacksonian Age
Jazz Age
Jet Age
Mauve Decade
Middle Ages
Modern Age
Naughty Nineties
Postmodernism
Prohibition Era
Reconstruction Era
Reformation
Renaissance
Roaring Twenties
Roman Empire
Silver Age
Space Age
Steel Age
Stone Age
Technological Age
Victorian Age ☙

aggravate: aggrieve, anger, annoy, enlarge, exacerbate, exasperate, gall, heighten, incense, increase, inflame, irritate, magnify, nag, nettle, peeve, rile, rouse, upset

aggravate, make worse: exacerbate

aggravating problem: teaser

aggregate: accumulate, all, amount, blend, bulk, bunch, composite, gross, mass, sum, summation, total, unite, whole

aggregation: assembly, association, cluster, combination, company, crowd, cumulation, flock, gang, gathering, group, herd, nest, quantity

aggression: antagonism, assault, attack, fight, forceful, hostility, injury, invasion, offense, provocation, push, raid

aggressive: ambitious, barbaric, bellicose, flip, intense, militant, pugnacious, scrappy, zealous

aggressive and energetic: assertive, combative

aggressive and lively: feisty

aggressive and obnoxious: bumptious

aggressive flirt: wolf

aggressive, antisocial person: psychopath, sociopath

aggressively seeking power: self-aggrandizing

aggressor: antagonistic, assailant, attacker

aggrieve: afflict, aggravate, annoy, distress, hurt, injure, maltreated, mournful, oppress, pain, persecute, trouble, try, woeful, wrong

aghast: afraid, anxious, appalled, astounded, horrified, shocked, startled, stunned, stupefied, terrified

agile: active, athletic, brisk, dexterous, dextrous, fast, fleet, keen, light, limber, lithe, nimble, quick, springy, spry, zippy

agile deer: roe

aging, growing old: senescent

aging, study of: geriatrics, gerontology

agitate: activate, alarm, bother, churn, convulse, debate, discompose, discuss, disquiet, drive, excite, fluster, goad, harass, harry, inflame, irk, irritate, liven, move, perturb, provoke, rattle, rile, rock, rouse, ruffle, seek, stir, trouble, upset

agitate a liquid: slosh

agitate violently: churn

agitated: distraught, flustered, fluttered, roiled, seething

agitated state: flap, snit

agitated style used as a musical direction: agitato

agitating violently: turbulent

agitation: bustle, commotion, confusion, emotional, ferment, flurry, flutter, fury, rampage, snit, storm, trepidation, tumult, turbulence, turmoil, unrest, upheaval, violence

agitation of feelings: tumult

agitator: firebrand

aglet: shoelace tip

aglow: lit

agnate: affiliated, allied, connate, kindred, like, related

agnomen: alias, epithet, nickname, surname

agnostic: doubter, empiricist, freethinker, heathen, infidel, skeptic, unbeliever

ago: back, before, erst, gone, past, since

agog: awestruck, breathless, bursting, eager, excited, expectant, impatient, keen, lively, thrilled

agonize: ache, crucify, excruciate, fret, labor, lament, rack, strain, struggle

agonizing and painful: excruciating

agony: anguish, despair, distress, grief, heartache, misery, pain, pangs, sorrow, suffering, torment, torture, trial, tribulation

agony, place or time of great: Gethsemane

agora building: stoa

agrarian: agricultural, campestral, natural, pastoral

agree: accede, acquiesce, admit, allow, arrange, assent, attune, coincide, comply, concede, concur, congruous, consent, cooperate, equal, grant, harmonize, homologate, jibe, match, reconcile, square, submit, suit, unison, yes, yield

agree and comply: accede, acquiesce, yield

agree and match: accord, chime, coincide, comport, equate, harmonize, quadrate, square

agree in opinion: concur

agree or assent to: subscribe

agree silently: nod

agree to in patronizing way: condescend, deign

agree with: correspond

agree, concur: coincide

agree, informally: jibe

agreeable: acceptable, accord, alliance, amene, amiable, appealing, avowal, charming, charter, compliant, congenial, consentient, consonant, dulcify, pleasant, pleasing, promise, willing, writ

agreeable in manner: felicitous

agreeable to idea: amenable, receptive

agreeableness: complaisance

agreeably sharp: tart

agreed: assented, jibed, meshed

agreed to by all: unanimous

agreed to terms: met

agreed upon: settled

agreeing: congruent, in concert, in unison

agreeing and conforming: pursuant to

agreement: accord, accordance, arrangement, bargain, cartel, concurrence, consensus, consent, contract, covenant, deal, entente, indenture, lease, pact, partnership, rapport, treaty, understanding, unison

agreement among nations: pact

agreement among parts: compatibility, concord, conformity, congruity, consistency, consonance, coordination

agreement and harmony: consonance

agreement between church and state: concordat

agreement between disputing parties: arbitration, conciliation, mediation

agreement between rivals: accord, pact, treaty

agreement by general public, mutual: entente

agreement by two parties: bilateral, bipartite

agreement in isolated features, otherwise different: analogy

agreement of all: unanimity

agreement on parties' word: gentleman's agreement

agreement or contract: compact, covenant

agreement pending final accord: modus vivendi

agreement to partial payment: composition

agreement to raise for cost of living: threshold agreement

agreement, acceptance of: accession

agreement, break an: infringe, renege on, violate

agreement, contract or treaty: pact

agreement, discuss terms of: negotiate

agreement, express: assent

agreement, formally reject: denounce

agreement, general: consensus

agreement, informal: entente cordiale

agreement, person signing: signatory

AGRICULTURAL AND GARDENING TOOLS

baler	cultivator	hoe	pruning saw	sickle
billhook	dibble/dibber	lawn mower	rake	spade
binder	draw hoe	loy	reaper	spading fork
blower	edger	mattock	roller	sprinkler
brush cutter	flail	maul	rototiller	tiller
cant hook	grub hoe	pick	scuffle hoe	tractor
chisel plow	harvester	pickax	scythe	trowel
colter	hay rake	pitchfork	shears	weed trimmer
combine	hayfork	plow	shovel	wheelbarrow ❦
crop duster	hedge clipper	pruner	shredder	

agreement, set condition of: stipulate
agreement, summary of: aide-memoire
agreement, unspoken understood: tacit
agreement, willing: consent
agricultural: agrarian, rural
agriculture: agrology, agronomy, arviculture, dagan, farm, flora, gardening, grigit, grove, horticulture, orchard, picus, ranch, saturn, tillage, vacuna, vineyard
agriculture device: baler, binder, caterpillar, combine, cultivator, drill, harrow, header, mower, plow, reaper, seeder, separator, thrasher, thresher, tractor
agriculture goddess: Ceres
agriculture, concerning: geoponic
aground: beached, reefed, shipwrecked, stranded
ague: fever, malaria, shivering
aha: eureka
ahead: advanced, before, beforehand, early, fore, foremost, forward, leading, one up, onward, preceding
ahead of the times: avant-garde
ahead of time: early
aid: abet, advance, allay, alleviate, alms, assist, befriend, benefact, care, charity, coach, collaborate, facilitate, favor, forward, grant, help, relief, remedy, rescue, serve, subsidy, succor, uphold
aid a felon: abet
aid, subsidy: subvention
aide: apprentice, assistant, asst., coadjutant, deputy, helper, orderly, second, sidekick, subordinate
aiding and supporting: ancillary
ail: ache, affect, afflict, bother, decline, falter, pain, upset
ailing: ill, sick
ailing Biblical outcast: leper
ailment: acne, complaint, condition, disability, disease, disorder, ferment,

flu, food, illness, infirmity, malady, nourishment, nutriment, pabulum, pap, rash, sustenance, syndrome, weakness
ailment symptom: ague
ailurophobia: fear of cats
aim: address, ambition, attempt, bent, course, covet, design, destination, direct, essay, goal, intend, intent, intention, level, objective, plan, point, sight, strive, target, want
aim at: aspire
aim or goal: terminus ad quem
aimed at target: point-blank
aimed to the consumer: marketed
aimless: blind, careless, chance, drifting, erratic, goalless, haphazard, random, senseless, stray, undirected, vagabond, vagrant
aimless and random: desultory
aimless reverie: mooning
aimless wandering: meandering
aimlessly: idly
aims for: shoots at
ain't: is not, isn't
air: aerate, affectation, agitated, aloft, appearance, aria, aura, broach, broadcast, cachet, demeanor, deportment, display, divulge, exhibit, expose, haughtiness, manner, melody, mien, proclaim, publish, semblance, song, speak, tell, tune, unsettled, vanity, vent, voice
air-attack using low-flying planes: strafe
air-bag alternative: seat belt
air bubble: bleb
air conditioner chemical: Freon
air conditioning tube: duct
air cushion, support on: levitate
air deflector to increase drag, reduce lift: spoiler
air hole: spiracle
air maneuver: roll

AIR SPORTS

aerial skiing
aerobatics
aeromodeling
air racing
ballooning
bungy jumping
flying
freefalling
gliding
hang gliding
helicopter flying
hydroplane racing
kiting
microlighting
parachuting
paragliding
parasailing
parascending
skydiving
soaring
sport parachuting ❦

air of atmosphere: atmo, atmosphere, breeze, draft, draught, ephyr, ether, helium, krypton, neon, nitrogen, oxygen, ozone, sky, smog, welkin, wind, xenon
air of immediate area: ambient
air or gas from something, release: deflate
air pollutant: smog, soot
air-pressure indicator: barometer
air-quality watchdog agency: EPA
air raid: blitz
air-raid precaution: dimout
air sleeve: windsock
air speed, aerodynamic testing chamber for: wind tunnel
air swirl: eddy
air swirling around vertical axis: whirlwind
air through room, push fresh: ventilate

AIR FORCE RANK

Commissioned Officers
General of the Air Force
General
Lieutenant General
Major General
Brigadier General
Colonel
Lieutenant Colonel
Major
Captain
First Lieutenant
Second Lieutenant

Enlisted Personnel
Chief Master Sergeant
Senior Master Sergeant
Master Sergeant
Technical Sergeant
Staff Sergeant
Senior Airman
Airman First Class
Airman
Airman Basic ❦

---

air traffic control device: radar
air traffic, right of country to regulate its: cabotage
air turbulence: shear, wash
air vent: spiracle
air, bacterium that can live without: anaerobe
air, bacterium that needs: aerobe
air, death due to lack of: asphyxia
air, fear of fresh: aerophobia
air, foul or polluted: miasma

air, fresh: ozone
air, low-density: rarefied
air, relating to: pneumatic
air, very moist: humid, saturated
airborne: aloft
airs: arrogance, auras, front, hauteur, pomposity, pretense, songs, tunes, uppishness, vanity
airship basket or enclosure: gondola
airship, early self-propelled: dirigible
airship, nonrigid buoyant: blimp
airship, rigid long cylindrical: zeppelin
airstream driven backward behind aircraft: slipstream
airtight: closed, hermetic, impenetrable, sealed
airy: animated, breezy, cheerful, cool, debonair, empty, ethereal, fresh, graceful, happy, haughty, jocund, light, lively, merry, rare, spatial, sprightly, tenuous, thin, visionary, vivacious
airy fabric: mesh
aisle: alley, avenue, clearing, corridor, lane, passage, passageway, path, walk, walkway
aisle, covered: ambulatory
ait: islet
ajar: open, unlatched, unshut
akidded: slued
akin: affiliated, agnate, alike, allied, analogous, close, comparable, connate, correlated, kindred, related, similar
alabaster or selenite: gypsum
alacrity: avidity, briskness, celerity, dis-

patch, eagerness, enthusiasm, fervor, gaiety, nimbleness, rapidity, speed, willingness
alarm: disturb, disturbance, excite, fear, outcry, panic, scare, startle, stress, surprise, trepidation, unnerve, upset
alarm and upset: perturb
alarm or bell: alert, buzzer, clock, gong, signal, siren, tocsin, warning, yell
alarm, call to arms: alarum
alas: ach, alackaday, interjection, pity, welladay, woe
Alaskan bear: Kodiak
albacore: tuna
albacore, to a Briton: tunny
Albania monetary unit: qintar
albatross: gooney, handicap, hindrance, mallemuck, nelly, pelican, seabird
albeit: altho, although, though, whereas, while
Albion: Britannia, England, Great Britain
album: anthology, book, collection, index, memento, portfolio, record, register, scrapbook
albumen surrounds it: yolk
alchemist's finesse: Midas touch
alchemy: change, hermes, sorcery, transmutation, witchcraft, wizardry
alcohol: allyl, butanol, butyl, ethanol, ethyl, glycerol, methanol, methyl

RELATED TERMS

alcohol ban in U.S. 1920-1933: Prohibition
alcohol burner: etna

AIRCRAFT

aerodyne	carrier fighter	helicopter gunship	ornithopter	supersonic transport/ SST
aerostat	chopper	helium balloon	orthopter	tandem airplane
air cushion vehicle/ ACV	combat plane	high-altitude reconnaissance plane	parachute	tanker
air taxi	copter		parafoil	tilt-rotor
airliner	crop duster	hot-air balloon	paraglider	torpedo bomber
airplane	dirigible	hovercraft	pursuit plane	transport
airship	dive bomber	hydroplane	pusher plane	triphibian
amphibian	double-prop	interceptor	rotorcraft	turbojet
autogrio	fighter	jet	sailplane	turboprop
balloon	flying boat	jet bomber	seaplane	twin-prop
battleplane	glider	jet fighter	short takeoff and landing/STOL	ultralight
biplane	gyrodyne	jetliner	spy plane	vertical takeoff and landing/VTOL
blimp	gyroplane	jumbo jet	stealth bomber	
bogey	hang glider	kamikaze	stealth fighter	waterplane
bomber	heavier-than-air craft	kite	suicide plane	zeppelin ❦
business jet	helibus	lighter-than-air craft		
	helicopter	monoplane		

AIRCRAFT-RELATED TERMS

ability to fly faster than speed of sound: supersonic
aerial machine-gun attack: strafe
aerial maneuver: snaproll
aerial trick: barrel roll, buzz, dive, hedgehop, loop, nosedive, roll, sideslip, tailspin
aircraft: aerostat, airplane, balloon, blimp, chopper, copter, dirigible, drone, giro, glider, helicopter, jet, plane, whirlybird
aircraft carrier: flattop, wasp
aircraft circling at different altitudes, waiting to land: stack
aircraft load: payload
aircraft on single mission: sortie
aircraft shelter: hangar
aircraft for short: giro
airline regulator: FAA
airplane: aero, bomber, clipper, Enola Gay, fighter, glider, gyro, liner, mig, SST, transport, zero
airplane access: ramp
airplane seizure: skyjack
airplane's control: joystick
airport: aerodrome, airdrome, airfield, drome
airport area: runway, taxiway, tower
baton signaller for taxiing: marshaller
boom caused by aircraft traveling at or faster than speed of sound: sonic boom
compartment holding engines, guns, fuel: pod
condensed water vapor, ice crystals in plane's wake: condensation trail, contrail, vapor trail
conveyor for luggage, etc.: carousel
conveyor for pedestrians: moving sidewalk, walkway
course: vector

direct aircraft into crosswind: crab
electronic recorder: black box, flight recorder
empty aircraft: deadhead
flight on combat mission: sortie
flight path when awaiting clearance to land: holding pattern
fly low to the ground: hedgehop
funnel-shaped receptacle and probe towed behind aircraft: drogue
glide in with engine turned off: volpane
heavier-than-air aircraft: aerodyne
housing for engine: nacelle
instrument for measuring pressure changes caused by altitude: altimeter
landing beyond or past runway: overshoot
landing short of runway: undershoot
lighter-than-air aircraft: aerostat
movement on ground before takeoff, after landing: taxi
open-ended sleeve to indicate direction of wind: air sock, wind cone, wind sleeve, windsock
part affecting lift, stability: airfoil
paved parking for aircraft: apron
perfect landing: three-point landing
permission to proceed: clearance
quick takeoff to intercept enemy: scramble
seat that hurls crew during in-flight emergency: ejection seat
short for runway: tarmac
surveillance airplane: AWACS
training device: simulator
turn about vertical axis: yaw
wing's arched surface: camber ❧

---

alcohol drinking in moderation: temperance
alcohol drunkenness: inebriety
alcohol for drinking: aqua vitae, booze, cocktail, liquor, moonshine, spirits, whiskey, wine
alcohol in intoxicating beverages: ethanol, ethyl alcohol, grain alcohol
alcohol intake testing device: breathalizer
alcohol or drug addiction: dependence, substance abuse
alcohol or phenol compound: ester
alcohol secretly to drink, add: spike
alcohol shop in Prohibition: speakeasy
alcohol solution of medicine: tincture
alcohol to, add ethyl: denature
alcohol, abstain from: teetotal
alcohol, add to beverage: lace
alcohol, drink: imbibe

alcohol, licensed seller of: victualer
alcohol, refraining from drinking: abstinence
alcohol, to make, sell illegal: bootleg
alcohol, toxic: carbinol, methanol, wood alcohol
alcoholic: bibulous, brewed, fermented, inebriated, intoxicating, sot, spiritous
alcoholic appetizer: aperitif
alcoholic beverage with water, dilute: rectify
alcoholic drink: intoxicant, libation
alcoholic drink, small: snifter, snort
alcoholic drink, small measure for: jigger
alcoholic drinks, habitually take: tipple
alcoholic fit: delirium tremens, DTs
alcoholic person: dipsomanic, wino
alcoholic strength of spirits: proof
alcoholism: alcoholophilia, dipsomania

alcoholism-induced liver disease: cirrhosis ❧

alcove: arbor, compartment, corner, cranny, cubicle, dinette, niche, nook, recess, study
alder: alnus, arn, shrub
ale: beer, beverage, brew, lager, malt, nog, porter, stingo, stout, suds
ale mug: toby
ale/beer and ginger ale: shandygaff
alehouse: bistro, cabaret, cafe, nightclub, pub, saloon, taproom, tavern
alert: alive, awake, bright, eager, heedful, inform, keen, live, lively, nimble, observant, on one's toes, on the ball, on the qui vive, ready, sharp, spirited, up and doing, vigilant, wakeful, warn, wary, watchful
alert cat: mouser
alert watchman: argus
alert, method of: alarm, signal, siren
alfalfa: fodder, lucerne

alga, algae: algology, diatom, desmid, kelp, lichen, plankton, rockweed, seaweed, seawrack, stonewort

algebra symbol linking two or more terms into unit: vinculum

algebraic system of symbolic logic: Boolean algebra

Algerian dollar: dinar

Algerian governor: dey

Algerian native: Orani

algid: cold

Algonquian Indian: Arapahoe, Cree, Miami, Sac

alias: aka, anonym, epithet, handle, name, pen name, pseudonym

alias letters: a/k/a, aka

alias name: pseudonym

alias of a sort: stage name

alibi: excuse, explanation, pretext, proof, statement

alien: different, extraterrestrial, foreign, foreigner, hostile, immigrant, invader, opposed, outlander, outsider, refugee, remote, strange, stranger

alien craft: UFO

alienate: detach, devest, disaffect, disunite, estrange, hostility, remise, separate, transfer, wean

alienated: disaffected, estranged

alight: aglow, arrive, bright, deplane, disembark, dismount, land, lighted, perch, radiant, rest, roost, settle

align: adjust, affiliate, agree, join, level, marshal, regulate, straighten, true

align, on parade: oress

aligned with margin: flush

alignment of three celestial bodies: syzygy

alignment, in proper: register

alike: comparable, congruent, ditto, equal, homogeneous, identical, parallel, same, similar, uniform

alikeness by trait: common denominator

alimony: allowance, maintenance, provision, settlement, upkeep

aline: true

alit: landed

alive: abounding, active, alert, animate, animated, awake, aware, breathing, brisk, dynamic, eager, existent, extant, sprightly, spry, unexpired, vibrant, vigorous, vivid, zestful

alkali counter: acid

alkaline: alkali, antacid, borax, neutralizing, salty

alkaloid: caffeine, cocaine, codeine, ergot, eserin, harmine, heroin, morphine, quinidine, sinapin, strychnine

alkaloid, from cinchona bark: aricine

alkyl with five carbon atoms: pentyl

all: aggregate, alone, altogether, complete, completely, entirely, every, everyone, everything, exclusively, full, gross, group, quite, solely, sum, thoroughly, total, totality, whole, wholly

all around: everywhere, omnipresent, ubiquitous, under-the-sun

all at one time: holus-bolus

all-embracing: catholic

all-embracing view: panoptic

all-encompassing itinerary: grand tour

all-girl events: hen parties

all in: bleary, bushed, drained, exhausted, fatigued, pooped, spent, tired, weary

all-knowing: omniscient

all-male affair: stag

all-nighter, pulling an: pernoctation

all of ship's men: crew

all one's holdings: portfolio

all one's possessions: estate

all-or-nothing ultimatum: take it or leave it

all out: extensive, maximum, thorough, tooth and nail, unreserved

all-out determination: hammer and tongs

all over: concluded, ended, everywhere, finished, throughout, universal

all over again: anew

all possible: every

all-powerful: omnipotent

all right: adequate, agreed, average, good, hunky-dory, kosher, okay, roger, satisfactory, swell

all stirred up: agog

all the marbles: full deck

all the more: a fortiori

all the time: constantly

all thumbs: awkward, inept

all together: en bloc, en masse

all together, in music: tutti

all-weather covering: tarp

all welcome: open house

allay: abate, alleviate, appease, comfort, compose, diminish, ease, lull, mitigate, pacify, quiet, reduce, relieve, settle, soften, still

allege: advance, affirm, assert, asseverate, attribute, aver, avow, claim, declare, impute, maintain, offer, plead, present, profess, say, state, testify

allegiance: ardor, devotion, duty, faithfulness, fealty, homage, honor, loyalty, obedience, obligation, tribute

allegory: apologue, fable, moral, parable, story, symbol, tale

allegro or largo: tempo

allergic reactions, compound released in: histamine

allergic response: reaction

allergy indicator: hive, rash, urticaria

allergy medicine: antihistamine

allergy test on skin: scratch test

allergy that signals discontinuation of a medicine or treatment: contraindication

allergy, substance inducing: allergen

alleviate: abate, assuage, blunt, diminish, ease, help, lessen, mitigate, palliate, relieve, slake, soften, subdue

alley: byway, lane, oop, passage, passageway, path, slum, walk

alliance: accord, affiliation, affinity, agreement, axis, bloc, bond, coalition, compact, covenant, federation, fusion, league, marriage, pact, partnership, treaty, union

alliance of business concerns: consortium

alliance of nations: axis

alliance that is temporary: coalition, consortium

allied: agnate, akin, alike, bound, cognate, connate, connected, joined, linked, related, similar, unified, united

alligator pear: avocado

alligator relative, crocodile of tropical America: caiman, cayman

allocate: allot, allow, apportion, assign, distribute, divvy, earmark, give, mete, set apart, share, slice

allot: accord, allocate, appoint, apportion, assign, award, design, dispense, distribute, give, grant, mete, ordain, prescribe, present, provide, reserve, share, specify

allotment: quota, share

allow: accept, acknowledge, admit, approve, authorize, bear, concede, confess, consider, defer, enable, endure, grant, let, oblige, pass, permit, stand, suffer, suppose, tolerate

allow access: admit, let in

allow license to something that meets standards: accredit

allow oneself to satisfy whim: indulge

allow or enable: authorize, empower, warrant

allow or tolerate: countenance, sanction

allowable: licit

allowable and permissible: admissible, tolerable

allowance: alimony, annuity, cut, deduction, discount, fee, gift, margin, odds, part, pension, portion, quota, ration, rebate, reduction, salary, sanction, share

allowance for day's expenses: per diem

allowance for waste: tret

allowance for weight: tare

allowance or concession: edge, handicap, permission, tolerance

allowance or regular payment: stipend

allowance paid to former lover, court-ordered: palimony

allowance, salary: stipend

allowing extreme freedom: permissive

allowing for differences: mutatis mutandis

allows: enables, lets

alloy: adulterate, amalgamate, compound, fuse, reduce

alloy, black used to decorate other metal: niello

alloy, copper and tin: oreide, ormolu, oroide, pewter

alloy, copper and zinc: arsedine, tombac

alloy, fusible, used to join metal parts: solder

alloy, gold and silver: electrum

alloy, lead and tin: pewter, terne

alloy, main metal in: matrix

alloyed thing: blend, brass, composite, metal, mixture

allude: advert, connote, hint, imply, indicate, infer, insinuate, intimate, mention, point, refer, relate, suggest, touch on

allure: angle, attract, bait, beguile, blandish, cajole, captivate, charm, coax, court, draw, entice, glamor, induce, influence, lead, lure, magnetize, persuade, seduce, sway, tempt, woo

allurement: bribe

alluring ad: teaser

allusion: denotation, innuendo, insinuation, instance, intimation, mention, reference, remark

alluvial deposit at river mouth: delta

ally: accomplice, affiliate, assistant, associate, backer, colleague, comrade, confederate, connect, friend, helper, join, partner, relative, supporter, unite

ally with: side

almighty: absolute, creator, eternal, extreme, great, mighty, omnipotent, powerful, puissant, supreme

almond cookie: macaroon

almond drink: orgeat

almond-flavored liqueur: amaretto

almond or pistachio: nut

almond paste or confection: marzipan

almond, loosen skin by scalding: blanch

almond, pertaining to: amygdalaceous, amygdaloid

almonds, served with: amandine

almost: about, approximately, around, close, nearly, practically, quasi, roughly, virtually

almost perpendicular: sheer

alms: benefaction, charity, contribution, dole, donation, gift, handout, offering, pittance, relief

alms box: arca

alms, pertaining to: eleemosynary

almsman: beggar, panhandler, pauper

aloe: lily, vera

aloe derivative: aloin

aloft: above, airborne, high, overhead, risen, skyward

aloha: affection, farewell, goodbye, greeting, hello, love, salutation

aloha gift: lei

alone: aloof, apart, desolate, detached, exclusively, forlorn, hermit, incomparable, isolated, lonesome, one, removed, separate, single, solitary, solo, unescorted, unique, unparalleled

alone and remote: cloistered, incommunicado, insulated, isolated, sequestered

alone by choice: secluded, solitary

alone one: solo

alone (stage direction): solus

alone, person who lives: hermit, recluse

along: adjacent, ahead, also, approaching, beside, forward, lengthwise, likewise, near, onward, together, with

alongside: abreast, abutting, against, adjacent, beside, contiguous, juxtaposed, near, next to, parallel, tangential

aloof: alone, apart, arrogant, chilly, cold, cool, detached, distant, frosty, indifferent, offish, remote, reserved, uppity, withdrawn

aloof contempt: disdain

aloud: audible, clearly, lustily, noisily, oral, vocal

alough: mire

alp: mount, mountain, pike, summit

alpha: beginning, first, Greek letter, start

alpha and omega: first and last; beginning and end

alphabet: basics, elements, ideograph, letters, primer, rudiments, signs, symbols

alphabet character set with each representing syllable: syllabary

alphabet notches in reference book: thumb index

alphabet of ancient Germans: runes

alphabet of Celtics: ogham

alphabet of most Western and central European languages: Roman

alphabet of one language used for another: transliteration

alphabet of pictures representing entire words or phrases: pictography

alphabet of pictures used by ancient Egyptians: hieroglyphics

alphabet of runes: futhark

alphabet of symbolic characters representing entire words or ideas: ideography

alphabet, small letters: lowercase

alphabet, writing in letters of another: transliterate

alphabetic board and planchette for receiving telepathic messages: Ouija

alphabetic code used by radio operators: phonetic alphabet

alphabetic writing system: orthography

alphabetical: abecedarian

alphabetize: sort

Alpine farmhouse: chalet

Alpine goat: ibex

Alpine hogback: arete

Alpine primrose: auricula

Alpine refrain: yodel

Alpine region: Tirol, Tyrol

Alpine river: Rhone

Alpine sled: luge

Alpine wind: bise, bora, foehn

alpinist's gear: piton

already: before, beforehand, earlier, early, formerly, once, previously

also: again, and, besides, ditto, further, including, likewise, more, moreover, plus, similarly, too, with, yet

also known as: aka, alias

also known as inverted saucer, to a chartist: dome

also-ran: loser

altar: boys, chantry, sanctuary, shrine, tabernacle, table

altar approaches: aisles

altar area in Eastern Orthodox church: bema

altar back with ornaments, lights, etc.: reredos, retable

altar boy/girl: acolyte, thurifer

altar canopy: baldachin, tester

altar cloth: antependium, orale

altar decorative tapestry: dossal, frontal

altar for Mass: chantry

altar platform: altar rail, predella

altar screen: reredos

altar stone: mensa

altar vaulted canopy: ciborium

altar, in astronomy: ara

altarpiece of three parts: triptych

alter: adapt, adjust, amend, change, convert, ego, modify, mutate, neuter, redo, reset, revamp, revise, transform, turn, vary

alter a garment edge: rehem

alter deceptively: doctor

alter document to deceive: falsify

alter female with hysterectomy: spay

alter, as a manuscript: blue pencil

alter, change: mutate

alter, deter plans of another: dissuade

alteration of document to invalidate it, intentional: spoliation

alteration specialist: tailor

altercation: argument, brawl, controversy, dispute, fight, melee, quarrel, rift, row, run-in, scrap, spat, squabble, strife, tiff, wrangle

alternate: change, else, fluctuate, intermit, rotate, seesaw, shift, vary

alternate, change places: interchange

alternating: reciprocation

alternative: either, elective, loophole, option, other, preference

alternative plan: counterproposal

alters an itinerary: reroutes

alters form: reshapes

alters the text by insertion: interpolates

although: albeit, despite, whereas

altitude: ceiling, elevation, loftiness

altitude-measuring instrument: altimeter

altogether: collectively, completely, entirely, in all, quite, thoroughly, totally, utterly, wholly

altogether and entirely: in toto

altruism: benevolence, generosity, philanthropy

altruistic effort: labor of love

alum: grad

aluminum: alumina, epidote

aluminum, chief ore of: bauxite

always: constantly, continually, e'er, eternally, ever, everlastingly, evermore, forever, habitually, perpetually, uniformly

always prepared: semper paratus

always reliable one: standby

always, in poetry: e'er, eterne

amalgamate: alloy, blend, coalesce, combine, compound, consolidate, fuse, join, merge, mingle, unite

amalgamation: pool

amamentarium: inventory, stock, supply

amanuenses: stenos

amass: accumulate, assemble, collect, compile, gather, hoard, pile, stack, stockpile, store

amateur: admirer, beginner, dabbler, dilettante, greenhorn, neophyte, novice, tyro, votary

amateur professional: armchair general

amateur radio operator: ham

amatory: erotic

amaurotic: blind as a bat

amaze: astonish, astound, awe, confound, dumbfound, flabbergast, overwhelm, stagger, stun, stupefy, surprise

amazement, paralyzing: consternation

amazing: sensational

amazing and hard to believe: incredible

amazing and wonderful: prodigious

amazing thing: marvel

amazon: female, mythology, river, vixen, woman warrior

Amazon lily: Star of Bethlehem

amazon warrior: Hippolyta, Penthesilea

ambassador: deputy, diplomat, emissary, envoy, intermediary, legate, messenger

ambassador authorized to represent foreign government: plenipotentiary

ambassador of Vatican: nuncio

ambassador's document conveying credentials: letter(s) of credence

amber: yellow

ambiance: aura

ambience: atmosphere, environment, mood

ambiguity: doubtfulness, duplicity, entendre, evasion, obscurity

ambiguity due to poor grammar: amphibology

ambiguity from, remove: disambiguate

ambiguity in word: double entendre, polysemy

ambiguous: cryptic, doubtful, dubious, equivocal, indefinite, uncertain, unclear, unsettled, unsure, vague

ambiguous and oracular: delphic

ambiguous language: equivocation, prevarication, temporizing, tergiversation

ambiguous or evasive: equivocal

ambiguous remarks: weasel words

ambiguous talk: double-talk

ambit: boundary, bounds, compass, extension, extent, range, scope, space, sphere

ambition: aspiration, desire, dream, drive, end, goal, hope, intention, mark, plan, purpose, target

ambition thwarted: blight

ambition, excessive: folie de grandeur

ambitions: aims, ends, hopes

ambitious: ardent, aspiring, bold, demanding, eager, energetic, enterprising, keen

ambitious soul: striver

amble: dawdle, loiter, meander, mosey, pace, pad, ramble, rove, saunter, stroll

ambrosia: delicacy, nectar, perfume

ambrosial: aromal, delicate, delightful, fragrant, heavenly, luscious

ambulatory: nomadic, walking

ambush: ambuscade, assault, attack, await, camouflage, lurking, snare, surprise, trap, trick, waylay

ameliorate: advance, better, help, improve, progress, promote, recuperate, reform, set up, uplift

amen: approval, assent, certainly, exactly, response, so-be-it, truly, verily

amenable: accountable, complaisant, cooperative, docile, liable, pliant, responsive, subdued, subject, tractable, willing, yielding

amend: alter, better, change, correct, edit, improve, lift, polish, rectify, reform, repair, revise, right

amendment to bill, verdict, contract: rider

amends: alters, atonement, compensation, expiation, indemnity, payment, quittance, recompense, redress, reparation, requital, restitution

amends, make: recompense, recoup, reimburse, requite

amenities: comforts, conveniences, et-

AMERICAN INDIAN TERMS

arched hut of branches, bark, hides: wigwam
ax: tomahawk
baby: papoose
beads used as money, ornament: peag, wampum
cabin of logs and mud: hogan
communal feast in Northwest: potlatch
cone-shaped tent: tepee, tipi
leather shoe: moccasin
married male: sannup
ritual ceremony: powwow
temporary hut: wickiup
terraced dwelling: pueblo
tribe chief: sachem, sagamore
wife, woman: squaw ❦

---

iquette, formalities, geniality, luxuries, mildness, niceties, pleasantries, refinement
ament: catkin, cattail, idiot, imbecile, moron, simpleton
amerce: fine, penalize, punish
American: gringo, native, yankee
American Beauties: roses
American flag: Old Glory, Stars & Stripes
American flag maker: Betsy Ross
American idealized woman, 1890s: Gibson girl
American motto: Land of the Free
amethyst: onegite, purple, quartz
amiability: bon homie
amiable: affable, agreeable, charming, cordial, courteous, easy, engaging, friendly, genial, gracious, kind, pleasant, pleasing, polite, sociable, warm
amicable: benevolent, brotherly, empathic, friendly, harmonious, peaceable
amid: among, between, during, encompassed, midst, over, surrounded, throughout
amino and nitric: acid
amiss: askew, astray, awry, defective, erroneous, false, faulty, foul, haywire, ill, improper, inaccurate, incorrect, mistaken, unfair, wrong
amity: accord, brotherhood, friendship, goodwill, harmony, simpatico, sympathy
ammonia compound: amine, imide
ammonia derivative: amide, amine, imine
ammunition: arms, artillery, bombs, cannonball, cartridge, charge, fuse, grenades, materiel, missiles, powder, rockets, round, shells, shot, shrapnel
ammunition and weapons: munitions, ordnance
ammunition slung over shoulder on belt: bandolier
ammunition transport or two-wheeled horse-drawn vehicle: caisson
amnesia: blackout, fugue, stupor
amnesty: absolution, condonation, forgiveness, immunity
amoeba, ameba: animalcule, animalculum, bacteria, germ, organism, proteus, protozoan, virus
among: amid, amidst, between, midst, with
among other things: inter alia
amongst: amid
amor, amore, amour: Cupid, Eros, love
amorous: affectionate, aphrodisiac, ardent, attached, erotic, loving, lustful, passionate, sexy, tender
amorphous: formless, inchoate, irregular, nondescript, shapeless, undefined, vague
amorphous mass: blob, glob
amount: aggregate, bulk, chunk, comprise, cost, dosage, extent, lot, mass, measure, number, portion, price, quantity, store, sum, tab, total, unit, volume, whole
amount absorbed: intake
amount container lacks due to settling, leakage: ullage
amount of increase: increment
amount of medication: dose
amount paid: ante
amounting to: tantamount
amour propre: egoism, narcissism, pride, vanity
ampere unit: watt
ampersand: &, and
amphetamine: speed, upper
amphibian: caecilian, caudate, frog, hyla, newt, proteus, rana, salamander, toad
amphibian young: polliwog, tadpole
amphibians and reptiles, study of: herpetology
amphibole: edenite
amphitheater: arena, auditorium, cavea, coliseum, grandstand, oval, stadium
amphitheater or stadium passageway: vomitorium, vomitory
amphora: jug, ornament, urn, vase
amphora handle: ansa
ample: abundant, bountiful, broad, copious, extensive, full, galore, good, great, handsome, large, lavish, liberal, much, opulent, plentiful, plenty, rich, roomy, spacious, sufficient, vast, wide
amplified: added
amplify: augment, boost, dilate, expand, extend, increase, inflate, intensify, lengthen, pad, raise, swell, widen
amply: richly
ampoule: vial
ampule: vial
amputate: curtail, eliminate, excise, lop, remove, sever, truncate
amputation: avulsion
amputation pain or feeling where missing limb is: phantom limb
amputation, surgical: ablation
amulet: charm, fetish, luck, mojo, ornament, protection, saphie, talisman, token
amuse: beguile, cheer, delight, distract, divert, engage, entertain, exhilarate, fascinate, gratify, interest, kill, please, tickle
amuse greatly: slay
amuse oneself: disport
amuse with stories: regale
amused: diverted, entertained
amusement: disport, distraction, diversion, divertissement, fun, game, hobby, jest, lark, merriment, pastime, play, pleasure, recreation, relaxation, sport
amusement center: penny arcade, shooting gallery
amusement-park announcer of attractions: barker
amusement park car driving game: bumper car
amusement park elevated railway: roller coaster
amusement park item: ride
amusement park with theme: theme park
amusement, for short: rec
amusing: boffo, comical, delightful, droll, funny, humorous, laughable, ludicrous, merry, pleasant, priceless, ridiculous
amusing person: card
amusing story: anecdote
amusing time: picnic
anabasis: advance, expedition, headway, progress
anachronism, early date: prochronism
anachronism, late date: metachronism

anaconda or python: boa

anadem: chaplet, diadem, wreath

anagogic: mystical, occult, symbolical

anagram: cipher, game, logograph, puzzle

anal swelling, itching: hemorrhoids, piles

analgesic: anesthetic, anodyne, aspirin, codeine, opium, sedative, soother

analgesic tincture: arnica

analog of an allegory: apolog

analogize: liken

analogous: agreeing, akin, alike, allied, comparable, correlative, equivalent, kindred, like, related, resembling, similar

analogy: comparison, congruence, metaphor, parallel, resemblance

analysis: assay, audit, breakdown, brief, diagnosis, dissection, examination, finding, inquiry, reasoning, reduction, review, study, test

analysis after the fact: postmortem

analysis and attempted explanation of complex phenomena by comparison with simpler units: reductionism

analysis of word or work: exegesis

analysis opposite: synthesis

analytical and detached: clinical

analyze: assay, determine, dissect, evaluate, examine, inspect, parse, scrutinize, search, study, subdivide, weigh

analyze a sentence: parse

analyze in detail: anatomize, dissect

analyzed grammatically: parsed

analyzed ore: assayed

anarchist: agitator, anti, insurgent, malcontent, mutineer, nihilist, radical, revolter, revolutionary, terrorist

anarchy: chaos, confusion, disorder, lawlessness, nihilism, nongovernment, rebellion, revolt, turmoil

anathema: abhorrence, bane, censure, condemnation, curse, hate, imprecation, malediction, oath, pariah, phobia, taboo

anatomic sac: bursa

anatomical duct: vas

anatomical passage: iter, ostia

anatomical projection: lobe

anatomical tissue: tela

anatomy: analysis, biology, cytology, dissection, etiology, form, framework, histology, physiology, skeleton, structure, zoology

ancestor: Adam, antecessor, ascendant, elder, Eve, forebear, forefather, forerunner, patriarch, precursor, predecessor, primogenitor, procreator, progenitor, prototype, sire

ancestor but in different lines, descended from same: collateral

ancestor worship: manism

ancestor, animal or plant species sharing features derived from common: clade

ancestor, earliest known: primogenitor

ancestors and family tree, study of: genealogy, lineage

ancestors, derived from: hereditary

ancestral: aval

ancestral line: lineage, pedigree

ancestral spirits in ancient Rome: Manes

ancestry: antecedents, blood, derivation, descent, extraction, family, genealogy, heredity, heritage, lineage, line of descent, origin, parentage, pedigree, race, stock

anchor: ballast, grapnel, hook, killick, sea anchor, sheet anchor

anchor cable, hole in ship's bow for: hawse, hawsehold

anchor hanging clear of the bottom: aweigh

anchor or blight: stem

anchor or towing rope or cable: hawser

anchor place, available: anchorage

anchor position: atrip

anchor rope: rode

anchor something, to: attach, bind, connect, dock, fix, moor, plant, rivet, tie

anchor with three or more flukes for small vessel: grapnel

anchor, light, for positioning: kedge

anchor, lowest part: crown

anchor, raise: trip, weigh

anchor, sea: drogue

anchor, small: killick

anchorage: dock, harbor, haven, mooring, port, refuge, roadstead, slip, wharf

anchored: moored

anchovy: sardine

anchovy and meat dish: salmagundi

anchovy sauce: alec

ancient: aged, age old, ancestral, antiquated, antique, archaic, bygone, classical, eld, elderly, historic, hoary, old, olden, passé, patriarchal, primeval, primitive, relic, senior, timeworn

ancient and before Biblical flood: antediluvian

ancient and gray-haired: hoary

ancient and outmoded: antediluvian, antiquated, obsolete, passé

ancient and primitive: primeval, pristine

ancient and stale: hoary, musty

ancient artifact: antiquity, relic

ancient bird: dodo

ancient burial mound: tumulus

ancient Celtic harp: rotte

ancient chariot: essed

ancient Dead Sea kingdom: Moab

ancient drug of oblivion: nepenthe

ancient Egyptian gateway: pylon

ancient Egyptian rulers: pharaohs

ancient Egyptian writing system: hieroglyphics

ancient France: Gaul

ancient galley: trireme

ancient Greece or Rome, pertaining to: classical

ancient Greek coin: obol

ancient Greek jar: amphora

ancient Greek marketplace: agora

ancient harp: lyre

ancient Hebrew: Levite

ancient inscriptions, study of: epigraphy

ancient manuscript: codex

ancient measure of 18 inches: cubit

ancient Mesopotamian region: Sumer

ancient Mesopotamian writing system: cuneiform

ancient Persian governor: satrap

ancient Peruvians: Incas

ancient region of Asia Minor: Ionia

ancient region of Babylonia: Sumer

ancient region of Europe: Gaul

ancient remains: ruin

ancient road: iter

ancient Roman church: basilica

ancient Roman measure: pes

ancient Roman official: edile

ancient Roman portrait in wax: imago

ancient ship: bireme

ancient time indicator: dial

ancient times: antiquity, yore

ancient, before historical records: immemorial, prehistoric

ancillary: attendant, auxiliary, satellite, secondary, subordinate, subsidiary

and: also, besides, connective, further, furthermore, including, moreover, plus

and others: et al., et alii

and sign (&): ampersand

and so forth: etc.

Andean beast of burden: llama

andirons: fire dogs

Andorra monetary unit: centime, centimo, peseta

android: automaton

anecdotal collection: ana

anecdote: ana, chestnut, episode, narrative, reminiscence, sketch, story, tale, yarn

anemia fighter: iron

anemia with lowered capacity for making red blood cells: aplastic anemia, pancytopenia

anemic: bloodless, feeble, frail, lifeless, pale, watery, weak

anemone: buttercup, flower, windflower

anesthetic: analgesic, dope, drug, ether, general anesthetic, local anesthetic, morphine, narcotic, novocaine, opiate, palliative, sedative, spinal

anesthetic gas: laughing gas, nitrous oxide

anesthetic-induced state of semiconsciousness: twilight sleep

anesthetic injected by spinal cord: epidural

anesthetic, local: lidocaine, Novocain

anesthetic, strong formerly used: chloroform, ether

anew: afresh, again, de novo, fresh, lately, recently

angel: cherub, darling, dear, guardian, lamb, messenger, saint, seraph, spirit; backer, sponsor

angel appearance: visitation

angel hair: pasta

angel or cupid, chubby rosy-faced: amoretto, cherub, putto

angel or incorporeal being: intelligence

angel orders: angels, archangels, cherubim, dominations, dominions, powers, principalities, seraphim, thrones, virtues

angel topper: halo

angel, highest rank: seraph

angelic: beautiful, celestial, cherubic, divine, heavenly, holy, innocent, pure, saintly, seraphic, sweet

angels: cherubim

anger: acrimony, aggravate, annoy, antagonize, bile, bridle, burning, choler, cross, dander, displeasure, enrage, exasperate, fury, gall, goad, incense, inflame, infuriate, ire, irritate, mad, offend, outrage, provoke, rage, rancor, rankle, rile, ruffle, tantrum, temper, vex, vip, wrath

anger a little: irk, pique, rankle, vex

anger and resentment: dudgeon, hackles, umbrage

anger at injustice: indignation

anger from being wronged, feeling of: grievance

anger from disappointment, feeling of: chagrin

anger to point of breach: alienate, antagonize, envenom, exacerbate

anger, arouse: rankle

anger, arousing quick: inflammatory

anger, calming one's: allay

anger, feeling or display of: acrimony, animosity, rancor

anger, fit of: conniption, paroxysm, tantrum

anger, ire: rile, rip

anger, mild: asperity, irritability

angered: irate, ired, riled, sore

angered, easily: atrabilious, bilious, cantankerous, choleric, dyspeptic, fractious, inflammable, irascible, querulous, splenetic, volatile

angle: aspect, bend, bevel, bias, bow, cast, dogleg, jockey, lean, phase, position, slant, standpoint, turn, twist, viewpoint

angle added to another to measure 90 degrees: complement

angle between lateral organ and stem that bears it: axil

angle between lines or surfaces that is not ninety degrees: bevel, cant

angle formed by junction of two members or parts: crotch

angle formed by two intersecting planes: dihedral angle

angle of leafstalk: axil

angle of vision: slant

angle or rate of inclination: gradient, slope

angle, projecting: salient

angled: trawled

angler's basket: creel

angler's gear: bait, creek, creel, rod and reel, rods

angles in technical drawing, instrument for constructing: set square

angles, instrument for measuring and constructing: protractor

Anglo-Saxon person: atheling, esne, thane, thegn

Anglo-Saxon serf: esne

Anglo-Saxon tax: geld

Anglo-Saxon thorn: edh

angrily: hotly

angry: annoyed, cross, exasperated, furious, grim, heated, huffy, incensed, indignant, inflamed, irascible, irate, ired, ireful, livid, mad, outraged, perturbed, raging, resentful, riled, sore, upset

angry argument: altercation

angry behavior: bellicosity

angry color: red

angry criticism: invective, vituperation

angry dispute: wrangle

angry look: glare

angry speech: diatribe, harangue, jeremiad, philippic, tirade

angry stare: glower

angry, moderately: disgruntled

angry, sullen look: lower

angry, unreasonably: petulant

angry, very: apoplectic, incensed, in high dudgeon, livid

anguish: ache, agony, despair, distress, dole, dolor, grief, heartbreak, misery, pain, pang, sorrow, torment, woe

anguish, suffering: travail

anguished: torn

angular: abrupt, awkward, bony,

ANIMAL SPORTS

bronco busting
bullfighting
bull riding
calf roping
camel racing
carriage driving
cockfighting
dog racing
dogsled racing
dressage
equestrian sport
falconry
fishing
greyhound racing
harness racing
horseback riding
horse racing
hunting
pigeon racing
point-to-point
polo
rodeo
show jumping
sled-dog racing
steeplechasing
steer wrestling
three-day-event
trotting
vaulting ❦

ANIMAL TERMS

animal active at night: nocturnal
animal active during the day: diurnal
animal coat: fell, hair, hide, pelt, skin, wool
animal coat band or ridge: cingulum
animal disease that can be transmitted to humans: zoonosis
animal doctor: veterinarian
animal fat: lard, suet
animal for heavy work: beast of burden, draft animal
animal forms in art: zoomorphism
animal in earliest stage of development: embryo
animal life: fauna
animal living with another species: inquiline
animal missing its horns: pollard
animal moving from one region to another: migrant
animal naturalized in region: denizen
animal pouch: marsupium, sac
animal resembling plant: zoophyte
animal science: ethology
animal shell, as for turtle: carapace
animal skin: pelt
animal that lives by killing and eating victims: predator
animal track: spoor
animal without feet: apod
animal worship: zoolatry
animal/plant representative of new species: holotype
animal/plant surviving earlier period: relict
animals of a particular region or period: fauna

big, thick-skinned animal: pachyderm
body of dead animal: carcass
bred from two different species or varieties: hybrid
collection of animals: menagerie, zoo
concerning animals inhabiting land: terrestrial
concerning animals inhabiting trees: arboreal
concerning animals inhabiting water: aquatic, marine
concerning treatment of animal diseases or injuries: veterinary
enclosure for observation and research: vivarium
enclosure: cage, pen, pig sty
establishment of animal in new habitat: ecesis
external parasites: epizoa
harmful animal: vermin
individual animal development: ontogeny
mythical animal: centaur, dragon, griffin, hydra, loch ness, minotaur, phoenix, snark, sphinx, unicorn, yeti
nose and jaws: muzzle, snout
one-celled animal: amoeba, monad, protozoan
preservation of an animal after death: taxidermy
prevent female from reproducing: spay
process of survival and adaptation: natural selection
protective coloring: Batesian mimicry
single-celled animal: protozoan
study of animal behavior: ethology
to cause to multiply or breed: propagate
training to live among people: domestication
warm-blooded and milk-fed animal: mammal ❦

---

crooked, gaunt, lanky, lean, pointed, rawboned, rough, scraggy, scrawny, sharp, skewed, thin

angular distance from a fixed reference, horizontal: azimuth

anima: psyche, soul, spirit

animadversion: accusation, aspersion, blame, censure, criticism, faultfinding, flak, knock, observation, perception, slur

animate: actuate, alive, arouse, energize, enhearten, enliven, ensoul, excite, exhilarate, inspire, invigorate, liven, perk, prompt, quicken, rouse, spur, stimulate, stir, vitalize, vivify

animated: active, alive, brisk, dynamic, enliven, enthusiastic, glowing, happy, keen, live, lively, peppy, snappy, spirited, sprightly, vigorous, vivacious, vivid, zestful, zippy

animation: action, glow, life, sparkle, vigor, zap, zing

animation frame: cel

animosity: anger, animus, antagonism, dislike, hate, hostility, malice, rancor, resentment

animus: bile, hostility

anise liqueur: pernod

ankle: astragalus, talus, tarsus

ankle bone: talus

ankle bumps on either side: malleolus

ankle chains: fetters, manacles, shackles

ankle covering over shoe: gaiter, spat

anna: Indian coin

annals: archives, chronicles, history, journal, publication, records

annals entry: event

anneal: fuse, harden, heat, strengthen, temper, toughen

annelid: worm

annex: acquire, add, affix, appropriate, arrogate, attach, connect, ell, extension, fasten, hook, join, procure, secure, seize, tag, unite, win, wing

annihilate: crush, decimate, demolish, destroy, devour, eradicate, erase, exterminate, extinguish, kill, massacre, murder, negate, nullify, obliterate, rout, slay, squash

annihilation of a people: genocide

anniversary: celebration, commemoration, festival, recurrence

anniversary, hundredth: centennial

anniversary, thousandth: millenniary

annoint: anele

annotate: comment, define, explain, expound, footnote, gloss, illustrate, interpret, remark

annotate between lines: interline

announce: advertise, assert, blast, blazon, broadcast, declare, divulge, drum, foretell, herald, inform, introduce, post, present, proclaim, promulgate, publish, report, signify, sound, state, tell

announce officially: declare, herald, proclaim, promulgate

announce something secret: divulge

announcement: blurb, briefing, bulletin, communiqué, declaration, decree, manifesto, message, notice, notification, proclamation

announcement of new data: disclosure, revelation

announcement, official: communiqué, proclamation

announcer: anchorperson, broadcaster, emcee, newscaster

annoy: aggravate, agitate, badger, bait, bother, bug, chafe, displease, distress, disturb, exasperate, faze, fret, gall, get, harry, heckle, ire, irk, irritate, molest, nag, nettle, offend, peeve, pester, provoke, rile, tease, try, upset, vex

annoy or taunt: heckle

annoy or vex: irk

annoyance: bother, disturbance, fly in the ointment, headache, inconvenience, irritant, nuisance, pest, tailtwister, thorn, worry

annoyance, continuing: bugbear

annoyed: bothered, irked, miffed, sore

annoying: irksome, pesky, pestiferous, pestilential, pesty, vexatious

annoying insect: gnat

annoying person: gadfly

annoying tap sound: drip

annoying youngster: brat

annoyingly slow: poky

annual: anniversary, periodic, yearlong, yearly; flower, plant, weed

annual baseball game: all-star

annual golf classic: open

annual payment of dividends, allowance, or income: annuity

annual publication of reference data: almanac

annul: abolish, abrogate, annihilate, blank, cancel, countermand, disaffirm, dissolve, erase, invalidate, negate, nullify, recall, repeal, rescind, undo, void

annular coral island: atoll

anodyne: anesthetic, narcotic, painkiller, sedative, soother, tranquilizer

anoint: anele, bless, consecrate, crown, grease, rub, sanctify

anoint in olden times: anele

anointing in ritual: unction

anointing liquid: oil

anointing oil and balsam mixture: chrism

anomalous: aberrant, abnormal, bizarre, deviant, eccentric, incongruous, peculiar, rare, strange, unusual

anon: afterward, again, directly, ere long, immediately, later, presently, shortly, soon, then, tomorrow

anonymous: incognito, nameless, secret, unidentified, unknown, unnamed, unsigned

anonymous author for named author: ghostwriter

anorak: parka

anorexia, self-induced vomiting related to: binge-purge syndrome, bulimarexia, bulimia, bulimia nervosa

another: added, additional, different, extra, fresh, further, more, second

anpery: damask

anserine bird: goose

answer: acknowledge, argue, defense, fulfill, meet, plea, react, refute, reply, respond, response, retort, return, satisfy, say, serve, solution, suit, wisecrack

answer in kind: retaliate

answer in one syllable: monosyllable

answer or response: antiphon, replication

answer or retort: rejoinder, repartee, riposte

answer sharply: retort

answer, deliberately vague in: evasive

answer, witty, that occurs to one when it is too late: esprit d'escalier

answerable: accountable, amenable, chargeable, obliged, subject

answered: rejoined

answering objection or argument before it has been put forth: prolepsis

ant: amazon, atta, carpenter, driver, emmet, pismire, soldier, termite

ant adjective form: formic

ant-eating: myrmecophagous

ant genus: eciton

ant male: ergataner

ant mound: hill

ant nest: colony, drone, formicary, mound

ant queen: kelep, ponerine

antaean: huge

Antaeus father: Poseidon

Antaeus mother: Gaea

antagonism: animus, antipathy, competition, conflict, contention, dislike, friction, hatred, hostility, opposition, rancor, rivalry

antagonist: adversary, attacker, battler, competitor, enemy, foe, match, opponent, rival

antagonist, threatening: nemesis

antagonistic: bitter, clashing, contrary, counter, dissonant, hostile, opposed, unfriendly

antagonistic and hostile: inimical

antagonistic reaction: backlash

antagonize: oppose, set at odds

ante: pay, pot, price, stake, wager

anteater of Asia, Africa: pangolin

antebellum: prewar

antecedent: ancestor, blood, cause, earlier, foregoing, forerunner, former, line, past, precursor, predecessor, previous, prior, reason

anted up: paid

antedate: antecede, anticipate, backdate, precede

antediluvian: ancient, antiquated, archaic, obsolete, old, timeworn

antelope: agacella, blesbok, bongo, bushbuck, chamois, cnu, defassa, eland, gazelle, gnu, goa, grimme, hartebeest, impala, koba, lelwel, nagor, oribi, oryx, puku, reedbuck, springbok, takin, topi, tora, waterbuck

antelope, four-horned: chikara, chousingha

antelope, relative of the goral: elands, gnus, serow, serow antelopes

antenna: aerial, feeler, palp, receiver, wire

anterior: antecedent, atlantal, before, earlier, foregoing, former, forward, front, preceding, previous, prior

anterior forearm bones: radii

anthem: antiphony, chant, choral, melody, motet, music, psalm, responsory, song

anthill or ant farm: formicary

anthill, termite nest: termitarium

anthology: album, analect, book, choice, collection, compilation, excerpts, garland, miscellany, selection, treasury

anthology of literary extracts: chrestomathy

anthology of one author's works: omnibus

anthology of scholarly writings for occasion: festschrift

anthology of various writings: collectanea, miscellany

anthracite: coal

anthropoid: ape, chimpanzee, gibbon, gorilla, humanoid, monkey, orang, orangutan, primate

anti: adversary, against, antagonist, foe, opposed

anti-flood embankment: levee

anti-government: anarchic

anti-guerrilla government action: counterinsurgency

anti-intellectual: obscurant, philistine

anti-smoking view: misocapnia

antibody: lysin

antibody carrier: serum

antibody destruction of bacteria: lysis

antic: comic, dido, droll, escapades, gambado, jape, joke, lark, ludicrous, playful, prank, romp, shenanigan, stunt

anticipate: assume, augur, await, counter, expect, figure, forecast, foresee, forestall, foretaste, hope, obviate, outguess, precipitate, predict, prepare, see

anticipate and make unnecessary: obviate, preempt

anticipate before something starts: prolepsis

anticipation: augury, expectation, foresight, inkling, intuition, presentiment, readiness

anticipatory: prevenient

anticlimax: bathos

anticommunist movement of 1950s U.S.: McCarthyism

antidotal: alexipharmic

antidote: antitoxin, antivenin, corrective, negator, neutralizer, preventive, remedy

antidote to poison: mithridate

antidote to poison from blood of immunized animal: serum

antiestablishment: iconoclastic

antifeminists: misogynists

antifreeze chemical: ethylene glycol

antipasto garnish: olive

antipathy: abhorrence, allergy, animosity, antagonism, aversion, disgust, dislike, hatred, hostility, loathing, odium, rancor

antipodal: contrary, counter, diametric, opposed, opposite

antipodean avifauna type: emu

antiquated: aged, ancient, antediluvian, archaic, dated, elderly, hoary, old, outdated, outmoded, outworn, passé, primitive

antique: aged, artifact, classic, curio, heirloom, museum piece, old, relic, timeworn, venerable, vestige, vintage, virtu

antique store offering: curio

antiques expert: antiquary

antiques, knowledge of or taste for: virtu

antiques, pertaining to: antiquarian

antiquing material: ager

antiquity: eld, oldness

antiseptic: alcohol, disinfectant, germicide, hygienic, iodine, iodol, peroxide, phenol, pure, purifying, sterile

antisocial: alienated, anarchistic, hostile, introverted, misanthropic, rebellious, reclusive, solitary

antisocial person: cacogen

antisocial personality disorder, person with: psychopath, sociopath

antithesis: antipode, contrast, opposite, reversal

antitoxin: antibiotic, antidote, serum, vaccine

antler: deerhorn, horn, knob, point, rack, spike

antler branch: prong, tine

antler section: brow, crown, royal, snag, trestine

antler, falling off like an: deciduous

antler, flattened part of: palm

antlike wood-eating insect: termite

ants forcing ants of other group to do their work: helotism

ants, study of: myrmecology

ants, swarming like: formicate

anus-controlling muscle: sphincter

anus, area between genitals and: perineum

anus, surgical creation of: colostomy

anvil: bickern, converter, forge, includes, smithy, stithy

anxiety: anger, angst, anguish, apprehension, butterflies, chagrin, concern, disquiet, disquietude, doubt, dread, fear, foreboding, fuss, jitters, misgiving, panic, suspense, worry

anxiety about health, overactive: hypochondria

anxiety and agitation: dither

anxiety, persistently causing: niggling

anxiety, sense of evil: foreboding, premonition

anxiety, serving to reduce: anxiolytic

anxious: antsy, apprehensive, ardent, atip, concerned, distraught, disturbed, eager, expectant, fearful, fraught, hyper, impatient, keen, overwrought, perturbed, restless, solicitous, uneasy, uptight, watchful, yearning

anxious, in suspense: on tenterhooks

any: each, either, every, much, part, quantity, some, whatever

any which way: willy-nilly

anybody: everyone, masses, someone

anyhow: even so

anyplace: wherever

anything of value: asset

anything that can go wrong will go wrong: Murphy's Law

anyway: anyhow, nevertheless, random, regardless

aorta: artery

apace: posthaste, quickly, rapidly, speedily, swiftly

apart: alone, aside, asunder, detached, dissociated, distinct, divorced, enisled, freely, individually, isolated, reserved, secluded, separate, separately, split

apart and in pieces: piecemeal

apart from others: alone

apart or into pieces: asunder

apartment: abode, building, co-op, digs, dwelling, flat, pad, penthouse, rental, rooms, suite, tenement, unit

apartment building or apartment owned and operated by tenants: co-op, cooperative

apartment dweller: renter

apartment for occasional use: pied-à-terre

apartment house with separately owned units: condominium

apartment on three floors: triplex

apartment on top floor of larger building: penthouse

apartment on two floors: duplex

apartment with rooms in straight line: railroad apartment, railroad flat

apartment with tenant as owner of unit and joint owner of common elements: condo, condominium

apartment, one-room furnished: bedsitter

apartment, one-room with kitchenette, bathroom: efficiency

apartment, part-time or temporary: pied-à-terre

apathetic: blah, blase, cold, dull, flat, impassive, indifferent, inert, limp, listless, passive, phlegmatic, sluggish, stoic, unemotional, unfeeling, uninterested, unmoved

apathy: coolness, detachment, disregard, doldrums, heedlessness, impassivity, languor, lassitude, lethargy, phlegm, torpor, unconcern

ape: baboon, chimpanzee, gelada, gibbon, gorilla, orangutan, pongidae, simian; copy, emulate, imitate, impersonate, mime, mimic, mirror, parrot

ape, chimpanzee, or gorilla: troglodyte

ape, monkey, or human, pertaining to: primate

ape, pertaining to: pongid, simian

apelike and manlike: hominid

apercu: conspectus, glance, insight, outline, sketch, syllabus

aperitif: antipasto, appetizer, cocktail, drink

aperture: chasm, cleft, crack, fissure, gap, hole, leak, opening, orifice, outlet, perforation, puncture, slit, slot, vent, window

apes, group of: shrewdness, troop

apex: acme, climax, crest, crown, culmination, cusp, max, meridian, peak, pinnacle, point, quintessence, summit, tip, top, tops, vertex, zenith

aphid eater: earwig

aphorism: adage, apothegm, axiom, dictum, epigram, moral, motto, precept, proverb, saw, saying, slogan

aphoristic: gnomic

aphrodisiac made from beetles: cantharides, Spanish fly

apian abode: hive

apian matriarch: queen

apiary: beehive, beehouse, hive

apiary sound: hum

apiece: each, individually, per, respectively, severally, singly

apish: affected, emulative, slavish

aplomb: assurance, balance, confidence, coolness, equanimity, nerve, nonchalance, poise, surety, tact

apocalyptic: fateful, ominous, oracular, predictive, prophetic, revealing

apocopate: elide

apocryphal: counterfeit, disputed, doubtful, dubious, fabricated, false, fictitious, sham, unauthentic, unreal, untrue

apodal fish: eel

apogee: acme, apex, climax, crest, peak, pinnacle, summit, zenith

apologetic: atoning, contrite, deprecatory, expiatory, penitent, regretful, remorseful, supplicating, vindicatory

apologetic person: Milquetoast

apologue: allegory, fable, legend, parable, story

apology: amends, atonement, excuse, explanation, penitence, regret, remorse, vindication

apostate: deserter, disloyal, dissident, faithless, heretic, renegade, traitor, turncoat

apostatize: secede

apostle: Bartholomew, companion, disciple, evangelist, follower, James, Judas, Jude, Matthew, Matthias, messenger, Paul, Peter, Philip, pioneer, preacher, Silas, Simon, teacher, Thomas, witness

apothecary: dispenser, druggist, gallipot, pharmacist

apothecary unit: dram

apothegm: adage, aphorism, axiom, dictum, maxim, moral, proverb, saying, truism

apotheosis: ideal

apotheosize: adore

appall: astound, daunt, disgust, dismay, faze, frighten, horrify, insult, repel, revolt, shock, stun, terrify

appalling: alarming, awful, dire, dreadful, fearful, frightful, gross, outraged, shocking, terrible

appanage: adjunct, endowment, perquisite, prerogative, privilege, right

apparatus: appliance, contraption, device, doohickey, equipment, gadget, gear, gizmo, material, network, outfit, setup, tool, trappings, utensil

apparatus, self-running: automaton

apparel: adorn, attire, clothes, clothing, costume, dress, duds, embellish, furnishings, garb, garment, habit, robe, robes, suit, togs, vesture, wardrobe, wear

apparent: blatant, clear, discernible, distinct, evident, glaring, likely, manifest, noticeable, obvious, ostensible, overt, patent, plain, probable, supposed, unequivocal

apparent and obvious: manifest

apparent but not real: superficial

apparent meaning: purport

apparently: reputedly

apparently but not really: quasi

apparently true but not really: specious

apparition: appearance, bogeyman, bogie, delusion, eidolon, fantasy, ghost, haunt, hobgoblin, illusion, phantom, phenomenon, revenant, shadow, spirit, spook, wraith

apparition of live person: wraith

apparition or ghost: specter

apparition series: phantasmagoria

appeal: address, allure, approach, attraction, beauty, beg, beseech, bid, call, entice, implore, plea, plead, propose, request, seek, solicit, summon, supplicate

appeal for: invoke, solicit

appeal for help: SOS

appeal for urgently: adjure, beseech, entreat, exhort, implore, supplicate

appeal through mystery: mystique

appeal, earnest: cri de coeur

appeal, fascinating: allure, charisma

appealing: agreeable, attractive, cute, emanate, engaging, entrancing, lovable, nice, pleading, present, tempting

appealing to emotions: ad hominem, affective

appealing to greed: ad crumenam

appealing to prejudice: ad hominem

appealing to sentiment: ad populum

appeals court decision, person who: appellant

appear: arise, arrive, bob up, emerge, enter, issue, loom, materialize, occur, seem, show one's face

appear and materialize: manifest

appear between two things: intervene

appear ominously: loom

appear to do, falsely: purport

appearance: advent, arrival, aspect, attitude, countenance, debut, demeanor, disclosure, display, facade, front, guise, illusion, look, manner, mien, physiognomy, semblance, shape, show, sight, state, view

appearance changed by age, behavior, use: patina

appearance-improving: cosmetic

appearance of something else, adopt: mimic, simulate

appearance of truth or reality: verisimilitude

appearance or aspect: mien, visage

appearance, character revealed by: physiognomy

appearance, deceptive: façade, gloss, veneer

appearance, demeanor: mien

appearance, description of a person's: prosopography

appearance, false: guise

appearance, outward: guise, semblance

appearance, spoiled in: deformed, disfigured, misshapen

appearance, true: verisimilitude

appeared: arose, came, emerged, looked, seemed

appearing correct: specious

appease: allay, assuage, conciliate, diminish, ease, gratify, mitigate, mollify, pacify, placate, please, quell, quiet, satisfy, slake, soften, solace, subdue, tranquilize

appease and pacify: placate

appease and receive goodwill: propitiate

appease with lies: fob off

appellation: cognomen, designation, epithet, handle, label, moniker, name, nickname, title

append: add, add on, annex, attach, clip, fasten, fix, hang, join, subjoin

appendage: accessory, addition, adjunct, antenna, ear, extension, extra, extremity, leg, limb, member, offshoot, parasite, rider, suffix, supplement, tab, tag, tail, wing

appendix: addendum, addition, epilogue, organ, postscript, rider, supplement, table

appendix removal by surgery: appendectomy

appendix to will: codicil

appertain: apply, belong, concern, pertain, refer, relate, vest

appetite: craving, desire, gluttony, gusto, hankering, hunger, liking, longing, lust, passion, penchant, propensity, taste, tendency, urge, wanting, zest

appetite for living: zest

appetite for nonfood substances: pica

appetite impossible to satisfy: insatiable

appetite-stimulating drink: aperitif

appetite whetter: aroma

appetite, having a large: ravenous, voracious

appetite, increase: whet

appetite, indulge the: sate, satiate

appetite, voracious: edacity

appetizer: antipasto, canapé, cocktail, delicacy, hors d'oeuvre, munchies, sample, savory, snack, teaser, tidbit

appetizer consisting of meats, cheese, fish, vegetables: antipasto

appetizer of oysters wrapped in bacon on toast: angels on horseback

appetizer, bread or cracker and spread: canapé

appetizer, Italian: antipasto

appetizer, raw vegetable: crudités

appetizing: savory, succulent, toothsome

appetizing but out of reach: tantalizing

appetizing treat: bonne bouche

applaud: acclaim, approve, boost, cheer, clap, compliment, encourage, endorse, extol, hail, kudo, plug, praise, root

applause: accolades, bravos, cheers, clapping, hand, hurrahs, kudos, ovation, plaudits, praise

applause or praise: acclaim, accolade

applause, group hired to offer: claque

applause, long and enthusiastic: ovation

applause, reappearance of cast to acknowledge: curtain call

apple acid: malic

apple beverage: applejack, calvados, cider, juice

apple center: core

apple dessert: crisp, strudel

apple growth retardant: alar

apple of one's eye: darling, favorite, pet, pupil

apple or fruit with several seed chambers and flesh: pome

apple-pie maker: mom

apple-pitter: corer

apple pulp after pressing: pomace

apple salad with celery, walnuts, raisins, in mayonnaise: Waldorf salad

apple seed: pip

apple, unripe: codling

applesauce: baloney, bunk, fudge, hogwash, hokum, hooey, malarkey, nonsense, poppycock, pulp, rubbish

appliance: apparatus, device, fixture, gadget, instrument, tool, utensil

applicable: apposite, befitting, fit, fitting, germane, kosher, meet, pertinent, proper, relative, suitable, useful

applicable and pertinent: relevant

applicant: appellant, aspirant, candidate, prospect, suitor

applicant's preparation: resume

application: appeal, blank, claim, debate, diligence, effort, employment, form, industry, operation, petition, play, relevance, study, usage, use

application of branch of learning, practical: praxis

apply: address, administer, allude, appeal, bend, bestow, commit, conform, cover, direct, employ, exercise, exert, fit, impose, overlay, persevere, pertain, petition, relate, rub, solicit, suit, superimpose, use, utilize

apply an ax: hew

apply badly: misuse

apply bandages: dress

apply for formally: petition, solicit

apply force: exert

apply oneself: knuckle down

apply plaster: ceil

apply unction: anele

appoint: allot, arrange, assign, authorize, choose, commission, confirm, decree, delegate, designate, direct, elect, equip, furnish, inset, name, ordain, outfit, select, set, tap

appoint as one's representative: commission, delegate, depute

appoint or elect new member to group: co-opt

APPLES

Anna	Earliblaze	Jerseymac	Pippin	Spartan
Arctic	Early Harvest	Jonared	Porter	Starkrimson
Arkansas Black	Ein Shemer	Jonathan	Prima	Starr
Bailey Sweet	Empire	Lady Sweet	Priscilla	Stayman
Baldwin	English Sweet	Liberty	Rambo	Twenty Ounce
Belmont	Freedom	Lodi	Red Delicious	Tydeman's Red
Ben Davis	Gala	Longfield	Red Rome	Virginia Beauty
Blue Permain	Gideon	Macoun	Redfree	Wealthy
Braeburn	Golden Delicious	McIntosh	Rhode Island Greening	Williams
Bramley	Golden Harvest	McMahon		Winesap
Buckingham	Granny Smith	Missouri	Roman Stem	Winter Banana
Collins	Gravenstein	Monroe	Rome	Yellow Transparent
Cortland	Green Sweet	Mutsu	Rome Beauty	York Imperial ❦
Cox's Orange Pippin	Grimes Golden	Newton Pippin	Roxbury Russet	
Criterion	Hubbardston	Northern Spy	Russet	
Delicious	Idared	Oldenburg	Saint Lawrence	
Doctor	Ingram	Ortley	Sir Prize	
Dorset Golden	Jersey Black	Permain	Snowapple	

appoint to or recommend for office: name, nominate

appoint to position or to perform task: constitute, designate

appointment: assignment, berth, date, engagement, job, meeting, office, position, post, rendezvous, station, tryst; nomination, nominee

appointment and meeting place: rendezvous

appointment book: calendar

appointment for a specific time: date

appointment, secret lovers': tryst

apportion: allocate, allot, assess, assign, award, consign, deal, distribute, lot, mete, partition, prorate, quota, ration, share, split

apportion differently: reallocate

apportioned: dealt

apportionment: allotment, allowance, dividend, division, measure, part, share

apposite: germane, pertinent, relevant, suitable, timely

appraise: adjudicate, analyze, assess, check, estimate, evaluate, gauge, inspect, judge, rate, survey, value

appreciable: apparent, definite, discernible, evident, large, noticeable, obvious, tangible

appreciate: admire, adore, enjoy, esteem, gain, increase, judge, like, love, prize, realize, recognize, respect, treasure, understand, value, welcome

appreciation: admiration, enjoyment, gratitude, growth, recognition, testimonial, thanks, tribute

appreciation for fine art: virtuosity

appreciative: grateful

apprehend: anticipate, arrest, bust, capture, catch, collar, comprehend, detain, fathom, foresee, get, know, nab, nail, perceive, recognize, see, seize, take, view

apprehending: sensate

apprehension: alarm, anticipation, anxiety, arrest, concern, dismay, distrust, doubt, dread, idea, intellection, misgiving, mistrust, suspicion, taking, trepidation, uneasiness, worry

apprehension and doubt: misgiving

apprehension and dread: angst

apprehensive: afraid, anxious, conscious, fearful, jumpy, misgiving, morbid, nervous, stiff, suspicious, uneasy

apprentice: amateur, intern, learner, neophyte, novitiate, novice, pupil, rookie, student, tenderfoot, trainee

apprenticed: articled

apprise: acquaint, advise, disclose, enlighten, inform, notify, tell, value, warn

apprised of: in on

approach: access, address, adit, advance, approximate, avenue, come, feel, gate, impend, landing, loom, near, onset, overture, passage, procedure, reach, start, way

approach a point from different directions: converge

approach aggressively to speak to: accost

approach boldly: waltz up to

approach evasively: lead up to

approach involving trial and error, self-learning: heuristic

approach or bring up a problem: broach

approach or come close to: approximate

approach or proposal: overture

approach prey stealthily: stalk

approach slowly in trespass: encroach

approach, means of: access

approbation: admiration, applause, blessing, compliment, esteem, favor, praise, regard, respect, support

appropriate: applicable, apt, convenient, deserved, due, fit, fitting, germane, meet, pertinent, proper, related, relevant, suitable, timely, worthy

appropriate and applicable: relevant

appropriate beforehand: preempt

appropriate for purpose or time: felicitous, opportune, seemly

appropriate ideas: plagiarize

appropriate, to: annex, borrow, claim, confiscate, co-opt, earmark, embezzle, grab, pilfer, pirate, pocket, preempt, purloin, reserve, take, use, usurp

appropriation: allotment, allowance, budgeting, seizure, stipend, subsidy, takeover

approval: approbation, assent, blessing, consent, favor, liking, okay, permission, sanction, seal, support

approval and praise: approbation, commendation, kudos, plaudits

approval, official, of artistic work: nihil obstat

approve: accept, accredit, admire, adopt, agree, allow, applaud, authorize, back, compliment, consent, endorse, favor, handle, initial, like, okay, pass, ratify, sanction, sign, uphold, validate

approve and support: countenance

approve formally: endorse, ratify, sanction, validate

approve of belief: subscribe

approximate: about, almost, approach, close, estimate, guess, near, reach, resemble, similar, surmised

approximated abbr.: est.

approximately: about, almost, around, bordering, circa, generally, nearly, or so, practically, relatively, roughly, virtually

approximately 18 inches: cubit

approximation: ballpark figure

appurtenance: accessory, addition, annex, apparatus, appendage, appendix, attachment, component

apron: airstrip, cover, pinafore, protection, shield, smock, stagefront, tier

apropos: about, appropriate, apt, concerning, correct, fit, fitting, meet, proper, relevant, seemly, suitable, timely

apropos of: aline, in re

apse: chevet

apt: able, adept, alert, appropriate, apropos, astute, capable, competent, disposed, fitting, gifted, inclined, keen, likely, pat, pertinent, proficient, prone, quick, ready, savvy, skillful, talented, tendency

aptitude: ability, capacity, disposition, flair, genius, gift, inclination, knack, leaning, propensity, talent

aquainted, familiar with subject: conversant

aquarium: fishbowl, pool, tank

aquarium sediment in tank bottom: mulm

aquatic grass: reed

aqueduct: canal, channel, conductor, conduit, passage, pipeline, watercourse, waterworks

arable: cultivable, farmable, plowable, tillable

arachnid: harvestman, mite, scorpion, spider, tarantula, tick

arachnid's creation: web

Aran coal: peat

arbiter: judge, maven, middleperson, moderator, referee, umpire

arbitrary: absolute, autocratic, bossy, capricious, chance, erratic, high-

ARABIAN TERMS

Arab chieftain: emir
Arab garment: aba, burnoose
Arab headdress band: agal
Arab marketplace: suk
Arab provincial governor: vali
Arab quarter of Algiers: Casbah
Arab sailing vessel: zebec
Arabian arroyo: wadi
Arabian confection: marzipan
Arabian drink: boza
Arabian gazelle: ariel
Arabian kettledrum: atabal
Arabic diacritical mark like apostrophe: hamza
Arabic name for the supreme being: Allah ❦

___

handed, imperious, irrational, offhand, random, tyrannical, unreasonable, willful
arbitrary decree: ukase
arbitrate: decide, determine, intercede, mediate, negotiate, settle, smooth
arbitrator: conciliator, mediator, moderator, referee, umpire
arbor: axle, beam, bower, gazebo, pavilion, pergola, retreat, spindle, summerhouse
arbor bower: pergola
arbor with latticework roof: pergola
arbor, in Spain: ramada
arboreal marsupial: koala
arc: arch, azimuth, bend, bow, curve, half-moon, halo, orbit, rainbow
arc, ninety-degree: quadrant
arcade: colonnade, gallery, passageway, skywalk
arcade open on one side: loggia
Arcadia: Eden, paradise, utopia, Zion
arcane: cabalistic, enigmatic, esoteric, mystic, occult, secret
arch: bend, bow, bridge, curve, hump, ogee, ogive, span
arch and lintel, recessed space between: tympanum
arch essential: keystone
arch or arbor, latticework: trellis
arch rib: ogive
arch that curves in reverse before the point: ogee arch
arch, narrow and pointed: lancet arch
archaeological excavation: dig
archaeological find: ruins
archaeological mound: barrow
archaeological research location: site

archaeological tool: trowel
archaic: ancient, antiquated, antique, dated, historic, obsolete, old, outmoded, passé, venerable
archaic age: eld
archaic cave: antre
archaic cows: kine
archaic miss: spinster
archaic rascal: varlet
archangel: Gabriel, Michael, Raphael, Uriel
archbishop, relating to: archiepiscopal
archdeacon, relating to: archidiaconal
arched building or part of building: arcade
arched handle: bail
arched like bow: arcuate
arched structure or covering: vault
arched structure or fold, as brain, cave etc.: fornix
arched surface of airfoil, road, ski, ship deck: camber
archer: bowman, toxophilite
archer's wood: yew
archery contest: main
archery target center: bull's-eye, clout
archetype: example, exemplar, idea, ideal, model, original, paradigm, pattern, prototype
archfiend: Satan
archipelago member: isle
architect: artist, author, builder, creator, designer, draftsperson, engineer, founder, innovator, planner
archival unit: annal
archive: chronicle, document, library, museum, papers, record, registry, scrolls, writings
arcing throw: lob
arctic: bitter, boreal, chilly, cold, cool, freezing, frigid, frosty, gelid, glacial, hyperborean, icy, nippy, polar
Arctic abode: igloo
Arctic fish: char
arctic gear: snowshoe
Arctic group: Inuits
arctic gull: xema
Arctic phenomenon: ice cap
arctic region between ice cap and treeline: tundra
arctic transportation: reindeer, sled
arctic, frigid: hyperborean
ardent: ablaze, avid, devoted, eager, earnest, enthusiastic, feeling, fervent, fervid, fiery, flaming, fond, impetuous, intense, keen, passionate, shining, spirited, steadfast, torrid, vehement, warm, zealous

ARCHITECTURAL TERMS

architectural drawing: rendu
architectural order, Greek fluted colums, simple capitals: Doric
architectural order, Greek ornate, bell-shaped capitals: Corinthian
architectural order, Greek scrolled capitals: Ionic
architectural style: Adam, Doric, Ionic, Romanesque, Tudor
architectural views: cross sections
architecture: building, constitution, design, framework, planning
architecture and design, science of: architectonics
band: fascia
block on which column/statue stands: plinth
block that projects: dentil
border: orle
column: anta
curve: groin
dovetails: tenons
fillet: orle, reglet
gable: pediment
harmony: eurhythmy
leaf: acanthus
moldings: ogees, tori
person skilled at architectural drawing: draftsman, draftsperson
pier: anta
relating to architecture: tectonic
relating to architecture style of region, culture, period: vernacular
rooflike fronting or gable: pediment ❦

___

ardent admirers: fans
ardent and fervid: perfervid
ardent and impetuous: vehement
ardent and passionate: torrid
ardor: animation, desire, devotion, élan, enthusiasm, feeling, fire, glow, gusto, heat, intensity, keenness, love, oomph, passion, spirit, verve, vivacity, zeal, zest
ardor, intense: fervor
arduous: backbreaking, difficult, exacting, exhausting, laborious, lofty, murder, steep, strenuous, tight, tiring, tough, trying, uphill
arduous journey: trek
arduous work: toil
area: bailiwick, block, city, county, district, expanse, extent, field, locale, neighborhood, parcel, province,

ARCHITECTURAL STYLES

academic	Colonial Revival	French Colonial	Jacobean Style	Perpendicular
American colonial	Decorated Style	Style	Japanese	Persian
American Georgian	early American	French Renaissance	Jesuit	postmodernism
Anglo-Saxon	early Christian	functionalism	kinetic	Queen Anne Style
Art Deco	early English	Georgian	Louis Quatorze Style	Regency
Art Moderne	early Gothic	German	Louis Quinze	Renaissance
Art Nouveau	early Renaissance	German Renaissance	Mannerism	rococo
baroque	earthwork	Gothic	Mayan	Roman
Bauhaus	ecological	Greco-Roman	Medieval	Romanesque
Beaux Arts	Edwardian Style	Greek	Mesopotamian	Romanesque Revival
brutalism	Egyptian	Greek Revival	Minoan	Romantic
Byzantine	Elizabethan	high Renaissance	Modernism	Spanish
Carolingian	Empire Style	hi-tech	Moorish	transitional
Chicago School	English	Incan	Mudejar Style	Tudor
Chinese	English Georgian	Indian	neoclassical	Utopian
churrigueresque	English Renaissance	International Style	neo-Gothic	Victorian
classical	Federal Style	Islamic	new brutalism	Victorian Gothic ❦
Classical Revival	flamboyant style	Italian	Norman	
colonial	French	Italian Gothic	Palladianism	

range, realm, region, scene, section, sector, size, space, state, territory, township, tract, turf, vicinity, zone

area controlled by someone: bailiwick, domain, dominion, fiefdom, parish, realm

area drained by river, body of water: catchment

area east of the nave: chancel

area enclosed in a larger area: enclave

area of activity: arena

area of authority or competency: bailiwick

area of competition: arena

area of influence: sphere

area of land: acreage, demesne, expanse, tract

area served by school, hospital, etc.: catchment area

area unclaimed and indefinite: no-man's-land

area unit: acre

area where event occurred: locale

area without trees: clearing

arena: amphitheater, battlefield, bowl, coliseum, court, field, gridiron, hippodrome, oval, province, ring, rink, sphere, square, stade, stadium, stage

arena bull: toro

arena cheer: olé

arena combatant of ancient Rome: gladiator

arena for circus, horse shows: hippodrome

arena for jousting: list

arena for sports, spectacles: amphitheater

areola: halo, stoma

arête: crag, crest, ridge

argent: shining, silver, silvery, white

argot: cant, dialect, idiom, jargon, ling, lingo, patois, slang, vernacular

arguable: disputable

arguable, subject to debate: moot

argue: battle, bicker, claim, clash, conflict, contend, contest, cross, debate, disagree, discuss, dispute, expostulate, hassle, induce, maintain, moot, persuade, plead, quarrel, quibble, reason, remonstrate, spar

argue a case: plead

argue against: rebut

argue against and disprove: rebut, refute

argue and deny: controvert, gainsay, oppugn, repudiate

argue and quarrel: bicker

argue and reason against: expostulate, remonstrate

argue back: counter, retort

argue earnestly: contend

argue earnestly about bad plan: expostulate

argue in court: plead

argue needlessly: cavil, quibble, split hairs

argue noisily: wrangle

argue price: haggle

argue with: reason

arguer about trivia: stickler

arguer for the sake of argument: devil's advocate

arguer over small details: stickler

arguing and proving irrelevant: ignoratio elenchi

arguing with new evidence or on minor point: special pleading

argument: altercation, beef, brawl, case, combat, controversy, debate, defense, difference, discourse, fight, flap, fuss, hassle, plea, plot, polemic, quarrel, reason, rhubarb, run-in, scene, spat, squabble, statement, stew, summary, tiff, words

argument emphasizing single aspect of issue: special pleading

argument fine point: quodlibet

argument from general to particular, relating to: a priori, analytical, deductive

argument from particular to general, relating to: a posteriori, empirical, inductive, pedagogical

argument is based, proposition upon which an: premise

argument of philosophical or theological issue: quodlibet

argument of work, indicated in title: lemma

argument on facts, to base an: predicate

argument or debate rhet.: agon, tune

argument or investigation, something said to be true for the purpose of: hypothesis, working hypothesis

ARMOR TERMS

arm covering: rerebrace, vambrace
armor: bulwark, covering, defense, guard, mail, plate, protection, sheath, shield, tace
armor and full equipment of warrior: panoply
armor for horse's head: chamfron
armor for horse's neck: crinet, serene, tasse
armor piece: tace
bearer of armor for knight: armiger, squire
chain mail garment: hauberk
chest armor: breastplate, cuirass

foot armor: poulaine
garment worn over armor and bearing coat of arms: tabard
helmet: armet, beaver, brow reinforce, crest, gorget, nose, skull, ventail, visor
hinged piece on helmet: beaver
hook-and-loop clasp: agraffe
leg armor: greave, poleyn
padded tunic worn under armor: gipon, jupon
waist armor: tasset, tunic ❦

---

argument over doctrine, principle: polemic
argument that is illogical, spurious, or complicated: casuistry, choplogic, sophistry
argument that is series of incomplete syllogisms: sorites
argument with implied premise or conclusion: enthymeme
argument, able to withstand powerful: incontrovertible, irrefutable, unassailable
argument, acknowledgment of a good: touché
argument, convincing as in: cogent, compelling, incisive, trenchant
argument, disprove or weaken an: invalidate, nullify, vitiate, void
argument, false or illogical: paralogism
argument, formal: debate
argument, heated: altercation, confrontation, contretemps
argument, intended to trap as in: insidious
argument, involved in an: embroiled
argument, irrefutable as an: ironclad, watertight
argument, maintainable in: tenable
argument, noisy: ruction
argument, proposition maintained by: thesis
argument, relating to: eristic
argument, to cite as example or proof in: adduce
argument, to put forward for the sake of: posit, postulate
argumentation: forensics
argumentative: agonistic, belligerent, contrary, disputatious, eristic, indicative, rhetorical, scrappy, shrill, testy, touchy
arguments to arrive at truth, use of logical: dialectic

arguments, someone who likes to start: breedbate
argus-eyed: alert
argyles: socks
aria: excerpt, melody, solo, song, tune
aria, for one: solo
arid: bald, bare, barren, boring, desiccated, dry, dull, dusty, flat, jejune, lean, lifeless, moistureless, parched, sere, spiritless, sterile, waterless, withered
arid land: desert
arietta: song, tune
arise: accrue, appear, ascend, awake, begin, come up, derive, develop, emanate, emerge, happen, lift, mount, originate, proceed, raise, soar, spring, stand, stem, surge
aristocracy: gentry
aristocrat: blueblood, gentleperson, noble, nobleman, patrician, peer, ritzy
arithmetic procedure to solve problem in finite number of steps: algorithm
arithmetic result: quotient, sum, total
arithmetic skills, to have: numeracy
arithmetic, to solve problems in: calculate, cipher
arm: bough, branch, extension, hook, inlet, instrument, limb, projection, spur, wing
arm bone: humerus, radius, ulna
arm (elbow to fingertip), ancient measure of length based on: cubit
arm from shoulder to elbow: brachium
arm in arm, walk: oxter
arm joint: elbow, wrist
arm long bone: humerus
arm muscle: biceps, triceps
arm or wing, relating to: brachial
arm, to: enable, equip, fortify, furnish, pack, power, prepare, protect, strengthen, support; weapon

armada: fleet, flotilla, force, squadron, warships
armadillo: apar, apara, mulita, pangolin, peludo, pichiciago, poyou, quirquincho, tatou, tatouay, tatu
armament: defense, heat, munitions, ordnance, safeguard, security, shield, weapons
armamentarium: apparatus, armory, arsenal, collection, equipment, store
armband: armlet, brassard, brassaro, crape, crepe
armchair back covering: antimacassar
armchair strategists: retired generals
armchair, upholstered: fauteuil
armed attack: sortie
armed band: posse
armed conflict: war
armed forces: ranks
armistice: cessation, truce
armlike extension on squid, octopus, etc.: tentacle
armlike wing or flipper: brachium
armoire: clothespress, repository, wardrobe
armory: arsenal, center, depot, factory, field house, magazine, plant, range, warehouse
armpit: axilla, oxter, underarm
armpit, inflamed lymph node in: bubo
armpit, relating to: alar, axillary
arms bent outward with hands on hips: akimbo
arms bound and helpless: pinioned
arms cache: arsenal
arms storage: arsenal
aroma: bouquet, flavor, fragrance, odor, opdor, perfume, redolence, savor, scent, smell, spice
aromatic: ambrosial, fragrant, fruity, odorous, olent, pungent, redolent, savory, scented, spicy, sweet
aromatic case: sachet

ARMY TERMS

army: array, band, battalion, crowd, force, gang, horde, host, legion, militia, pack, soldiers, troops, warriors
army composed of ordinary citizens: militia
army food: mess
army law enforcers: military police, MP
army officers planning, coordinating, supervising operations: general staff
army operations dealing with materiel and personnel: logistics
army post: camp, fort
army unit: brigade, company, detachment, detail, division, outfit, platoon, regiment, squad, troop
camp follower peddling provisions: sutler

department providing food and supplies: commissariat
dismiss from army for disciplinary reasons, to: cashier
eatery: mess hall
enlisted man: doughboy, joe, NCO, private
foot soldiers: infantry
force into army, to: impress, press, press-gangforemost position in an army going into battle: vanguard
government by the army: stratocracy
officer: captain, colonel, general, lieutenant, major, sergeant
officer responsible for food, clothing, equipment: quartermaster
prohibit army or military control: demilitarize
relating to army: martial, military ❦

ARMY RANK

Commissioned Officers
General of the Army
General
Lieutenant General
Major General
Brigadier General
Colonel
Lieutenant Colonel
Major
Captain
First Lieutenant
Second Lieutenant

Warrant Officers
Chief Warrant Officer Five
Chief Warrant Officer Four
Chief Warrant Officer Three
Chief Warrant Officer Two
Warrant Officer One

Enlisted Personnel
Sergeant Major of the Army
Command Sergeant Major
Sergeant Major
First Sergeant
Master Sergeant
Sergeant First Class
Staff Sergeant
Sergeant
Corporal
Specialist
Private First Class
Private ❦

aromatic drink: tea
aromatic fragrance: balm
around: about, circa, encircling, encompassing, enveloping, everywhere, nearby, surrounding, through

arouse: actuate, agitate, alarm, alert, animate, awake, bestir, call, challenge, excite, fire, foment, incite, inflame, kindle, pique, provoke, raise, rally, stimulate, stir, summon, thrill, whet
arouse a memory or emotion: evoke
arouse and thrill: intrigue
arouse curiosity: pique
arouse enthusiasm: wow
arouse from sleep: waken
arouse great enthusiasm: wow
arouse interest or curiosity: intrigue
arouse pleasurably: titillate
aroused easily: hair-trigger
arousing strong emotion: inflammatory, provocative
arpeggio: division, flourish, roulade, scale
arraign: accuse, blame, challenge, charge, cite, impeach, incriminate, indict
arrange: adapt, adjust, align, aline, alphabetize, array, catalog, classify, codify, collocate, conclude, design, devise, edit, file, instrument, negotiate, orchestrate, order, organize, plan, position, prepare, rank, scheme, score, seriate, set, settle, sort, tabulate, tidy
arrange beforehand: preset
arrange elements for desired effect: orchestrate
arrange in an order: align, catalog, codify, digest, dispose, organize
arrange in correspondence with another: coordinate, correlate
arrange in design or layout: format
arrange in groupings: collocate
arrange in soft folds: drape
arrange together, side by side: collocate
arranged in layers: laminar

arranged in symbols for brevity: coded
arranged in threes: tern, ternate
arranged strategically: deployed
arranged under subjects: topical
arrangement: allocation, chart, composition, contract, design, disposition, distribution, format, grouping, index, layout, order, scheme, setup, terms, treaty
arrangement by time: chronology
arrangement of a project's details: logistics
arrangement of elements by rank: hierarchy
arrangement of elements of a set, ordered: permutation
arrangement of five things (square and middle): quincunx
arrangement of literary, artistic, or architectural elements: ordonnance
arrangement of logs: raft
arrangement of parts: configuration, conformation, posture
arrangement of parts, harmonious: concinnity
arrangement of troops: array
arrangement or plan of book, entertainment: format
arrangement, lack an organization or: arbitrary, haphazard, random
arrangement, orderly and gradual: gradation
arranger's container: vase
arranges systematically: files
arrant: blatant, brazen, downright, flagrant, gross, notorious, rascally, shameless, unmitigated, utter, vagrant, wicked
array: adorn, apparel, arrange, assemblage, attire, clad, clothe, deck,

drape, dress, equip, furnish, garb, grouping, host, marshal, order, outfit, parade, robe, series, set, show

array or classify: arrange

arrears: claim, debt, indebtedness, IOUs, liability, obligation

arrest: apprehend, bust, can, capture, collar, custody, detain, deter, grab, halt, hinder, imprison, incarcerate, intercept, jail, nab, nail, net, obstruct, pinch, restrain, run-in, secure, seize, stay, stem, stop

arrest warrant: capias

arrest with legal writ: attach

arrest, informally: nab

arrest, judicial writ to make an: warrant

arrested, the state of being: custody

arrival: advent, coming

arrive: appear, approach, attain, come, dismount, flourish, land, occur, prosper, reach, set in, show, succeed, visit

arrive at: get to, reach

arrogance: affectation, bluster, conceit, egotism, haughtiness, hauteur, hubris, insolence, nerve, pomposity, pride, vanity

arrogant: bossy, cocky, conceited, contemptuous, disdainful, egotistic, haughty, highfalutin, imperious, insolent, insulting, lofty, lordly, on one's high horse, overbearing, overweening, presuming, presumptuous, proud, snooty, supercilious, superior, uppity, vainglorious

arrogant and domineering: imperious, peremptory

arrogant and forward: bumptious, overweening, presumptuous

arrogant in beliefs: dogmatic

arrogant person new to higher status: nouveau riche, parvenu, upstart

arrogate: assume, claim, commandeer, confiscate, demand, preempt, seize, sequester, take, usurp

arrow: bolt, dart, direction, indicator, missile, pin, pointer, reed, rod, shaft, sprite, weapon

arrow case: quiver

arrow dart: shaft

arrow for crossbow: quarrel

arrow maker: fletcher

arrow poison: curare

arrow, blunt, used for target practice: butt arrow

arrow, to feather an: fledge, fletch

arrowlike: sagittal

arrowroot: canna

arrow's barbed head: fluke

arrow's feather: vane

arrow's notch at end that fits onto bowstring: nock

arroyo: brook, channel, creek, gorge, gully, ravine, stream, watercourse

arsenal: armory, depot, dockyard, magazine, stock, stockpile, storehouse, supply, weapons

arsenal stockpile: ammo

arsenate of copper: erinite

arsenic: chemical, poison

arson: set fires

arsonist: firebug, incendiary, pyromaniac

art: baroque, business, classical, contrivance, craft, cubism, cultivation, cunning, expertise, faculty, fauvism, finesse, genre, humanities, impressionism, ingenuity, knack, learning, magic, methods, objectivism, oils, primitivism, profession, realism, renaissance, romanticism, science, skill, surreal, trade, vocation, wile

RELATED TERMS

art aficionado: aesthete

art and literary movement concerning subconscious mind: surrealism

art and technique of motion picture photography: cinematography

art as an end in itself: autotelism

art created by pasting objects on one larger object: collage

art created directly on wall: mural

art exhibit area: salon

art exhibition covering artist's career: retrospective

art expert, of a kind: restorer

art for art's sake: ars gratia artis, l'art pour l'art

art gallery or museum keeper: curator, custodian

art grouping: genre

art made by firing earthenware, porcelain, or brick at high temperatures: ceramics

art movement departing reality and expressing feelings: Expressionism

art movement of the 1950s and 1960s: pop art

art movement to create moods through glimpses of subject: Impressionism

art movement with curvilinear designs: art nouveau

art movement with geometric forms and strong outlines: art deco

art movement, expressionist and bright colors: Fauvism

art movement, foremost position in an: vanguard

art not representing external reality: abstract, nonobjective, nonrepresentational

art object collector: curioso

art of defense: judo

art style from 1550 to 1700 in Europe: Baroque

art style from the eastern part of the Roman Empire: Byzantine

art style of early twentieth-century with geometrics: cubism

art technique of carving a design below the surface of material: intaglio

art transfer: decal

art, appreciation of fine: virtuosity

art, category of: genre

art, cheap and sentimental: kitsch

art, dabbler in: dilettante

art, excessively sentimental: schmaltz

art, expert in: connoisseur

art, one highly sensitive to and appreciative of: aesthete

artist: actor, composer, dancer, expert, master, painter, performer, professional, sculptor, singer, star, virtuoso

artist or literary group: cenacle

artist or writer not working for one employer: freelance

artist studio: atelier

artist, complete works of: corpus, oeuvre

artist, unconventional: Bohemian

artistic arrangement of elements: composition

artistic article: objet d'art

artistic category: genre

artistic circle: clique, coterie

artistic ethical or moral code: integrity

artistic freedom: poetic license

artistic imitator: epigone

artistic merit, natural or nonartistic object found to have: objet trouvé

artistic merit, object of: objet d'art

artistic people, as a class: intelligentsia

artistic premise of literary work: donnée

artistic realism: verismo

artistic rebirth: renaissance, renascence

artistic work critically acclaimed but unsuccessful commercially: succes d'estime

ART MOVEMENTS

abstract expression- ism	concrete art	geometric art	naturalism	postimpressionism
action painting	constructivism	Gothic art	Neapolitan	postmodernism
American	cubism	graffiti art	neoclassicism	prehistoric art
Art Deco	Dada	Harlem Renaissance	neoexpressionism	Pre-Raphaelitism
Art Nouveau	de Stijl	Hellenistic art	neoimpressionism	primitive art
Ashcan school	divisionism	Hudson River school	neoplasticism	primitivism
Barbizon school	Dutch	impressionism	neoromanticism	Quattrocento
baroque	early Christian art	International style	New Objectivity	rayonism
Bauhaus	earth art	Italian	New York	realism
Blaue Reiter, Der	environment art	Jugendstil	nonrepresentational art	representational art
body art	Etruscan art	junk art	Northern Renaissance art	Raphaelitism
Bolognese	expressionism	kinetic art		rococo art
British	fauvism	kitsch	op art	Roman
Brucke, Die	figurative art	Luminism	Origine	Romanesque art
Byzantine art	Flemish	Madrid	Parisian	romanticism
Carolingian art	Florentine school	mannerism	perceptual abstrac- tion	Scottish
Celtic art	fluxus	metaphysical art	photorealism	social realism
classical abstraction	folk art	Milanese	plein-air	surrealism
classicism	Fontainebleau school	minimal art	pointillism	symbolism
color-field painting	funk art	modernism	pop art	tachisme
conceptual art	futurism	Nabis		Venetian
	genre painting	narrative art		vorticism ❦

artistic work of drama, music, poetry, etc.: Gesamtkunstwerk

artistic works of person, early: juvenilia

artistic worth (or taste for artistic objects): vertu, virtu

artistically thought-of ordinary object: objet trouvé

artistically unifying: esemplastic

artistry and great technical skill: virtuosity

artists ahead of their time, experimental: avant-garde

artist's garment: smock

artist's ideal: ethos

artist's model, at times: nude

artist's stand: easel

artist's work as a whole: oeuvre ❦

arteries in neck: carotid

arteries, hardening of: sclerosis

artery: aorta, canal, carotid, conduit, coronary, course, highway, maxillary, passage, path, road, route, street, tube, vein

artery beneath collarbone: subclavian

artery going from heart: aorta

artery going to head and neck: carotid

artery layers: elastica

artery of lower limbs: iliac

artery wall thickening: atherosclerosis

artery wall, fatty deposit on: atheroma

artful: clever, contriving, crooked, cunning, deceitful, deceptive, deft, dexterous, foxy, gifted, imaginative, slick, slippery, sly, smart, smooth, stealthy, suave, tricky, underhand, vulpine, wily

artful strategy: finesse, maneuvers

artichoke center: choke, heart

artichoke's cousin: cardoon

article: item, matter, object, particular, piece, point, thing; column, composition, doctrine, essay, feature, paper, piece, report, story; condition, stipulation, term, terms

article alteration: revision

article first sentence or paragraph: lead

article in constant use: the

article of food: viand

article of property: chattel

article on specific, limited subject: monograph

article originally contained in larger publication: offprint

article, a or an, that makes the noun unidentified: indefinite article

article, biographical: profile

article, the, that makes the noun identified: definite article

article, writer's name appearing above: byline

articles needed for movie scenes: props

articles of little value, miscellaneous: trantles, trantlums

articles of merchandise, pottery: ware

articles, cartoons as sold by agency to numerous publications: syndication

articulate: clear, convey, distinct, eloquent, enunciate, express, fluent, formulated, intelligible, link, pronounce, speak, state, utter, verbal, vocalize

articulate clearly: enunciate

articulated: spoken

articulated speech: enunciation

artifice: cageyness, chicanery, cunning, deceit, deception, gimmick, hoax, intrigue, ploy, ruse, tactic, trick, wile, wiliness

artificial: assumed, bogus, counterfeit, ersatz, factitious, fake, false, feigned, fictitious, hollow, imitation, insincere, mock, phony, pretended, pseudo, sham, simulated, spurious, synthetic, unnatural

artificial and counterfeit: postiche

artificial and imitation: ersatz

artificial and not spontaneous: contrived, factitious, mannered, studied

artificial bank: levee

artificial behavior: affectation, pretentiousness

artificial environment, grown in: in vitro

artificial gem: paste

artificial grass: Astroturf, synthetic turf

artificial human being: android, automaton, golem, humanoid

artificial limb or body part: prosthesis

artificial male sopranos: castrati

artificial sweetener: aspartame, cyclamate, saccharin

artificial voice range: falsetto

artificial, not natural: factitious

artificially elegant speech or writing: euphuism

artillery: battery, bazooka, cannon, force, guns, missiles, ordnance, rockets, weaponry

artillery salute: salvo

artillery vehicle: caisson

artisan: builder, carpenter, craftsperson, master, plumber, professional

artisan's workplace: shop

artless: candid, childlike, direct, frank, guileless, humble, ingenuous, innocent, naïf, naive, natural, open, plain, pure, trusting, unaffected, unschooled, unsophisticated

artocarpus altilis: breadfruit

arts and crafts: decorative arts

arts and social science academic disciplines: humanities, liberal arts

arts, fine: beaux arts

arts, three-dimensional: plastic arts

artwork considered bad taste: kitsch

artwork used to illustrate text: graphics

artwork with three panels hinged together: triptych

artwork, critique or conceptualization of an: exegesis, interpretation

arty: dainty, highbrow, imitative, imposing, overblown, popular, pretentious, superficial, tasteless

arty person: aesthete

arum-family plant: aroid

as: because, being, equal, equally, essentially, like, now, similar, since, that, therefore, thus, when, while

ascend: arise, aspire, climb, escalate, mount, progress, rise, scale, slope up, soar, sprout, tower

ascendancy: control, domination, dominion, influence, mastery, power, prestige, success, superiority, supremacy, sway

ascending: upward

ascent: advancement, elevation, grade, incline, progress, ramp, rise, slope, spring, stairs, upgrade, uplifting

ascertain: determine, discover, doublecheck, identify, learn, unearth, verify

ascetic: abstinent, anchorite, celibate, disciplined, eremite, essene, fakir, hermit, monk, recluse, severe, stark, stoic, strict, stylite, yogi

ascot: scarf, tie

ascribable: owing

ascribe: accuse, allege, attach, attribute, blame, charge, cite, impute, infer, refer, reference

ascribe and attribute: impute

ascus: sac

asea: addled, adrift, befuddled, bewildered, confused, puzzled, sailing, uncertain

aseptic: barren, clean, lifeless, purifying, restrained, shrinking, sterile

asexual: agamic, agamogenetic, parthenogenetic

ash: cinder, clinker, ember, residue, soot, tree

ash left from burned coal, charcoal: breeze

ash or coal, smoldering: embers

ash, larger pieces of residue left with: clinker

ash, partially burned material not reduced to: cinders

ash, pertaining to: cinerous

ashamed: abashed, contrite, discomfited, embarrassed, flustered, humbled, humiliated, mortified, out of countenance, remorseful

ashamed-looking: hangdog, shamefaced

ashen: blanched, faded, ghastly, gray, pale, pallid, paly, pasty, wan, waxen

ashes of cremated body: cremains

ashes of dead, vault with niches for urns of: columbarium

ashes, place for cremated body: cinerarium

ashes, vase for cremated body: urn

Asia rainy season: monsoon

Asia and East in general: Orient

aside: afar, alone, alongside, aloof, apart, away, beside, gone, obliquely, private, reserved, secretly, separate, tangent

aside alone: apart, separate

aside from: barring, besides, except, excluding

aside to person or thing: apostrophe

asinine: absurd, dense, doltish, idiotic, imbecilic, inept, lamebrained, mindless, senseless, silly, simple, simpleminded, stupid

ask: adjure, beseech, call, claim, crave, demand, enquire, entreat, exact, expect, grill, implore, inquire, interrogate, petition, pray, press, question, quiz, request, seek, solicit, summon, utter

ask for humbly, pray for: supplicate

ask for or order needed supplies: requisition

ask for urgently: adjure, beseech, entreat, exhort, petition, solicit, supplicate

ask insistently: importune

ask payment: bill

ask questions and examine: interrogate

ask questions for investigation: catechize

ask special consideration: seek favor

askance: askew, critically, crooked, cynically, doubtfully, sideways, skeptically

asked: bade

asked for and commanded by: at the behest of

askew: ajar, amiss, aslant, asquint, atilt, awry, bent, cockeyed, crooked, distorted, knotted, lopsided, twisted, wry, zigzag

asking: inquisitive, querying

asking humbly: suppliant, supplicant

asks for payment: duns

asleep: dead, dozing, hibernating, idle, inactive, latent, motionless, napping, numbed, resting, slumbering, unaware, unconscious, unfeeling

asleep or inactive for a time: dormant

asocial person: loner

asp: viper

asparagus stalk: spear

aspect: angle, appearance, bearing, carriage, countenance, face, facet, feature, form, look, mien, outlook, phase, point, prospect, semblance, side, situation, view

aspect or side of subject: facet

aspect, best or most appealing: beauty part

aspen: poplar, quaking, quivering, trembling, wood

aspen's shady cousin: cottonwood

asperity: acrimony, bitterness, briskness, crabbiness, difficulty, hardness, harshness, hostility, sourness, tartness, unevenness

aspersion: abuse, backbiting, baptism, calumny, innuendo, insult, invective, reproach, slander, slur

asphalt: bitumen, blacktop, uintaite

asphyxia: apnea

asphyxiate: drown, smother, strangle, suffocate

aspic: gel

aspirant: applicant, candidate, competitor, hopeful

aspirant to the throne: pretender

aspiration: ambition, craving, desire, dream, goal, hope, ideal, pursuit, wish, yearning

aspire: ascend, desire, hanker, long, mount, rise, seek, soar, thirst, tower, want

aspirin alternative: acetaminophen, codeine, paracetamol

aspirin poisoning: salicylism

ass: burro, jackass, jenny

ass or donkey, pertaining to: asinine

ass, wild, in central Asia: onager

assail: abuse, accuse, assault, beat, belabor, beset, bombard, encounter, invade, lambaste, malign, pelt, pound, scathe, set at, stone, storm, strike, whack

assailant: aggressor, antagonist, assaulter, attacker, mugger

assassin: executioner, gunman, gunwoman, hatchet man, hit man, hit woman, killer, murderer, slayer, triggerman, triggerwoman

assassinate: slay

assassination by government (secret): executive action

assassination order euphemized: extreme prejudice

assault: advance, aggression, assail, attack, beat, beset, bombardment, breach, bushwhack, charge, fight, incursion, invade, jump, onset, onslaught, push, raid, siege, slug, smite, storm, violate

assault and rob: mug

assay: analyze, appraise, check, determine, estimate, evaluate, examine, experiment, eyeball, offer, prove, rate, survey, test, undertake

assayer: evaluator

assemblage: aggregation, assembly, batch, bunch, cluster, collage, congregation, convoy, crew, crowd, gathering, herd, mass, pack, stock, swarm, throng, turnout

assemble: build, call, collect, congress, construct, convene, couple, flock, gather, huddle, join, make, mass, meet, muster, piece, rally, recruit, summon

assembled: amassed, massed, met

assembly: audience, auditorium, body, company, conclave, congress, convention, convocation, diet, forum, group, hall, junta, legislature, meeting, parliament, party, rally, session, society, tribunal, troop

assembly in ancient Greek marketplace, place of: agora

assembly of church officials: convocation, synod

assembly, summon an: convene, convoke

assent: accede, acknowledge, acquiesce, adhesion, admission, admit, agree, amen, aye, chorus, compliance, comply, concur, condescend, consent, endorsement, grant, nod, permission, sanction, yes, yield

assert: advance, advocate, allege, argue, assure, aver, avouch, avow, champion, cite, claim, declare, defend, depose, emphasize, maintain, plead, pose, predicate, protest, state, stress, submit, support, uphold, utter, vaunt, vindicate, voice

assert ownership: stake out a claim

assertion: say-so

assertion by negation of opposite: litotes

assertion, arbitrary and not factually based: dictum, dogma, ipse dixit

assertive: absolute, affirmative, aggressive, confident, dogmatic, forceful, positive, pragmatic, pushy, strident, sure

assess: account, evaluate, rate, weigh

assess a tax: levy

assessment: dues, duty, fine, impost, reckoning, surtax, tariff, tax, valuation

asset: advantage, benefit, credit, distinction, help, plus, treasure

asset and money interchangeability: liquidity

asset or property, extremely valuable: blue chip

asset that cannot be perceived by senses: intangible

assets: belongings, capital, credit, equity, estate, goods, money, property, resources, riches, valuables, wealth, worth

assets into money, convert property or: realize

asseverate: aver, avow

assiduous: active, determined, devoted, diligent, earnest, hardworking, industrious, laborious, painstaking, persevering, persistent, plugging, steady, unwearied

assign: adjudge, advance, affect, allocate, allot, allow, appoint, apportion, appropriate, ascribe, attribute, charge, choice, consign, convey, deed, delegate, depute, designate, detail, dispose, distribute, give, grant, order, rate, seal, select, set, sign, specify, tag, transfer

assign and give out: allocate

assign roles: cast

assign to cause or source: affix, ascribe, attribute, impute, predicate

assign work or duty: delegate, depute

assignation: affair, appointment, engagement, meeting, rendezvous, tryst

assigned functions: duties, tasks

assigned period: term

assigned task: stint

assignment: authorization, chore, homework, mission, selection, task

assignment, production: quota

assimilate: absorb, adopt, alter, appropriate, blend, comprehend, grasp, integrate, learn, merge, metabolize, resemble, transform, understand

assimilate mentally: digest

assimilation of thoughts gradually: osmosis

assist: abet, abetment, aid, avail, back, befriend, benefit, boost, collaborate, comfort, facilitate, help, plug, reinforce, support, sustain, uphold

assist in wrongdoing: abet

assistance or money to start a venture: grubstake

assistance, emergency: succor

assistance, financial: subvention

assistant: abettor, adjutant, aide, aider, ally, apprentice, associate, colleague, confederate, deputy, hand, helper, henchman, lackey, partner, second, secretary, subordinate

assistant and attendant: acolyte

assistant doing wide range of duties: factotum

assistant in enterprise or scheme: accomplice, collaborator, confederate

assistant temporarily substituting for superior: deputy

assistant to magician, scholar: famulus

assistant to superior officer: aide-de-camp

assisting: ancillary, auxiliary, subsidiary, supplementing

assize: assembly, court, decree, enactment, hearing, inquest, measure, ordinance, regulation, rule, session, trial, tribunal

associate: adjunct, aide, ally, assistant, bracket, buddy, chum, cohort, colleague, companion, confidant, consort, counterpart, crony, federate, friend, helper, intimate, partner, peer, sidekick; connect, fraternize, hobnob, identify, join, link, mingle, relate, socialize

associate closely with someone: consort, fraternize, hobnob

associated with word or thing, idea: connotation

association: affiliation, assemblage, bond, cabal, cartel, clan, club, coalition, combination, company, confederacy, conjunction, connection, converse, co-op, council, fraternity, gang, guild, intimacy, league, lodge, lyceum, order, partnership, pledge, pool, ring, society, sorority, syndicate, union

association for business purposes: syndicate

association of organisms of different species of mutual benefit: symbiosis

association or fellowship: sodality

association, word, nonliteral: connotation

assort: categorize, clasify, class, group, rank, suit, type

assorted: different, hybrid, motley, varied

assortment: array, batch, collection, combo, diversity, group, kind, lot, medley, mélange, miscellany, mishmash, potpourri, set, variety

assortment of type: fonts

assuage: abate, alleviate, appease, comfort, diminish, ease, fill, lessen, lull, mitigate, modify, mollify, quiet, reduce, relieve, salve, slake, soften, solace, soothe, sweeten, tranquilize

assume: accept, acquire, adopt, affect, appropriate, arrogate, believe, cloak, counterfeit, deduce, deem, endue, expect, guess, infer, mask, raise, simulate, speculate, suppose, surmise, take, take over, think, undertake, usurp

assume control: take charge

assume or assert truth of: posit, postulate, premise

assume the character of: impersonate, pose

assumed: affected, bogus, expected,

false, fictional, fictitious, hypothetical, putative, supposed, supposititious, tacit, understood

assumed appearance or disguise: incognito

assumed attitude: pose

assumed character or part: role

assumed name: alias

assumed name or identity: incognito

assuming: arrogant, brazen, egotistic, lofty, overbearing, presumptuous, pretentious, rude, superior

assumption: premise

assumption on evidence, facts: extrapolation

assumption provisionally accepted: assurance, hypothesis

assurance: affirmation, audacity, belief, boldness, brass, certainty, cockiness, confidence, coolness, credit, effrontery, faith, impudence, insurance, nerve, oath, promise, say-so, surety, trust, word

assurance, give personal: attest to, vouch for

assurance, written: guarantee, warranty

assure: assert, attest, avouch, clinch, confirm, declare, encourage, lock, secure, strengthen, underwrite

assure or guarantee: vouch

assured air: élan

assured person, in law: promisee

asterisk: star

astern: aft, back, behind, rear

asteroid: meteorite

asthmatic: pursy

astir: about, active, afoot, alert, awake, moving, roused

astonish: amaze, boggle, confound, daze, dazzle, flabbergast, floor, impress, perplex, startle, stun, surprise

astonishing: breathtaking, confusing, eye-popping, fabulous, incredible, miraculous, shocking, spectacular, wonderful, wondrous

astound: amaze, appall, astonish, confound, dumbfound, electrify, flabbergast, shock, stagger, stun, terrify

astral: celestial, remote, sidereal, starlike, stellar, stellular, visionary

astral bear: Ursa

astray: abroad, adrift, afield, amiss, aside, awry, errant, faulty, lost, mistaken, wandering, wrong

astringent: acerb, alum, binding, compressive, constrictive, contracting, elum, harsh, severe, sour, stern, styptic, tannin, tart

astringent fruit: sloe

astringent mineral salt: alum

astrologer's fortune-telling chart: horoscope

astrologer's table of planet and star positions: ephemeris

astrological aspect: trine

astrological signs, point of transition between: cusp

astrology diagram: zodiac

astrology, configuration of planets at one's birth in: constellation

astrology, horoscope for the time of one's birth in: nativity

astrology, relative configuration of stars and planets at a given moment in: horoscope

astrology, relative configuration of stars and planets in: aspect

astrology's 12 divisions of the heavens: house, mansion, sign

astrology's 12 divisions of the heavens bearing a name for a constellation: zodiac

astronaut container: capsule

astronaut from Russia: cosmonaut

astronaut's return: reentry

astronomer: stargazer

astronomer's almanac: ephemeris

astronomical alignment of three celestial bodies: syzygy

astronomical altar: ara

astute: acute, canny, crafty, cunning, discerning, foxy, keen, quick, sagacious, sharp, shrewd, skilled, smart, wily

astute watchfulness: weather eye

asunder: divided, riven, separated, split

asylum: bedlam, cover, harbor, haven, institution, refuge, retreat, sanctuary, shelter

asymmetric: distorted

atelier: studio

atheist: agnostic, heathen, nonbeliever, pagan

atheist for particular religion: infidel

atheist who is uncertain about existence of gods: agnostic

atheistic: nullifidian

atheistic belief that humans control their own destiny: humanism

atheistic belief that reason is spiritual truth: rationalism

athlete: jock

athlete who shows off: hot dog

athlete's black pigment under eyes: lampblack

athlete's foot: dermatophytosis, ring-worm, tinea

athletic: acrobatic, brawny, burly, energetic, muscular, powerful, robust, strong, vigorous, vital

athletic body structure: mesomorphic

athletic club: gym

athletic competition of cross-country skiing and rifle marksmanship: biathlon

athletic competition of swimming, bicycling, and distance running: triathlon

athletic competition with automobile or horse steeplechase: gymkhana

athletic competition with five events: pentathlon

athletic competition with ten track events: decathlon

athletic or gymnastic club: turnverein

athletically vigorous: sthenic

athletics: exercise, sport

athodyd: ramjet

athrob: sore

athwart: across, against, crosswise

atilt: alist

Atlantic Ocean, this side of: cisatlantic

atlas book of maps: missile

atmosphere: aer, air, ambiance, aura, background, climate, envelope, environment, mood, nimbus, scene, sense, sky, spirit, tone
RELATED TERMS
atmosphere and weather science: meteorology
atmosphere based on harmonious feelings: vibes, wavelength
atmosphere of gloom: pall
atmosphere of place, situation: ambience
atmosphere of special power or mystery: mystique
atmosphere over nation: airspace
atmosphere starting around seven miles: stratosphere
atmosphere, absorption of solar radiation heating the earth's: greenhouse effect
atmosphere, cheerful and warm: amiable, congenial
atmosphere, party: convivial
atmosphere, poisonous: miasma
atmosphere, thin and low-density upper: rarefied
atmospheric balloon probe: sonde
atmospheric pressure indicator on map: isobar, isopiestic
atmospheric pressure, measuring instrument for: barometer

atmospheric pressure, unit of: millibar 🐚

atoll: island, isle, reef

atom: crumb, dot, fragment, infinitesimal, iota, jot, little, mite, molecular, mote, shade, speck, trace, whit

atom or group of atoms with an electric charge by gaining or losing one or more electrons: ion

atom or group of atoms with at least one unpaired electron: radical

atom or radical with other atoms, combining capacity of: valence

atom splitting: nuclear fission

atomic: energy, fission, fusion, granular, submarine, tiny

atomic accelerator: betatron

atomic clock that defines the second: cesium atomic clock

atomic fusion at high temperatures, concerning: thermonuclear

atomic nuclei and releasing energy, combining: fusion

atomic nuclei in reaction, splitting heavy: fission

atomic particle, negative charge: electron

atomic particle, no charge: neutron

atomic particle, positive charge: proton

atomic reactor part: core

atomize: destroy, grate, pulverize, reduce, smash, spray, vaporize

atomizer, to convert liquid to spray in: nebulize

atom's combining capacity: valence, valency

atom(s) electrically charged: ion

atoms having same atomic number but different mass numbers: isotope

atoms held together by chemical forces: molecule

atom's total protons and neutrons in nucleus: mass number

atom(s) with at least one unpaired electron: radical

atonal: unkeyed

atone: answer, compensate, correct, expiate, repent, square

atonement: amends, apology, expiation, penance, recompense, redemption, redress, reparation, restitution, satisfaction

atonement, making: piacular

atop: onto, up on, upon

atop, poetically: o'er

atrium: cavity, chamber, court, entrance, passage, room

atrocious: abominable, awful, cruel, dark, diabolical, evil, fiendish, foul, frightful, gross, heinous, horrible, inhuman, loathsome, rank, rotten, ruthless, savage, terrible, ungodly, vile, violent, wicked

atrocious actor: ham

atrocious and wicked: flagitious, heinous

atrophy: decaying, decline, deterioration, diminution, downfall, emaciation, wither

atrophy's aftermath: weakening

attach: addict, adhere, affiliate, affix, allocate, annex, append, appoint, arrest, associate, attribute, bind, cement, connect, fasten, fix, glue, hitch, indict, join, link, pin on, put, raid, seize, tether, tie on, weld

attach a yoke or harness: inspan

attach an atom: smash

attach falsely: asperse

attach property for paying debt: garnishee

attached directly at base: sessile, stalkless

attachment: accessory, affection, affinity, allegiance, amore, clamp, devotion, engagement, extension, fixture, inclination, lien, liking, love, loyalty

attachment because of resemblance to parent: anaclisis

attachment, immature, to something: fixation

attack: accuse, action, affray, aggression, ailment, assail, assault, assay, bash, battle, begin, beset, besiege, blame, blitz, bombard, bout, charge, criticize, denounce, fight, fray, incursion, offense, onset, onslaught, paroxysm, raid, rush, set on, skirmish, slander, sortie, storm, strike, stroke, thrust

attack from all sides: beleaguer, beset

attack from low-flying aircraft: strafe

attack in print: coup de plume

attack in speech or writing: hatchet job

attack in the back: stab

attack on another's beliefs: polemic

attack on custom, belief, institution held sacred: lèse majesté, lese majesty

attack or invasion: incursion, irruption

attack or set upon: sic

attack out of revenge: reprisal, retaliation

attack verbally: tear into

attack violently and suddenly: assail, foray

attack with criticism: flay

attack with snowballs: pelt

attack, armed: fusillade, offensive, sally, salvo, sortie

attack, armed, from the side: enfilade

attack, biblically: stone

attack, face an: bear the brunt

attack, forceful: onslaught

attack, harsh and critical in: blistering, scathing

attack, in danger of: vulnerable

attack, swift in war: blitzkrieg

attack, violent: onslaught

attacked or embroiled in controversy: embattled

attacker: besieger

attain: accede, accomplish, achieve, acquire, aspire, earn, fulfill, gain, hit, obtain, procure, reach, rise, secure, snag, strike, succeed, touch, win

attainment: finish, mastery, reaping, skill, talent, wisdom

attempt: aim, assay, begin, effort, endeavor, essay, experiment, seek, shot, stab, start, strive, trial, try, undertake, venture, wage

attend: accompany, appear, assist, await, chaperon, come, consort, convoy, follow, guard, harken, hear, heed, listen, mind, minister, see, serve, shadow, tend, treat, wait, watch

attend matins: pray

attend regularly: frequent, haunt

attendance: application, attention, company, crowd, gate, number, presence, regard, turnout

attendant: assistant, associate, chamberlain, companion, escort, follower, guide, helper, maid, orderly, page, porter, related, servant, squire, subsequent, usher, valet, waitperson

attendants of important person: cortege, entourage, retinue

attention: concentration, consideration, courtesy, ear, heed, mindfulness, note, notice, obedience, observation, regard, respect, study, thought, vigilance

attention diverter: red herring

attention-getter: ahem, cry, hey, hist, psst, yo

attention-getting: arresting, flashy

attention-grabbing: upstaging

attention, focused and exclusive: fixation

attention, public: limelight

attentive: alert, assiduous, awake, careful, circumspect, courteous, gallant, glued, intent, interested, listening, on the qui vive, polite, respectful, studious, vigilant, wary, watchful

attentive and hovering: solicitous

attenuate: constrict, decrease, dilute, diminish, lessen, reduce, shrink, slender, tapering, thin, undermine, water, weaken

attest: affirm, authenticate, aver, avow, concentration, confirm, consideration, corroborate, courtesy, diligence, indicate, invoke, mindfulness, observation, prove, show, subscribe, support, swear, testify, verify, vigilance, vouch, witness

attic: cockloft, garret, loft, mansard

attic under pitched roof: garret

attire: apparel, clad, clothe, clothes, dress, garb, outfit, robe, threads, wardrobe

attitude: action, angle, approach, behavior, disposition, feeling, frame of mind, manner, mind-set, mood, perspective, point of view, pose, position, posture, set, slant, stand, standpoint, tone, view

attitude or inclination toward something, having: disposed, orientated, oriented

attitude or posture: bearing, carriage, deportment

attitude, having arrogant: cavalier

attitude, reversal of: volte-face

attitudes and character: ethos

attitudinize: pose

attorney: advocate, agent, barrister, chaser, counselor, factor, lawyer, proxy, solicitor

attorney's sobriquet: esq

attract: allure, bait, beckon, captivate, catch, charm, draw, enchant, engage, enthrall, entice, fascinate, influence, interest, invite, lure, pull, seduce, tempt

attraction: affinity, allure, appeal, charisma, chemistry, draw, glamour, lure, magnet

attraction, moving toward in: gravitate

attractive: alluring, appealing, beautiful, bonny, captivating, cute, elegant, graceful, handsome, lovely, pleasant, pretty, sexy, winsome

attractive and appetizing: succulent, toothsome

attractive and bewitching: alluring, beguiling, captivating

attractive and pleasing: personable, prepossessing, winsome

attractive and unusual: picturesque

attractive but vulgar: garish, glossy, meretricious, specious

attractive, flashily: meretricious

attractive, photographically: photogenic

attractive, sexually: foxy

attractiveness, sensual: animal magnetism

attribute: aspect, badge, feature, grace, idiosyncrasy, mark, peculiarity, property, quality, reputation, sign, symbol, talent, virtue

attribute and ascribe: impute

attribute without reason: arrogate

attribute, to: allege, assert, bestow, blame, charge, place, point, refer

attrition: friction, grief, penance, regret, remorse, repentance, rubbing, sorrow, thinning, weakening, wear

attune: accord, adapt, adjust, agree, balance, compensate, harmonize, tailor, tune

attuned to: hep

atypical: novel, rare

au courant: latest

au naturel: naked, nude, undressed

auburn-haired: henna, strawberry blonde, titian

auction: barter, bidding, block, offering, public sale, sale, sell, trade, vendue

auction action: bid

auction bidder who raises prices for the owner: by-bidder

auction of one collection of varied items: job lot

auction participant: bidder

auction where prices keep going lower: Dutch auction

auction, lowest price fixed and announced at: reserve price

auctioneer hammer: gavel

auctioneer's word: going, sold

audacious: adventurous, arrogant, brash, brazen, courageous, daredevil, daring, defiant, fearless, gutsy, hardy, imprudent, impudent, insolent, presumptuous, reckless, risky, rude, shameless, spirited, uncurbed, venturesome, wild

audacity: assurance, boldness, brass, chutzpah, cockiness, courage, effrontery, fearlessness, gall, grit, guts, imprudence, insolence, moxie, nerve, sauciness, spirit, spunk

audacity and boldness: chutzpah, effrontery

audible: aloud, aural, discernible, distinct, hearable, heard, plain, resounding

audible bounce: echo

audible protest: plaint

audibly: aloud

audience: assembly, audition, clientele, crowd, ear, following, gallery, house, interview, listeners, market, patrons, public, spectators

audience grabber: grandstand play

audience poll on TV or radio program popularity: ratings

audio: sound

audio component: speaker, tape deck

audio quality: tone

audit: accounting, analysis, balance, check, estimate, examine, investigate, probe, reckon, report, review, scrutinize, survey

audition: hearing, reading, test, trial, tryout

audition disk or tape: demo

auditioned for a role: tried out

auditor: accountant, actuary, bookkeeper, CPA, hearer, listener

auditorium: amphitheater, arena, coliseum, room, theater

auditory: otic

auger: bore, borer, drill, gimlet, grill, tool

aught: anything, cipher, nothing, zero, zilch

augment: add to, amplify, build, deepen, develop, dilate, enhance, enlarge, exalt, expand, grow, heighten, improve, increase, inflate, multiply, rise, swell

augmented: eked

augur: anticipate, betoken, bode, conjecture, divine, forebode, foresee, foreshow, foretell, forewarn, harbinger, herald, indicate, intimate, omen, predict, predictor, presage, prophet, seer, signify

augury: ceremony, forecast, forerunner, omen, portent, prognostic, ritual, sign, sortilege, token, warning

august: baronial, brilliant, dignified, eminent, exalted, grand, majestic, monumental, noble, regal, solemn, splendid, stately, venerable

auk genus: alca

auntlike: amitular

aura: air, ambience, aroma, aspect, atmosphere, emanation, feeling, glow, halo, mood, mystique, nimbus, odor, quality, scent, tone

aura of power or mystery to something: mystique

aura or atmosphere, distinctive: karma

aura or halo: nimbus

aural: otic

aurally incapable: deaf

aureate: brilliant, flowery, golden, ornate, overblown, splendid, yellow

aureole: corona, halo

auricle: ear

auricular: audible, hearsay, otic, phonic

auricular projections: lobes

auriculate: eared

aurify: gild

aurora: dawn, eos

auspices: advocacy, aegis, backing, care, egis, guidance, influence, patronage, protection, signs, sponsorship, support

auspicious: advantageous, encouraging, favorable, fortunate, golden, good, happy, hopeful, propitious, prosperous

Aussie ratite: emu

austere: ascetic, astringent, bitter, bleak, earnest, forbidding, formal, grave, hard, harsh, puritanic, relentless, rigid, rigorous, rough, serious, severe, sharp, spartan, stern, stiff, strict, unadorned

austere person: ascetic

austerity: rigor

Australian eucalyptus: ironbark

Australian wild dog: dingo

Australia's back country: bush, outback

authentic: actual, authorized, bona fide, certain, correct, credible, legitimate, original, proper, real, reliable, sure, true, trustworthy, valid

authenticate: attest, confirm, document, endorse, guarantee, justify, prove, validate, verify, vouch

authentication: seal

authenticity lacking: apocryphal

author: architect, compiler, creator, founder, ghostwriter, inventor, journalist, maker, novelist, playwright, poet, producer, scribe, source, wordsmith, writer

author, list of works by or about: bibliography

author, pertaining to: auctorial

author, pertaining to unnamed: anonymous

authored for another: ghostwrote

authoritarian and nondemocratic form

of government: absolutism, autarchy, autocracy, despotism, dictatorship, totalitarianism, tyranny

authoritarian order: ukase

authoritarian person, rigid: martinet

authoritative: authentic, commanding, conclusive, dictatorial, dogmatic, effectual, factual, imperious, imposing, learned, legitimate, magisterial, official, proven, ruling, scholarly

authoritative and complete: definitive

authoritative and dogmatic: magisterial

authoritative and urgent: imperative

authoritative by rank or office: ex cathedra

authoritative order: decree, mandate, ukase

authoritative principle, unsupported: dictum, dogma, ipse dixit

authoritative rule of law: ordinance

authoritative sayings: dicta

authoritative spokesperson: oracle

authorities, transfer of power from central to regional or local: devolution

authority: command, competence, control, dominion, expert, force, government, importance, jurisdiction, kingpin, might, potence, power, regent, right, rule, say, say-so, scepter, source, sovereignty, strength, sway

authority in fatherly way: paternalism

authority of one's position, with the: ex cathedra

authority, absolute: imperium

authority, complete: carte blanche, supremacy

authority, extent of: jurisdiction

authority, former, now replaced: ancient regime

authority, rod or staff carried as emblem of: verge

authority, shared: collegiality

authorization: fiat, mandate

authorization to sell: dealership

authorize: accredit, allow, approve, commission, delegate, empower, endorse, legalize, legitimize, let, license, okay, permit, ratify, rubberstamp, sanction, vest, warrant

authorize and empower: warrant

authorize to receive: agent, entitle

authorized and officially recognized: accredited

authorized representative: agent

authors: scribes, sires

author's abbreviation: ibid

author's assumed name: nom de plume

author's complete works: canon, corpus, oeuvre

authorship, of questionable: apocryphal

autobiographical records: memoirs

autobiography: diary, journal, letters, life, memoir, vita

autochthonous: aboriginal, earliest, endemic, native

autocracy: tsarism

autocrat: czar, despot, dictator, mogul, monarch, ruler, sovereign, tsar, tzar

autocratic: absolute, arbitrary, arrogant, despotic, oppressive, tyrannous

autograph: endorsement, ink, John Hancock, name, pen, sign, signature

autograph collector: philographer

automatic: habitual, instinctive, intuitive, mechanical, natural, Pavlovian, predictable, robotic, routine, unconscious

automatic and lifeless: mechanical

automatic reaction: knee-jerk reaction

automatic regulating device: servomechanism

automatic response to stimulus: tropism

automatically, device that controls machines: electric eye, photocell, photoelectric cell

automation: android, computerization, golem, machine, robot

automobile: car, convertible, coupe, heap, hot rod, jalopy, jeep, machine, racer, roadster, sedan

RELATED TERMS

automobile accident, minor: fender bender

automobile air deflector: spoiler

automobile air valve: choke

automobile clamp for illegal parking: Denver boot

automobile long-distance race: rally

automobile maneuver: U-turn

automobile mishap: dent

automobile modified for racing: stock car

automobile one-piece back and window: hatchback

automobile option: power steering

automobile or demo follower: crat

automobile outing: spin

automobile race: drag

automobile shelter: carport, garage

automobile signal: blinker, signal light, turn signal

automobile steeplechase: gymkhana

automobile, defective since bought: lemon

automobile's radar detector: fuzzbuster

automobiles taken as part payments: trade-ins ☜

autonomous: independent, self-governed, separate, sovereign, uncontrolled

autumn: fall, harvesttime, Indian summer, season

autumn beverage: cider

autumn implement: rake

autumnal phenomenon: harvest moon

auxiliary: accessory, additional, adjutant, aide, ally, ancillary, assistant, backup, branch, emergency, helper, partner, reserve, secondary, spare, subordinate, supporting

auxiliary structure: annex

avail: account, advantage, assistance, benefit, help, meet, profit, serve, suffice, use, utilize, value, work

available: accessible, attainable, convenient, disposable, efficacious, feasible, free, handy, in hand, obtainable, on call, on tap, open, possible, present, procurable, ready, up for grabs, usable

available money: funds

available resources, make or provide from: improvise

available supply: pool

available, easily: accessible

availing: using

avalanche: cataclysm, deluge, flood, inundation, landslide, mudslide, slide, snowslide, torrent

avant-garde: innovative, leaders, new, offbeat, original, pioneers, progressive, trailblazing, trendsetting, van, vanguard

avant-garde artist: arp

avant-garde's antonym: arrière-garde

avarice: avidity, cupidity, frugality, greed, rapacity, stinginess

avarice and greed: cupidity

avaricious: greedy

avenaceous cereal: oats

avenge: chasten, injure, punish, redress, retaliate, revenge, vindicate

avenging: vindicatory

avenue: access, alee, allée, approach, artery, drive, entry, gate, mall, means, opening, outlet, passageway, road, street, way

aver: affirm, assert, avouch, claim, contend, declare, emphasize, insist, justify, maintain, predicate, proclaim, prove, state, swear, verify

average: common, fair, humdrum, mean, medial, median, mediocre, medium, middle, norm, normal, ordinary, par, proportion, respectable, rule, so-so, standard, typical, usual

average from the sum total divided by number of items: arithmetic mean, mean

average out: equate

average person: homme moyen sensuel

average value in set of values: median

averages: norms, pars

avers: says, states

averse: afraid, against, antagonistic, contrary, disinclined, hesitant, loath, opposed, reluctant, unfavorable

averse to: allergic

aversion: abomination, antipathy, disdain, disgust, dislike, distaste, dread, enmity, hatred, hostility, repugnance

avert: avoid, deflect, deter, dodge, evade, foil, forestall, frustrate, halt, preclude, prevent, thwart, turn, veer

avert and prevent: obviate

avian abode: aerie, nest

avian aggressor: bird of prey

avian cooler: bird bath

avian delight: suet

AUTOMOBILE AND MOTOR SPORTS

autocross
automobile racing
demolition derby
dirt car racing
drag racing
formula one racing
go-carting
Grand Prix
GT/grand touring
hot-rod racing
Indy car racing
midget racing
motocross/scrambling
motorcycle racing
off-track racing
rallying and cross-country racing
sports car racing
sprint car racing
stock-car racing
track-racing
vintage car racing ☜

avian feature: beak, wing

aviary: birdhouse, columbary, dovehouse, ornithon, volary

aviate: fly

aviation: aeronautics, navigation, piloting

aviator: airman, airwoman, barnstormer, birdman, flier, flyboy, hotshot, pilot

avid: anxious, ardent, covetous, craving, eager, grasping, greedy, hungry, impatient, insatiable, keen, ravenous, voracious, warm

avidity: avarice, cupidity, enthusiasm, fervor, greediness, longing

avocado: alligator pear

avocado paste: guacamole

avocation: amusement, diversion, hobby, occupation, pastime, recreation, sideline, thing

avoid: abstain, avert, boycott, bypass, caress, circumvent, disregard, ditch, dodge, duck, elude, evade, forsake, preclude, refrain, shirk, shun, sidestep, skirt, withdraw

avoid and escape: elude, parry

avoid and outwit: circumvent

avoid capture: elude

avoid deceitfully: evade

avoid doing: balk, eschew, shrink

avoid gathering moss: roll

avoid giving direct answers: fence, hedge

avoid work: malinger

avoid, as an issue: sidestep

avoidable: evitable

avoidance: annulment, eluding, evasion, flight, preventing, runaround, withdrawal

avoidance of extremes: golden mean

avoidance techniques: crisis management

avoided a trial: settled

avoider of paying: deadbeat

avoiding publicity: inconspicuous, low-profile, unobtrusive, unostentatious

avow: acknowledge, affirm, announce, assert, avouch, concede, confess, grant, maintain, proclaim, profess, state, swear

await: abide, anticipate, attend, expect, impend, pend, stay, sweat

awaiting: in store, pending

awake: active, alert, alive, arouse, attentive, careful, conscious, excite, heedful, mindful, rouse

awake and aware: alert

awake and doing: astir

awaken: alert, rouse

awakening: arousal, enlivening, eye-opener, rebirth, revival, stimulating

award: accolade, accord, appoint, assign, bestow, booby prize, citation, decoration, diploma, grant, honor, judgment, kudos, laurels, medal, present, prize, scholarship, sheepskin, tribute

award a rating: evaluate

award or honor: citation, commendation

award, propose for: nominate

aware: alert, alive, apprised, cognizant, conscious, groovy, informed, intelligent, knowing, mindful, onto, sentient, upon, vigilant, watchful, wise

aware and informed: cognizant, mindful

away: abroad, absent, along, apart, aside, begone, directly, distant, elsewhere, endlessly, gone, missing, not in, off, out, tirelessly

away from body part, carrying: efferent

away from center: centrifugal

away from shore: asea

away from the land: seaward

away from the wind: alee

awe: alarm, amaze, bewilder, fascinate, fear, fright, intimidate, overcome, overpower, panic, quivering, regard, respect, scare, showboat, terrorize, trembling, wonder

awe-inspiring: august, numinous, sublime

awesome: amazing, appalling, breathtaking, dreaded, ghostly, grand, hairy, imposing, majestic, solemn, uncanny

awesome and imposing: august, formidable, portentous

awful: appalling, awesome, dire, fearful, frightful, gross, horrendous, horrible, horrid, horrific, impressive, lousy, nasty, revolting, shocking, terrible, tremendous, ugly

awful dream: nightmare

awfully: badly, dreadfully, extremely, greatly, poorly, quite

awkward: angular, backhanded, blundering, bumbling, bungling, butterfingers, clumsy, cumbersome, difficult, embarrassing, gauche, gawky, inconvenient, inept, klutzy, lubberly, lumbering, maladroit, ponderous, rustic, stilted, uncoordinated, uncouth, uneasy, ungainly, ungraceful, unskillful, unwieldy, wooden

awkward or problematic situation: plight

awkward person: bumpkin, galoot, hobbledehoy, lout

awkward person on ship: landlubber

awkward to move or use: cumbersome, ponderous, unwieldy

awkwardly heavy: clunky

awn: arista, seta

awning: canopy, covering, marquee, protection, screen, shade, shelter, tent, velarium

awry: agee, alop, amiss, askew, cockeyed, crooked, distorted, faulty, haywire, improper, oblique, off-center, slanting, snafu, uneven, wrong

ax: can, cleaver, discharge, dismiss, fire, hatchet, poll, sack, tomahawk, twibil, twibill

ax, notch in wood made by: kerf

axed: fired

axel: leap

axillary: alar

axiom: adage, aphorism, dictum, maxim, motto, precept, principle, proposition, rule, saying, sentence, truism, truth

axiomatic and terse: sententious

axis: alliance, axle, coalition, deer, fulcrum, hinge, pivot, pole, spindle, stem, support

axle: arbor, axis, gudgeon, mandrel, pin, rod, shaft, spindle, wheel

axle pin holding wheel on: linchpin

axle pivot around which wheel turns: gudgeon

axlike tool: adz

ax-shaped: dolabriform

ayah: chambermaid, governess, nurse, nursemaid

aye: affirmative, always, continually, okay, vote, yes

azure: celeste, cerulean, cloudless, cobalt, sky blue

azure gem: lapis lazuli

Bb

babassu or bacaba: palm

Babbitt: alloy, boob, bourgeois, conformist, materialist, metal, philistine

babble: blab, blabber, blat, blather, chat, chatter, coo, drivel, gab, gibber, gibberish, gossip, jabber, murmuring, mutter, nonsense, prat, prate, prattle, rant, rattle, talk, twaddle, yak

babe in the wood: naïf

babel: bedlam, clang, confusion, din, discord, hubbub, hullabaloo, jargon, pandemonium, racket, tower, tumult, turmoil

babies or children, nursery for: day-care center

babies, produce: procreate, reproduce

babies, produce many: philoprogenitive, prolific

baboon: ape, babuina, chacma, mandrill, monkey

babushka: kerchief, scarf, veil

baby: babe, bambino, child, coddle, doll, fondle, humor, infant, kid, little, nestling, newborn, nipper, nurse, pamper, papoose, sissy, small, spoil, tot, wee, youthful
RELATED TERMS
baby and parent formation of close relationship: bonding
baby basketlike bed: bassinet
baby bed: bassinet, cradle, crib
baby birth, blood and tissue discharged after: afterbirth, lochia
baby birth, excrement discharged by baby just after: meconium
Baby Boomer: baby born between 1946 and 1965
baby carriage: buggy, perambulator, pram, stroller
baby clothing and accessories: layette
baby delivered by surgery: Caesarean section

baby delivery: parturition
baby develops, membranous organ in which: placenta
baby develops, membranous sac enclosing embryo in which: amnion, chorion
baby feet or bottom first, delivery of: breech
baby fetus, procedure to test for genetic abnormalities of: amniocentesis
baby fine downy hair: lanugo
baby food: pap
baby from conception to end of 8th week: embryo
baby from end of 8th week till birth: fetus
baby less than one month old: neonatal
baby off mother's milk, to get: wean
baby plastic nipple for sucking: pacifier
baby powder: talc
baby problem: colic
baby rocker: cradle
baby secretly exchanged for another: changeling
baby-sits: minds
baby-sitter: nana
baby tightly in clothes or strips of cloth, wrap: swaddle
baby to mother's placenta, cord linking: umbilical cord
baby up and down on knee, bounce: dandle
baby, carry unborn: gestate
baby, deserted: foundling
baby, Italian: bambina, bambino
baby, Native American: papoose
baby, surgical delivery of: Caesarian, Cesarean, Cesarean section, Cesarian

baby, temperature-controlled apparatus for premature: incubator
babyish: childish, immature, infantile, puerile, silly, simple
babylike cupid: amoretto
baby's first cry when born: vagitus
baby's footwear: bootee ❧

baccalaureate: address, bachelor, degree, sermon

baccarat variation: chemin de fer

bacchanal: carnival, debauch, feast, frolic, merrymaking, orgy, party, reveler

bacchant: satyr

bachelor: celibate, eligible, oner, single, unattached, unmarried

bachelor party: stag

bachelor, desirable and worthy: eligible

bachelor's degree: B.A., baccalaureate

bachelors, group of: score

bacillus: bacterium, bug, germ, microbe, virus

back: abaft, abet, aft, arear, astern, dorsum, extremity, final, fro, hind, lumbar, posterior, postern, rear, spine, stern, tail

back a loan: co-sign

back-and-forth movement: alternation, reciprocation

back and forth, send: shuttle, shuttlecock

back and sides between lowest ribs and pelvis, concerning: lumbar

back away and retreat: recede

back away in fear: blench, flinch, recoil, wince

back country: boondocks, hinterland, outback

back down: admit, back off, balk, ebb, move away, recant, renege, retract, retreat, surrender, welsh, withdrawn, yield

back end: rear, stern
back end of a ship: stern
back financially: stake
back gate: postern
back in anatomy: dorsal
back of head: occiput
back of horse (etc.) between shoulder blades: withers
back of neck: nape, nucha
back of skull: inion
back out: renege
back pain: dorsodynia, lumbago
back part of limb or organ: dorsum
back problem area: iliac
back talk: cheek, lip, mouth, sass
back up a statement: corroborate, substantiate, validate
back when standing or sitting, position of the: posture
back, get: regain, retrieve
back, pertaining to the: dorsal
back, sprain or strain: rick, wrench
back, upper, or dorsal surface of body segment of arthropod or insect: tergum
backbite: abuse, abusive, backstab, badmouth, defame, denigrate, gossip, hurtful, lie, malicious, slander, spite, vilify
backbone: character, courage, foundation, grit, guts, heart, mainstay, nerve, spirit, spunk, stamina, support, tenacity, will; spine, vertebrae
backbone or spine, having: vertebrate
backbone or spine, having no: invertebrate
backbone, animal at some stage having a notochord: chordate
backbreaker, supposed: straw
backcombs hair: teases
backcountry: boondocks, boonies, bush, farm, hinterlands, rural, sticks
backdrop: scenery, scrim
backed: endorsed, seconded
backer: advocate, ally, angel, investor, patron, promoter, protagonist, sponsor, supporter, to it
backer of cause: proponent
backfire: backlash, boomerang, crash, fail, fizzle, flop, miscarry, react
background: backdrop, credentials, culture, deeds, distance, education, experience, history, landscape, past, rear, rebound, scenery, setting, training, upbringing
background music of entertainment: incidental music
background of a lace design: fond

background or preceding cause, event: antecedent
background or setting of event, text, or statement: context
background, forming the immediate: ambient
background, in the: inconspicuous, low-profile, unobtrusive, unostentatious
backing: abetment, aegis, aid, assistance, auspices, endorsement, financing, grant, help, lining, support
backlash: fizzle, reaction, recoil, retaliation, snag, tangle
backless slippers: mules
backlog: accumulation, assets, excess, inventory, reserve, stockpile, store, surplus
backpack: haversack, hike, knapsack, pack, pouch
backpack basket: pannier
backside: behind, bottom, buns, butt, buttocks, can, derriere, fanny, hiney, keister, rear, seat, tush
backslide: desert, deteriorate, fall, lapse, regress, relapse, return, revert
backup: alternate, help, second, second string, spare, standby, substitute, supporting, understudy
backward: arear, astern, bashful, behind, behindhand, dense, dimwitted, dull, fro, hesitant, laggard, loath, recessive, reluctant, retarded, retral, retrospective, reverse, shy, slow, sluggish, stupid, unapt, undeveloped, unwilling, withdrawn
backward and remote place: backwater
backward as forward, word(s) reading same: palindrome
backward flow over propeller or of wave at beach: backwash
backward in a ship: astern
backward-looking: retrospective
backward looking or bending: retroversion
backward mentally: retarded
backward movement: recoil, regression
backward or reverse: recessive, regressive, retrograde, retrogressive
backward reasoning: hysteron proteron
backward students, for helping: remedial
backward tending: retrograde
backwater: bayou, ebb, holdback, retract, retreat, slack
backwoodsman: bumpkin, hick, hillbilly, yokel

bacon: flitch, gammon, loin, pig, pork, pork bellies, porkslab, rasher
bacon and egg sauce, served with: alla carbonara
bacon or ham, thin slice of: rasher
bacon, cured Italian: pancetta
bacon, salted and cured side of: flitch
bacon's partner: eggs
bacteria: aerobe, bacilli, bacterium, bug, cocci, germ, microbe, organism, spirilla, virus
bacteria away from external stimulus, responsive movement of: taxis
bacteria by the antibody lysin, destruction of: lysis
bacteria colony or growth for research: culture
bacteria growth, point of: nidus
bacteria that grows, feeds on organism: parasitic
bacteria, capable of being decomposed by: biodegradable
bacteria, disease-causing: pathogen
bacteria, elongated spiral-shaped: spirillum
bacteria, rod-shaped: bacillus
bacteria, round or ovoid pathogenic: streptococcus
bacteria, sewage tank in which waste is decomposed by anaerobic: septic tank
bacteria, spherical parasitic: staphylococcus
bacteria, spherical-shaped: coccus
bacteria, spiral pathogenic: spirochete
bacteria, substance that can destroy or inhibit: antibiotic
bacterium that can live without oxygen: anaerobe
bacterium that cannot live without oxygen: aerobe
bactrian: camel
bad: abandoned, aggravated, annoying, arrant, atrocious, awful, baleful, baneful, big, blemished, contaminated, contrite, corrupt, criminal, cruddy, dangerous, defective, deplorable, depraved, dire, disagreeable, displeasing, distressed, dreadful, evil, faulty, flagrant, foul, grave, gross, harmful, hazardous, hurtful, ill, immoral, inadequate, inauspicious, ineffective, inferior, lewd, lousy, mal, melancholy, misbehaving, nasty, naughty, no good, offensive, perverted, poor, repulsive, rotten, severe, sick, sinful, sorry, spoiled, tain-

ted, troublesome, unfavorable, unlucky, unpleasant, unruly, vicious, vile, wicked, worthless

bad actor: ham

bad air: smog

bad and contemptible: abject

bad and disappointing: meager, paltry

bad and disgraceful: ignominious, sordid, squalid

bad and evil: vile

bad and hateful: obnoxious, odious, vile

bad and improper: infelicitous, untimely, untoward

bad and inferior: abysmal, deplorable, lamentable

bad behavior: delinquency, misconduct, misdemeanor

bad blood: anger, bitterness, enmity, feud, hate, rancor, resentment

bad breath: halitosis

bad buy: lemon

bad check: kite

bad cut: gash

bad ending: doom

bad faith, in: mala fide

bad handwriting: cacography

bad in behavior: discreditable, reprehensible

bad loser: sorehead

bad luck: ambsace, hoodoo, misadventure, mischance, misfortune, mishap

bad luck, something bringing: hoodoo, jinx, Jonah

bad mood: pique

bad-mouth: criticize, disparage, insult, slur, smear

bad news, someone bringing: stormy petrel

bad or stale: putrid, rancid

bad person: caitiff, charlatan, knave, miscreant, rapscallion, rascal, reprobate, rogue, villain

bad play: flop

bad points: demerits

bad spelling: cacography

bad temper: bile, ire

bad-tempered: atrabilious, cantankerous, snarly, splenetic, surly, waspish

bad-tempered outburst: tantrum

bad-tempered person: crosspatch

bad thing: bane

bad to the core: rotten

bad verse: doggerel

bad, conspicuously: egregious, flagrant

bad, extremely: abominable, atrocious, diabolic, evil, execrable, flagitious, heinous, iniquitous, nefarious, pernicious, unredeemable

bad, incorrigible person: blackguard, rotten apple

badge: brand, emblem, ensign, insignia, kudos, laurels, mark, medallion, motto, pin, plaque, scepter, sign, symbol, token

badge of rank or office: insignia

badgelike rosette or ribbons: cockade

badger: annoy, bait, bandicoot, bother, brock, bully, chivy, harass, heckle, hound, huckster, irritate, nag, need, needle, pester, ride, tease, torment, worry

badger burrow: sett

badger group: cete

badgerlike animal: ratel

badinage: banter, fool, joking, joshing, kidding, raillery, repartee, ribbing, teasing

badly: awry, carelessly, corruptly, crudely, defectively, dreadfully, faultily, feebly, harshly, ill, imperfectly, inadequately, ineptly, poorly, seriously, severely, shamefully, shoddily, unfavorably, unskillfully, unwell

badminton object of play: shuttlecock

badness: evil

Baedeker: guidebook

baffle: amaze, astonish, astound, balk, bewilder, circumvent, confound, confuse, confusion, daze, deceive, defeat, discomfit, disconcert, dumbfound, elude, evade, faze, foil, frustrate, mystify, outwit, perplex, puzzle, rattle, stump, thwart

baffling problem: poser, puzzler

bag full of treats: grab

bag or suitcase: valise

bag with shoulder strap, for back carrying: haversack, knapsack, rucksack

bag, small, for carrying books: satchel

bag, small, for carrying supplies: ditty bag

bag, worn over one shoulder: haversack

bag, worn over the back: knapsack

bag, worn strapped on the back: backpack

bagatelle: game, knickknack, toy, trifle, trinket

baggage: arms, belongings, carriage, gear, impedimenta, luggage, munitions, packages, refuse, suitcases, tote, trunks, utensils

baggage carrier: porter

baggage handler at station: redcap

baggage, army: impedimenta

baggy: bloated, droopy, flabby, limp, loose, puffed, roomy, sagging, unpressed

baglike structure: sac

bagnio: bath, bordello, brothel, cathouse, hothouse, prison, whorehouse

bagpipe: doodlesack, drone, instrument, musette, zampogna

bagpipe finger hole part: chanter

bagpipe high shrill wail: skirl

bagpipe monotone drone: bourdon, burden

bagpipe pipe producing a single tone: drone

bail: bailsman, bond, bucket, bulwarks, collateral, custody, deliver, dip, guarantee, hoop, lade, ladle, pawn, pledge, release, ring, scoop, secure, security, surety, throw

bailed, as water: laded

bailiff: agent, bobby, constable, deputy, magistrate, marshall, overseer, sheriff, steward

bailiff's demand: silence

bailiff's jurisdiction: bailiwick

bailiwick: area, beat, diocese, district, domain, jurisdiction, neighborhood, province, realm, territory

bait: allure, allurement, attack, badger, bite, bribe, chum, decoy, draw, entice, enticement, exasperate, feed, fulcrum, halt, harass, inducement, irk, lure, provoke, tempt, temptation, torment, trap

bait and enticement: gudgeon

bake: boil, broil, cook, dry, fire, fry, grill, harden, heat, parch, roast, simmer, stew, toast

bake eggs: shirr

bake meat: roast

baked clay slab: tile

baked ham garnish: cloves

baker: chef, cook, roaster

baker's dozen: thirteen

baker's long-handled oven shovel: peel

bakery emanation: aroma

bakery item: bun, éclair, pie, roll, tart, torte

bakery or bread shop: boulangerie

bakery, in France: patisserie

baking dish: pan

baking dish, earthenware: terrine

balance: adjust, antithesis, composure, due, equality, equalize, equate, equilibrium, even, excess, hang, leftover, level, neutralize, offset, parity, pay, poise, recoup, remainder, residue, rest, scale, square, stability, steadiness, total, weigh

balance and compensate: offset

balance and counteract: neutralize

balance and offset: countervail, equiponderate

balance as an opposite: counterpose

balance exactly: poise

balance in metabolism: homeostasis

balance of forces: equilibrium, equipoise, stasis

balance or counterbalance: equiponderate

balance out: equate

balance precariously: teeter

balance sheet item: asset, cost

balance, mental: equilibrium

balance, movements to maintain: compensation

balance, to adjust a: redress

balanced: poised

balanced and harmonious: Apollonian

balanced arrangement of parts: symmetry

balanced very delicately: precarious

balancing point: fulcrum

balcony: brattice, catwalk, deck, foyer, gallery, mezzanine, mirador, pergola, piazza, platform, porch, stoop, terrace, veranda

balcony area: loge

balcony for singers: cantoria

balcony in theater: mezzanine

balcony in theater, open: loggia

balcony with extensive view: mirador

bald: bare, barren, callow, crude, exposed, hairless, literal, naked, plain, shaven, sheared, simple, smooth, stark, unadorned, uncovered, undisguised

balderdash: bosh, bull, bunk, claptrap, crock, drivel, jargon, malarkey, nonsense, poppycock, rigmarole, rot, trash, tripe

balding from forehead back: receding

baldness: alopecia, hairlessness, phalacrosis

baldness on top of head: calvities

baleful: apocalyptic, bad, calamitous, cold, coldhearted, deadly, destructive, evil, harmful, malicious, malign, ruinous, sinister, vindictive, wretched

balk: baffle, bar, beam, bilk, block, check, cramp, defeat, demur, discomfit, falter, foil, frustrate, hinder, hunch, impede, inhibit, loft, outwit, quibble, recoil, refuse, shy, stall, stumble, thwart, waver

balky: contrary, loath, mulish, negative, obstinate, ornery, rebellious, stubborn, wayward

ball before it bounces, strike a: volley

ball in football or soccer, steal or gain back: intercept

ball of fire: dynamo, genius, whiz

ball of yarn, thread: clew

ball or formal dance: promenade

ball-shaped: conglobate

ball where people wear masks: masque, masquerade

ball, curved flight path of: trajectory

ballad: canzone, ditty, lay, lied, poem, serenade, song, sonnet

ballast: balance, brace, load, poise, sandbag, stabilizer, steady, stone, support, trim, weight

ballet: choreography, dance, drama, pantomime

RELATED TERMS

ballet clothing: costume, leotards, tights, toe shoes, tutu

ballet dance for one: pas seul

ballet dance for three: pas de trois

ballet dance for two: pas de deux

ballet dance performed on tiptoes: pointes, sur les pointes

ballet dancer in groups only: figurant

ballet dancer just below soloist: coryphée

ballet dancer ranked below soloist, above corps: coryphée

ballet dancer, female: ballerina

ballet dancer, male: danseur

ballet dancer, principal female: prima ballerina

ballet dancer, principal male: danseur noble, premier danseur

ballet dancers who perform as a group: corps de ballet

ballet finale: coda

ballet full turn on toe: pirouette

ballet knee bend: plié

ballet leap: entrechat, jeté, sauté

ballet leap from one leg to the other: jeté

ballet leap from one leg, with legs beating together before landing: brise, pas de brise

ballet leap with alternating leg crosses: entrechat

ballet leap with calves beating together: batterie, battu

BALL-AND-STICK SPORTS

bandy
baseball
bowls
cricket
croquet
field hockey
golf
hurling
lacrosse
petanque
polo
roller hockey
rounders
shinty
softball
stickball ❦

ballet leap with legs wide apart in midair: ciseaux, pas ciseaux

ballet leap with one leg beating against the other: cabriole

ballet leap with the appearance of being suspended in midair: elevation

ballet leap, degree of height in a: elevation

ballet lover: balletomane

ballet pose on one leg, other behind: arabesque

ballet pose on one leg, other behind at right angle: attitude

ballet position: arabesque, batterie, fouette, pointe

ballet position, tiptoe: en pointe

ballet sequence: adagio

ballet short performance as interlude: divertissement

ballet small steps on point: bourrée, pas de bourrée

ballet stage director: regisseur

ballet star: étoile

ballet step: pas

ballet step of gliding and bringing feet together: glissade

ballet step of quick gliding step: chasse, pas chasse

ballet that tells a tragic story: ballet d'action

ballet traveling step: pas de bourrée

ballet turns: double, pirouette, single, tours, triple

ballet warmup: battement ❦

ballistic missile housing: silo

balloon: airship, bag, billow, blimp, distend, expand, gasbag, inflate, swell, zeppelin

balloon basket, hot-air: gondola

balloon for increased stability, heavy material in: ballast

balloon-held instrument for gathering weather data: radiosonde

balloon pilot: aeronaut

balloon, cord to release gas from a: ripcord

ballot: choice, elect, lineup, poll, tally, ticket, voice, vote, yea

ballpark figure: estimate

ball's horizontal twist/spin: English

balls of fiber, become covered with: pill

ballyhoo: advertise, buildup, hoopla, hype, plug, promote, propaganda, publicity, tout, trumpet

balm: comfort, cream, cure, fragrance, lotion, lull, medicine, oil, ointment, perfume, potion, relief, solace, soother, spice, unction

balmy: aromatic, bland, calm, fragrant, gentle, healing, mild, moist, pleasant, refreshing, soft, soothing, spicy, sunny, sweet, tropical

baloney: bull, bunk, flapdoodle, hogwash, hooey, humbug, nonsense; sandwich

balsam: copaiba, cream, fir, ointment, resin, storax, tolu, tree

balustrade: handrail, post, rail

bamboo sticks, fencing with: kendo

bamboolike grass: reed

bamboozle: buffalo, cajole, cheat, con, deceive, defraud, dupe, flimflam, fool, grill, hoax, humbug, puzzle, rook, snow, swindle

ban: bar, block, boycott, condemn, denounce, denunciation, enjoin, exclude, exclusion, execrate, forbid, halt, interdict, invoke, malediction, outlaw, prevent, prohibit, proscribe, suppress, taboo, veto

ban or exclude from participating: blackball, debar, excommunicate, ostracize

banal: blah, clichéd, commonplace, corny, dull, flat, hackneyed, humdrum, inane, insipid, mundane, ordinary, pedestrian, silly, stale, trite, trivial, watery

banal remark: cliché, platitude

banana: bunch, ensete, musa, plantain, saba

banana fiber: abaca

banana-like fruit: plantain

band: aggregate, bevy, bunch, bundle, collection, combo, company, crew, gang, garland, group, merge, orchestra, outfit, pack, posse, ring, set, symphony, troop

band between moldings: fascia

band of black worn for mourning: crape

band of color on insect, plant: fascia

band of decoration on upper wall of room: frieze

band of musicians, singers, dancers, or actors performing together: ensemble

band of people: cohort

band of ribbon or metal worn as headband: fillet

band of Zulu warriors: impi

band together: herd

band worn around the upper arm, cloth: brassard

band, small jazz: combo

bandage: bind, blind, blindfold, cast, cincture, clout, compress, dress, fillet, gauze, ligate, plaster, swaddle, swathe, tape, truss

bandage of overlapping spirals to immobilize digit or limb: spica

bandage or bind tightly: swaddle, swathe

bandage to check bleeding, tight encircling: tourniquet

bandaged: dressed, fasciate

bandanna: handkerchief, kerchief, scarf, silk

bandeau: bra, brassiere, fillet, strip

bandit: bandido, banish, bravo, brigand, caco, crook, cutthroat, desperado, gangster, highwayman, marauder, outlaw, pirate, robber, thief

band's stint: gig

bandy: banter, barter, carriage, cart, discuss, exchange, spar, swap, toss, trade

bane: blight, curse, death, downfall, evil, harm, injury, mischief, murder, nemesis, nuisance, pest, poison, ruin, torment, undoing, woe

baneful: bad, deadly, dire, evil, fatal, harmful, hurtful, ill, malevolent, noxious, pestilent, poisonous, ruinous, venomous, vile

bang: beat, blow, bounce, clap, clash, collide, crash, detonation, dock, drive, drub, echo, energy, excel, explosion, force, hit, kick, pound, rap, slam, sound, strike, thrash, thump, thwack, whack, wow

bang of aircraft flying faster than speed of sound: sonic boom

banger: firecracker

banging door sound: slam

bangle: bracelet, charm, droop, fritter, knickknack, ornament, roam, tinsel, trinket, waste

banish: abandon, ban, bar, condemn, deport, dismiss, dispel, displace, eject, exclude, exile, expatriate, expel, ostracize, oust, proscribe, relegate, rid

banish or exclude: ostracize

banish or exile: deport, expatriate, relegate

banish or outlaw: proscribe

banister: balustrade, handrail, railing, support

banister, post supporting handrail at landing of: newel

banister, posts of: baluster

bank: acclivity, anthill, banco, bay, bench, brew, brink, coast, dike, dune, edge, elevation, embankment, fence, hill, levee, margin, mass, mound, pile, platform, ramp, ridge, rive, river, row, sand, shallow, shelf, shore, slope, stack, stage, strand, tier

bank account, overdrawing a: O.D., O/D, overdraft

bank aide: clerk, teller

bank holding back river or irrigated field: levee

bank loan, lowest rate of interest on: prime rate

bank of earth to prevent floods: dike, embankment

bank of earth to support roadway: embankment

bank of protection or defense: barricade, bastion, breastwork, bulwark, earthwork, parapet, rampart

bank of river, pertaining to: riparian

bank of seats: tier

bank on: rely

bank paper: note

bank room: vault

bank, a check's passing through a: clearing

bankroll: back, capitalize, currency, finance, funds, grubstake, stake, subsidize, wad

bankroller: angel

bankrupt: belly-up, broke, busted, default, depleted, destitute, devour, drain, failure, impoverished, insolvent, liquidation, on the rocks, penniless, ruin, ruined, sap, strip

bankrupt business or person, settle affairs of: liquidate

banned: illegal, outlawed, taboo

banned goods: contraband

banner: banderole, colors, ensign, flag, foremost, gonfalon, headline, jack, pennant, standard; exemplary, leading, profitable, salient, surpassing

banner feature: spangle

banner on crosspiece: gonfalon

banquet: carousal, dine, dinner, feast, festival, fete, jamboree, junket, meal, reception, regale, treat

banquet with mock attacks on guest of honor: roast

banquet, concerning a lavish: Lucullan

banquet, person proposing toasts and introducing speakers at: toastmaster

bantam: chicken, cock, combative, diminutive, dwarf, hen, little, petite, saucy, small, teeny, tiny

banter: badinage, chaff, chitchat, fool, jest, jive, joke, jolly, josh, kid, mockery, persiflage, playfulness, pleasantry, rag, raillery, rib, ride, satirize, tease

bantling: child

banzai: attack, charge, cry, hello

baobab: tree

baobab fruit: monkey bread

baptism: beginning, christening, cleansing, dunking, immersion, initiation, purification, ritual, sacrament

baptism by pouring water on head: affusion

baptism by sprinkling of water: aspersion

baptism by total submersion in water: immersion

baptism oil and balsam anointment: chrism

baptism or church rite: sacrament

baptism robe worn by baby: chrisom

baptism tank or font: baptistry

baptism, instruction received before: catechism

baptismal receptacle: font

baptize: admit, christen, cleanse, dip, dub, full, name, purify, sprinkle, term

bar and restaurant: brasserie

bar connecting wheels: axle

bar during Prohibition: speakeasy

bar fastened into loop or strap: toggle

bar for ballet exercises: barre

bar inside motor vehicle roof to prevent injury in rollover: roll bar

bar manager or saloon keeper: publican

bar of gold or metal made for storage, shipment: ingot

bar or barroom: lounge, saloon, taproom, tavern

bar or pub, small private room in: snug

bar used to brace a structure against side forces: strut

bar with sink: wet bar

bar, legally: estop

bar, upright and principal support: stanchion

barb: awn, beard, bristle, bur, burr, clip, cut, dart, file, hook, horse, insult, jag, jagg, kingish, point, projection, ridge, sarcasm, scoff, shaft, snag, spike, thorn

barbarian: alien, boor, brute, bully, clod, goth, hoodlum, hooligan, hun, philistine, punk, rude, savage, uncivilized, untutored, vandal, vicious, wild

barbarians, of old: huns

barbarism: atrocity, brutality, cant, catachresis, corruption, cruelty, misuse, savageness, solecism

barbarity: atrocity, boorishness, brutality, cruelty, ferocity, inhumanity, rudeness, ruthlessness, savagery

barbarous: brutal, cruel, fell, ferocious, heartless, hunnish, ignorant, impolite, inhumane, mean, outlandish, primitive, rough, rude, ruthless, slavish, truculent, uncivil, uncivilized, uncultivated, unholy, unpolished, wild

barbarous female: ogress

barbecue: bake, broil, cookout, fireplace, grill, party, picnic, rotisserie, spit

barbecue coal: briquette

barbecue-style Japanese food: hibachi

barbecue, rotating: rotisserie

barbed spear: gaff

barbed wire with points: razor ribbon

barbed wire, obstacle composed of: cheval-de-frise, fraise

barber: beautician, chirotonsor, coiffeur, cosmetologist, cut, haircutter, hairdresser, poller, scraper, shave, stylist, tonsor, tonsure, trim

barber, pertaining to a: tonsorial

bard: druid, minstrel, musician, poet, scald, scop, singer, troubadour, writer

bare: all, alone, austere, bald, bare-skinned, barren, callow, clear, cold, defenseless, desolate, disclose, divert, divest, divulge, empty, expose, exposed, meager, mere, naked, nude, paltry, plain, reveal, scanty, simple, stark, strip, stripped, threadbare, un-

adorned, unarmed, unclad, uncover, uncovered, undraped, undress, unfurnished, worn, worthless

bare rocks: scars

barefaced: audacious, blatant, blunt, bold, brash, brazen, candid, flagrant, frank, glaring, impudent, open, sassy, shameless, undisguised

barefoot or wearing sandals: discalced

barefooted: discalced, shoeless, unshod

barely: almost, faint, hardly, just, narrowly, only, poorly, scantily, scarcely, slightly

barely adequate: mere, scanty, so-so

barely discernible or visible: faint

barely perceptible: liminal

barest trace: modicum, semblance

barfly: alcoholic, carouser, drunk, lush, sot, stiff, tippler

bargain: agreement, barter, buy, cheap, closeout, contend, contest, contract, covenant, deal, dicker, discount, giveaway, haggle, negotiate, pact, sale, steal, stipulate, struggle, trade, transaction

bargain for: anticipate, contemplate, expect, imagine

bargain-priced: bon marché

bargain, secure a: clinch

bargaining unit: union

barge: ark, boat, dory, ferry, flagship, flatboat, lighter, lumber, lunge, lurch, raft, scow, ship, thrust, tow, vessel

barhopping: popination

barium oxide: baryta

bark: abrade, arf, bag, bay, cough, cry, holler, howl, roar, rub, shout, snap, solicit, woof, yap, yell, yelp; cortex, covering, rind, shell, skin

bark like a dog: latrate

bark, growing or living on: corticolous

barley: food, grain, malt, seed

barley appendage: arista

barley bristle: awn

barmy: flighty, foamy, foolish, frothy, loco, screwy, silly

barn: bay, corral, hayloft, loft, outbuilding, shed, stable, stall, storehouse

barnacle: appendage, bloodsucker, crustacean, freeloader, hanger-on, leech, parasite

barnstorm: campaign, pilot, tour, troupe

barnstormer: actor

barometer based on changes in atmospheric pressure: aneroid barometer

baron: capitalist, king, magnate, mogul, noble, peer, tycoon

baronet's wife: lady

baroque: bizarre, elaborate, extravagant, flamboyant, gilt, grotesque, irregular, ornate, rococo

barrack: base, camp, dormitory, garrison, hut, quarters

barracks for military: casern, garrison

barracks for slaves: barracoon

barracuda: barry, becuna, fish, guaguanche, pelon, picuda, sennet, spet

barrage: attack, barrier, bombardment, broadside, burst, cannonade, deluge, fire, hail, onslaught, outpouring, salvo, shower, torrent, volley

barrel: butt, cask, cistern, container, cylinder, drum, fat, hogshead, hoop, hurry, keg, receptacle, rundlet, tub, tun, vat, vessel

barrel bulge: bilge

barrel for drawing or tapping, hole in: bunghole

barrel maker or repairer: cooper, hooper

barrel of gun, front of: muzzle

barrel or cask holding around 100 gallons: hogshead, puncheon

barrel or cask, stopper: spigot, spile

barrel organ: hurdy gurdy

barrel part: hoop, stave

barrel rim, lip: chime

barrel stave: lag

barrel strips of wood forming sides: staves

barrel support for when it is on its side: gantry

barrel, drawing off or tapping from: draft

barrel, small: firkin, kilderkin

barrel, to draw off by piercing hole in: broach

barrel, very large: tun

barren: arid, badland, bare, childless, depleted, desert, desolate, dry, dull, effete, empty, exhausted, fallow, fruitless, impotent, infertile, jejune, meager, stark, sterile, stern, treeless, unfruitful, unproductive, useless, vain, vapid, waste, yeld

barren and bleak: stark

barren and fruitless: infecund, sterile

barricade: bar, barrier, block, blockade, bulwark, close off, defend, fence, fortify, obstruction, stockade, stop, wall

barrier: bar, barricade, bound, boundary, chain, confines, dam, defense, door, drawback, fence, fortress, gate, gurdle, handicap, hedge, hurdle, limit, line, moat, obstruction, palisades, parapet, rail, railing, restraint, roadblock, screen, stockade, trench, wall

barrier of floating logs: boom

barrier of stakes: palisade

barrier, curtain, or screen: traverse

barrier, incapable of being overcome, as a: insuperable, insurmountable

barring: besides, but, excepting, excluding, saving

barrister: advocate, attorney, counsel, counselor, lawyer, solicitor

barroom: cafe, dramshop, lounge, pub, saloon, taproom, tavern

barrow: bank, dune, grave, gurry, hill, hog, mote, mound, mountain, pile, pushcart, trolley, tumulus

bartenders, group of: blarney

barter: bargain, chop, commerce, dicker, exchange, haggle, hawk, permute, reciprocate, sell, swap, trade, traffic, truck, vend

basal: basic, beginning, easy, elementary, fundamental, initial, lowest, necessary

base and degraded: ignoble, sordid

base argument on facts: predicate

base-forming compound: amine

base of column, statue: pedestal, plinth

base of the thumb: thenar

based on earlier example: derivative

based on eight: octal

baseless: false, gratuitous, groundless, idle, pointless, reasonless, unfounded, untenable, unwarranted

baseness and vileness: turpitude

bash: bat, beat, blast, blow, blowout, clobber, dent, mash, party, smash, strike, swat, wallop, whop, wingding

bashful: blushing, coy, daunted, demure, diffident, dismayed, embarrassed, humble, modest, reserved, retiring, sheepish, shrinking, shy, timid, unassertive

basic: abecedarian, central, chief, elemental, essential, fundamental, inherent, key, main, primary, rudimentary, underlying, vital

basic beliefs: ethos

basic component of matter: atom

basic constituent: element

basic cultural character: ethos

basic element of a word: root

basic element or skill of subject: rudiment

basic facts: data

basic metal: ore

basic nature of something: hypostasis, quintessence

basic neutralizer: acid

basic structure of organization or system: infrastructure

basic underlying principle: axiom, elixir, postulate, premise

basically: at least, au fond, essentially, firstly, fundamentally, mostly, primarily, radically

basil: herb, ocimum, plant, royal, tulasi

basilica: church, shrine, temple, title

basilica part: apse, nave

basin: bay, bowl, crater, depression, dish, dock, font, lagoon, lavatory, marina, pan, receptor, reservoir, sink, stoup, tank, tub, valley, vessel, washbowl, watershed

basin for ceremonial ablution: piscina, sacarium

basin for holy water: font, stoup

basin for washing private parts: bidet

basis: antecedent, axiom, bed, bottom, cause, core, essence, footing, foundation, ground, groundwork, heart, motive, premise, principle, proof, reason, root

basis and fundamental principle: hypostasis

basis for action or belief: rationale

basis for discussion or conclusion: premise

basis for plot development: donnee

basis or fundamental principle: anlage, bedrock, substratum

basis, conceptual structure or system built from a: superstructure

bask: bathe, delight, enjoy, indulge, laze, loll, lounge, rejoice, relax, relish, revel, sun, wallow, warm

basket: ark, barrel, bassinet, bin, canasta, cesta, chest, container, cradle, crate, dosser, hamper, pannier, receptacle, scull, scuttle, skep

basket carried on back: pannier

basket for fishermen, wicker: creel

basket for picnic: hamper

basket material: osier, reed

basket of flowers or fruit, architectural ornament of: corbeil

basket of hot-air balloon: gondola

basket over bicycle wheel: pannier

basket weaving, fiber from palm for: raffia

basket weaving, fiber from wood and other materials for: chip

BASEBALL TERMS

advance to first base after four balls: base on balls, walk

baseball terms: assist, bag, bat, batter, battery, bean, bench, blooper, bottom, bullpen, bunt, circuit, cleanup, count, curve, delivery, diamond, double, drive, dugout, error, fan, field, force, foul, full count, grounder, high, hit, home, homer, infield, inside, knuckler, lob, mound, out, outfield, outside, peg, pinch hit, pitch, plate, pole, popout, popup, putout, RBI, run, sacrifice, save, score, sidearm, single, sinker, slide, spitball, squeeze, stance, stretch, strike, strikeout, swing, triple, walk, wild, windup

baseballs caught in practice: shagging

batter stance with front foot closer to plate: closed stance

batter stance with front foot farther from plate: open stance

batter, fourth in lineup: cleanup

batter, not playing field: designated hitter, DH

blunder: error

catcher error allowing runner to advance: passed ball

decision to put out runner rather than batter: fielder's choice

diamond inside: infield

face mask flap hanging down over neck: goat's beard

game portion with two teams coming to bat: inning

games between same teams on one day, two: doubleheader

glove: mitt

hit back to pitcher: comebacker

hit in practice, tossing ball up and hitting it: fungo

hit that bounces into stands or is interfered with by spectator: ground rule double

hit that is an out but advances a runner: sacrifice

hit, between infield/outfield: Texas Leaguer

hit, hard and horizontal: line drive

hit, rolling on ground: ground ball, grounder

hit, weak: blooper

hitter that hits right- and left-handed: switch hitter

home run with runners on all bases: grand slam

intentionally batted softly into infield: bunt

minor league: bush league

officials: ump, umpire

out when runner is out when forced from his base by a hit
and fails to reach next base safely: force-out

outfield between center/left and center/right: power alleys

oversock: stirrup sock

pitch by right-hander that curves right or left-hander that
curves left: screwball

pitch error allowing runner to advance: wild pitch

pitch in the strike zone: strike

pitch outside strike zone and not swung at: ball

pitch that curves sharply down as it approaches home plate:
sinker

pitch that is fast and curves slightly: slider

pitch that suddenly drops as it approaches home plate: split-
fingered fastball

pitch thrown fast but is slow in movement: changeup

pitch thrown intentionally close to batter: brushback pitch

pitch thrown wide to catcher to entice runner to steal:
pitchout

pitcher: hurler

pitcher and catcher team: battery

pitcher illegal motion: balk

pitcher that relieves early in game: long man, long reliever

pitcher who replaces another: reliever

pitcher's area: bullpen

play catching runner off base: pickoff

play to not swing at pitch: take

play trapping runner between bases: rundown

play where third-base runner tries to score as soon as pitch
is thrown: suicide squeeze, squeeze play

player bench in shelter: dugout

player intercepting throw in from outfield: cutoff man

player who bats for pitcher: designated hitter

player, substitute: utility player

positions: catcher, center-field, first-base, left-field, pinch-
hitter, pitcher, right-field, second-base, shortstop, third-
base

rule applicable when there are runners at 1st, 2nd or 1st,
2nd, 3rd with fewer than two outs that catchable infield
fly is automatic out: infield fly rule

runner advancing while pitching in progress: stolen base

strip in outfield: warning track ❦

---

basket weaving, plant shoots like willow for: wicker

basket weaving, willow twigs for: osier

basket, large and covered: hamper

basket, large wicker: pannier

basket, laundry: hamper

basketlike furniture, furnishings: wickerwork

basketry: caning

basketry twigs: osier

bass: alto, black, deep, fish, jewfish, low, singer, voice

bass accompaniment played on the keyboard instrument: basso continuo, figured bass, thoroughbass

bassinet: cradle, crib, perambulator, pram

bassoon and contrabassoon: reeds

bassoon's cousin: oboe

basswood: linden

bastard: adulterated, artificial, bantling, baseborn, fake, false, fatherless, galley, hybrid, illegitimate, impure, lowbred, mongrel, scoundrel, spurious

baste: batter, beat, cane, cook, lambaste, lard, pelt, punish, roast, season, sew, stitch, tack, thrash

bastion: citadel, fort, mainstay, pillar, rock, stronghold

bat: beat, beetle, billy, binge, blow, bludgeon, bop, brick, clobber, club, cudgel, flutter, hit, racket, sock, spree, stick, strike, stroke, swat

bat direction and distance sensory system: echolocation

bat winglike membrane: patagium

bat wood: ash

batch: array, assemblage, bunch, bundle, collection, group, lot, mass, mixture, parcel, quantity, sort, volume

bath: cleansing, dip, plunge, shower, spa, sponge, toilet, tub, wash

bath for sitting in: sitz bath

bath or hot tub: Jacuzzi

BASKETBALL TERMS

basketball nicknames: cager, hoopster
basketball terms: backboard, backcourt, cage, dribble, dunk, field goal, free throw, front court, jump ball, key, layup, pass, rebound, stuff, tap, timeout, tip-in
bouncing: dribble
defense with two players on side of free-throw lane and one man-to-man: box and one
dribbling violation: steps, traveling, walking
free throw: foul shot
goal made by thrusting ball forcefully down in basket: slam dunk
interference at backboard or rim: goaltending
loss of possession: turnover
marked area between free-throw line and basket: key, lane
man-to-man length of court defense: full-court press

offense moving ball quickly toward basket: fast break
offense with screen and turn to receive pass: pick and roll
officials: ref, referee, umpire
rule that offense must move to front court within 10 seconds: 10-second rule
rule that offense must try for a goal within 30 seconds of possession: 30-second rule
rule that players may not remain in key more than three seconds: 3-second rule
shot taken from line after a foul: free throw
shot, not touching backboard, rim, net: air ball
shot, one-handed close to basket: layup
shot, one-handed over head: hook shot
shot, while jumping in air: jump shot ❦

---

bath or toilet, communal: latrine
bath sponge: loofah
bath, cleansing: ablution
bath, Finnish steam: sauna
bath, steam: sauna, Turkish bath
bathe: bask, douse, immerse, irrigate, lave, permeate, pervade, rinse, shower, soak, submerge, suffuse, tub, wash, wet
bathhouse: cabana
bathing suit: bikini, maillot, one-piece, string bikini, swimsuit, trunks, two-piece
bathroom: can, commode, head, john, latrine, lav, restroom, sudatory, toilet, wc
baths in ancient Rome, room for hot: caldarium
baths of ancient Greece and Rome, public: thermae
baths or bathing, pertaining to: balneal
baths or bathing, science of: balneology
batiklike dyeing technique: tie-dye
baton: bend, billy, bourdon, cudgel, nightstick, rod, scepter, staff, stick, truncheon, wand
batrachian: amphibian, frog, toad
bats, pertaining to: chiropteran, vespertilian
batten: down, enrich, fix, gloat, prosper, thrive, tie
batter: assault, beat, bombard, bruise, clobber, concoction, cripple, crush, demolish, dent, destroy, hammer, hit, hitter, maim, paste, pound, pummel, ram, shatter
battered car: heap, jalopy
batter's position: stance

battery: army, artillery, assault, bombardment, brigade, cell, division, grid, group, ring, series, violence
battery cables used to start car: jumper cables
battery chemical action, referring to: galvanic, voltaic
battery conductor of electric current: electrode
battery ionizing substance: electrolyte
battery opposing magnetic points: poles
battery terminal: anode
battle: affray, blitzkreig, bombard, brush, campaign, carnage, clash, combat, competition, conflict, contend, contest, crusade, duel, encounter, engagement, fight, fray, hostilities, joust, meet, press, skirmish, sortie, strife, struggle, warfare
battle-ax with two sharp edges: twibil
battle characterized by bloodshed, carnage, of a: internecine
battle cry of a kamikaze pilot: banzai
battle flag: oriflamme
battle formation: deployment, phalanx
battle rallying point flag: standard
battle-ready: armed
battle, minor: skirmish
batty: crazy, deranged, foolish, insane, loco, nuts, silly, wacky
bauble: bead, doodad, gewgaw, gimcrack, knickknack, novelty, plaything, toy, trifle, trinket
bawdy: dirty, foul, lewd, obscene
bawl: bellow, boohoo, cry, howl, shout, weep
bawl out: rail, read the riot act
bay: bank, compartment, cove, creek,

enclose, fiord, fleet, gulf, haven, hole, indentation, inlet, recess, sinus, window; horse, roan; howl, yawp; laurel, tree
bay city: port
bay formed by shoreline, wide: bight
bay on shoreline of sea/river/lake, small: cove
bay tree: laurel
bay window: oriel
bay, stream leading into land: inlet
baylike body of water connecting larger bodies of water: sound
baylike body of water extending inland to meet mouth of river: estuary
baylike body of water partially enclosed by land: gulf
baylike body of water separated from sea by sandbars or coral reefs: lagoon
bayonet: knife, pierce, stab, weapon
bayou: backwater, brook, creek, outlet, river, stream
bazaar: canteen, emporium, exposition, fair, fete, market
bazaar stall: booth
bazoo: kazoo, mouth, talk
bazooka or onager: launcher
be-all and end-all: acme, aggregate, entirety, everything, ultimate
beach: bank, coast, ground, moor, ripa, sand, seaside, shingle, shore, strand
beach bag: tote
beach bathhouse/tent: cabana
beach cover: sand
beach gravel of large smooth pebbles: shingle
beach hazard: undertow
beach shoe: flip-flop, thong, water shoe

beach topography: dunes
beach washer: neap tide
beach, shoreline (in Latin): ripa
beached: ashore, on shore
beacon: cresset, flare, guide, lighthouse, mark, seamark, sign, signal, signpost, warning, watchtower
bead: bauble, bubble, chaplet, drop, foam, globule, prayer, rosary, sight, sparkle, trinket
bead at end of decade on rosary: paternoster
beads, group of ten prayer: decade
beads, Native American currency: peag, wampum
beads, rosary with five decades or string of: chaplet
beads, string of five to fifteen decades of prayer: rosary
beady starch from root of cassava: tapioca
beak: bill, mandible, neb, nib, nose, peak, proboscis, rostrum, schnozzle, snout, spout
beaker: bareca, cup, glass, vessel
beam: chevron, emit, flash, gleam, glow, laser, light, radiate, ray, shine, smile; bar, girder, joist, rafter, stud, support
beam-amplifying device: laser
beam as foundation or support for structure, heavy: pile
beam as main support, horizontal: girder
beam as support or connector, long heavy: stringer, summer
beam as upper member of window or door and supporting structure: lintel, summer
beam extending wall to wall: crossbeam
beam fastener: rivet
beam of light: ray
beam projecting beyond fulcrum and fixed at only one end: cantilever
beam supporting floor or ceiling, parallel horizontal: joist
beaming: aglow, cheerful, gay, joyous, lucent, radiant, rosy, shining
bean: caster, frijol, frijole, haricot, kidney, lentil, lima, soya; brain, head, noggin, skull
bean curd: tofu
bean sprout source: mung bean
beanery drink: java
bear: brown bear, bruin, cub, grizzly, koala, polar bear
bear a grudge against: resent

bear down: defeat, exert, overpower, push, stress
bear impact of: bear the brunt of
bear the cost: defray
bear witness: attest
bear young, as sheep: yean
bear, pertaining to: ursine
bear, to: abide, afford, allow, behave, breed, bring, carry, conduct, constellation, drive, endure, forebear, lug, press, produce, put up with, render, stand, suffer, support, sustain, thrust, tolerate, tote, transport, yield
beard: awn, barb, fuzz, goatee, stubble, whiskers
beard, long and rectangular: patrician
beard on chin only: goatee
bearded: barbate, barbed, hairy, hirsute, pogionate, shaggy, unshaven, whiskered
bearded plant or animal: barbate
beardlike hair by ears: sideburns
bearing: address, air, allure, aspect, attitude, behavior, birth, carriage, conduct, countenance, course, direction, front, habit, look, orient, poise, port, posture, pressure, producing, support, track, trend, way; aim, importance, influence, meaning, purport, relation, significance, thrust, weight
bearing multiple young: multiparous
bearing no trade name: generic
bearing or behavior: comportment, demeanor, deportment, manner, mien
bearing weapons: armed
bearing while walking: gait
bearing young by eggs that hatch outside the body: oviparous
bearing young by eggs that hatch within the body: ovoviviparous
bearing young not by eggs: viviparous
bearing, part of machine shaft or axle supported by: journal
bearings, finding one's: orientation
bearings, having lost one's: disoriented
bearlike: ursine
bears, concerning: ursine
bears, group of: sloth
beast: animal, barbarian, brute, cad, creature, demon, fiend, gargoyle, hun, lion, monster, pig, savage, tiger, varmint
beast of burden: ass, burro, camel, llama, mule, pack animal
beast, like a wild: theroid
beastlike: feral, theriomorphic
beastly: abominable, animal, awful, bad, boorish, brutal, brutish, disgust-

ing, dreadful, feral, foul, gross, inhuman, loathsome, nasty, obscene, offensive, sadistic, swinish, vulgar
beasts, concerning: bestial
beat: accent, area, assault, assignment, baff, bang, bash, bashed, baste, bat, batter, beatnik, beetle, belt, best, better, blister, blow, bolt, bray, buffet, cadence, cane, canvass, churn, clink, clobber, club, cob, conquer, cotton, crush, cudgel, defeat, ding, douse, drub, dump, excel, exhaust, exhausted, fan, fatigue, fatigued, fight, filch, flap, flax, flog, fluctuate, hammer, hamper, haze, hit, ictus, kaput, knock, lambaste, lash, lick, lump, malleate, maul, meter, outrun, overcome, pant, patrol, pelt, pound, pulsate, pulse, pulsed, pummel, quiver, raddle, repel, repulse, rhythm, ripple, round, rout, scat, scoop, shellac, shellack, slam, squash, strike, stroke, suppress, surpass, switch, tack, tap, thrash, thresh, throb, throbbing, thump, tired, top, trounce, trump, vanquish, wave, whip, whop, win, worst
beat around the bush: equivocate, hedge, prevaricate, temporize
beat back: repel
beat it: begone, fled, get out, go, leave, out, scat, scram, shoo, skedaddle, vamoose
beat or cudgel: fustigate
beat person running between them, punishment with two lines to: gauntlet
beat rapidly: palpitate
beat rhythmically: pulsate
beat severely: trounce
beat the odds: turn the tide, upset
beat to a story: scoop
beat with a stick: caned
beat with club: bludgeon, cudgel
beat with fists: pommel, pummel
beat with force: pelt
beat with hand, tool, weapon: smite
beat with stick: drub, flail, lambaste
beat with stick on soles of feet: bastinado
beat with whip: flagellate, flay, flog, scourge
beat, defeat: drub
beaten by the tortoise: hare
beating or rapping, repetitive: rataplan
beating or sound of beating: percussion
beatitude: blessedness, bliss, ecstasy, euphoria, exaltation, happiness, joy

beatnik: beat, bohemian, dropout, hippie, maverick, peacenik

beats a birdie: eagle

beats a deuce: three

beats decisively: shellacs

beau: admirer, beaux, blade, boyfriend, bravery, buck, caballero, coxcomb, cupidon, dandy, dude, escort, fellow, flame, gentleman, guy, honey, lover, spark, steady, suitor, sweetheart, truelove

beau ideal: example, model, standard

beau monde: aristocracy, elite, fashion, society

beautiful: angelic, attractive, belle, blithe, bonny, charming, choice, cute, decore, delicate, elegant, elite, exquisite, fair, fine, freely, gorgeous, graceful, handsome, lovely, poetic, pretty, radiant, ravishing, splendid, stunning

beautiful and delicate: exquisite

beautiful and sensual: voluptuous

beautify: adonize, adorn, bedeck, deck, decorate, embellish, enhance, garnish, gild, glamorize, grace, prune

beauty parlor: hairdresser, salon

beauty, concerning: esthetic

beauty, lover of: esthete

beauty, physical: pulchritude

beauty, study of: esthetics

beaver: kit, plew, skin

beaver den: lodge

beaver hat: castor

beaver project: dam

beaverlike animal: ratel

because: being, for, inasmuch, since, so, that, therefore, thus

because of: owing

because of one's official position: ex officio

beckon: ask, bid, bidding, bow, call, coax, command, curtsey, curtsy, entice, gesture, motion, nod, salutation, summon, tempt, wave

beck's partner: call

becloud: camouflage, conceal, confound, confuse, darken, fog, hide, muddy, mystify, obscure, overcast, perplex, puzzle

become: accord, adorn, augment, befall, befit, behoove, betide, change, enhance, evolve, flatter, get, grace, grow, heighten, pass, rise, shift, suit, turn into, wax

become accustomed to: enure

become apparent: emerge

become corroded: rust

become dim: fade

become envious: turn green

become ill: sicken

become indistinct: blur

become irate: get one's dander up

become limp: wilt

become motionless: freeze

become tiresome: pall

become too large for: outgrow

become visible: emerge

become weary: tire

become wedged: jam

becoming: appropriate, attractive, befitting, convenient, decorum, fit, flattering, gainly, good, handsome, right, suitable, tasteful, worthy

becoming larger: waxing

becoming old: aging

becoming passé: on the way out

bed: bassinet, berth, bunk, cot, couch, cradle, crib, davenport, double bed, feather bed, hay, king-size bed, lodging, mattress, pad, pallet, queen-size bed, rollaway, sack, stretcher, twin; base, basis, bottom, foundation, matrix; channel, layer, row, stratum; garden, plot

bed and couch, Japanese mattress: futon

bed board: slat

bed in the morning, dragging oneself out of: dysania

bed of canvas or netting suspended from supports: hammock

bed of coal: seam

bed of roses: ease

bed of straw mattress: paillasse, pallet, palliasse

bed on casters that rolls under another bed: trundle bed

bed that closes into wall: Murphy bed

bed-wetting: enuresis

bed, canopy over: tester

bed, confined or staying in: accouchement, confinement, lying-in

bed, decorative hanging from under mattress of: bedskirt

bed, narrow hard: pallet

bed, old-fashioned pan of coals or hot liquid for warming a: warming pan

bed, posture or position in: decubitus

bedazzle: astound, awe, bewilder, blind, captivate, daze, enchant, overwhelm, stagger, stun

bedbug family: cimex

bedding: afghan, bedclothes, bedspread, blanket, comforter, cover, duvet, linen, pillow, quilt, sham, sheets

bedeck: adorn, array, decorate, embellish, gem, grace, ornament, trim

bedevil: abuse, annoy, bewitch, harass, harry, hex, irk, muddle, pester, tease, torment, worry

bedight: clad

bedim: becloud, blur, cloud, darken, fade, fog, gloom, mist, obscure

bedlam: asylum, chaos, confusion, din, furor, lunatic, madhouse, madness, noise, racket, riot, tumult, turmoil, uproar

bedraggled: limp

bedridden: ailing, confined, disabled, feeble, ill, incapacitated

bedridden, not: ambulatory

bedrock: base, basis, bottom, ground, substratum

bedroom: berth, boudoir, chamber, compartment, cubicle, flat

bedroom clock type: alarm

bedsore: decubitus

bedspread: comforter, counterpane, quilt

bedspread case or covering: duvet

bee-eating: apivorous

bee fertilizing queen but doing no work: drone

bee food: flowers, nectar

bee genus: apis

bee group: colony, swarm

bee mixture of nectar (honey) and pollen as bee food: beebread

bee product: honey

bee substance secreted by workers that feed larvae: royal jelly

bee type: bumblebee, carpenter, cuckoo, honeybee, worker

bee young: grubs

bee, having a stinger as a: aculeate

beef cattle male: steer

beef cured by drying and smoking: biltong, charqui, jerky

beef cut from tenderloin, fillet of: tournedos

beef cuts: brisket, chuck, cutlet, flank, loin, porterhouse, quarter, roast, round, rump, shank, short rib, shoulder, side, sirloin, steak

beef cuts from brisket: brisket, shank crosscuts

beef cuts from chuck: blade steak, chuck short ribs, eye roast, pot roast, shoulder steak

beef cuts from flank: flank steak

beef cuts from rib: rib roast, rib steak, rib-eye steak

beef cuts from round: eye of round roast, round steak, rump roast, top round steak

beef cuts from short loin: Porterhouse steak, T-bone steak, tenderloin steak, top-loin steak

beef cuts from short plate: plate-skirt steak

beef cuts from sirloin: pinbone sirloin steak, sirloin steak, tip roast

beef fillet in sour cream sauce served on a bed of noodles: beef stroganoff

beef in bun, spicy ground: sloppy joe

beef industry: ranching

beef marinated in vinegar, water, wine, spices: sauerbraten

beef smoked and thinly sliced, dried: chipped beef

beef unit: side

beef, double sirloin cut of: baron

beef, raw: steak tartare

beef, thin strips of fat in: marbling

beefs: grievances

beefy: brawny, bulky, hefty, husky, robust, stolid

beehive: apiary, hive, skep

beehive of straw: skep

beekeeper: apiarist, apiculturist

beelike: apian

beep: honk, page

beeper: pager

beer: ale, barley, beverage, bock, bottled, brew, brewer, brewsky, case, dark, glass, grog, hops, keg, kvass, lager, liquor, malt, mug, near, pitcher, porter, stein, stout, suds, swanky, yard, yeast

RELATED TERMS

beer and bar mat collector: tegestologist

beer barrel: keg

beer brewing pulp: mash

beer can or coffee cup sleeve: zarf

beer flavoring: hops

beer foam: barm

beer from keg, draw: draft, tap

beer glass: stein, toby

beer hall: rathskeller

beer ingredient: barley, hops, malt

beer maker: brewer

beer mug which may have hinged lid: stein

beer without pausing, swallow: chugalug

beer, heating to kill microorganisms in: pasteurization

beer, low-hop: lager

beerlike: malty ☙

beet: beetrave, beta, borscht, chard, mangel, mangold, sugar, vegetable

beet soup: borscht

beet with large yellowish root: mangel-wurzel

beetle: battledore, bug, chafer, dor, drive, elater, firefly, golach, goldbug, Japanese, june bug, ladybug, meloe, prinoid, scarab, skipjack, stag, tumblebug, weevil

beetle sacred in ancient Egypt: scarab

beetle secretion: trehala

befall: bechance, become, betide, come, develop, gel, hap, happen, occur, pertain, transpire

befits: suits

befitting: appropriate, apt, becoming, conforming, correct, just, kosher, right, seemly, suitable

befog: cloud, conceal, confound, confuse, dim, enshroud, mystify, obscure, puzzle

before: afore, ahead, already, antecedent, anterior, avant, back, earlier, ere, facing, first, former, forward, front, heretofore, hitherto, past, preceding, previously, prior, rather, sooner, till, vanward

before and earlier: anterior

before another in a job, person who goes: predecessor

before another, person or thing that comes: forerunner, harbinger, herald, precursor

before birth: antenatal, prenatal

before birth, in uterus: in utero

before maturity: teenage

before noon: ante meridiem, antemeridian

before now: heretofore

before or introductory: prelatory, preliminary, preparatory

before the Civil War: antebellum

before the Flood: antediluvian

before, suggest or indicate: foreshadow, portend, presage

befoul: contaminate, corrupt, defile, dirty, malign, pollute, slander, soil, stain

befoul with mud: bemire

befriend: abet, advise, aid, assist, back, benefit, defend, embrace, favor, help, protect, support, sustain

befuddle: addle, baffle, confuse, daze, distract, fluster, inebriate, intoxicate, muddle, mystify, stun, stupefy, unsettle

beg: adjure, ask, beseech, bid, bum, cadge, coax, crave, entreat, hustle, mooch, nag, panhandle, petition, plead, pray, request, solicit, supplicate, urge

beg for for another: intercede

beg for persistently: importune

beg the question: evade

beg urgently: implore

beget: afford, bear, breed, bring, create, engender, father, generate, germinate, procreate, produce, sire, spawn, yield

beggar: almsman, almswoman, asker, bidder, bum, canter, deadbeat, freeloader, hobo, impoverish, indigent, leech, mendicant, moocher, palliard, panhandler, pauper, pleader, rogue, ruin, scrounger, sponger, suppliant, supplicant, vagabond, vagrant, wretch

beggarly: bankrupt, cheap, cheesy, despicable, indigent, infamous, low, mean, paltry, petty, poor, sorry, vulgar, wretched

begin: arise, attack, bud, commence, create, dawn, emanate, embark, enter, germinate, inaugurate, initiate, institute, introduce, lead, open, originate, rise, set, set in, setin, spring, start, trigger

begin a discussion: broach

begin officially: inaugurate

beginner: amateur, apprentice, candidate, debutante, entrant, fledgling, founder, freshman, greenhorn, neophyte, novice, postulate, recruit, rookie, student, tenderfoot, tiro, trainee, tyro

beginner in learning: abecedarian, novice

beginner in religion: novitiate

beginner's crucial test: pons asinorum

beginning: alpha, birth, cause, commencement, conception, dawn, day, day one, debut, egg, elementary, embryonic, entrance, foundation, genesis, germ, heart, inception, initial, initiation, kickoff, new, onset, origin, outset, rise, root, seed, spring, start

beginning and end: alpha and omega

beginning in development: embryonic, inchoate, incipient, nascent

beginning of a course of action or performance: debut

beginning of a word, phoneme or syllable added to: prothesis

beginning of project: inception, outset

BEERS

abbey ale	cream ale	home brew	mead	schwarzbier
ale	crystal malt	ice beer	melomel	specialty malt
all barley beer	dark beer	India pale ale	Munchener	spruce beer
all malt beer	diat pils	kellerbier	near beer	starkbier
altbier	doppelbock	kolsch	needled beer	steam beer
amber ale	dort	krausen	nonalcoholic beer	stout
barley wine	dortmunder	kriek	nonalcoholic malt	Trappist
Berliner weisse	draft beer	kristall weizen	beverage	tripel beer
Biere de Garde	draught beer	kruidenbier	nut brown ale	ur-bock
bitter	dry beer	Kulmbacher beer	oatmeal stout	Vienna beer
bitter stout	dunkel beer	kumiss	obergarig	weiss
bittersweet	dunkel weissbier	kvass	old ale	weizenbier
bock beer	eisbock	lager	oscura	wheat beer
brown ale	faro	lambic beer	pale ale	white beer
bruised beer	festbier	light ale	pilsener	witbier
caramel malt	fire-brewed beer	light beer	poker beer	zwickelbier ❧
cask-conditioned ale	framboise	loster bier	porter	
chicha	genuine draft	maibock	rauchbier	
copper ale	gueuze	malt liquor	saison	
craft-brewed beer	hefe weizen	marzen	Scotch ale	

beginning or first in time sequence, concerning: primordial

beginning or origin: conception, creation, genesis

beginning or source: seed

beginning or start: onset

beginning or starting point: terminus a quo

beginning to appear: incipient

beginning, from the: de novo

beginnings: alphas, kickoffs, onsets, origins, seeds

begins to knit: casts on

begone: away, depart, hightail, leave, off, out, scat, scoot, scram, shoo, skiddoo, vamoose

begrimes: smudges

begrudge: covet, envy, grumble, loathe, pinch, resent

beguile: amuse, bluff, burn, charm, cheat, coax, con, deceive, delude, divert, elude, entertain, entrap, evade, flatter, foil, fool, fox, gyp, lure, maneuver, manipulate, mislead, seduce, trick, vamp

begun, barely: inchoate

behalf: account, advantage, aid, assistance, benefit, defense, interest, matter, part, profit, sake, side, support

behave: act, bear, carry, comport, conduct, demean, deport, direct, function, gesture, handle, manage, manager, react, regulate, restrain, treat, work

behave different than normal: deviate

behave like someone is inferior: condescend, deign, patronize

behave theatrically: emote

behavior: action, air, attitude, bearing, code, comport, conduct, decorum, deed, demeanor, deportment, etiquette, guise, manner, mien, morals, port, routine, tact, tenue

behavior modification: conditioning

behavior principle: ethic

behavior standards: mores

behavior theory, cause-and-effect: determinism

behavior treatment with unpleasant stimuli connected to bad habits: aversion therapy

behavior, artificial: affectation, pretentiousness

behavior, code of: protocol

behavior, distinctive: eccentricity, foible, idiosyncrasy, mannerism, quirk

behavior, having or concerning bad: indecorous, insubordinate, restive, unbecoming, unruly, unseemly

behavior, noisy and rough: boisterous

behavior, overemotional: melodrama

behavior, proper: decorous

behead: behemoth, big, decapitate, decollate, execute, guillotine, kill

beheading device: guillotine

behemoth: beast, giant, huge, leviathan, mammoth, monster

behest: bid, command, decree, demand, desire, direction, edict, injunction, mandate, order, prompting, rule, solicitation, wish

behind: abaft, aft, after, afterward, arear, arrear, astern, backing, backward, buttocks, derriere, fanny, hiney, instigating, laggard, late, losing, past, posterior, rear, rump, seat, tardy, trailing, tush, ward

behind closed doors: in camera

behind in payment: arrears, in debt

behold: catch, consider, discern, earmark, ecce, eye, gaze, hold, look, maintain, notice, observe, perceive, regard, retain, scan, see, sight, view, voila, wait, watch, witness

beholden: accountable, bound, grateful, indebted, obliged, owing

behoove: befit, benefit, fit, need, ought, proper, require, suit, suitable

beige: brownish, camel, color, cream, ecru, khaki, tan

being: actuality, angel, animal, because, creature, entity, esse, essence, existence, human, life, living, matter, mortal, nature, one, ontology, organism, person, present, reality, self, soul, spirit, standing, subsistence, supreme, thing

belabor: assail, beat, buffet, cudgel, drub, hammer, lash, ply, pound, reiterate, thrash, work

belated: deferred, delayed, late, overdue, remiss, tardy

belch: burp, eruct, eructation, expel, hiccup, rasp, repeat, spew, vent, vomit

beldam: crone, hag

beleaguer: annoy, assault, beset, besiege, blockade, bother, harass, invest, nag, persecute, plague, surround

belfry: campanile, carillon, clocher, dome, tower, turret

belfry denizen: bat

belie: belong, besiege, betray, camouflage, color, contradict, contravene, counterfeit, deceive, defame, deny, disguise, disprove, distort, falsify, hide, negative, pertain, slander, surround

belief: admission, assurance, axiom, certainty, confidence, conviction, credence, credo, creed, doctrine, dogma, ethos, faith, feeling, gospel, hope, idea, -ism, mind, opinion, persuasion, position, reliance, religion, sect, tenet, theory, trust, view

RELATED TERMS

belief at variance with established beliefs: heresy, heterodoxy, unorthodoxy

belief considered to be absolutely true: article of faith, dogma

belief contrary to established doctrine: heresy

belief in a creator: deism

belief in a god: theism

belief in God without denying others: henotheism

belief in more than one god: polytheism

belief in supernatural: tabu

belief in the miraculous: supernaturalism

belief in virtue of hard work: work ethic

belief maintained as true: tenet

belief not substantiated: factoid

belief or strongly held opinion: conviction, persuasion

belief that is necessary: article of faith

belief that one is ill, false: hypochondria, valetudinarianism

belief with little evidence: credulity

belief, concerning: doxastic

belief, declare a: profess

belief, express approval of: espouse, subscribe

belief, express or declare personal: testify

belief, false: delusion

belief, unquestioning religious or ideological: fundamentalism

beliefs: creeds, -isms, tenets

beliefs and doctrines of a system: ideology

beliefs and values of a people: mythos

beliefs of others, respect for and recognition of: tolerance, toleration

beliefs or religious principles: creed, doctrine, tenet, credo, testament

beliefs, defense or justification of: apologia

beliefs, firmly established as: entrenched

believabilty: credence

believable: acceptable, authentic, conceivable, credible, likely, plausible, possible, straight, trustworthy

believe: accept, accredit, affirm, assume, buy, consider, credit, deem, hold, imagine, judge, opine, suppose, swallow, theorize, think, trust

believe, unwilling to: incredulous, skeptical

believer: adherent, admirer, apostle, devotee, disciple, supporter, zealot

believer in one god: theist

believer in strong central government: statist

believer or follower: adherent

believers in the here and now: realists

believing according to a religion or philosophy: sectarian

believing too easily: credulous, gullible, naive ❧

belittle: criticize, decry, denigrate, depreciate, detract, diminish, discredit, disdain, disparage, downgrade, knock, minimize, pan, put down, slight, sneer, squash

bell: chime, church bell, cowbell, curfew bell, dinner bell, doorbell, gong, school bell, tocsin, tower bell

RELATED TERMS

bell is suspended, wooden block from which: stock

bell regulating nighttime outings: curfew

bell ringer: campanologist, sexton

bell ringing, art of: campanology

bell-shaped: campanulate

bell-shaped cover for plants: cloche

bell signal or alarm: tocsin

bell sound: chime, dong, peal, ting

bell sounded regularly: tolling

bell tolling for death: knell

bell tower: belfry

bell tower, freestanding: campanile

bell, metal bar inside: clapper, tongue

bell, to ring slowly and solemnly: knell, toll

bells at morning, noon, night: angelus

bells, ringing of a set of: carillon, peal, tintinnabulation ❧

belles lettres: classics, literature

bellicose: belligerent, combative, hostile, mad, militant, pugnacious, rebellious, scrappy, warlike

belligerent: adversary, aggressive, antagonistic, aroar, bellicose, combative, contentious, fierce, fighting, hostile, hot, litigious, mean, nasty, ornery, pugnacious, quarrelsome, warlike, warring, wrangling

bellow: bark, bawl, bell, blare, bluster, call, clamor, cry, holler, roar, rout, saul, scream, shout, shriek, vociferate, yap, yawp, yell

bellowing: a roar

bellwether: doyen, forerunner, guide, lead, leader, sheep

belly: abdomen, breadbasket, bulge, gut, pot, stomach, tummy

belly button: navel, umbilicus

belly laugh: boff, ha ha

belly nerves and ganglia: solar plexus

belly of mammal: venter

belong: accord, affiliated, appertain, apply, bear, concern, correlate, fit, harmonize, in here, match, pertain, relate, set, vest

belong as essential part: inherent, integral, intrinsic

belong as part or adjunct: appertain, pertain

belongings: appendages, assets, effects, estate, family, gear, goods, household paraphernalia, possessions, property, things

beloved: admired, adored, boyfriend, cherished, darling, dear, flame, girlfriend, idol, inamorata, love, pet, precious, revered, spouse, steady, sweetheart, turtle dove, valentine

below: beneath, down, downstairs, downward, inferior, infra, less, lower, subordinate, under, underneath

below earth's surface: nether

below in text: infra

below the speed of sound: transonic

below-the-waist flounce: peplum

below threshold of conscious perception: subliminal

belt: area, band, bandoleer, bash, beat, blow, cincture, circle, circuit, clobber, conveyor, cummerbund, encircle, encompass, girdle, girth, highway, invest, mark, passage, region, ring, sash, strait, strap, strip, stripe, surround, tract, waistband, whack, zone

belt buckle loop for excess belt: keeper

belt buckle tongue: tang

belt carrying goods: conveyor belt

belt for hernia patient: truss

belt for sword or bugle: baldric

belt or sash for monk or nun habit: cincture

belt or sash worn with dinner jacket: cummerbund

belt with cartridge pockets: bandoleer

belt, encircle with a: gird

bemoan: deplore, grieve, lament, mourn, pity, regret, rue, sorrow, wail

bemoaning one's lot: singing the blues

bemuse: addle, confuse, distract, fluster, overwhelm, stun

bemused: pixilated

bench: bar, board, court, discard, ledge, pew, seat, settee, sideline, stool, tribunal

bench with storage underneath, high-backed: settle

bench, long upholstered: banquette

benchmark: criteria, example, gauge, model, standard, touchstone, yardstick

bend: angle, arch, bow, buckle, compel, crimp, crouch, curvature, curve, direct, divert, fasten, flex, incline, kink, lean over, loop, persuade, ply, refract, sag, stoop, submit, tilt, turn, twist, wind, zigzag

bend easily, able to: flexible, limber, lissom, lithe, malleable, pliable, pliant, supple

bend in a river: bight

bend in river, U-shaped: oxbow

bend in stream or river: meander

bend knees, as in worship: genuflect

bend of a body part: flexure

bend the elbow: tope

bend, curve in and out: sinuate

bend, sharp and elbowlike: dogleg

bend, twist: writhe

bendable and flexible: pliable

bender: binge, spree, toot

bending easily, limber: lithe

bending of joint: flexion

bending of light or heat ray: refraction

bending or bent part: flection

bending or winding: flexuous

bends in a mountain road: esses

bends in divers: aeroembolism, caisson disease, decompression sickness

beneath: below, inferior, lesser, lower, subordinate, under, underground

beneath one's dignity: inexpedient, infra dig, infra dignitatem

benediction: amen, approval, bless you, blessing, grace, gratitude, invocation, praise, prayer, thanks, thanksgiving

benefaction: alms, approbation, benevolence, charity, donation, endowment, gift, grant, gratuity, kindness, philanthropy, present

benefactor: aid, angel, donor, friend, grubstaker, helper, humanitarian, patron, promoter, savior, sponsor, usee

beneficial: advantageous, desirable, enjoyable, favorable, gainful, good, healthful, helpful, lucrative, profitable, remunerative, salutary, serviceable, useful, valuable

beneficiary: donee, heir, heiress, legatee, legatee, recipient, successor, usee, user

benefit: advance, advantage, aid, assist, avail, befriend, behalf, better, blessing, boon, boost, boot, concert, deserve, emolument, enhance, exhibition, gain, gift, help, improve, interest, performance, perk, profit, raffle, relieve, sake, service, use, utility, welfare

benevolent: altruistic, benign, caring, charitable, chivalrous, considerate, generous, good, humane, kind, liberal, loving, philanthropic, unselfish

benign: affable, amiable, benedict, benevolent, bland, charitable, favorable, genial, gentle, good, gracious, harmless, healthful, kind, mild, salutary, slight, tender, wholesome

bent: aim, angled, aptitude, bias, bound, bow, braced, contorted, course, crank, crooked, curvature, curved, decided, declined, determined, direction, flexed, hooked, hunched, insistent, leveled, pronate, prone, set, settled, stooped, swayed, turned; disposition, energy, flair, genius, gift, impetus, inclination, knack, leaning, nose, penchant, prejudice, proclivity, propensity, purpose, talent, taste, tendency, trend

bent backward: retroflex

bent beyond resiliency: sprung

bent in flight: arced

bent into a curve, in heraldry: enarched

bent like hook: uncinate

bent out of shape: cortorted

bent over: astoop

benumb: blunt, chill, cumber, daze, deaden, desensitize, numb, stun, stupefy

bequeath: bequest, bestow, commend, commit, demise, donate, endow, give, grant, leave, legate, offer, testament, transmit, will

bequest: bequeath, dower, endowment, estate, gift, heritage, inheritance, legacy, will

berate: abuse, blister, castigate, censure, chastise, chide, jaw, lash, nag, objurgate, rail, revile, sail into, scold, scorch, score, upbraid

bereave: deprive, dispossess, divest, leave, oust, rob, sadden, strip

bereavement: affliction, death, distress, sorrow

bereft: destitute, devoid, fleeced, forlorn, lacking, lorn, lost, missing, poor, robbed

beret: tam

berry-bearing: bacciferous

berry segment or division: acinus, drupe

berry used as medicine: cubeb

berry with thick leathery rind, as citrus fruit: hesperidium

berry, clustered as raspberry and mul-: aggregate

berrylike: baccate

berserk: amok, crazy, demented, distraught, enraged, frenzied, mad, maniacal, violent, wild

berth: appointment, bed, billet, bunk, dock, harbor, job, mooring, niche, office, place, position, profession, situation, slip, upper, wharf

berth or hand: upper

beryl: emerald, gem, green, jewel, yellow

beseech: adjure, appeal, ask, beg, entreat, implore, invoke, obsecrate, petition, plead, pray, solicit, sue, supplicate

beseeching: suppliant

beset: allot, arrange, assail, attack, beleaguer, besiege, blockade, bug, circle, harass, harry, hound, infest, obsess, obstruct, pester, plague, ply, sail, siege, spend, storm, surround

beset with trouble: in hot water

BERRIES

bilberry
bearberry
blackberry
black raspberry
blueberry
boysenberry
buffalo berry
candleberry
checkerberry
cloudberry
cranberry
currant
dangleberry
dewberry
elderberry
gooseberry
huckleberry
Juneberry
lingonberry
loganberry
mulberry
partridgeberry
raspberry
sala berry
serviceberry
shadberry
strawberry ❦
whortleberry ❦

---

beside: abreast, abutting, adjacent, adjoining, along, alongside, aside, by, contiguous, except, excluding, juxtaposed, near, next, opposite, tangential, with

besides: added, additional, also, and, beyond, but, else, except, extra, furthermore, moreover, otherwise, plus, then, too

besides and in addition: withal

besiege: annoy, assail, assault, attack, belay, beleaguer, beset, blockade, close in on, confine, embattle, girt, nag, pester, plague, siege, solicit, storm, surround, trap

besmirch: blacken, blot, defile, discolor, dishonor, slander, smear, smudge, soil, stain, taint

besotted: buzzed, cooked, drunk, inebriated, infatuated, intoxicated, sloshed, smashed, wasted, zonked

bespangle: adorn, decorate, dot, embellish, garnish, light, sequin, sprinkle, star, stud, trim

bespatter: blot, condemn, dash, dirty, malign, muddy, reproach, scatter, slur, soil, sparge, spot, sprinkle, stain, stigmatize

bespeak: accost, address, announce, argue, arrange, ask, attest, cite, discuss, engage, exclaim, foretell, hint, imply, indicate, request, reserve, show, speak, stipulate

best: ace, bad, boss, champion, choice, conquer, cream, defeat, edge, elite, exceed, excel, excellent, finest, foremost, greatest, largest, most, nonpareil, optimum, outdo, outmatch, outstrip, paramount, par excellence, peerless, pick, pip, preeminent, primo, surpass, top, topnotch, unsurpassed, utmost, vanquish

best of its kind: vintage

best of the best: crème de la crème

best or highest quality: gilt-edged

best part: highlight

best, the: elite

bestial: barbaric, brutal, brutish, cruel, depraved, filthy, low, ruthless, vile, wild

bestow: accord, add, allot, allow, apply, award, bequeath, beset, confer, deal, deliver, devote, dispense, dispose, divide, donate, entail, entrust, extend, gift, give, grant, harbor, present, put, quarter, render, tribute, use

bestow abundantly: rain down

bet: ante, chance, gamble, lay, lottery, odds, play, pledge, pot, raffle, risk, speculate, stake, staked, wage, wager, wagered

bet choosing 1st, 2nd place finishers: perfecta

bet choosing 1st, 2nd place finishers in no particular order: quiniela

bet choosing 1st, 2nd, 3rd place finishers: trifecta

bet doubling the stakes after a loss: martingale

bet on race in which backers share in total wagered: parimutuel

bet on winners in two races: daily double

bet original wager and its winnings on a subsequent event: parlay

bet taker or card dealer: croupier

bet with little chance of winning: long shot

bet, minimize loss by counterbalancing: hedge

bête noire: abomination, bogeyman, bugaboo, dread, hate, ogre, outcast, plague, terror

bethink: consider, deliberate, devise, mind, recall, recollect, reflect, remember, reminisce

betide: become, befall, befit, chance, develop, fall, happen, occur, presage, transpire

betimes: anon, early, occasionally, prematurely, seasonably, shortly, sometimes, soon, speedily

betoken: assert, bespeak, betide, denote, express, forebode, foreshadow, import, indicate, note, omen, presage, show, signify, symbolize, witness

betray: abandon, accuse, beguile, blab, blow, cross, deceive, delude, disclose, discover, divulge, expose, falsify, finger, mislead, peach, rat, reveal, seduce, sell, sing, snare, snitch, spill, squeal, tattle, tell, traduce, undo

betrayal: breach, chicanery, deception, dishonesty, disloyalty, perfidy, sellout, treason

betrayer: informer, Judas, nark, rat, skunk, stoolie, traitor, turncoat

betroth: affiance, assure, bind, contract, engage, espouse, pledge, promise, vow

better: advance, aid, ameliorate, amend, bigger, choice, correct, desirable, elevate, exceed, excel, excelling, finer, good, greater, half, healthier, improve, increase, more, outdo, preferable, promote, rectify, safer, superior, support, surpass, top, well, win, wiser, worthier

better from illness, get: convalesce, recuperate

better than average: above par

better than no loaf: half

better, make or become: ameliorate

betterment: correction, improvement, mastery, melioration, reform, revision

betterment of world: meliorism

betting consideration: odds

betting system where winners receive share of total bet: parimutuel, totalizator, tote

between: amid, amidst, among, average, betwixt, halfway, intermediate, intervening, within

between cities: interurban

between lines: interlinear

betwixt: amidst

bevel: angle, bezel, blow, cant, chamfer, diagonal, edge, incline, miter, mitre, oblique, ream, slanted, slope

bevel surface: chamfer

beverage: ade, ale, beer, cider, cocktail, cocoa, coffee, cola, cooler, cordial, draft, drink, eggnog, green tea, grog, ice tea, juice, lager, lemonade, liquid, liquor, malted, milk, nectar, negus, nog, pop, potable, potion, punch, seltzer, soda, tea, tonic, treat, water, wine

beverage of chocolate syrup, milk, soda water: egg cream

bevy: assembly, band, collection, company, covey, crew, crowd, flight, flock, gathering, group, herd, pack, party, school, swarm, troupe

bewail: bemoan, cry, deplore, grieve, lament, moan, mourn, repent, rue, sigh, sorrow, weep

beware: avoid, cave, eschew, heed, mind, notice, shun, spend, warning

bewilder: abash, addle, amaze, amuse, astonish, baffle, bother, buffalo, confound, confuse, daze, dazzle, distract, embarrass, floor, fluster, fog, foil, muddle, mystify, nonplus, obfuscate, perplex, puzzle, rattle, stun, stupefy, surprise, upset

bewildered: asea, bemused, at sea, lost, perplexed

bewildered and worried: distraught

bewitch: allure, attract, bedevil, captivate, charm, control, dazzle, delight, enchant, entice, fascinate, hex, hook, hypnotize, jinx, spellbind, spook, thrill, trick, voodoo, wile

beyond: above, across, after, aside, besides, free, further, hereafter, hope, moreover, otherwise, outside, over, past, question, remote, superior, ultra, yonder

beyond a doubt: proven

beyond improvement: ideal

beyond one's legal power: ultra vires

beyond ordinary perception: transcendent

beyond plump: obese

beyond reasonable limits: inordinate

beyond reclaim: lost

beyond the call of duty: supererogatory

beyond words: ineffable

bias: awry, bent, bigotry, color, declination, diagonal, disposition, favoritism, incline, influence, intolerance, leaning, narrowness, oblique, partiality, parti pris, preconception, predetermine, predilection, prejudice, prepossess, procedure, propensity, skew, slant, slope, standpoint, sway, tendency

biased: partial, partisan, tendentious

biased and intolerant: bigoted

bibelot: curio

Bible books accepted as Holy Scripture: canon

bible of information carried around: vade mecum

Bible study and interpretation: hermeneutics

biblical book of prayers: psalter

biblical critical interpretation: exegesis

biblical disclosure of God's will or religious truth: revelation

biblical interpretation: hermeneutics

biblical mystical interpretation: anagogy

bicker: altercate, argue, assail, attack, battle, brawl, contention, dispute, fight, haggle, quarrel, rattle, scrap, skirmish, spar, squabble, tiff, war, wrangle

bicuspid: tooth

bicycle: bike, cycle, mountain, racing, tandem, ten-speed, two-wheeler, wheel

bicycle basket fastened to rack over wheels: pannier

bicycle built for two: tandem

bicycle with big front wheel and tiny rear wheel: penny-farthing

bicycle with one wheel: unicycle

bicycle, old-fashioned, with pedals attached to front wheel: velocipede

bid: adjure, announce, ask, beckon, beg, call, charge, command, declare, direct, invitation, invite, offer, order, pray, price, proclaim, proposal, request, reveal, summon, warn, wish

bid made on goods or services: tender

biddy: hen

bide: await, continue, dwell, endure, face, linger, remain, reside, stay, suffer, tarry, tolerate, wait, withstand

bids, simultaneous, resolved by coin flip: matched and lost

bier: catafalque, coffin, grave, hearse, pyre, support

big: adult, altruistic, boastful, bold, bulky, chief, eminent, enormous, fat, generous, gigantic, grand, great, gross, heavyweight, hefty, huge, important, imposing, jumbo, large, leading, magnanimous, major, massive, mature, mighty, outstanding, pompous, pregnant, pretentious, roomy, tall, tremendous, vast

big bang, matter that may have existed before: ylem

big leaguer: pro

big piece: hunk, slab

big shot: bigwig, celebrity, magnate, mogul, somebody, titan, tycoon, VIP

big toe: hallux

big top: tent, three-ring circus

big-word user: lexiphanes

bigfoot: omah, sasquatch, yeti

bighearted: benevolent, charitable, generous, liberal, openhanded, unselfish

Bighorn sheep: argali

bight: angle, bay, bayou, bend, corner, curve, gulf, inlet, loop, noose, road

bignoniaceous tree: catalpa

bigot: hypocrite, intolerant, racist, zealot

bigotry: bias, ignorance, intolerance, prejudice, racism, sexism

bigwig: mogul, nabob, pooh-bah, VIP

bijou: gem

bike: cycle, pedal

biker's backrest: sissy bar

bikini top: bra

bilge: balderdash, bull, malarky, rot, rubbish, trash

bilk: balk, bamboozle, cheat, con, deceive, defraud, dodge, dupe, escape, fleece, flimflam, frustrate, gyp, hoax, shake, swindle, trick

bill: flyer, placard, post, poster, program, score; act, document, law, petition, statute; buck, dollar, fin, five, greenback, note, sawbuck, ten; beak, neb, nib

bill for goods or services: charge, check, debt, dun, fee, invoice, reckoning, statement, tab

bill for payment, submit: render

bill of exchange: trade acceptance

bill of fare: carte, menu

bill or account, settling of: reckoning

bill to legislators, presentation of: reading

bill to pay: debt

bill, clause added to legislative: rider

bill, legislator proposing or supporting: sponsor

billet: appointment, ballot, bar, bearing, berth, camp, canton, document, dwelling, enroll, firewood, harbor, house, hut, job, letter, lodge, log, loop, note, notice, office, order, pass, pollack, position, post, quarter, quarters, requisition, residence, slab, strip, ticket

billiard ball's recoil: draw

billiard shot, ball hits cushion first: bricole

billiard shot, cue ball strikes two balls: carom

billiard shot, cue held perpendicular: massé

billiard stick: cue

billiard table green cloth: baize

billiards term: break, bridge, cannon, carom, chalk, cue, cue ball, cushion, eight ball, english, massé, miscue, miss, pocket, rack, rotation, run, scratch, string

billingsgate: abuse

billionth of second: nanosecond

billow: bounce, breaker, crest, float, ripple, roll, sea, surge, swell, toss, wave

billowing sail: spinnaker

bills: duns, nebs, ones, paper money, tabs

billy club: bat, baton, bludgeon, nightstick, stick

bin: basket, bing, box, bunker, cart, container, crate, crib, frame, hamper, hutch, receptacle, stall, store, trough, within

bin for storing corn: crib

bin or bigerine lead-in: glo

binary: double, dual

binary compound of oxygen with an element: oxide

binary group: byte

binaural system: stereo

bind: bandage, cement, confine, constrict, difficulty, dilemma, fasten, fetter, gird, hogtie, hold, jam, join, lash, obligate, predicament, secure, stick, tape, tie, unite

bind books: oversew

bind tightly in bandage or cloth: swaddle, swathe

bind tightly in device: fetter, pinion, shackle

bind wheat: sheave

bind with rope: lash

binder: band, bond, cover, folder, frame, girder, guarantee, lever, notebook, tape

binding: astringent, belt, cord, edging, fastener, limiting, mandatory, necessary, obligatory, restraining, restrictive, ribbon, rope, stringent, tape, tether, tying, valid

binding, act of: ligature

bindlestiff: tramp

binge: affair, bat, bender, blow, blowout, bow, bust, carousal, cringe, fling, hit, indulge, indulgence, jag, obeisance, party, soak, splurge, spree, tear, toot

binge eating disorder: bulimia

biochemical catalyst of protein in cells: enzyme

biographical essay: profile

biography: account, bio, diary, history, journal, life, memoir, recount, saga

biography of one's own life: autobiography, memoirs

biography of person written by that person: autobiography

biological angle: axil

biological development of individual: ontogeny

biological factor: gene

biological groups: genera

biological similarity in form of organisms with different ancestry: isomorphism

biological unit: cell

biologically deteriorating, esp. in man: dysgenic

biologically occurring in different regions: allopatric

biologically occurring in same region: sympatric

biology and technology, study of: biotechnology, ergonomics, human engineering, human factors engineering

biology branch dealing with heredity in plants and animals: genetics

biology classification: taxonomy

biology classification, subdivision of genus: species

biology degeneration, the opposite of evolution: devolution

biota: life

bipartite: dual

biped: man

birch relative: alder

birchbark: canoe

bireme's propeller: oar

birth: bear, beginning, burden, delivery, extraction, genesis, lineage, naissance, nascence, nascency, natal, nativity, origin, parentage, spring

birth and circumstances of a birth: nativity

birth but not hereditary, concerning condition existing from: congenital

birth by abdominal surgery: Caesarean section

birth by eggs that hatch outside body: oviparous

birth by eggs that hatch within body: ovoviviparous

birth by sheep or goats: yean

birth control: condom, contraception, foam, pill, sponge, vasectomy

birth feet or butt first: breech

birth membranes and placenta expelled: afterbirth, logia, secundines

birth or beginning of something: genesis

birth to live offspring, not eggs: viviparous

birth to only boys, giving: arrhenotokous

birth to only girls, giving: thelyotokous

birth to prematurely, give: slink, slip

birth, amniotic sac covering baby's head at: caul

birth, buttocks first: breech delivery

birth, pertaining to: natal, puerperal

birth, pertaining to time after: postnatal, postpartum

birth, pertaining to time before: antenatal, prenatal

birth, pertaining to time just before birth (five months before, one month after): perinatal

birth, present from: innate

birth, referring to the place of one's: native

birthday calculation: genethialogy

birthmark: blemish, feature, hemangioma, mole, naeve, nevus, spiloma, strawberry mark

birthmark or congenital skin growth: nevus, stigma

birthplace: motherland

birthstone: gem

biscuit: bake, bun, cake, cookie, cracker, dog, gem, hardtack, muffin, pentile, pretzel, roll, scone, snap, wafer, zwieback

biscuit, brittle and salted, in knots and other shapes: pretzel

biscuit, hard, for military: hardtack

bisect: cross, divide, fork, furcate, halve, intersect, nalve, separate, split

bisexual in organs or characteristics: androgynous, hermaphrodite

bishop assisting another bishop or ordinary: suffragan

bishop district: diocese

bishop just below patriarch in Eastern Orthodox Church: metropolitan

bishop of certain sees in Eastern Orthodox Church: patriarch

bishop of highest rank in a province or country: primate

BIRDING TERMS

African birds: coly, fink, hammerhead, marabou, quelea, taha, tock, touraco, unbrette

Antarctic birds: penguin, skua

aquatic birds: auk, cob, cormorant, dabchick, duck, ern, flamingo, goose, grebe, gull, loon, mew, penguin, petrel, small, swan, tern, terne

Arctic birds: auk, dovekey, fulmar, guillemot, skua

Asian birds: brambling, courser, dotterel, fêng huang, funghwang, lapwing, mine, myna, parakeet, pitta

Australian birds: arara, bellbird, boobook, bushlark, bustard, cassowary, coachwhip, emu, friarbird, frogmouth, leipoa, lorikeet, lory, lyrebird, manucode, pardalote, pitta, roa, waybung

beak: rostrum

bird: ani, avis, blackbird, bluebird, bluejay, boatbill, bobolink, bobwhite, brant, bulbul, bullfinch, bustard, buzzard, catbird, chicadee, crow, daw, eagle, egret, emu, erne, falcon, finch, flicker, flier, goldfinch, grosbeak, halcyon, hobby, hoopoe, hummingbird, ibis, jackdaw, kingbird, kinglet, kite, lark, linnet, marten, mocker, nun, oriole, owl, partridge, peacock, pewee, pheasant, phoebe, pie, plover, raven, redstart, redwing, robin, rook, ruff, sandpiper, shrike, skylark, snipe, sparrow, starling, swallow, tanager, terek, tern, thrasher, thrush, tit, vireo, warbler, waxwing, woodpecker, wren

bird call: caw, cheep, coo, twee

bird class: aves

bird dog: setter

bird food: bread crumbs, seeds, suet

bird genus: alca, apatornis, certhia, crax, otis

bird house: aviary

bird marsh: coot, crane, rail, snipe, sora, stilt

bird of legend, rising from ashes: phoenix

bird of Paradise: apus, manucode

bird of peace: dove

bird of prey: accipiter, eagle, eaglet, elanet, erne, falcon, goshawk, harpy, hawk, kite, osprey, owl, owlet, raptor, vulture

bird of prey's claw: pounce, talon

bird parts: bill, knee, lora, lores, mala, neb, nib, pecten, pileum, pinion, rostra, syrinx

bird shelter: cote

bird sound: peep, tweet, twitter

bird stomach: gizzard, ventriculus

bird that cannot fly: ratite

bird that has just acquired flight feathers: fledgling

bird too young to leave nest: nestling

bird trill: tiralee

bird wing: pinion

bird with an eerie cry: loon

bird young: birdikin, chick, flapper, fledgling, gull, nestler, nestling, piper, poult, squab

birdlike: avian

birdlike reptile: pterodactyl

bird's beak: neb

bird's behind: curpin

bird's crop: craw

bird's egg expert: oologist

bird's head tuft: crest

bird's home: nest

birds (in Latin): aves

bird's rump: uropygium

bird's thumb: alula

birdwatcher looking for rare species: twitcher

birdwatcher shelter: blind

Central American birds: booby, corvine, crow, curassow, daw, guan, ibis, jacamar, macaw, magpie, puffbird, rave, raven, rook

clean feathers as a bird, to: preen

concerning being a helpless, naked and blind newborn bird: altricial

concerning bird active at twilight or before sunrise: crepuscular

concerning bird adapted for running: cursorial

concerning bird leaving nest a short time after hatching: nidifugous

concerning bird remaining in nest until ready to fly: nidicolous

concerning bird without flight feathers: callow, unfledged

concerning birds: avian, avine, ornithic, volucrine

concerning large order of perching birds and songbirds: passerine

concerning nonmigratory bird: sedentary

dip lightly and quickly into water, to: dap

distinctive color on throat of bird: gorget

diving birds: auk, dipper, grebe, merganser, petrel

fertilizer made of bird dung: guano

European birds: amsel, ani, avocet, bargoose, bittern, brambling, bustard, chepster, chiffchaff, darr, daw, dotterel, emeu, emu, gallinule, garganey, gled, godwit, goldfinch, goosander, haybird, kestrel, kite, lammegeyer, linnet, loriot, mag, mall, marten, martlet, mavis, merle, merlin, mew, missel, nun, nuthatch, ortolan, ouzel, peregrine, qua, redcap, redstart, rook, sakeret, serin, stag, starnel, tarin, terek, terin, turtledove, whaup, whewer, wheybird, whimbrel, whitterick, windle, winnel, witwall, yite

extinct birds: didus, dodo, mamo, moa, offbird, solitaire

feathers: plumage

flightless birds: apteryx, cassowary, dodo, emu, kakapo, kiwi, moa, ostrich, penguin, ratite, rhea

game birds: duck, goose, grouse, merganser, partridge, pheasant, quail, turkey, wildfowl, woodcock

Hawaiian birds: ava, iiwi, io, iwa, koae, mamo, moho, omao

Indian birds: adjutant, baya, bulbul, luggar, peacock

large enclosure for birds: aviary

male birds: cob, cock, drake, gander, peacock, rooster, tom

Mexican birds: jacamar, jacana, towhee

mythical birds: fêng huang, hansa, phoenix, roc, simurgh

New Zealand birds: apteryx, ihi, kaka, kakapo, kea, kiwi, kulu, moa, morepork, notornis, poe, ruru, titi, tui, weka

North American birds: bittern, coot, crane, egret, flamingo, junco, robin, stork, swift, wren

BIRDING TERMS *continued*

opening for intestinal, genital, urinary tract: cloaca
pertaining to birds: avian, ornithic
pouch for food storage in bird gullet: craw, crop
poultry birds: chicken, duck, goose, hen, pheasant, pigeon, rooster, turkey
rare birds: rara avis
sea birds: albatross, auk, avocet, curlew, eider, ern, erne, gannet, gony, gull, pelican, petrel, plover, puffin, rail, ree, ruff, sandpiper, seagull, shearwater, snipe, solan, sora, stilt, tern, wader
songbirds: bobolink, canary, cardinal, crow, finch, jay, lark, linnet, mavis, mocking, nightingale, oriole, oscine, restart, robin, shama, shrike, sparrow, starling, thrush, tit, vireo, whippoorwill, wren
sound of birds chirping and singing at once: chavish
South American birds: anna, ara, boatbill, caracara, cariama, chaja, guacharo, guan, hia, hoactzin, mina, myna, mynah, toco, toucan, trumpeter

sticky substance used to capture birds: birdlime
study of birds: ornithology
talking birds: myna, mynah, parrot
tropical birds: ani, barbet, cacique, manakin, motmot, quetzal, quezal, tody, toucan, trogon, waxbill
unfledged birds: eyas, gor, gorlin, nestling
upper or lower part of beak: mandible
wading birds: avocet, bittern, crane, egret, flamingo, heron, ibis, jacana, rail, sandpiper, snipe, stilt, stork
waxy beak swelling as of parrot: cere
web-footed birds: albatross, auk, avocet, avoset, drake, duck, gander, goose, loon, mure, puffin, razorbill, swan
West Indian birds: ani, tody
wrinkly skin hanging from the throat of a bird: wattle ❦

---

bishop of highest rank under pope: patriarch
bishop of Rome: pope
bishop robe: chimar, chimere
bishop throne: cathedra
bishop to another see, transfer: translate
bishop with ordinary jurisdiction over specified territory: ordinary
bishop with some power over suffragan: metropolitan
bishop, light blow on cheek given at confirmation service by: alapa
bishop, term or office of: episcopate
bishop, to make a: consecrate, miter, ordain
bishopric: episcopacy, episcopate, see
bishop's area of jurisdiction: diocese
bishop's assistant, esp. one who may succeed bishop: coadjutor
bishop's crosier: staff
bishop's district or churches: bishopric, diocese, see
bishop's headdress: mitre
bishop's seat in ancient churches: apse
bishop's staff: crosier
bishop's wear: alb
bishops, concerning: episcopal
bison: aurochs, buffalo, ox, oxen, urus, wisent
bison hybrid: catalo
bistro: bar, barroom, cabaret, café, discotheque, nightclub, restaurant, tavern
bit: ace, atom, bite, blade, bridle, check, chip, crumb, curb, drill, frac-

tion, fragment, iota, item, jiffy, jot, mite, molecule, morsel, ort, part, particle, portion, quantity, restraint, scatch, scrap, shred, smidge, smidgen, snap, snip, speck, spell, splice, tad, time, tittle, tool, trifle, wee, while
bit of burning coal: ember
bit of cloud: wisp
bit of color: tinct
bit of data: stat
bit of dust: mote
bit of fried bread: crouton
bit of gossip: item, ondit
bit of info: fact
bit of news: item
bit or small amount: driblet, modicum, moiety, pittance, sliver, snippet
bit part or role: cameo
bit, tiny: iota, scintilla, semblance, smidgen, soupçon, tincture, vestige
bite: bait, cheat, chew, chomp, corrode, crunch, cut, decay, eat, food, gash, gnaw, hold, impress, lacerate, meal, mouthful, nibble, nip, pierce, pinch, puncture, rust, seize, smart, snack, snap, sting, taste, trick, wound; allotment
biting: acid, acrid, astringent, bitter, caustic, cold, corrosive, cutting, incisive, mordant, nipping, penetrating, pungent, raw, sarcastic, scathing, severe, sharp, stinging, trenchant
biting comment: barb
biting in speech: acerbic, caustic, incisive, mordant, pungent

biting in taste: acrid, pungent
biting insect: gnat
biting one's fingernails, habit of: onychophagy
biting wit: irony
bits of noodle dough: farfel
bitter: acerb, acid, acrid, acrimonious, afflictive, austere, bad, bleak, caustic, crabby, cruel, distasteful, grievous, harsh, hostile, irate, keen, malicious, nasty, offensive, painful, piercing, poignant, resentful, sardonic, severe, sharp, sore, sour, stinging, tart, unpleasant, virulent
bitter accusation in return: recrimination
bitter alcoholic liquid used in cocktails or as tonic: bitters
bitter and critical: scathing, virulent, vitriolic, vituperative
bitter attitude: animus
bitter beer: ale
bitter in attitude or speech: acrimonious, caustic, rancorous
bitter in taste or smell: acrid, astringent
bitter or tart: acerbic, acetous, acidulous, sour
bitter orange: Seville orange
bitter plant: aloe
bitterness: acerbity, acrimony, agony, anguish, animosity, antagonism, asperity, enmity, hostility, malevolence, malice, poignancy, rancor, rue, scorn, severity, sourness, virulence, wormwood
bitterness, to cause: fester, rankle

BLACK

blue black
Brunswick black
carbon
coal black
ebony
ink
jet
jet black
lampblack
night black
pitch black
pure black
raven
sable
sloe black
soot ❦

---

bituminous: coal
bivalve: brachipod, clam, cockle, mollusk, mussel, oyster, scallop, spat
bivouac: camp, encamp, encomp, etape
bizarre: absurd, antic, curious, eccentric, extravagant, fanciful, fantastic, grotesque, kinky, odd, offbeat, outlandish, outré, peculiar, queer, ridiculous, strange, weird, wild
bizarre quality: oddness
blab: babble, betray, blabber, chat, chatter, gab, gossip, jabber, rat, reveal, sing, snitch, spill the beans, squeal, tattle, tell, tell on, yak
blabbermouth: bigmouth, busybody, chatterbox, magpie, tattletale, windbag
black: atrocious, dark, dirty, dismal, dusky, fuliginous, forbidding, gloomy, grim, inky, mournful, murky, oppressive, sinister, sooty, spotted, subfusc, sullen, swarthy, unclean
black-and-blue mark: bruise, ecchymosis
black-and-green tea: oolong
black and white: achromatic
black-and-white animal: zebra
black-and-white cutout or drawn portrait outline: silhouette
black-and-white mix: gray
black-and-white whale: orca
black and white, spotted or patched: piebald, pinto
black and white, with shading: chiaroscuro
black box ending article: end slug
black box of aircraft: flight recorder

black cloud: pall
black cuckoo: ani
black culture pride: negritude
black currant liqueur: cassis
black evening jacket: dinner jacket, tuxedo
black eye: shiner
black-fin snapper: sesi
black fur: sable
black gold: oil
black hole boundary: event horizon
black ice: glaze ice
black-ink item: asset
black magic: diabolism, necromancy, obeah, occult, sorcery, voodoo, witchcraft, wizardry
black magic involving the dead: necrolatry
black magic practitioner: warlock, witch
black mark: blot, demerit
black or white or neutral: achromatic, monochrome
black out: censorship, conceal, darken, eclipse, erase, faint, shade
black performers, first publisher of music by: Motown
black person considered subservient to whites: Uncle Tom
black sheep: deviate, reprobate
black tea: pekoe
black, glossy: piceous
black, in poetry: ebon
blackball: ban, banish, bar, blacklist, boycott, exclude, expel, ostracize, shun, snub
blackberry or raspberry bush: bramble
blackbird: ani, daw, merl, merle, nerl, thrush
blackboard: slate
blackboard accessory: eraser
blacken: cloud, darken, defame, defile, disgrace, malign, slander, smear, soot, stain, stigmatize, sully, tar
blackest black: ebon
blackguard: cad, knave, louse, lowlife, rascal, scoundrel, shag, vagabond, vagrant, villain
blackhead: comedo
blackhearted: evil
blacklist: ban, banish, bar, blackball, boycott, exclude, expel, ostracize, shun, snub
blackmail: bleed, bribe, coerce, extort, payoff, ransom, shakedown, squeeze, threaten
blackmail by buying stock and threatening takeover: greenmail

BLACKSMITH TOOLS

anvil
ball peen hammer
blower
chisel
clinch cutter
clincher
clipping hammer
cold chisel
creaser
cross peen hammer
dipper
drift
drill
fileflatter
floor mandrel
forge
fuller
hammer
hardie
hoof gauger
hoof tester
hot chisel
mandrel
nipper
post drill
post vise
power hammer
pritchel
puncher
rasp
set hammer
sledgehammer
straight peen hammer
swage
swage block
swedge
swedge block
tongs
treadle hammer
vise ❦

---

blackness: nigrescence
blackout sketch: skit
blacksmith: anvil, horseshoer, plover, shoer, smithy
blacksmith furnace: forge
blacksmith hammer: fuller
blacksmith or horseshoer: farrier
blacksmith's equipment: anvil
blacksmith's stock in trade: horseshoes
blacksmith's workshop: smithy
blackthorn: sloe
bladder: bag, blister, inflate, pocket, pouch, sac, vesicle
bladder exam: cystoscopy
bladder inflammation: cystitis

bladder or bowel lack of control: incontinence

bladder or gallstone: cystolith, urinary calculus, urolith

bladder removal by surgery: cystectomy

bladder-shaped: ampullaceous

bladder, urinary or gall-: vesica

blade: bit, blow, bone, cutlass, cutter, edge, gallant, grain, knife, leaf, oar, propeller, razor, scapula, scythe, sickle, spear, spire, sword

blade of leaf, petal: lamina

blade of oar or paddle: palm

blade of propeller, turbine, windmill: vane

blade of skate or sled: runner

blade on stick for mixing batter or spreading: spatula

blade side: edge

blade surface of chisel: bezel

bladed tool: adze

blah: bland, boring, bunk, drab, dull, flat, humdrum, lifeless, monotonous, nonsense, tedious, uninspiring, vapid, yawn

blame: accusation, accuse, admonish, ascribe, call, castigate, censure, challenge, charge, chide, condemn, criticize, culpability, fault, guilt, hurt, impute, inculpate, liability, onus, rebuke, reprehension, reproach, reprobation, reprove, revile

blame for wrongful act: incriminate, inculpate

blame is mine: mea culpa

blame of others, one made to bear: scapegoat, whipping boy

blame or charge: censure, inculpate, reprehend, reproach, reprove

blame or guilt, pronounce free from: absolve, exculpate, exonerate, vindicate

blame or rebuke: censure, disapproval, reproof

blame, offer excuses to lessen: extenuate

blamed person who didn't do it: scapegoat

blameless: clear, faultless, good, immaculate, innocent, irreproachable, perfect, pure, righteous, spotless, unimpeachable, unstained, upright

blameworthy: culpable, deplorable, discreditable, heinous, imputable, reprehensible

blanch: argent, bleach, chalk, fade, lighten, pale, recoil, whiten, whitewash, wince

blanched: ashen, paled

bland: affable, amiable, benign, blah, courteous, dull, flat, gentle, gracious, ingratiating, insipid, kind, lenient, mild, oily, smooth, soft, suave, tasteless, tranquil, unexciting, urbane

bland diet: pap

blandish: allure, beguile, cajole, charm, coax, entice, flatter, urge, wheedle

blank: abyss, annul, bare, blind, break, clean, clear, colorless, empty, expression, form, fruitless, frustrate, hollow, idle, muddled, omission, scoreless, shot, skip, space, unfilled, vacant, void

blank and uncomprehending: glassy

blank check: carte blanche

blank disk to be stamped for coin: flan

blank space: lacuna

blanket: afghan, coat, comforter, cover, coverlet, film, layer, mask, poncho, quilt, serape, sheet, stroud, sweeping, throw, wrap

blare: blast, blaze, boom, fanfare, noise, peal, roar, scream, shout, toot, trumpet

blarney: butter, cajole, coax, exaggeration, flatter, flattery, line, softsoap, wheedle

blasé: apathetic, bored, casual, indifferent, nonchalant, sated, satiated, unexcited, weary

blaspheme: swear

blasphemous: impious

blasphemy: anathema, calumny, cursing, desecration, execration, impiety, irreverence, malediction, profanation, profanity, sacrilege, scoffing, shaming, swearing, violation, vituperation

blast: attack, bang, blight, blow, blowout, bluster, bomb, criticize, detonation, discharge, dynamite, explode, explosion, gale, gust, lambaste, outburst, party, pop, proclaim, ruin, shatter, shell, shindig, stunt, trumpet, wind

blatant: brawling, brazen, clamorous, coarse, conspicuous, deafening, flagrant, gaudy, gross, loud, noisy, obtrusive, obvious, overt, shameless, vocal, vociferous, vulgar

blatant publicity: ballyhoo

blather: babble, blither, chatter, nonsense, prattle, stir

blaze: bonfire, brilliance, burn, coruscate, declare, effulgence, fire, firebrand, flame, flare, flash, glare, gleam, glory, glow, holocaust, illuminate, pioneer, rush, shine, shot, sparkle, torch

blazer: coat, jacket

blazing: afire, aflame, fiery

blazing a trail: pioneering

blazon: adorn, announce, blare, boast, broadcast, deck, declare, depict, description, display, embellish, exhibit, inscribe, proclaim, publish, shield, show

bleach: blanch, decolor, etiolate, fade, lighten, purify, sun, whiten

bleach or dry in sun: insolate

bleach, oxygen used in: ozone

bleacherite: fan

bleachers: benches, boxes, grandstand, scaffold, seats, stand

bleaching vat: kier

bleak: austere, barren, bitter, blay, blighted, cold, cutting, depressing, desolate, dim, dismal, dour, drear, dreary, gloomy, gray, grim, joyless, melancholy, pale, pallid, raw, stark

bleak and barren: stark

blear: blur, darken, deceive, dim, dull, faint, fog, mislead, obscure, protrude

bleat: baa, blat, blather, bluster, cry, fuss, gripe, maa, whine

bled: ran

bleed: agonize, blackmail, drain, exhaust, extort, extract, exude, fleece, flow, gush, hemorrhage, leak, overtax, pity, run

bleeding, heavy: hemorrhage

bleeding, hereditary disorder of unstoppable: hemophilia

bleeding, pencil to stop: styptic pencil

bleeding, point to apply pressure to stop: pressure point

bleeding, stopping or slowing: astringent, hemostatic, styptic

bleep out: erase

blemish: birthmark, blackhead, blame, blister, blot, blotch, blur, breach, crack, defacement, defame, default, defect, deficiency, deformity, dent, discredit, disfigure, eyesore, failing, fault, flaw, freckle, hurt, impair, imperfection, injure, mar, mark, mole, pimple, pockmark, scar, slur, smirch, speck, spot, stain, stigma, sully, taint, vice, want, wart, zit

blemish or stain: maculation

blemishes: mars, scars, stains, taint

blend: amalgam, amalgamate, associate, blind, blot, brew, combine, commingle, compound, concoction, cream, dazzle, fit, fuse, fusion, harmonize, incorporate, integrate, join, meld, merge, mesh, mingle, mix, mixture, olio, pollute, shade, spoil, stain, synthesize, unite

blend and combine: coalesce, fuse, interlace

blend and reconcile schools of thought: syncretize

blend different readings of text: conflation

blend of two words, e.g. chortle: portmanteau word

blend or adjust alcohol by adding water or another liquid: rectify

blend two vowels: syneresis

blended, old style: admixt

blender: mixer, toner

bless: absolve, adore, anele, aneles, anoint, approve, baptize, celebrate, confirm, consecrate, cross, dedicate, eulogize, extol, favor, felicitate, give, glorify, grace, grant, guard, hallow, praise, preserve, protect, sanctify, thank

bless you in German: gesundheit

bless, old-style: anele

blessed: beata, benedict, blissful, consecrated, divine, endowed, exalted, hallowed, happy, holy, joyful, revered, sacred, sanctified, venerated

blessed with: endowed

blessedness: beatitude, nirvana

blessing: approval, benedicite, benediction, benison, boon, bounty, consent, felicity, gift, godsend, grace, okay, praise, thanks, windfall, worship

blessing or benefit: boon

blessing, act of: benedicite, benediction, benison

blight: affliction, bane, blast, cripple, destroy, disease, eyesore, frost, frustrate, kill, mar, nip, plague, rot, ruin, rust, smut, spoil, wither

blimp: airship, balloon, fatso, zeppelin

blind: aimless, ambush, bandage, benight, blank, blend, camouflage, cloak, concealed, dark, daze, dazzle, deceitful, decoy, defective, dull, eclipse, eyeless, front, hidden, hood, hoodwink, ignorant, incomplete, inebriated, insensate, intoxicated, involved, misleading, myopic, nearsighted, obscure, secret, senseless, shortsighted, shutter, sightless, unaware, unseeing

blind alley: blockade, cul-de-sac, dead end, impasse, standstill

blind components: slats

blind for window: jalousie, screen, shade

blind reading method: Braille

blind spot: scotoma, optic disk

blind with adjustable horizontal slats: jalousie

blind with adjustable, overlapping horizontal slats: venetian blind

blind, as a falcon or hawk: seel

blind, nearly: purblind

blinder: blindfold, bluff, flab, hood, obstruction, shade

blindfold: bandage, blinder, blink, concealed, dark, darken, heedless, obscure, reckless

blinding light: glare

blindly believing in theory: doctrinaire

blindness for blue and yellow: tritanopia

blink: bat, blindfold, blush, bypass, condone, falter, flash, flicker, glance, gleam, glimmer, ignore, neglect, nictate, nictitate, omit, overlook, peek, shine, shun, sparkle, squint, trick, twinkle, wink

blink quickly and involuntarily: palpebrate

blintze: crepe, pancake

blip: censor, echo, glitch, spot, tap

bliss: contentment, delight, ecstasy, eden, euphoria, gladden, gladness, glory, happiness, heaven, joy, jubilation, nirvana, paradise, pleasure, rapture, utopia

bliss, concerning a state of: connubial

blissful: blessed, blithe, divine, dreamy, ecstatic, elated, elysian, enchanted, euphoric, glorified, happy, holy, in seventh heaven

blissful and blessed: beatific

blister: abscess, beat, blain, bleb, blob, boil, bubble, bulla, canker, castigate, cyst, lambaste, lash, sac, scorch, vesicate, vesicle

blister-producing: vesicant

blister pus: serum

blister with pus: abscess, pustule

blistering: hot

blithe: bonny, carefree, cheerful, gay, glad, gleeful, happy, jocular, jolly, jovial, joyous, lively, merry, radiant, vivacious, winsome

blitz: attack, blitzkrieg, bombardment, football, offensive, raid, red dog, strike

blizzard: blow, gale, snowfall, snowstorm, squall, whiteout, wind

bloat: balloon, expand, inflate, puffy, swell

bloated: arrogant, pompous, stuffy, swollen, turgid

blob: blemish, blister, blobule, blot, boil, daub, dollop, drop, lump, mark, mass, pimple, postule, splash, splotch, wen

bloc: alliance, cabal, clique, coalition, combination, faction, group, party, ring, union

block: annex, bar, barricade, blockade, buckler, cake, check, clog, cob, cube, dam, deter, estop, fill, foil, frustrate, hamper, hinder, hindrance, impass, impede, inhibit, intercept, nudge, oblong, obstacle, obstruct, obstruction, occlude, oppose, outline, plug, prevent, road, row, spike, square, stonewall, stop, street, stump, stymie, thwart

block a blow or hit: parry

blockade: bar, barricade, barrier, beleaguer, beset, block, checkpoint, closure, dam, embargo, fence, obstruct, obstruction, restriction, roadblock, siege, snag, wall

blockbuster: hit

blocked with fluid: congested

blockhead: ass, beefhead, bonehead, bust, chump, dolt, dummy, dunce, fool, halfwit, hardhead, harebrain, idiot, jackass, knucklehead, moron, nincompoop, ninny, noodle, numskull, oaf, screwball, tomfool, yutz

blocking of thoughts or desires: repression, suppression

bloke: chap, gent, skate

blond: ash, bleached, blonde, color, fair, flaxen, gold, golden, light, platinum, sandy, straw, towheaded, yellow

blond-haired peoples of Scandinavia: Nordic

blood (family): brother, family, friend, kin, kinship, kinsman, lineage, pedigree, race, relation

blood (fluid): cell, clot, fluid, gore, hemoglobin, life, lifeblood, sap, serum, stock

RELATED TERMS

blood clot drifting in bloodstream and then getting lodged: embolus
blood clot in heart, blood vessel: thrombosis

blood clot that gets lodged in blood vessel or chamber of heart: thrombus

blood clotted from wound: gore

blood clotting: coagulation

blood component: plasma, serum

blood conveyer: aorta

blood deficiency: anemia

blood-filtering and -storage organ: spleen

blood flow of wound, to stop: stanch, staunch

blood flow, stopping or slowing: hemostatic, styptic

blood fluid: plasma

blood in arteries, concerning: arterial

blood in veins, concerning: venous

blood infection: septicemia

blood not immunologically compatible: incompatible

blood of the gods: ichor

blood or liquid, to be filled with excess: engorged

blood or liquid, to become clotted or curdled as: coagulate

blood or liquid, to become soaked: welter

blood poisoning: pyemia, septicemia, toxemia

blood pressure measuring instrument: sphygmomanometer

blood pressure, technique for regulating: biofeedback

blood pressure, very high: hypertension

blood pressure, very low: hypotension

blood purification by artificial means: hemodialysis, renal dialysis

blood-red: incarnadine

blood relationship: consanguinity

blood settling in lower part of organ: hypostasis

blood-sugar excess: hyperglycemia

blood-sugar shortfall: hypoglycemia

blood supply, death of tissue from obstruction of: infarction

blood vessel and nerve network: plexus

blood vessel dilation caused by weakening of vessel wall: aneurysm

blood vessel outer covering: adventitia

blood vessel, minute: capillary

blood vessel, larger: artery

blood vessels and heart, pertaining to: cardiovascular

blood, concerning: hemal, hematic, hemic

blood, consisting of: sanguinary

blood, injection or tranfer of: transfusion

blood, patient giving: donor

blood, presence of nitrogen bubbles in: decompression sickness, the bends

blood, problem-causing substance in: cholesterol

blood, study of: hematology

blood, to oxygenate the: ventilate

bloodbath: carnage, massacre, purge, slaughter, war

bloodless: anemic, cold, lifeless, pale, pallid, passionless, torpid, unfeeling

bloodletting: phlebotomy, venesection

bloodshed: death, gore, killing, murder, violence

bloodshed on large scale: carnage

bloodshed, pertaining to: sanguinary

bloodsucker: freeloader, leech, parasite, sponge, tick, vampire

bloodthirsty: barbaric, carnal, cruel, murderous, ruthless, sanguinary, sanguine, savage, vicious

bloody: bleeding, crimson, cutthroat, damned, ferocious, gory, murderous, wounded ❦

bloom: blossom, blow, blush, bud, develop, flare, floret, flourish, flower, flush, grow, luster, sprout, thrive

blooming: rosy

blooming of plants: anthesis

blooming twice or more per season: remontant

blooper: blunder, boner, bungle, error, goof, mistake

blossom: blob, bloom, bud, burgeon, develop, effloresce, flourish, flower, grow, mature, open, prosper, spike

blossoming: efflorescence, florescence

blossoming late: serotinous

blot: absorb, blemish, blend, blob, blotch, blue, daub, defect, discolor, disgrace, dry, eclipse, efface, flaw, impair, mar, obliterate, obscure, onus, reproach, smear, smudge, smutch, soil, speck, spot, stain, stigmatize, sully, tarnish

blot out: delete, erase, expunge

blotch: acne, blemish, blot, dab, eruption, mark, patch, smear, smirch, smudge, splotch, spot, stain, stigma

BLOOD DISEASES

anemia
aplastic anemia
blood poisoning
blue rubber bleb nevus syndrome
Cooley's anemia
decompression sickness/caisson disease/bends
edema/dropsy
hematic disease
hemolytic anemia
hemophilia
hemorrhagic anemia
Hodgkin's disease
internal bleeding
leukemia
lymphoma
pernicious anemia
Raynaud's disease
septicemia
sickle cell anemia
thalassemia
toxemia ❦

blotchy: mottled, spotted

blotto: oiled, stewed

blouse: casaque, middy, shell, shirt, smock, top, tunic, waist

blouse frills on front: jabot, ruffle

blouse or dress with fitted waist that blouses out: blouson

blouselike garment gathered at waist: tunic

blow: assault, bang, bash, beat, belt, blast, bluster, boasting, bump, calamity, clout, clump, concussion, conk, destroy, disaster, drub, hit, jab, jolt, knock, lash, misfortune, pop, punch, rap, shatter, shock, slam, slap, slug, sock, sound, storm, swipe, thump, wallop, whack

blow gently: waft

blow in puffs: whiffle

blow one's horn: brag, honk

blow one's mind: awe

blow one's top: rage, rant, rave

blow up: balloon, bomb, dynamite, exaggerate, explode, fly off the handle, inflate, outburst, rage, rave

blow up, as a volcano: erupt

blowhard: boaster, braggart, gascon, windbag

blowhole of whale: spiracle

blowout: bash, feast, gala, leak, meal, party, rupture, shindig, spree, valley

BLUE

air force blue	dark blue	ice blue	navy blue	sky blue
aquamarine	deep blue	Indanthrene	pale blue	slate blue
azure	Delft blue	indigo	peacock blue	smalt
baby blue	Dresden blue	jouvence	perse	smoke blue
blueberry	electric blue	kingfisher blue	powder blue	steel blue
bluebonnet	flag blue	lapis lazuli	Prussian blue	teal blue
bright blue	gentian	light blue	purple blue	turquoise
calamine blue	gray blue	lucerne	reddish blue	ultramarine
cerulean	greenish blue	lupine	robin's-egg blue	Venetian blue
cobalt blue	Havana lake	marine	royal blue	water blue
Copenhagen blue	Helvetia blue	midnight blue	sapphire	Wedgwood blue
cornflower	huckleberry	milori	saxe blue	wisteria
cyan	hydrangea	Napoleon blue	sea blue	woad zaffer ✺

blubber: blub, cry, fat, flab, flitch, nettle, seethe, sob, swell, swollen, thick, wail, weep, whale, whimper, whine

bludgeon: bat, clobber, club, coerce, cudgel, hit, stick, truncheon

blue (emotion): dejected, despondent, downcast, gloomy, glum, low, melancholy

blue blood: aristocrat, elite, noble, socialite

blue dye: anil, indigo, woad

blue flower: ageratum, cornflower, larkspur, scilla

blue-green: aqua

blue heron: crane

blue jean: dungaree

blue-pencil: abridge, alter, condense, cut, delete, edit, revise

bluefin or bonito: tuna

bluefish: shad

bluegrass instrument: banjo

bluenose: prig, prude

blueprint: chart, diagram, draft, map, plan, schematic, sketch, strategy

blues: depression, dumps, melancholy, music

bluff: abrupt, assume, bamboozle, bank, blunt, boast, brag, burly, candid, cliff, crusty, curt, deceive, facade, fool, fraud, front, gruff, hill, hoax, impolite, outspoken, pretend, rude, sham, trick

bluish gray: slate

bluish green: aqua

bluish, as skin: livid

blunder: balk, blooper, blotch, boggle, boner, botch, break, bull, bumble, bungle, confuse, disturbance, err, error, failure, fault, flounder, flub, goof, mess, mismanage, mistake, muddle, oversight, slip, stir, stumble, wallow

blunder or slip of the tongue: lapsus linguae

blunder or social mistake: faux pas, gaffe

blunder worth laughing about: boner, howler

blundering: maladroit

blunt: bald, bluff, curt, dampen, deaden, depressed, downright, dull, explicit, flat, frank, hebitate, insensitive, numb, obtuse, plain, point-blank, pointless, rounded, stupid, weaken

blunt and direct: point-blank

blunt and dull: obtuse

blur: blear, blemish, blob, blot, cloud, confuse, dim, disfigure, fog, mackle, mask, obfuscate, smear, smudge, soil, spot, stain, stigmatize, sully, taint

blurb: ad, advertisement, announcement, brief, commendation, puff, spot

blurry: indistinct

blurt out: blat

blush: appearance, color, crimson, glance, gleam, glow, pink, redden, rose, rouge, tinge

blush to face, apply: raddle, reddle, ruddle

blushing: bashful, coy, embarrassed, flushing, modest, red, rosaceous, rosy

blushing crow, e.g.: spoonerism

blushing, as skin: erubescence

bluster: babble, bellow, blast, blow, blubber, boast, bully, confusion, huff, intimidate, noise, rage, rant, roar, storm, swagger, swash, threaten, tumult, turbulence

blustering: stormy

Bo Peep's responsibility: sheep

boar: barrow, gore, hog, hoggaster, hogget, sanglier, sus, swine, wild

boar, pertaining to: procine, suidian

board: accommodate, house, keep, lodge, mount; authority, cabinet, commission, council, management, panel, tribunal; eats, food, meals, plank, provisions, table

board for a bed: slat

board-meeting list: agenda

board of thin wood sheets glued together: plywood

board used with planchette to spell out spiritualistic messages: Ouija

board with handle for holding plaster, mortar: hawk

board with one thicker edge, used for roofing and walls: clapboard, weatherboard

boarder: lodger, roomer

boarding house: pension

boardlike: rigid

boards arranged for nailing together into box, barrel: shook

boards with advertisement worn by a person: sandwich board

boast: blow, blow one's horn, bluster, bounce, brag, clamor, clamour, crow, display, exult, flaunt, flourish, gab, gasconade, glorify, glory, own, rave, shovel, strut, toot one's own horn, vaunt

boaster: blow off, blowhard, bouncer, braggart, cracker, crower, egotist, gascon, rodomont, ruffler, skite

boastful: arrogant, big, bragging, cocky, conceited, egotistic, gasconade, glorious, loudmouth, pompous, pretentious, rodomontade, swell-headed, vain, vainglorious

BOAT TERMS

anti-submarine boat disguised as merchant ship: Q-boat, Q-ship
boat or yacht club chairperson: commodore
boat servicing others at sea: tender
boat-shaped: scaphoid
boat with double hull and sails: catamaran
boat with triple hull and sails: trimaran
boatman: barger, canoeist, deckhand, gondolier, hobbler, huffler, mate, oarsman, paddler, poler, yachtsman
boat's designated spot: slip
bottom: keel
bumper: fender
carried in unnavigable waterway: portaged
Chinese or Japanese small flat-bottomed boat junk: sampan
Chinese flat-bottomed boat: junk
crane: davit
crosswise rower's seat: thwart
dock for pleasure craft: marina
dragging fishing net: trawler

fishing boat: smack
framework extending beyond gunwale: outrigger
front: fore, prow
gondolier's song: barcarole
interior wall: bulkhead
intersection of side and bottom: chine
landing: pier
name plate: escutcheon
narrow, light racing boat: scull
oarlock: rowlock, thole
open spaces at front and rear of seats: sheets
pole projecting from bow: bowsprit
propellers: oars
race: regatta
seat for oarsman: thwart
stairs between decks: companionway
steerman in rowing: cox, coxswain
triangular sail in front of mainsail: jib, spinnaker
upper edge of side: gunnel, gunwale ❧

---

boastfulness: braggadocio, jactitation, rodomontade
boasting: braggadocio, fanfaronade, gasconade, rodomontade
bob: ball, bounce, bow, buff, buffet, bunch, clip, curtsy, cut, dance, dib, duck, float, hop, jeer, jest, leap, mock, nid, pendant, refrain, seesaw, shake, shilling, sled, tap, trick, weight, wobble, worm; haircut, hairdo
bobbin: braid, coil, cord, cylinder, pin, quill, ratchet, reel, spindle, spool
bobble: error
bobby socks: anklets
bobolink: ortolan
bock and lager: beer
bode: augur, forecast, foreshow, foretell, herald, indicate, message, offer, omen, portend, predict, signify, stop
bodice tying behind neck, skimpy: halter
bodily: actual, carnal, completely, corporal, entirely, fleshly, physical, sensual, solid, somatic, substantial, tangible, totally
bodily desires, concerning sexual and: carnal, sensual
bodily form to something, giving of: avatar, embodiment, incarnation
bodily form, having: incarnate
bodily pouch: bursa
bodily processes 24-hour rhythm: circadian rhythm
body: anatomy, argument, assemblage, association, being, bulk, cadaver,

carcass, company, core, corporation, corpse, extent, flesh, form, foundation, frame, fuselage, group, heavenly, hull, majority, mass, nave, object, person, remains, stem, stiff, substance, torso, trunk
RELATED TERMS
body awareness: coenesthesis, kinesthesia
body between hip and neck: torso, trunk
body cavity of skull filled with air: sinus
body cavity or tube, saclike: cul-de-sac
body chemical that stimulates others: pheromone
body disorder caused by emotion: psychosomatic
body duct: vas
body duct or canal, minute: canaliculus
body fluid: humor
body frame: torso
body health and strength: constitution
body in time of disease: habitus
body into abnormal positions, person who can twist: contortionist
body language: kinesics
body organ or part, unnecessary but remaining from earlier human development: vestige
body organs, necessary: vitals
body part for healing, continuous stretching of: traction

body parts corresponding in evolutionary origin but not function: homologous
body parts corresponding in function but not evolutionary origin: analogous
body passage or channel: duct, vas
body process of energy production: metabolism
body processes replaced by electronic or mechanical components, of: bionic
body representation with skin removed, anatomical: ecorche
body side: flank
body structure and appearance: physique
body waste matter: egesta
body, affecting entire: systemic
body, big-boned and muscular: mesomorphic
body, broad and powerful: mesomorphic
body, concerning the abdomen or lower surface of: ventral
body, in zoology: soma
body, involving: corporal, corporeal, somatic
body, lacking a: disembodied, incorporeal
body, lean and frail: asthenic
body, one, or thing: some
body, pertaining to the: corporal, somatic
body, preoccupied by: carnal

TYPES OF BOATS AND SHIPS

airboat
aircraft carrier
amphibious landing
 craft
argosy
ark
banana boat
barge
bark
bark/barque
barkentine
bateau
battle cruiser
battleship
bilander
bireme
brig
brigantine
bucentaur
bullboat
bumboat
cabin cruiser
caique
canal boat
canoe
caravel/caravelle/
 carvel
cargo liner
cargo ship
carrack
carrack/carack
catamaran
catboat
clipper/clipper ship
coble
cockboat/cockleboat
cockleshell
collier
container ship
coracle
corsair
corvette
crabber
cruise ship

cruiser
currach/curragh
cutter
dahabeah/
 dahabeeyah/
 dahabiah
dandy
destroyer
dhow
dinghy
diving boat
dory
dreadnought
dredger
drift boat
dromond
dugout
escort vessel
faltboat
felucca
ferry
fishing boat
flagship
flatboat
foldboat
fore-and-after
freighter
frigate
galiot/galliot
galleass
galleon
galley
galliot
gig
gondola
gunboat
hermaphrodite brig
hospital ship
houseboat
hovercraft
hoy
hydrofoil/hydroplane
iceboat
icebreaker

inboard
Indiaman
inflatable
ironclad
jackass rig
jangada
jet boat
jolly boat
junk
kayak
keelboat
ketch
knockabout
lateen
launch
life raft
lifeboat
lighter
liner
longboat
longship
lugger
luxury liner
mailboat
man-of-war
medical ship
merchant ship/mer-
 chant vessel
minelayer
minesweeper
monitor
motorboat
motorized fishing ves-
 sel/MFV
nuclear-powered sub-
 marine
nuggar
ocean liner
oil tanker
oiler
outboard
outrigger
packet
paddle streamer

paddle wheeler
paddleboat
passenger steamer
patrol boat
pink/pinkie/pinky
pinnace
piragua/pirogue
pirate ship
polacre
pontoon
powerboat
pram
prison ship
privateer
proa/prau/prahu
PT/patrol torpedo
 boat/mosquito
 boat/motor torpedo
 boat
punt
Q-ship
quinquereme
racing boat
raft
randan
refrigeration ship
research vessel
riverboat
rowboat
runabout
sailboard
sailboat
sailer
sailing dinghy
sailing vessel
sampan
schooner
scow
scull
shallop
shell
sidewheeler
skiff
sloop

smack
speedboat
square-rigger
steamboat
steamer
steamship
stern-wheeler
submarine
submarine chaser/
 subchaser
supertanker
swamp boat
tall ship
tanker
tartan
tender
torpedo boat
towboat
tramp steamer
trawler
trimaran
trireme
troopship
tug
tugboat
U-boat
umiak/oomiak
underwater craft
vaporetto
vedette
warship
weather ship
whaleback
whaleboat
whaler
wherry
windjammer
workboat
xebec/zebec/zebeck
yacht ❦
yawl ❦

body, slight and slender:
 ectomorphic
body, stocky and round: pyknic
body's inherent timing or cycles: biological clock ❦

body of a vessel: hull
body of beliefs: ethos, lore
body of dead animal: carcass
body of dead person: cadaver, corpse

body of heavy or fatty build: endomorphic, pyknic
body of knowledge: lore
body of laws: codex
body of ore: lode
body of soldiers: array
body of strong and muscular build:
 mesomorphic
body of thin and weak build: ectomorphic, leptosomic

body of troops: force
body of water: bay, channel, gulf, lagoon, lake, ocean, pond, pool, reservoir, river, sea
body or form, rebirth in another:
 reincarnation
bodybuilding artificial hormone: anabolic steroid
bodybuilding by muscle contraction
 without moving limbs: isometrics

bog: backwater, cess, everglade, fen, gog, marsh, mire, moor, morass, ooze, quag, quagmire, sink, slough, slue, sump, swamp, wetlands

bog bird: snipe

bog down: delay, halt, impede, mire, stall

bog product: peat

boggle: alarm, baffle, balk, blunder, botch, bungle, dissemble, dumbfound, embarrass, falter, foil, frighten, hesitate, jib, muff, overwhelm, perplex, scare, shy, stagger

boggy: mossy

bogus: artificial, counterfeit, fake, false, fictitious, forged, imitation, phony, pseudo, sham, spurious

bogus gemstone: paste

bohemian: artsy, arty, beatnik, dilettante, eccentric, hippie, maverick, nonconformist

boil: abscess, blob, blotch, pimple, sore; bubble, burble, burn, cook, effervesce, fester, inflame, poach, simmer, steam, stew

boil and condense: decoct

boil and condense repeatedly: reflux

boil gently: simmer

boil or scald food briefly as a preliminary cooking step: blanch

boil partially: parboil

boil slowly: simmer, stew

boil, pus-filled: furuncle

boiled, hulled corn: hominy

boiler: cauldron, copper, furnace, geyser, kettle, retort

boiling, steep or soak without: infuse

boisterous: blustering, burly, clamorous, coarse, disorderly, excessive, excitable, furious, loud, loudmouthed, massive, mischievous, noisy, obstreperous, roaring, rough, rowdy, rude, stormy, strong, turbulent, unruly, unyielding, vehement, violent, vociferous, wild and wooly

boisterous and disorderly: raucous

boisterous declamation: rant

boîte: café

bold: abrupt, adventurous, arrogant, assured, audacious, big, bodacious, brash, brassy, brave, brazen, bright, colorful, confident, courageous, daring, dashing, dauntless, defiant, fearless, fierce, forward, fresh, hardy, haughty, heroic, immodest, imprudent, impudent, insolent, intrepid, large, manly, massive, powerful, pre-

sumptuous, resolute, rude, spunky, steep, stout, striking, strong, unafraid, undaunted, valiant, wise

bold and fearless: impudent, intrepid

bold and indecent: immodest

boldly against: defiant

boldness: assurance, audacity, bravery, brazenness, confidence, courage, daring, effrontery, grit, hardihood, hardiness, impudence, intrepidity, nerve, presumption, valor, vigor

bole: tree trunk

bolero: vest

bollix: misdo

bolster: aid, assist, boost, cushion, help, maintain, pad, pillow, prop, reinforce, strengthen, support, uphold

bolt: bar, fasten, fastener, latch, lock, nut, pin, rivet, rod, secure, shackle, shaft, toggle; lightning bolt, thunderbolt

bolt and spring-loaded toggle, threaded: molly, toggle bolt

bolt, to: consume, devour, gorge; dart, decamp, desert, flee, flight, run, rush, sprint, stampede

bomb: atom, blare, bombard, bust, destroy, device, dud, egg, failure, fiasco, flop, grenade, hydrogen, nuclear, pass, projectile, shell

RELATED TERMS

bomb dropped from air, releasing explosives widely: cluster bomb

bomb exploding into jagged pieces: fragmentation bomb

bomb from low-flying aircraft: strafe

bomb in bottle with flammable liquid: Molotov cocktail

bomb of flammable liquid and rag wick, makeshift: Molotov cocktail

bomb or charge: depth

bomb or shell fragments: shrapnel

bomb part containing explosive: warhead

bomb that destroys life but spares property: enhanced radiation bomb, neutron bomb

bomb used to break down gate or wall, small: petard

bomb working off fission of heavy atomic nuclei: atomic bomb, fission bomb

bomb working off fusion of light nuclei: fusion bomb, thermonuclear bomb

bomb, ancient fire: Greek fire

bomb, explode as a: detonate

bomb, fire: incendiary bomb, napalm bomb

bomb, remove fuse from: deactivate, defuse ☙

bombard: assault, attack, batter, beset, besiege, blitz, blitzkrieg, bomb, pelt, pound, shell, strike

bombardment, heavy: cannonade

bombast: bluster, boasting, cotton, exaggeration, pad, padded, rage, rant, rave, rhapsody, rhetoric, stuff, stuffed, turgidity

bombastic: balderdash, flamboyant, flatulent, flowery, fluent, grandiloquent, grandiose, heroic, highfalutin, inflated, overblown, pompous, ranting, rhetorical, tumid, turgid, vocal, wordy

bombastic language: fustian, rant

bombing mission: air raid

bombing, concentration of: saturation

bombing, sustained: barrage

bombs and bullets: ammo

bombs, rapid discharge of weapons or: salvo

bombycid, bombyx: eri

bon vivant: epicure, gourmet, hedonist, sport, sybarite

bona fide: authentic, genuine, legal, legitimate, real, valid

bonanza: eldorado, eureka, jackpot, mine, mint, windfall

bonbon: candy, caramel, confetti, cream, dainty, sweet

bond: adhesive, agreement, allegiance, association, bail, binder, blue, bound, cement, certificate, chain, composure, constraint, contract, covenant, duty, engage, fasten, friendship, guarantee, irons, knot, ligament, ligature, link, marriage, network, nexus, obligation, security, shackle, surety, tie, union, vinculum, vow

bond by governmental agency, unsecured long-term: debenture

bond earning: accrued interest

bond-issue span: average life

bond issue that may be redeemed before maturity: callable bond

bond or common relation: ligament, vinculum

bond possibly lacking pledge of assets: debenture

bond servant: slave

bond value on security: face value**

bond with low rating, high yield: junk bond

bond with principal and interest guaranteed by other company: guaranteed bond

bond without owner's name registered with issuing company, payable to any holder: bearer bond

bondage: captivity, chains, enslavement, helotry, restraint, serfdom, servitude, slavery, thrall, yoke

bondsman of old: esne

bone: acetabulum, astragalus, calcaneus, carpal, cervix, chorax, clavicle, coccyx, coxa, cranium, dorsa, femur, fibula, frontal, humerus, ilium, ischium, jugal, lumbar, malar, mandible, maxilla, metacarpal, metatarsal, nasal, occipital, os, parietal, patella, pelvis, phalange, pubis, radius, rib, sacrum, scapula, shin, skull, sphenoid, sternum, talus, tarsal, temporal, tibia, ulna, vertebrae, zygomatic

RELATED TERMS

bone: os

bone and teeth basis: calcium

bone at lower end of spine: coccyx

bone cavity: fossa

bone component: ossein

bone decay: caries

bone disease of elderly when bones become extremely porous: osteoporosis

bone formation: ossification, osteogenesis

bone-forming process: ossification

bone out of joint, to put a: dislocate

bone projection that attaches to muscle or tendon: tuberosity

bone surgery or grafting: osteoplasty

bone through which nerves or blood vessels pass, passage in: foramen

bone to correct deformity, surgical fracture of: osteoclasis

bone with porous structure, concerning: cancellate

bone, carved or engraved whale or ivory: scrimshaw

bone, cavity or chamber in: antrum

bone, consisting of: osseous

bone, end of long: epiphysis

bone, having a large rounded knoblike end like wrist: capitate

bone, having a small knoblike end: capitulum

bone, knobbed end of bone that fits together with another: condyle

bone, pertaining to: osteal

bone, shaft of long: diaphysis

bone, small cavity or depression in: fossa, fovea

bone, surgical division of: osteotomy

bone, thin layer of: lamella, lamina

bone, to creak as a: crepitate

bone, turn to: ossify

bone, very small: ossicle

bone/muscle surgery: orthopedics

bones and fossils, study of ancient: paleontology

bones and musculoskeletal system, medicine dealing with manipulation of: osteopathy

bones connected by muscles: syssarcosis

bones from fish or meat, to remove: bone, fillet

bones of dead are placed, building where: charnel, charnel house

bones of dead receptacle/vault: ossuary

bones, branch of medicine dealing with: orthopedics

bones, fibrous tissue connecting and moving: ligament

bones, study of structure and function of: osteology

bones, tissue at joints between: cartilage ❧

bonehead: blockhead, clod, dunce, fool, idiot, imbecile, moron, nincompoop, nitwit

boner: blooper, blunder, bungle, error, faux pas, goof, mistake, slip

boneyard: cemetery, dump, grave, stock, store

bonhomie: camaraderie

bonita or albacore: tuna

bonkers: bats, gaga

bonnet: blue, cap, capote, chapeau, coronet, cover, decoy, hat, headdress, headgear, hood, string

bonny: beautiful, fair, fine, gay, good-looking, handsome, healthy, merry, plump, pretty, ravishing, strong

bonsai tree: ming

bonus: allowance, award, benefit, boon, bribe, compensation, dividend, gift, gratuity, gravy, perk, premium, prize, reward, signing, subsidy, tip

bonus on top of salary: premium

bonus or benefit from investment or favor: dividend

bonus or tip: gratuity

bonus to one's job: fringe benefit, perk, perquisite

bony: angular, hard, lank, lanky, lean, osteal, sclerous, scrawny, skinny, stiff, thin, tough

bony head cavity: sinus

boo: catcall, decry, heckle, hiss, holler, hoot, jeer, raspberry

boob: ass, dunce, fathead, fool, goof, goon, idiot, imbecile, jerk, nitwit

booboo: gaffe, goof, lapse, slip

booby hatch: asylum, can, cooler, hoosegow, jail, madhouse

boodle: bilk, cheat, chisel, crowd, flimflam, graft, loot, plunder, swag

boogieman: ghoul

boohoo: coo, cry, fret, hoot, snivel, sob, weep

book, to: arrest, charge, indict; hire, reserve, schedule

bookish: academic, educated, highbrow, learned, pedantic, scholarly, studious

bookkeeper: accountant, auditor, clerk, CPA

bookkeeping record book: ledger

bookkeeping system with each transaction as credit and debit: double entry

bookmaking figures: odds

boom: bang, blast, clap, crash, expansion, explode, flourish, grow, jib, pole, prosperity, resound, roar, spar, support, thrive, thunder, upturn

boomerang: backfire, backlash, kalie, kiley, projectile, rebound, recoil, reverse, ricochet, wango

boom's antithesis: bust

boon: advantage, benefit, benign, blessing, bounty, congenial, donation, favor, favorable, festive, fun, gay, gift, godsend, good, grant, intimate, jovial, kind, merry, offering, prayer, present, prosperous, windfall

boondocks: backwoods, boonies, bush, country, hinterland, sticks, wilderness

boor: barbarian, buffoon, cad, churl, clod, clodhopper, clown, countryman, dork, goon, hick, lout, lummox, oaf, peasant, roughneck, rustic, slave, villein, yokel

boorish: awkward, bourgeois, churlish, cloddish, clownish, clumsy, coarse, crass, crude, gawky, inurbane, rough, rude, uncivil, uncouth, uncultured, uneducated, ungracious, unpolished, vulgar

boost: abet, advance, aid, amplify, as-

BONES, HUMAN

alveolar arch or bone
anklebone or talus or astragalus
anvil or incus
astragalus or anklebone or talus
backbone or spinal column or spine or vertebral column
big toe or hallux
breastbone or sternum
calcaneus or heel bone
calf bone
carpal bones or carpus or wrist
carpus or carpal bones or wrist
cheekbone or zygomatic bone or malar bone
chinbone
clavicle or collarbone
coccyx or tailbone
collarbone or clavicle
costa
cranium
cuboid bone
ethmoid bone
femur or thighbone
fibula
finger bones or phalanx/phalanges
floating rib
frontal bone
funny bone or olecranon process
gladiolus
hallux or big toe
hammer or malleus
haunch bone
heel bone or calcaneus
hipbone or innominate bone
humerus
hyoid bone
ilium
incus or anvil
innominate bone or hipbone
ischium
jawbone or mandible
kneecap or kneepad or patella
kneepad or kneecap or patella
lacrimal bones
lunate bone or semilunar bone
malar bone or zygomatic bone or cheekbone
malleus or hammer
mandible or jawbone
manubrium
mastoid bone or mastoid process
mastoid process or mastoid bone
maxilla
maxillary
metacarpal bones or metacarpus
metacarpus or metacarpal bones
metatarsal bones or metatarsus
metatarsus or metatarsal bones
nasal bone

navicular bone or scaphoid bone
occipital bone
olecranon process or funny bone
palate bone
palatine bones
parietal bone
patella or kneecap or kneepad
pectoral girdle or pectoral arch
pectoral arch or pectoral girdle
pelvic girdle
pelvis
periotic bone
petrosal bone or petrous bone
phalanx/phalanges or finger bones
pisiform
premaxillary
pterygoid bone
pubic bone or pubis
pubis or pubic bone
radius
rib
sacrum
scaphoid bone or navicular bone
scapula or shoulder blade
sesamoid bones
shinbone or tibia
shoulder blade or scapula
semilunar bone or lunate bone
skull
sphenoid bone
spinal column or spine or backbone or vertebral column
spine or backbone or spinal column or vertebral column
stapes or stirrup bone
sternum or breastbone
stirrup bone or stapes
styloid bone or styloid process
styloid process or styloid bone
tailbone or coccyx
talus or anklebone or astragalus
tarsal or tarsus bones
tarsus bones or tarsal
temporal bone
thighbone or femur
tibia or shinbone
trapezium
trapezoid
triquetrum
ulna
vertebra
vertebral column or spinal column or spine or backbone
vomer
wrist or carpus or carpal bones
xiphisternum or xiphoid or xiphoid process
xiphoid or xiphisternum or xiphoid process
zygomatic bone or malar bone or cheekbone ☙

BONE OR JOINT DISEASE

achondroplasia
arthritis
bursitis
degenerative joint disease
fibrodysplasia ossificans progressiva
fibrositis
fibrous dysplasia
frozen shoulder
gout
housemaid's knee
lumbago
muscular rheumatism
myeloma
osteoarthritis
osteogenesis imperfecta
osteomyelitis
osteoporosis
Paget's disease
Perthes disease
pulled muscle
repetitive strain injury (RSI)
rheumatism
rheumatic fever
rheumatoid arthritis
rickets
scoliosis
slipped disk
synovitis
tendonitis
tennis elbow ❧

---

sist, back, commend, elevate, encourage, endorse, exalt, foster, further, help, hoist, improve, increase, laud, lift, plug, praise, promote, promotion, push, raise, rise, up, upgrade

booster: promoter

boot: bootie, buskin, casing, covering, cowboy boot, footwear, galoshes, shoe, sock, waders, Wellington; discharge, dismissal, eject, evict, fire, kick, oust, punt

boot covering leg to knee: Wellington boot

boot metal spikes for rough terrain: crampons

boot of a British car: trunk

boot of seal or reindeer skin: mukluk

boot out: evict

booth: box, cabin, crame, cubbyhole, house, kiosk, loge, nook, shed, shop, stall, stand, table

booth or newstand: kiosk

booth or theater box: loge

bootleg: alcohol, booze, clandestine, hooch, illegal, illicit, liquor, moonshine, smuggle

bootless: fruitless, futile, idle, nouse, unavailing, useless, vain, worthless

bootlick: brownnose, fawn, flatter, grovel, toady

booty: gain, graft, loot, pelf, pickings, pillage, plunder, prize, spoils, swag

booze: alcohol, bout, cocktail, drink, grog, hooch, liquor, spree

booze by the yard: ale

boozer: alcoholic, drunk, drunkard, lush, sot, sponge, toper, wino

bordeaux: claret, wine

border: abut, bound, boundary, braid, brink, coast, costa, curb, dado, edge, edging, end, extremity, flank, frame, fringe, frontier, hem, impale, line, lip, margin, neighbor, outline, outskirt, periphery, plait, rim, side, sideline, skirt, strip, surround, threshold, trim, verge

border area: rimland

border-crossing certificate: carnet

border for a picture: frame

border in heraldry: orle

border marker: terminus

border of fabric, woven: selvage

border on: abut

border or contrasting edge: limbus

border or outskirts: periphery, precinct, purlieu

border or rim, raised to keep out water: coaming

border, evenly wavy: scalloped

bordering: abutting, adjacent, adjoining, contiguous, juxtaposed, tangential

borderline: ambiguous, ambivalent, inexact, marginal, unclear, undecided, vague, verge

bore: annoy, bummer, cloy, drag, fatigue, irk, nuisance, pall, tire, vex, wimp; auger, bit, caliber, drill, eagre, gauge, hole, penetrate, perforate, pierce, poke, prick, punch, size, tap, terebrate, thrust, tool, tunnel

boreal: arctic

boredom: apathy, disinterest, dullness, ennui, fatigue, lethargy, tedium, weariness

boring: blah, colorless, displeasing, drag, dry, flat, humdrum, irksome, mundane, piercing, tedious, tiresome, tiring, wearisome

boring and tedious: wearisome

boring routine: rut

boring speech pattern: singsong

boring tool: auger, awl, reamer

born: congenital, delivered, hatched, inbred, inherent, innate, nascent, natural, née

born out of wedlock: bastard, illegitimate, misbegotten, spurious, supposititious

born with: inherent

born, just having been: nascent

born, pertaining to region where one was: native

borne: braved, carried, endured, narrow, produced, rode, tolerated, toted

borne by the wind: eolic

boron compound: boride

borosilicate of aluminum: tourmaline

borough: burg, castle, citadel, county, district, fortress, parish, precinct, town, township, village

borrow: adopt, copy, hostage, loan, mooch, pawn, pirate, plagiarize, pledge, steal, substitute, surety, take, tap, use

borrowed money on: pawned

borrower's property pledged toward repayment: collateral

borrowing from a variety of previous ideas or works, work: pasticcio, pastiche, potpourri

borrowing from a variety of sources: eclectic

borscht base: beets

boscage: copse

bosh: tommyrot

bosom: beloved, breast, bust, cherished, chest, circle, close, dear, desire, embrace, emotions, heart, inclination, intimate

bosom friend: alter ego

boss: awesome, bully, bur, chief, cushion, direct, director, employer, excellent, foreman, groovy, head, headman, kingpin, knob, knop, leader, manage, manager, master, order, overseer, owner, pad, politician, shield, superior, supervise, supervisor

bossy: cow, dictatorial, domineering, tyrannical

botany: cytology, ecology, genetics, horticulture, phytography, phytology

botch: blow, blunder, boggle, bumble, bungle, err, fail, fiasco, flub, fumble, goof, hash, jumble, make a hash of, mar, mend, mess, misdo, mux, sore, spoil

both: alike, couple, equally, pair, two

both comb. form: ambi, amphi

BOOK TERMS

additional material added upon discovery of omission: addenda, addendum

additional material at end: appendix

address book to a person, to: dedicate

appearing in passages: passim

blank leaf in front or back: flyleaf

blank margin between two facing pages: gutter

book burner/destroyer: biblioclast

book carried as handy reference: vade mecum

book containing cases and resource material: casebook

book containing comprehensive articles on a wide range of subjects: encyclopedia

book containing Mosaic laws: deuteronomy

book dealing with earlier events than those in previous book: prequel

book dealing with events after those in previous book: sequel

book-devouring: bibliophagic

book for account recording: ledger

book for recording favorite quotes, passages, thoughts: commonplace book

book leaf: page

book of articles serving as a tribute or memorial: festschrift

book of defined words in alphabetical order: dictionary, glossary, lexicon

book of little value: pap

book of manuscripts: codex

book of maps: atlas

book of passages to be read at church service: lectionary

book of prayers, church service: breviary

book of synonyms and antonyms: thesaurus

book or article on single subject: monograph

book or Bible peddler: colporteur

book or passage missing a particular letter: lipogram

book printed before 1501: incunabulum

book producer that prepares works for publishers: packager

book providing step-by-step instructions: enchiridion, handbook, manual

book that achieves sudden success after a quiet beginning: sleeper

book with rules of punctuation, spelling, etc.: stylebook

book with various versions of a text: variorum

bookbinder's leather: roan, skiver

bookbinding cardboard: pasteboard

bookbinding fine parchment: vellum

bookbinding with leather on spine and corners: half binding

bookcase, double-faced: range

bookplate inscription "from the library of": ex libris

book's blank leaf at beginning, end: flyleaf

books dealing with unusual, often pornographic, topics: curiosa

book's leaves before binding: quire

books printed before 1500 AD: incunabula

bookseller of old and rare volumes: antiquarian

booksellers: colporteurs

bookworm: wonk

catalog: bibliotheca

children's reader: hornbook

classification number in library: call number

classification system for libraries: Dewey decimal system, Library of Congress classification

cloth hardcover: clothbound

collector or lover: bibliophile

commentary on book: apparatus criticus

cover ornamental lining: doublure

cover: jacket

criticism or review: critique

dealer in rare books: bibliopole

decorative design at beginning or end of chapter: vignette

dedication written in gift book: inscription

end section with explanation: epilogue

excessive book collecting: bibliomaniac

excessive devotion to books: bibliolatry

extract major parts, to: gut

gather material from sources, to: compile

hardcover: casebound

illustration facing title page: frontispiece

installment before publication: fascicle

jacket publicity notice: blurb

large, scholarly book: tome

layout, design, size: format

left-hand, even-numbered pages: verso

list of corrections: corrigenda, errata

listing of names, addresses, telephone numbers, and other data: directory

look rapidly through pages: riffle, skim

lurid or sensational book: pulp

notches for alphabetical reference: thumb index

older books kept in print by publisher: backlist

passage used in separate publication: excerpt, extract

published after author's death: posthumous

read carefully or study, to: peruse, pore over

remove objectionable material, to: bowdlerize, censor, expurgate

right-hand, odd-numbered pages: recto

shortened version of book: abridgment, condensation

surplus book, sold at discount: remainder

title, heading, or initial letter printed in red decorative lettering: rubric

Types of Books

almagest

almanac

annals

anthology

armorial

atlas

Baedeker

bestiary

Bible

bilingual dictionary

biographical dictionary

BOOK TERMS *continued*

breviary	incunabulum
cambist	index
catalog	lectionary
catechism	lexicon
chapbook	manual
children's book	missal
children's dictionary	monograph
classic	novel
coffee-table book	omnibus
college dictionary	pharmacopoeia/dispensatory
coloring book	picture book
commonplace book	primer
concordance	psalter
cookbook	reference book
dictionary	reprint
directory	rhyming dictionary
encyclopedia	Roget's Thesaurus
etymological dictionary	schoolbook
festschrift	sports book
field guid	storybook
foreign-language dictionary	telephone book
formulary	textbook
gazetteer	thesaurus
guidebook	trade book
handbook	trilogy
herbal	unabridged dictionary
hornbook	usage dictionary
how-to book	vade mecum
idioms dictionary	variorum ❧

both houses together: congress

both sides of something, be on: straddle

bother: ado, aggravate, ail, annoy, badger, bewilder, bug, confuse, disturb, fret, fuss, goad, harass, hassle, headache, irritate, molest, nag, nuisance, pain, perplex, pest, pester, provoke, puzzle, tamper, taunt, tease, trouble, try, upset, vex, worry

bother and disturb: discommode, fluster, incommode, pother

bother or inconvenience: incommode

bothered: irked, nettled, pestered

bothersome insect: gnat

bottle: ampul, canteen, carafe, carboy, container, cruet, decanter, ewer, flagon, flask, glass, jug, magnum, phial, preserve, restrain, vessel, vial

bottle adjunct: pourer, stopple

bottle for perfume, small: flacon

bottle for serving oil, vinegar, or salad dressing: cruet

bottle for serving water or wine: carafe, decanter

bottle for wine, large: flagon

bottle or container with stopper, small: phial, vial

bottle top with crimped edges: crown cap

bottle with two handles used by ancient Romans: ampulla

bottleneck: barrier, clog, congestion, gridlock, impasse, jam, logjam

bottom: abyss, basal, base, basis, bed, bedrock, butt, buttocks, can, derriere, dregs, essence, fanny, floor, foot, foundation, ground, groundwork, lowland, root, rump, seat, sediment, surface, underneath, underside

bottom facet of a gem: culet

bottom-heavy shape: pear

bottom layer: substratum

bottom line: end, net, payoff, total

bottom or foundation, solid: bedrock

bottom point of business cycle or statistical graph: trough

bottomless pit: abyss

bough: arm, branch, leg, limb, offshoot, sprig, twig

bought in a thrift shop: secondhand

bouillabaisse: stew

boulevard: avenue, concourse, drag, highway, road, street, way

bounce: boast, bob, bound, carom, discharge, eject, elasticity, evict, expulsion, fire, hop, jump, knock, leap, rebound, resilience, ricochet, sack, scold, spirit, spring, strike, terminate, thump, vault, vitality

bounce back: rebound, recoil

bounce off hard surface quickly: carom, ricochet

bounce or jolt: jounce

bounces, to hit a ball before it: volley

bouncing stick as toy: pogo stick

bound: certain, committed, compelled, confined, constrained, destined, going, liable, obligated, prepared, tied; apprenticed, indentured, inhibited, secured

bound by an oath: sworn

bound, as cotton: baled

boundary: ambit, barrier, border, confines, define, dole, edge, end, environs, extent, fence, frontier, hedge, horizon, limit, line, march, margin, mete, perimeter, precinct, rim, term, termination, verge, wall

boundary between adjacent things, common: interface

boundary between shore and ocean: strand line

boundary line of circle: circumference

boundary marker: terminus

boundary of figure, area: perimeter

boundary of language groups, dialects: isogloss

boundary or limit: pale, parameter

boundary or outer limits: outskirts, parameters, perimeter, periphery, purlieus

boundary separating conditions: threshold

boundary, external: ambit, bourn, circuit, compass

boundary, of sorts: pale

boundary, restrict within limit or: circumscribe

boundary, setting of: delimit, demarcate

boundary, sharing a: coterminous

bounder: cad, lout, roue

bounding main: ocean

boundless: endless, eternal, everlasting, great, immeasurable, infinite, limitless, measureless, unconfined, undending, unlimited, unmeasured, untold, vast

bountiful: abundant, ample, aplenty, fertile, free, galore, generous, good, lavish, liberal, lush, munificent, plentiful, plenty, rich

bounty: allowance, award, bonus, boon, charity, donation, fee, generosity, gift, goodness, grant, gratuity, kindness, largess, largesse, munificence, pay, premium, present, reward, subsidy, virtue

bouquet: aroma, arrangement, aura, balm, boutonniere, compliment, corsage, essence, fragrance, nosegay, odor, perfume, posy, scent, spray

bourgeois: boorish, capitalistic, common, commonplace, mediocre, middle-class, ordinary, stupid

bout: attack, attempt, binge, booze, carouse, circuit, clash, conflict, contest, essay, fight, fray, job, match, period, round, set to, siege, spell, spree, term, trial, turn

boutique: ship, shop, tara

boutonniere of a sort: corsage

bout of otalgia: earache

bovine: cow, oxen

bovine bunch: herd

bovine feature: dewlap

bow: arc, arch, archer, bend, bent, buckle, cave, concede, crescent, cross, crush, curtsy, curve, defer, dip, duck, fiddle, fold, greeting, inflict, knot, nod, rainbow, ribbon, salaam, stem, stoop, submit, succumb, tie, turn, weapon, yield

bow as greeting: salutation

bow by performers, second: curtain call

bow down in worship: genuflect

bow of stringed instrument rebounding: spiccato

bow or curtsy: obeisance

bow or lie down in worship or adoration: prostrate

bow part: hawse

bow-shaped: arced

bow, Indian: namaste

bow, low Chinese: kowtow

bow, low Muslim: salaam

bowdlerize: edit

bowed: arched, bent, bulging, curved, hunched, rounded

bowel or bladder lack of control: incontinence

bowels: belly, colon, depths, entrails, guts, innards, intestines, stomach

bowels, fiber-rich food for: roughage

bowels, medicine to move: cathartic, laxative, purgative

bowels, remove the: disembowel, eviscerate, exenterate

bower: abode, alcove, anchor, arbor, chamber, cottage, dwelling, jack, joker, knave, nook, pergola, retreat, shelter

bowl: amphitheater, arena, basin, beaker, container, crater, cup, helping, pan, saucer, stadium, tureen, urn, vessel

bowl for grinding to powder with pestle: mortar

bowl of fruit, to an artist: still life

bowl-shaped depression: crater

bowl-shaped stir-fry pan: wok

bowl with handle, shallow: porringer

bowler hat: derby

bowling terms: frame, ninepin, skittle, spare, split, strike, tenpins

bowwood: yew

box: barge, bin, boist, bunker, caddy, cage, carton, case, casket, chest, coffin, confine, container, crate, crib, encase, enclose, pack, package, receptacle, seat, stall, till, tray, trunk, wrap

box-elder genus: acer

box for practice: spar

box of stationery and writing materials: papeterie

box-office draw: star

box-office flop: bomb

box-office success: smash

box, strong: coffer

boxcars, in dice: sixes

box/case for tobacco or cigars: humidor

boxed: cased, crated, spared

boxer 112 pounds or less: flyweight

boxer 126-134 pounds: featherweight

boxer of lightest weight divisions: bantamweight, featherweight, flyweight

boxer or wrestler 113-118 pounds: bantamweight

boxer or wrestler 119-126 pounds: featherweight

boxer or wrestler 127-135 pounds: lightweight

boxer or wrestler 136-147 pounds: welterweight

boxer or wrestler 148-160 pounds: middleweight

boxer or wrestler 161-175 pounds: light heavyweight

boxer or wrestler over 175 pounds: heavyweight

boxer, professional: pugilist

boxer's combination: one-two punch

boxer's deformed ear: cauliflower ear

boxer's garb: robes

boxer's milieu: ring

boxes fitting into larger boxes: Chinese boxes

boxing: pugilism

boxing official: referee

boxing ring: arena

boxing terms: bantam, blow, bout, feint, fighter, fisticuffs, glove, heavyweight, jab, knockout, match, prizefighting, pug, pugilism, pugilist, punch, sparrer, TKO

boxing victory based on points: decision

boxing victory with fight stopped by referee: technical knockout

boxing, pertaining to: fistic

boy (Spanish): muchacho

boy: bat, buck, buddy, chap, child, junior, knave, lad, nipper, page, rascal, servant, son, tad, urchin, valet, waiter, youngster, youth

boy who has sexual relationship with man: catamite

boy who lied: Pinocchio

boy, homeless: gamin, urchin, waif

boycott: avoid, blackball, blacklist, embargo, exclude, ostracize, protest, reject, shun

boyfriend: beau, date, fellow, fiancé, flame, inamorato, lover, steady

boys and girls, giving birth to both: ampherotokous

boy's voice change: ponticello

boys, giving birth to only: arrhenotokous

brace: arm, bind, buttress, case, clench, couple, crutch, duo, fasten, fortify, gird, leg, mark, nerve, prop, rafter, reinforce, splint, stay, steady, steel, stiffen, strengthen, support, suspender, tie, truss, yoke; pair, two

brace counterpart: bit

brace oneself: bite the bullet

brace pair: prop, truss

bracelet: armlet, band, bangle, chain, charm, handcuff, ring, trinket

bracing: arousing, brisk, crisp, exhilarating, invigorating, quickening, refreshing, stimulating, tonic

bracken and maidenhair: ferns

bracket: ancon, category, class, classify, compare, corbel, couple, fixture, group, join, level, prop, sconce, shelf

bracket for candle, wall: sconce

bracket of stone, wood, brick to support arch or other architecture: cantilever, corbel, truss

bracket used for decoration and support for shelf or cornice: console

bracket, metal: gusset

brackets in punctuation ( ): parentheses

brackets in punctuation { }: braces

brackets in punctuation [ ]: square brackets

brackets in punctuation < >: angle brackets

brackish: saline

brad: nail

brae: hillside

brag: blow, blow one's own horn, blow your own horn, boast, bounce, braggart, crow, defy, display, exaggerate, exult, flourish, gasconade, hotdog, huff, pretense, strut, swagger, threaten, vaunt

braggadocio's forte: ego

braggart: bigmouth, blatherskite, blowhard, boast, boaster, brag, braggadocio, cracker, crower, egotist, gasbag, gascon, loudmouth, rodomont, windbag

bragging: thrasonical

bragging talk: gasconade

braid: band, border, cue, deceitful, entwine, fancy, interlace, interweave, knit, lace, mesh, moment, ornament, pigtail, plait, plat, pleat, reproach, ribbon, snatch, soutache, start, string, tress, trick, trim, trimming, twine, twist, weave

braid on military uniform: aiguillette

braid that trims fabric: soutache

braid, narrow flat and often plastic: gimp, guimpe, guipure

braid, narrow, for trimming: bobbin

braid, ornamental looped fastening: frog

braid, zigzag: rickrack

braided cord: sennit

braided cord on military uniform left shoulder, ornamental: fourragére

braided hairstyle: dreadlocks

braided linen tape: inkle

braise: sear

braised veal shanks, Italian: osso buco

brake: anchor, block, bridle, check, curb, decelerate, delay, drag, hinder, impede, rein, retard, skid, slow, stop

brake part: shoe

brake with friction pads pressing on disc of wheel: disc brake

brakes operated by compressed fluid: hydraulic brakes

bramble: brier, burr, bush, nettle, prickers, rough, sage, shrub, thorn

branch: affiliate, annex, arm, bough, bow, bureau, bush, creek, department, district, diverge, divide, fork, leg, limb, member, offshoot, out, outlet, part, ramification, section, snag, sprig, spur, stem, stream, twig

branch comes out of tree, point where: node

branch of biology dealing with form and structure of organisms: morphology

branch of chemistry dealing with brewing and fermentation: zymurgy

branch of geology dealing with rocks: petrology

branch of knowledge: discipline, subject

branch of linguistics dealing with speech sounds and their representation: phonetics

branch of linguistics studying meaning of words: lexicology

branch of mechanics dealing with effects of forces on motion of bodies: dynamics, kinetics

branch of mechanics studying motion but not forces or bodies' mass: kinematics

branch of medicine concerned with old age: geriatrics

branch of medicine concerning mouth and its diseases: stomatology

branch of medicine dealing with blood and blood-producing organs: hematology

branch of medicine dealing with bones: orthopedics

branch of medicine dealing with causes or origins of disease: etiology

branch of medicine dealing with classification of diseases: nosology

branch of medicine dealing with feet: podiatry

branch of medicine dealing with infants and children: pediatrics

branch of medicine dealing with nervous system: neurology

branch of medicine dealing with pregnancy and childbirth: obstetrics

branch of medicine dealing with skeletal system, muscles, joints, ligaments: orthopedics

branch of medicine dealing with the skin: dermatology

branch of medicine dealing with urinary tract and urogenital system: urology

branch of medicine dealing with women's health care: gynecology

branch of medicine interpreting or establishing facts for law case: forensic medicine

branch of medicine involving urinary system: urology

branch of medicine involving X rays and radiation: radiology

branch of medicine treating eyes: ophthalmology

branch of medicine treating the nose: rhinology

branch of philosophy studying the nature of knowledge: epistemology

branch of physical science: optics

branch of psychology studying pleasant and unpleasant states of mind: hedonics

branch of theology concerned with end of the world: eschatology

branch of theology dealing with the end of the world: eschatology

branch of zoology concerning fish: ichthyology

branch or twig used in basket weaving, flexible: wicker

BRAIN-RELATED TERMS

brain: bean, berebrum, cranium, intellect, mind, psyche, skull, wits
brain canal: iter
brain disorder with motor, sensory, psychic attacks: epilepsy
brain exam: EEG, electroencephalogram
brain half: hemisphere
brain inflammation: encephalitis
brain of vertebrate: encephalon
brain opening: pyla
brain parts: alba, aula, cerebrum, cortex, dura, encephalon, iter, lura, meninges, pericranium, pia
brain related: cerebellar, cerebral, encephalic
brain ridge between grooves: convolution, gyrus
brain sections: cerebrums
brain surgeon: neurosurgeon
brain wave of alert waking state: beta rhythm, beta wave
brain wave of awake and relaxed state: alpha rhythm, alpha wave
brain wave: brainchild, brainstorm, idea
brainless: asinine, dumb, foolish, mindless, senseless, silly, stupid, thoughtless, witless
brains or intellect: gray matter
brainstorms: ideates
brainwash: alter, control, convert, convince, influence, persuade
brainwashed assassin: Manchurian candidate
brainy: smart
electrical impulse-measuring instrument: EEG, electroencephalograph
hemorrhage causing stroke: apoplexy, cerebral hemorrhage
hormone that reduces pain sensations, affects emotions: endorphin
injury by jarring causing brief unconsciousness: concussion
pertaining to the brain: cerebral
surgery to sever nerve tract: lobotomy
technology's attempt to simulate brain functions in computers: artificial intelligence, bionics
three membranes enclosing brain and spinal cord in vertebrates: meninges
treatment with electric current: ECT, electroconvulsive therapy, electroshock therapy

Brain or Neurological Disease

Alzheimer's disease
amnesia
amyotrophic lateral sclerosis/Lou Gehrig's disease
Ataxia-Telangiectasia
atrophy
attention deficit disorder/ADD
autism
Batten disease
Bell's palsy
bilateral paralysis
catalepsy
catatonia
cerebral palsy
Charcot-Marie-Tooth
chorea
delirium tremens/DTs
dementia
diplegia
Down's syndrome/mongolism
dyslexia
encephalitis
epilepsy
general paralysis
general paresis
grand mal
Guillain-Barre syndrome
headache
hemiplegia
Huntington's disease/Huntington's chorea
hydrocephalus/water on the brain
leukodystrophy
meningitis
migraine
Moebius syndrome
motor-neuron disease
multiple sclerosis (MS)
muscular dystrophy
myasthenia gravis
narcolepsy
neuralgia
neurilemmitis
neuritis
neuropathy
numbness
palsy
paralysis
paraplegia
paresis
Parkinson's disease
partial paralysis
petit mal
poliomyelitis/infantile paralysis
porphyria
postural orthostatic tachycardia syndrome
quadriplegia
rabies/hydrophobia
sciatica
shingles/herpes zoster
spasm
spina bifida
spinal muscular trophy
stiff man syndrome
Sydenham's chorea/Saint Vitus' dance
thoracic outlet syndrome
tic
tic douloureux
Tourette's syndrome
tremor
trigeminal neuralgia
toxoplasmosis
trigeminal neuralgia
twitch ❦

branch out: divaricate, fork

branch out into numerous subdivisions without main axis: deliquesce

branch-trunk angle: axil

branch/twig, tough and flexible: withe

branched: ramose

branches, arrangement of: ramification

branches, having: brachiate, forked, furcate, ramate, ramose

branches, spreading out widely like: patent, patulous

branching into equal parts: dichotomy

branchlike: ramiform

brand: character, emblem, hallmark, kind, label, make, mark, name, sign, sort, species, stamp, trademark

brand ID: logo

brand marked on criminal or slave: stigma

brand name: trademark

brand new: mint, unused

brand, discounted, not made by major company: generic

branding: cautery

brandish: display, flash, flaunt, flourish, flutter, glitter, irradiate, shake, show, swagger, swing, wave, wield

brandy: Alexander, applejack, cognac, eau de vie, grappa, marc, sidecar, stinger

brandy distilled from grape residue: marc

brandy from white wine of France: cognac

brandy glass: pony

brandy measure: dram

brandy or whiskey: aqua vitae

brannigan: altercation, bender, brawl, fight, quarrel, ruckus, spree

bran or fiber in diet: roughage

brant: goose

brash: attack, bold, brazen, cocksure, cocky, forward, impetuous, impulsive, indiscreet, irascible, nervy, presumptuous, rash, reckless, sassy, storm, tactless, thoughtless, uppity

brass: audacity, brazen, confidence, effrontery, gall, impudence, nerve, officer, top; alloy

brass hat: bigwig

brass instrument: cornet, horn, tuba

brass rubbings expert: chalcotript

brass tacks: details, essentials, facts, meat

brass worker: brazier

brass, green coating forming on: patina, verdigris

brasserie: eatery

brassy: arrant, arrogant, blatant, bold, brazen, impudent, outspoken, showy

brat: apron, child, cloak, clothing, garment, holy terror, imp, infant, rascal, scum, spoiled, urchin

bravado: bluster, boasting, braggadocio, bravery, daring, gasconade, pomp, pride, storm, swagger

bravado, reckless: Russian roulette

brave: adorn, boast, bold, breast, cavalier, challenge, confident, courageous, dare, daring, dashing, dauntless, defiance, defy, endure, excellent, face, fearless, gallant, game, good, gutsy, hardy, heroic, intrepid, manly, soldier, stalwart, stomach, stout, stouthearted, superior, swagger, unafraid, undaunted, unflinching, valiant, venturesome, virtuous, warrior, withstand, yeomanly

brave and chivalrous: gallant, valiant, valorous

brave and daring: audacious, venturesome

brave and spirited: feisty

brave fighter: warrior

brave when drunk: pot-valiant

brave, very: stalwart, undaunted, unflinching

bravery: boldness, bravado, courage, fortitude, gallantry, grit, guts, heroism, spirit, spunk, valor, valour

bravery and daring: emprise

bravery and strong will: fortitude, tenacity

bravery in battle: prowess

bravery pretended: bravado

bravery, award or honor for: commendation

brawl: affray, altercation, argument, bicker, broil, complain, dispute, disturbance, dogfight, donnybrook, fight, fisticuffs, fracas, fray, free-for-all, melee, quarrel, revile, riot, row, ruckus, rumble, scuffle, shindy, spat, squabble, strife, tiff, tumult, upheaval, uproar, wrangle

brawn: breadth, clout, flesh, might, moxie, muscle, ruggedness, strength

brawny: beefy, bulky, husky, muscular, powerful, robust, stalwart, strong, sturdy, tough

bray: heehaw

brazen: arrogant, bold, brass, brassy, callous, chintzy, cocky, flashy, forward, immodest, impudent, loud, metallic, sassy, shameless, unashamed

Brazil parrot: ara

Brazilian ballroom dance of African origin: samba

Brazilian jazz and samba music blended together: bossa nova

Brazilian palm: assai

Brazilian timber tree: apa

breach: assault, blemish, breaking, chasm, chip, cleft, crack, dispute, disruption, dissension, flaw, force open, fracture, gap, harbor, hiatus, hole, infraction, infringement, inroad, interruption, interval, offend, opening, parting, pause, quarrel, rift, rupture, split, transgress, trespass, violate, violation, wound

breached: open

bread: brown, bun, corn, crouton, diet, dough, fare, food, French, Italian, lite, loaf, malt, multigrain, pita, potato, pumpernickel, roll, rye, soda, sourdough, squaw, staple, sustenance, toast, wheat, white, wholegrain, whole-meal, zwieback

RELATED TERMS

bread and butter: career, job, keep, living, profession, work

bread-and-butter: basic

bread baked, then sliced and toasted: zwieback

bread braided and eaten by Jews: challah, hallah

bread crumbs and cheese melted on dish: au gratin

bread dunked in gravy, sauce, etc.: brewis, sippet, sop

bread in French: pain

bread ingredient: yeast

bread made without yeast or leavening agent: unleavened

bread of cornmeal and baked soft: spoon bread

bread of Eucharist, consecrated: host

bread or bakery item oven shovel: peel

bread portion: slice

bread spread: butter, jam, jelly, marmalade, oleo

bread unit: loaf

bread, agent that causes batter or dough to rise for: leaven

bread, braided loaf of: challah

bread, crescent-shaped: croissant

bread, dark sour rye: pumpernickel

bread, flat cornmeal: corn pone, johnnycake, jonnycake

bread, flat round toasted: crumpet

bread, Genoese flat: focaccia

bread, Greek flat: pita, pitta

TYPES OF BREAD

bagel
brioche
brown bread
challah
cheese bread
corn bread
croissant
dinner roll
egg bread
English muffin
flatbread
French bread
Irish soda bread
Italian bread
matzo
nut bread
oatmeal bread
plain white roll
poppy-seed plait
potato bread
pumpernickel bread
raisin bread
rye bread
salt-rising bread
sliced white sandwich bread
soft roll
sourdough bread
starch-reduced bread
Vienna bread
white bread
whole-wheat bread ❧

bread, hard, of flour and water: hardtack, sea biscuit, sea bread, ship biscuit
bread, protein mixture substituted for flour in: gluten
bread, sweet: pannettone
bread, sweetened and toasted: zwieback
bread, toasted and crisp: croutons
bread, unleavened: matzo, matzoh, tortilla
bread, unleavened pocket: pita ❧

breadfruit: rima
breadnut tree: ramon
breadth: amplitude, broadness, diameter, dimension, extent, gamut, latitude, range, scope, span, spread, stretch, width
breadwinner: earner
break: alienation, alter, announce, blank, blunder, boon, breather, bruise, burst, bust, chip, cleave, cleft, crack, crackle, crevice, cripple, crumble, cut, cutoff, dash, defeat, destroy, disable, disrupt, division, down, eradicate, escape, exhaust, fissure, flee, fold, fraction, fracture, gap, hiatus, impair, in, intermission, interrupt, interruption, interval, invalidate, lapse, lull, off, opening, opportunity, out, pause, penetrate, pick, pierce, plow, pluck, point, rent, respite, rift, rupture, separate, separation, sever, shatter, shot, slip, smash, snap, stop, tame, tear, transgress, wound
break a code: decipher, decode, decrypt
break a habit: wean
break apart: fracture, reave, rend, rupture, sunder
break away: dissociate, part
break away from organization: secede
break bread: eat
break by splitting: cleave, rend, rift
break down into parts: decompose, disintegrate
break for schoolkids: recess
break hole in: stave
break in: burglarize, condition, interject, interrupt, intrude, invade, train, trespass
break in continuity: interregnum
break in continuity and return to earlier episode: flashback
break in the shoreline: ria
break into pieces: crumble, pulverize, spall
break into spray: atomize, vaporize
break loose: escape
break of day: dawn, daybreak, mourning, sunrise, sunup
break off: cease, snap
break off association: disaffiliate, dissociate
break open: burst, rupture
break or gap: hiatus, interval, lacuna
break or pause: caesura, intermission, interruption, recess, respite
break or split in layer: spall
break out: arise, bolt, escape, flee, flight, getaway, recrudesce, start
break/pause in line of verse: caesura
break suddenly: snap
break the cipher: decode
break the resistance: soften up
break the surface of soil: scarify
break through or explode: erupt
break up: crack, smash
break up group: disband
break up group into factions: Balkanize
break up into parts: resolve
break up surface of: scarify
break up, as a glacier: calve
break with: bolt, secede
breakable: brittle, delicate, flimsy, fragile, frail, weak
breakable and brittle: frangible, friable
breakdown: analysis, collapse, crash, diagnosis, failure, itemization, mishap, nervous, smashup
breakdown and ruin: debacle
breakdown of social order: anomie
breaker: billow, destroyer, roller, surf, wave
breakfast area: nook
breakfast fare: bagel, bran, cereal, Danish, eggs, flapjack, French toast, granola, oatmeal, omelet, pancakes, sausages, toast
breakfast, in France: petit dejeuner
breakfast, late: dejeuner
breakfast, pertaining to: jentacular
breaking a promise: reneging
breaking in: irruption
breaking the law: breach, contravention, infraction, infringement, transgression, violation
breaking the law by public official: malfeasance, malversation
breaking up or dividing: fissiparous
breakneck: daredevil, fast, quick, reckless, risky, speedy
breakout: escape
breakthrough: advance, boost, development, discovery, find, improvement, leap, progress
breakup: disband, divorce, part, separate, separation, split
breakwater: mole, seawall
breakwater or small jetty: groin, mole
breast: bosom, brave, bust, chest, emotions, encounter, heart, mammilla, udder
breast area that is darker around nipple: areola
breast/chest, pertaining to: pectoral
breast enlargement in male, abnormal: gynecomastia
breast examination for diagnosis: palpation
breast examination for diagnosis by X ray: mammogram, mammography
breast fluid preceding production of milk: colostrum, foremilk
breast of woman: poitrine
breast removal surgery: mastectomy
breast separation line: cleavage
breast, surgical removal of: mastectomy

breast, surgical removal of tumor of: lumpectomy

breastbone: sternum

breastfeeding, produce milk as in: lactate

breastplate of armor: cuirass, plastron

breasts, concerning the: mammary

breasts, hollow between woman's: cleavage

breath: aroma, blow, breeze, exhalation, gasp, huff, lifeblood, pant, pause, puff, respite, second, sigh, smell, vapor, wheeze, whiff, wind

breath, bad: halitosis, ozostomia

breath, having bad: saprostomous

breathe: articulate, aspire, emanate, exhale, exist, fan, inhale, instill, live, murmur, pant, puff, respire, sigh, speak, utter, whisper

breathe heavily: gasp, pant

breathe in: inhale

breathe noisily, as dog following scent: snuffle

breathe or blow into: insufflate

breathe or sigh: suspire

breathe out: exhale, expire

breather: break, lull, pause, recess, respite, rest

breathers: inhalers, lungs

breathing: alive, respiration

breathing and snoring, having heavy: stertorous

breathing apparatus: lungs, nares

breathing apparatus, underwater: aqualung

breathing difficulty due to swelling: emphysema

breathing hole in some fishes, insects: spiracle

breathing rattle: rale

breathing space: room

breathing that is interrupted: apnea

breathing that is labored: dyspnea

breathing, abnormally fast: hyperpnea, hyperventilation

breathing, abnormally slow: hypopnea

breathing, cutting of artificial opening for: tracheotomy

breathing, harsh vibrating: stridor

breathing, having difficulty in: labored

breathing, relating to: aspiratory

breathing, temporary absence or cessation of: apnea

breathing, unconsciousness or death from restricted: asphyxiation

breathless: agasp, airless, astounded, dead, eager, excited, exhausted, keen, spent, stale, tense

breathtaking: amazing, astonishing, awesome, hair-raising, impressive, stunning, thrilling

breeches: pants

breeches loose above knee and tight below: jodhpurs

breed: class, family, ilk, kind, lineage, lot, offspring, species, stock, strain, type, variety

breed by natural reproduction: propagate

breed created from two varieties or species: hybrid

breed rapidly and abundantly: pullulate

breed, to: bear, beget, create, cultivate, engender, hatch, multiply, nourish, nurture, originate, procreate, produce, raise, rear, reproduce, sire, spawn, train

breeding: behavior, civility, conduct, culture, descent, development, education, extraction, genealogy, instruction, line, manners, mating, origin, rearing, schooling, training, upbringing

breeding of special animals and plants: stirpiculture

breeding place of bacteria: nidus

breeding, horse or animal kept for: stud

breeding, study of improvement of human race by selective: eugenics

breeze: air, aura, blast, blow, breath, cruise, current, draft, freshen, gale, glide, gust, report, sail, stir, whisper, wind, zip; ease, pushover, snap, waltz

breezy: airy, brisk, carefree, debonair, easygoing, fresh, lively, racy, relaxed, sunny, vivacious, windy

brevity: briefness, conciseness, crispness, laconism, pointedness, shortness, succinctness, terseness

brew: ale, beer, beverage, blend, boil, concoct, distill, ferment, gather, grog, hatch, liquor, make, miscellany, mix, pour, potation, prepare, suds; contrive, devise, plot, prepare

brew coffee: perk

brew tea: steep

brewer's need: malt, vat

brewing and fermentation, branch of chemistry dealing with: zymurgy

brewing, fermentable mixture used in: mash

bribable and corrupt: venal

bribe: allurement, bait, blackmail, bonus, buy, corrupt, douceur, entice, extort, fee, fix, gift, graft, grease, hire, kickback, meed, offer, oil, payola, sop, steal, suborn, tempt

bribe as appeasement: sop

bribe into doing something illegal: suborn

bribe money fund: slush fund

bribe or conciliatory present: douceur

bribe to commit perjury: suborn

bribe to keep quiet: hush money

bribe to promote something: payola

bribe, small, or tip: baksheesh

bribery, open to: mercenary, venal

bric-a-brac: artifacts, knickknacks, ornaments, trinkets

brick: adobe, block, house, layer, oven, stone, tile

brick carrier: hod

brick laid parallel to wall face: stretcher

brick laid perpendicular to wall face: header

brick of charcoal, small: briquette

brick or stone worker: mason

brick, sun-dried: adobe

bricks, cement or mortar for filling in between: grouting, pointing

bricks, horizontal layer or row of: course

bridal: connubial, espousal, hymeneal, marriage, nuptial, shower, song, wedding

bridal attendant who is married: matron of honor

bridal attendant who is not married: maid of honor

bridal cache: hope chest

bridal wreath: spirea

bride: bridle, loop, newlywed, rein, tie, wife

bride's money or property turned over to new husband: dowry

bride's outfit: trousseau

bridge: auction, band, bascule, catwalk, connect, contract, cross, game, link, overpass, pont, pontoon, span, suspension, tie, traverse, trestle, union, viaduct, way

bridge counterbalanced so one end raises while the other is lowered: bascule

bridge fare: toll

bridge framework: trestle

bridge made of ropes, suspension: joola

bridge or stretch over: span

bridge over another roadway: overpass

bridge pillar at junction of spans: pier

bridge structure supporting conduit or canal: aqueduct

bridge supporting framework: trestle, truss

bridge supports, section between: span

bridge term: bid, rebid, ruff, slam

bridge that can be raised: drawbridge

bridgework: denture

bridle: bit, blinder, brake, bride, check, control, curb, direct, govern, guard, guide, halter, harness, leash, muzzle, rein, repress, restrain, restraint, rule, subdue, suppress, swagger

bridle adjuncts: blinders

bridle part: bit, martingale, rein

bridle-path debris: road apples

brief: abridge, abridgment, abrupt, advise, argument, blurb, case, charm, common, compact, compendium, compose, concise, condensation, condense, condensed, crisp, curt, few, fleeting, invoice, letter, limited, list, mandate, memorandum, momentary, outline, passing, quick, short, succinct, summary, syllabus, temporary, terse, transitory, update, writ

brief and curt: brusque

brief and meaningful: laconic, succinct

brief and pithy: terse

brief and without notice of detail: cursory

brief appearance in entertainment: cameo

brief attention: short shrift

brief comment: note

brief drama: playlet

brief nap: forty winks, siesta

brief pause: rest

brief period of time: moment

brief quarrel: spat

brief skirt: mini

brief summary: recap

brief swim: dip

brief talk: chat

brief treatise: tract

brief try: stab

brief view of a work: synopsis

briefcase: etui

briefness: brevity

brig: boat, guardhouse, jail, prison, ship, slammer, stockade, vessel

brigade: army, company, corps, crew, detachment, outfit, posse, regiment, squad, unit

brigadier general: one-star general

brigand: bandit, desperado, highwayman, hoodlum, marauder, outlaw, pillager, pirate, robber, soldier, thief

brigandage: banditry

bright: ablaze, acute, aglow, alert, animated, apt, beamy, blazing, brilliant, cheerful, cheery, clear, clever, cloudless, colorful, flashing, forward, fresh, gay, glad, gleaming, glistening, glittering, illustrious, intelligent, light, lively, lucent, lucid, luminous, optimistic, precocious, promising, psychedelic, quick, radiant, ringing, rosy, sharp, shining, smart, sparkling, splendid, sunny, transparent, twinkling, vivid, wise, witty

bright and clear: lucid, vivid

bright and flashy: garish, gaudy

bright-colored plaid: tattersall

bright from rubbing or polishing: burnished

bright idea: brainstorm

bright light: glare, neon

bright, brilliant: incandescent

brighten: animate, cheer, clear, enliven, gild, illuminate, intensify, irradiate, lift, light, lighten, liven, polish, shine

brighten by rubbing: furbish

brighter stars: novas

brightest star in the sky: Sirius

brightly colored birds: tanagers

brightly colored butterfly: red admiral

brightly colored lizard: agama

brightness: brilliance, clarity, clearness, éclat, flame, gleam, gloss, luster, radiance, sheen, shine, sparkle, splendor

brilliance in ability: virtuosity

brilliance or radiance: refulgence

brilliance, great: éclat

brilliant: bright, celebrated, clever, dazzling, distinguished, eminent, gay, genius, gifted, glittering, glorious, glossy, good, incandescent, keen, learned, lucent, luminous, pyrotechnic, radiant, shining, signal, smart, sparkling, wise

brilliant action or achievement: coup, masterstroke

brilliant and glowing: effulgent, incandescent, resplendent

brilliant and sparkling: coruscating, scintillating

brilliant coloring: flame

brilliant green: emerald

brilliant marine fish: wrasse

brilliant red: scarlet

brilliant star: nova

brilliant stroke: coup

brilliant young person: child prodigy, wunderkind

brilliantly colored fish: opah

brilliantly plumed bird: macaw

brim: bluff, border, brink, edge, hem, lip, margin, ocean, overflow, rim, sea, verge, water

brim on front of cap: visor

brimless hat: toque

brimming: crowded, flooded, flush, full, jammed, swelling

brine: alkali, blue, main, marinade, ocean, saline, salt, sea

brine for pickling: souse

brine ingredient: salt

bring: accompany, bear, carry, convey, deliver, escort, fetch, institute, lead, lug, procure, produce, summon, take, transport

bring a catch to shore: reel in

bring a price: sell

bring about: accomplish, achieve, attain, cause, create, do, effect, establish, evoke, make, organize, realize, start, transact

bring about quickly: precipitate

bring around: convert, convince, cure, get, induce, revive

bring back: effect, recall, recollect, remember, restore, retrieve, return, revive, surrender, transact

bring back to health: restore

bring back to life: reanimate, regenerate, resurrect, resuscitate, revitalize, revivify

bring cargo aboard: lade

bring down: drop, humble, level, overthrow

bring down on oneself: incur

bring forth: adduce, ean, originate, spawn, yean

bring forth young (animal): ean, yean

bring home the bacon: earn

bring in: acquire, earn, get, gross, import, realize, reap, report, usher, yield

bring in forcefully: intertrude

bring into accord: attune

bring into agreement: aline

bring joy to: elate

bring legal action: sue

bring off: accomplish, achieve, complete, execute, perform, succeed

bring on: incur

bring out: declare, display, educe, elicit, publish, state, tell

bring relief to: assuage

bring the cymbals together: clang

bring to a certain strength by concentration: gradate

bring together: accumulate, amass,

blend, combine, compile, conflate, consolidate, harmonize, join, rally, unite

bring up: discuss, educate, fear, foster, nurse, nurture, offer, raise, rear, regurgitate, train, vomit

bring up partly digested food: regurgitate

bring upon oneself: incur

brings in a fish: lands

brings into harmony: attunes

brink: bank, border, boundary, brim, edge, end, eve, limit, lip, margin, point, rim, sea, shore, verge

briny: ocean, saline, salty, sea

brisk: active, agile, alert, alive, animated, breezy, busy, chipper, crisp, energetic, fast, fresh, gay, keen, lively, nimble, nippy, perky, quick, refreshing, sharp, smart, snappy, spirited, spry, stimulating, vivacious, walk, yern, zippy

brisk and lively: jaunty

brisk run: trot

briskly: apace

briskly in music: vivace

bristle: anger, arista, barb, brush, feeler, fiber, fume, hair, ruffle, seta, strut, stubble, toast, whisker

bristle prefix: seti

bristled: awned

bristlelike appendage: arista

bristles: aristae, awns, seta, setae

bristles, covered with: barbellate

bristles, rough with: hispid

bristling of body hair: horripilation, piloerection

bristly: echinate, hispid, setaceous, setal, setose, spiny

Britain, poetically: Albion

British bag: portmanteau

British car trunk: boot

British dictionary, famous: OED, Oxford English Dictionary

British elevator: lift

British fellow: chap

British hood: bonnet

British late-morning snack: elevenses

British noblemen: peerage

British parliament member, not leader: backbencher

British prison: gaol

British pub: local

British railway vehicle: carriage

British sausage: banger

British streetcar: tram

British stroller: pram

British subway: tube

British truck: lorry

British TV: telly

British weapon: sten

brittle: brash, breakable, candy, crisp, crispy, crumbling, crunchy, delicate, eager, feeble, fickle, fragile, frail, irritable, nervous, perishable, prim, short, slight, weak

broach: approach, begin, cut, dress, drift, incision, interject, introduce, mention, moot, open, ouch, pierce, pin, prick, publish, spindle, spool, spur, stab, submit, suggest, tap, veer, violate, voice

broad: ample, coarse, deep, evident, expansive, extensive, full, general, large, liberal, nonspecific, obvious, plain, roomy, spacious, sweeping, thick, tolerant, universal, vast, wide

broad and inclusive: compendious, comprehensive

broad bean: fava, lima

broad expanse: acre, ocean

broad flat stone: slab

broad geological basin: tala

broad jump: long jump

broad-minded: flexible, latitudinarian, lenient, liberal, magnanimous, open, progressive, receptive, tolerant

broad pardon: amnesty

broad sash: obi

broad street: avenue, parkway

broad-topped hill: loma

broad valley: dale

broadcast: air, aired, announce, communicate, declare, newscast, program, publish, radio, report, send, show, sow, sown, strew, strewn, televise, television

broadcast again: replay

broadcast channel: airway

broadcast interruption: newsflash

broadcast on television and radio simultaneously: simulcast

broadcaster, news: anchor

broader: wider

broadheaded: brachycephalic

broadly elliptical: oval

broadside: poster

brobdingnagian: big, colossal, giant, gigantic, huge, immense, mammoth, tremendous

broccoli part: floret

brochure: book, circular, flyer, pamphlet, tract

brochure of institution: prospectus

brocket: deer

broil: bake, burn, char, grill, heat, roast, sear

broiled to excess: charred

broke: bankrupt, busted, destitute, down and out, flat, insolvent, penniless, poor, strapped

broken: arm, burst, busted, cracked, crushed, damaged, defective, disconnected, discouraged, dispersed, down, erratic, fractured, fragmentary, incomplete, injured, kaput, leg, rent, rough, ruined, ruptured, shaken, shattered, subdued, tamed, torn, weak

broken and destroyed: kaput

broken-arm support: sling

broken bits: debris, smithereens

broken down: decrepit, dilapidated

broken foundation stones: riprap

broken grain spike: chob

broken-hearted: inconsolable

broken husks of cereal grain: bran

broken-off piece: cantle

broken piece of pottery, glass: shard, sherd

broker: agent, broacher, dealer, factor, intermediary, jobber, marriage, merchant, middleperson, negotiator, realtor, scalper, stock

broker holding securities in his/her name rather than client: street name

broker on floor of stock exchange, working for others: two-dollar broker

brokerage, fraudulent: bucket shop

bromide: banality, cliché, commonplace, compound, platitude, saw, sedative, stereotype, trite

brontophobia: fear of thunder

bronze: aes, alloy, brownish, bust, copper, metal, statue, tan

bronze drinking bowl: mazer

bronze or silver gilt: vermeil

bronze, greenish coating on: patina, verdigris

brooch: bar, cameo, clasp, clip, jewelry, ornament, pin, shield

brooch with head in profile: cameo

brood: agonize, contemplate, daydream, dwell, eat one's heart out, fret, languish, meditate, mope, ponder, pout, sulk, weep, worry; breed, children, clutch, family, flock, fry, hatch, incubate, issue, litter, multitude, nest, offspring, progeny, race, young

brood of pheasants: nid, nide, nye

brooding: moody

BROWN

acorn	butternut	fox	nutria	sorrel
amber	café au lait	fulvous	oatmeal	tan
anthracene	camel	fuscous	orange brown	tanaura
auburn	chestnut	hazel	otter	taupe
autumn leaf	chocolate	khaki	pale brown	tawny
bay	cinnamon	leather	peat brown	terra-cotta
beaver	coffee	light brown	peppercorn	toast
beige	Cologne brown	liver brown	pongee	topaz
biscuit	copper	mahogany	putty	tortoiseshell
bistre	dark brown	manila	raffia	umber
brindle	doeskin	maple sugar	raw sienna	Vandyke brown
bronze	Dresden	Mars brown	raw umber	walnut
brunet	dun	mink	red brown	yellow-brown ❧
brunette	earth	mocha	rust	
buff	ecru	nougat	sandalwood	
burnt almond	fallow	nutbrown	seal	
burnt umber	fawn	nutmeg	sepia	

brook: creek, ghyll, gutter, rill, river, run, runnel, rush, stream, watercourse

brook or creek, small: beck, bourn, bourne, burn, creek, arroyo

brook or stream, small: rivulet, runnel

brook trout: char

brooklet: rill

broom: besom, brush, mop, splinter, swab, sweep, whisk

broth: bouillon, bree, consommé, soup, stock, water

broth garnished with vegetables cut in thin strips: julienne

broth, clear: bouillon

brothel: bawdyhouse, bordel, bordello, cathouse, crib, lupanar, stew, whorehouse

brothel manager: madam, pimp

brother: billy, blood, bro, bub, buddy, cadet, comrade, fellow, fra, friar, kin, mate, monk, pal, peer, relative, sibling, twin

brother or sister: sibling

brother, murder of: fratricide

brotherhood: association, clan, club, fellowship, fraternity, gang, guild, lodge, order, society, sodality, union

brotherly: affectionate, amicable, fraternal, friendly, kind, love, neighborly, tender

brouhaha: ado, fracas, melee, row, setto, to-do, uproar

brow: bound, brim, brink, eye, forehead, front, ridge, rim, slope, temple, top

brow of a hill, to Scots: snab

browbeat: bully, coerce, cow, depress, disconcert, frighten, harass, hector, henpeck, intimidate, nag

brown bag: sack

brown-haired: brunette

brown in fat: fry

brown paper wrapping: kraft

brown seaweed: kelp

brown-winged butterfly: satyr

browned bread: toast

brownie: cake, cooky; elf, fairy, Girl Scout, pixie

brownish gray: taupe

brownish purple: puce

brownish red: terra-cotta

brownish yellow: amber

brow's curve: arch

browse: brut, crop, feed, flip, forage, glance, graze, nibble, pasture, scan, shop, skim, thumb

bruise: abuse, bash, batter, black, breach, break, contusion, crush, dent, disable, ecchymosis, hurt, injury, maim, mangle, mar, maul, pound, pulverize, shiner, welt

bruise on impact: contuse

brume: fog, mist

brunette: brown, brown-haired, brunet, dark, swarthy, tanned

brunt: assault, attack, blow, burden, clash, crux, force, impact, jar, jolt, shock, stress, tension

brush: broom, clash, clean, comb, conflict, encounter, fight, fray, graze, groom, hair, paint, rub, scuffle, sideswipe, skim, skirmish, stroke, sweep, tooth, touch, undergrowth, whisk

brush aside: disregard, neglect, reject, slight, snub, spurn

brush off: cut, deny, dismissal, reject

brush up: cram, polish, refresh, reread, review, study

brusque: abrupt, bluff, blunt, cavalier, curt, discourteous, frank, gruff, harsh, impolite, rough, rude, short, snippy, surly, terse, violent

brusquely: tersely

brutal: atrocious, barbarous, beastly, bestial, bloody, caddish, callous, carnal, coarse, cruel, ferocious, gross, inhuman, ruthless, savage, severe, uncivil, unfeeling

brute: animal, beast, demon, feral, fiend, force, ogre, physical, ruffian, savage, scoundrel

brutish: insensate

bryophite: moss

bubble: air, bead, blister, blob, blubber, boil, deceive, delusive, effervesce, empty, fizz, foam, froth, globule, percolate, popple, sac, seed, seethe, simmer, slosh, speculation, suds, trifle

bubbliness: effervescence, élan

bubbling with excitement: ebullient, exuberant

bubbling, excited: aboil

bubbly beverage: champagne, club soda, mineral water, soda, soda water

buccaneer: corsair, freebooter, pirate, rifler, robber, rover, spoiler, viking

bucket: bail, barrel, cage, can, cheat, container, drench, hurry, kettle, pail, scoop, skeel, swindle, tub, vessel

bucket handle: bail

BUDDHIST TERMS

attainment of wisdom and compassion: nirvana

Buddhist disciple: ananda

Buddhist monk: arhat, dalai lama, lama, mahatma, poongee, talapoin, yahan

Buddhist or Hindu religious law: dharma

Buddhist terms: bhikku, bhikshu, bo tree, bodhi, bodhissatva, dharma, karma, krikaya, mani, mantra, nirvana, prayer wheel, raga, stupa, sutra, tantra, tope

concept of birth-death-rebirth: samsara

cylinder inscribed with prayers: prayer wheel

dome-shaped monument: stupa, tope

geometric design: mandala

high priest and ruler of Tibet and Mongolia: Dalai Lama

mystical literature: tantra

scriptural narrative: sutra, sutta

sect believing enlightenment is achieved through meditation, self-contemplation, intuition: Zen Buddhism

sum of person's lifelong actions, one's fate: karma

temple: wat

tower: pagoda

verbal formula repeated in meditation, prayer: mantra ❧

---

bucket, iron: kibble

buckle: bend, bow, clasp, contend, curl, distortion, down, fasten, grapple, kink, struggle, twist, under, warp, yield; belt, fastener

buckle down: work

buckle metal prong: chape

buck's mate: doe

buckthorn: cascara

buckwheat: kasha

bucolic: bumpkin, farmer, herdsman, hick, idyl, local, naive, pastoral, poetic, rural, rustic, simple

bucolic poem: eclogue

bud: blossom, bourgeon, bulb, button, child, develop, eye, flower, gem, germ, germinate, grow, incipient, pip, seed, shoot, sprout, youth

bud of plant embryo: plumule

buddy: brother, chum, companion, comrade, crony, friend, mate, pal, partner, sidekick

buddy-buddy: chummy, close, cozy, friendly, intimate

budge: convince, fur, move, movement, persuade, propel, push, stir

budget: allocate, allowance, amount, estimate, finances, funds, pack, plan, program, ration, resources, stock, store, wallet

buff: devotee, enthusiast, expert, fan; polish, rub, shine, smooth; bare, naked, nude

buffalo: anoa, arni, bamboozle, bewilder, bison, frustrate, gazelle, hamper, meat, ox, puzzle, stag, stump

buffalo and domestic cow hybrid: cattalo

buffer: backstop, bumper, cushion, fender, pad, safeguard, screen, zone

buffet: bar, batter, beat, blow, box, cuff, jolt, lambaste, slap, smite, spank, strike, thrash, toss; brunch, cupboard, dinner, lunch, meal, sideboard, smorgasbord, spread, supper

buffet or sideboard furniture: credenza

buffoon: antic, bozo, buffo, clown, comic, droll, fool, harlequin, humorist, idiot, jerk, jester, mime, mummer, playboy, prankster, ridicule, stooge, wag

buffoonery: japery

bug: ant, beetle, flea, fly, gnat, hemipter, insect, June bug, lightning bug, mite, mosquito, spider; bug, flaw, germ, virus

bug, to: annoy, bother, eavesdrop, harass, harry, irk, nag, needle, pester, rile, tease, wire, wiretap

bugaboo: alarm, bogey, bogeyman, bugbear, fear, goblin, hobgoblin, ogre, scare, scarecrow, specter

buggy: caboose, carriage, cart, demented, foolish, infested, nutty, pram, shay, vehicle, wagon

bugle: bead, call, clarion, cornet, horn, instrument, trumpet

bugle alert: call to arms

bugle call at sunset when flag is lowered: retreat

bugle call for lights out or at funeral: last post, taps

bugle call in evening to summon to quarters: tattoo

bugle call in morning to summon awake: reveille

build: assemble, body, construct, create, develop, engineer, erect, establish, expand, fabricate, fashion, form, found, frame, increase, make, manufacture, physique, put up, raise, rear, shape, undertake, up

build up: amass

builder: architect, artisan, carpenter, contractor, erector, maker, mason

builder's fastener: nail

building: apartment, architecture, barn, casa, casino, castle, church, construction, dwelling, edifice, fabric, factory, hotel, house, hut, library, museum, palace, pile, storehouse, structure, temple, tenement, theater

RELATED TERMS

building addition: ell

building and construction, relating to: tectonic

building and equipment for activity: facility

building beam: girder, I bar

building block: adobe, brick, stone

building circular and domed room: rotunda

building commemorating heroes: pantheon

building destruction: demolition

building floor: story

building front: facade

building housing library: athenaeum

building inspection: assessment, survey

building material of overlapping boards: clapboard, weatherboard

building material of sun-dried bricks: adobe

building material of twigs and clay: wattle and daub

building of sun-dried bricks or stone, Native American: pueblo

building or physical structure: fabric

building settling: subsidence

building site: lot

building supervisor: janitor, super, superintendent

building timber: beam

building with stone or brick: masonry

building with tiered seats around arena: amphitheater

building wood: timber

building, added section to: annex

building, foundation of stone: stereobate

building, front of: facade, frontispiece

building, historical and protected: landmark, national historic site

building, large and imposing: edifice

building, ready-made part of: module

building, run-down apartment: tenement

building, to declare open a: dedicate

building, to demolish: raze

building, to restore a: renovate

buildings and land: real estate, real property, realty

buildings, person who climbs: stegophilist ❦

buildup: accretion

buildup of tissue fluid: edema

built in advance and then assembled: prefabricated

built in at the supports: encastre

built poorly: jerry-built

built to specifications: custom-built

bulb: bud, corm, expansion, garlic, globe, knob, lamp, node, nub, onion, plant, root, seed, swell, tuber, tulip

bulb segment: clove

bulblike underground stem: bulblet, corm

bulbous lily plant: star of Bethlehem

bulge: appendage, bag, belly, bilge, billow, blister, bloat, bug, bump, cask, dilate, expand, extend, flask, growth, hump, knob, lump, pouch, projection, protrude, protuberance, swell, swelling, wallet

bulging: convex, protuberant

bulging and swollen: tuberous, tumescent, tumid, turgid

bulging eyes, with: ophthalmic

bulging rear of skull: inion

bulk: aggregate, amount, body, cargo, dimension, expand, extent, figure, heap, heft, hulk, largeness, lump, magnitude, majority, mass, massiveness, might, pile, power, quantity, size, substance, sum, swell, volume

bulky: awkward, beefy, big, burly, clumsy, corpulent, cumbersome, enormous, gross, heavy, hefty, huge, large, massive, obese, ponderous, stout, substantial, voluminous, weighty

bull, relating to: taurine

bulldoze: browbeat, bully, cow, dig, drive, flatten, force, grade, intimidate, level, push, ram, scoop, threaten, thrust

bulldozer: earthmover

bullet: ammunition, ball, cartridge, fast, hurry, lead, missile, pellet, shot, sinker, slug, tracer, zip

bullet, diameter of tube or bore of gun for: caliber

bullet, rebound off hard surface, like: ricochet

bulletin: announcement, communiqué, flash, memo, message, notice, poster, program, release, report, scoop, statement

bullets and guns, study of: ballistics

bullets, missiles, rockets, science of: ballistics

bullfight cheer: olé

bullfight locale: corrida

bullfight point at which kill is made: moment of truth

bullfight short red cape: capa, capote, muleta

bullfight wound: gore

bullfight, horseman who lances bull's neck in: picador

bullfighter: banderillero, matador, picador, toreador, torero

bullfighter who kills bull: matador

bullfighter with cape: capeador

bullfighter, principal: matador, toreador, torero

bullfighter's assistant inserting darts: banderillero

bullfighting fan: aficionado

bullfighting large dart: banderilla

bullfighting move of presenting and moving cape: pase, pass

bullfighting move of swinging cape slowly away from bull: veronica

bullhead: sculpin

bullheaded: headstrong, obstinate, pigheaded, stubborn

bullish: taurine

bullish trend: upturn

bull's-eye: center, precisely, pulley, target, window

bully: annoy, antagonize, bluster, boss, bounce, bravo, browbeat, bullock, coerce, dashing, domineer, dragoon, excellent, frighten, good, great, harass, huff, intimidate, meany, menace, oppress, punk, ride, ruffian, tease, terrorize, tyrranize, tyrant, victimize

bullying: despotic, domineering, imperious

bulrush: reed, tule

bulwark: bastion, breakwater, buffer, citadel, defend, defense, fence, fort, fortress, fortification, guard, parapet, protect, rampart, secure, shield, stronghold, support, wall

bum: drone, frolic, hobo, idle, idler, loafer, lounge, mooch, panhandler, sponge, tramp, vagabond

bumble: bee, blunder, bobble, botch, bramble, bungle, jumble, muffle, stumble, veil

bumbling: inept

bummer: beggar, flop, moocher, washout

bump: bang, blow, bounce, clash, collide, concussion, demote, dislodge, downgrade, hit, impact, jar, jolt, knock, lump, node, nodule, oust, pothole, protrusion, protuberance, replace, smash, strike, swelling, thud, thump

bump into: collide, encounter, hit, luck, meet, stumble

bump off: assassinate, finish, kill, liquidate, murder

bump or tiny nipplelike projection on tongue or other body part: papilla

bump, small: knurl, node, nodule

bumped, poker-style: upped

bumper label: sticker

bumpkin: clod, clodhopper, clos, country, hayseed, hick, lout, lummox, oaf, rube, yokel

bumptious: aggressive, arrogant, bold, brazen, cocky, conceited, insolent, obtrusive

bumpy: bouncy, jolting, rocky, rough, uneven

bun: biscuit, bread, roll

bun or knot of hair at back of woman's head: chignon

bunch: aggregate, assemble, assortment, batch, body, bouquet, bundle, clump, cluster, collection, crew, crowd, flock, glob, group, herd, lot, mass, mob, pack, quantity, scad, set, swarm, wad

bunch of flowers: bouquet, nosegay, posy

bundle: bag, bale, band, bind, bunch, collection, fortune, group, lade, lot, pack, package, packet, parcel, pile, roll, sheaf, tie, wad

bundle of hides: kip

bundle of twigs, sticks, branches: faggot

bundle, small: fascicle

bungle: blunder, boggle, botch, bumble, butcher, err, flub, foozle, fumble, goof, misdo, mismanage, mistake, muff, slip, spoil

bungling: inept

bunk: balderdash, baloney, bed, berth, billet, bull, cot, foolishness, hay, hogwash, hokum, hooey, lodge, malarky, nonsense, sleep, trough, twaddle

bunker: army, bin, dugout, hold, sandtrap, shelter, trap

bunkum: bunk, hooey, rot

bunt: bat, butt, meet, push, shove, spearhead, strike, tap

bunting: scrim

buoy: bell, dan, elate, elevate, float, marker, raise, signal, support, sustain, uplift

buoyancy: elasticity, resilience

buoyant: airy, animated, cheerful, elastic, floating, gay, happy, hopeful, joyous, light, lighthearted, lilting, lively, resilient, spirited, springy, unsinkable, vivacious, volatile

buoyant and optimistic: sanguine

bur: sticker

burble: babble, boil, bubble, chatter, confuse, gush, jabber, yak

burden: afflict, aggravate, albatross, bother, capacity, care, cargo, charge, clog, debt, duty, encumber, grievance, hamper, handicap, impede, impedimenta, imposition, lade, load, millstone, onus, oppress, overhead, pile, saddle, strain, stress, tax, trouble, try, vex, weight, worry

burden of proof: onus, onus probandi

burden or impediment: encumbrance

burden with: saddle

burden, discouraging: incubus

burdened: laden, loaded, taxed

burdens and drawbacks: impedimenta

burdensome: arduous, demanding, difficult, grievous, grinding, heavy, onerous, oppressive, troublesome, weighty

bureau: agency, branch, chest, chiffonier, department, desk, division, dresser, office

bureau of drawers, esp. with mirror: chiffonier

bureaucrat: apparatchik, civil servant, official, politician

bureaucratic routine: red tape

burgeon: bloom, blossom, bud, expand, flower, grow, increase, mushroom, prosper, snowball, sprout, thrive

burglar: crook, prowler, robber, safecracker, thief, yegg

burglar crowbar: jimmy

burglarize: rob

burglary: break-in, caper, crime, felony, heist, larceny, robbery, theft

burial: deposition, entombment, funeral, interment, rites, sepulture

burial chamber: grave, sepulcher, tomb, vault

burial chamber formed by two or more vertical stones supporting horizontal one: dolmen

burial chamber hidden underground: catacomb, hypogeum

burial chamber in large building: mausoleum

burial chamber under church: crypt, vault

burial ground: boneyard, catacomb, cemetery, grave, graveyard, necropolis, potter's field, pyramid, tomb

burial mound, beehive-shaped: tholos

burial mound, earth-covered: barrow, tumulus

burial site, ancient, of earth or stones: barrow, mound, tumulus

burial site, ancient, with large upright stones: cromlech, dolmen

burial wrap for body: shroud

buried mound of ancient refuse: kitchen midden, midden

burlap: bag, cloth, fabric, gunny, sacking, wrapping

burlap bag: gunnysack

burlap source: jute

burlesque: caricature, comedian, comedy, exaggerate, farce, lampoon, mime, mimic, mock, overact, parody, revue, ridicule, satire, slapstick, spoof, strip, takeoff, travesty, vaudeville

burlesque composition: amphigory

burlesque imitation of serious work: parody

burly: beefy, big, brawny, bulky, hearty, heavy, hefty, husky, imposing, muscular, portly, stocky, stout, sturdy

burn: anger, bake, beat, blaze, brew, broil, brown, cauterize, char, cheat, chisel, combust, consume, cremate, desire, fire, flame, flicker, incinerate, kindle, oxidize, parch, raze, scald, scorch, sear, singe, skin, smolder, squander, sting, sun, swindle, tan, tingle, waste

burn a bit: char

burn a corpse to ashes: cremate

burn balm: aloe

burn brightly: blaze, flare

burn intensely: deflagrate

burn low and unsteadily: gutter

burn midnight oil: lucubrate

burn tissue: cauterize

burn to ashes: incinerate

burn, cause to: ignite, kindle

burn, scab of: eschar

burned dummy: effigy

burned substance: cinder, clinker

burner for lab experiments: Bunsen burner

burning: ablaze, afire, aflame, alit, angry, ardent, arduous, blaze, boiling, combustion, consuming, desire, eager, exciting, fervent, fervid, feverish, fiery, fire, flame, flaming, glaring, glowing, hot, inflaming, intense, irritating, on fire, shining, sizzling, stinging, torrid, urgent

burning and caustic: vitriolic

burning at the stake: auto-da-fé

burning brightly: aflame

burning bush: wahoo

burning coal: ember

burning material to start fire: kindling, tinder

burning of fuel: combustion

burning of property, criminal: arson

burning readily: flammable, inflammable

burning, as a chemical: caustic, corrosive

burnish: brighten, buff, furbish, glaze, gloss, luster, polish, rub, shine, wax

burnt sugar: caramel

burp: belch, eruct

burr: accent, briar, buzz, circle, cut, halo, knob, notch, nut, pad, rib, ring, sticker, tunnel, washer, whetstone

burro: ass, donkey, jackass

burrow: cave, couch, delve, den, dig, excavate, hole, mine, mole, passage, root, shelter, tube, tunnel

burrowing canine: terrier

burrowing insectivore: mole

burrowing rodent: gopher

bursa: sac

bursar: cashier, cashkeeper, controller, paymaster, purser, treasurer

burst: blast, blew, blow, break, broken, bust, damage, erupt, explode, explosion, fit, flash, gush, injury, interrupt, out, outbreak, pop, puncture, rupture, rush, scat, shatter, spasm

burst along seam: dehisce

burst forth: erupt

burst in violently: irrupt

burst of energy: spasm

burst of flame: flare

burst of gunfire: barrage, fusillade

burst open: rupture

burst or discharge, quick: volley

burst or outburst: salvo

bursting forth: efflorescence

bursting in: irruption

bury: conceal, cover, embed, engross,

entomb, hide, immerse, inhume, inter, inundate, overwhelm, plant, repress, rivet, shroud, sink, stash, submerge

bus rider's ticket: transfer

bus station: depot

bus, large sightseeing: charabanc

bush: backcountry, backwoods, bosch, branch, clump, cluster, forest, grove, league, outback, plant, shrub, thicket

bush dog: dingo

bush fence: hedge

bushed: beat, exhausted, fatigued, pooped, spent, tired, worn

bushwa: baloney, bull, bunk, hogwash, hooey, nonsense, poppycock, rubbish, trash

bushwacker: bandit, guerilla, outlaw, pioneer, scythe, sniper

bushy: bushman, furry, hairy, shaggy, woolly

business: activity, affair, art, bag, beeswax, calling, capital, care, career, cause, commerce, concern, custom, disturbance, duty, employment, enterprise, establishment, field, firm, game, industry, job, occupation, office, outfit, partnership, patronage, profession, racket, situation, syndicate, task, trade, trading, traffic, transaction, venture, vocation, work

RELATED TERMS

business activities, undertake a variety of: diversify

business agent: factor

business as registered company, to form a: incorporate

business association for purpose of joint enterprise: consortium, syndicate

business association of companies to monopolize or control: cartel

business branch or licensee: franchise

business controlled by another: subsidiary

business controlling others: holding company

business corporation of different companies in diversified fields: conglomerate

business deal: transaction

business executives, recruitment of: head-hunting

business operation expenses: overhead

business organization's twelve-month accounting period: fiscal year

business owner or owner-manager: proprietor

business symbol or trademark: logo

business that hires nonunion members and requires union membership by a date: union shop

business venture launched or financed by issue of stocks or bonds: flotation

business, exclusive control over market or: monopoly

businesses, combining of separate: consolidation

businesslike: careful, diligent, earnest, efficient, intent, organized, professional, purposeful, routine, serious

businesslike and practical: pragmatic

businessperson between producer and retailer: middleman

businessperson who starts companies, develops ideas: entrepreneur

businessperson, important: magnate, tycoon

business's impressive and successful product: flagship ❦

buss: kiss

bust: arrest, bankrupt, break, burst, capture, fail, failure, flop, flunk, lemon, loser, nab, pinch, raid, reduce, ruin, tame; bosom, breast, bronze, chest, sculpture, statue

bustle: activity, ado, agitation, clamor, clatter, commotion, dash, flurry, frisk, furor, fuss, haste, hubbub, hustle, racket, rumpus, scamper, scurry, stir, to-do, tumult, turmoil, unrest, uproar, whirlwind

busy: absorbed, active, assiduous, at work, attentive, brisk, diligent, distracting, employed, energetic, engaged, hopping, humming, industrious, intent, laborious, lively, nosy, occupied, sedulous, swamped, tireless, unavailable, untiring, working

busy and energetic: dynamic, vibrant

busy and hectic: frantic

busy and persevering: assiduous, diligent, sedulous

busy one: ant, bee, doer, goer

busybody: blabbermouth, buttinsky, fussbudget, gossip, meddler, pragmatist, pry, quidnunc, rubberneck, snoop, snooper, yenta

but: besides, except, however, just, mere, nevertheless, nonetheless, only, otherwise, save, still, unless, yet

but as a word expressing opposition: adversative, disjunctive

but as a word joining others: coordinating conjunction

butcher: botch, bungle, executioner, kill, killer, merchant, murder, murderer, mutilate, ruin, slaughter, slay

butcher knife: cleaver

butcherbird: shrike

butler: valet

butlers, group of: sneer

butt: adjoin, behind, bottom, buck, buttocks, cart, cask, cigar, cigarette, derriere, end, fanny, flounder, goat, head, hinge, horn, in, joint, jolt, patsy, project, push, ram, rump, shaft, stub, stump, sucker, target, thrust, tush, victim

butte: mesa

butter: beurre, fat, flatter, food, ghee, ghi, margarine, oil, oleo, ram, spread

butter dab: pat

butter for pastry making: shortening

butter maker: churner

butter, clarified Indian: ghee

butter, pertaining to: butyraceous

butter, purify: clarify

buttercup: anemone

butterfat: cream

butterfingered: awkward, bungling, careless, clumsy

butterfinger's cry: oops

butterfly: admiral, alfalfa, aphrodite, apollo, arthemis, buckeye, christmas, giant, grayling, kiho, lepidopteran, monarch, morpho, red admiral, satyr, skipper, swim stroke, tiger, underwing, ursula, viceroy, zebra

butterfly in cocoon: chrysalis, pupa

butterfly kin: moth

butterfly or moth: lepidopteran

butterfly or moth expert: lepidopterist

butterfly transformation into moth: metamorphosis

buttery: dairy

buttinski: interloper, pest

buttocks: behind, bottom, breech, buns, butt, derriere, fanny, fundament, heinie, keister, nates, rear, rump, seat

buttocks, fat: steatopygia

buttocks, shapely: callipygian

button: badge, bauble, buckle, bud, chin, emblem, fastener, fasten, hook, knob, pearl, stud

button ridge: knurl

buttonhole: accost, approach, detain, eyelet, loop, slip, stop

buttonhole blossom: carnation

buttonhole site: lapel

buttress: abutment, bolster, boost, brace, pad, pier, pile, prop, reinforce, stay, strut, support, uphold

buttress that juts out: flying buttress

buxom: bosomy, bouncing, built, busty, curvaceous, full-figured, hefty, plump, robust, shapely, stacked, voluptuous

buy: acquire, bargain, bribe, chap, coup, gain, get, market, purchase, ransom, redeem, score, secure, shop, trade

buy a round or meal for: treat

buy back: redeem

buy now, pay later: charge it

buy or spend, itch to: emacity

buy things, uncontrollable desire to: oniomania

buyer: agent, client, consumer, customer, patron, prospect, purchaser, shopper, sucker, vendee

buyer beware: caveat emptor

buying and selling for quick profit, risky: speculation

buying and selling sacred things: simony

buying of goods for resale at profit: forestall

buyout strategy, at times: tender offer

buzz: call, drone, gossip, hearsay, hiss, hum, notion, phone, ring, rumor, saw, scandal, telephone, whir, whisper

buzz and hum: bombinate, drone

buzzard or hawk: buteo

buzzing in ear: tinnitus

by: along, alongside, apart, beside, close, concerning, handy, near, past, per, through, toward, via

by and by: anon, down the road

by chance: accidental, coincidental, fortuitous, haphazard, random, serendipitous

by degrees: gradual

by memory: rote

by-product: aftermath, offshoot, spin-off

by sight: ocular

by the very fact: ipso facto

by the way: apropos, en passant, incidentally, parenthetically

by virtue of one's official position: ex officio

by way of: via

bygone: ago, ancient, archaic, backward, departed, forgotten, former, obsolete, old, olden, oldfangled, past

bylaw: rule

bypass: avoid, detour, dodge, ignore, miss, omit, shun, shunt, sidestep, skip

bypath: byway, lane, pathway, shortcut, trail, way

byre: barn

bystander: eyewitness, observer, onlooker, passerby, spectator, witness

byword: adage, axiom, byname, catchword, dictum, epithet, motto, nickname, phrase, proverb, rule, saw, saying, slogan

Cc

caama fox: asse

cab: carriage, hack, hansom, locomotive, taxi

cabal: camarilla, camp, circle, clan, clique, collusion, conspiracy, coterie, council, faction, intrigue, junta, party, plot, ring, scheme

cabalistic: esoteric, mysterious, mystic, occult, strange, supernatural

caballero: cavalier, escort, gentleman, horseman, knight, lover, señor

cabaret: boîte, café, club, discotheque, nightclub, restaurant, speakeasy, tavern

cabbage: coleslaw, colewort, kale, sauerkraut

cabbage and mayonnaise salad: cole slaw

cabbage appetizer: egg roll

cabin: booth, boy, caboose, camp, coach, cottage, den, hut, lodge, log, shack, shanty, shed, stateroom

cabin, private, on ship or train: stateroom

cabin, ramshackle: shanty

cabinet: armoire, board, box, bureau, case, chest, chiffonnier, closet, committee, commode, console, council, cupboard, dresser, file, kitchen, ministry, vanity

cabinet for displaying objects: étagère

cabinet for stereo, TV: console

cabinet member's office or post: portfolio

cabinet of unofficial advisers to head of government: kitchen cabinet

cabinet with projecting front: breakfront

cable: boom, chain, coaxial, cord, link, rope, stitch, telegram, television, wire

cable car: tram

cable car of ski lift car: gondola

cable car, aerial: telpher

cable is wound, cylindrical apparatus on boat around which: capstan

cable railway: funicular

cable/rope for mooring, towing: hawser

cable/rope for steadying, securing: guy

cablegram: wire

cache: bury, conceal, cover, hide, hoard, kitty, reserve, secrete, stockpile, store, storehouse, treasure

cachet: capsule, design, distinction, prestige, seal, stamp, stature, status

cackle: babble, blab, chackle, chat, chatter, cluck, crow, gab, giggle, gossip, jaw, laugh, laughter, snicker, titter, twaddle

cacophonous: discordant, dissonant, harsh, noisy, off-key, raucous, sour, strident

cacophony: din, noise

cactus: agave, airampo, bleo, cereus, chaute, chende, chichipe, cholla, Christmas, cochal, easter, mescal, moon, nopal, peyote, plant, porcupine, rainbow, saguaro, snake, snowdrop, spider, succulent, sun, toad, xerophyte

cactus feature: spine

cactus or plant with water-storing leaves: succulent

cactus producing narcotic drug: mescal, peyote

cad: boor, bounder, creep, cur, dastard, heel, louse, lout, masher, rascal, rotter, scoundrel, villain, worm

cadaver: body, carcass, corpse, remains, stiff

cadaverous: corpselike, deathly, emaciated, gaunt, ghastly, haggard, pale, shadowy, wasted

caddishly: basely

cadence: beat, count, inflection, lilt, measure, meter, metre, modulation, pace, pulse, rhythm, sound, swing, tempo, tone

cadence call: hep

cadet: junior, midshipman, plebe, recruit, student, youth

cadge: beg, bum, hawk, huckster, mooch, panhandle, peddle, scrounge, sponge

cadre: core, force, frame, framework, group, infrastructure, nucleus, panel, staff, unit

caducity: age, feebleness, lapse, perishable, senility, transitory

caesura: break, interruption, interval, pause, rest, stop

café: bar, cabaret, cafeteria, coffeehouse, diner, estaminet, nightclub, restaurant, saloon, tavern, teahouse

café with entertainment: cabaret

café, small: estaminet

cafeteria or lunchroom at entertainment studio: commissary

caffeine or other agent causing increased activity: stimulant

caffeine-yielding tree: kola

cage: basket, box, brake, bucket, chantry, confine, coop, enclosure, imprison, incarcerate, jail, mew, pen, pound, prison

cage for molting hawks: mew

cage for small plants and animals: terrarium

cage, large, for birds: aviary

cagey: astute, canny, crafty, cunning, discreet, foxy, sharp, shrewd, sly, wary, wily

caisson: box, case, chamber, chest, float, wagon

caitiff: base, cowardly, dastard, despicable, louse, mean, rat, scoundrel, vile, wicked

cajole: beguile, blandish, brownnose,

coax, con, entice, flatter, jolly, lure, persuade, sweet-talk, tease, tweedle, wheedle

cake: bake, bar, block, bun, coagulate, coffeecake, compress, crust, cupcake, éclair, food, harden, lump, mass, pastry, patty, set, slab, solidify, thicken, torte, wedge

cake of cornmeal deep-fried: hush puppy

cake or bread mold filled with fruit, sponge: charlotte

cake or pastry, rich: torte

cake pastry filled with custard cream: napoleon

cake soaked in rum and syrup: baba au rhum

cake soaked in rum, sherry or brandy and layered with jam, jelly or custard: trifle

cake tier: layer

cake topping: icing

cake, almond-flavored sponge: angel food cake

cake, chocolate, dense and sometimes with nuts: brownie

cake, chocolate, with apricot jam and chocolate icing: Sacher torte

cake, coffee, with fruit and nuts: kuchen

cake, decorated small and square-cut: petit four

cake, elaborate sweet: torte

cake, fruit, for mid-Lent, Easter and Christmas: simnel

cake, rich and small, made in shell-shaped mold: madeleine

cake, rich, with many eggs, little flour, and chopped nuts: torte

cake, small piece of frosted and decorated pound or sponge: petit four

cake, unsweetened and soft: crumpet

cake, very light sweet: sponge cake

cake, yeast, with candied fruit peels and raisins: panettone

cakes and other sweets: confectionery

cakewalk: cinch, dance, march, prance, rout, strut

calabash: gourd

calaboose: brig, clink, cooler, hoosegow, jail, jug, lockup, pen, prison, slammer

calamitous: adverse, afflictive, bitter, cataclysmic, catastrophic, deadly, deplorable, dire, direful, disastrous, dismal, distressful, evil, fatal, miserable, ruinous, sad, tragic, unfortunate, unlucky, woeful, wretched

calamity: accident, adversity, affliction, blow, catastrophe, disaster, hardship, ill, misadventure, misery, misfortune, mishap, ruin, scourge, sorrow, storm, tragedy, wreck

calash: hat

calcium oxide: lime

calculate: add, aim, anticipate, assess, average, cipher, compute, consider, count, determine, devise, divide, enumerate, estimate, evaluate, expect, figure, forecast, multiply, number, plan, project, rate, subtract, tally, think

calculate again: recast

calculated: artful, careful, cautious, computed, computing, contriving, crafty, cunning, safe, scheming, sly, wily

calculating: deliberate, measured, planned, premeditated, risk, studied

calculating bead device: abacus

calculating procedure using a finite number of steps: algorithm

calculation: adjustment, answer, ciphering, computation, deduction, estimation, forecast, logistics, precaution, prediction, prudence, reckoning, result, totaling

calculation based on inference: dead reckoning, guesswork

calculator: abacus, computer, table

calculator of risks in insurance: actuary

calculator's register for counting and accumulating data: accumulator

caldron: boiler, cauldron, kettle, pot, vat

calembour: pun

calendar: agenda, almanac, annal, chronology, diary, docket, Gregorian, journal, Julian, log, menology, ordo, program, schedule, slate, timetable

calendar before the one with leap years: Julian calendar

calendar of a church: menology

calendar of events: docket

calendar of weather and tide information, etc.: almanac

calendar with leap years: Gregorian calendar

calendar, first day of the month in Roman: calends

calendar, most common: Gregorian

calendar, to insert a day into a: intercalate

calf: dogie, dolt, fatling, foreleg, maverick, muscle, veal, yearling, youth

calf meat: veal

calf or lamb skin, untanned: kip

calf prematurely born: slink

calf that is sterile born as twin of bull calf: freemartin

calf, female, between one to two years old: stirk

calf, inner lining of fourth stomach of: rennet

calf, of a hand-reared: cade

calf, stray or motherless: dogie

calf's cry: blat, bleat

caliber: ability, capacity, character, class, degree, dignity, grade, merit, prestige, prominence, quality, rank, scope, skill, stature, talent, value, weight, worth; bore, diameter, gauge

calico cat's adversary: gingham dog

calico pony: pinto

call: accuse, address, alarm, announce, appeal, appoint, arouse, assemble, baptize, bid, buzz, challenge, claim, collect, command, convene, cry, decree, demand, designate, dial, dub, elect, entitle, hail, identify, impeach, invite, invoke, muster, name, nominate, order, page, phone, plea, proclaim, reason, request, ring, rouse, shout, solicit, stop, style, subpoena, summon, telephone, title, utter, visit, vocation, waken, yell, yodel

call for: crave, demand, entail, need, page, request, require, suggest, want

call for aid or witness: invoke

call for earnestly: invoke

call for help: SOS

call for silence: shush

call forth: awaken, command, elicit, evoke, summon

call in question: dispute, oppugn

call off: cancel, end, halt, scrub

call on: visit

call on for help or inspiration: invoke

call or whistle, derisive: catcall

call out: cry, holler, muster, shout, yell

call to: address, greet, hail

call to account or chastise: call on the carpet

call to arms: alarum

call to order: begin, convene, open

call to the riders: all aboard

call to troops: muster

call together to meet: convoke

call upon: ask, invite, request, urge, visit

call, in poker: see

calla lilies: aroid, arum

caller to prayer: muezzin

calling: appellation, art, business, career, condition, convocation, craft, devotion, employment, function, job, lifework, métier, mission, naming, occupation, position, profession, pursuit, rank, shouting, station, summons, trade, undertaking, utterance, vocation, work

calling or summons to a type of work: vocation

callous: apathetic, brawny, cold, cruel, hard, hardhearted, horny, indifferent, insensitive, obtuse, stubborn, torpid, tough, unfeeling

callow: bald, bare, crude, green, immature, infantile, juvenile, marshy, naive, raw, shallow, tenderfoot, unfledged, youthful

callow youth: teen

calm: abate, allay, appease, assuage, charm, collect, collected, complacence, composed, cool, cool-headed, defuse, dispassionate, docile, ease, easy, easygoing, equable, fair, gentle, halcyon, harmonious, hush, impassive, levelheaded, low-key, lull, mild, nonchalant, pacify, passive, pastoral, patient, peace, peaceful, placate, placid, quell, quiescent, quiet, rest, restful, restrain, sedate, serene, silence, smooth, sober, soothe, steady, still, stoic, subdued, temperate, tranquil, tranquilize, unconfused, undisturbed, unexcited, unmoved, unruffled

calm and detached: aloof, indifferent, phlegmatic, staid

calm and quiet: halcyon, serene, tranquil

calm and rational: Apollonian, self-possessed, unruffled

calm and soothe: allay, assuage, quell

calm and tranquil: halcyon, impassive, placid, serene

calm and unemotional: dispassionate, impassive, imperturbable, placid

calm and well-behaved: sedate

calm down: abate, quell, subside

calm in difficult time: fatalistic, philosophical, stoical

calm or pacify: appease, conciliate, mollify, placate, propitiate

calm period: lull

calm personality: equanimity, eventemperedness, sangfroid

calm state: composure, repose

calm under pressure: cool

calming: ataractic, sedative

calming agent: bromide

calmly: evenly

calmness: ataraxia, composure, coolness, equanimity, peacefulness, placidity, poise, quietness, repose, sangfroid, serenity, stillness, tranquility

caloric output: heat

calories without nutrition: empty calories

calumet: peace pipe, pipe

calumniate: accuse, asperse, blacken, blaspheme, defame, libel, malign, revile, scandalize, slander, slur, smear, vilify

calyx: husk, leaf, petal, sepal

cam: askew, awry, cog, crooked, cylinder, disk, shaft, tappet, trippet

camaraderie: brotherhood, cheer, fellowship, friendliness, jollity, sociability

camarilla: advisers, cabal, clan, clique, council, junta, mob, ring

camber: arch

camel: ship of the desert

camel driver: camaleer, sarwan

camel relative: llama

camel, Arabian, with one hump: dromedary

camel, Asian, with two humps: bactrian

camel's hair fabric: aba

cameo ornament in low relief: anaglyph

camouflage: cloak, conceal, cover, deceptive, disguise, fake, hide, masquerade, screen, smokescreen

camouflage naturally existing in some animals: Batesian mimicry, protective coloring

camouflage or resemble closely, to: mimic, simulate

camouflage, concerning coloration serving as natural: apatetic

camouflaged: hidden

camouflaging: apatetic

camp: barrack, bivouac, etape, fire, ground, lodging, quarters, settlement, shelter, siege, tent; mod, pop, wild

camp bed: cot

camp structure: tent

camp, temporary, often without shelter: bivouac

campaign: barnstorm, canvass, crusade, drive, muckrake, offensive, operation, politick, run, solicit, warfare

campaign for a cause: crusade

campaign motto or catchphrase: slogan

campaign of revenge: vendetta

campaign to solicit votes: canvass

CAMERA TERMS

camera for filmmaking: cinematograph
camera stand with one leg: monopod
camera stand with three legs: tripod
camera that makes instant photograph: Polaroid
camera with view of finished print: single lens reflex, SLR
cameraman's lamp: arc
closeup without losing focus: zoom lens
device determining the distance of an object: range finder
device limiting the amount of light passing through lens: aperture
device regulating duration of exposure: shutter
device regulating light traversing the lens: diaphragm, stop
eye of the camera: lens
follow movement, to: pan
lens system receiving light from object and forming the image: objective
lens with 180-degree field of vision: fisheye lens
move a camera lens toward or away from a subject, to: zoom
picture-taking push button: shutter release
print made from film: photo, photograph, snapshot ❧

---

campanile: belfry, steeple, tower

camper's groundsheet: tarp

campfire leavings: ashes

campus: college, field, grounds, quad

campus accommodation: dorm, dormitory

campus area: quad

campus building: dorm, hall, lab

campus celebration: homecoming

campus greenery: ivy

campus-related: parietal

campus social organization: fraternity, sorority

can: container, cup, jug, receptacle, tin, vessel

can/cup, small: cannikin

can opener: key

canaille: commoners, masses, mob, rabble, riffraff, unwashed

canal: aqueduct, bottleneck, channel, conduit, ditch, drain, duct, erie, Panama, strait, Suez, towpath, trench, tube, watercourse

canal boat: gondola

canal dam to raise or divert water: weir

canal for water, artificial: sluice

canal or channel for water, bridgelike: aqueduct

canal or channel, stretch of water between bends in: reach

canal part: lock

canal used by animals towing boats, path along: bridlepath, towpath

canals connecting Superior and Huron: Soo

canapé spread: pâté

canard: exaggeration, fabrication, fib, hoax, lie, rumor, spoof, swindle

canary: bird, dance, fink, informer, singer, songbird, squealer, stoolie, wine, yellow

canary's kin: serin

cancel: abolish, abort, abrogate, annul, ax, call off, dele, delete, drop, efface, end, erase, invalidate, negate, nullify, omit, quash, recall, remit, remove, revoke, scrub, trash, vitiate, void

cancel a claim or belief: abjure, disavow, recant, renounce, retract

cancel a law: repeal, revoke

cancel a liftoff: scrub

cancel an order or command: countermand, rescind

cancel common factors in fraction's numerator and denominator: reduce

cancel or erase: delete, efface, expunge

cancel or postpone: remit

cancel or rescind: recall, revoke

cancel passenger's place: bump

cancelled as uncollectible: written off

cancer: carcinoma, chemotherapy, corruption, disease, malignancy, radiation, sarcoma, sickness, tumor

cancer-causing: carcinogen

cancer growth, secondary: metastasis

cancer moving to other parts of body: metastasis

cancer of blood: leukemia

cancer of cervix test: Pap smear, Pap test

cancer treatment by drugs: chemotherapy

cancer treatment by radiation: radiotherapy

cancer, of inoperable: terminal

cancer, subsiding or abatement of symptoms of: remission

cancer, with no: benign

cancerous and metastasizing: malignant

cancerous growth: carcinoma

cancerous molelike tumor: melanoma

candelabrum, Jewish 7-branch: menorah

candescent: dazzling, glowing, hot, luminescent, shine, white

candid: aboveboard, artless, blunt, clear, direct, fair, frank, genuine, guileless, honest, honorable, immaculate, impartial, just, open, outspoken, pure, sincere, splendid, straightforward, truthful, unconcealed

candidate: applicant, aspirant, bidder, campaigner, contender, nominee, postulant, prospect

candidate list: slate

candidate, unknown, who wins: dark horse

candied or iced: glacé

candied potato: yam

candle: bayberry, bougie, chandelle, dip, light, roman, stick, tallow, taper, wax

candle burning low or almost out: gutter

candle kept burning in church: vigil light

candle part: wick

candle, slender or small: taper

candle, to extinguish: douse, snuff

candleholder: candelabra, chandelier, girandole, lampad, menorah, pricket, sconce

candleholder for Jewish traditions, nine- or seven-branched: menorah

candleholder, large branched ceiling: chandelier

candleholder, ornamental branched: girandole

candlelight: glim

candlemaker or seller: chandler

candlenut tree: ama

candles, hard fat used to make: tallow

candlestick on wall bracket: sconce

candlestick with several branches: candelabrum

candlestick with spike for holding candle: pricket

candlestick, large ornamental: flambeau

candor: brightness, brilliance, fairness, frankness, honesty, impartiality, innocence, integrity, kindliness, kindness, openness, purity, sincerity, veracity

candy: bar, bonbon, brittle, caramel, chocolate, comfit, confection, congeal, crystallize, flatter, fondate, fudge, granulate, gumdrop, jawbreaker, jelly bean, kiss, licorice, lol-

CANCERS

anal cancer
benign tumor
bladder cancer
bone cancer
brain cancer
breast cancer
cancerous growth
cancerous tumor
carcinoma
cervical cancer
colon cancer
colorectal cancer
epithelioma
esophagus cancer
eye cancer
gall-bladder cancer
gastric cancer
Hodgkin's disease
innocent tumor
intumescence
kidney cancer
larynx cancer
leukemia
liver cancer
lung cancer
lymphoma
malignant tumor
melanoma
metastatic tumor
mouth cancer
multiple myeloma
nasopharynx cancer
neoplasm
neuroblastoma
oral cancer
ovarian cancer
pancreatic cancer
primary growth
prostate cancer
rectal cancer
salivary glands cancer
sarcoma
secondary growth
skin cancer
stomach cancer
testicular cancer
throat cancer
thyroid cancer
tumor
uterine cancer
uveal cancer
vaginal cancer
vulvar cancer ❧

lipop, mint, nougat, praline, rock, sourball, sugarcoated, sweet, sweeten, sweetmeat, taffy, toffee

candy coating: dragée

candy filled with cream, fruit, or nuts, chocolate: bonbon

candy stick: cane

candy with nuts and fruit: nougat

cane: bamboo, beat, birch, flog, hickory, hit, lance, pikestaff, pipe, pole, punish, rod, scourge, staff, stem, stick, strike, sugar, whip

cane-cutting knife: machete

cane used by armed forces officer: swagger stick

cane used for wickerwork etc.: rattan

cane used to punish: ferule

canine: chow, coyote, cur, dingo, dog, eyetooth, fox, hound, hyena, lobo, mutt, pooch, pup, wolf

canine neighbor: bicuspid

canine pest: flea

canine tooth: cuspid, eyetooth

canine with blue-black tongue: chow

canker: boil, cancer, consume, corrode, corrupt, decay, infect, lesion, pollute, sore, stain, tarnish, ulcer

cannabis: dope, grass, hashish, hemp, marijuana, pot, reefer, tea, weed

canned: fired

cannibal: anthropophagite, anthropophagus, brute, headhunter, maneater, primitive, savage

canning jar: Mason

cannon: artillery, ball, bastard, bit, crack, firearm, gun, howitzer, mortar, ordnance, pickpocket, pompom, robinet, thief

cannon emplacement in low-roofed building: pillbox

cannon pivots, pin on which: trunnion

cannon plug or cover: tampion

cannon with high trajectory, medium velocity: howitzer

cannon, artillery: ordnance

cannon, cluster of iron balls fired from: grapeshot

cannonade: barrage, battery, blitz, bomb, bombardment, burst, salvo, shower, volley

cannons are fired, platform or mounds from which: barbette

cannot be erased: indelible

canny: able, astute, cagey, careful, carefully, clever, cozy, cunning, dexterous, fortunate, frugal, gentle, ingenious, knowing, lucky, prudent,

sagacious, sharpwitted, shrewd, skillful, sly, thrifty, wary, watchful, wily, wise

canoe: almadia, ballam, birch, boat, bungo, coracle, currane, dugout, irogue, kayak, pitpan, proa, skiff, waka

canoe float: outrigger

canoe from tree trunk: pirogue

canoe with opening for paddler: kayak

canon: axiom, catalog, code, command, constitution, criterion, decision, decree, doctrine, dogma, edict, law, list, maxim, model, precept, principle, regulation, rule, standard, statute, tenet

canon mark: presa

canonical: accepted, authorized, customary, legal, orthodox, proper, sanctioned

canonical hour at dawn: matins, with lauds

canonical hour at nine A.M.: terce

canonical hour at noon: sext

canonical hour at six A.M.: prime

canonical hour at three P.M.: none

canonical hour just before bedtime: compline

canonical hour of early evening: vespers

canonical hours: nones

canonized woman: seton

canopy: awning, baldachin, cover, covering, hood, marquee, pavilion, shade, shelter, sky, tester, umbrella

canopy for bed or pulpit: tester

canopy for processions or over altar, dais, throne: baldachin

canopy or awning for boat, cart, wagon: tilt

canopy or large tent: pavilion

cans of film: reels

cant: argot, dialect, idiom, jargon, language, lingo, patter, pomposity, pretense, slang, vernacular, vocabulary, vulgarism

cantaloupe: fruit, melon, muskmelon

cantankerous: choleric, contentious, cranky, crochety, fretful, irritable, malicious, mean, ornery, sour, surly

cantata solo: aria

canteen: bar, bottle, cantina, commissary, flask, jug, k.t., p.x., thermos

canter: beggar, bum, drifter, gallop, jog, lope, pace, rack, run, trot, vagabond, whiner

canticle: ode

cantina snack: taco, tamale

canting: alist

canton: billet, corner, county, district, division, part, quarter, section, subdivision

cantor: chanter, hazan, leader, precentor, singer, soloist, vocalist

Canuck: Canadian, French Canadian

canvas: artwork, burlap, duck, oil, painting, picture, sail, sails, tarp, tarpaulin, tent

canvas as waterproof covering: tarpaulin

canvas cot suspended in the air: hammock

canvas holder: easel

canvas shelter: tent

canvass: agitate, analyze, campaign, case, check, debate, discuss, electioneer, examine, hawk, investigate, peddle, poll, scrutinize, search, seek, sift, solicit, study, stump, survey

canyon: arroyo, divide, glen, gorge, grand, gulch, gully, ravine, valley

caoutchouc: India rubber

cap: arrest, barrect, beanie, beret, best, better, bonnet, climax, coif, cork, cornet, cover, crest, crown, detonator, dome, excel, fez, hat, headgear, headpiece, helmet, hood, kepi, lid, montero, mortarboard, outdo, outshine, pass, seal, seize, summit, surpass, taj, tip, top, topee, trump, turban, yarmulke

cap back flap for neck protection: havelock

cap containing gunpowder that explodes when struck: percussion cap

cap part: earlap, visor

cap with a pompon: tam

cap with bells for jester: foolscap

cap, flat and round: beret

cap, flat top, with snap: touring cap

cap, knit and navy blue, for sailors: watch cap

cap, Moslem, felt with tassel: tarboosh

cap, Russian, covering head and neck: balaclava

cap, stiff and square, for clergy: biretta

capability: ability, aptitude, art, capacity, competence, craft, efficacy, knack, means, potential, skill, talent

capable: able, accomplished, adept, apt, can, competent, effective, experienced, expert, fitted, masterly, proficient, qualified, skilled, suited, up to

capable of being split apart: divisible

capable of being turned outward: reversible

capable of modification: adaptable
capable of working: viable
capable person: adept
capacious: abundant, ample, broad, commodious, comprehensive, considerable, expandable, extensive, full, generous, large, massive, plentiful, roomy, spacious, vast, wide
capacious bag: tote
capacitance unit: farad
capacity: ability, aptitude, bulk, burden, caliber, capability, competence, content, extent, faculty, full, gift, intellect, knack, limit, potential, power, room, size, skill, space, spread, strength, talent, volume
capacity to be reassigned: transferability
caparison: adorn, clothing, covering, deck, decoration, harness, trappings
cape: cloak, mantilla, mantle, poncho, shawl, stole, tabard
cape antelope: eland
Cape Cod architecture: salt box
cape fox: asse
caper: adventure, antic, cavort, dance, devilment, dido, escapade, fling, frisco, frisk, frolic, gag, gambado, gambol, hop, jump, lark, leap, mischief, monkeyshine, prance, prank, romp, shenanigans, skit, spring, stunt, trip
capillary: blood vessel, hairlike, minute, slender, tension, tube
capital: a-one, basic, cairo, cap, cash, central, chief, city, dominant, excellent, foremost, funds, good, great, headquarters, leading, letter, main, major, money, paramount, principal, prominent, resources, scrumptious, serious, stake, stock, supreme, top, vital, wealth, weighty
capital letter: majuscule, uppercase letter
capital letter, not: lowercase letter, minuscule
capital punishment: death penalty, electrocution, gas, guillotine, hanging, lethal injection, murder
capitalism: competition, democracy, economics, free enterprise, free market, government
capitalist: businessperson, entrepreneur, financier, investor, plutocrat, tycoon
capitalize: back, bankroll, exploit, finance, fund, gain, profit, sponsor, stake, subsidize

capitol: center, dome, legislature, statehouse
capitulate: agree, bow, cave, cede, concede, enumerate, fall, fold, headline, submit, succumb, surrender, yield
caprice: antic, capriccio, craze, crotchets, fad, fancy, humor, impulse, inconsistent, kink, mood, notion, quirk, sudden, temper, trait, vagary, whim, whimsey, whimsy, willfulness
capricious: arbitrary, changeable, crotchety, dizzy, doddy, erratic, fanciful, fantastic, fickle, flighty, fluky, iffy, impulsive, inconsistent, moody, quirky, unstable, unsteady, volatile, wavering, wayward, whimsical
capricious and willful: wayward
capsize: coup, invert, keel, overthrow, overturn, roll, upset
capsule: abridged, ampule, cartridge, case, cockpit, condensed, dose, membrane, outline, pill, pod, sheath, shell, tabloid, time
captain: boh, boss, centurion, chief, commander, foreman, governor, guide, head, headman, headwaiter, leader, manager, master, officer, pilot, principal, skipper
caption: cutline, explanation, heading, headline, legend, subtitle, title, underline
caption or description for map or chart: legend
captious: capricious, contrary, crabby, crafty, critical, cross, cynical, demanding, fault-finding, fretful, insidious, irascible, mean, nit-picking, ornery, peevish, perverse, petulant, sarcastic, severe, testy
captivate: allure, attract, bewitch, capture, catch, charm, dazzle, draw, enamor, enamour, enchant, entertain, enthrall, fascinate, hook, hypnotize, infatuate, lure, mesmerize, overtake, please, seduce, spellbind, subdue, take, win
captive: enslaved, hostage, imprisoned, incarcerated, oppressed, prisoner, slave
captivity: bondage, confinement, custody, duress, enslavement, imprisonment, serfdom, servitude, slavery, thrall, thralldom
capture: apprehend, arrest, bag, captivate, catch, collar, corral, cop, get, grab, hook, land, nab, nail, net, obtain, prize, seize, snag, snare, take, trap, win

car: armored, auto, automobile, basket, buggy, cable, chariot, coach, convertible, coupe, dragster, full-size, hardtop, hatchback, heap, hotrod, jalopy, jeep, limousine, midsize, motor, nash, race, railroad, roadster, sedan, station wagon, subcompact, trailer, train, trolley, vehicle, wheels
RELATED TERMS
car air deflector: spoiler
car blinker lights: hazard light
car collision exhibition: demolition derby
car electrical system that activates vehicle: ignition
car framework on which body is attached: chassis
car gears and associated parts: gear box, transmission
car loss of value through age, wear: depreciation
car old-fashioned footboard: running board
car passenger seat opening out from rear: rumble seat
car phone: cellular phone, mobile phone
car procession: motorcade
car springs and insulation: suspension
car stop in parking lots, concrete: bumper stop, car stop, curb bumper, tire stop, wheel stop
car traveler: motorist
car turn signal light: indicator
car with a rumble seat: roadster
car with folding roof: convertible
car with folding roof over rear seat: cabriolet, landau
car with front and back seats: sedan
car with souped-up engine: hot rod
car with two doors: coupe
car with upward-opening rear door: hatchback
car, airstream behind moving: slipstream
car, long: limousine
car, low framework on casters for working under: cradle, creeper
car, old and run-down: jalopy
car, to remove serviceable parts from: cannibalize, strip ❦

caravan: band, convoy, fleet, journey, line, motorcade, parade, procession, safari, travel, trek, trip
caravan stopping place: oasis

CARD GAMES

all fours	chemin de fer	five hundred	pinochle	seven-up
baccarat	clubs	gin	piquet	skat
beggar-my-neighbor	concentration	gin rummy	poker (blind, Carib-	slapjack
bezique	cooncan/conquian	go fish	bean stud, draw,	snap
Black Maria	crazy eights	hearts	knock, Pai Gow,	solitaire
blackjack/twenty-	cribbage	high-low-jack	straight, strip, stud)	solo
one/vingt-et-un	Earl of Coventry	loo	Pope Joan	speculation
Boston	écarté	Michigan	primero	tarok
brag	eights	monte	quadrille	war
bridge (auction, con-	euchre	nap/napoleon	racing demon	whist ❦
tract, duplicate)	fan-tan	old maid	rouge et noir	
canasta	faro	ombre	rummy	
casino	fish	patience	sevens	

caravansary: hostel, hostelry, hotel, inn, khan, lodge, resthouse, serai

carbohydrate: cellulose, complex, compound, dextrose, glucose, glycogen, maltose, simple, starch, sugar

carbon: charcoal, coal, coke, copy, element, graphite, lead, replica, soot

carbon compounds, referring to: organic

carbon copy: twin

carbon dioxide depletion: hyperventilation

carbon-producing: carboniferous

carbon residue: soot

carbonaceous: organic

carbonate: aerate, burn, char, scorch, sear

carbonated: effervescent

carbonized material: peat

carbuncle: abscess, boil, pimple, sore, stones

carcass: body, cadaver, carrion, corpse, stiff

carcinoma: cancer, malignancy, tumor

card: birthday card, business card, chart, map, menu, plan, postcard, program, schedule, tally, ticket; ace, trump, wild card; comedian, joker

card dealer at gambling table: croupier

card dealer's push: stuss

card for fortune-telling: tarot

card for learning: flash card

card-game authority: Hoyle

card game breaking a tie: rubber

card game for three: skat

card game for two: écarté, jass, war

card game observer who makes comments: kibitzer

card-game preliminary: cut

card-game situation when winner has double the opponent: lurch

card game terms: ace, auction, bid, book, bue, cat, check, cut, deal, deuce, draw, duplicate, flush, hand, holding, international, jack, joker, king, knave, pair, pass, pic, progressive, queen, raise, royal, skat, slam, straight, suit, ten, tenace, trump, widow, wild

card game, casino, played against bank: baccarat, chemin de fer

card of a suit that outranks other suits for a deal or game: trump

card that is jack, queen, king: court card

card that is the only one of its suit in player's hand: singleton

card, to play a trump: ruff

cardboard box: carton

cardboard on which a picture is mounted: mount

cardboard used in bookbinding: pasteboard

cardinal: basic, central, chief, cleric, cloak, essential, fundamental, head, highest, important, key, main, number, preeminent, principal, ruling, underlying, uppermost, vital; red

cardinals that elect the pope, body of: College of Cardinals, Sacred College

cardinals, assembly of: consistory

cards by releasing two piles into one, to shuffle playing: riffle

cards left on table after deal: stock, talon

cards of the trump suit, the four or five highest: honors

cards to increase chance of winning, to prearrange a deck of: stack

cards, fortune-telling by: cartomancy

cardsharp: blackleg

care: alarm, anxiety, attention, auspice, burden, business, caution, chagrin, cherish, concern, cure, desire, diligence, direction, dismay, distress, dole, duty, effort, enthusiasm, foster, grief, guard, guardianship, heartache, heed, keeping, lament, like, management, mind, minister, nurse, nurture, oversight, pains, reck, regard, sadness, safekeeping, solicitude, sorrow, tend, tension, thought, tribulation, trust, tutelage, watchfulness, wish, worry

care and attentiveness, offering: solicitous

care for: fancy, foster, guard, like, love, mind, minister, nurse, nurture, relish, tend

care or guardianship of a minor: custody, tutelage

careen: bend, cant, incline, keel, lean, list, lurch, pitch, slant, slope, stagger, sway, swing, tilt, tip, veer, weave

career: bag, business, calling, course, field, gallop, job, livelihood, occupation, path, profession, pursuit, racket, road, run, trade, vocation, walk of life, work

career advance: office promotion

career and education, summary of: curriculum vitae, CV, resume

career-determining test: aptitude test

career is promoted by influential person, one whose: protégé

carefree: blithe, breezy, careless, dégagé, easy, easygoing, gay, indifferent, insouciant, lighthearted, nonchalant, reckless, relaxed, sans souci, untroubled, wild

careful: accurate, advertent, alert, anxious, attentive, canny, cautious, chary, conservative, considerate, diligent, discreet, economical, exact,

CARDIOVASCULAR DISEASE

aneurism	heart attack
angina pectoris	heart disease
arteriosclerosis	heart failure
atheroma	heart trouble
athlete's heart	hypertension/high blood pressure
blood clot	hypotension/low blood pressure
Buerger's disease	infarction
cardiac arrest	low blood pressure
cardiac disease	mitral stenosis
cardiac hypertrophy	myocardial infarction
carditis	palpitation
chest pain	pericarditis
congenital heart disease	phlebitis
congestive heart failure	rheumatic heart disease
coronary heart disease	stroke
coronary thrombosis	tachycardia
dyspnea	valvular lesion
embolism	valvulitis
enlarged heart	vascular disease
fatty degeneration of the heart	weak heart ❦
hardening of the arteries	

exquisite, frugal, gingerly, guarded, heedful, intent, leery, meticulous, mindful, observant, painstaking, particular, provident, prudent, respective, safe, scrupulous, thorough, thoughtful, thrifty, vigilant, wary, watchful

careful and cautious: chary, judicious
careful and conscientious: assiduous, diligent, punctilious, scrupulous, sedulous
careful and precise, extremely: fastidious, meticulous
careful and tactful: circumspect, discreet, judicious, politic, prudent
careful and watchful: vigilant
careful consideration: advisement
careful financially: provident
careful in speech: circumspect, discreet, prudent, tactful
careful not to reveal feelings: noncommittal
carefully: gingerly
carefully picked jury: blue ribbon panel
carefully receive and consider seriously: take under advisement
carefully selected: handpicked
careless: absentminded, casual, cool, disorderly, easy, forgetful, haphazard, hasty, heedless, improvident, imprudent, inadvertent, inattentive, indifferent, injudicious, irresponsible, languid, lax, listless, messy, neglectful,

negligent, nonchalant, rash, reckless, regardless, remiss, slack, slipshod, slovenly, spontaneous, supine, thoughtless, unconcerned, unfit, unheeding, unmindful, untidy, unwary, wasteful
careless and impulsive: impetuous, precipitate
careless and negligent: reckless, lax, remiss
careless and unmindful: heedless
careless and untidy: slipshod, slovenly
careless in unintentional way: inadvertent
careless or sloppy person: sloven
carelessly done: negligent, remiss, slipshod
caress: coddle, cosset, coy, embrace, feel, flirt, fondle, hug, kiss, massage, neck, pat, pet, stroke, touch, toy
caretaker: concierge, curator, custodian, housekeeper, janitor, keeper, super, watchman
caretaker of building: concierge, custodian, janitor, porter, superintendent
caretaker of collection: conservator, curator, custodian
careworn: distressed, exhausted, fatigued, haggard, jaded, troubled, tuckered
cargo: bulk, burden, contents, freight, goods, haul, lading, load, payload, shipment, truckload
cargo and passengers of craft: payload

cargo and passengers, list of: manifest
cargo and wreckage floating in water: flotsam
cargo found washed ashore: jetsam
cargo in hold of ship, to stow or pack: steeve
cargo thrown into water with buoys for later recovery: lagan
cargo thrown overboard to lighten ship: jetsam
cargo, large reusable receptacle for: container
caribou or elk: deer
caricature: art, burlesque, cartoon, copy, exaggeration, farce, lampoon, mimic, mock, overdo, parody, satire, skit, takeoff, travesty
carillon: angelus, belfry, bell tower, bells, chimes, glockenspiel, peal
carmine: cherry, color, crimson, red, scarlet
carnage: annihilation, blitz, bloodshed, butchery, havoc, holocaust, massacre, murder, slaughter
carnal: animal, bodily, corporeal, earthly, erotic, fleshly, immoral, lewd, lustful, material, obscene, sensual, sensuous, sexual, temporal, wanton, worldly
carnation or pink: dianthus
carnelian, e.g.: gem
carnival: carny, circus, fair, festival,

fete, fiesta, jamboree, mardi gras, merrymaking, revelry, show, sideshow

carnival attraction: ride

carnival performer of disgusting acts: geek

carnivore: bear, cat, civit, coon, cougar, coyote, dingo, dog, easel, ermine, feline, ferret, fox, hyena, jackal, jaguar, leopard, lion, lynx, marten, mink, mongoose, ocelot, opossum, otter, panda, possum, puma, raccoon, sable, seal, skunk, tiger, tigress, weasel, wolf

carnivorous: flesh-eating, predatory, rapacious

carol: ballad, chorus, dance, ditty, hymn, noel, sing, song, warble

carom: bounce, bump, glance, graze, rebound, ricochet, skim, strike

carousal: banquet, bender, binge, carouse, debauchery, drunk, feast, festival, frolic, jamboree, orgy, revel, romp, shindy, spree

carouse: drink, hell, party, quaff, revel, riot, spree, wassail

carp: bother, cavil, censor, censure, chatter, complain, condemn, criticize, fuss, henpeck, knock, nag, nibble, nitpick, quibble, rant, scold, speak, talk; fish

carpe diem: seize the day

carpenter: artisan, builder, cabinetmaker, framer, joiner, mason, woodworker; carpenter ant, carpenter bee

carpenter's tool: adze, auger, awl, file, hammer, plane, rasp, sander, saw

carpentry groove: dado

carpentry joint: miter, tenon

carpet: covering, fabric, flying, indoor, magic, matting, outdoor, Persian, rug, shag, tapestry, tapis

carpet with thick, rough pile: shag

carpet, fringe around Oriental: selvage

carpet, long narrow: runner

carpet, pileless densely patterned: Aubusson

carpet's cut or uncut loops of yarn forming the surface: pile

carpet's underlayer for padding, resilience, or insulation: underlay, underlayment

carping remark: barb

carpus: wrist

carriage (attitude): air aspect, attitude, bearing, behavior, conduct, de-

meanor, deportment, execution, front, gesture, look, manner, mien, poise, posture

carriage (vehicle): buggy, chaise, chariot, coach, conveyance, hack, rig, stroller, transport, vehicle, wagon

RELATED TERMS

carriage trade: aristocracy, elite, quality, society, upper class

carriage, 2- or 4-wheeled, drawn by horse: buggy

carriage, 2-wheeled, drawn by horse: gig

carriage, 2-wheeled, drawn by horse with covered elevated driver's seat in rear: hansom

carriage, 2-wheeled, drawn by horse with folding top and rear groom platform: cabriolet

carriage, 4 horses, driven by one person: four-in-hand, tallyho

carriage, 4-wheeled and 2 seats facing forward: surrey

carriage, 4-wheeled and sideways seats: droshky

carriage, 4-wheeled, closed box with front driver's seat: brougham

carriage, 4-wheeled, facing seats, folding top, front driver's seat: barouche

carriage, 4-wheeled, simple flat platform: buckboard

carriage, 4-wheeled, with folding back section: landau ❦

carried: borne, carted, drifting, lugged, toted, transported, wafted

carried away: elated, rapt

carried on: kept it up, raged, transacts, waged

carried out (campaign): waged

carrier: aircraft, airline, barge, bearer, bus, car, courier, emissary, flattop, mail, mailman, mailwoman, messenger, pigeon, plane, porter, postman, postwoman, rack, railroad, ship, teamster, toter, train, truck, yoke

carrier of disease or germs: vector

carries on riotously: carouses

carrion: bones, cadaver, carcass, corpse, corrupt, loathsome, remains, rotten, vile

carrot: enticement, plant, reward, root, top

carrot-family plant: anise

carrot-top: redhead

carry: bear, behave, bolster, bring, cart, conduct, contain, continue, convey,

convoy, derive, extend, guide, haul, have, hold lead, lug, move, pack, poise, prevail, produce, schlepp, send, shoulder, stock, supply, support, sustain, take, tote, transfer, transmit, transport, undergo

carry along: bring

carry and drag: schlepp

carry away: abduct, kidnap, remove, steal, transport

carry away with delight: entrance

carry on: continue, endure, engage, horseplay, perform, persist, proceed, rage, rail, rant, rave

carry on board: lade

carry out: accomplish, act, complete, do, effect, enact, execute, fulfill, implement, obey, transact

carry out business: transact

carry person face down by arms and legs: frog march

carry weapon diagonally across body: port

carryall: satchel, tote, valise

carrying a weapon: armed

carrying electric current easily: superconductive

carrying inward or toward center: afferent

carrying outward or away from center: deferent, efferent

carrying, act or instance of: portage

cart: bring, carry, chariot, convey, dray, haul, lug, sulky, tote, trolley, truck, trundle, tumbler, vehicle, wagon, wain, wheelbarrow

cart for prisoners to be executed during French Revolution: tumbrel

cart with two wheels for passenger, pulled by person: ricksha, rickshaw

carte blanche: authority, freedom, license, permission, power

carte du jour: menu

cartel: bloc, challenge, contract, defy, federation, group, letter, mob, monopoly, pact, paper, pool, ring, ship, syndicate, trust

cartilage: gristle, tissue

cartilage under dog's tongue: lytta

cartograph: map

cartographer: mapper

carton: bin, box, case, container, crate, packet, receptacle

carton material: cardboard

cartoon: animation, caricature, comic strip, drawing, sketch

cartoon oval for printed words of character: balloon

CARVING, CUTTING, EDGED AND POINTED TOOLS

adz	butcher knife	gouge	masonry chisel	scissors
awl	carving knife	graver	paring chisel	scorper
ax	chisel	hardy	pick	scraper
bill	cleaver	hatchet	pinking shears	scythe
blade	clipper	hook	pipe cutter	shears
bodkin	cold chisel	jackknife	punch	sickle
bolster chisel	drove/boaster	knife	razor	square-end chisel
burin	firmer chisel	machete	router	wire cutter ❦

cartoon portrait: caricature

cartoon single scene: frame

cartoonlike drawing: caricature

cartridge: blank, bullet, capsule, case, cassette, cylinder, shell, tube

cartwheel: coin, handspring, somersault, tumble, turn a handspring

caruncle: comb

carve: chip, chisel, cut, dissect, engrave, etch, incise, mold, saw, sculpt, sculpture, sever, shape, slice, split, whittle

carved figure beneath surface of metal or stone: intaglio

carved gem: cameo

carved in relief: embossed

carved ivory, stone, shells: scrimshaw

carved post: totem pole

carving on an ornament in low relief: anaglyph

carving or engraving of gems: glyptics

casa: dwelling, house

Casanova: admirer, cad, Don Juan, ladies' man, lothario, lover, lover boy, paramour, romeo, roue, wolf, womanizer

cascade: cataract, falls, gush, rapids, spout, tumble, waterfall

case as an example, to mention a: cite

case establishing rights for suspects: Miranda

case for business papers: attaché, briefcase

case for carrying cosmetics: vanity case

case for carrying loose papers, etc.: diplomatic pouch, portfolio

case for small articles: etui

case history of patient, complete: anamnesis

case or example: instance

case used as a standard for subsequent legal cases: precedent

case with no loopholes or flaws, of a: ironclad, watertight

cash: backnote, brass, bread, capital, change, clink, coin, coinage, currency, dinero, dough, draw, funds, long green, money, principal

cash drawer: till

cash extraction: debit

cash in: redeem

cash payment made when client uses broker's credit for purchase: margin

cash, available: liquidity

cash, lacking: illiquid

cashews and pecans: nuts

cashier: boot, bursar, can, cast, clerk, discard, expel, fire, oust, purser, reject, teller, treasurer

casing: boot, coffin, covering, frame, lining, sheath, skin, tire

cask: barrel, bulge, butt, casket, casque, firkin, hogshead, keg, pipe, tub, tun, vat

cask material: oak

cask or barrel, small: firkin, kilderkin

cask stopper: bung

cask, half-barrel: kilderkin

cask, vent plug of: spigot, spile

casket: box, case, cask, chest, coffer, coffin, pall, tomb

casket platform: bier

casque: helmet

casserole: goulash, hash, potluck

casserole of white beans and meats or poultry: cassoulet

casserole, covered earthenware: marmite

cassiterite or cinnabar: ore

cassock: soutane

cassolette: ramekin

cassowary kin: emu

cassowary, for one: ratite

cast: actors, characters, company, players

cast about: contrive, hunt, search, seek

cast aspersions upon: slur

cast assignment: part

cast away: abandon, discard, jilt, reject, scrap, shed, strand

CASTLE TERMS

battlement's notch between merlons: crenel

battlement's toothlike part between crenels: merlon

castle: bastille, chateau, citadel, fort, fortress, manor, mansion, palace, rook, stronghold, villa

castle designs: concentric castle, motte-and-bailey castle, mound castle

castle feature: turret

castle impossible to capture or enter forcibly, of a: impregnable

castle keeper: castellan, chatelain, chatelaine, constable

castle or manor house: chateau

castle protecting city: citadel

castlelike: castellated

exterior defense: drawbridge, moat

ledge between parapet and moat: berm

opening in projecting battlement: machiocolation

projecting turret: bartizan

rear gate: postern

steep slope in front of castle: escarpment, glacis

tower at drawbridge/gate: barbican

tower or keep: donjon ❦

cast down: abase, dejected, depressed, disgraced, dispirit, droopy, humbled, humiliated, lower, sadden, sink

cast-iron frying pan, type of: spider

cast lots: ballot

cast metal: ingot

cast off: discard, free, repudiate, shed, unfasten, untie

cast off dead skin: molt, slough

cast off sweetheart: jilt

cast out: banish, eject, exile, expel, ostracize, oust

cast out evil spirit: exorcise

cast-out matter: ejecta, refuse

cast up: add, disgorge, measure, spew, total, vomit

castaway: derelict, leper, maroon, outcast, outlaw, renegade, shipwreck, waif

caste: breed, class, degree, grade, position, race, rank, standing, status

caste, highest Hindu: Brahman

castigate: admonish, bash, berate, censure, chasten, chastise, chide, criticize, flog, lambaste, lash, pummel, punish, ream, reprimand, revise, scare, scathe, subdue, thrash

casting matrix: mold

casting of spell: conjunction, incantation, invocation

casting, molding done in criminal investigation: moulage

castrate: alter, caponize, change, emasculate, fix, geld, mutilate, neuter, spay, sterilize

castrated and fattened male chicken: capon

castrated male horse: gelding

castrated male sheep: wether

castrated man: eunuch

castrated mature male pig: stag

castrated rooster: capon

castrated young pig: barrow

casts off: molts

casual: accidental, aloof, blasé, carefree, chance, contingent, dégagé, desultory, easygoing, fortuitous, free and easy, homey, idle, impromptu, incidental, indifferent, informal, insouciant, loose, natural, nonchalant, occasional, offhand, random, relaxed, stray, uncertain

casual and by chance: adventitious, contingent, fortuitous

casual and disorganized: haphazard, indiscriminate, lackadaisical

casual and hasty: cursory, perfunctory

casual and minor: incidental

casual and random: desultory

casual and spontaneous: impromptu, off-the-cuff

casual and unplanned: unpremeditated

casual carpeting: throw rug

casual greeting: hi

casual look: glance

casual onlooker: passerby

casual sex, having: promiscuous

casual way, walk in: meander, saunter

casual, relaxed: easygoing

casually: informally

casualties, prioritized: triage

casualty: accident, blow, chance, death, disaster, fatality, hazard, injury, loss, misfortune, mishap, victim, wounded

casualty of talking pictures: vaudeville

casuistry: chicanery, deceit, delusion, evasion, fallacy, sophistry

cat: cheetah, civet, cougar, feline, jaguar, kitten, kitty, leopard, lion, lynx, manx, panther, puma, puss, pussy, tiger, tigress

cat breed: alley, Angora, Calico, Cheshire, Civet, Himalayan, longhair, Maltese, Manx, Persian, shorthair, Siamese, tabby

cat burglar: robber

cat family: feline

cat female: grimalkin, lioness, queen, tigress

cat in heat, to cry like: caterwaul

cat purring or heavy trilling sound: hirrient

cat sound: meow, purr

cat whiskers: vibrissae

cat, adult female: catta, queen

cat, old female: grimalkin

cat, pertaining to: feline

cataclysm: calamity, cemetery, collapse, crypt, disastrous, ruin, tomb, tragic, vault

catacomb: chamber, passageway

catafalque: bier, box, casket, coffin

catalog: arrange, book, brief, catalogue, classify, directory, enumerate, file, flyer, index, inventory, itemize, list, price list, prospectus, record, register, roll, roster, schedule, sort, tally

catalog of literary works or paintings with critical notes: catalogue raisonne

catalyst: activator, goad, incentive, motivation, spark, spur, stimulus, synergist

catamaran: float, raft, sailboat, vessel

catamount: puma

catapult: ballista, fling, heave, hurl, launch, onager, propel, slingshot, throw

catapult, ancient: ballista, bricole, mangonel, onager, trebuchet

cataract: cascade, deluge, downpour, eye disease, falls, flood, rapids, waterfall

catastrophe: accident, blow, calamity, cataclysm, disaster, doom, emergency, fatality, fiasco, misfortune, mishap, tragedy

catastrophe, very destructive: Armageddon

catatonic state: coma

catcall: boo, bronx cheer, heckle, hiss, hoot, jeer, raspberry, razz

catch: apprehend, arrest, attract, bag, bait, bust, capture, clamp, clasp, clip, clutch, comprehend, corner, detect, develop, draw, drawback, entangle, entrap, get, grasp, haul, hitch, hoax, hold, intercept, ketch, knack, land, lasso, marry, nab, nail, net, overtake, pass, receive, seize, snag, snap, snare, snatch, stop, surprise, trap, trick, wed

catch a disease: contract

catch clothing on something sharp: snag

catch fire: ignite

catch fly balls: shag

catch on: assimilate, discover, fathom, get, grasp, learn, see, snag

catch or capture: apprehend, ensnare, nail

catch sight of: espy, spot, spy

catch up with (ship): forereach

catchall abbreviation: et al., etc.

catcher's gear: mitt

catches forty winks: naps

catching: captivating, communicable, contagious, epidemic, infectious, taking

catching (disease): infectious

catchphrase: jingle, motto, slogan

catchword: byword, cliché, cue, maxim, motto, phrase, slogan

catchy: appealing, captivating, fitful, popular, tricky

categorical: absolute, certain, emphatic, explicit, flat, specific, sure, unequivocal, unmitigated, unqualified

categorize: class, classify, pigeonhole, rate, sort

category: class, classification, division, family, genre, genus, grouping, heading, kind, order, rank, rubric, species, type

catena: chain

cater: feed, help, humor, indulge, pamper, provide, purvey, serve, spoil, supply

cater to someone's lower tastes: pander

caterpillar: aweto, butterfly, canker, larva, moth, tractor, woolly bear, worm

caterpillar limb: proleg

caterpillar or tadpole: larva

caterpillar track: tread

caterpillar, for a while: pupa

caterwaul: bawl, cry, scream, wail, whine, yell

catfight: tiff

CATHOLICISM TERMS

abode of unbaptized infants' souls and those who died before Christ was born: limbo

annual calendar with instructions for each day: ordo

authorized version of Bible: Vulgate

book of hymns, prayers for canonical hours: breviary

caps of Catholic clergy: biretta, calotte, zucchetto

Catholic doctrine that bread and wine of Mass become

body and blood of Christ: transubstantiation

church's central administration: curia

consecrated bread or wafer of Eucharist: host

division administering missions and missionaries: propaganda

ecclesiastical court: rota

laypeople's society or association: sodality

mass for deceased: requiem

meeting of cardinals

and pope to announce papal acts: consistory

meeting of cardinals to elect new pope: conclave

minor offense that does not cause damnation: venial sin

official appointed to present arguments against beatification or canonization: devil's advocate

proclamation of deceased as a saint: canonization

proclamation of de-

ceased to be blessed: beatification

proclamation that a book is not damaging: nihil obstat

recitation of prayers for 9 consecutive days: novena

remission of punishment still due for absolved sin: indulgence

rite for sick or injured in danger of dying: extreme unction, anointing of the sick

service manual: ordo

sin so horrible that it causes damnation: mortal sin

state in which dead souls expiate their sins and are purified: purgatory

title for first canonization: venerable

title for male cleric: Monsignor

title for person in first stage of canonization: Venerable

title of Benedictine and Carthusian monks: Dom

tribunal: rota ❦

---

catfish: bagre, banjo, cusk, flathead, mud, pout, raad, shal, sucker

catharsis: abreaction, cleansing, purgation, release

cathartic: cleansing, laxative, purgative, purifying, senna

cathedral: basilica, church, duomo, sanctuary, temple

cathedral and its grounds: close, precinct, purlieu

cathedral center: nave

cathedral feature: alcove, rose window

cathedral gallery over side: triforium

cathedral instrument: organ

cathedral section: apse

cathedral town: ely, see

cathedral upper wall with windows: clerestory

cathode's opposite: anode

catholic: broad, charitable, ecumenical, general, global, inclusive, liberal, papal, tolerant, universal, unsectarian, whole

cation: ion

catkin: ament

catkin producer: pussywillow tree

catlike: feline, quiet, silent, stealthy

catlike carnivore: civet

catnap: doze, forty winks, siesta, sleep, snooze

catnip: cataria, catnep, catwort, nep

cat's dismissal: scat

cat's-eye gem: chatoyant

cat's paw: pad

cat's-paw: breeze, bulrush, cloud, dupe, gull, matreed, patsy, pawn, rush, stooge, tool

cattail land: marsh

cattle: beasts, beefs, bovid, bulls, calves, cows, herd, kine, livestock, longhorn, neat, oxen, steers, stock

RELATED TERMS

cattle and other mammals that chew the cud and are hoofed: ruminant

cattle and sheep disease, serious: anthrax, murrain

cattle assemblage: drove, herd

cattle barrier: stile

cattle brand: buist, duff

cattle breed: Angus, Ayrshire, Beefmaster, Belted, Bradford, Brahman, Brangus, Brown Swiss, Charbray, Charollaise, Devon, Durham, Dutch, Dutch Belted, Guernsey, Hereford, Jersey, Longhorn, Red Polled, Shorthorn, Sussex, Water Buffalo, Zebu

cattle dealer or driver: drover

cattle enclosure: corral, kraal

cattle feed: mash, provender

cattle genus: bos

cattle herder: cowboy, cowhand, cowpuncher

cattle in panic-stricken rush: stampede

cattle movement, seasonal: transhumance

cattle of poetry: kine

cattle rope: lasso

cattle roundup: drift, rodeo

cattle stall: drib

cattle steal: rustle

cattle trough: manger

cattle viral disease: rinderpest

cattle with rod, to drive: goad

cattle, male: bull

cattle, pertaining to: bovine, taurine

cattle, young: calf, heifer, yearling ❦

cattleman: cowboy, cowpuncher, drover, gaucho, wrangler

catty: backbiting, bitchy, evil, feline, hateful, malicious, mean, nasty, spiteful, venomous

catwalk: bridge, footway, walkway

caucus: assembly, council, election, gathering, meeting, powwow, primary, session

caudal: back, posterior, rear

caudal appendage: tail

caudex: stem

caught in the act: in flagrante delicto, red-handed

caught off guard: startled

caulk or grout: filler

caulking agent: oakum

cause: agency, agent, aim, basis, belief, bring on, business, call, case, concern, conviction, create, disease, effect, effectuate, encompass, engender, goal, ideal, induce, key, lawsuit, let, mainspring, malady, motive, move, movement, object, occasion, origin, originate, precipitate, principle, produce, prompt, provoke, purpose, reason, root, source, spur, suit

cause a result: redound

cause and bring about: induce, invite, precipitate

cause-and-effect theory: determinism

cause and effect, undesirable and progressing: vicious circle

cause attrition: erode

cause external to the body, having a: exogenous

cause for discussion: topic

cause internal to the body, having a: endogenous

cause is independent of human will, philosophy that: determinism

cause of hay fever: allergy

cause of war: casus belli

cause or chief motivator: fountainhead, mainspring

cause or origin of disease, determination of: etiology

cause or precipitator of process or event: catalyst

cause or provoke: foment, instigate

cause trouble: agitate

cause, adopt or support a: espouse

cause, believer or supporter of: adherent

cause, militant zeal for a: evangelism

cause, person who argues for: apologist

cause, tending to: conducive, contributive

cause, without apparent external: spontaneous

causes and origins, study of: etiology

caustic: abrasive, acerb, acid, acrid, acrimonious, alkaline, astringent, biting, bitter, burning, corrosive, crisp, cutting, gnawing, ironic, lye, malevolent, mordant, pungent, rough, sarcastic, satirical, scathing, severe, sharp, stinging, tart, vitriolic

caustic and biting: pungent

caustic in tone: acrid

caustic substance: lye

cauterize: brand, burn, char, sear, singe

caution: admonish, admonition, advice, anxiety, attention, calculation, care, caveat, counsel, diligence, discretion, exhort, flag, forecast, forewarn, heed, hint, notify, providence, prudence, reservation, vigilance, wariness, warn, warning, watchfulness

caution color: amber

cautious: alert, canny, careful, chary, circumspect, conservative, discreet, guarded, leery, mindful, moderate, prudent, safe, scrupulous, vigilant, wary

cautiously: carefully, gingerly

cavalcade: caravan, column, drill, journey, march, parade, procession, safari, sequence, spectacle

cavalier: arrogant, brave, caballero, chevalier, cocky, curt, disdainful, escort, fine, frank, gallant, gay, haughty, horseman, knight, lofty, nonchalant, offhand, proud, rider, soldier, supercilious

cavalry: army, horsemen, horses, knighthood, lancers, rangers, soldiers, troops

cavalry horse: charger

cavalry mount: steed

cavalry soldier: hussar, lancer

cavalry sword: lance, saber, sabre

cave: antre, cavern, cavity, cellar, collapse, cove, crumple, crypt, den, give, grot, grotto, hole, hollow, lair, luster, overturn, plunge, rear, toss, upset

cave drawing or rock painting: pictograph

cave dweller: bat, bear, hermit, lion, troglodyte

cave entrance exposed to daylight: twilight zone

cave explorer: spelunker

cave icicle-like deposit growing up from floor: stalagmite

cave icicle-like deposit hanging down from roof: stalactite

cave in: buckle, collapse, crumple, founder, implode, sink, submit, succumb, yield

cave or cavern in a mountainside or cliffside: cove

cave or cavern, small: grotto

cave researcher: speleologist

cave study: speleology

cave underground chamber/passageway: catacomb

cave, large, or underground chamber: cavern

caveat: admonition, alarm, alert, beware, caution, don't, flag, notice, sign, warning

caveman: troglodyte

cavern: cave, cavity, croft, den, grotto, hole, hollow, subterrane

cavernous: broad, deep, gaping, hollow, huge, immense, vast, wide, yawning

caviar: delicacy, eggs, relish, roe

caviar makers: beluga, sturgeon

cavil: belittle, bicker, carp, criticize, exception, haggle, nitpick, objection, quibble

cavities in anatomy: antra

cavities in skull by nose: sinuses

cavities or cells, pitted with: faveolate, honeycombed

cavity: antrum, atrium, bag, bursa, cave, cavern, chamber, crater, decay, dent, depression, excavation, grotto, hole, hollow, mine, orifice, pit, pocket, sac, sink, sinus, vacuum, vein, vesicle, void

cavity filled with fluid around joints of body: bursa

cavity filled with fluid or gas bubble: vesicle

cavity with one opening: cecum

cavort: caper, frolic, gambol, horseplay, play, prance, revel, romp, sport

cay: ait, isle, islet

cayenne: red pepper

Cayuse: horse

CBer's name: handle

CD player sensor: laser

cease: abate, abstain, cessation, culminate, desist, discontinue, end, finish, halt, lapse, pause, peter, quit, refrain, rest, stop, suspend, terminate

cease-fire: armistice, truce

cease, at sea: avast

ceaseless: continual, endless, enduring, everlasting, incessant, nonstop, perpetual, unending, unremitting, untiring

cedar: deodar, evergreen, sabine, savin, tree, wood

cedar genus: cedrus, juniperus, thuja

cede: abandon, assign, award, fold, give, grant, leave, relinquish, renounce, resign, submit, surrender, transfer, waive, yield

ceding or surrendering: cession

ceiling: acme, covering, dome, lid, limit, lining, maximum, plafond, plaster, roof

ceiling and wall, curved junction between: cove, coving

ceiling beam: rafter

ceiling or vault, decorative sunken panel in: coffer

ceiling with painted or carved design: plafond

ceiling with recessed panels: lacunar

ceiling, arched: vault

ceiling, branched lighting fixture suspended from: chandelier

ceiling, decorated: plafond

ceiling, sculptured ornament suspended from Gothic: pendant

Celebes buffalo: anoa

celebrate: applaud, bless, cheer, commemorate, eulogize, extol, feast, glorify, honor, keep, laud, observe, paint the town red, praise, proclaim, rejoice, revel, ritualize

celebrate loudly: maffick, revel, roister

celebrated: distinguished, eminent, famed, famous, glorious, illustrious, important, kept, noted, observed, popular, prominent, renowned, venerable

celebration: anniversary, birthday, ceremony, exultation, festival, fete, fiesta, gala, jamboree, jubilance, jubilation, jubilee, party, rite, triumph

celebration or celebratory outing: junket

celebration, drunken or riotous: bacchanal, carousal, revelry, saturnalia, wassail

celebration, festive: shindig, shindy

celebration, solemn: commemoration

celebratory feast course: fatted calf

celebrity: dignitary, fame, heavyweight, hero, hotshot, lion, luminary, name, notable, personage, prestige, renown, repute, somebody, star, superstar, VIP

celebrity banquet with mock attacks on guest of honor: roast

celebrity, to treat like a: lionize

celerity: haste, hurry, hustle, legerity, quickness, rapidity, speed, swiftness, velocity

celery-like vegetable: rhubarb, udo

celery unit: stalk

celestial: angelic, astronomical, beatific, blissful, divine, empyreal, empyrean, ethereal, heavenly, holy, olympian, planetary, sky, spiritual, supernal, supernatural, uranic

celestial being: angel, cherub, god, goddess, seraph

celestial body: comet, moon, nebula, orb, planet, star, sun

celestial journey: ascension

celestial movement: rotation

celestial sighting: comet

celibacy: abstinence, chastity, purity, unwed, virginity

celibate: chaste, continent, pure, unmarried, virginal, virtuous

cell: bacterium, cellule, egg, embryo, germ; cage, chamber, compartment, cubicle, dungeon, group, hold, jail, lockup, prison, unit, vault

cell biology: cytology

cell constituent: DNA, RNA

cell destruction: cytolysis

cell division in sexually reproducing organism: meiosis, mitosis

cell division producing blastula from fertilized ovum: cleavage, segmentation

cell division that is asexual: fission

cell formed by union of two gametes: zygote

cell living matter: protoplasm

cell membranous tissue forming most surfaces of body and organs: epithelium

cell part: centriole, chloroplast, chromosome, cytoplasm, lysosome, membrane, nucleus, vacuole

cell study: cytology

cell substance: linin

cell tissue of fingernail, toenail, tooth: matrix

cell, blood: hemocyte, red, white

cell, reproductive: gamete

cell, sperm: spermatozoon, zoosperm

cellar: basement, cave, downstairs, storeroom, subterrane, vault

Celsius: centigrade, thermometer

cement: adhesive, bind, cohere, concrete, epoxy, fasten, glue, imbed, join, lime, lute, mastic, mortar, paste, putty, solder, solidify, stick, unify, unite, weld

cement mixture for filling and finishing masonry: grouting, pointing

cement mixture for waterproofing walls: pargeting

cement, tuff used in hydraulic: trass

cemetery: boneyard, catacomb, charnel, churchyard, golgotha, graveyard, litten, mortuary, necropolis, polyandrium, potter's field

cemetery, large: necropolis

cemetery, poor people's: potter's field

cenobite: celibate, monastic, monk, nun, religious

censor: bleep, blip, blue-pencil, control, critic, delete, edit, forbid, purge, restrict, suppress, withhold

censor a text: blue-pencil, bowdlerize, expurgate

censor or prohibit: interdict, proscribe

censor speech: muzzle

censorious: abusive, blameful, carping, critical, denouncing, disparaging, faultfinding, reproachful, severe

censure: accuse, admonish, attack, berate, blame, carp, castigate, challenge, charge, chasten, chide, condemn, criticize, disallow, disapproval, flame, impeach, judge, rebuff, rebuke, reprehension, reprimand, reproach, reprove, scold, tirade

censure and rebuke: inveigh, reprimand, reproach, upbraid

census: count, enumeration, list, number, poll, tally

census taker: enumerator

centaur: chiron, man-horse, nessus

Centennial State: Colorado

center: axis, capital, core, eye, focalize, focus, halfway, headquarters, heart, hotbed, hub, mean, mid, middle, midmost, midpoint, midst, nave, nucleus, pivot, point

center in common: concentric

center of attention: cynosure, focal point, foci, focus

center of power or energy: ganglion

center of wheel, fan, propeller: hub

center or core around which parts are grouped: nucleus

center part: core

center, branch out from: diverge

center, having a common: concentric

center, move toward a: converge

center, moving away from: centrifugal, efferent

center, moving toward: afferent, centripetal

center, not situated at or in the geometric: eccentric

center, without: acentric

centers of activities: hotbeds

centigrade: Celsius, degree, scale, thermometer

centipede: arthropod, boat, chilopoda, insect

central: among, basic, capital, chief, dominant, essential, focal, foremost, fundamental, inner, interior, key, leading, main, median, mid, middle, pivotal, primary, prime, significant

central cylinder of a stem: stele

central element: core, hub, linchpin, nucleus, omphalos

central part: core, focal point, gist, omphalos

central point: node, pivot

central star: sun

centralize: accumulate, assemble, concentrate, condense, focus, gather, streamline

centrally, asea: amidships

centrifugal: divergent, efferent, radiating, spiral, spreading

cents per ounce, for example: unit cost

century: age, one hundred, siecle, years

century-and-a-half observance: sesquicentennial

century plant: agave, aloe, pita, sect

century's end: fin de siecle

cephaloped: cuttlefish, mollusk

ceraceous: waxy

ceramic: brick, clay, earthenware, porcelain, pottery, stoneware, tile, tiles

ceramic oven: kiln

ceramic square: tile

ceramist's oven: kiln

cereal: barley, bran, buckwheat, corn, farina, food, grain, millet, mush, oat, oatmeal, oats, porridge, ragi, rice, rye, soybean, wheat

cereal addition: raisin

cereal container: bowl

cereal of untoasted rolled oats and dried fruit: muesli

cereal plant by air current, to separate the grains or seeds of: winnow

cereal plant fungus: ergot

cereal plant, to separate the grains or seeds of: flail, thresh

cereal seed coat: bran

cerebral: brain, highbrow, intellectual, mental, psychic

ceremonial: conventional, formal, lofty, mannered, ritual, stately

ceremonial act: rite

ceremonial drumroll and fanfare: ruffle and flourish

ceremonial garb: robe, vestment

ceremonial procession: cavalcade, cortege

ceremonial washing of hands: ablution

ceremonious: civil, dignified, exact, grand, grandiose, lofty, precise, proper, punctilious, respectful, solemn, stiff, studied

ceremony: accolade, celebration, custom, display, etiquette, formality, function, liturgy, marriage, observance, occasion, pageant, parade, prodigy, protocol, rite, ritual, show, sign, solemnity, state

ceremony and etiquette: decorum, propriety

ceremony as a memorial: commemoration

ceremony marking major life change: rite of passage

ceremony of admission: initiation

ceremony of conferring authority: induction, investiture

ceremony to show something new: unveiling

ceremony, formal opening: commencement, dedication, inauguration

ceremony, pretentious or hypocritical: mummery

ceremony, to perform a formal: solemnize

ceresin: wax

cerise: red

certain: actual, apodictic, bound, categorical, clear, cocksure, conclusive, exact, firm, fixed, indubitable, real, secure, stated, sure, true, unequivocal, unmistaken

certain and accurate: unerring

certain and incapable of failing: infallible

certain and unavoidable: inevitable

certain and unquestionable: apodictic, incontrovertible, indubitable

certainly: absolutely, hardily, indeed, really, san doute, surely, to be sure, truly, verily, without doubt, yes

certainty: actuality, assurance, certitude, confidence, conviction, credence, dogmatism, fact, faith, firmness, foregone, sureness

certificate: bond, check, credential, declaration, deed, diploma, document, license, permit, statement, testimony, ticket, verify, voucher

certificate for graduation: diploma

certificate of indebtedness: debenture

certificate of stock or money claim: scrip

certificate of transfer: bill of sale

certificate price: par value

certified to a standard: accredited

certifies by oath: attests

certify: affirm, approve, assure, attest, authenticate, avow, confirm, depose, determine, endorse, guarantee, license, notarize, swear, testify, verify, warrant, witness

cessation: armistice, ceasing, conclusion, ending, halt, intermission, interruption, interval, let up, letup, lull, pause, recess, remission, respite, rest, stop, stoppage, suspension, termination, truce

cessation of hostilities: truce

cessation of practice: disuse

cesspool or sewer: cloaca

cetacean: beluga, cete, dolphin, grampus, inia, mammal, narwal, orca, porpoise, whale

chafe: abrade, anger, annoy, banter, bother, excite, fret, friction, fume, gall, grind, harass, incense, inflame, injury, irk, irritate, nettle, rage, rub, scold, scratch, vex, wear

chafe with friction: rub

chaff: banter, bran, debris, jest, joke, josh, kid, rag, ride, taunt, tease, trash, waste

chagrin: dismay, displeasure, dissatisfaction, humiliation, irritate, mortify, shame

chain: bind, bond, bracelet, cable, chatelaine, collar, connect, constrain, embrace, enslave, fasten, file, gang, handcuff, iron, join, leash, link, manacle, moor, network, restrain, saw, secure, sequence, series, set, shackle, string, tether, tie, train; chain mail

chain crosspiece: toggle

chain of events, things: concatenation

chain of flowers, paper, ribbon in loops: festoon

chain or clasp for attaching keys, watch to waist: chatelaine

chain or connected series: catena

chain or outline of events: scenario

chain ring: link

chain together: catenate, concatenate

chains for confinement: fetters, manacles, shackles

chair: bench, office, preside, recliner, rocker, seat, sedan, stool, throne

chair back slat: splat

chair carried on poles by footmen, enclosed: sedan chair

chair fabric covering: upholstery

chair leg, rolling ball on: caster

chair on long pole used for punishment: ducking stool

chair part: arm, rung

chair rung: stave

chair with high spoked back and splayed legs: Windsor chair

chair, high back, high side pieces: wing chair

chair, leather, armless: Barcelona chair

chair, long reclining: chaise lounge

chair, thick deep upholstered: club chair

chairperson: director, emcee, executive, head, moderator, monitor, speaker, supervisor, toastmaster

chalcedony: agate, carnelian, gem, hematite, jasper, mineral, onyx, opal, opaline, quartz, sard, stone

chalet: cabin, cottage, house, hut

chalice: ama, calix, cup, goblet, grail

chalk: blanch, bleach, crayon, draw, sketch, talc, whiten

chalk up: achieve, acquire, earn, obtain, score, win

chalk used in paint, ink, putty: whiting

chalklike crayon: pastel

chalky: calcareous

chalky antacid: magnesia

chalky silicate: talc

chalky with calcium or calcium salts, process of becoming: calcification

challenge: accuse, appeal, arraign, brave, call, censure, charge, claim, confront, controvert, dare, defy, demand, exception, forbid, invite, objection, protest, provoke, query, question, reclaim, reproach, slap, stump, summons, test

challenge for inexperienced person: pons asinorum

challenge the validity, truth of: impeach, impugn

challenge to do battle, with thrown-down glove: gage

challenge to duel: throw down the gauntlet

challenger: contender, darer, defier, disputer

challenging: hard

chamber: alcove, apartment, assembly, atrium, bedroom, bower, caisson, camarilla, camera, cave, cell, compartment, crypt, cubicle, flat, hall, hollow, legislature, parlor, room, solar, vestibule

chamber music group: string trio

chamberlain: attendant, camerlengo, lord, officer, servant, steward, treasurer, wilt

chamberpot in chair or box: commode

chamois: antelope, chammy, cloth, fabric, leather, shammy, skin

champ at the bit: fret

champagne: bubbly, wine

champagne bottle's metal bands over cork: agrafe, coiffe

champagne bucket: icer

champagne designation, moderately dry: sec

champagne mixed with orange juice: mimosa

champagne, dry: brut

champion: ace, advocate, assert, backer, challenge, combatant, defend, defender, fighter, first-rate, greatest, hero, heroine, medalist, outstanding, protect, squire, titleholder, unbeaten, undefeated, victor, winner

champion of cause: advocate, proponent

championship: advocacy, crown, cup, defense, pennant, Stanley Cup, Super Bowl, supremacy, title, World Cup, World Series

chance: accident, accidental, adventitious, adventure, case, casualty, contingent, fate, fluke, fortuitous, fortuity, fortune, gamble, hap, haphazard, happen, happening, hazard, lot, lottery, luck, mishap, odds, opportunity, outcome, outlook, possibility, probability, raffle, random, risk, stake, stumble, unplanned, venture, wager

chance and unexpected: accidental, inadvertent, incidental, unplanned, unpremeditated

chance change: vicissitude

chance occurrence: happenstance

chance or speculation basis, on a: on spec

chance to buy, first: first refusal

chance, fortunate discoveries by: serendipity

chance, happening by: aleatory, arbitrary

chances: prospects

chancy: auspicious, dangerous, dubious, erratic, hairy, iffy, perilous, precarious, risky, rocky, touchy, tricky

chandelier: candelabrum, candleholder, fixture, light, luster

chandelier glass pendant: luster

chandelier lit by gas: gasolier

change: adapt, alter, alteration, amend, break, castrate, commute, conversion, convert, correction, deviate, deviation, difference, diversity, evolve, innovation, metamorphosis, modify, move, mutate, rearrange, remove, replace, revamp, reversal, revise, revision, shift, specie, substitute, swap, switch, transfer, transform, transition, transpose, turn, variation, vary, veer; cash, coin

change and adapt: acclimatize, orient, orientate

change and vary: diversify, variegate

change appearance of: transfigure

change channels: click, dial, zap

change course: reroute, veer

change form or quality of: transmute

change from preferred to common: conversion

change from wafer and wine to body and blood in Eucharist: transubstantiation

change in attitude or direction: 360, about-face, turnaround, U-turn, volte-face

change in form, character: metamorphosis

change in order of letters in word development: metathesis

change in tone or pitch: inflect, modulate

change into different shape: transmogrify

change of heart: conversion, reversal

change of life: climacteric, menopause

change of mind on impulse: caprice, whim

change one substance to another: transubstantiate

change or increase, big and sudden: quantum jump, quantum leap

change or movement, constant: flux

change or reverse in order or position: transpose

change or transform: commute, convert, mutate, transmute

change or vary often, irregularly: fluctuate

change places: alternate, interchange

change repeatedly back and forth: alternate, fluctuate, oscillate, vacillate

change sides: apostatize, defect, tergiversate

change someone's convictions by coercion: brainwash

change someone's plans by persuasion: dissuade

change that is completely opposite: about-face

change the order of: permute

change the wording: edit

change to another state: metamorphosis, transition

change to improve or adjust: modify, regulate

change tuxedo to tux, for example: apocopate

change, abrupt and radical: quantum leap, upheaval

change, complete: transformation, permutation

change, constant: flux

change, marked: metamorphosis, transfiguration, transmogrification

change, one that precipitates: catalyst

change, to bring about a: militate
changeable: alterable, ambivalent, amenable, capricious, convertible, erratic, fickle, fitful, giddy, impulsive, inconsistent, inconstant, irregular, irresolute, labile, mercurial, mobile, mutable, uncertain, unsettled, unstable, unsteady, variant, volatile
changeable and transformable: mutable
changeable in luster: chatoyant
changeable into other forms: protean
changeable person: chameleon
changed residence: moved
changeless: constant, enduring, fixed, invariable, regular, same, stable, steadfast, steady
changeover: alteration, conversion, shift, switch, transition
changes in life, sudden or unexpected: vicissitudes
changes opinions to prevailing ones, one who: opportunist, timeserver, trimmer
changes to better or more complex form, gradual process by which something: volution
changing and unstable: turbulent, vertiginous
changing-color animal: chameleon
changing course: digressive, tangential
changing easily to adapt: adaptable, pliable
changing in behavior or attitude: capricious, erratic, fickle, skittish, whimsical
changing in color: iridescent, opalescent
changing in shape, form, meaning: protean
changing land use: rezoning
changing pattern: kaleidoscope
changing rapidly, intricately: kaleidoscopic
changing set of colors: kaleidoscope
changing, constant: inconstancy, levity
changing, constantly: musical chairs
changing, not: changeless, immutable
changing, open to: labile, mutable
changing, shifting situation: musical chairs
changing, unpredictably: mercurial, quicksilver, volatile
channel: aqueduct, arroyo, artery, canal, canyon, chase, conduct, conduit, ditch, drain, drill, duct, flume, flute, furrow, gat, groove, guideway, gutter, inset, instrument, main, medium, passage, pipe, river, route, send, sinus, steer, strait, stream, tideway, transmit, trough, tube, vein, watercourse

channel cut in earth by running water: gully
channel for carrying water, artificial: flume
channel for conveying substance: duct
channel for drainpipes or wiring: chase
channel for sewer or drain crossing road or embankment: conduit, culvert
channel for water overflow: spillway
channel for water under road: culvert
channel into larger area: debouch
channel joining two large bodies of water: strait
channel of fast-moving water: race
chant: anthem, cant, canticle, cantillate, carol, chorus, croon, hallel, hymn, intone, intonation, intone, plainsong, psalm, sing, song, trill, tune, vocalize, warble, worship
chant of charms or spells: incantation
chant, Gregorian: plainsong
chanted hymn: canticle
chanticleer: rooster
chantilly: lace
chaos: anarchy, babel, bedlam, chasm, confusion, disorder, entropy, jumble, lawlessness, mess, pandemonium, shambles, snafu, turmoil, unruliness, uproar, void
chaos and disorder: Chinese fire drill
chaotic: confused, disordered, helter-skelter, muddled, riotous, turbulent
chap: baby, band, barter, bloke, boy, buyer, chink, chip, chop, cleft, cove, crack, customer, dry, fellow, fissure, gent, gentleman, jaw, knock, lad, lover, man, mash, redden, roughen, split, strike, stroke, trade, youth
chapeau: hat
chapel: bethel, chantry, church, oratory, sanctuary, shrine, tabernacle, vestry
chapel for masses and prayers for benefactor: chantry
chapel for seafarers: bethel
chapel, private prayer: oratory
chaperon: attend, companion, duenna, escort, governess, guard, guardian, guide, hood, matron, oversee, protector, safeguard
chaplain: clergyman, clergywoman, minister, padre, pastor, preacher, priest, rabbi, reverend

chaplet: band, bead, circle, coronet, crown, diadem, fillet, garland, necklace, ornament, rosary, wreath
chapman: buyer, dealer, merchant, peddler, trader
chapped: raw
chapter: affiliate, assembly, body, branch, episode, era, lodge, meeting, member, period, phase, section, topic
chapter lead-in: epigraph
char: blacken, broil, burn, carbonize, scorch, sear, singe, trout
character: appearance, aspect, attribute, bent, brand, card, constitution, courage, eccentric, engrave, essence, ethic, ethos, fame, fiber, figure, identity, impress, intelligence, kind, lead, letter, logo, mold, nature, oddball, original, part, personality, quality, reputation, repute, role, sign, sort, soul, spirit, stamp, star, style, symbol, temperament, tone, trait, type, weirdo
character assassination: smear
character or mark, distinctive: impress
character or personality: disposition, humor, temperament
character printed slightly above another: superior, superscript
character printed slightly below another: subscript
character who makes comments: raisonneur
characteristic: attribute, cast, distinctive, feature, inborn, inclination, individuality, inherent, mannerism, mark, nature, peculiarity, property, quality, special, symbolic, tendency, trademark, trait, typical, unique
characteristic making up for fault: mitigating factor, redeeming feature, saving grace
characteristic mark: stamp
characteristic practice: habit
characteristic quality: flavor, lineament, stamp, style
characteristic, typifying factor: parameter
characterization, often disparaging: epithet
characterize: define, delineate, depict, describe, designate, distinguish, imprint, indicate, mark, outline, pigeonhole, portray, represent, symbolize, typecast, typify
characterized by bribery: venal
characterized by volcanic eruptions: pelean

characterless: nondescript

characters in literary work: dramatis personae, personae

character's thoughts and feelings presented: stream of consciousness

charade: disguise, enigma, fake, game, picture, pretense, puzzle, riddle, trick

charcoal grill: hibachi

charcoal, pan for burning: brazier

charcoal, small block of: briquette

charge: accuse, allege, arraign, arraignment, attack, bid, burden, challenge, chastise, command, commission, credit, custody, demand, duty, fill, finger, gripe, impeach, impute, incriminate, indict, injunction, instruction, invade, levy, load, management, mandate, onset, onslaught, order, overload, penetrate, rush, saddle, sortie, storm, weigh; bill, cost, damage, debit, dues, expense, fee, price, rate, tab, tarrif, toll

charge at nightclubs for entertainment: cover charge

charge of wrongdoing: accusation, imputation

charge or accuse of crime: indict

charge or cost, extra: surcharge

charge or work for less than a rival: undercut

charge public official with crime: impeach

charge that weighs most heavily against accused, part of: gravamen

charge with an offense: indict

charge with wrongdoing: arraign, indict

charge, to clear of a: exculpate, exonerate

chargeable: answerable, burdensome, liable, responsible, troublesome

charged: accused, debited, emotional, excited, filled, laden, live, loaded, purposeful, tense

charged atom: anion, ion

charged meson: muon

charged with a crime: indicted

charger: accuser, biga, buggy, car, cart, char, dish, horse, instrument chariot, mount, platter, steed

charisma: allure, appeal, charm, dazzle, fascination, gift, glamour, magnetism, pizzazz, power

charitable: alms-giving, altruistic, beneficent, benevolent, eleemosynary, forgiving, generous, giving, humane, kind, kindly, lenient, liberal, philanthropic, sympathetic, thoughtful

charitable gift: benefaction, donation, oblation, offertory

charity: alms, almsgiving, assistance, compassion, donation, fund-raising, generosity, gift, goodwill, handout, kindness, love, mercy, philanthropy, pity, relief

charity for mankind: philanthropy

charity, one who offers: sponsor

charity, one who receives: beneficiary

charity, to pledge money to a: subscribe

charivari: serenade

charlatan: cheat, faker, fraud, imposter, medicaster, mountebank, phony, pretender, quack, sham

Charlotte dessert: russe

charm: agreeable, allay, allure, appeal, attract, attraction, bait, beauty, beguile, bewitch, calm, captivate, caract, charisma, conjure, control, delight, draw, enamor, enamour, enchant, enthral, enthrall, entice, entrance, fascinate, flatter, freet, freit, glamour, grace, lucky, magic, magnetism, melody, please, saphie, seduce, seduction, song, soothe, sorcery, spell, subdue, summon; amulet, fetish, juju, talisman

charm and sensual appeal: animal magnetism

charming: adorable, agreeable, alluring, attractive, beautiful, beguiling, captivating, cute, delicate, electrifying, enchanting, enticing, glamorous, inviting, lovely, ravishing, seductive, titillating, winning, winsome

charming and simple: naive, rustic

chart: blueprint, design, devise, diagram, document, draft, explore, graph, map, outline, plan, plat, platform, plot, project, record, scheme, table

chart of pie-shaped wedges: pie chart

chart of rectangular bars: bar chart, bar graph

chart or diagram with stages: flowchart

chart with growth, value changes in lines: graph

charter: agreement, commission, constitution, deed, grant, hire, lease, license, member, pact, permit, privilege, rent, sanction

chary: careful, cautious, dear, discreet, economical, frugal, guarded, hesitant, leery, prudent, reluctant, reserved, safe, scant, scrupulous, shy, sparing, suspicious, treasured, vigilant, wary

chase: catch, follow, gallop, harass, harry, hound, hunt, pursue, pursuit, quarry, shadow, shag, shoo, track

chase fly ball: shag

chasm: abyss, aperture, arroyo, blank, canyon, cavity, cleft, crater, crevasse, fissure, gap, gorge, gulf, hiatus, oversight, pit, rift, void

chasse: step

chaste: celibate, clean, continent, decent, honest, immaculate, incorrupt, innocent, moral, proper, pure, refined, spotless, undefiled, vestal, virginal, virtuous, wholesome

chasten: abase, castigate, censure, chastise, correct, discipline, humble, humiliate, punish, rate, refine, reprimand, reprove, scold, smite, subdue, upbraid

chastening rod: ferule

chastise: accuse, admonish, beat, berate, blame, cane, castigate, chasten, correct, discipline, flog, lash, pummel, punish, ream, rebuke, reprove, scold, scourge, spank, strap, taunt, thrash, whip

chastity: abstinence, celibacy, devotion, goodness, honor, innocence, integrity, modesty, morality, purity, virginity, virtue

chat: babble, cackle, causerie, chatter, chew the rag, confabulate, conversation, converse, coze, dally, dialogue, gab, gabble, gibber, gist, gossip, jabber, palaver, point, prate, prattle, rap, schmooze, speak, talk

chat or informal conversation: causerie

chateau: castle, estate, house, manor, mansion, villa

chateaubriand: beef, steak, tenderloin

chattel: belongings, capital, effects, gear, goods, property, slave, wares

chatter: babble, blab, blabber, brabble, cackle, chat, chipper, chitchat, clack, gab, gabble, gibber, goosecackle, gossip, jabber, jaw, palter, prabble, prate, prattle, rattle, schmoose, shake, talk, talk a blue streak, tattle, twaddle, verbiage, yak, yap

chatterbox: blabbermouth, busybody, clack, gossip, magpie, talkative, windbag

chatty: friendly, gabby, garrulous, gossipy, loquacious, talkative, verbose, windy, wordy

chauvinism: cheesy, chintzy, economical, fanatical, jingoism, nationalism, partiality, patriotism, petty, prejudice, worthless

cheap: abject, bargain, chintzy, common, depreciated, gaudy, inexpensive, inferior, poor, price, purchase, schlock, seedy, shabby, shoddy, sleazy, stingy, tacky, tight, trashy, vile

cheap and showy: brassy, brummagem, catchpenny, gaudy, tawdry

cheap cigar: stogie

cheap dress: frippery

cheap fiction: dime novel

cheap imitation: fake, pinchbeck

cheap talk: claptrap

cheap whiskey: red-eye

cheap wine: vin ordinaire

cheapen: adulterate, belittle, corrupt, debase, denigrate, devaluate, diminish, downgrade, reduce

cheapest in price: wholesale

cheat: artifice, baffle, bamboozle, beguile, bilk, chicanery, chisel, con, cozen, crib, crook, deceive, defraud, delusion, deride, dodge, doodle, dupe, euchre, fake, fiddle, finagle, finesse, flam, fleece, flimflam, fling, fool, fraud, gouge, gudgeon, gyp, hoax, hoodwink, humbug, imposter, jilt, liar, mislead, mountebank, mulct, plunder, quibble, renege, rogue, rook, scammer, scamp, scoundrel, screw, sham, shark, shaver, short, shyster, snooker, spoil, swindle, take, trick, victimize, welsh

cheat by reneging on agreement: double-cross

cheated, easily: credulous, gullible

cheating: chicanery, duplicity

cheating on taxes by concealing profits: skimming

check: abort, allay, arrest, audit, balk, block, brake, bridle, confirm, constrain, control, curb, daunt, defeat, delay, detain, deter, examination, frisk, hinder, hindrance, hold, impede, inhibit, leash, limit, mark, monitor, neutralize, oppose, probe, quell, quench, rein, repel, repress, reprove, restrain, restraint, review, setback, stall, stay, stem, stifle, still, stop, study, stunt, supervise, survey, taunt, test, verify, withhold; bill, certificate, stub, tab, tally

check and confirm: authenticate, corroborate, substantiate, validate, verify, vet

check design: checkerboard, hound's-tooth, plaid, tattersall

check earlier than date of writing, to date a: antedate

check endorser: payee

check flow of: stanch, staunch

check later than date of writing, to date: postdate

check off of list: tally, tick

check on: keep tabs on, monitor

check or other document, place one's signature of agreement on: endorse

check out and authenticate: vet

check someone's ID: card

check stub, money order stub: counterfoil

check, bad: kite

check, blank: carte blanche

checkered: diversified, mosaic, motley, patchwork, pied, plaid, quilted, tessellated, varied, variegated

checkmate: corner, countermove, defeat, frustrate, gain, outwit, stop, thwart, triumph, undo

cheddar shredder: grater

cheek: audacity, boldness, brashness, crust, effrontery, gall, impudence, nerve, sauciness, temerity

cheek meat: jowl

cheekbone: jugal, malar, zygoma, zygomatic bone

cheeks or mouth, concerning the: buccal

cheeky and arrogant: audacious, brazen, bumptious, impertinent, impudent, insolent, obstreperous, presumptuous, sassy, saucy, temerarious

cheep: chipper, chirp, chirrup, peep, pip, shrill, squeak, tattle, tweet, twitter, yap

cheer: acclaim, animate, applaud, bravo, brighten, cherish, clap, comfort, console, drink, elate, encourage, exhilarate, feast, food, gaiety, happiness, heart, hearten, hope, hospitality, hurrah, inspire, inspirit, invigorate, merriment, ole, ovation, rah, refresh, rejoice, root, shout, solace, support, uplift, yell

cheer and invigorate: enliven

cheer up: liven

cheer word: rah

cheerful: airy, blithe, bouncy, bright, buoyant, cadgy, cheery, chipper, chirpy, comfortable, contented, enlivening, gay, genial, glad, happy, hearty, jocund, jolly, lighthearted, lightsome, lively, merry, pleasant, riant, roseate, rosy, sanguine, sprightly, sunny, upbeat

cheerful in atmosphere: congenial, gemutlich

cheerful readiness: alacrity

cheerful tune: lilt

cheerleader tuft of material: pompom, pompon

cheerless: austere, bleak, cold, comfortless, dejected, depressing, dismal, dispirited, dreary, forlorn, gloomy, glum, gray, melancholy, sad, solemn, sullen

cheese and beer melt on toast: Welsh rabbit

cheese and bread crumbs and browned, covered with: au gratin

cheese-and-crumb crust: au gratin

cheese covering: rind

cheese dish: cake, fondue, omelet, rarebit, souffle

cheese eaten with bread etc., hot melted: fondue

cheese holder: crock

cheese hung in strips to cure: provolone

cheese in a red jacket: edam

cheese like Roquefort: gorgonzola

cheese made from ewes' milk and matured in caves: Roquefort

cheese made from skimmed or whole milk, white: Neufchatel

cheese-making byproducts: whey

cheese-making process: ageing

cheese making, ruminant stomach lining extract used in: rennet

cheese melted and eaten with bread: fondue

cheese melted over boiled potatoes and bread: raclette

cheese orginally made by Trappist monks, semihard: Port Salut

cheese pastry baked and served individually: ramekin, ramequin

cheese prepared or converted by special process: process cheese

cheese section: wedge

cheese served in lasagna, cottage: ricotta

cheese served on pizza: mozzarella

cheese types: hard, processed, semihard, soft, very hard

cheese with a creamy center, soft: Camembert

cheese with a whitish rind and soft center: Brie

CHEESE

American	Cottage cheese	Havarti	New England Sage	Sapsago
Banon	Cream cheese	Hoop cheese	Parmesan	Smoked cheese
Bel Paese	Danish blue	Jaalsberg	Pecorino	Stilton
Bleu cheese	Dolcelatte	Jack cheese	Pont l'Eveque	String cheese
Bleu de Bresse	Dunlop	Jarlsberg	Port Salut/Port du	Swiss
Blue cheese	Edam	Lancashire	Salut	Teleme
Blue Cheshire	Edelpilzkase	Leicester	Pot cheese	Tillamook
Boursin	Emmenthaler	Liederkranz	Provolone	Tilsiter
Brick	Epoisses	Limburger	Quargel	Tome au raisin
Brie	Feta	Liptauer	Rat cheese	Vacherin
Caciocavallo	Fontina	Livarot	Red Windsor	Velveeta
Caerphilly	Fromage	Maroilles	Ricotta	White
Camembert	Gloucester	Mimolette	Romano	Wensleydale ❦
Cheddar	Goat cheese	Monterey Jack	Roquefort	
Cheshire	Gorgonzola	Mozzarella	Saint Marcellin	
Chevre	Gouda	Muenster	Saint Nectaire	
Chevret	Gruyère	Neufchatel	Samsoe	

cheese with a wrinkled rind and blue-green mold: Stilton

cheese with large holes, Norwegian: Jarlsberg

cheese with small holes, Swiss: Emmenthaler, Gruyére

cheese with strong odor and flavor: Limburger

cheese, blue: bleu cheese

cheese, concerning: caseic, caseous

cheese, dessert: mascarpone

cheese, formation of: caseation

cheese, goat's milk: fromage de chevre

cheese, grated: Parmesan, parmigiano

cheese, hard and yellow English: Cheshire

cheese, Italian: Parmesan

cheese, Italian blue: Gorgonzola

cheese, mild cheddar: jack cheese, Monterey Jack

cheese, mild Limburger: Liederkranz

cheese, mild semisoft and creamy: Munster

cheese, milk or cream, beer, and seasoning melted on bread: Welsh rabbit, Welsh rarebit

cheese, protein that forms: casein

cheese, red-or yellow-rinded Dutch: Edam

cheese, semisoft, mild Italian: Bel Paese

cheese, smoked: provolone

cheese, turn into: casefy

cheeselike: caseous

cheesy: caseous, cheap, inferior, poor, shabby, sleazy, trashy, worthless

chef master: cordon bleu

chef's hat: toque, toque blanche

chemical: acid, alkali, amide, azine, base, boride, catalyst, compound, element, ester, imine, metamer, purin, sal, salt

chemical action, a burning or eating away by: corrosive, cuastic

chemical change with gain of electrons: reduction

chemical combination of substance with oxygen: oxidation

chemical compound: amide, amine, diene, diol, enol, ester, imine, isomer, oxide

chemical compound decomposition with electricity: electrolysis

chemical compound decomposition with water: hydrolysis

chemical compound formed from simpler compounds or elements: synthesis

chemical compound that reacts with acids to form salts: base

chemical compound with repeated linked units of molecules: polymer

chemical compound with same elements in same proportions but different atom arrangement: isomer

chemical compound's common name: trivial name

chemical compound's descriptive name: systematic name

chemical compounds, carbon: organic

chemical compounds, noncarbon: inorganic

chemical dispersion of solid particles in liquid: suspension

chemical dissolving or wearing away: corrosion

chemical element loses electrons and valence is increased: oxidation

chemical element's number of protons in nucleus: atomic number

chemical elements table: periodic table

chemical force holding atoms, ions together: chemical bond

chemical formula showing atoms' and bonds' arrangement: structural formula

chemical gradual absorption or assimilation: osmosis

chemical group 0 that is inert: argon, helium, inert gas, krypton, neon, noble gas, radon, xenon

chemical happening: reaction

chemical method of determining solution's concentration by adding reagent: titration

chemical mixture of liquids inseparable by distillation: azeotropic mixture

chemical reaction where hydrogen is added or oxygen removed: reduction

chemical reaction, something that slows: inhibitor

chemical substance affecting reaction but not itself changing: catalyst

chemical substance used to detect, measure, examine or produce substance in reaction: reagent

chemical suspension of fine particles in fluid: colloid

chemical warfare weapon: nerve gas

chemically inactive: inert

chemically refine or purify: rectify

chemise: camisole, dress, lingerie, shirt, smock, undergarment

chemistry dish for culture: petri dish
chemistry, medieval: alchemy
cherish: admire, adore, appreciate, caress, cling, coddle, comfort, cultivate, embrace, esteem, fondle, foster, guard, harbor, honor, hug, indulge, inspirit, like, love, nestle, nourish, nurse, nurture, pamper, pet, preserve, prize, protect, revere, save, support, sustain, treasure, value
cherry in fermented juice: maraschino
cherry red: cerise
cherry types: Amarelle, Bigarreau, Bing, Duke, Gean, Lambert, Marasca, Maraschino, Mazzard, Morel, Morello, Napoleon, Oxheart
cherry, dark sour: Morello
cherub: amoretto, angel, cupid, saint, seraph, spirit
chess moment with no advantageous move: zugzwang
chess moment with no safe move: stalemate
chess opening move with minor piece: gambit
chess piece exposed to possible capture, of a: en prise
chess pieces: bishop, castle, horse, king, knight, man, pawn, queen, rook
chess player, beginner: patzer
chess player's explanation of piece adjustment: j'adoube
chess position where king can move into check and no other piece can move: stalemate
chess position where king is attacked and has no move, thus ending game: checkmate
chess position where player is forced to make an undesirable move: zugzwang
chess terms: castle, checkmate, debut, draw, en prise, endgame, fianchetto, fidate, gambit, gardez, j'adoube, mate, move, opening, scacchic, stalemate, zugzwang
chest: arca, ark, basket, box, bureau, cabinet, casket, chiffonier, coffer, coffin, commode, container, cupboard, dresser, fund, hamper, hutch, locker, receptacle, safe, shrine, strongbox, treasury, trunk; bosom, breast, bust, front, thorax, trunk
chest between neck and abdomen: thorax
chest noise: rale
chest of drawers or cabinet, low: commode

chest of drawers, high with mirror: chiffonier
chest of drawers, short-legged: lowboy
chest of drawers, two-sectioned: highboy
chest pain from lack of oxygen in heart: angina pectoris
chest protector: bib, rib, ribcage
chest rattling, whistling sound: rhonchus
chest sound, high vibrating or whistling: stridor
chest, pertaining to the: pectoral
chesterfield: coat, overcoat, topcoat; couch, davenport, divan, sofa
chestnut: bay, brown, cliché, color, horse, joke, sorrel, tree
chestnut genus: castanea
chestnut horse: roan
chevalier: cadet, cavalier, gallant, gentleman, horseman, knight, lord, noble
chevron: badge, bar, beam, glove, insignia, mark, molding, stripe, zigzag
chew: bite, champ, chomp, crush, cud, deliberate, eat, gnaw, grind, manducate, masticate, mull, munch, nibble, ponder, ruminate
chew and swallow: eat
chew humble pie: eat one's words
chew noisily: champ, chomp, munch
chew out: berate, castigate, criticize, rail, scold, upbraid
chew the cud: ruminate
chew the fat: chat, chitchat, converse, gab, gossip, talk
chew the scenery: emote
chewable nut: betel
chewing gum ingredient: chicle
chewing muscle: masseter
chewy candy: caramel
chewy, lightly cooked (pasta): al dente
chic: chichi, classy, dapper, elegance, elegant, faddish, fashionable, modish, nifty, posh, smart, stylish, swank, trendy, trim, up-to-date, vogue
chicanery: artifice, cheating, cunning, deceit, deception, dishonesty, fraud, hocus-pocus, ploy, ruse, trick, trickery, wile
chichi: arty, flamboyant, frilly, grandiose, pompous, pretentious, showy, splashy, swank
chick: child, girl, moppet, sprout, woman, youngster
chickadee: titmouse
chicken: afraid, coward, gutless, sissy,

timid, yellow; biddy, broiler, capon, chick, chicky, cock, cockerel, fowl, fryer, hen, poultry, pullet, rooster
chicken-and-leek soup: cock-a-leekie
chicken and vegetables, Cantonese: moo goo gai pan
chicken cooked in red wine: coq au vin
chicken heart, liver, gizzard: giblets
chicken house: coop
chicken Italian style: chicken cacciatore, chicken parmighiana
chicken or veal layered with ham, cheese: cordon bleu
chicken pieces grilled on a skewer: yakitori
chicken pox: varicella
chicken wings and legs before cooking, to tie up: truss
chicken, castrated male: capon
chicken, few months old: spring chicken
chicken, pertaining to: gallinaceous
chicken, young: poulet, poult
chickpea and fava bean balls, fried: falafel
chickpea dip: hummus
chickpea plant: gram
chickpeas and fava beans patties, deep-fried: falafel, taameyya
chicks' mother: biddy, mother hen
chicle product: chewing gum
chicory: bunk, herb, plant, radicchio, root, witloof
chicory's cousin: endive
chide: admonish, berate, blame, castigate, censure, criticize, lecture, rail, rebuke, reprehend, reprimand, reproach, reprove, scold, upbraid, wrangle
chief: arch, big, bigwig, boss, capital, captain, central, cock of the walk, commander, crucial, dominant, duce, duke, elder, eminent, first, foreman, foremost, great, head, high, honcho, key, king, kingpin, leader, lord, main, major, master, paramount, pooh-bah, predominant, preeminent, premier, preponderant, president, prime, principal, prominent, rector, ring leader, ringleader, ruler, sachem, supreme, vital
chief commodity: staple
chief constituent of teeth: dentine
chief executive of a city: mayor
chief of Native American tribe: sachem
chief person: kingpin
chief support: mainstay
chiefly: mainly

chiffonier: bureau, cabinet, chest, commode, cupboard, dresser

chignon: bun, hairdo, knot, twist

child: adolescent, babe, baby, bambino, bantling, ben, boy, brat, bud, cherub, chick, cub, daughter, descendant, girl, imp, infant, kid, lad, lass, minor, moppet, offspring, orphan, page, progeny, scion, son, squirt, tad, tadpole, toddler, tot, tyke, urchin, waif, youngster, youth

RELATED TERMS

child as part of a family tree: descendant

child care center: day care, nursery

child guardianship: custody

child home alone: latchkey child

child in early adolescence, of a: pubescent

child murder: infanticide

child murder by parent: filicide

child of one's father by a previous marriage: half brother, half sister

child on a knee, to bounce: dandle

child or an heir: scion

child under legal guardianship: ward

child with extraordinary talent: prodigy

child, abandoned: foundling, waif

child, exceptional: prodigy, wunderkind

child, of an unusually mature: precocious

child, poor: guttersnipe, ragamuffin, urchin

child, unweaned: suckling

child, young: nipper, shaver, tyke, youngster ❦

childbirth: confinement, delivery, labor, lying-in, nativity, parturition, producing, travail

childbirth aide: midwife

childbirth discharge: afterbirth, placenta, secundines

childbirth incision to make delivery easier: episiotomy

childbirth pains: labor, travail

childbirth with drugs, hasten onset of: induce

childbirth, care of women before, during, and after: obstetric

childbirth, father's ritual simulating mother's: couvade

childbirth, involuntary shortening of abdominal muscles in: contraction

childbirth, relating to: puerperal

childbirth, serious condition involving coma and convulsions before or after: eclampsia

childbirth, time of: accouchement

childhood years: formative years

childish: asinine, babyish, childlike, credulous, foolish, frivolous, immature, infantile, juvenile, kiddish, naive, petty, puerile, puling, senile, silly, simple, young

childish comeback: is so

children and descendants of a person: offspring, posterity, progeny

children, aversion or dislike of: misopedia

children, producing many: philoprogenitive, prolific

children, to produce: procreate, reproduce

children's diseases, science of: pediatrics

child's bringer of sleep: sandman

child's food guard: bib

child's nurse: caretaker, nanny, nursemaid

child's relation to parents: filial

Chile capital: Santiago

chill: arctic, cold, coldness, cool, dampen, depress, dispirit, distant, fever, freeze, frigid, frosty, gelidity, glacial, hostile, ice, nip, raw, refrigerate, rigor, shake, shiver

chill out: relax

chill, shivering or trembling caused by a: rigor

chilled: iced

chilled brown dessert: chocolate mousse

chiller: eerie, frightening, horror show, shocker, thriller

chilling: frigorific, icy, on ice

chills and fever: ague

chilly: algid, aloof, arctic, biting, bleak, cold, cool, crisp, drafty, freezing, frigid, frosty, nippy, raw

chilly and wet: dank

chime: accord, agreement, bell, concord, cymbal, edge, gong, harmony, jingle, knell, melody, peal, ring, sound, ting, toll

chime in: declare, interrupt, offer, remark, state, tell

chimera: delusion, dream, fabrication, fantasy, illusion, mirage, monster

chimerical: absurd, delusive, fabulous, fanciful, fantastic, fictional, imaginary, mythical, unfounded, unreal, utopian, visionary, wild

CHINESE TERMS

Chinese ancient bow: kowtow

Chinese beverage: tea

Chinese boat: bark, junk, sampan

Chinese calculator: abacus

Chinese cooking pan: wok

Chinese decoration: chinoiserie

Chinese dog: chow

Chinese domino-like game: mah-jongg

Chinese dumpling: dim sum, shumai, wonton

Chinese female force: yin

Chinese fruit: kumquat, lichee, mandarin

Chinese language, culture, civilization study: sinology

Chinese masculine force: yang

Chinese medicine: acupuncture

Chinese philosophy: Tao

Chinese physical exercises: tai chi

Chinese puzzle with triangles, square, rhomboid: tangram

Chinese temple: pagoda

Chinese transliteration into Roman alphabet: Pinyin

Chinese weaponless self-defense: jujitsu ❦

chimney: fireplace, flue, funnel, furnace, gully, hearth, lum, pipe, smokestack, stack, tube, vent

chimney accumulation: soot

chimney duct: flue

chimney man: sweep

chimney, windscreen for: bonnet

chimp or gorilla: great ape

chimpanzee: animal, anthropoid, ape, bonobo, chimp, monkey, primate, troglodyte

chimp's relative: orang

chin: button, chat, chitchat, jaw, mandible, mentum, rap, talk

chin whiskers: goatee

chin, concerning the: genial, mental

chin, divided: cleft chin

chin, having a double: buccula

chin, having prominent: prognathous

chin, well-positioned: orthognathous

china: ceramic, crockery, dishes, earthenware, porcelain, pottery, service, tableware, ware

china, thin and delicate: eggshell china

chine: back, backbone, cleave, meat, spine

chink: aperture, bore, cash, chinkle,

cleft, coin, crack, cranny, crevice, fissure, gap, gash, jingle, money, rent, rift, rime, slit

chintzy: cheap, gaudy, mean, petty, sleazy, stingy, tight

chip: bit, chaff, chisel, chunk, clip, coin, crack, cut, damage, flake, flaw, fragment, hew, marker, money, nick, pare, piece, scrap, shard, shaving, splinter, token, whittle

chip from stone or ore: spall

chip in: ante, contribute, help, interpose, pay, subscribe

chipmunk: chippy, gopher, rodent, squirrel

chipmunk snack: acorn

chipped off: flaked

Chippendale: cabinetmaker

chipper: alert, alive, chatter, cheerful, chirp, cockey, energetic, frisky, gay, happy, lively, perky, pert, sprightly, spry, twitter

chirography: calligraphy, handwriting, penmanship, writing

chiromancer's reading matter: palm

chirp: call, cheep, chipper, chirrup, chirt, chitter, peep, pipe, sing, sound, tweet, twitter

chirp by rubbing body parts together: stridulation

chirrup: call, cheep, chipper, chirt, chitter, peep, pipe, sing, sound, tweet, twitter

chisel: bargain, bilk, carve, cheat, chip, cut, defraud, engrave, form, gouge, gyp, intrude, knife, rook, sculpture, shape, tool

chisel for rough hewing, stonemason's: drove

chisel handle: helve

chisel roughly: boast

chiseler: cheat, crook, fake, swindler

chisel's slanted surface: bezel

chit: bill, check, child, draft, infant, IOU, kid, memo, memorandum, moppet, note, offspring, sprout, tab, voucher

chitchat: babble, banter, bytalk, chatter, conversation, drivel, gossip, prattle, talk

chivalrous: brave, considerate, courageous, courteous, gallant, generous, gentle, heroic, honorable, knightly, noble, polite, valiant

chivalrous and idealistic: quixotic

chivalry: courage, fairness, knight≈ errantry, knighthood, valor

chive's relative: onion

chivy: annoy, badger, bait, bother, chase, chivvy, confusion, harass, hound, hunt, pursue, pursuit, race, scamper, tease, torment

chloride: chemical, compound, ester, muriate, salt

chlorine: bleach, disinfectant, element, halogen

chloroform: anesthetic, kill, poison, solvent, toxic

chocolate brown: mocha

chocolate substitute: carob

chocolate tree: cacao

choice: alternative, assortment, deciding, decision, druthers, election, judgment, option, pick, preference, selection, substitute, variety, verdict, voice, volition; best, better, cream, delicate, elite, excellent, exquisite, fine, flower, picked, popular, preferable, prime, rare, select, uncommon, winner

choice and excellent: vintage

choice between equally undesirable options: dilemma

choice between what is offered and nothing: Hobson's choice

choice gossip: tidbits

choice group or class: elite

choice stocks: blue chips

choice word: and/or, either, else, nor, or else

choice, of one's free: voluntary

choice, power to make a responsible: discretion

choir entering church: procession

choir gallery or balcony: loft

choir leader: cantor, precentor

choir leaving church: recession

choir music unaccompanied: a cappella

choir of four male a cappella voices: barbershop quartet

choir or chorus: chorale

choir performing short pieces, small: glee club

choir, singer in: chorister

choke: asphyxiate, block, clog, close, congest, constrict, crack, fail, fill, gag, hinder, impede, lose, neckcloth, obstruct, plug, silence, smother, stifle, stoppage, strangle, suffocate, suppress, throttle, wring

choke to death: strangle

choker: necklace

choler: anger, bile, ire, wrath

choleric: angry, belligerent, cranky, cross, enraged, grouchy, grumpy,

huffy, impatient, irascible, irate, mad, peevish, quarrelsome, testy, touchy, wrathful

cholesterol lowerer: bran

cholesterol raiser: fat

cholesterol source: eggs

chomp: bite, chew, crunch, masticate

Chong's partner: Cheech

choose: adopt, cull, decide, determine, elect, embrace, fancy, opt, pick, prefer, select, take, vote

choose actors: cast

choose as preference: elect, favor, single out

choose between: differentiate, discriminate, distinguish

choose from a collection: cull, select

choose with care: handpick

choosing based on need: triage

choosy: eclectic, fastidious, finicky, fussy, particular, picky, selective

chop: axe, barter, carve, change, chip, cleave, cleft, crack, cut, dice, gash, grade, hack, hew, knock, lop, meat, mince, quality, sever, slash, slit, split

chop finely: mince

chop up: hash

chop, frilly paper on end of meat: frill, papillote

chop-chop: fast, lickety-split, promptly, quickly, rapidly, tout de suite

chopper: axe, dicer, mincer, molar

chopper blade: rotor

choppy: chapped, jerky, ripply, rough, violent, wavy

choral love song: madrigal

chord: accord, cord, harmonize, major, minor, music, nerve, note, rope, string, tendon, tone, triad

chord tones played in rapid succession: arpeggio

chords moving in progression to a harmonic close: cadence

chore: assignment, duty, effort, errand, housework, job, scutwork, stint, task, work

choreography: composition, dancing

chores that have to be done, irksome: metutials

chorography: chart, diagram, mapmaking, mapping

chortle: cackle, chuckle, giggle, laugh, snicker, snort

chorus: accord, agreement, carolers, choir, concert, consensus, echo, ensemble, harmony, melody, refrain, response, singers, song, unison

chorus of song: burden, refrain

chosen: called, elect, elected, elective, elite, named, picked, preferred, selected, tabbed, voted

chosen few: elite

chosen freely: voluntary

chosen from a variety of sources: eclectic

chow: bye, dog, eats, food, grub, meal, mess, victuals

Christ: God, Jesus, Lord, Messiah, Savior, Son

christen: baptize, bless, immerse, name

Christian: charitable, devoted, disciple, faithful, pious, religious
RELATED TERMS
Christian 16th-century reform movement: Reformation
Christian 40-day period of penitence: Lent
Christian act, sacred: sacrament
Christian creed in Mass: Credo
Christian era: A.D., C.E., Common Era
Christian fellowship handshake: kiss of peace
Christian Holy Communion: Eucharist
Christian love: agape
Christian prayer in Mass starting "Glory be to God": Gloria
Christian prayer in Mass starting "Holy, holy, holy": Sanctus
Christian prayer in Mass starting "Lord have mercy": Kyrie
Christian prayer in Mass to Christ as Savior: Agnus Dei
Christian precept: Golden Rule
Christian sacrament of Eucharist: communion
Christian Science practitioner: healer
Christian teachings: gospel
Christian worship, pertaining to enthusiastic: charismatic, Pentecostal
Christianity, of one who rediscovers: born-again ❦

Christmas: festival, holiday, nativity, Noel, Xmas, yule, yuletide

Christmas carol: noel

Christmas display of Jesus' birth: crèche

Christmas message: good will to men

Christmas-tree decoration: star

chromosome constituent: DNA

chronic: confirmed, constant, continual, continuous, fixed, habitual, inbred, incessant, incurable, intense, lasting, lingering, prolonged, recurring, routine, severe, stubborn, usual

chronic illness: dysphoria

chronicle: account, annals, archives, describe, diary, epic, history, journal, narrative, record, register, saga, story, tell

chronological: classified, consecutive, dated, ordered, sequential, successive, tabulated

chronology of tree rings: dendrochronology

chronometer: clock, hourglass, metronome, timekeeper, timepiece, timer, watch

chrysanthemum leucanthemum: ox eye

chubby: chunky, flabby, fubsy, heavyset, overweight, plump, pudgy, roly-poly, rotund, round, tubby

chuck: cast, cluck, discard, dismissal, ditch, fling, food, hurl, jerk, junk, oust, pat, pitch, scrap, shed, throw, toss; beef, roast, stew meat

chuck-wagon fare: grub

chuckle: cackle, chortle, exult, giggle, laugh, snicker, teehee, titter

chum: associate, buddy, companion, comrade, confidant, crony, friend, mate, matey, pal, pard, sidekick

chump: blockhead, boob, dolt, fool, goof, lunkhead, oaf, sap, sucker

chunk: gob, mass, piece, portion, slab, slug, wad, whang

chunky: beefy, chubby, dumpy, husky, lumpy, plump, squat, stocky, stout, stubby

chunky part: slab

churl: boor, cad, carle, ceorl, chuff, countryman, haskard, husband, knave, lout, miser, niggard, peasant, rustic, serf, skimper, tightwad, villain, yokel

churlish: blunt, boorish, crabbed, crabby, crude, crusty, grouchy, gruff, lowbred, mean, ornery, rough, rustic, sullen, surly, uncivil, ungracious, violent, vulgar

churlish in sports: poor loser

churn: agitate, beat, ferment, foam, shake, stir, swirl, vessel, whip

churn up: rile

chute: cascade, channel, flume, parachute, ramp, rapid, rush, slide, slope, trough, tube, watercourse, waterfall

chutzpah: audacity, gall, nerve

cicada: locust

cicatrice, cicatrix: scar

cicerone: conductor, guide, mentor, pilot

cider: alcohol, apple, beverage

cigar: belvedere, boquet, bouquet, cheroot, claro, corona, Havana, panatela, perfecto, smoke, stogie, stogy, tobacco, toby, weed
RELATED TERMS
cigar band collector: brandophilist
cigar case: humidor
cigar end: ashtip, ette
cigar tobacco leaf case: wrapper
cigar, cheap and thin: stogy
cigar, dark and strong: maduro
cigar, high-quality Cuban: Havana
cigar, long and thin: panatela, panatella
cigar, long slim and inexpensive: stogie
cigar, square-cut at both ends: cheroot
cigar, strong and dark: maduro
cigar, tapered at both ends: corona, perfecto ❦

cigar-shaped shell: torpedo

cigarette: biri, butt, cubeb, fag, gasper, puff, reefer, smoke

cigarette breathing in: inhale

cigarette remains: ash

cigarette residue: tar

cigarfish: scad

cilium: eyelash, hair, lash

cinch: assure, belt, breeze, certainty, fasten, girth, grip, piece of cake, pushover, sash, snap

cincture: band, belt, collar, encircle, enclosure, girdle, girth, surrounding

cinder: ash, ashes, clinker, coal, dross, embers, gray, scoria, slag, soot

cinema: bijou, film, flick, motion picture, movie, moviehouse, picture, screen, show, theater

cinema, early: nickelodeon

cinema, early small: cinematheque

cinematic event: premiere, sneak preview

cinnabar: red

cinnamon bark: cassia

cinnamon stick: quill

cipher: aught, blank, code, cryptogram, decode, figure, letter, nada, naught, nil, nonentity, nothing, null, number, symbol, unravel, zero, zilch, zippo

circa: about, approximation, around, near, roughly

circle: bowl, circlet, circuit, circulate,

CHURCH TERMS

aisle: ambulatory
announcement: banns
arches above side aisles: triforium
architecture/decoration, study of: ecclesiology
area: apse, nave
area behind altar: retrochoir
assembly: synod
attendant and usher: verger
attendees: laity
baptism basin: font
bell: angelus
bell tower not attached to church: campanile
benches: pews
building with nave, clerestory, transept, apse, side aisles: basilica
calendar: ordo, rota
candle or light kept burning: altar light, vigil light
caretaker: sexton
ceremonial washing of hands: lavabo
ceremony or ritual: liturgy
chanting by monks: Gregorian chant
chapel dedicated to Virgin Mary: Lady Chapel
choir-sung reply: response
church: basilica, congregation, creed, edifice, faith, house of God, sanctuary, sect, synaxis, temple
church-and-state conflict: Kulturkampf
church fathers' writings: patristics, patrology
Church of England member: Anglican
church or cathedral with special privileges: basilica
church or chapel for prayer: oratory
church or temple, another name for: tabernacle
church workers: abbot, altarboy, beadle, bishop, clergyman, curate, deacon, dean, elder, lector, minister, ostiary, pope, prelate, presbyter, priest, primate, reader, reverend, sacrist, sexton, vicar, warden
churches derived from Byzantine Empire church: Eastern Orthodox Church, Orthodox Church
clergy stipend: prebend
code of law: canon
community of bishop: diocese
concerning: ecclesial, ecclesiastical
conference: convocation, synod
construction with altar on eastern end: orientation
council: rota, synod
corrupt buying of pardons: simony
crossing near choir: transept
devotional composition sung in liturgy as response: antiphon
dignitary of high rank, authority: prelate
division: diocese, episcopacy, episcopate, parish, prelacy, sacerdotum, see, synod
doorkeeper: ostiary
entrance hall at western end: narthex
faction split: schism
gallery over side aisle: triforium
garments of officials: vestments
grounds: precinct

group: choir, communion, confession, denomination, elders
instrument: organ
intersection of nave and transept in cruciform: crossing
jurisdicition: see
kneeling bench: prie-dieu
large Christian church: basilica
laws: canons
Mass that does change daily, parts of: proper
Mass that does not change daily, parts of: common, ordinary
membership: laity, laymen, laypeople, laypersons
membership, cut off from: excommunicate
midsection: nave
modernization of ideas: aggiornamento
niche for vessels: ambry, fenestella
nonreligious and inappropriate for, to make: defile, desecrate, profane
of or relating to the church: ecclesiastical
of or relating to the worldwide Christian church: ecumenical
office: chancellery, chancery
officer: elder
one-tenth of one's income contributed to church: tithe
parts of a church: aisle, altar, apse, apses, balcony, belfry, bell tower, bema, bench, cantoria, chancel, chapel, clerestory, font, galilee, narthex, nave, oratory, pew, pulpit, reredos, sacristy, solea, steeple, transept, vestry
plate: paten
platform or dais: tribune
projecting side, often vaulted: apse, chevet
property destruction: defilement, desecration, profanation, sacrilege
pulpit: ambo
room with vestments: sacristy, vestry
rule by prelates: prelacy
rule or custom: rubric
sacred, to declare something: consecrate, dedicate, sanctify
seat: pew
semicircular projection behind altar: apse
sentence spoken as reply to versicle: response
sentence spoken to be followed by response: versicle
service: baptism, communion, evensong, liturgy, mass, matin, nocturn, novena, rite, vespers
service asking for God's blessing: benediction
service of late afternoon or evening: vespers
service reading desk: lectern
spire at intersection of nave and transepts: fleche
stall's hinged seat: miserere, misericord
stone basin: piscina, sacrarium
symbol: icon
tower: steeple
tower with bell: belfry
tribunal: rota
upper wall with windows: clerestory
vault or underground chamber: crypt, undercroft
vestibule, portico: narthex
vow of faith to a church: covenant
wall with sacrament repository: ambry, aumbry
with high side aisle roofing: hall church ❧

circumference, collet, compass, cordon, corona, coronet, cycle, disc, disk, encircle, enclose, encompass, equator, girdle, globe, gyre, halo, hoop, lap, loop, orb, orbit, pivot, radius, realm, revolution, revolve, ring, ringlet, rink, rotary, rotate, round, set, sphere, spiral, surround, swirl, system, turn, twirl, wheel; associates, clique, companions, company, coterie, crowd, fraternity, friends, group, insiders, sorority

circle around a point: gyrate, spin

circle around, to draw a: circumscribe

circle boundary: circumference

circle dance: farandole, hora

circle of light: halo

circle of people with common interest: coterie

circle of prehistoric stone slabs: cromlech

circle of stone or wooden uprights, ancient: henge

circle on earth's surface passing through poles, imaginary: meridian

circle part: arc, curve

circle whose circumference rolls along circumference of fixed circle: epicycle

circle with locked arms in folk dance: hora

circle, flattened or elongated: elliptical

circle, trace the outline of a: describe

circle's circumference in relation to diameter: pi

circles having a common center, of: concentric

circles in diagram used to represent relationships between sets: Venn diagram

circles overlap, area where two overlapping: eccentric

circlet: band, bangle, bracelet, headband, hoop, ring, wreath

circuit: ambit, area, beat, boundary, circumference, compass, course, cycle, dap, district, excursion, hookup, jaunt, lap, loop, orbit, revolution, robert, round, route, tour, track, whirl, zone

circuit on microchip, electronic: integrated circuit

circuitous: ambiguous, circular, complicated, crooked, curved, deceitful, devious, indirect, labyrinthine, mazy, meandering, rambling, round about, roundabout, serpentine, turning, twisted, underhand, wandering, winding

circular: annular, bill, brochure, complete, curved, flyer, handbill, insert, leaflet, pamphlet, perfect, publication, ringed, round, roundabout, rounded, spheroid, spinning

circular Buddhist or Hindu design: mandala

circular graph divided into sections: pie chart

circular or revolving: gyral

circular or ring-shaped figure, part, marking: annulus

circular panels: roundels

circular plate: disc

circular wall: tambour

circular work of art: tondo

circulate: air, broadcast, disperse, distribute, flow, mix, move, promulgate, propagate, publish, radiate, report, rotate, rove, spread, turn

circumference: ambit, arc, border, boundary, bounds, circuit, edge, girth, limits, outline, perimeter, periphery, rim, surround, verge

circumference section: arc

circumference, as waist: girth

circumlocution: euphemism, periphrase, periphrasis, rambling, redundancy, roundabout, verbality, verbiage, winding, wordiness

circumscribe: bound, confine, curb, define, delineate, encircle, enclose, encompass, fence, impede, limit, restrain, restrict, surround, trammel

circumspect: alert, attentive, cagey, canny, careful, cautious, chary, deliberate, discerning, discreet, guarded, observant, safe, wary, watchful, wise

circumstance: affair, coincidence, condition, destiny, detail, element, environment, event, fact, factor, fate, happening, incident, item, occurrence, opportunity, particular, point, position, situation, state

circumstances reversed: peripeteia, peripetia, peripety

circumstantial: accurate, ceremonial, contingent, deduced, detailed, exact, incidental, inferential, minute, nonessential, particular, precise, presumed

circumvent: avoid, baffle, balk, bypass, cheat, check, deceive, defraud, detour, dupe, elude, encompass, entrap, evade, foil, fool, frustrate, mislead, outwit, overreach, prevent, stymie, surround, thwart, trick

circus: amphitheater, arena, bazaar, big top, carnival, cirque, hippodrome, ring, show, spectacle

circus bar: trapeze

circus big guy: strong man

circus canvas: big top, tent

circus covering: tarp

circus horseback performer: equestrian

circus launching springboard: teeterboard

circus ring: arena

circus star: ringmaster

cirque: basin, circle, circlet, circus

cistern: cavity, chest, reservoir, sac, tank, tub, vat, vessel, well

citadel: acropolis, bastion, castle, fastness, fort, fortification, fortress, manor, stronghold, tower

citation: award, encomium, honor, mention, notice; cite, excerpt, quotation, reference; allegation, summons, writ

cite: adduce, allege, arouse, arraign, call, credit, document, excerpt, extract, indicate, mention, name, note, notify, praise, quote, refer, repeat, specify, subpoena, summon, tell

cities making urban complex, group of large: conurbation, megalopolis

citified: urban

citizen: burgess, burgher, civilian, commoner, denizen, inhabitant, national, native, occupant, resident, settler, subject, taxpayer, villager, voter

citizen of world: cosmopolite

citizen, middle-class: burgher

citizens' proposition of a new law to electorate: initiative

citizens' rights, study of: civics

citizenship rights, to give: enfranchise

citizenship, to grant: naturalize

citric quality: tang

citron: cedrat, fruit, lemon, lime, rind, tree, watermelon, yellow

citrus drinks: ades

citrus-fruit unit: crate

city: megalopolis, metropolis, municipality

city area, poor: ghetto

city blight: slum

city center: downtown

city electoral division: district, precinct, ward

city map: plat

city-state: polis

city, concerning a: civic, municipal, urban

city, fortification guarding: citadel

CITRUS FRUIT

citron
clementine
grapefruit
kumquat
lemon
lime
mandarin
naartje
orange
ortanique
pomelo
satsuma
shaddock
tangelo
tangerine ❦

civet's cousin: genet
civic: borough, civil, community, local, national, public, urban, urbane
civic disorder: riot
civic pride: boosterism
civil: affable, civic, civilized, complaisant, cordial, courteous, courtly, cultivated, diplomatic, discreet, formal, gracious, laic, mannerly, obliging, polished, polite, politic, refined, respectful, suave, urbane
civil affairs magistrate: syndic
civil disorder: riot
civil liberties advocate: libertarian
Civil War, concerning period after U.S.: postbellum
Civil War, concerning period before U.S.: antebellum
civil wrong: tort
civilian: citizen, commoner, noncombatant, nonmilitant, pacificist, practitioner, subject
civilian clothes: civvies, mufti
civilians armed in military emergency: levy en masse
civility: affability, amenity, comity, compliance, courtesy, decorum, politeness, propriety, respect, tact
civilization: cultivation, culture, development, education, mores, people, progress, refinement, society
civilization, of the ancient Greek or Roman: classical
civilize: acquaint, cultivate, develop, educate, enlighten, humanize, idealize, improve, polish, refine, tame, teach, train, uplift
clack: babble, blab, cackle, chatter, clatter, cluck, gossip, jaw, prate, prattle, rattle, yak

clad: adorned, arrayed, attired, clothed, covered, dressed, face, garbed, robed, sheathed
clad, old style: drest
claim: acclaim, allege, ask, assert, aver, birthright, call, case, challenge, charge, declare, demand, dibs, elicit, exact, lien, maintain, mine, name, ownership, postulate, pretence, pretend, pretense, privilege, proclaim, profess, property, right, take, title, vindicate
claim as an attribute or quality of something: predicate
claim as being true or the basis of an argument: postulate, premise
claim as due: demand
claim on property as payment or security for debt: lien
claim positively: affirm, assert, asseverate, aver, avouch, avow
claim to a privilege or right: pretension
claim to have the intention of doing: profess, purport, purpose
claim voluntarily, to give up: relinquish, waive
claim without or before proof: allege
claim without permission: appropriate, arrogate
claim, to disprove a: invalidate
claim, to refuse to pay a: repudiate
claimant: petitioner, plaintiff, pretender
clairvoyance: cryptesthesia, discernment, ESP, extrasensory perception, feeling, insight, premonition, sixth sense, telepathy
clairvoyant: intuitive, medium, perceptive, prophet, psychic, seer, telepathic, visionary
clam: base, bivalve, clamp, clasp, crash, grasp, hush, mollusk, mussel, quahog, shellfish; dollar
clam type: cherrystone, geoduck, giant, hard, little neck, quahog, razor, round, soft, steamer, stuffed
clam, large littleneck: cherrystone
clam, young of quahog: littleneck
clamant: blatant, clamorous, dire, imperative, pressing, urgent
clammy: cool, damp, dank, moist, slimy, sticky
clamor: bellow, blare, boast, brouhaha, bunk, commotion, cry, din, discord, hubbub, hullabaloo, noise, outcry, racket, roar, ruckus, shout, tumult, uproar, wail, yell

clamorous: aroar, blatant, loud, noisy, rackety
clamp: block, bolt, brace, clasp, clench, fasten, fastener, grapple, grip, hold, holdfast, lock, nail, pin, secure, snap, vise
clamping device: chuck
clan: band, brotherhood, circle, class, clique, coterie, cult, family, fraternity, gang, gens, group, horde, house, kinfolks, party, race, ring, sect, sept, society, stock, tribe, unit
clan chief: thane
clan members: septs
clan or kinship group: phratry, tribe
clan symbol: totem
clandestine: artful, back stairs, cloaked, concealed, covert, foxy, fraudulent, furtive, hidden, illicit, secret, sly, sneaky, stealthy, surreptitious, undercover, underground
clandestine meeting: tryst
clandestine subversive organization: fifth column
clang: call, clank, ding, jangle, noise, peal, resounding, ring, sound
clangor: blare, noise, peal, plare
clangorous: loud
clank: bang, clang, clatter, clink, ring, sound
clannish: akin, close, exclusive, narrow, secret, sectarian, select, united
clap: applaud, bang, boom, chatter, cheer, clack, clink, crack, explosion, flap, peal, praise, roar, slap, smack, strike, stroke, thunder
clapper, clicking instrument: castanets
claptrap: baloney, bull, bunk, drivel, fustian, hogwash, hokum, hooey, humbug, insincerity, malarkey, nonsense, poppycock, pretension, trash
claret, for one: red wine
clarified butter, of India: ghee
clarify: analyze, clean, cleanse, clear, delineate, elucidate, enlighten, explain, illuminate, interpret, irradiate, purify, rarefy, refine, settle, simplify
clarinet: instrument, reed, wind, woodwind
clarinet low register: chalumeau
clarinet socket: birn
clarinet's cousin: oboe
clarion: acute, clear, definite, inspiring, ringing, sharp
clarity: accuracy, brightness, brilliance, clearness, explicitness, literacy, openness, precision, radiance
clash: affray, argue, bang, battle, brawl,

collide, collision, conflict, contrast, crash, differ, disagree, discord, dispute, dolt, feud, fight, impact, interfere, jar, melee, scandal, showdown, slam, strife, strike, struggle

clasp: brooch, buckle, clamp, clench, cling, clip, clutch, constrain, embrace, entwine, fasten, fastener, fold, grab, grasp, grip, hasp, hold, hook, hoop, hug, infold, lock, pin, secure, surround

class: bracket, breed, caste, category, circle, clan, denomination, description, division, family, fashionable, form, gauge, gender, genre, genus, grade, group, hierarchy, ilk, index, kind, order, position, race, rank, rating, sect, sort, species, standing, status, style, subject, type, variety

class-conscious insects: ants

class for slower learners, of a: remedial

class in society: caste

class member who isn't graded: auditor

class of travel: steerage

class or category of art, film, literature, music: genre

class or category title: rubric

class or level in hierarchy: stratum

class, individual instruction or: tutorial

class, of a higher: superordinate

class, of a lower: subordinate

class, poorest working: proletariat

classes: genera

classic: ancient, composition, flawless, ideal, masterpiece, model, old, perfect, prime, standard, time-honored, top, venerable, vintage

classical: academic, chaste, elegant, Greek, Latin, masterly, pure, Roman, scholastic, simple, standard, traditional

classical ballroom dance: waltz

classical music, lover of: longhair

classical pillar: stela

classification: analysis, arrangement, category, confidential, division, family, file, genre, genus, grade, group, niche, order, rank, rate, rating, sort, species, system, taxonomy

classification by status, rank, ability: hierarchy

classification in science: taxonomy

classification into categories: distribution

classification of diseases: nosology

classification of organisms based on shared ancestry: cladistics

classification or title of group: denomination, designation

classification that is scaled or stepped: gradation

classification, common name as opposed to taxonomic name of organism: vernacular name

classification, pertaining to an entire: general, generic

classification, system of Latin names in organism: binomial nomenclature, Linnaean nomenclature

classification, system of names in a: nomenclature

classification, uncapitalized Latin adjective or noun after genus name in organism: specific epithet, trivial name

classifications of organisms: class, division, family, genus, kingdom, order, phylum, species

classified: labeled, sorted, typed

classified according to naturalist Linnaeus' system: Linnaean

classified into a hierarchy: stratified

classify: alphabetize, arrange, assort, catalog, categorize, codify, distribute, divide, grade, group, label, list, number, pigeonhole, range, rank, register, segregate, size, sort, type

classify into a more comprehensive category: subsume

classify into systematic arrangement: catalog, codify, digest

classify too minutely: oversort

classify under: subordinate, subsume

classroom competition: spelling bee

classroom jottings: notes

classy: chic, elegant, fashionable, posh, slick, smart, stylish, tony

clatter: babble, bang, blatter, chatter, clack, clutter, commotion, disturbance, gabble, gossip, noise, prattle, rattle, roar, turmoil

clause: article, conclusion, condition, dependent, heading, independent, part, passage, phrase, point, provision, proviso, rider, sentence, stipulation, term, ultimatum

clause acting as a noun, dependent: noun clause

clause identifying modified noun or phrase: restrictive

clause modifying a noun or pronoun, dependent: adjective clause

clause modifying a verb, dependent: adverb clause

clause or amendment to document or record: rider

clause that can stand alone: independent clause, main clause

clause that cannot stand alone: dependent clause, subordinate clause

clause that describes but does not identify meaning of modified noun: nonrestrictive

clause, subordination of one to another: hypotaxis

clauses with no coordinating or subordinating conjunctions between: parataxis

clavicle: collarbone

claw: chela, clutch, dig, foot, grasp, griff, grope, hand, hook, lacerate, maul, nail, nipper, paw, scrape, scratch, seize, sere, slash, talon, tear, unguis, ungula

claw of bird of prey: pounce, talon

claw of lobster, crab, scorpion: chela, pincer

clay: adobe, ali, argil, bole, brick, clunch, cob, earth, galt, gault, kaolin, loam, loess, marl, mud, ochre, paste, pottery, rabat, tiles

clay and firing it at high temperatures, material made by shaping: ceramic, china

clay and sand, rock intermediate between: silt

clay or brown earth used as pigment: bole, sienna, umber

clay or clay mixture used in making porcelain or pottery, moist: paste, pate

clay pigeon shooting: skeet, trapshooting

clay pot: olla

clay pottery: ceramics

clay target: skeet

clay used by potters: argil, terra-cotta

clay used for ceramics: kaolin, terra alba

clay, potter's tool for shaping: pallet

clay, sun-dried: adobe

clay, thinned potter's: slip

clayey mixture: loam

clayey rock: shale

clayey soil: marl

claylike: fictile, marly

claylike substance used in materials: fuller's earth

clean: antiseptic, bathe, brightly, butterworth, chaste, cleanse, clear, clearly, dexterous, disinfected, dust, empty, entirely, guiltless, hygienic, immaculate, innocent, kosher, laundered, mop, perfect, pure, purify, renovate, sanitary, sanitized, scour, scrub, smart, smug, speckless, spotless, spruce, squeaky, sterile, swab, tidy, trim, unadulterated, undefiled, unsoiled, untarnished, vacuum, wash, wholesome, wipe

clean a pipe: ream

clean a windshield: defog

clean and flawless: immaculate

clean and restore: refurbish

clean and trim: preen

clean-cut: chiseled, defined, explicit, outlined, wholesome

clean furniture: dust

clean rugs: beat

clean slate: tabula rasa

clean the deck: swab

clean the skillet: scour

clean the slate: erase

clean, totally: immaculate, pristine, sterile

cleaner: abrasive, ammonia, antiseptic, bleach, borax, cleanser, detergent, janitor, polish, purer, soap, whiter

cleanse: absolve, baptize, brush, clarify, deterge, disinfect, erase, expurgate, free, heal, purge, purify, refine, rinse, scour, scrub, soap, sterilize, sweeten, wash

cleansing of a system: cathartic, purgative

cleansing of pity and fear: catharsis

cleansing substance: detergent

clear: absolve, acquit, alert, apparent, articulate, bright, brighten, candid, clarify, clarion, clean, cloudless, convinced, crystal, definite, discharge, disengage, disentangle, distinct, earn, elucidate, erase, evident, exempt, exonerate, explicit, extricate, free, gain, glaring, innocent, intelligible, legible, lighten, limpid, lucent, lucid, net, obvious, open, over, overt, pellucid, plain, positive, profit, purify, release, relevant, rid, settle, sharp, smooth, sunny, translucent, transparent, unblock, unconfused, unhampered, unmistakable, unobscured, vacate, vindicate, vivid, void

clear a profit: net

clear a tape: erase

clear a windshield: defog, deice

clear and comprehensible: intelligible, lucid, pellucid, perspicuous

clear and comprehensible in one way only: unequivocal

clear and intelligible: limpid

clear and intense: vivid

clear and loud: clarion

clear and obvious: evident, manifest, palpable, patent

clear and sharp: cogent, incisive, trenchant

clear and specific: manifest

clear and straightforward: explicit

clear and transparent: crystalline, diaphanous, limpid, lucid

clear and unambiguous: unequivocal

clear-cut: apparent, categorical, chiseled, concise, decisive, definite, distinct, evident, exact, explicit, lucid, obvious, open, sharp, trenchant, unconfused, unquestioned

clear from accusation: acquit

clear of a charge or blame: absolve, acquit, exculpate, exonerate, vindicate

clear of accusation: acquit, exonerate, vindicate

clear of the bottom, as an anchor: atrip

clear out: decamp, eliminate, hightail, remove, scram, skedaddle, sort, vamoose

clear profit: net

clear semantically, to make: disambiguate

clear sky: ether

clear the blackboard: erase

clear the throat audibly: hawk

clear up: brighten, decipher, explain, improve, resolve, settle, solve, untangle

clear, to make: clarify, elucidate

clearance: approval, authorization, consent, headroom, permission, sale

clearheaded: alert, astute, awake, perceptive, sensible

clearing: assart, glade, opening, tract

clearly: apparently, conspicuously, evidently, noticeably, obviously, plainly, seemingly, signally, surely, unmistakably

clearly described: graphic

clearly expressed: explicit, lucid, luminous, pellucid, perspicuous

clearness: clarity

cleat: batten, bitt, block, bollard, chock, metal, spike, spurlike, support, wedge, wood

cleavage: break, cleft, crevice, division, gap, schism, separation, slit, split

cleave: adhere, bisect, break, carve, chop, cleft, cling, clove, cut, divide, hack, join, link, part, pierce, remain, rend, rift, rip, rive, separate, sever, shear, slice, slit, split, sunder, tear, whack

cleaver: axe, foe, hatchet, knife, meat-ax, river

cleft: aperture, breach, break, chasm, chink, cleave, clove, crack, cranny, crevice, crotch, divide, divided, division, fissure, flow, forked, fracture, gap, gorge, indentation, opening, ravine, recess, reft, rift, rima, rive, riven, split, torn, trough

cleft into two parts: bifid

clemency: compassion, fairness, forgiveness, humanity, indulgence, kindness, leniency, mercy, mildness

clement: benevolent, benign, calm, easy, forgiving, gentle, indulgent, kind, lenient, merciful, mild, peaceful, warm

clench: clamp, clasp, clinch, clint, close, clutch, grapple, grasp, grip, grit, hold, tighten

clergy: canonry, cardinalate, clerics, cloth, deaconry, ministry, priesthood, rabbinate

clergy of rights, to strip: defrock, unfrock

clergy school: seminary

clergy, concerning: clerical

clergy, to authorize as: ordain

clergyman/woman: bishop, blackcoat, canon, cardinal, cassock, chaplain, cleric, clerk, deacon, dean, dignitary, ecclesiastic, evangelist, father, minister, missionary, monk, monsignor, nun, padre, parson, pastor, pontiff, preacher, presbyter, priest, rabbi, rector, reverend, vicar

clergyman's residence: manse

clergyperson assisting communion: concelebrant

clergyperson officiating service: celebrant

clergyperson's residence: rectory

clergyperson's salary: prebend, stipend

clerical calendar: ordo

clerical cap: biretta

clerical cloak: amice, orale

clerical cloak, clasped at neck: cope

clerical cloak, knee-length and white: surplice

clerical cloak, white: alb

clerical garment, sleeved, worn over alb: dalmatic

clerical garment, sleeveless as mantle at communion: chasuble

clerical garment, sleeveless, hanging from shoulders: scapular

clerical scarf: tippet

clerically garbed: in vestment

CLERGYPEOPLE

archbishop
archdeacon
archpriest
bishop
brother
canon
cardinal
chancellor
chaplain
cleric
confessor
curate
Dalai Lama
deacon
deaconess
dean
ecclesiastic
elder
eparch
evangelist
exarch
father
friar
imam
metropolitan
minister
monk
monsignor
Mother Superior
nun
ordinand
padre
parson
pastor
pontiff
pope
preacher
prebendary
precentor
prelate
primate
prior
proctor
provost
rabbi
rebbe
rector
reverend
rural dean
sexton
suffragan
swami
televangelist
vicar ❦

clerk: accountant, agent, assistant, auditor, bookkeeper, cashier, cleric, employee, layman, receptionist, recorder, registrar, salesman, salesperson, saleswoman, scholar, secretary, steno, stenographer, teller, typist

clever: able, active, acute, adroit, agile, alert, apt, artful, astute, bright, clean, clear, creative, cunning, cute, deft, dexterous, dextrous, discerning, foxy, funny, gifted, habile, handsome, handy, imaginative, ingenious, intelligent, inventive, keen, nimble, obliging, penetrating, perceptive, percipient, perspicacious, politic, pretty, quick, shrewd, skillful, slick, sly, smart, talented, witty

clever and intelligent: apt, astute, receptive

clever and inventive: cunning, ingenious, resourceful

clever and wise: judicious, prudent, sagacious, sapient

clever remark: bon mot, epigram

cleverly sly: arch

cleverly stylish: chic

cleverness and initiative: gumption, ingenuity

cleverness and insight: acumen

cliché: adage, banality, bromide, buzzword, hackneyed, motto, slogan, stereotyped, timeworn, trite, truism

cliché or catchword of group: shibboleth

cliché-ridden: sententious, trite

cliché that is self-evident truth: truism

cliché, unoriginal: bromide, commonplace, platitude

clichéd and moralizing talk: homily

clichéd and unused metaphor: dead metaphor

clichéd idea: received idea

click: agree, bang, beat, clack, match, succeed, tick

click beetle: dor, elater, elaterid

clicking musical instrument: castanets

client: buyer, consumer, customer, dependent, patient, patron, shopper, user

clientele: cortege, following, patronage, public, regulars

cliff: bluff, cleve, crag, escarpment, face, hill, hillside, ledge, rock, scar, scarp, slope, wall

cliff at rim of plateau: scarp

cliff chamber: cave

cliff edge: precipice

cliff high above body of water: headland, promontory

cliff made from erosion: escarpment

cliff on side of hill: scar

cliff projecting into water: headland

cliff, debris at base of: scree, talus

cliff, steep: bluff

cliffs, line of: palisades

climate: ambience, attitude, aura, condition, environment, feeling, mood, temper, tone, weather

climate good for one's health, of a: salubrious

climate with small temperature range, of a: equable, maritime

climate, adjust to a new: acclimatize

climate, of a mild: temperate

climax: acme, apex, apogee, ascend, cap, conclude, crisis, culmination, finish, gradation, highlight, peak, pinnacle, summit, top, zenith

climb: ascend, ascent, clamber, crawl, creep, escalate, mount, rise, scale, shin, soar, struggle

climb a pole: shin

climb awkwardly: clamber, scramble

climb by clasping with arms and legs: swarm

climb or scale a fortification: escalade

climb to top of: ascend, surmount

climber of buildings: stegophilist

climber's gear: piton

climber's goal: arête

climbing cactus: queen of the night

climbing palm: rattan

climbing plant: bine, bryony, creeper, ivy, liana, liane, vine

climbing plant is trained to grow, arbor or passageway on which: pergola

climbing plant is trained to grow, latticework on which: trellis

climbing plant threadlike structure for grasping: tendril

clinch: bind, clamp, clench, cling, clutch, complete, conclude, confirm, culminate, decide, embrace, establish, fasten, grapple, grasp, grip, hug, ice, nail, rivet, scuffle, seal, secure, seize, win

cling: adhere, bond, cherish, clasp, cleave to, clinch, cohere, cohesion, depend, embrace, fasten, hang, hold, hug, last, linger, maintain, persevere, stick, trust

clinging: adhesive, osculant, tenacious

clinging mollusk: limpet

clinic: dispensary, hospital, infirmary

clink: bang, beat, brig, calaboose, can,

clap, cooler, guardhouse, hoosegow, jail, jingle, latch, lockup, noise, pokey, prison, ring, sound, tinkle

clinquant: glittering, gold, showy, tinsel

clip: abbreviate, barb, block, bob, clasp, clutch, crop, curtail, cut, decrease, diminish, embrace, encompass, excise, fasten, fastener, hinder, hit, hold, hook, mow, nip, overcharge, pace, prune, punch, reduce, scissor, shave, shear, shorten, snip, sock, swindle, time, trim, truncate; rate

clipper: boat, sailboat, shearer, ship, vessel

clique: bloc, cabal, camarilla, camarilla, circle, clan, club, conclave, coterie, crew, crowd, faction, gang, group, insiders, mob, ring, set, site

cloak: aba, blind, burnoose, camouflage, cape, capot, capote, coat, conceal, cover, disguise, dissemble, garment, guise, hide, mant, manta, manteau, mantilla, mantle, mask, obscure, palliate, poncho, portmanteau, pretext, robe, screen, shawl, shelter, shield, shroud, tabard, veil, wrap

cloak with opening for head, blanket-like: poncho

clobber: beat, belt, defeat, drub, lick, pound, rout, shellac, slam, slug, smash, stomp, strike, trounce, wallop, whip, whop

cloche or toque: hat

clock: alarm, attain, Big Ben, chronometer, cuckoo, digital, grandfather, hit, hourglass, indicator, meter, odometer, ornament, punch, realize, recorder, speedometer, stopwatch, sundial, time, timepiece, timer, wallop, watch

clock clear cover: crystal

clock device emitting light when diode applies voltage: LED

clock display with electrically stimulated liquid crystals: LCD, liquid-crystal display

clock face: dial

clock mechanism in timepieces: escapement

clock that strikes the hour: repeater

clock with dripping water, ancient: clepsydra

clock with hand and dial display: analog

clock with number display: digital

clock, precision: chronometer

clock, subatomic accurate: cesium clock

clock, swinging device regulating a: pendulum

clocks and watches, study of or art of making: horology

clockwise: deasil

clockwork: consistency, precision, regularity

clod: blockhead, bumpkin, clown, dimwit, divot, dolt, dull, dummy, earth, fool, goop, lout, lump, moron, nerd, numskull, oaf, soil, stupid, yokel

clodhopper: boor, boot, bumpkin, hick, lummox, oaf, plowman, redneck, rustic, shoe

clog: barrier, block, blockage, check, choke, close, curb, dance, difficulty, encumbrance, fetter, gum, halt, hamper, hindrance, impede, jam, load, lump, obstruct, overload, overshoe, plug, restrain, restraint, shackle, snag, stop, stop up, trammel, weight; shoe

cloister: abbey, aisle, arcade, convent, enclosure, friary, hall, hermitage, lamasery, monastery, monastic, nunnery, order, passageway, retreat, sanctuary, seclude, sequester, shelter, stoa

cloister courtyard: garth

cloister resident: monk

cloister walkway: alure

cloistered: alone, confined, hermitic, isolated, recluse, secluded, sequestered, shielded, solitary, withdrawn

clone: android, copy, double, duplicate, replica

clone original: ortet

close: adjourn, bar, barricade, block, button, cap, cease, clench, complete, completion, conclude, conclusion, connect, context, culmination, discontinue, end, extreme, extremity, finale, finish, link, quit, seal, secure, shut, slam, snug, stop, termination, windup

close (adj.): accurate, adjacent, allied, approaching, avaricious, cheap, compact, congested, convenient, cramped, dense, familiar, friendly, imminent, intimate, loving, narrow, near, nearby, packed, parsimonious, precise, proximate, secretive, similar, snug, stagnant, stingy, thick, tight; airless, muggy, musty, stale

close again: reseal

close and touching: contiguous

close at hand: near

close attention: care, heed

close behind: at one's heels

close by: anear, near

close call: near miss

close connection: liaison

close friendship: intimacy

close meeting or session: adjourn

close observer: eyewitness

close of play, poem or speech at: epilogue

close of speech, formal summary as: peroration

close off: occlude, seal

close or climax of drama or narrative: denouement

close shave: squeaker

close tightly: seal

close to: abutting, adjacent, adjoining, contiguous, near

close to the action: ringside

close together: chockablock, juxtaposed

close watch: surveillance

closed: bankrupt, exclusive, folded, locked, private, resolved, settled, shut

closed carriage: landau

closed-minded: inflexible, obstinate, pigheaded, rigid, stubborn

closed or secret: in camera

closed session of commission, legislature: executive session

closed to other beliefs: intolerant

closed to outside influence: impervious

closefisted: cheap, clinging, near, stingy, tenacious, tight

closely: almost, barely, carefully, nearly

closely associated: intimate

closely contested: nip and tuck

closely packed: dense

closemouthed: bashful, quiet, reserved, secretive, sedate, silent, taciturn, withdrawn

closeness: intimacy, nearness, propinquity, proximity, secrecy, stinginess, strictness

closeness or nearness: propinquity, proximity, vicinity

closest relative: next of kin

closet: ambry, armary, cabinet, chamber, coatroom, conceal, confidential, cuddy, cupboard, hidden, locker, nearest, pantry, private, recess, room, safe, secret, storeroom, theoretical, wardrobe

closure: agreement, bound, cessation, conclusion, confinement, containment, cover, enclosure, end, finish, limit, plug, seal, sealing

clot: agulate, array, blockage, blockhead, clod, clodder, clump, cluster, coagulate, coagulum, concrete, congeal, curd, embolus, gel, gout, group, grume, jell, lump, mass, solidify, thicken, thrombus

clot formation: infarction

cloth: bolt, bunting, drapery, fabric, material, remnant, shroud, swatch, textile, upholstery

cloth for arms of sofa, chair: antimacassar

cloth in loose folds: drapery

cloth left over after roll has been used or sold: remnant

cloth on furniture: upholstery

cloth on lap of bishop at mass, ordination: gremial

cloth piece, sample: swatch

cloth roll: bolt

cloth scraps: oddment, offcut

cloth sewn at edge of garment as lining or decoration: facing, selvage

cloth strips hung as decoration: bunting

cloth wrapping corpse: shroud

cloth, diagonal cut across grain of: bias

cloth, knot or lump in: burl, slub

clothe: accouter, adorn, apparel, array, attire, bedrape, clad, couch, cover, deck, don, dress, endow, endue, garb, gown, guise, habilitate, habit, outfit, rig, robe, swathe, tog, vest, vesture

clothe richly: caparison

clothed sloppily: dishabille

RELATED TERMS

clothes: apparel, attire, baggage, bedclothes, casual, civvies, clothing, costume, dress, duds, formal, garb, garments, gear, habiliments, outfit, rags, raiment, regalia, sportswear, suit, threads, togs, vestments, vesture, wardrobe, wear, work

clothes designer: couturier, modiste

clothes for monk: habit

clothes for mourning: weeds

clothes for new baby: layette

clothes model or life-size dummy: mannequin

clothes of a theater or performing group: wardrobe

clothes of minister or priest: canonicals, vestments

clothes of opposite sex, person who wears: cross-dresser, transvestite

clothes of servants: livery

clothes on pointed object, to tear: snag

clothes rack: valet

clothes suitable for either sex: epicene, unisex

clothes, civilian: civvies, mufti

clothes, dealer of men's: haberdasher

clothes, high-fashion: haute couture

clothes, item to be worn with: accessory

clothes, matching set of: ensemble, outfit

clothes, nice: finery, regalia

clothes, relating to: sartorial

clothier: tailor

clothing: accoutrements, apparel, furnishings, garb, habiliments, togs, vests, wear

clothing and insignia of authority: investment

clothing-related: sartorial ❦

cloud: befog, befuddle, billow, blacken, blemish, blur, cirrus, confuse, cover, cumulus, darken, distort, dust, film, fog, gloom, haze, hide, mist, nebula, nimbus, obfuscate, obscure, ominous, overcast, perplex, screen, shade, shadow, smog, stigma, stratus, sully, swarm, taint, tarnish, thunderhead, vapor, veil

cloud-nine state: euphoria

cloud of dust or gas in outer space: nebula

cloud, fluffy or woolly as a: flocculent

cloud, to: obfuscate, obnubilate

cloudburst: deluge, downpour, rainstorm, storm, torrent

cloudless: azure, bright, clear, fair, sunny

cloudy: dark, dimmed, dismal, dreary, dull, filmy, gloomy, gray, hazy, indistinct, lowery, murky, nebulous, nubilous, obscure, opaque, overcast, shady, turbid, vague

cloudy radiance surrounding deity: nimbus

clout: bandage, bash, bat, beat, blow, clod, club, hit, influence, nail, power, pull, punch, slap, slug, smite, sock, strike, swat, target, thrash, whack

clover with four leaves: quatrefoil

clover with three leaves: shamrock, trefoil

clown: boor, bozo, buffoon, bumpkin, card, comedian, comic, cut up, Emmet Kelly, fool, harlequin, hick, ignorant, jester, joke, lout, merryandrew, mime, punchinello, rustic, stooge, wisecracker, zany

TYPES OF CLOUDS

cloud, before thunderstorm: thunderhead

cloud, dense and white with domed top and flat base: cumulus

cloud, fleecy and globular: cirrocumulus

cloud, globular and in groups: stratocumulus

cloud, hazy and fine: cirrostratus

cloud, long and fibrous, foretelling storm: mare's tail

cloud, low-forming and even at bottom: stratus

cloud, streaks of precipitation under: virga

clouds, study of: nephology

clouds, wind-driven: rack, scud ❦

clown around: play the fool

clowns, group of: pratfall

cloy: glut, gorge, nail, overdo, overfill, pall, sate, satiate, satisfy, saturate, surfeit

club: bat, baton, billy, blackjack, mallet, nightstick, staff, stick, truncheon, weapon, association, brotherhood, bunch, circle, clique, fraternity, gang, hangout, lodge, order, sorority, team, union

club for beating: bastinado, blackjack, bludgeon, truncheon

club membership, vote against someone for: blackball

club-shaped: clavate, claviform

club used by law enforcement: billy club, blackjack, nightstick, truncheon

club with spiked metal head: mace

club, local branch of: chapter

club, to: baste, fustigate

clubfoot: talipes

clublike weapon: mace

cluck: call, clack, click, dumb, hen, naive, nitwit, sound, stupid

clucking of turkeys: drintling

clue: answer, evidence, fingerprint, guide, hint, idea, indicate, inkling, innuendo, intimation, key, lead, notify, sign, suggestion, telltale, tip, trace, warn

clump: agglutinate, array, blob, bunch, bush, clunch, cluster, galumph, group, heap, hodgepodge, lumber, lump, mass, scuff, stomp, thud, thump

TYPES OF CLOTHES

Coats/Overgarments
academic gown
academic hood
academic robe
afghan
anorak
Aquascutum raincoat
bachelor's gown
balmacaan
benjamin
blazer
blouse
bolero
bomber jacket
box coat
Burberry
burnoose/burnous
bush jacket
caftan/kaftan
cagoule
camelhair coat
cape
capelet
capote
capuchin
car coat
cardigan
cardinal
cassock
chesterfield
chiton
chlamys
claw hammer
cloak
coach coat
combat jacket
cowl
cutaway
denim jacket
dinner coat/jacket
djellabah/djellaba/
   jellaba/galabia
doctor's gown
dolman
double-breasted
   jacket
doublet
down jacket
dress coat
duffle coat
duster
Eton jacket
fitted coat
flyaway jacket
frock
fur coat
fur-lined coat

gaberdine
greatcoat
hacking jacket
haik
happi coat
hauberk
himation
Inverness
jean jacket
jerkin
joseph
jubbah
judge's robe/gown
kimono
kirtle
longcoat
lounge coat
mackinaw
mackintosh raincoat
manteau
mantelet
mantilla
mantle
mantua
Mao jacket
maxicoat
mess jacket/monkey
   jacket/shell jacket
monk's robe
Norfolk jacket
pallium
parka
peacoat/pea jacket
pelerine
pelisse
peplos/peplus
peplum
petersham
pilot jacket
poncho
Prince Albert
raglan
raincoat
rebozo
redingote
reefer jacket
robe
roquelaure
safari jacket
serape
shawl
shell jacket
shooting jacket
single-breasted jacket
ski jacket
slicker
slop

smock
smoking jacket
soutane
spencer
spiketail coat
sport coat
sports jacket
stole
surcoat
swallow-tailed coat
tabard
tail coat
tails
tippet
toga
topcoat
topper
trench coat
tunic
tuxedo coat/jacket
ulster
watch coat
windbreaker
wraparound

Dresses and Skirts
A-line skirt
backless dress
backwrap
ball gown
ballet skirt
body dress
bouffant skirt
bridal gown
cage
cheongsam
chiton
coat dress
cocktail dress
crinoline
culottes
dinner dress/gown
dirndl
divided skirt
evening dress/gown
farthingale
fillebeg
flared skirt
flounce
formal
frock
full skirt
gathered skirt
gored skirt
gown
granny dress
grass skirt

gymslip
harem skirt
hobble skirt
hoop skirt
housedress
hula skirt
johnny
jumper
kilt
kirtle
lavalava
mantua
maternity dress
maxiskirt
microminiskirt
microskirt
midiskirt
miniskirt
Mother Hubbard
muumuu
overdress
overskirt
pannier
pantdress
pantskirt
party dress
peasant skirt
peplum
petticoat
pinafore
pleated skirt
princess dress
riding skirt
sack
sari
sarong
sheath
shift
shirtdress
slit skirt
split skirt
sport skirt
straight skirt
strapless dress
sundress
sweater dress
tank dress
T-dress
tea gown
tennis skirt
tent dress
tight skirt
tube dress
tunic dress
tutu
wedding dress/gown
wrap dress

wrap skirt
wraparound

Hosiery
ankle sock
anklet
argyles
athletic sock
bobbysocks
boot sock
boothose
crew sock
dress sheer
fishnet stocking
footlet
garter stocking
halfhose
knee-high
knee-hose
knee-sock
leg-warmer
lisle hose
maillot
mesh stocking
nylons
pantyhose
rayon stocking
seamless stocking
sheer stockings
sheers
shin sock
silk stockings
slouch sock
sock
stocking
stocking hose
stretch stockings
support hose
sweat sock
tights
trunk hose
tube sock
varsity sock

Religious Attire
alb
amice
capuche
cassock
chasuble
cincture
clerical collar
cope
cotta
cowl
dalmatic
Geneva bands

Geneva gown
habit
maniple
miter
mozzetta/mozetta
pallium
rochet
scapular
soutane
stole
surplice
tippet
tunicle
vestment
wimple

Shirts
aloha shirt
basque
blouse
blouson
body shirt
bush shirt
bustier
button-down shirt
camise
camp shirt
coat shirt
dashiki
dickey
doublet
dress shirt
evening shirt
flannel shirt
garibaldi
gipon
habit shirt
hair shirt
halter
Hawaiian shirt
hickory shirt
jersey
long-sleeved shirt
middy blouse
overblouse
plaid shirt
polo shirt
pourpoint
pullover
romper
rugby shirt
sark
shell
shirt-jacket
shirtwaist
short-sleeved shirt
sport shirt

sweatshirt
tank top
tee-shirt/T-shirt
top
tube top
turtleneck
work shirt

Suits
black tie
bodysuit
boiler suit
business suit
camouflage suit
casual suit
cat suit
double-breasted suit
dress suit
flight suit
foul-weather suit
gray flannel suit
jogging suit
jumpsuit/jumper
leisure suit
lounge suit
mod suit
monkey suit
one-piece suit
pants suit
pinstripe suit
playsuit
rain suit
riding suit
sack suit
seersucker suit
shirt suit
shirtwaist suit
single-breasted suit
ski suit
snowsuit
spacesuit
sports suit
summer suit
sun suit
sweat suit
swimsuit
tailored suit
tank suit
three-piece suit
town-and-country
   suit
track suit
tropical suit
trouser suit
tuxedo
tweed suit
two-piece suit

wet suit
zoot suit

Sweaters
bolero
bulky
cable-stitched
   sweater
cardigan
cashmere sweater
crewneck sweater
desk sweater
fisherman's sweater
hand-knit
Irish knit
jersey
knitted sweater
knittie
poor boy sweater
pull-on sweater
pullover
shoulderette
ski sweater
slip-on
slipover
Sloppy Joe
topper
turtleneck sweater
V-neck sweater
woolly

Swimwear
bathing suit
bikini
coverup
jams
maillot
monokini
one-piece bathing
   suit
string bikini
swimming trunks
swimsuit
swimwear
tank suit
thong
trunks
two-piece bathing
   suit
wetsuit

Undergarments
athletic supporter
baggies
bandeau
bikini underpants
bloomers

bodice
body stocking
bodywear
boxer shorts
bra
brassiere
breechclout/
   breechcloth/
   loincloth
briefs
bustle
BVDs
camisole
chastity belt
chemise
chemisette
combination
codpiece
corselet
corset
crinoline
crotchless panties
cup
diaper
drawers
farthingale
foundation garment
G-string
garter belt
girdle
halter-top
intimate apparel
Jockey shorts
jockstrap
knickers
leotard
liberty bodice
lingerie
loincloth
long underwear/long
   johns
merry widow
negligee
padded bra
pannier
pantalets/pantaletts
panties
panty-girdle
pantyhose
pasties
peek-a-boo
peignoir
petticoat
pettipants
push-up bra
scanties

shimmy
shorts
skivvies
slip
sports bra
spencer
step-ins
support garment
tank top
teddy
tee-shirt/T-shirt
thermal underwear
truss
underclothes
underdrawers
underpants
undershirt
undershorts
underskirt
undervest
undies
union suit
unitard
unmentionables
uplift brassiere

Uniforms
blues
clerical dress
clerical garb
continentals
dress blues
dress whites
fatigues
firefighter's uniform
full dress
khaki
military uniform
nauticals
nun's habit
nurse's uniform
olive-drab/OD
police officer's
   uniform
prison uniform
regimentals
sailor suit
school uniform
scrub suit
soldier suit
sports team uniform
stripes
undress
whites ❦

clump of grass: sod
clump of grass, hair: tuffet, tuft, tussock
clumsily handle: botch, bungle
clumsiness: butterfingers
clumsy: awkward, blundering, blunt, bulky, bumbling, bungling, cumbersome, gauche, gawky, ham-handed, heavy-handed, hulky, inept, inexpert, klutzy, lumbering, maladroit, ponderous, stiff, stumbling, tactless, ungainly, unhandy, unwieldy
clumsy in movement: awkward, gawky, uncoordinated, uncouth, ungainly
clumsy person: bumpkin, clodhopper, duffer, galoot, klutz, lummox, oaf, palooka, schlemiel, stumblebum
cluny or alençon: lace
cluster: accumulate, band, bunch, clump, cluther, collection, conglomerate, converge, flock, gather, group, heap, knot, lump, mass, package, swarm, tuft
cluster fruit: grape
cluster of flowers at end of stalk: truss
cluster of threads: tuft
clusters of flowers on a stem: racemes
clutch: catch, clam, clasp, claw, clench, clinch, control, coupling, embrace, fist, grab, grapple, grasp, grip, gripe, hold, nab, retain, seize, snatch, talon
clutter: bustle, confusion, dirty, disarray, disorder, hodgepodge, litter, mess, rummage, strew
coach: advise, adviser, direct, drill, guide, help, instruct, instructor, mentor, prepare, prime, ready, teach, train, tutor; bus, cabin, carriage, stagecoach, vehicle
coach dog's place of origin: Dalmatia
coadjutor: aide
coagulate: clabber, clod, clot, concrete, congeal, cotter, curd, curdle, gel, harden, jell, set, solidify, thicken
coagulates: curds, gels
coagulation: clot
coal: ash, carbon, char, charcoal, cinder, ember, fuel, smut, spark, stoke
RELATED TERMS
coal black: jet
coal-burning stove: brazier
coal deposit: seam
coal distillate: tar
coal grade: briquette, broken, chunk, duff, egg, lump, nut, pea, stove
coal layer: seam
coal lump: cob
coal mine: colliery, drift, seams, shaft, strip

coal mine car: tram
coal mine waste: slag
coal mine, combustible gas occurring naturally in: firedamp
coal miner: collier
coal mining by stripping off soil rather than sinking shaft: strip mining
coal residue used as fuel: coke
coal scuttle: hod
coal size: pea
coal types: anthracite, bituminous, cannel, hard, lignite, peat, pit, soft
coal, bituminous, with much smoke: cannel
coal, dense shiny: anthracite, hard coal
coal, inferior: culm
coal, mineral, with smoky yellow flame: bituminous coal, soft coal
coal, small block of: briquette
coal, smokeless fuel: coke
coal, soft brownish-black: brown coal, lignite
coal, solid residue from burning: clinker ❧

coal-producing: carboniferous
coalesce: amalgamate, associate, blend, combine, fraternize, fuse, incorporate, integrate, join, merge, mix, unite
coalition: alliance, association, bloc, combination, conjunction, faction, federation, fusion, league, merger, syndicate, trust, union
coarse: bawdy, birald, blatant, brutal, callow, common, crass, crude, dirty, disgusting, filthy, foul, gross, gruff, hard, harsh, homespun, immodest, impure, indecent, indelicate, inelegant, inferior, lewd, loose, loud, low, mean, obscene, offensive, rank, raucous, raunchy, raw, repulsive, ribald, rude, scatological, thick, unchaste, uncouth, unpolished, unrefined, vile, vulgar
coarse file: rasp
coarse wheat: emmer
coarse, glazed thread: gimp
coarse, matted wool: shag
coarse, stiff hair: seta
coarsely ground corn: meal
coast: bank, beach, border, land, littoral, seaboard, seashore, seaside, shore, strand; cruise, freewheel, glide, sail, skirt, sled, slide
coast feature: bleach, cave, cliff, dune, headland, lagoon, marsh, stack
coast indenture: cove

COAST GUARD RANK

Commissioned Officers
Admiral
Vice Admiral
Rear Admiral (upper half)
Rear Admiral (lower half)
Captain
Commander
Lieutenant Commander
Lieutenant
Lieutenant Junior Grade
Ensign

Enlisted Personnel
Master Chief Petty Officer
Senior Chief Petty Officer
Chief Petty Officer
Petty Officer First Class
Petty Officer Second Class
Petty Officer Third Class
Seaman
Seaman Apprentice
Seaman Recruit ❧

coastal inlet: estuary, firth
coastal sea inlet, narrow and between steep cliffs: fjord
coasts, concerning: littoral
coat: cape, chesterfield, cloak, cutaway, duster, garment, jacket, overcoat, parka, reefer, robe, swallowtail, tails, toga, tunic, vesture; rind
coat fabric: tweed
coat food with flour, etc., to: dredge
coat in one piece with sleeves: raglan
coat lapel: revers
coat metal for protection: anodize
coat of arms: crest, ensign, heraldry, insignia, pennant, shield
coat of arms, person entitled to: armiger
coat of arms, possessing: armigerous
coat of arms, shield bearing: escutcheon
coat of arms, tunic emblazoned with: tabard
coat of seed: tegmen
coat on material, to put a thin layer or: laminate, veneer
coat parts: collar, cuff, lapel, pocket, sleeve
coat with gelatinous or glutinous substance: size
coat with hood and fastened with toggles: duffle coat
coat with plaster, cement: parget, render
coat with soft, adhesive substance: daub

coat with tails: cutaway
coat worn over other garments, sleeveless: cloak, mantle
coat, living: bark, bloom, fur, hair, hide, husk, integument, mantle, membrane, pelage, pellicle, pelt, rind, shell, tegument, wool
coat, mammal: pelage
coat, nonliving: crust, daub, enamel, glaze, laminate, layer, overlay, plaster, plate, veneer
coated with carbon: sooty
coating: blanket, covering, crust, film, glaze, layer, patina, skin, veneer
coating of substance on surface of solid or liquid: adsorption
coating on new coins, waxy: bloom
coating on plums, etc., waxy: bloom
coating, membrane, or film on substance: pellicle
coats of arms, concerning: armorial
coats of arms, profession, study, or art involved with: heraldry
coax: beg, beguile, blandish, cajole, con, dupe, entice, flatter, hook, implore, induce, influence, inveigle, lure, manipulate, persuade, press, soothe, tease, tempt, urge, wheedle
cobalt: azure, blue, element
cobbler: botcher, chuckler, dessert, nag, pie, saddler, shoemaker, soler
cobra: asp, naja, snake, uraeus
cobweb: fiber, gossamer, labryinth, mesh, net, network, spiderweb, trap
cobweb mesh: gossamer
cocaine, streetwise: snow
coccyx: tailbone
cock: capon, chanticleer, chicken, fowl, rooster
cock-and-bull story: canard, fabrication, falsehood, fib, lie, untruth, whopper, yarn
cock spur in cockfights: gaff
cockapoos: dogs
cockatoo feature: crest
cockchafer: oakweb, oakwes
cocked (hat): arake
cocked items: hats
cocked or cracked: half
cockeyed: absurd, alop, askew, awry, crooked, drunk, goofy, inebriated, topsy-turvy, intoxicated, lopsided, ludicrous, tilted, weird
cockle: bivalve, mollusk, pucker, ripple, shell, wrinkle
cockpit: cabin, compartment, pit, quarters

cockpit transparent cover or window: canopy
cocksure: arrogant, brash, certain, cocky, conceited, confident, positive, sure, vain
cocktail: appetizer, Bloody Mary, boilermaker, daiquiri, drink, gimlet, highball, horse, Manhattan, margarita, martini, Molotov, piña colada, pink lady, sidecar, stinger, wine
cocktail drink made of tequila and salt around the rim of the glass: margarita
cocktail garnishment: olive
cocktail hour: happy hour
cocktail of sweet vermouth, whiskey, bitters: Manhattan
cocktail with onion: Gibson
cocky: arrogant, brash, cocksure, conceited, crouse, egotistical, hotdogging, jaunty, pert, presumptuous
cocoa: bean, beverage, brown, chocolate, hot
coconspirator: ally
coconut cookie: macaroon
coconut family: arecaceae, palmae
coconut husk fiber: coir
coconut meat, dried: copra
coconut product: milk, oil
cocoon: covering, encase, envelop, pod, swaddle, wrap
cocoon, pupa in: chrysalis
cod kin: hake
coda: end
coddle: baby, brew, caress, cook, cuddle, fondle, humor, indulge, mollycoddle, nurse, pamper, pet, poach, simmer, spoil
code: canon, cipher, codex, custom, ethics, instructions, law, precept, regulation, secret, signal, standards
code decipherment: cryptanalysis
code for radio operators, pilots: phonetic alphabet
code for words, Alpha through Zulu, in communication: alphabet code
code of laws, complete: legal code, pandects
code signaled with flags: semaphore
code talk where first consonant is put at end of word and "ay" is added: pig Latin
code types: area, blue, book, Morse, name, penal, red, zip
code, to break a: decipher, decode, decrypt
code, to put into: encipher
coded message decoded: plaintext

coded writing: cryptogram, cryptography
codes, study of: cryptography, cryptology
codfish, young: scrod
codger: crank, dodo, eccentric, elderly, fellow, galoot, miser
codicil: addition, appendix, modifier, postcript, rider, sequel, supplement
codify: arrange, categorize, classify, condense, digest, index, order, rank, summarize, systematize
coerce: blackmail, bulldoze, bully, compel, constrain, cow, dominate, dragoon, drive, enforce, extort, force, intimidate, make, menace, pressure, push, repress, restrain, restrict, suppress, terrorize, threaten, urge
coercion: compulsion, constraint, duress, force, intimidation, persuasion, violence
coercion, feeling: duress
coexistence: conjunction, harmony, order, peace
coffee: café, cappuccino, chicory, decaffeinated, demitasse, drip, espresso, instant, java, mocha
RELATED TERMS
coffee bean sediment: grounds, grouts
coffee cake with fruits and nuts: kuchen
coffee container, glass with black rim and top: hottle
coffee cup, holder for a handleless: zarf
coffee-flavored: mocha
coffee mixed or topped with steamed milk or cream, espresso: cappuccino
coffee or espresso, small cup of strong: demitasse
coffee or other drink with caffeine: stimulant
coffee pot: urn
coffee served with milk: café au lait
coffee stimulant substance: caffeine
coffee substitute or additive, plant used as: chicory
coffee with caffeine removed: decaffeinated
coffee with frothed milk or cream: cappuccino
coffee with milk: café au lait
coffee, black: café noir
coffee, high-quality: mocha
coffee, in a diner: java

COCKTAILS AND MIXED DRINKS

Adam and Eve
a day at the beach
after dinner cocktail
Alabama slammer
Alaska cocktail
alexander
Allegheny
Americana
angel's kiss
Bacardi cocktail
B & B
Bahama mama
banshee
Basin Street
bay breeze
beachcomber
bee stinger
Bellini
Bermuda Rose
Betsy Ross
between the sheets
B-52
bijou cocktail
black Maria
Black Russian
black velvet
bloody Caesar
Bloody Mary
blue Hawaiian
blue lagoon
blue margarita
blue whale
bocce ball
Bombay cocktail
Boston cocktail
bourbon and water
bourbon on the rocks
brandy Alexander
brandy fizz
brandy smash
Bronx cocktail
buck's fizz
bull and bear
bull's eye
bull's milk
bullshot
buttered rum

Cape Codder
caudle
cement mixer
champagne cocktail
champagne cooler
Chapel Hill
cherry blossom
chi-chi
clamato cocktail
classic cocktail
cobbler
coffee grasshopper
coffee old-fashioned
cooler
Cooperstown
    cocktail
Cuba libre
daiquiri
Daisy Dueller
damn-the-weather
    cocktail
death by chocolate
depth charge
dingo
dirty banana
dixie julep
dream cocktail
dry martini
eggnog
English highball
Fifth Avenue
firefly
fizz
flip
foxy lady
frappé
French connection
frozen daiquiri
frozen Margarita
fuzzy navel
gentleman's cocktail
Georgia mint julep
Georgia peach
Gibson
gimlet
gin and bitters
gin and sin

gin and tonic
gin fizz
gin highball
gin rickey
gin sling
gin sour
gluhwein
godfather
godmother
golden Cadillac
grasshopper
greyhound
grog
Harvard cocktail
Harvard cooler
Harvey Wallbanger
highball
hole-in-one
Hollywood
Honolulu cocktail
hot buttered rum
hot toddy
hurricane
income tax cocktail
Indian summer
Irish coffee
Jack Rose
kamikaze
Kentucky blizzard
Kentucky cocktail
King Alphonse
Kir
Kir royale
liberty cocktail
Long Island iced tea
look out below
Louisville lady
lover's kiss
madras
mai-tai
Manhattan
Margarita
martini
Mary Pickford
    cocktail
melon ball
merry widow

Mexican coffee
mimosa
mind eraser
mint julep
morning cocktail
Moscow mule
mudslide
Narragansett
negus
New York cocktail
nutcracker
nutty professor
old-fashioned
orange blossom
orgeat
passion mimosa
peach sangaree
peppermint pattie
Peter Pan cocktail
Pimm's cup
piña colada
pink lady
pink squirrel
planter's punch
platinum blonde
posset
pousse cafa
prairie oyster
presbyterian
Princeton cocktail
punch
quaalude
Ramos gin fizz
red death
rickey
Rob Roy
rum and coke
rum cooler
rusty nail
salty dog
sangre
sangria
San Juan cooler
Scarlett O'Hara
scotch and soda
scotch on the rocks
screwdriver

seabreeze
Seven and Seven
sex on the beach
shandy
shrub
sidecar cocktail
Singapore sling
slam dunk
slippery nipple
sloe gin fizz
smash
snake bite
snowball
sombrero
soother cocktail
southern lady
southern peach
spritzer
stinger
syllabub/sillabub
Tang
tequila sunrise
Thanksgiving special
thoroughbred cooler
toasted almond
toddy
Tom and Jerry
Tom Collins
to the moon
tropical special
velvet hammer
virgin Mary
vodka and tonic
vodka gimlet
vodka martini
Wassail
whiskey sour
white lady
White Russian
white satin
white spider
wild thing
wine cooler
wu-wu
Yale cocktail
zombie ❦

---

coffee, small cup of strong, black:
    demitasse
coffee, strong, brewed by forcing
    steam through ground beans:
    espresso
coffeepot basket holding grounds:
    biggin

coffeepot with hot water forced up
    through central tube to filter back
    down: percolator ❦

coffer: box, caisson, case, casket, chest,
    depository, hutch, strongbox, trea-
    sury, trunk

coffin: box, casing, casket, pall, pine
    box, sarcophagus, urn
coffin carrier at funeral: pallbearer
coffin of stone: sarcophagus
coffin platform: bier, catafalque
cog: cajole, cam, cheat, connect, de-
    ceive, fang, gear, lie, prong, subordi-

nate, tenon, tooth, wedge, wheedle, wheel

cogent: convincing, effective, forcible, influential, justified, legitimate, momentous, persuasive, potent, powerful, solid, strong, trenchant, valid

cogitate: brainstorm, consider, contemplate, deliberate, imagine, meditate, mull, muse, plan, ponder, reason, reflect, ruminate, speculate, study, think

cognate: affiliate, akin, alike, allied, close, common, kindred, related, similar, universal

cognizance: attention, awareness, bearing, cognition, grasp, heed, insight, jurisdiction, knowledge, mark, notice, observation, perception, recognition, regard

cognizant: alive, apprehensive, awake, aware, conscious, enlightened, hip, informed, intelligent, knowing, sensible, versed

cognomen: epithet, handle, moniker, name, nickname, surname, title

cognoscente: authority, connoisseur, critic, expert, insider, judge, specialist

cohere: agree, bind, blend, cement, cleave, cling, combine, concur, conform, connect, dovetail, fit, glue, join, relate, solidify, stick, suit, unite

coherent: clear, logical, lucid, orderly, rational, sound, understandable

cohort: accomplice, ally, associate, buddy, chum, comrade, fellow, friend, mate, partner, sidekick

coif: afro, arrange, cap, cover, hairdo, headdress, hood, skullcap

coiffure: afro, beehive, braids, buzz, da, dreadlocks, dreads, flattop, haircut, hairdo, hairstyle, perm, pigtails, ponytail, shag, trim

coiffure designer: stylist

coil: confusion, convolution, corkscrew, curl, difficulty, encircle, entwine, fuss, intertwine, loop, ringlet, roll, rotate, scroll, skein, spiral, spire, tense, tumult, twine, twist, whorl, wind, windup, wreathe

coil of yarn, thread, rope: hank, skein

coil on shell: volution

coiled: helicoid, tortile

coiled or ring-shaped: circinate

coiled together: convolute, convoluted

coin: besant, bezant, bezzo, bob, caramel, carolus, cash, castellano, cent, change, chink, currency, cuyne, dan-

diprat, daric, denarius, die, dime, disme, doit, doubloon, ducat, eagle, florin, groat, groschen, krugerrand, lap, louis d'or, metal, mint, moidore, nickel, noble, obol, ora, ori, pina, quarter, quoin, rap, real, rial, rosa, sequin, sesterce, solidus, sou, sovereign, specie, stater, striver, taler, tanner, tara, thaler, tickey, token, zecchino

coin blank: flan, planchet

coin chest at a mint: pyx

coin chute: slot

coin collecting: numismatics

coin collector: numismatist

coin fake: brummagem, counterfeit

coin grooves on edge: engrailing, fluting, milling, reeding

coin "heads" side: obverse

coin-in-the-slot restaurant of yore: automat

coin inscription: legend

coin part without lettering or design: flan

coin parts: head, obverse, tail, verso

coin space below central design, giving date and place of engraving: exergue

coin "tails" side: reverse, verso

coin unit of value: denomination

coin word: mint, neologize

coinage: coined, invention, mintage, neologism

coincide: accord, agree, coexist, concur, correspond, harmonize, jibe, sync, synchronize, tally

coincidence: accident, chance, concourse, concurrence, conjunction, fate, fluke, parallelism

coincidence in pitch: unison

coincidence of events that seem to be meaningfully related: synchronicity

coincident: ancillary, attending, concomitant, concurring, consonant, contemporary, coordinate, simultaneous

coincidental: accidental, casual, chance, circumstantial, unintentional, unplanned

coinciding in scope, meaning, time: coextensive, congruent, coterminous

coinciding or simultaneous occurrence: concurrence, conjunction

coined money: specie

coining money, engraved piece used for: die

coins and medals, study of: numismatics

coin's circular inscription: circumscription

coins, paper cylinder of: rouleau

coins, revenue from the minting of: seigniorage

colander: bowl-shaped, sieve, sifter, strainer, utensil

cold: algid, arctic, bleak, brisk, chilled, chilly, cool, crisp, freezing, frigid, frosty, frozen, gelid, glacial, hyperborean, nippy, penetrating, raw, refrigerated, shivers, unheated, wintry; flu, virus

cold Adriatic wind: bora

cold and austere: clinical

cold and gloomy in temperament: saturnine

cold and reserved: aloof

cold and unemotional: aloof, apathetic, distant, impassive, indifferent, insensible, phlegmatic, reserved, spiritless, unemotional, unfeeling, unfriendly

cold-blooded: brutal, callous, cruel, diabolical, evil, heartless, insensitive, poikilothermic, ruthless, satanic, savage, unfeeling

cold cuts, pickles, etc., informally: deli

cold feet: alarm, cowardice, doubt, fear, fright, nerveless, panic

cold or chilly: algid

cold plus wind: windchill factor

cold shoulder: ignore, refuse, scorn, shun, slight, snub

cold sore: herpes labialis

cold soup: gazpacho

cold spell: snap

cold sweat: anxiety, fear, jitters, nervousness, panic, shock, trepidation, worry

cold turkey: quitting, stop, withdrawal

cold water, shock of: curglaff

cold-weather response: brr

cold, abnormally low body temperature from exposure to: hypothermia

cold, freezing: hyperborean, icy

cold, head: coryza

coldlike condition of inflamed mucous membranes: catarrh

colic: bellyache, gripe, pain, stomachache

coliseum: amphitheater, arena, bowl, hippodrome, stadium, theater

collaborate: aid, assist, conspire, cooperate, interface, join

collaborating: colluding, in cahoots

collaborator with enemy: quisling

collapse: breakdown, buckle, cave, crash, crumple, debacle, deflate, disintegrate, downfall, failure, fall, fold, founder, prostration, ruin, ruination, topple, wilt, wreck

collapse inward violently: implode

collapse or sink down: cave in, founder, subside

collapse upon itself: telescope

collapsible plan, situation, structure: house of cards

collar: apprehend, assemble, capture, catch, chain, gill, grab, nab, nail, order, seize, shackle, sort, tackle, tree; band, Eton, jabot, neckband, necklace, neckpiece, ruff, torque, turtleneck, vandyke

collar necklace: choker

collar necklace of twisted metal: torque

collar piece to attach to leash: terret

collar stiffener: stay

collar, high stiff: mandarin

collar, ornamental: gorget

collarbone: clavicle

collate: arrange, bestow, bracket, compare, integrate, sort, verify

collateral: added, ancillary, bond, concomitant, guarantee, indirect, pledge, secondary, security, subordinate, subsidiary

collateral evidence: admincle

collation: meal, repast

colleague: aide, ally, assistant, associate, buddy, cohort, compatriot, confrere, consort, crony, partner, teammate

collect: accrue, accumulate, acquire, aggregate, amass, assemble, call, compile, congregate, contract, flock, garner, gather, get, glean, gropu, hoard, impound, levy, muster, obtain, pile, pool, raise, save, sheave, stockpile, tax

collect and gather: embody, garner

collect money: pass the hat

collect on a surface: adsorb

collected: aggregate, calm, clustered, composed, confident, cool, cool as a cucumber, levelheaded, peaceful, poised, quiet, serene, sober, unflappable

collected literary excerpts: analects

collection: acquisition, aggregate, ana, anthology, array, assemblage, assembly, assortment, batch, bevy, bundle, caboodle, cancionero, clan, cluster, collation, conger, crowd, gathering, group, mass, medley, olio, omnibus, pile, reportory, set, sorite, store, suite

collection during religious ceremony: offertory

collection of anecdotes: ana

collection of complete writings of author: corpus, oeuvre

collection of extracts to teach language: chrestomathy

collection of hay: bale

collection of miscellaneous items to be sold in one lot: job lot

collection of offerings at church: offertory

collection of Old Norse poems: edda

collection of performances: repertory

collection of poetry: epos

collection of things: congeries

collection of treasure: trove

collection of various items: accumulation, assemblage, compendium, congeries, conglomeration, miscellany, motley, potpourri, stockpile

collection of various writings: anthology, chrestomathy, collectanea, omnibus

collection, heterogenous: conglomerate

collective: aggregate, composite, consolidated, cumulative, group, joint, multiple, mutual, shared

collective farm, Israel: kibbutz

collective farm, Russia: kolkhoz

collector of antiques: antiquary

collector of art: connoisseur, virtuoso

collector of books: bibliophile

collector of butterflies, moths: lepidopterist

collector of coins, money, medals: numismatist

collector of matchbooks or matchboxes: phillumenist

collector of postcards: deltiologist

collector of stamps, postmarks: philatelist

college: academy, institution, lycee, school, university

college athlete's nonvarsity year for extended eligibility: redshirt

college dining hall: cafeteria, refectory

college education: tertiary education

college enrollment: matriculation

college financial officer: bursar

college first-year student: freshman

college fourth-year student: senior

college girl: coed

college graduate: alumna, alumnae, alumni, alumnus, bachelor, doctor, master

college second-year student: sophomore

college terms: academic, alma mater, class, collegiate, fraternity, lecture, major, minor, semester, seminar, sorority, term, tutorial

college third-year student: junior

collide: bang, bump, carom, clash, conflict, crash, disagree, hit, impinge, jolt, meet, strike

collision: accident, blow, butt, clash, contact, crackup, crash, encounter, impact, insurance, pileup, shock, smashup

collocate: arrange, collect, compile, gather, parallel, place, position

colloid: gel

colloquial: casual, common, conversational, familiar, informal, ordinary, particular, plain, vernacular

colloquy: chat, conference, conversation, converse, debate, dialogue, discussion, parley, talk

collude: abet, collaborate, connive, conspire, devise, plot, scheme

collusion: agreement, cahoots, complicity, connivance, conspiracy, fraud, graft, scheme

colon: colonist, farmer; intestine; line, punctuation

colonial: immigrant, pilgrim, pioneering

colonic or ileac: intestinal

colonization: settlement

colonize: establish, found, gather, migrate, populate, settle, transplant

colonnade: stoa

colony: band, community, dominion, group, outpost, province, satellite, settlement, swarm

colony type: penal

colophon: device, inscription

color: cast, dye, hue, paint, pigment, shade, stain, tincture, tinge, tint, tone; flag

color band on organism: fascia

color blending or gradation: sfumato

color blindness: achromatism, achromatopsia, daltonism, dichromatism, insensitive, monochromatism, oblivious

color blindness with confusion of green and red: daltonism, protanopia

color blindness with inability to see blue, yellow: tritanopia

color blindness, complete: monochromatism

color change: versicolor

color changing: iridescent, opalescent

color-changing lizard: chameleon

color knotted cloth: tie-dye

color matter mixed with material to form paint: pigment

color or shade: hue, tincture, tint

color permanently: tint

color primary: black, blue, red, white, yellow

color range: palette

color rings: areolas

color sensation produced by another sensation such as hearing: synesthesia

color separator: prism

color to make a hue, percentage of: saturation

color, achromatic: beige, black, gray, neutral, white

color, concerning: chromatic

color, light and delicate: pastel

color, secondary: green, orange, purple

color, slight trace of: cast, tinge

color, slight variation in: nuance

color, study of: chromatics

color, to spread with: suffuse

colorant: dye, pigment

colored: biased, bigoted, distorted, dyed, hued, misrepresented, painted, prejudiced, prismatic, stained, tinted

colored differently in various parts: particolored

colored flare: fusee

colored flower part: corolla

colored for identification purposes: color-coded

colored lithographs: chromos

colored minerals: spinels

colored ring: areola

colorful: animated, bright, brilliant, dynamic, flashy, gay, glamorous, jazzy, loud, psychedelic, vivid

coloring: coloration, complexion, guise, influence, quality, shading

coloring agent: dyer, smalt, toner

coloring chemical of body: melanin, pigment

coloring of animal, referring to protective: apatetic

coloring parts of cloth, technique for: tie-dye

coloring that protects animal: cryptic coloring

colorless: achromatic, albino, anemic, ashen, blanched, blank, bleached, drab, dull, faded, lifeless, neutral, pale, pallid, plain, prosaic, transparent, wan, white

colorless gas: argon, methane

colorless or neutral: achromatic

colorless or pale: pallid

colorless, odorless chemical: alum

colors mixed to make white or gray: complementary colors

colors of rainbow, changes in: iridescence

colors of the rainbow, having all: multicolored, prismatic

colors, having a variety of: motley, particolored, pied, polychrome, varicolored, variegated

colors, having blotches of different: piebald, pinto

colors, pertaining to: chromatic

colors, range of rainbow: spectrum

colossal: behemothic, big, enormous, gigantic, grand, great, huge, humongous, immense, mammoth, monstrous, monumental, vast

colt: beginner, filly, fledgling, foal, gun, horse, pistol, revolver, sapling, yearling, youngster

column: brace, file, formation, line, monolith, parade, pilaster, pillar, post, procession, row, shaft, stack, support, totem; article

column or page width: measure

column or pedestal base: socle

column or pillar, top part of: capital

column parts: base, capital, shaft

column shaped like female: caryatid

column types: Corinthian, Doric, Egyptian, Gothic, Ionic, Roman

column used, style of architecture based on: order

columnist: commentator, correspondent, journalist, newspaperman, newspaperperson, newspaperwoman

columns or tables, arranged in: tabular

columns, regularly spaced: colonnade

coma: blackout, insensibility, lethargy, sleep, slumber, somnolence, stupor, torpor, trance, unconsciousness

comatose: catatonic, drowsy, drugged, insensible, lazy, lethargic, listless, soporific, torpid, unconscious

comb: brush, card, clean, curry, groom, probe, rake, ransack, search, smooth, sweep, tease

comb for horse: currycomb

comb hair from ends toward scalp: tease

comb on animal, like wattle: caruncle

combat: action, argument, battle, bout, brush, clash, conflict, contend, contest, controversy, cope, duel, encounter, fight, fray, joust, oppose, repel, resist, scuffle, strife, struggle, war, withstand

combat between two persons: duel

combat between knights on horseback: joust, tilting match

combat pilot: ace

combatant: battler, champion, dueler, fighter, serviceman, serviceperson, servicewoman, soldier

combative: agonistic, antagonistic, bellicose, belligerent, hawkish, militant, pugnacious, scrappy

combed wool: carded

combination: affiliation, aggregate, alliance, amalgam, association, blend, bloc, brew, cartel, coalescence, coalition, combine, combo, composite, composition, composure, compound, concoction, confederacy, conjunction, consort, ensemble, faction, gang, key, lock, merger, mix, pact, party, pool, ring, synthesis, unification, union

combination of events, circumstances: conjuncture

combination of substances: amalgam

combine: add, affiliate, amalgamate, bind, blend, coalesce, combination, compound, condense, conjoin, conjure, consolidate, construct, cooperate, couple, dub, fuse, group, intermix, join, marry, merge, merger, mingle, mix, pool, splice, unite

combine and reconcile differing philosophies: syncretize

combine in proper order: collocate

combine or merge: incorporate, meld

combine with gas: aerate

combined action for greater effect: synergism, synergy

combined interests or corporations: amalgamation, consolidation

combines efforts or resources: pools

combining capacity of atom or radical: valence

combining separate elements to coherent whole: synthesis

comblike: ctenoid

combustible: burnable, excitable, explosive, fiery, flammable, fuel, gas, inflammable, volatile

combustible heap: pyre

combustible material: fuel

combustible pile: pyre

combustible substance: tinder

combustion: agitation, burning, candescence, consuming, cremation, fire, heat, ignition, incineration, oxidation, tumult, volatile

come: accrue, advance, amount, appear, approach, arise, arrive, befall,

COMBAT SPORTS AND MARTIAL ARTS

aikido	kenipo
arm wrestling/wrist wrestling/Indian wrestling	kick boxing
boxing	kung fu
capoeira	ninjutsu
fencing	professional wrestling
freestyle wrestling	savate
Greco-Roman wrestling	self-defense
Greek boxing	sumo wrestling
haphido	tae bo
Iaido	tae kwon do
jousting	t'ai chi
judo	tang soo do
jujitsu/jiujitsu	Thai kick boxing
karate	wrestling
kendo	wu shu/wushu ❦

develop, emanate, emerge, enter, extend, grow, happen, loom, mature, occur, proceed, reach, spring, transpire

come about: happen, occur, result

come across: discover, find, notice, uncover

come after: ensue, follow, succeed

come again: revisit

come along: accompany, attend, improve, mend, progress, recover

come apart: detach, disintegrate, rend, separate

come around: rally, slue

come at: achieve, attack, charge, grasp, reach, rush

come before: antecede, antedate, precede, predate, sooner

come before in time, order, rank: precede

come between: alienate, divide, interpose, meddle, part, separate

come clean: acknowledge, admit, confess, fess up, reveal

come forth: emanate

come forward: appear, emerge, volunteer

come from: arise, derive, emanate, result, stem

come in: arrive, enter, finish, intrude

come in first: best

come in third: show

come into office: accede

come into one's own: blossom

come into open: debouch, emerge

come into sight: emerge, loom

come into view: appear, emerge, show, surface

come into view ominously: loom

come last: lag

come off: break, click, develop, severed, succeed, transpire

come-on: bait, decoy, inducement, lure, seduction, teaser, temptation

come-on gesture: wink

come out: appear, conclude, disclosed, emerge, leak, protrude, revealed

come out of a toaster: pop up

come through: accomplish, achieve, deliver, endure, persist, prevail, succeed, survive, weather the storm

come to: awaken, recover, recuperate, total, waken

come to pass: betide, eventuate, happen, occur, transpire, turn out

come to terms: agree

come together: assemble, collide, gather, join, meet, unite

come upon: discover, find, identify, locate

comeback: answer, quip, rally, rebound, recovery, repartee, reply, response, resurgence, return, revival, triumph

comedian: actor, amuser, card, clown, comic, entertainer, fool, humorist, jester, joker, prankster, wag, wisecracker, wit

comedian's partner: stooge, straight man

comedown: anticlimax, collapse, crash, descend, dive, fall, land, letdown, reduce, setback, worsen

comedy: burlesque, farce, humor, revue, satire, sitcom, slapstick, travesty

comedy missile: coconut cream pie

comedy, boisterous: slapstick

comedy, exaggerated: farce

comeliness: prettiness

comely: agreeable, attractive, beautiful, becoming, bonny, charming, decent, fair, good-looking, gorgeous, graceful, gratifying, handsome, lovely, not hard to look at, personable, pleasing, pretty, proper, stunning, suitable

comestible: eatable, edible, esculent, food, provisions, victual

comet head center: nucleus

comet head, cloud around nucleus of: coma

comet, point farthest from sun in orbit of: aphelion

comet, point nearest sun in orbit of: perihelion

comfort: aid, alleviate, assist, cheer, console, ease, encourage, endure, enliven, gladden, help, pleasure, reassure, refresh, relief, relieve, serenity, solace, soothe, strengthen, succor, support, sympathize

comfort and relieve: allay, alleviate, assuage, palliate

comfort or sympathy: consolation, solace

comfort with refreshment and warmth: couther

comfortable: acceptable, adequate, ample, at home, cheerful, comfy, complacent, contented, cozy, easy, gratifying, pleasant, relaxed, rich, satisfied, snug, suitable, wealthy, well-off, well-to-do

comfortable and easy: cushy

comfortable and roomy: commodious

comfortable for living: habitable

comfortable spot: niche

comforter: afghan, blanket, cover, pacifier, puff, quilt, scarf, sympathizer

comforting: anodyne
comforts: amenities
comfy: homey, snug, soft
comic: card, comedian, droll, funny, humorist, ironic, joker, laughable, ludicrous, wag, wit
comic opera: bouffe, opera buffa
comic parody: spoof
comic playlet: skit
comic verse: doggerel
comical: amusing, capricious, crazy, droll, entertaining, farcical, funny, goofy, humorous, jocular, laughable, ludicrous, ridiculous, silly, ticklish, whimsical, witty, zany
coming: advent, approaching, arrival, certain, deserved, future, imminent, impending, likely, next, on the way, progressing, promising
coming from without: extraneous
coming in continually: influx
coming into existence: incipient
coming out: debut
coming together: concourse, confluence, crowd
coming up: ahead
comma: interval, mark, pause, punctuation
comma, error in use: comma fault, comma splice
comma, used much: close punctuation
command: adjure, appoint, authority, beck, behest, beken, bid, bidding, call, charge, commission, compel, conquer, control, demand, dictate, direct, direction, domineer, duty, edict, enjoin, exact, expertise, force, govern, impose, influence, instruction, knowledge, manage, mandate, master, might, officer, ordain, order, ordinance, power, prescribe, proclamation, regulate, request, restrain, rule, supremacy, sway, tell
command a horse: geed
command level: echelon
command or order: enjoin
command post: helm
command, old style: hest
commanded: bade
commandeer: appropriate, arrogate, confiscate, grab, hijack, seize, snatch, take, usurp
commandeer transportation: hijack
commander: boss, captain, chief, commandant, czar, emperor, general, guru, head, kingpin, leader, master, officer, ruler

commander of King David's army: Amasa
commanding: authoritative, magisterial, ordering
commandment: commanded, edict, law, mandates, mitzvah, order, precept, rule
commandment word: thou, unto
comme ci, comme ça: so-so
commemorate: celebrate, hail, honor, immortalize, keep, memorialize, observe, remember, salute, solemnize
commemoration: memorial
commemorative pillar: stele
commence: arise, begin, found, inaugurate, incept, initiate, launch, open, originate, set in, spring, start
commencement: admission, alpha, beginning, celebration, dawn, genesis, graduation, kickoff, onset, opening, outset, start
commencement headgear: mortarboard
commend: acclaim, adorn, applaud, approve, bequeath, bestow, boost, commit, compliment, entrust, eulogize, extol, give, ingratiate, laud, praise, recommend, relegate, support, yield
commendable: deserving, excellent, exemplary, honorable, laudable, notable, praiseworthy, worthy
commendation: acclamation, accolade, award, honor, plaudit, tribute
commendatory: laudatory
commensurate: adequate, appropriate, balanced, corresponding, equal, equivalent, even, parallel, proportional, square
comment: animadvert, annotation, commentary, criticize, discourse, discuss, editorial, explain, expound, illustrate, interject, notate, note, observe, opinion, reflection, remark, say, statement, talk, wisecrack, word
comment in book margins: annotation, marginalia
comment in interruptive way: interject, interpose
comment in passing: obiter dictum
comment on another's action or choice: second-guess
comment on in detail: descant, discourse, expound
comment, object getting: conversation piece
comment, very critical: animadversion
commentary: account, analysis, criti-

cism, critique, exegesis, explanation, explanatory note, exposition, gloss, review, treatise
commentary on text: gloss, scholium
commentary, formal: discourse, disquisition
commentator: analyst, annotator, announcer, columnist, correspondent, critic, expositor, observer, reporter, writer
commenting character: raisonneur
comments explaining a book, introductory: preface
comments written at the beginning of a book: introduction
commerce: barter, business, exchange, industry, marketing, retailing, trade, traffic
commercial: advertisement, exploited, mercantile, popular
commingle: amalgamate, blend, combine, fuse, integrate, join, merge, mix, unite
commiserate: compassionate, console, empathy, pity, sympathize
commiseration: empathy, pity
commission: agency, allowance, appoint, assignment, authorize, board, brokerage, charge, charter, command, compensation, consign, constitute, delegate, demand, deputize, dispensation, duty, establish, fee, hire, instruction, license, mandate, mission, obligation, office, ordain, order, payment, permit, royalty, stipend, task, trust, warrant, work
commissions and costs to purchaser of securities: load
commit: allot, assign, bequeath, bind, command, confide, consign, delegate, entrust, give, invest, perpetrate, place, practice, pursue, refer, relegate, write down
commit crime: perpetrate
commit irrevocably to course of action: cross the Rubicon
commit perjury: lie
commitment: bond, duty, guarantee, obligation, pledge, promise, warranty
committed: earnest, engage
committee: board, body, bureau, council, gathering, group, junta, jury, panel, trustees
committee business: agenda
committee for determining actions to follow: steering committee
committee for specific purpose: ad hoc committee

committee, number of people required for a vote by: quorum

commode: bathroom, cap, chiffonier, cupboard, dresser, toilet, washstand

commodious: ample, big, capacious, comfortable, convenient, fit, handy, roomy, serviceable, spacious, suitable, wide

commodities of exchange: market

commodity: article, asset, chattel, goods, lot, possession, product, quantity, staple, stock, ware

common: average, banal, base, bourgeois, cheap, coarse, conventional, current, customary, daily, everyday, familiar, frequent, general, generic, habitual, hackneyed, informal, joint, mean, mediocre, monotonous, mutual, normal, ordinary, ornery, plain, plebeian, popular, prevailing, prevalent, regular, shared, stale, trifling, trite, trivial, typical, universal, unrefined, usual, vulgar

common and frequent: predominant, prevailing, prevalent, regnant, rife, widespread

common and prevalent in area: endemic

common and shared: joint, mutual, reciprocal

common boundary or connection: interface

common commodity: necessity, staple

common conjunction: and, but, or

common contraction: aren't, didn't, hasn't, isn't, it's, tis

common everyday speech: vernacular, vulgate

common fund: pool

common good: commonweal

common law: custom, precedent, system, tradition

common name of organism: trivial name

common notion: received idea

common number or range in mathematical set: mode

common opinion or position: consensus

common or standard speech of people: demotic, vernacular, vulgate

common people: commonalty, hoi polloi, lowest common denominator, populace, proletariat, ruck

common people of Rome: plebeian, plebs

common people, concerning: demotic

common person indifferent to culture, style: philistine

common sense: judgment, mother wit, nous, prudence, realistic, reason, sensible, soundness, wisdom

common stock earnings affected by interest, dividends: leverage

commoner: citizen, civilian, peasant, pleb, plebe, student

commonly: frequently, generally, often, popular, regularly, routinely, usually, widely

commonplace: banal, clichéd, daily, dull, everyday, exoteric, garden, hackneyed, humdrum, mainstream, mundane, obvious, ordinary, plain, prosaic, stale, stereotyped, tolerable, trite, trivial, truism, uneventful, unimportant, usual, worn

commonplace and basic: bread-and-butter

commonplace and dull: stodgy

commonplace idea: cliché

commonplace statement: platitude

commonplace theme: motif, topos

commonwealth: community, nation, people, public, republic, res publica, society, state

commotion: ado, agitation, alarm, brouhaha, bustle, clatter, confusion, disorder, disturbance, excitement, flap, flare, flurry, fluster, fracas, fray, fuss, heat, hurry, mutiny, pandemonium, pother, racket, revolt, riot, row, stir, storm, tempest, to-do, tumult, turbulence, turmoil, unrest, upheaval, uprising, uproar

communal bath: hot tub

commune: advise, area, chat, collective, communicate, confer, consult, conversation, converse, cooperative, debate, discuss, divulge, kibbutz, parley, participate, reveal, share, talk

communicable: catching, contagious, expansive, infectious, pandemic, sociable, talkative, transferable, transmittable

communicate: answer, bestow, broadcast, converse, convey, correspond, disclose, dictate, divulge, impart, inform, interface, network, reach, reveal, signal, talk, tell, write

communicate with others, unable to: incommunicado

communication: bulletin, communiqué, connection, contact, conversation, directive, ESP, exchange, ideas, intelligence, language, letter, link, message, news, note, radiogram, report, telegram

communication between different groups within organization: liaison

communication between minds: telepathy

communication by beams sent through glass or plastic fiber: fiber optics

communication by gesture and expression, study of: kinesics

communication by gossip: grapevine

communication system for emergency: hotline

communication, extrasensory: telepathy

communication, nonverbal and unconscious: body language

communication, supplementing of verbal: paralinguistic

communication, without means of: incommunicado

communications system of teletypewriters: telex

communion: affinity, agreement, church, communication, concord, confession, conversation, converse, creed, denomination, eucharist, faith, fellowship, harmony, mass, religion, sacrament, sect, share, talk, union, unity

communion box for consecrated bread: ciborium, monstrance, ostensory, pyx

communion box for wine: ampulla, cruet

communion bread: Eucharist, host, Sacrament

communion bread in thin disk: wafer

communion breaking of bread: fraction

communion calling for bread, wine consecration: epiclesis

communion cloth covering chalice: pall

communion cloth for table: corporal

communion cloth for wiping celebrant's lips: purificator

communion consecrated bread, wine: species

communion cup for consecrated wine: ama, chalice

communion given to dying person: viaticum

communion kiss of peace: pax

communion lifting of bread, wine: elevation

communion of bread dipped in wine: intinction

communion of Eastern churches: liturgy

communion offering to God: oblation, offertory

communion plate: paten

communion plate for bread: paten

communion service: mass

communiqué: announcement, bulletin, cable, communication, dispatch, letter, message, note, report, wire

Communism: Bolshevism, Collectivism, Leninism, Marxism

Communism emblem: hammer and sickle

Communist: commie, comrade, Leninist, Maoist, Marxist, pinko, red

Communist party supporter: fellow traveler

Communists and sympathizers, persecution of suspected: McCarthyism, witch hunt

community: association, body, brotherhood, city, colony, commonwealth, district, enclave, fellowship, fraternity, hamlet, identity, likeness, nation, neighborhood, people, polity, population, province, public, society, sodality, state, town, township, village

commute: alter, change, convert, decrease, exchange, interchange, metamorphose, shorten, substitute, trade, transform; drive, fly, ride, travel

compact: agreement, alliance, bargain, bond, brief, case, close, compressed, concentrate, concise, concord, condense, consolidate, conspiracy, contract, covenant, cram, dense, federation, firm, hard, packed, pact, pithy, short, small, snug, solid, solidify, stuffed, succinct, tamp, terse, thick, tight, trim, understanding

compact body: phalanx

compact white gypsum: alabaster

companies grouped for a business interest: consortium, syndicate

companies grouped in a corporation, multi-interest: conglomerate

companion: accomplice, amigo, associate, attendant, buddy, chaperon, chum, cohort, comate, compadre, comrade, crony, escort, fellow, friend, husband, mate, matey, pal, partner, peer, playmate, sidekick, spouse, wife

companion, reliable: boon companion

companionship: camaraderie, esprit de corps, fraternity, society, sodality

company: actors, assembly, association, band, body, business, circle, clique, companionship, concern, concourse, consort, core, corporation, crew, crowd, enterprise, fellowship, firm, flock, gang, gathering, group, guest, horde, host, mob, outfit, parrots, partnership, party, society, squad, team, throng, troop, troupe, visitor

company association to control business: cartel, trust

company controlled by another: subsidiary

company/corporation breakup or selling of holdings: divestiture

company of theater actors: repertory

company of workmen: crew

company producing books or entertainment for another company: packager, producer

company trademark or symbol: logo

company using capital to invest in other companies: investment trust

company with, keep: consort, fraternize, hobnob

company, to form a: incorporate

comparable: analogous, close, corresponding, equivalent, like, parallel, similar, tantamount

comparative: approaching, approximate, equal, near, qualified, relative, rival, than

compare: analyze, assimilate, collate, confer, contrast, correlate, equate, estimate, examine, inspect, liken, match, ponder, relate, scale, weigh

compared with: vis-á-vis

comparison: allegory, analogy, collation, connection, contrasting, distinguishing, examination, likeness, metaphor, parable, similarity, simile

comparison degrees for adjectives, adverbs: comparative, positive, superlative

comparison for experiment, standard of: control

comparison not possible: disparate, dissimilar, incongruous

comparison showing similarities between different entities: analogy

comparison, test or standard used for: yardstick

compartment: alcove, bay, berth, bin, bunker, cell, chamber, cubicle, division, hold, locker, niche, nook, pigeonhole, section, stall

compass: area, boundary, bounds, circle, circuit, circumference, confine, enclose, environ, field, horizon, radius, range, reach, scope, sphere, surround; instrument

compass deflection by magnetic influence: deviation

compass holder on boat: binnacle

compass points icon: compass card, compass rose

compassion: benevolence, clemency, condolence, consideration, empathy, heart, humanity, lenity, mercy, pity, remorse, sorry, sympathy, tenderness

compassionate: humane

compassionate one: good samaritan

compatible: agreeable, congenial, congruous, consistent, fitting, harmony, reconcilable, simpatico, suitable, together

compatible, to make: reconcile

compel: bind, cause, coerce, command, constrain, dragoon, drive, enforce, enjoin, exact, extort, force, hale, impose, influence, make, move, necessitate, oblige, overpower, persuade, press, require, squeeze, tell, urge

compelling: fascinating, irresistible

compendium: abbreviation, abridgment, abstract, aperçu, brief, compilation, digest, epitome, handbook, list, outline, sketch, summary, syllabus, synopsis

compensate: agree, atone, balance, correct, indemnify, neutralize, pay, recompense, recoup, redeem, refund, reimburse, remunerate, repay, restore, reward, satisfy, square, tally

compensate and pay back: reimburse, requite

compensate and pay for: remunerate

compensate and right a wrong: redress

compensate for: countervail, offset

compensate for damage or loss: indemnify, recompense, reimburse

compensation: allowance, amends, bonus, counterpoise, damages, fee, income, indemnity, offset, pay, payment, redress, remuneration, restitution, reward, salary, satisfaction, settlement, stipend, wage, wages

compensation and repayment: amends, redemption, redress, reparations, restitution

compensation for damage, loss: indemnity

compensation for hurt feelings: solatium

compensation or pay: emolument

compete: battle, challenge, clash, contend, contest, encounter, face, fight, match, oppose, pit, rival, strive, vie

competent: able, adept, apt, capable, complete, effective, expert, fit, good, meet, proficient, qualified, sane, skilled, smart, sufficient, suitable, trained, worthy

competition: conflict, contention, contest, debate, emulation, game, match, opposition, race, rivalry, sport, struggle, tournament

competition with all competitors playing each other: round robin

competition with prize: sweepstakes

competition, athletics: gymkhana

competition, relating to: agonistic

competitor: adversary, antagonist, challenger, combatant, contestant, emulator, enemy, entry, foe, opponent, opposition, player, rival

competitor who fills in or is outsider: ringer

competitor finishing poorly: also-ran

compile: abridge, accumulate, add, amass, anthologize, arrange, assemble, collect, compose, consolidate, cull, edit, gather

complacent: calm, comfortable, confident, contented, egotistic, satisfied, self-assured, self-satisfied, serene, smug

complacently: smugly

complain: beef, bellyache, bemoan, bewail, brawl, carp, cavil, crab, criticize, deplore, fret, fuss, gripe, groan, grouch, grouse, grumble, grunt, kick, lament, moan, object, protest, rail, squawk, whine, yammer, yelp, carp, fret, kvetch, poor-mouth, repine, whine

complain bitterly: rail

complain or object: expostulate, remonstrate

complaining: querulous, whining

complaint: accusation, ailment, criticism, disease, disorder, exception, grievance, gripe, illness, infirmity, malady, objection, peeve, plaint, protest

complaint about injustice: grievance

complaint in literary form: jeremiad

complaint or protest to authorities: demarche

complaint, to register a: lodge

complaints to agency, investigator of: ombudsman

complement: addition, balance, completion, counterpart, crew, enrichment, gang, mate, obverse, supplement, whole

complete: absolute, accomplish, achieve, all, carry out, circular, close,

conclude, consummate, done, effect, end, end up, ended, entire, every, execute, fill, finish, flawless, full, fulfill, implement, implicit, mature, perfect, realize, ripen, settle, teetotal, terminate, thorough, total, uncut, utter, whole, wholehearted

complete and absolute: outright, unmitigated

complete and authoritative: definitive

complete and thorough: circumstantial, comprehensive, detailed, exhaustive

complete arms and armor: panoply

complete confidence: certitude

complete failure: fiasco

complete happiness: bliss

complete surprise: bolt from the blue

complete view: panorama

complete, absolute: plenary, unmitigated

complete, as a surrender: unconditional

completely: a fond, all, from the ground up, in all, in toto, thoroughly

completely active: full-fledged

completely addled: asea

completely exhausted: spent

completely opposite: polar

completeness: fullness, integrity, plenitude, plenum

completion of process, time needed for: turnaround

completion, steps toward: inroads

complex: anxiety, complicated, composite, compound, convoluted, cryptic, difficult, entangled, fear, hard, intricate, involved, knotty, labyrinthine, manifold, mixed, network, perplexed, phobia, puzzling, sophisticated, syndrome, tangled

complex and intellectual: metaphysical

complex of a boy for his mother or girl for her father, emotional: Oedipus complex

complexion: appearance, aspect, color, glow, hue, look, makeup, state, temper, texture, tinge, tint, tone

complexion problem: acne

complexion, ruddy: florid, flushed

complexion, sickly yellow: sallow

compliance: acquiescence, agreement, civility, concession, conformity, consent, docility, harmony, obedience, passivity, submission

compliant: docile, easy, flexible, manageable, meek, tractable, willing, yielding

complicate: arduous, bewilder, confound, confuse, embrangle, entangle,

intricate, involve, jumble, obfuscate, perplex, puzzle, ravel, tangle, troublesome

complicated: complex, convoluted, difficult, disordered, elaborate, embroiled, hard, intricate, involuted, knotty, labyrinthine, reticular, snarled, sophisticated

complicated state of affairs: imbroglio, plight, predicament

complication: catch, confusion, convolution, development, difficulty, dilemma, drawback, entanglement, fly in the ointment, hitch, illness, intricacy, involution, obstacle, problem, ramification, snag, snarl, tangle

compliment: adulation, applaud, commend, commendation, congratulate, eulogy, extol, flattery, gratuity, kudos, laud, notice, praise, respects, salute, sentiment, tribute

compliment that is not meant or is insulting: left-handed compliment

comply: abide, accede, accommodate, accord, acquiesce, agree, apply, bend, conform, courteous, fold, follow, mind, obedient, obey, observe, submit, yield

comply temporarily: procrastinate, temporize

component: basic, constituent, element, factor, fundamental, ingredient, inherent, item, member, part, piece, substance, unit, vector

compos mentis: sane

compose: accord, adjust, alleviate, arrange, author, brief, build, calm, compound, comprise, concoct, conform, constitute, construct, control, create, design, dispose, fashion, form, formulate, make, orchestrate, originate, pacify, pen, produce, quiet, redact, relax, restrain, settle, soothe, write

compose, printwise: typeset

composed: calm, collected, composite, compound, controlled, cool, demure, placid, poised, quiet, sedate, serene, staid, together, tranquil, unflappable, unruffled

composer: author, bard, compositor, elegist, lyricist, monodist, musician, odist, poet, wordsmith, writer

composer's works that are numbered: opus

composite: combo, compound, hybrid, medley, mixture, mosaic, synthesized

composition: accord, aggregate, architecture, arrangement, article, combination, compound, concerto, concoction, congruity, conjunction, constitution, construction, creation, design, ditty, drama, essay, étude, fantasia, formation, invention, lesson, makeup, manuscript, melody, mixture, opus, paper, piece, play, score, structure, style, symphony, synthesis, theme, thesis, work, writing

composition for eight instruments or voices: octet

composition for five instruments or voices: quintet

composition for four instruments or voices: quartet

composition for nine instruments or voices: nonet

composition for one's voice: scena

composition for seven instruments or voices: septet

composition for six instruments or voices: sextet

composition for three instruments or voices: trio

composition for two instruments or voices: duet, duo

composition in free and irregular form, often improvisatory: rhapsody

composition in three or four contrasting form movements for one to four instruments: sonata

composition intended to be used for practice: étude

composition intended to depict definite events, scenes, or images: program music

composition mimicking style of another: parody

composition or hymn for the dead: requiem

composition sung unaccompanied and based on sacred text: motet

composition that repeats the main theme at least three times and alternates subordinate theme: rondo

composition with melodic themes introduced systematically and contrapuntally: fugue

composition with the same melody being repeated by different voices starting at different times: canon, round

compost: blend, composition, compound, fertilizer, manure, mixture, mulch, pile, soil

composure: balance, calmness, collectedness, control, coolness, equanim-

ity, even temper, poise, posture, quiet, repose, sangfroid, serenity, stability, tranquility

compound: acerbate, aggregate, alloy, amalgam, amalgamate, augment, blend, combine, commixture, complex, compose, composite, compost, compute, concoction, confection, constitute, enclosure, ester, fusion, goulash, increase, join, jumble, link, meld, multiple, residence, settle, substance, synthesize, unite, worsen

compound having only hydrogen and carbon: hydrocarbon

compound made up of components: composite

compound, breaking down a: analysis

compound, forming a: synthesis

comprehend: absorb, appreciate, apprehend, assimilate, attain, click, comprise, conceive, conclude, contain, digest, discern, embody, embrace, fathom, get, get the drift, grasp, imagine, involve, know, perceive, read, realize, savvy, see, sense, understand

comprehensible: clear, coherent, conceivable, intelligible, lucid, unambiguous, understood

comprehension independent of senses: ESP, extrasensory perception

comprehensive: blanket, broad, compendious, complete, concise, copious, encyclopedic, expansive, extensive, full, grand, inclusive, large, thorough, umbrella, wide

comprehensive price: flat rate

compress: abbreviate, abridge, astringe, bale, bandage, bind, compact, condense, consolidate, constrain, contract, cram, cramp, crowd, crush, curtail, deflate, dehydrate, embrace, epitomize, firm, flatten, press, shrink, squeeze, stuff, summarize

compressed air, run by: pneumatic

comprise: compose, comprehend, constitute, contain, cover, embody, embrace, enclose, form, hold, imply, include, involve

compromise: agreement, compound, concession, deal, endanger, give and take, hazard, negotiate, risk, sellout, settle, truce

compromise, discuss or negotiate to buy time or to: temporize

compromise, temporary: modus vivendi

compromising out of weakness: accommodating, accommodationist

comptroller: accountant, auditor, controller, treasurer

compulsion: addiction, coercion, compelled, constraint, drive, duress, force, impulse, necessity, need, obligation, obsession, urge

compulsion to talk: logorrhea

compulsive and habitual: pathological

compulsive preoccupation: obsession

compulsively neat or detailed: anal-retentive

compulsory: binding, coercive, imperative, mandatory, obligatory, prerequisite, required, statutory, unavoidable

compulsory in requirement: involuntary

compulsory service: conscription

compunction: anxiety, concern, conscience, contrition, misgiving, penitence, pity, qualm, regret, remorse, repentance, sorrow, sympathy

compute: add, calculate, count, enumerate, estimate, figure, number, reckon, sum, tally

computer: brain, calculator, machine
RELATED TERMS

computer display area: screen

computer feature, often: data bank

computer illness: virus

computer information fed or entered: input

computer information printed: output, printout

computer linked to Internet, Web, service provider: online, on-line

computer machinery: hardware

computer products not yet existing: vaporware

computer program code written as a fix: patch

computer programs: software

computer science: cybernetics

computer-screen symbols: icons

computer symbol, moving and blinking: cursor

computer terms: access, analog, code, compatible, data, debug, digital, hardware, input, memory, output, program, programmer, silicon chip, simulation, software

computer, easily understood and used: user-friendly

computerized, robotic or mechanical autonomy: artificial intelligence

computers and human nervous system, study of: cybernetics

computers or computing devices that can be integrated, of: compatible 🐛

comrade: ally, associate, brother, buddy, chum, companion, confidant, crony, fellow, friend, mate, pal, partner, peer, sidekick, tovarish

con: against, anti, bamboozle, bilk, bluff, cheat, convict, deceive, direct, dupe, examine, fool, guide, gyp, know, learn, master, mislead, opposed, peruse, rap, regard, rook, scam, snooker, steer, study, swindle, trick, versus

con game: bunko, hoax, scam, sham

concatenation: chain, connection, coupling, integration, link, nexus, sequence, series, union

concave: arched, bowlike, cupped, depressed, dished, hollow, saddlebacked, scooped, sunken

conceal: bury, cache, camouflage, cloak, closet, couch, cover, disguise, dissemble, dissimulate, ensconce, feign, harbor, hide, mask, pretend, screen, secrete, shroud, stash, stow, veil, withhold

conceal flaw or failure: whitewash

conceal intentions or plans, actions to: smokescreen

concealed: abstruse, blind, blindfold, clandestine, covert, hid, hidden, incognito, latent, occult, perdue, privy, recondite, secret, unseen

concealed priority: hidden agenda

concealment of facts, calculated: subreption

concealment of profits: skimming

concealment of real activities: cover-up

concealment of wrongdoing by public official: misprision

concede: accord, acknowledge, admit, agree, allow, confess, grant, own, quit, recognize, relinquish, resign, surrender, vouchsafe, waive, yield

conceit: arrogance, ego, egotism, pomposity, pride, self-esteem, snobbery, vanity

conceited: arrogant, bragging, bumptious, cocky, egotistical, ham, loudmouth, narcissistic, opinionated, overweening, pompous, prideful, proud, self-opinionated, smug, snobbish, snooty, vain, vainglorious, whimsical

conceited person: egomaniac

conceive: apprehend, begin, comprehend, comprise, contrive, create, design, develop, devise, dream, envisage, envision, form, formulate, frame, ideate, imagine, make, plan, ponder, realize, start, suppose, suspect, think, understand, visualize

concentrate: accumulate, assemble, attend, center, centralize, compact, condense, conglomerate, consolidate, essence, examine, fixate, focus, gather, intensify, mass, meditate, pile, scrutinize, thicken, unify

concentrate and thicken: inspissate

concentrate, inability to: aprosexia

concentrated: condensed, deep, dense, engrossed, intense, intent, potent, real, reduced, robust, straight, undiluted, whole

concentrated essence of thing: quintessence

concentrated form to normal strength, to bring a: reconstitute

concentrating psychic energy on something: cathexis

concentration: absorption, application, array, convergence, diligence, extract, fixation, focusing, study

concentration of a solution, method of determining: titration

concentration on single subject or idea: idée fixe, monomania

concentration, excessive: hyperprosexia

concept: brainchild, conviction, idea, image, notion, opinion, slant, theory, thought

conception: apprehension, beginning, belief, comprehension, design, fertilization, genesis, idea, image, impregnation, impression, inception, invention, notation, origin, plan, purpose, start

conception in female who is already with child: superfetation

conceptualization: idea

conceptualize: ideate

concern: affair, affect, anxiety, apprehension, attentiveness, bear, behold, bother, burden, business, care, cause, charge, company, consideration, corporation, distress, disturb, establishment, firm, implicate, interest, involve, matter, misgiving, pertain, regard, solicitude, touch, trouble, unease, worry

concerned: active, affected, anxious, distressed, fearful, involved, solicitous, worried

concerned with knowledge: gnostic

concerned with public works: edilian

concerning: about, anent, as to, asto, in re, in the matter of, rem

concerning birth: natal

concerning finance: economic

concert: accord, agreement, chorus, collaboration, concord, cooperate, entertainment, gig, harmony, performance, plan, recital, show, tune, union, unite

concert circuit: tour

concert hall: auditorium, music hall, odeon, odeum, theater

concert performance by soloist: recital

concert series, purchase of tickets for: subscription

concert sponsor or producer: impresario

concerted: combined, joint, mutual, prearranged

concession: acquiescence, admission, allowance, assent, boon, buyback, compromise, condescension, favor, gambit, giveback, grant, lease, permit, privilege, rollback, yielding

conch or carapace: shell

concha: ear

concierge: attendant, doorman, janitor, porter

conciliatory: appeasing, calm, forgiving, gentle, giving, irenic, lenient, mollifying, placating, placid, reassuring

concise: abbreviated, abridged, brief, compact, compedious, comprehensive, condensed, crisp, curt, epigrammatic, in a nutshell, laconic, pithy, pointed, precise, short, succinct, summary, terse

concise in expression: aphoristic, compendious, elliptical, gnomic, laconic, pithy, succinct, terse, to the point

concise summary: abstract

conciseness: brevity

conclave: assembly, huddle, meeting, parley, secret meeting, session

conclude: achieve, arrange, cease, clinch, close, complete, confine, decide, deduce, determine, discontinue, end, figure, finish, gather, infer, judge, limit, reason, resolve, rule, settle, speculate, stop, suppose, terminate

conclude an argument: have the last word

conclude from evidence: infer

conclude from incomplete evidence: conjecture

concluding musical passage: coda

conclusion: closure, end, finale, finding, finish, opinion, outcome, period, result

conclusion by reasoning: deduction, inference

conclusion following stated condition: apodosis

conclusion is drawn, proposition from which: premise

conclusion on basis of evidence: generalization

conclusion that does not follow from evidence: non sequitur

conclusive: absolute, certain, cogent, compelling, convincing, decisive, definite, definitive, final, irrefutable, last, obvious, revealing, telling, ultimate

conclusive test: acid test, litmus test

conclusively, more: a fortiori

concoct: brew, compose, compound, cook, create, devise, fabricate, formulate, frame, hatch, intrigue, invent, originate, perfect, plan, plot, prepare, scheme, vamp

concocting secretly: hatching

concoction: brew

concomitant: accessory, accompanying, associate, attendant, belonging, coincident, companion, concurrent, conjoined, connected, consort, contributing, fellow, satellite, synchronous, synergistic

concord: accord, agree, agreement, amity, communion, concert, consensus, consent, consonance, cooperation, covenant, friendship, harmony, oneness, pact, peace, protocol, rapport, treaty, unison, unity

concourse: assemblage, company, concursion, confluence, conjunction, crowd, foyer, gathering, junction, linkage, merging, passageway, path, street, throng

concrete: actual, cement, coalesce, combine, compound, congeal, factual, firm, harden, material, particular, precise, real, solid, solidify, tangible, unite

concrete components: gravel, sand, water

concrete mineral materials: aggregate

concrete parking barrier: bumper stop, car stop, curb bumper, tire stop, wheel stop

concrete, not: abstract

concubine: harem, odalisque, slave

concupiscent: erotic

concur: accord, acquiesce, agree, approve, assent, band, chime, coincide, collaborate, combine, consent, cooperate, jibe, join, meet, unite

concurrent: allied, associated, coeval, coexistent, coincident, compatible, concomitant, consistent, mutual, parallel, simultaneous, synchronous, united

concurrent symptoms: syndrome

concussion: blow, bump, clash, collision, crash, impact, injury, jolt, pounding, trauma

condemn: adjudge, banish, belittle, blame, castigate, censure, convict, criticize, damn, decry, denounce, detest, disapprove, doom, judge, knock, proscribe, punish, reproach, sentence

condemn to penalty: sentence

condemnation: blaming, censure, denunciation, doom, judgment, rebuke, reprobation

condensation: abridgment, brief, digest, precipitate, rainfall, reduction, summary, synopsis

condense: abbreviate, abridge, boil down, capsulize, chop, compact, compress, concentrate, consolidate, constrict, contract, cut, decoct, digest, diminish, edit, epitomize, harden, inspissate, lessen, reduce, shorten, shrink, thicken, trim, unite

condensed compendium: digest

condenser for distillation: rectifier

condescend: concede, deign, oblige, patronize, stoop, submit, unbend, vouchsafe

condiment: catsup, herb, horseradish, ketchup, mustard, pepper, relish, salt, sauce, seasoning, soy, spice

condition: agreement, angle, article, case, cause, circumstances, estate, exception, fettle, limitation, mode, occasion, plight, position, predicament, premise, provision, proviso, rank, requisite, rote, situation, state, station, status, stipulation

condition implied, contained, or stated: conditional

condition in clause, leading to apodosis/conclusion: protasis

condition of agreement, to state as: stipulate

condition of being damp and heavy: sogginess

condition of difficulty: dilemma, plight, predicament, quandary

condition required or necessary, prior: prerequisite, presupposition

condition, clause in document making a: proviso

condition, existing: status quo

conditional: contingent, depending, iffy, qualified, tentative

conditional member of hypothesis: antecedent

conditional release: parole

conditional sentence, main clause of: apodosis, consequent

conditional sentence, subordinate clause of: antecedent, protasis

conditioning with immediate reward or punishment: operant conditioning

conditioning with stimulus inducing response: classical conditioning

condolence: comfort, commiseration, compassion, pity, ruth, solace, sympathy

condone: absolve, excuse, forget, forgive, ignore, overlook, pardon, remit, tolerate

condor's nest: aerie

conducive: accessory, beneficial, contributory, favorable, helpful, useful

conduct: accompany, action, administer, attitude, bear, bearing, behave, behavior, carriage, carry, channel, charge, comport, comportment, conduit, control, convey, convoy, deed, demeanor, deportment, direct, escort, execute, funnel, govern, government, guidance, guide, lead, manage, mien, move, operate, oversee, pilot, plan, proceeding, regimen, regulate, rule, send, show the way, steer, strategy, superintend, supervise, transact, usher, wage

conduct oneself inconspicuously: efface

conductor: aqueduct, bandleader, cathode, cicerone, collector, convoy, copper, director, escort, guard, guide, impresario, leader, maestro, material, motorman, propagator, transmitter

conductor's directing stick: baton

conductor's platform: dais, podium, rostrum

conduit: aqueduct, cable, canal, channel, conduct, drain, duct, gully, main, passage, pipe, sewer, trough, tube, watercourse, wire

cone: bobbin, conoid, container, fissure, funnel, object, pyramid, solid, spire, strobile

cone midsection: frustum

cone or pyramid with top sliced off: fulstrum

cone-shaped or funnel-shaped: infundibuliform

cone-shaped headdress: cornet

cone-shaped pile of straw or hay: cock

cone-shaped receptacle: cornucopia

cone-shaped roll or yarn or thread on spindle: cop

cone-shaped tent: teepee

cone-shaped or top-shaped: turbinate

conelike mound of volcano: cinder cone

Conestoga wagon: prairie schooner

confab: chat

confection: bonbon, candy, caramel, compound, dainty, delicacy, gum, icing, jelly, marmalade, mixture, praline, preparation, preserve, sherbert, sweet, sweetmeat, taffy

confection containing mixed fruits: tutti-frutti

confection, molded ground almond or almond paste: marzipan

confederate: abettor, accessory, accomplice, ally, assistant, associate, auxiliary, cohort, collaborator, colleague, comrade, conjure, conspire, leagued, pal, partner, reb, rebel, syndicated, unite

confederate soldier: reb, rebel

confer: advise, award, bestow, brainstorm, commune, compare, comprise, consult, contribute, converge, deliberate, discuss, donate, endow, give, grant, invest, meet, parley, powwow, present, provide, speak, talk, treat

confer a knighthood: dub

conference: association, collation, colloquy, comparing, congress, consultation, convention, conversation, council, discussion, forum, huddle, interview, league, meeting, organization, palaver, parley, powwow, seminar, symposium, talk

conference of highest level officials: summit

conference of scholars: colloquium, seminar, symposium

conference or conversation, formal: colloquy

conference's published transcripts: proceedings

confess: acknowledge, admit, attest, aver, avow, concede, confide, declare, disclose, divulge, grant, own, own up, recant, reveal, shrive, sing, unload

confess or hear confession: shrive

confession: admission, assertion, avowal, communion, creed, disclosure, profession, revelation, shrive, statement

confession heard by priest: shrift

confession of sin: mea culpa, peccavi

confessor: penitent

confidant or confidante: adviser, amigo, crony, friend, intimate

confide: admit, believe, commit, confess, entrust, intimate, relegate, tell, trust

confidence: aplomb, assurance, backbone, belief, boldness, conviction, courage, credence, credit, effrontery, faith, guts, hardihood, heart, hope, morale, nerve, personal, poise, reliance, secret, spirit, spunk, sureness, trust

confidence game: scam, sting

confidence man: sharper

confidence, cause to lose: demoralize, dishearten

confidence, lacking: diffident, shy, timid

confidence, to boost someone's: bolster

confident: assured, bold, brash, certain, cocksure, cocky, constant, courageous, determined, fearless, hardy, hopeful, intrepid, presumptuous, reliant, sanguine, secure, smug, sure, trustful, trusting, trustworthy, undaunted

confidential: classified, covert, esoteric, hushed, hush-hush, intimate, personal, private, privy, secret, trustworthy

confidential conversation: tête-à-tête

confidentially: between you and me, entre nous

configuration: apparatus, arrangement, contour, design, figure, form, gestalt, outline, pattern, shape

confine: astrict, bind, border, bottle up, bound, boundary, cage, circumscribe, constrain, coop, corral, cramp, dam, detain, encage, enclose, ground, hold, hurdle, immure, impound, imprison, incarcerate, intern, jail, keep, limit, lock, pen, regulate, repress, restrain, restraint, restriction, scope, seal, shorten, stint, tether, tie

confine in jail: incarcerate

confine with shackles: bind, pinion

confine within walls: immure

confined: bedridden, caged, hampered, ill, indisposed, limited, pent, sick

confinement: accouchement, captivity, childbirth, constraint, curb, custody, detention, durance, immuration, imprisonment, internment, isolation, limitation, lying-in, parturition, restraint

confines: boundary, bounds, dimensions, environs, limits, pens, range, region

confining item, rope: tether

confirm: affirm, approbate, approve, assure, attest, authenticate, bless, certify, clinch, corroborate, countersign, endorse, establish, firm, fortify, OK, prove, ratify, reinforce, sanction, seal, settle, strengthen, substantiate, sustain, uphold, validate, verify, vouch, warrant

confirm as genuine or true: attest, authenticate, sustain, verify, vouch for

confirm authorization: ratify, sanction, validate

confirm with evidence: corroborate, substantiate

confiscate: appropriate, arrogate, commandeer, impound, preempt, seize, sequester, take, usurp

confiscate for military use: commandeer

confiscate into legal custody: embargo, impound, levy, sequestrate

confiscate property: attach, expropriate

conflagrant: afire

conflagration: blaze, burning, conflict, fire, holocaust, inferno, war, wildfire

conflict: action, animosity, antagonism, argument, battle, bout, brush, clash, collision, combat, competition, contend, contest, contrast, controversy, difference, disagree, discord, dispute, dissension, duel, encounter, faction, fight, fray, friction, hostility, melee, mutiny, oppose, rebellion, rift, scuffle, setto, strife, struggle, tug-of-war, war, warfare

conflict and confrontation: crossfire

conflict and strife: discord, dissension

conflict between two laws: antinomy

conflict between two parties: discrepancy, disparity, dissonance, incongruity

conflict with blocked resolution: deadlock, stalemate

conflict within organization: faction, internal dissension

conflict, minor military: skirmish

conflicting: adverse, against the grain,

at cross purposes, at loggerheads, at variance, clashing, contradictory, contrary, discordant, in dispute, incompatible, inconsistent, opposing, warring

conflicting feelings or attitudes, having: ambivalent

conflicting natures, having two: diophysitic

conflicting tendency or movement: crosscurrent

conflicting, totally: incompatible, irreconcilable

confluence: assembling, concourse, conflux, conjunction, crowd, flowing, gathering, junction, meeting, union

conform: accommodate, acquiesce, adapt, adjust, agree, apply, assent, comply, compose, correspond, fit, follow, harmonize, obey, settle, submit, suit, tailor, toe the line, yield

conform strictly: toe the line

conform, forcing to: procrustean

conformable: agreeable, alike, amenable, matching, obedient, submissive, suitable

conformation: adaptation, configuration, figure, harmony, outline, shape, structure

conforming: congruent, in accordance with, in line, pursuant

conformity: accord, acquiescence, affinity, agreement, congruity, consistency, decorum, docility, harmony, likeness, obedience, resemblance, submission, willingness

confound: addle, amaze, astonish, astound, baffle, bewilder, confuse, consume, destroy, disconcert, dismay, dumbfound, embarrass, faze, flabbergast, frustrate, muddle, mystify, perplex, puzzle, rattle, refute, spoil, stun, stupefy, surprise, waste

confrere: comrade

confront: accost, beard, brave, challenge, dare, defy, encounter, face, meet, oppose, repel, resist, threaten

confrontation: battle, clash, conflict, contest, dispute, showdown

confuse: addle, amaze, baffle, befog, befuddle, bemuse, bewilder, blend, blunder, cloud, complicate, confound, daze, disarrange, discombobulate, discompose, disconcert, disorient, disrupt, distract, divert, dumbfound, embroil, fluster, frustrate, fuddle, jumble, maze, misin-

form, mislead, mix up, muddle, muddy, mystify, nonplus, obfuscate, obscure, perplex, puzzle, rattle, snarl, stump, stupefy, throw off, unhinge, upset

confuse in understanding: obfuscate, obscure

confuse or fluster: confound, discombobulate, discomfit, disconcert, discountenance

confused: addled, addlepated, asea, at sea, befuddled, bemused, bewildered, chaotic, discombobulated, disconcerted, disorganized, disoriented, foggy, hazy, helter-skelter, incoherent, indiscriminate, lost, misled, mistaken, muddy, mystified, nonplussed, obscure, perplexed, puzzled, random, stupefied, tumultuous, unglued, vague

confused and chaotic: haywire

confused and dazed: dizzy, woozy

confused fight: melee

confused situation: imbroglio, morass, predicament, quagmire, shambles, snafu

confused talk: galimatias

confusedly: helter-skelter, pell-mell

confusing place: maze

confusing situation: three-ring circus

confusion: agitation, anarchy, babble, bedlam, blunder, bluster, chagrin, chaos, Chinese fire drill, clutter, commotion, deray, disarray, disorder, disturbance, dither, farrago, flutter, fuss, havoc, hodgepodge, hubbub, huddle, hullabaloo, imbroglio, jumble, katzenjammer, maelstrom, mare's nest, mess, mix-up, moil, muck, muddle, pandemonium, perturbation, pother, razzle-dazzle, riot, rumpus, shambles, snafu, snarl, trepidation, tumult, turmoil, uproar, welter

confusion and dizziness: vertigo

confusion and fuss: bedlam, brouhaha, commotion, furor, havoc, hubbub, hullabaloo, mayhem, pandemonium, tumult

confusion of people: melee

confusion of words because of similar sound: malapropism

confusion, state of: tsimmes

confute: confound, contradict, counter, deny, disprove, expose, invalidate, negate, overcome, overwhelm, rebut, refute, silence

congeal: cake, clot, coagulate, con-

crete, condense, curdle, freeze, gel, gelalinize, harden, jell, refrigerate, set, solidify, stiffen, thicken

congenial: affable, agreeable, compatible, cordial, delightful, friendly, good, kindred, like, pleasant, simpatico, social, sympathetic

congenital: connate, hereditary, inborn, inbred, inherent, innate, intrinsic

conger: eel

congested: blocked, clogged, crowded, gridlocked, packed, plugged

congestion: bottleneck, crowding, gathering, jam, overcrowding, snarl, stoppage

conglomerate: accumulation, agglomerate, amass, assemblage, assemble, assorted, cartel, clustered, combine, composite, group, heap, mass, melded, pile, stack, trust, varied

congratulate: compliment, felicitate, laud, praise, salute, toast

congratulations for retort or point made: touché

congratulatory drink: toast

congregant's seat: pew

congregate: assemble, collect, convene, converge, flock, gather, mass, meet, muster, rendezvous, swarm, teem

congregation: assembly, audience, body, brethren, church, churchgoers, collection, flock, following, gathering, group, laity, mass, meeting, parish, parishioners, plovers, swarm

congregation, belonging to: lay, secular

congregation, religious: communion, confession, denomination

congregational response: amen

congress: assembly, brotherhood, caucus, conclave, convention, convocation, council, diet, fellowship, league, legislature, meeting, parliament, sisterhood, synod

congruity: accord, agreement, coherence, compatible, concord, conformity, consistency, consonance, harmonious, symmetry

conic section: ellipse

conical stone heap: cairn

conical utensil: funnel

coniferous tree: cedar, fir, larch

conjecture: assumption, belief, conceive, conclusion, deem, estimation, fancy, guess, hypothesize, idea, imagine, inference, judgment, opine, opinion, plot, presume, speculate, speculation, supposition, surmise, suspect, suspicion, theory, think, view

conjugal: bridal, connubial, hymeneal, marital, married, matrimonial, nuptial, spousal, wedded

conjunction: and, but, either/or, neither/nor, or

conjunction joining words, phrases of equal status: coordinating conjunction

conjunction omission: asyndeton

conjunction repetition: polysyndeton

conjunction that connects similar grammatical elements: coordinating conjunction

conjure: adjure, appeal, charm, combine, command, conspire, contrive, crave, exorcise, imagine, implore, importune, invoke, pray, raise, summon, supplicate, voodoo

conjure up spirit: evoke

conjurer: enchanter, juggler, mage, magician, sear, shaman, sorcerer, warlock, witch, wizard

conjurer's rod: wand

conk: decease, die, fail, faint, fungus, hit, knock, stall, straighten, swat

connect: affiliate, ally, associate, attach, bind, bridge, chain, cohere, combine, correlate, couple, fasten, interface, interlock, join, link, marry, meet, merge, network, rapport, relate, tie, unite, wed

connect in series: catenate, concatenate

connect neatly: dovetail

connect with a crime: implicate

connected with one another, to be: communicate

connecting pipe: header

connecting tissue: pons

connection: affiliation, affinity, alliance, association, attachment, bond, coherence, conjunction, contact, continuity, coupling, family, hookup, intermediary, junction, kinship, link, nexus, relationship, relative, relevance, seam, tie, union

connive: abet, blink, collude, conspire, finagle, foment, incite, intrigue, machinate, plan, plot, scheme, wink

connive with: abet

connoisseur: authority, bon vivant, buff, cognoscente, collector, critic, epicure, expert, gourmet, judge, maven, mavin, specialist, virtuoso

connoisseur of food, wine: bon vivant, epicure, gastronome, gourmet

connoisseur of the arts: virtuoso

connotation: coloring, essence, hint, implication, intent, meaning, overtone, spirit, suggestion

connote: imply, indicate, insinuate, signify, spell

connubial: bridal, conjugal, hymeneal, marital, married, matrimonial, nuptial, spousal, wedded

conquer: achieve, acquire, beat, best, checkmate, clobber, cream, crush, daunt, defeat, down, humble, lick, master, occupy, overcome, overpower, overthrow, prevail, rout, subdue, subjugate, succeed, surmount, tame, triumph, vanquish, victor, whip, win

conquer and occupy territory: annex

conqueror: champion, conquistador, hero, master, subjugator, victor, winner

conqueror, Spanish, of New World: conquistador

conquest: catch, defeat, enchantment, invasion, mastery, rout, score, victory

consanguinity: affilation, affinity, blood, brotherhood, kinship, lineage, relationship, sisterhood

conscience: compunction, heart, inwit, morals, principles, psyche, qualm, scruples, sense, thought, virtue

conscience, guilty: compunction, misgiving, qualm, scruple

conscience, not guided by: unconscionable

conscientious: assiduous, careful, diligent, dutiful, exact, fair, faithful, honest, just, meticulous, painstaking, pious, punctual, reliable, scrupulous, sedulous, upright

conscientious, extremely: meticulous, punctilious, scrupulous

conscious: alert, alive, attentive, awake, aware, cognizant, deliberate, feeling, felt, intentional, keen, knowing, perceptive, sensible, sentient

conscious and sane moment: lucid interval, lucid moment

conscious of being observed: self-conscious

conscious of information: cognizant, informed, knowledgeable

conscious perception: apperception

conscious perception, below the threshold of: subliminal

consciously done: wittingly

consciousness: awareness, concern, knowledge, mind, realization, sentience

consciousness to express subconscious, suspension of: automatism

consciousness, below the threshold of: subliminal

consecrate: anoint, bless, dedicate, deify, devote, exalt, glorify, hallow, honor, make holy, ordain, sanctify, seal, venerate, vow

consecrator: anointer

consecutive: after, continuous, ensuing, following, progressive, serial, succeeding, unbroken

consensus: accord, harmony, unanimity, unity

consent: accede, accord, acquiesce, acquiescence, agree, allow, allowance, approve, assent, authorization, blessing, comply, concede, permission, permit, submit, yield

consent, passive: sufferance

consequence: account, aftereffect, aftermath, cachet, concern, consecution, consideration, effect, end, event, fallout, fruit, importance, issue, moment, outcome, payback, prestige, prominence, rank, repercussion, result, sequel, sequela, stature, weight, worth

consequence, logical: corollary

consequent: ensuing, following, indirect, rational, resultant, sound

consequential: big, crucial, eventful, important, meaningful, pompous, substantial

consequently: ergo, therefore, thereupon, wherefore

conservation: care, cherishing, husbandry, managing, preservation, protection, saving, storage

conservative: bourgeois, cautious, diehard, guarded, moderate, old guard, old liner, reactionary, right-winger, safe, square, stable, traditional

conservative in politics: Tory

conservative person: fogy, mossback, prig

conservative, extremely: reactionary

conservatory: academy, glasshouse, greenhouse, nursery, school

conserve: guard, hoard, husband, maintain, preserve, protect, safeguard, save, scrimp, skimp, squirrel, sustain

conserves: jams

consider: adjudicate, analyze, believe, cogitate, consult, contemplate, debate, deem, deliberate, entertain, estimate, examine, expend, heed, impute, inspect, judge, meditate, mull, muse, note, ponder, reason, reckon, reflect, review, speculate, study, think, weigh

consider anew: rethink

consider carefully: ponder, reflect

consider real: hypostatize

consider seriously: take under advisement

considerable: abundant, ample, bountiful, capacious, important, large, major, notable, noteworthy, remarkable, several, significant, substantial, super

considerate: attentive, benevolent, careful, concerned, generous, gentle, heedful, kind, mild, mindful, observant, polite, prudent, respectful, sympathetic, tactful, thoughtful

consideration: advisement, aspect, attention, cause, commission, concern, importance, incentive, mercy, motive, notice, perk, point, reason, recompense, regard, respect, review, reward, scrutiny, thought

considered or called so by oneself: self-styled

consign: address, allot, assign, authorize, commission, commit, confide, delegate, deliver, deposit, devote, entrust, forward, give, mail, recommend, relegate, remand, remit, send, shift, ship, transfer, yield

consist: abide, comprise, contain, dovetail, exist, harmonize, hold, include, inhere, lie, reside, stand

consistency: adherence, body, coherence, composition, concord, congruity, consonance, density, firmness, harmony, regularity, stability, symmetry, uniformity, union, unity, viscosity

consistency and agreement: concord, concurrence

consistent: changeless, congruous, consonant, constant, dependable, even, expected, firm, harmonious, logical, persistent, regular, same, steady, suitable, unfailing, uniform, unvarying

consistent and agreeing: conformable, in unison

consistent and matching: congruous, consonant, coordinated, corresponding

consistent and unchanging: chronic, inveterate, reliable, steadfast, undeviating, unregenerate, unwavering

consistent relationship, of a: compatible

consistent, to make conflicting things: reconcile

consisting of a turbine: turbo

consisting of minute granular concretions: acinose

consolation: cheer, comfort, compassion, relief, solace, sympathy

console: allay, alleviate, cabinet, calm, cheer, comfort, encourage, lift, relieve, solace, soothe, support, table, tranquilize

consolidate: amalgamate, blend, centralize, coalesce, combine, compact, compress, concentrate, condense, fortify, fuse, harden, join, merge, pool, reinforce, solidify, strengthen, unify, unite

consonance: accord, agreement, chime, chorus, concord, harmony, unity

consonant: agreeable, alike, coincident, compatible, congruous, consistent, harmonious, letter, parallel, phoneme, resonant, similar, sonant, suitable, unified

consonant before vowel with high vowel sound: glide, semivowel

consonant directly following a vowel: postvocalic

consonant or combination with breath friction: spirant

consonant sound: apical, click, dental, frontal, glide, glottal, nasal, palatal, retroflex, spirant, trill, voiced, voiceless

consonant sound lengthened like a vowel: liquid

consonant sound repeated in stressed syllables: alliteration

consort: accompany, accord, agree, aide, assembly, associate, association, colleague, companion, concert, conform, conjunction, correspond, escort, fraternize, group, harmonize, husband, join, mate, mingle, partner, play, sidekick, spouse, tally, unite, wife

conspicuous: apparent, blatant, celebrated, clear, discernible, distinctive, distinguished, eminent, evident, famous, flagrant, flashy, important, loud, manifest, marked, notable, noticeable, notorious, obvious, outstanding, patent, plain, pointed, prominent, salient, signal, striking, visible

conspicuous public situation: limelight

conspicuously wrong: egregious, flagrant

conspiracy: agreement, cabal, collusion, confederacy, connivance, coup, covin, intrigue, machination, plan, plot, scheme, treason

conspiratorial group: cabal

conspire: agree, collude, complot, concur, confederate, conjure, connive, consort, contrive, cooperate, devise, join, league, machinate, plot, scheme

conspiring: in cahoots

constancy: adherence, allegiance, ardor, attachment, devotion, eagerness, earnestness, faithfulness, fealty, fidelity, fixedness, fortitude, honesty, integrity, loyalty, stability, tenacity

constant: certain, chronic, confident, continual, continuous, dependable, durable, endless, enduring, eternal, even, everlasting, faithful, firm, fixed, forever, habitual, incessant, invariable, lasting, loyal, nonstop, permanent, perpetual, persistent, regular, relentless, solid, stable, stalwart, staunch, steadfast, steady, sustained, true, uniform, unvarying, unwavering

constant and long-lasting: abiding, durable, persistent

constant and not stopping: incessant, unflagging, unremitting

constant and unchanging: invariable, regular

constant and uniform: chronic, inveterate, unregenerate

consternation: alarm, amazement, anxiety, confusion, dismay, distraction, distress, dread, fear, fright, horror, panic, shock, terror, trepidation, wonder

constipated: costive

constipation medicine: cathartic, laxative, purgative

constituent: citizen, component, division, element, factor, ingredient, integral, item, member, part, piece, portion, unit, voter

constitute: appoint, authorize, commission, compose, compound, comprise, create, determine, develop, draft, embody, enact, establish, fix, form, found, legislate, make, ordain, set, shape

constitution: being, build, character, composition, custom, enactment, essence, establishment, health, nature,

CONSTELLATIONS

constellation of the Air Pump: Antlia
constellation of the Altar: Ara
constellation of the Archer: Sagittarius
constellation of the Balance of Scales: Libra
constellation of the Berenice's Hair: Coma Berenices
constellation of the Bird of Paradise: Apus
constellation of the Bowl or Cup: Crater
constellation of the Bull: Taurus
constellation of the Centaur: Centaurus
constellation of the Chained Lady: Andromeda
constellation of the Chameleon: Chamaeleon
constellation of the Charioteer: Auriga
constellation of the Clock: Horologium
constellation of the Colt or Filly: Equuleus
constellation of the Crab: Cancer
constellation of the Crane: Grus
constellation of the Crow: Corvus
constellation of the Dolphin: Delphinus
constellation of the Dragon: Draco
constellation of the Eagle: Aquila
constellation of the Engraver's Chisel or Sculptor's Tool: Caelum
constellation of the Fabulous Bird: Phoenix
constellation of the Fishes: Pisces
constellation of the Fly: Musca
constellation of the Flying Fish: Volans
constellation of the Fox: Vulpecula
constellation of the Furnace: Fornax
constellation of the Gilthead of Swordfish or Goldfish: Dorado
constellation of the Giraffe: Camelopardalis
constellation of the Goat: Capricornus
constellation of the Great Dog: Canis Major
constellation of the Greater Bear or Big Dipper: Ursa Major
constellation of the Hare: Lepus
constellation of Hercules: Hercules
constellation of the Herdsman: Bootes
constellation of the Hero: Perseus
constellation of the Hunter: Orion
constellation of the Hunting Dogs: Canes Venatici
constellation of the Indian: Indus
constellation of the Keel: Carina
constellation of the King: Cepheus
constellation of the Lady in the Chair or Cassiopeia or Queen: Cassiopeia
constellation of the Lesser Bear or Little Dipper: Ursa Minor
constellation of the Lesser Dog or Little Dog: Canis Minor

constellation of the Lesser Lion or Little Lion: Leo Minor
constellation of the Lion: Leo
constellation of the Lizard: Lacerta
constellation of the Lynx: Lynx
constellation of the Lyre: Lyra
constellation of the Microscope: Microscopium
constellation of the Net: Reticulum
constellation of Noah's Dove or Dove: Columba
constellation of the Northern Crown: Corona Borealis
constellation of the Octant: Octans
constellation of the Painter's Easel: Pictor
constellation of the Pair of Compasses: Circinus
constellation of the Peacock: Pavo
constellation of the Ram: Aries
constellation of the River or Eridanus: Eridanus
constellation of the Sails: Vela
constellation of the Scorpion: Scorpius
constellation of the Sculptor's Shop or Sculptor: Sculptor
constellation of the Serpent: Serpens
constellation of the Serpent Holder or Serpent-Bearer: Ophiuchus
constellation of the Sextant: Sextans
constellation of the Shield: Scutum
constellation of the Ship's Compass or Mariner's Compass: Pyxis
constellation of the Southern Cross: Crux
constellation of the Southern Crown: Corona Australis
constellation of the Southern Fish: Piscis Austrinus
constellation of the Southern Triangle: Triangulum Australe
constellation of the Square or Rule or Straightedge: Norma
constellation of the Stern: Puppis
constellation of the Swan: Cygnus
constellation of the Table Mountain: Mensa
constellation of the Telescope: Telescopium
constellation of the Toucan: Tucana
constellation of the Triangle: Triangulum
constellation of the Twins: Gemini
constellation of the Unicorn: Monoceros
constellation of the Virgin: Virgo
constellation of the Water Bearer: Aquarius
constellation of the Water Serpent or Sea Serpent: Hydra
constellation of the Water Snake: Hydrus
constellation of the Whale: Cetus
constellation of the Winged Horse: Pegasus
constellation of the Wolf: Lupus ❦

---

organization, physique, stamina, state, structure, temper, vitality; charter, code, law
constitutional: congenital, essential, inborn, inherent, innate, intrinsic, lawful, legal, natural, organic, stroll, walk

constrain: check, clasp, coerce, compel, compress, confine, constrict, curb, deny, deprive, deter, distress, enforce, fain, force, impel, inhibit, limit, oblige, oppress, press, ravish, repress, restrain, restrict, secure, squash, stifle, subdue, urge, violate

constraint: bond, captivity, coercion, compulsion, confinement, distress, duress, force, modesty, necessity, obligation, pressure, reserve, restraint, shyness, suppression, timidity
constrict: astringe, bind, choke, compress, confine, constipate, constrain,

constringe, contract, cramp, curb, grip, hamper, inhibit, limit, restrict, shrink, squeeze, strangle, tense, tighten

construct: arrange, assemble, build, combine, compose, create, devise, engineer, envision, erect, fabricate, fashion, form, frame, make, originate, rear

construction: architecture, building, creation, design, development, inference, makeup, structure, version

construction, science of: tectonics

constructive: beneficial, effective, helpful, practical

construe: analyze, comprehend, decipher, deduce, explain, expound, infer, interpret, parse, render, resolve, translate

consul: delegate, emissary, envoy, magistrate, minister, official, representative

consult: advise, ask, brainstorm, confer, consider, counsel, decision, deliberate, determine, devise, discuss, huddle, meeting, negotiate, refer

consultants: advisors

consume: absorb, annihilate, burn, crush, deplete, destroy, devour, dissipate, down, drink, dwindle, eat, engage, engross, exhaust, expend, gulp, hoover, inhale, monopolize, perish, ravage, scarf, squander, swallow, use, use up, utilize, waste

consumer: buyer, client, customer, eater, purchaser, shopper, user

consumers persuaded by mass media: admass

consuming: eating

consummate: absolute, accomplish, achieve, complete, conclude, crown, culminate, effect, exquisite, finish, fulfill, ideal, perfect, perform, ripe, undisputed

consumption: decay, depletion, destruction, devouring, drinking, eating, expenditure, phthisis, TB, tuberculosis, use, waste

contact: abut, acquaintance, approach, collision, communication, connection, contiguity, contingency, get to, impact, join, junction, meet, meeting, network, rapport, reach, relate, touch, touching, union

contact and sharing, professional: networking

contact at single point: tangent

contact, spread by: communicable, contagious

contagion: contamination, corruption, disease, epidemic, illness, infection, miasma, pestilence, poison, pox, taint, virus

contagious: catching, communicable, epizootic, infectious, spreading, transmittable

contagious diseases, widespread: epidemic

contain: accommodate, bound, check, comprehend, comprise, control, embody, embrace, enclose, harness, have, hold, house, include, keep, restrain, retain, stifle, stop, subsume

contain and include: comprise, encompass, incorporate

contain sacred thing: enshrine

contain, include: comprise

contained as essential part of: implicit, inherent, integral

container: bag, barrel, basket, bin, bottle, box, bucket, cage, can, canister, canteen, capsule, carafe, carton, case, cask, casket, crate, crib, cup, decanter, drum, flask, hamper, hod, holder, inkwell, jug, keg, magnum, pail, pod, pot, pouch, purse, receptacle, sack, shaker, silo, tank, tin, tub, urn, vase, vat, vial

container for flowers: vase

container for fluid: ampulla, cistern, cruse, receptacle, reservoir

container for living organisms: terrarium

container for miscellanea: catchall

container for molten metal: crucible

container for oranges: crate

container for sacred thing: reliquary

container for tea: caddy

container of misfortunes: Pandora's box

container's weight deducted to find contents' weight: tare

containing iron: ferric

containing tin: stannic, stannous

contaminate: adulterate, befoul, blight, corrupt, debase, debauch, defile, deprave, desecrate, foul, infect, poison, pollute, soil, spoil, stain, sully, taint, tarnish, vitiate

contemn: abhor

contemplate: consider, deliberate, examine, inspect, meditate, muse, plan, ponder, probe, propose, reflect, regard, ruminate, scrutinize, speculate, study, survey, think, view, weigh

contemplation: awareness, consideration, deliberation, gazing, intention, meditation, musing, observation, prayer, purpose, scanning, speculation, study, thought

contemplation of navel: omphaloskepsis

contemplative: meditative, ruminant, thoughtful

contemporary: abreast, aversion, coetaneous, coeval, current, dispite, hatred, modern, newfangled, recent, stigma, voguish

contempt: disdain, disgrace, disrespect, hatred, indignation, mockery, odium, scorn, shame, slight, sneer

contempt, to show: depreciate, disparage

contemptible: abject, base, beggarly, cheap, crass, despicable, disgusting, dishonorable, evil, hateful, infamous, low, mean, paltry, petty, pitiful, revolting, sad, scummy, scurvy, shabby, sneaking, sordid, sorry, vile, worthless, wretched

contemptuous: arrogant, cavalier, condescending, derisive, disdainful, haughty, insolent, insulting, sardonic, scornful, supercilious

contemptuous behavior: contumacy

contemptuous expression: sneer

contend: argue, assert, avow, bargain, battle, brawl, buffet, bustle, claim, combat, compete, conflict, contest, cope, cross, debate, dispute, encounter, face, fight, maintain, oppose, quarrel, reason, skirmish, squabble, struggle, tug, vie, vindicate, wage

contend orally: argue

content: amount, capacity, essence, gist, meaning, text, volume; appeased, calm, cozy, ease, gratify, happy, peace, please, satiate, satisfy, smug

contention: altercation, argument, beef, combat, competition, conflict, contest, controversy, debate, difference, disagreement, discord, dispute, dissension, explanation, feud, fight, flak, friction, ground, opinion, rebellion, riot, rivalry, rumpus, scrap, squabble, strife, struggle, tiff, war, wrangle

contentious: argumentative, bellicose, belligerent, cantankerous, carping, disputatious, hostile, militant, perverse, pugnacious, quarrelsome, rabulisic, wrangling

contentment: bliss, comfort, complacency, ease, gladness, happiness, pleasure, satisfaction

contest: action, affray, agon, altercation, argue, argument, battle, bee, bout, challenge, clash, combat, compete, competition, conflict, contend, debate, defend, dispute, duel, encounter, feud, fight, fray, game, match, meet, oppose, pitt, protest, question, race, resist, rivalry, skirmish, spar, strife, strive, struggle, tiff, tournament, trial, vie, warfare

contest prizes: stakes

contest where all competitors play each other: round robin

contest won without much opposition: walkaway

contest, to forfeit a: default

contestant: adversary, candidate, challenger, combatant, competitor, contender, defendant, enterer, entrant, entry, finalist, participant, player, prospect, rival, warrior

context: background, climate, framework, matrix, meaning, situation, substance, vocabulary

contiguous: abutting, adjacent, besides, bordering, close, meeting, nearby, neighboring, touching

continent: abstinent, celibate, chaste, mainland, pure, restrained, restrictive, temperate

continents: Africa, Antarctica, Asia, Australia, Europe, North America, Oceania, South America

contingency: accident, chance, crossroads, emergency, event, fortuity, incident, juncture, likelihood, odds, possibility, predicament, prospect, uncertainty

contingent: accidental, body, casual, chance, conditional, delegation, dependent, detachment, empirical, fortuitous, likely, possible, provisional, unanticipated, unpredictable

continual: ceaseless, connected, constant, continuous, endless, enduring, eternal, everlasting, incessant, lasting, perennial, permanent, perpetual, recurrent, unbroken, unceasing, unremitting, unwaning

continuance: adjournment, continuity, duration, endurance, extension, extent, longevity, perseverance, postpone, procedure, sequel, stay, term

continuation, uncontrollable: perseveration

continue: abide, add, carry, connect, endure, exist, extend, go on, last, live, maintain, outlast, persevere, persist, proceed, prolong, pursue, reestablish, remain, renew, resume, run on, stay, survive, sustain

continue a subscription: renew

continue after break: resume

continue despite obstacles, setbacks: persevere, persist

continue steadily: persist

continue to exist: subsist, survive

continue unchanged: abide, subsist

continue, to cause to: perpetuate

continued story: serial

continuing: chronic, incessant, ongoing

continuing story: saga, serial

continuing through year: perennial

continuity: chain, cohesion, connection, endurance, flow, linking, progression, stamina, succession

continuity interrupted by previous episode: flashback

continuous: nonstop, pitiless, relentless

continuous belief: perseverance, steadfastness

continuous change: flux

continuous flow: stream

continuous procession: stream

continuum of four dimensions: space-time

contort: bend, coil, convolute, curve, deform, disfigure, distort, gnarl, knot, turn, twist, warp, wrest, writhe

contorted face: grimace

contour: characteristic, curve, figure, form, graph, line, lineament, outline, profile, shape, silhouette, structure

contour feather: penna

contraband: acquire, banned, bootleg, cause, deflate, develop, illegal, illicit, moonshine, piracy, prohibited, smuggled, unlawful

contraception, surgical cutting of sperm ducts for: vasectomy

contraception, surgical tying of fallopian tubes for: tubal ligation

contraception, withdrawal as: coitus interruptus

contraceptive: preventative, prophylactic

contraceptive for men: condom

contraceptive for women: birth-control pill, cervical cap, diaphragm, intra-uterine device, IUD, the Pill

contract: abbreviate, abridge, catch, concentrate, condense, constrict,

constringe, curtail, lessen, limit, narrow, reduce, restrict, shorten, shrink, shrivel, wrinkle; agreement, arrangement, bond, compact, convention, covenant, deed, lease, obligation, pact, pledge, promise, stipulation, treaty; come down with, incur, engage, get

contract between master and apprentice: indenture

contract for tenure: lease

contract invalid, to make a: invalidate, nullify, vitiate, void

contract stipulation: term

contract, amendment to: endorsement, rider

contract, section of a: clause

contract, something done, given, or promised that is in effect a: consideration

contract, to require as condition in: stipulate

contract, to run out, as a: expire

contradict: belie, call into question, controvert, counter, deny, differ, disaffirm, disclaim, disprove, dispute, gainsay, impugn, negate, oppose, oppugn, rebut, refute, repudiate

contradiction: antilogy, conflict, contravention, denial, disagreement, discrepancy, gainsaying, inconsistency, paradox

contradiction between two laws, conflict of authority: antinomy

contradictory: against, antagonistic, antipodean, contrary, diametric, incompatible, inconsistent, opposite, polar, reverse

contradictory feelings: ambivalence, cognitive dissonance, dissonance

contradictory phrase: oxymoron

contradictory statement that may be true, seemingly: antinomy, paradox

contraption: apparatus, contrivance, device, gadget, instrument, machine, thing, tool

contrary: adverse, antagonistic, antipodal, averse, balky, conflicting, converse, counter, disagreeable, discordant, discrepant, hostile, insubordinate, nonconforming, opposed, opposite, ornery, paradoxical, perverse, polar, rebellious, refactory, reverse, stubborn, unfavorable, unpopular, wayward

contrast: antithesis, comparison, deviate, differ, difference, dissimilarity, divergence, diversity, mismatch, opposite, separate, show up

contrast as literary technique: chiaroscuro

contravene: breach, contradict, defy, deny, disregard, gainsay, hinder, infringe, offend, oppose, overstep, repudiate, spurn, thwart, transgress, tresspass, violate

contribute: aid, assist, augment, bestow, cause, donate, endow, factor, furnish, further, give, help, provide, strengthen, submit, subscribe, subsidize, supply, tend, tender

contribution: alms, article, benefaction, charity, donation, gift, grant, handout, input, offering, payment, present, share, supplement, writing

contribution by persons unknown, of a: anonymous

contributor: donor

contributor to blood pressure reading: systole

contributor to result or process: factor

contrite: apologetic, compunctious, humble, penitent, regretful, remorseful, repentant, rueful, sorrowful, sorry

contrition: penitence

contrivance: apparatus, appliance, artifice, contraption, creation, design, device, doodad, doohickey, gadget, gear, gizmo, instrument, invention, machine, plan, project, scheme, shift, tool, widget

contrive: accomplish, achieve, agitate, brew, concoct, connive, conspire, construct, consult, contend, design, devise, engineer, fabricate, fake, fashion, finagle, fudge, intrigue, invent, machinate, make, manage, maneuver, manipulate, plan, plot, project, scheme, wangle

control: bridle, check, clout, command, conduct, contain, curb, direct, discipline, dominate, domination, dominion, govern, grasp, guide, handle, hold, influence, juice, jurisdiction, leash, manage, mangagement, manipulate, mastery, monopoly, ordinance, overlook, power, predominate, preside, regulate, regulation, rein, restrain, rule, steer, subdue, supervise, sway

control a force: harness

control artfully: manipulate

control completely: dominate, monopolize

control or authority: dominion, jurisdiction, sovereignty

control to a standard: regulate

control, bodily: continence

control, loss of bodily: palsy

control, resistive to: restive, turbulent

control, to bring under: subjugate, subordinate

controlled and prescribed course: regimen

controlling position: helm, preeminence, tiller

controversial: arguable, contended, debatable, disputatious, eristic, polemic, polemical, questionable, suspect

controversy: altercation, argument, beef, contention, debate, difference, disagreement, discussion, dispute, flak, quarrel, row, spat, strife, tiff, wrangle

controversy, major: cause célèbre

controvert: argue, belie, challenge, contest, contradict, counter, debate, deny, dispute, gainsay, moot, oppose, question, rebut, refute

contumacious: haughty, insolent, mutinous, ornery, riotous, unruly

contumely: abuse, arrogance, contempt, disdain, humiliation, insolence, insulting, remark, reproach, rudeness, scorn

contusion: bruise, bump, injury, knock, mouse

conundrum: enigma, mystery, paradox, poser, puzzle, question, riddle

convalesce: improve, mend, recover, recuperate, rejuvenate, restore, revive

convene: assemble, call, congregate, convoke, gather, meet, muster, open, rally, sit, summon, unite

convenience: amenity, appliance, availability, benefit, comfort, ease, enjoyment, leisure, luxury, preference, service, usefulness

convenient: accessible, adaptable, agreeable, appropriate, at hand, available, beneficial, favorable, handy, helpful, nearby, proper, ready, suitable, useful

convenient to one's self: expedient

conveniently arriving person or event in plot: deus ex machina

convent: abbey, cloister, community, easy, monastery, nunnery, priory, retreat, sanctuary

convent apartment: cell

convention: agreement, assembly, caucus, conference, congress, contract, convocation, custom, delegates, etiquette, gathering, meeting, members, practice, precept, protocol, rule, tradition, treaty, usage

convention address: keynote

convention attendee: delegate

convention site: hall

conventional: accepted, ceremonial, common, contractual, correct, customary, decent, developed, established, everyday, formal, middlebrow, normal, orthodox, proper, regular, routine, standard, traditional, trite, typical, usual

conventional image: stereotype

conventional in approach: academic

conventional medicine: allopathy

conventional trend: mainstream

conventionalize: stylize

conventions: mores

conventions, being in accord with: comme il faut

conventual: nun

converge: assemble, concentrate, concur, focus, gather, join, meet, merge, rally

conversant: abreast, acquainted, adept, au fait, awake, aware, cognizant, experienced, expert, familiar, hip, informed, practiced, proficient, skilled, versed

conversation: association, chat, chitchat, colloquy, communication, confabulation, conference, dialogue, discourse, discussion, exchange, gossip, interchange, palaver, parley, repartee, shoptalk, talk

conversation about trivial matters: small talk

conversation between two: dialogue, tête-à-tête

conversation by one: monologue

conversation marked by exchanging witty retorts: repartee

conversation or discussion, formal: colloquy

conversation participant: collocutor, interlocutor

conversation with wit: repartee

conversation, departure in observation from: aside, digression, excursus, parenthesis

conversation, informal: causerie, chat

conversation, lively: badinage, banter, gabfest

conversation, of a small-talk: phatic

conversation, person involved in: interlocutor

conversational: colloquial

conversationalist, boring: macrologist

conversationalist, dinner-table: deipnosophist

converse: antipode, antithesis, association, chat, chin, colloque, commune, confer, consort, convert, dialogue, exchange, obverse, opposite, palaver, parley, reverse, speak, talk

conversion: adaptation, alteration, change, flux, metamorphosis, mutation, switch

conversion of assets: liquidation

convert: acetalize, adapt, alter, amend, brainwash, change, commute, converse, disciple, follower, modify, neophyte, novice, persuade, proselytize, reform, renew, resolve, restore, reverse, revise, sway, transform, translate, transpose, turn

convert illegal monies to legal-looking form or place: launder

convert impulse to socially acceptable one: sublimate

convert in shape: transmogrify

convert or attempt to convert to a religion, cause: proselytize

convert to a religion: neophyte, proselyte

convert with indoctrination: brainwash

convertible furniture: sofa bed

convex: arched, bent, bowed, bulging, curved, gibbous, outcurved, protuberant, raised, rounded

convex moldings: ovoli, ovolos, tori

convey: alienate, assign, bear, bequeath, bring, carry, cart, communicate, conduct, convoy, deliver, devise, dispose, give, grant, guide, impart, import, lead, mean, move, project, relate, remove, reveal, send, steal, support, take to, tell, tote, transfer, transmit, transport, will

conveyance: airplane, auto, automobile, bus, car, carriage, carrying, cart, charter, conduct, deed, grant, railroad, sled, trailer, train, transfer, transit, transport, trolley, truck, vehicle, wagon

conveying a warning: monitory

conveyor of goods: dray

convict: adjudge, attain, attaint, captive, con, condemn, criminal, culprit, felon, find, inmate, jailbird, lifer, malefactor, prisoner, prove, sentence, timeserver

conviction: belief, certainty, confidence, creed, dogma, faith, fervor, mind, opinion, position, principle, sentiment, tenet, view; sentence

convince: assure, change, get across, persuade, prove, satisfy, sell, sway

convincing: authentic, believable, cogent, conclusive, evident, influential, persuasive, plausible, potent, powerful, sound, telling, valid

convivial: cheerful, entertaining, festal, festive, friendly, gay, genial, hilarious, jocular, jolly, jovial, joyous, lively, merry, vivacious

convocate: gather

convocation: assembly, calling, caucus, concourse, congress, convention, council, gathering, meeting, synod

convoke: assemble, call, cite, convene, gather, meet, muster, request, summon

convolute: cloud, coil, contort, intricate, loop, snaking, spiral, tangle, twist, wind

convoy: accompany, attend, carry, convey, escort, formation, guard, guide, lead, manage, pilot, protection, safeguard, usher

convulsion: attack, commotion, contraction, disturbance, epilepsy, fit, furor, laughter, paroxysm, seizure, shaking, spasm, throe, tottering, tumult, uproar

convulsive: spasmodic

convulsive breath: gasp

convulsive seizure while carrying unborn child: eclampsia

convulsive twitch: tic

coo: murmur, sound, utter, woo

cooing birds: doves

cook: bake, baker, barbecue, baste, boil, braise, broil, chef, concoct, contrive, curry, develop, fix, fry, grill, happen, heat, make, microwave, parboil, poach, prepare, process, roast, sauté, sear, servant, simmer, steam, stew

cook/boil gently in water: coddle

cook up: brew, contrive, devise, formulate, invent, plot, scheme

cooked simply or uncooked: au naturel

cookery and cooking, pertaining to: culinary

cookie: biscuit, brownie, cake, confection, gingersnap, macaroon, Oreo, snap, sugar, Toll House, wafer

cookie made with almond paste or coconut: macaroon

cookie with a lot of butter or shortening: shortbread

cookie, chewy, with coconut or almonds: macaroon

cookie, flat brittle, made with ginger and molasses: gingersnap

cooking: cordon bleu, cuisine, gastronomy, haute cuisine, magirics

cooking pot, airtight and fast: pressure cooker

cooking terms: al dente, au bleu, bake, bard, blanch, bouchée, bouillon, bouquet, broil, brûlé, chine, coddle, culinary, devil, dredge, farci, flambé, fry, garni, jardiniere, marinade, marinate, medallion, parboil, puree, sauté

cooking tools: broiler, casserole, colander, dutch oven, galley, griddle, kitchen, pan, pot, ramekin, range, roaster, rotisserie, skillet, spatula, steamer, stove, terrine, trivet, tureen, wok

cooking, high-quality: cordon bleu, haute cuisine

cooking, particular style of: cuisine, gastronomy

cooking, pertaining to: culinary

cookout: barbecue, barbeque

cool: algid, chill, chilly, cold, frigid, gelid, ice, nippy, refrigerate; moderate, temperate; assured, calm, collected, composed, confident, dandy, deliberate, poised, relaxed, sedate, serene; excellent, sensational

cool and indifferent: apathetic, indifferent, nonchalant, placid, unconcerned, unemotional, unexcited, unflappable, unfriendly, unmoved, unresponsive, unruffled, unsociable

cooler: ade, container, drink, icebox, icer, jail, lockup, prison, refrigerant, refrigerator

cooling substance: refrigerant

coolness: aplomb, assurance, calmness, cold, composure, indifference, nerve, sangfroid, serenity

coop: cage, confine, corral, cramp, enclosure, hutch, jail, pen, prison, yard; co-op, cooperative

cooperate: agree, assist, band, coadjute, collaborate, combine, concur, conduce, contribute, join, participate, play ball, tend, unite

cooperate secretly: collude, connive, conspire

cooperate with and indulge: gratify, pander to

cooperating: compatible, in tandem

cooperation: concert, partisanship, partnership, synergy, teamwork, union

cooperation, insincere: lip service

cooperative: accommodating, amenable, complaisant, compliant, considerate, helpful, obliging, synergetic, tractable

cooperative arrangement: reciprocity

cooperative farm in Israel: kibbutz

cooperative farm in Russia: kolkhoz

cooperative instinct: altruism, selflessness, symbiosis

coordinate: adapt, adjust, alike, arrange, correlate, equal, equivalent, harmonize, integrate, mesh, organize, reconcile, synchronize, tune

coordination: agility

coordination effort: liaison

coordination, lack of: apraxia, ataxia

cootie: crab louse

cop: officer, patrolman, patrolwoman, policeman, policewoman

cope: canopy, chapel, cloak, complete, confront, contend, cover, deal, dress, encounter, endure, equal, face, handle, manage, match, notch, strive, struggle, survive, vault, weather

cope with: grapple

copies' multiple pages in order, to put: collate, decollate

copies, to make three: triplicate

copious: abundant, affluent, ample, bountiful, exuberant, flowing, full, galore, generous, lavish, lush, numerous, overflowing, plenteous, plentiful, plenty, profuse, replete, rich, wordy

copper, greenish coating on: patina, verdigris

coppice: bosk, copse, firth, forest, grove, growth, regrow, thicket, underwood, wood, woodland

cop's club: billy

copse: grove, thicket

copulate: breed, cohabit, fornicate, join, mate, unite

copy: ape, carbon, cheat, clone, counterfeit, ditto, duplicate, echo, edit, effigy, emulate, facsimile, follow, forgery, image, imitate, imitation, issue, likeness, mime, mimeograph, mimic, mirror, parrot, personify, phony, plagiarize, redraft, remake, replica, reprint, reproduce, reproduction, simulate, takeoff, trace, tracing, transcribe, transcript, Xerox

copy in greatly reduced size: miniature

copy in longhand: engross

copy machine substance: toner

copy machine, old-fashioned: duplicator, mimeograph

copy manuscripts, person whose job is to: amanuensis, scribe, scrivener

copy of a bond: oyer

copy of academic record: transcript

copy of creator's work: replica

copy of proceedings: transcript

copy on smaller scale: replica, reproduction

copy or adapted from others: derivative, unoriginal

copy or exact reproduction: facsimile

copy or forge, to: counterfeit

copy process: photocopying, xerography, Xerox

copy someone's elses writings or ideas and pass off as one's own: plagiarize

copy, corrected clean: fair copy

copy, exact genetic: clone

copycat: ape, aper, mime

copying machine for diagrams: pantograph

copyright or patent, expired: public domain

copyrighted material, unauthorized use of: infringement, piracy, plagiarism

coquet or coquette: coy, dally, flirt, fool, philander, toy, trifle, vamp, wanton

coral: horny, limestone, madrepore, pink, polyp, red, skeleton, zoophyte

coral island: atoll, cay

coral island or reef that encircles lagoon: atoll

coral of a lobster: roe

coral or sea anemone: polyp

coral ridge: reef

coral rock parallel to coast, separated by lagoon: barrier reef

cord: band, bind, bond, cable, fabric, fiber, laniard, lanyard, line, measure, nerve, rope, sennet, spinal, string, tendon, thread, twine, wire, wood, yarn

cord for securing, binding: lashing

cord for trimming: bobbin

cord from fetus to placenta: umbilical cord

cord of Arab headdress: agal

cord on left uniform shoulder, braided: fourragere

cord or belt: cincture

cord unit: log

cord used to strangle: garrote

cord, elastic, for securing items: bungee cord, shock cord

cordage fiber: hemp, istle, jute, kenaf, pita, sisal

cordial: agreeable, amiable, courteous, drink, friendly, genial, gracious, hearty, hospitable, liqueur, polite, real, sincere, sociable, vigorous, vital, warm, zealous

cordial flavoring: anise

cordial liqueur: amaretto, anisette, Benedictine, Chartreuse, Cointreau, Grand Marnier, Kahlua, ouzo, sambuca, triple sec

cordiality: amenity, ardor, empressement, friendliness, geniality, heartiness, pleasantness, regard, sociability, sympathy, warmth

cordillera: range

cordlike decoration: piping

cordon: cord, group, guard, ribbon, shrub, stringcourse, tree

corduroy rib or ridge: wale

cordwood measure: stere

core: base, center, cob, essence, focus, gist, guts, heart, hub, kernel, meat, middle, nodule, nub, nucleus, pith, root, staple, substance

core group: cadre

core of anything: heart

core or central idea: gist, gravamen

cork: bobber, close, float, oak, phellem, plug, seal, shive, spike, stop, stopper, stopple

cork in bottle of champagne, wire cage holding down: agraffe, coiffe

cork tree: oak

cork, of or resembling: suberose

corker: crackerjack, dandy, excellent, humdinger, lulu, oner, remarkable, whiz

corkscrew: coil, entwine, spiral, twist, wind

cormorant: bird, gluttonous, gourmand, greedy, rapacious, ravenous

corn: cob, ear, grain, Indian, kernel, maize, mealie, mealy, nubbin, samp

corn bread or cake: pone

corn cover: husk

corn liquor, illegally distilled: mountain dew

corn meal: masa

corn or wart: papilloma

corn product: bread, grist, hominy, meal, pone, tortilla

corn unit: ear, kernel

corned-beef dish: hash

corner: angle, bend, cranny, edge, el-

CORDIALS AND LIQUEURS

absinthe	Chamborel	curaçao	Malibu	schnapps
alcohol blanc	Chartreuse	Drambuie	Mandarine Napoleon	sloe gin
amaretto	chocolate liqueur	Frangelico	Marachino	Southern Comfort
Amer Picon	Cointreau	Galliano	Midori	strega
anisette	créme de bananas	Goldschalger	mocha liqueur	Tia Maria
Asiago	créme de cacao	Grand Marnier	pastis	triple sec
B and B	créme de cassis	Irish cream	Pimm's	tuaca
Benedictine	créme de framboise	Irish Mist	ratafia	Vandermint ❦
bitters	créme de menthe	Kahlua	rock and rye	
Calvados	créme de noyeaux	Kir	Sabra	
cassis	créme de violette	kummel	sambuca	

bow, ell, junction, niche, nook, recess, retreat, spot, trap, veer; monopoly

corner of building, outer: cant

corner or nook by fireplace: inglenook

corner, cut off a: bevel, chamfer

cornered: at bay, treed

cornerstone: base, basis, coigne, foundation, marking, quoin, support

cornet: headdress, horn, instrument, trumpet

cornflower: bachelor's button, ixia

cornice: band, crown, drip, eave, frame, furnish, geison, molding

cornice molding: cyma

cornmeal: atole

cornmeal bread: johnny cake

cornmeal cake: pone

cornmeal dough deep-fried: hush puppy

cornmeal mush: polenta, porridge

cornrows: braids

cornstalks as fodder, hay made from clover: stover

cornucopia: abundance, horn, the horn of plenty, ornament, receptacle

corny: banal, clichéd, dated, sentimental, square, stale, stupid, trite

corolla component: petal

corollary: analogy, conclusion, consequent, deduction, effect, inference, proposition, result, theorem

corona: aureole, cigar, circle, crown, halo, light, ring, rosary, tiara, wreath

coronary tissue death: infarction

coronation: accession, ceremony, crowning, inauguration

coroner's investigation: inquest, inquiry

coronet: anadem, band, chaplet, circle, crown, diadem, headband, headdress, tiara, wreath

corporal: anatomical, bodily, corporeal, physical, punishment, rank, tangible

corporal's boss: platoon sergeant

corporate insignia: logo

corporation: association, business, combination, company, enterprise, firm, syndicate, trust

corporation holding other's securities: holding company

corporation ordinance: bylaw

corporation with varied industries: conglomerate

corporation's total securities issued: capitalization

corporeal: actual, bodily, carnal, corporal, material, physical, real, somal, somatic, substantial, tangible

corps: band, brigade, company, division, outfit, squad, troop, unit

corpse: body, cadaver, carcass, remains, stiff

corpse burning for disposal: cremation

corpse deep-freezing technique: cryonics

corpse examination: autopsy, necropsy, postmortem

corpse for research: cadaver

corpse from a grave, to remove: disinter, exhume

corpse of animal: carcass

corpse storage room or building: morgue, mortuary

corpse with chemicals, to preserve: embalm

corpses, feeding on: necrophagous

corpulent: blimp, bulky, chubby, fat, fleshy, heavy, husky, large, obese, overweight, plump, portly, rotund, stout, tubby, weighty

corpus: body, bulk, capital, compilation, mass, principal, whole, writings

corpuscle deficiency: anemia

corral: confine, coop, enclosure, fence, pen, round up, stockade, surround

correct: accurate, adjust, amend, better, castigate, change, chastise, check, edit, emend, exact, fit, fix, improve, inform, nice, perfect, precise, proper, punish, rectify, redress, reform, regulate, remedy, repair, reprove, revamp, revise, right, true, truthful, upgrade

correct and proper: comme il faut, kosher

correct text: emend

correct, always: infallible, unerring

correct, to confirm as: attest, corroborate

corrected or improved, capable of being: corrigible

correction: adjustment, alteration, discipline, modification, punishment

correction made for variation in judgment, reasoning: personal equation

correction, note to ignore: stet

corrections in book: corrigenda, errata

corrective: remedial, remedy, salutary

corrective action: disciplinary action, punishment

correctly inferred or deduced: valid

correctness of judgment: rectitude

correlate: associate, compare, coordinate, equate, match, parallel

correlation: analogue, correspondent, equivalence, relationship

correlative conjunction: nor

correlative of if and then: else

correspond: accord, agree, answer, coincide, communicate, complement, conform, equal, fit, harmonize, jibe, match, parallel, reply, resemble, respond, square, suit, tally, write

correspond to: comport with, conform with

correspondence: agreement, analogy, bulletins, coherence, congruity, correlation, epistle, letters, mail, messages, parallelism, similarity

correspondence and harmony: congruity, consistency, consonance

correspondence in math, rule of: function

correspondence of number, case, gender, and person between words: agreement

correspondence of set to set by rule: mapping

correspondent: conformable, contributor, correlation, equivalent, freelancer, journalist, match, pen pal, reporter, suitable, writer

corresponding and matching: coincident, coinciding

corresponding in function but not structure, origin: analogous

corresponding in position, value, structure, function: homologous

corresponding in size, extent, duration, degree: commensurate

corresponding person, thing: counterpart, vis-á-vis

corridor: aisle, areaway, couloir, foyer, gallery, hall, hallway, passageway, path

corroborate: attest, authenticate, back, confirm, establish, prove, strengthen, substantiate, support, sustain, validate, verify

corrode: bite, canker, consume, corrupt, decay, destroy, deteriorate, eat, eat away, erode, gnaw, oxidize, rust, scour, waste, wear away

corrosive: abrasive, acerbic, biting, caustic, destructive, erosive, mordant, sarcastic, venomous

corrugated: creased, crinkled, crumpled, folded, grooved, ridged

corrugated metal hut, arched: Quonset hut

corrupt: abusive, adulterate, bad, bribe, contaminate, corrode, crooked, debase, debauch, defile, defiled, degrade, demoralize, deprave, dishonest, evil, falsified, flagitious, fraudulent, immoral, impure, low, mar, on the take, pervert, poison, pollute, profligate, ravish, rot, rotten, spoil, stain, subvert, taint, underhanded, unethical, venal, vile, violate, vitiate

corrupt and degraded: peccant, putrid, rotten, scrofulous, venal

corrupt innocent person, to: debauch

corrupt official: highbinder

corruptible: venal

corrupting: evil, noxious, pernicious, pestiferous, pestilent

corrupting thing: blight, canker

corruption: debauchery, evil, fiddling, fraud, graft, impropriety, jobbery, payola, turpitude, vice

corruption in government or business: graft, malversation

corruption in public office: graft, jobbery

corruption, fund used for: slush fund

corruption, moral: depravity

corruption, source of spreading: canker

corsair: buccaneer, freebooter, marauder, picaroon, pirate, robber

corset: belt, bodice, control, girdle, laced, restrict, stays, support, undergarment

cortege: caravan, line, procession, retinue, train

cortex: bark, layer, peridium, rind

corundum: emery

coruscate: beam, blaze, flash, gleam, glint, glisten, glitter, radiate, sparkle

cosa nostra: mafia, mob, syndicate

co-sign: vouch

cosmetic: beautify, blush, cream, decorative, eye shadow, henna, liner, lipgloss, lipstick, makeup, maquillage, mascara, nail polish, pomade, powder, restorative, rouge, superficial

cosmic: catholic, cosmopolitan, global, huge, immense, infinite, limitless, planetary, universal, vast

cosmonaut: astronaut

cosmopolitan: cosmic, cultured, ecumenical, global, sophisticated, universal, urbane, worldly

cosmopolitan person: cosmopolite

cosmos: creation, earth, flower, galaxy, globe, harmony, nature, order, realm, scheme, stars, structure, universe, world

cosset: caress, cuddle, fondle, lamb, love, pamper, pet, spoil

cost: charge, damage, estimate, expenditure, expense, fee, harm, loss, pain, penalty, price, sacrifice, suffering, toll, value

cost, additional: surcharge

costly: damaging, dear, disastrous, exorbitant, expensive, extravagant, gorgeous, high, lavish, opulent, precious, priceless, rich, ruinous, splendid, steep, sumptuous, valuable

costs of operating a business: overhead

costs, cut back on: economize, retrench

costs, to undertake payment of: defray

costume: apparel, attire, clothes, clothing, disguise, dress, ensemble, garb, getup, guise, outfit, robe, suit, uniform

costume ball with masks: masquerade

costume department of theater: wardrobe

cot: bed, bedstead, berth, bunk, cabin, cottage, couch, covering, dwelling, house, hut, sheath, shelter, stall, stretcher

coterie: circle, clan, clique, club, gang, junto, ring, set, society

cottage: bungalow, cabin, chalet, dwelling, guesthouse, house, hut, lodge, maisonette, shack, shanty, shelter

cottage cheese: smearcase

cotton bundle: bale

cotton fabric: calico, canvas, chintz, denim, duck, etamine, leno, lisle, muslin, nankeen, organdy, percale, pima, sateen, terry

cotton for stuffing or lining: batting

cotton grass: sedge

cotton on stick for cleaning: swab

cotton refuse: lint

cotton seed-bearing capsule: boll

cotton thread: lisle

cotton thread, to treat and improve: mercerize

cottontail: hare, rabbit

couch: bed, chesterfield, cot, davenport, daybed, divan, floor, ottoman, sofa; express, word

couch made out of a folding mattress: futon

couch without armrests or back: divan

couch without arms or back: ottoman

couchlike chair with support for legs: chaise longue

cougar: cat, catamount, mountain lion, panther, puma

cough: ahem, bark, cold, hack, pertussis, tussis, whoop

cough drop: troche

cough medicine: linctus

cough medicine promoting expulsion: expectorant

cough-relieving: antitussive

cough up: ante, confess, deliver, disclose, relinquish

cough up and eject: expectorate

cough up phlegm: hawk

council: assembly, board, body, cabinet, committee, conclave, conference, congress, consistory, convocation, deliberation, discussion, diet, divan, federation, junta, meeting, ministry, panel, senate, synod

council, pertaining to a: conciliar

counsel: admonish, advice, advise, advocate, attorney, barrister, caution, confer, consultation, counsellor, counselor, deliberation, exhort, guidance, instruction, lawyer, prescribe, recommend, rede, rule, steer, suggest, urge, warn

counsel, of yore: rede

counselor: adviser, advisor, attorney, barrister, counsel, counsellor, instructor, lawyer, mentor, supervisor, teacher

count: add, await, bank, calculate, cast, census, compute, deem, depend, earl, enumerate, esteem, expect, figure, foot, impute, include, judge, matter, name, number, numerate, outcome, poll, rate, reckon, rely, result, score, signify, sum, tally, tell, total, tote

count off list: enumerate

countenance: abet, accept, advocate, aid, approve, aspect, back, befriend, encourage, endorse, favor, help, OK, sanction, show, support, uphold; face, feature, front, mien, physiognomy, semblance, visage; bearing, calmness, composure

counter: adverse, against, antipodal, asset, contend, contradict, contrary, current, marker, match, nullify, offset, oppose, opposite, rebut, respond, retaliate, reverse, token; stand, table

counter or retaliatory action: riposte

counter or ward off: parry

counteract: annul, antidote, balance, cancel, check, correct, foil, frustrate, hinder, negate, negative, neutralize, oppose, overcome, resist, thwart

counteractant: antidote

counterargument: rebuttal

counterbalance: check, compensate, correct, equalize, equiponderate, offset, rectify

countercharge: recrimination

counterclockwise: widdershins, withershins

counterculturist: rebel

counterfeit: affect, artificial, assume, bogus, brummagem, coin, copy, deception, disguised, dummy, fake, false, falsify, feigned, fictitious, forge, forged, forgery, fraud, fraudulent, fudge, imitate, impersonate, mock, phony, postiche, pretend, pseudo, reproduction, sham, simulate, spurious

counterfeit coin: slug

countermand: abrogate, annul, cancel, frustrate, override, recall, repeal, rescind, reverse, revoke, stop, void

counterpart: analog, carbon, complement, copy, correlate, double, duplicate, equal, equivalent, like, match, mate, obverse, parallel, twin, vis-à-vis

counterpoise: balance, ballast, compensate, counteract, counterweight, equalize, equilibrium, offset, stabilize

countersign: authorize, certify, confirm, corroborate, endorse, mark, password, seal, sign, signature, watchword

countertenor: alto

counting, process of: enumeration, numeration

countless: incalculable, infinite, innumerable, limitless, numberless, umpteen, untold

countrified: rural

countrified, become: rusticate

country: backwoods, boondocks, bush, citizens, commonwealth, district, farm, fatherland, home, homeland, land, motherland, nation, outland, pastoral, people, realm, region, rural, state, sticks, territory

country gentleman: squire

country house: manor

country inn: ferme auberge

country isolated from main part and surrounded by foreign territory, part of: exclave

country life, relating to: bucolic, pastoral, rural, rustic

country path: lane

country person, uncultured: bumpkin, yokel

country shindig: hoedown

country, dependent: client state

country, neutral, between opposed countries: buffer state

country, person from one's own: compatriot

country, person who has been driven from or left their: emigrant, émigré, exile, expatriate

country, relating to open: campestral

country, rural: boondocks, hinterland

country, to disown allegiance to one's: defect

country, to expel a foreigner from a: deport

county: borough, canton, district, division, parish, seat, shire, subdivision

county division: township

county official: sheriff

coup: achievement, attack, feat, mastery, overthrow, overturn, plan, plot, revolution, stratagem, strike, stroke, takeover

coup de grâce: clincher, deathblow, knockout, mercy stroke, quietus

coup d'état: mutiny, overthrow, revolt, revolution, stratagem

couple: assemble, bond, brace, bracket, combine, connect, copulate, duad, duo, dyad, fasten, harness, hitch, join, link, marry, mate, pair, team, tie, twin, two, twosome, unite, yoke

coupler: device, drawbar, fastener, link, ring, shackle

couplet: distich, pair, poem, unit, verse

coupon: advertisement, certificate, form, slip, stamp, stub, token, voucher

coupon for goods, to turn in: redeem

courage: audacity, backbone, boldness, braveness, bravery, chin up, daring, élan, fearlessness, firmness, fortitude, gallantry, gameness, grit, gumption, guts, hardihood, heart, the heart of a lion, heroism, mettle, nerve, pluck, prowess, resolution, soul, spine, spunk, tenacity, valor

courage from alcohol: Dutch courage

courageous: adventurous, bold, brave, daredevil, daring, fearless, gallant, game, gutsy, hardy, heroic, intrepid, lionhearted, mettlesome, red-blooded, spartan, stouthearted, unafraid, undaunted, valiant, valorous, venturous

courageous behavior: heroics

courier: attendant, carrier, envoy, gofer, guide, mailman, mailwoman, messenger, post, postman, postwoman, runner, scout, spy

course: artery, beeline, career, circuit, curriculum, class, conduct, cycle, design, direction, drift, flow, gallop, game, heat, highway, itinerary, lap, line, manner, method, movement, orbit, passage, path, pathway, plan, policy, procedure, proceeding, progress, race, rink, road, route, routine, run, running, scheme, sequence, series, stream, street, subject, system, tendency, track, trail, trend, way

COURT GAMES

badminton
basketball
court tennis
handball
jai alai
lawn tennis
paddleball
paddle tennis
pelota
platform tennis
racquetball
roller hockey
rugby fives
shuffleboard
squash racquets
squash tennis
table tennis
tennis
volleyball ❧

---

course chosen but not required, a: elective

course done on one's own: distance learning, extension program

course for updating: refresher course

course of action: plan, scenario

course of events: tide

course of study: curriculum, syllabus

course of thought or argument: tenor

course, side dish served in addition to main: entremets

course's learning unit: module

courteous: attentive, civil, complaisant, considerate, cordial, debonair, deferential, fair, gallant, genteel, gentle, gracious, kind, mannerly, polished, polite, refined, respectful, suave, thoughtful, urbane

courteous and gallant: chivalrous

courtesan: hetaera

courtesy: civility, comity, pleasantry

courtier: attendant, beau, courter, flatterer, wooer

courtly: aristocratic, civil, cultured, debonair, decorous, dignified, elegant, flattering, gracious, lofty, polished, polite, prim, refined, stately, suave

courtroom panel: jury

courtship: amour, dating, pursuit, romance, suit

courtyard: area, curtilage, enclosure, patio, quad, quadrangle, space

courtyard of church: atrium, parvis

courtyard surrounded by cloisters: garth

cousin: counterpart, coz, kin, kinsman, kinswoman, nobleman, relative

cousin, first: cousin-german

cousins separated by generations, of: removed

cove: basin, bay, bight, cave, cavern, creek, gulf, harbor, hole, inlet, lagoon, molding, nook, pass, recess, retreat, sound, valley

covenant: accord, agree, agreement, bargain, bind, bond, commitment, compact, concordat, condition, contract, convention, deal, document, engage, oath, pact, pledge, promise, stipulation, testament, treaty

cover: blanket, camouflage, cap, cloak, clothe, coat, conceal, defend, detail, disguise, drape, eclipse, hatch, hide, lid, mask, obscure, overlay, overlie, pave, protect, roof, sanctuary, screen, shade, shelter, shield, skin, span, tegmen, track, veil, wrap

cover up wrongdoing: whitewash

cover with clouds or fog: obnubilate

cover with hoarfrost: rime

cover with liquid or color: perfuse

cover with plaster: ceil

cover with thin plastic: laminate

coverage: analysis, broadcasting, description, inclusion, indemnity, insurance, observed, report, scope

coverall: jumpsuit

covered walk: arcade, stoa

covered with matted wool or hair: flocculent, tomentose

covered with soft hair: pilose

covered with viscous mud: slimy

covering: april, apron, aril, armor, awning, bark, bonnet, boot, canopy, capsule, case, ceiling, clothing, coverlet, crust, explanatory, helmet, hood, hull, husk, integument, jacket, lid, otitis, overlay, pall, quilt, robe, rug, screen, sheath, shell, shroud, smokescreen, tarp, testa, tile, toupee, umbrella, wig

covering for coffin: pall

covering or outer layer: cortex, mantle, pallium

covering that darkens, obscures: pall

covering, animal or plant: integument

covering, natural: integument

coverlet: afghan, blanket, comforter, quilt, spread, throw

covert: asylum, camouflaged, clandestine, concealed, confidential, covered, defense, disguised, feather, guarded, harbor, hidden, hush-hush, incognito, insidious, latent, masked,
private, privy, refuge, secret, sheltered, thicket, underbrush, undercover, underhanded

covet: ache, aspire, crave, desire, envy, hanker, lust, thirst, want, wish, yearn

coveted role: lead

covetous: acquisitive, avaricious, avid, desirous, eager, envious, gluttonous, grasping, greedy, itchy, jealous, keen, mercenary, ravenous, selfish, stingy

covey: bevy, brood, bunch, company, family, flock, group

cow: daunt, ruminant

cow about to give birth: springer

cow between 1 and 2 years old: stirk, yearling

cow habitat: barn, byre, corral, pasture, pen, vaccary

cow in stall, framework to secure: stanchion

cow or ox, like a: bovine

cow pasture: lea

cow shed: byre

cow snatcher: rustler

cow stomachs: omasa

cow tail bushy tip: switch

cow without calf: farrow

cow, female: farrow, milch, springer

cow, group: cattle, herd, kine

cow, not pregnant: farrow

cow, young: beef, bovine, calf, heifer, quadruped, ruminant, stirk

cow, young and not yet breeding: heifer

coward: caitiff, chicken, dastard, gutless, jellyfish, noel, poltroon, quitter, scaredy-cat, sissy, sneak, wimp, yellowbelly

cowardice: cold feet

cowardly: afraid, chicken-hearted, chicken-livered, craven, dastardly, fainthearted, fearful, frightened, lily-livered, nervous, pusillanimous, recreant, shy, spineless, timid, yellow

cowboy: broncobuster, buckaroo, cattleman, cattlewoman, charros, cowgirl, cowpoke, cowpuncher, driver, frontiersman, frontierswoman, gardian, gaucho, herder, herdsman, herdswoman, huasos, llanero, puncher, rider, roper, stockman, stockwoman, vanquero, waddy, wrangler

cowboy contest: rodeo

cowboy dressing: bandana, boots, chaps, hat, long johns, spurs

cowboy equipment: boleadoras, branding irons, gun belt, holster, lariat, pistol, quirt, rope, saddle, shotgun, six gun, whip

COURT & LEGAL TERMS

agenda: docket
applying to a court for aid: recourse
attempt to influence court of law: embracery
before a court of law: sub judice
break in court proceedings: recess
brief entry of court proceedings: docket
calendar of cases awaiting: docket
call to order: oyez
celebrated court case: cause célèbre
chief court clerk: prothonotary
contempt of court: contumacy
court action: appeal, plea, suit
court case: action, arraignment, hearing, litigation, moot, sitting, suit, trial
court case or lawsuit: litigation
court of appeals: appellate court
court of justice: forum, tribunal
court officials: advocate, amicus curiae, bailiff, crier, defendant, judge, jury, marshall, plaintiff, pleader
court order for imprisonment: committal, mittimus
court order for prohibiting something: interdict
court order to a lower court, higher: mandamus
court order to appear, testify: subpoena
court order to do or stop act: injunction, restraining order, writ
court order to produce documents, evidence: subpoena duces tecum
court order to send back to custody: remand
court to give testimony, writ requiring appearance in: subpoena, summons
court site: venue

court terms: bond, brief, citation, cognizance, committal, cross-examine, decree, embracery, finding, forensic, in camera, injunction, interdict, judgment, mandamus, oyez, perjury, recess, recognizance, recource, remand, session, subpoena, sue, summons, testify, testimony, verdict, ward, writ
court training exercise: moot court
court types: appellate, circuit, forum, judicature, judiciary, kangaroo, star chamber, tribunal
court's jurisdiction: cognizance
courts of law: judicature, judiciary
failure to make court appearance: default
give as evidence under oath in a court of law, to: testify
giving of evidence under oath in a court of law: testimony
giving of false testimony: perjury
judge in county court: circuit judge
of a court hearing held in private: in camera
party against which court action is brought: defendant
party bringing suit: plaintiff
person summoned to advise: amicus curiae
pleading guilty to lesser charge: plea bargain
promise or obligation to appear: bond, recognizance
question a witness, to: cross-examine, cross-question
refer a case to another court for further action, to: remit
relating to courts of law: forensic
relating to principles of law for courts: substantive
relating to rules or procedures of courts: adjective
summons to appear: citation
unauthorized court: kangaroo court
under a court's consideration: sub judice ❧

---

cowboy film: oater
cowboy trousers: chaps
cowboy, South American: gaucho
cowboy, southwestern U.S.: buckeroo, vaquero
cower: cringe, crouch, fawn, grovel, hide, quail, recoil, shrink, stoop, toady, tremble, wince
cowl: bonnet, cap, capuche, cloak, hood, monk, robe
cow's stomach: omasum
cows, of yore: kine
cows, relating to: bovine
coxa: hip
coxcomb: buck, cap, dandy, dude, fob, fool, fop, hinge, popinjay
coy: allure, arch, bashful, coquettish, demure, diffident, distant, evasive, hesitating, kittenish, modest, quiet, reserved, shy, skittish, still, timid, unassertive
coypu: nutria
cozen: bamboozle, beguile, bilk, cheat,

chisel, con, deceive, defraud, dupe, flimflam, fraud, gyp, hoodwink, swindle, trick
coziness: gemutlichkeit
cozy: buddy-buddy, comfortable, contented, covering, cushy, easy, familiar, friendly, homey, intimate, palsy-walsy, relaxing, safe, secure, snug, soft, toasty, warm
cozy place: den, lair, nest
CPA's report: audit
crab claw: chela
crab family: brachyura
crab or other 10-legged crustacean: decapod
crab terms: anthropod, arachnid, chela, crustacean, decapod, fiddler, hermit, horseshoe, nipper, pincer, robber, soft-shelled
crabby: bitter, cranky, cross, cynical, difficult, dour, glum, grouchy, huffy, irritable, sullen, surly, testy
crablike: cancroid

crack: blemish, break, chip, chop, cleave, cleft, cranny, craze, crevice, damage, division, fissure, flaw, fracture, gap, interstice, rend, rift, shatter, snap, split
crack or split, narrow: cleft, crevice, fissure
crack, deep: chasm, crevasse
cracked: bonkers, break, chinky, collapse, crazy, deranged, insane, mad, nuts, rimose, split, unbalanced
cracker: biscuit, saltine, wafer
crackerjack: ace, adept, excellent, expert, fine, nifty, skilled, splendid, super
crackle: break, brustle, crepitate, crinkle, noise, snap, sound, sparkle
crackpot: crank, eccentric, flake, insane, kook, lunatic, maniac, nut, oddball, screwball, wacko
cracks in painting: craquelure
cracks in pottery, intersecting: craze
cracks, covered with fine: crazed

crack up: amuse, breakdown, collapse, pileup, smash, wreck

cradle: bassinet, bed, cot, crib, cuddle, hug, infancy, lull, nestle, nourish, nursery, nurture, origin, tend, wellspring

craft: ability, aptitude, art, artifice, dexterity, employment, expertise, foxiness, job, occupation, profession, skill, talent, trade, vocation; airplane, boat, ship, spacecraft, vessel

craft wood: balsa

craftsperson: artificer, artisan, artist, carpenter, master, mechanic, smith, specialist, worker, writer

craftsperson not self-employed: journeyman

crafty: acute, adept, adroit, arch, astute, cagey, calculating, canny, clever, conniving, cunning, deceitful, designing, disingenuous, foxlike, foxy, fraudulent, ingenious, insincere, scheming, shrewd, slick, sly, smooth, snide, subtle, tricky, vulpine, wily

crafty one: finagler

craggy: harsh, rocky, rough, rugged, steep, unlevel

craggy hill: tor

cram: crowd, crush, drive, fill, force, glut, gorge, jam, load, pack

cramp: ache, bar, compress, confine, constraint, constrict, contraction, crick, crowd, frame, hamper, hinder, impede, interfere, iron, kink, limit, myalgia, pain, prevent, restrain, restrict, rigor, spasm, stiffness, stunt, stymie

cramp or appendage stiffness: charley horse

cramped: incommodious

crane: bird, davit, derrick, device, heron, hesitate, hoist, machine, raise, stretch, wader

crane on ship: davit

crane, mount for traveling: gantry

crane, raise or lower boom of: luff

crane's long arm: boom

cranial cavity: sinus

cranial nerve: vagus

cranium: braincase, brainpan, head, nob, skull

crank: bend, brace, bracket, crab, crackpot, eccentric, fanatic, grouch, handle, kook, sourpuss, start, turn, unstable, vigorously, winch, wind

cranky: cantankerous, crabby, cross, crotchety, difficult, disagreeable,

grouchy, irascible, irritable, ornery, out of sorts, perverse, stubborn, testy, touchy, ugly

cranny: byplace, cleft, corner, crack, crevice, fissure, hole, niche, nook, opening

crash: accident, bang, blast, bust, collapse, collide, collision, crack, crunch, crush, depression, fabric, failure, fall, lodging, noise, pileup, ram, shatter, shelter, shock, sleep, smash, smashup, sound, topple, wreck

crash into someone from side, unseen: blindside

crashing, as waves: plangent

crass: coarse, crude, gross, insensitive, raw, rough, rude, stupid, uncouth, unpolished, unrefined, vulgar

crass one: boor, yahoo

crate: aircraft, airplane, basket, box, car, carton, case, chest, container, cradle, jalopy, package, pallet, receptacle, vehicle

crater: abyss, bowl, caldera, cavity, depression, hole, hollow, mouth, opening, pit

crater formed by volcano: caldera

cravat: ascot, band, neckerchief, necktie, overlay, scarf, tie

crave: ache, ask, beg, beseech, covet, desire, dream, fancy, hanker, hunger, implore, long, lust, need, pray, request, require, solicit, supplicate, thirst, want, yearn

craven: afraid, chicken, cowardly, dastard, defeated, fainthearted, gutless, overcome, poltroon, recreant, scared, timid, weak, wimp, yellow

craving: appetence, itch, thirst, yen

craving for candy: sweet tooth

crawl: creep, cringe, drag, fawn, grovel, inch, lag, lollygag, pen, poke, slither, slow, swim, teem, writhe

crawl face down: grovel

crayon: chalk, charcoal, color, drawing, pastel, pencil, sketch, wax

crayon of dried paste: pastel

craze: bewilder, break, chic, derange, fad, fasion, frenzy, furor, infatuation, kick, loco, madden, mania, mode, novelty, obsession, passion, rage, style, trend, unbalance, vogue, wild

craze for one thing: monomania

crazy: absurd, amok, bananas, bats in the belfry, batty, bizarre, bonkers, cockamamie, cracked, crackpot, cuckoo, daffy, daft, demented, dotty,

erratic, fanatical, flaky, foolish, gaga, goofy, harebrained, haywire, inane, insane, loco, loony, lunatic, mad, maniac, meshuga, meshugga, nuts, preposterous, psycho, senseless, silly, strange, touched, unbalanced, wacky, weird

creak: complain, croak, grate, grind, groan, noise, rasp, screech, sound, squeak

creaking noises, to make: crepitate

cream: beat, best, choice, cosmetic, defeat, elite, emulsion, froth, lotion, moisturizer, ointment, pick, top, trounce, whip

cream of the crop: crème de la crème, elite

cream pastry: Napoleon

cream puff with chocolate sauce: profiterole

cream soup: potage

cream, thick and heavy: crème fraîche

creamery: dairy

creamy: ecru, fluffy, foamy, lush, rich, smooth, thick

crease: bend, crimp, crumple, fold, furrow, groove, line, pleat, ruck, ruffle, seam, tuck

crease or wrinkle: pucker, ruck

create: beget, build, cause, compose, conceive, concoct, design, establish, fashion, form, found, generate, imagine, invent, make, mold, originate, plan, procreate, shape, start

create one company from another: spinoff

creation: achievement, brainchild, cosmos, formation, genesis, macrocosm, masterpiece, nature, opus, production, universe, work, world

creation becoming uncontrollable: Frankenstein's monster

creation of idea: genesis, inception, procreation

creation theory of Bible: creationism

creative: artistic, clever, gifted, imaginative, innovative, inspired, inventive, original, productive, Promethean, seminal

creative impulse: afflatus

creativity of living things: élan vital

creator: architect, author, designer, father, founder, inventor, maker, mastermind, originator

creature: alien, animal, beast, being, giant, gnome, gremlin, human, individual, mammal, man, mermaid, monster, ogre, person, thing, tool, troll, varmint

credence: acceptance, belief, certainty, confidence, credit, faith, reliance, shelf, table, trust, trustworthiness

credentials: card, certificate, deed, documents, license, papers, permit, proof, reference, voucher

credible: aboveboard, authentic, believable, likely, plausible, probable, reliable, satisfactory, seeming, straight, trustworthy, valid

credit: ascribe, asset, assign, attention, attribute, belief, believe, charge, credence, deem, distinction, esteem, estimation, faith, glory, honor, kudos, loan, merit, on the plus side, points, recognition, thanks, trust, weight

credit for achieving: kudos

creditable: deserving, praiseworthy, reputable, suitable, worthy

credits, TV or movie: crawl

credo: belief, code, creed, philosophy, tenet

credulous: accepting, gullible, trusting, unsuspecting, unwary

credulous and simple: naive

creed: belief, canon, confession, credo, cult, doctrine, dogma, faith, ideology, ism, principles, tenet

creed of Christians: Nicene Creed

creek: arroyo, bay, bayou, brook, burn, channel, cove, crick, estuary, inlet, kill, race, ria, rill, rindle, rio, rivulet, spring, stream, watercourse

creep: crawl, grovel, gumshoe, inch, lurk, prowl, pussyfoot, skulk, slink, slither, snake, sneak, steal, tiptoe, writhe

creeper: vine

creepy: disgusting, eerie, ghoulish, macabre, nasty, ominous, scary, sinister, spooky

creepy look: leer

cremate: burn, char, incinerate, scorch

cremation pile: pyre

cremation remains, place for: cinerarium

creole or nonstandard speech: patois

crepe: band, crape, crinkled, fabric, paper, wrinkled; pancake

crescent: arch, concave, convex, curve, horn, concave, lunar, lune, meniscus, moon, semicircle

crescent point: cusp

crescent, crescent-shaped thing: lune, lunette, meniscus

crescent-shaped: bicorn, bicuspid, lunar, lunate, lunular, lunulate

crescent-shaped mark on fingernail: lunula

crest: acme, apex, apogee, arête, arms, bearing, climax, comb, crown, culmination, edge, emblem, escutcheon, height, helmet, insignia, noon, peak, pinnacle, plume, ridge, seal, summit, symbol, tip, top, tuft, whitecap

crested ridge: arête

crestfallen: blue, dejected, depressed, disappointed, dispirited, down, downcast, downhearted, low, sad

cretin: deformed, fool, idiot, imbecile, moron

crevasse: abyss, breach, chasm, crack, fissure, gully, rift, split

crevice: break, chink, cleavage, cleft, crack, cranny, crevasse, division, fissure, interstice, leak, nook, opening, rent, seam, slit

crevice from the Proterozoic Age: Grand Canyon

crew: assemblage, band, company, complement, covey, crowd, gang, group, hands, herd, horde, mariners, members, men, mob, party, posse, retinue, rowers, rowing, sailors, squad, team, throng, troop, workers

crewman: hand, oar

crib: basket, bed, bin, box, building, bunk, cot, cottage, crate, frame, hut, manger, rack, room, silo, stall, storehouse, trot; cheat, pilfer, plagiarism, plagiarize, pony, steal, theft

cribbage piece: peg

crick: ache, cramp, kink, pain, spasm, twinge

cricket positions: batsman, bowler, captain, cover, cover point, extra cover, fielder, fine leg, first slip, gully, leg slip, long leg, long off, long on, mid off, mid on, mid wicket, ons, second slip, short leg, silly mid, silly mid on, square leg, third man, wicket keeper

cricket score: run

cricket sound: chirp, stridulation

cricket terms: attack, bails, bat, bowl, bye, crease, lob, off, ons, over, pitch, rot, run, smick, strumps, yorker

crime: abomination, abuse, act, arson, atrocity, breach, caper, corruption, evil, felony, illegality, iniquity, misdeed, misdemeanor, murder, offense, scandal, sin, tort, transgression, vice, violation, wrong

RELATED TERMS

crime by public official: malfeasance

crime less serious than felony: delinquency, misdemeanor, violation

crime like murder, rape, burglary: felony

crime of being homeless and a nuisance: vagrancy

crime of bribing a jury member: embracery

crime of contempt of court: contumacy

crime of giving false testimony: perjury

crime of illegally obtaining or using someone's property, funds: defalcation, embezzlement, peculation

crime of illegally obtaining property, funds, patronage: extortion

crime of kidnapping: abduction

crime of maliciously setting a fire: arson

crime of marrying someone while already married: bigamy, polygamy

crime of not reporting a felony, by one who is not accessory: misprision

crime of persistently instigating lawsuits: barratry

crime of sex between close relatives: incest

crime of sex with person not of age of consent: statutory rape

crime of theft: larceny

crime of treason against ruler, state: lese majeste, lese majesty

crime or concealment of crime by government official: misprision

crime or sin: transgression

crime or treason against government: lèse-majesté, lese majesty

crime organization: Mafia, mob, syndicate

crime preventor, civilian: vigilante

crime syndicate chief: capo

crime syndicate chief's adviser: consigliere

crime syndicate chief's assistant: caporegime

crime syndicate low-ranking member: button, soldier

crime to someone, to attribute a: impute

crime, being accomplice to: complicity

crime, in the act of committing a: in flagrante delicto, red-handed crime, lack of state of mind to commit a certain: diminished capacity

crime, performance of a: commission, perpetration

crime, proof of a: corpus delicti

crime, shocking: atrocity

crime, study of: criminology

crime, tendency to go back to life of: recidivism

crime, time limit for prosecution or legal action for: statute of limitations

crime, to accuse formally of: charge, indict

crime, to cause to appear guilty of: implicate, incriminate, inculpate

crime, to choose to overlook a: condone, wink at

crime, to declare not guilty of: absolve, acquit, exculpate, exonerate, vindicate

crime, to lessen the seriousness of a: extenuate, mitigate

crime, to lure into committing a: entrapment

crime, to plan or conduct a: mastermind

crime, very evil: enormity

crimes such as murder, rape, arson, burglary: felony

criminal: con, convict, corrupt, crook, culpable, culprit, delinquent, deplorable, desperado, evildoer, felon, fugitive, gangster, guilty, hood, hoodlum, illegal, inmate, jailbird, lawless, malefactor, miscreant, mobster, outlaw, repeater, reprehensible, thug, wrongdoer

criminal assist: abet

criminal bandit: brigand

criminal behavior, antisocial personality disorder often with: psychopath, sociopath

criminal conditional release: parole

criminal gangster: mobster

criminal hunter who seeks the reward: bounty hunter

criminal informer: stool pigeon

criminal intent: mens rea

criminal on the run: fugitive

criminal rehabilitation and prison management, study of: penology

criminal to noncriminal life, to help restore: rehabilitate

criminal to place for trial, legal surrender of: extradition

criminal, bold: desperado

criminal's encourager or helper: accessory, accomplice ☙

crimp: bend, corrugate, cramp, crease, crinkle, curl, fold, frizz, hamper, mold, obstacle, pinch, plait, pleat, ruffle, snag, thwart, wave, wrinkle

crimson: beet red, bloody, blush, color, dye, maroon, red, redden, rose, rouge

cringe: bend, bootlick, cower, crawl, crinkle, crouch, dodge, flinch, grovel, quail, quiver, recoil, shrink, sneak, stoop, toady, tremble, truckle, wince

crinkle: bend, coil, crackle, crease, crimp, curl, fold, kink, pucker, ridge, ripple, rumple, rustle, seam, turn, twist, wrinkle

crinkled cloth: crepe, plissé, seersucker

cripple: crumpet, debilitate, disable, dismember, enfeeble, handicap, harm, hurt, immobilize, impair, incapacitate, injure, lame, maim, mar, mutilate, paralyze, sideline, weaken

crisis: apoplexy, catastrophe, climax, conjuncture, convulsion, crossroads, crux, dilemma, emergency, impasse, juncture, panic, paroxysm, pass, peril, pinch, predicament, seizure, trauma, trial, trouble

crisis between groups: confrontation

crisis situation less dangerous or tense, to make: defuse

crisp: biting, bracing, brisk, brittle, chilly, clear, clear-cut, cold, concise, crackling, cutting, firm, fresh, friable, incisive, invigorating, lively, nippy, plump, refreshing, sharp, short, spruce, terse

crisscross: awry, conflicting, confused, intersect, traverse

crisscross pattern: grid, lattice, tracery

crisscross pattern framework for plants: trellis

criterion: benchmark, canon, example, gauge, measure, norm, precedent, proof, rule, scale, standard, test, touchstone, yardstick

criterion for testing: touchstone

critic: analyst, antagonist, anti, authority, carper, censor, commentator, connoisseur, detractor, evaluator, expert, faultfinder, judge, muckraker, mudslinger, nitpicker, reviewer

critic, severe: Dutch uncle

critic, strict and fair: aristarch

critical: acute, captious, carping, censorious, crucial, cynical, dangerous,

decisive, dire, disapproving, exact, exacting, finicky, fussy, judgmental, pivotal, precarious, pressing, sarcastic, serious, significant, strategic, urgent

critical and biased writing: hatchet job

critical and harsh: acidulous, captious, hypercritical

critical and important: exigent

critical explanation or analysis of text or theory: exegesis, explication, exposition

critical in dispassionate way: clinical

critical revision of text: recension

critical time: climacteric, watershed

critical time before outbreak: flashpoint

critical, very: captious, carping, faultfinding, nitpicking

critically urgent: dire

criticism: animadversion, assessment, blame, censure, comment, critique, disapproval, evaluation, flak, judgment, knock, objection, review, strictures

criticism for failing: reproof

criticism from two sides: gantlet, gauntlet

criticism in speech or text: diatribe, invective, polemic

criticism of popular belief: iconoclasm

criticism, abusive: denunciation, execration, hatchet job, obloquy, vituperation

criticism, anything thought to be above: sacred cow

criticism, blunt: brickbat, broadside

criticism, literary or entertainment: appraisal, critique

criticism, long speech of: harangue, philippic, tirade

criticism, malicious: diatribe

criticism, of harsh: blistering, caustic, scathing, vitriolic

criticism, petty: quibble

criticism, severe: stricture

criticism, trivial: cavil

criticize: assess, bad-mouth, bash, blame, blast, carp, castigate, cavil, censure, comment, disparage, examine, interpret, judge, knock, pan, rap, rebuke, reprehend, reproach, review, roast, scarify, scathe, slam, slur

criticize and disapprove: condemn, denounce, deplore, execrate, reprobate

criticize as if an authority: admonish, moralize, sermonize

criticize in hindsight: second-guess

TYPES OF CRIMES

abduction	capital crime	extortion	misdemeanor	sexual assault
accessory after the fact	check forgery	false pretense	moral turpitude	sexual harassment
accessory before the fact	child abuse	felony	murder	shoplifting
accessory during the fact	child molestation	forgery	negligence	skip bail
aggravated assault	civil offense	fraud	obstruction of justice	slander
arson	coercion	graft	peculation	smuggling
assault	collusion	grand larceny	perjury	sodomy
automobile theft	concealment	harassment	petty larceny	statutory rape
battery	conspiracy	homicide	pickpocketing	subornation
blackmail	contempt of court	illegal gambling	racial harassment	treason
breach of contract	contributory negligence	involuntary manslaughter	racketeering	trespass
breaking and entering	counterfeiting	jury tampering	rape	undue influence
bribery	defamation	kidnapping	reckless endangerment	vagrancy
burglary	disorderly conduct	larceny	resisting arrest	vandalism
	drug trafficking	malicious mischief	robbery	voluntary manslaughter
	embezzlement	malpractice	sabotage	war crime
	espionage	manslaughter	sexual abuse	white collar crime ❦

criticize severely: castigate, chastise, crucify, excoriate, fly, pan, pillory, revile, scarify, vituperate

criticize verbally: belabor, berate, censure, decry, depreciate, derogate, disparage, reprehend

criticize, insatiable urge to: cacoethes carpendi

croak: caw, complain, die, gasp, grouch, grumble, grunt, hoarse, kill, moan, mutter, noise, quark, sound

crochet stitch: loop

crock: bull, container, earthenware, nonsense, pot, potsherd, smudge, soil, soot, vessel

crocodile of tropical America: caiman

crocodile type reptile of India: gavial, gharial

crocus or gladiolus: irid

crone: beldam, hag, ugly woman

crony: accomplice, ally, associate, buddy, chum, cohort, companion, confidant, friend, pal, partner, sidekick

crook: bend, burglar, cheat, criminal, curve, hook, meander, outlaw, robber, shyster, snake, swindler, thief, thug, turn

crooked: agee, alop, angled, askew, awry, bent, corrupt, crafty, curved, devious, dishonest, dishonorable, distorted, errant, false, fraudulent, irregular, knavish, lying, misleading, shady, shifty, skewed, snide, tortu-ous, tricky, turning, twisted, underhanded, unethical, unlawful, unscrupulous, winding, zigzag

croon: bellow, hum, lull, murmur, roar, sing, wail

crop: clip, curtail, cut, fruit, gather, grain, haircut, harvest, lop, maw, mow, produce, prune, reap, shear, top, trim, truncate, vegetable, whip, yield

crop of region, principle: staple

crop spraying, low: hedgehopping

crop up: arise, occur

croquet gear: mallet

croquet wicket: hoop

croquet, to hit another's ball in: roquet

cross: affliction, angry, annoyed, betray, bisect, blend, bridge, burden, combination, crabby, cranky, crotchety, crucifix, crux, delete, disagreeable, divide, emblem, ford, fretful, frustrate, grumpy, half-breed, hinder, hybrid, interbreed, intersect, irate, irritable, lace, mad, mix, navigate, petulant, rood, sign, snappish, span, sullen, symbol, tau, testy, thwart, touchy, transverse, traverse, trial

cross a line or space: intersect

cross-country motorcycle racing: motocross

cross-country race with obstacles: steeplechase

cross-country runner: harrier

cross-country ski run: langlauf

cross-country sport involving map and compass reading: orienteering

cross equator by ship: shellback

cross-examine: debrief, grill, interrogate, pump, question

cross-eye: esotropia, strabismus, walleye

cross-fertilization: xenogamy

cross like X: decussate, intersect

cross of the T: serif

cross out: cancel, dele, delete, eliminate, erase

cross-shaped: cruciate, cruciform

cross-shaped figure: chiasma

cross surmounted: crux ansata

cross surmounted by loop: ankh

cross threads in cloth: weft

cross to another side: transverse

cross with arms narrow in center, V-shaped ends: Maltese cross

cross with circle behind crossbeam: Celtic cross

cross, Jesus': holy rood, rood

crossbar: transom

crossbearer: crucifer

crossbones' accompaniment: skull

crossbow arrow: quarrel

crossbow missile: bolt

crossbred: hybrid

crossed eyes: strabismus

crossing: intersection, junction, loop, opposing, pass, passage, traverse

crosspiece of ladder: rung

crossroads: crisis, intersection, pass, turning point

crosswise: across, aslant, athwart, catercorner, diagonal, longways, oblique, perpendicular, sideways, transverse, vertically

crosswise path or movement: traverse

crossword diagram: grid

crossword puzzle devotee or expert: cruciverbalist

crotchet: eccentricity, fancy, notion, peculiarity, quirk, trait, vagary, whim

crotchety: cantankerous, cranky, cross, difficult, grouchy, irritable, obstinate, ornery, surly

crouch: bend, cower, cringe, dip, duck, grovel, squat, stoop

crow: bird, blackbird, corvine, grapnel, jackdaw, jay, magpie, raven, rook; boast, brag, cackle, caw, cry, exult, gloat, jubilate, sound, squawk, strut, swagger

crow kin: raven

crowbar: chisel, extract, jimmy, lever, pry, remove

crowd: assemblage, bunch, circle, clique, cluster, company, concourse, confluence, cram, cramp, crush, deluge, drove, flock, gang, gathering, group, herd, horde, host, huddle, jam, legion, mob, multitude, pack, party, posse, press, push, scores, sellout, set, shove, squeeze, stream, swarm, three, throng

crowd and shove: jostle

crowd of close-knit people: phalanx

crowd of moving people: drove

crowd or flock, tending to move in: gregarious

crowd or throng: concourse, ruck

crowd-scene actor: extra

crowd together: congregate, herd, serry

crowd, headlong rush of: stampede

crowded: close, compact, congested, dense, densely populated, filled, full, impacted, jam-packed, loaded, overflowing, populous, standing room only, stuffed, swarming, teeming, thick, tight

crowded, over-: congested

crowding or gathering at point: confluence

crowds, fear of: demophobia, ochlophobia

crowlike bird: daw

crown: adorn, apex, best, cap, chaplet, circle, climax, coin, corona, coronet, crest, diadem, dignify, enthrone, exalt, garland, headband, headdress, install, invest, king, knock, laurel, pate, peak, pinnacle, queen, reward, roof, sovereign, summit, surmount, tiara, tip, tooth, top, trophy, wreath, zenith

crown of pope: tiara

crown of royalty: diadem

crown of the head: pate

crown, small, for those of lower rank: coronet

crowning of royalty: coronation

crucial: acute, climatic, critical, decisive, difficult, dire, essential, final, grave, important, necessary, pivotal, serious, severe, telling, trying, urgent, vital

crucial test: acid test, ultimate test

crucially important: pivotal

crucible: affliction, dish, furnace, ordeal, test, trial, vessel

cruciferous plant: cress

crucifix: rood

crucifix letters: inri

crucify: browbeat, execute, hang, kill, lampoon, martyr, persecute, ridicule, smite, torment, torture

crude: callow, cheap, coarse, crass, dirty, foul, gross, harsh, ignorant, impolite, inartistic, incomplete, incult, indelicate, lewd, obscene, primitive, randy, raunchy, raw, rough, rude, savage, uncouth, uncultured, undeveloped, unpolished, unrefined, vulgar

crude and basic: rudimentary

crude and stupid person: Neanderthal, yahoo

crude bed: pallet

crude building: hovel, hut, lean-to, shed

crude mineral: ore

crude native platinum: platina

crude tartar: argol

cruel: atrocious, barbaric, bloody, brutal, brutish, callous, depraved, diabolical, evil, ferocious, fiendish, fierce, hard, hardhearted, harsh, heartless, indurate, inhuman, inhumane, insensitive, iron, mean, merciless, pitiless, ruthless, sadistic, savage, truculent, unfeeling, unjust, unkind, vengeful, vicious

cruel act: atrocity, enormity, outrage

cruel and perverted: sadistic

cruel in the extreme: draconian, fell, truculent

cruel treatment: persecution

cruel, very: bestial, flagitious, implacable, inexorable, remorseless

cruise: boat, coast, gallivant, glide, jaunt, sail, scud, ship, tom, trip, voyage, wander

crumb: bit, break, drop, fragment, little, loathsome, morsel, ort, particle, piece, remnant, scrap, shred, smidgen, speck

crumble: break, collapse, crush, decay, decompose, disintegrate, erode, molder, perish, powder, pulverize, rot, splinter, spoil, tumble

crumbly: brittle, fragile, frail, friable, pulverizable, worn

crumbly soil: marl

crumpet's accompaniment: tea

crumple: break, cave, collapse, corrugate, crease, crinkle, crunkle, crush, fold, ruck, rumple, shrivel, wad, wrinkle

crunch: bite, chew, chomp, confrontation, crisis, crush, crux, gnash, gnaw, grind, masticate, munch, press, ruminate, scrunch, tread

crural part: shin

crusade: campaign, cause, jihad, march, movement, push, rally, war

crusader: pilgrim, templar

crusading: messianic

crush: annihilate, break, compress, conquer, cram, crash, crowd, crumble, crunch, defeat, demolish, destroy, drove, dump, force, granulate, grind, hurt, infatuation, mash, mill, obliterate, oppress, overpower, overwhelm, passion, press, pulp, pulverize, quell, reduce, repress, smash, squash, squelch, subdue, suppress, tamp, thwack, trample, tread, tread on

crush an action or movement: quash, quell, repress, scotch, subdue, suppress

crush into powder: comminute, pulverize, triturate

crushing implement: pestle

crust: caking, coating, film, harden, hull, layer, rind, scab, shell

crustacean: barnacle, crab, lobster, louse, pillbug, prawn, shrimp, squilla, water flea

crustacean part: alima, antenna, chela, claw, endite, exite, feeler, nauplius, pincer, pleopod, podite, podomere

crusty: abrupt, blunt, brief, choleric, crabbed, crabby, curt, dour, gruff, hard, harsh, irascible, irritable, morose, peevish, snappish, stern, surly, testy; crisp

crux: basis, core, cross, crunch, difficulty, essence, gist, kernel, matter, meat, moment, nub, point, problem, puzzling

cry: acclamation, advertise, bark, bawl, bellow, blame, blubber, boo, boo hoo, broadcast, cackle, call, caw, clamor, complain, coo, demand, exclaim, fret, groan, hawk, hoot, howl, hurrah, hype, keen, lament, lamentation, meow, moan, ouch, plead, proclaim, protest, puff, rage, rumor, scream, screech, shout, shriek, snivel, sob, sound, squall, squeal, tears, utter, vogue, wail, weep, whimper, whine, yammer, yell, yelp

cry from the heart: cri de coeur, lament

cry heard on the diamond: play ball

cry of a dog: yelp

cry or screech like cat in heat: caterwaul

cry, impassioned: cri de coeur

crybaby: bawler, whiner

crying: action, annoyance, astonishment, attention, burning, desperate, dire, heinous, imperative, insistent, pressing, teary, urgent

crying or shouting together: conclamant

crying, inclined to: lachrymose, tearful

crypt: catacomb, cave, cavern, cavity, cell, chamber, grave, grotto, pit, recess, tomb, undercroft, vault

cryptic: ambiguous, apocryphal, camouflage, dark, enigmatic, esoteric, hidden, murky, mysterious, mystical, obscure, occult, of codes, secret, vague

cryptogram: cipher, code, figure, representation, writing

cryptologize: encode

crystal: clear, crystalline, diamond, glass, hard, ice, limpid, lucid, mineral, oscillator, pellucid, quartz, transparent, unblurred

crystal added to solution to start crystallization: seed

crystal and liquid, intermediate between: mesomorphic, nematic, smectic

crystal angles, instrument for measuring: goniometer

crystal ball gazer: seer

crystal ball, to see the future with a: scry

crystal branching or treelike: dendrite

crystal exposed to air, of a hydrated: efflorescing

crystal gazing: soothsaying

crystal that converts between mechanical and electrical energy: piezoelectric

crystalline mineral: feldspar, quartz

crystalline structure of two or more substances, similarity of: isomorphism

crystalline structure, lacking distinct: amorphous

crystallization of compound in two or more distinct forms: pleomorphism, polymorphism

crystallize: candy, coat, form, granulate, jell, solidify, sugar

crystals lining rock cavity, crust of: druse

crystals, rock lined with: geode

cub: bear, fox, giraffe, lion, moose, novice, pup, reporter, scout, shark, tiger, whelp, wolf, youngster

cubbyhole: category, cranny, cubicle, niche, nook

cube: block, cubicle, dice, die, hexahedron

cube, four-dimensional equivalent of: tesseract

cubic meter: stere

cubicle: chamber, compartment

cuckoo: ani, batty, bird, clock, crazy, daffy, fool, insane, nuts, screwball, silly, wacky

cuckoolike bird: ani

cucullate: hooded

cucumber used for pickling: gherkin

cud: bolus, chew, food, quid

cud-chewing mammal: ruminant

cud, chew the: ruminate

cuddle: caress, embrace, fondle, hug, kiss, love, nestle, nuzzle, pet, snuggle, touch

cudgel: bastinado, bat, baton, beat, blackjack, bludgeon, cane, club, drive, drub, nightstick, shillelagh, staff, stave, stick, truncheon, weapon

cue: catchword, clue, gesture, hint, intimation, nod, notion, prod, prompt, queue, reminder, rod, sign, signal, suggestion, tip, warning, wink

cue cards: prompters

cuff: band, belt, blow, box, buffet, clobber, clout, handcuff, hit, pummel, scuffle, slam, slap, slug, smack, smite, spank, strike, swat, wallop

cuirass: lorica

cuisine: cookery, fare, food, menu

cul-de-sac: cavity, dead end, impasse, pocket, tube

culex specimen: mosquito

cull: choose, collect, elect, extract, gather, glean, opt, pick, prefer, reject, remove, select, separate, sift, sort, weed

culminate: climax, conclude, end, finish, result

culminating point: solstice, zenith

culmination: acme, apex, apogee, completion, consummation, crown, end, finale, maximum, ne plus ultra, noon, peak, pinnacle, summit, zenith

culpable: answerable, blamable, blameworthy, censurable, criminal, guilty, responsible

culprit: convict, criminal, delinquent, malefactor, miscreant, offender, transgressor, villain

cult: church, clan, clique, creed, faction, faddish, faith, followers, obsessive, religion, ritual, school, sect, worship

cultivable: arable

cultivate: acquire, bolster, cherish, civilize, develop, educate, encourage, farm, foster, grow, hoe, improve, labor, nourish, nurse, plant, plow, prepare, raise, rear, sow, study, tend, till, work

cultivate favor deliberately: ingratiate

cultivated estate: plantation

cultivation: advancement, advocacy, agriculture, agrology, culture, gentility, horticulture, husbandry, manners, nurture, polish, refinement, tillage

cultivation of land for crops: tillage, tilth

cultivation of plants: horticulture

cultivation of plants without soil: aquiculture, hydroponics

cultural change brought by another culture: acculturation

cultural group, relating to a distinct: ethnic

culture: agronomy, art, breeding, civilization, education, farming, folklore, knowledge, learning, lifestyles, literature, mores, music, polish, refinement, savoir faire, society

culture and human thought, branches of knowledge involving: humanities

culture modification through contact with other cultures: acculturation

culture of peoples, study of: ethnology

culture passed down from preceding generations: heritage, tradition

culture, revival of a: renaissance, renascence

cultured: educated, elegant, enlightened, genteel, literate, polished, sophisticated

cultured people: cognoscenti, intelligentsia

cultured, highly: highbrow, intellectual

cultureless or rootless: deracinated, deracine, displaced

cultures form integrated society, place where: melting pot

culvert: channel, conduit, drain, gutter, sewer

cumbersome: awkward, bulky, burdensome, clumsy, cumbrous, heavy, massive, ponderous, weighty

cummerbund: sash

cumulation: accruing, amassed, augmenting, collective, heap, increasing, multiplying

cunning: adroit, arch, art, artful, astute, chicanery, clever, crafty, deceit, deceptive, designing, devious, dextrous, disingenuous, finesse, foxy, guile, imaginative, ingenious, insidious, keen, Machiavellian, pretty, savvy, sharp, shifty, shrewd, skillful, slick, slippery, sly, sly as a fox, smart, smooth, subtle, wary, wile, wily

cunning and intricate: daedal, insidious, treacherous, wily

cunning in politics: Machiavellianism

cup/glass filled to brim: bumper

cup/glass for measuring hard liquor: jigger

cup holder for handleless mug: zarf

cup of Arthurian legend: Holy Grail

cup of tea: forte

cup or goblet: chalice

cup or plate of Last Supper: grail, Holy Grail, Sangrail

cup parts: beaker, calix, cannikin, chalice, demitasse, ear, glass, goblet, grail, Holy Grail, jorum, kantharos, lug, mug, noggin, pannikin, porringer, shot, stein, stirrup, stoup, tankard, tig, tyg, vessel, zarf

cup-shaped: calathiform, cotyloid, cupulate

cup with handle, shallow: porringer

cup, concerning: oalicular

cup, large and with hinged cover: tankard

cup, small, for strong coffee: demitasse

cupboard: ambry, armoire, buffet, bureau, cabinet, chiffonier, closet, cuddy, dresser, locker, pantry, sideboard

cupidity: avarice, covetousness, craving, desire, greed, lust, passion, rapacity, yearning

cur: bum, cad, canine, coward, dog, mongrel, mutt, rotten, scoundrel, stinker, toad, villain, yellow dog

curate: abbe, assistant, clergyman, cleric, dominie, minister, pastor, priest

curative: beneficial, curing, healing, healthful, invigorating, medicinal, remedial, restorative, salutary, therapeutic

curator: caretaker, custodian, director, guardian, keeper, manager, overseer

curb: abstain, arrest, barrier, border, brake, bridle, brink, check, constrain, control, curve, edge, hamper, hinder, inhibit, limit, moderate, rein, repress, restrain, restrict, shackle, suppress, tame, thwart, withhold

curdle: change, clabber, clot, coagulate, condense, congeal, curd, ferment, quail, quarl, sour, spoil, thicken, turn

curds, watery part of milk that separates from: whey

cure: agent, antidote, care, correct, heal, help, mend, physic, recover, rectify, remedy, restore, save, solution, therapy, treatment; age, dry, kipper, preserve, salt, season, smoke, tan

cure-all: balm, catholicon, elixir, medicine, panacea, remedy

cure that is counteractive: antidote

cure, doubtful: nostrum

cure, miraculous: magic bullet

cured and smoked side of pig: bacon

cures or alleviates grief, something that: dolorifuge

curfew: bell, regulation, restriction, signal, time

curing: healing, sanative

curio: antique, bauble, bibelot, bric-a-brac, collectible, curiosity, keepsake, knickknack, relic, souvenir, trinket

curiosity: concern, curio, interest, marvel, meddling, nosiness, objet d'art, snooping, wonder

curiosity, person with no: fysigunkus

curiosity, to arouse one's: pique

curious: eager, exotic, inquisitive, intrusive, nosy, novel, odd, peculiar, peeping, prying, queer, rare, singular, snoopy, strange, unique, unorthodox, unusual, weird, wondering

curious, offensively: inquisitorial

curl: bend, coil, convolution, corkscrew, crimple, crisp, frizz, intort, kink, lock, loop, meander, ringlet, ripple, roll, spiral, swirl, tress, twist, wave, wind, writhe

curled design: volute, whorl

curling broom or brush: besom

curling stone: clint

curls or waves, to press into tight: crimp

curly canine: poodle

curly- or wavy-haired: cymotrichous

currencies, to let currency find a level of relationship to other: float

currency: bills, bread, cabbage, cash, change, circulation, coin, dinero, dough, greenbacks, money, moolah; prevalence

currency equivalent at official rate of exchange: parity

currency exchanger: agiotage

currency not based on gold or silver, of a: fiat, fiduciary

currency, legally valid: circulating medium, legal tender

currency, to lower the exchange value of a: devaluation

current: accepted, common, contemporary, counter, customary, general, instant, latest, living, modern, now, ongoing, popular, present, prevailing, prevalent, recent, topical, trend, trendy, usual; course, draft, drift, electricity, flow, flux, motion, moving, rapid, rife, run, running, rush, stream, tide, torrent

current fashion: mode

current moving contrary to main current: eddy

current style: trend

current that flows one direction, electrical: DC, direct current

current that reverses its direction periodically, electrical: AC, alternating current

curry: clean, comb, condiment, favor, groom, powder, prepare, relish, sauce, seasoning

curse: affliction, anathema, bane, blasphemy, burden, condemn, cuss, damn, denounce, denunciation, execrate, execration, expletive, fulmination, hex, imprecate, imprecation, jinx, malediction, malison, oath, obscenity, plague, profanity, spell, swear, swearword, voodoo, whammy

curse or excommunication, formal: anathema

cursed: blankety-blank, blighted, con-

CURRENCIES OF THE WORLD (EQUIVALENT OF U.S. DOLLAR)

Afghanistan: afghani
Albania: lek
Algeria: dinar
Andorra: French franc, Spanish peseta
Angola: kwanza
Antigua and Barbuda: East Caribbean dollar
Argentina: peso
Armenia: dram
Australia: Australian dollar
Austria: euro, schilling
Azerbaijan: manat
Bahamas: Bahamian dollar
Bahrain: Bahrain dinar
Bangladesh: taka
Barbados: Barbados dollar
Belarus: Belarusian ruble
Belgium: euro, Belgian franc
Belize: Belize dollar
Benin: Franc CFA
Bhutan: ngultrum
Bolivia: boliviano
Bosnia and Herzegovina: dinar
Botswana: pula
Brazil: real
Bulgaria: lev
Burkina Faso: Franc CFA
Burma: kyat
Burundi: Burundi franc
Cambodia: riel
Cameroon: Franc CFA
Canada: Canadian dollar
Cape Verde: Cape

Verdean escudo
Central African Republic: Franc CFA
Chad: Franc CFA
Chile: peso
China: yuan
Colombia: peso
Congo: Franc CFA
Costa Rica: colon
Croatia: kuna
Cuba: peso
Cyprus: Cyprus pound
Czech Republic: koruna
Denmark: krone
Dominican Republic: peso
Ecuador: sucre
Egypt: Egyptian pound
El Salvador: colon
Equatorial Guinea: Franc CFA
Eritrea: birr
Estonia: kroon
Ethiopia: birr
Fiji: Fiji dollar
Finland: euro, markka
France: euro, franc
Gabon: Franc CFA
Georgia: coupon
Germany: euro, deutsche mark
Ghana: cedi
Greece: drachma
Grenada: East Caribbean dollar
Guatemala: quetzal
Guinea: Guinean franc
Guinea-Bassau: Guinea-Bassau peso
Guyana: Guyana dollar
Haiti: gourde
Honduras: lempira

Hungary: forint
Iceland: krona
India: rupee
Indonesia: rupiah
Iran: rial
Iraq: Iraqi dinar
Ireland: euro, Irish pound
Israel: shekel
Italy: euro, lira
Jamaica: Jamaican dollar
Japan: yen
Jordan: Jordanian dinar
Kazakhstan: tenge
Kenya: Kenyan shilling
Kuwait: Kuwaiti dinar
Kyrgyzstan: som
Laos: kip
Latvia: lats
Lebanon: Lebanese pound
Lesotho: loti
Liberia: Liberian dollar
Libya: Libyan dinar
Liechtenstein: Swiss franc
Lithuania: litas
Luxembourg: euro, Luxembourg franc
Macedonia: dinar
Madagascar: Malagasy franc
Malawi: kwacha
Malaysia: ringgit
Mali: Franc CFA
Malta: Maltese lira
Mauritania: ouguiya
Mauritius: Mauritian rupee
Mexico: peso
Moldova: Moldovan lem
Monaco: euro,

French franc
Mongolia: tugrik
Morocco: dirham
Mozambique: metical
Namibia: Namibian dollar
Nepal: Nepalese rupee
Netherlands: euro, guilder
New Zealand: New Zealand dollar
Nicaragua: cordoba
Niger: Franc CFA
Nigeria: naira
North Korea: won
Norway: krone
Oman: Omani rial
Pakistan: Pakistan rupee
Panama: balboa
Papua New Guinea: kina
Paraguay: guarani
Peru: inti
Philippines: peso
Poland: zloty
Portugal: euro, esudo
Principe: dobra
Qatar: Qatari riyal
Romania: leu
Russia: ruble
Rwanda: Rwanda franc
Sao Tome and Principe: dobra
Saudi Arabia: riyal
Senegal: Franc CFA
Sierra Leone: leone
Singapore: Singapore dollar
Slovakia: koruna
Slovenia: Slovenian tolar
Somalia: Somali shilling
South Africa: rand
South Korea: won

Spain: euro, peseta
Sri Lanka: Sri Lanka rupee
Sudan: Sudanese pound
Suriname: Suriname guilder
Swaziland: lilangeni
Sweden: krona
Switzerland: Swiss franc
Syria: Syrian pound
Taiwan: New Taiwan dollar
Tajikistan: Tajik ruble
Tanzania: Tanzanian shilling
Thailand: baht
Togo: Franc CFA
Tonga: pa'anga
Trinidad and Tobago: Trinidad and Tobago dollar
Tunisia: Tunisian dinar
Turkey: Turkish lira
Uganda: Ugandan shilling
Ukraine: karbovanets
United Arab Emirates: U.A.E. dirham
United Kingdom: pound sterling
Uruguay: peso
Uzbekistan: som
Vanuatu: vatu
Venezuela: bolivar
Vietnam: dong
Western Samoa: tala
Yemen: rial
Yugoslavia: Yugoslav new dinar
Zambia: kwacha
Zimbabwe: Zimbabwean dollar ✎

---

founded, damned, doggone, execrable, foredoomed, hateful, infamous, loathsome, vile
cursory: brief, careless, depthless, desultory, fast, haphazard, hasty, hur-

ried, passing, quick, rambling, rapid, scant, shallow, short, sketchy, sloppy, speedy, superficial
cursory, as a hearing: summary
curt: abrupt, bluff, blunt, brief, concise,

condensed, gruff, pithy, rude, short, snappy, snippy, succinct, summary, tart, terse
curtail: abbreviate, abridge, chop, clip, crop, cut, decrease, diminish, dock,

downsize, halt, lessen, lop, reduce, restrict, retrench, shorten, slash, stop, water down

curtain: backdrop, barrier, blind, boom, conceal, decoration, drape, mask, purdah, screen, shade, shroud, shutter, veil, wall

curtain at rear of stage: backdrop

curtain hung across top edge, ornamental: valance

curtain on doorway: portiere

curtain separating women in India: purdah

curtsy: bending, bob, bow, curtsey, dip, gesture, obeisance

curvaceous: attractive, buxom, curvy, endowed, shapely, stacked, voluptuous, well-built

curvature: arc, arch, bend, curve, deflection, ratio

curvature of the spine: kyphosis, lordosis

curve: arc, arch, bend, bight, bow, circuit, concave, contour, crook, crump, curb, curl, curvature, deviate, ellipse, ess, hairpin, hook, parabola, sinus, spiral, sweep, swerve, swirl, turn, twist, veer

curve bounding plane area, closed: perimeter

curve crosses itself, point at which: cusp, spinode

curve in and out: sinuate

curve in ship's timber: sny

curve inward: concave, incurvate

curve of body part: flexure

curve of flight: trajectory

curve on geometric graph: hyperbola, parabola

curve outward: convex, flare

curve that circles to a central point, axis: spiral

curve, line considered limit to: asymptote

curved: aquiline, arced, arched, arciform, arcuate, arrondi, bent, crooked, declinate, elliptical, essed, humped, looped, round, snaky, turned

curved furniture leg with ornamental foot: cabriole

curved mark over vowel for "short" sound: breve

curved surface of liquid: meniscus

curved surface of vehicle or road: camber

curved sword: scimitar

curved trajectory: arc

curved wall or screen of pictures: cyclorama

curved, as a leaf: acinaciform

curved, bent part: flection

curves touching, of two adjoining: osculate

curves, draftman's tool for: French curve

cushion: bolster, buffer, hassock, insole, insulate, mat, mitigates, pad, pillow, protect, quiet, seat, soften, squab, upholster

cushion, long narrow: bolster

cushioned footstool: ottoman

cusp: angle, apex, corner, end, flap, fold, horn, peak, point, tip, tooth

custard apple: papaw

custard-filled pastry: napoleon

custard or other bland food: flummery

custard served in a tall glass, layers of frozen: parfait

custard topped with caramel: crème caramel, flan

custard with glazed carmelized sugar top: crème brûleé

custard with whipped cream, flavored egg: Bavarian cream

custardlike pie with vegetables, cheese, etc.: quiche

custodian: attendant, caretaker, cerberus, cleaner, curator, guard, guardian, janitor, keeper, protector, steward, warden

custodian of museum collection: curator

custody: arrest, care, charge, confinement, control, keeping, protection, safekeeping, supervision, trust, watch

custom: business, consuetude, convention, costume, duty, fashion, form, formality, groove, habit, law, method, mode, more, observance, practice, rite, ritual, routine, rule, style, system, tailor-made, toll, usage, use, way, wont

custom for change of status: rite of passage

customary: accepted, accustomed, common, conventional, established, familiar, general, habitual, nomic, normal, orthodox, popular, regular, standard, traditional, understood, usual

customary practice: convention, habit, wont

customer: buyer, client, clientele, consumer, patron, prospect, purchaser, regular, shopper, user

customs: duty, inspection, levy, mores, rate, tariff, tax, toll, uses

customs and folkways: mores

customs, to seize at: confiscate, embargo, impound

cut: affront, allotment, bisect, bite, carve, chip, chisel, chop, cleave, clip, condense, curtail, delete, dice, dilute, dissever, divide, dock, excise, fell, form, gash, hack, hew, hewed, hewn, ignore, incise, incision, insult, kickback, knife, lacerate, lance, lessen, lop, lopped, lowering, mince, mode, mow, mown, nick, nip, opening, part, piece, prune, raze, reduce, retrench, saw, sawn, section, segment, sever, severed, share, shave, shear, shorten, slash, slashed, slice, slight, slit, sned, snip, snub, split, stab, tear, trim, type, whittle

cut across: divide, intersect, transect

CYCLES

all-terrain vehicle/ATV
bicycle
bicycle-built-for-two
bike
BMX bike
chopper
dandy
dirt bike
hog
hybrid bike
minibike
monkey bike
monocycle
moped
motor scooter
motorbike
motorcycle
mountain bike
off-road bike
ordinary
pedicab
quadricycle
racing bike
scooter
sidewalk bike
tandem
ten-speed
touring bike
trail bike
tricycle
trike
trishaw
unicycle
velocipede ❦

cut-and-dried: cut-and-dry, ordinary, routine, settled, trite

cut at angle, but not right angle: bevel

cut back on spending: curtail, economize, retrench

cut down: clear, clip, diminish, fell, kill, level, limit, pare, pared, reduce, slain, slaughter, slay

cut groove in: chamfer, chase, flute

cut in small pieces: mince

cut into long thin pieces: sliver

cut off: amputate, block, clip, deprive, detach, discontinue, disinherit, halt, insulate, interception, isolate, lop, nip, prevent, sequester, severed, snip, trim

cut off by authority: excommunicate

cut off from outside influence: cloistered, hermetic, insulated, isolated

cut off limb: dismember

cut on the diagonal: bias

cut or notch by saw, ax: kerf

cut or notch on border: indent

cut out: cancel, delete, deprive, eliminate, escape, excise, exit, exscind, fit, remove, scram, suit, supplant

cut short: abbreviate, abort, clip, crop, curtail, dock, end, nip in the bud, shear, snip, terminate, truncate

cut the lawn: mow

cut through object showing inner structure: cross section

cut to pieces: shred

cut up: carve, chop, clown, criticize, crucify, divide, horseplay, joke, knock, misbehave, ridicule, scissor, split

cut up a whale: flense

cut up or open to examine or do surgery: dissect

cut with a sickle: reap

cut wool from: shear

cut, pencil to stop bleeding of: styptic pencil

cutaway: coat, diagram, dive, model

cutback: clip, curtail, decrease, economize, lower, prune, reduction, reversal, shorten, trim

cute: adorable, attractive, beautiful, clever, coy, cunning, dainty, precious, pretty, sharp, shrewd

cutlass: machete, sword, weapon

cutlery: silverware

cutlet, veal: schnitzel

cutoff of service by accident: outage

cutout decorating art: decoupage

cutter: boat, clipper, editor, hewer, saw blade, sled, sleigh, slicer, sloop, tailor, vessel

cutthroat: cruel, hoodlum, murderer, relentless, ruffian, ruthless

cutting: barbed, biting, bitter, chilling, crisp, curt, edged, hateful, incisive, malicious, nasty, penetrating, piercing, pointed, raw, sarcastic, sardonic, scission, severe, sharp, tart; editing

cutting and intersecting: secant

cutting criticism: slam

cutting edge: blade, cusp, element, forefront, quality

cutting for planting: scion, slip

cutting off: abscission

cutting teeth: dentition, teething

cutting up animals for research: vivisection

cuttlefish pigment: sepia

cycle: aeon, age, bicycle, bike, chain, circle, circuit, course, eon, era, orbit, period, phase, revolution, ring, round, sequence, series, time, vehicle, wheel

CYCLE SPORTS

bicycling
BMX racing
cycle racing
cyclocross
in-line skating
mountain biking
road cycle racing
roller derby
roller hockey
roller-skating
skateboarding
track cycle racing ❦

cycle of human emotion or physical condition: biorhythm

cycling arena: velodrome

cyclone: blast, gale, gust, storm, tornado, twister, typhoon, weather, whirlwind, wind, windstorm

cygnet: swan

cylinder: tube

cylinder with top cut at angle: ungula

cylindrical: circular, coordinates, round, terete, tubular

cylindrical and tapering: terete

cylindrical Buddhist mound: stupa

cymbals worked by foot pedal: high-hat

cynic: doubter, misanthrope, misogamist, mocker, pessimist, skeptic, unbeliever

cynical: disabused, disenchanted, disillusioned, doubtful, ironic, sarcastic, sardonic, scornful, snarling, suspicious, wry

cyst: bag, blister, pouch, sac, sore, spore, vesicle, wen

czar: autocrat, baron, emperor, king, monarch, ruler, tycoon

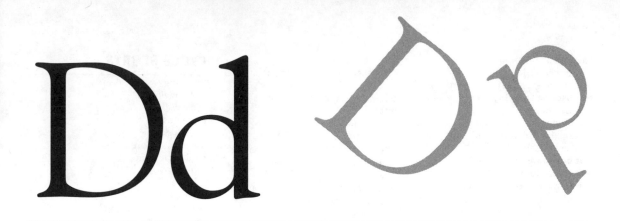

dab: blotch, daub, drop, flatfish, flounder, hit, lump, pat, peck, portion, smear, smidgen, spot, swab, wipe

dabble: dally, fiddle, idle, meddle, moisten, putter, spatter, splash, sprinkle, tinker, trifle

dabbler: amateur, beginner, dilettante, novice

dabbler with superficial interest: dilettante

dactylogram: fingerprint

dactyls: toes

dad: father, old man, papa, pop, poppy

daddy longlegs: harvestman

daffodil: narcissus

daffodil crown-shaped part: corona

daft: absurd, barmy, cracked, crazy, cuckoo, daffy, demented, foolish, fried, frolicsome, giddy, goofy, idiotic, imbecile, insane, loco, loony, mad, nutty, silly, stupid, unsound, wild

dagger: anlace, blade, bodkin, dirk, knife, misericord, stiletto, weapon

dagger formerly used in Scotland: skean

dagger haft: hilt

dagger mark, double: diesis

dagger with wavy blade: kris

dagger, in printing: obelus

daily: circadian, diurnal, periodic, quotidian, regularly, routine; journal, newspaper

daily account: diary

daily account of events: chronology

daily allowance for expenses: per diem

daily Catholic prayers: breviary

daily routine: rut

daily walk: constitutional

daily, recurring: diurnal, quotidian

daintily pleasing: cute

dainty: airy, attractive, beautiful, choice, cute, delicacy, delicate, ele-

gant, exquisite, fastidious, finicky, fragile, frail, graceful, nice, persnickety, pretty, rare, select, trim

dainty and prim: fastidious, mincing

dairy: creamery, farm

dairy product: cheese, butter, cottage cheese, cream, eggnog, milk, yogurt

dais: bench, platform, podium, rostrum, seat, stage, table, terrace

daisy: black-eyed Susan, oxeye

daisy dense disk cluster: capitulum

daisy flower head: composite

daisy small reduced flower head: floret

daisylike flower: aster

dale: dell, dene, dingle, glen, ravine, spout, trough, vale, valley

dally: chat, dabble, dawdle, delay, drag, flirt, fool, frivol, frolic, idle, linger, loiter, lollygag, play, romp, sport, toy, trifle

dam: bar, barricade, barrier, block, blockade, check, choke, clog, dike, hinder, impede, levee, obstacle, obstruct, plug, repress, restrain, slow, stem, stop, weir

dam channel or apron to divert flow: spillway

dam for electricity generation: hydroelectric dam

dam in stream: weir

dam wall: barrage

damage: accident, award, bill, blemish, charge, cloud, corrupt, cost, defile, deleterious, destruction, detriment, disadvantage, disservice, expense, harm, harm done, hurt, impair, indemnity, injury, loss, maim, mar, pollute, reparation, ruin, sabotage, scathe, scratch, spoil, tarnish, undermine, vandalism, weaken, wound

damage appearance: deface, disfigure

damage by perforation: riddle

damage impossible to repair, of: irreparable

damage of neglect: blight

damage or corrupt: vitiate

damage or maim: mutilate

damage or weaken: disable, impair, incapacitate, mar

damage property maliciously: vandalize

damage reputation: discredit, disgrace, dishonor

damage to reputation in false written statement or representation: libel

damage, deliberate: sabotage

damage, severe: devastation, havoc, ravage

damages awarded in excess of actual loss: exemplary damages

damaging: deleterious, noxious

dame: female, gal, lady, matron, miss, title, woman

damn: attack, castigate, condemn, curse, cuss, darn, denounce, doom, penalize, punish, sentence

damnable: atrocious, blamed, culpable, detestable, execrable, hateful, odious, wicked

damnation: hell, perdition

damned: accursed, cursed, doggone, doomed, dratted, fallen, infamous, loathsome, revolting

damning and faint praise: diasyrm

damp: clammy, dank, dewy, drenched, drizzly, fog, hinder, humid, mist, moist, moisture, muggy, musty, rainy, saturated, soaked, soggy, wet

damp and moist: dank, humid

dampen: bedew, cloud, deaden, depress, discourage, dispirit, dull, moisten, muffle, ret, spray, wet

damsel: demoiselle, female, girl, lass, maid, maiden, miss, princess, woman

dandelion: color, plant, weed, yellow

dandelion tuft of fluff: pappus

DANCE TERMS

ballroom dance: beguine, carioca, cha-cha, fox-trot, lancers, mambo, merengue, polka, quickstep, rumba, samba, shimmy, tango

dance: ball, cotillion, fox-trot, frug, hoedown, hoof, hop, hula, jig, prom, reel, samba, shag, stomp, tango, tarantella

dance in duple meter: galop

dance notation: choreology

dance of Brazil: bossa nova, maxixe, samba

dance performed by rhythmic heel stamping: zapateado

dance performed by women featuring high kicking while holding skirt front: can-can

dance professional: choreographer

dance with alternating squatting kicks: kazatsky

dance with castanet accompaniment: fandango

dance with locking arms: hora

dancer: terpsichorean

dancers approach, circle back-to-back, and return to original position in square dancing: do-si-do

dancer's handrail: barre

dancers in a ballet company who perform together: corps de ballet

dancing girl: almah, alme

dancing girls all in a line: chorines

dancing mania: tarantism

design of dances: choreography

dip: corte

folk dance: belly, fling, hoedown, hornpipe, hula, jig, morris, reel, square, streathspey, sword

footwear: pumps, slippers, taps, toe shoes

formal dance: ball, promenade

French dance: farandole, galop, tambourin

garment: leotard, tights, tutu

historical dance: allemande, bourrée, chaconne, Charleston, cotillion, courante, ecossaise, galliard, gavotte, minuet, passacaglia, passepied, pavane, quadrille, rigadoon, sarabande, schottische, turkey trot, volta

Hungarian dance: czardas

Indian dance: nautch

Israeli dance: hora

Italian dance: courante, rigoletto, saltarello, tarantella

Latin American dance: carioca, cha-cha, conga, criolla, limbo, mambo, maxixe, rumba, samba, tango

modern dance: boogie, bop, break, go-go, hustle, jitterbug, mashed potato, rock 'n' roll, salsa, shuffle, twist

person unwilling to dance: wallflower

pertaining to dance: terpsichorean

Peruvian dance: cueca

Polish dance: mazurka, polonaise

skirt: tutu

slow polka dance: schottische

Spanish dance: bolero, cachucha, fandango, flamenco, malaguena, seguidilla, zapateado

square dance going counterclockwise in circle: promenade ❦

---

dander: anger, ire, provoke, scurf, temper

dandified man: fop

dandle: caress, cuddle, love, nuzzle, pamper, rock

dandling site: knee

dandruff: flakes, furfur, scurf, seborrhea

dandruff, covered with: furfuraceous, scurfy

dandy: capital, crackerjack, excellent, exquisite, fine, grand, great, humdinger, nifty, peachy, splendid, superb, swell, terrific

danger: adventure, crisis, emergency, fear, hazard, jeopardy, menace, peril, pitfall, risk, threat, uncertainty

danger at work: occupational hazard

danger from two sides: Scylla and Charybdis

danger signal: alarum

danger, disregard for: temerity

danger, looming: pitfall, sword of Damocles

danger, susceptible to: exposed, vulnerable

danger, to prevent or ward off: avert

danger, to put in: imperil, jeopardize

dangerous: chancy, deadly, hairy, hazardous, insecure, nasty, parlous, perilous, precarious, speculative, touchy, treacherous, unsafe, unsound

dangerous and evil: pernicious, pestiferous, pestilent

dangerous and risky: forbidding, hazardous, insidious, perilous, threatening, treacherous

dangerous and uncertain: parlous

dangerous current: riptide

dangerous in speed: breakneck

dangerous situation, potentially: powder keg, tinderbox

dangerous spot: line of fire

dangerous to society: pestilent

dangerous, risky project: venture

dangerously lacking in security or stability: precarious

dangle: droop, entice, hang, hover, loll, lure, suspend, swing, tempt

dank: chilly, clammy, cold, damp, dripping, humid, moist, soggy, wet

dapper: chic, classy, dashing, natty, neat, prim, sharp, spiffy, spruce, stylish, swank, trim

dappled: calico, dotted, flecked, freckled, mottled, multicolored, piebald, speckled, spotted, variegated

dare: attempt, brave, challenge, confront, defy, disregard, face, gamble, goad, hazard, risk, speculate, take a risk, undertake, venture

daredevil: adventurous, bold, daring, reckless, stuntman, stuntwoman, swashbuckler

daring: adventurous, audacious, audacity, bold, brave, cocky, courageous, daredevil, dashing, dauntless, death-defying, derring-do, devilish, fearless, gutsy, hardihood, heroic, impudence, intrepid, nerve, rash, valiant, venturesome

dark: abstruse, aphotic, black, brown, brunet, caliginosity, cloudy, dim, dingy, dismal, dreary, dusky, ebony, forbidding, gloomy, grim, hidden, inky, lowering, murky, mysterious, mystifying, nighttime, obscure, occult, ominous, opaque, overcast, secretive, shady, sinister, sombre, stygian, sunless, swarthy, unlit

dark ale: stout

dark and damp: dank

dark and drab: subfusc

dark and gloomy: calignous, cimmerian, funereal, somber, stygian, tenebrous

dark brown: sepia

dark cloud: pall

dark-colored in poetry: swarth

dark-complexioned: swarthy

dark granular corundum: emery

dark in pigmentation: melanoid

dark profile with light background: silhouette

dark red: puce

dark yellow: ocher, ochre

dark, hard, heavy wood: ebony

darken: bedim, benight, blacken, cloud, deepen, dim, dull, eclipse, gloom, obfuscate, obscure, opacate, overcast, overshadow, shade, shadow, tarnish, tint, umber

darkened: obnubilated

darkened with brown: infuscate

darkest area, as in shadow: umbra

darkish area: penumbra

darkness: blackness, concealment, dusk, isolation, murk, night, privacy, secrecy, shadow, twilight, unawareness, wickedness

darling: adorable, attractive, beloved, cute, dear, dearest, deary, favorite, honey, honeybunch, lamb, love, pet, precious, sugar, sweet, sweetheart, sweetie, truelove

darn: cussed, damn, downright, heck, mend, patch, repair, stitch, weave

dart: arrow, bolt, bound, dash, flechette, fling, flit, hasten, hurry, launch, leap, missile, movement, propel, race, scoot, scurry, speed, spring, sprint, stinger

dash: animation, élan, energy, flair, oomph, panache, pizzazz, spirit, verve, vigor, vim, vivacity, zip; bolt, dart, lunge, race, run, rush, scamper, speed, sprint

dashing: bold, chic, courageous, dapper, daring, debonair, fashionable, fearless, flamboyant, gallant, gay, jaunty, lively, rakish, showy, spanking, spirited, stylish, vivacious

dashingly smart: chic

dastard: cad, chicken, coward, craven, malicious, poltroon, recreant, sneak, wimp, yellow

dastardly: base, cowardly, despicable, foul, mean, rotten, vile

data: charts, compilations, facts, figures, info, information, input, material, scoop, stats, statistics, values

date: age, anniversary, appointment, century, day, duration, epoch, era, moment, time, year; companion, escort, lover, steady; court, escort, rendezvous, tryst, woo; fruit

date a bond or loan is due: maturity

date earlier than date of writing: antedate

date later than date of writing: postdate

date, about or approximately on a: circa

dated: aged, antiquate, archaic, behind the times, demode, faded, obsolete, old-fashioned, outmoded, passé

dates of history, ordering of: chronology

dating of trees by radioactive carbon: carbon dating, radiocarbon dating

daub: apply, besmear, blot, blur, coat, cover, dab, fleck, grease, paint, plaster, smear, smudge, soil, splatter, splotch, sully

daughter sexually attached to father: Electra complex

daughter, pertaining to a: filial

daunt: alarm, awe, break, bully, check, conquer, control, cow, depress, deter, disconcert, discourage, dishearten, dismay, dispirit, faze, foil, frighten, horrify, intimidate, stun, stupefy, subdue, tame, terrify

daunt archaic: amate

dauntless: aweless, bold, brave, courageous, daring, fearless, intrepid, lionhearted, stouthearted, unafraid, valiant

davenport: bed, chesterfield, convertible, couch, desk, sofa

dawdle: dally, delay, diddle, dillydally, idle, lackadaisical, linger, loaf, loiter, lollygag, lounge, mope, mosey, piddle, poke, procrastinate, putter, vacillate, waste time

dawdler: loiterer, poke

dawn: aurora, beginning, birth, cockcrow, daybreak, emerge, genesis, morn, morning, occur, rise, start, sunrise, sunup, understand, unfold

day: age, cycle, date, epoch, era, generation, lifetime, period, sunlight, time

day added to calendar: intercalary

day and night are of equal length, time when: equinox

day before a Jewish holiday: erev

day beginning new season or quarter: quarter day

day laborer: peon

day of the year, shortest or longest: solstice

day, active during the: diurnal

day, pertaining to biological cycles that take place in a: circadian

daybreak: aurora, dawn, morn, morning, sunrise, sunup

daydream: envision, fantasize, imagine, muse, reverie, vision, wish

daydreamer: luftmensch, Walter Mitty

daydreaming: brown study, reverie, woolgathering

daytime dramas: soaps

daytime movies: matinees

daze: befuddle, bemuse, benumb, bewilder, confuse, disorient, dizzy, dumbfound, fog, muddle, numb, overwhelm, puzzle, shock, stun, stupefy, stupor, trance

dazed: addled, confused, dazzled, dopey, groggy, punch drunk, punchy, woozy

dazed and confused: groggy, stupefied, woozy

dazed state: trance

dazzle: amaze, awe, bewilder, blind, blur, eclipse, electrify, excite, impress, outshine, shine

dazzling: breathtaking, bright, brilliant, foudroyant, fulgent, glaring, glowing, gorgeous, meteoric, radiant, resplendent, sparkling, vivid

dazzling effect: éclat

de-emphasize: minimize, understate

de facto: actual, existing, real, tangible, truly

de novo: afresh, again, anew, beginning, newly

de rigueur: becoming, correct, fashionable, fitting, obligatory, proper, required, right

de trop: excess, superfluous, surplus

deacon: cleric, elder, layperson, vicar

dead: absolute, asleep, barren, beat, bleak, bloodless, breathless, buried, cold, complete, deceased, defunct, demised, departed, discharged, doomed, drained, dull, exactly, exhausted, expired, extinct, extinguished, fallen, flat, gone, inactive, inanimate, indifferent, inert, inoperative, lackluster, lapsed, lifeless, lost, motionless, numb, obsolete, perished, quiet, slain, spent, spiritless, stiff, unexciting, unproductive, useless, utter

dead animal body: carcass

dead animal feeder: scavenger

dead animal flesh: carrion
dead animal stuffing: taxidermy
dead as a species: extinct
dead at birth: stillborn
dead end: close, cul-de-sac, deadlock, impasse, rowdy, stop, tough
dead-end street: cul-de-sac
dead flesh: carrion
dead heat: tie
dead or not working: defunct
dead person: decedent, the deceased
dead person gravestone inscription: epitaph
dead person, hymn or service for: requiem
dead person, speech or poem written for: elegy, epitaph, eulogy
dead skin, cast off: molt, slough
dead, pretend to be: play possum
deadbeat: bum, freeloader, lazy, loafer, sponger, vagrant
deaden: anesthetize, benumb, blunt, damp, desensitize, diminish, dope, dull, freeze, incapacitate, kill, lessen, muffle, numb, obtund, paralyze, petrify, quiet, repress, retard, soothe, stun, stupefy, weaken
deadfall: snare, trap
deadlock: dilemma, draw, gridlock, impasse, predicament, stalemate, standstill, tie
deadly: awful, carcinogenic, dangerous, destructive, dire, extreme, fatal, ghostly, harmful, implacable, lethal, mortal, pernicious, pestilent, poisonous, ruinous, ruthless, tedious, terrible, toxic, venomous, violent, virulent
deadly compound: toxin
deadly fly: tsetse
deadly pale: ashy
deadly poison: bane
deadly viper: asp
deadpan: blank, expressionless, impassive, unemotional, vacant
deaf-mute alphabet: dactylology
deal: administer, agreement, allot, apportion, arrangement, bargain, barter, behave, bestow, board, compromise, control, deliver, dispense, distribute, divide, dole, hand, handle, manage, negotiate, pact, part, plank, portion, sale, separate, share, swap, trade, transaction, treat, treatment, wield, wrestle
deal out: allot, mete
deal with: cope, treat
dealer: agent, broker, businessman, businessperson, businesswoman, distributor, jobber, marketer, merchant, middleman, middleperson, middlewoman, monger, negotiator, operator, retailer, seller, trader, tradesman, tradesperson, tradeswoman, trafficker, vendor
dealings: affairs, business, commerce, doings, matters, proceedings, relations, traffic
dealt out: meted
dean: authority, dignitary, doyen, headmaster, principal, senior
dean, concerning a: decanal
dear: affectionate, angel, beloved, cherished, costly, darling, esteemed, expensive, fond, heartfelt, high, honey, honeybunch, important, lovable, love, loved, near, pet, precious, prized, scarce, special, steep, sweetheart, treasure, valuable, worthy
dearly: affectionately, deeply, earnestly, heartily, profoundly, yearningly
dearth: deficiency, famine, insufficiency, lack, need, paucity, poverty, scantiness, scarcity, shortage, sparsity, want
death: bane, biolysis, curtains, decay, decease, demise, departure, doom, end, euthanasia, exit, expiration, extinction, fatality, grim reaper, loss, murder, passage, passing, sleep

RELATED TERMS

death and end of world, study of: eschatology
death as relief: quietus
death blow: coup de grace
death by disintegration: dissolution
death caused to relieve suffering: euthanasia
death-defying: audacious, bold, daredevil, daring, rash, risky
death house: charnel house
death notice: obit, obituary
death of body tissue: gangrene, mortification, necrosis
death of one million people: megadeath
death omen: knell
death penalty cancellation or postponement: pardon, reprieve, respite
death reminder: memento mori
death resulting from accident or disaster: fatality
death, apparition of living person seen just before: wraith
death, at the point of: in extremis, moribund
death, capable of causing: internecine
death, causing or relating to: fatal, lethal
death, certain to end in: terminal
death, hospital for those near to: hospice
death, medical specialist looking into cause of: coroner
death, muscle stiffening following: rigor mortis
death, occurring after: postmortem
death, of a premature: untimely
death, painless and peaceful, during terminal illness: euthanasia
death, preoccupied with: morbid
death, relating to: mortal, mortuary
death, relating to time after a: posthumous, post-obit
death, suggestive of: macabre
death, very upset by: bereaved, bereft
deathless: eternal, everlasting, immortal, undying
deathlike condition, restoring to life from: anabiotic
deathlike state: suspended animation
deathly: appalling, cadaverous, extremely, fatal, ghastly, grim, grisly, gruesome, lethal, macabre, mortal, sepuchral, terrible
deathly pale: cadaverous ☙

debacle: breakdown, cataclysm, catastrophe, collapse, crash, defeat, disaster, downfall, failure, fiasco, flood, havoc, rout, washout, wreck
debar: blackball, deny, deprive, exclude, forbid, hinder, preclude, prevent, prohibit, refuse, reject, suspend
debase: adulterate, cheapen, contaminate, corrupt, debauch, defile, degenerate, degrade, demean, deprave, deteriorate, disgrace, dishonor, humble, humiliate, impair, lower, pervert, pollute, reduce, revile, shame, sink, spoil, stoop, vilify, vitiate
debatable: arguable, controversial, disputable, dubious, moot, questionable, uncertain, unsure
debatable or hypothetical: moot
debate: argue, argument, canvass, consider, contend, contest, controversy, deliberate, discuss, dispute, examine,

fight, moot, oppose, parley, ponder, quarrel, question, reason, rebut, spar, wrangle

debate by law students: moot court

debate ending in parliament: closure, cloture

debate of fine point: quodlibet

debate, formal: disputation

debate, study of formal: argumentation, forensics

debater's response: rebuttal

debauch: abuse, bacchanal, contaminate, corrupt, debase, defile, demoralize, deprave, lure, mislead, orgy, pollute, revel, seduce, spree, taint, violate, vitiate, warp

debauched: abandoned, dissolute, immoral, lecherous, lewd, profligate, wanton, wicked

debauchee: rake

debauchery: dissipation, excess, indulgence, riot

debilitated: decrepit, enervated, enfeebled, feeble, frail, incapacitated, infirm, sapped, weakened

debility: affliction, disease, fatigue, feebleness, infirmity, languor, malaise, sickliness, weakness

debit: charge, debt, detriment, drawback, liability, obligation

debonair: affable, charming, dapper, dashing, elegant, gracious, jaunty, smooth, suave, urbane

debouche: discharge, emerge, exit, issue, opening, outlet

debris: garbage, junk, litter, pieces, refuse, remains, rubbish, rubble, trash, waste, wreckage

debt: arrear, arrears, baggage, bill, commitment, debit, deficit, liability, note, obligation, offense, owed, sin, wrong

debt-acknowledging certificate: debenture

debt and unable to pay, in: bankrupt, insolvent

debt cancellation: remittal

debt demand for payment: dun

debt discharged: quittance, recompense

debt payment as part of series: installment

debt payment, authorization for suspension of: moratorium

debt payment, to make a: amortize

debt recorded in ledger: debit

debt security: lien, note

debt that remains unpaid: arrears

debt to someone, in: beholden, indebted, obliged

debt, discharge from: quietus, quittance

debt, to fail to pay a: default, welsh

debt, to pay a: liquidate, settle

debt, to reduce the amount of a: commute

debt, to refuse to recognize or pay a: repudiate

debt, to run up a: incur

debt, value of property beyond: equity

debtor as security or payment, right to take property of: lien

debunk: disprove, expose, lampoon, mock, ridicule, sham, strip, unmask

debut: beginning, entrance, intro, introduction, launching, open, opener, opening, premiere, presentation

debutante group: Junior League

decade: ten years

decadence: corruption, decay, decline, deterioration, downfall, perversion, regression

decadent: degenerate, depraved, effete, immoral, self-indulgent, sinful, wanton, wicked

decamp: bolt, depart, desert, escape, evacuate, flee, hightail, leave, move, scoot, skedaddle, take French leave, vamoose

decampment: disappearing act

decant: pour

decanter: bottle, carafe, flagon, vessel

decapitate: behead, execute, guillotine, kill

decay: atrophy, caries, collapse, corrode, crumble, death, decadence, decline, decompose, decrease, destruction, deteriorate, dilapidation, disintegrate, dwindle, fade, fail, fester, mildew, molder, putrefy, rot, ruin, rust, sour, spoil, waste, wither

decay in art, morals: decadence

decay of teeth, bones: caries

decay or rot: putrefy

decay or waste away: atrophy

decay, spreading: canker

decayed organic matter: humus

decayed, as the teeth: carious

decaying: decrepit, dilapidated

decaying animal flesh: carrion

decaying matter's odorous fumes: effluvium

deceased: dead, defunct, departed, expired, finished, gone, late, succumbed

deceit: chicanery, cunning, deception,

dishonesty, entrapping, flimflam, fraud, guile, hoax, misleading, swindle, trickery

deceitful: crafty, crooked, cunning, dishonest, double-dealing, fallacious, false, foxy, fraudulent, insidious, insincere, lying, Machiavellian, mendacious, shifty, slick, sly, sneaky, treacherous, underhanded

deceitfulness: double-dealing, duplicity, knavery, wile

deceive: baffle, bamboozle, beguile, betray, bilk, bluff, buffalo, catch, cheat, con, cozen, defraud, delude, doublecross, dupe, equivocate, finagle, flimflam, fool, gull, gyp, hoax, hoodwink, humbug, jilt, lie, mislead, misrepresent, scam, swindle, take in, trap, trick, victimize

deceive as to true nature: dissemble, masquerade

deceive with cheap trick or fraud: cozen

deceived, easily: credulous, gullible, naive

deceiving sight: optical illusion

decelerate: brake, slow, slow down

decency: civility, courtesy, decorum, etiquette, propriety, virtue

decent: acceptable, adequate, appropriate, average, chaste, clean, common, competent, conforming, correct, ethical, fair, fitting, good, honest, kind, modest, moral, proper, pure, respectable, sufficient, suitable, thoughtful

deception: artfulness, artifice, camouflage, cheat, chicanery, collusion, contrivance, counterfeit, covin, craft, cunning, deceit, dishonesty, duplicity, fallacy, falsehood, fraud, guile, hocus-pocus, humbug, hustle, hypocrisy, illusion, imposture, intrigue, jive, magic, mirage, misleading, ruse, scam, sham, sleight, slyness, sophism, sting, subtlety, treachery, trick, trickery, wile

deceptive: crafty, cunning, dishonest, fallacious, false, feigned, illusory, misleading, phony, slick, snide, specious

deceptive appearance: gloss, veneer

deceptive in answer: equivocal

deceptive movement: feint

deceptive scheme: subterfuge

deceptive trick: legerdemain, sleight of hand

deceptively true or attractive: specious

decide: choose, conclude, determine, establish, judge, opt, resolve, rule, select

decide and judge: adjudicate, arbitrate

decided: absolute, certain, decisive, definite, emphatic, firm, fixed, formed, intent, positive, prearranged, sure, unequivocal

decided in advance: predetermined

deciding statement or factor: clincher

deciding vote: casting vote

decimal base: ten

decimal point: radix point

decimal system: algorism, Arabic system

decimate: annihilate, demolish, destroy, kill, massacre, reduce, slaughter, wreck

decipher: analyze, break, decode, decrypt, deduce, explain, interpret, read, reveal, solve, translate, understand, unravel

deciphering of codes: cryptanalysis

decision: adjudication, agreement, choice, conclusion, crisis, culmination, decree, determination, diagnosis, epilogue, finding, inference, judgment, opinion, perseverance, precedent, probability, resolution, result, ruling, selection, sentence, settlement, summation, termination, verdict, volition

decision already arrived at: parti pris

decision maker in dispute: arbiter

decision or judgment, left to one's own: discretionary

decision taken by judges previously: res judicata

decision used as standard: precedent

decision, agree to: underwrite

decision, conclusive: determination

decision, deliberate: volition

decision, of a hasty: impetuous, impulsive, precipitate

decision, of an unchangeable: irrevocable

decision, to reverse a: disallow, invalidate, overrule, overturn, quash, rescind

decisions independently, inability to make: abulia, aboulia

decisive: absolute, categorical, conclusive, critical, crucial, definite, definitive, final, firm, intent, peremptory, resolute, unequivocal, unmistakable

decisive defeat: rout, waterloo

decisive factor: clincher, trump card

decisive trial: acid test

decisive vote to break tie: casting vote

decisively forceful thing: sockdologer

decisively important: fatal

deck: adorn, apparel, array, beautify, blazon, cards, clothe, cover, decorate, dress, drop, embellish, equip, fall, festoon, floor, orlop, outfit, pack of cards, platform, present, tog, trim

deck on bow forward of foremast: forecastle

deck on stern superstructure of ship: poop deck

deck out: adorn, array

deck out, old style: bedight

deck, structure of ship above main: superstructure

declaim: attach, denounce, harangue, inveigh, lecture, orate, perorate, pontificate, proclaim, rant, rave, recite, speak

declamation: oration

declaration: admission, affidavit, affirmation, allegation, announcement, assertion, charge, deposition, disclosure, document, edict, oath, oracle, pitch, proclamation, statement, ultimatum, word

declaration in writing under oath: affidavit

declaration, to make a: enunciate

declare: acknowledge, admit, advertise, advocate, affirm, allege, announce, annunciate, assert, asseverate, assure, attest, aver, avouch, avow, bid, broadcast, certify, confess, confirm, describe, divulge, express, herald, indicate, indict, maintain, manifest, notify, proclaim, profess, promulgate, pronounce, relate, reveal, show, signify, state, tell, testify, vent, voice

declare falsely: misstate

declare frankly: avow

declare seriously: affirm, asseverate, aver

declare untrue: deny

declare without proof: allege

decline: abstain, cheapen, chute, decadence, decay, declivity, decrease, depression, descend, descent, deterioration, diminish, dip, downslide, droop, drop, dwindle, ebb, fade, fail, failure, fall, forbear, languish, lapse, lessen, lower, recession, refuse, reject, repudiate, sag, shrink, sink, slant, slide, slip, slope, slump, stoop, wane, weaken, wilt, withdraw

decline in art, morals: decadence

decline or regress to poor health: relapse

declining: retrograde

declining in morals: decadent

declining market: bear market

declivitous: steep

declivity: cliff, decline, descending, descent, downgrade, drop, fall, gradient, plunge, slope

decoct: boil

decode: decipher, decrypt

decoded message: plaintext

decoding: cryptanalysis

decompose: decay, disintegrate, dissolve, fester, molder, putrefy, rot, separate, spoil

decomposed by bacteria, capable of being: biodegradable

decomposing naturally: biodegradable

decor: adornment, background, colors, furnishings, scenery, setting

decorate: adorn, beautify, cite, color, deck, dress, embellish, emboss, enhance, festoon, furbish, garnish, ornament, paint, parget, redo, trim

decorate border, edge: purfle

decorate food: garnish

decorate lavishly: array, bedeck

decorate manuscript: illuminate

decorate with embedded material: inlaid

decorate with engraving or inlay: enchase

decorate with jewels: encrust, incrust

decorate with ornaments: adorn

decorated tinware: tole

decorating by placing one material on the surface of another: appliqué

decoration: accolade, award, citation, embellishment, frill, furniture, garnish, lace, laurels, lights, medal, ornament, paintings, plaque, ribbon, spangle, tinsel, trim, trimming, trinket

decoration of cloth or streamers: bunting

decoration of silver strands on Christmas tree: tinsel

decoration suspended between two points: festoon

decoration, Chinese: chinoiserie

decoration, glitter: diamanté

decoration, glued or sewed on: appliqué

decorations and furniture: decor

decorative art style from 1925 to 1940: art deco

decorative art style from late nineteenth century to early twentieth century: art nouveau

decorative chain: festoon

decorative grating: grille
decorative inlaid floor: marquetry
decorative inlay: intarsia
decorative needle cases: etuis
decorative openwork: tracery
decorative rather than functional: cosmetic
decorative wall strip: frieze
decorous: appropriate, befitting, calm, composed, decent, demure, dignified, fitting, good, mannerly, modest, moral, nice, orderly, polite, prim, proper, quiet, regular, respectful, sedate, seemly, settled, sober, staid, steady, suitable, unruffled
decorticate: pare, peel, skin
decorum: civility, decency, etiquette, formality, gentility, propriety, protocol, tact
decoy: allure, bait, camouflage, drill, entice, entrap, fake, inveigle, lure, mislead, plant, seduce, shill, tempt, trap
decrease: abate, curb, curtail, cutback, decline, decrement, devaluate, diminish, diminution, discount, drop, dwindle, fall, lessen, loss, reduce, shrink, sink, slacken, subside, subtract, taper, wane, waste
decrease from standard: declension, declination
decrease or amount lost: decrement, diminution
decreasing yield after a certain point: diminishing returns
decree: act, adjudge, adjudicate, announcement, appoint, authorize, canon, command, decision, determine, dictum, directive, edict, enact, enactment, fiat, impose, indict, irade, judgment, law, mandate, ordain, order, ordinance, proclamation, regulation, require, rule, sentence, statute, tenet, ukase
decree and authorize: ordain
decree taking effect, of a: nisi
decree, formal: edict, rescript
decrepit: battered, bedridden, creaky, dilapidated, failing, feeble, flimsy, fragile, frail, lame, rickety, rundown, shabby, unsound, weak, worn
decry: asperse, belittle, blame, censure, condemn, criticize, degrade, deprecate, depreciate, derogate, diminish, disapprove, discredit, disparage, lessen, lower, slur, undervalue

dedicate: anoint, assign, consecrate, devote, direct, donate, hallow, inscribe, pledge, present, sanctify
dedicate or sign a book: inscribe
dedicatory stanza or portion: envoy
deduce: analyze, comprehend, conclude, derive, draw, evolve, extract, gather, infer, presume, reason, surmise, trace
deduce by logic: ratiocinate
deduce from evidence: conclude, infer
deduce from information known: extrapolate
deduct: abate, abstract, discount, dock, reduce, remove, subtract, take, withdraw
deducted the weight of the box: tared
deduction: calculation, conclusion, conjecture, exemption, illation, inference, markdown, rebate, understanding, write-off
deduction in payment: discount, rebate
deduction opposite: induction
deductive: a priori
deductive reasoning: logic, syllogism, synthesis
deed: achievement, act, action, adventure, crusade, exploit, fact, feat, gest, geste, performance, quest; certificate, charter, contract, document, escrow, proof, title, transfer
deed to property: title deed
deed, brilliant or heroic: exploit, gest
deem: account, allow, believe, consider, esteem, expect, feel, hold, hope, judge, judgment, opine, proclaim, reckon, regard, rule, say, sense, suppose, surmise, tell, think, view
deep: absorbed, abstruse, abysmal, below, bottomless, complete, complex, cunning, dark, entangled, focused, grave, heavy, insidious, intense, intent, involved, low, ocean, penetrating, philosophical, profound, serious, sly, thorough, vivid; abyss, sea
deep and vast: cavernous
deep brown: sepia
deep cut: gash
deep enough for vessels: navigable
deep fissure: chasm
deep-freezing of the dead: cryonics
deep glossy black: jet
deep in feeling, intellect: profound
deep in thought: pensive
deep involvement: immersion
deep mud: mire
deep red-purple: carmine

deep-rooted: endemic, ingrained, inveterate
deep-rooted grass: brome
deep-sea chamber: bathyscaphe, bathysphere
deep-sea inlet: fiord
deep-seated: congenital, entrenched, inbred, ingrained, inherent, innate, lasting, rooted
deep sleep: sopor
deep thought or study: brown study, reverie
deep, as in color: intense
deep, extremely: fathomless
deepen: broaden, enhance, expand, intensify, strengthen, thicken
deepest: inmost, nethermost
deepest point: nadir
deer: cervid, cervine, does, dow, elk, mammal, roebuck, roes, ruminant, stags
deer family: cervidae
deer horn: antler
deer in second year before antlers branch: pricket
deer meat: charqui, jerky, venison
deer of India: axis
deer or animal with two to four toes on foot: artiodactyl
deer tail: flag
deer track: slot
deer young: fawn, kid, pricket, spay, spitter
deer, African: okapi
deer, Asian: chevrotain, chitra, hangul, maha, napu, sambar, sika
deer, Eurasian: caribou, fallow, red, reindeer, roe
deer, female: doe, hind
deer, male: buck, hart, roebuck, spay, stag
deer, North American: caribou, elk, moose, mule, reindeer, white-tailed
deer, pertaining to: cervine
deer, South American: brocket, guemal, pudu, vanada
deface: blemish, damage, deform, disfigure, distort, impair, injure, mar, mark, mutilate, ruin, scar, spoil, tarnish, vandalize
defamation: backstabbing, calumny, derogatory, libel, slander, slur
defamation, spoken: obloquy, slander
defame: asperse, besmirch, blacken, blemish, calumniate, damage, degrade, denigrate, disgrace, dishonor, disparage, foul, injure, libel, malign,

revile, scandal, slander, slur, smear, smirch, stigmatize, traduce, vilify, vilipend

default: blemish, delinquency, dereliction, fail, failure, forfeit, imperfection, mistake, negligence, nonpayment, omission, omit, shirk, skip, slight, want, welsh

defeat: baffle, beat, best, break, check, conquer, crush, decimate, defeasance, deprive, destroy, disappoint, eclipse, excel, floor, foil, frustrate, lick, loss, master, outplay, overcome, overpower, overthrow, overwhelm, prevail, quell, reverse, rout, ruin, setback, shellac, subjugate, surpass, thwack, triumph, trounce, undo, vanquish

defeat abruptly: rebuff

defeat and nullify: override, prevail over

defeat but sustain heavy losses: Cadmean victory, Pyrrhic victory

defeat completely: annihilate, checkmate, cream, crucify, crush, devastate, drub, pulverize, rout, shellac, trounce, vanquish, whop

defeat narrowly: edge

defeat purposes, plans: discomfit, vanquish

defeat with cleverness: outwit

defeated incumbent in office: lame duck

defect: abandon, birthmark, blemish, blotch, break, damage, deficiency, deformity, desert, drawback, error, fault, flaw, forsake, glitch, imperfection, injury, reject, renounce, shortcoming, vice, want

defect from birth: congenital defect

defect in machine: malfunction

defective purchase: lemon

defend: advocate, assert, back, champion, conserve, contest, exculpate, go to bat for, guard, hedge, justify, maintain, preserve, protect, rationalize, repel, safeguard, save, screen, secure, shelter, shield, support, uphold, vindicate, watch, wear

defend and deflect: parry

defendable: defensible, tenable

defendant: accused, appellant, defense, litigant, offender

defendant in divorce action: respondent

defendant's excuse: alibi

defendant's statement: plea

defender: advocate, champion, guardian, patron, protector, sponsor, upholder

defender of plebeian rights: tribune

defense: aegis, alibi, answer, armament, armor, barricade, bastion, boundary, bulwark, covert, excuse, explanation, fence, fort, guard, justification, outpost, plea, protection, rampart, safeguard, security, shelter, stronghold, wall

defense and justification: apologia

defenseless: bare, exposed, helpless, naked, powerless, unarmed, unprotected, untenable, vulnerable

defensible: tenable

defensive: territorial

defensive bank: breastwork, bulwark, bunker, enceinte, parados, parapet, retrenchment, revetment, stockade, traverse

defensive emergency measures: civilian defense

defensive structure: fort

defer: adapt, capitulate, delay, postpone, procrastinate, prorogue, protract, put off, shelve, stall, stay, submit, suspend, table, wait, waive, yield

deference: attention, homage, honor, obedience, obeisance, regard, respect, submission, veneration

deferentially: humbly

deferment or deferral: delay, extension, pause, procrastination, stay, suspension

defiance: audacity, boldness, contempt, disobedience, disregard, hostility, insolence, insurgency, rebellion, revolt

defiance to established doctrine: heresy

defiance, boastful: bravado

defiant: truculent

deficiency: dearth, defect, flaw, frailty, glitch, imperfection, inadequacy, insufficiency, lack, minus, need, scarcity, shortage, shortcoming, want, weakness

deficit: arrears, default, disadvantage, impairment, inadequacy, shortage, shortfall

defile: abuse, adulterate, besmirch, contaminate, corrupt, debase, degrade, deprave, desecrate, dirty, discolor, disgrace, dishonor, gorge, maculate, pollute, ravish, smear, soil, spot, sully, taint, tarnish, violate

define: assign, bound, characterize, clarify, construe, decide, describe,

detail, determine, distinguish, explain, expound, fix, illustrate, interpret, label, limit, outline, prescribe, set, specify, state, term

define limit or boundary: circumscribe, delimit, demarcate

defined word or expression: definiendum

defining factor: constraint, parameter

definite: categorical, certain, clear, conclusive, determinate, distinct, exact, explicit, fixed, limited, positive, precise, settled, sharp, specific, sure, unequivocal, unmistakable

definite no: never

definition: clarity, description, explanation, interpretation, terminology, translation

definition by example: ostensive definition

definition in dictionary entry: definiendum

definition, by: ipso facto

definitive: absolute, complete, conclusive, decisive, explicit, final, specific

definitive and judicial: decretory

deflate: devaluate, diminish, humble, humiliate, lessen, puncture, reduce

deflect: avert, bend, bounce, carom, detour, deviate, distract, divert, refract, ricochet, swerve, veer

defoliant: Agent Orange

deform: contort, deface, disarrange, disfigure, distort, flaw, impair, maim, mangle, mar, misshape

defraud: bamboozle, bilk, cheat, con, cozen, deceive, embezzle, fleece, gyp, mulct, rob, rook, skin, swindle, trick, victimize

defrost: melt, thaw

deft: able, adroit, agile, clever, dexterous, dextrous, expert, fleet, handy, neat, nimble, proficient, quick, skillful

defunct: dead, deceased, extinct, finished, inactive, inoperative, kaput, lifeless

defy: beard, brave, challenge, dare, face, flout, front, frustrate, ignore, jeer, mock, oppose, resist, scoff, scorn

defy authority: rebel

dégagé: casual, detached, easy, free, informal, relaxed, uninvolved

degenerate: corrupt, debase, decadent, decay, depraved, deteriorate, effete, immoral, perverted, regress, rot, sink, vitiate, worsen

degradation: degeneration, demotion, depravity, descent, disgrace, ignominy

degrade: abase, belittle, bust, cheapen, corrupt, debase, decline, demean, demote, depose, depreciate, deteriorate, diminish, discredit, dishonor, disparage, humble, humiliate, lessen, lower, reduce, shame, unfrock, vilify

degraded: dishonorable, guilty, hangdog, ignoble, scrofulous, shamefaced

degree: class, grade, honor, level, notch, order, phase, pitch, rank, rate, rung, step, term, tier, unit

degree awarded as honor: honorary degree

degree awarded though student not there: in absentia

degree of excellence: caliber

degree of feeling, action: intensity

degree of occurrence: incidence

degree of road inclination: grade

degree of speed: rate

degree point: caliber, extent, interval, measure, quantity, ratio, scale, stage, title

degree relation: attainment, classification, gradation, standing, temperature

degree "with greatest praise": summa cum laude

degree "with high praise": magna cum laude

degree "with praise": cum laude

degree, present or bestow a: confer

degree, student about to receive: graduand

degrees of comparison for adjective, adverb: comparative, positive, superlative

degree's research report: dissertation, thesis

dehydrate: anhydrous, desiccate, drain, dry, evaporate, parch, preserve

dehydrated: sere

deification: apotheosis

deify: adore, elevate, exalt, glorify, idolize, immortalize, revere, venerate, worship

deign: condescend, patronize, stoop, vouchsafe

deity: almighty, baal, celestial, creator, demigod, demigoddess, divinity, god, goddess, godhead, idol, immortal, supreme being, tutelary

deity appearance: epiphany

déjà vu: familiarity, illusion

dejected: blue, chapfallen, cheerless, crestfallen, dampened, depressed, despondent, disconsolate, discouraged, disheartened, dismal, dispirited, down, downhearted, gloomy, glum, humbled, hurting, inconsolable, low, melancholy, sad, saddened, somber, sorrowful, spiritless, unhappy, woebegone, wretched

dejection: despair, despondency, slough of despond

Delaware capital: Dover

Delaware cities: Newark, Trenton, Wilmington

Delaware nicknames: Diamond State, First State

delay: arrest, block, check, dally, dawdle, defer, deferment, demurral, detain, detention, deter, dillydally, drag, filibuster, hesitate, hinder, impede, inhibit, interruption, lag, lingering, logjam, loiter, lose time, moratorium, obstruct, postpone, prevent, procrastinate, prolong, reprieve, retard, shelve, slow, stall, stay, stop, stoppage, suspension, table, tarry, temper, wait, weaken

delay and hinder: impede, retard, stonewall

delay by preventing or holding back: detain

delay decision: temporize

delay development: retard

delay legislation or voting by speech: filibuster

delay of action, at law: stay

delay or lag behind: loiter, tarry

delay or suspension of activity: moratorium, respite

delay, temporary: abeyance, reprieve, respite

delay, to cause a: dillydally, dither, vacillate

delayed: late, retarded, sat on, tardy

delayed reaction to situation, joke: double take

delayed scientific effect: hysteresis

delaying: dilatory, procrastinating

delectable: appetizing, delicious, delightful, divine, enjoyable, exquisite, heavenly, palatable, pleasing, pleasurable, satisfying, savory, scrumptious, tasty

delegate: agent, appoint, assign, authorize, commit, consign, depute, deputy, designate, devolve, emissary, empower, entrust, legate, name, pass on, proxy, relegate, send, transfer

delegation: appointment, commission, committee, contingent, mission, nomination

delete: annul, bleep, cancel, edit, elide, eliminate, erase, excise, expunge, obliterate, omit, purge, remove

delete objectionable material: expurgate

deleterious: damaging, destructive, detrimental, harmful, hurtful, injurious, pernicious, prejudicial, ruining

deliberate: advise, calculated, confer, consider, consult, cool, debate, designed, determine, examine, intentional, leisurely, meant, measured, meditate, meticulous, planned, ponder, premeditated, purposeful, reflect, slow, study, think, unhurried, voluntary, weigh

deliberate and planned: premeditated

deliberate decision: volition

deliberate distraction: red herring

deliberately done: wittingly

deliberately ignore: close one's eyes to

deliberation: attention, care, counsel, discussion

deliberation, under: sub judice

delicacies, eating of: opsophagy

delicacy: daintiness, delight, elegance, exactness, finesse, frailty, goody, luxury, nicety, pleasure, precision, propriety, refinement, savoir faire, slenderness, tact, taste

delicacy in dealing with others: tact

delicacy of artisanship or performance: finesse

delicate: airy, beautiful, cautious, charming, choice, considerate, critical, dainty, delightful, diplomatic, elegant, ethereal, exquisite, faint, fine, fragile, frail, graceful, lacy, light, luscious, nice, persnickety, petite, pleasant, precarious, refined, sensitive, sickly, silky, slight, soft, susceptible, tender, tenuous, touchy, volatile, weak

delicate and refined: ethereal, exquisite, subtle

delicate fabric: gossamer, lace

delicate, interlacing work: tracery

delicatessen specializing in cooked meats: charcuterie

delicious: ambrosial, appetizing, delectable, delightful, divine, enticing, exquisite, heavenly, luscious, nectarous, savory, scrumptious, tasteful, tempting, toothsome, yummy

delicious and sweet: luscious

delicious drink: nectar

delicious food: ambrosia
delicious meal: repast
delight: amuse, bliss, charm, ecstasy, elate, elation, enchant, enjoyment, enrapture, entertain, fascinate, feast, gladden, gladness, glee, gratify, happiness, joy, jubilation, mirth, please, pleasure, rapture, regale, rejoice, relish, revel, satisfy, savoring, thrill, transport, treat, wow
delight and entertain: regale, revel
delight and please: gratify
delight in others' misfortune: gloating, schadenfreude
delighted: elated, enraptured, glad, pleased
delightful: adorable, alluring, delectable, delicate, delicious, dreamy, elysian, enchanting, engaging, idyllic, lovely, nice, pleasant, ravishing, refreshing
delineate: chart, depict, describe, design, draft, draw, etch, limn, map, outline, picture, portray, represent, sketch, survey, trace
delinquency: default, dereliction, failure, misbehavior, misconduct, misdeed, misdemeanor, neglect, offense, violation, wrongdoing
delinquent: behind, criminal, culprit, hoodlum, irresponsible, late, lax, negligent, overdue, punk, remiss, tardy
delirious: crazed, demented, deranged, ecstatic, excited, frantic, frenzied, hysterical, insane, irrational, lightheaded, lunatic, mad, raving, thrilled, unreasonable, unsettled, wild
delirium: aberration, enthusiasm, fever, furor, hallucination, mania
delirium tremens: DTs, horrors, shakes, trembling, withdrawal
delirium, wild look of: periblepsis
deliver: announce, bring, broach, carry, cart, convey, deal, dispatch, distribute, emancipate, free, give, inflict, liberate, pitch, present, pronounce, redeem, release, render, rescue, resign, save, send, serve, speak, supply, surrender, tell, throw, transfer, transmit, transport, voice
deliver or surrender accused person: extradite
delivery: accouchement, address, birth, diction, drop, elocution, emphasis, labor, parturition, rescue, salvation, shipment

dell: dale, dingle, glade, glen, vale, valley
Delphi shrine: oracle
delta's makeup: silt
delude: beguile, bilk, cheat, cozen, deceive, dupe, fool, hoodwink, mislead, trick
deluge: cataclysm, downpour, drown, engulf, flood, inundate, niagara, overflow, overload, overpower, overwhelm, soak, submerge, swamp, torrent
delusion: aberration, apparition, deception, dream, fallacy, fantasy, figment, ghost, hallucination, illusion, mare's nest, mirage, misconception, phantom, trick, vision, will-o'-the-wisp, wishful thinking
delusion of two associated people: folie à deux
delusions of grandeur: folie de grandeur
delusions of grandeur or persecution: paranoia
delusive: deceptive, false, fanciful, illusory, imaginary, misleading, quixotic, unreal
deluxe: choice, elegant, exclusive, grand, luxurious, opulent, palatial, plush, posh, ritzy, sumptuous, superior
delve: dig, examine, explore, inquire, investigate, mine, probe, research, search, seek
demagnetize: degauss
demagogue: agitator, fanatic, fomenter, hothead, inciter, instigator, leader, rabble-rouser, radical, troublemaker
demand: call, challenge, charge, claim, coerce, command, compel, crave, exact, expect, force, implore, inquire, insist, mandate, need, order, plea, question, request, require, requisition, summon, urge
demand as condition: stipulate
demand in writing for supplies, equipment: requisition
demand insistently: hector, importune
demand or summons: requisition
demand payment: dun
demanding: exacting, exigent, niggling, taxing
demanding and insistent: importunate
demanding and rigorous: exacting
demanding person: stickler
demarcate: bound, define, delimit, detach, distinguish, divide, limit, separate, split
demarcation: line

demean: abase, appearance, attitude, bearing, behavior, belittle, carriage, comportment, conduct, countenance, debase, degrade, deportment, disparage, disposition, humble, humiliate, lower
demeanor: manner, mien, poise, treatment
demise: collapse, death, decease, dying, expire, fall, ruin, termination
demobilize: demilitarize, disband, discharge, disperse
democracy: commonwealth, equality, freedom
democratic: autonomous, egalitarian, popular, self-ruling
demolish: bulldoze, consume, crush, decimate, destroy, devastate, level, obliterate, pulverize, rase, raze, ruin, tear down, total, waste, wreck
demon: devil, diligent, evil, fiend, genie, ghoul, goblin, hag, imp, incubus, ogre, satan, skillful, succubus, vampire, villain, warlock, witch
demon having intercourse with sleeping woman: incubus
demon possessing person: dybbuk
demon, someone possessed by: demoniac, energumen
demon, to drive out a: exorcise
demon, to summon a: conjure
demonlike figure: gargoyle
demonstrably true: apodictic
demonstrate: attest, bespeak, betoken, display, evince, exhibit, explain, flaunt, illustrate, manifest, parade, picket, protest, prove, rally, show, strike, validate
demonstrating: deictic, ostensible, ostensive, professed
demonstration or protest: picket, rally
demonstration, public: manifestation
demonstrative: affectionate, conclusive, definite, effusive, emotional, expansive, expressive, frank, open, outgoing, unrestrained
demonstrative pronoun: those
demoralize: corrupt, dampen, daunt, deject, deprave, depress, discourage, dishearten, dispirit, pervert, undermine, unnerve, upset, vitiate, weaken
demote: bench, break, bump, bust, degrade, dismiss, downgrade, reduce
demur: challenge, delay, disagree, doubt, hesitate, linger, object, oppose, pause, protest, question, resist, scruple, vacillate

demure: affected, bashful, composed, coy, decorous, earnest, modest, prim, reserved, shy, staid, timid, unassertive

demurring politely: begging to differ

den: burrow, cabin, cave, cavern, couch, dwelling, grotto, haunt, hideaway, hole, hollow, lair, library, nest, playroom, retreat, room, shelter, snuggery, study, workroom

denial: abstinence, contradiction, never, rebuttal, refusal, rejection, repudiation, retraction

denigrate: asperse, belittle, defame, degrade, disdain, disparage, libel, malign, pan, ridicule, slander, smear, stigmatize

denizen: citizen, dweller, inhabitant, native, occupant, resident

denomination: appellation, category, church, class, classification, creed, cult, faith, kind, name, persuasion, religion, second base, sect, size, title, value

denominational: sectarian

denotation: description, explanation, meaning, sign, signifying, symbol

denote: betoken, connote, denominate, designate, express, imply, indicate, insinuate, intend, mark, mean, name, represent, show, signal

denouement: result

denounce: accuse, announce, arraign, attack, blame, condemn, criticize, decry, denunciate, execrate, fulminate, knock, rail, stigmatize, upbraid

dense: close, compact, crowded, deep, firm, foggy, heavy, opaque, solid, substantial, thick; ignorant, obtuse, simple, slow, thickheaded

dense growth: mat

dense thicket, out West: chaparral

dense woods: forest

density: bulk, complexity, consistency, mass, weight

dent: blemish, chip, depress, depression, dimple, ding, dint, gouge, hallow, headway, impression, indent, nick, notch, progress, tooth

dental-drill part: bur

dental filling: inlay

dental plate replacing teeth: bridge, bridgework

dentalgia: toothache

dentist helper cleaning teeth: dental hygienist

dentist straightening teeth: orthodontist

dentistry of gum, bones: periodontics

dentistry of tooth irregularities: orthodontics

dentists, group of: wince

denude: bare, dismantle, divest, erode, expose, strip, unclothe, undrape

denunciation: accusation, castigation, censure, commination, condemnation, criticism, denounce, diatribe, fulmination, invective, reprimand, reprobation, tirade

deny: abjure, contradict, contravene, decline, deprive, disaffirm, disagree, disavow, disclaim, disown, dispute, forbid, forsake, gainsay, impugn, negate, negative, recant, refuse, refute, reject, renege, renounce, restrain, traverse, veto, withhold

deny absolutely: categorical

deny and contradict: contradict, controvert, gainsay, negate

deny and reject validity of: disaffirm, rebut, refute, repudiate

deny formally in lawsuit: traverse

deny knowledge of or responsibility for: disavow, disclaim, disown

deny oneself: abnegate, abstain

deny or retract a statement or belief: abjure, forswear, recant, renounce

depart: abandon, abscond, bygone, decamp, deviate, die, digress, disappear, divide, exit, expire, farewell, forsake, go, leave, pass, perish, recede, retire, retreat, secede, separate, split, stray, succumb, sunder, vacate, vamoose, vary, veer, withdraw

depart from danger: evacuate, vacate

depart one's country: emigrate

depart quickly: abscond, flee, hightail, skedaddle, vamoose

depart secretly: abscond, absquatulate, decamp

depart secretly to get married: elope

department: agency, assignment, branch, bureau, commission, division, domain, niche, office, part, province, realm, section, specialty, unit, went, word

department store: emporium

departure: abandonment, aberration, change, death, deviation, divergence, egress, evacuation, exit, exodus, farewell, going, goodbye, shift, twist

departure from norm: deviation, divergence

departure in mass: exodus

departure without permission: AWOL, French leave

depend: bank, conditioned, confide, contingent, count, hang, hinge, lean, rely, rest, trust

dependable: constant, faithful, loyal, reliable, responsible, secure, solid, stable, staunch, steadfast, steady, sure, tried, trustworthy

dependency: addiction, colony, need, reliance

dependency on something for existence, value, significance: function

dependent: clinging, conditional, contingent, helpless, provisional, reliant, secondary, sequacious, susceptible; child, minion, relative, subject, subordinate, vassal, ward

dependent country: client state

dependent on chance: aleatory

dependent relationship: symbiosis

dependent relationship of clauses: hypotaxis

dependent upon: conditional, contingent, provisional

depict: characterize, delineate, describe, detail, draft, draw, etch, express, illustrate, image, limn, paint, picture, portray, represent, sketch

depilate: shave

deplete: bankrupt, bleed, consume, diminish, drain, empty, enervate, exhaust, impoverish, reduce, sap, squander, waste

depleted of energy: spent

depletion of talent: brain drain

deplorable: calamitous, distressing, dreadful, grievous, intolerable, pitiful, reprehensible, sad, sickening, terrible, tragic, unfortunate, woeful, wretched

deplore: abhor, bemoan, bewail, condemn, disapprove, grieve, hate, lament, moan, mourn, regret, rue, wail

deploy: arrange, display, position, redistribute, unfold

deport: banish, bearing, behave, dismiss, displace, eject, exile, expel, extradite, transport

deportment: action, address, air, appearance, bearing, behavior, carriage, conduct, demeanor, gest, manner, mien, posture, presence

deportment and manner: demeanor

depose: assert, aver, bounce, degrade, dethrone, dismiss, divest, impeach, oust, remove, subvert, testify, unseat

deposit: accumulation, bank, consign,

dump, entrust, fund, hock, lay, pawn, payment, place, pledge, retainer, security, sediment, settle, silt, squirrel, stash, store

deposit as security: gage, pledge

deposit eggs, roe: spawn

deposit of sediment: alluvium, silt

deposit rich in heavy metals: placer

deposit, money as a: earnest

deposition: affidavit, allegation, declaration, evidence, opinion, statement, testimony; burial; sediment; overthrow, removal

depository: archives, bank, cache, locker, repository, safe, strongbox, tomb, trustee, vault

depot: annex, armory, arsenal, base, entrepot, junction, magazine, station, storehouse, terminal, terminus, warehouse, yard

depraved: abandoned, base, bestial, corrupt, debauched, degenerate, demoralized, evil, immoral, incorrigible, lewd, mad, perverted, rotten, vicious, vile, vitiated, wicked

depravity: debauchery, evil, turpitude, vice

deprecate: belittle, denigrate, deplore, depreciate, derogate, disapprove, downgrade, pooh-pooh, underrate

deprecating attitude: sneering, sour grapes

depreciate: abase, belittle, cheapen, decry, degrade, deprecate, depress, derogate, devalue, diminish, disparage, downgrade, lessen, reduce, ridicule, shrink, smear, undervalue

depredation: crime, devastation, looting, marauding, pillage, plunder, raid, rapine, ravage, stealing, theft

depress: abase, cheapen, crush, dampen, dash, degrade, deject, dent, depreciate, diminish, discourage, dishearten, dismay, dispirit, droop, enfeeble, fall, indent, lessen, lower, sadden, sink, slump, trouble, weaken

depressant: downer

depressed: blue, bummed, crestfallen, dejected, despondent, destitute, dispirited, down, downbeat, downcast, downhearted, gloomy, glum, hollow, in a funk, in the dumps, low, melancholy, sad, somber, spiritless, under a cloud, unhappy

depressed state: doldrums, funk

depressed urban area: slum

depressing: bleak, dismal, distressing, dreary, joyless, melancholic, upsetting

depression: basin, blahs, blowout, cavity, crater, dejection, dent, despair, despondency, dimple, dip, dismay, doldrums, downturn, dumps, ennui, fall, gulley, hole, hopelessness, impression, malaise, melancholia, pit, pocket, ravine, recession, slough of despond, slump, vale, valley

depression or hysteria disorder: the vapors

deprivation: denial, destitution, hardship, loss, need, poverty, privation, want, withholding

deprive: bereave, deny, despoil, disinherit, dismantle, dispossess, divest, dock, remove, rob, stiff, strip

deprive as punishment: amerce

deprive of courage: unman

deprive of food: starve

deprive of hearing: deafen

deprive of meaning or essential part: eviscerate

deprive of possession: commandeer, confiscate, divest, expropriate, rob, strip

deprive of rights: disenfranchise, disfranchise, divest

deprive of strength: enervate

depth: abstruseness, abyss, bottom, deepness, insight, intensity, measure, penetration, perspective, pitch, profoundness, sense, strength, wisdom

depth of feeling, intellect, meaning: profoundness, profundity

depth of water, instrument measuring: bathometer, sonar

depth of, measure the: fathom, plumb, sound

depth relationships in space: perspective

deputation: committee, delegation

deputy: agent, aide, appointee, assistant, bailiff, delegate, envoy, minister, proxy, second, stand-in, substitute, surrogate, vicar

deputy chief: second-in-command

deputy for disagreeable tasks: hatchet man

deranged: berserk, crazy, delirious, demented, disturbed, had, insane, irrational, loco, mad, nuts, unbalanced

derelict: abandoned, bum, careless, castaway, delinquent, deserted, dilapidated, dingy, drifter, forsaken,

hobo, negligent, outcast, remiss, seedy, shabby, tramp, uncouth, vagabond, vagrant, wino

deride: chaff, fleer, gibe, hoot, insult, jape, jeer, mock, rally, razz, ridicule, scoff, scorn, sneer, taunt, twit

derision: contempt, disdain, disrespect, insult, mockery, ridicule, scorn

derisive: snide

derisive sound: raspberry, snort

derivation: ancestry, beginnings, etymology, genealogy, origin, root, source, wellspring

derivations, study of word: etymology

derivative: adapted, borrowed, copied, evolved, fluxion, offshoot, outgrowth, secondary, unoriginal

derive: acquire, arrive, conclude, deduce, determine, draw, evolve, extract, gather, glean, infer, obtain, originate, reach, receive, stem, trace

derive by reasoning: infer

dernier cri: chic, craze, fad, last word, latest, latest cry, latest thing, mode, rage, style, vogue

derogatory: belittling, damaging, decrying, defamatory, degrading, depreciatory, detract, diminish, disparaging, malicious, offensive, pejorative, snide, unflattering

derrick: crane, hoist, lift, machine, rig

derring-do: audacity, courage, daring, feat, nerve, reckless

dervish: fakir

descant: comment, counterpoint, criticism, discourse, melody, observation, remark, sing

descend: decline, derive, dive, drop, fall, incline, land, lower, originate, penetrate, sink, slope, stoop

descend a mountain: rappel

descendant: advance, child, heir, invasion, lowering, offshoot, offspring, origin, raid, scion, seed

descendants of ancestor: lineage, posterity

descended from same language, parent: cognate

descended from same male ancestor: agnate

descended in direct line from ancestor: lineal

descending slope: declension, declination, decline, declivity

descent: ancestry, assault, breeding, chute, decline, declivity, degradation, downfall, drop, extraction, fall,

DESERTS

An Nafud (Saudi Arabia)	Kyzyl Kum (Uzbekistan and Kazakhstan)
Arabian or Eastern (Egypt)	Libyan (Libya, Egypt and Sudan)
Atacama (Chile)	Lut (Iran)
Black Rock (United States)	Mojave (United States)
Chihuahuan (United States and Mexico)	Namib (Namibia)
Colorado (United States)	Negev (Israel)
Dahna (Saudi Arabia)	Nubian (Sudan)
Dasht-e-Kavir (Iran)	Painted Desert (United States)
Dasht-e-Lut (Iran)	Patagonian (Argentina)
Death Valley (United States)	Rub' al Khali (Saudi Arabia, Oman, Yemen and United
Eastern or Arabian (Egypt)	Arab Emirates)
Gibson (Australia)	Sahara (North Africa)
Gobi or Shamo (Mongolia)	Shamo or Gobi (Mongolia)
Great Arabian (Saudi Arabia)	Simpson (Australia)
Great Australian (Australia)	Sinai (Egypt)
Great Basin (United States)	Sonoran (United States)
Great Indian or Thar (India and Pakistan)	Sturt Stony (Australia)
Great Salt Lake (United States)	Syrian (Syria, Iraq, Jordan and Saudi Arabia)
Great Sandy (Australia)	Takla Makan (China)
Great Victoria (Australia)	Thar or Great Indian (India and Pakistan)
Iranian (Iran)	Turfan Depression (China)
Kalahari (South Africa, Nambia and Botswana)	Yuma (United States and Mexico) ❧
Kara Kum (Turkmenistan)	

generation, inclination, issue, lineage, onslaught, pedigree, slope, stock

descent or origin: derivation, source

descent, study of one's: genealogy

describe: characterize, construe, define, depict, designate, detail, discourse, explain, express, illustrate, interpret, limn, narrate, outline, picture, portray, recite, recount, rehearse, relate, report, represent, state, tell

describe and draw: limn

describe grammatically: parse

describe, hard to: nondescript

description: account, brief, category, chronicle, class, definition, ilk, kind, nature, order, recital, sort, type, variety, vignette, write up

description, brief: profile, thumbnail sketch

description, exact: specification

descry: behold, detect, determine, discern, disclose, discover, espy, note, observe, perceive, reveal, see, sight, spot

desecrate: abuse, blaspheme, defile, dishonor, pollute, profane, ravage, violate

desert (abandon): abscond, bolt, decamp, defect, deserved, flee, forsake, leave, merited, punishment, relinquish, renege, renounce, reward, split, tergiversate

desert (wasteland): barren, sand

RELATED TERMS

desert basin floor: playa

desert fertile area: oasis

desert hot wind: simoom

desert plant: agave, cactus, yucca

desert tabletop: mesa

desert wanderer: nomad

desert with eroded ridges, peaks: badlands

desert, illusion of water in: mirage

desert, of a: arid, xeric

desertlike: arid ❧

desert to another side: apostatize, tergiversate

deserted: abandoned, AWOL, bare, desolate, forlorn, forsaken, lonely, lonesome, marooned, neglected, uninhabited, vacant

deserter: apostate, betrayer, bolter, defector, fugitive, rat, renegade, runaway, traitor, truant, turncoat

deserter of allegiance: apostate, renegade

desertion of faith, principles, cause: apostasy

deserve: claim, earn, merit, procure, rate, warrant

deserved as punishment: condign

deserving: admirable, fitting, worthy

desiccate: dehydrate, deplete, devitalize, dry, evaporate, parch, sear, shrivel, wither

desiccated: sere

desideratum: need

design: architecture, arrange, blueprint, chart, conceive, contemplate, contrive, create, decor, delineate, device, diagram, draft, draw, end, fashion, goal, idea, intend, intent, intention, invent, layout, map, model, motif, motive, object, outline, pattern, perspective, plan, plot, project, proposal, purpose, scenario, shape, sketch, strategy, tailor

design and structure, having: architectonic

design carved beneath surface: intaglio

design cut on gem: glyptograph

design done on object with tools: tooling

design having five sides made of converging arcs: cinquefoil

design in a particular fashion: stylize

design in architecture, repeated: motif

design in nature, study of: teleology

design in relief: repousse

design made by carving, etching, or cutting a hard surface: engraving

design of five leaves, petals, lobes: cinquefoil

design of four leaves, petals, lobes: quatrefoil

design of interlaced flora: arabesque

design of three leaves, petals, lobes: trefoil

design on embroidery or object: device, emblem

design on wall or ceiling: mural

design or layout: format

design or purpose in natural phenomena, study of: teleology

design that is simplified or abstract: conventionalized, stylized

design using initial letters: monogram

design using overlapping pictures, etc.: collage, montage

design, original: archetype, prototype

design, superimposing of repetitive: moiré effect

designate: allocate, appoint, assign, authorize, call, characterize, choose, commission, denominate, denote, dub, elect, entitle, identify, indicate, intend, label, mark, mean, name, select, set, settle, show, specify, style, term, title

designation: appellation, appointment, indication, label, moniker, name, nomination, selection, term, title

designed leather: tooled

designer: artificer, stylist

designing: artful, astute, conniving, crafty, cunning, devious, foreseeing, planning, scheming, sharp

desirable: advantageous, advisable, agreeable, alluring, attractive, beneficial, eligible, gratifying, luring, pleasing, seductive, suited, tantalizing, welcome, worthwhile

desirable reward: plum

desire: appetence, appetency, appetite, ardor, aspire, care, covet, crave, craving, cupidity, fancy, fantasy, hankering, hope, hunger, inclination, itch, longing, lust, mania, need, passion, petition, prefer, preference, request, thirst, urge, want, will, wish, yearning, yen

desire and crave: covet, desiderate, hanker, yearn

desire and other behavior directed toward action, change: conation

desire ardently: long

desire eagerly: relish

desire for wealth, strong: avarice, covetousness, cupidity

desire greatly: crave

desire something that belongs to another: covet

desire that remains a wish: velleity

desire to achieve something: aspiration

desire wrongfully: covet

desire, compulsive and harmful: cacoethes, mania

desire, deep intense: craving, hankering, longing, yearning, yen

desire, deliberate denial of: repression, suppression

desire, natural: appetence

desire, of an unsatisfiable: insatiable

desire, strong sexual: concupiscence, lust

desire, to indulge a: gratify, sate, satiate

desired thing: desideratum

desires, pertaining to: orectic

desirous: acquisitive, ambitious, ardent, aspiring, avid, eager, envious, greedy, hopeful, solicitous, wishful

desist: abandon, abstain, cease, discontinue, forbear, halt, pause, quit, stop, suspend, yield

desk: ambo, booth, carrel, counter, davenport, escritoire, furniture, lectern, pulpit, secretary, table, tambour, vargueno

desk with small bookcase on top: secretary

desk with storage: console

desk, rolling top of rolltop: tambour

desk, small: davenport

desolate: abandoned, alone, bare, barren, bleak, depopulate, depressed, deprived, deserted, destitute, destroy, devoid, disconsolate, dismal, dreary, empty, forlorn, forsaken, gaunt, gloomy, heartbroken, lifeless, lonely, lorn, melancholy, plunder, ravage, ruin, solitary, uninhabited, unoccupied, unused, woebegone

despair: burden, dejection, depression, desperation, despondency, discouragement, gloom, hopelessness, melancholy, pain, slough of despond, surrender

despair, spiritual: accidie, acedia, ennui

desperado: bandit, gangster, hoodlum, lawbreaker, outlaw, ruffian, thug

desperate: audacious, critical, dangerous, despairing, despondent, dire, drastic, extreme, frantic, futile, headlong, hopeless, lost, outrageous, precipitate, rash, reckless, urgent, vain

desperation: anguish, concern, despair, frenzy, hopelessness

despicable: abject, base, caitiff, cheap, contemptible, detestable, hateful, loathsome, low, mean, miserable, pitiful, scurvy, shabby, slimy, sordid, unworthy, vile, wretched

despise: abhor, abominate, contemn, detest, disdain, disregard, hate, loathe, misprize, nora, repudiate, scorn, scout, shun, slight, spurn, vilipend

despite: although, regardless

despoil: depredate, deprive, destroy, disarray, divest, loot, mar, pillage, plunder, raid, ravage, ravish, remove, rifle, rob, ruin, sack, strip, vandalize

despoiler of property: vandal

despondency: depression, despair, desperation, gloom, hopelessness, melancholy, misery, sadness

despondent: blue, bummed, dejected, depressed, disconsolate, discouraged, dispirited, doleful, down, forlorn, hopeless, low, sad, woebegone

despondently: glumly

despot: autocrat, czar, dictator, monarch, monocrat, oppressor, ruler, tsar, tyrant

despotic: absolute, arbitrary, authoritarian, dominant, oppressive, tyrannical

dessert: apple pie, brown Betty, cake, cheesecake, cherry pie, cookie, éclair, final course, fruit, ice cream, mousse, pastry, pie, pudding, sherbet, strudel, sweet, tart, torte

dessert glazed with carmelized sugar: brûlée

dessert of custard with caramel topping: flan

dessert of egg yolks, sugar, wine beaten until thick: zabaglione

dessert of fruit juice or fruit puree, frozen: sorbet

dessert of pudding, light and fluffy: mousse

dessert shredded topping: jimmies, sprinkles

dessert, layered in glass: parfait

destination: aim, end, fate, goal, objective, purpose, target, terminal, terminus ad quem

destination of some pilgrims: mecca

destination or goal: bourn

destine: certain, decree, direct, intend, ordain, predetermine, preordain, purpose

destiny: design, doom, expectation, fate, fortune, inevitability, karma, kismet, lot, stars

destitute: abandoned, bankrupt, bereft, broke, defaulted, defeated, deprived, desolate, devastated, devoid, down and out, empty, exhausted, forsaken, homeless, impoverished, indigent, insolvent, lacking, needy, penniless, poor, underprivileged, wanting, wasted

destroy: abolish, abrogate, annihilate, blight, blow, break, consume, damage, decimate, deface, defeat, demolish, depredate, desolate, devastate, dismantle, dissolve, dynamite, end, eradicate, erase, erode, expunge, exterminate, extinguish, extirpate, famish, finish, ruin, kill, level, liquidate, mutilate, neutralize, nuke, nullify, obliterate, overrun, overturn, quell, rase, ravage, raze, rescind, retract, ruin, rush, sabotage, scratch, slay, smash, smite, spoil, total, undo, vaporize, waste, wreck

destroy a large part of: decimate

destroy affection: disaffect

destroy and erase: efface

destroy and put an end to: abolish

destroy building: demolish, raze

destroy by fire: gut

destroy by making invalid: annul, invalidate, nullify, vitiate, void

destroy by taking apart: dismantle

destroy completely: annihilate, eradicate, expunge, exterminate, extinguish, extirpate, obliterate, subvert, wipe out

destroy effectiveness of: gut

destroy gradually: corrode, erode

destroy inside of: gut

destroy oneself or itself: self-destruct

destroy or ruin: scuttle

destroy population: decimate

destroy to the ground: raze

destroyed, completely: fordone

destroyer: iconoclast, razer, saboteur, terrorist, vandal, vessel, warship

destroyer of religious images: iconoclast

destroying others for one's own gain: predatory

destruction: bane, carnage, decay, demolition, devastation, doom, downfall, extinction, genocide, havoc, holocaust, massacre, ruin, shambles, subversion, waste, wreckage

destruction by decomposing: disintegration, dissolution

destruction by fire: holocaust

destruction by secret workings: subversion

destruction in war: devastation, havoc

destruction of a people or group: genocide, holocaust

destruction of bacteria by antibody: lysis

destruction of document: spoliation

destruction of political and social institutions, belief in: nihilism

destruction of property and normal operations: sabotage

destruction of property, deliberate: vandalism

destruction of regime or institution: Gotterdammerung

destruction of religious objects: iconoclasm

destruction or loss: depredation

destruction, of unnecessary: gratuitous, wanton

destruction, source of: nemesis

destruction, violent upheaval causing: cataclysm

destruction, wanton: mayhem

destructive: baleful, baneful, cataclysmic, damaging, deadly, deleterious, detrimental, discredit, fatal, harmful, hurtful, internecine, lethal, noxious, pernicious, pestilent, poisonous, ruinous, shattering, truculent, vicious, wasteful

destructive effects: ravages

destructive thing: blight, canker, juggernaut

desuetude: disuse, inactivity

desultory: aimless, casual, chance, disconnected, erratic, haphazardly, incidental, inconstant, irregular, rambling, random, roving, sporadic, unsettled, unsteady, wavering

detach: disassociate, disconnect, disengage, disjoin, dismount, disunite, divorce, isolate, separate, sever, sunder, unfasten, unhitch, unsnap

detach from: wean

detachable motor: outboard

detached: alone, aloof, apart, disinterested, dispassionate, distant, emancipated, free, impartial, insular, isolated, neutral, remote, removed, unbiased, unconcerned, unconnected, uninvolved, withdrawn

detached and unbiased: objective

detachedly analytical: clinical

detachment: coolness, detail, disinterest, division, indifference, patrol, separation, unit

detail: account, appoint, article, aspect, assign, detachment, elaborate, element, expound, fact, feature, fine distinction, item, itemize, minutia, narrate, nicety, particular, point, rehearse, relate, specify, stipulation; squad, unit

detail important only to specialist: technicality

detail of etiquette: punctilio

detail, add or enliven with great: embellish, embroider

detail, described in great: graphic

detail, examine in: canvass, scrutinize

detail, overattention to: pedantry

detailed: accurate, circumstantial, comprehensive, full, itemized, meticulous, minute, particular, precise, thorough

detailed analysis: dissection

detailed and clearly expressed: explicit

detailed and thorough: circumstantial, comprehensive, definitive

details: specifications, specifics, specs

details, done with great attention to: elaborate, expatiate

details, overly concerned with: hairsplitting, meticulous, nitpicking

details, trivial: minutiae, quibble, trivia

detain: arrest, check, confine, delay, hinder, hold, impede, imprison, inhibit, keep, mire, restrain, retard, stop

detained during hostilities: interned

detect: ascertain, catch, descry, discern, discover, espy, expose, find, identify, notice, reveal, scent, see, spot, uncover, unmask

detection system: radar

detective: bull, dick, flatfoot, gumshoe, hawkshaw, investigator, operator, PI, private investigator, scenter, shamus, sleuth, spotter, tek, tracer

détente: easement, passivity, pause, policy, precaution

detention: confinement, custody, delay, detainment, hindrance, imprisonment, incarceration, quarantine, restraint

detention by police: custody

deter: avert, block, check, dampen, debase, decline, degenerate, delay, divert, frighten, obstruct, prohibit, spoil, stop, weaken

deter or alter someone's plans: dissuade

detergent: cleanser, soap

deteriorate: corrode, crumble, decompose, go bad, go to pot, go to seed, regress, wane, worsen

deteriorated: ramshackle, rickety

deteriorating in hereditary qualities: dysgenic

deterioration from everyday use: wear and tear

determination: conclusion, conviction, decision, fortitude, grit, heart, judgment, persistence, resolve, settlement, spunk, tenacity, verdict, wile, will

determine: adjudicate, analyze, appoint, arbitrate, arrange, ascertain, assess, assign, award, calculate, choose, conclude, control, decide, decree, define, deliberate, dictate, discover, end, establish, fix, predestine, regulate, resolve, settle

determine a value: assess

determined: bent, decided, decisive, dogged, driven, firm, foregone, indomitable, intent, mulish, obstinate, persistent, pigheaded, resolute, serious, set, set on, settled, single-minded, stalwart, steadfast, steeled, stubborn, tenacious, unyielding

determined effort: endeavor

deterrent: block, curb, hindrance, hurdle, impediment, obstacle, restraint

deter's opposite: abet

detest: abhor, abominate, curse, damn, despise, dislike, execrate, hate, loathe, reject

detestable: despicable, disgusting, execrable, foul, heinous, horrid, loathsome, lousy, obnoxious, odious, repulsive, revolting, shocking, vile

detestable thing: anathema

detestation: odium

dethrone: depose, displace, oust, remove, uncrown

detonate: bang, blast, discharge, explode, fire, ignite

detour: avoid, branch, bypass, circumvent, deviation, divert, reroute, skirt, turn

detract: belittle, cheapen, decry, depreciate, derogate, diminish, disparage, divert, lessen, minimize, underrate, vilify

detraction: backbiting, calumny, damage, innuendo, libel, ridicule, slander, traducement

detriment: cost, damage, disability, disadvantage, drawback, harm, hurt, impairment, impediment, injury, liability, loss

detrimental: adverse, baleful, damaging, deleterious, destructive, evil, negative, pernicious

detritus: debris, fragments, garbage, matter, rubbish, scree, silt, tuff, waste

devalue: cheapen, debase, decrease, defile, degrade, depreciate, lower

devastate: demolish, desecrate, desolate, destroy, overwhelm, pillage, plunder, ravage, ruin, stun, waste, wreck

devastation: confusion, destruction, havoc, ruin

develop: advance, augment, blossom, broaden, disclose, discover, educate, elaborate, emerge, evolve, expand, expound, flourish, flower, form, generate, grow, happen, manifest, materialize, mature, occur, prosper, refine, reveal, ripen, strengthen, transpire, uncover, unfold, unfurl, untwist

develop and breed: propagate

develop and help to grow: foster, nurture

develop buds, sprouts: pullulate

develop gradually: evolve, germinate, gestate, incubate

develop into: become

develop into reality: materialize

develop or enlarge: amplify, elaborate

develop or provoke: foment

develop rapidly: burgeon, flourish

develop to utmost: optimize

developed and advanced: precocious

developing: nascent

developing countries: third world

developing one's personality: formative

developing outside the body: exogenous

developing unusually early: precocious

developing within the body: endogenous

development: dwellings, elaboration, evolution, expansion, formation, growth, incident, increase, phase, progress, situation

development by natural means: evolution

development of a species through evolution: phylogenesis, phylogeny

development of an individual: ontogenesis, ontogeny

development, in the earliest stage of: embryonic, germinal, seminal

development, something that promotes: nutriment

develops a liking for: takes to

deviant: abnormal, atypical, different, errant, irregular, wayward

deviate: change, deflect, depart, detour, digress, diverge, drift, lapse, meander, sheer, sidetrack, stray, swerve, vary, veer, wander, warp

deviate from course momentarily: yaw

deviating: aberrant

deviating from generally accepted: perverse

deviating from normal: anomalous

deviation: aberration, abnormality, anomaly, deflection, departure, error, perversion

deviation from main current: eddy

device: accessory, angle, apparatus, appliance, artifice, concoction, contraption, contrivance, design, doohickey, emblem, equipment, expedient, fastener, figure, gadget, gimmick, insignia, instrument, invention, machine, maneuver, means, mechanism, meter, motto, pattern, plan, project, scheme, shift, symbol, technique, thingamajig, tool, vehicle

device adopted as means to an end: expedient

device for an efficiency expert: stopwatch

device used to promote learning through individual investigations: heuristic

devices allowing rotation in one direction: pawls

devices in a pipe to regulate flow: valves

devil: adversary, amaimon, annoy, apollyon, archfiend, azazel, Beelzebub, demon, diablo, dickens, error, fiend, haze, imp, knave, Lucifer, Mephist, Mephisto, Old Nick, pester, rascal, ruler, Satan, scoundrel, tease, torment, villain, wicked

devil-may-care: bold, heedless, jovial, rakish, rash, risky

devil worship: diabolism

devilfish: manta

devilish: atrocious, demoniac, demonic, deuced, diabolic, diabolical, evil, excessive, extreme, fiendish, hellish, infernal, malicious, mischievous, nefarious, satanic, unhallowed, wicked

devious: ambagious, crafty, crooked,

cunning, deceitful, dishonest, errant, foxy, fraudulent, indirect, misleading, rambling, roundabout, shifty, sly, sneaky, tortuous, tricky, underhand, wily, winding

devious idea: scheme

devise: appoint, arrange, bequeath, chart, coin, concoct, conspire, construct, consult, contrive, convey, create, design, dream up, excogitate, fabricate, forge, form, formulate, frame, imagine, invent, plan, plot, prepare, scheme, suppose, will

devise as one goes along: improvise

devitalize: deaden, destroy, diminish, enervate, weaken

devoid: barren, bereft, destitute, empty, lacking, needed, vacant, wanting, without

devote: address, ally, apply, appropriate, attach, bestow, commit, consecrate, dedicate, depute, destine, direct, entrust, give, pledge, resign, venerate, vow

devote life or time to something: consecrate, dedicate

devoted: adoring, affectionate, ardent, arduous, assiduous, attached, constant, dedicated, devout, dutiful, earnest, faithful, loyal, pious, religious, true, unwavering, wholehearted, zealous

devoted in religious way: devout, pious

devoted to wife, excessively: uxorious

devoted, blindly: idolatrous

devotee: admirer, advocate, aficionado, amateur, believer, booster, buff, disciple, enthusiast, fan, fanatic, follower, groupie, supporter, votary, zealot

devotion: adherence, adoration, allegiance, commitment, dedication, faithfulness, fealty, fidelity, love, loyalty, passion, piety, prayer, reverence, sanctity

devotion to books, extreme: bibliolatry

devotion to God: reverence, veneration

devotion, excessive: hero worship, idolatry

devour: annihilate, consume, eat, engulf, gobble, gorge, guzzle, ravage, relish, stuff, swallow, waste

devout: ardent, cordial, devoted, earnest, faithful, heartfelt, hearty, holy, pious, religious, reverent, righteous, serious, sincere, solemn, spiritual, venerating, warm

devoutness: piety

dew: condensation, fresh, moisture, pure, renewing, tears, water, wet

dew formation: dewfall

dewlap: jowl

dewy: moist, roric

dexterity: ability, adeptness, adroitness, agility, aptitude, art, cleverness, craft, cunning, deftness, expertise, facility, finesse, hand, knack, nimbleness, proficiency, quickness, readiness, skill, sleight, tact, touch

dexterous: active, adroit, agile, deft, handy, nimble, smooth

dharma: Buddhism, conduct, enlightenment, Hinduism, law, obligation, principle, teachings

diabetes high sugar level: hyperglycemia

diabetes low sugar level: hypoglycemia

diabetes, hormone deficiency creating: insulin

diablerie: black magic, devilish, devilry, deviltry, satanism, sorcery, witchcraft

diabolical: cruel, demoniac, devilish, evil, fiendish, heinous, hellish, infernal, satanic, serpentine, vicious, vile, wicked

diacritical: discriminating, distinguishing, marking

diacritical mark: caret, cedilla, tilde

diadem: anadem, coronet, crown, dignity, fillet, halo, headband, tiara

diagnosis: analysis, conclusion, examination, identification, opinion

diagnosis by stethoscope: auscultation

diagnosis by tapping: percussion

diagnostic sign: stigma

diagnostic substance sent through bodily system: tracer

diagonal: angled, beveled, bias, catercorner, catercornered, crosswise, oblique, slanted, transversal

diagonal punctuation mark: backslash, oblique, slant, slash, solidus, virgule

diagonal route: traverse

diagram: blueprint, chart, description, design, drawing, graph, illustration, layout, map, outline, plan, plat, schema

diagram of divided circle: pie chart

diagram of stages or sequence: flowchart, schema

diagram of structure showing parts separately: exploded view

diagram with components in blocks and lines showing relationships: block diagram

diagram with covering cut away: cross section, cutaway

dial: knob

dial showing changing numbers: digital

dial showing numbers with hands: analog

dialect: accent, argot, cant, idiom, jargon, language, lingo, patois, slang, speech, vernacular

dialect closest to standard language: acrolect

dialect dictionary: idioticon

dialect farthest from standard language: basilect

dialect midway from standard language: mesolect

dialect mixed with English: pidgin English

dialect of region becoming language of larger area: koine

dialect study: dialectology

dialect, provincial: patois

dialogue: chat, composition, conference, conversation, discussion, interlocution, parley, passage, script, speech, talk

dialogue in literary composition: colloquy

dialogue, person taking part in: interlocutor

diameter: breadth, caliber, thickness, width

diameter-measuring device: calipers

diameter of tube: caliber

diametrical: conflicting, contrary, contrasting, counter, opposed, polar

diametrically opposed: antipodal

diamond: brilliant, corundum, gem, gemstone, ice, jager, jewel, lozenge, rhombus, rock, solitaire

diamond, fake: rhinestone, schlenter, zircon, zirconia

diamond, industrial: balas, black diamond, bort, bortz, carbonado

diamond or rhombus: lozenge

diamond set by itself: solitaire

diamond-studded socks: argyles

diamond weight: carat

diamond, large unflawed: paragon

diamond, transparency and luster of: water

diamondlike: adamantine

diamondlike mineral: zircon, zirconia

diamondlike shape: lozenge, rhombus

diamonds, pertaining to or similar to: diamantine

diaphanous: airy, clear, delicate, fine, flimsy, gauzy, gossamer, insubstantial, lucid, sheer, transparent, vague

diarrhea: collywobbles, flux

diarrhea in Mexico: Montezuma's revenge

diarrhea of the tourist: tourista, turista

diary: chronicle, journal, log, minutes, record, register

diatribe: abuse, castigation, criticism, denunciation, harangue, invective, screed, tirade

dice: bones, chop, cube

dice dot: one

dice throw of lowest score: ambsace, craps

dicey: chancy, dangerous, iffy, risky, tricky, uncertain

dichotomize: sever

dicker: bargain, barter, chaffer, deal, exchange, haggle, negotiate, quibble, swap, trade

dictate: command, communicate, compose, control, decree, impose, mandate, ordain, order, prescribe, record, require, rule, say, tell, utter

dictation, one who takes: amanuensis, scribe, secretary

dictator: autarch, authoritarian, autocrat, czar, despot, duce, fascist, fuhrer, totalitarian, tsar, tyrant

dictator, military: caudillo

dictatorial: absolute, arbitrary, arrogant, authoritative, bossy, despotic, doctrinaire, dogmatic, domineering, imperious, lordly, magisterial, masterful, oppressive, overbearing, peremptory, pompous, positive, tyrannical

dictatorial system: absolutism, totalitarianism

dictators, group of military: junta

diction: articulation, enunciation, fluency, intonation, language, oratory, phraseology, phrasing, rhetoric, style, verbiage, vocabulary, wording

dictionary: glossary, lexicon, onomasticon, reference, vocabulary, wordbook, words

RELATED TERMS

dictionaries for great words, searching: perquesting

dictionaries, art and science of compiling: lexicography

dictionary and wordbook collector: lexiconophilist

dictionary compilation: lexicography

dictionary compiler: lexicographer

dictionary definition: definiens

dictionary editor or compiler: lexicographer

dictionary entry word: headword

dictionary headword or entry word: definiendum

dictionary notches on side: thumb index

dictionary of synonyms: thesaurus

dictionary quotation or example of use: citation

dictionary within textbook, small: glossary, lexicon, vocabulary

dictionary words at top of pages: guide word, running head

dictionary, geographical: gazetteer

dictionary, polygot: calepin

dictionary, proper name: onomasticon

dictionary, to put together a: compile ☙

dictum: adage, apothegm, axiom, declaration, decree, edict, moral, motto, pronouncement, proverb, saying, say-so, statement, truism

didactic: academic, educational, homiletic, instructive, moralistic, pendantic, preachy, sermonic, tutorial

diddle: cheat, dawdle, gyp, jiggle, loiter, swindle, worthless

dido: antic, caper, prank

die: abate, cease, croak, decease, degenerate, demise, depart, dwindle, ebb, expire, finish, languish, perish, stop, succumb, vanish, wane, wither, yearn; cube; mold

die-hard: conservative, hardnose, inflexible, mossback, obstinate, pigheaded, reactionary, resisting, standpat, stubborn, tory, uncompromising

diesel engine: compression-ignition engine

diesel fuel rating: cetane number

diet: drink, fare, fast, food, nourishment, provisions, reduce, regimen, starvation, viands; assembly, convention, legislature

diet and food, study of: nutrition

diet deficiency, substance for: supplement

diet of plant products with or without dairy products: vegetarian

diet of plant products without dairy products: vegan

diet of whole grains and beans: macrobiotics

dietary laws, conforming to Jewish: kosher

differ: clash, conflict, contend, debate, disagree, discord, dissent, dissimilar, distinct, oppose, vary

difference: alteration, antithesis, argument, conflict, controversy, disagreement, discord, discrepancy, disparity, dispute, dissension, dissimilitude, distinction, divergence, hassle, heterogeneity, quarrel, squabble, unlikeness, variation

difference between facts or claims: discrepancy, inconsistency

difference from norm: deviation, divergence, eccentricity

difference in brightness: contrast

difference of opinion: discord, dissension, divergence, personal equation, quarrel

difference, subtle: nuance

different: alien, another, assorted, atypical, contrary, disparate, dissident, dissimilar, distinct, divergent, divers, diverse, else, heterogeneous, incomparable, novel, offbeat, other, peculiar, separate, several, strange, sundry, unalike, unique, unlike, unrelated, unusual, variant, various

different and various: diverse, manifold, miscellaneous, sundry

different colors, having many: motley, multicolored, particolored, variegated

different directions, move in: diverge

different from standard: variant

different in unexpected way: heterogeneous, incongruous

different names that have a relationship: heteronymous

different, completely: disparate

differentiate: alter, change, comprehend, contrast, discriminate, distinguish, modify, separate

differentiating: diacritical

difficult: arduous, complex, complicated, cranky, demanding, fussy, hairy, hard, intricate, involved, knotty, labored, laborious, painful, puzzling, rough, stubborn, tough, troublesome, trying, uphill

difficult and demanding: exacting, exigent, onerous

difficult and futile: Sisyphean

difficult and stubborn: intractable, unruly

difficult course or experience: Via Dolorosa

DIGESTIVE OR GASTROENTEROLOGICAL DISEASE

acidity	colitis	enteritis	irregularity	stomach ulcer
acidosis	constipation	flatulence	liverishness	stomachache
bellyache	cramps	flatus	nausea	trichinosis
biliousness	Crohn's disease/re-	food poisoning	peptic ulcer	typhoid/enteric fever
botulism	gional enteritis	gas	peritonitis	ulcer
cardialgia	diarrhea	gastritis	ptomaine poisoning	upset stomach
celiac disease	diverticulitis	gastroenteritis	pyrosis	vomiting ☙
cholera	duodenitis	gripes	salmonelosis	
cirrhosis	dysentery	heartburn	stomach cancer	
colic	dyspepsia	hyperacidity	stomach flu	

difficult journey: trek

difficult question: poser

difficult situation: imbroglio, morass, quagmire, stickler, sticky wicket

difficult to accomplish: arduous, Herculean, strenuous

difficult to define or describe: elusive

difficult to interpret: delphic, oracular

difficult to manage: intractable, scabrous

difficult to understand: abstruse, convoluted, impalpable, incomprehensible, intricate, opaque, recondite, unfathomable, unintelligible

difficult to undertake or defeat: formidable

difficulties on both sides: gantlet, gauntlet

difficulty: ado, aggravation, barrier, complication, controversy, dilemma, dispute, fight, fix, frustration, hardship, hassle, hindrance, hole, impediment, jam, mess, nodus, obstacle, obstruction, paradox, pickle, pinch, pitfall, problem, quagmire, quarrel, rigor, scrape, setback, snag, struggle, trouble, vicissitude

difficulty, add to a: compound

difficulty, in grave: in extremis

difficulty, painful: ordeal, tribulation

difficulty, serious: plight, predicament, quandary, straits

difficulty, to overcome: surmount

diffidence: apprehension, bashfulness, doubt, fear, hesitation, humility, insecurity, meekness, modesty, reserve, shyness, timidness

diffuse: circulated, copious, disperse, disseminate, dissipate, divide, expanded, expatiate, extend, full, irradiate, palaverous, prolix, propagate, rambling, scatter, soften, spread, strewn, verbose, waffling, widespread, wordy

diffuse gradually: seep

diffuse throughout: permeate

diffusion of liquid through membrane: osmosis

dig: bulldoze, burrow, crack, delve, discover, enjoy, excavate, exhume, explore, extricate, get, gibe, grasp, groove, hoe, hole, insult, investigate, jab, like, mine, nudge, pion, plunge, poke, probe, prospect, quarry, quip, root, shovel, spade, taunt, thrust, till, tunnel, understand, unearth

dig out facts: plumb

dig up artifacts: excavate

dig up dead body: disinter, exhume

dig up weeds: sarcle

digest: abridge, absorb, analyze, assimilate, code, codify, comprehend, condense, conspectus, dissolve, endure, epitome, grasp, organize, pandect, ponder, precis, stomach, summary, synopsis, tolerate

digestion, concerning: peptic

digestion, concerning food, nutrition, or: alimentary

digestion, good: eupepsia

digestion, poor: dyspepsia, indigestion, malnutrition

digestive autonomic contractions: peristalsis

digestive catalyst: enzyme

digestive enzyme: lipase, pepsin

digger: miner, mole, spade

digit: extremity, finger, pinkie, thumb, toe; figure, number, numeral, one, symbol, unit

digital watch display: LCD, LED, light-emitting diode, liquid crystal display

dignified: august, courtly, distingué, ennobled, exalted, grant, honorable, lofty, majestic, noble, prim, regal, respected, sedate, staid, stately, statuesque, upright

dignify: adorn, distinguish, elevate, ennoble, glorify, honor, promote, raise

dignitary: eminence, leader, luminary, notable, official, VIP

dignity: character, decorum, elegance, etiquette, excellence, grace, honor, majesty, nobleness, poise, prestige, pride, rank, standing, stature, virtue, worth

dignity, attack another's: impugn

dignity, beneath one's: infra dig

dignity, do something beneath one's: condescend, deign

digress: deviate, divagate, diverge, drift, meander, roam, shift, stray, swerve, veer, wander

digression: apostrophe, aside, deflection, detour, episode, excursion

digressive: excursive, rambling, tangential

digs in one's toes: balks

dike: bank, barrier, causeway, channel, ditch, dyke, embankment, levee, watercourse

dilapidated: battered, damaged, decrepit, dingy, neglected, ramshackle, run-down, shabby, shot, threadbare

dilate: amplify, augment, broaden, enlarge, expand, expatiate, expound, extend, inflate, lengthen, prolong, protract, stretch, swell, widen

dilatory: delaying, inactive, laggard, lazy, leisurely, poky, procrastinating, remiss, slack, slow, sluggish, tardy, unhurried

dilemma: bind, complication, crisis, fix, Hobson's choice, mess, mire, pickle, predicament, problem, quandary, spot

dilemma, unresolvable: double bind

dilettante: admirer, amateur, connoisseur, dabbler, dabster, rookie, superficial, trifler

dilettantish: arty

diligence: application, assiduity, attention, dedication, earnestness, effort, heed, industry, intensity, perseverance, vigor, zeal

diligent: active, assiduous, busy, careful, eager, hardworking, heedful, industrious, operose, painstaking, persistent, sedulous, steadfast, studious, thorough, unflagging

diligent and careful: painstaking

diligent and persevering: sedulous

dill seed: anet

dilly: beaut, dandy, doozer, humdinger, lollapalooza, lulu, peach, pip

dillydally: dawdle, delay, idle, lag, linger, loaf, loiter, stall, vacillate

dilute: adulterate, alter, attenuate, cut, diminish, lessen, reduce, thin, water, weaken

dim: bleak, blear, blur, blurred, cloudy, darken, darkish, dense, depressing, disapproving, dreary, dull, dusky, eclipse, efface, fade, faint, foggy, gloomy, hazy, lackluster, mist, mysterious, negative, obfuscate, obscure, obtuse, overcast, pale, shadowy, soft, somber, subdued, tarnish, unclear, unfavorable, unlit, vague

dim of twilight: crepuscular

dim or faint: wan

dim-witted: dull, dumb, feebleminded, idiotic, slow, stupid

dimension: aspect, bulk, capacity, element, extent, height, importance, length, magnitude, mass, measure, proportion, quality, range, scope, size, thickness, time, volume

diminish: abate, abridge, alleviate, bate, cheapen, condense, curtail, decrease, deplete, derogate, detract, dilute, dwindle, ease, ebb, erode, extenuate, fade, lessen, lower, minimize, moderate, narrow, peter, recede, reduce, retrench, shrink, sink, slake, subside, subtract, taper, wane, wither

diminish by degrees: erode, tail off

diminution: abatement, curtailment, decay, decline, decrease, decrement, lessening

diminutive: bantam, dwarf, ette, lilliputian, little, miniature, minuscule, petite, pintsized, pocket-size, slight, small, teeny, tiny

dimming of lights: brownout

dimness of vision: mist

dimple: fossette

din: babble, clamor, clangor, clatter, commotion, confusion, hubbub, hullabaloo, instill, loud, noise, pandemonium, racket, rattle, riot, sound, steven, tumult, turmoil, uproar

dine: breakfast, consume, dinner, eat, feast, lunch, partake, sup

diner: café, canteen, eater, eatery, greasy spoon, guest, luncheonette, patron, restaurant, train car

ding: beat, clang, dash, dent, drive, knock, nick, pound, ring, stroke, thrust, thump

dinghy: boat, life raft, lifeboat, rowboat, skiff

dingle: dale, dell, glen

dingy: dark, dilapidated, dirty, discolored, drab, dreary, dusty, gloomy, grimy, seedy, shabby, smoky, soiled, squalid, tacky

dining hall: refectory

dining out of doors: al fresco

dining room, small upper-floor: cenacle

dining segments: seatings

dining, artful or learned conversation while: deipnosophy

dining, science of: aristology

dinky: cute, insignificant, miniature, minor, petite, poor, shabby, small, tiny

dinner: banquet, entrée, feast, food, meal, potluck, supper

dinner course: appetizer, dessert, entrée, hors d'oeuvre, main dish, salad, soup, vegetable

dinner selection: main course

dinner with complete meal price: table d'hôte

dinner with item prices: à la carte

dinner, concerning: cenatory, prandial

dinner, just after: postprandial

dinnerware: china

dinosaur walking on two legs: tyrannosaur

dinosaur with long neck and small head: brontosaur

dinosaur with three horns and fanlike crest: triceratops

dinosaur with toothlike bony plates along back and tail: stegosaurus

dinosaur, flying: pterodactyl

dint: dent, drive, effort, energy, force, impression, indentation, nick, power, strength, will

diocese: benefice, bishopric, district, episcopate, jurisdiction, prelacy, see

dip: bail, browse, candle, dabble, decline, decrease, delve, depression, descend, douse, downturn, droop, drop, duck, dunk, fade, immerse, lade, ladle, lower, moisten, plunge, sag, sauce, sink, slope, soak, souse, submerge, swim, veer

dip and throw: bail

dip into liquid: souse

dip into water by bird: dap

diphtheria test: Schick test

diploma: award, certificate, charter, degree, document, honor, sheepskin

diplomacy: artfulness, delicacy, dexterity, graciosity, poise, savoir-faire, skill, statesmanship, tact

diplomat: agent, ambassador, attaché, consul, envoy, mediator, minister, nuncio, representative

diplomat of high rank, just below ambassador: minister

diplomat representing a nation's commercial interests and assisting its citizens abroad: consul

diplomat sent on special mission: emissary, envoy

diplomat standing in for ambassador or minister: charge d'affaires

diplomat who is an expert assigned for a specific capacity: attaché

diplomatic: discreet, judicious, politic, prudent, tactful

diplomatic etiquette: protocol

diplomatic mission: embassy

diplomatic mission headquarters: chancellery, consulate

diplomatic mission ranked below embassy: legation

diplomatic move or position: démarche

dipsomania: alcoholism, craving

dire: apocalyptic, awful, calamitous, critical, crucial, desperate, devastating, dismal, doleful, drastic, dreadful, fearful, grave, grim, horrendous, horrible, ominous, terrible, tragic, urgent, woeful

direct: blank, blunt, candid, clear, compendious, even, frank, honest, immediate, lineal, nonstop, point-blank, straight, straightforward, utter

direct elsewhere: reroute

direct insult: slap, stab

direct opposite: antithesis

direct relationship: immediacy

direct, to: address, administer, advise, aim, apply, appoint, bend, coach, command, conduct, control, dedicate, ensign, even, focus, govern, guide, head, helm, instruct, lead, manage, marshall, order, oversee, point, preside, prompt, refer, regulate, rein, steer, superintend, superscribe, sway, train, turn

directed firmly: intent, unwavering

direction: bearing, bent, care, command, control, course, east, gist, guidance, inclination, information, instruction, label, leadership, management, mandate, north, outlook, path, plan, regulation, road, route, rule, south, tendency, tenor, toward, trajectory, trend, way, west

direction and supervision: aegis, auspices

direction plant goes to light, heat: tropism

direction when guided by radio: vector

direction, general: tenor

direction, having lost a sense of: disoriented

directional guide: arrow

directions from a point, moving in different: diverging

directions, coming from different: converging

directive: behest, bulletin, communication, decree, edict, injunction, instruction, memo, order, ruling, ukase

directly: candidly, exactly, immediately, instantly, literally, now, presently, promptly, quickly, shortly, soon, straight, totally

directly opposite: antipodal

director: administrator, boss, chairman, chairperson, chairwoman, chief, coach, commander, conductor, governor, head, leader, manager, prefect, supervisor

director of ballet or theater: regisseur

director of museum or gallery: curator

directory: almanac, atlas, guide, index, lineup, list, ordo, register, roster, telephone book, yellow pages

dirge: chant, elegy, epicedium, hymn, keen, lament, poem, requiem, song, threnody

dirigible: aerostat, zeppelin

dirndl: skirt

dirt: clay, dregs, dust, earth, filth, grime, muck, mud, rumo, sand, scum, smut, soil, soot

dirty: base, begrime, bemire, clouded, corrupt, defile, despicable, dingy, dishonest, distasteful, filthy, foggy, foul, greasy, grimy, grubby, illicit, impure, low, messy, muddy, nasty, obscene, polluted, raunchy, risqué, sloppy,

smutty, soil, soiled, sordid, squalid, stain, stormy, sullied, tarnish, unclean, unsanitary, vile, vulgar

dirty and untidy: bedraggled

dirty child: ragamuffin

dirty language: coprolalia

dirty look: glare

dirty or corrupt: defile, sully, tarnish

dirty, extremely: feculent

dirty, to: adulterate, besmirch, contaminate, pollute

disability: affliction, defect, deficiency, disadvantage, drawback, handicap, impediment, incapacity, malady

disable: cripple, damage, disarm, hamstring, hinder, hog-tie, immobilize, inactivate, incapacitate, lame, maim, undermine, weaken, wreck

disabuse: correct, debunk, disenchant, disillusion, enlighten, expose, free, liberate, rectify, rid

disadvantage: damage, deprivation, detriment, difficulty, disability, drawback, encumbrance, handicap, hardship, hindrance, hurt, liability, loss, obstacle, penalty, prejudice, weakness

disadvantaged: deprived, impoverished, underprivileged

disadvantaged person: underdog

disadvantageous: deleterious, detrimental, harmful, hurtful, prejudicial, slighting, unfavorable, wrong

disaffected: alienated, disloyal, estranged, faithless, mutinous, perfidious, rebellious, recreant, resentful, treacherous, withdrawn

disaffirm: annul, contradict, deny, disclaim, gainsay, negate, renounce, repudiate, reverse

disagree: argue, clash, conflict, contend, counter, differ, dispute, dissent, oppose, quarrel, vary, wrangle

disagreeable: annoying, awful, cross, foul, grouchy, harsh, hateful, nasty, offensive, peevish, sour, unsavory, vile

disagreeable person: crab

disagreeing: at loggerheads

disagreement: argument, bickering, clash, conflict, contention, controversy, debate, difference, difficulty, discord, discrepancy, disharmony, displeasure, dispute, dissension, dissidence, diversity, estrangement, falling-out, fight, odds, rift, spat, squabble, strife, variance

disagreement in opinion: dissension, dissent, dissidence, variance

disagreement or contradiction: discord, discrepancy, disparity, dissonance, incompatibility, incongruity, inconsistency, irreconcilability

disallow: ban, censor, censure, deny, exclude, forbid, nix, prohibit, refuse, reject, repudiate, veto

disappear: cease, depart, diminish, dissolve, evanesce, evaporate, fade, flee, leave, vamoose, vanish, withdraw

disappear after breaking up: disperse, dissipate

disappear gradually: evanesce, wither

disappear in bodily form: dematerialize

disappearance of celestial body during eclipse: occultation

disappearing and decomposing naturally: biodegradable

disappoint: baffle, bungle, dash, defeat, disenchant, dishearten, disillusion, dismay, dissatisfy, fail, fall, frustrate, sadden, shoot down, thwart

disappointing: underwhelming, unimpressive

disappointing outcome: anticlimax, bathos

disappointment: anticlimax, blow, defeat, delusion, displeasure, failure, fiasco, letdown, obstacle, regret, setback, washout

disappointment or unease: chagrin

disapproval: animadversion, blame, boycott, catcall, censure, criticism, disapprobation, disliking, dissent, grumble, hiss, rejection

disapprove: condemn, denounce, deplore, deprecate, disallow, discountenance, expostulate, protest, reject, veto

disapprove of strongly: condemn, deplore, reprehend, reprobate

disapproving or disparaging: depreciatory, pejorative

disapproving sound: Bronx cheer, raspberry

disapproving word: bah, tut

disapproving, hypocritical: pharisaical

disarm: allure, charm, convince, cripple, defuse, demilitarize, demobilize, disable, fascinate, immobilize, incapacitate, influence, subdue

disarmament by one nation: unilateral

disarrange: confuse, disconcert, dishevel, dislocate, disorganize, disturb, jumble, muss, ruffle, scramble, unsettle, upset

disarray: anarchy, chaos, confusion, disorder, mess, muddle, pandemonium, turmoil

disarrayed: dishabille

disassemble: disband, dismantle, rends, scatter, separate, undo

disassemble weapon to clean: field strip

disassociate: disaffiliate, disconnect, divorce, part, separate, uncouple

disaster: accident, adversity, bale, blight, blow, calamity, casualty, cataclysm, catastrophe, debacle, devastation, fatality, fiasco, holocaust, misadventure, misfortune, mishap, ruin, tragedy

disaster with widespread destruction: apocalypse, Armageddon, cataclysm

disaster, to ward off: avert

disastrous: devastating, dire, hapless, harmful, horrendous, ruinous, terrible, unfortunate

disastrous failure: debacle, fiasco, rout

disavow: abjure, contradict, deny, disclaim, forswear, gainsay, negate, recant, refuse, reject, renounce, repudiate, retract

disband: disassemble, disintegrate, dismiss, disperse, dissipate, dissolve, part, scatter, separate

disbelief or denial of customs' purpose: nihilism

disbelieve: distrust, doubt, mistrust, question, reject, skeptical, suspect

disbeliever: agnostic, atheist, cynic, dissident, doubter, infidel, skeptic

disbelieving: doubting, incredulous, skeptical

disburden: rid

disburse: allocate, defray, dispense, distribute, divide, divvy, expend, mete, outlay, spend

discard: abandon, cashier, chuck, ditch, divest, divorce, dump, eliminate, fling, jettison, jilt, junk, oust, reject, remove, repudiate, scrap, shed, shuck, toss, unload

discard hampering thing: jettison

discard sweetheart: jilt

discarded item: reject

discern: anticipate, ascertain, behold, descry, detect, discover, distinguish, espy, foresee, observe, perceive, see, spot, uncover, understand

discernible: apparent, comprehensible, distinct, evident, noticeable, obvious, perceptible, tangible, visible

discernible by touch: tangible

discerning: acute, astute, clairvoyant, clever, discriminating, insightful, keen, perceptive, perspicacious, sagacious, sapient, sensitive, wise

discernment: sagacity, tact, taste, wisdom

discharge: absolve, acquittal, blast, boot, bounce, can, cashier, defray, detonate, disgorge, dismiss, dispense, displace, dump, egest, eject, emit, emptying, evacuate, execute, execution, exempt, exonerate, expel, explosion, exude, fire, free, launch, liberation, liquidate, ooze, oust, pardon, performance, pour, quash, release, relieve, sack, seepage, shoot, supplant, terminate, unload, void

discharge cargo: unlade

discharge from duty: quietus

discharge of emotion: catharsis

discharge suddenly, quickly: ejaculate

discharge violently: spew

discharge, as a debt: pay

discharged debt: quittance, recompense

disciple: adherent, apostle, believer, chela, epigone, follower, imitator, -ite, scholar, student

disciplinarian: authoritarian, chastener, czar, enforcer, martinet, ramrod, reprover, taskmaster, tyrant

disciplinarian, military: martinet

disciplinary: corrective, ordered, punishing, punitive

disciplinary action, swift: crackdown

discipline: area, chasten, chastise, control, correct, drill, education, flog, instruct, obedience, penalize, punish, regiment, restrain, school, self-control, specialty, strictness, teach, train, training, whip, willpower

discipline and chastise: call on the carpet, call to account

discipline by self-denial: mortify

discipline stressing spiritual insight and tranquillity: yoga

discipline to correct: chasten

disclaim: abjure, abnegate, contradict, deny, disavow, disown, gainsay, negate, recant, renounce, repudiate, retract

disclose: acknowledge, admit, bare, bestow, betray, bring to light, confess, discover, display, divulge, exhibit, expose, give vent to, impart, indicate, leak, make known, open, publish, reveal, spill, squeal, tell, unbosom, uncover, unveil, utter

disclose, poetically: ope

disclosure: admission, arrival, declaration, enlightenment, exposé, revelation

disclosure at trial by defendant: discovery

disco light: strobe

discolor: besmirch, bleach, blot, defile, fade, smear, spot, stain, streak, sully, tarnish

discolor by fungi: mildew

discoloration: stain

discolored, as a book: foxed

discombobulated: addled, shaken, thrown, undone

discomfit: abash, annoy, baffle, bother, confound, confuse, defeat, disconcert, disturb, embarrass, fluster, frustrate, humiliate, irk, outwit, rattle, thwart, upset

discomfort: ache, agony, annoyance, dismay, displeasure, disquietude, distress, disturb, embarrass, irritation, malady, malaise, pain, soreness, trouble, uneasiness

discommode: bother, burden, fluster, inconvenience, trouble, upset

discompose: agitate, confuse, disarrange, disarray, disconcert, disorder, disorganize, displace, disquiet, disturb, fluster, perturb, pester, provoke, rattle, ruffle, unhinge, unsettle, upset

disconcert: abash, baffle, bewilder, complicate, confound, confuse, disarrange, discomfit, discompose, discountenance, disturb, embarrass, faze, frustrate, nonplus, perplex, perturb, rattle, ruffle, unbalance, unsettle

disconcerted: aback, abashed

disconnect: detach, disengage, interrupt, separate, sever, sunder, uncouple, undo, unlink, unplug

disconnected: abstracted, broken, desultory, disjointed, illogical, incoherent, irrational, loose, muddled, rambling, random, removed

disconnected and separate: discrete, off-line, unhooked

disconnected in sound: staccato

disconsolate: blue, cheerless, dejected, depressed, despairing, dispirited, down, dreary, forlorn, gloomy, hopeless, melancholy, miserable, pessimistic, sad, somber, unhappy, woebegone

discontent, chronic: dysphoria

discontented: bored, displeased, disappointed, disenchanted, disillusioned, dissatisfied, malcontent, miserable, peeved, restless, unhappy

discontented and alone: alienated, disaffected

discontented person: malcontent

discontinue: abandon, break, cease, desist, drop, end, gap, halt, interrupt, pause, quit, scrub, stop, suspend, terminate

discontinuous: intermittent, periodic

discord: animosity, antagonism, atony, cacophony, clash, conflict, contention, differ, difference, disagreement, disharmony, dissension, dissonance, enmity, friction, hostility, noise, static, strife, variance

discordant: absonant, ajar, conflicting, contrary, discrepant, dissonant, harsh, heterogeneous, hoarse, incompatible, incongruous, inconsistent, inharmonious, jangling, jarring, mismated, quarrelsome, untenable

discordant sound: cacophony, din, jangle

discount: allowance, decrease, deduction, depreciation, dismiss, disregard, exemption, forget, ignore, lessen, mark down, minimize, rebate, reduction, rollback, subtract

discount notes not paying interest: zero coupon bonds

discount or partial refund: rebate

discourage: dampen, daunt, deject, demoralize, depress, deter, dishearten, dispirit, dissuade, frighten, hinder, inhibit, intimidate, restrain

discourse: address, argument, chat, colloquy, comment, conversation, converse, descant, description, dialogue, discuss, discussion, dissert, dissertation, eulogy, expatiate, expound, homily, lecture, monologue, narration, orate, oration, paper, parley, preach, prelect, rhetoric, sermon, soliloquy, speak, talk, tell, thesis, treatise

discourteous: crude, disrespectful, illbred, ill-mannered, impolite, inaffable, rude, uncivil, uncouth, ungracious, unmannerly

discourteous manner: incivility

discover: ascertain, confess, define, descry, detect, determine, discern, disclose, divulge, espy, explore, expose, find, identify, learn, locate, observe, perceive, pioneer, realize, recognize, reveal, see, spot, spy, turn up, uncover, unearth, unmask

discover and bring out: unearth

discover by careful observation: descry, detect

discover the meaning of: fathom

discover with certainty: ascertain

discoveries made by accident: serendipity

discovery: analysis, breakthrough, diagnosis, espial, invention, method, origination, revelation, sighting, strike, treasure, trouvaille

discovery as learning experience: heuristics

discovery, cry of: eureka

discredit: asperse, belittle, blame, blemish, damage, decry, defame, disbelieve, disgrace, dishonor, disparage, distrust, doubt, expose, ignominy, impeach, question, shame, slander, slur, smear, suspect, taint

discreet: careful, cautious, circumspect, civil, controlled, guarded, judicious, modest, polite, politic, prudent, reasonable, reserved, sensible

discrepancy: conflict, difference, disagreement, disparity, error, gap, inconsistency

discrete: detached, distinct, diverse, individual, separate, various

discretion: caution, choice, diplomacy, judgment, maturity, privacy, prudence, restraint, secrecy, sense, tact, wisdom

discriminate: contrast, demarcate, differentiate, discern, distinguish, favor, hate, perceive, segregate, separate, victimize

discriminate against: blacklist, distinguish, secern

discriminate and bully: victimize

discriminating: analytical, astute, bigoted, careful, choosey, critical, distinctive, finicky, perceptive, prejudiced, selective, shrewd

discriminating taste: gourmet

discrimination: acumen, bias, hatred, heed, inequity, injustice, keenness, partiality, sagacity, taste, understandment

discrimination against blacks: Jim Crow

discrimination against elderly: ageism

discrimination against group allegedly practicing discrimination: reverse discrimination

discriminatory: invidious

discursive: digressive, meandering, rambling, roving, verbose

discuss: agitate, air, argue, confer, consider, consult, contend, debate, discourse, dispute, elaborate, examine, explain, expound, hash over, parley, talk over, treat

discuss or debate: deliberate, moot

discuss thoroughly: canvass

discussing informally: cracker-barrel

discussion: argument, canvass, colloquy, confabulation, conference, conversation, deliberation, descant, dialogue, exposition, huddle, meeting, palaver, parley, powwow, rap, symposium, talk

discussion by two: dialogue, tête-à-tête

discussion by writers: cenacle

discussion group: panel

discussion on a theme: descant

discussion or conference: colloquium, powwow, symposium

discussion participant: collocuter, interlocutor

discussion to arrive at a truth: dialectic

discussion, expose to public: ventilate

discussion, informal: causerie

discussion, public meeting for: forum

discussion, to arrange or settle by: negotiate

discussion, to bring up for: broach

disdain: abhor, arrogance, contemn, contempt, derision, despise, detest, flout, hate, haughtiness, indifference, loathe, ridicule, scorn, slight

disdainful: arrogant, supercilious

disease: ailment, complaint, debility, epidemic, ergot, illness, infirmity, malady, pandemic, sickness, virus

RELATED TERMS

disease affecting entire body: systemic

disease and its causes, study of: pathology

disease caused from work: occupational disease

disease caused or aggravated by mental problems, of: psychosomatic

disease-causing agent: pathogen

disease causing jerky movements: chorea, Saint Vitus' dance

disease-causing microorganisms, organism that carries: carrier, vector

disease causing tics, outbursts, twitches: Tourette's syndrome

disease classification: nosography

disease corrected by bodily manipulation: osteopathy

disease developing or caused outside body: exogenous

disease developing or caused within body: endogenous

disease existing from birth but not hereditary, of a: congenital

disease finding: diagnosis, prognosis

disease from eating undercooked meat, pork: trichinosis

disease in dormancy, of a: latent, quiescent

disease indicator: symptom

disease moving to various body parts: metastasis

disease not manifesting typical symptoms, of a: subclinical

disease occurring suddenly and severely, of a: foudroyant

disease of animals that can be transmitted to humans: zoonosis

disease or disorder, genetic predisposition to: diathesis

disease-preventing: prophylactic

disease-preventing treatment: prophylaxis

disease-producing: morbific

disease resistant to treatment, of a: refractory

disease spread from one part to another in the body: metastasis

disease spread, isolation to prevent: quarantine

disease spreading uncontrolled, of a: insidious, malignant, virulent

disease treatment by causing incompatible condition: allopathy

disease with vaccine, to protect against: inoculate, vaccinate

disease, abatement or subsiding of symptoms of: remission

disease, branch of medicine dealing with causes or origins of: etiology

disease, condition results from a: sequela

disease, gradual subsiding of symptoms of acute: lysis

disease, identification of a: diagnosis

disease, medical testing of group for: screening

disease, of a localized: endemic

disease, of a transmittable: communicable, contagious, infectious, notifiable

disease, prediction of course and outcome of a: prognosis

disease, regress after partial recovery from: recrudescence, relapse

disease, relating to: morbid, pathological

disease, slow and lingering: chronic disease

disease, study of: pathology

disease, sudden and severe: acute disease

disease, sudden and widespread: epidemic

disease, susceptibility to a: predisposition

disease, susceptible to a: at risk

disease, symptoms that characterize: syndrome

disease, to catch a: contract

disease, widespread: epidemic, pandemic

diseased: infectious, pestiferous, pestilent, poxy

diseased thing: blight, canker

diseases, branch of medicine dealing with classification of: nosology ❦

disembark: arrive, deplane, dismount, land

disembowel: eviscerate, exenterate

disenchanted: blasé, disappointed, disillusioned, enlightened, knowing, mundane, undeceived, unhappy, worldly-wise

disencumber: alleviate, disengage, lighten, relieve, rid, unburden, unload

disengage: clear, detach, draft apart, extricate, free, liberate, loosen, release, sever, undo, unfasten, wean, withdraw

disentangle: comb, disconnect, evolve, extricate, free, loose, ravel, separate, solve, sunder, unravel, unsnarl, untie, untwist

disfavor: aversion, disapproval, disesteem, disgrace, dislike, displeasure, odium, repulsion

disfigure: blemish, deface, defile, deform, distort, injure, maim, mangle, mar, mark, mutilate, scar

disfranchised: voteless

disgorge: spew

disgrace: abase, blot, contempt, debase, degradation, degrade, desecrate, discredit, disfavor, dishonor, disrepute, embarrass, humiliate, humiliation, ignominy, infamy, mock,

obloquy, odium, reproach, scandal, shame, slander, slur, spot, stain, stigmatize

disgrace to person, group: infamy, obloquy, stigma

disgrace, extreme: ignominy, infamy, odium, opprobium

disgrace, mark of: stigma

disgrace, to banish in: ostracize

disgraceful: appalling, base, flagrant, inglorious, shady, shameful, shoddy, unbecoming, unworthy

disgracing: opprobrious

disgruntled: dissatisfied, grumpy, irritated, malcontent, peevish, sore, unhappy

disguise: alter, artifice, belie, camouflage, charade, cloak, conceal, cover, dissemble, dissimulate, facade, falsify, feign, hide, incognito, mask, masquerade, obscure, pretend, pretense, veil, veneer, whitewash

disguise like environment: camouflage

disguise oneself as someone else: impersonate

disguise or shelter: coverture

disguised: incognito

disguised attack: ambush

disguised enemy: fifth column, Trojan horse

disgust: abhorrence, abomination, antipathy, appall, aversion, dislike, distaste, loathing, nauseate, offend, outrage, repel, repugnance, repulsion, revolt, revulsion, shock, sicken, surfeit

disgust or extreme dislike: abhorrence, loathing

disgust or sicken, to: nauseate

disgusting: abhorrent, abominable, awful, beastly, creepy, detestable, foul, gross, hateful, hideous, loathsome, nasty, nauseating, noisome, obscene, odious, offensive, rebarbative, repugnant, repulsive, revolting, shocking, vile, yucky

disgusting and offensive: noisome, noxious, odious, repugnant

disgusting degree, to a: ad nauseam

disgusting to the taste: fulsome

dish: basin, bowl, casserole, ceramic, charger, china, container, course, cup, dispense, entrée, favorite, food, helping, plate, platter, recipe, saucer, serve, tray, tureen

dish for baking and serving: casserole

dish for lab culture: petri dish

KINDS OF DISEASE

acute disease/condition
allergy/allergic disease
atrophy
autoimmune disease
bacterial disease
blood disease
bone disease
brain disease
cardiopulmonary disease
cardiovascular disease
childhood/pediatric disease
chronic disease/condition
circulatory disease
collagen disease
communicable disease
congenital disease
contagious/infectious disease
deficiency disease
degenerative disease
dermatological disease
digestive disease
ear disease
eating disorder
endemic disease
endocrine disease
endocrine gland disease
environmental disease/occupational disease
epidemic disease
eye disease
febrile disease
functional disease
fungus/fungal disease
gastric/stomach disease
gastroenterological disease
gastrointestinal disease
genetic disease
geriatric disease
glandular disease
heart disease

hematopoietic disease
hepatic/liver disease
hereditary disease
hypertrophy
iatrogenic disease
infectious disease
intestinal disease
joint disease
kidney disease
liver disease
malignant disease
mental disorder
metabolic disease
muscular disease
musculoskeletal disease
neoplastic disease
neurological disease
nutritional disease
occupational disease
ophthalmic disease
organic disease
pandemic disease
parasitic disease
poisoning
psychiatric disease
psychogenic/psychosomatic disease
pulmonary disease
radiation disease
renal/kidney disease
respiratory disease
sexually transmitted disease/STD/venereal disease
skin disease
substance abuse
traumatic disease
tropical disease
urinogenital/urogenital disease
virus/viral disease
wasting disease
worm disease ❧

---

dish on hotplate or warmer: chafing dish
dish out: ladle, mete
dish, appetizer or following meal: savory
dish, covered soup: tureen
dish, main: entrée
dish, small, for baking and serving: ramekin
dishabille: careless, disarray, disorder, undress
disharmony: chaos, clash, conflict, disarray, discord, dissension, friction
dishearten: abash, crush, dampen, daunt, deject, demoralize, depress, deter, discourage, dispirit, humble, sadden

disheartened: abject
dishes, side or dessert: entremets
dishevel: muss, tousle
disheveled: disarranged, disorderly, frowsy, messy, ratty, ruffled, sloppy, slovenly, straggly, tousled, uncombed, unkempt, untidy, wrinkled
dishonest: cheating, corrupt, crooked, deceitful, deceptive, devious, false, fraudulent, knavish, lying, mendacious, misleading, shady, shifty, underhanded, unscrupulous, untrustworthy, untruthful
dishonest ploy: dirty trick, subterfuge
dishonestly crafty: disingenuous
dishonestly, to use language: equivocate, prevaricate

dishonesty: chicanery, cunning, double-dealing, duplicity, fraud, hankypanky, improbity, knavery, mendacity, stealing
dishonor: blemish, debauch, defame, defile, degrade, discredit, disgrace, disrepute, humiliate, ignominy, infamy, obloquy, opprobrium, shame, smirch, stain, tarnish
dishonorable: base, contemptible, corrupt, cowardly, degraded, despicable, foul, ignoble, ignominious, reprehensible, shady, shameful, unethical, unprincipled
dishonorable discharge, to give a: cashier
dishwashing room: scullery

disillusioned: disabused, disappointed, disenchanted, enlightened, shattered, wakened

disinclination: antipathy, aversion, disinterest, dislike, hatred, reluctance, resistance, unwillingness

disinclined: averse, balking, bashful, indisposed, loath, protesting, reluctant, uneager, unwilling

disinfect: cleanse, fumigate, purify, sanitize, sterilize

disinfect with spray: fumigate

disinherit: cut off, deprive, disaffiliate, disown, exclude

disintegrate: crumble, decay, decompose, dissolve, erode, fragmentize, melt, pulverize, rust, shatter, splinter

disintegrating: fissiparous

disintegrative: erodent

disinter: delve, dig, disclose, exhume, expose, uncover, unearth

disinterested: apathetic, detached, fair, impartial, indifferent, neutral, nonpartisan, passive, unbiased, uninfluenced, uninvolved

disjoin: detach, dislocate, luxate

disjointed: apart, chaotic, confused, disconnected, dislocated, disordered, incoherent, loose, muddled, tangled, unattached, unhinged, unorganized

disjointed and confusing: incoherent

disjointed, separated by incident: episodic

disk of semiconducting material: wafer

disk used as ornament in architecture: bezant

disk, shiny, as ornament: sequin

dislike: animosity, antagonism, antipathy, aversion, despise, detest, disaffection, disrelish, distaste, hate, hatred, loathe, prejudice, resent

dislike intensely: abhor, abominate, execrate, hate, loathe

dislike of argument, reasoning: misology

dislike of children: misopedia

dislike, intense: animosity, animus, antipathy, aversion, enmity, repugnance, revulsion

dislike, rousing: invidious

disliked, one that is particularly: bête noire

dislocate: disjoint, displace, disrupt, luxate, move, separate, transfer, uproot, upset

dislodge: disturb, expel, extricate, oust, remove

disloyal: faithless, false, perfidious, recreant, subversive, traitorous, treacherous, treasonable, undutiful, unfaithful, untrue

disloyal person: rat, recreant

disloyalty: apostasy, betrayal, infidelity, insurrection, mutiny, perfidy, rebellion, treason

dismal: black, bleak, blue, calamitous, cheerless, cloudy, dark, depressing, dire, disheartening, doleful, drear, dreary, dull, funereal, ghastly, gloomy, glum, gray, grim, hopeless, joyless, lonesome, melancholy, ominous, sad, somber, sorrowful, sullen, unhappy

dismantle: annul, denude, deprive, destroy, disassemble, dismount, divest, level, raze, rescind, strip, take apart, undo, unmake

dismay: affright, alarm, anxiety, appal, appall, apprehension, confound, consternation, daunt, deprive, disappoint, discomfort, discourage, disenchantment, disillusion, dread, fear, fright, horrify, panic, rattle, shake, subdue, terrify, terror, trepidation, unhinge, upset

dismember: amputate, disjoint, dissect, maim, mangle, mutilate, sever, sunder

dismiss: banish, boot, bump, can, cashier, clear, delegate, disband, discard, discharge, dispel, drop, eject, expel, fire, free, oust, reject, release, remove, sack, send packing, terminate, write off

dismissal: adjournment, congé, deportation, disregard, expulsion, layoff, leavetaking, marching orders, release, removal, waiver

dismissal from position: congé, firing, heave-ho, layoff, pink slip

dismount: alight, deplane, descend, dismantle, unhorse

disobedient: contrary, contumacious, defiant, disorderly, dissenting, factious, froward, insubordinate, insurgent, mischievous, mutinous, naughty, noncompliant, perverse, rebellious, recalcitrant, refractory, stubborn, undisciplined, unruly, wayward, willful

disobey: defy, disregard, ignore, misbehave, rebel, resist

disobey a law with contempt: flout, outface

disobey or violate a rule: contravene, infringe, transgress

disorder: affliction, ailment, anarchy, chaos, clutter, commotion, complaint, confuse, confusion, disarrange, disarray, disconcert, disease, dishevel, disorganize, disturb, fracas, fuss, illness, jumble, malady, mayhem, mess, misconduct, mucker, muddle, riot, ruffle, shambles, sickness, syndrome, tousle, trouble, tumult

disorder and destruction: shambles

disorder and lawlessness: anomie

disorder from no leadership or plan: anarchy

disorder, state of: aflunters

disordered system: entropy

disorderly: disobedient, hugger-mugger, messy, pell-mell, rambunctious, raucous, rowdy, uncontrollable, ungovernable, unkempt, unlawful, unmanageable, unruly, unsettled, untidy

disorderly profusion: riot

disorderly struggle: scramble

disorganized: chaotic, confused, disorderly, fragmental, haphazard, helterskelter, muddled, scatterbrained, unmethodical, upset

disorientation in different environment: culture shock

disoriented: addled, confused, lost, unbalanced, unstable

disown: abandon, abdicate, deny, disavow, disinherit, expel, forsake, reject, renounce, repudiate

disparage: abuse, belittle, blacken, criticize, decry, defame, degrade, demean, demoralize, denigrate, derogate, discredit, disdain, dishonor, minimize, rap, ridicule, slight, slur, underrate, vilipend

disparagement of the unattainable: sour grapes

disparaging: derogatory, snide

disparaging remark: slur, tut

disparaging term for something inoffensive: dysphemism

disparaging term for wealth: pelf

disparity: contrast, difference, discrepancy, dissimilarity, gap, imbalance, inequality, unevenness

dispassionate: calm, clinical, collected, composed, cool, fair, impartial, just, levelheaded, moderate, serene, unbiased, unemotional, unexcited, unfeeling, unflappable, unimpaired, unmoved, unprejudiced, unruffled

dispassionately critical: clinical

dispatch: accelerate, bulletin, celerity, communication, communiqué, consume, deliver, devour, expedite, finish, flash, free, haste, hasten, hurry, instruction, message, note, post, promptness, quickness, report, send, sendout, slay, speed, story, swiftness, transmit; assassinate, dispose, eliminate, kill, murder, slay

dispatch boat: aviso

dispel: allay, banish, dismiss, disperse, dissipate, drive away, eject, expel, scatter, squander, waste

dispensable: disposable, expendable, minor, needless, superfluous, trivial, unessential

dispensary: clinic

dispensation: allotment, arrangement, decree, distribution, exemption, management, permission, relief, scheme, system

dispense: absolve, administer, arrange, assign, deal, direct, distribute, divide, dole out, excuse, exempt, exonerate, manage, manipulate, measure, prepare, provide, release, spare

dispense with: abandon, discard, dump, eliminate, omit, relinquish, scarp, shelve

disperse: circulate, diffuse, disappear, disband, dispel, disseminate, dissipate, distribute, melt, scatter, separate, spread, strew, vanish

dispirited: blue, bummed, cheerless, crestfallen, dejected, demoralized, depressed, disheartened, down, downcast, flat, forlorn, low, melancholy, sad, woebegone

displace: banish, depose, discharge, dislocate, dislodge, evict, exile, move, remove, shift, supersede, supplant, unsettle, uproot, usurp

displace a bone or limb: dislocate

displaced turf: divot

displacement from office: deposal

display: advertise, affectation, blazon, boast, ceremony, demonstrate, disclose, discover, emblazon, example, exhibit, exhibition, expose, extend, flaunt, flourish, indicate, manifest, model, pageant, parade, pomp, promote, reveal, sample, show, sight, spectacle, splendor, sport, stage, uncover, unfold, unveil, wear

display brazenly: flaunt, flourish

display medium: showcase

display on digital watch or clock: LCD

display showily: blandish

displaying obtuseness: missing the point

displease: aggravate, anger, annoy, bother, dissatisfy, disturb, exasperate, irritate, miff, offend, pall, pique, provoke

displeasure: anger, aversion, disapproval, discomfort, discontent, disgust, dislike, distaste, indignation, offense, resentment, sorrow, umbrage, unhappiness, vexation, wrath

disport: amusement, entertain, frolic, merriment, play, recreation

disposable: expendable

disposal: arrangement, authority, clearance, command, conclusion, discarding, dumping, jettison, power, riddance, settlement

dispose: abandon, adjust, arrange, array, bend, bestow, determine, dispatch, distribute, give, incline, order, organize, place, prepare, regulate, settle, systematize

dispose of: dispatched, make short shrift of, make unnecessary, obviate

disposed: prone

disposed to love: amative

disposed to stay with one's own clique: clannish

disposition: adjustment, affection, aptitude, arrangement, attitude, bent, bias, character, concept, constitution, direction, heart, humor, idiosyncrasy, inclination, leaning, makeup, management, mood, nature, organization, personality, proclivity, propensity, temper, temperament, tendency

dispossession, unlawful: disseizin

disproportion: difference, disparity, imbalance, inadequacy, inequality, mismatch

disproportionate: asymmetric, excessive, inadequate, incommensurate, irregular, unbalanced, unequal, uneven, unrelative

disproportionate portion: lion's share

disprove: belie, call in question, challenge, confute, controvert, discredit, impugn, invalidate, negate, oppugn, puncture, rebut, refute, weaken

disprove claim or argument: invalidate

disputable: arguable, debatable, doubtful, dubious, fallible, moot, questionable, uncertain, unsure

disputation: argument, controversy, debate, discussion, dissension, mooting, polemic

dispute: altercation, argue, argument, bicker, brawl, challenge, contend, contest, contradict, contravene, controversy, controvert, debate, deny, differ, disagreement, discuss, doubt, encounter, faction, feud, fuss, gainsay, haggle, moot, oppose, oppugn, polemic, quarrel, question, rebut, repudiate, resist, squabble, wrangle

dispute and argument: altercation, contretemps, ruction

dispute and difference of opinion: dissention, variance

dispute and fight: skirmish

dispute settlement by third party: adjudication, arbitration, mediation

dispute truth or validity: impugn

dispute, causing: divisive

dispute, involved in a: embroiled

dispute, mediator in: arbitrator, intermediary, moderator

dispute, to act as mediator in: intercede

dispute, to settle or resolve: arbitrate, conciliate, mediate

disqualification: disability, elimination, ineligibility

disqualify: debar, exclude, incapacitate, invalidate, outlaw, prohibit, suspend

disquiet: agitate, anxiety, discompose, discontent, distress, disturb, excite, fear, fluster, fret, pain, restlessness, trouble, turmoil, uneasiness, unrest, upset, worry

disregard: close one's eyes to, defiance, discount, disobey, forget, forgetfulness, ignore, inattention, indifference, lassitude, neglect, oblivion, omit, overlook, oversight, passover, skip, slight, waive

disregard for rules to achieve artistic effect: poetic license

disreputable: base, contemptible, disgraceful, dishonorable, lowly, notorious, raffish, ratty, seamy, seedy, shady, shameful, sleazy, sordid, tawdry, unsavory, vulgar

disreputable urban area: slum

disrespect: boldness, contempt, discourtesy, dishonor, incivility, rudeness

disrespectful: impertinent, impolite, impudent, insolent, insulting, rude, uncivil, ungracious

disrobe: denude, divest, remove, shed, strip, undress

disrupt: break, disorder, disorganize, disturb, interrupt, unsettle, upset

disrupt a nap: roust

dissatisfaction: annoyance, discontent, dislike, displeasure, distaste, frustration, unhappiness

dissatisfied: disappointed, disenchanted, disgruntled, irked, malcontented, peeved, unfulfilled

dissatisfied in relationship: alienated, disaffected

dissect: analyze, anatomize, carve, dichotomize, examine, investigate, pick apart, probe, separate, study, sunder

dissect the language: parse

dissemble: camouflage, cloak, conceal, counterfeit, cover, disguise, feign, hide, mask, pretend, screen, simulate, veil

dissembler: liar

disseminate: blazon, broadcast, circulate, diffuse, disperse, distribute, promulgate, propagate, publicize, scatter, sow, spread, strew, transmit

dissension: conflict, contention, disagreement, discord, disharmony, friction, odds, static, strife

dissent: buck, differ, disagreement, dissidence, divide, exception, nonconformity, objection, oppose, protest, vary

dissenter: dissident, heretic, maverick, mutineer, nonconformist, protestor, rebel, recusant, schismatic, sectary

dissertation: critique, debate, discourse, discussion, essay, exposition, lecture, monograph, thesis, tract, treatise

disservice: damage, harm, injury, injustice, outrage, unkindness, wrong

dissident: agitator, disagreeing, dissenter, fractious, heretic, nonconformist, rebel, schismatic, sectary

dissimilar: contrary, different, difform, disparate, distinct, diverse, heterogeneous, unique, unlike, unrelated

dissimulate: camouflage, cloak, conceal, disguise, dissemble, feign, hide, pretend

dissipate: consume, deplete, diffuse, disappear, dispel, disperse, dissolve, evanesce, evaporate, expend, fritter, misuse, overindulge, scatter, spend, squander, waste

dissipation: amusement, debauchery, diversion, entertainment, intemperance, wantonness

dissociate: alienate, disconnect, distance, estrange, separate, sever

dissociated: apart

dissolute: abandoned, corrupt, debauched, immoral, lax, loose, lustful, profligate, rakish, slack, unprincipled, unrestrained, wanton, wild

dissolute one: roué

dissolution: annulment, breakup, death, decay, decease, demise, disintegration, dismissal, division, divorce, end, extinction, liquefaction, ruin, rupture, separation, termination

dissolve: adjourn, annul, decompose, destroy, disappear, disband, discontinue, disintegrate, dissipate, divorce, dwindle, evanesce, fade, fuse, invalidate, liquefy, melt, relent, separate, thaw, undo, vanish, void

dissolve and absorb moisture in air: deliquesce

dissolve and filter: leach, percolate

dissolved in another substance, substance: solute

dissolved, capable of being: soluble

dissolved, substance in which another substance is: solvent

dissonance: conflict, difference, disagreement, discord, jarring, noise, strife

dissonant: atonal, cacophonous, discordant, grating, harsh, incongruous, inconsistent, inharmonious, irregular, jangling, raucous, strident, unmelodious

dissuade: caution, deter, discourage, disincline, divert, prevent, restrain, stop, talk out of, thwart

distance: aloofness, coldness, degree, depth, difference, disagreement, dissociate, extent, farness, horizon, interval, latitude, length, longitude, mileage, outrun, outstrip, period, radius, range, remoteness, space, span, yardage

distance 3,280 feet: kilometer

distance around edge of object: circumference

distance around thing: circumference

distance between limits: span

distance light travels in vacuum in year: light-year

distance measured with angles: telemetry

distance of ⅛ mile: furlong

distance traveled measuring instrument: odometer

distant: afar, aloof, away, cold, far, far-away, isolated, remote, removed, reserved, separated, unfriendly, unsociable, withdrawn

distant unknown region: Ultima Thule

distaste: abhorrence, aversion, disgust, dislike, displease, disrelish, hate, hostility, loathing, offend, opprobrium, repugnance

distasteful: bitter, detestable, disagreeable, flat, hateful, nauseating, objectionable, offensive, repulsive, undesirable, unpalatable, unpleasant, unsavory

distemper: affliction, ailment, disease, disorder, disturbance, illness, infection, malady, paint, testiness

distend: augment, balloon, bloat, bulge, dilate, elongate, enlarge, expand, increase, inflate, spread, stretch, swell, widen

distended and swollen: turgid

distill: condense, drop, extract, exude, ferment, purify, separate, trickle

distillation, to refine or purify by: rectify

distillation, to separate into components in: fractionation

distillery mixing tank: mashtun

distillery sediment: draff

distinct: apparent, categorical, clear, different, discrete, dissimilar, distinguish, diverse, explicit, individual, obvious, particular, plain, recognizable, separate, special, unique, unmistakable, unusual, vivid

distinct taste: tang

distinct, to make: differentiate

distinction: differentiation, eminence, excellence, feature, glory, greatness, honor, laurels, mark, merit, nicety, nuance, prominence, rank, renown, reputation, separation, significance, subtlety

distinctive: characteristic, discriminating, original, outstanding, peculiar, typical, uncommon, unique

distinctive atmosphere: aura

distinctive mark(s): cachet, indicia

distingué: cultivated, cultured, distinguished, polished, refined

distinguish: admire, ascertain, characterize, classify, define, designate, differentiate, discern, distinct, exalt, identify, note, perceive, praise, punctuate, secern, separate, stamp

distinguished: acclaimed, brilliant, celebrated, dignified, distinct, distingué, eminent, famous, grand, illustrious, imposing, marked, notable, prestigious, prominent, renowned, secerned, shining, special, stately

distinguishing character: ethos

distinguishing characteristic: diagnostic, feature, landmark, lineament

distort: alter, belie, bend, deceive, deform, disfigure, doctor, falsify, garble, mangle, misrepresent, misstate, pervert, skew, twist, warp

distorted: anamorphic, askew, awry, bargled, cockeyed, colored, crooked, gnarled, perverted, wry

distortion of shape: anamorphism

distortion of vision: astigmatism

distract: addle, agitate, amuse, bewilder, confound, confuse, deflect, disturb, divert, entertain, fluster, harass, perplex, puzzle, stall, unnerve, upset

distraction: aberration, commotion, disturbance, diversion, interruption, preoccupation

distraction from real issue: red herring

distraught: crazed, deranged, distressed, flustered, frantic, frenzied, hysterical, troubled, unglued, upset, worried

distress: adversity, afflict, affliction, agonize, aggrieve, anger, anguish, annoy, anxiety, calamity, constrain, constraint, danger, discomfort, distraught, dolor, grief, grieve, harass, heartbreak, hurt, misery, necessity, need, pain, perplex, soreness, sorrow, suffer, suffering, torment, torture, travail, tribulation, trouble, upset, woe, worry

distress signal: alarm, broadcast, flag, flares, mayday, siren, SOS

distress the mind: harrow

distress, cause of: wormwood

distress, great: suffering, tribulation

distressing: deplorable, dreadful, fearful, frightening, nagging, painful, poignant, regrettable, sad, troublesome, woeful

distribute: administer, allocate, allot, apportion, arrange, assign, circulate, classify, deal, deliver, dispense, disperse, dispose, disseminate, divide, dole, donate, group, issue, mete, parcel, pass around, ration, separate, share, sort, spread, supply

distribute cards: deal

distribute proportionately: admeasure, allocate, apportion, parcel out, prorate

distribute widely: diffuse, disperse, disseminate, propagate, scatter, strew

distributor: businessperson, cap, dealer, jobber, merchant, publisher, seller, wholesaler

district: area, canton, community, diocese, locality, neighborhood, parish, precinct, province, quarter, region, sector, territory, tract, turf, vicinity, ward, zone

distrust: doubt, fear, qualm, question, skepticism, suspect, suspicion

distrust of mankind: misanthropy

distrustful: cynical, disbelieving, dubious, leery, suspicious

distrustfully: askance

disturb: agitate, alarm, annoy, arouse, bother, disarrange, discomfit, discommode, discompose, disconcert, disrupt, distemper, distract, distress, harass, harrow, incommode, inconvenience, interfere, interrupt, intrude, ire, nettle, perturb, rile, roil, ruffle, tamper, trouble, unnerve, unsettle, upset

disturb or annoy: agitate, discommode, roil, stir up

disturb smoothness: ruffle

disturb the mind: harrow

disturb the peace: discompose, violate

disturbance: ado, affray, brawl, civil disorder, commotion, confusion, cyclone, derangement, disorder, distemper, distraction, eruption, excitement, ferment, fracas, hubbub, hurricane, insurrection, interruption, perturbation, quake, riot, row, rumpus, storm, to-do, tornado, trepidation, tumult, turmoil, uproar, violence

disturbance of the mind, sudden: brainstorm

disturbance, sudden: upheaval

disturbing: vexatious

disunite: alienate, detach, disband, disconnect, disengage, disjoin, dissociate, dissolve, divide, divorce, estrange, part, separate, sever, sunder

disuse: desuetude

ditch: abandon, canal, channel, chuck, dike, discard, excavation, forsake, foss, foxhole, gully, gutter, jettison, junk, moat, reject, scrap, skip, trench, trough

ditch for running water, as rain: gully

ditch or moat, artificial: fosse

ditch, drainage: dike

ditchlike depression in desert: wadi

dither: agitation, babble, confusion, flap, fluster, hesitate, irresolute, panic, shake, shiver, tizzy, tremble, vacillate, waver, whiffle

dithyrambic: boisterous, elevated, euphoric, unrestrained, wild

ditto: agreement, alike, copy, duplicate, repeat, same

ditto, in citations: ibid

ditty: ballad, ephemeral, poem, song, tune

diurnal: daytime, diary, journal

divagate: deviate, digress, drift, ramble, stray, wander

divan: book, chamber, coffeehouse, couch, davenport, lounge, seat, sofa, tribunal

dive: belly flop, cannonball, descent, dump, fall, gainer, hangout, jackknife, jump, leap, lunge, plummet, plunge, spring, submerge, swan, swoop, tailspin

dive facing forward, back somersault, and entering water feet first: gainer

dive quickly and deep: sound

dive with back flip and enter headfirst facing board: half gainer

dive with body folded and then straightened before entering water: jackknife

dive, perilous: brodie

diver: aquanaut

diver breathing apparatus: aqualung

diver condition in extreme pressure: decompression sickness, the bends

diver with breathing apparatus: scuba diver

diverge: branch, contrast, deflect, deviate, differ, digress, disagree, divide, oppose, split, spread, swerve, vary, veer

diverge and branch out: divaricate

divergence: variation

divergent: aberrant, atypical, conflicting, different, separate, unequal, variant

diverging from a point: digressive, tangential

divers: many

diver's affliction: bends

diver's apparatus: scuba

diver's sickness, nitrogen in bloodstream: caisson disease, decompression sickness, nitrogen narcosis, the bends

diverse: assorted, different, distinct, heterogeneous, motley, multifarious, opposite, separate, several, sundry, varied

diverse in sources: eclectic

diversify: change, expand, rotate, variate, vary

diversify, add something different: interlard

diversion: amusement, deflection, departure, detour, digression, distraction, entertainment, game, hobby, levity, merriment, pastime, play, recreation, red herring, relaxation, relief, sideshow, sport

diversity: assortment, change, difference, multiformity, variegation, variety

divert: amuse, avoid, beguile, deflect, distract, entertain, redirect, relax, stall, swerve, tickle, veer

divest: bare, bleed, denude, deprive, despoil, dethrone, dismantle, dispose, dispossess, disrobe, free, spoil, strip, unclothe, uncover, unload

divest of office: depose

divide: alienate, allocate, allot, apportion, bisect, branch, carve, categorize, classify, cleave, cleft, deal, dichotomize, differ, dissent, dissever, distribute, disunite, diverge, divvy, fissure, fork, fraction, graduate, halve, intersect, isolate, parcel, part, partition, quarter, ramify, ridge, section, segment, separate, sever, share, slice, split, sunder, trisect

divide 50-50: halve

divide by cutting or passing across: intersect

divide in proportion: prorate

divide into distinct classes: compartmentalize, pigeonhole

divide into marked intervals: graduate

divide into three parts: trisect

divide into two contrasting positions: polarize

divide into two equal parts: bisect

divide or branch into two: bifurcate

divide territory into hostile units: balkanize

divide up: dismember, fragment, partition, segment, sort

divide voting area for interests of a political party: gerrymander

divided: apart, asunder, branched, cleft, detached, disunity, incomplete, partite, prorated, reft, split, unattached

divided in half: dichotomize, dimidiate

divided into classes: hierarchical, segregated, stratified

divided into segments: partite

divided into two equal lobes: bifid

divided or forked: bifurcate

divided, quantity by which another is: denominator, divisor

divided, quantity to be: dividend, numerator

dividend: bonus, carrot, earning, profit, return, reward, share

divides masses of tissue, membrane that: septum

dividing evenly into another number: aliquot

dividing into parts: fissiparous

dividing not evenly into another number: aliquant

dividing one quantity by another, number obtained by: quotient

divination: augury, clairvoyance, forecast, fortune-telling, guess, insight, intuition, omen, prediction, premonition, prognosis, prophecy

divination on a crystal ball: scrying

divination on consulting ghosts: sciomancy

divination on drawing lots: sortilege

divination on dreams: oniermancy

divination on fire: pyromancy

divination on numbers: numerology

divination on tarot cards: cartomancy

divination on the palm: chirmancy, palmistry

divination on the planets: horoscope

divination on the stars: astrology

divination with divining rod: rhabdomancy

divine: angelic, blessed, celestial, conjecture, deific, delightful, godlike, heavenly, holy, immortal, magnificent, mystical, perfect, pious, religious, sacred, spiritual, superhuman, supernatural, wonderful; minister, theologian

divine intervention: theurgy

divine manifestation: epiphany, revelation, theophany

divine nature: deity

divine or supernatural: numinous

divine, to: anticipate, discern, dowse, forebode, foreknow, foresee, foretell, guess, perceive, portend, predict, prognosticate, understand

divinely supplied nourishment: manna

diviner's card: tarot

diving bird: auk, grebe, loon

diving duck: scaup, smew

diving vessel for research: bathyscaphe, bathysphere

divinity: deity, god, goddess, godhead, religion, sanctity, theology

divisible: cantonal

division: allotment, bifurcation, border, branch, breach, category, cleavage, compartment, department, disconnection, discord, disharmony, disjunction, district, dole, fission, group, part, partition, realm, reduction, rift, rupture, schism, scission, section, sector, separation, share, split, territory, unit

division according to a plan: allocation

division into opposing factions: schism

division into two parts: dichotomy

division of a long poem: canto

division of a shield, in heraldry: enté

division of cells in genetics: meiosis, mitosis

division of church or organization into factions: schism

division of Hindu society: caste

division of mankind: race

division sign: obelus

division within organization, dissenting: faction

divisions of a cricket match: overs

divisions of a race: heats

divorce: annul, dissolve, disunion, disunite, nullify, separate, separation, sever, split, sunder

divorce action is brought, person against whom: respondent

divorce action, adulterer cited in: corespondent

divorce action, person bringing: applicant

divorce settlement paid to former spouse: alimony, maintenance

divorce, guardianship awarded in: custody

divorce, right to see children in: visitation rights

divulge: bare, blab, broadcast, confess, confide, disclose, expose, gossip, impart, proclaim, publish, reveal, show, spill, squeal, tattle, tell, uncover, voice

dizziness: vertigo

dizzy: awhirl, bewildered, confused, crazy, flighty, foolish, giddy, groggy, harebrained, haste, lightheaded, rapid, reeling, scatterbrained, silly, swimming, tipsy, unsteady, vertiginous, wobbly, woozy

DNA: acid, deoxyribonucleic acid, double helix, gene, nucleic

DNA structure: double helix

do away with: abolish, annihilate, banish, cancel, discard, discontinue, dissolve, drop, eliminate, erase, exterminate, kill, liquidate, murder, revoke, slay

do-gooder: altruist

do in: bankrupt, destroy, eliminate, exhaust, finish, kill, liquidate, murder, ruin, slay, tire

docent: guide, instructor, lecturer, teacher

docile: agreeable, calm, compliant, gentle, manageable, meek, mild, obedient, resigned, submissive, tame, tractable, willing

dock: anchor, basin, berth, couple, landing, marina, moor, pier, platform, quay, slip, wharf; clip, shorten, withhold

dock fitting: cleat

dock for mooring ship: bollard

dock for small boats: marina, pier

dock on river, waterway: embarcadero

dock worker: lader, longshoreman, stevedore

docket: agenda, calendar, card, label, list, program, roster, schedule, slate, tally, timetable

doctor: expert, healer, internist, medic, medico, Ph.D., physician, professor, sawbones, scholar, scientist, surgeon

RELATED TERMS

back doctor: chiropractor
blood doctor: hematologist
bone doctor: orthopedist
cancer doctor: oncologist
care for as a doctor, to: administer, rebuild, repair, treat
childbirth doctor: obstetrician
doctor certified as specialist: diplomate
doctor for animals: veterinarian
doctor in apprenticeship: intern
doctor pursing occupation: practitioner
doctor receiving clinical training: resident
doctor specializing in clinical studies or practice: clinician
doctor specializing in digestive system: gastrologist
doctor specializing in disease: pathologist
doctor specializing in heart health and disease: cardiologist
doctor who treats children: pediatrician
doctoral candidate's exam: oral

doctor's listening instrument: stethoscope
doctor's oath: Hippocratic oath
doctor's organization: AMA
ear doctor: otologist
ear, nose and throat doctor: otolaryngologist
eye doctor: ophthalmologist, optometrist
family doctor: G.P., general practitioner
female reproductive system doctor: gynecologist
foot doctor: podiatrist
gland doctor: endocrinologist
kidney doctor: nephrologist
mental health doctor: psychiatrist
negligence or misconduct of doctor: malpractice
recent graduate from medical school: intern
skin doctor: dermatologist
specialized training for medical student: resident
staff doctor in hospital: attending physician
symbol of intertwined snakes on staff: caduceus
technician administering anesthesia: anesthesiologist
throat doctor: laryngologist
tooth doctor: dentist, orthodontist
urinary tract doctor: urologist
X-ray technician: radiologist ☜

doctrine: article, attitude, belief, canon, concept, credo, creed, discipline, dogma, fundamental, gospel, ism, maxim, philosophy, precept, principle, ritual, rule, statement, teaching, tenet, theory

doctrine of axioms: noetics

doctrine that life is sacred: ahimsa

doctrine that reality is independent of mind: objectivism

document: bill, book, contract, covenant, deed, diploma, evidence, indenture, lease, license, manuscript, mortgage, paper, passport, record, report, testimony, voucher, writ

document addendum: appendix, codicil, postscript, rider, supplement

document compiled under oath: affidavit

document examination for authenticity: bibliotics

document in a roll: scroll

document in handwriting of person signing it: holograph

document introduction: preamble

document of conveyance of property: deed

document to deceive, alter: falsify, forge

document transmitted telegraphically: facsimile, fax

document written in the signer's handwriting: holograph

document, to: certify, confirm, substantiate, validate, verify, vouch

document, to sign a: endorse, underwrite

documents on subject: dossier

documents, study of ancient official: diplomatics

doddering: aged, decrepit, feeble, infirm, old, senile, shaky, trembling, weak

dodge: artifice, avert, avoid, cheat, deceive, ditch, duck, elude, equivocate, escape, evade, hedge, prevaricate, pussyfoot, shift, shirk, sidestep, skirt, swerve, trick

dodger: circular, dishonest, evader, haggler, handbill, shifty, trickster

doe: deer, fawn, female

doer: activist, actor, dynamo, go-getter, hustler, performer, worker

doff: discard, disrobe, remove, shed, strip, tip, undress, unhat

dog: canine, cur, hound, mongrel, mutt, pooch, pug, pup, puppy

RELATED TERMS

dog breeds: Afghan, Airedale, Basset, Beagle, Belgian Sheepdog, Bloodhound, Borzoi, Boxer, Bulldog, Chihuahua, Cocker Spaniel, Collie, Corgi, Dachshund, Dalmatian, Dane, Dingo, Doberman, Elkhound, Heeler, Husky, Keeshond, Kelpie, Labrador, Malamute, Mastiff, Pekingese, Pinscher, Pointer, Pomeranian, Poodle, Retriever, Saluki, Setter, Sheepdog, Shepherd, Spaniel, Wolfhound
dog constellation: Canis
dog ear flap: leather
dog family member: canine
dog functionless claw: dewclaw
dog lips, as for bloodhound: flews
dog lover: philocynic
dog paddle: tread
dog rump: croup
dog snout: muzzle
dog with blue-black tongue: chow
dog, Australian outback: dingo

dog, having a face like a: cynocephalous

dog, mongrel: cur

dog, pertaining to: canine

dog, to give birth to: whelp

dogfight: melee

dogged: adamant, determined, insistent, obstinate, persevering, persistent, staunch, steadfast, stubborn, tenacious, unshakable, unyielding

doggedness: pertinacity, stamina, tenacity

doggone: blasted, confounded, damn, darn, heck, shucks

doglike: cynoid

doglike mammal: jackal

dog's infectious viral disease: distemper

dogs, fear of: cynophobia

dogs, group of: kennel, pack

dogs, keeper of: fewterer

dogs, relating to: canine

dogs, study of: cynology

dogsled, to drive a: mush ☃

dogma: belief, canon, credo, creed, doctrine, gospel, philosophy, principle, rule, statement, teachings, tenet

dogmatic: arbitrary, arrogant, authoritative, biased, despotic, dictatorial, doctrinal, fanatical, intolerant, opinionated, pedantic, pompous, pontifical, prejudiced, scholastic, totalitarian

dogmatic assertion: ipse dixit

doldrums: apathy, blues, boredom, depression, dumps, ennui, lassitude, listlessness, melancholy, slump, stagnation, tedium

dole: allot, alms, charity, dispense, distribute, donation, give, grief, handout, mete, relief, share, sorrow, welfare

doleful: bleak, depressed, dismal, dour, down, downcast, dreary, forlorn, gloomy, lugubrious, melancholy, mournful, plaintive, sad, somber, sorrowful, unhappy, woebegone

doll: baby, darling, figure, figurine, mannequin, mistress, moppet, puppet, sweetheart, toy, woman

doll collecting: plangonology

doll collector: plangonologist

dollar: bean, buck, currency, greenback, money, one, simoleon

dollop: bit, blob, dab, dash, lump, modicum, splash

dolls nesting one within another: matrushka

dolly: car, cart, locomotive, mobile platform, Parton, tool, truck

dolor: anguish, distress, grief, heartbreak, misery, sadness, sorrow, suffering

dolorous: dismal, doleful, grievous, lamentable, melancholy, morose, mournful, painful, sad, woeful

dolphin's cousin: orca

dolt: ass, blockhead, blubberhead, bonehead, chowderhead, chump, clod, dork, dullard, dummy, dunce, fool, goof, idiot, ignoramus, imbecile, jughead, lunkhead, meathead, moron, ninny, numskull, oaf, pinhead, schmo, simp, simpleton

domain: area, authority, bailiwick, dominion, empire, estate, field, jurisdiction, kingdom, land, property, province, realm, sphere, territory, turf

domain of authority: bailiwick

domain or realm: demesne

dome: bubble, cap, ceiling, cupola, mosque, roof, vault

dome of polygons: geodesic dome

dome-shaped roof or ceiling: cupola

dome, circular building with: rotunda

dome, sunken panel in: caisson, coffer, lacuna

domed domicile: igloo

domed projection of a church: apse

domelike Buddhist shrine: stupa

domestic: chamberperson, common, homebred, homemade, homeworker, household, maid, native, servant, tranquil

domesticate: adapt, break, habituate, housebreak, master, naturalize, subdue, tame, teach, train

domicile: abode, castle, dwelling, habitation, home, house, pad, palace, residence

dominance: advantage, ascendancy, edge, power, rule, superiority, supremacy

dominant: ascendant, authoritative, bossy, central, chief, commanding, controlling, despotic, foremost, master, outweighing, paramount, preeminent, preponderant, prevailing, prevalent, primary, principal, regnant

dominant theme: motif

dominate: browbeat, control, dictate,

direct, domineer, enslave, govern, intimidate, manage, monopolize, overshadow, reign, rule

dominate thoughts: engross, preoccupy

dominated by spouse: henpecked

dominating: domineering, imperious, magisterial

domination: ascendency, command, influence, mastery, might, power, preeminence, prepotency, repression, sovereignty, subjection, supremacy, sway, tyranny

domination of one state over another: hegemony

domineer: boss, bulldoze, bully, command, control, dominate, henpeck, intimidate, oppress, rule, tyrannize

domineering: arrogant, autocratic, bossy, despotic, dictatorial, egotistic, imperial, imperious, insolent, lordly, masterful, overbearing, tyrannical

dominion: ascendancy, authority, bailiwick, command, control, domain, empire, field, jurisdiction, kingdom, land, ownership, privilege, realm, right, rule, sovereignty, sphere, supremacy, sway, territory, turf

domino feature: pip

don: assume, clothe, dress, put on, slip on, take on, title, wear; tutor, instructor, professor

donate: award, bequeath, bestow, contribute, dole, give, grant, present, provide, supply

donation: alms, assistance, benefaction, bequest, charity, contribution, endowment, gift, offering, relief

done: accomplished, completed, concluded, cooked, depleted, doomed, ended, exhausted, finished, over, past, prepared, ready, rendered, settled, spent, through

done and unchangeable: fait accompli

done for: beaten, dead, defeated, ended, goner, kaput, licked, ruined, sunk, wrecked

done in: beat, drained, exhausted, frazzled, murdered, pooped, slain, spent, tired

done openly: overt

donkey: ass, burro, fool, imbecile, jackass, jenny, moke, mule, numskull

donkey as pack animal: burro

donkey driver: muleteer

donkey sound: bray

donor: backer, benefactor, contributor, donator, giver, humanitarian, patron, philanthropist

doodle: dolt, draw, fiddle, putter, scribble, tinker, trifle

doohickey: doodad, gadget, gizmo, thing, thingamajig, trinket, widget

doom: calamity, condemn, curse, damn, death, decision, destine, destiny, destruction, disaster, fate, fortune, judgment, kismet, ordinance, predestine, ruin, sentence, statute, tragedy

doomed: abandoned, fatal, fated, fey, forlorn, hopeless, up the creek

doomed one: goner

door: barrier, egress, entrance, entry, exit, gate, hatchway, opening, opportunity, passage, portal

door divided horizontally for separate opening: Dutch door

door hole for viewing visitors, one-way: peephole

door keyhole plate: escutcheon

door latch: hasp

door or window upper part and supporting structure: lintel

door upright post: jamb, stile

door, back: postern

door, glass and in pairs: French door

doorkeeper in a church: ostiary

doorman: concierge, porter

doorway: threshold

doorway curtain: portiere

doorway or window top-half curtain: lambrequin

dope: dummy, dunce, fool, idiot; cocaine, downers, drug, heroin, marijuana, narcotic, opiate, opium, stimulant, substance, uppers

dopey: asinine, comatose, dazed, doltish, dumb, foolish, lethargic, silly, sluggish, stupid, torpid

doppelganger: apparition, double, ghost, spirit

dormant: asleep, hibernating, idle, inactive, latent, motionless, passive, quiescent, quiet, resting, sleeping, suspended, torpid, unaroused

dorsum: back, posterior

dose: amount, capsule, draft, dram, draught, measure, part, pill, potion, prescription, quantity, remedy, slice, spoonful

dot: dowry, freckle, iota, mark, mote, particle, period, pimple, point, speck, speckle, spot, sprinkle

dot dot dot: ellipsis

dot setting off items in list: bullet

dotage: decrepitude, elderliness, feebleness, old age, senility

dote on: admire, adore, fancy, idolize, indulge, lavish, pamper, revere, spoil, treasure, worship

doting: affectionate, dear, devoted, fatuous, fond, gaga, loving, serving, struck

dots as painting: pointillism

dots or dashes leading eyes horizontally across page: leader

dots, three, for omitted words: ellipsis, points of ellipsis

dots, two, over adjacent vowels for separate pronunciation: dieresis

dotted: punctate, stippled

dotted fabric: polka dot

dotty: absurd, crazy, eccentric, enamored, feebleminded, insane, ridiculous, unbalanced, wacky

double: alter ego, analog, bend, binary, binate, clone, copy, counterpart, diploid, doppelganger, dual, duple, duplex, duplicate, enlarge, fold, geminate, impersonator, increase, paired, reciprocal, second, twice, twin, twofold, understudy, wraith

double agent: mole, spy

double beat per heartbeat: dicrotic

double-breasted coat: reefer

double-cross: betray, cheat, deceive, defraud, mislead, swindle, trick

double-dealing: betrayal, chicanery, deceit, devious, dishonest, disloyal, duplicity, hypocritical, sneaky, treachery, trickery

double-edged sword: kopis

double entendre: ambiguity, equivocation, innuendo, pun

double in meaning: ambiguous, equivocal

double meaning: amphibology, equivocalness, equivocation, equivoque, pun

double meaning, word or phrase having: double entendre

double-reed instrument: oboe

double seat, small sofa: love seat

double sirloin of beef: baron

double speech sound, complex: diphthong

double-spouted bottle: gemel

double tablet or picture, often religious: diptych

double-talk: balderdash, baloney, bull, bunk, doublespeak, drivel, gibberish, hokum, jazz, nonsense, rigmarole, twaddle

double vision: diplopia

double, ghostly: doppelganger

double, to: geminate

doubling of syllable or sound in word: reduplication

doubling stakes in gambling to recover loss: martingale

doubly curved molding: cyma

doubt: apprehension, demur, difficulty, disbelieve, discredit, distrust, fear, hesitation, indecision, misgiving, mistrust, qualm, question, skeptical, suspect, suspicion, uncertainty, unlikely, waver

doubt on, to cast: discredit

doubter: agnostic, cynic, headshaker, skeptic, Thomas, unbeliever

doubtful: ambiguous, apprehensive, distrustful, dubious, equivocal, fearful, hazy, hesitating, iffy, improbable, irresolute, moot, questionable, shaky, suspect, suspicious, uncertain, unclear, unconvinced, undecided, undetermined, unsure, vague

doubtful and insecure: precarious

doubtful authenticity, of: apocryphal

doubtful nature, of a: ambiguous, equivocal

doubtful state: apprehension, dubiety, incertitude, misgiving, negativism, qualm, quandary

doubting: disbelieving, incredulous, skeptical

doubting and noncommittal: agnostic

doubting conscience: scruples

doubtless: sure

douceur: bonus, bribe, gift, gratuity, present, tip

dough: batter, bread, cabbage, cash, money, moola

dough balls fried and coated with sugar: poffertjes

dough raiser: yeast

dough to rise, agent that causes: leaven

doughnut: cruller, Danish, dunker, pastry, sinker

doughnut-shaped: toric

doughnut-shaped figure: torus

doughnut, long and twisted: cruller

doughnut, square and no hole: baignet, bang, beigne, beignet

doughty: awesome, bold, brave, courageous, fearless, heroic, intrepid, stouthearted, valiant

dour: bleak, cheerless, dismal, forbidding, gloomy, glum, grim, inflexible, morose, obstinate, severe, sour, stern, sullen, unyielding

douse: deluge, doff, downpour, drench,

duck, dunk, extinguish, immerse, plunge, rinse, saturate, slosh, smother, soak, splash

douse to remove soap: rinse

dove's home: cote

dovetail: agree, combine, connect, correspond, fit, harmonize, interlock, jibe, join, mesh, tally, tenon

dowager: elderly woman, matriarch, matron, widow

dowdy: antiquated, dated, dingy, drab, frumpy, homely, shabby, slatternly, slovenly, tacky, unkempt, unstylish, untidy

dowel: pin, peg

down: ailing, beat, below, blue, crestfallen, defeat, dejected, depressed, destroy, dispirited, drink, eat, fell, floor, fuzz, level, overthrow, plumage, sad, suppress, underneath, unhappy

down-and-out: beaten, broke, destitute, incapacitated, needy, outcast, penniless, prostrate

down-at-the-heels: seedy, ratty

down feather: plumule

down in spirits: chapfallen, dejected, dispirited, down in the dumps, down in the mouth, sad

down source: eider

down-to-earth: casual, easy, elemental, nice, plain, practical, pragmatic, realistic, reasonable, sensible, simple

downbeat: bleak, cheerless, grim, inactive, negative, pessimistic, stagnate

downcast: blue, chapfallen, dejected, depressed, discouraged, disheartened, dispirited, forlorn, gloomy, low, melancholy, moody, morose, sad, unhappy, woebegone

downer: barbiturate, bummer, depressant, predicament, sedative

downfall: abyss, atrophy, cloudburst, collapse, decline, degeneration, deluge, descent, destruction, disgrace, disintegration, drop, ruin, shower, storm, topple, undoing

downgrade: belittle, bump, debase, declass, decline, decrease, demote, denigrate, depreciate, descent, devalue, drop, hill, lessen, lower, pitch, reduce, slope

downhearted: blue, dejected, depressed, discouraged, sad, unhappy, woebegone

downless peach: nectarine

download: move, transfer, unload

downpour: deluge, flood, monsoon, rain, shower

downright: aboveboard, absolute, absolutely, arrant, blunt, candid, categorical, complete, direct, entirely, forthright, frank, honest, open, plain, positive, pure, stark, sure, thoroughly, undisguised, unequivocal, unmitigated, utterly

downstairs: basement, below, cellar

downstairs, nautically: alow

downtrend: decline, dip, downslide, downturn, drop, fall, plunge, sag, setback, slide, slip, slump

downward sloping or bending: declension, declination

downward stock market prices: downside

downward vertical stroke in handwriting: minim

downwind: alee

downy: feathery, fluffy, lanuginous, light, nappy, placid, plumage, quiet, silky, soft, soothing

dowry, man's: bride price, lobola

dowry, woman's: dot

doze: catnap, drowse, nap, siesta, sleep, slumber, snooze

doze off: nap, nod

drab: bleak, boring, cheerless, colorless, commonplace, dingy, dismal, dreary, dull, faded, flat, lackluster, lifeless, monotonous, mousy, prostitute, slattern, subfusc, uninspired, whore

drab color: olive

draft: beverage, drink, potion, swig, swill, toot; breeze, gust, wind; compose, design, devise, diagram, draught, drawing, formulate, outline, pattern, plan, prepare, project, redact, sketch, version; induct, lottery, pick, registration, selection

draft, military: conscription

drafting: mechanical drawing

drag: anchor, bore, bother, brake, bummer, burden, crawl, delay, draw, drawback, dredge, haul, linger, loiter, lug, nuisance, pull, road, schlepp, search, street, tediously, tiresome, tow, tug, yank; inhalation

drag one's feet: lag, stall

dragon: basilisk, hydra, monster, quaviver, tarragon, wyvern

dragon breathing fire: firedrake

dragon in the sky: draco

dragon slayer: Beowulf, Cadmus, Perseus, Sigurd

dragons, pertaining to: draconic

dragoon: cavalryman, coerce, intimidate, persecute, pressure, soldier, subjugate, trooper

drain: canal, channel, gutter, leak, outlet, pipe, pump, sewer, sink, spout, trench, tube, watercourse

drain hole: sump

drain or sewer under road or embankment: conduit, culvert

drain plug: stop

drain, to: aspirate, bankrupt, bleed, burden, deplete, dry, dwindle, empty, exhaust, fade, sap, siphon, tire, weaken

drainage or sewage, covered pit for receiving household: cesspool

drainage pipe: tile

drained: beat, bushed, depleted, devoid, leeched, pooped, spent, used up, weary, worn out

drainer for washed foods: colander

drains, device for unblocking pipes or: plumber's helper, plunger

dram: draft, drink, drop, measure, mite, nip, quantity, sip, slug, smidgen, snifter, swig, weight

drama: acting, climax, composition, conflict, excitement, movie, opera, play, program, show, tension, theater, tragedy

drama exaggerating emotions: melodrama

drama of satire and light humor with happy resolution: commedia dell'arte

drama of shocking black humor: black comedy

drama or play introductory speech: prologue

drama performed by masked players: masque

drama set to music: opera

drama with music and dancing, Japanese: Kabuki

dramatic: breathtaking, emotional, histrionic, moving, powerful, scenic, spectacular, stagy, striking, suspenseful, theatrical, thespian, thrilling, vivid

dramatic behavior, overly: histrionics

dramatic change or increase: quantum jump, quantum leap

dramatic pause: cesura

dramatic recitative: scena

dramatic suspenseful situation at end of episode: cliffhanger

dramatic work combining tragedy and comedy: tragicomedy

dramatic work in which main character suffers: tragedy

dramatic work using irony and wit to expose wickedness and folly: satirc

dramatics, relating to: thespian

dramatist: author, dramaturge, playwright, writer

drape: adorn, cloak, clothe, cover, curtain, dangle, deck, don, dress, enwrap, hang, shroud, sprawl, suspend, swathe

drapery on top of window: valance

drastic: dangerous, desperate, dire, extreme, harsh, radical, rash, severe

draw: allure, attract, attraction, captivate, catch, charm, color, compose, deadlock, deduce, delineate, depict, derive, design, drag, earn, entice, etch, express, extend, extract, gain, haul, hook, induce, influence, inhale, lead, lug, lure, paint, portray, pull, select, sketch, stalemate, standoff, tie, tow, trace, train, tug

draw and scribble: doodle

draw attention from: steal the show, upstage

draw away: detract

draw back: blench, flinch, quail, recede, recoil, retreat, sheathe, shrink

draw back in, able to: retractable

draw forth: educe, elicit, evoke

draw from information: infer

draw into folds: gather

draw line around: circumscribe

draw off: drain, pump, siphon, untap

draw on: approach, cause, convince, employ, prompt

draw or derive from a source: extract

draw or paint: limn

draw or paint with dots: stipple

draw or tie: deadlock, stalemate, standoff

draw out: attract, drag, educe, elicit, extend, extract, lengthen, protract, stretch

draw parallel line shading to show slope, elevation: hachure

draw short lines to show projection, extension in space: foreshorten

draw up: compose, diagram, draft, formulate, halt, prepare, write

draw, in a tourney: bye

drawback: burden, detriment, disadvantage, fault, flaw, handicap, hindrance, impediment, impedimenta, obstacle, refund, shortcoming

drawer slides, support on which: runner

drawers: bloomers, panties, pants, shorts, underpants, underwear

drawing: art, attracting, captivating, cartoon, delineation, depiction, doodle, draft, graphics, hauling, illustration, lottery, magnetic, picture, plan, pulling, sketch, storyboard

drawing completed with rulers, scales, and compasses: mechanical drawing

drawing conclusion from general to particular reasoning: deduction

drawing lots: casting lots, sortition

drawing of humorous situation: cartoon

drawing of item's structure with parts separated: exploded view

drawing or model with exterior removed: cutaway

drawing or writing on wall of public place: graffiti

drawing power: appeal, fascination, lure, magnetism, pull

drawing rapidly: sketching

drawing room: parlor, reception room, salon, stateroom

drawing to scale of structure: elevation

drawing together: rapprochement, reconciliation

drawing with fine lines, shading a: hatching

drawing with parallel lines, shading a: cross-hatching

drawing with side cut away to reveal inside: cutaway

drawing, person skilled at technical: draftsperson

drawing, the art of detailed or technical: graphics

drawl: accent, intone, lengthen, southern, utter

drawn: fatigued, haggard, sapped, stressed, tense, tired, wan, worn

dray: cart, sled, vehicle, wagon

dread: alarm, angst, anguish, anxiety, apprehension, awe, cringe, fear, fright, horror, panic, shudder, terror, trepidation

dread or fear, persistent and abnormal: phobia

dreaded, hated thing: bête noire, bugbear

dreadful: abominable, appalling, awful, dire, distasteful, fearsome, formidable, frightful, ghastly, grim, grisly, hideous, horrendous, horrible, horrid, revolting, shocking, terrible, tragic, unpleasant

dreadnought: battleship, gunboat, warship

dream: apparition, aspiration, chimera, desire, expectation, fancy, fantasy, goal, hallucination, hope, ideal, illusion, image, nightmare, reverie, surreal, trance, vision, wish

dream interpreter: oneirocritic

dream state: reverie

dream up: conceive, create, imagine, invent

dreamer: fantast, idealist, ideologist, romanticist, visionary

dreamlike: hypnagogic, surreal

dreamlike illusion: hallucination

dreamlike sequence of imagery: phantasmagoria

dreamlike state: trance

dreams, movement of eyes during: rapid eye movement, REM

dreams, relating to: oneiric, visionary

dreamy: absentminded, abstracted, airy, beautiful, delightful, divine, ethereal, fantastic, great, hazy, ideal, imaginative, marvelous, moony, pensive, preoccupied, romantic, serene, soft, soothing, super, unreal, utopian, vague

dreamy composition: nocturne

dreamy, romantic piano instrumental composition: nocturne

dreary: blah, bleak, boring, cheerless, damp, depressing, dismal, distressful, doleful, drab, dull, forlorn, gloomy, glum, lonely, melancholy, monotonous, oppressive, sad, somber, sorrowful

dreary routine: rut

dredge: coat, deepen, dig, drag, excavate, fish, net, scoop, sift

dredging output: silt

dregs: deposit, draff, dross, grounds, lees, rabble, refuse, residue, riffraff, scum, sediment, settling, slags, trash

dregs of wine, liquor: draff, lees

drench: deluge, dose, douse, draft, drown, dunk, flood, hose, imbrue, immerse, inundate, permeate, saturate, soak, souse, steep, submerge, waterlog, wet

dress: accoutrement, adorn, apparel, array, attire, clothe, clothes, clothing, don, frock, garb, garment, gear, getup, gown, habiliment, habit, invest, ornament, outfit, preen, primp, rig, robe, rog, toggery, toile, train, vestiture, vestment

dress as opposite sex: cross-dress

dress down: berate, castigate, lash, reprimand, scold, tongue-lash, upbraid

dress part trailing wearer: train

dress showily: engaud, preen, primp, titivate
dress up: adorn, clothe, embellish, enhance, perk, preen, primp, tog
dress, casual or partial: dishabille
dress, Japanese robelike: kimono
dress, loose-hanging: chemise
dress, loose unbelted: Mother Hubbard
dress, loose, with wild patterns: muumuu
dressed person, poorly: beagle, callet, dratchell, drazel, jeeter, shabbaroon, slammock, slubberdegullion, tatterdemalion
dressed to the nines: all dolled up
dresser: bureau, cabinet, chest, chest of drawers, chiffonier, commode, cupboard
dressing: bandage, gauze; fertilizer, sauce, stuffing
dressing as opposite sex: transvestism
dressing gown: negligee, peignoir, robe
dressing room: boudoir, bower
dressmaker: couturier, couturiere, modiste, seamstress, sewer, tailor
dressmaking, high-quality: couture, haute couture
dressy: chic, classy, elegant, fancy, fashionable, formal, showy, smart, stylish
dressy and stylish person: clotheshorse
dribble: bounce, drip, drool, drop, fritter, move, seep, slaver, slobber, trickle
dried coconut meat: copra
dried from removal of water: dehydrated, desiccated
dried meat ration: pemmican
dried or concentrated food by adding water, to restore: reconstitute
dried orchid tuber: salep
dried plum: prune
dried seaweed: wrack
dried strips of meat: biltong, charqui, jerky
dried up: sere, sered, withered, wizened
drift: accumulation, cluster, dune; amble, bat around, coast, course, deviation, float, flock, flow, linger, meander, mosey, ramble, waft, wander; design, gist, intention, meaning, purport, scheme, tendency, tenor, tide, trend
drift gently: waft
drifter: bum, hobo, roamer, tramp, vagabond, vagrant, wanderer
drill: auger, bit, bore, borer, channel, exercise, hit, instruct, locating, ma-

DRILLING TOOLS

auger
bench drill
bit
bore
bow drill
breast drill
broach
cordless drill
corkscrew
countersink
diamond drill
drill press
eggbeater drill
electric drill
gimlet
hand drill
portable drill
power drill
push drill
reamer
rose reamer
seed drill
twist drill
wimble
woodborer ❦

neuvers, perforate, pierce, practice, punch, puncture, rehearse, repetition, teach, tool, train, tutor, workout
drill bit socket: pod
drill bit, clamp for holding a: chuck
drill handle: bitstock, brace
drill run by compressed air, of a: pneumatic
drill, hand: brace and bit
drilling oil wells, apparatus for: rig
drink: absorb, alcohol, beverage, booze, brew, carouse, chaser, cocktail, coffee, consume, draft, draught, grog, gulp, guzzle, highball, imbibe, lap, libation, liquid, liquor, mead, potable, potion, punch, quaff, salute, shot, sip, slurp, snort, swallow, swig, tea, tiff, tipple, toast, wine
drink before a meal, alcoholic: aperitif
drink daintly: sip
drink eagerly: gulp, quaff, swig, swill
drink excessively: carouse, tope
drink greedily: guzzle, ingurgitate, quaff
drink like a cat: lap
drink made of milk or cream and eggs, often mixed with rum: eggnog
drink noisily: slurp

drink of alcohol, tiny: shot, snort
drink of chocolate syrup, milk, soda water: egg cream
drink of sweetened cream with sherry or wine and fruit juice: syllabub
drink of the gods: nectar
drink or act of drinking: potation
drink or food with stimulating effect: stimulant
drink to your health: toast
drink vending machine: dispenser
drink, before-dinner: preprandial libation
drink, citrus piece to flavor a: twist
drink, drugged: Mickey Finn
drink, excluding water: beverage
drink, fit to: potable
drink, like beer or water, taken after hard liquor: chaser
drink, mat or disk to place under: coaster
drink, stick for stirring: swizzle stick
drink, to add alcohol: spike
drinkable: potable
drinker: alcoholic, bibber, boozer, drunk, drunkard, imbiber, lush, quaffer, sponge, toper, tosspot, wino
drinker, excessive: alcoholic, drunkard, lush, tippler
drinking bowl, large: jorum
drinking cup: mug
drinking cup, goblet: mazer
drinking glass, large for beer: schooner
drinking glass, rounded with narrow top: snifter
drinking in quantity: bibulous
drinking party of ancient Greeks: symposium
drinking problems, organization for: AA, Alcoholics Anonymous
drinking salutation: toast
drinking session, afternoon: downdrins
drinking sparingly: abstemious
drinking vessel filled to brim: bumper
drinking vessel for beer: stein, tankard
drinking vessel holding 2 quarts: pottle
drinking vessel with loops to attach to belt: costrel
drinking vessel with stem and base: goblet
drinking vessel with wide mouth: beaker
drinking vessel, originally with rounded bottom: tumbler
drinking water flask: canteen
drinking, act of: draft
drinks at reduced price in bar: happy hour

drinks, not drinking alcoholic: abstinence, teetotalism, temperance

drip: bore, dribble, drop, exude, jerk, klutz, leak, seep, trickle

drip-edge: eave

dripping into vein, of medicine: intravenous

drive: attack, bang, butt, campaign, chauffeur, commute, compel, constrain, excursion, force, get-up-and-go, goad, hammer, herd, hurry, impel, impulse, initiative, momentum, motor, move, operate, outing, plunge, pound, press, propel, push, ride, roll, run, shove, spin, spur, stamp, steamroll, suggest, surge, thrust, urge, vigor

drive a nail aslant: toe

drive away: alienate, banish, chase, deter, dispel, disperse, dissipate, exile, expatriate, repel, shoo

drive away or expel foreigner: deport

drive back: rebuff, repel, repulse

drive cattle with rod: goad

drive dangerously close to another vehicle: tailgate

drive from one's homeland: exile

drive-in employee: carhop

drive on (back) roads rather than highways: shunpike

drive out evil spirit: exorcise

drive out of hiding: ferret out

drive out or expel: evict

drive sharp stake through: impale

drive to action: impel

drive to distraction: enrage

drive, as from bed: roust

drivel: babble, bunk, gibberish, maunder, mush, nonsense, prating, rubbish, slaver, slobber, twaddle

driven by zeal: messianic

driver: autoist, cabbie, charioteer, chauffeur, coachman, cowboy, engineer, golf club, hackie, hammer, jockey, mallet, motorist, operator, propeller

driving force: impetus

driving forward: propulsion

driving impulse: compulsion

driving very close behind another: tailgating

drizzle: mist, rain, shower, spray, sprinkle

drizzly fog: smur

droll: absurd, amusing, buffoon, comic, comical, eccentric, farcical, funny, humorous, jocular, laughable, ludicrous, odd, offbeat, queer, ridiculous, strange, whimsical, zany

dromedary: camel

dromedary feature: hump

drone: bagpipe, bee, bum, bumble, buzz, drum, humming, idler, leech, loiterer, lubber, parasite, shirker, slug, sound, speaker

drone of bagpipes: burden

drool: desire, dribble, drivel, froth, gush, salivate, slaver, slobber

droop: bend, dangle, decline, diminish, drop, fade, flag, hang, languish, lower, sag, sink, slouch, slump, stoop, wilt, wither

droop and weaken: flag, languish, loll, lop

drooping: alop, flaccid, limp, nutant

drooping, of plants: cernuous

drop: abandon, abyss, bead, blob, certain, collapse, dash, decrease, descent, discontinue, dismiss, down, dribble, drip, droop, dump, fall, forsake, fumble, globule, incline, knock, let fall, lower, omit, plop, plummet, plunge, release, relinquish, sack, shed, sink, slope, slump, stop, terminate, unload

drop and flop: flump

drop back: lag

drop bait gently: dap

drop cloth: tarp

drop heavily: plop

drop in: arrive, call, come over, stop by, surprise, visit

drop of liquid (pharmacy): gutta

drop off: decline, deliver, doze, dwindle, nod, sag, slacken, slide, slip, snooze, unload

drop out: leave, quit, resign, withdraw

drop straight down: plummet, plunge

drop the jaw: gape

droplet: bead, globule, tear

droplike: guttate

dropping sound at beginning of word: apheresis

dropping sound at end of word: apocope

dropping sound at middle of word: syncope

droppings from nuclear explosion: fallout

dropsy: edema

dross: cinder, cinders, commonplace, dregs, impurity, lees, recrement, refuse, remains, scoria, scum, sediment, sinter, slag, trash, waste, worthless

drought: aridity, dearth, dryness, lack, scarcity, shortage, thirst

droughty: arid, aris

drove: assemblage, chisel, collection, crowd, flock, following, herd, horde, mob, motored, press, swarm

drover: cowboy, cowpoke, shepherd

drown: deluge, drench, flood, immerse, inundate, muffle, overwhelm, soak, submerge, suffocate, swamp

drowning execution: noyade

drowsy: comatose, dull, indolent, lazy, lethargic, listless, lulling, oscitant, sleepy, sluggish, somnolent, soporific, supine, tired

drub: baste, beat, belabor, berate, defeat, drum, flay, flog, instill, lambaste, lick, pound, pummel, shellac, stamp, thrash, throb, whip

drudge: grind, grub, hack, hireling, labor, menial, moil, peon, plod, scrub, slave, slavey, toiler, workhorse

drudgery: chore, grind, labor, moil, struggle, tedious job, toil, work

drug: acid, aloe, amphetamine, analgesic, anesthetize, barbiturate, cocaine, desensitize, dope, downer, generic, hallucinogen, hashish, heroin, LSD, marijuana, medication, medicine, narcotic, numb, opiate, opium, peyote, pharmaceutical, pill, poison, prescription, relaxant, sedative, stupefy, upper

drug addiction: dependence, narcotism

drug adverse effect: reaction

drug dealer: pusher

drug-induced distorted perception: hallucination

drug-induced stupor or unconsciousness: narcosis

drug interfering with another: antagonist

drug into vein, inject illegal: mainline

drug overcoming sedative's effects: analeptic

drug producing sensory distortion: hallucinogen, hallucinogenic, psychedelic

drug slipped into someone's drink secretly: knockout drops, Mickey Finn

drug that shrinks the pupils: miotic

drug used by bodybuilders, athletes: anabolic steroid, steroid

drug, addictive and illegal: narcotic

drug, discontinuation of using addictive: withdrawal

drug, immediate complete discontinuation of using addictive: cold turkey

COMMONLY ABUSED DRUGS

Hallucinogens	Hemp Products	Opiates	ataraxic drug	Benzedrine/benny
blotter	Acapulco gold	big H	barbital	Biphetamine
datura/locoweed	bhang	codeine	barbiturate/doll/	black beauty
diethyltryptamine/	cannabis	diacetylmorphine	goofball	blow
DET	Colombian	H	betel	caffeine
ecstasy	dagga	heroin	chloral hydrate	cocaine/coke/snow
LSD/acid/lysergic	doobie	horse	Demerol	crack
acid diethylamide	ganja	junk	downer	crank
magic mushroom/	grass	laudanum	nitrous oxide/laugh-	crystal
sacred mushroom	hashish/hash/hash oil	methadone	ing gas	crystal meth
mescal	hooch	morphine	Quaalude	cubeb
mescaline	Indian hemp	O	sleeping pill	Dexamyl
morning glory seed	joint	opium	sodium pentothal/	diet pill
Owsley's acid	marijuana	paregoric	truth drug	doll/pop pill
peyote	Mary Jane	poppy	tranquilizer	freebase
phencyclidine/PCP/	Mary Warner	scag/skag	Valium	methamphetamine
angel dust	Maui wowie	smack	yellow jackets	methyldiamphetam-
psilocybin	Panama red	tar		ine/MDA
purple haze	pot	white stuff	**Stimulants**	pep pill
shroom	reefer		amphetamine	speed
STP	Thai stick	**Sedatives**	amyl nitrite/popper	speedball
windowpane	weed	analgesic	anabolic steroid	upper ❦

drug, pleasant intoxication from a: buzz, high, rush

drug, unharmful and unhelpful: adiaphorous

drugged: dosed, freaked, high, loaded, spaced out, stoned, turned on, wasted, zonked

drugging: narcotic, stupefacient

druggist: apothecary, pharmacist

drugs collectively in medicine: pharmacopoeia

drugs, science of: pharmacology

drum: barrel, beat, bongo, capstan, cask, cylinder, drone, gather, instrument, keg, pulsate, reiterate, strum, tabor, tambour, tambourine, tap, throb, thunder, timbrel, tom-tom

drum major stick: baton

drum major's headwear: shako

drum of India, small hand: tabla

drum played by fifer: tabor

drum player, kettle-: tympanist

drum that reverberates, small double-headed: side drum, snare drum

drum-type instrument: percussion instrument

drum, African or Latin American: bongo, conga drum, kettledrum, timbal

drum, Indian/Asian hand: tabla

drum, to deaden the sound of: muffle

drumbeat: dub, flam, rataplan

drumbeat with sticks hitting simultaneously: flam

drumbeat, continuous even: tattoo

drumbeat, continuous loud: drumroll

drumbeat, continuous low: ruffle

drumhead: tympan, vellum

drumhead with jingles on rim: tambourine

drumlike: tympanic

drumming continuously: tattoo

drumming monotonously: thrum

drumming with fingers, feet: devil's tattoo

drums played by the hands, small double: bongo, tomtom

drums played by the hands, tall tapered: conga

drums, set of kettle-: timpani

drunk: besotted, bibulous, crapulent, drunken, high, inebriated, intoxicated, polluted, sot, tipsy

drunk without ice or anything added: neat, straight

drunkard: alcoholic, barfly, bibber, boozer, dipsomaniac, drinker, inebriate, lush, soak, sot, souse, sponge, stiff, tippler, toper, tosspot, wino

drunken: buzzed, gone, groggied, inebriated, intoxicated, loaded, pickled, plastered, sloshed, tanked, tight, tipsy, totaled, wasted

drunken party: bacchanalia, carousal

drunkenly brave: pot-valiant

drunkenness, causing: intoxicating

dry: arid, baked, bare, barren, biting, boring, cynical, dehumidify, dehydrate, depleted, desiccate, drain, drinkless, droll, dull, dusty, empty, evaporated, fruitless, harden, moistureless, monotonous, parched, rainless, sapless, sarcastic, sec, sere, shriveled, siccaneous, teetotaler, thirsty, towel, uninteresting, unproductive, vapid, waterless, wipe, withered, wizen, xeric, xerothermic

dry and crumbly: mealy

dry and withered: sere

dry and without rainfall: arid

dry-area plants: cacti

dry by heat: parch, torrefy

dry creek bed: arroyo

dry dock ledge: altar

dry from water removal: dehydrated

dry goods: cloth, clothing, fabrics, soft goods, textiles

dry gulch in western U.S.: coulee

dry habitat, of an extremely: xeric

dry hay: ted

dry land: terra firma

dry mouth sensation: thirst

dry out: desiccate

dry red wine: claret

dry red wine of Spain: rioja

dry run: maneuver, rehearsal, test, trial

dry sherry from Spain: fino

dry state: aridity

dry steam bed: wadi

dry up: dehydrate, desiccate, evaporate, exsiccate, parch, sear, shrivel, welter, wilt, wither

dry up and wrinkle: sear, shrivel, wither

dry, as champagne: brut

dry, as in wine: sec

dryer debris: lint

dryer filter stuff: lint

drying: siccative

dual: binary, coupled, double, duplex, paired, reciprocal, twin, twofold

dualism in theology: ditheism

dualistic in philosophy, religion: Manichaean

dub: baptize, bestow, boggle, botch, bungler, call, copy, designate, duffer, entitle, flub, fluff, knight, label, muff, name, nickname, poke, rerecord, thrust, title

dubious: ambiguous, chancy, disputable, doubtful, equivocal, fishy, iffy, indecisive, questionable, shady, shaky, skeptical, suspicious, uncertain, unclear, undecided, undetermined, unsure, vague

dubious possession: white elephant

duck: avoid, blackjack, bob, bow, canard, dabbler, dive, dodge, drake, duckling, eider, elude, evade, gadwall, mallard, mandarin, merganser, Peking, pintail, plunge, scaup, shelduck, shirk, shoveler, sidestep, smee, smew, tal, teal, wigeon

duck feathered bedding: eiderdown

duck genus: anas

duck group: brood, skein, sord, tea

duck soup: breeze, cinch, easy, picnic, pushover, snap

duck toes, of webbed: palmate

duck wing, bright color on: speculum

ducks, flock of: skein

duct: canal, channel, chute, conduit, outlet, passage, pipe, tube, vas

duct opening: via

ductile: adaptable, compliant, docile, flexible, malleable, manageable, moldable, plastic, pliable, pliant, responsive, soft, supple, tractable, yielding

ductlike: vasal

dud: bomb, bummer, bust, debacle, drag, flop, lemon, loser, turkey, washout

dude: Beau Brummell, buck, chap, clotheshorse, coxcomb, dandy, easterner, fellow, fop, hotshot, popinjay, swell

dudgeon: anger, bitterness, fury, huff, ire, irritation, malice, rage, resentment, umbrage, wrath

duds: apparel, attire, belongings, clothing, garb, gear, threads, togs

due: adequate, appropriate, attributable, becoming, collectible, compensation, debt, deserts, deserved, directly, earned, fitting, justified, mature, merit, owed, owing, payable, proper, revenge, rightful, rights, scheduled, suitable, unpaid

duel: afaire d' honneur, combat, conflict, contest, dispute, engagement, fence, fight, joust, oppose, spar

duel between knights on horseback: joust, tilting match

dueling sword, sharp pointed and no cutting edge: épée

dues: ante, assessment, collection, contribution, debt, duty, fee, initiation, payment, tax, toll

duet: duo, pair, piece for two

duff: buttocks, coal, pudding, slack

duffel coat fastener: toggle

duffer: dope, dub, dullwitted, dunce, incompetent, peddler, useless, worthless

dugout: abri, boat, canoe, cave, cellar, foxhole, hollow, pirogue, shelter

duke, pertaining to a: ducal

dukedom: duchy

dulcet: agreeable, charming, soothing, harmonious, melodious, musical, pleasing, soft, sonorous, sweet, tuneful

dull: apathetic, arid, banal, blah, blind, blunt, boring, brainless, cloudy, colorless, common, deaden, dense, depressed, desensitize, dim, dimwitted, dingy, dismal, dispirited, down, drab, drear, dreary, drowsy, dry, dumb, flat, foggy, gloomy, gray, grey, heavy, humdrum, inactive, inanimate, inert, insensible, insensitive, insipid, lackluster, lethargic, lifeless, listless, logy, matte, miffle, monotone, monotonous, murky, muted, numb, obtuse, overcast, pedestrian, perfunctory, pointless, prosaic, prosy, routine, shallow, simple, slow, sluggish, square, stagnant, stale, stodgy, stolid, stuffy, tame, tedious, tiresome, torpid, trite, uneventful, unexciting, unimaginative, uninspired, vacuous, vapid, weaken, zestless

dull and austere: aseptic, clinical

dull and colorless: blah

dull and dark: drab, subfusc

dull and laborious: pedestrian, plodding, ponderous

dull and lifeless: arid, desiccated, lackluster, pallid

dull and mediocre: banal, humdrum, monotonous, mundane, ordinary, pedestrian, prosaic, trite, uninspired, unoriginal

dull and nondistinctive: banal, faceless, nondescript, stereotyped

dull and not sensing: insensible, obtuse

dull and routine: banausic, monotonous, repetitious, tedious

dull and sluggish: stagnant

dull and tasteless: bland, flat, insipid, vapid

dull and unexciting: anodyne, bland, insipid, vapid

dull blue: livid

dull enough to induce sleep: soporific, stultifying, stupefying

dull finish: mat, matte

dull gray: pewter

dull in outlook: gray

dull life, to lead a: stagnate, vegetate

dull menial work: drudgery

dull or blunt: obtuse

dull or make stupid: hebetate

dull pain: ache

dull sound: thud

dullard: boor, clod, dimwit, dodo, dolt, dumbbell, dummy, dunce, fool, idiot, moron, nitwit, simpleton

dulled: exhausted, jaded, sated, worn-out

dullness: apathy, bluntness, evenness, insensibility, languor, lassitude, lethargy, monotony, sluggishness, spiritlessness, tedium, torpor

duly: accordingly, appropriately, befittingly, justly, mannerly, properly, punctually, rightly, suitable

dumb: asinine, dense, dull, foolish, idiotic, ignorant, inane, inarticulate, moronic, mum, mute, senseless, silent, speechless, stupid, taciturn, unintelligent, unintentional, voiceless

dumb and speechless: tongue-tied

dumbbell: blockhead, boob, clown, dolt, dope, dullard, fool, idiot, ignoramus, lunkhead, moron, nitwit

dumbfound: amaze, astonish, astound,

bewilder, boggle, confuse, daze, flabbergast, nonplus, overwhelm, perplex, stagger, startle, stun, surprise

dumbfounded: agape, aghast, amazed, astounded, overcome, puzzled, shocked, speechless

dummy: copy, dimwit, doll, dolt, dunce, effigy, fake, fool, front, idiot, ignoramus, imitation, klutz, mannequin, puppet, simpleton, stooge, substitute

dummy for fashion or art: lay figure, mannequin

dummy representing hated person: effigy

dummy voice projection: ventriloquism

dump: beat, cast, chuck, deposit, discard, ditch, drop, empty, eyesore, hole, hovel, junk, junkyard, landfill, pigsty, reject, scrap, transfer, unload

dump, as for military supplies: depot

dumpling filled with meat or seafood: quenelles

dumplings made with potatoes: gnocchi

dumplings, Chinese: dim sum

dumpy: disreputable, ninny, pudgy, shapeless, short, squat, stocky, stout, stubby

dunce: ass, blockhead, bonehead, boob, buffoon, chump, dolt, dope, dumbbell, dummy, dunderhead, fool, goof, goon, hammerhead, idiot, ignoramus, jackass, jughead, lunkhead, nincompoop, numskull, oaf

dune: bank, hill, ridge, sandbank

dung: excrement, ordure, scat

dung beetle: scarab

dung-eating: coprophagous, scatophagous

dung of sea birds for fertilizer: guano

dung, relating to: stercoraceous

dungarees: jeans

dungeon: cell, chamber, donjon, jail, oubliette, prison, stockade, vault

dungeon with trap door: oubliette

dungeonlike: dank

dunghill: midden, refuse heap

dunk: baptize, dip, douse, drench, duck, immerse, saturate, slam, soak, souse, submerge

duo: combo, couple, duet, dyad, pair, twosome

dupe: baffle, bamboozle, betray, bilk, cat's-paw, cheat, chump, con, deceive, delude, flimflam, fool, gull, hoax, hoodwink, lamb, mislead,

patsy, pigeon, pushover, sap, shaft, snooker, sucker, swindle, tool, trick, victim

duped: taken

duple: binary, double, dual, two

duple-time dance: samba

duplicate: alike, carbon, clone, copy, counterpart, ditto, double, echo, facsimile, identical, imitate, mate, mirror, parallel, photocopy, repeat, replica, reproduce, spare, transcript, twin

duplicate of original: replica

duplicate the foregoing: ditto

duplicity: chicanery, cunning, deceit, deception, dishonesty, double-dealing, duality, fraud, guile, perfidy, treachery, twofold

durability: constancy, endurance, fortitude, grit, reliability, stamina

durability of clothes: wear

durable: constant, dependable, enduring, hard, hardy, lasting, permanent, stable, staple, strong, sturdy, tough

durable and permanent: perdurable

duration: continuance, endurance, length, lifetime, longevity, period, persistence, run, span, stretch, term, time

duress: captivity, coercion, compulsion, confinement, constraint, detention, force, pressure, stranglehold, threat

during: along, amid, meanwhile, midst, throughout, when, while

dusk: darken, darkness, evening, gloaming, gloom, nightfall, sundown, sunset, twilight

dusky: blackish, bleak, cloudy, dark, dim, ebon, gloomy, murky, obscure, overcast, shadowy, shady, swart, swarthy, tawny

dust: agitation, ashes, clean, coat, commotion, confusion, cover, dirt, earth, eburine, film, flour, particles, pollen, powder, remains, sift, soot, sprinkle, strew, turmoil

dust speck: mote

dust, to crumble to: molder

dusty: arid, chalky, dim, dry, powdery, pulverulent, stale, timeworn, unswept

Dutch cheese: Edam

duties of a pastor, relating to: pastoral

duties of an office, to perform the: officiate

duties, to assign: delegate, depute

dutiful: assiduous, compliant, conscientious, devout, diligent, docile,

faithful, loyal, obedient, obligatory, respectful, reverent, sedulous, trustful

dutiful and respectful: deferential

duty: allegiance, assignment, burden, calling, chore, commitment, devoir, excise, function, job, mission, objective, obligation, office, onus, pledge, promise, purpose, respect, responsibility, role, service, shift, station, stint, task, undertaking

duty imposed on imported, exported goods: charge, customs, levy, tariff, tax, toll

duty or allegiance: homage

duty owed by vassal to feudal lord: fealty

duty payment: impost, levy

duty to behave honorably: noblesse oblige

duty, beyond the call of: supererogatory

duty, burdensome: onus

duty, discharge from: quietus

duty, failure to perform: delinquency, dereliction, negligence

duty, imposed as obligation or: incumbent, obligatory

duty, period or turn of: trick, watch

duty, release from post or: relief

duty, to free from: exempt, exonerate

duty, to shirk work or: goldbrick, goof off, malinger, skive

dwarf: bantam, belittle, diminish, elf, gnome, goblin, homunculus, leprechaun, lilliputian, midget, miniature, minimize, overshadow, peanut, peewee, pygmy, runt, small, stunt, tiny, Tom Thumb, tower over, troll

dwarf buffalo: anoa

dwarf cattle: nata

dwarf or race of dwarfs: pygmy

dwarf poultry: bantam

dwarf shrub or tree: bonsai

dwarfism, condition causing: achondroplasia

dwell: abide, brood, expatiate, harp, linger, live, occupy, reside

dwell on: harp

dwell temporarily: sojourn

dweller: resider, tenant

dwelling: abode, apartment, building, bungalow, cabin, casa, castle, chalet, chateau, condo, cottage, domicile, duplex, flat, habitation, haunt, home, house, hovel, hut, igloo, manor, mansion, nest, pad, palace, residence, shanty, split-level house, tenement, tent, tepee, trailer, villa

dwindle: abate, decline, decrease, di-

minish, ebb, fade, lessen, peter, recede, shorten, shrink, taper, wane,
waste

dye: anil, color, colorant, eosin, imbue,
litmus, pigment, ruddle, shade, stain,
tincture, tinge, tint, tracer

dye, black: lampblack, nigrosine

dye, blue-violet: anil, cyanine, indigo,
ultramarine, woad

dye, brown: bister, sienna, umber

dye container: vat

dye, green: sumac, terre-verte, viridian

**dye parts of cloth while other parts are
tied:** tie-dye

dye, red: brazilin, cinnabar, henna,
kermes, madder, orcein

dye, white: titanium

dye, yellow-orange: annatto, flavin,
fustic, saffron

dyed-in-the-wool: devoted, ingrained,
sworn, thoroughgoing

**dyeing fabric method with parts that are
not to be dyed protected with removable wax:** batik

dyeing, to fix colors in: mordant

dying: in extremis, moribund

dying coal: ember

dying declaration: last words

dying on the vine: withering

dying work of artist: swan song

dying, hospital for the: hospice

dynamic: active, charismatic, compelling, driving, energetic, forceful, influential, intense, kinetic, live, progressive, vigorous, vital

dynamite: blast, demolish, destroy, exciting, explosive, shatter, superb,
TNT, trinitrotoluene, wonderful

dynamite inventor: Alfred Nobel

dynamo: doer, generator, go-getter,
hustler, mover

dynasty: control, dominance, dominion, empire, realm, regime, reign,
rule, supremacy

dyspeptic: crabby, grouchy, irritable,
mean, ornery

dysphoria: anxiety, depression, melancholy, restlessness

Ee

e, upside-down: schwa

each: apiece, apop, every, everyone, individually, per, separate, specific

eager: agog, antsy, anxious, ardent, athirst, avid, desirous, enthusiastic, excited, expectancy, fervent, hardworking, impatient, impetuous, intense, intent, itchy, keen, ready, restless, sharp, spirited, vigorous, willing, yearning, zealous

eager and hopeful: agog, expectant, atip

eager and willing: solicitous

eager for food: voracious

eager to please: complaisant, compliant, obliging, obsequious, servile

eager to start: chafing at the bit

eagerness: alacrity, ardor, avidity, élan, enthusiasm, fervency, fervor, gusto, hunger, impatience, readiness, thirst, urgency, zeal

eagle: aquila, bataleur, crow, ern, erne, falcon, gier, hawk, pygargus, raptor

eagle nest: aerie, eyrie

eagle's claw: talon

eagles, relating to: aquiline

ear: aural, auris, cob, cochlea, concha, drum

ear: auricle, lobe, neb, pinna, stapes

ear bone: ossicle, stapes

ear deformed from blows: cauliflower ear

ear disease, study of: otology

ear disorder: otitis

ear doctor: otologist

ear-inspecting instrument: otoscope

ear, nose and throat specialist: otorhinolaryngologist

ear of animal, to clip: crop

ear of wheat: spica

ear opening, fleshy wedge in front of: tragus

ear opening, notch under tragus of: intertragic notch

ear part important to balance and coordination, inner: saccule, utricle

ear part transmitting sound, inner: organ of Corti

ear-shaped: auriculate

ear-shaped part: auricle

ear, innermost cavity of external: concha

ear, relating to the: aural, auricular, otic

ear, ringing in the: tinnitus

ear, vegetable: capes, cob, mealie, nubbin, risom, rizzom, spica, spici, spike

earache: otalgia

eardrum: tympanic membrane, tympanum

earl: British, lord, nobleman, peer

earlier: already, antecedent, anterior, before, beforehand, formerly, preceding, previous, prior, sooner

earlier and before: anterior

earlier event inserted in narrative: flashback

earlier in time, to come: antedate

earliest: archetypal, first, original, primal, primeval, primitive

earliest example: archetype, prototype

earliest stages of development: beginnings, incunabula

earliest time, pertaining to the: primordial, pristine

earlike projections on pot: lugs

earl's wife: countess

early: advanced, ancient, betimes, first, immature, immediately, initial, matutinal, nascent, premature, primal, primitive, prior, soon, timely, unexpectedly, untimely

early anesthetic: ether

early in development: embryonic, germinal, nascent, seminal

early in the morning: cockcrow, matutinal, small hours

early newspaper edition: bulldog edition

early show: matinee

early spring, pertaining to: primaveral

early, developing or maturing: precocious

early, happening too: premature, previous, untimely

early, to do something too: anticipate

earmark: aspect, attribute, band, distinction, feature, identification, label, quality, signature, stamp, tag, trait

earn: achieve, acquire, attain, clear, collect, deserve, gain, get, gross, make, merit, net, obtain, procure, profit, realize, reap, win

earnest: affectionate, ardent, determined, devoted, diligent, engage, fervent, grave, heartfelt, honest, industrious, intent, meaningful, resolute, sedate, serious, sincere, sober, solemn, staid, token, wholehearted, zealous

earnest request: entreaty, plea

earnestly appeal: adjure, pray

earnings: dividends, gate, income, pay, proceeds, profits, salary, wages

earnings of common stock affected by bond interest, preferred stock: leverage

earnings on a bond: dividend

ear's large shell-like hollow: concha

ears, buzzing or ringing in: acouasm, tinnitus

ears, having big: macrotous

ears, of hearing with both: binaural

earsplitting: blaring, deafening, loud, piercing, shrill

earth: alluvium, clay, dirt, dust, globe, ground, land, layer, loam, loess,

EAR, EYE OR MOUTH DISEASE

acoustic neuroma	pink eye	labyrinthitis	ophthalmic disease	sty
anophthalmia	deafness	macular degeneration	otalgia	tinnitus
aural atresia	dizziness	mastoiditis	otic disease	trachoma
blepharitis	dry eye	Meniere's disease	otitis media	tympanitis
cataract	earache	microphthalmia	otosclerosis	usher syndrome
chorioretinitis	gingivitis	microtia	pyorrhea	vascular occlusion
color blindness	glaucoma	myopia	retinitis pigmentosa	vertigo ❦
conjunctivitis/	keratoconus	nystagmus	strabismus	

planet, soil, telluric, terra, terra firma, terrestrial, topsoil, turf, vale, world

earth between Arctic and Tropic of Cancer, Antarctic and Tropic of Capricorn: Temperate Zones

earth between North Pole and Arctic Circle, South Pole and Antarctic Circle: Frigid Zones

earth between Tropics of Cancer and Capricorn: Torrid Zone

earth color: ocher

earth inhabitant: tellurian

earth (in Latin): terra

earth mover: bulldozer

earth satellite: moon

earth study: geodesy, geography, geology

earth, outside of: extraterrestrial

earth, pertaining to: planetary, telluric, terrestrial

earth, point where moon is farthest from: apogee

earth, point where moon is nearest to: perigee

earth, to travel around: circumnavigate

earthen jar: olla

earthenware: biscuit, ceramics, china, crockery, crocks, delft, faience, jugs, majolica, porcelain, pottery, stoneware

earthenware decorated with opaque glazes: faience

earthenware, broken: potshard, potsherd, shard, sherd

earthenware, glazed blue and white: delft

earthly: bodily, conceivable, global, human, imaginable, material, mortal, mundane, physical, possible, secular, telluric, temporal, terrestrial, worldly

earthquake: aftershock, movement, seism, shock, temblor, trembler, tremor, upheaval

earthquake after main shock, mini: aftershock, tremors

earthquake center: epicenter

earthquake detecting instrument: seismograph

earthquake magnitude scale: Richter scale

earthquake measuring instrument: seismograph

earthquake preliminary tremor: foreshock

earthquake science: seismology

earthquake's energy on scale: magnitude

earthquakes, relating to: seismic

earth's atmosphere trapping solar radiation: greenhouse effect

earth's crust deformation into landforms: diastrophism

earth's crust, theory of movement of: plate tectonics

earth's girdle: equator

earth's physical structure, study of: geology

earth's size and shape, study of: geodesy

earth's spinning on axis: rotation

earth's structural features, study of: tectonics

earth's surface above sea level, study of: hypsography

earthwork: embankment, fortification

earthworm: annelid

earthy: bulwark, coarse, crude, excavation, folksy, gross, hearty, indecent, natural, obscene, practical, realistic, simple, terrestrial, uninhibited, unrefined, vulgar, worldly

earthy pigment: ocher, ochre, umber

earwax: cerumen

ease: abate, affluence, allay, alleviate, appease, breeze, calm, comfort, comfortable, composure, content, contentment, diminish, enjoyment, expertise, facilitate, facility, faculty, freedom, guide, inch, knack, leisure, let up, liberty, lighten, loosen, maneuver, mitigate, moderate, naturalness, pacify, palliate, quiet, readiness, reduce, relax, relaxation, relief, relieve, relieved, rest, satisfaction, security, simplify, smooth, snap, soften, soothe, tranquility, unburden

ease in doing: facility

ease up: abate

easily: certainly, coolly, decidedly, effortlessly, freely, handily, hands down, indubitably, readily, simply, smoothly, undeniably

easily achieved: facile

easily obtained: accessible

easily taken advantage of, person: pushover

easing of tension between rivals: détente

East Indian palm used in fans: talipot

East Indian pepper: betel

Easter season: Lent

Easter, relating to Passover or: paschal

eastern Asia countries: Orient

Eastern sandal: zori

Eastern sash: obi

easy: amiable, basic, calm, carefree, careless, cinch, comfortable, complaisant, compliant, cozy, cushy, effortless, facile, familiar, friendly, gentle, glib, lenient, light, manageable, mild, moderate, natural, obvious, painless, relaxed, secure, simple, smooth, snap, soft, susceptible, tolerant, tractable, tranquil, unconcerned, unforced, unhurried

easy and elementary: rudimentary

easy basket: layup, tap-in

easy for consumer to learn, use: user-friendly

easy gait: amble, lope, trot

easy to accomplish, something: cinch

easy to approach: affable

easy to understand: lucid, perspicuous, transparent

easy victim: gull, patsy

easygoing: calm, carefree, careless, casual, collected, composed, dégagé, flexible, happy-go-lucky, lenient, nonchalant, patient, placid, relaxed, unaffected, unhurried

eat: absorb, banquet, bite, breakfast, chow, consume, corrode, destroy, devour, dine, dinner, erode, feast, feed, forage, fret, gnaw, gobble, gormandize, graze, ingest, lunch, munch, nibble, nosh, ravage, rust, snack, sup, supper, swallow, taste

eat away: erode, gnaw

eat by candlelight: sup

eat greedily: devour, engorge, gorge, gormandize, gourmandize, guttle, ingurgitate, wolf

eat in style: dine

eat or drink: ingest

eat ravenously with ugly noises: glunsh, gruzzle, yaffle

eat with someone: break bread

eat, excessive desire to: polyphagia

eatable: appetizing, comestible, delicious, edible, esculent, palatable, savory, succulent, tasteful

eater, hearty: barathrum, gormandizer, gourmand, trencherman, trencherwoman

eating animal and vegetable products: omnivorous

eating at same table: commensal

eating disorder, bingeing: bulimia

eating disorder, loss of appetite: anorexia nervosa

eating excessively: crapulent, gluttonous, intemperate, overindulgent

eating implements: cutlery

eating many different foods: pleophagous

eating meat: carnivorous

eating place: automat, beanery, café, cafeteria, canteen, chophouse, delicatessen, diner, drive-in, hotel, inn, luncheonette, lunchroom, mess, mess hall, pizzeria, restaurant, tavern, tearoom

eating plants: herbivorous

eating regimen: diet

eating sparingly: abstemious

eating, art of good: gastronomy

eating, fast: tachyphagia

eating, full after: sated, satiated

eavesdrop: bug, listen, overhear, snoop, spy, tap, wiretap

ebb: abate, decline, decrease, diminish, diminution, languish, recede, reflux, regression, retire, retreat, sink, subside, tide, wane, withdraw

ebb, flow back: reflux

ebbing: refluent

ebony: inky, jet, raven, wood

ebullience: animation, elation, enthusiasm, excitement, exhilaration, exuberance, ferment, gaiety, vitality, zestful

ebullient: agitated, agog, bouncy, bubbling, ecstatic, effervescent, excited, gushing, high-spirited, joyous, lively, overflowing

eccentric: abnormal, anomalous, bizarre, capricious, character, crackpot, dotty, erratic, flaky, irregular, kooky, nonconformist, odd, oddball, off, offbeat, outre, peculiar, queer, quizzical, screwball, singular, strange, unconventional, unusual, weird, whimsical

eccentricity: aberration, deviation, hereticism, idiosyncrasy, kink, oddity, quirk

ecclesiastic: abbe, abbot, chaplain, cleric, divine, minister, parson, pastor, preacher, prelate, priest, religious, reverend

ecclesiastic painting: pieta

ecclesiastical armband: maniple

ecclesiastical bread plate: paten

ecclesiastical council: synod

ecclesiastical court: rota

ecclesiastical linen neckwear: amice

ecclesiastical monologue: sermon

ecclesiastical vestment: alb

ecdysiast: peeler, stripper, stripteaser

echelon: class, formation, hierarchy, level, position, rank, tier

echo: ape, copy, duplicate, imitate, imitation, impersonate, iterate, mimic, mirror, parrot, reiterate, repeat, resound, response, reverberate, revoice, ring, second

echo sounder: ASDIC, sonar

echoic words: onomatopoeic, onomatopoetic

echolocation: sonar

eclectic: assorted, broad, choosy, combined, comprehensive, diverse, heterogeneous, jumbled, mingled, mixed, selective, universal, varied

eclipse: blot, cloud, conceal, cover, darken, dazzle, exceed, extinguish, hide, mask, obscuration, obscure, occultation, outdo, overshadow, shade, sully, transcend, veil

eclipse where moon is silhouetted by ring of sun: annular eclipse

eclipse where three celestial bodies are aligned: syzygy

eclipse, flaming gas of sun during total solar: prominence

eclipse, full shadow during: umbra

eclipse, partial shadow during: penumbra

eclogue: idyl, idyll, poem

ecological interrelationships, study of: synecology

ecological stage: sere

ecological transitional zone: ecotone

ecology: bionomics

ecology basic unit of environment, organisms: ecosystem

economic: commercial, efficient, financial, material, productive, profitable

economic decline with serious unemployment: depression

economic decline, three quarters of falling GNP: recession

economic policy of self-sufficiency: autarky

economic theory of tax reduction to stimulate business: supply-side

economic theory stimulating employment, business: Keynesian

economical: careful, chary, cost-effective, frugal, inexpensive, meager, modest, penurious, practical, provident, prudent, sound, sparing, thrifty, tight

economically short-term and unfunded, of debt that is: floating

economics: arbitrage, bond, credit, deflation, equity, fund, futures, inflation, interest, loan, macroeconomics, management, plutonomy, portfolio, recession, securities, stock, system, treasury

economize: conserve, entrench, husband, manage, pinch, save, scrape, scrimp, skimp, squeeze

economy: austerity, discretion, frugality, plan, prudence, saving, thrift

economy of resources: conservation, husbandry

economy, careful money management: husbandry

economy, overall aspects of national: macroeconomics

ecru: beige, tan

ecstasy: bliss, delight, elation, euphoria, exaltation, happiness, heaven, joy, paradise, pleasure, rapture, transport

ecstasy, religious: theopathy

ecstatic: delirious, dionysiac, dionysian, dreamy, enchanted, enraptured, entranced, excited, happy, rhapsodic

ecstatic joy: transport

ecstatic, to become: swoon

ecumenical: general, global, inclusive, liberal, planetary, unifying, universal, worldwide

eczema: dermatitis, inflammation, rash, tetter

eddy: counter, countercurrent, current, gyrate, maelstrom, reverse, shift, swirl, turn, vortex, whirlpool

edema: dropsy

Eden: bliss, garden, heaven, innocence, paradise, utopia

edentate: aardvark, anteater, armadillo, sloth, toothless

edge: adjoin, bank, bevel, blade, border, boundary, brim, brink, brow, crest, flange, fringe, grind, hem, hone, inch, keeness, ledge, line, lip, margin, molding, nip, outline, perimeter, periphery, rim, selvage, sharpen, sharpness, side, sidle, threshold, trim, valance, verge, whet; advantage

edge a handkerchief: tat

edge of a cask: chime

edge of a roof: eave

edge of a sail: leech

edge of paper, ragged: deckle edge

edge or border, finish: purfle

edge or farthest point: extremity

edge or fringe of group: periphery

edge or margin: verge

edge or outer limit: perimeter

edge sewn to prevent unraveling: selvage

edge, sloping: bevel

edging indented with small curves: engrailed

edging with embroidered loops: picot

edgy: anxious, excitable, impatient, irritable, jittery, nervous, restless, tense, touchy, uneasy, uptight

edible: comestible, digestible, eatable, esculent, food, viand

edible bulb: onion, shallot

edible fungus: morel, truffle

edible part of fruit or nut: meat

edible root: oca, parsnip, radish, taro, yam

edict: announcement, ban, bull, command, decree, dictum, directive, enactment, fiat, irade, law, mandate, notice, order, ordinance, proclamation, program, regulation, ruling, statute, ukase, writ

edification: direction, education, enlightenment, illumination, improvement, knowledge, teaching

edifice: building, cathedral, monument, skyscraper, structure

edifice for drama presentation: theater

edify: educate, elevate, enlighten, illuminate, improve, inform, instruct, teach, uplift

edit: adapt, blue-pencil, censor, check, compile, copyedit, copyread, correct, delete, emend, modify, prepare, proofread, publish, redact, review, revise, rework, rewrite

edit a soundtrack: redub

edit and revise: redact

edit with prudence: bowdlerize

editing, critical revision and: recension

edition: copy, impression, issue, kind, number, printing, version, volume

edition with editorial and scholarly notes: variorum

editor's insertion mark: caret

editors, group of: erudition

educate: civilize, coach, cultivate, develop, discipline, edify, enlighten, explain, foster, indoctrinate, inform, instruct, nurture, rear, school, teach, train

educated: bred, broadened, enriched, experienced, knowledgeable, learned, lettered, literate, nurtured, scholarly, taught, trained

educated class: clerisy, intelligentsia, literates, literati

education: apprenticeship, background, breeding, discipline, erudition, learning, pedagogy, schooling, study, training, tutelage

education and career report: curriculum vitae, resume, vita

education method: heuristic, Montessori, Socratic

education world: academia

education, college or university: tertiary education

educational basics: arithmetic, reading, RRR, writing

educational method stressing child's initiative and natural abilities: Montessori

educe: arrive, conclude, deduce, derive, elicit, evoke, evolve, extract, procure, wrest

eel in postlarval transparent state: elver, glass eel

eel-shaped: anguilliform

eel, bright-colored marine: moray

eel, scaleless marine: conger

eelgrass: sea hay

eel's relative: lamprey

eerie: bizarre, creepy, eery, eldritch, frightening, ghostly, gloomy, macabre, mysterious, ominous, scary, spooky, strange, supernatural, uncanny, unearthly, weird

efface: cancel, delete, destroy, eliminate, eradicate, erase, expunge, indistinct, obliterate, raze, remove, undo

effect: accomplish, achieve, acquire, advantage, avail, cause, complete, conduce, consequence, emotion, enact, execute, expression, fulfill, generate, hypothesis, impact, import, impression, influence, initiate, intent, invoke, make, mark, operate, outcome, perform, phenomenon, produce, purport, ramification, realize, redound, result, sequel, upshot

effect, to have an: redound

effective: able, active, actual, adequate, capable, causal, cogent, competent, direct, effectual, efficacious, efficient, forceful, incisive, influential, moving, operant, operative, persuasive, potent, powerful, productive, striking, telling, trenchant, valid, vigorous

effective and producing desired result: efficacious, valid

effective as possible, to make as: optimize

effective from a specified past time: retroactive

effectiveness: efficacy

effects: assets, belongings, chattels, commodities, goods, movables, possessions, property, things

effectual: adequate, authoritative, capable, effective, efficacious, efficient, fulfilling, functional, influential, potent, practicable, useful, valid

effeminate: emasculated, epicene, feminine, gentle, mincing, prissy, sissified, sissy, soft, timid, unmanly, weak, womanish, womanly

effervescent: airy, animated, bouncing, breezy, bubbly, buoyant, carbonated, ebullient, enthusiastic, exuberant, fizzy, foaming, frothy, happy, lively, mirthful, spirited, vivacious, volatile, zestful

effete: anemic, barren, consumed, decadent, drained, exhausted, infertile, sere, spent, sterile, unfruitful, unproductive

efficacious: active, capable, effective, effectual, efficient, forcible, potent, powerful, prevalent, useful, valid, vigorous, virtuous

efficacy: advantage, effectiveness, potency

efficient: able, able to, adept, businesslike, capable, competent, economic, effective, effectual, expert, organized, productive, skillful

effigy: dummy, figure, idol, image, likeness, model, representation

efflorescence: anthesis, blooming, developing, flowering, folding, rash, redness, sprouting

effluence: emanation

effluvium: aura, byproduct, exhalation, exhaust, fumes, odor, scent, smell, vapor, waste

efflux: discharge, effluence, emanation, outflow

effort: achievement, application, arduous, attempt, battle, chore, dint, drive, endeavor, energy, exercise, exertion, force, labor, nisus, pains, power, push, strain, stress, struggle, sweat, task, toil, trial, trouble, try, undertaking, work

effort or hard work: application, assiduity, diligence, exertion, sedulousness, travail

effort to depress stock price: bear raid

effort, done with great: labored

effort, requiring much: arduous, strenuous

effortless: easy, facile, flowing, fluent, graceful, painless, simple, smooth, snap

effrontery: arrogance, audacity, boldness, brashness, brass, brazenness, cheek, gall, hardihood, insolence, nerve, presumption, sassiness, temerity

effulgence: blaze, brightness, brilliance, dazzle, luster, radiance, splendor

effulgent: beaming, bright, glowing, luminous, radiant, resplendent

effusive: bubbling, demonstrative,

ebullient, emotional, expressive, exuberant, gushy, overflowing, profuse, talkative, unrestrained

egg: chicken, embryo, ovule, ovum, seed, spawn

egg at a time, producing one: uniparous

egg by baking, cook unshelled: shirr

egg cell or ovum, to produce: ovulate

egg cell, mature unfertilized female: gamete

egg cell, unfertilized female: ovum

egg cooked in water just below boiling point: coddled

egg dish, fluffy baked: soufflé

egg fertilization by sperm: conception, impregnation

egg following cleavage, fertilized: embryo

egg-laying mammal: monotreme, platypus

egg-laying tube of insects, fish: ovipositor

egg on: abet, encourage, goad, incite, instigate, prod, spur, urge

egg parts: air space, albumen, chalaza, embryo, membrane, shell, vitellus, yolk

egg-producing gland: ovary

egg-shaped: elliptical, oblong, oval, ovate, oviform, ovoid, rounded

egg white: albumen

egg white glaze: glair

egg wrapped in sausage meat, hard-boiled: Scotch egg

egg yolk: parablast, vitellus

egg, fertilized ovum or: zygote

egghead: brain, highbrow, intellectual

eggplant: aubergine

eggs and ham on English muffins with hollandaise sauce, poached: eggs Benedict

eggs baked until set: shirred eggs

eggs before hatching, warming: brood, incubate

eggs laid at one time: clutch

eggs of fish: roe

eggs of fish, mollusk, amphibian: spawn

eggs scrambled on toast with anchovies: Scotch woodcock

eggs simmered slowly: coddled

egg's sunny side: yolk

eggs, carrying: gravid

eggs, sit on and hatch: incubate

eggshell color: ecru

eggy drink: nog

ego: conceit, personality, psyche, self

egocentric: narcissistic

egotist: snob

egotistic: boastful, cocky, conceited, egotistical, self-centered, stuck-up, superior, vain, vainglorious

egregious: blatant, deplorable, flagrant, gross, heinous, outrageous, shocking

egress: departure, exit, outlet, passage

egret cousin: heron

Egypt animals: adda, apis, bubal, cerastes, gazelle, genet, haje, hyena, ibis, icyneumon, jackal, jerboa, lynx, saluki, scarab, sicsac, skink

Egypt boats: baris, dahabeah, felucca

Egypt cosmetic: kohl

Egypt cotton: pima

Egypt monarch: pharaoh

Egypt monument: obelisk

Egypt paper: papyri, papyrus

Egypt stone: Rosetta

Egypt symbol: ankh, aten, lotus, scarab, uta

Egypt tomb: mastaba, pyramid

Egyptian beetle and charm: scarab

Egyptian cobra: asp, haje

Egyptian cross: ankh

Egyptian four-sided pillar with pyramid top: obelisk

Egyptian headwear: fez

Egyptian monument/tomb for pharaohs: pyramid

Egyptian monument with body of lion and unknown head: sphinx

Egyptian picture writing system: hieroglyphics

Egyptian stone tablet used for decipherment: Rosetta stone

Egyptian tomb with sloping sides, flat roof: mastaba

eight bits: byte

eight degrees between notes of music: octave

eight furlongs: mile

eight-sided: octagon, octagonal, octahedral, octahedron

eight-sided figure: octagon

eight singers or musicians: octet

eight-year period: octennial

eighteen-wheeler: semi

eightfold: octonary, octuple

eighth Arabic letter: dal

eighth planet from the Sun: Neptune

eighty-six (86): discard, eject, refuse, throw out

eighty to eighty-nine years old: octogenarian

ejaculate: call, discharge, eject, exclaim, howl, utter, yell

ejaculation: bellow, exclamation, shout, utterance

eject: banish, boot, bounce, cast, disbar, discharge, disgorge, dismiss, dispossess, eighty-six, ejaculate, emit, erupt, evict, exclude, expel, extrude, jilt, ostracize, oust, remove, shun, spew, spurt, void, vomit

eke: also, augment, economize, fill, husband, increase, lengthen, magnify, stretch, supplement

elaborate: adorn, clarify, comment, complicated, detailed, develop, elegant, embellish, enhance, expand, expatiate, explain, fancy, flashy, intricate, involved, ornate, painstaking, plush

elaborate celebration: gala

elaborate display: éclat

elaborate encomium: panegyric

elaborate party: fete

elaborate production: extravaganza, pageant, spectacle

élan: ardor, dash, eagerness, enthusiasm, flair, gusto, liveliness, panache, spirit, style, verve, vigor, zeal, zest

élan vital: life force

elapse: expire, glide, go by, pass, skip, transpire

elastic: bouncy, buoyant, ductile, expansive, extensile, flexible, limber, pliant, rebounding, resilient, springy, stretchy, tolerant

elasticity: resilience, tone

elate: buoy, cheer, delight, elevate, exalt, excite, exhilarate, gladden, heighten, inflate, inspire, lift, liven, please, raise

elated: animated, aroused, cock-a-hoop, ecstatic, enthused, glad, happy, jocular, jovial, joyful, jubilant, on top of the world, overjoyed, proud, spirited

elbow: angle, bend, jab, joint, jostle, nudge, push, shove

elbowroom: leeway, range, room, space, sweep

elbow's bony tip: olecranon

elder: ancestor, forefather, head, matriarch, oldster, patriarch, presbyter, senior, shrub, superior, tree, veteran

elderly: aged, ancient, gray, hoary, old, superannuated, venerable

elderly woman of high social status: dowager

eldest child, state of being: primogeniture

eldest member of group: doyen, doyenne

elect: assume, call, choose, decide, designate, determine, embrace, legislate, name, nominate, opt, pick, prefer, select, vote

election: alternative, balloting, choice, primary, referendum, voting

election by majority, but not more than half: plurality

election campaigning: stumping

election slate: ticket

election to choose candidates: primary

election, authorization given representatives through vote in: mandate

election, political party beliefs drawn up for: platform

election, to admit defeat in: concede

election, to campaign for: canvass

electioneering: barnstorming, whistle-stop tour

elections, study of: psephology

elective: constituent, discretionary, electoral, optional, voluntary

electoral district: constituency, precinct, ward

electorate: voters

electric: magnetic, static

electric capicitance unit: farad

electric catfish: raad

electric charge unit: coulomb

electric charge, ability to store: capacitance

electric circuit controller of current: resistor

electric circuit element holding temporary charge: capacitor, condenser

electric conductance unit: siemens

electric current: AC, alternating, DC, direct

electric current as medical treatment: ECT, electroconvulsive therapy, electroshock therapy, EST

electric current circuit transfer, measure of: conductance, conductivity

electric current in one direction, device sending: diode

electric current modulator: coder

electric current or voltage, sudden increase of: surge

electric current unit: amp, ampere

electric current without resistance, flow of: superconductivity

electric current, conductor of: electrode

electric current, generator for direct: dynamo

electric current, nonconductor of: dielectric, insulator

electric current, opposition to flow of alternating: impedance, reactrance, resistance

electric device: alternator, ammeter, amplifier, anode, arc, battery, booster, capacitor, cathode, circuit, coer, coil, condenser, conductor, diode, dynamo, electrode, fuse, galvanometer, generator, meter, motor, plug, rectifier, resistor, rheostat, semiconductor, superconductor, switch, transformer, voltmeter

electric device converting AC to DC: rectifier

electric device converting DC to AC: inverter

electric energy in form of magnetic field, ability to store: inductance

electric inductance unit: henry

electric motor or generator's rotor: armature

electric or magnetic fields, creation of voltage or current by means of: induction

electric power unit: watt

electric resistance unit: ohm

electric service, loss of: outage

electric terminal: anode

electric unit: amp, ampere, coulomb, farad, henry, rel, siemens, volt, watt

electric voltage of alternating current signal, device changing: transformer

electric wires and cables channel: conduit, duct

electrical cable: cord

electrical conductivity substance: semiconductor

electrical or acoustical noise: white noise

electrical plug connecting other plugs to socket: adapter

electrical plug's third prong: grounding prong

electrical power network: grid

electrical rectifier: diode

electrical sparks from friction: static

electrical wave changing or regulating for transmitting sound or data: modulation

electrical wires, tower supporting: pylon

electrically positive or negative, condition of being: polarity

electricians, group of: ohm

electricity: juice

electricity created by running water: hydroelectricity

electricity, concerning direct-current chemical: galvanic, voltaic

electricity, solution conducting: electrolyte

electricity, substance with intermediate conductivity of: semiconductor

electricity, to prevent passage of: insulate

electrified: live, wired

electrified particle: ion

electrify: amaze, amplify, astonish, astound, charge, dazzle, energize, excite, galvanize, jolt, startle, stimulate, stun, thrill, wire

electrode: anode

electrode gap discharge: arc

electrode, negative: cathode

electrode, positive: anode

electromagnetic amplifier: maser

electromagnetic force unit: abvolt

electromagnetic unit: weber

electromotive force unit: volt, voltage

electron: atom, subatomic particle

electron tube: diode

electronic beam: laser

electronic detecting system: radar

electronic device eliminating unwanted noise: Dolby

electronic device with semiconductors: solid state

electronic loudspeaker reproducing high-pitched sounds: tweeter

electronic loudspeaker reproducing low-pitched sounds: woofer

electronic navigation device: Loran

electronic snooper: bug

electronic solid-state circuit part: transistor

electronic vacuum tube for screen: cathode-ray tube, CRT

eleemosynary: benevolent, charitable, gratuitous, philanthropic

elegance: beauty, chic, class, concinnity, courtesy, cultivation, dignity, grace, gracefulness, grandeur, luxe, luxury, polish, refinement, splendor, style, taste, urbanity

elegant: attractive, beautiful, chic, chichi, classy, courtly, cultivated, dainty, dapper, delicate, exquisite, fashionable, fine, genteel, graceful, grand, handsome, lapidary, lavish, majestic, polished, posh, refined, soigne, stately, stylish, swank, tasteful, urbane

elegant and grand: lavish, stately, statuesque, sumptuous

elegant in manner: genteel, urbane

elegy: dirge, lament, monody, poem, requiem, song, trenody

element: air, aspect, basic, component, constituent, detail, domain, earth, environment, essential, factor, feature, fire, fundamental, group, ingredient, iron, line, material, matter, member, metal, particle, plane, point, principle, quality, unit, water

elemental: basic, primitive, primordial

elemental metal: ore

elementary: abecedarian, basal, basic, crude, easy, elemental, essential, fundamental, initial, original, plain, preliminary, primary, primitive, rudimental, rudimentary, simple, underlying

elementary book: primer

elementary in instruction: propaedeutic

elements by atomic number etc., tabular arrangement of: periodic table

elephant: boar, mammoth, mastodon, pachyderm, tusker

elephant boy of early movies: Sabu

elephant-like extinct mammal: mastodon

elephant, female: cow

elephant, male: bull

elephant period of sexual aggressiveness: must, musth

elephant rider: mahout

elephant rider's seat: howdah

elephant trunk: proboscis

elephant with tusks: tusker

elephant, young: calf

elephant, extinct proboscidian mammals resembling: mastodon

elephant, pertaining to: elephantine

elephant, rhinocerous, hippopotamus: pachyderm

elephantine: clumsy, colossal, enormous, gigantic, huge, immense, mammoth, strong, ungainly

elevate: advance, boost, dignify, elate, enhance, erect, exalt, exhilarate, glorify, heighten, hoist, honor, idyllize, improve, lift, promote, raise, rear, rise, uphold, uplift, upraise

elevate in rank: exalt

elevated: aerial, dignified, elated, eminent, ethical, formal, great, high, lifted, lofty, majestic, noble, prominent, raised, righteous, steep, tall, towering

elevated region: upland

elevation: acclivity, advancement, altitude, ascent, eminence, exaltation, height, hill, mountain, platform, prominence, promotion, ridge, rise, sublimity, top

elevator: cage, dumbwaiter, hoist, lift, silo

elevator cage: car

elevator for food: dumbwaiter

elevator in England: lift

eleven-sided figure: hendecagon

eleventh-hour effort to complete something: charrette

elf: brownie, dwarf, fairy, fay, gnome, goblin, gremlin, hob, imp, kobold, leprechaun, nisse, ouph, ouphe, peri, pixie, pixy, puck, sprite

elfin: fairylike, mischievous, small, sprightly, tiny, wee

elicit: bring out, deduce, derive, discover, draw, educe, entice, evoke, exact, extort, extract, induce, wrest, wring

elide: abbreviate, abridge, annul, curtail, delete, eliminate, erade, ignore, nullify, omit, skip, slur

eligible: acceptable, available, competent, desirable, entitled, fitted, meet, qualified, suitable, worthy

eliminate: abolish, annihilate, banish, cancel, dele, delete, destroy, disqualify, drop, eradicate, erase, except, exclude, excrete, expel, expunge, ignore, liquidate, omit, oust, purge, remove, sift, wipe out

elite: best, blue blood, choice, cream, crème, flower, gentry, quality, royalty, select, society, top, topflight, upper class, upper crust, wealthy

elite group in organization: cadre

elite group or place: pantheon

elixir: arcanum, cure-all, medicine, nostrum, panacea, potion, principle, remedy, solution, tonic

elixir sought by alchemists: arcanum

elk, American: wapiti

ellipses, instrument for drawing: trammel

ellipsoid: oval

elliptical: abridged, concise, egg-shaped, oblong, oval, ovate, ovoid

elliptical path: orbit

elocution: articulation, eloquence, expression, oratory, rhetoric, speech

elongate: extend, lengthen, prolong, protract, stretch

elongated fish: eel, gar

elope: abscond, flee, go secretly, run away, run off

eloquence: articulation, discourse, elocution, expression, fervor, fluency, oratory, rhetoric

eloquent: ardent, expressive, facund, fervid, forceful, impassioned, lofty, moving, passionate, persuasive, poetic, vivid, voluble

else: additional, also, besides, different, extra, instead, more, other, otherwise

elsewhere: away, formerly, gone, outside

elucidate: clarify, clear, describe, detail, enlighten, explain, expound, illume, illustrate, interpret

elude: avoid, baffle, ditch, dodge, duce, escape, evade, flee, foil, frustrate, hide, outwit, sidestep, slip

elusive: cagey, cunning, eely, evasive, fleeting, foxy, lubricous, mysterious, slippery, subtle, tricky, wily

emaciate: macerate, make thin

emaciated: anorexic, bony, famished, gaunt, lean, scrawny, sickly, skinny, starving, thin, underfed, wasted, wizened

emaciation: marasmus

emanate: arise, discharge, effuse, emerge, exude, flow, initiate, issue, originate, proceed, radiate, spring, stem

emanation: aura, efflux, odor

emanation, nasty-smelling: effluvium

emancipate: enfranchise, free, liberate, loose, manumit, release, unchain, unfetter

emasculate: alter, castrate, devitalize, fix, geld, soften, weaken

embalm: freeze, immortalize, perfume, preserve, wrap

embankment: banquette, dike, fill, levee, mound, quay, ravelin, wall

embargo: ban, barrier, blockade, blockage, edict, order, prohibition, restriction, stoppage

embark: begin, board, commence, depart, engage, enlist, enter, entrain, invest, launch, sail, start

embarrass: abash, annoy, bewilder, chagrin, confound, confuse, contretemps, demean, discomfit, disconcert, discountenance, dumbfound, faze, flummox, fluster, humiliate, mortify, nonplus, rattle, shame, stun, tease, upset

embarrass and put down: deflate, demean

embarrassed: abashed, ashamed, discountenanced, out of countenance, redfaced

embarrassing mistake: boner

embarrassing situation: contretemps, pickle

embarrassment: awkwardness, bewilderment, chagrin, confusion, contretemps, discomfort, discomposure, distress, humiliation, mistake, mortification, perplexity, scandal, shame, unease

embassy: ambassador, consulate, delegation, diplomat, envoy, mission

embassy official place of business: chancellery

embassy, diplomatic mission ranking below: legation

embattled: at war, beset, crenelated, embroiled, fighting, fortified, prepared

embed in surface for decoration: inlay

embedded: deep-seated, enclosed, entrenched, fixed, ingrained, inserted, installed, nested, planted, set in

embellish: adorn, apparel, beautify, bedeck, blazon, brighten, color, deck, decorate, dress, elaborate, emboss, embroider, enhance, enrich, exaggerate, garnish, gild, grace, grim, lard, magnify, ornament, polish

embellish speech, writing: lard

embellish with ornamental writing: flourish

ember: ash, brand, cinder, coal, slag

ember goose: loon

embezzle: bilk, defalcate, defraud, forge, misappropriate, misuse, peculate, purloin, steal, swindle, thieve

embitter: acerbate, acidulate, aggravate, anger, envenom, exacerbate, rankle, sour, upset

emblem: allegory, arms, badge, banner, colophon, colors, crest, cross, device, figure, flag, image, insignia, logo, mace, monogram, motto, scepter, sign, symbol, token, trademark

emblem of authority: mace

emblem or trademark, publisher's: colophon

emblematic: typic

embodied: incarnate

embodiment: avatar, epitome, example, incarnation, inclusion, integration, manifestation, personification, realization, representation

embodiment of idea: avatar

embodiment of quality in person: personification

embody: absorb, actualize, assimilate, blend, coalesce, contain, embrace, fuse, incarnate, include, incorporate, materialize, merge, mirror, organize, represent, symbolize, typify

embolden: abet, bolster, encourage, excite, hearten, inspire, liven, motivate, spur, stimulate, support

embosom: embrace, enclose, envelope, surround

emboss: adorn, carve, chase, decorate, embellish, engrave, ornament

embossing tool: die

embrace: accept, adopt, caress, cherish, clasp, clinch, cling, clip, clutch, comprehend, comprise, cradle, cuddle, embody, encircle, enclose, encompass, enfold, espouse, fold, grasp, huddle, hug, in arm, include, incorporate, love, reach, snuggle, squeeze, support, twine, welcome

embrocate: anoint

embroider: adorn, beautify, decorate, dramatize, elaborate, embellish, exaggerate, lace, ornament, overdo, romanticize, sew, stitch

embroidered decoration on sock, stocking: clock

embroidered hole: eyelet

embroidery: appliqué, couching, crewel, lace, needlepoint, needlework, orphrey, purl, smocking, tambour, tapestry

embroidery frame: tambour

embroidery in a variety of stitches, example of: sampler

embroidery loop: picot

embroidery on canvas: petitpoint

embroidery thread: floss

embroidery yarn: crewel

embroidery, elaborate: orphrey

embroidery, finish an edge with: purl

embroil: complicate, confuse, ensnarl, entangle, implicate, involve, mire, muddle, tangle, trap

embroilment: altercation, argument, brawl, clash, conflict, dispute, fight, fray, quarrel, spat, squabble, tiff

embryo: egg, fetus, germ, organism, seed, voule

embryo of a wheat kernel: germ

embryonic form, early: blastosphere, blastula

embryonic membrane: serosa

embryo's home: womb

emcee: host

emend: better, correct, edit, improve, rectify, redact, reform, revise

emerald: beryl

emerge: appear, arise, dawn, develop, emanate, evolve, issue, loom, materialize, rise, show, surface, surge

emergence: egress

emergency: accident, crisis, crunch, exigency, fix, flashpoint, juncture, pinch, squeeze, urgency

emergency education: crash course

emergency measure: expedient, quick fix, stopgap

emergency medical squad member: paramedic

emergency or temporary: jury-rigged

emergency repairman: troubleshooter

emergency situation: exigency, flashpoint

emergency treatment: first aid

emergency, a future: contingency

emergent: resulting, rising, urgent

emeritus: retired

emery board: file

emigrant: alien, colonist, émigré, foreigner, immigrant, pilgrim, pioneer, refugee, settler

emigration of scientists, intelligentsia for better pay, jobs: brain drain

émigré: exile

eminence: bluff, distinction, elevation, greatness, height, hill, honor, knoll, loftiness, note, projection, promontory, rank, renown, rise, standing, stature, summit

eminent: acclaimed, celebrated, distinguished, dominant, exalted, famous, formidable, glorious, great, high, illustrious, important, imposing, lofty, noble, noted, noteworthy, outstanding, paramount, prestigious, prominent, renowned, towering

emir: chieftain, governor, leader, prince, ruler, title

emissary: agent, ambassador, consul, delegate, deputy, envoy, intermediary, legate, messenger, representative

emission: discharge, ejection, emitting, fumes, issuance, radiation

emit: beam, cast, discharge, disembogue, eject, emanate, exhale, expel, expire, express, exude, give, glow, issue, pour, radiate, reek, release, send, spew, transmit, utter, vent, voice

emit a foul odor: reek

emit lava: spew

emollient: balm, lotion, mollifying, ointment, salve, softening, soothing

emolument: compensation, earnings, fee, income, pay, payment, profit, recompense, salary, stipend, wage

emotion: affection, agitation, agony, anger, anxiety, concern, despair, despondency, ecstasy, empathy, fear, feeling, grief, happiness, hate, ire, jealousy, joy, love, melancholy, mental state, passion, pity, pride, relief, remorse, sadness, satisfaction, sensation, shame, sorrow, surprise, warmth

emotion attributed to inanimate objects or nature: pathetic fallacy

emotion felt by reader: objective correlative

emotion separate from thought, action: affect

emotion, devoid of: dispassionate, objective

emotion, excessive: hysteria

emotion, forcefully release an: vent

emotion, intense: white heat

emotion, joyful: ecstasy, rapture, transport

emotion, of the open expression of: demonstrative

emotion, outburst of: paroxysm

emotion, without: impassive

emotional: affective, arousing, distraught, effusion, heartwarming, hysterical, moving, mushy, nervous, neurosis, sensitive, sentimental, stirring, touching, trauma, upset, vulnerable

emotional affinity: rapport

emotional and theatrical: histrionic

emotional conflict, deeply agitated from: distraught

emotional discharge: catharsis

emotional disorder: neurosis

emotional highs: ups

emotional injury, susceptible to: vulnerable

emotional intensity: ardor, fervor

emotional or prejudicial in appeal: ad hominem

emotional outburst: scene

emotional shock with lasting damage: trauma

emotional tension after overwhelming experience, release of: catharsis

emotional, excessively: effusive, gushing, histrionic

emotional, tearfully: maudlin

emotionless: affectless, apathetic, cold, deadpan, dispassionate, distant, heartless, impassive, impersonal, indifferent, reserved, staid, stolid, unfeeling, unmoved

emotions, drama of exaggerated: melodrama

emotions, identification with another's: empathy

emotions, purifying or figurative cleansing of: catharsis

emotions, range of: gamut

emotions, resulting from: affective

emotions, unrestrained outpouring of: effusion

emotions, very distressing to: poignant

empathy: caring, compassion, insight, pity, rapport, ruth, sensitivity, sympathy, understanding

emperor: autocrat, caesar, czar, dictator, imperial, kaiser, king, monarch, ruler, sultan, tsar

emperor of Holy Roman Empire, Germany: kaiser

emperor of Japan: mikado, tenno

emperor of Russia: czar, tsar

emperor, relating to an: imperial

emphasis: accent, attention, focus, importance, prominence, strength, stress, weight

emphasis by contrast: relief

emphasize: accent, accentuate, amplify, feature, hammer, highlight, impress, italicize, pinpoint, punctuate, reiterate, stress, underline, underscore

emphasize a point: belabor

emphatic: absolute, categorical, certain, decided, decisive, definite, distinct, earnest, explicit, forceful, insistent, marked, positive, stressed, unequivocal, vehement

empire: control, domain, dominion, dynasty, federation, kingdom, realm, reign, rule, sovereignty, territory

Empire State: New York

empire, relating to an: imperial

empirical: experimental, factual, hypothetical, observational, practical, provable, verifiable

employ: apply, bestow, engage, exercise, hire, involve, manipulate, occupy, operate, procure, retain, service, supply, use, utilize

employee: apprentice, assistant, factotum, hand, help, jobholder, laborer, worker

employee among many: minion

employee barring until accepting of employer's terms: lockout

employee cutback: downsizing, retrenchment

employee cutback by retirement, resignation, death: attrition

employee doing variety of duties: factotum

employee extra benefits: fringe benefits

employee hourly record: time card

employer: boss, business, company, corporation, entrepreneur, firm, hirer, manager, organization, owner, user

employer hiring more workers than needed: featherbedding

employer, demanding: slave driver

employment: adoption, business, calling, craft, job, line, occupation, operation, profession, task, trade, usage, use, utilization, vocation, work

emporium: bazaar, boutique, galleria, market, marketplace, mart, shop, store

empower: allow, authorize, commission, delegate, deputize, enable, entitle, grant, invest, license, warrant

empress: czarina, maharani, queen, ruler

emptiness: bareness, blankness, hollowness, hunger, inanition, vacancy, vacuity, vacuum, void

empty: bare, barren, blank, clear, deplete, deserted, devoid, discharge, drain, dump, evacuate, exhaust, expel, fruitless, idle, inane, meaningless, pour, release, starving, unload, unoccupied, vacant, vacate, vacuous, void

empty flattery: flummery

empty-headed: brainless, dizzy, fatuous, featherbrained, flighty, harebrained, ignorant, scatterbrained, silly, simple, stupid, vapid

empty out: disembogue, dump

empty space: vacuity, void

empty tomb: cenotaph

empyrean: celestial, cosmos, ether, firmament, heavenly, paradise, sky

emu, ostrich, or rhea: ratite

emulate: compete, contend, copy, equal, excel, follow, imitate, rival, strive

en masse: all together, as a group, ensemble, in a group, jointly, together

en route: bound, midway, on the road, on the way, travelling

enable: activate, actuate, allow, authorize, capacitate, empower, entitle, permit, prepare, ready

enact: appoint, approve, constitute, decree, effect, establish, execute, legislate, ordain, pass, perform, personate, proclaim, ratify, represent

enactment: decree, edict, law, ordinance, portrayal, regulation, representation, statute

enamel: cloisonne, coating, finish, glaze, gloss, japan, lacquer, paint

enamel, glossy black: japan

enameled metalware: tole

enamelware of Italy: majolica

enamelware technique filling grooves with colored enamel: champleve

enamelware with colors separated by thin strips of metal: cloisonne

enamored: attracted, captivated, charmed, enchanted, enthralled, entranced, fascinated, gaga, in love with, infatuated, loving, smitten

enamored with acting: stagestruck

encamp: billet, bivouac, quarter, settle, tent

encased: sheathed, wrapped

enceinte: expecting, fortification, gestate, pregnant

enchant: allure, attract, bewitch, captivate, charm, delight, enamor, enthrall, fascinate, hypnotize, mesmerize, spellbind

enchanted: fey

enchanting: charming, delightful, glamorous, intriguing, ravishing, seductive, winsome, wonderful

enchiridion: guidebook, handbook, manual

enciphered: coded

encircle: band, belt, cincture, circumscribe, contain, embrace, enclose, encompass, engird, environ, enwind, fence, gird, loop, orbit, ring, surround, wreathe, zone

encircling fortification: enceinte

enclose: bind, blockade, bound, box, cage, circle, circumscribe, comprise, conclude, contain, coop, corral, embosom, embrace, encase, encircle, encompass, envelop, enwrap, fence, harness, hedge, hem, house, imprison, insert, pale, pen, surround, wall

enclose within walls: confine, immure, imprison, surround

enclosed feeling: cabin fever

enclosed space by cathedral: close, garth

enclosing border: frame

enclosure: aviary, barrier, bawn, cell, cincture, cloister, cofferdam, corral, cote, court, courtyard, crawl, fence, fold, garden, kennel, paddock, pale, pen, pound, prison, quadrangle, runway, stall, stockade, sty, trap, weir, yard, zone

enclosure with definite limits: precinct

encomium: accolade, commendation, compliment, eloge, eulogy, laudation, panegyric, praise, salutation, tribute

encompass: achieve, belt, beset, circle, circulate, circumscribe, circumvent, clip, comprise, constitute, contain, embody, embrace, encircle, enclose, engird, envelope, environ, gird, include, incorporate, involve, ring, span, surround

encore: again, anew, bis, cheers, reappearance, recall, repeat, repetition, return

encounter: action, address, affray, affront, assail, attack, battle, bout, brush, close, collision, combat, conflict, confront, contest, detect, dispute, engagement, espy, face, fight, meet, oppose, rendezvous, skirmish, struggle, suffer, undergo

encourage: abet, advance, advise, animate, applaud, assure, back, bolster, boost, buoy, cheer, comfort, confirm, console, elate, embolden, energize, exhort, foment, forward, foster, further, hearten, help, incite, induce, inspire, inspirit, instigate, nurture, promote, push, rally, reassure, restore, spur, stimulate, strengthen, support, sustain, uphold, urge

encourage and fill with spirit: animate, embolden, inspirit, invigorate

encourage and promote: advance, foster, nurture

encourage and support: abet, advocate, champion, promote

encourage with cheers: root

encouragement: approval, confidence, faith, hope, incentive, incitement, inducement, lift, motivation, patronage, praise, push, reassurance, relief, stimulus

encouragement of illegal act: abetment, connivance

encouragement or support: countenance, endorsement, patronage, sanction

encouraging: exhorting, hortative, hortatory, urging

encroach: impinge, infringe, intrude, invade, meddle, motivation, overstep, trespass, usurp

encrusted: caked

encumber: beset, burden, clog, embarrass, entangle, hamper, handicap, hinder, impede, load, obstruct, oppress, overburden, overload, saddle, tax

encumbered debtor: lienee

encumbrance: lien

encyclopedic: broad, complete, comprehensive, exhaustive, extensive, general, scholarly, thorough, universal

end: abolish, accomplishment, achieve, achievement, aim, boundary, butt, cease, cessation, close, closure, complete, completion, conclude, conclusion, culmination, death, define, design, destruction, determine, discontinue, dissolve, edge, expiration, expire, expiry, extinction, extreme, extremity, finale, finish, goal, intention, lapse, limit, objective, omega, outcome, period, point, position, purpose, quash, remainder, remnant, result, rump, scrap, sever, stop, tail, terminate, termination, terminus, tip, upshot, windup

end decisively: quash, scotch

end-of-semester exams: finals

end of the world: apocalyptic, Armageddon, crack of doom, death knell, doomsday, eschatology, finality, Gotterdammerung, knell

end-of-the-world battle: Armageddon

end of the world, branch of theology dealing with: eschatology

end of the world, relating to the: apocalyptic

end of, complete or reach the: accomplish, consummate

end or farthest point: extremity

end or reach completion: culminate

end or reach successful conclusion: resolve

end parliamentary session: prorogue

end result: denouement, fate

end unexpectedly: abort

end, add to the: annex, append, suffix

end, directed toward a specific: telic

endanger: chance, compromise, expose, hazard, imperil, jeopardize, put at risk, risk, threaten

endearing: affectionate, charming, engaging, lovable, sweet, winsome

endeavor: affair, aim, attempt, business, effort, enterprise, exert, exertion, fling, job, labor, pursuit, seek, strife, strive, struggle, study, try, undertaking, venture, vocation, work

ended: completed, destroy, done, finished, over, past, through

ending battle between good and evil: Armageddon

ending or ceasing of existence: demise

ending section of book with explanation: epilogue

ending, unsurprising and disappointing: anticlimax

endless: boundless, continual, continuous, enduring, eternal, everlasting, forever, immortal, indefinite, infinite, interminable, measureless, perpetual, unceasing, uninterrupted, unlimited, untold

endless and futile: Sisyphean

endless time: eon

endorse: advocate, affirm, approve, attest, authorize, back, bless, certify, countersign, guarantee, notarize, okay, pledge, recommend, second, sign, support, validate, vouch

endorse a motion or nomination: second

endorsement: acceptance, amendment, approbation, backing, fiat, okay, ratification, rider, sanction, signature

endow: award, bequeath, bestow, contribute, endue, enrich, equip, finance, fund, furnish, grant, invest, leave, provide, supply, support, will

endowed position: benefice

endowment: ability, appanage, aptitude, chantry, donation, dower, dowry, foundation, gift, inheritance, quality, talent, trust

endowment to an institution: patrimony

ends touching: abutting

endurance: capacity, continuance, durability, fortitude, hardihood, lastingness, longevity, patience, perseverance, persistence, pluck, stamina, strength, suffering, tenacity, tolerance, vigor, vitality

endurance test: marathon, ordeal

endurance, physical or moral: stamina

endure: abide, allow, bear, bide, brade, continue, goon, last, live, outlast, persist, prevail, remain, stand, stay, stomach, strengthen, suffer, survive, sustain, tolerate, toughen, undergo, weather, withstand

endure, capacity to: tolerance

enduring: biding, continuing, durable, eternal, lasting, perennial, permanent, sinewy, sound, staunch, steadfast, stubborn, sturdy, wiry

enema: colonic

enemy: adversary, antagonist, combatant, detractor, foe, nemesis, opponent, rival, roe

enemy-aiding internal group: fifth column

enemy encroacher: invader

enemy expansion, checking: containment

enemy position: beachhead, bridgehead, salient

enemy to maintain peace, granting concessions to potential: appeasement

enemy, associating with an: fraternization

enemy, harsh settlement imposed on defeated: diktat

enemy, maneuver deceiving an: decoy, diversion

enemy, relating to an: inimical

energetic: active, brisk, charged, dynamic, enterprising, enthusiastic, fast, forcible, hardworking, hearty, industrious, lively, peppy, robust, sprightly, spry, strenuous, tireless, up-and-coming, vibrant, vigorous, virile, vital, vivacious

energetic enterprise and determination: initiative

energetic hardworking person: dynamo, fireball, firebrand

energetic person: ball of fire

energetic, in music: vigoroso

energize: activate, animate, electrify, fuel, invigorate, prime, stimulate, vitalize

energy: activity, atomic, bang, brio, current, drive, effort, elan, electricity, enthusiasm, fire, force, fortitude, friction, fuel, geothermal, heat, juice, might, numen, pep, pizzazz, power, solar, spirit, stamina, steam, strength, verve, vigor, vim, vitality, voltage, zest, zip

energy and force as explanation for universe: dynamism

energy and matter, science of: physics

energy and spirit used as a musical direction: con brio

energy from internal heat of earth, of: geothermal

energy of body because of motion: kinetic energy

energy source, of an inexhaustible: renewable

energy used by a body at rest: basal metabolism

energy, concentration of emotional: cathexis

energy, control and direct: harness

energy, creative: genius, numen

energy, means of release for: outlet

energy, requiring great: strenuous

energy, unit of radiant: quantum

enervate: debilitate, deplete, devitalize, drain, enfeeble, exhaust, fatigue, sap, tire, weaken

enfant terrible: brat, embarrassment, hellion, rascal, scamp, troublemaker

enfeeble: attenuate, cripple, debilitate, deplete, disable, drain, enervate, exhaust, impair, incapacitate, soften, weaken

enfold: clutch, cover, cuddle, drape, embrace, encase, encircle, enclose, envelop, enwrap, hug, lap, surround, swathe, wrap

enforce: administer, coerce, compel, demand, exact, execute, implement, impose, invoke, prosecute, require, stress, support

enfranchise: deliver, emancipate, free, liberate, manumit

engage: absorb, affiance, agree, arrest, battle, betroth, book, conduce, contract, embark, employ, engross, entangle, enter, fascinate, fasten, hire, interest, interlock, involve, join, lock, mesh, occupy, participate, persuade, pledge, promise, rent, reserve, secure, undertake

engage a gear: mesh

engaged: affianced, betrothed

engagement: affair, appointment, assignation, battle, betrothal, booking, commitment, contest, date, employment, encounter, fight, gig, involvement, job, meeting, rendezvous, skirmish, stint, tryst, vow

engaging: attractive, captivating, charming, fascinating, interesting, likable, pleasant, sweet

engender: beget, breed, cause, create, cultivate, develop, excite, generate, incite, originate, procreate, produce, propagate

engine: beam, booster, bypass, combustion, diesel, donkey, fuel injection, gasoline, induction, ion, jet, lenoir's, locomotive, motor, newcomen, outboard, plasma, radial, ram, ramjet, retrorocket, steam, sustainer, synchronous, thruster, turbine, turbojet, turboprop, V, vernier, wankel

engine blower or compressor that supplies high-pressure air: booster, supercharger

engine clanking noise: knock

engine cooling device: radiator

engine electrical contact: point

engine electrical current conveying device: distributor

engine for boat, external: outboard motor

engine housing: pod

engine on rear of small boat: outboard motor

engine purr: idle

engine regulating valve: throttle

engine seal: O-ring

engine used to drive external propeller, turbojet: propjet, turboprop

engine with a turbine-driven compressor, jet: turbojet

engine with fuel burned internally: internal-combustion engine

engine with vaned shaft rotated by pressure, rotary: turbine

engine without carburetors, internal-combustion: fuel-injection engine

engine, electrical system activating an: ignition

engine, small rocket: thruster

engine, to start an: crank

engineer: arrange, builder, conductor, construct, constructor, contrive, designer, driver, inventor, manage, maneuver, manipulate, motorperson, negotiate, operate, pilot, plan, planner

England conservative: Tory

England nobility titles: baron, baroness, baronet, countess, dame, duchess, duke, earl, king, knight, lady, lord, marchioness, marquess, marquis, noble, peer, prince, princess, queen, viscount, viscountess

England, pertaining to: Anglican, Anglophile, Anglo-Saxon, British, Briton, English

English in form or style, to make: anglicize

English-speaking person: Anglophone

English sponge cake soaked in liquor and topped with cream, jam, custard: trifle

engrave: carve, chase, chisel, cut, etch, impress, imprint, incise, inscribe, mark, ornament, print, sculpture, stamp, stipple

engraved stone pillar: stela, stele

engraver: etcher, pye

engraver of precious stones: lapidary

engraving: cameo, cerograph, drypoint, enchase, glyptic, hyalography, intaglio, mezzotint, stamp, stylography, xylograph

engraving in relief: cameo

engraving on precious stones: glyptography

engraving opposite relief, sunken: intaglio

engraving tool: burin, stylet

engraving, relating to: glyptic

engraving, to decorate by: chase, enchase

engross: absorb, captivate, consume, engage, enthrall, fascinate, grip, hold, immerse, monopolize, occupy, preoccupy, rivet, submerge

engrossed: enrapt, into, lost in, rapt

engulf: bury, consume, deluge, drown, flood, inundate, overflow, overwhelm, submerge, swallow, swamp, whelm

enhance: add to, adorn, amplify, augment, beautify, deepen, elevate, embellish, enlarge, exaggerate, heighten, improve, increase, intensify, lift, magnify, raise, sharpen

enigma: conundrum, crux, inexplicable, mystery, problem, puzzling, rebus, riddle, secret

enigmatic: ambiguous, baffling, cryptic, elusive, equivocal, inexplicable, inscrutable, mysterious, mystical, obscure, perplexing, puzzling, recondite

enjoin: admonish, ban, bid, command, decree, deny, direct, forbid, impose, order, outlaw, plead, prohibit, restrict

enjoy: appreciate, benefit, command, fancy, have, like, own, pleasurable, possess, relish, savor

enjoy profits: reap

enjoy the flavor of: relish, savor

enjoyment: amusement, delectation, delight, entertainment, felicity, fun, gusto, happiness, liking, merriment, pleasure, possession, recreation, relish, satisfaction, zest

enjoyment of life: joie de vivre

enjoyment of possession: fruition

enlarge: add, aggrandize, amplify, augment, boost, broaden, develop, dilate, elaborate, enhance, exaggerate, expand, expatiate, extend, fatten, greaten, grow, increase, inflate, intumesce, lengthen, magnify, multiply, ream, spread, stretch, swell, widen

enlarge upon: expatiate

enlargement: accretion, addition, amplification, elongation, expansion, extension, growth, magnification

enlarging: increscent, waxing

enlarging gradually: evase

enlarging implement: reamer

enlighten: advise, apprise, disclose, edify, educate, guide, illuminate, inform, instruct, preach, teach, uplift

enlightened people: illuminati

enlightenment: awareness, bodhi, insight, knowledge, nirvana, truth, understanding, wisdom

enlightenment for Buddhists, Hindi: nirvana

enlist: draft, employ, engage, enroll, enter, hire, induct, join, recruit, register, secure, serve, volunteer

enliven: animate, brighten, cheer, excite, exhilarate, inspire, invigorate, refresh, rejuvenate, renew, revive, rouse, spice, stimulate, vitalize, vivify, warm

enmesh: catch, entangle, implicate, involve, snare, tangle, trammel, trap

enmity: acrimony, animosity, animus, antagonism, antipathy, aversion, bad blood, bitterness, dislike, hatred, hostility, ill feeling, loathing, malevolence, malice, rancor, resentment, spite

ennui: apathy, blues, boredom, dissatisfaction, doldrums, fatigue, languor, lassitude, listlessness, melancholy, tedium, weariness

enormity: abomination, depravity, evilness, heinousness, horribleness, immensity, massiveness, monstrosity, wickedness

enormous: abnormal, behemoth, big, colossal, elephantine, excessive, gargantuan, gigantic, great, Herculean, huge, immense, large, mammoth, massive, monstrous, ponderous, prodigious, stupendous, titanic, tremendous, unwieldy, vast

enough: acceptable, adequate, ample, fairly, fully, passably, plenty, quite, satisfactory, sufficient, suitable, tolerably, very

enrage: anger, annoy, exasperate, incense, incite, inflame, infuriate, ire, madden, needle, provoke, retainer

enrapture: allure, bewitch, captivate, charm, delight, elate, enchant, enthrall, entrance, fascinate, please, ravish, spellbind, thrill, transport

enrich: adorn, ameliorate, augment, decorate, embellish, enhance, fatten, fertilize, improve, lard, ornament, supplement, upgrade

enroll: accept, engross, enlist, enter, induct, inscribe, join, list, matriculate, record, recruit, register, subscribe

enrollment office: registry

ensconce: conceal, cover, embed, establish, hide, nestle, seat, settle, shield, stash

ensemble: aggregate, altogether, band, collection, company, costume, gathering, getup, group, outfit, suit, suite, troupe

enshrine: cherish, consecrate, idolize, sanctify

ensign: banner, flag, gonfalon, insignia, officer, oriflamme, pennant, rank, sign, standard, symbol, title

ensiled: alone, apart, capture, chain, imprison, isolated, oppress, segregated

enslave: oppress, shackle, subjugate, suppress

enslavement: bondage, serfdom, servitude, slavery, thralldom

ensnare: capture, catch, enmesh, entangle, entrap, hook, mesh, net, noose, snag, snarl, springe, trap

ensue: appear, emanate, flow, follow, proceed, result, stem

ensuing: after, later, next, resultant, subsequent, succeeding

ensure: assure, certify, clinch, guarantee, protect, safeguard, secure

enswathe: wrap

entail: bestow, cause, demand, encompass, evoke, impose, involve, necessitate, require

entangle: bewilder, catch, complicate, confuse, embarrass, embrangle, embroil, enmesh, ensnarl, entrap, entwine, impede, implicate, intertwine, involve, knot, mat, mesh, mire, muddle, perplex, puzzle, ravel, snare, snarl, trap, twist

entanglement: affair, difficulty, intrigue, involution, jumble, knot, liaison, maze, morass, obstacle, problem, web

entente: accord, agreement, alliance, coalition, harmony, treaty

enter: admit, appear, arrive, begin, come, engage, enlist, enrol, enroll, go in, infiltrate, initiate, inscribe, insert, introduce, intrude, invade, irrupt, join, list, penetrate, pierce, post, record, register, submit, trespass

enter by force to conquer: intrude, invade

enter by force, impossible to: impregnable

enter gradually and surreptitiously: infiltrate

enter illegally: encroach, impinge, infringe, intrude, trespass

enter in a burst: irrupt

enterprise: action, adventure, attempt, boldness, business, campaign, cause, company, courage, drive, effort, endeavor, exploit, firm, initiative, operation, project, pursuit, push, spirit, undertaking, venture, vigor, zeal

enterprise and determination: gumption, initiative

enterprising: active, aggressive, alert, ambitious, aspiring, bold, busy, courageous, daring, driving, energetic, enthusiastic, hardworking, industrious

enterprising businessperson: entrepreneur

entertain: amuse, beguile, comfort, consider, contemplate, dine, distract, divert, fete, harbor, host, occupy, ponder, receive, regale, stimulate, treat

entertainer: actor, actress, artist, artiste, comedian, comedienne, contortionist, dancer, emcee, geek, host, hostess, juggle, magician, mime, minstrel, musician, performer, player, singer, troubadour, trouper, ventriloquist

entertainers in group: troupe

entertainment: amusement, banquet, celebration, cheer, concert, diversion, enjoyment, extravaganza, fair, feast, festivity, function, gala, hobby, merriment, opera, party, pastime, performance, play, pleasure, reception, recreation, revue, show, sport, treat

enthrall: absorb, captivate, charm, enchant, enrapture, enslave, fascinate, hold, hook, intrigue, mesmerize, spellbind, subjugate, thrill

enthuse: elate

enthusiasm: ardor, dash, devotion, eagerness, éclat, élan, energy, esprit, excitement, exuberance, fanaticism, fervor, fire, gusto, intensity, kindle, love, mania, passion, spirit, verve, vivacity, zeal, zest

enthusiasm and zeal: ardor, fervor, gusto

enthusiasm, extreme: fanaticism

enthusiasm, to arouse: kindle

enthusiast: admirer, aficionado, buff, devotee, fan, fanatic, follower, lover, maniac, nut, optimist, rooter, supporter

enthusiastic: afire, ardent, avid, eager, ebullient, emotional, fervent, gung ho, interested, keen, obsessed, perfervid, rabid, rhapsodic, wholehearted, zealous

enthusiastic review: rave

enthusiastic supporter: fan

enthusiastic vigor: brio, élan, vivacity

enthusiastic, extremely: ebullient, evangelistic, exuberant, rhapsodic

entice: allure, attract, bait, cajole, charm, coax, decoy, fascinate, incite, induce, inveigle, invite, lure, persuade, seduce, solicit, tempt, wheedle, wile

entire: absolute, all, choate, complete, every, full, gross, intact, integral, perfect, plenary, sound, thorough, total, unbroken, uncut, undiminished, undivided, unimpaired, unmarred, whole

entire range: gamut

entirely: all, alone, altogether, exclusively, in toto, only, quite, reservedly, solely, tout à fait, undividedly, utterly

entitle: allow, appoint, authorize, call, designate, dub, empower, enable, label, name, nominate, permit, qualify, term

entity: being, body, essence, existence, individual, life, material, matter, one, presence, structure, substance, thing, unit

entomb: bury, confine, cover, inhume, inter, inurn, sepulture

entourage: associates, attendants, companions, escort, following, groupies, procession, retainers, retinue, staff, train

entrails: innards, viscera

entrails of deer: numbles, umbles

entrails of fowl: giblets

entrance: access, adit, admission, admittance, appearance, approach, beginning, debut, door, doorway, foyer, gate, gateway, hall, hallway, induc-

tion, ingress, introduction, lobby, mouth, opening, portal, threshold, vestibule

entrance hall: antechamber, anteroom, foyer, lobby, vestibule

entrance or doorway: threshold

entrance or passage: adit

entrance stair or porch: stoop

entrance to a hangar: apron

entrance to temple: propylaeum

entrance to theater or club: marquee

entrance walkway or porch with columns: portico

entrance, right of: access, ingress

entrance, to: bewitch, captivate, charm, delight, enrapture, fascinate, hypnotize, mesmerize, ravish

entrant: candidate, competitor, contestant, participant, player

entrap: allure, ambush, bait, beguile, capture, catch, decoy, entangle, hook, inveigle, lure, nail, snare, tangle, tempt

entreat: adjure, appeal, ask, beg, beseech, coax, conjure, crave, exhort, implore, importune, invoke, persuade, petition, plead, pray, request, seek, solicit, supplicate

entreaty for assistance: invocation

entreaty on behalf of another: intercession

entrechat: leap

entrée: access, admission, admittance, entrance, entry, induction; main course

entrench: anchor, embed, establish, fix, fortify, implant, infringe, ingrain, invade, protect, trespass

entrepreneur: businessperson, employer, enterpriser, executive, manager, operator, organizer

entrust: assign, authorize, commend, commit, confide, consign, delegate, depend, deposit, encharge, give, permit

entry: access, account, adit, adjustment, candidate, contestant, door, entrance, entrée, foyer, ingress, item, lobby, memo, note, opening, participant, passage, passageway, record, register, vestibule

entry, right of: entrée

entry's reverse: exit

entryway: portal, stoop

entwine: braid, coil, encircle, interlace, interweave, lace, spiral, twist, weave, wind

enumerate: calculate, catalog, com-

pute, count, detail, estimate, figure, itemize, list, number, recite, reckon, recount, tally, tell, total

enunciate: announce, articulate, declare, express, intone, proclaim, pronounce, speak, state, vocalize, voice

envelop: blanket, cage, cloak, cocoon, conceal, cover, encase, enclose, encompass, enfold, engulf, environ, enwrap, hide, mask, overlie, sheath, shroud, surround, swaddle, swathe, veil, wrap

envelope: covering, jacket, pocket, pouch, shell, wrapper

envelope markings instead of stamps: indicia

envious: begrudging, covetous, greedy, green, green-eyed, jealous, resentful, spiteful

environ: circumscribe, encircle, enclose, encompass, envelop, fence, limit, surround

environment: ambience, atmosphere, background, climate, conditions, element, matrix, medium, milieu, neighborhood, setting, surroundings, terrain

environment and organisms: ecosystem

environment and organisms, science of: ecology

environment for organism: habitat

environment, adjustment to new: orientation

environment, protection of: conservation

environment, to adjust to new: acclimatize

environmental atmosphere: ambiance, ambience

environmental concern: ozone

environmental conditions, capable of living in varying: facultative

environmental influences on organism: nurture

environs: area, areas, district, outskirts, precinct, suburbs, territory, turf, vicinity

envisage: confront, consider, image, picture, regard, visualize

envision: conceive, conceptualize, dream, foresee, imagine, picture, predict

envoy: agent, ambassador, attaché, consul, courier, deputy, diplomat, emissary, legate, messenger, minister, representative

envy: begrudge, covet, discontent, jealousy, resentment

ENVIRONMENTAL AND OCCUPATIONAL DISEASES AND DISORDERS

aeroembolism/caisson disease/decompression sickness/
   diver's palsy/the bends
allergies
altitude sickness
anoxemia
anoxia
anoxic anoxia
anthrax/pulmonary anthrax/woolsorter's disease
asthma
birth defects
cadmium poisoning
cancer
carpal tunnel syndrome
chilblain
chronic fatigue immune dysfunction syndrome
dermatitis
emphysema
fibromyalgia
frostbite
goiter
headache
heart disease
housemaid's knee

immersion foot
jet lag
job-related illnesses
kidney disease
lead poisoning
mercury poisoning
migraine
Minamata disease
motion sickness
nervous system disorders
pneumoconiosis/black lung
queensland fever
radiation sickness
radionecrosis
red-out
repetitive strain injuries
sensory integration dysfunction
sunstroke
toxic polyneuropathy
trench foot
uranium poisoning
writer's cramp ❦

---

envy something someone else has: covet

envy the possession of: begrudge

enzyme: adenase, amylase, ase, catalyst, diatase, lipase, olease, pepsin, protease, protein, racemase, renin

eon: aeon, age, era, eternity, time

ephemeral: brief, evanescent, fleeting, momentary, passing, short, temporary, transient, transitory, unenduring, vague

epic: composition, epos, grand, great, heroic, imposing, legendary, majestic, narrative, noble, poem, saga, tale

epic narrative: saga

epic poem, ancient Greek: rhapsody

epicure: connoisseur, gastronome, glutton, gourmand, gourmet, hedonist, sybarite, voluptuary

epidemic: catching, communicable, contagious, infectious, outbreak, pestilence, plague, rash, widespread

epidemic disease, usually fatal: pestilence

epidemic over wide geographical area: pandemic

epidemic, animal: epizootic

epidemiologist's concern: disease

epidermis: skin

epigram: adage, poem, saying, statement, witticism

epigrammatic: concise, pithy, terse, witty

epilated: bald

epilepsy, mild: petit mal

epilepsy, severe: grand mal

epileptic seizure, sensation that precedes onset of: aura

epilogue: afterword, appendix, conclusion, ending, postlude, summation

episode: adventure, event, experience, incident, occurrence, passage, scene, story

episode or serial: installment

episode, minor: incident

epistle: communication, composition, letter, message, note

epistolary afterthought: postscript

epitaph: eulogy, inscription, memoriam, remembrance

epithet: appellation, description, expletive, insult, label, name, nickname, phrase, sobriquet, term, title

epitome: abbreviation, abridgment, abstract, brief, condensation, digest, exemplar, ideal, illustration, model, resume, summary, synopsis

epoch: age, era, event, interval, period, time

epoxy: resin

equable: calm, consistent, constant, easygoing, even, methodical, placid, regular, serene, smooth, stable, steady, tranquil, unchanging, unflappable, unruffled

equal: abreast, adequate, alike, balanced, coextensive, commensurate, comparative, compeer, corresponding, counterpart, equivalent, even, fair, fifty-fifty, hess, identical, level, like, match, mate, meet, on a par, par, parallel, peer, rival, same, similar, symmetrical, tantamount, unbiased

equal according to law or position: peer

equal exchange or substitution: quid pro quo

equal in amount, status, value: parity

equal in dimensions: isometric

equal in effect, value: constituting, tantamount

equal in number of parts: isomerous

equal in size, extent, duration: coextensive, commensurate, coterminous

equal in social, political status: egalitarian

equal in time intervals: isochronal

equal political power in government: isocracy

equal rights, affirming or promoting: egalitarian

equal time given in media: fairness doctrine

equality: balance, egalitarian, equity, equivalence, evenness, fairness, impartiality, isonomy, parity, uniformity

equality among racial, ethnic groups: integration

Equality State: Wyoming

equalize: balance, coordinate, equate, handicap, level, square

equanimity: aplomb, calmness, composure, control, cool, evenness, patience, poise, sang-froid, serenity, steadiness, tranquility

equate: associate, balance, compare, correspond, equalize, liken, match, relate

equestrian: horseback, horseman, horsewoman, rider

equestrian sport: polo

equestrian trotting slowly in place: piaffe

equidistant: center, central, halfway, middle

equilibrium: balance, composure, poise, stability, steadiness, symmetry

equilibrium of organism: homeostasis

equine: horse, roan

equip: accouter, appoint, arm, array, attire, deck, dress, endow, furnish, gear, outfit, prepare, provide, qualify, ready, rig, stock, supply

equipment: accessories, apparatus, armament, contraptions, fixtures, gear, goods, instruments, machinery, machines, material, outfit, paraphernalia, provisions, rig, supplies, tackle, tools

equipment and buildings: facilities

equipment and clothing: accouterments

equipment for activity: appurtenances, gear, paraphernalia

equipment for carrying on a business: stock-in-trade

equipment of medical institution or physician: armamentarium

equipped with excessive weaponry: armed to the teeth

equitable: equal, ethical, even, fair, honest, impartial, just, moral, reasonable, righteous, unbiased

equity: assets, fairness, funds, honesty, integrity, investment, justice, law, stock, value

equivalence: correspondence, equation, symmetry

equivalent: alike, comparable, counterpart, equipollent, identical, match, parallel, parity, peer, proportionate, reciprocal, same, similar, substitute, synonymous, tantamount

equivalent in effect: tantamount

equivalent person: counterpart

equivocal: ambiguous, ambivalent, clouded, doubtful, dubious, evasive, hazy, inconclusive, indecisive, muddled, obscure, questionable, uncertain, unclear, undetermined, vague

equivocate: avoid, be evasive, con, deceive, dodge, elude, escape, evade, fib, hedge, hesitate, lie, palter, parry, prevaricate, pussyfoot, quibble, sidestep, spar, tergiversate, waffle, weasel

era: age, cycle, date, epoch, generation, period, stage, term, time

era of cultural refinement: belle epoque

eradicate: abolish, annihilate, delete, demolish, deracinate, destroy, eliminate, erase, expunge, exterminate, extirpate, obliterate, raze, remove, trash, uproot

erase: abolish, annul, blank, blot, cancel, de-, dele, delete, destroy, efface, eliminate, eradicate, expunge, negate, neutralize, obliterate, remove, rub out, scratch, undo, wipe

ere: before, prior, rather

erect: assemble, build, construct, create, elevate, establish, exalt, fabricate, make, perpendicular, put up, raise, rear, rigid, standing, stiff, straight, upended, upright, vertical

erection, persistent and painful: priapism

ergo: consequently, hence, then, therefore

erode: abrade, corrode, crumble, decay, destroy, deteriorate, disintegrate, rust, wear

erotic: amatory, ardent, bawdy, carnal, erogenous, fleshy, hot, indecent, kinky, lewd, passionate, prurient, romantic, salacious, seductive, sensual, sexy, spicy, stimulating

err: blunder, bungle, deviate, flub, goof, lapse, miscalculate, misdo, misjudge, mistake, muff, sin, slip, stray, stumble, transgress, wander, wrong

errand: assignment, chore, mission, task

errand-runner: gofer

errant: astray, deviating, drifting, erratic, meandering, misbehaving, roaming, roving, shifting, straying, wandering

errata: correction, corrigenda, error list, typos

erratic: aberrant, arbitrary, bizarre, capricious, eccentric, errant, fluctuant, inconsistent, irregular, peculiar, queer, strange, uncertain, unpredictable, unstable, unusual, volatile, wacky, wandering, wayward, wild

erratically: off and on

erring: fallible

erroneous: fallacious, false, faulty, inaccurate, incorrect, inexact, misguided, misleading, mistaken, untrue, wrong

erroneous name: misnomer

erroneous placement in time: anachronism

error: blooper, blunder, boner, boot, default, fallacy, falsity, fault, flub, fluff, fumble, gaff, inaccuracy, lapse, misconception, miscue, misplay, mistake, muff, offense, oversight, slip, slipup, transgression, trespass, typo, violation, wrong

error in judgment: hamartia

error in printing of a book that will be corrected: corrigenda, erratum

error in speaking thought to disclose true feelings: Freudian slip

error in speaking, reading lines: fluff

error in typing: typo, typographical error

error or problem is attributed, imaginary creature to which: gremlin

error, to add to an: compound

errorless: impeccable

ersatz: artificial, bogus, counterfeit, fake, imitation, phony, sham, substitute, synthetic

erstwhile: bygone, earlier, former, formerly, once, preceding, previous, whilom

erudite: cultured, educated, intelligent, learned, scholarly, studious, wise

erudition: education, knowledge, learning, literacy, lore, refinement, scholarship, studiousness, wisdom

erupt: boil, burst, detonate, discharge, eject, emit, expel, explode, gush, release, spew, spout, spurt, vent

eruption: blast, commotion, ejection, explosion, inflammation, outbreak, outburst, outpouring, rush, storm

escalate: advance, amplify, ascend, broaden, climb, enlarge, expand, extend, grow, heighten, increase, intensify, mount, rise

escalator: moving staircase

escalator, flattened: conveyor, moving sidewalk

escapade: adventure, antic, caper, fling, folly, lark, prank, romp, stunt, vagary

escape: avoid, bolt, breakout, decamp, desertion, disappear, diversion, dodge, duck, elope, elude, emerge, eschew, evade, evasion, flee, fly the coop, getaway, lam, leak, liberation, miss, outflow, outlet, rescue, shake, shun, sidestepping, skip, slip, spill, tone, vamoose, vent

escape artfully: evade

escaped criminal: fugitive

escapes, entertainer who practices: escapologist

escargot: snail

eschew: abandon, abstain, avoid, escape, refrain, renounce, shun

escort: accompany, attend, attendant, beau, bodyguard, cavalier, chaperon, companion, conduct, convoy, date, entourage, gigolo, guard, guide, lead, outrider, safeguard, see, show, squire, steer, usher

escort for unmarried young women: chaperon

escort to person of rank: retinue

escort vehicles for protection, to: convoy

escritoire: davenport, desk, secretary, writing table

escutcheon: arms, crest, shield

Eskimo boot: mukluk

Eskimo ice house: igloo

Eskimo knife: ulu

Eskimo large open boat: umiak

Eskimo pullover jacket: anorak

Eskimo sled dog: husky, malamute, Siberian husky

esne: serf, slave

esoteric: abstruse, arcane, confidential, mysterious, mystic, obscure, occult, private, recondite, secret

ESP: clairvoyance, insight, intuition, perception, precognition, extrasensory perception, second sight, sixth sense, telepathy

especial: characteristic, chief, distinguished, exceptional, extraordinary, important, intimate, notable, outstanding, particular, peculiar, significant, uncommon, unique

especially: conspicuously, eminently, exclusively, expressly, mainly, primarily, principally, remarkably, singularly, specifically

espionage: reconnaissance, spying, surveillance

espouse: adopt, advocate, back, betroth, boost, champion, defend, embrace, further, marry, mate, pledge, promote, support, unite, uphold, wed

espresso topped with steamed and foamy milk or cream: cappuccino

esprit: cleverness, élan, intelligence, morale, spirit, sprightliness, vigor, zest

esprit de corps: camaraderie, fellowship, morale, solidarity

espy: detect, discern, discover, find, glimpse, notice, observe, see, sight, spot, view, watch

essay: article, composition, critique, dissertation, editorial, exposition, narrative, paper, piece, story, theme, thesis, treatise, writing

essays by colleagues as tribute to scholar: festschrift

esse: being

essence: aroma, attar, being, character, cologne, constitution, core, crux, element, existence, extract, fiber, fragrance, fundamental, gist, heart, indispensable, life, meaning, nature, odor, perfume, point, principal, quality, requisite, root, scent, significance, sine qua non, soul, spirit

essence of a thing, purest: elixir, hypostasis, quiddity, quintessence

essence of accusation: gravamen

essence of something written or spoken: burden, crux, gist, gravamen, nub, purport, tenor

essence of something, abstracted form: distillation

essence of something, concentrated: quintessence

essence or foundation: anlage, bedrock, substratum

essence or perfect example: epitome, personification

essence or pure form: distillate

essence, in Hinduism: rasa

essential: basic, chief, constitutive, elementary, fundamental, imperative, important, inherent, integral, intrinsic, key, must, prerequisite, requirement, substantive, vital

essential and basic: primordial, rudimentary

essential and obligatory: imperative, incumbent, irremissible

essential and required: compulsory, de rigueur, mandatory, prerequisite, statutory

essential as a part: indispensable, inherent, integral, intrinsic

essential element or condition: prerequisite, sine qua non

essential facts: brass tacks, core, nitty-gritty

essential part: alpha and omega, cornerstone, crux, essence, gist, heart, linchpin, pith

essential to whole: part and parcel

essentially: au fond, basically, fundamentally

establish: accomplish, appoint, approve, ascertain, base, build, clarify, colonize, confirm, constitute, corroborate, create, decree, determine, discover, document, erect, found, generate, ground, identify, initiate, install, instate, institute, organize, originate, plant, predicate, prove, provide, ratify, secure, settle, setup, show, situate, start, substantiate, validate, verify

establish definitely: determine

establish in surrounding matter: embed

establish or base (an action, etc.): predicate

established: accepted, authenticated, based, certain, ensconced, entrenched, firm, fixed, fixture, stable, substantive, underlying

established firmly and indelibly: ingrained

established firmly and long: inveterate

established norm: par

established person or thing: fixture

established rule: canon

establishment: authority, bureaucracy, business, company, concern, corporation, elite, enterprise, factory, government, house, institution, old guard, organization, plant, ruling class, the system

estate: acres, assets, belongings, bequest, bracket, class, demesne, domain, echelon, effects, endowment, fortune, ground, grounds, hacienda, holdings, home, inheritance, latifundium, legacy, manor, money, order, plantation, position, property, rank, situation, standing, status, villa, will

estate of ancient Romans: latifundium

estate of Spanish-speaking country: hacienda

estate, to limit inheritance of: entail

estate's main house: manor

esteem: account, admiration, admire, appreciate, approval, believe, cherish, consider, count, credit, deem, estimation, face, favor, high regard, honor, judge, pride, prize, reckoning, regard, repute, respect, reverence, treasure, value, venerate, worth

esteemed teacher: guru

estimable: admirable, commendable, deserving, good, honorable, laudable, meritorious, praiseworthy, respected, solid, venerable, worthy

estimate: appraisal, approximate, assay, assess, assessment, average, believe, calculate, computation, compute, consider, critique, evaluate, figure, forecast, gauge, guess, judge, opinion, prize, projection, quotation, rank, rate, reckon, surmise, survey, value

estimate based on a guess: guesstimate

estimate from evidence at hand: extrapolate

estimate of costs, prices: quote

estimate too highly: overrate

estimate value: appraise, assay, evaluate

estimate, rough: approximation

estimation: arithmetic, belief, esteem, honor, impression, judgment, regard, valuation, view

estop: bar, impede, obstruct, plug, preclude, prevent, prohibit

estrange: alienate, antagonize, disaffect, disunite, divert, divorce, part, separate, sever, split

estrangement: falling-out

estrangement by one partner: alienation of affections

estuary: arm, creek, inlet, ria

estuary, sea inlet: firth

et cetera: and, and so on, et al., etc., what not

etch: carve, draw, eat, engrave, impress, imprint, inscribe, portray, stamp

etcher's medium: acid

etching done in stages to produce several tones: aquatint

eternal: ageless, always, boundless, changeless, constant, continual, deathless, endless, enduring, everlasting, forever, immortal, infinite, interminable, lasting, neverending, perdurable, perpetual, timeless, unceasing, undying, uninterrupted

eternal damnation: hell, perdition

eternity: aeon, afterlife, age, blue moon, eon, forever, immortality, olam, perpetuity, timelessness

ether: air, anesthetic, atmosphere, compound, element, gas, heavens, skies, sky, solvent

ethereal: aerial, aery, airy, celestial, delicate, divine, filmy, fragile, heavenly, intangible, light, refined, spiritual, unearthly, vaporous

ethical: aboveboard, conscientious, equitable, honorable, just, moral, righteous, virtuous

ethical consequences of life acts: karma

ethically indifferent: amoral

ethics: belief, conduct, customs, deontology, ideal, integrity, morals, mores, principles, standards, values

ethics and moral obligation, science of: deontology

ethics philosophy that happiness is produced by active, rational life: eudemonism

ethnic: background, cultural, heathen, pagan, racial

ethnic or racial slur: ethnophaulism

etiquette: amenities, behavior, conduct, courtesy, decorum, form, formalities, manners, politeness, propriety, protocol, punctilio, usage

etiquette fine point: punctilio

etiquette of diplomats: protocol

etiquette violation: solecism

etymology: derivation, history, origin, word origin

eucalyptus eater: koala

eucalyptus secretion: larp

Eucharist: communion, oblation, sacrament

Eucharist celebration: mass

Eucharist container: ampulla, chalice, ciborium, cruet, monstrance, ostensory, pyx

Eucharist just before death: viaticum

Eucharist plate: paten

Eucharist wine flagon: ama

Euclidean statement: axiom

eulogize: bless, celebrate, exalt, extol, glorify, honor, laud

eulogy: acclaim, address, commendation, encomium, homage, oration, paean, panegyric, praise, salutation, tribute

euphemism antonym: dysphemism

euphony: accord, harmony, melody, rhythm, sound

euphoria: bliss, ecstasy, elation, exhilaration, happiness, jubilation, well-being

Europe and Western Hemisphere: Occident

evacuate: abandon, clear, decamp, desert, empty, expel, flee, hightail, leave, remove, vacate

evade: avert, avoid, bypass, ditch, dodge, duck, elude, equivocate, escape, eschew, hedge, hide, maneuver, parry, pussyfoot, shirk, shun, sidestep

evade an obligation: shirk

evaluate: appraise, ascertain, assess, check, consider, criticize, estimate, grade, judge, rank, rate, survey, test, weigh

evaluate a metal sample: assay

evaluate expertly: vet

evaluation: analysis, appraisal, assay, critique, estimation, interpretation, judgment, opinion

evaluation as response: feedback

evaluation, subjective: value judgment

evanesce: disappear, dissipate, dissolve, evaporate, fade, vanish

evanescent: ephemeral, evasive, fleeting, fugitive, melting, temporary, transient, transitory, vanishing

evangelist: apostle, disciple, missionary, preacher, revivalist

evaporate: dehydrate, disappear, dissolve, dry up, evanesce, melt, steam, vaporize

evaporating and thickening: inspissated

evaporating at normal temperature: volatile

evasion by explanation or justification: song and dance

evasion of painful emotion with unconscious mental devices: defense mechanism

evasion of truth by using trivia: quibble

evasion that gains time, avoids argument, postpones decision: temporization

evasive: ambiguous, cagey, deceitful, devious, elusive, elusory, noncommittal, prevarication, shifty, slippery, sly, tricky, unclear, vague

evasive language: double-talk

evasiveness: equivocation, prevarication, tergiversation

eve: dusk, evening, sundown, sunset

even: abreast, aline, balanced, consistent, continuous, direct, equal, equitable, exact, fair, flat, flatten, flush, grade, homogeneous, impartial, indeed, just, level, match, moderate, on a par, parallel, placid, proportional, regular, smooth, square, stable, steady, still, tie, tied, uniform

even along margin: flush

even chance: toss-up

even horizontally: complanate, level

even if, for short: tho

even temper: equilibrium

even the score: avenge, reciprocate

evening: bedtime, dusk, eve, eventide, nightfall, sundown, sunset, twilight

evening meal: supper

evening party: soiree

evening prayers: vespers, vigils

evening star: Hesperus, Venus

evening, pertaining to: crepuscular, vespertine

evenly divided, in card playing: easy honors

event: achievement, adventure, affair, case, catastrophe, celebration, competition, consequence, contest, disaster, doing, experience, fact, fate, feat, game, happening, incident, landmark, match, meet, milestone, miracle, occasion, occurrence, offshoot, outcome, phenomenon, result, scenario, tournament

event in one's life or history, important: landmark, milestone

eventful: busy, crucial, exciting, fateful, important, memorable, momentous, newsy, notable, significant

eventual: concluding, ensuing, final, future, inevitable, later, possible, resulting, ultimate

eventually: finally, in the end, someday, sometime, ultimately, yet

eventuate: come true

ever: always, anytime, consistently, constantly, continually, eternally, forever, invariably, perpetually, usually

everday speech: vernacular, vulgate

evergreen: conifer, enduring, holly, mistletoe, oleander, pine

evergreen variety: cedar, fir, heath, hemlock, juniper, larche, laurel, rhododendron, savin, spruce, yew

everlasting: ageless, constant, continual, durable, endless, enduring, eternal, eternity, forever, immortal, imperishable, incessant, infinite, lasting, perdurable, perennial, perpetual, tedious, timeless, unceasing, undying, uninterrupted

everlasting, poetically: eterne

every: all, each, entire, equally, whole

every two months: bimestrial

every two weeks: biweekly

everybody in agreement: unanimous

everyday: common, commonplace, customary, daily, mundane, ordinary, plain, routine, unimaginative, usual

everyday language: prose

everyday speech: vernacular, vulgate

everything: aggregate, all, total

everything about one thing, person who knows: monomath

everywhere: all along the line, all over the world, extensively, high and low, near and far, omnipresent, prevalent, throughout, worldwide

everywhere, present: omnipresent, ubiquitous

evict: bounce, dismiss, dispossess, eject, expel, oust, remove

evidence: attest, clue, display, documentation, exhibit, goods, hearsay, illustrate, indicate, manifest, proof, show, testament, testimony, token, trace, witness

evidence appropriate for legal case: forensic evidence

evidence at trial disclosed by defendant: discovery

evidence based on reports of others: hearsay

evidence establishing a fact if uncontested: prima facie evidence

evidence given under oath: deposition

evidence impossible to dispute, of: incontrovertible

evidence not bearing directly on the fact in dispute: circumstantial evidence

evidence of a fact, condition: sign, symptom

evidence of wrongdoing: smoking gun

evidence of, to supply or be: attest, testify

evidence or information, written or printed: document

evidence submitted in court: exhibit

evidence under oath, giving of false: perjury

evidence without proof or reasoning: prima facie

evidence, strengthen or support with other: corroborate, substantiate

evidence, to support with: document

evident: apparent, certain, clear, conclusive, conspicuous, glaring, manifest, noticeable, obvious, overt, patent, plain, transparent, unmistakable, visible

evil: affliction, bad, baleful, bane, base, calamity, corrupt, crime, curse, damnable, demoniac, depraved, devilish, disaster, flagitious, foul, harm, heinous, heinousness, hideous, hurtful, immoral, iniquity, malefic, malevolent, malicious, mean, mischief, misfortune, nefarious, offensive, pernicious, satanic, sin, sinful, sinister, vice, vicious, vile, wicked, wickedness, worthless, wrong

evil and treacherous person: shaitan, snake in the grass

evil eye: hex, jinx, leer, stare, whammy

evil influence, having: maleficent, malevolent, malicious, malign, malignant, pernicious

evil notoriety: infamy

evil omen: foreboding, portent

evil spirit: cacodemon, daemon, demon, devil, incubus, Satan, succubus

evil spirit, cast out: exorcise

evil spirit, person possessed by: demoniac, energumen

evil, a monstrous: enormity

evil, extremely: flagitious, heinous, infamous, nefarious

evil, intended to ward off: apotropaic

evil, portending: baleful

evil, spreading: canker

evildoer: criminal, crook, felon, malefactor, miscreant, sinner, transgressor, villain

evildoing: foul play

evilness: depravity, iniquity, turpitude

evince: demonstrate, disclose, display, exhibit, express, indicate, manifest, prove, reveal, show

evoke: arouse, awaken, call, educe, elicit, excite, induce, recall, rouse, stimulate, summon

evolution: advancement, change, development, flowering, growth, metamorphosis, ontogeny, phylogeny, progress, transformation

evolution theory of Bible: creationism

evolutionary development of individual: ontogeny

evolutionary development of species: phylogenesis, phylogeny

evolve: derive, develop, devise, emerge, emit, expand, germinate, grow, increase, mature, ripen, unfold

evolving at standard rate: horotelic

evolving faster: tachytelic

evolving slowly: bradytelic

ewe: female sheep

ewer: container, decanter, jug, pitcher, urn, vessel

exacerbate: aggravate, anger, annoy,

enrage, exasperate, increase, infuriate, ire, irritate, provoke, tease, worsen

exact: accurate, careful, certain, command, compel, correct, critical, demand, distinct, elicit, enforce, even, explicit, extort, extract, fine, formal, identical, levy, literal, methodical, meticulous, painstaking, precise, punctilious, require, scrupulous, sharp, specific, square, true, verbatim, wreak, wrest

exact copy: clone, facsimile, reproduction

exact divisor or factor of quantity: aliquot

exact in detail: punctilious, scrupulous

exact in words: literal

exact opposite: antipode

exact statement of particulars: specifications, specs

exacting: arduous, burdensome, demanding, difficult, direct, finicky, fussy, onerous, particular, picky, pressing, rigorous, severe, stern, strict, stringent, taxing, trying

exactly: absolutely, accurately, altogether, assuredly, certainly, entirely, faithfully, fully, just, literally, positively, quite, right, specifically, truly

exactly right: on target

exactly upright: perpendicular

exaggerate: amplify, boast, brag, color, distort, embellish, embroider, enlarge, fabricate, inflate, magnify, overdo, overstate

exaggerate illness or incapacity: malinger

exaggerate story: embroider

exaggerated: histrionic, lied, melodramatic, overblown, overdone, tall

exaggerated drawing: caricature

exaggerated in emotion: histrionic, melodramatic

exaggerated masculinity: machismo

exaggerated praise: puffery

exaggerated statement: hyperbole

exaggerated trait or behavior: eccentricity, idiosyncrasy, mannerism

exaggeration: aggrandizement, hyperbole

exalt: acclaim, aggrandize, applaud, commend, dignify, distinguish, elate, extol, glorify, heighten, honor, inspire, intensify, laud, magnify, praise, promote, raise, uplift, worship

exaltation: bliss, delight, ecstasy, euphoria, jubilation, rapture, transport, veneration

exalted: high, noble, sublime

examination: analysis, assay, audit, autopsy, biopsy, blue book, catechism, checkup, comparison, exam, exploration, final, inquiry, inspection, interrogation, introspection, investigation, midterm, oral, quiz, research, review, scrutiny, survey, test, X ray

examination in detail: canvass

examination of complete event: post mortem

examination of one's feelings: introspection, soul-searching

examination of prospective witnesses, jurors: voir dire

examination of tissue removed: biopsy

examination or investigation: inquisition

examination, oral: viva voce

examination, study intensely for impending: cram

examination, to supervise: invigilate, monitor, proctor

examine: ask, canvass, check, dissect, explore, grill, inquire, inspect, look at, observe, palpate, peruse, ponder, scan, screen, scrutinize, search, sift, study, test, view, weigh

examine and authenticate: vet

examine by touching for diagnosis: palpate

examine carefully: peruse, scrutinize, traverse, winnow

examine for value: appraise, assess

examine formally or officially: cross-examine, interrogate

examine good and bad parts: sift, winnow

examine in detail: dissect, plumb

examine surreptitiously: case

examiner: analyst, appraiser, auditor, censor, coroner, critic, inquirer, inspector, interrogator, investigator, reviewer, teacher, tester

example: case, copy, description, epitome, ideal, illustration, instance, lesson, model, paradigm, pattern, precedent, prototype, sample, specimen, standard

example in practical terms: object lesson

example in similar circumstance, action or instance used as: precedent

example of class, type, quality: byword

example of excellence: paragon

example of, to be a good: embody, epitomize, exemplify, typify

example or ideal: archetype, avatar, epitome, exemplar, incarnation

example that is standard: paradigm

example, to cite as an: adduce

examples, used to introduce: vidielicet, viz

exasperate: aggravate, agitate, annoy, bother, disturb, enrage, exacerbate, excite, gall, incense, inflame, irritate, nettle, provoke, rile, ruffle, tire, upset

excavate: burrow, dig, dredge, hollow, mine, scoop, shovel, tunnel, unearth

excavation, archaeological: dig

exceed: beat, best, better, excel, outdo, outgo, outrun, outshine, overdo, overshoot, overstep, overtake, pass, preponderate, surmount, surpass, transcend

exceed and excel: outstrip, surpass, trump

exceeding all bounds: exorbitant, extortionate

exceedingly: enormously, everso, exceptionally, excessively, extremely, greatly, remarkably, strikingly, very

excel: best, better, exceed, outclass, outdo, outrival, outstrip, shine, star, superior, surpass, take the cake, transcend

excellence: class, distinction, greatness, marksmanship, merit, perfection, quality, superiority, supremacy, virtue, worth

excellence, example of: paragon

excellent: admirable, A1, blue-chip, bravo, bully, capital, classic, famous, fine, first rate, generous, good, great, magnificent, matchless, nifty, outstanding, peerless, prime, select, spiffy, sterling, stupendous, super, superb, superior, superlative, terrific, top-notch, tops, transcendent, unparalleled, unrivaled, valuable, wonderful, worthy

excellent and first-rate: copacetic

excellent and wonderful: stupendous, sublime

excellent as example: exemplary

excellent in quality: vintage

excellent review: rave

excelling: outstanding, preeminent, transcendent

except: ban, bar, besides, eliminate, exclude, exempt, however, omit, only, reject, save, than, unless

exception: allowance, anomaly, complaint, demur, exclusion, oddity, offense, omission, quirk

exceptional: A1, abnormal, extraordinary, fine, irregular, noteworthy, outstanding, phenomenal, prodigious, rare, remarkable, special, superior, unique, unparalleled, unprecedented, unusual, wonderful

exceptional performance: tour de force

excerpt: cite, extract, part, passage, portion, quote, sample, section, selection

excerpts, literary: analects

excess: extra, flood, glut, gravy, intemperance, lavishness, nimiety, over, overabundance, overboard, overflow, overindulgence, overkill, plethora, plus, prodigality, profusion, remainder, residue, slack, superfluity, superfluous, surfeit, surplus

excess eating, drinking: surfeit

excess money, value, or merchandise: overage

excess word, phrase: pleonasm

excessive: copious, enormous, exorbitant, extravagant, extreme, exuberant, fulsome, immoderate, indulgent, inordinate, intemperate, needless, overdone, overmuch, overweening, redundant, supererogatory, superfluous, supernumerary, too, ultra, unconscionable, undue, unreasonable, wanton

excessive attention, object of: fetish

excessive response: overkill, overreaction

excessive talking: logorrhea

excessively anxious: neurotic

excessively enthusiastic: gaga

excessively fat: obese

excessively flattering: fulsome

excessively sentimental: schmaltz

exchange: bandy, barter, commerce, commute, conversion, deal, dicker, market, network, quid pro quo, reciprocate, replacement, store, substitute, swap, switch, trade, traffic, transpose, truck

exchange and mutual granting: reciprocity

exchange goods or services directly: barter

exchange or interchange: reciprocate

exchange premium: agio

exchange, even: quid pro quo

exchange, informally: swap

exchange, public place for: forum

exchange, to make an: commute

excise: assessment, charge, dele, delete, duty, edit, eradicate, erase, exscind, extirpate, extract, levy, omit, remove, surcharge, tariff, tax, toll

excitable: emotional, enthusiastic, hysterical, jumpy, skittish, volatile, volcanic

excite: agitate, animate, arouse, awaken, elaye, electrify, elicit, energize, fire, foment, galvanize, incite, inflame, inspire, invigorate, kindle, move, prime, provoke, rouse, spur, stimulate, stir, thrill, titillate, upset

excite and enliven: galvanize, quicken, whet

excite interest: pique

excite pleasurably: titillate

excite to frenzy: intoxicate

excite with chemical substance: inebriate, intoxicate

excited: agog, aroused, atip, charged, delighted, eager, ecstatic, elated, fevered, frantic, frenzied, gaga, heated, hot, piqued

excited and confused: frantic, frenetic, frenzied, hectic

excited, very: ebullient, exuberant

excited, wildly: frantic, frenetic, frenzied

excitement: action, ado, adventure, commotion, confusion, disturbance, fillip, flap, flurry, furor, hubbub, hullabaloo, hysteria, stir, tingling, turmoil

exciting: breathtaking, dazzling, exhilarating, heady, provocative, spicy

exclaim: assert, blurt, declare, ejaculate, proclaim, roar, shout, utter, vociferate

exclamation: aha, ahem, alas, bah, boo, bravo, drat, egad, eureka, expletive, fie, gee, hallelujah, hosanna, humph, hurrah, indeed, interjection, man alive, o ho, oh, outcry, pah, phew, pish, pshaw, rats, ugh, ughs, wow

exclamation mark: bang, screamer

exclamation mark and question mark: interrobang

exclamation point: ecphoneme

exclamation, obscene or vulgar: expletive

exclamation, one-word: interjection

exclude: ban, banish, bar, blackball, blacklist, boycott, debar, eject, eliminate, except, expel, omit, ostracize, preclude, prohibit, reject, relegate, shut out

exclude from church membership: excommunicate

exclude from church sacraments and services: interdict

exclude from group: blackball, blacklist, ostracize

exclude or exile: relegate

exclusion: ostracism, purdah

exclusion from one's mind: repression, suppression

exclusive: alone, aloof, chic, cliquish, complete, discriminative, elite, esoteric, expensive, independent, limitative, monopoly, posh, private, rare, rarefied, restricted, select, selective, single, snobbish, sole, swank, undivided, whole

exclusive control by one group: monopoly

exclusive control of service, product: monopoly

exclusive group of friends, associates: clique

exclusive right claimed: perquisite

exclusive treatment: elitism

excommunicate: anathema, ban, banish, defrock, expel, unchurch

excoriate: abrade, assail, chafe, chastise, condemn, criticize, denounce, flay, gall, lambaste, scold, strip

excrement: dejecta, feces

excrement of animals: scats

excrement of insects: frass

excrement, fossilized: coprolite

excrement, human, used as fertilizer: night soil

excrement, pertaining to: stercoraceous

excrement, study of: scatology

excrescence: accretion, enlargement, knob, lump, outgrowth, pimple, wart

excrete: defecate, egest, emit, evacuate

excruciating: acute, agonizing, extreme, grueling, harrowing, intense, painful, severe, shooting, tormenting, torturous, unbearable

exculpate: absolve, acquit, amnesty, clear, dismiss, excuse, exonerate, forgive, free, pardon, release, vindicate

excursion: cruise, digression, diversion, expedition, hike, jaunt, journey, junket, outing, ride, safari, sail, sortie, tour, trek, trip, voyage, walk

excusable: allowable, forgivable, justifiable, pardonable, permissible, venial, warrantable

excuse: absolve, acquit, alibi, apology, condone, defend, discharge, exculpate, exempt, exonerate, explain, forgive, indulge, justify, out, pardon, plea, pretext, release, remit, vindicate

excuse from regulation: dispense, exempt

excuse offered: pretext

excuse or clear of accusation: acquit, exempt, exonerate, vindicate

excuse or explanation to avoid blame: alibi

excuse or reason for existing: raison d'être

excuse or reason, to devise self-satisfying: rationalize

excuse or saving clause: salvo

excuse that clears from blame: exculpation

excuse, in law: mise

excuse, to devise an: concoct

excuses, to lessen or attempt to lessen blame with: extenuate, mitigate

execrable: abhorrent, abominable, atrocious, awful, bad, base, deplorable, detestable, foul, hateful, heinous, horrifying, repulsive, revolting, sickening, vile

execrate: abhor, curse, damn, denounce, despise, detest, hate, imprecate, loathe

execute: accomplish, act, administer, cause, complete, conduct, direct, enact, enforce, finish, implement, manage, obey, perform; assassinate, behead, electrocute, gas, guillotine, hang, kill, lynch, murder, slay

execution: completion, consummation, doing, fulfillment, garrote, killing, realization, strangulation, transaction

execution by beheading: guillotine

execution by strangulation: garrote

execution platform: scaffold

executive: administrator, businessperson, CEO, dean, director, entrepreneur, governing, head, manager, officer, official, president, ruling, supervisor, VIP

executive's lavish severance benefits: golden parachute

executor: administrator, agent, doer, enforcer

exegesis: analysis, critique, explanation, exposition, interpretation

exemplary: admirable, admonitory, classical, commendable, honorable, ideal, illustrative, model, praiseworthy, sterling, typical

exemplify: clarify, demonstrate, depict, embody, epitomize, personify, represent, symbolize, typify

exempt: absolved, clear, discharge, excepted, exclude, excuse, exonerate, free, immune, pardoned, release, relieved, spare

exemption due to being diplomat: diplomatic immunity

exemption from legal duties, penalties, liability: immunity

exemption from legal liability for damages: indemnity

exemption from punishment, penalty: impunity

exemption from rule, obligation: dispensation

exercise: activity, aerobics, athletics, bestow, calisthenics, ceremony, condition, discipline, display, drill, effort, employ, exert, exertion, exhibition, gymnastics, isometrics, lesson, maneuver, operation, parade, performance, practice, praxis, prepare, problem, provoke, push-up, school, sit-up, study, task, train, utilize, workout, yoga

exercise for cardiovascular conditioning: aerobics

exercise for muscle tone, grace: calisthenics

exercise preparation: warm-up

exercise ropes: longes

exercise system: regimen

exercise system for body and mind control: yoga

exercise with muscle contraction while lengthening: isotonic exercise

exercise with muscle pushing against object, no motion: isometric exercise

exercise, heavy stuffed ball used in conditioning: medicine ball

exercise, to work at: condition

exert: apply, drive, employ, exercise, expend, force, strain, strive, thrust, wield

exertion: action, attempt, dint, effort, elbow grease, endeavor, energy, labor, pains, power, pull, strength, struggle, toil, trouble, work

exertions: dints

exhale: breathe, emit, evaporate, expel, expire, puff, respire, steam

exhaust: bankrupt, deplete, discharge, do in, drain, empty, expend, fatigue, fumes, gases, impoverish, overdo, squander, tire, tucker, use up, weaken, wear

exhaust duct: vent

exhaust emitted into air: emission

exhaust system reducing pollution: catalytic converter

exhausted: all in, beat, bushed, consumed, dead, debilitated, depleted, dog-tired, done, drained, effete, emptied, enervated, finished, frazzled, jaded, pooped, ran out, spend, spent, tired, used up, weakened, weary, worn

exhausted and lying flat: prostrate

exhaustive: complete, comprehensive, extensive, intensive, sweeping, thorough

exhibit: air, demonstrate, disclose, display, evidence, evince, expose, fair, feature, flaunt, manifest, ostend, parade, perform, performance, present, reveal, show, showcase, viewing

exhibit ostentatiously: flaunt

exhibit to advantage: showcase

exhibit, three-dimensional: diorama

exhibition: ceremony, contest, display, drill, event, expo, exposition, march, offering, pageant, showcase, sight, spectacle

exhibition covering a career or history: retrospective

exhilarate: animate, cheer, delight, elate, enliven, excite, inspire, invigorate, stimulate, uplift

exhilaration: ecstasy, euphoria, gaiety, gladness, jollity, joyousness, liveliness, refreshment

exhort: admonish, advise, caution, encourage, goad, incite, persuade, plead, preach, press, prod, spur, urge, warn

exhume: dig, disinter, unbury, uncover, unearth

exigency: crisis, difficulty, dilemma, emergency, fix, jam, juncture, necessity, need, pickle, pinch, plight, quandary, requirement

exigent: critical, crucial, demanding, dire, imperative, necessary, pressing, rigorous, taxing, urgent, vital

exiguous: diminutive, inadequate, little, meager, petty, scanty, skimpy, slender, small, spare, sparse, tiny

exile: banish, banishment, deport, eject, expatriate, expel, expulsion, fugitive, nonperson, ostracize, oust, outcast, outlaw, proscribe, refugee

exist: are, breathe, continue, endure, in here, last, lie, live, maintain, remain, survive

existence: actuality, animation, being, entity, esse, essence, journey, life, reality

existence to, ascribe material: hypostatize

existence, fact of: being, entity

existence, having actual: objective

existence, keep in: maintain, sustain

existence, to treat as having material: reify

existing: alive, extant, surviving

existing at the same time: contemporaneous

existing state of affairs: status quo

exists as discrete unit, something that: entity

exit: avenue, departure, door, egress, evacuation, exodus, gate, going, leave, opening, outlet, passage, retire, retreat, split, vent, way out, withdrawal

exodus: emigration, escape, exit, flight, leaving, migration

exonerate: absolve, acquit, clear, clearn, disburden, dismiss, exculpate, excuse, exempt, forgive, free, pardon, release, vindicate

exorbitant: abnormal, enormous, excessive, expensive, extravagant, outrageous, overpriced, preposterous, steep, undue, unreasonable

exorbitant charge: extortion

exotic: alien, alluring, different, elaborate, enticing, fantastic, foreign, kinky, mysterious, outlandish, romantic, strange, striking, unusual

expand: add, amplify, augment, balloon, broaden, develop, dilate, distend, diversify, elaborate, enhance, enlarge, escalate, expatiate, explicate, extend, grow, increase, inflate, lengthen, magnify, multiply, mushroom, open, spread, stretch, swell, unfold, widen

expand and explain: amplify, elaborate, expatiate

expand interests or activities: diversify

expand or widen: dilate

expand step-by-step: escalate

expanding with age, after flowering: accrescent

expanse: acres, area, breadth, distance, domain, extent, gulf, ocean, plain, range, reach, region, scope, sea, space, span, spread, stretch, sweep, territory, tract

expansion: development, dilatation, enlargement, extension, growth, increase, proliferation, widening

expansive: ample, broad, communicative, comprehensive, demonstrative, effusive, elastic, extensive, extroverted, free, generous, genial, grand, great, gregarious, large, lavish, outgoing, spacious, talkative, vast, widespread

expatiate: amplify, descant, elaborate, enlarge, expound, ramble, rant, sermonize, wander

expatriate: banish, deport, displace, emigrant, exile, expel, oust, outcast, refugee, relegate

expect: anticipate, assume, await, calculate, deem, demand, envision, feel, forecast, foresee, guess, hope, look forward to, presume, reckon, sense, suppose, think, want

expectant: agog, alert, atip, eager, hopeful, pregnant, waiting, watchful

expectantly: with bated breath

expectation: anticipation, belief, hope, likelihood, possibility, prospect

expectorated matter: sputum

expedient: advantageous, advisable, appropriate, beneficial, makeshift, method, opportune, politic, possible, profitable, proper, resource, scheme, stopgap, useful, wise, worthwhile

expedient and wise: politic

expedite: accelerate, advance, dispatch, ease, efficient, facilitate, hasten, hurry, press, quicken, rush, speed

expedition: advance, anabasis, crusade, excursion, exploration, haste, jaunt, journey, mission, patrol, promptness, quest, safari, speed, tour, trek, trip, voyage

expeditious: fast

expeditiously: in short order

expel: banish, deport, discharge, dislodge, dismiss, drive, eject, eliminate, evict, exclude, exile, expatriate, oust, pass, remove, spew

expel from one's native land: exile

expend: consume, disburse, dissipate, distribute, drain, exhaust, indulge, spend, squander, use, waste

expendable: disposable, excess, forgoable, nonessential, replaceable

expenditure: cost, disbursement, expense, outgo, outlay, payment

expenditures, regulated: sumptuary

expense: charge, cost, debt, expenditure, forfeiture, loss, outlay, overhead, price, risk, sacrifice, upkeep

expense allowance for day: per diem

expense of running business: overhead

expenses, of minor: incidental

expensive: costly, dear, exorbitant, extravagant, high-priced, lavish, overpriced, posh, pricey, steep, upscale, valuable

expensive possession that is financial burden to maintain: white elephant

experience: adventure, affair, background, behold, encounter, endure, event, exposure, feel, feeling, have, involvement, know, know-how, knowledge, live, maturity, ordeal, seasoning, sense, skill, suffer, sustain, taste, training, trial, undergo, view, wisdom

experience again: relive

experience and intuition as independent entities: transcendental

experience as source of knowledge: empiricism

experience in saying and doing the right thing: savoir faire

experience of unexpected change or shift in life: vicissitude

experience, difficult or painful: ordeal

experience, familiar with by: au fait, conversant

experience, unpleasant: mauvais quart d'heure

experienced: able, accustomed, adept, competent, expert, familiar, knew, old, practiced, professional, qualified, seasoned, sophisticated, tested, tried, veteran, wise, worldly, worldly-wise

experienced person: trouper, veteran

experienced through another: vicarious

experiment: analyze, assay, check, exercise, investigate, observation, probe, research, search, test, trial

experiment subject: guinea pig

experiment, derived from: a posteriori, empirical, inductive

experimental: contingent, developmental, empirical, exploratory, preliminary, tentative

expert: ace, adept, adroit, artist, authority, capable, connoisseur, consultant, deft, experienced, gourmet, master, maven, oner, past master, pro, professional, proficient, pundit, schooled, skilled, specialist, virtuoso

expert adviser: consultant

expert in fine food and drink: connoisseur, gourmet

expert in the arts: maestro

expert information, source of: authority

expert person: connoisseur, maven, mavin

expert with specialized knowledge: cognoscente

expertise, superficial: sciolism

experts who serve as advisers or planners, group of: brain trust

expiate: amend, appease, atone, forgive, reconcile, rectify

expiration: death, elapsing, exhalation, finish, passing, termination

expire: cease, die, emit, end, expel, lapse, perish, quit, stop

explain: annotate, clarify, construe, decipher, define, describe, elaborate, elucidate, expand, explicate, expound, illuminate, interpret, justify, manifest, rationalize, simplify, translate, unfold, unravel

explain actions in self-satisfying way: rationalize

explain in detail: elaborate, expatiate

explainer, critical and scholarly: exegete

explanation: account, answer, apology, brief, cause, commentary, exegesis, explication, exposition, history, meaning, motive, reason, statement

explanation for unknown should be attempted in terms of what is already known: law of parsimony, Ockham's razor

explanation of a statement: construction

explanation of a text, critical: exegesis

explanation of broad subject: rubric

explanation that awaits proof: hypothesis, theorem, theory, working hypothesis

explanation, detailed: explication

explanatory: exponent, expository

explanatory comment: parenthesis

explanatory material: epexegesis

explanatory note: commentary, definition, gloss, glossary

explanatory part of map, chart, illustration: legend

expletive: curse, exclamation, oath, swear

explicate: annotate, clarify, construe, expand, explain, expound, interpret, unfold

explicit: absolute, accurate, categoric, categorical, clear, definite, defini-

tive, direct, exact, express, frank, obvious, open, plain, pointed, positive, precise, specific, unambiguous, unequivocal, unmistakable

explode: blast, burst, deflate, detonate, discharge, disprove, dynamite, erupt, mushroom, pop, refute, shatter, spring, thunder

exploding star: nova

exploit: abuse, achievement, act, adventure, advertise, bilk, bleed, coup, deed, feat, gest, geste, manipulate, milk, misuse, promote, stunt, take advantage of, use, utilize

exploration: recce, reconnaissance

exploration, military-like: reconnaissance

explore: analyze, chart, examine, investigate, probe, prospect, question, research, scout, search, survey, test, try

explore for minerals or ore: prospect

explorer by water: navigator

explosion: blast, bomb, clap, detonation, discharge, eruption, ignition, outburst, pop

explosive: amatol, ammunition, bomb, charge, cherry bomb, critical, dangerous, dynamite, eruptive, fireworks, fulminate, grenade, guncotton, lyddite, mine, missile, nitroglycerin, payload, powder, propellant, stormy, strained, tense, tetryl, TNT, unstable, volatile

explosive force of one million metric tons of TNT: megaton

explosive liquid: nitroglycerin

explosive place or situation: powder keg, tinderbox

exponent: advocate, backer, booster, example, illustration, protagonist, supporter, symbol

expose: bare, broadcast, detray, disclose, discover, display, divulge, endanger, exhibit, feature, flaunt, jeopardize, open, publish, reveal, risk, strip, unclothe, uncover, unearth, unfold, unmask

expose corruption or possible corruption: muckrake

expose to public abuse: pillory

expose to sunlight: insolate

expose wrongdoing: blow the whistle

exposed: bared, liable, overt, prone, susceptible, unprotected, vulnerable

exposition: account, analysis, article,

bazaar, commentary, editorial, essay, exegesis, exhibition, explanation, fair, mart, piece, report, show

expository essay: treatise

expostulate: argue, debate, demand, discuss, dispute, dissuade, object, oppose, protest, remonstrate

exposure: confession, danger, discovery, divulgence, hazard, liability, orientation, outlook, publicity, revelation, unmasking, vulnerability

expound: clarify, construe, define, describe, elucidate, explain, explicate, express, illustrate, interpret, state

express: articulate, certain, convey, couch, declare, definite, denote, depict, describe, dictate, exhibit, expatiate, explicit, expound, manifest, phrase, show, signify, speak, state, symbolize, vent, ventilate, voice; direct, fast, nonstop, rapid, swift

express an opinion: opine

express effusively: emote

express in coherent verbal form: articulate, enunciate, verbalize

express in gestures: gesticulate

expressing by negating something's opposite: litotes

expressing much in a word or phrase: holophrastic

expression: assertion, atticism, cliché, communication, delineation, diction, emotion, euphemism, form, frown, gesture, grimace, grin, idiom, intonation, laconism, language, manifestation, modulation, motto, phrase, remark, show, sign, smile, smirk, sneer, statement, symbol, term, token, trope, voice, wince, word

expression in everyday language: colloquialism

expression of solemn ratification: amen

expression or inflection of voice: modulation

expression or manner: mien

expression used by particular person or group: locution

expression, choice of: diction

expression, concise: atticism

expression, figurative: trope

expression, manner of speaking or: parlance, phraseology

expression, overused: cliché

expression, roundabout: circumlocution, periphrasis

expressionless: blank, deadpan, dull, empty, enigmatic, impassive, inscrutable, poker-faced, stolid, stony, unfathomable, vacant, vacuous, wooden

expressive: colorful, demonstrative, dramatic, eloquent, evocative, graphic, lively, meaningful, passionate, poetic, revealing, significant, telling, vivid

expressive and demonstrative: effusive, gushing

expressly: clearly, definitely, explicitly, just, plainly, purposely, specially, unequivocally

expressway: freeway, highway, interstate, road, superhighway, thruway, turnpike

expropriate: commandeer, confiscate, impound, seize, take, usurp

expulsion: banishment, debarment, dismissal, ejection, eviction, exile, ousting, removal, suspension

expunge: annihilate, cancel, dele, delete, destroy, efface, eliminate, eradicate, erase, obliterate, remove

expunged, as from a record: stricken

expurgate: bleep, blip, blue-pencil, bowdlerize, censor, dele, edit, purge, screen

exquisite: attractive, beautiful, careful, charming, choice, dainty, delicate, delicious, elegant, excellent, flawless, impeccable, intense, keen, nice, outstanding, precious, rare, recherché, refined, striking

extant: alive, existing, present, surviving

extemporaneous: ad-lib, impromptu, improvised, informal, offhand, spontaneous, unpremeditated

extemporize: ad-lib

extend: accord, adulterate, amplify, augment, bestow, broaden, bulge, come, continue, deepen, dilate, display, elongate, enlarge, expand, grant, grow, holdout, increase, lengthen, offer, outstretch, perpetuate, proffer, prolong, protract, protrude, range, rise, span, spread, stretch, supplement, unbend, widen

extend or bridge: span

extended trip: tour

extension: addition, amplification, annex, area, arm, branch, delay, duration, enlargement, outgrowth, postponement, reach, reprieve, scope, spread, stay, wing

extensive: ample, broad, capacious, comprehensive, immense, large, major, prevalent, sizable, spacious, sweeping, thorough, vast, wide, widespread

extensive plain in South America: llano

extent: amount, area, assessment, body, breadth, bulk, degree, dimension, distance, duration, encompass, expanse, increase, intensity, latitude, limit, magnitude, measure, quantity, range, reach, scope, size, space, spread, sweep, territory, width, writ

extent of loss: toll

extent of power, function: purview, scope

extenuate: alleviate, palliate

extenuating: diminishing, justifying, lessening, mitigating, palliating, qualifying

exterior: coating, ectal, external, facade, outer, outermost, outside, rind, shell, surface

exterior angle of wall: coign, quoin

exterminate: abolish, annihilate, decimate, destroy, eliminate, eradicate, extinguish, extirpate, fumigate, kill, massacre

extermination, systematic and planned: genocide

external: exterior, extrinsic, foreign, out, outer, outside, peripheral, superficial, visible

external origin, of: exogenous, extraneous, extrinsic

extinct: antiquated, archaic, bygone, dead, defunct, disappeared, extinguished, gone, lost, obsolete, vanished

extinct bird: dodo, moa

extinct elephant-like mammal: mastodon

extinct, not: extant

extinguish: abolish, annihilate, cancel, destroy, douse, eclipse, eliminate, end, expunge, nullify, quash, quell, quench, smother, snuff, stifle, suffocate, suppress, trample

extirpate: abolish, annihilate, demolish, destroy, eradicate, erase, excise, expel, exterminate, extract, remove, uproot, weed

extol: applaud, bless, celebrate, commend, compliment, eulogize, exalt, glorify, laud, praise

extort: cheat, coerce, elicit, exact, extract, flay, force, intimidate, squeeze, wrench, wrest

extortion: blackmail, chantage, graft, payoff, pressure, racket, ransom, shakedown

extra: accessory, added, additional, ancillary, lagniappe, leftover, more, odd, over, plus, reserve, spare, special, stand-in, superfluous, superior, supervenient, supplemental, supplementary, surplus, unusually

extra card in a deck: joker

extra charge: surcharge

extra day of leap year: bissextile day

extra or excessive: supererogatory, superfluous

extra or unexpected gift: lagniappe

extra payment: bonus

extra personnel or equipment sent: reinforcements

extra text added: addendum, afterthought, annex, appendix, postscript, supplement

extra time: leeway

extra tire: spare

extra work benefit: fringe benefit, perk, perquisite

extract: cite, concentrate, cull, decoction, deduce, draw, educe, elicit, elute, essence, evoke, exact, excerpt, exhaust, extort, gather, obtain, quotation, quote, remove, select, separate, squeeze, withdraw, wring

extract flavor by boiling: decoct

extract from Bible: pericope

extract from publication or entertainment: excerpt

extract or chunk: gobbet, snippet

extract usable or reusable substances: recovery, recycling

extract with effort: pry

extract, pure: quintessence

extracted elements: derivatives

extracted, as a cork: drawn

extraction: ancestry, breeding, descent, lineage, origin, parentage, race, stock

extramarital sex: adultery, infidelity, unfaithfulness

extraneous: adventitious, exotic, extrinsic, foreign, immaterial, impertinent, inapplicable, irrelevant, needless, outer, pointless, supererogatory, superfluous

extraordinary: abnormal, amazing, bizarre, exceptional, fantastic, gnarly, incredible, monstrous, notable, outstanding, phenomenal, prodigious, rare, remarkable, signal, singular, special,

EYE-RELATED TERMS

above the eyebrow: superciliary
black eye: shiner
branch of medicine treating eyes: ophthalmology
colored part of eye with pupil inside: iris
concentrated focus: fixation
constricted coordination of eyes to focus at short range: convergence
corner of the eye: canthus, commissure
dark part within iris: pupil
defect in focus: squint, strabismus
difficulty seeing in dimness and darkness: night blindness, nyctalopia
double vision: diplopia
examination of refraction of eye: retinoscopy, skiascopy
eye: blinker, cornea, iris, lamp, ogle, orb, orbit, peeper, pupil, retina
eye disease: astigmatism, cataract, conjunctivitis, glaucoma, iritis, myopia, strabismus, stye
eye disease of pressure in eyeball: glaucoma
eye disease with imbalance of eye muscles: strabismus
eye disease with opacity of eye lens: cataracts
eye doctor: oculist, ophthalmologist
eye examiner: optometrist
eye exercises: orthoptics
eye of insect or crustacean: compound eye
eye of snail, on stalk: ommatophore
eye part: cornea, irido, iris, lens, pupil, retina, sclera, uvea
eye pigment sensitive to red light: rhodopsin
eye pigment sensitive to violet: iodopsin
eye socket: orbit
eyeball involuntary motion: nystagmus
eyeball movement when dreaming: REM
eyeglass: monocle
eyeglass sidepieces: temples
eyeglasses: contacts, goggles, lenses, lorgnette, monocles, specs, spectacles
eyeglasses and contact lens dealer: optician
eyeglasses and contacts prescriber: ophthalmic optician, optician, optometrist

eyeglasses clipped to bridge of nose: pince-nez
eyeglasses with handle: lorgnette
eyeglasses, three-part: trifocals
eyeglasses, two-part: bifocals
eyelid: palpebra
eyepiece: loupe
eye's ability to bend light to focus it on retina: refraction
eyesight: tunnel vision
farsightedness: hypermetropia, hyperopia
faulty curvature of lens: astigmatism
fold of skin covering inner corner of eyelid: epicanthic fold, epicanthus
having eyelids: palpebrate
lens of a compound eye: facet
make eye pupil larger, to: dilate
mucous or watery discharge: rheum
nearly blind: purblind
nearsightedness: myopia
on outer edges of eyesight: peripheral vision
opacity of lens of eye: cataract
perfect eyesight: emmetropia, twenty-twenty vision
pertaining to eye and sight: ocular
protruding eyeballs: exophthalmic
rapid movement of the eyes: saccade
relating to both eyes: binocular
relating to eyelids: palpebral
relating to eyesight: ocular, optical, visual
relating to one eye: monocular
relating to the eye: ocular, ophthalmic, optical
simple eye of invertebrates: ocellus
specks seen with eyes closed: muscae volitantes
substance used to dilate eye pupils: atropine
transparent coating of eye: cornea
transparent inner eyelid of birds and some other animals: nictitating membrane
unequal surface of eye: astigmatism
wrinkles around eyes: crow's feet ❧

---

strange, stupendous, superhuman, surpassing, terrific, tremendous, uncommon, unique, unusual, wonderful
extrasensory: paranormal
extrasensory perception: clairvoyance, cryptesthesia, ESP, telesthesia
extrasensory perception of distant stimuli: telesthesia
extraterrestrial: alien
extravagance, prodigality: conspicuous consumption
extravagant: bizarre, costly, excessive, exorbitant, expensive, fanatic, fancy, fantastic, flamboyant, generous, grandiose, lavish, luxurious, ornate,

outre, overpriced, pompous, preposterous, prodigal, profuse, reckless, ridiculous, unreasonable, unrestrained, wasteful, wild
extravagant and wasteful: prodigal
extreme: advanced, arrant, ceiling, conclusive, culmination, desperate, dire, drastic, excessive, faraway, farthest, final, greatest, harsh, highest, immoderate, intense, last, limit, maximum, nth degree, outermost, outward, peak, radical, severe, sheer, terrible, terrific, ultimate, ultra, utmost, violent, zenith
extreme degree: nth

extreme excellence: ne plus ultra
extreme fear: terror
extreme greed: rapacity
extreme in belief or position: intransigent, uncompromising
extreme in devotion: fanatical, rabid
extreme in opinion: radical
extremely: beyond measure, conspicuously, especially, very
extremely cold: gelid
extremely pale: ashen
extremes, divide into two: polarize
extremist: anarchist, fanatic, maximalist, nihilist, radical, revolutionary, zealot

extremity: apex, arm, backside, border, boundary, brink, crisis, danger, disaster, distress, end, finger, foot, hand, leg, limb, limit, outermost, tail, terminus, toe, verge

extricate: clear, disengage, disentangle, extract, free, liberate, loose, remove, rescue, untangle

extrinsic: adventitious, alien, external, extraneous, foreign, outside, unessential

extroverted: friendly, gregarious, outgoing, sociable

extrude: eject, evict, expel, project, protrude, spew

exuberance: eagerness, effervescence, élan, energy, enthusiasm, exhilaration, extravagance, life, liveliness, profusion, spirit, vigor, vitality, vivacity, zest, zestfulness

exuberant: abounding, animated, cheerful, effusive, excessive, excited, fertile, flamboyant, fruitful, happy, lavish, lively, passionate, plentiful, vivacious

exude: discharge, display, emit, excrete, exhibit, ooze, perspire, secrete, seep, sweat

exult: crow

exult maliciously: gloat

exultant: delighted, ecstatic, elated, happy, joyous, on top of the world, overjoyed, triumphant

exuviate: molt, peel

eye-catching: attractive, conspicuous, marked, noticeable, showy

eye-deceiving trick: optical illusion

eye-for-an-eye punishment: lex talionis, reprisal, talion

eye-popping: amazing, astonishing, exciting, thrilling, wonderful

eye tooth: canine

eyeful: beauty, knockout, looker, view

eyelash makeup: mascara

eyelet, reinforced ring of: grommet

eyelike spots: ocelli

eyesore: blemish, blight, dump, mess

eyespot of peacock: ocellus

eyewitness: bystander, observer, onlooker, spectator, witness

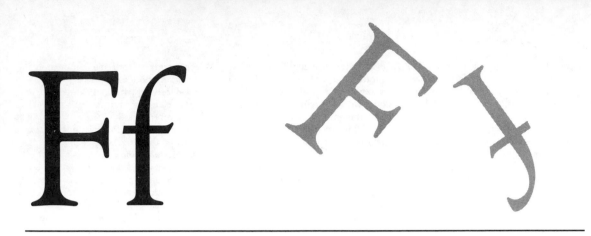

fable: allegory, apologue, concoction, exemplum, falsehood, fantasy, fiction, legend, lie, myth, narrative, parable, story, tale

fable ending: moral

fable of abstract ideas: allegory

fable or tale with moral: apologue

fable payoff: ethic

fable used to make a point: exemplum

fabled baby transport: stork

fables, composer of: fabulist

fabricate: build, coin, concoct, construct, contrive, create, devise, falsify, fashion, formulate, frame, invent, lie, make, manufacture, produce, weave

fabrication: coinage, fiction, figment, lie

fabulous: amazing, astonishing, astounding, awesome, fantastic, incredible, legendary, marvelous, mythical, outrageous, phenomenal, remarkable, terrific, wonderful

facade: disguise, face, fake, front, guise, mask, pretense, veneer

facade, elaborate: false front, Potemkin village

face: bear, border, brave, confront, countenance, cover, dare, defy, dial, dignity, encounter, envisage, expression, exterior, facade, feature, front, frown, grimace, honor, kisser, map, mask, mug, oppose, paint, pan, physiognomy, profile, puss, semblance, silhouette, stand, stare, surface, tolerate, visage

face courageously: brave

face downward: prone, prostrate

face in specified direction: orient, orientate

face of building: facade

face-to-face: affront, confront, direct, opposite, vis-á-vis

face-to-face meeting: confrontation, mano a mano

face value of security: nominal value, par value

face with stone: revet

face, flat on your: agroof

face, straight or blank: deadpan, poker face

facedown on stomach: prone

facelift: cosmetic surgery

facet: angle, aspect, feature, pane, part, phase, side

facetious: amusing, clever, comic, comical, funny, humorous, jesting, jocular, laughable, sarcastic, wisecracking, witty

faceup on back: supine

facial expression: countenance, smile, sneer, visage

facial features: countenance, lineaments, physiognomy

facial spasm: tic

facile: able, adept, adroit, easy, effortless, expert, fluent, glib, pat, proficient, quick, simple, skillful, slick

facilitate: aid, assist, ease, expedite, foster, further, help, promote

facility: ability, address, adroitness, amenity, aptitude, capability, dexterity, ease, east, expertness, knack, pliability, poise, readiness, skill

facing an impinging glacier: stoss

facing the observer: obverse

facing the pitcher: at bat

facsimile: copy, duplicate, fax, imitation, likeness, replica, reproduction

fact: actuality, basis, certainty, circumstance, data, datum, deed, event, evidence, ipso facto, point, proof, reality, specific, statistics, truth

fact itself, by the: by definition, ipso facto

fact, accomplished: fait accompli

faction: band, bloc, cabal, circle, clan, coalition, confederacy, coterie, denomination, dispute, dissension, group, intrigue, junto, party, quarrel, rebellion, ring, schism, sect, side, slique

factious: conflicting, contentious, dissident, fighting, insurgent, seditious

factitious: artificial, bogus, phony, sham, synthetic, unnatural

factor: agent, antecedent, aspect, author, cause, circumstance, component, constituent, detail, determinant, element, gene, ingredient, point, reason

factor making up for deficiency: mitigating factor, offset, redeeming feature, redeeming quality

factor ruling out treatment: contraindication

factory: building, business, cooperative, establishment, manufactory, mill, plant, shop, sweatshop, workshop

factory assembly belt: conveyor belt

factory line of workers or step-by-step operating: assembly line, production line

factory owned collectively by workers or users: cooperative

factory with poor working conditions, pay: sweatshop

factotum: do all, handyman

facts admissible as evidence: res gestae

facts and circumstances, concerned with: practical, pragmatic

facts and figures: data

factual: accurate, authentic, correct, genuine, literal, objective, real, true

faculty: ability, aptitude, capability, capacity, department, flair, gift, instinct, instructors, knack, power, professors, propensity, skill, staff, talent, teachers, wits

fad: amusement, chic, craze, fashion, hobby, quirk, rage, thing, trend, whim

fade: abate, decay, die, dim, diminish, disappear, discolor, dissolve, dull, ebb, evanesce, languish, lighten, pale, recede, shrivel, swindle, taper, vanish, wane, weaken, wilt, wither

fail: abandon, bankrupt, bomb, bungle, default, desert, disappoint, exhaust, falter, flop, flunk, fold, founder, languish, lose, miscarry, sink, sora, unsuccessful, wane, welsh

fail to pay debt, keep promise: default, welsh

fail to use efficiently: waste

failing: deficiency, drawback, fault, flaw, in a decline, inadequate, insufficient, poor, shortcoming, weakness

failure: abortion, bankruptcy, bomb, breakdown, bust, collapse, debacle, decay, decline, default, deficiency, delinquency, disappointment, downfall, dud, fault, fiasco, fizzle, flop, frustration, insolvency, lapse, lemon, loser, loss, miscarriage, neglect, omission, slump, washout

failure of institution: Gotterdammerung

failure to attain goal: shortfall

failure to do duty: dereliction, nonfeasance

failure to keep obligation: default

failure, complete: fiasco

fain: lief

faineant: idle

faint: blackout, collapse, dark, delicate, dim, distant, dizzy, faded, feeble, fuzzy, gentle, giddy, hushed, languid, languish, light, lightheaded, listless, muffled, obscure, pale, pass out, sickly, slight, sluggish, soft, swoon, syncope, thin, timid, unclear, vague, weak, woozy

faint and unclear: obscure

faint wish: inclination, tendency, velleity

faint, tending to: lipothymia

fair: aboveboard, adequate, average, bazaar, beautiful, blond, blonde, calm, carnival, charming, clear, decent, deserved, distinct, enchanting, equal, equitable, even, evenhanded, exhibit, exhibition, exposition, festival, fete, gala, handsome, honest, impartial, indifferent, judicious, just, light, mart, mediocre,

middling, mild, objective, pageant, pleasant, reasonable, right, so-so, square, sufficient, unbiased, unprejudiced

fair and unbiased: disinterested, dispassionate, impartial, unprejudiced

fair-haired and -skinned: xanthochroid

fair-skinned: Caucasian

fair to middling: so-so

fair weather indicator: rising barometer

fairly: absolutely, actually, courteously, distinctly, favorably, fully, gently, legitimately, properly, quite, rather, somewhat, tolerably

fairness: duty, equality, equity, honesty, impartiality, justice, justness, legitimacy, objectivity

fairy: banshee, brownie, dwarf, elf, enchantress, fay, genie, gnome, goblin, gremlin, leprechaun, peri, pixie, puck, spirit, sprite, sylphid

fairy-tale bad guy: ogre

fairylike: elfin, ethereal

faith: acceptance, belief, confidence, conviction, creed, dogma, hope, loyalty, pledge, promise, reliance, trust; church, cult, denomination, persuasion, religion, sect

faith and beliefs, statement of: creed

FABRIC TYPES AND TERMS

coarse fabric: burlap, crash, gunny, hopsack, mat

corded fabric: calico, corduroy, pinwale, pique, poplin, rep, repp

cotton fabric: chambray, chino, drill, galatea, gingham, jean, madras, nainsook, percale, susi, swiss

edge woven so it won't fray or ravel: selvage

fabric: bunting, cloth, construct, felt, fiber, grain, linen, lining, material, nap, Orlon, rayon, satin, shirting, structure, textile, texture, voile, web, weft, woof

fabric colorist: dyer

fabric dealer: draper, mercer

fabric from West Indian tree: guana

fabric gathered in parallel rows: shirring

fabric plaid: madras, tartan

fabric resembling velvet, closely napped: velour

fabric sample: swatch

fabric that is crinkly, light, often striped: seersucker

fabric with a design: print

fabric with a wrinkled effect: plissé

fabric with diagonal lines: twill

fabric with fuzzy surface: napped

fabric with triangular insert for expansion: gusset

flag fabric: bunting

linen fabric: barras, buckram, cambric, carde, crash, drabbet, ecru, lockram, sinelon

lustrous fabric: lamé, moiré, poplin, sateen, satin, silk, surah, taffeta

printed fabric: batik, calico, challis, chintz, damask, jacquard, toile

satin fabric: étoile, panne, pekin

sheer fabric: batiste, chiffon, dimity, gauze, lawn, organdy, organza, Swiss, tissue, voile

silk fabric: alamode, carded, chiffon, crepe, ninon, pongee, samite, sarsenet, satin, shantung, surah, taffeta

striped fabric: aba, abba, algerine, galatea, pekin, seersucker, ticking

surface of plush, velvet, corduroy or carpet: pile

synthetic fabric: acrilan, acrylic, Dacron, nylon, Orlon, plastic, polyester, rayon

wool fabric: baize, beige, Bolivia, burnet, caddis, camlet, casha, cataloon, catalowne, debeige, delaine, droguet, duffel, frisado, frisca, frizado, gabardine, grenadine, harrateen, hernani, loden, mackinaw, melton, merino, montagnac, moreen, rattinet, serge, tweed, witney, woolen, woollen, worsted, zibeline, zibelline

woven fabric: blanket, damasse, textile, tricot, tweed, twill, weft

Fabrics and Fibers

acetate
acrylic
alpaca
angora
astrakhan
baize
balbriggan
baldachin
barathea
batik
batiste
bayadere
bengaline
bombazine
bouclé
brilliantine
broadcloth
brocade
brocatel/brocatelle
buckram
bunting
burlap
byssus
calico
cambric
camel hair/camel's
  hair
candlewick
Canton crepe
canvas
cashmere
cassimere/casimere
castor
cavalry twill
challis
chambray
charmeuse
cheesecloth
chenille
cheviot
chiffon
chinchilla
chino
chintz
cire
cloque
cloth
combing wool
cord
corduroy
cotton
Courtelle
crash
crepe de Chine

cretonne
Crimplene
crinoline
Dacron
damask
denim
dimity
doeskin
Donegal tweed
drill
drugget
duck
duetyn/duvetyne
duffel/duffle
dungaree
ecru
faille
felt
flannel
flannelette
fleece
foulard
frieze
fustian
gabardine
galatea
gauze
Georgette
gingham
gossamer
grenadine
grogram
grosgrain
gunny
haircloth
Harris tweed
herringbone
homespun
honan/Honan
hopsack
horsehair
huckaback/huck
jaconet
jacquard
jardiniere
jean
jersey
jute
Kendal green
kersey
khaki
lace
lamé
lawn
leatherette

leno
linen
linsey-woolsey
lisle
lisse
loden
Lurex
mackinaw
mackintosh/
  macintosh
madras
maline/malines
marocain
marquisette
marseille/marseilles
mat
melton
merino
mesh
messaline
mohair
moiré
moleskin
monk's cloth
moquette
mousseline
muslin
nainsook
nankeen
net/netting
ninon
nylon
oilcloth
oilskin
organdy
organza
organzine
Orlon
paisley
panne
paramatta
percale
percaline
petersham
Pima
pique
plaid
plush
polyester
pongee
poplin
prunella
ragg
ratine
rayon

rep
russet
sackcloth
sacking
sailcloth
samite
sarcenet
sateen
satin
scrim
seersucker
serge
shalloon
shantung
sharkskin
Shetland wool
sheer
shoddy
shot silk
silk
spandex
stockinette
suede
surah
swansdown
swanskin
tabaret
tabby
taffeta
tapestry
terry cloth
ticking
tiffany
toile
toweling
tricot
tricotine
tulle
tussah
tweed
twill
velour
velure
velvet
velveteen
Venetian cloth
vicuna
voile
webbing
whipcord
wool
worsted ❦

faith, person without: agnostic, nullifidian

faith, to make declaration of: testify

faith, unquestioning in: implicit

faithful: constant, dependable, devoted, fast, firm, honest, leal, loving, loyal, patriotic, pious, reliable, sincere, staunch, steadfast, steady, tried, true, true to, trustworthy, trusty, unwavering, upright, veracious

faithful adherent: believer

faithful forever: semper fidelis

faithfulness to obligations: fealty, fidelity, loyalty

faithless: atheist, deceptive, disaffected, disloyal, false, fickle, hollow, inconstant, perfidious, punic, recreant, shifting, skeptical, traitorous, treacherous, unbelieving, unjust, unstable, untrue, wavering

fake: bogus, cheat, counterfeit, fabrication, false, falsify, fictitious, forged, fraudulent, fudge, hoax, imitation, imposter, invented, manufacture, phony, pretend, scam, sham, spurious, supposititious, swindle

fake gems: paste

fake identity: imposture

fake or imitation: artificial, ersatz, simulated, synthetic

fake or insincere: contrived, factitious

fake or pretend, to: dissemble, feign, simulate

fake, cheap: brummagen, gimcrack, pinchbeck

faked sorrow: crocodile tears

fakes a smile, person who: eccedentesiast

fakir: ascetic, dervish, hindu, mendicant, monk, moslem, yogi

falcon: bird, cannon, hawk, kestrel, lanner, merlin, musket, peregrine, saker, sparrow hawk, tiercel

falcon popular in falconry: duck hawk, peregrine falcon

falcon young enough to be trained for falconry: eyas

falcon, small: merlin, pigeon hawk

falconry, male hawk used in: tiercel

falcons release by falconer as pair: cast

fall: abate, backslide, buckle, capitulate, cascade, cataract, collapse, crash, decline, decrease, degrade, depreciate, depress, descend, destruction, die, disappoint, dive, drip, drop, fail, flop, lapse, occur, overthrow, perish, plop, plummet, plunge, precipitate, recede, ruin, sag, settle, sink, slip, slump, spill, stumble, submit, subside, surrender, topple, trip, tumble

RELATED TERMS

fall back: recede, recoil, retract, retreat

fall behind: lag, straggle

fall by drops: trickle

fall downward: gravitate, subside

fall guy: chump, dupe, fool, goat, patsy, pawn, scapegoat, sucker, tool

fall heavily: plop

fall in voice pitch: cadence, falling intonation

fall into disuse: lapse

fall off: bite the dust, come a cropper, measure one's length

fall out of place: prolapse

fall over: topple

fall over steep rocks, water: cascade

fall straight down quickly: hurtle, plummet, precipitate

fall upon: impinge ❦

fallacious: beguiling, deceitful, deceptive, delusive, erroneous, false, fraudulent, illusory, misleading, mistaken, untrue, wrong

fallacious argument or conclusion: paralogism

fallacy: error, false notion, falsehood, flaw, illusion, misconception, mistake, preconception

fallen: dead, deposed, disgraced, immoral, lost, ousted, shamed, sinful, slain

fallible: erratic, erroneous, faulty, human, imperfect, mortal, questionable, unreliable, unsure

falling back to former ill state: relapse

falling off, shedding leaves, fruit: deciduous

falling out: argument, disagreement, dispute, fight, resultant, spat

fallopian or eustachian tube: salpinx

fallout: by-product, debris, dust, radioactive

fallow: idle, inactive, lea, undeveloped, unseeded, unused

fallow female deer: doe

fallow land year for Jews: Sabbatical year

false: apocryphal, artificial, bogus, concocted, counterfeit, crooked, deceitful, deceptive, devious, disaffected, dishonest, disloyal, erroneous, faithless, fake, feigned, fictious, groundless, guise, hollow, hypocritical, illusive, imaginary, inaccurate, incorrect, inexact, insincere, mendacious, misleading, mistaken, not so, perfidious, phony, postiche, pretended, pseudo, recreant, sham, spurious, treacherous, unreal, untrue, untruthful, wrong

RELATED TERMS

false and invented: bogus, fictitious, spurious

false and made-up: concocted, trumped-up

false appearance: facade, guise, pretense, simulation

false appearance of, to give a: dissemble, feign, simulate

false argument: sophistry

false behavior or speech: duplicity

false but represented as otherwise: ostensible

false but seemingly true or plausible: meretricious, sophistic, specious

false charge: aspersion, slander

false conception: illusion

false conclusion or argument: paralogism

false evidence against, to use: frame

false evidence, deliberate giving of: perjury

false god: idol

false image or representation: simulacrum

false impression, presentation to give: window dressing

false information: bum steer

false lead: red herring

false notion: fallacy

false notion of proof that misses point: ignoratio elenchi, sophism

false notion that sequence of events implies causative connection: ergo propter hoc, post hoc

false or questionable: apocryphal

false perception: delusion, hallucination, illusion, mirage

false professing of beliefs, feelings, virtues: hypocrisy

false publication that damages person's reputation: libel

false remark or statement: aspersion, calumny, canard, defamation, libel, rumor, slander

false step or error in etiquette: faux pas

false teeth holder: bridge, bridgework

false teeth set: denture

false thought, idea, notion: misapprehension, misconception, misconstruction, misunderstanding

false verdict: bum rap

false, insincere pathos: bathos

false, slanderous story used for political purpose: roorback

false, to prove: confute, rebut, refute

falsehood: canard, deception, dishonesty, fable, fabrication, fallacy, fib, fiction, fraud, inaccuracy, lie, mendacity, misstatement, perfidy, perjury, story, tale, treachery, untruth

falsehood, to free from a: disabuse

falsely, to picture: belie, misrepresent

falsify: adulterate, alter, belie, betray, counterfeit, doctor, fake, forge, fudge, lie, mislead, misrepresent, twist ❦

falter: bobble, boggle, err, fail, flounder, hesitate, reel, shudder, stagger, stumble, stutter, totter, tremble, vacillate, waver

fame: acclaim, celebrity, distinction, éclat, glory, greatness, honor, kudos, notoriety, popularity, prestige, reclame, recognition, renown, report, reputation, repute, rumor, stardom, stature

fame, conspicuous: éclat

famed: noted, renowned

familial pole: totem

familiar: accustomed, acquaintance, acquainted, affable, aware, bold, buddy, chummy, close, common, confidential, conversant, cozy, customary, easy, free, frequent, friendly, habitual, intimate, known, ordinary, routine, snug, sociable, usual, versed

familiar with: au fait, conversant

familiarize: orient, orientate

family: ancestry, brood, category, children, clan, class, descendants, genealogy, generation, group, household, kin, kindred, kinsmen, line, lineage, offspring, progeny, relatives, tribe

family name: cognomen, patronymic, surname

family of parents, children: nuclear family

family of parents, children, and other close relatives: extended family

family of rulers for generations: dynasty

family side of father: spear side

family side of mother: distaff side, spindle side

family tree: genealogy, lineage, pedigree

family, in the: en famille

family's line of descendants: stirps

famine: dearth, hunger, scarcity, shortage, starvation

famous: acclaimed, celebrated, distinguished, eminent, excellent, grand, great, illustrious, known, legendary, notable, noted, notorious, prominent, recognized, renowned, storied, successful

famous and elite: beau monde, glitterati, jet set

famous and legendary: fabled, storied

famous and of high rank: distinguished, eminent, prominent

famous and worthy of reverence: august, venerable

famous for unfavorable reason: infamous, notorious

famous person: celebrity, luminary

fan: admirer, aficionado, blower, booster, buff, cool, devotee, enthusiast, flabellum, follower, groupie, punkah, rooter, spread, windmill, winnow; blower, cool, propeller

fan following entertainer: groupie

fan for drawing air out of room: extractor, ventilator

fan magazine: fanzine

fan operated by servant: punkah

fan rib: brin

fan-shaped: flabellate

fan-shaped anatomical structure: flabellum

fanatic: activist, bigot, crazy, devotee, energumen, enthusiast, extravagant, extremist, fiend, maniac, radical, ultra, zealot

fanatical: rabid

fanatical enthusiast: energumen, zealot

fanatical following: cult

fanciful: bizarre, capricious, chimerical, dreamy, fantastic, ideal, illusory, imaginary, imaginative, in the clouds, mythical, quaint, romantic, stronge, unread, visionary, whimsical

fanciful and improbable: chimerical

fanciful humor: whimsy

fanciful idea: conceit, crotchet, notion, whim, whimsy

fancy: admire, capriccio, caprice, chimera, conceit, conjecture, crave, desire, dream, fad, fantasy, humor, idea, illusion, imagination, imagine, impression, inclination, lavish, liking, love, notion, picture, pleasure, preference, romance, taste, vagary, vision, whim, whimsy; decorative, deluxe, elaborate, elegant, embellished, expensive, ornamental, ornate

fandango: dance, nonsense, tomfoolery, tune

fanfare: ceremony, cheering, display, éclat, fireworks, panoply, pomp, show, tantara

fanfare of trumpets: flourish, tucket

fanfare on trumpet or horn: tantara

fanfare or showy passage: flourish

fanny: behind, buttocks, derriere, heinie, hiney, rump

fantasies or dreams, having the nature of: visionary

fantasize: daydream, dream, envision, imagine, invent

fantastic: absurd, amazing, bizarre, capricious, chimerical, enormous, excellent, exotic, extravagant, fabulous, fanciful, grotesque, huge, imaginary, imaginative, incredible, massive, sensational, strange, terrific, unbelievable, unreal, weird, whimsical, wonderful

fantastic daydreams, person with: Walter Mitty

fantastic notion: bee in one's bonnet

fantasy: apparition, chimera, desire, dream, fancy, hallucination, idea, illusion, imagination, invention, mirage, reverie, romance, vision, whim

fantasy or notion: figment

far: considerably, deep, distant, greatly, inaccessible, long, miles, much, outlying, remote, wide, widely

far and wide: everywhere, far and near

far away: outlying, remote

far away and difficult to reach: inaccessible

far below the surface: deep

far-fetched: bizarre, cockamamie, doubtful, dubious, forced, improbable, strained, unbelievable, unlikely, unrealistic

far from point of attachment or reference: distal

far-reaching: broad, deep, extensive, universal, wide

faraway: abstracted, distant, dreamy, oblivious, preoccupied, remote, removed, yon

farce: burlesque, comedy, joke, mime, mockery, nonsense, parody, satire, slapstick, stuffing

farcical: absurd, amusing, comical,

funny, humorous, laughable, ludicrous, nonsensical, outrageous, ridiculous, silly

fare: charge, fee, price, rate, ticket, token, toll; customer, passenger; diet, eats, food, provision; get on, happen, manage, proceed, progress, prosper; journey, passage, path, travel

farewell: adieu, adios, aloha, ave, bon voyage, bye, cheerio, conge, departure, goodbye, parting, salutation, sayonara, sendoff, so long, swan song, tata, vale, valediction, valedictory

farewell or final act: swan song

farewell speech: valedictory

farina: cereal, flour, meal, mush, starch

farinaceous: floury

farm: cooperative, croft, cultivate, dairy, field, garden, grange, harvest, hatchery, homestead, kibbutz, kolkhoz, land, orchard, oyster, plant, plantation, plow, ranch, rancho, range, spread, till, vineyard

farm animal: boar, calf, ewe, goat, hog, horse, livestock, mare, oxen, pig, ram, sheep, sow

farm growing vegetables for market: truck farm

farm machine: baler, planter, plow, seeder

farm operated cooperatively: collective

farm or farm buildings: grange

farm owned by workers or users: cooperative

farm structure: barn, cowbarn, shed, silo, sty

farm, Israel collective: kibbutz

farm, Russian collective: kolkhoz

farm, Spanish type: hacienda

farmer: agriculturist, breeder, cultivator, granger, grower, harvester, husbandman, planter, plowman, plowwoman, producer, rancher, sharecropper, sower, tiller, yeoman

farmer cultivating his/her own land: yeoman

farmer managing a ranch: grazier, rancher

farmer, tenant: sharecropper

farmhouse and adjoining buildings, land: homestead

farming: agriculture, gardening, grazing, husbandry

farming and rural life, pertaining to: georgic

farming where farmer consumes produce: subsistence farming

farming with increased capital and labor, little land: intensive farming

farming with little labor and capital, more land: extensive farming

farming, of animal husbandry: pastoral

farming, of cultivatable land and: arable

farming, relating to: agrarian, agricultural

farms land owned by another, one who: tenant farmer

farouche: fierce, savage, sullen, surly, wild

farrago: mess, mishmash, olio

farsighted: clairvoyant, perceptive, provident, prudent, sagacious, shrewd, wise; hyperoptic

farsightedness: hypermetropia, hyperopia

farsightedness with aging: presbyopia

farther: beyond, futher, longer, remoter, yonder

farthest: endmost, extreme, last, lattermost, longest, outmost, utmost

farthest down: deepest, nethermost

farthest point or portion: extremity

farthest possible point: ultima Thule

fascicle: bunch, bundle, cluster, collection

fascinate: absorb, allure, attract, beguile, captivate, charm, compel, draw, enamor, enchant, engross, entrance, interest, intrigue, mesmerize, rivet, spellbind, thrill

fascinating: astonishing, enchanting, eye-popping, irresistible, spectacular

fascinatingly foreign: exotic

fascination: allure, astonishment, attraction, magnetism, obsession, wonder

fascism: autocracy, dictatorship, Nazism, totalitarianism

fashion: air, appearance, attitude, build, compose, construct, contrive, craze, create, custom, design, etiquette, fabricate, fad, form, frame, guise, invent, look, make, manner, method, mode, model, modes, mold, pattern, rage, shape, style, tailor, trend, vogue

fashion, high: haute couture

fashion, prevailing: dernier cri, vogue

fashion, relating to tailoring and: sartorial

fashionable: à la mode, chic, contemporary, dashing, de rigueur, hip, hot, mod, modern, modish, newfangled, popular, posh, smart, soigne, stylish, swank, tony, trendy

fashionable and pretentious: chichi

fashionable group: salon

fashionable person: clotheshorse, fashion plate

fashionable resort: spa

fashionable society: beau monde, grand monde

fast: abstain, active, apace, brisk, easy, enduring, expeditious, fleet, flying, hasty, hurried, in no time, loose, promiscuous, pronto, quick, rapid, reckless, refrain, speedy, swift; faithful, firm, held, immovable, loyal, permanent, secure, stable, stationary, steadfast, stuck, true, unyielding

fast, rhythmic Latin American ballroom dance: cha-cha

fasten: adhere, affix, anchor, attach, batten, bend, bind, bolt, bond, brace, cement, chain, clamp, clasp, clinch, cling, clip, connect, couple, direct, fix, focus, glue, hitch, hook, join, lace, latch, link, lock, moor, nail, padlock, paste, pin, rivet, rope, seal, secure, set, sew, solder, staple, strap, tether, tie, tighten, truss, weld, wire

fastener: bolt, brace, bracket, buckle, button, catch, clamp, clasp, clip, cotter pin, hasp, latch, leash, lock, nail, nut, padlock, peg, pin, rivet, screw, snap, staple, strap, stud, tack, toggle bolt, Velcro, zipper

fastidious: choosy, critical, dainty, delicate, demanding, difficult, elegant, exacting, exquisite, fine, finical, finicky, fussy, meticulous, nice, particular, refined, sensitive, squeamish

fasting and self-denial: mortification

fasting period: Lent

fat: adipose, blubber, broad, cellulite, chubby, corpulent, cushy, elephantine, fertile, flab, fleshy, fruitful, grease, heavy, lard, large, obese, obesity, oil, olein, opulent, overweight, paunchy, plump, portly, potbellied, profitable, prosperous, pudgy, rich, rotund, stocky, stout, suet, thick, tubby

fat by heating gently, to remove impurities in: clarify

fat by heating, to melt down: render

fat from animals used in candles, soap, etc.: tallow

fat of beef, mutton: tallow

fat of hogs: lard

fat of sperm whale: spermaceti

fat of thighs, buttocks: cellulite

fat of whale: blubber

fat stomach: corporation, paunch

fat stomach, having: abdominous, adipose, pinguid

fat streaks in meat: marbling

fat, like butter or lard: shortening

fat, relating to animal: adipose

fat, smell of decomposing: rancid

fat, solid form of: stearin

fat, state of being: embonpoint

fat, very: obese

fatal: calamitous, catastrophic, critical, crucial, deadly, destined, destructive, disastrous, doomed, fateful, final, incurable, lethal, mortal, pernicious, ruinous, terminal

fatal, ruinous act: kiss of death

fatality: accident, casualty, death

fate: chance, consequence, destiny, doom, end, fortune, karma, kismet, lot, outcome, portion, predestination, result

fate (in Buddhism): karma

fateful: critical, crucial, deadly, decisive, destructive, disastrous, eventful, important, inevitable, predestined, ruinous, significant

father: abbot, adopt, beget, confessor, create, creator, dad, dada, daddy, founder, friar, generate, inventor, minister, old man, originate, padre, papa, parent, parson, pastor, pater, paternity, patriarch, pop, priest, procreate, reverend, sire

father going through motions of birth with mother: couvade

father or ruler of family, clan, tribe: patriarch

father, founding: patriarch

father, looking more like your: patroclinous

father, murder of: patricide

father, of or relating to descent from a: patrilineal

father, of or relating to name of one's: patronymic

father, relating to a: paternal

father, to: beget, sire

fatherhood: paternity

fatherland: birthplace, homeland, motherland

fatherly: benevolent, kindly, parental, paternal, patriarchal, protective, supportive

father's side of family: agnate

fathom: comprehend, delve, discern, grasp, measure, penetrate, solve, understand

fatigue: bore, languor, tire

fatigued: all in, beat, bushed, drained, exhausted, foredone, jaded, languid, spent, tired, weakened, wearied

fatlike substance: lipoid

fatness: embonpoint

fats in living cells: lipid

fatten: batten, enrich, feed, lard, plump, stuff, swell, thrive

fatty: adipose, blubbery, greasy, lardy, oily, oleaginous, pinguid, pinguide, sebaceous, suety, unctuous

fatty acid in animal and vegetable fats: stearic acid

fatty secretion of skin: sebum, smegma

fatty substance linked to health problems: cholesterol

fatty material: cellulite

fatty tissue: suet

fatuous: asinine, brainless, delusive, foolish, idiotic, imbecile, inane, moronic, ridiculous, silly, stupid, unintelligent, unreal, witless

faucet: hydrant, nozzle, spigot, tap, valve

faucet with a bent-down nozzle: bibcock

faucet, valve reducing pressure: petcock

fault: blame, blemish, blunder, culpability, default, defect, deficiency, drawback, dysfunction, error, failing, flaw, flub, foible, frailty, glitch, imperfection, liability, mistake, neglect, offense, shortcoming, sin, slip, transgression, vice, weakness, wrong

fault of character, minor: foible

fault or small sin: peccadillo

fault, distance between two sides of: dislocation, displacement

fault, minor: foible, peccadillo

fault, my: mea culpa

fault, technical: bug, glitch, malfunction

faultfinder: carper, censor, critic, cynic, momus, nitpicker, scolder

faultfinding: berating, captious, carping, caviling, censorious, niggling, querulous, vituperating

faultless: blameless, correct, exemplary, flawless, foolproof, immaculate, impeccable, irreproachable, perfect, precise, pure, right, sinless, spotless, stainless, unimpeachable, whole

faulty: amiss, bad, broken, damaged, defective, erroneous, impaired, imperfect, inaccurate, incorrect, malfunctioning, marred, wrong

faulty reasoning: paralogism

fauna and flora: biota

faux pas: blooper, blunders, boner, bull, bungle, error, gaffe, goof, indecorum, mistake, slip, slip of the tongue, slip-up, solecism

favor: accommodate, advance, advocacy, approbation, approval, assistance, befriend, bless, boon, concession, courtesy, esteem, gift, go for, goodwill, grace, help, indulgence, kindness, letter, like, oblige, patronage, prefer, privilege, reward, service, subscribe, support, uphold

favor a foot: limp

favor with others, to bring oneself into: fawn, ingratiate, kowtow, truckle

favor, something owed for a: obligation

favor, trying to win: fawning, ingratiating, obsequious, servile, sycophantic, unctuous

favorable: advantageous, approving, auspicious, benefic, beneficial, benign, benignant, complimentary, convenient, encouraging, friendly, good, gracious, hopeful, kind, opportune, pleasant, pleasing, positive, propitious, reassuring, towardly, welcoming

favorable factor: plus

favorable impression, way of falsely creating: window dressing

favorable mention: plug

favorable review: rave

favorable thing: boon

favoring a view: partisan, tendentious

favoring one side: partial

favorite: adored, beloved, choice, darling, idol, minion, pet, popular, preference, special, treasured

favorite place to go: haunt

favoritism: bias, discrimination, nepotism, partiality, prejudice

favoritism shown to relatives by offering jobs: nepotism

favors, equal exchange of: quid pro quo

favors, to ask for: hector, importune

fawn: buck, cower, crawl, cringe, deer, flatter, grovel, ingratiate, kowtow, slaver, sycophant, toady, truckle, wheedle, yearling

fawning: obsequious

faxed matter, unsolicited: faxraff

faze: abash, bother, confuse, daunt, disconcert, embarrass, irritate, perplex, puzzle, rattle

TYPES OF FEAR

fear of animals: zoophobia	fear of loneliness: eremiophobia
fear of bees: apiophobia	fear of marriage: gametophobia
fear of being buried alive: taphephobia	fear of mice: musophobia
fear of blood: hemophobia	fear of mirrors: eisoptrophobia
fear of cats: ailurophobia	fear of money: chrometophobia
fear of childbirth: tocophobia	fear of night: nyctophobia
fear of choking: pnigophobia	fear of nothing: zerophobia
fear of confined spaces: claustrophobia	fear of old age: gerascophobia
fear of crossing bridges: gephyrophobia	fear of open spaces: agoraphobia
fear of crowds: ochlophobia	fear of pain: algophobia
fear of darkness: nyctophobia	fear of particular thing: phobia
fear of death: necrophobia	fear of poisoning: toxicophobia
fear of dirt: mysophobia	fear of poverty: peniaphobia
fear of dogs: cynophobia	fear of pregnancy: maieusiophobia
fear of drafts: aerophobia	fear of public speaking: lalophobia
fear of dust: amathophobia	fear of salad dressings: mayophobia
fear of fear: phobophobia	fear of sharks: galeophobia
fear of fire: pyrophobia	fear of sleep: hypnophobia
fear of future: apprehension, dread	fear of snakes: ophidiophobia
fear of germs: microbiophobia	fear of spiders: arachnaphobia
fear of ghosts: phasmophobia	fear of strangers: xenophobia
fear of heights: acrophobia	fear of thirteen: triskaidekaphobia
fear of illness: nosophobia	fear of thunder: brontophobia, tonitrophobia
fear of injury: traumatophobia	fear of travel: hodophobia
fear of insects: entomophobia	fear of water: hydrophobia
fear of lawyers: ipsophobia	fear of work: ergophobia
fear of lightning: astrapophobia	fear of worms: helminthophobia ❧

fealty: allegiance, constancy, devotion, divined, duty, faithfulness, fidelity, loyalty, obligation

fear: affright, agitation, alarm, anxiety, apprehension, awe, concern, consternation, dismay, distrust, doubt, dread, fright, horror, panic, phobia, reverence, suspicion, terror, trepidation, uneasiness, venerate

fear and apprehension: angst, presentiment, trepidation

fear or concern, exaggerated or obsessive: complex

fear, a shudder of: frisson, palpitation

fear, arousing: fearsome, formidable, redoubtable

fear, feeling of: anxiety, misgiving, qualm

fear, irrational: phobia

fear, move away in: blench, cower, cringe, flinch, quail, recoil, wince

fear, paralyzing: consternation

fear, state of: funk, panic, trepidation

fear, state of paralyzing: consternation

fear, to calm a: allay, quell

feared: formidable, redoubtable

feared thing: bugbear

fearful: afraid, aghast, alarmed, appalling, apprehensive, awful, chicken, concerned, dire, distressing, dreadful, frightened, frightful, ghastly, horrendous, horrible, jittery, leery, nervous, panicky, scared, shocking, terrible, terrified, timid, timorous, trembling, tremulous, worried

fearful person: scaredy-cat

fearfully suspicious: paranoid

fearless: adventurous, audacious, bold, brave, courageous, daring, dauntless, gallant, heroic, intrepid, unafraid, undaunted, valiant

fearsome thing or creature: bogey, bugaboo, bugbear, chimera, hobgoblin

feasible: achievable, attainable, cinch, conceivable, doable, likely, possible, reasonable, suitable, viable, workable

feast: banquet, carnival, celebration, delight, dine, dinner, eat, festival, fete, fiesta, gala, holiday, indulge, luau, meal, regale, repast, spread, stuff, treat

feast, relating to a: festal

feat: accomplishment, achievement, act, action, adventure, attainment, conquest, deed, exploit, masterstroke, miracle, stunt, tour de force, trick, trim, triumph

feat of strength or virtuosity: tour de force

feather: adorn, character, down, fledge, fletch, fluff, osprey, panache, penna, pinion, pinna, plumage, plume, quill, species, vane, wing

RELATED TERMS

feather beginning to emerge: pinfeather

feather of bird, primary: pinion

feather on helmet: panache

feather part: barb, barbicel

feather plume on woman's hat: osprey

feather shaft: rachis, scape

feather-shaped: pinnate

feather with barbs on sides: vane

feather, filaments projecting from main shaft of: barbs

feather, hollow shaft of: barrel, calamus, quill, rachis, scape

feather, opening in shaft of: umbilicus

feather, weblike part of: vane, vexillum, web

featherbrained: brainless, emptyheaded, flighty, foolish, giddy, silly, simple

feathered object in badminton: shuttlecock

feathers: plumage

feathers around neck of animal or bird: frill, hackles, ruff

feathers of bird, mouth: vibrissae

feathers of bird, outermost: contour feathers

feathers of bird, smaller: covert, tectrix

feathers of duck used for bedding: eiderdown

feathers of rooster tail, long: sickle feature

feathers or tuft of plumes: aigrette

feathers that are different color from rest of bird body: mantle

feathers with the beak, to clean: preen

feathers, to cover with: fledge

feathers, to erect: ruffle

feathers, to shed: molt

feathers, without: callow, unfledged ❦

featherweight: boxer, trivial, unimportant, wrestler

feature: angle, aspect, attribute, character, characteristic, column, component, countenance, detail, element, facet, factor, hallmark, headline, highlight, idiosyncrasy, lineament, mark, outline, story, trait

feckless: aimless, careless, feeble, ineffective, irresponsible, meaningless, purposeless, remiss, slack, unreliable, useless, weak, worthless

fecund: fertile, fruitful, productive, prolific

fed up: annoyed, bored, disgusted, dissatisfied, sated, surfeited

federal funds helping political representative and constituents: pork barrel

federation: alliance, association, coalition, consortion, league, partnership, syndicate, union

fee: allowance, assessment, charge, commission, compensation, cost, dues, emolument, expense, fare, gratuity, honorarium, payment, percentage, price, rate, recompense, retainer, reward, salary, stipend, tab, tariff, tax, toll, tuition, wage

fee paid for instruction: tuition

fee paid for job done: compensation, emolument

fee paid for service done out of kindness: honorarium

fee paid to retain professional adviser: retainer

fee paid to salesperson for services rendered: commission

feeble: ailing, debilitated, decrepit, disabled, faint, flimsy, fragile, frail, helpless, impotent, inadequate, ineffective, inferior, infirm, invalid, lame, languid, poor, puny, senile, sickly, weak

feebleminded: anile, dotty, foolish, halfwitted, irresolute, moronic, senile

feed: aggravate, bran, dine, dispense, eat, fatten, feast, fodder, foster, fuel, furnish, grass, grub, hay, indulge, meal, nourish, nurse, nurture, oats, provide, replenish, satiate, satisfy, strengthen, supply, sustain

RELATED TERMS

feeding on all kinds of food: omnivorous, polyphagous

feeding on ants: myrmecophagous

feeding on corpses: necrophagous

feeding on dung: coprophagous

feeding on fish: piscivorous

feeding on fruit: carpophagous, frugivorous

feeding on grasses, grains, seeds: graminivorous, granivorous

feeding on insects: entomophagous, insectivorous

feeding on leaves: phyllophagous

feeding on meat: carnivorous

feeding on other animals: predatory

feeding on plants: herbivorous, phytophagous

feeding on plants only: herbivorous

feeding on wood: xylophagous ❦

feed a fire: stoke

feed for cattle: fodder, stover

feed the pot: ante, bet

feed to excess: surfeit

feeding through stomach tube: gavage

feeding trough: manger

feel: air, ambience, atmosphere, aura, believe, conclude, deem, discern, experience, explore, gather, grope, handle, know, mood, perceive, sense, stroke, suppose, texture, think, tingle, touch, understand

feel and explore by touching: palpate

feel and return same emotion: reciprocate

feel anxiety: dread

feel around for: grope

feel guilt: rue

feel indignant: resent

feel of environment: ambiance, ambience

feel, ability to: sensibility, susceptibility

feeler: antenna, barbel, hint, palp, probe, proposal, prospectus, question, tentacle, test, trial balloon

feelers near mouth: palpi, palps

feelers on insect, crustacean: antennae

feeling: atmosphere, attitude, awareness, emotion, enthusiasm, experience, heart, humor, hunch, inclination, intuition, morale, notion, opinion, pain, passion, perception, pity, pleasure, sensate, sensation, sense, sensitivity, sentient, sentiment, suspicion, sympathy, touch, warmth

feeling as distinguished from perception, thought: affect, sentience

feeling for appropriate language: sprachgefuhl

feeling of bodily discomfort: malaise

feeling of doubt or suspicion: misgiving, qualm, scruple

feeling of dread: angst

feeling of great joy: ecstasy, rapture, transport

feeling of having an experience before: déjà vu

feeling of impending event: foreboding, premonition, presentiment

feeling, capable of: passible, sensitive

feeling, depth of: profundity

feeling, examine or diagnose by: palpate

feeling, showing no: impassive

feeling, used for: tactile

feeling, vague: hint, inkling, intimation, intuition

feelings for family shifted to psychiatrist or another: transference

feelings openly, showing one's: demonstrative

feelings, identification or understanding of another's: empathy

feelings, to have specific: entertain, harbor

feelings, to hide: dissimulate
feelings, to hurt someone's: scarify
feet: extremities, hoofs, hooves, paws
feet and toenails, care of: chiropody, pedicure, podiatry
feet or ankles, binding on: fetters, shackles
feet turned outward, of: splay
feet, branch of medicine dealing with: podiatry
feet, hands: extremities
feet, having huge: sciapodous
feign: act, affect, assume, avoid, bluff, conceal, concoct, counterfeit, devise, disguise, dissemble, fabricate, fake, imagine, invent, personate, pose, pretend, sham, simulate
feint: artifice, bait, bluff, deceit, dodge, expedient, gambit, hoax, mask, ploy, pretense, ruse, stall, trick, wile
feisty: aggressive, energetic, frisky, lively, sassy, spirited, spunky
felicitate: commend, congratulate, greet, hail, praise, salute
felicitous: delightful, inspired, suitable
felicity: bliss, ecstasy, happiness, joy
feline: cat, cheetah, civet, jaguar, leopard, lion, lynx, puma, tiger, tom, wildcat
feline fight sound: caterwaul
fellow: associate, beau, bloke, boy, brother, buster, cadet, chap, colleague, companion, comrade, friend, gent, gentleman, guy, hombre, lad, mac, man, match, mate, partner, peer, person
fellow countryman: compatriot
fellow member: confrere
fellowship: alliance, association, brotherhood, camaraderie, company, corporation, familiarity, fraternity, freemasonry, friendship, grant, guild, membership, order, partnership, sisterhood, society, sodality, union
felon: convict, criminal, crook, cruel, culprit, evil, gangster, jailbird, lawbreaker, malefactor, offender, outlaw, whitlow
felony: arson, burglary, crime, kidnapping, murder, offense, rape, robbery, sin
female: daughter, feminine, femme, girl, grandmother, lady, ladylike, lass, miss, mom, mother, sister, woman
RELATED TERMS
female airhead: fizgig, frippet
female and male organs, having: hermaphrodite

female assistant, efficient: gal Friday, girl Friday
female ballet dancer: ballerina, danseuse, prima ballerina
female club at university: sorority
female demon: lamia, succubus
female external genitals: pudendum
female figure on column, pillar: caryatid
female flier: aviatrix
female genitals orally stimulated: cunnilingus
female germ: ovum
female hormone: estrogen
female inner personality in man's unconscious: anima
female line of descent, of the: matrilineal
female nightclub singer: chanteuse
female sex hormone: estrogen
female side: distaff side, spindle side
female side, related on: uterine
female singer of note: cantatrice, diva, prima donna
female spirit, Gaelic folklore: banshee
female sterilization in which the fallopian tubes are tied or cut: tubal ligation ❦

feminine: dainty, effeminate, female, girlish, ladylike, soft, tender, womanish, womanly
femme fatale: charmer, seductress, siren, temptress, vamp
femur: thighbone
femur-tibia connection: knee
fen: bog, marsh, mire, moor, quagmire, wetland
fence: backstop, barricade, barrier, coop, defend, defense, dodge, duel, encircle, enclosure, gird, guard, hedge, palisade, picket, post, rail, stockade, surround, wall
fence marking boundary: perimeter
fence of crossed rails in zigzag pattern: worm fence
fence of moat, ditch: ha-ha
fence of pales for fortification: palisade, stockade
fence of pointed upright stakes: paling, picket fence
fence of pointed upright stakes or barbed wire: fraise
fence or row of trees: windbreak
fence part: pale, post, stile
fence, temporary wooden: hoarding
fence, top railing of: ledger board

fenced enclosure for horses: corral, paddock
fenced enclosure for livestock: corral
fencing attack with short jump forward: balestra
fencing defensive move: parade, parry
fencing false move: feint
fencing guard for protecting hand: coquille
fencing hit acknowledgment: touché
fencing move to avoid thrust: volt
fencing pierce or stab: thrust
fencing position: tierce
fencing quilted body covering: plastron
fencing running attack: flèche
fencing stamping of foot: appel
fencing sword: épée, foil, saber, sabre
fencing sword strong half near handle: forte
fencing sword weak half near point: foible
fencing sword with arched guard and flexible blade: saber
fencing sword with bowl-shaped guard and narrow blade: épée
fencing sword with circular guard and flexible blade: foil
fencing terms: appel, balestra, barrage, coquille, cut, duel, en garde, épée, feint, flèche, foible, foil, parry, piste, plastron, remise, reprise, riposte, saber, sword, swording, thrust, touché, volt
fencing thrust after parrying opponent's lunge: riposte
fencing warning: en garde
fend: avert, avoid, defend, guard, parry, protect, provide, repel, resist, safeguard, support
fender: buffer, bumper, cushion, frame, guard, mudguard, screen, shield, splashboard
feral: barbarous, brutal, ferocious, fierce, savage, untamed, wild
ferile and productive: fecund, prolific
ferment: agitate, barm, boil, brew, catalyst, churn, commotion, disorder, enzyme, exasperate, excite, excitement, fever, froth, heat, provoke, seethe, simmer, stew, tumult, turbulence, turn, uproar, yeast
fermentation: zymolysis
fermentation agent: yeast
fermentation in brewing: zymurgy
fermented honey drink: mead
fermented rice beverage: sake
fermented Russian beverage: kvass
fermented sour malt: alegar

fern frond petiole: stipe
fern leaf: frond
fern root: roi
fern seed: spore
fern spore: sorus
fern, coiled frond of: crosier, fiddlehead
fern, feathery: maidenhair
fern, single-celled reproductive body of: spore
fern, weedy coarse: bracken
ferocious: barbaric, bloodthirsty, brutal, cruel, extreme, fell, feral, fierce, grim, inhuman, malevolent, merciless, murderous, ravenous, relentless, ruthless, sanguinary, savage, truculent, untamed, vicious, violent, wild
ferret out: ascertain, elicit, follow, hunt, probe, seek, trace, track, trail, uncover
ferret, pertaining to: musteline
ferrous metal: iron
ferrule: tip
ferry: barge, carry, shuttle
fertile: abundant, bountiful, exuberant, fecund, feracious, flowering, fruitful, generous, hearty, lush, luxuriant, plentiful, pregnant, productive, profitable, progenitive, prolific, rich, teeming, virile
fertile part of desert: oasis
fertilization in artificial environment, of: in vitro
fertilization of one plant by another: cross-fertilization, xenogamy
fertilization of plant, self-: autogamy
fertilize: enrich, fecundate, fructify, impregnate, inseminate, lime, make pregnant, pollinate
fertilize an egg: impregnate
fertilize by pollen: pollinate
fertilized egg, cell capable of fusing with opposite sex to produce: gamete
fertilized egg, ovum: zygote
fertilizer: dung, manure, marl, mulch, niter
fertilizer component: nitrates
fertilizer compound: nitrate, phosphate, potash, urea
fertilizer of bird, bat droppings: guano
fertilizer of human excrement: night soil
fertilizer or protective covering: mulch
fertilizer, decayed vegetable or animal matter that acts as: humus
fervent: animated, ardent, blazing, burning, eager, emotional, enthusias-

FERNS

adder's-tongue fern
basket fern
bead fern
beech fern
bladder fern
Boston fern
boulder fern
bracken
bristle fern
buckler fern
chain fern
Christmas fern
cinnamon fern
cliff brake
climbing fern
curly grass fern
grape fern
hart's-tongue
hay-scented fern
holly fern
lady fern
lip fern
maidenhair
male fern
marsh fern
moonwort
mosquito fern
New York fern
oak fern
osmund
ostrich fern
polypody
rattlesnake fern
resurrection fern
rock brake
royal fern
seed fern
sensitive fern
shield fern
snuffbox fern
spleenwort
tree fern
walking fern
walking leaf
wall fern
water fernwood fern
woodsia ❦

tic, fierce, fiery, glowing, hot, impetuous, intense, passionate, raging, vehement, warm, zealous
fervid: ardent, impassioned
fervid to extreme: perfervid
fervor: ardor, eagerness, earnestness, ecstasy, enthusiasm, excitement, fire, gusto, heat, intensity, love, passion, relish, vehemence, warmth, zeal
fescue: grass
fester: blister, decay, fret, grow, inflame, rankle, rot, suppurate, ulcerate
festering anger: slow burn
festering sore: ulcer
festival: ale, banquet, carnival, cavalcade, celebration, fair, feast, festa, fete, fiesta, gala, holiday, jamboree, jubilee, pageant
festive: celebratory, decorated, frolicsome, gala, gay, happy, jocular, joyous, merry, mirthful, playful, sportive, upbeat
festivity: celebration, conviviality, entertainment, fanfare, gaiety, gala, hoopla, jollity, joyfulness, merrymaking, mirth, revelry, whoopee
festoon: adorn, swag
fetch: achieve, apparition, attract, bring, deliver, elicit, get, ghost, go for, inhale, obtain, realize, retrieve, strategem, sweep, trick
fetching: alluring, appealing, attractive, beautiful, captivating, charming, lovely, pleasing
fete: ball, banquet, bazaar, carnival, celebrate, entertain, fair, feast, festival, fiesta, gala, holiday, party, regale
fetid: corrupt, foul, fusty, malodorous, mephitic, moldy, musty, noisome, noxious, offensive, olid, putrid, rancid, rank, repulsive, rotten, stinking
fetish: amulet, charm, desire, fixation, idol, image, juju, mania, obeah, obsession, passion, sorcery, talisman, totem, voodoo
fetor: reek
fetter: bind, block, bond, chain, confine, hamper, handcuff, hobble, hold, impede, manacle, restraint, shackle, trammel
fetus murder: feticide
fetus's connection to uterus: placenta
feud: argument, broil, conflict, contest, disagreement, dispute, duel, enmity, fight, fray, grudge, hostility, quarrel, row, strife, tiff, vendetta, war
feud, family: vendetta
feudal dependent: vassal
feudal estate: fief
feudal lord of Japan: daimyo
feudal ruler: seignior
feudal slave: esne

The Writer's Digest Flip Dictionary

fever: ague, craze, delirium, desire, excitement, ferment, fire, frenzy, heat, pyrexia, temperature
fever and chills: ague
fever and inflammation, of: inflammatory, phlogistic
fever-reducing: antipyretic
fever, confused from a high: delirious
fever, relating to a: febrile, pyretic
fever, very high: hyperpyrexia, hyperthermia
feverish: ardent, burning, bustling, excited, febrile, fiery, flushed, frantic, hectic, intense, obsessive, overeager, pyretic, restless, warm
feverless: afebrile
few: handful, infrequent, less, limited, meager, occasional, rare, scant, scarce, seldom, skimpy, some
few and far between: sparse
few words, using: laconic
fey: clairvoyant, dead, elfin, fairylike, otherworldly, visionary, whimsical
fiancé: betrothed, engaged, fiancée, intended, steady
fiasco: blunder, bomb, catastrophe, debacle, disaster, failure, flop, screwup, washout
fiat: announcement, command, decree, dictum, edict, mandate, order, ordinance, proclamation, rule, sanction, ukase, writ
fib: canard, equivocate, fabrication, half-truth, hedge, lie, prevaricate, story, tale, taradiddle, untruth
fiber: acrylic, arnel, character, coir, cord, cotton, Dacron, essence, fabric, filament, flax, floss, fortitude, grain, hair, hemp, jute, lint, nature, nylon, polyester, quality, rayon, root, rope, roughage, sisal, string, texture, thread, tissue, wool
RELATED TERMS
fiber for making linen: flax
fiber for rope: abaca, manila, manila hemp, sisal
fiber for sacking: hemp, jute
fiber for telecommunications: fiber optics, optical fiber
fiber for twine: cantala, maguey
fiber from cellulose: rayon
fiber health food: bran
fiber in diet: roughage
fiber ingredient: cellulose
fiber knot: nep
fiber of agave plant: sisal
fiber of cotton, maize, silkworm: floss
fiber of flax or hemp for yarn: tow

fiber of hemp, jute: oakum
fiber of silk-cotton tree: kapok
fiber on coconut: coir
fiber on palm leaf: raffia ❦

fibrous: pulpy, ropy, sinewy, stringy, tough
fibrous protein: keratin
fibula: brooch, clasp, leg bone, lower leg
fichu: scarf
fickle: capricious, changeable, critical, erratic, faithless, flighty, fluctuating, frivolous, inconsistent, inconstant, labile, mercurial, shifting, shifty, skittish, transient, unsettled, unstable, unsteady, vacillating, variable, volatile, wavering, whimsical
fiction: book, concoction, contrivance, drama, fable, fabrication, falsehood, fantasy, figment, invention, legend, myth, narrative, novel, pretense, romance, tale, yarn
fiction set in castle or abbey: gothic novel, gothic romance
fictional wonderful place: cockaigne, Shangri-la, utopia
fictitious: apocryphal, artificial, assumed, bogus, chimeric, counterfeit, created, fake, false, fanciful, feigned, imaginary, invented, made, mythical, phony, sham, spurious, unreal, untrue
fictitious name: Doe, pen name, pseudonym, Roe
fiddle: bow, cheat, dabble, doodle, fidget, guardrail, putter, swindle, tamper, tinker, touch, trifle, violin
fiddle-shaped: pandurate
fidelity: adherence, allegiance, constancy, dependability, devotion, faithfulness, fealty, honesty, honor, integrity, love, loyalty, oath, reliability, troth
fidgety: antsy, anxious, apprehensive, fussy, hyper, impatient, jittery, jumpy, nervous, restive, restless, squirmy, uneasy, wired
fiduciary: curator, depositary, guardian, trustee
field: area, compass, competitors, contestants, course, department, discipline, domain, entries, occupation, orbit, profession, racket, range, realm, scope, specialty, sphere, track, tract; acre, area, background, battleground, catch, clearing, course, garden, grassland, gridiron, grounds, lea,

mead, meadow, pasture, patch, playground, plot, range, stadium, terrain, track, tract, vineyard
field, cover briefly: tarp
field day: success, triumph
field glasses: binoculars
field hand of yore: esne
field mouse: vole
field of competition: arena
field of fabricating devices used in production lines: tool & die
field of main activity: bailiwick, domain, preserve
field of study: discipline
field or scope of activity: ambit, compass, orbit, reach
fiend: addict, barbarian, beast, brute, demon, devil, fanatic, incubus, maniac, monster, obsessed, savage, scoundrel, succubus
fiendish: atrocious, barbarous, cruel, demoniac, demonic, devilish, diabolical, difficult, evil, satanic, sinister, vicious, wicked
fierce: aggressive, ardent, bold, brutal, cruel, cutthroat, fell, feral, ferocious, fervent, fiery, furious, intense, merciless, overpowering, passionate, raging, relentless, ruthless, savage, terrible, truculent, uncontrolled, unpleasant, untamed, violent, wild
fierce and cruel: fell, malicious, vicious
fierce and wild: farouche
fiery: ablaze, ardent, blazing, burning, choleric, enthusiastic, excitable, fervent, fervid, feverish, fierce, flaming, flammable, glowing, heated, hot, hotheaded, impetuous, impulsive, inflamed, inflammable, intense, irascible, irritable, mettlesome, passionate, peppery, spirited, spunky, tempestuous, torrid, violent
fiesta: carnival, celebration, feast, festival, fete, gala, holiday, party
fifteenth day of March, May, July, October in ancient Roman calendar: ides
fifth: quinary
fifth anniversary: quinquennial
fifth canonical hour: nones
fifty-fifty: divided, equally, even, shared, toss up
fifty to fifty-nine years old: quinquagenarian
fig: eleme, fico, fruit, ginger, mamme, pipal, rig, sinconus, syconium, syconus
fig-bearing tree: banyan

fig fruit: syconium

fig-shaped: caricous, sycosiform

fight: affair, affray, altercation, argue, argument, attack, battle, bicker, bout, box, brawl, brush, clash, combat, conflict, confrontation, content, contest, controversy, debate, disagreement, dispute, duel, encounter, exchange, feud, fracas, fray, grapple, grit, hassle, joust, melee, mettle, oppose, quarrel, resist, rivalry, row, rumble, scrap, scuffle, skirmish, spar, spat, spirit, squabble, struggle, tiff, war, withstand, wrangle

fight back: retaliate

fight between mounted knights: joust, tilting match

fight for breath: gasp

fight for two: duel

fight in which outsiders get stuck: crossfire

fight off: resist

fight or campaign for cause: crusade

fight over words: logomachy

fight, angry: altercation, confrontation, contretemps, tussle

fight, loud: donnybrook, fracas, melee

fight, minor: skirmish

fight, noisy: brawl, fracas, fray, melee

fight, petty: spat, tiff

fight, very involved in: at loggerheads, embroiled

fighter: battler, boxer, bruiser, combatant, competitor, contender, duelist, gladiator, pug, pugilist, scrapper, soldier, warrior

fighter in raiding band: guerrilla

fighting or disagreement, bitter: dissension, friction, strife

fighting, easily provoked into: fractious, pugnacious, truculent

fighting, imaginary: sciamachy, shadow boxing

figment: dream, fabrication, fantasy, fiction, illusion, invention, phantom

figuration: contour, form, outline, shape, symbolism

figurative: allegorical, descriptive, emblematic, florid, flowery, metaphorical, ornate, symbolic

figurative use of word: trope

figure: amount, character, cost, digit, emblem, form, gargoyle, number, numeral, price, quotation, rate, sum, symbol, topiary, total, value

figure-eight bandage: spica

figure of grotesque creature on building: gargoyle

figure of speech: adage, allegory, alliteration, allocution, amplification, analogy, antiphrasis, aphorism, aporia, atticism, brachylogy, cliché, color, conceit, echoism, euphemism, flowery, hyperbole, image, imagery, irony, litotes, malapropism, meiosis, metaphor, metonymy, onomatopoeia, oxymoron, paradox, periphrasis, personification, platitude, pleonasm, simile, syllepsis, synecdoche, tmesis, trope, troupe, zeugmaa

figure of speech describing event as happening before it actually could: prolepsis

figure of speech using "and" between two words instead of usual wording: hendiadys

figure of speech using "as" or "like" in making comparison: simile

figure of speech using attribute as substitute for thing's name: metonymy

figure of speech using combination of contradictory words: oxymoron

figure of speech using comparison: metaphor

figure of speech using embodiment of quality in person: personification

figure of speech using modifier with two words which acquires different meanings : syllepsis

figure of speech using negation of assertion's opposite: litotes

figure of speech using reversal of natural order: hysteron proteron

figure of speech using word with two others but it agrees grammatically with only one: zeugma

figure of speech, exaggerated: hyperbole

figure of speech, overused: dead metaphor

figure of speech, such as metaphor, hyperbole: trope

figure on cards: pip

figure or letter above and to right of character: superscript

figure or letter below and to right of character: subscript

figure out: calculate, crack, decide, decipher, decode, discover, resolve, solve, unravel, unscramble, untangle

figure, geometric: circle, cone, crescent, cube, diagram, ellipse, gnomon, hexafoil, isagon, isogon, lozenge, lune, oblong, pelcoid, pentacle, prism, rectangle, rhomb, rhombus, sector, solid, spheroid, square, triangle

figure, shapely: hourglass

figurehead: dummy, front, mouthpiece, nonentity, puppet, stooge

figurehead site: prow

figures of speech, based on or using: figurative, metaphorical

filament: fiber, hair, harl, stalk, strand, tendril, thread, wire

filbert: nut

filbert's cousin: pecan

filch: cop, embezzle, heist, lift, pilfer, pinch, rob, snitch, steal, swipe

file: archives, arrange, cabinet, case, catalog, classify, column, drawer, folder, index, line, list, order, rank, record, register, row, store, tool; grind, rasp, sharpen, smooth

file with detailed information: dossier

filibuster: adventurer, delay, opposition, orate, stonewalling, talkathon, tirade

fill: accomplish, capacity, caulk, charge, complete, cram, crowd, distend, earth, enlarge, execute, feed, gorge, inflate, load, occupy, pack, padding, permeate, pervade, plug, replenish, sate, satiate, satisfy, stock, stuffing, sufficiency, suffuse, supply

fill again: replenish

fill in: brief, complete, inform, interject, replacement, substitute

fill or spread throughout: riddle

fill throughout: impregnate, infuse, saturate, suffuse

fill to excess: glut

fill to overflowing: brim

fill to the brim: sate

fill with delight and wonder: entrance

fill with joy: elate

filled or full: fraught, glutted, gorged, laden, replete, sated, satiated

filled tortillas: tacos

filled with anger: livid

filled with freight: laded

filled with light: luminous

filled with righteous wrath: indignant

filler or glaze made for porous materials: size

fillet: band, bandeau, boneless, chaplet, crown, fish, garland, headband, listel, meat, molding, ribbon, ridge, slice, snood, strip, tape, wreath

fillet a fish: bone

filling: amalgam, center, content, custard, inlay, mixture, wadding, weft

fillip: boost, charge, excite, flip, incentive, stimulus, tap

film: blur, coating, deposit, haze, layer, mist, pellicle, scum, skin, transparency, veil; celluloid, cine, cinema, flick, footage, movie, negative, photograph, record, transparency, X ray

film adding of soundtrack: dub

film assistant to gaffer: best boy

film at the ends, to join: splice

film award: Oscar, Golden Globe

film buff: cineast

film camera: cinematograph

film camera platform on wheels: dolly

film camera toward or away from subject, quick move of: zoom

film category: genre

film change of scenes with one fading out as next appears: dissolve

film director known for style: auteur

film documentary, realistic: cinema verité

film dramatization based on fact: docudrama

film electrician or lighting technician: gaffer

film footage: reel

film gradual appearance or disappearance of image or sound: fade-in, fade-out

film hinged board with take number: clapper board

film lamp providing intense light: klieg light

film library: cinematheque

film list of performers and workers: credits

film presenting factual or historical subject matter in informative way : documentary

film scene that is short: vignette

film scene, unedited print of: rush

film scene, uninterrupted camera shot of: take

film scenes edited out: outtake

film screening early in the day: matinee

film script, full narrative version of: treatment

film segment: clip

film sequence of shots or scenes depicting different aspects of theme or event: montage

film sequence or part: footage

film set and camera worker: grip

film single frame repeated to simulate static picture: freeze-frame

film site outside a studio: location

film technique of changing scenes as if obliterating old scene: wipe

film technique of following a moving object or viewing a panorama: pan

film technique of photographing a slow process in intervals: time-lapse

film with earlier events than in a previous film: prequel

film with events following those in previous film: sequel

film, biographical: biopic

film, commentary of unseen narrator on: voice-over

film, passage or segment taken from a: excerpt

film, single picture on roll of: frame

film, tiny: microfiche, microfilm

film, to move the camera and follow action in making: track

film, trial: pilot film

filming technique with series of static drawings to simulate movement: animation

filmmaking: cinematography

film's first public showing: premiere

film's script with camera directions and scene descriptions: screenplay

film's script, final version of: shooting script

filmy: clouded, dainty, finespun, fragile, gauzy, gossamer, hazy, milky, misty, wispy

filter: clean, drain, infiltrate, leach, percolate, purify, refine, screen, seep, sieve, sift, strain, strainer

filter, claylike substance used as: fuller's earth

filth: corruption, dirt, dung, garbage, grime, muck, obscenity, pollution, pornography, refuse, sewage, silt, slime, slop, smut, trash

filthy: dirty, disgusting, foul, grimy, gross, grubby, impure, lewd, nasty, obscene, offensive, polluted, raunchy, repulsive, revolting, rotten, scatological, scummy, sleazy, sordid, squalor, unclean, vile, vulgar, wreched

filthy abode: Augean stables, pigsty, sty

filthy literature, art: coprology, scatology

filthy lucre: pelf

fin: airfoil, appendage, arm, dorsal, flipper, hand, pinna, stabilizer, vane

fin on bomb or missile, stabilizing: vane

fin, fish's bony spine supporting: ray

finagle: cheat, connive, deceive, rook, scheme, swindle, trick

final: absolute, concluding, conclusive, crowning, decisive, definitive, end, extreme, farewell, imperative, last, latter, peremptory, supreme, telic, terminating, ultimate, unalterable

final and perfected state of an insect: imago

final appearance or act: swan song

final authority: say-so

final battle: Armageddon

final decisive event: coup de grâce

final degree: nth

final end, development toward: teleology

final part: end piece, homestretch

final part of composition that closes action: coda

final part of play, poem or speech as: epilogue

final part of speech, summary as: peroration

final passage: coda

final poem stanza: envoy

final point in progression: climax, culmination

final relay race contestant: anchor

final resolution of plot: denouement

final sonnet lines: sestet

final statement of terms dictated to another: "or else," ultimatum

final word: amen, never, omega, tata

final, deciding election: run-off

final, to make: clinch

finale: climax, closing, coda, conclusion, culmination, end, ending, epilogue, finis, windup

finalize: agree, conclude, consummate, finish, settle

finally: at last, certainly, decisively, eventually, irrevocably, lastly, once and for all, ultimately

finance: back, banking, bankroll, business, economics, endow, float, fund, money, sponsor, stake, subsidize, underwrite

finance a project, to: subsidize

finances: affairs, budget, cash, resources, revenue, wealth

finances, pertaining to: fiscal

financial: economic, fiscal, markets, monetary, pecuniary

financial aid, grant of: subvention

financial aid, one who gives: benefactor, benefactress

financial independence: easy street

financial obligation: liability

financial obligations, capable of meeting: solvent

FIRE TERMS

catching fire by localized heat-increasing reaction: spontaneous combustion
causing or capable of causing fire: incendiary
combustible heap for funeral fire: pyre
combustible material used to start fire: kindling, punk, spunk, tinder, touchwood
cover a fire with ashes or fresh fuel, to: bank
crime of setting fires: arson
criminal fire setter: arsonist, incendiary
destroy interior of with fire, to: gut
great and destructive fire: conflagration
large blazing fire: conflagration, holocaust, inferno

of or relating to fire: igneous
put out a fire, to: douse, extinguish, quench
sensing device for fire: pyrostat, smoke detector
set or catch fire, to: ignite
sit idly by a fire, to: cloffin
smoldering ash or coal of dying fire: embers
sparks and embers rising from fire: izles
tending to catch fire: flammable, incendiary, inflammatory
water main spout for fighting fire: fire hydrant, fireplug, hydrant
wood or rolled paper to start fire: spill ☙

---

financial office of college: bursar, bursary, treasurer

financial officer of corporation or governmental body: comptroller, controller

financial responsibility for, to assume: underwrite

financial restriction, of a: stringent

financial settlement paid to former lover: palimony

financial supporter or backer: angel, patron, sponsor

financier: backer, capitalist, entrepreneur, sponsor, staker, underwriter

finch: fringillid, junco, linnet, serin, snowbird, sparrow

finch family: oscine

find: ascertain, bonanza, catch, dig up, discovery, judge, locate, recover, solve, spot, treasure, uncover, unearth

find a solution: resolve

find again: rediscover

find by careful observation or scrutiny: descry, detect

find fault: blame, carp, pan

find guilty: condemn, convict, indict

find innocent: absolve, acquit, exonerate, vindicate

find out: ascertain, detect, discover, fathom, hear, identify, learn, realize, reveal, unearth

find the answer: solve

find the meaning or nature of: fathom

finding one's bearings: orientation

findings by accident, making fortunate: serendipity

fine: absolute, admirable, amerce, assessment, beautiful, bonny, bright, capital, choice, clear, consummate, dainty, damages, dandy, delicate, elegant, excellent, exceptional, expensive, forfeit, fragile, frail, good, granular, great, handsome, levy, magnificent, minute, mulct, nice, nifty, okay, outstanding, penalize, penalty, pleasant, powdery, precise, pulverized, punishment, pure, reparation, sharp, sheer, silky, skillful, slight, splendid, subtle, superior, swell, tender, tenuous, thin, topgrade

fine detail: punctilio

fine food, of old: cate

fine lines on the ends of letters: serifs

fine point: nicety, subtlety

fine point of etiquette: punctilio

fine-tuned: honed

fine, lacelike ornamentation: filigree

fine, penalty of a: mulct

fine, punishment by: amercement

fine, to impose a: levy

finery: adornment, apparel, array, clothes, elegance, frills, frippery, gaudery, gewgaws, regalia, Sunday best, trappings

finesse: adeptness, artfulness, artifice, craftiness, cunning, delicacy, dexterity, guile, maneuver, manipulate, operate, refinement, savvy, sensitivity, skill, stratagem, subtlety, tact

finger: appendage, choose, dactyl, designate, digit, feel, handle, identify, index, indicate, make, paw, pinky, pinpoint, strum, thumb, touch

finger bones: phalanges

finger of glove or protective sheath: stall

finger-operated: digital

finger or toe: dactyl, digit

finger or toe, little: minimus

finger- or toenail, ingrown: acronyx

finger snap: fillip

finger, fleshy end of: pad

fingerboard, movable bar on guitar: capo

fingerhole on flute: ventage

fingerless: adactylous

fingerless glove: mitten

fingernail hardened skin at base and sides: cuticle

fingernail white crescent: lunula

fingerprint: dab, dactylogram, identify, mark

fingerprint pattern: arch, loop, whorl

fingerprint smudges on clean surface, to leave: climp

fingerprints, study of: dactylography

fingers, snap the: lirp, thrip

finial: epi, spire

finicky: choosy, difficult, fastidious, finical, fussy, meticulous, nitpicking, particular, picky, prissy, scrupulous

finis: end

finish: accomplish, achieve, be done, cease, close, coating, completion, conclusion, culminate, defeat, deplete, destroy, devour, die, end, execute, finalize, finis, fulfill, glaze, kill, lacquer, limit, mop up, perfect, perfection, stain, stop, surface, terminate, wind up

finish line: tape

finish off: dispatch, dispose of, kill

finish quickly: make short work of

finished: at an end, closed, completed, concluded, consumed, consummated, done, done for, done with, ended, exhausted, gone, kaput, ornate, over, perfected, polished, refined, ripe, ruined, terminated, through

finishing layer of wood: veneer

finishing touch or stroke: coup de grâce

finite: bounded, definable, exact, fixed, impermanent, limited, measurable, restricted

fir: alpine, cedar, conifer, Douglas, evergreen, pine, wood

fire: animate, ardor, arouse, arson, attack, blaze, burn, combustion, conflagration, detonate, discharge, drive, element, enthusiasm, excite, explode, fervor, fervour, flames, fling, glow, heat, holocaust, ignite, illuminate, incite, inferno, inflame, inspire, intensity, kindle, launch, light, shoot, spirit, torch, vigor, vivacity, zeal; can, discharge, dismiss, sack, terminate

fire-breathing monster: Chimera

firearm: gun, musket, piece, pistol, repeater, rifle, weapon

firearm charge: load

firearm cleaning rod: ramrod

firearm diagonally across body, carry: port

firearm discharge from side of warship: broadside

firearm sighting line in eyepiece: crosshair

firearms simultaneously, discharge of several: barrage, fusillade

firebomb: Greek fire, incendiary bomb, Molotov cocktail, napalm bomb

firebug: arsonist, incendiary, pyromaniac

firecracker, loud: petard

firecracker, small: squib

fireflies' light: luciferin

firelike: igneous

fireplace: furnace, grate, hearth, ingle

fireplace cover: bonnet

fireplace frame or facing, and its protruding shelf: mantel

fireplace log holder: andiron, dog, dog iron, firedog

fireplace screen: fender

fireplace-to-chimney pipe: flue

fireplace, incombustible residue of coal in: clinker

fireplace, nook beside an open: inglenook

fireplace, the back of an open: reredos

fireproof: incombustible, noncombustible, nonflammable

fires, uncontrollable urge to start: pyromania

fireworks: girandole, pyrotechnics, rocket display, Roman candle, sparkler, trouble

fireworks, rotating display of: girandole

fireworks, smoldering substance used to light: punk

firkin: pail

firm: adamant, anchored, backboned, certain, compact, confirm, consistent, constant, decided, definite, dense, determined, durable, established, exact, faithful, fastened, fixed, hard, hearty, house, immovable, inelastic, inflexible, intent, iron, loyal, neve, outfit, resolute, rigid, secured, set, settled, solid, sound, stable, staunch, steadfast, steady, stiff, stout, strict, strong, sturdy, substantial, sure, tight, unmoved, unshaken, unwavering, unyielding; business, company, conglomerate, corporation, enterprise, establishment, partnership

firm and durable: impregnable, indissoluble, unshakable, unyielding

firm and having solid basis: substantive

firm and loyal: staunch

firm dealing in securities: investment trust

firm foundation: bedrock, hardpan

firm in chewing (pasta): al dente

firm, in music: risoluto

firmament: empyrean, ether, heavens, sky, universe, vault

firmly committed: deep-rooted, dyed-in-the-wool, inveterate

firmly entangled or involved: inextricable

firmly entrenched: enrooted

firmly faithful: steadfast, unwavering

firmly fixed: anchored, fast

firmly holding: tenacious

firmly settled: entrenched

firmness: consistency, density, immobility, impenetrability, iron, resolve, solidity, stability, steadiness, strength, tanacity, toughness

first: aboriginal, ahead, alpha, archetypal, beginning, chief, debut, earliest, eldest, foremost, fundamental, head, high, highest, initial, leading, maiden, main, onset, original, premier, primal, primary, prime, primeval, primitive, primordial, principal, unveiling

first achievement toward success: beachhead, bridgehead, foothold, salient

First Amendment: academic freedom

first among equals: prima inter pares, primus, primus inter pares

first appearance: dawn, debut

first cardinal number: one

first-class: A1, best, excellent, exclusive, finest, first-rate, five-star, prime, shipshape, superior, tip-top, top-drawer, topflight, top-notch

first cousin: cousin-german

first experience in combat or ordeal: baptism of fire

first Hebrew letter: alef

first in position: premier

first mention, make: broach

first move: initiative

first or earliest stages of development, in: embryonic, germinal, inchoate, incipient, nascent

first or fundamental principle, element: rudiment

first or original model: archetype, prototype

first play, in bridge: lead

first prize: blue ribbon

first public display: unveiling

first public presentation: premiere

first-rate: A1, classy, dandy, super, top-notch, tops

firstborn: eigne, eldest, heir, oldest, primogeniture

firstborn, state of being the: primogeniture

firstborn's ancient inheritance right: esnecy

firsthand: direct, eyewitness

fiscal: budgetary, economic, monetary

fish: angle, bass, carp, cast, dab, dace, dap, drail, eel, gill, gudgeon, ide, ling, net, poisson, quab, scrod, scup, seine, shad, smelt, snapper, sole, spet, troll, trout, tuna

fish out of water: misfit

fishy: cold, doubtful, dull, farfetched, implausible, improbable, shady, suspicious, unlikely

fissile rock: shale

fission: breaking, reaction, reproduction, scission, splitting

fissure: aperture, blemish, break, chink, cleavage, cleft, crack, cranny, crevasse, crevice, division, flaw, furrow, gap, groove, leak, lesion, opening, rift, rima, rime, schism, seam, slit, split, vein

fissure or chasm: crevasse

fissured, cracked: rimose

fist: clench, clutch, grasp, grip, hand, hold, strike

fit: able, accommodate, adapt, adapted, adept, adequate, adjust, alter, applicable, appropriate, apt, attack, become, becoming, befitting,

FISH AND FISHING TERMS

branch of zoology concerning fish: ichthyology
catfish: bullhead, hassar, hornpout, sheatfish, stonecat
cod: bacalao, beardie, bib, burbot, cusk, gadoid, hake, ling, pollock, tomcod, torsk
concerning fish: ichthyic, piscatory, piscine
dish of deep-fried squid: calamari
dish of dried salted lizardfish: Bombay duck, bummalo
eel-like fish: conger, cuchia, eelpout, lamprey, link, moray, opah
electric fish: raad, stargazer, torpedo
female fish: henfish, raun
fin types: adipose, anal, caudal, dorsal, median, paired, pectoral, pelvic, ventral
fish-eating: piscivorous
fish eggs: roe
fish hook: barb, gaff
fish illegally: poach
fish net: seine, trawl
fish sperm: milt
fish split and air-dried: stockfish
fish stew: bouillabaisse
fish story: lie
fish tank: aquarium
fish with cartilage skeleton: cartilaginous fish
fish with sucking disk: remora
fish without fins: eel
fisherman: angler, eeler, harpooner, piscator, seiner, spearer, trawler, troller, whaler
fisherman's basket: creel
fishery: cannery, hatchery, piscary, weir
fishing bait or decoy: lure
fishing boat's anchored chair: fighting chair
fishing cord: line
fishing from a moving boat: troll
fishing spear: gig, leister

flat fish: bream, brill, butt, dab, dace, flounder, fluke, halibut, plaice, ray, sanddab, skate, sole, sunfish, torpedo, turbot
game fish: bass, grilse, marlin, perch, pickerel, pike, salmon, swordfish, tarpon, trout, tuna
herring: alewife, pilchard, sardine, shad, sprat
large fish net, hanging vertically at surface: seine
large school of fish: run, shoal
large tapered fishing net towed along sea bottom: trawl net
of fish recently spawned: shotten
of or relating to fish: piscine
opening for intestinal, genital, urinary tracts: cloaca
period during which it is illegal to fish: closed season
period during which it is legal to fish: open season
raw fish: sashimi, sushi
relating to fishing: piscatorial
sauce served with fish: alec, tartar
shellfish: clam, crab, langouste, langoustine, lobster, mussel, oyster, shrimp
small or young fish: fingerling, fry
types of fish: alewife, anchovy, barbel, blenny, bream, brill, caribe, carp, catfish, cod, dab, dogfish, dolphin, eel, flounder, gar, gass, haddock, hake, herring, hiku, jocu, lamprey, lance, lant, machete, mackerel, mado, marlin, masu, meat, midge, opah, orfe, otter, pega, perch, peto, pike, piranha, pogy, porgie, pout, ray, salmon, scrod, scup, seine, shad, shark, skate, smelt, sole, sturgeon, sunfish, sword, tarpon, trout, tuna, turbot, ulua, umbra, wahoo, wrasse
types of fish caught for food: alewife, baleen, barracuda, bass, carp, catfish, caviar, cod, eel, flounder, grouper, haddock, hake, halibut, herring, mackerel, pompano, salmon, sardine, scup, sea trout, shad, skate, smelt, snapper, sole, swordfish, tautog, tile, trout, tuna, wrasse
young fish: alevin, fingerling, fry, grilse, larva, parr, smolt ❦

---

belong, bout, capable, competent, conform, convenient, convulsion, correct, correspond, deserving, dovetail, eligible, equip, felicitous, frenzy, furnish, hale, happy, healthy, in the pink, match, meet, opportune, outbreak, outburst, paroxysm, pertinent, prepare, proper, qualified, qualify, rage, ready, right, ripe, robust, seemly, seizure, shape, spasm, stroke, strong, suit, suitable, suited, tantrum, timely, toned, well, whim
fit inside others: nest
fit neatly together: dovetail
fit of anger: snit
fit of shivering: ague
fit to be ingested: edible
fit to drink: potable
fit to eat: edible

fit with sails: rig
fit, emotional frenzy or: nympholepsy
fit, sudden: apoplexy, convulsion, ictus, paroxysm, seizure, spasm
fitful: capricious, convulsive, erratic, haphazard, impulsive, intermittent, irregular, periodic, random, restless, spasmodic, sporadic, variable
fitness: aptitude, capacity, competence, condition, decency, decorum, health, readiness, shape, suitability
fitted piece: tenon
fitting: accessory, adjustment, applicable, appropriate, apt, attachment, becoming, due, happy, instrument, meet, part, proper, seemly, suitable, warranted
fitting to proportion: commensurate
five children born at once: quintuplets

five-hundredth anniversary: quincentenary
five in cards or dice: cinque
five-line rhyme scheme: limerick
five-line stanza: cinquain
five objects around rectangle or square and one in the center: quincunx
five parts or units, having: quintuple
five-pointed star: pentacle, pentagram, pentangle
five-sided or -lobed design: cinquefoil
five-sided polygon: pentagon
five-year anniversary: quinquennial
five-year period: lustrum, quinquennium
five, group of: pentad
fivefold: quinary, quintuple
fivesome: pentad
fix: adjust, amend, anchor, appoint, ar-

FISHING

angling
big-game fishing
bottom fishing
bowfishing
coarse fishing
deep-sea fishing
drift fishing
float fishing
fly-fishing
freshwater fishing
game fishing
ice fishing
kite fishing
lake fishing
margin fishing
match fishing
reef fishing
saltwater fishing
sportfishing
still fishing
stream fishing
trolling ❦

---

range, arrest, assign, attach, attribute, bind, bribe, cement, concentrate, confirm, corner, correct, couple, determine, direct, establish, fasten, filemma, focus, glue, hold, imbed, influence, limit, mend, moor, nail, neuter, patch, prepare, recondition, reconstruct, redo, renovate, repair, restore, revamp, scrape, seal, secure, set, settle, spay, spot, stabilize, station; difficulty, dilemma, jam, mess, pickle, predicament

fix in time: date

fix up: arrange, beautify, equip, furnish, mend, refurbish, renovate, repair, restore

fixation: addiction, craze, fascination, fetish, infatuation, mania, obsession, quirk

fixed: agreed, arranged, ascertain, attached, capture, certain, constant, definite, embedded, explicit, fast, fastened, firm, frozen, immobile, immovable, incessant, inflexible, intent, permanent, prearranged, resolute, rigid, sessile, set, stable, staid, stationary, steady, still, stubborn, unbending, unwavering

fixed amount of work to be done: stint

fixed and impossible to get rid of: ineradicable, inextricable

fixed firmly: embedded, entrenched

fixed idea: idée fixe
fixed in place: stabile
fixed intention: resolve
fixed look: stare
fixed machine part: stator
fixed or attached, permanently: sessile
fixed or impressed deeply: engraved
fixed price for whole meal: prix fixe, table d'hôte
fixed procedure: rote
fixed relation: ratio
fixture: apparatus, appliance, attachment, counters, equipment, furnishing, regular, shelves
fizz: bubble, carbonation, effervescence, foam, sparkle
fizzle: bomb, collapse, fail, failure, fiasco, flop, hiss, misfire
fizzy water: carbonated drink, seltzer water, soda water
fjord: arm, inlet, ria
flabbergast: amaze, astonish, awe, confound, floor, overcome, overwhelm, shock, stun, surprise
flabby: doughy, fat, feeble, flaccid, lax, limp, loose, sagging, sloppy, soft, toneless, unfit, weak
flaccid: drooping, flabby, hanging, limp, weakened, yielding
flag: banderole, banner, blue peter, burgee, cattail, colors, emblem, ensign, gesture, guidon, iris, jack, Jolly Roger, masthead, motion, Old Glory, oriflamme, pendant, pennant, pennon, signal, standard, Stars and Stripes, streamer, symbol, yellow jack
flag carried by military unit, small: guidon
flag cloth: bunting
flag collector: vexillologist
flag for streamers, strips of cloth in colors of: bunting
flag hung on crosspiece, not pole: gonfalon
flag in salute or surrender, to lower a: strike
flag of college or sports team: pennant
flag of military unit or branch: ancient, banner, ensign, standard
flag of ship indicating nationality, small: jack
flag of yacht: burgee
flag or streamer, narrow often forked: banderole, bannerol, pencel, pennoncel
flag support: pole
flag, a signal with a: waft, waif

flag, ecclesiastical: gonfalon
flag, rope to raise and lower a: halyard
flag, to: decline, deteriorate, droop, fade, fail, falter, languish, pine, slump, tire, wilt
flag, to roll up and secure a: furl
flag, to unroll or open a: unfurl
flag, to wave grandly as a: flaunt
flag, triangular: pennant, pennon
flagellate: beat, cudgel, flog, impel, lash, punish, scourge, thrash, whip
flagging: tired
flagitious: atrocious, corrupt, criminal, flagrant, heinous, infamous, rotten, scandalous, vicious, villainous, wicked
flagon: bottle, cup, mug, stein, vessel
flagrant: atrocious, bad, blatant, brazen, conspicuous, dreadful, egregious, flagitious, glaring, gross, hateful, heinous, nefarious, noticeable, notorious, obvious, odious, offensive, outrageous, rank, reprehensible, shameful, shocking, violent, wicked
flags, relating to: vexillary
flags, study of: vexillology
flail: beat, flog, hit at, lash, strike, swing, thrash, whip
flair: ability, aptitude, bent, dash, élan, elegance, feel, gift, keenness, knack, nose, panache, style, talent, taste
flak: abuse, artillery, complaint, criticism, dissension
flake: bit, chip, crumble, fleck, lamina, nut, oddball, peel, scale, screwball, shred, sliver, snow, strip
flaky delight: croissant
flaky material: mica
flamboyant: dazzling, extravagant, flashy, florid, flowery, glamorous, loud, ornate, ostentatious, resplendent, rococo, showy, swank, theatrical
flame: ardor, beau, blaze, boyfriend, burning, fire, flare, flash, girlfriend, glare, glow, kindle, lover, passion, spark, sweetheart
flame about to go out: gutter
flame for lab experiments: Bunsen burner
flame glowing gently, of a: lambent
flame, hot gases around: mangle
flame, to extinguish a: douse, quench, snuff
flaming: ablaze, afire, flambé, ignescent, on fire
flaming French pancakes: crêpe suzettes
flaming torch: flambeau

flaming, served: flambé

flank: border, meat, side, thigh

flap: alarm, clap, commotion, disturbance, flack, flounce, flutter, fly, fuss, ruckus, slap, strike, tongue, waff, wave; appendage, lapel, tab, wing

flap of a shoe: tab

flap while losing wind, to: luff

flap, as sails: slat

flapdoodle: nonsense

flapjacks: pancakes

flapper hairdo: bob

flaps on some caps: earlaps

flare: balloon, blaze, broaden, dilate, erupt, expand, flame, flash, fleck, flicker, glare, light, outburst, pass, signal, splay, spread, torch, widen

flash: beam, blaze, bolt, burst, coruscate, coruscation, dart, flame, flare, flicker, fulgurate, glance, gleam, glimmer, glimpse, glint, glisten, glitter, glow, instant, jiffy, scintillate, second, shake, shimmer, sign, signal, spark, sparkle, streak, twinkle, vision

flash like lightning: fulgurate

flashy: brazen, cheap, dazzling, fiery, flamboyant, flaunting, garish, gaudy, glitzy, jazzy, loud, ornate, showy, sleek, snazzy, sporty, tacky

flashy, as a jacket: loud

flask: alembic, bottle, canteen, carafe, container, crock, ewer, flacon, frame, matrass, vial

flask-shaped: lageniform

flat: absolute, apart, apartment, banal, bland, blunt, boring, colorless, dead, decided, deflated, downright, dreary, dull, dwelling, even, fade, fixed, flashy, flush, horizontal, insipid, lackluster, level, lifeless, low, mat, monotonous, pad, plane, prone, prostrate, sluggish, smooth, stale, tasteless, tenement, uniform, unvarying, vapid

flat and dull: insipid, vapid

flat and even: flush

flat and parallel to horizon: horizontal

flat-bottomed boat: barge, dory, punt, scow

flat-bottomed boat, e.g.: keelless

flat bread: pita

flat disk: paten

flat elevated land: plateau

flat finish: matte

flat hat: beret

flat instrument for spreading, stirring: spatula

flat on one's back, lying: supine

flat on one's front, lying: prone, prostrate

flat stretch of ground: terrace

flat stretch of pavement, grass: esplanade

flat-topped elevation: mesa

flat, lying: recumbent

flat, open country: champaign

flatten: compress, deck, defeat, deject, depress, floor, level, oblate, prostrate, raze, roll, squash, step on, trample

flattened: complanate

flattened at the poles: oblate

flatter: adorn, adulate, become, beguile, blandish, blarney, bootlick, cajole, charm, coax, compliment, court, enhance, grovel, hammer, praise, scratch one's back, smooge, soothe, wheedle

flatter to pursuade or gain favor: cajole, fawn, kowtow, truckle

flatterer: apple-polisher, eulogist, lickspittle, panegyrist, sycophant, toady

flatterers, group of: claque

flattering review: rave

flattering talk: blarney

flattering, overly: obsequious, servile, unctuous

flattery: adulation, blandishment, bosh, butter, compliment, gloze, palaver, praise, puffery, salve, snow job, taffy

flaunt: advertise, boast, brag, brandish, display, exhibit, flash, hotdog, parade, reveal, show, strut, vaunt, wave

flavor: aroma, aura, essence, extract, fragrance, odor, perfume, piquancy, quality, relish, salt, sapid, sapor, savor, scent, season, spice, style, tang, taste, touch, zest

flavor enhancer: salt

flavor enhancer, Chinese: monosodium glutamate, MSG

flavor, color, or odor pervading thing: tincture

flavor, having: sapid

flavorful: sapid, savory, tasty

flavoring: additive, anise, capers, cola, condiment, grenadine, herb, orgeat, pepper, sage, salt, sauce, seasoning, spice, vanilla

flavorless: bland, dull, flat, insipid, stale, tasteless, vapid

flavorsome: palatable, sapid, tasty

flaw: blemish, cleft, crack, default, defect, deformity, error, fault, fissure, flake, fracture, fragment, glitch, hole, imperfection, mark, mistake, rift, scratch, shortcoming, spot, squall, stain, vice, weakness, wind

flaw, tragic: hamartia

flawless: exquisite, faultless, ideal, immaculate, impeccable, intact, perfect, sound, spotless, undamaged, unexceptionable, unmarred

flawless serve: ace

flay: assail, attack, castigate, chafe, criticize, decorticate, excoriate, flail, fleece, lash, peel, reprove, skin, slash, strip, whip

fleas, infested with: pulicose

flèche: spire

fleck: dapple, dot, flake, freckle, jot, mark, particle, speck, speckle, spot, streak

fledgling: apprentice, beginner, chick, inexperienced, novice, squab, tenderfoot, untried

flee: abscond, bolt, decamp, disappear, elude, escape, evade, fly, jump, lam, liberate, run, scamper, scoot, scram, skedaddle, skip, take to one's heels, vamoose, vanish

flee secretly: abscond, absquatulate, decamp, hightail

flee secretly to marry: elope

fleece: bilk, cheat, clip, deceive, defraud, dupe, fabric, fell, flay, fleck, plunder, rook, shear, steal, swindle, wool

fleecy: fluffy, lanose, soft, woolly

fleecy mass: flocculus

fleeing from bad situation, person: refugee

fleeing from homeland, person: émigré

fleeing from law, person: fugitive

fleer: grimace, grin, jeer, laugh, mock, scoff, smirk, sneer, taunt

fleet: abound, agile, argosy, armada, brisk, caravan, drift, evanescent, fast, float, flotilla, formation, hasty, navy, nimble, occasional, quick, rapid, sail, speedy, spry, swift, unit, vanish

fleet of ships: argosy, armada

fleet of small craft: flotilla

fleeting: brief, elusive, ephemeral, evanescent, fading, fugacious, fugitive, impermanent, momentary, passing, short-lived, temporary, transient, transitory, volage, volatile

flesh: beef, body, humanity, kin, man, mankind, meat, muscle, plumpness, pulp, race, realty, sensuality, skin, stock, substance

flesh-colored: incarnadine

flesh-eating: carnivorous, creophagous
flesh-eating mammal: carnivore
flesh of dead rotting animal: carrion
fleshly: carnal
fleshy: beefy, bodily, carnal, chubby, corpulent, fat, gross, heavy, obese, overweight, plump, portly, pulpy, stout
fleshy part of palm: thenar
fleshy part under jaw: jowl
flex: bend, contract, curve, stretch, tense
flexible: adaptable, adjustable, bendable, ductile, elastic, limber, limp, lissom, lithe, lush, malleable, manageable, pliable, pliant, resilient, responsive, soft, springy, supple, tractable, versatile, willowy, yielding
flexible and easily molded or shaped: ductile, malleable, pliable
flick: blow, fillip, film, flip, hit, movie, picture, propel, snap, toss
flicker: blink, flash, fluctuate, glimmer, gutter, movie, oscillate, sparkle, vacillate
flickering: lambent
flickering low: butter
flier: ace, airman, airwoman, aviator, pilot; circular, leaflet, pamphlet
flies, relating to: muscid
flight: agitation, bolt, escape, exodus, fleeing, flock, floor, flying, getaway, hegira, lam, migrate, migration, mission, rout, scrap, shuttle, soaring, stairs, stampede, story, swarming, trajectory, trip, voyage
flight across a long distance, disruption of body rhythms from: jet lag
flight by visual observation of horizon and landmarks: contact flight, contact flying
flight feather: remex
flight of Mohammed: hegira
flight overnight, late at night: red-eye
flight path of plane waiting to land: holding pattern
flight path of projectile: trajectory
flight segment: leg, step
flight to escape danger: exodus, hegira
flightless bird: dodo, emu, moa, penguin, rhea
flightless birds, pertaining to: ratite
flighty: anile, barmy, capricious, ditzy, dizzy, fickle, fleeting, foolish, giddy, harebrained, impulsive, irresponsible, lightheaded, mercurial, skittish, swift, transient, unstable

flighty one: flibbertigibbet, social butterfly
flimflam: bamboozle, cheat, chicane, deception, deceptive, defraud, dupe, fool, hoax, humbug, nonsense, swindle, trick, trifle
flimsily build: jerrybuild
flimsy: delicate, dilapidated, feeble, fragile, frail, gaudy, gossamer, inadequate, insubstantial, lame, limp, shoddy, sleazy, slight, superficial, tenuous, thin, transparent, weak
flinch: avoid, blench, blink, cower, cringe, feign, quaver, recoil, retreat, shrink, shudder, start, wince, withdraw
fling: affair, binge, cast, catapult, chuck, dart, dash, discard, emit, fire, flip, flirt, flounce, heave, hurl, hurtle, launch, overthrow, pitch, plunge, scatter, sling, spirit, splurge, spree, throw, toss, whirl
flinty: callous, hard, rigorous, steely, stern, unyielding
flip: browse, fillip, flap, flick, leaf, propel, snap, somersault, spin, throw, thumb, toss, turn, twist; glib, pert
flip a coin: toss
flip-flop: do an about-face
flippant: airy, brassy, chatty, disrespectful, fresh, glib, irreverent, pert, rude, talkative
flippant manner: persiflage
flippant talk: jive, lip
flipper: fin
flirt: coquet, coquette, dally, dart, flick, fling, flip, gibe, jest, make eyes at, mock, ogle, ogler, philander, play, spring, tease, throw, toss, toy, trifle, trifler, vamp, vixen
flirtation: dalliance
flirtatious: amorous, arch, coquettish, coy, provacative
flirting glance: oeillade
flit: dart, fleck, fleet, flicker, flow, flutter, hover, hurry, move, nimble, quick, run, rush, scoot, scurry, swift, whiz
float: bob, bobber, buoy, cork, drift, drink, fleet, flood, flow, fly, glide, hover, launch, levitate, natant, negotiate, pontoon, raft, ride, sail, soar, swim, waft
float and move gently: waft
float in defiance to gravity, to rise or cause to: levitate
float in liquid or rise in gas, tendency to: buoyancy

float in the air: hover, levitate
floating body of ice: berg, floe
floating objects on water: flotsam, waveson
floating or living on water's surface: asea, emersal
floating or swimming in water: natant
floating structure that closes dock or canal lock: caisson, camel
floating structure that supports a bridge: pontoon
flock: aggregation, assembly, bevy, brood, bunch, church, collection, company, congregation, converge, crowd, drift, drove, flight, gaggle, gang, gather, gathering, group, herd, legion, mob, multitude, pack, rush, swarm
flock of geese or similar birds in flight: skein
flock of quails: covey
flock or crowd: confluence
flock or herd being driven in body: drove
flog: beat, belt, cane, castigate, chastise, cotton, fight, flagellate, flail, hide, larrup, lash, paddle, scourge, strike, switch, tan, thrash, trounce, whip, wool
flood: abundance, alluvion, bore, cataclysm, deluge, downpour, engulf, excess, flow, flux, glut, gush, inundate, outpouring, overflow, overwhelm, rush, saturate, spate, submerge, surplus, swamp, torrent
flood barrier embankment: dike, levee
flood from heavy rain, sudden and violent: flash flood
flood of tide in estuary: eagre
flood, devastating: cataclysm
flood, occurring before the biblical: antediluvian
flood, overwhelm: inundate
flood, relating to a: diluvial
floodgate: sluice
flooding: alluvion, inundation
floor: ground floor, level, linoleum, parquet, story, tiles; deck, defeat, drop, fell, flatten
floor of mosaic wood blocks or strips: parquet, parquetry
floor, smooth final surface of: screed
flooring beam: header
flop: bomb, bust, collapse, disaster, dud, fail, failure, fall, fizzle, lemon, loser, lounge, plop, rest, tumble, washout
flora and fauna: biota

floral: blooming, blossoming, decorative, flowery

floral bit: sprig

floral essence used for perfume: attar

florid: baroque, blooming, embellished, figurative, flamboyant, flowery, healthy, ornate, rhetorical, rococo, ruddy, rufous, showy, vigorous

floridity: redness

flounce: bounce, flap, fling, flounder, leap, prance, spring, stomp, struggle; ruffle

flounder: blunder, bobble, falter, flounce, fumble, grovel, keep, muddle, plounce, roll, struggle, stumble, toss, trip, wallow; flatfish, fluke

flour filter: sifter

flour substitute: gluten

flour, to coat with: dredge

flourish: adorn, arrive, bloom, blossom, boast, boom, brag, brandish, burgeon, curlicue, decoration, develop, display, embellish, expand, fanfare, flaunt, garnish, grow, increase, multiply, ornament, parade, prosper, quirk, rise, shake, show, succeed, thrive, vaunt, wave

flourish on signature: paraph

flourishing: lush, luxuriant, palmy, verdant, verdurous

flourishing, period of major activity and: floruit

flout: affront, deride, disregard, fleer, gibe, insult, jeer, mock, outrage, ridicule, scoff, scorn, scount, sneer, taunt

flow: alluvion, cascade, circulate, continuity, course, current, debouch, deluge, discharge, drain, drift, ebb, emanate, float, flood, flutter, flux, glide, gush, influx, inundate, issue, movement, oozing, outpouring, pour, progress, ripple, river, roll, run, rush, sequence, spill, spurt, stream, streaming, tide, torrent, well, wind

flow into larger area: debouch

flow of water: stream

flow out of: disembogue, empty

flow to or toward an area: afflux

flower: anemone, annual, aster, azalea, azalia, bloom, bloomer, blossom, bluebell, bluet, bud, buttercup, camellia, carnation, chrysanthemum, crocus, daffodil, dahlia, gardenia, geranium, gladiolus, hepatica, hibiscus, honeysuckle, hyacinth, hybrid, iris, jonquil, lilac, lily, lobelia, lotus, marigold, narcissus, orchid, pansy, peony, perennial, phlox, pink, posy, primrose, rose, tulip, violet

flower and bloom: blossom, effloresce

flower and ornamental plant cultivation: floriculture

flower arranging, art of Japanese: ikebana

flower attached firmly at base: sessile

flower bred from two varieties: hybrid

flower bunch: bouquet

flower cluster: cyme, inflorescence, raceme

flower cluster at end of stalk: truss

flower cluster bracts: involucre

flower cluster, compacted head: glomerule

flower cluster, convex or flat-topped: cyme

flower cluster, dense and drooping: ament, catkin

flower cluster, head-shaped: capitate

flower for buttonhole: boutonniere

flower garden, ornamental: parterre

flower garland: lei

flower is fully open, period during which: anthesis

flower opening during day and closing at night, of a: diurnal

flower opening during the evening, of a: vespertine

flower outer part of calyx or corolla: floral envelope, perianth

flower part: anther, calyx, carpel, filament, nectar, nectary, ovary, peduncle, perianth, pericarp, petal, petiole, pistil, sepal, stalk, stamen, stigma, style

flower part lasting past maturity and not falling off: persistent

flower part withering or falling off early: fugacious

flower petals, collectively: corolla

flower pollinated by insects, of a: entomophilous

flower pollinated by windblown pollen, of a: anemophilous

flower-secreted liquid: nectar

flower turning toward the sun: heliotrope

flower, clustered as in a: aggregate

flower, leaflike part just below: bract

flower, pull dead blossoms off: deadhead

flower, small: floret

flower, small bouquet: nosegay

flower, small bouquet for buttonhole: boutonniere

flower, small or reduced: floret

flower, stem supporting a: peduncle

flower, to become limp or droop like a: wilt

flowering: abloom, efflorescence, florescence, flourishing, in bloom, inflorescence

flowering plant: angiosperm, lantana, lobelia, oleander, rue

flowering plant lasting a few years: perennial

flowering plant lasting one year: annual

flowering shrub: azalea, bixa, camellia, itea, lilac, mimosa, oleander, spirea

flowering throughout the growing season: perpetual

flowerless: ananthous

flowerless seedless plant: fern

flowerlike design: rosette

flowers arranged in ring: wreath

flowers in vase such as sponge, support for: frog

flowers worn on woman's clothes, small bouquet of: corsage

flowers, bunch of: bouquet, nosegay, posy

flowers, garland of Hawaiian: lei

flowers, pertaining to: botanical, floral

flowers, science or art of cultivating: horticulture

flowers, string or garland of: festoon

flowers, wreath or crown of: chaplet, coronal, garland

flowery: embellished, euphuistic, fancy, figurative, florid, grandiloquent, ornate, rococo, windy, wordy

flowery in speech, writing: euphuism

flowing: abounding, abundant, afflux, continuous, copious, current, cursive, discharge, effortless, emanating, fluent, fluid, flux, gushing, rolling, rushing, smooth, spouting, tidal, uninterrupted

flowing back: ebb (ebbing), reflux (refluent)

flowing in: influent, influx

flowing out: effluence, effluent, efflux

flowing spring: fount

flowing together: confluence, confluent

flowing water, swift-: torrent

flowing with sweetness: mellifluent, mellifluous

flub: blunder, boner, botch, bungle, err, error, fat, fluff, muff

fluctuate: alternate, change, flutter, os-

FLOWERS AND FLOWERING PLANTS

acacia
adder's tongue
African violet
agave
alstromeria
amaranth
amaryllis
American Beauty
 rose
anemone
arbutus
arethusa
arrowhead
artemisias
asphodel
aster
azalea
baby's breath
baby-blue eyes
bachelor's button be-
 gonia
balloon flower
bay laurel
begonia
bird of paradise
bitterroot
black-eyed Susan
blazing star
bleeding heart
bloodroot
blue poppy
bluebell
bluebonnet
bluet
boxwood
bridal wreath
broom
burnett
buttercup
cactus
calendula
camas
camellia
camomile
campanula
candytuft
cardoon
carnation
cat's-paw
cattail
century plant
chicory
Chinese lantern
Christmas rose
chrysanthemum

cineraria
clematis
clethra
cockscomb
columbine
cornel
cornflower
cosmos
cowslip
crocus
cyclamen
daffodil
dahlia
daisy
damask rose
dandelion
daylilies
delphinium
desert mallow
dogwood
duckweed
Dutchman's-
 breeches
edelweiss
eglantine
elderflower
fireweed
flax
forget-me-not
forsythia
foxglove
foxtail
freesia
fuchsia
gardenia
gas plant
gentian
geranium
ghostplant
gladiolus
globe flower
goatsbeard
goldenrod
groundsel
guelder rose
harebell
hawthorn
heather
heleconia
hepatica
hibiscus
holly
hollyhock
honeysuckle
horehound

hyacinth
hydrangea
ice-plant
impatiens
Indian paintbrush
indigo
iris
jack-in-the-pulpit
japonica
jasmine
jonquil
kalanchoe
kangaroo paw
kingcup
knotweed
lady's-slipper
larkspur
lavender
leopard's bane
lilac
lily
lily of the valley
lobelia
lotus
love-lies-bleeding
lupine
magnolia
mallow
marguerite
marigold
marsh marigold
marshmallow
mayflower
Michaelmas daisy
mignonette
mimosa
moccasin flower
mock orange
monkshood
morning glory
moss rose
motherwort
mountain laurel
mourning widow
myrtle
narcissus
nasturtium
oleander
opium poppy
orchid
oxalis
oxeye daisy
pansy
parrot's flower
passion flower

pelargonium
penstemon
peony
periwinkle
petunia
phlox
pink
pinxter flower
plume poppy
poinsettia
polyanthus
poppy
portulaca
primrose
priula
purple top
Queen Anne's lace
ragged robin
ragwort
rambler rose
ranunculus
resurrection plant
rhododendron
rose
shasta daisy
shooting star
silkweed
smilax
snapdragon
snowball
snowberry
snowdrop
solidago
spiraea
stock
storksbill
strawflower
sunflower
sweet alyssum
sweet pea
sweet william
tick trefoil
tiger lily
toad lilly
trailing arbutus
trillium
trumpet vine
tulip
twayblade
twinflower
umbrella plant
valerian
Venus's-flytrap
verbena
vetch

viburnum
viola
violet
wake-robin
wallflower
water hyacinth
water lily
water milfoil
water pimpernel
wax flower
waxplant
white clover
white rosebay
windflower
wisteria
wolfsbane
wood anemone
wood hyacinth
woody nightshade
yarrow
yellow ox-eye
yellow scabious
yellow water lily
yucca
zinnia ❧

cillate, seesaw, shift, sway, undulate, unsteady, vacillate, vary, veer, vibrate, waver

flue: barb, channel, chimney, fishnet, funnel, net, organ, passage, pipe, stack, tube, tunnel

flue valve: damper

fluent: articulate, copious, effortless, eloquent, facile, flowing, fluid, glib, graceful, liquid, natural, polished, smooth, smooth-spoken, talkative, verbose, voluble

fluff: blunder, botch, down, entertainment, err, error, flub, flue, froth, fuzz, lint, miscue, mistake, puff, soft

fluffy: airy, creamy, downy, feathery, frivolous, furry, fuzzy, light, soft

fluffy mass or tuft: flocculus

fluffy or woolly: flocculent

fluid: adaptable, changeable, flexible, floating, flowing, fluent, fluible, fluxible, fluxile, gaseous, graceful, ink, juice, liquid, milk, pliable, rasa, runny, shifting, unstable, variable, water, watery

fluid accumulation: edema

fluid around embryo and fetus: amniotic fluid

fluid-containing sac or cavity: cistern, cisterna, reservoir

fluid-filled sac: cyst

fluid rock: lava

fluid, body: humor

fluid, device regulating flow of: baffle

fluid, involving or operated by: hydraulic

fluid, pouch of plant or animal with: sac

fluidless: aneroid

fluke: accident, blade, blessing, fish, flounder, oddity, quirk, trematode

fluky: capricious, chance, shifting, uncertain, unsteady, variable

flunky: attendant, drudge, footman, gofer, lackey, servant, steward, toady

fluorine or iodine compound: halide

fluoroscope: Xray

flurry: ado, agitation, alarm, bother, burst, bustle, commotion, confuse, confusion, excitement, fluster, flutter, gust, haste, hubbub, panic, scurry, shower, snowfall, spurt, squall, stir, whirl, wind

flush: abounding, abundant, affluent, blush, cleanse, color, even, excite, flat, flood, frighten, glow, lavish, level, mantle, opulent, overflowing,

prosperous, redden, redness, rinse, rose, rosiness, rouge, smooth, square, thrill, vigor, wash

flushed: aglow, animated, crimson, embarrassed, feverish, florid, pink, prosperous, red, rosed, rosy, ruby, ruddy

fluster: agitate, befuddle, bewilder, bother, confuse, discompose, disturb, flurry, frustrate, fuddle, muddle, perplex, puzzle, rattle, ruffle, shake, unhinge, upset

fluster or fuss: pother

flute: chamfer, channel, crimp, fife, flautino, furrow, goffer, instrument, ocarina, piccolo, pipe, tube, wineglass, zuffolo, zufolo

flute finger hole: ventage

flute player: flautist, flutist

flute with eight fingerholes, whistlelike mouthpiece: recorder

flutelike: reedy

flutelike instrument: flageolet

flutter: flap, flicker, flit, flitter, fluctuate, flurry, hover, pulsate, quiver, shake, thrill, tingling, vibrate, wave

flutter and beat: palpitate

flux: additive, discharge, flood, flow, flowing, fluctuation, fuse, fusion, melt, motion, resin, rush, stream, substance, unrest

fly alone: solo

fly ball: looper

fly-by-night: brief, questionable, shady, undependable, unreliable, unscrupulous, unsure, untrustworthy

fly high: soar

fly in the ointment: catch, drawback, hindrance, hitch, snag

fly the coop: bolt, escape, flee, hightail, skedaddle

fly, bloodsucking African: tsetse fly

fly, insect: bug, dipteron, gnat, hackle, horse, house, midge, sedge, tsetse

flycatcher: pewee, phoebe, scissortail

flyer: ace, aviator, erne, pilot; insert, leaflet, pamphlet, throwaway

flying: aloft, volant, volitant

flying aircraft, profession or pastime of: aviation

flying apparatus like kite: hang glider

flying boat: seaplane

flying buttress: arc-boutant

flying saucer: spacecraft, spaceship, UFO, unidentified flying object

flying, exhibition of stunt: barnstorming

flying, not having feathers necessary for: unfledged

foal: colt, filly, fledgling, offspring

foal's mother: dam, mare

foam: aerate, bubble, cream, effervesce, fizz, frost, froth, fume, head, lather, scud, scum, spume, suds, whip, yeast

foam for insulation: polystyrene

foam from soap: lather

foam on fermenting beer or malt liquor: barm

foam or froth: spume

fob: chain, cheat, deceive, flimflam, ornament, pocket, ribbon, trick

fob off: foist

focal: central, important, main, nucleus, principal

focus: adjust, center, concentrate, converge, core, direct, fireplace, fixate, hearth, point, spotlight, train

focusing ability of eye: refraction

focusing disability: astigmatism

fodder: alfalfa, barley, corn, feed, food, forage, hay, oats, provender, provisions, silage, soilage, stover, straw

fodder preserved in a silo: ensilage

fodder trough: crib, manger

foe: adversary, antagonist, competitor, enemy, opponent, rival

fog: bedim, bewilderment, brume, cloudiness, confusion, daze, film, gloom, grass, haze, mist, moisture, muddy, murk, nebula, obscure, smog, stream, stupor, vapor, whiteout

fog with ice: ice fog, pogonip

fog, heavy polar: whiteout

foggy: blurred, brumous, cloudy, confused, dark, dense, dull, gray, groggy, hazy, marshy, misty, muddled, murky, nubilous, obscure, overcast, shadowy, soupy, unclear, vague

foible: defect, deficiency, failing, fault, frailty, imperfection, infirmity, quirk, shortcoming, weakness

foil: baffle, balk, beguile, blade, blunt, boggle, counter, curb, defeat, defile, disgrace, elude, evade, frustrate, metal, obscure, outwit, overthrow, prevent, repulse, setback, stooge, thwart, track, trail; épée, sword; aluminum

foil and frustrate: thwart

foist: cheat, deceive, dupe, fob off, fool, fudge, gull, hoax, hoodwink, impose, palm off, swindle, thrust

fold: bend, buckle, clasp, close, collapse, corrugate, crease, crimp, crinkle, crumple, double, drape, fail, flap,

FOOD TERMS

art or science of good food and cooking: gastronomy

coarse and fibrous food: roughage

concentrated food or flavoring: extract

decorate food, to: garnish

digest and metabolize food, to: assimilate

discourse on food: bromatology

eater of any and every type of food: grandgousier

eater of good food: gastrophile

eating all types of food: omnivorous

eating only a few kinds of food: oligophagous

excessive spending on food and drink: abligurition

food allowed by Jewish dietary law: kosher

food eaten before main course: antipasto

food expert: epicure

food lover: epicure, gourmand, gourmet

food mix of oats, fruit, nuts, sugar: granola

food not allowed by Jewish dietary law: tref

food of the gods: ambrosia, amrit

food or anything that promotes salivation: sialagogue

food poisoning: ptomaine poisoning

food-poisoning bacteria: ptomaine

food poisoning from improperly stored or undercooked food: salmonella poisoning, salmonellosis

food prepared elaborately and skillfully: haute cuisine

food scrap: crumb, ort

food seller: grocer, provisioner, purveyor

food storage place: larder, pantry

food without nutritive value: junk food, lubber-wort

French food prepared lean-style versus rich-style: cuisine maigreure, nouvelle cuisine

full from eating: replete, sated, satiated

ill from overindulgence: crapulent, crapulous, cropsick

inexpensive and quickly prepared food: fast food

mass of chewed food: bolus

necessary food: sustenance

nourishing ingredient of food: nutrient

obsessively loving food: opsomanic

partially digested food in stomach: chyme

person appreciating fine food and drink: connoisseur, epicure, gastronome, gourmand, gourmet

picnic basket: hamper

reheated food: réchauffé

relating to food and nutrition: alimentary

relating to food in the diet: dietary

savory aroma of cooked food: nidor

science of food and nourishment: nutrition

search for food, to: scavenge

semiliquid or soft food: pap

severe food poisoning: botulism

ship's officer in charge of food: steward

store selling prepared foods, sandwiches, etc.: deli, delicatessen

style or manner of food preparation: cuisine

substance added to food to improve or preserve it: additive

table scraps for animals: slop, swill

take in food, to: ingest ✋

---

groove, intertwine, lap, lapel, layer, loop, plait, pleat, plicate, ply, pucker, ridge, rimple, surround, tuck, turn, withdraw, yield; embrace, enclosure, envelope, flock, group, pen

fold of skin, membrane, shell: plica

fold of tissue under the tongue: frenum

fold tightly: crimp

folded backward: replicate

folded by doubling back: pleated

folded fanlike: plicated

folded in long parallel ridges: corrugated

folded insert or section: foldout

folder: binder, brochure, case, cover, leaflet, pamphlet

folds of brain: convolutions, gyri, sulci

foliage: growth, leafage, leaves, vegetation, verdure

foliage decaying on forest floor: duff

folk: clan, family, friends, kindred, people, relatives

folk music originated by rural southern African-Americans: blues

folklore: belief, custom, history, legend, myth, superstition, tales, tradition

folks: family, parents, people, relatives

folksy: ethnic, quaint

folkways: lore, mores

follow: accompany, act on, adopt, after, alternate, chase, comply, comprehend, conform, copy, dog, ensue, fathom, hound, hunt, imitate, next, obey, observe, pursue, replace, result, sequel, shadow, spy, stalk, succeed, supervene, supplant, support, tag, tail, trace, track, trail, understand

follow closely: tag, tail

follow immediately after: ensue, supervene

follower: acolyte, adherent, aficionado, apostle, attendant, believer, claque, copycat, devotee, disciple, enthusiast, entourage, fan, groupie, henchman, -ist, minion, parasite, partisan, pupil, pursuer, retainer, retinue, satellite, successor, sycophant, toady, votary

follower or devout adherent: votary

follower or fan: aficionado, devotee

follower or imitator, second-rate: epigone

follower or servant, devoted: myrmidon

follower or subordinate, loyal: henchman, myrmidon

follower who flatters or is servile: minion, sycophant, toady

followers or attendants: entourage

following: after, afterward, audience, below, clientele, consequent, consequential, ensuing, gathering, group, later, next, posthumous, resulting, sect, sequent, sequential, serial, subsequent, succeeding, successive, trailing, train

following as effect: consequential

following Hiroshima: post-atomic

following in order: consecutive, sequential, serial, seriatim, succeeding

following in time: subsequent

following logically or naturally, of something: consequential

follows tirelessly: dogs

follows, something that: continuation, sequel

folly: absurdity, craziness, daffery, foolery, foolishness, frivolity, idiocy, imprudence, levity, lunacy, madness, mistake, nonsense, revue, silliness, wantonness, whim

FOOTBALL TERMS

blocking from behind of someone without ball: clipping

catch signalled with arm, where receiver may not advance or be tackled: fair catch

corner of end zone: coffin corner

defense with five backs or back instead of linebacker: nickel defense

defense with six backs or two backs instead of linebackers: dime defense

football field: grid

football kicked as it bounces up from ground: drop kick

football kicked before touching ground: punt

football official: ref, referee, umpire, zebra

football official tending sidelines: linesman

football officials on sideline: box-and-chain crew

football positions: center, cornerback, end, fullback, guard, halfback, kicker, linebacker, punter, quarterback, running back, safety, split end, tackle, tailback, tight end

football terms: block, clipping, conversion, defense, down, drive, end zone, field goal, flare, fumble, gridiron, holding, huddle, interception, interference, kickoff, lateral, offense, offside, pass, punt, rushing, sack, safety, scrimmage, secondary, tackle, touchback, touchdown, uprights

four chances for offense to gain ten yards: downs

imaginary line where ball rests and teams line up for play: line of scrimmage

kick beginning half or after touchdown: kickoff

kickoff that is low and oblique: onside kick

other names for a football: pigskin, rugger

pass caught by opposing team's: interception

pass parallel to goal line: lateral

pass starting with faked handoff: play-action pass

pass, high and long: Hail Mary pass

penalty for being ahead of ball before the snap: offside

play change at line of scrimmage: audible

play grounding ball behind goal line: touchback

play looking like a pass but handed off to back: draw play

play of throwing to a receiver: pass

play with lateral or handoff and forward pass: flea-flicker

point after touchdown: extra point

putting football in play: snap

rush by several defenders: blitz

score made by kicking ball between uprights of goal: field goal

score made by moving ball into opposing team's end zone: touchdown

score of one to two points made after touchdown: conversion

scoring area between goal and end line: end zone

touch or catch behind own goal line, costing two points: safety ❧

---

folly or vice attacked by irony, wit in work: satire

foment: abet, agitate, arouse, encourage, excite, foster, goad, incite, instigate, provoke, rouse, spur, start, stir, stir up, stupe

fond: affection, affectionate, amorous, ardent, beguile, caress, cherished, credulous, dear, desirous, devoted, doting, enamored, foolish, inclination, indulgent, infatuated, insipid, kind, liking, loving, partial, passionate, sanguine, silly, tender, trifling, warm

fond of husband, overly: maritorious

fond of others' company: gregarious

fond of wife, overly: uxorious

fondle: caress, clasp, coddle, cosset, cuddle, embrace, feel, grope, hug, love, neck, nestle, pamper, pet, snuggle, stroke

fondness: affection, attachment, dearness, devotion, foolishness, kindness, love, preference, regard, taste, tenderness, weakness

font: basin, fountain, fource, receptacle, spring, stoup, type, well

font for holy water: stoup

food: aliment, bite, bread, cheer, chow, comestibles, diet, eats, edibles, fare, fodder, grub, handout, meat, morsel, nosh, nourishment, nurture, nutriment, nutrition, pabulum, provisions, sustenance, viand, viands, victuals

foofaraw: ado, stir, to-do

fool: ass, bamboozle, blockhead, bluff, blunderer, bonehead, boob, buffoon, butt, cheat, chump, clown, comedian, coxcomb, cretin, deceive, dimwit, dolt, dope, dumbbell, dunce, dunderhead, dupe, fake, fathead, goose, hoax, hoodwink, idiot, imbecile, jerk, jest, joke, kid, meathead, mislead, moron, nincompoop, ninny, nitwit, nudnick, numskull, oaf, outwit, pretend, sap, scam, schlemiel, silly, simp, simpleton, spoof, stooge, sucker, tamper, tease, toy, trick, victim

fool around: dally, dawdle, dwadle, futz, lallygag, lark, lollygag, play, putter, shilly-shally, waste time

fool, boring: morologist

foolhardy: bold, daredevil, daring, impetuous, rash, reckless, temerity, unwise, venturesome

foolish: absurd, anile, anserine, asinine, batty, boneheaded, brainless, cockeyed, crazy, daft, dizzy, doddering, dumb, fatuous, goofy, harebrained, heedless, idiotic, imprudent, inane, indiscreet, inept, insensate, irrational, loony, ludicrous, nonsensical, nutty, preposterous, rash, ridiculous, senseless, silly, simple, stupid, unwise, wiless, witless, zany

foolish love: infatuation

foolish talk: drivel

foolish, appearing: stultified

foolishness: absurdity, balderdash, bunk, drollery, horseplay, insanity, lunacy, nonsense, senselessness, stupidity

foolproof: certain, effective, infallible, sure

foolscap: paper

foot: base, bottom, dance, defray, dog, extremity, flipper, hoof, nadir, pad, paw, pay, ped, pes, speed, tootsy; ft., measurement

foot ailment: gout

foot and toenail cosmetic treatment: pedicure

foot care by doctor: chiropody, podiatry

foot flat and turned out: splayfoot

foot lever: pedal, treadle

foot-operated machine lever: treadle

foot part above arch on upper side between ankle and toes: instep

foot parts of human: Achilles tendon, ankle, arch, ball, digit, hallux, heel, instep, minimus, second toe, sole, tarsal, toe, toenail

foot soldiers: infantry

foot-sole beating: bastinado

foot-travel gauge: pedometer

foot, animals that walk on whole: plantigrade

foot, misshapen: clubfoot, talipes

foot, relating to the sole of the: plantar, volar

foothold, temporary: toehold

footing: balance, base, basis, condition, foothold, foundation, groundwork, place, position, rank, relationship, standing, status, support, surface

footless: apod, apodal

footlike organ: pes

footloose: carefree, free, unattached

footnote: afterthought, explanation, reference

footnote symbols: asterisk, dagger, diesis, double dagger, obelisk

footnote word: ibid, ibidem, idem

footpad: bandit, highwayman, mugger, robber, thief, thug, yegg

footprint: footstep, mootmark, moulage, spoor, step, trace, track

footprint mold for criminal investigation: moulage

footprint or track of animal: spoor

footrest: hassock, ottoman, stool

fop: Beau Brummell, buck, cavalier, coxcomb, dandy, dasher, dude, exquisite, man-about-town, pipinjay, swell

for a still stronger reason: a fortiori

forage: alfalfa, barley, clover, corn, fodder, grass, hunt, millet, oat, plunder, provisions, raid, ravage, raven, rummage, rye, scour, search, wheat

foray: attack, attempt, incursion, inroad, invasion, pillage, raid, ravage, sortie

forbear: abstain, ancestor, avoid, cease, decline, desist, endure, forego, forgo, help, omit, refrain, resist, shun, withstand

forbearance: abstinence, fortitude, mercy, moderation, patience, tolerance

forbearing: clement, easy, forgiving, gentle, lenient, mild, patient, restraint, sympathetic, tolerant

forbid: ban, block, censor, debar, defend, defy, deny, deprive, disallow, enjoin, fend, gainsay, halt, impede, inhibit, interdict, preclude, prevent, prohibit, proscribe, refuse, stop, taboo

forbidden: banned, denied, prohibited, taboo, tabu, ultra vires, unlawful, verboten, vetoed

forbidden from disclosing details as reporter: court order

forbidden from use or mention: taboo

forbidding: disagreeable, fierce, gaunt, grim, harsh, menacing, odious, offensive, ominous, prohibiting, sinister, stern, strict, threatening, unpleasant

force: ability, army, bang, cause, clout, coaction, coerce, command, compel, compress, constrain, constraint, constringe, corps, cram, demand, detachment, determination, dint, drive, effort, energy, exert, extort, gumption, hammer, impact, impel, impetus, impulse, influence, insist, make, might, momentum, muscle, necessitate, obligate, oblige, persuade, pound, power, press, pressure, pry, push, ravish, regiment, repel, require, restraint, strength, stress, stuff, unit, validity, violence, wrest

force a payment or yielding of: exact, extort

force acting on body in curvilinear motion away from center or axis: centrifugal force

force acting on body in curvilinear motion directed toward center or axis: centripetal force

force and coercion: duress

force back: repel

force balancing another: counterpoise

force-feeding through tube: gavage

force of a blow: brunt

force of body in motion: impetus, momentum

force on, to use physical: bulldoze, strong-arm

force onward: urge

force or impose on another: foist, obtrude

force or incite to action: actuate, goad, impel, spur

force or influence: vector

force or pack down: tamp

force or push out: extrude

force out and substitute another: supplant

force out from power, office: depose, oust

force out of position or location: dislodge

force someone to do something: coerce, dragoon, press-gang, railroad, shanghai

force that draws item into interior space: suction

force to action: impel

force to leave: eject, evict, expel

force, body at rest until affected by external: inertia

force, driving or propelling: propulsion

force, impelling, or stimulus: impetus

force, overpowering: act of God, force majeure, juggernaut

force, the moment or measure of a: torque

force, to control or put down by: repress, subdue, subjugate, suppress

force, to seize and hold by: usurp, wrest

force, turning or twisting: torque

forced: artificial, begrudging, compulsory, constrained, contrived, farfetched, involuntary, labored, mandatory, recherché, reluctant, slave, stiff, stilted, strained

forced and strained: agonistic, contrived

forced hard labor: penal servitude

forced labor, esp. for roadwork: corvée

forced or restricted state or situation: constraint

forceful: assertive, cogent, dominant, dynamic, effective, emphatic, energetic, forcible, mighty, potent, powerful, strong, vigorous, violent, virile

forceful and bullying: dictatorial, domineering, imperious, overbearing, tyrannical

forceful in emotion: fervid, vehement

forceful in speech: cogent, compelling, incisive, trenchant

forceful or powerful: potent, virile

forces at work in a sphere: dynamics

forces of nature, manifestation of: act of God

forces, stable or balanced: equilibrium

forcible: aggressive, compulsory, emphatic, energetic, forceful, impressive, incisive, intense, mighty, obligatory, persuasive, potent, powerful, puissant, stout, telling, valid, weighty

forcible seizure of property: pillage, rapine

forcibly take away: wrest

fore: advanced, ahead, antecedent, earlier, former, forward, front, near, previously, prior

forearm: radius, ulna

forebear: ancestor, parent

forebode: augur, divine, foresee, foretell, omen, portend, predict, presage, prognosticate, prophesy, warn

foreboding: anxiety, apprehension, augury, fear, feeling, gloomy, omen, prediction, premonition, presage, presagement, presentiment, sinister

forecast: anticipate, bode, calculation, callo, conclude, conjecture, estimate, foresee, foretell, fortune, guess, horoscope, infer, meteorology, outlook, predetermine, predict, prediction, presage, prognosis, prognostic, prognosticate, prognostication, projection, prophesy, surmise

forecast according to indications: foretell, predict, prognosticate, prophesy

forecast of future based on planets' and stars' positions: horoscope

forecaster: astrologer, meteorologist, Nostradamus, prophet, seer, soothsayer

forecasting, weather: meteorology

forefather: ancestor, antecedent, elder, forbear, founder, originator, primogenitor, progenitor, sire

forefront: beginning, front, lead, prominence, van, vanguard

forefront of technology: cutting edge

forego: forfeit, forsake, neglect, precede, refrain, relinquish, renounce, sacrifice, waive

forehead: brow, frons, front, metopic, sinciput

forehead losing hair, of a: receding

forehead mark of Hindus: tilak

forehead of animal, bird: frontlet

forehead, pertaining to the: frontal, metopic

forehead's flat area: glabella

foreign: alien, barbaric, different, distant, exiled, exotic, extraneous, extrinsic, faraway, impertinent, inapplicable, incompatible, inconsistent, irrelevant, outlandish, overseas, peregrine, remote, strange, unaccustomed, unexplored, unknown

foreign policy based on advancement of national interest: realpolitik

foreign policy based on regaining lost territory or standing: revanchism

foreign resident of country, unnaturalized: alien

foreign to an environment: adventive

foreigner: alien, barbarian, greenhorn, immigrant, outlander, outsider, stranger

foreigner who resides in another country: expatriate

foreigner, to expel a: deport

foreignness or uncertainty: culture shock

foreknowledge: intuition, premonition, prescience

foreknowledge held by God: predestination

foreman: boss, captain, chairperson, chief, forewoman, gaffer, headman, leader, manager, overseer, spokesperson, steward, supervisor, taskmaster

foremost: banner, chief, first, forme, front, head, high, highest, leading, main, preeminent, prime, principal, supreme

forensic: argumentative, debatable, disputation, judicial, legal, rhetorical

forensic medic: coroner

foreordained: destined

forepart of the alimentary canal: maw

forerunner: ancestor, augury, forebear, forefather, harbinger, herald, messenger, omen, originator, portent, precursor, predecessor, prelude, presager, progenitor, prognostic, sign, symptom, trailblazer, warning

forerunner in field, position: antecedent, precursor, predecessor

foresee: anticipate, divine, envisage, envision, forecast, foretell, predict, prognosticate, prophesy

foreshadow: adumbrate, bode, hint, imply, indicate, portend, prefigure, presage, suggest, warn

foresight: anticipation, caution, clairvoyance, discretion, forethought, prescience, providence, prudence, vision, wisdom

foresight, having: visionary

foreskin: prepuce

foreskin, removal of: circumcision

forest: backwoods, boscage, bush, cover, glade, jungle, park, shelter, silva, taiga, thicket, timber, trees, wilderness, woodland, woods

forest clearing: glade

forest converted into stony fossilized replica: petrified forest

forest fire advancing in treetops: crown fire

forest fire burning humus layer: ground fire

forest fire burning surface undergrowth: surface fire

forest floor decay: duff, underbrush

forest floor, uppermost layer of: litter

forest humus: mor

forest or trees of a region: silva

forest, pertaining to: sylvan

forestall: anticipate, avert, delay, deter, hinder, preclude, prevent, thwart

forestry: silviculture

foretell: anticipate, augur, bespeak, bode, divine, figure, forecast, forewarn, portend, predicate, predict, prefigure, presage, prognosticate, prophesy, read, soothsay, vaticinate, warn

foretell based on signs: augur, forecast, prognosticate, prophesy, vaticinate

foretell or be a sign of: adumbrat, bespeak, betoken, bode, foreshadow, indicate, prefigure, presage

foretell or warn: forebode, portend

foretelling events, the power of: clairvoyance, precognition, prescience

foretelling with omens: augury

forethought: anticipation, beed, calculation, canniness, caution, consideration, foresight, judgment, planning, premeditation, preparation, provident, prudence, sense

foretold: boded, presaged

forever: ad infinitum, always, ceaselessly, constantly, continually, endless, endlessly, eternally, eternity, ever, everlasting, interminably, permanently, perpetual, unincreasingly, world without end

forever, poetically: eterne

forewarn: alert, augur, caution, flag, notify, portend, signal

foreword: introduction, overture, preamble, preface, prelude, proem, prologue

forfeit: abandon, default, fine, forego, lose, loss, penalty, relinquish, sacrifice, surrender

forge: advance, bloomery, copy, counterfeit, drive, fabricate, falsify, fashion, manufacture, pound, reproduce, shape, smithy

forged: counterfeit, fake, spurious

forgery: counterfeit, deception, fabrication, fake, feigning, fiction, fraud, imposture, phony, sham

forget: disregard, disremember, fluff, ignore, neglect, omit, overlook, skip, unlearn, unmindful

forgetful: absentminded, abstracted, amnesic, careless, distracted, heedless, inattentive, negligent, oblivious, preoccupied, remiss, sloppy

forgetfulness: disregard, lapse, lethe, oblivescence, oblivion, obliviousness

forgetfulness-inducing potion: nepenthe

forgetting one's past, accidental: amnesia

forgetting word temporarily: lethologica, tip-of-the-tongue syndrome

forgivable (sins): remissible, venial

forgive: absolve, acquit, amnesty, cancel, clear, commute, condone, exculpate, excuse, exonerate, overlook, pardon, release, remit, shrive

forgiving: charitable, clement, compassionate, kind, merciful, placable, tolerant

forgiving disposition: clemency, indulgence, leniency

forgo: forfeit, forsake, give up, neglect, precede, refrain, relinquish, renounce, sacrifice, waive

forgotten or neglected condition: limbo

fork: angle, bifurcation, bisect, branch, crotch, divaricate, divide, pierce, prong, split, stab, tine, tuner, utensil

fork prong: tine

fork with three broad tines and cutting edge: runcible spoon

fork with three prongs: trident

fork, to: bisect

forked: branching, furcate

forked into two: bifurcate

forklift platform: pallet, skid

forklike body part: fourchette, furcula, wishbone

forlorn: abandoned, abject, alone, cheerless, depressed, deserted, desolate, desperate, despondent, destitute, disconsolate, dispirited, forsaken, friendless, helpless, hopeless, inconsolable, lonesome, lost, miserable, rejected, sad, solitary, tragic, wretched

form: appearance, arrangement, being, body, build, configuration, conformation, contour, design, expression, fashion, figuration, figure, frame, framework, guise, image, likeness, manner, mode, model, mold, outline, pattern, physique, shape, skeleton, structure

form and structure of organisms, branch of biology dealing with: morphology

form in imagination: ideate

form in which divine being is revealed: manifestation

form, to give a definite: crystallize

formal: academic, affected, ceremo-nial, ceremonious, conventional, correct, dressy, established, fancy, methodical, nominal, official, orderly, precise, prim, proper, punctilious, regular, reserved, solemn, stately, stiff, stilted, systematic

formal affirmation: oath

formal and proper: ceremonious, decorous

formal approval: confirmation, ratification, sanction, validation

formal argument: debate

formal ceremony: rite

formal closing at the end of a composition or movement: coda

formal code of correct conduct: protocol

formal dance: ball, prom

formal jacket: dinner jacket, tux, tuxedo

formal offer: tender

formal order: writ

formal social dance: ball

formal White House affair: state dinner

formal, artificially: pompous, stilted

formalism, traditional: academicism, academism

formality: ceremony, conventionality, custom, gesture, procedure, protocol, rite, tradition

formally withdraw: secede

format: arrangement, pattern, plan, scheme, shape, size, style

formation: composition, construction, deposit, development, form, makeup, organization, parade, procession, rank, spread, structure

formation of troops in ranks: echelon

formative: impressionable, plastic, pliant

formative years: teens

formed into a series: seriate

formed into columns: tabulated

formed into rounded mass: glomerate

former: ancient, antecedent, creator, departed, earlier, erst, erstwhile, foregoing, late, maker, old, once, onetime, past, previous, prior, quondam, some time, sometime, whilom

formidable: alarming, awesome, awful, challenging, dangerous, difficult, fearful, fierce, hard, horrible, imposing, impressive, menacing, mighty, powerful, redoubtable, terrible, threatening, tough

formless: amorphous, anidian, aplastic, arupa, chaotic, crude, disorganized, inchoate, indistinct, nebulous, shapeless, vague

forms, occurring in different: polymorphic

formula: blueprint, code, direction, equation, maxim, method, plan, procedure, recipe, rule, theory

formula showing arrangement of atoms and bonds, chemical: structural formula

formulate: coin, concoct, define, develop, devise, draft, express, frame, invent, originate, plan, state

forsake: abandon, abdicate, avoid, deny, desert, discard, disclaim, disown, flee, forego, forgo, leave, quit, refuse, reject, relinquish, renounce, resign, shun, spurn, surrender, waive, withdraw

forsaken: abandoned, deserted, desolate, forlorn, ignored, jilted, lorn, neglected, rejected

forsaking faith or principles: apostasy

forsooth: indeed

forswear: abandon, abjure, abnegate, deny, disavow, gainsay, perjure, recant, reject, renounce, retract

fort: base, bastille, bastion, blockhouse, bulwark, camp, castle, citadel, fortify, fortress, garrison, protection, stronghold

forte: ability, aptitude, bag, knack, metier, skill, specialty, strength, talent, thing

forth: abroad, away, forward, into, onward, outward

forthcoming: anticipated, approaching, expected, imminent, impending, in store, inevitable, pending

forthright: aboveboard, candid, direct, foursquare, frankly, honest, open, plain, straightforward, truthfully

forthwith: directly, immediately, instantly, now, presently, pronto, quickly, straightaway, therewith

fortification: barricade, barrier, bastion, buffer, bulwark, castle, citadel, defense, entrenchment, fastness, fortress, garrison, moat, palisade, parapet, protection, rampart, redan, retrenchment, shield, stockade, stronghold, tower, wall

fortified position: bastion, fastness, stronghold

fortified wall or barrier: enceinte, traverse

fortify: arm, barricade, bastille, beef up, boost, brace, confirm, embattle, energize, enrich, entrench, invigorate, man, prepare, reinforce, sara, secure, steel, strengthen, stronghold, support, sustain

fortitude: backbone, bravery, courage, determination, endurance, grit, guts, heart, perseverance, resolution, spunk, stamina, strength, valor

fortnightly: biweekly

fortress: barrier, bastille, castle, citadel, fort, garrison, rampart, redoubt, stronghold

fortuitous: accidental, casual, chance, contingent, fluky, incidental, lucky, random, serendipitous, unplanned

fortunate: advantageous, auspicious, blessed, blest, dexter, favorable, favored, golden, good, gracious, happy, lucky, profitable, promising, prosperous, successful, thriving, timely, well

fortune: accident, bonanza, bundle, chance, destiny, doom, estate, fate, hap, inheritance, lot, luck, possessions, pot, prosperity, riches, success, treasure, wealth, windfall, worth

fortune-teller: astrologer, clairvoyant, gypsy, medium, palmist, psychic, seer, sibyl, soothsayer

RELATED TERMS

fortune-telling by casting or drawing lots: sortilege

fortune-telling by consulting spirits: necromancy, sciomancy

fortune-telling by crystal ball: scrying

fortune-telling by dream interpretation: oneiromancy

fortune-telling by omens or the supernatural: augury, divination, soothsaying

fortune-telling by palm lines: chiromancy, palmistry

fortune-telling by planets' and stars' positions: horoscope

fortune-telling by random Bible verse: bibliomancy

fortune-telling by tarot or playing cards: cartomancy

fortune-telling by visions: clairvoyance

fortune-telling card: tarot ❦

fortune, sudden change in: vicissitudes

forty winks: nap, siesta, sleep, snooze

forum: court, marketplace, medium, symposium, tribunal

forward: advance, advanced, aggressive, ahead, along, before, coming, eager, earnest, encourage, extreme, forth, front, further, hasten, hasty,

leading, onward, progressive, radical, ready; deliver, relay, remit, send, ship, transmit

forward and overconfident: arrogant, audacious, bold, brash, brazen, impudent, obtrusive, precocious, presumptuous, pushy

forward mezzanine: loge

forward-moving: posigrade

forward pass: aerial

fossil: ammonite, antiquated, antique, conodont, coprolite, fogy, ichnite, impression, relic, skeleton

fossil dating technique: carbon dating

fossil fuel: coal

fossil is embedded, solid matter in which: matrix

fossil shell of extinct mollusk: ammonite

fossilized excrement: coprolite

fossilized resin: amber

fossils, study of: palaeontology, paleontology

foster: advance, advocate, assist, back, befriend, breed, cherish, cultivate, encourage, feed, food, further, harbor, help, house, nourish, nurse, nurture, promote, rear, shelter, support, sustain

foul: abusive, base, bawdy, blocked, contaminated, corrupt, defaced, defame, detestable, dirty, disgusting, dishonorable, entangled, filthy, grimy, gross, horrid, illegal, impure, indecent, lewd, loathsome, muddy, nastiness, nasty, nauseating, obnoxious, obscene, odious, offensive, polluted, profane, putrid, raunchy, repulsive, revolting, rotten, scatalogical, smeared, smelly, soiled, stinking, sully, unclean, unfair, unsportsmanlike, vicious, vile, vulgar, wicked, wretched

foul or fecal in nature: feculent

foul play: crime, illegal, killing, murder, violence

foul-smelling: fetid, malodorous, mephitic, olid, rancid

foul-up: glitch, snafu, snag

foul up: blunder, botch, bungle, goof, mismanage

foulmouthed: dirty, lewd, obscene, offensive, profane, rude, scurrilous, vulgar

found: base, begin, board, build, cast, create, depart, detected, endow, equipped, erect, establish, gather,

initiate, institute, isolate, launch, located, organize, originate, provided, rest, start, supported

foundation: base, basis, bed, bedding, bedrock, bottom, cellar, charity, corporation, donation, endowment, foot, fund, goundwork, institute, organization, pedestal, pile, pilotis, raft, roadbed, root, sill, society, staddle, substratum, substructure, support

foundation of community, organization: infrastructure

foundation of stone building: stereobate

founder: architect, author, collapse, creator, fail, fall, forefather, inventor, miscarry, organizer, originator, patriarch, precursor, progenitor, sink, stumble, submerge, supporter

foundling: orphan

fountain: beginning, bubbler, fount, geyser, jet, reservoir, source, spray, spring, stream, well, wellspring

fountain treat: float, malt, shake, soda, sundae

fountainhead: origin, originator, source

four children born at one time: quadruplets

four-dimensional continuum: space-time

four-dimensional equivalent of cube: tesseract

four-hundredth anniversary: quadricentennial, quatercentenary

four-in-hand: necktie, tie

four-leafed plant: clover

four-legged animal: quadruped, tetrapod

four-line poetry or stanza: quatrain

four notes: chord

four or more dimensions, space that has: hyperspace

four-page sheet: rolio

four parts, having: quadruple

four pecks: bushel

four quarts: gallon

four-sided closed figure: quadrilateral, tetragon

four-year period: quadrennium

four, group of: tetrad

fourfold: quadruple, quaternary

fourpence, once: groat

fourscore: eighty

fourth Jewish month: tebet

fowl: bird, capon, chick, chicken, cock, duck, game, goose, hen, hens, pheasant, rooster, turkey

fox: attractive, baffle, clever, confuse, crafty, fool, intoxicate, outwit, reynard, sly, tod, trick, vixen, vulpine

fox genus: vulpes

fox, female: vixen

fox, pertaining to: vulpine

fox, young: cub, kit, pup

foxglove family: digitalis

foxy: astute, crafty, cunning, sexy, shifty, shrewd, slick, sly, sneaky, vulpine

foyer: anteroom, entrance, hall, lobby, vestibule

fracas: altercation, brawl, brouhaha, commotion, dispute, disturbance, donnybrook, flight, melee, quarrel, row, rumpus, scrap, squabble, uproar

fraction: bit, break, breaking, chunk, component, division, fragment, little, part, piece, portion, proportion, ratio, section, slice

fraction to decimal, converting a: reduction

fraction, canceling of common factors in: reduction

fraction, line in: dividing line

fraction, number above line in: dividend, numerator

fraction, number below line in: denominator, divisor

fractional: insignificant, partial, small

fractious: cranky, cross, fretful, grouchy, irritable, mean, ornery, peevish, perverse, quarrelsome, rebellious, snappish, testy, unruly

fracture: breach, break, crack, fault, flaw, gap, rend, rift, rupture, separation, split, wound

fracture of bone to reset it, surgical: osteoclasis

fracture, thin and clean: hairline fracture

fragile: breakable, brittle, dainty, delicate, feeble, fine, flimsy, frail, frangible, friable, slender, slight, unsound, weak

fragment: atom, bit, chip, chunk, crumb, flake, flinder, fraction, grain, morsel, parcel, part, particle, piece, portion, remnant, scrap, shard, shatter, shrapnel, shred, sliver, snip, splinter, trace

fragment of food: ort

fragment of pottery, glass, etc.: potsherd, shard, sherd

fragment or flake of stone or ore: spall

fragmentary: broken, incomplete, partial, scattered, unsystematic

fragments: debris, detritus, orts, rubble, shreds, smithereens

fragments of explosive shell: shrapnel

fragments worn away from rock: detritus

fragrance: aroma, attar, balm, bouquet, flavor, incense, odor, perfume, redolence, scent, smell, spice

fragrant: ambrosial, aromal, aromatic, balmy, delectable, nectarous, odoriferous, odorous, olent, perfumy, redolent, scented, spicy, sweet

fragrant and suggestive: redolent

fragrant oil: attar

fragrant pine: cedar

frail: breakable, brittle, delicate, feeble, fine, flimsy, fragile, infirm, puny, reedy, sickly, slender, vulnerable, weak, weedy

frailty: blemish, defect, delicate, fallibility, fault, flaw, foible, imperfection, peccadillo, vice, weakness

frame: adjust, arrange, attempt, binder, body, border, build, casement, casing, chassis, construct, draft, encase, enclose, fabric, fashion, form, furnish, manage, mold, outline, panel, physique, plan, portray, prepare, proceed, raise, serve, shape, shell, structure, support, tenter, truss

frame for a papermaker's mold: deckle

frame for sleeping: bedstead

frame for supporting or showing a painting: easel

frame of mind: attitude, bent, disposition, mood, posture

frame used for sawing wood: sawhorse

frame, bridgelike: gantry

frame, to: calculate, contrive, devise, fabricate, formulate, incriminate, invent

framework: cadre, constraints, fabric, foundation, gantry, lattice, plan, rack, sill, skeleton, stroma, structure, studwork, system, trestle

framework for vines: trellis

framework of stall or goalpost: stanchion

framework or guidelines: constraints, limits, parameters

framework, crisscrossed: lattice

France delicatessen: charcuterie

France divisions: arrondissement, canton, commune, department

France drink: bordeaux, burgundy, champagne, cognac

France food: boeuf, brie, Camembert, canapé, crêpe, croissant, escargot, Meunster, mousse, Napoleon, pâté, quiche, Roquefort, soufflé

France people: Franks

franchise: authorization, charter, grant, license, permission, privilege, right, suffrage, team, territory

frangible: brittle

Frank: Frenchman

frank: aboveboard, bluff, blunt, brusque, candid, carefree, curt, direct, explicit, forthcoming, forthright, foursquare, free, honest, ingenuous, natural, open, outright, outspoken, plain, profuse, sincere, straight, straightforward, truthful, unreserved, up-front

Frankenstein's helper: Igor

frantic: berserk, delirious, deranged, desperate, distracted, distraught, distressed, excited, frenzied, hectic, insane, mad, rabid, raving, violent, wild

frantic or frenzied: demoniac

fraternal: brotherly, friendly, social

fraternity: association, brotherhood, circle, club, fellowship, frat, order, society, union

fraternity neophyte: pledge

fraternize: affiliate, associate, consort, keep company with, mingle, socialize

fraud: artifice, charlatan, cheat, chicanery, crook, deceit, deception, duplicity, fake, faker, flimflam, gaff, guile, hoax, hustle, imposition, impostor, imposture, knave, mountebank, phony, pretender, quack, rogue, scam, sham, swindle, trick, trickery, wile

fraudulent: bogus, cheating, clandestine, counterfeit, criminal, crooked, cunning, deceitful, deceiving, deceptive, dishonest, fake, false, misleading, snide, spurious, treacherous, underhand, wily

fraudulent taking or use: defalcation, embezzlement, peculation

fraught: abounding, charged, filled, laden, loaded, stuffed, upsetting

fray: alarm, altercation, assail, attack, battle, brawl, broil, chafe, clash, combat, commotion, conflict, contest, dispute, donnybrook, feud, fracas, frazzle, frighten, melee, panic, ravel, riot, rumpus, scuffle, shred, skirmish, spat, strain, tumult, unravel

frazzle: exhaustion, fray, prostrate, shred, tire, upset

freak: aberration, addict, bizarre, caprice, chimera, crochet, eccentric, enthusiast, fanatic, fancy, fiend, fleck, flimflam, frolic, geek, humor, monster, monstrosity, mutant, oddity, prank, rarity, rave, sport, vagary, whim, whimsy

freak of nature: lusus naturae, monster

freakish: abnormal, arbitrary, capricious, odd, outlandish, peculiar, screwy, strange, unusual, weird, whimsical

freckle: lentigo, macula

freckle of old age, larger: liver spot

free: able, absolve, abundant, acquit, autonomous, available, bail, clear, communicative, complimentary, deliver, democratic, detached, devoid, discharge, disencumber, disengage, disentangle, emancipate, enfranchise, exculpate, exempt, exonerate, expedite, extricate, footloose, generous, gratis, gratuitous, handout, handsome, idle, immune, independent, in the clear, leisure, liberal, liberate, liberated, loose, loosen, manumit, off-the-hook, open, pardon, parole, ready, release, relieve, remove, rescue, rid, self-ruling, separate, separated, sovereign, spare, spontaneous, spring, unattached, unbind, unbound, unbridled, unburden, unchecked, uncommitted, unconfined, uncontrolled, unfasten, unfettered, unimpaired, unimpeded, unleased, unoccupied, unreserved, unrestrained, unrestricted, unshackled, untie, untrammeled, vacant, void, willing

free access: entrée

free advance to next round of competition: bye

free-for-all: battle, brawl, brouhaha, donnybrook, fight, fray, melee, riot, ruckus, scrap, set-to

free from a danger: deliverance

free from a difficulty: extricate

free from blame: exculpate

free from bondage: enfranchise

free from fever: afebrile

free from obligations or slavery: affranchise, emancipate, enfranchise, manumit

free from restraint: emancipate, untie

free from slavery: manumit

free hand: laissez-aller

free of a burden, problem: disembarrass, disencumber

free of a responsibility or duty: exempt, exonerate

free of charge: gratis, gratuitous

free prisoner with provisions: parole

free prisoner without bail: release on their own recognizance

free time: leisure

free to do as one pleases: footloose, unencumbered

free trade: laissez-faire

free will: choice, consent, freedom, volition, voluntary

freebie: pass, perk, sample

freedom: abandon, autonomy, carte blanche, ease, emancipation, exemption, facility, flexibility, frankness, generosity, immunity, independence, latitude, leeway, leisure, liberation, liberty, license, openness, readiness, release, right, salvation, sovereignty, sweep, willingness

freedom from punishment, harm: impunity

freedom from restraints, limitations: latitude, leeway

freedom of speech, religion, etc.: civil liberties

freedom, total: carte blanche

freelance journalist: stringer

freeloader: barnacle, leech, moocher, parasite, sponge

freely: bountiful, cleanly, easily, generously, intentionally, unchallenged, unhindered, voluntarily

freely and without preparation: ad lib

freely, bestowed: ungrudging, unstinting

freethinker: agnostic, atheist, infidel, libertine, radical, skeptic

freeze: anesthetize, chill, coagulate, congeal, frost, halt, harden, ice, numb, preserve, refrigerate, solidify, stop

freezing: arctic, bitter, cold, frigid, gelation, gelid, icy, nippy, raw

freezing dead for revival or future cure: cryonics

freezing rain: sleet

freight: bulk, cargo, contents, goods, haul, lading, load, merchandise, payload, shipment, transport

freight allowance: tare

French-American: creole

French borrowings from English: Franglais

French bread: pain

French cooking school with light, low-calorie sauces: nouvelle cuisine

French phrase or idiom appearing in another language: gallicism

French pronunciation of final consonant when next word begins with vowel: liaison

French quotation marks (>>): guillemets

French-speaking person: francophone

French, relating to ancient France or the: Gallic

frenetic: crazy, delirious, demented, distracted, distraught, excited, fanatic, frantic, frenzied, furious, insane, mad, obsessive, passionate, rabid, violent, wild, zealous

frenzied: amok, amuck, berserk, delirious, excited, feverish, frantic, frenetic, furious, hectic, hysterical, madding, manic, raging, ramage, uncontrolled

frenzy: craze, delirium, distraction, excitement, fit, frantic, furor, hysteria, insanity, lunacy, mad, madness, mania, maniacal, rage, rampaging, ruckus, turmoil

frequency: number, persistence, recurrence, regularity, repetition

frequency beyond human hearing: ultrasonic

frequency distribution: ogive

frequency measurement: hertz

frequency or extent of occurrence: incidence

frequent: assiduous, common, continual, current, familiar, habitual, hourly, numerous, often, persistent, predominant, prevailing, prevalent, recurrent, repeated, usual

frequent and repeated: habitual, persistent, recurrent

frequent visitor: habitué

frequent, to: attend, habituate, haunt, patronize, visit

frequently, poetically: oft

fresh: added, additional, anew, bold, brazen, breezy, bright, brisk, chipper, clean, cool, crisp, current, different, energetic, green, hot, impudent, inexperienced, invigorating, lively, modern, more, new, novel, presumptuous, pure, racy, recent, rested, rude, sassy, smart-alecky, sparkling, straight, sweet, unspoiled, untried, unused, vibrant, vivid, wise

fresh and lively: vibrant, vivid

fresh and springlike: vernal

fresh condition: verdure

freshen: air, cleanse, deodorize, purify, renew, sweeten, ventilate

freshet: spate

freshman: apprentice, beginner, frosh, neophyte, newcomer, novice, plebe, recruit, rookie, student, tenderfoot, tyro

fret: abrade, agitate, agonize, brood, chafe, consume, corrode, disturb, erode, fray, fume, fuss, gnaw, grate, harass, headdress, irritate, mope, nettle, pout, rile, ripple, rub, ruffle, stew, strait, sulk, trouble, vex, wear, worry

fretful: angry, captious, contrary, crabby, cranky, cross, gnawing, huffy, impatient, irascible, irritable, jittery, ornery, peevish, pettish, plaintive, querulous, repine, restive, restless, testy, troublesome

Freudian emotional and sexual energy: Eros, libido

Freudian psychological treatment: psychoanalysis

friable: brittle, crimp, crisp, crumbly, flaky, fragile, mealy

fribble: fritter, frivolity, frivolous, trifle

friction: antagonism, chafing, clash, conflict, disagreement, disharmony, dissension, grinding, hostility, resistance, rubbing

friction and lubrication, study of: tribology

friction-reducing substance: lubricant

friction, adhesive: traction

friction, wearing away through: attrition

fridge adornment: magnet

fried lightly in fat: sauté, sautéed

friend: acquaintance, ally, ami, amie, amiga, amigo, associate, attendant, bonne amie, buddy, chum, cohort, compadre, companion, comrade, confidant, confidante, crony, pal, partner, playmate, relative, sidekick, wellwisher

friend, intimate: alter ego, confidant, confidante, intimate

friendless: outcast

friendliness: amicability, empressement, gemulichkeit

friendly: affable, amiable, amicable, amical, benevolent, brotherly, chummy, civil, comforting, companionable, congenial, cordial, favorable, fond, genial, gracious, hospitable, intimate, kind, neighborly, open door, peaceful, platonic, sisterly, sociable, warm, warmhearted

friendly agreement: entente, entente cordiale, mutual understanding

friendly and sociable: affable, convivial, cordial, debonair, expansive, gregarious

friendly and sympathetic: congenial, hail-fellow-well-met, simpatico

friendly atmosphere, having a: cozy, gemutlich

friendly nature: bonhomie, geniality

friendly outgoing person: extrovert

friendly relationship: amity, camaraderie, rapport

friendly to guests: hospitable

friends, exclusive circle of: clique

friendship: accord, alliance, amity, asociation, attachment, coalition, federation, goodwill, harmony, love, pact, platonic

friendship and help among females: old girl network

friendship and help among males: old boy network

friendship ignoring sexuality: platonic

friendship weakened: disaffection

friendship, to reestablish a: reconcile

frigate: boat, sailboat, ship, vessel, warship

fright: alarm, anxiety, awe, consternation, dismay, dread, fear, funk, horror, panic, scare, shock, startle, strange, terror, trepidation, unsightly

frighten: alarm, appal, appall, cow, discomfit, discourage, hazen, horrify, intimidate, panic, petrify, rattle, scare, spook, startle, terrify, terrorize, unnerve, upset

frighten or make nervous: discomfit, unnerve

frighten with threats: intimidate

frightened: afraid, alarmed, chicken, fearful, frozen, scared, skittish, terrified, timid

frightened easily: skittish

frightening: daunting, disheartening, fearsome, formidable, rebarbative, redoubtable

frightening exclamation: boo

frightful: alarming, awful, daunting, dire, distressing, dreadful, excessive, extreme, fearful, fearsome, gashful, ghastly, grim, grisly, hairy, hideous, horrendous, horrid, horrific, horrifying, morbid, scary, shocking, sinister, terrific, terrifying, wicked

frigid: arctic, chilly, cold, freezing,

frosty, frozen, hyperborean, icy, passionless, raw, stiff, straitlaced, unresponsive

frill: air, amenity, flounce, furbelow, luxury, pleated, ruffle

frill on blouse or shirt front: jabot

fringe: border, brim, brink, edge, edging, hem, limit, outskirts, perimeter, periphery, rim, trimming, verge

fringe of group: periphery

frippery: finery, flashiness, nonsense, ostentation, pretentious, regalia, trivial, waste

frisk: brisk, caper, caracole, cavort, curvet, dance, disport, examine, frolic, gambol, lark, leap, prance, romp, search, shake down, skip

frisky: active, chipper, coltish, frolicsome, kittenish, lively, peppy, pert, playful, spirited, spry

fritter: bangle, cake, consume, dally, dawdle, deplete, idle, pancake, shred, spend, squander, trifle, waste

fritter, seafood: baignet, bang, beigne, beignet

frivolity: coquetting, flummery, folly, fribble, fun, jest, levity, nonsense

frivolity, inappropriate: levity

frivolous: carefree, childlike, featherbrained, flighty, flippant, fribble, futile, giddy, impractical, inane, insignificant, petty, pointless, senseless, shallow, silly, trivial, worthless, yeasty

frizzle: curl

frock: apron, dress, gown, habit, mantle, robe, smock, tunic, wrap

frog: amphibian, anuran, batrachian, bullfrog, croaker, newt, peeper, ranine, salientian, toad

frog or toad, relating to: anuran, batrachian, batrachoid, ranine, salientian

frolic: amusement, caper, carouse, cavort, curvet, dally, disport, frisk, fun, gaiety, gambol, lark, masquerade, merriment, play, prance, prank, ramp, revel, romp, scamper, skylark, sport, spree, tomfoolery, wassail

frolicsome: frisky, gamesome, jocular, jovial, lively, mischievous, playful, rollicking, sportive, waggish

from that place: thence

from the beginning: ab initio, ab ovo, de novo

frond producer: fern

front: anterior, appearance, before, beginning, bow, brow, cover, demeanor, dickey, disguise, display, ef-

FRUIT-RELATED TERMS

bear fruit, to: fructify
berry fruit: blackberry, blueberry, boysenberry, cranberry, loganberry, strawberry
citrus fruit: citron, clementine, kumquat, lemon, lime, maartje, mandarin, mango, orange, ortanique, pomelo, satsuma, tangelo
colloidal carbohydrate of fruit: pectin
depression or dimple on bottom: basin
exotic fruit: breadfruit, cantaloupe, cherimoya, durian, gooseberry, granadilla, guava, kiwi, litchi, longan, loquat, mangosteen, melon, papaw, passion fruit, persimmon, pomegranate, rambutan, sapodilla, tamarind
fleshy fruit like apple: pome
fruit-bearing: fructiferous, fruition
fruit blown down by wind: windfall
fruit created only through breeding: cultivar
fruit derived from several flowers that combine into one structure, like pineapple: aggregate fruit, collective fruit, multiple fruit

fruit-eating: carpophagous, frugivorous
fruit of fir tree: cone
fruit of the blackthorn: sloe
fruit of the oak: acorn
fruit of the palm: date
fruit of various evergreen like lemon, orange: citrus fruit
fruit part: pulp, rind, seed
fruit rind: peel
fruit seed: pip
fruit skin as decoration: zest
fruit stew: compote
fruit with single hard stone: drupe, stone fruit
pulpy material after pressing: marc, pomace
study of fruit: pomology
white covering under rind of citrus fruit: albedo ❦

---

frontery, exterior, facade, face, facing, fore, forehead, foremost, forward, head, lead, manner, obverse, oppose, outlook, show, van

front formed when a cold front blocks a warm front: occluded front
front of building: facade, frontispiece
front of something, relating to the: anterior, frontal
front position: vanguard
front side of leaf of paper: recto
front side of something: obverse
frontier: backlands, backwoods, border, borderline, bound, boundary, edge, march, outpost, outskirts, perimeter, unsettled
frost: blight, chill, freeze, hoar, ice, nip, rime
frost that is frozen dew: hoarfrost, white frost
frost, coating of: rime
frosty: arctic, chilling, cold, cool, freezing, frigid, frozen, gelid, glacial, icy, rimed, rimy
froth: barm, fizz, foam, lather, scum, spume, suds, surf
froward: adverse, balky, contrary, cross, disobedient, headstrong, obstinate, ornery, peevish, perverse, petulant, stubborn, unfavorable
frown: disagree, disapprove, fret, glare, gloom, glower, grimace, lower, pout, scowl, sulk

frowsy: disheveled, disordered, frowzy, musty, seedy, slovenly, smelly, stale, unkempt
frozen: arctic, chilled, cold, cold-hearted, congealed, cooled, fixed, frappé, frigid, frostbitten, frosted, gelid, hardened, iced, immobile, numb, refrigerated, stiff, stopped, suspended
frozen dessert: bombé, ice, ice cream, mousse, sherbet
frozen dew: rime
frozen ground, permanently: permafrost
frozen rain: sleet
frozen state: gelidity
frozen subsoil and treeless area: tundra
frugal: austere, canny, careful, chary, economical, inexpensive, meager, parsimonious, penny-pinching, provident, prudent, saving, sparing, spartan, stingy, thrifty, tight, unwasteful
fruitful: abundant, ample, blooming, fecund, feracious, fertile, flourishing, inventive, plenteous, plentiful, pregnant, procreant, productive, profitable, prolific, rewarding, successful, worthwhile
fruition: accomplishment, achievement, actualization, attainment, delight, fulfillment, maturation, pleasure, realization, satisfaction
fruitless: abortive, barren, futile, geld, idle, ineffective, ineffectual, infer-

tile, pointless, profitless, rewarding, sterile, unproductive, unprofitable, unsuccessful, useless, vain
fruits, seeds, nuts, eater of only: fruitarian
frump: dowdy, dull, flout, plain, prim, sedate, snub, sulk, unfashionable, unstylish
frustrate: as is, baffle, balk, blight, block, check, checkmate, circumvent, confound, countermand, cramp, crimp, cross, crush, dash, defeat, disappoint, discomfit, disconcert, dishearten, elude, exasperate, fluster, foil, hinder, impede, neutralize, nullify, outwit, prevent, stymie, thwart, unsettle, useless, vain, void
frustrate and defeat plans: discomfit
frustrate by holding something desirable: tantalize
frustration: bottleneck, disappointment, discomfiture, irritation, letdown, setback, vexation
fry: brown, cook, destroy, electrocute, grill, sauté, sizzle
frying pan: browner, griddle, skillet, spider, wok
frying pan with long handle: spider
fuddle: confuse, drink, intoxicate, jumble
fudge: candy, cheat, contrive, dodge, evade, exaggerate, fake, falsify, humbug, hunch, misrepresent, nonsense, substitute

FRUIT TYPES

apple	clementine	jackfruit	olive	prune
apricot	coconut	jujube	orange	quince
atemoya	crabapple	kiwi	papaya	quinoa
avocado	currant	kumquat	passion fruit	raisin
banana	custard apple	lemon	pawpaw	rambutan
berry	damson	lime	peach	sapodilla
black currant	date	longan	pear	sapote
breadfruit	durian	loquat	pepino	satsuma
bullace plum	fig	mandarin orange	Persian melon	sea grape
calmyrna	granadilla	mango	persimmon	soursop
canistel	grape	May apple	pineapple	tamarillo
cantaloupe	grapefruit	medlar	plantain	tamarind
carambola	greengage	melon	plum	tangelo
cherimoya	ground cherry	muskmelon	pomegranate	tangerine
cherry	guava	navel orange	pomelo	tomato
citron	haw	nectarine	prickly pear	watermelon 🍉

fuel: ammunition, charcoal, charge, coal, coke, combustible, energize, energy, ethane, ethanol, feed, gas, gasoline, ignite, incite, inspiration, juice, kerosene, nourish, oil, peat, petrol, petroleum, propellant, reb, stoke, sustain, wood

fuel derived from prehistoric living matter: fossil fuel

fuel in rocket: propellant

fuel, colorless gas: butane, propane

fugitive: AWOL, brief, criminal, deserter, dodger, elusive, ephemeral, escapee, evanescent, exile, fleeing, fleeting, fugacious, outlaw, refugee, renegade, roaming, runaway, transient, transitory, vagabond, wanted

fulfill: accomplish, achieve, answer, complete, effect, effectuate, execute, finish, full, meet, perform, reach, realize, redeem, satisfy, suit

fulfillment: attainment, consummation, crowning, fruition, gratification

fulgent: bright, brilliant, dazzling, flashing, luminous, radiant, shining

full: adequate, ample, brimming, bursting, capacious, clear, complete, copious, crammed, crowded, entire, exhaustive, filled, glutted, good, laden, overflowing, packed, perform, plenary, plentiful, plump, replete, resonant, rich, round, sated, satisfied, stocked, stuffed, surfeited, teeming, thorough, total, uncut

full and blocked: congested

full and rounded in voice: orotund, sonorous

full-blooded: florid, genuine, purebred, rubicund, ruddy, thoroughbred

full-blown: adult, aged, all-out, blossomed, developed, lush, mature, ripe

full-bodied: flavorful, intense, potent, rich, robust

full development of one's talents: self-realization

full extent: range

full-fledged: developed, expert, genuine, mature, plumage, proficient

full force: brunt

full-grown: developed, mature, ready, ripe

full-length: unabridged

full length, at: in extenso

full moon, time of the: plenilune

full of emotion or tension: charged, fraught

full of food or drink: replete, sated, satiated, satisfied

full turn ballet movement standing on the point of the toe: pirouette

full, complete: plenary

fullness: abundance, aggregate, amplitude, breadth, completeness, completion, entirety, perfection, plenitude, plentitude, plenty, plenum, plumpness, satiety, scope

fully: abundantly, amply, clearly, completely, enough, entirely, outright, perfectly, plenteously, plentifully, positively, quite, sufficiently, totally, utterly, wholly

fully expressed: explicit

fully grown: mature

fully stopped, as consonants k, p, t: lene

fulminate: berate, castigate, detonate, explode, fume, rant, roar

fulsome: abundant, copious, disgusting, flattering, foul, glib, gross, ingratiating, insincere, nauseating, offensive, overfed, plump, repulsive, satiating, sickening, slick, suave, unctuous, wanton

fumble: bobble, boot, botch, bumble, bungle, error, flounder, flub, goof, grope, memble, mishandle, mismanage, muff, stammer

fume: anger, boil, emit, exhalation, exhale, foam, fumigate, odor, rage, rant, rave, seethe, smell, smoke, steam, stew, storm, vapor

fun: amusement, antic, ball, blast, clowning, diversion, enjoyment, entertainment, festivity, gaiety, game, glee, happy, hilarity, horseplay, jest, joke, laughter, merriment, mirth, nonsense, play, pleasure, recreation, sport, tomfoolery

function: action, activity, affair, benefit, business, capacity, celebration, ceremony, duty, feast, festivity, gathering, goal, job, mission, object, occasion, occupation, office, operate, operation, party, profession, providence, purpose, reception, role, service, task, use, work

functional: operative, practical, useful, utile, working

functioning of substance within living body: metabolism

functioning properly: operational, operative

functioning, impaired: dysfunction
functionless: otiose
fund: accumulation, back, bankroll, capital, deposit, endow, finance, foot the bill, foundation, pool, reserve, source, stock, store, subsidize, supply, support, trust
fund for bribes and corruption: slush fund
fund for emergency or future use: contingency
fund invested so its gradual increase will pay a debt: sinking fund
fundamental: basal, basic, cardinal, central, chief, component, crucial, element, elementary, essential, first, important, integral, major, necessary, organic, original, paramount, primary, principle, radical, real, rule, theorem, underlying, vital
fundamental character of a culture: ethos
fundamental principle: hypostasis
fund-raiser: benefit
funds: assets, capital, cash, currency, money, profits, resources, savings, wealth
funds for risky new venture: venture capital
funds, misuse or theft of: defalcation, embezzlement, misappropriation, peculation
funds, to appeal for: solicit
funeral: burial, ceremony, cortege, cremation, exequies, mass, obsequies, rite, rites, sepulture, services, wake
RELATED TERMS
funeral bell ring: knell
funeral bugle call: last post, taps
funeral coffin carrier: pallbearer
funeral director: mortician, undertaker
funeral hymn: dirge, epicedium, lament, threnody
funeral notice: obit
funeral oration: eloge, encomium, eulogy, panegyric, salutation, tribute
funeral procession: cortege
funeral rites: obsequies
funeral song: chant funebre, dirge, elegy, lament, requiem, taps, threnody
funeral vehicle: hearse
funeral watch or party before burial: wake
funeral wood pile for cremation: pyre ❦

funereal: bleak, depressing, dirgeful, dismal, doleful, dreary, gloomy, grave, grieving, grim, mournful, solemn
fungi reproductive body: spore
fungus: agaric, amanita, cepe, chitin, ergot, mildew, mold, morel, mushroom, oidium, organism, puffball, rust, smut, stinkhorn, telium, tinea, toadstool, truffle, yeast
fungus eaten as delicacy, underground: truffle
fungus, substance that kills: fungicide
funk: coward, depression, despondency, flinch, fright, frighten, gloom, misery, music, odor, panic, rage, recoil, shrink, smell
funnel: channel, conduct, cone, convey, focus, move, pipe, siphon, transmit
funnel-shaped: infundibuliform
funniness at inappropriate time: flippancy, frivolity, levity
funny: amusing, bizarre, clever, comic, comical, curious, droll, entertaining, hilarious, humorous, hysterical, jocose, jocular, laughable, mysterious, offbeat, outlandish, puzzling, queer, silly, slapstick, strange, uproarious, weird, zany
funny and coarse: bawdy
funny and ridiculous: comical, ludicrous, risible
funny bone: olecranon
funny, extremely: hilarious, hysterical, priceless, riotous, sidesplitting, uproarious
funny, mildly: amusing, diverting
fur: brush, coat, hair, hide, lapin, pelage, pell, pelt, pile, sable, sealskin, skin, stole, wool
fur hat, tall, worn by British army, etc.: busby
fur of mammal: pelage
fur of white weasel: ermine
fur scarf: boa, tippet
fur wrap: stole
fur, kind of: beaver, fox, lamb, mink, otter, rabbit, raccoon, sable, seal, squirrel
furbelow: falbala, flounce, frill, ornament, ruffle, trimming
furbish: clean, improve, polish, recondition, restore, revive, scour, shine
furious: angry, blustery, boiling, boisterous, crazed, enraged, fierce, frantic, frenzied, fuming, impetuous, incensed, irate, livid, mad, mad as a

March hare, rabid, raging, seething, steamed, steaming, stormy, tempestuous, turbulent, upset, vehement, violent
furl: bundle, coil, curl, enfold, fold, roll, truss, wrap
furlough: layoff, leave, permit, vacation
furnace: boiler, forge, gas heater, heater, incinerator, kiln, oven, reverberatory, stove
RELATED TERMS
furnace floor: hearth
furnace for baking and firing ceramics: kiln
furnace for burning waste: incinerator
furnace for heating metal: forge, smithy
furnace part adjusting airflow or draft: damper
furnace residue: cinder, scoria, sinter, slag
furnace residue that is metallic: salamander
furnace-to-chimney pipe: flue
furnace with combustion intensified by air blast: blast furnace
furnace with deflection of heat onto material: reverberatory ❦

furnish: accommodate, afford, apparel, appoint, arm, array, bestow, cater, clothe, decorate, endow, equip, feed, garnish, give, insure, lend, outfit, prepare, provide, purvey, render, stock, store, supply, transfer
furnish weaponry: arm
furnishing food: catering
furnishings: accessories, appliances, appointments, equipment, fittings, fixtures, furniture, habiliments, trappings
furnishings, having full: well-appointed, well-equipped
furniture: appointments, armoire, bed, bookcase, bureau, cabinet, chair, chesterfield, chiffonier, couch, credenza, davenport, decoration, desk, dresser, embellishment, equipment, furnishings, hutch, oak, ottoman, sofa, table, tallboy
furor: bustle, commotion, craze, enthusiasm, excitement, fad, fashion, frenzy, fury, hysteria, ire, madness, mania, rage, stir, uproar, whirlwind
furrow: channel, crease, crumple,

FURNITURE TERMS

artificially aged: distressed
curved and tapered leg: cabriole
furniture component that is interchangeable: module
furniture fabric: upholstery
furniture of early-eighteenth-century England: Queen Anne
furniture of early-nineteenth-century England: Regency
furniture of mid-eighteenth-century England: Chippendale
furniture of nineteenth-century Germany: Biedermeier
furniture or art as focus of room: conversation piece
furniture styles: Adam, Biedermeier, Boulle, Chippendale,
  Colonial, Elizabethan, Queen Anne, Regency, Second

Empire, Sheraton
furniture that cannot be moved: fixture
high, narrow chest of drawers: chiffonier
large cabinet or wardrobe: armoire
large sofa: davenport
set of open shelves for items: étagère
sofa for two: love seat
upholstered bench, no arms: banquette
wheel on swivel: caster, castor
wickerwork furniture: rattan ❧

ditch, drill, fold, groove, hollow, plow, rimple, rut, stria, trench, wrinkle

furrow, deep: sulcus

further: abet, accelerate, additional, advance, advantage, again, aid, also, and, another, assist, besides, beyond, contribute, farther, forward, foster, help, more, moreover, other, promote, push, serve, supplemental, yet

furtherance: advancement, advocacy, assistance, facility, help, progress, promotion, pursuit

furthermore: additionally, again, also, and, besides, likewise, moreover, too, yet

furthest point: ne plus ultra

furtive: clandestine, covert, crafty, evasive, foxy, mystical, secret, shifty, sly, sneaking, sneaky, stealthy, surreptitious, undercover, wily

fury: anger, bluster, Erinys, fierceness, force, frenzy, furiosity, furor, indignation, intensity, ire, madness, outburst, passion, rage, rigor, vehemence, violence, vixen, wrath

fuse: amalgamate, bind, blend, coalesce, combine, flux, incorporate, join, link, meld, melt, merge, mingle, smelt, solder, unite, weld

fuse by applying heat: weld

fuse that is string of gunpowder: train

fusing material: solder

fusion: alliance, blending, coalition, flux, liquefying, melting, merger, mixture, music, reaction

fusion bomb: hydrogen bomb, thermonuclear bomb

fuss: ado, annoy, argument, bother, bustle, commotion, complain, confusion, crab, disconcert, dispute, disturbance, fanfare, fidget, flap, fret, fume, gripe, hassle, hoo-ha, nag, nitpick, palaver, pother, production, protest, quarrel, rave, row, spat, sputter, squawk, stew, stir, to-do, trouble, tumult, upset, whine, worry

fuss over trifling matter: foofaraw

fussily attentive to details: punctilious, scrupulous

fussily dainty: precious, prissy

fussy: chary, choosy, demanding, difficult, fastidious, fidgety, finicky, meticulous, niggling, nit-picking, painstaking, particular, persnickety, picky, quibbling

fussy attention to details or rules: pedantry

fussy in tastes: discerning, discriminating

fussy person: precisian, stickler

fustigate: beat, castigate, criticize, cudgel, lash, strike, whip

futile: exhausted, forlorn, fruitless, hopeless, idle, ineffective, ineffectual, nouse, otiose, pointless, trifling, trivolous, unavailing, unsuccessful, useless, vain, worthless

futile endeavor: wild-goose chase

futile hope: will-o'-the-wisp

future: coming, ensuing, eventual, forthcoming, hereafter, impending, later, latter, projected, prospect, to be

future event referred to as having happened: prolepsis

future expectations, impression of: prospect

future generations: posterity

future happening, indication of: foreboding, portent

future happening, person indicating or ushering in: harbinger, herald, precursor

future period of joy, peace, justice, prosperity: millennium

future possibility, think of as: envisage, envision

future, about to occur in near: imminent, impending

future, likely to happen in the: prospective

future, possibility for: contingency, eventuality

future, sense of something to occur in the: premonition, presentiment

fuzz: down, fiber, fluff, hair, lint, officer of the law, pile, plainclothesman, police

fuzzy: bleary, blurred, faint, hazy, linty, out of focus, unclear, unfocused, vague, woolly

G g

gab: blabber, chat, chatter, chin, conversation, gabble, gossip, jabber, prate, prattle, rap, talk, yackety yak, yak, yap

gabble: babble, blab, cackle, chatter, chitchat, clatter, drivel, gab, gossip, jabber, patter, prate, talk, twaddle, yak, yap

gaberdine: cloak, coat, frock, garment, gown, smock

gad: gallivant, meander, prowl, ramble, roam, rove, stray, tool, traipse, wander

gadabout: social butterfly

gadfly: bother, busybody, critic, goad, nuisance, pest

gadget: appliance, contraption, contrivance, device, doodad, doohickey, gimmick, gizmo, invention, novelty, thingamajig, tool

Gaelic: Celt, Celtic, Erse, Gael, Goidel, Highlander, Irish, Kelpie, Scot, Sept

gaffe: blooper, blunder, boner, error, faux pas, goof, misjudgment, mistake, slip

gag: hoax, joke, trick, wisecrack; choke, constrain, heave, hush, muffle, muzzle, obstruct, quiet, restrain, silence, suppress, vomit

gaiety: animation, celebration, elation, festivity, finery, frolic, fun, geniality, glee, happiness, hilarity, jollity, joy, levity, merriment, mirth, vavacity

gain: accretion, accumulation, achieve, acquire, acquisition, addition, advance, advantage, attain, benefit, clear, dividend, earn, effect, get, good, growth, improvement, income, increase, increment, land, lucre, net, obtain, plus, prevail, procure, profit, progress, reach, realize, reap, return, secure, win

gain control over: harness

gain knowledge: learn

gain matched to loss in system, game: zero-sum

gainsay: contradict, controvert, deny, disagree, disclaim, dispute, impugn, negate, oppose, refute, resist

gait: amble, canter, gallop, lope, march, pace, rack, step, stride, strut, tread, trot, walk

gaiter: boot, chaps, legging, overshoe, puttee, shoe, spat

gala: affair, ball, bash, carnival, celebration, colorful, feast, festal, festival, fete, fiesta, function, merry, party

galaxy other than Milky Way: nebula

gale: blast, flurry, gust, hurricane, outburst, squall, storm, tempest, typhoon, wind, windstorm

gall: abrade, acerbity, annoy, bitterness, boldness, brashness, bug, burn, chafe, cheek, effrontery, exasperate, excoriate, fret, harass, impudence, inflame, irk, irritate, nerve, pester, rancor, rile, rub, ruffle, spite, temerity, vexation

gallant: attentive, beau, blade, bold, brave, cavalier, chivalrous, conduct, courageous, courteous, courtly, daring, dashing, dignified, fearless, game, gentlemanly, handsome, heroic, intrepid, lover, noble, polished, polite, showy, spark, splendid, stately, suave, suitor, swain, valiant, wooer

gallantry: attention, bravery, chivalry, courage, courtesy, courtliness, grit, heroism, spirit, valor

gallbladder removal: cystectomy

gallery: arcade, assortment, audience, balcony, collection, exhibit, grandstand, loggia, mezzanine, museum, passageway, piazza, porch, portico, promenade, salon, spectators, veranda

gallery or arcade, usually roofed, on front or side of building: loggia

gallery or balcony, usually roofed, on outside of building: veranda

galley: bireme, boat, cookroom, cuddy, kitchen, proof, rowboat, scullery, ship, tray, trireme, vessel

gallinipper: mosquito

gallivant: flirt, ramble, roam, traipse, travel, wander

gallop: bolt, dart, fly, gait, hasten, hurry, jog, race, run, scoot, speed, sprint, stride, tantivy, trot

gallop, fast and furious: tantivy

gallows: gibbet, hanging, noose, potence, rope, scaffold

gallstone: calculus, concretion, cystolith

galore: abundant, aplenty, copious, lots, plentiful, plenty

galosh: boot, overshoe, rubber, shoe

galvanize: arouse, coat, electrify, energize, excite, inspire, jolt, motivate, prime, provoke, rally, spur, startle, stimulate, stir, zinc

gambit: design, gimmick, maneuver, move, opener, plan, plot, ploy, remark, ruse, strategem, trick

gamble: bet, brave, chance, dice, game, hazard, hedge, jeopardize, play, risk, speculate, stake, uncertainty, venture, wager

gambler: bookie, darer, dicer, gamester, hustler, player, risker, shark, sharper, speculator

gambling establishment: casino

gambling game in many states: lottery

gambling in which stakes are doubled after loss: martingale

gambling table attendant who collects and pays bets: croupier
gambling, characterized by: aleatory
gambling, unable to stop: compulsive
gambol: caper, cavort, frisk, frolic, jump, lark, leap, play, prance, rollick, romp, skip, tumble
game on court with curved basket strapped to wrist: jai alai
game on horseback: polo
game or games to break tie: playoff
game or hunted animals: prey, quarry
game where one team fails to score: shutout
game, ball: baseball, basketball, billiards, catch, cricket, croquet, football, golf, handball, hockey, ping-pong, polo, rugby, soccer, softball, squash, tennis
game, board: backgammon, bingo, checkers, chess, cribbage, lotto, Monopoly, Parcheesi, Scrabble
game, card: accordion, all fours, argington, auction, authors, belotte, bezique, big forty, blackjack, blind tiger, Bolivia, boodle, bridge, calculation, canasta, canfield, cassino, Chicago, Chile, chouette, cinch, clubby, concentration, conquian, crapette, crazy eights, crazy jacks, cribbage, dealer's choice, deuces wild, Earl of Coventry, eights, euchre, fan tan, faro, fish, five finger, five hundred, five or nine, forth thieves, forty-five, frog, garbage, gin rummy, hearts, hombre, kalabrias, kaloochi, kalougi, kaluki, klaberjass, klondike, low ball, memory, Michigan, Michigan rummy, monte bank, Napoleon, newmarket, Oklahoma, old maid, old sledge, ombre, pan, panguingue, parliament, pedro, pig, pinochle, piquet, pitch, play or pay, poker, pool nap, pounce, put and take, red and black, red dog, rummy, russian bank, sam, samba, saratoga, schafskopf, sevens, seven-up, shasta, sheepshead, shotgun, sir garnet, sixty-six, skat, slapjack, slough, smudge, solitaire, spider, spite and malice, spoil five, stops, stud poker, tournament, trio, tunk, twenty-one, Uruguay, vingt-et-un, war, whist, wipe-off, zioncheck
game, court: badminton, basketball, handball, jai alai, pelota, squash, tennis, volleyball

game, racket: badminton, bandy, lacrosse, racquetball, squash, tennis
game, spiritual board: Ouija
game, word: acrostic, anagram, crossword, ghost, ludi, Scrabble
gameness: pluck
gamete: egg, oosphere, ovum, sperm, spermatozoon, zygote
gamut: compass, continuum, extent, field, orbit, range, reach, scale, series, span, spectrum
gang: band, cabal, circle, clan, clique, club, company, crew, crowd, friends, group, horde, mob, outfit, pack, posse, ring, syndicate, team
gang ending: -ster
gangling: awkward, gangly, lanky, rangy, skinny, tall
gangrenous: sphacelate
gangster: bandit, criminal, crook, desperado, goon, gunman, hood, hooligan, mobster, moll, punk, racketeer, ruffian, thief, thug
gap: aperture, blank, breach, break, chasm, cleft, clove, crack, crevice, defile, disparity, divide, fissure, flaw, gully, hiatus, hole, inconsistency, interruption, lacuna, lapse, lull, notch, opening, pass, pause, ravine, rift, separation, space, vacuum, void

RELATED TERMS

gap between nerve cells: synapse
gap between teeth: diastema
gap from splitting, cleaving: cleavage, discontinuity, void
gap in body part: foramen
gap or channel, narrow: canyon, couloir, gulch, gully, ravine, wadi
gap or interruption: hiatus, lacuna
gap or interval: adjournment, intermission, recess, respite
gap or omission: loophole
gap or opening, small: cleft, cranny, crevice, fissure, rift
gap or pass, narrow: defile
gap or space, small: interstice
gap or void, deep: abyss, chasm
gap, narrow gorge in mountain: flume
gap, unbridgeable: gulf ☙

gape: eye, gasp, gawk, gaze, goggle, ogle, oscitate, peer, rubberneck, stare, yawn
gaping: astare, broad, cavernous, great, open, ringent, vast, wide open
garage hand: mechanic
garb: apparel, appearance, array, attire,

bundle, clothe, clothing, costume, custom, dress, fashion, gear, getup, guise, outfit, raiment, style, threads, togs, vestment
garbage: debris, junk, litter, meaningless, offal, refuse, rubbish, sewage, trash, waste
garbage, large container: Dumpster
garble: color, cull, disguise, distort, jumble, mangle, misrepresent, misstate, scramble, sift, slur, twist
garden: arbor, bed, conservatory, cultivate, eden, enclosure, field, greenhouse, lawn, nursery, park, parterre, patch, plot, terrace, tract, yard
garden cultivation: horticulture
garden party: fete champetre, fete galante
garden plot: bed
garden protective covering of straw, peat, leaves: mulch
garden structure or summerhouse: belvedere, gazebo
garden structure, secluded: alcove, arbor, bower
garden tool: dibber, dibble, edger, hoe, spade, trowel
garden-variety: usual
garden with paths in pattern: parterre
garden, secluded: pleasance
garden, variety of: cactus, english, floating, flower, formal, hanging, herb, kitchen, rock, rose, vegetable, victory, water, zoological
gardener: caretaker, hoer, horticulturist, landscaper
gardeners, group of: sprinkling
gardening: horticulture
gardening with clipped shrubs in designs: topiary
gargantuan: colossal, enormous, giant, gigantic, huge, immense, mammoth, massive, titanic, vast
gargle: irrigate, mouthwash, swish
garish: bright, cheap, flashy, gaudy, glaring, loud, ostentatious, showy, tasteless, tawdry
garland: accolade, anadem, anthology, band, bay, chaplet, circlet, corona, coronal, coronet, crown, decorate, festoon, glory, headband, laurel, lei, rosary, wreath
garlic plant: allium
garlic segment: clove
garliclike or onionlike: alliaceous
garment: accouterment, adorn, apparel, attire, blouse, cape, cloak, clothe, clothes, clothing, coat, cov-

GAS TYPES AND TERMS

cause gas to change state but not to liquid, to: sublimate
chemically inert and monatomic gas: inert gas, noble gas
compressed gas in aerosol: propellant
convert into gas: vaporize
gas given off by waste or decaying matter: effluvium
gas in digestive tract: flatulence, flatus
gas laboratory burner: Bunsen burner
gas of ions, electrons, neutral particles: plasma
gas supposedly composing the heavens: ether
gas that is breathed out: effluvium, exhalation
gas that smells like garlic: arsine
give off gas, to: emit
inducing expulsion of digestive gas: carminative
not penetrated by gas: impermeable, impervious
of a thin and less dense gas: rarefied
pertaining to gas: gaseous
poisoning and foul-smelling earth gas: mephitis
release contained gas, to: deflate
that can be penetrated by gas: permeable, porous
very irritating gas in intestines: colic

Gases
acetylene
air gas
ammonia
argon
blackdamp
butane
carbon dioxide
carbon monoxide
chlorine
chlorofluorocarbon
coal gas
cyanogen
ethane
ether/diethyl ether
ethylchloride
ethylene
ethylene oxide
firedamp
fluorine

fluorocarbon
formaldehyde
Freon
helium
hydrogen
hydrogen bromide
hydrogen chloride
hydrogen cyanide
hydrogen fluoride
hydrogen iodide
hydrogen sulfide
krypton
lacrimator/lachrymator
laughing gas
liquid oxygen
Mace
marsh gas
methane
mustard gas
natural gas
neon
nerve gas
nitric oxide
nitrogen
nitrogen dioxide
nitrous oxide
oxyacetylene
oxygen
ozone
phosgene
poison gas
producer gas
propaneradon
rocket fuel
sewer gas
swamp gas
tear gas
war gas
water gas
xenon ❧

---

erall, don, dress, frock, garb, garment, gear, getup, gown, habiliment, habit, invest, jacket, jeans, jersey, jumper, ornament, outfit, overalls, pants, preen, primp, robe, shift, shirt, skirt, sweater, tog, toggery, toile, train, trousers, vestiture, vestment, wrap
RELATED TERMS
garment for gymnastics or ballet, one-piece: leotard
garment of office or state: vestment

garment that dries unwrinkled: drip-dry
garment tightly covering and one-piece: body stocking
garment wearable without ironing: wash-and-wear
garment, ancient: chiton, kirtle, palla, rochet, simar, stola, tabard, toga
garment, one-piece work: coverall
garment, religious: cloth, habit, robe, vestment ❧

garner: accumulate, acquire, amass, collect, gather, hoard, reap, stockpile, store
garnish: adorn, beautify, deck, decorate, embellish, enhance, equip, furbish, furnish, improve, jardiniere, ornament, trim
garnish of diced, cooked vegetables: jardiniere
garret: attic, loft, turret, watchtower
garrison: fort, post, regiment, secure, station, troops

garrulous: babbling, gabby, gossipy, loquacious, rambling, talkative, talky, voluble, wordy

gas: acetylene, ammonia, butane, carbon dioxide, carbon monoxide, cyanogen, ethane, ethene, ether, ethylene, fuel, helium, hydrogen, hydrogen sulfide, inert, ketene, krypton, laughing, marsh, methane, mustard, nitrous oxide, noble, oxane, oxygen, ozone, propane, radon, tear, xenon

gasconade: brag

gases, radioactive: emanation

gash: carve, cleft, cut, incision, laceration, slash, slit, split, wound

gasoline jelly bomb: napalm

gasoline rating: octane number

gasoline vaporizing at low temperature: high-octane, high-test

gasp: blow, breathe, exclaim, gulp, heave, huff, inhale, pant, wheeze

gastronome: bon vivant, connoisseur, epiture, gourmet

gastropod: cowrie, limpet, mollusk, pteropod, slug, snail, volute

gate: access, attendance, bar, barbican, dam, door, entrance, exit, hatch, hole, opening, pass, passage, postern, receipts, take, threshold, turnstile, valve, way

gate controlling canal, lock, etc.: head gate

gate controlling water: penstock, sluice

gate or carriage entrance leading to enclosed courtyard: porte-cochere

gate that revolves for admitting fare payers: turnstile

gatekeeper: guard, porter, sentinel, sentry, warden, watchman

gate's grating of slats raised and lowered: portcullis

gateway: arch, entrance, entry, portal, pylon, toran

gather: accumulate, amass, assemble, assume, bunch, bundle, collect, compile, compress, concentrate, conclude, congregate, convene, convoke, crowd, cull, deduce, derive, draw, flock, garner, glean, group, harvest, herd, huddle, imagine, infer, marshal, mass, meet, muster, pick, reap, reckon, recruit, select, shirr, stack, swarm, take, think, understand

gather a sail: furl

gather and arrange in order: enlist, marshal, mobilize, muster, rally

gather and collect: cull

gather and store: accumulate, amass, collect, garner

gather data or text from various sources: compile

gather from data: infer

gather grain left after harvesting: glean

gather into an ordered whole: collate

gather into mass or whole: aggregate, conglomerate

gather into wrinkles or folds: pucker, purse

gather or come together: convene, convoke

gather together: amass, assemble, congregate, forgather

gathered into mass: agglomerate

gathering: accumulation, affair, assemblage, assembly, bevy, collection, company, concourse, congregation, convention, convocation, crowd, flock, function, meet, meeting, multitude, party, rally, roundup, stag, trove, turnout

gathering of people, things: bunch, clutch

gauche: awkward, blundering, bumbling, bungling, clumsy, crude, inept, maladroit, tactless, uncouth, unrefined

gaudy: brazen, bright, cheap, crude, festival, flashy, flaunting, flimsy, garish, glaring, loud, ornate, ostentatious, pretentious, showy, splashy, tasteless, tawdry, vulgar

gauge: barometer, benchmark, criterion, estimate, evaluate, guideline, instrument, judge, measure, meter, norm, scale, size, standard, test, yardstick

gauge or pattern used as guide to make accurately: template

gaunt: angular, anorexic, barren, bleak, bony, cadaverous, desolate, emaciated, forbidding, ghastly, grim, haggard, hollow, lank, lanky, lean, meager, rawboned, scraggy, scrawny, skeletal, skinny, slender, slim, thin

gauntlet: armor, challenge, glove, onslaught, ordeal, test, trial

gauzy: delicate, filmy, flimsy, gossamer, lucid, sheer, transparent

gavel: hammer, mallet, maul, rent, tribute

gawk: eyeball, gape, gaze, glare, goggle, klutz, lout, oaf, ogle, rubberneck, simpleton, stare

gawky: awkward, bumbling, bungling, clumsy, lumbering, maladroit, ungainly

gay: airy, animated, blithe, bright, brilliant, brisk, carefree, cheerful, chipper, colorful, dissolute, festive, flamboyant, flashy, frisky, frolicsome, glad, gleeful, happy, jocular, jocund, jolly, jovial, joyful, licentious, lighthearted, lively, merry, mirthful, playful, riant, showy, sportive, sprightly, vavacious, vivid; homosexual, lesbian

gay blade: roue

gaze: admire, behold, contemplate, eye, gape, gawk, glance, glare, leer, look, observe, ogle, peek, peer, scan, scrutinize, sight, stare, study, survey, view, watch

gazelle: admi, ariel, cora, goa, mohr

gazette: journal, newspaper, paper, publication

gazetteer: atlas, dictionary, guide, index

gear (machine): apparatus, appliance, cam, cog, cogwheel, derailleur, machine, mechanism, pinion, sprocket, tackle

RELATED TERMS

gear arrangement for wheel rotation on curves: differential gear

gear arrangement with one revolving around another: epicyclic train

gear mechanism allowing motion in one direction only: ratchet

gear part: cog, teeth

gear shifting system with gear synchronization: synchromesh

gear teeth, engagement of: mesh

gear that lowers ratio and power output: overdrive

gear wheel, smaller: pinion

gear wheel, toothed bar that meshes with: rack

gear, toothlike part of: dent, dentation, denticle

gears and associated parts of auto: gearbox, transmission

gears on bicycle, device for shifting: derailleur

gears with teeth to connect unparallel gear shafts: bevel gear ☙

gear (supplies): accessory, apparel, baggage, belongings, clothing, dress, duds, equip, equipment, garb, garments, goods, implements, instrument, luggage, materiel, outfit, paraphernalia, personal effects, possessions, prepare, property, reverse, rig, rigging, stuff, supplies, tackle, things, tools, trappings

geese in the air, flock of: skein

geese on land, flock of: gaggle

geese, pertaining to: answerine

gelatin: agar, dessert, isinglass, Jell-O, jelly, membrane, protein, sericin

gelatin mold: aspic

gelatinizing agent: pectin

gelatinous: coagulated, gummy, jelly-like, viscous

gelato: ice

geld: alter, castrate, emasculate, fix, neuter, spay, tax, weaken

gelid: chilly, cold, freezing, frozen, iced, icy

gem: agate, alexandrite, amber, amethyst, amulet, aquamarine, asteria, bijou, cameo, citrine, diamond, emerald, garnet, gasper, gemstone, hyalithe, intaglio, jade, jewel, lapis lazuli, marquise, moonstone, morganite, onyx, opal, pearl, peridot, ruby, sapphire, sardonyx, stone, tiger-eye, topaz, turquoise, zircon

RELATED TERMS

gem brilliance and ability to reflect light: luster, water

gem cut in oblong: baguette

gem cutting, engraving, or polishing: lapidary

gem is set, flange or rim in which: collet

gem made of leaded glass, artificial: paste, strass

gem polishing machine: tumbler, tumbling barrel, tumbling box

gem set alone: solitaire

gem surface: facet

gem unit of weight (200 mg): carat

gem, colorless artificial: rhinestone

gem, highly polished and round: cabochon

gem, shell, or stone carved in relief: cameo

gem, thin metal layer put under: foil

gem, upper faceted part of cut: bezel

gems, relating to engraving or carving: glyptic

gems, study of: gemology

gemstone associated with particular month: birthstone

gemstone support or backing: mounting

gemstone with changeable luster: chatoyant

gemstones, carving or engraving: glyptography ❦

gemsbok: oryx

gemutlich: agreeable, cheerful, comfortable, congenial, cozy, friendly, genial, pleasant, warm

gendarme: police officer, soldier

gender: class, epicene, female, identity, male, neuter, sex, sort

gender of nouns that apply to either sex: common gender

gender, of neither: epicene, neuter

genderless: neuter

gene causing feature only when paired with identical gene: recessive gene

gene causing feature whether paired with identical or dissimilar gene: dominant gene

genealogies, study or tracing of: heraldry

genealogy: ancestry, descent, family tree, heredity, lineage, pedigree

general: all-embracing, anesthetic, approximate, average, basic, broad, catholic, common, customary, diversified, endemic, epidemic, everyday, generic, hospital, inexact, ordinary, pandemic, popular, prevailing, prevalent, public, routine, true, typical, universal, unspecific, widespread; commander, leader, officer, rank

general agreement: consensus

general and comprehensive: macroscopic, panoramic, synoptic

general and comprehensive view: conspectus, overview

general and uncommitted: free-floating

general and widespread: pandemic

general apathy: ennui

general assembly, meeting: plenary session, plenum

general class, higher rank than: superordinate

general class, lower rank than: subordinate

general direction: trend

general drift: tenor

general employee or assistant: factotum

general follower: exod

general good: weal

general handyperson: factotum, jack-of-all-trades

general idea: concept, notion

general or abstract concept or term: abstraction

general pardon: amnesty

general principle, classify under: subsume

general store: emporium

general to the particular, in reasoning: deduction

general, state of being: generality

generalization from a particular: a priori, deductive

generalize: derive, extend, hypothesize, infer, spread, theorize

generally: about, as a rule, broadly, commonly, customarily, largely, mainly, mostly, normally, often, overall, primarily, principally, roughly, typically, usually

generate: beget, breed, cause, create, develop, engender, form, induce, initiate, make, originate, procreate, produce, propagate, sire, spawn, yield

generation: age, creation, descendants, era, family, lifetime, offspring, peers, period, posterity, procreation, progeny, span, time

generator: alternator, dynamo

generator of some ignition systems: magneto

generator producing direct output: dynamo

generator, device providing unidirectional current from: commutator

generator, electrostatic: Van de Graaf generator

generator, rotating part of: armature

generic: common, comprehensive, general, universal, unspecified

generic ordinal: nth

generosity: benevolence, charity, heart, hospitality, kindness, largesse, unselfishness

generous: abundant, altruistic, ample, benevolent, bighearted, bounteous, bountiful, charitable, considerate, excellent, fertile, freehanded, good, gracious, helpful, humanitarian, kind, kindhearted, liberal, magnanimous, munificent, noble, openhanded, openhearted, philanthropic, plenteous, spirited, thoughtful, ungrudging, unselfish, warmhearted

generous and charitable: altruistic, philanthropic, selfless

generous in forgiving: magnanimous

generous in giving, spending: lavish, munificent

generous, too: lavish, prodigal, profuse

genes, strand of DNA carrying: chromosome

GENETIC DISEASES AND DISORDERS

achondroplasia	lipid histiocytosis
achromatic vision	Long QT syndrome
achromatopsia	Klinefelter syndrome
acid maltase deficiency	Krabbes disease
adrenoleukodystrophy	Marfan syndrome
albinism	mental retardation
Alpha-1 antitrypsin deficiency	Milroy's disease
arrhythmogenic right ventricular dysplasia	Moebius syndrome
ataxia telangiectasia	mongolism
Barlow's syndrome	mucopolysaccharidosis
bleb nevus syndrome	mucoviscidosis
blue rubber	muscular dystrophy
celiac disease	Nail-Patella syndrome
Christmas disease	nephrogenic diabetes insipidus
color blindness	neurofibromatosis
Cooley's anemia	Niemann-Pick disease
cretinism	osteogenesis imperfecta
cri du chat syndrome	pancreatic fibrosis
cystic fibrosis	porphyria
Dercum's disease	Prader-Willi syndrome
dichromatic vision	proteus syndrome
Down's syndrome	retinitis pigmentosa
dwarfism	Shwachman syndrome
dysautonomia	sickle-cell anemia
Fanconi anemia	Smith-Magenis syndrome
fibrodysplasia ossificans progressiva	Stickler syndrome
fragile X syndrome	Tay-Sachs disease
galactosemia	thalassemia
Gaucher disease	Treacher Collins syndrome
Hartnup's disease	triose phosphate isomerase deficiency
hemophilia	trisomy
Huntington's disease/Huntington's chorea	tuberous sclerosis
Hurler syndrome	Turner's syndrome
hypohidrotic ectodermal dysplasia	urea cycle disorder
ichthyosis	Waardenburg syndrome
Langer-Giedion syndrome	Werdnig-Hoffmann disease
leukodystrophy	Williams syndrome ❧

genesis: alpha, beginning, birth, creation, dawning, inception, origin, origination, seed

genetic: ancestral, hereditary

genetic code letters: DNA

genetic composition from mixed tissues or cells: chimera

genetic copy: clone

genetic factor: RNA

genetic information transfer: transcription

genetically different or changed: mutant, sport

genetically identical cells descended from single common ancestor: clone

genetics, laws of: Mendel's laws

genial: amiable, benign, cheerful, congenial, cordial, festive, friendly, gemutlich, gracious, happy, jovial, kindly, mild, nice, pleasant, sociable, sunny, warm

genital area: crotch

genital area of male: groin

genital display in public: exhibitionism

genital opening of birds, fish, reptiles: cloaca

genital sore, nonsyphilitic: chancroid, soft chancre

genital sore, syphilitic: chancre

genitals and anus, area between: perineum

genitals, external woman's: pudenda

genitals, relating to: pubic, venereal

genius: ability, aptitude, brain, brilliance, creativity, flair, gift, imagination, ingenuity, insight, intellect, knack, mastermind, talent, whiz

genre: category, classification, description, gender, genus, group, kind, order, species, style, type, variety

genteel: courteous, cultivated, cultured, elegant, formal, graceful, mannerly, nice, polished, polite, prim, refined, stylish, urbane

gentle: amene, amiable, benign, bland, calm, chivalrous, clement, compassionate, considerate, courteous, docile, easy, faint, fair, feeble, gradual, harmless, honorable, kind, lenient, meek, mellow, mild, moderate, pat, peaceful, placid, pleasant, polite, quiet, sensitive, serene, soft, soothing, sweet, tame, tamed, tender, tranquil

gentle breeze: aura

gentle elevation: rise

gentle flute sound: tootle

gentle warning: admonition

gentleman: aristocrat, caballero, cavalier, esquire, gallant, lord, mister, nobleman, senor, sir, squire

gentlemanly: chivalrous

gentleman's gentleman: valet

gentleness: mansuetude, mildness

gentlewoman: attendant, considerate, gracious, lady, polite

gently criticize: admonish

gentry: aristocracy, elite, landowner, nobility, society, upper class

genuflect: kneel

genuine: actual, authentic, bona fide, certified, earnest, heartfelt, honest, intrinsic, kosher, legitimate, natural, open, original, plain, pukka, pure, real, sincere, sterling, substantive, true, trustworthy, unadulterated, unfeigned, veritable

genuine and authentic: kosher, pukka

genuine and truthful: veridical

genuine but not, seeming: specious

genuine (for short): legit

genuine, not: spurious

genus: category, classification, description, gender, genre, group, kind, order, species, style, type, variety

genus-and-species classification: Linnaean, taxonomic

genus, of a: generic

geographic angular distance in east to west parallels: longitude

geographic angular distance in north to south parallels: latitude

geographical features of region: topography

geography reference work: atlas

geologic faults, elongated depression between: graben, rift valley

geological debris: scree, talus

geological depression of earth, extensive: geosyncline

geological fine-grained deposit: loess

geological fold dipping inward from both sides: syncline

geological fold sloping down on both sides from crest: anticline

geological folding and faulting: orogeny

geological fracture: fault, shift

geological groundwater source: aquifer

geological mass between two faults: horst

geological period of time: stade

geological time divisions: age, eon, epoch, era, period

geological uplift or depression affecting large areas: epeirogeny

geology: earth science, paleontology

geology branch dealing with rocks: petrology

geometric figure etc. used to solve problem: construction

geometric figures coinciding exactly: congruent

geometric line: secant

geometric quantity measurement: mensuration

geometry of 3-dimensional figures: solid geometry

geometry, device for drawing circles or arcs in: compass, pair of compasses

geometry, device for measuring and drawing angles in: protractor

geranium family: pelargonium

germ: bacterium, beginning, bud, bug, disease, embryo, microbe, nucleus, organism, origin, parasite, pathogen, seed, spore, sprout, virus

germ cell: ovule, spore

germ-free: axenic, sterile

germ killer: germicide

germ stimulating production of an antibody: antigen

germ, disease-causing: pathogen

germane: applicable, appropriate, fitting, material, pertinent, related, relative, relevant, true

Germany food: bratwurst, kase, knackwurst, limburger, pumpernickel, sauerbraten, stollen, torte, Wiener schnitzel, wurst

germinate: pullulate, sprout

germs, organism carrying disease-causing: carrier, vector

germs, protein substance produced to destroy or weaken: antibody

gesture of respect: bow, curtsy, obeisance

gesture of respect, Chinese: kowtow

gesture of respect, Muslim: salaam

gesture of thumbing one's nose: snook

gesture of worship: genuflection

gesture, gracious: beau geste

gesture, greeting: salutation

gesture, symbolic: tokenism

gestures and facial expressions, study of: kinesics

gestures and voice quality supplementing speech, of: paralinguistic

gestures while speaking, to make: gesticulate

gestures without words: pantomime

gestures, facial expressions, and postures of person: body language

get-rich-quick scheme with investors presuming doubling of returns with increasing membership: pyramid scheme

get rid of law: abrogate, annul, nullify, repeal, rescind, revoke

get rid of or disown: repudiate

get rid of or end: abate, abolish

get rid of or throw out: discard, dispose of, jettison

ghost: apparition, eidolon, phantasm, phantom, presence, revenant, shade, specter, spirit, spook, visitant

ghost appearing during seance: ectoplasm

ghost but having no soul, person revived as: zombie

ghost that makes noise or mess: poltergeist

ghost, appearance of: visitation

ghost, to appear suddenly as: materialize

ghostly: eerie, ghoulish, spectral

ghostly double of living person: doppelganger

ghostly likeness: wraith

giant: colossus, ogre, tital, titan

giant cactus: saguaro

giant tea urn: samovar

giant timber tree from down under: eucalyptus

giants, race of one-eyed: Cyclops

gibberish: abracadabra, galimatias, gobbledegook, jargon, mumbo jumbo

giblets: gizzards

gift (aptitude): ability, aptness, bent, faculty, flair, genius, head for, knack, nose for, set, talent

gift (present): award, benefaction, benevolence, bestowal, boon, contribution, donation, favor, grant, lagniappe, presentation, remembrance, reward, tip, token

RELATED TERMS

gift given as apology, tip, bribe: douceur

gift given at beginning of New Year: handsel

gift of money: gratuity, perquisite, tip

gift of speech: eloquence

gift or acknowledgment: favor, tribute

gift or favor, Hindu: enam

gift or honor, to present as: accord, bestow, confer, endow with, invest with

gift or payment in return for favor or service: consideration, recompense

gift or small bribe: sop

gift recipient: donee

gift that serves as reminder of past: keepsake, memento

gift to beggar: alms, handout

gift to charity: contribution, donation

gift, small, offered by poor person: widow's mite

gifts of the Magi: frankincense, gold, myrrh

gifts, liberality in bestowing: largesse ❧

gifted: talented

gigantic: Brobdingnagian, Herculean, huge

giggle: tehee, titter

gilded silver, bronze, copper: vermeil

gill cover of some fishes: operculum

gimlet flavoring: lime

gin or vodka with dry vermouth: martini

gin or vodka with lime juice: gimlet

giraffe: camelopard

giraffe or camel: ruminant

gird with lines: truss

girl or young woman, innocent: ingenue

girl, homeless: gamine, urchin, waif

gist: meat, nub, pith, the long and short

give off gradually: emanate, emit, exhale, exude

give out in shares: allocate, allot, apportion, dispense, distribute

give over for custody or sale: consign

give rise to: generate, spawn

give up: cede, forgo, lay down one's arms, quit, throw in the towel, yield

give up claim or right voluntarily: abstain from, disclaim, forgo, forswear, relinquish, renounce, waive

give up for a while: lend

give up or surrender something: forfeit

give up (possession): abdicate, cede, consign, forgo, relinquish, waive, yield

give up power or responsibility: abdicate

give up rights, claim: abnegate, renounce

GLASSMAKING TERMS

glass by heating and cooling, harden and strengthen: anneal, temper

glass components: borax, quartz, silica, silicon dioxide

glass imperfection: sandiver

glass is shaped and worked, iron rod on which molten: pontil, punty

glass source: sand

glass with lump left in center, old-fashioned: crown glass

glass, person who cuts and fits: glazier

glass, pertaining to: vitreous

glass, to change or make into: vitrify

glass, waste, reused and remelted: cullet

glasslike: glassy, hyaline, vitreous

glassmaking furnace: leer ❧

give up something held dear: abjure, abnegate, forsake, renounce

given willingly: ungrudging

given without obligation: gratuitous

glacial deposit: esker, kame, moraine, osar

glacial hill: paha

glacial ice mass: serac

glacial lake deposit: marl

glacial mountain peak: nunatak

glacial ridge: arete, asar, esker, osar, reels

glacial snow that becomes ice: neve

glacially affected: stoss

glaciated rock line: stria

glacier, elongated hill formed by drift of: drumlin

glacier, erosion reducing a: ablation

glacier, sand or gravel deposited by melting: kame

glaciers, study of: glaciology

glad rags: finery

glance at or over: scan, skim

glancing contact in billiards: kiss

gland substance for physiological activity: hormone

glands, pertaining to: adenoidal

glands, secretion of sebaceous: sebum, smegma

glands, study of: endocrinology

glandular fever: infectious mononucleosis

glandular internal secretion: endocrine

glare shield in car or of hat: visor

glass container with black rim and top for keeping coffee: hottle

glass for one eye, eye-: monocle

glass inset: pane

glass laboratory or measuring tube: pipet, pipette

glass laboratory vessel with outlet tube: retort

glass of 1900s, stained or iridescent: Tiffany glass

glass-paneled cabinet for display: vitrine

glass parallelogram: prism

glass used to make artificial gems: paste, strass

glass vial of medicine: ampule

glass with no handle, foot, stem: tumbler

glass, communications fiber made of plastic or: optical fiber

glass, cup, filled to brim: bumper

glass, disk to put under: coaster

glass, for measuring liquor: jigger

glass, ice, and mixer: set-up

glass, large beer: schooner

glass, large drinking: rummer

glasswort: kali, samphire

glassy: vitreous

glassy black rock: obsidian

glaze: size

glaze made of egg white: glair

glaze or wax on material: luster

gleam: glint, glow, shine

glen: dale, vale, valley

glide: sail, scud, skate, ski, soar

glide like snake: slither

glide over water: skim, skitter

glide to earth with engine cut off: volplane

gliding in waves: undulation

glisten: gleam

glitter: luster, scintillate, spangle, sparkle

glittering: clinquant, diamante

glittering Christmas string: tinsel

glittering metallic fabric: lamé

glittering ornament: diamante

glitzy affair: gala

gloat: crow, exult

globe: ball, orb

globe's metal semicircle with calibrations at pole: meridian

globular: conglobate

globule: bead, blob, drop

gloomy: cimmerian, dark, dour, drear, dreary, morne, morose, saddened, saturnine, sepulchral, stygian, tenebrous

gloomy and depressed: disconsolate, dyspeptic, morose, saturnine, somber

gloomy feeling: angst

TERMS RELATED TO GODS AND GODDESSES

appearance of a god to humans: epiphany, manifestation, theophany
attribution of animal features to a god: zoomorphism
attribution of human features to a god: anthropomorphism, theanthropism
belief in a god as creator and ruler of the world: theism
belief in a god as creator of world but no longer influences it: deism
belief in a god as ever-present in world: pantheism
belief in and worship of all gods: pantheism
belief in more than one god: polytheism
belief in one god: monotheism
cloud around god or goddess: nimbus
disbelief that any god exists: atheism
disclosure of a god's will: revelation
disrespectful of a god: blasphemous, profane
drink of gods: nectar
food of gods: ambrosia
god does or does not exist: agnosticism
god or goddess: deity, divinity
godliness: sanctity
group of related gods: pantheon
household gods of ancient Rome: lares, penates
minor god: demigod
of gods of ancient Greek pantheon: Olympian
of gods that protect: tutelary
offering to a god: propitiation
question of existence of any god: agnosticism
respect for a god: reverence, veneration
revelation from a god: oracle
worship or revere as a god: apotheosize, deify, exalt, glorify ☙

glorification: apotheosis, deification, exaltation, translation
glorify: canonize, exalt, extol, transfigure
glory: halo, honor, kudos, laurels
gloss-making machine for paper, fabric: calender
gloss over: gild, whitewash
glossy: sleek, slick
glossy fabric: sateen, satin
glove: gauntlet, mitt
glove leather: kidd, mocha, napa, suede
glove of medieval armor: gauntlet
glove part joining back and front sections of fingers: fourchette
glove with thumb and section for other fingers: mitt, mitten
glove, finger of: stall
glow: radiance, radiate

glow of some fungi on rotting wood: foxfire
glow, having gentle: lambent, luminous
glower: glare, scowl, stare
glowing: aflame, ashine, lambent, luminous, radiant
glowing after stimulation by radiation: phosphorescence
glowing by high temperature: incandescence
glowing by living organism: bioluminescence
glowing caused by chemical, biochemica, crystallographic changes: luminescence
glowing caused by temperature of emitting body: bioluminescence, fluorescence, phosphorescence
glowing celestial rings: coronae

glowing coal fragment: ember
glowing during stimulation by radiation: fluorescence
glowing review: rave
glowing with heat: incandescent
glowing with its own light: luminous
glowing with light: lucent
glue or sticky substance: adhesive, mucilage
glue, thermosetting resin in: epoxy
gluey: glutinous, gummy, sticky, viscid, viscous
glum: morose, sour, sullen
glut: gorge, sate, satiate
gnat: midge
gnawing mammal: rodent
gnome: dwarf, elf, imp, kobold, troll
go along with or comply with someone's wishes: humor, indulge

GOLF TERMS

allowance of number of strokes player is expected to exceed par in round: handicap
ball's position: lie
cause ball to veer, to: fade
club: brassie, iron, mashie, spoon, wood
competition decided by number of holes won by each side: match play
distance ball travels through air: carry
fairway leading to green: apron
golf ball indentation: dimple
golf ball ingredient: balata gum
golf club equivalent to no. 2 wood: brassie
golf club equivalent to no. 5 iron: mashie
golf club equivalent to no. 8 or 9 iron: niblick
golf club equivalent to no. 10 iron: wedge
golf hazard: trap
golfing standard: par
holing of ball from sand trap: golden ferret
obstruction by another player's ball: stymie
one stroke over par on hole: bogey
one stroke under par on hole: birdie
peg: tee
person carrying player's clubs: caddie
score of three strokes under par for hole: double eagle
score of two strokes under par for hole: eagle
scrape the ground with club before hitting the ball, to: sclaff
short and lofted shot used to approach green: chip shot
stroke on green: putt
three strokes under par: double eagle
turf dug up by club: divot
two strokes over par: double bogey
warning cry: fore ☙

go back on promise or commitment: renege

go back over: retrace

go back to former state: regress, relapse, revert

go bad: rot, sour, spoil

go before: antecede

go in peace: vade in pace

go it alone: solo

go off course: stray, yaw

go off on a tangent: veer

go off or explode: detonate

go on the road: tour

go out of business: close down, fold

go without sleep: keep vigil, watch

goad: ease, egg on, incite, instigate, needle, prod, spur, tease

goal: aim, bourn, consummation, destination, end, ideal, intention, objective, target, terminus ad quem

goal, directed toward: purposeful, telic

goal, personal: mecca, Zion

goal, purposeful development toward final: teleology

goat hair: angora, mohair

goat or sheep, newborn: yeanling

goat skin used for writing or painting: parchment

goat, female: nanny goat

goat, like a: caprine, hircine, hircinous

goat, male: billy goat

goat, pertaining to: capric, hircine

goat, young: kid, yeanling

go-between: agency, agent, arbitrator, broker, deputy, intermediary, internuncio

go-between for prostitute: panderer, pimp, procurer

goblet of metal or wood: mazer

goblet with narrowed top: snifter

goblet, pear-shaped: snifter

goblin: gremlin, sprite

godspeed: farewell

going before: preceding, prevenient

gold and silver alloy: electrum

gold bar or block: ingot

gold before refinement: ore

gold by washing, to separate matter from: pan

gold content, chemical analysis of: assay

gold imitations using copper, zinc, tin alloys: ormolu

gold in water or waste piles, to search for: fossick

gold measure: karat

gold or gold leaf, to cover with layer: gild, gold-plate

gold or metal resistant to oxidation, corrosion: noble metal

gold or silver thread, fabric of: lamé

gold ore, trough for separating: sluice

gold place symbol: date mark

gold-plated silver, bronze, copper: rolled gold, vermeil

gold purity mark: hallmark, plate mark

gold twisted wire in ornamental work: filigree

gold, alchemist's attempt to change metal to: transmutation

gold, before refinement: ore

gold, containing: auriferous

gold, medieval chemical philosophy that metals could be turned into: alchemy

gold, substance thought to turn metal to: elixir, philosophers' stone

gold, to search for: prospect

goldlike: aureate, gilded, gilt

gondolier's need: pole

gondolier's song: barcarole

goo: muck, slime

goober: peanut

good and admirable person: mensch

good and helpful: advantageous, beneficial

good and of high quality: vintage

good and praiseworthy: commendable, creditable, estimable, laudable, meritorious

good-bye: adieu, adios, aloha, arrivederci, au revoir, auf Wiedersehen, ciao, farewell, hasta la vista, leave-taking, sayonara, tata, valediction

good faith, information guaranteeing: bona fides

good luck: mazel tov

good luck, animal or object thought to bring: mascot

good-natured: affable, amiable, beneficient, benign, convivial, cordial, friendly, genial, humane, jolly, jovial

good-natured dwarf: rumpelstiltskin

good-natured remark: pleasantry

good-naturedness: bonhomie

good reputation, having: honorable, reputable, sterling

good, very: copacetic, top-notch

goodness: integrity, probity, rectitude, virtue

goods and services produced by a country in a year: GDP, gross domestic product

goods in reserve: stockpile

goods not ordered, of: unsolicited

goods on hand: inventory

goods that may not be imported or exported: contraband

goods, miscellaneous, sold in collection: job lot

goods, personal: chattels

goods, tradable or salable: commodity

goodwill: altruism, philanthropy

goodwill or asset that cannot be perceived by senses: intangible

goof: blunder, bobble, err, faux pas, misdo, social blunder

goose genus: anser

goose liver paste and truffles: pâté de foie gras

goosebumps: goose flesh, horripilation, piloerection

gooselike: anserine

gorge: canyon, chasm, ravine, sate

gorge with stream, narrow: flume

gorge, narrow: defile

gorge, narrow and often steep: canyon, couloir, gulch, gully, wadi

gorilla: ape

gospel, spreading of: evangelism

gospels of New Testament, of first three: synoptic

gossamer: cobweb

gossip: chat, confabulate, dirt, hen, hearsay, on-dit, schmooze, tale, tale-bearer, talk, tittle and tattle

gossip tidbit: cite, item

gossiper: busybody, quidnunc, tattle-tale, yenta

Gothic type: black letter, Old English

goulash: olio, stew

gourd fruit: pepo

gourd smoking pipe: calabash

gourmet: connoisseur, epicure, gastronome

govern badly: misrule

governance: regime

governess: duenna

governing: dominant

governing body of the United Nations: General Assembly

governing itself: autonomous

governing principle: ethos

governing with expected obedience: authoritarian

grab: nab, seize, take

grab greedily: hog

grace: benedicite, benison, elegance, politeness, thanks

grace or embellishing note: appoggiatura, trill

graceful: eurythmic, fluent, limber, lissom, lithe

graceful and sleek: slinky, willowy

GOVERNMENT TYPES AND TERMS

attempt to overthrow a government, to: subvert

command or authorization by electorate to government representative: mandate

concerning a governor: gubernatorial

delegation of powers from central government to local: devolution

form of funds obtaining by borrowing rather than taxation: deficit spending

government: authority, dominion, jurisdiction, sovereignty, supremacy

government by absolute power: autarchy, autocracy

government by few: oligarchy

government by men: patriarchy

government by military: stratocracy

government by military officers after a takeover: junta

government by old: gerontocracy

government by religious leaders: hagiarchy, hagiocracy, hierocracy

government by rich: plutocracy

government by two: duumvirate

government by women: gynarchy

government of a nation or organization: polity

government office abroad: embassy

government opponent: dissident

government report: white paper

government takeover with violence: coup d'état

government that no longer exists: ancient regime

government use of force or threat of force: intervention

government with central authority and constituent political units: federal

government with distributed power and with a legal system that rulers must follow: constitutionalism

government with people owning and controlling production and distribution: collectivism

governor of country, province, or colony who represents sovereign: viceroy

grant of land in return for something: concession

inflexible government administration: bureaucracy

influence of one government over another: hegemony, suzerainty

one acting as governor or ruling in absence of monarch: regent

organization funded by government but acts independently: quango

policy of national interest above all: realpolitik

power to appoint people to government positions: patronage

spending financed by borrowing: deficit financing, deficit spending

theory that power should be held by one: absolutism

time between two successive governments' reign: interregnum

unofficial government advisers: kitchen cabinet

Government Systems

absolute monarchy
absolutism
anarchy
aristocracy
autarchy/autarky
authoritarianism
autocracy
autonomy
caretaker government
collectivism
coalition government
communism
constitutionalism
constitutional monarchy
crown
democracy
despotism
diarchy
dictatorship
duarchy
duumvirate
dyarchy
fascism
federalism
feudalism
gerontocracy
gynarchy
gynecocracy
hagiarchy/hagiocracy
hierocracy
isocracy
junta
matriarchy
meritocracy
militarism
mobocracy
monarchy
monocracy
ochlocracy
oligarchy
one-man rule
pantisocracy
parliamentary government
patriarchy
pentarchy
pluralism
plutocracy
presidential government
protectorate
provisional government
regency

republic
self-government
self-rule
socialism
state government
statism
stratocracy
technocracy
thearchytheocracy
timocracy
totalitarianism
triarchy
triumvirate ❦

GRAMMATICAL TERMS

abrupt change in sentence: anacoluthon
abstract underlying structure: deep structure
affixation of verb changing tense, number, etc.: inflection
analyze grammatical structure of sentence: construe, parse
case for indirect object: dative
case for object of a preposition: dative
case indicating direction away from: ablative
case indicating place: locative
case indicating possession: genitive, possessive
case indicating separation, direction away from or cause for
  certain verbs: ablative
case of noun, pronoun, adjective that is direct object of verb
  or preposition: accusative
case of the noun or pronoun serving as the object of the verb:
  objective
case of the subject: nominative
case that is the direct object of the verb: accusative
case to indicate person or thing being addressed: vocative
cases: nominative, objective, possessive
change of vowel: gradation, ablaut
characteristic of word determined by its function in sentence:
  case
component of verb that accompanies main verb and shows
  mood, voice, aspect, or tense: auxiliary verb
concerning grammar change through time: diachronic
construction expressing question: interrogative
construction of two nouns or noun phrases, one as explanation:
  apposition
construction showing mood of command or request: imperative
construction showing mood of normal verb: indicative
creation of new word by removing affix: back-formation
form of verb ending in -ed or -ing forming tenses or adjective:
  participle
formal sentence arrangement: surface structure
grammar dealing with inflections: accidence

grammar establishing norms and correct usage: normative
  grammar, prescriptive grammar
grammar of sentence broken down into components: parsing
grammar that accounts for new constructions from transformations and phrase structures: transformational grammar
grammatical correctness: purism
grammatical error out of attempt to be correct: hypercorrection
grammatical error: solecism
inflection of noun, pronoun, adjective: declension
inflection of particular verb: conjugation
modifier or qualifier like "any" or "both": determiner
mood of verb contingent on hypthetical action: subjunctive
nonreducible text element: token
nonstandard use of grammar: solecism
noun case expressing possession, measurement, source: genitive
noun case that is subject of verb: nominative
noun or noun equivalent: substantive
participle that has no clear relation to subject: dangling participle
process in which word acquires negative meaning over time:
  pejoration
rules for producing well-formed sentences: generative grammar
shortening of word: clipping
slightly different in grammatical form: variant
study of structure and form of words including inflection, derivation, and compound formation: morphology
unit capable of conveying distinction of meaning: phoneme
unit constituting minimum for word: morpheme
unit of verb and its objects as distinct from subject: predicate
verb form that is uninflected and often preceded by "to": infinitive
verb having direct object: transitive
verb having identical subject and direct object: reflexive
verb tense describing past action, state: preterit
verb with no direct object: intransitive
verbal noun created by adding -ing: gerund
word(s) used after verb to complete predicate: complement ❧

---

gracious: benignant, genial, genteel,
  polished, refined, suave, urbane
gracious gesture: beau geste
grackle: daw
gradation in word meaning: nuance
grade: class, degree, hill, mark, rank,
  rate, slope
graded series: hierarchy
gradual absorption or assimilation:
  osmosis
gradual appearance, in a film: fade-in
gradual change in a trait: cline
gradual development or change:
  evolution
gradual growth: accrual
gradual impairment: wear
gradual reduction of debt, liability:
  amortization
gradual successive stages: gradation

gradually: inchmeal, piecemeal
gradually shrink: taper
graduate: alum, alumna, grad; pass
graduated series: scale
graduates collectively: alumni
graduates of college gathered:
  convocation
graduation address: baccalaureate
graduation ceremony: commencement
graduation farewell speech: valedictory
Graf Zeppelin: airship
graft: boodle
grafting, shoot or twig used for: scion
grain beard: awn
grain bin: silo
grain bundle: sheaf
grain by air, separate chaff from:
  winnow

grain by beating, separate chaff from:
  flail, thresh
grain debris: chaff
grain fungus or disease: ergot
grain left by reapers, to gather: glean
grain or fuel, funnel for dispensing:
  hopper
grain stacked upright, sheaves of:
  shock, stook
grain stalk: straw
grain storehouse: granary
grain, coarsely ground: grits
grain, concerning: frumentaceous
grain, feeding on: graminivorous,
  granivorous
grain, ground into meal: grist
grain, small: granule
grain's outer layer, cereal: bran
grainy: granular

GRAPES

Alicante
Almeria
Cabernet Sauvignon
Cardinal
Champion
Chardonnay
Chenin Blanc
Concord
Delaware
Franconian
Hamburgh
Isabella
Italia
Labrusca
Lady Finger
Malaga
Martha
Merlot
Muscadet
Muscat
Pinot Blanc
Pinot Noir
Riesling
Superb
Thompson seedless
Tokay
White Corinth
Woodbury
Zinfandel ❦

---

grammar accounting for linguistic transformations and study of this: transformational grammar

grand: grandiose, imposing, impressive, stately, thou

grand and elegant: stately, statuesque

grand and luxurious: expansive, extravagant, lavish, sumptuous

grand and of high rank: august, venerable

grand and showy: ostentatious, pretentious

grand-jury report on offense based on jury's knowledge: presentment

grand or lofty: exalted, imposing, rarefied, sublime

grande dame: matriarch

grandeur: mightiness

grandiloquent: turgid

grandiloquize: orate

grandiose movie: epic

granite: igneous rock

grant: admit, cary, cede

grant by government to property in exchange for something: concession

grant of money: subsidy

grant temporary use: lend, loan

grant to charity: contribution, donation

grant with condescension: vouchsafe

granted: accorded, ceded

granular snow: firm, neve

granular tissue: acestoma

grape: uva

RELATED TERMS

grape bunch, shape of a: aciniform

grape cultivation for wine: viniculture

grape growing: viticulture

grape jam: uvate

grape juice fermenting into wine: must, stum

grape juice syrup: sapa

grape pomace: rape

grape refuse after juice extraction in winemaking: rape

grape residue after pressing: marc

grapefruit: pomelo, shaddock

grapes, bunch of: acinus

grapes, fungus attacking ripe: noble rot ❦

---

graph as circle divided up: pie chart

graph background: grid

graph flat section: plateau

graph numbers or measurements: coordinates

graph of cumulative frequencies: ogive

graph showing statistics in curve: bell-shaped curve

graph statistics shown in intervals: frequency distribution

graph using rectangular columns: bar chart, bar graph

graph, circular and divided into sections: pie chart

graphic symbol representing object, idea: ideograph

graphite: plumbago

grapple: claw, grope, wrestle

grasp: comprehend, see, span, understand

grasping: avid, greedy, holding, prehension, rapacious

grass bristles: awns

grass brought up by golf club or horse hoof: divot

grass clump: hassock, sod, tuffet, tussock

grass-covered land: sward

grass-eating: graminivorous

grass growing after mowing: aftermath, rowen

GRAY

ash
battleship gray
blue gray
charcoal gray
cinder
cinereous
cloud
dark gray
dove
flint
granite
gray white
greige
iron
lead
light gray
merle
moleskin
mouse
mushroom
neutral
nutria
obsidian
pale gray
pearl gray
pelican
plumbago
powder gray
salt-and-pepper
silver
silver gray
slate gray
smoke gray
steel gray
taupe ❦

---

grass path cut by mower: swath

grass spike part: palea

grass stem: culm

grass to be eaten by livestock: herbage, pasturage, pasture

grass, artificial: Astroturf, synthetic turf

grass, eat or graze off: crop

grass, new growth after cutting: fog

grasshopper chirp: stridulation

grasshopper relative: cricket, katydid

grassland: lea, meadow, prairie

grassland, Russia and Eastern Europe: steppe

grassland, South Africa: bushveld, veld

grassland, South American: campo, llano, pampa

grassland, treeless and uncultivated: prairie

grassland, tropical: savanna

GREEK TERMS

ancient Greek dialect: Aeolic, Attic-Ionic, Doric, Koine	goddess of injustice: Adikia
ancient Greek party: symposium	goddess of justice: Dike
chief god: Zeus	goddess of love and beauty: Aphrodite
citadel of ancient Greek city: acropolis	goddess of marriage: Hera
citizen assembly in ancient Greek state: ecclesia	goddess of memory: Mnemosyne
civic center: agora	goddess of night: Nyx
colonnade: stoa	goddess of pathways: Hecate
commune: deme	goddess of peace: Irene
cordial: ouzo	goddess of practical art: Athena
devotee of Greek civilization: Hellenist	goddess of rainbows: Iris
god of agriculture: Apollo	goddess of sorcery: Hecate
god of commerce and invention: Hermes	goddess of spring: Hebe
god of cunning and theft: Hermes	goddess of the earth: Gaia
god of death: Thanatos	goddess of the moon: Artemis, Hecate, Selena
god of dreams: Morpheus	goddess of the underworld: Persephone
god of fertility: Dionysus, Kronos	goddess of vegetation: Demeter
god of fire: Hephaestus	goddess of vengeance: Ara
god of forests: Pan	goddess of vengeance and justice: Nemesis
god of healing: Apollo	goddess of victory: Nike
god of herds and flocks: Pan	goddess of war: Athena
god of light: Hyperion	goddess of wisdom: Athena
god of light and truth: Apollo	goddess of youth: Hebe
god of love: Eros	goddess who served as a messenger: Iris
god of metalworking: Hephaestus	goddess, chief: Hera
god of mockery: Momus	Greek alphabet (in order): alpha, beta, gamma, delta, epsi-
god of oaths: Horkos	lon, zeta, eta, theta, iota, kappa, lambda, mu, nu, xi, omi-
god of reason: Logos	cron, pi, rho, sigma, tau, upsilon, phi, chi, psi, omega
god of sleep: Hypnos	Greek and Latin literature: classics
god of strength: Kratos	Greek and Roman aesthetics: classicism
god of the east or southeast wind: Eurus	Greek architecture, elaborate inverted bell-shaped capitals:
god of the north wind: Boreas	Corinthian
god of the sea: Poseidon	Greek architecture, ornamental scrolls on capitals: Ionic
god of the sky: Zeus	Greek architecture, plain capitals: Doric
god of the south wind: Zephyrus	Greek cheese: feta
god of the sun: Apollo	Greek culture, art, or thought: Grecism
god of the underworld: Hades	Greek Orthodox pulpit: ambo
god of the west wind: Aquilo	group of Greek goddesses: Fates, Horae
god of the winds: Aeolus	largest subdivision of Greek city-state: phratry, phyle
god of war: Ares	leather flask: olpe
god of wine: Dionysus	marketplace: agora
god who served as a messenger: Hermes	modern colloquial Greek: demotic
goddess of blind impulse: Ate	mythological creature with head/trunk of man, body/legs of
goddess of discord: Eris	horse: centaur
goddess of fertility: Hecate	peak: athos, ossa, pelion
goddess of harvest: Demeter	political state: deme
goddess of health: Hygeia	restaurant: taverna
goddess of hearth: Hestia	theater: odea, odeon
goddess of hunting: Artemis	wine: retsina ❧

---

grasslike: gramineous
grasslike plant: sedge
grassy turf: greensward
grate: abrade, rasp, scrape, shred
grateful: beholden, indebted, obliged
gratify: please, sate

gratify desires: indulge
grating: grid, harsh, raspy, strident
grating of crossed bars: grid
gratis: free
gratitude: testimonial, tribute
gratuity: honorarium, lagniappe, tip

grave: burial vault, repository, sepulcher, tomb; solemn
grave crime: felony
grave danger: peril
grave harvest, yield: vintage
grave marker: headstone

grave mound, ancient: barrow, tumulus
grave robber: ghoul, resurrectionist
grave, dig up: disinter, exhume
gravelly deposit or ridge: esker
graven image: idol
gravestone inscription: epitaph, hic jacet, RIP
gravestone slab laid flat: ledger
graveyard shift at newspaper: lobster shift
graveyard, underground: catacomb, hypogeum
gravitate: tend
gravity, to float and defy: levitate
gravy holder: boat
gravy-soaked bread: brewis, sippet, sop
gravy, in its own: au jus
gray or graying: grizzled, hoary
gray or white from age: hoary
gray wolf: lobo
gray, painting in shades of: grisaille
grayish and mottled: griseous, grizzled
grayish color: ash
grayish tan: beige
grayish yellow: ecru
graylags: geese
graze: browse, feed, feed upon
grazing land: herbage, lea, pasturage, pasture, range
grease: lard, lubricant, lubricate, oil
greasy: fatty, oily, oleic, pinguid, sebaceous, unctuous
great deal: a lot, scad
great disparity: chasm
great enthusiasm: mania
great foolishness: idiocy
great in size: vast
great lack: dearth, famine
great profusion: riot

great quantity: mort, ocean, oodles
great work: magnum opus, masterpiece
greatness: eminence, fame, stature
Greece, city-state of ancient: polis
Greece, of ancient: Hellenic
greed: avarice, craving, cupidity, excess, indulgence, mommonism
greed for food: gluttony, gulosity
greedy: acquisitive, avaricious, avid, covetous, eager, edacious, ensurient, envious, gormandize, immoderate, insatiable, mercenary, piggish, rapacious, ravenous, self-indulgent, selfish, stingy, voracious
greedy or hungry: edacious, esurient, insatiable, rapacious, ravenous, voracious
greedy person: cormorant, harpy
greedy woman looking for man: gold digger
green all year long: evergreen
green and grassy: verdant
green crops for fodder: soilag
green-eyed: envious, jealous
green in military uniform: olive drab
green light: approval, clearance, OK, permission, yes
green material on gaming tables: baize
green mineral: malachite, verditer
green paste of avocado used for dip: guacamole
green patina or crust on metal objects: verd antique, verdigris
green plant pigment involved in photosynthesis: chlorophyll
green quartz: plasma, prase
green shot: putt
green side dish: salad
green spaghetti sauce: pesto

green spot in a desert: oasis
green vegetation: verdure
greenback: bank note, bill, bread, cash, currency, dough, money, paper money
greenery: leafage
greenhorn: amateur, apprentice, inexperienced, neophyte, newcomer, recruit
greenhouse: conservatory, hothouse, nursery, orangery
greenhouse for oranges: orangery
greenish layer forming on copper, bronze: patina
greenish yellow: luteous
greet: acknowledge, hail, recognize, salute
greeting: all hail, aloha, compliments, curtsy, good day, hello, introduction, kiss, nod, ovation, salutation, toast
greeting of civility: compliments, devoirs
greeting with right palm on forehead: salaam
gregarious: social
Gregorian chant: plainsong
Gregorian plainsong melody with voices added: cantus firmus
gremlin: elf, fairy, fay, goblin, kobold, sprite, troll
grenade: bomb, explosive, fireball, missile, pineapple, shell
grid: bars, framework, grate, gridiron, mesh, network
griddle biscuit: scone
griddle cake: bannock, battercake, flannel cake, flapjack, hotcake, pancake

GREEN

absinthe	corbeau	jade	moss	spruce
aqua	cucumber	jungle green	myrtle	teal
avocado	cypress	kelly green	Niagara green	terre verte
bay	dark green	Kendal green	Nile green	tourmaline
beryl	drake	leaf green	olive	turquoise
bice	eau de Nile	leek green	pale green	verdigris
blue green	emerald	light green	parrot	vert
bottle green	fir green	lime	patina	virescent
brewster	flagstone	Lincoln green	pea green	viridian
Brunswick green	forest green	lizard	pistachio green	willow green
cadmium green	grass green	loden	reseda	yellow green
celadon	gray green	lotus	sage green	yew ☙
chartreuse	gunpowder	malachite	sea green	
chrome green	holly green	marine	serpentine	
clair de lune	ivy green	mint	shamrock	

gridiron: field, football, framework, grating, grid, network, structure

grief: affliction, agony, anguish, annoyance, bereavement, care, chagrin, depression, despair, distress, dolor, emotion, frustration, grievance, hardship, harm, heartache, heartbreak, hurt, lamentation, pain, regret, sadness, sorrow, suffering, tears, trial, trouble, woe

grief, false show of: crocodile tears

grief, free oneself of: disburden

grief, to cause: aggrieve

grief, to reduce: allay, alleviate, assuage

grief, to waste away from: pine

grief, unaffected by: stoical

grievance: affliction, beef, complaint, gravamen, grief, gripe, hardship, indignation, injury, injustice, plaint, protest, stink, wrong

grieve: ache, afflict, bemoan, distress, harm, hurt, lament, mourn, pain, pine, rue, sadden, sorrow, suffer, wail, weep

grieve or sympathize with: condole

grievous: atrocious, bitter, burdensome, calamitous, deplorable, dire, distressing, grave, heinous, hurtful, intense, painful, sad, serious, severe, shocking, sore, sorry, tragic, woeful

grifter: bunco-steerer, con artist, con man, fraud, scammer, swindler

grill: barbecue, broil, cook, cross-examine, grate, griddle, grille, hibachi, inquisition, interrogate, probe, pump, question, sear, third-degree

grim: adamant, angry, bleak, brutal, cruel, dire, dismal, dour, dreadful, ferocious, fierce, fixed, forbidding, furious, ghastly, gloomy, glum, grisly, harsh, hideous, hopeless, horrible, horrid, inexorable, loathsome, merciless, ominous, relentless, repulsive, rigid, ruthless, savage, sinister, somber, stern, sullen, unrelenting, unyielding

grim reaper: angel of death

grimace: expression, face, fleer, frown, make a face, mock, moue, mug, rictus, scowl, smirk, sneer

grimace, gaping: rictus

grime: crud, dirt, filth, gook, gunk, smut, soil, soot

grin: beam, expression, fleer, smile, smirk

grind: abrade, beat, chew, chore, compress, crunch, crush, disintegrate, drudge, gnash, grate, grit, groove, la-

bor, learn, mill, mull, oppress, overeat, overfill, plod, polish, pound, powder, press, pulverize, review, routine, rut, sand, shape, sharpen, smooth, squeeze, study, stuff, triturate, weaken, whet

grind and crush: comminute, pulverize, triturate

grind as teeth: gnash

grinding bowl: mortar

grinding machine: mill

grinding of teeth: bruxism

grinding tool: pestle

grindstone: hone

grip: brace, clamp, clasp, cleat, clench, clinch, clutch, comprehension, constrict, control, embrace, fascinate, grab hold, grapple, grasp, handle, handshake, hold, mastery, mesmerize, perception, rivet, seize, vise

grip in theater, film: stagehand, valise

grip to move something or keep it from slipping: purchase

gripe: annoy, beef, bellyache, complain, complaint, fret, fuss, grasp, grievance, groan, grouse, grumble, irritate, objection, protest, squawk, whine

gripping: intense

gripping device: grapnel, grapple, pincers, tongs

gripping or clinging: tenacious

gripping, ridges or grooves on handle to assist: knurl

grisly: abominable, awful, bloody, dreadful, frightful, gory, grim, gruesome, hideous, horrible, macabre, terrifying

gristle: cartilage

grit: backbone, bravery, courage, determination, dirt, fortitude, gravel, guts, moxie, nerve, pebbles, perseverance, pluck, resolution, sand, spunk, tenacity

gritty: arenose, sabulous, sandy

groan: bellow, complain, gripe, grumble, grunt, lament, moan, sigh, whine

grocery: market

grocery holdall: sack

grocery-shelf info: unit pricing

grog: alcohol, drink, liquor, rum

groggy: confused, dazed, dizzy, drunk, punch-drunk, shaky, sleepy, sluggish, stupefied, tipsy, tired, unsteady, wobbly, woozy

groin, of the: inguinal

grommet: eyelet

GRIPPING AND FASTENING TOOLS

adjustable bar clamp
band clamp
bar clamp
bench dog
bench vise
bent-nose pliers
brace
C-clamp
channel-type pliers
chuck
clamp
claw
clip
corner clamp
cutting pliers
diagonal-cutting pliers
electric riveter
forceps
glue gun
grip
hand vise
holddown clamp
joint fastener
lineman's pliers
locking pliers
long-nose pliers
nail puller
needlenose pliers
pincers
pinchcock
pipe clamp
plate joiner
pliers
power nailer
pucellas
puller
riveter
screw clamp
slip-joint pliers
snap ring pliers
spring clamp
staple gun
stapler
toggle clamp
tongs
tweezers
vise
vise grip
web clamp ❧

grommet of rope: strop

groom: assistant, brush, clean, comb, dress, educate, equerry, horsekeeper, hostler, marshal, nurture, preen, prepare, servant, shave, tend, tidy, train; husband, spouse

groove: canal, chamfer, channel, chase, crease, dado, excavation, flute, furrow, grind, gutter, hollow, indentation, rabbet, routine, rut, shaft, slot, sulcus

groove for a sliding door: regle

groove in a road: rut

groove in building: chamfer, coulisse, feather, glyph, kerf, mortise, rabbet, spline, tenon

groove in column, vertical: glyph

groove of brain: sulcus

groove or indentation: flute, notch

groove or notch: chase

groove or slot: spline

groove under nose: philtrum

grooved: ridged, striate, strigose

grooved and striped: striated

grooved with long rounded channels: fluted

grooves on coin: fluting, milling

grooves or notches, square: crenellations

grooves or series of teeth: serration

groovy: cool, copacetic, excellent, hep, modern, neat, wonderful

grope: examine, explore, feel, fondle, grabble, handle, paw, poke, probe, search

gross: all, big, bulk, burly, entire, great, heavy, large, mass, massive, total; beastly, brutal, brutish, burly, callous, carnal, cloddish, coarse, crass, crude, egregious, filthy, flagrant, foul, glaring, greasy, impure, indecent, lewd, obese, obscene, offensive, outrageous, plain, rank, repulsive, rough, rude, scurrilous, sleazy, sum, swinish, ugly, uncouth, unrefined, vulgar, whole; apparent, obvious; dense, thick

gross amount: total

grossly overweight: obese

grotesque: abnormal, absurd, antic, bizarre, deformed, eerie, fanciful, fantastic, freakish, hideous, incongruous, preposterous, ridiculous, ugly, weird

grotesque architectural ornament: gargoyle

grotesque representation: caricature

grotto: burrow, cave, cavern, den, hole, hollow, recess, vault

grouch: bellyacher, churl, complainer, crab, crank, crosspatch, grouse, grumble, grump, sourpuss

grouchy: cantankerous, crusty, irritable, surly, testy, touchy

ground: beach, bottom, country, dirt, earth, estate, field, foundation, land, landscape, mother earth, root, soil, strand, terrain, terrane, territory, turf

ground corn: samp

ground nuts: mast

ground plan of building: ichnography

ground squirrel: gopher

ground zero: site, target

ground, hard and unbroken: hardpan

ground, physical features of: topography

groundless: flimsy, idle, illogical, unjustified, unprovoked, untrue

grounds: basis, campus, domain, dregs, evidence, information, lees, park, premise, pretext, proot, property, reason, sediment, zone

grounds improved by gardens, plantings: landscaping

groundwork: base, basis, cornerstone, foundation, fundamentals, planning, practice, preliminaries, preparation, root, source, support, training

group: aggregation, arrange, assemblage, assemble, assembly, assort, band, batch, bevy, bunch, bundle, cabal, category, circle, class, classify, clique, club, clump, cluster, collect, collection, combine, company, conglomerate, congregate, consort, crew, division, drove, faction, family, file, flock, galaxy, gang, gather, genus, herd, huddle, link, lot, mob, organization, organize, party, pool, ring, sect, set, size, sort, squad, team, tribe, unit

RELATED TERMS

group active in new techniques: avant-garde

group assembled for ceremony: convocation

group assisting peace officer: posse

group character: ethic, ethos

group crowded together: concourse, confluence, drove, phalanx

group living together: commune

group of attendants for person: retinue

group of badgers: cete

group of components gathered together: aggregate, assemblage, congeries, conglomeration

group of contemporaries: coevals, peer group

group of eight: octad, octet

group of experts: brain trust

group of five: pentad

group of geese: gaggle

group of girls: bevy

group of larger organization, central: cadre

group of lions: pride

group of men, social: fraternity, sodality

group of musicians, small: combo

group of organizations working on common interest or cause: alliance, bloc, coalition, confederacy, league

group of people living in an area and under the same government: community

group of people who associate with one another frequently: coterie

group of people with common interests: clique, cohort, guild

group of plotters: cabal, junto

group of poems: epos

group of pueblos: tano

group of quail: covey

group of relatives: clan

group of representatives: delegation, deputation

group of seals: pod

group of seven: heptad

group of ships: flotilla

group of similar or related items gathered together: battery, compendium, ensemble, suite

group of six: sextet

group of songs played together: medley

group of songs, plays that artist or company can perform: repertoire

group of twenty: score

group of two or more business concerns for venture: consortium

group of vehicles traveling together: convoy

group of voters: constituency

group of whales: gam, pod

group of women, social: sorority

group of words containing a subject and predicate and forming a sentence: clause

group ordered by rank: hierarchy

group pulling away from larger group: enclave, faction, sect

group sharing interest(s): coterie

group spirit: esprit de corps

group to pursue business as monopoly: cartel, trust

group to pursue business interests: consortium, syndicate

group together: collate, collocate, coordinate

group trip: tour
group unity: solidarity
group with others of same kind, tending to form a: gregarious
group with political or business interest: cartel
group, highly regarded: pantheon
group, large: battalion, horde, multitude, throng
group, referring to an entire: generic
group, relating to a number of people acting as a: collective, communal
group, small: covey
group, spirit of comradeship in: esprit de corps
group, to break up a: disband ❦

grouper: bass
groupie: fan, follower, supporter
groups coexisting in one nation, diversity of: pluralism
groups, separation of ethnic or religious: segregation
grouse: bellyache, bird, complain, fret, grievance, gripe, grouch, grumble, pheasant, ptarmigan, quail, squealer
grouse of cold regions: ptarmigan
grouse's courtship dance: lak
grove: boscage, brake, bush, coppice, copse, orchard, pinery, thicket, wood, woodland
grove of trees: coppice, copse, spinney
grovel: abase, beg, bootlick, brownnose, cower, crawl, cringe, fawn, kowtow, sycophancy, toady, wallow, wheedle
grow: advance, age, augment, become, blossom, bud, cultivate, develop, edify, enlarge, evolve, expand, extend, flourish, germinate, increase, mature, multiply, mushroom, nourish, raise, rise, skyrocket, sprout, swell, thrive, wax, widen
grow buds or sprouts: pullulate
grow choppers: teethe
grow crops in sequence: rotate
grow dim: wane
grow dull: drag
grow faint: fade
grow less: decrease
grow like a plant: vegetate
grow old: age
grow quickly: burgeon, flourish, proliferate
grow slowly: gestate, incubate
grow together: accrete, amalgamate, coalesce, knit
grow wearisome: pall

grow weary: tire
grow, help to: foster, nurture, propagate
growing and enlarging: increscent
growing "fence": hedge
growing in pairs: binate
growing in series of steps: cumulative
growing indefinitely, not seasonal: perennial
growing irregularly: straggly
growing old: aging, senescence, senescent
growing on ground: decumbent
growing outward: enate
growing plants in solution, not soil: hydroponics
growing profusely: rank
growing together: concretion
growing white: albescent
growing with age: accrescence
growing years: teens
growl: bark, gnar, gnarl, grumble, grunt, gurr, howl, mutter, rumble
growler: iceberg
grown together: adnate
grown together, botanically: accrete
grown-up: adult
growth: advancement, augmentation, cancer, development, enlargement, evolution, expansion, increase, lump, parasite, polyp, progress, prosperity, rise, surge, swell, swelling, tumor
growth by addition: accretion, buildup, increment
growth from within: endogeny
growth in a field, as corn: stand
growth in a force: groundswell
growth of mucous lining: polyp
growth of species or organism: phylogeny
growth or development, agent causing: nutriment
growth rings on trees, study of: dendrochronology
growth, abnormal: excrescence, hypertrophy
growth, arrested: atrophy
growth, of the earliest stage: embryonic, germinal, nascent, seminal
growth, small: nodule, tubercle
grub: bum, chow, comb, dig, drudge, eat, feed, food, larva, maggot, mooch, plod, provisions, root, scour, search, sponge, stump, uncover, victuals, worm
grub around: forage

grubby: dirty, disheveled, filthy, foul, grimy, grungy, scruffy, seedy, shabby, slovenly, soiled, unkempt
grublike young of insect: larva
grudge: animosity, complain, envy, hatred, malice, pique, rancor, resentment, spite, spitefulness
grudge, bear a: harbor
gruel: mush, potage
grueling: arduous, brutal, demanding, difficult, fierce, hard, punishing, strenuous, taxing, tiring
gruesome: awful, ghastly, gory, grisly, gross, horrible, horrid, macabre, morbid, repugnant, repulsive, revolting, ugly
gruff: abrupt, bluff, blunt, brusque, crusty, curt, harsh, hoarse, impolite, rough, rude, severe, short, snippy, sour, surly, throaty
grumble: begrudge, bellyache, carp, complain, crab, croak, fret, fuss, gripe, groan, grouch, grouse, growl, mumble, murmur, protest, repine, rumble, snarl, squawk, whine
grumbling: muttering
grump: crab, curmudgeon, sourpuss
grumpy: cantankerous, crabby, cross, crotchety, irritable, moody, surly, testy
grungy: dirty, grimy, rundown, shabby
grunt: dessert, fish, groan, infantryman, snort, sound
guarantee: agreement, assurance, assure, bail, bond, certificate, certify, contract, covenant, earnest, endorse, guaranty, insurance, insure, make sure, pledge, promise, seal, security, stipulate, surety, swear, token, undertaking, vouch, vouchsafe, warrant, warranty, word
guarantee against loss, damage, default: security, surety
guarantee financially, to: underwrite
guarantee, in a way: insure
guarantee, to: vouch for
guaranteed: assured, ensured, good as gold
guarantor: backer, bailsman, bondsman, insurer, patron, sponsor, underwriter
guard: care, chaperon, conserve, custodian, defend, defense, escort, fend, garrison, herd, jailer, keep, keeper, lineman, lookout, mind, patrol, police, preserve, protect, protector, re-

strain, security, sentinel, sentry, shield, tend, ward, warden, warder, watch, watchdog, watchman

guard during the night or sleep: vigil, watch

guard duty: watch

guard go off-duty, to let: relieve

guard, safe-: palladium

guarded: careful, cautious, defended, discreet, leery, protected, reserved, safe, shrouded, supervised, suspicious, tentative, wary

guardian: angel, argus, attendant, caretaker, chaperon, conservator, curator, custodian, defender, escort, fiduciary, keeper, parent, protector, shepherd, trustee, warden, watchdog

guardian spirit of person or place: daemon, genius, genius loci

guardian spirits: genii, lares

guardian, legal: tutor

guardian, relating to: tutelary

guardianship: care, custody, safekeeping, trust, tutelage, tutorship

guards of Roman emperor, elite: praetorian guard

guards, line of: cordon

guerrilla: fighter, partisan, saboteur, soldier

guerrillas, military action against: counterinsurgency, pacification

guess: assert, assume, believe, conclude, conjecture, deduce, estimate, fancy, hunch, hypothesize, imagine, infer, prediction, presume, shot, speculate, speculation, stub, suppose, surmise, suspect, think

guess by intuition: divine

guess correctly: surmise

guess from what is known, to: deduce, extrapolate, infer

guess, to offer a: hazard, venture

guessing game with pantomimes: charades

guesswork: dead reckoning

guesswork, pertaining to: stochastic

guest: boarder, caller, client, customer, friend, lodger, patron, visitor

guest that takes too much: cadger, freeloader, sponger

guest, frequent: frequenter, habitue

guff: balderdash, baloney, humbug, lip, malarkey, mouth, nonsense, sass

guffaw: cachinnation, ha-ha, heehaw, horse laugh, howl, laughter, roar

guidance: advice, auspice, conduct, control, counsel, direction, help, hint, instruction, leadership, management, suggestion, supervision

guide: adviser, bellwether, bridle, buoy, captain, chaperon, cicerone, clue, conductor, control, convey, convoy, direct, director, escort, example, govern, guru, influence, inspiration, instruct, instructor, itinerary, landmark, lead, leader, lodestar, manage, manipulate, mark, marshal, master, mastermind, mentor, model, monitor, navigate, pathfinder, pilot, polestar, regulate, regulator, reign, rein, rudder, rule, scout, shepherd, show, steer, superintend, teach, teacher, tutor, usher

guide by radio instructions: vector

guide for sightseers: cicerone

guide in Turkish, Arabic, Persian country: dragoman

guide or sign: beacon, warning

guide to conduct: maxim, motto

guide vehicle, to: navigate

guide, speculative formulation serving as: heuristic

guidebook: Baedeker, catalog, directory, handbook, instructions, itinerary, manual, text

guidebook for ready reference: vade mecum

guidelines: constraints, parameters

guiding device: rudder

guiding doctrine: gospel

guiding in learning: heuristic

guiding light: lodestar

guiding principle: gospel, lodestar, motto, polestar

guiding spirit: daemon, genius, numen

guild: alliance, association, brotherhood, club, federation, fellowship, fraternity, league, order, profession, sisterhood, society, sorority, trade, union

guile: cheat, chicanery, cleverness, craft, craftiness, cunning, deceit, duplicity, fraud, slyness, strategem, treachery, trickery, wile

guileless: aboveboard, artless, candid, genuine, honest, innocent, naive, natural, truthful

guillotine: behead, decapitate, execution, lop, maiden

guillotine hole for head: lunette

guilt: blame, compunction, criminality, culpability, fault, liability, offense, regret, remorse, shame, sin, wickedness

guilt implied: incrimination

guilt, to clear of: exculpate, exonerate

guilt, to free oneself of: disburden

guilt, to pronounce free of: absolve

guilt, to try to lessen seriousness of: extenuate, mitigate

guiltless: blameless, clean, clear, free, immaculate, innocent, pure, sinless, spotless

guilty: ashamed, blamable, condemned, convicted, culpable, incriminated, liable, nocent, responsible

guilty of a sin: peccant

guilty person: culprit

guilty plea in exchange for reduced charge: plea bargaining

guilty, to appear or make appear: incriminate, inculpate

guinea pig family: cavy

guise: air, appearance, aspect, attire, behavior, cloak, color, costume, cover, dress, fashion, garb, habit, hue, manner, mask, masquerade, mien, pretense, semblance, shape

guitar movable bar on fingerboard: capo

guitar neck's movable bar to control pitch: capotasto

guitar thin disk for plucking strings: pick, plectrum

guitar without electric amplification: acoustic guitar

guitar's cousin: banjo, lute

gulch: arroyo, canyon, chasm, ditch, divide, gorge, gully, hollow, ravine, rift, valley

gulf: abyss, basin, bay, bayou, chasm, cove, gap, inlet, opening, separation, sound, whirlpool

gulfweed: sargasso

gull: bamboozle, bird, cheat, cheater, cozen, deceive, defraud, dupe, fool, gyp, hoodwink, mew, mislead, sucker, teaser, tern, trick, victim

gull genus: lari

gull kin: tern

gull-like: larine

gullet: craw, esophagus, maw, neck, throat

gullibility: credulity

gullible: green, innocent, naive, sucker, trusting, unsuspecting

gullible person: dupe, greenhorn, gull, sap, sucker

gully: arroyo, channel, chasm, couloir, ditch, gorge, gulch, hollow, ravine, valley, watercourse

gully in desert: wadi

gully in East India: nullah

gully, deep and dry: arroyo

gulp: choke, devour, gobble, guzzle, quaff, scarf, swallow, swig, swill

gulp down: xertz

gum: acacia, adhesive, bilsted, cheat, chewing, chicle, eucalyptus, frankincense, gingiva, glue, hive, kino, mastic, masticatory, mucilage, myrrh, resin, stick, tissue, trick

gum arabic: acacia

gum inflammation: gingivitis, pyorrhea

gum of sapodilla tree: chicle

gum of some plants: mucilage, resin

gum of teeth: gingiva

gum resin: frankincense, gamboge, mastic, myrrh

gumbo vegetable: okra

gummy: adhesive, glutinous, gooey, sticky, viscid, viscous

gumption: courage, enterprise, guts, initiative, nerve, sense, spine, spirit, spunk

gumshoe: cop, detective, dick, flatfoot, investigator, sleuth, sneaker, tec

gun: accelerate, cannon, Colt, Derringer, equalizer, firearm, forty-five, Gatling, heater, howitzer, magnum, musket, piece, pistol, Remington, rev, revolver, rifle, rod, shotgun, Smith and Wesson, speed, thirty-eight, tommy, uzi, weapon, Winchester

gun a motor: rev

gun-cleaning device: ramrod

gun plug: tampion

gun prepared position: emplacement

gun shot: report

gun, revolving piece on tank for: turret

gun, to determine caliber of: calibrate

gun, to spring back as a: recoil

gunfire: barrage, fusillade, salvo, volley

gunfire across trench or troop: enfilade

gung ho: avid, eager

gunk: goop

gunman: assassin, gunslinger, gunwoman, hit man, hit woman, killer, sniper, torpedo, triggerman, triggerwoman

gunman, well-concealed: sniper

gunner: artilleryman, marksman, rifleman, shooter, soldier, warrant officer

guns and ammunition of army: materiel

guns on side of warship: broadside

guns, heavy military: artillery, battery, ordnance

guns, study of: ballistics

gurgle: babble, bubble, burble, murmur, sound, sputter, swash

gurgling sound of flow from vessel with narrow aperture: blodder, glink

guru: guide, master, mentor, mystic, swami, teacher

guru, Hinduism: maharishi, mahatma

gush: blather, burst, cascade, chatter, effuse, flood, flow, outpouring, pour, prate, rush, spate, spew, spout, spurt, stream, surge

gushing: demonstrative, effusive, emotive, gooey, overdemonstrative

gushing, overdemonstrative: sentimental

gusset: gore

gussied up: dressy

gust: blast, blow, breeze, draft, explosion, flurry, gale, outburst, paroxysm, puff, rush, squall, surge, waft, whiff, wind

gusto: appetite, appreciation, delight, élan, enthusiasm, exhilaration, fervor, heart, passion, pleasure, relish, taste, zeal, zest

gut: abdomen, belly, clean, disembowel, eviscerate, innards, innate, instinctive, intuitive, level, midsection, paunch, plunder, ravage, stomach, strip, tummy

gut feeling, based on: visceral

gutless: chicken, cowardly, spineless, timid, weak, wimpy

guts: boldness, courage, fortitude, grit, moxie, nerve, spirit, spunk

gutsy: audacious, bold, brave, courageous, fearless, gallant, game, intrepid, plucky, robust, spunky, undaunted, uninhibited, valiant

gutter: channel, cullis, ditch, drain, duct, eaves, groove, gully, rainspout, trench, trough

gutter or latrine: cloaca, flume

gutter, roof: cullis

guttural: deep, grating, gravelly, gruff, harsh, hoarse, rasping, throaty, velar

GYMNASTICS

balance beam
floor exercises
high bar
horizontal bar
individual all-around
mini-trampolining
parallel bars
pommel horse
rhythmic gymnastics
rings
sports aerobics
still rings
team competition
trampolining
tumbling
uneven parallel bars
vaulting ❧

guy: bloke, bozo, buddy, cable, chain, chap, cord, fellow, guide, kid, male, man, person, rope

guy rope: stay

guzzle: bolt, devour, drink, gorge, gormandize, gulp, imbibe, quaff, slop, slosh, swig, swill, tipple

gymnast: acrobat, athlete, jumper, tumbler

gymnastic apparatus: balance beam, parallel bars, pommel horse, rings, vaulting horse

gymnastic association: turnverein

gymnastic physical fitness exercise: calisthenics, floor exercise

gymnastics: acrobatics, calisthenics, competition, exercise, sport, tumbling

gymnastics equipment: balance beam, horizontal bars, horse, mat, parallel bars, rings, trampoline, uneven bars

gynecological test: Pap smear, Pap test

gyp: bamboozle, bilk, burn, cheat, deceive, defraud, overcharge, rip off, steal, swindle, swindler

gypsy: bohemian, cale, calo, cziganz, gitana, gitano, nomad, roamer, rom, romany, tzigane, vagrant, wanderer, zingara, zingaro

gypsy gentleman: rom

gypsy lady: rani

gyrate: circulate, revolve, rotate, spin, spiral, turn, twirl

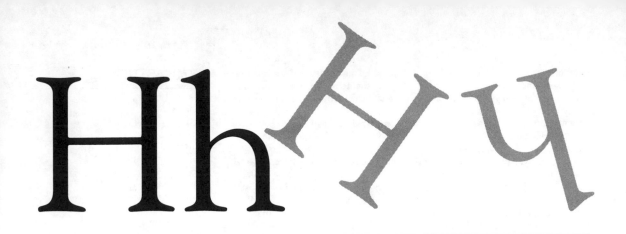

habeas corpus: deed, judgment, mandamus, mandate, order, writ

habiliment: apparel, attire, clothes, clothing, dress, garb, gown, trappings

habit: addiction, bearing, custom, demeanor, disposition, groove, guise, idiosyncrasy, mannerism, mode, pattern, practice, propensity, rote, routine, rut, second nature, tendency, usage, use, vice, way, wont; apparel, attire, clothes, costume, dress, garb, garment, gown, suit

habit, odd or exaggerated: aberration, eccentricity, idiosyncrasy, mannerism

habitant: denizen, dweller, resident

habitat: abode, apartment, cave, condominium, den, environment, flat, haunt, home, house, locality, nest, place, territory

habitat prefix: eco-

habitat, animal/plant adjustment to new: ecesis

habitation: abode, residence

habits of social group: mores

habitual: accustomed, chronic, common, confirmed, customary, established, familiar, fixed, hardened, inborn, inveterate, natural, ordinary, persistent, regular, routine, traditional, usual, wonted

habitual and irrational: pathological

habitual manner: disposition, tendency

habitual path: beat

habitual postponement: procrastination

habitual practice: usage

habitual procedure: rote

habituate: acclimate, accustom, addict, enure, familiarize, instill, inure, prepare, school, season, teach, train, unure, use

habitue: denizen, inhabitant

hacienda: casa, estate, farm, house, plantation, ranch

hack: butcher, chop, cut, hew, mangle, mutiliate, slash; cab, cabbie, hireling, lackey, taxi, taxicab; cough; writer

hackneyed: banal, clichéd, common, commonplace, everyday, outdated, outmoded, routine, stale, stereotyped, threadbare, tired, trite, vapid, worn

haddock, smoked: finnan haddie, finnan haddle, finnan haddock

haddock's young: scrod

Hades: abyss, Avernus, Dis, Gehenna, hell, netherworld, Orcus, pit, Pluto, Sheol, Tartarus, Tophet, underworld, Yama

Hades' river: Lethe, Styx

hag: beldam, biddy, bog, crone, demon, hellcat, marsh, nag, quagmire, shrew, sorceress, swamp, witch

haggard: bony, careworn, drawn, exhausted, fatigued, gaunt, harrowed, lank, lean, pale, scraggy, scrawny, spent, suffering, thin, tired, wasted, worn

haggle: badger, bargain, barter, bicker, cavil, chaffer, chisel, deal, dicker, dispute, hack, higgle, negotiate, quarrel, stickle, wrangle

hail: acclaim, accost, ahoy, applaud, ave, barrage, batter, call, compliment, greet, honor, originate, praise, precipitation, salutation, salute, shout, signal, summon, torrent, volley; sleet

hair and its diseases, study of: trichology

hair grows, cavity from which: follicle

hair in nostrils: vibrissa

hair of animal's neck: frill, hackles, ruff

hair of genitals: pubic hair

hair of newborn, downy fine: lanugo

hair plait (archaic): tress

hair-raising: breathtaking, eerie, exciting, terrifying, thrilling

hair-removing lotion: depilatory

hair roots with electric current, destruction of: electrolysis

hair, erection of body: goosebumps, gooseflesh, horripilation, piloerection

hair, root of: follicle bulb, papilla

hairiness, abnormal: pilosism

hairless: bald, depilous, glabrous, smooth, tonsure

hairlike: capillaceous, capillary

hairlike outgrowth: villus

hairlike thread on microscopic organism: cilia

hairs: pili

hairs or whiskers of animal: vibrissae

hairs standing on end: hystriciasis, piloerection

hairs, covered with barbed: barbellate

hairs, having soft fine: crinite, lanate, pilose

hairy: bristly, bushy, chancy, comate, comose, dangerous, difficult, fluffy, furry, fuzzy, harrowing, hazardous, hirsute, pileous, pilose, risky, shaggy, treacherous

hairy Himalayan goat: serow

hairy monster of North America: Bigfoot, Sasquatch

hairy social insect: bumblebee

hairy, in botany: comate

halcyon: bird, calm, carefree, contented, golden, happy, kingfisher, peaceful, placid, prosperous, quiet, serene, tranquil, unruffled

hale: drag, energetic, hardy, healthy, hearty, hoist, pull, robust, sound, stout, strong, vigorous

half: divided, division, fifty-fifty, fraction, incomplete, moiety, part, partial

HAIR STYLES AND RELATED TERMS

arrange the hair, to: coif
bushy, frizzy hair: Afro
chemical to make hair blond: peroxide
curl or wave hair tightly: crimp
cut or trim hair, to: clip, poll
false hair: fall, hair extension, hair implant, hair weaving
female hairdresser: coiffeuse
fringe across forehead: bangs
hair added in pieces: extensions
hair and skin, having fair: xanthochroid
hair clasp: barrette, bobby pin
hair cluster: tuft
hair coming to point on forehead: widow's peak
hair cream or wax: pomade
hair cut short and even around head: bob
hair cut very short and stiffly upright: crew cut
hair in knot or bun in back: chignon
hair in long twisted locks or braids: dreadlocks
hair in tight braids: cornrows
hair in tight waves or curls: crimped
hair loss: alopecia, psilosis
hair opposite direction, to comb: backcomb, tease
hair piece: rat, switch, toupee, wig
hair piled up by backcombing: beehive
hair puffed out by backcombing: bouffant
hair sticking up naturally: cowlick
hair sweeping up from the forehead: pompadour
hair swept back at sides to meet in upturned point at back: ducktail
hair tint: henna, rinse
hair with strip of hair left on shaven head: Mohawk

hairdo: Afro, beehive, bob, bouffant, bowl, butch, coif, cornrows, crew cut, do, dreadlocks, ducktail, flattop, marcel, Mohawk, moptop, pageboy, perm, pigtail, pompadour, ponytail, pouf, Prince Valiant, shingle
hairdresser: barber, beautician, coiffeur, coiffeuse, colorist, friseur, stylist
hairdressing place: beauty parlor, salon
hairline of balding person: receding
lighter streaks in hair: highlight
line dividing hair: part
long hair: tresses
male hairdresser: coiffeur
mass of tangled matted hair: litch
matted or tangled hair: shag
of flat and limp hair: lank
of messy hair: disheveled, rumpled, tousled, unkempt
person who cuts his/her own hair: autotonsorialist
pigment coloring hair: melanin
protein layer of hair: keratin
related to hairdressing: tonsorial
remove hair, to: depilate
rub hair the wrong way: fruzz
shed hair, to: molt
single curl of hair: ringlet
smooth and straight hair: leiotrichous, lissotrichous
thick mass of hair: shock
thin or trim hair by tapering, to: feather
tufts of unruly hair: feesks
very soft hair: velutinous
woolly and crisp hair: ulotrichous
woolly and matted hair: tomentose ❦

---

half-and-half ingredient: cream

half-bottle: split

half-breed: hybrid

half-brother or -sister, referring to: uterine

half-diameter: radius

half-line of verse: hemistich

half-man, half-horse: centaur

half-moon: arch, crescent, curve, semilunar

half-moon shape: lunette

half-wit: blockhead, dolt, dummy, dunce, fool, idiot, moron, nitwit, numskull, simpleton

half-witted: asinine, dull, feebleminded, foolish, senseless, stupid

halfhearted: blasé, faint, indifferent, listless, lukewarm, neutral, passive, tepid, unenthusiastic, uninspired

halfway: almost, center, compromising, incomplete, intermediate, middle, midmost, midpoint, midway, moderate, nearly, partially

halite: mineral, NaCl, rock salt, salt

hall: anteroom, arean, atrium, auditorium, chamber, corridor, dormitory, entrance, entry, foyer, gallery, hallway, lobby, manor, odeum, parlor, passage, passageway, room, theater, vestibule

hall for performance: auditorium

hall rug: runner

hallmark: characteristic, seal, sign, stamp, symbol

hallowed: anointed, blessed, consecrated, holy, revered, sacred, sanctified, venerated

hallowed place: shrine

Halloween pumpkin: jack-o'-lantern

hallucination: aberration, delusion, dream, fantasy, illusion, mirage, vision

hallucinations and tremors from alcoholism: delirium tremens, the DTs

hallucinatory: psychedelic

halo: aura, aureole, cincture, circle, corona, crown, gloria, gloriole, glory, glow, light, nimbus, radiance, ring, vesica piscis

halo light around celestial body: corona

halogen: astatine, bromine, chlorine, element, fluorine, iodine

halt: arrest, block, cease, desist, discontinue, end, foil, hamper, hesitate, hitch, hobble, inhibit, interrupt, lame, limp, pause, stand, stay, stem, stop, suspend, terminate, waver

halt, at sea: avast

halter: bodice, bridle, fetter, leash, noose, restrain, rope, strap

ham: bad actor

ham, Italian cured spiced: prosciutto

ham, smoked or cured: gammon

hamlet: burg, dorp, hamel, moray, thorp, thorpe, town, village

hammer: bang, batter, beat, clobber, defeat, drive, hit, maul, mell, nail, pound, pummel, punch, ram, reiterate, shape, sledge, strike, tack, tamp, wallop

HAMMERS AND MALLETS

ball peen hammer
beetle
blacksmith's hammer
brick hammer
bushhammer
chipping hammer
claw hammer
cross peen hammer
demolition hammer
double-claw hammer
drywall hammer
electric hammer
engineer's hammer
framing hammer
fuller
joiner's mallet
long-handled hammer
machinist's hammer
maul
peen hammer
pile hammer
rip hammer
rubber mallet
scutch
shingler's hammer
shoemaker's hammer
sledgehammer
small anvil
soft-faced hammer
soft-faced mallet
stonemason's hammer
tack hammer
tilt hammer
trip-hammer
Warrington hammer
wooden mallet ❦

RELATED TERMS

hammer doctors use on knees, rubber-headed: plexor
hammer handle: helve
hammer head: peen
hammer-shaped: malleiform
hammer type: air, ball-peen, beetle, claw, fuller, gavel, hatchet, jack, mallet, plexor, pneumatic, rip, sledge, tilt, Warrington
hammer with forked-end head: claw hammer
hammer, blunt end of: poll
hammer, heavy forge: tilt hammer
hammer, heavy long-handled: maul
hammer, metalworking: forge hammer
hammered in design: incuse ❦

hammock cords: clews
hamper: block, clog, confine, cramp, curb, embarrass, encumber, fetter, foil, frustrate, halter, handcuff, handicap, hinder, hobble, impede, inhibit, load, manacle, obstruct, restrain, restrict, shackle, slow, stymie, trammel; basket, container, crate, pannier
hand: ability, applause, assistance, craftsperson, employee, grasp, handwriting, help, helper, knack, laborer, ovation, participant, penmanship, player, pledge, power, share, signature, transmit, worker, workman; appendage, claw, extremity, fin, fist, flipper, manus, mitt, paw; indicator, pointer
hand between thumb and forefinger: purlicue
hand down: bequeath
hand grinding stone: mano
hand lines of palm: fate, head, heart, life
hand measure with thumb and little finger spread: span
hand mill: quern
hand-operated musical organ: barrel organ, hurdy-gurdy
hand out: alms, bestow, charity, dispense, distribute, give, mete
hand over: cede, consign, donate, present, release, relinquish, surrender, waive
hand over criminal: extradite
hand-shaped: palmate
hand, distance between thumb and little finger on spread: span
hand, fleshy base of thumb on: thenar
hand, muscle below thumb on: heel
hand, to: give, lift, pass, reach; clap
handbag: clutch, etui, gripsack, pochette, pocketbook, purse, reticule, satchel, tote, valise
handbill: advertisement, bulletin, circular, dodger, flyer, leaflet, pamphlet
handbook: directory, enchiridion, guidebook, manual, text, vade mecum
handcuffs: chains, fetters, irons, manacles, shackles
handed down, something: bequest, legacy
handful: difficult, few, quantity, scattering, some, sprinkling
handicap: barrier, burden, defect, disability, disadvantage, drawback, embarrass, encumber, hinder, hindrance, impede, impediment, liability, limitation, obstacle; advantage, edge, head start, odds
handicap aid: ramp
handicap race, weight horse must carry in: impost
handicap in foreign travel: language barrier
handicap, to: burden, encumber, hinder, penalize
handicapped: at a disadvantage
handicraft: artwork, metier, skill, trade, vocation, workmanship
handkerchief: bandana, hankie, neckerchief, scarf
handle: ansa, anse, bail, control, cope, crank, deal, direct, doorknob, feel, finger, grasp, grip, grope, guide, haft, handgrip, helve, hilt, hold, holder, knob, lever, lug, manage, maneuver, manipulate, nob, operate, paw, ply, shaft, steer, stem, swipe, touch, treat, use, wield; moniker, name, nickname
handle of tool: helve
handle of weapon, knife: haft, hilt
handle of whip, fishing rod, some tools: stock
handle on bucket, kettle: bail
handle ridges: knurls
handle roughly: maul, paw
handle skillfully: manipulate
handle, ear-shaped: lug
handle, having a: ansate
handrail supported on balusters: balustrade
handrail supporting post: baluster
hands, able to work with both: ambidextrous
hands, feet: extremities
hands, good with one's: adroit, deft, dexterous
hands, referring to: manual
hands, skill with: legerdemain, prestidigitation, sleight of hand
handsome: abundant, ample, appropriate, attractive, beautiful, becoming, bonny, bountiful, comely, copious, dapper, dexterous, elegant, exquisite, fair, fashionable, fine, fitting, gallant, generous, good-looking, gracious, liberal, plentiful, pretty, sizable, stunning, stylish, suitable
handsome man: Adonis
handwriting: amanuensis, autograph, calligraphy, chirography, cursive, griffonage, longhand, majuscule, manuscript, minuscule, penmanship, script, shorthand, uncial

handwriting analysis: graphanalysis, graphology

handwriting downward stroke: minim

handwriting in capital letters: majuscule

handwriting in code: shorthand

handwriting in full: longhand

handwriting in rounded capital letters, medieval: uncial

handwriting in small letters: minuscule

handwriting or spelling that is bad: cacography

handwriting slanting to the left: backhand

handwriting that is flowing: cursive, longhand

handwriting that is printed: block lettering, block printing

handwriting, art of: calligraphy

handwriting, bad: cacography

handwriting, fancy: flourish

handwriting, good: calligraphy, chirography, penmanship

handwriting, illegible: griffonage

handwriting, of hard to read: crabbed, illegible

handwriting, of readable: legible

handwriting, poor: cacography, hieroglyphics

handwriting, scribe using: amanuensis

handwriting, sloppy illegible: griffonage

handwriting, study of: graphology

handwriting, the art of: chirography

handwritten by signer: holograph

handwritten document: autograph, manuscript ✇

handy: accessible, adept, adjacent, adroit, available, central, clever, close, close-by, convenient, deft, dexterous, dextrous, helpful, near, nearby, ready, skilled, skillful, useful

handyman: fixer, jack-of-all-trades

hang: append, await, dangle, deck, depend, drape, droop, execute, hinge, hover, inclination, lynch, nail, noose, pend, pin, rest, sag, slope, stick, stretch, suspend, swing, tack

hang around: dawdle, frequent, hover, idle, loiter

hang down: lop, sag

hang in folds: drape

hang on: cling, clutch, continue, endure, persevere, persist

hang out: fraternize, hobnob, idle, loiter

hang suspended: hover

hang up: delay, halted, hinder, impede, snagged, suspend

hang-up: dilemma, fixation, inhibition, obsession, obstacle, phobia, preoccupation, problem, snag

hangar: barracks, garage, shed, shelter

hangar area: apron

hangdog: ashamed, cowed, defeated, downcast, groveling, guilty, intimidated, shamefaced, shifty, sneaking

hanger-on: adherent, dangler, dependent, flunky, follower, freeloader, groupie, lackey, leech, minion, parasite, scrounger, sponge, sycophant, toady

hanging: dangling, pendent, pendulous, pensile

hanging decoration: tassel

hanging limply, drooping: flaccid

hanging loosely: pendulous, pensile

hanging ornament: pendant

hanging part of garment, like sleeve or hood: tippet

hangnail, infected: paronychia

hangout: bar, den, dive, haunt, joint, nest, rendezvous, stamping grounds

hangover: aftereffect, headache, holdover, letdown, vestige

hankering: craving, desire, hunger, itch, longing, thirst, urge, want, wishing, yearning, yen

hanky-panky: chicanery, devious, mischievous, trickery

haphazard: accidental, aimless, arbitrary, careless, casual, chance, chaotic, disorderly, helter-skelter, hit-or-miss, random, reckless, shipshod, undirected, unorganized

hapless: cursed, jinxed, luckless, star-crossed, unfortunate, unlucky, wretched

happen: arrive, befall, betide, chance, come, come to pass, develop, eventuate, fall, materialize, occur, perhaps, result, stumble, supervene, take place, transpire

happen as a result: ensue, eventuate, follow, supervene

happen at same time: synchronize

happen, come to: materialize

happening: affair, afoot, episode, event, experience, incident, milestone, occasion, occurrence, phenomenon, thing

happening at same rate: synchronous

happening at same time: concurrent, simultaneous

happening intermittently: spasmodic

happiness: beatitude, bliss, contentment, delight, ecstasy, elation, elysium, enjoyment, eudaemony, euphoria, exaltation, felicity, gaiety, gladness, glee, joie de vivre, joy, mirth, pleasure, prosperity, rapture, rhathymia, satisfaction, seventh heaven, transport, weal

happiness in life of moderation: eudemonia

happiness, actions evaluated in terms of their production of: eudemonism

happiness, inability to experience: anhedonia

happiness, place of: Elysium

happy: apt, blessed, blithe, buoyant, carefree, cheerful, chipper, content, contented, cosh, elated, enthusiastic, euphoric, exuberant, felicitous, fitting, fortunate, gay, glad, gracious, gratified, gratifying, jubilant, lucky, merry, mirthful, nice, overjoyed, pleased, prosperous, providential, radiant, satisfied, sunny, willing

happy and healthy: eupeptic

happy-go-lucky: carefree, casual, easygoing, lighthearted, nonchalant, unconcerned, untroubled

hara-kiri: seppuku

harangue: accost, address, diatribe, hassle, jeremiad, lecture, orate, oration, perorate, rant, rave, scolding, screed, sermon, speech, spiel, tirade

harass: afflict, agitate, annoy, assail, attach, badger, bait, beleaguer, beset, bother, bully, chafe, chase, distract, distress, disturb, exhaust, fatigue, fret, harry, hassle, haze, heckle, hector, hound, impede, intimidate, irritate, jade, molest, nag, obsess, perplex, persecute, pester, plague, provoke, raid, ride, scrape, tantalize, tease, tire, torment, trouble, try, vex, weary, worry

harass or taunt: chivvy, chivy, heckle, importune

harass persistently: ride

harbinger: angel, forerunner, herald, indication, messenger, omen, portent, precursor, presage, shelter, sign, signal, symbol, usher

harbinger of spring: robin

harbor: basin, bay, believe, billet, cove, dock, foster, gulf, haven, hide, hold, imagine, inlet, landing, lodging, mooring, nurse, nurture, port, protect, quarter, refuge, retreat, sanctuary, seaport, shelter, withhold

harbor with breakwater: mole

harbor, to clean a: dredge

hard: adamant, adverse, arduous, backbreaking, bad, bitter, callous, close, coarse, cold, compact, complicated, comportment, cruel, dear, definite, demanding, dense, difficult, diligent, distressing, durable, earnest, energetic, firm, fit, frozen, granitic, grasping, harsh, impenetrable, impregnable, inclement, indisputable, inflexible, insensitive, intense, intoxicating, intricate, iron, laborious, lasting, marble, mean, obdurate, oppressive, penetrating, perplexing, persevering, persistent, petrified, practical, real, relentless, repelling, resentful, resistant, rigid, rigorous, robust, rocky, rough, rugged, ruthless, severe, solid, sour, stable, steely, stern, stiff, stony, strenuous, strict, stringent, strong, strongminded, stubborn, true, unassailable, unfeeling, unremitting, unyielding, uphill, violent, wearisome

hard coal: anthracite

hard-core: dedicated, devoted, explicit, graphic, intransigent, loyal, staunch, uncompromising

hard-hearted: callous, cold, cruel, indifferent, insensitive, mean, obdurate, pitiless, uncaring, unfeeling

hard problem for beginner: pons asinorum, stumbling block

hard-shelled: testaceous

hard to believe: amazing, incredible, unlikely

hard to come by: rare, sparse

hard-to-express quality or attribute: je ne sais quoi

hard to please: fastidious, hypercritical

hard to understand: abstruse, elusive

hardcover: casebound, clothbound, hardback

harden: acclimate, accustom, bake, cake, cement, climatize, coagulate, concrete, condense, congeal, endure, enure, firm, fossilize, freeze, gel, indurate, inure, ossify, petrify, season, set, settle, solidify, steel, stiffen, strengthen, temper, thicken, toughen

harden and solidify: clot, coagulate, congeal, set

harden glass, metal: anneal, temper

harden or toughen: indurate

harden rubber: vulcanize

harden to something: inure

hardened: calloused, enured, indurate, inured, steeled, unfeeling

hardened lava: basalt

hardened, emotionally: callous, unfeeling

hardened, having been: sclerous

hardening: calcification

hardening of the arteries: arteriosclerosis

hardening of tissue: sclerosis

hardheaded: inflexible, keen, mulish, poised, pragmatic, realistic, sagacious, shrewd, stubborn, unbending, willful

hardheaded persons: realists

hardihood: audacity, boldness, confidence, courage, daring, effrontery, fortitude, gravery, grit, guts, impudence, insolence, intrepidity, pluck, potency, stoutness, strength, vigor, will

hardly: barely, faintly, harshly, infrequently, just, not, painfully, rarely, scarcely, severely, somewhat, unfairly

hardness: callosity

hardness of metals and alloys: Brinell hardness

hardness of minerals: Mohs scale

hardship: accident, adversity, affliction, asperity, calamity, catastrophe, difficulty, disaster, endurance, grief, handicap, injury, injustice, misfortune, peril, privation, rigor, suffering, trial, tribulation

hardware: appliances, computer, fittings, fixtures, tools, weapons

hardwood: alm, ash, beech, birch, cherry, elm, hickory, mahogany, maple, oak, sycamore, teak, walnut

hardworking: assiduous, conscientious, dedicated, diligent, persevering, sedulous

hardy: audacious, bold, brave, burly, courageous, daring, durable, firm, healthy, intrepid, mighty, resolute, robust, rugged, solid, spartan, stout, strong, sturdy, tough, vigorous

hare, pertaining to: leporine

hare, very young: leveret

harebrained: absurd, asinine, crazy, foolish, insane, mindless, senseless, stupid, wacky

harem: concubines, purdah, seraglio, serai, serail, zenana

harem chamber: oda

harem, concubine or slave in: odalisque

harem, large: seraglio

hari-kari: suicide

hark: attend, hear, heed, listen, notice, obey, whisper

harlequin: buffoon, clown, jester

harlot: base, beggar, doxy, jezebel, prostitute, rogue, slut, vagabond, wanton, whore

harm: abuse, bane, damage, detriment, disservice, evil, hurt, ill, impair, infliction, injure, injury, maim, mar, misfortune, mistreat, pain, punish, sabotage, undermine, wound, wrong

harm reputation: discredit

harmful: adverse, bad, baneful, catastrophic, damaging, deadly, deleterious, destructive, detrimental, fatal, hazardous, hurtful, maleficent, malicious, nasty, noisome, noxious, pernicious, pestilent, poisonous, ruinous, toxic, unhealthy, unsafe

harmful and damaging: deleterious, detrimental, injurious

harmful and toxic: virulent

harmful and treacherous: insidious, maleficent, malevolent, malicious, malign, malignant, pernicious

harmful or unfavorable: adverse, inimical

harmful thing: bane

harmless: benign, gentle, innocent, innocuous, innoxious, inoffensive, naive, nontoxic, peaceable, pure, safe

harmless substance given as cure or as test control: placebo

harmonious: agreeable, amicable, Apollonian, attuned, balanced, compatible, concordant, conformable, congruous, cooperative, coordinated, cordial, corresponding, dulcet, en rapport, euphonious, friendly, in tune, in unison, melodious, musical, peaceful, proportional, rhythmical, sonorous, spheral, symmetrical, tuneful, unified, uniform

harmonize: accordance, agreement, amity, attune, blend, concert, concord, conformity, consonance, cooperation, correlate, gee, integrate, jibe, jube, match, melody, mesh, music, orchestrate, peace, rapport, sing, togetherness, tone, tune, unify

harmonizing: henotic

harmonizing singing: barbershop

harmony: accord, balance, chorus, compatibility, concinnity, consonance, friendship, order, symmetry, tranquility, unity

harmony in arrangement of parts: concinnity

harmony in music: chord, concord, consonance

harmony of parts: compatibility, concurrence, congruence, consistency, symmetry

harness: belt, bridle, channel, collar, control, enclose, equipment, gear, hitch, muzzle, rein, saddle, tackle, tame, trappings, utilize, yoke

harness bit types: double bridle, double-jointed snaffle, egg-butt snaffle, fulmer-snaffle, kimblewick, loose-ring snaffle, pelham

harness part: bellyband, billet, bit, blinder, breastband, bridle, collar, crownpiece, crupper, flap, hame, martingale, rein, ridgeband, saddle, skirt, swell, terret, trace

harp: dwell, harmonica, instrument, lyre, nag, reiterate, repeat, trigon

harpsichord: cembalo, spinet

harpsichord or clavichord plectrum: quill

harridan: crone, hag, nagger, shrew, strumpet, virago, vixen, woman

harrowing: chilling, dangerous, disturbing, frightening, terrifying, tilling, traumatic, upsetting

harry: agitate, annoy, assault, attack, badger, bedevil, bother, distress, disturb, harass, harrow, hector, hunt, pester, pillage, plague, plunder, raid, ravage, sack, steal, tease, torment, worry

harsh: acerb, acerbate, acrid, acrimonious, astringent, austere, bitter, brazen, brute, caustic, clashing, coarse, crude, cruel, curt, discordant, dissonant, district, drastic, fell, glaring, grating, grim, gruff, guttural, hard, hoarse, inclement, jarring, mean, nasty, pungent, rasping, raspy, raucous, relentless, repellent, rigorous, rough, scathing, severe, sharp, sour, stark, stern, strict, strident, truculent, unfeeling, ungentle, unkind, unpleasant

harsh and austere: spartan

harsh and bleak: desolate, grim, stark

harsh and relentless: implacable, inexorable, unremitting

harsh and severe: draconian, draconic, rigorous, stringent

harsh in manner: brusque, curt, gruff

harsh-sounding: cacophonous, grating, raucous, strident

harsh, very: draconian

harshly pungent: acrid

harshness in tone, as an out-of-tune instrument: wolf

hart: moss, stag

harum-scarum: careless, flighty, foolish, harebrained, irresponsible, rash, reckless, wild

harvest: accumulate, amass, autumn, cache, collect, crop, fall, gather, hoard, pick, produce, reap, yield

hash: chop, consider, hodgepodge, jumble, mangle, mess, mince, mixture, mix-up, review

hash mark: stripe

hasp: clasp, close, fastener, gird, latch, lock

hassle: altercation, argument, beef, bother, commotion, discussion, dispute, fight, flap, harass, hound, problem, quarrel, rhubarb, row, squabble, struggle, trouble, try

hassock: cricket, cushion, footrest, footstool, grass, ottoman, pess, pouf, tussock

haste: beeline, bustle, celerity, dash, dispatch, expedition, flurry, hectic, hurry, impetuousness, nimbleness, precipitance, quickness, rapidity, rush, scamper, scurry, speed, swiftness, tear

hasten: accelerate, advance, barrel, bolt, dart, drive, expedite, fleet, gallop, hie, hurry, precipitate, press, push, race, run, rush, scamper, scurry, speed, trot, whisk

hasty: abrupt, brash, brief, careless, cursory, eager, expeditious, fast, fleet, fleeting, hurried, hurrisome, impatient, impetuous, impulsive, irritable, nimble, precipitate, precipitous, quick, rapid, rash, speedy, sudden, swift, thoughtless, urgent

hasty and brief: cursory

hat rosette or ribbons: cockade

hat with flat square, academic: mortarboard

hat with high crown and wide brim: Stetson

hat, broad-brimmed Spanish: sombrero

hat, derby: bowler

hat, high creased crown and curled brim edge: homburg

hat, soft felt with low creased crown: fedora

hat, soldier or bandleader, tall cylindrical with visor and plume: shako

hat, stiff round wide-brimmed: pith helmet, topee

hat, three-sided: tricorn

hatch: breed, brood, compartment, concoct, contrive, cover, create, door, floodgate, gate, generate, incubate, invent, opening, originate, parent, plan, produce, sire

hatchet: axe, tomahawk

hatchet man: assassin, critic, goon, henchman, killer, murderer, myrmidon

hatchet- or ax-shaped: dolabriform

hatching, keep eggs warm before: brood, incubate

hatchway: door, scuttle

hate: abhor, abominate, animosity, animus, antagonism, aversion, condemn, despise, detest, detestation, disdain, dislike, enmity, hostility, loathing, malignity, rancor, revile, scorn

hate intensely: abhor, abominate, execrate, loathe

hated object: bête noire

hated one: anathema

hateful: abhorrent, abominable, bitter, detestable, disgusting, evil, flagitious, foul, heinous, loathsome, malignant, mean, nasty, obnoxious, odious, offensive, ornery, repellent, reprehensible, repugnant, revolting, rotten, ugly, vicious, vile

hater of children: misopedist

hater of government and authority: misarchist

hater of learning, wisdom: misophist

hater of math and science: misomath

hater of practicing piano: misodoctakleidist

hater of reason, enlightenment: misologist

hater of smoking: misocapnist

hater of the unknown: misotramontanist

hatred: abhorrence, abomination, animosity, animus, antipathy, aversion, bitterness, contempt, detestation, enmity, grudge, hostility, ill will, malice, malignity, odium, prejudice, rancor, repugnance, revulsion, spite, vitriol

haughtiness: airs, arrogance, conceit, condescending, hauteur, highfalutin, lordly, patronizing, pride, uppity

haughty: airy, aloof, arrogant, bold,

Brahmin, cavalier, condescending, contemptuous, disdainful, distant, dogmatic, egotistic, fastidious, hoity toity, imperious, lofty, magisterial, noble, overbearing, patronizing, pompous, pontifical, proud, scornful, snooty, stately, supercilious

haul: bring, cargo, cart, catch, drag, draw, freight, harvest, heave, load, lug, move, pull, schlepp, spoils, tote, tow, transport, truck, tug

haunch: buns, buttocks, hindquarters, hip, leg, loin, posterior, rump, thigh

haunt: clubhouse, custom, den, dive, frequent, frighten, ghost, habitat, hang around, hang out, infest, lair, manifest, nest, obsess, pervade, pester, resort, skill, spirit, spook, terrify, trouble, visit, worry, wraith

haunt, personal: purlieu

haut monde: aristocracy, blue blood, elite, high society

hautboy: oboe

hauteur: arrogance, conceited, disdain, haughtiness, pride, snobbery, snootiness, uppity

have: accept, acquire, allow, bear, become, beget, comprise, contain, deceive, endure, enjoy, experience, fool, gain, get, hold, include, need, obtain, own, permit, possess, receive, retain, swindle, undergo

haven: anchorage, asylum, cover, harbor, hideout, hope, inlet, oasis, port, refuge, relief, retreat, roadstead, sanctuary, shelter

havoc: chaos, confusion, destroy, destruction, devastate, devastation, disorder, disruption, mayhem, pillage, ravage, ruin, upheaval, waste

Hawaii bird: goose, nene

Hawaii flower: hibiscus, lehua

Hawaii food: kalo, poi, taro

Hawaii tree: candlenut, kukui

Hawaiian beverage: kava

Hawaiian dance with undulating hip movement and hand and arm gestures: hula, hula-hula

Hawaiian farewell: aloha

Hawaiian feast: luau

Hawaiian flower garland: lei

Hawaiian house: hale

Hawaiian loose dress: muumuu

Hawaiian winter wind: kona

hawk: accipiter, astur, bush, buteo, buzzard, caracara, falcon, harrier,

jingo, kite, militant, noble, osprey, peddle, puttock, sell, shark, spit, vend, vulture, warmonger

hawk cage: mew

hawk group: cast, leash

hawk or buzzard: buteo

hawk, adult: haggard

hawk, female: formel

hawk, male: tercel

hawk, young: eyas

hawker: crier, vendor

hawser: line, rope, tow rope

hay: chaff, feed, fodder, forage, grass, herbage, money, provender, swath

hay fever: pollenosis

hay fever medicine: antihistamine

hay for animals: herbage, provender

hay pile: rick

hay, second crop of: aftermath, rowen

haying machine: tedder

haying tool: pitchfork

hayseed: bumpkin, countryman, greenhorn, hick, rube, rustic, yokel

hazard: accident, adventure, bet, chance, danger, dare, endanger, gamble, guess, imperil, jeopardy, luck, mishap, obstacle, peril, possibility, risk, stake, threat, venture

hazardous: chancy, dangerous, dicey, hairy, insecure, perilous, precarious, risky, uncertain, unhealthy, unsafe

haze: beat, brume, cloud, daze, devil, dream, drizzle, film, fog, frighten, harass, initiate, mist, obscure, persecute, reverie, scold, smog, trance, vapor

hazel: brown, brownish, bush, cobnut, filbert, nut

hazy: ambiguous, blurred, cloudy, dull, filmy, foggy, fuzzy, groggy, indistinct, misty, murky, nebulous, obscure, smoky, uncertain, unclear, vague

hazy and confused: nebulochaotic

head and neck injury from sudden jerk: whiplash

head bob: nod

head cold: coryza

head englarged by fluid: hydrocephalus

head-shaped: capitate

head to foot: cap-a-pie

head waiter: maître d', maître d'hôtel, majordomo

head, back of: occiput

head, broad: brachycephalic

head, classification based on shape and size of: cephalic index

head, crown of: pate

head, front of: sinciput

head, relating to: cephalic

head, top of: corona, vertex

headache: annoyance, cephalagia, cephalodynia, cerebralgia, difficulty, megrim, migraine, pain, problem, trouble

headache on one side: hemicrania, migraine

headache, overall: galea

headband: agal, bandeau, coronet, diadem, fillet, frontlet, snood, tiara

headdress: bandore, biretta, bonnet, busby, cap, coiffure, coronet, crown, hat, helmet, hood, miter, tiara, toque, turban

headdress worn by bishop, pointy: miter

headdress, Arab: kaffiyeh

headdress, crownlike: tiara

headdress, Moslem: turban

headdress, woman's scarf: babushka

heading: course, direction, headline, introduction, lemma, rubric, subtitle, title, topic

heading or chapter title: rubric

heading, classified under general: subsume

headland: bluff, cape, cliff, ness, peak, promontory, ras, ridge, spit, strip

headless: acephalous

headlike end, having a: capitate

headlike part: capitulum

headline: banner, caption, feature, heading, streamer, title

headline across page width: banner, headline, streamer

headline on every or every other page: running head

headlong: abrupt, asprawl, breakneck, dangerous, foolhardy, hasty, heedless, impetuous, impulsive, pell-mell, precipitate, precipitous, rash, reckless, sheer, slambang, steep

headman: boss, captain, chief, commander, foreman, leader, manager, ringleader, supervisor

headmaster: administrator, dean, principal

headquarters: base, center, command, depot, operations, post, precinct

headstone: gravestone, keystone, marker, monument, tombstone

headstrong: bullheaded, determined, froward, mulish, obstinate, persistent, rash, stubborn, ungovernable, unruly, violent, willful

headway: dent, distance, ground, improvement, progress

heady: cagey, clever, domineering, exhilarating, impetuous, intoxicating, overbearing, precipitate, prudent, rash, smart, stimulating, stirring, stupefying, swift, thrilling, willful

heal: alleviate, convalesce, cure, free, mend, recover, recuperate, regenerate, rehabilitate, remedy, repair, restore, treat

heal or cure: physic

heal with a scar: cicatrize

healing: curative, remedial, sanative, therapeutic

healing plant: aloe

healing quickly, not: dysepulotic

heals, something that: salve

health: condition, constitution, disposition, euphoria, fettle, fitness, hardiness, moor, shape, soundness, spirits, stamina, strength, vitality, vigor, well-being

health, improve dramatically in: rally

health, improve in: convalesce, recuperate

health, person overly concerned with: hypochondriac, valetudinarian

health, restoration of: rehabilitation

health, restoring: curative, salutary

health, state of: constitution

healthful: holistic, salubrious, wholesome

healthful part of grain: bran

healthy: active, athletic, firm, fit, hale, hardy, hearty, nourishing, nutritious, prosperous, robust, salubrious, salutary, sound, spry, strong, sturdy, trim, vigorous, well, wholesome

healthy and happy: eupeptic

healthy and nourishing: nutritious

healthy condition: verdure

heap: abundance, accumulation, amass, bank, bulk, bundle, burrow, clump, clunker, cluster, collection, congeries, congestion, crowd, dump, gather, gobs, hill, jalopy, jumble, lots, lump, mass, mound, much, multitude, overflowing, pile, plenty, slew, stack, stockpile

hear: attend, catch, consider, detect, discover, eavesdrop, feel, harken, hearken, learn, listen, obey, participate, perceive, permit, receive

hearing: arraignment, audience, audition, auditory, conference, discussion, ear, earshot, examination, inquiry, interview, knowledge, meeting, probe, report, sense, sound, test, trial

hearing-afflicted: deaf

hearing beyond normal perception: clairaudience

hearing due to old age, loss of: presbycusis

hearing or sound, relating to: acoustic

hearing range: earshot

hearing, perceptible to: audible

hearing, relating to: auditory, auricular

hearsay: gossip, grapevine, information, report, rumor, scuttlebutt, talk

heart of the matter: crux

heart-related: cardiac

heart-shaped: cordate, cordiform

heartache: anguish, despair, grief, misery, pain, pang, regret, rue, sadness, sorrow, woe

heartbreak: agony, despair, disappointment, grief, misery, regret, sorrow, suffering

hearten: arouse, cheer, embolden, encourage, energize, inspire, rally, reassure, solace, spirit, stimulate, uplift

heartfelt: ardent, dear, deep, earnest, genuine, honest, profound, real, sincere, true

heartfelt cry: cri de coeur

hearth: brazier, fireplace, fireside, grate, home, house, ingle

heartless: callous, cold, cruel, hard, hopeless, insensitive, mean, merciless, ruthless, uncaring, unfeeling, unsympathetic

heartthrob: beauty, flame, honey, infatuation, sweetheart

hearty: abundant, active, ample, cheerful, cheery, complete, comrade, cordial, devout, eager, earnest, energetic, enthusiastic, firm, hale, hardy, healthy, nourishing, rich, robust, sincere, sound, staunch, strong, substantial, thorough, unequivocal, vigorous, wholesome

hearty repast: square meal

heat: ardor, bake, caloric, chafe, cook, degree, energy, excite, excitement, fever, fire, firearm, gun, hotness, ignite, inflame, intensity, ire, passion, pressure, rage, roast, simmer, steam, stress, temperature, toast, warm, warmness, warmth, zeal

heat and cold sensitivity: thermesthesia

heat and spice a wine or drink: mull

heat by circulation of currents, transfer of: convection

heat by rays, transfer of: radiation

heat energy employed after nuclear fusion: thermonuclear

HEART-RELATED TERMS

abnormally fast heartbeat: palpitation

concerning the heart: cardiac, cordial, coronary

disturbance of heart rhythm: extrasystole

double heartbeat: dicrotic

fast heartbeat: tachycardia

heart attack: coronary thrombosis

heart exam: EKG, electrocardiogram

heart murmur: bruit

heart muscle: myocardium

heart muscle twitching: fibrillation

heart specialist: cardiologist

heart-starting machine: defibrillator

heart wall: paries

heart, in anatomy: cor

heartbeat: force, impulse, pulsation, pulse, throb, tick, time

heartbeat very fast: palpitation, tachycardia

heartburn: cardialgia, indigestion, pyrosis

implanted device regulating heartbeat: pacemaker

irregular heartbeat: arrhythmia, palpitation

normal heartbeat: pulsate

pertaining to heart and blood vessels: cardiovascular

rhythmic contraction of heart: systole

rhythmic relaxation of heart: diastole

slow heartbeat: bradycardia

substance blamed for heart disease: cholesterol

tissue death from obstruction: infarction

weak and irregular heartbeat: fibrillation ❦

---

heat given out when something changes state: latent heat

heat measurement: calorimetry

heat medical therapy: diathermy

heat of earth's interior, concerning: geothermal

heat of female mammals: estrus, rut

heat or calories, measuring: caloric, calorific

heat or light ray bent in transit: refraction

heat-producing: calefacient, calorific, pyrogenic

heat-resisting magnesium: meerschaum

heat through static body or medium, transfer of: conduction

heat treatment of liquids to kill germs: pasteurization

heat, concerning: thermal

heat, oppressive: sweltering

heated: angry, ardent, bitter, emotional, excited, fierce, furious, hot, intense, passionate, sizzling, stormy, vehement, warmed

heated argument: rhubarb

heated dissension: strife

heated dry-air room: sauna

heater: boiler, convector, etna, fastball, furnace, gat, oven, pistol, radiator, stove

heater of ancient Roman house: hypocaust

heater using current circulation: convector

heater using water or steam: radiator

heathen: agnostic, atheist, ethnic, gentile, infidel, nonbeliever, pagan, paynim, skeptic, unconverted

heating and air conditioning control: thermostat

heating and cooling to glass, steel for strengthening: annealing

heating element for cup or tank: immersion heater

heating of earth's atmosphere by solar radiation: greenhouse effect

heating vessel: crucible, etna

heatproof, to make: insulate

heave: bulge, elevate, fling, gag, groan, haul, heft, hoist, hurl, launch, lift, pant, pitch, propel, pull, push, raise, regurgitate, retch, send, throw, toss, utter, vomit

heave in irregular manner: popple

heave or strain to vomit: retch

heaven: above, Abraham's bosom, afterworld, Canaan, Eden, Elysium, empyrean, eternity, ether, firmament, glory, happiness, hereafter, kingdom, nirvana, Olympus, paradise, promised land, Shangri-la, sky, utopia, Valhalla, welkin, Zion

heaven help us: absit omen

heaven, branch of theology dealing with: eschatology

heaven, Virgin Mary's ascent to: Assumption

heavenly: angelic, angelical, beautiful, blissful, celestial, delicious, divine, empyreal, enchanting, ethereal, holy, lovely, lush, pleasant, sacred, supernal, sweet, yummy

heavenly being: angel, archangel, cherub, seraph

heavenly body: celestial body, comet, equant, galaxy, moon, planet, satellite, sphere, star, sun

heavy: afflictive, arduous, beefy, broad, bulky, burdened, burdensome, burly, coarse, complex, complicated, cumbersome, deep, dense, despondent, difficult, doleful, dull, excessive, gloomy, grievous, gross, hard, hearty, hefty, huge, important, inactive, indulgent, intense, laborious, large, leaden, lethargic, lifeless, loud, massive, obese, onerous, oppressive, overcast, overweight, ponderous, popular, pregnant, profound, rough, serious, slow, sluggish, stodgy, strong, thick, villain, weighty

heavy and awkward: cumbersome, ponderous

heavy and clumsy: lumbering

heavy book: tome

heavy breathing, of: labored

heavy cart: dray

heavy club: mace

heavy-handed: awkward, bumbling, bungling, clumsy, harsh, indiscreet, oppressive, tactless

heavy hydrogen: deuterium

heavy or oppressive: onerous

heavy pressure: duress

heavy, stamping folk dance performed while wearing clogs: clog dance

heavyhearted: dejected, depressed, despondent, doleful, melancholy, sad, unhappy

heckle: badger, bait, bother, chaotic, confused, disrupt, embarrass, flushed, frenzied, gibe, harass, hector, hound, jeer, mock, needle, pester, ride, taunt, tease, torment, unsettled, wild

hectic: exciting, fervid, feverish, frantic, restless

hector: badger, bait, bluster, browbeat, bully, dominate, harass, heckle, intimidate, irritate, nag, plague, ride, swagger, tease, torment, worry

hedge: avoid, barrier, beg the question, block, bound, boundary, bush, cage, coop, dodge, enclose, evade, fence, guard, hinder, hurdle, obstacle, obstruct, protect, pussyfoot, separate, sidestep, straddle, surround, waffle

hedge shrub: box, yew

hedge to break force of wind: windbreak

hedge trimming in shapes: topiary

hedgehog, concerning a: erinaceous

hedonist: bon vivant, epicure, libertine, pleasureseeker, rake, sybarite

heed: attend, attention, beware, care, caution, cognizance, concern, consider, diligence, ear, harken, hear, listen, mind, note, notice, obey, observation, observe, reck, regard, remark, respect, study, thought, watch

heedful: advertent, alert, attentive, aware, careful, cautious, considerate, diligent, mindful, observant, wary, watchful

heedless: careless, deaf, disregardful, foolish, hairbrained, impetuous, imprudent, inadvertent, inattentive, incautious, indiscreet, mindless, negligent, oblivious, rash, reckless, regardless, remiss, thoughtless, unaware, unmindful, unobservant, unthinking, unwary

heel: cad, cant, careen, dastard, end, incline, knave, knob, lean, list, oppression, rascal, rogue, scoundrel, slant, swine, tilt, tyranny

heel bone: calcaneus

heel of shoe, high pointed: stiletto

heel of shoe, solid thick: wedge

heel-stamping Spanish flamenco dance: zapateado

heelless slipper: mule

hefty: ample, beefy, big, brawny, bulky, burly, cumbersome, extensive, heavy, husky, massive, powerful, substantial, weighty

hegemony: authority, control, dominance, influence

height: acme, altitude, apex, ceiling, climax, crest, culmination, dimension, elevation, eminence, magnanimity, maximum, peak, pinnacle, stature, summit, zenith

height of aircraft measuring instrument: altimeter

height of land above sea level measuring instrument: orometer

heighten: accent, advance, aggravate, amplify, augment, bolster, boost, elevate, enhance, enrich, expand, increase, intensify, lift, mangify, raise

heights, fear of: acrophobia, cremnophobia, hypsophobia

heinous: abominable, atrocious, awful, crying, detestable, evil, flagrant, grisly, hateful, hideous, horrifying, malicious, monstrous, nefarious, odious, outrageous, shocking, sickening, terrible, unspeakable, wicked

heir: beneficiary, daughter, firstborn, heiress, heritor, inheritor, legatee, offspring, scion, son, successor

heir, as entitled by law: heir presumptive

heir, indefeasible: heir apparent

heir, joint: coparcener, parcener

heir, passing to an: hereditary

heir, to deprive an: disinherit

held or sustained to full value in music: tenuto

helical: spiral

helicopter: aircraft, chopper, eggbeater, gyro, whirlybird

helicopter propeller: rotor

hell: abyss, agony, avernus, Gehenna, Hades, hereafter, holocaust, inferno, misery, netherworld, perdition, pit, purgatory, sheol, suffering, tartarus, tophet, underworld

hell in Vedic mythology: asat

hell, relating to: infernal

Hellene: Greek

hellion: brat, demon, imp

hellish: brutal, detestable, devilish, diabolic, diabolical, dreadful, stygian, unpleasant, vile, wicked

helm: direct, helmet, leadership, steer, tiller, wheel

helmet: basinet, burgonet, casque, crest, galea, head gear, headpiece, heaume, morion, salade, sallet

helmet hinged front: beaver, ventail, visor

helmet plume: panache

helmet, pith: topee, topi

helmetlike structure: casque

help: abet, accommodate, adminicle, advance, advice, aid, alleviate, assist, assistance, avail, back, befriend, benefit, boost, champion, contribute, cooperation, cure, employee, favor, guidance, hand, improve, laborer, lend a hand, lift, ment, promote, relief, relieve, remedy, repair, rescue, SOS, servant, servants, serve, stead, strengthen, succor, support, sustain, treat, worker

help and make easier: expedite, facilitate

help by pleading on another's behalf: intercede

help financially: lend, subsidize

help or support, to call on for: invoke

help, service, or aid: ministration

help, turning to a person or thing for: recourse

helper: abettor, adjutant, aide, ally, apprentice, assistant, associate, benefactor, coadjutant, coadjutor, co-worker, deputy, employee, samaritan, servant, server, striker, subordinate, volunteer

helpful: adjuvant, advantageous, auxiliary, beneficial, caring, considerate, constructive, cooperative, friendly, good, kind, neighborly, practical, supportive, useful, valuable

helpful person: Good Samaritan

helping: adjunct, adjuvant, ancillary, auxiliary, considerate, cooperative, obliging, subsidiary, supplementing

helping and promoting: conducive, contributive

helpless: defenseless, destitute, feeble, forlorn, futile, hopeless, impotent, incapable, incompetent, ineffective, involuntary, lost, numb, powerless, unable, unprotected, vulnerable, weak

helpless, distraught person: basket case

helpless, vulnerable person: sitting duck

helter-skelter: carelessly, confused, disordered, disorderly, flighty, haphazard, hastily, pell-mell, random, turmoil

hem: border, brim, circle, confine, cough, edge, edging, enclose, encompass, environ, fringe, hedge, margin, seam, sew, skirt, surround, trimming

hem in: fence, gird, straiten

hemlock: conium, herb, poison, tree, tsuga

hemp: abaca, ambary, bang, bhang, cannabis, fennel, fiber, flax, hashish, jute, kaif, kef, kif, manila, marijuana, plant, pua, rine, sizal, tow

hemp fiber: oakum

hen, spayed and fattened: poulard, poularde

hen, unconfined: free-range

hen, very young: pullet

hence: accordingly, away, consequently, ergo, leu, onward, since, therefore, thus

henchman: adherent, attendant, bodyguard, criminal, follower, goon, lackey, minion, myrmidon, page, shill, supporter, thug

henchman for dirty deed: hatchet man

henpeck: carp, dominate, harass, nag

herald: announce, bode, broadcast, courier, crier, declare, forerunner, foreshadow, foretell, greet, harbinger, messenger, omen, outrider, proclaim, runner, sign, signal, spokesperson, symbol, trumpet, usher

heraldic blue banner with three fleurs-de-lis: oriflamme

heraldic border: orle

heraldic device above shield in coat of arms: crest

heraldic vertical band through shield: pale

herbage: grass, greens, pasture, vegetation

herbs, seasoning: fines herbes

Herculean: colossal, enormous, giant, gigantic, huge, immense, mammoth, mighty, muscular, powerful, strong, titanic, vast

herd: assemblage, brood, bunch, clan, congregate, crew, crown, drift, drive, drove, flock, gaggle, gang, gather, group, guardian, guide, horde, lead, mob, pack, rabble, shepherd, swarm, tribe

hereafter: afterlife, beyond, eventually, future, heaven, hell, hence, underworld

hereditary: ancestral, congenital, descended, family, genetic, inborn, inherited, innate, lineal

hereditary estate: demesne

hereditary factor: gene

hereditary transmission, laws of: Mendel's laws

hereditary, existing from birth but not: congenital

heredity: ancestry, inheritance, tradition

heredity study to improve humans: eugenics

heredity through DNA: genetic code

heresy: blasphemy, defection, dissent, iconoclasm, infidelity, nonconformity, opinion, schism, unorthodoxy

heresy, tribunal to suppress: Inquisition

heretic: apostate, dissenter, iconoclast, infidel, miscreant, nonconformist, rebel, renegade, schismatic, skeptic, unbeliever

heretic burning at stake: auto-da-fe

heretical: heterodox

heritage: ancestry, birthright, custom, inheritance, legacy, patrimony, tradition

hermetic: airtight, alchemist, mystical, occult, sealed, secret, shut

hermit: anchoress, anchoret, anchorite, ascetic, cookie, eremite, loner, recluse, solitary, stylite

hermitage: abbey, cloister, hideaway, monastery, retreat

HERBS

abscess root	camas	figwort	lungwort
acacia bark	candlenut tree	finochio	lupine
adder's tongue	cannabis	Florence fennel	mandrake
agave	caraway	French tarragon	marijuana
agrimony	cardamom	garlic	marjoram
alecost	carob	ginger	marshmallow
alfalfa	cashew	ginkgo	May apple
alkanet	castor-oil plant	ginseng	mint
allspice	catmint	gnemon tree	monarda
aloe vera	catnip	goat's rue	monkshood
angelica	centella	greater galangal	motherwort
anise	chamomile	guava	mugwort
anise hyssop	charlock	gynura	mullein
arnica	chervil	gypsywort	mustard
arrowroot	chicory	harebell	neem tree
bacopa	cinnamon	heliotrope	nutmeg
balm	clove pink	hemlock	oregano
balsam fir	clover	hemp	oriental ginseng
baobab	coconut palm	hemp nettle	papaya
basil	coleus	henbane	papyrus
bead tree	coltsfoot	herb bennet	parsley
belladonna	columbine	herb Paris	parsnip
bergamot	comfrey	horehound	pennyroyal
betel nut palm	common alder	horse chestnut	peppermint
betony	comomile	horsemint	perilla
big love medicine	coriander	horseradish	pineapple
birthwort	corydalis	hound's-tongue	pink mempat
bistort	cow parsnip	houseleek	pleurisy root
bitter orange	cowbane	hyssop	pokeweed
bitterroot	Cretan dittany	jackfruit	polpala
black cohosh	cumin	Jacob's ladder	quince
black tea tree	datura	java almond	rattlesnake weed
bladderwort	deadly nightshade	kapok	rock samphire
blood root	death camas	kra chaai	rosemary
blue curls	dill	lady's mantle	rudbeckia
boneset	dittany	lady's smock	rue
borage	dropwort	large-flowered cala-	sacred lotus
buckthorn	durian	mint	safflower
bugle	dyer's chamomile	lawn daisy	sage
bugleweed	echinacea	leadwort	Saint John's wort
burdock	elecampane	lemon balm	salvia
butterbur	elephant apple	lespedeza	samphire
butterwort	eucalyptus	licorice	sanicle
button snakeroot	fennel	lipstick tree	savory
calamint	fenugreek	liverwort	self-heal
calendula	feverroot	lovage	sesame

sickle hare's ear
silverweed
smallage
soapwort
sorrel
soursop
southernwood
spearmint
spiderwort
star anise
star fruit
strawberry tree
sugar maple
sugar palm
sweet basil
sweet bay
sweet chestnut
sweet cicely
sweet flag
sweet vernal grass
sweet woodruff
tamarack
tansy
tarragon
tea bush
teasel
thyme
tobacco
turmeric
wall rue
water hemlock
wild amaranth
wild bergamot
wild ginger
wild marjoram
wintergreen
wood sorrel
woodruff
wormwood
woundwort
yarrow
yellow locust 🐛

hernia supportive device: truss

hernia with part of stomach pushing through diaphragm: hiatal hernia, hiatus hernia

hero: ace, actor, celebrity, champion, conqueror, demigod, heroine, idol, leading man, legend, male, martyr, paladin, protagonist, star

hero in literary work: protagonist

hero sandwich: grinder, sub

heroes in field of endeavor: pantheon

heroic: bold, brave, colossal, courageous, daring, enormous, epic, extreme, fearless, gallant, great, gutsy, illustrious, intrepid, lionhearted, magnanimous, mighty, mythological, noble, outstanding, unafraid, valiant

heroic narrative: saga

heroic poem: epic, epos, ode

heroin: drug, fix, H, horse, junk, narcotic, scag, smack

heroine: ace, actress, celebrity, champion, conqueror, demigoddess, female, idol, leading lady, legend, myrtyr, protagonist, star

heroism: bravery, chivalry, courage, gallantry, intrepidity, nobility, valor

heron kin: egret, ibis

herring: shad, sprat

hesitant: afraid, chary, halting, indecisive, irresolute, loath, reluctant, shy, skeptical, tentative, uncertain, unsure, vacillating, waiting, wavering

hesitant and jerking: faltering, halting

hesitate: avoid, balk, dally, delay, demur, doubt, equivocate, falter, flounder, hedge, pause, procrastinate, pussyfoot, sidestep, stall, stammer, straddle, vacillate, waffle, wait, waver

hesitate and postpone: delay, procrastinate, put off

hesitate on principle or because of conscience: scruple

hesitate to do: pussyfoot, shilly-shally

hesitate to speak: hem and haw

hesitating: irresolute

heterogeneous: assorted, different, dissimilar, diverse, miscellaneous, mixed, motley, piebald, varied

hew: axe, carve, chip, chop, cleave, cut, fashion, fell, hack, hold, prune, shape, strike, stroke

hex: bewitch, curse, evil eye, jinx, spell, voodoo, whammy

hiatus: aperture, break, gap, interim, interruption, interval, lacuna, lull, opening, pause, time off

hibernate: dormant, hide, inactive, sleep, torpid, vegetate

hibernation in summer: estivation

hiccup: singultus

hick: bumpkin, gullible, jake, provincial, rube, rustic, unsophisticated, yokel

hickey-giving: dermagraphism, love bites, passion purpura

hidden: abstruse, arcane, buried, clandestine, cloistered, concealed, covered, covert, cryptic, esoteric, invisible, latent, masked, mysterious, obscure, perdu, profound, recluse, recondite, secluded, secret, shrouded, undetected, undisclosed, unseen, veiled

hidden and secret: clandestine, covert, furtive, subterranean, surreptitious

hidden place: hermitage, recess, retreat

hidden resource: ace in the hole

hidden stage, in: latent

hidden store of something: cache, hoard, stash

hidden, half-: imperceptible, indistinct, obscured, unobtrusive

hidden, secret, and mystical: arcane, esoteric, occult

hide: abscond, bury, cache, camouflage, cloak, conceal, cover, disguise, ditch, duck, eclipse, harbor, mask, palliate, protect, screen, secrete, shroud, smuggle, stash, stow, suppress, take cover, veil, withhold; camouflage, cloak, coat, cover, leather, pelt, shroud, skin

hide and lie in wait: lurk, skulk

hide away safely: closet, ensconce, stash

hide onboard vehicle: stowaway

hide or cover with drape: enshroud, mantle

hide or disguise: dissemble

hide or mask: veil

hide or obscure: camouflage

hideaway: den, escape, hermitage, hideout, lair, nest, refuge, retreat, secluded

hideous: abominable, appalling, awful, detestable, dreadful, ghastly, grim, grisly, grotesque, gruesome, horrendous, horrible, loathsome, macabre, monstrous, nasty, revolting, shocking, sick, terrible, terrifying, ugly

hideous being: ogre

hideout: cave, covert, den, haven, hermitage, hideaway, lair, refuge, retreat, sanctuary, shelter

hides, person who: hermit, recluse

hie: expedite, haste, hasten, hurry, rush, scurry, speed

hierarchical system: totem pole

hieroglyphics' decipherment key: Rosetta stone

hieroglyphics' oblong frame: cartouche

hieroglyphics, cursive style of: hieratic

hieroglyphics, simplified style of: demotic

high: acute, admirable, advanced, alpine, cheerful, chief, costly, crucial, dear, elevated, eminent, euphoric, exalted, expensive, extending, favorable, foremost, grand, important, intoxicated, lofty, luxurious, main, malodorous, noble, piercing, prominent, psyched, raised, remote, sharp, shrill, soaring, steep, stoned, tall, towering, tumultuous, violent

high-altitude measuring device: sonde

high and dry: helpless, marooned, stranded

high and harsh in sound: strident

high and impressive: commanding, imposing, soaring, towering

high and level land formation: plateau

high-and-mighty: arrogant, conceited, imperious, lordly, overbearing, pompous, superior, vain

high class: elite

high clear sound: ting

high degree: nth

high dudgeon: ire, rage, wrath

high fashion: haute couture

high-handed: arbitrary, arch, arrogant, bossy, domineering, lordly, oppressive, overbearing

high-hat: aristocratic, condescending, haughty, la-di-da, snobbish, supercilious

high in degree, altitude, rank: elevated, lofty

high in pitch: alt

high in rank: august

high inaccessible place: aerie

high jinks: antics, pranks, rowdiness

high-minded: ethical, generous, honest, honorable, magnanimous, moral, noble, principled, righteous

high mountain: alp

high-pitched: acute, clarion, piercing, shrieky, shrill, treble

high plateau: mesa, puna

high platform raised by truck: cherry picker

high point: acme, apex, apogee, climax, meridian, peak, pinnacle, summit, vertex, zenith

high point in intensity: climax, culmination

high point in life: peak experience

high-pressure: aggressive, compelling, forceful, insistent, persistent

high-priced: costly, dear, exorbitant, expensive, precious

high-ranking person: dignitary, grandee, magnifico

high society: beau monde, elite, haute monde, upper crust

high-spirited: effervescent, exuberant, fiery, gallant, jolly, lively, merry, peppery, pert, vivacious

high spirits: élan, joie de vivre, zip

high-strung: edgy, excitable, hyper, jittery, jumpy, nervous, restless, stressed, taut, tense, uneasy, uptight, wired

high voice: falsetto

high-wire acrobat: aerialist, equilibrist, funambulist

high, craggy hill: tor

highborn: noble

highbrow: Brahmin, cultured, egghead, intellectual, scholarly

higher education: tertiary education
higher in status: superior, superordinate
highest female voice: soprano
highest honors at graduation: summa cum laude
highest in quality, degree: gilt-edged, paramount, superlative
highest male and lowest female voice: alto
highest point: acme, apex, apogee, capstone, culmination, meridian, ne plus ultra, pinnacle, solstice, tip top, zenith
highest rank or level: apotheosis
highfalutin: aureate, euphuistic, florid, grandiloquent, magniloquent, rhetorical, tumid
highlight: climax, emphasize, feature, focus, play up, stress
highway: artery, boulevard, causeway, course, expressway, freeway, interstate, parkway, path, pike, road, street, thoroughfare, thruway, turnpike
highway access: ramp
highway around a city or metropolitan area: beltway
highway interchange with overpass and curved ramps: cloverleaf
highway, German: autobahn
highwayman: bandit, brigand, criminal, crook, desperado, outlaw, rider, robber, thief
hike: backpack, boost, increase, journey, march, raise, ramble, snap, tour, traipse, travel, trek, trip, walk
hilarious: amusing, comical, entertaining, funny, humorous, jocular, jovial, ludicrous, merry
hilarity: cheer, comedy, gaiety, glee, happiness, hysteria, joviality, laughter, merriment, mirth
hill: acclivity, ascent, bank, bluff, brae, butte, cliff, cover, dune, elevation, eminence, fell, heap, highland, hillock, hogback, holt, incline, kame, knob, knoll, mesa, morro, mound, mountain, pile, slope, tor
hill formed by glacial drift: drumlin, esker, kame, os
hill runoff: rill
hill with flat top, steep sides: butte, mesa
hill with steeply sloping sides: hogback
hill, rocky: tor
hill, rocky debris at foot of: scree, talus

hill, small rounded: holt, knoll, hummock
hillock: hill, hummock, knob, knoll, morro, mound, tuffet
hillside hollow as shelter: abri
Himalayan guide: sherpa
Himalayan holy man: lama
Himalayan legend: yeti
hinder: arrest, bar, block, burden, check, choke, clog, cramp, crimp, curb, dam, debar, delay, deprive, detain, deter, embarrass, encumber, foreclose, forestall, frustrate, hamper, hamstring, handcuff, handicap, harass, impede, inhibit, interfere, obstruct, prevent, prohibit, restrain, restrict, retard, slow, stall, stifle, stop, straitjacket, stymie, tie down, trammel
hinder by delaying tactics: stonewall
hinder by long speech: filibuster
hinder, in law: estop
hinder plans: baffle, discomfit, foil, frustrate, stymie, thwart
hinder progress: delay, retard
hinder rather than serve purpose, tending to: counterproductive
hindmost: concluding, final, last, rear
hindquarters of animal: haunches, rump
hindrance: barrier, block, check, clog, curb, delay, deterrent, difficulty, drawback, handicap, hitch, impediment, interference, interruption, liability, limitation, obstacle, obstruction, restraint, snag, stop, stumbling block, trammel
hinge: axis, contingent, depend, elbow, hang, joint, link, mount, pin, pivot, rest, stand, turn
hint: advice, allude, catchword, clue, cue, forewarn, help, imply, indication, infer, inkling, innuendo, insinuate, insinuation, intimation, mention, moment, notion, overtone, reminder, suggestion, tinge, tip, touch, trace, warn, whiff
hint at: adumbrate, foreshadow, imply, inkle, intimate, signify
hint of something: inkling, notion, smack, soupçon, trace
hint or passing mention: allusion
hint, to: intimate
hint, usually derogatory: innuendo
hint, veiled and possibly offensive: aspersion, imputation, innuendo, insinuation
hip: aware, cognizant, coxa, fashion-

able, groovy, haunch, huckle, knowledgeable, loins, modern, onto, pelvis, stylish, wise
hipbone: coxa, ilia, innominate bone
hipbone socket: acetabulum
hippie: beatnik, Bohemian, longhair, rebel
hippodrome: arena, coliseum, stadium
ho-hum routine: rut
hobnob: associate, fraternize, mingle, mix
hobo: beggar, bum, drifter, migrant, tramp, vagabond, vagrant, wanderer
hockey championship: Stanley Cup
hockey enclosure for violators of rules: penalty box
hockey feint: deke
hockey foul for entry into zone ahead of puck: offside
hockey foul touching with stick held in both hands: cross-check
hockey goal: cage, net
hockey movement hitting puck in light taps: dribble
hockey pass, deceptive, to trailing teammate: drop pass
hockey rink rectangle in front of goal: crease, goal crease
hockey score: goal
hockey shot: slap
hockey starting play: face-off
hockey substitution without timeout: changing on the fly
hocus-pocus: abracadabra, cheat, chicanery, deception, delusion, flimflam, foolishness, juggler, legerdemain, magic, spell, trickery, trickster, wizardry
hodgepodge: combination, gallimaufrey, hash, hotchpotch, jumble, katzenjammer, medley, mélange, mess, miscellany, mishmash, mixture, olio, potpourri, salmagundi, stew
hog: barrow, boar, boschvark, glutton, motorcycle, pig, razorback, sheep, sow, swine
hog fat: lard
hog-tie: curb, disrupt, fetter, hamper, impede, rope, shackle
hoggish or swinish: porcine
hogshead: barrel, cask, drum, keg, vat, vessel
hogwash: baloney, bull, bunk, nonsense, poppycock, rubbish, slop, swill
hoi polloi: dregs, masses, mob, populace, rabble, riffraff, the common people, the masses, the multitude

HINDU TERMS

chant: mantra
clothing: jama, jamah, saree, sari
god of chaos: Vritra
god of creation: Brahma
god of crops: Soma
god of disease: Rudra
god of fire: Agni
god of journeys: Pusan
god of knowledge: Surya
god of love: Krishna
god of luck: Ganesha
god of monkeys: Hanuman
god of music: Narada
god of order, sea, and sky: Varuna
god of plague: Hardaul
god of rain and thunder: Indra
god of snakes: Manasa
god of support: Dhara
god of the destructor and restorer of the world: Shiva
god of the moon: Candra
god of the protection and preservation of the world: Vishnu
god of the sun: Dhatar, Surya, Vivasvan
god of victory: Vijaya
god of war, weather: Indra
goddess of beauty: Lakshmi
goddess of brightness: Dipti
goddess of desire: Candika

goddess of destruction: Kali
goddess of disease: Malhal Mata
goddess of fertility: Parvati
goddess of fortune: Abhijit
goddess of justice: Dharma
goddess of misfortune: Ardra
goddess of moonlight: Kaumudi
goddess of plague: Didi Thakrun
goddess of power: Kali
goddess of sacrifice: Hotra
goddess of success: Siddhi
goddess of war: Durga
goddess of wealth: Lakshmi
goddess of wrath: Indrani
Hindu class structure: caste
Hindu sacred literature: veda
Hindu title: baboo, sahib, sri
languages: Hindi, Hindustani, Pali, Sanskrit, Tamil, Urdu
loin cloth: dhoti
mystic: swami
nobleman: maharaja, maharajah, raja, rajah
pilgrimage center: puri
prince: rana
princess: ranee, rani
salutation: namaste
soul: atman ☙

---

hoist: boost, crane, davit, derrick, elevate, heave, jack, lift, raise, setup, uplift, winch, windlass

hoity-toity: arrogant, dizzy, flighty, giddy, partronizing, pompous, pretentious, silliness, snooty, thoughtless

hold: adhere, arrest, bear, behold, bind, brace, carry, catch, clasp, clench, clinch, cling, clutch, consider, contain, continue, control, defend, detain, embrace, entertain, feel, fill, function, grasp, grip, guard, harbor, have, hook, influence, interest, keep, leverage, maintain, mesmerize, occupy, own, pause, possession, postpone, preserve, pull, rely, remain, retain, rivet, spellbind, stay, steady, support, suppress, sustain

hold back: abstain, check, constrain, contain, curb, dam, detain, deter, inhibit, refrain, rein, repress, restrain, stall, stay, stem, stop

hold fast: clinch, cling, cohere, secure, stick

hold forth: bloviate, continue, descant, discuss, exhibit, expound, maintain, orate, talk

hold off: avert, defer, delay, postpone, refrain, repel, stay, stop, suppress

hold on: cling, continue, persist, wait

hold out: continue, endure, last, refuse, tender

hold someone's arms: pinion

hold spellbound: enthrall

hold sway: reign, rule

hold up: boost, burglarize, check, cope, delay, detain, endure, halt, impede, interrupt, laten, lift, manage, obstruct, postpone, prop, raise, rob, robbery, stay, support, sustain

holding of money or property by third property temporarily: escrow

holding, property or term of office: tenure

holdings: assets, capital, estate, land, property, stocks

hole: abyss, aperture, brig, burrow, cave, cavern, cavity, chamber, chasm, cove, cranny, crater, deep, defect, depression, difficulty, dump, dungeon, excavation, fault, fix, flaw, gap, grotto, hollow, inlet, jail, jam, leak, mess, mine, niche, nook, opening, orifice, passage, perforation, pit, pocket, predicament, prison, recess, rent, shaft, slot, tunnel, vacuum, vent, void

hole for fumes, gas, liquid to pass through: vent

hole-in-the-wall: dive

hole or pit for collecting water: sump

hole-punching tool: awl

hole, small: perforation

hole, to enlarge or shape: ream

hole, to hollow out: excavate

holes in a ship, make: scuttle

holes, to pierce with: riddle

holiday: celebration, feast, festival, festive, fete, fiesta, gala, holy day, leave, liberty, merry, outing, vacation

holiday spent similarly to work life: busman's holiday

holier-than-thou: sanctimonious

holiest part of sacred place: sanctuary

holiness: blessedness, consecration, devotion, divinity, faith, godliness, piety, reverence, righteousness, saintliness, sanctity, sanctuary, unction

holiness, feigning: pietistic, sanctimonious, unctuous

holler: bellow, complain, gripe, protest, shout, yell

hollow: alcove, alveolus, basin, cave, cavern, cavernous, cavity, chamber, chase, concave, cove, crater, cupped, curved, deceitful, deep, den, dent, depressed, depression, dip, empty, faithless, false, ghostly, glen, groove, hole, meaningless, muffled, pit, pocket, pointless, resounding, scoop, sepulchral, sinus, socket, specious, sunken, thunderous, unsound, vacant, vain, valley, void, worthless

hollow in wall for item: niche

hollow or cavity of body: sinus

hollow stone: geode

hollow, small: indentation, recess

hollowed-out recess: cavern, grotto

holly bush: ilex

hollyhock: althaea

Hollywood: Tinseltown

Hollywood light: kleig

holocaust: carnage, destruction, disaster, fire, genocide, inferno, massacre, sacrifice, slaughter

holy: angelic, blessed, blissful, consecrated, devine, devoted, devout, hallowed, immaculate, inviolable, moral, perfect, pious, religious, revered, reverent, sacral, sacred, sacrosanct, sainted, saintly, sanctimonious, sanctuary, spiritual, venerated

Holy Communion: Eucharist, sacrament, viaticum

Holy Communion bread plate: paten

Holy Communion close to death: viaticum

Holy Communion wafer plate: pyx

Holy Communion's bread dipped in wine: intinction

holy image: icon

holy men, government by: hagiarchy, hagiocracy

holy objects' repository: reliquary

holy of holies: sanctum sanctorum

holy oil: chrism

Holy One: Allah, Christ, God, Jehovah, Jesus, Messiah, Mohammed

holy person: saint

holy person who begs: mendicant

holy place: sanctuary

holy place of saint: shrine

holy place, spoiling or destruction of: desecration, profanation, sacrilege, violation

holy war of Christians: crusade

holy war of Muslims: jihad

holy water basin: aspersorium, font, stoup

holy water sprinkler: aspergillum

holy, make or declare: consecrate, sanctify

holy, to regard as: hallow, revere, venerate

homage: admiration, adoration, devotion, esteem, honor, loyalty, obeisance, ovation, praise, regard, respect, reverence, tribute, veneration

hombre: fellow, man, ombre

home: abode, address, apartment, asylum, birthplace, bungalow, castle, condominium, den, domestic, domicile, dwelling, estate, family, farm, habitat, habitation, haunt, house, neighborhood, nest, orphanage, residence, village

homeland, person from one's: compatriot

homeland, to give up or be driven from one's: emigrant, exile, expatriate

homeland, to return someone to their: repatriate

homeless: nomadic

homeless person, due to homeland war or upheaval: displaced person

homeless wanderer: vagabond, vagrant, waif

homeless woman: bag lady

homeless youngster: gamin

homely: comfortable, cozy, domestic, familiar, friendly, homey, intimate, kindly, natural, ordinary, plain, simple, ugly, unpretentious, unsightly

homemade goods business: cottage industry

homeopathy, opposite of: allopathy

homes for pet lizards, snakes, etc.: terraria

homespun: coarse, folksy, handwoven, modest, plain, simple, unpretentious

homicide: assassination, killing, manslaughter, murder

homily: assembly, discourse, exhortation, lecture, oration, sermon, talk

homogeneous: alike, comparable, compatible, consistent, equal, same, similar, solid, uniform

honcho: boss, chief, head man, leader, manager, top dog

hone: edge, hanker, moan, sharpen, smooth, tool, whetstone, whine, yearn

honest: aboveboard, bona fide, candid, chaste, conscientious, creditable, decent, equitable, ethical, fair, faithful, forthright, frank, genuine, honorable, just, legitimate, open, plain, plain-dealing, proper, reliable, repu-

table, respectable, rightful, scrupulous, sincere, square, straight, straightforward, trustworthy, truthful, upright, veracious, virtuous

honesty: decency, equity, fairness, fidelity, goodness, honor, integrity, justice, loyalty, probity, rectitude, soundness, uprightness, veracity, virtue

honey: darling, dear, dearie, deary, fine, flattery, nectar, precious, sweet, sweetheart, sweetness

honey and water, drink of fermented: mead

honey in pharmacy: mel

honey types: comb, eucalyptus, extracted, goldenrod, mountain, sage, sycamore, wild

honey, liquid used by bees for making: nectar

honeycomb pattern embroidery: smocking

honeycomb unit: cell

honeycombed: alveolate, faveolate

honeyed: charming, dulcet, ingratiating, melleous, sugary, sweet

honeysuckle: azalea, columbine, plant, shrub, trumpet flower, vine

honky-tonk: bar, dive, music, nightclub, tawdry

honor: accolade, adore, award, celebrate, character, commendation, courage, credit, decoration, deference, dignify, dignity, distinction, ennoble, esteem, exalt, fame, fete, glorify, glory, homage, honesty, integrity, kudos, laud, laurels, obeisance, praise, recognition, regard, reputation, respect, revere, reverence, tribute, trust, worship

honor or distinction, worthy of: laureate

honor or respect shown homage: reverence, tribute

honor or tribute: testimonial

honor or virtue: integrity, probity, rectitude

honor proportionate to owned property: timocracy

honor the memory of with ceremony: commemorate

honor with feast, festival, etc.: fete, lionize

honor, challenge or attack someone's: discredit, impeach, impugn

honor, to present an: bestow, confer

honor, to regard with: beatify, exalt, hallow, reverence, venerate

honorable: admirable, commendable,

creditable, elevated, ethical, honest, illustrious, just, moral, noble, reputable, respectable, sterling, title, upright, worthy

honorable behavior of persons of high rank: noblesse oblige

honorarium: compensation, gratuity, payment, reward, tip

honors, graduate with: cum laude

hoo-ha: row, stir, to-do

hood: almuce, blind, bonnet, canopy, cap, chapel, chaperon, cloak, coif, cover, covering, cowl, hat, helmet, hide, mask, scarf, tippet, top

hood-shaped: cucullate, hooded

hoodlum: bully, criminal, crook, delinquent, gangster, goon, gorilla, hooligan, mobster, punk, rowdy, ruffian, thug

hoodwink: bamboozle, blindfold, bluff, cheat, con, cozen, deceive, delude, dupe, fool, mislead, rook, seel, swindle, trick

hoof: cleft, cloven, foot, paw, tramp, unguis, ungula

hoof, to: dance, walk

hoof divided in two, of a: bisulcate, cleft, cloven

hoof sound: clop

hoof, claw, nail: unguis

hoofed mammal: tapir, ungulate

hoofer: chorine, dancer

hook: anchor, angle, arc, bend, crotchet, curve, fastener, gaff, hitch, hold, link, lock; captivate, capture, catch, enticement, net, pilfer, snare, steal, trap

hook from fish after catching, remove: disgorge

hook on pole, large iron: gaff

hook-shaped: unciform

hooked: addicted, aquiline, bent, compelled, devoted, hamate, unciform

hooked anchor: grapnel

hooked like eagle's beak: aquiline

hooked, as a beak: adunc

hookey player: truant

hooligan: bully, delinquent, hood, hoodlum, punk, ruffian

hoop: band, basket, circle, circlet, circumference, clasp, encircle, ring, surround, wicket

hoop in skirt: farthingale

hoop toy: hula hoop

hoopla: excitement, hype, publicity

hoot: boo, criticize, hiss, howl, jeer, raspberry, razz, shout, sound, taunt, utter, whoop, yowl

Hoover Dam's lake: Mead

hop: bounce, flight, gambol, hitch, hobble, jump, leap, limp, move, skip, spring, trip, vine; ball, dance, prom

hope: ambition, anticipation, aspiration, aspire, belief, bob, desire, dream, expect, faith, longing, optimism, prospect, reliance, trust, want, wish

hopeful: auspicious, budding, bullish, buoyant, cheerful, confident, encouraging, enthusiastic, expectant, optimistic, promising, sanguine, upbeat

hopeless: crushed, depressed, despairing, desperate, despondent, disconsolate, downcast, forlorn, futile, gloomy, impossible, incorrigible, incurable, ineffectual, irredeemable, pessimistic, pointless, sunk, useless, vain

horde: army, clan, crowd, drove, gang, gathering, group, multitude, pack, swarm, throng, tribe

horizon: border, edge, future, outlook, prospect, purview, reach, realm, skyline, sphere

horizontal: endwise, flat, flush, level, parallel, plane, prone

horizontal beam in building: stringer, summer

horizontal beam in window, door: lintel, summer, transom

horizontal movement: yaw

hormone: ACTH, adrenaline, autacoid, auxin, cortisone, estrone, insulin, steroid

hormone of females: estrogen

hormone of males: androgen, androsterone, testosterone

hormone regulating blood sugar: insulin

hormone regulating pulse and blood pressure: adrenaline, epinephrine

hormone taken by some bodybuilders, athletes: anabolic steroid, steroid

hormone that regulates metabolism of carbohydrates and fats: insulin

hormone used to treat allergies, arthritis: cortisone

horn: antenna, antler, cornucopia, protuberance, spike, tusk; bugle, clarinet, cornet, instrument, saxophone, siren, trombone, trumpet, tuba

horn filled with fruit, vegetables: cornucopia, horn of plenty

horn on older cars, loud electric: klaxon

horn-shaped: cornute

horn, fanfare on: tantara, tantivy

horn, to pierce or stab with: gore

hornets or wasps, group of: colony, vespiary

hornless animal: pollard

hornlike: ceratoid, corneous, horny

horns, having: corniculate, cornute

horns, having hollow: cavicorn

hornswoggle: bamboozle, cheat, deceive, dupe, fool, snow, swindle, trick

horny: calloused, ceratoid, hard, tough

horny plate: scute

horny prominence in horse hoof: frog

horoscope division: cusp

horrible: appalling, atrocius, awful, cruel, despicable, detestable, dreadful, fearful, ghastly, grim, grisly, gruesome, harrowing, heinous, hideous, horrendous, horrid, horrific, loathsome, mean, nasty, obnoxious, repulsive, revolting, shocking, terrible, ugly, unbearable, ungodly, unpleasant, unspeakable, vile

horrible and hateful: abominable, horrendous, loathsome, unspeakable

horrible to endure: harrowing

horrify: alarm, appal, appall, dismay, frighten, scare, shock

horripilation: goosebumps

horror: abhorrence, abomination, alarm, aversion, disagreeable, disgust, dislike, dread, fear, fright, hatred, panic, repugnance, revulsion, terror, trepidation, unpleasant

horror, to draw back in: recoil

hors d'oeuvre: antipasto, appetizer, canapé, caviar, crudités, dip, food, pâté, relish, tapas

hors d'oeuvre of raw vegetables: crudités

horsemen symbolizing pestilence, war, famine, death: Four Horsemen of the Apocalypse

horseplay: buffoonery, clowning, roughhousing

horseshoe-shaped: hippocrepiform

horticultural talent: green thumb

horticulture: agriculture, farming, floriculture, gardening

hose: breeches, drench, hosiery, sock, stockings, tights, tube, wash, water

hose measure: denier

hosiery thread: lisle

hospitable: charitable, cooperative, cordial, courteous, friendly, gracious, gregarious, kind, neighborly, receptive, sociable, warm

HORSE TERMS

boarding shelter: livery stable
brownish or brownish orange horse: sorrel
castrated horse: gelding
castrated male horse: gelding
circular movement of horse: volt
command to horse to turn left: haw
command to horse to turn right: gee
concerning a horse: hippic
draft horse: aiver, aver, Clydesdale
feed: mash, oats
feeder: nose bag
female donkey and male horse: hinny
female foal horse: filly
female parent: dam
golden or tan horse with lighter tail and mane: palomino
groom: saddler
groom a horse, to: curry
hair on neck: mane
half man and half horse: centaur
having hooves, as a horse: ungulate
heavy horse with brushlike pasterns, fetlocks: Clydesdale
horny wedge in horse hoof: frog
horse: bronc, bronco, caballo, cavallo, cavalry, charger, clipper, colt, courser, draft, equine, filly, foal, gee, gelding, hack, hackney, hobby, jade, mare, mount, mustang, nag, pacer, palomino, pinto, plug, pony, prad, roan, saddler, sheltie, sire, sleeper, stallion, steed, stepper, stud, trotter
horse ancestor: eohippus
horse blanket: manta
horse breeds: Arab, Arabian, Barb, Belgian, Clydesdale, Galloway, Hunter, Morgan, Normandy, Nubian, Percheron, Shetland, Shire, Suffolk, Tarpan
horse colors: bay, calico, chestnut, dapple, dun, morel, palomino, piebald, pied, pinto, roan, schimmel, sorrel
horse comb: currycomb
horse-drawn two-wheeled vehicle for one: sulky
horse enclosure: corral, paddock
horse equipment: bit, blinder, harness, longe, rein, saddle, sidesaddle, tack
horse farm: dobbin
horse genus: equus
horse hoof: coffin
horse less than year old: foal
horse lover: hippophile
horse measure: hand
horse thief: rustler
horse urine: stale
horse used as a lead pony: pinto
horse with gray or white in coloring: roan
horseback riding: equitation
horseman: buckaroo, caballero, cavalier, cowboy, equestrian, equestrienne, gaucho, jockey, knight, rider, roughrider
horseman of Russia: cossack
horsemanship: equitation, manege, riding

horsemanship competition: gymkhana
horsemanship jump: capriole, curvet
horsemanship movements: dressage
horsemanship side walk: volt
horsemanship trotting slowly in place: piaffe
horsemanship turn: caracole, pirouette
horsemanship, pertaining to: equestrian
horses' ankles: hocks
horses at inn, tender to: hostler, ostler
horse's gait: amble, canter, gallop, lope, pace, rack, run, trot, vott, walk
horses, oxen in pair: span
horseshoe maker: blacksmith, smithy
horseshoe spur: calk
horseshoer: blacksmith, farrier
hybrid of male horse and female donkey: hinny
left front horse rider in front of coach: postilion
male horse: colt, entire, gelding, stallion, stud
male horse under four years old: colt, foal
male parent: sire
mature female horse: mare
mature male horse: stallion
movements of trained horse: manege
old horse: hack, jade, nag
ornamental covering for horse: caparison, trappings
pertaining to horse: equine
race across open country or obstacle course: steeplechase
race informant, bet taker: tout
race term for weight carried in handicap race: impost
race track: hippodrome
race with competitors selected well in advance: futurity
race with one starter: walkover
reddish horse with white or gray hairs: roan
rising and falling of rider in saddle: post
rope or halter restricting horse: tether
rope or strap to lead or secure: halter
saddle for second rider: pillion
saddle horse: Appaloosa, cob, English, mount, palfrey
section connecting hindquarters to forequarters: coupling
shelter: stable
small compact horse: sheltie, shelty, Shetland pony
small horse: bidet, cayuse, cob, galloway, garron, genet, nag, pony, Shetland, tit
spirited horse: steed
spotted or patched with white horse: skewbald
spotted or patched with white on black horse: piebald, pinto
stocky short-legged horse: cob
strap binding saddle, blanket, or pack to horse: surcingle
striking a hind foot against a forefoot as a horse: overreach
stumble and go lame as a horse, to: founder
training horse to do complex maneuvers: dressage
troops on horseback: cavalry
trot with legs high: piaffer
uncastrated male horse: entire, stallion

useless and worn-out horse: rip
war horse: charger, courser, destrier, steed
white spot on horse forehead: blaze, star
wild horse: bronco, brumby, mustang, tarpan
wild or semiwild horse of America: bronco, mustang
young horse: colt, filly, foal, yearling

Horse Racing Vocabulary
accumulator
across the board
added money
also-ran
antepost bet
at the post
back stretch
bell
blind bet
blinders
bookie
boxed-out
break away
break stride
daily double
double
each way
exacta
fast track
favorite
feature race
finish line
forecast
form
handicap
hedge
home stretch
jockey
left at the post
long odds
long shot
maiden
mudder
nap
neck-and-neck
nose
nursery stakes
odds
odds on
pacer
pari-mutuel
parlay
perfecta
photo finish
place
point-to-point
post

post time
pulling
quarter horse
quirt
racing form
rail
ringer
scratched
short odds
show
silks
stable
stake
starting price
steeplechase
steward
straightaway
stretch
string
thoroughbred
ticktack
tipster
totalizator
tote
trifecta
Triple Crown
turf
turn
win
winner's circle
wire

Horsemanship Vocabulary
aids
balk
canter
capriole
caracole
cavaletto
cavesson
cues
currying
curvet
dressage
equestrianism
equestrianship
gait
gambado
hand
haute école
jib
leap
levade
lunging rein
manège

HORSE TERMS *continued*

martingale
oxer
passage
piaffe
prance
puissance
rack
singlefoot
tack
tittup
trot
volt ☙

hospital: clinic, hospice, infirmary, institution, lazaretto, sanatorium, sickbay
hospital attendant: orderly
hospital for contagious disease: lazaretto
hospital or clinic: infirmary
hospital or hospital area for terminally ill: hospice
hospital section with medical supplies: dispensary
hospital stretcher with wheels: gurney
hospital unit for gravely ill: intensive-care unit
hospital young nursing aide: candy striper
hospitality: amicability, cordiality, friendliness, gemutlichkeit, warmth, welcome
hospitality, pertaining to: xenial
hospital's equipment: armamentarium
host: army, assemblage, company, crowd, emcee, entertainer, flock, guest, horde, hostess, innkeeper, interviewer, landlord, legion, maître d', manager, multitude, myriad, owner, proprietor, sparrows, swarm, throng
hostage: captive, guarantee, pawn, prisoner, security
hostage beginning to identify with or like captor: Stockholm syndrome
hostel: caravansary, hotel, inn, lodge, shelter
hostile: adverse, antagonistic, belligerent, bitter, contentious, contrary, dissonant, enemy, hateful, incongruous, inimical, malevolent, mean, militant, opposed, rebellious, sour, unfriendly, venomous, vicious, warlike
hostile and bitter: malevolent, rancorous, virulent

hostile and eager to fight: aggressive, bellicose, belligerent, combative
hostile and opposed: antagonistic, antipathetic, averse, implacable, inimical, irreconcilable, oppugnant
hostile and unruly: truculent
hostile behavior: animus, bad blood, bellicosity, enmity, ill feeling
hostile groups, divide into: polarize
hostile one: foe
hostile reaction: backlash
hostile subversive organization: fifth column
hostile to prefix: anti-
hostility: aggression, animosity, animus, antagonism, antipathy, argument, bitterness, clash, enmity, feud, fighting, friction, hatred, ill will, open opposition, opposition, rancor, resentment, resistance, unfriendliness, war, warfare
hostility, deep: animosity, animus, antipathy, aversion, enmity
hostility, of becoming subject to another's: incur
hot: angry, ardent, aroused, attractive, biting, blazing, blistering, boiling, burning, eager, erotic, excitable, excited, fervent, fervid, fiery, glowing, heated, intense, lustful, passionate, peppery, piping, popular, pungent, raging, scalding, sizzling, spicy, stolen, strong, sultry, sweltering, torrid, trendy, tropical, vehement, violent, warm
hot-air bath: sauna
hot and humid: muggy, sultry, sweltering, torrid, tropical
hot coal: ember
hot days of July, August: dog days
hot-dish holder: trivet
hot-dog holder: roll
hot dry wind: simoon, sirocco
hot sauce: salsa, tabasco
hot spring: thermal spring
hot spring shooting column of water: geyser
hot-tempered: cranky, excitable, hotheaded, peppery, testy
hot water: difficulty, fix, jam, pickle, predicament, trouble
hotcakes: flapjacks
hotel: caravansary, fleabag, flophouse, hospice, hostel, imaret, inn, lodge, motel, roadhouse, spa, tavern
hotel entrance: lobby, vestibule
hotel in Europe, small: pension

hotel in Near or Far East, large: caravansary
hotel in Spain or Latin America: parador
hotel or resort with therapeutic baths or mineral springs: spa
hotel price including only room, service, but no meals: European plan
hotel price including room, service, and meals: American plan
hotheaded: fiery, hasty, impetuous, quick-tempered, rash, touchy
hothouse: greenhouse, orangery
hotness or heat, relating to: thermal
hound: addict, annoy, badger, bait, basset, bedog, bother, canine, chase, dog, harass, harry, hassle, heckle, hunt, mutt, persecute, ride, stalk, track
hound dog breed: afghan, basset, beagle, bloodhound, dachshund, deerhound, foxhound, greyhound, harrier, otterhound, staghound, whippet, wolfhound
hour, pertaining to an: horary
house: abode, accommodate, ancestry, apartment, audience, building, bungalow, burrow, cabin, casa, casino, castle, chateau, church, condominium, congress, convent, cot, cottage, council, cover, domicile, dorm, dormitory, dump, duplex, dwelling, family, firm, flat, four-storied, gingerbread, grange, habitation, harbor, heartbreak, home, hovel, hut, igloo, legislature, live, lodge, manor, mansion, monastery, nest, palace, parliament, quarter, rectory, reside, residence, roof, senate, shack, shanty, shell, shelter, split-level, store, stow, structure, synagogue, temple, tenement, theater, villa
house assembled in sections, of a: prefabricated
house comprised of several buildings and enclosed: compound
house for clergy: manse, rectory, vicarage
house in poor condition, of a: dilapidated, ramshackle, rickety
house in Spanish-speaking countries, large: hacienda
house with each floor half a story above or below another: split-level
house with steep triangular roof or shape: A-frame
house, dome-shaped Eskimo: igloo
house, of a large spread-out: rambling, sprawling

house, run-down: hovel

house, to fix up or repair a: refurbish, remodel, renovate

housebreak: burglarize, rob, steal, subdue, tame, train

household: common, domestic, familiar, family, folks, home, menage, ordinary

household, male head of: paterfamilias

household, management of a: menage

housework: chore, cleaning, cooking, drudgery, dusting, ironing, laundering, sweeping, washing

housing: accommodations, box, casing, covering, dwelling, frame, lodging, niche, pad, protection, shelter

hovel: burrow, cabin, dump, dwelling, hole, hut, hutch, lodge, pigpen, pigsty, shack, shanty, shed, sty

hover: flit, float, flutter, hang, linger, loom, suspended, waver

however: although, but, despite, except, nevertheless, nonetheless, notwithstanding, still, though, yet

howitzer: cannon

howl: bark, bawl, bay, bellow, complaint, cry, lament, protest, roar, scream, squeal, ululate, yell, yowl

hub: center, core, focal point, focus, heart, middle, nave, pivot

hub of wheel: nave

hubbub: ado, brouhaha, clamor, clatter, commotion, confusion, din, disorder, disturbance, flap, fuss, noise, pandemonium, racket, rumpus, stir, tumult, turmoil, uproar

huckster: adman, dicker, haggler, hawker, hustler, peddler, salesperson, sell, vendor

huddle: assemble, confer, conference, confusion, consult, converge, crouch, crowd, cuddle, discussion, embrace, gather, group, hug, hurry, jumble, meeting, mingle, scrunch, snuggle

hue: appearance, aspect, cast, color, complexion, depict, form, outcry, shade, shout, tinge, tint, tone

huff: anger, blow, bluster, boasting, brag, dudgeon, expire, gasp, inflate, pant, pique, puff, rage, storm, temper, tiff

huffy: annoyed, arrogant, conceited, crabby, cross, grumpy, haughty, indignant, irritated, moody, offended, pettish, snappy, superior, touchy, windy

hug: affection, caress, cherish, clasp, clinch, cling, cradle, cuddle, embrace, hold, huddle, huggle, press, snuggle, squeeze, welcome

huge: behemoth, big, Brobdingnagian, colossal, elephantine, enormous, epic, gargantuan, giant, gigantic, great, Herculean, heroic, humongous, immense, imposing, jumbo, large, leviathan, mammoth, massive, monster, monstrous, monumental, oversize, titanic, towering, tremendous, vast, vasty

huge and vast: boundless, immeasurable, incalculable, limitless

huge animal or thing: behemoth, leviathan

huge number of individuals: horde

huge statue: colossus

huge, archaically: enorm, vasty

hugger-mugger: clandestine, concealment, confused, confusion, covert, disorderly, hush-hush, jumbled, muddle, secrecy, secret

hulk: bulk, clumsy, hull, loom, shambles, ship, unwieldy

hull: body, case, casing, covering, frame, hulk, husk, mold, rind, shed, shell, skeleton, structure

hull part: keel

hullabaloo: ado, din, excitement, hubbub, noise, pandemonium, racket, tumult, uproar

hum: blur, buzz, croon, drone, murmur, purr, sing, sound, speed, vibrate, whiz, zoom

hum and buzz: bombinate

human: being, child, earthling, hominoid, homo sapiens, individual, man, mortal, person, woman

human behavior, study of: praxeology

human being, diminuitive: homunculus, manikin, pygmy

human being, early form of: Cro-Magnon

human character, study of: ethology

human characteristics to inanimate thing, attributing: anthropomorphism, pathetic fallacy, personification, prosopopoeia

human embodiment: incarnation

human flesh eater: cannibal

human identical to another: clone

human in form and nature: embodied, incarnate, personified

human in shape or appearance: anthropoid, anthropomorphic

human knowledge, study of: epistemology

human-made object: artifact

human manifestation of supernatural being: avatar, embodiment, incarnation

human nature attributed to God: anthropophuism

human or related mammal: primate

human race improvement through improved living conditions: euthenics

human race improvement through selective breeding: eugenics

human settlements, study of: ekistics

human-shaped: android

human soul: psyche

human traits ascribed to inanimate things: personification

human trunk: torso

human with processes aided by mechanical devices: cyborg

humane: altruistic, benevolent, charitable, compassionate, forgiving, kind, merciful, philanthropic, sympathetic, tender

humanitarian: benefactor, benevolent, charitable, generous, philanthropist

humanitarian effort: philanthropy

humanity: compassion, goodwill, kindness, life, man, mankind, mercy, mortality, people, race, species, woman

humankind, aid to: charity, philanthropy

humans and humanlike ancestors: hominid

humble: abase, bashful, deferent, deject, demean, demure, disgrace, embarrass, humiliate, ignoble, little, low, lower, lowly, mean, meek, mild, modest, mortify, poor, quiet, reduce, reserved, shame, sheepish, simple, submissive, unassuming, unpretentious

humble abode: cabin, cot, hut, shanty

humble oneself: bow and scrape, grovel, truckle

humble, very: abject, servile

humbly asking: suppliant

humbug: balderdash, bamboozle, bluff, bosh, bull, bunk, bunkum, cheat, deceive, deception, faker, flam, flimflam, flummery, fraud, fudge, gammon, guff, gyp, hoax, impostor, imposture, kid, malarkey, mislead, nonsense, phony, phooey, pretense, rot, rubbish, sham, strategem, swindle, trick

humdinger: dandy, doozy, extraordinary, lollapalooza, lulu, nifty, remarkable, ripsnorter

humdrum: blah, boring, commonplace, drab, dreary, dull, everyday, indifferent, monotonous, mundane, prosaic, routine, so-so, trite, uneventful, unexciting

humerus neighbor: ulna

humid: clammy, damp, dank, moist, muggy, sticky, sultry, wet

humidity measuring instrument: hygrometer, psychrometer

humiliate: abase, abash, belittle, degrade, demean, denigrate, derogate, disgrace, disparage, embarrass, humble, insult, mortify, shame

humiliating experience: bitter pill

humiliation of oneself: self-abasement

humility: humble, meekness, mildness, modesty, reserve, shyness

humming: brisk, bustling, busy, buzzing, hopping, lively

humongous: immense, prodigious

humor: accommodate, amusement, baby, banter, caprice, cater, clowning, comedy, disposition, drollery, fancy, fluid, funniness, gratify, inclination, indulge, jesting, joke, levity, lightness, makeup, merriment, mood, pamper, personality, satisfy, temper, temperament, whim, wittiness, wisecrack, wit

humor and seriousness, combination of: jocoseriosity

humor oneself: indulge

humor or appease someone, something used to: placebo

humor using words with two meanings: double entendre

humor with a twist: irony

humor, feeble attempt at: witzelsucht

humorist: card, clown, comedian, comic, jester, joker, nye, wag, wit

humorous: amusing, comic, comical, droll, entertaining, facetious, funny, hilarious, ironic, jocose, jocular, laughable, pleasant, protuberance, sardonic, satirical, sidesplitting, waggish, whimsical, witty, wry

humorous and flippant: facetious

humorous effect of using word in opposite from literal meaning: irony

humorous offering: skit

humorous performer with expressionless face: deadpan

humorous remark or act: jest, pleasantry

humorous treatment of grave situation: gallows humor

humorous writing: facetiae

humorous, coarsely: Rabelaisian

humorous, cynically: sardonic

humorous, deceptively: tongue-in-cheek

humorous, dryly: wry

humors of body: black bile, blood, choler (yellow bile), phlegm

humors, of the body's: choleric, melancholic, phlegmatic, sanguine

hump: bulge, bump, hill, hummock, hunch, lump, mound, projection, protuberance, ridge, swelling

humpback: gibbous, hunckback, kyphosis, whale

hunch: clue, feeling, forecast, hint, idea, inkling, intuition, notion, premonition, suspicion

hunch, to: arch, bend, crouch, huddle, hump, lump, squat

Hunchback of Notre Dame's character: Quasimodo

hundred: centenary, centennial, century

hundred years old: centenarian

hundredfold: centuple

hundredth anniversary: centenary, centennial

Hungarian stew: goulash

hunger: ache, appetite, craving, desire, famine, greed, hankering, longing, starvation, thirst, want, yearning, yen

hunger, sharp feeling of: pang

hunger, to satisfy: assuage

hungover: crapulent, crapulous

hungry: avaricious, avid, barren, craving, eager, empty, esurient, famished, greedy, hollow, insatiable, ravenous, starving, unfed, unsatisfied, voracious

hungry, very: famished, ravenous, voracious

hunk: batch, block, chunk, clod, clump, glob, gob, hump, lump, mass, nugget, piece, portion, slab, wad

hunker down: squat

hunky: attractive

hunt: chase, delve, drive, ferret, follow, forage, hawk, hound, inquest, inquiry, inquisition, investigation, persecute, probe, pursue, quest, rummage, search, seek, shoot, stalk, track, trail

hunt or fish illegally: poach

hunter: chaser, chasseur, marksman, stalker

hunter in mythology: Orion

hunter of dangerous people or animals: bounty hunter

hunting dog: hound, setter, terrier

hunting permitted, time of year when: open season

hunting prohibited, time of year when: closed season

hunting trek: safari

hunting with dogs to chase game: coursing

hunting, act or sport of: the chase, venery

hunting, concerning: venatic

hunting, something providing artificial scent in: drag

hunting, something pursued in: chase, quarry

huntress of Greek mythology: Atalanta

huntsman, chief: master of foxhounds, MFH

huntsman's alert that the fox has been seen: view halloo

huntsman's assistant: whipper-in

huntsman's call: tallyho

huntsman's scarlet coat: pink

hurdle: bar, barricade, barrier, bound, clear, complication, handicap, hazard, hedge, impediment, jump, leap, obstacle, obstruction, overcome, roadblock, snag, spring, surmount, throw, wall

hurdy-gurdy: barrel organ

hurl: cast, catapult, chuck, fire, fling, heave, hurtle, launch, pitch, propel, send, sling, throw, toss

hurl from a height: precipitate

hurly-burly: action, activity, bustle, commotion, confusion, hubbub, tumult, turmoil, uproar

hurrah: applaud, approve, bravo, cheer, commotion, encouragement, enthusiasm, excitement, fanfare, huzza, joy, rah, shout, zeal

hurricane: cyclone, gale, monsoon, storm, tempest, tropical storm, typhoon, wind, windstorm

hurricane center: eye

hurry: accelerate, ado, barrel, beeline, bolt, dart, dash, dispatch, drive, expedite, fly, haste, hasten, hie, highball, hustle, make tracks, motion, pass, posthaste, quicken, race, run, rush, scoot, scurry, speed, step on it, trot, tumult, urge, urgency, whir, whisk, zip

hurry away: decamp, hightail, hotfoot, scamper, scarper, skedaddle, vamoose

hurry or speed up: expedite, precipitate

hurt: abuse, ache, afflict, agony, battered, bleeding, bruise, cripple, damage, detriment, distress, grief, harm, harmed, heartbroken, impair, injure, injury, maim, mangled, offend, pain, punch, punish, scathe, smart, sore, sting, strike, suffering, tarnish, torture, upset, weaken, wound

hurt or offend, to: alienate, antagonize, estrange

hurt with harsh criticism, to: lacerate, scarify

hurtful: baneful, cruel, damaging, deadly, deleterious, destructive, detrimental, evil, harmful, injurious, malicious, mean, noxious, pernicious, poisonous, unkind

hurtle: charge, clash, collide, dash, fling, hurl, lunge, plunge, race, rush, scamper, throw, whirl

hurtle through air: catapult

husband: bridegroom, conserve, economize, groom, helpmate, hoard, hubby, keep, man, manage, mate, partner, save, spouse, steward, store

husband at a time, more than one: bigamy, polyandry, polygamy

husband at a time, one: monandry

husband murdering of wife: uxoricide

husband of reigning female sovereign: prince consort

husband of unfaithful wife: cuckold

husband or wife of monarch: consort

husbandry: agriculture, conservation, cultivation, economy, farming, frugality, management, thrift

husband's right to the company, help, affection of wife: consortium

hush: appease, calm, lull, mute, muzzle, quiet, shush, silence, soothe, still, suppress, tranquility

hush-hush: cloak-and-dagger

hush money: sop

hush up: conceal, cover, squash, suppress

husk: bark, bran, case, coat, covering, envelope, framework, harvest, hulk, hull, peel, pod, rind, scale, shell, shuck, skin, strip

husky: beefy, big, brawny, burly, deep, gigantic, growling, gruff, hefty, hoarse, loud, overweight, solid, stocky, strong, throaty

husky-voiced: hoarse, roupy

hussy: adulteress, female, harlot, jade, minx, prostitute, slut, tramp, wench, woman

hustle: bolt, bustle, dash, deceit, drive, fraud, hasten, hie, hurry, jostle, move, press, push, race, scramble, shove, solicit

hustler: dynamo, hooker, peeler, prostitute, streetwalker, vendor

hut: bungalow, cabana, cabin, camp, chalet, cottage, crib, house, hovel, hutch, lean-to, lodge, shack, shanty, shed, shelter, wickiup

hut for sportspeople: lodge

hutch: bin, cage, chest, coffer, coop, cupboard, hut, nest, pen

hyalite: opal

hybrid: blend, composite, cross, crossbreed, mixture, mongrel

hybrid of stallion and ass: hinny

hydrant: faucet, fireplug, spigot

hydrogen bomb: fusion bomb, thermonuclear bomb

hydrogen combined with compound, reaction of: reduction

hydrogen isotope with atomic mass 1: protium

hydrogen isotope with atomic mass 2: deuterium

hydrometer scale: Baume

hydrophobia: rabies

hygienic: asceptic, clean, disinfected, good, healthy, salubrious, sanitary, sterile

hymenopterous insect: ant

hymn: anthem, canticle, carol, chant, chorale, dirge, glorify, introit, laud, paean, prayer, processional, psalm, recessional, requiem, sing, song

hymn for deceased: requiem

hymn of praise: psalm

hymn or composition sung as response in liturgy: antiphon

hymn or song of praise: laud, magnificat

hymn or verse praising God: doxology

hymn sung at the opening of a church service: introit

hymn sung in Eucharistic liturgies: Sanctus

hymn while clergy and choir enter: processional

hymn while clergy and choir leave: recessional

hymn, frenzied ancient Greek: dithyramb

hymn, harmonized: chorale

hymn, song, chant often from biblical text: canticle

hype: advertise, boost, buildup, deceive, exaggerate, mislead, plug, promote, publicity, puffery

hyperbole: distortion, embellishment, exaggeration, magnification, overstatement

hypercritical: captious, carping, faultfinding, fussy, overcritical, scrupulous

hypnotic: comatose, enticing, sleepy, somnifacient, soothing, soporific, spellbinding

hypnotic power: animal magnetism

hypnotic state: trance

hypnotize: allure, captivate, charm, entrance, induce, mesmerize, spellbind

hypochondriac: ailer, valetudinarian

hypocrisy: bigotry, cant, deceit, insincerity, pharisaism, phoniness, pretense, sanctimony

hypocrite: bigot, charlatan, dissembler, faker, humbug, phony, poseur, pretender, quack, two-face, Uriah Heep

hypocritical: artificial, bigoted, canting, captious, deceitful, deceptive, dishonest, dissembling, false, insincere, pharisaical, pietistic, pretending, sanctimonious, two-faced

hypocritical and insincere: disingenuous

hypocritical behavior: dissemblance, mummery

hypocritically self-righteous person: pharisee, whited sepulcher

hypothesis: assumption, belief, deduction, guess, proposal, supposition, system, theory, thesis

hypothesis without proof: premise, thesis, working hypothesis

hypothetical: abstract, assumed, conjectural, contingent, imaginary, inferred, moot, notional, presupposed, supposititious, theoretical

hypothetical machine: perpetual motion

hypothetical unit in theory of relativity: fourth dimension

hysteria: delirium, excitement, frenzy, madness, panic, the vapors

hysterical: berserk, comical, crazed, distraught, emotional, excited, frantic, funny, hilarious, histrionic, hysteriform, melodramatic, overemotional, overwrought, raving, unnerved, uproarious, wild

hysterical outburst: conniption

ice: chill, congeal, cool, flow, freeze, frost, geal, glacier, gloe, gorge, icicle, permafrost, refrigerate, rime, rink, sleet; crystal, diamonds, jewels

ice cream: cassata, dessert, parfait, sherbet, soda, sorbet, sundae, tofutti

ice cream enclosed in sponge cake and meringue and baked: baked Alaska

ice cream layered and frozen in a rounded mold: bombe

ice cream or ice, Italian: gelato

ice cream served in a tall glass, layers of: parfait

ice cream topped with macaroons and almonds, rich: tortoni

ice cream with chopped and candied fruits: tutti-frutti

ice cream with layers of fruits and nuts: spumone, spumoni

ice cream with various toppings: sundae

ice cream, frozen fruit puree or syrup similar to: sorbet

ice cream, served with: à la mode

ice driven together into mass, floating: pack ice

ice game with heavy stones: curling

ice hockey disk: puck

ice house: igloo

ice mass formed from compacted snow and flowing slowly over land mass: glacier

ice mass obstructing narrow passage: gorge

ice more than 5 miles long, expanse of floating: ice field

ice on body of water, broken or half-formed: sludge

ice on river, breaking up of: debacle

ice on roads or sidewalks, thin almost invisible: black ice

ice on rock, thin coating of: verglas

ice pinnacle: serac

ice skating jump: axel, lutz, salchow

ice smaller than ice field, expanse of floating: ice floe

ice sport: curling, hockey, skating, speed skating

ice where aquatic mammals come to breathe, hole in: blowhole

ice, beverage poured over shaved: frappé

ice, compacted snow not yet glacial: firn, neve, old snow

ice, dessert of sweetened crushed: ice

ice, fruit-flavored frozen: sorbet

ice, harmless floating: drift ice

ice, spikes or cleats for walking on: clamper, climbing iron, crampons

ice, of a drink with: on the rocks

ice, of a drink without: neat, straight up

iceberg, small: growler

iced dessert similar to sherbet: frappé

iced with sugar glaze: candied, glacé

Icelandic tale: saga

Icelandic tale collection: edda

ichnography: floor plan, ground plan, map

icing: coating, frosting, glacé, marzipan, topping

icing applied from tube with nozzle: piping

icing of almond paste: marzipan

icky: disgusting, distasteful, gooey, gross, offensive, revolting, sticky, vile

icon: command, idol, illustration, image, picture, portrait, representation, symbol

iconoclast: dissenter, individualist, nonconformist, radical, rebel, revolutionary

icy: aloof, arctic, chilling, cold, distant, freezing, frigid, frosty, frozen, gelid, polar, unemotional

icy rain: sleet

idea: belief, brainchild, brainstorm, concept, essence, feeling, hint, insight, notion, object, perception, philosophy, plan, point, principle, reaction, scheme, slant, suspicion, theory, view

idea as a concrete thing, to treat an abstract: reify

idea based on incomplete evidence: conjecture, guesswork, surmise

idea conference: brainstorming, ideation

idea derived from specific instances, general: apprehension, concept, notion

idea having been accepted as true or worthy, of an: received

idea having general application: abstraction, generalization

idea immune from criticism: sacred cow

idea in the mind, to conceive of an: gestate

idea into words, to put an: articulate, formulate

idea only, existing as an: hypothetical, notional

idea produced in the mind rather than learned, of an: innate

idea used as basis for argument or theory: axiom, postulate, premise

idea, compulsive preoccupation with: fixation, idée fixe, obsession

idea, concrete: construct, working hypothesis

idea, sudden: caprice, fancy, whim

idea, sudden clever: brainstorm

idea, vague: hunch, inkling, intimation, intuition

idea, wild: vagary

ideal: absolute, abstract, appearance, aspiration, classic, cogitation, conception, conceptual, design, dream, embodiment, example, exemplar, exemplary, fancy, fantasy, figure, flawless, goal, image, imaginary, impression, inkling, model, norm, notion, opinion, optimal, paragon, pattern, perfect, perfection, prototype, reflection, satisfactory, standard, theoretical, thought, visionary

ideal example of a type: archetype, exemplar, prototype

ideal example of virtue or vice: embodiment, incarnation, personification

ideal place: utopia

ideal, statement expressing an: motto

idealess: inane

idealism: meliorism, philosophy, principle

idealist: dreamer, optimist, romantic, utopian, visionary

idealistic: quixotic, utopian, visionary

idealize: deify, exalt, glorify, transfigure

idealized image of someone: imago

ideas, medium for conveying: vehicle

ideas, person or place for testing new: sounding board

identical: alike, corresponding, double, duplicate, equal, equivalent, matching, same, self, selfsame, tantamount, twin, uniform

identical counterpart: twin

identical in appearance, person almost: ringer

identical organism, genetically: clone

identical twins, of: monozygotic

identical, twins not: fraternal twins

identification: badge, classifying, description, earmark, fingerprint, ID, labelling, passport, recognition, verification

identification of disease, problem: diagnosis

identification of journalistic resource: attribution

identification with another's situation, feelings, etc.: empathy

identification with other people, objects: introjection

identify: associate, brand, describe, designate, diagnose, discover, establish, find, finger, label, mark, name, pinpoint, recognize, tag, verify

identity: characteristics, homogeneity, individuality, name, oneness, personality, self

identity or public image: persona

identity, loss of personal: alienation, anomie

identity, person who takes another's: impersonator, impostor

ideology: beliefs, creed, culture, doctrine, dogma, ideals, outlook, philosophy, principles

ideology, to try to instill an: brainwash, indoctrinate

idiocy: amentia

idiograph: logogram, symbol, trademark

idiom: argot, dialect, expression, idiosyncrasy, jargon, slang, speech, style, vernacular

idiom or speaking style: parlance

idiosyncrasy: characteristic, eccentricity, habit, idiom, mannerism, oddity, peculiarity, quirk

idiot: ament, blockhead, bonehead, booby, cretin, dimwit, dolt, dope, dork, dullard, dunce, fathead, fool, imbecile, jerk, moron, nitwit, simpleton, stupid, twit

idiotic: asinine, crazy, daffy, daft, fatuous, foolhardy, foolish, inane, ridiculous, senseless, silly, stupid

idle: aimless, barren, baseless, dally, dawdle, deserted, dormant, empty, fallow, futile, inactive, ineffectual, laze, lazy, loaf, loiter, motionless, otiose, relax, slothful, stationary, still, trifling, trivial, unfounded, unoccupied, unused, useless, vacant, vacuous, vain, waste, worthless

idle talk: gossip, palaver, prate

idler: bum, do-nothing, drone, faineant, flaneur, lazybones, loafer, loiterer, slacker, sluggard, tramp, trifler

idol: god, goddess, hero, icon, image, star, symbol

idolize: admire, adore, canonize, cherish, glorify, honor, revere, spiritualize, venerate, worship

idyllic: bucolic, carefree, halcyon, pastoral, peaceful, pleasing, rural, rustic, simple, unspoiled

if: assuming, granting, in case, on condition that, protasis, provided, supposing, suppositive, whenever, whether

if clauses: antecedent, apodosis, conditional clause, protasis, suppositive

iffy: capricious, chancy, dicey, doubtful, risky, uncertain, undecided, unsettled, unsure

ignite: blaze, burn, detonate, excite, fire, glow, inflame, kindle, light

ignoble: base, common, cowardly, degenerate, despicable, disgraceful, dishonorable, infamous, lewd, low, mean, plain, shameful, unworthy, vile, wretched

ignominy: shame

ignoramus: dolt, dunce, fool, idiot, moron, nitwit, numbskull, simpleton

ignorant: benighted, callow, dense, green, illiterate, misinformed, naive, nescient, shallow, stupid, unaware, uncultured, uneducated, unenlightened, uninformed, unknowing, unlearned, unskilled, untaught, untutored, unwitting, young

ignore: avoid, bypass, circumvent, discount, disregard, elide, forget, look the other way, neglect, omit, overlook, pretermit, slight, snub

ignore as insignificant: discount

ignore correction and let original stand (proofreading): stet

ignoring complexity of problems: oversimplifying, simplistic

ilk: breed, class, family, genus, kind, nature, same, sort, type

ill: adverse, adversity, affliction, ailing, ailment, amiss, bad, baneful, condition, cruel, defective, diseased, disorder, evil, harm, harmful, hostile, indisposed, malady, misfortune, noxious, plague, poor, poorly, queasy, sick, sickly, trouble, under the weather, unfriendly, unhealthy, unlucky, unwell, wicked, wrong

ill-advised: brash, dumb, foolhardy, foolish, hasty, imprudent, misguided, rash, reckless, shortsighted, thoughtless, unwise

ill at ease: awkward, discomfited, fidgety, nervous, restless, uncomfortable, uneasy, unsure

ill-behaved child: brat

ill-boding: apocalyptic, dire, evil, inauspicious, unfavorable, unlucky

ill-bred: boorish, churlish, crude, discourteous, impolite, rude, uncivil, uncultured, vulgar

ill-defined: clouded, dim, fuzzy, indistinct, murky, obscured, unclear, vague

ill-fated: disastrous, doomed, jinxed, misfortunate, unfortunate, unlucky

ill-favored: objectionable, offensive, ugly, unattractive, unsightly

ill health: ailment, malady, sickness

ill health unnecessarily, person worried about: hypochondriac

ill humor: bile

ill-humored: cranky, cross, gloomy, grouchy, grumpy, irritable, morose, sulky, surly, testy

ill-mannered: discourteous, disrespectful, impolite, rude, uncouth, ungracious

ill-natured: crabby, cranky, cross, disagreeable, irritable, malicious, nasty, ornery, spiteful, surly, touchy

ill-omened: inauspicious, ominous

ill-smelling: fetid

ill-starred: dire, disastrous, fateful, luckless, ominous, unfortunate, unlucky

ill-suited: inappropriate, incompatible, mismatched, unbecoming, unfit

ill-tempered: angry, bilious, crabby, cranky, cross, crotchety, curly, dour, irritable, mean, sour, sulky, surly

ill-tempered woman: shrew

ill-timed: awkward, inappropriate, inopportune, malapropos

ill treatment: abuse, harm, maltreatment, molestation

ill person, chronically: invalid

ill will: acrimony, animosity, animus, bitterness, dislike, grudge, hatred, hostility, maleficence, malevolence, malice, rancor, resentment, spite, spleen, spitefulness, venom

ill will, having: malevolent, malicious

ill will, tending to rouse: invidious

illegal: banned, bootlegged, contraband, criminal, crooked, felonious, illegitimate, illicit, lawless, outlawed, prohibited, shady, smuggled, ultra vires, unconstitutional, unlawful

RELATED TERMS

illegal act by public official: malfeasance, malversation

illegal coin: slug

illegal commerce in goods: contraband

illegal influence of jury, judge: embracery

illegal interest: usury

illegal liquor: moonshine, mountain dew

illegal operation: scam

illegal payment: kickback

illegal resident: illegal alien

illegal ticket sale: scalp

illegal whiskey: moonshine ❦

illegible: faint, hieroglyphic, scribbled, unclear, undecipherable, unreadable

illegible handwriting: griffonage

illegitimate: bastard, counterfeit, illegal, illogical, improper, invalid, spurious

illegitimate, as person: bastard, misbegotten, spurious

illiberal: biased, bigoted, greedy, hidebound, mean, myopic, narrowminded, partial, prejudiced, stingy, vulgar

illicit: clandestine, contraband, criminal, crooked, forbidden, illegal, improper, prohibited, unlawful

illiterate: ignorant, uneducated, unlearned, unlettered, unread, unschooled, untutored

illness: affliction, ailment, breakdown, colic, complaint, disability, disease, disorder, distemper, flu, infirmity, malady, sickness, syndrome

RELATED TERMS

illness having emotional or mental causes, of an: psychomatic

illness or poor health, one obsessed: valetudinarian

illness with great weakness: infirmity

illness, chronic feeling of: dysphoria

illness, decline after apparent recovery from: relapse

illness, fear of: hypochondria

illness, gradual return to health after: convalescence

illness, slight: indisposition

illness, sudden attack of: ictus

illness, sudden feeling of faintness or: dwam

illness, to regain health after: convalesce, recuperate ❦

illogical: absurd, contradicting, crazy, groundless, inconsistent, invalid, irrational, nutty, preposterous, senseless, unreasonable, unreasoned, unsound, unsubstantial

illogical conclusion or statement: non sequitur

illogical reasoning, argument: fallacy, faulty reasoning, paralogism, sophism

illuminate: adorn, brighten, celebrate, clarify, emblaze, enhance, enlighten, explain, expound, fire, glow, highlight, ignite, irradiate, kindle, light, lighten, spotlight, uplift

illuminated beetle: firefly

illumination: awareness, brightness, brilliance, enlightenment, gleam, information, insight, knowledge, light, lighting

illuminator: lamp

illusion: apparition, chimera, déjà vu, delusion, dream, fallacy, fancy, fantasy, hallucination, invention, mirage, misconception, myth, phantasm, phantom, vision

illusion of disturbed mind: aberration, chimera, specter

illusion of reality in art: trompe l'oeil

illusion that experience happened before: déjà vu

illusion, visual: optical illusion

illusive: apparent, deceitful, deceptive, fake, false, illusory, imaginary, misleading, seeming, sham, unread

illusory: Barmecidal, tricksy

illusory hope: pipe dream

illustrate: clarify, decorate, demonstrate, draw, elucidate, emphasize, exemplify, explain, highlight, picture, portray, represent, show, sketch

illustration: analogy, cartoon, demonstration, drawing, example, figure, image, instance, model, painting, picture, vignette

illustration of something showing parts separately: exploded, view

illustration opposite title page of book: frontispiece

illustration with side cut away: cross-section, cutaway

illustration within illustration: inset

illustrations accompanying text: graphics

illustrative: exemplary

illustrious: brilliant, celebrated, distinguished, eminent, exalted, exemplary, famed, famous, glorious, great, honorable, magnificent, noble, noted, outstanding, prominent, renowned, splendid, striking

image: appearance, concept, copy, double, effigy, eidolon, emblem, facsimile, figure, form, icon, idol, ikon, illustration, impression, likeness, memory, mirror, phantasm, photocopy, photograph, picture, portrait, reflection, replica, representation, semblance, specter, statue, symbol, vision

image on a radar screen: blip

image or likeness of disliked person: effigy

image or representation: simulacrum

image or type that is oversimplified: stereotype

images associated with theme of art: iconography

images or pictures to represent objects and ideas: imagery

images, having extraordinarily vivid recall of: eidetic

imaginable: earthly, possible, secular

imaginary: assumed, chimerical, dreamlike, fancied, fantastic, fictitious, hypothetical, ideal, illusive, illusory, insubstantial, invented, make-believe, mythical, mythological, notional, supposed, unreal, unrealistic, visionary

imaginary and sought-after thing: will-o'-the-wisp

imaginary fear or thing: chimera, specter, nonentity

imaginary illness: hypochondria

imaginary line: axis

imaginary line south of the equator: Antarctic Circle

imaginary semblance: simulacrum

imaginary troublemaker: gremlin

imagination: creativity, fancy, fantasy, figment, ingenuity, insight, originality, thought, vision

imagination, idea credited to: figment

imagination, lively: whimsy

imagination, state of being lost in one's: reverie

imaginative: clever, creative, dreamy, fanciful, ingenious, innovative, inventive, original, visionary

imaginative verse: poesy

imagine: believe, comprehend, conceive, conceptualize, conjecture, conjure up, create, devise, dream, envisage, envision, fancy, fantasize, ideate, picture, presume, realize, suppose, surmise, suspect, think, understand, visualize

imagined: Barmecidal, eidetic, unreal

imbalance: vertigo

imbalance of movement: disequilibrium, instability

imbalance of parts: asymmetry

imbecile: dimwit, dolt, dumbbell, dummy, dunce, fatuous, fool, idiot, jerk, moron, ninny, nitwit, silly, simpleton, stupid

imbibe: absorb, assimilate, consume, down, drink, guzzle, partake, quaff, soak, swallow, swig, tipple, tope, wet one's whistle

imbroglio: altercation, ambroilment,

argument, brawl, disagreement, dispute, fight, quarrel, row, ruckus, spat, squabble

imbue: animate, charge, color, dye, infuse, inoculate, inspire, instill, invade, permeate, saturate, soak, stain, steep, tinge

imitate: ape, assume, bogus, clone, copy, counterfeit, duplicate, echo, emulate, impersonate, lampoon, mime, mimic, mirror, mock, parody, parrot, pretend, resemble, simulate

imitate, impossible to: inimitable, matchless

imitated: aped, copied, emulated, parodied

imitation: copy, emulation, ersatz, fake, impression, phony, replica, reproduction, resemblance, sham, spurious, substitute, substitution, synthetic, travesty

imitation gold leaf: ormolu

imitation in writing or art: mimesis

imitation marble: scagliola

imitation of literary work: travesty

imitation of literary, musical work as humor: parody

imitation of person or thing: clone, copy, ectype

imitation, exaggerated: mockery, parody, travesty

imitation, mocking: burlesque, lampoon, spoof

imitation, satirical: parody, pastiche

imitative: à la, apish

imitative of sound: echoic

imitator: aper, copycat

immaculate: chaste, clean, faultless, flawless, innocent, perfect, pure, sinless, spotless, unblemished, uncorrupted, undefiled, unsoiled, unspoiled, unstained, unsullied, untarnished

immanent: inherent, innate, instinctive, internal, intrinsic, subjective

immaterial: bodiless, celestial, impertinent, inappropriate, incorporeal, inessential, insignificant, insubstantial, intangible, irrelevant, meaningless, metaphysical, shadowy, spiritual, trifling, trivial, unearthly, unimportant, unsubstantial

immature: adolescent, callow, childish, green, inchoate, inexperienced, infantile, jejune, juvenile, puerile, sophomoric, undeveloped, unfledged, unripe, unsophisticated, verdant, young, youthful

immature frog: tadpole

immature insect stage: pupa

immature mushroom: button

immature seed: ovule

immaturity: nonage

immaturity, prolonged: neoteinia

immeasurable: boundless, countless, endless, immense, incalculable, indefinite, inestimable, unfathomable, unlimited, vast

immediate: abrupt, anon, close, critical, directly, instant, instantaneous, near, next, presto, straightaway, sudden, urgent

immediately: at the drop of a hat, forthwith, instantaneous, instanter, instantly, promptly, rapidly, shortly, tout de suite

immediately available: on tap

immediately following: hereupon

immediately upon: as soon as

immemorial: ancient, archaic, dateless, old, prehistoric

immense: colossal, enormous, excellent, extensive, gigantic, good, grand, great, huge, immeasurable, large, mammoth, massive, mighty, monstrous, prodigious, titanic, tremendous, vast

immerse: absorb, baptize, bathe, bury, christen, dip, douse, drench, dunk, engross, merge, occupy, plunge, saturate, soak, submerge, wet

immigrant: alien, foreigner, newcomer

immigrant adjustment to new place: assimilation

immigrant limit: quota

immigrants are integrated, place where: melting pot

immigrate: colonize, migrate, settle

imminent: approaching, around the corner, brewing, close, due, expecting, immediate, impending, inescapable, inevitable, looming, near, ominous, threatening, unavoidable

immobile: anchored, firm, fixed, frozen, immovable, inert, motionless, stable, stationary, steadfast, still

immoderate: boundless, excessive, exorbitant, extravagant, extreme, inordinate, unconscionable, unreasonable, unrestrained

immodest: arrogant, boastful, bold, brazen, coarse, conceited, indecent, shameless, unabashed, unchaste, vain

immoral: bad, corrupt, debased, debauched, degenerate, depraved, dirty, dishonest, dissolute, evil, impure, indecent, licentious, loose, nefarious, reprobate, sinful, unethical, unscrupulous, vicious, wrong

immoral behavior: depravity, turpitude

immoral overindulgence: debauchery, dissipation, intemperance

immoral, quite: libertine, profligate, wanton

immortal: ceaseless, deathless, divine, endless, enduring, eternal, everlasting, famous, forever, imperishable, indestructible, neverending, undying

immortality: athanasia

immovable: adamant, fast, firm, fixed, heartless, immobile, implanted, inflexible, obdurate, permanent, rigid, rooted, set, stationary, steadfast, stubborn, stubborn as a mule, stuck, unshakable, unyielding

immune: exempt, free, guarded, insusceptible, invulnerable, protected, resistant, safe, unresponsive

immunity: amnesty, exemption, exoneration, freedom, privilege, release

immunity from foreign government's prosecution: extraterritoriality

immunity from government prosecution: amnesty

immunity from penalty, punishment, harm: impunity

immunity in body, protein substance that is basis for: antibody

immunity system, severe noncongenital disorder causing lack of: AIDS

immunity to disease, study of: immunology

immunize: inoculate, protect, vaccinate

immunizing agent: antigen, serum

immure: cloister, confine, coop, entomb, imprison, incarcerate, jail, seclude, wall

immutable: constant, enduring, eternal, firm, fixed, invariable, permanent, solid, sure, unaltered, unchangeable, unchanging

imp: brat, demon, devil, elf, fay, fiend, gnome, goblin, gremlin, hobgoblin, pixie, puck, rascal, scamp, sprite, troll, urchin

impact: bang, blow, brunt, collision, concussion, consequences, contact, crash, crush, effect, force, implication, impression, jolt, pound, rock, shack, significance, smash

impair: afflict, blemish, cripple, damage, decrease, devalue, diminish,

harm, hinder, hurt, impede, injure, lessen, mar, reduce, spoil, undercut, undermine, vitiate, weaken

impair secretly or slowly: undermine

impaired: afflicted, broken, damaged, faulty, flawed, imperfect, unsound

impale: gore, lance, pierce, puncture, skewer, spear, spike, spit, stab, transfix

impart: admit, announce, bestow, communicate, confer, convey, direct, disclose, discover, divulge, expose, give, inform, inspire, lend, offer, render, reveal, share, tell, yield

impartial: detached, disinterested, dispassionate, equitable, evenhanded, fair, indifferent, just, neutral, objective, unbiased, unprejudiced, unslanted

impartiality: equity, fairness, justness

impasse: blind alley, box, cul-de-sac, dead end, deadlock, dilemma, gridlock, jam, pickle, stalemate, standoff, standstill

impassioned: ardent, excited, fervent, fervid, feverish, fiery, intense, passionate, romantic, rousing, stirring, zealous

impassive: apathetic, callous, calm, collected, cool, emotionless, expressionless, impassible, insensible, insensitive, motionless, poker-faced, still, stoic, stoical, stolid, unemotional, unfeeling, unflappable

impatient: antsy, anxious, eager, edgy, fidgety, footloose, fretful, hasty, hot, hurried, intolerant, irascible, irritable, itchy, nervous, peevish, restive, restless, testy

impeach: accuse, blame, censure, challenge, charge, denounce, discredit, dismiss, incriminate, indict

impeachment of an attorney: disbarment

impeccable: exquisite, faultless, flawless, perfect, right, unblemished

impecunious: broke, destitute, impoverished, indigent, needy, penniless, poor

impede: block, check, clog, curb, delay, deter, disrupt, hamper, harass, hinder, interfere, obstruct, slow, stop, stymie, thwart

impede with useless addition: encumber

impediment: barrier, defect, detriment,

difficulty, drawback, flaw, handicap, hindrance, hitch, hurdle, malady, obstacle, obstruction, snag, trammel

impedimenta: baggage, gear, luggage, supplies

impel: compel, constrain, drive, encourage, excite, force, goad, incite, induce, influence, inspire, instigate, motivate, move, press, prompt, propel, push, send, stimulate, urge

impending: approaching, close, coming, forthcoming, imminent, inevitable, looming, menacing, nearing, threatening

impenetrable: adamant, adamantine, airtight, bulletproof, dense, hard, impassable, impermeable, impervious, mysterious, sealed, thick, unfathomable

imperative: absolute, command, commanding, compulsory, critical, crucial, duty, essential, indispensable, mandatory, necessary, order, peremptory, pressing, required, rule, stern, urgent, vital

imperceivable by touch: impalpable

imperceptible: faint, inappreciable, indiscernible, insensible, insignificant, intangible, invisible, scant, slight, small, subtle, unapparent, undetectable, unnoticeable

imperfect: blemished, damaged, defective, disfigured, faulty, flawed, ill, impaired, incomplete, unfinished

imperfect item that is discarded: reject, second

imperfection: blemish, blot, defect, deficiency, failing, fault, flaw, inadequacy, kink, mar, shortcoming, wart, weakness

imperial: domineering, kingly, lordly, magisterial, majestic, regal, royal, sovereign, stately

imperil: compromise, endanger, expose, hazard, jeopardize, risk

imperious: arrogant, authoritative, bossy, commanding, despotic, dictatorial, domineering, haughty, lordly, magisterial, oppressive, overbearing, peremptory, pressing, tyrannical, urgent

impermanent: ephemeral, evanescent, fleeting, passing, perishable, temporary, transient

impersonal: cold, detached, general, impartial, neutral, objective, unfriendly

impersonate: ape, copy, imitate, mimic, mirror, portray, pose

impertinence: audacity, boldness, brazenness, crust, forwardness, incivility, insolence, relevance, rudeness, sass

impertinent: arrogant, audacious, discourteous, disrespectful, fresh, ill-mannered, impolite, impudent, meddling, rude, sassy, saucy

imperturbable: calm, collected, composed, cool, levelheaded, placid, serene, stable, tranquil, unexcitable, unflappable, unruffled

imperturbable poise: aplomb

impervious: hermetic, impassable, impenetrable, impermeable, inaccessible, watertight

impervious to fluids: waterproof

impetuosity: élan

impetuous: abrupt, ardent, brash, eager, fervid, fierce, fiery, flashy, forcible, furious, hasty, headlong, heady, heedless, hurried, impulsive, precipitate, rash, rushing, spontaneous, sudden, unplanned, unthinking

impetuous and forceful: vehement

impetus: ambition, catalyst, drive, élan, force, impulse, incentive, momentum, push, spur, stimulus

impetus of body in motion: momentum

impiety: blasphemy, disrespect, heresy, reprobation, sacrilege, undutifulness, ungodliness

impinge: abut, collide, disturb, encroach, infringe, intrude, strike, trespass

impious: blasphemous, godless, iniquitous, irreligious, irreverent, profane, sinful, undevout, unfaithful, ungodly, unholy

impish: devilish, elfish, elvish, fresh, mischievous, naughty, playful, puckish

implacable: cruel, immitigable, inexorable, iron, ironfisted, merciless, relentless, ruthless, unappeasable, unrelenting

implant: embed, enroot, establish, graft, impregnate, impress, inculcate, infuse, ingrain, inoculate, insert, inset, instill, introduce, root, sow

implant ideas: inseminate

implanted heart regulator: pacemaker

implausible: doubtful, dubious, farfetched, fishy, flimsy, improbable, ridiculous, suspect, unbelieveable, unlikely, weak

implement: agent, apparatus, appliance, contraption, device, gadget, instrument, machine, tool, utensil

implement with broad flexible blade for mixing: spatula

implement, to: accomplish, complete, enforce, execute, fulfill, realize; begin, start

implicate: accuse, charge, connect, embroil, frame, imply, incriminate, involve, link, suggest

implication: association, assumption, inference, overtone, presumption, ramification, suggestion

implication of word, writing: connotation

implicit: absolute, complete, fixed, implied, inherent, real, suggested, tacit, understood, unquestioning

implied: assumed, hinted, implicit, indicated, inferred, insinuated, intended, intimated, meant, suggested, tacit, understood, unspoken

implied word or thought: subaudition

implore: adjure, appeal, ask, beg, beseech, entreat, petition, plead, pray, solicit, supplicate, urge

imply: blunt, comprise, connote, hint, indicate, infer, insinuate, intimate, mean, predicate, presume, presuppose, signify, suggest, unrefined

imply falsely: purport

imply or involve: entail

imply slyly: insinuate

impolite: crude, discourteous, disrespectful, ill-bred, indecorous, inelegant, mannerless, rough, rude, uncivil, unmannerly, unpolished

import: convey, denote, indicate, introduce, mean, signify; drift, intent, meaning, purpose, sense, significance, substance, tenor, thrust, value, worth

import duty: tariff

import illegally: smuggle

importance: attention, consequence, dimension, emphasis, gravity, influence, magnitude, moment, position, prestige, priority, prominence, rank, relevance, salience, significance, standing, stature, urgency, weight, worth

importance in rank or position: magnitude

importance increase in power, influence, stature, reputation: aggrandizement

importance, item of principal: staple

importance, minimize something's: soft-pedal

importance, priority claimed because of superiority or: precedence

important: big, consequential, considerable, critical, decisive, earthshaking, eminent, epochal, essential, grave, great, influential, major, meaningful, momentous, necessary, noted, noteworthy, pivotal, pompous, powerful, preeminent, prominent, salient, serious, significant, strategic, striking, urgent, valuable

important and eminent person: bigwig, celebrity, dignitary, eminence, high muck-a-muck, kingpin, luminary, VIP, worthy

important and highly regarded: prestigious

important and influential: consequential, considerable, exalted, formidable, prominent, redoubtable

important and real: substantive

important and urgent: imperative

important and wealthy person: magnate, magnifico, nabob, tycoon

important in affecting future events: fateful, momentous, portentous

important part, most: alpha and omega, core, essence

important work, one's most: magnum opus

important, essential matter: bottom line

important, extremely: cardinal, crucial, earthshaking, epochal, momentous, monumental, pivotal, seminal, signal, significant, vital

important, most: foremost, overriding, paramount, predominant, preponderant

importune: annoy, appeal, ask, beg, beseech, demand, entreat, implore, insist, petition, plead, press, solicit, supplicate, tease, urge, vex

impose: apply, burden, charge, command, create, demand, dictate, force, generate, infringe, intrude, levy, obtrude, order

impose discipline: lower the boom

impose tax, fine, fee: assess, levy

impose unwelcomely: foist

imposing: august, awesome, burly, commanding, grand, grandiose, impressive, magnificent, majestic, massive, outstanding, royal, stately, striking

imposing structure: edifice

imposition: burden, deception, demand, duty, fine, fraud, intrusion, levy, tax

impossible: absurd, hopeless, insoluble, unacceptable, unattainable, unbearable, unfeasible, unimaginable, untenable, unthinkable

impossible to undo: inextricable

impost: assessment, charge, custom, duty, fee, levy, surtax, tariff, tax, toll, tribute, weight

impostor: charlatan, cheat, fake, faker, humbug, imitator, impersonator, mountebank, pettifogger, phony, pretender, quack, sham

imposture: artifice, cheat, copy, counterfeit, deceit, deception, fake, falsehood, fraud, imitation, imposition, masquerade, pretension, quackery, ruse, sham, swindle, trick

impotent: barren, feeble, helpless, inadequate, incapable, inept, powerless, sterile, weak

impound: accumulate, collect, confine, retain, seize, store

impoverish: bankrupt, beggar, deplete, drain, exhaust, reduce, ruin, weaken

impoverished: barren, bereft, broke, destitute, empty, indigent, needy, pauperized, penurious, poor

impractical: idealistic, illogical, quixotic, romantic, unattainable, unfeasible, unrealistic, unusable, unwise, utopian, visionary

impractical idealist: do-gooder, Don Quixote

impractical theory, person attached to: doctrinaire

impractically romantic: quixotic

impregnable: firm, hard, invincible, invulnerable, secure, shielded, strong, sturdy, unshakable

impregnate: charge, drench, fecundate, fertilize, imbue, infuse, inseminate, leaven, penetrate, permeate, saturate, soak

impresario: director, manager, producer

impress: affix, brand, drive, effect, electrify, emphasize, etch, hammer, indent, inspire, move, opinion, pound, print, reach, reaction, stamp, stress, sway, thrill, touch

impress on mind: inculcate, instill

impression: belief, dent, feeling, hunch, image, impact, imperson-ation, influence, inkling, intimation, intuition, percept, print, sense, stamp, takeoff, thought, trace, view

impression, of an unforgettable: indelible

impression, person trying to make an: poseur

impressionable: gullible, plastic, responsive, susceptible, teachable, vulnerable

impressive: august, formidable, grand, imposing, lavish, luxurious, magnificent, majestic, memorable, moving, powerful, redoubtable, solemn, stirring, striking, telling

impressive and grand: baronial, lofty, stately

impressive array: panoply

impressively great: epic

imprint: brand, effect, engrave, etch, impression, inscribe, mark, press, signature, stamp, symbol

imprint in the memory: embed

imprison: arrest, cage, confine, detain, embar, enclose, entomb, hold, immure, incarcerate, intern, jail, limit, mure, restrain, shackle

imprisonment: confinement, durance, duress

imprisonment and forced labor: penal servitude

imprisonment, temporary: custody, detention

imprisonment, writ to release from unlawful: habeas corpus

improbable: doubtful, farfetched, inconceivable, questionable, slim, unbelievable, unconvincing, unlikely

improbable person or event to resolve situation: deus ex machina

impromptu: ad-lib, extemporary, improvised, impulsive, offhand, off-the-cuff, spontaneous, sudden, unexpected, unprepared, unrehearsed

improper: amiss, crude, erroneous, ill-advised, illegal, illegitimate, illicit, ill-suited, impolite, inappropriate, incorrect, indecent, indecorous, indelicate, irregular, out of place, unbecoming, unbefitting, undue, unethical, unfit, unjust, unseemly, unsuitable, untoward, vulgar, wrong

improper use of word(s): solecism

impropriety: barbarism, blunder, corruption, error, faux pas, gaffe, indiscretion, solecism

improve: advance, ameliorate, amend, augment, benefit, better, correct, cultivate, develop, edify, elevate, emend, enhance, enrich, gain, grow, help, lift, meliorate, mend, recover, recuperate, reform, strengthen, upgrade, uplift

RELATED TERMS

improve a text: emend

improve and enliven with colorful details: embellish, embroider, garnish

improve and remedy: make amends, make restitution, redress

improve and repair: refurbish, remodel, renovate, revamp

improve and restore: regenerate, rehabilitate, revitalize

improve appearance of deceptively: gild, gloss

improve dramatically in appearance, form, etc.: transfigure, transform

improve in health: convalesce, recuperate

improve intelligence, morals, spirit: edification

improve to the greatest degree: optimize

improve value, beauty, reputation of: augment, enhance ❧

improvements to property: capital expenditure

improvident: careless, extravagant, imprudent, incautious, negligent, prodigal, rash, reckless, shortsighted, spendthrift, thriftless, wasteful

improvisational U.S. music style derived from blues, ragtime and gospel music: scat

improvise: ad-lib, contrive, devise, extemporize, invent, jam, wing

improvised: ad-libbed, extemporaneous, extemporary, extempore, impromptu, makeshift, offhand, off-the-cuff, spontaneous, temporary, unrehearsed

improvised musical passage: cadenza

improvised substitute for need: stopgap

imprudent: crazy, foolish, heedless, ill-advised, impolitic, improvident, inadvisable, incautious, indiscreet, injudicious, negligent, rash, reckless, unwise, unwise

impudence: audacity, brass, brassiness, chutzpah, effrontery, gall, sass

impudent: arch, bold, brash, brazen, disrespectful, flippant, forward, fresh, impertinent, impolite, insolent, mal-apert, offensive, pert, rude, sassy, saucy, shameless, wise

impudent talk: lip, sass

impugn: attach, denounce, doubt, knock, question

impulse: catalyst, drive, force, impetus, instinct, motion, motive, propulsion, push, resolve, stimulus, tendency, throb, thrust, urge

impulse, creative: afflatus

impulsive: forceful, hasty, headlong, impellent, impetuous, impromptu, involuntary, offhand, quick, sponta-neous, sudden, unpredictable

impune: assail, challenge, contradict, deny, fight, gainsay, resist

impunity: clearance, exception, free-dom, immunity, privilege

impure: adulterated, alloyed, base, blemished, carnal, coarse, contami-nated, corrupt, defiled, desecrated, diluted, dirty, filthy, foul, gross, inde-cent, inferior, lewd, maculate, ob-scene, polluted, smutty, tainted, un-chaste, unclean, unhallowed, unholy, unrefined, unwholesome, vile

impure substances, to add: adulterate

impurity: dross

impute: accuse, allege, ascribe, attri-bute, blame, charge, consider, count, credit, impart, implicate, intimate, refer

in addition: also, and, as well, besides, else, further, more, plus, supplemen-tal, to boot, too, withal

in advance: ahead, before, earlier, sooner

in any case: anyway, at all, ever, none-theless, regardless

in arrears: behind, delinquent, due, overdue, owing

in due course: eventually, soon, ultimately

in effect: absolutely, activated, really

in essence: basically, essentially, funda-mentally, practically, ultimately

in existence: alive, extant, surviving

in line: aligned, aplomb, arrow, bal-anced, straight

in line one behind the other: single file

in line with: anent

in memoriam: as a memorial to, com-memorating, honoring, in memory of, recognizing

in motion: active, astir, moving, traveling

in perpetuum: always, eternally, forever

in pieces: asunder, broken, busted, damaged, destroyed, ruined, shat-tered, smashed

in place of: for, in lieu of, instead, stead

in place of parent: in loco parentis

in place or proper position: in situ

in plain sight: open, out in the open, overt

in re: about, anent, as to, concerning, in regard to, in the case of, in the matter of, regarding

in reserve: aside, on ice, on tap

in the act: in flagrante delicto, red-handed

in the air: above, overhead, skyward, up

in the bag: assured, certain, clinched, definite

in the black: profitable, prosperous, successful, thriving

in the dark: confused, uninformed

in the end: eventually, finally, in con-clusion, sooner or later

in the know: aware, cognizant, hep, hip, knowledgeable

in the matter of: concerning, in re

in the neighborhood: about, almost, ap-proximately, around, close

in the place cited: loco citato

in the style of: à la

in the way: bothersome, disturbing, im-peding, meddlesome, nagging

in toto: altogether, completely, en-tirely, fully, totally

in use: functioning, operational

in vain: fruitless, futilely, hopeless, lost, purposelessly

in vogue: à la mode, chic, current, fash-ionable, popular, stylish

in which case: then, when, whereupon

inability: failure, helplessness, impo-tence, inaptitude, incapacity, incom-petence, ineptitude, weakness

inability to decide or act: abulia

inability to feel happiness: anhedonia

inability to swallow: aphagia

inability to understand objects: apraxia

inaccessible: aloof, closed, distant, elu-sive, remote, unattainable, unavail-able, unreachable

inaccuracy: blunder, error, fallacy, goof, imprecision, mistake

inaccurate: defective, discrepant, erro-neous, false, faulty, incorrect, inex-act, misleading, unreliable, untrue, wrong

inaccurate title: misnomer

inaction: deferral, idleness, inactivity, indolence, suspension

inactive: abrogated, at rest, dormant, dull, idle, in abeyance, indolent, in-ert, languid, latent, lethargic, mo-tionless, otiose, passive, quiescent, sedentary, slack, sleeping, slothful, slow, sluggish, static, still, supine, torpid, unemployed, unoccupied

inactive and seated: sedentary

inactive and still: quiescent

inactive as chemical: inert

inactive as volcano: extinct

inactive but potentially active: dor-mant, latent

inactive in winter: hibernating

inactive stages of insects: pupae

inactivity or stagnation: doldrums, en-nui, listlessness, slump

inadequacy: deficiency, flaw, inability, inefficiency, insufficiency, lack, shortage, shortcoming

inadequate: deficient, disproportion-ate, exiguous, imperfect, incommen-surate, incomplete, ineffective, little, meager, scant, scanty, short, skimpy, small, sparse, unfit, unqualified, wanting, weak

inadmissible: disallowed, immaterial, irrelevant, unacceptable, unallow-able, unqualified, unwelcome

inadvertent: accidental, careless, heed-less, unintended, unwitting

inadvisable: foolish, impolitic, impru-dent, rash, risky, unsensible, unwise

inalienable: absolute, basic, defended, inbred, inherent, inviolable, natural, sacred

inamorata: ladylove, lover, mistress, paramour, sweetheart, woman

inane: asinine, daft, dumb, empty, fatu-ous, foolish, frivolous, idiotic, illogi-cal, jejune, nonsensical, pointless, ri-diculous, senseless, silly, stupid, vacant, vacuous, vapid, worthless

inanimate: dead, dull, exanimate, flat, inert, inorganic, insensate, insensi-ble, lifeless, stolid, unfeeling

inanimate objects possessing souls, be-lief in: animism

inanity: absurdity, emptiness, foolish-ness, frivolity, hollowness, nonsense, senselessness, triviality, vacuity, vapidity

inapplicable: immaterial, impertinent, inapposite, irrelevant, unfit

inappropriate: ill-timed, improper, inapposite, inapt, incongruous, inconvenient, inopportune, malapropos, out of place, unapt, unbecoming, unfitting, unseasonable, unsuitable, unsuited, untimely

inappropriate as remark, humor: indecorous, infelicitious, untasteful, untoward

inapt: amateurish, awkward, clumsy, flat, gauche, ill-timed, improper, inadequate, inappropriate, inept, undue, unsuitable

inapt, in English upper society: non-U

inarticulate: blurred, dumb, garbled, hesitating, incoherent, inexpressive, muffled, mute, speechless, stammering, tongue-tied, unvocal

inartistic: graceless, inelegant, tasteless

inasmuch as: because, considering, for, since, while

inattention: carelessness, disregard, dreaminess, negligence

inattentive: absent, absentminded, abstracted, bored, careless, deaf, distracted, distrait, forgetful, heedless, lax, negligent, preoccupied, remiss, unaware, unheeding, unmindful, unnoticing, unobserving

inaudible: infrasonic

inaudible for humans: ultrasonic

inaugurate: auspicate, begin, commence, induct, initiate, install, institute, introduce, launch, open, start, undertake, usher in

inauguration: commencement, coronation, inception, induction, opening

inauspicious: adverse, dire, disastrous, foreboding, foul, ominous, sinister, threatening, unfortunate, unlucky, unpromising, unpropitious

inborn: basic, hereditary, inbred, ingrained, inherent, inherited, innate, instinctive, intuitive, natural

inbred: congenital, deep-seated, inborn, innate, intrinsic, native, natural, primal

incalculable: countless, immeasurable, immense, incomputable, inestimable, infinite, innumerable, limitless, measureless, uncertain, uncountable, unpredictable

incandescent: aglow, bright, brilliant, electric, glowing, intense, lucid, luminous, radiant, shining

incantation: abracadabra, chant,

charm, conjuration, jinx, magic, mantra, rite, sorcery, spell, utterance, voodoo, witchery

incantation of nonsense: mumbo jumbo

incantation to conjure evil spirit: invocation

incapable: helpless, inadequate, incompetent, inept, notable, powerless, unable, unequipped, unfit, unqualified, untrained

incapable of being passed through: impervious

incapable of being satisfied: insatiable

incapable of being transferred, removed: inalienable

incapacitate: cripple, damage, disable, disarm, disqualify, handicap, hinder, lame, maim, sideline

incarcerate: cage, commit, confine, constrain, detain, immure, imprison, jail

incarnate: actualize, embody, exteriorized, manifest, materialize, personified, tangible

incarnation of deity: avatar, embodiment, manifestation

incautious: bold, careless, hasty, impetuous, improvident, imprudent, indiscreet, negligent, rash, reckless, throughless

incendiary: agitator, arsonist, firebug, inflammatory, insurgent, pyromaniac, rebel, subversive

incense: anger, aroma, balm, elemi, enrage, essence, fragrance, frankincense, homage, incite, infuriate, irritate, myrrh, perfume, provoke, rile, scent, smell, spice

incense container: censer, thurible

incense stick: joss stick

incensed: enraged, irate, wroth

incentive: allurement, carrot, catalyst, encouragement, enticement, fillip, goad, impetus, impulse, incitement, inducement, inspiration, lure, motivation, motive, spark, spur, stimulus, urge

incentive for achievement: reward

inception: arrival, beginning, commencement, dawn, kickoff, onset, origin, source, start

incertitude: doubt, insecurity, instability, skepticism, uncertainty

incessant: ceaseless, constant, continuous, endless, eternal, nonstop, perpetual, persistent, relentless, steady, unending, unremitting

inch: creep, length, measurement, move, unit

inchoate: amorphous, incipient, incohesive, incomplete, rudimentary, shapeless, unformed, unorganized, unshaped, vague

incident: accident, contingent, episode, event, happening, occasion, occurrence, prone, scene

incidental: accessory, ancillary, casual, chance, contingent, contributing, fortuitous, minor, nonessential, occasional, related, secondary

incidental and lucky: adventitious, contingent, fortuitous

incidental and not relevant: marginal, peripheral, tangential

incidental or secondary: accessory, adjunct, adscititious, ancillary, auxiliary, subsidiary, supplementary

incidental remark: obiter dictum

incidental thing or occurrence: contingency

incidentally: apropos, by the way, en passant, parenthetically

incidents, broken into: episodic

incinerate: burn, consume, cremate, fire, parch

incipient: beginning, budding, commencing, developing, inceptive, inchoate, initial, nascent

incipient flower: bud

incise: carve, chisel, cut, engrave, etch, mold

incised carving: intaglio

incision: cut, gash, notch, scar, slash, slit, wound

incisive: acute, biting, clear, concise, crisp, cutting, intelligent, keen, mordant, penetrating, precise, sarcastic, sharp, steeltrap, trenchant

incite: abet, agitate, animate, arouse, coax, compel, drive, egg on, encourage, entice, excite, foment, goad, impel, induce, inflame, influence, instigate, lash, motivate, move, prod, prompt, provoke, spur, stimulate, stir up, trigger, urge

incite to do bad thing: entice, lure, seduce, solicit, suborn

incivility: churlishness, discourtesy, disrespect, impertinence, misbehavior, rudeness, uncivil

inclement: brutal, foul, hard, harsh, nasty, rainy, raw, rough, ruthless, severe, stormy, unmerciful

inclination: acclivity, affection, affinity, angle, appetite, ascent, attachment, bent, bias, descent, desire, disposition, druthers, fancy, fondness, grade, gradient, hill, leaning, liking, mind, mindest, mood, partiality, penchant, pitch, preference, proclivity, proneness, propensity, rise, slant, slope, tendency, trend, urge, will, wish, wont

inclination or slope: versant

inclination or tendency: bent, propensity

incline: bend, bias, bow, cant, dip, grade, hill, lean, leaning, pitch, ramp, slant, slope, tend, tilt, upgrade

incline from the vertical: rake

inclined plane on which ships are built: slip

inclined shaft: chute

inclined to copy: imitative

inclined to one side: alist, heeled

include: comprehend, comprise, consist of, contain, cover, embed, embody, embrace, encompass, enfold, incorporate, insert, involve

include and take in: comprehend, embrace, subsume

include as part of whole: embody, incorporate

include within or beneath: subordinate, subsume

including many things, parts: compendious, omnibus

inclusive: broad, comprehensive, embracing, general, global, surrounding, umbrella, universal

inclusive abbreviation: et al., etc.

incognito: anonymous, concealed, disguised, nameless, undercover, unidentified, unknown

incognizant: ignorant, oblivious, unaware, uninformed, unknowing

incoherent: disconnected, disjointed, illogical, inarticulate, incongruous, inconsistent, indistinct, muddled, muttered, rambling, unclear, unconnected, unintelligible

incoherent talk: gibberish

income: cash, commission, compensation, earnings, emolument, gain, interest, means, proceeds, profit, receipts, return, revenue, royalty, salary, take, wages

income after necessities paid for: discretionary income

income after taxes paid: disposable income, net income

income earned but not paid: accrued interest

income from trust, bequest: endowment

income of government: revenue

income to live modestly: competence, sufficiency

income to pay for necessities: subsistence level

income, individual, adjusted for inflation: real income

incomparable: excellent, incommeasurable, matchless, peerless, superior, superlative, supreme, surpassing, unequalled, unparalleled, unrivaled, unsurpassed

incompatible: adverse, antagonistic, clashing, conflicting, contradictory, contrary, disagreeing, discordant, dissonant, incongruous, inharmonious, irreconcilable, mismatched, opposite, warring

incompetence, rising to one's level of: Peter Principle

incompetent: bungling, helpless, incapable, inefficient, inept, lacking, unable, unequipped, unfit, unqualified, unskilled, useless

incomplete: broken, defective, deficient, divided, fragmentary, imperfect, inadequate, insufficient, lacking, partial, rough, undeveloped, undone, unfinished, wanting

incomplete and broken: fragmentary

incompleted pitch: balk

incomprehensible: abstruse, baffling, confusing, impenetrable, inconceivable, inscrutable, mysterious, perplexing, unclear, unfathomable, unimaginable, unreadable, unthinkable

inconceivable: improbable, incredible, strange, unbelievable, unlikely, unthinkable

inconclusive: indefinite, open, uncertain, undecided, undetermined, unfinished, unresolved, unsettled, vague

incongruous: absurd, alien, conflicting, contrary, disagreeable, discordant, dissonant, imcompatible, inappropriate, inconsistent, inharmonious, ironic, mismatched, unsuitable

inconsequential: insignificant, irrelevant, meaningless, measly, minor, negligible, paltry, petty, picayune, slight, trifling, trivial, unimportant

inconsiderably: little, minor, scanty, slight, small

inconsiderate: careless, impolite, improvident, incautious, indiscreet, in-

sensitive, neglectful, rash, rude, selfish, thoughtless, uncivil, ungracious, unkind

inconsistency: disagreement, discrepancy, disparity, variance

inconsistent: capricious, conflicting, contradictory, discordant, discrepant, dissonant, divergent, erratic, fickle, incompatible, incongruous, irreconcilable, irregular, uncongenial, unpredictable, unstable

inconsistent statement: paradox

inconsolable: comfortless, crushed, dejected, despondent, disconsolate, forlorn, heartbroken

inconspicuous: low-profile, unobtrusive, unostentatious

inconstant: capricious, changeable, disloyal, elusive, erratic, faithless, fickle, fluctuating, uncommitted, unsettled, untrue, vacillating, variable, wayward

incontinent: licentious, lustful, unchaste, uncontrolled, unrestrained

incontrovertible: certain, incontestable, indisputable, irrefutable, true, undeniable, unequivocal, unquestionable

inconvenience: annoy, annoyance, awkwardness, bother, discomfort, discommode, disoblige, disturb, disturbance, hindrance, incommode, nuisance, trouble, uneasiness

inconvenient: annoying, awkward, burdensome, embarrassing, inaccessible, inappropriate, inopportune, troublesome, unhandy, unreasonable, unseasonable, untimely

incorporate: absorb, assimilate, associate, blend, combine, embody, form, fuse, include, integrate, join, link, merge, unite

incorporeal: airy, bodiless, disembodied, immaterial, spiritual, supernatural, unearthly, unsubstantial, unworldly

incorrect: erroneous, false, inaccurate, mistaken, not so, untrue, wrong

RELATED TERMS

incorrect concept or opinion based on misinformation: fallacy

incorrect conclusion, unintended: paralogism

incorrect interpretation: misapprehension, misconception, misconstruction, misunderstanding

incorrect name: misnomer

incorrect though plausible: sophistic, specious

incorrect use of a word: catachresis

incorrect use of a word grammatically: solecism

incorrect use of a word that is close in sound or spelling to correct one: malapropism

incorrect, to prove something: confute, rebut, refute ❦

incorrigible: hardened, hopeless, ineradicable, intractable, irreparable, rooted, unmanageable, unreformed

incorruptible: honest, honorable, loyal, pure, righteous, trustworthy, untouchable

increase: accelerate, accrue, accumulate, add, addition, advantage, aggrandize, aggravate, amplify, appreciate, augment, boost, broaden, build, compound, development, dilate, double, enhance, enlarge, enlargement, enrich, escalate, exaggerate, expand, expansion, extend, extension, flourish, further, gain, gather, grow, growth, heighten, hike, increment, inflate, intensify, irrupt, jump, magnify, markup, multiply, proliferate, quadruple, raise, rise, soar, step up, strengthen, surge, swell, triple, upgrade, wax

RELATED TERMS

increase and expand: amplify, augment, wax

increase and intensify: escalate, flare up, inflame, spiral

increase and puff: inflate

increase as a result of growth: accrue

increase in force: groundswell

increase in loudness: crescendo

increase in power, influence, stature, reputation: aggrandize, elevate, enhance, exalt

increase in problem: aggravate, exacerbate

increase in rank or power: aggrandize

increase in size: dilate, distend, expand, inflate, swell

increase in time: extend, prolong, protract

increase naturally: grow

increase or addition: increment

increase or amassing: accretion, accumulation

increase or multiplication: propagation

increase or spread at rapid rate: burgeon, proliferate

increase rapidly and irregularly: irrupt

increase step-by-step: escalate

increase suddenly: surge

increase to the highest degree: maximize

increasing: increscent

increasing by successive addition: cumulative

increasing rapidly: exponential ❦

incredible: absurd, amazing, astounding, awesome, extraordinary, fabulous, impossible, outlandish, questionable, remarkable, unbelievable, unlikely, wonderful

incredulous: disbelieving, doubting, dubious, mistrustful, skeptical, suspicious, uncertain

increment: accrual, accumulation, addition, advancement, augmentation, gain, growth, increase, raise

incriminate: accuse, blame, charge, implicate, inculpate, involve

incriminating: in flagrante delicto, red-handed, telltale

incubus: burden, demon, nightmare, spirit

inculcate: drill, impart, implant, impress, indoctrinate, infuse, instill, program, propagate, teach

inculpable: blameless, clean, clear, exemplary, innocent

inculpate: accuse, blame, charge, implicate, incriminate, involve

incur: acquire, assume, encounter, gain, obtain, sustain

incurable: chronic, deadly, hopeless, incorrigible, inoperable, irredeemable, irremediable, irreparable, terminal, uncorrectible, unremediable

incurable optimist: Pollyanna

incursion: assault, attack, foray, infiltration, inroad, invasion, penetration, raid

indebted: appreciative, beholden, bound, grateful, liable, obligated

indebtedness: arrears

indecent: coarse, dirty, foul, gross, immodest, immortal, improper, impure, indelicate, lewd, nasty, obscene, offensive, raunchy, risqué, scabrous, scurrilous, smutty, unbecoming, unseemly, vulgar

indecipherable: cryptic, hieroglyphic, illegible, scrawled, unreadable

indecision: anxiety, doubt, hesitation, irresolution, uncertainty, vacillation, wavering

indecisive: ambivalent, dubious, equivocal, hesitant, inconclusive, indefinite, irresolute, namby-pamby, shaky, uncertain, unclear, vacillating, waffling, wavering

indecorous: coarse, distasteful, gross, impolite, improper, inappropriate, inelegant, offensive, rude, unbecoming, uncivil, unfitting

indeed: absolutely, actually, admittedly, certainly, honestly, naturally, positively, really, surely, truly, undeniable, undoubtedly, yea

indefatigable: diligent, dogged, energetic, industrious, inexhaustible, perservering, persistent, relentless, tenacious, tireless, untiring, unwearying, vigorous

indefensible: inexcusable, invalid, pregnable, unpardonable, unprotected, untenable, vulnerable

indefinable quality: je ne sais quoi

indefinite: ambiguous, doubtful, endless, equivocal, inconclusive, indecisive, inexact, infinite, intangible, loose, nubilous, tentative, uncertain, undetermined, unlimited, unspecific, unsure, vague

indefinite and lacking form: amorphous

indefinitely: sine die

indelible: enduring, fast, fixed, ineffacable, inexpungible, lasting, permanent, uneradicable, unerasable, unremovable

indelicate: brash, coarse, gross, impolite, improper, indecent, lewd, offensive, raw, tactless, unbecoming, uncouth, unrefined, unseemly, vulgar

indemnifies: pays

indemnify: atone, compensate, insure, pay, protect, recompense, reimburse, remunerate, satisfy

indemnity: compensation, exemption, insurance, protection, reparation, restitution

indent: bruise, depress, dint, inlay, mark, nick, notch, press, recess, serrate, space, stamp

indentation: cavity, dimple, ding, groove, impression, indenture, notch, pocket, recess

indentation of lines after first: hanging indent

indenture: agreement, contract, document, indentation

INDIAN TRIBES

Central/South American: Ande, Arawak, Aymara, Aztec, Bravo, Carib, Cuna, Guarani, Inca, Kechua, Maya, Olmec, Ona, Quechua, Toltec, Uro, Zapotec

Native American: Abenaki, Aleut, Algonquin, Apache, Apalachee, Apalachi, Arapaho, Arikara, Banak, Blackfoot, Caddo, Cayuga, Cherokee, Cheyenne, Chickasaw, Chilkat, Chinook, Chippewa, Choctaw, Comanche, Cree, Creek, Crow, Dakota, Dakotah, Delaware, Erie, Hitchiti, Hopi, Huron, Illinois, Ioni, Iowa, Iroquois, Kania, Kansas, Kaw, Keresan, Kiowa, Klamath, Lenape, Maidu, Massachuset, Menominee, Miami, Mohave, Mohawk, Mohegan, Mohican, Mojave, Munsee, Muskhogean, Narragansett, Natchez, Navaho, Navajo, Nez Perce, Nootka, Ojibwa, Omaha, Oneida, Onondaga, Osage, Oto, Otoe, Ottawa, Paiute, Pawnee, Pima, Pontiac, Potawatomi, Pueblo, Sac, Sagamore, Sambos, Sauk, Seminole, Seneca, Shawnee, Shoshoni, Sioux, Siwash, Tana, Taos, Tlingit, Tuscarora, Ute, Winnebago, Yuma, Zuni ❦

---

independence: autonomy, emancipation, freedom, liberty, self-government, sovereignty

independent: alone, autonomous, exclusive, free, liberated, nonaligned, self-governing, self-reliant, self-sufficient, self-supporting, separate, sovereign, unconnected, uncontrolled, unrestricted

independent in existence or function: substantive

independent melodic lines combined to make a harmonic relationship: contrapunto, counterpoint

independent-minded person: individualist, maverick

independent of order in math: commutative

indescribable: indefinable, ineffable, overwhelming, unexpressible, unspeakable

indestructible: durable, enduring, immutable, lasting, nonperishable, permanent, unbreakable, unchangeable

indeterminate: ambiguous, inconclusive, indefinite, inexact, obscure, uncertain, unclear, unresolved, vague

index: alphabetize, catalog, file, glossary, guide, indicator, list, mark, measure, pointer, symbol, table, tabulate

India butter: ghee, ghi

India castes: agarwal, ahir, brahman, brahmin, dhobi, harijan, jat, kshatriya, lohar, mali, maratha, rajput, shudra, singh, sudra, untouchable, vaishya, vaisya

India clothing: burga, saree, sari

India educated woman: pundita

Indian child: papoose

Indian curtain concealing women from view: purdah

Indian housing: hogan, lodge, teepee, tepee, wickiup, wigwam

Indian meeting: powwow

Indian money: sewan, wampum

Indian peace pipe: calumet

Indian stringed musical instruments: sarod, sitar, tamboura, vina

Indian, male: brave, buck, chief, sannup

indicate: attest, augur, bespeak, betoken, bode, demonstrate, denote, designate, disclose, display, evidence, evince, exhibit, gesture, hint, imply, import, infer, intimate, manifest, mark, mean, particularize, point, point out, prove, read, register, reveal, show, signify, specify, suggest, symbolize, testify

indicate and reveal: disclose, evidence, evince, manifest

indicate approach: harbinger, herald, presage

indication: auspice, clue, designation, evidence, expression, forewarning, hint, index, inkling, intimation, note, notion, omen, proof, sign, signal, suggestion, symptom, telltale, token, trace, warning

indicative: emblematic, expressive, representative, significant, suggestive, symbolic

indicator: bellwether, forerunner, index, sign

indict: accuse, arraign, charge, impeach, incriminate, inculpate, prosecute, summon

indifference: aloofless, apathy, callousness, carelessness, coldness, disdain, disinterest, iciness, insensitivity, languor, lassitude, lethargy, negligence, unconcern

indifferent: aloof, apathetic, blasé, careless, casual, cold, cool, detached, frigid, heedless, impervious, incurious, insensible, insouciant, lackadaisical, listless, lukewarm, mediocre, neutral, nonchalant, phlegmatic, po-cocurante, so-so, stoic, uncaring, unconcerned, unfeeling, uninspired, uninterested, unmindful, unmoved

indifferent and cool: nonchalant

indifferent in feeling: apathetic

indifferent to pain or pleasure: stoical

indigence: destitution, penury

indigenous: aboriginal, autochthonous, congenital, domestic, enchorial, endemic, homegrown, inborn, inherent, innate, native, natural, original

indigenous language: vernacular

indigent: beggarly, destitute, homeless, impecunious, impoverished, lacking, needy, penniless, poor, wanting

indigestion: dyspepsia, flatulence, gas, heartburn

indignant: angry, annoyed, disgruntled, exasperated, furious, incensed, infuriated, irritated, miffed, sore, steaming, up in arms, wrathful

indignation: anger, animosity, animus, disdain, displeasure, fury, ire, pique, rage, resentment, umbrage

indignity: abuse, affront, discourtesy, dishonor, embarrassment, humiliation, injustice, insult, offense, outrage, slight, wrong

indigo blue: anil

indirect: abstruse, circuitous, circular, crooked, devious, dishonest, erratic, evasive, incidental, meandering, misleading, oblique, rambling, roundabout, secondary, shifty, sneaky, subtle, twisting, underhand, vague, zigzag

indirect expression: circumlocution, periphrasis

indirect mention: allusion

indirect or secondhand: vicarious

indirect route: detour

indiscernible: evanescent, faint, impalpable, imperceptible, indistinct, insignificant, invisible, unnoticeable

indiscreet: brash, careless, foolish, heedless, ill-advised, impolitic, improvident, inconsiderate, injudicious, imprudent, rash, tactless, uncautious, unwise

indiscretion: carelessness, folly, foolishness, lapse, mistake, slip, stumble, unwariness

indiscretions of youth: wild oats

indiscriminate: assorted, broad, chaotic, confused, disorganized, haphazard, jumbled, mingled, mixed, motley, random, unplanned, unrestrained, unselective, wanton, wholesale

indiscriminate sexually: promiscuous

indispensable: basic, cardinal, crucial, essential, imperative, integral, necessary, needed, needful, obligatory, required, requisite, unavoidable, vital

indispensable thing: sine qua non

indisposed: ailing, averse, confined, disinclined, hesitant, ill, reluctant, sick, sickly, uneager, unwell, unwilling

indisposition: affliction, ailment, discomfort, dislike, disorder, illness, infirmity, malady, malaise, reluctance, resentment, sickness

indisputable: apodictic, apparent, certain, conclusive, definite, incontrovertible, indubitable, irrefragable, irrefutable, obvious, positive, sure, uncontestable, undeniable, unmistakable, unquestionable

indisputable evidence: smoking gun

indissoluble: binding, enduring, firm, imperishable, lasting, permanent

indistinct: ambiguous, blurred, cloudy, confused, dark, dim, faint, hazy, inaudible, indefinite, misty, muddy, obscure, shadowy, unclear, undefined, vague, weak

indistinguishable: identical, imperceptible, same, unclear, vague

indite: compose, dictate, pen, write

individual: alone, being, distinctive, entity, exclusive, explicit, mortal, one, particular, person, private, self, separate, single, sole, solitary, solo, somebody, special, specific, thing, unique, unit

individual and separate: discrete, distinct, diverse

individual detail: particular

individual in a directory: listee

individual or personal: subjective

individual speech pattern: idiolect

individual tendency: bent

individual uniqueness in hostile universe, philosophy of: existentialism

individuality: character, distinction, feature, habit, identity, indivisibility, makeup, mannerism, nature, personality, seity, singularity, temperament, uniqueness

individually: alone, apart, independently, personally, separately

individually in order: respectively

individuals chosen to be representative of group: random sample

Indo-European: Aryan

indoctrinate: brainwash, educate, imbue, instill, instruct, program, school, teach, train

indolent: idle, inactive, inert, lackadaisy, lazy, lethargic, listless, slothful, sluggish, torpid

indomitable: courageous, dogged, intrepid, invincible, invulnerable, persevering, spunky, stalwart, staunch, steadfast, unbeatable, undaunted, undefeatable, unyielding

indoor swimming pool: natatorium

indubitable: apparent, assured, certain, conclusive, evident, indisputable, irrefragable, open, positive, sure, undeniable, unequivocal, unquestionable

induce: actuate, cause, coax, convince, draw, elicit, encourage, generate, get, impel, incite, influence, lure, motivate, persuade, press, prompt, sway, tempt, urge

inducement: attraction, bait, carrot, consideration, enticement, hook, incentive, instigation, motive, reason, spur, stimulus

inducing nausea: emetic

induct: admit, draft, enlist, enroll, inaugurate, initiate, install, instate, recruit, register

indulge: accommodate, baby, cherish, coddle, cosset, delight, enjoy, favor, gratify, humor, mollycoddle, oblige, pamper, please, satisfy, spoil

indulge appetite: sate, satiate

indulge freely: give rein to

indulge in luxury: live high

indulge oneself: luxuriate, revel, wallow

indulge whim: gratify

indulgence: allowance, clemency, compassion, excess, fondness, forgiveness, gratification, hedonism, lenience, luxury, petting, spree, tolerance

indulgence, excessive: dissipation

indulgence, immoral: debauchery, depravity, dissipation, dissoluteness, intemperance

indulgent: benign, charitable, compliant, easy, easygoing, gentle, good, kind, pardoning, permissive, tender

industrial class: proletariat

industrial diamond: bort

industrial settlement: adjudication, arbitration, conciliation, mediation

industrial worker: blue-collar worker

industrialist: magnate, tycoon

industrious: active, ambitious, assiduous, busy, busy as a bee, diligent, dynamic, eager, energetic, enterprising, hardworking, laborious, operose, painstaking, persevering, productive, sedulous, zealous

industrious insects: ants

industry: activity, business, bustle, commerce, determination, effort, energy, field, ingenuity, labor, manufacturing, occupation, pursuit, toil, work, zeal

industry from government to private ownership, change: privatize

inebriated: bombed, drunk, intoxicated, loaded, plastered, smashed, stoned, tanked, tipsy, wasted

inedible part of meat: gristle

ineffable: celestial, devine, empyreal, ethereal, indescribable, inexpressible, sacred, taboo, transcendent, unspeakable, unutterable

ineffective: faineant, fruitless, futile, idle, impotent, inadequate, incompetent, ineffectual, inefficient, inept, neutralized, otiose, pathetic, useless, vain, void, weak, worthless

ineffective, make: invalidate, nullify, vitiate, void

ineffectual: futile, hopeless, idle, impotent, inadequate, ineffective, inefficient, insufficient, unable, unavailing, unproductive, useless, vain, weak

inefficient: disorganized, incompetent, ineffective, ineffectual, inept, slipshod, unfitted, unprepared, unproductive, unskilled, wasteful

inelastic: inflexible, rigid, stable, stiff, unadaptable, unbending, unyielding

inelegant: awkward, clumsy, coarse, common, crass, crude, gauche, graceless, ungenteel, unrefined, vulgar

ineligible: disqualified, unacceptable, unfit, unqualified, unsuitable, unworthy

ineluctable: certain, doomed, indubitable, inescapable, inevitable, sure, unavoidable, unevadable

inept: absurd, awkward, bumbling, bungling, clumsy, foolish, gauche, improper, inane, inappropriate, inapt, incompetent, ineffectual, inefficient, pointless, slow, unbecoming, unfit, unseemly, unskilled, unsuited

inept sportsman: duffer

inequality: bias, difference, discrimination, disparity, disproportion, diversity, imparity, prejudice, unevenness, unfairness

inequity: injustice, unfairness, wrong

inert: apathetic, dead, idle, immobile, impassive, inactive, indolent, languid, lazy, lethargic, lifeless, motionless, neutral, passive, phlegmatic, quiet, slack, slow, sluggish, static, stationary, still, supine, torpid

inert gas: argon, neon, radon, xenon

inertia: idleness, inactivity, indolence, lassitude, oscitancy, passivity, quiescence, stillness

inescapable: ineluctable, inevitable

inessential: expendable

inessential and supplementary: extraneous, extrinsic

inestimable: exquisite, incalcuable, invaluable, precious, priceless, unmeasurable, valuable

inevitable: assured, certain, decided, destined, doomed, fatal, fated, fateful, imminent, impending, in the cards, ineluctable, inescapable, necessary, sure, unavoidable, unpreventable

inexact: erroneous, false, inaccurate, rough, undetermined, vague

inexcusable: blameworthy, indefensible, intolerable, reprehensible, unallowable, unforgivable, untenable, wrong

inexhaustible: boundless, infinite, tireless, unflagging, unlimited, wearied

inexorable: adamant, determined, dogged, harsh, inflexible, intractable, ironclad, relentless, resolute, rigid, rigorous, stiff, stony, strict, unalterable, unbending, uncompromising, unrelenting, unyielding

inexpedient: detrimental, futile, impolitic, imprudent, inadvisable, injudicious, inopportune, unwise

inexpensive: bargain, cheap, economical, frugal, low-priced, reasonable, thrifty

inexpensive opera: threepenny

inexperienced: callow, green, inexpert, naive, raw, rookie, shortsighted, sophomoric, unaccustomed, unfamiliar, unfledged, unpracticed, unskilled, unsophisticated, untrained, untried, unversed, unworldly, verdant, wet behind the ears, young

inexperienced person: babe, beginner, greenhorn, greeny, neophyte, newcomer, novice, rookie, tenderfoot, tyro

inexpert: awkward, crude, green, inexperienced, unpracticed, unskilled, untrained

inexplicable: abstruse, ambiguous, enigmatic, inexplainable, mysterious, obscure, peculiar, strange, unaccountable, unfathomable

inexpressive: blank, devoid, dull, empty, flat, impassive, vacant

infallible: certain, dependable, divine, exact, faultless, flawless, foolproof, impeccable, perfect, reliable, sure, unerring, unfailing

infamous: atrocious, base, contemptible, corrupt, degenerate, despicable, detestable, dishonorable, evil, hateful, heinous, loathsome, miscreant, nefarious, notorious, odious, scandalous, shady, shameful, villainous

infamy: discredit, disesteem, disgrace, dishonor, ignominy, immorality, odium, reproach, scandal, shameful

infamy and disgrace: obloquy

infancy: babyhood, beginning, childhood, immaturity, inception, outset, start

infant: babe, baby, bambino, bantling, child, kid, minor, neonate, newborn, toddler

infantile: babyish, childish, immature, juvenile, sophomoric, youthful

infantryman: dogface, doughboy, foot soldier, soldier

infatuated: besotted, captivated, charmed, enamored, enchanted, enraptured, enthralled, fond, foolish, gaga, inflamed, obsessed

infatuation: attachment, craze, crush, fascination, folly, love, madness, obsession, passion

infect: affect, afflict, contaminate, damage, invade, poison, pollute, spoil, taint

infection: contagion, corruption, defilement, disease, illness, malady, plague

infection-fighting protein: antibody

infection main site: focus, nidus

infection-preventing technique: antisepsis

infection, spread of: zymosis

infectious: catching, communicable, contagious, epidemic, noxious, pestiferous, pestilential, poisonous, spreading, transferable, transmissible, transmitted, vitiating

infectious and spreading disease: pestiferous, pestilent

infectious, extremely: virulent

infective agent: virus

infer: ascertain, assume, conclude, construe, deduce, drive, educe, gather, glean, guess, hint, imply, interpret, opine, reason, speculate, suppose, surmise

infer from general principle: deduce, extrapolate

inference: assumption, conclusion, conjecture, corollary, deduction, illation, judgment, suggestion, understanding

inference drawn from misconception: subreption

inference from incomplete evidence: conjecture

inference of general from specific: induction

inferior: auxiliary, base, below, bum, cheap, common, cull, feeble, impure, inadequate, jerrybuilt, less, lesser, lower, mediocre, minion, minor, nether, peon, petty, poor, secondary, second-rate, shoddy, subaltern, subordinate, substandard, underling, underneath, unequal, unworthy, worst

inferior as substitute: ersatz

inferior in quality: mean, poor, shoddy

inferior, greatly: execrable, paltry, pitiable, sorry

infernal: abominable, avernal, awful, chthonian, cursed, damnable, demonic, devilish, diabolical, evil, fiendish, hellish, horrible, satanic, stygian, tartarean, underworld, vicious

inferno: abyss, fire, Hades, hell, holocaust, netherworld, pit, underworld

infertile: barren, depleted, drained, fruitless, impotent, infecund, sterile, unbearing, unproductive

INFECTIOUS, VIRAL, OR PARASITIC DISEASE

ague
AIDS/Acquired Immune-Deficiency Syndrome
AIDS-related complex/ARC
amebiasis/amoebiasis
amebic dysentery/amoebic dysentery
anthrax
bascillary dysentery
Black Death
blackwater fever
bovine spongiform encephalopathy
brucellosis
bubonic plague
chicken pox/varicella
cholera/Asiatic cholera
cowpox/vaccinia
Creutzfeldt-Jakob disease
dengue fever/dengue/breakbone fever/dandy fever
diphtheria
dumdum fever
dysentery
ebola
elephantiasis
encephalitis lethargica/sleeping sickness/sleepy sickness
enteric fever/typhoid fever
erysipelas/Saint Anthony's fire
fifth's disease
frambesia/yaws
German measles
glandular fever/infectious mononucleosis/mononucleosis
gonorrhea
grippe/grip/influenza
Hansen's disease/leprosy
hantavirus
helicobacter pylori
hepatitis
herpes
histoplasmosis
hookworm/uncinaria
influenza/grippe/grip
jail fever
kala-azar
Lassa fever
Legionnaires' disease
leishmaniasis/Dumdum fever/kala-azar
leprosy
leptospirosis/swamp fever
Lyme disease
malaria/paludism/swamp fever/malaria fever
measles/rubeola
meningitis
mononucleosis/infectious mononucleosis/kissing disease

mumps
ornithosis
otitis media
paratyphoid fever/salmonella
parotitis/parotiditis
plague
pneumonia
poliomyelitis/polio/infantile paralysis
prion disease
psittacosis/parrot fever
Q fever
rabies/hydrophobia
rat-bite fever
relapsing fever/recurrent fever
rheumatic fever
ringworm
Rocky Mountain spotted fever
rubella/German measles
rubeola/measles
scarlet fever/scarlatina
schistosomiasis/bilharziasis/snail fever
scrub typhus/Japanese river fever/tsutsugamushi disease
sexually transmitted diseases
shigellosis
shingles
sleeping sickness/African sleeping sickness
smallpox/variola
spotted fever
strep throat/septic sore throat
tetanus/lockjaw
thrush
tick fever
tinea
toxic shock syndrome
trachoma
trench fever
trench mouth/Vincent's angina/Vincent's infection
trypanosomiasis/sleeping sickness
tuberculosis
tularemia/rabbit fever
typhoid fever/typhoid/enteric fever
typhus/prison fever/ship fever/typhus fever
undulant fever/brucellosis/Gibraltar fever/Malta fever/Mediterranean fever/Rock fever
valley fever
variola/smallpox
venereal disease/VD
whooping cough/pertussis
yaws/frambesia
yellow fever/yellow jack
zoster/herpes zoster/shingles ❧

infest: beset, defile, flood, invade, overrun, pester, plague, ravage, swarm

infidel: agnostic, atheist, heathen, heretic, pagan, skeptic, unbeliever

infidelity: adultery, betrayal, breach, disloyalty, falsity, treason, violation

infiltrate: foist, impregnate, leak, penetrate, permeate, seep

infiltrator: mole, spy

infinite: boundless, countless, endless, eternal, illimitable, immeasurable, immense, interminable, limitless, perpetual, timeless, tremendous, unlimited, vast

infinitesimal: insignificant, little, microscopic, minuscule, minute, small, tiny, unnoticeable

infinitive with adverb between "to" and verb: split infinitive

infirm: ailing, anile, brittle, debilitated, decrepit, disabled, doddering, failing, feeble, fragile, frail, lame, sickly, unsound, vacillating, weak, worn

infirmary: clinic, dispensary, hospital

infirmity: affliction, ague, ailment, condition, confinement, debilitation, decay, deficiency, disease, feebleness, flaw, frailty, illness, malady, sickness, weakness

inflame: aggravate, anger, annoy, arouse, boil, burn, chafe, electrify, enrage, exasperate, excite, fire, heat, impassion, incense, infuriate, irritate, kindle, provoke, rile, stir

inflammable: ardent, burnable, combustible, excitable, fiery, hazardous, ignitable, incendiary, irascible, irritable, volatile

inflammation: acne, arthritis, boil, bursitis, chafing, conflagration, fire, gout, infection, irritation, phlegmasia, swelling

inflammation and fever, concerning: phlogistic

inflammation, reducing: anti-inflammatory, antiphlogistic

inflate: amplify, augment, balloon, bloat, blow, boost, dilate, distend, elate, enlarge, expand, increase, magnify, overestimate, pump, swell

inflate an expense account: pad

inflated: blown, bombastic, exaggerated, flatulent, flowery, overloaded, plethoric, pompous, rhetorical, swollen, tumid, turgid, wordy

inflated in speech: overblown, tumid, turgid

inflation: deficit finance, deficit financing

inflation caused by increased demand for limited goods and services: demand-pull

inflation caused by increased production costs: cost-push

inflation guide: retail price index

inflation, means of protection as against: hedge

inflection: accent, articulation, bend, curve, emphasis, enunciation, intonation, sound, timbre, tone, variation

inflection of words: accidence

inflexible: adamant, adamantine, dogged, firm, fixed, hard, headstrong, immovable, implacable, inelastic, inexorable, iron, obdurate, relentless, rigid, rigorous, steadfast, stiff, strict, stringent, stubborn, unadaptable, unbending, uncompromising, unyielding

inflict: administer, deliver, dispense, dump, force, impose, perpetrate, strike, unload, wreak

influence: affect, alter, ascendancy, aspect, attract, authority, clout, command, compel, connections, control, dominion, effect, fame, force, govern, gravity, hold, impel, impress, induce, inducement, inspire, lead, leverage, lobby, magnetism, mastery, money, motive, move, persuade, power, pressure, prestige, prominence, prompt, pull, rule, sway, weight

influence and stimulus: encouragement, incentive, incitement, motivation

influence dictating ethical choice: sanction

influence legislators, people with cause trying to: lobby

influence of charm and personality: charisma

influence over another, person exerting evil or forceful: Svengali

influence over others: clout, leverage, manipulation

influence with an ideology, forceful: brainwashing, indoctrination

influence, position of: ascendancy, dominance, preeminence

influence, susceptible to: biddable, cooperative, docile, ductile, flexible, malleable, pliable, tractable

influenced: actuated, guided, impelled, instigated, led, swayed

influenced, easily: docile, flexible, malleable, pliable, prone, susceptible

influential: dominant, effective, important, instrumental, leading, momentous, potent, powerful, significant, strong

influential behind-the-scenes person: eminence grise

influential person: luminary, magnate, tycoon

influential unofficial advising group: kitchen cabinet

influx: arrival, flow, increase, incursion, infiltration, inflow, inpouring, inrush, invasion, tide

inform: acquaint, advertise, advise, anile, apprise, betray, blab, brief, communicate, enlighten, familiarize, forewarn, instruct, notify, post, preach, snitch, squeal, talk, tattle, tell, train, update

inform formally: notify

informal: casual, colloquial, easygoing, frank, homey, loose, natural, relaxed, simple, unceremonious, unofficial

informal discussion: chat

informal in language: colloquial, conversational

informal language: slang

informal poll: straw vote

informant: canary, fink, informer, nark, rat, sneak, snitch, source, stoolie, tattletale, tipster

information: clue, data, direction, documents, dope, facts, feedback, instruction, intelligence, knowledge, lowdown, material, news, notice, poop, report, scoop, tidings, wisdom, word

RELATED TERMS

information about a process or activity, return of: feedback

information added at end: afterthought, appendix, postscript

information announcement: disclosure, revelation

information announcement, formal: bulletin, communiqué

information bit by bit, to gather: glean

information exchange among professionals: networking

information gathered on person, subject: dossier

information or mental stimulation that is pointless: pabulum

information overheard: hearsay

information processes in artificial systems, study of: cybernetics

information store: database

information to further a cause: propaganda

information, exchange or distribution point for: clearinghouse

information, of secret: classified

information, policy of withholding: obscurantism

information, to reveal: divulge, impart, relate

information, to supply with vital: brief, prime

informative: descriptive, educational, enlightening, illuminating, instructive, revealing

informed: abreast, apprised, aware, cognizant, conversant, hep, hip, knowing, notified, told, up on, versed, warned, well read, wise

informed on current events: au courant

informed on facts: au fait

informer: canary, informant, plant, sneak, source, stool pigeon, stoolie, tattletale, tipster ❦

infraction: breach, crime, encroachment, error, infringement, misdemeanor, transgression, violation

infrastructure: base, foundation, framework, ground, root, substructure, support

infrequent: intermittent, irregular, isolated, occasional, rare, scant, scarce, seldom, sparse, sporadic, uncommon, unusual

infringe: breach, break, contravene, disobey, encroach, impinge, infract, intrude, invade, meddle, offend, overstep, trespass, violate

infringe on a copyright: pirate

infuriate: aggravate, anger, enrage, incense, inflame, ire, irritate, outrage, rile, umbrage, vex

infuse: fill, imbue, impart, implant, inculcate, inspire, instill, introduce, leaven, pervade, plant, saturate, soak, steep

-ing form of verb acting as adjective or indicating tense: participle

-ing form of verb acting as noun: gerund

ingenious: able, acute, adroit, bright, brilliant, canny, clever, crafty, creative, cunning, daedal, gifted, imaginative, innovative, intelligent, inventive, original, refined, resourceful, sharp, skillful, smart, subtle, talented, witty

ingenuous: artless, candid, childlike, frank, guileless, honest, innocent, naif, naive, natural, open, simple, sincere, trustful, unaffected, undisguised

ingest: absorb, consume, drink, eat, swallow, take

inglorious: base, corrupt, degrading, disgraceful, dishonorable, ignominious, infamous, obscure, odious, scandalous, shabby, shameful

ingot: bar, block, ironbar, mold

ingrained: chronic, congenital, deepseated, established, firm, fundamental, inborn, inbred, inherent, innate, native, rooted

ingratiating: affable, agreeable, appealing, fawning, flattering, friendly, gushing, obsequious, oily, pleasing, servile, silken, soft, swarmy, sweet, sycophantic, unctuous, winsome

ingredient: additive, component, constituent, element, essence, factor, item, piece

ingress: access, door, entrance, entry, gate, opening, penetrate

inhabit: dwell, live, lodge, occupy, people, populate, reside, settle, tenant

inhabitant: boarder, citizen, colonist, denizen, dweller, habitue, inmate, native, occupant, resident

inhabitant from earliest times: aboriginal, autochthon

inhale: breathe, consume, devour, drag, inspire, puff, respire, smell, sniff

inharmonious: dissonant, incongruous

inherent: basic, characteristic, congenital, deeprooted, essential, fundamental, genetic, hereditary, inborn, inbred, indwelling, ingrained, innate, intrinsic, natural

inherit: acquire, get, obtain, receive

inheritance: bequest, birthright, endowment, estate, gift, heirloom, heritage, legacy, patrimony

inheritance from father: patrimony

inheritance or right to it: succession

inheritance right of eldest son: primogeniture

inheritance right to an estate: reversion

inheritance shared: coparcenary, parcenary

inheritance to a particular party, to limit the: entail

inherited item of value: heirloom

inherited traditions, customs: heritage

inherited, as disease: genetic, hereditary

inhibit: avert, bar, check, cramp, curb, deter, discourage, forbid, hinder, impede, prevent, prohibit, repress, restrain, restrict, stop, suppress

inhibited: cold, controlled, frigit, guarded, reserved, unresponsive

inhibition: barrier, hang-up, obstacle, restraint, suppression

inhospitable: hostile, impolite, rude, unfriendly, unsociable, unwelcoming

inhuman: barbaric, barbarous, beastly, bestial, brutal, brutish, cold, cold-hearted, cruel, diabolical, ferocious, heartless, insensate, insensible, malicious, merciless, monstrous, ruthless, savage, vicious

inimical: adverse, antagonistic, contrary, harmful, hostile, hurtful, injurious, repugnant, unfavorable, unfriendly

inimitable: rare

iniquitous: corrupt, evil, immoral, nefarious, sinful, unjust, wicked

iniquity: depravity, evil, immorality, infamy, miscreancy, offense, sin, vice, wrong

initial: basic, beginning, earliest, elementary, first, fundamental, inceptive, incipient, leading, maiden, opening, original, primary; letter

initial letter or sound dropped from word: apheresis

initial letter or sound repeating in words: alliteration

initial letters of lines forming word: acrostic

initial letters of words used to make word: acronym

initial TV show: pilot

initials in design: monogram

initiate: admit, begin, cause, commence, establish, found, haze, inaugurate, indoctrinate, induct, install, introduce, launch, open, originate, start, trigger

initiation: admittance, baptism, beginning, ceremony, commencement, enrollment, entrance, induction, introduction, investiture, onset, rite

initiation by first painful ordeal: baptism of fire

initiation ceremony or occurrence: rite of passage

initiation into group: induction

initiative: action, ambition, aptitude, creativity, drive, eagerness, energy, enterprise, enthusiasm, get-up-and-go, gumption, moxie, pluck, push, spunk

inject: force, imbue, inoculate, insert, instill, introduce, mainline, pump, put, shoot, vaccinate

injection in vein, of an: intravenous

injection of blood, etc.: transfusion

injection of medicine into rectum: clyster, colonic, enema

injection under skin: hypodermic, subcutaneous

injection vial holding liquid: ampoule, ampul, ampule

injection, additional dose: booster

injection, administered by: parentcral

injection, slow: infusion

injudicious: dumb, foolish, imprudent, inadvisable, indiscreet, unsound, unwise

injunction: behest, charge, command, decree, directive, edict, mandate, order, precept, ruling, writ

injure: abuse, affront, assault, bruise, damage, disfigure, harm, hurt, impair, insult, maim, maltreat, mar, offend, spoil, wound, wrong

RELATED TERMS

injured feeling: resentment, umbrage

injured or wronged, resentment from being: grievance

injurious: abusive, deleterious, detrimental, harmful, hurtful, libelous, malicious, nocuous, noxious, pernicious, slanderous, unhealthy

injury: affliction, blow, break, bruise, contusion, cut, damage, detriment, fracture, gash, hardship, harm, hurt, impairment, injustice, insult, laceration, lesion, mayhem, mutilation, sprain, stab, swelling, trauma, whiplash, wound, wrong

injury by violence or accident: trauma

injury in law: tort

injury or harmful action: disservice

injury, susceptible to: vulnerable ❦

injustice: bias, breach, crime, discrimination, favoritism, grievance, harm, hurt, inequality, inequity, iniquity, injury, miscarriage, prejudice, unfairness, violation, wickedness, wrong

ink, permanent: indelible ink

inkblot test for personality: Rorschach test

inkling: clue, glimmering, glimpse, hint, hunch, idea, indication, intimation, lead, notion, scent, suspicion

inky: black, dark, ebon, ebony, murky, raven, stained

inland region: backcountry, hinterland

inland, confined: landlocked

inlay work: damask, marquetry, mosaic, tessellation

inlet: arm, basin, bay, bayou, bight, channel, cove, creek, entrance, estuary, fiord, firth, fjord, gulf, harbor, inlay, narrows, opening, orifice, passage, ria, sound, strait, stream, waterway

inlet of sea between steep cliffs: fjord

inlet of sea or river mouth where tide, current meet: estuary

inmate: con, convict, felon, inhabitant, lifer, occupant, prisoner

inmost: central, deepest, intestinal, intimate

inmost nature: core, essence

inn: albergo, auberge, caravansary, fonda, hospice, hostel, hostelry, hotel, house, khan, lodge, motel, pub, resort, roadhouse, tavern

inn of East and Near East: caravansary, khan

inn of Spain: posada

innards: bowels, guts, insides, stuffing, viscera

innate: born, congenital, essential, hereditary, inborn, inbred, ingrained, inherent, inherited, instinctive, internal, intrinsic, native, natural

inner: central, close, concealed, deep, esoteric, hidden, inside, interior, internal, inward, middle, personal, private

innkeeper: boniface, host, hosteler, landlord, proprietor, publican, taverner, victualler

innocence: blamelessness, chastity, freshness, guiltlessness, naiveté, purity, sinlessness, spotlessness, virtue

innocence of rural life: pastoral

innocence-proving: exculpatory

innocent: artless, blameless, chaste, childlike, clean, exemplary, free, greenhorn, guileless, guiltless, harmless, ignorant, inculpable, ingenuous, lawful, naive, pristine, simple, unaware, unblamable, uncorrupt, uninvolved, unworldly, upright

innocent woman: ingenue

innocent, to declare: exculpate, exonerate

innocuous: harmless, inoffensive, insipid, jejune, pallid, unoffending

innocuous medication: placebo

innovation: change, departure, introduction, invention, novelty, vicissitude

innovative: contemporary, creative, ingenious, inventive, original

innuendo: clue, hint, implication, insinuation, intimation, overtone, reference, suggestion

innumerable: countless, incalculable, infinite, legion, many, myriad, numerous

inoculate: imbue, immunize, implant, infuse, leaven, protect, steep, vaccinate

inoffensive: harmless, innocuous, neutral, safe, unobtrusive

inoperative: countermanded, dead, idle, inactive, unworkable

inopportune: contrary, ill-timed, impractical, inappropriate, inconvenient, unfortunate, unseasonable, untimely

inopportune occurrence: contretemps

inordinate: copious, disorderly, excessive, exorbitant, extravagant, extreme, immoderate, lavish, outrageous, overmuch, superfluous, surplus, undue, unrestrained, wanton

inorganic: artificial, azoic, inanimate, lifeless, mineral

inquest: assize, delving, examination, finding, hearing, inquiry, investigation, probe, search

inquire: ask, examine, explore, grill, interrogate, investigate, pry, query, question, quiz, scrutinize, search, seek, study

inquiring: curious, investigative, searching, wondering

inquiry: analysis, audit, check, examination, hearing, inquest, inquisition, interview, investigation, probe, query, question, research, scrutiny

inquisition: hunt, inquest, inquiry, investigation, prosecution, search, trial, tribunal

INSECT TERMS

adult stage: imago
antenna: feeler
antenna knob: capitulum
back or upper surface of insect: tergum
change of form or habits after embryonic stage: metamorphosis
chirping by grasshopper, cricket: stridulation
egg: nit
excrement: frass
fear of insects: entomophobia
feeding tube: proboscis
insect carrying germs: carrier, vector
insect-eating: entomophagous, insectivorous
insect-eating plant: pitcher plant, Venus's-flytrap

insect in cocoon stage: chrysalis, pupa
insects that infest books: bibliophage, bookworm
insects, crustaceans, arachnids, etc.: arthropods
larva: maggot
larva living in water: naiad
larva not going through pupal stage: nymph
nest: nidus
noise made by insect: fritiniency
secondary part of insect: appendage
shedding of insect's skin: cast, casting
stage between larva and adult: chrysalis, pupa
study of insects: entomology
substance to repel insects: repellent 🐝

---

inquisitive: challenging, curious, interested, intrusive, meddlesome, meddling, nosey, nosy, prying, snooping

inroad: advance, encroachment, foray, incursion, intrusion, invasion, raid

ins and outs: details, particulars, quirks, ropes

insane: batty, bizarre, crazed, crazy, cuckoo, daffy, daft, delirious, demented, deranged, eccentric, frenetic, immoderate, irrational, loco, loony, lunatic, mad, maniac, manic, nuts, paranoid, psychopathetic, psychotic, screwy, touched, unbalanced, wacky

insane, to allege or prove: stultify

insanity: aberration, craziness, delirium, dementia, derangement, folly, foolishness, hysteria, lunacy, madness, mania, psychosis, vesania

insanity, temporary: amentia

insatiable: greedy, unsatisfied, voracious

inscribe: brand, carve, chisel, dedicate, engrave, enroll, enter, etch, impress, imprint, indite, list, print, scroll, sign, stamp, write

inscribe with symbols: blazon

inscribed pillar: stela, stele

inscription: autograph, caption, dedication, epigram, epitaph, label, legend, motto, signature, title, writing

inscription at the beginning of a book: dedication

inscription on tomb or monument: epigraph

inscriptions on walls: graffiti

inscriptions or decipherment, study of: epigraphy

inscriptions, study of ancient: epigraphy

inscrutable: abstruse, arcane, baffling, blank, cabalistic, hidden, impenetrable, inexplainable, inexplicable, mysterious, secret, sphinxlike, unfathomable, unrevealing

inscrutable one: sphinx

inscrutable person: enigma

insecure: afraid, apprehensive, dangerous, flimsy, frail, hazardous, loose, perilous, precarious, rickety, risky, shaky, uncertain, unconfident, unprotected, unsafe, unstable, unsure, vulnerable

inseminate: fertilize, implant, impregnate, promulgate, seed, sow

insensate: brutal, dull, fatuous, foolish, inanimate, insensible, senseless, unconscious, unfeeling, witless

insensibility: analgesia, apathy, coma, dullness, inactivity, indifference, lethargy, torpor, trance

insensible: cold, imperceptible, inanimate, inappreciable, indifferent, insensate, numb, obdurate, oblivious, unaware, unconscious, unfeeling, unintelligible, unmindful

insensitive: anesthetized, blasé, callous, cold, crass, deadened, hardened, impervious, indifferent, numb, unconcerned, unresponsive

inseparable: attached, connected, entwined, indivisible, inextricable, unified, united

inseparable and essential: inherent, integral, intrinsic, part and parcel of

insert: embed, engraft, enter, foist, imbed, implant, infuse, inlay, inset, intercalate, interpolate, interpose, introduce, set in

insert day in calendar: intercalate

insert organ in body: implant

insert sound or letter in word: epenthesis

insert unacknowledged addition in text: interpolate

insertion: intromission

insertion mark: caret

inside: confidential, indoors, innards, inner, interior, intramural, intrinsic, lining, middle, private, surrounded

inside of curved surface: concavity

inside or part of essence: immanent, implicit, inherent, intrinsic

inside out: backward, evert, inverted, reversed

inside out, to turn: evert

inside out, to turn a body part: evaginate

insider: cognoscente

insidious: alluring, artful, concealed, cunning, deceitful, deep, devious, foxy, fraudulent, guileful, harmful, sneaky, snide, treacherous, tricky, underhanded

insight: acumen, awareness, discernment, idea, intuition, observation, penetration, perception, understanding, vision, wisdom

insightful impression: apercu, intuition

insignia: badge, crest, decoration, emblem, mark, medal, stripe, symbol

insignia or ensigns: heraldry

insignia, V-shaped: chevron

insignificant: contemptible, dinky, immaterial, inferior, irrelevant, little, meaningless, minor, minuscule, minute, negligible, nonessential, nugatory, paltry, petty, puny, small, tiny, trifling, trivial, unimportant, unsubstantial, worthless

insignificant amount: drop in the bucket, iota, tad

insignificant person, thing: nonentity

insincere: ambiguous, backhanded, deceitful, dishonest, disingenuous, false, feigned, guileful, hollow, hypocritical, left-handed, phony, untruthful

insincere support: lip service

insincere sympathy: bathos

insincere talk of morality, religion: cant

insincerely charming: ingratiating, unctuous

insinuate: allude, foist, hint, hint at, implant, imply, indicate, infuse, insert, intimate, introduce, penetrate, suggest

insipid: arid, banal, blah, bland, boring, commonplace, dead, dry, dull, flat, hohum, jejune, lackluster, lifeless, monotonous, mundane, ordinary, pointless, prosaic, prosy, spiritless, stale, tame, tasteless, unappetizing, uninteresting, vapid

insipid remark: platitude

insist: assert, claim, contend, demand, expect, maintain, press, require

insistent: assertive, dogged, emphatic, firm, forceful, importunate, incessant, pushy, resolute, strident, unyielding

insolence: arrogance, audacity, backtalk, boldness, brazenness, contempt, disrespect, effrontery, gall, haughtiness, hauteur, impertinence, impudence, incivility, insult, nerve, presumption, sass

insolent: abusive, arrant, arrogant, audacious, bold, brazen, contumacious, defiant, impolite, impudent, overbearing, rude, sassy, saucy, ungracious, unmannerly

insoluble: baffling, inexplicable, mysterious, unexplainable, unresolved

insolvent: bankrupt, broke, busted, foreclosed, impoverished, penniless, ruined

insomnia: agrypnia, ahypnia, anhypnosis, indisposition, restlessness, sleeplessness, wakefulness

insouciant: carefree, casual, easygoing, heedless, indifferent, lighthearted, nonchalant, unconcerned, untroubled

inspect: audit, canvass, check, examine, eye, investigate, observe, probe, scan, scout, scrutinize, study, supervise, survey, view

inspection: appraisal, checkup, examination, frisk, investigation, parade, review, surveillance

inspection of building: assessment, survey

inspection or exploration of area: reconnaissance, reconnoitering

inspection, cursory, for quality: spot check

inspiration: animus, brainstorm, creativity, flash, genius, idea, impulse, incentive, motivation, revelation, spark, spur, stimulus, thought, vision

inspiration, divine: afflatus

inspire: affect, animate, arouse, cause, encourage, enliven, exalt, excite, fire, galvanize, influence, inspirit, invigorate, motivate, move, prompt, provoke, stimulate, stir, touch

inspire with ideas: imbue, permeate, pervade

instability: changeability, fluctuation, flux, imbalance, inconstancy, insecurity, shakiness, uncertainty, unpredictability, unsteadiness, volatility, wavering

instability, physical: disequilibrium, imbalance

install: establish, furnish, inaugurate, induct, initiate, instate, invest, lay, place, position, seat

installment: chapter, episode, part, payment, section

installment ceremony: investiture

installments, to pay in: amortize

instance: case, detail, example, exemplify, illustration, occasion, occurrence, precedent, proof, refer, request, show, specimen, suggestion, suit, time

instant: breath, direct, fast, flash, immediate, jiffy, minute, moment, pressing, quick, rapid, second, speedy, swift, trice, urgent, wink

instantly: directly, immediately, now, pronto, urgently

instantly at a given signal: at the drop of a hat

instead: alternatively, equivalent, in lieu, preferably, rather, substitute

instigate: abet, encourage, excite, foment, goad, incite, influence, initiate, motivate, move, needle, plot, prod, prompt, provoke, push, spur, stimulate, urge

instigate evil: suborn

instill: engender, imbue, impart, implant, impress, inculcate, infix, infuse, insert, introduce, pour

instinct: feeling, hunch, idea, intuition, sense, tendency

instinctive: automatic, congenital, gut, inborn, inbred, ingrained, inherent, innate, intuitive, involuntary, natural, spontaneous, unacquired, visceral

instinctive knowledge: intuition

instincts defined by Freud: Eros, libido, Thanatos

institute: begin, custom, edict, enact, establish, found, inaugurate, launch, ordain, organize, originate, rite, rule, start, tradition

institute legal proceedings: prosecute, sue

institution immune from criticism: sacred cow

institution, someone confined in: inmate

institution, within bounds of: intramural

instruct: advise, apprise, brief, coach, command, counsel, direct, discipline, drill, educate, enlighten, guide, indoctrinate, inform, lead, show, teach, tell, train, tutor

instruct in doctrines, principles: indoctrinate

instruct thoroughly: drill

instruction: advice, directions, edification, education, formula, lesson, lore, method, recipe, schooling, teaching, training, tuition, tutelage

instruction in church principles: catechesis, catechism

instructional: didactic, pedagogical

instructor: coach, guide, guru, lecturer, mentor, professor, teacher, trainer, tutor

instrument for determining a horizontal plane: spirit level

instrument recording travel distance: odometer

instrument to measure diameter, thickness: calipers

instrument, mute for: damper, sordino

instrumental: assisting, conducive, contributory, crucial, essential, helpful, influential, useful, vital

instrumental and choral composition with many solos: cantata

instrumental composition: sonata

instrumental composition in the same key consisting of different dance forms: suite

insubordinate: defiant, disobedient, dissentious, factious, fractious, insurgent, mutinous, rebellious, recalcitrant, refractory, riotous, seditious, ungovernable, unruly, unyielding

insubstantial: airy, delicate, fine, flimsy, fragile, frail, imaginary, immaterial, intangible, small, weak

insubstantial and spiritual: incorporeal

insufferable: agonizing, dreadful, excruciating, hateful, intolerable, painful, unbearable, unendurable

insufficient: deficient, drained, incomplete, inadequate, lacking, meager, scanty, scarce, short, sparse, wanting

insular: biased, bigoted, clannish, confined, isolated, narrow, prejudiced, provincial, restricted, secluded

insulate: cover, enisle, isolate, protect, segregate, sequester, shield, tape

insult: abuse, affront, barb, belittle, blackguard, degrade, deride, derogatory, disgrace, humiliate, indignity, malign, mock, offend, outrage, revile, ridicule, roast, scorn, shame, slander, slap, slur, snub, taunt, tease

RELATED TERMS

insult and criticize: affront, anathematize, contemn, decry, denigrate, denounce, depreciate, deride, derogate, disparage, execrate, vilipend, vituperate

insult and slander: calumniate, malign, stigmatize, traduce, vilify

insult and taunt: bait, fleer, flout, ridicule, tease, torment

insult to God or religion: blasphemy, sacrilege

insult to reputation: aspersion, calumny, character assassination, defamation, libel, slander, slur, smear

insult, condition of disgrace after: ignominy, obloquy

insulting curse: denunciation, invective, vituperation

insulting remark or act: calumny, contumely

insulting, deliberately: derogatory, disparaging ❧

insurance: assurance, coverage, indemnity, protection, safeguard, security, warranty

insurance coverage for specified period but void upon expiration: term insurance

insurance coverage, wide-ranging: comprehensive

insurance fixed annual payments for lump sum return: annuity

insurance payment: premium

insurance policy are to be paid, time when proceeds of: maturity

insurance policy, amendment to: endorsement

insurance risk and premium calculator: actuary

insurance risk of death, injury, loss to others: personal liability

insure: cover, guarantee, guard, indemnify, underwrite

insurgent: dissident, insubordinate, mutineer, mutinous, radical, rebel, rebellious, resister, revolter, revolting, revolutionary

insurmountable: hopeless, impassable, impossible, insuperable, invincible, overwhelming

insurrection: coup, insurgence, mutiny, rebellion, revolt, revolution, riot, uprising

intact: complete, entire, inviolate, sound, together, unbroken, undamaged, undefiled, unharmed, unimparied, uninjured, unmarred, unscathed, whole

intangible: abstract, ethereal, immaterial, impalpable, indefinite, unapparent, unreal, unsubstantial, vague

integral: basic, complete, component, constituent, entire, essential, finished, full, fundamental, indispensable, necessary, whole

integrate: blend, combine, coordinate, desegregate, harmonize, join, link, merge, mesh, mix, organize, unite

integrity: candor, character, decency, honesty, honor, probity, virtue, wholeness

integrity, lack of: dishonesty, improbity

integrity, to challenge someone's: discredit, impeach

integument: aril, coat, covering, envelope, hide, pelt, skin

intellect: acumen, brain, genius, intelligence, mentality, mind, smarts, thinker, understanding, wit

intellect and wit, person of refined: bel esprit

intellectual: brainy, cerebral, egghead, genius, highbrow, literati, mental, scholar, studious

RELATED TERMS

intellectual and cultured: highbrow

intellectual class: intelligentsia, literati

intellectual class gathering: salon

intellectual perception of something senses cannot perceive: noumenon

intellectual rather than emotional: cerebral

intellectual teacher: guru

intellectually apprehended: noetic

intellectually unsatisfying: jejune

intellectuals' research center: think tank ❧

intelligence: acumen, aptitude, brainpower, brilliance, horse sense, information, learning, news, notice, report, sense, smarts, understanding, wisdom, wit, word

intelligent: acute, alert, astute, bright, brilliant, cognizant, exceptional, ingenious, logical, quick, sensible, smart, wise

intelligible: apparent, clear, definite, distinct, lucid, perspicuous, plain, unmistakable

intemperance: dissipation

intemperate: drunkenness, excessive, extravagant, immoderate, inclement, severe, unrestrained, violent

intend: aim, attempt, contemplate, dedicate, design, determine, expect, mean, plan, propose, signify, strive

intended: aimed, calculated, contemplated, deliberate, fiancé, fiancée, meant, planned, projected, proposed, purposed

intended by fate: destined, predestined, preordained

intense: acute, ardent, blistering, burning, consuming, deep, earnest, extreme, fervent, fierce, hard, keen, passionate, powerful, profound, rabid, severe, strained, strong, vehement, violent, vivid, zealous

intense dislike: hatred

intense fear: dread, terror

intensify: accentuate, aggrandize, aggravate, bolster, boost, deepen, elevate, enhance, escalate, exalt, heighten, increase, magnify, mount, quicken, rise, sharpen, strengthen

intensity: concentration, depth, emotion, energy, fervor, fire, force, passion, power, strength, vigor, zeal

intent: absorbed, aim, bent, decided, design, determined, diligent, eager, engrossed, firm, fixed, goal, industrious, meaning, preoccupied, purpose, rapt, resolute, riveted, steadfast, tense, watchful, will

intention: aim, animus, designation, drift, end, goal, hope, impulsion, motive, object, objective, plan, point, purpose, struggle

intention, concealed: hidden agenda, ulterior motive

intentional: calculated, deliberate, meant, planned, premeditated, voluntary, willing

inter: bury, entomb, inhume, inurn, plant

interact: communicate, cooperate, coordinate, interface, join, mesh, unite

interbreed: cross, hybridize, mix

intercede: arbitrate, interpose, intervene, mediate, negotiate

intercept: ambush, block, catch, deflect, grab, hijack, interrupt, seize, stop, take

interchange: alternate, barter, commute, convert, exchange, junction, network, permutate, reciprocate, substitute, swap, switch, trade, transposal

interchangeable: compatible, convertible, equivalent, fungible, reversible, synonymous, transposable

intercourse: business, commerce, communication, communion, connection, contact, conversation, dealings, networking; coitus, copulation, sex

interdict: ban, forbid, halt, inhibit, outlaw, prevent, prohibit, proscribe, stop, taboo, veto

interest: advantage, appeal, attraction, behalf, benefit, concern, curiosity, enthusiasm, excite, fascinate, grab, hobby, influence, part, passion, pursuit, recreation, sympathy, welfare; credit, earnings, investment, points, share, stake

interest-bearing certificate: registered bond

interest on bank loans, lowest rate of: prime rate

interest paid on principal and accumulating interest: compound interest, cumulative interest

interest paid only on original principal: simple interest

interest to protect, one's special: vested interest

interest, obsessive: fixation, idée fixe

interest, of widespread or universal: catholic

interest, to accumulate over time as: accrue

interested: absorbed, attentive, committed, drawn, hooked, involved, lured, rapt, taken

interested and concentrated on: absorbed, engrossed, immersed, intent, preoccupied, rapt

interesting: captivating, challenging, compelling, enchanting, entertaining, intriguing, stimulating

interesting and engaging: sapid

interesting, extremely: arresting, beguiling, bewitching, captivating, compelling, enchanting, engaging, enthralling, gripping, mesmerizing, riveting, spellbinding, tantalizing

interests, group with common: community

interfere: block, clash, conflict, disturb, foil, frustrate, hamper, hinder, impede, intervene, intrude, jam, meddle, mess in, obstruct, sabotage, tamper

interference, broadcast: static

interfering person: buttinsky, interloper, intruder, meddler

interim: acting, break, breather, hiatus, interlude, interval, makeshift, meantime, pause, pro tempore, spell, temporary

interim replacement: loaner

interior: center, core, domestic, heartland, inland, inner, inside, midst, within

interior covering: lining

interior scene: decor

interject: include, insert, interpose, interrupt, introduce

interjection: ah, ahem, alas, amen, boo, cheers, egad, er, exclamation, golly, hello, hey, hooray, huh, hurrah, jeepers, oh, oops, ouch, phew, phooey, pooh, psst, rah, rats, shucks, ugh, um, whoopee, wow, yipes

interlace: alternate, braid, entwine, intertwine, interweave, knit, mix, twine, weave

interlock: mesh

interlocked: dovetailed

interloper: busybody, intruder, meddler, trespasser

interlude: break, breather, episode, farce, hiatus, interim, intermission, interval, pause, recess, respite, rest

intermediary: agent, ambassador, arbitrator, broker, channel, delgate, gobetween, intercessor, mediator, medium, negotiator, referee, umpire

intermediate: average, between, common, fair, halfway, intervening, mean, median, middle, moderate

intermediate in law: mesne

intermediate place or state: limbo

intermediate point between two extremes: mean, medium

intermediate thing or factor: tertium quid

interminable: boundless, ceaseless, constant, continuous, endless, eternal, everlasting, incessant, infinite, perpetual, timeless, unlimited

intermingle: associate, blend, intermix, network, socialize

intermission: break, cessation, hiatus, interim, interval, pause, recess, respite, rest, stop, suspension, wait

intermittent: alternating, broken, cyclical, episodic, fitful, hesitant, irregular, occasional, on and off, periodic, recurrent, rhythmic, spasmodic, sporadic

intern: apprentice, doctor, immure, resident, student, trainee

internal: centralized, domestic, enclosed, home, inherent, inner, intrinsic, inward, within

internal clandestine subversive organization: fifth column

internal falling or slipping out of place by organ: prolapse

internal in origin: endogenous

internal organs: innards, viscera

internal to an institution: intramural

internal to being or force: immanent, implicit, inherent, intrinsic

international: cosmopolitan, global, universal, worldly, worldwide

international agreement: pact, peace agreement, treaty

international calm: détente

international conference of government officials: summit

international negotiating tactic of entering crisis rather than concede: brinkmanship

international relations: diplomacy

international, multicultural: cosmopolitan

interpolate: add, alter, change, estimate, foist, inject, insert, intercalate, introduce

interpose: arbitrate, insert, intercede, interfere, interject, intervene, introduce, mediate, moderate, negotiate

interpret: clarify, commentate, construe, decipher, decode, define, describe, diagnose, explain, explicate, expound, paraphrase, read, render, translate, understand, unravel

interpret from rational standpoint: rationalize

interpret or explain in detail: construe, elucidate, expound

interpret or read code, cipher: decipher, decode, decrypt

interpretation: analysis, exegesis, explanation, intent, meaning, rendition, translation, understanding, version

RELATED TERMS

interpretation of Bible: hermeneutics

interpretation of expression or statement: construction

interpretation of text or theory: explication, exposition

interpretation of text, critical: exegesis

interpretation of text, mystical: anagoge, anagogy

interpretation or performance of text, role: rendition

interpretation, open to more than one: ambiguous

interpretation, purposefully misleading: gloss

interpretation, science and methodology of: hermeneutics ❦

interpreter: exegete

interpreter, Middle East: dragoman

interrogate: ask, cross-examination, examine, grill, inquire, investigate, query, question, quiz

interrogation: catachism, inquest, inquisition, probe

interrupt: arrest, bother, break, cease, check, discontinue, disturb, halt, hinder, inject, interfere, stall, stop, suspend, thwart, upset

interrupt progress: disrupt, intercept, intervene, supervene

interrupt with comments: heckle, interject, interpose

interrupted: discontinuous

interruption: cessation, delay, distraction, disturbance, gap, hiatus, interference, intermission, interregnum, intrusion, lacuna, lapse, pause

interruption of utility service: outage

intersect: converge, crisscross, cross, cut, divide, meet, separate

intersect to form X: decussate

intersecting: secant

intersection: corner, crossroads, decussation, junction

intersperse: bestrew, distribute, pepper, scatter

interstellar gas cloud: nebula

interstellar space measurement: parsec

interstice: aperture, areola, areole, chink, crack, cranny, crevice, hole, interval, opening, orifice, pore, slit, space

intertwine: braid, crisscross, enlace, interlace, interweave, knit, lace, link, twist

interval: breach, break, delay, gap, hiatus, interim, interlude, intermission, pause, period, phase, recess, respite, rest, space, span, term, time

interval between acts, events, activities: intermission, recess

interval between end of one's reign and beginning of another: interrenum

interval between events, periods: interim

interval decreased by semitone, of musical: diminished

interval increased by semitone, of musical: augmented

interval, peaceful: lull, respite

intervene: arbitrate, intercede, interpose, mediate, negotiate, settle

intervention: conciliation, intercession, mediation

interview: audience, audition, communication, conference, consult, conversation, dialogue, hearing, meeting, question, talk

interweave: blend, braid, darn, enlace, fuse, interlace, intertwine, knit, link, mingle, mix, plait, pleach, twist

intestinal: enteric

RELATED TERMS

intestinal divisions: ilea

intestinal fortitude: backbone, courage, endurance, grit, guts, nerve, spirit, spunk

intestinal inflammation: colitis

intestinal malady: cholera

intestinal milky fluid: chyle

intestinal muscular contractions: peristalsis, vermiculation

intestinal pain: colic, gripes

intestinal pouch or sac, abnormal: diverticulum

intestinal pouches: caeca

intestinal vascular projections: villus ❦

intestines: bowels, entrails, guts, innards, insides, viscera

intestines of pigs as food: chitterlings

intimacy: affection, closeness, fondness, friendship, tenderness, warmth

intimate: acquaintance, announce, associate, bosom, buddy, chummy, close, companion, confidant, confidential, cozy, crony, dear, devoted, direct, familiar, friendly, hint, imply, informal, inmost, insinuate, loving, near, pal, personal, private, secret, signify, snug, suggest, trusted

intimate apparel: lingerie

intimate ballad or song: chanson

intimately: cheek by jowl

intimately with another: à deux

intimation: announcement, clue, cue, declaration, hint, indication, inkling, innuendo, notice, scent, suggestion, telltale, warning

intimidate: abash, badger, bludgeon, browbeat, bully, coerce, cow, daunt, dominate, faze, frighten, hector, overawe, ride, scare, swagger, terrify, terrorize, threaten

into: against, among, condition, divisor, form, inside, interested, toward, until

intolerable: abhorrent, excruciating, impossible, insufferable, offensive, unacceptable, unbearable

intolerant: biased, bigoted, comtemptuous, disdainful, dogmatic, fanatical, hidebound, hostile, impatient, narrow, outraged, prejudiced, sectarian

intolerant one: bigot, racist, sectarian

intone: articulate, cant, chant, croon, modulate, recite, sing, utter

intoxicant: alcohol, beer, booze, bourbon, dope, drug, gin, liquor, narcotic, rum, vodka, whiskey, wine

intoxicated: bombed, buzzed, drunk, ecstatic, euphoric, excited, high, high as a kite, inebriated, loaded, plastered, polluted, smashed, soused, stewed, stoned, tanked, tipsy, wasted, zonked

intractable: cantankerous, difficult, disobedient, headstrong, indocile, intransigent, mulish, obdurate, obstinate, ornery, perverse, pigheaded, stubborn, surly, ungovernable, unmanageable, unruly, unteachable, unyielding, willful

intransigent: inflexible, iron-willed, obdurate, pertinacious, stubborn, uncompromising, unmovable, unyielding, willful

intrepid: adventurous, bodacious, bold, brave, courageous, daring, doughty, fearless, gallant, game, gutsy, heroic, nervy, resolute, undaunted, valorous, vigilant

intricate: arduous, complex, complicated, convoluted, daedal, difficult, elaborate, entangled, hard, involved, knotty, labyrinthine, perplexing, tangled

intrigue: absorb, affair, allure, amour, angle, appeal, artifice, cabal, charm, conspiracy, conspire, design, excite, fascinate, hook, interest, liaison, machinate, machination, plot, puzzle, rivet, romance, scheme

intrinsic: basic, essential, fundamental, genuine, inborn, inbred, ingrained, inherent, inmost, innate, inner, natice, natural, necessary, real, true

intrinsic nature: essence

introduce: announce, begin, broach, debut, enter, establish, herald, inaugurate, induct, initiate, innovate, insert, insinuate, institute, interlarded, interpolate, launch, meet, originate, pioneer, precede, preface, presage, present, recommend, show, sponsor, start, submit, unveil, usher

introduce between things: intercalate, interject, interpolate, interpose

introduce cunningly: insinuate

introduce formally: induct, invest

introduce inventive thing: innovate

introduce subtly: insinuate

introduce to new field, activity: initiate

introduction: beginning, commencement, entrance, foreword, inception, insertion, intrada, lead, opening, overture, preamble, preface, prelude, preparation, primer, proem, prologue

introduction or theme: lemma

introduction to field of study: isagoge

introduction to Greek or Roman drama: protasis

introduction to text: foreword, preface, proem, prologue

introductory: beginning, elementary, first, initial, precursory, prefatory, preliminary, preludial, prelusive, preparatory

introductory comments for a book written by someone other than author: foreword

introductory course: induction, orientation

introductory discussion: prolegomenon, prolusion

introductory explanation: rubric

introductory part of treatise or speech: exordium, preamble

introductory section in music: overture, prelude

introductory tape: demo

introductory to an art or science: propaedeutic

introspection: contemplation, meditation, reflection, self-analysis, self-examination

introvert: brooder, inward, loner, solitary

intrude: bother, disturb, encroach, impose, infringe, interfere, interlope, interpose, interrupt, meddle, obtrude, overstep, press in, trespass

intrude on privacy, time, property: infringe, trespass

intrude one's opinion: obtrude

intruder: trespasser

intrusive: aggresive, curious, impertinent, meddlesome, nosy, officious, prying

intuition: apercu, clairvoyance, cryptesthesia, ESP, extrasensory perception, feeling, hunch, insight, instinct, premonition, second sight, sense, sixth sense

intuitive: clairvoyant, inherent, innate, instinctive, perceptive, psychic, visceral

Inuit: Eskimo

Inuit house: igloo, iglu

inundate: deluge, drown, engulf, flood, overflow, overrun, overwhelm, submerge, swamp

inure: acclimatize, accustom, adapt, desensitize, discipline, habituate, harden, season, teach, toughen, train, use

invade: assail, assault, attack, encroach, enter, infest, infringe, interfere, intrude, overrun, penetrate, raid, seize, storm, trespass

invalid: cripple, feeble, infirm, sickly, weak; ineffective, null, unfounded, unreasonable, useless, void, worthless

invalid and false: inauthentic, spurious

invalid and sickly: valetudinarian

invalid and without force: nugatory, powerless

invalidate: abolish, annul, cancel, negate, neutralize, nullify, offset, quash, revoke, undermine, undo, vitiate, void

invaluable: beyond price, costly, expensive, inestimable, precious, priceless, rare

invariable: consistent, constant, immutable, inflexible, same, steady, unchanging, unfailing, uniform, unvarying, unwavering

invariably: always, forever, perpetually, regularly

invasion: assault, attach, encroachment, foray, incursion, influx, inroad, intrusion, irruption, offensive, onslaught, raid

invective: abusive, berating, billingsgate, contumely, denunciatory, diatribe, insult, reproach, scurrile, tirade, venom, vituperation

inveigh: adminish, belittle, blame, castigate, condemn, declaim, harangue, lambaste, protest, rail, scold, upbraid

inveigle: allure, cajole, charm, coax, decoy, entice, entrap, influence, lure, manipulate, persuade, seduce, tempt, wheedle

invent: coin, conceive, concoct, contrive, create, design, devise, discover, engineer, envision, evolve, fabricate, fashion, form, frame, imagine, improvise, innovate, originate, patent, pioneer, vamp

invent and plan in mind: contrive, devise, excogitate, originate

invent details when memory fails: confabulate

invent to deceive: concoct, fabricate

invent word: coin, mint, neologize

invent, produce, perform without preparation: improvise

invented: fictitious

invention: brainchild, contraption, creation, discovery, fantasy, fiction, gadget, idea, innovation, lie

inventive: adept, clever, creative, demiurgic, fertile, ingenious, innovative, resourceful, skillful

inventor obtaining exclusive rights: patentee

inventor's exclusive right or title: patent

inventor's share of proceeds for right to use invention: royalty

inventory: accounting, backlog, catalog, checklist, evaluation, itemize, list, record, register, reserve, roll, stock, stockpile, store, summary, survey, tally

inverse: backward, contrary, inverted, opposite, reciprocal, reverse

inversion in second phrase/clause of the first's words: chiasmus

inversion of word order: anastrophe, hyperbaton

invert: alter, flip, inverse, reverse, transpose, turn, upside-down

inverted V indicating insertion: caret

invest: adorn, bankroll, beseige, clothe, confer, cover, crown, dress, endow, endue, envelop, gird, gown, imbue, install, instate, lend, ordain, robe, surround, wrap

investigate: analyze, audit, check, delve, dissect, examine, explore, inquire, inspect, probe, question, research, scrutinize, search, sift, sound, study, survey

investigation: analysis, hearing, inquest, inquiry, inquisition, inspection, legwork, probe, review

investigation for learning: heuristics

investigation, formal: inquest, inquiry, inquisition

investigator: agent, auditor, detective, examiner, inquisitor, inspector, police, researcher, sleuth

investiture: investment

investment: asset, backing, capital, financing, loan, money, property, share, speculation, stake, stock, venture

investment company offering new shares and buying existing shares on demand: mutual fund

investment readily convertible to cash: liquidity

investment shareholder: bondholder, rentier

investment sold without a sales charge: no-load fund

investment vehicle: money market fund

investment yield: return

investment, risky: speculation

investments and assets: portfolio

investments in stocks or bonds: securities

investor, optimistic: bull

investor, pessimistic: bear

inveterate: avid, chronic, confirmed, deep-rooted, deep-seated, enduring, entrenched, established, fixed, habitual, hardened, ingrained, innate, inured, settled

invidious: defamatory, detestable, discriminatory, envious, hateful, jealous, odious, repugnant, spiteful, vicious

invigorate: animate, energize, enliven, excite, exhilarate, fortify, freshen, pep up, refresh, rejuvenate, renew, revitalize, stimulate, stir, strengthen

invigorating: bracing, brisk, charged, crisp, healthful, hearty, lively, tonic, uplifting, zestful

invigorating drink: tonic

invincible: indestructible, invulnerable, powerful, unbeatable, undefeatable

inviolable: chaste, consecrated, divine, hallowed, holy, impregnable, pure, sacred, stable, unbreakable

invisible: covert, disguised, hidden, imperceptible, inconspicuous, indiscernible, indistinct, unapparent, unobservable, unseen

invisible emanation: aura

invisible radiation between light and microwaves: infrared

invisible radiation between light and X rays: ultraviolet

invitation: bid, call, challenge, date, lure, offer, overture, proposal, proposition, request, temptation

invite: allure, ask, attract, bid, call, court, draw, entice, include, solicit, summon, urge, welcome

invocation: benediction, calling, conjuring, incantation, litany, plea, prayer, sermon

invoice: account, bill, inventory, list, receipt, statement

invoke: appeal, beseech, call, conjure, entreat, initiate, muster, petition, pray, request, solicit, supplicate

involuntary: accidental, automatic, begrudging, compulsory, conditioned, forced, impulsive, instinctive, reflex, reluctant, spontaneous, unconscious, unintended, unrehearsed, unwilling, unwitting

involuntary response: reflex

involve: associate, commit, complicate, comprehend, comprise, concern, embrace, embroil, engage, entail, hook, implicate, imply, include, incorporate, link, snare, tangle, touch, wrap

involve as necessary consequence: entail

involved: absorbed, complex, elaborate, entangled, immersed, interested, into, intricate, participating, preoccupied

involved and committed: engage

involved and complicated: convoluted, intricate

involved and wasteful procedure: rigmarole

involved in argument, contention: embroiled

involved in mess: enmeshed, entangled

involving effort: operose

involving just one operand: unary

invulnerable: formidable, immune, impregnable, indestructible, invincible, unbeatable

inward: familiar, inbound, inflowing, ingoing, inner, inside, interior, internally, intimate, intrinsic, penetrating, spiritual

inward carrying or conducting to central organ: afferent

inward-moving or -directed: centripetal

inward-turning feet, of: pigeon-toed

inward, violent collapse: implosion

iodine source: kelp

ion, positive: cation, kation

ion, negative: anion

iota: atom, bit, crumb, grain, jot, particle, shred, smidgen, speck, trace, whit

ipso facto: by the fact of

irascibility: bile

irascible: angry, belligerent, cantankerous, choleric, crabby, cranky, fretful, hot-tempered, huffy, impatient, irate, ireful, ornery, passionate, quick-tempered, snappish, snappy, surly, testy, touchy

irate: angry, annoyed, enraged, fuming, furious, incensed, indignant, irascible, irked, livid, mad, provoked, riled, sore, wrathful, wroth

ire: anger, annoy, conniption, exasperate, fury, heat, infuriate, rage, resentment, spleen, vehemence, vexation, wrath

iridescent: bright, colorful, kaleidoscopic, lustrous, nacreous, opalescent, pearly, prismatic, rainbow-colored, shiny, versicolor

iridescent gem: opal

IRISH TERMS

ancient Irish mystic: druid
Celtic language of Ireland: Irish Gaelic, Erse
concerning Ireland: Gaelic, Hibernian, Irish, Milesian
floral symbol of Ireland: shamrock
Irish accent: brogue
Irish cudgel: shillelagh

Irish native: Gael, Celt
Irish sprite: leprechaun
Irish tobacco pipe: dudeen
Irish whiskey: poteen, usquebaugh
Irish writing system: ogam, ogham
kissing stone: Blarney stone ❦

---

iris: ixia
iris, white: fleur-de-lis
irk: abrade, aggravate, agitate, annoy, bother, bug, chafe, disturb, irritate, loess, nettle, peeve, pique, rile, ruffle, tire, upset, vex
irksome: annoyance, boring, dull, painful, pesky, rankling, tedious, troublesome, unpleasant, vexation, weariness
iron: appliance, ferric, ferrum, fetter, firmness, golf club, handcuffs, hard, hardy, harpoon, inflexible, manacles, metal, press, robust, shackles, steel, strong, stubborn, tough, unyielding
RELATED TERMS
iron for welding or bars: fagot
iron forger: blacksmith
iron in blocks, crude: pig iron
iron in the rough: ore
iron ore: hematite, limonite, magnetite, pyrite
iron sheet, ridged: corrugated iron
iron with zinc, to coat: galvanize
iron, tasting like: chalybeate ❦

iron out: agree, compromise, negotiate, reconcile, resolve, settle, simplify, smooth over
ironclad: fixed, immutable, inflexible, irrefutable, permanent, rigid, strict, unalterable, warship
ironhanded: controlled, despotic, firm, rigid, strict
ironic: clever, contrary, cynical, facetious, funny, mordant, sarcastic, sardonic, satirical, surprising, tongue-in-cheek, witty, wry
ironic and mocking: sardonic
ironic and nasty: caustic, mordant, sarcastic
ironic remark: sarcasm
ironic use of word in unusual sense: antiphrasis
ironically humorous: wry
ironlike: ferrous
ironworks: smithy

irony: antiphrasis, humor, mockery, paradox, sarcasm, satire, twist
irrational: absurd, crazy, demented, fanatical, foolish, illogical, insane, mad, mindless, preposterous, ridiculous, senseless, stupid, unfounded, unreasonable, unstable, unwise
irrational and bizarre: surreal
irrational and habitual: pathological
irrational and supernatural: transcendental
irrational fear or hatred: phobia
irrational number: surd
irrationally devoted: fanatical
irreclaimable: abandoned, hopeless, incorrigible, irredeemable, irreparable, lost
irreconcilable: conflicting, discrepant, incompatible, incongruous, inconsistent, opposed, uncompromising
irrefutable: certain, conclusive, inarguable, indubitable, ironclad, positive, undeniable, unimpeachable
irregular: aberrant, abnormal, aimless, amiss, anomalous, asymmetrical, atypical, bent, broken, changeable, crooked, cursory, desultory, devious, eccentric, elliptical, erose, erratic, fitful, haphazard, immoderate, imperfect, inconsistent, lopsided, nonconforming, occasional, odd, patchy, peculiar, random, sporadic, spotty, uncontrolled, unconventional, unequal, uneven, unlike, unsettled, unstable, unsteady, unsystematic, variable, wayward, weaving, zigzagged
irregular and abnormal: aberrant, anomalous, deviant
irregular and occasional: episodic, fitful, intermittent, periodic, spasmodic, sporadic
irregular and rambling: desultory
irregular and unbalanced: asymmetrical
irregularity: aberration, abnormality, anomaly, arrhythmia, disorder, flaw, helter-skelter, illegality, imperfection, intermittently, occasionally, periodically, unevenness, variation

irregularly edged: corrugated, jagged, pinked, serrated
irregularly notched: erose
irrelevant: foreign, immaterial, impertinent, inapplicable, inapposite, incidental, inconsequent, insignificant, marginal, moot, nihil ad rem, nonessential, peripheral, pointless, tangential, unapt, unconnected, unessential, unimportant, unrelated, wide of the mark
irrelevant and unimportant: extraneous, immaterial, impertinent, inapplicable
irrelevant remark: non sequitur
irreligious or disrespectful: sacrilege
irreparable: broken, destroyed, hopeless, incorrigible, incurable, irredeemable, irreversible, ruined
irrepressible: bubbling, ebullient, effervescent, enthusiastic, uncontainable, uncontrollable, vivacious
irreproachable: blameless, errorless, exemplary, faultless, flawless, immaculate, impeccable, inculpable, innocent, perfect, spotless, unblemished, unimpeachable
irresistible: alluring, charming, compelling, enchanting, fascinating, powerful, seductive, spellbinding, stunning
irresolute: doubtful, fickle, fluctuating, hesitant, indecisive, infirm, tentative, uncertain, undecided, undetermined, unsure, waffling, wavering, wishy-washy
irresponsible: carefree, careless, foolish, harum-scarum, immature, impetuous, impulsive, independable, reckless, thoughtless, unreliable
irreverent: blasphemous, disrespectful, flippant, impious, sassy, satirical, undevout, ungodly
irreverent remarks about God, religion: blasphemy
irrevocable: conclusive, constant, fated, final, firm, fixed, intractable, irreversible, unalterable

ITALIAN TERMS

appetizers: antipasto
dessert of eggs, sugar, wine: sabayon, zabaglione
eatery: trattoria
Italian food: antipasto, frittata, gelato, gnocchi, lasagna, linguine, manicotti, minestrone, pasta, pizza, ravioli, salami, scampi, spumoni, tortoni
Italian food developed in China: pasta
Italian for connoisseur: cognoscente

Italian for the good life: la dolce vita
layered ice cream: spumoni
low-fat ice cream: gelati, gelato
man: signor
milk: latte
rice dish: risotto
sauce: pesto, salsa
woman: signorina ❦

irrigate: flood, inundate, moisten, water

irritable: annoyed, atrabilious, bilious, cantankerous, choleric, crabby, cranky, cross, disagreeable, dyspeptic, edgy, excitable, fiery, fractious, fretful, grouchy, impatient, inapet, irascible, moody, ornery, peevish, petulant, querulous, quick-tempered, splenetic, tense, testy, tetchy, touchy

irritable person: crosspatch, curmudgeon

irritable state: snit

irritable temperament: asperity

irritableness: peevishness, petulance

irritate: abrade, acerbate, aggravate, anger, annoy, badger, bait, bother, bug, burn, chafe, disturb, enrage, exascerbate, exasperate, excite, fret, gall, goad, harass, harry, hector, hurt, incense, inflame, irk, madden, miff, nag, needle, nettle, peeve, pique, provoke, rankle, rasp, rib, rile, roil, ruffle, stimulate, sting, tease, upset

irritate by rubbing: chafe

irritate, constantly: fester, rankle

irritating: annoying, galling, irksome, pesky, pestiferous, vexatious

irritation: annoyance, chafing, discomfort, itch, rash, sore, vexation

Islamic shrine: Kaaba

Islamic greeting: salaam

Islamic holy city: Mecca

Islamic person: Moslem, Muslim

Islamic potentate: ameer, emir

Islamic text: Koran

island: ait, archipelago, atoll, cay, enclave, haven, isle, isolate, key, refuge, retreat, sanctuary, skerry

island of coral, low and by coast: cay, key

island of coral, ring-shaped: atoll

island, concerning an: insular

island, small rocky: skerry

isolate: confine, detach, disconnect, enisle, insulate, island, maroon, quarantine, remove, seclude, segregate, sequester, set apart

isolate a thought: prescind

isolated: alone, apart, hidden, insular, lone, lonely, private, random, remote, scattered, separated, singled out, solitary, sporadic, unrelated

isolated and withdrawn: cloistered, sequestered

isolated hill: mesa

isolated in occurrence: occasional, sporadic

isolated room: sanctum

isolation: solitude

isolation of sick or possibly sick: quarantine

issue: argument, arise, broadcast, concern, controversy, debouch, declare, deliver, distribute, edition, emanate, emerge, emit, flow, focus, hot potato, matter, offspring, outcome, question, result, spread, stem, supply, topic; brood, children, descendants; copy, printing, publication, release, version

issue of special stamps: commemorative

itch: appetite, burn, craving, desire, hankering, hunger, irritation, longing, scratching, sensation, thirst, tingling, urge, yearning, yen

itch or mania: cacoethes

itchiness, as from ants: formication

itching or hives: urtication

itching, severe: pruritus

item: account, article, aspect, clause, commodity, component, conversation, detail, entry, feature, object, paragraph, part, particular, point, product, story, thing, topic, unit

itemize: catalog, count, document, enumerate, inventory, list, number, record, tally

iterate: echo, repeat, resay, retell

itinerant: ambulatory, migrant, nomadic, peripatetic, roaming, roving, transient, traveler, traveling, vagabond, vagrant, wandering wayfaring

itinerary: account, course, guidebook, outline, plan, route, schedule, tour

ivory source: tusk

ivory tower: dreamy, impractical, lofty, retreat, unrealistic, visionary

ivory, bone, shell decorated with carving or incision: scrimshaw

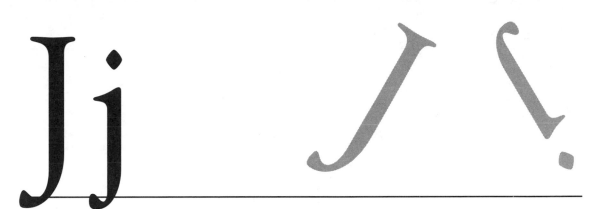

J-shaped: unciform

jab: blow, hit, pierce, poke, price, prod, punch, strike, swing, thrust

jabber: babble, chat, chatter, drivel, gibberish

jackanapes: ape, conceited, coxcomb, impudent, mischievous, monkey

jackass: blockhead, burro, dolt, donkey, dunce, fool, idiot, jerk, mule

jacket: blazer, bolero, cardigan, casing, chaqueta, coat, combat, covering, denim, dinner, dolman, doublet, envelop, Eton, folder, guernsey, habergeon, hide, parka, peacoat, pelt, reefer, safari, shell, ski jacket, skin, spencer, tuxedo, wammus, wampus, windbreaker, woolly, wrapping

jacket with binding arms for restraint: straitjacket

jacket with hood for winter: parka

jacket with hood not zipping all the way down: anorak

jacket with wide lapels, short: Eton jacket

jacket, very short: bolero

jacket, wide sash to wear with dinner: cummerbund

jack-in-the-pulpit: arad, aroid, arum

jack-of-all-trades: factotum, handyman, pantologist, tinker

jackpot: award, bonanza, kitty, pool, prize, reward, windfall

jackrabbit: hare

jade: fatigue, gem, hussy, jadeite, jewel, Jezebel, mineral, nag, narass, nephrite, pall, plug, slut, spiritless, tire, tramp, weary, wench

jaded: blasé, dulled, exhausted, indifferent, satiated, spent, tired, wearied, worn, worn-out

jagged: barbed, bristled, cutting, erose, harsh, indented, irregular, nicked, notched, pointed, ragged, rough, serrated, sharp, spiked, spiny, tattered, toothed, uneven

jai alai ball: pelota

jai alai basket: cesta

jai alai building: fronton

jai alai court: cancha, fronton

jai alai exclamation: olé

jail: arrest, bastille, book, brig, calaboose, can, cell, clink, cooler, dungeon, hoosegow, imprison, incarcerate, joint, jug, keep, lockup, pen, penitentiary, pokey, prison, reformatory, sentence, slammer, stockade

jailer: guard, keeper, turnkey, warden, warder

jam: bind, cease, clog, compress, congestion, corner, cram, crowd, crush, dilemma, hole, pack, pickle, pinch, predicament, press, push, quandary, scrape, squeeze, stop, stuff, tie up, trouble

jam, jelly or preserve: confiture, marmalade

Jamaican fruit: ugli

Jamaican popular music: reggae

jambalaya ingredient: rice

jamboree: fete

jangle: altercation, bicker, chime, clang, clatter, discord, hubbub, irritate, noise, quarrel, racket, rattle, reverberate, ring, uproar

Japan aborigine: Ainu

Japan baron: daimio, daimyo

Japan clothing: geta, haori, kimono, mino, mompei

Japan dancing girl: geisha

Japan drama: kabuki, noh

Japan drink: mate, sake, saki

Japan food: ansu, ayu, chirimen, fugu, fuji, sashimi, sukiyaki, tai, tempura, teriyaki, ume

Japan martial arts: judo, jujitsu, karate

Japan musical instruments: fuye, koto, samisen, tarko, truyume

Japan religion: Buddhism, Confucianism, Shinto, Shintoism, Tendai

Japan suicide: hara-kiri, hari-kari, kamikaze, seppuku

Japan title: kami, shogun

Japan vehicles: jinricksha, jinrikisha, ricksha, rickshaw

Japan writing: hiragana, kana, katakana

jape: fool, jeer, jest, joke, mock, prank, quip, trick

jar: agitate, bump, clash, clatter, collision, conflict, crash, discord, grate, impact, jangle, jolt, quake, rattle, rock, shake, shiver, shock, startle, stun, tremor, unsettle; bottle, container, cruet, jug, olla, urn, vase, vat, vessel

jar for mummy's entrails: canopic jar

jar or pot with wide mouth, ancient: olla

jar used as capacitor, ancient: Leyden jar

jar used for medications, ancient small: gallipot

jar with two handles, ancient Greek or Roman: amphora

jargon: argot, babble, balderdash, baloney, bull, bunk, cant, dialect, drivel, gibberish, gobbledygook, hogwash, idiom, jabberwacky, lingo, malarkey, nonsense, palaver, patois, pidgin, poppycock, shoptalk, slang, vocabulary

jargon where first consonant is put at end of word and "ay" is added: pig Latin

jarring: discordant, dissonant, grating, harsh, incongruous, rough, rude

jaundice: icterus

jaundice-causing liver disease: hepatitis

JAPANESE TERMS

artistic dwarfed tree: bonsai	legislature: diet
assassin: ninja	marinated chicken: yakitori
bedding on raised frame: futon	martial art like judo: aikido
broad sash with bow in back: obi	outcast class: eta
clogs: geta	paper folding art: origami
cooking pan: wok	poem: haiku, tanka
dish of meat, bean curd, vegetables fried together: sukiyaki	prince or noble: daimyo
dish of raw fish: sushi	ritual suicide by disembowelment: hara-kiri, suiseki
dish of thin-sliced raw fish: sashimi	robelike dress: kimono
fencing with poles: kendo	samurai code of honor: Bushido
floor mat: tatami	sandal: zori
flower arranging art: ikebana	upright wrestling: sumo
grill: hibachi	warrior: samurai, shogun
hereditary army commander until 1867: shogun	weaponless self-defense: jujitsu
instrument like zither: koto	

jaundiced: biased, bigoted, envious, hostile, jealous, prejudiced, skeptical, tainted, yellow

jaundiced point of view: cynicism

jaundice's yellow bile substance: bilirubin

jaunt: cruise, excursion, expedition, hike, journey, junket, outing, picnic, ramble, ride, spin, stroll, trip, voyage

jaunty: airy, animated, carefree, dapper, debonair, frisky, lively, perky, pert, playful, rakish, showy, sprightly, spruce, vivacious

java: coffee

javelin: dart, harpoon, lance, spear, sport, weapon

jaw: babble, berate, chat, chatter, converse, criticize, jabber, prate, scold, talk, yakety-yak; chops, jowl, mandible, maxilla

jaw muscles, paralysis of: lockjaw, tetanus, trismus

jaw, concerning the: gnathic

jaw, lower: mandible

jawbone points: gonions

jaws in position, of: orthognathous

jaws of carnivore: maw

jaws or flesh under them: jowls

jaws, of jutting: prognathous

jazz: animation, bebop, cool, Dixieland, enthusiasm, improvisation, jive, miscellaneous, nonsense, progressive, ragtime, scat, swing

jazz performer or devotee: hepcat

jazz, early style: barrelhouse

jazz, improved singing of: scat

jazz, relatively fast instrumental: Dixieland

jazzy: exciting, fancy, flashy, lively, sexy, snazzy

jealous: apprehensive, bitter, covetous, envious, green-eyed, possessive, protective, resentful, suspicious, wary, watchful

jealously possessive: territorial

jeans: blue jeans, denims, dungarees, Levis, pants

jeer: catcall, deride, fleer, flout, gibe, heckle, hiss, hoot, jabe, mock, razz, ridicule, scoff, sneer, taunt, tease

jejune: arid, aris, banal, barren, bland, childish, dull, empty, flat, immature, inane, innocuous, insipid, juvenile, meager, sterile, trite, unexciting, vapid

jell: clot, coagulate, congeal, crystallize, harden, materialize, set, shape, solidify, thicken

jell foods, carbohydrate used to: pectin

jelly becoming fluid, of: thixotropic

jelly of meat or fish stock: aspic

jellyfish: coelenterate, coward, invertebrate, man of war, medusa, medusoid, milksop, pantywaist, sissy, weakling

jellyfish, like a: discophoran

jellylike: gelatinous, viscous

jeopardize: compromise, endanger, expose, imperil, risk, venture

jeopardy: chance, danger, hazard, liability, peril, risk, trouble

jerk: ass, dope, dunce, fool, idiot, jiggle, jolt, lurch, nerd, oaf, quiver, reflex, schmo, snatch, spasm, tic, twist, twitch, wriggle, yank

jerkiness as nervous disorder: chorea, Saint Vitus' dance

jerky: beef, bouncy, charqui, fidgety, fitful, foolish, intermittent, meat, silly, spasmodic, sporadic, twitching

jerky in speech: halting, hesitant

jerry-built: cheap, flimsy, inadequate, shaky, sleazy, tacky, unsound

jest: banter, clown, drollery, fool, fun, gag, hoax, jape, japery, joke, josh, kid, laugh, prank, quip, razz, roast, sport, tease, trick, trifle, wisecrack

jester: buffoon, clown, comedian, comic, fool, harlequin, humorist, japer, jokester, merry-andrew, mime, prankster, trickster, zany

jester's cap: cockscomb, coxcomb, foolscap

jester's headgear: fool's cap

jester's multicolored clothes: motley

jesting: banter, facetitious, jocose, playful

Jesus' crucifixion marks: stigmata

Jesus' sayings not in Gospels: agrapha

jet: aero, aircraft, airplane, black, dark, ebony, flow, gush, nozzle, plane, raven, rush, spout, spray, spurt, SST, stream

jet black: onyx

jet engine power-augmenter: afterburner

jet lag: dysrhythmia

jet plane's trail of smoke: contrail

jettison: abandon, discard, dump, eject, eliminate, hurl, scrap, shed, unload

jetty: berth, black, breakwater, dock, ebony, groin, mole, pier, slip, spur, wharf

JEWISH TERMS

candelabrum, seven- or nine-branch: menorah
ceremonial dinner: seder
commandment of law: mitzvah
confession: alhet, ashamnu
diet: kashrut
disparaging term for non-Jew: goy
disparaging term for non-Jewish girl: shiksa, shikse
doorpost faith symbol: mezuzah
female coming-of-age ceremony: bas mitzvah, bat mitzvah, math mitzvah
greeting: shalom
group of ten Jewish men required for religious service: minyan
historical language: Yiddish
impure or unfit according to Jewish dietary laws: tref
Jewish breads: afikomen, challah, echem, hallah, matzo, matzoh, matzoth
Jewish communities outside Israel: Diaspora
Jewish community: aljama, kehillah
Jewish doctrine: kodashim, mishna, mishnah
Jewish laws: chok, chukah, halacha, halakah, kashruth, Talmud, tora, Torah
Jewish mystical philosophy based on Old Testament: cabala

Jewish prayers: alenu, geullah, shema
Jewish prophets: Amos, Daniel, Elias, Elisha, Ezra, Habakkuk, Haggai, Hosea, Jeremiah, Jonah, Micah, Nahum, Zechariah
Jewish school, college: yeshiva
Jewish toast: mazel tov
Jewish women's group: hadassah
Jews, mass killing of: pogrom
Jews, prejudiced against: anti-Semitic
leather box holding scripture: phylactery
men's prayer shawl: tallis, tallith
prayer book: machzor, mahzor, siddur
prayer in daily synagogue: Kaddish
prepared without milk, meat or derivatives, according to dietary laws: kosher
scarf: abnet
seven-day period of mourning: shivah
skullcap: kippah, yamilke, yarmulke
teacher: rabbi
temple: synagogue
toylike top: dreidel
unleavened bread eaten at Passover: matzo ❦

---

jewel: adorn, birthstone, brilliant, charm, darling, dear, emerald, gem, masterpiece, ornament, pearl, precious, prize, stone, winner
jewel-studded crown: tiara
jeweler's cup: dop
jeweler's magnifying glass: loupe
jeweler's weighing system: troy weight
jewelers, group of: ring
jewelry: accessory, amulet, anklet, band, bangles, beads, bijouterie, bracelet, brooch, chain, costume, crown, diamonds, earrings, gems, gold, lavalier, locket, necklace, pendant, ring, tiara
jewelry box: casket
jewelry charm: amulet
jewelry collection: bijouterie
jewelry, fake: bauble, brummagem, gewgaw, trinket
jewels set close so no metal shows: pave
jewels, decorated in: encrusted
jezebel: hussy, jade, prostitute, slattern, slut, strumpet, tramp, trollop
jib: arm, balk, boom, foresail, sail, stop
jibe: agree, conform, dovetail, harmonize, match, mesh, shift, square, tack, tally
jiffy: flash, hurry, instant, minute, moment, second, shake, trice, wink
jiggle: agitate, bounce, jerk, rock, shake, wiggle

jihad: campaign, crusade, holy war, strife, struggle, war
jilt: abandon, betray, deceive, desert, discard, drop, dump, forsake, leave
jimmy: crowbar, force, lever, open, pry
jingle: chime, chinkle, clank, clatter, ditty, limerick, noise, rhyme, ring, song, sound, tune, verse
jinx: bewitch, curse, damn, evil eye, hex, nemesis, spell, voodoo, whammy
jitters: anxiety, butterflies, dither, fidgety, heebie-jeebies, nervousness, shakes, shivers, uneasiness, willies
jittery: edgy, goosey, jumpy, nervous, restless, tense, uneasy
jive: bunk, dance, deceitful, jargon, jazz, kid, music, nonsensical, swing, talk
job: assignment, career, chore, craft, deed, duty, employment, function, grind, livelihood, mission, occupation, performance, position, post, profession, pursuit, racket, responsibility, stint, task, trade, vocation
job content: workload
job experience summary: C.V., curriculum vitae, resume
job loss by downsizing: attrition, redundancy, retrenchment
job permanence: tenure
job plus: perk

job recruiter: headhunter
job requiring little work: gravy train, sinecure
job suited to person's abilities, interests: métier, niche
job, of a sitting: sedentary
job, of a tough: exacting
job, of an easy: cushy
job, sloppy: hack
jobber: dealer, middleperson, wholesaler
jockey: beguile, cheat, direct, maneuver, manipulate, outwit, trick; driver, rider
jockey's clothing: silks
jockey's whip: bat
jocose: cheerful, frolicsome, funny, humorous, jocular, joking, merry, playful, witty
jocular: airy, amusing, animated, blithe, cheerful, comical, elated, entertaining, facetious, festive, frolicsome, funny, gleeful, happy, humorous, jesting, jocose, jocund, joking, jolly, jovial, joyous, lively, merry, mirthful, playful, rollicking, silly, sportive, vivacious, waggish, witty
jocund: blithe, cheerful, elated, jocose, jocular, jolly, lighthearted, sprightly
jog: activate, jiggle, jostle, nudge, poke, prod, prompt, push, refresh, remind, stimulate; canter, exercise, pace, run, trot

johnnycake: pone

joie de vivre: élan

join: abut, accompany, affiliate, ally, amalgamate, annex, associate, attach, bind, blend, bond, border, bridge, cantle, cement, coalesce, combine, connect, consolidate, consort, couple, engage, enlist, enroll, enter, fasten, fuse, glue, interlock, knee, knit, knot, link, marry, mate, meet, merge, mingle, mix, participate, piece, pool, relate, solder, splice, stitch, suture, team, tie, touch, unite, volunteer, wed, weld, yoke

join and attach: affix, appose, clamp, fasten, rivet, tether, yoke

join as metals: solder, weld

join businesswise: amalgamate, consolidate, incorporate, merge

join by hinge or joint: articulate

join by tie: colligate, lash

join from different directions: converge

join into cluster: constellate

join neatly: dovetail

join or blend texts: conflate

join or stick: cling, cohere

join parts to build whole: assemble

join smaller thing to larger: annex, append

join together in a league: federate

join together or fuse: accrete, agglomerate, agglutinate, aggregate, coalesce, conglomerate

join two pieces at ends: splice

join up: enlist, enroll

joined as pair: conjoint, conjugate, conjunct

joined in alliance: confederate, league

joined into one from components: composite, compound, integrated, synthesized

joined together, writing with letters: cursive

joining and touching: abutting, adjacent, contiguous, juxtaposed

joint: ankle, articulation, bend, butt, combined, communal, connection, cooperative, coupling, crux, dive, dwelling, elbow, hangout, hinge, hip, junction, knee, knuckle, mutual, point, prison, seam, shared, shoulder, union, united, wrist

RELATED TERMS

joint inflammation: arthritis

joint of a groove and fitted piece: rabbet, rebate

joint of fan-shaped tenons and interlocking mortises: dovetail

joint of notch and fitted projection: joggle

joint of tonguelike strip fitting into a groove on another piece: tongue-and-groove joint

joint of two abutting surfaces placed squarely together: butt joint, carvel-built

joint of two beveled edges forming forty-five-degree angle corner: miter joint

joint or point on plant where leaf is attached: node

joint pain: gout

joint stiffness: ankylosis

joint with knob moving freely in cavity: ball-and-socket joint

joint, bending of: flexion

joint, bushing to secure pipe: ferrule

joint, cavity or notch to attach to tenon in: gain, mortise

joint, fluid-filled cavity around: bursa

joint, projection for insertion into mortise: cog, feather, tenon

joints, tough elastic fibrous tissue found in: cartilage ❦

joist: beam, brace, stud, support

joke: antic, banter, buffoon, clowning, crack, escapade, farce, fool, fun, gag, goof, hoax, jape, jest, josh, kid, lampoon, parody, pleasantry, prank, quip, rib, sally, satire, stunt, tease, wisecrack, witticism

joke or tease at someone's expense: gibe, taunt

joke, meant as: jocular

joke, straight-faced when telling: deadpan

joker: card, clown, comedian, comic, cutup, farceur, humorist, jester, prankster, stand-up comedian, stooge, wag, wit

joker in card deck: mistigris

jokes, stock of: repertoire

joking, given to: good-humored, jocose, jocund, jolly

joking, playfully: facetious

jollity: amusement, cheer, festivity, frolic, fun, gaiety, glee, hilarity, jocundity, joviality, merriment, merrymaking, mirth, revel, revelry, whoopee

jolly: bouncy, cheerful, chipper, convivial, delightful, jocose, jocular, jovial, joyful, jubilant, kid, laughing, merry, playful, splendid, sportive

jolt: blow, bump, collision, concussion, floor, impact, jar, jog, jostle, knock, rock, setback, shake, shock, startle, surprise

jolt of neck in car accident: whiplash

josh: banter, jape, jest, jive, joke, kid, needle, razz, rib, spoof, tease

jostle: bulldoze, bump, collide, crowd, elbow, jar, jog, jolt, nudge, push, shake, shove, vie

jot: atom, bit, grain, iota, minum, record, scribble, smidgen, speck, tittle, whit, write

jounce: bounce, bump, collision, impact, jolt, shake, shock

journal: account, almanac, annals, blotter, chronicle, daily, diary, gazette, ledger, logbook, magazine, memoir, newspaper, observation, organ, paper, periodical, publication, record, scrapbook, tabloid, yearbook

journal article printed as excerpt: offprint

journal of learned society's meetings: annals

journal record: entry

journalism profession: fourth estate, the press

journalism, exaggerated and outrageous: gonzo journalism

journalism, irresponsible: yellow journalism

journalist: broadcaster, columnist, commentator, correspondent, editor, newsperson, reporter, writer

journalist, part-time or freelance: stringer

journey: adventure, circuit, course, drive, excursion, expedition, hike, jaunt, junket, migration, odyssey, passage, pilgrimage, ride, roam, route, safari, sojourn, tour, travel, trek, trip, voyage, wend

RELATED TERMS

journey at lower fare: excursion

journey place to place on foot: peregrination

journey segment: leg

journey to escape: hegira

journey to Mecca: hadj, pilgrimage

journey, extended adventurous: odyssey

journey, laborious: trek

journey, of a roundabout: circuitous

journey, short and pleasurable: jaunt

journey, supplies for a: viaticum

journey's interruption: stopover

journey's plan: itinerary ❦

joust: bout, combat, contest, duel, tilt, tournament, tourney

jouster's weapon: lance

jovial: cheery, chipper, convivial, delightful, elated, festive, genial, happy, hearty, humorous, jocose, jocular, jocund, jolly, joyous, jubilant, merry, mirthful, sociable

jowl: cheek, dewlap, jaw, mandible, wattle

joy: amusement, beatitude, bliss, cheerfulness, delight, ecstasy, elation, enjoyment, excitement, exhilaration, felicity, festivity, gaiety, gladness, glee, happiness, jubilation, mirth, pleasure, rapture, satisfaction, solace

joy of living: joie de vivre

joyless: blue, cheerless, depressed, dismal, doleful, forlorn, funereal, gloomy, glum, melancholy, miserable, unhappy, woebegone

joyous: blessed, blithe, cheerful, delighted, ecstatic, exuberant, festive, glad, gleeful, happy, heartwarming, jocular, jolly, joyful, jubilant, merry, mirthful, pleased, spirited, upbeat, vigorous, wonderful

jubilant: celebrating, elated, excited, exultant, glad, happy, jolly, joyful, joyous, pleased, rejoicing, thrilled, triumphant

judge: adjudicate, appraiser, arbiter, arbitrate, arbitrator, assess, assessor, bench, chancellor, conclude, condemn, connoisseur, consider, court, critic, criticize, critique, decide, deem, determine, estimate, expert, find, gather, gauge, honor, intermediary, justice, magistrate, mediator, rank, rate, ref, referee, review, rule, sentence, settle, suppose, try, ump, umpire, weigh

RELATED TERMS

judge or court, before a: sub judice

judge's bench: banc

judges collectively: judicature, judiciary

judge's determination: sentence

judge's disqualification of juror: recuse

judge's garment: robe

judge's hammer: gavel

judge's incidental opinion: obiter dictum

judge's order prohibiting a party from a specific action: injunction

judge's private chamber: camera

judge's refusal to concur with majority: dissent, dissenting opinion

judge's room: chambers

judge's summary to jury: charge, instruction

judges, concerning: judicial, judiciary ❦

judgment: analysis, appraisal, assessment, astuteness, award, common sense, conclusion, criticism, decision, decree, discretion, evaluation, fate, insight, opinion, prudence, punishment, reason, ruling, sense, sensibility, sentence, shrewdness, summary, taste, verdict, view, wisdom

Judgment Day: crack of doom, day of reckoning, doomsday, end of the world

judgment used as standard, legal: precedent

judgment, good: discretion

judgment, lacking: injudicious

judgment, overturning of: abrogation, annulment, cassation

judgment, personal: value judgment

judgment, showing good: astute, discerning, discreet, discriminating, judicious, politic, prudent, sagacious

judgment, standard used for making: criterion, precedent, yardstick

judgments, to make moral: moralize, sermonize

judicial: constitutional, critical, decretory, distinguished, impartial, lawful, legal, official

judicial order to do or refrain from action: injunction

judicious: calculating, careful, cautious, diplomatic, discerning, equitable, fair, just, knowing, prudent, rational, reasonable, sagacious, senseful, sensible, sound, thoughtful, wise

judo expert: judoka

judo levels of proficiency: dan

judo or karate attire: gi, judogi

judo or karate school: dojo

jug: bottle, calaboose, can, canteen, carafe, container, cooler, crock, demijohn, ewer, flagon, growler, jail, jar, lockup, olla, pitcher, prison, stir, toby, vessel

juggle: alter, change, disguise, falsify, manipulate, mislead, modify, reorganize, shuffle

juggling wooden clubs: Indian club

juice: alcohol, cider, electricity, essence, fluid, fuel, funds, gasoline, gossip, liquid, liquor, money, nectar, oil, sap, succulence, vitality

juice, to squeeze out: extract

juice, unfermented grape: must

juices from evergreen: sap

juicy: dripping, exciting, intriguing, luscious, moist, oozy, provocative, racy, runny, saturated, spicy, succulent, tantalizing

juicy gossip: dirt

jukebox: nickelodeon

julep garnish: mint

jumble: assortment, chaos, clutter, confuse, disarray, disorder, hash, heap, hodgepodge, medley, mess, mishmash, mixture, muddle, olio, potpourri, scramble, shake, shuffle, slew, welter

jumbo: colossal, elephantine, enormous, gigantic, huge, large, mammoth, monstrous, titanic

jump: ambush, boost, bounce, bound, caper, charge, clear, dive, escalate, evade, flinch, hop, hurdle, hustle, increase, leap, lunge, lurch, parachute, plunge, rise, skip, skyrocket, spring, start, startle, upturn, vault

jump around playfully: caper, cavort, frisk, frolic, gambol, romp, sport

jumped over: leapfrogged

jumper: dress, frog, jacket, kangaroo, shot, sled, smock, toad

jumping from one thing to another: desultory, disconnected

jumping-off place: springboard

jumping or leaping: saltation

jumping pole: pogo stick

jumping sheet attached to frame: trampoline

jumping, concerning: saltatorial

jumps in equestrianism: capriole, curvet, gambado

jumpy: antsy, anxious, apprehensive, excitable, frightened, jittery, nervous, restless, skittish, spooked, tense, uneasy, uptight

junction: conflux, connection, contact, crossing, crossroads, gathering, interface, intersection, joint, juncture, meeting, seam, transition, union

juncture: choice, condition, crisis, crossroads, emergency, hinge, instant, joint, junction, linkup, moment, pass, point, position, seam, time, union

June bug: beetle, dor, dorr, scarab

Jungian feminine side of male: anima

Jungian idea derived from collective unconscious: archetype
Jungian masculine side of female: animus
Jungian social front: persona
jungle: bush, forest, jumble, labrynth, maze, wilderness, zoo
junior: lesser, namesake, puisne, second, son, student, subordinate, younger
juniper: cade, cedar, evergreen, red cedar, retem, sabine, savin, shrub, tree
junk: boat, clutter, debris, discard, dope, dreck, dump, flotsam, garbage, jetsam, jettison, litter, refuse, rubbish, salvage, scrap, ship, trash, waste
junket: banquet, excursion, feast, jaunt, outing, party, picnic, tour, trip
junkie: addict, user
junta: cabal, committee, coterie, council, faction, government, tribunal
jurisdiction: area, authority, bailiwick, beat, bounds, command, control, county, diocese, district, domain, dominion, field, law, parish, power, precinct, province, reach, scope, territory, venue, zone
jurisdiction, having immediate: ordinary
juror group: panel

jury: committee, judges, makeshift, panel, peers, tribunal
jury member, defendant's right to reject: peremptory challenge
jury selected by each party striking off names: struck jury
jury unable to agree on verdict: hung jury
jury, attempt to corrupt a: embracery
just: accurate, befitting, correct, decent, deserved, due, equitable, ethical, even, exact, fair, fairminded, firm, fitting, hardly, honest, impartial, legal, legitimate, meet, normal, objective, purely, right, simply, solid, suitable, true, trustworthy, unbiased, undistorted, upright, valid; almost, barely, mere, merely, narrowly, only, recently
justice: atonement, code, court, equity, fairness, hearing, honesty, impartiality, judge, litigation, magistrate, reparation, righteousness, truth, virtue
justice system: judicature, judiciary
justice where good is rewarded and evil punished: poetic justice
justice, court or seat of: tribunal
justice, failure to administer: miscarriage

justice, prudence, fortitude, temperance: cardinal virtues
justice, to administer: dispense, mete out, render
justification: apologia, apology, defense, excuse, exoneration, explanation, grounds, proof, rationale, reason, redemption, vindication
justify: account, approve, authorize, defend, exculpate, excuse, explain, legitimate, legitimize, rationalize, sanction, substantiate, support, uphold, validate, vindicate, warrant
justify and acquit: vindicate
justify and provide sufficient grounds: warrant
jut: beetle, bulge, butt, elongate, extend, extrude, jetty, lengthen, overhang, projection, protrude, shoot
jutting rock: tor
juvenile: adolescent, callow, childish, green, growing, immature, infant, minor, pubescent, puerile, tender, undeveloped, unripe, young, youthful
juxtaposition: abutment, adjacency, contact, nearness, proximity, touching
juxtaposition of words for explanation: apposition

Kk

kaiser: emperor, monarch, ruler, title

kale: cabbage, cole, colewort, collard

kaleidoscopic: changeable, colorful, diverse, fluctuating, motley, protean, variable, vivid

kangaroo and pouched animals: marsupial

kangaroo pouch: marsupium

kangaroo, baby: joey

kangaroo, female: blue flier, doe

kangaroo, male: boomer, buck

kangaroo, pertaining to: macropine

kaput: broken, destroyed, incapacitated, over, ruined, shot, wrecked

karate: martial art, self-defense

karma: atmosphere, aura, destiny, fate, feeling, kismet, power, vibrations

keel over: capsize, collapse, faint, fall, overturn, swoon

keen: acute, alert, ardent, astute, avid, awake, bewail, boned, clever, cunning, devoted, eager, enthusiastic, fervent, fierce, incisive, intelligent, intense, interested, penetrating, perceptive, pungent, sensitive, severe, sharp, shrewd, solicitous, strong, trenchant, vivid, wail, zealous

keen and perceptive: perspicacious

keenness of mind: acuity, acumen

keep: amass, celebrate, confine, contain, control, delay, detain, deter, endure, fulfill, guard, have, hold, maintain, manage, observe, obstruct, possess, preserve, prevent, reserve, restrain, retain, safeguard, shackle, stock, store, tend, withhold

keep an eye on: watch

keep at: continue, endure, finish, grind, persevere, persist

keep back: check, delay, detain, forbid, hold, postpone, reserve, save, stifle, suppress, withhold

keep company: associate, consort, date, fraternize

keep for future use: mothball, store

keep from destruction: preserve

keep hold of: retain

keep or preserve: conserve

keep out: bar, blacklist, debar, detain, evade, reject, restrict

keep safe: safeguard

keeper: attendant, caretaker, chaperon, constable, curator, custodian, escort, guard, guardian, jailer, janitor, manager, sentinel, sentry, warden, warder, watchman

keepsake: knickknack, memento, relic, reminder, souvenir, token, trophy

keg: barrel, cade, cag, cask, container, drum, hogshead, vat

kegler: bowler

keister: behind, bottom, buttocks, derriere, fanny, rump, tush

kelp and sargasso: algae, seaweed

ken: admit, cognizance, grasp, insight, knowledge, lore, perception, recognition, scope, sight, understanding, view, vision, wisdom

kennel: den, doghouse, drain, enclosure, flock, gutter, lair, pound, shelter

kerchief: babushka, bandana, bandanna, handkerchief, hankie, headrail, scarf, shawl, veil

kernel: center, core, essence, germ, grain, heart, issue, meat, nucleus, nut, pit, pith, seed, stone, substance

kettle: cauldron, flambeau, hollow, kettledrum, pan, pot, stewpot, teapot, vat, vessel

kettledrum: naker, tabla, tabor, tambour, timbal, timpano

kettledrum set: timpani

key: address, answer, atoll, cay, central, code, critical, digital, essential, explanation, guide, important, island, isle, islet, main, opener, password, pitch, pivotal, quay, reef, scale, skeleton, solution, ticket, tonality, vital

key collector: cagophilist

key for many locks: master key, passepartout, passkey, skeleton key

key on a map, chart: legend

key, write or perform in a different musical: transpose

keyboard instrument: accordion, carillon, celesta, clavichord, clavier, harpsichord, organ, piano, spinet, synthesizer

RELATED TERMS

keyboard, dulcimer: cembalo, clavicembalo, harpsichord

keyboard instrument whose strings are plucked by plectrums or quills: harpsichord

keyboard instrument, electronic: synthesizer

keyboard instrument, organlike: harmonium

keyboard instrument, soft-sounding: clavichord

keyboard or stringed keyboard instrument: clavier

keyboard with pleated bellows, portable: accordion

keyboard, mechanically operated piano with paper roll activating: player piano

keyboard, piano with pedal: pedal piano

keyboard, small harpsichord with one: spinet

keyboard, tower bells played by: carillon ☙

keyed up: eager, excited, nervous, stimulated, tense

keyhole ridge corresponding to key ridges: ward

keyhole-shaped: clithridiate

keyhole, doorknob, door lock metal plate: escutcheon

keynote: basis, essence, feature, gist, heart, idea, measure, standard, theme, tone, topic

keystone: base, cornerstone, crown, foundation, headstone, mainstay, principle, root, support, wedge

khaki cotton twill: chino

khan: agha, caravansary, chief, emperor, hostelry, inn, official, ruler

kibbutz: collective, commune, farm, hora, settlement

kibitzer: busybody, buttinsky, meddler, snoop, spectator

kibosh: veto

kick: bang, blow, boost, boot, complain, eject, fret, fuss, gripe, growl, grumble, jolt, object, power, protest, punch, punt, recoil, snap, stop, strength; abandon, enjoyment, sensation, thrill

kick downstairs: demote

kick in: add, contribute, donate, give

kick off: begin, commence, inaugurate, launch, open, start

kick out: bounce, can, discharge, dismiss, eject, evict, expel, fire, remove

kickback: bribe, gift, graft, payoff, payola, repercussion

kid: baby, banter, bluff, child, deceive, dupe, fool, hoax, joke, josh, juvenile, rag, razz, rib, ride, spoof, tease, trick, youngster, youth; goat

kid leather: suede

kidnap: abduct, capture, grab, hijack, nobble, shanghai, snatch

kidnap for compulsory service: shanghai

kidnap victim's sympathy for captor: Stockholm syndrome

kidnapper: captor

kidney and other edible beans: haricot

kidney disease: nephritis

kidney machine: dialyzer, hemodialyzer

kidney pain: nephralgia

kidney removal by surgery: nephrectomy

kidney-shaped: reniform

kidney stone: calculus, concretion, nephrolith

kidneys, concerning: nephritic, renal

kidneys, edible: offal

kill: annihilate, asphyxiate, assassinate, cancel, croak, crucify, cull, deaden, destroy, dispatch, do in, electrocute, execute, exterminate, extirpate, finish, garrote, halt, hang, liquidate, lynch, massacre, murder, numb, poison, ruin, shoot, silence, slaughter, slay, strangle, suffocate, suppress, veto, waste, wipe out

RELATED TERMS

kill by beheading: decapitate

kill by cutting off air supply: asphyxiate, burke, strangle

kill for sacrifice: immolate

kill or destroy large portion of: decimate

kill public figure: assassinate

kill summarily: dispatch

kill time: dally, dawdle, fool around, idle, procrastinate, stall

kill to reduce animal herd: cull

kill without due process of law: lynch

killer: assassin, butcher, difficult, exterminator, gangster, gunman, hangman, hit man, murderer, slayer, sniper, tough

killer, pathological and repeated: serial killer

killing: carnage, execution, fatality, homicide, lethality, manslaughter, martyrdom, murder, slaughter, slaying

killing action: quietus

killing of brother, sister or countryman: fratricide

killing of father or of both parents: patricide

killing of god, goddess: deicide

killing of human by another: homicide

killing of mercy: euthanasia

killing of mother: matricide

killing of racial, ethnic, national group: genocide

killing of ruler: regicide

killing of self: suicide

killing of sister: sororicide

killing of wife: uxoricide

killing on large scale: carnage, holocaust, massacre, pogrom, slaughter

killing that is not deliberate but is unlawful: manslaughter ☙

kill a veto: override

killer whale: grampus, orca

killjoy: complainer, crape hanger, malcontent, party pooper, pessimist, sourpuss, spoilsport, wet blanket, worrywart

kiln: bake, fire, furnace, glaze, hearth, oast, oven, stove

kimono sash: obi

kin: aunt, aunts, blood, clan, connection, family, flesh, flesh and blood, folk, kindred, race, related, relation, relations, relative, sib, sibling, tribe

kind: affable, affectionate, amiable, amicable, benevolent, benign, blithe, brotherly, charitable, clement, compassionate, congenial, considerate, cordial, favorable, friendly, generous, genial, gentle, good, goodly, gracious, humane, humanitarian, lenient, loving, merciful, mild, neighborly, obliging, philanthropic, polite, simpatico, sisterly, soft, sympathetic, tendency, tender, warm, warmhearted; brand, breed, class, description, essence, fiber, gender, genre, genus, ilk, make, nature, order, sort, species, type, variety

kind act: favor

kind and charitable: altruistic, beneficent, benevolent, eleemosynary, philanthropic

kind and gentle: benign

kind and lenient: indulgent

kind and sympathetic: compassionate, humane, humanitarian, magnanimous

kind forbearance: mercy

kindle: animate, arouse, awaken, brood, excite, fire, fire up, flock, glow, ignite, incite, inflame, inspire, light, move, provoke, rise, start, stimulate, stir

kindling: firewood, fuel, paper, punk, sticks, tinder, touchwood, twigs

kindly and gracious: propitious

kindness: assistance, beneficence, benevolence, bounty, charity, compassion, courtesy, generosity, goodwill, help, mercy, philanthropy, sympathy, understanding

kindred: affiliated, affinity, allied, ancestry, blood, congenial, connection, family, flesh, folk, kin, lineage, race, related, relationship, similar, tribe

king: czar, emperor, leader, lion, majesty, master, monarch, rex, ruler, sovereign, tzar

RELATED TERMS

king ascending throne, of a: acceding

king relinquishing throne, of a: abdicating

king, one replacing king during illness or absence: regent

king, queen, or czar: potentate

KNIVES

anlace	cheese knife	fruit knife	misericord	skean
barlow	clasp knife	hunting knife	palette knife	skean dhu
bayonet	cleaver	jackknife	panga	snickersnee
bistoury	dagger	kard	parazonium	steak knife
blade	dirk	kirpan	pocketknife	stiletto
bolo knife	drawknife	kris	poniard	Swiss Army knife
bowie knife	dudgeon	kuttar	puntilla	switchblade
butter knife	fish knife	lancet	scalpel	trench knife ❦
carving knife	flick knife	machete	shiv	

kingdom: commonwealth, country, domain, dynasty, empire, monarchy, realm, scepter, territory, throne

kingly: imperial, imperious, lordly, majestic, noble, regal, royal, sovereign, splendid, stately

king's attendants: retinue

king's baron: thane ❦

kink: bizarre, complication, corkscrew, crick, crimp, crinkle, curve, defect, far-out, flaw, hitch, imperfection, knot, odd, outlandish, spasm, strange, twinge, wrinkle

kinky: curled, deviant, frizzy, perverse, twisted, warped, weird

kiosk: newsstand, stand

kismet: circumstance, destiny, doom, fate, fortune

kiss: buss, caress, embrace, French, greet, neck, osculate, peck, salute, smack, smooch

kiss in greeting: osculation, salutation

kiss of betrayal: Judas kiss

kiss of peace: pax

kissing with eyes closed: typhlobasia

kit: bag, collection, container, equipment, gear, instruments, knapsack, lot, outfit, pack, rig, set, supplies, tackle, things, utensils

kitchen: canteen, cuisine, galley, mess, scullery

kitchen on ship or aircraft: galley

kitchen servant: scullion

kitchen where chores are done, room adjoining: scullery

kitchen, relating to the: culinary

kite: bird, check, elanet, hang glider, hawk, sail, soar

kite type: box, Chinese, conyne, deltawing, eddy bow, hexagonal

kitelike glider: hang glider

kittenish: childish, coquettish, coy, flirtatious, frisky, mischievous, playful

kittens, group of: kindle, litter

kitty: cat, jackpot, kitten, pool, pot, pussy, stakes

kitty comment: meow, miaou

kitty treat: catnip

kiwi: apteryx, roa

kleptomaniac: criminal, pilferer, shoplifter, thief

klutz: blockhead, clumsy, lout, lummox, nerd, oaf, schlemiel, stupid

knack: ability, adroitness, aptitude, art, dexterity, expertise, feel, flair, forte, gift, head, nose, skill, talent, trick

knapsack: backpack, bag, kit, pack, rucksack

knave: blackguard, cad, cheat, churl, fraud, jack, lowlife, miscreant, rapscallion, rascal, rogue, scamp, scoundrel, trickster, varlet, villain

knave, of a notorious: arrant

knead: aerate, blend, fold, manipulate, massage, mix, press, stretch, work

knee and back-of-thigh tendon: hamstring

knee-ankle connector: tibia

knee-bend in ballet: plié

knee breeches: britches, knickers, shorts

knee inflammation: bursitis, housemaid's knee

knee jerk: automatism, patellar tendon reflex, reflex

knee-jerk: automatic, expected, predictable, reflex, spontaneous

knee, soft area behind: popliteal

knee, to bounce affectionately on: dandle

kneecap: patella

kneel: bow, curtsey, genuflect, kowtow, stoop

kneel on one knee: genuflect

kneeling cushion: hassock

kneeling stool: faldstool

knell: bell, chime, proclaim, ring, signal, sound, summon, toll, warning

knickknack: bauble, bibelot, bric-a-brac, curio, decoration, gadget, gewgaw, gimcrack, novelty, ornament, showpiece, souvenir, toy, trifle, trinket

knife: blade, shiv, sword, tool, utensil, weapon; carve, cut, lacerate, lance, pierce, slash, slice, stab, wound

RELATED TERMS

knife blade: bit

knife handle: haft, hilt

knife maker: cutler

knife of old: snee

knife point: tang

knife sharpener: hone, whetstone

knife types: bayonet, bolo, bowie, bread, butter, cutlass, dagger, dirk, hunting, lancet, machete, pen, pocket, putty, scalpel, shiv, sickle, snee, surgical, Swiss Army, switchblade

knife with folding blade that springs open: switchblade knife

knife, to sharpen a: hone, whet ❦

knit: bind, conjoin, connect, consolidate, crochet, fasten, furrow, heal, intermingle, intertwine, join, mend, plait, purl, stitch, unite, weave, wrinkle

knitted cloth fineness or density: gauge, tension

knitted shoe: bootie

knitting pattern with diamonds: argyle

knitting stitch: cable, purl

knives, forks, spoons: cutlery, flatware, silverware, utensils

knob: bulge, bump, button, dial, handle, heel, hill, knoll, knot, lever, lump, mountain, node, nodule, pommel, protuberance, switch

knobby: torose

knoblike part: capitulum, tubercle, umbo

knock: abuse, beat, belittle, blame,

blow, bounce, bump, clank, collide, criticize, defeat, denounce, hit, jolt, lick, pan, ping, pound, push, rap, reprehend, set back, slam, slur, smack, strike, thump, topple, whack

knock down: deck, drop, fell, flatten, floor, level, thrash, trample

knock knees: valgus, varus

knock off: achieve, assassinate, complete, copy, deduct, desist, discontinue, eliminate, finish, imitation, kill, murder, slay, steal, stop, subtract, waste

knock out: deck, floor, kayo, stun

knockout: beauty, dish, eyeful, kayo, looker, stunner

knoll: hill, hillock, hummock, knell, knob, mound, ring, sound

knot: bond, bow, braid, burl, contortion, crowd, entangle, entanglement, gnarl, group, hitch, knob, knur, knurl, link, loop, lump, mesh, node, nodule, protuberance, puzzle, rosette, snag, snarl, tangle, tie

knot in cloth: burl

knot in wood: knar, nur

knot in wool: nep

knot lace: tat

knot of short hair: noil

knot or bun of hair: chignon

knot types: blackwall hitch, bowline, carrick bend, figure eight, fisherman's, flat, granny, half hitch, rolling hitch, seizing, sheepshank, shroud, slide, slipknot, square, stevedore's, surgeon's

knotted lace work: macramé

knotty: bumpy, bunched, complex, difficult, gnarled, hard, intricate, nodal, nodule, perplexing, puzzlingly, tricky, troublesome

knotty problem: poser

know: associate, cognize, comprehend, discern, discriminate, distinguish, experience, fathom, grasp, identify, ken, profess, realize, recognize, see, understand

know by intuition: divine

know-how: ability, aptitude, capability, experience, expertise, flair, ingenuity, knack, knowledge, mastery, savoir faire, skill, talent

know-it-all: brash; maven, smarty, wiseacre, wisenheimer

know more than they do, person who pretends to: philosophaster, philosophunculist

knowing: alive, aware, bright, brilliant, cagey, clever, cognition, cognitive, conscious, deep, deliberate, educated, experienced, gnostic, informed, intelligent, intentional, knowledgeable, observant, perception, perceptive, scholastic, sensible, sharp, shrewd, smart, sophisticated, wise, witty, worldly

knowing all things: all-knowing, omniscient

knowing before occurrence: prescience

knowledge: ability, awareness, cognition, cognizance, comprehension, data, education, enlightenment, erudition, experience, expertise, facts, familiarity, grasp, information, inkling, instruction, intelligence, ken, know-how, learning, lore, revelation, science, understanding, wisdom

RELATED TERMS

knowledge and the arts, movement to advance: humanism

knowledge bit by bit, to gather: glean

knowledge from sense perception: percept

knowledge of an event after it has occurred: hindsight

knowledge of right thing to say or do: savoir faire

knowledge of something in advance of occurrence: clairvoyance, cryptesthesia, ESP, extrasensory perception, precognition

knowledge, belief in experience as the source of: empiricism

knowledge, belief in reason as the source of: rationalism

knowledge, deep: erudition

knowledge, gradual absorption of: osmosis

knowledge, instinctive: intuition

knowledge, pretended: sciolism

knowledge, relating to familiarity or deep: intimate

knowledge, relating to intuitive: transcendental

knowledge, seeker of: philonoist

knowledge, study of the nature of: epistemology

knowledge, to spread: disseminate

knowledge, total: omniscience

knowledgeable: acquainted, apprised, au fait, aware, bright, clever, cognizant, conversant with, educated, experienced, expert, familiar, informed, knowing, posted, proficient, smart, versed, well-versed, wise

knowledgeable of subject: conversant

knowledgeable person: savant

knowledgeable person in many subjects: polyhistor, polymath

knowledgeable, made aware of: enlightened ❦

known: acknowledged, familiar, famous, noted, notorious, obvious, popular, prominent, recognized, renowned

known only to a few: arcane, esoteric, occult

knuckle under: acquiesce, capitulate, cave, give in, submit, succumb, surrender, yield

kook: crazy, crackpot, demento, eccentric, flake, lunatic, nut, screwball, wacko

kosher: accepted, authentic, clean, ethical, genuine, legitimate, permissible, proper, pure

kosher food laws: kashruth

kosher, Muslim equivalent of: halal

kosher, non-: tref

kowtow: bootlick, brownnose, cower, fawn, grovel, kneel, stoop, toady

kudos: acclaim, accolade, admiration, award, citation, credit, decoration, esteem, fame, glory, honor, laurels, praise, prestige

kyphosis: curvature, humpback, hunchback

Ll

l substituted for r: lallation
lab medium: agar
lab tube used to measure liquids: pipette
label: band, brand, call, characterize, classify, define, design, designate, hallmark; description, identification, insignia, logo, mark, name, sticker, tab, tag, ticket
labium: lip
labor: agonize, childbirth, contractions, drudgery, effort, employees, endeavor, exertion, grind, industry, parturition, slave, stress, strive, struggle, sweat, task, toil, travail, undertaking, work, workers
labor union for all workers of an industry: industrial union, vertical union
labor union for specialized workers of an industry: craft union, horizontal union
labor union is on strike, person who works while: scab
labor-union representative: shop steward
labor union, business where employees are not required to be in: open shop
labor union, business where employees are required to be in: closed shop, union shop
labor union, worker who refuses membership in: scab
labor, being in: parturient
labor, of a drug inducing or facilitating: oxytocic
labor, to bring about or stimulate: induce
labored: awkward, difficult, forced, heavy, ponderous, strained, strenuous, unnatural
laborer: blue-collar worker, coolie, esne, hand, navvy, peon, plebe, serf, toiler, worker, workhand, workman
laborious: arduous, assiduous, back-

breaking, burdensome, difficult, diligent, effortful, hard, hardworking, industrious, onerous, painstaking, rigorous, strenuous, tough, uphill
labyrinth: complexity, entanglement, intricacy, jungle, knot, maze, mesh, network, snarl, tangle, web
labyrinth monster of ancient Greece: Minotaur
lace: adorn, border, braid, cord, decorate, edging, embroidery, entwine, fabric, fasten, intertwine, lash, net, netting, plait, ribbon, shoestring, string, thread, tie, trimming, twine, unite

RELATED TERMS

lace made by interlacing thread with pins: bobbin lace, pillow lace, point
lace made by looping and knotting, handmade: tatting
lace made of coarse thread twisted in geometric patterns: torchon lace
lace made on paper patterns with needle: needlepoint, point lace
lace tip, shoe: aglet
lace work of woven and knotted cord: macramé
lace, background of a design in: fond
lace, large-patterned coarse: guipure
lace, net or mesh foundation for: reseau
lace, ruffle of: ruche, tucker
lace, small embroidery edging on some: picot
lace, to finish or edge with: purl ❧

lacelike metalwork: filigree
lacerate: cut, distress, gash, harrow, knife, lance, mangle, pierce, slice, slit, stab, tear, wound
lachryma: tear
lachrymose: crying, sad, tearful, teary, weeping, weepy
lack: absence, dearth, deficiency, defi-

cit, emptiness, failure, famine, fault, inadequacy, insufficiency, loss, minus, need, paucity, poverty, privation, scarcity, shortage, sparsity, want
lack of agreement: discord
lack of basic necessities: destitution, privation
lack of bodily fluid control: incontinence
lack of energy: anergy
lack of good taste: indecorum
lack of marriage laws: agamy
lack of maturity: nonage
lack of movement: inertia
lack of parity: inequality
lack of power: impotence, impuissance
lack of sight: anopia
lackadaisical: apathetic, blah, careless, halfhearted, idle, languid, lazy, lethargic, listless, spiritless, uninspired, unmotivated
lackey: attendant, flunky, footman, gorilla, page, servant, thug, toady
lacking: absent, deficient, deprived, impaired, inadequate, insufficient, minus, missing, needy, short, shy, wanting, without
lacking character or distinction: nondescript
lacking coloration: albino
lacking ethics: amoral
lacking firmness: limp
lacking precision: inexact
lacking principles: amoral
lacking refinement: crude
lacking sensitivity: crass
lacking understanding: purblind
lacking, completely: destitute, devoid
lackluster: blah, bland, boring, colorless, drab, dull, flat, humdrum, lifeless, uninspired

LAKES

Aral Sea (Kazakhstan, Uzbekistan)	Manzala (Egypt)
Athabaska (Canada)	Maracaibo (Venezuela)
Baikal (Russia)	Martin (United States)
Balkhash (Kazakhstan)	Mead (United States)
Bangweulu (Zambia)	Michigan (United States)
Bear (United States)	Mobutu Sese Seko (Uganda)
Becharof (United States)	Moosehead (United States)
Biwa (Japan)	Ness (Scotland)
Caspian Sea (Azerbaijan, Russia, Kazakhstan, Turkmenistan, Iran)	Nettilling (Canada)
Chad (Chad, Niger, Nigeria)	Nicaragua (Nicaragua)
Champlain (United States, Canada)	Nipigon (Canada)
Chapala (Mexico)	Nyasa (Malawi, Mozambique, Tanzania)
Derwent Water (England)	Okeechobee (United States)
Edward (Uganda, Zaire)	Onega (Russia)
Erie (United States, Canada)	Ontario (United States, Canada)
Eyre (South Australia)	Patos (Brazil)
Finger Lakes (United States)	Pontchartrain (United States)
Flathead (United States)	Reindeer (Canada)
Gairdner (Australia)	Rudolf (Kenya)
Garda (Italy)	St. Clair (United States, Canada)
George (United States)	Superior (United States, Canada)
Great Bear (Canada)	Tahoe (United States)
Great Lakes (United States, Canada)	Tanganyika (Tanzania, Congo)
Great Salt (United States)	Texcoco (Mexico)
Great Slave (Canada)	Titicaca (Bolivia, Peru)
Huron (United States, Canada)	Torrens (South Australia)
Issyk-Kul (Kyrgyzstan)	Trasimeno (Italy)
Katrine (Scotland)	Tung-t'ing (China)
Kioga (Uganda)	Turkana (Kenya, Ethiopia)
Kivu (Zaire, Rwanda)	Urmia (Iran)
Koko-Nor (China)	Utah (United States)
Ladoga (Russia)	Vanem (Sweden)
Lake of the Woods (Canada)	Victoria (Tanzania, Uganda)
Leech (United States)	Volta (Ghana)
Lochy (Scotland)	Winnebago (United States)
Loch or Lomond (Scotland)	Winnipeg (Canada)
Maggiore (Italy, Switzerland)	Winnipegosis (Canada)
Malawi (Malawi, Mozambique, Tanzania)	Yellowstone (United States)
Manitoba (Canada)	Zurich (Switzerland) ❧

laconic: blunt, brief, compact, concise, condensed, crisp, curt, pithy, pointed, short, succinct, terse

lacquer: coating, finish, gloss, shellac, varnish

lacuna: break, cavity, depression, gap, hiatus, interim, interval, opening, pause, space

lacy: delicate, elegant, fancy, frilly, netlike, ornate, sheer, transparent, weblike

lacy openwork: tracery

lad: adolescent, boy, juvenile, kid, shaver, son, stripling, youngster, youth

ladder rung: rundle, spoke, stave, step

ladder vertical post or strut: stile

ladder, rope: accommodation ladder, Jacob's ladder

laden: burdened, hampered, saddled, taxed, weighted

ladle: bail, calabash, cyathus, dip, dipper, pour, scoop, serve, spoon

lady: baroness, countess, dame, duchess, female, gentlewoman, girl, madam, mistress, noblewoman, princess, queen, woman

ladylike: elegant, feminine, genteel, mannerly, matronly, polished, polite, proper, refined, respectable

lag: dawdle, delay, dillydally, drag, flag, linger, loiter, procrastinate, slacken, slow down, stave, straggle, tarry, tire, trail

lag behind: drag, drop back, trail

lager: ale, beer, brew

laggard: dawdler, dilatory, idler, loiterer, mope, remiss, slow, slowpoke, sluggish, straggler

lagniappe: benefit, bonus, gift, gratuity, largess, present, tip

lagomorph: hare

lagoon border: atoll

laic: amateur, layman; secular

lair: burrow, cavern, den, habitat,

LAND-RELATED TERMS

connected to mainland by isthmus; land extending into water: peninsula

every seven years when Jewish land remains fallow: sabbatical year

high point of land extending into water: promontory

land area increase by river deposits: alluvium

land capable of being cultivated: arable

land cleared or plowed to stop spread of fire: firebreak, fireguard

land cultivation and scientific agriculture: agronomy

land gained by recession of water line: dereliction

land leveling: gradation

land projecting into body of water and connected to mainland by isthmus: peninsula

land reserved for minority community: reservation

land that is plowed but unseeded, of: fallow

land, buildings, immovable property: real estate, real property, realty

low-lying land along river: intervale

measure of land: acre, are, rood, stere

narrow extension of land or territory: panhandle

narrow point of land extending into water: spit

narrow strip of land connecting two larger masses of land: isthmus

perpetual ownership of land: mortmain

pertaining to land tenure and ownership: agrarian

physical features of land: topography

plan, map or chart of a piece of land: plat

possession and use of one's own land: demesne

private ownership of land and real estate: fee simple

reversion of feudal land to manor: escheat

right of government to appropriate land for public use: eminent domain

right-of-way part of piece of land: easement

something living on or relating to land, of: terrestrial

stretch of land: tract

title: deed

triangular piece of land: gore

wide-open extent of land: expanse ❧

---

haunt, hideout, nest, refuge, retreat, sanctuary, shelter

laissez-faire: inactive, indifferent, tolerant, unconcerned

lake or pond, shallow and near larger body of water: lagoon

lake, bow-shaped from river: oxbow, oxbow lake

lake, small: mere

lake, small mountain: tarn

lakes and fresh water, scientific study of: limnology

lakes, pertaining to: lacustrine

lam: bash, beat, escape, flight, flog, hit, strike, thrash, wallop

lamb or beef and sliced eggplant layered, Greek: moussaka

lamb or mutton, leg of: gigot

lamb's mother: ewe

lambaste: assail, beat, berate, castigate, clobber, criticize, drub, flay, hammer, pound, pummel, punish, scold, slog, thrash, whip, whop

lambent: bright, brilliant, flickering, glowing, luminous, lustrous, radiant, shining

lambskin, untanned: kip

lame: crippled, decrepit, defective, deformed, disabled, feeble, flimsy, game, gimpy, halt, halting, handicapped, hurt, incapacitate, limping, maim, stiff, unconvincing, weak

lamebrain: blockhead, dope, dunce, fool, imbecile, moron, ninny, nitwit, stupid

lameness: claudication, halting, limp

lament: alas, bemoan, bewail, complaint, condole, cry, deplore, dirge, dolor, elegize, grief, grieve, howl, jeremiad, keen, moan, monody, mourn, outcry, pine, plaint, regret, repent, repine, requiem, rue, sign, sorrow, wail, weep

lament or mourning hymn: dirge, elegy, keen, monody, threnody

lamentable: dire, distressing, grievous, miserable, sad, unfortunate, upsetting

lamp: arc, bulb, chandelier, davy, electric, floor, gas, incandescent, lantern, light, oil, table, torch

lamp with light directed upward: torchier

lamplight: glim

lampoon: burlesque, caricature, farce, mock, parody, pasquinade, roast, satire, spoof, squib, takeoff; satirize

lamp's metal frame around light bulb: harp

lampshade framework: spider

lance: cut, dart, hurl, javelin, launch, pierce, point, skewer, spear, weapon

land-and-water animal or vehicle: amphibian

landing of airplane past the runway: overshoot

landing of airplane short of the runway: undershoot

landing of airplane using only electronics: instrument landing

landing of spacecraft on water: splashdown

landlord: host, innkeeper, lessor, owner, proprietor

landmark: achievement, cornerstone, crisis, event, feature, guidepost, remnant, signpost

landscape: countryside, mural, painting, panorama, picture, scene, scenery, view, vista

landslide: avalanche, eboulement, lopsided, sweep, victory, win

lane: aisle, alley, approach, byway, course, footpath, passageway, path, pathway, race, road, street, strip, track, way

languid: apathetic, drooping, dull, enervated, feeble, inactive, indifferent, indolent, lackadaisical, lethargic, listless, slow, sluggish, spiritless, supine, wan, weak

languish: ail, decline, deteriorate, diminish, droop, fade, fail, faint, flag, linger, pine, repine, sink, stagnate, suffer, wallow, waste, wilt, wither; neglected

languor: apathy, blues, boredom, ennui, lassitude, lethargy, listlessness, stagnation, torpor

lanky: angular, gangling, gangly, gaunt, gawky, lean, meager, rangy, scraggy, scrawny, skinny, slender, slim, tall, thin

lanyard: cord, gasket, gimp, line, rope, string

LANGUAGE-RELATED TERMS

anthology used in language study: chrestomathy

being good in another language, of: fluent

commonly used language, of: colloquial, demotic, informal, vernacular

concerned with language as it changes through time: diachronic

customary language or grammar: usage

elaborate, pretentious and insincere language: rhetoric

everyday spoken language of area: vernacular, slang

formal system of syntax, phonology: structural linguistics

geographic boundary line showing where language feature occurs: isogloss

gradual change in language: drift

hybrid language for communication: lingua franca

informal and substandard language: slang

knowing only one language: monoglot, monolingual

knowing several languages: multilingual, polyglot

knowing two languages: bilingual

language and speaking style: parlance

language as it is actually used by a community: usage

language being taught: target language

language derived from pidgin but more complex: creole, creolized language

language distinguishing word meanings by variations in pitch, tone: tone language

language expert: linguist, logogogue

language for study, collection of: corpus

language formerly pidgin that becomes native language: creole

language from which translation is made: source language

language into which translation is made: target language

language of a particular community: langue

language of a trade, profession, or other group: argot, cant, jargon

language of an individual: idiolect

language that is hypothetical ancestor of another: protolanguage

language that is mixture of two or more languages: pidgin

language to describe language: metalanguage

language unit that cannot be divided into smaller meaningful units: morpheme

language used in specific social setting: register

language used to communicate by people with different languages: koine, lingua franca

language using inflectional affixes to express syntax: synthetic

language using morphemes that retain forms and meanings: agglutinative

language using word order or function words to express syntax: analytical

language well, using: articulate

language with regular changes in word form: inflected language

long-winded and indirect language: circumlocution, periphrasis, prolixity

meaning in language, relating to: semantic

mix of language: polyglot

mixture of two or more languages, of a: macaronic

persuasive and powerful language: eloquence

pertaining to language: linguistic

pompous language: bombast, euphuism, fustian, grandiloquence

regional variety of a language: dialect

science and study of language: linguistics, philology

science and study of language sounds: phonemics, phonetics, phonology

science and study of language use: pragmatics

science and study of meaning: semantics

sign language: semiology

smallest unit of language: morpheme

spoken common language, of the: colloquial, vernacular, vulgate

strict correctness in language: purism

study of grammar development in language: descriptive linguistics

study of internal structure of a language: structuralism

study of language evolution: historical linguistics, philology

study of language similarities and differences: comparative linguistics

study of patterns of sentence and phrase formation in language: syntax

system of rules for language: grammar

way in which words and phrases are used: diction, phraseology

wordy and indirect language: circumlocution, periphrasis ❧

---

lap: bathe, circle, circuit, course, drink, enfold, lick, loop, orbit, round, slosh, slurp, splash, swathe, wash, wrap

lapel or cuff's reverse side shown: revers

lapidary: engraver, jeweler

lapse: backslide, blooper, blunder, boner, break, deteriorate, disregard, err, error, expire, failure, fall, fault, gap, goof, infraction, lull, mistake, oversight, regression, revert, sink, slide, slip

larceny: absconding, burglary, crime, embezzlement, looting, pilfering, purloining, robbery, stealing, theft, thievery

larceny degree: grand, petty

lard: coat, cover, embellish, enrich, fat, garnish, grease, lace, oil, shortening, tallow

larder: buttery, cellar, cupboard, pantry, provisions, storeroom

large: ample, big, booming, broad, bulky, burly, capacious, coious, colossal, considerable, enormous, exorbitant, extensive, extravagant, far-reaching, fat, generous, giant, gigantic, grand, great, heavy, hefty, huge, hulky, immense, jumbo, liberal, mammoth, massive, monstrous, monumental, plentiful, pompous, roomy, sizable, substantial, sweeping, titanic, vast, whopping

large and grand: grandiose, imposing, monumental

large and spacious: capacious, commodious, extensive, roomy, voluminous

large beer mug: seidel

large capital letters: majuscule

large enough to be seen with unaided eye: macroscopic

large number: host, many, passel, scad, slew

large piece: hunk, slab

large system based on one of its parts: macrocosm

large, extensive, indiscriminate: blanket, wholesale

large, noisy gathering: corroboree

largely: chiefly, considerably, generally, mainly, mostly, predominantly, primarily

largess: charity, contribution, donation, generosity, gift, gratuity, lagniappe, perk, present, tip

largest planet in solar system: Jupiter

lariat: lasso, noose, reata, riata, rope, tether

lariat end: noose

lark: adventure, antic, bird, carousal, dido, escapade, frolic, outing, prank, romp, spree

larks, group of: exaltation

larrup: beat, clobber, flog, lambaste, thrash, whip

larval form of certain bivalve mollusks: spat

larval form of certain insects: naiad, nymph

lascivious: coarse, fleshy, indecent, lecherous, lewd, libertine, licentious, lustful, obscene, salacious, seductive, sensual, steamy, voluptuous, wanton

laser-made 3-D image of object: hologram, holograph

lash: assail, attack, beat, berate, blister, blow, castigate, chastise, criticize, fasten, flog, hammer, horsewhip, lace, pummel, secure, slash, smack, smite, strike, stroke, thrash, whip

lass: colleen, damsel, female, gal, girl, maid, maiden, miss, missy, sweetheart, woman

lassitude: apathy, blues, doldrums, drowsiness, enervation, ennui, exhaustion, fatigue, languor, lethargy, listlessness, sluggishness, torpidity, torpor, weariness

last: climactic, concluding, end, endmost, eventual, extreme, farthest, final, furthest, hindmost, latest, newest, omega, tail, ultimate, utmost

last drink of the day: nightcap

last in a series: omega

last or inferior part: rump

last part: end, fag end, omega

last resort: final recourse, pis aller, trump card

last resort, as a: faute de mieux, in extremis

last syllable heavily accented: oxytone

last, second from: penultimate

last, third from: antepenultimate

last, to: abide, continue, endure, persevere, persist, remain, stand, survive, wear

lasting: chronic, classical, constant, continual, deep-rooted, durable, eternal, everlasting, forever, immortal, incessant, perennial, permanent, stable, sturdy, unceasing, unending

lasting condition: perpetuity

lasting imprint: stamp

lasting long time: chronic

lasting only briefly: ephemeral, fleeting, transitory

lasting throughout year: perennial

latch: bolt, button, catch, clamp, close, fasten, fastener, hook, lock, secure

late: behind, behindhand, belated, delayed, lagging, overdue, postponed, recent, tardy, unpunctual; dead, deceased, departed, former, past; contemporary, new

late autumn mild weather: Indian summer

late or delay, to be: procrastinate, tarry

late or past the expected time: overdue

latent: abeyant, concealed, covert, dormant, hidden, inactive, inferred, passive, potential, quiescent, secret, undeveloped, unrealized

later: after, afterward, anon, behind, ensuing, following, hereafter, newer, posterior, soon, subsequently, succeeding

lateral: flanking, oblique, pass, side, sidelong, sideward, sideways

laterally: sidewise

latest in technology: cutting edge

latest trend, fashion: dernier cri

lathe, clamp holding material on: chuck

lather: agitation, bubbles, bustle, commotion, cream, foam, froth, fuss, hassle, soap, suds, wash

Latin American ballroom dance: tango

Latin American of mixed ancestry: ladino, mestizo

Latin American popular dance music: salsa

Latin American quickstep: cha cha

Latin American, concerning: Hispanic

Latin edition of Bible: Vulgate

latitude: breadth, degree, distance, elbowroom, extent, freedom, independence, leeway, liberty, measure, play, range, room, scope, width

latke ingredient: potato

latrine: bathroom, lavatory, privy, restroom, toilet

latter: concluding, final, latest, modern, recent, subsequent, succeeding

lattice: configuration, door, frame, gate, grid, mesh, structure, trellis

lattice part: lath, slat

laud: acclaim, admire, adore, applaud, commend, compliment, eulogize, exalt, extol, glorify, honor, praise, revere, venerate; hymn, song

laudable: admirable, commendable, deserving, estimable, exemplary, praiseworthy, sterling

laugh: cachinnate, cackle, chortle, chuckle, crow, giggle, guffaw, haha, hee-haw, howl, mock, nicker, roar, scream, snicker, snort, titter

laugh, loud: belly laugh, cachinnation, guffaw, horse laugh, roar

laugh, snide: snicker, snigger

laughable: absurd, amusing, bizarre, comic, comical, derisory, droll, entertaining, facetious, farcical, foolish, funny, hilarious, humorous, ludicrous, merry, mocking, outrageous, ridiculous, risible, silly, strange, witty

laughing gas: nitrous oxide

laughingstock: butt, dupe, fool, mockery, sport

laughter: ha ha, hahas, joviality, merriment, mirth, risibility

laughter, given to idiotic: abderian

laughter, relating to or causing: risible

launch: begin, bombard, catapult, commence, discharge, eject, fire, fling, heave, hurl, introduce, open, premiere, propel, start, throw, toss

launch from machine: catapult

launch site: pad

laurels: accolade, award, commendation, credit, decoration, distinction, glory, honor, kudos, praise, recognition, tribute

lava: ashes, basalt, cinders, coulee, latite, magma, obsidian, scoria, slag

lava rock, black glassy: basalt, obsidian

lava, cinderlike fragments of: cinders, scoriae, slag

lava, molten rock making up: magma

lava, rocks formed by solidification of: igneous

lava, sheet of solidified or stream of molten: coulee

lavaliere: pendant

lavatory: basin, bathroom, comfort station, head, john, latrine, little boys' room, little girls' room, privy, restroom, toilet, washroom

lavatory, military: latrine

lavatory, outdoor: outhouse, privy

lavatory, ship: head

lavender: lilac, purple, violet

lavish: bestow, bountiful, copious, excessive, expensive, extravagant, exuberant, free, generous, gorgeous, grand, immoderate, impetuous, lush, luxurious, magnificent, munificent, opulent, overindulge, plush, princely, prodigal, profuse, reckless, shower, spend, splendid, squander, unrestrained, unstinting, waste, wild

lawn: glade, grass, grounds, park, plot, turf, yard

lawn game: badminton, bocci, horseshoes

lax: careless, casual, delinquent, disregardful, easy, inactive, lazy, lenient, loose, negligent, oblivious, open, permissive, relaxed, remiss, slack, sloppy, tardy, unconfined, unmindful, unrestrained, unstructured, vague

laxative: aperient, cathartic, evacuant, physic, purgative

lay bare: strip

lay concrete: pave

lay down: assert, define, dictate, give up, specify, succumb, surrender, wager, yield

lay into: assail, attack, criticize, lambaste, scold

lay low: camouflage, cover, disappear, duck, hide, sneak

lay off: cease, discharge, fire, halt, release, stop, terminate

lay up: accumulate, amass, confine, disable, hide, hospitalize, incapacitate, injure, lay away, save, stock, store

lay waste: annihilate, desolate, destroy, devastate, ravage, ruin, wreck

layer: atratum, bed, bedding, blanket, coat, coating, covering, crust, depth, film, floor, fold, hen, lamina, level, lining, ply, scale, seam, sheet, skin, slab, story, stratum, substratum, tier, veneer

layer in archaeological pit: stratum

layer in organisms, thin: lamella, lamina

layer of green oxide on metal: patina, verdigris

layer of material: ply

layer of rocks: sima

layer, external: cortex

layers like onion, having concentric: tunicate

layers, composed of bonded: laminated

layman: amateur, churchperson, follower, laic, novice, parishioner, secular

layoff: cutback, dismissal, furlough

layout: arrangement, blueprint, design, diagram, disburse, draft, format, invest, map, model, outline, plan, spend

laziness: acedia, ennui, idleness, indolence, languor, lassitude, sloth, torpor

laziness of attitude: apathy, hebetude, indifference, lethargy

lazy: careless, fainéant, idle, inactive, indolent, insouciant, lackadaisical, lax, lethargic, loafing, logy, otiose, remiss, shiftless, slack, slothful, sluggish, torpid, unconcerned, unindustrious

lazy and sluggish: costive, inert

lazy in work habits: fainéant, shiftless, shirking, truant

lazy person: couch potato, dawdler, fainéant, idler, layabout, loafer, sluggard

lazy physically: languid, lethargic, listless, torpid

lazy, unemotional: lymphatic, phlegmatic

lead: advantage, ahead, carry, clue, command, conduct, convey, direct, escort, evidence, excel, first, govern, guide, head, headliner, influence, instruct, manage, persuade, pilot, pioneer, precede, principal, protect, shepherd, sign, spearhead, star, steer, surpass, usher; element, graphite, lode, metal

lead astray: beguile, corrupt, deceive, delude, entice, lure, seduce

lead line: leash

lead on: bait, encourage, entice, flirt, goad, lure, seduce

lead or escort: convoy

lead poisoning: plumbism, saturnism

lead sulfide: galena

lead weight on line: plumb

lead, material used in pencil: graphite, plumbago

leaden: depressed, downcast, dreary, dull, gloomy, gray, heavy, inert, languid, listless, sluggish

leader: bellwether, bishop, boss, cantor, captain, cardinal, chairperson, champion, chief, chieftain, coach, commander, conductor, duke, elder, foreman, general, guide, guru, head, honcho, line, lion, maestro, pilot, pope, president, priest, principal, rabbi, ruler, shogun, spark plug, trailblazer, warlord

leader appealing to emotions, prejudices: demagogue

leader in field: groundbreaker, guru, initiator, innovator, pioneer, trailblazer, trendsetter

leader in name only: figurehead, front man

leader or leading indicator of future trends: bellwether

leaderless: acephalous

leader(s) of new movement: avant-garde

leadership: authority, command, direction, guidance, helm, initiative, skill

leading: ahead, arch, capital, central, chief, controlling, dominant, first, foremost, guiding, head, headmost, initial, main, motivating, paramount, premier, prime, principal, stellar, unparalleled

leading actor: star

leading character in drama, literary work: protagonist

leading or opening move: initiative

leading or supreme: ascendant, dominant, foremost, paramount, predominant, preeminent, preponderant, primary

leading position in movement: vanguard

leaf: blade, bract, browse, foil, folio, frond, glance, insert, needle, page, petal, scale, scan, sepal, skim, spathe, stalk, thumb

RELATED TERMS

leaf at base of a flower: bract

leaf blade: lamina

leaf blade system of veins: venation

leaf-covered: foliate

leaf division: lobe

leaf-eating: phyllophagous

leaf interstice: areole

leaf of book: folio

leaf of fern, palm: front

leaf on Corinthian column: acanthus

leaf pores: stoma

leaf stalk attaching to stem: leafstalk, petiole

leaf-stem angle: axil

leaf tapering to a sharp point, of a: acuminate, apiculate, cuspidate

leaf that is stalkless and attached at base: sessile

leaf vein branch: venule

leaf vein or rib: nervure

leaf with fine woolly hairs, of a: ciliate, lanate, villous

leaf with low rounded projections, of a: crenate, crenulate, repand, sinuate

leaf with rough wrinkled surface, of a: rugose

leaf with stiff bristly hairs, of a: strigose

leaf, indentation between lobes of: sinus

leaf, of a dry withered: sere

leaf, rounded projection on: lobe

leaf, shaft of compound: rachis

leaf, three-part: trefoil

leaf, to give off water through stoma of: transpire

leafless stem: scape

leaflets, clover with three small: shamrock

leaflike: phylloid

leaflike bract holding flower cluster or spike: spathe

leafstalk appendages as for roses: stipule

leafstalk sheath: ocrea

leafy: abundant, foliate, green, layered, lush, shady, verdant

leafy shelter: arbor, bower

leaves and organic matter in gardens and yards, dead: kibble

leaves on a stem, arrangement of: phyllotaxy

leaves or snow heaped by wind: windrow

leaves that don't fall off after withering, of: persistent

leaves that fall off seasonally, of: deciduous

leaves' use of light with chlorophyll: photosynthesis

leaves, arrangement of three or more: whorl

leaves, bundle or cluster of: fascicle, fascicule

leaves, green pigment in: chlorophyll

leaves, of puckered or wrinkled: bullate

leaves, relating to: foliaceous, foliate

leaves, to strip of: defoliate ❦

leaflet: booklet, brochure, circular, flier, handbill, handout, pamphlet, pinna, tract

league: alliance, association, brotherhood, circuit, class, coalition, confederacy, conference, division, federation, fellowship, guild, network, order, sisterhood, union

leak: channel, crack, discharge, divulge, drain, drip, escape, fissure, flow, ooze, reveal, rupture, seep, spill, trickle, vent; hole, seepage

leakage, liquid lost from container: ullage

leaky: porous

lean: bare, bend, cant, curve, deficient, depend, emaciated, gaunt, inadequate, incline, lank, lanky, meager, nonfat, poor, prefer, pressure, rawboned, recline, rely, scant, scanty, scrawny, skinny, slender, slim, slope, spare, stoop, tend, thin, tilt, unproductive, wiry

lean back: recline

lean body structure: ectomorph

lean to one side: capsize, careen, heel over, keel over, list

lean toward: tend

lean-to: hut, shack, shanty, shed, shelter

leaning: alist, aptitude, bent, bias, desire, inclination, liking, preference, prejudice, propensity, reclining, recumbent, tendency, trend

leaning or reclining: recumbent

leaning or resting on: incumbent

leaning or tendency: inclination, proclivity

leap: ascend, bounce, bound, buck, caper, capriole, catapult, cavort, clear, fly, frisk, gallop, gambol, hop, hurdle, increase, jump, lunge, plunge, prance, skip, soar, spring, surge, upswing, vault

leap year: bissextile year, intercalary year

leap year's extra day: bissextile day

learn: acquire, apprentice, ascertain, detect, discover, find, grasp, hear, master, memorize, study, uncover, understand

RELATED TERMS

learn and understand: apprehend, assimilate, digest

learn bit by bit: glean

learn by heart: con, learn by rote, memorize

learn facts: fathom, plumb

learn through examination or experimentation: ascertain ❦

learned: academic, astute, cultivated, deep, educated, erudite, informed, intellectual, lettered, literary, read, scholarly, versed, wise

learned discourse on subject: tome, treatise

learned person: pedant, pundit, sage, savant, scholar

learned person in many subjects: polyhistor, polymath

learned response: conditioned reflex

learned, ostentatiously: inkhorn

learner: abecedarian, apprentice, beginner, disciple, novice, pupil, scholar, student, trainee

learner in life, late: opsimath

learning: comprehension, culture, discipline, education, erudition, experience, information, knowledge, literature, lore, philosophy, scholarship, science, wisdom

RELATED TERMS

learning by memorization: rote learning

learning by tape during sleep: hypnopedia

learning through investigation: heuristics

learning, a branch of: discipline

learning, early and long-lasting: imprinting

learning, methods to strengthen: reinforcement ❦

lease: charter, contract, grant, hire, let, rent, rental

lease, person granting: lessor

leaseholder: lessee

leash: bind, bridle, burb, chain, choker, control, cord, harness, lead, rein, restrain, rope, strap, tether

leash ring: terret

least: fewest, lowest, merest, minimal, minimum, shortest, slightest, smallest, tiniest, trivial, unimportant

least amount: iota, minimal, whit

least amount possible: amsace

leather: hide, oxhide, skin, strap, tan, thrash, whip
RELATED TERMS
leather by mineral tanning, to convert: taw
leather flask: olpe
leather for bookbinding: skiver
leather hides, one who prepares: currier
leather hides, to prepare: curry
leather of goat antelope, soft: chamois
leather of goatskin tanned with sumac, fine soft: morocco
leather of horsehide or goatskin, fine: cordovan
leather of untanned hide: rawhide
leather sheet for writing or painting: parchment
leather strap for sharpening razor: strop, strope
leather strip: strap, thong
leather to make smooth, rub: dub
leather treated to look used or antique: distressed
leather types: buckskin, buff, cabretta, calfskin, chamois, chevrette, cordovan, cowhide, deerskin, horsehide, kid, morocco, nappa, pebble grain, rawhide, scotch grain, skiver, split, suede
leather whip: cat-o'-nine-tails
leather, gilded designs on: tooling
leather, glossy black: patent leather
leather, tallow and oil for dressing: dubbin
leather, to bend or mold: crimp
leatherlike: coriaceous ❦

leave: abandon, allowance, assign, bequeath, cede, dash off, decamp, depart, desert, embark, emigrate, endow, escape, evacuate, exclude, exit, flee, forgo, forsake, furlough, getaway, goest, hit the road, holiday, liberty, license, move, omit, part, permission, permit, quit, relinquish, retire, sabbatical, scram, split, vacate, vacation, vamoose, will
leave behind: abandon, desert, forsake, relinquish
leave of absence: furlough
leave one's motherland: emigrate
leave-taking: farewell, valediction
leave, absence without: AWOL, French leave
leaven: activator, catalyst, enzyme, ferment, imbue, infuse, raise, yeast

leavening agent: yeast
leavetaking: congé, dismissal
leavetaking in mass numbers: exodus
leaving faith, party, principles: apostasy
lecherous: carnal, corrupt, goatish, lawd, lewd, lustful, raunchy, salacious
lectern: desk, platform, podium, stand
lecture: address, admonish, berate, class, discourse, hearing, lesson, orate, oration, preach, prelect, rebuke, reprimand, scold, sermon, sermonize, spiel, talk
lecture, formal discourse or: disquisition
lecture, moralizing: homily
lecture, short: briefing
lecturer: docent, instructor, lector, professor, reader, speaker, teacher
ledge: berm, edge, mantle, platform, ridge, shelf, sill, vein
ledger: book, entry, headstone, record, tombstone
leech: barnacle, bloodsucker, parasite, sponge, worm
leek or relative: allium
leer: eye, fleer, goggle, grimace, look, lust, ogle, smirk, stare
leery: cautious, distrustful, guarded, skeptical, suspicious, uncertain, wary
lees: dregs, residue
leeway: clearance, cushion, drift, elbowroom, flexibility, latitude, margin, play, room, space, tolerance
left: abandoned, departed, exited, gone, larboard, liberal, port, quit, remaining, went
left- and right-handed: ambidextrous
left-hand book page: verso
left-handed: awkward, clumsy, dubious, gauche, insincere, maladroit, sinistral, southpaw
left-handedness: mancinism
left-hander: southpaw
left over: extra, residual
left side in heraldry: sinister
left side of boat, plane (facing forward): port
left side of ship: larboard, port
left unharmed: spared
left-winger: leftist, liberal, radical, socialist
leftover: excess, extra, leavings, oddment, ort, remainder, remanent, remnant, residue, scraps, surplus
leftover food reheated, of: réchauffé
leftovers mixed together: gallimaufry, hash

leftovers or remainder: remains, remnants, vestiges
leftward at sea: aport
leg: appendage, bender, brace, cabriole, circuit, column, course, drumstick, gam, limb, pole, prop, run, shank, stage, stake, support; walk
RELATED TERMS
leg between knee and foot: crus, shank
leg bone: femur, fibula, metatarsals, patella, tarsals, tibia
leg coverings: chaps, gaiter, gambado, legging, puttee
leg kicks from squat in Slavic dance: kazatsky
leg muscle: biceps femoris, gastrocnemius, psoas, rectus femoris, tibialis anterior, vastus lateralis
leg muscle, large upper-: hamstring
leg vein, of a swollen: varicose vein, varix
leg, relating to the: crural ❦

legacy: bequest, birthright, devise, foundation, gift, heirloom, heritage, inheritance
legate: agent, ambassador, consul, delegate, deputy, emissary, envoy, nuncio, representative
legatee: heir
legator: testator
legend: code, fable, fiction, folklore, key, lore, motto, myth, saga, story, table, tale, tradition
legendary: celebrated, fabled, famous, fictitious, immortal, invented, mythical, noted, storied
legendary account: saga
legerdemain: artfulness, conjuring, deceit, deception, magic, trickery
legible: apparent, clear, discernible, distinct, neat, readable
legion: countless, flock, many, multitude, numerous, various; army, troops
legislation: act, bill, charter, enactment, law, ordinance, regulation, ruling, statute
legislative: nomothetic
legislative bill: measure
legislative errand runner: page
legislative group with common interest: bloc, lobby
legislator: assemblyperson, congressperson, delegate, lawgiver, lawmaker, politician, representative, senator

LEGAL TERMS

according to law: de jure
administer law, to: dispense
against the law: illegal, illegitimate, illicit, unlawful
alteration of legal document: spoliation
ambiguity in wording of a law: loophole
authorized by law: legal
branch of government enforcing laws: administration,
  executive
branch of government making laws: legislature
breaking a law: breach, contravention, infraction,
  infringement, transgression, violation
breaking law or pledge: infraction
breaking of law involving liability and not breach of
  contract: tort
by law: de jure
complete body of laws: canon, legal code, pandects
controversial legal case: cause célèbre
courts of law, relating to: forensic
create or pass laws, to: legislate
doorkeeper of law court or legislature: sergeant, sergeant
  at arms, usher
engage in legal proceedings,to: litigate
exemption from a law: dispensation
exemption from law for foreign diplomats: diplomatic
  immunity
formally approve a law, to: ratify, sanction
habitual lawbreaker: scofflaw
hypothetical case argued by law students: moot
law: act, assize, canon, decree, derectum, edict, fiat,
  institute, ordinance, precept, prescript, prescription,
  proclamation, regulation, rule, statute, stipulation,
  ukase (axiom, fundamental, principle, theorum)
law based on judicial decision and precedent: case law
law based on usage, not legislation: unwritten law
law courts: judicature, judiciary
law derived from custom, usage, and court decisions:
  common law
law enacted by legislature: statute
law enforcement officer for U.S. county: sheriff
law governing Sunday activities: blue law
law having little or no force, of a: nugatory
law no longer valid or enforced: dead letter law
law of city government: ordinance
law setting a time limit on legal action in certain cases:
  statute of limitations
law student: stagiary
law violation less serious than felony: misdemeanor
law violation that is grave crime (murder, rape,
  burglary): felony
lawbreaker: criminal, crook, delinquent, felon, offender,
  outlaw, violator
law-establishing: legislative, nomothetic
lawful: authorized, constitutional, due, established, just,
  kosher, legal, legit, legitimate, licit, official,
  permissible, rightful

lawless: anarchical, barbarous, chaotic, disorderly, illegal,
  illegitimate, insurgent, lewd, mutinous, riotous, ungoverned,
  unruly
laws against drinking, dancing: blue laws
laws to a code, to organize: codify
lawsuit on behalf of group: class action
lawsuit: accusation, action, case, claim, litigation
lawyer: advocate, attorney, barrister, commoner, counsel,
  counselor, defender, shyster
lawyer expelled: disbarred
lawyer for the state: public prosecutor
lawyer in a court case: counsel
lawyer's fee: retainer
legal: allowable, authorized, constitutional, contractual, juridical,
  juristic, lawful, legitimate, licit, permissible, statutory, valid
legal administrator: trustee
legal age: major
legal authority to act for another: power of attorney
legal claim: lien, title
legal code: pandect
legal document of contract or conveyance of property:
  deed
legal document with facts and point of specific case: brief
legal document: deed, lease, will, writ
legal jargon: grimgribber, legalese
legal matter: res, tort
legal obligation to return to court or perform court-ordered act:
  recognizance
legal order preventing wrong or enforcing right: remedy
legal order prohibiting party from specific action: injunction,
  restraining order
legal proceeding where third party with custody is ordered to hand
  over item: garnishment
legal restriction: entail
legal right of ownership for literary and artistic property: copyright
legal right of ownership: title
legal right of passage: easement
legal right to take property of debtor as security or payment: lien
legal right to use and profit from another's property: usufruct
legal right: droit, lien
legal rights advisory read to suspect: Miranda warning
legal scholar: jurist
legal seller: transferor
legal setting: venue
legal tender: cash, coin of the realm, currency, money
legal term for beneficiary of action: usee
legal writ requiring appearance in court to give testimony:
  subpoena
legal wrong: tort
legalize: allow, authorize, enact, license, permit, sanction, validate
legally accepted: admissible, competent, eligible
legally based: de jure
legally establishing validity of will: probate
legally obligated: liablemaking or giving laws: prescriptive

LEGAL TERMS
continued

one with knowledge of the law: juristordei having force of law: decree, edict, fiat, proclamation, prescript, ukase

party against which law action is brought: defendant

party instituting suit in law court: plaintiff

put a law into effect by announcement,to: promulgate

release of prisoner before sentence is completed: parole

require by law or agreement: stipulate

right and power to interpret and apply law: jurisdiction

science or philosophy of law: jurisprudence

someone taking law into one's own hands: vigilante

start legal proceedings, to: litigate

strict adherence to law: legalistic

unlawful execution of lawful act: misfeasance

unscrupulous lawyer: pettifogger, shyster

void a law: annul, repeal, rescind, revoke

willful negligence in pursuing legal claim: laches ❧

---

legislature: assembly, body, congress, council, diet, house, parliament, senate

RELATED TERMS

legislature with full attendance: plenum

legislature with two houses, chambers: bicameral

legislature's bills on hold: hopper ❧

legitimate: accepted, authentic, cogent, fair, genuine, just, lawful, legal, proper, real, recognized, rightful, sound, square, true, valid, warranted

legitimize illegal money through intermediate agent: launder

legume: bean, pea

leisure: chance, convenience, ease, freedom, holiday, opportunity, recreation, relaxation, rest, spare time, vacation; idle

leisure activity: avocation, hobby, play, sport

leisurely: calmly, casually, deliberately, gradually, idly, languidly, relaxed, slowly, unhurried

lemon rind as flavoring: zest

lemur: ape, loris

lend: accommodate, afford, extend, furnish, give, grant, impart, loan, permit, provide, supply

lender who charges illegally high interest: loan shark

lender's written safeguard: collateral note

length: compass, diameter, dimension, distance, duration, interval, longitude, period, radius, range, reach, span, term, time

length of time something persists, continues: duration

length, concerning: longitudinal

lengthen: augment, continue, eke, elongate, expand, extend, increase, produce, prolong, protract, stretch

lengthy: extended, long, padded, protracted, tedious, wordy

lenient: assuasive, benevolent, charitable, clement, condoning, easy, emollient, forgiving, gentle, indulgent, kind, lax, merciful, mild, pardoning, permissive, relaxing, soothing, sparing, sympathetic, tolerant

lenitive: mitigable

lens: bifocal, contact, glass, meniscus, monocle, optic, spectacles, trifocal

RELATED TERMS

lens covering watch: lunette

lens curved inward: concave

lens curved outward: convex

lens defect: aberration

lens for close-ups: zoom lens

lens for one eye: monocle

lens gathering light and directing it: condenser

lens imperfection causing faulty image: distortion

lens in microscope: object glass, object lens, objective, objective lens

lens irregularity causing faulty image: astigmatism

lens setting, camera: F-stop

lens with two prescriptions: bifocal

lens, concave-convex: meniscus

lens, device in optical instrument limiting light to: aperture ❧

lentigo: freckle, spot

leopard: cheetah, panther

leopard spot: maculation

leopard, pertaining to: pardine

leprechaun: dwarf, elf, fairy, sprite

lesbianism: sapphism, tribadism

lesbianism, concerning: sapphic

lesion: abscess, cut, flaw, gash, injury, sore, tumor, ulcer, wound

less: diminished, fewer, inferior, little, lower, minus, reduced, shortened, smaller

lessee: renter, tenant

lessen: abate, abridge, alleviate, assuage, attenuate, bate, belittle, condense, contract, curtail, cut down, decrease, degrade, deplete, depreciate, dilute, diminish, disparage, downsize, dwindle, ease, impair, lighten, lower, minify, minimize, mitigate, narrow, reduce, relieve, retrench, shrink, soften, subside, truncate, wane, weaken

lessen a reputation, tending to: derogatory, disparaging, pejorative

lessen dramatically: plummet, slump

lessen gradually: abate, dwindle, ebb, pare down, subside, taper off, wane, whittle

lessen greatly or empty: decimate, deplete

lessen guilt of offense: extenuate

lessen in importance: belittle, debase, demean, depreciate, derogate, detract, devalue, disparage, minimize

lessen intensity of: allay, alleviate, assuage, palliate, slacken

lessen or withdraw: recede

lessen scope or freedom: constrict

lessen size of herd: cull

lessen strength or purity: attenuate, dilute

lessen the extent of: abbreviate, abridge, curtail, truncate

lessen the seriousness of: extenuate, mitigate

lessen the value of: downgrade

lessen volume or size: compress, condense, contract, shrink

lessening of yield in proportion to outlays of capital, labor, time: diminishing returns

lesser: inferior, lower, minor, reduced, secondary, smaller

lesson: assignment, class, deterrent, education, example, exercise, experience, instruction, lecture, message, model, moral, practice, reading, rebuke, reprimand, reproof, study, task, text, warning

lesson preparation: homework

lessor: grantor, landlord, owner

let: allow, approve, authorize, cause, charter, grant, hire, lease, leave, license, permit, release, rent, suffer, tolerate; rented

let go: dismiss, emit, fire, free, release, relinquish, sack

let it stand (proofreading): stet

let off: absolve, acquit, drop, ease, emit, excuse, exonerate, forgive, free, pardon, spare, vent

let on: acknowledge, admit, confess, disclose, divulge, hint, indicate, pretend, suggest

letdown: anticlimax, bathos, blow, disappointment, drawback, frustration, setback, slump

lethal: dangerous, deadly, fatal, harmful, mortal, poisonous, toxic

lethargic: apathetic, comatose, dull, enervated, heavy, inactive, inert, lackluster, languid, lazy, listless, sleepy, slothful, slow, sluggish, torpid

lethargy: apathy, hebetude, impassivity, inactivity, inertia, languor, lassitude, laziness, sleep, sluggishness, sopor, stupor, torpor

letter (document): billet-doux, dispatch, epistle, memorandum, memo, message, missive, note, post card, report, telegram, wire
RELATED TERMS
letter delivered from post office it was posted at: drop letter
letter of recommendation: testimonial
letter requesting that copies of original be sent to others: chain letter
letter sent via telegraph: telegram, wire
letter sent with haste: dispatch
letter, afterthought at end of: postscript, PS
letter, interoffice: memo, memorandum
letter, long: epistle, missive
letter, love: billet-doux
letter, postage mark on: frank
letter, short: note, postcard
letter, threatening: poison-pen letter
letters, concerning the writing of: epistolary ❦

letter (of alphabet): capital, character, logograph, majuscule, miniscule, symbol
RELATED TERMS
letter dropped at beginning of word: aphaeresis, aphesis
letter dropped at beginning or end in pronunciation: elision
letter dropped at end of word: apocope
letter dropped in middle of word: syncope
letter embellishment: serif
letter for letter: literatim
letter going above body e.g. b, part of a: ascender
letter going below body e.g. p, part of a: descender
letter in red in manuscript: uncial
letter or design cut out: stencil
letter representing entire word or phrase: logogram, logograph
letter representing neutral unstressed vowel: schwa
letter that represents more than one sound: polyphone
letter, capital: majuscule, uppercase letter
letter, finishing line off main stroke of a: serif
letter, large: capital, majuscule, uppercase
letter, not capital: lowercase letter, minuscule
letter, pronunciation sign added to a: accent, diacritic
letter, small: lowercase, miniscule
letter, upright stroke of a: stem
letters as design, initial: monogram
letters for readability, space between: kern
letters joined together in writing or printing: ligature
letters of a language, arranged in an order: alphabet
letters of Greek and Latin, rounded capital: uncial
letters paired to represent speech sound: digraph
letters repeated at start of words: alliteration
letter(s) that represent one sound: grapheme ❦

lettuce types: bibb, Boston, chalk, cos, garden, iceberg, Romaine, water

letup: abatement, break, cessation, diminish, ease, lull, pause, reduction, slacken, slowdown, stop, wane

levee: bank, berth, burbar, dike, dock, embankment, jetty, landing, pier, quay, ridge

level: aligned, balanced, consistent, direct, equal, even, flat, flush, horizontal, matched, parallel, proportionate, same, smooth, steady, straight, true, uniform; aboveboard, degree, floor, grade, layer, plane, point, position, rank, stage, story, stratum, tier

level below which the ground is saturated with water: water table

level expanse of land: plateau

level in series: stratum

level land with few/no trees: savanna

level of responsibility or authority in hierarchy: echelon, rank

level or flat, aligned: flush

level or parallel to horizon: horizontal

level or row in seating: terrace, tier

level prefix: plani-

level surface, having a: plane, tabular

level, instrument for determining if surface is horizontal or: level, spirit level

level, relatively stable: plateau

level, to: aim (demolish, destroy, equalize, flatten, rase, raze, reduce

levelheaded: collected, composed, cool, poised, practical, rational, reasonable, sane, sensible, sound, together

leveling of land: gradation

leveling wedge: shim

lever: bar, binder, crowbar, jack, jimmy, lam, machine, peavey, peavy, pedal, pry, tool, treadle

lever pivots, point on which: fulcrum

leverage: advantage, clout, credit, influence, power, weight

leviathan: creature, dragon, ship, whale; enormous, giant, large

levitate: float, hover, lift, rise, suspend

levity: amusement, buoyancy, foolishness, frivolity, fun, hilarity, humor, humour, inconstancy, laughs, lightness, silliness

levy: assess, assessment, burden, charge, collect, duty, exact, extent, fee, fine, impose, tariff, tax, tithe, toll, wage

lewd: base, bawdy, coarse, filthy, indecent, ithyphallic, lascivious, lecherous, licentious, lubricious, lustful, obscene, pornographic, racy, randy, rude, salacious, suggestive, unchaste, vulgar, wanton, wicked

lexicographer: author, compiler, definer, editor, lexicologist, linguist

lexicon: dictionary, glossary, language, onomasticon, vocabulary, wordlist

liability: accountability, blame, burden, debt, drawback, duty, exposure, hindrance, minus, obligation, proneness, responsibility, shortcoming

liability for another, person assuming: guarantor, surety

liability or debt gradually worked off: amortized

liability to conviction, punishment: jeopardy

liable: accountable, answerable, apt, bound, contingent, exposed, inclined, likely, penetrable, possible, prone, responsible, subject, susceptible, vulnerable

liable to err: fallible

liable to injury, attack, criticism: vulnerable

liable, to become: incur

liaison: affair, amour, bond, contact, encounter, fling, intermediary, intrigue, link, mediator, relationship

liar: cheat, deceiver, exaggerator, fabricator, fibber, perjurer, prevaricator, pseudologue

libel: calumniate, defame, denigrate, discredit, lampoon, malign, slander, smear, vilify; calumny, defamation, scandal

liberal: abundant, ample, benevolent, bounteous, bountiful, broad, broad-minded, charitable, flexible, free, freehanded, generous, giving, handsome, lavish, lenient, magnanimous, munificent, open, openhanded, plentiful, profuse, progressive, radical; latitudinarian

liberal arts, four highest: arithmetic, astronomy, geometry, music, quadrivium

liberal arts, lower three: grammar, logic, rhetoric, trivium

liberal in political belief: leftist

liberal, tolerant in religious belief: latitudinarian

liberality: largess

liberate: acquit, clear, deliver, discharge, emancipate, free, loosen, manumit, redeem, release, rescue, set free, unbind, unchain, unfetter, unshackle

libertine: debauchee, dissolute, freethinker, immoral, lascivious, lewd, libidinous, licentious, lustful, rake, roué, sensualist

liberty: autonomy, choice, emancipation, freedom, furlough, independence, leave, license, permission, privilege, right, sovereignty

libidinous: carnal, lascivious, lewd, libertine, lustful, satyric, wanton

library: athenaeum, archive, bibliotheca, books, gallery, institution, reading room

RELATED TERMS

library book added to collection: accession

library books reduced on photographic film: microfiche

library classification number: call number

library classification system: Dewey decimal system, Library of Congress classification

library nook for study: carrel

library reading room: athenaeum

library shelves of books: stack ❦

lice, infestation with: pediculosis, phthiriasis

lice, relating to: pedicular

license: allow, authority, authorize, certificate, charter, empower, entitlement, excise, franchise, freedom, laxity, leave, liberty, looseness, pass, passport, patent, permission, permit, proof, sanction, unrestraint, variance

license or certify something that meets standards: accredit

license plate, specially selected: vanity plate

license to distribute company's goods or services in an area: franchise

license to publish, official: imprimatur

licensing charge for certain privileges: excise

licentious: amoral, carnal, depraved, dissolute, free, immoral, lascivious, lewd, libertine, libidinous, loose, lustful, obscene, profligate, promiscuous, satyric, uncontrolled, unprincipled, unrestrained, unruly, wanton

lichen kin: moss

licit: authorized, lawful, legal, licensed, permissible, sanctioned

lick: beat, clobber, conquer, defeat, flog, hit, overcome, punch, shellac, smack, speed, surmount, thrash, trace, trounce, whip, win; graze, lap, stroke, taste, tongue

lickety-split: fast, jiffy, quickly, rapidly, speedily, swiftly

licorice flavoring: anise

lid: cap, cover, curb, hood, limit, maximum, plug, restraint, roof, top

lie: canard, deceit, deceive, deception, dishonesty, distort, equivocate, equivocation, exist, fabricate, fabrication, falsehood, falsify, falsity, fib, fudge, invent, inveracity, mendacity, misinform, mislead, misrepresentation, misstate, palter, perjury, prevaricate, prevarication, story, subreption, tale, untruth; bask, languish, loll, lounge, position, prostrate, recline, remain, repose, rest, situated, sprawl

lie detector: polygraph

lie down: recline, repose

lie face downward: grovel

lie in and enjoy: bask

lie in court: perjure

lie in wait and surprise: ambush, lurk, waylay

lie relaxed: languish

lie, to: equivocate, fabricate, fudge, palter, prevaricate, temporize, tergiversate

lie, trivial: white lie

lien: charge, claim, mortgage, right

lien on personal property: chattel mortgage

lieu: instead, place, stead, substitution

life: animation, being, biosis, energy, enthusiasm, essence, existence, soul, spirit, vigor, vitality, zest

RELATED TERMS

life fluid of the gods: ichor

life force: élan vital

life from nonliving matter, hypothetical creation of: abiogenesis, autogenesis, spontaneous generation

life processes and organisms, study of: physiology

life, concerning: vital

life, length of a: longevity

life, parts of universe supporting: ecosphere

life, processes of cell or organism necessary for maintenance of: metabolism

life, restore: resurrect, resuscitate

life, view that all matter has: hylozoism ❦

life history written by another: biography

life insurance double payment in case of accidental death: double indemnity

life, Buddhist and Hindu belief in the sacredness of all: ahimsa

lifeless: amort, automatic, barren, bloodless, cold, dead, deal, deceased, defunct, dull, empty, extinct, flat, inactive, inanimate, inert, lackluster, lethargic, listless, mechanical, spent, spiritless, static, stiff, torpid, uninhabited, vapid, wooden

lifeless state: abiosis

lifelike: accurate, graphic, naturalistic, real, realistic, simulated

lifelike three-dimensional image produced by laser: hologram

life's work of artist: oeuvre

lifesize drawing or representation: macrograph

lifetime: age, being, day, duration, endurance, existence, forever, period, span

lifework: calling, career, occupation, profession, purpose, pursuit, vocation, work

lift: aid, ascend, aspire, boost, crane, elevate, encourage, enhance, exalt, hand, heave, help, hoist, improve, jack, levitate, mount, pilfer, pry, purloin, raise, rear, repeal, rescind, revoke, ride, rise, steal, support, swipe, take, transport, upgrade; derrick, elevator, ligament, theft

lift up your hearts: sursum corda

ligature: band, bandage, binding, bond, connection, cord, filament, link, tie, wire

light (action): land on, perch

light (illumination): beacon, beam, brighten, bulb, candle, dawn, daybreak, fire, flame, flare, flash, fluorescent, glimmer, glow, ignite, illuminate, illumine, kindle, lamp, lantern, lucent, luminary, luminc, luminous, moon, neon, radiance, shine, spark, sunny, sunrise, torch

light amplification by stimulated emission of radiation: laser

light and airy: ethereal

light and shade in art: chiaroscuro

light around celestial object: aureole, corona, nimbus

light at the end of day, fading: crepuscle, crepuscule, twilight

light brown: ecru, sorel

light bulb with filament: incandescent lamp

light bulb working on electromagnetic radiation: fluorescent lamp

light contact in billiards: kiss

light emission at low temperatures: fluorescence, luminescence, phosphorescence

light emission from heating: incandescence

light emission through biochemical process in organisms: bioluminescence

light energy by plant as energy source, use of: photosynthesis

light fixture's frosted covering or reflector: diffuser

light for moviemaking: klieg light

light from organism: bioluminescence

light from something exposed to radiation: phosphorescence

light-headed: delirious, dizzy, faint, flighty, giddy, silly, unsteady, woozy

light in wavelengths: spectrum

light inside car: courtesy light, map light

light intensity measurement based on candle in one square foot: foot-candle

light into spectral rays, to separate: disperse

light meal on fasting days: collation

light measure: candela, lumen, lux, photon

light on fire: conflagrate

light or heat ray bent in transit: refraction

light or sound wave change when source and observer in motion: Doppler effect

light phenomenon of night sky: aurora

light-producing: luminiferous

light pulses, lamp with: strobe light

light radiation, electronic device varying in response to: electric eye, photocell, photoelectric cell

light rain: sprinkle

light reflected by celestial body: albedo

light-rejecting: opaque

light up: illume, illuminate, irradiate

light wave, turning or bending of: refraction

light waves into colors of rainbow, breaking up of: diffraction

light when struck by radiation, substance capable of emitting: phosphor

light, allowing passage of: translucent, transparent

light, as gases: aeriform

light, as gauze: gossamer

light, brief blaze of: flare

light, brilliant: luster, radiance, scintillation

light, buoyant wood: balsa

light, concerning: photic

light, early type of stage: calcium light, limelight

light, emitting self-generated: fluorescent, luminous, phosphorescent

light, flickering with: lambent

light, fluffy baked egg dish: soufflé

light, giving off: radiate

light, having no: aphotic

light, not allowing passage of: opaque

light, powerful carbon-arc lamp making intense: klieg light

light, semiconductor diode that converts voltage to: LED

light, signal: beacon, Bengal light, flare, lighthouse, Very light

light, study of: optics

light, to put out a: douse, extinguish, quench, snuff

RELATED TERMS

light (of mood): carefree, casual, cheerful, dainty, deft, delicate, easy, ethereal, faded, fragile, frivolous, gentle, graceful, happy, lively, merry, mild, nimble, pastel, petty, portable, simple, slender, small, soft, trifling, trivial, undemanding, untaxing, weightless ❦

lightbulb, threadlike glowing conductor in: filament

lighten: allay, alleviate, bleach, brighten, decrease, dilute, ease, fade, gladden, gleam, illuminate, jettison, lessen, reduce, relieve, shine, trim, unburden, unload

lighthearted: blithe, buoyant, carefree, cheerful, gay, glad, happy, insouciant, jovial, lively, merry, rollicking, spirited, unconcerned, untroubled, upbeat, vivacious, volatile

lighting technician on film: gaffer

lighting technician on film, assistant: best boy

lightly: daintily, easily, effortlessly, faintly, gently, gingerly, mildly, softly, subtly, tenderly

lightness and gaiety: levity

lightning in sheetlike illumination: sheet lightning

lightning in single discharge: bolt, flash, streak

lightning without thunder: heat lightning

likable: amiable, attractive, charming, congenial, friendly, genial, nice, personable, pleasant

like: admire, adore, approve, cherish, choose, endorse, enjoy, favor, love, prefer, preference, relish, wish; akin, as, as if, compatible, equal, equivalent, homogenous, identical, parallel, quasi, related, resembling, same, similar, synonymous, uniform

likelihood: appearance, chance, possibility, probability, prospect

likely: achievable, apt, attainable, believable, conceivable, destined, expected, feasible, hopeful, inclined, liable, plausible, possible, presumably, probable, prone, suitable

likely to become or be: prospective

liken: compare

likeness: affinity, copy, double, duplicate, effigy, equivalence, facsimile, guise, image

likeness of disliked person: effigy

likening thing to another using "like" or "as": simile

likewise: also, and, besides, ditto, furthermore, moreover, similarly, too

liking: affection, affinity, appetite, appreciation, delight, fancy, favor, fondness, gusto, inclination, lust, penchant, pleasure, preference, propensity, shine, taste, tendency, whim

liking, special fondness or: partiality, predilection

lilliputian: diminutive, dwarf, little, midget, petty, small, teeny-weeny, tiny, trivial

lilt: air, intonation, move, refrain, sing, song, tune

lily: aloe, arum, butterfly, calla, celestial, climbing, flamingo, flower, glory, ixia, magic, mariposa, meadow, mountain, orange, pad, panther, plant, pond, rain, sego, spider, tiger, toad, tomlin, water, western, yucca

lily family: liliaceae

lily-livered: afraid, chicken, cowardly, fainthearted, gutless, timid, yellow

limb: appendage, arm, bough, branch, edge, extension, extremity, fin, flipper, leg, member, offshoot, projection, prosthesis, twig, wing

limb by amputation, loss of: avulsion

limb by some animals, regrowth of lost: regeneration

limb falling asleep, tingling of: obdormition

limb, deprive of: dismember, maim, mutilate

limb, displace: dislocate

limb, illusory: phantom limb

limber: agile, elastic, flexible, graceful, lithe, pliable, pliant, resilient, spry, supple; loosen

limbo: dance, neglect, nowhere, oblivion

lime: calcium oxide, citrus

lime growing up in cave: stalagmite

lime hanging down in cave: stalactite

limestone, concerning: calcareous

limit: absolute, ambit, barrier, border, bound, boundary, brink, ceiling, check, circumscribe, closure, conclude, confine, constrain, contract, curb, curfew, deadline, define, edge, end, extent, extreme, extremity, fence, finish, fix, goal, inhibit, maximum, mete, parameter, quota, ration, restrain, restrict, set, stint, term, ultimate, verge

limit above which something goes into effect: threshold

limit legal inheritance: entail

limit of damage or loss: damage control

limit on bringing a legal action, law setting time: statute of limitations

limit or modify, to: qualify

limit or outer boundary: perimeter, periphery

limit or range of one's knowledge, experience, interest: horizon

limit or range of power, action: tether

limit or restriction: restraint, stint, straightjacket, stricture, tether

limit or restriction that begins at a specified time: curfew

limit set forth in document clause: proviso

limit that may be admitted or needs to be reached: quota

limit to a locality: localize

limit, leeway beyond a: play, tolerance

limit, to establish a: circumscribe, delimit, demarcate

limit, to go beyond a: transgress

limited: confined, few, finite, having bounds, inadequate, local, ltd., narrow, reserved, restricted, scanty, short

limited allotment: ration

limited and narrow: parochial

limited by conditions: finite

limited in growth, development: stunted

limited in possibility for change: inflexible

limited or excluding most: esoteric, exclusive, rarefied, restricted, select

limitless: ad infinitum, bottomless, boundless, countless, endless, eternal, immeasurable, infinite, unending, unrestricted, vast

limn: delineate, depict, describe, draw, paint, represent

limp: dodder, droopy, enervated, falter, feeble, flabby, flaccid, flexible,

flimsy, floppy, gimp, hitch, hobble, lame, limber, loose, soft, stagger, weak, wilted, wobble

limpid: bright, clear, comprehensible, crystalline, distinct, lucid, pellucid, pure, serene, translucent, transparent, untroubled

line: axis, barrier, border, boundary, cable, carrier, column, configuration, contour, cord, course, dash, division, draw, file, formation, goods, groove, letter, march, mark, message, method, pattern, policy, principle, procedure, queue, rank, rope, route, row, rule, scratch, seam, stitch, stock, streak, string, stripe, stroke, suture, system, tier, track, wire, wrinkle

line bounding plane area in math: perimeter

line considered limit to a curve: asymptote

line finishing off main strokes of letter: serif

line in which each successive word has one more s: ropalic

line joining two points on a curve: chord

line meeting a curve: secant

line of bold cliffs: palisades

line of cliffs: scarp

line of latitude: parallel

line of longitude: meridian

line of people or vehicles stationed to guard area: cordon

line of verse: stich

line on a crystal: stria

line on ship showing how much it may be loaded: load line, Plimsoll line, Plimsoll mark

line or dash over vowel for "long" sound, horizontal: macron

line or lines, concerning: linear

line with weight for determining depth, verticality: plumb line

line, containing a common: coaxial, collinear

line, making contact at a point along a: tangent

line, slanted: forward slash, virgule

line, to cut across or through a: intersect

line, very thin: hairline

lineage: ancestry, background, birth, blood, breed, clan, descent, family, forebears, genealogy, heredity, kindred, pedigree, race, stirps, stock, tribe

lineament: feature

linear measure, ancient: cubit

linen: articles, barras, bedding, brabant, brin, cambric, cloth, damask, dornick, fabric, garments, lawn, napery, paper, sheets, thread, toile

linen source: flax

linen, household: napery

liner's path: sea lane

lines beginning with same word/phrase: anaphora

lines in which certain letters form a name or message: acrostic

lines meeting at the same point, of: concurrent, convergent

lines of printed or written material, number of: linage, lineage

lines of verse ending with pause: end-stopped

lines of verse running over to following line: enjambed

lines on light background, squares of dark: tattersall

lines on map, horizontal: latitude

lines on map, vertical: longitude

lines shading a drawing, fine: hatching

lines spoken by different characters, ancient Greek dialogue with alternate: stichomythia

lines that can be read left to right and alternately right to left, writing: boustrophedon

lines that serve as reference for plotting points: axis

lines used to find x-y coordinate, intersecting: crosshairs

lines, of straight: rectilinear

lines, ornamental work of branching: tracery

lineup: list, roster, schedule, slate

linger: cling, dawdle, delay, dillydally, drag, dwell, fritter, idle, lag, loiter, mosey, poke, remain, stay, survive, tarry, trifle, wait

lingo: argot, cant, dialect, idiom, jargon, language, patter, slang, vernacular, vocabulary

lingua franca: koine

linguist: grammarian, interpreter, lexicographer, pantoglot, philologist, polyglot

linguistic elements, arrangement of: collocation, syntax

linguistic feature boundary line: isogloss

linguistic study of form and structure of words or language: morphology

linguistics: philology

linguistics as it has changed through time, study of: diachronic

linguistics at specific stage of development, study of: descriptive, synchronic

linguistics branch dealing with speech sounds and their representation: phonetics

linguistics dealing with meaning of words, branch of: lexicology

liniment: arnica, balm, embrocation, lotion, oil, ointment

lining folded out: revers

lining inside the cover of a book: doublure

lining up of earth, sun, moon: syzygy

link: associate, band, bond, braced, catenate, chain, combine, component, concatenate, conjoin, connect, connection, contact, couple, course, fastener, fuse, group, hitch, hook, hookup, implicate, interface, involve, join, joint, linkage, network, nexus, tie, unite, vinculum

link in series: catenate, concatenate

linked series: catenas, concatenation

linking word: and

lion: cat, celebrity, cougar, feline, king, notable, puma, simba, star, wildcats

lionhearted: bold, brave, courageous, fearless, intrepid, valiant

lionlike: leonine

lions, group of: pride

lip: border, brim, brink, edge, kiss, labellum, labium, margin, mouth, nozzle, rim, spout, tip; backtalk, insolence, sass

lip deformity with cleft: harelip

lip-related consonant: labial

lip, groove from nose to upper: philtrum

lip, ring on: labret

liplike: labiate

lips: labia

lips, concerning: labial

lips, having thick: labrose

lips, to wrinkle the: pucker, purse

liquefy: melt

liquescent: runny

liqueur: alcohol, amaretto, anisette, benedictine, cordial, kahlua, triple sec

liqueur, aniseed-flavored Greek: ouzo

liqueur, licorice flavored: sambuca

liquid: aqueous, available, beverage, convertible, dissolved, extract, fluent, fluid, juice, liquor, melted, nectar, solution, solvent, watery

liquid and crystal, state of matter between: mesomorphic

liquid becoming soft solidified mass: clot, coagulate, curdle

liquid between fine suspension and solution: colloid

liquid butter: ghee, ghi

liquid cloudy by stirring up sediment, to make: roil

liquid flavoring for soaking meat: marinade

liquid from wound: ichor, pus

liquid in religious ritual: libation

liquid into gas, change from: evaporate

liquid mixed with finely ground cement, plaster of Paris, clay: slurry

liquid part of fat: olein

liquid poured as religious ritual: libation

liquid property of having stretched elastic membrane top: surface tension

liquid surface distortion when interacting with solid: capillarity, capillary action

liquid suspension in pharmacology: magma

liquid that cannot be mixed, of a: immiscible

liquid that leaks from container: ullage

liquid through semipermeable membrane, diffusion of: osmosis

liquid under pressure, operated or moved by: hydraulic

liquid waste: effluent

liquid when shaken or stirred, becoming: thixotropic

liquid, able to absorb: permeable, porous

liquid, boil down: decoction

liquid, change from gas into: condense

liquid, curved upper surface of: meniscus

liquid, material settling at bottom of: dregs, foots, grounds, lees, sediment

liquid, of a sticky thick: viscid, viscous

liquid, regulator for flow of: baffle

liquid, solid particles dispersed in: suspension

liquid, suspension of globules of one liquid in a second: emulsion

liquidate: abolish, amortize, auction off, clear, dissolve, eliminate, kill, murder, repay, settle, square, terminate

liquor: alcohol, ale, beer, beverage, bitters, booze, bourbon, brandy, brew, cocktail, cordial, drink, firewater, gin, grog, hooch, intoxicant, lager, moonshine, rum, rye, sake, saki, scotch, spirits, stout, vodka, whiskey, wine

liquor distilled from fermented grain, potatoes, or corn: vodka

liquor distilled from potatoes or grain, Scandinavian: aquavit, schnapps

liquor distilled from the fermented mash of the Agave tequilane plant: tequila

liquor fermented from palm trees: toddy

liquor with water or carbonated beverage in tall glass: highball

liquor, whiskey or brandy, strong: aqua vitae, eau-de-vie

lissome: agile, athletic, flexible, graceful, limber, lithe, nimble, pliant

list: arrange, bill, brief, canon, cant, catalog, catalogue, census, chart, count, dictionary, directory, docket, enumeration, file, glossary, incline, index, inventory, itemize, lexicon, manifest, record, register, roll, roster, rota, schedule, slate, table, tabulate

list extender abbreviation: et al

list in detail: particularize, specify

list of acknowledgments on TV show moving vertically: crawl

list of articles on hand with quantity: inventory

list of candidates: slate, ticket

list of dead: necrology

list of events: agenda

list of investments held: portfolio

list of merchandise or services purchased: invoice

list of mistakes: errata

list of names: roster, rota

list of names, reading a: muster, roll call

list of performances, skills that one can draw upon: repertoire

list of petty procedures: rigmarole, rigamarole

list of potential murder victims: hit list

list of prayers and fixed responses: litany

list of printing errors: errata

list of specific requirements: specifications, specs

list of things to do: agenda

list of things wanted or hoped for: wish list

list of words with definitions: glossary

list of workers on TV show or film: credits

list of writings: bibliography

list one by one: detail, enumerate, itemize, tally

list unit: item

list, to: careen, heel, keel, lean, slope, tilt, tip

list, to enter a name on a: enroll, register

listen: attend, audit, auscultate, concentrate, eavesdrop, hark, harken, hear, heed, monitor, note, obey, overhear

listen secretly: eavesdrop

listen, call to: oyez

listener: auditor, ear

listener, patient and helpful: sounding board

listening: auscultation

listening distance: earshot

listening instrument for doctor: stethoscope

listing of names, addresses, other data: catalog, directory

listless: anemic, apathetic, bored, careless, drowsy, dull, enervated, faint, heartless, heedless, inattentive, lackadaisical, languid, lazy, lethargic, sleepy, sluggish, spiritless, supine, uninterested

listlessness: ennui

lists or tables, to arrange in: codify, tabulate

litany: chant, invocation, list, prayer, recital, refrain, rogation, supplication

literacy for the ability and use of language but not in reading and writing, equivalent to: oracy

literacy for the ability to do numerical calculations, equivalent to: numeracy

literal: accurate, actual, authentic, exact, factual, precise, prosaic, real, unerring, verbatim

literal translation from one language to another: calque, loan, translation

literal, not: figurative

literary: bookish, educated, erudite, intellectual, lettered, pedantic, scholarly, versed

literary burlesque: parody

literary circle: cenacle, clique, coterie, salon

literary club: atheneum

literary collection: ana

literary commentary: apparatus criticus, critical apparatus

literary composition with character revealing character in speech: dramatic monologue

literary movement, early part of 20th century: imagism

literary movement, mid-19th century: realism

literary or artistic imitator: epigone

literary or artistic principles, premise: donnée

literary passage cited as illustration or instance: locus classicus

literary passage of inner thoughts, emotions of character: interior monologue

literary passages by one author, selection of: chrestomathy

literary patchwork: cento

literary professional: litterateur

literary selections: ana, analects, anthology, digest

literary sketch: cameo

literary study, classical scholarship: philology

literary subjects, writings on: belles lettres

literary theft: plagiarism

literary work evaluation: literary criticism

literary work judged by its emotional effect: affective fallacy

literary work on a specific subject, scholarly: monograph

literary work, first copies of a: first edition

literary work, humorous interlude in: comic relief

literary work, note about: annotation, gloss

literary work, short and descriptive: vignette

literary works intended for a particular group: esoterica

literary works intended to stimulate sexual desire: erotica

literate: educated

literature: article, belles lettres, biography, books, epode, essay, fiction, letters, nonfiction, novel, pamphlet, poetry, prose, thesis, writings

literature, category of: genre

literature, people with knowledge of: literati

literature, popular or sentimental: kitsch

lithe: agile, clever, flexible, graceful, lean, limber, lissome, nimble, pliant, slender, slim, supple, svelte

litigate: sue

litigation: action, case, contest, dispute, lawsuit, suit, trial

litter: clutter, debris, disorder, garbage, junk, mess, pile, refuse, rubbish, rummage, trash, waste; brood, offspring, young; bed, bier, couch, straw, stretcher

litter of pigs: farrow

little: crumb, dash, diminutive, dinky, insignificant, mean, microscopic, miniature, minor, petite, petty, pinch, puny, rich, seldom, slight, small, speck, stunted, tiny, trace, unimportant, wee

little bit: droplet, iota, mite, modicum, particle, pittance, shred, smidgen, soupçon, tittle

liturgy: ceremony, rite, ritual, sacrament, service, worship

livable: acceptable, bearable, comfortable, cozy, endurable, habitable, snug, suitable, tolerable

live: abide, active, animate, are, blazing, board, breathe, burning, continue, dwell, dynamic, energetic, exist, experience, glowing, in person, inpropria persona, maintain, occupy, reside, room, subsist, survive, unexploded, vigorous, vivid

live and survive: subsist

live dully: stagnate, vegetate

live in: inhabit, reside

live in the country: rusticate

live off: sponge

live together: cohabit

livelihood: bread, business, career, craft, employment, job, living, occupation, profession, subsistence, sustenance, trade, vocation

liveliness: alacrity, brio, effervescence, esprit, pep, sparkle, spirit, tittup, vim, vivacity

lively: active, agile, airy, alert, alive, animated, blithe, bright, brisk, buoyant, bustling, busy, buzzing, cheery, chipper, chirpy, eager, effervescent, energetic, enthusiastic, exuberant, feisty, fresh, frisky, humming, industrious, jaunty, mercurial, nimble, peppy, pert, piquant, rambunctious, snappy, sparkling, spirited, sprightly, spry, stimulating, vibrant, vigorous, vivacious, volatile

lively and rapid movement with leaps, jumps, and turns: allegro

lively and stimulating: exhilarating, invigorating

lively Bohemian round dance for couples: polka

lively Spanish bullfighting dance: paso doble

lively Spanish dance in triple time: bolero

lively Spanish dance performed in triple time: fandango

lively, musically: allegro

liver: gland, hepar, organ, tomalley

liver disease: biliousness, cirrhosis, hepatitis

liver paste, goose: pâté de foie gras

liver, concerning the: hepatic

lives, area where organism: habitat

lives, place where one: domicile, residence

livid: angry, ashen, bleak, bruised, colorless, discolored, enraged, fuming, furious, incensed, irate, pale, purple

living: alive, animated, being, bread, income, lifestyle, livelihood, means, realistic, subsistence, sustenance, vital, vivid, work

living biologically in different regions: allopatric

living biologically in same region: sympatric

living on both land and water: amphibious

living on its own, capable of: viable

living organism, in: in vivo

living organism, of: organic

living organisms developing only from living organisms: biogenesis

living plant or animal: organism

living together and benefitting, organisms: symbiosis

living together but not married: cohabitation, concubinage, shacking up

living together harmoniously, capable of: compatible

lizard that changes color: chameleon

lizard types: adda, agama, anole, chameleon, dab, dabb, eft, flying, galliwasp, gecko, gila, goana, horned toad, iguana, Komodo dragon, monitor, newt, saurian, skink, tuatera, uta, worrell

lizard, like a: lacertilian, saurian

lizardlike amphibian: salamander

lizard's regrowth of cut-off tail: regeneration

lizard's shedding of tail when necessary: autotomy

lizard's skin hanging from throat: wattle

llama relatives: alpaca, guanaco, vicuna

load: bear, bundle, burden, cargo, carriage, clog, contents, drag, drain, encumber, flood, freight, goods, hamper, haul, lade, oppress, pack, pressure, saddle, shipment, stow, stuff, tote, weigh, weight

loading wharf: staithe

loaf: dawdle, dillydally, idle, laze, lazy, loiter, lounge, slack, take it easy; bread

loafer: bum, deadbeat, drone, goldbricker, idler, layabout, lazybones, lounger, shoe, slouch, vagabond, vagrant, wastrel

loamy deposit: loess

loan: accommodation, advance, credit, mortgage; borrow, lend

loan for property with the deed as security: mortgage

loan of funds for services rendered to government: imprest

loan repayable upon demand: call loan, demand loan

loan translation in language: calque

loan, property acceptable as security for: collateral

loan, to pay off a: redeem

loans, agency accepting accounts receivable as security for short-term: factor

loath: against, averse, counter, disinclined, hesitant, inimical, odious, reluctant, resisting, unwilling

loathe: abhor, abominate, deplore, despise, detest, dislike, hate, scorn, spurn

loathing: abhorrence, odium

loathsome: abhorrent, abominable, cloying, deplorable, detestable, disgusting, distasteful, foul, hateful, hideous, horrible, mean, nauseating, obnoxious, odious, offensive, repugnant, revolting, ugly, undesirable, vile

lob: heave, hit, launch, propel, throw, toss

lobby: advance, anteroom, doorway, entrance, entrance hall, foyer, hall, room, vestibule; influence, persuade, pitch, promote, solicit

loblolly: pine

lobster: crustacean, decapod

lobster claw: chela, nipper, pincer

lobster eggs: roe

lobster family: decapod

lobster liver: tomalley

lobster shell: mail

lobster trap or basket: creel

lobster types: American, black, European, grasshopper, Maine, Norway, rock, spiny

lobster unfertilized eggs, red when cooked: coral

local: confined, endemic, homegrown, insular, limited, narrow, native, neighborhood, provincial, regional, restricted, topical

local and restricted: endemic, native

local boy: native son

local dialect: patois

local in application: topical

local in origination: aboriginal, autochthonous, indigenous

local language: vernacular

local political level: grass roots

locale: area, place, region, scene, site, venue

locate: detect, discover, dwell, espy, establish, find, pinpoint, position, seat, see, settle, site, situate, spot, stand, trace, uncover

locate with precision: pinpoint

location: area, bearings, habitat, place, point, position, scene, site, situation, spot, whereabouts

location finder: Loran

lock: bolt, cage, clamp, confine, fasten, fastener, grip, hook, latch, link, seal, secure; curl, ringlet, tress, tuft, wisp

lock part that key presses to shoot bolt: talon

lock part that releases bolt when moved by key: tumbler

lock with hinged slotted part, secured by pin, bolt, padlock: hasp

lock, revolving part in: spindle

lock, springless bolt turned by key: dead bolt

locking mechanism, as a pawl or catch: detent

lockjaw: tetanus, trismus

lock's edge plate with slot for bolt: selvage

lock's metal surrounding plate: escutcheon

lock's ridge that corresponds to key's notch: ward

lockup: calaboose, clink, cooler, hoosegow, jail, penitentiary, pokey, prison, slammer

loco: mad, crazy

locomotive: diesel, engine, iron horse, ironhorse

locomotive front triangular frame: cowcatcher

locomotive, power-collecting trolley above: pantograph

locust: cicada, grasshopper

locust tree: carob

locust types: bald, greenstriped, hellow, Rocky Mountain, seventeen-year, water

lode: deposit, fissure, lead, reef, strike, vein

lodge: accommodate, bestow, board, brotherhood, cabin, camp, chapter, club, cottage, couch, domicile, dwell, encamp, harbor, hostel, hotel, motel, shelter

lodging: abode, barracks, bed, camp, chambers, dormitory, dwelling, habitation, hostel, hostelry, hut, inn, longhouse, nest, quarters, residence, room, roost, tavern, teepee, tent, wigwam

lodging of soldiers in private home: billet

loft: attic, balcony, dormer, gallery, garret, raise, studio

lofty: aerial, aery, arduous, arrogant, condescending, dignified, distinguished, elevated, eloquent, eminent, epic, exalted, generous, grand, haughty, high, imposing, majestic, mighty, noble, overbearing, pompous, proud, raised, soaring, stately, steep, tall

log: account, billet, diary, journal, record, register, stump, timber, wood

log-and-mud dwelling: hogan

logarithm decimal part: mantissa

logarithm integer part: characteristic

logic: analysis, connection, deduction, philosophy, rationale, reason, reasoning, sense

logic argument with two or more alternatives that contradict original contention: dilemma

logic proposition with two alternatives but only one true: disjunction

logic syllogism in which a premise or conclusion is not stated explicitly: enthymeme

logic that is series of incomplete syllogisms: sorites

logic, error in: fallacy

logic, faulty: choplogic

logic, intuitive reasoning as opposed to: lateral thinking

logic, major or minor proposition in syllogism of: premise

logic, something made the basis of a proposition in: predicate

logic, subsidiary proposition used to demonstrate principal proposition in: lemma

logical: analytical, clear, coherent, intelligent, legitimate, perceptive, rational, reasonable, sensible, sound, valid, wise

logical argument: dialectic, syllogism

logical disproof of proposition by showing absurdity of conclusion: reductio ad absurdum

logical rather than intuitive: dianoetic

logical reasoning: ratiocination

logical reasoning from general premise to particular conclusion: deduction, synthesis

logical reasoning from particular instances to general truths: induction

logical reasoning with major and minor premise and conclusion: syllogism

logically conflicting: incompatible, mutually exclusive

logically false: faulty, invalid

logically from what preceded it, statement that does not follow: non sequitur

logically self-evident: a priori, analytic, apodictic, tautologous

logrolling: birling

logrolling contest: roleo

logs in fireplace, stand for: andiron, firedog

logs, floating barrier of: boom

logs, trough for carrying: sluice

loincloth: dhoti, lavalava, pareu

loiter: dawdle, delay, dillydally, hesitate, idle, lag, laze, linger, loaf, loll, lounge, saunter, slough, stroll, tarry

loll: dangle, dawdle, droop, idle, loaf, loiter, lounge, recline, relax, slouch, sprawl, tarry

London native: Brit, Cockney, Londoner

lone: alone, apart, individual, isolated, secluded, single, sole, solitary, solo, unique

lonely: abandoned, alone, apart, deserted, desolate, forlorn, forsaken, homesick, isolated, lonesome, secluded, solitary

lonely and sad: bereft, desolate, forlorn, forsaken

lonely and withdrawn: alienated, estranged

long: ache, crave, desire, hope, hunger, lust, miss, pine, thirst, want, yearn;

elongated, extended, extensive, interminable, lengthy, prolix, protracted, tedious, tiresome, unending

long ago: lang syne, once upon a time, yore

long and drawn-out: prolonged, protracted, sustained

long and indirect: circuitous

long and stretched: elongated, extended, rangy

long and tedious: interminable, marathon

long and wordy: prolix

long-established: inveterate

long explanation, narrative: megillah

long for: ache, crave, desire, hanker, miss, pine, yearn

long jump: broad jump

long-lasting: abiding, durable, enduring, resilient

long-lasting, as illness: chronic, persistent

long-standing: continual, durable, enduring, lasting, perpetual, persistent, rooted

long-suffering: enduring, forbearing, lenient, patient, tolerant

long time: ages, coon's age, eon, month of Sundays

long upholstered seat: sofa

long-winded: diffuse, garrulous, lengthy, loquacious, periphrasis, prolix, rambling, redundant, spiel, verbose, wordy

long-windedness: circumlocution, periphrasis, prolixity, spiel

long wooden bench: settle

long, deep cut: gash

long, light sled: toboggan

long, narrow valley: canyon

long, slow journey: trek

longing: hope, itch, wistful, yearning, yen

longing for past: nostalgia

longitude line: meridian

look: air, appearance, aspect, behold, characteristic, demeanor, expect, expression, face, fleer, focus, gander, gape, gawk, gaze, glance, glare, glimpse, glower, goggle, inspect, leer, notice, observation, ogle, peek, peep, peer, reconnaissance, review, scan, scout, scrutinize, search, see, sight, snoop, squint, stare, surveillance, view, visage, watch

look after: attend, guard, mind, nurse, protect, see to, support, tend, watch

look down on: condescend, despise, dominate, patronize, spurn

look for: await, expect, hunt, pursue, research, search, seek

look forward to: anticipate, await, expect

look into: check, examine, explore, inspect, investigate, probe, research, sift, study

look like: resemble, seem

look or countenance: semblance, visage

look over: browse, disregard, eye, ignore, scan, skim, survey

look sullen: pout

look up: discover, improve, progress, recuperate, refer, research, seek

looker-on: audience, bystander, observer, spectator, witness

looking back: hindsight, retrospect

lookout: beacon, crow's nest, guard, observer, patrol, perspective, post, scout, sentinel, sentry, surveillance, vigil, watch, watchtower, widow's walk

loom: appear, brew, dawn, emanate, emerge, gather, hulk, impend, implement, materialize, near, rise, threaten, tower, weave; machine

loony: crazy, demented, deranged, foolish, insane, lunatic, nuts, silly, wacky

loop: arc, bend, billet, bow, circle, circuit, coil, curl, curve, eye, fold, kink, knot, noose, picot, spiral, surround, turn, twirl

loop-shaped handle: ansa

loop, string or garland suspended in a: festoon, swag

loophole: alibi, aperture, escape, excuse, opening, out, outlet, slit

loops forming edging: picot

loops that form pile of fabric, uncut: terry

loose: apart, baggy, careless, coarse, detached, disconnected, dissolute, easy, fast, flabby, flaccid, free, immoral, indefinite, insecure, lax, liberated, limber, movable, open, promiscuous, random, relaxed, sagging, separate, slack, unattached, unbound, unbridled, uncaged, unchained, unchecked, unconfined, undone, unfastened, unhitched, unlash, unleash, unrestrained, unstable, untied, untightened, vague, wild, wobbly

loosen: disconnect, ease, extricate,

free, liberate, relax, relieve, slacken, unbind, unchain, undo, unfasten, unpeg, unpin, unstrap, untie

loot: booty, dough, haul, money, pelf, pilfer, pillage, plunder, prize, ravage, rob, sack, snatch, spoils, steal, strip, swag, swipe

lop: clip, crop, cut, dangle, droop, eliminate, flop, hang, prune, slice, sned, snip, trim, truncate

lopsided: cockeyed, crooked, irregular, leaning, skewed, tipped, unbalanced, unequal, uneven, unsteady, unsymmetrical, warped

loquacious: babbling, chattering, gabby, garrulous, jabbering, noisy, talkative, wordy

lord: aristocrat, bishop, earl, governor, king, landowner, marquis, master, nobleman, peer, prince, royalty, ruler, seigneur

lordly: arrogant, august, bossy, cavalier, condescending, despotic, dictatorial, dignified, domineering, gracious, grand, grandiose, haughty, high-and-mighty, honorable, lofty, magisterial, magnificent, majestic, masterful, noble, overbearing, proud, regal, snobbish, stately, superior, uppity

lore: belief, custom, erudition, fable, history, knowledge, learning, legend, myth, superstition, tale, tradition, wisdom

lorgnette: eyeglass, opera glass

lose: bereave, default, defeat, displace, elude, fail, forfeit, mislay, misplace, miss, stray, surrender, wander, waste

lose as punishment: forfeit

lose color: fade

lose focus: blur

lose force: flag, wane

lose freshness: droop

lose one's nerve: chicken out

lose strength: pall, weaken

lose through failure to appear: default

loser: also-ran, bomb, bust, deadbeat, failure, flop, lemon, nerd, schlemiel, underdog

loss: accident, affliction, bereavement, calamity, casualty, cost, damage, death, decrease, defeat, deficit, deprivation, destruction, disaster, failure, injury, leak, misfortune, price, privation, ruin, sacrifice, waste

loss for words, pretending to be at a: apophasis

loss from sale of assets: capital loss

loss in value from age, wear: depreciation

loss of consciousness, brief: syncope

loss of experts or scientists to another country: brain drain

loss of memory: amnesia

loss of merchandise, as through theft: shrinkage

loss of muscle coordination: ataxia

loss of speaking ability: aphasia

loss of tasting ability: ageusia

loss of unaccented vowel at word's beginning: aphesis

loss, to make amends for: compensate

loss, to make up for a: recoup

lost: abandoned, absent, absorbed, abstracted, astray, at sea, confused, dead, defeated, destroyed, disappeared, doomed, dreaming, engrossed, extinct, forfeited, forgotten, gone, hidden, irrevocable, mislaid, missing, obscured, perished, perplexed, preoccupied, rapt, ruined, squandered, strayed, wasted

lot: allotment, allowance, amount, assortment, batch, bunch, bundle, chance, clearing, clump, destiny, doom, fate, field, fortune, group, hazard, heap, land, luck, number, parcel, percentage, plat, plot, portion, quantity, ration, share, tract

lotion: ablution, balm, cleanser, cream, embrocation, emollient, liniment, moisturizer, oil, ointment, salve

lots: acres, fates, galore, gobs, legion, loads, lucks, many, oodles, plentitude, realty, reams, scads, slew, tons, wad

lottery: chance, contest, drawing, gamble, lotto, raffle, sweepstake, sweepstakes

lotto's relative: keno

loud: bigmouthed, blaring, blatant, blustering, boisterous, brassy, brazen, colorful, deafening, earsplitting, emphatic, flashy, garish, gaudy, glaring, noisy, obnoxious, obvious, offensive, ostentatious, piercing, raucous, roaring, showy, sonorous, splashy, stentorian, strident, thundering, tumultuous, turbulent, unrefined, uproarious, vehement, vociferous, vulgar

loud and clear: clarion

loud and deep: plangent, resonant, resounding, sonorous

loud and shrill: strident

loud enough to be heard: audible

loud pedal on piano: reverberation pedal, sustaining pedal

loud person: stentor

loud ringing: peal

loud, extremely: blaring, stentorian

loud, guitar-based rock music with violent lyrics: heavy metal

loudly in music: forte, fortissimo

loudness measure: decibel

loudness, gradual decrease in: decrescendo, diminuendo

loudness, gradual increase in: crescendo

loudspeaker reproducing high-pitched sounds: tweeter

loudspeaker reproducing low-pitched sounds: woofer

loudspeaker system: PA system, public-address system

loudspeaker, partition preventing interference in: baffle, diffuser

Louisiana cooking: creole

Louisiana, person from southern: Cajun

lounge: bar, club, couch, idle, loaf, lobby, loiter, loll, parlor, pub, recline, rest, saloon, slouch, sofa

louse: cad, cootie, insect, knave, rat, scoundrel

louse egg: nit

lousy: awful, bad, dirty, horrible, pediculous, poor, rotten, terrible

lout: bend, boor, bow, bumpkin, clod, clodhopper, clown, curtsy, dolt, dumbbell, fool, klutz, lummox, oaf, stoop, twit

louver: blind, slat

lovable: adorable, captivating, charming, cuddly, dear, endearing, enthralling, sweet, tender, winning

love: admire, adoration, adore, affection, agape, amor, caress, charity, cherish, dear, devotion, embrace, enamor, enthusiasm, fancy, feeling, flame, fondness, goodwill, idolize, infatuation, like, precious, romance, sweetheart, valentine

love affair: amour, enthusiasm, liaison, relationship, romance

love affair, secret: amour, intrigue, liaison

love affair, to carry on casual: fool around, philander

love apple: tomato

love as friends without sex: platonic

love feast: agape

love for your offspring: geneity, storge

love god: Amor, Cupid, Eros

love goddess: Aphrodite, Astarte, Hathor, Ishtar, Venus

love letter: billet-doux

love not returned: unrequited

love of others: altruism

love of women: philogyny

love out of selfishness: cupboard love

love poem: amoret, sonnet

love potion: aphrodisiac, philter

love seat: settee

love song: serenade, torch song

love, believing one is in: besotted, infatuated

love, Christian: agape

love, concerning: amatory, amorous, erotic

love, foolish: infatuation

love, in: enamored, smitten

love, intense: adulation, ardor, rapture

lovely: adorable, angelic, attractive, beautiful, captivating, charming, cute, delicious, enchanting, exquisite, graceful, ideal, irresistible, nice, pleasant, pretty, sweet, tender

lover: admirer, adorer, beau, boyfriend, buff, Cassanova, Don Juan, enthusiast, fan, fiancé, fiancée, flame, girlfriend, husband, lothario, mistress, paramour, Romeo, suitor, sweetheart, wife

lover kept by older woman: gigolo

lover of animals: philotherian

lover of arguments or debate: philopolemicist

lover of beauty: esthete, philocalist

lover of good food: gourmand

lover of learning: philomath

lover of literature, language: philologist

lover of married woman: cicisbeo

lover of math and science: philomath

lover of myths: philomythist

lover of trends and fads: philoneist

lover of truth: philalethist

lover, illicit: paramour

lover, live-in: concubine, significant other

lover, promiscuous: Don Juan, ladykiller, rake

lover, promiscuous lady: floozy, moll, prostitute

lover, secondary: concubine

lover, to discard a: jilt

lover, to run away to marry: elope

lover's song: serenade

lovers, meeting of: assignation, rendezvous, tryst

lovesick: languishing, longing, moonstruck, yearning

loving: affectionate, amorous, benevolent, caring, considerate, devoted, erotic, faithful, fond, passionate, tender, warm

loving devotion: reverence, veneration

loving expression: endearment

loving flirtation: dalliance

loving, longing look: belgard

low: base, bass, beneath, bestial, blue, coarse, common, contemptible, crude, cruel, deep, degraded, dejected, depressed, destitute, dirty, down, economical, faint, filthy, glum, gross, humble, hushed, ignoble, inferior, mean, melancholy, miserable, moo, muffled, murmured, nasty, nominal, offensive, plebian, quiet, reduced, rude, shallow, short, slight, small, sordid, under, undignified, unethical, unfavorable, unhappy, unworthy, vile, vulgar, weak, whispered, woebegone

low at neckline, cut: decolleté

low blood sugar: hypoglycemia

low bow: salaam

low-calorie descriptive: lite

low-calorie sweetener: saccharine

low-down: base, contemptible, depressed, despicable, mean, vile

low-key: easygoing, laid-back, relaxed, softened, subdued, subtle

low-minded: coarse, crude, lewd, offensive, vulgar

low point: base, bottom, foot, nadir, worst

low point on graph: trough

low-priced: bargain, cheap, discounted, economical, inexpensive

low sandhill: dune

low ship deck: orlop

low-spirited: blue, crestfallen, dejected, depressed, discouraged, down, forlorn, gloomy, melancholy, woebegone

low tide: ebb, neap

low voice: alto

low, hard baseball hit: line drive

low, sturdy cart: dray

lowbred: boorish, coarse, common, crude, unrefined, vulgar

lower: abase, abate, below, beneath, cheapen, debase, decreased, degrade, demean, demit, demote, depreciate, depress, descend, devalue, diminish, dip, disparage, downgrade, droop, drop, fall, glare, glower, humble, immerse, inferior, less, lessen, mute, nether, reduce, scowl, sink, submerge, subside, under

lower-class person: pleb, plebeian

lower in rank: demote; secondary, subaltern, subordinate

lower in status, to: degrade, demote, downgrade, relegate

lower jaw: mandible

lower middle class: petite bourgeoisie

lower or working class: proletariat

lower part of a ship's hull: bilge

lowest class or underclass: lumpenproletariat

lowest deck of a ship: orlop

lowest layer: bedrock

lowest point: nadir

lowest point in orbit: perigee

lowland: bottoms, flat, holm, marsh, swamp, vale, valley

lowly: base, commonplace, humble, ignoble, mean, meek, modest, mundane, ordinary, plain, prosaic, simple, unassuming

lox's companion: bagel

loyal: dependable, devoted, dutiful, faithful, feal, firm, liege, patriotic, reliable, staunch, steadfast, true, true blue, trustworthy

loyal person: liegeman, myrmidon, partisan, trouper

loyalty: adherence, allegiance, bond, constancy, devotion, faith, faithfulness, fealty, fidelity, honor, piety, steadfastness, troth

loyalty destroyed: disaffection

loyalty to group: esprit de corps, fellowship

loyalty, expression of: fealty, homage

lozenge: pastille, tablet, troche

lubricate: anoint, grease, moisten, oil, smooth

lubrication, study of: tribology

lucid: beaming, bright, brilliant, clear, cogent, crystal, evident, intelligible, luminous, obvious, pellucid, radiant, rational, sane, sensible, shining, translucent, transparent

lucid and transparent: limpid

lucid and understandable: perspicuous

luck: accident, advantage, blessing, break, chance, destiny, fate, fluke, fortuity, fortune, handsel, hit, kismet, lot, opportunity, prosperity, success, win

luck, bad: ambsace

luck, dependent on: aleatory

luck, fortunate discoveries by: serendipity

luck, sudden change of: vicissitudes

luck, sudden good: godsend, windfall

lucky: auspicious, beneficial, boding well, canny, charmed, fortuitous, fortunate, golden, happy, opportune, propitious, prosperous, providential, successful, timely

lucky charm: amulet, periapt, talisman

lucky discovery: serendipity

lucky gain: fluke, windfall

lucrative: fruitful, gainful, moneymaking, paying, productive, profitable, remunerative, worthwhile

ludicrous: absurd, antic, awful, bizarre, comic, comical, crazy, farcical, foolish, funny, laughable, nonsensical, ridiculous, risible, silly, zany

lug: box, buck, carry, drag, draw, haul, nut, pull, schlep, tote, tow, transport, tug, worm

luggage: baggage, bags, gear, suitcase, truck, valise

luggage conveyor belt: carousel

lugubrious: bleak, depressing, dismal, doleful, dour, funeral, gloomy, melancholy, morose, mournful, sad, sorrowful, woebegone

lukewarm: cool, halfhearted, indifferent, tepid, unenthusiastic, unresponsive

lull: allay, breather, calm, compose, ease, hush, interval, pacify, pause, quell, quiet, serenity, settle, soothe, still, stop, subside, tranquilize, wane

lullaby: berceuse, cradlesong, croon, music, sleepsong, song

lumber: blunder, boards, burden, log, plod, shuffle, timber, trudge, useless, wood

lumberjack: cutter, logger, lumberman, woodchopper

luminary: bigwig, celebrity, dignitary, eminence, light, notable, planet, somebody, star, sun, VIP

luminescent: bright, fluorescent, gleaming, glimmering, glistening, glowing, luminous, radiant, shining, twinkling

luminous: beaming, bright, brilliant, clear, evident, glowing, illuminated, inspiring, intelligent, lucid, luminescent, obvious, radiant, shining, translucent, transparent, vivid

luminous radiation: aura

luminous with heat: incandescent

lummox: boor, bungler, clumsy, klutz, lout, oaf, stupid

lump: aggregate, bear, beat, blob, bulge, bulk, bunch, burl, cake, clot, clump, dollop, endure, glob, gob, gobbet, growth, heap, hunk, knob, knot, knurl, mass, node, nodule, nugget, protrusion, protuberance, swelling, tumor, wad, wedge, welt, withstand

lump in yarn: slub

lump of chewed food: bolus

lump of earth: clod

lump of metal: nugget

lump, small: node, nodule, swelling

lumpish: awkward, bulky, clumsy, cumbersome, dull, heavy, sluggish, stupid

lunacy: absurdity, craziness, derangement, folly, foolishness, idiocy, ineptitude, insanity, madness, mania, silliness, stupidity

lunar depression: rill, rille

lunatic: bananas, batty, bonkers, crackpot, crazy, cuckoo, demoniac, deranged, insane, irrational, kooky, loco, loony, mad, madman, maniac, maniacal, neurotic, nutty, psycho, psychopath, psychotic, screwball, unsound, wacky, zany

luncheonette: café, cafeteria, diner, restaurant, sandwich shop, snack bar

lung disease, infectious: consumption, phthisis, TB, tuberculosis

lung sac where exchange of oxygen and carbon dioxide takes place: air sac, alveolus

lung, membrane of: pleura

lunge: attack, barge, burst, charge, dive, jump, leap, lurch, plunge, pounce, rush, stab, surge, thrust

lungs, abnormal sound of diseased: crepitate, rale

lungs, concerning the: pneumonic, pulmonary

lungs, tubes of trachea leading to: bronchi

lupine: fierce, plant, rapacious, ravenous, wolfish

lurch: blunder, careen, flounder, jerk, jolt, lunge, pitch, plunge, reel, rock, roll, stagger, stumble, sway, swerve, teeter, totter, weave

lurch side to side: careen

lure: allure, allurement, appeal, attract, attraction, bait, beguile, cajole, camouflage, captivate, capture, charm, chum, coax, decoy, draw, entice, fascinate, hook, inveigle, seduce, solicit, tempt, trap, trick

lure, bird or animal used as: decoy

lurid: appalling, ashen, fiery, gaudy, ghastly, gloomy, gory, graphic, grim, gruesome, hideous, horrible, livid, macabre, pale, sallow, savage, sensational, shocking, terrible

lurk: ambush, creep, hide, prowl, skulk, slink, sneak, snoop, unsuspected

luscious: appetizing, aromatic, delicate, delicious, delightful, divine, exquisite, flavorful, heavenly, juicy, opulent, ornate, rich, ripe, savory, scrumptious, sensual, sensuous, succulent, sweet, tasty, tempting, voluptuous, yummy

lush: alcoholic, ambrosial, delectable, deluxe, drunk, elaborate, epicurean, fancy, grand, luxurious, mellow, posh, profuse, rich, ritzy, sensual, soft, succulent

lust: ache, aphrodisia, appetite, concupiscence, craving, cupidity, desire, eroticism, hunger, long, passion, thirst, urge, want, yearning

luster: beauty, brightness, brilliance, distinction, glaze, glint, glory, gloss, iridescence, polish, radiance, sheen, shine, sparkle, splendor

lusterless: dead, dim, drab, dull, faded, flat, gloomy, lifeless, prosaic, tarnished, wan

lustful: amorous, concupiscent, dissolute, fulsome, itching, lascivious, lecherous, lewd, libertine, libidinous, passionate, prurient, randy, salacious, wanton

lustfully looking at someone: oculoplania

lustrous: bright, brilliant, dazzling, glistening, glossy, glowing, illustrious, luminous, polished, radiant, sheeny, shining, sparkling, splendid

lustrous cotton fabric: sateen

lusty: dynamic, energetic, hardy, hearty, joyous, merry, mighty, potent, powerful, robust, rugged, sound, strong, sturdy, vigorous, virile

luxuriant: deluxe, elegant, extravagant, fancy, lavish, lush, opulent, ornate, plush, posh, rank, rich, sensuous, sumptuous

luxuriate: bask

luxurious: affluent, costly, elaborate, elegant, expensive, extravagant, grand, indulgent, lavish, lush, magnificent, opulent, plush, posh, rich, sensuous, splendid, sumptuous, voluptuous

luxurious situation: bed of roses

luxury: amenity, bliss, comfort, delicacy, ease, extravagance, frill, hedonism, indulgence, splendor

luxury-loving: epicurean, hedonistic, prodigal, profligate, sybaritic

lying: deceitful, dishonest, false, fibbing, fraudulent, medacious, misleading, treacherous, untruthful

lying down: decumbent, flat, prone, reclining, recumbent, supine

lying down and growing on ground: decumbent

lying down or reclining: recumbent

lying face down: prone, prostrate

lying face upward: supine

lying flat: prostrate

lying next to: adjacent, contiguous, tangential

lying under oath: perjury

lying with limbs out to the sides: spread eagle

lynch: execute, hang, kill, murder, string up

lynx: bobcat, caracal, cat, catamount, wildcat

lyric: alba, dithyramb, madrigal, melic, musical, ode, odic, poem, poetic, rondeau, rondel, sonorous, verse, words

lyric poem: epode, ode

Mm

macabre: deathlike, dreadful, eerie, ghastly, grim, grisly, gruesome, horrible, sick

macabre being: ghoul

macadamize: pave, tar

macaw: ara, arara

mace: baton, club, mallet, rod, spice, staff, weapon

macerate: emaciate, liquefy, mash, permeate, ret, saturate, soak, soften, steep

machete: blade, bola, bolo, knife, sickle, weapon

Machiavellian: ambitious, crafty, cunning, deceitful, devious, foxy, sly, treacherous, tricky, unscrupulous

machination: conspiracy, contrivance, design, intrigue, maneuver, plan, plot, ruse, scheme

machine: apparatus, appliance, auto, automobile, car, computer, contraption, contrivance, device, engine, gadget, instrument, mechanism, robot, tool, vehicle

machine gun: Bren, Browning, Chatterbox, Garrand, Gatling, Maxim, Sten, Strafe, Thompson, Tommy gun

machine re-creating conditions of environment or bigger machine: simulator

machinelike person: automaton, robot, zombie

machines, person who does not like: Luddite

macho individual: he-man, machismo

macrocosm: cosmos, nature, totality, universe, world

maculate: blemish, blotched, defiled, impure, polluted, speckled, spotted, stained

mad: agitated, angry, distraught, enraged, fuming, furious, incensed, infuriated, irate, ired, irked, livid, outraged, rabid, ticked

mad and overpowered by emotion: fanatical, obsessed

mad or crazy: bananas, certifiable, daft, demented, deranged, desperate, distracted, distraught, fanatical, foolish, frantic, frenetic, insane, irrational, loco, loony, maniacal, meshuga, non compos mentis, psychotic, rabid, rage, unbalanced, unhinged, unreasonable, unstable, wild

madam: chatelaine, donna, frau, lady, mdm., mistress, mme., mrs., salutation, senora, title, woman

madcap: brash, crazy, flighty, foolish, impetuous, impulsive, rash, reckless, stupid, wild

madcap escapade: caper

madden: anger, bother, derange, enrage, incense, infuriate, outrage, provoke, rile, unhinge, upset

made: artificial, built, compiled, constructed, contrived, created, invented, manufactured, produced

made-up: created, fabricated, fictional, imaginary, invented, painted, unreal

madhouse: asylum, bedlam, chaos, funny farm, pandemonium, sanitarium, uproar

madman, madwoman: deranged, loon, lunatic, maniac, psycho, psychopath, psychotic

madness: amazement, bedlam, delirium, delusion, dementia, derangement, ecstasy, frenzy, furiosity, furor, fury, insanity, lunacy, mania, paranoia, psychosis, rage, schizophrenia

maelstrom: confusion, current, eddy, storm, swirl, turmoil, upheaval, vortex, whirlpool

maestro: bandleader, composer, conductor, master, teacher

magazine advance order: subscription

magazine copies distributed: circulation

magazine for devoted fans: fanzine

magazine for weapons: arsenal, cache, chamber, compartment, depository, depot, storehouse, warehouse

magazine sales stall: kiosk

magazine shape and layout: format

magazine staff and circulation list: masthead

magazine summary article: digest

magazine, cheap and sensational: pulp

magazine, expensive and classy: glossy

magazine, printed: digest, gazette, journal, monthly, periodical, publication, repository, review, weekly

maggot: bug, grub, larva, worm

magic: charm, conjuration, conjury, deception, enchantment, fairy, hocus-pocus, illusion, legerdemain, mystic, necromancy, occult, rune, sorcery, sortilege, spell, supernatural, theurgy, voodoo, witchcraft, witchery, wizardry

RELATED TERMS

magic object: amulet, charm, fetish, juju, rabbit's foot, relic, talisman, wishbone

magic potion: philter

magic rod: wand

magic sign: rune

magic spell: incantation

magic trick: hocus-pocus, legerdemain, prestidigitation, sleight of hand

magic word(s): abracadabra, incantation, open sesame, presto

magic, black: necromancy

magical: charming, enchanted, fascinating, marvelous, mysterious, occult, spellbinding, spooky

magical and occult, pertaining to: mermetic

magical arts: occult

magician: charlatan, charmer, conjurer, enchanter, entertainer, fortuneteller, genie, illusionist, juggler, mage, magus, mandrake, medium, necromancer, shaman, sorcerer, thaumaturge, thaumaturgist, warlock, witch, wizard ❧

magisterial: arrogant, august, authoritative, bossy, dictatorial, dignified, dogmatic, domineering, highhanded, imperious, judicial, lofty, lordly, overbearing, pompous, stately, stuffy

magistrate: administrator, alcade, archon, bailiff, chief, consul, court, governor, judge, justice, official

magistrate, concerning a: magisterial

magnanimous: altruistic, benevolent, big, chivalrous, eschewing, forgiving, free, generous, heroic, high-minded, honorable, liberal, lofty, noble, unselfish, unstinted

magnate: baron, bigwig, industrialist, lord, mogul, nabob, noble, titan, tsar, tycoon

magnesium silicate: talc

magnet, soft iron bar linking poles of horseshoe: armature, keeper

magnetic: alluring, captivating, charismatic, drawing, hypnotic, mesmerizing, pulling, seductive

magnetic disk, to erase information from: degauss

magnetic force driving bodies apart: repulsion

magnetic mineral: lodestone

magnetic physically: polar

magnetic poles of opposite charge in close proximity: dipole

magnetism or charm, personal: charisma

magnetization, maximum: saturation

magnificent: august, beautiful, brilliant, dazzling, elegant, epic, exalted, excellent, glorious, gorgeous, grand, grandiose, great, imposing, lavish, majestic, noble, opulent, outstanding, palatial, proud, regal, resplendent, splendid, stately, striking, sublime, superb, wonderful

magnifier for jeweler: loupe

magnify: aggravate, amplify, augment, boost, dilate, embellish, enhance, enlarge, eulogize, exaggerate, expand, increase, inflate, intensify, multiply, overemphasize, overstate, swell

magniloquent: boastful, bombastic, flowery, grandiloquent, lofty, pompous, turgid

magnitude: bigness, breadth, bulk, dimension, eminence, extent, greatness, importance, intensity, mass, measure, proportion, quantity, range, significance, size, space, volume, weight

magnum opus: achievement, classic, epic, masterpiece, one's great work

magus: magi, magician, sage, seer, sorcerer, wizard

maid: attendant, domestic, housekeeper, servant

maiden: damsel, earliest, first, girl, inaugural, lass, lassie, missy, new, unmarried, untried, virgin

maiden lady: spinster

maiden name of married woman, indicating: née

mail: armor, communication, dispatch, express, forward, letter, package, parcel, post, postcard, send, ship

mail boat: packet

mail called for by addressee: general delivery

mail chute opening: slot

mail, undeliverable: nixie

mailing privilege: frank

maim: batter, cripple, damage, disable, disfigure, dismember, injure, lame, mangle, massacre, maul, mutilate

main: absolute, capital, central, chief, critical, direct, duct, essential, first, foremost, grand, head, important, leading, major, paramount, predominant, preeminent, preponderant, prime, principal, purpose, supreme, vital

main artery: aorta

main axis of flower: rachis

main body of the church: nave

main course of meal: entrée

main element or feature: staple

main idea: burden, gist, gravamen

main or pipe: conduit, line

main vein of ore: mother lode

mainstay: backbone, brace, crutch, key, pillar, rope, supporter

mainstream: middle of the road

maintain: affirm, allege, argue, assert, aver, avouch, avow, claim, contend, declare, defend, hold, insist, justify, stand firm, state, sustain, uphold, vindicate, warrant

maintain physically: conserve, control, keep, manage, preserve, retain, supply, support

maintainable: defendable, tenable

maintenance: alimony, care, conservation, keep, livelihood, preservation, repairs, sustenance, upkeep

maintenance and repair: upkeep

maintenance man: janitor

maize: corn, milo, yellow

majestic: august, ceremonious, courtly, dignified, elegant, epic, grand, grandiose, imperial, impressive, kingly, lofty, magnificent, noble, princely, regal, royal, splendid, stately, stunning, sublime

major: big, chief, considerable, critical, crucial, extensive, foremost, great, important, leading, paramount, predominant, primary, principal, serious, significant, sizable, superior, vital

majority: adulthood, age, bulk, edge, generality, margin, mass, seniority; greater, more, most

majority in election that is not more than half: plurality

majority, understood and accepted by: lowest common denominator

make: accomplish, achieve, acquire, appoint, assemble, attain, bear, build, cause, coerce, coin, compel, compose, comprise, constitute, construct, create, earn, effect, erect, establish, fabricate, fashion, force, forge, form, formulate, frame, generate, invent, manufacture, mark, mold, originate, prepare, press, produce, render, require, secure, shape, suppose, synthesize

make amends: atone, compensate, expiate, reconcile, settle, square

make aware: disclose, enlighten, inform, notify, reveal, tell

make-believe: charade, dream, fake, fantasy, fiction, imaginary, imagined, invention, magic, playacting, pretend, sham, simulate, unreal

make by mixing ingredients: concoct, confect, cook up

make certain: assure, check, ensure, examine, guarantee, investigate

make do: accept, eke, employ, endure, improvise, suffice, survive

make-do meal: potluck

make effort: attempt, strive, try, undertake, venture

make exaggerated claims: oversell

make fun of: deride, embarrass, imitate, jape, mimic, parody, rib, ridicule, tease

make getaway: bolt, escape, flee

make good: accomplish, achieve, arrive, compensate, fulfill, justify, reimburse, repay, succeed

make headway: achieve, advance, improve, progress

make hostile: alienate, antagonize, provoke

make ill: afflict, disgust, nauseate, repulse, revolt, sicken

make indistinct: blur

make ineffective: negate

make insensitive: deaden

make into: alter, change, convert, reform, transform

make into law: enact

make known: advertise, advise, announce, broadcast, declare, disclose, divulge, expose, impart, notify, proclaim, publicize, publish, reveal, tell, uncover, unveil

make light of: belittle, disparage, pooh, underestimate

make marginal notes: annotate

make merry: celebrate, revel

make off: abscond, bolt, decamp, depart, escape, flee, run away, scamper, skedaddle, skip

make or achieve gradually: evolve

make or become better: ameliorate

make or create: fabricate, innovate, invent, originate, pioneer

make or create from available materials: improvise

make or fashion: forge, mold

make or think up: contrive, devise, excogitate

make out: accomplish, achieve, detect, determine, discern, espy, fare, gather, kiss, manage, neck, notice, observe, see, spot, succeed, understand

make statement: comment, explain, expound, remark

make sure: ascertain, check, determine, review, secure

make uneasy: discomfort, disturb, trouble, upset

make unnecessary: obviate

make up: arrange, assemble, atone, coin, complete, compose, conciliate, concoct, consist, constitute, create, devise, fabricate, formulate, improvise, invent, mend, pretend, reconcile

make up for: atone, compensate, counterbalance, countervail, offset

maker: author, builder, composer, creator, inventor, manufacturer, originator, producer

makeshift: alternative, emergency, extemporaneous, impromptu, improvised, provisional, replacement, rude, slapdash, stopgap, substitute, temporary

makeshift item from available materials: bricolage

makeup: character, complexion, composition, configuration, constitution, fiber, format, plan, shape, structure, style

makeup artist: visagiste

makeup for actors: greasepaint

makeup for face: blush, cosmetics, lipstick, mascara, powder, rouge

mal de mer: seasickness

maladroit: awkward, blundering, bumbling, bungling, clumsy, floundering, gauche, impolitic, inept, inexpert, tactless, ungraceful

malady: affliction, ailment, complaint, debility, disease, disorder, distemper, illness, infirmity, sickness

malaise: anxiety, depression, despair, disease, illness, lassitude, melancholy, sickness

malapropos: improper, inappropriate, inopportune, irrelevant, untimely

malaria: ague, jungle fever, miasma, paludism, sickness

malaria carrier: anopheles, mosquito

malaria-infested: paludal

malarkey: balderdash, drivel, foolishness, hogwash, nonsense

malcontent: agitator, anarchist, complainer, discontented, disgruntled, dissatisfied, grouch, grumbler, insurgent, rebel, rebellious, revolter, troublemaker, uneasy

male: guy, man, manful, mankind, manlike, manly, mannish, masculine, paternal, virile

male ant: aner

male ballet dancer: danseur

male ballet dancer, principal: premier danseur

male bee: drone

male club: fraternity

male cosmic principle: yang

male counterpart of ballerina: danseur noble

male creature with pointed ears, goat horns and legs: satyr

male deer: hart, roebuck, stag

male dominance: androcentrism, male chauvinism

male duck: drake

male features on a woman: virilism

male figure on pillar: telamon

male genital oral stimulation: fellatio

male head of household: father, paterfamilias

male hormone: androgen, testosterone

male line of descent, of a: patrilineal

male menopause: male climacteric

male of beef cattle: steer

male pig: boar

male plant organ: stamen

male pride: machismo, macho

male sex chromosome: Y chromosome

male sheep: ram, tup

male side of family: agnate

male sterilization surgery: vasectomy

male swan: cob

male turkey: tom

male, fussy: fribbler, twiddlepoop

malediction: anathema, curse, cuss, damnation, denunciation, imprecation, jinx, malison, slander, whammy

malefactor: convict, criminal, culprit, delinquent, felon, knave, offender, rascal, scoundrel, villain, wrongdoer

maleficence: evil, mischief

maleness, to deprive of: emasculate

males-only party: stag

malevolence: animosity, antagonism, bitterness, despiteful, enmity, evil, grudge, hateful, hatred, hostility, malice, malicious, malign, rancor, sinister, spite, spleen, vicious, wicked

malfeasance: crime, delinquency, misconduct, wrongdoing

malfunction: breakdown, failure, flaw, foul-up, glitch, problem, snag

malice: bane, bitterness, despite, enmity, grudge, hate, malevolence, meanness, rancor, resentment, spite, spitefulness, spleen, vengefulness, venom

malicious: bitter, catty, despiteful, evil, felonious, harmful, hateful, malevolent, malignant, mean, nasty, pernicious, poisonous, rancorous, resentful, revengeful, sinister, snide, spiteful, venomous, vicious, virulent, wicked

malicious destruction: sabotage

malign: antagonistic, asperse, backbite, baleful, belittle, calumniate, defame, denigrate, derogate, detrimental, evil, foul, hateful, hurtful, injurious,

TYPES OF MAMMALS

aquatic mammals: cetacean, desman, dolphin, dugong, hippopotamus, manatee, manati, narwhal, otter, platypus, porpoise, rytina, sea lion, seal, shark, sirenian, walrus, whale

arboreal mammals: ai, banxring, fisher, glutton, kinkajou, lemur, monkey, opossum, orangutan, raccoon, sloth

bovine mammals: bison, bos, bull, calf, cow, longhorn, ox, steer, taurine, zebu

burrowing mammals: armadillo, badger, gopher, mole, squirrel, suricate, wombat

carnivorous mammals: badger, bear, carnivore, cat, coyote, dingo, dog, fox, lion, mongoose, otter, panda, raccoon, skunk, tiger, weasel, wolf

cud-chewing mammals: ruminant

domestic mammals: cat, cattle, dog, horse, sheep

edentate mammals: ant bear, anteater, armadillo, pangolin, sloth, tamadau

equine mammals: colt, filly, foal, horse, mare, stallion, zebra

extinct mammals: mastodon, quagga, rytina, stegodon

feline mammals: bobcat, cat, cougar, jaguar, leopard, lion, lynx, ocelot, ounce, panther, puma, serval, tiger

flying mammal: bat

gnawing mammals: beaver, rat, rodent, squirrel

herbivorous mammals: bovine, daman, dugong, equine, hippopotamus, manatee, orangutan, rhinoceros, ruminant, tapir

highest order of mammal: primate

horned mammals: antelope, bison, buffalo, cow, deladang, gaur, goat, ox, reem, reindeer, rhinoceros

insectivorous mammals: bat, hedgehog, mole, shrew, tenrec

lagomorph mammals: hare, rabbit

lowest order of mammals: marsupial, Marsupialia

marsupial mammals: bandicoot, kangaroo, koala, opossum, possum, tait, wallaby, wombat

nocturnal mammals: bat, hyena, kinkajou, lemur, macaco, platypus, raccoon, ratel, tapir, tarsier, wombat

porcine mammals: boar, hog, peccary, pig, swine

primate mammals: baboon, chimpanzee, gibbon, gorilla, lemur, marmoset, monkey, orangutan

ruminant mammals: alpaca, antelope, bison, buffalo, camel, cattle, chewer, deer, giraffe, goat, llama, moose, okapi, ox, sheep, steer, vicuña, yak

toothless mammals: armadillo, edentate, pangolin, sloth

tropical mammals: coati, coatimodi, coati-mundi, peccary, rhino, rhinoceros

ursine mammals: bear, panda

vulpine mammals: fox, wolf

mammal with backbone: vertebrate

mammal with even number of toes, such as pigs: artiodactyl

mammal with four stomachs, such as cattle: ruminant

mammal with gnawing incisor teeth, such as rat: rodent

mammal with hooves, such as horse: ungulate

mammal with odd number of toes, such as horse: perissodactyl

mammals giving birth: viviparous ❦

---

libel, malevolence, mudsling, pernicious, revile, sinister, slander, slur, smear, stain, tarnish, traduce, vilify, virulent

malignant: evil, fiendish, hateful, injurious, invidious, malicious, pernicious, rancorous, spiteful, vicious, wicked

malignant physically: cancerous, diseased, fatal, noxious, poisonous, venomous, virulent

malignity: venom

malinger: dodge, evade, fake, loaf, sham, shirk

mall: alley, arcade, concourse, court, plaza, promenade, square, walk

malleable: adaptable, compliant, ductile, flexible, impressionable, plastic, pliable, pliant, supple, tractable

mallet variety: carpenter's, croquet, maul, metal, plastic, rubber, wooden

malnutrition: beriberi, cachexia, emaciation, scurvy, starvation

malnutrition from lack of protein: kwashiorkor

malnutrition from lack of vitamin B: beriberi

malnutrition from lack of vitamin C: scurvy

malodorous: fetid, foul, funky, noisome, offensive, putrid, rank, reeking, rotten, smelly, stenchy, stinking, vile

malpractice: carelessness, misconduct, negligence

malt beverage: ale, beer

malt vinegar: alegar

maltreat: abuse, damage, harm, injure, mishandle, misuse, victimize

mammal: beast, bovine, carnivore, cat, coati, edentate, equine, feline, marsupial, ovine, primate, rodent, ruminant, swine, ungulate

mammary gland: udder

mammon: avarice, gain, possessions, riches, wealth

mammoth: behemothic, colossal, enormous, gargantuan, giant, gigantic, great, huge, large, massive, monumental, stupendous, titanic

mammoth and ponderous: elephantine

mammoth kin: mastodon

man: anthropos, biped, bloke, boyfriend, buck, chap, chiel, creature, fellow, gent, guard, guy, hombre, homme, homo sapiens, human, husband, male, mensch, mister, mortal, valet

RELATED TERMS

man as center of universe: anthropocentric

man supported by woman (unmarried): gigolo

man to man: mano a mano

man wearing woman's clothes: drag

man, castrated: eunuch

man, concerning: human, humane, mortal

man, hater of: misandrist, misanthrope

man, primitive: savage, urmensch

man, resembling: android, anthropoid, anthropomorphic

man, rich: billionaire, capitalist, croesus, magnate, millionaire, nabob, plutocrat, tycoon

MANIAS BY OBSESSION OR ADDICTION

activity: ergasiomania
alcohol: dipsomania
animals: zoomania
Beatles: Beatlemania
bed rest: clinomania
bees: apimania
birds: ornithomania
books: bibliomania
bridges: gephyromania
buying: oniomania
cats: ailuromania
counting and numbers: arithmomania
crowds: demomania, ochlomania
dancing: choreomania
dead bodies: necromania
death: thanatomania
demonic possession: cacodemonomania
dogs: cynomania
drinking: potomania
drinking water: hydrodipsomania
drugs: narcomania
eating: phagomania, sitomania
erotica: eroticomania
fire, arson: pyromania
fish: ichthyomania

flowers: anthomania
food: sitomania
food, eating: phagomania
foreigners: xenomania
foul speech: coprolalomania
freedom: eleuthromania
fur: doramania
gaiety: cheromania
great wealth: plutomania
hair: trichomania
home: oikomania
horses: hippomania
imagined disease: nosomania
insects: entomomania
islands: nesomania
joy from complaining: paramania
light: photomania
listmaking: glazomania
lying and exaggerating: mythomania
marriage: gamomania
medicines: pharmacomania
men: andromania
mice: musomania

money: chrematomania
murder: homicidomania
music: celomania, musicomania, melomania
nakedness: gymnomania
narcotics: letheomania
night: noctimania
noise or sound: phonomania
nudity: nudomania
one's own wisdom: sophomania
oneself: egomania
open spaces: agoramania
penis: mentulomania
plants: florimania
pleasure: hedonomania
politics: politicomania
pornography: pornographomania
postage stamps: timbromania
power: megalomania
railroad travel: siderodromomania
religion: entheomania, theomania
reptiles: ophidiomania
riches, great wealth: plutomania
running away: drapetomania
sea: thalassomania
second coming of Christ: parousiamania
self-importance: megalomania
sex: erotomania, nymphomania, satyromania
sexual desire: aphrodisiomania, erotomania
sexual desire in females: nymphomania
sexual desire in males: satyromania
sin: hamartomania
single idea or thing: monomania
sitting: kathisomania
sleep: hypnomania
snow: chionomania
solitude: automania
speech: lalomania
spending: squandermania

stealing: kleptomania
stillness: eremiomania
suicide: autophonomania
sun: heliomania
surgery: tomomania
talking: logomania, verbomania
testicles: orchidomania
theater: theatromania
thinking: phronemomania
traveling: dromomania, hodomania, poriomania
wandering: ecdemiomania
washing, bathing: ablutomania
water: hydromania
wine: enomania, oinomania
woods: hylomania
words: verbomania
work: ergomania
writing: graphomania, scribblemania, scribomania ❧

---

man, sciences of: anthropology, ethnology

man, short: homunculus, shrimp, squirt

man, young: boy, lad, springal, stripling, varlet, youth ❧

man-made: artificial, synthetic, unnatural

man-made bank: levee

man-made fiber: acetate

man-woman friendship, pertaining to: platonic

manacle: band, bond, chains, confine, control, cuff, fetters, handcuff, irons, restraint, shackle

manage: accomplish, administer, boss, conduct, contrive, control, cope, deal, designate, direct, dominate, engineer, execute, fare, finagle, govern, guide, handle, head, husband, lead, maintain, maneuver, manipulate, muddle, operate, order, oversee, regulate, rule, run, steer, superintend, supervise, survive

manage by skillful or tricky acts: contrive, engineer, maneuver

manage to live: subsist

management: administration, agency, brass, care, charge, conducting, executives, generalship, governance, guidance, helm, intendance, ordinance, overseer, policy, steerage, superintendence

manager: boss, curator, director, doer, executive, executor, foreman, forewoman, gerent, handler, steward, supervisor

manager or agent of another: procurator

manager or producer of entertainment: impresario

mandate: behest, brief, charge, command, decree, directive, edict, injunction, order, precept, referendum, requisition, rule, sanction, warranty, word, writ

mandatory: compulsory, essential, forced, imperative, necessary, obligatory, required

mandible: beak, jaw, jawbone

maneuver: contrive, deploy, drill, engineer, exercise, exploit, finagle, finesse, jockey, manipulate, move, navigate, outflank, pilot, plot, ploy, scheme, steer, stratagem, stunt, tactic, trick

maneuver for advantage: jockey, stratagem

maneuver in diplomacy: démarche

maneuver to outwit another: ploy

maneuvers to gain end or advantage: gamesmanship, tactics

manger: cradle, crib, rack, stable, stall, trough

mangle: batter, butcher, calender, cripple, cut, deform, disfigure, dismember, garble, hack, iron, ironer, lacerate, maim, mar, maul, mutilate, presser, ruin, spoil

mangy: dirty, filthy, mean, rundown, scruffy, scurvy, seedy, shabby, squalid

mangy one: cur

manhandle: abuse, bully, maul, mistreat, paw, push, rough up

manhood: virility

mania: addiction, cacoethes, compulsion, craze, delirium, derangement, disorder, fascination, fear, fetish, fixation, frenzy, hangup, infatuation, insanity, lunacy, madness, obsession, passion, rage

maniac: crackpot, crazed, deranged, enthusiast, fanatic, insane, lunatic, madman, madwoman, nut, psychotic, psychopath

maniacal: demoniac, lunatic

manic-depressive condition, mild: cyclothymia

manicure board: emery

manifest: apparent, approve, bare, clear, conspicuous, declare, demonstrate, develop, disclosed, discover, display, embody, evident, evince, exhibit, expose, express, glaring, indicate, indisputable, indubitable, mark, materialize, noticeable, obvious, open, overt, palpable, patent, plain, prove, reveal, seem, show, signify, undisguised, unmistakable, visible

manifest in writing: index, list

manifestation: display, epiphany, example, expression, meaning, presentation, proof, revelation, sign, symptom

manifestation of divine being: epiphany

manifesto: declaration, edict, intentions, order, placard, policies, principles, proclamation, statement, writ

manifold: abundant, diverse, many, multifold, multiform, multiple, numerous, sundry, various

maniple: fanon, orale

manipulate: control, exploit, finagle, handle, influence, manage, maneuver, operate, rig, scheme, shape, swing, use, wield, work

manipulated for an advantage, person: pawn

manipulation of body parts to treat disease: osteopathy

manipulator of another: Svengali

mankind: flesh, homo sapiens, humanity, humans, male, people, race

manlike: android, humanoid

manly: bold, brave, courageous, daring, fearless, gallant, lionhearted, male, manful, masculine, resolute, strong, undaunted, valiant, virile

manna: bonanza, boon, delicacy, gift, windfall

mannequin: dummy, figure, manikin, model

manner: air, appearance, aspect, attitude, bearing, behavior, breed, category, character, conduct, course, custom, demeanor, deportment, etiquette, fashion, form, formalities, habit, kind, look, method, mien, mode, practice, protocol, sort, species, style, system, technique, tone, way

manner in which someone behaves: demeanor, deportment

manner of feeling: attitude

manner of governing: governance

manner of operating: modus operandi

manner of speaking: façon de parler, idiom, locution, parlance

manner of walking: gait

manner, harsh in: abrasive, brusque, curt

manner, overrefined in: precious

manner, peculiar: mannerism

mannered: affected, artificial, formal, posed, self-conscious

mannerism: affectation, bearing, eccentricity, habit, idiosyncrasy, individuality, peculiarity, pose, quirk, tic, trait

mannerly: civil, courteous, decorous, genteel, polished, polite, respectful, well-behaved

manners: amenities, behavior, conduct, courtesy, decorum, etiquette, formalities, miens, modes, protocol

manners, fine point of: punctilio

manners, improper: solecism

manor: castle, chateau, estate, house, land, mansion, villa

manservant: attendant, butler, footman, garçon, steward, valet

mansion: abode, castle, chateau, dwelling, estate, hall, home, house, manor, palace, residence, villa

manslaughter: crime, homicide, killing, murder

mantilla: scarf

mantle: cape, capote, cloak, coat, cover, envelope, filament, glow, hood, mantilla, robe, screen

manual: book, enchiridion, guide, guidebook, handbook, physical, primer, text

manual labor, concerning: blue-collar

manual skill: handicraft, handiness

manual worker: blue-collar worker

manual worker, skilled: artisan, craftsperson

manufacture: assembly, build, concoct, create, fabricate, fake, forge, invent, make, mold, prepare, produce, synthesize

manufactured item: ware

manumission: emancipation, freedom, liberation, release, rescue

manure: compost, dung, excrement, fertilizer

manuscript: codex, composition, copy, document, draft, handwriting, writing; typewritten

manuscript bound as a book: codex

manuscript copier: amanuensis

manuscript with decoration: illuminated manuscript

manuscript written on more than once: palimpsest

manuscript, to correct and prepare: copy-edit

manuscripts are worked on, room where: scriptorium

manuscripts, professional copyist of: scribe

manuscripts, unsolicited: slush pile

many: a lot, bountiful, countless, diverse, gobs, legion, lots, manifold, much, multi, multifarious, multiple, multiplex, multiplied, multitude, myriad, numerous, scores, several, sundry, tons, varied, various

many-eyed giant: argus

many, very: countless, innumerable, multitudinous, myriad, umpteen

map: atlas, blueprint, cartograph, chart, delineate, design, diagram, draft, explore, globe, graph, image, outline, picture, plan, plat, plot, projection, sketch, survey

map book: atlas

map circle-and-star symbol: compass rose

map collector: cartomaniac

map for tax purposes: cadaster

map key explaining symbols: legend
map of a region: chorography
map of earth with latitude, longitude lines: Mercator projection
map of sphere on plane surface, system of: projection
map representation of surface features, positions, elevations: topography
map showing changes in atmospheric pressure, line on weather: isobar
map showing elevations and surface configuration: contour map, relief map
map, symbols used to pinpoint a position on a: coordinates
maple genus: acer
maple tree sap spike: spile
mapmaking: cartography
map's lines for distance east or west of prime meridian: longitude
map's lines for distance north or south of equator: latitude
map's pattern of vertical and horizontal lines: grid
mar: blemish, blot, botch, bruise, damage, deform, disfigure, flaw, harm, hurt, impair, injure, mangle, mark, nick, ruin, scar, scratch, spoil, tarnish
marathon: activity, contest, enduro, event, race
maraud: attack, foray, pillage, plunder, raid, ransack, ravage, rove, steal
marauder: bandit, buccaneer, desperado, looter, pillager, pirate, plunderer, raider, ravager, robber
marble: agate, ball, basalt, cold, dolomite, game, granite, hard, mib, mid, mig, rock, sculpture, smooth, stone, taw, unfeeling
marble, concerning: marmoreal
marble, large playing: alley, shooter
march: advance, advancement, course, drill, file, hike, journey, move, parade, procession, progress, step, stride, strut, tramp, travel, traverse, trek, walk
march doggedly: slog
marching practice: close order drill
marching with legs swinging straight out, knees locked: goose-step
mare's nest: complication, deception, fraud, hoax, lie, trick
margarine: oleo
margin: allowance, border, boundary, brim, brink, edge, fringe, hem, indentation, latitude, leeway, lip, perimeter, rim, room, shore, side, verge

margin note of explanation: marginalia, scholium
margin of variation: latitude, leeway
margin, having lines printed straight along one: justified
marginal: borderline, insignificant, minimal, negligible, peripheral, small, unimportant
marginalia: notes
marigold genus: tagetes
marijuana: cannabis, dope, drug, ganja, grass, hemp, herb, joint, loco weed, marihuana, Mary Jane, moocah, pot, reefer, tea, weed
marina: basin, boatyard, dock
marinade: brine
marinate: soak, souse
marinated seafood, Latin style: escabeche
marine: aquatic, leatherneck, marinal, mariner, maritime, nautical, naval, oceanic, oceanographic, pelagic, seafaring, seagoing, water; sailor
marine alga: seaweed
marine and freshwater organisms that can swim freely: nekton
marine color: aqua
mariner: gob, navigator, sailor, salt, seafarer, seaman, seawoman, shipmate, swabbie, tar, yachtsman, yachtswoman
marionette: puppet
marital: conjugal, connubial, married, matrimonial, nuptial, spousal, wedded
mark: ambition, attribute, badge, betoken, blemish, brand, character, chart, criterion, dent, distinction, dot, dupe, emblem, feature, fool, gauge, goal, grade, heed, identity, image, importance, impress, impression, imprint, indication, influence, inscription, label, letter, line, logo, manifest, measure, nick, note, notice, number, objective, pock, point, rating, scar, score, seal, sign, spare, speckle, spot, stamp, standard, strike, symbol, symptom, tag, target, trace, track, trait, victim, yardstick
mark as verb: denote, designate, distinguish, observe
mark between compounded word: hyphen
mark boundaries: delimit, demarcate
mark down: cut, devaluate, lower, reduce, slash
mark extent or limits: circumscribe
mark for a Spanish ñ: tilde

MARINE CORPS RANKS

Commissioned Officers
General
Lieutenant General
Major General
Brigadier General
Colonel
Lieutenant Colonel
Major
Captain
First Lieutenant
Second Lieutenant

Warrant Officers
Chief Warrant Officer Five
Chief Warrant Officer Four
Chief Warrant Officer Three
Chief Warrant Officer Two
Warrant Officer One

Enlisted Personnel
Sergeant Major of the Marine Corps
Sergeant Major
Master Gunnery Sergeant
First Sergeant
Master Sergeant
Gunnery Sergeant
Staff Sergeant
Sergeant
Corporal
Lance Corporal
Private First Class
Private ❦

mark for identification, to: flag
mark for omission: dele
mark impressed on paper, identifying: watermark
mark in Arabic like apostrophe: hamza
mark like hook under ç: cedilla
mark of a wound: scar
mark of authenticity: cachet, hallmark
mark of disgrace: stigma
mark of distinction: cachet
mark of identification: earmark
mark of insertion: caret
mark on domino, die, playing card: pip
mark over a short vowel: breve
mark over a Spanish letter: tilde
mark used to punctuate text: punctuation mark, reference mark
mark with grooves: striate
mark, accent, on foreign letters: diacritical mark
marked: apparent, branded, clear, conspicuous, destined, distinct, empha-

MARKING AND MEASURING TOOLS

bevel	compass	line level	protractor	steel rule
butt gauge	depth gauge	marking gauge	rafter square	straight edge
caliper	dividers	mason's level	rule	studfinder
carpenter's level	electronic level	micrometer	ruler	tape measure
carpenter's pencil	feeler gauge	miter box	scale	torpedo level
carpenter's square	folding rule	miter square	scratch awl	T square
center punch	framing square	mortise gage	scriber	turning caliper
chalk liner	gauge	plumb bob	slide caliper	wing divider ❦
combination square	level	plumb rule	square	

sized, evident, fated, identified, noted, noticeable, obvious, prominent, pronounced, stained, striking, tabbed, traced

marked with gradations: calibrated

marked with lines: lineate, striped

marker: arrow, counter, flag, gravestone, guide, indicator, monitor, notch, peg, pole, rag, recorder, scorer, signal, stone, tombstone

market: advertise, agora, bazaar, boutique, delicatessen, emporium, exchange, mall, mart, outlet, peddle, plaza, rialto, sale, shop, square, store, vend, wholesale

market ahead of time: presell

market on decline: bear market

market on rise: bull market

market with few producers/sellers: oligopoly

market, outdoor: flea market

marketable: bankable, salable, sellable, vendible, wanted, wholesome

marketing and supplying goods: distribution

marketing privilege within certain premises: concession, franchise

marketing studies: demographics

marking spots on animals or plants: maculation

marks indicating insert: carets

marks on a score: rests

marks with fine lines: striates

marksman: deadeye, sharpshooter, shot, sniper, straight shooter

marmalade: jam, jelly, orange peel, preserve

marmite: casserole, earthenware, kettle, pot

marmoset: monkey, tamarin

maroon: abandon, desert, enisle, forsake, isolate, leave, peer, shipwreck, strand

maroon as color: cerise, magenta, purple, purplish, red, reddish

marquee: awning, canopy, signboard, tent

marriage: alliance, association, betrothed, connubial, espousal, link, match, matrimony, nuptials, unikon, union, wedding, wedlock

RELATED TERMS

marriage after death or divorce of first spouse: deuterogamy, digamy

marriage between different races: miscegenation

marriage between incompatible partners: heterogamosis

marriage between royal and partner of lower rank: morganatic

marriage between well-matched persons: nomogamosis

marriage broker: matchmaker, schatchen, shadchan

marriage by mutual agreement but without ceremony: common-law marriage

marriage ceremony, to celebrate in: solemnize

marriage estrangement: alienation of affections

marriage late in life: opsigamy

marriage outside the tribe, clan, caste: exogamy

marriage partner, right to affection and sexual relations with: consortium

marriage performed by justice of peace, civil official: civil marriage

marriage to inferior person: mesalliance

marriage to one person: monogamy

marriage to two or more people: bigamy, polygamy

marriage trousseau, chest for: hope chest

marriage vows, in violation: adulterous, extramarital, illicit

marriage with sexual relations, fulfillment of: consummation

marriage within the tribe, clan, caste: endogamy

marriage, announcement of impending: banns

marriage, ceremony or state of: matrimony

marriage, concerning: conjugal, connubial, hymeneal, marital, matrimonial, nuptial

marriage, forced: shotgun wedding

marriage, living together without: cohabitation

marriage, money or property brought by bride to groom in: dowry

marriage, possessions the bride assembles for: trousseau

marriage, run away with lover to have secret: elope

marriage, to end a: annul, dissolve, divorce

marriage, to reestablish a broken: reconciliation

marriage, trial: companionate marriage

marriage, unsuitable: misalliance

marriageable: eligible, nubile

married or engaged: betrothed, espoused

married parents, born of: legitimate

married woman's legal status: coverture

marry: associate, couple, espouse, hitch, join, link, pledge, splice, tie the knot, unite, wed, yoke

marry secretly: elope

marry someone above one's social status, wanting to: hypergamy ❦

marrow: core, essence, essential, inmost, medulla, pith, substance, vitality

Mars, study of: aerology

marsh: bayou, bog, everglade, fen,

glade, mire, moor, morass, palude, quagmire, slashes, slough, swale, swamp, wetland

marsh bird: heron, rail, snipe, sora, stilt

marsh gas: methane

marsh growth: reed, sedge

marsh, concerning a: paludal

marsh, poisonous atmosphere of: effluvium, miasma

marsh, sluggish stream through: bayou

marshal: align, arrange, array, assemble, deploy, direct, gather, guide, lead, mobilize, muster, usher

marshal as person: constable, officer, sheriff

marshy ground: morass, ooze, swale, wash

marsupial: bandicoot, euro, kangaroo, koala, opossum, possum, wallaby, wombat

mart: bazaar, emporium, exchange, fair, mall, market, shop, store

martial: aggressive, bellicose, belligerent, combative, hostile, militant, military, warlike

martial art: aikido, judo, jujitsu, karate, kendo, kung fu, sumo, tae kwon do

martial art, Chinese karatelike: kung fu

martial art, Chinese meditative: tai chi chuan

martial art, Japanese nonresistance: aikido

martial art, Korean aggressive karatelike: tae kwon do

martial art, self-defense: judo

martial arts weapon of sticks joined by rope or chain: nunchaku, nunchakus, nun-chucks

martinet: authoritarian, dictator, disciplinarian, ramrod, tyrant

martini ingredient: olive

martini served with pickled onion: Gibson

martyr: persecute, sacrifice, torment; saint, sufferer, victim

martyrdom: affliction, anguish, suffering, torment, torture

marvel: admire, astonish, astonishment, curiosity, gape, goggle, miracle, portent, sensation, surprise, wonder

marvelous: amazing, astonishing, awesome, excellent, extraordinary, fabulous, fantastic, great, incredible, magnificent, outstanding, prodigious, sensational, spectacular, splendid, stupendous, super, superb, terrific, wonderful, wondrous

masculine: brave, macho, male, manlike, manly, potent, powerful, robust, strong, vigorous, virile

mash: cream, crush, flirt, grind, mess, mixture, mush, pulp, pulverize, scramble, smash, squash

mashed and strained food: puree

mask: camouflage, cloak, conceal, cover, curtain, disguise, facade, face, front, guise, hide, masquerade, screen, shield, veil, visor

mask providing protection or air: inhalator, respirator

mask worn with hooded robe: domino

masked: concealed, covert, disguised, incognito, larvated, latent

masked ball or costume party: masquerade

masked merrymaker: mummer

masochism, sadism: algolagnia

masonry: ashlar, brickwork, stonework, trade

mason's carrier: hod

mason's tool: trowel

masquerade: camouflage, charade, disguise, guise, impersonate, mask, masque, party, pretend, pretense

masquerade ball: bal masque

mass: accumulate, agglomerate, aggregate, assemblage, assemble, batch, blob, body, bulk, bunch, bundle, clot, collection, composition, congeries, congregate, congregation, consolidate, crowd, gather, gob, gross, group, heap, horde, jam, knot, liturgy, lump, magnitude, majority, matter, measurement, mob, mound, mountain, pile, prayer, rite, service, stockpile, store, substance, sum, volume, whole

mass book: missal

mass confusion: chaos

mass-market advertising to public: admass

massacre: annihilation, bloodbath, butchery, carnage, decimation, genocide, murder, slaughter, slay

massacre, Jewish: pogrom

massage: caress, knead, manipulation, press, rub, rubbing, stimulate, stroke

massage-giver: masseur, masseuse

massage system on feet for body parts: reflexology

massage with acupressure points: shiatsu

massage, deep muscular: Rolfing

massage, therapeutic: physical therapy, physiotherapy

masses, pertaining to: demotic

masses, the: canaille, common people, hoi polloi, mob, plebs

massive: boisterous, bulky, colossal, enormous, giant, gigantic, gross, heavy, huge, immense, jumbo, large, mammoth, monumental, ponderous, substantial, titanic, vast, weighty, whopping

mast lookout: crow's nest

mast rigging: stay

mast supporting sails, rigging: spar

mast type: fore, jigger, jury, lower, main, mizzen, top, topgallant

mast, to lower a: strike

master: artist, best, boss, captain, champion, chief, commander, connoisseur, craftsman, doctor, educator, expert, guru, headman, lord, maestro, matriarch, overseer, paramount, patriarch, prevail, professional, ruler, sahib, sire, swami, teacher, tutor, wizard

master, to: acquire, best, dominate, down, get, govern, learn, lick, overpower, overcome, prevail, regulate, rule, subdue, subjugate, surmount, tame, triumph, understand

master in an art: maestro, virtuoso

master key: passe-partout

master of ceremonies: emcee, host, MC, performer, speaker, toastmaster

master of many jobs: jack-of-all-trades

master pattern: template

master violinist: auer

master, relating to a: magisterial

masterful: able, adept, arbitrary, authoritative, clever, commanding, crackerjack, dictatorial, domineering, expert, forceful, imperial, imperious, overbearing, preeminent, proficient, skilled

mastermind: artist, author, brains, expert, genius, planner; organize, plan

masterpiece: brainchild, chef d'oeuvre, classic, creation, jewel, magnum opus, masterwork, objet d'art, perfection, pièce de résistance, tour de force, treasure

masterstroke: coup

mastery: command, conquest, control, domination, expertise, grasp, grip, influence, knack, proficiency, rule, skill, supremacy, victory

masthead crosstree: jack

masticate: chew, chomp, crunch, crush, gnash, grind, knead

mast's angle of slant: rake

mast's lookout: crow's nest

mast's lower end: heel

masturbation: autoeroticism, onanism

mat: border, carpet, cushion, doily, pad, rug, tatami

mat of straw for floor covering: tatami

mat on chair or sofa back: antimacassar

mat, decorative and lacy: doily

mat, to: entangle, interweave, snarl, tangle

matador: bullfighter, toreador, torero

matadors' prey: toro

matador's red cape: capa, muleta

match: companion, compare, coordinate, correlate, correspond, counter, counterpart, couple, duplicate, equal, even, fit, lookalike, marriage, marry, mate, oppose, pair up, parallel, partnership, peer, pit, pout, rival, side, spar, spouse, team, tie, twin, union, vesta, wick

match or competition: bout, contest, event, game, meet, race, tournament

match to determine winner: playoff

match, at poker: call

match, slow-burning: fusee, vesuvian

matchbook collector: phillumenist

matchbook striking surface: friction strip

matched pair, part of: companion piece, pendant

matching clothing pieces: coordinates

matchless: alone, exemplary, exquisite, incomparable, inimitable, nonpareil, peerless, superior, unbeatable, unequalled, unparalleled, unrivaled, unsurpassed

matchmaker: marriage broker, schatchen, shadchan

mate: associate, breed, buddy, chum, cohort, colleague, companion, comrade, confidant, consort, couple, equal, fellow, friend, husband, join, marry, match, pair, pal, partner, peer, procreate, sidekick, spouse, twin, wed, wife

mate or complement: counterpart

material: apparatus, cloth, data, equipment, fabric, facts, gear, goods, information, ingredient, linen, matter, metal, stuff, substance, things, tool

material in nature: bodily, corporeal, essential, important, meaningful, objective, pertinent, physical, real, relevant, significant, tangible

materialism: heterodoxy, physicism, pragmatism, utilitarianism

materialistic: acquisitive, banausic, greedy, mercenary, possessive, sensate, unspiritual, worldly

materialize: appear, concretize, emanate, emerge, energize, evolve, happen, loom, manifest, reify, rise, shape, show

matériel: apparatus, arms, equipment, gear, machinery, provisions, supplies, tackle

maternal: motherly, protective

maternal side family name: matronymic

maternally related: enate

maternity: childbearing, gestation, motherhood, pregnancy

math power to which a base must be raised to produce a given number: log, logarithm

math progression with difference remaining constant: arithmetic progression

math progression with ratio remaining constant: geometric progression

math quantity with fixed value: constant

math ratio: sine

math statement showing equality of two expressions: equation

math term indicating parts into which the whole is to be divided: denominator

math theorem about right-angled triangles: Pythagorean theorem

mathematics branch dealing with limits, differentiation and integration of functions of variables: calculus

mathematics branch dealing with sides and angles of triangles: trigonometry

mathematics branches: algebra, analysis, arithmetic, calculus, computing, geometry, logarith, mechanics, statistics, trigonometry

mathematics symbols: multiplicand, operand

mathematics terms: cosine, decimal, derivate, digit, fraction, graph, pi, problem, quaternion, root, scalar, sector, sine, surd, theorem, vector

mathematics types: applied, pure

matinee: entertainment, movie, performance, play, show

matriarch: dowager, female, matron, mother, queen, ruler

matriculate: admit, enroll, enter, join, register

matrimonial: betrothed, bridal, conjugal, connubial, marital, married, nuptial

matrimony: connubiality, marriage, nuptials, union, wedlock

matrix: cast, die, form, gangue, groundmass, mat, model, mold, pattern, shape, womb

matron: dame, dowager, female, housekeeper, matriarch, mother, overseer, widow

matter: affair, business, concern, content, difficulty, discharge, issue, obstacle, problem, source, subject, text, thesis, topic, trouble, waste, worry

matter and energy, science of: physics

matter-of-fact: calm, cold, direct, dull, frank, impersonal, literal, objective, practical, pragmatic, prosaic, realistic, unaffected, unemotional

matter, physical: being, body, constituent, elements, entity, mass, material, object, solid, stuff, substance, thing

mattress covering: ticking

mattress holder: bedstead

mattress stuffing: batt, kapok

mattress support: bedspring

mattress, Japanese: futon

mattress, straw-filled hard: paillasse, pallet

mature: adult, age, aged, blossom, complete, considered, develop, developed, evolve, flower, grown, mellow, prime, ripe, ripen, season, seasoned, settled

mature insect: imago

maturity: adulthood, development, experience, manhood, maturation, womanhood

maturity, approach to: puberty

maturity, showing early: precocious

maudlin: bathetic, corny, emotional, lachrymose, mawkish, mushy, sentimental, tearful, tipsy, weepy

maul: abuse, bash, batter, beat, bruise, club, gavel, hammer, injure, mace, mallet, mangle, manhandle, pound, pummel, staff, stomp

maunder: babble, blather, drift, drivel, mumble, mutter, ramble, stray, wander

mausoleum: catacomb, monument, tomb

mauve: lavender, lilac, plum, purple, violet

maven: connoisseur, expert

MEASUREMENT TERMS

act or process of measuring: mensuration
area measurement: acre, are, area, decare, foot, hectare, inch, length, meter, mile, quantum, yard
capacity measurement: barrel, bushel, cask, fluidram, gallon, gill, liter, minim, orna, peck, pint, quart
cloth measurement: ell, yard
concerning measurement: mensural, metrical
electrical measurement: ampere, ergon, horsepower, joule, ohm, volt, watt
energy measurement: BTU, calorie, erg, joule, thermal unit
item of measurement: caliper, clock, odometer, rule, ruler, scale, standard, tape, time, yardstick
land measurement: acre, ar, are, area, decare, hectare, kiliare, mile, rod, rood
length measurement: centimeter, cubit, decimeter, digit, dra, ell, foot, hectometer, inch, kilometer, knot, league, meter, micron, mile, millimeter, nail, pik, rod, yard
light measurement: candela, candlepower
liquid measurement: aam, barrel, gallon, gill, hogshead, keg, kiloliter, liter, magnum, minims, pint, pipet, pipette, quart, rundlet, runlet, tierce
measure: act, amount, benchmark, cadence, calculate, criterion, degree, estimate, gauge, girth, law, mete, quota, ration, rhyme
measure the depth of: fathom, sound
measure up to the mark: toe
measure used in comparison or judgment: criterion, yardstick
measure water depth: plumb, sound

measured: calculated, careful, computed, deliberate, exact, gauged, meted, restrained, standardized, timed, uniform, weighed
measured amount of medicine: dose
measured in relation to the stars: sidereal
measured out: allotted
measurement: amount, area, assessment, calculation, dimension, distance, frequency, height, length, magnitude, mass, measuration, quantity, size, volume, weight
measuring instrument: actinometer, baroscope, caliper, calorimeter, colorimeter, densimeter, gage, gauge, gravimeter, meter, pluviometer, protractor, ruler, seismograph, sextant, tape, vinometer, yardstick
measuring instrument with two arms hinged together: divider, sector
medicinal measurement: dram, minim, ounce, scruple
metrical measurement: centigram, dekagram, gram, kilogram, milligram, quintal, ton, tonne
nautical measurement: fathom, knot
practical, not scientific measurement: rule of thumb
side-to-side measurement: breadth
sound measurement: decibel, phon
temperature measurement: calorie, calory, celsius, centigrade, degree, Fahrenheit, kelvin, therm, therme
time measurement: century, day, decade, hour, microsecond, millenium, millisecond, minute, moment, month, nanosecond, score, second, week, year
weight measurement: bale, carat, dram, grain, hectoliter, kiloliter, liter, ounce, pound, scruple, ton, troy ❦

---

maverick: bohemian, dissenter, loner, nonconformist, stray, unbranded
maw: craw, gullet, jaws, mouth, stomach
mawkish: bathetic, emotional, gushy, insipid, maudlin, mushy, nostalgic, sentimental, sickening, teary
maxim: adage, aphorism, apothegm, axiom, catchword, doctrine, gnome, moral, motto, precept, proverb, rule, saw, saying, truism, word
maximum: apex, ceiling, climax, culmination, greatest, highest, limit, most, optimum, paramount, peak, ultimate, utmost, zenith
may: allowed, can, hawthorn, likelihood, might, must, permitted, possible, shrub, wish
maybe: conceivable, feasible, perchance, perhaps, possibility, possibly
mayhem: chaos, commotion, confusion, pandemonium, violence
maze: bewilder, confound, confusion, hodgepodge, jungle, labyrinth, mesh, network, perplex, puzzle, stupefy, tangle, web

meadow: bed, field, grassland, heath, lea, mead, park, pasture, prairie, sward, vega, veldt
meager: bare, exiguous, feeble, gaunt, insufficient, lacking, lean, lenten, little, measly, mere, poor, puny, scant, scanty, skimpy, slim, small, spare, sparse, starved, thin
meager salary: stipend
meal: banquet, board, breakfast, brunch, chow, cookout, dinner, feast, feed, flour, food, grain, grub, lunch, menu, potluck, repast, snack, supper, victuals
meal at fixed price, full-course: prix fixe, table d'hôte
meal combining breakfast, lunch: brunch
meal- or dinner-related: prandial
meal served in the late afternoon or early evening, large: afternoon tea, high tea, tea
meal where guests serve themselves: buffet
meal where items are separately priced, of a: a la carte

meal with a variety of foods: smorgasbord
meal, after a: postprandial
meal, appetizer before: hors d'oeuvre
meal, light: collation, refection
meal, main dish of: entree
meal, of an outdoor: alfresco
meal, side dish of: entremets
meals and room included in rate: American plan
mean: abject, average, base, beggarly, coarse, common, contemptible, cruel, evil, excellent, hostile, humble, ignoble, intermediate, irascible, low, malicious, median, medium, mid, middle, midpoint, miserly, narrow, nasty, niggardly, norm, ornery, paltry, par, penurious, petty, poor, selfish, snide, sordid, spiteful, stingy, truculent, ugly, unkind, unpleasant, vile, vindictive
mean as verb: allude, denominate, denote, designate, express, get at, imply, import, indicate, intend, intimate, propose, purport, purpose, show, signify, specify, stand for, suggest, symbolize

mean behavior: cheeseparing, doggery
mean sea level: geoid
meander: amble, curve, drift, ramble, roam, rove, snake, stray, turn, twist, wander, wind, zigzag
meaning: acceptation, aim, content, context, definition, designation, drift, essence, gist, hint, import, indication, intent, intention, knowledge, message, point, purport, purpose, sense, significance, signification, spirit, substance, tenor, translation, understanding
meaning equivalent to another word, word with a: synonym
meaning of language forms, study of: semantics
meaning of literary text, implicit: subtext
meaning of, to explain or figure out the: construe
meaning opposite that of another word, word with a: antonym
meaning or purpose: aim, intent
meaning suggested or associated with something: connotation
meaning to word, going from: onomasiology
meaning, accepted: acceptation
meaning, depth of: profundity
meaning, direct and specific: denotation
meaning, doubtful: ambiguity
meaning, exact: literal
meaning, explicit: denotation
meaning, full lexical: notional
meaning, general: drift, gist, gravamen
meaning, having hidden: cryptic, enigmatic
meaning, having more than one: polysemous
meaning, having more than one interpretation or: ambiguous
meaning, having one: monosemous, univocal
meaning, implicit: connotation
meaning, intended: import, purport, significance, tenor
meaning, linguistic item in its capacity of referring to a: referent
meaning, of or relating to: semantic
meaning, subtle difference of: gradation, nuance
meaning, text around word or passage determining its: context
meaning, to misinterpret: distort, misconstrue, pervert

meaning, word with a second underlying: double entendre
meaningful: consequential, deep, eloquent, expressive, heavy, important, pithy, pointed, significant, useful, worthwhile
meaningful linguistic unit, smallest: morpheme
meaningful sign: omen
meaningless: aimless, blank, empty, hollow, insignificant, nugatory, senseless, shallow, unimportant, useless, worthless
meaningless or sociable talk: phatic
means: assets, avenue, budget, channel, funds, income, instrument, manner, method, mode, path, resources, road, system, way, wealth, wherewithal
meantime: interim, interval, temporary, while
measles' skin rash: roseola
measles, German: rubella
measly: contemptible, insignificant, meager, paltry, puny, skimpy, unimportant, worthless
measurable by common standard: commensurable, commensurate
meat: beef, brawn, comestibles, core, essence, fare, flesh, food, gist, heart, lamb, marrow, muscle, mutton, nourishment, nutriment, pork, veal, venison, viande, victuals

RELATED TERMS

meat and tomato sauce, served with: alla bolognese
meat and vegetable dish, boiled: pot-au-feu
meat and vegetables dish: stew
meat and vegetables grilled on a skewer: shish kabob, shish kebab, shish kebob
meat cut: chop, chuck, crown roast, cutlet, filet, flank, ham, joint, leg, liver, loin, rib, roast, round, rump, shoulder, sirloin, steak
meat dish: giblets, pot roast, ragout, rissole, stem, stew, veal cutlet
meat-eating: carnivorous, creophagous, zoophagous
meat foods, cooked and processed: charcuterie
meat grade: choice, commercial, first, grade A, prime, second, top
meat in liquid before cooking, to soak: marinate
meat jelly: aspic

meat or fish, boneless strip of: filet, fillet
meat or poultry grilled and served in a tortilla: fajita
meat or poultry simmered in gravy: fricassee
meat pie: pasty
meat pie topped with mashed potatoes: shepherd's pie
meat portion, small: collop
meat surface, to char: sear
meat, beef or ox: boeuf
meat, beef tenderloin: chateaubriand, chateaubriant
meat, beefsteak: bifteck
meat, duck or duckling: canard, caneton
meat, egg, onion, anchovy dish: salmagundi
meat, rotating spit for roasting: rotisserie
meats and vegetables boiled: pot-au-feu ❧

meaty: heavy, interesting, rich, significant, solid, substantial
mechanic: artisan, craftsman, machinist, operator, worker
mechanical: automatic, emotionless, instinctive, involuntary, reflex, routine, unconscious, uninspired
mechanical way of doing something: rote
mechanically done: perfunctory
mechanics studying motion but not forces or bodies' mass: kinematics
mechanism: apparatus, appliance, catch, component, device, engine, gadget, gear, instrument, machinery, means, method, motor, operation, process, system, technique, tool
mechanize: automate
medal: award, badge, decoration, laurel, plaque, purple heart, trophy, wreath
medal as emblem of honor: decoration
medal worn on chest: pectoral
medal, back of: reverse, verso
medal, front of: obverse
medal, Olympic: bronze, gold, silver
medalist: winner
medals, study or collection of: numismatics
meddle: butt in, dabble, impede, interfere, interlope, intervene, intrude, kibitz, mess with, pry, snoop, tamper, tinker

meddler: busybody, buttinsky, kibitzer, snoop, tattletale

meddlesome: busy, curious, impudicity, interfering, intrusive, nosy, officious, prying, snooping

media: cable, communications, magazines, news, newspaper, press, publishing, radio, television

medial: average, center, central, mean, median, middle, ordinary

median: average, center, intermediate, mean, medial, middle, midpoint, midway, norm

mediate: arbitrate, conciliate, intercede, interpose, intervene, moderate, negotiate, referee, resolve, umpire

mediator: agent, arbitrator, broker, go-between, intercessor, intermediary, judge, moderator, negotiator, ombudsman, peacemaker, referee, umpire

medic: doc, doctor, intern, physician, practitioner, surgeon

medieval: antiquated, Dark Ages, feudal, Gothic, Middle Ages

medieval association of merchants or artisans: gild, guild

medieval chemistry: alchemy

medieval helmet: armet, sallet

medieval liturgical music: plainchant, plainsong

medieval merchants' guild: hanse

medieval minstrel: jongleur, troubadour

medieval municipal corporation: commune

medieval peasant: serf

medieval political and economic system with vassals: feudal system, feudalism

medieval serf: esne

medieval tax: geld, murage, scutage, tithe

medieval tournament: carousel, joust

medieval trade organization: Hanseatic League

medieval weapon: crossbow, lance, mace, sword

mediocre: acceptable, adequate, average, common, commonplace, fair, indifferent, inferior, mean, medium, middling, moderate, normal, ordinary, passable, pedestrian, presentable, prosaic, second-rate, serviceable, so-so, tolerable

mediocre and everyday: ordinary, run-of-the-mill, undistinguished, unexceptional, uninspired

mediocre in character: bland, insipid

mediocre performer: hack

meditate: consider, contemplate, deliberate, dream, mull, muse, ponder, pore, reflect, revolve, ruminate, speculate, study, think, weigh

meditation: cogitation, contemplation, examination, mysticism, prayer, thought, TM, yoga

meditation chant: mantra

meditation folded leg position: lotus

meditation, westernized: transcendental meditation

medium: average, fair, mean, medial, midst, midway, moderate, normal, ordinary

medium or channel: agent, atmosphere, channel, clairvoyant, climate, diviner, environment, fortuneteller, genre, instrument, intermediary, magazine, mediator, music, newspaper, organ, painting, radio, sculpture, setting, television, tool, vehicle, writing

medley: assortment, blend, collection, combo, conglomeration, farrago, gallimaufry, hodgepodge, jumble, melange, miscellany, mixture, olio, patchwork, potpourri, salmagundi

meek: docile, fawning, gentle, humble, lowly, mild, moderate, modest, patient, peaceful, reserved, resigned, servile, sheepish, spineless, subdued, submissive, sycophantic, timid, tolerant, unassertive, unassuming, weak, yielding

meet: appropriate, assemble, battle, bump, chance, clash, collide, competition, comply, confer, confront, congregate, connect, contact, contend, contest, convene, converge, cross, duel, encounter, equal, event, face, find, fit, fitting, fulfill, gather, greet, happen, intersect, join, match, moderate, proper, rendezvous, satisfy, sit, suitable, touch, tournament, tryst

meet expectations: cut the mustard

meet face to face: confront

meet former classmates: reune

meet halfway: bargain, compromise, deal, middle, settlement

meeting: assembly, caucus, conclave, conference, congress, convocation, encountering, huddle, junction, moot, rally, rendezvous, sess, session, union

meeting at agreed-upon place: rendezvous

meeting at same point: concurrent

meeting chairperson: convener, moderator

meeting for academic discussion: colloquium, convention, seminar, symposium

meeting for consultation and discussion: conference, powwow

meeting for decisions on political delegates, policy, leadership: caucus

meeting for decisions on religious policy: consistory

meeting for discussion: conversazione, forum

meeting for working on ideas: brainstorming

meeting of church officials: synod

meeting of lovers: assignation, tryst

meeting of representatives, formal: congress

meeting of the minds: agreement, approval, collection, confrontation, consultation, date, encounter, engagement, forum, gathering, harmony, powwow, rapport, showdown, summit, symposium, tryst

meeting offering counsel or instruction: clinic, workshop

meeting or assembly for a cause: rally

meeting or interaction point: interface

meeting program: agenda

meeting to confer on subject: symposium

meeting with all members present: plenum

meeting with leader, formal: audience

meeting, minimum number of members needed for formal: quorum

meeting, recorded proceedings of a: minutes

meeting, secret: conclave

meeting, secret, of lovers: tryst

meeting, to call a: convene, convoke

meeting, to suspend or end a: adjourn

meeting, unplanned: encounter

megrim: blues, caprice, depression, dizziness, fancy, flounder, headache, melancholy, migraine, unhappiness, vertigo, whim

melancholy: atrabilious, blue, cheerless, dejection, depressing, depression, desolation, despair, despondent, disconsolate, dismal, doleful, downcast, downhearted, dreary, dull, dumps, funereal, gloomy, glum, low, moody, pensive, plaintive, sad, sadness, sepulchral, somber, sorrowful, tristful, unhappy, woebegone, woeful

MEDICAL TERMS

assistant or emergency technician: paramedic
branch for women's health matters: gynecology
case history: anamnesis
check-up: physical
cure-all medicine: panacea
equipment and supplies of physician or institution: armamentarium
health: rehabilitate
inactive substance given to hypochondriac or test subject: placebo
insertion of tube into body passage: intubation
instrument to hold open a body cavity: speculum
large medicinal pill: bolus
medical: aesculapian, corrective, curative, healing, iatric, medicinal, therapeutic
medical and biological technology: bioengineering
medical branch dealing with blood and blood-producing organs: hematology
medical branch dealing with infants and children: pediatrics
medical branch dealing with nervous system: neurology
medical branch dealing with pregnancy and childbirth: obstetrics
medical branch dealing with skeletal system, muscles, joints, ligaments: orthopedics
medical branch dealing with the skin: dermatology
medical branch dealing with urinary tract and urogenital system: urology
medical branch dealing with women's health care: gynecology
medical branch easing irritation: abirritant
medical branch interpreting or establishing facts for law case: forensic medicine
medical branch studying disease: pathology
medical branches: cardiology, chiropractic, dermatology, diagnostics, endocrinology, general practice, geriatrics, gynecology, internal, neurology, obstetrics, ophthalmology, oral surgery, orthopedics, osteopathy, pathology, pediatrics, psychiatry, psychotherapy, radiotherapy, surgery, therapy, urology, veterinary
medical center: clinic
medical drugs collectively: pharmacopoeia
medical instruments: aspirator, audiometer, cannula, CAT scanner, defibrillator, electrocardiograph, endoscope, forceps, iron lung, kymograph, lancet, osteoclast, otoscope, polygraph, retractor, scalpel, speculum, stethoscope
medical knowledge relating to legal questions: forensic medicine
medical preparation protected by trademark: patent medicine, proprietary medicine
medical specialist with diploma: diplomate
medical student in supervised practical training: intern
medical treatment: paramedic
medication inserted in body cavity: suppository
medicinal: aesculapian, curing, healing, medical,

medicative, pharmaceutic, remedial, salutary, therapeutic
medicinal amount: dosage, dose
medicinal beverage: tisane
medicinal pill: lozenge, pastille, perle, troche
medicinal plant or medicine obtained from it: simple
medicine: analgesic, antacid, antibiotic, anticoagulant, antidote, antihistamine, antitussive, capsule, cathartic, decongestant, diuretic, emetic, expectorant, hypnotic, injection, laxative, medicament, ointment, paregoric, pill, potion, prescription, sedative, serum, soporific, steroid, tablet, tincture, tranquilizer, vaccine
medicine available without prescription: officinal, over-the-counter
medicine causing flow of urine: diuretic
medicine causing vomiting: emetic
medicine for allergies: antihistamine
medicine for anxiety: diazepam, tranquilizer, valerian, Valium
medicine for arthritis, gout, rheumatism: cortisone
medicine for bacterial infection: amoxicillin, antibiotic, sulfonamide, tetracycline
medicine for blocked nasal passages: decongestant
medicine for blood clotting: anticoagulant, warfarin
medicine for causing vomiting after poison ingestion: emetic
medicine for constipation: cathartic, laxative, purgative
medicine for cough: antitussive
medicine for cough, pain, insomnia: codeine
medicine for diabetes: insulin
medicine for diarrhea, intestinal pain: paregoric
medicine for expulsion of phlegm, mucus: expectorant
medicine for fever: antipyretic
medicine for heart disorder: digitalis, digoxin
medicine for increasing urine discharge: diuretic
medicine for insomnia: hypnotic, soporific
medicine for malaria: quinine
medicine for pain: analgesic
medicine for Parkinson's disease: L-dopa, levodopa
medicine for particular ailment, disorder: specific
medicine for shock: noradrenaline, norepinephrine
medicine for skin rash: calamine
medicine for stomach gas: antacid
medicine given by injection: parenteral
medicine man: healer, priest, shaman, witch doctor
medicine prepared according to doctor's prescription: ethical, magistral
medicine to restore health: restorative
medicine with secret ingredients: nostrum, quack remedy
oath of ethics: Hippocratic oath
office or institution where medicines are dispensed: dispensary, pharmacy
person receiving clinical training in medical specialty: resident
prescription that is mixed: compound

MEDICAL TERMS *continued*

preventative measure: prophylactic
professional symbol: caduceus
purgative: enema
side effect showing treatment, procedure to be inadvisable: contraindication
sweet solution added to medicine to make it taste better: elixir
technique involving physical treatment of disorder: modality
technique with needle insertion to relieve pain: acupuncture
therapy: modality
treatment based on observation and experiment, of: empirical
unorthodox medical treatment: alternative medicine ☙

---

melancholy and pessimism: weltschmerz

melancholy, profound: lypothymia

mélange: assortment, combo, hodgepodge, medley, mishmash, mixture, olio, pasticcio

melanoma: cancer

meld: amalgamate, blend, combine, fuse, incorporate, join, merge, unite

melee: affray, battle, brawl, clash, commotion, dogfight, donnybrook, fight, fracas, fray, riot, row, ruckus, scuffle, skirmish

meliorate: better, improve, soften

mellifluous: golden, honeyed, musical, pleasant, smooth, sugared, sweet, syrupy

mellow: age, aged, developed, juicy, mature, matured, relaxed, rich, ripe, ripen, softened, soothing, tender, unhurried

melodic: ariose, arioso, canorous, dulcet, melodious

melodic material added above or below existing melody: counterpoint, polyphony

melodious: agreeable, arioso, canorous, dulcet, harmonious, lyrical, melodic, musical, pleasing, tuneful

melodramatic: corny, emotional, exaggerated, sensational, showy, theatrical

melody: air, aria, ditty, harmony, lay, lyric, music, refrain, resonance, rhythm, song, strain, theme, tune

MELONS

cantaloupe
casaba
Crenshaw
honeydew
muskmelon
Persian
watermelon
winter melon ☙

melody added to melody: counterpoint

melody or counterpoint sung higher than the main melody: descant

melt: bake, blend, burn, colliquate, cook, deliquesce, disintegrate, dissipate, dissolve, dwindle, flow, flux, fuse, heat, liquefy, perspire, render, scorch, smelt, soften, sweat, thaw, yield

melt gradually: deliquesce

melt ore and extract metal: smelt

melted and clarified: rendered

melting: liquescent

melting metal, vessel for: crucible

member: affiliate, branch, chapter, component, constituent, division, element, fellow, part, piece, portion, section, segment

member of body: arm, extremity, leg, limb

member of group represented by public official: constituent

member of legislative body: legislator

member of legislative body in charge of attendance, discipline: Whip

member of legislative body, presiding officer: Speaker

member or founder of organization, an original: charter member

members, not leaders, of organization: rank and file

members, to acquire new: enlist, enroll, recruit

membership: affiliation, association, brotherhood, club, enrollment, fellowship, group, seat, sisterhood, society

membership ceremony of admission: initiation

membership trial period: probation

membership, end of: expiration

membrane around fetus or embryo: amnion, chorion

membrane dividing two cavities or masses of tissue: septum

membrane lining abdominal cavity: peritoneum

membrane lining closed body cavity: serosa, serous membrane

membrane occluding vagina: hymen

membrane of inner eyelid: nictitating membrane

membrane separating abdominal and thoracic cavities: diaphragm

membranous: telar

memento: keepsake, relic

memoir: account, autobiography, biography, commentary, confessions, diary, journal, narrative, recollection, record, report

memorable: celebrated, distinguished, eventful, extraordinary, historic, illustrious, important, impressive, lasting, notable, noteworthy, remarkable, remembered, reminiscent, special, unforgettable

memorable point on landscape: landmark

memorandum: agenda, announcement, brief, chit, diary, directive, dispatch, letter, message, minute, notation, note, reminder, report

memorandum of major points: aide≈mémoire

memorial: cairn, ceremony, commemorative, mausoleum, memento, memoir, monument, plaque, record, relic, remembrance, shrine, souvenir, statue, testimonial, token, trophy

memorial or marker of stone heap: cairn

memorize by repetition, routine: rote

memorized materials, saying: recitation

memory: cognizance, image, mind, prompt, recall, recapture, recollection, remembrance, reminiscence, retention, retrospection, rote

memory aid: aide≈mémoire, mnemonic, mnemonic device, tickler

memory book: album, diary, journal, scrapbook

memory loss: amnesia, fugue, lethe, oblivion

memory of event: anamnesis, recollection, reminiscence

memory of experience, confusion of fantasy with: paramnesia

memory of precise visual images: photographic memory

memory of visual images, distinct: eidetic

memory of, in: in memoriam

memory, capacity for: recall, retention, retrieval

memory, commit to: con, memorize

memory, fixed in one's: engraved, inscribed

memory, tending to retain: retentive, tenacious

memory, to exclude painful: repress

memory, very vivid: hypermnesia

men, hatred of: misandry

menace: bother, danger, hazard, impend, jeopardy, peril, pest, threat, threaten, torment, troublemaker

menacing: formidable, frightening, imminent, intimidating, looming, minacious, minatory, threatening

menagerie: zoo

mend: ameliorate, amend, bar, better, convalesce, correct, cure, darn, doctor, fix, heal, help, improve, knit, patch, rebuild, rectify, recuperate, refurbish, remedy, renew, renovate, repair, resew, restore, sew

mendacious: deceitful, dishonest, false, fibbing, lying, untrue, untruthful

mendicant: beggar, friar, monk, panhandler, pauper, vagabond

menial: base, degrading, demeaning, humble, ignoble, lowly, mean, servant, servile, slavish, sordid, subservient, sycophantic

menial worker: peon

menstruation blood: menses

menstruation cessation: menopause

menstruation, abnormal suppression of: amenorrhea

menstruation, first: menarche

menstruation, membrane shed during: decidua

mental: cognitive, crazed, deranged, disturbed, insane, intellectual, intelligent, mind, psychotic, unstable

mental age tested, divided by chronological age, multipled by 100: intelligence quotient, IQ

mental anguish: dolor

mental as opposed to physical: psychogenic

mental block: inhibition

mental conception: idea

mental confusion: amentia

mental discomfort: malaise

mental disorder: aphasia, delusion, hypochondria, insanity, megalomania, neurosis, oddity, paranoia, psychosis, quirk, schizophrenia

mental disorder involving withdrawal from reality: schizophrenia

mental ennui: acedia

mental estrangement: alienation

mental image, illusory: phantasm, phantasma

mental institution: asylum, funny farm, loony bin, madhouse, sanatorium, sanitarium

mental institution, consignment to: commitment, committal

mental lapse: aberration

mental powers impaired: dementia

mental quickness: acumen

mental telepathy: cryptesthesia, ESP

mentality: acumen, attitude, brainpower, discernment, intelligence, makeup, mind, rationality, reasoning, sense

mentally alert: agile

mentally deficient: backward, retarded

mentally deficient person: ament, imbecile

mentally imagined, vividly: eidetic

mentally retarded person with one brilliant talent: idiot savant

mentally sound: compos mentis, sane

mentally unsound: non compos mentis

mention: allude, allusion, citation, cite, comment, denote, hint, honor, imply, indication, inform, name, notice, observation, quote, record, refer, reference, remark, speak, specify, statement, tribute

mention for first time: broach

mention indirectly: allude

mention individually: specify

mention saying something will not be mentioned: apophasis

mentor: adviser, coach, counselor, guru, instructor, master, teacher, trainer, tutor

menu: bill of fare, card, carte, cuisine, dishes, list, meal, options, program

menu special: blue plate

menu with separately priced items: a la carte

mephitic: foul, noxious, offensive, poisonous, smelly, stinking

mercenary: covetous, greedy, hack, hireling, legionnaire, soldier, sordid, venal, vendible, warrior

merchandise: commodities, goods, line, product, staples, stock, wares

merchandise, taking back defective: rehibition

merchandise, to: advertise, sell

merchandising event: sale

merchant: broker, businessman, businesswoman, buyer, dealer, exporter, jobber, peddler, purveyor, retailer, salesman, saleswoman, seller, shopkeeper, storekeeper, trader, vendor, wholesaler

merchant ship: argosy, oiler

merciful: benign, charitable, clement, compassionate, forgiving, humane, kind, lenient, pardoning, sparing, sympathetic, tender

merciless: cruel, ferocious, fierce, grim, hard-hearted, harsh, heartless, implacable, inhumane, mean, relentless, ruthless, savage, unyielding, wanton

mercurial: adroit, changeable, clever, cunning, flighty, fluctuating, inconstant, lively, quick, quicksilver, shrewd, volatile

mercy: benevolence, blessing, charity, clemency, compassion, forgiveness, generosity, goodwill, grace, humanity, kindness, leniency, lenity, pity, ruth, sympathy, tenderness, tolerance

mercy killing: euthanasia

mere: absolute, bare, boundary, entire, insignificant, limit, little, negligible, only, pure, scant, sheer, simple, slight, small, sole, stark, unadulterated, utter

merely: barely, just, only, quite, simply, solely, utterly

meretricious: blatant, cheap, deceptive, flashy, glaring, gaudy, junky, loud, misleading, showy

merge: absorb, amalgamate, assimilate, blend, coalesce, combine, commingle, consolidate, converge, fush, incorporate, integrate, join, meld, pool, unify, unite

merger: alliance, coalition, combination, takeover, unification, union

meridian: acme, apex, apogee, circle, climax, culmination, curve, noon, peak, pinnacle, summit, zenith

merit: award, credit, desert, deserts, deserve, dignity, earn, excellence, rate, reward, stature, virtue, warrant, worth

merited or deserved: condign

meritorious: admirable, commendable, deserving, exemplary, honorable, laudable, worthy

meritorious award: honor

merriment: amusement, celebration, cheerfulness, conviviality, enjoyment, festivity, frolic, fun, gaiety, glee, jocularity, jollity, joviality, laughter, merry-making, mirth, revelry

merry: blithe, cheerful, festive, frolicsome, gay, glad, gleeful, happy, hilarious, jocose, jocular, jocund, jolly, jovial, joyful, joyous, lighthearted, lively, mirthful, pleasant, sprightly, sunny, vivacious

merry-go-round: carousel

merrymaking: amusement, carousal, celebration, conviviality, enjoyment, festive, festivity, frolic, jolly, merriment, pleasure, revelry

mesa: butte, loma, mountain, peak, plateau, tableland

mesh: agree, connect, coordinate, engage, ensnare, entangle, grid, harmonize, interlock, net, netting, network, screen, skein, snare, tangle, web

mesmerize: captivate, charm, control, enthrall, fascinate, hold, hypnotize, spellbind

mesmerize or stun: petrify, stupefy

mess: botch, bungle, clutter, commotion, confusion, crisis, crumple, dabble, debris, difficulty, dilemma, dirty, disarray, dishevel, disorder, eyesore, fiasco, fiddle, hodgepodge, jumble, litter, meal, muddle, mull, pickle, predicament, rations, scramble, shambles, snafu, soil, trouble, wreckage, wrinkle

mess around: dabble, dawdle, experiment, fiddle, flirt, fool, play, putter, tinker

mess up: blunder, botch, bungle, confuse, dirty, disorganize, err, goof, muff

message: bulletin, cable, code, communication, communiqué, dispatch, epistle, information, letter, meaning, memo, memorandum, mission, missive, moral, news, note, point, report, telegram, wire, word

message, implied: subtext

message, interrupt a: intercept

message, pass along a: relay

messenger: ambassador, angel, apostle, carrier, courier, crier, delegate, dispatcher, emissary, envoy, evangelist, go-between, gofer, harbinger, herald, intermediary, legate, mercury, minister, page, pigeon, prophet, runner

messy: cluttered, dirty, disheveled, jumbled, sloppy, unkempt, unpleasant, untidy

metal alloy of silver and gold: electrum

metal alloy of tin and lead, antimony, or copper: pewter

metal-and-enamel work: cloisonné

metal by heating and beating, to form: forge

metal by heating and cooling, to strengthen or harden: anneal, temper

metal capable of being drawn out in length, of a: ductile, tensile, tractile

metal capable of being shaped, of a: malleable, workable

metal decorated by inlaying wavy patterns: damascening

metal decorating technique where hollowed out areas are filled with enamel and fired: champlevé

metal disk: paillette, paten

metal disk to be stamped for coin: flan

metal fragments from high-explosive shell: shrapnel

metal highly resistant to oxidation, corrosion: noble metal

metal in alloy, principal: matrix

metal in bar or block: ingot

metal into thin leaf or foil, hammer or cut: foliate

metal is melted and molded, factory where: foundry

metal or ore deposit: lode, vein

metal piece: dross, filings, gad, ingot, lemel, lode, nugget, paten, pig, scissel, scoria, seam, slag, slug, solder, spline, stope, swarf, vein

metal protection: armor, chain mail, mail

metal refuse: slag

metal sheet: lames, lamina, leaf, plate, tagger

metal types: cadmium, cerium, cobalt, copper, erbium, gold, iridium, iron, lead, lutecium, mercury, osmium, pewter, platinum, potassium, radium, silver, solium, terbium, tin, uranium, yttrium, zinc

metal with wavy inlay or etching, decorate: damascene

metal worker: blacksmith, coppersmith, goldsmith, riveter, silversmith, smith, tinsmith

metal, concerning: metallic, metalliferous, ory, tinny

metal, dissolve or wear away: corrode

metal, engrave or emboss: chase, enchase

metal, impurity on molten: dross

metal, nonprecious: base metal

metal, precious: gold, platinum, silver

metal, weakness in: fatigue

metallic ore, mass left over from smelting: scoria, slag

metallic parts, fusible alloys used to join: solder

metallic sound: clang, clank, clink, ting

metals and alloys, science of: metallurgy

metals by applying heat, join: weld

metals shaped by hammering: wrought

metals, mixture of two or more: alloy

metals, vessel for melting: crucible

metalware with enamel or lacquer design: tole

metamorphose: alter, change, mutate, transfigure, transform, transmute

metamorphosis: alteration, change, conversion, evolution, modification, mutation, permutation, rebirth, reformation, transfiguration, transformation, translation, transmogrification, transmutation, transubstantiation

metaphor: allegory, analogy, comparison, figure of speech, image, simile, symbol, trope

metaphor is identified, word or phrase with which the vehicle of a: tenor

metaphor or exaggerated comparison: conceit

metaphorical: figurative

metaphysical: abstract, abstruse, esoteric, immaterial, intangible, philosophical, supernatural, transcendental, unearthly

mete: administer, allocate, allot, apportion, bound, boundary, disburse, dispense, distribute, dole, give, limit, measure

meteor: falling star

meteor shower, celestial origin of: radiant

meteor that is as bright or brighter than planets: bolide, fireball

meteoric: blazing, brief, celestial, dazzling, flashing, rapid, spectacular, sudden, swift

meteorologist: forecaster, weatherman, weatherwoman

meteors, study of: aerolithology

meter: arrangement, beat, cadence, measure, measurement, music, pattern, rhythm, swing, time, verse

meter, one-hundreth: centimeter
meter, one-tenth: decimeter
meter, one-thousandth: millimeter
method: approach, fashion, form, formula, manner, means, mode, modus operandi, order, pattern, plan, procedure, process, routine, rule, science, strategy, style, system, technique, usage, way
method based on observation or experiment, of a: empirical
method of learning by discovery, educational: heuristic
method of operating: MO, modus operandi
method of teaching reading and spelling based on phonetic interpretation: phonics
method of transporting oil: pipage
method planned to achieve specific goal: strategy, tactics
method, therapeutic: modality
methodical: deliberate, exact, meticulous, orderly, organized, precise, systematic
meticulous: careful, detailed, exact, fastidious, finical, fussy, methodical, neat, painstaking, persnickety, precise, punctilious, scrupulous, thorough
métier: business, calling, career, craft, forte, line, occupation, profession, specialty, trade, work
metric: ampere, candela, carat, centigram, centiliter, centimeter, decigram, deciliter, decimeter, dekagram, dekaliter, dekameter, gram, hectare, hectogram, hectoliter, hectometer, hour, kelvin, kilogram, kiloliter, kilometer, liter, meter, micromillimeter, milligram, milliliter, millimeter, minute, radian, second, steradian, stere, ton, tonne
metric prefixes: atto, billi, centi, deci, deka, femto, giga, hecto, kilo, mega, micro, milli, nano, pico, tera
metrical patterns, analysis of verse into: scansion
metrical time unit, minimal: mora
metropolitan: bishop, city, cosmopolitan, municipal, urban
mettle: bravery, character, courage, fire, guts, nerve, quality, spirit, spunk, vigor
mettlesome: alley, ardent, brave, courtyard, fiery, hideaway, meow, peppery, plucky, seagull, spirited, spunky, street, valiant

Mexican blanket-like shawl: serape
Mexican cactus: mescal
Mexico food: arepa, atole, chile, enchilada, frijoles, guacamole, quesadilla, salsa, taco, tamale, tortilla, tostada
mezzanine: balcony, entresol
microbe: bacillus, bacteria, germ, microorganism, organism, parasite
microchip: integrated circuit
microcosm: small world
microfilm sheet: fiche, microfiche
microorganism: aerobe, bacillus, bacterium, germ, microbe, protozoan, spirillum, virus
microorganism carrier: vector
microphone interference-preventer: baffle
microphone receiver converting sound to signal: diaphragm
microphone return of output as input: feedback
microphone, long movable arm used for: boom
microscope eyepiece: ocular
microscope lens or lenses: objective
microscope slide, thin specimen for: section
microscope slide, to put a specimen on a: mount
microscope with high-intensity illumination: dark-field microscope, ultramicroscope
microscope, visible without: macroscopic
microscopic: atomic, infinitesimal, little, minute, small, tiny
microscopic organism: amoeba, animalcule
microscopic protozoan, oval ciliate: paramecium
microscopic single-celled organism: protozoan, protozoon
microwave tube creating power: magnetron
midday rest period: siesta
middle: average, belly, between, center, central, core, halfway, intermediate, intervening, marrow, mean, medial, median, midst, midway, waist
Middle Ages: medieval
middle-class: bourgeois, common, ordinary
middle ear: tympanum
middle ear bone: anvil
Middle East cone-shaped felt hat with tassel: fez
middle finger: medius
middle finger's tip: dactylion

middle ground: juste-milieu
middle number in distribution: median
middle of sequence of events: in medias res
middle of word, letters inserted in: infix
middle or average, ideal: golden mean
middle or intermediate factor: tertium quid
middle way: via media
middle, in the: intermediate
middleman: agent, broker, dealer, distributor, factor, go-between, huckster, intermediary, liaison, middlewoman, retailer, salesperson, trader
middling: average, common, fair, indifferent, mediocre, medium, moderate, okay, ordinary, so-so
midget: dwarf, homunculus, manikin, miniature, munchkin, pygmy, small, tiny
midmorning tea/coffee with snack: elevenses
midst: among, between, center, core, depth, halfway, heart, mean, medium, middle, midpoint, thick
midwife: accoucheuse, assistant, practitioner
mien: air, appearance, aspect, attitude, aura, bearing, behavior, carriage, conduct, countenance, demeanor, deportment, guise, look, mannerism, ostent, presence, semblance, style
miff: anger, annoy, bother, displease, irritate, offend, spat, upset
might: ability, capability, clout, control, domination, drawn, may, muscle, power, strength, supremacy
mighty: able, courageous, enormous, extensive, forceful, great, heroic, huge, imposing, massive, monumental, omnipotent, potent, powerful, puissant, stalwart, strong, towering, tremendous, vast, vigorous, violent
migraine: headache, megrim
migrant: drifter, itinerant, mover, nomad, transient
migrate: drift, move, relocate, roam, rover, trek, travel, wander
migration: diaspora, exodus, flight, journey, movement, passage
migratory: mobile, moving, nomadic, roving, seasonal, transient, wandering
migratory, non-: sedentary
mild: balmy, benign, bland, clement, cool, delicate, docile, easy, easygoing, forbearing, forgiving, gentle, indulgent, kind, lenient, medium,

meek, moderate, pleasant, smooth, soft, soothing, tame, temperate, tranquil, unassuming, warm

mild cigar: claro

mild climate, of a: temperate

mild reproof: admonition

mild substitute for offensive word: euphemism

mildew: blight, fungus, mold, must

mildness: lenity

milestone: achievement, anniversary, breakthrough, event, landmark, milepost, plateau, step

milieu: ambience, atmosphere, climate, environment, scene, setting, surroundings

militant: aggressive, belicose, combative, defiant, fighter, martial, soldier, warlike, warring, warrior

milk fermented by bacteria: yogurt

milk heated to kill microorganisms: pasteurized

milk included: au lait

milk made uniform in consistency: homogenized

milk of camel or mare, fermented: kumiss

milk of cow, first: beestings, colostrum

milk plant: dairy

milk sugar: lactose

milk types: condensed, cream, dried, evaporated, formula, goat's, homogenized, low fat, mother's, pasteurized, powdered, skim, two-percent, whole

milk watery part: serum, whey

milk with sugar added, reduced thick: condensed milk

milk, concentrated unsweetened: evaporated milk

milk, concerning: lacteal, lactic

milk, sour curdled: clabber

milk, to: bleed, drain, draw, elicit, empty, exhaust, exploit, nurse, siphon, squeeze, suckle

milk, to get baby off mother's: wean

milk, to produce: lactate

milk, to squeeze out: express

milkshake: cabinet, frappé, milk shake, shake, velvet

milksop: chicken, coward, jellyfish, lightweight, milquetoast, mollycoddle, pansy, pantywaist, sissy, weakling, wimp, yellowbelly

milky: chalky, cloudy, lacteal, lactescent, opaline, pearly, white

milky liquid: emulsion

mill: beat, box, crush, device, dress,

fight, finish, granulate, grind, knurl, polish, powder, pulverize, roam, shape, thrash, transform

millennium: golden age, happiness, paradise, prosperity, serenity, thousand years, utopia

million metric tons of TNT: megaton

million million: tera-, trillion

million million million: exa-, quintillion

million million millionth: pico-

million millionth: micro-

millstone: affliction, burden, load, responsibility

mime: actor, ape, apery, buffoon, clown, copy, farce, imitate, impersonate, jester, mimic, represent

mimic: actor, actress, ape, burlesque, comedian, copycat, copying, counterfeit, echo, imitate, impersonate, impressionist, mime, mock, parrot, ridicule, simulate, thespian, trouper

mimic bird: myna

mimicry of a work: parody, pastiche

mince: chop, cut, grind, hash

minced sheep or calf innards cooked in the animal's stomach, Scottish: haggis

mincing: affected, dainty, delicate, fussy, genteel, la-di-da, persnickety, pretentious

mind: belief, brain, concentration, faculty, feeling, inclination, instinct, intellect, intelligence, memory, mentality, opinion, outlook, psyche, reason, recollection, regard, sanity, senses, sentiment, spirit, thoughts, view, will

mind and soul, cosmic: logos, nous

mind-expanding: psychedelic

mind on the body, concerned with the influence of the: psychosomatic

mind over matter: psychokinesis

mind reading: cryptesthesia, telepathy

mind, bringing to: presentative

mind, of sound: compos mentis, sane

mind, originating in the: psychogenic

mindful: alert, attentive, awake, aware, careful, cautious, cognizant, conscious, observant, sensible

mindless: asinine, foolish, forgetful, idiotic, inattentive, insane, negligent, oblivious, regardless, silly, stupid, thoughtless, unattuned, unintelligent

mine: cache, cavity, colliery, deposit, excavation, explosive, gallery, hole, lode, passage, pit, quarry, sap, scoop, shaft, supply, tunnel, vein

mine access: adit

mine and its physical plant, coal: colliery

mine car: tram

mine deposit: lode

mine excavation by steps: stope

mine levels, inclined shaft between: winze

mine parallel to vein, almost horizontal entrance to: drift

mine roof, prop to support: gib, sprag

mine shaft, hole at lowest point: sump

mine shaft, rigging for hauling and lifting in: headgear

mine, to: burrow, delve, dig, drill, unearth

mine types: coal, copper, diamond, gold, iron, open pit, quartz, silver, strip, surface

mine ventilation partition: brattice

mine ventilation shaft: upcast

mine with seams and outcrops close to ground level, open: strip mine

miner: collier, digger, dredger, excavator, prospector, sapper

mineral deposit: lode, nest, placer, reef, seam, vein

mineral deposits, to search for: prospect

mineral ores, divination to find: rhabdomancy

mineral spring: spa

mineral water: seltzer water

mineral, nonmetallic: asbestos, boron, gangue, graphite, gypsum, halite, iodine, spar

mineral, soft: gypsum, talc

minerals into a mine to deceive, to place: salt

miner's lamp: Davy lamp, safety lamp

mines after fire or explosion, asphyxiating gases in: afterdamp, blackdamp, chokedamp

minesweeping equipment: paravane

mingle: amalgamate, associate, blend, circulate, coalesce, combine, commingle, compound, fuse, immix, intermix, join, meld, merge, mix, network, socialize, unite

miniature: diminutive, lilliputian, little, microscopic, midget, mini, miniscule, minute, petite, pocket, small, teeny, tiny, toy

miniature Japanese tree: bonsai

miniature people: pygmy

miniature representative system: microcosm

MILITARY TERMS

aircraft with single mission: sortie
ancient Roman unit of 3000–6000 troops: legion
ancient Roman unit of 300–600 troops: cohort
ancient Roman unit of 60–120 troops: maniple
attack: blitzkrieg, incursion, raid
braided cord on left shoulder of uniform: fourragère
bugle call in morning: reveille
cap with flat circular top and visor: kepi
civilians organized in military fashion, of: paramilitary
commanding officer of military organization: CO, commandant
commendation for outstanding service: citation
compulsory military service: conscription
concerning the military: martial, warlike
decoration for wounded in action: Purple Heart
dismiss from service for disciplinary reasons, to: cashier
extra military forces sent in: reinforcements
force into military service, to: commandeer, impress, press-gang, shanghai
heavy military equipment: hardware
hierarchy: chain of command
high-ranking military officer: brass hat
important military message: dispatch
leave of absence: furlough
lodging for military troops: billet, quarter
menial labor in the military: fatigue
military academy freshman: plebe
military base and training center: depot
military base in another country: outpost
military detachment for particular job: detail
military equipment: caisson, camion, catapult, jeep, matériel, ordnance, tank
military expedition: anabasis
military green: olive drab
military group: army, battalion, cadre, camp, cavalry, company, corps, division, drill, echelon, file, force, formation, guard, legion, line, parade, platoon, regiment, reserve, review, squad, troop, unit
military intervention used in diplomacy: gunboat diplomacy
military operation times: h-hours
military operations dealing with matériel and personnel: logistics
military person: adjutant, aide, brigadier, captain, colonel, commander, constabulary, estafet, gendarmes, general, Green Beret, guard, lieutenant, major, marshal, MP, patrol, subaltern
military planning: logistics
military prisoner: POW
military unit of troops or ships on special mission: detachment, task force
minor battle: skirmish
nonmilitary person: civilian
officer such as corporal, sergeant, petty officer: NCO, noncommissioned officer
officer trainee: cadet
officer who is second lieutenant or higher: commissioned officer
officer's assistant: adjutant, aide-de-camp
officers planning operations: general staff
position established in enemy territory: beachhead, bridgehead, foothold, salient
post: garrison
post in western U.S.: presidio
promotion in rank with no pay raise: brevet
reduction or abolition of military forces and armaments: disarmament
remove military forces or installations: demilitarize
request for military supplies: requisition
required sign-up for military duty: conscript, draft, levy
service stripe: hashmark
shops on base: post exchange, PX
sign up for military duty: enlist, enroll, recruit
small military fighting force: commando
smallest military unit: squad
student at military school: cadet
subdivision of military force: echelon
switch from military control to civilian control: demilitarize
system for supplying an army with food: commissariat
temporary encampment: bivouac
to discharge military service: demobilize
trial by military court: court-martial
troops contributed to a military effort: contingent
unit fighting on sea and land: marine
unit that fights from vehicles or horseback: cavalry
unit that fights on foot: infantry
unit trained to parachute: paratroopers ❦

---

minimal: bare, basic, insignificant, least, littlest, minimum, slightest, smallest, token

minimal amount of an element: atom

minimize: belittle, decrease, depreciate, diminish, disparage, downplay, lessen, reduce

minimize importance: play down, soft-pedal

minimum: least, littlest, lowest, mere, minimal, slightest, smallest, speck

minimum means needed to sustain life: subsistence

minimum members needed to conduct official business of organization: quorum

mining of coal by stripping off soil rather than sinking shaft: strip mining

mining tool, rock-boring: trepan

minion: dainty, darling, delicate, dependent, favorite, follower, idol, retainer, subordinate, sycophant

minister: agent, ambassador, attendant, chaplain, clergy, clergyman, clergywoman, cleric, divine, ecclesiastic, evangelist, father, padre, parson, pastor, preacher, priest, rabbi, reverend

minister's charge: pastorate

minister's or priest's residence: manse, parsonage, rectory

minister's spot: pulpit

MINERALS

acanthite	cassiterite	goethite	mineral wax	silica
actinolite	celestite	graphite	molybdenite	silicate
alabaster	cerussite	gummite	monazite	silicon
albite	chalcedony	gypsum	muscovite mica/isin-	smaltite/smaltine
allanite	chalcocite	halite	glass	smithsonite
alunite	chalcopyrite	hatchettine	natrolite	sodalite
amblygonite	chlorite	hematite	nepheline/nephelite	soda niter
amphibole	chromite	hemimorphite	niccolite	spar
anadalusite	chrysoberyl	heulandite	obsidian	sperrylite
analcime	cinnabar	holosiderite	olivenite	sphalerite
anglesite	clay	hornblende	olivine	sphene
anhydrite	coal	hypersthene	orpiment	spinel
antimony	cobaltite/cobaltine	idocrase	orthoclase	spodumene
apatite	coke	ilmenite	ozokerite	stannite
aplite	colemanite	iolite	peat	staurolite
apophyllite	columbite	iron pyrites	pentlandite	stibnite
aragonite	cordierite	jadeite	perlite	stilbite
argentite	corundum	jet	phenakite/phenacite	strontianite
argillite	covellite	kaolinite	phlogopite	sulfur
arsenic	crocoite/crocoisite	kernite	phosphate rock	sylvanite
arsenopyrite	cryolite	kyanite	phosphorus	sylvite/sylvine/
asbestos	cuprite	lazulite	pitchblende	sylvinite
asphalt	cyanotrichite	lazurite	polybasite	talc
augite	dendrite	lepidolite	psilomelane	tantalite
autunite	diamond	leucite	pumice	tellurium
aventurine/aventurin	diaspore	lignite	pumicite	tetrahadrite
azurite	diatomite	lime	pyrargyrite	thorite
barite	diopside	limonite	pyrite (fool's gold)	topaz
bauxite	dolomite	magnesite	pyrolusite	torbernite
beryl	dumortierite	magnetite	pyromorphite	tourmaline
biotite	elaterite	malachite	pyrophyllite	tremolite
bismuth	emery	maltha	pyroxene	tripoli
bitumen	enstatite	manganite	pyrrhotite/pyrrhotine	trona
blue john	epidote	marcasite	quartz	ulexite
borax	epsomite	marl	realgar	uraninite
bornite	erythrite	meerschaum	red clay	vanadinite
boron	feldspar	mica	rhodochrosite	vermiculite
brimstone	fluorite	microlite	rhodonite	willemite
bromine	fluorspar	millerite	rock	witherite
brookite	franklinite	mineral charcoal	rock salt	wolframite
brucite	gadolinite	mineral coal	rutile	wollastonite
calcite	galena	mineral oil	scapolite	wulfenite
carbon	garnet	mineral salt	scheelite	zeolite
carnallite	garnierite	mineral tallow	serpentine	zincite
carnotite	glauconite	mineral tar	siderite	zoisite ☙

ministry school: seminary

minor: incidental, insignificant, lesser, little, petty, secondary, slight, small, subordinate, superficial, trivial, unimportant

minor cut: nick

minor god or inferior deity: demigod

minor in age: adolescent, child, dependent, infant, juvenile, nonage, teenager, underage, youth

minor league: bush league

minor mistake: lapse

minor planet: asteroid

minority: adolescence, group, immaturity, nonage, youth

minority group gradually adopting ways of prevailing culture: assimilation

minstrel: bard, entertainer, gleeman, harper, jongleur, musician, performance, player, poet, show, singer, troubadour

mint condition: brand-new, excellent, fresh, new, undamaged

mint family plant: basil

mint flavoring: menthol

mint for specimen coins, chest at: pyx

mint, as money: bundle, coin, fortune, heap, money, stamp

mint, to: fabricate, invent, manufacture, mold

minting of coins, revenue from: seigniorage

minus: defect, deficiency, diminished, from, lacking, less, negative, subtract, without

minuscule: diminutive, insignificant, microscopic, minute, small, tiny, unimportant

minute: atomic, blow-by-blow, detailed, exact, flash, immaterial, in re, insignificant, instant, jiffy, lilliputian, little, meticulous, microscopic, minuscule, mite, petty, piddling, precise, record, second, shake, slight, small, teeny, thorough, tiny, trifling, unimportant, wee

minute arachnid: mite

minute groove: stria

minute particle: atom

minutes: acta, notes, proceedings, record, summary

minutiae: details, ins and outs, items, odds and ends, particulars, trivia

minx: coquette, flirt, hussy, jade, slut, woman

miracle: feat, marvel, mystery, phenomenon, portent, sign, wonder

miracle substance for turning metal into gold: philosophers' stone

miracles, performer of: thaumaturgist

miraculous: amazing, astonishing, divine, extraordinary, magical, marvelous, mysterious, spectacular, supernatural, wonderful, wondrous

miraculous solution: magic bullet

mirage: delusion, dream, fata morgana, hallucination, illusion, optical illusion, phantasm, vision

mire: bog, define, delay, embroil, entangle, fen, glar, marsh, muck, mud, ooze, quag, quicksand, slough, sludge, stall, swamp, tangle

mirror: ape, copy, echo, emulate, exemplar, exemplify, image, imitate, looking glass, mimic, model, reflection, speculum

mirror mounted on swiveling frame: cheval glass

mirror, inversion of left and right as seen in: lateral inversion

mirror, reflective metal coating on back of glass: foil, tain

mirror, signaling with sun on: heliograph

mirrors, relating to: catoptric

mirth: amusement, cheerfulness, delight, festivity, frivolity, fun, gaiety, gladness, glee, happiness, hilarity, jocularity, jollity, joy, joyousness, levity, merriment, playfulness, pleasure, spleen

misadventure: accident, adversity, blow, blunder, boner, catastrophe, debacle, disaster, error, faux pas, lapse, mishap

misanthrope: hater

misanthropic: antisocial, cynical, distrustful, unfriendly, unsociable

misappropriate: defalcate, embezzle, misuse, steal, swindle

misbegotten: fatherless, illegitimate, unlawful

misbehave: act up, disobey, transgress

misbehavior: disrespect, impropriety, misconduct, misdeed, shenanigans

miscalculate: blunder, err, miscount, misinterpret, misjudge, overestimate, overshoot, underestimate

miscarriage: botch, failure, malfunction, misdeed, mishap, mismanagement, mistake, spontaneous abortion

miscarry by animal: slink

miscellaneous: assorted, diverse, heterogeneous, mixed, motley, random, scattered, sundry, varied

miscellany: ana, anthology, assortment, blend, collection, combination, compilation, hodgepodge, medley, melee, mixture, olio, omnium-gatherum, potpourri, variety

mischance: accident, catastrophe, misadventure, misfortune, mishap

mischief: damage, devilment, devilry, deviltry, espièglerie, evil, harm, hob, hurt, injury, knavery, misbehavior, misdeed, naughtiness, prank, rascality, roguery, shenanigans, trouble, waggery

mischief-maker: gremlin, hellion, imp, pixie, rogue, scamp

mischievous: apish, devilish, elfin, elfish, evil, harmful, impish, injurious, knavish, naughty, playful, prankish, roguish, sly, sportive, teasing, tricky, vexing, waggish, wicked

mischievous activity: hanky panky

misconception: delusion, error, fallacy, misjudgment, mistake

misconduct: disorder, impropriety, malfeasance, misbehavior, misdoing, mismanage, offense, transgression, wrongdoing

misconduct in public office: malversation, misprision

misconstrue: distort, miscalculate, misconceive, misinterpret, misjudge, misunderstand

miscreant: blackguard, evildoer, heretic, infidel, knave, malefactor, rapscallion, rascal, scalawag, scamp, scoundrel, transgressor, unbeliever, villain, wretch

miscue: blooper, err, error, fluff, mistake, slip

misdeed: crime, delinquency, fault, indiscretion, mischief, misdemeanor, offense, sin, transgression, violation, wrongdoing

misdemeanor: criminality, violation

mise-en-scène: ambience, atmosphere, climate, environment, locale, site, stage setting, surroundings

miser: cheapskate, churl, curmudgeon, hoarder, niggard, pennypincher, Scrooge, skinflint, tightwad

miserable: abject, depressed, despicable, discomfort, disconsolate, doleful, feeble, forlorn, gloomy, hopeless, melancholy, pitiful, poor, shabby, sorrowful, sorry, woebegone, woeful, wretched

miserly: avaricious, cheap, close, close-fisted, covetous, frugal, greedy, iron-fisted, mean, near, parsimonious, penurious, scrimping, stingy, tight

miserly person: curmudgeon, pennypincher, Scrooge, skinflint, tightwad

misery: ache, adversity, affliction, agony, ailment, anguish, burden, calamity, depression, desolation, despair, distress, gloom, grief, melancholy, misfortune, pain, sadness, sorrow, suffering, torment, tribulation, trouble, unhappiness, woe, wretchedness

misfortune: accident, adversity, affliction, ambsace, bad luck, catastrophe, calamity, curse, disaster, dole, harm, misadventure, mischance, misery, mishap, tragedy, trouble, woe

misgiving: alarm, apprehension, distrust, doubt, qualm, suspicion, uncertainty, unease

misguided: confused, foolish, misdirected, misinformed, misled, mismanaged

mishandle: abuse, botch, bungle, fumble, maltreat, mismanage, muff

mishap: accident, blunder, boner, casualty, disaster, error, fiasco, misadventure, misfortune, tragedy

mishmash: heterogeneity, hodgepodge, jumble, medley, mélange, mixture, olio, pasticcio, pastiche

misinform: deceive, lie, misdirect, misguide, mislead, misstate

misinterpret: distort, err, misunderstand, miscalculate, misconceive, misconstrue, misread, pervert

misjudge: err, miscalculate, misconceive, misconstrue, misinterpret, misthink, overestimate, presume, underestimate

mislay: displace, lose, misplace

mislead: bait, bamboozle, beguile, betray, bilk, bluff, cheat, deceive, delude, dupe, equivocate, fool, hoodwink, inveigle, misdirect, misguide, misinform, mismanage, seduce

misleading: ambiguous, confusing, deceiving, deceptive, distorted, equivocal, factitious, false, fraudulent, illusory, inaccurate, sham

misleading information, deliberately: disinformation

misled: hoodwinked

mismanage: botch, bungle, misgovern, mishandle, misinterpret, muff

misplace: disarrange, displace, lose, mislay, unsettle

misplay: bobble, error, fumble, miscue, muff, renege

misprint: typo

misrepresent: belie, bend, deceive, disguise, distort, falsify, feign, lie, mislead, misstate, twist, wrench

misrepresentation: chicanery, exaggeration, pretense, untruth

miss: avoid, desire, disregard, err, escape, fail, failure, fault, flub, forget, ignore, lack, miscue, misfire, mistake, muff, neglect, omission, omit, overlook, skip, want, yearn

missile: arrow, bomb, bullet, dart, ICBM, minuteman, nike, patriot, projectile, rocket, scud, sidewinder, spear, torpedo, trajectile, weapon

missile guided by gyroscopic device: buzz bomb, flying bomb, robot bomb

missile housing: silo

missile launched from ground against airborne target: surface-to-air missile

missile part containing explosives, etc.: warhead

missile path or course: trajectory

missile system with multiple warheads launched by one rocket: MIRV

missile with freefalling descent, self-powered ascent: ballistic missile

missile, self-propelled: projectile

missile, self-propelled underwater: torpedo

missile, unmanned aircraft serving as self-contained: cruise missile

missile's explosive charge: payload

missile's lateral deviation: azimuth

missile's turning about vertical axis: yaw

missiles, simultaneous release of several: salvo

missing: absent, AWOL, gone, lacking, lost, misplaced, omitted

missing person: absentee

mission: assignment, calling, charge, commission, duty, embassy, errand, goal, legation, ministry, objective, purpose, task, undertaking

mission, agent sent on a: emissary

mission, government representative sent on a: envoy

mission, to question about knowledge or intelligence gained during: debrief

missionary: apostle, converter, evangelist, promoter, propagandist

missive: billet, dispatch, epistle, letter, memorandum, message, note, report

misspelling: cacography

misspellings used to represent dialect, nonstandard speech (e.g. luv): eye dialect

misspent: frittered, misapplied, squandered, wasted

misstate: color, confuse, distort, misrepresent, twist, warp

misstatement: falsehood, falsity, prevarication, tale, untruth

misstep: blooper, bungle, error, faux pas, miscue, mistake, slip, slipup, stumble, trip

mist: blur, brume, cloud, condensation, damp, dew, drizzle, film, fog, haze, mist, moisture, murk, obscure, precipitation, rain, smog, sprinkle

mistake: balk, bloomer, blooper, blunder, bobble, boner, bungle, err, erratum, error, faux pas, folly, miscalculate, misconceive, miscue, misinterpret, misstep, omission, oversight, slip, slipup

mistake in argument or conclusion: paralogism

mistake in grammar: misconstruction, solecism

mistake in printed text: typo

mistake one thing for another: confound, mix up

mistake revealing unconscious thought or emotion, verbal: Freudian slip, lapsus linguae, slip of the tongue

mistake, likely to make a: fallible

mistake, social: faux pas, gaffe

mistake, stupid: boner, clanger, howler, pratfall

mistaken: confused, erroneous, false, in error, inaccurate, incorrect, misguided, misinformed, wrong

mistaken idea, to free from a: disabuse

mistaken thought or idea: misapprehension, misconception, misunderstanding

mistaken use of word or phrase: catachresis, malapropism

mistaken, to prove someone: confute, rebut, refute

mistakes noted for book: corrigenda

mistreat: abuse, harm, injure, mishandle, outrage, violate

mistress: chatelaine, concubine, courtesan, dozy, hostess, housekeeper, kept woman, ladylove, lover, paramour, sweetheart

mistress of fashionable household: chatelaine

mistress, abandoned: grass widow

mistrust: apprehension, concern, doubt, dubiety, question, skepticism, suspect, wonder

mistrusting: disbelieving, leery, skeptical

misty: bleary, blurred, clouded, dim, filmy, foggy, hazy, indistinct, musky, nebulous, obscure, sentimental, vague, vapory

misunderstand: misapprehend, misconstrue, misinterpret

misunderstanding: argument, conflict, confusion, difference, disagreement, dispute, feud, misconception, mistake, quarrel, spat, squabble

misunderstanding between generations: generation gap

misuse: abuse, exploit, maltreat, misapplication, misappropriate, mistreat, negligence, outrage, pervert

mite: acarid, atom, bit, bug, insect, iota, minim, minute, nit, parasite, particle, smidgen, speck, tick

mites, infestation with: acariasis

mitigate: abate, allay, alleviate, appease, assuage, bate, calm, cushion, diminish, ease, lessen, lighten, moderate, pacify, palliate, placate, quell, reduce, relax, relieve, slake, soften, soothe, sweeten, temper, tone

mix: alloy, amalgamate, associate, blend, coalesce, combine, commingle, compound, concoct, confuse, consort, cross, crossbreed, fuse, fusion, hybridize, incorporate, interbreed, intermingle, join, jumble, link, merge, mingle, shuffle, socialize, stir, toss, unite, whip

mix and combine: blend, meld

mix and combine to make new whole: homologize, synthesize

mix and unite: assimilate, integrate, merge

mix by inserting: interlard, intersperse

mix into social situation or crowd: fraternize, mingle

mix to uniform consistency: homogenize

mix up: addle, confound, confuse, disorder, disrupt, disturb, fluster, muddle, perplex

mix-up: confusion, disorder, melee, mess, mistake, snafu, tangle

mix up ingredients: concoct

mixed: assorted, blended, diverse, heterogeneous, hybrid, impure, inconclusive, intermingled, miscellaneous, mongrel, motley

mixed and varied: miscellaneous

mixed feelings: ambivalence

mixed in interests: diversified

mixed in origin: half-breed, hybrid

mixed metaphor: catachresis

mixed or dissimilar elements, having: diffuse, heterogeneous, multifarious, omnifarious

mixed origin or composition, of: hybrid, mongrel

mixed race relationship: miscegenation

mixing paint board with thumb hole: palette

mixing reagents to determine concentration of a solution: titration

mixing, counteract in: neutralize

mixing, something added by: admixture

mixing, unable to undergo: immiscible

mixture: admixture, amalgam, assortment, batch, blend, brew, collection, combination, composite, compound, concoction, conglomeration, fusion, hash, hodgepodge, medley, melange, mess, miscellany, mishmash, olio, potpourri, stew, variety

mixture of cement, sand and water: mortar

mixture of chemical elements: compound

mixture of dissimilar ingredients: alloy, amalgam, farrago, gallimaufry, hodgepodge, hybrid, jumble, medley, melange, miscellany, mishmash, motley, olio, olla podrida, omnium-gatherum, pasticcio, pastiche, patchwork, potpourri, salmagundi

mixture of substances with different consistencies: colloid, emulsion, suspension

moan: complain, cry, deplore, grieve, groan, grumble, lament, sob, sough, wail, weep, whimper, whine

moat: barrier, channel, ditch, fosse, trench

moat, walled ditch, or hedge: ha-ha

mob: clique, crowd, drove, flock, gang, gathering, group, herd, masses, multitude, pack, populace, rabble, ring, surround, swarm, syndicate

mob rule: mobocracy, ochlocracy

mobile: changeable, fluid, locomotive, migratory, movable, portable, sculpture, traveling, unstable

mobilize: activate, assemble, gather, marshal, muster, prepare, rally

mobster: criminal, gangster, hood, hoodlum, mafia

mock: ape, parody, artificial, banter, burlesque, caricature, copy, counterfeit, deceive, deride, disappoint, fake, false, farce, fleer, flout, imitate, imitation, insult, jape, jeer, jibe, joke, lampoon, mimic, ridicule, scoff, scorn, sham, sneer, stimulated, taunt, tease

mock attack: feint

mock or criticize: pillory

mock or ridicule: deride, derogate, gibe, heckle, jeer, make fun of, scoff at, taunt

mock trial: kangaroo court, moot court

mock-up: model

mockery: burlesque, derision, farce, imitation, irony, joke, laughingstock, parody, ridicule, sarcasm, satire, sham, spoof, travesty, trifle

mocking piece of writing: burlesque, caricature, lampoon, parody, pasquinade, pastiche, satire, spoof, travesty

mocking whistle: catcall

mocking, cynically: sardonic

mod: chic, fashionable, latest, modern, offbeat, stylish, up-to-date

mode: appearance, approach, attitude, chic, custom, fad, fashion, flair, form, look, manner, method, modus, order, rage, state, style, system, technique, trend, variety, vogue, way

model: archetype, avatar, blueprint, build, copy, design, display, effigy, example, exemplar, exemplary, facsimile, fashion model, figure, form, gauge, ideal, imitate, manikin, mannequin, miniature, mirror, mockup, mold, parade, paradigm, paragon, pattern, perfect, plan, portrait, poser, prototype, replica, reproduction, shape, sitter, standard, symbol, type, typical, version, wear

model cut to show interior: cutaway

model for clothes display: mannequin

model for larger system, small system regarded as: microcosm

model literary passage: locus classicus

model of greatly reduced size: miniature

model of intended work in sculpture, architecture: maquette

model of solar system, mechanical: orrery

model plane wood: balsa

model, old astronomical: armillary sphere

moderate: abate, alleviate, arbitrate, average, balanced, bate, bland, calm, conservative, control, decrease, diminish, ease, even, fair, gentle, lessen, lower, mediate, mediocre, medium, middle of the road, mild, ordinary, prudent, qualify, reasonable, slacken, slight, sober, soft, soften, temper, temperate

moderation: abstinence, balance, control, diminution, limitation, measure, prudence, restraint, restriction, steadiness, temperance

moderation, quality of wise: sophrosyne

moderator: arbitrator, bater, chairman, chairwoman, judge, mediator, peacemaker, umpire

modern: avant-garde, contemporary, current, fashionable, latter-day, neoteric, new, novel, prevailing, recent, up-to-date

modern and of the highest level of development: high-tech, state-of-the-art

modern, extremely: avant-garde, futuristic

modern, needlessly new and: newfangled

modern, opposite of: classical

modernization: aggiornamento

modernize: improve, refresh, refurbish, rejuvenate, renovate, reorganize, update

modest: average, bashful, chaste, coy,

decent, demure, diffident, humble, meek, mild, moderate, plain, prim, reasonable, reserved, retiring, shy, simple, unassuming, unexcessive, unobtrusive, unpretentious, unshowy, virtuous

modest about one's value: self-deprecating

modest and in background: self-effacing, unobtrusive

modesty: bashfulness, coyness, demureness, humility, pudency, reserve, shyness, virtue

modicum: iota, tinge

modify: adapt, alter, amend, change, etude, influence, lessen, limit, mitigate, moderate, reduce, reorganize, revise, rework, soften, transform, vary

modish: chic, contemporary, dashing, fashionable, happening, snazzy, stylish, swank, trendy, voguish

modulate: adjust, change, harmonize, regulate, temper, tone, tunc

modus operandi: method, operation, organization, procedure, system, way

mogul: autocrat, baron, bump, lord, magnate, mongol, mongolian, mound, personage, ruler, tsar, tycoon

moiety: affiliation, component, element, fraction, half, part, piece, portion, share

moist: clammy, damp, dank, dewy, humid, rainy, wet

moist medicinal mass: poultice

moist, sticky stuff: muck

moisten: anoint, bedew, dabble, dampen, dip, humidify, irrigate, saturate, soak, sparge, sprinkle, water, wet

moisten with oil: embrocate

moisten while cooking: baste

moisture: dampness, dew, drizzle, humidity, liquid, mist, precipitation, rain, vapor, water, wetness

moisture-absorbing: deliquescent

moisture in air, measurement of: hygrometry

moisture, promoting retention of: humectant

moisture, soaked with: saturated

moisture, without any: dehydrated

mold: adapt, cast, character, devise, die, fashion, form, fungus, humus, knead, make, mildew, model, moulage, must, pattern, plot, sculpture, shape, stamp, transform

mold for casting: matrix

mold in which objects are cast: die

molding around door, window: architrave

molding around walls and near ceiling: cornice

molding as design, horizontal: cornice, stringcourse, table

molding edge: arris

molding of footprints, etc. at crime scene: moulage

molding projecting from panel surface: bolection

molding, concave: cavetto, conge, cove

molding, lengthwise groove in: quirk

molding, narrow convex: astragal, baguette, bead, beading, chaplet, reeding

molding, partly concave and partly convex: cyma, cymatium, ogee, talon

moldy: dated, decaying, fusty, hoary, mildewed, musty, rotten, stale

mole: birthmark, fault, growth, mark, nevus

mole, malignant: melanoma

mole, pertaining to: talpine

molecule: atom, bit, fragment, ion, iota, part, particle, speck, unit

molecule component: atom

moles, group of: company, labor, movement

molest: abuse, accost, annoy, assail, attack, bother, disturb, encroach, harass, harm, interfere, misuse, tease, torment, trouble, vex

mollify: abate, alleviate, appease, calm, conciliate, cushion, ease, lessen, lull, mitigate, moderate, pacify, placate, quiet, relax, relieve, smooth, soften, soothe, sweeten, temper, tranquilize

mollusk: abalone, chiton, clam, cuttlefish, limpet, snail, whelk

mollusk cephalopod: argonaut

mollusk classes: amphineura, bivalvia, cephalopoda, gastropoda, monoplacophora, scaphopoda

mollusk shell: bivalve, chambered, cockle, cowrie, cowry, test, testa, testae, univalve

mollusk shell concretion: pearl

mollusk teeth: radula

mollusk types: abalone, argonaut, chama, chiton, clam, coat-of-mail, cockle, cuttlefish, etheria, leda, limpet, murex, mussel, octopus, oyster, pearly nautilus, razor shell, scallop, seaslug, shipworm, slug, snail, spat, squid, tellin, whelk, winkle

mollusk young: spat

mollusk, eight-armed: octopus

mollusk, gastropod: abalone, slug, snail, taenioglossa, whelk

mollusk, marine: abalone, asi, murex, nautilus, scallop, whelk

mollusk, one-shell: snail, univalve

mollusk, shell-less: slug

mollusk, ten-armed: squid

mollusk, two-shell: bivalve, chama, clam, cockle, leda, mussel, oyster, scallop, spat

mollycoddle: baby, indulge, milsop, overprotected, pamper, recreant, spoil, weakling

molt: cast, change, discard, exuviate, shed

molten: glowing, liquefied, melted, seething

molten metal: solder

molten rock: lava, magma

moment: consequence, element, import, importance, magnitude, significance, stage, weight

moment in time: flash, instant, jiffy, minute, point, second, tick, time, twinkling, wink

moment of truth: test

momentary: brief, ephemeral, fleeting, immediate, passing, quick, short, transient, transitory

momentous: crucial, decisive, epochal, eventful, fateful, grave, historic, important, meaningful, paramount, pivotal, serious, significant, unparalleled, weighty

momentum: drive, energy, force, impetus, motion, thrust, tide, velocity

monad: atom, one, unit

monarch: autocrat, butterfly, czar, despot, emperor, empress, king, majesty, prince, princess, queen, ruler, sovereign

monastery: abbey, cloister, convent, friary, hospice, lamasery, minister, nunnery, prior, priory, retreat, sanctuary

monastery head: abbé, abbot, prior

monastery of Eastern Orthodox Church, head of: archimandrite

monastery of lamas: lamasery

monastery room for copying, writing, illuminating manuscripts: scriptorium

monastery, layperson living in: oblate

monastic: ascetic, austere, celibate, contemplative, monkish, oblate, recluse, secluded, solitary

monetary: budgetary, commercial, financial, fiscal, pecuniary

monetary value of currency, government reduction of: devaluation

money: argent, bankroll, bill, blunt, boodle, booty, brass, bread, cabbage, capital, cash, cent, change, chattel, chips, clink, coin, coinage, currency, cush, dinero, dough, dubs, dump, finances, folding green, funds, gelt, gilt, gold, green stuff, greenbacks, grig, handsel, hansel, hard cash, jack, jake, kale, lettuce, livre, long green, loot, lour, lucre, mammon, maneh, mazuma, mina, moola, moolah, moss, noters, oof, ooftish, pelf, resources, rhino, riches, rocks, scratch, stipend, swag, tender, tin, wad, wampum, wealth, wherewithal

RELATED TERMS

money and asset interchangeability: liquidity

money and possessions, motivated by: materialistic, mercenary

money and worldly concerns, focus on: materialism

money as bribe: hush money

money as evil influence: mammon

money as income: revenue

money bet with privileged information: smart money

money by intimidation, to obtain: blackmail, extort

money derived from fundraising or commercial venture: proceeds

money dishonestly acquired: pelf

money drawer: till

money exchange rate: agio

money factory: mint

money for contingencies: mad money

money for incidental expenses: pin money

money for new risky venture: venture capital

money for new venture: seed money

money for or associated with a murder: blood money

money from account, written order for payment of: draft

money fund for entertainment: slush fund

money gain, unexpected: windfall

money gift: alms, bequest, charity, endowment, largesse

money given as gift for service: gratuity, pourboire, tip

money given for new venture in exchange for promised profits: grubstake

money held until certain conditions fulfilled: escrow

money in coins or currency, concerning: numismatic

money in pool or reserve: kitty

money lender: banker, loanshark, pawnbroker, shylock, usurer

money not backed by gold or silver, government-authorized: fiduciary

money obligations, capable of meeting: solvent

money of a fund or estate, principal or capital sum of: corpus

money or financial resources: coffers, exchequer, funds, treasury

money or property bequeathed in will: bequest, legacy

money or property in custody of third party for delivery upon fulfillment of conditions: escrow

money paid in advance to get contract or bargain: earnest

money paid out: disbursement, expenditure

money paid to keep secret: bribe, hush money

money paid upon termination: golden handshake, severance pay

money paid, return of some: rebate

money recipient: payee

money returned due to pressure, coercion, or secret agreement: kickback

money set aside for a purpose: appropriation

money short of what is needed or expected: deficit, shortfall

money supply, economic theory based on regulation of: monetarism

money transport: armored car

money withdrawn from bank in excess of credit: overdraft

money worth less, decline in prices: deflation

money, coined: coin, specie

money, concerning: monetary, pecuniary

money, counterfeit: bogus, boodle, queer

money, legally valid: legal tender

money, low, for new venture: shoestring

money, making much: lucrative, profitable, remunerative

money, necessary: wherewithal

money, of a small amount of: nominal, trifling

money, small amount of: peanuts, pittance

money, to convert assets into: liquidate, realize

money, to disguise the source of illegal: launder

money, to forge: counterfeit

money, to misuse or embezzle: misappropriate

money, to pay: remit

money, trade goods or services without: barter

moneyed: affluent, loaded, opulent, prosperous, rich, wealthy

moneylender: usurer

moneylender, extortionist: shylock

moneymaking: gainful, lucrative, profitable, successful, worthwhile ❧

monger: dealer, hawker, merchant, peddler, trader, trafficker, vender

mongrel: crossbred, cur, dog, halfbreed, hybrid, mixed, mutt, tyke

monition: admonition, caution, caveat, citation, forewarning, hint, intimation, notice, order, summons, warning

monitor: adviser, check, control, counselor, device, guard, mentor, observe, police, reminder, survey, track, warship, watch

monk: abbot, anchorite, archoret, brother, cenobite, clerk, eremite, fakir, fra, friar, lama, monastic, votary

RELATED TERMS

monk haircut: tonsure

monk or nun candidate: neophyte, novice, postulant

monk orders: Benedictine, Capuchin, Carthusian, Cistercian, Dominican, Franciscan, Trappist

monk, Buddhist: arhat, bhikhu, bodhisattva, bonze, lama

monk, Eastern Orthodox: caloyer, hegumen, startis

monk, Hindu: guru, sannyasin

monk, Islamic: mystic, sufi ❧

monkey business: foolishness, highjinks, shenanigans, silliness

monkey family member: primate

monkey, New World: acari, ateles, beelzebub, capuchin, coaita, couxia, grison, howler, marmoset, miriki, ora-bassu, ouakari, sai, saki, samari, sapajou, spider, squirrel, tamarin

monkey, Old World: baboon, bandar, douc, grivet, jocko, langur, macaque, patas, potto, quenon, rhesus, toque, vervet

monkey, pertaining to: simian

monkeyshine: antic, caper, lark, prank, tomfoolery, trick

monocle: eyeglass, lorgnon, pince-nez

monogram: character, cipher, design, identification, initials, symbol

monograph: discourse, dissertation, essay, thesis, tract, treatise

monolith: block, column, menhir, monument, pillar, statue, stone

monologue: address, discourse, lecture, oration, soliloquy, speech

monopolize: absorb, consume, control, corner, dominate, engross, hog, manage, preoccupy, sew up

monopoly: cartel, consortium, control, corner, domination, exclusivity, syndicate, trust

monopoly by a few purchasers: oligopsony

monopoly by single purchaser: monopsony

monopoly, anti-: antitrust

monotone: drone

monotonous: boring, drab, dull, flat, humdrum, mundane, repetitious, repetitive, routine, same, tedious, unchanging, uniform, unvaried, wearisome

monotonous routine: grind, rut

monotony: boredom, humdrum, redundancy, sameness, tedium, uniformity

monster: afreet, barbarian, beast, behemoth, bogeyman, bogie, brute, centaur, cerberus, chimera, colossus, creature, cyclops, demon, devil, dragon, fiend, frankenstein, freak, gargoyle, giant, gigantes, gila, gorgon, harpy, hippocampus, huge, hydra, kraken, lamia, medusa, naiad, nereid, ogre, orc, savage, scoundrel, scylla, sphinx, vampire, werewolf, yeti, zombie

monster with many heads: Hydra

monsters, study of: teratology

monstrosity: abortion, freak, malformation, miscreation, teratism

monstrous: abnormal, atrocious, awful, Brobdingnagian, colossal, deformed, diabolical, enormous, fantastic, frightful, gargantuan, ghastly, gigan-tic, heinous, hideous, horrible, huge, immense, large, mammoth, massive, outrageous, overwhelming, revolting, shocking, stupendous, titanic, tremendous, unnatural, vast

monstrous act: enormity, wickedness

month, of or in the following: proximo

month, the current: instant

monthly: mensal

monument: cairn, gravestone, headstone, marker, mausoleum, memento, memorial, monolith, record, remembrance, reminder, shrine, statue, testament, token, tomb, tombstone, tribute

monument ceremony: dedication, unveiling

monument commemorating heroes and heroines of nation: pantheon

monument for dead buried elsewhere: cenotaph

monument inscription: epigraph

monument plate: plaque

monument, tall four-sided: obelisk

monumental: astounding, awesome, enduring, enormous, epic, epochal, gigantic, great, historic, huge, immense, important, impressive, mammoth, massive, memorable, significant, stupendous

mooch: beg, bum, cadge, drift, filch, skulk, sneak, steal, wander

mood: ambiance, atmosphere, attitude, aura, caprice, disposition, emotion, feeling, frame of mind, humor, inclination, spirit, spirits, strain, temper, temperament, tone, vein, whim

mood shifts, suffering from extreme: manic-depressive

moody: angry, atrabiliar, brooding, capricious, crabby, depressed, fickle, gloomy, grumpy, melancholy, moping, sulky, sullen, surly, temperamental, touchy

moolah: bread, gelt, kale, paper money

moon, concerning: lunar, lunate, selenian, selenic

RELATED TERMS

moon after harvest moon: hunter's moon

moon in thick convex shape: gibbous moon

moon in thin convex shape: crescent moon

moon near autumnal equinox: harvest moon

moon parts: cleft, crater, mare, maria, rill, rille, scar, sea

moon phases: apogee, apsis, crescent, cusp, dark, first quarter, full, half, last quarter, menisci, meniscus, new, octant, perigee, phasis, waning, waxing

moon, first or last quarter: crescent

moon, four-day period between old and new: interlunar

moon, half: demilune

moon, having two cusps like crescent: bicuspid

moon, more than half: gibbous

moon, points of crescent: cusp

moon, ring of light around: aureole, corona

moon, study of: selenography, selenology

moon, sun, Earth lined up: syzygy

moon, waning: decrescent

moon, waxing: increscent

moonlight on water, reflection of: moonglade

moonlighter's business: sideline

moon's dark area: mare

moon's decrease in size: wane

moon's increase in size: wax

moon's orbit is closest to center of Earth, point when: perigee

moon's orbit is most distant from center of Earth, point when: apogee ❦

moonshine: alcohol, bathtub gin, bootleg, eyewash, homebrew, hooch, liquor, sauce, whiskey, white lightning

moonshiner's factory: still

moor: berth, dock, heath, tether, wasteland

mooring: wharf

moot: argue, argument, broach, contestable, debatable, debate, discuss, dispute, litigation, meeting, plead, problematic, questionable, speak, uncertain, undecided, unresolved, unsettled

mope: brood, despair, droop, fret, grump, linger, pine, pout, stew, sulk

moppet: child, kid, toddler, tyke, youngster

moral: aboveboard, axiom, chaste, decent, ethic, ethical, good, homily, honest, honorable, just, lesson, maxim, message, motto, noble, point, principled, proverb, pure, righteous, scrupulous, truism, upright, virtuous

moral code, adherence to: integrity, probity, rectitude

moral conduct: ethics

moral conduct, Buddhism: dharma

moral conscience: scruples

moral corruption: baseness, decadence, depravity, dry rot, turpitude

moral decay, in: decadent

moral improvement: edification, enlightenment

moral lapse: sin

moral law that applies to all, unconditional: categorical imperative

moral maxim: precept

moral obligation: duty

moral obligation, study of: deontology

moral or immoral, neither: amoral

moral or religious belief, repudiation of all: anarchism, nihilism

moral principles permitting greater liberty to one over another: double standard

moral restraint, lacking: dissolute, libertine, licentious

moral standards and values, erosion of: anomie

moral truth told in story: exemplum

morale: attitude, confidence, disposition, esprit, esprit de corps, mood, outlook, spirit, state, zeal

morality: ethics, goodness, honor, integrity, mores, principles, righteousness, scruples, standards, uprightness, virtue

morality play role: everyman

moralizing: didactic, pedantic, sententious, trite

moralizing lecture: homily

morally bad: degenerate, noxious, pernicious, pestiferous, pestilent, scrofulous, unsavory

morally good: decent, virtuous

morally instructive: didactic

morally neutral: adiaphorous

morally unrestrained: libertine

morass: bog, fen, marsh, mess, quag, quagmire, snarl, swamp, tangle, wetlands

moratorium: ban, cessation, delay, halt, suspension

morbid: corrosive, dark, diseased, dreadful, gloomy, grim, grisly, gruesome, horrible, malicious, melancholic, morose, painful, pathological, saturnine, sick, sullen, tenchant, unhealthy

mordant: acid, biting, burning, keen, pungent, sarcastic, sharp

more: added, additional, again, also, another, better, else, expanded, extra, further, greater, increased, plus

moreover: additionally, also, and, besides, further, likewise, too, yet

moribund: death, decaying, doomed, dying, fading, obsolete, regressing, terminated

morning: A.M., aurora, cockcrow, dawn, daybreak, forenoon, sunrise, sunup

morning bugle or drum call: reveille

morning moisture: dew

morning or dawn, song about: aubade

morning prayer: ave, matins

morning, in the: antemeridian, matutinal

moron: blockhead, boob, dimwit, dolt, dull, dunce, fool, idiot, ignoramus, imbecile, numskull, stupid, supposition

morose: blue, choleric, churlish, crusty, depressed, dolorous, dour, gloomy, glum, gruff, grum, melancholy, moody, moping, morbid, sad, saturnine, sour, splenetic, sulky, sullen, surly, unhappy

morpheme that retains meaning alone (e.g. cat): free form

morpheme, various forms of a: allomorph

morsel: bit, bite, crub, delicacy, fliver, fragment, mouthful, nibble, piece, scrap, slice, snack, snap, taste, tidbit

mortal: animal, being, conceivable, deadly, deathly, deep, destructive, dire, earthling, extreme, fatal, finite, grave, grim, human, lethal, man, terminal, terrible, unrelenting, woman

mortal blow: coup de grâce

mortality: bloodshed, carnage, death, ephemerality, fatality, humankind

mortar between brick or tiles: grout

mortarboard adornment: tassel

mortar's club-shaped tool: pestle

mortgage: contract, deed, hock, lien, loan, obligation, pawn, pledge, trust

mortgage in installments, to pay: amortize

mortgage on property: lien

mortgage or claim on property: encumbrance

mortgage something, to: hypothecate

mortgaged property, to repossess: foreclose

mortify: humble, torment, shame, humiliate, disgrace, discipline, chagrin, embarrass, humble, humiliate, shame, snerd, torment

mortise insertion: tenon

mortuary: charnel, funeral parlor

mortuary notice: obit, obituary

mosaic: design, diapered, intarsia, patchwork

mosaic piece: tessera, tile

mosaic woodwork style: intarsia

mosaic work: inlay

mosey: amble, linger, ramble, saunter, shuffle, stroll

mosque: church, hall of prayer, masjid, shrine, temple

mosque balcony: maqsura

mosque leader: imam

mosque lectern: kursi, minbar

mosque niche indicating direction to Mecca: mihrab

mosque south wall: giblah

mosque tower: manara, minaret

mosque, person calling others to prayer in: muezzin

mosquito: aedes

mosquito carrying disease-causing microorganisms: vector

mosquito netting fabric: marquisette

mosquito, common: culex

moss: bog, lichen, morass, swamp, treebeard

moss which decomposes into peat: sphagnum

moss, single-celled reproductive body in: spore

moss, study of: bryology

mote: atom, dot, iota, may, might, particle, speck

moth-eaten: decayed, decrepit, worn

moth genus: arctia

moth larva: caterpillar

moth or butterfly: lepidopteran

moth pupa in cocoon: chrysalis

moth relative: butterfly

moth spot: chloasma, fenestra

moth types: clothes, corn earworm, forester, hawk, luna, mattet, miller, silkworm, tinea, tineid

mothball substance: naphthalene

mother: dam, foster, mamma, mater, matron, nurse, nurture, parent, wellspring

mother alligator: cow

mother as head of family: matriarchy

mother as head of household: materfamilias

mother-of-pearl: nacre

mother-of-pearl shellfish: abalone

mother ruling a clan, family, tribe: matriarch

mother, concerning a: maternal

mother, derived from name of: matronymic

mother, different father but same: uterine

mother, looking more like your: matroclinous

mother, murder of: matricide

motherhood: maternity

mothering child for pay, woman: surrogate mother

mother's depression, new: postpartum

mother's side of family: distaff side, enate

mother's side, of descent through: matrilineal

mother's uterus as source of offspring: venter

motif: theme

motion: agitation, gesture, impulse, inclination, move, movement, signal, stir

motion picture advance showing: sneak preview

motion picture art and production: cinematography

motion picture computerized process for black-and-white coloring: colorization

motion picture effect of jumping to later action: jump cut

motion picture effect of still image: freeze frame

motion picture effect of stopping camera while change is made: stop-action, stop-motion

motion picture effect where scene is edged off by next scene: wipe

motion picture fast, blurred shot: flash pan

motion picture–making blackboard with hinged top: clapper

motion picture run of camera or recorder: take

motion picture sequence following for panoramic effect: pan, pan shot

motion picture sequence made by camera or track or dolly: dolly shot, tracking shot, traveling shot

motion picture shot combining live action and fake background: matte shot

motion picture shot with camera following moving object: running shot

motion picture studio cafeteria or lunchroom: commissary

motion picture transfer of recording to another medium: dubbing

motion picture transition fading former scene into new scene: dissolve, lap dissolve

motion picture translated dialogue: subtitle

motion picture with rebirth and discovery: film noir

motion, concerning: kinetic

motion, impetus of body in: élan, momentum

motion, resistance to: inertia

motionless: at rest, breathless, dead, immobile, inert, rigid, sedentary, stagnant, stagnate, static, still, transfixed

motivate: foster, impel, induce, influence, inspire, move, provoke, stimulate, stir

motivation: cause, impetus, incentive, incitement, inducement, influence, stimulus

motive: cause, end, impulse, incentive, object, purpose, reason, sake, spur, stimulus

motive kept secret: ulterior motive

motley: assorted, dappled, diverse, diversified, heterogeneous, hodgepodge, miscellaneous, mixed, mottled, multicolored, pastiche, piebald, pied, varied, varigated

motor: auto, automobile, buggy, car, device, drive, engine, instrument, machine, ride

motor on outside of boat: outboard motor

motor race for skill and speed: autocross

motor types: compound, diesel, electric, rotary, steam, turbine, wankel

motor, stationary part of: stator

motor, turning part of: rotor

motorboat skimming surface at high speed: hydroplane

motorcycle seat for extra rider: pillion

motorcycle, customized: chopper

mottled: blotched, checkered, dappled, diverse, motley, piebald, speckled, splotched, spotted, variegated

mottled in black and white: piebald

motto: adage, aphorism, axiom, byword, catchword, expression, maxim, phrase, precept, proverb, saying, slogan, truism, watchword

motto in beginning of book: epigraph

mound: bank, barrow, bulwark, butt, cairn, dune, elevation, embankment, heap, hill, hump, knoll, mass, mogul, pile, stack, tuffet, tumulus

mound of stones as memorial or marker: cairn

mound over ancient burial: barrow, tumulus

mounds and hills, with: tumulose

mount: advance, ascend, aspire, augment, climb, escalate, frame, grow, hill, increase, intensify, mountain, position, prepare, rise, scale, seat, stage, straddle

mountain: alp, aret, arête, barrow, ben, berg, bundoc, bundocks, butte, chain, cone, crest, dagh, everest, fell, kop, mesa, mont, onlay, orogency, peak, ridge, sawbuck, sierra, spur, summit, volcano

RELATED TERMS

mountain areas, concerning: montane

mountain base: foot, piedmont

mountain climber at end of rope, to secure: belay

mountain climbing: mountaineering

mountain climbing boot spikes: crampons

mountain climbing metal ring for attaching rope to something: carabiner, snap ring

mountain climbing spike: piton

mountain forests: arctice, boreal, coniferous, deciduous, ice pack, low alpine, snow line, temperate, tree line, tropical, tundra

mountain lake, small: tarn

mountain lion: cougar

mountain mass with separate peaks: massif

mountain on sea floor: seamount

mountain or range, lateral ridge projecting from: spur

mountain pass: col, cove, gap, gate, ghat, gorge

mountain peak: pinnacle

mountain peak, sharp pointed: aiguille

mountain-range backbone: massif

mountain reflection: alpenglow

mountain ridge: aret, arête, crest, peak, sawbuck, sierra, spur, summit

mountain run-off: rill

mountain science: orogenesis, orography, orology

mountain sickness: veta

mountain snow: jokul, névé

mountain sport: alpestrian, alpinism

mountain study: orography, orology

mountain valley, steep hollow in: cirque, cwm

MOTOR VEHICLES

ambulance	dragster	hearse	panel truck	station wagon
amphibian	DUKW/duck	hook and ladder	pantechnicon	steamroller
armored car	dump truck	hot rod	pickup truck	stock car
autobus	dune buggy	jalopy	police car	streetcar
automobile	eighteen-wheeler	Jeep	race car/racer/racing	stretch limousine/
beach buggy	fastback	jitney	car	limo
brougham	fire engine	juggarnaut	ragtop	subcompact car
cab	flatbed	limousine/limo	recreation vehicle/	tanker truck
cabriolet	float	lowrider	RV	taxicab
camion	forklift	microbus	rig	touring car
camper	four-by-four/4x4	minibus	roadster	tow truck
caravan	four-door car	minicar	rocket car	town car
cement mixer	garbage truck	minivan	runabout	tractor truck
compact car	go-kart	moon buggy	scrambler	two-door car
convertible	golf cart	motor coach	sedan	utility
coupé	grader	motor home	semitrailer	van
crawler	grand touring car	moving van	six-by-six	victoria ❦
dodgem car	hardtop	off-road vehicle	sports car	
double-decker bus	hatchback	paddy wagon	squad car	

mountain with steep sides and level top: butte

mountain, broad gently sloping base of: pediment

mountain, concerning: alpen, alpestrine, alpine, etiolin, mountainous, orological

mountain, flat-topped submarine: guyot

mountain, lower oneself from: abseil, rappel

mountain, of a steep: precipitous

mountain, steep slope of: escarpment

mountain, steeply projecting mass from: crag

mountaineer shoe plate for ice: crampon

mountaineering descent with rope: rappel

mountains or mountain ranges, chain of: cordillera

mountains, from the far side of the: tramontane, transalpine, ultramontane

mountains, high jagged range of: sierra

mountainside gorge or gully: couloir

mountainside rock pile: scree ❦

mountebank: charlatan, cheat, faker, fraud, hawker, hustler, impostor, phony, pretender, quack, swindler

mounted sentinel in advance of outpost: vedette

mourn: ache, anguish, bemoan, cry, grieve, keen, lament, long, melancholy, regret, rue, sigh, wail, weep, yearn

mournful: depressing, dolorous, elegiac, grievous, lugubrious, plaintive, plangent, sad, saddened, somber, sorry, unhappy, woebegone

mournful sound: groan, moan

mourning: anguish, bereavement, despair, dolor, garb, grieving, sadness

mourning black band: crape

mourning clothes: weeds

mourning song: dirge, elegy, lament, monody, threnody

mourning watch before burial: wake

mouse: murine, rodent, vermin

mouse family: rodent

mousy: bashful, drab, quiet, shy, timid

mouth: aperture, beak, cavity, crevice, crow, delta, entrance, estuary, funnel, gab, kisser, mug, orifice, spokesman, spokeswoman, stoma, voice

mouth and its diseases, branch of medicine concerning: stomatology

mouth cavity or cheeks, concerning the: buccal

mouth of river: embouchure, estuary

mouth or an opening: os

mouth or body opening: orifice

mouth or gullet of animal: maw

mouth organ: harmonica, kazoo

mouth part: alveoli, floor, gums, jaw, lips, pharynx, roof, teeth, tongue, uvula

mouth the words: lip sync

mouth-watering: appealing, appetizing, delicious, inviting, palatable, tasty

mouth, concerning the: oral

mouth, congenital fissure in roof of: cleft palate

mouth, open expanse of: rictus

mouthful: bite, gulp, morsel, piece, portion, taste

mouthlike opening as in nematode: stoma

mouthpiece: adviser, attorney, counselor, lawyer, spokesman, spokesperson, spokeswoman

mouthpiece of wind instrument: embouchure, reed

movable: ambulatory, changeable, detachable, loose, mobile, motile, portable, transportable, unstable, unsteady

movable properties: chattels

move: act, action, advance, affect, alpestrine, alpine, animate, arouse, budge, cause, change, crawl, deed, drift, drive, evacuate, excite, flow, glide, go, goad, huge, impel, incite, induce, influence, inspire, instigate, kindle, lead, leave, migrate, motion, motivate, mountainous, persuade, proceed, prompt, propel, propose, relocate, rouse, rugged, run, shift, spur, start, step, stimulate, stir, stratagem, suggest, sway, touch, transfer, turn, walk

RELATED TERMS

move about: stir

move across: traverse

MOUNTAINS AND MOUNTAIN RANGES

Aconcagua (Argentina)
Adirondack Mountains (United States)
Alaska Range (United States)
Aleutian Range (United States)
Allegheny Mountains (United States)
Alps (France, Switzerland, Italy, Austria)
Andes (South America)
Annapurna I (Nepal)
Annapurna II (Nepal)
Appalachian Mountains (United States)
Ararat (Turkey)
Athos (Greece)
Balkan Range (Bulgaria)
Batian (Kenya)
Ben Nevis (Scotland)
Bighorn Mountains (United States)
Blue Mountains (Jamaica)
Blue Mountains (New South Wales and Australia)
Blue Mountains (Papua New Guinea)
Blue Mountains (United States)
Blue Ridge Mountains (United States)
Bonete (Argentina)
Brazilian Atlantic Coast Range (Brazil)
Broad Peak (Kashmir)
Byachung Kang (Nepal)
Cantabrian Mountains (Spain)
Carmel (Israel)
Carstensz (New Guinea)
Catskill Mountains (United States)
Central New Guinea Range (New Guinea)
Cho Oyo (Nepal)
Communism Peak (Tajikistan)
Cook (New Zealand)
Cordillera de Los Andes (South America)
Cotopaxi (Ecuador)
Dhaulagiri (Nepal)
Duwoni (Uganda)
Eiger (Switzerland)
El Condor (Argentina)
Elbrus (Republic of Georgia)
Ellsworth (Antarctica)
Fuji (Japan)
Gasherbrum (Kashmir)
Golan Heights (Israel)
Gosainthan (Tibet)
Grand Teton (United States)
Granite Peak (United States)
Great Dividing Range (Australia)
Great Smoky Mountains (United States)
Green Mountains (United States)
Gurla Mandhata (Tibet)
Helicon (Greece)
Highlands (Scotland)
Himalayas (South Asia)
Huascaran (Peru)
Hymettus (Greece)

Jagerhorn (Switzerland)
Jongsong Peak (Nepal)
Jungfrau (Switzerland)
K2 or Godwin Austen (Kashmir)
Kanchenjunga (Nepal, Sikkim)
Kilimanjaro (Tanzania)
Kungur (China)
Lebanon Mountains (Lebanon)
Lenin Peak (Tajikistan, Kyrgyzstan)
Lhotse I (Nepal, Tibet)
Lhotse II (Nepal, Tibet)
Libertador (Argentina)
Logan (Yukon)
Makalu (Nepal, Tibet)
Manaslu (Nepal)
Masherbrum (Kashmir)
Matterhorn (Switzerland, Italy)
Mont Blanc (France)
Mount Elbert (United States)
Mount Erebus (Antarctica)
Mount Etna (Sicily)
Mount Everest (Nepal, Tibet)
Mount Hood (United States)
Mount Kirkpatrick (Antarctica)
Mount Kosciusko (Australia)
Mount McKinley (United States)
Mount Mitchell (United States)
Mount of Olives (Israel)
Mount Olympus (Greece)
Mount Ossa (Greece)
Mount Parnassus (Greece)
Mount Rainier (United States)
Mount Rosa (Italy, Switzerland)
Mount Rushmore (United States)
Mount Saint Helens (United States)
Mount Shasta (United States)
Mount Vesuvius (Italy)
Mount Whitney (United States)
Mourne Mountains (Ireland)
Mulhacen (Spain)
Nanga Parbat (Kashmir)
Nuptse (Nepal)
Ojos del Salado (Argentina, Chile)
Olympic Mountains (United States)
Orizaba (Mexico)
Ozark Mountains (United States)
Pikes Peak (United States)
Pissis (Argentina, Chile)
Popocatepetl (Mexico)
Pumasillo (Peru)
Pyramid (Nepal)
Revolution Peak (Tajikistan)
Rocky Mountains (United States)
Sierra Madre (United States and Mexico)
Sierra Nevada Range (Spain)
Sierra Nevada Range (United States)

MOUNTAINS AND MOUNTAIN RANGES *continued*

Snowdon (Wales)	Tupungato (Argentina and Chile)
Snowy Mountains (Australia)	Vinson Massif (Antarctica)
Teide (Canary Islands)	Washington (United States)
Tent Peak (Nepal)	Weisshorn (Switzerland)
Teton Range (United States)	West Sumatran-Javan Range (Sumatra-Java)
Tien Shan (Kyrgyzstan-China)	White Mountains (United States)
Toubaki (Morocco)	Yerupaja (Peru) ❦
Trans-Antarctic Mountains (Antarctica)	

move ahead steadily: forge

move aimlessly: gallivant, maunder, meander, ramble, roam, rove, traipse, wander

move along in easy gait: amble, lope, mosey, saunter

move backward and withdraw: recede

move backward to inferior condition: retrogress

move boat with long pole: punt

move clumsily: lumber

move crablike: sidle

move faster: accelerate

move in a circle: gyre

move in a stream: flow

move in bouncy way: flounce

move in different directions from a point: diverge

move in headlong rush: stampede

move in wavelike motion: undulate

move irregularly at sea: yaw

move like advancing waves: surge

move like clouds: flit, scud

move nimbly: flit

move or go around: circumvent, skirt

move out: evacuate, leave, vacate, withdraw

move quickly: flit, hie, scamper, scurry, skedaddle, spank

move rapidly along surface: skitter

move rapidly and out of control: careen, career

move shakily: dodder

move slightly: budge

move slowly: dawdle, inch, lag, loiter, wade

move smoothly: glide

move sneakily: prowl, sidle, slink

move spontaneously, having the power to: motile, tactic

move swiftly: dart, flit, scud, zip

move swiftly and forcefully: hurtle

move through mud: slosh

move to a new place: relocate

move to gain advantage: gambit

move toward from different points: converge

move toward or downward: gravitate

move up: advance, ascend, boost, climb, hoist, promote, raise

move upward: arise

move with effort: slog

move without lifting feet much: shuffle

move without propelling power: coast

move, animal refusing to: restive

move, market-wise: sell

move, to be unable to: paralyzed ❦

movement: action, activity, campaign, crusade, drive, gesture, locomotion, mobility, motion, rhythm, steps, stirring, trend, unrest

movement by mental powers: psychokinesis, telekinesis

movement of particles suspended in fluid or gas: Brownian motion

movement perceived due to different observational position: parallax

movement toward or away from external stimulus: taxis

movement, concerning: kinetic, motive

movement, expression by body: gesture

movement, forward: headway

movement, graceful and rhythmic: eurythmic

movement, to impede: immobilize

movement, total or partial loss of: apraxia

movie: cine, cinema, film, flick, picture, screen, show

movie award: Oscar

movie theater, squalid: fleapit

movie, low-budget: B movie, B picture

moviemaking: cinematography

moving: affecting, arousing, astir, emotional, exciting, gripping, impressive, inspirational, on the go, pathetic, poignant, provoking, stimulating, stirring, touching

moving about: ambulant, ambulatory

moving in different direction: divergent

moving in emotional way: poignant

moving inward: afferent, centripetal

moving outward: centrifugal, efferent

moving sideways: laterigrade, sidling

moving stairway: escalator

moving water, living in: lotic

moving with grace: agile, flexible, limber, lissome, lithe, supple

mow: clip, crop, cut, heap, lay, level, mass, pile

moxie: backbone, courage, energy, grit, guts, heart, initiative, nerve, skill, spirit, spunk

much: about, abundance, alot, ample, considerable, exceedingly, great, greatly, heaps, loads, lots, many, mire, most, multitude, plenty, quantity, remarkable, scores, sizable, sufficient, uncommon, very

mucilage: adhesive, glue, gum, paste, substance

muck: complicate, dirt, drudge, dung, filth, garbage, goo, gook, gunk, manure, mud, ooze, refuse, sewage, slime, sludge, trash, waste

mucus: slime

mucus coughed up from respiratory tract: sputum

mucus from eyes or nose: rheum

mucus in breathing passages: phlegm

mud: dirt, mire, mush, ooze, roil, silt, slime, sludge, soil

mud or silt deposited by water flow: sullage

mud, depression filled with: slough

muddle: addle, befuddle, bewilder, blunder, boggle, botch, bungle, chaos, complicate, confound, confuse, daze, disorder, embroil, flounder, fluster, fuddle, fumble, humble, mess, mishmash, mismanage, mix,

TYPES OF MURDER

killing without express or implied intent but not necessarily murder: manslaughter
mercy killing: euthanasia
murder by secret government order: executive action
murder done with some planning, of a: premeditated
murder of baby: infanticide
murder of brother: fratricide
murder of father: patricide
murder of god: deicide
murder of king/queen: regicide

murder of mother: matricide
murder of parent: parricide
murder of prominent person: assassinate
murder of self: suicide
murder of sister: sororicide
murder of spouse by spouse: mariticide
murder of wife: uxoricide
murder victims, list of potential: hit list
planned murder: premeditated
ritual murder: hara-kiri, seppuku ❦

---

muddy, muff, obfuscate, obscure, perplex, pother, roil, snafu, snarl, stumble, stupefy, tangle

muddled: bemused, bewildered, cloudy, foggy, fuzzy, incoherent, tipsy, turbid, unorganized

muddy: besmeared, blurred, clouded, cloudy, confused, dirty, drab, filthy, grimy, hazy, miry, mucky, murky, obscure, roil, slushy, soily, spattered, squalid, turbid, unclear, vague

muff: blow, botch, bungle, error, flub, fumble, fur, warmer

muffin, light and hollow: popover

muffle: cushion, dampen, deaden, dull, envelope, hush, lessen, mute, muzzle, shroud, shush, silence, smother, soften, stifle, suppress, wrap

muffler: cover, mask, scarf, silencer

mug handle: ear

mug in shape of man with three-cornered hat: toby

mug or cup, small: noggin

mug with lid: flagon, stein, stoup

mugger: assailant, attacker, crocodile, thief, thug

muggy: clammy, damp, dank, humid, moist, sticky, sweltering

mulch: compost, litter, manure, straw

mulct: balk, cheat, deceive, defraud, fine, fleece, forfeit, penalize, penalty, punish, rook, steal, swindle

mule: burro, crossbreed, donkey, hinny, hybrid, jack, jackass, slipper, spinner

mules, driver of: muleteer

mules, group of: barren, pack, rake, span

mulish: balky, determined, headstrong, intractable, obstinate, ornery, pigheaded, recalcitrant, stubborn

mull: cloth, consider, contemplate,

dawdle, deliberate, loiter, muse, ponder, pore over, powder, reflect, ruminate, think, weigh

mulled beverage: cider

mulled port with oranges, sugar, cloves: bishop

multicolored: checkered, dappled, motley, mottled, particolor, piebald, pied, polychrome, variegated

multifarious: assorted, diverse, heterogeneous, miscellaneous, mixed, motley, multiple, versatile

multilingual: polyglot

multiple: assorted, manifold, many, multifarious, numerous, several, varied

multiplication sequence that works independent of order: commutative

multiply: augment, breed, burgeon, compound, enlarge, grow, increase, magnify, procreate, reproduce, spread

multiply or breed, cause organism to: propagate

multisided figure: polygon

multitalented: versatile

multitude: army, array, bevy, collection, crowd, drove, flock, heap, horde, host, legion, many, mass, mob, myriad, pack, populace, public, scores, sea, swarm, throng

multitudinous: abundant, considerable, countless, crowded, many, numerous, populous, voluminous

mum: mute, silent, speechless, still

mumble: chew, grumble, mouth, murmur, mutter, patter, whisper

mumbo jumbo: baloney, bugaboo, confusion, gibberish, hocus pocus, jargon

mummies, study of: momiology

mummy entrails, jar for: canopic jar

mumps: parotitis

munch: bite, champ, chew, chomp, crunch, eat, grind, masticate

mundane: commonplace, cosmic, everyday, humdrum, ordinary, prosaic, routine, secular, terrestrial, unearthly, worldly

municipal: borough, city, civic, community, town, urban

municipal map: plat

munificent: altruistic, benevolent, bountiful, charitable, free, generous, humanitarian, kindly, lavish, liberal, openhanded, philanthropic

munitions: ammunition, armament, equipment, weapons

murder: asphyxiate, assassinate, butcher, crows, destroy, do in, electrocute, eliminate, execute, exterminate, guillotine, hang, homicide, kill, killing, lynch, manslaughter, massacre, slaughter, slay, strangle, waste

murder, lack of ability to achieve state of mind necessary for: diminished responsibility

murderer: assassin, criminal, executioner, killer, slaughterer, slayer

murderous: arduous, bloodthirsty, bloody, brutal, cruel, deadly, destructive, difficult, ferocious, homicidal, lethal, monicidal, ruinous, savage

murky: ambiguous, black, cheerless, cloudy, dark, dense, dim, dismal, dreary, foggy, fuzzy, gloomy, gray, mirky, misty, muddy, obscure, unclear

murmur: babble, brool, buzz, complain, coo, drone, fret, groan, grumble, hum, moan, mumble, mutter, purr, repine, report, sound, susurration, undertone, utter, whisper

murmuring softly: susurrant

murmuring sound: curr, purl, sough

muscle: beef, brawn, clout, flesh, force, influence, meat, might, power, sinew, strength

MUSCLES OF THE BODY

abdominal
anterior tibial
biceps brachii
biceps femoris
crural ligaments soleus
deltoid
erector
external oblique
extensor
fascia lata
flexor
gastrocnemius
gluteus maximus
gracilis
hamstring
latissimus dorsi
pectoralis major
pectoralis minor
quadriceps
rectus abdominis
rectus femoris
rotator cuff
sartorius
sternomastoid
tendon of Achilles
trapezius
triceps brachii ❦

RELATED TERMS

muscle and bones, branch of surgery
for: orthopedics
muscle condition: tonus
muscle contraction: convulsion
muscle coordination loss: ataxia
muscle fibers, rapid twitching of:
fibrillation
muscle furrow: stria
muscle pain, cramp: myalgia
muscle protein: actin
muscle rigidity or flexibility, extreme: catatonia
muscle rigidity: catalepsy, rigor
muscle strength: brawn
muscle strength measurer: ergometer
muscle to bone, fibrous tissue connecting: tendon
muscle tone: tonicity, tonus
muscle twitching: fibrillation
muscle weakness: atony
muscle, fibrous tissue supporting a:
ligament
muscle, prominent fleshy part of:
vente
muscle, shortening and thickening of
working: contraction

muscles, fibrous connective tissue
holding, separating, or binding:
fascia
muscles, outline of well-developed:
definition
muscles, sense that detects movement of: kinesthesia
muscles, study of: myology ❦

muscular: athletic, brawny, burly, fibrous, hardy, husky, lean, mighty,
powerful, robust, sinewy, stalwart,
strong, thewy, vigorous
muscular contraction: spasm
**muscular contraction against resis-
tance:** isometric
**muscular contraction, intense involun-
tary:** convulsion
muscular contractions, wavelike:
peristalsis
muscular loss: ataxia
musculature of body shown in picture:
ecorche
museum: archive, atheneum, collection, foundation, gallery, institution,
library, repository
museum collection manager: curator
museum exhibit, three-dimensional:
diorama
museum piece: relic
mush: amorousness, cornmeal, crush,
drivel, flattery, goo, journey, march,
porridge, pudding, sentimentality,
slush, travel, trek
mush or mash: pap
mush, cornmeal: polenta
mushroom: cèpe, champignon, chanterelle, fungi, fungus, morel, spore,
toadstool
mushroom caps: pilei
mushroom cap's thin skin: pellicle
mushroom-like edible fungi: truffle
mushroom parts: annulus, basidiospore,
basidium, cap, gill, hymenium, pi-
leus, stem, sterigma, stipe
mushroom poison: amanita, mycetism,
toadstool
mushroom-shaped: fungiform
mushroom species: agaric, champignon, chanterelle, morel
mushroom yielding a dark fluid: inky
cap
mushroom, edible Asian: Chinese black
mushroom, golden oak mushroom,
Oriental black mushroom, shiitake
mushy: corny, gooey, gushy, mawkish,
pulpy, romantic, sentimental, slushy,
soft, spongy, spoony

musical composition: arioso, ballad,
ballade, boutade, cabaletta, cantata,
cento, chanson, concerto, étude,
fugue, glee, interlude, intermezzo,
monody, motet, nocturne, nonet, opera, operetta, opus, oratorio, piece,
prelude, rondo, scherzo, serenade, sonata, sonatas, sonatina, symphony
RELATED TERMS
composition about morning: aubade
composition based on story or ideal:
symphonic poem, tone poem
composition featuring point of technique: étude, study
composition for 1–4 instruments
with 3–4 independent movements:
sonata
composition for full orchestra and
small group of solo instruments:
concerto grosso
composition for gondolier: barcarole
composition for instrument or voice,
written form of: score
composition for instrumental chamber orchestra: divertimento
composition for mass of deceased
person: requiem
composition for orchestra and one or
more solo instruments: concerto
composition for orchestra and solo
instruments: concerto
composition for organ or keyboard
instrument with full composition
for small ensemble, like suite and
sonata: serenade
composition for three unaccompanied males: glee
composition for voices and orchestra
telling sacred story: oratorio
composition improvised on solo instrument: voluntary
composition in 3/4 time: scherzo
composition made up to suit composer's fancy: fantasia, fantasy
composition of choruses, solos, recitatives: cantata
composition of composer, numbered:
opus
composition performed by small
group or quartet: chamber music
composition serving as introduction:
prelude
composition suggestive of rural life:
pastorale
composition telling religious story:
oratorio
composition to perfect a technique:
étude

MUSIC TERMS

12-tone music: dodecaphony

animated: allegro, vivace, vivo

appreciative of music: philharmonic

arrangement of music for performance by orchestra: orchestration

beat: ictus, meter, pulse, rhythm, tempo, time

change from one key or tonality to another by progression: modulation

chord: augmented, diminished, dominant, tonic, triad

combination of parts at same pitch or in octaves: unison

device keeping time: metronome

embellished music: arpeggio, cadenza, flourish, grace note, mordent, roulade, run, trill, turn

exercise: scale

humorous medley of music: quodlibet

instrumental music: concerto, étude, fantasia, fugue, jazz, march, minuet, overture, polka, ragtime, rhapsody, serenade, sonata, suite, swing, symphony, waltz

mark made above or below staff to show notes beyond range: ledger line

melodic phrase: leitmotif, leitmotiv

melodies for two or more voices: polyphony

morning song: aubade

music between stanzas of hymn: interlude

music characterized by trills and runs: coloratura

music dealing with daybreak or sunrise: aubade

music dominated by single melodic line: homophony, monody, monophony

music for eight players: octet

music for five players: quintet

music for four players: quartet

music for nine players: nonet

music for one player: soli, solo

music for seven players: septet

music for six players: sestolet, sextet

music for three players: trio

music for two players: duet, duo

music group: band, choir, chorus, combo, ensemble, orchestra, quartet, symphony, trio

music hall: odeon

music mania: melomania

music or hymn played while clergy enter a church: processional

music or hymn played while clergy exits a church: recessional

music played during the offering of communion: offertory

music syllables (in order): do, re, mi, fa, so, la, ti

music symbols: accidental, alla breve, bar, brace, clef, cleft, fermata, flat, key, ligature, natural, note, presa, rest, segno, sharp, slur, staff, tie, turn

music teacher, composer, conductor: maestro

music that is invented without preparation: improvisation

music timer: metronome

music with two or more independent melodies played together: polyphony

musical: canorous, choral, harmonious, lyrical, melodious, operatic, revue, rhythmic, show, songful, symphonious, tonal

musical accompaniment that is integral: obbligato

musical afterthought: postlude

musical aptitude: ear

musical bell sound: chime

musical break: rest

musical closing: coda

musical composition: anthem, aria, chorale, étude, hymn, madrigal, postlude, psalm, requiem, solo, suite

musical flourish: roulade

nonelectric music: acoustic

passage: coda

popular music of spoken or chanted rhyming lyrics: rap

ragtime music with tinny-sounding piano: honky-tonk

school of music: conservatory

school of music with extreme simplification and trancelike effect: minimalism

showy passage in music: fanfare, flourish

sounds chosen by performer of music: aleatory

stock of music that person or group can perform: repertoire

swelling in loudness: crescendo

vocal music: anthem, aria, ballad, canon, cantata, chanson, chant, chorale, hymn, madrigal, opera, round, serenade ☙

composition with bodily movement, interpreting: eurythmics

composition with choruses, solos, recitatives: cantata

composition with improvisatory style and free form: capriccio

composition with melody repeated in one or more voices overlapping: canon

composition with reiterated harmonic pattern: chaconne, passacaglia

composition with theme occurring three or more times between subordinate themes: rondo

composition with theme repeated contrapuntally: fugue

composition, dreamy instrumental: nocturne

composition, improvisatory: rhapsody

composition, improvised irregular: rhapsody

composition, light orchestral: extravaganza

composition, lullaby: berceuse

composition, short: bagatelle

composition, short movement separating major sections of: intermezzo

composition, short whimsical: arabesque

composition, whimsical: humoresque

composition, words of a: lyrics

compositions: cantatas, études, fugues, sonatas, suites

compositions depicting or defining incident or idea: program music

compositions not defining idea or incident but being solely rhythmic or melodic: absolute music

composition's separation by short movement: intermezzo ☙

musical conductor: maestro

musical counterpoint: descant

MUSIC DIRECTIONS AND NOTATIONS

as written: sta

bass accompaniment: continuo, figured bass, thorough bass, thoroughbass

bold: audace

disconnected: staccato

dying away: calando

emotional: appassionato

evenly: equalmente

excited: agitato, spiritoso

fast: allegro, presto, tostamente, tosto, veloce, vivace, vivo

faster: stretto

for string instruments: tablature, tabs

freely: ad libitum

full time value or sustained: tenuto

gayly: giocoso

gently: dolce

half: mezzo

heavy: pesante

held: tenuto

hurried: agitato

joyous: giocoso

leap: salto

less: meno

little, a: poco

lively: allegro, animato, giocoso, vivace

loud: forte, fortissimo

louder: crescendo

lovingly: amabile, amoroso

majestic: maestoso

moderate: andante, moderato

musical direction dignified: maestoso

muted: sorda, sordo

passionless: freddo

plaintive: dolente, doloroso

playful: giocoso, scherzando

plucked: pizzicato

quick: allegro, presto, schnell, tostamente, tosto, veloce, vite, viva, vivace

quickening: affrettando

repeat: ancoro, bis, segno

repeat a passage, to: bis

repeated: represa

sad: dolente

sadly: doloroso

sharp: sforzando, staccato

silence: tacet

silent: tacet

sliding: glissando

slow: adagio, andante, grave, larghetto, largo, lento, tardo

slowing: rallentando, rit, ritard, ritardando

smooth: dolee, grazioso, legato

soft: dolce, pianissimo, piano

softening: diminuendo

softer: decrescendo

solemn: grave

spirited: animato, spiritoso

stately: maestoso, pomposo

strong: forte, fortissimo

sustained: sostenuto, sustenuto, tenuto

sweet: dolce

tender: amabile ❦

---

musical counterpoint, concerning: contrapuntal

musical instrument, distinctive tone of a: timbre

musical instrument, entire range of a: diapason, register

musical instrumental composition, improvisatory: capriccio

musical material added above or below existing melody: counterpoint

musical passage in rhythm of natural speech: recitative

musical performance, brilliant technique in: bravura

musical production lighter than opera: operetta

musical production or variety show: revue

musical shift of accent in passage or composition: syncopation

musical shift to different key: transposition

musical sound, theory or study of physical properties of: harmonics

musical stringed instrument like zither but with buttons: autoharp

musical study piece: étude

musical style of nonsense words with jazz: scat singing

musical syllables representing tones: solfeggio, solmization

musically unaccompanied: acapella

musician: artist, bard, baritone, cellist, composer, conductor, drummer, entertainer, flutist, guitarist, maestro, minstrel, organist, performer, pianist, piper, player, saxophonist, serenader, singer, soprano, tenor, troubadour, violinist, virtuoso, vocalist

musician with master's ability, technique, style: virtuoso

musician, eminent: maestro

musicians and music publishers, district with many: Tin Pan Alley

musicians, job or performance for: gig

music's metric unit between two bars on staff: measure

music's tonal system consisting of seven tones in fixed relationship: key

musing: absorbed, daydreaming, introspective, meditative, pensive, pondering, reflective, reverie

musket: carbine, firearm, fusil, gun, matchlock, rifle, weapon

muss: chaos, disarrange, dishevel, disorder, disorganize, jumble, mess, ruffle, rumple, shambles, turmoil

must: duty, erato, essential, mold, necessity, need, need to, obligation, ought, prerequisite, requirement, shall, should, stum, want

mustache, bushy drooping: walrus mustache

mustache, long curved: handlebar mustache

mustard gas or other blistering agent: vesicant

mustard plaster: poultice, sinapism

muster: accumulate, amass, assemble, call, collect, congregate, crowd, en-

MUSIC GENRES, VARIETIES, AND STYLES

acid rock	circus music	heavy metal	primitive	semiclassical music
acoustic rock	classical music	hillbilly music	program music	shockabilly
aleatory music	concerto	hip-hop	progressive jazz	show tunes
alternative rock	country-and-western	honky-tonk	progressive rock	ska
ambient music	music	house music	progressive soul	soft rock
anthem	country music	hymn	protest music	soul music
art music	country rock	inspirational music	psychedelic music	soundtrack
art rock	dance hall	instrumental music	psychobilly	spiritual
atonal music or aton-	dance music	jazz	punk rock	stadium rock
alism	deca-rock	jazz rock	punkabilly	steel band
ballet music	Delta blues	karaoke	R&B or rhythm-and-	surf music
ballroom music	disco	Latin rock	blues	swing
baroque music	Dixieland	march	raga-rock	symphony music
beach music	doo-wop	martial music	ragtime	synthesized music
bebop	easy listening music	metal	rap music	synthpop
big band	electronic music	military music	rave	technopop
bluegrass	elevator music	modern jazz	reggae	theater music
blues	ensemble music	Muzak™	rhythm-and-blues or	thirdstream music
boogie	field music	New Age	R&B	thrash metal
boogie-woogie	folk music	new wave	rock-and-roll	through-composed
cabaret	folk rock	opera music	rock music	music
Cajun	funk	operetta music	rock 'n' roll	twelve-tone music or
calypso	fusion	party music	rockabilly	serialism
cathedral music	gangsta rap	piped music	romantic music	vocal music
chamber music	glitter rock	political rock	sacred music	wind music
chant	gospel music	polyphonic music	salon music	Zopf music
choral music	grunge	pop music	salsa	zydeco ❦
church music	hard rock	power pop	scat	

list, gather, generate, invoke, marshal, mobilize, organize, rally, roster, roundup, summon

musty: aged, antiquated, damp, dank, dirty, dull, filthy, mildewed, moldy, rank, rotten, smelly, sour, spoiled, squalid, stale, timeworn, tired, trite

mutable: alterable, changeable, erratic, fickle, fluctuating, inconstant, mercurial, unreliable, vacillating, variable, wavering

mutate: alter, anomaly, change, convert, modify, mutant, mutation, vary

mutation that drastically alters genetic makeup of organism: saltation

mute: deaden, dumb, muffle, mum, muzzle, quiet, silent, soften, speechless, unspoken, voiceless

mute for instrument: sordino

mutilate: batter, butcher, cripple, damage, deface, destroy, disfigure, hack, hurt, injure, lame, maim, mangle, mar

mutilation of legal document: spoliation

mutineer: insurgent, malcontent, radical, rebel, revolter, subversive

mutinous: lawless, disaffected, insubordinate, intractable, rebellious, riotous, seditious, tumultuous, turbulent, uncontrollable, unruly

mutiny: defiance, insurrection, rebellion, resistance, revolt, riot, strife, upheaval, uprising

mutt: dog, mongrel, pooch

mutter: complain, growl, grumble, moan, mumble, murmur, patter, whisper

muttonchops: burnsides, sideburns, whiskers

muttonhead: blockhead, dunce, fool, idiot, stupid

mutual: associated, bilateral, collective, common, interactive, joint, reciprocal, related, shared

mutual reliance: interdependence

muzzle: censure, cork, cover, gag, harness, nose, quiet, repress, restrain, silence, snout, squelch

myopic: astigmatic, blind, blurred, nearsighted, presbyopic, shortsighted

myriad: army, countless, endless, flood, host, innumerable, legion, lots, scores

myrmidon: attendant, cohort, follower, henchman, henchwoman, minion, servant, sycophant

mysterious: abstruse, arcane, cabalistic, concealed, cryptic, curious, dark, enigmatic, esoteric, inexplicable, inscrutable, magical, mystic, occult, puzzling, recondite, runic, secret, strange, supernatural, unfathomable, unknown

mysterious and known to few: arcane, esoteric

mysterious or supernatural: numinous

mysterious, one who is: enigma

mystery: arcanum, cliffhanger, conundrum, craft, enigma, novel, puzzle, riddle, secret, stickler, story, stumper, thriller, trade, whodunit

mystery story: whodunit

mystery with police investigation: police procedural

mystic: cabalistic, cryptic, enigmatic, esoteric, magic, magical, mystical, obscure, occult, paranormal, recondite, secret, seer, sorcerous, spiritual, supernatural, symbolic, visionary, wizardly

mystical: anagogic, arcane, cryptic, esoteric, hermetical, magical, occult, orphic

MUSICAL INSTRUMENTS

Brass Wind Instruments
alpenhorn/alphorn
althorn
ballad horn
baritone horn
bass horn
bombardon
bugle
clarion
cornet
cornopean
double-bell
  euphonium
E-flat horn
euphonium
flugelhorn
French horn
hand horn
helicon
horn
hunting horn
key trumpet
lituus
lur
mellophone
nyas taranga
ophicleide
orchestral horn
pocket trumpet
post horn
sackbut
saxcornet
saxhorn
saxtuba
serpent
slide trombone
sousaphone
tenor horn
tenor tuba
tromba
trombone
trumpet
tuba

Keyboard Instruments
accordion
baby grand
barrel organ
calliope
cembalo
clarichord
clavichord
clavicittern
clavicymbal

clavicytherium
clavier
concert grand
concertina
console piano
digital piano
grand piano
harmonichord
harmonium
harpsichord
hurdy-gurdy
lyrichord
manichord
melodion
melopiano
monochord
organ
pair of virginals
parlor grand
pianette
piano
pianoforte
pipe organ
player piano
reed organ
spinet
square piano
squeezebox
street piano
synthesizer
upright piano
virginal
vocoder

Percussion Instruments
anvil
barrel drum
bass drum
bata
bells
bodhran
bones
bongo
bull roarer
carillon
castanets
celesta/celeste
chime
cimbalom/cymbalom
clappers
claves
conga drums
conical drum
cowbell

cylindrical drum
cymbals
double drum
footed drum
gamelan
glass harmonica
glockenspiel
gong
hackbrett
hand bells
high-hat cymbals
humming top
Jew's harp
jingling Johnny
kazoo
kettledrum
lithophone
maraca
marimba
membranophone
metallophone
musical glasses
musical saw
naker
orchestral bells
pedal drum
peyote drum
rattle
rhythm stick
santir
side drum
sistrum
sleigh bells
slit-drum
snappers
snare drum
spoons
steel drum
tabla
tabor
tam-tam
tambourin
tambourine
tenor drum
thumb piano
thunder stick
timbale
timbrel
timpani
tintinnabula
tom-tom
triangle
Turkish crescent
vibraharp
vibraphone

washboard
wood block
xylophone

String Instruments
acoustic guitar
archlute
autoharp
balalaika
bandore
banjo
banjorine
bass fiddle
bass guitar
bass viol
bouzouki
cello
centerhole guitar
cithara
cittern
classical guitar
concert guitar
contrabass
crowd
double bass
dulcimer
electric guitar
fiddle
gittern
guitar
gutbucket
harp
Hawaiian guitar
Irish harp
kit
kithara
koto
lute
lyre
mando-bass
mando-cello
mandola
mandolin
mandolute
mandore
oud
pandora
pochette
psaltery/psaltry
rebec/rebeck
rote
samisen
sarod/sarode
sitar
Spanish guitar

steel guitar
string bass
tamboura/tambura
theorbo
troubadour fiddle
ukulele/uke
viele
viol
violin
zither

Woodwind Instruments
bagpipe
bass oboe
bassanello
bass clarinet
basset horn
bassoon
bombard
bombardon
clarinet
contrabassoon
double bassoon
English horn
fife
fipple flute
flageolet
flute
hautboy/hautbois/
  oboe
heckelphone
hornpipe
krummhorn/
  crumhorn
musette
nose flute
oaten pipe
oboe/hautboy/
  hautbois
ocarina
Pandean pipe
panpipe
penny whistle
piccolo
pipe
pommer
recorder
saxophone
shawm
syrinx
tabor
tenoroon
whistle ❦

MUSLIM TERMS

annual fast: Ramadan
ascetic: dervish, fakir, fekeer, sufi
call to prayer: azan
cap: kulah, kullah, taj
crusade: jahad, jehad, jihad
expert on Koran: mufti
holy cities: Mecca, Medina
house of worship: masjid, mosque
monastery: khankah, ribat, tekke
mosque: masjid
Muslim: Abadite, Islam, Islamic, Mahometan, Mohamma-
dan, Moor, Moro, Muslim, Mussulman, Paynim, Saracen,

Shiite
Muslim calendar: Jumada, Mulharram, Rabia, Rajab, Ramadan, Safar, Shaban, Shawwal, Zu'lhijah, Zu'lkadah
official summoning faithful to prayer: muezzin
sacred book: Koran, Qur'an
scholar of holy law: mullah
sects: Abadite, Ahmadiya, Dervish, Isawa, Senusi, Shiite,
Sifatite, Sunnite, Wahabi
spiritual guide: pir
student: softa
teacher: alim, imam, mujtahid, mulla, mullah, pir ❦

---

mystical interpretation: anagoge
mystical or secret teachings: cabala
mystify: baffle, bamboozle, befuddle,
confound, confuse, bewilder, muddle, perplex, puzzle, stump
mystifying: cryptic

myth: allegory, fable, fantasy, folklore,
legend, parable, saga, story, tale,
tradition
mythic lamp-dweller: genie
mythical: fabled, fabricated, fictitious,
imaginary, invented, legendary,

unreal
mythical creature, part lion, part eagle:
griffin, gryphon
mythical multiheaded serpent: hydra
**myths explained as being based on real
events:** euhemerism

MYTHOLOGICAL AND LEGENDARY CHARACTERS

abominable snow-man/yeti	blunderbore	Deianira	gnome	King Arthur
Achilles	bogeyman/bogyman/ boogeyman/ boogyman	Diomedes	goblin	King Kong
Adapa		Don Juan	Godzilla	kobold
Adonis	Bragi	Dracula	Gog	Kraken
Aegir	Brobdingnagian	dragondryad/ hamadryad	golem	Kriss Kringle
Aeneas	brownie	Echo	Goliath	Lachesis
afreet/efreet	bugbear	Electra	Gorgon	lamia
Agamemnon	bunyip	Enceladus	gremlin	Lares
Aladdin	Cacus	Erato	Grendel	leprechaun
Ali Baba	Calliope	Euterpe	griffin/gryphon	Leviathan
Alifanfaron	Callisto	Fafnir	Guinevere	Lilith
Amazons	Calypso	Fates	Harpy	Loch Ness monster
Amon	Cassandra	Faust	Hecate	Lorelei
Amphion	Cassiopeia	Ferragus	Hecatoncheires	Magog
amphisbaena	Castor	firedrake	Helen	manticore
Antaeus	Cecrops	Fortuna	Hercules/Heracles	Medusa
Argonauts	centaur	Frankenstein's monster	hippocampus	Melpomene
Argus	Cephalus		hippogriff/ hippogryph	Merlin
Asclepius	Cerberus	Furies/Eumenides/ Erinyes	hobbit	mermaid
Atlas	Charybdis		Hydra	merman
Atropos	Chimera/Chimaera	Galapas	Hyperion	Midas
Azazel	Cinderella	Galatea	Icarus	Midgard serpent
Baba Yaga	Circe	Galligantus	Iris	Mimir
Babe the Blue Ox	Clio	Gargantua	Jack Frost	Minotaur
banshee/banshie	Clotho	genie	Jason	Muses
barghest	Clytemnestra	Geryon	jinni/jinnee/djinni/ djinny	naiad
basilisk	cockatrice	ghost		Narcissus
Beowulf	Cupid	ghoul	John Henry	nereid
Bigfoot/Sasquatch	Cyclops	giant	Jotun	Nibelungs
Blob, the	Daphne	Gigantes	kelpie	Nymphs
				Oceanus

Odnir	Peter Pan	Romulus	siren	vampire
Odysseus	Phoenix	Rumpelstiltskin	Sleeping Beauty	Vidar
Oedipus	Pied Piper	salamander	Sphinx	werewolf
ogre	Pollux	Santa Claus	stork	William Tell
ogress	Polyhymnia	Sasquatch/Bigfoot	Styx	windigo
orc	Polyphemus	Satyr	succubus	witches
oread	Priam	Scheherezade	Titan	wolfman
Orion	Prometheus	Scylla	tooth fairy	wyvern/wivern
Pandora	Puck	sea serpent	Triton	yeti/abominable
Pantagruel	Pygmalion	Siegfried	troll	snowman
Parsifal	Python	simurgh	Typhon	Ymir
Paul Bunyan	Rip Van Winkle	Sinbad	Ulysses	zombie 🐛
Pecos Bill	Robin Hood	Sir Galahad	unicorn	
Pegasus	roc	Sir Lancelot	Urania	

nab: apprehend, arrest, bust, capture, catch, collar, grab, nail, pinch, seize, snatch

nabob: bigwig, deputy, dignitary, governor, magnate, nawab, notable, tycoon, viceroy

nag: ache, aggravate, annoy, badger, berate, bother, fuss, goad, hackney, harangue, harass, harp, heckle, hector, henpeck, horse, importune, irritate, jade, needle, nudge, pester, plug, prod, racehorse, ride, scold, torment, urge

nagging: niggling

naiad: nymph

nail: arrest, capture, catch, collar, detect, expose, seize, trap

nail by bending protruding end, secure a: clinch

nail container: keg

nail file: emery board

nail head: stud

nail in hardware: affix, brad, fasten, fastener, hammer, join, pound, secure, spike, stud, tack

nail of animal: claw, talon

nail or brad without a head: sprig

nail with tiny head, thin: brad

nail, claw, or hoof: unguis

nail, crescent-shaped mark of: cuticle

nail, formative tissue or cells of: matrix

nail, painful dead skin around: hangnail

nail, painful sore around: agnail

nails, flesh under finger-: quick

naive: artless, candid, childish, green, guileless, gullible, inexperienced, ingenuous, innocent, natural, simple, trusting, unaffected, unassuming, unschooled, unsophisticated, unworldly

naive and immature: jejune

naive or innocent girl: ingenue

naïveté, falsely showing: faux-naïf

naked: au naturel, bare, barren, defenseless, disclosed, discovered, disrobed, exposed, manifest, nude, obvious, pure, revealed, stripped, unclad, unclothed, uncovered, undressed, unprotected, vulnerable

namby-pamby: banal, inane, innocuous, insipid, sapless, sentimental, spineless, weak, wishy-washy

name: agnomen, alias, appellation, appoint, baptize, brand, byline, call, celebrity, choose, christen, cite, classify, cognomen, delegate, denomination, deputize, designate, designation, distinction, dub, entitle, epithet, family, handle, headliner, identity, label, moniker, nomenclature, nominate, personage, pseudonym, race, reputation, select, signature, sobriquet, style, tab, tag, term, title

name as different from specific name, common: trivial name, vernacular

name at baptism: christen

name at birth, identifying word for: neé

name before article, writer's: byline

name-calling: revilement

name derived from a thing or place, personal: eponym

name derived from father's side: patronymic

name derived from mother's side: matronymic, metronymic

name derived from place or region: toponym

name for class or group: denomination, designation

name in support of, to lend one's: endorse

name on a check, to write one's: endorse

name only, in: nominal, titular

name or identity, assumed: incognito

name or initials, to have printed with one's: personalize

name or nickname, assumed: sobriquet

name or nickname, personal: moniker

name or surname, family: cognomen

name or title, descriptive substitute for: epithet

name replaced by epithet or title: antonomasia

name spelled backward as pseudonym: ananym

name substituted for another with which it is closely associated: metonymy

name system: nomenclature

name taken by a writer, assumed: allonym

name unknown, condition of having one's: incognito

name used by an author, another: nom de plume, pen name, pseudonym

name, assumed: alias, sobriquet

name, common rather than scientific: vernacular

name, erroneous: misnomer

name, false: alias, nom de guerre, nom de plume, pen name, pseudonym

name, family or last: cognomen, surname

name, fictitious: anonym, nom de guerre, pseudonym

name, first or given: praenomen

name, good: euonym

name, having an unknown or unacknowledged: anonymous, incognito

name, having the same: homonymous

name, historical, assumed by a writer: allonym

name, pet: hypocorism

name, place: toponym

name, preposition used as mark of noble rank before a: nobiliary particle

name, secret: cryptonym

name, substitution of epithet or title for proper: antonomasia

name, taxonomic: tautonym

name, to give a: designate, dub, nominate, style

name, unknown: anonym

name, woman's family: maiden name

nameless: anonymous, incognito, indescribable, innominate, obscure, unknown, unmentionable, untitled

namely: especially, i.e., id est, noted, particularly, sc., scilicet, specifically, that is, that is to say, to wit, videlicet, viz.

nameplate for professional: shingle

names in taxonomy, procedure for assigning: nomenclature

names, concerning: onomastic

names, having two: binomial

names, study of: onomastics, onomatology

naming of journalistic source: attribution

nanny: au pair, caregiver, governess, maidservant, nurse

nap: break, doze, fluff, forty winks, fuzz, nod, pile, pour, respite, rest, shag, shut-eye, siesta, sleep, slumber, snooze, wink

nap-raising device: teasel

nape of neck: nucha, scruff

napery: linens

napkin: cloth, diaper, doily, handcloth, linens, serviette, towel

narcissistic: conceited, egotistical, self-loving, vain, vainglorious

narcotic: anesthetic, anodyne, coca, cocaine, dope, downer, drug, ether, hashish, heroin, hypnotic, junk, LSD, marijuana, medication, morphine, opiate, opium, painkiller, quaalude, sedative, soporific, tranquilizer, valium

narcotic law enforcer: lark, narc

narcotic seller: candy man, dealer, peddler, pusher, source

narrate: characterize, chronicle, depict, describe, detail, discourse, recite, recount, relate, report, spin, state, tell

narrative: account, anecdote, comment, conte, dialogue, epic, episode, history, legend, myth, narration, saga, statement, story, tale

narrative or tale with moral: fable

narrative poem: epic, epos, idyl

narrow: biased, bigoted, close, confining, constrict, cramped, definite, eliminate, hidebound, illiberal, inexorable, inflexible, lessen, limited, little, meager, mean, pinched, prejudiced, reactionary, reduce, restricted, rigid, scant, select, slender, slim, small, sound, strait, strict, taper, tight

narrow and limited: parochial, provincial

narrow board: slat

narrow canyon: gorge

narrow channel: stria

narrow elevated walkway: catwalk

narrow flag: streamer

narrow foyer: hall

narrow furrow: stria

narrow glacial ridge: eskar

narrow inlet: ria

narrow land strip connecting two larger land masses: isthmus

narrow-minded: biased, bigoted, hidebound, inflexible, insular, intolerant, limited, parochial, petty, prejudiced, provincial, sectarian, shallow

narrow-minded teacher: pedant

narrow-mindedness: tunnel vision

narrow opening: slit, slot

narrow piece: strip

narrow space, margin: hairbreadth

narrow street: alley

narrow the eyes: squint

narrower, to become gradually: taper

narrowing of a passage: stenosis

narrowing of passage, abnormal: stricture

narrowly: almost, barely, just, nearly

nasal: rhinal

nasal cavity: sinus

nasal obstruction: adenoid

nasal-sounding: adenoidal, twangy

nastily insinuating: snide

nasty: abominable, awful, cruel, dirty, disgusting, evil, filthy, foul, gross, harmful, hateful, horrible, indecent, loathsome, malicious, mean, nauseating, obscene, offensive, raunchy, repugnant, repulsive, sickening, squalid, ugly, unpleasant, vicious, vile, vulgar, wicked

nation: commonwealth, community, country, land, people, race, republic, sovereignty, state, territory, tribe, union

nation uncommitted to superpower: neutral nation, nonaligned nation

national: citizen, countrywide, domestic, ethnic, federal, nationwide, political, public

nations advocating intermediate position: third force

nation's desire to reduce tensions with former rival: détente

nation's goods and services: GNP, gross national product

nation's recognition of another's laws and institutions: comity of nations

native: aboriginal, autochthonous, citizen, congenital, constitutional, domestic, endemic, inborn, inbred, indigene, ingrained, inhabitant, inherent, innate, local, natal, natural, original, regional, resident

native country: fatherland, motherland

native language: vernacular

native of one country who resides in another country: expatriate

native or originating where found: aboriginal, autochthonous, enchorial, indigenous

native to area or people: endemic

natty: chic, dapper, fashionable, neat, posh, smart, spruce, tidy, trim

natural: accepted, anticipated, artless, candid, common, congenital, easy, expected, general, genuine, illegitimate, inborn, inbred, inherent, innate, instinctive, intuitive, naive, native, normal, open, organic, plain, primitive, pure, regular, rustic, sincere, unaffected, unrefined

natural and healthful: holistic

natural and rough: agrestic

natural and unrefined: earthy

natural attraction: affinity

natural attribute: appanage

natural environment of organism: habitat

natural from birth: inborn, innate, native

natural gift or ability: endowment

natural good qualities: cardinal virtues

natural inclination, arising from: spontaneous, unrehearsed

natural resources, controlled use and protection of: conservation

natural resources, reduction of: depletion

natural response to stimulus: instinct

naturalize: acclimatize, accustom, adapt, adopt, character, conform, disposition, essence, kind, nature, sort, structure, temperament, type, universe

nature: attributes, category, constitution, environment, makeup, outdoors, property, quality, style

NAVY RANKS

Commissioned Officers
Fleet Admiral
Admiral
Vice Admiral
Rear Admiral (upper half)
Rear Admiral (lower half) (Commodore is part of Rear Admiral lower half)
Captain
Commander
Lieutenant Commander
Lieutenant
Lieutenant Junior Grade
Ensign

Warrant Officers
Chief Warrant Officer (W-4)
Chief Warrant Officer (W-3)
Chief Warrant Officer (W-2)

Enlisted Personnel
Master Chief Petty Officer of the Navy
Master Chief Petty Officer
Senior Chief Petty Officer
Chief Petty Officer
Petty Officer First Class
Petty Officer Second Class
Petty Officer Third Class
Seaman; Airman; Fireman
Seaman Apprentice; Airman Apprentice; Fireman Apprentice
Seaman Recruit ❦

---

nature area for wildlife: sanctuary

nature, purposeful development in: teleology

nature, to relate closely as with: commune

nature's influences on an organism's development: nurture

naught: cipher, insignificant, nonexistence, nothing, useless, worthless, zero, zilch

naughty: bad, disobedient, disorderly, evil, fiendish, immoral, improper, lewd, mischievous, obscene, playful, unruly, vulgar, wayward, wicket

naughty or difficult: incorrigible

nausea: disgust, dizziness, hatred, loathing, queasiness, revulsion, sickness, vomiting

nauseate: bother, disgust, loathe, repel, revolt, sicken, upset

nauseated: queasy, seasick, sick

nauseated easily: prudish, squeamish

nauseating: disgusting, distasteful, fulsome, loathsome, offensive, qualmish, repugnant, sickening

nautical: aquatic, marine, maritime, Naval, oceanic, pelagic, seafaring

nautical acknowledgment: aye, aye

nautical direction: abeam, aft, alee, aport, leeside

nautical guy line: stay

nautical man: bosun, salt

nautical measure: fathom, knot

nautical mop: swab

nautical rope: lanyard

nautical signaling flag: Blue Peter

nautical whistle: boatswain's whistle

naval detection method: sonar

naval fleet, small: detachment, flotilla, squadron

naval jail: brig

naval petty officer with clerical duties: yeoman

naval petty officer with navigation duties: quartermaster

nave: body, center, core, hub, middle

navel: omphalos, umbilicus

navel, contemplation of one's: omphaloskepsis

navigate: cruise, direct, guide, journey, keel, maneuver, operate, pilot, sail, steer

navigation: nautics, piloting, sailing, seamanship, shipping, traveling, voyaging, yachting

navigation aid: loran, radar, sextant

navigation based on position estimates, not based on celestial bodies: dead reckoning

navigation based on the positions of celestial bodies: astronavigation, celestial navigation

navigation by the horizon or landmarks, aircraft: contact flight, contact flying

navigational instrument measuring celestial bodies: astrolabe, sextant

navigator: airman, aviator, copilot, explorer, mariner, pilot, sailor, seaman

navy: armada, fleet, flotilla

nay: against, denial, deny, moreover, negative, no, not, refuse

ne'er-do-well: bum, idler, incompetent, loafer, loser, shiftless, wastrel, worthless

near: about, adjacent, advance, almost, alongside, approach, approaching, approximately, around, beside, circa, close, close in on, contiguous, convenient, dear, handy, immediate, imminent, intimate, looming, neighboring, nigh, rival, similar, touch, vicinal

near future, in the: imminent, impending

near in space or relationship: vicinity

near or next to: abutting, adjacent, adjoining, contiguous, verging on

nearby: about, accessible, adjacent, close, convenient, handy, in close, nigh

nearly: almost, circa, roughly, virtually, well-nigh, within an inch of

nearness: contiguity, propinquity, proximity

nearsighted: astigmatic, myopic, shortsighted

neat: adroit, clean, clever, concise, dapper, dexterous, exact, exciting, great, immaculate, kempt, meticulous, natty, nice, nifty, orderly, organized, precise, prim, pure, refined, shipshape, skillful, spick-and-span, spotless, spruce, swell, tidy, tosh, trig, trim, uncluttered, undiluted

neat and compulsive: anal-retentive

nebula: galaxy, nimbus, vapor

nebulous: ambiguous, cloudy, foggy, hazy, indefinite, indistinct, misty, murky, obscure, uncertain, unclear, vague

necessarily: accordingly, certainly, indubitably, inevitably, naturally, perforce, unavoidably, undoubtedly

necessary: crucial, essential, fundamental, imperative, important, indispensable, inevitable, integral, mandatory, needed, paramount, required, requisite, unavoidable, vital

necessary and essential: inherent, integral, intrinsic

necessary and required: binding, compulsory, de rigueur, imperative, incumbent, indispensable, inescapable, mandatory, obligatory, statutory

necessary changes have been made: mutatis mutandis

necessary consequence or accompaniment, to have as: entail

necessary element or condition: prerequisite, sine qua non

necessary means for existing: subsistence

necessary, something considered: desideratum

necessitate: command, compel, demand, entail, force, impel, oblige, require

necessity: clothing, essential, food, must, need, prerequisite, requirement, shelter, want, water

neck: cape, cervix, collar, column, isthmus, nape, scruff, strait

neck arteries: carotid

neck cloth off back of hat: havelock

neck enlargement, noncancerous: goiter, struma

neck feather: hackle

neck injury caused by abrupt jerking: whiplash

neck muscle contraction, unnatural: torticollis, wryneck

neck or neck-shaped anatomical structure: cervix

neck-related: cervical, napal

neck sinking into shoulders, look of: hunksit

neck, back of: nape, nucha, scruff

neck, loose skin hanging from: dewlap

neck, wrinkled skin of: wattle

neckerchief: bandanna, handkerchief, kerchief, scarf

necklace: band, beads, carcanet, chain, choker, collar, jewelry, locket, pearls, pendant, rivière, rope, torque

necklace of twisted metal: torque

necklace with pendant and long chain: lavaliere

necklace worn on throat: choker

necklace, jewelry attached to: pendant

neckline, low, of dress: décolletage

necktie: ascot, band, bolo tie, bow tie, clip-on tie, cravat, foulard, four-in-hand, string tie

necktie cord with clasp: bolo tie

necktie in bowknot: bow tie

necktie made of scarf: cravat

necktie with simple slip knot: four-in-hand

necktie with wide simple slip knot: Windsor

necrology: obituary

necromancy: conjuration, enchantment, goety, magic, sorcery, thaumaturgy, witchcraft, wizardry

necropolis: boneyard, cemetery, graveyard

nectar: ambrosia, amrita, drink, honey, wine

née: born

need: compulsion, crave, demand, dependence, desire, distress, emergency, essential, exigency, extremity, hanker, hunger, lack, longing, must, necessity, obligation, pinch, poverty, require, requirement, requisite, shortage, thirst, urgency, want, weakness, yearn

needle: annoy, badger, bother, get at, goad, harass, irk, prod, provoke, ride, taunt, tease, twit

needle case: etui

needle hole: eye

needle injected beneath skin, of a: hypodermic

needle-pricking medical procedure: acupuncture

needle-shaped: acerate, acerose, aculeate

needle-shaped drill or mountain peak: aiguille

needle, phonograph: stylus

needle, phonograph arm holding: tone arm

needlelike part or structure: acicula

needless: excessive, gratuitous, inessential, pointless, superfluous, unnecessary, useless

needlework: appliqué, crochet, embroidery, knitting, quilting, sampler, sewing, stitching, tatting

needlework frame, wooden: tambour

needlework made by looping thread with hooked needle: crochet

needlework on canvas, decorative: needlepoint

needy: destitute, disadvantaged, down and out, impoverished, indigent, penniless, poor

nefarious: atrocious, base, corrupt, depraved, despicable, detestable, evil, gross, heinous, horrible, infamous, miscreant, rank, rotten, sinful, treacherous, vicious, vile, villainous, wicked

negate: abolish, annul, deny, gainsay, impugn, invalidate, nullify, quash, repudiate, retract, revoke, undo, veto

negative: adverse, blank, contradict, detrimental, film, minus, nay, neutral, nil, not, pessimistic, resisting, skeptical, unfavorable, veto

negatively charged atom: anion

neglect: abandon, bypass, carelessness, default, discount, disregard, fail, failure, fault, forget, ignore, inattention, laxity, omission, omit, overlook, oversight, pretermit, reject, shirk, slight, slip

neglect to fulfill obligation: default, dereliction, laches, nonfeasance

neglected: dilapidated, untended

neglected condition: desuetude

neglectful: careless, heedless, inattentive, remiss, slack, thoughtless, unmindful, unwatchful

negligee: camisole, kimono, nightgown, nightie, peignoir, robe

negligence: laxity, laxness

negligent: careless, delinquent, derelict, forgetful, heedless, inattentive, inconsiderate, indifferent, lax, remiss, slack, slipshod, thoughtless

negligent, heedless: careless

negligible: insignificant, minute, piddling, remote, slim, small, trifling

negotiate: arrange, bargain, barter, contract, deal, debate, dicker, discuss, haggle, hurdle, manage, settle, surmount, transact, traverse, treat

negotiation: compromise, deal, mediation, treaty

negotiation between employer and representatives of organized workers: collective bargaining

negotiation with hard bargaining: horse-trading

negotiations, final statement of terms in: ultimatum

neigh: nicker, whinny

neighbor: abut, address, adjoin, border, friend, nearby, touch, verge

neighborhood: area, block, community, district, environs, locality, parish, precincts, region, section, street, suburb, turf, vicinity, zone

neighboring: vicinal

neighborly: amicable, civil, cordial, friendly, helpful, hospitable, kind, polite, sociable

nemesis: antagonist, avenger, bane, destruction, downfall, enemy, opponent, rival

neophyte: beginner, catechumen, convert, greenhorn, learner, newcomer, novice, proselyte, rookie, student, tiro, trainee, tyro

nepenthe: drug, narcotic, opiate

nephritic: renal

Neptune god of: sea

Neptune planet order: eighth

Neptune's spear: trident

nerd: creep, drip, misfit, oaf, sap, twerp

Nero killed: Agrippina, Lucan, Octavia, Seneca

Nero's kingdom: Rome

Nero's mother: Agrippina

Nero's successor: Galba

Nero's wife: Octavia, Poppaea

nerve: audacity, backbone, boldness, brass, bravery, brazenness, coolness, courage, daring, effrontery, encourage, energy, fearlessness, fortitude, gall, gameness, grit, guts, hardihood, heart, moxie, pluck, presumption, spirit, spunk, stamina, strength, temerity, tendon, vigor

RELATED TERMS

nerve cell: neuron

nerve cell process: axon

nerve cells forming nerve center, group of: ganglion

nerve ending carrying impulse to organ: effector

nerve ending responding to stimuli: receptor

nerve fibers, bundle of: fascicle, fasciculus

nerve fibers, starlike bundle of: peduncle

nerve inflammation: neuritis

nerve network: rete

nerve networks: retia

nerve sensing pain, pressure, heat, cold: protopathic

nerve sensing touch, temperature intensity: epicritic

nerve, cranial: abducens, facial, glossopharyngeal, hypoglossal, oculomotor, olfactory, optic, statoacoustic, trigeminal, trochlear, vagus

nerveless: calm, collected, controlled, cool, cowardly, dead, fearful, inert, powerless, spineless, spiritless, weak

nerves: jitters

nerves carrying impulses from brain or spinal cord: deferent, efferent

nerves carrying impulses to brain or spinal cord: afferent

nerves, network of: plexus ❦

nervous: anxious, apprehensive, concerned, edgy, excitable, fearful, fidgety, jittery, jumpy, nervy, neurotic, querulous, sensitive, shaky, skittish, tense, touchy, unstrung, upset, uptight

nervous and upset: fraught, overwrought

nervous disorder like a phobia, mania, depression: neurosis

nervous disorder with fatigue, memory loss: neurasthenia

nervous disorder with irregular and uncontrollable muscle movement: chorea

nervous excitement: agitation, dither

nervous feeling: butterflies

nervous one: fidgeter, fraidcat

nervous sign: tic, twitch

nervous system: brachial, cervical, coccygeal, digital, femoral, intercostal, lumbar, mandibular, maxillary, median, ophthalmic, peroneal, radial, sacral, sciatic, thoracic, tibial, ulnar

RELATED TERMS

nervous system or a nerve, of the: neural

nervous system parts reducing digestive secretions, speeding the heart, contracting blood vessels: sympathetic nervous system

nervous system parts regulating involuntary actions: autonomic nervous system

nervous system parts stimulating digestive secretions, slowing the heart, dilating blood vessels: parasympathetic nervous system

nervous system, brain and spinal cord of: central nervous system

nervous system, parts not including brain and spinal cord of: peripheral nervous system

nervous system, study of: neurology ❦

nervous unease, of: fretful, high-strung, jittery

nervously excited: fevered, overwrought

nervously move: fidget

nervousness: anxiety, heebie-jeebies, jitters, willies

nervousness, hormone secreted in response to: adrenaline, epinephrine

nervousness, in a state of: anxious, on tenterhooks

nervy: bold, brash, brazen, cheeky, gutsy, impudent

nest: abode, aerie, aery, brook, cave, den, eyrie, fit, group, hive, home, hount, lair, nide, nidus, swarm

nest just after hatching, leaving the: nidifugous

nest of bird in high place: aerie, eyrie

nest of boxes: inro

nest of insect, spider: nidus

nest of predatory bird, high: aerie

nest until ready to fly, staying in: nidicolous

nest, to build a: nidify

nestle: bundle, caress, cuddle, embed, embrace, lodge, nuzzle, shelter, snuggle

NERVE PAIRS

first pair of cranial: olfactory nerve

second pair of cranial: optic nerve

third pair of cranial: oculomotor nerve

fourth pair of cranial: trochlear nerve

fifth pair of cranial: trigeminal nerve

sixth pair of cranial: abducens nerve

seventh pair of cranial: facial nerve

eighth pair of cranial: statoacoustic nerve

ninth pair of cranial: glossopharyngeal nerve

tenth pair of cranial: vagus nerve

eleventh pair of cranial: accessory nerve

twelfth pair of cranial: hypoglossal nerve ❦

net: bag, capture, catch, ensnare, entangle, entrap, hook, lace, mesh, network, reticulum, seine, seize, trap, trim, web

net in money, to: clear, gain, make, profit, realize, take, yield

net or mesh foundation for lace: reseau

net or network, open spaces in: interstice, mesh

net profit: bottom line

net type: drift, drop, gill, grawl, keep, landing, seine, snood, trammel

net, large fishing: seine

net, three-layer fishing: trammel

net, to entangle or catch in: enmesh

nether: below, beneath, inferior, lower, under

Netherlands people: Dutch, Flemish, Frisian, Hollander

netlike: cancellate, cancellous, lacy, reticular, reticulate, retiform

netlike cap worn on hair: snood

nettle: agitate, aire, annoy, bother, fret, irk, irritate, peeve, pique, provoke, rile, ruffle, splice, trouble, upset, vex

network: chain, circuitry, grid, labyrinth, matrix, maze, mesh, nexus, organization, plexus, reseau, rete, reticulation, reticulum, structure, system, web

network or grid: reticle, reticule

neurotic: anxious, compulsive, erratic, nervous, obsessive, unstable, uptight

neurotic anxiety: angst

neurotic condition: inferiority complex, insecurity

neuter: alter, asexual, balanced, castrate, detached, disinterested, expressionless, fix, flat, impartial, intransitive, neuter, neutral, nonpartisan, objective, spay, sterilize, unallied, unbiased, undecided

neutral: achromatic, colorless, gray, indifferent, nonaligned

neutral and sexless: epicene, neuter

neutral person working out dispute: arbitrator, go-between, intermediary, ombudsman

neutralize: abrogate, annul, balance, block, cancel, counteract, frustrate, negate, nullify, offset, stop, undo

never-ending: constant, continual, eternal, everlasting, immortal, infinite, lasting, perpetual, unceasing, uninterrupted

nevertheless: although, anyhow, but, however, howsoever, notwithstanding, regardless, still, tho, though, withal, yet

new: additional, contemporary, current, fresh, green, improved, inexperienced, latest, modern, novel, original, rebuilt, recent, regenerated, remodeled, renovated, restored, revived, unaccustomed, unexplored, unfamiliar, untested, untried, unused

new and fresh: novel, vernal

new and modern: neoteric

new and primitive: pristine

new birth: rebirth, renascence

new word, expression, usage: neologism

newborn child: neonate

newcomer: baby, beginner, fledgling, greenhorn, immigrant, neophyte, novice, rookie, settler, tenderfoot, tyro, upstart

newcomer to organization: initiate

newcomer to success, ambitious: arriviste

newcomer to wealth, power, importance: nouveau riche, parvenu, upstart

newfangled: contemporary, fresh, latest, modern, novel, stylish, unique

newly conceived: nascent

newly introduced element: innovation

newly made: in mint condition

newly rich: nouveau riche, parvenu

news: account, announcement, bulletin, canard, communique, description, dirt, dispatch, flash, gossip, information, intelligence, lowdown, poop, release, report, revelation, scoop, tidings, word

news correspondent, freelance: stringer

news of current interest, of: topical

news story gotten by luck or initiative: exclusive, scoop

news story, misleading: canard

news summary: update, wrapup

news, journalism that exaggerates and distorts: yellow journalism

newsmonger: busybody, gossip, reporter, tabloid, tattler

newspaper: biweekly, community, daily, gazette, herald, journal, metropolitan, periodical, publication, sheet, tabloid, weekly

newspaper archive: morgue

newspaper headline across width of page: banner, streamer

newspaper late-night shift: lobster shift

newspaper list of staff, circulation: masthead

newspaper section with light entertainment (Europe): feuilleton

newspaper with sensational stories, small-format: tabloid

newspapers sold or distributed, number of: circulation

newspapers, the selling of features, comic strips, etc. for publication in range of: syndication

newsprint, large continuous roll of: web

next: adjoining, after, behind, closest, ensuing, following, immediate, nearest, proximate, subsequently, succeeding, then

next to: abutting, adjacent, adjoining, almost, alongside, beside, bordering, contiguous, juxtaposed, neighboring, practically, side by side, tangential

next to last: penult, penultimate

next to nothing or worthless: ambsace

next to the last syllable is acutely accented: paroxytons

nexus: bond, center, connection, core, link, network, tie, union

nibble: bite, chew, crumb, eat, gnaw, morsel, peck, snack, speck

nice: accurate, agreeable, appealing, charming, choosy, considerate, cordial, correct, courteous, dainty, decent, delicate, delightful, discerning, elegant, exact, exacting, exquisite, fastidious, fine, finical, friendly, fussy, genteel, gentle, good, gratifying, helpful, likable, lovely, particular, peachy, picky, pleasant, pleasing, polite, precious, precise, profligate, proper, refined, respectable, skillful, subtle, swell, wanton, warmhearted

niche: alcove, apse, corner, cranny, cubbyhole, hollow, nook, place, recess, retreat, slot, space

nick: chip, cut, dent, dint, indentation, mark, notch, scratch, slit

nickname: agname, agnomen, andy, byword, cognomen, handle, label, len, minicker, moniker, sobriquet, tag

nickname, descriptive: cognomen, epithet

nickname, humorous: sobriquet

nifty: cool, excellent, fashionable, marvelous, natty, neat, peachy, sharp, smart, stylish, super, swell, terrific

niggard: avaricious, cheap, closefisted, mean, miser, miserly, niggardly, scanty, scrimper, skinflint, stingy, tight

niggardly: frugal, greedy, grudging, meager

niggling: finicky, fussy, petty, picayune, trifling

nigh: about, adjacent, almost, beside, close, near, nearly, neighboring, practically

night: bedtime, darkness, dusk, evening, sundown, twilight

night and day of equal length: equinox

night before: eve

night blindness: nyctalopia

night person: owl

night-sky streaks in northern hemisphere: aurora borealis, northern lights

night watch over body before burial: wake

night, concerning: nocturnal

night, deadline to be inside at: curfew

nightclub: bar, boîte, cabaret, cafe, copa, disco, discotheque, honky-tonk, hot spot, spot, tavern

nightclub female singer: chanteuse

nightclub with recorded music: discotheque

nightdress: negligee, nightgown, peignoir

nightfall: dusk, eve, evening, gloaming, sundown, sunset, twilight

nightingale: florence, philomel, songbird, thrush, warbler

nightmare: apprehension, demon, dream, fancy, fiend, horror, incubus, spirit, succubus, vision

nightstick: baton, billy, bludgeon, club, cudgel, staff

nihilism: anarchy, antheism, chaos, disorder, lawlessness, renunciation, repudiation, skepticism

nil: naught, nihil, nonexistent, nothing, zero

nimble: active, adroit, agile, alert, brisk, clever, deft, dexterous, fleet, limber, lithe, lively, quick, spry, swift

nimbus: atmosphere, aura, aureole, cloud, halo, vapor

nincompoop: ass, blockhead, boob, clod, fool, idiot, imbecile, jerk, lummox, moron, ninny, nitwit, simpleton

nine days of prayer for Catholics: novena

nine inches: span

ninefold: nonuple, novenary

ninepin: skittle

ninety to ninety-nine years old, from: nonagenarian

ninth day before the ides: nones

ninth hour: none

nip: bite, blast, check, chill, clip, compress, curtail, cut, dart, dash, dram, drink, hurry, morsel, pinch, remove, sever, shot, sip, snag, snatch, snort, squeeze, steal, sting, stop, thwart, twitch

nipper: biter, boy, child, lad, youngster

nipple: mamilla, pap, teat

nipple coverings for showgirls: pasties

nipple dark circle: areola

nippy: biting, brisk, chilly, cold, crisp, cutting, freezing, sharp

nirvana: bliss, compassion, condition, emancipation, harmony, joy, paradise, seventh heaven, stability, wisdom

nitid: bright, glossy, glowing, lustrous, radiant, resplendent, shiny, spruce

nitpick: carp, cavil, criticize, quibble

nitpicking: captious, hairsplitting

nitrogen, concerning: azotic

nitty-gritty: brass tacks, crux, essence, essentials, heart, lowdown, meat

nitwit: blockhead, bonehead, coot, dolt, dope, dunce, fool, idiot, imbecile, nincompoop, ninny, oaf, pinhead, simpleton

nix: forbid, no, nothing, refusal, sprite, veto

no: any, denial, disagree, naw, nay, negative, never, nix, not, refusal, veto

no-nonsense: businesslike, demanding, direct, efficient, grave, hard, practical, rigid, serious, stern, strict

nobility: aristocracy, dignity, eminence, exaltedness, integrity, magnanimity, peerage, peers, prestige, royalty

noble: aristocratic, august, cavalier, dignified, distinguished, elevated, eminent, epical, ethical, exalted, excellent, fine, free, gallant, generous, good, grand, grandiose, heroic, honorable, ideal, idealistic, illustrious, imperial, just, kingly, lofty, lordly, magnanimous, majestic, moral, peer, peeress, precious, princely, principled, proud, pure, pureblooded, queenly, regal, renowned, righteous, splendid, stately, sterling, sublime, venerated, worthy

noble in mind and heart: magnanimous

noble or distinguished: distingué, majestic, stately, sterling

noble title or rank, person without: commoner

noble, grand: baronial

nobleman: archduke, aristocrat, baron, baronet, count, duke, earl, emperor, gentleman, grandee, knight, lord, magnifico, marquis, patrician, peer, prince, valet, viscount

nobleman below duke but above earl and count: marquess, marquis

nobleman or prince, Anglo-Saxon: atheling

nobleman, German medieval: burgrave

nobleman, high Russian: boyar

nobleman, highest Spanish or Portuguese: grandee

nobleman, lower French: chevalier

nobleman, lower Spanish: hidalgo

nobleman, medieval German: landgrave

noblewoman: archduchess, baroness, contessa, countess, duchess, empress, gentlewoman, lady, marquise, marquises, princess, queen

nobody: cipher, jackstraw, nonentity, pipsqueak, punk, scrub, upstart

noctambulism: sleepwalking, somnambulism

nocturnal: night, nightly, nighttime

nocuous: damaging, dangerous, deadly, harmful, injurious, noxious

nod: acceptance, acknowledge, agree, approval, beckon, bend, bow, doze, drift, drowse, gesture, greeting, motion, salute, signal, signify, sleep, yes

nodding, head: nutation

node: bump, complication, dilemma, granule, growth, joint, knob, knot, lump, nodule, point, protuberance, swelling

nodose: lumpy

noel: carol, yuletide

noggin: cup, dome, head, mug, noddle, pate

noise: babel, bang, blare, blast, boom, bruit, clamor, commotion, din, explosion, fanfare, fuss, gossip, hubbub, pandemonium, racket, shouting, sound, talk, thunder, uproar, yelling

noise-absorber: baffle, muffler

noise like snoring, coarse rattling: rhonchus

noise measure: decibel

noise of crashing waves: plangent

noise of crickets: stridulation

noise of great crowd: tumult

noise, crackling popping: crepitation

noise, discordant: cacophony, discord, dissonance

noise, gradual decrease in: decrescendo, diminuendo

noise, gradual increase in: crescendo

noise, grating shrill: stridor

noise, loud sustained: clamor, hubbub, racket

noise, loud wailing: keening, ululation

noise, metal tinkling: jangle, tintinnabulation

noise, murmuring rustling: froufrou, purl, sough, susurration

noise, repeated clanging: clangor

noise, repeated echoing: reverberation

noise, shrill: stridor

noise, shrill clear: clarion

noise, to interrupt a: stifle

noiseless: deadened, hushed, inaudible, mute, quiet, silent, still

noisemaker: baneful, bell, clapper, dangerous, distasteful, horn, nasty, noisome, noxious, putrid, rancid, rank, rattle, repulsive, revolting, vile, whistle

noisome: destructive, disgusting, fetid, foul, harmful, hurtful, offensive, pernicious, stinking, unwholesome

noisy: aroar, blatant, boisterous, clamorous, clattery, deafening, lively, loud, rackety, rambunctious, screaming, squeaky, thunderous, tumultuous, turbulent, uproarious, vociferous

noisy and exuberant: boisterous, rumbustious

noisy and harsh-sounding: blaring, grating, jarring, raucous

noisy and vehement: clamorous, strident, vociferous

noisy argument, to have: caterwaul

noisy breath: rale

noisy celebration: revelry

noisy celebration for newlyweds: charivari, shivaree

noisy commotion: tumult

noisy confusion: babel, bedlam, fracas

noisy dance: stomp, tap

noisy disturbance: brouhaha, commotion, furor, hullabaloo, riot, ruckus, ruction, rumpus

noisy fray: riot

noisy laughing: cachinnation

noisy mock serenade: charivari, shivaree

noisy place: babel, bedlam

noisy salute: salvo

noisy scene: havoc, mayhem, pandemonium

noisy sleeper: snorer

noisy, extremely: stentorian

noisy, making loud sounds: clamorous

nom de plume: alias, elia, pen name, pseudonym

nomad: Arab, Bedouin, itinerant, migrant, roamer, rover, roving, vagabond, wanderer

nomadic: drifting, itinerant, migratory, peripatetic, traveling, wandering

nomenclature: appellation, catalogue, classification, designate, designation, glossary, language, list, name, taxonomy, terminology, vocabulary

nominal: formal, inexpensive, insignificant, mere, minimal, ostensible, professed, small, supposed, titular

nominate: appoint, call, choose, designate, elect, name, offer, propose, select, slate, specify, submit, tap

nominee: applicant, candidate, hopeful

non compos mentis: demented, deranged, incompetent, insane, not of sound mind

nonage: childhood, immaturity, infancy, youth

nonalcoholic drinks: mocktails

nonappearance excuses in British law: essoins

nonbeliever: agnostic, atheist, doubter, heathen, infidel, pagan, skeptic, unbeliever

nonchalant: airy, blasé, calm, careless, causal, collected, cool, easy, easygoing, imperturbable, indifferent, lethargic, offhand, unemotional

noncommittal: ambiguous, evasive, indecisive, indefinite, middle of the road, neutral, reserved, tentative, vague

noncompliant: belligerent, disobedient, rebellious, stubborn, unorthodox, unruly

nonconformist: beatnik, bohemian, dissenter, dropout, eccentric, hippie, maverick, oddball, orthodox, radical, rebel, recusant, renegade, weirdo

nonconformity: anomaly, disbelief, discordance, dissent, dissidence, heresy, peculiarity, recusancy

nondescript: commonplace, dull, mousy, ordinary, unexceptional, unimpressive, unmemorable

nondrinker: teetotaler

nondrinking: abstinent, temperate

nonentity: cipher, nobody, nonexistence, nothing, small fry, strawman, zero, zilch

nonessential: deadwood, dispensable, expendable, extrinsic, incidental, insignificant, trivial, unimportant, unnecessary

nonesuch: matchless, paradigm, paragon, unequaled, unparalleled, unrivaled

nonetheless: even so, however, nevertheless, still, though

nonexistent: baseless, extinct, fictional, groundless, imagined, missing, mythical, null

nonfading: colorfast

nongraduate: dropout

nonhuman or inanimate: insensate, insensible

noninterference in government, business: laissez-faire

nonmaterial and spiritual: incorporeal

nonmetrical hymn, song, or chant using words taken from the bible: canticle

nonmilitary: civilian

nonobservance: disregard, failure, laxity, negligence, slight, violation

nonpareil: A-one, ideal, oner

nonpartisan: equitable, fair, impartial, independent, just, neutral, objective, unbiased, unprejudiced

nonplus: baffle, balk, bewilder, blank, confound, confuse, disconcert, dumbfound, embarrass, faze, fluster, frustrate, perplex, puzzle, rattle, stump, stymie

nonproductive: barren

nonprofessional: amateur, dabbler, laic, layman, layperson, laywoman, tyro

nonreligious: profane, secular

nonresistant: meek, passive, submissive, tolerant, yielding

nonsense: absurdity, amphigory, antics, applesauce, babble, balderdash, baloney, bilge, blah, blarney, blather, bosh, bull, bunk, bunkum, craziness, drivel, drool, faddle, fandangle, fiddle-faddle, flapdoodle, flummery, folder, folderol, folly, foolishness, footle, frivolity, garbage, gibberish, gobbledygook, guff, hogwash, hokum, hooey, horsefeathers, inanity, jabberwocky, jive, junk, malarkey, moonshine, muck, mumbo jumbo, poppycock, rot, rubbish, shenanigans, silliness, tomfoolery, tosh, trash, tripe, triviality, trumpery, twaddle

nonsense and empty talk: bunk, claptrap, flimflam, hokum, malarkey, rigmarole, waffle

nonstop: constant, continuous, direct, endless, incessant, uninterrupted

nonverbal expression: sigh

nonviolent: irenic, pacifist, passive, peaceful

nonviolent methods of Buddhists and Hindus: ahimsa

nonviolent methods of Mahatma Gandhi: satyagraha

nonviolent methods, refusal to obey civil laws by: civil disobedience

nonviolent methods, resistance by: passive resistance

nonviolent resistance: civil disobedience, passive resistance, satyagraha

nonworking: idle

nook: alcove, angle, byplace, cavity, corner, cove, cranny, crevice, glen, hideaway, hole, niche, recess, retreat

nook or alcove for informal meals: dinette

noon: apex, eight bells, meridian, midday, twelve o'clock

noon, after: postmeridian

noon, before: antemeridian

noose: ensnare, entrap, hang, hitch, lariat, lasso, loop, snare, tie, trap

norm: average, benchmark, gauge, mean, median, model, par, pattern, rule, scale, standard

norm, to depart from a: deviate

normal: average, common, compos mentis, conventional, expected, natural, ordinary, orthodox, reasonable,

TYPES OF NOSES

broad flat: leptorrhinian, platyopic
bumpy: kyphorrhinos
curved or hooked: aquiline
hawklike: accipitrine
high prominent-bridged: Roman nose
short: pug nose, snub nose
straight: Grecian nose
turned-up: retroussé ❦

regular, routine, sane, sound, standard, together, traditional, typical, usual
normal according to custom, fashion: established, prevailing, wonted
normal breathing: eupnea
normal consequence: corollary
normal custom or usage: consuetude
normal customs, person adhering to: conformist
Norse epic or saga: edda
north: arctic, cold, polar
North Star: polar star, polaris, polestar
north, concerning the: boreal
north, of the far: arctic, hyperborean
northeaster: gale, storm, wind
northerly habitable world according to ancient Greeks: Thule, Ultima Thule
Northerner who went South after Civil War: carpetbagger
nose: beak, bill, busybody, conk, detect, flair, gift, investigate, knack, meddle, muffle, muzzle, nozzle, poke, proboscis, pry, scent, schnoz, schnozz, schnozzle, smell, smeller, sniff, sniffer, sno, snoop, snoot, snout, spy
nose blockage: congestion
nose congestion medicine: decongestant
nose-dive: dip, drop, plummet, plunge, skid
nose out: edge
nose partition: septum
nose plastic surgery: nose job, rhinoplasty
nose red from drunkenness: coppernose
nose ridge above lip, separating nostrils: columella
nose, branch of medicine treating the: rhinology
nose, concerning the: nasal, rhinal
nosebleed: epistaxis
nosegay: bouquet, flowers, posy, sprigs
nosh: eat, snack
nostalgia: homesickness, loneliness, longing, reminiscence, sentimentality, yearning

nostril: nare, naris
nostrils' side bulbs: alae
nostrils, bone of wall between: vomer
nostrils, cavity close to: sinus
nostrils, wall between: septum
nostrum: elixir
nosy: curious, inquisitive, intrusive, meddlesome, prying, snooping
not: denial, hardly, nay, negative, neither, nought, prohibition, refusal
notable: aileron, baron, celebrity, chief, distinguished, eminent, eventful, fabled, famous, heavyweight, historic, kingpin, leader, luminary, memorable, mogul, noteworthy, personality, remarkable, storied, superstar, VIP
notarize: attest, certify, validate
notation: annotation, entry, marking, memo, memorandum, record, system
notational sign, in music: segno
notch: cut, degree, dent, dint, gash, groove, incision, indent, indentation, jab, level, mark, nick, pass, record, score, scotch, serrate, step, tally, undercut
notch cut by saw or ax: kerf
notch for inserted part: feather, gain, mortise, rabbet, tenon
notch or groove: chamfer, chase, indentation, kerf
notched: erose, serrate
notched as a leaf: erose
notched at edge: crenelated, indented, serrated
notched at edge of fabric: pinked
notches for keeping count: tally
notches on coin: fluting, milling
notches or teeth, set of: serration
note: annotate, comment, commentary, eminence, enter, epistle, heed, indicate, indication, inscription, jot, key, letter, line, mark, memo, memorandum, message, minute, missive, notice, observation, observe, perceive, pitch, record, remark, reminder, report, reputation, scale, scribble, song, sound, symbol, thank you
note as legal tender: bill, certificate, chit, currency, draft, greenback, I.O.U., loan, money, promissory, token, voucher
note at bottom of page: footnote
note group in music: chord
note individually: enumerate, itemize, particularize, specify

note, explanatory or critical: annotation, commentary, gloss
note, reminder: aide-mémoire, memo, memorandum
note, whole: semibreve
notebook: diary, journal, log, record, register
notebook of quotes, literary excerpts: commonplace book
noted: celebrated, distinguished, eminent, famous, illustrious, marked, prominent, recognized, renowned, seen
notes in margin: marginalia
notes (music) lengthened or shortened arbitrarily: rubato
notes (music) short and detached: staccato
notes of chord played in quick succession: arpeggio
notes played without a break and linked to each other: appoggiato
noteworthy: considerable, eminent, epic, exceptional, important, meaningful, memorable, notable, observable, outstanding, prominent, remarkable, significant, special
nothing: bagatelle, blank, cipher, free, nada, naught, nihil, nil, nix, none, nought, null, trifle, useless, zero, zilch
nothingness: death, emptiness, naught, nihility, nonentity, nonexistence, oblivion, vacuum, void
notice: acknowledge, apprisal, attention, ban, billet, care, caution, caveat, civility, cognizance, consideration, discern, espy, greet, heed, mark, mind, observe, recognize, regard, see, sense
notice or announcement: advertisement, advice, announcement, article, brochure, bulletin, citation, comment, disclosure, leaflet, memorandum, mention, news, note, obituary, pamphlet, poster, remark, sign, warning
noticeable: clear, conspicuous, distinct, evident, marked, noteworthy, obvious, outstanding, prominent, remarkable, salient, sensational, striking, unmistakable
noticeable and observable: apparent, discernible, evident, explicit, manifest
noticeable and perceivable: appreciable, palpable

noticeable, immediately: conspicuous, glaring, patent, prominent, pronounced, unmistakable

notify: acquaint, advise, announce, apprise, brief, broadcast, circulate, clue, declare, divulge, inform, post, promulgate, publish, report, signal, tell, warn

notion: belief, caprice, clue, conceit, concept, desire, fancy, hint, idea, image, inclination, inkling, insight, intention, intimation, opinion, theory, thought, understanding, vagary, view, whim

notoriety: celebrity, fame, infamy, publicity, reputation, scandal, stigma

notorious: acclaimed, apparent, arrant, bad, blatant, celebrated, dishonorable, disreputable, famous, flagrant, infamous, known, scandalous, villainous

notwithstanding: against, although, aside, despite, even, howbeit, however, nevertheless, nonetheless, regardless, spite, though

nought: zero

noun: name, person, place, thing
RELATED TERMS
noun affected by the action verb: object

noun expressing direction from or cause in some Indo-European languages: ablative

noun expressing possession, measurement, or source in some Indo-European languages: genitive

noun for both male and female forms: epicene

noun for person or thing being addressed in some languages like Latin: vocative

noun formed with -ing, verbal: gerund

noun functioning as an explanatory equivalent: appositive

noun identifying a specific person, place or thing: proper name, proper noun

noun inflection for case, number, gender in some languages: declension

noun or noun equivalent, designating: substantive

noun or pronoun and its modifiers: noun phrase

noun or pronoun following linking verb: predicate nominative

noun preceded by the article representing all members of a class: common noun

noun representing idea, concept, quality: abstract noun

noun representing physical thing: concrete noun

noun representing substance or concept that is indivisible: mass noun, noncount noun

noun representing substance that can form a plural: count noun

noun representing unique individual, place, event: proper name, proper noun

noun that denotes a group: collective noun

noun that is direct object of verb or preposition: accusative

noun that is indirect object of verb in some languages like Latin: dative

noun that is subject of verb in some languages like Latin: nominative

noun to designate a class or group, substitution of personal name for common: antonomasia

noun to which a pronoun refers: antecedent

noun types: common, personal, pronoun, proper

noun, adjective, pronoun complementing a verb: objective complement

noun, concerning a: nominal ❧

nourish: administer, cherish, cultivate, develop, feed, foster, maintain, nurse, nurture, promote, rear, stimulate, strengthen, supply, support, sustain

nourishes, something that: nurture, nutriment, sustenance

nourishing: beneficial, healthful, hearty, nutritious, wholesome

nourishment: ailment, food, meat, nutrient, nutriment, provisions, support, sustenance

nourishment, providing: alimentary

nourishment, source of: food, nutrient, nutrition

nouveau riche: newly rich, parvenu, upstart

nova: star

novel: avant-garde, contemporary, daring, different, fresh, innovative, modern, new, newfangled, odd, original, uncommon, unique, unusual

novel (book): fiction, paperback, romance, story
RELATED TERMS
novel about actual persons with fictional names: roman à clef

novel about adventures of roguish hero: picaresque novel

novel about moral, intellectual development of youth: bildungsroman

novel about several generations of family, community, or society: roman-fleuve, saga novel

novel continuing work of previous novel: sequel

novel in the form of a series of letters: epistolary

novel published in installments: feuilleton

novel with events preceding previous novel: prequel

novel, brief, with a moral: novella

novel, short additional section at end of: afterword, epilogue, postscript ❧

novel's introductory chapter: prologue

novelty: bauble, change, contraption, fad, gewgaw, innovation, knick-knack, oddity, trinket

novice: abecedarian, amateur, apprentice, beginner, colt, convert, fledgling, greenhorn, learner, neophyte, newcomer, plebe, punk, pupil, rookie, student, tenderfoot, tiro, trainee, tyro

now: at present, directly, forthwith, immediately, in our time, instantly, modern, present, promptly, pronto, soon, straightaway, today

now and then: infrequently, occasionally, periodically, seldom, sometimes

noxious: baneful, dangerous, deadly, destructive, evil, fetid, harmful, hurtful, injurious, lethal, nocent, nocuous, noisome, pernicious, poisonous, putrid, revolting, stinking, toxic, unhealthy, unwholesome, virulent

noxious atmosphere: miasma

nuance: degree, gradation, nicety, refinement, shade, soupçon, subtlety, suggestion, touch, variation

nub: bulge, bump, core, crux, essence, gist, kernel, knob, knot, lump, nucleus, point, substance

nuclear bomb with lessened physical damage: neutron bomb

nuclear capacity exceeding amount needed to destroy enemy: overkill

nuclear detonation point: ground zero

nuclear explosion's cloud: fireball, mushroom

nuclear explosion's released energy: yield

nuclear fuel, elements used in: plutonium, uranium

nuclear means of discouraging enemy attack: deterrent

nuclear reaction with heavy nucleus split into fragments: fission

nuclear reaction with nuclei combining to make massive nuclei: fusion

nuclear reactor: pile

nuclear reactor that slows fast neutrons, substance in: meltdown

nuclear weapons or energy, means other than: conventional

nuclear weapons, calling for an end to acquisition or deployment of: nonproliferation

nucleus: cadre, center, core, crux, focus, kernel, nub, ring, seed, spark

nude: au naturel, bare, exposed, naked, raw, stark, stripped, unclad, unclothed, uncovered, undressed

nudge: bump, elbow, jab, jog, jostle, poke, prod, push, shove, touch

nudism: naturism

nugatory: futile, hollow, idle, ineffectual, invalid, trifling, trivial, useless, vain, worthless

nugget: chunk, clump, gold, hunk, lump, mass

nuisance: annoyance, bother, burden, exasperation, headache, imposition, inconvenience, irritation, pest, plague, problem, thorn

null: ineffectual, insignificant, invalid, nonexistent, nothing, nullify, useless, void, worthless, zero

null and void: diriment, invalid

nullify: abolish, abrogate, annul, cancel, counteract, invalidate, negate, neutralize, null, offset, renege, repeal, rescind, revoke, squash, undo, veto, void

nullity: cipher, naught, nonentity, nothing, zero, zilch

numb: anesthetized, blunt, dead, deaden, desensitize, different, dull, freeze, insensible, insensitive, paralyze, stun, stupid, torpid, unfeeling

number: aggregate, amount, array, bunch, bundle, calculate, compute, count, crowd, flock, fraction, group, herd, horde, host, many, multitude, myriad, numerate, percentage, proportion, quantity, quota, scads, score, several, slew, sum, swarm, tally, total

number or numeral: cardinal, cipher, decimal, denominator, digit, factor, figure, integer, numeral, numerator, prime, symbol

number admitted, maximum: quota

number assigned to library book: call number

number by which another number is to be divided: divisor

number expressed as an integer or quotient of integers: rational number

number from which another number is to be subtracted: minuend

number in numbering system, character indicating: digit, figure

number indicating position in sequence (1st, 2nd, 3rd): ordinal number

number indicating quantity: cardinal number

number midway between highest and lowest numbers of series: median

number multiplied in multiplication problem: factor

number multiplying a variable: coefficient

number needed to make up a whole: complement

number obtained by dividing one quantity by another: quotient

number obtained by multiplying two or more numbers: product

number obtained when another number is divided into one, e.g. 7 of 1/7: inverse, reciprocal

number of steps, problem-solving procedure with finite: algorithm

number or range of numbers occurring most frequently in a set: mode

number sequence in which each is formed by adding a constant to the preceding number, e.g. 2,5,8 or 1,3,5: arithmetic progression

number showing how many times a number is used as factor in calculation: exponent, power

number slightly above another: superscript

number slightly below another: subscript

number that divides exactly into another number: aliquot

number that divides into another without a remainder: factor

number that is integer or quotient of integers, whole number or fraction: rational number

number that is result of multiplying: factorial

number the pages of a book: foliate, paginate

number to be divided: dividend

number to be multiplied: multiplicand

number to be subtracted from another: subtrahend

number used in counting (1,2,3): cardinal number

number written using base 10: decimal

number, positive or negative whole: integer

number, vast: multitude, myriad

numbered: doomed, fated, limited, marked, specified, totalled

numbered musical composition: opus

numbering system: numeration, reckoning

numberless: endless, immeasurable, incalculable, infinite, myriad, numerous, unlimited

numbers used to determine position of something: coordinates

numbers, amount obtained by adding: sum

numbers, concerning: numerical

numbers, relation between two: proportion, ratio

numbers, study of the occult meanings of: numerology

numeral: cipher, digit, figure, integer, letter, number, symbol

numerate: calculate, count, list, number, tally, total

numeration system using only 0 and 1: binary number system, binary system

numerous: abundant, copious, diverse, extensive, infinite, large, lots, many, multiple, multitudinous, plentiful, several, untold, voluminous

numskull: blockhead, bonehead, dolt, dunce, fool, idiot, imbecile, jerk, knucklehead, nincompoop, ninny, nitwit

nun: abbess, anchorite, devotee, postulant, prioress, sister, vestal, votaress

nun or monk: votary

nun who is superior of convent: abbess, prioress

nun, candidate for: neophyte, novice, novitiate, postulant

nun, to become a: take the veil, take vows

nun, woman living in religious community living without vows of: canoness

nuncio: ambassador, delegate, diplomat, messenger, representative

nuncupative: oral

nunnery: abbey, convent, monastery, order, sisterhood

nun's cone-shaped headdress: cornet

nun's donation as candidate: dowry

nun's dress: habit

nun's starched neck-and-shoulder piece of habit: guimpe

nun's white headdress: wimple

nuns, group of: superfluity

nuptial: bridal, connubial, espousal, hymeneal, marital, matrimonial, wedding

nurse: attend, care, cherish, cradle, feed, foster, harbor, nanny, nourish, nurture, rear, Sisterkenny, suckle, tend

nurse who raises child: dry nurse

nursery: crèche, greenhouse, playroom, preschool

nurse's teenaged helper: candy striper

nurture: bolster, cherish, cultivate, develop, educate, feed, foster, mother, nourish, nurse, raise, rear, strengthen, support, teach, tend, train, uphold

nut: acorn, almond, betel, bur, cashew, core, filbert, hazel, hickory, kiik, kola, peanut, pecan, pistachio

nut confection: nougat

nut fitting over bolt: lug nut

nut of the Americas, two-part bumpy: peanut

nut, hazel-: filbert

nut, oval thin-shelled U.S.: pecan

nut, round hard-shelled Australian: macadamia

nut, smooth hard-shelled North American: hickory

nuthatch genus: sitta

nutriment: aliment, diet, food, nourishment, nutrition, provisions, support, sustenance

nutrition and diet, science of: sitology

nutrition, defective: dystrophy

nutrition, pertaining to: trophic

nutritious: balanced, healthy, nourishing, salubrious, wholesome

nutritious snack: gorp

nutritive meal: salep

nuts: bananas, batty, bonkers, crazy, demented, deranged, eccentric, insane, loco, loony, mad, masts, nutty, touched, wild

nutty liqueur: amaretto

nuzzle: caress, cuddle, fondle, nestle, nudge, push, snuggle

nymph: damsel, deity, fairy, female, girl, houri, maiden, mermaid, naiad, oread, siren, sprite, sylph, woman

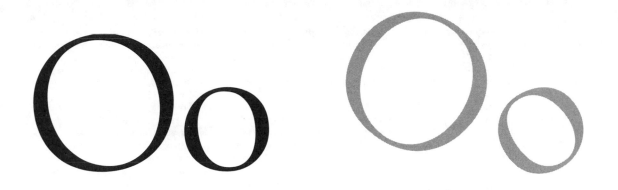

oaf: blockhead, bonehead, boob, boor, clod, clown, dolt, dumbbell, dunce, fool, foundling, goof, goon, idiot, jerk, lout, lummox, lump, moron, nincompoop, nitwit, simpleton

oak fruit: acorn

oak variety: bear, black, blackjack, bluejack, bur, canyon, chestnut, holly, huckleberry, laurel, live, poison, Red, scarlet, scrub, Western, white, willow

oar: blade, paddle, pole, propel, row, rower, scull, sweep

oar blade horizontal between strokes, to turn an: feather

oar in position that acts as fulcrum, device holding: oarlock

oar in position, device holding: becket

oar or paddle blade: palm

oar types: needle, spade

oarlock: thole

oarsman: gondolier, helmsman, rower, sculler

oasis: garden, haven, refuge, relief, sanctuary, spa, wadi

oasis, illusion of: mirage

oath: adjuration, affidavit, affirmation, appeal, bond, contract, curse, expletive, obligation, pledge, profanity, promise, swear, swearword, testimony, vow

oath of fidelity to feudal lord: fealty, homage

oath of new physicians: Hippocratic oath

oath, declaration given in place of an: affirmation

oath, one who testifies in writing under: deponent

oath, testimony under: deposition

oath, to make declaration under: testify

oath, written statement under: affidavit

oaths, one legally empowered to administer: notary, notary public

oatmeal: cereal, food, porridge

oatmeal cake: scone

obdurate: adamant, callous, cruel, firm, hard, hardened, hardhearted, headstrong, immovable, impenitent, inflexible, insensible, intractable, iron, obstinate, persistent, pigheaded, rigid, rough, rugged, stubborn, unbending, unemotional, unfeeling, unshakable, unyielding

obedience unsupported in reality, verbal: lip service

obedience, person of unquestioning: apple-polisher, bootlicker, flunky, lacky, minion

obedient: abiding, acquiescent, amenable, attentive, compliant, docile, duteous, dutiful, heedful, loyal, mindful, obeying, obsequious, respectful, submissive, tame, tractable, yielding

obedient and easily managed: amenable, biddable, compliant, governable, obeisant, pliable, tractable

obedient, overly: acquiescent, deferential, docile, obsequious, servile, submissive, sycophantic, unctuous

obeisance: bow, curtsy, deference, esteem, fealty, gesture, homage, honor, kowtow, loyalty, reverence, salaam, salutation, submission

obelisk: column, dagger, mark, monolith, monument, needle, pillar, pylon, shaft, tower

obese: chubby, corpulent, fat, fleshy, heavy, overweight, plump, pudgy, rotund

obey: accept, acquiesce, comply, conform, follow, heed, mind, observe, respect, submit, yield

obey and comply: abide by, acquiesce in, adhere to, conform to, defer to, humor, indulge, toe the line

obey to gain favor: fawn, kowtow, truckle

obfuscate: bewilder, blur, cloud, confuse, darken, dim, garble, hide, muddle, obscure, perplex, puzzle

obiter dictum: comment, opinion, remark

obituary: announcement, death notice, eulogy, necrology

obituary commemoration: epitaph

object: aim, design, doodad, duty, end, essence, expostulate, function, gadget, goal, intent, item, mark, mission, motive, oppose, point, principle, purpose, reason, target, thing, thingamajig, victim

object affected by the action verb: indirect object

object as guide to travelers: landmark

object believed to have magical powers: fetish

object beyond or real only to senses and unknowable through reasoning: phenomenon

object made by humans: artifact

object of attention: cynosure

object of worship: icon, idol

object understood only by intellect and not by senses: noumenon

object with magical, spiritual power: fetish, juju, relic, talisman

object, to: argue, cavil, challenge, demur, disapprove, dispute, protest, take exception

objection: argument, cavil, challenge, demural, exception, gripe, oppose, protest

objection or disagreement: dissent, dissidence

objection or uneasy feeling about something: qualm, scruple

objection, irrelevant or petty: quibble

objection, to affirm validity of: sustain

objectionable: abhorrent, deplorable, disagreeable, exceptional, loathsome, offensive, repellent, reprehensible, revolting, unacceptable, undesirable, unpleasant, vile

objective: aim, detached, disinterested, dispassionate, duty, end, fair, goal, impartial, just, mission, motive, purpose, straight, target, unbiased

objective and representative of reality: realistic

objective and unbiased: disinterested, dispassionate, impartial

objet d'art: bauble, bibelot, curio, gewgaw, trinket, virtu

objurgate: abuse, berate, castigate, chide, execrate, rebuke, reprove, scold

oblation: gift, offering, presentation, sacrifice

obligated: beholden, bound, committed, forced, indebted, required

obligation: agreement, bond, burden, commitment, compulsion, contract, debt, duty, guarantee, indebtedness, liability, loan, mortgage, must, need, oath, onus, pledge, promise, requirement, responsibility, vow, warranty

obligation owed: fealty

obligation to honorable behavior by nobility: noblesse oblige

obligatory: binding, compulsory, enforced, essential, imperative, incumbent, irremissible, mandatory, necessary, required, unavoidable

oblige: accommodate, assist, compel, constrain, contribute, favor, force, gratify, help, necessitate, obligate, please, require

oblique: angled, askance, askew, aslant, awry, backhanded, bent, crooked, cross, diagonal, evasive, inclined, indirect, out of kilter, pitched, roundabout, sidelong, sideways, sidewise, skew, slanting, sloped, tilted, underhand, vague

oblique or diagonal line: bias

obliterate: abolish, annihilate, blot, cancel, delete, destroy, efface, eliminate, erase, expunge, extinguish, raze, waste

oblivion: amnesty, emptiness, forgetfulness, lethe, limbo, nonexistence, nothingness, obscurity, pardon

oblivious: absentminded, blind, disregardful, inattentive, preoccupied, unaware, unconscious, unnoticing, unwitting

oblong: angular, elliptical, elongated, oval, rectangular

oblong figure: quadrilateral, tetragon

oblong-shaped cut gem: baguette

obloquy: aspersion, calumny, censure, contempt, defamation, disgrace, dishonor, ignominy, infamy, invective, odium, shame, vilification

obnoxious: abhorrent, annoying, detestable, foul, hateful, liable, loud, nasty, offensive, reprehensible, repugnant, repulsive, unpleasant, vile

obscene: bawdy, coarse, crude, dirty, disgusting, fescennine, filthy, foul, foulmouthed, gross, immoral, impure, indecent, lascivious, lewd, licentious, loathsome, lurid, nasty, offensive, pornographic, profane, rank, raunchy, repugnant, repulsive, salacious, scatological, smutty, vulgar

obscene material: pornography

obscene talk: bawdry, coprolalia

obscenity, interest in: scatology

obscure: ambiguous, becloud, bedim, befog, bemist, blanket, blind, block, blot, blurred, caliginous, camouflage, cloak, cloud, cloudy, complicated, conceal, confuse, cover, cryptic, dark, darken, deep, difficult, dim, disguise, enigmatic, equivocal, falsify, foggy, forgotten, gloomy, hazy, hidden, hide, incomprehensible, indistinct, mask, murky, mystic, mystical, overshadow, puzzling, remote, screen, secluded, secretive, shadowy, shield, uncertain, unclear, undefined, unimportant, unknown, unnoticeable, vague, veil

obscure and foggy: cloudy, misty, obnubilate

obscure except to expert: arcane, esoteric, recherché

obscure or muddle: eclipse, obfuscate

obscure person: quidam

obscure saying or riddle: enigma

obscured at twilight: crepuscular, murky

obsequies: ceremony, funeral, rites, service

obsequious: attentive, bootlicking, compliant, cowering, fawning, groveling, kowtowing, menial, obedient, servile, slavish, slick, submissive, subservient, sycophantic, toadying

observable: aboveboard, open, overt

observance: attention, celebration, ceremony, custom, form, formality, mark, observation, practice, regard, rite, ritual, service, tradition

observant: alert, attentive, aware, discerning, keen, mindful, perceptive, vigilant, watchful

observation: attention, autopsy, comment, commentary, discovery, espial, examination, finding, monitoring, note, notice, probe, remark, scrutiny, study, surveillance, survey, view

observation area on roof of house: widow's walk

observation as the basis: a posteriori

observation or experiment, based on: empirical

observation, close: surveillance

observatory: catbird seat, lookout, tower, watchtower

observe: adhere, behold, catch, celebrate, commemorate, comment, comply, detect, discern, espy, eye, follow, heed, honor, keep, look, mark, monitor, note, notice, obey, perceive, regard, remark, respect, see, sight, solemnize, spot, study, take notice, to see, view, watch, witness

observe carefully: scrutinize

observer: bystander, eyer, onlooker, spy

observing one's own thoughts: introspection

observing post, favorable: coign of vantage

obsessed: beset, consumed, controlled, dogged, dominated, engrossed, fixated, haunted, hooked, infatuated

obsession: amnia, attraction, compulsion, craving, craze, fascination, fetish, fixation, idée fixe, infatuation, mania, passion, phobia, preoccupation

obsessively anxious: neurotic

obsolete: ancient, antiquated, archaic, dated, extinct, old, old-fashioned, out, out-of-date, outdated, outmoded, outworn, passé, superannuated, timeworn

obsolete thing, to get rid of: pension off, put out to pasture

obsolete thing, to replace: supersede

obstacle: bar, barrier, block, blockade, bump, catch, difficulty, handicap, hindrance, hitch, hurdle, impediment, obstruction, snag, stumbling block, vicissitude

obstinate: bulky, bullheaded, cantankerous, contrary, crotchet, deter-

OCEANS AND SEAS

Adriatic Sea	Barents Sea	Greenland Sea	Mediterranean Sea	Sea of Galilee
Aegean Sea	Bay of Bengal	Gulf of Alaska	Molukka Sea	Sea of Japan
Amundsen Sea	Beaufort Sea	Gulf of California	North Atlantic	Sea of Marmara
Andaman Sea	Bellingshausen Sea	Gulf of Guinea	Ocean	Sea of Okhotsk
Antarctic Ocean	Bering Sea	Gulf of Mexico	North Pacific Ocean	South Atlantic
Arabian Sea	Black Sea	Hudson Bay	North Sea	Ocean
Arafura Sea	Caribbean Sea	Indian Ocean	Pacific Ocean	South China Sea
Aral Sea	Caspian Sea	Inland Sea	Persian Gulf	South Pacific Ocean
Arctic Ocean	Celebes Sea	Ionian Sea	Philippine Sea	Tasman Sea
Atlantic Ocean	China Sea	Irish Sea	Red Sea	Timor Sea
Baffin Bay	Chukchi Sea	Java Sea	Ross Sea	Tyrrhenian Sea
Bali Sea	Coral Sea	Kara Sea	Sargasso Sea	Weddell Sea
Baltic Sea	East China Sea	Laptev Sea	Savu Sea	White Sea
Banda Sea	Flores Sea	Ligurian Sea	Sea of Azov	Yellow Sea ❦

mined, dogged, headstrong, inflexible, intractable, muleheaded, mulish, obdurate, opinionated, persistent, pertinacious, perverse, pigheaded, recalcitrant, refractory, staunch, steadfast, stubborn, sullen, tough, unbending, unruly, willful

obstinately resistant: diehard, hardheaded, hidebound, refractory, unregenerate

obstreperous: boisterous, clamorous, defiant, loud, noisy, raucous, unruly, vociferous

obstruct: arrest, bar, barricade, barrier, beset, block, block up, blockade, check, choke, clog, close, congest, crimp, curb, dam, delay, encumber, filibuster, foil, hamper, hinder, impede, inhibit, interfere, interrupt, oppose, plug, prevent, retard, screen, shroud, stonewall, stop, stymie, thwart

obstructed section: bottleneck

obstructing: in the way, obstruent

obstruction: barrier, dam, delay, difficulty, encumbrance, gridlock, hindrance, hitch, hurdle, impediment, obstacle, restriction, roadblock, snag, stumbling block

RELATED TERMS

obstruction of blood supply, death of tissue due to: infarction

obstruction of blood vessel by mass: embolism

obstruction of duct, passage: occlusion, stricture

obstruction of normal operations: sabotage

obstruction, serious: deadlock, impasse, logjam

obstructionist tactic: filibuster ❦

obtain: accomplish, achieve, acquire, attain, capture, collect, compass, earn, encompass, gain, gather, get, procure, purchase, reach, reap, receive, secure, sponge, succeed, take, win

obtain by force or threat: extort

obtain or receive from a source: derive

obtrude: impose, infringe, interfere, intrude

obtrusive: aggressive, brash, forward, impertinent, intrusive, meddlesome, noticeable, obvious, officious, presumptuous, protruding, pushing, pushy

obtrusive plants: weeds

obtuse: blunt, crass, dense, dull, ignorant, insensitive, opaque, round, stupid

obverse: complement, counterpart, face, front, opposite

obviate: avert, avoid, circumvent, dodge, forestall, interfere, intervene, preclude, prevent, ward

obvious: apparent, blatant, clear, conspicuous, distinct, evident, glaring, lucid, manifest, open and shut, overt, palpable, patent, plain, self-explanatory, unmistakable, unsubtle, visible

obvious and following necessarily: analytic, tautologous

obvious and needing no proof: axiomatic, self-evident, self-explanatory

obvious and noticeable: conspicuous, salient

obvious and plain: clear, evident, manifest, patent

obvious remark or statement: commonplace, platitude, truism

obvious, concerned only with what is: superficial, trivial

obvious, totally: blatant, glaring, gross, palpable

occasion: celebration, ceremony, chance, condition, event, excuse, function, gathering, grounds, happening, hint, incident, instance, instant, milestone, moment, opportunity, reason, time

occasional: infrequent, intermittent, irregular, odd, periodic, random, rare, scarce, scattered, sporadic, stray

occasionally: from time to time, hardly, irregularly, now and then, periodically, rarely, sometimes

occlude: absorb, block, clog, close, impede, obstruct, plug, prevent, seal

occult: arcane, concealed, cryptic, eerie, esoteric, hidden, inscrutable, magic, mysterious, mystical, psychic, recondite, secret, supernatural, underground, voodoo, weird

occupancy: habitation, occupation, tenancy, tenure

occupant: denizen, dweller, inhabitant, inmate, lessee, renter, resident, tenant

occupation: business, calling, career, control, employment, habitation, industry, job, line, livelihood, métier, profession, pursuit, racket, seizure, takeover, tenure, trade, vocation, work

occupation for which one is suited: métier

occupied: absorbed, busy, engaged, engrossed, in use, inhabited, populated, rented, settled, taken

occupy: amuse, busy, dwell, employ, engage, establish, fill, fulfill, immerse, inhabit, involve, overrun, populate, possess, reside, seize, take, tenant

occupy completely: absorb, engross

occupy oneself in amusing way: disport

occur: appear, arrive, befall, betide, chance, come, eventualize, exist, hap, happen, materialize, pass, result, strike, transpire

occur as result: ensue, eventuate, follow

occur at same time, to: synchronize

occur between two points in time: intervene, supervene

occurrence: accident, affair, case, circumstance, condition, development, encounter, episode, event, happening, incidence, incident, occasion, situation

occurring at same time as something else: concurrent, simultaneous

occurring intermittently: spasmodic

occurring repeatedly: frequently, recurrently

occurring together: concomitant

ocean or water that is not reached by sunlight: aphotic

ocean route: lane, sea lane

ocean spray blown by wind: spindrift

ocean wave, destructive: tsunami

oceanic: aquatic, marine, maritime, nautical, pelagic, seafaring, thalassic, vast

octave: cask, eight, interval, note, scale, tone

octopus: cephalopod, devilfish, mollusk

octopus arm, for one: tentacle

octopus, tapeworm, leech sucker: acetabulum

ocular: eye, ophthalmic, optic, sight, visible, visual

odd: aberrant, abnormal, atypical, bizarre, curious, deviant, different, droll, eccentric, fanciful, freakish, funny, irregular, lone, occasional, offbeat, peculiar, quaint, queer, rare, strange, uncommon, uneven, unique, unmatched, unpaired, unusual, weird

odd and confined to small group: abstruse, esoteric

odd and inconsistent: anomalous, discordant, erratic, incongruous, out of place

odd and supernatural: eerie, uncanny

odd and unconventional: bizarre, eccentric, freakish, grotesque, idiosyncratic, ludicrous, outlandish, outré, pixilated, quirky, singular, whimsical

odd and unnatural: inexplicable, preternatural

odd item: curio

odd notion: vagary

odd-numbered page: recto

odd on purpose: capricious, perverse, weird

odd, comically: bizarre, kooky, zany

oddball: batty, crackpot, eccentric, kook, misfit, oddity, peculiar, strange, weirdo

oddity: abnormality, anomaly, curiosity, eccentricity, idiosyncrasy, irregularity, phenomenon, quirk, unnaturalness

odds: advantage, chance, chances, degree, edge, likelihood, percentage, probabilities

odds and ends: assortment, bits, hodgepodge, jumble, leftovers, miscellany, mixture, motley, olio, paraphernalia, potpourri, remnants, scraps, sundries

odds and ends, discarded: flotsam, jetsam

ode: poem, psalm, ratio, song, variance, verse

odious: abhorrent, abominable, detestable, disgusting, evil, forbidding, foul, hateful, heinous, hideous, horrible, horrid, infamous, loathsome, mean, obnoxious, offensive, putrid, rancid, repugnant, revolting, rotten, sickening, terrible, vile

odium: antipathy, blot, condemnation, contempt, disapprobation, disesteem, disgrace, dishonor, hate, hatred, malice, shame, spot, stain, stigma

odor: aroma, bouquet, effluvia, essence, esteem, estimation, flavor, fragrance, fume, fumet, funk, nidor, perfume, redolence, reputation, repute, scent, smell, stench, stink, tang

odor of decay: effluvium

odorless gas: argon

odorous: aromatic, balmy, dank, fragrant, pungent, rank, smelly

odyssey: epic poem, trek, trip

oeuvre: opus, output, work

of: about, concerning, from, like, regarding

off: abroad, absent, apart, aside, astray, away, canceled, crazy, distant, eccentric, farther, gone, incorrect, launched, postponed, remote, removed, slack, slim, unlit, wrong

off-balance: lopsided, topsy, uneven, unsteady

off base: erroneous, incorrect, mistaken, wrong

off-center: alop, askew, eccentric, irregular, strange, unbalanced, unsteady

off-color: blue, dirty, indelicate, lewd, obscene, offensive, purple, racy, risque, salty, smutty, spicy, suggestive, vulgar

off course: amiss, errant

off the cuff: ad lib, adlib, extemporaneous, impromptu, spontaneous

off the record: confidential, private, restricted, secret, undisclosed

off the wall: crazy as a loon, goofy, wacky

offal: carrion, debris, garbage, junk, leaving, refuse, remains, rubbish, trash, waste

offbeat: bizarre, different, eccentric, odd, peculiar, strange, unique, unusual, weird

offend: abuse, aggravate, anger, annoy, appall, attack, dishonor, displease, disturb, harm, hurt, insult, irritate, miff, mortify, nettle, outrage, pique, repel, revolt, shock, sin, transgress, trespass, upset, vex, zing

offend and hurt: alienate, antagonize, estrange

offend one's pride: pique

offended, to be: take exception, take umbrage

offender: criminal, crook, culprit, sinner

offense: affront, aggression, assault, attack, breach, charge, crime, delictum, delinquency, fault, felony, guilt, huff, indignity, misdeed, misdemeanor, onslaught, peccadillo, sin, tort, trespass, umbrage, violation, wrongdoing

offense against ruler: lèse-majesté, lese majesty

offense not as bad as felony: misdemeanor

offensive: appalling, assault, attack, coarse, fetid, foul, fulsome, gross, gruesome, hideous, horrible, horrid, invading, invasion, invidious, loathsome, nasty, noisome, noxious, obnoxious, obscene, off-color, push, rank, rude, storming, unsavory, vile

offensive and belittling: derogatory

offensive and foul: noisome

offensive and unnecessary: gratuitous

offensive by acting superior: condescending, patronizing

offer: advance, attempt, bid, commend, extend, feeler, furnish, pledge, present, proffer, propine, propose, reward, show, submit, suggest, tender

offer for acceptance: proffer, tender

offer of a price: bid

offer, invitation: approach, overture

offering: alms, charity, contribution, donation, gift, oblation, present, sacrifice, tribute

offering fulfilling vow or pledge, of an: votive

offering of worship or thanks: oblation

offering to a god, conciliatory: propitiation

offhand: abrupt, careless, casual, cavalier, chance, curt, extemporaneous, extempory, hasty, impromptu, improvised, informal, spontaneous, unplanned, unrehearsed

office: agency, appointment, bailiwick, berth, building, bureau, business, capacity, commission, department, duty, function, job, occupation, place, position, post, responsibility, service, shop, situation, station, workstation

office employee: bookkeeper, clerk, data processor, keypuncher, pencil pusher, receptionist, secretary, typist

office-supply seller: stationer

office work, concerning: clerical, secretarial

office, act or condition of holding: incumbency, occupation, tenure

office, advancing to higher: preferment, promotion

office, badge of: insignia

office, formal induction into: inauguration, induction, investiture

office, to install to public: inaugurate, induct, invest, swear in

office, to remove from: depose, dethrone

office, to select or set aside for an: designate

officeholder remaining until inauguration though not reelected: lame duck

officeholder, current: incumbent

officer: administrator, agent, aide, captain, director, executive, general, manager, official, president, secretary, treasurer

RELATED TERMS

officer between noncommissioned officer and commissioned officer: warrant officer

officer investigating death: coroner

officer keeping order in organization: sergeant, sergeant at arms, usher

officer of military organization, commanding: commandant

officer that is second lieutenant or above: commissioned officer

officer, army: adjutant, brigadier, chaplain, colonel, lieutenant, major, quartermaster, sergeant, surgeon general

officer, federal court: marshal

officer, law-enforcement: bailiff, chief, constable, cop, detective, marshal, patrolman, patrolwoman, policeman, policewoman, sheriff

officer, navy: admiral, captain, commander, commodore, ensign, lieutenant, mate, mister

officers, group of: mess ❦

official: administrator, agent, aide, alderman, alderwoman, ambassador, bureaucrat, chairman, chancellor, commissioner, comptroller, constable, councilman, councilwoman, dean, dignitary, director, envoy, executive, functionary, judge, leader, magistrate, manager, mayor, minister, notary public, officer, president, referee, representative, selectman, selectwoman, umpire

RELATED TERMS

official and orthodox: canonical

official announcement: communiqué, proclamation

official approval or permission: authorization, fiat, ratification, sanction, validation

official approval to publish: imprimatur

official deadline for coming in at night: curfew

official denial: dementi

official document: writ

official document for authority: credentials

official documents, language of: officialese

official empowered to witness and certify documents: notary, notary public

official in bureaucracy: bureaucrat

official in courtroom during trial: bailiff

official investigating complaints and mediating settlements: ombudsman

official opening ceremony: commencement, dedication

official order: edict

official questioner: inquisitor

official record: register

official report: compte rendu, white paper

official seal: cachet, stamp

official, misconduct of public: malfeasance, malversation

officially recognized: accredited, legitimate

officials, corruption of public: graft, jobbery ❦

official, being: approved, authentic, authoritative, authorized, bona fide, canonical, certified, endorsed, formal, genuine, legitimate, sanctioned

officiate: chair, command, direct, govern, head, moderate, oversee, preside, ref, referee, regulate, umpire

officious: arrogant, busy, efficacious, impersonal, impertinent, impudent, informal, interfering, intrusive, meddlesome, meddling, pushy, snooping, unofficial

offset: account, balance, compensate, compensate for, complement, counteract, counterbalance, countervail, equalize, ledge, neutralize, recess, redeem

offshoot: arm, branch, by-product, consequence, derivative, descendant, outgrowth, ramification, scion, spin-off, sprout, subsidiary, twig

offshore: asea, seaward

offspring: brood, child, children, daughter, descendant, family, fruit, generation, heir, issue, kid, litter, outcome, produce, product, progeny, result, scion, seed, son, young, youngster

RELATED TERMS

offspring of mixed races: half-breed

offspring of stallion and female ass: hinny

offspring that hatch inside body, having: ovoviviparous

offspring that hatch outside body, having: oviparous

offspring, create: beget, procreate, reproduce

offspring, having live: viviparous

offspring, having many: philoprogenitive, prolific

offspring, having more than one: multiparous ❦

often: common, constantly, continually, frequent, frequently, generally, much, repeatedly

ogle: eye, gape, gaze, glance, leer, look, stare

ogre: beast, brute, demon, fiend, giant, monster, troll, tyrant

oil: anoint, attar, balm, chrism, coat, cream, fat, fuel, gas, grease, lanolin, lube, lubricate, smear

oil and balsam used in church sacraments: chrism, holy oil

oil and vinegar holder: cruet

oil from flax seed: linseed

oil from lemon-scented Asian grass: citronella

oil in crankcase, rod for measuring: dipstick

oil job, for short: lube

oil or fat with long-chain carbon compounds: polyunsaturated

oil or petroleum processing plant: refinery

oil or similar substance that reduces friction: lubricant

oil-producing rock: shale

oil products: bitumen, chemicals, diesel fuel, gasoline, kerosene, lubricants, natural gas

oil to as in ceremony, to apply: anoint

oil types: animal, butter, castor, cod-liver, cooking, corn, cottonseed, crude, fatty, linseed, lubricating, machine, mineral, motor, olive, palm, sesame, soybean, vegetable, whale

oil used in dyeing: aniline

oil well that is overflowing: gusher

oil well, sudden escape of gas or liquid from: blowout

oil well, tall framework supporting equipment over: derrick, oil platform

oil wells, apparatus used for digging: rig

oil, concerning: oleaginous, unctuous

oil, gas etc., substance from earth that is separated into: petroleum

oil, remains settling or filtered out when refining: foots

oils and inhalants, promotion of health using fragrant: aromatherapy

oily: bland, fatty, flattering, fulsome, glib, greasy, oleaginous, oleose, pinguid, plausible, rich, sebaceous, slick, slippery, smooth, suave, unctuous

oily substance from wool: lanolin

ointment: balm, cerate, chrism, cream, dressing, embrocation, liniment, lotion, medicine, nard, remedy, salve, spikenard, unction, unguent

okay: acceptable, agreed, amen, approve, assent, authorize, blessing, consent, fine, jake, ok, pass, permission, ratify, yes

okra's edible pods as soup or vegetable: gumbo

old: aged, ancient, antediluvian, antiquated, antique, archaic, bygone, dated, elderly, experienced, former, hoary, lifelong, mature, medieval, obsolete, outdated, passé, past, seasoned, senile, senior, stale, timeworn, traditional, venerable, vintage, worn-out

old age: caducity, decrepitude, dotage, maturity, senectitude, senescence, senility

old age, branch of medicine concerned with: geriatrics

old age, metaphorically: sunset

old age, of yore: eld

old age, resulting from or concerning: geriatric, senile

old age, to shake from: dodder, totter

old and commanding respect: venerable

old and grayish-white: hoary

old and rare items dealer: antiquarian

old and worn-out: decrepit, dilapidated

old and wrinkled: wizened

old-fashioned: aged, ancient, antediluvian, antiquated, antique, archaic, behind the times, bygone, cocktail, corny, dated, démodé, dowdy, drink, fossilized, fuddy-duddy, fusty, obsolete, old hat, ossified, out of date, outdated, outmoded, passé, primitive, quaint, stagnated, stale, traditional, vieux jeu, vintage

old-fashioned person: antediluvian, diehard, fogy, fuddy-duddy, mossback

old hat: antiquated, archaic, behind the times, cliché, dated, obsolete, outdated, passé, shopworn, stale, timeworn, trite, vintage

old or past: erstwhile, ex-, former, previous, quondam, whilom

old or rare books, dealer in: antiquarian

old, very: ancient, antiquated, archaic, superannuated

olio: collection, hash, hodge podge, hodgepodge, jumble, medley, mélange, miscellany, mishmash, mixture, potpourri, salmangundi, stew

olive genus: olea, Oleo europaea

olla: container, crock, earthenware, jar, jug, pot

olla-podrida: stew

omelet with ham, onion, green pepper: western omelet

omelet with tomato, onion, green pepper: Spanish omelet

omen: a straw in the wind, augury, auspice, bode, bodement, forebode, foreshadow, harbinger, indication, portent, prediction, premonition, presage, prophecy, sign, token, warning

omen of death: knell

ominous: apocalyptic, baneful, dangerous, dark, dire, dismal, doomed, dour, fateful, fearful, foreboding, gloomy, grim, menacing, portentous, sinister, threatening, unlucky

omission: blank, chasm, elision, ellipsis, error, exclusion, failure, lapse, negligence, overlook, oversight, skip

omission of similar or adjacent syllable: haplology

omission of sound(s) at beginning of word: aphaeresis, aphesis

omission of sound(s) at end of word: apocope

omission of sound(s) in middle of word: syncope

omission of understood word(s): ellipsis

omission of unstressed vowel or syllable: elision

omission, act of: preterition

omit: alide, avoid, bypass, cancel, cut, dele, delete, disregard, drop, edit, elide, eliminate, except, exclude, forget, ignore, miss, neglect, overlook, skip, slip, spare

omnibus: anthology, compilation, including, vehicle, whole

omnipotent: all-powerful, almighty, deity, godlike, great, mighty, powerful, supreme, unequaled, unlimited

omnipresent: allover, everywhere, infinite, simultaneous, ubiquitous

omniscient: all-knowing, knowledgeable, learned, pansophical, wise

on: about, above, against, ahead, along, atop, covering, forward, over, touching, upon, with, within

on guard: alert, careful, cautious, vigilant, wary, watchful

on hand: accessible, available, convenient, stocked

on the ball: able, alert, competent, qualified, skilled, smart

on the contrary: au contraire, but, contrasting, conversely, inversely, oppositely

once: already, back, before, earlier, erst, former, past, previously, quondam

once-over: checkup, examination, inspection, look, survey

oncoming: approaching, expected, imminent, impending, looming

one: alone, chosen, different, digit, individual, number, numeral, person, same, separate, single, sole, solitary, undivided, uni, unique, unit, unite, united, uno

one-billionth: nano

one-colored: monochrome

one-eyed giant: Cyclops, Polyphemus

one-horse sleigh: cutter

one hundred years: centenary, centennial

one-seeded fruit: drupe

one-sided: biased, lopsided, partial, prejudiced, uneven, unfair, unilateral, unjust

one-sided surface, continuous: Mobius strip

one-sided topologic surface having no inside or outside: Klein bottle

one-time: former, past, previous, prior, quondam

one-way conversation: monolog

one-wheeled vehicle: unicycle

oneness: accord, concord, harmony, identity, indivisibility, integrity, sameness, singularity, uniformity, union, unity, wholeness

onerous: arduous, backbreaking, burdensome, demanding, difficult, exacting, exhausting, grueling, hard, heavy, laborious, oppressive, pressing, rigorous, strenuous, taxing, toilsome

ongoing: advancing, continuous, current, endless, evolving, improving, operating, unfolding, uninterrupted

onion before development of bulb: scallion

onion family: allium

onion family plant: leek

onion genus: Allium cepa

onion types: Bermuda, Danvers, green, leek, scallion, shallot, Spanish, white, wild

onion with long, pointed, pear-shaped bulb: shallot

onion, having a layered bulb as an: tunicate

onion, resembling: alliaceous

onions, cooked with: lyonnaise

onlooker: bystander, eyewitness, gazer, observer, rubberneck, sightseer, spectator, viewer, witness

only: barely, but, entirely, except, exclusively, however, individual, just, lone, mere, merely, nevertheless, nothing but, simply, single, singly, singular, sole, solely, solitary, totally, unparalleled, unrivaled, yet

onomatopoeia: echoism

onrush: assault, attack, deluge, flood, flow, gush, onset, onslaught, race, surge, tide

onset: assault, attack, attempt, beginning, birth, charge, commencement, dash, dawning, encounter, onrush, onslaught, origin, outbreak, push, raid, start

onslaught: assault, attack, blitz, invasion, offensive, onrush, onset, storm

onto: above, atop, aware, informed, over, toward, upon

onus: blame, burden, duty, liability, load, obligation, responsibility, stigma, task, weight

onward: advancing, ahead, along, away, beyond, forward

oodles: abundance, gobs, heap, heaps, loads, lot, lots, rafts, scads, slew, slews, tons

oomph: attraction, dash, drive, élan, energy, pizzazz, spirit, stamina, strength, vigor, vitality

ooze: bleed, discharge, drip, emanate, emit, escape, exude, gook, leak, marsh, mire, muck, mud, overflow, secrete, sediment, seep, seepage, slime, slob, sludge, spew, weeze

opal type: black, chalcedony, fire, geyserite, girasol, harlequin, hyalite, menilite, milky, noble, precious, white

opaque: blurred, clouded, concealed, dark, dense, dull, muddy, nubilous, obscure, obtuse, stupid, unclear, unintelligible, vague

open: accessible, agape, airy, ajar, apparent, available, begin, blatant, candid, clear, cleared, commence, crack, direct, disclose, expand, explicit, expose, extended, extroverted, flagrant, forthright, frank, free, gaping, hole, honest, initiate, naked, objective, obvious, originate, outdoors, overt, patent, plain, prone, release, revealed, sincere, start, susceptible, unbolt, unclose, unconcealed, uncovered, undecided, undo, unfasten, unfold, unlace, unlatch, unlocked, unplug, unreserved, unseal, unstop, untie, untwine, unwrap, vacant, vacated, wide

open-air: alfresco, outdoor, outside, spacious

open air, in the: alfresco

open and observable: overt

open-and-shut: apparent, clear, evident, obvious

open area in a forest: glade

open audition: cattlecall

open country: bush, range, veld

open-handed blow: slap

open-minded: fair, flexible, just, liberal, objective, tolerant, unbiased

open or begin use formally in ceremony: dedicate, inaugurate

open stretch of pavement or grass: esplanade, promenade

open surface, land, sky: expanse

open to action or influence: exposed, vulnerable

open to admitting substances: permeable, porous

open to question: arguable, disputable, moot

open to the sky: hypethral

open up discussion on: broach

open wide: gape, yawn

openhanded: altruistic, benevolent, bountiful, charitable, free, generous, kind, liberal, receptive

openhearted: frank, honest, kindly, sincere, warm

opening: aperture, beginning, breach, break, cave, chance, cleft, commencement, crack, cranny, crevice, debut, door, fissure, gap, gash, gate, hiatus, hole, lacuna, launch, mouth, opportunity, orifice, outlet, pass, pore, portal, possibility, rift, slit, slot, space, span, start, threshold, vent, width, window

opening for coins: slot

opening in a mold for molten metal: sprue

opening in chess or other endeavor: gambit, initiative

opening in wall for door or window: embrasure

opening left for attaching a sleeve: scye

opening motto or quotation: epigraph

opening of a dead end street: cul

opening of letter or greeting: salutation

opening of the mouth: rictus

opening or slit in clothing: placket

opening or space, small: interstice

opening oration at commencement: salutatory

opening performance: premiere

openly acknowledge: avow, confess

openly and clearly expressed: explicit, forthright

openly oppose: defy

openmouthed: aghast, amazed, astonished, awestruck, confounded, gaping, insistent, surprised, vociferous

openwork barrier: grille

openwork fabric: mesh

opera: aida, libretto, musical, theater

RELATED TERMS

opera company, director of: impresario

opera female lead: diva, prima donna

opera interval entertainment: divertissement, entr'acte

opera singer's vibrato: tremolo

opera solo song: aria, arietta

opera song text or spoken part: libretto

opera voice: basso, casso, heldentenor

operatic singing of tonal lyricism: bel canto

operatic singing style: bel canto ❧

operate: drive, function, man, manage, maneuver, manipulate, perform, pilot, run, use, work

operation: action, agency, business, engagement, exercise, function, influence, overseeing, procedure, process, production, surgery, transaction, undertaking, use

operation, management and details of an: logistics

operative: active, agent, detective, effective, efficient, hand, in use, manipulative, open, spy, workable

operator: agent, broker, computer, conductor, dealer, driver, emergency, manager, motorist, speculator, switchboard, telephone, user

operose: arduous, diligent, hard, industrious, laborious

opiate: deaden, depressant, dope, downer, drug, hypnotic, narcotic, opium, sedative, soporific, tranquilizer

opine: conclude, deem, hold, judge, offer, regard, state, suppose, surmise, think, view

opinion: advice, attitude, belief, concept, conclusion, conjecture, conviction, decision, dictum, doctrine, estimate, estimation, evaluation, expression, feeling, guess, hypothesis, idea, impression, judgment, notion, persuasion, say, say-so, sentiment, tenet, theory, think, thought, view, viewpoint

RELATED TERMS

opinion at variance with established beliefs: heresy, heterodoxy

opinion based on emotion or feeling: sentiment

opinion based on inconclusive evidence or guess: conjecture, speculation, supposition, surmise

opinion contrary to established doctrine: heresy

opinion for or against that affects judgment: bias, parti pris, prejudice

opinion formed in advance: preconception

opinion generally held, of majority or group as a whole: consensus

opinion opposed to established views: heresy

opinion or conception, conventional oversimplified: stereotype

opinion or idea serves as measure of acceptability, person whose reactions to: sounding board

opinion poll: survey

opinion taker: pollster

opinion, disagreeing in: dissident

opinion, fixed or strong: conviction, dogma, persuasion

opinion, gathering of force of public: groundswell

opinion, of a fixed: entrenched

opinion, to deliver an: render

opinion, to form beforehand: preconceive

opinionated: adamant, biased, bossy, bullheaded, dictatorial, dogmatic, inflexible, obstinate, overbearing, pigheaded, stubborn, uncompromising

opinionated and immature: sophomoric

opinionated theorist or exponent of ideology: ideologue

opinions, division into two contradictory: dichotomy ❧

opium: chandu, codeine, cryptopine, dope, drug, heroin, hops, intoxicant, laudanine, laudanum, opiate, poppy, soporific

opium addiction: meconism

opponent: adversary, antagonist, anti, assailant, challenger, combatant, competitor, enemy, foe, nemesis, opposition, rival

opponent for the sake of argument: devil's advocate

opponent, troublesome: nemesis

opportune: advantageous, appropriate, auspicious, convenient, favorable, fitting, fortunate, pat, ready, seasonable, suitable, timely, well-timed

opportune time to carry out something: window of opportunity

opportunity: advantage, break, chance, exploit, fortuity, hope, occasion, opening, room, shot, stab, turn

opportunity, to take best advantage of: capitalize on, cash in on, exploit, utilize

oppose: argue, battle, block, buck, combat, conflict, confront, contest, contradict, contrast, controvert, counter, cross, debate, defy, deny, differ, disagree, dispute, duel, encounter, face, fight, front, gainsay, match, meet, object, obstruct, oppugn, pit, protest, rebel, repel, resist, traverse, vie, withstand

oppose and balance out: counterbalance, counterpose, countervail, offset

oppose and stand up to: challenge, confront, defy, protest, remonstrate

oppose, in a debate: rebut

oppose, to: contradict, controvert, deny, dispute, gainsay, oppugn, repudiate

opposed: anti, averse, repugnant

opposed and unharmonious: contradictory, incompatible, inconsistent

opposed to change or progress: conservative, reactionary

opposed to usual beliefs: heterodox

opposed to verso: recto

opposed, diametrically: antipodal

opposed, unchangeably: implacable, irreconcilable

ORANGE

apricot	chrome orange	mikado	pumpkin	tangerine
aurora	copper	ocher	realgar	terra cotta
brass-colored	dark orange	old gold	red-orange	titian
burnt Roman ocher	helianthin	orange-red	Rubens' madder	yellow-orange ❦
cadmium orange	hyacinth	orange-yellow	saffron	
carotene	mandarin	pale orange	Spanish ocher	
carrot	marigold	peach	tan	

opposing: adverse, anti, at variance, conflicting, rival

opposing and contradicting: contrary, perverse

opposing attitudes or feelings, having: ambivalent

opposing or antagonistic: adversarial

opposing sides, shared by: reciprocal

opposite: across, adverse, antagonistic, antipodal, antipodean, antipole, antithesis, antithetical, antonym, contra, contradictory, contrary, contrast, converse, counter, counterpoint, diametrical, different, face to face, facing, inverse, paradox, polar, reverse, vis-à-vis

opposite in meaning: antonym

opposite terms combined in a phrase: oxymoron

opposite that completes a whole: complement

opposite, direct: antithesis, converse, inverse

opposite, exactly: antipodal, contrary, diametrical, dilemmatic, polar

opposition: animosity, antagonism, antis, clash, competition, contention, contrariety, defiance, encounter, enemy, hostility, resistance, rivalry, strife, struggle

opposition group: faction

opposition or unlikeness: antinomy, contradiction, discrepancy, disparity, incongruity

opposition to authority: contumacy, dissent

opposition, hostility resulting in: antagonism

opposition, nonviolent: passive resistance

opposition, of a feeling of: adversative, antipathetic, averse, oppugnant

opposition, to induce: polarize

oppress: abuse, afflict, burden, constrain, crush, depress, dishearten, distress, harass, harrow, overpower, overthrow, overwhelm, persecute, pressure, ravish, repress, smother, subdue, subjugate, suppress, trample, trouble, weight, wrong

oppression: affliction, dullness, injustice, lassitude, misery, suffering, tyranny

oppressive: bleak, burdensome, cruel, depressing, dismal, distressing, gloomy, hard, hardhanded, harsh, heavy, heavyhanded, muggy, onerous, overbearing, overwhelming, severe, stifling, suffocating, taxing, vexing

oppressive thing: burden, incubus

oppressor: authoritarian, autocrat, czar, despot, dictator, martinet, tyrant

opprobrious: abusive, contemptuous, despicable, disgraceful, hateful, infamous, invective, malicious, notorious, scornful, shameful

opprobrium: abuse, contempt, disdain, disgrace, dishonor, disrespect, ignominy, infamy, odium, offense, reproach, scorn, scurrility, shame

oppugn: attack, contend, contradict, dispute, oppose, question, resist

opt: choose, decide, elect, pick, prefer, select, take, vote

optical illusion: mirage

optimist, naive: Pollyana

optimistic: bright, cheerful, confident, enthusiastic, happy, hopeful, hoping, idealistic, promising, roseate, rosy, sanguine, sunny, upbeat

optimistic about rising prices: bullish

optimistic, naively: Panglossian

optimum: best, greatest, height, ideal, maximum, peak, supreme, zenith

option: alternative, choice, decision, druthers, feature, item, prerogative, privilege, right, selection, vote

optional: alternative, available, contingent, discretionary, elective, facultative, nonobligatory, unforced, voluntary

opulent: abundant, affluent, book, composition, elegant, extravagant, gaudy, lavish, luscious, luxurious, opus, plentiful, plush, profuse, rich, showy, study, swank, wealthy, work

opus: brainchild, creation, masterpiece

or: alternative, either, else, ere, instead, oppositely, rather, substitute, uncertainty

oracle: augury, clairvoyant, maxim, medium, prediction, prophecy, revelation, sage, seer, sibyl, soothsayer

oracular: cryptic, delphic, diving, enigmatic, esoteric, foreseeing, mysterious, mystical, obscure, prophetic, vatic

oral: acroamatic, aloud, articulate, lingual, narrated, phonetic, sonant, spoken, unwritten, uttered, verbal, vial, voiced

oral defamatory statement: slander

oral sex, reciprocal: 69, sixty-nine

oral teaching: catechesis

oral, not written: nuncupative

orange and related fruits: citrus

RELATED TERMS

orange container: crate

orange decorated with cloves: pomander

orange rind as flavoring: zest

orange seed: pip

orange variety: bergamot, blood, China, Florida, Maltese, mandarin, navel, Seville, sweet, tangerine, Temple, wild

orange, and others: pekoes

orange, bitter: bigarade, bitter orange, Seville orange, sour orange

orange, spongy white tissue of: pith

orangelike fruit of tangerine tree: mandarin orange ❦

orangutan: anthropoid, ape, mias, primate, satyr

orate: address, declaim, filibuster, harangue, lecture, recite, sermonize, speak, spiel, spout

oration: address, discourse, eulogy, lecture, sermon, soapbox, speech

orator: demagogue, lecturer, rhetorician, speaker, spellbinder, spokesperson

oratorical: articulate, eloquent, rhetorical

oratory: chapel, discourse, elocution, eloquence, preaching, public speaking, rhetoric

orb: ball, circle, circuit, earth, eye, eyeball, globe, ocular, planet, ring, sphere

orbit: circle, circuit, course, cycle, dominion, ellipse, influence, path, radius, range, realm, revolution, rotation, scope, track

RELATED TERMS

orbit around moon closest to moon's center, point of: perilune

orbit around moon farthest from moon's center, point of: apolune

orbit east to west, opposite of most celestial bodies: retrograde

orbit of celestial body closest to the sun, point of: perihelion

orbit of celestial body farthest from sun, point of: aphelion

orbit of celestial body from center of attraction, closest or farthest point in: apse, apsis

orbit of moon or satellite closest to earth, point of: perigee

orbit of moon or satellite farthest from earth, point of: apogee

orbit, of a noncircular: eccentric, elliptical

orbiting manmade body: satellite ❧

orchard: arbor, farm, garden, grove, plantation, trees

orchestra: band, chamber, ensemble, gamelan, group, instruments, maestro, philharmoic, philharmonic, string, symphony

orchestra instrument: bass, bells, cello, clarinets, cornet, drum, flute, French horn, gong, harp, oboe, oboes, piano, piccolo, saxophone, timpani, trombone, trumpets, tuba, viol, viola, violin, xylophone

orchestra section: brass, percussion, reed, reeds, string, strings, woodwind

orchestra, small: chamber orchestra

orchestral composition based on a theme and consisting of one movement: symphonic poem, tone poem

orchestral composition in at least three movements: symphony

orchestra's first violinist and assistant conductor: concertmaster

orchestra's place: pit

orchestrate: arrange, compose, coordinate, harmonize, organize, score

orchid root: salep

orchid variety: baby, butterfly, buttonhole, calypso, Christmas, cobra, cradle, cymbidium, Easter, hyacinth, moth, rainbow, scarlet, snowy, spider, vanda

ordain: allot, appoint, arrange, authorize, command, commission, conduct, consecrate, constitute, decree, deem, destine, enact, establish, install, name, order, predestine, prepare

ordeal: experience, grief, nightmare, suffering, test, tragedy, trial, tribulation, trouble

order as group: association, brotherhood, caste, category, class, club, fellowship, genus, grade, lodge, rank, sisterhood, society

order by authority: decree, edict, fiat, proclamation, ukase

order by legislature or ruler: law, ordinance, regulation, rule, statute

order by virtue of authority: decree, ordain, prescribe

order from the premises: evict

order of events: sequence

order of players: lineup

order of rank or authority: chain of command

order of rank or preference: precedence

order of, to reverse or change the: transpose

order or authorize task or job, to: commission

order or command: directive, mandate

order or command, to: adjure, enjoin, exhort

order or equivalence between parts: proportion, symmetry

order or hierarchy: pecking order

order or request for something, formal: requisition

order or send back: remand

order prohibiting course of action, court: injunction

order to appear before judge: habeas corpus

order to appear in court: subpoena, summons

order to buy or sell stocks or commodities at prevailing market price: market order

order to perform a specified duty: mandamus

order to perform or refrain from action: injunction

order to refrain: monition

order, a particular: disposal, distribution, placement

order, act or process of following in: succession

order, arbitrary: fiat

order, authoritative: behest, ukase

order, having no: aleatory, arbitrary, haphazard, random

order, having the nature of an: imperative, peremptory

order, in: acceptable, all right, hunkydory, kosher, proper

order, in working: functional, operational, operative

order, rearrangement of an: permutation

order, to issue an: dictate, lay down, stipulate

order, to place in particular: arrange, dispose

order, to put carefully in: arrange, codify, collate, collocate, systematize, tabulate

ordered arrangement of elements in set: permutation

ordered or in sequence: consecutive, sequential, serial, successive

orderly: businesslike, controlled, cosmic, exact, formal, manageable, methodical, neat, obedient, peaceable, peaceful, precise, quiet, regulated, ruly, shipshape, snug, systematic, tidy, tranquil, trig, trim, uncluttered, uniform, well-behaved

orderly whole of universe: cosmos

ordinance: act, canon, code, enactment, order, ruling, statute

ordinary: average, banal, common, commonplace, conventional, customary, day-to-day, everyday, exoteric, familiar, frequent, garden variety, habitual, hackneyed, mediocre, mundane, natural, normal, prosaic, quotidian, regular, routine, so-so, traditional, trivial, typical, uneventful, unexceptional, usual

ordinary and plain: anonymous, inconspicuous, prosaic, unexceptional

ordinary and unpretentious: homespun

ordinary everyday language: colloquial, vernacular

ordinary language: prose

ordinary person as opposed to specialist: layman, layperson, laywoman

ordnance: ammunition, armaments, armor, artillery, cannon, equipment, firearms, guns, supplies, torpedoes, weapons

ore: blende, bronze, copper, gold, iron, lead, metal, mineral, platinum, rock, silver, tin, zinc

ore analysis: assay

ore deposit: bonanza, lode, metal, mine, vein

organ: agency, channel, console, forum, instrument, journal, magazine, means, medium, melodeon, newspaper, periodical, publication, tool, vehicle, voice

organ for transplant, one who gives: donor

organ out of place: prolapse

organ pipe: flue, reed

organ pipe similar to the clarabella: melodia

organ pipes, group of matched: register

organ stop: bombardon, bourdon, quint, reed

organ through wall that normally holds it, protrusion of: hernia, rupture

organ wall, body: paries, parietes

organ, desklike part of: console

organ, human: brain, ear, eye, heart, intestine, kidney, liver, lung, nose, pancreas, stomach, tongue

organ, main part of bodily: corpus

organ, musical: accordion, Calliope, harmonica, harmonium, hurdy-gurdy, melodeon

organ, normal firmness of body: tone

organ, pathological change in: lesion

organ, small reed: melodeon

organ, two principal stops on pipe: diapason

organic: basic, constitutional, fundamental, healthful, inborn, inherent, interconnected, living, natural, nonsynthetic, simple

organic compound: amide, amine, enol, ester, imide, steroid

organic equilibrium: homeostasis

organic salt: ester

organic soil: peat

organic substance providing nutrients for plants: humus

organic wholes are greater than sum of parts: holism

organism: amoeba, animal, bacterium, being, cell, entity, fungus, germ, individual, life, microbe, monad, person, plant, protist, protozoan, virus

organism derived asexually from ancestor: clone

organism's body: soma

organisms in relation to environment: ecology

organisms of different species for mutual benefit, association of: symbiosis

organisms, single-celled microscopic eukaryotic: protozoan, protozoon

organist's finale: postlude

organization: agency, alliance, arrangement, association, band, brotherhood, business, circle, club, coalition, company, confederation, configuration, constitution, cooperative, coordination, corporation, disposition, establishment, fellowship, firm, format, framework, group, guild, institute, league, lodge, order, partnership, planning, profession, setup, sisterhood, system, team, trade, union

RELATED TERMS

organization financed by a government but run independently: quango

organization, criminal: Cosa Nostra, gang, mafia, syndicate

organization, political: bloc, machine, party

organization's members, not leaders: rank and file ❦

organize: arrange, catalog, create, edify, establish, formulate, found, index, marshal, neaten, plan, set up, sort, start

organized persecution of a minority group: pogrom

organized protest: sit-in

organizer, entertainment: impresario

organs, concerning internal: splanchnic, visceral

organs, internal: entrails, innards, viscera

orgiastic: Dionysian, pagan

orgy: bacchanal, Bacchanalia, bash, binge, carousal, debauch, feast, fling, frolic, indulgence, merry-making, party, rampage, revel, romp, saturnalia, spree

orient: acclimatize, accommodate, accustom, adapt, adjust, align, conform, familiarize, locate

orifice: aperture, crack, hole, inlet, mouth, opening, outlet, pore, slit, slot, vacity, vent

origin: alpha, ancestry, anture, basis, beginning, birth, blood, cause, commencement, conception, creation, embryo, evolution, extraction, family, genesis, inception, inspiration, lineage, maternity, parent, parentage, paternity, provenance, provenience, root, seed, source, spring, start

origin and development of humans, scientific study of: anthropogenesis

origin of word: etymology, word history

origin of word, incorrect: folk etymology

origin or descent: ancestry, derivation, extraction, family tree, lineage, parentage, paternity, pedigree

origin or source: fountainhead, originator

origin, biological point of: radix

origin, place of: derivation, provenance, starting point, terminus a quo

original: aboriginal, archetypal, authentic, creative, earliest, eccentric, first, first generation, forerunner, fresh, fundamental, genuine, initial, innovative, inventive, native, new, novel, oddity, pioneer, primal, primary, primeval, primitive, primordial, pristine, prototype, unique

original and creative: Promethean

original and first: primal, primitive, primordial

original condition, brand new: mint condition

original form, concerning something in: endemic, native

original inhabitant: arborigine, native

original model or type: archetype, blueprint, prototype

original population, concerning the: aboriginal, autochthonous, indigenous

originality: cleverness, creativeness, freshness, ingenuity, innovation, novelty, unorthodoxy

originate: arise, begin, birth, cause, coin, commence, contrive, create, develop, devise, discover, emanate, establish, father, formulate, found, generate, hatch, inaugurate, initiate, institute, introduce, invent, launch, make, produce, rise, spawn, spring, start, stem

originate, concerning or having power to: creative, seminal

originating externally: exogenous

originating in an area or environment: aboriginal, autochthonous, indigenous

originating internally: endogenous

originator: author, causer, creator, designer, father, fountainhead, initiator, innovator, inventor, mother, pioneer, precursor, progenitor, trailblazer

origins and causes, study of: etiology

origins and forms of proper names, study of: onomastics

ornament: adorn, amulet, attire, bead, beautify, brooch, deck, decorate, decoration, design, embellish, emboss, embroider, enrich, festoon, figurine, finery, flower, furbish, furnishing, garnish, gewgaw, jewel, trim

ornament carved in low relief: anaglyph

ornament-holding furniture piece: étagère

ornament made by setting pieces into surface: inlay

ornament on arch, arched structure: finial

ornament that hangs: pendant

ornament with raised design: emboss

ornament, small: bauble, bric-a-brac, gewgaw, gimcrack, knickknack, novelty, trinket

ornamental: chichi, decorative, dressy, elaborate, elegant, fancy, florid, frilly, rococo

ornamental graphical element, e.g. bullet: dingbat

ornamentation done with tools: tooling

ornamentation having raised work: embossment

ornamentation of metal with wavy patterns: damascene

ornamentation, art style marked by: rococo

ornamentation, bizarre: baroque

ornate: baroque, bombastic, cantankerous, contrary, dazzling, elaborate, fancy, flamboyant, flashy, florid, flowery, glitzy, irritable, lush, luxurious, mean, opulent, ornery, rococo, showy, stubborn

ornate writing: purple prose

ornery: cranky, cross as a bear, crotchety, grouchy, mean, nasty, surly

orotund: bombastic, clear, loud, pompous, resonant, resounding, rich, showy, sonorous, stentorian

orphan: forsaken, foundling, waif

orthodox: accepted, approved, canoni-cal, conservative, conventional, correct, customary, devout, pious, proper, standard, traditional

oscillate: flicker, fluctuate, palpitate, pulsate, rock, sway, swing, unsteady, vacillate, vary, vibrate, waver

oscitate: yawn

osculate: buss, contact, kiss, peck, touch

osmosis: absorption, assimilation, diffusion, passage

osprey: ossifrage

osprey cousin: erne

ossify: barden, fossilize, petrify, set, stiffen, thicken

ossuary: receptacle, tomb, urn, vault

ostensible: alleged, apparent, clear, illusory, implied, likely, obvious, pretended, professed, purported, seeming, supposed

ostentation: display, eclat, exhibition, flare, flashiness, flaunting, flourish, pageantry, parade, pomp, pomposity, pretense, pretentious, show, spectacle, splash

ostentatious: chichi, dashing, elaborate, extravagant, flamboyant, flashy, flaunting, gaudy, grandiose, loud, overdone, pompous, pretentious, showy, splashy, sporty, swanky

ostentatious display of knowledge: pedantry

ostracize: avoid, banish, blackball, blacklist, exclude, exile, expatriate

ostrich: bird, rhea

ostrich cousin: emu

ostrich or emu: ratite

ostrich, concerning an: struthious

other: added, additional, alternative, different, distinct, else, former, further, more, opposite, spare

otherwise: alternatively, contrarily, differently, else, oppositely, variously

otiose: empty, futile, hollow, idle, inactive, indolent, ineffective, laggard, lazy, slothful, sterile, superfluous, surplus, useless, vain

otitis: earache

otter family: musteline

otter, pertaining to: lutrine

ouch: blazes, brooch, clasp, cry, darn, displeasure, oops, pain, setting, shoot

ought: anything, behoove, cipher, desirability, duty, likelihood, must, obligation, should, want

oust: banish, bar, depose, dethrone, discharge, dismiss, eject, evict, expel, fire, ostracize, remove, topple, unseat

out: absent, away, exterior, external, extinguished, forth, gone, not in, public, published, revealed

out-and-out: absolute, arrant, complete, downright, entire, frank, notorious, outright, perfect, pure, sheer, thoroughgoing, unequivocal

out loud: oral

out of business: defunct

out of control: amok, amuck, crazy, doomed, lost, rampant, ruined, runaway, wild

out-of-date: antiquated, archaic, obsolete, old hat, old-fashioned, outmoded, passé, superannuated, vieux jeu

out of fashion: antiquated, dated, démodé, passé, unfashionable

out of hand: disorderly, uncontrolled, unmanageable, unruly, wild

out of kilter: askew, crooked, uneven

out of line: crooked, exorbitant, uneven, unreasonable

out of order: awry, broken, defective, faulty, inoperative, kaput, malfunctioning

out of place: inapposite, inappropriate, inept, inopportune, lost, malapropos, mislaid, unsuitable

out of practice: rusty, stale

out of the blue: sudden, unanticipated, unexpected, unforeseen

out of the ordinary: different, extraordinary, phenomenal, rare, remarkable, unique, unusual

out-of-the-way: distant, far-off, isolated, obscure, remote, removed, secluded

out of touch: disoriented, estranged, unaware, unstable

out of tune keyboard or stringed instrument: wolf

outage: blackout, brownout, failure, interruption

outback: bush, country, remote, rural, wilderness

outbreak: beginning, burst, commotion, conflict, epidemic, eruption, explosion, fury, insurrection, mutiny, onset, plague, revolt, riot, ruckus, uprising

outbreak, renewed: recrudescence

outbuilding: barn, garage, outhouse, shed, stable, storehouse

outburst: access, attack, blast, blow-up, discharge, disturbance, eruption, explosion, frenzy, gale, gust, paroxysm, rage, scene, tantrum, tiff, tirade, torrent

outcast: banished, bum, derelict, exile, expatriate, expelled, fugitive, harijan, leper, pariah, refugee, rejected, runaway, untouchable, vagabond, vagrant

outclass: bast, exceed, excel, outdo, surpass

outcome: aftermath, causatum, conclusion, consequence, denouement, effect, end result, fallout, fate, issue, payoff, reaction, result, score, upshot

outcome of plot: denouement

outcome, possible: eventuality

outcry: alarm, bawl, clamor, complaint, hubbub, noise, objection, protest, racket, scream, screech, shout, shriek, upheaval, uproar, yell

outdated: antiquated, archaic, corny, démodé, obsolete, old, passé, square, superannuated, unfashionable

outdo: beat, best, better, cream, defeat, exceed, excel, outclass, outshine, overcome, surpass, top, transcend, worst

outdoor meal: barbeque, fête champêtre, picnic

outdoors: alfresco, country, fresh air, in the open, outside, surroundings

outer: alien, beyond, ectal, exposed, exterior, external, extraneous, foreign, peripheral, remote, space

outer covering or coat, natural: integument

outer edge: perimeter, rim

outer end of a spoon: toe

outer feather: penna

outer layer of body organ: cortex

outer layer of the skin: derma

outermost: extreme, farthest, final, last, periphery, remotest, utmost

outermost part or region: periphery

outfit: array, attire, clothing, dress, duds, equipment, furniture, garb, gear, getup, kit, provisions, rig, suit, trappings

outfit or team: company, corps, ensemble, enterprise, organization, party, squad, team, unit

outfit, to: clothe, equip, furnish, supply

outflow: drainage, effluent, issue

outgoing: cordial, demonstrative, exiting, extroverted, former, friendly, genial, gregarious, leaving, open, retiring, sociable, warm

outgoing and sociable: gregarious

outgoing person: extrovert

outgrowth: branch, bulge, consequence, culmination, derivative, issue, node, offshoot, offspring, product, projection, result, sequel, sprout

outgrowth of organ or part: apophysis

outgrowth, unnatural: excrescence

outhouse: latrine, lavatory, outbuilding, privy, toilet

outing: clambake, day trip, drive, excursion, hike, jaunt, junket, picnic, ride, spree, trip, vacation

outlandish: alien, barbarous, bizarre, eccentric, exotic, extravagant, fantastic, foreign, odd, outrageous, peculiar, remote, strange, unorthodox, unusual, weird, wild

outlast: endure, persist, prevail, remain, survive

outlaw: ban, bandit, banish, condemn, criminal, crook, desperado, felon, forbid, fugitive, gangster, hoodlum, miscreant, prohibit, proscribe, stop

outlaw-seeker for reward: bounty hunter

outlay: charge, cost, disbursement, expenditure, expense, payment

outlet: aperture, channel, door, egress, escape, exit, market, opening, orifice, passage, shop, spillway, store, vent

outline: blueprint, border, chart, configuration, conformation, contour, delineate, describe, draft, figuration, figure, form, frame, fringe, limits, limn, lineament, map, perimeter, plan, preplan, profile, prospectus, rundown, shape, silhouette, skeleton, sketch, summary, syllabus, synopsis, trace

outline in black or filled with color: silhouette

outline of plot: scenario, treatment

outline of study, course: syllabus

outline sketchily: adumbrate

outline, to draw an: delineate, depict, describe, sketch

outlook: angle, aspect, attitude, direction, expectation, exposure, forecast, perception, perspective, probability, prognosis, prospect, slant, view, viewpoint, vista

outlook of narrator: point of view

outlying: afar, distant, external, faraway, outer, remote, removed

outlying area: purlieu

outmoded: antiquated, archaic, by-

gone, dated, démodé, horse and buggy, obsolete, old-fashioned, outdated, passé

outpatient part of hospital: polyclinic

outpost: boundary, frontier, position, settlement, station

outpouring: deluge, effusion, flood, gush, outburst, overflow, spate, stream

output: achievement, energy, gain, harvest, power, production, profit, take, turnout, yield

outrage: abuse, affront, anger, atrocity, enormity, evil, harm, illtreat, incense, iniquity, insult, mistreat, misuse, offend, offense, ravish, rile, shock, wrongdoing

outrageous: abominable, atrocious, base, brutal, crazy, debauching, despicable, dreadful, excessive, exorbitant, extreme, flagrant, gross, heinous, horrible, horrid, obscene, shocking, ungodly, unreasonable, unspeakable, vile, wicked

outrageous person: enfant terrible

outrageous wickedness: villainy

outrageously bad: egregious, flagrant

outrageously scandalous: scabrous

outré: bizarre, eccentric, extravagant, strange, unconventional

outrigger canoe: proa

outright: absolute, complete, dead, direct, entire, flat, forthwith, instantly, openly, sheer, thoroughly, total, unconditional, undeniable, unmitigated, whole

outrun: beat, defeat, distance, elude, exceed, surpass

outset: beginning, birth, commencement, dawning, origin, start

outshine: eclipse

outside: alfresco, covering, distant, exterior, external, facade, faint, farthest, remove, slender, slight, slim, small, unlikely

outside angle of wall: coign, quoin

outside normal perception: transcendent

outside something's nature: extrinsic

outside the jurisdiction of an area: extraterritorial

outside, coming from the: exogenous, extraneous, extrinsic

outside, external: peripheral

outside, state of being or feeling: alienation, disassociation, estrangement

outsider: alien, foreigner, odd man out, outcast, outlander, stranger

outskirts: boundary, edge, environs, fringes, limit, outpost, purlieus, sticks, suburbs

outspoken: artless, blunt, brash, candid, direct, explicit, frank, free, honest, open, opinionated, oral, unreserved, vocal

outspread: broad, expanded, free, opened, unfolded, unlimited, unrestrained, widespread

outstanding: celebrated, distinguished, dominant, eminent, excelling, exceptional, famed, famous, foremost, great, impressive, major, marked, notable, noted, noticeable, overdue, preeminent, prominent, remarkable, renowned, standout, superb, superlative, transcendent, uncollected, unpaid, unsettled

outstanding accomplishment: pièce de résistance, showpiece

outstanding and prominent: salient

outstanding example: paragon

outstanding feature: highlight

outstrip: best, defeat, exceed, excel, outdo, overtake, pass, surpass, top, transcend, win

outward: apparent, ectad, evident, exterior, external, formal, noticeable, obvious, ostensible, overt, perceivable, superficial, visible

outward carrying, directed away: efferent

outward-directed: centrifugal, deferent, efferent

outward, push or thrust: protrude

outward, spread or turned: splayed

outweigh: compensate, dominate, exceed, offset, override, overshadow, prevail, surpass

outwit: baffle, bamboozle, best, circumvent, dupe, euchre, finagle, foil, fool, fox, frustrate, jockey, outmaneuver, thwart

ouzo flavor: anise

oval: egg-shaped, ellipse, elliptical, oblong, ocoid, ovate, spherical

oval- or almond-shaped: amygdaloid

ovary cavity: follicle

ovary removal from female animal: spaying

ovation: acclaim, applause, broiler, cheering, hand, homage, laudation, praise

oven: baker, furnace, hearth, kiln, oast, range, stove

oven for baking or firing ceramics: kiln

oven or stove with space for cooking several things at one time: range

over: above, across, additionally, again, also, anew, atop, beyond, clear, completed, concluded, done, elapsed, ended, excess, excessive, extra, finished, hurdle, leap, midst, past, terminated, through, throughout, too, upon, vault

over and above: additional, besides, beyond, super

overabundance: excess, glut, plethora, profusion, superfluity, surfeit, surplus

overall: comprehensive, extensive, generally, head-to-foot, largely, mainly, mostly, primarily, sweeping, total

overattentive: officious, solicitous

overbearing: arrogant, bossy, bullying, cockey, dictatorial, disdainful, dominant, domineering, egotistical, haughty, high-handed, imperious, insolent, lordly, overpowering, overweening, peremptory, pompous, proud, superior

overblown: bombastic, excessive, flowery, inflated, pretentious, profuse, superfluous, windy

overboard, to cast: jettison

overburden: encumber, exhaust, oppress, overloaded, overwhelm

overcast: cloudy, dark, darken, dull, foggy, gloomy, gray, hazy, heavy, lowering, nebulous, obscure, sullen

overcharge: cheat, clip, embellish, extortion, fleece, gyp, nick, pad, soak, stick

overcoat: capote, Chesterfield, great coat, inverness, parka, raincoat, reglan, surtout, topcoat, ulster

overcome: appall, awe, beat, best, conquer, crush, daunt, defeat, exceed, hurdle, lick, master, overpower, overwhelm, prevail, prostrate, speechless, suppress, surmount, triumph, vanquish

overcome, impossible to: insuperable, insurmountable

overconfident: arrogant, brash, cocky, presumptuous

overdevelopment: hypertrophy

overdo: exaggerate, exceed, exhaust, fatigue, overstate, overwork

overdue: arrears, behind, belated, delayed, delinquent, late, outstanding, tardy, unpaid

overeat: gluttonize, gorge, indulge, satiate, stuff

overeating with self-induced vomiting: binge-purge syndrome, bulimarexia, bulimia nervosa

overexcited: high-strung, hyper

overflow: abundance, alluvion, cascade, deluge, drain, ebullient, engulf, excess, exuberant, flood, inundate, outlet, overrun, pour, slop, soak, spate, spill, submerge, surplus, swim, torrent

overflow of stream, sudden: freshet

overflow of water, channel for: spillway

overflowing: exuberant, inundant, swarming, teeming

overgrown: colossal, dense, excessive, huge, jungly, lush, rank, wild

overgrowth of shrubs or undergrowth: brake, copse, thicket

overhang: bulge, drape, eaves, extend, jetty, jut, overlap, project, protrude, suspend

overhaul: doctor, examine, mend, rebuild, recondition, redo, renovate, repair, restore, revamp

overhead: above, aerial, aloft, cost, cover, expenses, insurance, outlay, rent, roof, upkeep

overindulgence: debauchery, depravity, dissipation, excess, gluttony, intemperance, overdrinking, overeating, spoiling, satiation

overindulgent: immoderate

overjoyed: charmed, delighted, ecstatic, elated, euphoric, happy, jubilant, thrilled

overkill: destruction, excessive, genocide, slaughter, surplus

overlap: cover, flap, imbricate, intersect, overhang

overlapping in regular arrangement: imbricate

overlapping planks or boards, built with: clinker-built, lapstrake

overlay: coat, cover, glaze, pave, plate, spread, superimpose, veneer

overload: burden, encumber, excess, glut, inundate

overlook: absolve, chaperon, chaperone, condone, disregard, excuse, forget, forgive, ignore, inspect, manage, miss, neglect, omit, pardon, pass, pretermit, skip, slight, supervise

overlook from a height: command, dominate

overlord: chief, czar, despot, emperor, ruler, suzerain, tyrant

overpower: beat, bulldoze, clobber, conquer, cream, crush, dazzle, defeat, deluge, master, overbear, overcome, overthrow, overwhelm, rout, stun, subdue, subjugate, trounce, vanquish

override: annul, cancel, defeat, nullify, quash, reverse, revoke, veto

overrule: abrogate, disallow, invalidate, overturn, supersede, veto

overrun: crush, defeat, devastate, exceed, infest, inundate, invade, massacre, overwhelm, raid, ravage, swarm, teem

overseas: abroad, alien, exotic, foreign, ultramarine

oversee: direct, examine, inspect, manage, monitor, rule, run, shepherd, supervise, survey, watch

overseer: administrator, boss, chaperon, chaperone, chief, curator, director, foreman, guardian, head, inspector, manager, superintendent, supervisor

overshadow: cloud, cover, darken, dominate, dwarf, eclipse, obfuscate, obscure, outshine, rule, shade

overshadowing: adumbral

oversight: blunder, carelessness, disregard, error, failure, inadvertence, inattention, lapse, mistake, neglect, negligence, omission, skip, slipup

oversimplifying: simplistic

oversleeping: hypersomnia

overspread with color, light: suffuse

overstate: amplify, brag, color, embellish, exaggerate, exceed, expand, inflate, magnify, overdo

overstatement: hyperbole

overstep: encroach, exceed, infringe, transgress, trespass, violate

overt: apparent, clear, manifest, obvious, open, public, unconcealed, undisguised, visible

overtake: apprehend, approach, attain, catch, overhaul, pass, reach

overtax: burden, exceed, exhaust, overload, overwork, strain, tire

overthrow: confound, conquer, defeat, demolish, depose, destroy, destruction, dethrone, discomfit, dismiss,

downfall, fell, foil, oust, overcome, overpower, overturn, overwhelm, prostrate, raze, rebellion, remove, rout, ruin, subvert, topple, tumble, undermine, unseat, upset, vanquish

overthrow government: coup d'état

overtone: association, hint, implication, inference, innuendo, insinuation, intimation, meaning

overture: approach, beginning, composition, foreword, intro, introduction, invitation, opening, poem, preface, prelude, prologue, proposal, proposition, tender, ultimatum, volunteer

overturn: capsize, countermand, invalidate, overthrow, reverse, spill, subvert, tilt, tip, topple, upend, upset, void

overuse, commonplace through: banal, clichéd, hackneyed, shopworn, trite

overweening: arrogant, brash, egotistical, haughty, highhanded, insolent, pompous, presumptuous, pushy, vain

overweight: ample, chubby, corpulent, fat, heavy, hefty, huge, obese, plump, portly, pudgy, tubby

overweight state: embonpoint

overwhelm: amaze, astonish, bury, confuse, conquer, crush, defeat, deluge, devastate, engross, engulf, floor, inundate, massacre, oppress, overcome, overpower, overrun, overthrow, overturn, puzzle, rout, sink, smother, steamroll, submerge, swamp, whip

overwhelming: awing, domineering, overbearing, staggering

overwork: burden, exhaust, exploitation, labor, strain, tax, tire

overwrought: agitated, emotional, excited, flustered, frenzied, hysterical, nervous, ornate, overdone, shaken, weary

ovine female: ewe

ovule: egg, embryo, integuments, nucellus, seed, seedlet

ovum: egg, egg cell, gamete, oosphere, seed, spore

ovum develops by meiosis, cell from which: oocyte

owing: attributable, beholden, due, in debt, indebted, mature, obligated, outstanding, payable, unpaid

owl family: Strigidae, Strigiformes, Tytonidae

owl-like: strigine

owl, kind of: barn, boobook, eagle, hawk, hoot, horned, pigmy, screech, snow, spotted

own: acknowledge, admit, allow, avow, confess, control, have, hold, individual, maintain, possess, recognize, rejoice in, retain

own up: accept, acknowledge, admit, confess

owned, land exclusively: domain

owned, privately: proprietary

owner: buyer, landlady, landlord, landowner, proprietor, titleholder

owner's certificate: deed

ownership: claim, deed, dominium, holding, possession, tenancy, title

ownership of private land and real estate: fee simple

ownership, full: freehold

ox: aver, banteng, beast, bison, bovine, buff, buffalo, bugle, bull, bullock, cow, gaur, gayal, musk, oaf, seladang, taurine, yak, zebu

ox tail: ide

ox, extinct: aurochs, urus

oxen harness: yoke

oxen, concerning: bovine, taurine

oxide, iron: ferric, limonite, magnetite, rust

oxidize: burn, corrode, heat, rust

oxygen removed from compound, reaction in which: reduction

oxygenate: aerate, oxygenize

oyster: bivalve, mollusk, shellfish

oyster hors d'oeuvre: angels on horseback

oyster product: pearl

oyster type: blueprint, flat, native, rock, saddlerock, tonged, wild

oyster's pearly internal layer: mother-of-pearl, nacre

P p   P a

pabulum: diet, food, fuel, nourishment, nutrient, nutriment, support, sustenance

pace: amble, canter, clip, count, gait, gallop, lick, march, measure, motion, move, progress, rate, speed, step, strait, stride, tempo, time, tread, trot, walk

pachyderm: elephant, hippopotamus, mammoth, mastodon, rhinoceros

pacific: appeasing, calm, gentle, harmonious, irenic, mild, peaceable, peaceful, placid, quiet, serene, smooth, tranquil

pacifist: appeaser, dove, flower child, passive resister, peacemonger

pacify: abate, allay, alleviate, appease, assuage, calm, conciliate, lull, mitigate, moderate, mollify, palliate, placate, propitiate, quiet, reconcile, salve, sedate, serene, settle, soften, soothe, subdue, tame, tranquilize

pack: baggage, bale, band, bunch, bundle, carry, compact, container, crowd, deck, fill, flock, gang, group, heap, horde, jam, knapsack, load, mob, parcel, pile, squeeze, store, stow, stuff, swarm, tote, truss

pack animal: ass, burro, mule, sumpter

pack down with repeated pressure: tamp

pack of cards: deck

package: box, bundle, container, crate, encase, packet, parcel, wrap

package or message deliverer: courier

package with plastic affixed to cardboard: blister pack, bubble pack

packed: congested, full, jammed, loaded, overcrowded, overflowing, stuffed, tamped

packet: boat, bundle, container, envelope, folder, package, parcel, pouch

packet as of sugar, small sealed: sachet

packing or stuffing material: dunnage

pact: agreement, alliance, arrangement, bargain, bond, cartel, contract, covenant, deal, tract, treaty, understanding

pad: abode, amplify, bolster, buffer, cushion, embellish, embroider, exaggerate, fatten, fudge, inflate, mat, muffle, notebook, overcharge, overstate, pillow, plod, protect, quilt, stuff, tablet, tramp, trudge, wad, walk

pad, medicine: compress

padding: filler, lining, packing, protection, stuffing, wadding

padding in pillows, mattresses: flock, kapok

padding of feathers: down

padding or stuffing in furniture: upholstery

paddle: ally, blade, dabble, oar, racket, row, scull, spank, thrash

paddle, blade of: palm

paddy plant: rice

padre: chaplain, father, minister, monk, pastor, priest

paean: acclamation, anthem, hymn, laud, laudation, ode, praise, psalm, song

paella ingredient: rice

pagan: agnostic, gentile, heathen, hedonist, heretic, idolator, infidel, nonbeliever, skeptic, unbeliever

page: announce, attendant, bellboy, bellhop, footboy, gofer, messenger, servant, usher, valet

page at start of book: frontispiece

page not slit or trimmed: uncut

page number and heading at top: header, running head

page number in book: folio

page size, formerly: sexto

page that folds out: foldout, gatefold

page, left-hand: verso

page, right-hand: recto

page, to: beep, call, summon

pageant: celebration, display, exhibition, parade, pomp, pretense, procession, show, spectacle, tableau

pages facing each other: spread

pages in order, to arrange: collate

pages of book, to thumb through: riffle

pages of multipart continuous paper form, to separate: decollate

pages of, to number the: paginate

pages, blank space of margins on: gutter

pagoda: alcove, gazebo, memorial, pavilion, shrine, temple, tower

paid: anted, compensated, indemnified, refunded, reimbursed, rewarded

pail: bucket, can, container, piggin, receptacle, vessel

pail or bucket wire handle: bail

pain: ache, afflict, affliction, agony, anguish, annoy, bother, cramp, crick, discomfort, disquiet, distress, grief, grieve, gripe, harm, heartache, hurt, injury, irritation, malaise, nuisance, pang, pest, punishment, soreness, sting, strain, suffering, torment, torture, travail, trouble, twinge, unhappiness, upset, wound

pain along nerve(s): neuralgia

pain due to anesthetic, insensibility to: analgesia, anesthesia

pain felt in another body part though problem is elsewhere: referred pain

pain infliction on others as source of sexual pleasure: sadism

pain of lost limb felt by amputee: phantom limb pain

pain or illness, imaginary: humdudgeon

pain reliever: acetaminophen, anodyne, aspirin

pain-relieving hormone: endorphin

pain spasm, severe: throe

pain, absence of: analgesia

PAINTING TECHNIQUES

applying thick layers: impasto
pigment mixed with egg yolk or glue: tempera
splattering, dripping, etc: action painting
varicolored dots: pointillism
drying oil as vehicle: oil painting
opaque watercolors mixed with gum: gouache

resin-based paint: acrylic
shades of gray only: grisaille
watercolors on wet plaster: fresco
dribbling or splashing for effect: action painting
painting on wall: fresco, frieze, mural, putto ☙

---

pain, deriving sexual pleasure from inflicted: masochism
pain, indifferent to: stoical
pain, marked by: dolorous
pain, minimum level for tolerating: threshold
pain, of a piercing: fulminant, lancinating
pain, of stinging: smarting, tingling
pain, relieving: analgesic, anodyne, lenitive
pain, severe abdominal: colic, gripes
pain, shrink or flinch in: wince
pain, spasm of: pang, throe
pain, to inflict severe: excruciate
pain, to relieve: allay, alleviate, mitigate, palliate
painful: acute, agonizing, angry, annoying, awful, difficult, dolorous, excruciating, grueling, hurting, irksome, irritated, laborious, piercing, raw, sharp, sore, stinging, throbbing, troublesome, uncomfortable
painful and embittering experience: wormwood
painful course or experience: Via Dolorosa
painful effort: agony, anguish, suffering, travail
painful experience: ordeal
pains in the face, shooting: tic douloureux, trigeminal neuralgia
painstaking: assiduous, careful, conscientious, diligent, exacting, fussy, laborious, methodic, meticulous, precise, punctilious, scrupulous, sedulous, strenuous, thorough
paint: brush, coat, color, daub, decorate, depict, enamel, gaud, limn, makeup, picture, pigment, portray, pretend, represent, rouge, stain, tint, varnish
RELATED TERMS
paint applied in thick layers on a canvas or painting surface: impasto
paint atomizer for delicate work: airbrush
paint in dots or short strokes: stipple

paint in which vehicle is drying oil: oil paint
paint layer: coat
paint made with pigment mixed with beeswax and heated: encaustic
paint-mixing board: palette
paint of water-soluble pigment: watercolor paint
paint pigments are mixed for application, oil or other substance in which: base, vehicle
paint stroke: daub
paint that dries to hard, glossy finish: enamel
paint thinner: turpentine
paint to promote drying, substance added to: drier, siccative
paint with latex binder: latex paint, rubber-base paint
paint, dry coloring matter mixed with a base to make: pigment
paint, dull rough finish of: mat, matte
paint, priming coat of: couch, sizing
paint, quick-drying semigloss: acrylic paint
paint, undercoat of: primer
painted or carved panels hinged together, two: diptych
painter: artisan, artist, illustrator
painters, group of: illusion
painting: art, canvas, composition, design, drawing, mural, oil, picture, portrait, seascape, watercolor
painting cracks: craquelure
painting in different shades of same color: monochrome, monotint
painting or photograph of inanimate objects: still life
painting placed in certain parts of a book: vignette
painting prop: easel
painting schools: abstract, Dutch, expressionist, Flemish, Florentine, French, impressionist, pop, postimpressionist, Spanish, surrealism, symbolism, Venetian
painting, blurring or softening of: scumble

painting, plaster of Paris and glue as base for: gesso
painting, small detailed: miniature
painting, to depict by: limn
paintlike glaze used for paper, cloth, wall surfaces: size ☙

pair: brace, couple, deuce, duad, duo, dyad, match, mate, set, span, team, twins, two, twosome, unite, yoke
pair of matched horses or oxen: span
pair of objects considered as single unit: duad
pair of things: brace, doublet
paired: binary, dichotomized, double, mated
paired horses: span
pairs, forming: jugate
pairs, to arrange in: geminate
pal: ally, amigo, associate, buddy, chum, cohort, companion, comrade, confidant, crony, friend, mate, partner, sidekick
palace: alcazar, castle, chateau, manor, mansion, seraglio, villa
palace of sultan: seraglio
palace, concerning a: palatial
paladin: champion, douzeper, hero, knight, supporter
palatable: acceptable, agreeable, appetizing, delectable, delicious, delightful, heavenly, pleasing, sapid, savory, tasty, toothsome
palatial: elegant, grandiose, imposing, lush, luxurious, magnificent, majestic, opulent, ornate, plush, posh, regal, ritzy, splendid, stately
palaver: babble, blab, chatter, chitchat, clack, conference, conversation, debate, dialogue, discussion, flatter, flummery, gab, jolery, parley, talk, wheedle
pale: anemic, ashen, ashy, blanch, bleak, bloodless, cadaverous, chalky, colorless, deathlike, diminish, dull, encircle, enclose, fade, faint, feeble, fence, ghastly, haggard, insipid, light,

lily, lurid, pallid, pastel, peaked, picket, sick, sickly, stake, wan, weak, white, whiten, whitish

pale and sickly yellow complexion, of: sallow

pale complexion, of: ashen, cadaverous, etiolated, livid, pallid, pasty, peaked

pale, to become: blanch, bleach

palisade: barrier, bluff, cliff, defense, enclosure, fence, fortify, furnish, slope, stockade, surround

pall: bore, cloak, cloud, cloy, coffin, covering, damper, disgust, gloom, insipid, satiate, shadow, tire, weary

pallet: bed, blanket, cot, mattress, palette, platform

palliate: allay, alleviate, calm, cloak, conceal, conciliate, cover, diminish, disguise, ease, excuse, extenuate, glaze, gloss, hide, lessen, mitigate, mollify, relieve, soften, soothe, sugarcoat, whitewash

pallid: anemic, ashen, ashy, blah, bleak, bloodless, boring, colorless, dull, lifeless, monotonous, wan

palm: areca, atap, betel, nipa, pale, talipot, thin, wan, white

palm of hand or sole of foot, concerning: volar

palm reading: chiromancy, fortunetelling, palmistry

palm variety: bamboo, betel, butterfly, cabbage, coconut, date, doom, fan, feather, funeral, hemp, ivory, mangrove, needle, oil, palmyra, petticoat, pignut, rock, royal, silver, snake, umbrella, wax, weddell, wine, yellow

palm's fleshy pads as in palmistry: mount

palm's rounded part below thumb: thenar

palmy: booming, delightful, glorious, pleasant, rosy, serene, successful,

palooka: clumsy, idiot, lug, lummox, stupid

palpable: apparent, blatant, certain, clear, concrete, discernible, distinct, evident, manifest, material, noticeable, obvious, ostensible, patent, perceptible, plain, real, recognizable, tactile, tangible

palpate: feel

palpitate: atonic, beat, crippled, flutter, palsied, pound, pulsate, pulse, quiver, shake, spastic, throb, tremble, vibrate

palpitatingly: pitapat

palsied: paralyzed, shaking, trembling

palsy-walsy: chummy, friendly, intimate

palter: babble, bargain, cheap, deceive, equivocate, falsify, fib, haggle, lie, meager, paltry, piddling, poor, prevaricate, quibble, shabby, trifle, wretched

paltry: bare, base, contemptible, flimsy, insignificant, mere, petty, picayune, pitiful, puny, rubbish, sorry, trash, trashy, trifling, trivial, unimportant, vile, worthless

pamper: baby, caress, cherish, coddle, cosset, cuddle, dandle, fondle, gratify, humor, indulge, mollycoddle, pet, satiate, spoil

pamphlet: booklet, brochure, bulletin, ephemeron, flyer, folder, handbill, handout, leaflet, manual, tract

pan: basin, container, kettle, skillet, vessel

pan-fry: sauté

pan in picture, to: follow, scan

pan or flat metal surface for cooking: griddle

pan out: click, happen, succeed, work

pan, to: criticize, denounce, review, ridicule

panacea: catholicon, cure, cure-all, cureall, elixir, nepenthe, nostrum, remedy

panache: charisma, dash, élan, flare, plume, style, swagger

pancake: bannock, blin, blini, blintz, blintze, crêpe, flapjack, fritter, griddlecake, hotcake, slapjack

pancake turn: flip

pancake with flaming orange sauce, thin: crêpe suzette

pancake, small light Russian: blini

pancake, thin with filling: crêpe

pandemonium: bedlam, chaos, clatter, commotion, confusion, craziness, disorder, hell, noise, racket, riot, tumult, turmoil, uproar

pander: bawd, cater, gratify, pimp, procurer

panegyric: acclamatory, citation, complimentary, eloge, encomium, eulogy, laudation, priase, tribute

panel: board, committee, gore, group, insert, jury, partition, section

panel head: moderator

panel on lower part of inner wall: wainscot

panel truck: van

paneling: wainscoting

panels, work consisting of two painted or carved: diptych

pang: ache, agony, anguish, cramp, pain, smart, spasm, stab, tang, throb, throe, torment, twinge, twitch

panhandle: beg, bum, cadge, hustle, solicit

panic: alarm, anxiety, chaos, confusion, consternation, crash, dismay, dread, fear, frenzy, hysteria, overreact, scare, slump, stampede, terror, trepidation, unnerve

panic, paralyzing: consternation

panorama: compass, horizon, overview, perspective, picture, radius, range, scene, scenery, scope, survey, sweep, view, vista

panoramic camera eye: wide-angle lens

pansy-like bloom: viola

pant: ache, beat, blow, gasp, heave, palpitate, puff, pulsate, throb, yearn

panther: cat, cougar, jaguar, leopard, puma

pantomime performer: mime artist, mummer

pantry: ambry, buttery, closet, cupboard, larder, pannier

pants: bellbottoms, blue jeans, britches, capri, chaps, chinos, corduroys, denims, drawers, jeans, knickers, slacks, trousers

pants ending just below knee: capri, clamdiggers, pedalpushers

pants ending just below knee and wide: knickerbockers, knickers

pants, wide-hipped riding: jodhpurs

pantywaist: milksop, sissy, weakling, wimp

papa: dad, daddy, father, pa, pop

papal: apostolic, papistic, pontifical

papal ambassador: nuncio

papal bull's round seal: bulla

papal cape: orale

papal court: curia, rota, see

papal court over other authority, supporting the: ultramontane

papal letter not as formal as bull: brief

papal letter to bishops of a country or countries: encyclical

papal letter with decision on point of law: decretal

papal vestments: alb, cassock, chasuble, crosier, cross, miter, mozzetta, sash, stole, zuchetto

paper: article, assignment, composition, critique, deed, diploma, dissertation, document, essay, examination, exposition, foolscap, monograph, report, sheet, stationery, theme, thesis, tissue, treatise, vellum, wallpaper, writing

paper 8½ × 13 inches: legal cap

paper 13 × 16 inches: foolscap

paper 23 × 31 inches: imperial

paper bag paper: kraft

paper bound in a book, sheet of: leaf

paper connecting a book's cover to its contents, folded: end leaf, end paper, flyleaf

paper cover on book: dust jacket

paper cutouts, decoration with: decoupage

paper decorated with raised design: embossed

paper for printing newspaper, inexpensive: newsprint

paper frill on meat chop or cutlet: papillote

paper hole covering for loose-leaf sheets: reinforcement

paper imitating sheep- or goatskin sheets: parchment

paper money: bills, cash, greenbacks, notes, scrip

paper or newspaper: daily, folio, gazette, journal, periodical, publication, tabloid

paper or newsprint, large continuous roll of: web

paper pasted to front or back binding of book: end paper

paper pieces thrown on festive occasions: confetti

paper pulp and glue or paste that can be molded: papier-mâché

paper resembling fine parchment: vellum

paper reused: recycled

paper screen, Japanese rice-: shoji

paper sizes: atlas, copy, crown, demy, elephant, emperor, folio, foolscap, imperial, legal, medium, royal

paper strip of telegraphic printer: ticker tape

paper unit of 480–516 sheets: ream

paper used as pH or acid-base indicator: litmus paper

paper used for printing, superior grade: bond paper

paper, 24–25 sheets of: quire

paper, ancient: papyrus

paper, carbohydrate important in making: cellulose

paper, cellulose mixture used to make: pulp

paper, crinkled tissue: crepe paper

paper, heading at top of: letterhead

paper, Japanese art of folding: kirigami, origami

paper, opaque thick printing: Bible paper, India paper

paper, rough grainy feel of: pebble

paper, strong yellow: manila paper

paper, to reprocess: recycle

paper, very thin: rice paper

papermaker's symbol: watermark

papers on a subject, collection of: dossier

papoose: baby, child, infant

par: average, balance, equal, equality, equivalence, norm, normal, parity, sameness, standard

par excellence: excellent, preeminent, superior, supreme

parable: allegory, apologue, fable, legend, moral, myth, story, tale

parachute of spacecraft or satellite: drogue parachute

parachute opening to catch the air, part of: canopy

parachute ropes connecting harness and canopy: rigging, shrouds

parachute to body, straps holding: harness

parachute, cord pulled to release: ripcord

parachute, sport of jumping from airplane with: skydiving

paraclete: advocate, aider, comforter, consoler, Holy Spirit, intercessor

parade: advertise, array, caravan, cavalcade, ceremony, demonstration, display, exhibit, exhibition, flash, flaunt, flourish, grandeur, march, march past, marshal, masquerade, motorcade, pageant, pageantry, pomp, procession, promenade, review, show, spectacle, stroll, strut, ticker-tape

parade for heroes: ticker-tape parade

parade of cars: motorcade

parade of slaves, etc. fastened together: coffle

parade, funeral procession or: cortege

paradigm: example, ideal, model, pattern, prototype, sample, yardstick

paradise after death: Elysian fields, Elysium, happy hunting ground, Valhalla

paradox: absurdity, anomaly, antinomy, contradiction, enigma, puzzle

paraffin: wax

paragon: cream, epitome, example,

ideal, jewel, model, nonesuch, nonpareil, paradigm, pattern, quintessence, tops, ultimate, unequaled

paragraph set in: indent

paragraph symbol: pilcrow

parallel: abreast, agree, alike, alongside, analog, analogue, collateral, compare, correlation, correspond, counterpart, equal, equate, equivalent, even, like, match, relation, similar

parallelogram: oblong, plane, rectangle, rhomb, square

parallelogram with oblique angles and equal opposite sides: rhomboid

paralyze: cripple, deaden, demolish, destroy, disable, freeze, gorgonize, halt, immobilize, incapacitate, maim, numb, petrify, stun, transfix

RELATED TERMS

paralysis involved in physical and psychological disorders: catalepsy

paralysis of arms or legs: quadriplegia

paralysis of jaw: lockjaw, tetanus, trismus

paralysis of lower half of body: paraplegia

paralysis of one side of the body: hemiplegia

paralysis of schizophrenia: catatonia

paralysis of single limb or muscle group: monoplegia

paralysis, complete or partial: palsy

paralysis, partial: paresis

paralyze with fear: petrify ❧

paramount: cardinal, chief, commanding, crowning, dominant, foremost, highest, master, predominant, preeminent, premier, prime, principal, ruler, superior, supreme, utmost

paramour: amoret, concubine, courtesan, gallant, leman, lover, mistress, suitor

paranormal ability, briefly: ESP

parapet: barricade, battlement, breastwork, bulwark, embankment, embattlement, railing, rampart, wall

paraphernalia: accessories, accoutrements, apparatus, appurtenances, belongings, equipment, furnishings, gear, materials, supplies, tackle, things

paraphrase: interpret, recapitulate, rephrase, restatement, revise, reword, summarize, synopsis, translate

parasite: bacteria, barnacle, bloodsucker, bug, deadbeat, dependent, freeloader, hanger-on, hangeron, leech, moocher, moss, opportunist, organism, sponge, sponger, sycophant, toady, virus

parasite in or on, to live as a: infest

parasitic insects: lice, nits

parasitic larva: bot

parasitic worm: helminth, trematode

parasol: canopy, sunshade, umbrella

parboil: blanch

parcel: acreage, apportion, box, bunch, carton, company, crew, deal, distribute, divide, dole, fragment, group, land, lot, pack, package, packet, part, piece, plat, plot, portion, property, ration, section, tract, wrap

parcel out: mete

parch: blister, burn, char, dehydrate, desiccate, dry, roast, scorch, sear, shrivel, wither

parched: arid, dry, sere, torrid

parchment: diploma, paper, papyrus, scroll, sheepskin, vellum

parchment made from animal skin, fine: vellum

parchment or tablet reused: palimpsest

pardon: absolution, absolve, acquit, amnesty, clear, commute, condone, exculpate, excuse, exempt, forgive, free, grace, liberate, mercy, overlook, release, remission, remit, reprieve, spare, tolerate, vindicate

pardon by confessing, to obtain: shrive

pardon granted by government: amnesty

pardonable: remissible, venial

pardons, buying or selling of religious: simony

pare: clip, curtail, cut, decrease, diminish, flay, peel, prune, reduce, remove, shave, shear, skin, trim

parent: ancestor, author, begetter, cause, dad, daddy, father, forbear, forebear, forefather, generate, guardian, mama, mater, mom, mother, origin, papa, produce, progenitor, protector, rear, sire, spawn

parent killing: parricide

parent, female four-legged: dam

parent, in the position or place of: in loco parentis

parentage: filiation

parenthetical: bracketed, explanatory, incidental, qualifying

pariah: outcast, scapegoat, undesirable, untouchable

parish: archdiocese, brethren, churchgoers, community, congregation, diocese, flock, fold, parishioners

parity: analogy, balance, closeness, consistency, equity, likeness, similarity

park: commons, forest, grounds, meadow, playground, preserve, refuge, sanctuary, stop, woodland

park employee: ranger

parlance: conversation, diction, idiom, language, lingo, phrasing, speech, talk, tongue, verbiage

parley: confab, confer, conference, consult, conversation, debate, discuss, discussion, huddle, palaver, speak, talk, treat

parliament: assemblage, assembly, congress, council, court, diet, gathering, legislature, senate

parlor: lounge, reception, room, salon

Parmesan cheese, served with: alla parmigiana

parochial: biased, bigoted, insular, limited, narrow, petty, prejudiced, provincial, restricted

parody: ape, burlesque, caricature, copy, exaggerate, farce, imitate, lampoon, mimic, mock, pastiche, satire, spoof, takeoff, travesty

paronomasia: pun

paroxysm: agitation, attack, convulsion, eruption, frenzy, fury, outbreak, outburst, pang, rage, rapture, seizure, spasm, tantrum, throe

parrot: ape, aper, bird, copy, echo, imitate, kaka, kea, mimic, polly, repeat

parrot disease: psittacosis

parrot variety: cockatoo, conure, kakapo, lory, lovebird, macaw, parakeet, quetzal, trogon

parroting speech: psittacism

parrots, concerning: psittacine

parry: avert, avoid, block, circumvent, deflect, dodge, elude, evade, fend, shirk, sidestep, ward

parsimonious: avaricious, cheap, chintzy, close, economical, frugal, illiberal, meager, mean, miserly, niggardly, penny-pinching, penurious, skimpy, stingy, thrifty, tightfisted

parson: clergyman, cleric, clerk, minister, pastor, preacher, priest, rector, reverend

parsonage: manse

part: allotment, behalf, bit, character, chip, chunk, component, constituent, cut, department, detail, division, element, factor, fraction, fragment, half, incomplete, ingredient, item, member, parcel, piece, portion, quota, ration, region, role, section, sector, segment, share, side, slice, some, subdivision, unit

part considered in relation to the whole: percentage, proportion

part extending from main body: branch, offshoot, ramification, subdivision

part of speech expressing emotion: interjection

part of speech shift, e.g. noun used as verb: functional shift

part of whole: component, constituent, element, ingredient

part standing for the whole: synecdoche

part-time amusement: diversion

part-time lodging: pied-à-terre

part-time news correspondent: stringer

part, small: modicum, snippet

part, to: allot, apportion, break, cleave, cut, detach, disjoin, disperse, disunite, divide, ration, segment, separate, sever, slice, split, sunder

partake: consume, divide, drink, eat, engage, participate, sample, share, taste

parti-colored: checkered, motley, piebald, pied, variegated

partial: biased, colored, favored, fractional, halfway, inclined, incomplete, limited, one-sided, partisan, prejudiced, sectional, slanted, unfair, unfinished

partiality: affinity, bias, fancy, favoritism, fondness, inclination, interest, leaning, preference, slant, taste, tendency

partiality, predetermined: predilection

participant: accomplice, actor, ally, associate, cohort, collaborator, colleague, contributor, fellow, helper, player

participate: assist, complete, concur, contribute, cooperate, engage, enter, join, partake, perform, play a part, share

participle lacking clear relation to sentence subject: dangling participle

particle: ace, anion, atom, atomon, bit, crumb, dot, drop, element, fleck, fragment, grain, granule, ion, iota, mite, molecule, morsel, mote, pellet, piece, ray, scrap, shred, smidgen, speck, tittle, trace

particular: accurate, careful, choosy, circumstance, definite, detail, detailed, distinct, especial, exacting, exceptional, extraordinary, fact, fastidious, finicky, fussy, individual, item, itemized, lone, minute, notable, noteworthy, peculiar, persnickety, picky, point, precise, scoop, selective, separate, special, specific, uncommon, unique, unusual

particularize: individuate

parting: adherent, adieu, biased, breakup, departure, devotee, division, factionary, farewell, follower, goodbye, partisan, separation, split

partisan: advocate, backer, champion, defender, disciple, doctrinal, fanatic, guerilla, sectarian, stalwart, supporter, sympathizer, zealot

partition: allotment, apportionment, barrier, compartment, detachment, distribution, divide, division, fence, panel, portion, screen, section, separate, separation, septum, severance, wall

partition in aircraft, ship, spacecraft: bulkhead

partly: comparatively, halfway, incompletely, notably, noticeably, partially, slightly, somewhat

partly frozen rain: sleet

partly melted snow: slush

partly open, as a door: ajar

partner: accomplice, ally, assistant, associate, buddy, chum, cohort, colleague, companion, compeer, comrade, confederate, crony, fellow, friend, helper, husband, mate, pal, sidekick, spouse, teammate, wife

partner at home: helpmate, helpmeet, spouse

partner at work: associate, collaborator, colleague, confrere, consociate

partner in activity: bedfellow, cohort, crony, sidekick

partner in contest or practice: sparring partner

partner in criminal activity: accessory, accomplice, confederate, henchman

partnership: affiliation, alliance, association, business, cahoots, cartel, company, conglomerate, firm, gang, marriage, organization, ring, union

partnership of dissimilar organisms: symbiosis

partnership, secret: cahoots, collusion

partridges, group of: brace, covey

parts that fit and complete each other, one of two: complement, counterpart

parts to make a whole, combining of: synthesis

parts, consisting of dissimilar: heterogeneous

parts, consisting of similar: homogeneous

parts, having distinct and varied: composite, compound

parts, having two: bipartite

parts, to break down into: decompose, deconstruct

parturition: birth, childbirth, delivery

party: affair, bacchanal, ball, banquet, bash, carouse, celebration, dance, festivity, fiesta, gala, gathering, occasion, orgy, picnic, reception, shindig, shindy, shower, social, soiree, spree, stag, tea, wingding

party to something: alliance, association, body, cabal, clan, coalition, company, crew, defendant, detachment, faction, force, group, individual, outfit, person, plaintiff, ring, sect, side, squad, troop, troupe

party for men only just before wedding: bachelor party, stag party

party for special occasion, especially as welcome or greeting: reception

party for women only: hen party, ladies' night

party or gathering of social or intellectual crowd: conversazione, salon

party or reception, evening: soiree

party, life of the: tummler

party, orgylike: bacchanal

party, outdoor: barbeque, clambake, cookout, fête champêtre, picnic

party, tea: tea dance, thé dansant

party, to move about at a: circulate, socialize, work the room

parvenu: arrogant, newcomer, nouveau riche, snob, upstart

pasquinade: burlesque, farce, lampoon, parody, satire

pass as law: abjudicate, advance, approve, authorization, bequeath, convey, decree, enact, give, happen, permission, permit, proceed, progress, qualify, ratify

pass away: cease, decease, depart, die, discontinue, elapse, end, expire, furlough, leave, perish, succumb

pass between two mountain peaks: col

pass beyond limits of: transcend

pass by: abandon, disregard, elapse, ignore, neglect, omit, overlook, skip

pass guaranteeing safe journey: safe-conduct

pass imperceptibly to another state: gradate

pass in land: canyon, col, gap, gorge, juncture, passage, pathway, ravine

pass in lieu of passport: laissez-passer

pass in round of competition: bye

pass off: eject, foist, palm, pretend, vanish

pass on: convey, relay, transmit

pass on in a will: devise

pass or slip by: elapse

pass or wander from one subject to another: discursive

pass out: black out, circulate, distribute, faint, swoon

pass over: dismiss, disregard, elide, forget, ignore, miss, neglect, omit, overlook, skip, wipe

pass through tissue: transpire

pass thrown by other team, to catch a football: intercept

passable: acceptable, accessible, adequate, admissible, clear, crossable, fair, mediocre, navigable, negotiable, okay, open, satisfactory, so-so, tolerable, travelable, unobstructed

passage: access, adit, aisle, alley, aorta, aqueduct, atrium, avenue, belt, burrow, channel, corridor, course, crossing, door, duct, egress, enactment, entry, estuary, excerpt, exit, fare, gangway, gate, gorge, hall, journey, lane, legislation, pass, path, permission, piece, quotation, ratification, reading, road, route, selection, strait, text, transit, transition, transmission, travel, tunnel, verse, voyage

passage from Bible: pericope

passage from literary work: excerpt, extract

passageway: adit, aisle

passageway connecting two structures: breezeway

passageway of amphitheater or stadium: vomitory

passageway open on one side: loggia

passageway, especially with shops: arcade

passageway, heavily traveled: thoroughfare

passageway, intricate: labyrinth, maze

passé: aged, ancient, antiquated, archaic, bygone, dated, demoded, extinct, faded, lapsed, obsolete, old-fashioned, outdated, outmoded, past, superannuated

passenger: commuter, fare, hitchhiker, pilgrim, rider, stowaway, traveler, wayfarer

passenger being cancelled: bump

passenger list: manifest

passenger vessel: liner

passing: adequate, brief, cursory, death, demise, elapsing, ephemeral, exceeding, fleeting, illusive, momentary, quick, temporary, transitory

passing down through successive stages of time or a process: devolution

passing of a soul into another body after death: metempsychosis, reincarnation, transmigration

passing or fleeting: migratory, transient

passion: adoration, amour, anger, appetite, ardor, craving, craze, dedication, desire, devotion, distress, eagerness, ecstasy, élan, emotion, enthusiasm, feeling, fervor, fire, fury, gusto, heat, hunger, infatuation, intensity, ire, love, lust, obsession, rage, sensuality, temper, thirst, zeal

passion for flowers: anthomania

passion for religion: evangelism

passion, foolish: infatuation

passion, great: ardor, fervor, rapture

passion, unreturned: unrequited

passionate: affectionate, aflame, amorous, ardent, avid, emphatic, enthusiastic, fervent, fervid, fierce, fiery, flaming, frenetic, heated, hotheaded, hot-tempered, hotblooded, impassioned, intense, lustful, peppery, perfervid, romantic, sensual, steamy, stimulated, sultry, torrid, vehement

passionate and angry speech: diatribe, tirade

passionate and excitable: incensed, inflammable

passionate and happy: ecstatic, rhapsodic

passionate leader: demagogue

passive: apathetic, compliant, docile, dormant, inactive, inert, lethargic, lifeless, phlegmatic, quiescent, quiet, stoic, stolid, submissive, unassertive, yielding

passive consent: acquiescence, sufferance

passive resistance: satyagraha

passivity, marked by: supine

passkey: master key, passe-partout

passport: conge, credentials, identification, key, license, safeguard, ticket, visa, voucher

password: catchphrase, countersign, open sesame, password, shibboleth, watchword

past: after, ago, antecedents, antiquity, beyond, bygone, ended, expired, foregone, former, gone, history, latter, over, preceding, previous, prior, yesterday, yore

past episode or scene used in entertainment or literature: flashback

past events, perception of significance of: hindsight

past events, sequence of: chronology

past participle of verb, e.g. had learned: pluperfect

past period, influencing or applying to a: retroactive, retrospective

past, review or contemplation of the: retrospect

past, something handed down from the: heritage, legacy

pasta: fettuccini, gnocchi, lasagna, linguine, macaroni, manicotti, orzo, ravioli, rigatoni, shells, spaghetti, tortellini, vermicelli, ziti

RELATED TERMS

pasta cooked firm: al dente

pasta in the form of potato dumplings: gnocchi

pasta layered between cheese, meat, and sauce, wide strips of: lasagna

pasta made from steamed semolina wheat: couscous

pasta made of wheat particles: semolina

pasta pressed and dried into tubes or other shapes: macaroni

pasta stuffed with meat or cheese, ring-shaped: tortellini

pasta tubes stuffed with meat or cheese: cannelloni

pasta with pockets stuffed with cheese, meat, or seafood: ravioli

pasta, concerning: farinaceous

pasta, large ribbed macaroni: rigatoni

pasta, long narrow ribbon: fettuccine, linguine

pasta, long string: spaghetti

pasta, long, thin: vermicelli

pasta, medium tubular: ziti

pasta, short tubular: penne

pasta, small ring-shaped filled: tortellini ☜

paste: affix, attach, batter, beat, cement, cream, fasten, glue, patch, pate, punch, seal, stick, strass

paste gem: rhinestone

paste, avocado: guacamole

paste, mashed chickpeas: hommos, hummus, humus

paste, meat: pâté

paste, sesame seed: tahini

pasted on surface, artwork of materials and objects: collage

pastel: assortment, color, crayon, delicate, light, mishmash, pale, pastiche, tint

pastiche: hodgepodge, jumble, medley, olio

pastille: lozenge, troche

pastime: activity, amusement, diversion, entertainment, game, hobby, leisure, recreation, relaxation, sport

pastor: clergyman, clergywoman, ecclesiastic, minister, padre, parson, preacher, priest, rabbi, rector, reverend, shepherd

pastoral: agrarian, bucolic, country, ecclesiastical, idyllic, picturesque, poem, rural, rustic

pastoral poem: idyl, idyll

pastor's place: manse

pastry: baba, baklava, cake, Danish, delicacy, éclair, flan, fritter, goodies, phyllo, pie, puff, strudel, tart

pastry filled with custard or whipped cream, chocolate-covered: éclair

pastry for Greek foods, very thin sheets of: phyllo

pastry into ridged edge, pinch: crimp

pastry of fruit rolled in thin dough and baked: strudel

pastry stuffed with meat or fish: vol-au-vent

pastry with nuts and honey, very thin: baklava

pastry, bakery specializing in: patisserie

pastry, biscuitlike: scone

pastry, fat used in making: shortening

pastry, in: en croûte

pastry, ridged edge of: fluting

pasturage: eatage

pasture: agist, feeding, grass, grazing, herbage, lea, meadow, range, retirement

pasture chip: cowpie

pasture grass: grama

pasture land: lea

pasty: adhesive, ashen, bloodless, chalky, dull, gluey, pale, pallid, sickly, unhealthy; meat pie

pasty mass: magma

pat: apropos, aptly, caress, dab, exactly, fitting, ideal, opportunely, pertinent, piece, readily, rehearsed, relevant, soothe, strike, stroke, suitable, tap, timely, touch

patch: area, blotch, chunk, clump, cover, darn, doctor, emblem, fix, insignia, mend, piece, plot, reinforcement, repair, restore, revamp, scrap, settle

patch to glue or sew on: appliqué

patchouli: mint

patchwork: fragments, hodgepodge, jumble, mélange, medley, mess, miscellany, mishmash, mixture, olio, pastiche

patchy in color: brindled, piebald, pied, pinto, skewbald, splotched

pate: brain, crown, dome, head, intellect, meat, noggin, paste, pie, spread

patella: kneecap

paten: disk

patent: apparent, clear, conspicuous, distinct, evident, flagrant, gross, manifest, obvious, open, overt, plain, rank, unobstructed

patent granted: control, copyright, franchise, grant, invention, license, protection

paternal: benevolent, fatherly, protective, tender

paternity: fatherhood

path: access, alley, artery, avenue, byway, fare, lane, line, orbit, road, route, track, trail, walk, way

path along beach or waterfront: boardwalk

path along river or canal for animals to tow boats: towpath

path cut by mower: swath

path of projectile: trajectory

path or trail for horseback riding: bridle path

path, heavily traveled: thoroughfare

path, narrow elevated: catwalk

pathetic: affecting, doleful, heartbreaking, lamentable, miserable, moving, pitiful, poor, rueful, sad, useless, worry

pathos: emotion, feeling, pity, poignancy, sentiment, sympathy, tenderness

patience: calm, composure, cool, diligence, endurance, fortitude, perseverance, poise, resignation, resolution, stoicism, submission, tenacity, tolerance

patient: case, enduring, forgiving, long-suffering, meek, mild, persistent, subject, tireless, understanding

patient receiving transplant, blood etc.: donee, recipient

patient treated at hospital but not staying there: outpatient

patient under duress: forbearing, long-suffering

patient, of direct observation of: clinical

patient, suit for restraining violent: straightjacket

patient's case history: amamnesis

patio: courtyard, deck, lanai, piazza, porch, terrace

patois: argot, cant, dialect, idiom, jargon, lingo, slang, vernacular

patriarch: ancestor, chief, elder, father, founder, head, leader, male, ruler, sire, venerable

patrician: aristocrat, blueblood, highborn, lordly, noble, stately, upper-class

patrimony: ancestry, bequeathal, endowment, estate, heritage, inheritance, legacy

patriot: chauvinist, flag-waver, jingoist, loyalist, nationalist, partisan, volunteer

patrol: detachment, garrison, guard, inspect, protect, safeguard, scout, sentinel, watch

patrol wagon: black maria

patrolman's milieu: beat

patron: advocate, angel, backer, benefactor, champion, client, customer, guardian, guest, host, manager, owner, protector, shopper, sponsor, supporter, user

patron, person protected by: protégée, protégé

patronage: aegis, assistance, auspice, backing, business, buying, clientele, custom, customers, egis, encouragement, favor, help, nepotism, protection, sponsorship, subsidy, trade

patronize: assist, condescend, deign, frequent, promote, snub, stoop, support, talk down to

patsy: chump, dupe, goat, pawn, pigeon, sap, sucker, victim

patter: babble, cant, chatter, drum, glib, jabber, jargon, move, mumble, rattle, scuttle, sound, speak, talk, tapping, utter

pattern: archetype, arrangement, configuration, conformation, copy, design, diagram, emulate, example, exemplar, figure, form, format, guide, ideal, imitate, markings, method, model, mold, motif, order, paradigm, plaid, plan, prototype, sample, sequence, specimen, stencil, system, template, trend

RELATED TERMS

pattern in embroidery, decorative: device

pattern made by setting pieces into a surface: inlay

pattern of behavior, distinctive: syndrome

pattern of dark-lined squares on light background: tattersall

pattern of elements in literary, artistic or architectural composition: ordonnance

pattern of fibers in leather, wood, stone: grain

pattern of short parallel slanted lines in alternating directions: herringbone

pattern of swirled abstract shapes: paisley

pattern of symmetrical figures, repeated: fret, key, meander

pattern of varicolored diamond shapes: argyle

pattern or example: exemplar, paradigm

pattern or gauge for accurate copying: template

pattern or method of operating: modus operandi

pattern or system of doing things: regimen, routine

pattern that is model for a process or system: paradigm

pattern, Chinese blue-on-white: willow pattern

pattern, having wavy rippled: moire

pattern, overlap in regular: imbricate

pattern, repeated: motif

patterns in relief, decorated with: repoussé ❦

paucity: dearth, guilty, insufficiency, lack, poverty, scantiness, scarcity, shortage, sparsity

paunch: abdomen, belly, breadbasket, bulge, gut, potbelly, stomach, tummy

pauper: almsman, bankrupt, beggar, destitute, indigent, insolvent

pause: break, breath, breather, caesura, cease, cessation, comma, delay, demur, halt, hesitate, hesitation, hiatus, hover, intermission, interruption, interval, layoff, letup, lull, recess, respite, rest, stay, stop, wait

pause between acts of play: intermission
pause for rest or relief: recess, respite
pause in continuity or governments: interregnum
pause in space, time, continuity: break, hiatus
pause indicator: comma
pause or interruption in verse or conversation: caesura
pause or suspension in proceedings: adjournment
pause temporarily: intermit
pave: asphalt, blacktop, cover, floor, macadamize, overlie, prepare, smooth, surface, tile
paved outdoor space adjoining residence: patio
pavement: concrete
pavilion: awning, canopy, covering, dome, gazebo, kiosk, litter, structure, tent
paw: foot, hand, pad, toe
pawn: counter, dupe, flunk, fool, guarantee, guaranty, hock, hostage, impignorate, patsy, pledge, puppet, stooge, sucker
pay: allowance, ante, atone, clear, commission, compensate, compensation, defray, fee, foot, grant, hire, income, indemnify, liquidate, outlay, profit, reciprocate, recompense, refund, reimburse, remit, remunerate, retribution, return, reward, salary, satisfy, settlement, spend, stipend, tip, tribute, wage, wages, yield
pay attention: heed, mind, note
pay back: compensate, compound, rebate, reimburse, remunerate, retaliate, return
pay costs or expenses: defray
pay in installments: amortize
pay out from fund: disburse, expend
pay rate or price, difference in: differential
payable: due, mature, obligatory, outstanding, owed, owing, receivable, unpaid
payback: revenge
payload: cargo, charge, haul, weight
paymaster: bursar, cashier, purser, treasurer
payment: alimony, allowance, amends, annuity, award, cash, compensation, debt, defrayal, discharge, dues, duty, expenditure, fee, fine, honorarium, levy, money, pension, premium,

price, rebate, recompense, remittance, requital, return, reward, stipend, tariff, tax, toll, tuition
RELATED TERMS
payment able to be used as needed or desired: discretionary
payment as acknowledgment of gratitude, respect, admiration: tribute
payment as favor, for free: ex gratia
payment as percentage of sale or as agent for services rendered: commission
payment by each party for his own: Dutch treat
payment extorted to prevent disclosure: blackmail
payment for employment: compensation, emolument
payment for periodical or series of performances over specified time: subscription
payment for release of seized person, property: ransom
payment for service rendered: consideration, recompense, remuneration
payment for services or as allowance, fixed and regular: stipend
payment for something not ordinarily reimbursed: honorarium
payment in addition to salary: fringe benefit, perquisite
payment made to author: royalty
payment made to professional adviser: retainer
payment of an allowance or income: annuity
payment of an obligation: tender
payment or charge: rate
payment or reward: guerdon, recompense
payment to clergyman: prebend
payment to dismissed employee, generous: severance pay
payment to former lover: palimony
payment to former spouse: alimony, maintenance
payment to induce action or motivate effort: bonus, incentive
payment to influence someone's views or conduct: bribe
payment to offset or make reparation: compensate
payment to shareholders from corporation earnings: dividend
payment upon termination: severance pay

payment, done without expecting: voluntary
payment, reduction in or return of some: rebate
payment, to force a: blackmail, exact, extort ☙

payoff: bribe, climax, conclusion, culmination, fee, graft, outcome, payola, profit, result, retribution, reward, settlement
payola: bribe, bribery, bribes, graft, payoff
pea container: pod
pea family: legume
peace: agreement, amity, armistice, ataraxia, calm, concord, contentment, ease, equanimity, harmony, neutrality, order, pacification, pact, quiet, repose, rest, serenity, tranquility, treaty, truce
RELATED TERMS
peace agreement: treaty
peace be with you: pax vobiscum
peace branch: olive
peace of mind: ataraxia, equanimity, tranquillity
peace pipe: calumet
peace terms decided by dominant country: Pax Romana
peace, granting concessions to maintain: appeasement
peace, person advocating: dove
peace, person advocating military force over: hawk
peace, promoting: conciliatory, irenic, Pacific, placatory
peace, reestablishment of: détente, rapprochement
peace, temporary: armistice, truce ☙

peaceable: amiable, amicable, friendly, gentle, irenic, nonviolent, Pacific, peaceful, placid, undisturbed
peaceful: calm, halcyon, irenic, neutral, nonviolent, pacific, peaceable, placid, quiet, serene, silent, steady, still, tranquil, undisturbed
peaceful in purpose: irenic
peacemaker: ambassador, arbitrator, conciliator, diplomat, mediator, negotiator, pacifist, placater
peach genus: Prunus persica
peach or other fruit that adheres to its stone: clingstone
peach or other fruit that does not adhere to its stone: freestone
peach pit: stone

PEACHES

Clingstone
Elberta
Freestone
Greensboro
Heath
Late Crawford
Lovell
Mountain Rose
Muir
nectarine
Phillips
Susquehanna
Triumph
Yellow ❦

PEARS

Anjou
Bartlett
Bosc
Clapp Favorite
Comice
Kieffer
Le Conte
Sheldon
Wilder Early
winter nellis ❦

peach, for one: drupe
peachy: dandy, divine, excellent, fine, marvelous, nice, splendid
peacock eyespot: ocellus
peacock, concerning a: pavonine
peacocks, group of: muster, ostentation, pride
peak: acme, aiguille, alp, apex, apogee, climax, cone, crag, crest, crown, culmination, maximum, meridian, mountain, perfection, pinnacle, point, roof, summit, tip, top, tor, ultimate, visor, zenith
peaked: ailing, anemic, ashen, drawn, emaciated, pale, sharp, sickly, spiked, thin, wan, weak
peal: bells, blast, bong, boom, chime, clap, noise, resound, reverberate, ring, thunder, toll
peanut: Arachis hypogaea, earthnut, goober, groundnut, mani, petty, pinda, pindal, plant, puny, seed, small
pear-shaped: obconic, pyriform
pear-shaped instrument: mandolin
pearl: color, gem, jewel, lustrous, margaric, nacre, orient, paragon, seed

pearl found in: oyster
pearl of high quality, luster of: orient
pearl that is irregular in shape, of: baroque
pearl, artificially produced: cultured pearl
pearl, concerning: margaric
pearl, large spherical: paragon
pearl, small imperfect: seed pearl
pearly: clear, ivory, milky, nacreous, opalescent, shining
pearly inner surface of some mollusk shells: mother-of-pearl, nacre
peasant: boor, bumpkin, churl, cotter, countryman, esne, farmer, fellah, kern, knave, kulak, laborer, lowlife, muzhik, peon, rustic, ryot, serf, sharecropper, swain, toiler, villain
peat moss: sphagnum
peccadillo: blunder, error, fault, misdeed, mistake, offense, sin, transgression, violation, wrongdoing
peccant: corrupt, erring, guilty, sinful
peck: beak, bill, bite, buss, carp, dot, hole, jab, kiss, nag, nose, pick, prick, tap
peculate: embezzle, steal
peculiar: abnormal, bizarre, characteristic, curious, distinctive, distinguishing, eccentric, exclusive, idio, odd, offbeat, outlandish, queer, wacky, singular, strange, unique, unusual, weird
peculiar to a locality, people: endemic
peculiarity: attribute, character, crotchet, feature, idiosyncracy, kink, mark, oddity, oddness, stamp, trait, twist
peculiarity of behavior: eccentricity, foible, idiosyncrasy, mannerism, quirk
pecuniary: economic, financial, fiscal, monetary
pedagogic: academic, educational, instructional, instructive, scholastic, tutorial
pedagogue: educator, instructor, pedant, schoolmaster, teacher, tutor
pedal of piano, right: loud pedal, reverberation pedal, sustaining pedal
pedal of potter's wheel or sewing machine: treadle
pedantic: academic, bookish, didactic, donnish, hairsplitting, learned, precise, scholastic, schoolish
pedantic effort: lucubration
pedantic teacher: pedagogue, prig
pedantic word: inkhorn word

pedantic writing: lucubration
peddle: canvas, dispense, hawk, huckster, piddle, pitch, push, retail, sell, solicit, vend
peddler of provisions to soldiers: sutler
peddler of religious literature: colporteur
peddler's item: ware
pedestal: anta, base, column, foot, foundation, leg, pillar, podium, stand, support
pedestal between base and cornice / surbase: dado
pedestal on which statue or column stands: plinth
pedestrian: banal, commonplace, dull, everyday, humdrum, mundane, ordinary, prosaic, so-so, unexciting, unimaginative, uninteresting
pedestrian person: hiker, stroller, walker, wayfarer
pedestrian crosswalk: zebra crossing
pedestrian disregarding traffic rules: jaywalker
pedestrian shopping street or complex: arcade, mall
pedicel: stem
pediculosis problem: lice
pedigree: ancestry, bloodline, breed, descent, genealogy, heredity, heritage, line, lineage, purebred, stock, thoroughbred
peduncle: stalk, stem
peek: gander, glance, glimpse, look, peep, snoop, watch
peel: bark, cover, flake, flay, hull, husk, pare, remove, rind, scale, shovel, shuck, skin, strip, uncover
peep: chatter, cheep, chirp, chirrup, glance, hoot, look, peek, peer, snoop, spy, squeak, tweet, watch
peep show: raree
peephole: crevice, eyehole, eyelet, judas, opening, slit, slot
peephole, one-way: judas
peeping Tom: voyeur
peer: associate, baron, companion, comrade, contemporary, equal, juror, lord, mate, nobleman
peerage: gentry, jurisdiction, nobility, rank, title
peerless: excellent, incomparable, matchless, superlative, supreme, unequaled, unparalleled, unrivaled
peeve: aggravate, annoy, bother, bug, disturb, exasperate, irk, irritate, nettle, provoke, rile, vex
peevish: bilious, cantankerous, cap-

tious, carping, contentious, contrary, cranky, critical, cross, crotchety, crusty, discontented, disgruntled, dyspeptic, fractious, fretful, huffy, irascible, irritable, mean, obstinate, ornery, pettish, petulant, querulous, snappish, sullen, surly, testy, touchy, waspish

peevishness: bile, ill temper, petulance, spleen

peewee: diminutive, dwarf, lilliputian, little, miniature, reese, small, teeny, tiny

peg: attach, dowel, fix, join, leg, nob, notch, pin, plug, prong, spike, stake, throw, tooth

peg or pin fitting in corresponding hole: dowel

pegs on boat that are oarlocks: thole pin

pejorative: belittling, debasing, demeaning, derogatory, disparaging, irreverent, negative, slighting

pelagic: aquatic, marine, oceanic, thalassic

pelf: loot, lucre

pell-mell: chaos, confusion, disarray, disorder, haphazard, headlong, heedlessly, helter-skelter, hurriedly, impetuously, in a rush, pandemonium, recklessly, turmoil

pellet: ball, bolus, bullet, mass, pebble, pill, rock, shot, stone, wad

pellucid: bright, clear, comprehensible, crystalling, explicit, limpid, luminous, plain, simple, translucent, transparent

pelt: assail, batter, beat, belt, blow, cast, clobber, fur, hair, hide, hurl, hurry, pepper, pound, pummel, rawhide, skin, stone, strike, thrash, thrust, wallop, whack

pelvic: ilial

pelvis part: coccyx, ilium, ischium, pubis, sacrum, symphysis

pen: cage, confine, coop, corral, crib, draal, encage, enclose, enclosure, fence, fold, hutch, imprison, jail, kennel, penitentiary, prison, stockade, yard

pen made from feather shaft: quill

pen name: alias, nom de guerre, nom de plume, pseudonym

pen point: nib

pen types: ball point, desk, drawing, felt-tip, fountain, highlighter, marker, quill, reed, stylograph

pen, fluorescent marking: highlighter

pen, to: author, compose, quill, stylus, write

penal: corrective, disciplinary, punishing, punitive, punitory, retributive

penalize: amerce, castigate, discipline, fine, handicap, punish

penalty: amercement, damages, disadvantage, fine, forfeit, hardship, loss, mulct, penance, punishment, retribution, suffering

penalty in which something is given up or taken away: forfeit

penalty or obligation demanded: imposition

penalty remission: pardon

penalty that ensures compliance or conformity: sanction

penalty to a less severe one, to change a: commute

penalty, punish with arbitrary: amerce

penance: absolution, atonement, compunction, contrition, expiation, forgiveness, mortification, penalty, remorse, repentance, suffering

Penates' partner: Lares

penchant: affinity, attraction, bent, bias, fancy, fondness, inclination, knack, leaning, liking, partiality, predilection, proneness, propensity, taste, tendency

pencil to check bleeding: styptic

pencil writing matter: graphite, plumbago

pend: await, hang

pendant worn on chain around neck: lavaliere

pendent ornament: tassel

pending: awaiting, dependent, during, hanging, undecided, unresolved, unsettled

pendulate: swing

pendulous: dangling, droopy, hanging, pendent, suspended, tentative

pendulum's length of swing: rating

penetrate: absorb, bore, comprehend, discern, drill, drive, enter, fathom, imbue, infiltrate, insert, insinuate, invade, perforate, permeate, pervade, pierce, prick, puncture, stab, stick, thrust, understand

penetrate completely: permeate

penetrating: acute, astute, caustic, cutting, deep, discriminating, harsh, incisive, insightful, into, intrusive, keen, knowing, mordant, perceptive, pervasive, sagacious, sharp, shrewd, stinging, trenchant

penguin feature: flightless

penicillin and other bacterial infection medicine: antibiotic

penicillin source: mold

peninsula: cape, chersonese, headland, neck, point

penis canal for urine and semen: urethra

penis gland controlling urine and secreting fluid as part of semen: prostate

penis head: glans

penis, fold of skin covering head of: foreskin, prepuce

penis, having erect: ithyphallic

penis, representation of: phallus, priapus

penis, representation of erect: ithyphallic

penislike: phallic

penitence: anguish, attrition, compunction, contrition, distress, expiation, grief, penance, qualm, regret, remorse, repentance, scruple, shame, sorrow

penitent: atoner, compunctious, contrite, regretful, remorseful, repentant, ruer, shamed, sinner, sorry

penitent period: lent

penitentiary: brig, can, clink, cooler, coop, jail, joint, jug, pen, poky, prison, slammer, stir, stockade

penitent's sentiment: remorse

penmanship: handwriting, longhand, script, writing

penmanship, beautiful: calligraphy

penmanship, the art of: chirography

pennant: banner, color, emblem, ensign, flag, jack, pendant, pennon, streamer, symbol

penniless: bankrupt, broke, busted, destitute, impecunious, impoverished, insolvent, needy, poor, stone broke

pennon: banner, color, ensign, flag, gonfalon, jack, pennant, pinion, streamer, symbol

penny-pinching: miserly, niggardly, parsimonious, penurious, stingy, tight

pension: allowance, annuity, IRA, payment, social security, subsidy, support

pension drawn while holding another job: double-dipping

pension recipient: pensioner

pension, to allow to retire on: superannuate

pensive: absorbed, blue, contemplative, dreamy, introspective, meditative, melancholy, pondering, preoccupied, reflective, ruminating, sober, solemn, thinking, thoughtful, wistful

pent-up: bridled, checked, inhibited, repressed, stored, suppressed

pentad: five

pentagram: star

penurious: barren, destitute, frugal, indigent, miserly, niggardly, parsimonious, penny-pinching, poor, stingy, tight

penury: barrenness, dearth, destitution, indigence, insufficiency, need, poverty, privation, scantiness

peon: drudge, footman, hand, laborer, messenger, pawn, peasant, serf, servant, slave

people: citizens, clan, commoners, community, electorate, family, folk, humanity, humans, individuals, inhabit, inhabitants, kin, laity, mankind, men, multitude, nation, ones, persons, plebeians, plebs, populace, populate, proletariat, public, rank and file, society, stock, subjects, tribe, women

people forced by circumstances to listen: captive audience

people-loving: philodemic

people outside specific occupation: laity

people with common interests: birds of a feather

people, elite: crème de la crème

pep: animation, briskness, dash, energy, enthusiasm, getup, ginger, gusto, hardihood, invigorate, liveliness, oomph, snap, spirit, verve, vigor, vim, vitality, zip

pepo variety: cantaloupe, cucumber, gourd, pumpkin, squash, watermelon

pepper: condiment, exercise, fruit, hot, plant, spice

pepper plant: capsicum, kava

pepper variety: black, cayenne, cherry, chili, green, jalapeno, paprika, pimiento, red, sweet

pepper, pungent red: cayenne

pepper, red garden: pimiento

pepper, served with: au poivre

peppermint camphor: menthol

peppery: biting, choleric, cranky, fiery, hot, irascible, keen, lively, passionate, poignant, pungent, sarcastic, sharp, snappy, spicy, spirited, spunky, stinging, vivid, zesty

peppy: active, alert, animated, lively, perky, spirited, spry, vigorous, vivacious

per: apiece, by, each, for, through, to, via

per day: per diem

per person: per capita

per se: alone, essentially, fundamentally, intrinsically, solely

per year: annually, per annum

perambulate: mosey, promenade, ramble, roam, stroll, tour, walk

perceive: apprehend, behold, comprehend, deduce, descry, detect, discern, discover, distinguish, divine, feel, grasp, hear, identify, know, mind, note, notice, observe, realize, recognize, see, sense, smell, spot, taste, touch, understand

perceive as different: discern

perceived by sight or hearing: sensate

perceived under the threshold of consciousness: subliminal

percentage: allotment, cut, division, interest, odds, part, piece, portion, probability, profit, proportion, rate, ratio, share, split

perceptible: apparent, appreciable, clear, cognizable, detectable, discernible, lucid, noticeable, obvious, palpable, recognizable, sensible, tangible, visible

perception: acumen, awareness, concept, idea, image, insight, intuition, judgment, ken, sensation, tact, thought, understanding

perception after an event: hindsight

perception independent of senses: ESP, extrasensory perception

perception of a fact: cognizance

perception of distant stimuli by extrasensory means: telesthesia

perception of one's own consciousness: apperception

perception, below threshold of conscious: subliminal

perception, extraordinary: clairvoyance, cryptesthesia, ESP, extrasensory perception, telesthesia

perception, false or distorted, that seems real: hallucination

perception, keen: sensibility

perception, something known through intellect not sense: noumenon, thing-in-itself

perception, something known through sense: phenomenon

perceptive: acute, alert, astute, aware, insightful, keen, observant, perspicacious, sensitive, sharp, wise

perch: alight, bar, fish, land, peg, pike, pole, rod, roose, roost, seat, sit, squat, staff, stick

percolate: brew, drip, filter, leach, ooze, penetrate, permeate, seep, sift, strain, transfuse, trickle

percussion: blow, collision, impact, jolt, shock, sound

percussion instrument: bones, bongo, castanets, chime, chimes, claves, conga, cymbal, drum, glockenspiel, gong, kettle drum, kettledrum, lithophone, maraca, marimba, piano, rattle, tambourine, tabor, timbal, timpani, triangle, vibraphone, xylophone

percussion instrument of board with metal ridges: washboard

percussion instrument of gourd with pebbles or beans: maraca

percussion instrument of metal bars played with two hammers: glockenspiel

percussion instrument of small drum head with jingles: tambourine

percussion instrument of wooden bars on chromatic scale played with two mallets: xylophone

percussion instrument with resonators and resembling xylophone: marimba

percussion instrument with resonators and metal disks: vibraharp, vibraphone

percussion section of orchestra: battery

perdition: condemnation, damnation, destruction, doom, downfall, hell, loss, ruin

peregrination: expedition, hiking, jaunt, journey, roaming, roving, travels, traversing, trip

peremptory: absolute, authoritative, bossy, commanding, decided, decisive, dictatorial, dogmatic, domineering, final, harsh, imperative, imperious, masterful, overbearing, positive, rigid, rigorous, uncompromising, urgent

perennial: annual, changeless, constant, continual, durable, enduring, fixed, geophyte, lifelong, neverfailing, permanent, perpetual, plant, recurrent, timeless, unceasing

perfect: absolute, accomplish, accurate, blameless, complete, consummate, correct, culminating, entire, exact, excellent, expert, exquisite, faultless, fine, finish, finished, flawless, fulfill, holy, ideal, immaculate, impeccable, improve, infallible, irreproachable, masterly, precise, pure, realize, right, sinless, sound, stainless, suitable, thorough, unblemished, unerring, unimpaired, unimpeachable, unmarred, untarnished, utopian, whole

perfect example: archetype, avatar, epitome, exemplar, paragon, phoenix

perfect example of characteristic or idea: embodiment, incarnation, personification

perfect state or excellence: ne plus ultra

perfect tennis serve: ace

perfection: acme, excellence, fullness, fulness, ideal, integrity, maturity, ne plus ultra, paragon, pink

perfectly: absolutely, altogether, entirely, quite, superbly, totally

perfidious: deceitful, disaffected, dishonest, disloyal, faithless, false, shifty, traitorous, treacherous, unfaithful, untrue, untrustworthy, venal

perforate: bore, drill, penetrate, permeate, pierce, pounce, prick, punch, puncture, sieve, stamp

perforations on postage stamp sheets or rolls: roulette

perform: accomplish, achieve, act, at, complete, dramatize, effect, enact, execute, exert, exhibit, fulfill, furnish, gesture, operate, play, present, render, stage, transact, work

perform functions of an office: officiate

perform on the spur of the moment: extemporize, improvise

perform or be responsible for a crime: perpetrate

perform or conduct business: transact

perform with formal ceremony: solemnize

performance: accomplishment, act, acting, benefit, ceremony, completion, concert, consummation, deed, depiction, effect, efficiency, exhibition, feat, fulfillment, function, matinee, play, portrayal, presentation, recital, rendition, review, show, spectacle, stint, stunt, test, work

performance added after audience demand: encore

performance and interpretation of text or role: rendition

performance by solo performer: recital

performance of musical or dramatic work: rendering, rendition

performance of musical or dramatic work in daytime: matinee

performance that is a triumph: star turn

performance, brilliant technique in: bravura

performance, demand for additional: encore

performer: actor, actress, artist, artiste, doer, entertainer, impersonator, mime, musician, player, star, thespian, trouper, worker

performer, veteran: trouper

performer's stock of pieces, songs, or skills: repertoire, repertory

performers' waiting room: green room

perfume: aroma, attar, aura, balm, bouquet, cense, chypre, cologne, essence, flavor, fragrance, incense, myrrh, odor, patchouli, potpourri, redolence, sachet, scent, smell, spice, sweeten

perfume bottle: phial

perfume floral essence: attar

perfume from evaporating, liquid added to keep: fixative

perfume sprayer: atomizer

perfume to slow rate of evaporation, substance added to: ambergris

perfumed bag: pomander, sachet

perfumed ointment: pomade

perfumed powder: talc

perfumed stick or substance that is burned: incense, joss stick

perfumes, oil used in: attar, bergamot, citronella, musk, patchouli

perfunctory: automatic, careless, cursory, disinterested, indifferent, lackadaisical, listless, mechanical, passionless, routine, standard, superficial, unthinking

perhaps: conceivably, feasibly, imaginably, likely, maybe, perchance, possibly, probably, suppose

peril: adventure, crisis, danger, endanger, exposure, hazard, insecurity, jeopardy, liability, menace, pitfall, risk, threat, trap

peril, imminent: sword of Damocles

perilous: chancy, dangerous, dicey, hairy, hazardous, precarious, risky, touchy, treacherous, unsafe, unstable, unsteady

perimeter: border, boundary, brim, circumference, edge, edges, fringe, margin, outline, periphery

period: age, century, close, conclusion, cycle, date, day, decade, dot, duration, ending, eon, epoch, era, finis,

generation, hear, interval, point, season, semester, siècle, span, stop, term, termination, time

period just before a holiday: eve

period of decline: sunset

period of development of new life in uterus: gestation, pregnancy

period of existence or persistence: duration

period of history, particular: epoch, era

period of joy and prosperity: millennium

period of nonwork: downtime

period of power and popularity: heyday, prime

period of woman: menses, menstruation

period, early harmonious: honeymoon

period, intervening: interlude

periodic: intermittent

periodic rise and fall: tide

periodical: annual, cyclical, daily, infrequently, intermittent, journal, magazine, newspaper, occasionally, recurring, review, routinely, seasonal, tabloid

periods used to indicate word(s) omitted: ellipsis

peripatetic: ambulatory, itinerant, migrant, mobile, nomadic, rambling, roving, traveling, wandering

peripatetic person: nomad, rover

peripheral: distant, external, incidental, minor, outermost, secondary

periphery: ambit, border, boundary, brim, circumference, edge, edges, environs, fringe, limit, outside, outskirts, perimeter, rim, surface

perish: croak, crumble, decay, decease, depart, die, disappear, expire, fade, pass away, ruin, succumb, vanish

perjure: deceive, equivocate, falsify, forswear, lie, mislead, prevaricate, suborn

perk: appanage, benefit, bonus, extra, fringe benefit, gain, gratuity, percolate, perquisite

perk up: animate, brighten, convalesce, improve, invigorate, rally, recuperate, refresh, revive

perky: alert, animated, bouncy, brisk, bubbly, cheerful, happy, lively, pert, spirited, vivacious

permafrost area: tundra

permanent: constant, diurnal, durable, endless, enduring, eternal, everlasting, fixed, imperishable, in perpetuity, indelible, indestructible, lasting, sempiternal, stable, unending

permanent and lasting for eternity: forever, perdurable, perennial, perpetual

permanent and unchanging: immutable, indelible, indissoluble, irreversible, irrevocable, substantive

permanent apparatus, appliance: fixture

permanent basis, job status that has: tenure

permanent physically: abiding, enduring, imperishable, indestructible

permanent reminder: scar

permanent, making: perpetuate

permanently beautiful: amaranthine, everlasting

permeable: absorbent, passable, penetrable, porous, spongelike

permeate: diffuse, drench, fill, filter, imbue, infiltrate, leaven, ooze, penetrate, pervade, saturate, seep, soak

permeation and absorption, gradual: osmosis

permissible: acceptable, admissible, allowable, endorsed, lawful, legitimate, licit, permitted, unprohibited

permission: allowance, approbation, approval, authorization, consent, endorsement, fiat, grant, leave, liberty, license, permit

permission implied: sufferance

permission to leave: conge, exeat, nunc dimittis

permission to proceed: clearance

permission, granting: facultative

permit: admit, allow, authorize, condone, consent, countenance, empower, enable, furlough, grant, have, leave, legalize, let, license, pass, passport, permission, ratify, sanction, suffer, tolerate, visa, warrant

permit issuer: licenser

permitted by law: legal, licit

permutation: alteration, change, modification, shift, transformation

pernicious: baleful, baneful, deadly, deleterious, destructive, detrimental, evil, fatal, harmful, hurtful, malign, mortal, noxious, ruinous, toxic, wicked

perorate: address, declaim, lecture, orate, rant, speak

perpendicular: erect, horizontal, plumb, sheer, straight, upright, vertical

perpetrate: commit, enact, execute, perform, pull, wreak

perpetual: constant, continual, continuous, endless, enduring, eternal, ever, everlasting, incessant, perennial, permanent, unceasing, unending, uninterrupted

perpetuate: continue, eternalize, immortalize, keep, maintain, preserve, prolong, sustain

perplex: amaze, astonish, astound, baffle, bamboozle, bedevil, beset, bewilder, boggle, complicate, confound, confuse, cumber, diffuse, distract, dumbfound, embroil, entangle, muddle, mystify, nonplus, obfuscate, puzzle, snarl, stump, thwart

perplexing situation: quandary

perquisite: appanage, due, fee, gain, gratuity, income, perogative, privilege, proceeds, profit, reward, right, tip

persecute: abuse, afflict, annoy, badger, bait, crucify, harass, harry, heckle, hound, maltreat, martyr, molest, oppress, pester, torment, torture, victimize, wrong

persecution complex: paranoia

persecutory campaign: witch-hunt

perseverance: constancy, continuance, dedication, determination, diligence, drive, endurance, grit, insistence, patience, persistence, resolution, spunk, stamina, steadfastness, tenacity

persevere: abide, endure, last, maintain, persist, prevail, pursue, stick

persevering: assiduous, dogged, indefatigable, indomitable, persistent, pertinacious, stubborn, tenacious, unremitting

persiflage: banter, chaffing, flippery, frivolity, mockery

persist: abide, continue, endure, insist, last, linger, perdure, persevere, prevail, remain, survive

persistent: assiduous, consistent, constant, continuing, continuous, determined, diligent, dogged, durable, enduring, fixed, gritty, insistent, obdurate, persevering, pertinacious, relentless, resolute, sedulous, steadfast, stubborn, sustained, tenacious, unshakable

persistent pain: ache

persistent striving: perseverance

persnickety: choosy, finicky, fussy, particular, picayune

person: being, body, chap, child, creature, earthling, entity, fellow, guy, human, individual, life, man, mortal, one, self, soul, woman

RELATED TERMS

person apart from others: loner, odd man out, outsider

person being addressed: second person

person coming into new country to live: immigrant

person from whom a family is descended: stirps

person granted exclusive right: patentee

person in whom another confides: confidant

person named after another: namesake

person other than speaker or person being addressed: third person

person typifying quality or idea: personificaiton

person who buys and sells for another, on commission: broker

person who corrects and prepares book for publication: copy editor

person who focuses solely on others: alterocentric

person who has admirable qualities: mensch

person who has refined tastes: bon vivant

person who has superior specialized knowledge: cognoscente

person who has two or more distinct personalities: multiple personality

person who has undergone sex change: transsexual

person, admirable: mensch

person, animal, plant living off another: parasite

person, bad: anathema, blackguard, cad, caitiff, heel, knave, toad

person, crazy: lunatic, monomaniac, nut, psychopath, psychotic

person, engaged: fiancé, fiancée

person, foolish: clown, dotard, halfwit, simpleton, sop, zany

person, in: in propria persona, live

person, middle-class: bourgeois, bourgeoisie

person, mixed blood: half-breed, mestizo, metis, mulatto, octoroon

person, nonJewish: gentile

person, skilled: adept, artisan, artist, master, mechanic, talent person, small: dwarf, midget, poppet, runt, sprat

person, stupid: ass, blockhead, bonehead, boob, boodle, clod, coot, dolt, duffer, dullard, dumbbell, dunce, fool, gump, imbecile, moron, nitwit, simpleton

person, wealthy: capitalist, millionaire, nabob, nob, plutocrat ✺

personable: affable, amiable, attractive, charming, easygoing, friendly, handsome, likable, pleasant, shapely, sociable, warm

personage: being, bigwig, celebrity, dignitary, heavyweight, individual, magnate, notable, tycoon, VIP

personal: confidential, individual, intimate, particular, private, privy, secret

personal and biased: subjective

personal and private: intimate

personal belongings: chattels, dunnage, effects, estate, peculium

personal charm: charisma

personal experience summary: curriculum vitae, CV, résumé, vita

personal verbal attack to destroy reputation: character assassination

personality: behavior, celebrity, character, charisma, disposition, ego, emotions, humor, identity, makeup, nature, psyche, self, star, temperament, trait

personality feature: facet, quality, trait

personality test: inkblot test, Rorschach test

personality, aggressive and competitive: Type A

personality, having a changeable: mercurial, volatile

personality, relaxed and tolerant: Type B

personification: prosopopeia, role

personify: characterize, embody, epitomize, exemplify, externalize, imitate, incarnate, represent, symbolize, typify

personnel: crew, employees, people, staff, troops, workers

personnel nucleus: cadre

personnel reduction through retirement, etc.: attrition

personnel specialist for executives: headhunter

person's name which is source of another place/thing's name: eponym

perspective: angle, context, expectation, mindset, outlook, panorama, relativity, viewpoint, vista

perspicacious: acute, alert, astute, clearheaded, discerning, keen, observant, perceptive, savvy, shrewd, wise

perspicacity: acumen

perspicuous: apparent, clear, conspicuous, crystal, distinct, intelligible, keen, lucid, luminous, manifest, obvious

perspiration: hidrosis

perspiration, excessive: diaphoresis

perspiration, smelly: bromidrosis, kakidrosis, osmidrosis

perspire: excrete, exude, secrete, sweat

persuadable: acceptive, amenable, ductile, flexible, impressionable, malleable, obliging, pliant, tractable

persuade: allure, argue, brainwash, coax, convert, convince, entice, incite, induce, influence, inveigle, lead, lure, prompt, seduce, sell, sway, tempt, urge

persuade by deceit: finagle, wangle

persuade or force with threats: coerce, dragoon, induce, prevail upon

persuade or influence legislators etc., to try to: lobby

persuade with flattery: cajole, coax, inveigle, smooth-talk, soft-soap, wheedle

persuade, talk or speech intended to: spiel

persuasion: affiliation, belief, character, church, class, conviction, creed, cult, denomination, enticement, faction, faith, mind, pull, religion, school, sentiment, type, view

persuasive and insincere flattery: snow job

persuasive: cogent, compelling, convincing, effective, eloquent, impelling, incisive, influential, seductive, slick, smooth, trenchant

persuasive pressure: jawbone

pert: active, alert, alive, animated, arch, audacious, bold, brazen, brisk, chipper, dapper, energetic, fresh, frisky, insolent, jaunty, lively, naughty, perky, sassy, saucy, smart, spirited, sprightly, spry, vivacious

pertain: apply, associate, befall, belong, concern, connect, refer, regard, relate, touch

pertinacious: bullheaded, determined, dogged, firm, headstrong, inflexible, obstinate, persistent, stubborn, tenacious, unshakable

pertinent: applicable, apposite, appropriate, apropos, apt, connected, fitting, germane, material, proper, related, relative, relevant, suitable, timely

perturb: agitate, annoy, bother, confuse, disconcert, disorder, disturb, fluster, irritate, pester, trouble, unsettle, upset, vex, worry

peruse: analyze, examine, inspect, read, scan, scrutinize, search, study, survey

pervade: animate, charge, fill, imbue, inform, penetrate, permeate, saturate, spread, suffuse

pervasive: common, dominant, extensive, general, prevalent, universal, widespread

pervasive atmosphere: aura

perverse: awkward, backward, balky, contentious, contrary, corrupt, cranky, crotched, degenerate, depraved, determined, deviant, difficult, diverse, forward, fractious, obstinate, ornery, petulant, stubborn, vicious, wayward, wicked, wrongheaded

pervert: abuse, adulterate, contort, corrupt, debase, degenerate, demoralize, deprave, desecrate, deviant, distort, divert, garble, misapply, misconstrue, misdirect, misinterpret, misrepresent, misuse, poison, ruin, subvert, twist, undermine, warp, weirdo

perverted: abnormal, corrupt, distorted, immoral, kinky, twisted, unnatural, wicked

pervious: accessible, approachable, open, penetrable, permeable, porous

pesky: annoying, bothersome, disagreeable, disturbing, irksome, obnoxious, troublesome, vexatious

pessimism: cynicism, despair, gloom, hopelessness, melancholy, weltschmerz

pessimist: bear, complainer, crapehanger, cynic, killjoy, misanthrope, sourpuss, worrier

pessimistic: bleak, cynical, despairing, disbelieving, doubting, gloomy, hopeless, negative, skeptical

pest: annoyance, bane, bother, bug, creep, gnat, heckler, insect, irritation, louse, nuisance, pestilence, plague, trouble, vermin

pester: aggravate, annoy, annoyance, badger, bait, bother, bug, devil, earse, get at, harass, harry, hound, irk, irritate, nag, plague, rib, ride, tease, torment, trouble

pester for payment: dun

pestiferous: annoying, bothersome, diseased, harmful, pernicious, toxic, unhealthy, virulent

pestilence: blight, destruction, disease, epidemic, evil, pest, plague, scourge

pestilent: contagious, dangerous, deadly, harmful, infectious, lethal, noxious, pernicious

pestle grinds, bowl in which: mortar

pet: caress, cherish, cherished, coax, coddle, cosset, cuddle, embrace, fondle, hug, indulge, kiss, neck, pamper, stroke

pet, one's: beloved, darling, dear, favorite, idol, jewel, lover

petals from single node, three or more: whorl

petals that drop off quickly, of: fugacious

peter out: diminish, dwindle, fade, fizzle, stop, wane

petite: dainty, delicate, demure, diminutive, lilliputian, little, small, tiny, wee

petition: address, appeal, application, apply, ask, beg, beseech, call, entreat, entreaty, implore, invoke, plea, plead, pray, prayer, proposal, request, solicit, sue, supplicate

petri dish contents: agar

petrify: appall, daze, deaden, fossilize, frighten, horrify, immobilize, numb, paralyze, startle, stun

petticoat: clothes, female, feminine, kilt, slip, undercoat, underskirt, underwear, waistcoat

petty: base, childish, chintzy, contemptible, diminutive, frivolous, inconsiderable, inessential, inferior, insignificant, irrelevant, little, mean, measly, minor, nagging, niggling, nugatory, paltry, picayune, piddling, puny, shallow, slight, small, trifling, trivial, unimportant

petty criticism: carping, nitpicking

petty quarrel: spat, tiff

petulant: crabby, cranky, cross, crotchety, displeased, fretful, grouchy, gruff, hoity-toity, huffy, impatient, insolent, irascible, irritable, moody, peevish, pettish, querulous, snappish, sulky, sullen, testy

pew: bench, seat, slip, stall

phantasm: apparition, dream, eidolon, fancy, fantasy, illusion, image, mirage, nightmare, shade, shadow, specter, spirit, vapor, vision

phantom: eidolon, figment, hallucination, idol, phantasm, specter, vision, wraith

pharmacist: apothecary, chemist, druggist

phase: angle, aspect, chapter, condition, facet, feature, hand, leg, look, part, period, position, side, stage, step, time

Ph.D. submission: dissertation, oral exam, thesis, viva voce

phenomenal: exceptional, extraordinary, fantastic, incredible, outstanding, rare, remarkable, sensational, super, unique, unprecedented, unusual

phenomenon: abnormality, actuality, event, experience, fact, happening, incident, marvel, miracle, paradox, sensation, wonder

pheromone: animal chemical, scent

philanderer: adulterer, debaucher, flirt, lover, swinger, tomcat, womanizer

philanthropic: altruistic, benevolent, charitable, generous, giving, humane, humanitarian, kindhearted, magnanimous, openhanded

philanthropist: altruist, benefactor, contributor, donor, humanitarian, patron

philatelist's interest: stamps

philippic: diatribe, exchange, reproach, screen, tirade

Philippines capital: Manila

philosophers, group of: wrangle

philosophical: abstract, calm, composed, deep, learned, logical, metaphysical, profound, rational, reflective, resigned, serene, stoic, temperate, thoughtful, wise

philosophical issue that is formally addressed: quodlibet

philosophical thought, concerning: noetic

philosophies, to reconcile and unite: syncretize

philosophy: axiology, belief, conviction, doctrine, epistemology, ethics, ideology, metaphysics, principles, psychology, reasoning, school, theory, values, wisdom

RELATED TERMS

philosophy and ethics, concerning: deontological

philosophy based on the teachings of Confucius: Confucianism

philosophy dealing with nature of knowledge, branch of: epistemology

philosophy dealing with nature of reality, branch of: metaphysics

philosophy fields: aesthetics, logic

philosophy of law: jurisprudence

philosophy of the condition of a thing whose essence is fully realized: entelechy

philosophy of the principles and standards of human conduct: ethics

philosophy of the world and life, comprehensive: weltanschauung

philosophy, school of: Eleatic, epicurean, Gnostic, idealism, materialism, modern, nihilism, Platonic, Pythagorean, realism, Sophist, Stoic, tabula rasa, yoga

philosophy, unformed featureless infant mind of: tabula rasa ❦

phlegmatic: aloof, apathetic, calm, cold, composed, cool, dull, impassive, indifferent, lethargic, listless, slow, sluggish, spiritless, unemotional

phobia: anxiety, apprehension, dread, fear, neurosis, obsession

phoenix: bird, paragon, statue, symbol

phoneme, various forms of a: allophone

phonetic: oral, spoken, vocal, voiced

phonetic notation system for hearing-impaired: visible speech

phonetic unit capable of a distinction in meaning, smallest: phoneme

phonograph: gramophone, hi-fi, machine, stereo, turntable, victrola

phonograph needle: stylus

phonograph record collector: discophile

phonograph recording catalog: discography

phony: artificial, bogus, counterfeit, fake, false, fictitious, fraud, imitation, impostor, sham, spurious, unread

phony appearance: facade

phony corporation: dummy corporation

photocopying: xerography, Xerox

phrase: cliché, couch, diction, idiom, motto, present, proverb, saying, slogan, state, term, verbiage, voice, word

RELATED TERMS

phrase formed by reordering another phrase: anagram

PHILOSOPHIES

aestheticism	Cynicism	Hinduism	Neo-Hegelianism	rationalism
agnosticism	Cyrenaics	historicism	Neo-Platonism/	realism
ahimsa	deconstructionism	Hobbism	Neoplatonism	reductionism
altruism	deism	holism	Neo-Scholasticism	relativism
animism	deontology	humanism	nihilism	Sankhya
anthroposophy	descriptivism	Humism	nominalism	Satyagraha
antinomianism	determinism	hylomorphism	noumenalism	scholasticism
apriorism	dialectical material-	hylotheism	objectivism	Scotism
Aristotelianism	ism	hylozoism	occasionalism	secular humanism
asceticism	Donatism	idealism	ontology	secularism
atheism	dualism	immaterialism	optimism	sensationalism
atomism	dynamism	individualism	ordinary language	Shintoism
Augustinianism	eclecticism	instrumentalism	philosophy	Sikhism
Averroism	egoism	intuitionism	organicism	skepticism
axiology	Eleaticism	Jainism	pacifism	socialism
Baconism	empiricism	Jansenism	panlogism	Socratic philosophy
behaviorism	Epicureanism	Judaism	panpneumatism	solipsism
Benthamism	epiphenomenalism	jurisprudence	pantheism	Spencerianism/
Bergsonism	epistemology	Kantianism	Parmenidean school	Spencerism
Berkeleianism	essentialism	logical positivism	personalism	Spinozism
Bonaventurism	estheticism	Manichaeism/	perspectivism	spiritualism
Bradleianism	ethics	Manichaeanism	pessimism	Stoicism
Brahmanism	eudaemonism/	Marxism	phenomenalism	structuralism
Buddhism	eudemonism	materialism	phenomenology	subjectivism
Cartesianism	euhemerism	mechanism	physicalism	syncretism
Catholicism	existentialism	mentalism	Platonism	Taoism
communism	Fabianism	metaphysics	pluralism	theism
Comtism	fatalism	Mimamsa	positivism	Thomism
conceptualism	Fichteanism	Mithraism	pragmatism	transcendentalism
Confucianism	functionalism	Modernism	prescriptivism	utilitarianism
consequentialism	Gnosticism	monasticism	probabilism	utopianism
contextualism	hedonism	monism	Protestantism	vitalism
cosmotheism	Hegelianism	Mormonism	Puritanism	voluntarism
creationism	Heideggerianism	mysticism	Pyrrhonism	yoga ❦
critical philosophy	Heracliteanism	naturalism	Pythagoreanism	

phrase in wide popular use:
catchphrase

phrase occurring only once in language: hapax legomenon

phrase or watchword of group:
shibboleth

phrase with syntax independent of context, qualifying: parenthesis

phrase, arrangement of words to form meaningful: construction

phrase, newly invented: coinage, neologism

phrase, shortened or condensed:
brachylogy

phrase, word, etc. inserted to add explanation or comment:
parenthesis ❦

phraseology: diction, language, locution, manner, parlance, style, syntax, wording

phraseology peculiar to a language or region: idiom

phylactery: amulet, charm, reminder, talisman

physic: cathartic, cure, drug, heal, medicine, treat

physical: bodily, brute, carnal, concrete, corporeal, examination, material, natural, real, somatic, substantial, tangible, violent

physical characteristics of individual, esp. as related to disease: habitus

physical desires, concerning: carnal, sensual

physical fitness exercises: calisthenics

physical fitness exercises for cardiovascular health: aerobics

physical fitness exercises for muscles using resistance: isometrics

physical science of the static and dynamic behavior of fluids: fluid mechanics, hydraulics

physical, not spiritual or conceptual: corporeal, objective, tangible

physician: consultant, curer, doc, doctor, healer, intern, medic, medico, quack, sawbones, specialist, surgeon

physician's training time at hospital: residency

physiognomy: appearance, aspect, countenance, expression, face, fea-

PHOTOGRAPHY TERMS

affix photograph on backing for display, to: mount
brown tint for photographs: sepia
clarity of detail: definition
composite of photographs: mosaic
film coating: emulsion
improving a photograph: retouching
medium that scatters light: diffuser
old photography process: daguerreotype
one who photographs attractively, of: photogenic
photograph: blowup, candid, film, image, likeness, mug, picture, pinup, portrait, record, slide, snap, snapshot, still, tintype
photograph of person's face: head shot, mug shot

photograph with light and dark patches, of a: grainy
photographer of celebrities: paparazzo (paparazzi)
photographic: cinematic, exact, lifelike, picturesque, precise
photographic plate or piece of film: exposure
photographic print on smooth shiny paper: glossy
photographic slide viewed with light: transparency
screen of three colors used in: reseau
small print for preliminary viewing: contact print
three-dimensional photograph: hologram
unbordered photograph: vignette
written explanation for photograph: caption ❦

PHYSICS TERMS

abrupt change from one energy level to another: quantum jump
branch of physics dealing with action of forces on matter: mechanics
branch of physics dealing with equilibrium mechanics of stationary bodies: statics
branch of physics dealing with relation of heat to other forms of energy: thermodynamics
physical constant relating the energy of a photon to its frequency: Planck's constant
physical phenomenon in which surface of liquid is a stretched elastic membrane: surface tension
physical phenomenon of body's tendency to resist acceleration: inertia
physical phenomenon of constant erratic motion of tiny particles suspended in fluid or gas: Brownian motion
physical phenomenon of force's tendency to produce turning or twisting: moment of force, torque
physical phenomenon of time required for half the nuclei

of radioactive material to undergo decay: half-life
physical phenomenon that frequency of waves changes when source and observer are in motion relative to each other: Doppler effect
physical principle that at constant temperature the volume of a gas varies inversely with its pressure: Boyle's law
physical principle that body's loss of weight in fluid is equal to the weight of fluid displaced: Archimedes' principle
physical principle that energy of isolated system remains constant: conservation of energy
physical principle that equal volumes of gasses under same conditions have same number of molecules: Avogadro's law
physical theory that radiant energy is transmitted in discrete units: quantum theory
physical variable, such as mass, length or speed, that has distance but no direction: scalar
physical variable that has distance and direction: vector ❦

ture, look, mien, portrait, visage
physique: anatomy, body, build, constitution, figure, form, frame, makeup, muscles, shape, stature
piano: clavichord, clavier, grand piano, instrument, pianoforte, Pianola, player, spinet, upright piano
piano adjuster: tuner
piano family: keyboard
piano inventor: Cristofori
piano-key wood: ebony
piano, largest grand: concert grand
piano, mechanically operated: player piano
piano, small upright: spinet
pianolike instrument: celesta, clavichord
piazza: balcony, colonnade, patio, porch, portico, square, veranda

picaroon: adventurer, buccaneer, freebooter, knave, pirate, rogue
picayune: little, mean, measly, petty, piddling, small, small-time, trivial, unimportant
pick: bargain, best, choice, choose, cream, cull, druthers, elect, elite, gather, harvest, jimmy, opt, pluck, prefer, preference, prize, select, take
pick on: badger, bull, criticize, goad, tease, torment
pick up: acquire, apprehend, collect, gain, garner, gather, improve, learn, procure
pick up the tab: treat
picket: boycott, fence, guard, lookout, pale, patrol, post, protester, rail, sentinel, stake, strike, striker, tether
picket-line crosser: scab

pickle: bind, crisis, dilemma, jam, mess, plight, predicament, quandary, trouble
pickle juice: brine
pickle relish: chow chow
pickle, food: capers, chutney, cucumber, cure, dill, garlic, gherkin, marinate, sweet
pickled vegetable: beet
pickpocket: cannon, cutpurse, digger, dipper, fingersmith, friskers, jostle, riffle, robber, thief
pickup: acceleration, boost, impromptu, stimulant
pickup truck part: cab
picky: choosy, finicky, fussy, meticulous, particular, persnickety
picnic: barbecue, barbeque, cookout, fête champêtre, outing

picnic basket: hamper

pictorial composition by juxtaposing or superimposing pictures: montage

picture: canvas, cartoon, conceive, copy, delineate, depict, describe, draw, drawing, envision, etching, explain, film, flick, icon, idea, illustrate, illustration, image, imagine, impression, likeness, mosaic, movie, painting, panorama, pastel, photo, photograph, pictorial, portrait, portray, portrayal, print, represent, scene, shot, show, sketch, snapshot, tableau, vignette, watercolor

RELATED TERMS

picture framed with a mat border: passe-partout

picture holder: album, frame

picture in box or 3-D setting: diorama

picture made by juxtaposing pictures or designs: collage, montage

picture made of small colored pieces set into a surface: mosaic

picture on computer representing command or program: icon

picture on interior of cylindrical room, composite: cyclorama

picture or graphic description: tableau

picture or image of sacred person: icon

picture or symbol representing word, meaning, or sound: hieroglyph, hieroglyphic, pictograph

picture with blurry edges: vignette

picture writing: hieroglyphics

picture, represent in a: depict, limn

picture, written explanation of: caption

pictures or symbols representing words, puzzle with: rebus

pictures, concerning: pictorial

picturesque: alluring, artistic, beautiful, charming, graphic, idyllic, photographic, quaint, scenic, striking, vivid ❦

piddling: insignificant, little, measly, paltry, petty, picayune, small, trifling, trivial

pie: blackbird, cobbler, crustade, dessert, pastry, tart, turnover

pie filled with meat, seafood, or vegetables, custard: quiche

pie filled with molasses and brown sugar: shoofly pie

pie with a mashed potatoe crust, meat, baked: shepherd's pie

pie with ice cream: à la mode

piebald: dappled, heterogeneous, mixed, motly, mottled, multicolored, pinto, spotted, varicolored, variegated

piece: article, assemble, bit, component, creation, crumb, cut, essay, exposition, flake, fraction, fragment, hunk, join, lot, mend, morsel, painting, paper, parcel, part, patch, percentage, portion, sample, section, segment, shred, slab, slice, sliver, snack, story, strip, unit

pièce de résistance: accomplishment, centerpiece, main dish, masterpiece, roast, roti, showpiece

piece together: assemble, combine, create, form, make

piece, cut or broken off: cantle

piecemeal: fragmentary, gradual, intermittent, patchy, partly, spotty

pier: anta, berth, breakwater, buttress, column, dock, jetty, landing, pilaster, pile, pillar, quay, slip, support, wharf

pier or wharf protecting harbor or shoreline: jetty

pierce: bite, bore, break, broach, cleave, cut, drill, enter, gash, gore, hole, impale, lance, penetrate, perforate, probe, puncture, slash, spear, spike, stab, stick, sting, tunnel, wound

pierce with a horn: gore

pierce with a stake: impale

pierce with numerous holes: perforate, riddle

piercing: acute, agonizing, blaring, clear, cutting, deafening, earsplitting, high, intense, keen, loud, painful, poignant, pungent, roaring, screeching, sharp, shrill

piercing tool: awl

piety: ardor, devotion, devoutness, faith, fealty, fervor, fidelity, godliness, holiness, loyalty, religion, reverence

pig: hog, mammal, porcine, porker, slob, swine

pig castrated after reaching maturity: stag

pig castrated while young: barrow

pig family: Suidae

pig food: bacon, chap, chitlins, ham, pettitoes, pork, sausage, trotters

pig just after weaning: shoat

pig litter: farrow

pig or swine, like a: porcine

pig paddock: pen, sty

pig that has not farrowed: gilt

pig, female: sow

pig, male: barrow, boar

pig, young: barrow, farrow, gilt, piglet, runt, shoat, shote

pigeon family: Columbidae

pigeon house: cote

pigeon kin: dove

pigeon that can puff itself up: pouter

pigeon that rolls while flying: roller, tumbler

pigeon types: carrier, crowned, fantail, fruit, homing, isabel, pouter, turtledove

pigeon used as decoy: stool pigeon

pigeon, clay: bird, disk, skeet, target

pigeon, young: squab

pigeonhole: arrange, assort, catalog, compartment, compartmentalize, cubbyhole, cubicle, label, niche, rank, recess, shelf, slot, store, type

pigeonhole in dovecote: columbarium

pigeons, concerning: columbine

pigheaded: dense, headstrong, insistent, obstinate, perverse, stubborn, unyielding, willful

piglike: porcine

pigment: color, colorant, dye, paint, shade, stain, tint

pigment and beeswax fixed with heat: encaustic

pigment, earthy: ocher, sienna, umber

pigmentation, lacking any: albinism

pigmented skin areas: nevi

pigpen: dump, hole, mess, sty

pigs as food, small intestines of: chitlings, chitlins, chitterlings

pigs, food and liquid mixed to feed: slop, swill

pigs, food of nuts for: mast

pigs, litter of: farrow

pigtail: braid, plait, queue

pike: drive, expressway, freeway, highway, lance, parkway, point, road, thruway, tollgate

pilaf ingredient: rice

pilaster: alette, anta, column, pier, pillar, post, support

pile: accumulate, amass, boodle, bundle, cock, collection, fortune, gob, hair, heap, hill, hoard, jam, load, mass, money, mound, nap, pyre, shag, stack, wad, wealth, wool, yarn

pile of stones as marker or grave: cairn

pile of wood for burning dead body: pyre

pile, mound, heap: cumulus

piles: hemorrhoids

pileup: accident, accumulation, collision, crash, stack

pilfer: filch, finger, hook, loot, pillage, purloin, rob, snitch, steal, swipe, take, thieve

pilgrim: crusader, hadji, palmer, pioneer, settler, sojourner, traveler, wanderer, wayfarer

pilgrimage: crusade, expedition, hadj, hajj, journey, mission, sojourn, trip, voyage

pilgrimage to Mecca: hadj, hajj

pilgrimage to Mecca, one who has made: hajji

pill: ball, bolus, capsule, lozenge, medicine, pastille, pellet, pilule, placebo, tablet, troche

pillage: appropriate, booty, confiscate, depredate, desecrate, despoil, devastate, lift, loot, maraud, pilfer, pinch, plunder, raid, ransack, ravage, rifle, steal, swipe, trespass

pillager: freebooter, looter, marauder, plunderer, vandal

pillar: anta, colonnade, leader, mainstay, obelisk, pedestal, pier, pilaster, pile, post, prop, shaft, stele, support

pillar as monument or gravestone: stele

pillar marking boundary: terminus

pillar shaped like female: caryatid

pillar shaped like male: telamon

pillar with capital and base: pilaster

pillar with Native American symbols: totem pole

pillar with pyramid top, four-sided Egyptian: obelisk

pillar, female figure as supporting: caryatid

pillar, rectangular, supporting arch or roof: pier

pillarlike stone, large: dolmen, megalith, menhir, monolith

pillars and one across top, two large stone: dolmen, trilithon

pillars, ring of stone: cromlech, henge

pillars, row of regularly placed: colonnade

pillow: bolster, cushion, headrest, padding, support

pillow cover: sham

pillow stuffing: eider, kapok, ticking

pillow, long hard: bolster

pilot: ace, airman, airwoman, aviator, conductor, coxswain, director, flier, fly-boy, fly-gal, guide, helmsman, helmswoman, leader, operate, scout, steer, steerer

pilot of aircraft: aviator, aviatrix

pilot of balloon or lighter-than-air craft: aeronaut

pilot, suicide: kamikaze

pilot's seat designed for emergencies: ejection seat, ejector seat

pimple: abscess, acne, blackhead, blemish, boil, papule, pustule, whelk, whitehead, zit

pimple of keratin and sebum in pore: blackhead, comedo

pimple of sebaceous gland: milium, wen, whitehead

pimple on eyelid: sty

pimple, break out in a: erupt

pimplelike projection at root of hair: papilla

pimples, goose: goose bumps, horripilation, piloerection

pin: affix, attach, badge, bind, bolt, brooch, clasp, clip, confine, cotter, dart, dowel, fasten, fastener, fix, jewelry, join, ornament, peg, rivet, secure, stake, thole

pin a medal on: decorate

pin fitting into corresponding hole to fasten adjacent pieces: dowel

pin in form of clasp: safety pin

pin in shaft, locking: linchpin

pince-nez: eyeglasses, lorgnette, lorgnon, spectacles

pincers: forceps, pliers, tongs

pincers, small: tweezers

pinch: contract, cramp, grab, grasp, nip, snip, squeeze, tweak, vellicate

pinch into tight folds or curls: crimp

pinchbeck: counterfeit, fake, imitation, spurious

pine: ache, agonize, brood, crave, desire, dwindle, flag, fret, grieve, hunger, lament, languish, long, moon, mope, mourn, repine, want, waste, wither, yearn

pine cone petal: scale

pine-cone shape: pineal

pine family: conifer

pine fruit: cone

pine variety: Apache, blue, Buddhist, cedar, cypress, evergreen, fir, foxtail, giant, gray, hickory, jack, loblolly, mahogany, mountain, Norwegian, nut, pinon, pond, red, Scotch, spruce, stone, sugar, Weymouth, white

pineapple: piña

PINK

begonia
blush
cameo
carnation
casino pink
coral-pink
deep pink
fiesta
flamingo
flesh-pink
hot pink
incarnadine
livid pink
mallow pink
nymph
ombre
orange-pink
orchid rose
pale pink
peach
petal pink
reddish pink
rose
royal pink
salmon
shell pink
shocking pink
tea rose ❦

pineapple-shaped: pineal

ping: clink, knock, noise, sound, ting

pinhead: clown, dunce, fool, insignificant, small, stupid, tiny

pinnacle: acme, apex, belfry, climax, crest, crown, height, peak, serac, spire, summit, top, turret, zenith

pinnacle of glacial ice: serac

pinniped: seal

piñon seed: pine nut

pinpoint: aim, diagnose, distinguish, exact, finger, fix, identify, locate, point, precise, spot

pinto: horse, mottled, piebald, pied

pioneer: colonist, discover, experimental, explorer, first, initial, innovator, invent, original, pathfinder, pilgrim, settler, trailblazer

pious: commendable, dedicated, devine, devout, faithful, godly, holy, loyal, priestly, religious, reverent, saintly, sanctimonious, spiritual, worthy

pious, hypocritically: holier-than-thou, sanctimonious, self-righteous

pipe: aqueduct, briar, canal, cask, conductor, conduit, drain, duct, flue, flute, hookah, hose, instrument, leader, main, outlet, passage, peep, reed, sewer, siphon, spout, stack, supply, trough, tube, tweet, whistle

pipe adapter to fit different-sized pipes together: bushing

pipe cleaning device of rubber suction cup on wooden handle: plumber's helper, plunger

pipe collar: flange

pipe connecting smaller pipe: header

pipe dream: fantasy, hope, illusion

pipe fitting: elbow, ell, tee

pipe for hot air or smoke: flue

pipe or channel for rainwater: conduit, culvert

pipe with multiple apertures for connections: manifold

pipe with S- or U-bend: trap

pipe's bowl and shank: stummel

pipe's bowl of magnesium silicate: meerschaum

pipsqueak: nobody, runt, small, twerp

piquancy: salt, spice, tang, zest

piquant: biting, bitter, flavorful, peppery, poignant, provocative, pungent, racy, salty, sharp, snappy, sparkling, spicy, stimulating, stinging, tangy, tart, zestful, zesty

pique: aggravate, anger, annoy, annoyance, arouse, bother, displeasure, exasperate, excite, fret, grudge, incense, ire, irritate, irritation, miff, nettle, offend, offense, peeve, pout, pride, provoke, resentment, rile, snit, stimulate, sting, strunt, umbrage, vexation

pirate: buccaneer, corsair, freebooter, marauder, picaroon, plagiarize, plunderer, privateer, raider, robber, sea dog, sea wolf, steal, thief

pirate flag: Jolly Roger, skull-and-crossbones

pirate ideas, writings, music: plagiarize

pirate sword: cutlass

pistils of flower: gynoecium

pistol: automatic, derringer, firearm, gat, gun, handgun, revolver, rod, six-shooter, weapon

pit: abaddon, abyss, cavern, cavity, chasm, crater, depression, downfall, foxhole, grave, gully, hell, hole, hollow, indentation, mine, pockmark, seed, shaft, sump, trap, trench, underworld, well

pit in which water is collected: sump

pit of stomach: solar plexus

pitch black: ebon

pitch in: contribute, cooperate, egin, help, participate, volunteer, work

pitch in sound: accent, frequency, intonation, sound, tone

pitch of musical instrument, adjust: temper

pitch or slant: angle, cant, cast, changeup, curve, degree, fastball, fling, forkball, heave, hurl, incline, knuckler, line, lunge, lurch, plunge, raise, rate, rock, roll, seesaw, slant, slider, slope, spitball, throw, tilt, toss, totter

pitch to sell: sales talk, snow job, spiel

pitch, concerning: piceous

pitcher: carafe, container, creamer, decanter, ewer, jar, jug, olla, vessel

pitcher part: ear

pitcher plant: flytrap

pitcher's place: bullpen

piteous: merciful, miserable, pathetic, pitiful, pitying, ruined, woeful

pitfall: danger, drawback, hazard, peril, risk, snag, snare, springe, trap, traps

pith: center, core, corey, crux, essence, fiber, force, gist, gist of the matter, heart, importance, marrow, meat, nucleus, pulp, significance, soul, strength, substance, sum and substance, vigor

pith helmet: topee, topi

pithy: brief, compact, concise, crisp, forceful, laconic, meaningful, meaty, pointed, short, significant, succinct, terse

pithy saying: apothegm, motto

pitiable: sorry

pitiful: commiserable, contemptible, despicable, dismal, forlorn, heart-rending, mean, miserable, moving, pathetic, piteous, pitiable, sorrowful, sorry, suffering, woeful, wretched

pitiless: brutal, callous, cruel, ferocious, hardhearted, harsh, heartless, inhuman, insensitive, merciless, obdurate, relentless, ruthless, savage, stony, unfeeling, unmerciful, unsympathetic

pittance: alms, bit, dole, little, mite, peanut, scrap, smidgen, trace, trifle

pituitary gland: hypophysis

pity: charity, clemency, comfort, commiserate, compassion, crime, forbearance, kindliness, lament, mercy, pathos, piety, shame, solace, sympathy, tenderness, understanding

pity for, to feel: commiserate, sympathize with

pity, arousing: pathetic

pivot: avert, axis, center, focus, fulcrum, hinge, rotate, shirl, slue, spin, swing, swivel, turn

pivotal: central, critical, crucial, decisive, determining, essential, important, vital

pivotal point: center of gravity, hinge

pivoted part of electric machine: armature

pivoting, capable of: trochoid

pixie: brownie, elf, fairy, goblin, imp, leprechaun, rascal, sprite

pizzazz: dazzling, élan, energy, excitement, exuberance, flair, flamboyance, oomph, pep, spirit, zing

placard: advertisement, affiche, announce, bill, bulletin, notice, plaque, poster, sign

placate: appease, calm, conciliate, humor, mollify, pacify, quiet, sooth, tranquilize

place: allocate, area, assign, base, bestow, city, community, deposit, dispose, duty, dwelling, gait, home, identify, install, invest, lay, lieu, locale, locality, locate, location, locus, niche, plant, point, posit, position, post, put, rank, region, residence, responsibility, room, seat, second, set, site, situate, situation, space, spot, standing, station, status, stead, stick, store, tract, vicinity, village, where

place a bet: wager

place in reference to particular event: locale, locus, setting

place in society or profession: prestige, status

place inside something else: embed, insert

place name or name derived from a place: toponym

place nearby: locality, neighborhood, vicinity

place on map, find a: locate, pinpoint

place or scene where something takes place: venue

place over or on top of: superimpose

place's distinctive atmosphere: genius loci

placid: calm, collected, composed, contented as a cow, even, gentle, irenic, mild, peaceful, quiet, serene, still, tame, tranquil, undisturbed, unruffled

placing in time erroneously: anachronism

plagiarize: appropriate, copy, forge, lift, pirate, steal, thieve

plague: affliction, annoyance, badger, bane, bedevil, bother, calamity, chafe, contagion, curse, disease, epidemic, fret, gall, harass, harry, hassle, importune, infestation, irritate, nuisance, outbreak, pest, pester, pestilence, pox, rash, scourge, suffering, tease, teast, torment, trouble, worry

plague spread by rats: black death, bubonic plague

plain: apparent, austere, average, bald, bare, basic, blunt, bovious, broad, campaign, candid, clear, coarse, direct, distinct, downright, even, evident, explicit, fair, frank, genuine, glaring, gross, guileless, homely, homemade, homespun, homey, honest, humble, ingenuous, legible, level, manifest, mere, modest, moor, nondescript, obvious, open, ordinary, outspoken, patent, primitive, pure, simple, straight, straightforward, transparent, unadorned, unaffected, unassuming, unattractive, undisguised, unembellished, unmistakable, unvarnished

plain and clear: unambiguous, unequivocal

plain-cooked: au naturel

plain to see: conspicuous, evident, manifest, obvious, salient

plain where most of the rain falls: llano

plain, flat treeless grassy: steppe

plain, land: champaign, flatland, heath, meadow, plateau, prairie, savanna, steppe, tundra, wold

plainsong: Gregorian chant

plainsong beginning: intonation

plaintiff: accuser, complainant, litigant, prosecutor, suer, usee

plaintive: cross, doleful, dolorous, elegiac, fretful, lamenting, mournful, piteous, pitiful, rueful, sad, sorrowful, woebegone

plait: braid, crease, fold, interweave, knit, pigtail, pleach, pleat, tress, tuck, twine, weave

plaited straw: sennit

plan: agenda, aim, arrange, arrangement, blueprint, brainstorm, budget, calculate, chart, conception, conspire, contemplate, contrive, design, devise, diagram, draft, drawing, engineer, foresee, form, formulate, frame, game, idea, intend, layout, map, method, order, organize, outline, platform, plot, policy, premeditate, program, project, proposal, proposition, purpose, schedule, scheme, shape, sketch, stratagem, strategy, system, think

plan for radio program: format

plan for trip: itinerary

plan in mind: concoct, contrive, design, devise, formulate, invent, scheme

plan into effect, to put: carry out, execute, implement

plan not fully worked out, of a: makeshift, stopgap, tentative

plan or intend: contemplate, destine, envisage, mediate, purpose

plan or model: blueprint, prototype

plan or order: arrangement, disposition

plan or rough drawing: draft, sketch

plan, description of a: specification, specs

plan, impediment to a: hitch, snag

plan, overall or long-range: strategy

plan, realization of: fruition

plan, to make sketchy outline of: adumbrate

plane: aero, aircraft, jet

plane and level: degree, even, flat, flush, grade, horizontal, smooth

planet: celestial body, earth, globe, heavenly body, world

planet at closest point to Sun: perihelion

planet at farthest point from Sun: aphelion

planet closer to Sun than Earth is: inferior planet

planet farther from Sun than Earth is: superior planet

planet or celestial body, very small: asteroid, minor planet, planetoid

planet orbit that is not circular, of a: eccentric

planet path: orbit

planet viewing and measuring device: planetarium

planet, dark area on: mare

planetarium: orrery

planetary: earthly, erratic, global, nomadic, terrestrial, universal, wandering, worldly

planets and stars' positions, predictions based on birth date in relation to: horoscope

planets, Moon, Sun in imaginary band: zodiac

plank: board, deal, duckboard, lumber, platform, slab, support, timber

plank alongside of a ship: wale

plank as removable footway: gangplank, gangway

planking, continuous line of: strake

planks, built of edge-to-edge: carvel-built

planks, built of overlapping: clinker-built, lapstrake

planks, promenade made of: boardwalk

planned and deliberate: premeditated

planned for, possibility that must be: contingency

planned or intended: projected

planner: administrator, architect, creator, designer, executive

planning beforehand: forethought, preparation

planning details of an operation: logistics

planning for future: providence

planning large project with tasks, milestones, schedules and their interrelations: critical path analysis, critical path method

planning to achieve an end, aim, goal: tactics

planning, having some degree of: premeditated

plans: blueprints, intentions, maps

plant adapted to extreme changes of weather: tropophyte

plant adjustment to new habitat: ecesis

plant and animal comparisons, science of: biostatics

plant and animal periodic phenomena, science of: phenology

plant and animal processes, science of: physiology

plant and structures, science of: morphology

plant angiosperm: dicot, monocot

plant appendage: awn

plant body: cormus, stem, thallus

plant branch: ramus

plant bred from two varieties or species: hybrid

plant bristle: awn, beard

plant cell containing starch grains: statocyst

plant coloring: carotene, chlorophyll, endochrome, xanthophyll

plant cultivation not in soil: aquaculture, hydroponics

plant cultivation, science or art of: horticulture

plant deprived of sunlight, whitening of: etiolation

plant disease: blight, blister, edema, ergot, gall, mildew, mold, mosaic, rot, rust, scab, smut

plant-eating: herbivorous, phytophagous

plant food-conducting tissue: phloem

plant green pigment using sunlight for photosynthesis: chlorophyll

plant growing from self-sown or accidentally dropped seed: volunteer

plant growing in mineral solutions: hydroponics

plant growing on another plant for support but not nutrients: aerophyte, air plant, epiphyte

plant growth determined by external stimulus: tropism

plant growth determined by internal stimulus: nastic

plant growth, herb not woody: herbage

plant having branching parts: dichotomy

plant into another region, introduce: domesticate, naturalize

plant juice: sap

plant life of a region: flora

plant naturalized in region: denizen

plant or animal as representative of new species: holotype

plant or animal membranes: septa

plant or animal occupying area from initial stage to climax: sere

plant or animal surviving from earlier period: relict

plant originating or growing in area, of a: indigenous

plant part just below flower or on flower stalk, leaflike: bract

plant parts: appendage, axil, bine, boll, bract, bud, bulb, bur, burr, button, cambium, caulis, cellulose, cholorophyll, cormus, cutin, flower, fruit, grain, lenticel, medula, meristem, node, nut, palet, phloem, pip, pith, pod, radicle, radix, rhizome, rod, root, scion, shaft, sprig, stalk, stamen, stem, stems, stipel, stolon, stoma, stomata, tendril, trunk, xylem

plant pest: aphid, aphis, mite

plant plot: bed

plant pore: stoma

plant pot or stand, large decorative: jardiniere

plant process using carbon dioxide, water, and sunlight: photosynthesis

plant runner: stolon

plant sheath: ocrea

plant shoot, twig, or cutting: cion, scion, slip

plant specimens, case for: vasculum

plant that originated and persisted only through cultivation: cultivar

plant water-conducting tissue: xylem

plant whose flowers retain color when dried: everlasting, immortelle

plant with single embryonic seed leaf: monocotyledon

plant with two embryonic seed leaves: dicot, dicotyledon

plant, arrangement of 3+ leaves on: whorl

plant, aquatic: cattail, lotus, need, papyrus, sedge, water lily, watercress

plant, bulbous: camas, hyacinth, jonquil, lily, narcissus, onion, quamash, tulip

plant, cactus: cereus, dildo, mescal, nopal, opuntia, prickly pear, saguaro

plant, carnivorous: butterwort, pitcher plant, sundew, Venus's flytrap

plant, climbing: betel, bignonia, byrony, creeper, derris, ivy, jasmine, liana, morning glory, philodendron, smilax, vetch, vine, wisteria

plant, concerning a: agamic, botanic, botanical, vegetal, vegetative

plant, cone-bearing: cedar, conifer, cypress, fir, gingko, pine, redwood, spruce, yew

plant, desert: agave, alhagi, aloe, brittlebush, cactus, cholla, mesquite, paloverde

plant, evergreen: boxberry, clubmoss, fir, pine, spruce, wintergreen

plant, flowerless: alga, clubmoss, fern, fungus, horsetail, kelp, lichen, liverwort, moss, seaweed

plant, foreign: exotic

plant, garden: amaryllis, anemone, aster, begonia, bletia, bluebell, calla, canna, carnation, celery, celosia, chrysanthemum, clarkia, clivia, cosmos, crocus, daffodil, daisy, delphinium, dianthus, forget-me-not, gardenia, gazania, geranium, gerbera, gypsophila, hollyhock, hyacinth, iris, ixia, jonquil, larkspur, lily, lobelia, lupine, marigold, muscari, myosotis, oxalis, pansy, pentunia, peony, phlox, poppy, primrose, rhododendron, rose, scabiosa, snapdragon, statice, stock, sweetpea, tulip, verbena, viola, zinnia

plant, grain: barley, buckwheat, corn, maize, millet, oat, rice, rye, teff, wheat

plant, marsh: bulrush, cattail, juncus, reed, sedge

plant, medicinal: aconite, aloe, boneset, camomile, camphor, caraway, chamomile, dandelion, fennel, garlic, gentian, ginger, hemlock, henbane, ipecac, juniper, licorice, lobelia, monkshead, mullein, mustard, nettle, parsley, peppermint, poppy, saffron, sage, senna, simple, wormwood

plant, microscopic: bacterium, diatom, microphyte, mold, spore

plant, native: indigene

plant, onionlike: chive, leek, scallion, shallot

plant, poisonous: amanita, atis, belladonna, castor, cowbane, datura, foxglove, larkspur, nightshade, oleander, poke, sumac, tobacco, upas

plant, succulent: agave, aloe, bitterroot, gasteria, herb, houseleek

plant, thorned: briar, cactus, cocklebur, nettle, rose, teasel, thistle

plant, to breed: propagate

plant, to go limp as a: droop, wilt

plant, young: cion, cutting, scion, seedling, shoot, sprout, vinelet

plantation: colony, estate, farm, ranch

plants indoors, place for raising: vivarium

plants living or growing for only one year or season: annual

plants living three or more years: perennial

plants of a region: flora, plant life, vegetation

plants taking two growing seasons to complete life cycle: biennial

plants turning toward the sun or light, phenomenon of: heliotropism

plants, bell-shaped cover for: cloche

plants, concerning: vegetal

plants, cone-bearing evergreen: cycad

plants, cutin layer covering epidermis of: cuticle

plants, invertebrate animals resembling: zoophyte

plants, science or study of: botany, phytology

plaque: badge, brooch, decoration, disk, medal, memorial, nameplate, patch, plate, slab

plaster: adhere, ceil, cement, coat,

cover, gesso, glue, grout, gypsum, mortar, paste, salve, smear, spackle, stucco

plaster and pebble rough finish for outside walls: pebble dash, rock dash

plaster application, strip as guide for smooth: screed

plaster finish for interior wall: stucco

plaster finish for walls and ceilings, thin: grout

plaster level or smooth, to make: float

plaster of lime, pebbles, shells for wall: roughcast

plaster of paris and glue: gesso

plaster used to coat walls and line chimneys: pargeting

plaster, painting on dry: secco

plaster, painting on moist: fresco

plaster, to coat with: render

plasterer's tool: trowel

plasterlike surface for painting: gesso

plastic: acrylic, adaptable, ductile, elastic, flexible, formative, malleable, moldable, pliable, pliant, soft, synthetic, waxy, yielding

plastic capable of polarizing light passing through it: Polaroid

plastic fiber: saran

plastic in die, to shape: extrude

plastic made of resin, lightweight: acrylic

plastic of synthetic resin, laminated: Formica

plastic polymer, rigid thermo-: polystyrene

plastic surgery: anaplasty

plastic surgery to improve looks: cosmetic surgery

plastic, tough flexible shiny: vinyl

plastic, trademarked synthetic: Bakelite

plastic, transparent thermoplastic acrylic resin: lucite

plasticlike durable floor covering: linoleum

plastics, compounds of many repeated linked units making up: polymer

plate: armor, base, coat, cover, denture, disc, dish, disk, lamina, layer, pane, panel, paten, saucer, scale

plate of bone or tissue: lamella, lamina

plate on tortoise underside: plastron

plate or platter on which food is carved or served: trencher

plate or warmer, hot: chafing dish

plate used in a church service: paten

plateau: elevation, highland, mesa, milestone, table, tableland, uplands

plateau, small and steep-walled: mesa

plates or scales, bony: cuirass

plates, covered with bony scales or: scutate, scutellate

platform: altar, base, boardwalk, chart, dais, deck, estrade, floor, forum, gangplank, ledge, pallet, podium, pulpit, ramp, rostrum, scaffold, skid, soapbox, stage, stand, terrace

platform for coffin: bier

platform for speaker, conductor: dais, podium, rostrum, tribune

platform for storing or moving cargo, portable: pallet, skid

platform or raised framework, often temporary: scaffold

platform with steps at entrance of building: stoop

platform, low and wheeled: dolly

platform, political: objectives, plan, policy, position, program, soapbox, stand

platitude: banality, bromide, cliché, commonplace, corn, shibboleth, triteness, triviality, truism

platonic: idealistic, quixotic, spiritual, theoretical, transcendent, utopian, visionary

platoon: battery, company, crew, detachment, division, force, formation, group, outfit, patrol, squad, team, unit

platter: charger, disc, dish, disk, lanx, plate, record, salver, tray, trencher

platypus family: monotreme

plaudit: acclaim, acclamation, applause, approbation, approval, cheer, compliment, kudo, ovation, praise

plausible: acceptable, believable, colorable, credible, logical, reasonable, specious, valid

play (performance): amusement, comedy, drama, entertainment, hit, musical, opera, performance, show, tragedy

RELATED TERMS

play act: emote

play or scene with two actors speaking: duologue

play performed in the afternoon: matinee

play, characters of a: dramatis personae

play, climax or resolution of: denouement

play, conversation between characters in a: dialogue

play, discourse revealing character's thoughts in a: soliloquy

play, scenery and props: mise-en-scène

play, section end with explanation: epilogue

play, short performance as interlude to a: divertissement, entr'acte

play, to test or try out for: audition

play's stage articles, not costumes or scenery: property

play's opening performance: premiere

plays, asked to play the same kind of part repeatedly in: typecast

plays, organization performing a season of different: repertory company

plays, writer or adapter of: dramatist, dramaturge, playwright ❧

play a musical composition in a different key: transpose

play at or undertake superficially: dabble

play down: belittle, deemphasize, minimize, soft-pedal, soften, underrate

play on words: equivoque, paranomasia, pun

play to gain time: temporize

play with something: toy, trifle

play, to: act, amuse, carouse, cavort, contend, delight, disport, enact, engage, execute, farce, fiddle, flirt, flop, frolic, gamble, gambol, impersonate, jest, joke, manipulate, margin, merrymaking, oppose, pantomime, participate, perform, portray, recreate, relax, romp, swing

play, word: paranomasia, punning

playboy: Casanova, Don Juan, flirt, ladykiller, libertine, lothario, philanderer, profligate, rake, Romeo, swinger, wolf, womanizer

played out: beat, bushed, depleted, drained, ended, exhausted, finished, pooped, spent, tired

player: actor, actress, adversary, athlete, competitor, contestant, entertainer, gambler, jock, opponent, participant, performer, star, thespian

playful: blithe, coltish, coy, elfin, frisky, frolicsome, funny, gamesome, humorous, jocose, jocular, jolly, kittenish, larkish, lively, merry, mischievous, prankish, rollicking, spirited, sportive, sprightly

playful in music: scherzo

playful or whimsical composition: humoresque

playful talk: banter, bantering, repartee

playful teasing: badinage

playfully, move about: caper, cavort, frisk, frolic, rollick, romp, sport

playfulness or playing, concerning: ludic

playing card spot: pip

playmate: amigo, buddy, chum, companion, comrade, friend, pal

plaza: common, court, green, marketplace, park, square

plea: alibi, apology, appeal, argument, entreaty, excuse, explanation, overture, petition, prayer, pretext, request, solicit, suit, supplication

plead: advocate, appeal, argue, ask, beg, beseech, entreat, implore, importune, petition, pray, solicit, supplicate, urge

plead for another: intercede

plead poverty: poor-mouth

pleasant: affable, agreeable, amiable, appealing, charming, congenial, cordial, delightful, engaging, enjoyable, fair, favorable, felicitous, fine, friendly, genial, good, gracious, grateful, gratifying, humorous, jocular, joyous, likable, lovely, merry, mild, nice, pleasing, refreshing, sunny, sweet, warm, welcome, winsome

pleasant-sounding: euphonious

pleasant-tasting: sapid

pleasant, quality of being: amenity

pleasantry: banter, fun, gesture, greeting, jest, jocularity, joke, quip, remark, salutation, wit, witticism

please: agree, amuse, content, delight, elate, enjoy, gladden, grab, gratify, humor, humour, indulge, like, placate, satisfy, suit, thrill, tickle, titillate, will, wish

please, trying hard to: fawning, obsequious, servile, sycophantic, toadying, unctuous

pleased, very: ecstatic, enraptured, transported

pleasing: agreeable, attractive, charming, delectable, delightful, desirable, ducky, enchanting, enjoyable, favorable, fawning, glad, inviting, likable, liking, nice, palatable, pleasant, pleasurable, prepossessing, winsome

pleasurable: delightful, enjoyable, entertaining, gratifying, pleasing, satisfying, sensual

pleasurable to the senses: sensual

pleasure: amusement, bliss, cheerfulness, choice, comfort, contentment, delectation, delicacy, delight, desire, diversion, enjoyment, fancy, felicity, fruition, fun, gladness, gratification, haiety, happiness, hedonism, hobby, jollity, joy, like, merriment, mirth, preference, relish, selection, treat, will

pleasure as way of life: primrose path

pleasure craft: yacht

pleasure from one's own suffering or pain: masochism

pleasure from others' misfortune: schadenfreude

pleasure-loving: epicurean, hedonistic

pleasure through others' achievements, gaining: vicarious

pleasure trip: jaunt, junket

pleasure, person devoted to: sybarite, voluptuary

pleasure, pursuit of or devotion to: hedonism

pleasure, to amuse oneself to gain: disport

pleat: crease, crimp, fold, gather, kilt, ruffle, shir, tuck

pleated edge to garment or curtain: flounce

plebe: cadet

plebeian: base, coarse, common, commoner, everyday, homely, ignoble, lowborn, lowly, ordinary, unrefined, vulgar

pledge: assurance, assure, betroth, bind, certainty, collateral, commit, contract, covenant, engage, gage, guarantee, guaranty, impignorate, insurance, I.O.U., mortgage, oath, pawn, promise, seal, security, surety, swear, toast, troth, vouch, vow, wage, warrant, word

pledged property to ensure repayment of loan: collateral

pledged securities as collateral for loan: hypothecation

plenary: absolute, complete, entire, full, inclusive, whole

plenipotentiary: agent, ambassador, diplomat, emissary, spokesperson

plentiful: abounding, abundant, affluent, ample, bounteous, bountiful, copious, extravagant, exuberant, fertile, fruitful, full, galore, generous, large, lavish, liberal, lush, opulent, overflowing, plenteous, plenty, profuse, rich, rife, swarming

plentiful in appearance: barmecidal

plentiful supply, overly: embarrassment of riches

plentiful, endlessly: bottomless, inexhaustible, infinite, untold

plentiful, extremely: brimming, flush, oversupplied, populous, replete, rife, teeming

plenty: abundance, affluence, ample, amplitude, copious, enough, exuberance, fullness, galore, generous, gobs, heaps, loads, lots, much, oodles, opulence, plenitude, plentiful, plentitude, prosperity, reams, slew, sufficiency, wealth

plenty in offspring, production: fecund, fertile, fruitful, profuse, prolific

plenty, horn of: cornucopia

plethora: excess, flood, glut, many, overabundance, overflow, repletion, surfeit, surplus

plexus: mesh, network, rete, system, web

pliable: adaptable, bendable, compliant, docile, ductile, easy, flexible, limber, lithe, malleable, manageable, moldable, plastic, pliant, responsive, soft, supple, tactile, tractable, workable, yielding

pliant: elastic, flexible, limber, lissome, malleable, pliable, soft, supple, yielding

plight: betroth, bind, condition, crisis, difficulty, dilemma, fix, impasse, jam, pickle, pinch, pledge, predicament, promise, quandary, situation, state

plod: drag, drudge, flounder, grind, grub, labor, moil, plow, plug, schlepp, slog, stomp, struggle, toil, tramp, trudge, work

plot: acre, cabal, calculate, chart, collaborate, collude, connive, conspiracy, conspire, contrive, design, devise, diagram, engineer, grave, intrigue, land, lot, machination, map, mark, outline, parcel, patch, plan, plat, scenario, scheme, setup, story, theme, tract

plot of literary or dramatic work: scenario

plot or conspiracy: complot, intrigue, machinations

plot resolution: denouement

plot to foil another: countermine

plot to incriminate innocent person: frame-up

plot, secret: collusion, connivance

TYPES OF POEMS

crude, irregular poem: doggerel
Japanese 3-line 17-syllable poem: haiku
Japanese 5-line 31-syllable poem: tanka
lament for deceased: elegy, monody, threnody
long lyric poem: ode
morning poem: aubade
narrative poem meant to be sung: ballad, lay
poem about rural life: bucolic, eclogue, idyll, pastoral
poem expressing thoughts and feelings: lyric
poem for bride and bridegroom: epithalamium, prothalamion
poem in which first letters of lines spell something: acrostic
poem of 10 or 13 lines with two rhymes: rondeau

poem of 14 lines with conventional rhyme scheme: sonnet
poem of 19 lines with two rhymes: villanelle
poem of 4 lines: quatrain
poem of 7 lines: heptastich
poem of 8 lines and two rhymes with two lines repeated: triolet
poem of three stanzas: ballade
poem on heroic figure: epic, heroic poem
poem retracting something said in earlier poem: palinode
poem with final letters of lines forming word: telestich
poem with middle letters of lines forming word: mesostich
short and pastoral poem: eclogue
short witty poem: epigram ❧

---

plotters: cabal, confederacy, conspiracy

plover: bird, killdeer, lapwing, turnstone, wader

plover's cousin: sandpiper

plow: break, bulldoze, cultivate, dig, farm, forge, furrow, mole, plough, press, smash, till

plow, blade or wheel attached on front of: coulter

plow, ridge between furrows made by: list

plow, trench made by: furrow

plowed ground, farm implement to even off: harrow

plow's track: furrow

ploy: frolic, gambit, gimmick, joke, maneuver, move, ruse, scam, scheme, strategy, tactic, trick

pluck: backbone, bravery, courage, daring, finger, fortitude, gameness, grit, guts, hardihood, jerk, mettle, moxie, nerve, pick, plunder, pull, remove, resolution, snatch, spirit, spunk, strip, strum, tear, tug, yank

pluck eyebrows: tweeze

plucker for clavichord-type instrument: quill

plucker for guitar: pick, plectrum

plucking, played by: pizzicato

plucky: bold, brave, courageous, daring, fearless, game, unafraid, undaunted, valiant

plug: advertise, block, boost, bung, clog, close, cork, dam, fitting, hack, mention, persevere, plowhorse, push, seal, stopper, stopple, stuff, wad

plug connecting more than one device to electrical socket: adapter

plug for muzzle of cannon, gun: tampion

plug of cask, vent: spigot, spile

plug of tobacco: chaw

plug or seal edges and crevices: caulk

plug up: estop

plum: carrot, catch, dividend, find, prize, reward, windfall

plum variety: American, black, cherry, Damson, date, European, ground, hog, Indian, Oklahoma, sloe, wild

plumb: delve, explore, fathom, probe, search, solve, sound

plumb or perpendicular: straight, vertical

plumber's tool: plunger, snake

plumbers, group of: flush

plume: crest, egret, feather, panache, preen, pride, prize, quill, token

plummet: buxom, chubby, crash, decline, descend, dip, downturn, drop, fall, fleshy, nose-dive, obese, plop, plumb, plunk, portly, rotund, sink, stout, support

plump: abundant, ample, back, obese, round, tubby, zaftig

plump body structure: endomorphic, pyknic

plunder: booty, depredate, devastate, fleece, forage, foray, goods, loot, maraud, peach, pilfer, pillage, pirate, pluck, prey on, raid, ransack, rape, rapine, ravage, raven, ravish, rifle, rob, sack, spoils, steal, swag

plundered goods: booty, loot, spoils

plunderer: bandit, freebooter, looter, marauder, pillager, raider, rapparee, ravager, thief, vandal

plundering: rapacious

plunge: absorb, descend, dig, dip, dive, douse, drive, duck, dump, engulf, fall, fling, immerse, jump, lunge, plummet, rush, sink, souse, submerge, swim, thrust, tumble

plunk: drop, place, pluck, plump, sink, sound, strike, strum, throw, toss

plurality: advantage, bulk, majority, most, multitude, variety

plus: added, added to, addition, advantageous, also, and, asset, augment, beneficial, bonus, expand, helpful, increase, more, perk, positive

plush: deluxe, elegant, fancy, lavish, lush, luxurious, opulent, palatial, posh, ritzy, sumptuous, swank

plutocrat: capitalist, magnate, moneybags, tycoon

plutonic: abyssal, Cimmerian, igneous, infernal

pluvial: rainy

ply: bend, comply, employ, exercise, exert, fold, handle, importune, maneuver, manipulate, mold, pursue, shape, steer, urge, wield, work

ply of material: fold, layer, thickness

poach: encroach, filch, pilfer, plunder, steal, trample, trespass

pocket: cavity, compartment, pouch, sack, sinus

pocket billiards: pool

pocket for watch: fob

pocketbook: bag, billfold, handbag, poke, pouch, purse, satchel, wallet

pockmark: scar

pod: bag, boll, capsule, case, cocoon, flock, hull, husk, pouch, sac, sheath, shell, shuck, silicle

pod, split ripened: dehisce

podiatrist's concern: feet

podium: base, dais, lectern, pedestal, platform, pulpit, stage, wall

poem: acrostic, ballad, composition,

dimeter, ditty, doggerel, elegy, epic, epithalamium, epode, epos, idyll, ionic, jingle, limerick, lyric, madrigal, ode, poetry, rhyme, rime, rondeau, rondo, rune, song, stanza, sulogy, tercet, threnody, verse

poem's line in iambic hexameter with caesura after third foot: alexandrine

poem's set of verses: canto, stanza, stave

poet: artist, author, balladist, bard, idyllist, lyricist, lyrist, minstrel, muse, odist, rhymer, rimer, scop, writer

RELATED TERMS

poet, eminent: laureate

poet, poor untalented: poetaster

poet, woman: poetess ☙

poetic: beautiful, dramatic, dreamy, epical, epodic, idyllic, imaginative, lyrical, odic, rhythmic, romantic

poetic image, exaggerated: conceit

poetic measure: meter, spondee

poetic metrical foot of one accented and two unaccented syllables: dactyl

poetic metrical foot with middle syllable of three accented: amphibrach

poetic metrical foot with one long syllable followed by a short: trochee

poetic metrical foot with one short syllable: mora

poetic metrical foot with one short syllable followed by a long: iamb, iambus

poetic metrical foot with two long accented syllables: spondee

poetic metrical foot with two short followed by one long syllable: anapest

poetic short closing stanza: envoy

poetic structure, study of: prosody

poetic unit of two rhymed lines in iambic pentameter: heroic couplet

poetic upbeat: arsis

poetic verse of variable, usu. unrhymed, lines: free verse

poetic writing: verse

poetric rhythm imitating speech: sprung rhythm

poetry, book of: anthology, chrestomathy

poetry, two successive rhyming lines in: couplet

poignant: acute, affecting, astute, biting, bitter, cutting, distressing, incisive, keen, moving, painful, piercing, piquant, pungent, sharp, sour, stinging, touching, urgent

point-blank: blunt, close, direct, frank, plainly, straight

point in a drawing in which parallel lines appear to converge: vanishing point

point in an eccentric orbit: apsis

point in argument, acknowledgment of effective: touché

point in drawing where parallel lines converge: vanishing point

point of contact: interface

point of intersection: node

point of intersection by three or more lines: concurrence

point of no return: Rubicon

point of origin: starting point, terminus a quo

point of view: angle, attitude, opinion, outlook, perspective, position, standpoint

point of view beforehand, forming: preconceive

point on body to stop bleeding: pressure point

point on which something rotates: pivot

point or condition relevant only to a specialist: technicality

point out: denote, indicate, show

point that is no longer meaningful: moot point

point the finger at: accuse

point, to approach an intersecting: converge

point, to go different directions from a common: diverge

point, to the: poignant, relevant

pointed: accurate, actuate, acuate, aculeate, acuminate, acute, barbed, biting, concise, conspicuous, cultrate, direct, fine, keen, marked, penetrating, picked, piercing, piked, poignant, pronged, sarcastic, sharp, stinging, striking

RELATED TERMS

pointed arch: ogee, ogive

pointed end or point: cusp

pointed heel: stiletto

pointed in shape: acerate, acerose, aculeate, acuminate

pointed instrument for writing or engraving: stylus

pointed tool: awl, punch, stylar ☙

pointer: arm, dial, dog, gauge, hand, index, indicator, rod, stick

pointer or hint: clue, suggestion, tip

pointless: absurd, academic, blunt, futile, hypothetical, idle, inane, inept, insignificant, ridiculous, senseless, silly, unnecessary, useless

poise: aplomb, assurance, balance, bearing, calm, calmness, composure, confidence, dignity, elegance, equilibrium, grace, maintain, stability, steady, support, suspend, tact

poised bearing: presence

poison: anee, arsenic, bacteria, bane, botulin, botulism, cancer, contagion, contaminate, corrupt, curare, cyanide, debase, debauch, envenom, evil, harm, inee, infect, kill, murder, pervert, plague, pollute, salmonella, taint, toxin, venom, virus, vitiate

poison affecting entire body, of a: systemic

poison antidote: mithridate, theriaca

poison, deadly: bane

poison, immunity or tolerance to a: mithridatism

poison, remedy to counteract effects of: antidote, antitoxin, antivenin

poisoning often from inadequately cooked or washed food, food: salmonella poisoning, salmonellosis

poisoning, former term for food: ptomaine poisoning

poisoning, severe food: botulism

poisonous: baneful, deadly, fatal, harmful, lethal, noxious, toxic, venomous, virulent

poisonous gas in coal mine: afterdamp, firedamp

poisonous metallic element, extremely: arsenic

poisonous secretion of animal: venom

poisonous snake: adder, asp, rattler, viper

poisonous substance that stimulates production of antibody: antigen

poisonous white alkaloid, extremely: strychnine

poisonous, extremely: virulent

poisons and treatment of poisons, study of: toxicology

poisons, substance once considered antidote to all: mithridate

poke: awaken, blow, bonnet, bulge, dally, dawdle, delay, dig, drag, intrude, jab, job, jog, lag, loiter, meddle, mosey, nudge, probe, prod, pry, punch, push, putter, sack, shove, snoop, stir, thrust

poke around: root

poke for water: dowse

poke fun at: jibe

poker for fireplace: salamander

POISONOUS PLANTS

Aconite	Corn Cockle	Glory Lily Bulb	Milo	Sheep Laurel
Alsike Clover	Corn Lily	Golden Chain	Monkey Agaric	Sierra Laurel
Amanita	Cow Cockle	Great Lobelia	Monkshood	Singletary Pea
Angel's Trumpet	Cowbane	Ground Ivy	Moonseed	Snow-on-the-
Arrowgrass	Cowslip	Groundsels	Morning Glory	Mountain
Arrowhead	Creeping Charlie	Hairy Vetch	Mountain Fetterbush	Sorghum
Baneberry	Crowfoot	Halogeton	Narrow-leaved Vetch	Spurges
Banewort	Crown Vetch	Hellebore	Nephytis	Squirrel Corn
Bearded Darnel	Daphne	Hemlock	Nightshade	St. John's Wort
Belladonna	Datura	Henbane	Nux Vomica	Star-of-Bethlehem
Birdsfoot Trefoil	Deadly Nightshade	Horse Chestnut	Oak Trees	Stinging Nettle
Bitter Cherry	Death Angel Mush-	Horse Nettle	Oleander	Sudan Grass
Black Cherry	rooms	Horsebrush	Opium Poppy	Swamp Onions
Black Locust	Death Camas	Horsetail	Panther Cap	Sweet Pea
Black Nightshade	Death Cap	Indian Tobacco	Periwinkle	Tall Fescue
Bleeding Heart	Delphiniums	Irises	Philodendron	Tangier Pea
Bloodroot	Desert Potato	Jack-in-the-Pulpit	Pigweed	Thorn Apple
Boston Ivy	Devil's Trumpet	Japanese Pieris	Pin Cherry	Tobacco
Bouncing Bet	Dock	Jessamine	Poinsettia	Tree Tobacco
Bracken Fern	Dogbane	Jimsonweed	Poisonberry	Tung Oil Tree
Broad Beans	Doll's-eyes	Johnson Grass	Poison Hemlock	Upas
Buckeye	Downy Thornapple	Laburnum	Poison Ivy	Water Hemlock
Buffalo Bur	Drooping Leucothoe	Lambkill	Poison Oak	West Indian Lantana
Buttercups	Dutchman's Breeches	Lamb's Quarters	Poison Sumac	White Camas
Caley Pea	Eastern Skunk Cab-	Lantana	Pokeweed	White Clover
Calla Lily	bage	Larkspur	Ponderosa Pine	White Snakeroot
Cardinal Flower	Elderberry	Lily-of-the-Valley	Prickly Poppy	Wild Cherries
Castor Bean	Ergot	Locoweed	Purging Nut	Wild Onions
Castor-Oil Plant	Euphorbia	Lucerne	Purple Vetch	Wisteria
Celandine	Everlasting Pea	Lupine	Ragworts	Wolfsbane
China berry	False Hellebore	Mandrake	Red Angel's Trumpet	Yellow Sage
Choke Cherry	Fiddleneck	Marijuana	Red Clover	Yellow Star Thistle
Christmas Rose	Flax	Marsh Marigold	Red Sage	Yew ❧
Cocklebur	Foxglove	Mayapple	Rhubarb leaf	
Common Nightshade	Gastrolobium	Mescal Bean	Rosary Pea	
Common Oleander	Gill-over-the-	Mexican Poppy	Senecio	
Common Vetch	Ground	Milkweed	Sensitive Fern	

POKER TERMS

demand for hand disclosure: call
game with first card face down, four others face up: stud poker
hand of five cards of the same suit: flush
hand of five cards of the same suit in numerical sequence: straight flush
hand of five consecutive cards not all of same suit: straight
hand of five highest cards of same suit: royal flush
hand of four cards in one suit: four flush

hand of three of a kind and a pair: full house
increase a bet, to: raise
initial contribution to pot: ante
kitty: pot
laying down of cards to determine winner: showdown
poker-faced: neutral, serious, sober, somber, stolid
poker varieties: baseball, bluff, draw, jack, straight, strip, stud
withdraw from game by laying one's hand down, to: fold ❧

poky: confined, cramped, dawdling, dull, frumpish, jail, pokey, prison, shabby, slammer, slow, small
polar: arctic, contradictory, diametric, freezing, opposite

polar region phenomenon: midnight sun
polar weather condition of heavy cloud cover over snow: whiteout
pole: axis, bar, beam, boom, caber, guide, mast, pike, post, rod, spar,

staff, wand
pole a boat forward: punt
pole of a ship for sails or rigging: spar
pole raising and lowering bucket in well: sweep, swipe

pole, carved and painted Native American: totem pole

polecat, pertaining to: mustelid, musteline

police: bobby, constable, constabulary, cop, detective, flatfoot, fuzz, gendarme, govern, guard, heat, law, marshal, MP, officer, patrol, patrolman, patrolwoman, policeman, policewoman, protect, sheriff, watch

police informer or spy: stool pigeon

police matters into one's own hands, one who attempts to take: vigilante

police officer: bobby, cop, copper, flatfoot, roundsman, the fuzz, the heat

police officer in training: cadet

police officer's club: billy club, nightstick

police on navy vessel: master-at-arms

police organized like military unit: constabulary

police record book: blotter

police surveillance: stakeout

police tactical squad: SWAT team

police to secure an area, rope or line used by: cordon

police unit, district under jurisdiction of specific: precinct

police van: paddy wagon

police, detained or held under guard by: custody

policies of group, declaration of political: manifesto

policy: action, code, contract, course, custom, line, method, plan, platform, principle, procedure, program, sagacity, strategy, system, tactics, wisdom

policy reversal: about-face, volte-face

policy, long-range: plan, strategy

poliomyelitis vaccine: Sabin vaccine, Salk vaccine

polish: brighten, buff, burnish, gloss, luster

polish or cultivation: poise, refinement

polished: buffed, shiny, smooth, suave, waxed

polishing rock, porous: pumice

polite: attentive, bane, civil, complaisant, considerate, correct, courteous, courtly, cultivated, cultured, decorous, gallant, genteel, gentle, mannerly, neighborly, polished, proper, refined, respectful, suave, thoughtful, urbane

polite act: courtesy

polite and proper, extremely: ceremonious, punctilious

polite utterance: civility, pleasantry

polite, of speech that is: phatic

politeness, generally accepted: convenances, convention, etiquette, protocol

politesse: propriety

politic: adroit, artful, astute, calculating, crafty, cunning, diplomatic, discreet, expedient, judicious, prudent, sharp, shrewd, tactful, tactical, wise, wuave

political: civic, governmental, legislative

political activist: anarchist, demagogue, dissident, extremist, guerrilla, hawk, lobbyist, nihilist, peacenik, radical

political appearance, brief: whistle-stop

political beliefs, extreme in: intransigent

political campaign speeches, location of: hustings

political candidate or party's motto: slogan

political candidate unexpectedly nominated: dark horse

political cause, actively committed to: engage

political change, favoring revolutionary: radical

political clean-up: purge

political coalition: bloc

political concern: issue

political corruption: malversation

political dinner, lecture tour: rubber chicken circuit

political extremist: anarchist, Jacobin, leftist, nihilist

political favors, exchange of: logrolling

political group causing dissention: faction

political group's declaration of principles: manifesto, platform

political group's pamphlet of appeal or declaration: tract

political ideas, one with ambitious: utopian, visionary

political issue or policy, person actively against: activist, dissident, insurgent, militant, protestor, Young Turk

political laws and principles of a government: constitution

political leader emotionally appealing to populace: demagogue

political league or association: federation

political meeting for decisions on political delegates, policy, leadership: caucus

political pact between church and state: concordat

political parties or groups with political cause, alliance of: coalition

political party: Communist, Democratic, GOP, Green, Labor, Republican, Socialist, Tory

political party but is not a member, one who sympathizes with: camp follower, fellow traveler

political party, to unfairly divide districts to favor a: gerrymander

political party, zealots forming core of revolutionary: cadre

political patronage: pork barrel

political philosophy: anarchism, capitalism, collectivism, communism, conservatism, democracy, extremism, laissez-faire, liberalism, Maoism, Marxism, nihilism, socialism

political philosophy supporting people vs. privileged elite: populism

political platform part: plank

political policy, refusal to obey laws to try to change: civil disobedience

political power: clout

political power to appoint to governmental positions: patronage

political propaganda found in entertainment: agitprop

political risk to limit to seek advantage: brinkmanship, brinksmanship

political slander: character assassination

political slant: spin

political speeches, to travel and give: stump

political system that no longer exists: ancien regime

political tactic of getting rid of undesirable people or opponents: purge

political theory that Communist nation will cause neighbors to become Communist: domino theory

political underground movement: apparat, apparatus

politically amoral: Machiavellian

politically divide voting area for interests of a political party: gerrymander

politically neutral person: mugwump

politician: congressperson, lawmaker, leader, legislator, officeholder, politico, senator, statesperson, statist

politician charged with enforcing party discipline and attendance: whip

politician who uses impassioned appeals: demagogue

politicians, group of: odium

politicking around countryside: barnstorming

politics or business, dishonesty in: graft

poll: ballot, canvass, census, clip, count, counting, head, list, listing, opinion, shear, survey, tally, trim

poll, first public opinion: Gallup poll

poll, unofficial: straw poll

pollen: dust, microspores

pollen-bearing organ: stamen

pollen from one plant to another, transfer: cross-pollination, xenogamy

pollens and spores, study of: palynology

pollex: thumb

pollinate: breed, fertilize

pollinated by insects: entomophilous

pollinated by wind-dispersed pollen: anemophilous

pollination among flowers by same plant: endogamy

pollination in plants, self-: , autogamy

pollute: contaminate, corrupt, debauch, defile, desecrate, dirty, foul, poison, profane, smear, soil, stain, taint

pollution: contamination, desecration, impurity, smog, uncleanness, waste

polo match period of play: chukker

poltergeist: apparition, ghost, phantasm, specter, spirit

poltroon: chicken, coward, craven, dastard, milksop, varlet, weakling, wetch, yellowbelly

polygon, eight-sided: octagon

polygon, five-sided: pentagon

polygon, four-sided: tetragon

polygon, nine-sided: nonagon

polygon, seven-sided: heptagon

polygon, six-sided: hexagon

polygon, ten-sided: decagon

polygon, three-sided: triangle

polygon, twelve-sided: dodecagon

polyhedron that bends light rays: prism

polyp: anemone, coelenterate, coral, growth, hydra, hydroid, tumor

polysyllabic: sesquipedalian

pomegranate sweet syrup: grenadine

pommel: beat, finial, handle, knob, pound, pummel, saddlebow, strike

pomp: ceremonial, ceremony, cortege, display, fanfare, fare, form, glitter, grandeur, pageantry, parade, pride, ritual, show, spectacle, splendor, state, strut

pompous: affected, aloof, arrogant, bloated, bombastic, condescending, consequential, disdainful, egotistic, flaunting, grandiose, haughty, high-faluting, hoity-toity, huffish, insolent, la-di-da, large, lofty, officious, orotund, ostentatious, overbearing, patronizing, pontifical, portentous, pretentious, proud, puffy, pushy, self-important, sniffy, snobbish, snooty, snotty, stately, stilted, stuck-up, supercilious, swaggering, tumid, uppish, uppity, vain, vainglorious

pompous gait: strut

pompous language: fustian, grandiloquence

pompous moralizing, given to: canting, holier-than-thou, pious, pontifical, preachy, punctilious, sanctimonious, sententious, sermonizing

pond: basin, lagoon, lake, mere, pool, tarn

ponder: appraise, brood, chew the cud, consider, contemplate, deliberate, dwell, evaluate, examine, mediate, meditate, mull, muse, pore, reason, reflect, ruminate, speculate, study, think, weigh, wonder

ponderous: awkward, bulky, cumbersome, dreary, dull, heavy, hefty, humdrum, labored, large, massive, monotonous, tedious, weighty

pongid: ape

pontiff: bishop, pontifex, pope

pontifical: arrogant, dogmatic, overbearing, papal, pompous, pretentious, puffy

pontificate: orate

pony: cayuse, crib, glass, horse, mustang, nag, pinto, racehorse, trot

pooh-pooh: boo, catcall, deride, disdain, dismiss, hiss, knock, raspberry, razz, sneer

pool: basin, billiards, car, cartel, combination, combine, cooperative, funds, game, group, jackpot, kitty, lagoon, lake, mere, merge, natatorium, pond, pot, puddle, reservoir, resources, salina, share, tank, tarn

pool and billiard table green cloth: baize

pool frame: rack

pool shot, curving: massé

poop out: exhaust, fatigue, tire

poor: abject, bankrupted, bare, barren, base, broke, cheap, cheesy, defective, depleted, deprived, destitute, disadvantaged, emaciated, empty, feeble, fruitless, humble, hungry, ill, impecunious, impoverished, inadequate, indigent, inferior, infertile, insignificant, insolvent, insufficient, lacking, lean, meager, mean, necessitous, needy, paltry, penniless, penurious, pinched, pitiful, scanty, seedy, shabby, sorry, sparse, squalid, strapped, subpar, underprivileged, unfortunate, unlucky, unsatisfactory

pop: bang, burst, explosion, hit, shoot, shot, snap, sock, strike

pope: otho, pius, pontiff, Vicar of Christ, vicegerent

pope and a government, agreement between: concordat

pope over national authority, supporting: ultramontane

pope, assembly of cardinals by: consistory

pope, concerning the: papal

pope, formal meeting with: audience

pope, meeting held to elect new: conclave

pope, office and jurisdiction of: papacy

pope's ambassador or representative: nuncio

pope's central administration of church: curia

pope's decree on canon law: decretal

pope's formal letter: bull

pope's incapability of error: infallibility

pope's informal letter: brief

pope's letter addressed to bishops: encyclical

pope's official representative: emissary, legate

pope's secular affairs, cardinal managing: camerlengo

poplar: abele, alamo, aspen, balsam, cottonwood, downy, tree, tulip tree

poppy variety: black, California, horned, Mexican, opium, oriental, snow

poppycock: balderdash, baloney, bosh, gibberish, hogwash, jive, malarkey, nonsense, rot, rubbish, trash

populace: commonality, demos, masses, mob, multitude, people, plebeians, plebs, public, society

popular: accepted, admired, celebrated, cheap, common, current, democratic, demotic, famous, fashionable, favored, favority, noted, preferred, prevailing, prevalent, sought, trendy

popular everyday speech: vulgate

popularity: acclaim, celebrity, esteem, fame, favor, notoriety, vogue

populate: colonize, inhabit, live, occupy, people, settle

population: citizens, denizens, inhabitants, people, residents, society

population, general: canaille, commonality, hoi polloi, plebeians, plebs, populace, proletariat, riffraff, the masses

population, sample meant to be representative of: cross section

population, science of: demography

population, to increase rapidly in: irrupt

populous: crowded, jammed, multitudinal, numerous, populated, swarming

populous region of several large cities: megalopolis

porcelain: ceramic, china, crackleware, earthenware, nankeen

porcelain made of clay mixed with bone ash: bone china

porcelain material: frit

porcelain, pale grayish-blue glaze applied to: clair de lune

porch: balcony, breezeway, colonnade, deck, entrance, gallery, lanai, plaza, portico, solarium, stoa, stoop, terrace, veranda, verandah

porch with roof supported by columns: portico

porch's step at entrance of building: stoop

porcine: hoggish, piggish, rapacious

porcupine spine: quill

pore: brood, examine, foramen, gaze, meditate, opening, ponder, search, stare, study

pore: stoma

pork: bacon, food, funds, ham, hamhog, jowl, loin, meat, pig, shoulder, sowbelly, swine

pornographic: dirty, indecent, lewd, obscene, offensive, raunchy, smutty, steamy

pornographic movie: adult movie, blue movie, stag film, X-rated movie

pornography: erotica, smut

pornography, mild: soft-core

pornography, study of: coprology

porous: absorbent, leaky, penetrable, permeable, pervious, spongy

porous volcanic rock: pumice

porpoise: cetacean, dolphin, mammal, seahog, whale

porridge: burgoo, crowdie, frumenty, grits, grout, gruel, loblolly, mush, oatmeal, polenta, pottage, putu, samp, skilly

porridge of uncertain temperature: pease

port: boatyard, carriage, city, deportment, destination, dock, entrance, exit, gate, harbor, haven, landing, larboard, mooring, opening, portal, porthole, refuge, shelter, town, transport

port and sherry: wines

port side of ship: larboard

portable: convenient, handy, light, manageable, mobile, movable, pocket

portal: adit, arch, augur, bode, door, doorway, entrance, gate

portend: bode, entry, gateway, herald, omen, opening, passage, port, predict

portent: caution, clue, foreboding, foretoken, marvel, miracle, omen, premonition, prodigy, sign, vibes, warning, wonder

portentous: exciting, foreboding, looming, ominous, pompous, pretentious, significant, weighty

porter: ale, bearer, beer, bellhop, carrier, carry, doorkeeper, gateman, hamal, redcap, skycap, stout, transport

porterhouse's cousin: sirloin

portico: arcade, atrium, balcony, colonnade, patio, piazza, porch, stoa, terrace, veranda, verandah, walkway

portion: allocation, allotment, allowance, apportion, bit, bite, cut, deal, destiny, distribute, division, divvy, dole, dollop, dose, dowry, endow, fate, helping, kismet, lot, measure, moiety, parcel, part, percentage, piece, quantity, quota, ratio, ration, section, segment, serving, share, slice

portion, biggest: lion's share

portly: beefy, bulky, burly, chubby, chunky, corpulent, dignified, fat, fate, grand, hefty, majestic, obese, plump, pudgy, stately, stocky, stout, striking

portmanteau: bag, gladstone, luggage, suitcase, valise

portrait: account, drawing, image, likeness, painting, photograph, picture, similitude, sketch

portrait, exaggerated or comical: caricature

portray: act, copy, delineate, depict, describe, draw, duplicate, enact, frame, image, imitate, impersonate, limn, paint, picture, play, represent, reproduce, show

portrayal of rural life: bucolic, eclogue, idyll, pastoral

pose: affectation, air, attitude, expression, guise, mannerism, position, posture, stance, state

poser: facer, problem, puzzle, question, riddle, stickler

posh: chic, elegant, exclusive, luxurious, opulent, ritzy, smart, swanky, tony

posing customer working with con: shill

posing under false identity: imposture

position: affirmation, angle, assignment, bearings, belief, class, condition, disposition, importance, job, judgment, locale, location, locus, niche, office, opinion, outlook, place, placement, point, pose, post, posture, rank, rating, seat, set, side, site, situation, slot, spot, stance, stand, standing, standpoint, station, stature, status, tenet, viewpoint

position in relation to direction or weather conditions: aspect, exposure

position in, to enjoy a controlling: dominate

position of control: helm

position of something in space, two or more numbers determining: coordinates

position of things, to reverse or transfer the: transpose

position of, to determine: locate, pinpoint

position on a scale: ranking, rating

position relative to surroundings: bearings, orientation

position side by side: juxtapose

position that requires little or no work: sinecure

position with respect to a point of reference, to: orient, orientate

position, advantageous: bully pulpit

position, occupying the same: coincident

position, to force out of a: dislodge

positive: absolute, actual, affirmative, assertive, assured, beneficial, categorical, certain, clear, cocksure, complete, conclusive, confident, convinced, decided, decisive, definite, dogmatic, downright, emphatic, empirical, explicit, firm, genuine, helpful, plus, practical, real, sure, undisputed, unequivocal, unmistakable, unqualified, useful

positive and dictatorial: peremptory

positive assertion of opinion: dogmatic

positive declaration: asseveration

positive electrode: anode

positive particle: ion

positive with no qualifications: categorical

posse: band, gang, search party, vigilante

possess: acquire, bear, bewitch, control, dominate, have, hold, inhabit, maintain, occupy, own, retain

possessed: cursed, demoniac, haunted

possessed, to free from being: exorcise

possessing a will: testate

possession: asset, belongings, control, goods, mastery, ownership, property, territory, title, wealth

possession by which prestige is measured: status symbol

possession that's more trouble than it's worth: white elephant

possessions, excessive regard for: materialism

possessions, treasured household: lares and penates

possessive case in grammar: genitive

possessive pronoun: her, hers, his, its, our, ours, their, whose, your

possibility: chance, contingency, eventuality, feasibility, likelihood, odds, potential, probability, prospect

possible: attainable, conceivable, earthly, feasible, imaginable, likely, manageable, practicable, probable, realistic, viable, workable

possible but not certain: contingent, facultative, latent, potential

possible outcome: eventuality, scenario

possibly: maybe, perchance, perhaps, probably

possibly valid or acceptable: credible, plausible

possum: coon

post: advertise, advise, announce, assign, base, beat, brief, circulate, courier, dispatch, inform, notify

post as foundation: pile, spile

post at end of staircase handrail: newel

post exchange: canteen, PX

post or position: fort, job, lookout, office, place, position, situation, station

post or support: beam, column, leg, mast, picket, pillar, pole, stake, stilt, stud

postage stamp design: spandrel

postage stamps and marks, collection and study of: philately

postage stamps, book of: carnet

postcard collecting: deltiology

postcard collector: deltiologist

poster: advertisement, affiche, an-

nouncement, banner, bill, billboard, broadside, notice, placard, sign, sticker

poster material: oaktag

poster with printing on one side: broadside

posterior: after, back, backside, behind, butt, buttocks, derriere, dorsal, fanny, following, hind, hinder, keester, rear, retral, seat, subsequent, succeeding, tush

posterity: children, descendants, family, heirs, offspring

posthaste: expeditious, fast, pronto, quickly, rapidly, speedy, swiftly

postmortem investigation: inquest

postmortem law officer: coroner

postmortem medical examination: autopsy

postmortem medical specialist: pathologist

postpone: adjourn, defer, delay, hold in abeyance, mothball, pigeonhole, procrastinate, prorogue, put off, put on the back burner, remand, remit, reprieve, shelve, stay, suspend, table, wait, waive

postpone a decision, act evasively to: temporize

postpone and waste time: procrastinate

postpone indefinitely: table

postpone or avoid making a statement or giving an answer: equivocate, prevaricate

postpone or forgo a right: waive

postpone proceedings, to: adjourn

postponed offer or promise: rain check

postponement: respite, stay

postponement or cancellation of punishment: reprieve, respite

postponement or suspension of planned activity: moratorium

posts supporting handrail: baluster

posts, defensive barrier of: palisade, stockade

postscript: appendage, appendix, attachment, footnote, rider, sequel, supplement

postulate: assert, assume, assumption, axiom, claim, demand, element, hypothesis, posit, premise, presume, presuppose, principle, require, suppose

posture: attitude, bearing, carriage, demeanor, display, feeling, manner, mien, outlook, pose, position, shape, stance, standing, state, status

posy: blossom, bouquet, corsage, flower, motto, nosegay, sentiment, verse

pot: basin, basket, bet, bowl, caldron, cauldron, container, crock, cup, decay, deteriorate, drink, fortune, kettle, kitty, pan, pool, shoot, tankard, toilet, urn, vessel, wager

pot for cooking over fire: caldron

pot with tight lid for slow cooking: Dutch oven

pot, airtight, cooking quickly under pressure: pressure cooker

pot, earthenware broad-mouthed: olla

pot, small earthenware: pipkin

potable: clean, fresh, pure, unpolluted

potage: soup

potage, sometimes cold: consommé

potassium hydroxide: potash

potassium nitrate: niter

potato: murphy, plant, spud, tater, tuber, vegetable, yam

potato bud: eye

potato dumplings: gnocchi

potato pancake: latke, lefse

potato soup, thick: vichyssoise

potato types: baked, chip, French fries, Idaho, Maine, mashed, Russet, scalloped, sweet, white

potato, for example: tuber

potatoes baked in casserole with sauce: scalloped

potatoes cooked with cheese and browned bread crumbs: au gratin

potatoes cooked with finely sliced onions: Lyonnaise

potatoes in a casserole, thin sliced: potatoes Anna

potatoes strips deep-fried: chips, French fries, frites

potbelly: abdominal, paunch, stomach, stove

potency: authority, efficacy, energy, force, hardihood, influence, kick, might, muscle, power, strength, vigor, virtue, vitality

potency, male: virility

potent: able, cogent, control, effective, efficient, forceful, influential, mighty, powerful, robust, strong, sturdy, vigorous, virulent

potential: ability, aptitude, capability, concealed, latent, manque, possibility, possible, promising, undeveloped, unfulfilled, unrealized

pother: ado, agitation, annoyance, bother, bustle, commotion, confusion, controversy, disturbance, flap, fuss, harass, hassle, stir, to do, turmoil, uproar, worry

potion: brew, dose, draft, dram, drink, drug, medicine, mixture, philter, remedy, tonic

potpourri: assortment, blend, hash, hodgepodge, jumble, medley, melange, miscellany, mishmash, mixture, olio, pastiche, salmagundi, stew

potter: ceramicist, ceramist, cotter, dabble, dawdle, fiddle, idle, loiter, mess, poke, putter, saunter, tinker, trifle

potter's clay fired once but not glazed: biscuit

potter's clay used for decorating and coating ceramics, thin: slip

potter's mixing and shaping tool: pallet

potter's wheel, to shape or form on a: throw

pottery: ceramics, china, crockery, deftware, delft, earthenware, porcelain, stoneware, ware

pottery before glazing, coloring or decoration applied to: underglaze

pottery fired at low temperatures: earthenware

pottery fragment found by archaeologist: potsherd, shard, sherd

pottery kiln in which pots are fired without direct flame: muffle

pottery or ceramics before firing, coating applied: glaze

pottery oven: kiln

pottery with pale green glaze: celadon

pottery with surface of fine cracks, glazed: crackleware

pottery, blue and white glazed: delft

pottery, glazed colorful opaque: faience

pottery, hard unglazed: basalt

pottery, hard waterproof ceramic clay used in: terra cotta

pottery, hard white: ironstone

pottery, heavy nonporous: stoneware

pottery, richly colored and decorated Italian: majolica

potterylike: fictile

pouch: bag, container, cyst, handbag, marsupium, pocket, pocketbook, pod, purse, sac, saccule, sack, sporran

pouch branching from hollow organ: diverticulum

pouch mammal: marsupial

pouch of female marsupial: marsupium

pouch or pouchlike structure of organism: sac

pouch-shaped: bursiform

pouch worn on front of kilt: sporran

pouchlike cavity with one opening: cecum

poultice: cataplasm, compress, dressing, fomentation, plaster

poultry: chicken, duck, fowl, geese, goose, grouse, hen, partridge, pheasant, pigeon, pullet, quail, rooster, turkey

pounce: attack, claw, dart, leap, plunge, pound, powder, punch, spring, stamp, strike, surge, swoop, talon

pound: bang, bash, batter, beat, blow, buffet, clobber, clout, crush, ezra, grind, hammer, knock, malleate, maul, powder, pulverize, pummel, quid, smack, sock, stamp, stomp, strike, tamp, thrash, thump, unit, wallop, weight

pour: cascade, decant, deluge, discharge, drain, drench, effuse, emit, empty, flood, flow, gush, inundate, issue, rain, spew, spill, spout, stream, teem, vent

pour liquid from one container to another: decant, transfuse

pourboire: gift, gratuity, lagniappe, tip

pouring of liquid in religious ritual: affusion, libation

pout: brood, fish, fret, frown, grump, mope, moue, pique, sulk

pouting face: moue

poverty: dearth, destitution, dire straits, impoverishment, inadequacy, indigence, lack, need, pauperism, pennilessness, penury, privation, rags, scantiness, scarcity, shortage, want

poverty area: slum

poverty-stricken: broke, destitute, impoverished, indigent, needy, penniless, penurious, poor

powder: cosmetic, dust, explosive, film, medicine, pollen, pounce, snow, sprinkle, talc, talcum

powder in a mortar, to crush into a: bray

powder, case containing face: compact

powder, to grind or crush to a: bray, crush, comminute, granulate, grind, pulverize, triturate

powdery: dusty, pulverized, pulverulent

powdery coating on some fruits, newly minted coins: bloom

powdery texture, having a: farinaceous

power: ability, agency, arm, authority, brawn, capacity, clout, command, control, dominance, domination, do-

minion, effort, empire, energy, fight, force, guns, hand, influence, intensity, jurisdiction, leverage, mastery, might, money, muscle, potency, prestige, right, rule, sovereignty, stamina, status, steam, strength, supremacy, sway, sword, throne, vigor, virility, vis, weight

power and control: ascendancy, authority, dominance, domination, dominion, jurisdiction, predominance, preeminence, sovereignty, supremacy

power and influence: clout, sway

power and unconditional authority, unrestricted: carte blanche

power bike: moped

power failure: blackout, outage

power formally, to relinquish: abdicate, renounce

power from central government to local units, transfer of: devolution

power from the earth's internal heat, of: geothermal

power group: elite

power in a hierarchy, level of: echelon

power in time of shortage, cutback or reduction in electrical: brownout

power is exercised, territory in which one's: bailiwick, domain, fiefdom, parish, realm

power network: grid

power of 1000 watts: kilowatt

power of a physical object in motion: impetus, inertia, momentum

power of choosing: volition, will

power of microscope or fineness of detail that can be shown of an image: resolution

power of one state over another: hegemony, suzerainty

power of thought, feeling: intensity

power or ability, inherent: aptitude, faculty

power or status, categorization according to: hierarchy, pecking order

power that is left to one's judgment and not based on laws, of a: discretionary

power that is unlimited, of a: plenary, plenipotentiary

power to a representative, to assign: delegate, depute

power to produce desired effect: efficacy

power without legal authority, to seize and hold: usurp, wrest

power, absolute: autarchy, autocracy, despotism

power, government by person with absolute: tyranny

power, having supreme: omnipotent, sovereign

power, muscular: sinew, thew

power, one in a position of: overlord

power, person with delusions of: megalomaniac

power, position of: driver's seat

power, to have or get controlling: predominate, prevail

power, to make greater in: aggrandize

power, to remove from: depose

power, without: nugatory, powerless

powered bicycle: moped

powerful: able, brawny, convincing, dominant, dominating, effacious, effective, great, Herculean, important, influential, invincible, leonine, mighty, omnipotent, passive, potent, puissant, stout, strong, supine, versatile

powerful and convincing: cogent, compelling, incisive, trenchant

powerful person: magnate, mogul, nabob, potentate

powerful person who influences candidate selection: kingmaker

powerful, arrogantly: dictatorial, domineering, imperious

powerless: crippled, defenseless, frail, impotent, impuissant, ineffectual, nugatory, unable, unfit, vulnerable, worthless

powwow: assembly, confer, conference, congress, council, discussion, forum, huddle, meeting, talk

practicable: accessible, attainable, doable, feasible, possible, realistic, usable, viable, workable

practical: bandy, efficient, feasible, functional, possible, pragmatic, pragmatical, proficient, realistic, seasoned, sensible, skilled, sound, suable, useful, utile, utilitarian, veteran, workable

practical and routine: banausic

practical experience, guided by: empirical

practical, not theoretical: pragmatic

practicality: common sense, gumption, horse sense

practically: almost, basically, essentially, most, nearly, virtually

practice: drill, exercise, perform, play, preparation, process, rehearse, repeat, train, use

practice boxing: spar

practice or business: clients, profession, trade

practice or custom: habit, manner, method, praxis, procedure, rote, routine

practice or test exercise: dry run, rehearsal, trial

practice, state of being out of: desuetude

pragmatic: active, busy, busybody, dogmatic, logical, meddlesome, practical, realistic, sensible, skilled, systematic, utilitarian

prairie: grassland, llano, meadow, pampa, plain, quamash, savanna, steppe

prairie schooner: wagon

prairie wolf: coyote

praise: acclaim, accolade, admiration, adore, adulate, adulation, applaud, appraise, approbation, bless, blessing, celebrate, commend, commendation, compliment, congratulate, esteem, eulogize, eulogy, exalt, extol, extoll, flatter, glorify, glory, hail, homage, honor, hosanna, kudos, laud, magnify, panegyrize, plaudit, proclaim, revere, salute, tout, tribute, vaunt, worship

praise expressed publicly: acclaim, accolate, bouquet, compliment, encomium, eulogy, homage, laudation, panegyric, tribute

praise or promote, to: endorse, puff, tout

praise to God, short hymn or expression of: doxology

praise, enthusiastic: approbation, plaudits

praise, shout of worshipful: hosanna

praise, song of: paean

praiseworthy: admirable, commendable, complimentary, deserving, exemplary, laudable, meritorious, stellar

praline ingredient: pecan

prance: caper, cavort, dance, flounce, frolic, gambol, parade, romp, sashay, strut

prank: adorn, antic, caper, caprice, curvet, decorate, dido, entic, escapade, frivolity, frolic, gambol, hijinks, horseplay, joke, lark, mischief, monkeyshine, shenanigans, tomfoolery, trick, whim

prate: babble, blab, boast, brag, chat, chatter, clash, drivel, gab, jabber, prattle, runon, talk, tongue, utter, yack

praxis: custom, exercise, habit, practical, practice

pray: appeal, ask, beg, beseech, conjure, implore, invoke, petition, plead, request, supplicate

prayer: appeal, application, ave, benediction, blessing, chant, complin, compline, confession, epiclesis, grace, invocation, litany, matin, orison, paternoster, petition, plea, request, suit, supplication, thanksgiving, vesper, worship

RELATED TERMS

prayer beads: rosary

prayer book: bible, breviary, hymnal, liturgy, missal, ordo

prayer ending: amen

prayer expressing a wish or vow, of a: votive

prayer folding bench or stool: faldstool

prayer in church, psalm or other piece sung as invitation to: invitatory

prayer kneeling bench with space for book: prie-dieu

prayer on behalf of others: intercession

prayer opening ceremony: invocation

prayer or hymn sung at opening of church service when minister enters: introit

prayer shawl of some Jews: tallith

prayer with list of supplications having responses: litany

prayers or religious texts: devotions

prayers or services in evening: vespers

praying figure: orant ❦

preach: advocate, evangelize, exhort, humilize, lecture, moralize, proclaim, profess, sermonize, teach

preach, traveling to: itinerant

preacher: ecclesiastic, evangelist, minister, missionary, parson, pastor, pulpiteer, reverend

preachy: moralizing, pontifical, sententious, sermonizing

preamble: foreward, introduction, preface, prelude

precarious: chancy, dangerous, doubtful, dubious, hazardous, insecure, perilous, risky, rocky, touch and go, tricky, uncertain, unstable, unwarranted

PRECIOUS AND SEMIPRECIOUS STONES

agate	carbuncle	gemstone	olivine	smoky quartz
alexandrite	carnelian/cornelian	girasol	onyx	spinel
almandine	cat's-eye	heliotrope	opal	star sapphire
amazonite	chalcedony/	hematite	pearl	sunstone
amber	calcedony	hyacinth	peridot	tiger-eye
amethyst	charoite	jade	quartz	topaz
andradite	chessylite	jadeite	red jasper	touchstone
aquamarine	chrysoberyl	jasper	rhodonite	tourmaline
aragonite	chrysolite	jet	rose quartz	turquoise
aventurin	chrysoprase	kunzite	rubasse	unakite
azurite	citrine	lapis lazuli	rubellite	water sapphire
basanite	coral	lazurite	ruby	white sapphire
beryl	demantoid	malachite	rutile	zircon ✇
black opal	diamond	melanite	sapphire	
bloodstone	emerald	moonstone	sard	
brilliant	fire opal	morganite	sardius	
cairngorm	garnet	nephrite	sardonyx	

precaution: care, carefulness, foresight, prudence, safeguard

precautions, taking: circumspect, prudent

precede: announce, antecede, antedate, forego, introduce, lead, outrank, pace, predate, preface, surpass

precede in history: antedate

precedence: importance, preference, priority, rank, superiority

precedent: custom, decision, example, guideline, instance, model, preceding, ruling, standard

precedent establisher: test case

preceding: above, anterior, before, earlier, first, former, heretofore, precursory, prevenient, previous, prior

precept: axiom, behest, brief, canon, code, command, commandment, decree, direction, doctrine, document, dogma, edict, fundamental, injunction, law, mandate, maxim, motto, order, ordinance, principle, regulation, rule, statute, tenet, writ

preceptor: expert, guru, instructor, mentor, specialist, teacher, tutor

precinct: area, beat, boundary, district, domain, environs, quarter, sector, subdivision, territory, ward

precious: adorable, beloved, cherished, choice, costly, darling, dear, delicate, expensive, exquisite, fastidious, favority, fragile, inestimable, loved, overrefined, particular, picky, priceless, prized, rare, treasurable, treasured, valuable, valued

precipice: bluff, cliff, crag, declivity, drop, ledge, steep

precipitate: abrupt, accelerate, brash, expedite, fall, hasten, hasty, headlong, hurl, hurried, hurry, impatient, impetuous, impulsive, madcap, precipitous, rash, reckless, sleet, speed, sudden, throw, unexpected

precipitation: condensation, downpour, drizzle, hail, hastening, impetuosity, mist, moisture, rain, sleet, snow

precipitous: abrupt, hasty, precipitate, quick, rapid, rash, sheer, steep

precis: abridgement, abstract, condensation, digest, epitome, summary, synopsis

precise: accurate, careful, definite, detailed, even, exact, explicit, fastidious, faultless, fixed, formal, fussy, immaculate, literal, meticulous, neat, nice, painstaking, particular, proper, punctilious, rigid, specific, stiff, strict, stringent

precise detail: minutia, trifle, trivia

precise person, extremely: perfectionist, purist, stickler

precise statement of particulars: specifications, specs

precision: accuracy, attention, care, correctness, exactness

preclude: avert, bar, cease, close, debar, discontinue, exclude, forbid, hinder, impede, inhibit, prevent, prohibit, stop

precocious: advanced, bright, fresh, gifted, intelligent, premature, sassy, smart

preconceived judgment: parti pris

preconception: assumption, bias, nation, prejudice, presumption

precook in water: parboil

precursor: ancestor, forerunner, harbinger, herald, messenger, predecessor, trailblazer, vanguard

predatory: carnivorous, marauding, pillaging, plundering, predacious, preying, rapacious, raptorial, ravenous, vulturine

predecessor: ancestor, forbear, forebear, forefather, foremother, precursor

predestination: destiny, doom, fate, foredoom, fortune, preordination

predetermined: agreed, decided, deliberate, fixed, planned, prearranged, premeditated

predetermined fate: predestination

predicament: bind, condition, corner, crisis, difficulty, dilemma, emergency, fix, hole, jam, pickle, pinch, plight, quandary, scrape, situation, spot, state

predicament with no way out: impasse

predicate: affirm, assert, aver, base, declare, establish, imply, proclaim, profess, rest

predict: anticipated, augur, call, certain, conjecture, divine, envision, expected, forbode, forebode, forecast, foresee, foretell, guess, likely, omen, portend, predictable, prognosticate, prophesy, read, soothsay, suppose

prediction: forecast, foresight, guest, hunch, insight, prognosis, prophecy

predilection: bent, bias, druthers, leaning, mindset, partiality, penchant, predisposition, preference, prejudice, proclivity, propensity, tendency

predisposed: biased, prone, willing

predisposition: inclination, leaning, likelihood, predilection, susceptibility, tendency, willingness

predisposition to certain diseases: diathesis

predominant: chief, controlling, dominating, important, influential, leading, main, paramount, prevailing, prevalent, primary, principal, reigning, ruling, superior

predominate: command, domineer, govern, lead, manage, master, prevail, rule, sovereign

preeminent: best, capital, chief, distinguished, dominant, famed, honored, incomparable, main, outstanding, prominent, renowned, star, stellar, superior, supreme, towering, unequalled, unparalleled, unrivalled, unsurpassed

preempt: acquire, appropriate, arrogate, bump, confiscate, displace, obtain, seize, sequester, take, usurp

preen: adorn, clean, dress, groom, neaten, perk, plume, press, pride, primp, prune, smooth, spruce, trim

preface: begin, commence, explanation, front, introduce, introduction, overture, preamble, precede, prelude, proem, prologue

preface or introduction: proem, prolegomenon

prefer: advance, choose, desire, elect, fancy, favor, like, opt, pick, promote, raise, rather, select

preference: advancement, bias, choice, cup of tea, druthers, favoritism, partiality, predilection, prejudice, priority, propensity, selection, upgrading

prefigure: adumbrate, foreshadow, foretell, hint, imagine, indicate, presage, suggest, symbolize, type, typify

pregnancy: gestation
RELATED TERMS
pregnancy for genetic abnormalities and sex of fetus, test during: amniocentesis
pregnancy occurring in already-pregnant animal: superfetation
pregnancy outside the uterus: ectopic pregnancy

pregnancy, 8th week+ unborn young of human: fetus
pregnancy, childbirth and post childbirth, branch of medicine providing care for women in: obstetrics
pregnancy, concerning: antenatal, prenatal
pregnancy, imagined: false pregnancy, pseudocyesis, pseudopregnancy
pregnancy, non-Western cultural practice where husband takes to bed in: couvade
pregnancy, premature expulsion of fetus ending: miscarriage, spontaneous abortion
pregnancy, technique for determining position of fetus in: ballottement
pregnancy, toxic condition of: eclampsia
pregnancy, woman who has had only one: primipara
pregnant: abounding, creative, enceinte, expectant, expecting, fecund, fertile, fruitful, gestating, gravid, heavy, hopeful, meaningful, momentous, potential, prolific, replete, rich, significant, teeming, weighty
pregnant, to make: fecundate, fertilize, impregnate, inseminate ❦

prehistoric: ancient, immemorial
RELATED TERMS
prehistoric hominids or primates resembling humans: protohuman
prehistoric human being of Africa: australopithecine
prehistoric human being of Europe: Cro-Magnon
prehistoric human being of Europe, Africa, Asia: Neanderthal man
prehistoric human being, ancestor of Homo sapiens: Homo erectus, sinanthropus
prehistoric large block of stone, often upright: monolith
prehistoric monument in England: Stonehenge
prehistoric monument of monoliths: cromlech
prehistoric monument of one capstone atop two megaliths: dolmen
prehistoric monument of one monolith: menhir
prehistoric very large block of stone, often upright: megalith ❦

prejudice: bent, bias, bigotry, damage, discrimination, distort, favoritism, harm, hatred, hinder, hurt, impair, inclination, influence, intolerance, parti pris, partiality, preconception, predetermine, predilection, predisposition, prejudgment, prepossess, racism, sexism, slant, taint

prejudice and inflexibility, characterized by: doctrinaire, dogmatic

prejudiced: biased, jaundiced, myopic, narrow-minded, parochial, partial

prejudiced individual: bigot, racist

prejudicial: biased, contrary, damaging, detrimental, discriminatory, harmful, injurious, undermining, unjust

prelate: abbess, abbot, archbishop, bishop, cardinal, dignitary, ecclesiastic, hierarch, priest

prelate with highest rank in country, province: primate

preliminary: antecedent, basic, beginning, exploratory, fundamental, inductive, initial, introductory, precursory, preface, prefatory, preparatory, previous, prior, qualifying

preliminary draft or record of transaction: protocol

prelude: beginning, foreward, fugue, introduction, opening, overture, preface, proem

premature: early, immature, incomplete, precocious, undeveloped, unready, unripe

premature babies, device for: incubator

premature news disclosure: leak

prematurely: untimely

premeditated: calculated, conscious, contrived, deliberate, intended, intentional, planned, predetermined, studied

premeditation: malice aforethought, malice prepense

premiere: beginning, debut, inaugural, opening, performance

premise: argument, assumption, hypothesis, postulate, presume, proposition, supposition, thesis

premise, and conclusion, major premise, minor: syllogism

premise, to assert the truth of a: hypothesize, posit, postulate

premises: bounds, campus, grounds, land, layout, property, site

premium: agio, award, bonus, bounty, carrot, choice, excellent, gravy, installment, payment, prime, prize, recompense, reward, superior

premium on money exchanged: agio

premonition: apprehension, feeling, foreboding, forewarning, hunch, misgiving, omen, prediction, sign, vibes, warning

preoccupation: fixation, idée fixe, obsession

preoccupied: absent, absentminded, absorbed, bemused, distracted, engaged, engrossed, immersed, lost, oblivious

preordain: destine

preparation: alertness, arrangement, composition, concoction, foresight, foundation, groundwork, readiness, readying, training

preparatory work for project: homework, spadework

prepare: adapt, address, adjust, alert, arm, arrange, braced, coach, concoct, condition, construct, cook, devise, dispose, draft, edit, equip, finished, fit, fix, frame, furnish, groom, instruct, make, outfit, pave, plan, prime, process, provide, qualify, ready, rehearse, settle, strengthen, supply, train

prepare hide: tan

preponderance: ascendancy, command, dominance, most, predominance, prevalence, superiority, supremacy, weight

preposition: for, from, into, onto, per, to, unto, upon

preposition (e.g. de, van) in name indicating noble rank: nobiliary particle

prepossess: bias, influence, predetermine, prejudice, preoccupy

prepossessing: attractive, charming, enchanting, handsome, pleasant

preposterous: absurd, bizarre, crazy, foolish, insane, irrational, ludicrous, nonsensical, outrageous, ridiculous, senseless, silly, unbelievable, unreasonable

prerequisite: condition, essential, mandatory, must, necessary, postulate, requirement

prerogative: advantage, birthright, choice, exemption, gift, grant, immunity, option, preeminence, privilege, right

presage: apprehension, augur, augury, betoken, bode, feeling, forebode, forecast, foretell, forewarn, harbinger, indicate, indication, intuition, omen, portend, portent, predict, prediction, premonition, prescience,

presentiment, prognostic, prognosticate, prophecy, prophesy, sign, soothsay, token, warning

prescience: foreknowledge, foresight, omniscience, prediction, presage

prescribe: allot, appoint, assign, authorize, command, control, define, designate, dictate, direct, enjoin, establish, guide, limit, ordain, order, recommend, rule

prescribed form: rite

prescript: command, decree, law, regulation, rule, statute

prescription: direction, dose, drug, formula, medicine, mixture, recipe, remedy

prescription only, by: ethical, magistral

prescription, available without: officinal, over-the-counter

presence: air, alertness, apparition, appearance, aspect, aura, bearing, being, calmness, character, closeness, company, cool, demeanor, deportment, influence, look, manner, mien, occupancy, poise, proximity, sangfroid, spirit

present and modern: being, contemporary, current, existing, here, immediate, nearby, now, nowadays, ready, today

present but not active or evident: latent

present everywhere at once: omnipresent, ubiquitous

present for consideration or payment: render

present or gift: award, bonus, bounty, donation, endowment, gift, grant, gratuity, lagniappe, largess

present tense describing past events: historical present

present time: nonce

present, to: address, allege, bestow, confer, contribute, demonstrate, display, donate, give, introduce, manifest, offer, perform, render, serve, show, tender

presentable: acceptable, appropriate, decent, okay, proper, respectable, satisfactory, stylish, suitable

presentation: appearance, award, debut, delivery, demonstration, gift, lecture, performance, pitch, production, show

presentiment: apprehension, expectation, feeling, foreboding, intuition, premonition, presage, vibes

presently: anon, currently, directly, immediately, now, shortly, soon, today

preservation: care, defense, maintenance, protection, safeguard, safekeeping, saving, storage

preservative: alcohol, chemical, formaldehyde, salt, saltpeter, vinegar

preservatives, to treat a corpse with: embalm

preserve: can, compote, cure, defend, dehydrate, dry, embalm, freeze, govern, guard, jam, jelly, keep, maintain, mummify, pickle, refrigerate, retain, safeguard, salt, save, season, secure, shield, smoke, spare, store, uphold

preserve by removing moisture: desiccate

preserve by salting, smoking, or aging: cure

preserve in brine: corn

preserves, something that: fixative

preside: administer, chair, conduct, control, direct, handle, head, manage, moderate, oversee, regulate, run

presidential prerogative: veto

press: bear, bind, bother, bunch, compel, compress, constrain, cram, crowd, crunch, crush, drive, embrace, emphasize, entreat, express, flatten, force, gather, hasten, horde, hug, impact, importune, impress, imprint, iron, jam, knead, mash, mob, pack, pile, pressure, push, ram, roller, rush, smooth, squash, squeeze, steam, stuff, tax, throng, thrust, urge, wring

press clothes: iron

press conference: announcement, briefing, hearing, interview

press food or drinks on someone: ply

press or media: correspondent, journalist, reporter

press, sensational exaggerated: yellow journalism

pressing: acute, burning, critical, crucial, exacting, immediate, imperative, important, importunate, serious, urgent

pressure: anxiety, burden, compression, constraint, difficulty, duress, force, heat, impression, mass, oppression, power, pull, push, squeeze, stress, tension, urge, weight

pressure of liquids and gases, measuring instrument for: manometer, sphygmomanometer

pressure points: brachial artery, common carotid artery, facial artery, femoral artery, subclavian artery, temporal artery

pressure prefix: piezo-

pressure, condition caused by sudden change of deep-sea: caisson disease, decompression sickness, the bends

pressure, feeling of tightness and: constriction

pressure, measuring instrument for atmospheric: barometer

pressure, measuring instrument for variations in: kymograph

pressure, moved or operated by fluid: hydraulic

pressure, unit of atmospheric: millibar

pressure, weather map line for meeting points of equal atmospheric: isobar, isopiestic

pressurized vessel for sterilization: autoclave

prestidigitation: magic

prestige: cachet, dignity, distinction, eminence, esteem, fame, honor, importance, influence, position, power, prominence, rank, renown, respect, stature, status

prestigious: distinguished, eminent, famed, honored, influential, prominent, renowned, respected

presto: fast, instantaneous, magic, quickly, rapidly, suddenly

presumably: apparently, credible, doubtlessly, indubitably, likely, ostensibly, probably, supposedly, unquestionably

presume: believe, conjecture, consider, deduce, gather, guess, impose, infringe, postulate, reason, speculate, suppose, surmise, venture

presumption: audacity, belief, boldness, brass, cheek, chutzpah, daring, effrontery, forwardness, gall, nerve, speculation, suspicion

presumptuous: arrogant, assuming, audacious, bold, brash, brazen, conceited, confident, familiar, forward, haughty, insolent, pompous, pushy, rude, smug, uppity

presuppose: assume, believe, infer, posit, reckon, speculate, surmise

pretend: acknowledge, act, affect, assume, bluff, claim, counterfeit, deceive, disguise, dissemble, dissimulate, fake, feign, imagine, imitate, impersonate, let on, mislead, pose, proclaim, profess, put on, sham, simulate

pretend illness: malinger

pretend to be sleeping or dead: play possum

pretend to be someone else: impersonate, masquerade, mimic

pretended: bogus, false, ostensible, sham, specious

pretended blow: feint

pretender: actor, charlatan, deceiver, dissembler, fake, faker, fraud, hypocrite, imitator, impostor, phony, quack, snob

pretending: disingenuous

pretense: affectation, appearance, assumption, brazenness, charade, claim, cloak, cover, deceit, deception, disguise, excuse, fabrication, facade, fake, false front, falsehood, feint, fiction, flam, fraud, guile, guise, humbug, hypocrisy, imagined, insincerity, mask, occasion, ostentation, pose, pretext, sham, show, simulation, smugness, trick, trickery

pretense as part of scheme: artifice, dodge, ruse, stratagem, subterfuge, wile

pretension: airs, charade, claim, hypocrisy, ostentatious, pretext, showiness, snobbishness, title

pretentious: arrogant, arty, conceited, extravagant, flamboyant, flashy, flowery, gaudy, grandiose, highflown, highfaluting, inflated, insincere, lofty, ornate, ostentatious, overblown, pompous, presuming, showy, smug, splashy, turgid

preternatural: abnormal, atypical, exceptional, extraordinary, ghostly, miraculous, mysterious, supernatural, uncommon, unnatural, unusual

pretext: cover, device, disguise, excuse, front, locus standi, mask, masquerade, pretense

pretty: adroit, alluring, appealing, attractive, beautiful, captivating, clever, comely, cunning, cute, dainty, darling, dollish, elegant, fair, graceful, handsome, ingenious, lovely, moderately, skillful, terrible

prevail: beat, conquer, control, dominate, obtain, overcome, reign, rule, succeed, surmount, triumph, win

prevailing style: trend

prevalent: accepted, accustomed, common, current, dominant, established, frequent, general, influential, pervasive, popular, prevailing, rampant, regnant, rife, ruling, superior, usual, widespread

prevaricate: deceive, dodge, equivocate, evade, exaggerate, falsify, fib, lie, mislead, misrepresent, palter

prevarication: deception, dishonesty, fabrication, falsehood, fib, lie, tale, untruth

prevent: anticipate, arrest, avert, balk, bar, bind, block, dam, debar, defend, deter, estop, foil, forbid, forestall, frustrate, gag, guard, hamper, hinder, impede, inhibit, intercept, interrupt, nip in the bud, obstruct, obviate, parry, preclude, preempt, prohibit, repress, resist, restrain, stave off, stop, thwart, veto, ward, ward off, warn

prevent from continuing: abort, arrest, balk, curb, frustrate, thwart

prevent from joining social organizatin: blackball, ostracize

prevent from moving: immobilize, paralyze

prevent legally: estop

prevent or hold back: stifle, suppress

prevent something, acting to: prophylactic

preventive: anticipatory, prevenient

preview: foretaste, sample, show, trailer

previous: ante, antecedent, anterior, before, beforehand, bygone, earlier, early, erstwhile, fore, foregone, former, heretofore, onetime, past, preceding, precipitate, premature, prior, quondam, unfounded

previous to consideration: a priori

previously: already, back, before, earlier, heretofore, once

prey: food, game, quarry, underdog, victim

prey, seeking and taking: predacious, predatory, rapacious, raptorial, ravening

prey, to: capture, depredate, hunt, kill, plunder, ravage, seize

preying on others, organism: predator

price: amount, ante, appraisal, assessment, charge, cost, damage, estimation, evaluate, expense, fare, fee, penalty, punishment, rate, sacrifice, value, worth

price fall caused by decrease of money in circulation: deflation

price fixed and announced as minimum for item being auctioned: reserve price

price fixed for whole meal: prix fixe

price last reported for stock or security: market price

price rise combined with fall in money value: inflation

price, amount added to selling: markup

price, of an unfairly high: exorbitant, extortionate

priceless: amusing, cherished, costly, funny, hilarious, inestimable, invaluable, irreplaceable, precious, prized, rare, treasured, valuable

prick: bore, broach, cactus, cut, goad, jag, nettle, perforate, pierce, ping, pinhole, pink, point, prod, prompt, puncture, smart, spur, stab, stick, stimulate, sting, thorn, urge

prickle: acantha, barb, bristle, chill, point, sensation, spiculum, spike, thorn, tingling

prickly: burry, coarse, complicated, irritable, scratchy, sharp, spined, spinous, spiny, thorny, touchy, troublesome

pride: amour propre, arrogance, best, boast, cockiness, conceit, crow, dignity, disdain, egoism, egotism, elite, enjoyment, esteem, glory, haughtiness, hauteur, honor, huff, insolence, jewel, loftiness, lordliness, mettle, plume, prime, respect, satisfaction, self-assurance, self-esteem, smugness, spirit, splendor, vainglory, valor, vanity

priest: abbé, bishop, chancellor, churchman, churchwoman, clergyman, clergywoman, cleric, dignitary, divine, ecclesiastic, father, flamen, friar, lama, minister, padre, pastor, pontifex, pontiff, preacher, presbyter, rabbi, rector, shaman, vicar

priest jointly officiating communion: concelebrant

priest officiating communion: celebrant

priest, confession to: shrift

priest, residence of Catholic: presbytery

priestly: churchly, ecclesiastical, hieratic, sacerdotal

priest's abstention from sex: celibacy

priest's calling: vocation

priest's forgiveness of sin: absolution

priests, group of: mass, pontificality

priest's home: manse

priest's residence: rectory

priest's sacrament for critically ill or injured: extreme unction, last rites

priest's vestment: alb, amice

priggish: complacent, pompous, prim, smug, straitlaced, stuffy, vain

prim: ceremonial, decorous, demure, formal, genteel, neat, nice, particular, precise, prissy, proper, prudish, sedate, shipshape, snug, staid, stiff, straight, straitlaced, stuffy, tidy, trim, wooden

prima donna: actress, diva, lead, star

prima facie: first blush

primary: basic, central, chief, direct, dominant, earliest, elementary, essential, first, fundamental, immediate, initial, leading, main, primal, prime, primitive, principal, underlying, vital

primary where public selects candidates: direct primary

primate: anthropoid, ape, archbishop, baboon, bishop, chimpanzee, gorilla, Homo sapiens, human, lemur, mammal, man, monkey, orangutan, prosimians

prime: best, chief, choice, coach, cream, elite, essential, excellent, greatest, important, main, original, pick, prep, prepare, primary, principal, ready, size, superior, supreme, tutor, undercoat

prime of day: dawn, daybreak, morning, sunrise

primer: basal, book, hornbook, reader, textbook

primitive: aboriginal, ancient, antiquated, archaic, barbaric, basic, crude, early, elemental, elementary, first, fundamental, original, prehistoric, primal, primary, primeval, primordial, pristine, simple, uncivilized, uncultured, undeveloped

primitive state, reversion to: atavism

primordial: early, elementary, first, fundamental, original, primal, primary, primeval

primp: adorn, beautify, dress up, groom, gussy up, preen, spruce up

prince: archduke, atheling, emeer, emir, monarch, nobleman, potentate, raja, rajah, royalty, ruler, sovereign

princely: grand, lavish, lordly, magnificent, noble, regal, royal, sovereign, stately

principal: administrator, arch, capital, cardinal, champion, chief, dean, dominant, essential, first, foremost, head, headmaster, high, highest, important, leader, main, money, outstanding, paramount, predominant, preeminent, preponderant, primal, primary, prime, star, stellar

principal commodity: staple

principal female ballet dancer: premiere danseuse

principal male ballet dancer: premier danseur

principle: axiom, belief, canon, code, credo, creed, dictum, doctrine, dogma, element, essence, ethics, foundation, fundamental, honor, integrity, law, morals, precept, rule, standards, teaching, tenet, theorem, truth, uprightness

principle maintained as true: tenet

principle prescribing course of action or conduct: precept

principle upon which judgment is based: criterion, standard

principle, brief statement expressing a: motto

principle, self-evident: axiom, postulate

principle, truth, or rule of conduct, succinct formulation of: maxim

principle, underlying: foundation, groundwork, substratum

principle, unquestioned: gospel

principles and practices of a discipline: methodology

principles or ideas upon which work is based: donnée

principles that provide greater opportunity to one group and not another, set of: double standard

print: copy, edition, engrave, fabric, film, fond, impression, lithograph, magazine, newspaper, picture, publication, publish, stamp, text, type, write

print made by treating printing area to retain ink and nonprinting area to repel ink: lithograph

print made from a carved plate or block: engraving

print made from raised portion of a design: block print

print or type style, straight: roman

print, blurred: mackle

print, one that sets written material into: compositor, typesetter

printed at one time from same set of type, copies of publication: impression

printed character joining two or more letters: ligature

printed document, dots or dashes leading eye across: leaders

printed document, space between lines of type in: leading

printed document, to adjust spacing between letters of: kern

printed document, to adjust spacing in lines of: justify

printed document, white space of margin in: gutter

printed in thick heavy type: boldface

printed letter, fine line finishing a main stroke of: serif

printed letter's part extending down: descender

printed letter's part extending up: ascender

printed material, trial sheet of photos or: proof

printed matter for errors, to read: proofread

printed matter of short-lived interest: ephemera

printed matter to form sequence of pages, arrangement of: imposition

printed matter, last line of paragraph appearing at top of page of: widow

printed matter, symbol to indicate insertion of: caret

printed matter, to nullify a correction or deletion in: stet

printed running head: catchword, guide word

printed works produced on office computers: desktop publishing

printer: compositor, linotyper, lithographer, machine, pressman, presswoman, typesetter, typographer

printing by indirect image transfer: offset

printing done with plate bearing an image carved into surface: gravure, intaglio

printing even with outside margin: flush

printing frame holding pages or columns of type: chase

printing from a raised inked surface, process of: letterpress

printing from plate treated so that some areas take ink and others repel it: lithography

printing from raised surfaces: letterpress

printing or typing error: errata, typo, typographical error

printing process reproducing by photography on plates in relief: photoengraving

printing process with impression transferred to roller and then paper: offset

printing proof: galley

printing sign of hand pointing right: index fist

printing style of black letters, German: fraktur

printing style with letters slanting to the right: italic

printing type of one size and face: font

printing type of the same design: typeface

printing type with thicker darker lines: boldface

printing type with thin light lines: lightface

printing type with two or more characters, single piece of: logotype

printing, trial impression or sheet made in: proof

prior: antecedent, anterior, before, earlier, erstwhile, former, past, preceding, precursory, preexisting, previous, retroactive

prior, poetically: ere

priority: ascendancy, order, position, precedence, preference, rank, seniority, superiority, urgency

prism: crystal, cylinder, figure, gem, spectrum, stone

prison: bastille, big house, brig, calaboose, can, cell, clink, cooler, dungeon, guardhouse, hole, hoosegow, jail, keep, lockup, pen, penitentiary, pokey, quod, slammer, stir, stockade, tank

prison camp, enclosed area of: compound

prison cell, dark underground: dungeon, oubliette

prison for political dissidents: gulag

prison for those awaiting trial: custody, detention, detention center, jail, lockup

prison head: warden

prison on condition of payment of security, release from: bail

prison or jail, military base: stockade

prison sector: cell

prison sentence, pardon from: remission

prison terms running one after another, of: concurrent

prison, rehabilitation center for after: halfway house

prison, resident of: inmate

prison, ship used as: hulk

prisoner: captive, con, convict, detainee, hostage, jailbird, lifer

prisoner granted special privileges: trusty

prisoner is isolated from other prisoners, condition when: solitary confinement

prisoner of captors who set terms for his/her release: hostage

prisoner to return to criminal habits, tendency of a former: recidivism

prisoner transfer or delivery to another place: extradition

prisoner, early release of: parole

prisoner, guarding of: custody

prisoner, restraining garment for: straitjacket

prisoners are permitted outside employment, program where: work release

prisonlike institution for discipline and training of young or first offenders: reformatory

prisons and punishment, study of: penology

prison's keeper of keys: jailer, turnkey

prissy: effeminate, finicky, fussy, prim, prudish, sissified, squeamish, straitlaced, stuffy

pristine: clean, early, fresh, new, original, primitive, pure, uncorrupted, unspoiled, untouched, untrod

privacy: isolation, privity, retreat, seclusion, secrecy, solitude

private: clandestine, closet, concealed, confidential, covert, desolate, discreet, hidden, hushed, inside, intimate, nonpublic, personal, privy, reclusive, remote, secluded, secret, sequestered, soldier, solitary, unofficial

private and personal: intimate

private conversation between two: tête-a-tête

private matters are disclosed, one to whom: confidant, confidante

private property: peculium

private room: sanctum

private, in: in camera

private, knowing something: privy to

privateer: buccaneer, corsair, distress, freebooter, lack, pauperism, penury, pirate, privation, ship, vessel

privately: sub rosa

privately and exclusively owned: proprietary

privately said: sotto voce

privately with one other person: a deux

privation: absence, deprivation, destitution, hardship, loss, misery, need, poverty, want

privilege: advantage, allowance, birthright, boon, charter, concession, entitlement, exemption, favor, freedom, grace, grant, honor, immunity, liberty, permission, perquisite, prerogative, right

privilege entails responsibility: noblesse oblige

privilege, exclusive: prerogative

privileged: allowed, authorized, confidential, eligible, elite, immune, privy, secret, special

privy: aware, clandestine, concealed, confidential, conscious, covert, hidden, informed, in on, private, privileged, secret

privy or bathroom: head, latrine, lavatory, outhouse, toilet

prize: appreciate, award, best, bonus, booty, carrot, catch, choice, cream, crown, elite, esteem, gem, goal, jackpot, jewel, leverage, loot, medal, payoff, pick, plate, plum, premium, prime, purse, reward, seized, spoil, stake, treasure, trophy, value, winnings

prize for arts or sciences, one honored with: laureate

prize for inferiority: booby prize

prize for loser or worthy competitor: consolation prize

prize money: loot, purse

prize, biggest possible: jackpot

prize, second: proxime accessit

prizefight: bout, boxing match, contest, fisticuffs, match

pro: advocate, authority, expert, favoring, for, master, professional, supporting, whiz, with

pro tempore: interim, pro tem, temporarily

probability: chances, credibility, likelihood, odds, possibility, prospect, shot

probability, having same or equal chances or: random

probable: apt, believable, conceivable, logical, possible, presumable, reasonable, seeming

probable and possible: feasible

probable or expected to happen: prospective

probable or valid: plausible

probably: apparent, feasible, imaginably, likely, presumably, supposedly

probe: analysis, delve, examine, exploration, explore, inquiry, instrument, investigate, investigation, penetrate, poke, query, quiz, research, scout, scrutinize, search, seek, sift, snoop, test

probity: goodness, honesty, honor, integrity, morality, righteousness, sincerity, uprightness, virtue

problem: complication, difficulty, dilemma, enigma, issue, knot, obstacle, poser, puzzle, quandary, question, riddle, situation, sum, trouble, unmanageable

problem of choice between unpleasantries: dilemma

problem solving by trial and error: heuristic

problem-solving or research center: think tank

problem, difficult: conundrum, enigma, poser

problem, intricate: Gordian knot, imbroglio, labyrinth, mare's nest, morass, quagmire

problem, intuition used to solve: lateral thinking

problem, unforeseen: hitch, snag

problem, unsolvable: deadlock, dilemma, impasse, quandary, stalemate

problematic: ambiguous, debatable, disputable, doubtful, dubious, moot, questionable, tricky, uncertain, unsettled

problematic situation: difficulty, dilemma, distress, plight, predicament

problems that together indicate a condition: syndrome

problems, imaginary cause of: gremlin

proboscis: beak, nose, organ, snoot, snout, trunk

procedure: approach, course, custom, formula, measure, method, mode, policy, process, program, routine, step, technique

procedure or system followed daily: regimen

procedure, operating: MO, modus operandi

proceed: advance, arise, begin, commence, continue, derive, emanate, flow, go on, march, move, pass, progress, spring, start, wend

proceed smoothly: amble

proceed without pause, musically: segue

proceedings: account, acta, activity, business, dealings, doings, litigation, matters

proceeds: earnings, gate, income, loot, profit, receipts, return, revenue, split, take, winnings

process: cook, course, evolution, function, manner, method, mode, notice, operation, order, outgrowth, passage, policy, practice, prepare, procedure, progress, routine, step, summons, system, technique, usage, writ

process of development: evolution

processes of an organism that maintain life: metabolism

procession: caravan, cavalcade, column, cortege, course, file, formation, line, litany, march, parade, series

procession of motor vehicles: motorcade

procession of riders or horse-drawn carriages: cavalcade

procession out of church by clergy and choir: recession

procession, ceremonial or funeral: cortege

procession, spectacular: pageant

proclaim: advertise, announce, assert, avow, blare, blazon, broadcast, call, celebrate, declare, divulge, exhibit, glorify, herald, mark, outcry, praise, preach, promulgate, publish, show, sound, state, tell, toot, trumpet, utter, ventilate, voice

proclaim loudly: trumpet

proclaim widely: blazon, bruit

proclaimed unfit for use: condemned

proclamation: announcement, ban, declaration, decree, edict, mandate, manifesto, notice, promulgation, pronunciamento, publication, statement, ukase

proclivity: bent, disposition, inclination, leaning, partiality, penchant, predilection, predisposition, prejudice, propensity, talent, tendency

procrastinate: dally, defer, delay, loiter, postpone, prolong, stall, wait

procreate: bear, beget, conceive, father, mother, multiply, parent, produce, reproduce, sire, spawn

proctor: agent, delegate, monitor, representative, supervise, supervisor

procure: aar, acquire, attain, bring, earn, effect, find, gain, get, induce, land, obtain, promote, score, secure, win

prod: egg, elbow, encourage, excite, goad, incite, move, nudge, poke, prompt, provoke, push, shove, spur, urge

prodigal: abundant, excessive, extravagant, gluttonous, lavish, lush, luxurious, opulent, profligate, profuse, spender, spendthrift, squanderer, squandering, wasteful, wastrel

prodigious: astonishing, colossal, enormous, epic, extraordinary, fabulous, fantastic, giant, gigantic, grand, huge, immense, impressive, large, mammoth, marvelous, mighty, monumental, portentuous, spectacular, stupendous, tremendous, wonderful

prodigy: genius, marvel, miracle, natural, phenomenon, portent, wizard, wonder

produce: bear, beget, breed, build, cause, create, cultivate, effect, elicit, engender, evoke, exhibit, fabricate, generate, grow, harvest, induce, make, manufacture, multiply, offspring, originate, parent, present, procreate, reveal, shape, show, spawn, stage

produce as food: fruits, harvest, staples, vegetables, yield

produce egg: ovulate

produce or come forth with idea or discovery, about to: parturient

produce or obtain from a source: derive

produce sound by vibration: resonate

producing many, much: prolific

producing or capable of producing desired effect: efficacious

product: consequence, device, effect, goods, item, merchandise, offshoot, outgrowth, output, produce, result, yield

product grown in region, principal: staple

product or article of trade or commerce: commodity

product or service of company, chief: flagship

production: assembly, manufacturing, movie, output, performance, play, show, yield

production of goods and services by nation: GNP, gross national product

productive: active, busy, creative, energetic, fecund, fertile, fruitful, germinal, pregnant, prolific, rich, seminal, useful, valuable, worthwhile

proem: foreword, introduction, opening, preface, prelude, prologue

profane: abuse, blasphemous, coarse, crude, debase, defile, desecrate, dirty, filthy, foul, godless, impious, irreverent, lay, lewd, obscene, raunchy, sacrilegious, secular, smutty, temporal, ungodly, unhallowed, unholy, uninitiated, unsanctified, vulgar, wicked, worldly

profanity: curse, cuss, expletive, oath, obscenity, swear

profess: admit, affect, affirm, announce, assert, avow, claim, confess, declare, purport, state, vouch

profession: art, business, calling, career, craft, declaration, employment, endeavor, faith, forte, job, métier, occupation, skill, trade, vocation, work

profession, members of a learned: faculty

profession, one who practices a: practitioner

profession, resources habitually called on in a: stock-in-trade

professional: ace, adept, expert, hired, master, paid, pro, proficient, shark, skilled, trained

professional contact-sharing: networking

professional or clerical worker: white-collar worker

professor: don, educator, instructor, lecturer, teacher, tutor

professor retired but retaining honorary title: emeritus

proffer: extend, give, offer, present, proposal, submit, suggest, tender

proficiency: ability, adeptness, advance, aptitude, capability, competence, dexterity, efficiency, expertness, know-how, knack, mastery, skill

proficient: able, adept, competent, efficient, expert, master, professional, skilled, skillful, versed

profile: configuration, contour, description, figuration, form, outline, review, side, silhouette, sketch

profile, drawing or portrait of human: silhouette

profit: advantage, avail, benefit, earnings, gain, good, help, improve, income, increase, interest, killing, lucre, money, net, proceeds, remuneration, return, revenue, surplus, take, yield

profit after deductions and expenses: bottom line, net

profit amount added to original price: markup

profit anticipated but not yet realized: paper profit

profit before deductions and expenses: gross

profit from: cash in

profit from commercial or fundraising venture: proceeds, yield

profit from employment: emolument

profit from sale of assets: capital gain

profit, something that can be used for advantage or: grist

profitable: advantageous, beneficial, fruitful, gainful, lucrative, productive, prosperous, remunerative, rewarding, useful, worthwhile

profitable and easy work: gravy train, sinecure

profligate: corrupt, depraved, dissolute, extravagant, immoral, lavish, libertine, licentious, prodigal, reprobate, roue, sinful, spender, spendthrift, squandering, wasteful, wastrel

profound: abysmal, bottomless, deep, emotional, enlightened, exhaustive, far-reaching, heavy, intellectual, intense, moving, penetrating, philosophical, recondite, sagacious, sage, serious, thoughtful, unfathomable, wise

profound and hidden: recondite

profuse: abundant, ample, bountiful, copious, excessive, extravagant, exuberant, galore, generous, hearty, lavish, lush, luxuriant, munificent, opulent, plentiful, prodigal, replete, riotous

progenitor: ancestor, forefather, founder, originator, parent, precursor, sire

progeny: blood, breed, brood, child, children, descendants, family, fruit, generation, issue, lineage, offspring, posterity, product, race, seed, sons, strain

prognosis: diagnosis, forecast, prediction, prophecy

prognosticate: augur, divine, forebode, forecast, foreshadow, foretell, portend, predict, presage, prophesy

prognosticator: augur, divine, diviner, fortuneteller, prophet, seer, soothsayer

program: agenda, broadcast, bulletin, calendar, card, catalog, course, docket, list, notice, outline, plan, playbill, presentation, prospectus, schedule, scheme, show, slate, syllabus, timetable

program of courses offered by educational institution: curriculum

program or system of diet and exercise: regimen

program simultaneously on radio and television, to broadcast: simulcast

program, recorded radio or television: transcription

program, spoken matter that links parts of radio or television: continuity

program, to transmit a radio or television: relay

progress: advance, breakthrough, circuit, course, develop, development, evolution, expedition, fare, grow, growth, headway, improve, improvement, journey, march, move, passage, proceed, promotion

progress to new level: graduate

progress toward goal: headway

progressing equally: pari passu

progression: chain, continuation, course, development, evolution, growth, improvement, order, sequence, series, stage, string, succession

progression, orderly or gradual: gradation

progressive: active, advancing, continuing, forward, gradual, growing, liberal, rising

progressive in political party, young: Young Turk

prohibit: ban, bar, block, debar, disallow, forbid, hinder, impede, inhibit, interdict, outlaw, prevent, proscribe, restrict, stop, veto

prohibit and forbid by law: enjoin, interdict, restrain

prohibit from church membership: excommunicate

prohibited: banned, forbidden, illegal, illicit, restricted, taboo, tabu, unlawful, verboten

prohibited by convention or tradition: taboo

prohibited by law, goods: contraband

prohibited goods, to make or sell: bootleg

prohibiting party from course of action, court order: injunction, writ

prohibition: ban, injunction, taboo

prohibition by a government on trade with a foreign nation: embargo

prohibition law: estoppel

prohibition of disclosure of details of legal case: gag order

prohibitive: expensive, forbidding, limiting, oppressive, restrictive

project: activity, assignment, enterprise, feature, goal, idea, intention, pattern, plan, proposition, scheme, task, undertaking, venture, vision, work

project on basis of facts: extrapolate, infer

project that is daring or having uncertain outcome: undertaking, venture

project, management of the details of a: logistics

project, to: beetle, bulge, extend, extrude, fling, hurl, launch, propel, protrude, shoot, throw

projected sequence of events: scenario

projectile: arrow, bomb, bullet, dart, impelling, missile, rocket, shaft, shell, shot, spear, torpedo, weapon

projectile, diameter of large: caliber

projecting: extruding, jutting, protruding, salient

projecting rim, edge, collar for strength, attachment etc.: flange

projecting structure with only one end supported: cantilever

projecting transparencies or opaque objects on screen, device for: epidiascope

projection: abutment, approximation, arm, bulge, cornice, eminence, empathy, estimate, extension, forecast, guess, hook, ledge, overhand, point, prediction, protrusion, protuberance, ridge, tab, tusk

projection on piece of wood for mortise insertion: tenon

projector, movie: cinematograph

projects, something that: protuberance

proletariat: commonalty, commoners, masses, plebs, rabble, working class

proliferate: burgeon, escalate, grow, increase, multiply, mushroom, procreate, propagate, spawn, spread, sprout

prolific: abounding, abundant, fecund, fertile, fruitful, lush, plentiful, productive, proliferous, reductive, rich, spawning, swarming

prolific, childrenwise: philoprogenitive

prolix: diffuse, lengthy, prolonged, protracted, redundant, tedious, tiresome, verbose, wearisome, wordy

prologue: foreward, introduction, opening, preamble, preface, prelude, proem, prolusion

prolong: endure, extend, increase, last, lengthen, perpetuate, persist, protract, stall, stretch

prolonged: continued, delayed, drawn-out, extended, lengthened, prolix, protracted, spun out, sustained

promenade: ball, boardwalk, cakewalk, dance, deck, gallery, mall, marina, parade, party, reception, stroll, walk

prominence: bump, celebrity, crest, distinction, eminence, fame, greatness, importance, nobility, notoriety, pinnacle, popularity, prestige, protrusion, rank, renown, salience, standing

prominent: celebrated, conspicuous, distinguished, eminent, famed, famous, great, illustrious, important, leading, marked, notable, noticeable, obvious, outstanding, popular, projecting, protruding, renowned, salient, striking, unmistakable

promiscuous: casual, confused, diverse, fast, immoral, indiscriminate, loose, random, unchaste, wanton

promise: ability, agree, assurance, assure, band, betroth, commitment, contract, covenant, declaration, engage, ensure, grant, guarantee, oath, obligation, outlook, pawn, pledge, plight, potential, stipulate, swear, troth, vow, warranty, word

promise despite resistance, to obtain a: extract

promise of marriage: plight one's troth

promise to human race, God's: covenant

promise, fail to fulfill: renege, welsh

promised land: Canaan, heaven, paradise, utopia, Zion

promising: apt, bright, budding, encouraging, happy, hopeful, rising, rosy, talented, up-and-coming

promising to be favorable: auspicious, boding well, propitious

promising young actress: starlet

promontory: bill, head, headland, jutty, mount, ness, peak, point, projection, ridge, scaw, spit

promote: abet, advance, advocate, aid, better, bolster, boost, champion, elevate, encourage, endorse, enhance, exalt, forward, foster, further, help, move up, patronize, plug, prefer, publicize, push, sponsor, translate

promoter: advocate, agent, booster, lobbyist, organizer, proponent, supporter

promoter or backer: angel, patron, sponsor

promoting oneself or one's own: boosterism

promoting or tending to cause: conducive, contributive

promotion: advancement, advertising, buildup, elevation, fanfare, hype, preferment

promotion, sensational: ballyhoo, puffery

prompt: active, alert, assist, cue, cuent, excite, fast, forward, goad, hint, induce, instantaneous, motivate, move, needle, nudge, on time, prod, provoke, punctual, quick, ready, remind, reminder, responsive, spur, swift, timely, urge

promptness: alacrity, dispatch

promulgate: advertise, announce, broadcast, communicate, declare, decree, notify, proclaim, sound

prone: apt, disposed, exposed, flat, horizontal, inclined, liable, likely, open, passive, pronated, prostrate, ready, reclining, recumbent, supine, susceptible, willing

prong: fork, hook, horn, nib, point, spike, spine, spur, tine

pronoun: her, hers, him, its, itself, one, our, she, that, thee, them, these, they, this, those, who, who so, your, you

pronoun ending in -self: reflexive pronoun

pronoun refers, word or phrase to which: antecedent

pronoun that introduces a relative clause: relative pronoun

pronoun, concerning a: pronominal

pronounce: affirm, announce, articulate, declare, decree, deliver, enunciate, phonate, say, sound, speak, utter, verbalize, vocalize

pronounce, phrase or sentence that is difficult to: tongue twister

pronounced: apparent, clear, conspicuous, distinct, evident, marked, noticeable, unmistakable

pronounced with back of tongue touching soft palate: guttural, velar

pronounced with sound omitted: elide

pronounced without stress when followed by another word: proclitic

pronounced without stress when preceded by another word: enclitic

pronouncement: announcement, broadcast, declaration, decree, dictum, edict, judgment, proclamation, promulgation, statement

pronouncing "r" like "l" or "l" like "r" or "w": lallation

pronto: fast, immediately, now, promptly, quickly, soon

pronunciation: accent, articulation, drawl, elocution, phonology, speech, twang

pronunciation and speech sounds, study of: phonemics, phonetics, phonology

pronunciation mark over or under letter: diacritical mark

pronunciation of a word, insertion of a sound in the: epenthesis

pronunciation of usually silent final consonant of a word when followed by word starting with vowel: liaison

pronunciation of words, study of the: orthoepy

pronunciation produced out of desire to be correct, mis-: hypercorrection

pronunciation, agreeable: euphony

pronunciation, clarity and distinctness of: articulation, diction, elocution, enunciation

pronunciation, conforming to: phonetic

pronunciation, misuse of a word based on similar: malapropism

pronunciation, omission of initial or final sound in: elision

proof: argument, authentication, certification, confirmation, credentials, edit, evidence, exhibit, galley, indication, probate, reason, test, testimony, trial, validation, verification

proof by mathematical process: derivation

proof for another proposition, proposition that follows using existing: corollary

proof of crime: corpus delicti, smoking gun

proof of property ownership: title deed

proof or disproof of proposition by showing absurdity of inevitable conclusion: reductio ad absurdum

proof, burden of: onus probandi

proof, real or substantial as: substantive, tangible

proof, self-evident: axiomatic

proof, something that is tangible: testament

proof, supposed but without: alleged, hypothetical

proof, to clear of blame or suspicion with: vindicate

proofreading mark to ignore correct and let original stand: stet

proofs of a book's text: galley proofs, galleys

prop: bolster, brace, buttress, lean, leg,

shore, staff, stand, stay, stilt, strengthen, support, sustain, tip up, truss

propaganda: agitprop, brainwashing, doctrine, hoopla, hype, indoctrinate, publicity

propaganda distribution, means for: agitprop

propagandist: activist, advocator, apostle, missionary, proponent

propagate: breed, broadcast, develop, diffuse, disseminate, fecundate, generate, grow, multiply, proclaim, procreate, publicize, reproduce, spawn, spread, transmit

propel: drive, force, hurl, launch, move, prompt, push, send, shove, sling, spur, throw, thrust, urge

propeller: blade, driver, fan, fin, oar, paddle, prop, screw

propeller blade: vane

propeller, turbulent flow of air driven back by: slipstream

propensity: affection, affinity, appetence, aptness, bent, bias, disposition, fancy, inclination, leaning, liking, partiality, penchant, predilection, prejudice, proclivity, proneness, susceptibility, taste, tendency

proper: able, acceptable, accurate, advisable, allowable, appropriate, becoming, befitting, chaste, comme il faut, convenient, conventional, correct, decent, decorous, due, ethical, fine, fitting, formal, good, honest, just, ladylike, meet, moral, polite, prim, respectable, right, seeming, seemly, strict, suitable, true, useful

proper and appropriate: comme il faut, expedient

proper and conventional: orthodox

proper and orthodox: canonical

proper behavior: etiquette, good manners, protocol

proper in behavior: decorous

proper or customary act or procedure: formality

properness in usage: propriety

property: acre, acreage, appropriate, asset, assets, attribute, belongings, characteristic, chattel, domain, dominion, effects, estate, feature, goods, holdings, homestead, land, lot, ownership, possessions, premises, quality, real estate, realty, riches, trait, wealth

property acceptable as security for loan: collateral

property as long as it is not damaged, the right to enjoy: usufruct

property beyond mortgage or liability, residual value of: equity

property claim: lien

property for public use, right of government to appropriate private: eminent domain

property held back for a special government purpose: reservation

property held for life: freehold

property improvement: capital expenditure

property or money fraudulently and in violation of trust, to take or use another's: defalcate, embezzle, peculate

property owned: asset

property ownership tied to political power: timocracy

property returned to the grantor or grantor's heirs after grant has expired: reversion

property reverting to government in absence of legal heirs: escheat

property seizure in legal proceeding: attachment

property set aside by man for widow: jointure

property that is transferrable to another, of: alienable

property to certain heirs, to limit inheritance of: entail

property to oneself, to transfer another's: expropriate

property to which one has absolute ownership: domain

property transfer: conveyance

property transferee: alienee

property transferer: alienor

property, condition of holding: occupation, tenure

property, extensive piece of landed: demesne, estate

property, law granting a use of another's: servitude

property, legal claim or right to: title

property, legal document of contract or transfer of: deed

property, lien or claim on: encumbrance

property, movable personal: chattel, chose

property, to deprive of rights or: dispossess, divest

property, to repossess mortgaged: foreclose

property, to seize and hold: distrain, distress, levy

property, to stealthily intrude on another's: encroach, trespass ☙

prophecy: bodement, declaration, divination, forecast, foretelling, portent, prediction, prognosis, revelation, vision

prophesy: augur, divine, forebode, forecast, foreshow, foretell, predict, presage, prognosticate, soothsay, vaticinate, warn

prophet: augur, clairvoyant, diviner, forecaster, fortuneteller, medium, oracle, predictor, seer, soothsayer, sorcerer, visionary

prophet, major: Baruch, Daniel, Ezekiel, Isaiah, Jeremiah

prophetess: Cassandra, pythoness, seeress, sorceress

prophetic: apocalyptic, clairvoyant, divinatory, fateful, fatidic, foreshadowing, foretelling, mantic, mysterious, mystic, oracular, predictive, prognostic, pythonic, sibylline, signifying, vaticinatory, vatic, vatical

prophetic disclosure: apocalypse, revelation

prophetic response given through a medium: oracle

prophetic sign: harbinger, omen, portent, presage

propinquity: affinity, closeness, connection, continuity, kinship, nearness, proximity, relationship, solidarity, togetherness, vicinity

propitiate: adapt, appease, calm, conciliate, conform, mediate, pacify, placate, reconcile, soothe

propitious: advantageous, auspicious, beneficial, benign, encouraging, favorable, friendly, good, gracious, helpful, kindly, opportune, promising, prosperous, rosy, timely

proponent: booster, champion, defender, protector

proportion: balance, correlation, degree, dimension, harmony, measure, part, percentage, portion, rate, ratio, relation, share, symmetry

proportion, in: pro rata

proportional: commensurate, comparative, correlative, corresponding, equal, equivalent, even, reciprocal, relative, symmetrical

proportional share: quota

proportionate: commensurate

proportionate configuration: symmetry

proposal: affirmation, bid, design, draft, gesture, idea, motion, offer, outline, overture, plan, project, prospectus, question, recommendation, scheme, statement, undertaking

proposal in outline form: prospectus

proposal, detailed: specifications, specs

propose: allege, contemplate, design, hope, intend, invite, mean, move, nominate, offer, plan, propound, purpose, start, state, submit, suggest, tender

propose as a candidate: nominate

propose for consideration: propound

proposition: affirmation, approach, offer, overture, point, post, premise, project, proposal, question, solicit, statement, suggestion, task, undertaking

proposition on which argument is based or a conclusion drawn: premise

proposition presenting two or more alternative terms: disjunction

proposition that can be demonstrated as true: theorem

proposition that follows necessarily, of a: analytic

proposition, subsidiary: lemma

propositions that can be simultaneously true, of: dilemmatic, incompatible

proprietor: landlord, manager, master, owner, titleholder

propriety: aptness, attribute, behavior, code, conduct, courtesy, customs, decency, decorum, etiquette, manners, rule, suitability

propulsion: drive, force, push, thrust

prorate: allot, apportion, assess, distribute, divide, portion

prosaic: actual, colorless, common, commonplace, drab, dull, everyday, factual, flat, humdrum, insipid, lackluster, literal, mundane, straightforward, tedious, tiresome, trite, unexciting, unimaginative, uninspiring, uninteresting

prosaic and dull: mediocre, pedestrian

proscribe: ban, banish, condemn, denounce, exclude, exile, expatriate, forbid, outlaw, prohibit, sentence, taboo

prose: composition, edda, essay, story, written

prosecute: accuse, arraign, charge, continue, indict, litigate, persevere, press, pursue, sue

proselyte: conscript, convert, neophyte, recruit

prospect: applicant, buyer, candidate, chance, customer, delve, explore, hope, likelihood, mine, outlook, possibility, proposal, scene, sift, view, vision, vista

prospective: anticipated, coming, destined, eminent, expected, forthcoming, future, likely, possible, potential

prospector: forty-niner, miner, sourdough

prosper: augment, batten, benefit, blossom, boom, flourish, flower, gain, increase, progress, succeed, thrive

prosperity: abundance, affluence, boom, easy street, florescence, fortune, growth, riches, success, thrift, weal, wealth, welfare

prosperous: affluent, blooming, booming, bright, favorable, flourishing, flush, fortunate, halcyon, happy, in the money, lucky, opulent, palmy, promising, propitious, rich, roaring, rosy, successful, thriving, timely, wealthy

prostitute: abuse, bawd, bimbo, call girl, catamite, chippy, cocotte, corrupt, courtesan, debase, demean, doxy, fille de joie, floozy, gigolo, harlot, hooker, hussy, hustler, licentious, madam, moll, slut, streetwalker, streetwalker, strumpet, tramp, trollop, wench, whore, working girl

prostitute of men of rank or wealth: courtesan, demimonde, demondaine, hetaera

prostitute, one who finds customers for: pander, panderer, pimp, procurer

prostitute, to approach with offer of: accost, hustle, importune, solicit

prostitutes as group: demimonde

prostitute's customer: john, trick

prostitution of talent for gain: venality

prostitution, woman kidnapped for: white slave

prostrate: abase, beaten, bow, exhaust, fallen, fell, flatten, floor, helpless, horizontal, overcome, overthrow, overwhelm, paralyze, powerless, prone, reclining, recumbent, submissive, supine, weak

prosy: colorless, commonplace, dull, humdrum, jejune, prosaic, stale, tedious, trite

protagonist: actor, advocate, champion, defender, hero, heroine, leader, proponent, spokesman, spokeswoman, star, warrior

protect: advocate, backer, bulwark, champion, cherish, conserve, cushion, defend, fend, guard, harbor, hedge, hide, insure, police, preserve, proponent, safeguard, save, screen, shade, shelter, shield, supporter, watch over

protect against damage, loss, injury: indemnify, insure

protect and bring up: foster, nurture

protect and cushion: buffer, buttress, insulate, shield

protect and ensure safety: harbor, safeguard, shelter

protect from attack: secure

protect from disease by producing immunity: immunize, inoculate, vaccinate

protect from loss or harm: conserve, preserve

protected against malfunctioning: fail-safe

protected by influential person, one whose welfare or career is: protégée, protégé

protected by trademark or patent: patent, proprietary, trademarked

protected legally as ownership of originator: proprietary

protected position or defensive stronghold: bastion, bulwark, outpost, rampart

protection: aegis, armor, asylum, auspice, auspices, barrier, bribe, buffer, care, conservation, defense, egis, extortion, fort, graft, guard, haven, immunity, moat, patent, preservation, safeguard, safety, sanctuary, security, shakedown, shelter, shield, smock

protection against loss, means of: hedge

protection and preservation from loss, damage, neglect: conservation

protection and safety, place of: asylum, haven, refuge, sanctuary, shelter

protection of guardian or court, person under care or: ward

protection, care, supervision granted by court: custody

protection, payment to nation for: tribute

protection, under: under the aegis of, under the auspices of

protective: prophylactic

protective and watchful: vigilant

protective animal coloring: Batesian mimicry

protective charm: amulet, talisman

protective covering: armor, bandage, tarp

protective covering, structure of organism: armature, integument

protective of one's area: defensive, territorial

protective spray: mace

protector: advocate, angel, armor, benefactor, caretaker, champion, defender, guard, guardian, paladin, patron, shield, sponsor, supporter, tutelary

protector and defender of cause: paladin

protector in social situations: chaperon, duenna

protector of the people: tribune

protects, something that preserves and: fixative

protégé: apprentice, pupil, student, ward

protein: albumen, albumin, beans, casein, cheese, creatine, egg, enzyme, fibrin, globulin, histon, macromolecules, meat, milk, mucedin, prolamin

protein-digesting enzyme: protease

protein in cheese: casein

protein-laden bean: soya

protein of blood plasma, milk, muscle, plant seeds: globulin

protein of egg white, blood serum, milk etc.: albumin

protein substitute for meat: textured vegetable protein, TVP

protein used to make food, drugs, film: gelatin

protein, organic compound linking to peptide bonds to form: amino acid

proteins of organisms that are biochemical catalysts: enzymes

protest: affirm, assert, assure, aver, avow, beef, boycott, challenge, combat, complain, contest, declare, demur, deny, disagree, dispute, dissent, dissidence, expostulate, fight, grievance, gripe, kick, object, objection, picket, profess, rebel, remonstrate, revolt, sit in, strike

RELATED TERMS

protest of government policy or legislation by passive resistance: civil disobedience

protest speech: declamation, harangue, philippic, tirade

protest vehemently: inveigh, vociferate

protest, circumstance regarded as just cause for: grievance

protest, diplomatic: démarche

protest, expression of: clamor, outcry

protest, person or group expressing a: picket

protest, to abstain from buying or using as a: boycott

protest, to express: lodge, register ❦

Protestant churches, 16th-century movement resulting in establishment of: reformation

protestor: activist, dissident, militant

protocol: behavior, code, custom, decorum, etiquette, manners, order, rules

protoplasm as continuous body process: metabolism

prototype: archetype, forerunner, model, original, predecessor, sample

protozoan: ameba, amoeba, cell, ciliate, euglena, flagellate, organism, paramecium, plasmodium, sporozoan, stentor

protract: continue, defer, delay, detract, drag, elongate, extend, lengthen, procrastinate, prolong, stall, stretch

protracted falling-out: feud

protrude: bulge, distend, extrude, interfere, jut, poke, project, swell

protruding: exsertile

protruding eyes, having: exophthalmic

protrusion of internal organ: intusseption, invagination

protuberance: bulge, bump, hump, knob, node, outgrowth, projection, protrusion, swelling, tuberosity, wart

proud: dignified, honorable, imposing, impressive, lofty, lordly, majestic, noble, satisfying, splendid, stately, valiant

proud and conceited: aloof, arrogant, boastful, cavalier, cocky, haughty, imperious, inflated, narcissistic, ostentatious, overbearing, overweening, pompous, presumptuous, smug, snooty, stuffy, supercilious, uppity, vain

proud and selfish: egocentric, full of oneself, self-centered

prove: argue, ascertain, attest, confirm, convince, corroborate, demonstrate, establish, indicate, justify, manifest, substantiate, sustain, test, validate, verify

prove correct, true, genuine: attest, authenticate, testify, validate, verify, vouch for

prove false: belie, confute, contradict, disprove, rebut, refute

prove one's ability: win one's spurs

prove or exemplify: evidence, manifest

prove the worth of: vindicate

prove with evidence: bear out, corroborate, substantiate, verify

prove wrong: confute

prove, impossible to dis-: incontrovertible

proved, which was to be: QED, quod erat demonstrandum

proven beyond question: apodictic, incontrovertible, irrefutable

provender: chow, feed, fodder, food, forage, grain, hay, oats, provisions, straw, viands

proverb: adage, allegory, aphorism, apothegm, axiom, byword, cliché, epigram, gnome, maxim, motto, parable, precept, saw, saying, truism, word

proverbial: acknowledged, common, customary, famous, legendary, traditional, unquestioned

proverbs, tending to speak in: sententious

provide: afford, cater, contribute, endow, endue, equip, fend, furnish, give, maintain, offer, outfit, prepare, ration, render, replenish, stipulate, stock, store, supply, support, yield

providence: economy, foresight, guidance, husbandry, precaution, prudence, thrift

provident: canny, careful, discreet, economical, foresighted, frugal, prepared, prudent, saving, shrewd, sparing, thrifty, wise

province: area, arena, colony, county, domain, field, range, realm, region, role, scope, tract, work, zone

provincial: awkward, bigoted, bucolic, countrified, crude, homespun, limited, local, narrow, one-horse, parochial, regional, rural, rustic, uncultured, unpolished

provincial in outlook: insular, limited, narrow, parochial

provincial regarding group as central: ethnocentric

proving charge or allegation, responsibility of: burden of proof

proving directly by argument: deictic

proving indirectly by argument: elenctic

provision: catch, clause, condition, food, prerequisite, proviso, rider, stipulation, term

provisional: conditional, contingent, dependent, experimental, iffy, interim, makeshift, temporary, tentative

provisions: board, chow, fare, feed, fodder, food, forage, groceries, provender, rations, stores, supplies, viands, victuals

provisions for a journey: viaticum

provisions, supplier of: sutler, victualler

proviso: article, clause, condition, prerequisite, provision, restriction, rider, stipulation, term

provocation: annoyance, grievance, incentive, incitement, insult, irritation, offense, vexation

provocation, responding to the slightest: hair-trigger

provocative: aggravating challenging, alluring, arch, erotic, exciting, fascinating, seductive, sexy, tantalizing

provoke: aggravate, anger, annoy, arouse, bait, bother, bug, cause, chafe, challenge, excite, foment, galvanize, generate, goad, harass, incense, incite, inflame, infuriate, inspire, instigate, insult, ire, irritate, madden, move, outrage, perturb, prompt, rile, rouse, ruffle, spur, start, stimulate, stir, tease, upset, vex

provoke, tending to: incendiary, inflammatory

provoked: irate, irked, taunted

provoker of punishable acts: agent provocateur

provoking anger through discrimination: invidious

provoking person: gadfly

provost: administrator, chief, director, executive, head, jailer, keeper, magistrate, officer, official, supervisor

prow adornment: figurehead

prow of ship: bow, fore, forepart, front, nose, rostrum, stem

prowess: ability, address, boldness,

PSYCHIATRIC DISORDERS

affective disorder	disorder	delusional disorder	neurasthenia	reactive attachment
alcoholism	eating disorder	Kleine-Levin	neurosis	disorder
amnesia	emotional disorder	syndrome	obsessive-	Rett syndrome
anorexia nervosa	emotional shock	male orgasmic	compulsive disorder	schizophrenia
antisocial personality	enuresis	disorder	oppositional defiant	seasonal affective
disorder	female orgasmic	mania	disorder	disorder
anxiety disorder	disorder	manic-depressive	panic attack	self injury
autism	female sexual arousal	psychosis	panic disorder	sexual addiction
avoidant personality	disorder	melancholia	paranoia	sexual disorder
disorder	fetishism	mental disorder	personality-type	sexual dysfunction
binge eating	gambling addiction	mental illness	disorder	sleep disorder
bipolar disorder	hypoactive sexual	mood disorder	phobias	sleepwalking disorder
borderline	desire disorder	multiple personality	pica	smoking addiction
personality disorder	hypochondria	disorder	pornography	social maladjustment
bulimia nervosa	impotence	Munchausen's	addiction	sociopathy
clinical depression	impulse-control	syndrome	postpartum	split personality
codependency	disorder	narcissistic	depression	stress
debt addiction	insanity	personality disorder	post-traumatic stress	substance abuse
depression	insomnia	narcolepsy	disorder	zoophilia ✃
dissociative disorder	Internet addiction	narcotics addiction	psychopathy	
dissociative identity	jealous-type	nervous breakdown	psychosis	

bravery, courage, daring, dexterity, grit, heroism, power, skill, strength, talent, valor

prowl: creep, hunt, lurk, roam, rove, sneak, stalk

proximate: close, direct, forthcoming, imminent, near, nearby, next

proximity: closeness, contiguity, immediacy, juxtaposition, locality, nearness, propinquity, togetherness, vicinity

proxy: agent, alternate, assignee, authority, delegate, deputy, proctor, procurator, representative, substitute, vicar, vote

prude: bluenose, goody-goody, prig, priss, puritan

prudence: calculation, caution, discretion, economy, foresight, forethought, frugality, sense, thrift, wisdom

prudent: advisable, canny, careful, cautious, circumspect, diplomatic, discerning, discreet, economical, expedient, frugal, guarded, judicious, levelheaded, politic, provident, rational, reserved, sagacious, sage, sensible, shrewd, tactful, wary, wise

prudish: priggish, prim, prissy, puritanical, smug, square, squeamish, stern, straightlaced, stuffy, timid, Victorian

prune: clip, crop, pare, shave, shear, snip, thin, trim

prurient: bawdy, carnal, coarse, erotic, foul, goatish, impure, lascivious, lewd, lustful, passionate, sensual

pry: butt, force, inquire, interfere, intrude, jimmy, lever, leverage, lift, meddle, move, nose, open, peek, peep, peer, prize, raise, scrounge, separate, snoop, spy, twist

prying: inquisitive, inquisitorial, nosing, nosy

psalm: anticle, chant, eulogy, glorify, hymn, ode, poem, praise, song, verse

psalm chanted or sung in response in liturgy: antiphon

psalms, book of: psalter

pseudo: artificial, bogus, counterfeit, fake, false, fictitious, forged, imitation, mock, phony, pretended, sham, simulated, spurious

pseudonym: alias, ananym, anonym, nickname, nom de guerre, nom de plume, pen name

pseudonym by spelling name backwards: ananym

psyche: ego, id, mind, personality, self, soul, spirit, subconscious, superego

psychiatrist: analyst, doctor, psychoanalyst, shrink, therapist

psychiatrist testifying to mental competence of people in legal case: alienist

psychiatrist's patient: analysand

psychic: cerebral, clairvoyant, medium, mental, mystic, paranormal, sensile,

spiritual, supernatural, telepathic

psychic ability: ESP, extrasensory perception

pub: bar, ginmill, grogshop, rummery, saloon, taproom, tavern

puberty: adolescence, juvenility, pubescence, youthfulness

puberty change of voice: ponticello

public: accessible, citizens, civic, civil, common, communal, community, general, known, masses, municipal, mutual, national, obvious, open, overt, people, plain, popular, shared, society, state, voters, widespread

RELATED TERMS

public announcement for immediate release: bulletin

public announcement, official: communiqué, proclamation

public announcement, put law into effect by: promulgate

public attention: limelight, spotlight

public building design: civil architecture

public funds designated for purpose: appropriation

public good, for the: pro bono publico

public highway: thoroughfare

public meeting, presentation, or meeting place: forum

public not a part of the clergy, of the general: lay, secular

PSYCHOLOGY TERMS

achievement in one area to make up for real or supposed defect in another: compensation
antisocial personality disorder: psychopath, sociopath
attribution of one's own attitudes and feelings to others: projection
conscious that deals with external reality: ego
defense mechanism with unconscious shift of feelings to a substitute: displacement
delusions of persecution or grandeur: paranoia
desire of child for parent of opposite sex: Oedipus complex
desire of daughter for father: Electra complex
dreamlike period with memory loss: fugue
idealized image of person: imago
inkblot personality test: Rorschach
IQ test: Binet-Simon, Stanford-Binet, Terman
modification of impulse into socially acceptable one: sublimation
persuasion by pretending opposite of desire: reverse psychology
psychoanalysis patient: analysand
psychoanalytical arrested development: fixation
psychological attachment manifested in neurotic behavior: fixation
psychological cause of physical symptoms or disorder: psychosomatic
psychological elements so unified that parts cannot be distinguished: gestalt
psychological school based on observation and experimentation: behaviorism
psychotherapy analyzing personal relationships and interactions: TA, transactional analysis
psychotic: crazy, demented, disordered, insane, loony, lunatic, mad, nuts, psychopathic, schizoid, unhinged, unreasonable
reaction that is programmed: conditioned response
restraint of a behavior, desire, impulse: inhibition
sexual energy and desire: libido
shifting of emotions from one person to another person: transference
slang for psychoanalyst or psychiatrist: shrink
unconscious that deals with instinct and satisfaction of biological needs: id
unconscious that restrains and censors ego: superego

Psychological, Mental, and Educational Tests
ACER test of basic skills
achievement test
AGCT or Army General Classification Test
alpha test
apperception test
aptitude test
Army General Classification Test or AGCT
association test
attention deficit disorder evaluation scale
Babcock-Levy test
basic inventory of natural language

Bender-Gestalt test
Bernreuter personality inventory
beta test
Binet test or Binet-Simon test
Brigance diagnostic assessment of basic skills
Brigance diagnostic comprehensive inventory of basic skills
Brown personality inventory
Cattell's infant intelligence scale
CAVD test
College Boards
controlled association test
English language skill assessment
free association test
Gesell's development schedule
GMAT or Graduate Management Admission Test
Goldstein-Sheerer test
Graduate Management Admission Test or GMAT
Graduate Record Examinations or GRE
graduated reciprocation in tension reduction
GRE or Graduate Record Examinations
Holtzman technique
House-Tree-Person Projective Test
IDEA oral language proficiency test
inkblot test
intelligence quotient or IQ
intelligence test
interest inventory
Iowa test of basic skills
IQ test
Kaufman test of education achievement
Kent mental test
Law School Admission Test or LSAT
LSAT or Law School Admission Test
Luscher color test
MCAT or Medical College Admission Test
Medical College Admission Test or MCAT
Minnesota Multiphasic Personality Inventory or MMPI
Minnesota preschool scale
MMPI or Minnesota Multiphasic Personality Inventory
nonstandardized test
Oseretsky test
performance test
personality inventory
personality test
Phelps kindergarten readiness scale
placement test
Preliminary Scholastic Aptitude Test or PSAT
PSAT or Preliminary Scholastic Aptitude Test
psychometric test
Rorschach test
Rotter incomplete sentences blank
SAT or Scholastic Aptitude Test
Scholastic Aptitude Test or SAT
school attitude measure
scientific aptitude test
standardized test

The Writer's Digest Flip Dictionary

PSYCHOLOGY TERMS *continued*

Stanford revision
Stanford scientific aptitude test
Stanford-Binet test
Szondi test
TAT or thematic apperception test
Test of English as a Foreign Language or TOEFL
thematic apperception test or TAT
TOEFL or Test of English as a Foreign Language
unstructured test

verbal test
WAIS or Wechsler Adult Intelligence Scale
Wechsler Adult Intelligence Scale or WAIS
Wechsler Intelligence Scale for Children or WISC
Wechsler-Bellevue intelligence scale
WISC or Wechsler Intelligence Scale for Children
Woodcock language proficiency battery
Woodcock-Munoz language survey
word association test ❦

---

public office as reward for partisan service: spoils system
public office, misconduct in: malversation
public opinion survey: canvass, poll
public record, court or office of: chancery
public sale or auction: vendue
public scorn as punishment: pillory
public service like electricity, transportation, water: utility
public speaking, art of: elocution, oratory, rhetoric
public square: agora, forum, green, piazza, plaza
public statement, give approval or support in: endorse, publicize, sanction
public, to make: divulge, reveal ❦

public-spirited: patriotic
publication: annals, announcement, book, booklet, declaration, digest, gazette, information, journal, magazine, newspaper, notification, pamphlet, paper, periodical, proclamation, tabloid
publication not protected by copyright: public domain
publicity: advertising, attention, ballyhoo, buildup, hoopla, ink, limelight, notoriety, plug, press, promotion, puffery, réclame, release, spotlight, type, write-up
publicity, a taste or flair for: réclame, showmanship
publicity, attracting little: inconspicuous, low-key, low-profile, unobtrusive, unostentatious
publicize: advertise, broadcast, expose, hype, pitch, plug, promote, promulgate, propagandize, push, spread, tout
publish: advertise, announce, broadcast, declare, divulge, expose, issue, print, proclaim, promulgate, propagate, release, vent

published after author's death: posthumous
publisher of books at author's expense: vanity press
publisher's list of older titles kept in print: backlist
publisher's trademark: colophon
publishing right to quote or reprint without permission when done fairly: fair use
puck: elf, fairy, fay, goblin, hobgoblin, imp, prankster, sprite
pucker: bind, bulge, cockle, contract, crease, crinkle, fold, gather, plait, purse, tuck, wrinkle
puckish: impish, mischievous, mysterious, naughty, playful, wicked
pudding: custard, dessert, mousse, tapioca
pudding baked under a roast: Yorkshire pudding
pudding, light and fluffy: mousse
pudding, starch used in: sago, tapioca
puddle: plash, pond, pool, quagmire
pudgy: chubby, chunky, dumpy, fat, hefty, obese, plump, roly-poly, rotund, squat, tubby
puerile: babyish, callow, childish, green, immature, infantile, jejune, juvenile, naive, sophomoric, trivial, young, youthful
puff: admire, bloat, blow, boast, brag, drag, draw, fluff, gust, pant, plug, quilt, smoke, whiff
puff pastry: napoleon, vol-au-vent
puffery: hype, praise, publicity
puffy: bloated, bouffant, enlarged, expanded, inflamed, pompous, soft, swollen, tumescent, turgid
puffy baked egg dish: soufflé
puffy part: tumefaction
pug: boxer, clay, dog, footprint, knead, track
pugilist: boxer, bruiser, fighter, prizefighter

pugnacious: aggressive, antagonistic, bellicose, belligerent, cantankerous, combative, contentious, defiant, militant, quarrelsome, rebellious, truculent, warlike
puissance: clout, energy, force, influence, might, muscle, potency, power, strength, sway, vigor
pulchritude: appeal, beauty, comeliness, grace, handsomeness, loveliness
pule: complain, cry, repine, snivel, weep, whimper, whine
pull apart: criticize, detach, divide, rend, separate, split, tear
pull away by violent twisting: wrest
pull down: annihilate, demolish, destroy, dismantle, lower, raze, wreck
pull heavily: drag
pull off: accomplish, achieve, detach, execute, manage, yank
pull out: depart, evacuate, leave, quit, retreat, withdraw
pull out with effort: extract
pull through: rally, recovery, survive, triumph, weather
pull up: arrive, halt, pause, stop, uplift
pulley: block, machine, ring, sheave, wheel
pulley block, lower part of: breech
pulley or pulleys set in a casing: block
pulley wheel with grooved rim: sheave
pulleys, system of ropes and blocks for raising and lowering weights of: tackle
pulling power of animal or machine: draft, traction
pulp: crush, curd, mash, mush, pith, pomace, pulverize, sheap, smash, squash
pulpit: ambo, chair, dais, desk, lectern, ministry, platform, podium, rostrum, stage, stand
pulpit of synagogue: almemar, bema
pulpit or church desk: ambo
pulpy: pultaceous

pulpy fruit: drupe, pome
pulpy residue after fruit juice is pressed: marc, pomace
pulsate: beat, fluctuate, flutter, oscillate, pant, pound, pulse, quiver, throb, vibrate, waver
pulsatory: sphygmic
pulse: beat, oscillation, palpitation, pulsate, rhythm, throb, vibration
pulverize: annihilate, atomize, beat, comminute, crunch, crush, decimate, demolish, destroy, flour, grind, levigate, mash, mince, powder, ruin, shatter, smash, triturate
puma: catamount, cougar, mountain cat, mountain lion, panther
pummel: batter, beat, hammer, maul, pelt, pommel, pound, thrash, wallop
pump: drain, draw, inject, jack, shoe, siphon, stirrup, syringe
pump for information: grill, interrogate, question, quiz
pump used to create partial vacuum: aspirator
pump using downward water flow to force flow upward through pipe: hydraulic ram
pump without pistons working off pulsed condensation of steam: pulsometer, vacuum pump
pumpkin: fruit, gourd, jack-o'-lantern, pepo, squash, vine
pun: calembour, conundrum, double meaning, equivoque, joke, knock, paronomasia, play on words, quibble, quip, witticism
punch: bash, blow, box, clobber, cuff, hit, hook, jab, prod, smack, sock, strike, swat, uppercut, vigor
punch-drunk boxer: stumblebum
punch hole in: drill, perforate, pierce, poke, puncture
punchy: confused, dazed, groggy
punctilious: careful, ceremonial, conscientious, correct, exact, finicky, formal, fussy, meticulous, painstaking, particular, precise, proper, punctual, scrupulous
punctual: exact, on time, precise, prompt, punctilious, reliable, timely
punctuate: accent, break, divide, emphasize interrupt, mark, point, separate, stress
punctuation mark: apostrophe, asterisk, brace, bracket, bullet, colon, comma, dash, diacritic, dot, ellipsis, exclamation, hyphen, obelisk, parenthesis, period, quote, semicolon, slash

punctuation, the art of: stigmeology
puncture: bore, deflate, depression, drill, gore, hole, pierce, prick, riddle, rupture, slit, stab, vent, wound
pundit: critic, emtor, expert, guru, intellectual, sage, scholar, swami, teacher
pungent: acrid, acrimonious, acute, aromatic, biting, bitter, caustic, cutting, flavorful, hot, keen, penetrating, peppery, piercing, piquant, poignant, pointed, provocative, racy, rich, salty, seasoned, sharp, smart, snappy, spicy, stimulating, stinging, strong, tangy, tart, tez, witty
punish: abuse, admonish, avenge, cane, castigate, chasten, chastise, consume, correct, discipline, dismiss, excommunicate, fine, flog, hurt, incarcerate, penalize, revenge, scold, sentence, spank, strap, strike, torture, whip
punish by arbitrary penalty: amerce
punish by exile or removal to obscure position: banish, relegate
punish in retribution: avenge
punishing: brutal, grueling, hard, punitive, tough
punishment: castigation, chastisement, correction, damages, disciplinary action, discipline, forfeiture, judgment, lesson, loss, lumps, ostracism, penalty, penance, retribution, revenge, suffering, vengeance

RELATED TERMS

punishment and prison management, study of: penology
punishment as repayment: retribution, revenge
punishment by attack from all sides: gauntlet
punishment corresponding to nature of crime: talion
punishment for evil: retribution
punishment identical to offense: eye for an eye, lex talionis, talion
punishment of having to stay after school: detention
punishment of head and hands in wooden framework: pillory, stocks
punishment or penalty, exemption from: impunity
punishment ordained by God: visitation
punishment that one deserves: comeuppance, just deserts
punishment, cancellation or reduction of: reprieve, respite

punishment, means of inflicting: scourge
punishment, of a deserved appropriate: commensurate, condign
punishment, relating to: penal
punishment, something surrendered as a: forfeit
punishment, to cancel or reduce a: remit
punishment, to correct by: chasten, take to task
punishment, to inflict severe: castigate, chastise ❦

punitive: avenging, disciplinary, penal, punishing, revengeful, vindicatory, vindictive
punk: beginner, bully, delinquent, gangster, hood, hoodlum, hooligan, incense, inferior, kindling, novice, prostitute, rookie, ruffian, thug, tinder, worthless
punt: boot, indentation, kick, propel
puny: feeble, frail, inferior, little, measly, minor, petty, shrimp, sickly, slight, small, tiny, trivial, weak
pupa: chrysalis, cocoon
pupil: apprentice, cadet, disciple, freshman, junior, learner, neophyte, novice, scholar, senior, sophomore, student, trainee, tyro, undergraduate
pupil absent from school without permission: truant
pupil and tutor relationship: tutelage
puppet: doll, dupe, figurehead, flunky, manikin, marionette, pawn, slave, stooge
puppet on strings: marionette
puppies, group of: litter
puppy: animal, canine, dog, whelp
purchase: acquire, acquisition, asset, buy, earn, investment, obtain, procurement, property
purchaser: buyer, consumer, customer, patron, shopper, user
purchasing power of individual: real income
pure: absolute, authentic, blameless, chaste, clean, clear, complete, elemental, faultless, filtered, fine, fresh, genuine, good, guiltless, immaculate, innocent, moral, neat, nice, perfect, pristine, refined, simple, sincere, sinless, stainless, straight, true, unadulterated, unalloyed, unblemished, uncorrupted, undefiled, unmixed, unsullied, utter, virgin, virtuous
pure air: ozone

PURPLE

amaranth	clematis	indigo	pansy	royal purple
amaranthine	dahila	lavender	periwinkle	rubine
amethyst	damson	light purple	phlox	salferino
amethystine	dark purple	lilac	plum	tulip
Argyle	deep purple	magenta	prune	Tyrian purple
aubergine	fuchsia	maroon	puce	violaceous
blue-violet	grape	mauve	purple-blue	violet
bluish purple	gridelin	monsignor	purple-red	violetta ❧
bokhara	heliotrope	mulberry	raisin	
campanula	hyacinth	orchid	raspberry	
cerise	imperial purple	pale purple	reddish purple	

pure and absolute: unmitigated, veritable

pure and perfect: impeccable, irreproachable, unimpeachable

pure and uncorrupted: immaculate, pristine, unadulterated, unblemished

pure essential part: quintessence

pure profit: net

pure sexually: chaste

puree: blend, mush, paste, pulp, soup

purely: absolutely, completely, essentially, fully, just, simply, totally, wholly

purgatory: expiation, hell, limbo, misery, suffering

purge: absolve, cleanse, clear, eliminate, erase, exculpate, exonerate, exterminate, liquidate, oust, purify, remove, rid, unload

purging of emotions: catharsis

purify: absolve, baptize, clean, cleanse, clear, decontaminate, deodorize, depurate, disinfect, distill, exonerate, filter, fumigate, purge, rarefy, refine, sanitize, wash

RELATED TERMS

purification: atonement, baptism, catharsis, cleansing, distillation, freeing, rebirth, redemption, salvation, washing

purify a text: bowdlerize, expurgate

purify and make holy: consecrate, hallow, sanctify

purify by ceremony: lustrate

purify by exposing to air: aerate

purify by washing, decanting, settling: elutriate

purify liquid: distill

purifying: depurative

purifying phenomenon: alembic

purifying plant for crude substance: refinery ❧

puritanical: austere, blue-nosed, genteel, prim, proper, prudish, rigid, stern, straitlaced, strict, stuffy, Victorian

puritanical, as a law: blue

purity: chastity, cleanliness, continence, holiness, innocence, piety, sanctitude

purlieu: area, environ, fringe, hangout, haunt, neighborhood, outskirts, periphery

purloin: appropriate, filch, finger, pilfer, pinch, rob, steal, swipe, thieve

purple-dye snail: murex

purport: connotation, core, drift, gist, implication, import, intent, intention, maintain, mean, meaning, object, point, profess, purpose, rationale, sense, significance, substance, tenor, thrust

purpose: aim, ambition, animus, aspiration, aspire, design, destination, determination, duty, end, function, goal, impulsion, intend, intent, intention, mean, mission, motive, object, objective, plan, point, proposal, purport, reason, resolution, resolve, sake, use

purpose, concealed: arrière-pensée, hidden agenda, ulterior motive

purpose, professed: pretext

purposeful: telic

purposeless: aimless, floundering, haphazard, insignificant, meaningless, pointless, random, senseless, unnecessary, unplanned, useless

purposelessness: anomie

purposely: consciously, deliberately, expressly, intentionally, knowingly, willfully

purposes, unintentionally conflicting: cross-purposes

purr: hum, murmur, noise, sing, sound

purse: bag, handbag, pocketbook, poke, pouch, wallet

purse of winnings: money, prize, stake

purser: bursar, cashier, comptroller, treasurer

pursue: address, badger, chase, continue, court, date, ensue, follow, harass, hound, hunt, persist, proceed, prosecute, seek, stalk, tail, track, trail

pursuit: business, calling, career, chase, following, occupation, pleasure, quest, undertaking, vocation, work

pursuit of pleasure: hedonism

purvey: assist, cater, circulate, equip, furnish, procure, provide, sell, serve, supply, vend

purview: ken

pus-filled inflamed elevation: pustule

pus, concerning: purulent

pus, to discharge: fester, maturate, suppurate

push: advance, advertise, bear, boost, bulldoze, bunt, butt, coerce, cram, crowd, ding, drive, effort, elbow, energy, expand, extend, force, forge, goad, gumption, heave, hunch, hustle, impel, incentive, increase, initiative, inspire, jostle, launch, motivate, move, nudge, peddle, plug, press, pressure, prod, promote, prompt, propel, ram, sell, shove, stimulus, thrust, urge, vigor, vitality

push around: bully, intimidate, threaten

push aside: shunt

push back: repel

push forward: impel

push gently: jostle, nudge

push in inappropriately: intrude

push off: depart, exit, launch, leave, start, withdraw

push on: continue, journey, proceed

push oneself or ideas on others: obtrude

push out: exert, extrude

pushcart: handcart, trolley, wagon, wheelbarrow

pushover: breeze, chump, cinch, fool, snap, softy, sucker

push's partner: shove

pushy: aggressive, ambitious, assertive, bossy, brash, brazen, bumptious, insistent, intrusive, obnoxious, obtrusive, officious, persistent, presumptuous, self-aggrandizing, strident

pusillanimous: afraid, chicken, cowardly, fearful, gutless, tame, timid, timorous

puslike discharge: ichor

puss: cat, child, face, girl, kisser, kitten, mouth, mug, tabby, woman

pussyfoot: avoid, dodge, evade, hedge, sidestep, tiptoe

put aside: deposit, forget, inferred, shelve, store, table

put aside for specific use: appropriate

put away: ate, bury, commit, confine, consume, devour, discard, down, finish, incarcerate, jail, kill, ryans, stash, store, stow

put back: demote, reinstate, restore, restored, return

put down: belittle, condemn, consume, criticize, defeat, degrade, dis, disparage, disparate, enter, humiliate, laid, log, quash, quell, record, reject, repress, silence, sited, subdue, suppress

put down by force: allay, quash, quell

put forth: constitute, exert, form, offer, posited, possited, produce, propose, show

put forward as basis of argument: posit, postulate

put off: defer, delay, discard, linger, offend, postpone, repulse, shelve, stall, stalled

put off doing: defer, procrastinate

put on: act, add, apply, attach, bluff, deceive, don, donned, endue, fake, hoax, masquerade, parody, present, pretend, pretense, satire, send up, sham, spoof, stage, staged, tease, trick, wear, wore, worn

put out: anger, annoy, bother, discard, discomfit, displace, disturb, douse, egest, emit, expel, extinguish, inconvenience, irritate, oust, provoke, quench, rile, smother, trouble

put out fire: douse, extinguish, quench

put the kibosh on: nix

put through: connect, finish, manage, undergo

put together: amass, assemble, build, construct, create, erect, join, made, merge, produce, unite

put together in bits and pieces: cut-and-paste

put up: accommodate, ante, build, bunk, can, construct, erect, harbor, house, lodge, make, rear, rig

putative: accepted, alleged, assumed, believed, inferred, reputed, supposed

putrefy: corrupt, crumble, decay, decompose, deteriorate, disintegrate, rot, spoil, taint

putrid: bad, contaminated, depraved, disagreeable, foul, malodorous, noisome, offensive, polluted, rancid, rotten, smelly, spoiled, stinking, vile

putter: dabble, dawdle, doodle, fiddle, fool around, fritter, loaf, loiter, tinker

puzzle: addle, amaze, anagram, baffle, bamboozle, bewilder, brainteaser, charade, code, confound, confuse, conundrum, crossword, difficult, disconcert, distract, disturb, dumbfound, enigma, entangle, frustrate, intrigue, jigsaw, labyrinth, maze, muse, mystery, mystify, nonplus, paradox, perplex, ponder, poser, rattle, rebus, riddle, stump, upset

puzzle in pictures and symbols: rebus

puzzle of intricate patterns of lines: labyrinth, maze

puzzle solution: key

puzzle, difficult: conundrum, dilemma, enigma, plight, poser, predicament, quandary

puzzling: ambiguous, bewildering, complicated, confusing, cryptic, difficult, enigmatic, inscrutable, intricate, involved, knotty, mysterious, mystifying, unclear, unfathomable

pygmy: chimpanzee, dwarf, elf, gnome, lilliputian, midget, pigmy, pixy, runt, short, shrimp, small, tiny, trivial, unimportant

pyknic: fat

pyramid: accrue, heap, monument, pile, shrine, stack, tomb, ziggurat

pyramid of Assyria, Babylonia: ziggurat

pyramid with top sliced off: fulstrum

pyre: bonfire, fuel, heap, suttee

pyromaniac: arsonist, firebug, incendiary

pyrosis: heartburn, indigestion

pyrotechnics: fireworks, pyrotechny, rockets, sparklers

python: anaconda, boa, boa constrictor, snake

pyx: binnacle, box, case, casket, chest, ciborium, container, pix, tabernacle, vessel

Qq Pp

quack: charlatan, cheat, counterfeiter, faker, fraud, impostor, mountebank, phony, pretender, sham, snake-oil salesman

quad: quadrangle, quadrant, quadraphonic, quadruplet

quadrangle: campus, court, enclosure, forum, square, yard

quadrangle surrounded by cloisters: garth

quadrangular: tetragonal

quadrate: adapt, adjust, agree, balanced, conform, correspond, suit

quadrille: square dance

quaff: down, drink, guzzle, imbibe, ingest, swallow, swig, tipple

quagmire: bog, impasse, marsh, morass, mudhole, quicksand, swamp, trap

quahog: clam

quail: blench, cower, cringe, flinch, quake, recoil, shake, shrink, shudder, squealer, tremble, tremor, wince

quail, group of: bevy, covey, flock

quaint: antique, archaic, bizarre, charming, colonial, curious, ethnic, fanciful, folksy, nice, odd, offbeat, peculiar, picturesque, strange, unfamiliar, unusual, weird, whimsical

quake: aftershock, earthquake, jitter, oscillate, quail, quiver, shake, shiver, shudder, spasm, tremble, tremor, vibrate, waver

qualification: ability, aptitude, attribute, capability, capacity, competence, condition, credential, endowment, experience, makings, prerequisite, requirement, skill, talent

qualified: able, capable, certified, eligible, equipped, licensed, limited, restricted, skillful, trained

qualified and in accordance with standards: legitimate

qualified or entitled to be chosen: eligible, worthy

qualifier: adjective

qualify: adapt, alter, assuage, authorize, certify, change, commission, condition, diminish, empower, enable, equip, habilitate, lessen, license, limit, mitigate, modify, permit, ready, restrain, restrict, soften, temper

qualifying word, phrase: parenthesis

quality: attribute, blood, caliber, capacity, character, characteristic, class, element, essence, excellence, excellent, factor, feature, grade, merit, nature, nobility, position, power, property, rank, rate, sort, stature, status, superior, taste, trait, value, virtue, worth

quality or degree of worth: caliber

quality or excellence, mark indicating: cachet, hallmark

quality, distinctive: accent, atmosphere, aura, character, ethos

qualm: anxiety, apprehension, doubt, faintness, feeling, hesitation, indecision, insecurity, misgiving, nausea, pall, regret, reluctance, reservation, scruple, sickness, suspicion, twinge, uncertainty, unease

qualm due to ethics, morals: scruple

quandary: bind, crisis, difficulty, dilemma, fix, impasse, jam, pickle, plight, quagmire, scrape

quantity: allotment, allowance, amount, amplitude, batch, atom, bit, body, bunch, bushel, degree, dosage, dose, dram, drop, extent, grain, handful, iota, length, lot, magnitude, mass, morsel, multitude, number, portion, proportions, shred, size, slew, smidgen, some, speck, sum, ton, total, unit, volume, weight

quantity by which a container falls short of being full: ullage

quantity by which another is divided: denominator, divisor

quantity produced at one time: batch

quantity to be divided: dividend, numerator

quantum: amount, measure, portion, quantity, sum, total, unit

quarantine: ban, confine, exclude, interdict, isolate, restrain, restrict

quarantine station in building, ship: lazaretto

quarrel: altercation, argue, argument, beef, bicker, brawl, clash, conflict, contention, contretemps, controversy, difference, disagree, disagreement, discord, dispute, dissension, estrangement, faction, falling out, falling-out, feud, fight, fracas, fray, fuss, hassle, miff, rhubarb, row, ruckus, run in, spat, squabble, strife, tiff, variance, vendetta, war, words, wrangle, wrangling

RELATED TERMS

quarrel go-between: adjudicator, arbitrator, intermediary, mediator, moderator, ombudsman

quarrel or call into question: contradict, controvert, dispute, gainsay, oppugn, repudiate

quarrel with words, to: flite

quarrel, feud or long-time: vendetta

quarrel, involved in: embroiled

quarrel, noisy: commotion, ruction, uproar

quarrel, petty: bicker, squabble, wrangle

quarrel, to settle or end a: compose, conciliate, determine, reconcile

quarrel, to try to settle: intercede

quarreling: at loggerheads, at odds, at variance, conflicting, disputing quarrels, causing: divisive

quarrelsome: antagonistic, argumentative, bellicose, belligerent, brawling, cantankerous, choleric, combative, contentious, disputatious, fiery, hostile, irritable, litigious, militant, ornery, petulant, pugnacious, rancorous, scrappy, termagant, unruly ❧

quarry: chase, dig, game, mine, pit, prey, shape, side, source, square, victim

quarter: coin, fourth, period, phase, quad, quadrant, section, sector, time, tract, zone

quarter of a circle: quadrant

quarters: barracks, camp, chambers, digs, dormitory, home, lodging, pads, residence, room, shelter, space, station

quartz type: agate, amethyst, bloodstone, carnelian, chalcedony, chert, crystal, flint, jasper, onyx, opal, rose, sard, sardonyx, smoky, topaz

quash: abate, abolish, abrogate, annul, beat, cancel, crush, defeat, destroy, extinguish, invalidate, nullify, overthrow, quell, repeal, retract, smother, squash, stop, subdue, suppress, undo, vacate, void

quaver: falter, note, oscillate, quake, quiver, shake, shiver, shudder, sway, tremble, tremor, trill, vacillate, vibrate, waver, wobble

quay: berth, dock, jetty, key, landing, levee, slip, wharf

queasy: carsick, dizzy, groggy, nauseated, qualmish, queer, seasick, sickening, squeamish, timid, troubled, uncertain, uncomfortable, uneasy, unsettled, upset, woozy

queen: czarina, empress, matriarch, monarch, ranee, regina, ruler, sovereign

queen, concerning a: regal

queen, to relinquish the title of: abdicate

queen's husband, king's wife: consort

queer: abnormal, atypical, bizarre, curious, disrupt, doubtful, eccentric, eerie, erratic, faint, fanciful, fantastic, funny, giddy, odd, peculiar, puzzling, qualmish, queasy, questionable, singular, spurious, squeamish, strange, suspicious, touched, unconventional, unorthodox, unusual, weird

quell: allay, assuage, calm, check, con-

quer, cool, crush, curb, defeat, destroy, extinguish, kill, obtund, overcome, overpower, overwhelm, pacify, quash, quench, quiet, reduce, repress, silence, soothe, stop, subdue, suppress

quench: allay, alleviate, destroy, douse, extinguish, quell, satisfy, slake, smother, squelch, suppress

querulous: cantankerous, complaining, cross, discontented, fretful, grouchy, grumbling, irritable, peevish, petulant, touchy, whiny

query: ask, catechize, challenge, doubt, examine, inquiry, inquisition, interrogate, investigation, mistrust, probe, question, quiz

quest: adventure, crusade, delving, examine, expedition, goal, hunt, investigation, journey, mission, odyssey, probe, pursuit, search, seek, seeking, voyage

question: ask, catechize, challenge, debate, debrief, demand, demur, dispute, doubt, drill, examination, examine, grill, inquire, inquiry, interrogate, interrogation, interview, investigation, mystery, objection, poll, probe, problem, proposition, pump, query, quiz, scruple, suspect

RELATED TERMS

question-and-answer book on Christian principles: catechism

question-and-answer instructional method: Socratic method

question asked for effect and not an answer: rhetorical question

question closely and methodically: catechize, interrogate

question insistently: ply

question mark: eroteme

question mark and exclamation mark combined: interrobang

question method of Socrates, concerning the: maieutic

question that suggests answer sought: leading question

question the other side's witness: cross-examine

question to be disputed: quodlibet

question to obtain intelligence or knowledge gained on mission: debrief

question to which no answer is expected: rhetorical question

question within a sentence, like 'can I?': tag question

question, difficult: conundrum, poser

question, word or construction used to ask a: interrogative

questionable: ambiguous, arguable, controversial, disputable, dubious, equivocal, iffy, improbable, moot, shady, shaky, suspect, suspicious, uncertain, unconfirmed, undecided, unreliable, unsure

questioning the existence of God: agnosticism

questioning with harshness: inquisition

questions, inclined to ask many: inquisitive

questions, overwhelming number of: barrage ❧

queue: braid, chain, column, file, line, order, pigtail, plait, sequence, succession

quibble: argue, bicker, carp, cavil, complaint, criticism, dispute, dodge, equivocate, equivocation, evade, haggle, niggle, nitpick, objection, palter, pettifog, spat, split hairs, squabble, wrangle

quibbling: captious, casuistic, hairsplitting, sophistic

quick: able, abrupt, active, acute, agile, alert, alive, animated, apt, asap, brisk, clever, deft, dexterous, eager, expeditious, fast, fiery, fleet, hasty, immediate, impatient, instantaneous, intense, keen, live, moving, nimble, perceptive, prompt, rapid, ready, sensitive, sharp, skillful, snappy, speedy, sprightly, sudden, swift, vigorous, volant, wise

quick and without ceremony: summary

quick-tempered: angered, choleric, cross, excitable, fiery, impatient, inflammable, irascible, snappish, temperamental, touchy, volatile

quick-witted: acute, alert, astute, bright, brilliant, canny, clever, keen, savvy, sharp, slick, smart, wise

quick, excessively: impetuous, precipitate, precipitous

quicken: accelerate, animate, arouse, energize, enliven, excite, expedite, hasten, hurry, incite, invigorate, motivate, move, press, provoke, refresh, revive, rush, sharpen, speed, stimulate, stir, vivify

quicker than normal: accelerated

quickly: apace, at once, briefly, fast, instantly, lickety-split, presto, promptly, pronto, rapidly, soon, speedily, subito, tout de suite

quickly and efficiently, done: expeditious

quickly and nimbly, moving: agile, volant, volitant

quickly and with little care: cursory, perfunctory

quickly in music: subito, vivace

quickness: acumen, agility, alacrity, briskness, celerity, dexterity, dispatch, haste, pace, speed, velocity

quickness of mind: acumen

quicksand: mercurial, quagmire, quicksilver, snare, syrt, trap, unpredictable

quid pro quo: equivalent, exchange, substitution, tit-for-tat, trade

quidnunc: busybody, gossip, rumormonger

quiescent: calm, dormant, inactive, latent, motionless, passive, placid, quiet, serene, sleeping, still, tranquil, undisturbed

quiet: collected, docile, ease, idle, inaudible, mellow, muffle, mute, passive, reposeful, quell, relaxation, reserved, secretive, sequestered, serene, shush, silence, soft, stable, tranquil

RELATED TERMS

quiet and inactive: inert, passive, quiescent, still

quiet and low in volume or pitch: undertone

quiet and not speaking: dumbstruck, mute

quiet and reluctant to speak: reticent

quiet and restrained: reserved, reticent, taciturn, uncommunicative

quiet consent: acquiescence

quiet down: abate, mitigate, mollify, pacify

quiet isolated place: backwater

quiet manner, having a: inconspicuous, low-key, low-profile, subdued

quiet retreat: den ❦

quietly thoughtful: contemplative, introspective, meditative, pensive, reflective

quietus: acquittance, death, decease, discharge, dissolution, end, extinction, release, repose

quill: bobbin, calamus, feather, instrument, pen, pinion, spine

quill or feather, hollow shaft of: calamus

quill- or needle-shaped object: acicula, aculeus

quilt: bedspread, blanket, comforter, counterpane, cover, coverlet, duvet, pad, patchwork

quilt of irregularly shaped, multicolored pieces: crazy quilt

quilt with washable cover: duvet

quilting with raised effect: trapunto

quintessence: core, epitome, essence, gist, heart, pith, soul, spirit, substance

quintessential: classic, ideal, model, typical, ultimate

quip: banter, curious, gag, gibe, jest, joke, odd, pun, quibble, remark, sally, spoof, taunt

quirk: aberration, band, caprice, crook, deviation, eccentricity, equivocation, groove, idiosyncrasy, kink, knack, mannerism, oddity, peculiarity, quibble, trait, turn, twist, vagary

quisling: puppet, traitor, turncoat

quit: abandon, abdicate, acquit, alleviate, appease, avoid, cease, clandestine, depart, desert, desist, discontinue, drop, end, leave, release, relieve, relinquish, renounce, resign, resigned, retire, retired, rid, secede, secluded, stop, surrender, terminate, withdraw

quite: absolutely, actually, altogether, completely, considerably, entirely, exactly, fully, most, perfectly, positively, purely, really, reasonably, somewhat, thoroughly, totally, truly, very, well, wholly

quitter: ceder, chicken, coward, deserter, dropout, shirker, slacker

quiver: beat, convulse, flutter, jerk, oscillate, palpitate, quake, quick, shake, sheaf, shudder, spasm, tremble, twinkle

quivering: aspen

quixotic: capricious, dreamy, fanciful, idealistic, imaginary, impractical, impulsive, romantic, unread, utopian, visionary, whimsical

quiz: ask, exam, examination, examine, inquire, probe, pump, question, test

quizzical: amusing, bantering, comical, curious, eccentric, inquisitive, mocking, probing, questioning, skeptical, teasing

quoin: angle, cornerstone, keystone, wedge

quondam: bygone, former, once, one-time, past, sometime

quota: allocation, allotment, allowance, divide, dividend, part, portion, proportion, quantity, ration, share, slice

quotation: estimate, excerpt, offer, passage, price, quote, reference, selection

quotation at beginning of work or chapter: epigraph, motto

quotation from authoritative source for substantiation: citation

quotation from standard work cited as illustration: locus classicus

quotation in dictionary entry: citation, illustrative example

quotation mark, British: inverted comma

quotation mark, French: guillemets

quote: adduce, cite, cost, excerpt, extract, passage, quotation, recite, refer, reference, repeat, retell, select

quote as example or authority: cite

quote is correct, indication that: sic

quotidian: commonplace, daily, everyday, ordinary, trivial, usual

rabbi: clergyman, master, priest, rabbin, Talmudist, teacher

rabbit: buck, bunny, capon, coney, cony, cottontail, doe, hare, lapin, rodent

rabbit dwelling: warren

rabbit family: Leporidae

rabbit with long white hair: Angora

rabbit, like a: leporine

rabbit, pertaining to: oryctolagine

rabbits, colony of: warren

rabbit's tail: scut

rabble: coarse, commonality, crowd, dregs, herd, mob, ragtag, riffraff, scum, swarm, trash

rabble-rouser: agitator, demagogue, firebrand, incendiary

rabid: berserk, crazy, delirious, demented, deranged, eager, enthusiastic, extreme, fanatical, frantic, frenzied, insane, irrational, mad, maniacal, raging, uncontrollable, violent, wild, zealous

rabies: hydrophobia

rabies or other animal disease transmitted to humans: zoonosis

race: chase, competition, contest, course, dart, dash, hasten, hurdle, hurry, marathon, meet, pursuit, rally, regatta, relay, rivalry, run, running, rush, scamper, slalom, speed, sprint, track

race arena of Greece, Rome: hippodrome

race bet of original wager and its earnings on a subsequent event: parlay

race bet with winners sharing total amount bet: pari-mutuel

race competitor: entrant, entry

race course section farthest from spectators: backstretch

race course section from last turn to finish line: homestretch

race in which compensations and advantages are given to even out chances of winning: handicap

race of mankind: blood, breed, brood, clan, class, culture, descendants, dynasty, family, generation, kindred, line, lineage, nation, nationality, pedigree, people, species, stock, strain, tribe, type

race of water: channel, course, creek, passageway, river, stream, watercourse

race on horseback on obstacle course: steeplechase

race or ethnic group membership, treatment based on: bigotry, discrimination

race or series of races, boat: regatta

race segment: lap

race which determines winner of lottery: sweepstake

races and ethnic groups, study of: ethnology

races, mixture of: miscegenation

racetrack: course, hippodrome, oval, paddock, path, racecourse, ring, track, turf

racetrack betting board: tote board

racetrack enclosure for horse, car preparations: paddock

racial and ethnic groups in unrestricted association and equality: desegregation, integration

racial improvement by selective breeding, study of: eugenics

racial segregation in South Africa: apartheid

racial separation in a society: segregation

racial sharing of unconscious mind, memory: collective unconscious

racing boat: shell

racism: apartheid, bias, bigotry, discrimination, prejudice, segregation

rack: afflict, agonize, excruciate, oppress, pain, persecute, strain, suffering, torment, torture, wrench

rack used in carpentry: sawhorse

racket: babel, blare, business, bustle, clamor, clatter, commotion, din, disturbance, fuss, hubbub, noise, outcry, roar, shouting, trick, turbulence, uproar, voise

racket, making a big: polyphloisboian

racketeer: criminal, crook, gangster, hood, mobster

raconteur: anecdotist, narrator, storyteller

racy: brisk, crude, fiery, fresh, indecent, lewd, lively, obscene, piquant, pungent, ribald, risque, salty, saucy, sharp, spicy, spirited, strong, suggestive, vigorous, vulgar, zesty

radar and microwaves, electron tube of: magnetron

radar antenna domelike shell: radome

radar beacon: racon

radar-screen mark: blip

radarlike measuring device for water: echo sounder, sonar

radarlike sensory system of bats and dolphins: echolocation

radiance: beam, brightness, brilliance, delight, effulgence, glare, gleam, glitter, glory, glow, happiness, light, luminescence, luster, refulgence, sheen, shine, splendor, warmth

radiance around head or body of holy person: aureole

radiant: beaming, beamy, blissful, bright, brilliant, cheerful, glowing, happy, incandescent, lambent, lucent, luminous, refulgent, resplendent, shining

radiate: beam, burn, circulate, diffuse,

emit, extend, exude, glisten, illuminate, manifest, scatter, send, shine, sparkle, spread, transmit

radiating: stellate

radiation between light and microwaves, invisible: infrared

radiation between light and X-rays, invisible: ultraviolet

radiation measurement instrument: Geiger counter

radiation unit: REM

radiation, impenetrable by certain types of: opaque

radiation, permeable to certain electromagnetic: transparent

radiation, to give off: emit

radical: agitator, anarchist, basal, basic, cardinal, complete, drastic, essential, extreme, extremist, firebrand, fundamental, iconoclast, leftist, leftwinger, liberal, nihilist, nonconformist, primal, primary, rebel, renegade, revolutionary, root, subversive, ultra

radical form, having: actinoid

radical political figure: leftist

radicle: root

radio: AM, boom box, broadcast, CB, FM, portable, receiver, shortwave, signal, transistor, walkman, wireless
RELATED TERMS
radio and television, broadcast simultaneously on: simulcast
radio broadcast facilities available for public use: public access
radio broadcast, live: relay
radio channel, capable of receiving two messages on same: diplex
radio frequency band for private communications: CB, citizens band
radio operator: ham
radio or television program, spoken matter that links parts or: continuity
radio program, prerecorded: transcription
radio receiver that beeps when contacted: beeper, pager
radio receiver, early: crystal set
radio signals and converting to sound, device getting incoming: receiver
radio system accurately reproduces sound, degree to which: fidelity ☜

radioactive gases produced by radioactive decay: emanation

radioactive particles slowly descending in atmosphere: fallout

radioactive substance that can be followed through process or system: tracer

radioactivity duration measure: half-life

radioactivity, to expose to: contaminate

radius: boundary, compass, extent, field, line, orbit, range, reach, span, spoke, sweep

raffish: carefree, cheap, flashy, rakish, showy, tawdry, unconventional, uncouth, unkempt, vulgar, wild, worthless

raffle: chance, debris, drawing, gambling, game, lottery, refuse, rubbish, sweepstake

raft: barge, catamaran, craft, float, mat, pontoon, transport

raft of logs lashed together: catamaran

rag: annoy, banter, harass, jive, joke, josh, kid, mock, needle, razz, remnant, rib, scold, scrap, shred, tatter, tease

ragamuffin: beggar, bum, hobo, orphan, panhandler, scarecrow, tatterdemalion, tramp, vagabond, vagrant, waif

rage: acerbity, acrimony, anger, animosity, boil, chafe, choler, craze, emotion, enthusiasm, fad, fashion, fervor, frenzy, fume, funk, furor, fury, hysteria, indignation, ire, irritation, latest, livid, madness, mania, outburst, paroxysm, passion, rant, rave, rese, squall, storm, style, tantrum, temper, vehemence, violence, wrath

rage or fit of emotion: conniption, conniption fit

rage, filled with: furious, livid

ragged: battered, defective, dilapidated, dingy, erose, frayed, frazzled, imperfect, irregular, patched, seedy, shabby, shaggy, strident, tattered, threadbare, torn, uneven, unkempt

ragged edge of handmade paper: deckle edge

raging: angry, blustering, fanatical, ferocious, fervent, fierce, frenzied, furious, incensed, irate, madding, rabid, rampant, stormy, uncontrolled, violent, wild

ragout: goulash, hash, pot-au-feu, stew

ragtime: blues, jazz, music, swing

ragtime music on tinny-sounding piano: honky-tonk

rah: approve, cheer, encouragement, hurrah

raid: assault, attack, bombard, bust,

forage, foray, harass, harry, incursion, inroad, invade, invasion, loot, maraud, onslaught, pillage, pirate, plunder, predation, ravage, roundup, sack, seizure, sortie, storm

raid on defensive position: foray, sally, sortie

raider: bandit, buccaneer, freebooter, highwayman, hijacker, looter, marauder, pilferer, pillager, pirate, plunderer, privateer, rustler, thief

raiding force: commando

rail and posts that support it: balustrade

rail of staircase, hand-: banister

rail support: stanchion

railing: banister, bar, barrier, fence, grate, paling, posts, siding, support

railing around vessel's stern: taffrail

railing of roof or balcony: parapet

raillery: badinage, bantering, chaffing, derision, irony, joking, kidding, lampoonery, parody, persiflage, razzing, ridicule, roasting, satire, sport, teasing

railway in amusement park, high-speed: roller coaster

raiment: apparel, attire, clothing, dress, duds, garb, garments, habiliments, threads

rain: cloudburst, deluge, downpour, drizzle, flood, mist, mizzle, pour, precipitation, shower, sprinkle, storm, thunderstorm

rain downpour: cataract, deluge

rain gauge: pluviometer, udometer

rain, of heavy: torrential

rain, to sprinkle a cloud with chemicals to make: seed

rainbow: arc, assortment, band, bow, fantasy, illusion, spectrum

rainbow, having all colors of: prismatic, spectral

rainbowlike colors, having: iridescent

raincoat: mac, mack, mackintosh, overcoat, poncho, slicker, trench coat

raincoat with opening for head, hooded: poncho

rainfall, study of: hyetography

rainy: damp, hyetal, moist, pluvious, stormy, wet

rainy season in Asia: monsoon

raise: addition, advance, aggrandize, amass, arouse, ascend, augment, awaken, boost, build, collect, construct, crane, elevate, erect, establish, evoke, excite, gather, heighten, hike, hoist, incite, increase, inflate, intensify, introduce, jump, leaven, levy, lift, muster, pump, resurrect, rise, spur, stir, transcend, upheave, uplift

raise or care for: breed, create, cultivate, enhance, foster, grow, nourish, nurture, procure, produce, promote, propagate, rear

raise anchor: trip, weigh

raise from dead: resuscitate, revive

raise in rank, status: elevate, exalt, prefer, promote

raise trivial objections: carp, cavil

raise up and unearth: dredge

raise with a machine: hoist, winch

raised figures as decoration: embossing

raised platform: dais, podium, rostrum, stage, tribune

raised sculpture: bas-relief

raisin: dried grape

raisin grapes: sultanas

raising agent for dough: leaven, leavening

rake: Casanova, debauchee, libertine, playboy, rascal, roué, swinger, womanizer

rakish: chic, dapper, dashing, debonair, dissolute, immoral, jaunty, lewd, licentious, raffish, sporty, streamlined, wild

rally: arouse, assemble, attack, awaken, challenge, charge, comeback, convene, convention, drag, encourage, improvement, kindle, meet, mobilize, mock, muster, organize, race, recovery, recuperate, refresh, rejuvenate, restore, reunite, revival, revive, rouse, stir, strengthen, unite

ram: batter, buck, bulldoze, bump, butt, collide, cram, crash, drive, force, hammer, hit, plunger, pound, strike, stuff, tamp, tap, thrust

ramble: babble, chatter, digress, drift, excursion, gad, gallivant, meander, roam, rove, saunter, spatiate, stray, stroll, travel, walk, wander

rambling: cursory, desultory, digressive, disconnected, discursive, excursive, incoherent, lengthy, meandering, rolling, sprawling, wandering, wordy

rambunctious: active, boisterous, disorderly, loud, raucous, rough, rowdy, tumultuous, unruly, untamed, wild

ramification: arm, branch, complication, consequence, development, divergence, division, extension, offshoot, ramus, result

ramp: access, apron, easing, gangplank, grade, gradient, hill, incline, platform, rage, slope, walk

ramp that curves and ascends: helicline

rampage: binge, frenzy, rage, spree, storm, uproar, violence

rampant: dominant, epidemic, excessive, extravagant, fierce, prevailing, prevalent, profuse, raging, rife, threatening, unchecked, uncontrollable, unrestrained, violent, widespread

rampart: agger, barricade, barrier, bastion, breastwork, bulwark, defense, embankment, fortification, parapet, protection, wall

ramshackle: crumbling, decrepit, dilapidated, dissipated, flimsy, rickety, seedy, shabby, shaky

ranch: estancia, farm, grange, hacienda, plantation

rancher: cattleman, cowboy, cowgirl, cowhand, cowpoke, farmer, gaucho, hand, shepherd

rancid: malodorous, musty, nasty, odorous, offensive, putrid, rank, repugnant, repulsive, rotten, smelly, sour, spoiled, stale, stinking, unpleasant

rancor: animosity, bitterness, enmity, gall, grudge, hatefulness, hatred, hostility, malice, resentment, spite, vengeance

random: accidental, aimless, aleatory, arbitrary, chance, desultory, fortuitous, haphazard, hit-or-miss, indiscriminate, occasional, purposeless, stochastic, stray, unplanned

random and not inherent: adventitious

random and whim, according to: capricious, fickle, impulsive

random occurrences, based on: stochastic

random or by accident, happening at: fortuitous

random or left to one's own judgment: discretionary

random, lucky discovery made at: serendipity

randomly, occurring irregularly or: intermittent, sporadic

randy: carousal, coarse, crude, disorderly, lascivious, lecherous, lewd, libertine, licentious, lustful, uninhibited, vulgar

range: align, ally, ambit, appliance, area, arrange, assortment, bounds, classify, compass, diapason, distance,

domain, explore, extent, farm, field, gamut, grassland, highlands, horizon, latitude, lea, length, limits, line, orbit, order, parameters, pasture, plain, province, purview, ramble, rank, reach, realm, ridge, roam, rove, scope, series, sierra, sort, space, span, spectrum, sphere, stove, stray, stretch, stroll, sweep, tether, variety, wander

range of a musical instrument or voice: compass, diapason, register

range of performance possibilities: repertoire

range of understanding: cognizance, ken

range or extent, complete: gamut

range or field of activity: bailiwick, domain, preserve, province, sphere

range, sphere, or scope: ambit, orbit, radius

ranger: policeman, policewoman, rover, soldier, trooper, wanderer, warden

rangy: gangling, lanky, lean, roomy, skinny, slim, spacious, spindling

rank: ancestry, arrange, arrangement, array, assort, caliber, caste, class, classification, classify, column, condition, coordinate, degree, dignity, distinction, division, downright, echelon, estate, evaluate, formation, gentry, genus, gradation, grade, gross, hierarchy, line, order, place, position, precede, prestige, quality, range, rate, rating, row, score, seniority, series, sort, space, standing, station, stature, status, tier, type, value

rank and file: commonality, commoners, masses, militia, plebes, proletariat, troops

rank in organization: chain of command, hierarchy, pecking order

rank of tournament competitors: seed

rank or preference, order of: precedence

rank, being: dirty, fetid, filthy, foul, malodorous, obscene, offensive, rancid, raunchy, revolting, smelly, smutty, strong

rankle: annoy, embitter, fester, fret, gall, inflame, irk, irritate, nettle, plague, rile, torment, vex

ransack: comb, loot, pillage, plunder, raid, rake, ravage, ravish, rifle, rummage, search, vandalize

ransom: atone, compensation, deliver,

emancipate, expiate, free, liberate, price, redeem, release, rescue, retrieve, save

ransom, person held for: hostage

rant: bellow, berate, fume, harangue, huff, orate, rage, range, rave, storm, tirade, yell

rap: blame, blow, chat, communicate, conversation, criticism, criticize, discussion, hit, knock, punishment, rebuke, reprehend, reprimand, sentence, smite, snatch, speak, strike, swat, talk, tap, thwack, utter, whack

rapacious: avaricious, ferocious, fierce, greedy, plundering, predatory, ravening, ravenous, voracious, vulturous, wolfish

rapacity: avarice, covetousness, cupidity, greed, thievery

rape: abuse, assault, attack, defile, despoil, file, offense, pillage, plunder, ravage, ravish, spoil, violate, violation

rape, intercourse with underaged girl considered: statutory rape

rapid: abrupt, agile, brisk, fast, fleet, hasty, hurried, nimble, prompt, quick, speedy, swift, winged

rapid recovery: sea change

rapid, in music: mosso, presto, veloce

rapidity: acceleration, celerity, pace, promptness, quickness, speed, swiftness, velocity

rapidly: apace, on the double

rapids: river, whitewater

rapine: plunder, seize

rapport: accord, affinity, bond, compatibility, connection, harmony, relationship, unity

rapscallion: rascal, rogue, scamp, villain

rapt: absorbed, captivated, charmed, deep, delighted, dreaming, ecstatic, enchanted, engrossed, enraptured, entranced, fascinated, immersed, intent, lost, preoccupied, spellbound, transported

rapture: bliss, contentment, delight, ecstasy, elation, enchantment, euphoria, exhilaration, happiness, rhapsody

rare: antique, beautiful, choice, distinctive, excellent, exceptional, exotic, exquisite, extraordinary, fine, infrequent, invaluable, isolated, limited, occasional, odd, precious, priceless, raw, scarce, seldom, select, spe-

cial, thin, uncommon, uncustomary, undercooked, underdone, unique, unlikely, unusual

rare and known to only a few: abstruse, arcane, recherché

rare book dealer: bibliopole

rare person or thing: rara avis

rarefied: attenuated, diluted, diminish, esoteric, lofty, reduced, refined, tenuous, thin

rarely: exceptionally, extra, hardly, infrequently, occasionally, once in a blue moon, seldom, unusually

raring: anxious, eager, impatient, keen, ready

rarity: anomaly, antique, curiosity, oddity, scarcity, wonder

rascal: blackguard, cad, devil, imp, knave, miscreant, ne'er-do-well, rake, rapscallion, rogue, roué, scalawag, scamp, scapegrace, scoundrel, trickster, troublemaker, villain

rash: abrupt, adventuresome, adventurous, bold, brash, careless, daring, desperate, epidemic, eruption, flood, foolhardy, foolish, hasty, headlong, headstrong, heady, heedless, hotheaded, impetuous, improvident, imprudent, impulsive, incautious, irrational, irresponsible, precipitate, precipitous, reckless, sudden, temerarious, thoughtless, unadvised, unthinking, unwary, unwise, venturesome, venturous, wave

rash, skin: eczema, hives, roseola, stigma

rasher: bacon slab

rashly, behaving: headlong, impetuous, impulsive, madcap, overhasty, precipitate, reckless

rasp: abrade, abrasive, file, grate, hoarseness, irritate, scrape, wheeze

raspberry: boo, catcall, hiss, razz, sound

raspberry feature: drupelet

raspberry genus: rubus

raspberry sections: acini

raspberry stem: cane

rasping: abrasive, grating, harsh, hoarse, raspy, raucous, rough

rat: betrayer, defect, deserter, fink, inform, informer, scab, snitch, snot, stool pigeon, stoolie, traitor, turncoat; pest, rodent, vermin

rat or mouse, like a: muriform, murine, myomorphic

rate: account, amount, appraise, assess, assessment, charge, class, classify, clip, cost, degree, earn, estimate,

evaluate, expense, fare, fee, grade, judge, merit, pace, percentage, price, proportion, quality, rank, ratio, scale, scold, speed, standard, tariff, tax, tempo, value, velocity

rate of activity: tempo

rate of body processes: metabolism

rather: accurately, alternatively, choice, contrary, enough, exactly, instead, moderately, preferably, preference, quite, relatively, significantly, somewhat, sooner, than

ratify: affirm, approve, authorize, bless, confirm, consent, endorse, establish, pass, sanction, seal, uphold, validate, verify

rating: class, classification, evaluation, grade, mark, rank, rebuke, reprimand, scolding, score, standing

ratio: correlation, degree, distribution, fraction, percent, percentage, proportion, quota, quotient, rate, relation, share

ratiocinate: argue

ration: allocate, allot, allotment, allowance, distribute, divide, divvy, dole, helping, measure, mete, portion, quota, serving, share

rational: balanced, calm, collected, cool, intelligent, levelheaded, logical, prudent, realistic, reasonable, sane, sensible, sound, stable, wise

rational and easily understood: lucid

rationale: basis, explanation, grounds, logic, motive, reason

rationalization of questions of right and wrong: casuistry

rationalize: explain, justify, reason, think

rattle: annoy, babble, chat, chatter, clack, clapper, clatter, confound, confuse, faze, fluster, jabber, jangle, jar, jiggle, noise, perplex, prate, rale, shake, sound, stun, toy, unnerve, upset

rattle, gourd-shaped: maraca

rattlebrained: dizzy, flighty, foolish, frivolous, giddy, irrational, silly, stupid, talkative

rattlesnake tail tip: button

rattlesnake, like a: crotaline

ratty: decayed, dilapidated, old, shabby, unkempt, worn

raucous: blaring, boisterous, braying, cacophonous, coarse, disorderly, gruff, harsh, hoarse, loud, noisy, piercing, rasping, rough, rowdy, strident, tumultuous, unruly

raunchy: coarse, dirty, explicit, filthy, foul, grimy, gross, lewd, obscene, smutty, unkempt, vulgar

ravage: annihilate, consume, crush, demolish, desolate, despoil, destroy, devastate, devastation, devour, forage, foray, harry, havoc, loot, overrun, pillage, plunder, raid, ransack, ruin, sack, scourge, spoil, trample, waste, wreck

rave: babble, blurb, bluster, declaim, enthuse, jabber, rage, ramble, rant, roar, storm, talk

ravel: complicate, crumble, disentangle, entangle, fray, free, loosen, muddle, perplex, separate, sleave, snarl, tangle, undo, unsew, untangle, untwist, unwind

raven: bird, black, blackbird, corvus, crow, ebony, jet

raven, concerning a: corvid

ravenous: desirous, edacious, famished, gluttonous, greedy, hungry, insatiable, lupine, predatory, rapacious, starved, voracious

ravine: abyss, aroyo, arroyo, canon, canyon, chasm, coulee, crevice, cut, dell, ditch, flume, gap, glen, gorge, gulch, gully, kloof, notch, pass, rift, valley, wadi, wady

raving: berserk, delirious, frenzied, fuming, irrational, mad, ranting, violent, wild

ravish: abuse, defile, deflower, despoil, force, pillage, plunder, raid, rape, seize, transport, violate

raw: abrade, basic, biting, bleak, chilly, coarse, cold, crude, cruel, cutting, damp, fresh, green, harsh, immature, inexperienced, naked, natural, nude, rare, rude, sore, stark, uncivilized, unclothed, uncooked, uncultivated, unexposed, unfair, unfinished, unprepared, unprocessed, unrefined, unripe, unseasoned, unskilled, untested, untrained, untried

rawboned: angular, gaunt, lanky, lean, scrawny

ray: alpha, beam, beta, emanation, fish, flair, flash, gamma, gleam, indication, irradiate, light, line, manta, moonbeam, particle, radial, radiate, radiation, shaft, shine, skate, streak, stripe, sunbeam, trace, vision

rays, concerning: radial

raze: bulldoze, decimate, demolish, destroy, dismantle, efface, erase, flatten, level, obliterate, overthrow, ruin, scrape, scratch, shave, smash, subvert, tear down, wreck

razor: blade, knife, shaver

razor leather strap for sharpening: strop

razz: banter, chaff, heckle, jest, joke, kid, needle, raspberry, rib, ridicule, taunt, tease

reach: accomplish, achieve, affect, ambit, amount, approach, arrive, attain, come, compass, contact, expanse, extend, extent, find, fulfill, gain, get at, grasp, influence, move, penetrate, purview, range, scope, span, stretch, strive, sway, touch

reachable: accessible, answer, impression, influence, obtainable, possible, reaction, response

react: answer, behave, counter, reply, respond

reaction: allergy, backlash, feedback, opinion, opposition, reflex, reply

reaction that is trained: conditioned reflex

reaction, antagonistic: backlash

reaction, automatic unthinking: knee-jerk reaction

reaction, involuntary physical: reflex

reaction, of an automatic: Pavlovian

reactionary: conservative, diehard, orthodox, traditionalist

reactions are measure of effectiveness or acceptability, person whose: sounding board

read: browse, comprehend, decipher, describe, descry, discern, express, foresee, foretell, grasp, interpret, learn, peruse, pore, predict, proof, recite, relate, scan, show, skim, study, tell, translate, understand

read aloud: recite

read and interpret: decipher, decode

read and write, able to: literate

read and write, unable to: illiterate

read as it stands: sic, stet

read carefully: peruse, pore, scrutinize

read hastily: glance at, scan, skim

read too much, people who: bibliobibuli

readable: clear, coherent, comprehensible, eloquent, engaging, intelligible, legible, pleasing

reader: anthology, bookworm, editor, elocutionist, lector, lecturer, proofreader, reciter, scholar; primer

reader of manuscript to determine publishability: referee

reader of scriptural passages at church: lector

reader, of an eager: avid, insatiable, voracious

readily: easily, freely, immediately, promptly, quickly, soon, speedily, willingly

readily convertible to cash, investment: liquid

readiness: address, alacrity, dexterity, eagerness, expedition, facility, preparedness, promptness, prowess, quickness, volubility

reading: declamation, lecture, lesson, perusal, recital, rendition, review, version

reading desk: lectern

reading disability: alexia, dyslexia

reading printed text into electronic form: optical character recognition, scanning

reading room: athenaeum, den

reading test where words are deleted at intervals: cloze

reading text with musical accompaniment: declamation

ready: active, adept, adroit, alert, all set, apt, arranged, attentive, available, convenient, dexterous, dextrous, eager, equipped, expeditious, facile, fit, fluent, fortify, game, handy, in the wings, likely, mature, on standby, on tap, organize, poised, prep, prepare, prepared, prime, primed, prompt, ripe, set, skillful, willing

ready for use: on tap, operational, ripe

ready-reference handbook: vade mecum

ready to go: alert, all set, set

ready-to-wear: pret-a-porter

real: actual, being, certain, factual, genuine, honest, literal, material, pure, serious, sincere, solid, substantive, tangible, true, valid

real and material: corporeal, palpable, tangible

real and not imaginary: actual, substantial, substantive

real and verifiable: authentic, authoritative, bona fide, genuine, reliable, true, veritable

real, quality of appearing to be: verisimilitude

realistic: down-to-earth, genuine, graphic, lifelike, matter-of-fact, practicable, practical, rational, reasonable, representative, sensible, sound, viable

realistic in art, writing: naturalistic, representational

reality: being, concreteness, existence, fact, substance, tangibility, truth

reality or fact, in: actually, de facto

reality to, to ascribe: hypostatize

reality, having: objective

reality, lacking material form or: disembodied, incorporeal

reality, painting with photographic: trompe l'oeil

reality, treat or regard as if having: reify

reality, underlying: essence, hypostasis, substance

realization: achievement, awakening, awareness, culmination, fulfillment, understanding

realization, accomplishment of things worked for: fruition

realize: accomplish, achieve, acquire, appreciate, apprehend, complete, conceive, fulfill, gain, obtain, reap, sense, think, understand

realize as profit: net

realized condition, fully: entelechy

really: actually, indeed, truly

realm: area, circle, country, demesne, department, division, domain, dominion, dynasty, empire, jurisdiction, kingdom, land, province, range, region, sphere, territory

reap: acquire, collect, garner, gather, glean, harvest

rear: breed, build, construct, educate, elevate, erect, lift, nurse, nurture, raise

rear, of the: aft, back, behind, end, last, stern, tail

rear car of train: caboose

rear of boat: stern

rear of boat, toward: abaft, aft

rear of horse, etc.: croup, crupper, haunches, rump

rear of ship, at the: astern

rear or tail part: caudal, posterior

rear skull bulge: inion

rearing on hind legs: rampant

reason: argument, brain, cause, discourse, explanation, intellect, intellectualize, logic, meaning, mind, motive, ponder, rationale, rationality, rationalize, sanity, sense, think, understanding, wherefore, why

reason and knowledge: nous

reason methodically and logically: ratiocinate

reason or justification for existing: raison d'être

reason, against: illogical, irrational

reason, concerning: rational

reason, for a still stronger: a fortiori

reason, of a seeming or professed: ostensible, ostensive, purported, specious

reason, seeming or professed: pretext

reason, to: argue, converse, debate, discourse, expostulate, remonstrate

reasonable: affordable, equitable, fair, feasible, inexpensive, just, legitimate, levelheaded, logical, moderate, modest, plausible, practical, prudent, rational, sane, sensible, sound, tenable, tolerable, valid, wise

reasoning: analysis, argument, basis, logic, rationale, thinking, thought

reasoning from general to specific: deduction, synthesis

reasoning from specific to general: induction

reasoning from specific to general, concerning: a posteriori, empirical, inductive

reasoning in a circle, of: circular

reasoning or intuition opposite: phenomenon

reasoning or intuition, something known by: noumenon

reasoning that is plausible but fallacious: sophistry

reasoning to arrive at truth, logical: dialectic

reasoning to conclusion, rather than intuition: discursive

reasoning with major and minor premise and conclusion: syllogism

reasoning, appealing to powers of: cogent, compelling, convincing, incisive, trenchant

reasoning, arrive at by: deduce, derive, infer

reasoning, based on abstract or speculative: metaphysical

reasoning, complicated: choplogic

reasoning, drawing of a conclusion by: deduction

reasoning, excessively subtle but plausible: casuistry, sophistry

reasoning, illogical: paralogism

reasoning, incorrectness of: fallacy

reasoning, using deduction in: a priori, deductive

reassure: cheer, comfort, convince, encourage, guarantee, uplift

rebate: abatement, deduction, diminish, discount, kickback, lessen, reduce, reduction, refund, reimbursement

rebel: adversary, anarchist, antagonist, arise, demagogue, denounce, dissenter, iconoclast, insubordinate, insurgent, mutineer, mutiny, nonconformist, radical, recusant, renegade, revolt, revolutionary, revolutionist, riot, rise, secede

rebel against church dogma: heretic

rebellion: defiance, disturbance, insurrection, mutiny, outbreak, revolt, revolution, sedition, upheaval, uprising

rebellion against authority, open: mutiny

rebellion, instance of: insurgence, insurrection, revolt, sedition, uprising

rebellion, suppression of: pacification

rebellion, to start a: foment, instigate

rebellious: alienated, contumacious, cranky, defiant, disobedient, fractious, incorrigible, insolent, insubordinant, insubordinate, insurgent, irritable, mutinous, obstinate, recalcitrant, refractory, restive, rioting, seditious, unruly

rebellious overthrow, sudden: coup, coup d'état, putsch

rebels against system, one who: agitator, firebrand, incendiary, malcontent, subversive

rebels or terrorists, military action against: counterinsurgency

rebirth: regeneration, reincarnation, rejuvenation, renaissance, renascence, renewal, resurrection, revival

rebirth, political: risorgimento

reborn thing: phoenix

rebound: boomerang, bounce, carom, echo, recoil, recovery, reflect, resilience, resound, retrieve, return, reverberate, ricochet, spring, stot

rebound after hitting surface at angle: ricochet

rebuff: brushoff, check, chide, disregard, ignore, rebuke, rebut, refusal, refuse, reject, repel, reprimand, reprove, repulse, scold, slap, slight, snub, spurn

rebuke: admonish, admonition, beat, berate, castigate, chastise, check, chide, criticize, lecture, lesson, objurgate, reprehend, repress, reprimand, reproach, reproof, reprove, restrain, scold, slap, snub

rebut: confute, contradict, disprove, invalidate, rebuff, refute, repel, reply, repulse

recalcitrant: defiant, disobedient, headstrong, obstinate, rebellious, resisting, stubborn, undisciplined, unmanageable, unruly, wild, willful

recall: annul, awaken, cancel, cite, countermand, elicit, extract, memory, nullify, place, recognize, recollect, reconvene, remember, remind, reminisce, repeal, rescind, restore, retain, retrace, retract, retrieve, revoke, withdraw

recall of past events: anamnesis, reminiscence, retrospection

recant: abandon, abjure, abrogate, annul, cancel, disavow, disclaim, renege, renounce, repudiate, retract, revoke, unsay, withdraw

recapitulate: paraphrase, recap, recount, rehash, reiterate, repeat, restate, review, summarize, synopsize

recapitulation: peroration, reprise, summary

recede: abate, decrease, depart, diminish, dwindle, ebb, fade, regress, retract, retreat, retrograde, subside, withdraw

receipt: acceptance, admission, arrival, bill, notice, release, scrip, slip, stub, voucher

receipts: cash, earnings, gate, income, money, payments, proceeds, profits, revenue

receive: accept, acquire, admit, catch, collect, derive, earn, endure, experience, get, greet, inherit, obtain, support, take, take in, welcome

receiver: addressee, beneficiary, collector, fence, heir, recipient, telephone

receiver of benefits, property: beneficiary

receiver of stolen goods: fence

recent: contemporary, current, fresh, late, modern, neo, neotenic, new, newfangled

receptacle: basket, bin, bottle, box, bucket, can, canister, carton, case, cell, chest, container, crate, cup, font, holder, jar, pitcher, repository, tank, tray, tub, urn, vase, vat, vessel

reception: acceptance, admission, admittance, affair, at home, entertainment, function, gathering, greeting, levee, meeting, ovation, party, soiree, tea, welcome

receptive: amenable, friendly, hospitable, interested, open, responsive, sensitive, sympathetic

recess: alcove, apse, cave, cavity, cleft, closet, cove, cranny, crypt, depression, hole, niche, nook, sinus

recess or break: adjournment, breather, hiatus, intermission, interval, respite, rest, retreat, suspension, vacation

recess in wall: niche

recession: bust, decline, depression, off year

recherché: choice, exceptional, exotic, exquisite, forced, fresh, novel, overblown, precious, pretentious, rare, superior, uncommon, unusual

recipe: directions, formula, instructions, pattern, prescription, process, rule

recipient: awardee, beneficiary, donee, heir, legatee, receiver

reciprocal: changeable, complementary, correlative, corresponding, duplicate, equivalent, exchanged, interdependent, mutual, shared, twin

reciprocate: alternate, correspond, equal, exchange, interchange, match, recompense, repay, requite, retaliate, return, swap, trade

recital: account, concert, description, musical, narration, narrative, performance, presentation, program, rehearsal, report, story, tale

recite: address, chant, communicate, describe, enumerate, explain, list, narrate, quote, read, recapitulate, recount, relate, speak, tell

recite in singing tone: cantillate, intone

reckless: adventurous, bold, carefree, careless, dangerous, daredevil, daring, devil-may-care, feckless, foolish, hasty, headlong, heedless, impetuous, imprudent, impulsive, indifferent, irresponsible, madcap, neglectful, negligent, precipitate, rash, regardless, remiss, temerarious, thoughtless, unadvised, unheeding, wild

reckless ride: joyride

recklessness: abandon, desperation, disregard, foolhardiness, temerity

reckon: account, add, aret, assume, calculate, cipher, compute, consider, count, deem, determine, enumerate, estimate, figure, guess, judge, number, numerate, opine, rate, regard, rely, repute, sum, suppose, surmise, tally, tell, think, total, understand

reckoning: bill, charge, computation, cost, count, debt, invoice, rate, score, settlement, statement, summation, tally

reclaim: recall, recover, reform, refurbish, regenerate, repair, resolve, restitute, restore, salvage, save, tame, train

recline: accumbent, lay, lean, lie, loll, lounge, recumbent, relax, reposing, rest, slope, sprawl, stretch

reclining: flat, loner, recluse, recumbent, troglodyte

recluse: anchoress, anchorite, cloistered, eremite, hermit, hidden, loner, monk, nun, secluded, sequestered, solitary, troglodyte

recognition: acceptance, attention, awareness, credit, gratitude, identification, notice, remembering

recognize: accept, acknowledge, admit, appreciate, apprehend, approve, distinguish, greet, honor, identify, know, note, notice, perceive, recall, remark, remember, review, revise, salute, see, spot, understand

recognize as different: discern

recognized generally: acknowledged, received

recognized officially: accredited

recoil: backlash, blench, blink, dodge, flinch, jerk, kick, quail, retreat, reverse, shrink, shy, wince, withdraw

recollect: arouse, awaken, bethink, cite, recall, remember, reminisce

recollection: anamnesis, memory, recall, remembrance, reminiscence, retrospection

recommend: advise, advocate, counsel, encourage, endorse, entrust, praise, prescribe, propose, refer, sanction, second, tout, urge

recommendation: advice, direction, ent, instruction, reference, suggestion, urging

recompense: amends, atonement, award, bounty, compensate, compensation, indemnify, pay, premium, reciprocate, recover, reimburse, renumerate, reparation, repay, repayment, restitution, retribution, reward, salary, wage, wages

reconcile: absolve, accord, adapt, adjust, arbitrate, atone, conciliate, conform, expiate, harmonize, intercede,

RED

alizarin crimson	coral-pink	murrey	Turkey red	fulvous
alpenglow	cranberry	old rose	Venetian red	ginger
annatto	crimson	orange-red	vermeil	henna
beet red	crimson lake	oxblood	vermilion	light red-brown
blood red	damask	paprika	wild cherry	liver
bois de rose	dark red	peach	wine	mahogany
bougainvillea	deep red	Persian red		nutmeg
Bourdeaux	faded rose	pinkish red	**Red-Brown**	ocher
brick red	fire-engine red	ponceau	auburn	oxblood
bright red	fuchsia	poppy	baize	piccolopasso
brownish red	garnet	Prussian red	bay	roan
cadmium red	geranium	puce	brick	rubiginous
cardinal	grenadine	purple-red	burgundy	rust
carioca	gules	rhodamine	burnt ocher	russet/rufous
carmine	Indian red	rose madder	burnt sienna	sand
carnelian	iron red	rubious	caramel	sedge
Castilian red	jockey	ruby	Castilian brown	sepia
cerise	light red	rust	chestnut	sienna
cherry	lobster	scarlet	chocolate	sorrel
Chinese red	madder lake	solferino	cinnamon	terra cotta
cinnabar	magenta	stammel	cocoa	titian
claret	maroon	strawberry	cordovan	Venetian red
cochineal	Mars red	tile red	ferruginous	vermilion/vermiel ❦

---

mediate, moderate, pacify, placate, propitiate, rectify, resolve, restore, reunite, satisfy, settle, square

reconcile and blend: syncretize

recondite: abstruse, ambiguous, arcane, concealed, cryptic, dark, deep, difficult, esoteric, hidden, mysterious, mystic, obscure, occult, profound

reconnaissance: exploration, inspection, observation, scouting, survey

reconnoiter: examine, explore, inquire, inspect, look, probe, scout, survey

reconsider: amend, modify, reevaluate, reexamine, reflect, replan, rethink, revise

reconstruct: copy, mend, overhaul, patch, reassemble, rebuild, recondition, renovate, reorganize, repair, restore

record: account, achievement, album, annal, ark, background, calendar, catalog, catalogue, chart, chronicle, date, diary, directory, disc, disk, document, enscroll, enter, entry, experience, file, history, journal, legend, list, log, memo, memoir, minutes, note, preserve, register, report, score, show, tab, tape, transcribe, transcript, videotape

record album or CD collector: discophilist

record for later broadcasting: transcribe

record in detail, to: document

record item by item: list, tally

record of a transaction in first draft: protocol

record of business carried on by organization or at conference: proceedings, transactions

record of employment and education: curriculum vitae, CV, résumé, vita

record of events, daily personal: diary, journal

record of happenings worth remembering: memorabilia

record of historical events, extended: annals, chronicles

record of line of ancestors: pedigree

record of proceedings: acta

record of proceedings at meeting: minutes

record player: gramophone, phonograph

record player needle: stylus

record player, moving arm of: pickup, tone arm

recorder (musical): blockflote, flute

recorder, whistlelike mouthpiece on: fipple

recording media on laser-read disc: CD, compact disc

recording on record, tape, disk: digital

recording, rapid fluctuation in pitch of sound: flutter

recording, slow fluctuation in pitch of sound: wow

recordings of an artist or group: discography

records, one in charge of official: registrar

records, place or collection of historical: archive, dossier

recount: convey, describe, enumerate, explain, narrate, portray, recite, rehash, rehearse, relate, repeat, state, tell

recoup: regain, retrieve

recover: amend, balance, compensate, convalesce, mend, rally, reclaim, recoup, recruit, recuperate, redeem, reform, regain, reimburse, repossess, rescue, restore, retake, retrieve, salvage, snap out of it

recover health, something that helps one: restorative

recover or restore, help to: resuscitate, revive

recover ownership of by paying: redeem

recover personal property unlawfully taken, help to: replevin, replevy

recover quickly, ability to: buoyancy, resilience

recover to good condition or useful life: rehabilitate

recoverable goods, at sea: ligan

recovering to good health: convalescent, recuperating, valetudinarian

recovery: comeback, convalescence, cure, gain, heal, improve, improvement, mend, procure, rebound, recuperation, redeem, rehabilitate, revive, upturn

recreant: apostate, betrayer, coward, cowardly, craven, deserter, disloyal, faithless, spiritless, traitor, unfaithful, untrue, yellow

recreation: amusement, diversion, entertainment, exercise, frolic, game, hobby, leisure, pastime, picnic, play, pleasure, relaxation, sport

recruit: assemble, beginner, draft, draftee, enlist, enroll, inductee, muster, neophyte, newcomer, novice, reinforce, rookie, soldier, tyro, volunteer

recruit forcibly: impress, shanghai

rectangle: figure, oblong, parallelogram, plane, square

rectify: adjust, amend, correct, cure, emend, fix, improve, purify, rebuild, redress, refine, reform, remedy, repair, right, straighten

rectitude: decency, goodness, honesty, integrity, morality, righteousness, uprightness, virtue

rector: clergyman, clergywoman, cleric, headmaster, minister, pastor, priest, principal, proctor

rectory: benefice, manse, parsonage, presbytery, vicarage

rectum or other body cavity, plug of medicine put into: suppository

rectum, liquid medicine injected into: enema

recumbent: flat, idle, inactive, lying, prone, prostrate, reclining, resting, supine

recuperate: convalesce, heal, improve, mend, recover, regain

recur: iterate, persist, reappear, reiterate, repeat, return

recurrence in mind of a tune, thought: perseveration

recurrent: chronic, cyclical, habitual, reappearing, recurring, regular, repeating, repetitive, returning

recurring at regular intervals: intermittent, periodic

recyclable text: boilerplate

recycled or unoriginal substance: rehash

red and white horse: roan

red-blooded: energetic, healthy, robust, spirited, strong

red-handed: blatantly, caught, in flagrante delicto, openly

red-hot: burning, glowing, heated, hippest, new, popular, scorching, sizzling, sweltering

red initial letter in manuscript: uncial

red ink item: debit, debt, loss

red-letter: banner, happy, memorable, notable, noteworthy

red pepper: capsicum, cayenne, pimiento

red table wine: claret

red tape in government: bureaucracy

red-wrapped cheese: Edam

redact: edit

redden: blush, color, crimson, flush, glow, rouge, ruddy

redeem: atone, balance, cash, compensate, convert, defray, exchange, free, fulfill, ransom, reclaim, recover, regain, release, repay, rescue, restore, save

redemption: ransom, salvation

redistrict for political advantage: gerrymander

redolent: aromatic, balmy, fragrant, perfumed, reminiscent, savory, scented, spicy, suggestive

redouble: augment, breastwork, enhance, fort, fortification, heighten, intensify, magnify, reinforce, repeat, retrace, stronghold

redoubtable: awesome, dreadful, fearful, fearsome, formidable, frightening, illustrious, imminent

redound: accrue, cause, contribute, recoil, resound, return, reverberate

redress: adjust, amend, atone, change, compensation, correct, counteract, help, indemnity, negate, offset, payment, recompense, rectify, reform, relief, relieve, remedy, reparation, vindicate

reduce: abase, abate, abridge, annihilate, bate, change, condense, conquer, contract, curb, curtail, cut, debase, decrease, defeat, degrade, demote, deplete, depreciate, diet, dilute, diminish, discount, downgrade, dwindle, emaciate, humble, humiliate, impair, lessen, level, lower, minimize, overcome, pare, rebate, recede, scale, shorten, slash, slow, subdue, subjugate, thin, trim, weaken

reduction: abatement, attrition, contraction, curtailment, cut, cutback, decline, degradation, devaluation, discount, downgrading, markdown, rebate, shrinkage, subtraction

reduction in membership or personnel, natural: attrition

reduction of debt or liability in gradual manner: amortization

redundant: copious, excessive, extra, exuberant, irrelevant, loquacious, overabundant, overflowing, prolix, reiterating, repetitious, superfluous, surplus, tautological, verbose, wordy

redundant words: pleonasm

redundant, to make: obviate, preempt

redwood: coniferous, evergreen, sequoia, tree

reed: arrow, cane, dart, grass, instrument, oboe, pipe, plant, spear, stalk, stem, tule

reef: atoll, bank, bar, bioherm, coral reef, key, ledge, lode, ridge, sandbar, shoal, vein

reef near coastline: barrier reef

reef or island, small rocky: skerry

reef, body of water separated from sea by: lagoon

reef, ringlike coral island or: atoll

reek: emanate, emit, exude, fume, funk, odor, smell, smoke, steam, stench, stink, vapor, vent

reel: bobbin, careen, dance, drum, lurch, rock, roll, rotate, spin, spindle, spool, stagger, stumble, sway, swim, swing, teeter, totter, turn, waver, windlass, wobble

reel for holding thread, yarn, magnetic tape: bobbin, quill, spindle

refer: advert, allude, appeal, ascribe, assign, attribute, cite, commit, confer, consult, direct, guide, identify, ipute, mention, name, quote, recommend, relate, send, specify, submit, transfer

refer a matter or case elsewhere: remit

referee: adjudge, arbiter, arbitrator, conciliator, determine, intermediary, judge, mediate, mediator, moderator, official, umpire

reference: aspect, associating, connection, credentials, footnote, implication, innuendo, meaning, mention, quote, recommendation, remark, respect, source, testimonial

reference at bottom of page: footnote

reference book: almanac, atlas, dictionary, encyclopedia, manual, thesaurus

reference for plotting points: axis

reference manual: vade mecum

reference or personal recommendation: testimonial

reference point: datum line, starting point

reference to authoritative source: citation

references, list of: bibliography

referendum: election, mandate, poll, vote

referring to, concerning, pertaining to: anent, apropos of

refine: better, clarify, cleanse, cultivate, distill, edit, elevate, filter, finish, groom, improve, perfect, polish, purify, rarefy, smelt, smooth, strain

refine, as ore: smelt

refined: civilized, courteous, cultured, delicate, elegant, fastidious, genteel, gentlemanly, graceful, highbred, ladylike, polished, polite, processed, recherché, suave, urbane

refined affected word or phrase: genteelism

refined, highly: ethereal

refinement: civility, clarification, culture, elegance, filtering, finesse, finish, gentility, good breeding, grace, polish, purification, taste

reflect: cast, cogitate, consider, contemplate, deflect, deliberate, divert, echo, express, image, imitate, meditate, mirror, muse, ponder, reason, ruminate, shine, study, think

reflecting light: glaring, relucent

reflecting raised tiles as dividers on highways: Botts dots

reflection: absorption, appearance, cogitation, contemplation, deliberation, idea, image, impression, light, likeness, meditation, opinion, rumination, sentiment, thinking, thought, view

reflective: meditative, pensive, pondering, ruminative, thoughtful

reflector in optical instruments: speculum

reflex movement of organism toward stimulus: taxis

reflex or involuntary functioning: automatism

reflex-testing rubber hammer: plexor

reflux: ebb

reform: alter, amend, better, change, convert, correct, emend, improve, mend, rebuild, reclaim, rectify, redress, rehabilitate, remedy, renew, reorganize, repair, restore, revise

refractory: bullheaded, cantankerous, contrary, difficult, disobedient, headstrong, incorrigible, intractable, mullish, obstinate, opinionated, perverse, rebellious, stubborn, ungovernable, unmanageable, unresponsive, unruly, unyielding, willful

refrain: abstain, avoid, cease, check, curb, desist, forbear, forego, forgo, halt, inhibit, restrain, withhold; chorus, music, song, tune

refresh: cheer, cool, energize, enliven, freshen, invigorate, jog, modernize, prompt, reanimate, recreate, rejuvenate, renew, renovate, replenish, rest, restore, revise, revive, stimulate, strengthen, update

refreshing: balmy, bracing, crisp, different, enervating, exhilarating, invigorating, tonic, unique

refreshment: beverage, collation, drink, food, regale, snack, treat

refrigerant: freon, icer

refrigerate: air-condition, chill, cool, freeze, ice

refrigeration regulating device: thermostat

refuge: ark, asylum, cover, covert, harbor, haven, hideout, home, hospital, immunity, lair, oasis, port, protection, relief, resort, resource, retreat, sanctuary, shelter, shield

refugee: defector, DP, émigré, exile, expatriate, foreigner, fugitive, runaway

refugee from native country: émigré

refulgent: bright, brilliant, glowing, luminous, radiant, resplendent, shining

refund: indemnify, kickback, rebate, reimburse, remunerate, repay, retribution, return

refurbish: brighten, clean, freshen, recondition, redo, remodel, renew, renovate, restore, revamp, update

refusal: contradiction, declination, denial, nay, negation, option, rejection, turndown

refusal, blunt: rebuff, repulse, snub

refuse: debris, dross, excrement, garbage, junk, litter, offal, rubbish, scrap, slag, trash, waste

refuse barge: scow

refuse to acknowledge as one's own: disown, repudiate

refuse to buy or use as part of protest: boycott

refuse to include: ostracize

refuse, to: balk, decline, defy, deny, disallow, disavow, disdain, dissent, evade, forbid, prohibit, rebuff, reject, repel, repudiate, scorn, spurn, veto, withhold

refusing to move: restive

refutation: argument, elenchus, rebuttal

refute: answer, avoid, confute, contradict, counter, deny, disclaim, discredit, disprove, invalidate, overthrow, rebut, silence

refute false statements or opinions: debunk

regain: recapture, recoup, recover, recuperate, redeem, repossess, retake, retrieve

regal: august, grand, imperial, imposing, kingly, lordly, magnificent, majestic, noble, princely, queenly, royal, splendid, stately

regal residence: palace

regale: amuse, banquet, delicacy, delight, dinner, entertain, feast, party, refreshment, spread

regard: adjudge, admiration, admire, affection, air, appearance, aspect, assay, attend, attention, behold, care, concern, consider, contemplate, contemplation, deem, esteem, estimate, estimation, eye, gaze, glance, heed, hold, homage, honor, interest, look, mind, note, notice, observe, reference, relation, remark, respect, revere, sake, think, treat, value, view, watch

regard highly: esteem

regard worshipfully: adore

regard, high: deference, respect, reverence

regarding: about, anent, apropos, apropos of, as to, concerning, in re, pertaining to, relating to

regardless: although, anyhow, careless, despite, inattentive, indifferent, irrespective, neglectful, negligent, nevertheless, unconcerned, willy-nilly

regards: beholds, compliments, good wishes, salutations

regenerate: exhilarate, invigorate, reborn, recreate, redeem, reform, refresh, renew, renovate, reproduce, restore, revitalize, revive

regent: director, governor, minister, official, ruler, viceroy

regimen: administration, control, diet, government, menu, procedure, process, regime, rule, system

regiment: cadre, control, corps, order, soldiers, troops

region: area, belt, climate, country, district, division, domain, field, kingdom, neighborhood, part, place, precinct, province, realm, scope, section, sector, sphere, terrain, territory, tract, vicinity, zone

regional: local, parochial, provincial, sectional, territorial

region's surface features: topography

register: agenda, annal, archives, blotter, book, calendar, catalog, certify, chronical, diary, docket, enlist, enrol, enroll, enter, entry, file, indicate, join, list, membership, record, roll, roster, schedule, show, tally

register in a college as candidate for degree: matriculate

regnant: predominant, prevalent, reigning, ruling, sovereign, widespread

regress: back, deteriorate, recede, relapse, retreat, retrograde, return, reverse, revert, rollback, withdraw

regret: anguish, apologize, bitterness, compunction, demur, deplore, disappointment, distress, grief, grieve, heartache, heartbreak, lament, lamentation, mourn, pang, qualm, remorse, repent, repentance, repine, rue, scruple, sorrow, sorry, woe

regretful: apologetic, contrite, deplorable, disappointed, penitent, remorseful, repentant, rueful, sorry, woeful

regular: automatic, common, complete, consistent, constant, continual, customary, daily, dependable, established, even, everyday, faithful, fixed, formal, general, genuine, habitual, methodical, natural, normal, orderly, ordinary, periodic, proper, recurrent, rhythmic, routine, serial, standard, stated, steady, systematic, thorough, typical, uniform, usual, utter

regular and recurring: intermittent, periodic

regular and repeating: continual

regular and uniform: consistent

regular customer: patron

regulate: adjust, administer, allocate, arrange, balance, clock, conduct, control, correct, direct, discipline, establish, gauge, govern, guide, man-age, modulate, monitor, order, organize, pace, rectify, rule, settle, standardize, temper, time

regulation: canon, code, codification, decree, edict, law, order, ordinance, precept, regiment, requirement, rule, statute

regulator: director, governor, manager, switch, thermostat, valve

rehabilitate: improve, recondition, recover, reinstate, renovate, restore

rehash: reiterate, repeat, summarize

rehearsal: dry run, trial run

rehearse: describe, detail, drill, enumerate, exercise, instruct, narrate, practice, prepare, recapitulate, recite, recount, reenact, repeat, retell, review, study, test, train

reheated: réchauffé

reign: authority, command, control, dominance, dominate, dominion, empire, govern, influence, kingdom, monarchy, power, predominate, prevail, regime, rule, sovereignty

reigning: regnant, ruling

reigns, period between two: interregnum

reimburse: compensate, indemnify, offset, pay, recompense, recoup, recover, refund, remunerate, repay, return

rein: bridle, check, compose, control, curb, deterrent, guide, harness, leash, repress, restrain, slow, stop, strap, suppress

reincarnation: metempsychosis, transmigration

reindeer: caribou

reinforce: augment, back, bolster, brace, buttress, energize, fortify, pillar, prop, shore, strengthen, supplement, support, toughen

reinstate: recall, reestablish, rehabilitate, rehire, reinstitute, restore, revive

reintroduce: reestablish, reinstitute, renew, revive

reiterate: harp, recapitulate, rehash, repeat, resume, stress

reject: adjure, blackball, cancel, cashier, castaway, decline, deny, disallow, discard, disdain, dismiss, disown, eject, eliminate, forsake, jettison, jilt, ostracize, rebuff, refuse, renounce, repel, reprobate, repudiate, repulse, scorn, scrap, snub, spurn, veto

reject and throw away: discard, jettison

reject commitment or responsibility: disavow, disown, forsake

reject lover: jilt

reject or shun: ostracize

reject or treat with contempt: disdain, spurn

reject validity or authority of: abjure, forswear, renounce, repudiate

rejection: denial, disallowance, exclusion, ostracism, rebuff, refusal, repulse, snub, turndown

rejection of moral and religious values: anarchism, nihilism

rejoice: celebrate, delight, elate, enjoy, exult, gladden, glory, jubilate, please, relish, triumph

rejoin: answer, assemble, reply, respond, retort, reunite

rejuvenate: recondition, refresh, regenerate, reinvigorate, renew, restore, revitalize, revive

rekindle: relight, renew, revitalize, revive

relapse: backslide, decline, degenerate, deteriorate, recurrence, regress, revert, setback, sink, slip, weaken

relate: appertain, apply, associate, belong, commune, connect, convey, correlate, describe, detail, disclose, express, link, narrate, pertain, recite, recount, refer, report, reveal, speak, state, tell, touch

relate to intimately: commune

related: affiliated, akin, associated, cognate, connected, correspondent, enate, germane, interconnected, intertwined, joint, kin, kindred, mutual, parallel, pertinent, synonymous, told

related but separated by generations: removed

related but subordinate or auxiliary: adjunct

related by blood: akin, consanguineous, kindred

related in structure and evolutionary origin: homologous

related on father's side: agnate

related on mother's side: enate

related or same in meaning: synonymous

related superficially: divergent, tangential

related to a subject: germane, pertinent, relevant

relating harmoniously: compatible, on the same wavelength

relating to: anent, apropos, concerning, pertaining, referring to

relation: account, affiliation, affinity, association, bond, connection, correlation, family, kin, kinship, kinsman, kinswoman, ratio, reference, relative, sibling

relation in degree or number between two things: proportion, ratio

relation to others, position or rank in: footing, standing

relation to, in: regarding, vis-à-vis

relations, friendly: détente, rapprochement

relationship: affiliation, alliance, association, blood, bond, connection, correlation, friendship, kinship, link, marriage, rapport, tie in, tie-in

relationship break: rift

relationship by nature or character: affinity, kinship

relationship of aspects of subject to each other and to whole: perspective

relationship of correspondence, equivalence, or identity: symmetry

relationship of mutual trust or affinity: communion, rapport

relationship that is free of physical desire, having: platonic

relationship to each other, having the same: mutual, reciprocal

relationship, close: affinity, liaison

relationship, formation of close human: bond, bonding

relationship, political, social, psychological forces in a: dynamic

relationship, reciprocal: correlation, mutuality, reciprocity

relationships within a group, study of: sociometry

relative: ancestor, aunt, brother, cousin, dad, daughter, dependent, family, father, grandchild, granddaughter, grandfather, grandmother, grandparent, grandson, in-law, kin, kindred, kinsman, kinswoman, mom, mother, nephew, niece, parent, relation, sib, sibling, sister, son, tribe, uncle

relative, being: associated, comparable, comparative, connected, contingent, correlative, corresponding, pertinent, proportionate, relevant

relatives in jobs, favoritism shown to: nepotism

relax: abate, clam, divert, ease, idle, languish, lessen, let one's hair down, loll, loose, loosen, lounge, meditate, mellow, mitigate, recline, reduce, relieve, rest, simmer, slack, slacken, soften, take it easy, unbend, unclench, unwind

relaxation: amusement, calmness, diversion, ease, entertainment, hobby, leisure, pleasure, recreation, repose, rest, tranquility

relaxing: sedative

relaxing of tension: détente, rapprochement

relaxing of law or obligation: dispensation

relay: carry, communicate, deliver, forward, post, race, shift, station, transfer, transmit

relay race last person: anchor

relay race stick: baton

relay race unit: leg

release: absolve, acquit, bail, clear, commute, deliver, disband, discharge, disengage, eliminate, emancipate, emit, exempt, exonerate, extricate, free, freedom, let go, liberate, loosen, manumit, mitigate, news, pardon, parole, publication, publish, ransom, relieve, relinquish, remit, rescue, spring, story, trip, turn loose, unbind, unchain, uncork, undo, unfasten, unleash, untie, vent, yield

relegate: assign, banish, charge, classify, commit, deport, dismiss, downgrade, entrust, exile, expel, ostracize, remove, shun

relent: abate, acquiesce, bend, comply, dissolve, ease, melt, moderate, slacken, soften, subside, wane, yield

relentless: adamant, continuous, determined, ferocious, fierce, hard, harsh, incessant, inexorable, inflexible, merciless, persistent, rigid, rigorous, severe, steady, stern, strict, tenacious, unbending, unstoppable, unyielding

relevant: ad rem, admissible, allowable, applicable, apposite, appropriate, apropos, apt, associated, connected, correlated, fitting, germane, material, pertinent, related, significant, timely, to the point, Weser

relevant relationship, interconnection: bearing

relevant superficially: tangential

relevant to occasion or time: opportune, seasonable, timely, well-timed

reliable: constant, credible, devoted, faithful, honest, loyal, proven, responsible, solid, sound, stable, true, trusty, verified

reliable and honest: reputable

reliable and loyal: dependable, stalwart, steadfast, trusty

reliance: credence, loyalty, mainstay, trust

relic: artifact, heirloom, keepsake, memento, oldie, ruin, token

relief: aid, antidote, assistance, break, breather, cure, diversion, easement, food, lift, map, remedy, respite, succor, support

relief design on metal: repoussé

relief in sculpture: bas-relief, basso-relievo, low relief

relieve: absolve, assuage, dismiss, exempt, help, palliate, relax, rescue, soothe, spell, sub, substitute

relieve of problem: disembarrass, disencumber

relieve oneself of thoughts or feelings: confess, unbosom

religion: affiliation, belief, church, creed, denomination, orthodoxy, spirituality, theology

RELATED TERMS

religion and the nature of God, study of: theology

religion based on one god: monotheism

religion based on several gods: polytheism

religion believing in a self-sufficient lifestyle that rejects influences of modern life: Amish

religion believing in a simple way of life with communal property: Shakers

religion believing in Ali and his descendents as the successor to Muhammad: Shiites

religion believing in baptism by total immersion during early teens and older: Baptists

religion believing in Calvinism: Presbyterian Church

religion believing in devotion to the Hindu god Vishnu: Hare Krishna

religion believing in faith healing and founded by Mary Baker Eddy: Christian Science

religion believing in finding enlightenment through meditation: Buddhism

religion believing in holiness or Christian perfection: Pentecostal Church

religion believing in individual responsibility and bible study: Methodists

religion believing in Islam: Black Muslims, Moslems

religion believing in Islamic mysticism: Sufism

religion believing in Judaism but adapting it to modern life: Conservative Judaism

religion believing in reincarnation: Hinduism

religion believing in simplicity and plain living: Mennonites

religion believing in strict interpretation of the Torah as in the Talmud: Orthodox Judaism

religion believing in strict rituals, joyous worship, mysticism: Chasidim, Hasidim

religion believing in the authority of the bible: Protestantism

religion believing in the doctrine and discipline of the Church of England: Anglicans

religion believing in the episcopal form of church government: Episcopalians

religion believing in the first four caliphs as the successor to Muhammad: Sunni

religion believing in the Gospels, faith, grace over sacraments: Evangelicals

religion believing in the immortality and transmigration of the soul: Jainism

religion believing in the primacy of the patriarch of Constantinople: Eastern Orthodox

religion believing in the second coming of Christ, preached door-to-door: Jehovah's Witnesses

religion believing in the second coming of Christ, Sabbath on Saturday: Seventh-day Adventists

religion believing in the teachings of Lao-tzu: Taoism

religion believing in the universal struggle between light and darkness: Zoroastrianism

religion believing in worshipping nature and ancestors, native to Japan: Shinto

religion believing that all people can perceive God in their soul: Quakers, Society of Friends

religion founded by Joseph Smith: Church of Jesus Christ of the Latter-day saints, Mormon Church

religion in affected way, devoted to: holier-than-thou, pharisaical, religiose, sanctimonious

religion name given to French Protestants in the 16th and 17th century: Huguenots

religion on the basis of disbelief in the existence of God or gods, rejection of: atheism

religion on the basis that there is no proof that God exists, rejection of: agnosticism

religion rejected: atheism

religion that mixes Hinduism and Islam: Sikhism

religion that rejects the doctrines of the Trinity: Unitarianism

religion that was founded by Martin Luther in the 16th century: Lutheran Church

religion, affirm belief in: profess

religion, cut off from membership in: excommunicate

religion, devoted to: devout, pious

religion, devout follower of: devotee, votary

religion, one who has no: heathen, pagan

religion, recent convert to: neophyte, proselyte

religion, sixth century, believing in adult baptism, church-state separation, nonviolence: Anabaptists

religion, unbeliever with respect to particular: infidel ❧

religions, movement promoting unity among: ecumenicalism, ecumenism

religious: believing, ecclesiastical, ethical, monk, moral, nun, pontifical, priestly, reverent, righteous, sacred, sanctimonious, staunch, theological

RELATED TERMS

religious anointing: unction

religious belief other than orthodox: heresy, heterodoxy

religious belief that God created world and controls it: theism

religious belief that God created world and then left: deism

religious belief that God knows all and ordains fate of souls: predestination

religious beliefs or religion: persuasion

religious beliefs, recognition of rights of those with different: toleration

religious career, inclination to: calling, vocation

religious ceremony or rite, person participating in or officiating: celebrant

religious ceremony where penis foreskin is removed: circumcision

religious ceremony, formal: consecration, solemnization

religious ceremony, to put oil on during: anoint

religious denomination, adhering to strict limits of: partisan, sectarian

religious devotion: piety

religious devotion, one who leads life of: ascetic

religious ecstasy: theopathy

religious envoy: missionary

religious faith, abandonment of one's: apostasy

religious hermit: anchoress, anchoret, anchorite, eremite, recluse

religious image: icon

religious life, layperson dedicated to: oblate

religious literature: hierology

religious matters, having broad tolerant views of: latitudinarian

religious matters, referring to non-profane, secular, temporal religious meeting, secret or illegal: conventicle

religious observance, one who is strict about the rules of: precisian

religious offering: oblation

religious order but has not taken final vows, person in: novice

religious order candidate: postulant

religious place, violation of a: defilement, desecration, profanation, sacrilege

religious principle or beliefs: catechism, creed, doctrine, dogma, gospel, tenets

religious ritual: liturgy, rite

religious ritual marking life transition: rite of passage

religious ritual's pouring of fluid: libation

RELIGIONS, SECTS, AND BELIEFS

Adventist	Copt	Karaites	Nazarite	Sikhism
Albigensian	Covenanters	Lamaism	Nichiren Buddhism	Soka Gakkai
Amish	Docetism	Latter-day Saint/	Orphism	Buddhism
Anabaptist	Druses	Mormonism	Orthodox Judaism	Sufism
Anglican	Dunker	Lollard	Parseeism	Sunni
anthroposophy	Eastern Orthodoxy	Lutheranism	Plymouth Brethren	Swedenborgian
antinomian	Episcopalianism	Magianism	Protestantism	Taoism
Assemblies of God	Ethical Culture	Mahayana Buddhism	Puritan	theosophy
Babism	Evangelicalism	Mahdism	Quaker	Tractarian
Bahaism	Gnostic	Mandaeism	Rastafarianism	Trappist
Baptist church	Gnosticism	Manichaeism	Reconstructionism	Uniate
Brahmanism/	Greek Orthodoxy	Maronite	Reform Judaism	Unitarianism
Brahminism	gymnosophy	Mazdaism/	reincarnationism	Vaishnav Hinduism
Buddhism	Hare Krishna	Zoroastrianism	Roman Catholicism	Wahhabism
Calvinists	Hasidism	Melchite	Rosicrucianism	Yoga/Yogism
Catholicism	Hinduism	Mennonite	Sabbatarianism	Zen Buddhism
charismatic	Huguenot	Mithraism	Saivism	Zoroastrianism/
Christadelphian	Hussite	Monophysite	Salvation Army	Mazdaism
Christian Scientist	iconoclasm	Moravian	Seventh-day	Zwinglian ❦
Christianity	Illuminati	Mormonism/Latter-	Adventist	
Confucianism	Islam	day Saints	Shaker	
Congregationalism	Jainism	Moslem	Shamanism	
Conservative	Jehovah's Witness	Mozarab	Shiite	
Judaism	Judaism	Muslim	Shintoism/Shinto	

---

religious sacrament of confession, acceptance of punishment, absolution: penance

religious sayings: logia

religious school: seminary

religious song: hymn

religious song or chant: canticle

religious story: parable

religious system or code of divine commands: dispensation

religious tradition or rite: sacrament

religious truth, manifestation of: revelation

religious use, to set apart for: consecrate, dedicate, sanctify

religious washing of hands: ablution

religious work not accepted by Protestants: Apocrypha

religious work of Anglicans: Book of Common Prayer

religious work of Christians: Bible

religious work of Christians and Jews: Old Testament

religious work of Christians, not Jews: New Testament

religious work of Confucians: analects

religious work of first 4 books of New Testament: gospels

religious work of first 5 books of Hebrew Scriptures: Pentateuch

religious work of first 5 books of Old Testament to Jews: Torah

religious work of first 5 books of Old Testament, translated to Greek: Septuagint

religious work of Hindus: Vedas

religious work of Jesus Christ of the Latter-day Saints: Book of Mormon

religious work of modern version of Bible: Revised Standard Version

religious work of Muslems: Koran

religious work of Vedas: Bhagavad Gita

religious worship or service, person bound by vows to life of: votary ❦

relinquish: cede, forgo, give up, hand over, part with, release, vacate, waive

relinquishment of office, function: demission

reliquary: arca, feretory

relish: appreciate, desire, enjoy, fancy, love, pleasure, savor, wish; condiment, herb, sauce, spice, zest

relish made from fruits, spices, herbs: chutney

reluctant: afraid, averse, cautious, chary, grudging, loath, shy, uneager, unwilling, wary

rely: bank, believe, confide, count, depend, expect, hope, lean, reckon, rest, trust

remain: abide, bide, continue, dwell, endure, last, linger, persist, reside, rest, stand, stay, tarry, wait

remain beyond the time limit: overstay

remain but be idle: dawdle, hang about, linger, loiter

remain in a place: abide, endure, withstand

remainder: balance, excess, leavings, leftovers, remnant, residual, residue, residuum, rest, surplus

remainder after expenses, outlay: net

remaining temporarily or fleetingly: itinerant, migrant, transient

remains: ashes, corpse, dust, leftover, oddment, relic, remainder, remnant, scrap, stays

remains after processing, removal, etc.: residue

remains from a past culture: artifact, relic

remains that show something once existed: evidence, sign, trace, vestige

remark: animadvert, annotation, barb, comment, commentary, express, expression, note, notice, observation, observe, opine, perceive, regard, say, see, state, word

remark as one is leaving: Parthian shot

remark departing from theme: digression, parenthesis

remark in, to throw a: comment, interject, interpose

remark made in passing: obiter dictum

remark made in undertone and pretended to be inaudible: aside, stage whisper

remark or answer made when leaving: Parthian shot

remark that does not follow logically from what preceded it: non sequitur

remark that removes initial awkwardness: icebreaker

remark to an audience: aside

remark, concise and clever epigram: zinger

remark, critical: animadversion

remark, cutting: barb

remark, incidental: obiter dictum, passing comment

remark, insightful: aperçu

remark, ironic: sarcasm

remark, of a belittling: derogatory, disparaging

remark, of a forceful and effective: cogent, incisive, mordant, to the point, trenchant

remark, of an inappropriate: infelicitous

remarkable: awesome, darb, exceptional, extraordinary, notable, noticeable, prodigious, singular, strange, surpassing, unaccountable, uncommon, unusual, wonderful

remarriage: deuterogamy, digamy

remedial: curative, therapeutic

remedy: amend, antidote, assistance, catholicon, correct, corrective, curative, cure, cure-all, drug, elixir, heal, help, medicine, nostrum, panacea, placebo, rectify, redress, relief, relieve, repair, salve, treacle, treatment

remedy for particular ailment or disorder: specific

remedy, quack: nostrum

remedy, universal: catholicon, panacea

remember: bethink, commemorate, memorize, mention, recall, recognize, recollect, record, remind, reminisce, retrieve, reward, treasure

remember and keep in mind: retain

remember and tell of past events: reminisce

remember consciously: go back over, retrace

remember or return to the memory: recur

remember the memory of with ceremony: commemorate

remembering: amamnesis, recall, recollection, retrospection

remembering important events and experiences, objects kept for: memorabilia

remembering in complete detail: total recall

remembering through routine or repetition: rote

remembering, formula or rhyme used as an aid to: mnemonic, mnemonic device

remembrance: gift, keepsake, memento, memorial, memory, mention, recall, recollection, relic, reminder, reminiscence, souvenir, testimonial, token, trophy

remind: alert, call to mind, caution, emphasize, hint, nudge, prompt, recall, stress, suggest

reminder: aide-mémoire, hint, keepsake, memento, memo, note, prod, relic, sign, souvenir, string, token, warning

reminder note: aide-mémoire, memorandum

reminder of death, mortality: memento mori

reminder, tending to serve as: evocative, redolent, reminiscent, suggestive

reminisce: mull, recall, recollect, reflect, remember, revive

reminiscent: nostalgic, recollective, remindful, retrospective

remiss: careless, delinquent, derelict, dilatory, forgetful, heedless, idle, inactive, inattentive, indifferent, indolent, irresponsible, laggard, languid, lax, lazy, neglectful, negligent, relaxed, slack, sloppy, slothful, tardy, thoughtless, unmindful

remission: abatement, absolution, break, cessation, diminution, forgiveness, lessening, lull, pardon, pause, release, relief, subsidence

remission of sin: absolution

remit: abandon, abate, abrogate, absolve, cancel, compensate, defer, desist, excuse, forgive, free, liberate, mail, mitigate, moderate, pardon, postpone, relax, release, resign, re-

store, return, route, send, shelve, ship, slacken, spend, stop, submit, surrender, suspend, transmit

remnant: ash, balance, crumb, dreg, end, fragment, leftover, ort, part, piece, portion, rag, relic, remainder, remains, residual, residue, rump, scrap, shred, stub, tag end, trace, vestige

remodel: change, rebuild, recondition, reconstruct, redo, refurbish, renovate, revamp

remonstrance: challenge, complaint, demur, objection, protest, rebuke, reproach

remonstrate: argue, challenge, combat, complain, criticize, dispute, expostulate, fight, object, oppose, profess, protest, rebel, reproach

remorse: anguish, compassion, compunction, contrition, grief, guilt, penance, penitence, regret, rue, shame, sorrow

remorse, sincere: contrition, penitence, repentance

remorseful: apologetic, ashamed, contrite, guilty, penitent, regretful, repentant, sorrowful

remote: afar, alien, cold, cool, detached, distant, faint, far, faraway, foreign, improbable, inaccessible, isolated, obscure, off, old, removed, secluded, separate, slender, slight, slim, small, solitary, unlikely, unrelated, unsettled, vague, withdrawn

remote and unapproachable: inaccessible

remote country: boondocks, boonies, hinterland, outback

remote from a center: outlying

remote outside chance: long shot

remote territory or destination: ultima, Thule

remote, set apart: cloistered, secluded, sequestered, solitary

removal of women from society: purdah

remove: amputate, assassinate, bench, cancel, deduct, dele, delete, depose, disconnect, dislodge, dismiss, displace, doff, eliminate, eradicate, erase, evict, expel, exterminate, extract, fire, free, kill, move, murder, oust, purge, retire, sack, separate, strip, transfer, uncover, unseat, uproot, void, weed, withdraw

remove a part of the body, as in surgery: amputate

remove all traces of: eradicate, exterminate, extirpate, obliterate

remove burden: disburden, disembarrass, disencumber, divest, relieve

remove by cutting: excise

remove by surgery: abscission

remove by the roots: deracinate, extirpate, uproot

remove clothing: doff

remove for separate consideration or publication: excerpt, extract

remove from office or power: depose, displace, oust, supplant

remove objectionable or erroneous text: excise, expunge, expurgate

remove or isolate from main body or group: segregate

remove rejected members or parts from: cull

remove soluble or other constituents with percolating liquid: leach

remove the cream: skim

remove to another place to conceal: eloign

remove with a solvent: elute

remove without permission: abstract, filch

removed: afar, alone, aloof, apart, away, detached, distant, faraway, isolated, obscure, remote, separate, took, withdrawn

removed from consideration: tabled

removed from others: cloistered, remote, secluded, sequestered, solitary

remunerate: award, compensate, indemnify, pay, recompense, reimburse, reward, settle, vouchsafe

remuneration: bounty, commission, compensation, emolument, gratification, honorarium, pay, payment, reimbursement, requital, satisfaction, stipend, wages

remunerative: advantageous, beneficial, gainful, lucrative, profitable, useful

renaissance: reawakening, rebirth, reconstruction, reemergence, revival

rend: break, cleave, crack, cut, disintegrate, disrupt, disturb, divide, fracture, lacerate, mangle, pierce, pull, rip, rive, rupture, separate, sever, shatter, slit, split, sunder, tear, wrest

render: administer, contribute, deliver, depict, explain, furnish, give, grant, inflict, interpret, make, pay, payment, perform, portray, present, provide, relinquish, represent, restore, return, show, submit, translate, treat, yield

rendezvous: affair, appointment, assemble, date, engagement, gather, gathering, hangout, haunt, meet, muster, retreat, tryst

rendition: delivery, depiction, edition, explanation, interpretation, performance, portrayal, translation, version

renegade: apostate, deserter, fugitive, heretic, insurgent, mutineer, outlaw, radical, rebel, recreant, rogue elephant, traitor, turncoat

renege: decline, disown, renounce, revoke, welsh, withdraw

renew: continue, extend, freshen, invigorate, maintain, modernize, rebuild, redintegrate, reestablish, refresh, regenerate, rejuvenate, renovate, repair, repeat, replace, replenish, restore, resume, resuscitate, revamp, revitalize, revive, stimulate, update

renew spiritually or morally or with life: regenerate, rejuvenate, resuscitate, revitalize, revivify

renew stock or supply: refill, replenish

renew to good health or useful life: rehabilitate, reinstate

renewal of culture: renaissance, renascence

renewed activity after inactivity: recrudescence

renounce: abandon, abdicate, abjure, abnegate, cease, defect, deny, desert, disavow, discard, disclaim, disown, forego, forgo, forsake, forswear, give up, quit, recant, redo, reject, relinquish

renovate: furbish, invigorate, make over, modernize, overhaul, recondition, redecorate, redo, refresh, refurbish, restore, revamp, spruce up

renown: acclaim, celebrity, distinction, éclat, eminence, fame, honor, kudos, note, notoriety, popularity, prestige, prominence, reputation, status

renowned: celebrated, distinguished, eminent, esteemed, famed, famous, great, illustrious, known, notable, noted, prestigious, prominent

rent: dues, hire, income, lease, let, payment, profit, revenue, share, sublease, sublet, toll

rent-paying group: tenantry

rent, exorbitant: rack-rent

rent, person who gets income from: rentier

rent, very low: peppercorn rent

renunciation: abandonment, abjurement, denial, disclaimer, eschewing, forgoing, forswearing, rejection

repair: correct, darn, doctor, fix, heal, improve, journey, mend, overhaul, patch, rebuild, refit, remedy, renew, renovate, restore, retire, retread, revamp, revive, service, travel

repair and improve: ameliorate, amend

repair and rebuild: furbish, reconstitute, reconstruct, refurbish, renovate

repair malfunction, search for and: debug

repair or set right: rectify, redress, remedy

repair, impossible to: irreparable

repairs, make extensive: overhaul

reparation: amends, atonement, compensation, damages, expiation, indemnity, recompense, redress, remuneration, repairing, requital, restitution, retribution, reward, satisfaction, settlement

reparation for wrongdoing: penance

repartee: answer, banter, comeback, humor, irony, reply, retort, sarcasm, satire, wit

repast: banquet, dinner, eating, feast, feed, food, meal, refreshment, snack, treat, viands, victuals

repay: avenge, award, balance, compensate, indemnify, offset, reciprocate, recompense, refund, reimburse, remunerate, require, restore, retaliate, return, reward, square

repay for loss or injury: compensate, indemnify, recompense, reimburse

repay in kind: compensate, requite, retaliate

repayment: amends, atonement, compensation, indemnification, quittance, recompense, redress, reparation, requital, restitution

repeal: abolish, abrogate, amend, annul, cancel, countermand, invalidate, lift, nullify, recall, renounce, rescind, retract, reverse, revocation, revoke, scrub, void, withdraw

repeat: ditto, duplicate, echo, harp, iterate, make copy, mimic, parrot, quote, recap, recapitulate, recite, recount, recur, reiterate, repetition, replay, reproduce, reshowing, restate, resume, retell

repeat in concise form: recap, recapitulate, summarize

repeat meaningless words: verbigerate

repeat or bring back without significant alteration: rehash

repeated phrase or verse: burden, chorus, refrain

repeated song or part of song: reprise

repeated theme: leitmotif, motif, motto

repel: beat, check, combat, decline, defend, deflect, disgust, drive back, drive off, nauseate, offend, oppose, rebuff, refuse, reject, repulse, resist, scatter, sicken, spurn, stop

repellent: foul, hateful, loathsome, nauseating, offensive, pugnant, repulsive, revolting, sickening

repent: apologize, atone, deplore, grieve, lament, penitent, reform, regret, rue

repentance: atonement, attrition, compunction, contrition, grief, guilt, penance, penitence, remorse, ruth, sorrow

repentance motivated by fear of punishment: attrition

repentance motivated by love of God: contrition

repentance, forgiveness given for: absolution

repentance, making good after: amends, expiation, redemption, redress, restitution

repentance, self-punishment as: penance

repentant: contrite, penitent, regretful, remorseful, rueful, sorry

repercussion: action, backlash, consequence, echo, effect, fallout, flak, impact, rebound, recoil, reflection, result, reverberation

repetition: copy, duplication, echo, iterance, iteration, practice, recital, recurrence, redundancy, rehearsal, repeat, reproduction, rote

repetition of a response, uncontrollable: perseveration

repetition of conjunctions for rhetorical effect: polysyndeton

repetition of initial sound in series of words: alliteration

repetition of last word of sentence at beginning of next sentence: anadiplosis

repetition of phrase or verse: reprise

repetition of same sense in different words, needless: pleonasm, redundancy, tautology

repetition of word or phrase in successive verses or paragraphs: anaphora

repetition of word(s) ending previous phrase, rhetorical: anadiplosis

repetitious: boring, dull, iterant, redundant, tedious, wordy

repetitive or monotonous: belabored, one-note

repetitive, needlessly: redundant, verbose

repine: complain, fret, grumble, lament, languish, moan, mope, mourn, regret, whimper, wish, yearn

replace: alter, change, oust, refund, reimburse, relieve, renew, repay, replenish, reset, restitute, restock, restore, substitute, succeed, supersede, supplant

replace by formation of new tissue: regenerate

replace or follow after in office or position: succeed

replace something inferior or antiquated: supersede

replacement: stand-in, substitute

replacement or substitute in parental, family, or educational role: surrogate

replay, of sorts: encore

replenish: fill, freshen, refill, refresh, reload, renew, restock, restore, stock, supply

replete: abounding, abundant, bloated, brimming, complete, filled, full, glutted, gorged, rift, sated, satiated, stocked, stuffed, surfeited

replica: carbon, copy, duplicate, facsimile, image, likeness, model, reproduction, twin

replicate: clone

reply: answer, comeback, correspond, counter, feedback, reaction, rebut, rejoin, rejoinder, repartee, repeat, replication, respond, response, retort, return, solution

report: account, advice, announce, article, brief, bulletin, comment, crackle, describe, detail, digest, disclose, document, grapevine, hearing, hearsay, information, message, narrate, narrative, news, noise, notice, recital, recite, record, relate, release, reputation, rumor, state, statement, story, summary, tattle, tell, word

report of proceedings: cahier

report on technical topic or proposing draft specification: white paper

report or revelation of something discreditable: exposé

report sent over distance, news: dispatch

report, false: canard, hoax

reporter: anchorperson, commentator, journalist, newshound, newsman, newsperson, stringer

reporter or photographer dogging celebrities, freelance: paparazzo

reporter, freelance: stringer

reporter's assurance: confidentiality

repose: calm, calmness, comfort, compose, ease, inactivity, leisure, lie, loaf, lounge, peace, quiet, quietness, recline, relaxation, requiescence, rest, serenity, sleep, tranquillity

repository: capsule, chest, closet, depository, depot, file, magazine, museum, safe, storehouse, tomb, treasury, vault, warehouse

repossess mortgaged property when payment is not made: foreclose

reprehend: admonish, berate, censure, chide, criticize, denounce, disprove, rebuke, reprimand, reprove, scold

reprehensible: base, blamable, condemnable, criminal, culpable, foul, heinous, inexcusable, shameful, sinful

represent: act for, characterize, delineate, denote, depict, describe, embody, enact, epitomize, exemplify, exhibit, express, illustrate, image, interpret, limn, mean, personify, picture, portray, produce, show, signify, simulate, stand for, symbolize, typify

represent as a model or typical example: embody, epitomize, incarnate, personify, typify

represent in words: delineate, describe, limn, portray, realize, render

representation: account, chart, delegation, diagram, effigy, embodiment, graph, icon, illustration, image, likeness, map, model, picture, portrayal, protest, sample, sketch, statement, symbol

representative: agent, ambassador, assignee, attaché, commissary, congressman, congresswoman, consul, delegate, deputy, diplomat, emissary, envoy, example, executor, illustrative, legate, legislator, messenger, minister, proxy, sample, senator, spokesperson, stand-in, substitute, symbolic, typical

representative as spokesperson: mouthpiece

representative dealing with difficult situations: point man

representative filling in for another: surrogate

representative holding property and administering it to beneficiaries: trustee

representative in business dealings: broker, factor, go-between, intermediary, middleman, syndic

representative lacking real power: figurehead

representative managing household affairs of large estate: steward

representative of special-interest group talking with legislators: lobbyist

representative or symbol of cause: exponent

representative sent on mission: emissary, envoy, legate

representative serving in wide range of duties: factotum

representative to conference, convention: delegate

representative trained to do the work or performance of another: understudy

representative used as cover for another person: dummy, front, front person

representative who carries out wishes of will: executor, executrix

representative, one that is typical or: archetype, avatar, epitome, example, exemplar, incarnation, personification

representative, to appoint or authorize as: depute

representative, to authorize and send as one's: delegate

represented by a figure, resemblance: emblematic, figurative, symbolic

representing another or others, person or group: delegation, deputation

representing as something really is: realistic

representing someone, performed or experienced by: substituted, vicarious

repress: bridle, bury, check, compose, conceal, constrain, control, cover, crush, curb, holdback, hush, inhibit, mask, muffle, overpower, quell, rein, restrain, squash, squelch, stifle, stop, subdue, suppress, withhold

repression: constraint, control, inhibition, restraint, smothering, suppression

reprieve: absolve, amnesty, breather, clemency, defer, delay, pardon, postpone, relief, respite, stay, suspend

reprimand: admonish, berate, castigate, censure, chasten, chastise, chide, criticize, discipline, lecture, punish, rebuff, rebuke, reprehend, reproach, reprove, scold

reprint or excerpt of article: offprint

reprisal: counterblow, requital, retaliation, retribution, revenge

reproach: abuse, admonish, besmirch, blame, blot, braid, censure, chide, condemn, contempt, criticize, degradation, denounce, discredit, disgrace, dishonor, disrepute, rebuke, reprimand, reprove, revile, shame, slur, stigmatize, taunt, twit, upbraid, vilify

reprobate: abandon, blamable, castaway, condemned, corrupt, criticize, denounce, depraved, disapproved, evil, immoral, miscreant, rascal, reprehend, reprehensible, scalawag, scamp, scoundrel, sinful, sinner, spurn, unprincipled, vicious

reproduce: breed, cline, copy, duplicate, generate, imitate, multiply, procreate, proliferate, propagate, repeat, replicate, represent, spawn

reproduce by making new tissue, parts, cells: proliferate, propagate

reproducing by fission or splitting: fissiparous

reproducing eggs that hatch outside the body: oviparous

reproducing eggs that hatch within the body: ovoviviparous

reproducing live offspring: viviparous

reproducing without sexual union: agamic, agamogenetic, asexual, parthenogenetic

reproduction: copy, counterpart, duplicate, facsimile, likeness, photostat, procreation, proliferation, propagation, replica

reproduction of original: ecotype

reproduction, asexual: apogamy, apomixis, parthenogenesis

reproduction, incapable of further: barren, effete, infertile

reproduction, sexual: amphimixis

reproductive cell: gamete, ovum, spore

reproductive female organ: ovary

reproductive male organ: testis

reproductive organ of animals: gonad

reproductive organs that are external: genitalia, genitals

reprove: admonish, berate, blame, castigate, censure, chastise, chide, condemn, criticize, disprove, lambaste, rebuff, rebuke, refute, reprehend, reprimand, reproach, reprobate, scold, shame, upbraid

reptile, like a: herpetiform, herpetoid

reptiles and amphibians, study of: herpetology

republic: commonwealth, democracy, nation, state

repudiate: abandon, abjure, abrogate, annul, banish, belie, cancel, contradict, deny, disaffirm, disavow, discard, disclaim, disinherit, disown, forsake, recant, refuse, reject, renounce, retract, revoke, spurn, void

repugnant: abominable, disagreeable, disgusting, foul, horrid, nasty, obnoxious, odious, offensive, repulsive, revolting, sickening, unpleasant, vile

repulse: defeat, deny, disdain, disgust, nauseate, rebuff, refuse, reject, repel, revolt, sicken, snub, spurn

repulsive: abhorrent, abominable, detestable, disgusting, distasteful, foul, fulsome, hateful, hideous, horrendous, loathsome, nasty, nauseating, odious, offensive, repellent, repugnant, revolting, sickening, slimy, ugly, unpleasant, unspeakable, vile

repulsive and gross: disgusting, grisly, gruesome, nauseating, offensive, sickening

repulsive thing or person in appearance: eyesore

repurchase agreement: repo

reputable: acclaimed, celebrated, creditable, distinguished, famous, honorable, notable, respectable

reputation: character, credit, distinction, éclat, fame, glory, honor, name, notoriety, odor, prestige, prominence, regard, renown, repute, respect, respectability, standing, stature

reputation-damaging campaign: character assassination

reputation, achieved: standing, stature, stock

reputation, damage to: disrepute, notoriety

reputation, evil: infamy

reputation, good: cachet, esteem, prestige

reputation, to damage a: defile, discredit, profane, sully, tarnish

repute: fame

reputed: assumed, believed, considered, hypothetical, putative, regarded, said, supposed

request: appeal, apply, ask, ask for, demand, entreat, inquiry, invitation, invite, offer, order, petition, plea, pray, solicit, sue, suit, supplicate, wish

request that succeeds: impetration

requiem: chant, composition, dirge, hymn, mass, service, song, threnody

requiescat: prayer, wish

require: ask, bid, claim, compel, crave, demand, desire, exact, force, lack, need, order, want

require and claim: postulate

require as condition: stipulate

required: compulsory, essential, forced, imperative, mandatory, necessary, needed, obligatory, requisite

required as duty: incumbent

required by custom: prescriptive

required by law: compulsory, mandatory, obligatory

required earlier: prerequisite

requirement: condition, criterion, essential, formality, fulfillment, must, necessity, need, prerequisite, terms

requisite: condition, essential, indispensable, must, necessity, need, needed, precondition, required, vital

requisition: application, call, claim, demand, form, order, postulate, request

requital: redress, reprisal, retaliation, retribution, revenge, vengeance

requite: atone, avenge, compensate, indemnify, reciprocate, recompense, reimburse, repay, retaliate, return, revenge, reward, satisfy

res publica: commonwealth, republic, state

rescind: abolish, annul, cancel, countermand, invalidate, lift, nullify, renege, repeal, retract, reverse, revoke, void

rescue: deliver, deliverance, extricate, free, help, liberate, ransom, recovery, redeem, redemption, release, retrieve, salvage, save

rescue and bring back to proper course: reclaim

rescue from destruction, difficulty, evil: deliverance, salvation

rescue from loss, waste, destruction: salvage

rescue from sin: redeem

research: analysis, delving, examination, experiment, inquiry, investigation, probe, R&D, study

research for academic degree, original: dissertation, thesis

research room: laboratory

research to improve efficiency of business, management, government: operations research

resemblance: affinity, analogy, closeness, comparison, correspondence, counterpart, likeness, parallel, similarity, simile, similitude

resemblance in some respects to otherwise dissimilar things: analogy

resemble: favor, like, match, mirror, parallel, similar

resemble closely: imitate, mimic, simulate

resembling: bogus, ersatz, quasi

resembling or correlative thing: counterpart

resent another's property or enjoyment: begrudge, envy

resentful feeling: grudge

resentful, very: in high dudgeon, jealous

resentment: acrimony, anger, animosity, animus, bitterness, choler, displeasure, dudgeon, grudge, hate, hatred, hostility, huff, indignation, malice, malignity, pique, rancor, spite, umbrage, wounded pride

resentment at supposed insult: pique, umbrage

resentment, tending to arouse: invidious

reservation: booking, condition, doubt, provision, proviso, sanctuary, stipulation, terms, territory

reservation, mental: salvo

reserve: alternate, assets, backlog, book, caution, coldness, conserve, discretion, exception, hold, keep, modesty, nest egg, preserve, reservoir, resources, retain, reticence, save, savings, shyness, spare, standby, stock, store, substitute, supply, surplus, withhold

reserve of goods: stockpile

reserved: aloof, backward, bashful, cautious, cold, collected, constrained, demure, distant, inhibited, modest, onice, qualified, reticent, saved, sedate, shy, silent, taciturn, unsociable, withdrawn

reserved area for birds, animals: sanctuary

reserved for opportune moment, key resource: trump card

reservoir: basin, container, fountain, fund, inventory, lake, pond, pool, reserve, source, stockpile, store, supply, tank, well

reside: abide, dwell, endure, exist, habit, habitat, live, lodge, occupy, remain, room, settle, stay

residence: abode, apartment, castle, condominium, digs, domicile, dwelling, habitat, habitation, home, house, household, lodging, mansion, occupancy, palace, villa

resident: citizen, denizen, dweller, habitant, inhabitant, ite, lessee, native, occupant, tenant

residual: extra, leftover, remainder, remaining, surplus

residue: ash, ashes, balance, cinder, debris, dregs, excess, foots, grounds, leavings, lees, relics, remainder, remains, remnant, residuum, scraps, sediment, silt, slag, sludge, soot, waste

resign: abandon, abdicate, demit, forsake, quit, relinquish, renounce, submit, surrender, vacate, withdraw, yield

resignation: departure, endurance, modesty, notice, patience, submission, withdrawal

resignation of office: demission

resigned: calm, compliant, gentle, passive, reconciled, subdued, submissive, yielding

resilient: adaptable, buoyant, elastic, flexible, hardy, rebounding, resistant, springy, stretchy, strong, tough

resin: acrylic, aloe, amber, ambrite, balm, balsam, colophony, copal, elemi, epoxy, frankincense, gum, gum arabic, lac, myrrh, olibanum, pitch, rosin, shellac, syrup, tar, tolu

resin used in stringed instrument bows, pine: rosin

resin, wine flavored with pine: retsina

resist: buck, combat, contest, defend, defy, dispute, endure, fend, forbear, frustrate, impugn, obstruct, oppose, prevent, rebel, refuse, repel, thwart, traverse, wither, withstand

resistance: defense, defiance, fight, movement, opposition, rebellion, rebuff, struggle

resistance by nonviolent methods: passive resistance

resistance to disease or harmful influence: immunity

resistance to drug or something unpleasant: tolerance

resistance to established government: insurrection

resistance, unit of electrical: ohm

RESPIRATORY DISEASE

acute respiratory distress syndrome
Alpha-1 antitrypsin deficiency
asbestosis
asthma
black lung disease
bronchitis
bronchopneumonia
bronchopulmonary dysplasia
catarrh
chronic obstructive pulmonary disease
cold
common cold
coryza
cough
cystic fibrosis
diphtheria
emphysema
flu
Goodpasture syndrome
head cold
influenza
laryngitis
Legionnaires' disease
lung disease
lymphagioleiomyomatosis

mononucleosis/glandular fever
pharyngitis
pleurisy
pneumoconiosis
pneumonia
psittacosis/parrot fever
quinsy
respiratory distress syndrome
respiratory syncytial virus
rhinitis
rhinorrhea
runny nose
sarcoidosis
silicosis
sinusitis
sleep apnea
sleep disorder breathing
sore throat
sudden infant death syndrome/SIDS
tonsillitis
tuberculosis/TB/consumption/phthisis
upper respiratory infection
valley fever
whooping cough ❦

---

resistant: immune, insusceptible, unassailable

resistant and not yielding: impregnable, refractory

resistant to change: conservative, moderate

resolute: adamant, ardent, determined, faithful, firm, fixed, loyal, obstinate, persistent, resolved, stalwart, staunch, stout, stubborn, unbending, undaunted, unflagging, unwavering

resolution: answer, backbone, conviction, courage, decidedness, decision, determination, firmness, fortitude, goal, grit, hardihood, heart, intent, judgment, mettle, nerve, objective, perseverance, proposal, purpose, resilience, resoluteness, resolve, solution, spirit, spunk, steadfastness, stoutness, strength, tenacity, verdict, will

resolve: analyze, answer, breakdown, change, clear, conclude, conclusion, decide, decision, determine, dispel, dispose, dissolve, explain, intention, remove, resolution, separate, settle, solve, unfold, willpower

resolve or solve: decipher, unravel

resonant: bellowing, booming, deep, echoing, enhanced, full, intensified, loud, powerful, profound, reboant, resounding, reverberant, rich, ringing, rotund, sonorous, thunderous, vibrant

resort: apply, direct, refer, repair, turn, visit; haunt, hotel, inn, lodge, refuge, retreat, spa

resound: celebrate, clang, echo, extol, peal, praise, reverberate, ring

resource: ability, asset, capital, device, expedient, reserve, stopgap, supply, wealth

resourceful: apt, artful, capable, clever, creative, enterprising, imaginative, ingenious, innovative, sharp, talented

resources: assets, capital, funds, means, money, possessions, property, reserves, revenue, riches, savings, wealth

resources, conserve: husband

resources, financial: wherewithal

respect: admiration, admire, adoration, attention, concern, deference, dignity, esteem, homage, honor, obeisance, observe, recognition, regard, revere, reverence, tribute, value, venerate, worship

respect deeply: venerate

respect demanded for person or idea: sacred cow

respect shown, special honor or: homage

respect, attitude of: obeisance, reverence

respect, commanding: venerable

respect, gift or acknowledgment of: tribute

respect, inspiring: formidable, redoubtable

respect, profound: reverence, veneration

respectable: aboveboard, adequate, admirable, appropriate, becoming, decent, decorous, good, honest, honorable, legitimate, on the up-and-up, presentable, proper, reputable, sufficient, upright, worthy

respectful: civil, considerate, courteous, deferential, dutiful, gracious, mannerly, polite, subservient, upholding

respects: civility, compliments, devoirs

respiration: breathing, exhalation, inhalation, process

respiration, excessive rate of: hyperventilation

respire: breathe, exhale, inhale, oxidate

respite: break, breather, cessation, deferment, delay, intermission, leisure, lull, pause, recess, reprieve, rest, stay, suspension, truce

resplendent: blazing, bright, brilliant, dazzling, glittering, glorious, glowing, lustrous, magnificent, radiant, refulgent, shining, shiny, splendid

respond: acknowledge, answer, behave, correspond, feel, field, react, rejoin, reply, response, retort, return, write

respond excessively: overreact

response: answer, comeback, echo, reaction, replication, reply, respond, retort

response elicited by stimulus after conditioning: conditioned reflex, conditioned response

response sung or chanted in church: antiphon

response to unsatisfactory plan: counterproposal

response, evaluative: feedback

responsibility: accountability, authority, blame, burden, capacity, care, charge, duty, fault, function, liability, obligation, onus, sphere

responsibility for all one's acts: karma

responsibility, relinquish: abdicate, renounce

responsible: accountable, amenable, answerable, dependable, levelheaded, liable, mature, reliable, reputable, sensible, trustworthy

responsible for crime or offense, person: culprit

responsive: active, amenable, aware, compassionate, conscious, kindhearted, receptive, sensitive, sentient, sympathetic, warm

responsive evaluation: feedback

responsive singing or chanting: antiphony

responsive to change or persuasion: amenable

rest: breather, caesura, cessation, doze, ease, hibernation, holiday, inactivity, interlude, intermission, interval, leisure, loll, lounge, lull, nap, pause, peace, quiet, R and R, recess, recline, relax, relaxation, repose, respite, retire, siesta, sleep, slumber, spell, stillness, stop, tranquility, unwind, vacation

rest, of bodies at: static

rest, tendency of body to remain at: inertia

restaurant: automat, barbecue, beanery, bistro, brasserie, café, cafeteria, canteen, chophouse, diner, eatery, hashhouse, inn, luncheonette, pizzeria, porterhouse, rathskeller, rotisserie, steakhouse, tavern, tearoom, trattoria

RELATED TERMS

restaurant in Greece, small: taverna

restaurant owner: restauranteur, restaurateur

restaurant serving alcoholic beverages: brasserie

restaurant serving beer, often underground: rathskeller

restaurant serving steaks and chops: chophouse, steakhouse

restaurant where meats are roasted to order: rotisserie

restaurant with entertainment: cabaret

restaurant with food in vending machines: automat

restaurant with meals set up on counter or table: buffet

restaurant, coffeehouse, or bar, small: café, estaminet

restaurant, small: bistro, brasserie

restaurant, small and informal, in Italy: trattoria

restaurant, small inexpensive unsanitary: greasy spoon

restaurant, small informal: bistro ❦

restful: calm, comfortable, peaceful, quiet, relaxed, reposeful, serene, soothing, tranquil

resting: abed, nonactive, repose, static, upon

resting and inactive: dormant, oatent

restitution: amends, atonement, compensation, indemnity, recompense, redress, reimbursement, reparation, repayment, restoration

restless: anxious, edgy, feverish, fidgety, footloose, impatient, itchy, jumpy, nervous, ornery, restive, tense, uneasy, uptight, worried

restless and nervous state: disquietude, fantods, inquietude, the fidgets

restlessness in bed, extreme: jactitation

restoration: healing, rehabilitation, remodeling, renovation, reparation, restitution, revival

restoration as compensation: amends, reparation

restoration of deteriorated urban property: gentrification

restorative: analeptic, corrective, curable, healing, medicinal, remedy, therapeutic, tonic

restore: cure, heal, mend, rebuild, recondition, reconstruct, recover, rectify, redeem, redintegrate, refresh, refurbish, regenerate, rehabilitate, reinstate, remedy, renew, renovate, repair, repay, replace, resuscitate, return, revitalize, revive, right, save, update

restore friendship: reconcile

restore honor, worth, reputation: redeem

restore life or energy to: regenerate, revitalize, revivify

restore to condition or rank: rehabilitate

restore to confidence: reassure

restore to good condition: recondition, revamp

restore to normal strength: reconstitute

restore to serviceable or attractive condition: furbish, refurbish, renovate

restore to vigor: rejuvenate

restore youthful vigor: rejuvenate

restoring taken or lost property to rightful owner: restitution

restrain: abridge, abstain, arrest, bar, bate, bind, bridle, chain, check, circumscribe, clog, coarct, command, confine, constrain, contain, control, cool, cramp, curb, curtail, dam, detain, deter, estop, fetter, gag, govern, halter, hamper, harness, hinder, hold, impede, imprison, inhibit, jail, leash, limit, muzzle, pinion, prevent, prohibit, regulate, rein, repress, restrict, rule, shackle, stay, stem, stop, suppress, tether, trammel, withhold

restrain expression: check, stifle, suppress

restrained: abstemious, bated, calm, controlled, cool, disciplined, discreet, moderate, quiet, reserved, slowed, subdued, temperate, tied, withdrawn

restraining garment: straitjacket

restraining rope: leash, tether

restraint: abridgment, abstinence, confinement, constraint, continence, control, curb, embargo, leash, limitation, moderation, rein, temperance

restrict: bar, bind, bound, circumscribe, confine, construct, contract, cramp, curb, hamper, impede, limit, prohibit, ration, repress, restrain, tie

restricted in thought: hidebound, inflexible

restricted number that may be admitted: quota

restricted to elite membership: arcane, esoteric, exclusive, rarefied, select

restricting force: stranglehold

restriction: ban, check, condition, confinement, cramp, curb, limit, limitation, regulation, restraint, rule, stipulation

restriction and ban: embargo

restriction goes into effect, time at which: curfew

restriction in document: proviso

result: aftermath, answer, arise, conclude, conclusion, consequence, decision, effect, end, ensue, finding, finish, follow, happen, judgment, opinion, outcome, proceed, product, ramification, resolution, rise, score, sequel, stem, sum, supervene, total, upshot

result coming from and complicating a problem, plan: ramification

result of a process or activity, return of information about: feedback

result of disaster or misfortune: aftermath, backwash

result of event or action, indirect: fallout, repercussion, reverberation

result of or reaction to earlier action, antagonistic: backlash

result regarded as inevitable: foregone conclusion

result to its cause, relation of: consequence, corollary, sequel

result ultimately: eventuate

result, end: denouement, outcome, upshot

result, following as a: consequential

result, normal: corollary

result, secondary: byproduct, fallout, side effect, spinoff

resume: continue, proceed, recapitulation, recommence, recover, regain, renew, reopen, restart

résumé of experience: biography, C.V., curriculum vitae, epitome, recapitulation, review, summary, synopsis

resurgence: rebirth, renewal, revival

resurrection: rebirth, restoration, revival, transformation

resuscitate: restore, resurrect, revive, save

retail: barter, dispense, distribute, hawk, market, peddle, sell, trade

retain: absorb, commission, contain, employ, grasp, have, hire, hold, keep, maintain, memorize, possess, preserve, recollect, remember, reserve, restrain, save, withhold

retainer: appliance; attendant, employee, minion, servant; fee

retaining wall: curb, revetment

retaliate: avenge, counter, reciprocate, repay, requite, return, revenge, settle

retaliation: payback, reprisal, requital, retribution, tit for tat, vengeance

retard: baffle, brake, clog, delay, fetter, hamper, hinder, impede, inhibit, obstruct, prevent, slow, stunt

retarded person with one brilliant skill: idiot savant

retelling of event, interesting or humorous: anecdote

retention: holding, keeping, memory, recall, recognition, recollection, remembering

retentive in memory: tenacious

reticent: discreet, quiet, reluctant, reserved, restrained, retiring, secretive, silent, subdued, unwilling, withdrawn

retinue: attendants, band, cortege, crew, entourage, escort, following, harem, personnel, procession, retainers, service, staff, suite, train

retire: depart, exit, hit the sack, leave, pension, quit, recede, resign, rest, retreat, sleep, vacate, withdraw

retire-early incentive: golden handshake

retired but retaining honorary title: emeritus

retired on a pension: superannuated

retired person: pensioner

retiring: bashful, demur, diffident, meek, modest, quiet, reserved, reticent, shy, timid, unassertive, unassuming, withdrawn

retort: answer, comeback, counter, crack, quip, rebut, repartee, repay, reply, reprisal, respond, response, return, riposte

retract: abjure, back, cancel, deny, disavow, disown, recall, recant, remove, renege, renounce, repeal, repudiate, rescind, retreat, reverse, revoke, withdraw

retraction, statement of: palinode

retreat: abandon, asylum, back, bolt, den, departure, draw in one's horns,

dropback, escape, evacuation, flee, getaway, harbor, haven, hightail, lair, leave, nest, port, privacy, recede, recess, refuge, resort, retire, sanctuary, seclusion, shelter, shrink, solitude, withdrawal

retreat to worse condition: retrogress

retreat, place or attitude of: ivory tower

retrench: abridge, curtail, decrease, delete, diminish, economize, eliminate, lessen, omit, reduce, remove, save, shorten, slash

retribution: compensation, justice, payback, punishment, recompense, reprisal, requittal, retaliation, return, revenge, reward, vengeance

retrieve: fetch, recall, reclaim, recoup, recover, recuperate, regain, remember, rescue, restore, revive, salvage, save

retroactive: ex post facto

retrograde: backslide, backward, catabolic, contrary, decline, degenerate, deteriorate, inverse, inverted, lapse, recede, regress, retrogress, reversed, revert, sink, slip, worsen

retrogress: backslide, degenerate, retrograde, revert, worsen

retrospect: afterthought, contemplate, flashback, hindsight, recollection, remember, reminiscence, review

retrospective: backward, remembrance, retroactive, review

return: advert, answer, comeback, coming, earnings, gain, gross, income, profit, reappear, reappearance, reciprocate, recompense, recover, recrudesce, recur, recurrence, reinstate, rejoin, render, repay, repayment, reply, report, reprise, requital, respond, response, restoration, restore, retaliate, retort, revenue, reverse, revert, revisit, send back, statement, summary, yield

return in kind: reciprocate

return of trait after period of absence: atavism

return or restoration to previous state or position: restitution

return to country of birth or citizenship: repatriate

return to former condition: revert

return to previous behavior, often criminal: recidivism

return to wrongdoing: backslide, regress

return, send, or order back: remand

return, show or give in: reciprocate, requite

returns from the dead, one who: revenant

returns to criminal habits, one who: recidivist

reunite: reconcile, reconvene, rejoin

revamp: recondition, reconstruct, rejuvenate, renew, renovate, repair, replenish

reveal: admit, announce, bare, betray, blab, communicate, confess, confide, decipher, declare, develop, disclose, discover, disinter, display, divulge, evince, exhibit, exhume, expose, impart, leak, manifest, open, proclaim, publish, show, spill, squeal, tell, uncover, unearth, unmask, unveil, unwrap

revel: bacchanal, bask, carnival, carousal, carouse, celebrate, delight, enjoy, eye-opener, feast, festival, festivity, frolic, gloat, indulge, inspiration, merrymaking, rejoice, relish, revelation, roister, rollick, romp, shocker, sign, spree, spress, telling, whoopee

revelation: apocalypse, disclosure, discovery, manifestation, prophecy, vision

revelation of something discreditable: exposé

revelation or manifestation of divine being: theophany

revelation or realization, sudden: epiphany

reveler: bacchant, carouser, merrymaker, ranter, roisterer

revelry: carousal, celebration, festivity, high jinks, jollity, merriment, merrymaking, saturnalia, whoopla

revenant: apparition, ghost, phantom, repay, reprisal, revenge, settle, specter, spirit, vengeance, vindicate

revenge: avenge, lex talionis, nemesis, requital, retaliate, retaliation, retribution, revanche, revanchism, vengeance

revenge for injury or loss: redress, reprisal, requittal, retribution

revenge for, exact: avenge, vindicate

revenge, feud with acts of: vendetta

revengeful: spiteful, vindictive

revenue: assets, compensation, earnings, gains, income, interest, proceeds, profit, receipts, return, salary, taxation, wages, yield

reverberate: echo, rebound, reflect, repel, resonate, resound, ring, thunder, vibrate

revere: admire, adore, cherish, esteem, exalt, honor, idolize, love, respect, treasure, value, venerate, worship

reverence: admiration, awe, deference, devotion, fear, homage, honor, obeisance, piety, praise, regard, respect, worship

reverend: clergy, clergyman, clerical, divine, holy, minister, monsignor, parson, priest, sacred, venerable

reverent: devout, dutiful, humble, pious, religious, solemn

reverie: abstraction, brown study, contemplation, daydream, dream, fantasy, meditation, musing, pipe dream, thought, trance

reversal: setback, turnaround

reversal of circumstances, literary: peripeteia, peripetia

reversal of natural order of words, figure of speech involving: hysteron proteron

reverse: annul, antithesis, backtrack, backward, cancel, change, contrary, converse, counter, countermand, defeat, disaster, exchange, invert, misfortune, nullify, opposite, overturn, recessive, regressive, renege, repeal, rescind, retract, retrograde, retrogressive, revoke, shift, transpose, turn, turnabout, undo, upset

reverse count of time: countdown

reverse or back of coin or medal: verso

reverse order or place of: interchange, transpose

reverse position, order, condition: invert

reverse reading of word or sentence that is the same as forward: palindrome

reversion of land to the state law: escheat

reversion to more primitive form: atavism, throwback

revert: backslide, lapse, react, recover, regress, retrograde, retrogress, return, reverse, turn, undo

review: analysis, analyze, assessment, audit, brush up, compt, rendu; criticism, criticize, critique, edit, evaluation, examination, inspection, journal, magazine, parade, periodical, reassess, recap, recapitulate, reconsider, reevaluate, rehash, rethink, retrospect, revision, study, summarize, survey, synopsis

review of completed event: postmortem

review, critical: critique, notice

reviewing past occurrences: retrospection

revile: abuse, belittle, berate, blaspheme, castigate, criticize, debase, hate, libel, malign, reproach, scold, slander, slur, upbraid, vilify

revise: alter, amend, change, correct, edit, emend, improve, modify, redact, redo, redraft, reform, renovate, revamp, rewrite, update, upgrade

revision: alteration, amendment, change, correction, rewriting

revision of a text, critical: recension

revival: anabiosis, comeback, invigoration, reawakening, rebirth, rejuvenation, renaissance, renascence, renewal, resurgence, resurrection, resuscitation

revive: arouse, energize, enliven, freshen, galvanize, invigorate, rally, reanimate, reawaken, recover, recuperate, refreshen, regenerate, reinvigorate, rejuvenate, rekindle, remember, renew, restore, resurrect, resuscitate, return, revivify, stimulate, wake

revocable: repealable

revoke: abjure, abolish, abrogate, annul, cancel, check, countermand, disclaim, erase, invalidate, lift, nullify, recall, recant, renege, renounce, repeal, rescind, restrain, retract, reverse, void, withdraw

revoke a command: countermand

revolt: arise, boycott, coup, disgust, insurrection, mutiny, nauseate, offend, opposition, rebel, rebellion, renounce, repel, repulse, resist, revolution, riot, sedition, uprising

revolting: appalling, awful, disgusting, execrable, gross, hideous, horrible, loathsome, nasty, nauseating, offensive, repugnant, repulsive, shocking, sickening, ugly, vile

revolution: bloodshed, circuit, cycle, gyration, gyre, insurrection, outbreak, overthrow, rebellion, retation, revolt, turn, unrest, uprising

revolution about a center: spiral, volution

revolutionary: extremist, fanatic, insurgent, radical, rebellious

revolve: circle, consider, deliberate, gyrate, gyre, meditate, orbit, ponder, reflect, roll, rotate, ruminate, spin, swing, turn, twirl, wheel, whirl

revolve around fixed point or axis: gyrate

revolver: firearm, gun, handgun, pistol, six-shooter, weapon

revolving: gyral, vertiginous, whirling

revolving food serving stand: dumbwaiter, lazy Susan

revolving part of electrical or mechanical device: rotor

revolving passageway: turnstile

revulsion: abhorrence, abomination, aversion, detestation, distaste, hate, loathing, repugnance, repulsion, withdrawal

reward: award, bonus, bounty, carrot, compensation, crown, fruit, gift, guerdon, honor, indemnify, medal, meed, merit, perks, plum, premium, prize, profit, recompense, remuneration, repay, requital, return, ribbon, salary, success, trophy, wages

reward by government for acts beneficial to the state: bounty

reward for job: emolument

rewarding: beneficial, fulfilling, gratifying, pleasing, profitable, satisfying, worthwhile

rewarding partisan service with public office: spoils system

rewording: abstract, paraphrase, precis, summary

rework: adapt, alter, edit, emend, modify, redo, redraft, redraw, reshape, revamp, revise, rewrite

rhapsodic: ecstatic, elated, emotional, enthusiastic, excited, exhilarated, overjoyed

rhetoric: bombast, discourse, elocution, eloquence, flamboyance, oratory, pomposity, speech, verbosity, wordiness

rhetorical: articulate, bombastic, eloquent, embellished, figurative, flamboyant, florid, flowery, fluent, forensic, oratorical, ornate, showy, sonorous, wordy

rhetorical inversion of second of two parallel structures: chiasmus

rhinoceros, pertaining to: rhinocerotic

rhinoceroses, group of: crash, herd

rhizopod: ameba, amoeba

rhubarb: argument, controversy, discussion, dispute, fight, hassle, quarrel

rhubarb genus: rheum

rhyme: harmony, jingle, measure, meter, poem, poetry, rune, song, tune, verse

rhyme at beginnings of words: alliteration

rhyme in which final syllable is unstressed: feminine rhyme

rhyme made on a single stressed syllable: masculine rhyme

rhyme of similar spellings but different sounds: eye rhyme, sight rhyme

rhyme or light singsong verse: jingle

rhyme scheme: aba, abab, ababa

rhyme with internal word rhyming with final word of line: leonine rhyme

rhyming game: crambo

rhythm: accent, beat, cadence, flow, lilt, meter, movement, music, pace, pulse, sound, swing, tempo, time

rhythm and number, in regular: measured

rhythm or relative speed at which music should be played: tempo

rhythm with irregularly stressed beat: syncopation

rhythmic activity cycle of 24 hours for many organisms: circadian rhythm

rhythmic beat: cadence, lilt

rhythmic flexibility: rubato

rhythmic pattern: meter

rhythmic pendulum for keeping beat: metronome

rhythmic shift of accent not coinciding with metric accent: syncopation

rhythmical body movement, interpreting music with: eurythmics

rib: banter, bone, costa, jest, joke, needle, purl, razz, ridge, stay, tease, wale

rib in Gothic vaulting: lierne

rib of fabric like corduroy: wale

ribald: bawdy, coarse, crude, filthy, gross, irreverent, lewd, obscene, offensive, racy, raunchy, risqué, rogue, rude, uncouth, vulgar

ribbon: award, band, bandeau, banderole, binding, bow, braid, cordon, corse, decoration, fillet, prize, riband, streamer, strip, stripe, tape, taste, trimming, trophy

ribbon knot worn as badge: cockade

ribbon worn as badge of honor or decoration: cordon

ribbon worn as badge, rose-shaped: rosette

ribbon worn as headband: fillet

riblike part: costa

ribs, between the: intercostal

rice dish: biryani, jambalaya, pilaf, pilau, pudding, risotto

rice dish with meat, fish, chicken, vegetables, Spanish: paella

rice dish with meat, fish, or vegetables: pilaf, pilaff, pilau

rice dish with saffron, cheese, sometimes meat: risotto

rice drink: sake, saki

rice field: paddy, padi

rich: abounding, absurd, abundant, affluent, ample, amusing, bountiful, comfortable, copious, costly, creamy, dark, elaborate, eloquent, expensive, fecund, fertile, filling, flavorful, flush, fruity, funny, golden, hearty, heavy, humorous, laughable, lavish, loaded, luscious, lush, luxuriant, luxurious, mellow, moneyed, opulent, ornate, orotund, plentiful, posh, potent, powerful, prosperous, ridiculous, substantial, sumptuous, sweet, upscale, valuable, vivid, wealthy, well-heeled, well-to-do

rich and fashionable young people: jeunesse dorée

rich and luxurious: opulent, sumptuous

rich class controlling government: plutocracy

rich or ambitious newcomer: arriviste

rich people, newly: nouveau riche, parvenu

rich powerful person: magnate, mogul, tycoon

riches: affluence, assets, booty, fortune, gold, lucre, mammon, money, opulence, pelf, possessions, property, resources, treasure, wealth, worth

rickets: rachitis

rickets, curing or preventing: antirachitic

rickety: dilapidated, feeble, flimsy, infirm, ramshackle, shaky, tottering, unsafe, unsound, unstable, unsteady, weak, wobbly

ricochet: bounce, carom, glance, rebound, reflect

rid: abolish, cleanse, clear, deliver, disencumber, divested, eliminate, empty, expel, free, liberate, loosen, purge, relieve, remove, shake, shed, unburden

riddle: charade, conundrum, crux, dilemma, enigma, maze, mystery, perforate, perplex, pierce, problem, rebus, sieve, sift, teaser

riddle based on pun: conundrum

riddle in pictures or symbols: rebus

riddle or ambiguous saying: enigma

riddle, Zen Buddhist: koan

ride: commute, cruise, drift, drive, excursion, float, journey, outing, spin, travel, trip; badger, harass, heckle, hound, needle, oppress, ridicule, tease, torment, torture

ride out: weather

rider: addendum, addition, amendment, appendix, clause, endorsement, supplement; motorist, passenger; cowboy, driver, equestrian, horseman, horsewoman, jockey

rider for free: deadhead

ridge: arête, back, balk, bank, bluff, chine, corrugation, costa, crease, crest, dune, elevation, esker, hill, hogback, hump, ledge, levee, moraine, range, reef, rib, ruck, seam, spine, spur, stria, summit, wale, wave, weal, wedge, welt, wrinkle

ridge bordering irrigated field: levee

ridge in fabric like corduroy: wale

ridge of earth's crust lying between two faults: horst

ridge of glacial drift: drumlin

ridge of gravel or sand left by glacier: esker, kame, os

ridge of land jutting out into water: cape, headland, ness, promontory

ridge of land jutting out into water, narrow: spit

ridge of sand: dune

ridge of sand and gravel: esker

ridge or crest: chine

ridge or mound, low: hummock, knoll

ridge with steeply sloping sides: hogback

ridged: striate, strigose

ridges on edges of coins: fluting, milling

ridges on fingerboard of stringed instrument: frets

ridges, series of: serration

ridicule: absurd, banter, belittle, burlesque, caricature, deride, farce, lampoon, parody, pillory, roast, satire, skit, spoof, squib, travesty

ridicule or mock: ape, caricature, mimic, parody, pastiche, satirize

ridicule the falseness or sham claims of: debunk

ridicule, object of: butt, laughingstock

ridiculous: absurd, asinine, comical, crazy, deride, droll, foolish, funny, gibe, guy, haze, humiliate, idiotic, inane, irrational, jeer, kid, lampoon, ludicrous, mock, mockery, nonsense, outrageous, parody, pillory, preposterous, putdown, rage, raillery, razz, rib, ride, roast, sarcasm, satire, satirize, silly, sneer, stupid, taunt, tease, twit, unbelievable

ridiculous and laughable: absurd, bizarre, derisory, farcical, incomprehensible, ludicrous, outlandish, outré, preposterous, risible, strange

ridiculous and stupid: asinine, fatuous, inane

ridiculous situation: farce

riding clothes: habit

riding crest of wave on sailboard: windsurfing

riding crest of wave on surfboard: surfing

riding pants flare at thighs and tight below knees: jodhpurs

riding school: manège

riding whip: quirt

rife: abounding, abundant, active, alive, common, current, numerous, overflowing, prevailing, prevalent, profuse, raging, rampant, swarming, teeming, widespread

riffraff: dregs, garbage, masses, mob, rabble, refuse, rubbish, scum, trash

rifle: arm, despoil, firearm, gun, loot, pillage, plunder, ransack, ravage, rob, search, steal, weapon

rifle marksmanship and skiing competition: biathlon

rifle types: automatic, carbine, Garand, Johnson, Mauser, Minie, Remington, repeating, Sharps, Sober, Springfield, Winchester

rifle with short barrel: carbine

rift: aswarm, blemish, breach, break, chasm, chink, cleave, cleft, crack, cranny, crevasse, disagreement, divide, division, fault, fissure, flaw, fracture, gap, opening, quarrel, rent, rupture, split

rig: apparatus, arrange, carriage, cheat, clothe, contraption, costume, derrick, dress, equip, equipment, fittings, fix, furnish, gear, machinery, manipulate, outfit, quip, semi, supply, tackle, tamper, tractor, trick, truck

right: aboveboard, acceptable, accurately, amend, appropriate, authentic, authority, becoming, clear, common, correct, deserved, directly, due, easement, emend, equity, ethical, exactly, fair, faultless, favorably, fit, fitting, genuine, good, just, lawful, legal, moral, normal, obligation, precisely, proper, real, rectify, redress, restore, sane, sound, square, straight, sufficient, suitable, thoroughly, true, valid, vindicate, virtu-

ous, well; franchise, liberty, license, patent, perquisite, privilege, prerogative

right a wrong: redress

right- and left-handed, being both: ambidextrous

right angles, intersecting at or forming: perpendicular

right away: directly, immediately, instantly, now, presently, urgently

right-hand book page: recto

right-hand side of ship, aircraft, as you face forward: starboard

right-handed or on the right side: dextral

right of eldest child to inherit entire estate: primogeniture

right of government to take private property for public use and compensate owner: eminent domain

right of spouse to company, help, affection, sexual relations of mate: consortium

right of way on another's property: easement

right or claim, legal: droit

right or option to buy, first: first refusal

right or privilege held, exclusive: prerogative

right or wrong, not caring about: amoral

right side in heraldry: dexter

right side of a ledger: credit

right that cannot be withdrawn or transferred to another, of a: inalienable

right that grants use of another's property: easement, servitude

right to buy or sell something within specified time at set price: option

right to rule coming directly from God: divine right

right to set up a subsidiary business within certain premises: concession

right to speak: say

right to use another's property as long as it is not damaged or altered: usufruct

right to vote: franchise, suffrage

right triangle's side opposite the right angle: hypotenuse

right voluntarily, to give up a: relinquish, waive

right-wing: conservative, reactionary

right word or expression: mot juste

righteous: blameless, conscientious, devout, ethical, faithful, godly, good, guiltless, holy, honest, just, moral, pious, principled, pure, religious, reverent, sinless, smug, upright, virtuous, worthy

righteous as pretense: sanctimonious

rightful: appropriate, correct, deserved, due, fair, fitting, honest, just, lawful, legal, legitimate, proper, true

rights gradually or stealthily, to take another's: encroach

rights of citizens, system of laws concerning: constitution

rights of the citizens: civil liberty, civil rights

rights, protector and champion of: tribune

rights, to defend or maintain one's: assert

rights, to deprive of: divest, strip

rigid: adamant, austere, exacting, firm, fixed, formal, hard, immovable, inflexible, ironhanded, rigorous, set, severe, sharp, solid, stern, stiff, strait, strict, stringent, stubborn, taut, tense, unbending, unyielding

rigid and uniform: monolithic

rigid disciplinarian: martinet

rigidity of muscles after death: rigor mortis

rigmarole: amphigory, drivel, nonsense

rigor: austerity, cruelty, difficulty, exactitude, exactness, fury, hardship, harshness, inflexibility, precision, severity, sharpness, sternness, stiffness, strictness, trial

rigorous: accurate, ascetic, brutal, burdensome, challenging, correct, exact, hard, harsh, inclement, onerous, oppressive, precise, relentless, rigid, rugged, severe, stern, stiff, strict, stringent, trying

rile: agitate, anger, annoy, bother, bug, disturb, gall, irk, needle, nettle, peeve, roil, upset, vex

rill: brook, channel, creek, rille, rivulet, stream, trench, valley

rim: bank, border, boundary, brim, brink, circumference, edge, flange, fringe, horizon, ledge, lip, margin, perimeter, ring, skirt, tire, verge

rime: freeze, frost, hoar, ice

rind: bark, cortex, covering, crust, epicarp, hull, husk, integument, peel, shell, skin

rind end of a cheese: heel

rind or bark: cortex

ring: arena, aureole, band, belt, bezel, border, bracelet, cartel, chock, cincture, circle, circlet, circus, clique,

collar, collet, corona, coterie, encircle, enclosure, eye, gang, gasket, girdle, group, halo, henge, hoop, mob, monopoly, organization, party, rim, ringlet, surround, syndicate

ring (sound): bell, buzz, call, chime, clang, clank, ding, echo, jangle, jingle, knell, peal, resound, reverberate, summon, telephone, tingle, tinkle, toll, vibrate

ring appearing around celestial body: corona

ring flange or rim into which gem is set: collect

ring for attaching leash to collar: terret

ring or halo around holy person's head: aureole, gloria, gloriole, glory, nimbus

ring reinforcing an eyelet: grommet

ring-shaped: annular, annulus, circinate, circular, coiled, toroid, torus

ring-shaped coral island: atoll

ring-shaped roll of bread: bagel

ring to make water- or gas-tight: gasket

ring types: band, class, earring, engagement, key, napkin, nose, wedding

ring with pointed oval stone(s): marquise

ring, lip: labret

ringing in the ears: tinnitus

ringing of bells: tintinnabulation

ringing of set of chimes or bells with all possible variations: change ringing

ringleader: boss, instigator, mastermind

ringlet: curl, hair, lock, tress

ringlike figure, part, structure, marking: annulus

ringlike molding around capital of pillar: annulet

ringlike muscle: sphincter

rings of different kinds of gold, three: Russian wedding ring

rings or ringlike segments, made of: annulate

rings, two or more interlocked: gimmal

ringworm: athlete's foot, dermatophytosis, tinea

rinse: bathe, cleanse, douse, flush, gargle, lave, sluice, soak, wash, water

riot: affray, bedlam, brawl, card, carousal, commotion, confusion, disorder, distemper, disturbance, donnybrook, fight, howl, melee, mutiny, outbreak, outburst, pandemonium, protest, quarrel, rage, rampage, revel, revelry, revolt, rumble, scream, tumult, turmoil, uprising, uproar

riotous: boisterous, disorderly, loud, luxuriant, noisy, profuse, rampant, rebellious, stormy, turbulent, unrestrained, unruly, violent, wanton, wild

rip: belittle, cleave, cut, estuary, lacerate, rend, rent, rive, shred, slit, split, sunder, tear, torn

ripe: adult, aged, as brown as a berry, complete, consummate, developed, enlightened, enriched, experienced, favorable, finished, fit, grown, ideal, mature, matured, mellow, opportune, perfected, primed, ready, seasonable, seasoned, skilled, suitable, timely, wise

ripen: age, bloom, develop, evolve, flower, fruit, grow, heighten, improve, maturate, mature, mellow, perfect, season

riposte: comeback, maneuver, repartee, reply, retort, return, thrust

ripple: comb, crinkle, curl, dimple, fret, motion, popple, purl, riff, riffle, rimple, ruffle, wave, wrinkle

rippling or waving: undulation

rise: addition, advance, amount, appear, arise, ascend, ascent, aspire, attain, augment, awake, begin, boost, climb, elevate, elevation, emanate, emerge, flourish, flow, gain, go up, grade, grow, growth, hike, hill, increase, intensify, levitate, lift, loom, mount, multiply, originate, promotion, prosper, raise, reach, rebel, revolt, skyrocket, soar, stand, start, stem, succeed, surface, surge, swell, thrive, tower, transcend, well

rise above: overcome, surmount, surpass, transcend

rise and defy gravity: levitate

rise and fall regularly: heave, surge, swell, undulate

rise rapidly and abruptly: skyrocket, soar, spiral, upsurge

rise some from water when moving at high speed: plane

risible: amusing, comical, droll, funny, humorous, laughable, ludicrous, ridiculous

rising again: resurgent

rising and setting of star: acronical

rising from the dead: anabiosis, resurrection, resuscitation

rising market: bull market

rising of water: tide

rising on hind legs: rampant, rearing up

rising up against: insurgence

risk: adventure, brave, chance, danger, dare, endanger, expose, exposure, gamble, hazard, imperil, jeopardize, jeopardy, liability, menace, peril, plunge, possibility, speculate, stake, threat, uncertainty, venture, wage

risk assessor: underwriter

risk associated with job: occupational hazard

risk to insurance company because of question on insured's honesty: moral hazard

risk, disregard of: temerity

risks taken to get advantage: brinksmanship

risky: bold, chancy, dangerous, dicey, hairy, hazardous, insecure, perilous, precarious, shaky, speculative, ticklish, touch-and-go, uncertain, unhealthy, unsafe, unstable

risky business transactions, engagement in: speculation

risky venture: crapshoot, long shot

risqué: bawdy, blue, crude, daring, dirty, indecent, lewd, lurid, naughty, obscene, off-color, provocative, racy, salty, scabrous, sexy, spicy, suggestive, vulgar

rite: celebration, ceremonial, ceremony, cult, formality, initiation, liturgy, observance, occasion, ordinance, procedure, ritual, sacrament, service, tradition

rite instituted by Jesus: sacrament

ritual: ceremony, cult, custom, formality, liturgy, obsequy, observance, practice, rite, routine

ritual for new member: initiation

ritual Mohammedan prayer: salat

ritual of ancient Greeks and Romans, sexual and drinking: bacchanal, orgy

ritual recitation of verbal charms or spells: incantation

ritual signifying major life event: rite of passage

ritual washing or cleansing: ablution

ritual, pouring of liquid in religious: libation

ritzy: chic, classy, elegant, expensive, fancy, fashionable, luxurious, posh, snobbish, spiffy

rival: adversary, antagonist, anti, challenger, compete, competing, competitor, contender, contending, contest, contestant, emulate, enemy, equal, feuding, match, opponent, oppose, peer, strive, struggle, vie

rivalry: battle, competition, contention, contest, jealousy, opposition

river: plata

river bank: ripa

river bank, concerning a: riparian

river bed material: sediment

river but migrating to marine water to breed, living in a: anadromous

river embankment to prevent flooding: levee

river empties into slower-moving body of water, triangular area where: delta

river flowing into a larger river: tributary

river flowing out of a larger body of water: effluent

river mouth: debouchure, embouchure, estuary, inlet

river mouth of plain and streams: delta

river mouth where stream current meets sea: estuary

river or other running water, gorge or chasm cut by: canyon, gulch, ravine

river or stream, concerning a: fluvial

river part that meets with tides: estuary

river source: headwaters

river that flows away from it, branch of: distributary

river that flows through area that is dry except in rainy season: wadi

river used by animals towing boats, path along: towpath

river, circular and contrary current in a: eddy, purl

river, dam placed across: weir

river, extremely fast-moving part of: rapids

river, formation of land by deposition of a: alluvion

river, of a muddy: turbid

river, rippling water of: purl

river, search bottom of: drag, dredge

river, sediment deposited by: silt

river, stretch of water visible between bends in: reach

river, to emerge as a: debouch, issue

river, to flow out or empty as a: disembogue

river, to follow winding course as a: meander

river, U-shaped bend in: oxbow

river, very small: rill, rivulet, runlet, runnel, stream, streamlet

river's position or direction determined by original earth's slope, of a: consequent

rivers, pertaining to: fluvial

rivet: attach, bolt, engross, fasten, fastener, fix, pin, secure

rivulet: brook, channel, creek, rill, river, runlet, stream, streamlet

road: agger, alley, artery, avenue, beltway, boulevard, career, causeway, concourse, course, drive, expressway, fare, freeway, highway, interstate, journey, lane, parkway, passage, path, pavement, pike, railroad, railway, ride, route, speedway, street, throughway, track, trail, turnpike, viaduct, way

road affording access to and from area: access road

road courtesy: right of way

road designed for high-speed travel: expressway, freeway, interstate, superhighway, throughway, thruway

road edge: wayside

road ice that is difficult to see: black ice

road in Europe, high-speed expressway or: autobahn, autoroute, autostrada

road interchange with series of four entrance and exit ramps: cloverleaf

road into which secondary roads flow, major: arterial road, artery, trunk road

road marker: mile post, sign post

road of logs laid crosswise: corduroy

road or public highway, main: thoroughfare

road or thoroughfare, broad: concourse

road pavement: macadam, tarmac

road raised over marsh: causeway

road that ascends steep incline and zigzags: switchback

road that goes around congested or obstructed area: belt highway, beltway, bypass

road that links to a larger road, secondary: feeder

road used temporarily instead of main route: detour

road, bridge of spans and arches carrying a: viaduct

road, crushed rock as bed of: ballast

road, dead-end: cul-de-sac, impasse

road, high-speed high-traffic: expressway, freeway, parkway

road, relating to a: viaduct

road, sharp bend or turn in: hairpin

road, side: byroad, byway

road, small narrow street or: alley, mews

roadblock: barricade, barrier, blockade, obstruction

RIVERS

Alabama (North America)
Allegheny (North America)
Amazon (South America)
Amu Darya (Asia)
Amur (Asia)
Androscoggin (North America)
Apalachicola or Chattahoochee (North America)
Apurimac (South America)
Avon (Europe)
Big Sioux (North America)
Bow (North America)
Brahmaputra (Asia)
Brazos (North America)
Cape Fear (North America)
Catawba (North America)
Chang Jiang or Yangtze (Asia)
Chattahoochee or Apalachicola (North America)
Cheyenne (North America)
Churchill (North America)
Colorado (North America)
Colorado (South America)
Columbia (North America)
Congo or Zaire (Africa)
Connecticut (North America)
Cooper Creek (Australia)
Coppermine (North America)
Danube (Europe)
Darling or Murray (Australia)
Daugava (Europe)
Delaware (North America)
Des Moines (North America)
Dnieper (Europe)
Dniester (Europe)
Don (Europe)
Douro (Europe)
Ebro (Europe)
Elbe (Europe)
Elster (Europe)
Euphrates (Asia)
Fraser (North America)
Gambia (Africa)
Gan or Kan (Asia)
Ganges (Asia)
Garonne (Europe)
Glomma (Europe)
Godavari (Asia)
Green (North America)
Guadalquivir (Europe)
Guadiana (Europe)
Hawkesbury (Australia)
Housatonic (North America)
Huang or Yellow (Asia)
Hudson (North America)
Hwai (Asia)
Illinois (North America)
Indigirka (Asia)

Indus (Asia)
Irrawaddy (Asia)
James (Europe)
James (North America)
Jordan (Asia)
Kan or Gan (Asia)
Kansas (North America)
Kemi (Europe)
Kennebec (North America)
Khatanga (Asia)
Khotan or Tarim (Asia)
Kistna (Asia)
Klamath (North America)
Kolyma (Asia)
Lena (Asia)
Liao (Asia)
Little Bighorn (North America)
Little Colorado (North America)
Little Missouri (North America)
Loire (Europe)
Lualaba (Africa)
Lule (Europe)
Mackenzie (Australia)
Mackenzie (North America)
Magdalena (South America)
Mekong (Asia)
Merrimack (North America)
Mezen (Europe)
Milk (North America)
Minnesota (North America)
Mississippi (North America)
Missouri (North America)
Mobile or Tombigbee (North America)
Mohawk (North America)
Murray or Darling (Australia)
Narbada (Asia)
Nelson (North America)
Neva (Europe)
Niemen (Europe)
Niger (Africa)
Nile (Africa)
Northern Dvina (Europe)
Ob (Asia)
Oder (Europe)
Ohio (North America)
Olenek (Asia)
Onega (Europe)
Orinoco (South America)
Parana (South America)
Parnaíba (South America)
Peace (North America)
Pechora (Europe)
Penobscot (North America)
Po (Europe)
Raritan (North America)
Red or Song Koi (Asia)

RIVERS *continued*

Rhine (Europe)	St. Johns (North America)
Rhone (Europe)	St. Lawrence (North America)
Rimac (South America)	Susquehanna (North America)
Rio Bravo or Rio Grande (North America)	Tagus (Europe)
Rio de la Plata (South America)	Tarim or Khotan (Asia)
Rio Grande or Rio Bravo (North America)	Tennessee (North America)
Roanoke (North America)	Thames (Europe)
Saco (North America)	Tiber (Europe)
Sacramento (North America)	Tigris (Asia)
Salween (Asia)	Tombigbee or Mobile (North America)
San Joaquin (North American)	Trinity (North America)
Santee (North America)	Ural (Asia)
Sao Francisco (South America)	Urubamba (South America)
Saskatchewan (North America)	Uruguay (South America)
Savannah (North America)	Vistula (Europe)
Seine (Europe)	Volga (Europe)
Senegal (Africa)	Volta (Africa)
Severn (Europe)	Xingu (South America)
Severn (North America)	Yalu (Asia)
Shannon (Europe)	Yangtze or Chang (Asia)
Shatt a Arab (Asia)	Yellow or Huang (Asia)
Shenandoah (North America)	Yenisey (Asia)
Snake (North America)	Yukon (North America)
Song Koi or Red (Asia)	Zaire or Congo (Africa)
St. John (North America)	Zambezi (Africa) ❧

roadhouse: hostel, hotel, inn, nightclub, restaurant, tavern

road's incline: gradient

roads meet, place where two or more: crossroads, intersection

road's slightly arched surface: camber

road's traffic circle: rotary

roadway crossing above another roadway: overpass

roam: gad, gallivant, meander, prowl, ramble, range, rove, straggle, stray, stroll, travel, wander

roaming: nomadic

roar: bawl, bell, bellow, boom, clamor, cry, din, growl, holler, hoot, howl, laugh, noise, outcry, scream, shout, shouting, shriek, sound, thunder, yell

roast: banter, criticize, lambaste, lampoon, razz, ridicule; bake, broil, burn, cook, fry, grill, parch, swelter

roasting meat, spit or skewer for: broach, brochette

roasting on rotating spit, meat: rotisserie

rob: bereave, bilk, bribe, burglarize, cop, defraud, deprive, despoil, dispossess, embezzle, filch, heist, hijack, hustle, lift, loot, mug, pilch, pilfer, pillage, pinch, pirate, pluck, plunder, purloin, reave, relieve, rifle, roll, snatch, snitch, spoil, steal, strip, swindle, take, thieve, touch

rob a vehicle in transit: hijack

rob of goods esp. in wartime: despoil, loot, maraud, pillage, plunder, ransack, ravage

robber: bandit, bandolero, brigand, buccaneer, burglar, catman, crook, desperado, ghoul, highwayman, hijacker, marauder, mugger, outlaw, pickpocket, privateer, rustler, swindler, thief, yegg

robber as part of outlaw band: brigand

robber of road travelers: highwayman

robber smuggling goods from store: shoplifter

robber who assaults or threatens victim: mugger

robbery: burglary, heist, theft

robbery at sea: piracy

robbery of funds: embezzlement, malversation, peculation

robbery of property left in one's care: conversion

robe: array, cape, chimere, cloak, clothe, clothing, costume, cover, dress, garment, gown, habit, housecoat, invest, kimono, mantle, muumuu, negligee, smock, toga, tunic, vest, vestment, wrap

robot: android, draoid, Golem, humanoid, machine

robot like human: android

robot-operated mechanism: automaton, zombie

robotlike or electronic components, having parts replaced by: bionic

robotlike or electronic components, human with some: cybernetic organism, cyborg

robust: athletic, brawny, built, energetic, firm, flourishing, hale, hard, hardy, healthy, hearty, lusty, muscular, potent, prosperous, roaring, rugged, sinewy, sound, stalwart, stout, strapping, strong, sturdy, thriving, vigorous

rock-hurling mechanism or weapon: ballista, catapult, mangonel, onager, trebuchet, trebucket

rock or stone used in architecture, large: monolith

rock painting, drawing, carving: petroglyph

rock protruding through soil, bed-: outcrop

TYPES OF ROCK

rock altered by extreme heat, pressure, chemicals: metamorphic

rock and soil layers, cross section showing: profile

rock bed or layer: stratum

rock composed of small calcareous grains: oolite, oolith

rock composed of volcanic fragments: agglomerate

rock consisting of stone fragments: breccia

rock debris on slope or at base of steep incline: scree, talus

rock deposits of springs, lakes, ground water: tufa

rock derived from magma: extrusive

rock far removed from original position, sheetlike: nappe

rock filled with secondary minerals in cavity: amygdule

rock forced while molten into cracks or between rock layers: intrusive

rock formation, fracture in the continuity of a: fault

rock formation, projecting part of: overhang

rock formed from molten state: igneous

rock forming cliff or headland, steeply projecting: crag

rock-forming minerals part of earth's crust: feldspar

rock fragment 64mm–256mm: cobble

rock fragment or grain: clast

rock fragments, collection of large: debris, rubble, scree

rock in layers, medium- to coarse-grained metamorphic: schist

rock lacking crystalline structure: amorphous

rock lined with crystals: geode

rock of fine-grained claylike layers: shale

rock of igneous or magmatic origin: plutonic

rock of mixed inseparable minerals: aggregate

rock of pebbles and gravel embedded in cement: conglomerate, puddingstone

rock of porous glassy lava: pumice

rock of sharp-angled fragments: breccia

rock of volcanic black glass: obsidian

rock stratum overlying archaeological stratum to be studied, sterile: verburden

rock underlying soil, sand, clay, gravel: bedrock

rock with mineral or metal deposits: lode

rock, dark dense volcanic: basalt

rock, very magnetic: lodestone ❦

---

rock salt: halite, sodium chloride

rock the boat: make waves

rock worn or rubbed away by friction, process of: attrition

rock, cavity in volcanic: vesicle

rock, drill for: aiguille

rock, loose fragments worn away from: detritus

rock, lump of minerals found by a: nodule

rock, narrow bed of: lamina

rock, protruding and isolated: scar

rock, wear down or rub away by friction as a: abrade, corrade

rocker: chair, cradle; musician, singer

rocket: agena, ascend, climb, firecracker, missile, projectile, satellite, soar, spacecraft, starship, tower, whiz, zoom

rocket engine used to retard or reverse motion of vehicle: retrorocket

rocket for launch and liftoff: booster

rocket for takeoff, scaffolding holding: gantry

rocket fuel: propellant

rocket in space, path of: trajectory

rocket launcher: bazooka

rocket part containing explosive: warhead

rocket turning about vertical axis: yaw

rocket with two or more propulsion units that fire in succession: multistage rocket, step rocket

rocks formed by deposition of sediment: sedimentary

rock(s) on top of hill, high: tor

rocks' structure and composition, study of: lithology

rocks, study of: petrology

rocky: discouraging, doubtful, shaky, stubborn, uncertain, unstable, unsteady, weak; craggy, firm, hard, inflexible, obdurate, rough, rugged, solid, stony

rocky cliff, extended: palisades

rococo: arty, extravagant, flamboyant, gaudy, ornate

rod: axle, bamboo, bar, baton, bolt, cane, crowbar, fasces, pin, pole, scepter, scion, shaft, skewer, spike, spindle, spoke, staff, stick, strip, support, switch, toggle, twig, wand, whip

rod for surveying: ranging pole

rod holding and turning meat for cooking: spit

rod holding meat, etc. for cooking: skewer

rod-shaped: bacillary, bacilliform, virgate, virgulate

rodent: aguti, beaver, biting, cavy, chincha, chinchilla, chipmunk, cypu, gerbil, gnawing, gopher, guinea pig, gundie, hamster, hare, hutia, kangaroo rat, leporide, leveret, marmot, mole, mouse, murine, muskrat, porcupine, prairie dog, rabbit, rat, ratel, squirrel, vole, weasel, woodchuck, zokor

rodent, like a: gliriform

rodent, mass-drowning: lemming

rodeo: competition, enclosure, exhibition, festival, roundup

rodeo events: broncobusting, bullriding, bulldogging, calf-roping, cutting, re-riding, steer-wrestling

rodeo rope: lasso

rodomontade: bluster, boast, boastful, bombast, brag, braggart, crow, exaggeration, grandiloquence, pretension, pride, rant

rods with ax as emblem of authority, bundle of: fasces

roe: caviar, coral, deer, eggs, hart, hind, milt, spawn

roe of female lobster which turn reddish when cooked: coral

roe of large fish, salted and eaten as delicacy: caviar

rogation: chant, decree, law, litany, prayer, rite, supplication, worship

rogue: beggar, blackguard, cad, cheat, cheater, criminal, culprit, delinquent, devil, harlot, knave, lowlife, miscreant, picaro, picaroon, pirate, rapscallion, rascal, scalawag, scamp, scoundrel, shark, swindler, tramp, trickster, vagabond, vagrant, villain, wander

---

roguish: aggravate, arch, bother, deceitful, devilish, dishonest, mischievous, pawky, playful, prankish, provoke, sly, sportive, unprincipled, unscrupulous, wanton

roil: agitate, anger, annoy, foul, muddy, rile, stir, vex

role: appearance, aspect, bit, business, cameo, capacity, character, duty, function, guise, job, lead, office, part, performance, portrayal, task, title

role close to one's own personality or appearance, cast in acting: typecast

role of organism in ecological community: niche

role that one assumes in public or society: persona

roll: bagel, bread, bun, croissant, Danish, Parkerhouse

roll back: lower, reduce, retreat

roll call response: here, present

roll of cloth, large: bolt

roll of coins, paper: rouleau

roll of film or magnetic tape in casing: cassette

roll of money: wad

roll of paper or newsprint, large continuous: web

roll of parchment or papyrus for document: scroll

roll of sliced meat with filling: roulade

roll or cylinder in printer, typewriter: platen

roll up and secure a flag, sail: furl

roll, sandwich on a long hard: grinder, hero, submarine

rollaway: cot

rolled or coiled together: convolute, convoluted

roller, small wheel or: trundle

rollicking: boisterous, cheerful, frisky, frolicsome, gay, happy, jocular, jovial, joyful, joyous, lighthearted, lively, merry, playful, romping, wild

roly-poly: chubby, dumpy, fat, obese, plump, portly, pudgy, rotund

romance: adventure, affair, amour, charm, court, courtship, exaggerate, fable, fancy, fantasy, fiction, fling, gest, geste, liaison, love, novel, sentiment, story, tale

romance novel: bodice ripper

romance of noble deeds, idealistic about: quixotic

romantic: amorous, ardent, dreamy, enchanting, exotic, fictitious, idealistic, imaginary, mushy, passionate, poetic, quixotic, unreal, visionary

romantic song or musical piece to express love to someone: serenade

Rome and Greece civilization, pertaining to ancient: classical

Rome and Greece, languages and literature of ancient: humanities

romp: caper, carousal, carouse, cavort, celebrate, frolic, gambol, gammock, play, prance, roil, rollick, run, skip, win

roof: canopy, ceiling, covering, crown, dome, gambrel, house, palate, shelter, slate, summit

RELATED TERMS

roof edge: eave

roof for attaching rafters, horizontal beam at ridge of: ridgepole

roof of a building, dwelling or apartment on: penthouse

roof of mouth: palate

roof or ceiling supported by columns: hypostyle

roof with downward slant: pitched

roof with ridge and two gables: saddle roof

roof with single slope or pitch: lean-to

roof with two slopes on all four sides (lower vertical, upper horizontal): mansard

roof with two slopes on each side: curb roof, gambrel roof, mansard roof

roof, arched structure supporting a ceiling or: vault

roof, crescent-shaped opening in vaulted: lunette

roof, domed: cupola

roof, gutter or groove in: cullis

roof, horizontal beam supporting rafters of: purlin

roof, low wall or railing on edge of: parapet

roof, metal reinforcing and weatherproofing the joints and angles of: flashing

roof, ornamental ridge on: cresting

roof, rigid framework supporting: truss

roof, room under a pitched: attic, garret

roof, space between two slopes of a: gable

roof, turret or spire on: pinnacle ❦

roofing slate with one rough surface: rag

rooftop landing area: heliport

rook: bamboozle, bilk, castle, cheat, deceive, defraud, fleece, steal, swindle

rookie: apprentice, beginner, buck private, greenhorn, newcomer, novice, tenderfoot, trainee, tyro

room: accommodation, allowance, apartment, area, atrium, attic, auditorium, boudoir, cabinet, capacity, cell, chamber, clearance, compartment, cubicle, den, digs, dining, divan, dormitory, expanse, flat, foyer, gallery, hall, kitchen, latitude, leeway, library, living, lobby, lodge, lodging, margin, nursery, opening, opportunity, parlor, place, play, quarters, range, rotunda, salon, scope, space, studio, study, suite, theater

room and board: pension

room apartment, one-: efficiency, efficiency apartment, studio, studio apartment

roomer: boarder, dweller, guest, lodger, renter, tenant

rooms, to connect two: communicate

roomy: ample, baggy, broad, bulky, capacious, commodious, extensive, generous, huge, large, sizable, spacious, spacy, voluminous, wide

roost: abode, alight, land, lodging, nest, perch, perch on, settle, sit, sleep

rooster: capon, chanticleer, chicken, cock

rooster, castrated: capon

rooster's beard: wattle

rooster's comb: caruncle

root: amole, applaud, base, basis, beet, beginning, bottom, bulb, burrow, carrot, center, cheer, clap, core, derivation, dig, elihu, encourage, entrench, essence, establish, fasten, foundation, fundamental, groundwork, grout, grub, heart, motive, nucleus, origin, plant, radical, radish, reason, rise, rummage, sassafras, search, settle, soul, source, stem, support, tuber, turnip

root bearing buds, underground stem or: tuber

root of a number, calculate: extract

root of a plant, main: taproot

root out: abolish, annihilate, demolish, destroy, eradicate, extirpate, extract, remove, stub, unearth

root, arising from the: radical

root, part of plant embryo that develops into: radicle

rooted and fixed: ingrained, sessile

rootless: alienated, deracinated

rootlike: rhizoid

rope: bight, bind, binder, binding, bob-

ROMAN TERMS

army of 100: century
assembly: comitia, forum, senate
chariot: essed
clothing: palla, sagum, stola, stole, toga, tunic
concerning Rome: classical, Italian, Latin
court of appeal: rota
date: calends, ides, kalends, nones
dining room: triclinium
military formation: ala, alares, cohort, legion, maniple, phalanx
official: aedile, augur, censor, consul, edile, irenarch, lictor, Nestorian, praetor, prefect, quaestor, tribune

Gods and Goddesses
chief god: Jove, Jupiter
chief goddess: Juno
god of crops: Promitor
god of death: Mors
god of fertility: Bacchus
god of fire: Vulcan
god of harvest: Occator
god of healing: Apollo
god of herding: Silvanus
god of infants: Edusa
god of love: Amor
god of loyalty: Fides
god of martial honor: Honus
god of metalworking: Vulcan
god of sleep: Somnus
god of the dead: Pluto
god of the forest: Silvanus
god of the sea: Neptune
god of the sky: Jupiter

god of the sun: Apollo, Sol
god of the underworld: Dis, Orcus, Pluto
god of trade: Mercury
god of war: Mars
god of wine: Bacchus
goddess of abundance: Abundantia
goddess of agriculture: Ceres
goddess of beauty: Venus
goddess of childbirth: Diana
goddess of dawn: Aurora
goddess of dissent and strife: Discordia
goddess of fertility: Ceres, Diana, Egeria
goddess of flowers: Flora
goddess of fruit: Pomona
goddess of good fortune: Fortuna
goddess of grain: Ceres
goddess of healing: Meditrina
goddess of hearth: Vesta
goddess of hope: Spes
goddess of hunting: Diana
goddess of invention: Minerva
goddess of love: Venus
goddess of marriage: Juno, Unxia
goddess of martial prowess: Minerva
goddess of peace: Pax
goddess of safe travel: Abeona
goddess of the arts: Minerva
goddess of the earth: Maia
goddess of the moon: Diana, Luna
goddess of the underworld: Proserpina, Proserpine
goddess of wisdom: Minerva
goddess of woods and plants: Fauna ❦

stay, cable, chord, cord, cordage, corral, fast, fasten, guy, halter, halyard, hawser, hemp, hobble, inveigle, lanyard, lariat, lasso, leash, lifeline, line, longe, marline, noose, painter, riata, shroud, stay, string, tether, thread, tie, tow, towline, twine, vang
RELATED TERMS
rope can be wound around, projecting piece that: cleat
rope fiber: coir, hemp, jute, sisal
rope for fastening or securing, short: lanyard
rope for holding animal in place: tether
rope for leading or securing animal by neck: halter
rope for securing, binding: lashing
rope of loosely twisted strands: marline
rope on boat for tying up: painter
rope on pin or cleat, secure a: belay

rope passed through overhead pulley for hoisting: gantline
rope passing through overhead pulley, hoist with: whip
rope rigged as handrail on gangplank, ladder: manrope
rope running from peak of gaff to deck of boat: vang
rope sling for rolling cylinders on inclined plane: parbuckle
rope through hole, ring, pulley, block, to pass a: reeve
rope to prevent slipping, to tighten, or to hold something, pin or piece on: toggle
rope to steady or secure something: guy, stay
rope used in mooring or towing ship: hawser, towline, warp
rope used to impede progress of animal: hobble

rope used to raise or lower flag, sail: halyard
rope used to steady or secure something: guy
rope with noose for animals: lariat
rope with rigid rungs: Jacob's ladder
rope with weights attached to catch cattle or game: bola
rope, concerning: funicular
rope, lower oneself with: abseil
rope, middle or slack part of: bight
rope, one of the strands twisted together to make: ply
ropelike elastic cord: bungee cord
ropes and cables from masthead to vessel sides to support mast: shrouds
ropes by interweaving strands, join: splice
rope's frayed or unraveled ends: feazings
ropes in rigging of ship: cordage

TYPES OF ROOMS

room exposed to sun, glassed-in: solarium
room for bones of the dead: charnel, charnel house
room for freedom or variation: latitude, leeway, play
room for play, parties: rumpus room
room for receiving and entertaining guests: salon
room for sacred items of church: sacristy, vestry
room for sleeping a number of people: dorm, dormitory
room for sweat baths: sudatorium, sudatory
room for wardrobe: garderobe
room for washer, dryer, furnace, etc.: utility room
room off kitchen for chores, small: scullery
room on upper floor, small dining: cenacle
room or cabin on ship, private: stateroom
room or compartment for work or study, small: cubicle
room or nook in library for private study: carrel
room that is private, free from intrusion: den, sanctum
room to live, develop, function: lebensraum
room under pitched roof: attic, garret
room where meals are served at an institution: refectory
room with records, historical documents: archive
room with therapeutic dry heat: sauna
room, entrance: antechamber, anteroom, foyer, lobby, vestibule
room, large round: rotunda
room, reading: athenaeum
room, separate: compartment
room, small: cubbyhole, cuddy
room, woman's private sitting or dressing: boudoir ❦

---

rope's loop: bight
ropes on ship's shrouds forming ladder: ratline
ropes, chains, tackle supporting and controlling masts, sails, etc. of vessel: rigging ❦

---

rosary: beads, chaplet, prayers
rosary beads: aves
rose: blush, flush, pink, red, rosette, rouge
rose class: floribunda, noisette, polyantha, rambler, tea, wild
rose essence: attar
rose family: Rosaceae

rose-shaped design or object: rosette
roseate: bright, cheerful, hopeful, optimistic, pink, promising, red, rosy
roses with prickles or thorns, of: aculeate
roses with single or double flowers, hybrid: floribunda
roster: agenda, catalog, index, list, muster, record, register, roll, rota, schedule, slate
rostrum: dais, lectern, platform, podium, pulpit, snout, stage, tribune
rosy: blushing, bright, cheerful, encouraging, favorable, florid, flushed, fresh, hopeful, optimistic, pink, promising, reddish, roseate, rubicund, ruddy, sunny
rot: bosh, breakdown, bull, chaff, contaminate, corrode, decay, decline, decompose, degenerate, deteriorate, fester, nonsense, perish, poppycock, putrefy, rubbish, spoil, trash, twaddle, warp
rot, gas emanating from: effluvium
rotary current: eddy
rotary motion of a pitched ball: sidespin
rotate: alternate, circle, gyrate, orbit, pivot, revolve, roll, spin, swivel, turn, twirl, wheel, whirl
rotate around fixed point: gyrate
rotating device: centrifuge
rotating fireworks display: girandole
rotating force: torque
rotating machine part: cam
rotating motion of fluid in drain, whirlpool: vortex
rotation: cycle, eddy, revolution, spin, torque, turn, vortex
rotation takes place, something around which: axis
rote: automatic, instrument, learn, list, memorizing, memory, repeat, repetition, routine, sound, system
rotor housing: stator
rotten: abominable, bad, carious, corrupt, crooked, decayed, decomposed, depraved, dishonest, disintegrated, evil, festering, fetid, foul, inferior, lousy, nasty, offensive, perished, putrefied, putrid, rank, smelling, sour, spoiled, tainted, unlucky, unpleasant, unsound, vicious
rotten and bad-smelling: decomposed, feculent, fetid, off, putrid, putrified, rancid, rank
rotten flesh: carrion
rotten or rotting body tissue: gangrene, necrosis

rotting of bone or tooth: caries
rotund: beefy, chubby, chunky, fat, obese, plump, portly, potbellied, pudgy, roly-poly, round, sonorous, spherical, stocky, stout, vibrant
rouge: blush, color, cosmetic, flush, paint, pink, red, redden
rough: abrupt, approximate, austere, basic, blunt, boisterous, boorish, bristly, broken, bumpy, choppy, churlish, coarse, craggy, crude, curt, difficult, erose, gruff, hairy, hard, harsh, hazy, hoarse, imperfect, inclement, incomplete, inexact, jagged, lumpy, manhandle, outline, raspy, raucous, rocky, rowdy, rude, ruffled, rugged, scabrous, severe, sketchy, stern, stormy, tough, tumultuous, turbulent, uncivil, uncouth, uncut, uneven, unpleasant, unpolished, unrefined, violent, vulgar, wild
rough in vocal sound: guttural, rasping, throaty
rough out: delineate, draft, outline, plan, sketch
rough protuberance: burr, snag
rough sketch: draft, esquisse
rough to the touch: grainy, scabrous
rough up: bash, manhandle, thrash
roughneck: bully, hood, punk, rowdy, ruffian, tough
roughness: acrimony, asperity, bumpiness, coarseness, crudity, gruffness, irregularity, unevenness, wooliness
round: ammunition, ample, annular, approximate, arched, ball, band, beat, bend, bullet, chubby, circle, circuit, circular, complete, curved, cycle, full, globe, globular, looped, nearly, orbed, orbit, oval, perfect, plump, resonant, revolution, ring, rotation, rotund, shape, sonorous, spherical, turn, wheel
round and plump: rotund
round building or hall: rotunda
round but flatter and concave at poles: oblate
round off: approximate, climax, complete, conclude, culminate, finish
round up: assemble, collect, corral, gather, herd, marshal, rally
roundabout: ambiguous, circuitous, circular, curving, detour, devious, evasive, excursion, indirect, meandering, rotary, runaround, tour, verbiage, winding, wordy, zigzag
rounded: approximated, balanced, bowed, circular, complete, convex,

curved, estimated, globular, labialized, orbicular, oval, rotund, spherical

rounded mass: glomeration

rounded outward: convex, gibbous, protuberant

rounded, circling shape: helix, spiral, volute, whorl

roundup: assembly, branding, collection, gathering, herding, muster, summary

rouse: agitate, alarm, animate, arouse, awake, awaken, bestir, call, challenge, disturb, enliven, excite, exhilarate, foment, galvanize, goad, intensify, kindle, motivate, move, provoke, raise, rally, revive, roust, start, startle, stimulate, stir, trigger, urge, wake, waken

roust: motivate, provoke, rouse, rout, stimulate, stir

rout: band, beat, clobber, confuse, confusion, conquer, cream, crowd, debacle, defeat, demoralize, discomfit, disturbance, dregs, drive, eject, expel, furrow, gouge, knock, lick, mob, multitude, outmaneuver, overpower, overthrow, overwhelm, rabble, ream, retreat, riot, romp, root, rummage, scoop, shellac, stampede, thrashing, uncover, vanquish, wallop

route: beat, beeline, channel, circuit, course, detour, direction, guide, highway, itinerary, lane, line, parkway, passage, path, pilot, plans, road, rounds, send, ship, track, trail, turnpike, way

route into which local routes flow, major: artery

route of communications or transportation system, main: trunk line

route or proposed route of journey: itinerary

route used temporarily instead of main route: detour

routine: boring, course, customary, cycle, drill, dull, everyday, grind, groove, habit, habitual, mechanical, method, mundane, ordinary, perfunctory, practice, procedure, regular, rote, rut, standard, system, treadmill, typical, usual

routine or mechanical: banausic

routine way of doing things: modus operandi, regimen

routine, monotonous: treadmill

routinely done: perfunctory

rove: drift, gad, gallivant, meander, move, prowl, ramble, range, roam, straggle, stray, stroll, wander

rover: drifter, freebooter, itinerant, maverick, migrant, nomad, pirate, traveler, vagrant, wanderer

roving: aimless, cursory, desultory, errant, itinerant, mobile, nomadic, rambling, straying, wandering

row: altercation, argument, beef, brawl, commotion, dispute, disturbance, fight, fray, fuss, noise, propel, pull, quarrel, rhubarb, ruckus, rumpus, scrap, spat, squabble, uproar; aisle, column, file, line, list, order, rank, sequence, series, tier

row house: brownstone

row of columns at regular intervals: colonnade

rowboat: canoe, dinghy, dory, scull, skiff, vessel, wherry

rowboat with high sides and flat bottom: dory

rowboat, small light racing: scull

rowboat, spaces at front and back of: sheets

rowdy: boisterous, bully, disorderly, hoodlum, hooligan, noisy, punk, rebellious, rough, roughneck, rude, ruffian, tough, unruly, wild

rower directing crew: cox, coxswain

rower nearest coxswain or stern, setting tempo: stroke

rower's seat: thwart

royal: august, easy, elite, eminent, excellent, grand, grandoise, imperial, kingly, lavish, magnificent, majestic, monarchal, noble, princely, regal, sovereign, splendid, stately, superb

royal and lower rank partner, marriage between: morganatic

royal authority, signs of: diadem, regalia, scepter

royal household, attendant to: equerry

royalty: dividend, dominion, eminence, kingdom, kingship, majesties, nobility, percentage, power, princesses, queenship, rank, regality, share, sovereignty

rub: abrade, annoy, anoint, buff, caress, chafe, difficulty, fret, friction, glaze, gloss, grind, hindrance, hurdle, impediment, irk, irritate, massage, nettle, obstacle, polish, problem, scour, scrape, scrub, shine, smear, smooth, snag, stroke, swab, vex, wear, wipe

rub away: abrade

rub body with oil: embrocate

rub down a horse with currycomb: curry, groom

rub elbows: associate, mingle, mix, socialize

rub hard: scour

rub or polish to fine finish: burnish, levigate

rub or wipe out: efface, erase

rub out: annihilate, assassinate, cancel, delete, destroy, efface, eliminate, erase, kill, massacre, murder, obliterate

rub the wrong way: irk

rubber: band, elastic, flexible, galoshes, material, overshoe, resilient, stretching

rubber and plastic globules in water, emulsion of: latex

rubber band: elastic

rubber from plants, natural: caoutchouc, India rubber

rubber implement to remove water from windows: squeegee

rubber-improving process: vulcanization

rubber on end of pencil: eraser

rubber overshoe: galoshes

rubber suction cup on stick for clearing drain or pipe: plumber's helper, plunger

rubberneck: gape, look, snoop, stare, survey

rubbery substance used in golf balls: gutta-percha

rubbing against another for sexual satisfaction: frottage

rubbing away by friction: abrasion, attrition, corrasion

rubbing one object against another: friction

rubbing or wearing off: detrition

rubbing, wear away by: abrade, chafe, erode, fray, frazzle

rubbish: balderdash, bilge, bosh, crap, debris, dreck, drivel, dross, foolishness, garbage, garble, gibberish, hogwash, junk, leavings, litter, nonsense, offal, offscouring, pish, poppycock, refuse, riffraff, rubble, rummage, slop, Tommy rot, trash, tripe, waste, worthless

rubbish for salvageable material, search through: scavenge

rubbish heap or dunghill: midden

rubbish, furnace for burning: incinerator

rubble: brash, debris, fill, scree

rubdown: massage

rube: boor, bumpkin, clodhopper, dolt, hayseed, hick, hillbilly, jake, redneck, yokel

rubicund: color, florid, flushed, healthy, red, reddish, rosy, rubescent, ruddy

ruby: color, crimson, flushed, gem, jewel, mineral, pinkish, red, rubicund, sanguine, scarlet, stone

ruckus: ado, altercation, brawl, brouhaha, commotion, confusion, dispute, disturbance, donnybrook, fight, fracas, fray, free-for-all, melee, row, rowdydow, ruffle, rumpus, to do, uproar

rudder control: tiller

ruddy: blushing, florid, flushed, red, reddish, rosy, sanguine

rude and disrespectful: impertinent, insolent, irreverent

rude language: expletive, profanity

rudeness: arrogance, contumely, impertinence, incivility, insolence, sass

rudimentary: basic, beginning, elemental, elementary, fundamental, initial, primary, simple, undeveloped, vestigial

rue: afflict, anguish, bewail, compassion, deplore, dolor, grief, grieve, lament, mourn, pity, regret, remorse, repent, repentance, sorrow, suffer, sympathy

rueful: contrite, depressed, doleful, lamentable, melancholy, mournful, penitent, pitiful, plaintive, sad, sorrowful, sorry, woeful

ruffian: brute, bully, cutthroat, gangster, hood, hoodlum, hooligan, punk, roughneck, rowdy, scoundrel, thug, tough

ruffle: abrade, agitate, annoy, bother, brandish, commotion, confusion, crimp, crinkle, derange, disarrange, discompose, dishevel, disorder, disturb, drumbeat, fluster, flutter, fray, fret, intimidate, irk, irritate, jabot, nettle, plait, pleat, provoke, riffle, ripple, roil, ruche, ruckus, shake, swagger, unsettle, upset, vex, wrinkle

ruffle at neckline or front of shirt: jabot

ruffle used for trim on woman's garment: peplum, ruche

rug: carpet, cover, drugget, mat

rug of India: dhurrie

rugged: arduous, brawny, brutal, bumpy, burly, craggy, demanding, difficult, fierce, hard, hardy, harsh, healthy, jagged, mountainous, muscular, rigorous, robust, rocky, rough, rude, severe, stern, stormy, strong, sturdy, surly, tough, tour hale, trying, uncivil, uncouth, uneven, unkempt, unpolished, vigorous, violent, weathered, worn, wrinkled

ruin a plan: scuttle

ruin and impoverishment: destitution

ruin or doom: downfall, undoing

ruin or impair: spoil, vitiate

ruin property: ravage, vandalize, wreck

ruin, great: cataclysm, debacle

ruined: derelict, dilapidated, fordone, irremediable, irreparable, shot, spoilt, undid, undone

ruinous: adverse, calamitous, catastrophic, damaging, destructive, devastating, dire, disastrous, fatal, pernicious, shattering

ruinous or fatal act: kiss of death

ruins, investigated archaeological: excavation

rule by the privileged: aristocracy

rule by which judgment can be made: criterion

rule cruelly: tyrannize

rule no longer in effect: dead letter

rule of conduct: precept

rule of thumb: axiom

rule on which judgment or decision can be based: criterion, norm, touchstone, yardstick

rule or authority: dominion, sovereignty, supremacy

rule or code of laws: canon

rule or direction, authoritative: rubric

rule or law, established: article, bylaw, statute

rule or principle, recognized: axiom, creed, maxim, precept, tenet

rule out: bar, eliminate, except, exclude, forbid, omit, preclude, prevent, refuse, reject

rule with force of law: decree, dictum, ordinance, prescript

rule, breaking of: breach, infraction, infringement, transgression, violation

rule, exemption from: dispensation

rule, obey a: comply

rule, of an exceedingly harsh: draconian, ironclad, stringent

rule, statement of a mathematical: formula, theorem

rule, to set down a: enjoin, prescribe

rule, violating a: erring, peccant

ruler: amir, autocrat, boss, chief, commander, czar, despot, dictator, dominator, dynast, emir, emperor, empress, gerent, governor, king, leader, lord, matriarch, monarch, pharaoh, potentate, president, prince, princess, queen, regent, satrap, shah, sheik, sovereign, straightedge, sultan, tsar, tyrant, viceroy

RELATED TERMS

ruler during absence of monarch: regent

ruler for punishment: ferule

ruler from office, to remove: depose

ruler, harsh: despot, dictator, tyrant

ruler, supreme: sovereign

rulers in one line of descent: dynasty ✿

rules of social behavior: customs, etiquette, mores, protocol

rules, grammar: syntax

rules, making or giving: normative, prescriptive

rules, one who is strict about following: precisian

rules, statement of: guidelines

ruling: central, controlling, decision, decree, directive, dominant, edict, enactment, finding, judgment, leading, popular, predominant, prevailing, prevalent, regnant, reigning, resolution, statute, ukase, verdict, widespread

ruling by hereditary right: legitimate

ruling itself: autonomous

ruling military after takeover: junta

rum cake: baba

rum drink: daiquiri, grog, mai tai

rum drink with lemon/lime juice and sugar: planter's punch

rum types: Bacardi, dark, Jamaica, light, Puerto Rican, spiced

rumble: boom, clap, crack, crash, fight, gossip, growl, grumble, melee, murmur, noise, polish, resound, reverberate, roar, roll, rumor, seat, thunder, uproar

rumbling sound of distant thunder: brontide

rumbling, stomach: borborygmus

ruminant: antelope, bison, bovine, buffalo, camel, cattle, chewing, contemplative, cow, deer, giraffe, goat, llama, meditative, moose, oxen, sheep, steer, yak, zebra

ruminate: brainstorm, brood, chew, consider, contemplate, deliberate, masticate, meditate, mull, muse, ponder, reflect, spew, think

rummage: clutter, collect, comb, confusion, disarrange, disorder, disturb, examine, explore, forage, gather, hunt, junk, litter, muddle, poke, ransack, rubbish, search, searching, trash, upheaval

rummage around: fossick

rumor: bruit, buzz, canard, fabrication, gossip, grapevine, hearsay, idle talk, innuendo, message, murmur, news, noise, ondit, prattle, report, scandal, scuttlebutt, spread, story, talk, tidings, whisper, word

rumor, false: canard, hoax

rumor, to put an end to a: scotch

rumor, to spread a: bruit, circulate, disseminate

rumor, transmission of: bush telegraph, grapevine

rumor, unconfirmed report or: hearsay

rump: backside, behind, bottom, butt, buttocks, derriere, duff, fanny, haunches, keister, rear, seat, tush

rumple: crease, crimp, crinkle, crumple, crush, dishevel, fold, muss, plait, ruffle, scrunch, tousle, wrinkle

rumpus: argument, barney, brawl, clamor, commotion, confusion, disturbance, fracas, fray, hubbub, melee, rhubarb, row, ruckus, scuffle, stir, uproar

run away: bolt, decamp, desert, elope, escape, flee, flow, leave, scram, skedaddle, split, stampede, take to one's heels, vamoose

run away and hide: abscond, absquatulate, decamp, hightail

run away to wed: elope

run away, urge to: drapetomania

run down: belittle, capture, chase, collide, criticize, denigrate, depreciate, detract, disparage, hunt, pursue, ridicule, seize, stop, trace, vilify

run-down: abandoned, debilitated, deserted, dilapidated, enervated, exhausted, fatigued, neglected, ratty, seedy, shabby, squalid, tattered, tired, weary, worn out

run easily: jog, lope

run-in: altercation, argument, battle, brush, confrontation, dispute, encounter, fight, skirmish, tiff

run into: bump, collide, crash, encounter, meet, see

run naked in public as stunt: streak

run-of-the-mill: average, common, everyday, mediocre, ordinary, regular, typical, usual

run out: abandon, elapse, empty, exhaust, expire, fail, finish, flow, lapse, leave, lose, peter, spill, stop, terminate, tire, waste, weaken

run, but go nowhere: idle

runaround: avoidance, detour, diversion, postponement, roundabout

runaway: delinquent, eloper, escaped, fleeing, fugitive, truant, wild

rundown: briefing, outline, recap, review, seedy, summary, synopsis

rung: bar, crossbar, crosspiece, rod, round, spoke, step, tread

runic alphabet: futhark

runner: agent, collector, courier, messenger, page, smuggler; blade, ski; carpet, rug; hurdler, jogger, marathoner, racer, sprinter; vine

running: continuous, flowing, functioning, going, operating, uninterrupted, working

running down of a system: entropy

running together of final and initial sounds of two adjacent words: sandhi

running, adapted or specialized for: cursorial

runt: dwarf, homunculus, lilliputian, midget, peewee, pygmy, shrimp

runway: airstrip, channel, groove, passageway, path, platform, ramp, road, strip, tarmac, track

runway, land past end of: overshoot

runway, land short of: undershoot

rupture: breach, break, burst, disagreement, disrupt, divide, division, divorce, fracture, hernia, open, part, puncture, quarrel, rend, rent, separate, split, sunder, tear

rupture of body organ through wall: hernia

rural: agrestic, arcadian, bucolic, country, geoponic, idyllic, natural, pastoral, rustic, simple, unspoiled

rural affairs, pertaining to: georgic

rural area: boondocks

ruse: artifice, deceit, deception, feint, fraud, gimmick, hoax, maneuver, ploy, scheme, trick, twist, wile

rush: assault, attack, blitz, bolt, bustle, charge, chase, course, dart, dash, defeat, flood, flow, haste, hasten, hie, hurry, hurtle, hustle, onslaught, overpower, plunge, press, pressure, race, rampage, reed, scamper, scoot, scramble, scud, scurry, speed, stampede, storm, streak, surge, tear, urgent, zoom

Russian dance with alternating squatting kicks: kazatsky

Russian denial: nyet

Russian drink: kvass, quass, vodka

Russian food: beluga, borscht, caviar, ikary, ikra

Russian nesting wooden dolls: matrushka

Russian or Polish: Slavic

Russian pancake: blin

Russian policy of candor about social problems: glasnost

Russian vehicle drawn by three horses: troika

rust: blight, canker, color, corrode, corrosion, decay, eat, erode, erosion, oxidation, oxide, oxidize, rot, tarnish

rust-resistant zinc, coat with: galvanize

rustic: agrarian, agrestian, agrestic, arcadian, artless, backwoodsman, boor, bucolic, bumpkin, bushman, churl, clod, clodhopper, clownish, coarse, country, countryman, crude, farmer, greenhorn, hayseed, hick, hillbilly, inelegant, jake, natural, pastoral, peasant, picturesque, plain, plowboy, plowman, redneck, rough, rube, rude, rural, simple, sturdy, sylvan, uncouth, unpolished, yokel

rustle: crackle, crinkle, forage, haste, noise, sound, steal, stir, swish, swoosh

rustle of silk: scroop

rustler: bandit, desperado, driver, robber, thief

rustling: sough, susurrant, susurration, susurrus

rustling leaves, wind whispering: psithurism

rusty: corroded, decayed, discolored, eroded, rough, rugged, sluggish, unpracticed, unused

rut: channel, ditch, furrow, grind, groove, habit, indentation, pattern, pothole, routine, track, trench

rutabaga: turnip

ruth: compassion, grief, mercy, penitence, pity, regret, remorse, repentance, sadness, sorrow, sympathy

ruthless: brutal, cold, cruel, cutthroat, ferocious, heartless, mean, merciless, pitiless, relentless, savage, unsympathetic, vicious

ruthless disregard for individuality: procrustean

rye: cereal, feed, grain, grass, whiskey, whisky

S-shaped: sigmate, sigmoid

S-shaped curve, molding in architecture: ogee

sabbatical: holiday, leave, vacation

saber: cutlass, scimitar, sword

sable: black, dark, ebony, jet

sable or its fur: zibeline

sabotage: block, damage, destroy, disable, disrupt, incapacitate, subvert, undermine, vandalize, wreck

sac: bag, bursa, cavity, cyst, pocket, pouch, sack, vesicle

saccharine: candied, cloying, honeyed, ingratiating, sentimental, sugary, sweet, syrupy

sacerdotal: apostolic, clerical, ministerial, priestly, religious, sacred

sachet: bag, fragrance, perfume, potpourri, pouch, scent

sack: bag, burlap, container, duffel bag, duffle bag, gunny, pouch, purse, sac

sacrament: baptism, ceremony, communion, confirmation, covenant, eucharist, liturgy, marriage, matrimony, penance, pledge, rite, ritual, sign, symbol

sacred: blessed, cherished, consecrated, divine, godly, guarded, hallowed, holy, inviolable, pious, protected, pure, religious, reverend, sacrosanct, saintly, sanctified, spiritual, undefiled, venerated

sacred beetle: scarab

sacred bird: ibis

sacred image: icon

sacred musical composition with voices and orchestra without costumes, action, and scenery: oratorio

sacred object protecting city or state: palladium

sacred place: sacrarium, sacristy, sanctuary

sacred place for venerated person: shrine

sacred relics, place for: reliquary

sacred song: motet, psalm

sacred, make or set apart as: consecrate, sanctify

sacred, opposite of: profane, secular

sacred, violation of something: sacrilege

sacredness: sanctity

sacredness maintained: inviolate

sacredness of, violate: desecrate, profane

sacrifice: bunt, concession, deed, devote, endure, forfeit, forgo, give, hecatomb, homage, immolate, loss, martyr, oblation, offering, surrender, victim

sacrifice or slaughter, large-scale: hecatomb

sacrificial site: altar

sacrilege: blasphemy, crime, desecration, impiety, iniquity, irreverence, profanation, sin, violation

sacrilege, atonement for: piacular

sacrilegious: blasphemous, impious, irreligious, irreverent, profane, sinful

sacrosanct: blessed, divine, esteemed, hallowed, inviolable, regarded, religious, reverent, sacred

sad: bad, bleak, blue, calamitous, cheerless, dark, dejected, deplorable, depressed, depressing, desolate, despondent, disconsolate, dismal, dispirited, doleful, dolorous, down, downcast, dreary, gloomy, glum, grave, grievous, heartbroken, heavyhearted, joyless, low, melancholy, miserable, mournful, pathetic, pitiable, pitiful, sober, solemn, somber, sorrowful, sorry, tragic, triste, unfortunate, unhappy, woebegone, woeful, wretched

sad and discouraged: crestfallen, dejected, depressed, despondent, disconsolate, dispirited, downcast

sad and morose: dour, dyspeptic, glum, resentful, sullen

sad and mournful: bereft, desolate, dolorous, elegiac, forlorn, funereal, lugubrious, melancholy, plaintive, plangent, somber, tristful, wistful, woebegone

sad and tearful: lachrymose

sad and thoughtful: brooding, pensive

sad for one's sins, offenses: contrite, penitent, remorseful, rueful

sad, looking: baleful, doleful, gloomy, lugubrious

sad, very: heartbroken, inconsolable

sadden: burden, crush, deject, depress, discourage, dishearten, dispirit, upset

saddened by love: lovelorn

saddened through loss: bereaved

saddle: howdah, montura, packsaddle, pillion, seat

saddle or seat on elephant or camel: howdah

saddle parts: branch, cantle, eye, girth, horn, pommel, skirt, stirrups, tread

saddle room for a second rider: pillion

saddle types: cowboy, English, sidesaddle, western

saddle's hind part that sticks up: cantle

saddle, bicycle or motorcycle: pillion

saddle, leather gaiters attached to: gambadoes, gambados

saddle, light and padded, with no pommel horn: English saddle

saddle, ornamental covering for: caparison, trappings

sadism involving pain: algolagnia

sadistic: barbarous, brutal, cruel, vicious

sadness: anguish, blues, dejection, depression, dolor, dumps, funk, gloom, heartache, melancholy, sorrow, unhappiness

sadness over evils of world: weltschmerz

sadness, causing: heartrending

sadness, inclined to: atrabiliar, atrabilious

safari: excursion, expedition, exploration, hunt, journey, tour, trek, trip

safe: careful, cautious, clear, conservative, dependable, discreet, guarded, harmless, impregnable, innocuous, invulnerable, nontoxic, preserved, protected, prudent, secure, sheltered, shielded, sound, stable, sure, trustworthy, unharmed, unhurt, unscathed, untouched, wary; armory, chest, depository, strongbox, vault

safe and unharmed: unscathed

safe from attack: impregnable, invulnerable, secure, unassailable

safe place, harbor: asylum, haven, refuge, sanctuary, shelter

safecracker: yegg, yeggman

safeguard: armament, bulwark, convoy, defend, defense, escort, harbor, preserve, protect, protection, secure, security, shield, umbrella

safeguard and guarantee: backstop, backup, fail-safe feature, safety net

safekeeping: care, conservation, custody, preservation, protection, security

safekeeping place: depository, repository, safe deposit box, storage, vault

safety: assurance, asylum, cover, freedom, protection, refuge, sanctuary, security, shelter; touchback

safety, person entrusted with something's: depositary, depository, trustee

saffron rice mixed with vegetables, meat, poultry, and seafood, Spanish: paella

sag: bend, dangle, decline, deflate, diminish, downtrend, downturn, droop, drop, flag, flop, languish, lull, settle, sink, slide, slouch, slump, weaken, wilt

saga: adventure, edda, epic, history, legend, myth, narrative, story, tale, yarn

sagacious: acute, astute, cagey, clever, cunning, discerning, insightful, intelligent, judicious, knowing, penetrating, perceptive, prudent, quick, sage, sapient, sensible, sharp, shrewd, smart, wise

sagacity: acumen, cleverness, discernment, intelligence, perception, prudence, sapience, shrewdness, wisdom, wit

sage: guru, master, oracle, philosopher, pundit, savant, scholar, seer; discerning, judicious, learned, perceptive, profound, prudent, sapient, sensible, shrewd, solemn, sound, wise; herb, mint, salvia, seasoning, spice

saguaro plants: cacti

sail: boat, canvas, cruise, dart, drift, excursion, float, fly, gaff, jib, journey, kaul, keel, lateen, move, navigate, scud, sheet, skim, soar, trip, voyage

RELATED TERMS

sail on mast of square-rigged ship, lowest: course

sail support: mast, spar

sail that swings out opposite mainsail on racing yachts: spinnaker

sail types: balloon, foresail, jib, mainsail, mizzen, spanker, spinnaker, staysail, topsail

sail, bulging part of: bag

sail, corner of: clew, head, tack

sail, large triangular, swinging opposite mainsail on: spinnaker

sail, middle pouchlike part of: bunt

sail, ring or grommet on edge of: cringle

sail, rope or chain attached to lower corners of: sheet

sail, rope to raise and lower: halyard

sail, strap to secure furled: gasket

sail, to haul down or lower a: strike

sail, to relieve pressure of wind on: spill

sail, to roll up and secure a: furl

sail, to secure or bind a: frap, lash

sail, triangular, ahead of foremast: jib ❦

sailboat: catamaran, craft, ketch, schooner, skiff, sloop, vessel, yacht, yawl

RELATED TERMS

sailboat spar for foremast: bowsprit

sailboat with three parallel hulls: trimaran

sailboat with two parallel hulls: catamaran

sailboat, light with flat hull: sailboard

sailboat, single-masted fore-and-aft rigging: sloop ❦

sailing, person unfamiliar with: landlubber

sailor: bluejacket, deckhand, jack, mariner, middy, midshipman, midshipwoman, pirate, salt, seafarer, seaman, seawoman, swab, tar, yachtsman, yachtswoman

sailor of lowest grade in merchant marine: ordinary seaman

sailor, of fiction: Sinbad

sailor, veteran: old salt, shellback

sailor's belongings bag: ditty bag

sailors' hard biscuit or bread: hardtack, sea biscuit, sea bread, ship biscuit

sailor's navy blue knit cap: watch cap

sailors' work song: chantey, shanty

sails and yards to receive wind, adjust: trim

sails nearer the wind: luffs

sails, masts, and yards, system holding and controlling: rigging

sails, masts, spars on sailing vessel, arrangement of: rig

sails, spar supporting: yard

saint: altruist, canonize, enshrine, holy, martyr, paragon

saint protecting a place, craft, activity, class, person: patron saint

saint, declare a person a: canonize

saint, honor person in first step toward declaring them a: beatify

saint, image of: icon

saint, personal item of: relic

sainthood, title at first level of: venerable

sainting a person, Catholic official arguing against: devil's advocate

saintliness: holiness, sanctity

saintly: angelic, beatific, blessed, devout, divine, godly, good, heavenly, holy, pious, religious, righteous, spiritual, upright, virtuous

saints accepted by Catholic church, list of: canon

saints, biography of: hagiography

sake: account, advantage, behalf, benefit, end, gain, good, interest, motive, objective, purpose, reason, regard, respect, welfare; beverage, drink, saki, wine

salaam: bend, bow, genuflect, greeting, obeisance, salutation, salute

salacious: bawdy, lascivious, lecherous, lewd, lustful, obscene, wanton

salad: aspic, greens, slaw

salad dressing of oil-and-vinegar: vinaigrette

salad, toasted bread square in: crouton

salamander: amphibian, axolotl, eft, lizard, mudpuppy, newt, poker, reptile, spirit, stove, triton, urodele

salary: allowance, compensation, earnings, emolument, fee, hire, honorarium, income, pay, recompense, remuneration, stipend, wage, wages

salary limit: cap

salary, to deduct from: dock, garnishee

sale: bargain, clearance, deal, demand, discount, exchange, market, purchase, reduction, rummage, transaction, transfer

sale in one lot, miscellaneous items for: job lot

sale item used to attract customers: loss leader

salesperson: agent, clerk, hawker, peddler, salesman, saleswoman, vendor

salient: conspicuous, flagrant, glaring, important, jumping, marked, moving, noticeable, obvious, projecting, prominent, pronounced, protruding, signal, springing, striking

saline: brackish, briny, salty

saliva: drool, phlegm, salivation, slaver, slobber, spit, spittle, sputum, water

sallow: anemic, ashen, jaundiced, pale, pallid, sickly, unhealthy, wan, yellowish

sally: attack, burst, charge, dash, erupt, excursion, jaunt, joke, journey, leap, outburst, outing, quip, retort, rushing, sortie, spring, start, trip, witticism

salmagundi: assortment, hash, hodgepodge, jumble, medley, mishmash, mixture, potpourri, salad

salmon after spawning: kelt

salmon between parr and grilse: smolt

salmon enclosure: weir, yair

salmon genus: oncorhynchus, salmo

salmon migrating up rivers from the sea to breed, of: anadromous

salmon on its first return from sea to fresh water: grilse

salmon under two years old, living in fresh water: parr

salmon variety: Atlantic, blueback, chinook, coho, humpback, Pacific, quinnat, redback

salmon, female: baggit, blackfish, raun

salmon, male: kipper, redfish

salmon, smoked: lox

salmon, young: alevin, grilse, parr

salon: assemblage, gallery, gathering, group, hall, parlor, reception, room, shop, showroom

saloon: alehouse, bar, barroom, cabin, groggery, hall, pub, taproom, tavern

salt: brine, compound, condiment, corn, cure, element, flavor, gob, humor, piquant, preservative, sailor, sal, saline, seaman, season, seasoning, sharp, spice, tar, wit, witty

salt for animals, a deposit of natural: lick

salt water: brine, saline

salt, to remove the: desalinate

saltation: leap

saltlike flavor enhancer: monosodium glutamate, MSG

salts, medicinal: Epsom salts

salty: alkaline, brackish, briny, colorful, flavored, racy, risqué, saline, spicy, witty, zestful

salubrious: beneficial, bracing, curative, desirable, good, healthful, healthy, helpful, invigorating, restorative, salutary, sanitary, wholesome

salutary: advantageous, nutritious, remedial, salubrious, useful

salutation: address, aloha, ave, bow, curtsy, greeting, hail, hello, howdy, kiss, salaam, salute, toast

salutation portending bad news: Dear John

salute: accost, address, applaud, cheer, greet, hail, heil, honor, praise, recognize, signal, wave

salvage: reclaim, recover, rescue, restore, save

salvage something usable from waste: scavenge

salvation: conservation, deliverance, emancipation, liberation, mainstay, preservation, redemption, rescue

salve: alleviate, anoint, assuage, balm, cerate, cream, ease, flattery, heal, lotion, medicine, ointment, relieve, remedy, soothe, unguent

salvo: barrage, bombardment, burst, cannonade, gunfire, outburst, reservation, volley

same: alike, comparable, consistent, ditto, duplicate, equal, equivalent, exact, ibid, identical, invariable, like, parallel, self, similar, synonymous, unchanging, very

same age or duration, around: coetaneous, coeval, contemporary

same as original: clone, copy, double, duplicate

same as previous reference: ibid.

same boundaries, contained in: coextensive, conterminous, coterminous

same form or configuration around an axis or center, having: symmetrical

same importance or rank, around: coordinate

same in amount or value: parity

same in effect or value: tantamount

same kind/class/group, member of: congener

same or corresponding to: congruent

same or equal to, to be: constitute

same or similar meaning, having the: synonymous

same place, in the: ibid., ibidem

same scope or range of meaning, around: coextensive, coterminous

same size or extent, around: commensurate

same when exchanged or substituted: interchangeable

same, literally: idem

sameness: equivalence, identity, likeness, monotony, oneness, parity, similarity, uniformity, unity

samovar: urn

sample: example, illustration, inspect, instance, model, pattern, piece, segment, specimen, taste, test, try

sample fabric piece: swatch

sample meant to be representative of population: cross section

sanctified: blest, consecrated, hallowed, holy, inviolable, sacrosanct, venerated

sanctify: anoint, bless, consecrate, dedicate, glorify, purify

sanctimonious: canting, holier-than-thou, holy, hypocritical, insincere, pharisaic, pharisaical, pious, preachy, smug

sanction: abet, accredit, allow, approbate, approve, assent, authorization, authorize, boycott, confirm, confirmation, consent, decree, embargo, encourage, encouragement, endorse, endorsement, fiat, legalize, let, okay, penalty, permission, permit, ratification, ratify, support

sanctity: godliness, holiness, inviolability, piety, purity, righteousness, sacredness, saintliness, solemnity, virtue

sanctuary: asylum, bemata, chapel, church, convent, cover, den, harbor, haven, hideaway, holy of holies, monastery, mosque, oasis, port, preserve, protection, refuge, retreat, safe harbor, safety, sanctum, sanctum sanctorum, shelter, shrine, tabernacle, temple

sanctuary of church: sacrarium, sacristy

sand and clay, material intermediate between: silt

sand hill: dene, dune

sand, living or growing in: arenaceous, arenicolous

sandal: clog, espadrille, flip-flop, huarache, moccasin, shoe, slipper, talaria, thong, zori

sandals of rubber with thong toe: flipflops

sandbar: dune, reef, shoal, spit

sandpiper: beachrobin, bird, dunlin, fiddler, knot, ree, reeve, ruff, teeter, terek, triddler

sand's crystalline compound: silica

sandstone for scouring ship deck: holystone

sandwich: canapé, cheeseburger, club, grinder, hamburger, hero, hoagie, lunch, sloppy joe, sub, submarine

sandwich made in pita bread, lamb or chicken: gyro

sandwich of corned beef, Swiss cheese, sauerkraut on rye: Reuben

sandwich on a long hard roll: grinder, hero, submarine

sandwich with three pieces of bread and two layers of filling: club, double-decker

sandwich, mini open: canapé

sandy: blond, brownish, granular, gritty, plucky, porous, powdery, sabulous, shifting, unstable

sandy deposit: loess

sandy desert area: erg

sandy elevation in body of water: sandbank, sandbar, shoal

sandy ridge: esker

sandy whirlwind: dust devil

sane: balanced, coherent, compos mentis, healthy, levelheaded, logical, lucid, rational, reasonable, sagacious, sensible, sober, sound, sound of mind, wise

sangfroid: aplomb, calmness, composure, coolness, equanimity, poise

sanguine: buoyant, cheerful, confident, enthusiastic, expectant, flushed, fond, happy, hopeful, lively, optimistic, passionate, upbeat, warm

sanitary: aseptic, clean, disinfected, healthful, hygienic, purified, sterile

sanity: balance, competency, intelligence, lucidity, mind, rationality, reason, saneness, sense, soundness, stability

sap: debilitate, deplete, destroy, devitalize, drain, enervate, exhaust, subvert, tire, undermine, weaken

sapid: engaging, flavorable, palatable, savory, tasty, zestful

sapient: discerning, intelligent, knowing, knowledgeable, learned, sagacious, sage, wise

sapless: devitalized, dry, lazy, shriveled, spineless, withered

sapling: seedling, tree, young, youth

sappy: foolish, juicy, lush, mawkish, moist, plump, sentimental, silly, slushy, succulent, watery

sarcasm: acerbity, acridity, banter, criticism, gibe, humor, irony, jeer, lampooning, mockery, needling, ridicule, satire, scorn, taunt

sarcastic: acerb, acrimonious, biting, caustic, corrosive, cutting, cynical, disparaging, ironic, ironical, mocking, mordant, sardonic, sassy, satirical, scornful, sharp, snide

sarcastic literary style: irony

sarcastic, humorously: facetious, sardonic

sash: band, belt, casement, cincture, corset, cummerbund, frame, girdle, obi, ribbon, scarf, waistband

sash for a geisha: obi

sash worn across chest and holding sword, bugle: baldric

sash worn with dinner jacket: cummerbund

sashay: excursion, flounce, glide, mince, move, prance, strut, swagger, walk

sassy: bold, brash, brazen, cheeky, discourteous, disrespectful, forward, fresh, impudent, jaunty, pert, rude, sarcastic, saucy, smart, snippy, wise

satanic: cruel, demonic, devilish, diabolical, evil, fiendish, heinous, malicious, sadistic, wicked

satchel: bag, case, handbag, pouch, purse, reticule, suitcase, valise

sate: cloy, glut, gorge, gratify, overfill, satiate, satisfy, stuff, surfeit

satellite: ancillary, asteroid, luna, moon, rocket, spacecraft, subsidiary

satellite path: orbit

satellite that rotates with Earth: geostationary orbit satellite, geosynchronous orbit satellite

satiate: cloy, glut, gorge, gratify, overfill, quench, sate, satisfy, stuff, surfeit

satire: banter, burlesque, caricature, irony, lampoon, mockery, parody, ridicule, sarcasm, spoof, takeoff

satirical: caustic, comical, cynical, farcical, ironical, lampooning, mocking, sarcastic, sardonic, witty

satirical burlesque of heroic style: mock-heroic

satirical comedy: farce

satirical imitation: mock-heroic, skit, spoof, takeoff

satirical imitation of literary or artistic work: parody, pastiche, travesty

satirical representation in art or literature: caricature

satirical writing or speech: lampoon, pasquinade, squib

satirize: caricature, criticize, deride, lampoon, mimic, mock, parody, ridicule, spoof

satisfaction: amends, atonement, bliss, comfort, compensation, contentment, enjoyment, fulfillment, gratification, happiness, justice, payment, pleasure, recompense, relief, renumeration, reparation, restitution, vindication

satisfaction from another's troubles: schadenfreude

satisfaction from feelings or experience of another: vicarious

satisfactory: acceptable, adequate, average, decent, enough, fair, good, okay, passable, sufficient, tolerable, valid

satisfied with past achievements, self-: resting on one's laurels

satisfied, self-: complacent

satisfy: accommodate, answer, appease, assuage, clear, compensate, content, convince, defray, discharge, fill, fulfill, gratify, indemnify, indulge, meet, pacify, pay, persuade, placate, please, quench, remunerate, reparate, repay, sate, satiate, serve, settle, slake, suffice, suit, supply, surfeit

satisfy another's whims: pander to

satisfy thirst: quench, slake

satisfy whim: gratify, indulge

saturate: dampen, drench, fill, glut, imbrue, imbue, impregnate, ingrain, penetrate, permeate, soak, sop, souse, steep, submerge, waterlog, wet

saturated: imbued, sodden, soggy, sopped

Saturday as the Sabbath, one who observes: Sabbatarian

saturnalia: bacchanal, feast, festival, orgy, party, revelry, spree

saturnine: bitter, dour, dull, gloomy, glum, grave, heavy, melancholy, morose, passive, sardonic, solemn, somber, sullen

sauce: condiment, dressing, flavor, gravy, relish, seasoning

sauce for fish, wine: matelote

sauce of a pungent mustard family plant: horseradish

sauce of butter, egg yolk, herbs, vinegar or wine: béarnaise

sauce of butter, egg yolk, vinegar or lemon juice: hollandaise

sauce of chicken stock, cream, egg yolks: suprême

sauce of garlic mayonnaise: aioli

sauce of garlic, basil, tomato, Parmesan, olive oil: pistou

sauce of hot red pepper, trademarked: Tabasco

sauce of lemon, butter, and spices, sautéed and served in: piccata

sauce of mayonnaise, onion, olive, pickles, capers: tartar

sauce of mayonnaise, pickles, capers, anchovies, herbs: remoulade

sauce of meat stock thickened with flour, cream, egg yolk, butter: velouté

sauce of onion, capers, herbs, vinegar: ravigote

sauce of pine nuts, garlic, basil, cheese, olive oil: pesto

sauce of red Bordeaux wine: bordelaise

sauce of vinegar or lemon juice and herb-flavored oil: vinaigrette

sauce or mixture of chestnuts, maraschino cherries, candied fruits, liquer, dessert: Nesselrode

sauce thickener of flour and fat: roux

sauce with cheese, white: Mornay

sauce with herbs, white: bechamel

sauce with onions, white: soubise

sauce, Burgundy-based: bourguignonne

sauce, peanut: satay

sauce, spiced Indian: curry

sauce, spiced New Orleans: creole

sauce, white cream: bechamel

saucy: arch, audacious, bold, brash, brazen, cheeky, cocky, defiant, disrespectful, flippant, forward, fresh, impertinent, impudent, insolent, malapert, pert, relapert, rude, sassy, smug

saunter: amble, dally, dawdle, drift, frank, idle, loiter, lounge, meander, mosey, promenade, ramble, roam, rove, ruminate, sashay, straggle, stray, stroll, walk, wander

sausage: banger, bratwurst, frankfurter, kielbasa, liverwurst, pepperoni, rolliche, rollichie, wienerwurst, wurst

sausage in England: banger

sausage-shaped: allantoid

sausage, German: bratwurst, braunschweiger, knackwurst, liverwurst

sausage, mild: bologna, mortadella

sausage, mild smoked: frankfurter, wiener, wienerwurst

sausage, Polish: kielbasa

sausage, pork: bratwurst

sausage, pork and beef: pepperoni

sausage, spicy: chorizo, pepperoni, salami, saveloy

sausages and other processed meat foods: charcuterie, variety meat

sauté: fry, pan fry

savage: barbarian, barbaric, beastly, bloodthirsty, bloody, brutal, brute, brutish, cannibal, crude, cruel, demoniac, feral, ferocious, fierce, grim, harsh, heartless, inhuman, merciless, murderous, native, primitive, rabid, rough, rude, ruthless, sadistic, truculent, uncivilized, unrestrained, untamed, vicious, violent, wild

savage beast: brute

savanna: grassland, plain, savannah

savant: expert, genius, intellectual, master, sage, scholar, wise man

save: accumulate, amass, bank, conserve, defend, deliver, deposit, economize, extricate, free, guard, hoard, husband, keep, lay by, maintain, preserve, reclaim, redeem, rescue, reserve, retain, safeguard, salvage, scrimp, skimp, spare, stockpile, store, stow

save and conserve: husband

save by not spending: scrimp

save for one's pleasure or profit: amass, garner, stockpile

save from loss or destruction: salvage

save from loss or harm: conserve

save from sin: redeem

save usable substances from waste: reclaim, salvage

saved material after destruction: salvage

saved money for future: nest egg

saving: barring, careful, conservation, economical, frugal, preservation, prudent, rescue, thrifty

saving from sin: deliverance, redemption, salvation

saving grace: mitigating factor, redeeming quality

saving occurrence or thing: godsend

savings: account, funds, investment, means, nest eggs, provisions, reserves

savior: defender, emancipator, guardian, hero, knight, liberator, messiah, protector, redeemer, rescuer

savoir-faire: adroitness, composure, diplomacy, elegance, finesse, grace, manners, poise, style, tact, worldliness

savor: aroma, enjoy, essence, experience, flavor, fragrance, odor, piquancy, quality, relish, scent, sensation, smack, smell, taste, tinge, trait, zest

savory: agreeable, alluring, appetizing, aromatic, delectable, flavored, inoffensive, palatable, piquant, pleasing, pungent, salty, sapid, scrumptious, spicy, tasty

savory tomato jelly: aspic

say: advertise, advise, affirm, announce, answer, articulate, assert, asseverate, aver, call, claim, comment, communicate, convey, declare, deliver oneself of, dictate, enunciate, express, imply, indicate, inform, insinuate, intimate, mention, pronounce, quote, recite, relate, remark, repeat, report, respond, show, speak, state, talk, tell, testify, utter, verbalize, vocalize, voice, vote

say publicly: disclose, divulge

say seriously: affirm, asseverate

saying: adage, aphorism, apothegm, axiom, byword, cliché, epigram, expression, maxim, mot, motto, phrase, proverb, saw, slogan, truism

saying expressing a principle or rule: maxim, motto, precept, slogan

saying expressing a truth or opinion: adage, aphorism, apophthegm, axiom, dictum

saying expressing an insight: aperçu

saying or precept: dictum

saying that's been used for a while: adage

saying, concise and clever: aphorism, epigram, gnome, mot

saying, overused: bromide, byword, cliché, commonplace, platitude, saw, truism

sayings ascribed to Jesus but not in Bible: agrapha

SAWS

backsaw
band saw
bench saw
bucksaw
butcher's saw
buzz saw
chain saw
circular saw
compass saw
coping saw
crosscut saw
crown saw
cutoff saw
diamond saw
dovetail saw
dry-wall saw
electric saw
flooring saw
flush cut saw
folding saw
frame saw
fretsaw
hacksaw
hand saw
jeweler's saw
jigsaw
keyhole saw
log saw
lumberman's saw
meat saw
one-man crosscut saw
pad saw
panel saw
pit saw
plumber's saw
portable circular saw
power saw
radial arm saw
reciprocating saw
ripsaw
saber saw
scroll saw
stationary circular saw
table saw
tree saw
two-handed saw
two-man crosscut saw
utility saw
vertical saw ☙

sayings of Jesus: logia
scab: apostate, blackleg, scoundrel, strikebreaker
scab forming on burn: crust, eschar
scabbard's metal tip: chape

scabby: base, blotchy, contemptible, crusty, despicable, mangy, mean, scurvy, shabby, vile
scabrous: coarse, difficult, knotty, rough, rugged, scaly, treacherous
scaffold: staging
scalawag: black sheep, miscreant, ne'er-do-well, rapscallion, rascal, reprobate, rogue, scamp, scapegrace, scoundrel, trickster
scald: blanch, burn, char, criticize, excoriate, heat, parboil, scorch
scale: ascend, balance, calibration, climb, continuum, covering, degree, escalate, film, gamut, gradation, hierarchy, instrument, measure, mount, order, proportion, ranking, rate, ratio, regulate, rule, size, spectrum, spread, weight
scale calibrating the measurements of a larger scale: vernier
scale down: decrease, diminish, downsize, limit, restrict, shorten, trim
scale drawing of side, front, rear of structure: elevation
scale for colors by hue, value, chroma: Munsell color scheme
scale for comparison: index
scale for earthquake magnitude: Richter
scale for hardness of metals and alloys: Brinell
scale for hardness of minerals: Mohs
scale for industrial, medical use: platform scale
scale for specific gravity of liquids: Baume
scale for wind velocities: Beaufort
scale of gradual successive stages: gradation
scale of organism: coating, covering, crust, flake, husk, lamella, lamina, peel, shed, skin, squama
scale of 12 semitones in music: chromatic, dodecaphonic, twelve-tone
scale of Western music using only 8 tones or major or minor scale: diatonic, mode
scale standard, to check or adjust in comparison with: calibrate
scale up: advance, augment, increase, lengthen
scale with protractor, draw to: plot, protract
scale, position assigned on a: rating, standing

scale, syllable system representing musical: solfeggio, solmization, tonic sol-fa
scales for IQ: Binet-Simon, Stanford-Binet
scales, having: mailed, scabrous, scutate, scutellate
scallion relative: leek, onion, shallot
scallops: coquilles St. Jacques
scaloppine, generally: veal
scalpel: knife
scaly skin: scurf
scamp: cheat, imp, knave, prankster, rapscallion, rascal, reprobate, rogue, scalawag, scoundrel, villain
scamper: bolt, dart, dash, flee, hasten, hurry, lope, race, rolic, run, scoot, scurry, skedaddle
scan: browse, contemplate, examination, examine, glance, inspect, observe, peruse, read, scrutinize, search, skim, study, survey, view
scandal: aspersion, calumny, defamation, detraction, discredit, disgrace, embarrassment, exposé, gossip, ignominy, infamy, odium, opprobrium, outrage, reproach, shame, slander, stain
scandal facts made public: exposé
scandal involving famous people: cause célèbre
scandalize: appall, calumniate, disgrace, dishonor, embarrass, offend, revile, shock, slander, smear, vilify
scandalmonger: talebearer
scandalous: defamatory, disgraceful, disreputable, flagitious, heinous, libelous, offensive, outrageous, shameful, shocking, slanderous
Scandinavian: Dane, Nordic, Norse, Norseman, Swede
Scandinavian buffet: smorgasbord
scanty: exiguous, inadequate, meager, skimpy, sparse
scapegoat: butt, fall guy, whipping boy
scar: blemish, cicatrix, cliff, crack, cut, damage, deface, disfigure, flaw, injury, mark, pockmark, scab, scratch, wound
scar on healing wound: cicatrice, cicatrix
scar or birthmark: stigma
scar, red fibrous: keloid
scarab: beetle
scarce: deficient, hardly, infrequent, insufficient, meager, occasional, rare, scant, seldom, short, sparse, uncommon, unusual

scarcity: dearth, deficiency, famine, inadequacy, infrequency, insufficiency, lack, rareness, scantiness, shortage, sparsity, uncommonness, want

scare: affright, alarm, dread, fear, fright, frighten, horrify, intimidate, panic, shock, spook, startle, terrify, terrorize, threaten

scared: afraid, alarmed, fearful, frightened, startled, terrified

scared and cowardly: craven, lily-livered

scared and timid: fearful, timorous, tremulous

scared by threat: intimidated, unnerved

scared or nervous: apprehensive, fretful, ill at east, jittery

scared suddenly: startled

scared, extremely: panic-stricken, petrified

scared, extremely and unreasonably: paranoid

scarf: ascot, babuska, bandanna, boa, comforter, cover, cravat, groove, muffler, neckerchief, necktie, sash, shawl, stole, tie, tippet, wrap; consume

scarf as necktie: cravat

scarf for woman tied under chin: babushka

scarf of fluffy material, long: boa

scarf worn as semi-coat: stole

scarf, lace, worn on comb: mantilla

scarlet fever: scarlatina

scary: alarming, chilling, creepy, eerie, fearful, frightening, ghostly, hairy, horrifying, spooky, terrifying

scat: beat, flee, scoot, scram, shoo, singing, vamoose

scathing: biting, brutal, burning, caustic, harmful, harsh, mordant, pointed, scalding, scorching, scornful, severe, sharp, stinging

scatter: bestrew, cast, circulate, decentralize, deflect, diffuse, disband, dispel, disperse, disseminate, dissipate, distribute, diversity, divide, fling, fritter, rout, separate, shower, sow, splatter, spray, spread, sprinkle, squander, strew, waste

scatter among other things: interlard, intersperse

scatterbrained: absent-minded, careless, dizzy, flighty, forgetful, frivolous, giddy, irresponsible, silly, zany

scattered: erratic, infrequent, intermittent, interspersed, irregular, isolated, occasional, semé, sparse, sporadic, spotty, strewn, widespread

scattered remains: detritus

scattering of people outside of native land: diaspora, dispersion

scavenger: collector, hyena, magpie, rat, vulture

scenario: outline, plan, plot, rundown, screenplay, script, summary, synopsis

scene: arena, backdrop, background, culture, display, episode, incident, landscape, locale, locality, location, picture, place, scape, setting, sight, site, spectacle, spot, tableau, venue, view, vista

scene or commotion: quarrel, tantrum

scene in 3-D setting: diorama

scene of a crime: venue

scene on stage with people motionless as if in picture: tableau vivant

scene or distant view: prospect, vista

scenery: backdrop, decor, furnishings, landscape, props, sets, setting, surroundings, terrain, view

scenery and play props: mise-en-scéne

scenic: beautiful, breathtaking, dramatic, panoramic, picturesque, spectacular

scent: aroma, bouquet, clue, detect, essence, flavor, fragrance, nose, odor, perfume, redolence, smell, sniff, spoor, track, trail, whiff

scented flower petals and spices in mixture: potpourri

scented liquid of alcohol and fragrant oils: cologne, eau de cologne, eau de toilette

scented mixture in bag or box: pomander, sachet

scepter: authority, baton, jurisdiction, rod, sovereignty, staff, stick, wand

schedule: agenda, arrange, calendar, card, catalog, chart, docket, inventory, itinerary, list, organize, plan, program, register, roster, routine, slate, table, time, timetable

scheme: aim, angle, arrangement, cabal, collude, concoct, concoction, conspiracy, conspire, contrivance, contrive, design, device, devise, diagram, gimmick, intrigue, layout, list, machinate, maneuver, order, outline, pattern, plan, plant, plot, program, project, proposition, purpose, strategy, system, tactics, trick, web

scheming: artful, calculating, conniving, crafty, cunning, deceitful, foxy, sly

schism: breach, break, discord, disharmony, disunion, division, faction, rent, separation, split

schizophrenia: dementia praecox

schizophrenia starting in puberty: hebephrenia

schlemiel: bonehead, bozo, bungler, clod, dolt, fool, idiot, jerk, oaf

schlep: carry, drag, haul, jerk, lug, pull, tote

scholar: academic, bookman, bookwoman, bookworm, brain, egghead, intellectual, learner, pedant, professor, pundit, pupil, sage, savant, student

scholar of encyclopedic learning: polyhistor, polymath

scholar of law or theology: imam

scholarly: educated, erudite, intellectual, learned, lettered, schooled, studious

scholarly book: tome

scholarly celebratory publication: festschrift

scholarly knowledge: erudition

scholarly life: academe

scholarly person: savant

scholars' conference: colloquium

scholars' notes, edition of a work with: variorum

scholars, group of: brow

scholarship: education, erudition, knowledge, learning; aid, grant

scholarship ostentatiously displayed: pedantry

scholastic: academic, educational, learned, lettered, versed

school: academy, belief, coach, college, conservatory, convent, cultivate, doctrine, drill, educate, elementary, faith, guide, high, institute, institution, instruct, kindergarten, law, lead, middle, military, philosophy, prep, prepare, primary, private, public, secondary, seminar, seminary, teach, train, university, view, vocational

RELATED TERMS

school curriculum, occurring outside: extracurricular, extramural

school for discipline, training of young or first offenders: reform school, reformatory

school head: headmaster, principal, rector

SCIENCES

science and methodology of interpretation: hermeneutics
science and study of language: linguistics, philology
science and study of language meaning: semantics
science and study of language sounds: phonemics, phonetics, phonology
science and study of language use: pragmatics
science dealing with metal extraction and working: metallurgy
science experiment, derived from observation in: empirical
science of animal behavior: ethology
science of animal/plant comparison: biostatics
science of animal/plant processes: physiology
science of animal/plant structures: morphology
science of architecture and design: architectonics
science of atmosphere and weather: meteorology
science of baths or bathing: balneology
science of bullets, missiles, rocketry: ballistics
science of capital punishment: ktenology
science of caves: speleology
science of cells: cytology
science of children's diseases: pediatrics
science of construction: tectonics
science of cultivating flowers: horticulture
science of dining: aristology
science of drugs: pharmacology
science of earth's physical structure: geology
science of earth's surface and its characteristics: geography
science of earthquakes: seismology
science of energy and matter: physics
science of environment and organisms: ecology
science of ethics and moral obligation: deontology
science of fishing: piscatology
science of food and nourishment: nutrition

science of gardening, abbr.: hort
science of good eating: gastronomy
science of housekeeping: oikology
science of lakes and fresh water: limnology
science of language: linguistics
science of law: jurisprudence
science of matter and energy: physics
science of meaning of words: semantics
science of measuring time: horology
science of metals and alloys: metallurgy
science of museum curatorship: museology
science of nutrition and diet: sitology
science of old age: geriatrics
science of origin and development of humans: anthropogenesis
science of plant and animal comparisons: biostatics
science of plant and animal periodic phenomena: phenology
science of plant and animal processes: physiology
science of plant and structures: morphology
science of poisons: toxicology
science of population: demography
science of reasoning: logic
science of relationships between organisms and environments: ecology
science of soil: agrology, pedology
science of symptoms: symptomatology
science of systems of control and communications: cybernetics
science of time measurement: chronology
science of weather: meteorology
science of wind: anemology
science or philosophy of law: jurisprudence
science or study of plants: botany, phytology ❦

school of art developed in the early twentieth century in Paris: cubism
school of design, twentieth century German: Bauhaus
school of linguistics developed from the 1930's–1950's: structural linguistics
school of music or dramatic arts: conservatory
school of painting, post WWII: abstract expressionism
school subject, intended to correct deficient skills in: remedial
school supported by church parish: parochial school
school supported by public, government funds: public school
school supported by tabernacle: yeshiva
school without permission, absent from: truant

school, central European high: gymnasium
school, French public secondary: lycee
school, private secondary: prep school, preparatory school
school, program that is introduction to: kindergarten
school, student at military: cadet
school, surrounding area served by a: catchment area
school, within the same: intramural ❦

schoolbook: grammar, primer, reader, textbook
schooner: boat, clipper, glass, ship, tern, vessel, yacht
science: art, discipline, education, erudition, knowledge, skill, study, technique, technology

scientific: exact, experimental, methodical, skillful, systematic, technical
scientific agriculture: agronomy
scientific and objective: clinical
scientific philosophy, medieval: alchemy
scintilla: atom, flash, glimmer, iota, particle, ray, spark, speck, trace
scintillate: charm, coruscate, flash, gleam, glimmer, glitter, shine, sparkle, twinkle
scintillating: animated, bright, brilliant, dazzling, lively, stimulating, witty
scion: branch, bud, child, descendant, graft, heir, offshoot, offspring, progeny, seed, son, sprout, successor, twig
scissors: clippers, shears, trimmer
scissors with serrated blade: pinking shears

scoff: belittle, chide, deride, despise, devour, eat, fleer, gibe, gobble, gorge, jeer, jibe, knock, mock, razz, ridicule, sneer, steal, taunt, tease

scold: abuse, admonish, berate, castigate, censure, chastise, chide, criticize, dress down, haze, keelhaul, lambaste, lash, nag, objurgate, punish, rag, rail, rant, rate, rebuke, reprehend, reprimand, reproach, reprove, revile, shrew, tell off, upbraid, virago, vituperate

scold severely: berate, blister, flay, ream

scolded: bawled out, chid, rebuked

scolding: chewing out, talking to

scolding of husband by wife, private: curtain lecture

scolding woman: termagant, virago

sconce: bracket, candlestick, earthwork, fort, head, noggin, protection, shelter, skull

scoop: bail, beat, dig, dipper, dredge, excavate, exclusive, gather, gouge, hollow, lade, ladle, lift, news, shovel, spoon, story, vessel

scoot: bolt, dart, dash, flee, hie, hurry, hustle, run, rush, scram, scurry, skedaddle

scope: ambit, area, capacity, compass, dimension, distance, domain, extension, extent, field, goal, grasp, influence, intent, latitude, length, liberty, margin, orbit, outlook, purview, radius, range, reach, room, span, sphere, sweep, tether, vision

scope of freedom: latitude, leeway

scope of someone's awareness, knowledge: cognizance

scope or province of a certain person: bailiwick, domain, preserve

scorch: blister, burn, char, dry, excoriate, flay, lambaste, parch, scald, scathe, scourge, sear, shrivel, singe, toast, wither

score: accomplish, account, add, amount, arrange, attain, average, basket, calculate, composition, count, debt, evaluate, goal, grade, grievance, grudge, judge, line, number, obligation, orchestrate, outcome, point, rate, reason, reckoning, record, result, run, scotch, secure, succeed, summary, tab, tally, text, total

score a symphony: orchestrate

scorn: condemn, contemn, contempt, deride, derision, despise, disdain, flout, jeer, mock, ostracize, reject, ridicule, scoff, shun, sneer, snub, spurn

scorn publicly: pillory

scornful: abusive, arrogant, belittling, contemptuous, despicable, disdainful, disparaging, haughty, insolent, malicious, opprobrious, sarcastic, sardonic, supercilious

scorpion: arachnid, catapult, nepa, onager, scourge, stinger, vinegaroon, weapon

scorpion claw: chela

scorpion or spider: arachnid

scot-free: unpunished

Scotland clothing: arisard, balmoral, fecket, kilt, maud, tam, tam o'shanter, tartan, toosh

Scottish hill: brae

Scottish lake: loch

Scottish landlord: laird

scoundrel: blackguard, cad, cheat, crook, heel, knave, miscreant, rapscallion, rascal, rat, reprobate, rogue, rotter, scalawag, scamp, thief, varlet, villain, weasel

scour: brighten, buff, clean, cleanse, comb, forage, hurry, polish, rake, rub, rummage, scrub, scurry, search, swab, traverse, wash

scourge: afflict, affliction, bane, beat, castigate, chastise, curse, epidemic, excoriate, flay, flog, infliction, lambaste, lash, pest, plague, punish, punishment, slash, switch, thrash, torment, whip

scouring substance: abrasive

scout: adventurer, despise, explore, explorer, guide, informer, investigate, lookout, observe, patrol, pioneer, reconnoiter, scoff, search, spy, survey, vanguard, watch

scout badge: merit

scout or forerunner: outrider, sentinel, sentry, vedette

scowl: disapprove, expression, frown, glare, glower, grimace, lour, lower

scrabble: clamber, grope, scape, scribble, slimb, struggle

scraggly: battered, coarse, irregular, patched, ragged, shabby, shoddy, tattered, unkempt, untidy

scram: decamp, depart, flee, lam, leave, scat, scoot, shoo, skedaddle, vamoose

scramble: blend, clamber, climb, confuse, contend, disarrange, distort, garble, haste, hike, hustle, jostle, jumble, mishmash, mix, move, muddle, push, race, rush, scatter, shuffle, struggle, upset

scrap: bit, chip, crumb, drop, fraction, fragment, grain, leftover, morsel, ort, piece, remnant, shred, snippet, speck, waste

scrape: abrade, amass, claw, corrode, cut, difficulty, dig, dilemma, erase, feed, fight, gash, gather, grate, graze, hole, mar, mess, pickle, predicament, rasp, remove, row, rub, scratch, scrimp, scuffle, shave, spot, trouble

scraps: oddments, orts, remnants

scratch: abrasion, eliminate, erase, exclude, expunge, incision, injury, mar, money, scotch, scrape, scrawl, scribble, withdraw, write

scratch slightly: abrade, scarify, scrape, scuff

scratching the ground in search of food, habitually: rasorial

scrawl: doddle, handwriting, scabble, scratch, scribble, squiggle, write

scrawny: bony, gaunt, lanky, lean, meager, rawboned, scragy, skinny, thin

scrawny animal: scrag

scream: bellow, cry, holler, howl, joker, roar, shout, shriek, shrill, wail, yell, yowl

screech: howl, outcry, scream, shout, shriek, shrill, squeal, yell

screen: analyze, censor, evaluate, examine, filter, pick, separate, sieve, sift

screen or blind: camouflage, canopy, conceal, cover, curtain, divider, mesh, partition, shade, shelter, shield, veil

screen to separate women from men in India: purdah

screen, rice paper: shoji

screw: bolt, clamp, fasten, rivet, spiral, thread, tighten, turn, twist

screw or nail something until it is flush with or below surface: countersink

screw thread, tool for cutting internal: tap

screw thread width: pitch

screw-type ancient apparatus for raising water: Archimedean screw, Archimedes' screw

screw with two intersecting slots: Phillips

screwball: blockhead, bonehead, bozo,

SCREWDRIVERS

auger screwdriver
cabinet-pattern screwdriver
clutch-head tip screwdriver
cordless screwdriver
electric screwdriver
flat-head screwdriver
impact driver
magnetic screwdriver
offset screwdriver
Phillips screwdriver
ratcheting screwdriver
screw gun
spiral ratchet screwdriver
stubby screwdriver
Yankee screwdriver ❦

---

character, crackpot, dingbat, dumb-bell, eccentric, fanatic, goof, kook, lunkhead, numbskull, nut, saphead

screwdriver-like tool with head having six sides: Allen key

screwdriver, slanting surface on: bezel

screwy: absurd, batty, cracked, crazy, daft, doodle, draw, eccentric, flaky, impractical

scribble: insane, mark, nuts, peculiar, scrabble, scratch, scrawl, unbal-anced, wacky, whacky, write

scribble artfully: doodle

scribble on wall: graffiti

scribbled handwriting: griffonage

scribe: amanuensis, author, clerk, copier, copyist, editor, journalist, penman, reporter, scrivener, secre-tary, transcriber, writer

scrimmage: battle, contest, fight, game, play, practice, skirmish

scrimp: economize, eke, make do, save, scanty, skimp, stint

script: calligraphy, chirography, hand-writing, manuscript, penmanship, scenario, score, screenplay, text

scroll: document, list, papyrus, parch-ment, roll, schedule, scrawl, streamer, volute, writing

scroll-like ornament: cartouche, volute

scrounge: beg, bum, forage, freeload, search, sponge

scrub: abort, buff, cancel, clean, drop, erase, mop, rub, runt, scour, stop, swab, wash

scruffy: mangy, messy, rough, scraggly, seedy, shabby, unkempt, untidy

scrumptious: appetizing, delicious, de-lightful, exquisite, heavenly, lus-cious, succulent, tasty, yummy

scruple: anxiety, balk, conscience, de-mur, doubt, iota, misgiving, part, pause, qualm, question, reluctance, uneasiness, weight, worry

scrupulous: careful, cautious, conscien-tious, dutiful, exact, fussy, honest, honorable, meticulous, painstaking, particular, precise, principled, proper, punctilious, reluctant, upright

scrutinize: analyze, audit, canvass, check, comb, examine, eye, peruse, probe, scan, sift, survey, view

scrutiny: analysis, examination, in-spection, investigation, observe, sur-veillance, watch

scud: cloud, dart, fly, go before the wind, gust, run, skim, wind

scuff: mar

scuffle: affray, brawl, fight, fracas, how, melee, row, scrap, shuffle, strife, tus-sle, wrestle

sculptor: artist, carver, chiseler

sculptural relief that projects very little from background: bas-relief, basso-relievo, low relief

sculpture: art, bust, carve, chisel, he-roic, mold, sculpt, shape, statue, totem

sculpture like mobile but having no moving parts, abstract metal: stabile

sculpture made of gold and ivory: chryselephantine

sculpture of equilibrated parts that move: mobile

sculpture opposite of intaglio: relief

sculpture with design carved into or be-neath surface, opposite of relief: intaglio

sculpture, chip from stone carving of: spall

sculpture, framework for clay: armature

sculpture, plaster of Paris and glue as base for low-relief: gesso

sculpture, small model of intended: maquette

sculpture, wax casting process for metal: ciré perdue, lost-wax process

sculptured basket of fruit or flowers in architecture: corbeil

sculptured slab: stele

scum: algae, dregs, film, foam, froth, rabble, refuse, residue, slime, snake, trash, waste

scurrilous: abusive, coarse, derogatory, dirty, disparaging, filthy, foul, gross, indecent, insulting, lewd, obscene, offensive, raunchy, vile, vulgar

scurry: base, bustle, contemptible, dart, dash, disease, flit, harry, hasten, hie, hurry, hustle, mean, race, run, rush, scoot, scorbutic, scuttle, shabby, ske-daddle, speed, sprint, vile, whisk

scurvy, concerning: scorbutic

scuttlebutt: chitchat, common talk, gossip, hearsay, rumor, talk

sea anemone or animal attaching to sur-faces and looking like plants: antho-zoan, zoophyte

sea arm, long and narrow with high banks: fjord

sea barrier to protect harbor: break-water, bulwark, groin, mole

sea by sandbars or coral reefs, body of water separated from: lagoon

sea cow: manatee

sea from mainland, land strip projecting into: peninsula

sea- or yellowish-green: glaucous

sea organisms at surface, microscopic: plankton

sea partially enclosed by land, large area of: gulf

sea robber: buccaneer, corsair, freeboo-ter, pirate, privateer

sea through another country, strip of land allowing inland country access to: corridor

sea water, to remove salt and chemicals from: desalinate, desalinize

sea with numerous islands: archipelago

sea, concerning the: marine, maritime, nautical, pelagic, thalassic

sea, high ridge of land jutting into a: promontory

sea, narrow inlet of the: estuary, firth

sea, person unfamiliar with the: landlubber

sea, wreckage at: flotsam, jetsam

seal: assurance, assure, attest, authenti-cate, brand, cachet, cap, clinch, close, confine, consummate, cork, fasten, finalize, guarantee, hallmark, insignia, pledge, plug, ratify, secure, shut, sigil, sign, signet, stamp, sticker, symbol, token, validate, waterproof

seal-like aquatic mammal: manatee

seal male fur: seecatch

seal on pope's bull: bulla

seal pipe joints, substance used to: lute, luting

seal seams of ship with tar or asphalt: pay

seal to make watertight, airtight: caulk

seal, young: pup

seal, pertaining to: phocid, phocine

sealed medicine vial: ampoule
sealed with a cork: bunged
sealed, completely: airtight, hermetic
seals and signets, study of: sphragistics
seals, group of: pod, school
sealskin: sculp
seam: bond, cleft, connection, coupling, crack, crevice, fissure, fold, groove, hem, join, joint, layer, line, mark, pleat, ridge, scar, sew, stitching, stratum, suture, wrinkle
seaman: gob, mariner, mate, salt, tar
seamlike joint of articulation in fruit, shell, bones: suture
seamstress: dressmaker, needleworker, sewer, tailor
seamy: base, corrupt, rough, seedy, sordid, unpleasant, unwholesome
seance: gathering, haven, meeting, ritual, seaport, session, sitting, town
sear: broil, brown, burn, char, cook, dry, mark, parch, scar, scorch, singe, sizzle, wither
search: canvass, check, comb, delve, drag, dragnet, examine, exploration, explore, ferret, forage, frisk, hunt, inquire, inspect, investigate, learn, look, manhunt, probe, prospect, pursuit, quest, rake, ransack, research, rifle, rummage, scavenge, scour, scout, scrounge, scrutinize, seek, sift, survey
search bottom of body of water: drag
search deeply and laboriously: delve, probe
search for food, supplies: forage, scavenge
search for game animals: hunt
search for information: delve, ferret, investigate
search for management employees: head-hunt
search for the meaning or nature of: fathom
search rapidly: skirr
search someone for something concealed: frisk
search thoroughly: comb, ransack, root
search, judicial writ authorizing: warrant
search, make preliminary: reconnoiter
seas', lakes', rivers' navigation, study of: hydrography
seas, waterway linking two: strait
seashore: beach, coast, seaboard, seacoast, seaside
seasickness: dizziness, mal de mer, nausea, queasiness, wooziness

season: accent, acclimatize, accustom, harden, inure, mature, prepare, refine, ripen, soften, temper, train
season food: add, age, embellish, enliven, flavor, marinate, pepper, salt, savor, spice
season of the year: autumn, fall, spring, summer, winter; interval, period
season of warm hazy weather in late autumn: Indian summer
seasonable: appropriate, apropos, apt, favorable, mature, opportune, relevant, suitable, timely
seasonal activity: spring cleaning, spring training
seasoned: aged, experienced, veteran
seasoning: allspice, basil, cardamom, celery, cloves, condiment, dill, dressing, garlic, ginger, gravy, herb, mace, marjoram, mustard, nutmeg, onion, oregano, paprika, parsley, pepper, relish, rosemary, sage, salt, sauce, seasoner, spice, thyme, vinegar, zest
seat: backside, banquette, base, behind, bench, bleacher, bottom, buttocks, capital, center, chair, cushion, derriere, floor, foundation, fulcrum, home, house, hub, install, keister, locality, location, lounge, membership, ottoman, pew, place, posterior, residence, rest, room, rump, settle, sit, site, situate, station, stool, throne, usher
seat for elephant or camel riders: howdah
seat for second rider: pillion
seat for two people: love seat
seat in aircraft, emergency: ejection seat
seat in car, extra folding: jump seat
seat in nook by fireplace: inglenook
seat on rowboat: thwart
seat or sofa, backless upholstered: ottoman
seat, boxlike (horizontal), for carrying with poles by litter bearers: palanquin
seat, boxlike (upright), for carrying with poles by litter bearers: sedan chair
seated and inactive: sedentary
seaward current of water beneath the surface: undercurrent
seaward pull of waves after breaking: undertow
seaweed: agar, agar-agar, algae, carrageen, delisk, desmid, desmidian,

dulse, gulfweed, Irish moss, kelp, nori, reit, rockweed, sargasso, talgae, tangle, varec
seaweed and vegetation cast ashore: wrack
seaweed ash: kelp
seaweed jelly: agar
seclude: cloister, conceal, evict, exclude, hide, isolate, quarantine, recess, remove, retire, retreat, screen, segregate, separate, sequester, withdraw
secluded: alone, aloof, cloistral, deserted, isolated, lone, lonesome, private, reclusive, remote, secret, sequestered, sheltered, solitary, withdrawn
secluded for season: hibernating
second: abet, additional, advocate, aid, aide, another, assist, assistant, back, confirm, deputy, double, encourage, endorse, flash, forward, help, inferior, instant, jiffy, moment, next, other, ratify, stand-in, subordinate, substitute, succeed, support, supporter, time, understudy, uphold, wink
second-hand: reused, used, worn
second-rate: cheap, common, inadequate, inferior, mediocre, shabby
second-time feeling for an experience: déja vu
second-year student: sophomore
secondary: accessory, affiliated, ancillary, appendant, appurtenant, attendant, auxiliary, backup, borrowed, bye, dependent, derivative, derived, incidental, indirectly, inferior, lesser, minor, satellite, small, subordinate, tributary, unessential
secondary in rank: subaltern, subservient, subsidiary
secondary response or idea: afterthought, footnote, postscript
secondary school exam, in Britain: A level
secondary tone produced by fundamental tone: harmonic, overtone
secondhand: hand-me-down, used
secrecy: closeness, concealment, covertness, mystery, privacy, silence, stealth
secret: arcane, camouflaged, clandestine, classified, closet, clouded, concealed, concealment, confidence, confidential, covert, cryptic, dark, discreet, disguised, enigma, esoteric, furtive, hidden, hide, mysterious,

mystery, mystical, obscure, occult, private, privy, remote, retired, secluded, seclusion, shrouded, sneaky, stealthy, surreptitious, undercover, underhand, unknown, veiled

secret agent: collaborator, courier, emissary, mole, operative, saboteur, spy

secret agreement for illegal or deceitful purpose: connivance, collusion

secret and hidden: covert, subterranean

secret and personal: intimate, private

secret and with intrigue: cloak-and-dagger

secret communications or exchange, predetermined place for: drop

secret doctrine: cabala

secret except to authorized persons: classified

secret fund used for corruption: slush fund

secret group pursuing interest: cabal, junta, junto

secret hiding place: cache, stash

secret information: intelligence

secret jargon: cant

secret key resource or weapon: ace in the hole, trump card

secret laboratory: skunk works

secret means of relaying information: grapevine

secret meeting: conclave

secret meeting of lovers: assignation, tryst

secret meeting of organization: executive session

secret name: cryptonym

secret or concealed, knowing something: privy

secret session: in camera

secret stealthy means, done or obtained by: furtive, surreptitious

secret things: penetralia

secret writing system or message: cipher, cryptographic system

secret, disclosing of: disclosure, disinterment, divulgement, revelation

secret, in: confidentially, in camera, in confidence, privately, sub rosa

secret, kept or done in: backstair(s), clandestine, furtive

secret, known to only a few: arcane, cryptic, esoteric, occult

secret, performed or occurring in: undercover

secret, security status offering more access than: restricted

secretary: aide, amanuensis, assistant, chancellor, clerk, desk, officer, official, recorder, steno, typist

secretary in ancient times: scribe

secrete: bury, cache, conceal, discharge, exude, filch, hide, ooze, screen, stash

secretion: bile, gum, hormone, juice, laap, latex, milk, mucus, saliva, sap, sweat, tears

secretive or stealthy way, working in: insidious

secretly: sub rosa

secretly informed: privy

secretly into enemy territory, to enter: infiltrate

secretly meeting or planned: clandestine

secretly or concealed: incognito

secretly provoking another to do illegal act, person: agent provocateur

secrets are disclosed, one to whom: confidant, confidante

sect: caste, church, clan, cult, denomination, faction, faith, group, order, party, persuasion, religion, school

sectarian: bigoted, dissenter, factional, heretic, limited, narrow-minded, non-conformist, parochial, partisan, zealot

section: area, branch, category, division, leg, locality, parcel, part, piece, portion, region, sector, segment, slice, sphere, territory, tract, vicinity, zone

section of document, distinct: clause

sector: area, district, division, quarter, section, zone

secular: civil, earthly, laic, laical, lay, layperson, material, nonclerical, nonspiritual, profane, temporal, worldly

secure: acquire, anchor, assure, attach, bind, bolt, cement, chain, clamp, clasp, clinch, constrain, defend, fasten, get, guarantee, guard, insure, land, lock, moor, nail, obtain, procure, protect, safeguard, tie, tighten

secure a boat: anchor, moor

secure or settle: clinch

secure, being: assured, certain, confident, dependable, easy, fast, firm, on ice, shielded, solid, sound, stable, strong, unharmed

secure, make certain: ensure

secure, valuable shareholdings: blue chip stocks

securities held: portfolio

securities pledged as collateral: hypothecation

securities purchase in one market for immediate resale on another market at a higher price: arbitrage

securities, buy or sell order good only on day it is entered: day order

securities, buying at intervals in fixed amount: monthly investment plan

security: armament, assurance, bail, confidence, defense, freedom, gage, guarantee, guard, hostage, insurance, lien, pledge, police, protection, safeguard, safety, sanctuary, shelter, shield, stability, surety, trust, warranty

security against loss, damage, default: guarantee, security, surety

security against obligation: gage, pledge

security for debt without transfer of title, pledge as: hypothecate

security for loan or other obligation: collateral

security having a maturity of less than a year with no interest and sold at a discount, U.S. Treasury: Treasury bill

security transferable by delivery: negotiable

sedate: calm, collected, composed, cool, dignified, dope up, drug, earnest, grave, placid, proper, quiet, serene, serious, settled, sober, solemn, staid, still, subdued, tranquil, unruffled

sedative: barbiturate, depressant, downer, drug, lenitive, narcotic, opiate, pacifier, palliative, relaxing, soothing, tranquilizer

sedentary: inactive, inert, lazy, motionless, seated, settled, sluggish, stationary

sediment: crap, debris, deposit, dregs, grounds, gunk, lees, refuse, residue, scum, settling, silt, slag, sludge, soot, trash, waste

sediment at bottom of liquid like coffee: grounds

sediment at bottom of liquid like wine: dregs, foots, lees

sediment of very fine particles: silt

sedition: coup, dissension, insurrection, lawlessness, mutiny, protest, rebellion, revolt, revolution, strife, subversion, treason, uprising

seditious: treasonous

seduce: allure, charm, coax, corrupt, debauch, deflower, draw, entice, lure, mislead, tease, tempt

seductive: alluring, attractive, captivating, charming, desirable, enchanting, enticing, flirtatious, provocative, sexy, voluptuous

seductress: Jezebel, Lorelei, seducer, siren, temptress, vamp

sedulous: active, assiduous, busy, busy as a bee, diligent, industrious, laborious, painstaking, persevering, persistent, untiring, vivacious

seed: acorn, ancestry, beginning, bud, bulbs, children, conception, core, descendants, egg, embryo, germ, grain, kernel, offspring, origin, pea, pip, plant, posterity, progeny, samara, scatter, source, sow, spark, sperm, spore, voule

RELATED TERMS

seed coat: aril, hull, testa

seed or pod of pea, bean: legume, pulse

seed part that develops into root: radicule

seed part that develops into stem: seminal

seed plant, embryonic part of: ovule

seed plant, leaf of the embryo of: cotyledon

seed pod seam: raphe, suture

seed to speed germination, slit: scarify

seed with ovary, stalk connecting: funiculus

seed's scar where it was attached to stem: hilum, umbilicus

seed, grow from: germinate

seed, hairs on a: coma

seed, inner coat of: tegmen

seed, opening for pollen to fertilize: micrypyle

seed, two-winged: dipterous

seed, wall of fruit: pericarp

seed-bearing: seminiferous

seed-bearing capsule of cotton, flax, etc.: boll

seed-bearing part of flowering plant: pistil

seedless plant: fern

seeds germinating on parent plant: viviparous

seeds in rows, sow: drill, furrow

seeds of flowering plants, nutritive tissue: endosperm

seeds, feeding on: granivorous

seeds, outgrowth on certain: caruncle ❦

seedy: bedraggled, debilitated, decaying, decrepit, mangy, messy, neglected, ratty, shabby, slovenly, tacky, tattered, unkempt, untidy, worn

seeing everything in one view: panoptic

seek: aspire, comb, court, delve, endeavor, examine, explore, hunt, inquire, investigate, probe, pursue, quest, request, scout, search, sniff, solicit, trace, undertake

seem: appear, imply, insinuate, intimate, look, pretend, sound

seeming: apparent, evident, illusory, ostensible, presumed, professed, purported, quasi, supposed

seeming to exist: nominally

seemingly: quasi, reputedly

seemingly attractive or true: specious

seemly: acceptable, appropriate, becoming, befitting, compatible, correct, decent, decorous, fitting, meet, pleasing, proper, right, suitable, suited

seep: dribble, drip, exude, flow, infiltrate, leak, ooze, percolate, permeate, spread, trickle

seer: astrologer, augur, clairvoyant, diviner, forecaster, medium, mystic, oracle, predictor, prognosticator, prophet, psychic, soothsayer, sorcerer, sorceress, sybil

seesaw: alternate, fluctuate, rock, sway, teeter, teeter-totter, vacillate, waver

seethe: boil, bubble, churn, foam, fret, fume, rage, sizzle, steam, steep, stew, teem

segment: cantle, divide, division, fragment, parcel, part, period, piece, portion, section, separate, share, slice

segregate: detach, divide, insulate, isolate, part, quarantine, seclude, separate, sequester

seism: earthquake, quake, tremor

seize: abduct, afflict, annex, apprehend, appropriate, arrest, arrogate, attack, bag, bind, capture, catch, claw, clinch, collar, commandeer, comprehend, confiscate, conquer, corral, gather, grab, grip, hijack, hook, impound, kidnap, nab, net, occupy, overtake, possess, prehend, secure, snatch, strike, take, trap, understand, usurp

seize and hold to compel payment: distrain, distress, sequestrate

seize and hold without legal authority: usurp

seize and incorporate territory: annex

seize and put in custody: impound, sequester

seize beforehand: preempt

seize by violence: grapple, wrest

seize for military use: commandeer, confiscate

seize neutral vessel in wartime: spoliation

seize on the way: intercept

seize or rob by force: pillage, rapine

seize something in mid-course: intercept

seize the day: carpe diem

seize without permission: appropriate, confiscate, levy

seizure: abduction, attack, capture, convulsion, episode, fit, paroxysm, spasm, spell, stroke

seizure of property in legal proceeding: attachment

seldom: hardly, infrequently, occasionally, rarely, scarcely, sporadically, uncommonly

seldom seen: rare, rarity

select: best, choice, choose, chosen, cull, decide, draw, elect, elite, excellent, exclusive, good, handpicked, name, nominate, opt, pick, pick out, prefer, preferred, rare, superior, take, topnotch

selected passages of writing: analecta, analects

selecting from diverse sources: eclectic

selection: choice, collection, draft, excerpt, option, passage, pick, preference, vote

selection of literary passages by an author: chrestomathy

selective: careful, choosy, discriminating, eclectic, finicky, fussy, particular, picky

self: being, character, ego, identical, identity, individuality, myself, oneself, own, personal, personality, psyche

RELATED TERMS

self-absorbed: egotistical, narcissistic, vain

self-absorbed person: omphalopsychite

self-acceptance, induced: autosuggestion

self-assertive: audacious, bold, bumptious, confident, immodest, pushy, sure

self-assurance: aplomb, poise

self-assured: calm, cocky, composed, confident, poised, pose, smug, unabashed

self-centered: egocentric, egotistical, narcissistic, selfish

self-centered as ethnic group: ethnocentric

self-composed: calm, collected, poised

self-confidence: aplomb, assurance, cockiness, conceit, pluck, poise

self-congratulatory: smug

self-conscious: awkward, insecure, nervous, uncomfortable, uneasy, unnatural, unsure

self-contradictory statement: paradox

self-control: calmness, composure, constraint, discipline, fighting, forebearance

self-defense or combat arts: martial arts

self-denial: abnegation, abstinence, ascetic, asceticism, selflessness

self-denial of indulging: abstemiousness, abstinence, temperance

self-determination: autonomy

self-discipline in religion: askesis

self-discipline, one living life of: ascetic

self-esteem: amour propre, confidence, ego, egotism, pride, self-respect, vanity

self-evident: apparent, axiomatic, clear, glaring, obvious, plain, prima facie, undeniable, unequivocal, unmistakable, visible

self-evident statement: axiom

self-examination of innermost feelings: heart-searching, introspection

self-explanatory: clear, distinct, evident, manifest, obvious, plain, unmistakable

self-generated: spontaneous

self-governing: autonomous, independent, sovereign

self-importance: conceit, ego, egoism, pomposity, vainglory

self-important: arrogant, conceited, egotistical, hoity-toity, pompous, pretentious, smug, stuffy

self-important old guard: Colonel Blimp

self-important person: panjandrum, snob

self-indulgence: debauchery, depravity, dissipation, dissolution, intemperance

self-indulgent: decadent, effete, greedy, hedonistic, miserly, parsimonious, sybaritic

self-interest, serving: expedient

self is the only thing that can be known, theory: solipsism

self-love: conceit, egotism, narcissim, narcissism, vainglory, vanity

self-operated machine: automaton

self part of psyche: ego

self-possessed: calm, collected, composed, confident, cool, easy, poised, reserved, tranquil

self-possession: aplomb, composure, countenance, poise, self-confidence

self-protective reaction: defense mechanism

self-reflecting: reflexive

self-reliant: hardy, independent, resolute

self-respect: confidence, dignity, pride, self-esteem, vanity, worth

self-restraint: continence, moderation

self-righteous: canting, holier-than-thou, moralistic, pharisaical, pompous, preachy, sanctimonious, smug

self-sacrificing: gallant, generous, helpful, heroic, noble, unselfish

self-satisfaction: contentment, pride, smugness

self-satisfied: complacent, content, egotistic, priggish, proud, smug, vain

self-service meal: buffet, cafeteria, smorgasbord

self-styled expert: maven

self-sufficient: arrogant, competent, confident, efficient, independent, smug

self-sufficient country or region: autarky

self-taught person: autodidact

self-training of body and mind: biofeedback

self, particular to the: subjective

self, second: alter ego

selfish: asocial, egocentric, grabby, self-aggrandizing, self-centered, self-seeking

selfless: altruistic ❦

sell: auction, bargain, barter, betray, cheat, convince, deal, deliver, dispose, dump, fetch, hawk, hustle, market, negotiate, peddle, persuade, push, retail, stock, supply, trade, transfer, unload, vend, wholesale

sell assets for cash: liquidate

sell by quiet persuasion: soft sell

sell contraband: fence

sell for quick profit: scalp

sell goods on street: hawk, peddle, vend

sell in large quantities at low cost: dump

sell off company or holdings: divest

sell out: betray, cross, deceive, mislead, trick

sell property for profit: realize

sell to consumers: retail

seller: agent, businessperson, dealer, merchant, peddler, pusher, retailer, salesman, salesperson, saleswoman, shopkeeper, storekeeper, trader, vender

seller of food: provisioner, purveyor

selling and buying, to carry on: trafficking

semblance: air, analogy, apparition, appearance, aspect, aura, bearing, copy, duplicate, feeling, guise, image, likeness, look, mask, modicum, pretense, pretext, representation, resemblance, showing, similarity, similitude

semicircle: arc, hemicycle

semiconductor: diode

semiconscious: hypnopompic

semifluid: viscous

semiskilled worker: blue-collar worker

senator: lawmaker, legislator, politician, statesman

send: address, bestow, broadcast, carry, commission, consign, convey, delegate, deliver, discharge, dispatch, drive, emit, fling, forward, hurl, inflict, issue, launch, mail, project, propel, relay, remit, route, ship, throw, transmit, wire

senile: aged, ancient, decrepit, doddering, doting, feeble, feebleminded, infirm, old, weak

senility: caducity, dotage

senility caused by disease: Alzheimer's disease

senior: ancient, doyen, elder, eldest, golden-ager, head, older, student, superior

senior member of group: doyen, doyenne

seniority: precedence, priority, quality, rank, standing, status, tenure

sensate: alive

sensation: bombshell, emotion, feeling, marvel, perception, phenomenon, scandal, sense, sensibility, thrill, tingle

sensation like vision, hearing: modality

sensation or sensibility, lacking: insensate

sensational: amazing, boffo, breathtaking, dramatic, electrifying, emotional, exciting, glorious, impressive, lurid, marvelous, outstanding, remarkable, shocking, smash, spectacular, startling, stunning, superb, thrilling

sense: anticipate, apprehend, aura, awareness, comprehend, consciousness, definition, feel, feel in ones bones, feeling, foresight, grasp, hearing, intelligence, intuition, judgment, meaning, message, mind, perceive, perception, point, prudence, realize, reason, sensation, sensibility, sight, smell, substance, taste, touch, understanding, wisdom, worth

sense of unhealth: malaise

senseless: absurd, comatose, deadened, dumb, foolish, idiotic, illogical, inane, insensible, irrational, meaningless, mindless, moronic, nonsensical, numb, nutty, oblivious, pointless, purposeless, ridiculous, silly, stupid, unconscious, unfeeling, unreasonable

senses are the only source of knowledge, view that the: empiricism

senses as source of pleasure: sensuous

senses, capable of being perceived by: perceptible

senses, occurrence or fact perceptible by: phenomenon

senses, something not perceived by the: noumenon

sensibility: affection, awareness, esthesia, feeling, insight, keenness, perception, rationale

sensible: aware, cognitive, cognizant, discerning, emotional, intelligent, judicious, keen, knowing, levelheaded, logical, moronic, painful, perceptive, prudent, psychic, rational, realistic, reasonable, reasoned, responsive, ridiculous, sane, sensitive, smart, sound, together, tricky, wise

sensitive: acute, delicate, impressionable, receptive, responsive, sore, susceptible, tender, touchy

sensitive flesh under fingernails: quick

sensitive to fine distinctions: subtle

sensitive, especially: passible, susceptible, thin-skinned, vulnerable

sensitivity and speed, perceiving with: quick

sensitivity in the extreme: hyperesthesia

sensitivity of body part, abnormal: erethism

sensitivity to heat and cold: thermesthesia

sensitivity when dealing with others: tact

sensory appendages on insect heads: antenna

sensory organs of mollusks, crustaceans, insects: palp, palpus

sensory organs on some fishes' heads: barb, barbel

sensory stimuli, cell or nerve endings responding to: receptor

sensual: adjudge, adjudication, carnal, coarse, condemn, decide, decision, decree, doom, erotic, fleshly, fleshy, judgment, lewd, licentious, lustful, passage, physical, proscribe, rap, seductive, sensuous, sexual, sexy, statement, steamy, voluptuous, worldly

sensual pleasures, indulgence in: debauchery, depravity, dissipation, dissolution, intemperance

sensual pleasures, person indulging in: hedonist, sybarite, voluptuary

sensual pleasures, place offering: fleshpot

sensualist: epicure, roue, voluptuary

sensuous: carnal, hedonistic, luxurious, passionate, pleasurable, sensual, sultry, sybaritic, voluptuous

sentence: condemnation, convict, doom, edict, penalize, penalty, punishment, stretch, term, verdict

sentence containing one independent and one or more dependent clauses: complex sentence

sentence difficult to say fast: tongue twister

sentence in paragraph stating main thought: topic sentence

sentence into component parts, break down a: parse

sentence is completed, release for good behavior before: parole, probation

sentence reading the same forwards and backwards: palindrome

sentence that declares a statement: declarative

sentence that differs in number but agrees in meaning: synesis

sentence using all the letters of the alphabet: pangram

sentence with carefully balanced clauses in formal writing: period

sentence with clauses joined by punctuation: parataxis

sentence with clauses joined with connectives: hypotaxis

sentence with main clause at the end: periodic sentence

sentence with two or more independent clauses: compound sentence

sentence with two or more independent clauses improperly joined: fused sentence, run-on sentence

sentence, abrupt change within a: anacoluthon

sentence, arrangement of words to make meaningful: construction

sentence, break in middle: aposiopesis

sentence, incomplete: fragment

sentence, sudden breaking of thought mid-: aposiopesis

sentence, to reduce to a less severe: commute

sentences' separation by comma rather than by correct semicolon or period: comma fault, comma splice, run-on sentence

sentences, rules for correct: syntax

sententious: abounding, aphoristic, brief, concise, meaningful, moralistic, pithy, pompous, pretentious, short, terse

sentient: aware

sentiment: attitude, conviction, disposition, emotion, feeling, inclination, leaning, meaning, notion, opinion, penchant, perception, tendency, thought, view

sentimental: affectionate, corny, emotional, gushy, idealistic, lovey-dovey, loving, maudlin, mawkish, moonstruck, mushy, nostalgic, romantic, sappy, tender, touching

sentimental and dull: insipid, namby-pamby

sentimental and overly sweet: cloying, saccharine

sentimental tale: tearjerker

sentimental, tearfully: maudlin, mawkish

sentimentality: bathos, hokum, schmaltz

sentimentality, false: mawkishness

sentinel: guard, keeper, lookout, patrol, sentry, soldier, watchman

sentry: guard, sentinel

separate: abstract, alienate, alone, apart, assort, break, cleave, cull, dependent, detach, detached, different, disassociate, discharge, disconnect, disconnected, discrete, disengage, disjoin, dismember, disparate, dispart, disperse, dissect, dissociate, distinct, distinctive, distinguish, distribute, disunite, diverse, divide, divorce, eliminate, estrange, extricate, free, halve, individual, isolate, isolated, part, partition, quarantine, remove, secede, secluded, segment, segregate, sequester, set apart, sever, sift, single, solitary, sort, space, split, strip, subdivide, sunder, unattached, unconnected, uncouple, undo, unlink, unravel, winnow

separate by boundaries: demarcate

separate chaff from grain with air: winnow

separate checks: Dutch treat

separate coarse from fine particles: sift

separate copies: decollate

separate directions from common point: branch out, divaricate, diverge

separate from a set course or norm: deviate, divaricate, diverge

separate from others or main body of group: segregate

separate from, to cause to be: cordon off, insulate, isolate

separate grain or seed by beating: flail, thresh

separate into categories: compartmentalize, pigeonhole

separate into opposing groups: polarize

separate into two parts: bifurcate, dichotomize, fork, ramify

separate or disperse: disband

separate or divide into parts, sections: break up, dismember, fractionate, fragment, partition, segment

separate or unfasten: detach, disjoin, dislodge

separate people, come between: interpose, intervene

separate the essential elements of: distill

separate to prevent disease from spreading: quarantine

separated in emotional relations: alienated, estranged

separated or kept apart: cloistered, secluded, sequestered

separated, divided: asunder, cleft, cloven

separately: apart, respectively

separately priced items on the menu: à la carte

separation: apartheid, breakup, detachment, discharge, disjunction, distance, division, divorce, fracture, gap, gulf, parting, partition, schism, segregation, severance, split, wall

sepulcher: bury, catacomb, crypt, entomb, grave, necropolis, repository, tomb, vault

sequel: aftermath, chain, conclusion, consequence, continuation, effect, offshoot, order, outcome, result, sequence, series, succession, upshot

sequence: chain, course, cycle, episode, flow, gamut, order, outcome, progression, rhythm, schedule, sequel, series, succession

sequence in logic or grammar: consecution

sequence of events, middle of: in medias res

sequence of priority, rank, superiority: precedence

sequence of those in line for title, throne, estate: succession

sequence of, reverse or change the: transpose

sequence, arrange in: codify, systematize, tabulate

sequence, assemble in logical or numerical: collate

sequence, change in: permutation

sequence, formed by: consecutive, ordered, sequential, serial, successive

sequence, lacking a: aleatoric, aleatory, arbitrary, haphazard, random

sequence, place in proper: collocate

sequential: chronological, consecutive, continuous, following, next, serial, succeeding

sequester: confine, confiscate, insulate, isolate, quarantine, seclude, segregate, seize, separate

sequoia: redwood

serape: shawl

seraphic: angelic, beatific, cherubic, heavenly, pure, sublime

sere: arid, burned, desicated, dried, droughty, dry, parched, scorched, shriveled, waterless, withered

serene: bright, calm, clear, collected, composed, cool, fair, impassive, peaceful, placid, poised, quiet, sedate, smooth, steady, still, tranquil, unclouded, undisturbed, unobscured, unruffled

serenity: balance, calm, composure, peace, peace of mind, peacefulness, quietude, stillness, tranquility

serf: bondman, churl, esne, helot, hireling, peasant, peon, servant, slave, thrall, vassal, villein

serial: consecutive, continual, ordered, recurring, sequential, succeeding, successive

serial installment: episode

series: category, chain, column, consecution, continuation, continuity, course, list, order, progression, scale, sequel, sequence, string, succession, train

series in which elements are graded or ranked: hierarchy

series of connected rooms, furniture pieces, or another set: suite

series of events with each influencing the next: causality, chain reaction

series of gradual, successive stages: gradation

series of melodies in one musical arrangement: medley

series of reactions where results become causes: chain reaction

series or chain, connect or link in: catenate, concatenate

series or continuous succession with indistinguishable divisions: cline, continuum, spectrum

series or range, complete: gamut

series opening show, TV: pilot

series, in a: seriatim

serious: austere, businesslike, critical, crucial, deep, determined, difficult, dire, earnest, ernest, grave, grim, hard, heavy, humorless, important, intense, intent, life and death, momentous, pensive, pressing, reflective, sedate, severe, sober, solemn, staid, unamusing, unsmiling, weighty

serious and dismal: grave, grim, pokerfaced, solemn, somber

serious and extreme: acute, drastic, grievous

serious and firm: determined, intent, resolute

serious and important: consequential, momentous

serious and sincere: fervent, heartfelt

serious and sober: dignified, sedate, staid

serious and thoughtful: introspective, pensive, reflective

serious face when telling a joke: deadpan

serious hard work: assiduity, conscientiousness, diligence

seriousness of, increase the: aggravate, compound, exacerbate

seriousness of, lessen the: extenuate, mitigate

sermon: address, discourse, harangue, homily, lecture, lesson, preaching, preachment, speech

sermon with moral: exemplum

sermon writing, study of: homiletics

sermonize: prelect

serpent: asp, creature, devil, fiend, krait, reptile, satan, snake, viper

serpentine: convoluted, crooked, devilish, devious, fiendish, meandering, sinuous, sly, snaky, sneaky, tempting, wily, winding

serrate: denticulate, erose, jagged, notched, toothed

servant: amah, attendant, chamberlain, chambermaid, chauffeur, cook, domestic, eunuch, factotum, flunkey, flunky, footman, garcon, girl, gofer, groom, handmaid, help, helper, housekeeper, maid, menial, minion, nurse, page, retainer, slave, squire, usher, valet, varlet, vassal

servant and child-care giver, foreign: au pair

servant in harem, castrated male: eunuch

servant in VIP household, highest-ranking: butler, chamberlain, chief steward, majordomo, seneschal

servant or attendant: acolyte, famulus, varlet, yeoman

servant or attendant in VIP household: familiar, retainer

servant or attendant, woman: handmaid

servant who does errands: gofer

servant, attendant, errand runner: bellhop, page

servant, horse- or automobile-tending: hostler, ostler

servant, hotel: chambermaid, femme de chambre

servant, household: ancillary, domestic, menial

servant, liveried: chasseur, flunky, footman, lackey

servant, man's male: valet

servants of household and their uniforms, male: livery

servants or attendants for VIP, group of: retinue, suite, train

serve: act, advance, aid, assist, attend, avail, benefit, cater, deliver, distribute, function, further, give, help, ladle, minister, offer, officiate, pass, requite, satisfy, succor, suffice, suit, supply, tend, treat, wait, wait on, work

service: agency, assistance, benefit, bureau, duty, employ, employment, help, liturgy, maintenance, setting, utility

service, offer: cater, help, maintain, repair, supply

service or ceremony: liturgy, mass, rite, sermon

serviceable: beneficial, dependable, durable, effective, functional, helpful, practical, tough, useful, utile, valuable

services or features of a place: amenities, facilities

services, units of armed: battalion, battery, brigade, command, company, corps, division, flight, group, platoon, regiment, squad, troop, wing

serviette: napkin

servile: abject, base, bootlicking, compliant, cringing, dependent, fawning, groveling, ignoble, mean, menial, obedient, obsequious, sequacious, slavish, submissive, subservient, sycophantic, toadying

serving: dollop, plate, portion

serving as means to an end: expedient, subservient

serving no good purpose: futile

serving or aiding, act or process: ministration

serving stand or table, portable: dumbwaiter

servitude: bondage, captivity, confinement, peonage, serfdom, slavery, subjection, subjugation, thralldom, vassalage

session: assemblage, bout, conference, discussion, gathering, meeting, round, semester, sitting, term

session fully attended: plenary

set apart: allocate, alone, distinguish, earmark, isolate, seclude, segregate, separate, sequester

set aside: abrogate, annul, cancel, discard, earmark, isolate, overturn, reject, reserve, saved, table, void

set back: delay, hinder, mire, reverse

set forth: begin, explain, leave, present, start, state

set free: emancipate, extricate, let go, liberate, loosen, pardon, release, unleash

set in one's ways: inflexible, intractable, monolithic, ossified, rigid

set of symptoms indicating disease or condition: syndrome

set of values: ethic, ethos

set off: activate, detonate, explode, start, trip

set straight: align, correct, disabuse, enlighten, revise

set-to: altercation, argument, brawl, dispute, fight, fracas, fray, quarrel, scuffle, skirmish, spat, squabble

set up: arrange, begin, build, create, erect, establish, found, generate, institute, launch, open, organize, pose, start

set up according to law or provision: constitute

set, in or as part of a: en suite

set, matching or coordinated: ensemble

setback: defeat, disappointment, hindrance, impediment, loss, obstacle, rebuff, relapse, reversal, reverse

sets type, person who: compositor, typesetter

sets, correspondence between elements of: mapping

setting: ambiance, backdrop, decor, environment, framework, hardening, locale, location, mounting, scene, scenery, surroundings

setting of film, etc.: mise-en-scéne

setting or scene: ambience, locale, milieu, surroundings

settle: accommodate, adjudicate, appoint, arrange, assign, calm, clarify, clear, colonize, compose, conclude, confirm, decide, deposit, designate, determine, dispose, establish, firm, habituate, land, live, locate, lodge, marry, nest, pacify, pay, perch, plant, populate, provide, quiet, reconcile, rectify, reduce, regulate, relieve, remit, render, resolve, sag, seat, secure, set, sink, solve, soothe, stabilize, subside, tranquilize

settle differences between other people: arbitrate, conciliate, mediate, moderate

settle or adjust: compose, determine, reconcile

settle securely: ensconce, entrench

settlement: agreement, arrangement, compensation, compromise, conclu-

SEVEN WONDERS OF THE ANCIENT WORLD

The Colossus of Rhodes
The Great Pyramids of Egypt at Giza
The Hanging Gardens of Babylon
The Lighthouse of Alexandria
The Mausoleum of King Mausolus at Halicarnassus
The Statue of Zeus at Olympia
The Temple of Artemis (Diana) at Ephesus ❦

---

sion, decision, determination, establishment, payment, regulation, reimbursement, resolution, sediment

settlement or camp: colonization, colony, community, habitation, hamlet, outpost, residence, village

settlement conditions: terms

settlement of accounts: reckoning

settlement of dispute by middle party chosen by sides: arbitration, mediation

settler: colonist, colonizer, habitant, homesteader, immigrant, pilgrim, pioneer, planter, sooner

settler without permission: squatter

seven days, occurring every: hebdomadal

seven things: heptad

seven years, continuing for or occurring every: septennial

sevenfold: septenary, septuple

seventy to seventy-nine years old, from: septuagenarian

sever: chop, cleave, cut, depart, detach, disassociate, dismember, dissociate, dissolve, disunite, divide, divorce, hack, lop off, nip, part, rend, separate, slice, slit, split, sunder

several: a few, assorted, different, distinct, diverse, handful, individual, many, miscellaneous, myriad, numerous, some, sundry, various

several languages, speaking, writing, and reading in: polyglot

several melodies arranged to form a piece of music: medley

severe: acute, afflictive, astringent, austere, biting, bitter, bleak, blistering, brutal, caustic, chronic, coarse, cold, crucial, cruel, cutting, dangerous, deadly, demanding, difficult, dour, drastic, exacting, excruciating, extreme, fierce, grave, grim, grueling, gruff, hard, harsh, hostile, inclement,

inflexible, intense, ironclad, oppressive, painful, relentless, rigid, rigorous, rough, scathing, sedate, serious, sharp, simple, sober, solemn, spartan, stern, stiff, strenuous, strict, stringent, tough, unpleasant, unsparing, violent

severe disciplinarian: martinet, ramrod

severe in criticism: scathing

severe self-discipline: austerity

severe, rigidly: demanding, draconian, rigorous

severity, to moderate in: alleviate, extenuate, mitigate, palliate

sew: baste, bind, darn, fasten, join, mend, needle, patch, seam, stitch, suture, unite

sew loosely with large running stitches: baste, tack

sewage: excrement, sludge, sullage, waste

sewage-disposal tank in which anaerobic bacteria decompose the material: septic tank

sewage-disposal underground system carrying off material: sewer

sewage from house, hole or pit for receiving drainage or: cesspool

sewage treatment semisolid material: sludge

sewing machine pedal: treadle

sewing thread treated to reduce shrinkage, increase luster and affinity for dye: mercerize

sewing together in surgery: suture

sex: coitus, copulation, fornication, intercourse, intimacy, love, lovemaking, reproduction; female, gender, male

sex bias: sexism

sex change, one who had: transsexual

sex partners sharing living quarters: cohabitation, common-law marriage, live-ins

sex, abstaining from: celibate

sex, inordinate interest in: prurience

sex, person who dresses as member of opposite: cross-dresser, transvestite

sexes united in one person: androgynous

sexes, having characteristics of both: androgynous, epicene, hermaphroditic, unisex

sexless: asexual, castrated, epicene, neuter, spayed, unisex

sexual: amatory, carnal, erotic, gamic, intimate, loving, passionate, reproductive, sensual, venereal

RELATED TERMS

sexual act, caught in an illicit: in flagrante delicto

sexual activity abstention: continence

sexual activity between men and boys: pederasty

sexual activity party: orgy

sexual activity, unwanted: molestation

sexual acts of others, one who gets gratification from viewing: peeping Tom, voyeur

sexual arousal of oneself: autoeroticism, masturbation

sexual arousal over inanimate object: fetishism

sexual attraction of adult to child: pedophilia

sexual behavior, unacceptable: deviance, perversion

sexual desire: concupiscence, Eros, libido

sexual desire in man, uncontrollable: erotomania, satyriasis

sexual desire in woman, uncontrollable: nymphomania

sexual desire, arousing: aphrodisiac, erogenous

sexual desire, lacking: anaphrodisia

sexual desires, given to expressing: concupiscent, debauched, lascivious, lecherous, lewd, libertine, libidinous, lubricious, lustful, salacious

sexual excitement period in female mammal: estrus, heat, rut

sexual excitement period in male deer: rut

sexual excitement period in male elephants, etc.: must, musth

sexual gratification by rubbing against another: frottage, grinding

sexual inactivity period for female mammals: anestrus, metestrus

sexual intercourse: carnal knowledge, coition, coitus, commerce, congress, conjugation, conjunction, consummation, conversation, copulation, union

sexual intercourse between partners not married to each other: fornication

sexual intercourse between people related but who could not marry: incest

sexual intercourse capacity: potency, virility

sexual intercourse deliberately interrupted: coitus interruptus

sexual intercourse with sleeping man, female demon who has: succubus

sexual intercourse with sleeping woman, male demon who has: incubus

sexual intercourse, abstaining from: ascetic, celibate, chaste, continent, virginal

sexual intercourse, averse to: frigid

sexual intercourse, incapable of: impotent

sexual intercourse, lacking interest in: asexual

sexual intercourse, transmitted by: venereal

sexual joining of sperm and egg: amphimixis

sexual love or desire, concerning: amatory, erotic

sexual maturing period: puberty

sexual organs: genitalia, genitals, private parts, privates, reproductive organs

sexual organs, concerning area of external: pubic

sexual organs, external: pudenda

sexual orientation to opposite sex: heterosexual

sexual orientation to same sex: gay, homosexual

sexual partner, unfaithfulness to: adultery, infidelity

sexual pervert: deviate

sexual potency of man: virility

sexual relations between closely related people: incest

sexual relations with spouse, right to: conjugal rights

sexual relations, indiscriminate or casual: promiscuity

sexual relationship between three people: ménage à trois

sexual relationship between women: lesbianism, tribadism

sexual relationship with boy, man who has: pederast

sexual relationship, adulterous: affair, liaison

sexual relationship, non: platonic

sexual reproduction, stage when one becomes physically capable of: puberty

sexual services, to offer: accost, proposition, solicit

sexual stimulant: aphrodisiac

sexual union of cells, occurring without: agamic, agamogenetic, agamous, asexual, parthenogenetic ❦

sexuality, suggesting: carnal, sensual

sexually arousing: erogenous, sensual

sexually attractive: nubile, voluptuous

sexually attractive, chemical secreted by animal making them: pheromone

sexually explicit materials: erotica, pornography

sexually promiscuous man: Don Juan, libertine, Lothario, philanderer, profligate, satyr, sleeze

sexually promiscuous woman: nymphomaniac, slut, whore

sexually provocative: arousing, erotic, titillating

sexually unrestrained: promiscuous, wanton

sexy: erotic, flirtatious, libidinous, racy, risqué, seductive, sensual, spicy, steamy, suggestive

shabby: beggarly, cheap, contemptible, decrepit, deteriorated, dilapidated, dingy, disgraceful, dowdy, faded, mangy, mean, neglected, poor, ragged, run-down, scrubby, scummy, scurvy, seedy, shoddy, sleazy, tacky, tattered, threadbare, unkempt, unworthy, worn, wrecked

shack: cabin, hovel, hut, lean-to, shanty

shackle: band, bind, bridle, chain, collar, confine, coupling, cuffs, curb, fetter, hamper, handcuff, hinder, hobble, hogtie, iron, irons, leash, manacle, pinion, restrain, ring, rope, secure, tie, yoke

shade: cast, color, coolness, dark, darken, darkness, degree, difference, dim, eclipse, gradation, hint, hue, nuance, obscure, overshadow, protect, protection, shadow, shelter, streak, suggestion, tinge, tint, tone, trace, umbrage, variation, vestige

shade or canopy: awning, cover, curtain, protection, screen, shield, veil

shade of meaning, subtle: nuance

shading a drawing with intersecting lines: cross-hatching, hachure

shadow: apparition, cloud, cover, darken, forecast, ghost, gloom, image, lurk, obscure, omen, penumbra, phantom, reflection, remnant, shade, shelter, shroud, suggest, tinge, trail, umbra, watch

shadow against light background: silhouette

SEXUALLY TRANSMITTED DISEASE (STD) OR VENEREAL DISEASE (VD)

acquired immune deficiency syndrome/AIDS

AIDS-related complex

bacterial vaginosis

cervicitis

chancre

chlamydia/lymphogranuloma venereum

clap

condyloma acuminatum

crabs

Cupid's itch/Venus's curse

cytomegalovirus

genital herpes

genital ulcer disease

genital warts

gonorrhea

granuloma inguinale

hepatitis B

herpes

herpes simplex

HIV/human immunodeficiency virus

HPV/human papilloma virus

NGU/nongonococcal urethritis

nonspecific urethritis

PID/pelvic inflammatory disease

pubic lice

sexual disease

social disease

syphilis

syphilitic sore

trichomonas

trichomoniasis

urethritis

vaginitis

venereal ulcer ❦

shadow as a sundial, object that projects shadow: gnomon

shadow, partial: penumbra

shadow's blackest part: umbra

shadowy: adumbral, cloudy, dark, dim, dreamy, faint, ghostly, hazy, imaginary, indistinct, obscure, shady, umbral, unsubstantial, vague

shady: adumbral, crooked, dishonest, doubtful, fishy, hidden, questionable, risqué, shadowy, suspect, suspicious, umbrageous, underhanded, unethical

shady bower: arbor, fenestra

shady with trees: bosky, umbrageous

shaft: arrow, axle, bar, barb, beam, chimney, column, conduit, cylinder, diaphysis, duct, flue, handle, hole, lance, missile, monolith, obelisk, pillar, pole, ray, rod, spear, spindle, tunnel, vent

shaft on which wheels rotate: axle

shaggy: bushy, furry, fuzzy, hairy, rough, ruffled, scrubby, straggly, uncombed, unkempt, whiskered, woolly

shake: agitate, avoid, brandish, chatter, convulse, disturb, dither, drink, elude, fluctuate, fluster, free, hustle, jar, jerk, jiggle, jog, joggle, jolt, jostle, move, palpitate, pulsate, quake, quaver, quiver, rattle, remove, rock, shudder, startle, stir, sway, swing, toss, totter, tremble, tremor, unnerve, unsettle, upset, vibrate, waggle, wave, waver, weaken

shake down: blackmail, extort, frisk, search, squeeze

shake or waver: fluctuate, oscillate, vacillate

shake rapidly and irregularly: flutter, judder

shake slightly: joggle

shake the body in a dance: shimmy

shake up: alarm, disturb, jar, remove, reorganize, shock, stir, unsettle, upset

shake violently: agitate, convulse

shaking fit: ague

shaking movement: tremor, trepidation

shaking violently: succussion, tremor

shaky: doubtful, fragile, infirm, insecure, jumpy, nervous, precarious, questionable, rickety, suspect, tottering, trembling, uncertain, unreliable, unsafe, unsettled, unsound, unstable, unsteady, unsure, weak, wobbly

shale: clay, rock, sediment, slate

shallow: depthless, empty, flimsy, shoal, slight, surface, weak

shallow and lacking depth: cosmetic, cursory, facile, superficial, token, trifling, trivial

shallow and superficial in expression: glib

shallow enough to be measured with weighted line, water: sounding

shallow lake: lagoon

shallow reading matter: pap

shallow sandy elevation: sandbank, sandbar, shoal

shalom: farewell, greeting, peace

sham: artificial, bluff, bogus, cheat, copy, counterfeit, deceit, deceive, deception, facade, fake, false, farce, feign, feigned, fictitious, flimflam, forgery, fraud, hoax, hypocrisy, imi-

tation, imposter, imposture, mock, mockery, phony, pretend, pretense, simulacrum, substitute, synthetic, travesty, trick, trickery

shaman: healer, medicine man, monk, priest, witch doctor

shambles: bedlam, chaos, confusion, disarray, disorder, havoc, mess, wreckage

shame: abase, abash, chagrin, contempt, degradation, degrade, disgrace, dishonor, embarrass, embarrassment, guilt, humiliate, humiliation, ignominy, infamy, mortify, stigma, unworthiness

shame, mark of: stigma

shameful: atrocious, base, brazen, contemptible, degrading, deplorable, disgraceful, dishonest, dishonorable, disreputable, ignoble, ignominious, indecent, mean, offensive, opprobrious, outrageous, scandalous, shocking, sinful

shameless: arrant, audacious, barefaced, bold, brash, brazen, immodest, impervious, impudent, unabashed, unblushing

shanghai: abduct, coerce, compel, induce, kidnap, seize

Shangri-la: heaven, paradise, Utopia

shank: crus, leg, meat, shaft, shin, stalk, stem

shanty: cabin, cottage, hovel, hut, lodge, shack, shed, tumbledown shack

shape: adapt, appearance, arrange, arrangement, aspect, bend, body, build, carve, cast, chisel, condition, configuration, conform, contour, contrive, create, design, determine, develop, devise, fabricate, fashion, figuration, figure, form, format, frame, health, image, look, make, model, mold, order, outline, pattern, physique, plan, posture, state, structure, tool, trim

shape distortion: anamorphism

shape or view from the side: profile

shape, capability to resume original: elasticity, resilience

shape, distinctive: lineament

shape, etc., marked change in: metamorphosis, transfiguration, transmogrification

shape, not in natural: distorted, misshapen

shaped abnormally: deformed, malformed

shapeless: amorphous, aplastic, de-

formed, distorted, formless, indistinct, irregular, misshapen, nebulous, unformed, unshaped

shapely: beautiful, built, comely, curvaceous, distorted, fit, neat, proportioned, symmetrical, trim

share: allotment, allowance, apportion, claim, commission, cut, deal, distribute, divide, dividend, division, divvy, dole, interest, lot, moiety, part, partake, participate, percentage, piece, plowshare, portion, proportion, quota, ratio, ration, split, stake

share of production assignment: quota

share, proportional: allocation, allotment, quota

shared: common, communal, joint, mutual

sharer of inheritance: coparcener, parcener

share's face value: nominal value, par value

shares for diversified securities, investment company using: mutual fund

shares free of charge to existing stockholders, issue of: bonus issue, scrip issue

shares of stock: common stock, equity, preferred stock

shares of stock, provisional certificate for: scrip

shares of stocks and bonds owned: portfolio

shares sold, less than round: odd lot, short sale

shares, total value of a company's: capitalization

sharing in involvement: complicity

sharing sensations as if one were actually participating: vicarious

shark: cheat, expert, fish, make, mako, maneater, predator, swindler, usurer

shark kinds: blue, great white, hammerhead, sand, shovelhead, tiger, whale, white

shark, like a: selachian

sharp: abrupt, acerb, acid, acrid, acrimonious, acute, angular, attractive, austere, barbed, biting, bitter, brisk, caustic, clear, cold, crisp, cute, cutting, distinct, drastic, edged, excruciating, handsome, harsh, horned, incisive, intense, jagged, painful, peaked, penetrating, piercing, piquant, pointed, precisely, prickly, promptly, punctually, pungent, salty,

SHAPES

almond-shaped: amygdaloid	lance-shaped: lanceolate
arrowhead-shaped: sagittate	lens or lentil seed-shaped: lenticular
bell-shaped: campanulate	lyre-shaped: lyrate
berry-shaped: aciniform/bacciform	needle-shaped: acerose/beloneform
boat-shaped: navicular/scaphoid	pear-shaped: pyriform
bow or arch-shaped: fornicate/arcuate	pine cone-shaped: strobilaceous
bristle-shaped: setiform/acicular/styliform	pouch or sac-shaped: bursiform/saccate
brush-shaped: penicilliform	ribbon or belt-shaped: cestoid
club-shaped: clavate/claviform	ring-shaped: annular/toroid
coil-shaped: circinate	rod-shaped: bacillary/bacilliform/virgate/virgulate
coin-shaped: nummular	S-shaped: sigmoid
comb-shaped: pectinate	sausage-shaped: allantoid
cone-shaped: fastigiate	scimitar-shaped: acinaciform
crescent-shaped: bicorn/lunular	shaped like a bunch of grapes: botryoidal
cross or X-shaped: decussate/cruciform/cruciate	shaped like a snail's shell: cochleate
cup-shaped: cotyloid/cupulate/acetabular	shaped like an eagle's beak: acquiline
diamond-shaped: rhomboidal	shaped like spokes of a wheel: rotate
dish or pan-shaped: patelliform	shaped like the teeth of a saw: runcinate/serrate
droplet-shaped: guttate/stilliform/globular	shield-shaped: scutate/scutellate/peltate/clypeate
ear-shaped: auriculate	sickle-shaped: falcate
eel-shaped: anguilliform	slipper-shaped: calceolate
egg-shaped: oval/ovoid	snake-shaped: anguiform/colubriform/colubroid/ophidiform
fan-shaped: flabellate	spearhead-shaped: hastate
feather-shaped: pinnate	spiral-shaped: helical/turbinal/volute
fingers-shaped: digitate/dactyloid	star-shaped: stellate/astroid
fish-shaped: pisciform	strap-shaped: ligulate
foot-shaped: pediform	string of beads-shaped: moniliform
fork-shaped: furcate/bifurcate	sword-shaped: ensiform/gladiate/xiphoid
funnel-shaped: infundibular	tongue-shaped: lingulate
hand-shaped: palmate/chiroform	tooth-shaped: dentiform
head-shaped: capitate	tree-shaped: dendriform/dendroid
heart-shaped: cordate	triangle-shaped: deltoid
helmet-shaped: galeate	urn-shaped: urceolate
hood or cowl-shaped: cucullate	violin-shaped: pandurate
hook-shaped: uncinate/unciform	wand or rod-shaped: virgate
horn-shaped: cornual	wedge-shaped: cuneal/sphenic
keel-shaped: carinate	wheel-shaped: rotary/rotate/trochal
kidney-shaped: reniform	whip-shaped: flagellate
knife blade-shaped: cultrate	wing-shaped: alary/aliform
ladder-shaped: scalariform	worm-shaped: vermicular/vermiform/lumbricoid ❦

severe, shrill, sour, steep, stinging, strong, stylish, sudden, swank, tangy, tart, violent

sharp-edged: cultrate

sharp emphasis in music: staccato

sharp fragment of glass, wood, etc.: sliver, splinter

sharp in intelligence: adept, adroit, alert, astute, bright, canny, classy, clever, crafty, cunning, discerning, expert, fast, ingenious, keen, perceptive, poignant, quick, quick-witted, savvy, shrewd, slick, sly, smart, vigilant, wise, witty

sharp in taste or smell: acrid, piquant, pungent

sharp pain: pang, twinge

sharp point on a leaf: mucro

sharp point, tapering to: acuminate, apiculate

sharp prong: tine

sharp-sighted: acute, alert, attentive, aware, keen, observant, penetrating, perceptive

sharp taste, odor, flavor: tang

sharp-witted: bright, clever, discerning, intelligent, keen, smart, wise, witty

sharp, cutting speech: acerbic, acrid,

caustic, incisive, mordant, pungent, trenchant

sharpen: edge, enhance, focus, grind, hone, intensify, point, stimulate, strop, taper, whet

sharpen to a point: spiculate

sharpener: carborundum, file, hone, honer, snakestone, steel, strop, whetstone

sharpness of perception: acuity

sharpness or clarity of detail: definition, resolution

sharpshooter: marksman, rifleman, sniper

SHAPING, SHAVING, AND SMOOTHING TOOLS

adz	disk sander	grindstone	putty knife	smoothing plane
anvil	double cut file	grooving plane	rasp	spokeshave
beading plane	drum sander	half-round file	round file	stone
belt sander	electric sander	hand sander	router	swage
bench plane	emery wheel	hone	router plane	swage block
block plane	file	jack plane	sander	tamper
brick trowel	finishing sander	lathe	sandpaper	thickness planer
buffer	flat file	machine tool	scraper	trimming plane
bullnose plane	flatter	multiplane	shaper	trowel
chamfering plane	float	oilstone	sharpener	trying plane
circular file	fore plane	plane	shavehook	waterstone
corner trowel	grinder	planer	single cut file	whetstone ❦
die	grinding wheel	power sander	slipstone	

shatter: annihilate, blast, break, burst, clatter, crack, crash, damage, dash, demolish, destroy, disable, dissipate, fragment, pulverize, quash, rend, rive, ruin, scatter, smash, splinter, split, wreck

shattering effect of explosion: brisance

shave: barber, brush, cheat, crop, cut, divide, glance, graze, mow, pare, portion, reduce, scrape, separate, shear, slash, slip, sliver, splinter, tonsure, trim, whittle

shaved monk's head: tonsure

shaving cut, stick for: styptic pencil

shawl: cape, cloak, cloth, fichu, manta, mantle, maud, scarf, serape, stole, tallith

shear: cleave, clip, crop, cut, fleece, lop, prune, remove, sever, shave, snip, strip, trim

shears: clippers, cutters, pruner, scissors, snippers, trimmers

sheath: capsule, case, coat, covering, dress, envelope, scabbard, skin, wrapper

sheath, metal tip or mounting on: chape

sheath, resembling or forming a: vaginate

shed, to: cast, cut, diffuse, discard, disperse, divest, divide, drop, emanate, emit, exuviate, jettison, molt, part, peel, pour, radiate, reject, rid, scatter, slough, sprinkle, strew, strip

shed: cabin, cottage, hut, lean-to, shelter

shed feathers or skin: molt

shed, dead layer of skin or other covering that is: slough

shedding foliage at end of growing season: deciduous

shedding limb when injured or attacked: autotomy

shedding of outer integument or skin: ecdysis, sloughing

shedding or molting: exuviation, slough

sheen: bright, brightness, finish, glaze, gleam, glisten, glitter, gloss, glossiness, glossy, luster, lustrous, polish, radiant, resplendent, shimmer, shine, shininess, shining

sheen on surface from age, use: patina

sheep: ewe, mutton, teg

RELATED TERMS

sheep breeds: Blackfaced, Cheviot, Cotswold, Delaine, Dorset, Galway, Horn, Iceland, Leicester, Lincoln, Merino, Mountain, Oxford, Romney, Shropshire, Somali, Suffolk, Welsh

sheep caretaker: drover, shepherd

sheep coat: fleece, wool

sheep family: bovidae

sheep genus: ovis

sheep meat: lamb, mutton

sheep of central Asia with curled glossy wool: broadtail, karakul

sheep of northern Africa with long curved horns: aoudad, Barbary sheep

sheep of Sardinia and Corsica: mouflon

sheep of Spain with long fine wool: merino

sheep or goat, baby: yeanling

sheep shelter: cote

sheep, castrated male: wether

sheep, concerning: ovine

sheep, male: bellwether, ram, wether

sheep, wild: aoudad, argal, argali, arui, bighorn, mouflon, urial

sheep, young: kid, lamb, shearling, teg, twinter, yeanling, yearling

sheep's wool by-product: lanolin ❦

sheepish: abashed, ashamed, bashful, chagrined, docile, embarrassed, meek, ovine, passive, shy, tame, timid, unassertive

sheepskin: bond, diploma, leather, mouton, parchment, roan

sheer: abrupt, absolute, altogether, completely, deflect, deviate, downright, mere, outright, pure, steep, swerve, total, turn, undiluted, unmixed, unqualified, upright, utter, utterly, veer

sheer as fabric: chiffon, clear, diaphanous, fine, gossamer, thin, transparent

sheer fabric: batiste, lawn, ninon, toile, voile

sheet: chain, coating, covering, layer, leaf, linen, newspaper, overlay, page, pan, pane, paper, plate, ply, rope, sail, shroud, surface, tabloid, tin

sheet of cotton: batt

sheet of glass: pane

sheet of material that is permeable to substances: membrane

sheet of paper folded into four leaves: quarto

sheet of paper folded once into four pages: folio

sheet of stamps: pane

sheet of standing water: mere

sheet, burial: shroud, winding sheet

sheets of material folded or glued together: ply

sheets, cover with thin: laminate

shelf: bank, bedrock, bracket, counter, jutting, layer, ledge, mantel, rack, reef, sandbank, sandbar, shoal, sill, slab, stratum

shelf behind altar: retable

shelf over fireplace: mantel, mantelpiece

shell (ammunition): bomb, bullet, cartridge, grenade, projectile, rocket
RELATED TERMS
shell fragments from high-explosive shell: shrapnel
shell handler: artilleryman, bombardier
shell, device for firing a: bazooka, Big Bertha, cannon, field gun, gun, howitzer, light anti-tank weapon (LAW), mortar, rocket launcher, tank
shell, diameter of large projectile: caliber
shell, to: blast, blitz, bomb, bombard, cannonade, strafe
shelling a position, an attack made mainly by: barrage, bombardment, broadside, burst, cannonade, drumfire, fusillade, hail, salvo, shower, storm, volley ❦

shell (exterior): armor, capsule, carapace, case, covering, crust, frame, hull, husk, pod, scale, shuck, skin
RELATED TERMS
shell attached to submerged surfaces, crustaceans with: barnacle
shell collector: conchologist
shell in some gastropod mollusks, hollow at base of: umbilicus
shell-like covering of turtle, crustacean: carapace
shell lined with mother-of-pearl: abalone
shell material of some arthropod exoskeletons: chitin
shell of bony plates and scales, protective: cuirass
shell of single valve: univalve
shell of some insects and amoebas: test
shell of some invertebrates like insects: cuticle
shell of some marine gastropods: cowrie
shell of two hinged valves: bivalve
shell- or pod-covered insect stage: chrysalis, pupa

shell or protective covering of an animal or plant: armature
shell that is spiral and cone-shaped: turbinate
shell, apex of coiled gastropod: spire
shell, coiled fossil: ammonite
shell, gastropod with ear-shaped: abalone, ear shell
shell, having or forming a: conchiferous
shell, knob near hinge of bivalve: umbo
shell, mollusk with radiating fluted: scallop
shell, mollusk with single coiled: gastropod, univalve
shell, mollusk with spiral pearly-lined: nautilus
shell, mollusk with two hinged valve: bivalve
shell, spiral formation of gastropod: volute, volution, whorl ❦

shell out: contribute, disburse, expend, give, pay, spend

shellac: batter, defeat, strike, trounce, varnish

shellac ingredient: lac, resin

shellfish: barnacle, clam, conch, crab, crawfish, crayfish, crustacean, lobster, mollusk, mussel, oyster, piddock, prawn, scallop, shrimp, snail, whelk

shellfish eaten by whales, tiny: krill

shellfish including lobster, crab, shrimp: crustacean

shellfish looking like small lobster: crawdad, crayfish, langouste

shellfish that eject inky fluid when in danger: cuttlefish

shellfish with jointed paired appendages and segmented bodies: arthropod

shellfish with soft unsegmented body and protective shell: mollusk

shells used by Native Americans as currency, beads made from: peag, wampum

shells, pearly internal layer of some mollusk: mother-of-pearl, nacre

shells, study of: conchology

shelter: abri, asylum, barn, burrow, camp, carport, cave, cote, cottage, cover, covert, coverture, defend, defense, den, disguise, dwelling, enclose, ensconce, fold, foxhole, garage, hangar, harbor, haven, hideaway, hideout, hospice, hostel, house, housing, hovel, hut, lean-to, lodging, port, protect, protection, quarters, refuge, retreat, roof, safeguard, safety, sanctuary, screen, security, shack, shade, shed, shield, tent, trailer, trench, umbrella

shelter or lodging for travelers or the destitute: hospice

shelter or shed with single-pitch roof attached to side of building: lean-to

shelter, prefabricated corrugated steel military: Nissen hut

sheltered: alee, cloistered, covered, hidden, private, secluded, sequestered

shelve: arrange, ledge, mantel, suspend

shelve, as a topic: defer, delay, dismiss, drop, hold, pigeonhole, postpone, retire, scrub, suspend, table

shenanigans: antic, game, hijinx, horseplay, mischief, monkey business, monkeyshine, nonsense, prank, stunt, tomfoolery, trick

shepherd: attend, caretaker, drive, escort, guard, guide, herd, herder, herdsman, keeper, lead, leader, minister, pastor, pilot, protector, teacher, tend, watch

shepherds, concerning: bucolic, pastoral

sherbet-like dessert: frappé, ice, sorbet

sheriff: constable, marshal, officer

sheriff aide: bailiff, deputy

sheriff to aid in law enforcement, group of people summoned by: posse

sherry: amoroso, brandy, fino, oloroso, port, wine

sherry from Spain, pale and dry: amontillado

sherry to which grape brandy has been added: fortified wine

sherry, pale very dry Spanish: Manzanilla

shibboleth: catchword, custom, password, phrase, practice, saying, slogan, truism, watchword

shield: aegis, armament, armor, badge, buckler, bumper, canopy, cloak, conceal, cover, defend, ecu, egis, escutcheon, fend, guard, harbor, hide, house, pavis, prevent, protect, protection, safeguard, screen, shade, shell, shelter, target

shield bearing coat of arms: escutcheon

shield for the entire body, medieval: pavis

shield or shield-shaped emblem for coat of arms: escutcheon

shield-shaped: clypeate, peltate, scutate, scutellate, scutiform

shield, knob at center of: boss, umbo

shield, oval, or oblong scroll for hieroglyph: cartouche

shield, small round: buckler, targe, target

shield, small square division of: canton

shields held over heads, overlapping: testudo

shift: alter, arrange, change, conversion, convert, dispose, divide, dodge, evade, exchange, expedient, fault, fluctuation, group, jump, move, period, rearrange, relay, replace, shuffle, spell, stint, stir, stratagem, substitute, subterfuge, swap, swerve, switch, tack, tour, transfer, transition, trick, turn, vacillate, vary, veer

shift of disease to a different part of body: metastasis

shift or period of duty as guard or sentinel: watch

shift or period of duty at helm of ship: trick

shiftless: idle, inactive, incompetent, indolent, inefficient, lazy

shifty: cagey, conniving, crafty, crooked, cunning, deceitful, devious, dishonest, elusive, evasive, lubricious, scheming, shady, slick, slippery, sly, sneaky, tricky, underhand

shilly-shally: blow hot and cold, dawdle, fluctuate, halting, hesitate, indecision, procrastinate, stall, vacillate, waver

shim: wedge

shimmer: blink, coruscate, flash, flicker, flutter, gleam, glimmer, glisten, glow, scintillate, shine, sparkle, twinkle

shimmy: chemise, dance, shake, vibrate, wobble

shin bone: shank, tibia

shindig: ball, bash, dance, fête, gala, party, shebang, shindy, spree

shindy: ball, bash, carousal, commotion, dance, disturbance, fracas, frolic, merrymaking, party, revel, shindig, spree, uproar

shine: beam, blaze, buff, burnish, coruscate, dazzle, excel, finish, flash, glare, gleam, glint, glisten, glitter, glitz, gloss, glow, illuminate, light, luster, polish, radiance, radiate, ray, reflect, rub, sheen, shimmer, sparkle, splendor, twinkle, wax

shiner: black eye, bruise, fish, mouse

shining: agleam, bright, coruscating, effulgent, irradiant, lambent, lucent, refulgent, relucent, resplendent, scintillating, sparkling, splendent

shiny: beaming, bright, brilliant, glaring, gleaming, glistening, glossy, lustrous, polished, radiant, sparkling

shiny coating: patina

shiny fabric: lamé, sateen

shipbuilding wood: teak

shipment: cargo, consignment, delivery, freight, goods, load, purchase

shipping container: carton, crate

shipping, concerning: marine, maritime

shipshape: neat, orderly, snug, spruce, tidy, trim

shirk: avoid, dodge, duck, elude, evade, neglect, sidestep, slack

shirt: blouse, dress, jersey, polo, pullover, sark, silk, sport, turtleneck

shirt tails tied in knot at waist: calypso

shiver: ague, break, chill, fragment, freeze, frisson, quake, quiver, shake, shatter, shudder, splinter, tremble, tremor, vibrate

shivering, fit of: ague, chill, rigor

shoal: bank, bar, crowd, flock, group, horde, mass, reef, sandbank, sandbar, school, shallow

shock: agitation, appall, astonish, astound, blow, bum, collect, collision, concussion, crash, daze, disgust, disturb, earthquake, electrify, excite, fight, horrify, impact, jar, jolt, offend, outrage, paralyze, scare, shake, startle, stun, surprise, terrify, trauma, tremor, upset

shock as treatment, electric: ECT, electroconvulsive therapy

shock to brain: concussion

shock to the body, serious: trauma

shock, temporary stiffness due to: rigor

shocked: aghast, amazed, appalled, astonished, stupefied

shocking: abominable, appalling, atrocious, awful, disgusting, dreadful, ghastly, grisly, heinous, hideous, horrible, horrid, lurid, outrageous, revolting, risqué, sensational, stunning, surprising, terrible, unspeakable

shockingly unscrupulous or excessive: unconscionable

shoddy: base, cheap, cheesy, dilapidated, dishonest, gaudy, inferior, poor, seedy, shabby, sleazy, sloppy

shoe: balmoral, blucher, boot, brodequin, brogan, brogue, buckskin, chopine, cleat, clodhoppers, clog, flat, galosh, gilly, larrigan, loafer, moccasin, mule, oxford, pack, pantofle, patten, platform, plight, pompootee, pump, sabot, sandal, slipper, sneaker, status, wader

RELATED TERMS

shoe upper front part: vamp

shoe, layer of material in heel of: lift

shoe, metal plate on sole or heel of: tap

shoe, spiked plate attached to: clamper, crampon ☜

shoelace end: aglet, tag

shoemaker: cobbler, crispin, snob, soler

shoot: bag, blast, bolt, bombard, cast, chute, dart, dash, discharge, drive, drop, eject, emit, explode, fire, fly, grow, hit, hunt, hurry, inject, kill, launch, move, photograph, plug, pop, project, propel, race, riddle, shell, snipe, spear, spurt, strike, throw, thrust, utter, wound

shoot cut from plant for grafting or planting: scion, slip

shooter from concealed place: sniper

shooting game: skeet

shooting is prohibited, time when: closed season

shooting season for game: open season

shooting star, after the fact: meteorite

shooting target clay disk: clay pigeon

shop: boutique, browse, business, buy, emporium, factory, hunt, market, mart, office, outlet, plant, purchase, store, studio, workplace

shopkeeper: businessman, businesswoman, merchant, retailer, storekeeper, vendor

shoplift: palm, pilfer, pinch, rob, steal, swipe

shopworn: cliché, faded, frayed, overused, stale, tarnished, trite

shore: bank, beach, bolster, brink, buttress, coast, coastline, land, seaboard, seaside, strand, waterfront, waterside

shore, concerning a: littoral

shoreline barrier to break waves: breakwater

short: abbreviated, abridged, abrupt, abruptly, brief, briefly, compact, compendious, concise, condensed, crisp, crumbling, curt, curtail, deficient, diminutive, hasty, inadequate, incomplete, insufficient, lilliputian, little, momentary, petite, rude, scant,

SHIPS AND SHIPPING TERMS (see also BOATS)

above main deck: topside
ancient ship: galleon, galley, knorr, trireme
armored ship: carrack, cruiser, destroyer, ironsides, submarine
attendant: steward
berth: dock, slip
bow decoration: fiddlehead, figurehead
capacity: ton, tonnage
cargo storage: hold
cargo thrown to sea attached to buoys: lagan
central part or backbone of ship: keel
cheapest accommodations: steerage
commercial ship: freighter, liner, oiler, tanker, trader
compass holder: binnacle
crew: boatswain, bosun, engineer, hand, helmsman, mate, navigator, purser, sailor, steerman, steward
deck: orlop
depth of ship's keel below water line: draft
fishing ship: hooker, lugger, smack, trawler
fleet: argosy, armada, flotilla, navy
frame or body: hull
government prohibition of foreign ships in and out of its ports: embargo
heavy material in hold of ship for stability: ballast
left side of ship, if facing forward: larboard, port
line on ship showing how much it may be loaded: load line, Plimsoll line, Plimsoll mark
lookout point: crow's nest
lower decks: steerage
lowest inner part of hull: bilge
mooring or towing cable: hawser
name plate on stern: escutcheon
navigation or trade in coastal waters: cabotage
oar: bireme, galley, pinnace, rowboat, sampan, trireme
of a ship that can be steered: navigable
officer below captain: first mate
officer in charge of equipment and deck crew: bosun, boatswain
officer in charge of money matters: purser
officer in charge of provisions and dining: steward
one who loads and unloads: stevedore
opening in floor or deck: hatch
passenger who snuck aboard: stowaway
permission to enter port: pratique
petty officer: bosun
pilothouse or observation post: conning tower
platform on main deck with the controls: bridge

prepare and equip ship for additional use: refit
put a ship into active service: commission
radio system: loran
rear of ship: abaft, aft, astern, stern
rigging and pulleys: tackle
right side of ship, if facing forward: starboard
rope: halyard, hawser, lanyard, line, painter, ratline
sailing close to wind: luff
sailing ship: brig, caique, caravel, chebec, galleon, ketch, lugger, saltie, schooner, sloop, xebec, yawl
seller of ship goods or equipment: chandler
ship abandoned at sea: derelict
ship accompanying another: consort
ship in repair: drydock
ship parts: bilge, boom, bow, bridge, brig, bulkhead, bulwark, capstan, carling, crane, davit, deck, galley, gangplank, gunwales, helm, hoist, hold, hull, keel, keelson, mast, port, porthole, prow, ram, rudder, sail, scupper, stateroom, stern, waist, wheel
ship that brought the Statue of Liberty: Isere
ship with two or more masts, fore-and-aft: schooner
ship, curved timbers forming rib of: futtock
ship, large private cabin on: stateroom
ship, list of cargo on: bill of lading, manifest, waybill
ship, rail around stern of: taffrail
ship, recreation area and dining room for commissioned officers on: wardroom
ship, shift at helm of: trick
ship, small opening or hatch on: scuttle
ship, steering apparatus of: steerage
ship, turbulence in water left by: wake
ship's floor: deck
ship's bearing calculated from fixed reference: azimuth
ship's journal: log
shipboard prison: brig
sloping surface on which ships are built: slipway
small boat: lifeboat, yawl
stairway between decks: companionway
structure above main deck: superstructure
submersible ship: bathyscaphe, submarine
upper front deck part: forecastle
vertical exhaust pipe: stack
warship: cruiser, destroyer, dreadnaught, flattop, sub, submarine
window: port, porthole
wooden strip forming hull: stave
wreckage of ship cast ashore: wrack ❦

---

scanty, scarce, skimpy, slight, small, spare, squat, stunted, succinct, summary, terse

short and pithy: terse
short and stocky: endomorphic, pyknic
short-fingered or -toed: brachydactylic
short-headed: brachycephalic

short hymn or song praising God: doxology
short literary sketch: cameo, vignette
short-lived: brief, ephemeral, evanescent, fleeting, fugacious, fugitive, momentary, passing, temporary, transient, transitory, unenduring, volatile

short pain: pang
short-tailed monkey: macaque
short-tempered: cranky, grouchy, grumpy, huffy, irascible, irritable, snappish, testy, touchy
shortage: dearth, deficiency, deficit, inadequacy, lack, need, paucity, spar-

TYPES OF SHOES

ankle-high work shoe: brogan
ankle-high, three-eyelet shoe: chukka
backless shoe or slipper: mule
bedroom slipper: pantofle
big, heavy shoe: clodhopper
heavy Oxford shoe: brogue
heavy, laced shoe: balmoral
heavy, often wooden-soled shoe: clog
leather boot or shoe of reindeer or seal skin: mukluk
low laced shoe: Oxford
moccasin with knee-high leggings: larrigan
shoe with fabric upper and rope or rubber bottom: espadrille
shoes with heel strap: slingback
shoes with no straps and higher heel: pump
shoes with spiked pieces to provide traction: cleats
soft leather slipper: moccasin
sports shoe with fringed laces: gillie
step-in casual shoe: loafer
waterproof hip-high boots: wader
waterproof knee-high boots: Wellingtons
waterproof overshoe: galosh
women's shoe with thin high heel: stiletto ❦

sity, underage
shortcoming: defect, deficiency, drawback, failure, fault, flaw, imperfection, inadequacy, lapse, vice, weakness
shorten: abbreviate, abridge, bob, chop, clip, condense, contract, curtail, cut, decrease, deprive, diminish, lessen, nip, reduce, shrink, slash, trim, truncate
shorten a text: abridge, condense, cut, summarize
shortened text: abridgment, abstract, digest, epitome, precis, summary, synopsis
shortened word form: clipped form
shortening: lard, oleo, suet
shorthand: stenography
shortly: anon, concisely, curtly, immediately, in a trice, presently, pronto, quickly, soon
shorts ending just above knee: Bermuda shorts

shortsighted: blind, careless, foolish, headlong, imprudent, myopic, nearsighted, rash
shot: ammunition, blank, blast, bullet, gunfire, jolt, missile, pellet, projectile, slug; attempt, chance, effort, fling, guess, opening, opportunity, try
shoulder blade: scapula
shoulder cord or braid on uniform: aiguillete, fourragère
shoulder joint prone to injury: rotator cuff
shoulder ornament on uniform: epaulet
shoulder wrap: shawl, stole
shoulders and has cowl, monk's sleeveless garment hanging from: scapular
shout: acclaim, bark, bawl, bellow, blare, call, cheer, clamor, crow, cry, fulminate, hoot, howl, hurrah, noise, rejoice, roar, root, scream, screech, shriek, vociferate, whoop, yell, yelp
shout of approval: bravo, ole
shove: bump, cram, drive, elbow, force, hustle, jostle, nudge, press, prod, push, ram, shunt
shove off: depart, go, leave, vamoose
shovel: digger, excavator, scoop, spade, trowel
shovel used by pizza makers: peel
show clearly: evidence, evince, express, register
show fear: cower, pale
show manager or producer: impresario
show no loss or profit: break even
show of mercy: leniency
show of skits, songs, etc.: revue
show off: attitudinize, boast, brag, display, exhibit, flaunt, grandstand, parade, pose, posture, put on an act
show up: appear, arrive, come, defeat, embarrass, expose, shame
show, afternoon: matinee
show, first public: premiere
show, spectacular entertainment: extravaganza
showcase: cabinet, display, exhibit, vitrine
showdown: clash, climax, confrontation, crisis, culmination, encounter
shower: barrage, bath, bathe, bestow, bombard, cloudburst, deluge, drizzle, lavish, party, pour, rain, salvo, scatter, spray, sprinkle, storm, volley, wash
showing-off person: exhibitionist, poseur
showing or proving directly: deictic, ostensible, ostensive

SHOVELS AND DIGGING TOOLS

bail
bar spade
bull tongue
coal shovel
cultivator
ditch spade
draw hoe
fire shovel
fork
garden spade
garden trowel
grub hoe
hoe
irrigating shovel
loy
mattock
peat spade
pitchfork
plow
posthole digger
power shovel
rake
scoop
scooper
spade
spatula
spud
trowel ❦

showmanship: public acclaim
showoff: boaster, braggart, exhibitionist, hotdog
showpiece: gem, jewel, masterpiece, pride, prize, treasure
showy: arty, brilliant, dashing, flamboyant, flashy, flaunting, garish, gaudy, glaring, gorgeous, grand, loud, opulent, ornate, ostentatious, overdone, pompous, pretentious, snazzy, splashy, splendid, striking, swanky
showy and cheap: brummagem, gaudy, junky, tawdry
showy and fancy: glitzy, ritzy
showy and overly decorated: emblazoned, florid, garish, gaudy, ornate, rococo, tawdry, tinsel
showy but worthless finery: bric-a-brac, trumpery
showy finery: falderal, frills and furbelows, frippery, froufrou
showy gesture: flourish, ostentation
showy public display: blazon, bravura, fanfare, razzle-dazzle, razzmatazz

showy, overly: flamboyant, obtrusive, ostentatious, pretentious

shred: bit, crumb, cut, fragment, grain, iota, ounce, particle, piece, prune, pulverize, ribbon, scrap, sliver, smidgen, snip, speck, strip, tatter, tear, trace, wisp

shredded and dried: desiccated

shrew: battleaxe, curse, hag, harpy, mammal, nag, scold, spitfire, termagant, virago, vixen, xanthippe

shrewd: acute, artful, astute, biting, cagey, calculating, canny, careful, clever, contriving, crafty, cunning, discerning, farsighted, foxy, harsh, ingenious, intelligent, judicious, keen, knowing, neat, penetrating, perceptive, perspicacious, piercing, politic, sagacious, sage, sensible, sharp, sharp-witted, slick, sly, smart, subtle, wily, wise

shriek: cry, holler, howl, scream, screech, shout, shrill, squawk, squeal, wail, yell

shrill: acute, biting, blaring, crustacean, dwarf, high, high-pitched, keen, loud, nasal, noisy, penetrating, piercing, piping, screech, seafood, sharp, shriek, sound, strident, stridulation, treble, vivid

shrimp: krill, peewee, runt, shellfish

shrimp class: crustacean

shrimp cousin: prawn

shrimplike food of whales: krill

shrine: altar, box, case, chapel, chasse, church, container, gleam, grotto, hallow, mausoleum, memorial, monument, naos, reliquary, sanctuary, sanctum, temple, tomb

shrine for sacred relics: reliquary

shrine, domelike Buddhist: stupa

shrink: atrophy, blench, cling, condense, construct, contract, cower, cringe, curtail, decrease, demur, flinch, hesitate, huddle, lessen, quail, recede, recoil, reduce, retire, retract, retreat, shorten, shrivel, shy, swindle, wane, weaken, withdraw, wither

shrinking: bashful, coy, declining, modest, retiring, shy, timid

shrive: absolve, acquit, atone, confess, forgive, free, pardon, purge, repent

shrivel: age, dehydrate, parch, shrink, wilt, wither, wizen, wrinkle

shroud: cerecloth, cerement, cloak, clothe, clothing, conceal, cover, covering, dress, enfold, envelop, gar-

ment, grave clothes, hide, obstruct, pall, screen, shade, shadow, sheet, shelter, vault, veil, wrap

shrub: beverage, bush, drink, hedge, lilac, plant, rose, sola, tree

shrub variety: allspice, aloe, azalea, barberry, blackberry, blueberry, buddleia, cassia, cinchona, coca, coffee, cranberry, cubed, elderberry, euonymus, forsythia, hemlock, hibiscus, holly, honeysuckle, hydrangea, jasmine, laurel, lilac, mistletoe, rosemary, sagebrush

shrubs and trees trimmed: topiary

shuck: discard, ditch, husk, jettison, peel, pod, remove, shed, shell, strip, worthless

shudder: convulse, flutter, frisson, jitter, quake, quiver, shake, shimmy, shiver, tremble

shuffle: change, dance, disorganize, equivocation, evade, gait, jumble, limp, mix, move, muddle, rearrange, scramble, scuff, shamble, shift, shunt, sidestep, walk

shuffle with two hands: riffle

shun: avoid, balk, dodge, duck, elude, escape, eschew, evade, ignore, ostracize, reject, snub

shut: bar, block, cage, close, confine, exclude, fasten, forbid, lock, seal, secure, snap

shut away: cloister, closet, immure, seclude, sequester

shut down: abandon, cease, close, idle, stop

shut in: cage, confine, enclose, fence, hemmed, imprison, pen, restrained, surrounded

shut off: isolate, occlude, refuse, stop

shut out: bar, blockade, evict, exclude, ostracize, preclude, screen

shut up: caged, gag, hush, interned, pent, quiet, shush, silence

shutter with adjustable horizontal slats: jalousie

shuttlecock: bird, birdie

shy: bashful, cautious, chary, cower, coy, demure, diffident, fearful, hesitant, humble, inadequate, incomplete, insufficient, introverted, lacking, meek, modest, nervous, reluctant, reserved, restrained, reticent, retiring, secluded, self-effacing, shamefaced, sheepish, short, skittish, taciturn, timid, timorous, tremulous, unassertive, unassuming, undemonstrative, unforthcoming, wary

shy and confused: tongue-tied

shy and distant: aloof

shy and hesitant: cautious, chary, constrained, tentative

shy and inward-directed: introverted

shy and unconfident: gauche, self-conscious

shy away: balk, blench, flinch, quail, recoil, shrink

shy nonparticipant: Milquetoast, shrinking violet, wallflower

shylock: loan shark, money-lender, usurer

sibling: brother, kin, kinfolk, relative, sib, sister

sick: afflicted, ailing, bedridden, confined, debilitated, depressed, diseased, disgusted, down, feverish, frail, gross, ill, impaired, indisposed, infected, infirm, insane, longing, lousy, morbid, nauseated, pale, pining, stricken, suffering, unfit, unhealthy, unsound, unwell, upset, weak, weary

sick and tired: fed up

sicken: affect, disgust, nauseate, offend, repulse, revolt, shock, upset

sickening to an extreme: ad nauseum

sickle-shaped: falcate

sickly: afflicted, ailing, bilious, diseased, down, faint, feeble, flagging, frail, ill, infirm, invalid, lackluster, languid, pale, peaked, poorly, sallow, unhealthy, unwholesome

sickly person, chronically: invalid, valetudinarian

sickness: affliction, ailment, bout, condition, disease, disorder, illness, infirmity, insanity, malady, nausea, syndrome

sickness from eating or drinking too much: crapulence

side away from a glacier: alee

side by side: abreast, cheek by jowl, collateral, juxtaposed, parallel, together

side by side and progressing together: pari passu

side entrance: postern

side exactly equal to others: equilateral

side of ship above water line: broadside

side sheltered from wind: leeward

side-to-side lurch: careen

side-to-side measurement: breadth

side track of railroad: spur track

side view: profile

side with: agree, back, champion, favor, help, join, support

side, concerning a: lateral
sidearm, of yore: saber
sideboard: buffet, cellarette, closet, credenza, cupboard, furniture, table
sideburns: burnsides
sideburns, long and wide: muttonchops
sidekick: assistant, chum, companion, comrade, deputy, friend, mate, pal, pard, partner
sideline: avocation, bench, boundary, hobby, interest
sides of, to be on both: bestride, straddle
sidesplitting: uproarious
sidestep: avoid, bypass, circumvent, dodge, duck, elude, escape, evade, skirt
sidetrack: delay, deter, detour, deviate, divert, shunt, stall, switch
sidewalk: boardwalk, footpath, pavement, walkway
sideways: alongside, askance, broadside, crabwise, indirectly, lateral, laterally, obliquely, sidelong, slanting
sideways glance, with a: askance, obliquely
sidle: ease, edge, inch, saunter, tilt, veer
siege: assault, attack, beleaguer, beseige, beset, blockade, bout, flock, offense, onslaught, spell
sieve: basket, colander, filter, mesh, riddle, screen, separate, sift, sifter, strain, strainer
sieve or strainer, run through a: puree
sievelike: cribriform, holey
sift: analyze, bolt, canvass, comb, examine, filter, inspect, investigate, probe, refine, riddle, screen, scrutinize, search, separate, sieve, sort, strain, winnow
sift through coarse sieve: riddle
sigh: ache, complain, crave, exhale, grieve, groan, lament, languish, long, lust, moan, mourn, pant, sob, sough, suspire, wail, yearn
sigh of relief: phew
sighing or rustling sound: sough, susurration
sight: aim, behold, display, espy, exhibition, eyesore, glance, glimpse, ken, look, mess, observation, observe, outlook, perception, scene, see, show, spectacle, spot, spy, view, visibility, vision, witness
sight of, catch: descry, detect, discern, espy, glimpse
sight-related: ocular
sighting lines: crosshairs

sighting of land: landfall
sightseer: observer, tourist, traveller
sign: advertisement, aries, auspice, authorize, autograph, badge, banner, beckon, billboard, brand, clue, constellation, cue, demonstration, denotation, earmark, emblem, endorse, enter, evidence, expression, extol, figure, gesture, guidepost, harmonize, hint, image, index, indication, indicator, initial, ink, inscribe, insignia, lullaby, mark, message, motion, neon, nod, note, omen, portent, poster, premonition, presage, proclaim, prognostic, proof, signal, signature, standard, subscribe, suggestion, symbol, tattle, token, trace, underwrite, vestige, vocalize, warning
sign a policy and assume liability: underwrite
sign a previously signed document: countersign
sign at end of a document in attestation, testimony, consent: subscribe
sign language: dactylology
sign of something to come: forerunner, harbinger, herald
sign or abbreviation representing word: logograph, logogram
sign or dedicate a book: inscribe
sign or endorse at the end of something: underwrite
sign or symbol for idea or thing: ideogram, ideograph
sign or symbol, particular meaning of: denotation
sign or trace of something absent: vestige
sign up: accept, enlist, enroll, enter, join, register, subscribe, take, volunteer
sign, of a favorable: auspicious, propitious
sign, of an obvious: patent
sign, prophetic: augury, auspice, omen, portent, presage, prodigy
signal: alarm, arrow, blinker, buzzer, command, communicate, cress, cue, extraordinary, flag, flare, gesture, horn, image, impulse, indicator, lantern, memorable, message, motion, notable, noticeable, notify, outstanding, password, presage, prominent, remarkable, sign, signify, siren, sound, tocsin, toot, warning, wave, whistle, wink

signal light: beacon, Bengal light, flare, Very lights, warning light
signaling system: heliograph, railway signal, semaphore, smoke signal
signature: autograph, hand, identification, ink, John Hancock, John Henry, mark, name, seal, sigil, sign, stamp, trademark
signature made by one person for another: allograph
signature on as contract or for legal transfer, to write one's: endorse
signature, one's own: autograph
signatures arranged in circle on petition to conceal order of signing: round robin
signature's decoration: curlicue, flourish, paraph
signboard for professional office: shingle
signet: impression, mark, seal, sign, stamp
signets and seals, study of: sphragistics
significance: bearing, consequence, gravity, importance, influence, intent, meaning, merit, pith, point, purport, purpose, relevance, seriousness, value, weight
significance or importance, subjective evaluation of relative: perspective
significant: compelling, consequential, critical, decisive, eloquent, expressive, great, important, key, knowing, large, main, major, meaningful, momentous, noteworthy, powerful, prominent, substantial, suggestive, symbolic, telling, valid, weighty
significant other: beau, companion, main squeeze, partner
significant sign: portent
signify: announce, betoken, communicate, compare, connote, convey, declare, denote, express, imply, import, indicate, insinuate, intend, intimate, manifest, matter, mean, nod, proclaim, represent, reveal, sign, signal, spell, suggest, symbolize, tell
signing an agreement, person bound by: signatory
signs and symbols, study of: semantics, semasiology, semiotics
silence: calm, deaden, death, defeat, destroy, gag, hush, kill, muffle, mute, muteness, muzzle, overcome, pacify, peace, quell, quiet, refute, repress, reticence, secrecy, shush, squash, squelch, still, stillness, stop, suppress, tranquility

silence in broadcast: dead air
silencing of rumor: quietus
silent: closemouthed, discreet, dumb, hushed, inactive, mum, mute, quiescent, quiet, reserved, reticent, secretive, speechless, still, tacit, taciturn, tightlipped, tranquil, unexpressed, unpronounced, unspoken, unuttered, voiceless
silent, being: passive, quiescent, reticent, taciturn, uncommunicative
silent, thoughtfully: contemplative, introspective, meditative, pensive, reflective
silhouette: contour, figuration, outline, portrait, profile, shadow, shape
silk: fabric, fiber, mantua, pongee, samite, sendal, taffeta, thread, tulle, tussah, tussore
silk fabric: chiffon, crepe, foulard, gossamer, moire, ninon, pekin, satin, surah, velvet
silk protective case of moth larvae: cocoon
silk-screen process: serigraphy
silk, drawing and spinning: filature
silky: elegant, fine, flossy, gentle, glossy, plush, satiny, sericeous, silken, silky, sleek, smooth, soft, sweet
silky fibrous substance or thread: floss
silliness: absurdity, craziness, folly, foolishness, goofiness, inanity
silly: absurd, asinine, brainless, childish, childlike, crazy, cuckoo, daft, dazed, dumb, fatuous, feather brained, foolish, foppish, frivolous, funny, giddy, goofy, harebrained, idiotic, imbecile, inane, irrational, loopy, ludicrous, pointless, preposterous, ridiculous, senseless, shallow, simple, simpleminded, simpleton, stupid, unwise, wacky, witless
silly and humorous: facetious, flippant, frivolous
silly and immature: childish, puerile
silly and unrealistic: fanciful, whimsical
silly and unthinking: empty, inane, vacuous
silly and unwise: injudicious
silly grin: simper
silly laugh: giggle
silly, utterly: asinine, laughable, ludicrous, ridiculous, risible
silver: argent, argentine, argentum, bullion, coin, color, element, gray, jewelry, lustrous, money, pale, plate, precious, sterling, tableware
silver articles, mark of quality or purity on: hallmark
silver that is 92.5 percent pure: sterling silver
silver, fine ornamental work of: filigree
silver-tongued: eloquent, fluent, glib, oratorical
silverware: cutlery, flatware
silverware pieces: fork, knife, ladle, nutpick, server, spatula, spoon, tablespoon, teaspoon
silvery strips for Christmas trees: tinsel
simian: anthropoid, ape, apish, chimpanzee, gorilla, monkey, orangutan, primate
similar: agnate, akin, alike, cognate, comparable, congruent, congruous, consistent, corresponding, harmonious, homogeneous, like, matching, parallel, related, resemblance, resembling, semblance, uniform
similar enough to be mistaken for another: doppelganger, dead ringer
similar in functions and characteristics to another, one that is: counterpart
similar in sound: assonant, consonant
similar or equivalent: akin, analogous, cognate, comparable
similar origin or nature, of: kindred
similar structure or composition, of: homogeneous
similarity: affinity, analogy, closeness, comparison, correlation, likeness, parity, relationship, sameness, similitude
similarity in some aspects between dissimilar things: analogy
similarity of two things, figure of speech directly conveying: simile
similarity of two things, figure of speech indirectly conveying: metaphor
similarity or correspondence between components of entity: symmetry
similarity, inherent: affinity, kinship
similarly: also, equally, likewise, thus
simile: analogy, comparison, metaphor, similitude
similitude: allegory, analogy, comparison, counterpart, likeness, parable, replica, resemblance, semblance, similarity, simile
simmer: boil, brood, bubble, coddle, cook, ferment, seethe, smolder, stew, warm

simple: absolute, austere, backward, bare, basic, candid, childish, childlike, cinch, common, easy, effortless, elemental, elementary, endless, genuine, gullible, homely, homemade, homespun, humble, idyllic, inexperienced, ingenuous, innocent, manageable, mere, modest, naive, naked, natural, nitwitted, ordinary, plain, primitive, pure, real, rustic, sincere, stark, trifling, unadorned, unaffected, uncluttered, uncomplicated, uncompounded, uneducated, unelaborate, unembellished, uninvolved, unmixed, unpretentious
simple and austere: clinical, frugal, spartan
simple and basic: elementary, rudimentary
simple and homely: homespun, modest, rustic, unpretentious, unsophisticated
simple and natural: artless, earthy, forthright, frank, guileless, uncontrived
simple and peaceful: pastoral
simple and plain: rustic
simple principles, attempt to explain complex phenomena with: reductionism
simple to understand: accessible, comprehensible, intelligible, lucid, perspicuous, transparent, understandable
simpleminded: artless, dull, dumb, idiotic, ignorant, imbecile, moronic, naive, silly, slow, stupid, thick, unintelligent
simpleton: ass, blockhead, boob, clod, daw, dodo, dolt, dullard, dumbbell, dunce, fool, goose, ignoramus, imbecile, loon, lout, moron, nincompoop, ninny, noodle, numskull, oaf, simp, zany
simplified: abstract, conventionalized, streamlined, stylized
simplified concept or image, over-: stereotype
simplified restatement of text: paraphrase
simplify: clarify, disentangle, ease, explain, expound, generalize, interpret, reduce, shorten, streamline
simply: absolutely, candidly, clearly, completely, frankly, honestly, merely, naturally, openly, plainly
simply, cooked: au naturel

simulate: act, affect, ape, copy, dissemble, feign, imitate, mimic, playact, pretend, reproduce, resemble, sham

simulated: artificial, fake, fictitious, imitation, manmade, phony, sham, synthetic

simultaneous: coexisting, coincident, coinciding, concurrent, contemporaneous, contemporary, synchronal, synchronize, together

sin: adultery, covetousness, debt, envy, err, error, evil, fault, felony, gluttony, guilt, immorality, iniquity, lust, misdeed, murder, offense, peccadillo, pride, slot, stray, transgress, transgression, trespass, vice, violate, violation, wrong, wrongdoing

sin or fault, small: peccadillo

sin so heinous it causes damnation: mortal sin

sin that has been absolved, cancelling of punishment for: indulgence

sin that is minor and may receive God's grace: venial sin

sin, act to show sorrow for: penance

sin, liable to: peccable

sin, pardon a: absolve, remit

sin, save from: redeem

sin, sincere remorse for: contrition, penitence, repentance

sin, study of: hamartiology

since: after, afterward, ago, already, as, because, considering, for, from, hence, inasmuch, later, now, past, subsequently, therefore, whereas

sincere: aboveboard, artless, authentic, candid, cordial, devout, earnest, faithful, frank, genuine, guileless, heartfelt, hearty, honest, open, pure, real, serious, true, truthful, unaffected, unfeigned, virtuous, wholehearted

sincerity: candor, earnestness, genuineness, goodwill, honesty

sine qua non: condition, element, essential, indispensable, necessity

sinew: force, muscle, potency, power, strength, tendon, thew, vigor, vitality

sinewy: athletic, brawny, elastic, firm, forceful, lean, muscular, robust, stringy, strong, tough, wiry

sinful: bad, blameworthy, corrupt, criminal, damnable, erring, evil, immoral, iniquitous, peccant, profligate, reprehensible, shameful, ungodly, unholy, unregenerate, vile, wicked, wrong

sing: cant, carol, chant, croon, hum, intone, lilt, rejoice, tweedle, warble, yodel

RELATED TERMS

sing in artificially high voice: falsetto

sing to express love for someone: serenade

sing with trills: warble, yodel

singing by monks: Gregorian chant

singing exercise: solfège, solfeggio, solmization, tonic sol-fa

singing group: choir, chorale, chorus, duet, ensemble, glee club, octet, octette, quartet, sextet, trio

singing in church, director of: cantor, precentor

singing in four-part harmony: barbershop

singing responsively: antiphony

singing that is like speech: recitative, sprechstimme

singing that is melodic and light: lyric

singing tone, recite in: cantillate, intone

singing voice between soprano and contralto: mezzo-soprano

singing voice between tenor and bass: baritone

singing voice in part music, highest: descant

singing voice of woman or young boy, highest: soprano

singing voice, deep bass: basso profundo

singing voice, highest female: soprano

singing voice, highest male: alto, countertenor, tenor, treble

singing voice, highest natural male: tenor

singing voice, highest young male: soprano

singing voice, low female: alto, contralto

singing voice, lowest male: bass

singing voice, strikingly dramatic tenor: heldentenor

singing with rich tonal lyricism, style of operatic: bel canto

singing with two or more melodic parts: polyphony

singing without instrumental accompaniment: a cappella ❦

singe: burn, char, scorch, sear

singer: alto, artist, artiste, bard, baritone, bass, basso, buffo, cantatrice, cantor, chanter, chanteuse, chorister, crooner, descanter, diva, entertainer, minstrel, musician, poet, soloist, songbird, soprano, tenor, troubadour, vocalist, warbler

singer-poet of medieval times: jongleur, minstrel, troubadour

singer, leading female opera: diva, prima donna

singer, woman: chanteuse

single: alone, bachelor, distinct, divorced, eligible, exclusive, individual, lone, mono, one, one-base-hit, part, separate, singular, sole, solitary, unattached, uniform, unique, unit, unitary, unmarried, unusual, unwed

single and undivided: unitary

single component: unit

single-celled microorganism: monad

single-colored: monochrome

single-combed fowl: Rhode Island Red

single-handedly: alone, courageously, unassisted

single-minded: determined, firm, inflexible, obsessed, persistent, relentless, resolute, rigid, staunch, steadfast, stubborn, unbending

single-set gem: solitaire

singled out for special honor: laureate

singular: alone, bizarre, curious, different, eccentric, exceptional, extraordinary, fantastic, individual, isolated, lone, marvelous, novel, odd, one, only, peculiar, queer, rare, remarkable, respective, separate, single, sole, solitary, solo, strange, uncommon, unique, unparalleled, unprecedented, unusual

sinister: apocalyptic, baleful, corrupt, dark, despicable, devilish, diabolical, dire, disastrous, dishonest, evil, frightening, grim, left, malicious, malign, menacing, ominous, portentous, underhand, wicked

sink: bog, capsize, debase, decline, decrease, degrade, depress, descend, destroy, deteriorate, diminish, dip, dive, drain, drench, drop, ebb, fail, fall, founder, humble, immerse, lower, merge, plummet, plunge, ruin, sag, slope, slump, stoop, submerge, submerse, subside, thrust, torpedo, wane

sink below the water: founder

sink by cutting or getting holes in: scuttle

sink or settle down: subside

sinless: chaste, good, holy, immaculate, innocent, innocent as a lamb, perfect, pure

sinner: adulterer, evildoer, miscreant, murderer, reprobate, scamp, thief, transgressor, trespasser, wrongdoer

sins, seven deadly: cardinal sins

sinuous: anfractuous, bending, circuitous, convoluted, crooked, curving, curvy, deviating, devious, indirect, meandering, sinuate, slinky, snaky, twisting, wavy, winding, zigzag

sinus: antrum, cavity, channel, depressing, hollow, opening, pocket, recess

sip: drink, drop, quaff, sample, savor, taste

siphon: drain, draw, funnel, pipe, pump, tube

sir: address, king, knight, lord, master, mister, monsieur, title

sire: alarm, ancestor, beget, begetter, breed, creator, father, forefather, lord, parent, pater, procreator, spawn, title

siren: alarm, bell, horn, signal, whistle

sirocco: wind

sisal plant: agave

sissy: baby, coward, effeminate, mama's boy, milksop, pantywaist, weakling, wimp

sister: companion, female, friend, nun, sibling, woman

sister killing: sororicide

sisterhood: bond, friendship, sisterly, sodality, sorority, unity

sister's daughter: niece

sister's son: nephew

sit: assemble, brood, convene, deliberate, endure, meet, occupy, perch, please, pose, relax, remain, repose, rest, roost, set, settle, squat, stay, unused, weigh

sit for a photograph or painting: pose

sit-in: demonstration, display, march, protest, strike

sit in the sun: bask

sit on and hatch eggs: incubate

sit quietly at anchor: lie to

site: area, field, locale, location, place, point, position, scene, sector, setting, spot

sitting duck: decoy, dupe, target, victim

sitting position of yoga, cross-legged: lotus position

sitting, characterized by much: sedentary

situate: establish, locate, place, position, settle

situation: arrangement, bargain, berth, case, circumstance, condition, dilemma, direction, emergency, job, locale, locality, location, need, place, plight, point, position, post, posture, predicament, problem, quandary, seat, site, spot, state, station, status, strait, vantage, whereabouts

situation from which extrication is difficult, troublesome: predicament

situation that requires choice between equally good or bad options: dilemma, double bind

situation, tricky: sticky wicket

six-line stanza: sestet

six-ounce bottle of beverage: split

six-pointed star: hexagram

six-sided figure: hexagon

six years, occurring every: sexennial

six, group of: hexad, sextet

sixfold: senary, sextuple

sixteen grains: dram

sixteenth of a cup: tablespoon

sixth part of a drachma: obol

sixth planet from the Sun: Saturn

sixth sense: clairvoyance, ESP

sixty to sixty-nine years old, from: sexagenarian

sixty, concerning the: sexagesimal

sizable: ample, big, considerable, extensive, hefty, large, roomy, spacious, substantial, whopping

size: amount, amplitude, area, breadth, caliber, capacity, cover, degree, diameter, dimensions, expanse, extent, grade, height, length, magnitude, mass, measure, proportions, scope, total, volume, width

size of type: agate, pica

size or extent: amplitude, dimensions, magnitude, proportions

size up: evaluate, eye

sizzle: burn, cook, crackle, fry, grill, hiss, sear, shrivel, sputter

skate blade: runner

skate type: figure, hockey, ice, roller

skedaddle: bolt, flee, hightail, leave, scamper, scoot, scram, scurry, split, vamoose

skeleton: bones, coral, draft, frame, framework, outline, past, shell, sketch, support

skeptic: agnostic, cynic, disbeliever, doubter, doubting Thomas, freethinker, infidel, questioner, sceptic, scoffer, unbeliever

skeptical: cynical, disbelieving, doubtful, doubting, dubious, incredulous, leery, questioning, sceptical, suspicious, uncertain, unconvinced, zetetic

skepticism: concern, disbelief, doubt, dubiety, suspicion, uncertainty

sketch: account, aperçu, blueprint, cartoon, chart, delineate, depiction, describe, description, design, diagram, doodle, draft, draw, drawing, jot, layout, limn, map, outline, paint, picture, plan, play, scene, skeleton, skit, story, summary, trace, vignette

sketch of humorous situation: cartoon

sketchily outline: adumbrate

sketchy: cloudy, crude, hazy, incomplete, preliminary, rough, shallow, superficial, unfinished, vague

skew: angle, biased, blunder, distort, glance, slant, slip, squint, swerve, turn, twist, veer

skewer: brochette, lance, pick, pierce, pin, prick, puncture, rod, skiver, spit, truss

skewer for broiling meat: brochette

skewered meat: kabob, kebab

skid: brake, coast, drag, glide, log, pallet, plank, platform, plummet, rail, runner, shoe, sideslip, skim, slide, slip, slue, spinout, support, swerve, timber, tumble, veer

skid produced by an icy road: fishtail

skier drawn by horse or vehicle: skijoring

skiff: boat, canoe, dinghy, rowboat

skill: ability, address, adeptness, adroitness, aptitude, art, artistry, capability, capacity, competence, craft, cunning, deftness, dexterity, efficiency, experience, expertise, expertness, facility, faculty, finesse, gift, knack, know-how, knowledge, mastery, method, occupation, profession, proficiency, science, talent, trade, training

skill at card tricks: sleight of hand

skill at particular thing: expertise, knack, prowess, virtuosity

skill in manipulation: sleight

skill in moving, acting, doing: facility

skill in not offending others: tact

skill in sailing: seamanship

skill or sensitivity: savoir faire, tact

skill, one's special: forte, métier

skilled enough for the purpose: competent

SKI TERMS

Alpine event: combined, downhill, freestyle, giant slalom, slalom, super G, super giant slalom

climbing ski slope with tips of skis pointed outward: herringbone

concerning cross-country ski racing: Nordic

cross-country ski run: langlauf

device for securing foot to ski: binding

disk on ski pole: basket

downhill and slalom racing: alpine

downhill turn: telemark

jump from crouching position: gelandesprung

leaning forward from ankles: vorlage

make fast straight downhill run: schuss

mark in snow by skier who fell backwards: sitzmark

mound or bump on skier: mogul

natural line of descent: fall line

Nordic event: combined, cross-country, ski jumping

of skiing on uncompacted snow: off-piste

performing stunts: hotdogging

ski and rifle marksmanship competition: biathlon

ski down straight steep slope: schuss

ski down zigzag course: slalom

ski lift: chair, gondola, helicopter, J-bar, poma, T-bar

ski technique: herringbone, parallel, pedaling, sideslipping, sidestepping, skating, snowplow, traverse

ski trail densely packed with snow: piste

ski with short zigzag turns: wedeln

slowing down by bringing tips of skis together: snowplow

turn: christy, parallel, stem, step, swing, wedeln

turn made by pushing weight to inside edge and bringing other ski parallel: stem turn

two-ski vehicle: skibob ❧

SKIN DISEASE

acne	dermatitis	hidradenitis suppurativa	pimple	scleroderma
Alagille's syndrome	dermatofibroma	ichthyosis	pityriasis rosea	seborrhea
albinism	dermatomyositis	impetigo	pityriasis rubra pilaris	serpigo/ringworm
athlete's foot	dhobi's itch	jock itch	pockmark	shingles
atopic dermatitis	eczema	keratoacanthoma	poison ivy	skin cancer
basal-cell carcinoma	Ehlers-Danlos syndrome	leishmaniasis	poison sumac	skin lesion
birthmark	epidermal nevus	leprosy	poison oak	smallpox
blackhead	erysipelas/Saint Anthony's fire	leukoderma/leucoderma	porphyria	sporotrichosis
blemish		lupus	prickly heat	tetter
blister	erythema	macula	prurigo	tinea corporis
bullous pemphigoid	formication	malignant melanoma	pruritus	tinea cruris
burn	frambesia/yaws	mange	pseudofolliculitis barbae	urticaria/nettle rash/hives
candidiasis/moniliasis/thrush	freckle	melanoma	psoriasis	vasculitis
cellulitis	gangrene	miliaria rubra	pustule	verruca
chickenpox	granuloma annulare	mole	pyoderma gangrenosum	vitiligo
chromomycosis	Hansen's disease	morphea		wart
cutaneous disease	heat rash	myxedema	rash	Wegener's granulomatosis
cyst	herpes	pemphigus vulgaris	rosacea	
Dego's disease	herpes zoster/shingles		scabies	xanthomas ❧

---

skilled worker: artificer, artisan, craftsperson

skillful: able, accomplished, adept, adroit, apt, artful, au fait, capable, clever, crafty, cunning, deft, dexterous, experienced, expert, gifted, good, handy, ingenious, learned, professional, proficient, qualified, sharp, tactical, talented, trained, veteran

skillful handling of situation: finesse

skillful of mind: ingenious, inventive

skillful with one's hands: adroit, deft, dexterous, habile, handy

skills or equipment needed: armamentarium

skim: browse, brush, carom, coast, examine, float, glance, glide, graze, ladle, ricochet, sail, scan, scoop, scud, shave, skate, skip, skitter, study, throw

skimp: economize, pinch, sacrifice, save, scrape, scrimp

skimpy: inadequate, insufficient, lean, meager, measly, scant, scanty, scrimpy, spare, sparse, stingy, thin, tight

skin: bark, callous, callus, case, cheat, coat, coating, covering, crust, cuticle, cutis, decorticate, defraud, derma, dermis, epidermis, exterior, exuviate, flay, fleece, fur, hide, husk, layer, membrane, overcharge, peel, pell, pellicle, pelt, planking, rack, rind, scale, scalp, scrape, sheath, sheathe, shed, shell, strip, surface, swindle, vellum

RELATED TERMS

skin and its diseases, study of: dermatology

skin around fingernail, piece of dead: hangnail

skin around fingernails and toenails, hardened: cuticle

skin blemish: birthmark, freckle, lentigo, macula, mole, nevus, rash, stigma, strawberry, wart, wen skin blueness due to lack of oxygen: cyanosis

skin bumps and itchiness: hives

skin disease: acne, dermatitis, eczema, formication, hives, itch, mange, pinta, prurigo, pruritis, psoriasis, rash, roseola, seborrhea, shingles

skin disorder: acne, eczema, psora

skin diver's breathing tube: snorkel

skin during pregnancy, patches on: chloasma

skin elevation with pus: pimple, pustule

skin fold: frenum, plica, wattle

skin grafts to correct defects: dermatoplasty

skin hanging loosely on neck of animals: dewlap, wattle

skin irritation from wind: windburn

skin layer: cirium, derma, dermis, epidermis, fat, subcutaneous tissue

skin lotion, medicinal: liniment, unguent

skin lotion, softening: emollient

skin markings in indelible ink: tattoo

skin of animal: hide, integument

skin of animal with fur: fell, pelt

skin of sheep or goat prepared as writing or painting material: parchment

skin outer layer: epidermis

skin parts: appilla, artery, capillary, hair follicle, hair shaft, melanocyte, nerve, pore, sweat gland, tissue, vein

skin peeling from sunburn: blype

skin piece under tongue: frenum

skin pigment: melanin

skin problem: acne, tinea, rash, roseola, wen

skin protuberance: wart

skin scab: eschar

skin secretion: sebum

skin shedding: ecdysis, slough

skin, as a whale: flense

skin, benign brownish patch on: lentigo, liver spot

skin, concerning: cutaneous, dermal

skin, dry shedded or scaly: furfur, scurf

skin, fibrous connective tissue of: fascia

skin, having chalky: cretaceous

skin, having scaly: squamulose

skin, horny growth on: keratosis

skin, injected beneath the: hypodermic

skin, just beneath the: subcutaneous

skin, minute opening in: pore

skin, of rough: scabrous, squamous

skin, of tough and leathery: coriaceous

skin, removing impurities from: despumate

skin, sensitive layer of: corium, cutis, derma, dermis

skin, shallow cut in: scarification

skin, strip off: flay

skin, thickened horny layer of: callosity, callus

skin, to appear on the: erupt

skin, to tear or wear off: excoriate

skin's goose bumps: horripilation ❦

skinny: bony, emaciated, lank, lanky, lean, malnourished, scant, scrawny, skeletal, slender, spare, thin, underweight

skip: abscond, avoid, bolt, bound, elide, escape, flee, gait, gambol, glance, hip, hooky, hop, jimp, leap, leave, miss, omit, overlook, pass, ricochet, skedaddle, skim, spring, trip, vault

skip a stone on water: dap, scoon

skip or rebound after hitting surface: ricochet

skipper: butterfly, captain, coach, commander, fish, leader, master, officer

skirmish: action, battle, brawl, brus, clash, combat, conflict, contest, dispute, encounter, fight, fray, melee, scrap, scrimmage, scuffle, spar, struggle

skirt: avoid, border, brim, bypass, dodge, duck, edge, envelope, evade, flank, periphery, rim, sidestep

skirt as clothing: A-line, culottes, dirndl, kilt, maxi, midi, mini, petticoat, sari, sarong, tutu, wraparound

skirt of bright cloth, Pacific Island woman's: sarong

skirt on whalebone framework, hoop: farthingale

skirt panel: gore

skirt support: farthingale, hoop, pannier

skirt to make it full, pad under back of woman's: bustle

skirt, Hindu woman's body cloth or wrapped: sari

skit: act, burlesque, caper, joke, parody, play, revue, sketch, story

skittish: bashful, coy, excitable, fickle,

fidgety, frivolous, irresponsible, jumpy, lightheaded, lively, mercurial, nervous, playful, restive, restless, shy, timid, unstable

skivvies: underwear

skulk: creep, evade, hide, lurk, malinger, prowl, pussyfoot, shirk, slink, sneak

skull: brain, cranium, head, mind, scalp

skull-and-crossbones pirate flag: Jolly Roger

skull as sign of mortality: death's-head, memento mori

skull for spinal cord, large orifice at base of: foramen magnum

skull protuberance: inion

skull, outermost projection of back of: inion

skull, spongy bony tissue of: diploe

skull, study of: craniology, phrenology

skull, upper half of: sinciput

skullcap: beanie, calotte, kappel, kipa, yarmulke, zucchetto

skullcap, Catholic: calotte, zucchetto

skullcap, Jewish: yarmulke

skullduggery: chicanery, crafty, trickery

skull's highest point: vertex

skull's joint line: suture

skunk: animal, cheat, defeat, knave, mammal, polecat, scoundrel, shellac, stinker

skunk cabbage: aroid

skunk genus: mephitis

skunk cousin: polecat

sky: air, empyrean, firmament, heavens, jump, space, vault, welkin

sky-blue: azure, celeste, cerulean, color

sky with streaks of clouds: mackerel sky

sky, concerning: celestial, empyreal, supernal

skylarking: antics, carousing, frolicking, hijinks, horseplay, playing, revelry, roughhousing

skylight: abat-jour

skylight, mall or court with: galleria

skylight, open room with: atrium

skyline: horizon, outline

slab: board, chunk, hunk, lump, piece, portion, slice, tablet, tile, wood

slack: careless, dilatory, easy, excess, flaccid, flexible, idle, inactive, inadequate, inattentive, indolent, lax, lazy, leeway, leisurely, lethargic, limp, loose, loosen, looseness, neglectful, negligent, play, relax, relaxed, remiss, shirk, sloppy, slothful, slow, sluggish, soft, tardy, unsteady

slacken: abate, decrease, diminish, ease, let up, loose, loosen, moderate, reduce, relax, relent, remit, retard, sag, slow, soften, subside, temper, untighten, weaken

slacker: dawdler, goldbrick, goof-off, idler, laggard, loafer, loser, shirker, sluggard

slacks: pants

slag: ashes, cinders, debris, dross, embers, lava, recrement, refuse, residue, scoria

slake: abate, allay, appease, assuage, compose, cool, crumble, decrease, disintegrate, gratify, lessen, loose, mitigate, moderate, quench, reduce, refresh, relax, relaxed, relieve, satisfy, slack, subdue

slam: abuse, bang, batter, beat, belt, blow, clash, clobber, crash, criticize, hit, impact, knock, pound, push, rap, slug, smack, smash, strike, swat, throw, thump, wallop

slammer: big house, calaboose, can, clink, cooler, hoosegow, jail, jug, pen, penitentiary, pokey, prison

slander: asperse, assail, backbite, belie, betray, calumniate, calumny, character assassination, defamation, defame, derogate, dirt, disgrace, dishonor, distort, libel, malediction, malign, misrepresent, muckrake, mudslinging, scandal, scandalize, slur, smear, sully, traduce, vilify, villify

slang: argot, cant, colloquialism, dialect, jargon, jive, language, lingo, patois, vernacular, vituperate, vulgarity

slant: angle, aside, band, bank, bevel, bias, decline, diagonal, distort, glance, grade, incline, lean, opinion, pitch, point, prejudice, sideways, skew, slope, tilt, tip, turn, veer, view, viewpoint, virgule

slant a nail: toe

slanted: aslope, atip, oblique

slanting typeface: italic

slap: blow, buffet, castigate, clap, crack, criticize, cuff, hit, insult, pat, rebuff, smack, spank, strike, swat, wallop, wham

slapdash: careless, haphazard, hasty, impetuous, reckless, slipshod, sloppy

slapstick: absurd, comedy, comical, farce, funny

slapstick troupe: Keystone Kops

slash: butcher, carve, criticize, curtail, cut, decrease, gash, hack, knife, laceration, lash, lessen, reduce, shorten, slice, slit, strike, stripe, wound

slash or oblique stroke (/) used between words or in fractions: diagonal, oblique, separatrix, shilling, slant, solidus, virgule

slate: ballot, list, record, register, roster, schedule; blackboard, chalkboard, tablet; stone, tile

slate-trimming tool: zat

slatted opening: louver

slaughter: annihilate, bloodbath, bloodshed, butcher, butchery, carnage, decimate, destroy, destruction, hecatomb, kill, killing, liquidation, maim, massacre, murder, mutilate, overwhelm, pogrom, rout, slay, trounce

slaughterhouse: abattoir, butchery, shambles, stockyard

slave: bond, bondman, bondsman, bondswoman, captive, chattel, drudge, esne, grind, helot, laborer, moil, serf, serfs, servant, thrall, toil, toiler, vassal, workhorse

slavelike: compliant, sequacious, servile, slavish, submissive

slaver: dribble, drivel, drool, fawn, saliva, slobber

slavery: bondage, captivity, drudgery, enthrallment, grind, helotry, labor, serfdom, servitude, thrall, thralldom, vassalage

slavery, to free from: emancipate, enfranchise, manumit

slavery's end: abolition

slavish: abject, bond, dependent, hard, imitative, menial, obsequious, oppressive, servile, submissive, subservient, uninspired, unoriginal

slay: annihilate, assassinate, butcher, destroy, do in, eliminate, execute, kill, massacre, murder, overwhelm, slaughter, snuff, strike

sleazy: cheap, dilapidated, disreputable, flimsy, seedy, shabby, shoddy, tacky, tawdry, thin, trashy

sled: bobsled, clipper, coaster, cutter, luge, pung, sledge, sleigh, toboggan

sled with curled front end: toboggan

sled, racing: luge

sled, to travel with: mush

sleek: adroit, attractive, chic, chisel, clever, crafty, cunning, fashionable, glistening, gloss, glossy, ingenious,

oily, polish, preen, satiny, shiny, silken, silky, slick, slide, slippery, smart, smooth, stylish, suave, unctuous

sleep: catnap, coma, crash, death, doze, dream, dreamland, drowse, estivate, hibernate, lethargy, nap, repose, rest, retire, siesta, slumber, snooze, sopor, stupor

sleep after lunch: siesta

sleep and dreams, god of: Morpheus

sleep cycle when dreaming takes place: rapid eye movement, REM

sleep-deterring: agrypnotic

sleep disorder: apnea

sleep-inducing: hypnagogic, hypnotic, narcotic, somniferous, somnolent, soporiferous, soporific

sleep-learning: hypnopedia

sleep noisily: snore

sleep-producing: hypnagogic, somniferous

sleep-producing medicine: soporific

sleep through summer: estivate

sleep through winter: hibernate

sleep, amnesiac: twilight sleep

sleep, deep: sopor

sleep, regular: orthodox sleep

sleep, REM: paradoxical sleep, rapid-eye-movement sleep

sleep, to induce: lull

sleep, uncontrollable desire for: narcolepsy

sleeper, late: slugabed

sleepiness: oscitancy

sleeping: abed, asleep, comatose, dormant, inactive, latent, unconscious

sleeping cap: biggin, nightcap, Pullman

sleeping car, European: wagon-lit

sleeping pill: hypnotic, narcotic, opiate, sedative, soporific

sleeping quarters for a number of people: dorm, dormitory

sleeping sickness: encephalitis lethargica, sleepy sickness

sleeping state: somnolence, torpor

sleeping, excessive: hypersomnia

sleepless: active, alert, ceaseless, insomnolent, restless, wakeful, watchful

sleepless period keeping vigil: watch

sleeplike state: trance

sleepwalking: noctambulation, noctambulism, somnambulism

sleepy: dozy, drowsy, dull, exhausted, fatigued, hypnotic, inactive, lethargic, listless, quiet, sluggish, slumberous, somnolent, soporific, tired

sleeve that is in one piece with neckline: raglan

sleeve, capelike: dolman

sleeve, extremely puffy: bouffant, leg-of-mutton sleeve

sleeveless apron: pinafore

sleeveless garment: aba, vest

sleigh: bobsled, cutter, luge, pung, sled, sledge, toboggan

sleight of hand: hocus-pocus, legedermain, legerdemain, magic, prestidigitation

slender: delicate, faint, feeble, frail, lank, lanky, lean, lithe, little, meager, minute, narrow, outside, remote, scant, skinny, slight, slim, small, svelte, tenuous, thin, trim, weak, willowy, wiry, wispy

slender thread: filament

sleuth: agent, bears, detective, gumshoe, investigator, private eye, shamus, tracker

slice: carve, course, cut, gash, part, piece, quota, segment, sever, share, shave, slit, wedge

slice thinly: shave, skive

sliced meat, vegetables, and bean curd fried together, Japanese: sukiyaki

slick: cagey, foxy, glib, greasy, neat, oiled, oily, sharp, slimy, smart, tidy, wily, wise

slide: chute, coast, decline, downswing, downturn, elide, fall, flow, glide, glissade, hurry, incline, scoot, skate, skid, skim, sled, sledge, slip, slither, slope, stream, veer

slide from building: chute

slide, controlled, on icy or snowy incline: glissade

slide, photographic: transparency

slight: dainty, delicate, flimsy, fragile, frail, insignificant, light, little, meager, minor, nominal, petty, remote, scant, scanty, skinny, slender, slim, small, superficial, thin, trifling, trivial, unimportant

slight, to: cut, discourtesy, neglect, offend, overlook, rebuff, snub

slight coloration: tinge, tint

slight depression: dent

slight error: lapse

slight suggestion: hint, inkling

slightly: delicately, hardly, marginally, slenderly, somewhat

slightly in music: poco

slightly open: ajar

slightly wet: moist

slightly-raised platform: estrade

slim: diet, gaunt, lean, meager, narrow, negligible, outside, reduce, reedy, remote, scanty, skinny, slender, slight, small, spare, sparse, svelte, tenuous, thin

slime: filth, gleet, glop, goo, gunk, mire, muck, mud, ooze, scum, slop, sludge

slimy: clammy, eely, filthy, foul, gooey, mucky, muddy, offensive, oozy, scummy, vile, viscous, vulgar

sling: cast, catapult, chuck, fling, heave, hurl, launch, send, slingshot, throw, toss, weapon

slink: creep, lurk, prowl, skulk, slither, sneak, steal, weasel

slip: blooper, blunder, bungle, chute, dock, elapse, elude, err, error, fall, fault, faux pas, flub, glide, goof, harbor, imp, jetty, lapse, miscue, mishap, misstep, mistake, muff, neglect, omit, oversight, pier, quay, skid, slide, slither, stumble, trip, voucher

slip and slide: skid

slip away, as time: elapse

slip into former condition: backslide, relapse

slip of the tongue: Freudian slip, lapsus linguae, parapraxis, spoonerism

slip-knot: noose

slip-up: blooper, blunder, bungle, error, flub, miscue, mishap, mistake, omission, oversight

slipper: mule, pantofle, pump, sandal, scuff, shoe

slippery: crafty, dishonest, eely, elusive, evasive, foxy, glib, greasy, icy, oily, shifty, slick, smooth, sneaky, tricky, uncertain, unreliable

slippery and smooth: lubricious

slippery-feeling: greasy, unctuous

slipshod: careless, disheveled, messy, neglected, seedy, shabby, shoddy, sloppy, slovenly, tacky, untidy

slit: aperture, crack, cut, fissure, gash, opening, rent, sever, slash, slice, split, tear

slither: crawl, creep, glide, grovel, lurk, prowl, slide, slink, snake, sneak

sliver: crumb, flake, fragment, shred, slice, splinter, thorn

slob: hog, pig, slattern, sloven

slobber: blubber, dribble, drivel, drool, froth, gush, kiss, salivate, slabber, slaver

slogan: catchword, expression, idiom, jingle, motto, phrase, watchword

slop: drivel, garbage, gulp, gush, guzzle, mash, muck, mud, mush, ooze, refuse, slobber, sludge, slush, spill, splash, swill, trash, waste

slope: acclivity, angle, ascent, bank, bend, bevel, cant, cliff, declivity, descent, deviate, grade, gradient, hill, hillside, inclination, incline, lean, obliquely, pitch, ramp, rise, slant, splay, tilt

slope diagonally, to go up or down a: traverse

slope of mountain: versant

slope of roof: pitch

slope or incline from perpendicular: rake

slope or rate of inclination: gradient

slope, descending: declension, declination, decline, declivity, descent

slope, gentle: glacis, incline

slope, steep: escarpment

slope, upward: acclivity

sloping: askew, aslant, declivous, downhill, inclined, leaning, oblique, pitched, slanting, supine, tilted

sloping edge: bevel, bezel

sloping entrance: ramp

sloping rock surface, broad gently: pediment

sloping sides, bank of earth with: terrace

sloping steeply: declivitous

sloping type style: italic

sloppy: careless, clumsy, dirty, disheveled, messy, muddy, slipshod, slovenly, slushy, unkempt, untidy

slosh: flounder, mud, slime, slush, spill, splash, splatter, wade, wallow

slot: chase, crack, gap, groove, hole, hollow, keyhole, niche, notch, opening, slit, space, track

slot-machine part: lever

sloth: animal, apathy, idleness, indolence, languor, lassitude, laziness, lazy, lethargy, listlessness, pack, slowness, sluggishness, tardiness, torpidity, torpor

sloth or anteater, like a: xenarthral

sloth, two-toed: unau

slothful: idle, inactive, indolent, lazy, lethargic, listless, sluggish

slothlike animal: loris

slouch: bend, droop, gait, hunch, idle, idler, laggard, loaf, lounge, posture, slacker, stoop, wilt

slovenly: careless, dawdy, dirty, disheveled, disorderly, grubby, grungy, lazy, messy, ragged, seedy, slatternly, slipshod, sloppy, tacky, unkempt, untidy

slow: backward, behind, boring, brake, decelerate, delay, delaying, deliberate, dilatory, dragging, dull, gradual, hamper, hinder, impede, inactive, lackadaisical, laggard, languid, late, lazy, leisurely, lingering, phlegmatic, plodding, poky, procrastinate, relaxed, retard, simple, slack, slacken, sluggard, sluggish, tardy, unhurried

slow and delaying: dilatory

slow and hinder: retard

slow and unhurried: deliberate

slow diffusion or absorption: osmosis

slow gallop: canter

slow in coming, going, doing: procrastinate, tarry

slow journey: trek

slow movement in music: adagio

slow-motion Chinese physical exercises: tai chi

slow or lengthened in duration: interminable, prolonged, protracted

slow person: dawdler, laggard, slowpoke

slow-witted: dense, dull, moronic, stupid, unintelligent

slow, as in music: andante, largo, lento, tardo

slowdown: brake, curb, deceleration, delay, falloff, inactivity, setback, slump, stoppage, strike

slowing or motionlessness: stasis

slowly: bit by bit, costive, leisurely, sluggish, tardy, unhurried

slowly but surely: inchmeal

slowly destroy: erode

slowpoke: dawdler, laggard, lingerer, slug, snail, straggler

sludge: filth, ice, mire, muck, mud, ooze, residue, sediment, slime, slop, slush, waste

slug: bat, belt, bullet, clobber, disk, drink, gastropod, hit, mollusk, punch, shack, shot, slam, slouch, slow, sluggard, smash, snail, sock, strike, swat, wallop

slug, like a: limacine

slug's kin: snail

sluggard: dawdler, drone, fainéant, idler, laggard, lazy, lazybones, loafer, slouch, slug, snail

sluggish: apathetic, dilatory, dragging, drowsy, dull, heavy, inactive, indolent, inert, laggard, lazy, leaden, lethargic, listless, lumpish, lymphatic, poky, slothful, slow, sluggard, stagnant, stiff, supine, torpid, unresponsive

sluggish creek: bayou

sluggishness: inertia, lethargy

sluice: channel, douse, flume, flush, gate, gush, pour, soak, stream, trough, valve, wash

slum: alley, barrio, dump, ghetto, skid row, tenement

slum rehabilitation: gentrification, urban renewal

slumber: coma, dormancy, doze, drowse, hibernate, languor, lethargy, nap, rest, sleep, snooze

slump: collapse, decline, depression, dip, downswing, downtrend, droop, drop, fall, lapse, plunge, recession, sag, sink, slide, slip, slouch, topple

slur: aspersion, blacken, blemish, blur, calumniate, calumny, criticize, defame, discredit, disgrace, disparage, elide, garble, innuendo, insinuation, insult, mumble, reproach, salign, slander, slide, slight, smear, soil, spot, stain, stigma, sully, traduce

slur in pronunciation: elide

slush: drench, drivel, ice, mire, mud, pulp, slop, sluice, snow

slut: bimbo, floozy, harlot, hooker, hussy, jade, jezebel, minx, slattern, tramp, wench, whore

sly: artful, astute, cagey, calculating, clever, crafty, cunning, deceitful, devious, evasive, foxy, furtive, guileful, ingenious, mischievous, roguish, secret, secretive, sharp, shifty, shrewd, skillful, slick, smooth, sneaking, sneaky, subtle, tricky, underhand, underhanded, weaselly, wily

sly and not straightforward: disingenuous

sly way, in a: clandestine, furtive, stealthy, surreptitious

smack, on the kisser: buss

small: cramped, diminutive, dinky, faint, humble, humiliated, insignificant, limited, little, meager, mean, microscopic, mignon, miniature, minimal, minor, minuscule, minute, modest, narrow, negligible, petite, petty, picayune, pocket size, puny, remote, scant, selfish, short, slender, slight, slim, teeny, thin, tiny, trifling, trivial, undersized, unimportant, wee

small alphabet letters: lowercase

small amount: bit, dab, dram, drop, gram, iota, modicum, ounce, paucity, scintilla, semblance, sliver, smattering, smidgen, some, soupçon, splash, spot, tad, tincture, trace, vestige

small and cramped: incommodious

small cubicle in library for private study: carrel

small in size, very: diminutive, lilliputian, midget, miniature, minuscule

small-minded: bigoted, intolerant, mean, narrow, petty, prejudiced, selfish

small talk: babble, chat, chitchat, civilities, courtesies, pleasantries, prattle

small-time: nickel and dime, two-bit

small, extremely: imperceptible, infinitesimal, lilliputian, microscopic, negligible, nominal

small, memorable acting part: cameo

small, ornamental bottle: flacon

smallness of head: microcephaly

smallpox: variola

smart: ache, active, acute, alert, astute, bright, brilliant, brisk, canny, chic, clever, dapper, elegant, energetic, fashionable, hurt, impertinent, insolent, intelligent, knowing, lively, natty, neat, pain, posh, precocious, pungent, quick, resourceful, sassy, sharp, shrewd, slick, smug, spirited, sporty, spruce, sting, stylish, swanky, throb, trendy, vigorous, wily, wise, witty

smart aleck: boaster, braggart, clown, wise guy, wiseacre, wisenheimer

smash: accident, annihilate, bang, bash, batter, belt, break, clobber, collapse, collision, crack, crash, crush, dash, defeat, demolish, destroy, hit, impact, jolt, press, pulverize, sensation, shatter, slam, slug, sock, strike, success, wallop, whack, wreck

smashed: buzzed, drunk, inebriated, intoxicated, plastered, soused, stewed, wasted, zonked

smashup: accident, collapse, collision, crash, defeat, pileup, wreck

smattering: dash, drop, few, smidgen, sprinkling

smear: bedaub, besmear, besmirch, blot, blotch, blur, coat, cover, dab, daub, defame, defeat, defile, degrade, grease, lambaste, malign, mar, plaster, rub, sample, slander, slur, smash, smirch, smudge, soil, spatter, splotch, spot, spread, stain, sully, taint, thrash, trounce, vilify

smell: aroma, aura, detect, discover, flair, fragrance, funk, fust, nose, odor, perfume, reek, savor, scent, sense, sniff, stench, stink, trace, whiff

smell of waste, decaying matter: effluvium

smell of wine or liqueur: bouquet

smell, bad: fetor, mephitis, stench

smell, concerning: olfactory, osmatic

smell, having sharp: acrid, pungent

smell, loss of the sense of: anosmia

smell, pleasant: aroma, fragrance, incense

smell, substance for masking: deodorant

smelling of decay or mildew: frowsy, fusty, mephitic, musty

smelling salts bottle: vinaigrette

smelling, pleasant-: aromatic, fragrant, odiferous, redolent

smelling, unpleasant-: fetid, gamy, malodorous, noisome, odoriferous, odorous, rancid, rank, reeking

smelly: fetid, foul, funky, noisome, olid, putrid, rank, rotten, stinking

smelly insect: stinkbug

smelting residue: cinder, scoria, sinter, slag

smidgen: atom, bit, crumb, dab, drop, iota, jot, mite, particle, pinch, shred, speck, trace

smile: beam, expression, grin, laugh, simper, smirk, sneer

smile with slightly upturned corners: archaic smile

smile, of an angelic: beatific

smirch: besmear, besmirch, bespatter, blacken, blemish, blot, blotch, contaminate, corrupt, country, degrade, dirty, discredit, disgrace, dishonor, pollute, smear, smudge, soil, stain, sully, taint, tarnish

smirk: beam, grimace, grin, leer, simper, smile, sneer

smite: afflict, attack, belt, buffet, chasten, chastise, clobber, dash, defeat, destroy, hit, knock, slap, smack, sock, strike, swat, wallop, whack

smithy's equipment: anvil

smitten: affected, afflicted, enamored, infatuated, stricken, taken

smog-like weather condition: smaze

smoke: cigar, cigarette, cure, fume, funk, haze, kill, loud, mist, murder, perform, pipe, puff, smog, smudge, steam, vapor

smoke conveyor: flue

smoke for extermination or disinfection, use: fumigate

smoke inhaled by nonsmokers: passive smoking

smoke, concerning: fumatory

smoked salmon: lox

smoky: blackened, burning, cloudy, dingy, fuliginous, fumid, fumy, hazy, murky, smoldering, sooty

smolder: bubble, burn, fester, fulminate, fume, seethe, simmer, smother

smooth: bland, calm, civilize, comfort, courteous, creamy, ease, easy, easygoing, effortless, equable, even, evenly, flat, flatten, flowing, fluent, gentle, glossy, hairless, harmonious, iron, level, methodical, mild, palliate, pave, persuasive, placid, pleasant, polish, polished, preen, press, satiny, serene, silky, sleek, slick, slick as a whistle, soft, soothe, soothing, suave, tranquil, undisturbed, uninterrupted, unruffled, unwrinkled

smooth and expressive: fluent

smooth and polished: glacé

smooth and slippery: ingratiating, unctuous

smooth and sweet: mellifluous

smooth baldness, of: glabrous

smooth flattering talk: blarney

smooth musical transition: segue

smooth- or straight-haired: lissotrichous

smooth polished surface of gem, bone, tooth: facet

smooth the way: expedite, pave

smooth-spoken: glib, suave

smooth, downless peach: nectarine

smooth, flowing style used as a musical direction: cantabile

smooth by rubbing with an abrasive: file, plane, sand

smoothly, flowing or moving: fluent

smorgasbord: buffet, hodgepodge, mishmash

smother: asphyxiate, choke, conceal, cover, extinguish, hide, overwhelm, quash, quench, repress, shower, solder, stifle, suffocate, suppress

smudge: blot, blotch, blur, dirty, grime, smear, smut, smutch, soil, soot, stain, sully

smug: complacent, confident, neat, pompous, priggish, self-righteous, spruce, stuffy, suave, tidy, trim

smuggle: bootleg, pirate, sneak

smuggled product, esp. liquor: bootleg, contraband

smut: dirt, filth, grime, muck, obscenity, porn, porno, pornography, smudge, soil, spot, stain, sully, taint

smutty: dirty, filthy, indecent, lewd, nasty, obscene, pornographic, raunchy, soiled, sooty, vulgar

snack: bit, bite, eat, goodies, morsel, munchies, nibble, nosh, refreshment, tea

snack, nutritious: gorp

snafu: chaos, complication, confusion, entangle, mess, muddle, predicament, snarl

snag: barrier, branch, catch, complication, damage, difficulty, drawback, fly in the ointment, glitch, hamper, hazard, hinder, hindrance, hitch, hurdle, impediment, knot, nail, obstacle, obstruction, pickle, problem, spot, stump, tear, tree

snail: escargot, gastropod, periwinkle, slowpoke, slug

snail shell, shaped like: cochleate

snail, edible: escargot

snake eyes: ace

snake scale: scute

snake skin shedding: ecdysis, sloughing

snake sound: hiss, siss

snake symbol of medical profession: caduceus

snake teeth: fangs

snake that coils around and asphyxiates prey: constrictor

snake worship: ophiolatry

snake, concerning: anguine, colubrine, ophidian

snakelike: anguiform, crawly, eely, serpentine

snakes, mammal known for killing venomous: mongoose

snaking and winding: sinuous

snaky: crafty, devious, evil, meandering, serpentine, sinuous, sly, sneaky, twisting, venomous, winding, wriggly, zigzag

snap, crackle, pop: crepitation

snappish: angry, cantankerous, crabby, cranky, cross, curt, edgy, grouchy, irascible, irritable, luffy, peevish, petulant, short, testy, touchy

snappy: brittle, chic, classy, dapper, energetic, fashionable, fast, hasty, irritable, lively, nasty, prompt, quick, rapid, smart, speedy, spiffy, stylish, sudden, swank, swift

snapshot: photo, print

snare: ambush, bag, bait, catch, deception, decoy, entangle, entanglement, enticement, entoil, entrap, gin, grasp, grin, inveigle, involve, land, lure, mesh, net, noose, pitfall, seize, tangle, trap, web

snarl: arr, bark, chaos, complicate, confuse, entangle, gnarl, growl, grumble, infusion, jam, kink, knot, maze, mesh, mess, muddle, predicament, quarrel, scold, snap, snare, tangle, twist, web

snatch: abduct, bit, catch, clutch, collar, fragment, grab, grabble, grasp, kidnap, nab, nail, piece, pluck, rescue, seize, snare, swipe, take, trap, wrest, yank

sneak: ambush, cheater, coward, cower, crawl, creep, knave, lurk, prowl, rascal, scoundrel, secret, skunk, slink, slither, snake, snoop, steal, tiptoe, underhand, worm

sneak a look: peek

sneaky: clandestine, conniving, devious, dishonest, furtive, shifty, sinister, sly, surreptitious, undered, underhanded

sneer: belittle, condemn, disdain, expression, fleer, flout, gibe, grimace, grin, insult, jeer, lampoon, leer, mock, ridicule, scoff, scorn, smile, smirk, snicker, snub, taunt

sneering: sardonic

sneering language: sarcasm

sneeze blessing: bless you, gesundheit

sneeze, sound of a: sternutation

sneezing, causing: sternutatory

snicker: chortle, chuckle, giggle, heehaw, laugh, sneer, snigger, sniggle, teehee

snide: base, contemptible, cynical, hateful, insincere, malicious, mean, nasty, sarcastic, sinister, sly, spiteful, tricky, underhand

sniff: detect, inhale, nose, scent, smell, sniffle, snoop, snuff, snuffle, whiff

snifter: dram, drink, goblet, shot, snort

snip: bit, clip, cut, easy, fragment, incision, piece, scrap, shear, shorten, shred, trim

snipe, plover or stork: wader

sniper: assassin, gunman, gunwoman, killer, marksman, markswoman, sharpshooter

snippet: bite

snippy: abrupt, bluff, blunt, brief, curt, gruff, mean, rude, sharp, short, snippety, snotty

snitch: betray, inform, informer, pilfer, pinch, rat, squealer, steal, stoolie, swipe, tattle, tattler, tell, thief

snivel: blubber, complain, cry, fret, shine, sniff, sniffle, sob, weep, whimper

snob: elitist, parvenu, toady, upstart

snobbish: aloof, arrogant, condescending, haughty, ostentatious, overbearing, pompous, pretentious, snooty, snotty, stuck up, uppity

snoop: busybody, meddle, meddler, peek, peep, poke, prowl, pry, search, sneak, spier, spy

snooty: aloof, conceited, egotistical, exclusive, haughty, pretentious, snobbish, snotty, stuck up, supercilious

snooze: doze, drowse, forty winks, nap, siesta, sleep, slumber

snoring sound like rattling or whistling: rhonchus

snoring, heavy: stertorous

snort: blow, breathe, drink, grunt, laugh, pant, puff, snore, sound

snotty: arrogant, dirty, haughty, impertinent, impudent, nasty, rude, snobbish, snooty

snout: beak, nose, nozzle, proboscis, rostrum, spout, trunk

snow in Scotland: sna

snow pellet: graupel

snow turning into glacial ice: firn, névé, old snow

snow, concerning: nival, niveous

snow, ice, and rain: sleet

snow, melted and refrozen into granular surface: corn snow

snowy: fluffy, nival, niveous, pure, soft, spotless, stormy, white, wintry

snub: cold shoulder, consure, cut, disregard, ignore, neglect, nip, ostracize, quell, rebuff, rebuke, remark, repress, reprimand, reproach, restrain, shun, slap, slight, stop

snuff: adequate, destroy, detect, extinguish, inhale, odor, scent, smell, sniff, snort, whiff

snug: close, comfortable, comfy, compact, cozy, cuddle, cushy, intimate, neat, nestle, safe, seaworthy, secure, sheltered, snuggle, tidy, tight, trim, warm

so: accordingly, afterward, apparently, because, consequently, ergo, exact, hence, indeed, likewise, quite, sic, similarly, then, therefore, thus, too, true, very, well

so-called: alleged, nominal, pretended, soi-disant, supposed

so-so: adequate, average, comme ci

comme ca, fair, fair to middling, mediocre, middling, OK, ordinary, passable, second rate, subpar, tolerable, tolerably, unmastered

soak: dip, douse, drink, dunk, flood, imbrue, imbue, immerse, impregnate, infuse, marinate, ooze, ret, saturate, seep, sop, souse, submerge, wet

soak flax, hemp, lumber: ret

soak in liquid: steep

soak meat in sauce before cooking: marinate

soak or steep to extract flavor, etc.: infuse

soak up sun: bask, tan

soaked: drenched, saturated, sodden, soggy, waterlogged, wet

soaking or steeping, make soft by: macerate

soap: castile, cleanser, detergent, lather, suds, wash

soapy: saponaceous

soar: ascend, aspire, climb, float, fly, glide, lift, mount, rise, sail, skyrocket, tower

sob: bawl, blubber, boohoo, cry, lament, moan, snivel, wail, weep, whimper

sobbed: wept

sober: abstemious, abstinent, ailing, calm, collected, composed, controlled, cool, disciplined, dull, earnest, gentle, grave, grim, humble, moderate, peaceful, placid, quiet, rational, realistic, reasonable, regular, reserved, sane, sedate, serious, solemn, somber, sound, staid, steady, subdue, subdued, unimpassioned, unruffled

sobriety: abstinence, continence, gravity, moderation, soberness, solemnity, temperance

sobriquet: alias, appellation, byname, epithet, handle, nickname

sociable: affable, agreeable, chummy, congenial, convivial, cordial, cozy, extroverted, friendly, genial, gracious, gregarious, hospitable, outgoing, pleasant, social, talkative

social: communal, companionable, convivial, cordial, entertaining, friendly, gathering, genial, gregarious, hospitable, neighborly, party, pleasant, public, sociable, tea

social climber: arriviste, bounder, nouveau riche, parvenu, snob, upstart

social clique: cenacle

social division: caste, classe, stratum

SNOW AND ICE VEHICLES

blade
bobsled
dogsled
drag
kibitka
luge
pung
skiddoo
skibob
skimobile
sled
sleigh
snowmobile
tobaggan
troika
weasel ❦

---

social error: faux pas, gaffe
social estrangement: alienation
social grace: diplomacy, savoir faire, poise, tact
social insect: ant, bee, wasp
social occasion for a foursome: double date
social or public image or personality, one's: front, persona
social ostracism or seclusion: Coventry, exile, purdah
social outcast: Ishmael, leper, pariah
social prestige is measured, possession or activity by which: status symbol
social standing, advancing in: upwardly mobile
social talk, not about information or ideas: phatic
socialize: associate, consort, entertain, fraternize, hobnob, mingle, mix, party
socially inexperienced young man: hobbledehoy
socially lower: déclassé
socially proper: comme il faut
society: alliance, aristocracy, association, brotherhood, circle, civilization, clan, club, community, companionship, cooperation, elite, fellowship, gang, gentry, guild, league, order, organization, people, public, sisterhood, sodality, union
Society of Friends member: Quaker
society, basic functioning parts of a: infrastructure
society, young woman making formal debut into: debutante
sock: beat, belt, blow, bop, clobber,

comedy, hit, punch, smack, smash, strike, wallop, whack; hose, hosiery, stocking
socklike wind direction item: windsock
sod: dirt, divot, earth, fellow, grass, peat, soak, soil, turf
soda: beverage, drink, mixer, pop, seltzer, tonic
soda water: carbonated water, club soda, seltzer water
sodality: association, brotherhood, fellowship, fraternity, league, order, society, union, unity
sodden: bloated, doughty, drenched, drunk, heavy, intoxicated, moist, mushy, saturated, soaked, soggy, soused, steeped, stewed, stupid, torpid, unimaginative, wet
sofa: banquette, chaise, chesterfield, confidante, couch, davenport, divan, lounge, meridienne, ottoman, pouf, sectional, settee, sociable, squab
sofa with high back: settee
sofa with low cushioned seat and arm rests: divan
soft: affectionate, balmy, bland, comfortable, comfy, compassionate, cottony, cushiony, cushy, delicate, doughy, downy, faint, feeble, flabby, flexible, fluffy, gentle, gently, hushed, lenient, lightly, limp, mealy, mild, mushy, pampered, peacefully, placid, pliant, quiet, silken, simple, smooth, snug, soothing, spongy, squashy, squishy, subdued, supple, sympathetic, temperate, tender, tranquil, velvety, weak
soft and crumbling: friable
soft and flexible: ductile, malleable, pliable
soft and limp: flabby, flaccid
soft ball: wad
soft drink: ade, cola, pop, soda, soda pop
soft mashed food: pap
soft palate: velum
soft sighing: susurration
soft tone or volume: undertone
soft tones, in: sotto voce
soft, in music: dolce, piano
soften: alleviate, appease, assuage, attemper, bend, calm, cushion, diminish, ease, lessen, macerate, mash, mellow, melt, mitigate, modulate, mollify, pacify, relax, relent, soothe, subdue, temper, tenderize, thaw, weaken, yield
soften by soaking: macerate

soften intensity of: mitigate, moderate, temper
softening: mollescent
softening to skin: emollient
softhearted: compassionate, forgiving, humane, kind, merciful, sympathetic, tender, warm
softly, in music: piano
soggy: damp, drenched, dull, heavy, humid, limp, mushy, saturated, soaked, sodden, waterlogged, wet
soigné: chic, elegance, fashionable, neat, polished, sleek, stylish, well-groomed
soil: befile, blacken, blot, defile, degrade, dirt, dirty, earth, foil, grime, ground, humus, land, loam, muck, mud, ruin, shame, smear, smut, soot, spolt, stain, sully, taint
soil abundant in organic materials: pinguid, unctuous
soil as a factor in organisms' life, pertaining to: edaphic
soil composed of sand, clay, silt, organic matter: loam
soil deposit: loess
soil deposited by flowing water: alluvion, alluvium
soil protector mix: mulch
soil science: agrology, pedology
soil, break the surface of: scarify
soil, relating to: edaphic
soil, remove soluble constituents of: leach
soil, very black top-: chernozem
soil, wearing away of: erosion
soiled: besmeared, blemished, dirty, faded, filthy, foul, grimy, stained, sullied, taint
soils, mineral salts in arid: alkali
soils, study of: pedology
sojourn: abide, abode, bide, delay, dwell, layover, lodge, rest, stay, stop, tarry, travel, trip, visit
solace: allay, alleviate, assuage, calm, cheer, comfort, consolation, console, entertain, lessen, mitigate, peace, relaxation, relief, soften, soothe
solar: celestial, cosmic, empyreal, heliacal, lunar, planetary, stellar
solar system model: orrery
sold: convinced, gone, impressed, marketed, pleased, retailed
solder: braze, fasten, fuse, join, mend, patch, unite, weld
soldier: airman, airwoman, cadet, cavalier, colonel, commando, doughboy, fighter, general, GI, grenadier, guer-

rilla, gunner, infantryman, infantry-woman, lieutenant, major, marine, mercenary, musketeer, officer, para-trooper, pilot, plebe, poilu, private, recruit, sergeant, serviceman, ser-vicewoman, trooper, vet, veteran, warmonger, warrior

soldier attending superior officer: orderly

soldier below commissioned or warrant officer: enlisted person

soldier for refuge, pit dug by: foxhole

soldier from duty, to dismiss a: cashier

soldier in irregular troop: guerrilla, partisan

soldier, concerning a: martial, military

soldier, drafted: conscript, draftee, recruit

soldier, person who is not a: civilian

soldier, person who refuses for moral or religious reasons to become: consci-entious objector

soldiers' lodging: barracks, billet, ca-sern, garrison

soldiers, army of ordinary citizens rather than: militia

soldiers, group of: cohort

sole: alone, desolate, exclusive, iso-lated, lone, lonely, one, only, single, solitary, unique, unmarried, un-matched, unshared

sole of a plow: slade

sole of the hand, relating to: volar

sole of the foot: plantar, thenar, volar

solecism: blooper, error, impropriety, incongruity, mistake, slip

solely: alone, barely, entirely, exclu-sively, merely, only, purely, simply, singly, totally, uniquely, wholly

solemn: august, ceremonial, ceremoni-ous, devout, dignified, distinguished, divine, earnest, formal, funereal, gloomy, grave, hallowed, holy, quiet, reflective, religious, ritual, sacred, sanctified, serious, sober, somber, staid, stately, weighty

solemn declaration: asseveration

solemn promise: oath

solemnize: bless, celebrate, commemo-rate, dignify, exalt, honor, mark, ob-serve, sanctify, venerate

solicit: accost, approach, ask, beseech, call, canvass, crave, demand, entice, evoke, hustle, implore, importune, inquire, panhandle, peddle, petition, plea, proposition, request, seek, supplicate

solicitous: anxious, ardent, careful,

concerned, considerate, desirous, ea-ger, keen, meticulous, thoughtful, troubled, worried

solicitude: anxiety, apprehension, at-tention, care, carefulness, caution, concern, heed, qualm, uneasiness, worry

solid: compact, consistent, constant, continuous, convincing, cubic, dense, dependable, durable, firm, full, hard, impermeable, lasting, level, reliable, rooted, rugged, secure, sound, stable, sterling, stiff, strong, sturdy, thick, thorough, trustworthy, unanimous, unbroken, uninter-rupted, valid, weighty

solid foundation: bedrock

solid glass with parallel sides: prism

solid ground: terra firma

solid hard mass: calculus, concretion

solidarity: cohesion, harmony, togeth-erness, union, unity

solidify: cake, cement, coagulate, com-pact, concrete, condense, congeal, consolidate, crystallize, dry, gel, harden, set, stiffen, thicken, unify

solidify into soft mass: clot, coagulate, congeal, curdle

soliloquy: address, discourse, mono-logue, speech

solitary: abandoned, alone, antisocial, deserted, desolate, eremite, her-metic, individual, isolated, lone, lonely, lonesome, only, recluse, re-clusive, remote, secluded, single, sole, unsocial, withdrawn

solitude: aloneness, desert, desolation, isolation, loneliness, privacy, quar-antine, reclusiveness, remoteness, re-tirement, seclusion, wilderness

solo: alone, aria, arietta, individual, monologue, one, single, single-handed, unaccompanied

solo opera piece: aria, arietta

solo organ music piece, usually short and improvised: voluntary

soloist in company, leading female: diva, prima donna

solution: analysis, answer, compound, discovery, explanation, key, mixture, resolution, result, solvent

solution for problems, favorite but un-tested: nostrum

solution to emergency: quick fix

solution to plot: denouement

solution, cause a solid to be separated from a: precipitate

solution, exclamation when one has found a: eureka

solve: decide, decipher, decode, disen-tangle, dissolve, explain, fathom, in-terpret, resolve, settle, undo, unfold, unlock, unravel, untangle, work

solve a puzzle: decipher

solve complicated problem: cut the Gor-dian knot

solve or convert from code: decipher

solve or learn the meaning or nature of: fathom, unravel

solved or dissolved, capable of being: soluble

solved or dissolved, incapable of being: insoluble

solvent: diluent, dissolvable, remover, soluble, solvent

somber: bleak, dark, depression, dis-mal, down, dreary, dull, dusky, ear-nest, funereal, gloom, gloomy, grave, melancholy, serious, sober, solemn, staid

some: any, approximately, bout, ex-traordinary, few, part, portion, quan-tity, remarkable, several, unknown

somebody: celebrity, dignitary, some-one, superstar, VIP

someday: anytime, eventually, finally, sometime, subsequently

somehow: anyhow, anyway, unspecified

sometime: former, formerly, late, once, previous, quondam, someday

somewhat: approximately, bearably, considerably, kinda, moderately, par-tially, partly, pretty, rather, slightly

sommelier's offering: wine

somnolent: drowsy, fatigued, languid, lethargic, sleepy, sluggish

son: ben, boy, child, descendant, disci-ple, fils, heir, lad, male, native, off-spring, relative

song: anthem, aria, arietta, ballad, blues, cabaletta, call, cant, canticle, canzone, carol, chant, chanty, chorus, composition, dirge, ditty, glee, hymn, lied, lilt, lullaby, lyric, melody, music, noel, number, pit-tance, poem, poetry, psalm, rock, roundelay, serenade, shantey, shanty, solo, sonnet, strain, threnody, tune, verse

song by lover under window: serenade

song for three or more voices, canonical seventeenth-eighteenth century: catch

song of joy or rejoicing: paean, pean

song of mourning: threnody

song or chant from Bible text: canticle

song that tells a narrative story: ballad

song without instrumental accompaniment: a cappella

song, chorus or refrain of: burden

song, eulogistic: panegyric

song, German art: lied

song, lullaby: berceuse

song, part-: madrigal

song, sailors': chantey, shanty

song, sentimental love: torch song

song, short and sweet: ditty

song, Venetian gondolier's: barcarole

song, verses repeated at intervals in: refrain

song, wedding: epithalamium, prothalamion

song, words of a: lyrics

songbird: canary, lark, oscine, pipit, serin, vireo, wren

songbird, repetitive melodic sound of: tirra-lirra

songlike: arioso, cantabile

song's middle part: bridge

songs that performer or group knows, stock of: repertoire

songwriter: composer, lyricist, songsmith, songster

sonnet part: sestet

sonnet's first 8 lines: octet

sonnet's last 6 lines: sestet

sonorous: deep, full, grandiose, imposing, impressive, noisy, orotund, resonant, resounding, ringing, rotund, vibrant

soon: anon, around the corner, ASAP, before long, directly, early, expeditiously, fast, forthwith, hastily, immediately, imminent, impending, instantly, later, looming, presently, promptly, proximate, quick, quickly, readily, shortly, speedily, speedy, willingly

soot: blacken, carbon, coom, dirt, grime, grit, residue, sediment, smoke, smudge, smut

soothe: allay, alleviate, appease, assuage, balm, calm, comfort, compose, console, ease, heal, hush, lull, massage, mitigate, mollify, pacify, pat, pet, placate, quiet, relax, relieve, salve, settle, soften, solace, stroke, tranquilize

soothing: anodyne, appeasing, balmy, bland, calming, comforting, demulcent, downy, dulcet, gentle, lenitive, mild, nervine, palliative, pleasant, relaxing, sedative, sweet, tranquilizing

soothing lotion: balm, embrocation, emollient, liniment, salve, unguent

soothing substance: anodyne, balm, narcotic, nepenthe, opiate, sedative, soporific

soothsay: forecast, portend, predict

soothsayer: augur, diviner, forecaster, fortune-teller, haruspex, oracle, prognosticator, prophet, seer, seeress, wizard

sooty: black, blackened, dark, dingy, dirty, fulginous, grimy, murky, smeared, smutty

sop: absorb, bribe, dip, douse, drench, dunk, milksop, saturate, soak, steep, weakling, wet

sophisticated: adulterated, advanced, civilized, complex, continental, cosmopolitan, cultivated, cultured, debonair, experienced, hep, highbrow, intricate, involved, mature, refined, seasoned, soigné, suave, uptown, urbane, worldly, worldly-wise

sophisticated as child: precocious

sophisticated, over-: chichi

sophistry: ambiguity, casuistry, deception, inconsistency, trickery

sophomoric: foolish, immature, inexperienced, infantile, naive, reckless

soporific: calming, drowsy, hypnotic, lethargic, narcotic, nodding, opiate, opium, sedative, sleepy, slumberous, somniferous

soprano: coloratura, falsetto, singer, treble

sorcerer: alchemist, charmer, conjurer, magi, magician, necromancer, occultist, warlock, witch, wizard

sorceress: enchantress, hag, hex, pythoness, sibyl, siren, witch

sorcery: diablerie, divination, enchantment, incantation, magic, necromancy, obeah, sortilege, spell, thaumaturgy, voodoo, witchcraft, witchery, wizardry

sordid: abject, base, cheap, contemptible, corrupt, degraded, despicable, dirty, filthy, foul, grasping, gross, ignoble, low, mean, nasty, rank, scurvy, selfish, servile, vile, wicked, wretched

sore: abrasion, abscess, aching, achy, affliction, angered, angry, annoyed, annoying, bitter, blain, bruise, discomfort, disgruntled, distressed, distressing, exatious, excoriation, grievous, hostile, hurting, infected, inflamed, irate, ired, irritated, lesion, pain, painful, raw, sensitive, severe, suffering, temperamental, tender, touchy, trauma, ulcer, uncomfortable, unpleasant, upset, vexed, weal, welt, wound

sore containing pus: abscess

sore hands, feet, ears from exposure to damp cold: chilblain

sore on finger or toe: felon, whitlow

sore on first joint of big toe: bunion

sore on mouth or lips: canker

sore or ulcer, festering: fester, gathering, pustule

sore throat, septic: strep throat

sore with pus, infected: carbuncle

sore, bed-: decubitus ulcer

sore, inflamed: bleb, bulla, papule, pustule, whelk

sore, wartlike: condyloma

sorely: badly, extremely, greatly, grievously, painfully, woefully

sore's scab: eschar

sorority: association, club, organization, sisterhood, society

sorority word: tau

sorrow: affliction, agony, ailment, anguish, bale, calamity, despair, discomfort, distress, dolor, grief, grieve, hardship, heartache, lamentation, loss, melancholy, misery, misfortune, moan, mourn, mourning, pity, regret, remorse, sadness, suffering, tribulation, trouble, unhappiness, weep, woe

sorrowful: afflicted, depressed, dismal, distressing, doleful, dolent, dolorous, dreary, forlorn, grievous, grieved, heartbroken, lamentable, lamenting, melancholy, miserable, mournful, painful, plaintive, rueful, sad, tragic, unhappy, woebegone

sorrows, potion making you forget: nepenthe

sorry: afflicted, apologetic, bad, cheap, cheesy, contemptible, contrite, disappointed, disgraceful, dismal, gloomy, grievous, mean, miserable, mournful, paltry, pathetic, penitent, pitiful, poor, regret, regretful, remorseful, repentant, sad, saddened, shabby, shoddy, unhappy, worthless, wretched

sorry for, feel: commiserate, sympathize with

sorry, be: deplore, regret, rue

sort: batch, brand, breed, class, collection, description, family, gender, genus, grade, group, ilk, kind, manner, nature, order, part, pigeonhole, race, rank, species, suit, type, variety

sort, by color: gradate

sort, to: allot, alphabetize, arrange, assign, batch, categorize, choose, class, classify, collate, conform, distribute, gradate, index, order, organize, screen, select, separate, sift, systematize, type, typecast

sortie: assault, attack, foray, mission, raid, sally

sortilege: augury, enchantment, sorcery, witchcraft, witchery

sorting of casualties: triage

soul: anima, being, body, conscience, courage, energy, essence, force, ghost, heart, human, individual, inspiration, life, marrow, person, personage, pneuma, psyche, saint, spirit, substance, vitality

soul into another body after death, passing of: metempsychosis, palingenesis, reincarnation, transmigration

soul or vital spirit: anima, animus, pneuma, psyche

soul, loss of the: eternal damnation, hell, perdition

souls, place for innocent but unbaptized: limbo

souls, place for sinning: purgatory

sound added to film, tape, medium: dub

sound and scene reproduction: audiovisual

sound capable of conveying a distinction in meaning, smallest unit of: phoneme

sound distinguishing it from others of same pitch and volume, quality of: timbre

sound frequency wave change: Doppler effect

sound from single chanel: monaural, mono, monophonic

sound from two channels: binaural, stereo, stereophonic

sound-imitating: echoic

sound in consecutive words or syllables, repetition of: alliteration

sound in enclosed space, effect of: acoustics

sound in pronunciation, omission of final: elision

sound level measure: decibel

sound loss from the end of the word: apocope

sound made with lips, teeth, and/or tongue: consonant

sound modified to become similar to adjacent sound: assimilation

sound modulation of the voice: cadence

sound navigation range: sonar

sound preceding accented syllable: pretone

sound produced by air passing over one or both sides of the tongue: lateral

sound produced by air passing through the nose: nasal

sound produced by closing or partly closing the lips: labial

sound produced by closing oral passage and releasing burst of air: explosive, plosive, stop

sound produced by closing the glottis and then releasing it: glottal stop

sound produced by creating free passage of air through the larynx and mouth: vowel

sound produced by obstructing the air stream past the speech organs: consonant

sound produced by the back of the tongue making contact with the soft palate while lips closed: click, suction stop

sound produced by the speech organs above the glottis: supraglottal

sound produced by the tip of the tongue touching the upper front teeth: alveolar, dental

sound produced by using the blade of the tongue: laminal

sound produced from a puff of breath: aspiration

sound produced in the back of the mouth: guttural, velar

sound produced in the back of the mouth and closing or partly closing the lips: lablovelar

sound produced with both lips: bilabial

sound produced with the front of the tongue near or against the hard palate: palatal

sound produced with the lower lip and upper teeth: labiodental

sound produced with the tip of the tongue: apical

sound produced with the tip of the tongue turned backward and pointed up toward the roof of the mouth: cacuminal, retroflex

sound produced with the tongue and other speech organs: lingual

sound-producing: soniferous

sound quality: timbre, tone

sound reproduction: audio

sound reproduction with two or more speakers: stereophonic

sound return: echo

sound stage: set

sound stopped and sharply released: affricative

sound system: hi-fi, stereo

sound that can be drawn out, consonant: continuant

sound transmitter for underwater: sonar

sound waves in speaker, preventer of interference of: baffle

sound waves repeatedly reflected: reverberation

sound waves to detect objects underwater, using: echolocation, sonar

sound waves, apparent change in frequency of: Doppler effect

sound, agreeable: euphony

sound, around the speed of: sonic

sound, cat crying: caterwaul

sound, concerning: acoustic, aural

sound, concerning audible: sonic

sound, discordant: cacophony, discordance, dissonance

sound, faster than the speed of: supersonic

sound, gradual decrease in: decrescendo, diminuendo

sound, gradual increase in: crescendo

sound, hissing: sibilation

sound, hissing or roaring broadcast: white noise

sound, hitting: percussion

sound, humanly audible: audio

sound, intensity and longness of: resonance

sound, multiple: polyphonic

sound, outpouring of harmonious: diapason

sound, responsive: antiphony

sound, scientific study of: acoustics

sound, sighing: sough

sound, stifle a: muffle, mute

sound, voiced speech: sonant

sound, voiceless: surd

sound, wailing or howling: ululation

sound, whispering or murmuring: susurration

sound, with a hissing: sibilant

sounding, agreeable-: dulcet, euphonious, melodious

sounding, rich-: resonant, sonorous

sounding, rough-: raucous

soundness: correctness, durability,

healthiness, heartiness, horse sense, integrity, solidity, stability, strength, truth, weight, wit

soundproof: anacoustic

soundproof, to: insulate

sounds in two or more words, transposition of: spoonerism

sounds of the things it describes, word imitating the: onomatopoeia

sounds repeated at beginning of words or in accented syllables: alliteration

sounds, alphabetic letter having two or more: polyphone

sounds, study of a language's speech: phonology

soundtrack, to insert a: dub

soup: bisque, black bean, bouillabaisse, bouillon, broth, chowder, consommé, food, gazpacho, modify, mulligatawny, oxtail, pea, pepper pot, potage, potato, predicament, puree, vichyssoise

soup bowl, broad deep: tureen

soup made with okra pods, thick: gumbo, okra

soup of chicken broth and leeks: cock-a-leekie

soup of curry-flavored meat, East Indian: mulligatawny

soup of meat or fish, creamy: bisque

soup of meat or vegetable stock, clear: consommé

soup of potatoes, leeks, onions that is cold: vichyssoise

soup of pureed vegetables: bisque

soup of tomatoes and vegetables, cold: gazpacho

soup of vegetables and pasta, thick Italian: minestrone

soup, beet: borsch, borscht, borsht

soup, soybean-based: miso

soup, thick creamy: potage

soup, thick fish: chowder

soupçon: dash, drop, hint, particle, pinch, smidgen, sprinkle, taste, tinge, trace

sour: acerb, acerbic, acetic, acetose, acetous, acid, acidulate, acidulous, acrid, astringent, beginning, bitter, crabby, cranky, curdled, disagreeable, distasteful, dour, dry, fermented, fount, fountain, fountainhead, grim, grouchy, irritable, keen, origin, parent, rancid, rot, rotten, seed, sharp, spoiled, spring, tangy, tart, turned, unhappy, unpleasant, vinegary, wellspring

sour cherry: morello

sour fermented cabbage: sauerkraut

sour juice of fruit: verjuice

sour, becoming: acescent

source: antecedent, author, authority, basis, cause, dawning, expert, font, fount, inception, informant, origin, provenance, rise, root, seed, springhead, start, well

source, poetically: fount

source, relating to a: seminal

sources, coming from a variety of: eclectic

sourness: acidity, acor, acrimony, asperity, bitterness, discontent, irritability, tartness

sourpuss: complainer, crab, crank, grouch, grump, killjoy, sorehead, spoilsport

souse: alcoholic, attack, brine, deluge, dip, douse, drench, drink, drunk, drunkard, duck, dunk, immerse, lush, pickle, plunge, pounce, preserve, saturate, soak, sop, steep, strike, submerge, thump, tippler, waterlog, wet

south, concerning the: austral, midi, southerly

souvenir: gift, keepsake, memento, memory, relic, remembrance, reminder, token, trophy

sovereign: absolute, autocrat, autonomous, chief, coin, controlling, emperor, empress, free, governing, imperial, independent, king, kingly, lord, majesty, master, monarch, monarchical, omnipotent, paramount, potentate, prince, princely, queen, queenly, regal, reigning, royal, ruler, sominant, superior, supreme, unmitigated

sovereignty: ascendancy, autonomy, control, domination, dominion, empire, independence, jurisdiction, masterdom, power, rule, supremacy, sway

sow: disseminate, germinate, grow, implant, plant, propagate, scatter, seed, spread

soybean curd: tofu

spa: bath, baths, oasis, resort, saratoga, spring

space: align, amplitude, apportion, area, arrange, berth, blank, breadth, capacity, cavity, clearance, distance, divide, duration, elbowroom, empty, ether, expanse, extent, freedom, gap, headroom, interval, leeway, margin, period, quantity, range, reach, re-

gion, reservation, room, scope, separate, sky, territory, time, track, universe, void, width

space around church altar: chancel

space between things or parts, small: interstice

space beyond earth's atmosphere: ether, heavens

space by which a moving object clears something: clearance

space for freedom: latitude, leeway

space from which something is missing: lacuna

space of four or more dimensions: hyperspace

space rocket, primary stage of: booster

space satellites, earliest Soviet: Sputnik

space, concerning outer: cosmic, extraterrestrial, spatial

space, speed to get outside of gravity in: escape velocity

spacecraft: capsule, module, probe, rocket, satellite, shuttle

spacecraft at launch site, structure supporting: gantry

spacecraft landing on water: splashdown

spacecraft passengers, crew, instruments, equipment: payload

spacecraft pilot: astronaut, cosmonaut

spacecraft self-contained unit: module

spacecraft, maneuvers performed outside: extravehicular activity

spacious: ample, baggy, broad, bulky, capacious, commodious, enormous, expansive, extensive, huge, immense, large, roomy, vast, voluminous, wide

spade: dig, shovel, tool; playing card, suit

spaghetti cooked to firm: al dente

spaghetti-like pasta: vermicelli

Spain, dances of: bolero, fandango, flamenco, tango

span: arch, bridge, connect, cover, cross, distance, duration, extension, extent, fasten, fetter, interval, length, link, measure, period, reach, rope, scope, spread, stretch, term, time, trestle

spangle: adorn, coruscate, decorate, flash, gleam, glimmer, glisten, glitter, ornament, sequin, shimmer, sparkle, sprinkle, star, trim, twinkle

Spanish conqueror of New World: conquistador

Spanish gentleman: caballero, cavalier, senor

Spanish lady: dama, dona, latina, senora

Spanish nobleman or man of high rank: grandee

Spanish nobleman, minor: hidalgo

Spanish noblewoman: eboli

Spanish-speaking community: barrio

Spanish-speaking country, political boss in: cacique

spank: belt, cane, flog, paddle, punish, slap, smack, sock, strike, switch, thrash, whip

spanking: brisk, dashing, exceptional, fresh, new, remarkable, swift, vigorous

spar: argue, bar, beam, bicker, boom, box, contend, contest, dispute, fight, gaff, mast, pole, quarrel, rafter, sprit, strike, timber, wrangle

spare: additional, duplicate, emergency, excess, extra, free, leftover, replacement, substitute, surplus

spare, to: accommodate, afford, avoid, deprive, exempt, favor, forbear, forgive, free, give, grant, preserve, release, relieve, reprieve, reserve, save, skimp, withhold

sparing: careful, chary, economical, forbearing, frugal, lenient, meager, merciful, parsimonious, prudent, saving, scant, scanty, stingy, thrifty, tightfisted

sparingly used: abstemious, restrained, temperate

spark: arc, beau, ember, excite, fire, flash, flicker, gallant, germ, glimmer, glint, glow, grain, incite, inflame, inspire, instigate, kindle, light, motivate, provoke, scintilla, scintillate, scintillation, seed, sparkle, stimulate, stir, suitor, trace

spark plugs, device sending electric current to: distributor

spark, engine system powered by: ignition

sparkle: brilliance, bubble, coruscate, dash, dazzle, effervesce, effervescence, flash, flicker, fulgurate, gleam, glimmer, glint, glisten, glitter, glow, illuminate, radiate, scatter, scintillate, scintillation, shimmer, shine, spangle, spark, twinkle, vivacity

sparkling: animated, bright, brilliant, bubbly, dazzling, effervescent, fizzy, flashing, gleaming, glistening, glittering, lively, scintillating, shimmering, shining, starry, twinkling

sparkling ornament like rhinestone or sequin: diamante

sparkling threads on Christmas tree: tinsel

sparkling wine: asti

sparkling with gold or tinsel: clinquant

sparkling with rainbow colors: iridescent

sparse: dispersed, inadequate, infrequent, meager, occasional, scant, scanty, scarce, scattered, skimpy, spare, sporadic, thin, uncrowded

spartan: austere, brave, courageous, disciplined, frugal, laconic, plain, rigorous, simple

spasm: attack, convulsion, cramp, crick, fit, pain, pang, paroxysm, seizure, spell, tic, twitch

spasm or fit: convulsion, paroxysm

spasm, muscle: clonus, hyperkinesia, myoclonus

spasm, pain: throe

spasmodic: convulsive, erratic, excitable, fitful, intermittent, irregular, jerky, sporadic, sudden

spat: altercation, beef, bicker, dispute, fight, flood, gaiter, gush, quarrel, rain, row, scrap, slap, smack, spate, squabble, strike, tiff

spate: flow, freshet, outpouring, rush, torrent

spatial or depth relationships of objects: perspective

spatter: dabble, defame, dirty, dribble, pepper, scatter, shower, slop, smear, smudge, soil, splash, spot, spread, sprinkle, spurt, sputter, sully

spawn: breed, create, eggs, engender, father, fungi, generate, germ, multiply, mushroom, offspring, originate, parent, procreate, produce, proliferate, reproduce, roe, seed, sire, source

speak: address, articulate, bespeak, blab, blurt, bluster, chat, comment, communicate, consult, converse, convey, declare, discourse, discuss, drawl, drone, enunciate, equivocate, expound, express, gabble, harangue, intonate, jabber, jibber, lecture, mention, mumble, murmur, mutter, orate, pontificate, proclaim, pronounce, rant, recite, remark, reveal, say, shout, sound, splutter, stutter, talk, tell, testify, utter, ventilate, verbalize, vocalize, voice, whisper, yammer

speak about and compare views: confer, consult

speak about evasively: equivocate, hedge, prevaricate, quibble

speak about in leisurely way: chat, chew the fat, confabulate, schmooze

speak about in public: ventilate

speak about with enthusiasm: rhapsodize

speak at great length: declaim, perorate, speechify

speak at length: perorate

speak at length in formal way: discourse

speak at length to delay: filibuster

speak bombastically: orate

speak distinctly and carefully: articulate, enunciate

speak dogmatically: pontificate

speak incoherently when angry or confused: splutter, stutter

speak incoherently, aimlessly: chatter, gibber, maunder, prate

speak opinions overconfidently: dogmatize, pontificate

speak or chant rhyming lyrics: rap

speak or write at length: dilate, elaborate, enlarge, expatiate, expound

speak pridefully: boast

speak rapidly: babble, blabber, chatter, jabber, palaver, prattle

speak readily and effortlessly, able to: fluent

speak simply and directly, unwilling to: mealy-mouthed

speak with lengthened vowels: drawl

speak without preparation: extemporize

speaker: announcer, demagogue, lecturer, mouthpiece, orator, preacher, rhetorician, speechmaker, spellbinder, spokesman, spokesperson, spokeswoman, talker, utterer

speaker's stand: dais

speaker's stand for notes: lectern

speaker, annoy or embarrass: heckle

speaker, eloquent: rhetorician

speaking ability, loss of: aphasia

speaking for puppet or dummy: ventriloquism

speaking in tongues: glossolalia

speaking multiple languages: multilingual

speaking style: parlance

speaking to another, someone: interlocutor

speaking to oneself: soliloquy

speaking two languages: bilingual

speaking, excessive: logorrhea

speaking, particular manner of: idiom, parlance

SPECIAL OLYMPICS SPORTS

alpine skiing
aquatics
athletics
badminton
basketball
bocce
bowling
cross country skiing
cycling
equestrian
figure skating
floor hockey
football (soccer)
golf
gymnastics
powerlifting
roller skating
sailing
softball
speed skating
table tennis
team handball
tennis
volleyball ❦

spear: bayonet, blade, bolt, bore, dart, gouge, harpoon, impale, javelin, lance, leister, penetrate, pierce, prick, puncture, shoot, skewer, spike, stab, strike, trident, weapon

spear, three-pronged: trident

spearhead: advance, begin, create, develop, direct, initiate, launch, lead, originate, pioneer, start

special: additional, chief, choice, dear, designated, distinct, distinctive, distinguished, exceptional, extra, extraordinary, extravaganza, favorite, gala, important, individual, limited, momentous, notable, noteworthy, particular, peculiar, primary, privileged, rare, remarkable, select, specific, uncommon, unique, unusual

specialist: ace, authority, connoisseur, consultant, doctor, expert, master, maven, professional, scholar, virtuoso

specialist opposite: generalist

specialize: concentrate, major, practice, pursue, train

specialized vocabulary: nomenclature, terminology

specialty: aptitude, career, concentra-

tion, earmark, feature, focus, forte, game, masterpiece, profession, pursuit, skill, talent, trademark

species: breed, brood, category, class, division, genre, genus, group, humankind, ilks, image, kind, nature, order, race, sort, type, variety

species improvement: eugenics

species (in Latin), as Acer saccharum: binomial nomenclature

species (in Latin), as saccharum in Acer saccharum: specific epithet, trivial name

species of modern humans: Homo sapiens

species, evolutionary development and history of a: phylogeny

species, gradual change of a: evolution

species, single mutation that alters a: saltation

specific: categorical, clear-cut, concrete, definite, detailed, distinctive, exact, explicit, individual, limited, particular, precise, special, unique

specific gravity: relative density

specific gravity measuring scale: Baumé scale, hydrometer

specify: assign, cite, concretize, define, describe, designate, detail, determine, enumerate, establish, individualize, itemize, list, name, request, state, stipulate, tell

specimen: case, examination, exhibit, illustration, individual, instance, mark, model, person, prototype, sample, type

specious: beguiling, colored, deceptive, fallacious, false, glossy, hollow, hypocritical, misleading, ostensible, plausible, questionable, showy, unsound, untrue

speck: atom, bit, blemish, blot, crumb, defect, dot, flaw, fleck, iota, mark, mite, molecule, mote, particle, pinch, point, smidgen, spot, stain, whit

spectacle: curiosity, display, event, example, exhibition, extravaganza, marvel, pageant, parade, phenomenon, scene, show, sight, wonder

spectacles: eyeglasses, glasses, lenses

spectacular: amazing, astonishing, breathtaking, dazzling, dramatic, elaborate, fabulous, fantastic, grand, magnificent, marvelous, miraculous, sensational, splendid, striking, stupendous, theatrical, thrilling, wonderful

spectacular parade: extravaganza, pageant

spectator: audience, beholder, bystander, eyewitness, fan, kibitzer, observer, onlooker, viewer, witness

spectator giving unwanted advice: kibitzer

specter: demon, ghost, illusion, image, phantasm, phantom, prospect, shade, spirit, spook, vision, wraith

spectral: creepy, eerie, ghostly, phantom, scary, shadowy, spooky, supernatural, unearthly

spectrum: array, colors, continuum, distribution, range, sequence, series, sphere

spectrum colors: blue, green, indigo, red, violet, yellow

speculate: brainstorm, chance, conjecture, consider, contemplate, deliberate, dream, gamble, guess, hypothesize, imagine, ponder, predict, reason, reflect, risk, ruminate, surmise, theorize, think, venture, wonder

speculation: conjecture, contemplation, gamble, guesswork, hunch, hypothesis, meditation, reasoning, review, risk, surmise, theory

speculative: conjectural, iffy, inquiring, insecure, reflecting, risky, theoretical, uncertain

speculative or theoretical: academic

speculator: explorer, gambler, investor, philosopher, theorist, venturer

speech: address, allocution, colloquy, conversation, dialect, dialogue, drivel, eulogy, expression, harangue, homily, idiom, jargon, jeremiad, keynote, language, lecture, lingo, monologue, narration, oration, oratory, prattle, rhetoric, salutation, sermon, slange, soliloquy, spiel, statement, talk, tirade, tongue, utterance, valedictory, verbalization, vernacular, vocalization, voice

speech ability, loss of: aphonia

speech at formal event: oration

speech blunder: solecism

speech by newly installed president, etc.: inaugural address

speech by one person, long: monologue, soliloquy

speech defect: impediment, lisp

speech form with its own meaning, undiscernible through individual word meanings: idiom

speech opening: salutation

speech or sales talk: spiel

speech or tribute, laudatory: encomium, eulogy, panegyric

speech or writing about a subject, formal: disquisition

speech or writing, expression: discourse

speech or writing, pompous: bombast

speech or writing, very enthusiastic: dithyramb

speech particular to a region: dialect, idiom, patois

speech particular to an individual: idiolect

speech patterns and forms, study of regional: dialect geography, geolinguistics, linguistic geography

speech revealing character's thoughts: soliloquy

speech sound beginning with one vowel sound and changing to another: diphthong

speech sound of "h": aspirate

speech sound produced: articulation

speech sound, smallest unit of: phoneme

speech sounds, study of: phonetics, phonology

speech that is unmeaningful and made up: glossolalia

speech units, study of language's distinct: phonemics

speech used in specific social setting: register

speech with nasal tone: twang

speech with recap, conclude: peroration

speech without preparation, give: ad-lib, extemporize, improvise

speech, angry: diatribe, harangue, philippic, tirade

speech, clarity of: articulation, diction, elocution, enunciation

speech, concerning: oral

speech, digression in: apostrophe, aside, excursion, excursus, parenthesis

speech, encouraging or advising: exhortation

speech, endowed with: articulate

speech, evasive: circumlocution, equivocation, periphrasis, prolixity

speech, everyday: colloquialism, demotic, vernacular, vulgate

speech, farewell: valediction, valedictory

speech, give long pompous: harangue

speech, grandiloquent: bombast, euphuism, flatulence, fustian

speech, harsh in: acerbic, acidulous, acrid, caustic

speech, hesitant in: halting

speech, important opening: keynote address

speech, impressive in style of: sonorous

speech, lamenting: jeremiad

speech, lengthy extravagant: spiel

speech, light good-natured: banter, persiflage

speech, long and tiresome: screed

speech, meaningless: glossolalia

speech, of logical: coherent

speech, outpouring of feeling in: effusion

speech, place or occasion for political: stump

speech, pretentious: oratory, rhetoric

speech, quick: patter, squib

speech, skilled at unrehearsed or unprepared: extemporaneous

speech, strong accent in: brogue

speech, study of the structure and nature of: glossology, glottology, linguistics

speech, tedious: homily

speech, way words and phrases are used in: diction, phraseology, style

speeches, leader who makes impassioned: demagogue, rabble-rouser

speechless: amazed, astounded, dumb, mum, mute, shocked, silent

speechmaking as delay tactic: filibuster

speechwriter, historian, chronicler: logographer

speed: accelerate, alacrity, barrel, briskness, celerity, clip, dash, dispatch, expedite, fare, gallop, haste, hasten, hie, hightail, hurry, hustle, informed, knot, pace, precipitate, propel, quickness, race, rapidity, rate, rip, run, rush, swiftness, tear, tempo, urgency, velocity, zip, zoom

speed and promptness: dispatch

speed at which a piece of music is to be played: tempo

speed contest: race

speed in music: tempo

speed in performance: dispatch, expedition, promptness

speed less than that of sound: subsonic

speed needed to leave gravitational pull: escape velocity

speed of motion: swiftness, velocity

speed of one nautical mile: knot

speed of sound, faster than: supersonic

speed specified by a magnitude and direction: vector

speed up progress: expedite, facilitate

speedy: brisk, expeditious, express, fast, fleet, hasty, hurried, nimble, prompt, quick, rapid, snappy, supersonic, swift

spell: abracadabra, bewitch, charm, conjuration, curse, enchantment, hex, incantation, jinx, magic, seizure, shammy, sorcery, trance, trap, trick, voodoo

spell or bout: duration, hitch, interlude, interval, period, relief, rest, shift, stint, streak, stretch, time, tour, while

spell out: clarify, define, describe, explain, expound, interpret, mean, suggest

spellbound: amazed, bewildered, bewitched, captivated, enchanted, enthralled, fascinated, hooked, possessed, transfixed

spelled the same: synorthographic

spelling close to the pronunciation: phonetic

spelling due to mistaken assumption about word, change in: folk etymology

spelling of same word, different: variant

spelling, bad: cacography

spelling, study of: orthography

spelunker's place: cave

spend: allocate, blow, consume, deplete, devote, disburse, dissipate, distribute, drain, elapse, exert, exhaust, expend, fatigue, give, lavish, lay out, occupy, outlay, pass, pay, sacrifice, splurge, spread, spring, squander, use, waste

spend generously: lavish, shower, splurge

spend wastefully: dissipate, squander

spending to impress others: conspicuous consumption

spendthrift: imprudent, prodigal, profligate, spender, squanderer, waster, wastrel

spendthrift's opposite: cheapskate

spent: all in, beat, consumed, depleted, drained, effete, enervated, exhausted, fatigued, finished, overtired, tired, used, used up, wasted, weary

sperm cell: gamete, spermatozoon

sperm duct removal: vasectomy

sperm whale substance: ambergris

spew: disgorge, eject, emit, exude, flood, gush, heave, ooze, regurgitate, scatter, spit, vomit

sphagnum moss: peat

sphere: ambit, area, arena, bailiwick, ball, business, circle, circuit, class, compass, domain, field, globe, influence, jurisdiction, orb, orbit, order, planet, range, rank, reach, realm, scope, sky, spheroid, star, stratum, territory

sphere of action: ambit, arena, compass, orb, orbit, range, reach, scope

sphere of activity, expertise: bailiwick, domain, preserve, province

sphere, elongated: spheroid

spheres: areas, orbs

spherical: celestial, circular, global, globate, globular, heavenly, orbic, orbicular, rotund, round, stellar

spherical but flattened or concave at poles: oblate

spheroid-shaped: prolate, oval, spheroidal

Sphinx body: lion

spice: accent, allspice, aroma, cinnamon, clove, condiment, curry, dash, excitement, flavor, fragrance, ginger, herb, hint, kick, mace, mustard, nutmeg, oregano, paprika, pepper, perfume, pizzazz, relish, sage, salt, scent, season, seasoning, taste, thyme, tinge, zest

spice and heat wine or cider: mull

spice or seasoning: condiment

spick-and-span: clean, fresh, neat, new, orderly, spotless

spicy: aromatic, balmy, erotic, fiery, flavorful, fragrant, hot, juicy, peppery, piquant, pungent, racy, risqué, salty, savory, scandalous, scented, seasoned, sharp, showy, snappy, spirited, suggestive, tangy, zesty

spicy beef, chilies, and beans: chile con carne

spicy condiment or appetizer: chutney, relish, salsa

spicy liquid for soaking meat before cooking: marinade

spider class: arachnid

spider legs: eight

spider nest: nidus

spider order: araneae

spider phylum: arthropod

spider, common: black widow, garden, hermit, jumping, tarantula, wolf

spider, large hairy: tarantula

spider's web-spinning organ: spinneret

spiel: line, oratre, patter, pitch, promote, speech

spiffy: chic, classy, dapper, dressy, fashionable, neat, sharp, slick, smart, snappy, snazzy, stylish

spigot: dossil, faucet, nozzle, outlet, plug, spile, spout, stopper, tap, valve, vent

spike: antler, bayonet, block, fasten, fortify, horn, impale, injure, lace, lance, mackerel, nail, peak, peg, pierce, pin, point, puncture, secure, skewer, spear, spit, stab, stake, stud, thwart, tine

spill: betray, blab, disclose, divulge, downpour, drip, drop, empty, fall, flow, leak, overflow, overrun, peg, pin, reveal, rod, roll, ruin, scatter, shed, slop, spile, splash, tell, tumble, upset, waste

spin: birl, drive, extend, gyre, narrate, oscillate, pirouette, prolong, protract, reel, revolution, revolve, ride, roll, rotate, spiral, swirl, trundle, turn, twirl, twist, whirl

spin around axis: gyrate, revolve, rotate

spin off: byproduct, divestiture, offshoot, outcome, outgrowth

spin on toe or ball of foot in ballet: pirouette

spinach, cooked with: Florentine

spinal column: axis, backbone, chine, rachis, spine, vertebrae

spinal column curvature: kyphosis, lordosis, saddleback, scoliosis, swayback

spinal column manipulation: chiropractic, osteopathy

spinal cord, concerning side of body with: dorsal, neural

spinal cord, small bone at base of: coccyx, tailbone

spindle: axis, axle, baluster, mandrel, pin, pivot, rachis, rod, shaft, stalk, stem

spindle-shaped: fusiform

spindly: elongated, frail, lank, lanky, rangy, skinny, slender, weak

spine: back, backbone, chine, courage, crest, needle, point, prickle, rachis, ridge, spicule, spinal column, spirit, thorn, vertebrae, willpower

spine consisting of five fused vertebrae, bone at base of: sacrum

spine on porcupine, hedgehog: quill

spine that supports skull, top vertebra of: atlas

spine-tingling: electrifying, exciting, suspenseful, thrilling

spine, abnormal bend to: curvature

spine, abnormal lateral curvature of: scoliosis

spine, curvature of the: kyphosis

spine, extreme curvature of: hunchback, kyphosis, lordosis, swayback

spine, having: vertebrate

spine, having no: invertebrate

spineless: cowardly, fearful, indecisive, invertebrate, meek, soft, timid, weak

spinning mass on base: gyroscope

spiny: hispid, pointed, prickly, sharp, spiked, thorny

spiny anteater: echidna

spiny lobster: langouste

spiral: circling, cochlear, coil, coiling, curl, curve, curving, gyrate, helical, helix, twisting, whorl, winding

spiral downward: tailspin

spiral motion of fluid: vortex

spiral structure: helicoid, helix, volute, whorl

spiral, revolve in: gyrate

spiraling current: eddy

spiraling or spinning like top: turbinate

spiraling structure: tendril

spirally twisted: cochleate

spire: apex, cone, curl, fleche, peak, pinnacle, point, shorl, sprout, steeple, summit, tower

spirit: animation, animus, apparition, atman, attitude, banshee, bravery, breath, character, cheerfulness, courage, dash, dedication, demon, determination, drive, dryad, élan, elf, encourage, energy, enterprise, enthusiasm, esprit, essence, fairy, fire, force, genie, ghost, ghoul, goblin, gremlin, gumption, guts, hag, heart, hobgoblin, imp, incubus, inspiration, intent, life, loyalty, meaning, mettle, mood, morale, motivation, moxie, oomph, oread, passion, pep, phantasm, phantom, pluck, pneuma, poltergeist, psyche, puck, purport, resolution, shode, soul, specter, spook, sprite, spunk, strength, substance, succubus, temper, tenacity, undine, vigor, vim, willpower

spirit attributed to object in nature: animism

spirit in a container: genie, jinni

spirit of a culture: ethos, peridot

spirit of a place: genius loci, numen

spirit of enterprise: gumption, initiative

spirit of the air: ariel

spirit speaking or acting through medium: control

spirit's medium: channel
spirit, appearance of a: visitation
spirit, attendant: daemon, genius
spirit, benevolent good: eudemon
spirit, migration of a: metempsychosis, palingenesis, reincarnation, transmigration
spirit, person possessed by: demoniac, energumen
spirit, revealing of a: manifestation, materialization, precipitation
spirit, to summon a: conjure, invoke
spirited: active, animated, audacious, bold, brave, brisk, cheerful, chipper, courageous, dashing, dauntless, eager, energetic, enthusiastic, exuberant, fearless, fiery, game, gritty, intrepid, lively, lusty, mettlesome, peppy, sprightly, spunky, valiant, vigorous, vital, vivacious, zealous
spirited war horse: steed
spiritless: apathetic, broken, cold, dejected, depressed, despondent, downcast, dull, examinate, heartless, inanimate, lackadaisical, languid, lifeless, listless, melancholy, vapid
spirits: alcohol, booze, liquor; condition, disposition, feeling, mood, morale, tone
spirits, belief in: mysticism
spirits, communicating with: necromancy
spirits, person thought to be able to communicate with: medium
spirits, to free from evil: exorcise
spiritual: angelic, celestial, cerebral, churchly, deific, devout, divine, ethereal, godly, holy, immaterial, incorporeal, insubstantial, intangible, material, metaphysical, nonmaterial, platonic, pneumatic, psychic, pure, religious, sacred, saintly, sanctified, song, spirited, supernatural, unearthly, unworldly
spiritual adviser: guru
spiritual apathy: acedia, ennui
spiritual communication with dead: séance
spiritual damnation: perdition
spiritual energy: divine power
spiritual force: numen
spiritual gathering: séance
spiritual leader: guru, mentor, rabbi
spiritual opposite: temporal
spiritual perfection in Buddhism: nirvana
spiritualistic medium, substance emanating from: ectoplasm

spiritualistic messages board: Ouija
spiritually elevated: numinous, sublime
spit out: discharge, eject, emit, expectorate, hawk, phlegm, saliva, secretion, slobber, spew, spittle, splutter, sputter, sputum
spit receptacle: cuspidor
spit, produce: salivate
spite: animosity, annoy, contempt, dislike, enmity, envy, grudge, hatred, hostility, humiliate, hurt, ill-will, malevolence, malice, malignity, offend, provoke, rancor, resentment, revenge, vengeance, venom
spiteful: annoying, antagonistic, bitter, catty, envious, evil, hateful, hostile, hurtful, malevolent, malicious, malignant, mean, nasty, ornery, rancorous, resentful, troublesome, vengeful, venomous, vicious, vindictive, viperous, virulent, wicked
spitting image: counterpart, double, duplicate, likeness, ringer, twin
splash: bathe, blotch, dabble, dash, display, douse, drench, impact, mark, moisten, plop, plunge, publicize, scatter, shower, slop, slosh, soak, spatter, splatter, spot, spray, sprinkle, squirt, stir, strike, wallow, wash
splashy: flashy, gaudy, loud, opulent, ornate, ostentatious, sensational, showy, snazzy, spectacular
splatter: dash, douse, slop, spatter, splash
splay: awkward, bevel, carve, clumsy, dislocate, display, expand, fanlike, obliquely, slant, slanting, slope, sloping, spread, widen
spleen: anger, caprice, dislike, grudge, hate, hatred, hostility, ire, lien, malice, melancholy, rancor, resentment, spite, whim, wrath
splendid: admirable, beautiful, bright, brilliant, costly, dazzling, elegant, excellent, exquisite, fantastic, fine, glorious, good, gorgeous, grand, grandiose, illustrious, impressive, lavish, lofty, luxurious, magnificent, marvelous, praiseworthy, regal, rich, showy, sumptuous, superb, surpassing
splendid and dazzling: resplendent
splendid generosity: munificence
splendor: array, beauty, bright, brightness, brilliance, dazzle, display, eclat, effulgence, elegance, excellence, gleam, glory, gorgeousness, grandeur, light, luminosity, luster, magnifi-

cence, opulence, pageantry, parade, pomp, radiance, refulgence, resplendence, shine, showiness
splice: attach, connect, entwine, fasten, insert, interweave, join, marry, merge, mesh, unite
splinter: break, chip, disintegrate, flake, fragment, rend, shatter, shiver, slice, sliver, smash, split
splinter group: sect
split: alienate, allocate, bisect, break, broken, burst, cleave, cleaved, cleft, crack, cut, deal, destroy, difference, distribute, divide, divided, divorce, fissure, fork, fractured, fragment, halve, isolate, lam, leave, mixed, opening, part, portion, reave, rend, rent, rift, rip, rive, rupture, schism, segregate, separate, separated, separation, shatter, slice, sliver, slopped, splinter, sunder, tear, tore, undecided
split in organization: schism
split in two: bifurcate
split open: dehisce
splitting compound word by injecting other words: tmesis
splitting of atomic nuclei: fission
splotch: blemish, blob, blot, blotch, dash, fleck, mark, smear, smudge, spot, stain
splurge: bender, binge, display, fling, indulgence, rampage, showy, spend, splash, spree
spoil: adulterate, baby, blemish, booty, coddle, contaminate, corrupt, cosset, crumble, damage, decay, decompose, deface, defile, destroy, foul, harm, hurt, impair, indulge, injure, loot, mar, mollycoddle, overindulge, pamper, perish, pickings, pillage, plunder, pollute, prize, ravage, rot, ruin, smear, sour, squash, taint, thwart, undo, vilate, vitiate, waste, wreck
spoil and corrupt: barbarize, bastardize, degrade, deprave, pervert
spoil and dirty: adulterate, alloy, blemish, contaminate, debase, defile, foul, pollute, soil, sully, taint, tarnish
spoil another or oneself: coddle, cosset, gratify, indulge, pamper, pander to
spoil appearance: deface, disfigure, mar, mutilate
spoiled: overprotected, self-indulgent, spoon-fed
spoiled from frequent exposure or indulgence: blasé, jaded
spoiling for fight: pugnacious

spoils: amenities, booty, bounty, goods, haul, loot, pickings, pillage, prize, rots, sway, trophy

spoken: announced, articulated, communicated, declared, expressed, mentioned, oral, said, told, unwritten, uttered, verbal, viva voce, vocal

spoken error disclosing true feelings: Freudian slip

spoken false statement: slander

spoken language and letters, unit of: syllable

spoken language, characteristic of: colloquial, informal

spokesperson: advocate, agent, champion, delegate, mediator, mouthpiece, prolocutor, representative, speaker, spokesman, spokeswoman, sponsor

sponge, dried fibrous loofah fruit as: dishcloth gourd, vegetable sponge

sponge, mouthlike opening in: oscule, osculum, ostium

spongelike framework of a red corpuscle: stroma

sponger: bloodsucker, chiseler, deadbeat, freeloader, moocher, parasite

spongy: absorbent, cushioned, porous, soft, soggy, springy

sponsor: advertiser, advocate, angel, back, backer, bankroll, benefactor, champion, defender, finance, godparent, guardian, patron, promoter, proponent, stake, supporter, surety

sponsorship: advocacy, aegis, aid, auspices, backing, egis, patronage, support

spontaneous: automatic, careless, free, impromptu, improvised, impulsive, instinctive, involuntary, knee-jerk, native, natural, off-the-cuff, offhand, reflex, unforced, unplanned, unpremeditated, unprepared, unrehearsed, unthinking

spontaneous and unnecessary: gratuitous, unjustified, unprompted

spontaneous connections during psychoanalysis: free association

spontaneous in action: spur-of-the-moment, unpremeditated, without forethought

spontaneous in speech, writing: ad-lib, extempore, impromptu, improvised, off-the-cuff

spontaneously acting: insightful, instinctive, intuitive

spontaneously put together: devised, makeshift, stopgap

spoof: bluff, cheat, deceive, fake, fool, hoax, joke, josh, lampoon, mockery, nonsense, parody, prank, satire, swindle, tomfoolery, trick, wisecrack

spook: apparition, frighten, ghost, goblin, haunt, hobgoblin, phantom, scare, specter, spirit, startle, terrorize

spooky: chilling, creepy, eerie, eery, frightening, ghostly, haunted, jumpy, mysterious, ominous, scary, uncanny, weird

spool: bobbin, cylinder, reel, spindle

spoor: footprint, odor, scent, trace, track, trail

sporadic: desultory, infrequent, intermittent, irregular, isolated, occasional, periodic, random, rare, scattered

sport: amusement, athletics, competition, contest, dally, diversion, entertainment, exercise, frolic, fun, game, hobby, pastime, play, recreation

sport types: archery, baseball, basketball, billiards, bobsledding, boccie, bowling, boxing, cricket, croquet, cycling, fencing, fishing, football, golf, gymnastics, handball, hiking, hockey, horseshoes, hunting, jai alai, lacrosse, pool, racing, racquetball, rowing, rugby, sailing, skating, skiing, soccer, squash, surfing, swimming, tennis, volleyball, weightlifting, wrestling, yachting

sporting game extra period to decide win: sudden death

sportive: festive, frisky, frolicky, frolicsome, game, jocular, lively, merry, sprightly, wanton

sports arena: amphitheater, coliseum, stadium

sports artificial grass: artificial turf, Astroturf

sports, synthetic hormone sometimes used in: anabolic steroid

sporty: casual, flashy, jazzy, showy, smart

spot: bind, blemish, blot, blotch, blur, corner, defect, detect, difficulty, dilemma, discolor, discover, dot, espy, fault, find, fix, flaw, fleck, freckle, handicap, identify, jam, job, locate, location, mark, molecule, particle, patch, pickle, pimple, pinpoint, place, point, position, post, predicament, quandary, recognize, scrape, see, site, smear, smidgen, smudge, soil, speck, splotch, spy, stain, stigma, sully, taint

spotless: blameless, chaste, clean, flawless, holy, immaculate, impeccable, pure, sanitary, stainless, unblemished, undefiled, unsullied, untarnished

spotlight: attention, beam, fame, floodlight, highlight, limelight, publicity

spotted: blemished, blotchy, dappled, espied, eyed, guttate, mackled, marked, mottled, noticed, patchy, pied, seen, smeared, smudged, speckled, stained, stippled, sullied, tarnished, variegated

spotted black-and-white: piebald

spotting on animal or plant: maculation

spotty: blotchy, dotty, erratic, irregular, patchy, splotchy, sporadic, uneven, unreliable

spouse: bride, bridegroom, companion, consort, groom, helpmate, husband, mate, partner, roommate, wife

spout: boast, brag, chute, conduit, declaim, discharge, eject, emit, expel, flow, fountain, gush, jet, nose, nozzle, orate, outlet, pipe, rant, shoot, snout, spew, spigot, spray, spurt, squirt, stream, trough, waterfall

sprain: injury, pull, strain, tear, turn, twist, wrench

sprawl: extend, flop, loll, lounge, recline, relax, slouch, slump, spread-eagle, stretch

spray: bouquet, branch, discharge, drizzle, dust, fumigate, hose, mist, moisture, nozzle, scatter, shoot, shower, spew, sprig, sprindrift, sprinkle, squirt, strew, treat, twig, volley

spray, convert into fine: atomize, nebulize

spread: branch, broadcast, broaden, circulate, coat, compass, cover, diffuse, dilate, disperse, distribute, divulge, enlarge, escalate, expand, extend, fan, multiply, overlay, permeate, plaster, proliferate, prolong, propagate, publish, radiate, scatter, seep, smear, stretch, strew, unfurl, unroll, unwind, widen

spread apart: splayed

spread by direct or indirect contact: communicable, contagious, infectious, transmissible

spread false charges: asperse

spread for a cause, material: propaganda

spread here and there: scatter, sprinkle, strew

spread in all directions: diffuse, divaricate, diverge, pervade, splay

spread in branches: divaricate, ramify

spread or distribute: circulate, disseminate, give out, peddle, promulgate, propagate

spread or distribution: gamut, spectrum

spread or flow throughout: diffuse, implant, instill, percolate, permeate, pervade

spread or increase at rapid rate: proliferate

spread or open out: unfurl

spread or turn out: splay

spread out: diffuse, dispersed, extend, rambling, splay, sprawling, straggly, widespread

spread out in waves or rays: radiate

spread through or over: imbue, infuse, interfuse, permeate, suffuse

spread to dry: ted, tedded

spread with soft adhesive substance: daub

spread, orderly impressive: array

spreading: patulous, permeating, radial

spreading from original site to other body sites: metastasis

spreading kitchen implement: spatula

spreading or opening outward: flare, widen

spreading rapidly and extensively: epidemic

spreading widely: rampant, rife, unrestrained

spree: bash, bat, bender, binge, bout, carousal, debauch, escapade, fling, frolic, indulgence, lark, orgy, rampage, revel, riot, romp, shindig, shindy, splurge, tear, toot, wassail

sprightly: active, agile, airy, alert, alive, animated, brisk, buoyant, chipper, clever, coltish, dynamic, energetic, fresh, frisky, frolicsome, fun, gay, jaunty, lively, merry, peppy, perky, pert, playful, quick, sharp, spirited, sportive, spry, vigorous, vivacious, zestful

spring: appear, arise, begin, birth, bolt, bounce, bound, dart, develop, elasticity, emanate, emerge, estuary, flexibility, font, fountain, fountainhead, head, hop, hurdle, jump, leap, motive, origin, pop, recoil, release, resilience, rise, shoot, skip, source, spa, start, stem, surge, trap, uncoil, vault, well, youth

spring from source: derive, originate

spring of the year: prime, vernal equinox

spring tide: neap

spring, natural hot: geyser, thermal spring

spring, pertaining to: vernal

spring, pertaining to early: primaveral

spring, sediment deposited by mineral: sinter

springy: bouncy, elastic, flexible, pliable, rebounding, resilient, stretchy, supple

sprinkle: asperse, bedew, dabble, dot, dredge, drizzle, dust, moisten, perfuse, powder, rain, scatter, shake, shower, sparge, sparkle, spatter, speckle, splash, spot, spray, squirt, strew, water, wet

sprinkling, moisten by: sparge

sprint: dart, dash, race, run, rush, scamper, scurry

sprite: apparition, ariel, brownie, demon, elf, essence, fairy, fay, genie, ghost, gnome, goblin, hobgoblin, leprechaun, peri, pixie, specter, spirit

sprout: bloom, bud, burgeon, develop, germinate, grow, offshoot, proliferate, pullulate, seedling, shoot, spout, sprig, spring, tendril, thrive

spruce fruit: cone

spry: active, agile, brisk, chipper, energetic, frisky, healthy, lively, nimble, perky, quick, robust, spirited, sprightly, vigorous, vivacious

spud: potato, tater

spume: foam, froth, scum, spray, suds

spunk: backbone, courage, determination, doggedness, flame, fortitude, get up and go, gleam, grit, gumption, guts, heart, liveliness, mettle, moxie, nerve, passion, pluck, spark, spirit

spunky: bold, brave, courageous, feisty, game, gutsy, plucky, spirited

spur: arouse, crampon, catalyst, cause, drive, encourage, excite, foment, galvanize, goad, impel, impetus, incentive, incite, instigate, motivate, move, needle, press, prick, prod, prompt, propel, provoke, push, ridge, spark, spike, stimulate, stimulus, stir, trigger, urge

spur of the moment: impromptu

spur or motivation: goad, incentive, incitement, stimulus

spur, toothed wheel inserted into: rowel

spurious: apocryphal, artificial, bastard, bogus, contrived, counterfeit, fake, false, feigned, fictitious, forged, fraudulent, illegitimate, imitation, phony, unauthentic, unreal

spurn: contemn, decline, despise, disdain, disregard, eschew, flout, ignore, kick, rebuff, refuse, reject, repudiate, scoff, scrape, shun, slight, snub, tread

spurt: burst, commotion, dart, discharge, emit, erupt, expel, flow, gush, jet, rush, spout, spray, sprout, squirt, stream, surge

sputter: falter, spit, stammer, stumble

spy: agent, behold, case, descry, detect, discover, espy, examine, informer, inspect, meddle, mole, notice, observe, peep, pry, saboteur, scout, scrutinize, search, secret agent, see, sleeper, sneak, snoop, snooper, stake out, stoolie, view, watch

spy meeting or safety place: safe house

spy or double agent operating within an organization: mole

spy planted in enemy country: sleeper

spy that incites others to commit illegal acts: agent provocateur

spy training: tradecraft

spy's entry into organization: infiltration

spy's last resort: poison pill

spy's return from mission, interrogation upon: debriefing

spying: espionage, following, intelligence gathering, surveillance, voyeurism, wiretapping

squabble: altercation, argue, argument, bicker, brawl, dispute, feud, fight, hassle, quarrel, spat, tiff, words, wrangle

squad: band, company, crew, group, squadron, team, unit

squad car: cruiser

squadron: armada, battalion, escadrille, fleet, squad, unit

squalid: base, dingy, dirty, disgusting, disheveled, filthy, foul, grimy, grubby, mangy, mean, miserable, nasty, offensive, repulsive, rotten, seedy, shabby, shoddy, slummy, sordid, ugly, unclean, unkempt, vile, wretched

squall: bawl, blast, bluster, commotion, cry, disturbance, flurry, gale, gush, gust, scream, shout, shower, shriek, squawk, storm, trouble, wind, windstorm, yell

squalor: dirt, filth, mire, neglect, poverty, seediness, squalidness, wretchedness

squamous: scaly

squander: blow, burn, consume, disperse, dissipate, extravagance, fool away, fritter, lavish, misspend, misuse, scatter, spend, waste

square: adjust, balance, equal, even, match, resolve, settle

square in shape: boxy, cubed, rectangular

square dance for eight: quadrille

square dance official: caller

square dancing when two dancers approach, circle, return to places: do-si-do

square or four-sided figure: quadrilateral, rectangle, tetragon

square-rigged, two-masted ship: brig

square root or root of quantity: radical

square, public: concourse, green, park, piazza, plaza

square, puzzling mathematical: magic square

squash: annihilate, beat, cram, crowd, crush, disconcert, fall, flatten, game, mash, pound, press, quash, quell, sit on, squeeze, squelch, squish, stop, suppress, undermine, vegetable

squash variety: acorn, banana, crookneck, cushaw, hubbard, pepo, summer, turban, winter, zucchini

squat: broad, chunky, cower, crouch, dumpy, hunch, kneel, pudgy, settle, stocky, stoop, stubby

squaw's responsibility: papoose

squawk: blare, cackle, crow, cry, fuss, gripe, grumble, hoot, protest, scream, screech, yammer

squeak: cheep, chirp, creak, cry, escape, inform, noise, peep, shriek, shrill, snitch, sound

squeak by: edge

squeal: betray, blab, fink, howl, inform, oink, rat, scream, shriek, shrill, sing, snitch, yell

squealer: canary, fink, informer, pigeon, rat, snitch, stoolie, third ear, traitor

squeamish: afraid, dainty, dizzy, fastidious, finical, finicky, fussy, modest, nauseated, nauseous, priggish, prissy, prudish, queasy, scrupulous, sensitive, shaky, sickened

squeezable container: tube

squeeze: bear, choke, clasp, clutch, compact, compress, compression, condense, constraint, constrict, cram, crown, crush, cuddle, eke, embrace, extort, extract, force, grip,

hug, influence, juice, oppress, pack, pinch, predicament, press, pressure, scrunch, squash, strangle, stuff, wring

squelch: crush, muffle, quash, quell, restrain, shush, silence, sit on, smother, squash, stamp, suppress

squib: filler, firecracker, lampoon, parody, satire, skit, spoof

squid: cephalopod, cuttlefish, loligo, mollusk, octopus

squid or other cephalopod mollusk: decapod

squid prepared as food: calamari, totani

squid secretes: ink

squid tentacles: ten

squid's internal shell: pen

squiggle: curl, squirm, twist, wiggle, wriggle, writhe

squiggle over some foreign letters: tilde

squiggle under foreign-letter c: cedilla

squint: bent, cast, deviate, goggle, look, peek, peer, skew, squinch, strabismus, trend

squire: accompany, assist, attendant, chaperon, escort, gallant, gentleman, guard, judge, landowner, lawyer, lover, title

squire's holding: estate

squirm: contort, fidget, shift, squiggle, toss, turn, twist, wiggle, worm, wriggle, writhe

squirrel away: cache, hide, hoard, stash, store

squirrel family: sciuridae

squirrel food: acorn

squirrel genus: sciurus

squirrel skin: vair

squirrels, concerning: sciurid, sciurine

squirt: eject, emit, gush, jet, runt, shower, spatter, splash, splatter, spray, spurt, stream, twerp

stab: attack, attempt, bayonet, cut, dab, dagger, dirk, fling, gash, gore, gourge, incision, knife, lance, lunge, pain, penetrate, pierce, plunge, poke, puncture, spear, stick, strike, thrust, try, whirl, wound

stab lightly: pink, prink

stability: balance, constancy, dependability, equilibrium, firmness, permanence, poise, reliability, security, stableness, steadfastness, steadiness, strength

stability, something providing: ballast, moorings

stabilize: balance, equalize, fixate, fixed, poise, regulate, secure, settle

stabilizer: airfoil, balance, ballast, gyro

stable: anchored, balanced, constant, dependable, durable, enduring, established, fast, firm, fixed, immutable, lasting, moored, permanent, poised, reliable, resistant, safe, secure, solid, sound, stationary, staunch, steadfast, steady, strong, sturdy, sure, together, trustworthy, unchangeable, unchanging, unvarying, unwavering

stable compartment: stall

stable fenced area: paddock

stable, horse: barn, hangar, livery stable

stables converted into dwellings: news

stack: bank, bunch, bundle, flue, group, heap, load, lump, mound, pile, rick, stow

stack of logs: woodpile

stadium: arena, ballpark, bleachers, bowl, coliseum, diamond, field, grandstand, gridiron, gymnasium, oval, period, ring, stage, stands

stadium benches not under roof: bleachers

stadium deck: tier

stadium passageways for entrance, exit: vomitorium, vomitory

staff: aides, assistants, associates, crew, employees, entourage, force, group, help, personnel, servants, team, workers

staff or club: baton, caduceus, cane, club, crosier, cudgel, flagpole, mace, pole, prod, rod, rung, scepter, stave, stick, support, verge, wand

staff of life: bread

staff with cross at end: crosier

stage: arena, arrange, condition, dais, degree, dramatize, enact, exhibit, floor, grade, leg, level, limelight, notch, orchestrate, organize, perform, period, phase, platform, play, point, present, produce, pulpit, rostrum, setting, show, spotlight, step, story, theater, tier

stage comment: aside

stage curtain: drop curtain, scrim, teaser

stage device: prop

stage direction: aside, enter, exeunt, exit, reenter

stage front: downstage

stage light cover: gel

stage of a journey: leg

stage performer without speaking part: supernumerary

stage setting: decor, mise-en-scène, scenery

stage side scenes: coulisse

stagehand: grip

stages, gradual successive: gradation

stages, passing down through successive: devolution

stagger: alternate, amaze, astonish, astound, dumbfound, flabbergast, hesitate, hobble, lurch, overpower, reel, rock, shake, shift, shock, startle, stumble, stump, stun, surprise, sway, totter, unsettle, waver, weave

stagnant: dormant, dull, foul, idle, inactive, inert, lethargic, monotonous, motionless, sluggish, stale, standing, static, stationary, still, unchanging

stagnate: decay, deteriorate, dull, fester, languish, rust, stifle, vegetate

staid: composed, cool, decorous, demure, dignified, earnest, fixed, grave, permanent, restrained, sedate, serious, settled, sober, solemn

stain: blemish, blot, blotch, blur, brand, color, contaminate, corrupt, debase, defile, discolor, discoloration, disgrace, dishonor, dye, flaw, mark, paint, pigment, ruin, smudge, soil, speck, spot, stigma, sully, taint, tarnish, tincture, tinge, tint, trace

stained glass lead dividing strips: breaker

stained or discolored, of a book: foxed

stainless: chaste, exemplary, immaculate, pure, spotless, unsoiled, unsullied, untainted

stair part: riser, tread

staircase support: string, stringboard, stringer

staircase underside: soffit

staircase, vertical support of: newel, spindle, stairpost

stairway, step in straight: flier

stairway, step in winding: winder

stake: ante, back, bankroll, bet, capitalize, chance, claim, finance, gamble, hazard, interest, investment, kitty, loot, marker, pale, picket, pile, play, pledge, pole, pool, post, pot, prize, purse, reward, risk, share, spike, sponsor, stick, take, venture, wager, winnings

stale: banal, cliché, commonplace, corny, decayed, dusty, flat, hackneyed, humdrum, insipid, moldy, monotonous, musty, not fresh, passé,

shopworn, sour, spoiled, stagnant, trite, unoriginal, vapid, worn, worn-out

stale in odor or taste: frowsy, fusty, musty

stale joke: chestnut

stale truism: platitude

stalemate: check, deadlock, draw, gridlock, impasse, standoff, standstill, tie

stalk: axis, chase, follow, hunt, menace, prey, pursue, reed, shaft, stem, straw, track, trail

stalk bearing one flower: peduncle

stall: bin, block, booth, brake, check, compartment, cubicle, delay, dillydally, filibuster, halt, hamper, hesitate, impede, manger, obstruct, pew, postpone, procrastinate, seat, stable, stand, stonewall, stop, suspend

stall for time: temporize

stalwart: bold, brave, brawny, courageous, dauntless, fearless, firm, forceful, gallant, mighty, muscular, powerful, resolute, robust, stout, strong, sturdy, tireless, upright, valiant

stamens of flower: androecium

stamina: backbone, courage, endurance, energy, fortitude, grit, heart, perseverance, strength, tolerance, vigor, vitality

stammer: falter, fumble, haw, hesitate, jabber, sputter, stumble, stutter

stamp: beat, cast, crush, die, drive, hammer, pound, stomp, strike, trample

stamp a piece of mail: frank

stamp collector: philatelist, timbromaniac

stamp indentation or hole: perforation

stamp out: scotch, stifle

stamp or seal: brand, character, earmark, hallmark, identity, impress, impression, imprint, kind, label, mark, mint, mold, postage, postmark, print, press, signature, signet, sticker, symbol, type

stamp sheet: pane

stamped cards: postals

stamped on articles indicating quality, mark: hallmark

stamped on envelope commemorating an event, design: cachet

stampede: bolt, charge, flight, inundate, overrun, panic, riot, rout, rush

stamps, disk making perforations in: roulette

stance: attitude, policy, pose, position, posture, stand, station, viewpoint

stanchion: beam, bolster, brace, framework, pole, post, prop, stay, support, upright

stand for: allow, endure, imply, mean, permit, represent, signify, symbolize

stand for a hot dish or for cooking vessels in hearth: trivet

stand for art: easel

stand for reading or to hold books: lectern

stand-in: alternate, backup, double, proxy, second, substitute, surrogate, understudy

stand on hind legs and stretch out forelegs: ramp

stand on with legs astride: bestride, straddle

stand out: beetle, bulge, conspicuous, emerge, loom, overhand, project, prominent, protrude, shine, star

stand up to: face, resist

stand, three-legged camera: tripod

standard: accepted, average, banner, barometer, base, benchmark, classic, common, criterion, customary, ensign, ethics, example, flag, gauge, gonfalon, grade, guideline, ideal, level, magnitude, mark, mean, measure, measurement, median, model, morals, norm, normal, ordinary, par, pattern, pennant, principle, regular, requirement, rule, sample, signal, touchstone, unit, yardstick

standard and usual: garden variety

standard-bearer: vexillary

standard for making judgment: criterion

standard image or conception: stereotype

standard of acceptability: norm

standard of comparison: control, measure

standard of excellence: ideal

standard of living, sub-: subsistence level

standard of pitch for tuning instruments: concert pitch, international pitch

standard of quality: benchmark, criterion, touchstone

standard of reference in surveying, mapping, geology: datum

standard on which judgment or decision may be based: benchmark, canon, criterion, litmus paper, touchstone, yardstick

standard or example: model

standard to which conformity is enforced, arbitrary: procrustean bed

standard, guiding: lodestar, polestar, principle

standard, measure up to a: pass muster

standing: capacity, character, continuing, dignity, dormant, duration, eminence, erect, esteem, fixed, footing, inactive, lasting, location, order, permanent, position, prestige, rank, reputation, settled, stagnant, stance, static, station, stationary, status, tenure, term, upright, verticle

standing out: conspicuous, salient

standoff: deadlock, draw, impasse, stalemate, tie

standoffish: aloof, antisocial, cold, cool, distant, haughty, reclusive, reserved, solitary, unfriendly, withdrawn

standpoint: angle, aspect, attitude, direction, opinion, outlook, perspective, point of view, position, side, slant, viewpoint

standstill: cessation, deadlock, delay, gridlock, halt, impasse, pause, stalemate, stop

stanza: division, stave, strophe, verse

staple: basic, chief, commodity, core, fasten, fastener, fiber, foundation, fundamental, goods, item, necessary, principal, resource, rice

star altitude, instrument for measuring: astrolabe, sextant

star and planet position chart or almanac: ephemeris

star as point of reference: lodestar

star at the end of the handle of the Little Dipper: Polaris

star brightness: magnitude

star cluster: nebula

star cluster smaller than constellation: asterism

star-crossed: damned, unfortunate, unlucky

star in Canis Major, brightest: Sirius

star in constellation Orion: Rigel

star in constellation, brightest: alpha

star in Orion, bright: Betelgeuse

star mapping: uranography

star-shaped: actinoid, asteroid, stellate

Star-Spangled Banner author: Francis Scott Key

star symbol in printing (*): asterisk

star system in the constellation Centaurus: Alpha Centauri

star system of formation, design: constellation

star system of universe: galaxy

star that becomes much brighter and then returns to normal: nova

star that does not go below horizon: circumpolar

star, five-pointed: pentacle, pentagram, pentangle

star, six-pointed Judaism: Magen David, Mogen David, Shield of David, Star of David

star, small cool: red dwarf

star, small hot: white dwarf

starch: backbone, drive, energy, formality, gumption, mettle, push, stiffen, stiffness, strength, vigor, vitality

starch from perennial herb: arrowroot

starch source: taro

starch, made of or rich in: farinaceous

starches, sugars, celluloses, gums: carbohydrate

starchy: formal, prim, proper, rigid, stiff

stare: eye, focus, gape, gawk, gaze, glare, glaze, goggle, leer, look, ogle, peer, squint, watch

stare at in petrifying way: gorgonize

stargazer: astrologer, astronomer, daydreamer

staring with curiosity: rubbernecking

staring, bulging sight organs: pop eyes

stark: absolute, austere, bare, barren, bleak, blunt, complete, crude, desolate, downright, dreary, empty, entire, entirely, extreme, firm, forsaken, grim, hard, harsh, naked, nude, plain, pure, rigid, robust, severe, stalwart, stiff, stripped, strong, tense, unadorned, unclad, unyielding, utter, vacant, vigorous, wholly

starlike object emitting blue light, radio waves: quasar

starry: astral, bright, celestial, glittering, luminous, lustrous, shimmering, shining, sidereal, spangled, sparkling, stellar

stars of a universe, like Milky Way: galaxy

stars on inner dome, device for projecting: planetarium

stars orbiting around common center of mass, two: binary star, double star

stars smaller than constellation, cluster of: asterism

stars, bespangled with: stellular

stars, building with telescopes for looking at: observatory

stars, concerning: astral, sidereal, stellar

stars, study of the effects of positions of: astrology

start: activate, advantage, begin, beginning, birth, bolt, broach, cause, commence, create, dart, dawn, embark, enter, establish, flinch, form, found, generate, genesis, head, ignite, inaugurate, inception, infancy, initiate, instigate, introduce, jump, kickoff, launch, lead, leap, onset, opening, opportunity, originate, outset, provoke, pulse, recoil, retreat, root, rouse, rush, seed, shy, source, spring, startle, turn, twitch, undertake, wince

start-up funding: venture capital

starting point: jumping-off place, springboard, tee

startle: alarm, excite, frighten, jump, rouse, scare, shock, start, stun, surprise, terrify, upset

startling experience: eye opener

starved: anorexic, emaciated, famished, hungry, macerated, malnourished, ravenous, undernourished

state as an attribute or quality of: predicate

state between two hostile countries, neutral: buffer state, buffer zone

state explicitly, in detail: enunciate, expound, propound, set forth, specify, spell out

state of affairs, existing: status quo

state of fullness: satiety

state of mind: attitude, mood, morale

state of the spirits of a person or group: morale

state or declare as truth or fact: attest, back up, certify, corroborate, postulate, premise, posit, testify

state over others, predominance of one: hegemony

state seriously, positively: affirm, asseverate, aver, avouch, avow, profess, warrant

state without proof: allege

state, concerning the governor of a: gubernatorial

stately: august, ceremonious, courtly, dignified, elegant, formal, gallant, grand, grandiose, imperial, imposing, impressive, kingly, lofty, lordly, magnificent, majestic, noble, regal, royal, statuesque

stately home: manor

statement: account, address, affidavit, agreement, allegation, article, assertion, audit, bill, certificate, claim, comment, declaration, deposition, dictum, epitome, expression, invoice, narrative, paradox, preface, presentation, record, remark, report, sentence, speech, summary, testimony, truism, utterance, voice, word

statement based on facts, to make: predicate

statement contrary to received opinion: paradox

statement of belief: credo, creed

statement of truth or opinion: adage, aphorism, maxim, saying

statement or protest addressed by citizens to public authorities: démarche

statement that does not follow logically from preceding statement: non sequitur

statement, self-evident: truism

statement, unsupported: dictum, ipse dixit

statesman or stateswoman: diplomat, lawmaker, leader, legislator, minister, official, politician

static: criticism, electricity, fixed, immobile, inactive, interference, motionless, noise, quiescent, stagnant, stationary, unchanging

station: assignment, base, berth, degree, depot, duty, footing, grade, headquarters, location, occupation, place, position, post, rank, settlement, site, spot, standing, stop, terminal

stationary: anchored, fixed, immobile, immovable, motionless, parked, permanent, riveted, sedentary, stabile, stagnant, stale, static, still, unchanging

stationary opposite: ambulant, ambulatory, migratory

statistical difference between one number in set and mean of the set: deviation

statistical distribution's set of intervals: frequency distribution, ogive

statistically random: stochastic

statistician of insurance risks, premiums: actuary

statistics and economic models in studying history, use of: cliometrics

statistics, simultaneous change in value of two random variables in: correlation

statistics, study of population: demography

statue: bronze, bust, colossus, figure, figurine, icon, image, likeness, memorial, monument, sculpture

statue base: socle

statue is placed, block on which: plinth

statue, huge: colossus

statue's inscription: epigraph

statuesque: beautiful, dignified, majestic, regal, shapely, stately, tall

statuette: figurine

stature: ability, cachet, eminence, greatness, height, importance, place, position, posture, prestige, prominence, rank, reputation, status

status: aspect, class, condition, degree, dignity, merit, position, posture, prestige, prominence, rank, situation, standing, state, stature

status benefit: perk

status in society: caste

status of holding one's position permanently: tenure

status of organism in ecological community: niche

status quo: as is

status, categorization according to: hierarchy, pecking order

status, raise in: elevate, exalt

statute: act, bill, decree, edict, enactment, law, measure, order, ordinance, precept, regulation, rule

staunch: ardent, dyed-in-the-wool, faithful, firm, loyal, reliable, resolute, rugged, solid, sound, stanch, steadfast, stem, strong, true, uncompromising

stave off: avert, block, repel, ward

stay: abide, appease, arrest, bide, block, brace, bunk, cable, column, continue, curb, defer, deferment, delay, detain, dwell, endure, fasten, halt, hold, linger, live, lodge, pause, permanence, persist, postpone, prop, remain, reprieve, reside, rest, restrain, rope, satisfy, secure, settle, sojourn, stand, stem, stop, stopover, strut, support, suspend, sustain, tarry, truss, visit, wait

stay around: hang around, linger, loiter

stay temporarily: sojourn, tarry

stay the course: endure, last

staying only a brief time: itinerant, migrant, migratory, transient

staying power: endurance, stamina

steadfast: adamant, ardent, constant, dependable, enduring, faithful, firm, fixed, inflexible, intent, loyal, relentless, resolute, stable, staunch, steady,

stubborn, sure, tenacious, true, unchanging, unflagging, unflinching, unswerving, unwavering, unyielding, wholehearted

steady: balanced, calm, careful, consistent, constant, continuous, coolheaded, deliberate, equable, even, faithful, firm, fixed, frequent, habitual, incessant, invariable, methodical, nonstop, poised, regular, reliable, resolute, sober, stabilize, stable, staunch, steadfast, sturdy, sure, unfaltering, unfluctuating, uniform, uninterrupted, unshaken, unswerving, untiring, unwavering

steady stream: influx

steak cuts: chateaubriand, chuck, cube, filet mignon, hamburger, minute, New York, Porterhouse, salisbury, sirloin, strip, T-bone, tenderloin

steal: abduct, appropriate, bargain, blackmail, bribe, burglarize, cheat, cop, creep, divert, embezzle, filch, grab, heist, hijack, hook, kidnap, lift, loot, nim, peculate, pilfer, pillage, pinch, pirate, plagiarize, poach, pocket, purloin, rob, rustle, shaft, shoplift, snatch, sneak, snitch, swindle, swipe, take, theft, thieve

steal another's ideas or writings: pirate, plagiarize

steal livestock: rustle

steal money: defalcate, embezzle, peculate

steal money in accounting or conceal profits: skimming

steal or use illegally: appropriate, convert, liberate, misappropriate

steal the show: upstage

steal, obsessive impulse to: kleptomania

stealthy: clandestine, covert, crafty, cunning, devious, furtive, quiet, secret, secretive, slippery, sly, sneaking, sneaky, surreptitious, undercover, underhanded, wily

steam: brew, cook, force, fume, heat, might, mist, power, smoke, vapor, vigor, water

steam bath: sauna

steam-heated vessel for laboratory work: autoclave

steam-whistle organ: calliope

steamed semolina: couscous

steamer: boat, clam, liner, paddleboat, ship, steamboat, steamship

steel: alloy, bathe, brace, brew, color,

encourage, firm, fortify, gird, gray, harden, high, hilly, nerve, rail, reinforce, smooth, soak, stew, strengthen

steel with zinc, coat: galvanize

steel, harden or strengthen: temper

steel, high-grade: crucible steel, drill steel

steelmaking furnace: open-hearth furnace, reverberatory furnace

steelmaking method using air: Bessemer process

steep: abrupt, declivitous, elevated, extreme, headlong, inclined, perpendicular, precipitous, raised, sheer, sloping

steep and rugged: craggy

steep descent: rappel

steep downward slope: declivity, escarpment, scarp

steep, as tea: brew, infuse

steeple: belfry, campanile, cupola, flèche, minaret, spire, tower, turret, ziggurat

steer: direct, drive, govern, guide, herd, lead, manage, pilot, show; bull, cattle

steer into the wind: luff

steering apparatus: helm, reins, rudder

stellar: astral, celestial, chief, cosmic, heavenly, leading, outstanding, principal, shining

stem: arrest, axis, base, body, branch, cane, check, contain, control, counter, curb, dam, deter, halt, hinder, impede, oppose, pedicel, penduncle, petiole, prevent, prow, reed, resist, restrain, rod, root, shaft, stall, stanch, stock, stolon, stop, trunk, tuber, withstand

stem from: arise, derive, develop, emanate, originate, spring

stem like the potato, fleshy underground: tuber

stem or stalk offering support: pedicel

stem that bends to ground or grows horizontally: runner, stolon

stem that sends out roots and shoots: rhizome, rootstalk, rootstock

stem where leaf is or was attached, point: node

stem with flowers: inflorescence

stem, central cylinder of: medulla, pith

stem, climbing and twining: bine

stem, food-storing underground: corm

stem, main: rachis

stem, stalk by which leaf is attached to: leafstalk, petiole

stemlike structure like mushroom: stipe

stench: fetor, funk, malodor, mephitis, odor, redolence, reek, smell, stink

stencil cutter: stylus

stencil instrument, intricate: French curve

stencil or pattern: template

stenography: shorthand, stenotype, tachography, transcribing

stentorian: blaring, loud, orotund, resounding, sonorous

step: action, advance, course, dance, degree, footprint, gait, gradation, grade, ladder, level, maneuver, measure, move, movement, pace, phase, plane, prance, procedure, proceeding, process, promotion, rank, round, rung, stage, stair, stride, strut, tread, walk

step down: leave, quit, reduce, resign, retire

step in: arrive, enter, intercede, interfere, intervene

step recorder for walking distance: pedometer

step up: accelerate, boost, escalate, hurry, increase, intensify

step, backward: retrograde, retrogression

stepmother, concerning a: novercal

steppe: grassland, plain, prairie, savanna

steps at entrance of building: stoop

stereo: gramophone, hi-fi, phonograph, record player

stereo cabinet: console

stereo effect, with: binaural, stereophonic

stereo with four channels or speakers: quadraphonic

stereo with one channel: monaural, monophonic

stereotype: categorize, convention, mold, pattern, standard, typecast

stereotyped: conventional, hackneyed, ordinary, trite

sterile: antiseptic, arid, aseptic, barren, bioclean, clean, dead, disinfected, fruitless, geld, hygienic, impotent, ineffective, infecund, infertile, sanitary, unfruitful, unproductive

sterilize: alter, castrate, change, disinfect, emasculate, fix, geld, neuter, purify, sanitize, spay

sterilize by snipping sperm ducts: vasectomy

sterilize by tying fallopian tubes: tubal ligation

sterilize female mammal: spay

sterilize male mammal: castrate

sterilized: axenic, uncontaminated

sterilizing steam-heated vessel: autoclave

sterling: admirable, authentic, excellent, flawless, genuine, honorable, noble, pure, true

stern: astringent, austere, authoritarian, cold, cruel, dour, fierce, firm, forbidding, gloomy, grim, hard, harsh, inexorable, inflexible, rear, relentless, resolute, rigid, rigorous, rough, serious, severe, stout, strict, sturdy, tough, tyrannical, unbending, uncompromising, unfeeling, unkind, unsympathetic, unyielding

stethoscope, listening with: auscultation

stew: anger, boil, brew, brood, commotion, confusion, cook, dither, excitement, fret, fume, fuss, goulash, hash, hodgepodge, hotchpotch, melange, mess, miscellany, mishmash, olio, olla, seethe, simmer, snit, soup, sweat, swelter, tizzy, turmoil, worry

stew made from eggplant, tomatoes, zucchini, peppers, onion: ratatouille

stew of meat or fish and vegetables: ragout

stew, beef: boeuf Bourguignon

stew, fish: bouillabaisse

steward: administrator, agent, attendant, bailiff, chamberlain, curator, custodian, director, foreman, guardian, magistrate, manager, officer, proctor, reeve, seneschal, waiter

steward of a monastery: manciple

stick for beating: bastinado, cudgel, truncheon

stick for fastening or aligning two adjacent pieces: dowel

stick for making notches to keep score or count: tally

stick for stirring drinks: muddler, swizzle stick

stick of incense: joss stick

stick out: beetle, bulge, extend, extrude, jut, poke, project, protrude

stick used by mountain climbers: alpenstock

stick used by orchestra or band conductor: baton

stick used for punishment: ferule

stick used to give prophesy, forked: divining rod, dowsing rod

stick with footrests for hopping: pogo stick

stick, pointed: pale, paling, picket, stake

stick-in-the-mud: conservative, mossback, square

stick-together fastening tape: Velcro

sticking or clinging: adhesive, tenacious

stickler: fanatic, mystery, paradox, puzzle, riddle, zealot

sticks for martial arts: nunchuku

sticky: adhesive, awkward, clammy, damp, difficult, embarrassing, gluey, glutinous, gooey, gummy, hairy, hard, humid, messy, muggy, oppressive, sultry, syrupy, tricky, uncomfortable, viscid, viscous

sticky stuff: glue, goo, gum, mucilage, paste

stiff as a board: inflexible, rigid, starched, tense, unbending, wooden

stiff collar: eton, rabato

stiff or artificially formal: stilted

stiff or rigid in thinking: inflexible, stubborn, unadaptable

stiff-necked: aloof, arrogant, bull-headed, obstinate, pigheaded, stubborn, unyielding

stiffen: benumb, bolster, brace, firm, harden, ossify, petrify, reinforce, set, solidify, tense, thicken

stiffness: rigidity, rigor

stiffness and inflammation, joint: arthritis

stifle: asphyxiate, check, choke, curb, gag, inhibit, interrupt, muffle, repress, restrain, silence, smother, stop, strangle, stultify, suffocate, suppress, trammel

stigma: blemish, blot, brand, cloud, disgrace, mark, odium, onus, scar, shame, spot, stain, taint

stigmatize: brand, censure, defame, denigrate, discredit, smear, tarnish

still: also, besides, but, even, however, likewise, moreover, nevertheless, nonetheless, though, yet

still and inactive: dormant, latent

still and motionless: immobile, inert, quiescent, stagnant, static, stationary

stilted: affected, artificial, awkward, flowery, formal, pompous, prim, stiff, stuffy, unnatural, wooden

stimulant: bracer, caffeine, catalyst, drug, energizer, fillip, incentive, motivation, tonic, upper

stimulate: activate, animate, arouse, brace, elate, encourage, energize, enliven, excite, exhilarate, foster, galvanize, goad, impel, incite, innervate, inspire, instigate, invigorate, jog, motivate, move, pep up, prod, provoke, quicken, rouse, spark, spur, sting, stir, thrill, trigger, urge, whet

stimulate appetite: whet

stimulate emotion: exhilarate, kindle

stimulate growth: foment

stimulate motion or activity: activate, actuate, animate, invigorate, vivify

stimulate or incite: egg on, instigate, provoke, spur on, urge on, whip up

stimulate to action: impel, motivate

stimulate with electric current: galvanize

stimulating: brisk, electrifying, erotic, exciting, interesting, intriguing, invigorating, provocative, refreshing, titillating

stimulus: boost, catalyst, cause, cue, fillip, goad, impetus, impulse, incentive, inducement, motivation, motive, propellant, provocation, spur, sting

sting: burn, hurt, impale, itch, nettle, pain, pierce, poke, prick, smart, tang, tingle, wound

stinger, having a: aculeate

stinging: acrimonious, aculeate, biting, bitter, burning, caustic, harsh, painful, piquant, sarcastic, scathing, sharp

stinging sensation: hives, urtication

stingy: biting, cheap, chintzy, close-fisted, economical, frugal, greedy, illiberal, meager, mean, miserly, near, niggardly, parsimonious, penurious, scanty, selfish, skimpy, thrifty, tight, tightfisted, ungenerous, varicious

stink: fetor, funk, odor, offensive, reek, smell, stench

stinking: fetid, foul, malodorous, mephitic, noisome, noxious, rank

stint: assign, assignment, chore, confine, duty, economize, job, limitation, quota, restrain, restraint, restrict, restriction, scant, scrimp, serve, shift, skimp, spell, stop, stunt, task, term, tour, withhold

stipend: allowance, compensation, emolument, fee, income, pay, payment, pension, recompense, salary, wage, wages

stipulate: agree, arrange, bargain, contract, covenant, designate, detail, guarantee, indicate, promise, require, specify, state, warrant

stipulation: agreement, arrangement, article, clause, condition, demand, detail, item, limit, precondition, prerequisite, provision, proviso, requirement, situation, terms

stir: activity, ado, agitate, animate, arouse, bestir, blend, budge, bustle, challenge, churn, commotion, displace, disturb, electrify, energize, excite, flutter, furor, fuss, galvanize, goad, hubbub, hurry, jail, kindle, mix, motion, motivate, move, movement, pen, poke, prison, prod, racket, rally, scramble, seethe, shake, shift, stimulate, to-do, toss, trigger, tumult, uproar, wake, whip

stir-crazy feeling: cabin fever

stir up: awake, awaken, enliven, excite, foment, incite, inspire, instigate, provoke, quicken, rile, roil, rouse, spur

stir up a furnace: stoke

stir up sediment: roil

stirring: active, afoot, animating, astir, bit, electrifying

stirring food over heat: stir fry

stitch: baste, sew, suture

stitching in surgery: suture

stitching, honeycombed: smocking

stitching, loose and temporary: basting

stock: accumulation, ancestry, animals, asses, assessment, assortment, backlog, banal, band, blood, breed, broth, brothedents, capital, carry, cattle, certificate, cling, commodities, common, commonplace, confidence, customary, descent, equip, estimation, family, folk, fund, goods, hackneyed, herd, hoard, hope, house, inventory, line, lineage, livestock, merchandise, ordinary, pedigree, post, produce, provide, provision, race, replenish, reserve, shares, staple, stem, store, supply, traditional, tribe, trunk, trust

stock amount of fewer than 100 shares: odd-lot

stock and preferred stock, common: equity, security

stock bought on margin, for instance: leverage

stock buying and selling in relatively low volume: thin market

stock buying and selling simultaneously in different markets: arbitrage

stock entitling owner to dividends after prior claims are paid: common stock

stock entitling owner to dividends before common stock's: preferred stock

stock expected to decline, borrowed to sell at higher price: short sale

stock in a warehouse: inventory

stock index on a formula, relative price: Dow Jones Average

stock market decline: bear market

stock market rise: bull market

stock market, illegal action with privileged information about: insider trading

stock not listed or available on officially recognized stock exchange: over-the-counter

stock of entertainment that person or company can perform: repertoire

stock or bond price above dollar value: premium

stock or securities not listed on a stock exchange: unlisted

stock price for customer using broker's credit for purchase: margin

stock priced high because of public confidence: blue chip, blue chipper

stock purchase by takeover target of raider's stock: greenmail

stock selling at less than $1 per share: penny stock

stock shares reissued in greater number but at lower individual share price: stock split

stock sold by individual who has not yet paid for it: short position

stockade: barrier, can, cooler, corral, enclosure, étape, fence, jail, kennel, pen, prison, protection

stockbrokers, group of: portfolio

stocking: hose, hosiery, nylons, sock

stockpile: accumulate, amass, backlog, heap, hoard, inventory, reserve, store

stock's (common) market price in a ratio to its earnings per share: price-earnings ratio

stocks or commodities bought or sold upon agreement for future delivery: futures

stocky: chubby, chumpy, chunky, fat, husky, obese, plump, solid, squat, stocky, stubby, sturdy

stocky, short physique: pyknic

stodgy: blah, boring, dreary, dull, flat, heavy, indigestible, lumpish, monotonous, pedantic, pompous, prim, starchy, sticky, stuffy, tacky, tedious, thick, thickset, unimaginative, uninspired, uninteresting

stoic: calm, cool, detached, impassive, indifferent, patient, philosophic,

phlegmatic, spartan, stolid, unconcerned, unflappable, unmoved, unruffled

stoicism: fortitude, impassiveness, impassivity, indifference, patience

stoke: feed, fuel, poke, stir, tend

stole: boa, cape, embezzled, fur, purloined, robe, scarf, swiped, took, vestment, wrap

stolen: embezzled, lifted, pilfered, poached, robbed, rustled, shanghaied, swiped, taken

stolen goods: booty, haul, loot, plunder, spoils, swag

stolen goods, person who knowingly buys or receives: fence, receiver

stolen jewelry: ice

stolid: apathetic, blunt, brutish, deadpan, dense, dull, impassable, impassive, insensitive, passive, phlegmatic, slow, stoic, unemotional, unexcitable, unfeeling

stomach: abdomen, abomasum, appetite, bear, belly, breadbasket, brook, craw, crop, desire, endure, gizzard, gut, inclination, maw, midriff, midsection, mindlow, omasum, paunch, potbelly, pouch, psalterium, reticulum, standt, taste, tolerate, tummy

stomach and intestines, rumbling sound coming from: borborygmus, gurgulation

stomach area: abdomen, belly, midriff, solar plexus

stomach inflammation: gastritis

stomach lining of ruminants: rennet

stomach of ruminant, first: rumen

stomach of ruminant, fourth: abomasum

stomach of ruminant, second: reticulum

stomach of ruminant, third: manyplies, omasum, psalterium

stomach or bowel pain: collywobbles

stomach pain, severe: colic

stomach pouch in birds: gizzard

stomach rumbling: borborygmus, gurgulation

stomach to duodenum passage: pylorus

stomach to pharynx passage: esophagus, gullet

stomach upset: dyspepsia, indigestion

stomach, concerning the: gastric

stomach, hernia involving: hiatal hernia

stomach, pit of the: solar plexus

stomachache from muscle spasms: colic

stomp: dance, jazz, music, stamp, trample, tread

stone: block, boulder, boundary, brick, cobble, crag, crystal, diamond, flint, gem, granite, gravel, jade, jewel, marble, market, mineral, monolith, onyx, opal, pebble, pelt, petrified, pit, quartz, rock, ruby, salte, sand, sapphire, seed

Stone Ages: Mesolithic, Neolithic, Paleolithic

stone as monument, inscribed upright: stele

stone atop two others in prehistoric monument: dolmen

stone chip, fragment, flake: spall

stone coffin: sarcophagus

stone cutter: lapidary

stone debris: rubble

stone decorative patterns, Gothic: tracery

stone extraction pit: quarry

stone figure or projection, grotesque: gargoyle

stone for knife sharpening: whetstone

stone implement of the Neolithic Period: neolith

stone laid flat over grave: ledger

stone of structure or wall, top: capstone

stone on top of column to support arch, lintel: summer

stone on which column or statue rests: plinth

stone protruding through soil level: outcrop

stone roughly with broad chisel, shape: boast

stone shaft tapering to pyramidal top: obelisk

stone tablet inscribed with three ancient scripts: Rosetta stone

stone to death: lapidate

stone used as abrasive, polisher: pumice

stone used for paving: flagstone

stone, ancient large: megalith

stone, concerning: lithic

stone, concerning the working of: lapidarian, lapidary

stone, four-sided Egyptian shaft of: obelisk

stone, small delicately worked: microlith

stone, worker or builder with: mason, stonemason

stoned: drugged, drunk, high, inebriated, intoxicated, plastered, zonked

stonelike: lithoid, petrous

stones as memorial or marker, mound of: cairn

stones in a circle, prehistoric monolithic: cromlech, henge

stones with capstone, ancient structure of upright: dolmen, trilithon

stonewall: filibuster, obstinate, rebuff, resist, stall, stubborn

stony: adamant, blank, cold, cruel, expressionless, firm, hard, hardened, inexorable, inflexible, jagged, lithic, obdurate, petrified, petrosal, pitiless, rigid, rocky, rough, stern, unfeeling, unyielding

stony meteorite: aerolite

stony, to become or cause to become: petrify

stool pigeon: decoy, fink, informer, nark, rat, stoolie, tattletale, weasel

stool, low: taboret

stoop: bend, bow, condescend, crouch, debase, decline, degrade, deign, descend, dip, duck, hunch, kneel, lean, lower, overcome, platform, resort, sag, sink, slant, slouch, slump, squat, submit, succumb, swoop, tilt, yield

stooped: round-shouldered

stop: adjourn, anchor, arrest, bar, barricade, behold, block, blockade, brake, break, caesura, calk, call, catch, caulk, cease, cessation, check, choke, clog, close, conclude, conclusion, cork, curb, cutoff, dam, defeat, delay, desist, detain, deter, discontinue, embar, end, finish, halt, hinder, hindrance, impede, intermission, interruption, layover, lull, obstacle, obstruct, obstruction, obturate, pause, period, plug, postpone, pretermit, prevent, prohibit, put an end to, quit, repel, restrain, roadblock, sojourn, stall, stanch, standstill, station, staunch, stay, stem, stifle, suppress, suspend, tarry, terminate, withhold

stop command: avast

stop during a journey: layover

stop proceedings for the time: adjourn, recess, table

stop progress or course of: intercept

stop, complete: standstill

stopgap: expedient, impromptu, makeshift, provisional, resort, resource, substitute, temporary

stoppage: blockage, cessation, curtailment, embargo, gridlock, halt, interruption, lockout, obstruction, shutdown, standstill, stasis, strike, walkout

stoppage in body fluid flow: stasis

stoppage of growth: atrophy

stopped for the time being: in abeyance

stopper: bung, cork, fill, lid, plug, wad

stopping at intervals: intermittent, periodic

storage: depository, depot, entrepot, repository

storage dispenser for grain or fuel: hopper

storage for defense weapons: armory

storage for newspaper or magazine articles: morgue

store: abundance, accumulate, amass, bank, bind, bottle, boutique, cache, can, collect, collection, commissary, deli, deposit, emporium, freeze, fund, garner, gather, hoard, hold, house, market, mart, outlet, pack, pile, provide, provisions, replenish, repository, reserve, reserves, reservoir, resources, save, secure, shop, shoppe, showroom, squirrel, stash, stock, stockpile, stow, supermarket, supplies, supply, treasure, warehouse

store a car: garage

store for the winter: ensile

store in sparsely settled area: trading post

store of money or valuables: stash

store of yore: dime store, five-and-ten

store on military base: commissary, post exchange, PX

store selling meat: boucherie

store specializing in fashionable items: boutique

store window dummy: mannequin

store, large retail: emporium, superstore, warehouse store

storehouse: armory, arsenal, barn, building, cache, commissary, depository, depot, étape, granary, magazine, repository, shed, silo, warehouse

storekeeper: businessperson, grocer, merchant, purveyor, shopkeeper

stories with skill, one who tells: raconteur

stories, collection of short: anthology

storm: ahil, anger, assail, assault, attack, barrage, besiege, blizzard, blow, bluster, bombardment, burst, charge, cloudburst, commotion, cyclone, disturbance, downpour, eruption, fume, gale, gust, hubbub, hurricane, lightening, monsoon, outburst, rage, raid, rain, rampage, rant, rave, roar, rush, shower, squall, strike, surprise, tempest, thunder, tornado, trouble, tumult, turmoil, twister, typhoon, upheaval, violence, wind

storm with sudden burst of wind: squall

storm with whirling column of air: cyclone, tornado

stormy: bitter, blustering, dark, foul, furious, gusty, howling, inclement, passionate, raging, rainy, rough, sleety, snowy, tempestuous, torrid, troublesome, tumultuous, turbulent, violent, wild, windy

story: account, alibi, allegory, anecdote, article, description, drama, epic, episode, fable, fabrication, falsehood, fib, floor, folktale, history, legend, lie, lore, myth, narrate, narration, narrative, news, novel, parable, play, plot, recital, record, report, rumor, saga, scenario, sequel, serial, statement, tale, version, yarn

story between two main floors: mezzanine

story for children: fairy tale

story illustrating lesson, simple: parable

story of humorous or interesting incident, short: anecdote

story of one's life written by another: biography

story of one's life written by oneself: autobiography, memoirs

story of past experiences: reminiscence

story of supernatural or heroes, traditional: myth

story of warning: cautionary tale

story with hidden meaning: allegory

story with moral: apologue, exemplum, fable, parable

story, deliberately misleading: canard

story, events of: plot

story, highly improbable: cock-and-bull story

story, long and chronicling: saga

story, long and pointless: shaggy dog story

storyteller: allegorist, author, bard, fibber, liar, minstrel, narrator, raconteur, writer

stout: ale, athletic, beer, bold, brave, brawny, bulky, burly, corpulent, courageous, defiant, determined, enduring, fat, fearless, firm, fleshy, forceful, gallant, hard, hardy, heavy, heroic, husky, insolent, lionhearted, muscular, obese, overweight, plump, portly, potbellied, powerful, proud, pudgy, resolute, robust, rotund, solid, stable, stalwart, staunch, steadfast, steady, stocky, strapping, strong, sturdy, substantial, thickset, tough, valiant, vigorous, weighty

stove: coal, electric, furnace, gas, heater, kiln, microwave, oven, potbelly, range, stave, wood

stove for heating or drying buildings under construction: salamander

stove like fireplace: Franklin stove

stove with spaces for cooking multiple items: range

stow: arrange, bundle, cache, contain, cram, crowd, fill, hide, hold, lade, load, lodge, pack, place, quarter, save, stack, stash, stop, store

straddle: bestride, hedge, mount, noncommittal, sprawl, stride

straggle: dawdle, drift, meander, ramble, roam, rove, stray, trail, wander

straight: aboveboard, accurate, aligned, beeline, blunt, candid, consecutive, continuous, continuously, conventional, correct, direct, directly, erect, even, factual, fair, frank, honest, honestly, honorably, immediately, level, linear, methodical, neat, nonstop, orderly, plain, reliable, rigid, sagittal, sequence, sound, square, successive, tidy, traditional, truthful, unbent, unbroken, undeviating, undiluted, uninterrupted, unmixed, unqualified, upright

straight and iceless drink: neat

straight edge: rule, ruler

straight line cutting a curve twice: secant

straight line over vowel for long sound: macron

straight lines, having: rectilineal, rectilinear

straighten: align, aline, arrange, compose, level, order, rectify, true, unbend, unravel, untwist

straightest route: beeline

straightforward: aboveboard, blunt, candid, clearcut, direct, directly, easy, even, frank, genuine, honest, ingenuous, outright, outspoken, plain, simple, sincere, trustworthy

strain: filter, puree, screen, separate, sieve, sift

strained: antagonistic, antagonized, contrived, explosive, farfetched, forced, intense, labored, overwrought, pretended, taut, taxed, tense, tensed, tight, uneasy, uptight, volatile, weakened, wrenched

strait: bind, channel, crisis, crossroad, difficulty, dilemma, inlet, isthmus, juncture, narrows, pass, pinch, plight, predicament, stressful

straitlaced: formal, prim, prissy, proper, prudish, puritanical, rigid, stiff, strict

strand: bank, beach, coast, desert, fiber, ground, leave, maroon, ply, shore, string, tress, wreck

strand of hair: tress

stranded: abandoned, aground, beached, castaway, enisled, helpless, high and dry, marooned, shipwrecked

strange: abnormal, alien, bizarre, curious, different, eccentric, eerie, eery, erratic, exceptional, exotic, extraordinary, fantastic, fishy, foreign, freaky, kooky, mysterious, new, novel, odd, oddball, offbeat, outlandish, peculiar, puzzling, quaint, queer, rare, singular, unaccustomed, uncanny, uncommon, unexplored, unfamiliar, unknown, unnatural, unusual, weird, wonderful

strange and abnormal: anomalous, deviating, inconsistent, irregular

strange and extraordinary: outlandish, unaccountable

strange and quirky: eccentric, idiosyncratic, odd, peculiar

strange and unique: individual, one of a kind, singular, sui generis

strange, very: bizarre, fantastic, freaky, inexplicable, outlandish, outre, preternatural, supernatural, uncanny

stranger: alien, drifter, foreigner, guest, immigrant, intruder, newcomer, novice, odder, outlander, outsider, visitor

strangers, person fearful or hating: xenophobe

strangle: asphyxiate, choke, garrote, garrotte, kill, muffle, quelch, quell, repress, restrict, smother, squelch, stifle, suffocate, suppress, throttle

stranglehold: choke, grip, monopoly, restrict, suppress

strap: band, beat, belt, bind, cord, flog, lash, leash, rein, strop, thong, whip

strap encircling animal body: cinch, girth, surcingle

strap on forehead supporting load on back: tumpline

strapping: brawny, burly, hefty, husky, powerful, robust, stout, strong, sturdy

stratagem: angle, artfulness, artifice, chicanery, deception, device, dodge, finesse, fraud, gimmick, intrigue, machination, maneuver, plot, ploy, ruse, scheme, slant, tactic, trepan, trick, wile

stratagem, brilliantly executed: coup, masterstroke

stratagem, deceptive: subterfuge

strategic: calculated, clever, critical, cunning, important, necessary, planned, tactical, vital

strategy: approach, artifice, course, design, intrigue, maneuvering, method, plan, policy, procedure, scheme, system, tactics

stratum: bed, class, division, group, layer, level, seam, tier

straw bedding for animals: hay, litter

straw-colored: flaxen

straw hat with flat crown: boater

straw mat, Japanese: tatami

straw or sawdust mattress: pallet, palliasse

stray: abandoned, aberrant, deviate, digress, drift, err, errant, homeless, isolated, lag, meander, occasional, ramble, random, range, roam, rove, runaway, sin, sporadic, straggle, straggler, swerve, veer, waif, wander

stray dog: cur, mutt

stray from main subject: digress

stray from script: ad lib

streak: band, blot, dash, fleck, hint, layer, line, mark, mottle, rush, series, shade, smear, smudge, speed, strain, strake, stripe, stroke, tinge, touch, trace, trait, vein, zoom

streaked: grooved, liny, ridged, striate, striated, strigose, tore

streaked with color: pied, variegated

stream: bourn, bourne, brook, burn, channel, continue, course, creek, current, drift, effluent, flood, flow, flume, flux, gush, issue, jet, pour, race, rill, river, rivulet, roll, run, runlet, runnel, rush, sluice, speed, spritz, succession, surge, water, watercourse

stream flowing out of body of water: effluent

stream leading into land from larger body of water: inlet

stream of fresh water emptying into salt water: freshet

stream of unconsciousness: lethe

stream source: fountainhead

stream, sluggish: creek

stream, small: brook, rill, rivulet, run, runnel, streamlet

streamer: banderol, banner, flag, headline, jet, pendant, pennant, pennon

streamlined: aerodynamic, modernized, simplified, sleek, smooth

street: alley, avenue, boulevard, court,

drag, drive, highway, lane, parkway, road, roadway, thoroughfare, turnpike, way

street awareness: street smarts

street musician, entertainer: busker

street show: raree

street with shops, closed to vehicles: mall

streetwalker: harlot, hooker, hustler, prostitute, strumpet, whore

strength: advantage, asset, backbone, beef, brawn, capacity, clout, durability, endurance, energy, firmness, force, forte, fortitude, influence, intensity, kick, might, muscle, potency, power, robustness, sinew, spirit, spunk, stability, stamina, stoutness, sturdiness, substance, thew, toughness, valor, vehemence, vigor, vitality, will

strength of a solution: titer

strength of character: backbone, determination, spunk

strength of mind: bravery, fortitude, valor

strength or degree of quality: intensity

strength to resist or withstand: endurance, stamina

strength to withstand tension: tensile strength

strength, having masculine: virile

strength, muscular: brawn

strength, requiring: strenuous

strength, return to: convalesce, recuperate

strengthen: add, back, beef, bind, bolster, brace, confirm, consolidate, encourage, endure, energize, enhance, fortify, heighten, help, improve, invigorate, nourish, prop, reinforce, revitalize, stabilize, steel, support, sustain, toughen

strengthen or harden: anneal

strengthen or harden by heating and cooling: temper

strengthen or support with evidence: corroborate, substantiate, underpin, verify

strengthening of conditioned response: reinforcement

strenuous: ardent, arduous, bard, demanding, difficult, energetic, exhausting, laborious, taxing, tough, uphill, vigorous, zealous

stress: accent, accentuate, anxiety, apprehension, assert, burden, distress, emphasis, emphasize, exertion, force, highlight, importance, intensity,

pain, press, pressure, resistance, significance, strain, tension, trauma, underline, underscore, urgency, weight, worry

stretch: bridge, course, crane, dilate, distance, distend, elasticity, elongate, exaggerate, expand, expanse, extend, extension, flexible, interval, length, lengthen, limber, period, prolong, range, rap, reach, run, scope, sentence, span, spell, sprawl, spread, stint, strain, tautness, tension, tighten, time, tract, walk, while

stretch or widen: dilate, distend, expand

stretch over in space or time: bridge, span

stretch vehicle: limo

stretch violently: rack

stretchable: ductile, elastic, extensible, extensile, tensile, tractile

stretched out, arms and legs: spread-eagle

stretcher: bed, cot, dooly, gurney, litter

stretcher with wheels: gurney

stretching and yawning when going to or getting up from bed: pandiculation

stretching out injured body part: traction

stricken: afflicted, disabled, harmed, hurt, incapacitated, injured, sick, smitten, wounded

strict: absolute, accurate, austere, authoritarian, complete, confining, disciplinary, exact, exacting, faithful, hard, harsh, inexorable, inflexible, narrow, oppressive, perfect, precise, punctilious, puritanical, restricting, rigid, rigorous, scrupulous, severe, stark, stern, stiff, straight, straitlaced, stringent, tense, tight, tough, true, undeviating, unsparing, upright

strict adherence to basic principles: fundamentalist, purist, stickler

strict and rigid: inexorable, ironclad

strict and unyielding: adamant, inflexible, obdurate, rigorous, unbending, uncompromising

strict authority: authoritarian, martinet, precisian, ramrod

strict, self-denying: ascetic, austere, puritanical

stride: advance, gait, headway, improvement, march, pace, progress, stalk, step, walk

stride, steady and easy: lope

strident: boisterous, cacophonous, dis-

cordant, grating, harsh, jarring, loud, noisy, piercing, raucous, shrill, vociferous

strife: altercation, argument, battle, brawl, combat, competition, conflict, contest, controversy, discord, dispute, dissension, feud, fight, fracas, fray, friction, hurling, quarrel, spat, squabble, static, struggle, turmoil, unrest, upheaval, war

strife within a group, of: internecine

strike: assail, assault, attack, attain, bang, bash, bat, batter, bean, beat, belt, box, boycott, buffet, bump, clap, clash, clout, collide, conk, crash, dint, discover, fan, find, flog, hammer, hit, hurt, knock, lash, pelt, penetrate, picket, pierce, poke, pop, pound, protest, punch, punish, rap, rout, ship, slam, slash, smack, smear, smite, sock, spank, stroke, struggle, swat, thrash, thrust, trend, uncover, walkout, wallop, whack

strike back: counter, retaliate

strike dumb: stun

strike made to gain advantage, of a military: preemptive

strike posted outside workplace, person on: picket

strike settlement by third party: adjudication, arbitration, conciliation, mediation

striking: arresting, attractive, beautiful, compelling, conspicuous, dazzling, handsome, noticeable, outstanding, powerful, prominent, remarkable, salient, showy, stunning, surprising, telling

striking difference: contrast

striking in appearance: dramatic

striking in brightness: vivid

striking together of two bodies, creating noise: percussion

string: band, chain, cord, file, line, queue, rope, row, series, strand, train, twine

string along: agree, bluff, cheat, dally, deceive, dupe, flirt, fool, hoax, toy

string around neck for whistle, etc.: lanyard

string instrument: banjo, cello, harp, lute, lyre, piano, viol

string instrument, Hindu: sitar

string instrument, plucker for: pick, plectrum, quill

string instrument, Russian: balalaika

string instruments of violin family: bass viol, kit, pochette, viol, viola d'amore, viola da gamba

string instruments, Greek: bouzouki, cithara, kithara, lyre

string instruments, medieval: gittern, hurdy-gurdy, lute, psaltery, rebab, rebec

string looped over fingers in intricate patterns: cat's cradle

string or cord, concerning: funicular

string to tighten or close an opening: drawstring

string, one of the strands making up: ply

stringent: binding, constricted, demanding, exacting, forceful, grim, hard, harsh, inflexible, restrictive, rigid, severe, stern, strict, tight

strings in keyboard, device deadening vibrations of: damper

stringy: fibrous, gluey, gummy, lanky, long, ropy, sinewy, slender, spindly, threadlike, tough, wiry

strip: band, bar, bare, clear, denude, deprive, despoil, dismantle, disrobe, divest, excoriate, expose, flay, husk, length, peel, pillage, pluck, plunder, ravage, reduce, remove, reveal, rob, runway, scale, segment, shed, shred, skin, slat, stripe, tear, unclothe, uncover, undress

strip of leaves, to: defoliate

strip of mown grass or cut grain: swath

strip of rights or possessions: deprive of, despoil, dispossess, divest

strip of wood: lath

strip or path of mown grass or grain: swath

strip skin or blubber from: flense

strip, continuous one-sided surface made from rectangular: Mobius strip

strip, decorative, on upper part of wall: frieze

stripe: band, blow, border, breed, chevron, decoration, design, division, flog, kind, lash, line, mark, pattern, ribbon, sort, streak, strike, strip, stroke, type

striped, grooved, ridged: striate, striated, strigose

stripling: adolescent, boy, fledgling, lad, minor, youngster, youth

stripped: bare, denuded, deprived, exposed, naked, nude, peeled, unclad, undressed

stripped of social position: déclassé

strips of meat or vegetables cut very thin: julienne

stripteaser: ecdysiast

stripteaser clothes: G-string, pasties

strive: aim, attempt, battle, buffet, compete, contend, emulate, endeavor, exert, fight, labor, press on, push, seek, strain, struggle, toil, try, undertake, vie, work

stroke: achievement, apoplexy, bat, beat, blow, caress, chop, effort, feat, fit, fluke, fondle, hit, impact, knock, lash, massage, movement, pat, pet, power, rap, rower, rub, shot, soothe, stride, swat, throb, walk, wallop, whack

stroke of luck: fluke

stroke or seizure: apoplexy, cerebral hemorrhage, ictus

stroll: amble, gait, linger, mosey, ramble, roam, rove, saunter, spatiate, stray, tramp, turn, walk, wander

stroller: actor, beggar, buggy, carriage, perambulator, performer, pram, tramp, vagabond, vagrant, wanderer

strong: able, active, ardent, athletic, biting, bold, brawny, burly, clear, cogent, concentrated, convincing, courageous, determined, difficult, distinct, durable, eager, effective, emphatic, energetic, explicit, fertile, firm, fit, forceful, forcible, forthright, great, hard, hearty, heroic, hot, important, intense, keen, mighty, muscular, outrageous, overpowering, persuasive, piquant, potent, powerful, pronounced, pungent, remarkable, resolute, resonant, robust, rugged, sharp, sinewed, sinewy, solid, sound, spicy, stable, stalwart, staunch, stout, strapping, sturdy, tart, tenacious, tough, undiluted, unmistakable, vehement, vigorous, violent, virile, zealous

strong accentuation used as a musical direction: marcato

strong ale: nog

strong and in good health: hardy, robust, rugged, vigorous

strong and long-lasting: durable

strong and manly: virile

strong and muscular: brawny, burly

strong and powerful: potent, puissant

strong and steadfast: stalwart, staunch

strong-arm: assault, browbeat, bully, coerce, force, intimidate, terrorize, violence

strong blast of wind: gust

strong brown paper: kraft

strong coffee: espresso

strong point: asset, forte, métier, strength, talent

strong, with no weak points: airtight, cast-iron, irrefutable, undeniable

strongbox: cault, coffer, depository, safe

strongest: predominant

stronghold: bastion, bulwark, bunker, castle, citadel, fort, fortify, fortress, garrison, redoubt

strongly marked: distinct, pronounced

structural component, standardized: module

structure: arrangement, bridge, building, complex, components, composition, conformation, construction, design, edifice, fabric, fabricature, form, format, frame, framework, house, makeup, morphology, network, organization, pattern, pyramid, scheme, skeleton, skyscraper, system, texture, tower

structure and design, having qualities of: architectonic

structure of organisms: morphology

struggle: agonize, attempt, battle, brawl, clash, combat, conflict, contend, contest, cope, duel, effort, endeavor, exertion, feud, fight, flounce, flounder, grapple, grind, hassle, labor, resist, scramble, scuffle, skirmish, strife, strike, strive, tangle, toil, try, tug, tussle, vie, war, warfare, wrestle

struggle awkwardly: flounder

struggle for air: gasp

struggle within organization, of a: internecine

struggle, agonizing: throes

strut: bluster, brace, brag, flaunt, flounce, gait, grandstand, parade, peacock, prance, sashay, stride, swagger, swank, walk

stub: bump, butt, counterfoil, crush, extinguish, receipt, remainder, remnant, snag, stump

stubborn: adamant, balky, bullheaded, contrary, determined, diehard, difficult, dogged, firm, fixed, hardheaded, headstrong, indomitable, inexorable, inflexible, intractable, mulish, obdurate, obstinate, opinionated, ornery, persevering, persistent, pertinacious, perverse, pigheaded, refractory, relentless, renitent, resolute, rough, sturdy, tenacious, tough, unbending, uncompromising, unreasonable, unyielding, willful

stubborn and disobedient: obdurate, recalcitrant, refractory, unmanageable

stubborn and persistent: inexorable, unremitting

stubborn and uncompromising: diehard, intransigent, unswerving

stubborn and unremovable: ineradicable, ingrained, persistent

stubbornly bad: impenitent, indurate, obdurate, unrepentant

stubbornly disobedient: contumacious, intractable, recalcitrant, refractory, unruly

stubbornly persistent: dogged, persevering, pertinacious, tenacious

stubbornly refusing: implacable

stubbornly willful: adverse, froward, headstrong, obstinate, unregenerate

stubby: chubby, dumpy, heavyset, puggy, short, squat, stocky, stout, stumpy, thickset

stuck: adhered, baffled, caught, fastened, fixed, frozen, glued, joined, mired, perplexed, puzzled, saddled, stumped, stymied

stuck-up: arrogant, bigheaded, cocky, conceited, condescending, disdainful, egocentric, haughty, patronizing, snobbish, supercilious, uppity, vain

stud: beam, brace, buck, button, dot, peg, pillar, pin, post

student: coed, pupil

student in college, final-year: senior

student in college, first-year: freshman

student in college, second-year: sophomore

student in college, third-year: junior

student of a college, former: alumna, alumnus

student organization, college: fraternity, sorority

student's attending course without permission: audit

studier at night: lucubrator

studies, outside regular: extracurricular, extramural

studio: atelier, bottega, den, library, office, salon, sanctorum, shop, study, workroom, workshop

studio or workshop, artist's: atelier

studious: academic, assiduous, attentive, bookish, contrived, deliberate, diligent, heedful, intellectual, learned, scholarly, studied

study: analysis, analyze, canvass, con, consider, consideration, contemplate, cram, dissect, examine, explore, eye, grind, inspect, learn, lesson, look, lucubration, meditate, memorize, office, perusal, peruse, ponder, pore, read, reflect, research, review, scan, schoolwork, scrutinize, survey, watch

study and science of writing systems: grammatology

study cubicle in library stacks: carrel

study hard for imminent exam: bone, cram, grind, pore

study in detail: anatomize, dissect, peruse, scrutinize

study of a specific limited subject: dissertation, monograph, treatise

study of amphibians and reptiles: herpetology

study of ancient inscriptions: epigraphy

study of ancient official documents: diplomatics

study of ancient writings: paleography

study of animal behavior: ethology

study of ants: myrmecology

study of beauty: aesthetics, kalology

study of bees: melottology

study of bells: campanology

study of biology and technology: biotechnology, ergonomics, human engineering, human factors engineering

study of birds: ornithology

study of blood: hematology

study of causes and origins: etiology

study of caves: speleology, spelunking

study of characteristics of human population: demography

study of Chinese language, culture, civilization: sinology

study of citizens' rights: civics

study of clocks and watches: horology

study of clouds: nephology

study of coats of arms: heraldry

study of codes: cryptography, cryptology

study of coins: numismatics

study of coins and medals: numismatics

study of color: chromatics

study of computers and human nervous system: cybernetics

study of crime: criminology

study of criminal rehabilitation and prison management: penology

study of culture of peoples: ethnology

study of deserts: eremology

study of design in nature: teleology

study of design or purpose in natural phenomena: teleology

study of diet and food: nutrition

study of disease and its causes: pathology

study of disease symptoms: symptomatology

study of ear disease: otology

study of earth's physical structure: geology

study of earth's size and shape: geodesy

study of earth's structural features: tectonics

study of earth's surface above sea level: hypsography

study of earthquakes: seismology

study of ecological interrelationships: synecology

study of elections: psephology

study of ferns: pteridology

study of fingerprints: dactylography

study of flags: vexillology

study of folk music: ethnomusicology

study of folklore and legends: storiology

study of formal debate: argumentation, forensics

study of fossils: palaeontology, paleontology

study of friction and lubrication: tribology

study of fruit: pomology

study of gems: gemology

study of genealogies: heraldry

study of gestures and facial expressions: kinesics

study of glaciers: glaciology

study of glands: endocrinology

study of guns: ballistics

study of guns and bullets: ballistics

study of hair and its diseases: trichology

study of handwriting: graphology

study of happiness: eudemonics

study of history using economic models and statistical methods: cliometrics

study of human behavior: praxeology

study of human character: ethology

study of human knowledge: epistemology

study of human settlements: ekistics

study of immunity to disease: immunology

study of inflection, derivation, compound formation of words: morphology

study of information processes in artificial systems: cybernetics
study of inscriptions or decipherment: epigraphy
study of insects: entomology
study of knowledge: epistemology
study of lakes and ponds: limnology
study of language: linguistics
study of life processes and organisms: physiology
study of light: optics
study of lubrication: tribology
study of meaning of language forms: semantics
study of meaning of words: semantics
study of metals: metallurgy
study of meteors: aerolithology
study of miracles: thaumatology
study of moss: bryology
study of mountains: orography, orology
study of mummies: momiology
study of muscles: myology
study of names: onomastics
study of nature of god: theology
study of nervous system: neurology
study of odors: osmics
study of one's descent: genealogy
study of oneself: autology
study of or tracing family tree: genealogy
study of organic tissues: histology
study of origins and causes: etiology
study of origins and forms of proper names: onomastics
study of place names: toponymics
study of plants: botany, phytology
study of poetic rhythms and forms: prosody
study of poisons and treatment of poisons: toxicology
study of political elections: psephology
study of pollens and spores: palynology
study of population statistics: demography
study of pornography: coprology
study of prehistoric animals: paleozoology
study of prisons and rehabilitation: penology
study of psychic phenomena: parapsychology
study of puzzles: enigmatology
study of races and ethnic groups: ethnology
study of racial improvement by selective breeding: eugenics
study of rainfall: hyetography

study of relationships within a group: sociometry
study of reptiles and amphibians: herpetology
study of rocks: petrology
study of rocks' structure and composition: lithology
study of saints: hagiography
study of seaweed and marine algae: algology
study of sermon writing: homiletics
study of shells: conchology
study of signets and seals: sphragistics
study of signs and symbols: semantics, semasiology, semiotics
study of skin and its diseases: dermatology
study of skull: craniology, phrenology
study of soils: pedology
study of sound: acoustics
study of sounds of speech: phonetics
study of speech sounds of a language: phonology
study of stars, celestial bodies: astronomy
study of structure and function of bones: osteology
study of supernatural phenomena: parapsychology
study of the body: physiology
study of the earth's surface water: hydrology
study of the heart: cardiology
study of the metrical structure of verse: prosody
study of the moon: selenology
study of the nature and structure of human speech: linguistics
study of the nature of being: ontology
study of the nature of knowledge: epistemology
study of the physical features of the moon: selenography
study of the skull: phrenology
study of the universe: cosmogony, cosmology
study of tissue and its structure: histology
study of trees: dendrology
study of two or more disciplines: interdisciplinary
study of UFOs: ufology
study of war: polemology
study of weather's effect on humans: biometeorology
study of whales: cetology
study of wines and winemaking: oenology

study of word origins: etymology
study of word structure and form: morphology
study of words and language forms: semantics
study of working conditions and environment: ergonomics
study offered by college, courses of: curriculum, syllabus
study or research, year of leave for: sabbatical
study, laborious: excogitation, lucubration
stuff: cash, cram, crowd, element, essence, fabric, fatten, fill, force, gear, jam, junk, load, material, matter, nonsense, objects, overeat, overfill, overindulge, overload, pack, pad, possessions, principle, ram, refuse, sate, squeeze, substance, things
stuffed, as meat or vegetables: farci
stuffing: dressing, feathers, filler, filling, forcemeat, innards, insides, padding, tomentum
stuffing and mounting of dead animals: taxidermy
stuffing in furniture: flock, upholstery
stuffy: airless, arrogant, close, conservative, crammed, dull, fusty, humid, muggy, musty, oppressive, pompous, prim, proper, puritanical, resolute, stagnant, stale, stifling, stodgy, stout, straitlaced, suffocating, sulky, uninteresting
stultify: cripples, impair, impede, inhibit, nullify, ridiculous, stifle
stumble: blunder, botch, bumble, chance, discover, encounter, err, error, failure, fall, falter, flounder, happen, hesitate, lurch, slip, spill, stagger, stammer, topple, trip, wallow
stumbling block: barrier, catch, complication, drawback, hindrance, hitch, hurdle, impediment, obstacle, problem, snag
stump: baffle, barge, bewilder, block, butt, challenge, clump, confuse, dare, end, foil, hobble, lumber, mystify, nonplus, orate, perplex, plod, puzzle, snag, stab, stub, stumble, stymie
stumper: oddity
stun: amaze, appall, astonish, astound, bewilder, daze, dazzle, deaden, dumfound, flabbergast, floor, numb, overpower, overwhelm, paralyze, petrify, shock, stagger, startle, stupefy, surprise
stunning: attractive, beautiful, daz-

zling, gorgeous, handsome, lovely, marvelous, pretty, shocking, smashing, spectacular, striking, stylish

stunning blow: rabbit punch

stunt: acrobatics, antic, deed, exploit, feat, performance, sketch, skit, stamp, trick

stunt, to: blunt, check, curb, curtail, dwarf, hinder, impede, shorten, suppress

stunted animal: runt

stunted in growth: depauperate

stupefy: amaze, astonish, astound, awe, bemuse, benumb, besot, bewilder, confound, confuse, daunt, daze, dazzle, dull, faze, flabbergast, nonplus, numb, overwhelm, rattle, shock, startle, stun, surprise

stupendous: amazing, astonishing, astounding, colossal, enormous, extraordinary, fabulous, fantastic, giant, gigantic, great, huge, immense, incredible, marvelous, massive, miraculous, monstrous, phenomenal, remarkable, spectacular, superb, terrific, tremendous, wonderful, wondrous

stupid: absurd, addled, asinine, blockish, brainless, brutish, clod, cloddish, crass, cretinous, daffish, dazed, dense, dimwitted, dizzy, doltish, dopey, dull, dumb, dumbbell, dunce, fatuous, foolish, footless, foppish, idiot, idiotic, ignorant, imbecile, imbecilic, inane, insensate, irrational, irresponsible, lethargic, meaningless, moron, moronic, oafish, obtuse, pointless, senseless, silly, simple, simpleton, slow, sluggish, stupefied, torpid, unintelligent, unwise, vacuous, witless, worthless

stupor: anesthesia, apathy, coma, daze, faint, fog, hypnosis, languor, lethargy, narcosis, sleep, slumber, swoon, torpor, trance

sturdy: athletic, brawny, courageous, determined, durable, firm, hardy, healthy, muscular, obdurate, powerful, resolute, robust, rugged, solid, sound, stable, stalwart, steady, stiff, stout, strapping, strong, stubborn, substantial, tough, unyielding, vigorous

sturdy and robust physique: mesomorph

Sturm und Drang translation: storm and stress

stutter: hesitate, sputter, stammer, stumble

sty: den, dump, hovel, pen, pigpen, shack

stye site: eyelid

style: air, appearance, class, craze, demeanor, design, elegance, fad, fashion, format, garb, genre, gnomon, grace, kind, manner, method, mode, name, pattern, rage, sort, taste, technique, title, tone, type, variety, vogue, way

style and verve: brio, chic, dash, élan, flair, panache, pizazz, smartness, swank

style, agreeably appropriate in: felicitous

stylish: à la mode, chic, chichi, classy, dapper, dashing, dressy, fashionable, hip, latest, modern, modish, nifty, posh, sharp, sleek, slick, smart, snazzy, spiffy, swagger, swanky, tony, trendy

stymie: block, cramp, foil, frustrate, hinder, impede, obstruct, prevent, puzzle, stonewall, stop, stump, thwart

suave: agreeable, bland, charming, civil, cordial, courteous, cultured, diplomatic, fulsome, gracious, mannered, pleasant, polished, polite, politic, refined, slick, smooth, sophisticated, svelte, tactful, unctuous, urbane, worldly

suave individual: smoothie

sub: alternate, auxiliary, backup, below, replacement, second, standby, under, understudy; submarine, U-boat

sub rosa: confidentially, covertly, obscurely, privately, secretly

subaltern: assistant, inferior, secondary, servile, subordinate

subatomic particle with half-integral spin: fermion

subatomic particle with integral spin: boson

subatomic particle, hypothetical: quark

subatomic particle, neutral: neutron

subatomic particle, stable and negative: electron

subatomic particle, stable and positive: proton

subatomic particles with strong interactions: baryon, hadron, kaon, meson, pion

subatomic particles with weak interactions: lepton, muon, neutrino, tau

subconscious: intuitive, mind, psyche, self, subliminal

subconscious mind exhibited in art, literature: surrealism

subdivision: branch, department, development, part, partition, sector, subclass, subsidiary

subdivision map: plat

subdue: allay, beat, break, calm, captivate, conquer, control, crush, defeat, diminish, disarm, dismay, floor, master, mellow, moderate, overcome, overpower, quash, quell, quench, reduce, repress, restrain, sober, soften, soothe, squelch, subjugate, suppress, surmount, tame, vanquish

subdued: controlled, cowed, humbled, mellow, mild, quiet, repressed, restrained, sober, sobered, soft, solemn, tame, tamed, tempered, toned down

subjacent: beneath, lower, underlying

subject: accountable, cause, conditional, contingent, core, dependent, discipline, discussion, disposed, expose, exposed, field, gist, governed, inferior, issue, liable, material, matter, motif, motive, obedient, point, prone, question, study, submissive, submit, subordinate, test, theme, topic

subject or citizen: follower, serf, subordinate, vassal

subject, formal discourse on: disquisition

subjective: abstract, biased, emotional, illusory, individual, internal, introspective, personal, prejudiced

subjugate: break, compel, conquer, crush, defeat, enslave, master, overcome, overpower, overthrow, subdue, suppress, tame, triumph, vanquish

sublime: dignify, divine, elevated, exalt, exalted, glorious, grant, great, heavenly, high, holy, ideal, impressive, lofty, magnificent, majestic, noble, spiritual, splendid, stately

submarine: boat, diver, submersible, U-boat, undersea, underwater; grinder, hero, hoagie, sandwich

submarine location system: echolocation, sonar

submarine optical instrument: periscope

submarine raised observation post: conning tower, sail

submarine research vessel: bathyscaphe, bathysphere

submerge: deluge, dip, dive, douse, drench, drown, dunk, engulf, flood, immerse, inundate, obscure, plunge, sink, souse, submerse, swamp

submission: acquiescence, compliance, humbleness, meekness, obedience, prostration, resignation, servility, surrender, yielding

submission to wishes, opinions of another: deference

submissive: accommodating, acquiescent, amenable, compliant, complying, dutiful, humble, meek, mild, obedient, obeying, passive, resigned, servile, slavish, subdued, subservient, tame, unassertive, yielding

submit: abide, acquiesce, agree, bend, bow, capitulate, cave, claim, comply, contend, defer, deliver, fall, give, knuckle, obey, offer, present, proffer, propose, resign, stoop, succumb, suggest, surrender, tender, urge, yield

subordinate: aide, ancillary, assistant, auxiliary, below, control, dependent, inferior, junior, lesser, lower, minor, secondary, servant, subaltern, subdue, subject, subservient, subsidiary, supplementary, under, underling, worker

subordinate relationship of clauses with connectives: hypotaxis

suborn: bribe, incite, instigate, procure

subscribe: accept, advocate, agree, approve, assent, attest, consent, contribute, endorse, give, pledge, sanction, sign, signature, support

subsequent: after, consecutive, ensuing, following, later, next, resultant, succeeding, successive

subsequently: after, afterwards, anon, consequently, following, later, since, then

subservient: accessory, acquiescent, ancillary, auxiliary, compliant, cringing, fawning, menial, obeisant, obsequious, resigned, secondary, servile, slavish, subject, submissive, subordinate, truckling, under

subside: abate, calm, decrease, descend, diminish, dwindle, ebb, fall, lessen, lower, lull, moderate, relapse, settle, shrink, sink, slacken, taper, wane, withdraw

subsidiary: accessory, affiliate, ancillary, auxiliary, back-up, branch, collateral, division, minor, secondary, subordinate, supplement, tributary

subsidiary business within certain premises: concession

subsidy: aid, allowance, appropriation, assistance, backing, endowment, gift, grant, help, honorarium, money, pension, sponsorship, subvention, support, tribute

subsidy for research: subvention

subsist: breathe, continue, endure, exist, live, maintain, manage, remain, stay, support, survive, sustain

subsistence: allowance, existence, hypostasis, keep, livelihood, living, maintenance, provisions, resources, support, survival, sustenance

substance: affluence, backbone, basis, being, body, burden, element, entity, essence, essentials, estate, fabric, focus, gist, heart, ingredient, marrow, mass, material, matter, meaning, means, meat, object, ore, pith, property, purport, reality, resources, riches, significance, solidity, soul, spirit, strength, stuff, tenor, thing, wealth, worth

substance produced chemically: synthetic

substantial: abundant, affluent, ample, big, considerable, corporeal, firm, full, generous, hearty, important, large, massive, material, meaningful, momentous, plentiful, significant, sizable, solid, sound, stout, strong, sturdy, tangible, valuable, weighty

substantiate: assure, attest, authenticate, confirm, corroborate, demonstrate, establish, justify, materialize, prove, support, validate, verify, vouch

substitute: alter ego, alternate, alternative, artificial, backup, deputy, double, ersatz, exchange, extra, imitation, improvised, makeshift, proxy, replace, replacement, reserve, second, sit-in, standby, stand-in, succedaneum, surrogate, swap, switch, understudy

substitute in job: locum tenens

substitute or agent: deputy, proxy, stand-in, surrogate, vicar

substitute, inferior: ersatz

substituted fraudulently: spurious, supposititious

substitutes on sports team: bench

substituting for another, done by one: vicarious

substituting milder word for harsh one: euphemism

subsume: classify, contain, include, incorporate, involve

subterfuge: artifice, cheat, chicanery, deception, device, dishonesty, evasion, fraud, plan, ploy, pretense, refuge, ruse, scheme, sham, stratagem, trick

subterranean: cave, cavern, concealed, hidden, secret, underground

subtitle shown above rather than below: supertitle, surtitle

subtle: abstruse, acute, analytic, artful, beguiling, cagey, clever, crafty, cunning, deceptive, deft, delicate, devious, elusive, expert, foxy, indefinable, indirect, ingenious, insidious, intricate, keen, logical, perceptive, quiet, sharp, shrewd, skillful, slick, sly, vague, wily

subtle difference in meaning: nuance

subtle distinction: fine point, nicety

subtle emanation: aura

subtle introduction: insinuation

subtract: deduct, diminish, discount, minus, remove, withdraw

subtracted from another, quantity to be: subtrahend

subtracted, quantity from which another quantity is to be: minuend

subversion: disruption, overthrow, sabotage, undermining

subversive: insurgent, rebellious, treasonous

subversive organization working to further enemy's aims: fifth column

subway: metro

succeed: accomplish, achieve, arrive, attain, click, ensue, flourish, follow, fulfill, get on, go far, make good, master, overcome, prevail, prosper, reap, replace, rise, score, surmount, thrive, triumph, win, work

succeed and thrive: flourish, prosper

succeed despite opposition: prevail

succeed in going over or coping with: negotiate

succeed in passing examination or inspection: pass muster

succeed to a position: accede to, supersede

succeed or work out: contrive, fructify

success: achievement, arrival, attainment, breakthrough, celebrity, fame, fortune, happiness, hit, prosperity, reward, rise, triumph, victory

success or attainment worked for or desired: accomplishment, fruition

success, brilliant: éclat

success, desire for: ambition, aspiration

success, sudden and removing obstacle: breakthrough

successful: accomplished, booming, flourishing, fruitful, on top, prosperous, proven, satisfied, smashing, thriving, triumphant, victorious, wealthy

successful and powerful: efficacious, potent

successful and smart young person: child prodigy, whiz kid, wunderkind

successful period: florescence

succession: chain, continuation, course, cycle, order, run, sequence, series, string, train

successive: consecutive, sequential, serial

succinct: blunt, brief, compact, concise, condensed, curt, direct, short, summary, terse

succor: aid, assist, befriend, comfort, help, mitigate, nurture, refuge, relief, relieve, rescue, support

succulent: appetizing, delicious, fresh, juicy, luscious, lush, mouthwatering, sappy, tasty, tender

succumb: accede, collapse, decease, die, drop, expire, fall, perish, quit, submit, surrender, yield

such: alike, comparable, equivalent, like, parallel, similar, some, specific, that

suck: absorb, draw, drink, engulf, extract, imbibe, inhale, nurse, sip, suction

sucker of tapeworm, leech, octopus: acetabulum

suckling: babe, baby, infant, unweaned

suction out gases or liquids, in medicine: aspirate

sudden: abrupt, fast, hasty, hurried, immediate, impetuous, impromptu, instant, precipitate, quick, rash, speedy, surprising, swift

sudden and forceful: headlong, impetuous, precipitate

sudden and spontaneous: spur-of-the-moment

sudden and unexpected: unannounced, unforeseen

sudden change of events: peripeteia

sudden change of mind: caprice, impetuosity

sudden collapse: crash

sudden exclamation: ejaculation

sudden increase: irruption

sudden inspiration: brainstorm

sudden leap: lunge

sudden manifestation of the meaning of something: epiphany, revelation

sudden outburst: flare, paroxysm, spurt

sudden outpouring: spate

sudden political takeover: coup d'etat

sudden rain: cloudburst

sudden reversal: about-face, U-turn, volte-face

sudden sharp feeling: pang

sudden terror: panic

sudden upheaval: cataclysm, disruption

sudden, brilliant, fast: meteoric

suddenly: abruptly, presto, quickly, swiftly, unawares, unexpectedly

suddenly, acting: impetuous, impulsive

suds: beer, bubbles, foam, froth, lather, soap

sue: appeal, beg, beseech, claim, contest, court, entreat, litigate, petition, plead, proceed, prosecute, seek, solicit, summon, supplicate, woo

suffer: accept, ache, agonize, ail, allow, anguish, bear, endure, experience, feel bad, grieve, hurt, lament, languish, permit, submit, tolerate, undergo

suffer humiliation: lose face

suffering: adversity, affliction, agony, ailing, anguish, discomfort, distress, dolor, grief, hurt, illness, loss, misery, misfortune, pain, sickness, sorrow, torture, travail

suffering and oppressed: downtrodden, persecuted

suffering for one's cause: martyrdom

suffering, exist in state of: languish

suffering, great: calvary, private hell, purgatory, tribulation

suffering, indifference to: fortitude, impassiveness, stoicism

suffering, scene of: Gethsemane

suffice: answer, appease, avail, enough, fulfill, meet, satisfy, serve, sufficient

sufficient: able, abundant, acceptable, adequate, ample, commensurate, competent, efficient, enough, good, plenteous, plentiful, plenty, qualified, satisfactory, substantial, suffice, valid

sufficient grounds: justification, warrant

suffocate: asphyxiate, burke, choke, destroy, drown, kill, smother, stifle, strangle, suppress, throttle

suffrage: ballot, consensus, franchise, petition, prayer, right, voice, vote

suffuse: bathe, charge, color, cover, fill, interject, introduce, overspread, permeate, saturate, spread, steep, tinge

sugar: candy, cane, caramel, dextrose, friose, fructose, fucose, glucose, gulose, lactose, maltose, maple, sucrose, sweeten, sweetener, tetrose, xylose

sugar apple: sweetsop

sugar cane and sugar beet sugar: saccharose, sucrose

sugar deficiency: hypoglycemia

sugar excess: hyperglycemia

sugar glaze, coated with: candied, crystallized, glacé

sugar in fruits and honey: fructose, fruit sugar, levulose

sugar in milk: lactose

sugar in plant and animal tissue: glucose

sugar in plant and animal tissue and derived synthetically from starch: dextroglucose, dextrose

sugar in wood: xylose

sugar levels in blood and urine, increased: diabetes mellitus

sugar processing plant: refinery

sugar substitute: allose, aspartame, cyclamate, glucose, saccharin

sugar, coat with: dredge

sugary: candied, flattering, granular, honeyed, pleasant, saccharine, sticky, sweet, syrupy

suggest: advise, allude, allude to, broach, connote, hint, imply, indicate, infer, insinuate, intimate, move, propose, propound, recommend, submit, theorize, urge

suggest clearly: evidence, exemplify, indicate, prove

suggest for first time: broach, propose, propound

suggest on another's behalf: advocate, commend, recommend

suggest or propose: advance, predicate, propound

suggested meaning: connotation

suggestion: advice, approach, hint, idea, implication, intimation, opinion, overtone, pointer, proposal, recommendation, shade, tinge, tip, touch, trace, undertone

suggestion or hint, indirect or subtle: aspersion, imputation, innuendo, insinuation

suggestion, underlying: implication, undercurrent, undertone

suggestive: dirty, erotic, evocative, expressive, indelicate, provocative, racy, risqué, seductive, sexy, symbolic, titillating, vulgar

suggestive of something: redolent

suggestive use of words: double entendre, double meaning

suggestive, delicately: subtle

suicidal: dangerous, deadly, depressed, destructive, fatal, lethal

suicidal game: Russian roulette

suicidal Japanese air attack: kamikaze

suicidal Japanese disembowelment: hara-kiri, seppuku

suicide: felo-de-se

suicide by Hindu widow: suttee

suing, person: plaintiff

suit: accommodate, adapt, adjust, agree, answer, appeal, arrange, become, befit, behoove, behove, conform, correspond, follow, group, harmonize, match, please, prayer, proceeding, satisfy, series, serve, suffice

suit or dress: attire, outfit, wardrobe

suit, law: litigation, petition

suitable: able, acceptable, adequate, apposite, appropriate, apropos, apt, becoming, befitting, comely, compatible, competent, consistent, consonant, convenient, due, eligible, expedient, fit, fitting, good, just, matching, meet, proper, relevant, right, seeming, timely, up one's alley, useful, worthy

suitable and adequate: condign

suitable and harmonious: congruent, congruous

suitable for farming: arable

suitable for marriage: nubile

suitable time, happening at: opportune, propitious

suitable to manners: becoming, decorous, seemly

suitable, be: appertain, pertain

suitcase: bag, grip, portmanteau, satchel, valise

suitcase with two hinged compartments: portmanteau

suitcase, small: valise

suite: attendants, band, entourage, followers, group, retinue, staff; apartment, chambers, flat, furniture; rooms, series, set

suitor: admirer, asker, beau, boyfriend, gallant, lover, wooer

sulk: brood, frown, glower, grumble, grump, mope, moue, pout

sulky: carriage, cart, dismal, gloomy, glum, grouchy, grouty, irritable, moody, peevish, poutish, sullen, surly

sullen: black, brooding, churlish, crabby, cross, depressing, dismal, dour, dull, forlorn, fretful, gloomy, glum, grim, grouchy, heavy, melancholy, moody, mopy, morose, peevish, petulant, pouty, saturine, serious, silent, slow, sluggish, somber, sour, sourpussed, sulky, surly

sully: befoul, blot, corrupt, debase, defile, disgrace, mar, pollute, smear, soil, stain, taint, tarnish

sultry: burning, close, hot, humid, lurid, muggy, oppressive, scorching, sensual, sexy, sizzling, stifling, sweltering, torrid, tropical, voluptuous

sum: add, addition, aggregate, amount, calculate, count, entirety, epitomize, extent, figure, gist, gross, height, integer, magnitude, mass, measure, number, numeral, quantity, result, summarize, summary, summation, tally, total, totality, value, whole, worth

sum, trivial: nominal

summarize: abridge, abstract, capsulize, condense, digest, epitomize, nutshell, recap, recapitulate, shorten, sum

summarized statement for preparing formal document: aide-mémoire

summary: abbreviation, abridgement, abstract, aperçu, breakdown, brief, compendium, concise, condensed, conspectus, digest, epitome, gist, inventory, outline, overview, précis, prospectus, recap, report, résumé, review, rundown, scenario, succinct, sum, summation, survey, syllabus, synopsis, terse

summary at beginning: conspectus, outline, synopsis

summary at end: recap, recapitulation, résumé, summation, wrap-up

summary of book: abridgment, compendium, condensation, digest

summary of course of study: curriculum, syllabus

summary of document: abstract

summary of dramatic plot: scenario

summary of law court proceedings: docket

summary of process: schema

summary of proposed work or venture: prospectus

summary of work experience: C.V., curriculum vitae, résumé, vita

summary, short succinct: encapsulation, overview, paraphrase, précis

summation: addition, aggregate, sum, summary

summer's beginning: summer solstice

summer's hottest days: dog days

summerhouse: alcove, belvedere, cottage, gazebo, pagoda, pavilion, retreat

summery: aestival, estival, sunny, warm

summery weather in fall: Indian summer

summit: acme, apex, apogee, cap, climax, crest, crown, culmination, height, meridian, mountain, peak, pinnacle, roof, tip, top, vertex, zenith

summon: assemble, beck, beckon, bid, call, cite, command, convene, evoke, gather, mobilize, motion, muster, notice, order, page, rally, rouse, signal, subpoena, warrant

summon a spirit: conjure, invoke

summon or call meeting: convene, convoke

summon to court to answer charge: arraign

summon, as a taxi: hail

summons: call, calls, citation, notification, pages, process, requisition, subpoena, writ

sumptuous: beautiful, costly, deluxe, elegant, expensive, extravagant, grand, grandiose, lavish, lucullan, lush, luxurious, magnificent, opulent, plush, rich, splendid

sun: daylight, shine, sol, star; apricate, bask, tan

sun at greatest distance from equator: solstice

sun being at center: heliocentric

sun-dried brick: adobe

sun-moon differential: epact

sun-related: heliacal, solar

sun worship: heliolatry

sun, blaze of light on: flare

sun, cloud of flaming gas rising from: prominence

sun, highest point of the: zenith

sun, layer of gas above chromosphere: corona

sun, layer of gas above photosphere of: chromosphere

sun, luminous ring around: aureole, corona

SUMMER OLYMPIC GAMES (MEN'S EVENTS)

Aquatics
50-meter freestyle; 100-meter freestyle; 200-meter freestyle; 400-meter freestyle; 1,500-meter freestyle; 100-meter backstroke; 200-meter backstroke; 100-meter breaststroke; 200-meter breaststroke; 100-meter butterfly; 200-meter butterfly; 200-meter individual medley; 400-meter individual medley; 4x100-meter freestyle relay; 4x200-meter freestyle relay; 4x100-meter medley relay; springboard diving (3 meters); platform diving (3 meters); synchronized diving (springboard diving; platform diving); water polo

Archery
individual round (90-70-50-30 m); team

Athletics
100-meter dash; 200-meter dash; 400-meter dash; 800-meter run; 1,500-meter run; 5,000-meter run; 10,000-meter run; 20-kilometer walk; 50-kilometer walk; marathon; 4x100-meter relay; 4x400-meter relay; 110-meter hurdles; 400-meter hurdles; 1,500-meter wheelchair; discus throw; hammer throw; running high jump; javelin throw; long jump; pole vault; shot put; triple jump; 3,000-meter steeplechase; decathlon (100-meter dash, long jump, shot put, high jump, 400-meter dash, 110-meter hurdles, discus, pole vault, javelin, 1,500-meter run)

Badminton
singles; doubles; mixed doubles

Baseball

Basketball

Boxing
light flyweight; flyweight; bantamweight; featherweight; lightweight; light welterweight; welterweight; light middleweight; middleweight; light heavyweight; heavyweight; super heavyweight

Canoe/Kayak
canoe single slalom/C-1, slalom; canoe slalom pairs/C-2, slalom; kayak slalom singles/K-1, slalom; canoe singles 500m/C-1, 500 meters; canoe singles 1,000m/C-1, 1,000 meters; canoe pairs 500m/C-2, 500 meters; canoe pairs 1,000m/C-2, 1,000 meters; kayak singles 500m/K-1, 500 meters; kayak singles 1,000m/K-1, 1,000 meters; kayak pairs 500m/K-2, 500 meters; kayak pairs 1,000m/K-2, 1,000 meters; kayak fours 1,000m/K-4, 1,000 meters

Cycling
track (one km time trial, individual pursuit, keirin, madison, olympic sprint, points race, sprint, team pursuit); mountain bike (cross-country); road (individual time, individual road race)

Equestrian
team dressage; individual dressage; team jumping; individual jumping; team three-day event; individual three-day event

Fencing
individual epee; individual sabre; individual foil; team epee; team sabre; team foil

Field Hockey

Gymnastics
team; all-around; horizontal bar; parallel bars; rings; pommel horse; vault; floor exercise; trampoline

Judo
extra-lightweight (60kg); half-lightweight (66kg); lightweight (73kg); half-middleweight (81kg); middleweight (90kg); half-heavyweight (100kg); heavyweight (+100kg)

Modern Pentathlon
shooting; fencing; swimming; show jumping; running

Rowing
coxless pairs; coxless four; single sculls; double sculls; lightweight double sculls; eight; quadruple sculls; lightweight coxless four

Shooting
10m air pistol; 10m air rifle; 10m running target; 25m rapid fire pistol; 50m free pistol; 50m free rifle 3-position; double trap; skeet shooting; trap

Soccer

Table Tennis
singles; doubles

Tae Kwon Do
less than 58kg; 58kg to 68kg; 68kg to 80kg; over 80kg

Team Handball

Tennis
tennis; doubles

Triathlon
1.5km swim; 40km cycle; 10km run

Volleyball
beach; indoor

Weightlifting
up to 56 kg; up to 62 kg; up to 69 kg; up to 77 kg; up to 85 kg; up to 94 kg; over 105 kg

Wrestling
freestyle; Greco-Roman

Yachting/Sailing
men's mistral; men's 470; open laser; open tornado; open soling; open star ☙

SUMMER OLYMPIC GAMES (WOMEN'S EVENTS)

Aquatics
50-meter freestyle; 100-meter freestyle; 200-meter freestyle; 400-meter freestyle; 800-meter freestyle; 100-meter backstroke; 200-meter backstroke; 100-meter breaststroke; 200-meter breaststroke; 100-meter butterfly; 200-meter butterfly; 200-meter individual medley; 400-meter individual medley; 4x100-meter freestyle relay; 4x100-meter medley relay; 4x200-meter freestyle relay; springboard diving (3 meters); platform diving (10 meters); synchronized diving (springboard diving; platform diving); synchronized swimming (duet, team); water polo

Archery
individual round (70-60-50-30m); team

Athletics
100-meter dash; 200-meter dash; 400-meter dash; 800-meter run; 1,500-meter run; 5,000-meter run; 10,000-meter run; 20-kilometer walk; 800-meter wheelchair; 100-meter hurdles; 400-meter hurdles; 4x100-meter relay; 4x400-meter relay; marathon; running high jump; long jump; triple jump; shot-put; discus throw; javelin throw; hammer throw; pole vault; heptathlon (100-meter hurdles, high jump, shot put, 200-meter dash, long jump, javelin, 800-meter run)

Badminton
singles; doubles; mixed doubles

Basketball

Canoe/Kayak
kayak slalom/K-1, slalom; kayak singles 500m/K-1, 500 meters; kayak pairs 500m/K-2, 500 meters; kayak fours 500m/K-4, 500 meters

Cycling
track (500m time trial, individual pursuit, points race, sprint, team pursuit); mountain bike (cross-country); road (individual time, individual road race)

Equestrian
team dressage; individual dressage; team jumping; individual jumping; team three-day event; individual three-day event

Fencing
individual epee; individual foil; team epee; team foil

Field Hockey

Gymnastics
team; all-around; balance beam; uneven bars; vault; floor exercise; rhythmic gymnastics (team & individual); trampoline

Judo
extra-lightweight (48kg); half-lightweight (52kg); lightweight (57kg); half-middleweight (63kg); middleweight (70kg); half-heavyweight (78kg); heavyweight (+78kg)

Modern Pentathlon
shooting; fencing; swimming; show jumping; running

Rowing
coxless pairs; single sculls; double sculls; eight; quadruple sculls; lightweight double sculls

Shooting
10m air rifle; 10m air pistol; double trap; 50m sport rifle three position; 25m sport pistol; trap; skeet shooting

Soccer

Softball

Table Tennis
singles; doubles

Tae Kwon Do
less than 49kg; 49kg to 57kg; 57kg to 67kg; over 67kg

Team Handball

Tennis
singles; doubles

Triathlon
1.5km swim; 40km cycle; 10km run

Volleyball
beach; indoor

Weightlifting
up to 48 kg; up to 53 kg; up to 58 kg; up to 63 kg; up to 69 kg; over 75 kg

Yachting/Sailing
women's mistral; women's europe; women's 470 ❦

---

sun, plants that turn toward: heliotrope, turnsole
sun, visible outer layer of: photosphere
sun, when planet is closest to: perihelion

sun, when planet is farthest from: aphelion
sunder: break, cleave, cut, disunite, divide, part, rend, rive, separate, sever, slice, split

sundial's upright blade: gnomon
sundown: dusk, evening, sunset, twilight
sundry: assorted, different, divers, diverse, manifold, many, miscellane-

ous, multifarious, myriad, numerous, separate, several, sundered, varied, various

sunglasses that darken when exposed to light: photochromic

sunken: below, depressed, hollow, lowered, submerged

sunken design and incised carving: intaglio

sunny: beaming, bright, cheerful, cheery, clear, fair, golden, happy, merry, optimistic, pleasant, shining, shiny, smiling, vivacious, warm

sunrise: dawn, daybreak, daylight, morn, morning, sunup

sunroom: solarium

sunset: dusk, eve, evening, nightfall, sundown, twilight

sunset, concerning: acronical

sunspot: macula

sunspot, darkest part of: umbra

sunspot, grayish outer part of: penumbra

sunstroke: insolation

super: A-one, cool, excellent, fantastic, great, keen, marvelous, neat, outstanding, sensational, superb, superintendent, terrific, tremendous, wonderful

superabundance: excess, flood, glut, overflow, plenty, plethora, superfluity, surplus

superannuate: retire

superannuated: aged, antiquated, obsolete, outdated, passé, senile

superb: A-one, elegant, excellent, exquisite, fine, glorious, grand, grandiose, imposing, lordly, luxurious, magnificent, majestic, marvelous, noble, outstanding, proud, regal, rich, sensational, splendid, standout, stately, supreme, wonderful

supercilious: arrogant, cavalier, condescending, disdainful, haughty, hoity toity, insolent, lofty, lordly, overbearing, proud, snobbish, snooty, superior, uppity

superficial: apparent, casual, cursory, desultory, flimsy, hasty, hollow, insignificant, pro forma, shallow, slight, surface, token, trite, trivial

superficial appearance: gloss, veneer

superficial beauty: gilt

superficially attractive: meretricious

superficially, done: cursory, perfunctory

superficially, person doing something: dabbler, dilettante

superfluity: abundance, excess, extravagance, luxury, overabundance, overflowing, plethora, superabundance, superfluous, surplus

superfluous: de trop, excess, excessive, excrescent, extra, extraneous, extravagant, gratuitous, inessential, needless, nonessential, redundant, spare, superabundant, supererogatory, superfluity, surplus, unnecessary, useless, worthless

superfluous person: fifth wheel

superfluous word: pleonasm

superhighway, European: autobahn, autoroute, autostrada

superhuman: bionic, divine, extraordinary, godlike, great, herculean, heroic, omnipotent, preternatural, supernatural, uncanny

superimpose: cover, overlap

superintendent: administrator, boss, caretaker, chief, custodian, director, foreman, forewoman, inspector, manager, overseer, super, supervisor, warden

superintendent of ancient Roman games: editor

superior: A-one, arrogant, best, better, boss, chief, choice, condescending, deluxe, dominant, elder, elevated, elite, exalted, exceeding, excellent, exceptional, exquisite, fine, greater, haughty, head, higher, higher up, insolent, marvelous, noteworthy, outstanding, predominant, preeminent, premium, senior, snobbish, supercilious, superlative, surpassing, transcendent, upper, uppity

superior in influence: preponderant

superior in rank, status, value: superordinate

superior of a convent: abbess

superlative: best, exaggerated, excellent, excessive, greatest, highest, optimum, outstanding, peak, peerless, supreme, unequaled, unmatched, unsurpassed, utmost

superlative suffix: -est

supernatural: abnormal, celestial, divine, extraordinary, magic, miraculous, mystic, mystical, mythical, occult, paranormal, phenomenal, preternatural, psychic, spiritual, superhuman, transcendental, uncanny

supernatural force, manifestation of: epiphany, revelation, visitation

supernatural or beyond normal experience or explanation: paranormal

supernatural phenomena, study of: parapsychology

supernatural powers: clairvoyance, cryptesthesia, ESP, extrasensory perception

supernatural powers, having: clairvoyant, psychic, visionary

supernatural practices, techniques: occult

supernumerary: extra

supersede: abandon, discard, displace, override, replace, succeed, supplant

superstition: fear, idolatry, irrationality, magic, notion, voodoo

superstitious belief or story of traditional folklore: old wives' tale

supervise: administer, boss, check, conduct, direct, govern, guide, inspect, manage, monitor, oversee, regulate, superintend

supervision: care, control, guidance, management, oversight

supervisor: administrator, boss, chief, foreman, forewoman, manager, overseer

supine: abject, apathetic, flat, horizontal, inactive, inattentive, inclined, indifferent, indolent, inert, languid, lethargic, listless, passive, prone, prostrate, reclining, sloping, sluggish

supplant: depose, displace, eject, oust, overthrow, remove, replace, substitute, succeed, supersede, undermine, usurp

supple: adaptable, agile, bendable, compliant, elastic, flexible, graceful, limber, lissom, lissome, lithe, malleable, nimble, plastic, pliable, pliant, resilient, springy, stretchy, versatile, yielding

supplement: accessory, add, addendum, addition, additive, annex, appendix, attachment, augment, complement, eke, enhance, extend, reinforce, rider, strengthen, subsidize

supplemental: adscititious, auxiliary, derivative, supporting

suppliant: asker, beggar, beseeching, petitioner, seeker, solicitor, suitor

supplicant appearing in early art: orant

supplication: appeal, entreaty, petition, plea, prayer, request, solicitation

supply: afford, aid, cache, cater, contribute, endue, equip, feed, fulfill, fund, furnish, give, help, hoard, inventory, load, lode, nourish, outfit, produce, provide, provision, purvey, reinforce, relief, replace, replenish, reserve, reservoir, satisfy, source, stock, stockpile, store, yield

supply commentary for: annotate

supply food: cater

supply oxygen: aerate

supply to excess: surfeit

supply, endless: cornucopia

supply, to re-: replenish

support: abet, abutment, adminicle, advocate, aid, alimony, anchor, assist, assistance, back, backing, base, beam, bear, bolster, boost, brace, buoy, buttress, carry, champion, cheer, cherish, column, comfort, confirm, console, corroborate, countenance, crutch, defend, embrace, encourage, endorse, endure, foster, foundation, friendship, help, hinge, keep, lift, living, maintain, nourish, nurture, patronize, pedestal, pillar, plint, post, prop, protect, protection, provide, reinforce, relief, sanction, second, shield, shore, side, stay, strengthen, subsidize, subsidy, substantiate, sustain, tolerate, tripod, trivet, uphold, verify, vindicate

support a cause: advance, advocate, champion, commend, espouse, propound

support a new cause: proselytize

support and sponsorship: patronage

support and unity of group: solidarity

support beam, heavy: pile

support financially: finance, patronize, sponsor, subsidize

support for lever that balances, lifts, moves: fulcrum

support for statue, column: pedestal, plinth

support for wood in fireplace: andiron, firedog

support from below: sustain, undergird, underpin

support or back up: confirm, corroborate, prove, substantiate, verify, vouch for

support or prop up: bolster, brace, buttress, reinforce

support or protection: aegis, auspices, patronage, sponsorship

support to ex-spouse: alimony, maintenance

support, financial: subsidy, subvention

support, one relying on another for: dependent

support, surgical: truss

support, upright: stanchion

supporter: abettor, abider, adherent, advocate, ally, bearer, booster, brace, exponent, follower, patron, proponent, seconder, suspender

supporter or pioneer, early: apostle

supporter or sympathizer: fellow traveler

supporter, athletic: jock, jockstrap

supporter, enthusiastic: aficionado, devotee, fan

supporter, enthusiastic cause: partisan, true believer

supporter, enthusiastic religious: votary

supporter, financial: angel, backer, patron, sponsor

supporter, hardworking: henchman, myrmidon, stalwart

supporters or patrons, group of: constituency

supporting: aiding, ancillary, auxiliary, collateral, corroborative

supporting balcony or cornice, bracket or block: cantilever

supporting beam: girder

supporting column, in man's form: telamon

supporting structure of bridge or arch: pier

suppose: allow, assume, believe, conceive, conclude, conjecture, consider, daresay, deem, expect, expectation, imagine, imply, intention, judge, opine, presume, suspect, think, understand

suppose from incomplete evidence: conjecture

supposed: alleged, assumed, conjectural, hypothetical, putative, reputed, supposititious, theoretical

supposition: assumption, conjecture, estimation, hypothesis, idea, implication, notion, postulate, proposition, surmise, theory

suppository: pessary

suppress: abolish, arrest, bridle, censor, check, choke, compose, conceal, crush, destroy, elide, exclude, extinguish, harass, hide, hugger-mugger, keep, keep back, kill, oppress, overpower, overthrow, prevent, prohibit, quash, quell, refrain, restrain, scotch, silence, smother, squelch, stifle, stop, stunt, subdue, withhold

supremacy: ascendancy, authority, control, dominance, domination, dominion, mastery, power, predominance, sovereignty, sway

supreme: best, chief, crucial, excellent, foremost, greatest, highest, last, maximum, paramount, peerless, preeminent, superb, ultimate, utmost

supreme good: summum bonum

surcease: cessation, defer, delay, desist, let up, postpone, refrain, respite, rest, stay, stop

surcharge: burden, impost, overcharge, tax

sure: assured, certain, confident, convinced, definite, dependable, enduring, fast, firm, indisputable, indubitable, inevitable, infallible, positive, reliable, rue, safe, secure, stable, steadfast, steady, strong, trustworthy, undoubted, unerring, unfailing, unfaltering

sureness: certitude

surety: assurance, bail, certainty, confidence, guarantee, guarantor, pledge, sponsor, surity

surf crashing on shore, roar of: rote

surf-n-turf item: fish, steak

surface: area, boundary, exterior, face, finish, outside, pave, skin, texture, top, veneer

surface depression: crater, dent

surface elegance: veneer

surface of a liquid, curved: meniscus

surface of gemstone, bone, tooth: facet

surface of substance, accumulation on: adsorption

surface, aged: burnish, patina

surface, break up: scarify

surface, on or near: superficial

surfeit: cloy, excess, glut, overabundance, overindulge, replete, sate, satiate, satiation, satiety, satisfy, superfluity, supply

surge: billow, pour, rise, rush, swell, tide, wave

surgery by freezing: cryosurgery

surgery of physical appearance: cosmetic surgery, plastic surgery

surgery on animals for research: vivisection

surgery, bone and muscle: orthopedics

surgery, breast removal: mastectomy

surgical cut: incision

surgical cutting for removal: ablation, amputation, excision, extirpation

surgical cutting or dividing of tissue: section

surgical knife: bistoury, scalpel

surgical method to close wound, join tissues: suture

surgical procedure removing all or part of the breast: mastectomy

surgical procedure removing all or part of the uterus: hysterectomy

surgical procedure using a dilator to expand cervix and a curette to scrape uterus: D&C, dilation and curettage

surgical replacement with artificial part: prosthesis

surgical thread: ligature, seton

surly: bearish, boorish, churlish, crabby, cross, crusty, discourteous, dour, glum, grouchy, gruff, grumpy, haughty, ill-humored, irritable, morose, rude, sour, sulky, sullen, testy, uncivil

surmise: assumption, attempt, believe, conclude, conclusion, conjecture, deduction, deem, guess, hypothesize, imagine, infer, inference, judge, notion, opinion, presume, speculation, suppose

surmount: ascend, best, clear, climb, conquer, defeat, exceed, excel, hurdle, leap, master, outdo, overcome, prevail, rise, scale, subdue, surpass, top, transcend, triumph, vanquish

surname: cognomen, family name

surname of father's side: patronymic

surname of mother's side: matronymic

surpass: beat, best, better, cap, eclipse, exceed, excel, outclass, outdo, outlive, outpace, outperform, outrank, outreach, outrun, outshine, overshadow, surmount, top, transcend, trump

surplus: excess, extra, leftover, over, overage, overflow, overstock, oversupply, plethora, remainder, reserve, spare, superfluity, surfeit

surplus merchandise: overage

surplus store: outlet

surprise: alarm, amaze, ambush, astonish, astound, bewilder, blow, bombshell, confound, curveball, dazzle, dumbfound, electrify, flabbergast, floor, fluster, miracle, nonplus, overcome, overwhelm, perplex, rattle, rivet, seize, shock, stagger, startle, storm, stun, unexpected, unsettle, wonder

surprise acquisition: trouvaille

surprise and confuse: disconcert, disorient, dumbfound, nonplus

surprise attack: ambush, coup de main, raid

surprise during wrongdoing, by: in flagrante delicto, red-handed

SURGICAL OPERATIONS

amniocentesis
apicectomy
appendectomy/appendicectomy
arterioplasty
autograft/autoplasty
cesarean section
cholecystectomy
cholelithotomy
colostomy
cordotomy
craniotomy
cryosurgery
cystectomy
D & C/dilatation and curettage
debridement
episiotomy
fenestration
gastrectomy
goniopuncture
hepatectomy
homograft/allograft/homoplasty
hysterectomy
ileostomy
iridectomy
labioplasty
laparotomy
laryngectomy
lithonephrotomy/nephrolithotomy
lobotomy/leukotomy
mastectomy
necrotomy
nephrectomy
neurotomy
oophorectomy/ovariectomy
orchidectomy/orchiectomy/
  testectomy
ostectomy
otoplasty
phlebotomy/venesection
pneumonectomy
rhinoplasty
rhizotomy
salpingectomy
thoracotomy
tracheostomy/tracheotomy
vasectomy ❧

---

surprise, shocking: bolt from the blue, bombshell, thunderclap

surprise, take by: ambush, waylay

surprise, taken by: caught napping, caught unawares, taken off guard

surprised: amazed, startled, taken aback

surprised and skeptical: disbelieving, incredulous

surprised, shocked: aghast, appalled, horrified

surprised, totally: flabbergasted, stunned, stupefied, thunderstruck

surprising character or event in plot: deus ex machina

surrender: abandon, acquiesce, capitulate, capitulation, cede, cession, concede, fall, foresake, relinquish, resign, submission, submit, succumb, vacate, waive, yield

surrender or relinquish: waiver

surrender or yield: capitulate, concede, submit

surrender possession of: cede

surrender without protest: acquiesce, kowtow, succumb

surrender, of absolute: unconditional

surreptitious: clandestine, concealed, covert, hidden, secret, sneaky, stealthy, undercover

surrogate: alternate, backup, delegate, deputy, expedient, proxy, replacement, substitute

surround: belt, beset, besiege, border, cincture, circle, circumscribe, circumvent, compass, corral, embosom, encase, encircle, enclose, encompass, engulf, envelop, environ, gird, hedge, hem in, inundate, invest, loop, ring, round, wrap

surround and include: comprise, embrace, encompass

surrounded by land: landlocked

surrounding: ambient

surrounding area: environs, outskirts, precincts, purlieus, vicinity

surrounding area of influence: ambit, compass, milieu, orbit, scope, sphere

surrounding band or ridge: cingulum

surroundings: ambience, area, atmosphere, climate, conditions, environment, environs, milieu, neighborhood, region, setting, vicinity

surroundings, adapt to: acclimatize

surveillance: espial, lookout, observation, spying, stakeout, track, vigil, watch

survey: analysis, assess, audit, canvass, compendium, consider, description, estimate, evaluate, examination, examine, exposition, gauge, inspect, inspection, measure, oversee, overview, poll, prospect, questionnaire, recce, reconnoiter, review, sample, scan, scrutinize, search, study, summarize, view

survey for information gathering: reconnaissance

survey of subject: conspectus

survey's printed form: questionnaire

surveyor's instruments: alidade, azimuth, level, range pole, tachymeter, target, tellurometer, theodolite, transit, vane

surveyor's map: plat

surveyor's mark of reference point: bench mark

survival: continuation, endurance, relic

survival of the fittest: natural selection

survive: continue, endure, exist, outlast, outlive, persevere, persist, remain, weather

survive and continue: subsist

surviving: extant, left over, remaining, residual, vestigial

surviving independently, capable of: viable

surviving item of history: artifact, relic, remnant

susceptibility or tendency toward something: predisposition

susceptible: affected, allergic, exposed, gullible, impressionable, inclined, influenced, liable, naive, open, prone, receptive, responsive, sensible, sensitive, subject, vulnerable

suspect: accused, believe, disbelieve, discredit, distrust, doubt, doubtful, dubious, fishy, guess, imagine, mistrust, presume, question, questionable, shaky, suppose, surmise, suspicious, theorize, think, uncertain, understand, wonder

suspend: adjourn, bar, cease, dangle, debar, defer, delay, discontinue, eliminate, expel, halt, hang, hold, hover, interrupt, postpone, shelve, stop, swing, table, waive, withhold

suspenders: braces, bretelles, galluses, garters, straps, supporters

suspense: anticipation, anxiety, apprehension, doubtful, mystery, tension, uncertainty, unease, worry

suspense, in: anxious, on tenterhooks

suspenseful last episode: cliffhanger

suspension: abeyance, delay, halt, intermission, interruption, moratorium, pause, postponement, remission, stay, stop, stoppage, termination

suspension of fine particles in fluid: colloid

suspension of liquid within liquid: emulsion

suspension of operation, temporary: abeyance

suspension of pain or punishment, temporary: reprieve

suspension of particles: dispersion

suspension or delay as a protest: moratorium

suspicion: apprehension, caution, concern, distrust, doubt, feeling, hint, hunch, inkling, intimation, jealousy, misgiving, mistrust, notion, shade, skepticism, surmise, tinge, touch, trace, uncertainty, uneasiness

suspicion, clear of: vindicate

suspicion, dispel: allay

suspicious: distrustful, doubtful, equivocal, farfetched, fishy, leery, mistrustful, questionable, shady, shaky, skeptical, suspect, wary

suspicious, being: chary, distrustful, doubting, leery, skeptical, wary

suspicious, overly: paranoid

sustain: abet, abide, back, bear, bolster, brace, comfort, confirm, console, contain, continue, corroborate, encourage, endure, experience, feed, foster, help, maintain, nourish, nurture, preserve, prolong, prop, strengthen, suffer, supply, support, survive, tolerate, undergo, uphold, withstand

sustenance: aliment, bread, living, maintenance, means, meat, nourishment, nutrition, provisions, subsistence, support, upkeep

suture: joint, line, seam, sew, stitch

svelte: graceful, lean, lissome, lithe, shapely, slender, slim, smooth, thin, trim

swab: clean, cotton, daub, mop, sailor, specimen, sponge, wash, wipe

swaddle: bandage, bind, restrain, restrict, swathe, warp, wrap

swag: booty, bundle, curtain, decoration, festoon, graft, loot, money, plunder, spoils

swagger: bluster, boast, boasting, brag, braggadocio, browbeat, bully, gasconade, gloat, hector, parade, pontificate, prance, sashay, strut, swank, swash, swashbuckle, swell

swallow: absorb, accept, bear, believe, take, tolerate, withdraw

swallow food or drink: chugalug, consume, devour, down, drink, eat, engulf, gulp, guzzle, imbibe, ingest, inhale, quaff, sip, swig, swill

swallowing: deglutition

swallowing difficulty: aphagia

swamp: deluge, engulf, flood, inundate, mire, overcome, overwhelm, saturate, submerge

swamp area: bayou, bog, everglades, fen, glade, marsh, marshland, mire, moor, morass, moss, muck, muskeg, quagmire, slough, slue, swale, vlei

swamp atmosphere: miasma

swamp gas: effluvium, methane

swamp, concerning a: paludial, paludinal, paludious

swamps, tree flourishing in: mangrove

swan family: anatidae

swan genus: cygnus, olor

swan, female: pen

swan, male: cob

swan, young: cygnet

swanky: chic, chichi, classy, elegant, exclusive, fancy, flashy, glamorous, luxurious, plush, posh, smart, snappy, snazzy, spiffy

swap: barter, exchange, substitute, switch, trade

swarm: army, assemble, congregate, crowd, drove, flock, group, horde, infest, mass, migrate, move, multitude, myriad, overrun, pack, pullulate, rush, shin, teem, throng, turnout

swarthy: dark, dark-skinned, darkish, dusky, swart

swashbuckler: adventurer, buccaneer, daredevil, pirate, ruffian, soldier, swordsman

swastika: fylfot, gammadion, hakenkreuz

swat: bash, bat, beat, belt, blow, hit, slug, smack, smash, strike, wallop, whack

swathe: bandage, bind, cover, drape, enfold, swaddle, wrap

sway: affect, authority, bend, bias, clout, command, control, direct, divert, dominance, dominion, fluctuate, fluctuation, oscillate, undulate, vacillate

swear: adjure, affirm, assert, attest, avow, declare, oath, pledge, promise, testify, threat, vouch, vow; blaspheme, curse, cuss, expletive

swear word: epithet, expletive, oath, profanity

sweat: emit, excrete, ooze, perspiration, perspire, seep, sudor, swelter, transude

sweat gland: eccrine gland

sweat-inducing: diaphoretic, sudorific

sweat-odor mask: deodorant

sweat, excessive: diaphoresis, hidrosis, sudation

sweat, smelly: bromidrosis, kakidrosis

sweater, collarless and buttoning: cardigan

sweater, long baggy: sloppy joe

sweaty: clammy, dripping, perspiring, soaked, sticky, wet

Sweden capital: Stockholm

sweep: bend, broom, brush, clean, compass, curve, dart, extend, extent, fly, glide, oar, orbit, range, remove, scope, scour, search, span, stretch, swoop, traverse, vacuum, whisk, zoom

sweeping: broad, complete, comprehensive, embracing, extensive, general, inclusive, large-scale, radical, vast, widespread

sweet: affectionate, agreeable, ambrosial, angelic, aromatic, attractive, beloved, candy, charming, confection, considerate, darling, dear, delectable, dessert, dulet, euphenic, fragrant, fresh, gentle, harmonious, heavenly, honeyed, kind, lovable, lovely, luscious, mellifluous, musical, pleasant, pleasing, pretty, scented, soothing, sugary, syrupy, thoughtful, wholesome, winsome

sweet potato: oca, ocarino, yam

sweet-smelling: fragrant

sweet-sounding: dulcet, euphonious, mellifluous, melodious

sweet talk: blarney, cajolery, coax, compliment, flattery

sweet, excessively: cloying, saccharine

sweeten: alleviate, appease, cleanse, conciliate, disinfect, enhance, freshen, honey, increase, mull, pacify, perfume, relieve, renew, soften, soothe, sugar, sugarcoat

sweetener, artificial: aspartame, cyclamate, saccharin

sweetheart: adorer, beau, boyfriend, companion, darling, dear, deary, doll, dreamboat, fiancé, fiancée, flame, girlfriend, honey, inamorata, inamorato, ladylove, lass, love, lover, paramour, rose, suitor, swain, truelove, valentine

sweets: candy, confectionery, desserts, goodies, preserves, sweetmeats

swell: accumulate, amplify, augment, awesome, balloon, bilge, billow, bloat, bulge, bulk, dandy, dilate, distend, enlarge, excellent, expand, extend, fabulous, fashionable, fine, good, grand, groovy, grow, heave, huff, increase, inflate, intensify, keen, marvelous, nifty, protuberance, puff, rise, stylish, super, surf, surge, terrific, wave, wonderful

swelling: abscess, boil, bubo, bulge, bump, contusion, corn, distention, edema, gibbous, growth, inflammation, intumescence, lump, node, puffiness, sty, tumefaction, tumor, wart

swelling in body tissues: edema

swelling in brain: hydrocephalus

swelling of an organ or part, natural: apophysis

swelling of lymph node: bubo

swelling of mucous membrane: polyp

swelling or knot: node, nodule, tubercle, tuberosity

swelling, reduction in: detumescence

swelter: boil, burn, fret, heat, languish, perspire, roast, stew, suffocate, sweat, wallow

sweltering: airless, burning, hot, humid, muggy, oppressive, scorching, sizzling, sticky, stifling, sultry, torrid

swerve: avert, deflect, deviate, digress, diverge, sheer, shift, sidestep, skew, stray, totter, turn, veer

swift: barrelling, brisk, expeditious, fast, fleet, flying, hasty, headlong, meteoric, prompt, pronto, quick, rapid, ready, reel, snappy, speedy, sudden

swig: draft, drink, gulp, guzzle, hoist, nip, swash, sway

swill: drench, drink, fill, flood, garbage, guzzle, mash, raft, rinse, slop, swash, wash

swim: abound, dip, float, paddle, reel, spin, wade

swimming: bathing, dizziness, floating, natation

swimming pool, indoor: natatorium

swimming stroke: back, breast, butterfly, crawl, dogpaddle, freestyle, side, trudgen

swimming underwater with equipment: skin diving

swimming with both legs kicking: scissors kick

swimming, dancelike: synchronized swimming

swindle: bamboozle, bilk, blackmail, bunco, cheat, con, con game, deceive, defraud, dupe, embezzle, fake, flimflam, fool, fraud, gip, gyp, hustle, mulct, rook, scam, shakedown, sham, shell game, skin game, spoof, steal, trick, victimize

swindle, money: defalcation, embezzlement, peculation

swindler: charlatan, cheat, chiseler, crook, finagler, forger, grifter, highbinder, imposter, knave, mountebank, rogue, scammer, shark, thief

swine: beast, boar, boars, brute, hog, pig, sow

swing: beat, dangle, fluctuate, flutter, handle, hang, knack, lurch, manage, maneuver, move, oscillate, pivot, rhythm, rock, rotate, stroke, suspend, sway, swivel, tempo, totter, trapeze, turn, undulate, vibrate, waver, whip, whirl, wobble

swing branch to branch: brachiate

swing to and fro: oscillate, waver

swinging: pendulous

swinging lever: pendulum

swipe: bash, blow, cop, filch, heist, hit, lever, lift, pilfer, snatch, steal, strike, swat

swirl: churn, curl, curve, eddy, roil, rotate, spin, turn, twirl, twist, whirl, whirlpool

swish: cane, classy, flog, hiss, posh, rustle, smart, sound, strike, swank, trendy, whip

switch: change, divert, exchange, rearrange, reversal, shift, sidetrack, substitute, swap, transfer, turn, turnabout

switch activated by electric signal: relay

switch, magnetic assembly used as a: solenoid

switch, to release a: trip

Switzerland's largest city: Zurich

swivel: pivot, rotate, spin, swing, turn, whirl

swiveling ball or wheel on furniture leg: caster

swollen: bloated, blown, bombastic, bulbous, bulging, bulgy, distended, enlarged, increased, inflamed, inflated, overblown, paunch, pompous, protuberant, puffy, tumescent, tumid, turgid, ventricular

swoon: blackout, coma, ecstacy, fade, faint, float, languish, overwhelmed, sleep, stupor, syncope

swoop: descend, dive, drop, grab, plummet, plunge, pounce, sweep

sword: bilbo, blade, brand, broadsword, claymore, creese, cutlass, dagger, dirk, dris, épée, falchion, foil, hanbger, rapier, saber, sabre, scimitar, toledo, weapon, yalaghan

sword belt worn across chest: baldric

sword blade, strong part of: forte

sword blade, weak part of: foible

sword combatant, ancient: gladiator

sword diagonally across body, carry: port

sword handle: haft, hilt

sword knob: pommel

sword-shaped: ensate, ensiform, gladiate, xiphoid

sword with one cutting edge: backsword

sword, pierce or stab lightly with: pink

swordsman: dueler, fencer, gladiator

sworn: affirmed, avowed, bound, confirmed

sworn statement: affidavit, deposition, oath

sworn written statement: affidavit

sybarite: epicure, hedonist, sensualist, voluptuary

sycophant: bootlicker, brownnoser, fawner, flatterer, flunky, hanger on, lackey, parasite, stooge, toady, yesman

syllable added to beginning of word: prefix

syllable added to end of word: suffix

syllable added to middle of word: infix

syllable deleted: apocope

syllable deleted at end: catalectic

syllable second to last: antepenult

syllable with an ictus: stress

syllable, accented: arsis

syllable, alphabet of characters with each representing a: syllabary

syllable, last: ultima

syllable, next to last: penult

syllable, of a stressed: accented, nuclear, tonic

syllable, omission of unstressed: elision

syllable, short: apocope, breve, elision, mora, systole

syllable, third from last in word: antepenult

syllable, unaccented: atonic

syllables for musical warmup: solfeggio, solmization

syllables into one, contraction of two: syneresis, synizesis

syllabus: abstract, compendium, digest, outline, plan, precis, program, statement, summary, synopsis

sylvan: forestlike, rustic, shady, wooded, woodsy, woody

sylvan deity: satyr

symbol: attribute, badge, breve, bullet, cedilla, centered dot, character, circumflex, creed, cross, dagger, diaeresis, diagram, dieresis, diesis, double dagger, em dash, emblem, en dash, figure, fist, gesture, hacek, hand, hieroglyph, icon, image, index, indication, letter, logo, macron, mark, mascot, motif, numeral, obelisk, paragraph mark, representation, sign, stamp, token, totem, trademark, type, umlaut, wedge

symbol &: ampersand

symbol *: asterisk

symbol ^: caret

symbol and its meaning: denotation

symbol in heraldry, embroidery: device

symbol in music, math, programming: notation

symbol of a company: logo, logotype

symbol of ancient Egyptian writing: hieroglyph

symbol of publisher on title page: colophon

symbol of upside-down e for pronunciation: schwa

symbol on a staff indicating pitch of notes: clef

symbol representing abstract idea: emblem

symbol representing idea or thing rather than sound: ideogram, ideograph

symbol representing word or phrase: logogram, logograph

symbol system for road signs: pasigraphy

symbol system for sounds and meanings, ancient: hieroglyphics

symbol used to represent a word, like @: grammalogue

symbol written above script: superscript

symbol written below script: subscript

symbol ~ representing word or word element previously spelled out: swung dash

symbol, nonverbal: glyph

symbol, venerated: totem

symbolic: emblematic, figurative, totemic

symbolic protection: security blanket

symbolic representation: allegory

symbolize: connote, emblemize, embody, epitomize, express, illustrate, mean, mirror, personify, represent, signify, suggest, typify

symbolize as something concrete or living: hypostatize, personify, reify

symbols and pictures, puzzle of: rebus

symbols and signs and what they represent, study of relationship between: semantics, semiotics

symbols in painting and poetry, use of: imagery

symmetrical: balanced, commensurable, equal, proportional, regular

symmetry: agreement, balance, beauty, conformity, congruity, equilibrium, evenness, harmony, order, proportion, rhythm

sympathetic: affectionate, altruistic, amenable, attuned, benignant, caring, comforting, compassionate, condolent, congenial, consonant, friendly, humane, kind, on the same page, on the same wavelength, pitying, responsive, sensitive, soft, tender, thoughtful, understanding, warm

sympathize: commiserate, condole, empathize, feel for, pity, support, understand

sympathy: accord, affinity, agreement, comfort, commiseration, compassion, condolence, empathy, favor, harmony, kindheartedness, kindness, mercy, pity, sensitivity, solace, sorrow, support, tenderness, understanding, warmth

sympathy and understanding: empathy, fellow feeling

sympathy for person in pain: commiseration, condolence

sympathy or pity, feelings of: pathos

sympathy, arousing: pathetic

symphony: band, concert, harmony, music, orchestra

symposium: banquet, conference, debate, discussion, forum, meeting, parley

symptom: ache, evidence, fever, indication, mark, sign, signal, syndrome, token, warning

symptom of attack or disease, early: prodrome

symptom of disease or condition: syndrome

symptoms of a disease, study of: symptomatology

symptoms, hysteria-caused: mimesis

symptoms, not manifesting: subclinical

synagogue: assembly, building, church, community, congregation, religion, schul, shul

synagogue area from which services are conducted: almemar, bema

synagogue singer: cantor

synchronize: agree, coincide, concur, simultaneous

synchronized lamp: strobe

synchronous: coexistent, concomitant, concurrent, contemporary, identical, simultaneous

syncopated early form of jazz: ragtime

syndicate: alliance, association, cartel, chain, coalition, committee, company, conglomerate, council, gang, group, organization, pool, ring, trust, union

syndrome: ailment, condition, disease, disorder, malady, problem, sickness, symptom

synod: assembly, body, committee, conclave, convocation, council, meeting

synonym book: thesaurus

synonymous: alike, correspondent, equivalent, identical, interchangeable, like, similar

synopsis: abridgement, abstract, aperçu, brief, compendium, digest, epitome, outline, plan, précis, review, rundown, summary, syllabus, view

synopsis of a process: schema

synopsis of dramatic plot: scenario

syntax: arrangement, order, pattern, rules, structure, system

syntax of words: collocation

synthesis: blend, combination, composition, deduction, forming, organization, structure, union, whole

synthesis of parts that constitute a whole not derived by a simple sum of the parts: gestalt

synthesize: amalgamate, blend, combine, fuse, incorporate, integrate, manufacture

synthetic: artificial, constructed, contrived, ersatz, fabricated, man-made, manufactured, nylon, Orlon, prepared, unnatural

syphillis lesion: chancre

syphillis, concerning: luetic, syphilitic

syringe, skin-injection: hypodermic

syrup: glucose, molasses, sorghum, sweetness, treacle

syrup of pomegranate for flavoring cordials: grenadine

system: aggregation, arrangement, classification, code, hypothesis, manner, method, network, operation, order, orderliness, organization, pattern, philosophy, plan, procedure, process, regimen, routine, rule, scheme, setup, strategy, technique, theory, whole

system of diet, exercise, etc.: regimen

system of fifteenth through nineteenth century Europe, political and economic: feudal system, feudalism

system of government: regime

system of inflections, syntax, and word formation of language: grammar

system of morals: ethics

system of phonetic notation for hearing-impaired: visible speech

system of symbols: notation

system, archetypical example as model for: paradigm

system, inevitable deterioration of a: entropy

systematic: analytical, businesslike, designed, efficient, logical, methodical, neat, ordered, orderly, organized, standardized

systematic procedure of natural phenomenon: regimen

systematize: alphabetize, arrange, catalog, classify, design, methodize, order, organize, plan, rationalize

Tt

tab: account, bill, check, cost, invoice, price, record, score, statement, tally; bookmark, clip, flap, label, loop, strip, tag

tabernacle: church, habitation, house of prayer, niche, reliquary, sanctuary, shelter, shrine, temple, tent

table: appendix, chart, graph, index, list, record, schedule, spread, synopsis, tabulation; bench, buffet, console, counter, desk, escritoire, furniture, lectern, secretary, sideboard, slab, stand; defer, delay, shelve

table of chemical elements: periodic table

table or column arrangement, concerning: tabular

table wine: claret, rosé, vin ordinaire

table with hinged sides or ends: drop-leaf table

table, insertion to increase size of: leaf

table, sideboard or buffet: credenza

table, thick rectangular with block legs: Parsons table

tableau: description, illustration, image, picture, scene, view

tables, graduated stacking: nest

tablet: book, notebook, pad, plaque, slab, slate; capsule, lozenge, medicine, pastille, pellet, pill, troche

tableware: bowl, China, cup, dish, dishes, disk, flatware, fork, glass, knife, plate, saucer, silver, silverware, spoon, utensils

taboo: anathema, ban, forbidden, illegal, ineffable, interdiction, no-no, outlaw, prohibited, proscribed, regulation, restraint, restriction, unacceptable, unmentionable

tabulate: arrange, categorize, chart, classify, figure, grade, index, list, order, rank

tacit: allusive, implicit, implied, inferred, intimated, silent, suggested, understood, unexpressed, unspoken

taciturn: aloof, close-mouthed, laconic, mute, quiet, reserved, reticent, silent, speechless, unexpressive, unvocal, withdrawn

tack on: add, append, brad, fasten, link, nail, pin, secure, thumbtack

tackle: accoutrements, apparatus, collar, derrick, equipment, gear, harness, linesman, material, outfit, paraphernalia, rigging, sack, tack, tools

tackle, to: attack, attempt, encounter, grapple, grasp, secure, undertake

tacky: adhesive, cheap, cheesy, crude, dowdy, gaudy, grubby, messy, ragged, ratty, shabby, slovenly, sticky, tasteless, unkempt, untidy, vulgar

tact: acumen, adroitness, delicacy, diplomacy, discernment, discretion, discrimination, finesse, judgment, perception, poise, refinement, savoir faire, sensitivity, smoothness, suavity

tact and refinement: finesse

tact in saying or doing right thing: savoir faire

tactful: careful, considerate, diplomatic, discreet, judicious, polished, politic, prudent, sensitive, skillful, suave, thoughtful

tactic: gambit, ploy, stratagem

tactical: approach, attack, diplomatic, expedient, maneuver, plan, policy, prudent, strategy, technique

tactless: brash, careless, clumsy, crude, discourteous, gruff, impolite, inconsiderate, indiscreet, insensitive, rude, thoughtless, undiplomatic

tag: accompany, add, affix, append, attach, badge, brand, designate, dog, fasten, flap, follow, game, identify, label, logo, mark, motto, nickname, pursue, shadow, sticker, strip, stub, tab, tail, ticket, title, touch, voucher

tail: appendage, back, backside, bottom, butt, buttocks, cauda, coda, conclusion, end, extremity, follow, last, posterior, pursue, rear, retinue, rudder, seat, shadow, stalk, tag

tail adapted for grabbing, of a: prehensile

tail of airplane: empennage

tail of some animals, bushy tip of: switch

tail, bushy: brush, bush

tail, clipped or bobbed animal: dock

tail, concerning a: caudal, caudate

tail, distinctly shaped or marked: flag

tail, fleshy part of animal: dock

tail, stubby erect: scut

tailless: acaudal

tailor: adapt, adjust, alter, conform, design, fashion, modify, sew, shape, style; clothier, dressmaker, sartor, seamster, seamstress

tailor, concerning a: sartorial

tails on coin or medal: reverse, verso

taint: blemish, blow, blur, cloud, color, contaminate, corrupt, damage, decay, defile, dirty, discredit, disgrace, harm, hurt, imbue, infect, poison, pollute, ruin, smear, smudge, soil, spoil, spot, stain, stigma, sully, tarnish, tinge, tint, touch, trace, vitiate

take: absorb, accept, accompany, adopt, affirm, apprehend, appropriate, attach, attack, attain, attempt, attract, avail, bear, bilk, booty, borrow, buy, captivate, capture, carry, catch, charm, cheat, choose, commandeer, conduct, confiscate, contract, convey, deceive, deduce, deduct, defraud, derive, detract, draw, enchant, endure, engage, extract, fascinate, gate, get, grab, grasp, grip, gross, gyp, haul, have, income, infer, kidnap, nab, net, obtain, pilfer, plunder, pocket, prefer, proceeds, profit, quantity, receipts, remove, revenue, rick, root, secure, seize, select, share, snare, snatch, steal, stomach, strike, submit, subtract, swallow, swindle, swipe, tolerate, touch, transport, trap, try, undergo, understand, usurp, win, withstand

take aback: astonish, overwhelm, startle, surprise

take advantage of: capitalize on, deceive, dupe, exploit, fool, hoodwink, use

take after: copy, emulate, follow, imitate, resemble, simulate

take apart: analyze, destroy, disassemble, dismantle, dismember, dismount, dissect, ruin, thrash, undo

take away: belittle, decrease, deduct, derogate, detract, diminish, discount, lessen, minus, reduce, seize, subtract

take away parts to repair another piece of equipment: cannibalize

take away possession: expropriate

take back: abjure, recall, recant, renege, repossess, restore, retract, return, reverse, withdraw

take back a statement: disavow, recant, retract, revoke

take care of: do for, foster, heed, mind, nurse, see to, tend, watch

take charge of: manage, operate

take down: disassemble, dismantle, humble, lower, note, record, reduce, transcribe

take exception: demur, disfavor, object, oppose, resent

take for oneself without permission: appropriate, arrogate

take-home pay: net, stipend

take in: absorb, accept, comprehend, digest, earn, embrace, grasp, include, inhale, see, understand, welcome

take notice: heed, note, observe, recognize, regard

take off: decamp, depart, doff, flee, hightail, leave, lessen, pare, remove, sail, strip, vamoose

take on: accept, acquire, add, adopt, assume, attack, battle, embrace, engage, face, fight, hire, oppose, shoulder, tackle, undertake

take on, as debt: incur

take over: commandeer, have, overthrow, seize, usurp

take pains: attempt, endeavor, strive

take place: happen, occur, supervene

take stock: appraise, audit, check, enumerate, examine, inventory, review, study, survey

take turns: alternate, rotate, share

take under advisement: consider

take up: adopt, commence, elevate, embrace, hoist, lift, occupy, raise, reduce, resume, shorten, start, tackle

takeoff: ascent, burlesque, caricature, climb, departure, imitation, lampoon, launch, mockery, parody, satire, spoof

tale: account, anecdote, canard, epic, exaggeration, fable, fabrication, falsehood, fib, fiction, gest, geste, gossip, history, legend, lie, myth, narration, narrative, novel, parable, report, romance, rumor, saga, speech, story, untruth, yarn

tale of lament or prophecy of doom: jeremiad

tale to teach moral or religious lesson: fable, parable

talent: ability, aptitude, aptness, art, attribute, capacity, charisma, endowment, expertise, faculty, feature, flair, forte, genius, gift, inventiveness, knack, nose, passion, performer, power, proficiency, skill, strength

talent, developed: bent, facility, flair, knack, penchant

talent, natural: aptitude, attribute, endowment, forte, gift, métier, specialty

talented: able, accomplished, adept, artistic, clever, gifted, skilled, smart

talented person: prodigy

talented, multi-: versatile

talisman: amulet, charm, fetish, grigri, jiji, lucky, mascot, rabbit's foot, scarab, symbol, token

talk: address, babble, banter, blab, bunk, chat, chatter, chitchat, colloquy, communicate, confer, conference, confess, consult, conversation, converse, council, debate, dialect, dialogue, discourse, discuss, discussion, express, gab, gabble, gossip, hearsay, huddle, inform, interface, interview, jargon, lecture, lingo, meeting, monologue, mumble, negotiate, noise, orate, palaver, patter, powwow, prate, pronounce, rant, rap, rave, reason, report, rumor, sermon,

speak, speech, spiel, symposium, tattle, tongue, utter, verbalize, verbiage, voice, yap

talk back: remark, reply, sass

talk big: boast, brag, crow, gloat

talk evasively: equivocate, hedge, waffle

talk to a crowd: address

talk to oneself: soliloquize

talk under one's breath: mutter

talk unfavorably about another: backbite

talk, insatiable urge to: cacoëthes loquendi

talk, rapid and incoherent: chatter, drivel, gabble, gibber, jabber, prate

talkative: chatty, diffuse, effusive, expansive, flippant, gabby, garrulous, gassy, glib, gossipy, long-winded, loquacious, mouthy, profuse, prolix, rambling, verbose, vocal, voluble, wordy

talkative bird: myna

talkativeness, excessive: logorrhea

talked-about object: conversation piece

talker: babbler, chatterbox, chatterer, debater, lecturer, magpie, orator, speaker

talker seen on television: talking head

talker, constant: blatteroon

talking and open: communicative, forthcoming

tall: elevated, gangling, giant, grand, great, high, lanky, large, lofty, long, rangy, skyhigh, towering

tall building: high rise

tallow: fat, smear, suet, wax

tally: account, add, agree, catalog, check, correspond, count, counterpart, estimate, grade, itemize, jibe, label, list, mark, match, notch, number, numerate, poll, reckon, reckoning, record, register, score, tab, tabulate, total

talon: claw, hook, nail

tame: amenable, bland, boring, break, bust, civilized, compliant, conquer, control, cultivated, curb, discipline, docile, domestic, domesticate, domesticated, dominate, dull, gentle, harmless, housebroken, humble, insipid, manage, master, meek, mild, obedient, prune, resigned, servile, subdue, submissive, suppress, timid, tractable, train, unexciting, uninteresting

tamper: alter, bribe, corrupt, fiddle, fix, influence, interfere, intervene, manipulate, meddle, rig, tinker

tan: beige, bronze, brown, color, cream, ecru, khaki, sun, sunburn, toast

tang: aroma, bite, flavor, hint, nip, odor, pang, pike, piquancy, prong, quality, relish, ring, scent, shank, smack, smattering, sting, taste, tinge, tongue, trace, twang, zest

tangible: actual, concrete, corporeal, material, palpable, perceptible, physical, real, solid, substantial, tactile, tactual, touchable, visible

tangle: altercation, argument, coil, complicate, embroil, enmesh, ensnare, ensnarl, entrap, intertwine, involve, jam, jungle, kink, knot, labyrinth, mat, maze, mesh, muddle, muss, ravel, skein, sleave, snare, snarl, trap, twist, web

tank: aquarium, basin, cauldron, cistern, container, jail, pond, pool, receptacle, reservoir, vat, vehicle, weapon

tank for solid waste: septic tank

tank or well for water: cistern

tankard: can, cup, flagon, flask, mug, stein, stoup

tantalize: allure, bail, captivate, charm, entice, frustrate, pester, provoke, taunt, tease, tempt, titillate, torment

tantamount: alike, comparable, equal, equivalent, identical, parallel, same

tantrum: anger, conniption, fit, hissy, outburst, rage, rampage, scene, storm

tap monotonously: thrum

tap on barrel: faucet, spigot

tap, valve regulating: stopcock

tape: band, bandage, bind, binding, ribbon, seal, video

tape for protecting surfaces during painting: masking tape

tape holder: reel

tape or material of safety belts: webbing

tape recording converting sounds to numbers: digital recording

tape recording distortion: flutter, wow

taper: abate, acuminate, candle, decrease, diminish, dwindle, lessen, light, narrow, reduce, wick

taper off: diminish, fade, recede, subside, wane, weaken

tapestry: arras, curtain, dosser, drapery, Gobelin, hanging

tapeworm: helminth

tapioca source: cassava, manioc

taproom: bar, barroom, lounge, pub, saloon, tavern

tar: asphalt, gob, mariner, pitch, sailor, salt, seadog, seafarer, seaman, taint, water dog

taradiddle: falsehood, lie

tardy: behindhand, belated, delayed, dilatory, lagging, late, overdue, remiss, slack, slow, sluggish, unpunctual

target: aim, ambition, bull's-eye, butt, center, destination, goal, intention, mark, object, objective, pigeon, quota, scapegoat, sight, victim

target with no chance: sitting duck

target, archery: clout

target's white center: blank, bull's-eye

tariff: assessment, charge, commission, duty, expense, fee, levy, price, rate, schedule, system, tax, toll

tarnish: besmirch, blemish, cloud, contaminate, corrode, corrupt, damage, darken, defile, dim, diminish, dirty, discolor, discredit, dull, fade, injure, mar, muddy, smear, smirch, smudge, soil, spoil, spot, stain, sully, taint

tarnish, as reputation: defile

taro plant or root: eddo, elephant ear

tarot card fortune-telling: cartomancy

tarpaulin: canvas, coat, cover, dropcloth, oilcloth, sailcloth

tarry: abide, bide, dally, dawdle, defer, delay, dwell, filibuster, lag, linger, lodge, loiter, loll, pause, procrastinate, remain, rest, sojourn, stay, visit, wait

tarsus: ankle

tart: acerb, acerbic, acid, bitter, cutting, girl, pastry, pie, piquant, poignant, prostitute, pungent, sever, sharp, snappy, sour, tangy, turnover, vinegary

Tarzan mate: Jane

task: assignment, burden, chore, duty, effort, employment, errand, function, job, labor, load, mission, objective, project, stint, study, tax, test, toil, undertaking, work

taskmaster: boss, disciplinarian, driver, foreman, forewoman, martinet, master, monitor, overseer

taste: appetite, bent, bit, bite, dash, delicacy, desire, discernment, eat, elegance, experience, flair, flavor, fondness, gusto, hint, hunger, inclination, judgment, liking, mouthful, nibble, palate, partake, partiality, preference, relish, sample, savor,

TARGET SPORTS

archery
biathlon
billiards
boccie
bowling
candlepin bowling
carom billards
clay pigeon shooting/skeet shooting/ trapshooting
croquet
crossbow archery
curling
darts
duckpin bowling
frisbee golf
golf
horseshoe pitching
lawn bowling
paintball
pistol shooting
pool
quoits
rifle and target shooting
shuffleboard
skeet shooting
skydiving
snooker
trapshooting ❦

---

scent, shade, sip, smack, spice, sprinkling, stomach, style, suggestion, tang, test, tinge, touch, trace, try, yearning, yen, zest

taste, concerning sense of: gustatory

taste, having good: discerning, discriminating

taste, salty or spicy to: savory

taste, sharp and spicy: piquant, tart

taste, sharp or harsh to: acrid, pungent

tasteful: attractive, classy, delectable, elegant, exquisite, pleasing, refined, savory, stylish

tasteful opulence: elegance

tasteful workmanship: artistry

tasteless: bland, crude, disgusting, dull, flat, flavorless, gross, inelegant, insipid, offensive, raunchy, tacky, tawdry, unpalatable, unrefined, vapid, vulgar

tasteless writing: pap

tastes, broad: catholic

tasty: appetizing, delectable, delicious, flavorsome, luscious, palatable, sapid, savory, scrumptious, toothsome, yummy, zestful

tattered: dilapidated, disheveled, disrupted, frayed, frazzled, ragged, ripped, shabby, shaggy, shredded, squalid, threadbare, torn

tattle: babble, blab, chat, chatter, hearsay, leak, prate, prattle, report, snitch, squeal, talk, tell

tattletale: bigmouth, blabbermouth, busybody, informer, squealer, stoolie, talebearer, tattler, whistleblower

taunt: bait, banter, bother, comeback, crack, deride, gibe, insult, jeer, jibe, mock, needle, offend, provoke, rag, razz, reply, reproach, ridicule, sneer, tease, tempt, torment, twit, upbraid

taut: close, drawn, firm, neat, rigid, snug, stiff, strained, stretched, tense, tidy, tight

tavern: bar, barroom, bistro, cabaret, drinkery, establishment, inn, lounge, pub, restaurant, roadhouse, saloon, taproom

tavern or bar, small, in Spain and Southwestern U.S.: cantina

tavern or restaurant, small: bistro, brasserie

tawdry: cheap, chintzy, crass, gaudy, gross, pretentious, showy, tacky, tasteless, vulgar

tawny: beige, bronze, brown, brownish, dusky, olive, swarthy, tanned

tax: accuse, assess, assessment, burden, cess, charge, contribution, custom, demand, deplete, difficulty, drain, dues, duty, excise, exhaust, expense, fee, fine, impost, levy, load, obligation, onus, overload, reproach, settle, strain, stress, tariff, tithe, toll, weight

tax deduction from income: withholding

tax on commodity within a country: excise

tax types: capital gains, cigarette, city, corporation, county, excise, federal, gas, geld, income, inheritance, luxury, property, sales, sin, Social Security, state, tallage, toll

tax which others pay, free from a: exempt

tax, impose or collect a: levy

taxable amount increases, decreasing proportionately as: regressive

taxable amount increases, increasing proportionately as: progressive

taxes, avoiding paying: evasion

taxes, repayment of part of paid: rebate, refund

taxicab: automobile, cab, car, hack, taxi, vehicle

taxing: burdensome, demanding, difficult, onerous, tiring, tough, troublesome, trying, wearing

tea: beverage, brew, Cha, drink, function, gathering, marijuana, Oolong, party, pekoe, reception, refreshment

tea urn: samovar

tea variety: Assam, bohea, cambric, Ceylon, Darjeeling, Earl Grey, ginger, ginseng, green, herb, Hyson, jasmine, Oolong, Paraguay, pekoe, sage, sassafras, Souchong, tisane

tea, to steep: infuse

teach: coach, demonstrate, develop, direct, discipline, drill, edify, educate, enlighten, explain, guide, inculcate, indoctrinate, inform, instill, instruct, nurture, preach, prepare, school, show, train, tutor

teach forcefully: inculcate, instill

teach forcefully new beliefs: brainwash, indoctrinate

teach to encourage improvement: edify, enlighten

teacher: coach, director, edifier, educator, guide, guru, instructor, lecturer, maestro, master, mentor, pedagog, pedagogue, preacher, preceptor, prof, professor, pundit, rabbi, schoolmaster, swami, trainer, tutor

teacher, itinerant: peripatetic

teacher, narrow-minded: pedagogue

teacher, non-faculty: docent

teacher, private: tutor

teacher, spiritual: guru

teaching: curriculum, didactics, discipline, education, instruction, pedagogy, schooling, training, tuition, tutelage; belief, doctrine, philosophy, precept

teaching by discovery: heuristics

teaching during sleep: hypnopedia

teaching for slower learners: remedial

teaching reading and spelling based on sound: acoustics, phonics

team: alliance, associate, association, ball club, brood, bunch, carriage, clique, club, coalition, collaborate

team animal: mascot

teammate: ally, collaborator, colleague, couple, crew, flock, foursome, gang, group, join, lineup, merge, pair, partner, partners, rig, side, squad, staff, string, unit, wagon, yoke

teapot cover: tea cozy

tear: claw, cleave, cut, damage, divide, fissure, gash, lacerate, rend, rip, rupture, separate, sever, shred, slit, snag, split, sunder

tear apart: asunder, rend, rip, rive

tear down: demolish, denigrate, destroy, level, raze, ruin, shatter, smash, wreck

tear into shreds: tatter

teardrop-shaped: guttiform

tearful: blubbering, crying, lachrymose, lamenting, maudlin, sad, snively, sobbing, sorrowful, weeping, weepy, whimpering

tears, concerning: lachrymal

tease: aggravate, annoy, badger, bait, banterer, bedevil, bother, card, chaff, coax, disentangle, disturb, gibe, harass, haze, heckle, importune, irk, irritate, josh, kid, nag, needle, pester, plague, provoke, rag, razz, rib, roast, ruffle, tantalize, taunt, torment, toy, twit, vex, worry

tease good-naturedly: josh, rag, rib

tease mockingly: gibe, taunt, torment

teasing way: persiflage

teasing, playful: badinage

technical: complicated, industrial, mechanical, scientific, specialized, technological

technical knockout: TKO

technical vocabulary: jargon, nomenclature, terminology

technique: approach, delivery, execution, fashion, formula, manner, method, mode, procedure, style, tactics, way

technologically, most advanced: cutting edge

technology hater: Luddite

technology, biological and medical: bioengineering

tedious: arid, bored, boring, boorish, dreary, dry, dull, exhausting, humdrum, irksome, laborious, long, monotonous, prolix, prosaic, prosy, slow, tiresome, tiring, unexciting, uninteresting, wearisome

tedium: boredom, dreariness, dullness, ennui, monotony, routine, tediousness

teed off: drove, irate, irked, mad, riled, sore

teem: abound, abundant, bristle, crawl, drain, empty, fill, full, gush, lead, overflow, pack, pour, produce, prosper, swarm

teeming: abounding, abundant, alive,

TEAM SPORTS

American football/ football	court tennis/royal tennis	flag football football	netball pelota	softball speedball
Australian-rules football	crew	Gaelic football	polo	stickball
bandy	cricket	handball	pushball	stoolball
baseball	croquet	hooverball	relay race	team handball
basketball	curling	hurling/hurley	roller hockey	touch football
beach volleyball	cycle polo	ice hockey	rounders	ultimate Frisbee
bobsledding	doubles tennis	jai alai	rugby/royal football	volleyball
Canadian football	Eton wall gamefield hockey	kickball	shinny/shinty	water polo
canoe polo	fives	korfball lacrosse	soccer/association football	whiffleball yachting ❦

bristling, bursting, bustling, crawling, crowded, full, overflowing, plentiful, prolific, replete, rife, swarming

teen maturing phase: adolescence

teeny: diminutive, microscopic, miniature, minute, small, tiny, wee

teeter: dangle, falter, flutter, lurch, quiver, reel, rock, saver, seesaw, stagger, stammer, sway, topple, totter, tremble, vacillate, wobble

teeth: canines, cogs, dentures, fangs, grinders, ivories, molars, pearly whites, sprockets, tusks

teeth arrangement: dentition

teeth fit with closed jaws: occlusion

teeth gap: diastema

teeth incrustation: tartar

teeth replacement, anchored: bridge, bridgework

teeth straightening, dentist for: orthodontist

teeth string: dental floss

teeth with sharp edges: carnassials

teeth, false: dentures

teeth, film of mucus and bacteria on: plaque

teeth, getting two sets of: diphyodont

teeth, grind: gnash

teeth, person with buck: gubbertush

teeth, pronounced gap between: diastema

teeth, ridged: serration

teeth, spaces between: embrasures

teeth, surrounding: periodontal

teeth, yellowish deposit of organic particles in salts on: tartar

teething: dentition

teetotaler: abstainer, prohibitionist

telegram: cable, letter, message, wire

telegraph signal: cable, dash, dot, Morse, signal, wire

telepathy: clairvoyance, cryptesthesia, ESP, extrasensory perception, foresight, insight, precognition, premonition, prescience, second sight, sixth sense, telesthesia

telepathy, study of: parapsychology

telephone: buzz, call, dial, glass, mouthpiece, ring, telescope

telephone book, e.g.: directory

telephone inventor: Bell

telephone link by computer: modem

telephone link for emergencies: 911, hot line

telephone part getting incoming signals: receiver

telephone part of curved metal clip, old-fashioned: finger stop

telephone part of two buttons on cradle, old-fashioned: plungers

telephone part that depresses to cut off connection: cradle switch

telephone part that vibrates in response to sound: diaphragm, tympanum

telephone pound key: octothorpe

telephone with television screen: videophone

telescope attached to larger one, small: finder

telescope building: observatory

telescope eyepiece: ocular

telescope inventor: Galileo

telescope lens nearest object being viewed: objective

telescope, small: spyglass

telescope's tube within a tube: drawtube

television: boob tube, box, cable, console, telly, tube, TV, video

television broadcast that is all text: teletext, videotex, viewdata

television cabinet: console

television captioning for hearing-impaired: closed captioning

television cuing device: TelePrompTer

television dramatization based on fact: docudrama

television facilities for use by public: public access

television horizontal scan lines: raster

television image unit: pixel

television live broadcast: relay

television program with factual or historical subject matter: documentary

television program, prerecorded: transcription

television program, spoken matter that links parts of: continuity

television ratings period: sweeps

television screen brightness: contrast

television screen sharpness: definition

television system for security or within building: closed-circuit television

television tape recording: videotape

television tube: cathode-ray tube

tell: acquaint, advise, announce, articulate, assure, betray, bid, blab, calculate, chat, command, communicate, confess, confide, decide, deem, describe, dictate, direct, discern, disclose, divulge, enumerate, explain, express, inform, instruct, mention, narrate, notify, order, post, publish, recite, recognize, recount, relate, repeat, report, request, reveal, say, speak, state, talk, tattle, utter, warn

tell a secret: disclose, divulge, reveal

tell a story: narrate, recite, recount, relate

tell and reveal: divulge

tell apart: differentiate, discriminate, distinguish

tell off: berate, chide, criticize, rebuke, reprimand, reprove, scold, upbraid

tell on: rat, tattle

teller: ATM, bank clerk, cashier, clerk

telling: cogent, conclusive, convincing, crucial, decided, definite, devastating, effective, forceful, important, powerful, significant, solid, sound, striking, valid

telltale: busybody, clock, gossip, hint, important, indication, informer, revealing, sign, squealer, suggestion, talebearer, tattler, tattletale

temblor: quake

temerarious: adventurous, bold, brash, daring, foolhardy, heedless, rash, reckless, venturesome

temerity: audacity, boldness, brass, carelessness, cheek, effrontery, foolhardiness, gall, heedlessness, nerve, rashness, venturesomeness

tempe: pagoda, ziggurat

temper: adapt, adjust, assuage, attune, chasten, compose, control, curb, dilute, ease, mitigate, moderate, modify, regulate, restrain, season, soften, soothe, tone; anger, asperity, calmness, complexion, composure, coolness, dander, disposition, ease, emotion, fit, fury, humor, ire, irritability, irritation, makeup, mind, mood, outburst, passion, rage, spirit, wrath

temper a material: anneal, harden, strengthen, toughen

temper tantrum: hissy fit, scene

temper, bad: ill humor, irascibility, pique

temperament: attitude, character, complexion, constitution, disposition, emotion, humor, makeup, mood, nature, outlook, personality, spirit, state, tendency

temperamental: emotional, excitable, explosive, fickle, irritable, moody, sensitive, touchy, undependable, unstable, volatile

temperance: abnegation, abstinence, constraint, control, moderation, prohibition, restraint, sobriety

temperate: abstemious, calm, clement, collected, continent, cool, easygoing, even, fair, fever, gentle, medium, mild, moderate, modest, pleasant, reasonable, restrained, sober, steady, temperature, unexcessive, unextreme, warm, warmth

temperate in eating and drinking: abstemious

temperature control: thermostat

temperature measurement for estimating energy needs: degree-day

temperature scales: Celsius, centigrade, Fahrenheit, Kelvin

temperature -459.67 Fahrenheit -273.15 Centigrade: absolute zero

temperature with wind index: wind chill, windchill

temperature, abnormally high body: hyperpyrexia, hyperthermia

temperature, abnormally low body: hypothermia

temperature-controlled container: incubator

tempered: moderated

tempered, quick-: hair-trigger, irascible, volatile

tempest: agitation, blizzard, commotion, furor, gale, hurricane, rage, squall, storm, thunderstorm, tumult, turmoil, upheaval, uproar, wind, windstorm

tempestuous: agitated, blustering, emotional, fiery, furious, heated, intense, raging, rough, stormy, tumultuous, turbulent, uncontrolled, violent, wild

temple: cathedral, chapel, church, fane, forehead, hieron, house of God, mosque, naos, pagoda, pantheon, sanctuary, shrine, synagogue, tabernacle, ziggurat

temple of Far East with curving stacked roofs: pagoda

temple shawl: talith

temple slave of ancient Greece: hierodule

temple, Jewish: tabernacle

tempo: beat, clip, meter, momentum, pace, pulse, rate, speed, time, timing

tempo and volume gradually decreased: calando

tempo-keeping device: metronome

tempo, moderately slow: andante

tempo, quick and lively: allegro

tempo, slow: adagio

temporal: civil, earthly, ephemeral, fleeting, laic, lay, material, momentary, mundane, passing, physical, profane, secular, temporary, transitory, worldly

temporarily: for a time, pro tem, pro tempore

temporary: acting, ad interim, brief, ephemeral, expedient, extemporaneous, fleeting, improvised, interim, limited, makeshift, provisional, short, stopgap, temporal, tentative, transient

temporary bridge: gangplank

temporary camp: bivouac

temporary craze: fad

temporary power suspension: outage

temporary quiet: lull

temporary residence or stay: sojourn

temporary suspension: abeyance, pause, respite

tempt: allure, attract, bait, coax, court, dare, decoy, entice, goad, incite, induce, intrigue, inveigle, lead, lure, provoke, risk, seduce, tantalize, try

temptation: allurement, attraction, bait, decoy, draw, enticement, fascination, hankering, incentive, inducement, lure, seduction

temptress: Delilah, enchantress, Jezebel, Lorelei, mermaid, seductress, siren, sorceress, vamp

Ten Commandments: Decalogue

Ten Commandments chest: Ark of the Covenant

ten decibels: bel

ten times: decuple, denary, tenfold

ten-year anniversary: decennial

ten-year period: decade, decennium

ten, based on the number: decimal, denary

tenacious: adamant, adhesive, cohesive, determined, dogged, fast, firm, indomitable, persevering, persistent, relentless, resolute, retentive, spunky, stalwart, staunch, steadfast, sticking, strong, stubborn, tough, unshakable, unyielding, viscid

tenacity: cohesiveness, courage, determination, diligence, doggedness, firmness, guts, heart, nerve, perseverance, persistence, resolution, strength, stubbornness, toughness

tenant: boarder, dweller, holder, inhabit, inhabitant, leaser, lessee, occupant, occupy, renter, sharecropper, vassal

tend: accompany, administer, attend, care, care for, contribute, cultivate, direct, favor, gravitate, guard, incline, intend, lead, lean, likely, listen, manage, mind, minister to, move, nurse, oversee, protect, provide, reach, safeguard, see to, serve, shepherd, supervise, supply, tendency, till, treat, watch, work

tendency: aim, appetency, aptness, bent, bias, course, custom, direction, disposition, drift, drive, habit, idiosyncrasy, inclination, instinct, leaning, liking, partiality, penchant, predisposition, preference, proclivity, proneness, propensity, reflex, relation, result, set, tenor, trend

tendency of a body to rest: inertia
tendency, inborn: instinct
tendency, individual: bent, disposition, inclination
tendency, strong: affinity, partiality, penchant, predilection
tender: aching, affectionate, bruised, careful, charitable, compassionate, considerate, delicate, extend, feeble, fond, fragile, frail, gentle, give, green, humane, immature, inexperienced, inflamed, kind, kindhearted, loving, merciful, mild, nice, offer, painful, pitiful, precious, present, proffer, proposal, propose, raw, sensitive, soft, softhearted, sore, sparing, submit, succulent, swollen, sympathetic, touchy, warm, warmhearted, weak, young
tenderness: affection, benevolence, compassion, gentleness, goodness, kindness, love, lovingness, sensitivity, sympathy, warmth, weakness
tenderness and love as a musical direction: con amore
tending to correct or improve: remedial
tending toward a point of view: partisan, tendentious
tendon: band, cord, hamstring, ligament, sinew, tissue
tendon behind knee and thigh: hamstring
tendril: cirrus, clasp, coil, curl, ringlet
tenebrous: dark, dusky, gloomy, murky, obscure, ominous, shadowy
tenet: belief, canon, conviction, credo, creed, doctrine, dogma, maxim, opinion, philosophy, position, principle, rule, teaching, view
tenfold: denary
tenor: copy, course, direction, drift, essence, gist, import, intent, meaning, nature, procedure, purport, purpose, sense, singer, substance, tendency, tone, transcript, trend, vein, voice
tense: agitated, anxious, aorist, conditional, edgy, excited, firm, future, intense, jittery, jumpy, keyed up, nervous, overwrought, past, perfect, pluperfect, present, preterit, queasy, restless, rigid, stiff, strained, stressful, stretched, taut, tight, uneasy, unnerved, uptight
tension: anxiety, apprehension, exertion, force, hostility, pressure, spring, strain, stress, tautness, tightness, uneasiness
tent: big top, camp, canopy, cover,

lodge, marquee, pavilion, plug, pup, shelter, tabernacle, tarpaulin, teepee, tepee, wigwam
RELATED TERMS
tent bed: cot
tent flap: fly
tent securing rope: guy
tent sticks: pegs
tent, large ornate: marquee, pavilion
tent, Native American: tepee, wigwam
tent, put up a: pitch
tent, take down a: strike
tent's horizontal pole: ridgepole ❧

tentacle: appendage, arm, feeler, limb
tentative: cautious, doubtful, experimental, hesitant, iffy, makeshift, proposed, provisional, speculative, temporary, trial, uncertain, undecided, unsure, vacillating
tenth part of something: tithe
tenuous: delicate, dilute, dubious, ethereal, flimsy, fragile, gossamer, insignificant, insubstantial, narrow, rare, shaky, slight, slim, subtle, thin, weak
tenure: clutch, grasp, grip, hold, occupation, possession, reign, term
tepid: cool, halfhearted, indifferent, lukewarm, mild, moderate, temperate, unenthusiastic, warm
tergiversate: apostatize, defect, equivocate, hedge, renounce, shift, shuffle
term: bound, boundary, condition, duration, era, interval, limit, limitation, period, semester, session, span, spell, state, stretch, stipulation, tenure, time, tour, trimester; call, definition, designate, detail, dub, entitle, expression, idiom, jargon, label, name, phrase, spell, state, word
term characterizing a person or thing: epithet
term more general than another: superordinate
term more specific than another: hyponym
termagant: disorderly, furious, harridan, hellcat, quarrelsome, raucous, scolding, shrew, tumultuous, turbulent, virago, vixen, Xanthippe
terminal: concluding, CRT, deadly, depot, end, extremity, fatal, final, finish, incurable, last, lethal, limit, monitor, screen, station, ultimate
terminally ill program or hospital: hospice

TENNIS TERMS

2-person game: singles
4-person game: doubles
tennis game with server one point from losing: break point
loss of point after two serving attempts: double fault
return ball before it touches ground: volley
action that puts ball into play: service
serve touching net before falling into opponent's court: let
hitting a ball out of turn: poach
winning against server: service break
failure to serve correctly: fault
return after ball has bounced: ground stroke
return arched high in air: lob
return where ball just clears net: drop shot
return where ball passes opponent: passing shot
returns back-and-forth: volley
unreturnable serve: ace
stroke crossing in front of body: backhand
stroke made on side of body holding racket: forehand
rushing net after each serve: serve-and-volley ❧

terminate: abolish, adjourn, call, cease, close, complete, conclude, confine, discharge, discontinue, dismiss, dissolve, drop, eliminate, end, expire, finish, fire, halt, quit, result, sack, stop
terminate early: abort
termination: boundary, cessation, close, completion, conclusion, end, expiration, finality, finis, finish, limit, outcome, period, result, stoppage, terminus, windup
termination of debate: cloture
terminology: nomenclature
terms: agreement, conditions, details, limitations, particulars, price, provisions, relationship, stipulations, understanding
terms of a field: jargon, nomenclature, terminology
terrace: balcony, bank, deck, gallery, patio, platform, porch, portico, promenade, roof
terrain: area, bailiwick, contour, coun-

tryside, domain, environment, ground, region, territory, topography, tract, turf

terrestrial: earthly, earthy, global, human, mundane, planetary, secular, terrene, worldly

terrible: alarming, appalling, atrocious, awful, brutal, cataclysmal, dire, disastrous, disturbing, dreadful, fearful, frightening, ghastly, grim, grisly, gruesome, harrowing, hideous, horrible, horrific, horrifying, intense, painful, revolting, severe, shocking, terrific, tough, tragic, unfortunate, unpleasant, upsetting, vicious

terrific: alarming, amazing, appalling, distressing, disturbing, dreadful, enormous, exciting, fabulous, fantastic, fearful, formidable, frightful, glorious, great, immense, intense, magnificent, marvelous, smashing, super, superb, terrible, terrifying, tremendous, upsetting, wonderful

terrified: afraid, aghast, alarmed, awed, frightened, frozen, scared

terrify: alarm, appall, frighten, gorgonize, haunt, horrify, intimidate, menace, petrify, scare, shock, startle, stun, terrorize, threaten, upset

terrifying: alarming, awful, frightening, ghastly, grim, hideous, horrible, horrid, scary

territory: area, bailiwick, colony, district, domain, empire, environs, ex-

tent, field, jurisdiction, land, neighborhood, province, region, sector, sphere, terrain, tract, turf, zone

RELATED TERMS

territory deemed necessary for nation, additional: Lebensraum

territory enclosed within a larger unit: enclave

territory into existing unit, incorporate: annex

territory into hostile units, divide: Balkanize

territory, policy intended to regain lost: irredentism, revanchism ❦

terror: affray, alarm, anxiety, awe, consternation, dread, fear, fright, horror, panic, pest, trepidation

terrorism: sabotage

terrorist: alarmist, bomber, goon, rebel, revolutionary, subversive, thug

terrorists, action against: counterinsurgency

terrorize: abash, browbeat, bully, coerce, frighten, intimidate, menace, oppress, scare, threaten

terse: abrupt, brief, clear-cut, compact, concise, crisp, curt, exact, laconic, neat, pithy, pointed, sententious, short, succinct

test: analyze, appraise, approve, assay, audition, authenticate, check, criterion, determine, evaluate, exam, examination, examine, experiment, experimental, explore, final, midterm,

oral, ordeal, probe, prove, quiz, refine, rehearse, sample, standard, taste, touchstone, trial, try, validate, verify

RELATED TERMS

test by severe ordeal: baptism of fire

test depth of water: sound

test for cancer of female genital tract: Pap smear

test for chemical acidity, basicity: litmus test

test for diphtheria: Schick test

test for judgment and comparison: criterion, touchstone, yardstick

test for part in entertainment: audition

test run: trial

test that is crucial and decisive: acid test

test to measure ability to develop skills: aptitude test

test with several possible answers to each question: multiple-choice test

test, critical: acid test

test, personality: inkblot test, Rorschach test ❦

testament: belief, covenant, credo, evidence, legacy, proof, testimony, tribute, will

tester: assayer, canopy, crown, examiner, frame, inspector, questioner, validator

testicle area: groin

testicle pouch: scrotum

THEATER TERMS

area above stage holding lights, curtains, etc.: flies

area between curtain and orchestra: proscenium

area for musicians: orchestra pit

attendant: usher

audience seating area: auditorium

backdrops: scenery

backstage area: coulisse

backstage bulletin board: callboard

company performing different works in alternation: repertory theater

district: rialto

drapery: teaser

front rows of mezzanine: box, loge

lowest balcony: mezzanine

outdoor theater: amphitheater

performers' waiting room: green room

projecting roof over entrance: marquee, marquise

serious theater: legitimate theater

set with ceiling and three walls: box set

stage area in front of the curtain: apron

stage objects: props

stagehand for scenery or cameras: grip

summer theater: straw-hat circuit

theater: arena, auditorium, battleground, Broadway, cinema, coliseum, drama, hall, hippodrome, house, movie, odeum, playhouse, stage

theater art: dramaturgy

theater in center of seating: arena theater, theater-in-the-round

theater parts: apron, auditorium, backstage, balcony, catwalk, footlights, gallery, green room, orchestra pit, proscenium, upstage, wings

theater section: loge, parterre, tier

touring company: troupe

writer for theater: dramaturge, playwright ❦

testicle sperm-bearing duct: vas deferens

testicle sperm duct system: epididymis

testicles: gonads

testifier in court: deponent, eyewitness

testify: affirm, assert, attest, certify, declare, depone, depose, express, indicate, proclaim, profess, prove, swear, witness

testify falsely: perjure

testimonial: citation, commendation, credential, endorsement, evidence, gala, honor, memorial, plaudit, recommendation, salute, salvo, testimony, tribute

testimony: affidavit, affirmation, attest, avowal, confirmation, declaration, deposition, evidence, facts, proof, witness

testimony under oath: deposition

testing idea or opinion, person for: sounding board

testing of idea on public: trial balloon

testy: cantankerous, choleric, cranky, cross, crusty, grouchy, grumpy, irascible, irritable, obstinate, ornery, peevish, snappish, touchy, uptight

tête-à-tête: chat, confidential, conversation, discussion, private, seat, sofa, talk

tether: band, cable, chain, fasten, leash, limit, manacle, moor, restrain, rope, scope, secure, shackle, tie

text: content, handbook, manual, motif, motive, passage, primer, schoolbook, subject, textbook, theme, topic, workbook

text of opera: libretto

text, classic or standard: locus classicus

text, commentary on: annotation, gloss

text, commonly accepted: vulgate

text, correct a: emend

text, critical analysis or explanation of: apparatus criticus, exegesis, variorum

text, cut a: delete, excise

text, different readings blended: conflation

text, edit a: redact, revise

textbook for teaching children to read, elementary: primer

textile: cloth, fabric, fiber, goods, yarn

textile dealer: mercer

texture: character, composition, consistency, constitution, essence, fabric, feel, fiber, grain, look, make, nature, quality, structure, surface

thank: acknowledge, appreciate, blame, bless, credit, praise

thankful: appreciative, contented, grateful, indebted, obliged

thankless: heedless, miserable, unappreciated, ungrateful, unrecognized, unrewarding

thanks: appreciation, blessing, credit, grace, gratefulness, gratitude, praise, recognition

thaumaturgy: alchemy, magic, sorcery, witchcraft

thaw: defrost, deice, dissolve, liquefy, melt, soften, warm

theater award: Obie, Tony

theatrical: affected, artificial, ceremonious, dramatic, exaggerated, extravagant, flashy, histrionic, melodramatic, scenic, showy, staged, stagy, superficial, thespian

theatrical behavior: histrionics

theft: burglary, caper, crime, embezzlement, filching, fraud, heist, larceny, mugging, pilferage, pilfering, piracy, plagiarism, purloining, robbery, shoplifting, stealing, thievery

RELATED TERMS

theft of another's property: larceny

theft of ideas, writings: piracy, plagiarism

theft of livestock: rustling

theft or misuse of entrusted property: conversion, defalcation, embezzlement, misappropriation, peculation

theft, minor: filching, lifting, pilferage, purloining ❦

theme: argument, article, composition, discourse, dissertation, essay, focus, idea, matter, melody, message, motif, paper, point, premise, song, subject, text, thesis, tune

theme or repeated verse: chorus, refrain

theme, music: subject

theme, recurrent: leitmotif, leitmotiv, motif, motto

then: accordingly, again, before, besides, consequently, formerly, hence, later, next, suddenly, therefore, thereupon

theologian: clergy, cleric, curate, divine, ecclesiastic, philosopher, scholar

theological: canonical, dogmatic, ecclesiastical, holy, religious, sacred, spiritual

theological school: seminary

theology of first things: etiology

theology of last things: eschatology

theology that defends and tries to prove Christian doctrines: apologetics

theology, study of: divinity

theorem: axiom, belief, doctrine, hypothesis, law, principle, theory, thesis

theorem to be demonstrated: proposition

theoretical: abstract, academic, analytical, conjectural, hypothetical, ideal, nominal, notional, philosophical, speculative, unpractical, unproved

theorize: conjecture, formulate, hypothesize, postulate, speculate, suppose, think

theory: analysis, assumption, belief, conjecture, doctrine, explanation, formula, guess, hunch, hypothesis, idea, ideology, nation, philosophy, principle, speculation, surmise, theorem, thesis

RELATED TERMS

theory as basis for investigation: hypothesis

theory for argument's sake: thesis, working hypothesis

theory of universe's origin: Big Bang theory

theory, believe in a: adhere, subscribe

theory, of an accepted: received

theory, person attached to impractical: doctrinaire

theory, religious: creed, doctrine, dogma

theory, unorthodox: heresy, heterodoxy ❦

therapeutic: beneficial, good, healing, medical, remedial

therapy: healing, remedy, treatment

RELATED TERMS

therapy administrating small doses of drugs to produce symptoms of disease being treated: homeopathy

therapy allowing screaming and aggression: primal scream therapy, primal therapy

therapy associating bad habit with pain: aversion therapy

therapy for disabled people, creative: occupational therapy

therapy for mental disorders: electroconvulsive therapy, electroshock therapy

therapy manipulating bones and joints: osteopathy

therapy manipulating spinal column and other body parts: chiropractic

therapy monitoring bodily function in order to get control of it: biofeedback

therapy using chemicals to treat cancer: chemotherapy

therapy using exercise: physical therapy, physiotherapy

therapy using fine needles: acupuncture

therapy using fragrant substances: aromatherapy

therapy using hypnosis: hypnotherapy

therapy using light: phototherapy

therapy using massage: reflexology

therapy using massage on acupuncture points: acupressure, shiatsu

therapy using natural remedies like sunlight, diet: naturopathy

therapy using radiation: irradiation, radiation therapy

therapy using water: hydrotherapy

therapy, medical: modality ✇

thereafter: accordingly, afterwards, consequently, following, subsequently

therefore: accordingly, because, consequently, ergo, hence, since, then, thence, thus, whence, wherefore

thereupon: directly, immediately, suddenly, then

thermometer: indicator, instrument, regulator, thermostat

thermometer degree marking: graduation

thermometer for very high temperatures: pyrometer

thermometer for very low temperatures: cryometer

thermometer instrument, two-: psychrometer

thermometer that records temperature: thermograph

thermometer types: Celsius, cryometer, Fahrenheit, mercury, pyrometer, thermoelectric, thermograph

thermoplastic resin: alkyd, saran

thesaurus: dictionary, lexicon, Roget, synonym book, word finder

thesis: argument, belief, composition, discourse, dissertation, essay, exposition, hypothesis, opinion, paper, point, postulate, premise, tenet, theme, theory

thespian: actor, actress, dramatic, performer, player, theatrical, trouper

thick: abundant, broad, brotherly, bulky, burly, chummy, chunky, cloudy, coarse, compact, concentrated, crowded, deep, dense, excessive, familiar, filled, friendly, gloppy, gross, hazy, heavy, husky, impenetrable, indistinct, intense, intimate, packed, plump, populated, pronounced, solid, squat, stodgy, substantial, swarming, tight, viscid, viscous, wide

thick and dense, as smoke or fog: turbid

thick-skinned: callous, hardened, tough, unfeeling

thick slice: slab

thicken: cake, clot, coagulate, condense, congeal, curd, curdle, deepen, freeze, gel, harden, incrassate, jell, set, solidify, stiffen

thicken in boiling, evaporation: inspissate

thickened end, with one: clavate

thickening of artery walls: arteriosclerosis

thicket: boscage, bosk, brake, brush, brushwood, bush, clump, coppice, copse, grove, growth, hedge, shrubbery, shrubs, underbrush, woods

thickheaded: blockheaded, boneheaded, dense, dull, dumb, idiotic, ignorant, stupid

thickness: consistency, density, diameter, dimension, girth, layer, ply, sheet, stratum, width

thief: bandit, burglar, criminal, crook, cut-purse, embezzler, filcher, ganef, gangster, grifter, highwayman, kleptomaniac, larcener, larcenist, looter, mugger, pickpocket, prowler, purloiner, robber, rustler, shoplifter, stealer

thigh: femur, flank, gammon, ham, hock, leg

thigh and pelvic area: loins

thigh and trunk junction: groin

thighbone: femur

thighs, concerning: crural

thin: acute, anorexic, attenuate, beanpole, bony, dilute, emaciated, extenuate, faint, fine, flimsy, gangly, gaunt, gossamer, hollow, inadequate, insufficient, lank, lanky, lean, meager, narrow, pale, poor, rare, rarefied, reduce, reedy, scant, scanty, scarce, scrawny, sheer, skeletal, skimpy, skinny, slender, slight, slim, spare,

sparse, stringy, tenuous, transparent, twiggy, unconvincing, unsubstantial, watery, weak, weaken, wiry

thin air: ether

thin and bony: angular, ectomorphic, gaunt, lank, scrawny

thin and flimsy: tenuous

thin and graceful: gracile, lithe, svelte, willowy

thin and light: chiffon, diaphanous, gossamer, papery, sheer, translucent

thin and slight: asthenic, wispy

thin coating: film, veneer

thin coating of glaze, paint, or ink: wash

thin cracker or cookie: wafer

thin disk: paten

thin flat strip: slat

thin-skinned: oversensitive, sensitive, sulky, touchy

thin, abnormally: anorexic, emaciated, skeletal

thing: act, action, affair, apparatus, article, circumstance, concern, contrivance, craze, creature, deed, detail, device, doing, doohickey, element, entity, event, fad, fashion, feat, feature, forte, gadget, gizmo, happening, idea, incident, item, junk, matter, notion, object, occurrence, oddity, phenomenon, point, property, quality, rage, reason, referent, shape, stunt, style, trait, vogue

thingamajig: contraption, device, doodad, doohickey, gadget, gizmo, thingamabob, widget

things: baggage, belongings, chattels, clothes, conditions, duds, effects, gear, goods, possessions, stuff

think: anticipate, believe, brood, cerebrate, cogitate, conceive, conclude, conjecture, consider, contemplate, deem, deliberate, entertain, expect, feel, formulate, guess, ideate, imagine, intellectualize, intend, invent, judge, meditate, mull, muse, opine, ponder, purpose, realize, reason, recall, reckon, reconsider, reflect, regard, remember, repute, resolve, ruminate, sense, speculate, study, suppose, surmise, suspect, understand, use the old noodle, visualize, weigh

think about at length: brood, mull, muse, ruminate

think and calculate: conjecture, estimate, speculate, theorize

think and plan in mind: devise

think by reasoning: deduce, figure

think carefully about: cogitate, contemplate, deliberate, excogitate, meditate, perpend, ponder

think methodically: excogitate, ratiocinate, reason

think up: conceive, concoct, contrive, devise, fabricate, fashion, formulate, ideate, invent

thinkable: believable, comprehensible, conceivable, feasible, imaginable, likely, possible, reasonable

thinker: brain, casuist, intellectual, mastermind, mind, philosopher, sage, scholar, sophist, student, theorist

thinking: bright, cerebration, deliberating, engrossed, intellection, introspective, judgment, meditation, rational, reasonable, reflective, studious, thought, understanding

thinness: meagerness, rarity, shallowness, slimness, tenuity

thinness from self-induced vomiting: bulimia

third estate: commonalty, commoners, populace

third finger: medius

third from the end: antepenultimate

third in place, order, degree: tertiary

third year, every: triennial

thirst: aridity, craving, desire, hankering, hunger, longing, lust, passion, wish, yearn, yen

thirst, satisfy: quench, slake

thirsty: adry, anxious, arid, avid, craving, dehydrated, desire, droughty, dry, eager, longing, parched, waterless

thirteen: baker's dozen

thirteen witches in group: coven

thirty-second note: demisemiquaver

thong: band, lace, lash, leash, rein, sandal, strap, strip, twitch, whip

thorn: annoyance, discomfort, irritation, pain, prickle, spike, spine, splint, spur, trouble, vexation

thorny: barbed, bristly, controversial, difficult, nettlesome, pointed, prickly, problematic, sharp, spined, spiny, sticky, tough, tricky, troublesome, unpleasant, vexatious

thorny bush: bramble, briar, brier

thorough: absolute, accurate, all-encompassing, careful, complete, comprehensive, detailed, exact, exhaustive, finished, full, ingrained, intensive, meticulous, painstaking, unmitigated, utter

thorough and painstaking: assiduous, conscientious, diligent, hardworking, industrious, sedulous

thorough and precise: meticulous, punctilious, scrupulous

thoroughbred: bloodstock, educated, full-blooded, horse, pedigree, pedigreed, purebred, trained, unmixed, well-bred

thoroughfare: artery, avenue, boulevard, causeway, channel, expressway, freeway, highway, lane, parkway, passage, path, road, roadway, strait, street, turnpike, waterway

thoroughfare for crowds: concourse

thoroughgoing: absolute, arrant, complete, out-and-out, unqualified

thoroughly: absolutely, carefully, completely, downright, efficiently, exhaustively, fully, in all, intensively, meticulously, throughout, totally, utterly

though: albeit, despite, granted, however, nevertheless, nonetheless, still, whereas, while

thought: anxiety, attention, belief, care, cerebration, cogitation, conception, concentration, concept, conception, consideration, deduction, deemed, deliberation, expectation, idea, image, imagination, inference, intellection, intention, judging, meditation, mind, musing, notion, opinion, outlook, plan, purpose, reasoning, reflection, sentiment, speculation, theory, trifle, view

thought and thinking: cerebration, cogitation, contemplation

thought broken off in mid-sentence: aposiopesis

thought transference: telepathy

thought, absorbed in: abstracted, concentrated, engrossed, immersed, intent, preoccupied

thought, deep in: cogitative, contemplative, meditative, pensive, ruminant

thought, reserved: arrière-pensée, reservation

thought, state of deep: brown study, lucubration, reverie

thoughtful: absorbed, attentive, careful, caring, charitable, considerate, contemplative, courteous, discerning, gracious, heedful, helpful, intellectual, introspective, kind, logical, meditative, mindful, pensive, philosophic, polite, prudent, reflective, regardful, ruminative, sensible, sensitive, serious, solicitous

thoughtful about consequences: circumspect, discreet, judicious, politic, prudent

thoughtless: brash, careless, discourteous, dull, foolish, hasty, heedless, impolite, inadvertent, inattentive, incogitant, inconsiderate, insensitive, neglectful, negligent, rash, reckless, remiss, rude, selfish, silly, stupid, uncaring, unthinking

thoughts clearly, unable to express: incoherent

thoughts of character in passage, inner: inner monologue

thoughts or cares, helping to escape: phrontifugic

thoughts or observation, literary: pensee

thoughts, contemplation of one's own: introspection

thousand million: trillion

thousand-year period: chiliad, millenary, millennium

thousand, concerning a: millenarian, millenary

thousandth: millesimal

thrall: bondage, bondman, captive, esne, serf, servitude, slave, slavery, subject, vassal

thrash: baste, batter, beat, belabor, belt, bray, cane, defeat, drub, flagellate, flail, flog, lace, lam, lambaste, lash, lick, maul, pelt, pound, pummel, punish, rout, shellac, spank, strike, swing, tan, trounce, wallop, whip

thread: attach, braid, connect, cord, cotton, fiber, filament, flax, floss, join, lisle, purl, reeve, silk, strand, string, twine, wire, wool, yarn

thread holder: spool

thread separated from fabric: ravel

thread, ball of: clew

thread, concerning: filar

thread, cone-shaped roll of: cop

thread, loose coil of: hank, skein

thread, loosely twisted: floss

thread, thin: filament

threadbare: banal, clichéd, corny, everyday, faded, frayed, hackneyed, ragged, seedy, shabby, stale, tattered, trite, used, worn

threadlike: filar, ropy

threadlike parts of a vine: tendrils

threads in woven fabric, crosswise or horizontal: weft, woof

threads in woven fabric, lengthwise: warp

threads, twisting into: filature

threat: caveat, commination, danger, hazard, intimidation, jeopardy, menace, peril, risk, warning

threat of future problem: omen, portent, presage

threat of penalty if terms are not accepted: ultimatum

threat or implied threat: saber rattling

threat words: or else

threat, constraint by: coercion, constraint, duress

threat, formal: commination

threaten: augur, bully, cow, endanger, expose, frighten, imperil, intimidate, jeopardize, menace, portend, pressure, scare, terrorize, warn

threatening: alarming, dangerous, imminent, impending, looming, lowering, menacing, ominous

threatening and dark: lowering, menacing, minacious, minatory

threatening evil: baleful, foreboding, menacing, minacious, minatory, ominous, portentous

threatening to occur: imminent, impending

threats, coerce or inhibit by: deter, intimidate

three-cornered hat: chapeaubras

three-cornered shoulder cape: fichu

three-dimensional appearance: perspective

three-dimensional effect, instruments creating: stereograph, stereoscope

three-dimensional figure: solid

three-dimensional image created by two-eyepiece optical instrument: stereoscopy

three-dimensional image created with laser: hologram, holograph

three-dimensional scene: diorama

three-fold: triune

three-horse carriage: troika

three-hulled boat with sails: trimaran

three in governing body: troika

three-leafed: trifoliate

three-legged stand: tripod, trivet

three-line verse: triole

three-masted schooner: tern

three miles: league

three months, period of: trimester

three-movement orchestra composition with one or more solo instruments: concerto

three-part painting: triptych

three-part period: trimester

three parts, division into: trichotomy

three people involved sexually: ménage à trois

three-pronged spear: trident

three related works: trilogy

three rhyming lines: tercet

three spots on card, domino: trey

three-syllable foot: anapest

three things, people: triad

three times: threefold, treble, triple, triplicate

three times daily in prescriptions: tid

three vowel sounds pronounced in a row: triphthong

three wise men: Magi

three-year anniversary: triennial

three years, every: triennial

three, group of: triad, trinity, trio, triumvirate, troika

threefold: ternary, treble, trinal, trine, triple

threesome: triad, trine, trio

threnody: dirge, elegy, poem, requiem, song

threshold: beginning, brink, dawn, door, doorsill, doorway, edge, entrance, eve, horizon, opening, outset, sill, verge

threshold of consciousness: limen

threshold of perception, below: subliminal

thrift: austerity, conservation, economy, frugality, husbandry, parsimony, prudence, saving, sparingness

thriftless: careless, extravagant, immoderate, lavish, prodigal, wanton, wasteful

thrifty: careful, conserving, economical, flourishing, frugal, industrious, parsimonious, prosperous, provident, prudent, saving, scrimping, skimping, sparing, thriving, useful

thrifty and regulating: sumptuary

thrifty management of resources: conservation, economy, husbandry

thrill: arouse, bang, charge, delight, elate, electrify, excite, flush, galvanize, glow, kick, please, quiver, stimulate, stir, tingle, tremble, tremor, vibrate

thrill of excitement: frisson

thrilled: atingle, elated, overjoyed

thrilling: awesome, breathtaking, electrifying, exciting, gripping, intense, riveting, sensational, stimulating, stirring, titillating

thrive: blossom, boom, burgeon, develop, flourish, grow, improve, progress, prosper, succeed

thriving: blooming, flourishing, flowering, healthy, prolific, prosperous, robust, succeeding, successful

thriving period: heyday

throat: esophagus, gorge, gullet, larynx, maw, neck, passage, pharynx, trachea, windpipe

throat and chest: thorax

throat by coughing loudly, attempt to clear: hawk

throat-clearing sound: ahem

throat irritation often with voice loss: laryngitis

throat of animal, color on: gorget

throat, concerning the: jugular

throat, hanging skin on: dewlap, wattle

throat, piece hanging down at back of: uvula

throaty: deep, gruff, guttural, hoarse, husky

throb: ache, beat, drum, flutter, pant, pound, pulsate, pulse, quiver, thump, vibrate

throe: ache, agony, anguish, disorder, pain, pang, spasm, struggle, turmoil

thrombus: clot, coagulation

throne: authority, cathedra, chair, dignity, power, rank, royalty, seat, sovereignty, toilet

throne, give up the: abdicate

throne, order to inherit a: succession

throne, remove from the: depose

throne, seize a: usurp

throne, take the: accede

throng: assemblage, bunch, concourse, converge, crown, drove, fill, flock, gag, group, herd, horde, host, jam, mass, mob, multitude, pack, press, push, scores, smother, stifle, swarm

throttle: accelerator, asphyxiate, choke, garrote, gun, strangle, suffocate, suppress

through: about, across, among, around, between, completed, concluded, direct, done, ended, finished, over, past, per, straight, terminated, thru, via, washed-up

throughout: about, amid, around, completely, during, everyplace, everywhere

throw: baffle, buck, cast, catapult,

chuck, confuse, discard, disconcert, dispose, fire, flick, fling, flip, force, heave, hurl, launch, lob, lose, nonplus, peg, pelt, project, propel, put, scarf, shawl, shed, shot, sling, submit, thrust, toss, unhorse, unseat, unsettle, whirl

throw away: abandon, cast, discard, dispose, ditch, dump, eject, fritter, jettison, reject, scrap, squander, waste

throw cargo overboard: jettison

throw forward: impel, launch, lob, project, propel

throw from great height: precipitate

throw in suddenly: inject, interject

throw off: confuse, derail, distract, divert, elude, emit, escape, evade, expel, lose, mislead, shake, slip, trick

throw out: banish, cast, chuck, discard, disengage, eject, emit, evict, expel, jettison, junk, oust, reject, remove, scrap, spew

throw out a window: defenestrate

throw up: barf, heave, puke, regurgitate, relinquish, retch, upchuck, vomit

throwback: atavism

thrown object, path of: trajectory

thrush, group of: mutation

thrust: assault, attack, barge, butt, charge, drive, impel, impetus, interject, interpose, intrude, jab, lunge, meaning, meat, onset, onslaught, penetrate, pierce, plunge, point, poke, press, pressure, protrude, push, ram, sense, shove, stab, stress

thud: bam, bang, blow, clonk, clump, clunk, fall, plop, smack, sound, strike, thump

thug: assassin, bully, criminal, cutthroat, gangster, goon, gunman, hood, hoodlum, hooligan, mobster, punk, ruffian, torpedo

thumb: browse, finger, hitch, hitchhike, pollex, scan

thumb and forefinger, flesh between: purlicue

thumb through pages of book: riffle

thumb, cushion at base of: heel, pad, thenar

thump: bang, beat, blow, bop, ding, drub, hit, knock, pound, punch, smack, sound, strike, stump, throb, thud, thwack, wallop, whack, whop

thunder: bang, boom, clap, cracking, crash, drumfire, fulminate, noise, peal, rage, roar, rumbling

thunder god: Thor

thunder, reverberating from: tonitruous

thunderbolt: boom, crack, flash, lightning

thus: accordingly, consequently, ergo, hence, sic, so, therefore, yet

thus (in Latin): ergo, sic

thwack: bang, blow, bop, drive, force, hit, knock, paddle, pound, rap, smack, smite, sock, strike, thrash, thump, wallop, whack

thwart: baffle, balk, block, counter, curb, defeat, foil, frustrate, hamper, hinder, impede, obstruct, oppose, outwit, prevent, resist, stop, stymie

thymus gland or pancreas of a young animal prepared as food: sweetbread

tiara: circlet, coronet, crown, diadem, headdress, miter

tic: contraction, jerk, spasm, twitch

tick: acarid, bloodsucker, insect, louse, mite, parasite, pest

tick-borne disease: Lyme

tick off: annoy, irk, miff, rile

ticked off: irate, ired, irked, sore

ticket: admission, ballot, card, certificate, check, choice, docket, document, ducat, fare, label, license, list, means, note, notice, pass, passport, permit, price, raincheck, receipt, record, slate, slip, sticker, stub, summons, tag, token, voucher

ticket remnant: stub

ticket selling above regular price: scalping

tickle: amuse, annoy, arouse, beat, caress, delight, divert, elate, excite, play, please, stimulate, stir, stroke, tease, thrill, tingle, titillate, touch

tickled pink: delighted, elated

tickling, feeling caused by: gargalesthesia

ticklish: chancy, changeable, complicated, dangerous, delicate, difficult, precarious, risky, sensitive, touchy, tricky, uncertain, unstable, unsteady, volatile

tidal wave: bore, tsunami

tidbit: bite, delicacy, goody, item, morsel, treat

tide: course, current, direction, drift, ebb, flood, flow, flux, movement, neap, opportunity, season, stream, surge, time, trend, undertow, wave

tide, dangerous: riptide

tide, falling or receding: ebb tide

tide, rising or incoming: flood tide

tides of new and full moon, maximum: spring tide

tides of new and full moon, minimum: neap tide

tidings: advice, greetings, information, intelligence, message, news, word

tidy: adequate, ample, clean, considerable, diligent, fair, good, groom, healthy, idiot, immaculate, large, methodical, neat, orderly, organized, satisfactory, shipshape, smug, spotless, spruce, substantial, tempt, trig, trim, uncluttered, well-groomed

tie feet and hands or all feet together: hog-tie

tie firmly with rope: lash

tie in game: draw, standoff

tie in race: dead heat

tie surgically: ligate

tie together: bind, relate

tie up: bind, delay, fasten, hinder, package, rope, secure, snarl, truss, wrap

tie-up: jam

tier: category, class, echelon, grade, grouping, layer, level, line, rank, row, stack, story, stratum

tiff: altercation, argument, disagreement, dispute, fight, fit, huff, outburst, quarrel, row, scrap, setto, snit, spat, squabble, tizzy, words

tiger: carnivore, cat, cougar, cub, feline, jaguar, leopard, lynx

tiger, pertaining to: tigrine

tight: bound, busy, cheap, close, compact, competent, concise, condensed, crowded, dense, difficult, drawn, faithful, fast, firm, fixed, full, hard, impervious, intimate, locked, narrow, neat, packed, parsimonious, sealed, severe, shapely, snug, solid, soundly, steady, stingy, stretched, taut, tense, tidy, trim, uncomfortable

tight-lipped: closemouthed, discreet, mum, quiet, reticent, secretive, silent, taciturn

tight spot: bind, jam, predicament, quandary

tight, pulled: taut

tighten: bind, clench, condense, constrict, contract, crush, squeeze, stiffen, stretch, tense

tightness, feeling of: constriction

tightrope walker: equilibrist, funambulist, schoenobatist

tightwad: cheapskate, miser, niggard, scrimp, scrooge, skinflint

tile: block, brick, drain, pantile, plate, shingle, slab, slate

tile-like: tegular

tile mortar: grout

tile of roof: shingle

tiles, make mosaic of: tessellate

till: cash register, drawer, tray, vault; cultivate, develop, dig, farm, hoe, labor, plough, plow, prepare, seed, sow, work

till now: as yet, so far, yet

tillable: arable, cultivatable, fertile, plowable, productive

tilt: bias, cant, gradient, inclination, incline, lean, list, pitch, seesaw, shift, slant, slope, tip, upend, upset

tilt of ship: cant, careen, heel, list

timber: balk, beam, board, cover, forest, frame, gate, girder, joist, logs, lumber, plank, rafter, rib, trees, wood, woodland, woods

timber supporting upright posts, horizontal: stringer, summer

timber wolf: lobo

timber, concrete, or steel beam as foundation or structure support: pile

timber, uncut and in stand: stumpage

timbre: character, intonation, miter, mood, pitch, quality, sound, tone

time: age, beat, book, break, century, chance, chronology, clock, continuum, cycle, date, day, decade, during, epoch, era, eternity, future, hour, instant, interim, interval, measure, millennium, minute, moment, month, opportunity, pace, past, period, phase, present, rate, rhythm, schedule, season, second, shift, shot, span, speed, spell, stint, stretch, tempo, term, tour, week, year

time 0100-2400 hours: military time

time allowed for accomplishing something: window

time along with length, width, thickness: fourth dimension

time and again: frequently, often, repeatedly

time being, for the: pro tempore

time between events: interim, interval, meantime

time counted in reverse: countdown

time erroneously given as earlier: prochronism

time erroneously given as later: metachronism

time erroneously given of thing: anachronism, parachronism

time flies: tempus fugit

time for working, employees setting their own: flextime

time-honored: accepted, classic, eminent, noble, respected, reverend, venerable, vintage

time limit: curfew, deadline

time limit for prosecuting: statute of limitations

time measurement, science of: chronology

time of greatest popularity, success: heyday, prime

time when work is stopped, equipment broken: downtime

time, arranged according to: chronological

time, beyond the limits of: immemorial

time, concerning: temporal

time, connected in: contiguous, uninterrupted

time, continuance in: duration

time, critical point in: juncture

time, happening at the same: coexisting, coincident, contemporaneous, contemporary, simultaneous

time, length, width, thickness: space-time

time, longest division of geologic: eon

time, most appropriate: psychological moment

time, science of measuring: horology

time, scientific measurement of: chronometry

time, spirit of the: zeitgeist

time, to pass by as: elapse

timeless: ageless, ceaseless, continual, continuous, dateless, endless, eternal, eterne, everlasting, immortal, imtemporal, lasting, permanent, perpetual, undated, unending, untimely

timely: appropriate, auspicious, contemporary, convenient, early, favorable, fitting, opportune, pertinent, promising, prompt, proper, punctual, relevant, seasonable, temporal, topical

timepiece: alarm clock, calendar, chronograph, chronometer, chronoscope, clock, dial, horologe, hourglass, metronome, pendulum, stopwatch, sundial, watch

timepiece covering: watchcase

timeworn: aged, ancient, antiquated, battered, dated, hoary, old, trite, weathered

timid: afraid, apprehensive, bashful, cowardly, coy, diffident, fainthearted, fearful, gentle, hesitant, indecisive, irresolute, meek, mild, modest, mousy, nervous, sheepish, shy, spineless, spiritless, tentative, timorous, tremulous, unassertive, unassuming, uncertain, vacillating, withdrawn

timorous: afraid, apprehensive, faint, fainthearted, fearful, hesitant, meek, shrinking, shuddering, shy, tentative, timid, tremulous, unassertive

tin and copper alloy: pewter

tin, concerning: stannic, stannous

tincture: cast, color, dye, elixir, extract, imbrue, imbue, pigment, shade, stain, taint, tinge, tint, trace, vestige

tinder: fuel, kindling, punk, wood

tinder of decayed wood: punk

tine: branch, fork, point, prong, spike

tinge: cast, color, coloring, dash, drop, dye, flavor, hint, hue, imbue, pigment, shade, smack, stain, suggestion, tincture, tint, tone, touch, trace

tingle: burn, itch, jingle, sensation, shiver, stimulate, sting, thrill, tickle, tinkle, tremble

tinker: dabble, fiddle, fuss, meddler, mend, mender, mess, patch, potter, putter, repair

tinkle: chime, chink, clink, dingle, jingle, plink, ring, signal, sound, tingle

tinsel: clinquant, decoration, flashy, gaudy, glossy, pretentious, sham, showy, tawdry

tint: cast, color, complexion, dash, dye, hint, hue, nuance, pigment, shade, stain, tincture, tinge, tone, trace

tintinnabulation: chime, clanging, clangor, jingle, noise, ringing, sound

tiny: diminutive, elfin, itty-bitty, lilliputian, little, microscopic, miniature, minuscule, minute, negligible, peewee, petite, pocket-size, small, teensy, teeny, teeny-weeny, wee

tip of metal on item: ferrule

tip-of-the-tongue phenomenon: lethologica

tip over: tilt, upset

tip, a: baksheesh, cumshaw, douceur, gratuity, pourboire

tipple: booze, drink, grog, imbibe, liquor

tipster: informer, nark, pigeon, snitch, squealer

tipsy: drunk, drunken, groggy, inebriated, intoxicated, loaded, plastered, shaky, smashed, soused, tight, unsteady, wobbly

tiptoe: cautious, cautiously, creep, quietly, sneak, stealthy, warily

tiptoe, spin on: pirouette

tiptoe, walking on: digitigrade

tiptop: best, elite, excellent, exceptional, extraordinary, first-rate, prime, superior, supreme, uppermost

tirade: berating, castigation, diatribe, harangue, invective, jeremiad, lecture, outburst, philippic, ranting, screed

tire: band, bore, drain, enervate, exasperate, exhaust, fag, fatigue, flag, hoop, jade, lag, overwork, recap, retread, rim, shoe, tax, teens, tucker, weaken, weary

tired: all in, beat, bored, bushed, dead, debilitated, depleted, drained, enervated, exasperated, exhausted, fatigued, flagging, jaded, lethargic, pooped, prostrate, run-down, sleepy, spent, tuckered, tuckered out, unrested, wearied, weary

tired and ready for sleep: somnolent, soporific

tired and without interest: blasé, jaded

tired from too much work: overextended, overtaxed

tired spiritually: decadent, effete

tiredness in general: ennui, lethargy, weltschmerz

tireless: busy, determined, energetic, enthusiastic, indefatigable, staunch, steadfast, unflagging, untiring, unwearied, weariless

tiresome: annoying, boring, demanding, difficult, dreary, dull, exasperating, hard, irksome, irritating, monotonous, tedious, tiring, uninteresting, wearisome

tiring: demanding, exacting, grueling, taxing

tissue and its structure, study of: histology

tissue covering most surfaces of body and organs: epithelium

tissue developing into nails, teeth: matrix

tissue for conducting fluids, plant: vascular tissue

tissue removed for examination: biopsy

tissue storing cellular fat: adipose tissue

tissue, abnormal new growth of: neoplasm, tumor

tissue, fibrous connective: fascia

tissue, permeable: membrane

tissue, wasting away of body: atrophy

tissues, fluid in body: lymph

tissues, study of organic: histology

titanic: colossal, earthshaking, enormous, gargantuan, giant, gigantic, great, huge, humongous, immense, large, mammoth, monstrous, vast

titillate: amuse, arouse, captivate, excite, stimulate, tantalize, tease, thrill, tickle

title conveying respect: honorific

title printed at the top of each page: running head, running title

title stating theme: lemma

title substituted for proper name: antonomasia

titular: in name only, nominal, so-called

to-do: agitation, brouhaha, commotion, excitement, fight, flap, furor, fuss, hoopla, hubbub, racket, rumpus, stir, turmoil, uproar

toad: amphibian, anuran, bufo, frog, peeper, polliwog, salientian, tadpole

toad, concerning a: anuran, batrachian, bufoniform, salientian

toady: bootlicker, brownnose, fawn, flatterer, flunky, kowtow, lackey, parasite, repulsive, stooge, sycophant, truckler, yes man

toast or bread dipped in sauce or gravy: sippet

toast to health: wassail

toast, thin crispy: melba toast

toasted bread square: crouton

toasted sweetened bread: zwieback

toastmaster: emcee, MC, officiator

tobacco: cigar, cigarette, crop, leaf, plant, shag, smoking, snuff, weed

RELATED TERMS

tobacco addictive chemical: nicotine

tobacco chewing wad: quid

tobacco holder: humidor

tobacco into pipe, tap: tamp

tobacco kiln: oast

tobacco leaf around cigar: wrapper

tobacco plug left in pipe: dottle

tobacco storage case: humidor 🌿

toboggan: bobsled, decline, luge, sled

tocsin: alarm, alert, bell, horn, sign, signal, siren, warning

toddler: child, infant, tot, tyke

toe: appendage, dactyl, digit, phalanx

toe joints, pain in big: bunion, gout

toe mammal, hoofed: artiodactyl

toe with joint bent downward: hammertoe

toe, big: hallux

toe, for one: digit

toeless: adactylous

toenail care: pedicure

toes turned inward: pigeon-toed

toes, animals that walk on: digitigrade

toes, stuff collecting between your: gronk, toe-jam

tofu: bean curd

together: as one, consecutively, en masse, fasten, in concert, integrated, joined, jointly, simultaneously, unison

together and cooperating: synergetic

together, occurring: concomitant, corollary

toil: battle, drudge, drudgery, effort, grind, industry, knell, labor, moil, overwork, pains, plod, plug, slave, snare, strain, strife, struggle, sweat, travail, work

toiler: laborer, peon, serf, slave, worker, workhorse

toilet: attire, bathroom, can, commode, costume, dress, head, john, latrine, lavatory, outhouse, privy, throne

toilet bowl for bathing genitals: bidet

toilet for many at camp: latrine

toilet in nautical terms: head

toilsome: arduous, difficult, hard, laborious, strenuous, tiring, uphill, wearisome

token: badge, emblem, evidence, expression, feature, gesture, gift, indication, keepsake, mark, medal, memento, minimal, nominal, omen, perfunctory, pledge, portent, proof, relic, remembrance, reminder, sign, signal, signify, souvenir, symbol, symbolize, trophy

token of appreciation: honorarium

token of solemn pledge: sacrament

tolerable: acceptable, adequate, allowable, average, bearable, decent, endurable, fair, livable, passable, permitted, satisfactory, so-so, sufferable, sufficient

tolerance: broadmindedness, compassion, endurance, fortitude, grit, hardiness, indulgence, leeway, leniency, mercy, patience, stamina, steadfastness, sufferance, sympathy, tacit consent, threshold, understanding

tolerant: broad-minded, compassionate, easy, enduring, forbearing, forgiving, indulgent, lenient, liberal, magnanimous, patient, permissive, soft, sympathetic

tolerate: abide, accept, allow, bear,

TOASTS AND CHEERS AROUND THE WORLD

Albania: Gezuar!
Austria: Prost!, Prosit!
Belgium: A votre sante!, Gezondheid!
Bulgaria: Nazdrave!
China: Gun-bei!
Denmark: Skal!
Finland: Kippis!, Skal!, Holkyn kolkyn!
France: A votre sante!
Germany: Prost!, Prosit!, Zum Wohl!
Greece: Stin yia ssas!
Hong Kong: Yum-sing!
Ireland: Slainte!
Israel: L'chaim!
Italy: Salute!, Ciao!
Japan: Kam pai!
Mexico: Salud!
Netherlands: Proost!, Santjes!
Norway: Skal!
Poland: Na zdrowie!
Portugal: Saude!
Romania: Noroc!
Scotland: Slainte mhath!
South Africa: Geluk!, Gesondheid!
Spain: Salud!
Sweden: Skal!
Switzerland: Prost!, Zum Wohl!, Sante!, Salute!
Thailand: Chokdee!
Turkey: Serefe!
U.S.S.R.: Na zdorovye!
Wales: Iechyd da!
Yugoslavia: Zieili! ❦

---

brook, condone, countenance, endure, let be, permit, sanction, stand, suffer, sustain, swallow, take, undergo
tolerate and endure: brook, stomach, withstand
tolerate offense: condone
toll: announce, assessment, casualties, charge, chime, cost, customs, damage, deaths, destruction, duty, expense, fee, knell, levy, loss, peal, ring, sacrifice, sound, strike, tariff, tax
toll road: pike
tomahawk: hatchet
tomato: love apple
tomato juice and vodka: Bloody Mary
tomato juice cocktail with no vodka: Virgin Mary
tomb: catacomb, cenotaph, chamber,

crypt, dolmen, grave, mastaba, mausoleum, monument, sepulcher, shrine, tumulus, vault
tomb material cover: pall
tomb, ancient Egyptian: mastaba
tomb, large stately: mausoleum
tomb, stone: sarcophagus
tomboy: gamine, girl, hoyden, meg, spitfire
tombstone: gravestone, market, memorial, monument
tombstone inscription: epitaph
tome: book, encyclopedia, portfolio, volume
tomfoolery: antics, caper, foolishness, frolic, horseplay, malarkey, nonsense, poppycock, prank, silliness
tone: accent, approach, atmosphere, attitude, balance, cast, character, color, drift, effect, elasticity, health, hue, humor, inflection, intonation, manner, modulate, mood, nature, note, nuance, pitch, quality, shade, sound, spirit, strength, style, temper, timbre, tint, trend
tone down: mitigate, moderate, mute, soften, subdue
tone quality distinguishing instrument or singing voice: timbre
tone within a range of musical sounds, relative position of: pitch
tone, subtle difference in: gradation, nuance
tones in a chord played in succession versus simultaneously: arpeggio
tones that have the same pitch but written differently: enharmonic
tongue: dialect, glossal, language, lick, lingo, lingua, lingula, speak, speech, talk, utter, vernacular
tongue bumps: papilla
tongue-lash: berate, castigate, rebuke, reprimand, reproach, scold, upbraid
tongue-shaped: lingulate
tongue-tied: nervous, silent, speechless
tongue to bottom of mouth, tendon holding: frenum
tongue, concerning the: glossal, lingual
tongue, flap under: frenum
tongue, relating to the: glossal
tongue, U-shaped bone under: hyoid bone
tongue, wooden stick: tongue depressor
tonic: astringent, bracer, bracing, invigorating, medicine, refreshing, restorative, roborant, soda, stimulant
tonsils' neighbors: adenoids
too: additionally, along, also, besides,

ever, exceedingly, excessively, extremely, furthermore, immensely, indeed, likewise, more, moreover, over, overly, very
too little: deficient, inadequate, insufficient, lacking, scarce, shortage
too much: excess, excessiveness, overabundant, overcharge, overflow, surplus
tool shaft: mandrel
tool, boring: auger, awl, bit, chuck, countersink, drill, gimlet, pick, reamer, zax
tool, bricklaying: float, hammer, hock, level, trowel
tool, carpentry: adz, auger, awl, bit, brace, chisel, edger, gimlet, hammer, handsaw, hatchet, lathe, level, plane, pliers, punch, rasp, router, sander, saw, square, vise
tool, cutting: adz, adze, ax, axe, bezel, billhook, bit, chisel, gouge, graver, hob, knife, razor, reamer, saw, scissors, shears
tool embedded into handle, part of: shank, tang
tool, engraving: burin, scauper
tool, garden: edger, hoe, mower, rake, sickle, spade, trowel, weeder
tool, gripping: clamp, pincer, pliers, screwdriver, tongs, tweezer, vise, wrench
tool, holding: clamp, vise
tool, prehistoric: celt, eolith, flint, palaeolith, paleolith
tool, striking: hammer, mallet, maul, pestle, punch, wedge
tool, woodworking: adz, adze, bevel, chisel, edgeman, grainer, hammer, plane, saw, scauper, scriber
toot: bender, binge, blow, declare, honk, proclaim, shout, sound, spree, trumpet, whistle
tooth: bicuspid, canine, cog, cuspid, dent, fang, grinder, incisor, ivory, laniary, molar, point, premolar, snag, tine, tusk
RELATED TERMS
tooth decay: caries
tooth enamel: dentine
tooth extraction: exodontia
tooth filling: inlay
tooth gnashing: bruxism
tooth powder: dentifrice
tooth socket in jawbone: alveolus
tooth standing alone: kag
tooth with two points: bicuspid
tooth, broad back grinding: molar

tooth, broken or projecting: snaggletooth

tooth, canine: cuspid

tooth, grinding two-crest: bicuspid, premolar

tooth, long pointed animal: fang

tooth, pointed tearing: canine, eyetooth, laniary

tooth, ridge or band around base of: cingulum

tooth, sharp front: incisor

tooth, to break through gum as a: erupt

tooth, to pull out a: extract ❦

tooth-shaped: dentiform

toothache: odontalgia

toothed device for perforating sheets of stamps: roulette

toothed projection on wheel: ratchet, sprocket

toothed wheel: cog, cogwheel, gear

toothless: edentate, futile, ineffectual, weak

toothlike part: dent, dentation, denticle

toothsome: appetizing, attractive, delicious, luscious, palatable, pleasant, pleasing, savory, spaid, tasty

top: ace, acme, apex, apogee, beginning, best, better, cap, ceiling, chief, choice, cork, cover, covering, cream, crest, crown, dome, dominate, elite, exceed, excel, excellent, foremost, head, highest, lead, leader, lid, maximum, meridian, notable, outdo, peak, pinnacle, preeminent, prime, prune, renowned, roof, summit, superior, surface, surmount, surpass, tip, toy, uppermost, vertex, zenith

top of something, put on: superimpose

top of something, reach: summit, surmount

top-shaped: turbinate

topic: argument, issue, item, material, matter, point, proposition, question, subject, text, theme

topical: confined, contemporary, current, limited, local, newsy, subjective, temporary, timely

topnotch: A-one, best, excellent, finest, first-rate, outstanding, prime, superior

topping: frosting, garnish, meringue, plunge, sauce

topple: capsize, defeat, fall, falter, overset, overthrow, overturn, stumble, teeter, tilt, totter, tumble, upend, upset

topsy-turvy: askew, chaotic, cluttered, cockeyed, confused, disordered, disorganized, head over heels, inverted, jumbled, on end, reversed, upside down, upside-down, upturned

torch: arsonist, beacon, blaze, brand, firebrand, firebug, flambeau, flare, flashlight, incendiary, lamp, lantern, light

torment: afflict, agitate, agonize, agony, anguish, annoy, badger, bait, bedevil, bother, browbeat, crucify, despair, devil, distress, grill, harass, harrow, harry, heckle, hector, irritate, misery, molest, nag, pain, persecute, pester, plague, punish, rack, rag, rib, smite, strain, suffering, tantalize, tease, tempest, torture, travail, trouble, vex

torn: damaged, divided, lacerated, mangled, rent, ripped, shredded, sliced, slit, split, undecided, wavering

tornado: cyclone, funnel, hurricane, squall, storm, thunderstorm, twister, typhoon, whirlwind, wind

torpedo: assassin, attack, cutthroat, damage, destroy, explode, explosive, firework, missile, projectile, ruin, sink, thug, wreck

torpid: apathetic, benumbed, dormant, drowsy, dull, hibernating, idle, inactive, lazy, lethargic, motionless, numb, sluggish, slumberous, static

torpor: apathy, coma, dormancy, dullness, inactivity, languor, lassitude, laziness, lethargy, listlessness, sleep, sluggishness, slumber, stagnation, stupor

torque: armband, collar, force, necklace, revolution, turn, twist

torrent: burst, cascade, cataract, channel, cloudburst, current, deluge, downpour, flood, flow, gush, inundation, outpouring, rush, spate, stream, tide, turbulent, waterfall

torrid: ardent, arid, blazing, burning, crime, fervent, fiery, heated, hot, hurried, impassioned, intense, oppressive, parching, passionate, rapid, scorching, sizzling, sultry, sweltering, zealous

tortilla dip: salsa

tortilla folded around a filling: taco

tortilla stuffed with cheese and meat, chicken, or seafood: enchilada

tortilla wrapped around a filling: burrito

tortoise: chelonian, emyd, laggard, terrapin, testudinal, turtle

tortoise breastplate: plastron

tortoise shell: carapace

tortoise, concerning: chelonian, testudinal

tortuous: anfractuous, bent, circuitous, complex, complicated, convoluted, crooked, curved, deceitful, devious, involved, labyrinthine, meandering, roundabout, sinuate, sinuous, snaky, spiral, twisting, winding, zigzag

torture: abuse, afflict, affliction, agonize, agony, anguish, annoy, beat, crucify, deform, distort, distortion, harrow, hurt, irritate, maim, mangle, mistreat, mutilate, pain, persecute, punish, punishment, rack, smite, torment, tribulation, wring

torture instrument: iron maiden, rack, thumbscrew, wheel

toss: agitate, agonize, bandy, cast, chuck, disturb, flick, fling, flip, flounder, heave, hurl, launch, lob, mix, peg, pitch, propel, roll, serve, sling, throw, turn, twist, upset

tossing and turning in bed: jactitation

total: absolute, accumulate, add, aggregate, all, amount, calculate, come to, complete, comprehensive, comprise, compute, concise, entire, entirety, equal, figure, full, gross, number, overall, sum, summary, summation, tally, thorough, tot, unconditional, utter, whole, yield; demolish, destroy, wreck

total emptiness: void

total withdrawal: cold turkey

totalitarian: absolute, authoritarian, autocratic, despotic, dictatorial, fascist, tyrannical

tote bag: carryall

totem: emblem, figure, pole, representation, symbol, token

touch: abut, affect, blow, border, brush, caress, contact, dab, dash, discuss, feel, feeling, finger, flair, fondle, grope, hand, handle, hint, hit, impinge, influence, inspire, knack, manipulate, meet, method, move, nudge, palpate, pat, paw, pet, reach, rub, scratch, sense, skill, stimulate, strike, stroke, style, suggestion, tactility, tag, tangible, tap, taste, texture, tickle, tincture, trace, trait, whiff

touch for diagnosis or therapy: manipulate, palpate

touch lightly: dab, skim

touch lovingly: caress, fondle

touch of pleasure or pain, slight: glisk

touch off: activate, cause, detonate, discharge, explode, ignite, initiate, light, start

touch or be next to: abut

touch or enter unwanted: impinge

touch up: enhance, improve, modify, polish, remodel, renovate, repair

touch, perceived through: palpable, tangible

touchable: palpable, perceptible, tactile, tactual

touching: abutting, adjacent, adjoining, against, bordering, contact, contacting, contiguous, tangent, upon

touching and affecting: poignant

touchstone: barometer, benchmark, check, criterion, example, gauge, guide, measure, precedent, standard, test, yardstick

touchy: cantankerous, crabby, cranky, cross, delicate, fragile, grouchy, grumpy, huffy, irascible, irritable, oversensitive, peevish, precarious, sensitive, sore, temperamental, testy, tetchy, thin-skinned, ticklish, umbrageous, uptight, volatile

tough: aggressive, bard, brutal, bullheaded, bully, callous, demanding, difficult, durable, enduring, flinty, goon, hardened, hardheaded, hardy, harsh, hoodlum, hooligan, laborious, leathery, mulish, obstinate, pigheaded, pugnacious, punk, resilient, resistant, resolute, rigid, robust, rough, rowdy, ruffian, rugged, ruthless, severe, stern, stiff, strenuous, strict, strong, stubborn, sturdy, taxing, thug, unfortunate, unyielding, uphill, vigorous, violent, viscous

tough and lasting: durable, enduring

tough and recovering readily: resilient

tough and spirited: feisty

tough and stubborn: adamant, hardnosed, impassive, stoical, stolid

toughen: acclimate, anneal, drill, enure, harden, inure, season, stiffen, strengthen, temper

toupee: carpet, hairpiece, periwig, rug, wig

tour: barnstorm, circuit, course, excursion, expedition, jaunt, journey, ride, shift, spell, stint, time, travel, trek, trip, turn, visit, voyage, watch

tour de force: accomplishment, achievement, exploit, feat, masterpiece

tourist: excursionist, globetrotter, rubberneck, sightseer, traveler, vacationist, visitor

tournament: competition, contest, event, joust, match, sport, tourny

tournament where everybody plays everybody: round robin

tourney placement: seed, seeding

tousled: disarrayed, disheveled, disordered, messy, ruffled, rumpled, sloppy, unkempt

tout: acclaim, advertise, ballyhoo, exalt, herald, importune, laud, plug, praise, proclaim, promote, publicize, recommend, solicit, toot, trumpet

tow: cable, drag, draw, ferry, haul, lug, pull, rope, trail, tug

toward: against, anent, approaching, apropos, beneficial, coming, concerning, facing, favoring, forward, into, near, obliging, propitious, regarding, willing

toward the center: centripetal, entad, inner, into, inward

toward the side: lateral

towel with uncut loops: terry, terrycloth

tower: ascend, belfry, brattice, campanile, castle, dominate, exalt, loom, minaret, monolith, mount, outshine, overlook, overtop, pillar, raise, rise, silo, skyscraper, soar, spire, steeple, surpass, transcend, turret, ziggurat

tower for fodder or grain storage: elevator, silo

tower of mosque: minaret

tower or tower-shaped projection: belfrey, turret

tower, bell: campanile

tower, pyramid-shaped temple: ziggurat

towering: dominant, excessive, gigantic, great, high, huge, imposing, intense, lofty, monstrous, outstanding, overpowering, preeminent, soaring, steep, supreme, tall, unequaled

towing vehicle's rear hook or bolt: pintle

town: bourg, burg, city, metropolis, municipality, settlement

town, concerning a: municipal, urban

town, remote and unknown: podunk

toxic: deadly, fatal, harmful, lethal, poisonous, venomous

toy: ball, bauble, blocks, cars, doll, gadget, game, gewgaw, knickknack, miniature, model, novelty, pastime,

pet, play, plaything, puzzle, rattle, sport, teddybear, top, trains, trifle, trinket, yoyo

trace: clue, dash, drop, evidence, flavor, hint, indication, iota, jot, mark, modicum, quantity, remains, remnant, scintilla, semblance, smidgen, soupçon, speck, tincture, tingue, tittle, token, vestige; establish, follow, hunt, locate, seek, track, trail, uncover; outline

trachea: tube, windpipe

track: artery, avenue, circuit, course, groove, oval, path, road, route, rut, slot, speedway, trail, tread

track-and-field leap over bar using pole: pole vault

track of turbulence left by vehicle, visible: wake

track official: starter, timer

track or trail of wild animal: slot, spoor

tract: area, brochure, course, essay, estate, expanse, extent, field, leaflet, lot, pamphlet, parcel, path, plot, portion, range, region, stretch, subdivision, terrain, territory, zone

tractable: amenable, complaisant, compliant, controllable, docile, flexible, gentle, governable, malleable, manageable, obedient, pliable, pliant, tame, workable

traction: adhesion, friction, power, resistance, stress

trade: action, bargain, barter, business, calling, career, clientele, commerce, craft, customers, deal, employ, exchange, handicraft, industry, job, métier, occupation, patronage, patronize, practice, profession, pursuit, sell, skill, substitute, swap, switch, track, traffic, trail, transaction, vocation, work

trade of goods and services: barter

trade prohibition: embargo

trade restrictions as protest of policy: sanctions

trade restrictions to protect from foreign competition: protectionism

trade, concerning: mercantile

trademark: brand, characteristic, emblem, feature, label, logo, logotype, symbol

trademark, protected by: patent, proprietary

trader: barterer, dealer, merchant, monger, salesperson, seller, ship, shopkeeper, stockbroker, tradesperson

TRACK-AND-FIELD EVENTS

1,500 meters
10 km walk
10,000 meters
100 meters
100-meter hurdles
110-meter hurdles
20 km walk
200 meters
3,000-meter steeplechase
400 meters
400-meter hurdles
4x100-meter relay
4x400-meter relay
5,000 meters
50 km walk
800 meters
cross-country running
decathlon
discus throw
fitness walking
hammer throw
heptathlon
high jump
hurdles
javelin throw
long-distance running
long jump
marathon
middle-distance running
modern pentathlon
pole vault
race walking
relay racing
shot put
sprinting
steeplechasing
triathlon
triple jump ❦

---

tradition: belief, code, convention, culture, custom, folklore, heritage, institution, legacy, legend, lore, myth, practice

traditional: acknowledged, ancestral, classical, common, customary, established, fixed, ivied, old, popular, rooted, unwritten, usual

traduce: calumniate, defame, denigrate, disgrace, malign, slander, slur, smear, vilify, violate

traffic: barter, bootleg, business, commerce, dealings, doings, exchange, freight, market, patronage, push, sell, smuggle, trade, truck

traffic obstruction: bottleneck, congestion, gridlock, jam

tragedy: accident, adversity, calamity, catastrophe, disaster, doom, hardship, misfortune, mishap, sorrow

tragedy's fatal flaw: hamartia

tragic: awful, catastrophic, dire, disastrous, dreadful, fatal, horrible, sad, terrible, unfortunate

tragic drama's purification: catharsis

trail: chase, course, dawdle, delay, dog, drag, draw, dwindle, follow, footpath, footprints, footsteps, hound, hunt, lag, linger, mark, path, plod, pursue, route, scent, shadow, spoor, stalk, straggle, stream, tail, tow, trace, track, train, traipse, trudge, wake

train: caravan, convoy, cortege, entourage, following; coach, locomotive, subway

train, to: accustom, breed, coach, condition, conduct, cultivate, develop, direct, discipline, educate, exercise, form, instruct, lead, practice, prepare, rehearse, teach, tutor

trained: aimed, bred, educated, equipped, prepared, qualified, schooled, skilled

trainee: apprentice, cadet, novice, pupil, student

trainee, contracted as: articled

trainer: coach, drillmaster, instructor, mentor, teacher, tutor

training: background, breeding, diet, discipline, drill, education, exercise, instruction, nurture, practice, preparation, schooling, supervision, teaching, upbringing

training device: simulator

training in a trade: vocational training

traipse: drag, drift, gad, meander, ramble, roam, trail, tread, trudge, walk, wander

trait: attribute, characteristic, custom, feature, habit, hallmark, idiosyncrasy, lineament, mannerism, mark, peculiarity, property, quality, quirk, tendency

traitor: apostate, Benedict Arnold, betrayer, defector, deserter, doublecrosser, informer, mole, quisling, rat, recreant, renegade, spy, turncoat

traitor of criminal world: stool pigeon

traitor operating for enemy: agent provocateur, collaborator, mole, plant, quisling, sleeper

traitor to country: defector

traitor to one's race: Uncle Tom

traitorous: disloyal, faithless, false, perfidious, renegade, treacherous, treasonable, unpatriotic, utinous

trajectory: arc, course, curve, missile, path, projectile

tram: cable car, car, gondola, street car, streetcar, thread, trolley

tramp: beggar, bum, crush, derelict, drifter, gallop, harlot, hike, hobo, march, panhandler, picaro, picaroon, plod, pound, prostitute, roam, rogue, slut, stamp, step, stomp, traipse, tread, trudge, vagabond, vagrant, vamp, walk, wander

trample: bruise, crush, defeat, destroy, flatten, infringe, injure, overwhelm, pound, squash, stamp, stomp, tread, tromp

trance: catalepsy, coma, daydream, daze, ecstasy, enchant, enrapture, hypnosis, muse, reverie, spell, stupor, swoon, transport

tranquil: balmy, calm, composed, cool, easygoing, equable, even, gentle, hushed, mild, motionless, Pacific, pastoral, peaceful, placid, quiet, restful, sedate, serene, soothing, steady, still, undisturbed

tranquility: ataraxia, calm, calmness, composure, harmony, order, peace, peacefulness, placidity, quiet, repose, rest, restfulness, serenity

tranquilize: assuage, calm, lull, pacify, quell, quiet, relax, sedate, soothe, subdue

tranquilizer: ataractic, opiate, sedative

tranquilizing hormone: endorphin

transact: accomplish, complete, conclude, conduct, finish, handle, negotiate, perform, transfer

transaction: affair, agreement, bargain, business, contract, covenant, deal, doing, exchange, pact, purchase, sale, trade, undertaking, venture

transcend: ascend, climb, elevate, exceed, excel, outdo, outshine, outstrip, raise, soar, surmount, surpass

transcendent: exceeding, preeminent, superior, supreme, surpassing

transcendental: boundless, mystical, spiritual, surpassing

transcendental meditation formula: mantra

transcribe: copy, decipher, duplicate, record, reprint, reproduce, rewrite, translate

transdermal medicine dispenser: patch

TRAIN AND RAILROAD TERMS

beams supporting rails of railroad track: crossties, ties

building for switching and repairs: roundhouse

car carrying fuel and water: tender

car that unloads through floor: hopper

cars owned by a railroad: rolling stock

device linking cars: coupler, coupling, drawbar

enclosed area at end of passenger car of railroad train: vestibule

freight car with low sides: gondola car

gravel forming bed for railroad track: ballast

locomotive front grid: cowcatcher

low open freight car: gondola car

parlor or sleeping car: Pullman

power-collecting trolley on electric locomotive: pantograph

rail car: caboose, coach, diner, engine, gondola, hopper, locomotive, parlor, Pullman, sleeper, tender

railroad: line, metro, push, railway, rush, track, train, transport

railroad or road bridge with many spans and arches: viaduct

railroad station: depot, terminal

railroad with single track: monorail

railroad's X-shaped warning symbol: crossbuck

rear car: caboose

signal to go: highball

sleeping berth: couchette

sleeping car in Europe: wagon-lit

striped bar that raises and lowers: crossing arm, gate arm

underground railroad: subway ❦

---

transfer: abalienate, assign, assignment, carry, cede, change, changeover, convert, convey, decal, deed, delegate, deliver, demise, dispose, give, move, orders, pass, relocate, sale, send, shift, substitution, trade, transform, transmission, transmit, transport

transfer of claim, right, interest, property: assignment

transfer of emotion to substitute for original: displacement

transfer of estate in will or lease: demise

transfer of title to property: conveyance

transferee, in law: alienee

transfix: astonish, astound, captivate, fascinate, hypnotize, impale, lance, mesmerize, penetrate, pierce, rivet, spear, spellbind, spike, stick

transform: alter, change, convert, metamorphose, mutate, reconstruct, remodel, resolve, revamp, switch, transfigure, transmogrify, turn

transformation: metamorphosis, permutation, sea change, transfiguration, transmogrification

transgress: disobey, err, infringe, lapse, offend, overstep, sin, trespass, violate

transgression: breach, crime, disobedience, error, infraction, infringement, misbehavior, misdeed, offense, sin, trespass, violation, wrongdoing

transient: brief, change, conveyance, ephemeral, evanescent, fleeting, fugitive, guest, impermanent, itinerant, migratory, momentary, passage, passing, temporal, temporary, transitory, traveler, volatile

transit: journey, movement, transportation, travel

transition: alteration, change, changeover, conversion, development, evolution, jump, passage, phase, shift

transition without pause: segue

transitional condition: limbo

transitional form: intergrade

transitory: brief, ephemeral, evanescent, fleeting, fly-by-night, fugacious, impermanent, passing, temporal, temporary, transient

translate: alter, change, convert, decipher, decode, explain, interpret, paraphrase, render, rephrase, restate, transcribe

translation: adaptation, explanation, gloss, interpretation, paraphrase, rendition, simplification, trot, version

translation to another language, literal: loan translation

translation word for word: metaphrase

translation, of a word-for-word: literal, verbatim

translucent: clear, diaphanous, limpid, lucid, obvious, opaque, pellucid, sheer, transparent, unblurred

transmission: broadcast, communication, conveyance, delivery, dispatch, gearbox, message, sending

transmit: broadcast, carry, channel, communicate, conduct, convey, dispatch, emit, funnel, relay, render, send, spread, televise, transfer, wire

transparent: airy, candid, clear, crystalline, evident, filmy, gauzy, glassy, gossamer, hyaline, limpid, lucent, lucid, luminous, obvious, open, pellucid, plain, sheer, translucent

transparent cellulose material: cellophane

transparent when wet: hydrophanous

transparent, not: opaque

transpire: befall, develop, emerge, happen, occur, result

transplant: displace, move, relocate, resettle, transfer, transport, uproot

transplant giver: donor

transplant receiver: donee, recipient

transplant, fail to accept: reject

transplants, drug for preventing rejection of: immunosuppressive

transport: banish, bear, boat, bring, carry, cart, convey, conveyance, deport, exile, expel, ferry, freight, haul, move, oust, piggyback, rapture, send, ship, smuggle, tote, transfer, transit, transplant, truck, vehicle

transport by carrying: portage

transport fee: haulage

transport of goods, people: conveyance, transit

transport of pedestrians, conveyor: people mover

transport service with bus, etc.: shuttle

transportation cost: fare

transpose: alter, change, convert, exchange, interchange, remove, reverse, shift, substitute, switch, transfer, transform

transposing letters of word to form another: anagram

transverse: across, alternate, cross, crosswise, diagonal, horizontal, oblique, pivot, shift, thwart, travel

trap: ambush, artifice, bag, bait, cage, capture, catch, confound, conspiracy, corner, deadfall, decoy, dragnet, ensnare, enticement, fool, hazard, inveigle, lure, maneuver, nail, net, pit, pitfall, ploy, roadblock, seal, seduce, snag, snare, stratagem, temptation, trick, web

trap another, animal used to: decoy

trap for large animals: deadfall

trap for small animals: snare, springe

trap that is feared: pitfall

trap, contradictory and self-defeating: catch-22

trap, intended to: insidious

trapeze acrobat: aerialist

TRAINS AND RAILROAD VEHICLES

air car	day coach	gondola	passenger car	steam locomotive
baggage car	diesel locomotive	handcar	passenger train	stock car
bar car	dining car	hopper car	piggyback car	streetcar
bogie truck	double-decked stock	local train	platform car	subway
booster	drawing room car	locomotive	pony engine	tank car
boxcar	electric car	log car	postal car	tender car
bullet train	electric train	lounge car	private car	tram
bunk car	elephant car	mail car	produce car	trolley
cable car	express car	milk car	Pullman car	trolley bus
caboose	express train	milk train	rack car	trolley car
chair car	flatcar	observation car	rail detector car	truck car
coach	fly coach	officers' car	refrigerator car	underground
coal car	freight car	outfit car	skeleton car	wagon-lit
container car	freight train	palace car	sleeping car	yard engine ❧
dandy cart	freightliner	parlor car	smoking car	

trappings: apparel, caparison, decorations, equipment, finery, gear, paraphernalia, regalia, things, trimmings

trapshooting: skeet

trash: balderdash, bilge, crap, debris, dirt, dregs, drivel, filth, garbage, hogwash, junk, litter, malarkey, muck, nonsense, rabble, refuse, riffraff, rubbish, rubble, scum, tramp, trumpery

trash collector in the U.K.: dustman

trash site: dump

trashy: cheap, flimsy, junky, paltry, riffraff, trumpery, useless, worthless

trashy art, literature: kitsch

trauma: anguish, injury, ordeal, shock, stress, suffering, wound

travail: agony, anguish, childbirth, distress, drudgery, effort, exertion, labor, pains, pangs, parturition, stress, struggle, suffering, toil, tribulation, woe, work

travel: coast, commute, cover ground, cruise, drive, excursion, expedition, explore, flay, jaunt, journey, junket, migrate, move, mush, passage, peregrinate, proceed, ramble, ride, roam, run, sightsee, sojourn, tour, traverse, trek, trip, visit, voyage, walk, wander, wend

travel across, over, or through: traverse

travel back and forth regularly: shuttle

travel from place to place: tour

travel place to place on foot: peregrinate

travel to sacred place or shrine: pilgrimage

travel, proposed route of: itinerary

travel, strong impulse and desire to: wanderlust

traveler: adventurer, commuter, explorer, globetrotter, goer, hobo, itinerant, nomad, pilgrim, rambler, salesperson, sightseer, tourist, tramp, vagabond, viator, voyager, wanderer, wayfarer

traveler of great distances: globetrotter, jetsetter

traveler on foot: wayfarer

travelers journeying together: caravan

traveling bag: etui, valise

traveling entertainer, medieval: jongleur, minstrel, troubadour

traveling in disguise: incognito

traveling library: bookmobile

traveling on foot: peripatetic

traveling place to place: itinerant, migrant

traveling, concerning: viatic

travels a distance to work, person who regularly: commuter

traverse: bridge, contradict, course, crisscross, cross, crosswise, deny, examine, hinder, negotiate, oppose, overpass, pass, rebut, refute, resist, span, swivel, thwart, transom, travel, zigzag

travesty: burlesque, caricature, distortion, exaggeration, imitation, lampoon, mimic, mockery, parody, perversion, ridicule, satire, sham

trawl: drag, dragnet, fish, line, net, seine, troll

tray: board, coaster, plate, platter, salver, server

tray for glass etc., small: coaster

tray for serving food and drink: salver, waiter

tray, circular revolving: dumb waiter, lazy Susan

treacherous: chancy, dangerous, deceptive, difficult, dirty, dishonest, disloyal, faithless, false, hairy, hazardous, insidious, perfidious, precarious, risky, snaky, traitorous, treasonous, tricky, undependable, unreliable, unsafe, unscrupulous, untrustworthy, wily

treacherous person: snake in the grass

treachery: betrayal, deceit, dishonesty, disloyalty, foul play, guile, infidelity, perfidy, treason, trickery

treacle: antidote, compound, molasses, remedy, syrup

tread: dance, footfall, footprint, footsteps, gait, groove, march, mark, pace, prance, press, repress, rush, stamp, step, stomp, stride, subdue, trace, trail, traipse, tramp, trample, walk

treason: betrayal, dishonesty, disloyalty, mutiny, perfidy, revolt, sedition, treachery

treason against sovereign: lèse-majesté, lese majesty

treason, accuse of: impeach

treasure: accumulate, appreciate, cache, cherish, collection, find, fortune, guard, hoard, jewels, money, pearl, preserve, prize, riches, store, trove, value, wealth, worship

treasurer: bursar, cashier, chamberlain, comptroller, curator, financier, officer, purser

treasury: archives, bank, chest, coffer, coffers, depository, exchequer, funds, museum, repository, security, storehouse, vault

treat: delight, goody, refreshment, snack, surprise

treatise: commentary, composition, discourse, discussion, disquisition, dissertation, essay, exposition, memoir, monograph, narration, paper, study, thesis, tract, writing

treatment: action, antidote, application, care, cure, handling, management, medication, method, procedure, remedy, strategy, surgery, therapy, usage

treatment of disease by joint manipulation: chiropractic

treaty: accord, agreement, arrangement, compact, concord, contract, deal, negotiation, pact, peace agreement, peace pact, settlement, understanding

treaty before ratification, copy of: protocol

treaty calling for an end to the acquisition of nuclear arms: nonproliferation treaty

treaty, approve a: ratify

treaty, one who has signed a: signatory

trek: excursion, expedition, hike, jaunt, journey, march, migrate, odyssey, travel, trip, voyage

trellis: arbor, framework, grille, lattice, latticework, pergola, screen

trellis for training fruit trees: espalier

tremble: dodder, fear, flutter, palpitate, quake, quaver, quiver, shake, shiver, shudder, totter, tremor, vibrate, wobble

tremendous: amazing, astounding, colossal, deafening, enormous, extraordinary, fabulous, fantastic, giant, gigantic, great, huge, immense, large, mammoth, marvelous, mighty, momentous, monstrous, overwhelming, powerful, stupendous, terrific, titanic, vast, whopping, wonderful

tremor: ague, earthquake, flutter, quake, quaver, quiver, shaking, shiver, shock, trembler, trembling, vibrating

tremulous: aquiver, aspen, cowardly, excited, fearful, jittery, nervous, palpitating, quavering, quivering, shaking, shivering, timid, timorous, trembling, wavering

trench: canyon, carve, channel, chase, cut, ditch, drain, earthwork, encroach, excavation, fosse, foxhole, furrow, gash, groove, gully, gutter, moat, slash, slice, trough

trench for drainpipes or wiring: chase

trenchant: acrid, biting, caustic, clear-cut, crisp, cutting, distinct, effective, energetic, explicit, forceful, incisive, intense, keen, mordant, penetrating, pointed, probing, sarcastic, scathing, sharp, vigorous

trend: bent, course, craze, current, direction, drift, fad, flow, inclination, mode, movement, rage, style, tendency, vogue

trendsetter: initiator, innovator, leader, pacesetter, stylist, trailblazer

trendy: chichi, chic, contemporary, faddish, fashionable, hip, in, popular, stylish

trepidation: agitation, alarm, anxiety, apprehension, butterflies, consternation, disturbance, dread, fear, fright, nervousness, panic, quaking, quivering, shaking, trembling, tremor, uneasiness

trespass: breach, encroach, encroachment, entrench, infraction, infringe, interlope, intrude, intrusion, invade, offend, offense, poach, sin, transgression, violation, wrongdoing

trespasser: encroacher, infringer, interloper, intruder, invader, offender, transgressor

tress: braid, curl, hair, lock, plait, ringlet

trestle: beam, brace, framework, horse, sawhorse, stand, support

trial: adversity, affliction, agony, anguish, attempt, crucible, hardship, misfortune, ordeal, pain, struggle, suffering, trouble, woe; analysis, attempt, endeavor, essay, experiment, probationary, sample, stab, test, trial, try, tryout, visitation; case, contest, evidence, examination, hearing, inquiry, lawsuit, proceedings, trial

trial and error: experiment, heuristic, method

trial and error approach, of a: heuristic

trial period in which to redeem oneself: probation

trial, preliminary session or inquest before: hearing

triangle opposite the right angle, side of: hypotenuse

triangle rule, right-angled: Pythagorean theorem

triangle side: leg

triangle theorem: Pythagorean

triangle types: equilateral, isosceles, right-angled, scalene

triangle with three equal sides: equilateral

triangle with three unequal sides: scalene

triangle with two equal sides: isosceles

triangle, intersection of three altitudes of: orthocenter

triangles, study of: trigonometry

triangular: cuneate, deltoid, hastate, trigonal, trilateral

triangular alluvial plain: delta

triangular architectural element: gable, pediment

triangular clothing insert: gore, gusset, wedge

triangular string instrument: balalaika

tribal priest-doctor: shaman

tribal symbol: totem

tribe: association, band, clan, division, family, folk, group, kindred, lineage, people, race, society, village

tribe consists of two or more clans, subdivision of: phratry

Tribe of Israel: Dan

tribulation: adversity, affliction, agony, anguish, burden, distress, grief, hardship, misery, ordeal, pain, persecution, sorrow, suffering, trial, unhappiness, woe

tribunal: assembly, bar, bench, board, committee, court, forum, rota, seat

tributary: accessory, ancillary, auxiliary, contributory, dependent, feeder, secondary, stream, subordinate, subsidiary

tribute: accoladetion, applause, assign, citation, commendation, compliment, declaration, duty, eulogy, gift, grant, gratitude, honoration, laudation, levy, memorial, obligation, ovation, panegyric, payment, praise, respect, salvo, tariff, tax, testimonial

trick: ambush, antic, artifice, bait, bamboozle, beguile, bilk, bluff, catch, cheat, chicanery, cozen, deceit, deceive, decoy, defraud, delusion, device, dodge, dupe, escapade, feat, feint, finagle, flimflam, fool, fox, fraud, gag, gimmick, guile, gull, hoax, hoodwink, hornswoggle, illusion, imposture, jape, jest, joke, knack, lark, legerdemain, maneuver, method, mislead, outwit, prank, pretext, ruse, scam, secret, shay, shift, skill, sleight, spell, spoof, stratagem, stunt, subterfuge, swindle, technique, trap, wile

trick by flattery: inveigle

TREES AND SHRUBS

acacia
abele
ailanthus/tree of
   heaven
alder
alerce
algarroba
allspice
almond
aloe
althea
American elm
annatto
apple
apple box
apricot
araucaria
arborvitae
arbutus
areca palm
ash
aspen
assegai/assagai
avocado/alligator
  pear
azalea
babassu
bald cypress
balsa
balsam
balsam fir
balsam poplar
banana
banksia
banyan
baobab
barbasco
barberry
basswood
bay tree
bay rum tree
bayberry
bead tree
beech
beefwood
betel palm
big tree
bigleaf maple
bignonia
bilberry
birch
black acacia
black alder
black ash
black cherry
black maple

black oak
black pine
black spruce
black walnut
blackberry
blackjack oak
blackthorn
blackwood
bladdernut
blue gum
blue spruce
blueberry
bo tree/peepul/pipal
bottle tree
bottlebrush
box elder
boxwood
bramble
Brazil nut
brazilwood
breadfruit
bristlecone pine
broom
buckeye
buckthorn
buddleia
buffalo berry
bunya-bunya
butcher's broom
butternut
buttonball
buttonwood
cabbage palm
cacao
calabash
California laurel
camphor tree
camwood
candleberry
candlewood
caper
carnauba
carob
cascarilla
cashew
cassia
casuarina
catalpa
cedar
cedar of Lebanon
celery pine
chaste tree
chaulmoogra
cherimoya
cherry
cherry plum

chestnut
Chilean pine
chinaberry tree/
   China tree
chinquapin
chittamwood
chokeberry
cinchona
cinnamon
citron
citrus
clematis
cleome
clove
cockspur
coco-de-mer
coconut
coffee
coffee tree
coffeeberry
coolabah
coquito
coral tree
cork oak
corkwood
cornel
cottonwood
crabwood
cranberry
croton
crowberry
cryptomeria
cucumber tree
currant
cycad
cypress
cypress pine
dahoon
daphne
date palm
dawn redwood
deodar/deodara
divi-divi
dogwood
Douglas fir
doum palm
dragon tree
durmast
Dutch elm
ebony
elder
elderberry
elm
eucalyptus
eucryphia
euonymus

false acacia
farkleberry
fever tree
ficus
fig
fir
firethorn
flame tree
flowering ash
forsythia
frankincense
fringe tree
fuchsia
funeral palm
gardenia
germander
giant sequoia
ginkgo
gomuti
gooseberry
grape
grapefruit
greasewood
greenheart
gru-gru palm
guaiacum
guava
guayule
gum
gumbo-limbo
hackberry
hawthorn
hazel/hazelnut
heath
heather
hemlock
hemp tree
henna
hibiscus
hickory
holly
holm oak/holly oak
honey locust
honeysuckle
hoop pine
hop tree
hornbeam
horse chestnut
horseradish tree
huckleberry
hydrangea
Indian mulberry
inkberry
ironwood
ivory palm
jacaranda

jack pine
Japanese cedar
Japanese maple
jarrah
jojoba
Joshua tree
Judas tree
juneberry
juniper
jute
kalmia
karri tree
kauri
kingwood
koa
kowhai
kumquat
kurrajong
laburnum
lacquer tree
lancewood
larch
laurel
lavender
leadwort
lehua
lemon
lignum vitae
lilac
lilly-pilly
lime
linden
liquidambar
litchi/litchi nut
loblolly pine
locust
logwood
longleaf pine
madrona/madrone/
   madrono
magnolia
mahogany
maidenhair tree
mallee tree
manchineel
mango
mangrove
manuka
manzanita
maple
marblewood
mastic tree
mate
mazzard
medlar
mesquite

TREES AND SHRUBS *continued*

milkwort	philodendron	sago palm	spicebush	walnut
mimosa	pine	sallow	spindle tree	wandoo
mistletoe	pistachio	sandalwood	spruce	Washington palm
monkey-bread tree	pitch pine	sandarac	stone pine	water elm
monkey puzzle	plane tree	sandbox tree	strawberry bush	wattle
monkeypod	plum	sapele	strawberry tree	wax palm
mountain ash	podocarpus	sapodilla	sugar gum	wax tree
mulberry	poinciana	sappanwood	sugar maple	wayfaring tree
myrtle	poison ivy	saskatoon	sugar palm	weeping willow
needle-flower tree	poison oak	sassafras	sugar pine	wellingtonia
neem	poison sumac	sasswood/sassy	swamp cypress	western hemlock
night jasmine	pomegranate	satinwood	sweet bay	western red cedar
ninebark	pond apple	savin	sweet cherry	white birch
nipa	poplar	scarlet sage	sweet gum	white cedar
Norfolk Island pine	prickly ash	screw pine	sycamore	white fir
Norway maple	privet	senna	tallow wood	white gum
Norway spruce	puriri	sequoia	tamarack	white oak
nut pine	pussy willow	seringa	tamarind	white pine
nutmeg	quassia	service tree	tamarisk	white poplar
nux vomica	quebracho	serviceberry	tamarugo	white spruce
oak	queen palm	shadbush	tan oak	whitebeam
ocotillo	quince	shagbark	tangerine	whitehorn
oil palm	raffia palm	shea tree	tea tree	wicopy
oleander	rain tree	sheepberry	teak	wild hydrangea
olive	raspberry	silk-cotton tree	terebinth	willow
orange	red cedar	silk oak	thorn tree	wine palm
Osage orange	red fir	silk tree	thuja	winterberry
osier	red gum	silver birch	titi	wintercreeper
pagoda tree	red oak	silver fir	tonka bean	witch hazel
palm	red pine	silver maple	toon	woolly butt
palmetto	redbud	silverberry	toothache tree	wych elm
palmyra	redwood	simarouba	torchwood	yaupon
papaw	rhododendron	sisal	toyon	yellow poplar
papaya	ribbonwood	slippery elm	trembling poplar	yellowroot
paper mulberry	roble	smoke tree	tulip oak	yellowwood/gopher
parlor palm	rose of Sharon	snowbell	tulip tree	wood
partridgeberry	rosebay	snowberry	tupelo	yew
paulownia	rosemary	snowdrop tree	Turkey oak	ylang-ylang
pawpaw	rosewood	soapbark	turpentine tree	yucca
peach	rowan	soapberry	umbrella tree	zebrawood
pear	royal poinciana	sorrel tree	upas	zenobia ☙
pecan	rubber plant	sour gum	varnish tree	
pencil cedar	rubber tree	sourwood	veronica	
pepper tree	sage	southern cypress	viburnum	
persimmon	sagebrush	Spanish cedar	wahoo	

trick game: con game, confidence game, confidence trick

trick or scheme: artifice, deception, evasion, finesse, gambit, maneuver, ploy, shift, stratagem, subterfuge

trick to divert attention: feint

trick, magic: legerdemain, prestidigitation, sleight of hand

trick, to obtain by: finagle

tricked, easily: credulous, gullible

trickery: artifice, cheating, chicanery, cunning, deceit, deception, dishonesty, double-dealing, dupery, duplicity, flimflam, fraud, guile, hanky-panky, ingenuity, knavery, machinations, quackery, scam, shenanigans, skulduggery, slyness, stratagem, tomfoolery, trumpery, underhandedness

trickle: distill, dribble, drip, flow, leak, ooze, percolate, seep

tricky: artful, craft, crafty, cunning, deceitful, delicate, devious, foxy, intricate, Loki, misleading, precarious, sensitive, shifty, slick, sly, sneaky, unstable, wily

tried: approved, demonstrated, dependable, endeavored, essayed, faith-

TREE-RELATED TERMS

art of cutting trees in decorative shapes: topiary
Buddha's tree: bodhi, bo tree
citrus trees: bergamot, calamondin, lemon, lime, orange
concerning trees: arboreal
crowns forming uppermost cover of trees: canopy, crown canopy
dwarf trees: abuscle, bonsai, chinquapin, scrub
evergreen trees: balsam, carob, carobe, cedar, fir, holly, juniper, madrona, olive, pine, pinyon, redwood, sequoia, tamarisk, titi, yew
flowering trees: acacia, dogwood, elder, mimosa, oleaster, redbud, sourwood, sumac
fruit trees: anona, araca, avocado, banana, biriba, capulin, cone, fig, lemon, lime, litchi, medlar, olive, papaw, pawpaw, sapota, tamarind, tangelo, tangerine
hardwood trees: beech, birch, cherry, chestnut, ebony, oak
large rounded outgrowth: burl
mass of small trees: coppice, copse
mass of trees: boscage, boskage, thicket
miniature Japanese tree or shrub: bonsai
needle-leaved evergreen: conifer
nut trees: almond, buckeye, cashew, cola, filbert, hazel, hickory, kola, pecan, pinon, pistachio
of a tree with spread-out branches: brachiate
of trees retaining their leaves: evergreen
of trees shedding their leaves: deciduous
oil-yielding trees: bel, ben, cajeput, ebo, eboe, shea, tung
palm trees: arengs, carnauba, coco, grugru, nipa, pinang, raffia, ratan, rattan

plantain tree: pala
shade trees: ash, elm, linden, maple, oak, poplar, sycamore
softwood trees: Alamo, ambay, balsa, black gum, cedar, corkwood, fir, lin, linde, pine, spruce, tupelo
study of trees: arboriculture, dendrology, silviculture
tree collection for scientific and educational purposes: arboretum
tree grown from seed: stand
tree or garden with variety: arboretum
tree parts: bark, bole, branch, knot, leaf, root, trunk, twig
tree plant type: dicot, dicotyledon
tree ring study: dendrochronology
tree spirit: dryad, hamadryad, wood nymph
tree trunk: bole
tree whose seeds are not inside ovary: gymnosperm
tree with top branches cut back: pollard
tree worship: dendrolatry
tree-bordered walk: alameda
tree's fluid: sap
trees or forests of a region: silva
trees serving to lessen the wind's force: windbreak
tree-shaped: arboreal, arborescent, dendriform, dendroid, ramate, treelike
tropical trees: acajou, allspice, areca, balsa, baobab, cacao, cherimoya, citrus, mangrove, ohia, palmyra, sago, sweetsop, teak
upper leafy part: crown
willow trees: osier, poplar, sauch, saugh
young tree: sapling ❦

---

ful, known, proved, reliable, tasted, tested, trustworthy, used
trifle: bagatelle, bauble, bit, dabble, dally, dash, dawdle, deceive, dessert, dibble, do it, doodle, drop, fiddle, fidget, flirt, fribble, frivol, gewgaw, gimcrack, hair, hint, jest, jot, knickknack, little, minutia, nothing, novelty, palter, pinch, play, plaything, putter, snippet, sou, speck, suggestion, touch, toy, trace, trick, trinket, triviality, waste
trifle with: coquet, flirt, toy
trifling: banal, frivolous, idle, immaterial, inane, insignificant, little, measly, mere, negligible, nominal, opuscule, petty, piddling, puny, shallow, slight, small, trivial, unimportant, worthless
trifling distinction: quibble, quiddity
trifling fault: peccadillo
trigger: activate, cause, generate, initiate, lever, prompt, provoke, release, spark, start, stimulate
trigonometric function: cosine, sine

trill: quaver, roll, shake, sound, tremolo, twirl, vibrate, vibrato, warble
trilling sound of grasshopper, bird: chirr
trillion prefix: tera-
trim or cut tree branches: lop
trimming: braid, border, decoration, edging, embellishment, embroidery, extras, flounce, frill, fringe, lace, ornament, piping, rickrack, ruffle, trapping
trinity: three, threesome, triad, trilogy, trine, trio, triune
trinity, religious: Father, Holy Ghost, Son
trinket: bagatelle, bauble, bibelot, bijou, curio, doodad, doohickey, fallal, gadget, gaud, gewgaw, gimcrack, jewel, kickshaw, knickknack, novelty, ornament, plaything, showpiece, tchotchke, thingamabob, thingamajig, toy, trifle
trio: threesome, triad, trinity, triune
trip: cruise, drive, errand, excursion,

expedition, hike, jaunt, journey, junket, outing, ride, safari, tour, trek, voyage
trip segment: leg
trip, short pleasurable: excursion, jaunt, junket, spree
trip, take short frivolous: gad about, gallivant
trite: banal, clichéd, common, commonplace, conventional, corny, dated, dull, everyday, hackneyed, inane, jejune, old, ordinary, passé, prosaic, routine, shopworn, silly, stale, stereotyped, threadbare, timeworn, tired, trivial, uninspired, unoriginal, vapid, worn
trite and worn-out: hack, hackneyed
trite remark: bromide, cliché, platitude
triturate: crush, grind, pound, pulverize, rub, thrash
triumph: achievement, beat, celebration, conquer, conquest, defeat, exult, exultation, flourish, glory, jubilation, mastery, overcome, pin one's

ears back, prevail, succeed, success, victory, win

triumphant: celebrating, elated, exultant, exulting, glorious, joyous, jubilant, successful, victorious

trivial: banal, bupkes, commonplace, featherweight, frivolous, inane, incidental, inconsequential, insignificant, little, meaningless, measly, minor, negligible, nominal, ordinary, paltry, peanuts, petty, picayune, slight, small, superficial, trifling, trite, unimportant, unimpressive

trivial things, person getting worked up about: microlipet

troll: dwarf, fairy, giant, gnome, goblin, gremlin, hobgoblin, ogre, sprite

trolley: tram

trollop: floozy, harlot, hussy, prostitute, slut, streetwalker, whore

trombone moving piece: glide, slide

troop: army, array, band, battery, cavalry, combatants, company, corps, crew, crowd, drove, flock, gang, gathering, group, infantry, legion, march, military, outfit, pack, soldiers, squad, troupe, unit

RELATED TERMS

troop formation: echelon, enfilade, phalanx
troop review or inspection: muster
troops at a military post: garrison
troops' lodging: billet, canton, quarters
troops out in front: vanguard
troops with civilian control, replace: demilitarize, disengage
troops, dismiss or discharge: demobilize, disband
troops, prepare and assemble: marshal, mobilize, muster
troops, selected unit of: detachment
troops, support: reinforcements
troops, to position: deploy, station ❦

trophy: award, booty, citation, crown, cup, honor, keepsake, laurel, medal, memento, memorial, prize, reward, ribbon, souvenir

trophy base: plinth

tropical: hot, steamy, sultry, sweltering, torrid, warm

tropical fruit: avocado, guava, mango, pineapple, ugli

tropical tree: date palm, ebo, eboe, palm, teak, ule

trot: canter, gait, hasten, hurry, jog, pace, pony, run, toddler, tot

troth: betrothal, declaration, engagement, fidelity, marriage, pledge, promise

troubadour: balladeer, bard, minstrel, musician, poet, singer

trouble: ado, adversity, afflict, aggrieve, agitate, ail, ailment, anger, annoy, anxiety, bother, burden, calamity, care, commotion, complaint, concern, crisis, danger, difficulty, dilemma, disability, discomfort, discommode, disorder, displeasure, dissension, distress, disturb, disturbance, dither, effort, exertion, fret, fuss, grief, harass, hardship, harm, heed, illness, impair, inconvenience, interfere, irk, labor, malady, matter, mess, mischief, misfortune, ordeal, pain, pains, perturb, pester, pickle, plague, plight, pother, predicament, scrape, snag, sorrow, spot, stir, strife, torment, travail, try, uneasiness, unrest, unsettle, upset, vex, woe, worry

trouble with constant demands: importune

trouble, make: raise Cain

troubled: afflicted, alarmed, asea, bothered, concerned, distraught, distressed, fazed, fearful, harassed, irritated, pained, plagued, puzzled, tormented, uneasy, upset, worried

troublemaker: agitator, enfant terrible, firebrad, firebrand, gremlin, incendiary, instigator, knave, miscreant, nuisance, punk, rascal

troublesome: annoying, arduous, belligerent, bothersome, burdensome, demanding, difficult, disturbing, fractious, inconvenient, irksome, onerous, oppressive, pesky, problematic, sticky, tiresome, trying, unruly, upsetting, vexing, wicked, worrisome

trough: basin, channel, chute, conduit, gutter, sluice

trounce: beat, clobber, conquer, cream, defeat, drub, flog, hammer, lick, overwhelm, pommel, rout, rush, scold, ship, thrash

troupe: actors, band, company, group, outfit, performers

trousers: breeches, britches, dungarees, jeans, knickers, pantaloons, pants, slacks

trousers cut to resemble skirt, woman's: culottes

trousers, heavy leather: chaps

truant: absent, idle, lazy, loafer, missing, neglectful, shirker, slacker, stray, straying

truce: armistice, break, breather, ceasefire, cessation, halt, letup, pause, peace, respite

truck: bargain, barter, business, cart, commerce, dealings, dolly, dray, exchange, handcart, lorry, move, negotiate, peddle, rig, rubbish, trade, traffic, transport, trash, van, vehicle

truck in V-shaped accident, tractor-trailer: jackknife

truck platform for raising worker: cherry picker

truck, large two-section: semi, tractor-trailer

truckle: apple-polish, bootlick, caster, fawn, grovel, kowtow, ringe, servile, submissive, submit, succumb, toady, trundle, yield

truculent: abusive, aggressive, antagonistic, barbarous, bellicose, belligerent, brutal, bullying, combative, cruel, ferocious, fierce, harsh, hostile, intimidating, militant, pugnacious, rough, rude, saage, scathing, scrappy, surly, vituperative

trudge: drag, hike, hobble, lumber, march, plod, schlep, slog, slug, toil, traipse, tramp, trek, walk

true: accurate, actual, authentic, bona fide, certain, constant, correct, dependable, devoted, dutiful, essential, exact, exactly, factual, faithful, fundamental, genuine, honest, honorable, just, kosher, lawful, legitimate, level, loyal, precise, proper, pure, real, reliable, resolute, right, rightful, sincere, staunch, steadfast, steady, trustworthy, truthful, unfeigned, upright, valid, veracious, veridical, veritable

true-blue: dependable, faithful, loyal, reliable, staunch

true or real, quality of being: verisimilitude

true or valid but open to doubt: credible, plausible

true to life: lifelike, naturalistic

true, acceptance as: credence

true, affirm to be: attest, corroborate, substantiate, validate, verify

true, demonstrably: apodictic, incontrovertible, veritable

true, quality of being: verity

truelove: beloved, lover, sweetheart

truism: adage, aphorism, axiom, cliché, maxim, motto, platitude, proverb, saying, self-evident truth

truly: absolutely, accurately, actually, as a matter of fact, certainly, definitely, exactly, genuinely, honestly, indeed, literally, positively, really, rightly, sincerely, surely, unequivocally, verily, very, well

trumpery: bosh, cheap, cheesy, deception, gaudy, malarkey, nonsense, paltry, rubbish, shoddy, showy, tawdry, trash, trickery, useless, worthless

trumpet: advertise, blare, herald, proclaim, publish, tout; bugle, clarion, cornet, horn, instrument

trumpet fanfare: tantara, tucket

trumpet mute: sordino

trumpet, medieval: clarion

truncate: abbreviate, abridge, condense, crop, curtail, cut, lessen, lop, prune, shear, shorten, trim

truncheon: bat, baton, bludgeon, stick, weapon

trundle: cart, caster, dolly, revolve, roll, roller, rotate, spin, turn, twirl, wheel, whirl

trunk: baggage, body, bole, box, case, chest, container, locker, luggage, proboscis, snoot, snout, stalk, stem, suitcase, tank, thorax, torso

trunk, body: torso

trunk, elephant: proboscis

trunk, tree: bole

truss: beam, bind, bracket, bundle, fasten, framework, hold, pack, prop, strap, strengthen, support, tie, tighten

trust: assign, assume, assurance, belief, believe, business, care, cartel, coalition, commission, confide, confidence, consign, credence, credit, custody, dependence, duty, faith, hope, loyalty, organization, presume, protection, reliance, rely, responsibility, safekeeping, security, stock, syndicate

trust, steal or misuse funds held in: defalcate, embezzle, peculate

trustee: administrator, bailee, custodian, depositary, depository, director, fiduciary, guardian, overseer

trustee or trusteeship, of: fiduciary

trustworthy: aboveboard, authentic, believable, confidential, credible, dependable, ethical, faithful, honest, loyal, reliable, responsible, safe, solid, sound, straight, tried, true, trusty, upright

trusty: credible, dependable, faithful, reliable, trustworthy

truth: accuracy, agreement, authenticity, axiom, candor, correctness, fact, fidelity, genuineness, gospel, honesty, integrity, lowdown, loyalty, realism, reality, scoop, sincerity, sooth, troth, truism, uprightness, validity, veracity, verity

truth by logical argument, arrival at: dialectic

truth, of plain: unvarnished

truth, universally accepted: axiom, maxim

truthful: aboveboard, accurate, candid, factual, frank, honest, open, sincere, square, trustworthy, trusty, veracious, verdical, veridical

try: adjudge, afflict, agonize, aim, annoy, assay, attempt, audition, bother, contest, crack, effort, endeavor, essay, examine, experiment, fling, harass, hear, irk, irritate, judge, opportunity, partake, prove, render, sample, screen, seek, stab, strain, strive, struggle, subject, taste, test, torment, torture, trial, trouble, turn, undertake, upset, venture, vex, whack, whirl

trying: annoying, arduous, bothersome, burdensome, demanding, difficult, exasperating, exhausting, hard, irksome, onerous, rough, strenuous, stressful, taxing, testing, tight, tough

trying experience: ordeal

tryst: agreement, appointment, assignation, date, engagement, meeting, rendezvous, union, visit

tub: barge, barrel, bath, bathe, boat, bucket, cask, crate, keeve, keg, scow, ship, tank, vat, vessel

tubby: chubby, fat, jumbo, large, plump, portly, pudgy, rotund

tube: cannula, chute, conduit, cylinder, duct, hose, pipe, pipeline, pipette, straw, subway, television, tunnel

tube between mouth and stomach: esophagus, gullet, throat

tube for draining body cavity: cannula, catheter

tube for transfer of liquid to lower-level container: siphon

tube-shaped optical instrument with colored pieces: kaleidoscope

tube, diameter inside of: caliber

tube, female: fallopian tube, oviduct

tube, small and often graduated: pipette

tuber: beet, bulb, jalap, potato, protuberance, root, salep, stem, swelling, taro, tubercule, turnip, yam

tuber trimmer: potato peeler

tuberculosis: consumption, phthisis, TB

tubular pasta: ziti

tuck: beat, cramp, enfold, fold, food, insert, pinch, pleat, save, shorten, stick, stuff, tap

tucker: exhaust, fatigue, poop, tire, wary, wilt

tuft: batch, beard, bunch, bundle, clump, cluster, feathers, goatee, group, mound, tassel, wisp

tuft of grass, hair: tussock

tuft of hair: cowlick

tuft of ribbon, yarn, feathers: pompom, pompon

tufted marsh plant: sedge

tug: chain, contend, contest, drag, draw, drudge, effort, haul, heave, labor, lug, pull, rope, strain, strap, strive, struggle, toil, tow, wrestle, yank

tuition: charge, cost, education, expenditure, instruction, teaching, tutelage

tumble: collapse, confusion, disarrange, disorder, fall, flatten, flip, jumble, level, overthrow, pitch, plummet, plunge, roll, rumple, somersault, spill, stumble, topple, toss, trip, twist, upset, whirl

tumid: bloated, bombastic, distended, bulging, enlarged, inflated, overblown, pompous, protuberant, puffy, swollen, tumescent, turgid

tummy noises: borborygmus

tumor: bombast, cancer, carcinoma, cyst, growth, gumma, hepatoma, lipoma, melanoma, neoplasm, papilloma, polyp, sarcocele, sarcoma, scirrhus, wart, wen

tumor of connective tissues, malignant: carcinoma, sarcoma

tumor that is a danger: malignant

tumor that is not a danger: benign

tumor, malignant: sarcoma

tumor, skin: melanoma

tumor, small usually benign: papilloma, polyp

tumult: ado, agitation, Babel, bedlam, biot, bluster, brawl, commotion, confusion, disorder, disturbance, dither,

excitement, fray, fuss, hassle, hubbub, hullabaloo, noise, outbreak,
outburst, outcry, pandemonium, paroxysm, racket, revolt, riot, stew, turbulence, turmoil, upheaval, uprising,
uproar

tumultuous: agitated, boisterous, chaotic, confused, disorderly, furious,
hectic, noisy, raucous, rough, rowdy,
stormy, turbulent, unruly, violent,
wild

tuna, canned: albacore

tune: accord, agreement, air, aria,
carol, concert, concord, disposition,
ditty, harmonize, harmony, jingle,
key, lilt, measure, melody, number,
piece, pitch, sonace, sound, strain,
string

tune an instrument: temper

tune, commercial: jingle

tune, humorous: quodlibet

tune, regularly repeated verse or: burden, chorus, refrain

tune, signature: theme song

tuneful: ariose, catchy, dulcet, harmonious, lyrical, melodious, musical,
rhythmic

tunic: blouse, chiton, coat, jacket, kirtle, robe, surcoat, toga

tuning fork: diapason, tonometer

tunnel: adit, bore, burrow, conduit,
crawlway, excavate, mine, passageway, shaft, subway, tube, underpass

turban: bandana, cap, hat, headdress,
lungi

turbid: cloudy, confused, dark, dense,
heavy, impure, muddled, muddy,
murky, obscure, polluted, roily, sedimentary, thick, unclear, unsettled

turbulence: agitation, bluster, commotion, disorder, disturbance, fight, fracas, frenzy, fury, havoc, tumult, turmoil, uproar

turbulent: agitated, blustering, boisterous, bumpy, chaotic, choppy, fierce,
furious, raging, rampant, rebellious,
restless, rough, rowdy, stormy, tempestuous, tumultuous, uncontrolled,
unruly, unsettled, unstable, violent,
wild

turbulent condition: maelstrom

turf: area, bailiwick, divot, earth, grass,
greensward, ground, neighborhood,
racetrack, region, sod, sods, soil,
sward, terrain, territory, track

turf piece: divot

turgid: bloated, bombastic, distended,
enlarged, grandiloquent, grandiose,

inflated, ornate, pompous, pretentious, puffy, swollen, tumescent,
tumid

turkey or chicken's fleshy neck growth:
caruncle, wattle

turmoil: ado, agitation, anxiety, bedlam, chaos, commotion, confusion,
disorder, disquiet, distress, disturbance, ferment, hubbub, pandemonium, riot, strife, toil, trouble, tumult, turbulence, unrest, upheaval,
uproar, upset

turn around: about-face, change, gyrate, reversal, revolve, rotate, shift,
spin, time

turn aside: avert, deflect, detour, digress, divert, shunt, skew, swerve,
veer, ward off

turn at an angle: skew

turn away: avert, deflect, desert, deter,
deviate, dismiss, distract, divert, repel, shunt, swerve

turn back: fold, halt, repel, retrace, retreat, retrogress, return, reverse, revert, stop

turn down: decline, lower, rebuff, refuse, reject, repudiate, scorn, spurn,
veto

turn from main subject: digress

turn inside out or outward: evert

turn into new form: metamorphose,
mutate, transform, transmogrify

turn inward: introvert

turn left: haw, veer

turn loose: release

turn off: alienate, bore, deflect, detour,
disgust, divert, halt, nauseate, repel,
repulse, stop, unplug, withdraw

turn on: activate, arouse, begin, enchant, energize, excite, initiate, start,
stimulate

turn on axis: spin

turn or bend in tubular organ: flexure

turn or go back to place or condition:
revert

turn over: assign, consider, contemplate, delegate, deliver, entrust, flip,
give, invert, keel, keep, ponder, reflect, relinquish, roll, rotate, spill,
surrender, topple, transfer, upend,
upset

turn palm to face down or back: pronate

turn palm to face up or forward:
supinate

turn to the right: gee

turn up: appear, arrive, detect, discover, emerge, find, increase, materialize, show, surface, uncover, unearth

turn upside-down or inside-out: invert

turn while fastened to something:
pivot, swivel

turncoat: apostate, betrayer, defector,
deserter, rat, renegade, spy, traitor

turning or twisting force: torque,
torsion

turning or winding: anfractuous, contorted, revolving, tortuous, twisting,
vertiginous

turning point: climax, crisis, critical
point, emergency, juncture, pivot,
watershed

turning point, ultimate: Rubicon

**turning thoughts, feelings toward one-
self:** introversion

turning to someone for aid, security:
recourse

turnip: neep, plant, rutabaga,
vegetable

turnout: attendance, audience, crowd,
gathering, output, productivity,
quota, volume, yield

turnpike: freeway, highway, parkway,
road, thruway, tollgate

turpitude: baseness, depravity, evil, immortality, vileness, wickedness

turquoise: aqua, aquamarine, blue-
green, color, gemstone, greenish-
blue, mineral, sea-green, stone

turret: belfry, gunhouse, gunmount,
lathe, minaret, spire, steeple, tower

turret, tower with excellent view:
mirador

turtle: chelonian, cooter, leatherback,
loggerhead, reptile, shagtail, slowpoke, snapper, terrapin, testudinal,
tortoise

turtle shell: carapace, mail

turtle, concerning a: chelonian,
testudinal

turtle, North American aquatic: terrapin

turtle's bony plate: breastplate, plastron

tusk: canine, fang, incisor, ivory,
tooth, tush

tussle: battle, brawl, conflict, contest,
fight, hassle, scrap, scuffle, skirmish,
spar, struggle, wrestle

tutelage: guardianship, guidance, instruction, schooling, teaching,
tuition

tutor: coach, direct, drill, educator,
guide, guru, instruct, instructor,
mentor, pedagogue, prepare, school,
teach, teacher, train

tutor without faculty rank: docent

tutorship: tutelage

tuxedo: black tie

TV award: Emmy

TV screen identifying the topic, box or window above newscaster's head: topic box

TV screen when a station is off the air, multicolored stripes on: color bars, colorburst

TV screen, typed information rolling along: crawl

twaddle: babble, balderdash, blabber, bosh, bunk, chat, chatter, drivel, gabble, jaber, nonsense, pap, poppycock, prate, rot, talk, tommyrot, tosh

twang: nasality, resonance, resound, sound, twank, vibration

tweak: adjust, jerk, pinch, pluck, pull, tease, twist

tweet: chirp, chirrup, peep, twitter

twelfth night: Epiphany

twelve times a year: monthly

twelve, concerning: duodecimal, duodenary

twentieth anniversary: vigentennial

twenty-five cents: two bits

twenty-four hour occurrence or cycle: circadian

twenty-six fortnights: year

twenty quires: ream

twenty years, every or lasting: vicennial

twentyfold: vigesimal

twice a week: semiweekly

twice a year: biannual, biennial, semiannual

twig: branch, limb, offshoot, scion, shoot, sprig

twig used for grafting or planting: scion, slip

twig, long rodlike: osier

twig, slender flexible: switch

twig, tough and supple: withe, withy

twiglike work or furniture: wickerwork

twilight: crepuscule, decline, dusk, eve, evening, eventide, gloam, gloaming, nightfall, sundown, sunset

twilight, concerning: crepuscular

twin: binate, clone, counterpart, couple, didymous, double, dual, duplicate, fraternal, identical, lookalike, pair, two

twine: braid, coil, cord, encircle, encurl, entangle, interlace, interweave, knot, rope, snarl, spiral, string, tangle, thread, twist, vine, weave, wind, wrap, wreathe

twinge: ache, apin, cramp, misery, pang, qualm, stitch, twitch

twinge of fear: qualm

twinkle: blink, flash, flicker, flit, flut-ter, gleam, glimmer, glint, glisten, glitter, glow, illuminate, scintillate, shimmer, shine, sparkle, wink

twirl: alter, braid, coil, convolute, falsify, gyrate, gyre, kink, knot, oddity, pirouette, pivot, ravel, revolve, rotation, slant, snake, spin, surprise, swivel, tangle, turn, twist, whirl, worm, wrap, wriggle, zigzag

twist: bend, coil, contort, corkscrew, crink, curve, deviation, distort, entwine, gnarl, intertwine, interweave, kink, meander, misrepresent, peculiarity, quirk, revolve, screw, spin, spiral, squiggle, squirm, tendril, thread, torsion, turn, tweak, twine, warp, wind, wrench, wrest, wring, writhe

twist and interweave: braid, plait

twist as in pain, struggle: writhe

twist out of shape: distort

twisted: awry, bent, braided, complicated, contorted, convoluted, crooked, curled, gnarled, intricate, involved, knurly, slewed, tangled, tortile, wound, wrenched, wry

twisted or corrupted: perverted

twisted or involved, very: convoluted

twisted or strained out of shape: contorted, distorted

twisted to one side: amiss, askew, awry

twister: cyclone, tornado, typhoon, whirlwind

twisting and winding: anfractuous, tortuous

twisting force: torque, torsion

twisting or curling: curlicue, helix, volute, whorl

twisting spiral: maelstrom, vortex, whirlpool

twitch: clutch, contraction, draw, grasp, jerk, lurch, pick, pluck, pull, shake, shudder, snatch, spasm, tic, tremble, tug, twinge, vellicate, yank

twitter: chat, chatter, cheep, chirp, chirrup, chitter, flutter, giggle, peep, sing, sound, titter, tweet

twittering or chirping of insects: fritinancy

two: binary, couple, dos, double, dual, duet, dyad, number, pair, twin

two chambers, having: bicameral

two contradictory parts or opinions, division into: dichotomy

two-dot mark: colon

two dots over Germanic vowel: umlaut

two dots over second of two vowels to indicate separate pronunciation: dieresis

two-faced: deceitful, devious, dishonest, false, hypocritical, treacherous, underhanded

two-footed: biped, bipedal

two-footed sloth: unau

two-hulled boat with sails: catamaran

two meanings to phrase, one risqué: double entendre

two minds, of: ambivalent

two months, every: bimonthly

two months in duration: bimestrial

two names or terms, relating to: binomial

two negatives in one sentence: double negative

two of a kind: brace, pair

two offspring, bearing: biparous

two opposed groups, parts: dichotomy

two or more distinct personalities disorder: multiple personality

two or more husbands at once: polyandry

two or more wives at once: polygamy

two-part division by opinion: dichotomy

two parts, divide into: bisect

two parts, divided into: bipartite

two points, in football: safety

two-purpose: dual

two-time: betray, cheat, deceive, double-cross, mislead

two tones rapidly alternated in music: trill

two trials for one offense: double jeopardy

two vowel sounds blended (e.g. boil, fine): diphthong

two vowels drawn together into one syllable: syneresis, synizesis

two-wheeled carriage: chaise

two-wheeled carriage with springs: trap

two-wheeler: bicycle, bike, caleche, cycle, tilbury

two-year period: biennium

twofold: bifold, binal, binary, diploid, double, dual, duple, duplex, paired

twosome: couple, duet, duo, dyad, pair

tycoon: baron, bigwig, financier, industrialist, magnate, mogul, nabob

tycoon, powerful and exploitive: robber baron

tying or binding: ligature

tying up for sexual pleasure: bondage

tyke: boy, child, cur, dog, mongrel, squirt

TYPE-RELATED TERMS

type aligned to a margin: justified
type in one size and style, complete set of: font
type measure: em, en, pica
type size and style: typeface
type size measure, ⅙ of inch: pica
type size measure, 1⁄12 of inch: point
type spacing between lines, measured in points: leading
type style, handwriting-like: cursive
type style, heavy and thick: boldface
type style, slanted: italic
type style, upright: roman
type that extends below line: descender
type that extends upward: ascender
type unit of measure 1⁄12 inch: point
type, half of width of square piece of: en
type, width of square piece of: em
typeface: agate, boldface, case, font, italic, pica, roman
typeface embellishment: serif
typeface, characters of a: font ☙

---

tympanic membrane: eardrum
type: breed, category, character, class, classify, emblem, example, family, form, genre, group, ilk, kind, mark, model, mold, nature, order, pattern, persuasion, race, sign, sort, species, specimen, stamp, strain, stripe, symbol, variety
type or kind in art, music, literature, film: genre
typesetter: compositor
typesetting methods: Linotype, Monotype, photocomposition
typewriter for dictation: stenotype
typewriter operated by telephone: telex
typewriter standard keyboard: QWERTY
typewriter's bar holding paper down: bail
typewriter's roller: platen
typhoon: cyclone, hurricane, storm, tornado, twister
typical: average, characteristic, classic, common, commonplace, conventional, everyday, exemplary, ideal, model, normal, ordinary, orthodox, regular, representative, standard, stereotypical, usual
typical and regular: average, commonplace, everyday, run-of-the-mill, stock
typical and standard: exemplary, paradigmatic, representative, textbook

typical example: embodiment, exemplar, image, incarnation, personification, quintessence
typical example of class, quality: byword, epitome, paradigm, type
typical of condition: symptomatic
typical or original: archetype, prototype
typical person for image or type: stereotype
typical standard, model, pattern: norm
typify: characterize, embody, epitomize, illustrate, personify, prefigure, represent, symbolize
typographical error: errata, typo
tyrannical: brutal, cruel, despotic, dictatorial, domineering, harsh, imperious, oppressive, totalitarian
tyrannize: dictate, dominate, oppress, trample
tyranny: absolutism, autocracy, despotism, dictatorship, fascism, oppression, repression, rigor
tyrant: autarch, autocrat, bully, Caesar, czar, despot, dictator, martinet, oppressor, overlord, persecutor, tsar
tyro: amateur, apprentice, beginner, greenhorn, neo, neophyte, newcomer, novice, rookie, tenderfoot, trainee

Uu Un

U-shaped: hippocrepiform, horseshoe
U-shaped lake: oxbow
U-turn: about-face, volte-face
ubiquitous: everywhere, omnipresent, pervasive, universal, widespread
ugly: appalling, awful, bad, base, beastly, crabbed, cranky, dangerous, despicable, disagreeable, disfigured, disgusting, foul, frightful, gloomy, grave, grisly, gross, grotesque, gruesome, hideous, homely, horrible, ill-favored, loathsome, nasty, offensive, ominous, repellent, repugnant, repulsive, revolting, servile, shocking, terrible, threatening, toady, troublesome, unattractive, unpleasant, vile, wretched
ugly and displeasing: unaesthetic, unsightly
ugly and monstrous: deformed, disfigured, grotesque, misshapen, mutilated
ugly structure or thing: abomination, eyesore
ulcer: abscess, boil, canker, lesion, sore
ulcer types: duodenal, gastric, peptic
ulterior: concealed, covert, enigmatic, guarded, hidden, later, obscure, privy, secret, selfish, shrouded, subsequent, undisclosed, undivulged
ultimate: absolute, best, capping, conclusive, elemental, end, eventual, extreme, farthest, final, fundamental, grand, greatest, last, maximum, paramount, peak, preeminent, primary, remote, supreme, transcendent, utmost
ultimatum: demand, offer, order, requirement, terms, threat
ultra: beyond, excessive, extravagant, extreme, fanatical, forward, outlandish, radical, ultimate
umber: brown, brownish, chestnut, color, darken, shadowy

umbilicus: navel
umbrage: anger, animosity, chagrin, displeasure, fury, grudge, hint, incense, infuriate, offend, offense, outrage, pique, protection, rage, resentment, shade, shadow, shelter, suspicion, trace, wrath
umbrella: brolly, guard, parasol, protect, screen, shade, shelter, sunshade
umbrella tip: ferrule
umbrella, sun: parasol
umpire: arbiter, arbitrator, decide, judge, mediator, moderator, negotiator, peacemaker, referee, rule
unable: cannot, helpless, impotent, inadequate, incapable, incompetent, inept, powerless, unqualified, weak
unable to act as desired: impotent
unable to deal with numbers: innumerate
unable to read: illiterate, unlettered
unabridged: complete, entire, full length, in extenso, intact, unabbreviated, uncut, whole
unacceptable: below par, deficient, inadequate, intolerable, lousy, poor, unsuitable, unwelcome, unworthy
unacceptable person: persona non grata
unaccompanied: abandoned, alone, deserted, detached, isolated, lone, single, solitary, solo, stag
unaccompanied part song: madrigal
unaccompanied singing: a cappella
unaccountable: baffling, curious, exempt, immune, inexplicable, irresponsible, mysterious, mystic, peculiar, puzzling, strange, unexplainable, unusual
unaccustomed: alien, curious, exotic, foreign, inexperienced, new, novice, rare, strange, uncommon, unfamiliar, uninstructed, unknown, unpracticed, unusual

unacquainted: ignorant, inexperienced, strange, unadorned, unaware, unfamiliar, unknown
unadorned: austere, bald, bare, barren, naked, plain, rustic, simple, stark, undecorated, unelaborate
unadulterated: clean, genuine, honest, pure, straight, unalloyed, uncorrupted, uncut, undiluted, unmixed, untainted, utter
unaffectedly simple: naive
unafraid: bold, brave, confident, courageous, daring, fearless, valiant
unalterable: firm, fixed, inalterable, inflexible, permanent, rigid
unambiguous: apparent, clear, distinct, explicit, obvious, plain, unblurred, univocal
unanimous: agreeing, collective, consensus, consentient, harmonious, solid, uncontested, undivided, unified, united
unannounced: surprise, unanticipated, undisclosed, unheralded, unpublished, withheld
unanticipated income: windfall profit
unappealing: disgusting, dreary, dull, plain, trite, unappetizing, unattractive, uninviting, unpleasant
unappetizing: disgusting, distasteful, gross, insipid, tasteless, unappealing, uninviting, unsavory
unapproachable: aloof, cold, distant, inaccessible, incomparable, superior, unequaled, unfriendly, unreachable, unsurpassed, withdrawn
unarmed: bare, clean, defenseless, disarmed
unaspirated consonant: lenes
unaspirated, voiceless plosive: tenues
unassuming: bashful, diffident, humble, meek, modest, reserved, shy, simple, unassertive

unattached: free, independent, loose, separate, single, uncommitted, unconnected, unmarried

unattractive: frumpish, homely, plain, rude, ugly, unappealing, unappetizing, undesirable, uninviting

unauthorized: banned, illegal, outlawed, prohibited, taboo, unallowed, unapproved, unlawful, unofficial, unpermitted, unsanctioned

unavailable: married, nonexistent, out, taken, unaccessible

unavoidable: fated, imperative, ineluctable, inescapable, inevitable, necessary, obligatory, unpreventable

unaware: heedless, ignorant, incognizant, oblivious, off-guard, unapprised, unfamiliar, uninformed, unknowing, unmindful, unsuspecting, unwitting

unbalanced: asymmetric, asymmetrical, lopsided, unequal, uneven, warped

unbearable: inadmissible, insufferable, intolerable, oppressive, unacceptable

unbecoming: disgraceful, homely, improper, inappropriate, indecent, indecorous, inelegant, lewd, malapropos, offensive, rude, tasteless, ugly, unattractive, unbefitting, unseemly, unsuitable, unworthy

unbelievable: absurd, amazing, astonishing, astounding, cockeyed, fabulous, fantastic, farfetched, harebrained, implausible, impossible, improbable, inconceivable, incredible, remarkable, unimaginable, unthinkable

unbending: firm, inelastic, inexorable, iron, obstinate, resolute, rigid, stern, stiff, strict, stubborn

unbiased: disinterested, dispassionate, equitable, even, fair, honest, impartial, indifferent, just, nonpartisan, objective, unbigoted, unprejudiced

unblemished: chaste, clean, flawless, immaculate, intact, perfect, spotless, stainless, unadulterated, undamaged, unmarred, unsullied, whole

unbound, unbounded: boundless, endless, free, freed, limitless, loose, open, released, unlimited, untied

unbreakable: infrangible, inviolable, irrefrangible

unbridled: loose, unchecked, uncontrolled, ungoverned, unleashed, unrestrained

unbroken: consecutive, continual, continuous, endless, entire, intact, sequential, sound, successive, undivided, unimpaired, uninterrupted, unmarred, unshattered, untamed, whole

unburden: admit, confess, dump, empty, free, relieve, relinquish, rid, unbosom, unload

uncalled-for: discourteous, disrespectful, foolish, gratuitous, groundless, impolite, needless, nonessential, rude, unessential, unjustified, unnecessary, unwarranted, wanton

uncanny: creepy, eerie, eery, exceptional, fantastic, incredible, mysterious, remarkable, spooky, strange, supernatural, unbelievable, unnatural, unusual, weird

unceremonious: abrupt, blunt, brief, casual, curt, familiar, hasty, inelegant, informal, short

uncertain: ambiguous, ambivalent, asea, chancy, changeable, doubtful, dubious, equivocal, erratic, fitful, hazy, hesitant, iffy, indecisive, indefinite, moot, precarious, questionable, speculative, tentative, touch-and-go, unclear, unconfirmed, undecided, undetermined, unpredictable, unresolved, unsettled, unsteady, unsure, vacillating, vague, variable

uncertain in number or size: incalculable

uncertain in one's mind: indecisive, irresolute, unresolved, wavering

uncertain in one's views: ambivalent

uncertain in precise meaning: ambiguous, equivocal

uncertain or impossible to foresee: unpredictable

uncertain outcome, of: inconclusive

uncertainty: ambiguity, ambivalence, concern, confusion, doubt, dubiety, gamble, hesitation, indecision, query, risk, skepticism, suspense, wonder, worry

unchangeable: constant, fixed, immutable, inflexible, invariable, rigid, steadfast, unalterable

unchanging: consistent, constant, eternal, fixed, invariable, permanent, persevering, resolute, same, stable, static, stationary, steadfast, steady, unfaltering, uniform, unvarying

unchanging and motionless: immobile, stabile, stable, static, stationary

unchecked: free, loose, rampant, unbounded, unrestrained, untamed, wild

uncivilized: abrupt, barbaric, barbarous, boorish, brutal, crass, crude, discourteous, disrespectful, ill-mannered, impolite, primitive, rough, rude, savage, uncouth, uncultivated, uncultured, ungracious, unmannerly, unpolished, unrefined, vulgar, wicked, wild

uncivilized person: yahoo

uncle, concerning an: avuncular

unclean: contaminated, defiled, dirty, filthy, foul, grimy, grubby, impure, messy, obscene, polluted, profaned, sloppy, soily, sullied, tainted, unchaste, unwholesome, vile

unclear: ambiguous, blurry, cloudy, confused, dim, elusive, fuzzy, hazy, imprecise, intangible, nebulous, obscure, shadowy, uncertain, unsettled, unsure, vague

uncomfortable: awkward, distressful, miserable, painful, prickly, stiff, suffering, troubled, uneasy, upset

uncommitted, politically: middle of the road

uncommon: abnormal, bizarre, exceptional, exotic, extraordinary, infrequent, novel, occasional, odd, peculiar, rare, remarkable, scarce, special, strange, unaccustomed, unique, unusual, unwanted, wonderful

uncommon thing: rarity

uncommunicative: closemouthed, dumb, quiet, reserved, reticent, secretive, silent, speechless, taciturn, unresponsive, unsociable, withdrawn

uncomplicated: basic, clear, easy, plain, simple

uncompromising: adamant, determined, firm, grim, inflexible, obdurate, rigid, stern, strict, stubborn, unbending, unyielding

unconcealed: aboveboard, apparent, bare, evident, exposed, obvious, open, overt, plain, revealed, visible

unconcerned: aloof, apathetic, carefree, cold, composed, cool, debonair, detached, distant, impervious, indifferent, insensitive, insouciant, nonchalant, uncaring, uninterested, unmoved

unconditional: absolute, categorical, complete, explicit, free, total, unmistakable, unquestionable

unconquerable: impregnable, innate, invincible, invulnerable, resistant, secure, unbeatable

unconscionable: criminal, excessive,

extreme, immoderate, immoral, inexcusable, inordinate, outrageous, unethical, unjustified, unreasonable, unscrupulous, unwarranted

unconscious: asleep, automatic, comatose, ignorant, inadvertent, insensate, insensible, involuntary, lethargic, repressed, stunned, stupefied, torpid, unaware, unintentional, zonked

unconscious in response: involuntary, reflex

unconscious mind shared by race, society, humankind: collective unconscious

unconscious part of psyche with instincts: id

unconscious, as a memory: repressed

unconsciously perceived: subliminal

unconsciousness caused by injury or disease: coma

unconsciousness from mental disturbance: catalepsy, catatonia

unconsciousness from substance abuse: narcosis

unconsciousness, brief: swoon, syncope

uncontrollable: free, hysterical, independent, irregular, unchecked, uncontrolled, undisciplined, ungovernable, ungoverned, unmanageable, unmanaged, unregulated, unrestrained, unruly, wild

uncontrolled in bodily function: incontinent

unconventional: alternative, atypical, bizarre, Bohemian, casual, crazy, eccentric, informal, loose, nutty, odd, offbeat, outré, peculiar, queer, strange, uncommon, unorthodox, unusual, weird

unconvincing: flimsy, implausible, lame, questionable, suspect, unbelievable, weak

uncooperative: contrary, perverse

uncouth: awkward, boorish, callow, clumsy, coarse, crass, crude, desolate, discourteous, disrespectful, gross, ignorant, impolite, inelegant, loud, loutish, mysterious, outlandish, raunchy, rude, strange, uncanny, uncivil, uncivilized, uncultivated, uncultured, ungainly, unpolished, unrefined, vulgar

uncover: bare, detect, disclose, discover, disinter, display, disrobe, divest, divulge, exhume, expose, open, remove, reveal, unbosom, unclothe, undress, unearth, unmask, unveil

uncritical: careless, casual, imprecise,

inaccurate, inexact, offhand, perfunctory, pleased, shallow, slipshod, superficial, undiscerning

unctuous: fatty, greasy, fulsome, oily, rich, slippery, smarmy, soapy, soft, suave

uncultivated: arid, barbaric, barbarous, coarse, crass, crude, fallow, lowbrow, rough, rude, savage, uncivil, uncivilized, uncouth, uncultured, undeveloped, unfarmed, unplowed, wild

uncultured: boorish, coarse, crass, crude, rude, uncivilized, uncouth, unpolished, unrefined, vulgar

undamaged: intact

undaunted: audacious, bold, brave, confident, courageous, fearless, gallant, heroic, intrepid, resolute, serene, stalwart, unafraid, unfazed, unflinching, valiant

undecided: ambivalent, doubtful, dubious, fluctuating, hesitant, indecisive, irresolute, moot, open, pending, tentative, uncertain, undetermined, unresolved, unsettled, unsure, up in the air, wavering

undecorated: austere, bare, plain, simple, unadorned, unembellished

undeniable: actual, certain, conclusive, decisive, definite, inarguable, incontestable, incontrovertible, indisputable, irrefutable, positive, proven, sure, true, unassailable, unequivocal

undependable: capricious, erratic, flighty, inconsistent, irresponsible, lesser, lower, pinned, secondary, unpredictable, unreliable, unsafe, unsound, unstable, untrustworthy

undependable person of group: weak link, weak sister

under: below, beneath, inferior, nether, sub, subordinate

under-floor or -roof space: crawl space

under-water detection aid: sonar

underage, legally: nonage

undercoat, apply: prime, size

undercover: clandestine, concealed, confidential, covert, disguised, furtive, hidden, incognito, secret, stealthy, surreptitious

undercurrent: atmosphere, aura, drift, eddy, flavor, mood, overtone, riptide, sense, undertow

underdeveloped: embryonic, immature, inchoate, nascent, rudimentary, undeveloped

underdeveloped countries: Third World

underdog with a chance: sleeper

underestimate: belittle, disparage, minimize, miscalculate, underrate, undervalue

undergo: bear, brave, encounter, endure, experience, feel, pass, serve, subject, suffer, sustain, take, tolerate, weather, withstand, yield

undergraduate: coed, freshman, junior, plebe, senior, sophomore, student, underclassman, upperclassman

underground: beneath, buried, clandestine, hidden, illegal, revolutionary, secret, subterranean, subversive, subway, surreptitious, undercover

RELATED TERMS

underground defensive position: bunker

underground drain: sewer

underground entrance: adit

underground passage: tunnel

underground passageway or rooms: catacomb, tunnel

underground urban railroad: metro, subway

underground vault: crypt, undercroft

underground water: aquifer, groundwater ❦

undergrown: stunted

undergrowth: brush, brushwood

underhanded: clandestine, crooked, cunning, deceitful, devious, dirty, dishonest, fraudulent, furtive, secret, shady, shifty, shorthanded, sly, sneaky, subversive, surreptitious, unethical, unfair, unscrupulous, wily

underhanded activity: intrigue, skullduggery

underline: accentuate, ascent, caption, emphasize, feature, mark, stress, underscore

underling: hireling, inferior, menial, minion, scrub, serf, servant, subordinate

underlying: basic, beneath, bottom, cardinal, crucial, elemental, essential, fundamental, implicit, latent, primary, vital

underlying layer: substratum

underlying meaning: subtext

underlying motive: ulterior motive

undermine: corrupt, cripple, debilitate, demoralize, destroy, disable, drain, erode, excavate, foil, frustrate, impair, ruin, sabotage, sandbag, sap, subvert, threaten, thwart, weaken, wreck

undermine a government, attempt to: subversion

underneath: below, beneath, bottom, covered, under, underside

underpinning: base, basis, foundation, ground, groundwork, substructure, support

underprivileged: deprived, destitute, disadvantaged, impoverished, needy, poor, unfortunate

underrate: belittle, depreciate, devalue, discount, minimize, underestimate, underprice, undervalue

underscore: accent, emphasize, heighten, italicize, mark, stress, underline

underside: belly, bottom, root, soffit, sole, underneath

undersized: little, miniature, petite, puny, short, small, stunted, tiny

understaffed: shorthanded

understand: absorb, accept, appreciate, apprehend, catch, compass, comprehend, conceive, conjecture, decode, deduce, dig, digest, discern, fathom, follow, gather, get, grasp, infer, interpret, ken, know, learn, penetrate, perceive, realize, reason, recognize, see, sense, solve, surmise, sympathize, think

understandable: acceptable, clear, coherent, comprehensible, intelligible, justifiable, logical, lucid, pellucid, plain, reasonable, recognizable, simple

understanding: acceptance, accepting, accord, acute, agreement, amity, attitude, awareness, belief, brain, compassion, compatible, comprehension, concept, deal, diagnosis, discerning, empathy, entente, forgiving, grasp, grip, idea, insight, insightful, intellect, intelligence, intuition, judgment, ken, kindly, knowing, knowledge, meaning, notion, open-minded, pact, perceptive, perspicacious, realization, reason, sagacious, sense, sensitivity, simpatico, sympathetic, sympathy, tolerance, treaty

understanding between governments: entente

understanding of another's situation: empathy

understanding or knowledge: awareness, cognizance, discernment, grasp, perception, savvy

understanding, of a broad: catholic

understatement: distortion, litotes, restraint, underestimate

understatement, rhetorical: meiosis

understood: accepted, assumed, clear, got, implicit, implied, inferred, knew, lucid, presumed, saw, seen, tacit, unsaid, unspoken

understood only by particular group: esoteric

understood, easily: accessible, lucid, luminous

understudy: alternate, backup, double, replacement, substitute

undertake: accept, assume, attempt, begin, commence, commit, contract, covenant, dare, endeavor, engage, execute, grant, guarantee, initiate, launch, overtake, perform, pledge, promise, seek, seize, shoulder, start, strive, tackle, try

undertaker: embalmer, funeral director, mortician

undertakers, group of: unction

undertaking: adventure, attempt, calling, charge, commitment, covenant, effort, endeavor, enterprise, experiment, project, promise, proposition, pursuit, struggle, task, venture

undertone: association, atmosphere, aura, buzz, feeling, flavor, hint, mood, mumble, murmur, overtone, sense, suggestion, whisper

undertone, in an: sotto voce

undertow: eddy, riptide, undercurrent, vortex, whirlpool

undervalue: belittle, depreciate, disparage, minimize, underestimate, underrate

underwater breathing apparatus: aqualung, scuba

underwater construction structure: caisson

underwater locator: sonar

underwater mountain: seamount

underwater reef: ledge

underwater research vessel: bathyscaphe, diving bell

underwater researcher: aquanaut, oceanaut

underwater stupor from excessive nitrogen: nitrogen narcosis

underwear: bloomers, bodice, boxers, bra, brassiere, briefs, camisole, chemise, corset, diaper, drawers, girdle, jockeys, lingerie, long underwear, panties, petticoat, shorts, skivvies,

slip, sports bra, T-shirt, teddy, underclothes, undergarment, underpants, undershirt, undies, union suit

underworld (crime): Cosa Nostra, gangland, Mafia, syndicate

underworld (Hell): abyss, Avernus, Erebus, Gehenna, Hades, hell, Hinnom, Jahannam, netherworld, Orcus, perdition, purgatory, Sheol, Tophet

RELATED TERMS

underworld dog, three-headed: Cerberus

underworld ferryman: Charon

underworld god: Anubis, Dis, Pluto, Thanatos, Yama

underworld goddess: Hecate, Nephthys

underworld, king condemned to: Tantalus

underworld river: Acheron, Cocytus, Lethe, Phlegethon, Styx

underworld, concerning: chthonic, infernal ❦

underwrite: back, bankroll, endorse, finance, guarantee, insure, sign, sponsor, subscribe, support

undesirable: disliked, displeasing, inappropriate, loathsome, objectionable, offensive, outcast, repugnant, unacceptable, unfit, uninviting, unpleasant, unsought, unsuitable, unwanted, unwelcomed

undetermined: doubtful, equivocal, faint, obscure, pending, unclear, undecided, unknown, unproven, unsettled, vague

undeveloped: archaic, backward, crude, green, immature, latent, primitive, primordial, uncultivated, uneducated, unevolved, unripe, untaught

undisciplined: amok, intractable, lax, mutinous, recalcitrant, uncontrolled, ungovernable, unmanageable, unruly, untrained, wanton, wayward, wild

undisclosed: concealed, confidential, hidden, sealed, secret, unrevealed

undisputed: accepted, acknowledged, conclusive, granted, irrefutable, recognized, sure, unchallenged, uncontested, undeniable, unquestioned

undistinguished: common, everyday, mediocre, ordinary, plain, unexceptional, unnotable, unnoteworthy

undistinguished writer: hack

undisturbed: calm, even, peaceful,

placid, quiet, serene, tranquil, undistracted, unmoved, unruffled, untouched

undivided: absorbed, complete, entire, exclusive, one, solid, total, unanimous, unbroken, undistracted, united, whole, wholehearted

undo: abolish, abrogate, annul, cancel, defeat, destroy, disconnect, disengage, disjoin, erase, free, invalidate, loose, negate, neutralize, nullify, offset, open, outwit, overturn, quash, release, reverse, ruin, unblock, uncover, undermine, unfasten, unravel, untie, unwrap, upset, void

undoing: blunder, cancellation, catastrophe, collapse, destruction, doom, downfall, error, misfortune, overthrow, ruin, weakness

undoubtedly: assuredly, certainly, indeed, indubitably, irrefutably, positively, really, surely, truly, undeniably, unmistakably, unquestionably

undress: disrobe, divest, doff, expose, peel, shed, strip, unclothe, uncover, undrape

undressed: dishabille

undue: excessive, exorbitant, extreme, illegal, immoderate, improper, inappropriate, needless, uncoming, undeserved, unfitting, unjustifiable, unnecessary, unreasonable, unsuitable, untimely, unwarranted, unworthy

undulate: fluctuate, ripple, roll, sway, swing, wave, weave

unduly: excessively, extravagantly, extremely, immoderately, inordinately, overly, unjustifiably, unnecessarily

undying: ageless, agelong, constant, continual, continuing, endless, enduring, eternal, everlasting, immortal, imperishable, permanent, perpetual, persistent, unceasing, unending, unfading

unearth: dig, disclose, discover, disinter, divulge, excavate, exhume, expose, find, learn, reveal, show, uncover, uproot

unearthly: awesome, eerie, ethereal, fantastic, ghostly, heavenly, miraculous, mysterious, preternatural, spectral, spooky, strange, superhuman, supernatural, uncanny, ungodly, weird

uneasiness: alarm, angst, anxiety, apprehension, disbelief, discomfort, discontent, displeasure, doubt, dread, embarrassment, fear, inquietude, in-

stability, malaise, misgiving, nervousness, qualm, restlessness, trouble, uncertainty, unrest, worry

uneasy: afraid, alarmed, anxious, apprehensive, awkward, concerned, difficult, edgy, fidgety, jumpy, nervous, nervy, perturbed, restless, tense, troubled, uncertain, uncomfortable, unsettled, unsure, uptight, worried

uneatable: inedible

uneducated: ignorant, illiterate, simple, unlearned, unlettered, unread, unschooled, untaught, untutored

unembellished: austere, bald, bare, modest, plain, simple, unadorned, undecorated, unelaborate

unemotional: apathetic, cold, coldhearted, cool, deadpan, detached, dispassionate, formal, heartless, impartial, impassive, impervious, indifferent, inexcitable, insensitive, objective, phlegmatic, reserved, stoic, stoical, unconcerned, unfeeling, unsympathetic

unemployed: canned, fired, idle, inactive, jobless, laid off, leisured, unoccupied

unencumbered: free, free as a bird

unending: ad infinitum, constant, continual, continuous, endless, eternal, ever, everlasting, infinite, lasting, perpetual, steady, timeless, unceasing, undying, uninterrupted

unenlightened: ignorant, uninformed, unlearned

unenthusiastic: apathetic, cool, indifferent, lackadaisical, languid, lukewarm, perfunctory, spiritless, tepid, unexcited, uninterested

unenviable state: odium

unequal: asymmetrical, different, disparate, dissimilar, fluctuating, inadequate, inequitable, irregular, lopsided, mismatched, unalike, unbalanced, uneven, unfair, unjust, variable, varying

unequaled: matchless, nonpareil, peerless, sans pareil, supreme, surpassing, unmatched, unparalleled, unprecedented, unrivaled, unsurpassed

unequivocal: absolute, categorical, certain, certainly, clear, decisive, definite, emphatic, explicit, indisputable, plain, positive, resounding, unambiguous, unmistakable

unerring: accurate, certain, dependable, exact, infallible, perfect, precise, reliable, sure, true, unfailing

unethical: amoral, corrupt, crooked, dishonest, disreputable, immoral, shady, sneaky, underhand, wrong

unethical situation involving public duty and personal interest: conflict of interest

uneven: alop, angled, bent, bumpy, crooked, discrepant, disparate, erose, fluctuating, ill-matched, irregular, jagged, lopsided, odd, rough, rugged, spotty, tilted, unbalanced, unequal, unfair, unjust, unlevel, varying

uneventful: boring, common, commonplace, dull, insignificant, monotonous, ordinary, prosaic, routine, unexceptional, unmemorable

unexceptional: common, commonplace, conventional, ordinary, prosaic, regular, satisfactory, typical, uneventful, usual

unexpected: abrupt, accidental, adventitious, aleatory, chance, fortuitous, impulsive, staggering, startling, sudden, surprising, unannounced, unanticipated, unforeseen, unplanned, unpredictable

unexpected gain: windfall

unexpected gift: bonus

unexpected lucky discovery: serendipity

unexpected outcome: upset

unexpected reverse: setback

unexpected welcome thing or occurrence: godsend

unexpectedly: out of the blue, unawares

unexplored area: terra incognita

unexplored or unused: virgin

unexpressed: tacit

unfailing: certain, consistent, continuous, dependable, faithful, inexhaustible, infallible, loyal, reliable, staunch, sure, surefire, true, trustworthy, unchanging, unerring, unflagging

unfair: biased, cheating, discriminatory, dishonest, dishonorable, foul, inequitable, partial, prejudiced, underhanded, unequal, unethical, uneven, unfavorable, unjust, unjustified, unwarranted, wrong, wrongful

RELATED TERMS

unfair and arrogant: high-handed
unfair and offensive: invidious
unfair attacker: cheap-shot artist
unfair attitude or action:
   discrimination

unfair judgment or accusation: bum rap

unfairly distributed: disproportionate

unfairly favored: biased, partial

unfairness: inequity ❦

unfaithful: adulterous, dishonest, disloyal, faithless, inaccurate, infidel, recreant, traitorous, treasonable, unloyal, unreliable, untrue, untrustworthy

unfaithful person: infidel, philanderer

unfaltering: dependable, enduring, firm, persevering, steadfast, steady, sure, true, wholehearted

unfamiliar: alien, curious, different, exotic, foreign, inexperienced, new, strange, unaccustomed, unacquainted, uninformed, unknown, unversed

unfamiliar things: exotica

unfashionable: antiquated, dated, frumpy, out, passé, unstylish

unfasten: detach, disengage, free, loosen, open, unbuckle, unbutton, undo, unhitch, unhook, unlace, unlock, unloosen, unpin, unsnap, untie

unfathomable: abstruse, abysmal, baffling, bottomless, complex, deep, mysterious, profound, ungraspable, vast

unfavorable: adverse, bad, contrary, damaging, detrimental, foul, hostile, ill, inauspicious, inimical, inopportune, negative, unfortunate, unkind, unlucky, untimely, untoward

unfavorable review: pan

unfavorable, most: worst-case

unfeasible: impossible, impractical, unachievable, unattainable, unworkable

unfeeling: apathetic, brutal, callous, cold, cruel, deadened, dispassionate, dull, hard, hardened, harsh, heartless, indurate, insensate, insensible, invulnerable, merciless, numb, numbness, obdurate, ruthless, senseless, stern, stolid, stony

unfeigned: genuine, heartfelt, honest, natural, real, sincere, true

unfermented grape juice: stum

unfettered: free, loose

unfilled orders or unfinished work: backlog

unfinished: crude, immature, imperfect, incomplete, raw, rough, rude, sketchy, unassembled, undeveloped, undone, unfulfilled, unpainted, unpolished, unstained

unfinished business: loose ends

unfit: blundering, disabled, faulty, feeble, handicapped, ill-suited, improper, incapacitated, incompatible, incompetent, ineffective, ineligible, inept, inexperienced, sick, sickly, unhealthy, unprepared, unqualified, unskilled, unsuited, untrained, weak

unflagging: constant, determined, firm, staunch, steadfast, steady, tireless, weariless

unflappable: calm, collected, composed, cool, relaxed, serene, unexcitable, unruffled

unflinching: determined, fearless, firm, gritty, relentless, resolute, staunch, steadfast, tenacious, undaunted, unwavering, unyielding

unfold: blossom, clarify, describe, develop, disclose, display, divulge, elaborate, evolve, expand, expiate, explain, explicate, flower, mature, open, release, resolve, reveal, show, solve, spread, uncover, uncurl, unfurl, unravel, unroll, untuck, unwind, unwrap

unforeseen: accidental, sudden, surprising, unanticipated, unexpected, unimagined, unpredicted

unforeseen but possible event: contingency

unforgettable: enduring, indelible, ingrained

unfortunate: afflicted, bad, calamitous, cursed, deplorable, dismal, doomed, hapless, inauspicious, inopportune, jinxed, luckless, miserable, poor, regrettable, sad, star-crossed, unhappy, unlucky, unsuccessful, wretch, wretched

unfounded: baseless, false, groundless, idle, misleading, unproven, unsubstantiated, untrue, vain

unfriendly: aloof, antagonistic, antisocial, cold, combative, cool, distant, forbidding, hateful, hostile, ill-disposed, inhospitable, inimical, malicious, remote, standoffish, unapproachable, ungracious, unneighborly, unsocial

unfriendly relations, of: alienated, estranged

unfriendly to outsiders: exclusive

unfruitful: arid, barren, fruitless, impotent, infecund, infertile, sterile, unproductive, unrewarding, useless, wasted

unfurl: develop, display, expand, open, spread, unfold, unroll, unwind

ungainly: awkward, clumsy, gawky, klutzy, lanky, lumbering, maladroit, stiff, uncouth, unwieldy

ungenerous: close, grudging, harsh, mean, miserly, petty, selfish, shabby, small, stingy

unglamorous one: plain Jane

unglazed pottery: rabat

ungodly: atrocious, blasphemous, corrupt, depraved, dreadful, hypocritical, immoral, impious, impure, outrageous, profane, rotten, sinful, unbelieving, uncivilized, unholy, wicked

ungovernable: disobedient, disorderly, fractious, intractable, mutinous, out-of-hand, rebellious, unbridled, uncontrollable, undisciplined, unmanageable, unruly, wild

ungraceful: awkward, clumsy, coarse, gawky, inelegant, rusty, vulgar

ungracious: churlish, discourteous, disrespectful, gruff, impolite, inhospitable, offensive, rude, short, thoughtless, uncivil, uncouth, unfortunate, unmannerly, unpleasant

ungrammatical usage: barbarism, catachresis, solecism

ungrateful: dissatisfied, grumbling, ingrate, repellent, repugnant, selfish, thankless, unappreciative

ungrateful person: ingrate

unguarded: careless, defenseless, imprudent, incautious, indiscreet, thoughtless, unalert, unmindful, unprotected, unwary, vulnerable

unguent: balm, cerate, cream, emollient, lotion, lubricant, ointment, salve

unguis or ungula: claw, nail

ungulate: buffalo, camel, cattle, cow, deer, elephant, giraffe, hippopotamus, hog, hoofed, hooflike, horse, llama, pig, rhinoceros, swine, tapir

unhandy: awkward, bumbling, clumsy, cumbersome, fumbling, inept, klutzy, maladroit, unskillful

unhappiness: dolor, grief, heartache, melancholy, misery, sadness, sorrow, woe, worry

unhappy: blue, bummed, dejected, depressed, discontented, disgruntled, dismal, dismayed, downcast, forlorn, gloomy, hurting, inappropriate, inauspicious, joyless, melancholy, miserable, pessimistic, sad, saddened, sorrowful, sorry, unfavorable, unfortunate, unlucky, woebegone, wretched

unharmed: harmless, intact, safe, unblemished, undamaged, unhurt, unmarred, unscathed, untouched, whole

unhealthy: chancy, dangerous, detrimental, diseased, feeble, frail, hazardous, ill, noxious, risky, sick, sickly, unsanitary, unsound, unwell, unwholesome

unhealthy condition: malady, malaise

unhealthy hue: pallor

unheard-of: extraordinary, novel, obscure, outrageous, rare, strange, unbelievable, uncommon, undiscovered, unique, unknown, unprecedented, unusual

unheeding: careless, deaf, disregarding, forgotten, heedless, ignored, inattentive, inobservant, unmindful, unnoticed, unwatchful

unhinge: detach, disconnect, disengage, distract, fluster, separate, unbalance, uncouple, unfasten, unhitch, unsettle, upset

unholy: amiss, atrocious, corrupt, depraved, evil, fiendish, immoral, impure, indecent, irreverent, malicious, sinful, unchristian, ungodly, unhallowed, unsanctified, wicked

unidentified: anonymous, mysterious, secret, unknown, unmarked, unnamed

unification: alliance, amalgamation, coalition, combination, hookup, joining, linkage, merger, union, unity

uniform: alike, comparable, compatible, consistent, constant, continual, equal, even, homogenous, invariable, level, like, orderly, regular, similar, systematic, unchanging; attire, costume, dress, livery, monkey suit, outfit, suit

uniform in structure: homogeneous

uniform of household help: livery

uniform, leather belt for dress: Sam Browne belt

uniform, not: heterogeneous

uniform, not a: civvies, mufti

uniformity: consistency, equality, harmony, homogeneity, monotony, oneness, sameness, unity

unify: ally, bind, centralize, combine, consolidate, couple, harmonize, integrate, merge, orchestrate, organize, systematize, unite

unifying: ecumenical

unifying treaty: pact

unilateral command: ukase

unimaginable: extraordinary, fantastic, improbable, inconceivable, incredible, indescribable, unbelievable, unthinkable

unimaginative: arid, dreary, dull, hackneyed, humdrum, pedestrian, predictable, prosaic, routine, trite, uncreative, unexciting, uninspired, unoriginal

unimpaired: free, intact, sound, unbroken, undamaged, unharmed, unhurt, uninjured, unscathed, whole

unimpassioned: calm, impassive, impersonal, phlegmatic, placid, serene, steady, tranquil, unemotional, unexcited

unimpeachable: blameless, clean, faultless, immaculate, impeccable, irreproachable, pure, spotless, stainless, unassailable, unblemished, unquestionable, untainted

unimportant: ancillary, dispensable, expendable, frivolous, immaterial, incidental, inconsequential, insignificant, irrelevant, little, marginal, meaningless, minimal, minor, minorleague, negligible, nonessential, nugatory, paltry, parenthetical, peripheral, petty, piddling, small, smalltime, subordinate, trivial, useless, worthless

unimportant happening: non-event

unimportant thing: bagatelle, cipher, non-entity, small beer

uninformed: in the dark, oblivious, unadvised, unaware, uneducated, uninstructed

uninhabited: abandoned, deserted, desolate, empty, forsaken, unoccupied, vacant

uninhibited: audacious, candid, flamboyant, free, heedless, impulsive, liberated, loose, outspoken, spontaneous, uncurbed, unhampered, unreserved, unrestrained, unsuppressed

uninjured: intact, sound, unbroken, undamaged, unharmed, unhurt, unscathed, whole

uninspired: bland, boring, dull, lack-

luster, stodgy, uncreative, unimpressed, uninteresting, unmoved, unoriginal

unintelligent: asinine, dense, dumb, foolish, idiotic, ignorant, obtuse, simple, stupid, unwise

unintelligible: ambiguous, illegible, inarticulate, incoherent, jumbled, meaningless, muddled, puzzling, unfathomable

unintended: involuntary

unintentional: accidental, fortuitous, haphazard, inadvertent, random, unanticipated, undesigned, unintended, unplanned, unwitting

uninterrupted: ceaseless, consecutive, continual, continuous, endless, sustained, unbroken, undisturbed, unending

uninviting: distasteful, unappealing, unappetizing, unpleasant, untempting, unwelcoming

union: alliance, association, bloc, brotherhood, club, coalition, confederation, connection, federation, fellowship, fraternity, group, guild, joining, league, local, marriage, merger, order, organization, partnership, syndicate, together, unification, unity

RELATED TERMS

union for a common purpose: alliance, bloc, confederacy, confederation, league

union of businesses, investors for projects: consortium, syndicate

union of plotters or intriguers: cabal

union of similar businesses to regulate pricing, etc.: cartel, trust

union of states with central authority, of a: federal

union or merger of corporations: amalgamation

union strike, non-member substitute in: scab

union, esp. temporary, of parties with common cause: alignment, coalition

union, political body established through federal: federation ❦

unique: alone, distinctive, exceptional, extraordinary, incomparable, individual, inimitable, lone, matchless, nonpareil, notable, odd, one, loner, only, peculiar, peerless, preeminent, rare, single, singular, sole, solitary, special, strange, sui generis, transcen-

UNITED NATIONS ORGANIZATIONS AND AGENCIES

Food and Agricultural Organization (FAO)
General Agreement on Tariffs and Trade (GATT)
Intergovernmental Maritime Consultative Organization (IMCO)
International Atomic Energy Agency (IAEA)
International Bank for Reconstruction and Development (World Bank)
International Civil Aviation Organization (ICAO)
International Development Association (IDA)
International Finance Corporation (IFO)

International Labor Organization (ILO)
International Monetary Fund (the Fund)
International Telecommunication Union (ITU)
United Nations Children's Fund (UNICEF)
United Nations Educational, Scientific and Cultural Organization (UNESCO)
United Nations Relief and Works Agency (UNRWA)
Universal Postal Union (UPU)
World Health Organization (WHO)
World Meteorological Organization (WMO) ❦

---

dent, uncommon, unequaled, unparalleled, unprecedented, unrivaled, unusual

unique and unheard-of: unprecedented

unison: accord, agreement, concert concord, concordant, consonant, harmony, together, union, unity

unit: ace, amp, atom, battalion, bite, brigade, BTU, bushel, carat, clan, company, component, decibel, degree, denomination, detachment, digit, entity, family, foot, gallon, gram, individual, item, length, liter, measure, measurement, meter, mile, minute, module, molecule, monad, one, ounce, outfit, part, pint, platoon, pound, quantity, quart, second, section, segment, squad, ton, tribe, troop, volt, watt, weight, whole, yard, year

unit name or designation for a class or group: denomination

unit, indivisible: monad

unite: adjoin, affiliate, affix, aggregate, ally, amalgamate, annex, assemble, associate, attach, band, bind, blend, bond, cement, coalesce, combine, compound, condense, connect, consolidate, consort, conspire, convene, cooperate, couple, federate, fuse, gather, hitch, incorporate, join, knit, link, marry, meld, merge, mingle, mix, organize, pool, rally, regulate, solder, solidify, splice, strengthen, tie, unify, wed, weld, yoke

united: allied, atone, banded, cemented, collective, cooperative, integrated, married, merged, one, unanimous, undivided, unified, wed, wedded

unity: accord, agreement, alliance, association, communion, concord, congruity, consent, continuity, harmony, one, oneness, peace, same-

ness, singleness, solidarity, unification, uniformity, union, unison, wholeness

unity in politics or interests: solidarity

universal: accepted, boundless, broad, common, comprehensive, constant, cosmic, customary, ecumenical, entire, general, global, omnipresent, pandemic, sweeping, total, ubiquitous, undisputed, unexcluding, unlimited, whole, widespread, worldwide

universal in religion: ecumenical

universe: cosmos, creation, earth, everything, macrocosm, nature, world
RELATED TERMS
universe in miniature: microcosm
universe was created by explosion and is still expanding theory: Big-Bang theory
universe was created gradually and is constantly expanding theory: steady-state
universe's Big Bang, matter before: ylem
universe, concerning the: cosmic
universe, inevitable and steady deterioration of the: entropy
universe, small system representative of whole or: microcosm
universe, study of the: cosmogony, cosmology ❦

university: academia, academy, college, institution, school
RELATED TERMS
university admission: matriculation
university community in assembly: convocation
university degree ceremony: commencement
university degree, first: baccalaureate
university education: tertiary education

university president: chancellor
university professor's paid leave: sabbatical
university professor's permanent status: tenure
university records officer: registrar
university society for high academic standing: Phi Beta Kappa
university speaker: lector
university teachers: faculty
university term: semester, trimester
university trustee: regent
university, first year student in: freshman
university, former student of: alumna, alumnus
university, fourth year student in: senior
university, second year student in: sophomore
university, third year student in: junior ❦

unjust: biased, cruel, dishonest, improper, inequitable, iniquitous, oppressive, partial, prejudiced, undeserved, unfair, wrongful

unjustifiable: inexcusable, insupportable, unconscionable, undue, unforgivable, unwarranted

unkempt: disarrayed, disheveled, disorderly, grubby, messy, neglected, ragged, ratty, rude, ruffled, scruffy, shabby, shaggy, sloppy, slovenly, tousled, uncombed, ungroomed, unpolished, untidy

unkind: bad, brutal, cruel, harsh, inconsiderate, inhumane, insensitive, malicious, mean, nasty, rough, severe, stern, uncaring, unfavorable, unfriendly, ungenerous, ungenial, ungracious, ungrateful, vile, wicked

unknown: alien, anonymous, concealed, foreign, incognito, inconspicuous, nameless, nobody, obscure, strange, uncelebrated, uncharted, undiscovered, unexplored, unfamiliar, unheard-of, unidentified, unsung

unknown and unnamed: anonymous, innominate

unknown except by few: esoteric

unknown territory: terra incognita

unlawful: banned, contraband, criminal, forbidden, illegal, illegitimate, illicit, lawless, outlawed, prohibited, taboo, unauthorized

unlearned: backward, ignorant, illiterate, instinctive, natural, uncivilized, uneducated, unscholarly, unschooled, untaught, untutored, unversed

unleash: discharge, free, release, vent

unleavened bread: pita

unleavened Jewish bread: matzo

unless: except, nisi, saving

unlike: clashing, contrary, different, disparate, dissimilar, distinct, diverse, heterogeneous, incompatible, opposite, uneven, unrelated

unlikely: absurd, doubtful, hopeless, improbable, questionable, remote, slight, unbelievable, unfit, unimaginable, unpromising, unsuitable

unlimited: boundless, complete, comprehensive, countless, endless, great, huge, immeasurable, indefinite, infinite, limitless, open-ended, total, unbounded, unconditional, undefined, undeterminate, universal, unmeasured, unrestricted, untold, vast, wide

unlimited money available: blank check

unload: deplane, deplete, disburden, discard, discharge, dump, eject, empty, jettison, lighten, liquidate, relieve, remove, rid, shed, trash, unburden, unpack

unlucky: cursed, doomed, hapless, ill, ill-fated, ill-omened, ill-starred, jinxed, miserable, misfortunate, star-crossed, unfortunate, unhappy, untoward

unlucky and threatening: inauspicious, ominous, portentous, unpropitious

unmanageable: disobedient, disorderly, fractious, incorrigible, rebellious, uncontrollable, ungovernable, unruly, wild

unmanly: cowardly, degrading, dishonorable, effeminate, gutless, sissy, unmasculine, womanish

unmannerly: boorish, coarse, crude, discourteous, impolite, rude, uncivil, uncouth, ungracious

unmarried: available, bachelor, celibate, chaste, divorced, eligible, single, spouseless, unattached, unwedded, widowed

unmarried and chaste: celibate

unmarried but living together: cohabit, common-law, shacking up

unmask: disclose, expose, reveal, show, uncloak, uncover, unshroud, unveil

unmatched: matchless, odd, peerless, supreme, unequaled, unique, unparalleled, unrivaled

unmerciful: bloodthirsty, brutal, cruel, evil, harsh, heartless, inhumane, merciless, pitiless, relentless, ruthless, severe, uncaring

unmindful: careless, forgetful, heedless, inattentive, neglectful, negligent, oblivious, remiss, thoughtless, unaware, unconscious, unobservant

unmistakable: apparent, certain, clear, definite, distinct, evident, explicit, obvious, plain, positive, undeniable, undisputable, unequivocal

unmitigated: absolute, arrant, clearcut, pure, sheer, unbroken, unmixed

unmixed: neat, pure, pureblood, purebred, sheer, simple, sincere, straight, unadulterated, unalloyed, unmitigated

unmoved: adamant, calm, cool, dispassionate, firm, impassive, indifferent, insensate, staunch, steadfast, stony, stubborn, unaffected, unemotional, unshaken, untouched

unmoving: immobile, inert, motionless, static, stationary, still, unemotional

unnamed: anonymous, incognito, nameless, unidentified, unknown, unmarked, unrevealed, unsigned

unnatural: aberrant, abnormal, affected, anomalous, artificial, fabricated, factitious, fake, forced, freakish, insincere, irregular, phony, strange, supernatural, synthetic, uncanny

unnecessary: dispensable, excess, expendable, extra, gratuitous, inessential, lavish, needless, nonessential, optional, redundant, supererogatory, superfluous, supernumerary, surplus, uncalled-for, unessential, unneeded, unrequired, useless

unnecessary and unjustified: extraneous, gratuitous, uncalled-for, unwarranted

unnecessary, render: obviate

unnerve: agitate, castrate, distract, emasculate, enervate, fluster, intimidate, rattle, shake, spook, undermine, unhinge, unman, unsettle, upset, weaken

unnoticed: disregarded, hidden, ignored, neglected, overlooked, undiscovered, unnoted, unobserved, unrecognized, unseen

unnoticed and spreading: insidious

unobservant: blind, heedless, inattentive, unseeing

unobstructed: clear, free, open, unhampered, unimpeded

unobtrusive: humble, inconspicuous, meek, modest, quiet, reserved, unassuming

unoccupied: abandoned, deserted, empty, free, idle, inactive, uninhabited, vacant

unofficial: casual, informal, unauthorized, unsanctioned

unofficial advisors: kitchen cabinet

unoriginal: derivative, imitative, stereotype, trite

unoriginal and overused: hackneyed, shopworn

unorthodox: abnormal, eccentric, heretical, heterodox, nonconformist, radical, schismatic, unconventional, unholy, unusual

unorthodox religious belief: heresy, heterodoxy

unpaid: delinquent, donated, due, gratuitous, honorary, outstanding, overdue, owed, unsettled, voluntary

unpaid debt: arrear, arrears

unpaid position: honorary, volunteer

unpalatable: bitter, disagreeable, distasteful, flat, repulsive, tasteless, unappetizing, uneatable, unpleasant, unsavory, weak

unparalleled: alone, exceptional, matchless, peerless, superlative, unequaled, unique, unmatched, unprecedented, unrivaled, unsurpassed

unperturbed: sedate

unplanned: accidental, adventitious, aleatory, fortuitous, haphazard, impromptu, random, spontaneous, undesigned, unexpected, unintended, unintentional

unplanned and self-generated: spontaneous, unprompted, unsolicited

unplanned and thrown together: ad hoc, extemporaneous, extempore, impromptu, improvised, makeshift, off-the-cuff, on the fly, unrehearsed

unplanned as a crime: unpremeditated

unpleasant: abhorrent, annoying, bad, disagreeable, displeasing, distasteful, irksome, lousy, nasty, obnoxious, odious, off-putting, offensive, repugnant, repulsive, ugly, unhappy, unpalatable, vexatious

unpleasant air: miasma

unpleasant to endure: insufferable, intolerable, unpalatable

unpolished: boorish, coarse, crude, discourteous, impolite, inelegant, rough, rude, rugged, tattered, uncivil, uncivilized, uncouth, uncultured, unfinished, unrefined

unpopular: avoided, detested, disliked, loathed, rejected, shunned, snubbed, unaccepted, undesirable

unpractical: idealistic, impracticable, quixotic, utopian, visionary

unprecedented: abnormal, exceptional, new, novel, original, uncommon, unheard-of, unique, unparalleled, unusual

unpredictable: arbitrary, capricious, erratic, fickle, iffy, incalculable, irregular, mercurial, quicksilver, random, temperamental, transient, uncertain, unstable, variable, volatile, whimsical

unpredictable event or act: quirk, vagary

unprejudiced: amenable, detached, disinterested, dispassionate, equitable, fair, impartial, just, nonpartisan, objective, receptive, straight, unbiased, unbigoted

unprepared: asleep, impromptu, improvised, napping, raw, spontaneous, surprised, unaware, uncooked, unguarded, unready, unrehearsed

unpretentious: discreet, humble, inelaborate, modest, plain, simple, unassuming, unobtrusive

unprincipled: amoral, corrupt, crooked, deceitful, dishonest, immoral, shady, unconscionable, unethical, unprofessional, unscrupulous

unproductive: barren, futile, idle, impotent, ineffective, infecund, infertile, sterile, unfruitful, useless

unprofessional: amateur, inexperienced, inexpert, shoddy, sloppy, unethical, unprincipled, unskilled

unprofitable: barren, fruitless, gainless, hopeless, pointless, unfruitful, unlucrative, useless, vain

unpromising: inauspicious

unpropitious: adverse, antagonistic, contrary, ill, inauspicious, ominous, threatening

unprotected: dangerous, defenseless, exposed, helpless, susceptible, unarmed, unguarded, unsafe, unsheltered, vulnerable

unpunished: scot-free

unqualified: absolute, bare, categorical, complete, definite, downright, firm, inadequate, incapable, incompetent, ineligible, inexperienced, outright, sheer, sure, thorough, unable, unfit, unmitigated, unprepared, unskilled, unsuited, untrained, utter

unquestionable: authentic, certain, clear, conclusive, decided, definite, established, evident, implicit, incontestable, indisputable, indubitable, obvious, positive, real, sure, true, undeniable, unmistakable, veritable

unquestioning: sure

unrattled: poised

unravel: decipher, disengage, disentangle, extricate, faze, resolve, separate, solve, undo, unfold, unlace, untangle, unwind

unreadable: illegible, indecipherable

unreal: aerial, artificial, chimerical, counterfeit, dreamy, fabled, fancied, fanciful, fantastic, fictitious, ideal, illusive, illusory, imaginary, imaginative, insubstantial, invented, mythical, nonexistent, pretended, surreal, unbelievable, visionary

unreal object: figment of the imagination, illusion, phantasm

unrealistic: absurd, foolish, idealistic, impracticable, impractical, improbable, silly, unfeasible, utopian, visionary

unreasonable: absurd, biased, excessive, exorbitant, extravagant, fanatical, foolish, headstrong, illogical, impractical, inflexible, irrational, mad, obstinate, senseless, silly, undue, unfair, unwarranted

unreasoning fear: panic

unreasoning passion or love: infatuation

unrefined: boorish, coarse, crass, crude, earthy, gross, inelegant, raw, rough,

rude, uncivilized, uncouth, uncultivated, uncultured, unpolished, vulgar

unrehearsed: extemporary, impromptu, improvised, informal, offhand, spontaneous

unrelated: accidental, discrete, disjoined, dissimilar, extraneous, independent, separate, unassociated, unconnected

unrelenting: constant, continuous, cruel, determined, implacable, inflexible, merciless, persistent, relentless, rigid, rigorous, severe, steady, tenacious, unabated

unreliable: capricious, disreputable, erratic, false, fly-by-night, irresponsible, questionable, shifting, tricky, undependable, unpredictable, unsafe, unstable, untrustworthy

unresolved: incomplete, indecisive, pending, questionable, speculative, tentative, unanswered, uncertain, unfinished, unsettled, unsolved, wavering

unresponsive: cold, cool, frigid, insensitive, passive, unemotional, unfeeling

unrest: anarchy, anxiety, chaos, commotion, confusion, discontent, disorder, disquiet, ferment, protest, rebellion, tension, tizzy, trouble, turbulence, turmoil, uneasiness, upheaval

unrestrained: abandoned, audacious, blunt, candid, dissolute, excessive, extravagant, frank, free, immoderate, incontinent, inordinate, intemperate, loose, rampant, unbounded, unbridled, unchecked, uncontrolled, uncurbed, ungoverned, unhampered, uninhibited, unlimited, unrestricted, wanton, wild

unrestrained revelry: riot, saturnalia

unrestricted: accessible, allowable, free, open, open-door, unlimited, unrestrained

unrestricted in action: carte blanche

unreturned serve: ace

unrivaled: peerless, superior, undisputed, unequaled, unique, unmatched, unparalleled

unroll: unfurl

unruffled: calm, collected, composed, cool, even, imperturbable, nonchalant, placid, poised, quiet, sedate, serene, smooth, undisturbed, unshaken, untroubled

unruly: boisterous, difficult, disobedient, disorderly, forward, fractious, headstrong, intractable, lawless, obstinate, obstreperous, ornery, rambunctious, raucous, rebellious, restive, riotous, rowdy, stormy, tumultuous, turbulent, ungovernable, unmanageable, violent, wayward, wild

unsafe: chancy, dangerous, exposed, hazardous, insecure, perilous, risky, shaky, unprotected, unreliable, unsound, untrustworthy, vulnerable

unsatisfactory: bad, disappointing, inadequate, inefficient, inferior, insufficient, poor, unacceptable, unfit

unsatisfiable: insatiable

unsavory: disagreeable, distasteful, flat, insipid, nasty, repugnant, revolting, sickening, tasteless, unappetizing, unpalatable, unpleasant

unscathed: intact, safe, sound, unharmed, unhurt, uninjured, unmarked, unscarred, untouched, whole

unschooled: green, ignorant, illiterate, naive, uneducated, uninformed, unlearned, unlettered, untaught, untrained, untutored

unscrupulous: corrupt, crafty, crooked, deceitful, devious, dishonest, dishonorable, immoral, ruthless, shady, sinister, unconscionable, underhanded, unethical, unprincipled, venal

unseasonable: abnormal, ill-timed, inappropriate, inopportune, malapropos, premature, unripe, untimely

unseasoned: bland, callow, green, immature, raw, untrained

unseat: depose, dethrone, remove, replace, upset

unseeable from smallness: imperceptible

unseemly: boorish, cheap, coarse, crude, distasteful, improper, inappropriate, indecent, indecorous, inelegant, inept, offensive, rough, unbecoming, unbefitting, unsuitable, vulgar

unseen: concealed, hidden, invisible, obscure, undetected, undiscovered, unnoticed, unobserved

unselfish: altruistic, benevolent, charitable, generous, giving, humanitarian, kind, magnanimous

unserviceable: impractical, unfunctional, unusable, useless

unsettled: anxious, bothered, debatable, distracted, dubious, indecisive, mobile, nervous, outstanding, pending, remote, restless, shaken, tense, uncertain, unclear, undecided, undetermined, unpaid, unpopulated, unresolved, unstable, up in the air, variable

unshakable: abiding, adamant, firm, fixed, steady, unflappable, unsinkable, unwavering

unsightly: deformed, hideous, homely, repulsive, revolting, sickening, ugly, unattractive

unsightly object: eyesore

unskilled: amateurish, awkward, bungling, clumsy, green, incompetent, inefficient, inept, inexperienced, inexpert, maladroit, uneducated, unhandy, unskillful, untrained

unsociable: antisocial, cold, cool, hostile, introverted, reserved, shy, solitary, unfriendly, withdrawn

unsolicited: free, undesired, uninvited, unrequested, unsought, voluntary, volunteered

unsophisticated: artless, callow, corny, cracker-barrel, crude, genuine, green, homespun, inexperienced, ingenious, innocent, naive, natural, provincial, pure, rustic, simple, uncomplicated, untutored, unworldly

unsophisticated and simple: ingenuous, naive, unworldly

unsound: chancy, crazy, dangerous, decayed, decrepit, defective, deranged, diseased, feeble, flawed, flimsy, foolish, fragile, frail, hairy, hazardous, impaired, imperfect, insane, insecure, rickety, risky, senseless, shaky, sick, tottering, treacherous, unbalanced, unfit, unsafe, unstable, unsteady, weak, weakened, wobbly

unsparing: abundant, bountiful, extravagant, generous, giving, liberal, munificent, openhanded

unspeakable: alarming, appalling, atrocious, awful, disgusting, hateful, heinous, inconceivable, indefinable, indescribable, ineffable, inexpressible, loathsome, outrageous, repulsive, revolting, shocking, sickening, unbelievable, unimaginable, unutterable, wicked

unspecified: general, undefined, undetermined, unmentioned, vague

unspoiled: fresh, natural, pristine, unblemished, uncorrupted, unmarred, unsullied, untapped, untouched, virgin

unspoken: implicit, implied, inarticulate, inferred, intimated, invoiced, mute, silent, tacit, unsaid, unstated, unuttered

unstable: changeable, eccentric, emotional, erratic, fickle, flighty, flimsy, fluctuating, fragile, inconsistent, inconstant, insecure, loose, precarious, rocky, shaky, shifting, shifty, tricky, turbulent, unhinged, unreliable, unsettled, unsteady, vacillating, variable, volatile, wavering, wobbly

unsteady: capricious, changeable, dizzy, erratic, fickle, fluctuating, giddy, groggy, inconstant, quivery, rickety, rocky, shaky, shifting, teetering, tippy, unreliable, unsettled, unsound, unstable, vacillating, variable, wavering, wayward, wiggly, wobbly

unstudied: artless, extemporary, instinctive, naive, natural, spontaneous

unsubstantiated: unattested, unconfirmed, unsupported, unverified

unsuccessful: abortive, failing, fruitless, futile, hapless, hopeless, ineffectual, manqué, unavailing, unfortunate, unlucky, unprofitable, vain, would-be

unsuitable: conflicting, improper, inadequate, inappropriate, inapt, incongruous, inept, infelicitous, inopportune, unacceptable, unbecoming, unbefitting, unfit, untimely, useless

unsuited: inappropriate, inapt, incompatible, unfitting, unseemly

unsullied: chaste, clean, immaculate, pristine, pure, spotless, unblemished, undefiled, unpolluted, unsoiled, untarnished

unsure: borderline, dangerous, doubtful, hazardous, hesitant, indecisive, insecure, mistrustful, shaky, timid, uncertain, unclear, unconvinced, undecided, unstable, unsteady, untrustworthy, vacillating, weak, wobbly

unsure and risky: precarious

unsurpassed: insuperable, matchless, peerless, unequaled, unexcelled, unparalleled, unprecedented, unrivaled

unsuspecting: credulous, gullible, innocent, naive, unaware, unwary

unswayed: far, firm, impartial, unbiased, unbigoted, unprejudiced

unswerving: dedicated, determined, devoted, firm, staunch, steadfast, steady, straight, true, undaunted, unfaltering

unsympathetic: aloof, callous, cold, coldhearted, cool, cruel, hardhearted, harsh, heartless, hostile, insensitive, mean, repellent, stony, uncaring, uncompassionate, unemotional, unfeeling, unlikable, unpleasant

unsympathetic treatment: short shrift

unsystematic: catch as catch can

untainted: fresh

untalkative: reticent, taciturn

untamed: barbaric, feral, rambunctious, savage, uncivilized, undisciplined, unsubdued, wild

untangle: disentangle, extricate, free, solve, unscramble, unsnarl, untie, untwist

untarnished: clean, immaculate, polished, pure, shiny, spotless, unblemished, unstained, unsullied, untainted

untaught: ignorant, illiterate, instinctive, natural, spontaneous, uneducated, uninstructed, unlearned, unschooled, untrained, untutored

unthinkable: absurd, extraordinary, impossible, inconceivable, incredible, outlandish, unbelievable, unique

unthinking: careless, foolish, heedless, impetuous, inadvertent, inconsiderate, insensitive, rash, senseless, stupid, thoughtless, unmindful, unwise

untidy: bedraggled, careless, dirty, disarranged, disheveled, disordered, haphazard, littered, messy, rumpled, scraggly, scruffy, slipshod, sloppy, slovenly, tousled, uncluttered, uncombed, ungroomed, unkempt

untie: before, continuously, disengage, disentangle, extricate, free, loosen, unbind, undo, unfasten, unhitch, unknot, unlace, untangle

untimely: early, improper, inappropriately, inapt, inopportune, mistimed, premature, unexpected, unfortunate, unseasonable, unseemly, unsuitable

untold: boundless, countless, endless, enormous, huge, immeasurable, innumerable, many, numerous, staggering, undisclosed, unimaginable, unrelated, unrevealed, vast

untouched: flawless, intact, perfect, pristine, pure, sound, unharmed, unspoiled, virgin, whole

untoward: adverse, awkward, difficult, improper, inconvenient, intractable, irritating, troublesome, unbecoming, undisciplined, unfortunate, ungovernable, unlucky, unmanageable, unpropitious, unruly, unseemly, vexatious, wild

untrained: amateurish, green, ignorant, inexperienced, inexpert, novice, raw, undisciplined, unprepared, unqualified, unskilled, untamed, untaught, wild

untrammeled: free

untransferable: inalienable

untried: callow, fresh, green, immature, inexperienced, new, unattempted, unproved, untested

untroubled: calm, carefree, easy, easygoing, halcyon, peaceful, placid, relaxed, serene, tranquil, unbothered, unruffled, unworried

untrue: deceptive, dishonest, disloyal, erroneous, faithless, false, fictitious, inaccurate, incorrect, misleading, not so, unfaithful, unloyal, untruthful, wrong

untrustworthy: corrupt, crooked, deceitful, devious, dishonest, disloyal, disreputable, irresponsible, questionable, shady, shifty, slippery, tricky, unassured, undependable, unethical, unreliable, unsafe, untruthful

untrustworthy person: snake in the grass

untruthful: deceptive, dishonest, false, fraudulent, insincere, lying, mendacious, misleading

untutored: ignorant, illiterate, naive, natural, uneducated, uninstructed, unlearned, unread, unschooled, untaught

untwist: ravel

untwist a rope: unlay

untypical: abnormal, bizarre, odd, strange, uncommon, unusual

unusable: impracticable

unused: brand-new, fresh, idle, mint condition, new, remaining, untapped, untried, vacant

unused and neglected condition: desuetude

unusual: abnormal, anomalous, bizarre, different, distinct, eccentric, exceptional, extraordinary, funny, novel, odd, offbeat, peculiar, phenomenal, rare, refreshing, remarkable, scarce, special, strange, surprising, typical, uncommon, unique, unorthodox, untypical, unwonted, weird

unusual happening: phenomenon

unusual item: curio, rarity

unvarnished: bald, bare, candid, frank, plain, simple, stark, unadorned, undisguised, unfinished

unvarying: constant, even, fixed, monotonous, plain, steady, unchanging, unfluctuating, uniform, uninterrupted

unveil: announce, disclose, divulge, exhibit, expose, reveal, uncloak, uncover, unmask

unwarranted: baseless, groundless, idle, pointless, uncalled-for, undue, unfair, unfounded, unjustified, unprovoked, unreasonable, wrong

unwary: brash, careless, credulous, heedless, imprudent, incautious, rash, reckless, thoughtless, unalert, unaware, unguarded, unsuspecting

unwavering: consistent, constant, dedicated, determined, firm, intent, persistent, stable, staunch, steadfast, steady, steely, true, unchanging, unfaltering, unflappable, unshakable, unshaken

unwelcome: barred, distasteful, excluded, intrusive, objectionable, unacceptable, unasked, undesired, uninvited, unpleasant, unpopular, unsought, unwanted

unwelcome person: persona non grata

unwholesome: baneful, corrupt, deleterious, detrimental, evil, foul, harmful, impure, insalubrious, noxious, offensive, pernicious, poisonous, repulsive, toxic, unclean, unhealthful, unhealthy, unsound

unwholesome atmosphere or influence: miasma

unwholesome condition: dyscrasia

unwieldy: awkward, bulky, burdensome, clumsy, cumbersome, heavy, ungainly, unmanageable, weighty

unwilling: against, averse, backward, disinclined, forced, grudging, hesitant, involuntary, loath, opposed, reluctant, uncooperative, uneager

unwilling to yield: stoic

unwind: loosen, recline, relax, rest, uncoil, undo, unravel, unroll, untangle

unwise: dumb, foolish, impolitic, impractical, imprudent, inadvisable, inane, indiscreet, inept, injudicious, irrational, irresponsible, misguided, naive, senseless, stupid, thoughtless, unintelligent, unsound, witless

unwitting: accidental, inadvertent, innocent, involuntary, unaware, unexpected, uninformed, unintended, unknowing, unplanned, unsuspecting

unworthy: base, beneath, blamable, contemptible, dishonorable, shameful, unbecoming, undeserving, unfit, unseemly, unsuitable, valueless, worthless

unwritten: accepted, customary, oral, traditional, understood, unsaid, unstated, verbal, vocal

unyielding: adamant, determined, fast, firm, fixed, grim, hard, headstrong, inelastic, inexorable, inflexible, intractable, intransigent, iron, ironclad, obdurate, obstinate, pigheaded, relentless, rigid, ruthless, solid, steadfast, steely, stern, stiff, stiff-necked, stony, strict, stubborn, tenacious, tough, truculent, unbending, unbudging, uncompromising, unsubmissive, unwavering, wooden

up: above, active, aloft, arisen, ascend, awake, boost, current, familiar, finished, higher, increase, jump, optimistic, raise, rise, risen, standing, versed; elapsed

up and about: ambulatory, astir

up-and-coming: active, alert, eager, enterprising, industrious

up-and-down: bobbing, perpendicular, seesaw, uneven, vacillating, vertical, yo-yo

up-to-date: abreast, au courant, au fait, current, mod, modern, with it

up to now: as yet, so far, yet

upbeat: arsis, cheerful, cheery, happy, hopeful, optimistic, positive, sanguine

upbringing: nurture, training

upcoming: approaching, forthcoming, future, imminent, impending, looming, nearing, next

update: amend, modernize, refurbish, rejuvenate, renew, renovate, restore, revise

upgrade: advance, ascent, boost, elevate, improve, incline, increase, raise, slope, uplift

upheaval: cataclysm, catastrophe, chaos, clamor, commotion, disaster, disturbance, overthrow, revolt, revolution, shakeout, storm, tumult, turmoil

upheaval, violent: cataclysm

uphill: arduous, ascending, difficult, exhausting, grueling, hard, laborious, rising, rugged, strenuous, tiring, toilsome, tough

uphold: advocate, assert, assist, back, bear, brace, carry, champion, confirm, defend, encourage, lift, maintain, promote, protect, raise, support, sustain, vindicate

upholder of long-established custom: traditionalist

upkeep: budget, expenses, maintenance, overhead, preservation, repair, support, sustenance

uplift: edify, elate, elevate, enlighten, enrichment, exalt, hoist, illuminate, improve, inspire, lift, raise, rehabilitation, rock, upgrade

upon: about, above, against, astride, atop, concerning, onto, over, stop, thereafter

upper: above, amphetamine, drug, elevated, elite, higher, important, over, overhead, senior, stimulant, superior, top, topmost

upper class: aristocracy, elite, highbred, society, upper crust

upper-class customers: carriage trade

upper hand: advantage, better, command, edge, superiority, supremacy

upper keyboard part of a piano duet: primo

upper or dorsal surface: tergum

upper part of a glacier: neve

uppermost: chief, dominant, foremost, greatest, highest, leading, loftiest, main, predominant, primary, senior, supreme, top, topmost

upright: aboveboard, elevated, equitable, erect, ethical, exemplary, fair, good, honest, honorable, just, moral, noble, on end, perpendicular, plumb, post, principled, prop, righteous, sincere, standing, steep, straight, true, trustworthy, vertical, virtuous

upright piece or pole: mullion, pillar, post, stanchion, stile

upright position: stance

uprightness: dignity, honesty, honor, integrity, virtue

uprising: ascending, ascent, commotion, disturbance, incline, insurgence, insurrection, mutiny, rebellion, revolt, revolution, riot, tumult, upheaval

uproar: ado, ballyhoo, bedlam, brawl, brouhaha, bustle, chaos, clamor,

commotion, confusion, din, disorder, disturbance, ferment, flap, fracas, fuss, hassle, hubbub, hullabaloo, mayhem, noise, pandemonium, racket, riot, stir, tumult, turmoil, violence

uproarious: boisterous, confused, hilarious, loud, noisy, turbulent, wild

uproot: annihilate, deracinate, destroy, dislocate, displace, eradicate, exterminate, extirpate, move, remove, transplant

upscale: posh

upset: agitate, anger, angry, annoy, asea, beat, bother, capsize, capsized, confuse, defeat, derange, discombobulate, discomfit, discompose, disconcert, disconcerted, disordered, disorganize, distressed, disturb, embarrass, enrage, fluster, flustered, incense, infuriate, ired, jar, jumbled, outcome, overthrow, overturned, overwrought, perturbed, rattle, reverse, rile, riled, ruffle, shock, subvert, surprise, throw off, topple, trouble, tumble, turn, unhinge, unnerve, unsettle, worry

upset and disturb: irritate, perturb, ruffle

upshot: aftermath, climax, conclusion, consequence, culmination, effect, ending, finale, finish, limit, outcome, result, sequel, termination

upside-down: backward, chaotic, confused, haywire, inverted, jumbled, reversed, topsy-turvy

upstanding: ethical, honest, honorable, moral, principled, trustworthy

upstart: comer, jackanapes, nouveau riche, parvenu, presumptuous, snob

upsurge: advance, boom, improvement, increase, recovery, rise, upswing, upturn

upswing: rally

uptight: edgy, jumpy, tense, tensed, uneasy

upward: above, ascending, greater, higher, lofty, skyward, uphill

upward slope: acclivity, rise

urban: central, city, civic, cosmopolitan, metropolitan, municipal, oppidan, town

urbane: affable, civil, civilized, cordial, cosmopolitan, courteous, cultivated, cultured, debonair, elegant, genteel, polished, polite, refined, smooth, sophisticated, suave

urchin: boy, brat, child, delinquent, elf, gamin, hedgehog, imp, scamp, waif

urge: abet, advocate, appeal, appetite, cajole, coax, demand, desire, drive, egg on, encourage, excite, exhort, force, goad, impel, importune, impulse, incentive, incite, induce, influence, insist, itch, motive, needle, passion, persuade, plead, press, pressure, prod, prompt, provoke, push, recommend, request, shove, solicit, spur, stimulate, suggest, sway, weakness, yearning, yen

urge a view, action: advocate, champion, commend, promote

urge and appeal: impel, induce, lobby, solicit, supplicate

urge on: encourage, exhort, hearten, impel, incite, motivate

urge strongly: adjure, beseech, entreat, exhort, importune

urge to succeed: ambition

urge, irrational: compulsion

urgency: desperation, exigency, importance, insistence, necessity, need, pressure, seriousness, stress

urgent: clamant, compelling, critical, crucial, demanding, dire, essential, exigent, grave, immediate, impelling, imperative, imperious, important, insistent, necessary, peremptory, pressing, required, serious

urgent plea: SOS

urgent request: appeal

urgent, as need: dire

urgent, troublesomely: importunate

urgently necessary: imperative

urinary system, branch of medicine involving: urology

urination increasing substance: diuretic

urination, excessive: diuresis

urine canal out of body: urethra

urine, causing increase in: diuretic

urine, lacking control of: incontinent

urine, releasing: micturate, urinate

urn: capsule, cistern, container, ewer, jar, ossuary, pitcher, samovar, vase, vessel

urn, shaped like a: urceolate

usable: accessible, applicable, available, beneficial, convenient, functional, handy, helpful, open, practical, serviceable, useful, valuable, working

usage: convention, custom, formula, grammar, habit, habitude, interest, manner, method, mode, practice, procedure, rule, system, tradition, treatment, wont

use: accustom, advantage, application, apply, avail, benefit, capitalize, consume, consumption, control, custom, demand, deplete, devour, duty, employ, employment, exercise, exhaust, expend, exploit, familiarize, function, gain, good, guide, habit, habituate, handle, handling, hire, incur, manage, manipulate, mileage, need, occupy, operate, practice, privilege, regulate, spend, treat, treatment, try, utility, utilize, value, wield, wont, work, worth

use to greatest advantage: capitalize on, exploit, parlay, utilize

use up: consume, deplete, exhaust, expend

use wastefully: squander

use, benefit, advantage: avail, recourse, resort

use, practical: application

used: accepted, consumed, old, secondhand, shopworn, utilized, worn

used to: acclimatized, accustomed, attuned, familiar, habituated, oriented, wont

useful: advantageous, beneficial, conducive, contributive, convenient, effective, functional, good, handy, helpful, multipurpose, practical, pragmatic, profitable, serviceable, utile, valuable, worthwhile

useful and practical: functional, utilitarian

useful as a means: instrumental, subservient

useful in many ways: versatile

useful thing or quality: asset

usefulness: advantage, benefit, efficiency, practicality, suitability, utility, value

useless: fruitless, futile, helpless, hopeless, idle, impracticable, incompetent, ineffective, ineffectual, inefficient, inutile, obsolete, otiose, outmoded, pointless, to no avail, unavailing, unproductive, unprofitable, unserviceable, unworkable, vain, void, worthless

useless and obsolete: obsolescent, outmoded, superannuated

useless and unproductive: fruitless, futile, ineffectual, unprofitable, vain

useless gift or possession: white elephant

useless thing or person: deadwood

useless, make: enfeeble, nullify

usher: attend, attendant, conduct, direct, doorkeeper, escort, gatekeeper, guide, herald, inaugurate, introduce, lead, officer, page, porter, precede, precursor, receive, seat, seater, servant, steer

usual: accustomed, average, common, conventional, current, customary, everyday, familiar, frequent, general, habitual, natural, normal, ordinary, predictable, prevailing, prevalent, regular, rife, routine, standard, traditional, trite, typical, wonted

usual and expected: customary, habitual, predictable

usual and standard: conventional, prescribed, staple

usurp: appropriate, arrogate, assume, commandeer, preempt, seize, steal, take, wrest

Utah capital: Salt Lake City

Utah cities: Ogden, Orem, Provo

Utah features: Arches, Bryce Canyon, Colorado Plateau, Great Basin, Mormon church

utensil: fork, implement, instrument, knife, silverware, spatula, spoon, tool

uterus: venter

uterus tissue removal: D & C, dilation and curettage

uterus tubes: fallopian tube, oviduct

uterus, organ where fetus develops in: placenta

uterus, surgical removal of part or all of: hysterectomy

utilitarian: economical, effective, efficient, functional, practical, pragmatic, realistic, sensible, usable, useful

utility: advantage, auxiliary, benefit, convenience, profit, secondary, service, substitute, use, usefulness

utilize: avail, capitalize, consume, employ, exercise, exploit, harness, use

utmost: absolute, best, extreme, farthest, final, greatest, highest, maximum, nth, paramount, ultimate

utopia: Eden, heaven, paradise, Shangri-la, Zion

utopian: Arcadian, ideal, idealistic, imaginary, impractical, perfect, unfeasible, visionary

utter: absolute, complete, downright, extreme, out-and-out, outright, peremptory, perfect, rank, sheer, stark, total, unmitigated, unqualified; articulate, assert, declare, deliver, disclose, divulge, emit, enunciate, exclaim, express, issue, mumble, mutter, pronounce, reveal, say, speak, state, talk, tell, vent, verbalize, vocalize, voice, whisper

utter disorder: chaos

utterance: announcement, articulation, dictum, discourse, expression, murmur, opinion, remark, revelation, speech, statement, talk, verbalization, vocalization, whisper, word

utterly: absolutely, all, altogether, assuredly, completely, diametrically, entirely, full, just, merely, perfectly, positively, quite, stark, thoroughly, totally, well, wholly

The Writer's Digest Flip Dictionary

Vv

V.I.P.: big shot, bigwig, celebrity, dignitary, leader, lion, notable, personage, someone

V-shaped emblem: chevron

vacancy: break, cavity, chasm, emptiness, opening, position, room, space, uninhabited, vacuity, vacuum, void

vacant: abandoned, absent, barren, blank, deadpan, deserted, devoid, disengaged, empty, expressionless, foolish, free, idle, inane, inexpressive, leisure, open, silly, unemployed, unfilled, uninhabited, unoccupied, untenanted, unused, vacuous, void

vacate: abandon, abrogate, annul, clear, countermand, depart, dissolve, empty, evacuate, leave, quit, relinquish, repeal, rescind, retire, void

vacation: furlough, holiday, intermission, leave, leisure, liberty, recess, rest, sabbatical, spite, trip

vacation home, shared ownership of: time sharing

vacation in Western ranch: dude ranch

vacation or paid leave of absence for one year, for research: sabbatical

vaccinate: immunize, inoculate, protect

vaccine additional dose: booster

vacillate: alternate, blow hot and cold, dither, fluctuate, flutter, hem and haw, hesitate, oscillate, rock, seesaw, shift, stagger, sway, teeter, totter, waver, whiffle, wobble

vacillating: changeable, fluctuating, hesitant, hesitating, oscillating, shifting, swaying, tentative, uncertain, unsure, vibrating, volatile, wavering

vacuous: clear, devoid, empty, inane, silly, vacant

vacuum: cavity, emptiness, nothingness, space, vacuity, void

vacuum tube: diode

vagabond: aimless, beggar, bohemian, bum, deadbeat, drifter, drifting, hobo, itinerant, nomadic, rogue, rover, scamp, stiff, stray, tramp, transient, unpredictable, vagrant, wander, wanderer, wandering, wayfarer, wayward, worthless

vagary: breach, caper, caprice, conceit, daydream, digression, divergence, fancy, fantasy, impulse, kink, notion, prank, quirk, rambling, roam, trick, waver, whim, whimsy

vagina examination instrument: speculum

vaginal examination using a magnifying device: colposcopy

vagrant: beggar, bum, hobo, homeless, idler, itinerant, nomadic, panhandler, roamer, rover, tramp, undesirable, unrestrained, vagabond, waif, wanderer, wayward

vague: ambiguous, bleary, blurry, cloudy, confused, dark, dim, dreamy, elusive, faint, foggy, fuzzy, hazy, ill-defined, imprecise, indefinable, indefinite, indeterminate, indistinct, intangible, loose, misty, muddy, nebulous, obscure, opaque, shadowy, sketchy, uncertain, unclear, undetermined, unexplicit, unfixed, unsettled, unspecified, unsure

vague concept: inkling, notion

vague feelings, having: ambiguous, ambivalent, equivocal

vague state: limbo

vagueness of mind: haze

vain: arrogant, boastful, cocky, conceited, egocentric, egotistic, egotistical, frivolous, narcissistic, ostentatious, otiose, petty, proud, proud as a peacock, snooty, stuckup, vainglorious

vain hope: pipe dream

vain, in: empty, fruitless, futile, hollow, hopeless, nugatory, senseless, to no avail, trivial, unavailing, unprofitable, unrewarded, useless, worthless

vainglorious: boastful, bragging, cocky, conceited, egotistical, insolent, narcissistic, pompous, proud, vain

vale: adieu, dale, dell, farewell, glen, valley

valedictory: adieu, departing, farewell, final, good-bye, parting, terminal

valentine: card, gift, letter, sweetheart

valet: attendant, dresser, equerry, manservant, servant, squire

valiant: adventurous, bold, brave, chivalrous, courageous, daring, excellent, fearless, gallant, gutsy, heroic, intrepid, noble, powerful, stalwart, steadfast, stout, stouthearted, strong, unafraid, undaunted, valorous, vigorous, worthy

valid: authentic, binding, certified, cogent, compelling, conclusive, confirmed, convincing, credible, effective, efficient, genuine, good, healthy, just, lawful, legal, legitimate, powerful, realistic, reasonable, right, satisfactory, satisfying, solid, sound, strong, sufficient, telling, true, verified, weighty

validate: authenticate, certify, confirm, establish, justify, legalize, prove, ratify, sanction, sign, substantiate, verify, vet

validation: proof

validity: cogency, effectiveness, force, genuineness, legitimacy, potency, soundness, strength, substance, weight

valise: bag, baggage, grip, haversack, luggage, satchel, suitcase

valley: basin, canyon, chasm, cirque,

combe, coulee, cove, dale, dell, depression, dingle, divide, glen, gorge, goyle, gulch, gully, hollow, ravine, rill, strath, swale, trough, vale

valley along crest of midocean ridge, wide: rift valley

valor: backbone, boldness, bravery, chivalry, courage, fearlessness, fortitude, gallantry, guts, heart, heroism, merit, mettle, nerve, prowess, resolution, spirit, spunk, tenacity, virtue

valorous: bold, brave, courageous, dauntless, fearless, gallant, heroic, intrepid, noble, stout, valiant

valuable: antique, asset, cherished, costly, dear, expensive, heirloom, important, precious, priceless, prized, rare, treasured, useful

value: account, admire, advantage, appraise, appreciate, apprise, apprize, assess, assessment, avail, cherish, cost, distinction, esteem, estimate, estimation, evaluate, expense, importance, merit, opinion, price, prize, quality, rate, respect, set store by, significance, treasure, usefulness, utility, valuation, weight, worth

RELATED TERMS

value of business or property beyond mortgage and liability: equity

value of nation's goods and services before deductions: GNP, gross national product

value of property beyond debt and liability: equity

value printed on bill or bond: face value, nominal value, par value

value, in proportion to the: ad valorem

value, loss in: depreciation

value, rise in: appreciation ☙

valued above its face value, amount something is: premium

valued possession passed down: heirloom

valued, highly: cherished, coveted, esteemed, prized

values of a people transmitted through arts, myths: mythos

values of group, moral: mores

values peculiar to a specific person, group, culture, people: ethos

valve: cock, faucet, flap, gate, outlet, regulator, shutoff, spigot, stopper

vamoose: begone, decamp, depart, hightail, leave, scat, scoot, scram, skedaddle, skiddoo

vamp: contrive, fabricate, flirt, improvise, mend, patch, repair, seduce, seductress, siren, temptress, tramp

vampire: bat, blackmailer, bloodsucker, Dracula, extortionist, lamia, monster

van: camper, cart, lead, truck, vehicle, wagon

vandal: hoodlum, looter, marauder, pillager, plunderer, raider, ravager, ruffian

vandalize: deface, destroy, mar, trash, wreck

vane: fan, feather, weathercock

vanguard: forefront, front, innovators, lead, leaders, leading, trailblazers

vanilla: bland, ordinary, unexciting, unoriginal

vanish: dematerialize, disappear, dissolve, evanesce, evaporate, exit, fade, melt, terminate, vaporize

vanish gradually: evanesce

vanity: cabinet, compact, conceit, egoism, egotism, emptiness, foppery, futility, idleness, narcissism, pomposity, pride, uselessness, vainglory, worthlessness

vanity case: etui

vanquish: beat, best, conquer, crush, defeat, expel, humble, master, overcome, overpower, overthrow, quell, reduce, rout, subdue, subjugate, subvert, suppress, surmount, trample

vapid: bland, boring, colorless, dull, flat, flavorless, inane, insipid, lame, lifeless, meaningless, pointless, spiritless, stale, tasteless, trite, unanimated, unexciting, unimaginative, uninspiring, uninteresting, weak

vapor: air, breath, cloud, dew, fog, fumes, gas, haze, humidity, mist, moisture, nimbus, smog, smoke, steam

vapor trail: contrail

vapor, convert or change into: evaporate

vaporize: aerate, boil, condense, dissipate, evaporate

vaporized, readily: volatile

vaporous: aerial, airy, ethereal, fleeting, hazy, insubstantial, misty, smoggy, vague, volatile, wispy

vapors: gas

variable: capricious, changeable, diverse, fickle, fitful, flexible, fluctuating, inconstant, irregular, shifty, spasmodic, uncertain, unequal, uneven, unstable, unsteady, variant, varying, volatile, wavering

variance: argument, change, conflict, deviation, difference, disagreement, discord, discrepancy, dispute, dissension, dissent, disunity, division, fluctuation, quarrel, variation

variation: alternative, change, departure, deviation, difference, disparity, modification, shade, variance, variety

variation in combination of elements: permutation

variation or change: vicissitude

variation, abrupt: saltation

variation, leeway for: latitude, play, tolerance

variation, subtle or slight degree of: nuance

varied: assorted, different, diverse, diversified, miscellaneous, mixed, motley, multiple, myriad, sundry, various

varied greatly: manifold, multifarious, multiform, omnifarious

variegated: calico, checkered, dappled, different, diversified, flecked, motley, mottled, multicolored, piebald, pied, speckled, spotted, varicolored, varied

variety: assortment, brand, breed, category, class, collection, diversity, family, genus, hodgepodge, kind, medley, sort, species, strain, subdivision, type, variation

variety of uses and functions, having: versatility

variety show, old-time: vaudeville

various: assorted, changeable, countless, different, differing, dissimilar, distinct, divers, diverse, manifold, many, miscellaneous, multitudinal, numerous, several, sundry, unalike, variable, variant, varied

varlet: attendant, blackguard, footman, helper, knave, page, rascal, scoundrel, servant, vassal

varnish: coat, embellish, enamel, finish, gloss, japan, lac, lacquer, polyurethane, shellac, stain, veneer

vary: alter, alternate, change, contrast, depart, deviate, differ, digress, disagree, dissent, diverge, diversify, divide, fluctuate, modify, modulate, oscillate, qualify, shift, swerve, variate

vary a business' products: diversify

vary tone or pitch: inflect, modulate

vase: amphora, container, crater, ewer, jar, jardiniere, krater, pot, urn, vessel

VEGETABLES

alfalfa sprout	chayote	jalapeño pepper	pinto bean	sorrel
artichoke	chickpea	kale	plantain	soybean
arugula	chicory	kidney bean	pokeweed	spinach
asparagus	Chinese cabbage	kohlrabi	potato	squash
bamboo sprout/shoot	chive	leek	pumpkin	string bean
bean	collard greens	lentil	radiccio	succotash
bean sprout	corn	lettuce	radish	sugar pea
beet	cress	lima bean	rampion	summer squash
bell pepper	cucumber	mung bean	red bean	sweet corn
black-eyed pea	dandelion	mushroom	red cabbage	sweet potato
Boston lettuce	eggplant	muskmelon	red pepper	tomato
broad bean	endive	mustard	rhubarb	truffle
broccoli	escarole	navy bean	rice	turnip
Brussels sprout	fennel	New Zealand spinach	romaine	water chestnut
butter bean	garbanzo bean	okra	rutabaga	watercress
cabbage	garlic	olive	sauerkraut	watermelon
cardoon	glasswort	onion	scallion	wax bean
carrot	globe artichoke	parsley	sea kale	white bean
cassava	gourd	parsnip	seaweed	yam
cauliflower	green bean	pea	shallot	yellow pepper
celery	green pepper	pepper	snap bean	yellow squash
chard	iceberg lettuce	petsai	snow pea	zucchini ☙

RELATED TERMS

vase handles: ansae

vase projections: ears

vase, cremation: urn

vase, device to support stems in flower: frog ☙

vassal: beneficiary, bondman, dependent, esne, helot, liege, peasant, serf, servant, servile, slave, subject, subordinate, tenant, thrall, varlet

vast: ample, boundless, broad, capacious, colossal, endless, enormous, extensive, far-reaching, giant, gigantic, great, huge, immense, large, massive, spacious, titanic, tremendous, unlimited, untold, whopping, wide

vast in number: infinite, innumerable, limitless, myriad

vat: basin, cask, container, pit, tub, tun

vaudeville: burlesque, entertainment, revue, show, skit, theater

vault: arch, bend, bound, box, case mate, casemate, catacomb, cave, cavern, ceiling, cellar, chamber, clear, crater, crypt, dome, dungeon, hurdle, jump, leap, mausoleum, mount, repository, roof, room, safe, soar, span, spring, storeroom, strongbox, strongroom, structure, tomb

vault, underground: crypt, undercroft

vaulted alcove: apse

vaults, junction of two: groin

vaunt: boast, brag, crow, display, exhibit, flaunt, gasconade, prate, strut

veal cutlet, breaded: wiener schnitzel

veal, thin sliced and sauteed: scaloppine

veer: alter, avert, bend, careen, change, deflect, depart, deviate, digress, dip, divert, dodge, shift, skew, slue, sway, swerve, tack, turn, twist, yaw

vegetable dish of cabbage and potatoes fried together: bubble and squeak

vegetable dish of fried ground spiced chickpeas and fava beans: falafel, felafel

vegetable dish of shredded, salted, fermented cabbage: sauerkraut

vegetable dish with rice and meat, saffron-flavored: paella

vegetable paste of avocado, tomato, peppers: guacamole

vegetable paste of chickpeas, tahini, oil, lemon, garlic: hommos, hummus, humus

vegetable paste of cornmeal: polenta

vegetable paste of sesame seeds: tahini

vegetable salad with bulgur wheat, scallions, tomatoes, mint, parsley: tabbouleh, tabbouli, tabooli

vegetable stew of corn, lima beans, tomatoes: succotash

vegetable stew, seasoned hot or cold: ratatouille

vegetable strips, long thin: julienne

vegetables and meats served with fried noodles, Chinese: chow mein

vegetables or seafood deep-fried, Japanese: tempura

vegetables served as side dish, diced cooked: jardiniere

vegetables, raw cut, with dip: crudités

vegetarian: fruitarian, herbivorous, plant-eating, vegan

vegetarian eating only plant products: vegan

vegetarian who eats both dairy products and eggs: lacto-ovo-vegetarian

vegetarian who eats dairy products: lactovegetarian

vegetarian, not strict: demi-veg

vegetate: blossom, decay, deteriorate, grow, hibernate, idle, languish, loaf, sprout, stagnate

vegetation: flora, greenery, growth, herbage, hibernation, inactivity, lethargy, listlessness, plants, verdure

vegetation of region or time: flora

vegetation, flourishing: herbage, verdure

vehemence: ire

vehement: angry, ardent, eager, emotional, emphatic, energetic, fervent, fervid, fierce, fiery, forceful, furious,

VERB TYPES AND TERMS

verb accompanying another to distinguish mood, voice, aspect, tense: auxiliary verb

verb and one or more particles acting as unit, e.g. *look up*: phrasal verb

verb characteristically used with other verb to indicate mood or tense: modal auxiliary

verb connecting predicate to subject (e.g. *be*): copula, linking verb

verb designating existence, like *be*: substantive

verb expressing past action: past participle, perfect participle

verb expressing present action: present participle

verb form changes showing mood or tense: inflection

verb form constructed by using an auxiliary word rather than inflected form, of a: periphrastic

verb form ending in *-ed* or *-ing* that can function independently as adjective: participle

verb form indicating time: tense

verb form often preceded by *to*: infinitive

verb formed from a noun: denominative

verb functioning as a noun: gerund

verb having same subject and direct object: reflexive

verb indicating contingent or hypothetical action: subjunctive

verb indicating ordinary objective statement: indicative

verb inflected: conjugation

verb like *be* or *seem* that links predicate to subject: copula, linking verb

verb mood that expresses a command or request: imperative

verb mood that expresses contingent or hypothetical action: subjunctive

verb mood that expresses ordinary objective statements: indicative

verb of active meaning but passive form: deponent

verb preceded by *to*: infinitive

verb tense used to express action completed before a specified past time: pluperfect

verb that does not require or cannot take a direct object: intransitive

verb that expresses action completed by a specific future time: future perfect

verb that requires direct object to complete meaning: transitive

verb used in speaking of action not yet occuring: future

verb used to indicate subject is the object of the action: passive

verb with participles ending in *-ed*, *-ing*: regular verb

verb with participles varying in spelling: irregular verb

verbal: articulate, oral, spoken, stated, talkative, unwritten, verbatim, vocal

verbal attack: philippic, slam, tirade

verbal diarrhea, to have: explaterate

verbal noun ending in *-ing*: gerund

verbs classified as to the relationship of action: aspect

verbs indicating relationship between subject and action: voice

verbs used to indicate speaker's attitude: mood ❦

---

heated, hot, impassioned, impetuous, intense, lively, opinionated, rabid, raging, stormy, strong, urgent, vigorous, violent, wild

vehicle on runners: sled

vehicle transporting passengers on route for small fare: jitney

vehicle, old broken-down: jalopy, rattletrap

vehicle, three-wheeled and pedaled: pedicab

vehicle, two-wheeled and pulled by one: ricksha, rickshaw

vehicles traveling together: caravan, convoy

veil: camouflage, cloak, cloud, conceal, cover, curtain, dim, disguise, drape, enfold, guise, hide, mantle, mask, netting, screen, shield, shroud, velum, yashmak

veil material: barege, tulle

veil-wearing, in India: purdah

vein: capillary, channel, duct, tube, vena, venule, vessel

vein conducting blood from digestive organs to liver: portal vein

vein of leaf or insect wing: costa

vein of ore: motherlode, roke

vein of upper extremities: subclavian vein

vein, into or in a: intravenous

vein, puncture of a: venipuncture

vein, surgical opening of: phlebotomy, venesection

vein, swollen leg: varicose vein, varix

vein, very small: venule

veinlike deposit: lode

veins draining into heart's right atrium: vena cava

veins of leaf or insect wing, area bounded by: areola

veins of leaf or insect wing, system of: venation

veins of neck: jugular vein

veins, concerning: venous

velocity: acceleration, celerity, expedition, haste, headway, momentum, motion, pace, quickness, rapidity, rate, speed, swiftness

velum: covering, membrane, palate, veil

velvet: plushy, velour, velveteen

velvet's fuzzy surface: nap, pile

velvety: velutinous

venal: bribable, buyable, corrupt, corruptible, crooked, dishonorable, greedy, hired, infamous, mercenary, salable, unscrupulous, vendible

vend: barter, hawk, huckster, market, peddle, sell, trade

vendetta: dispute, feud, fight, gripe, quarrel

vendor: businessperson, dealer, hawker, huckster, merchant, peddler, retailer, salesperson, seller, trader

veneer: coat, coating, cover, enamel, facade, facing, film, finish, front, gloss, layer, mask, overlay, surface, varnish, veil

venerable: aged, ancient, antique, hoary, honorable, old

venerate: admire, adore, cherish, honor, prize, regard, respect, revere, reverence, value, worship

veneration: admiration, adoration, awe, devotion, esteem, honor, repayment, respect, reverence, vengeance, worship, wrath

vengeance: reprisal, requital, retaliation, retribution, revenge

vengeance, inflict: exact, wreak

venial: allowable, excusable, forgivable, mild, minor, pardonable, slight, tolerable, trivial, unimportant

venison source: deer

venom: anger, animosity, hating, hatred, malice, poison, rancor, resentment, spite, toxin, vitriol

venomous: antagonistic, baleful, baneful, deadly, evil, hateful, hostile, lethal, malicious, malignant, mean, poisoned, poisonous, rancorous, spiteful, toxic, vicious, virulent

vent: air, aperture, avenue, discharge, eject, emit, flue, gush, hole, opening, orifice, outlet, pipe, release, slit, spout

vent, to: assert, communicate, express, expression, state, voice

ventilate: aerate, air, broadcast, circulate, debate, discuss, examine, expose, fan, freshen, oxygenate, publicize, state, voice

ventilator: transom

venture: adventure, attempt, bet, brave, challenge, chance, danger, dare, endeavor, enterprise, essay, experiment, feat, fortune, gamble, hazard, investment, project, risk, speculate, speculation, stake, try, undertaking, wager

venture out: sally forth

venturesome: adventurous, audacious, bold, brave, courageous, dangerous, daring, enterprising, fearless, foolhardy, hazardous, heroic, perilous, rash, reckless, risky, speculative, spirited

venue: ground, locale, place, scene, setting, site, thrust

veracious: accurate, direct, honest, precise, sincere, true, truthful, valid

veracity: accuracy, candor, correctness, credibility, exactness, fact, faithfulness, honesty, integrity, precision, sincerity, trueness, truth, truthfulness

veranda: balcony, lanai, patio, piazza, platform, porch, portico, stoop, terrace

verbalize: articulate, express, say, speak, state, talk, utter, vent, vocalize, voice

verbatim: accurately, exactly, literal, orally, precisely, verbal

verbiage: chatter, diction, floridity, logorrhea, parlance, redundancy, repetition, talk, verbosity, wordage, wordiness

verbose: flowery, gabby, grandiloquent, long-winded, loquacious, prolix, redundant, repetitive, talkative, tautologous, windy, wordy

verboten: banned, disallowed, forbidden, prohibited, taboo, tabu

verdant: blooming, fresh, grassy, green, inexperienced, innocent, lush, mossy, naive, vernal

Verdi opera: *Aida, Ernani, Il trovatore, La Traviata, Otello, Rigoletto*

verdict: assessment, decision, decree, deliverance, determination, finding, judgment, opinion, ruling, sentence

verdict of not guilty: acquittal

verdict, to give a: render

verdure: freshness, greenery, greenness

verge: approach, border, bound, boundary, brim, brink, edge, fringe, hem, horizon, incline, limit, line, lip, margin, point, range, rim, scope, slope, staff, tend, threshold, wand

verification: affirmation, averment, certification, confirmation, proof, validation

verify: affirm, attest, audit, authenticate, back, certify, check, confirm, corroborate, document, establish, maintain, prove, settle, substantiate, support, test, validate

veritable: actual, authentic, bona fide, factual, genuine, honest, indubitable, real, true, undoubted, valid, veracious

vermilion: antimony, cinnabar, color, red, scarlet

vermin: animal, ant, bedbug, centipede, flea, fly, foxes, insect, lice, mice, mosquito, pest, rat, rodent, snake, termite, weasel

Vermont capital: Montpelier

Vermont cities: Barre, Burlington, Rutland

Vermont features: Green Mountains

vernacular: cant, colloquial, dialect, endemic, idiom, jargon, language, lingo, parlance, patois, slang, speech, tongue

vernal: fresh, spring, springlike, verdant, young, youthful

versatile: able, adaptable, adjustable, adroit, changeable, flexible, gifted, handy, mobile, multifaceted, proficient, resourceful, skilled, talented, variable

verse: ballad, composition, jingle, limerick, meter, ode, poem, poesy, poetry, rhyme, stanza, stave, stich

RELATED TERMS

verse into metrical patterns, analysis of: scansion

verse mixing two or more languages: macaronic

verse of 5 anapestic lines, light humorous: limerick

verse of poem: stanza, stave, stich, strophe

verse repeated at intervals: burden, chorus, refrain

verse spoken by alternate speakers: stichomythia

verse, accent on stressed syllable in: ictus

verse, crude irregular: crambo, doggerel

verse, pause in a line of: caesura

verse, study of metrical structure of: prosody ❧

versed: abreast, accomplished, accustomed, acquainted, adept, au courant, aware, competent, experienced, familiar, informed, knowledgeable, learned, practiced, proficient, qualified, schooled, skilled, taught, trained

version: account, adaptation, depiction, description, edition, interpretation, paraphrase, rendition, report, side, statement, story, translation

version of a work, widely accepted: vulgate

verso's opposite: recto

versus: against, alternative, contrast, vs.

vertebra, vertebrae: back, backbone, chine, spinal column, spine, spondyl

vertebra, vertebrae parts: atlas, axis, caudal, cervical, coccyx, disk, lumbar, thoracic

vertebrate: chordate

vertex: apex, apogee, crown, culmination, node, peak, pinnacle, point, summit, top, zenith

vertical: acme, erect, perpendicular, plumb, sheet, standing, steep, summit, upright, vertex

vertical takeoff and landing: VTOL

vertiginous: dizzy, giddy, revolving, rotating, spinning, turning, unstable, whirling

vertigo: confusion, dizziness, giddiness, reeling, unsteadiness

verve: ability, animation, ardor, bounce, dash, éclat, élan, energy, enthusiasm, fire, gusto, life, liveliness, oomph, passion, pep, punch, spirit, spring, vigor, vitality, vivacity, zeal, zest, zing, zip

very: absolute, absolutely, actual, actually, authentic, awfully, bare, complete, deeply, eminently, emphatically, everso, exact, exactly, exceedingly, extremely, genuine, greatly, highly, hugely, ideal, identical, mere, mighty, most, much, notably, precise, precisely, quite, real, really, remarkably, same, special, strikingly, surpassingly, terribly, thoroughly, too, true, truly, truthful, utter, veracious, veritable

very much passion used as a musical direction: con molto passione

very seldom: once in a blue moon, rarely

vesicle: bladder, blister, cavity, cell, cyst, sac, utricle

vespers: evensong, orison, prayer, service

vessel: barge, barrel, basin, boat, bottle, bowl, caldron, can, canoe, carafe, cask, cogue, container, craft, crater, cresset, crucible, cruse, cup, cutter, drum, duct, ewer, flagon, flask, funnel, glass, goblet, jar, kettle, krater, liner, mug, olla, pail, pan, pitcher, pod, pot, pyx, receptacle, scow, ship, situlae, steamer, stein, tank, tub, tube, urn, utensil, vase, vat, vein, yacht

vessel for cooking in fireplace, large: caldron

vessels, concerning: vascular

vest: clothe, coat, drape, dress, endow, garment, jacket, jerkin, robe, waistcoat

vestal: chaste, nun, pure, virgin, virginal, virtuous

vestibule: antechamber, anteroom, cavity, channel, corridor, doorway, entrance, entry, foyer, hall, hallway, lobby, narthex, passage

vestige: evidence, footprint, footstep, hint, indication, mark, path, relic, remnant, scrap, shred, sign, tincture, tinge, trace, track

vestiges: ashes, traces

vestment: alb, amice, cassock, cincture, clothing, covering, dress, frock, garb, garment, gear, gown, habiliment, hood, orale, robe, stole, tunic, uniform, vesture

veteran: disciplined, experienced, expert, GI, longtimer, master, old hand, old timer, old-timer, practiced, professional, seasoned, skilled, weathered, wise

veto: defeat, deny, disallow, forbid, kill, negative, nix, nyet, override, overrule, quash, refuse, reject

veto by president by not signing a bill before Congress adjourns: pocket veto

vex: afflict, aggravate, agitate, anger, annoy, bother, bug, chafe, dispute, distress, disturb, disturbance, fret, fuss, gall, harass, harry, infuriate, ire, irk, irritate, miff, needle, nettle, offend, perplex, pester, plague, provoke, puzzle, rile, roil, rowel, ruffle, spite, tease, torment, toss, trouble, upset, worry

vexation: aggravation, agitation, annoyance, harassment, hassle, irritation, pique, weariness

vexatious: afflictive, aggravating, annoying, badgering, bothersome, distressing, disturbed, harassed, irritating, nagging, pesky, thorny, tormenting, troublesome, upsetting

via: along, by way of, over, per, through, with; passage, road, way

viable: applicable, doable, feasible, living, possible, practicable, reasonable, workable

viaduct: bridge, overpass, ramp

vial: ampoule, ampul, bottle, container, flask, phial

viands: chow, eats, edibles, fare, feed, food, grub, provisions, victuals, vittles

viands of Virginia: hams

vibrant: alive, animated, bright, brilliant, colorful, dynamic, eager, electrifying, energetic, enthusiastic, florid, glowing, pulsating, radiant, resonant, resounding, sonorous, throbbing, vigorous, vivacious, vivid

vibrate: agitate, beat, echo, fluctuate, flutter, jar, oscillate, pulsate, pulse, quake, quaver, quiver, resonate, resound, reverberate, ripple, rock, shake, shiver, swing, thrill, throb, tremble, tremor, trill, vacillate, waver

vibration: fluctuation, flutter, oscillation, pulsation, quake, quaver, quiver, reverberation, shake, thrill, trembling, tremor, vacillation, vibe

vibration caused by two bodies striking each other: percussion

vicar: clergyman, cleric, ecclesiastic, minister, pastor, priest, proxy, substitute

vicarious: delegated, empathetic, substituted, surrogate, sympathetic

vice: blemish, carnality, corruption, crime, defect, depravity, evil, failing, fault, flaw, foible, immorality, imperfection, iniquity, replacing, shortcoming, sin, weakness, wrong

vice versa: again, contrariwise, contrary, conversely, oppositely

viceroy: butterfly, governor, nabob, representative, ruler, satrap

vicinity: area, ballpark, close, district, environs, locality, nearby, neighborhood, proximity, region, surroundings

vicious: atrocious, bad, beastly, corrupt, corrupting, cruel, dangerous, debasing, depraved, diabolical, evil, ferocious, fiendish, fierce, foul, hateful, heinous, immoral, iniquitous, malicious, mean, nasty, nefarious, noxious, rotten, savage, severe, spiteful, terrible, vehement, vile, villainous, vindictive, violent, wicked, wild, wrong

vicissitude: alteration, change, difficulty, diversity, mutability, mutation, reversal, shift, switch, variation, variety

victim: casualty, chump, dupe, fatality, fool, goat, gull, patsy, prey, pushover, sacrifice, scapegoat, stooge, sucker, sufferer, underdog

victim of exploitation: fall guy, pawn, puppet, sacrificial lamb, scapegoat, whipping boy

victimize: bamboozle, burn, cheat, deceive, dupe, exploit, gull, hoodwink, persecute, prey, stiff, trick, use

victor: champ, champion, conquer, conqueror, master, subjugator, vanquisher, winner

victory: achievement, ascendancy, conquest, mastery, success, superiority, supremacy, triumph, win

victuals: chow, comestibles, eats, edibles, feed, food, meals, nourishment, provisions, rub, supplies, viands, vittles

vie: bet, compete, complete, contend,

content, contest, endure, fight, jostle, match, oppose, rival, stake, strive, wager

view: admire, aim, appearance, apprehend, aspect, attitude, behold, belief, believe, canvass, consider, contemplate, examination, examine, expectation, eye, feeling, gaze, glimpse, goal, inspect, inspection, judge, ken, landscape, look, notion, object, objective, observe, opinion, outlook, panorama, peek, perception, picture, plan, profile, regard, scan, scape, scene, scenery, scrutinize, scrutiny, seascape, see, sight, spy, standpoint, stare, summary, survey, theory, thought, vasta, vision, vista, watch, witness

view of the whole, offering general: synoptic

view with parts separated but shown in relation to each other: exploded view

view, broad: overview, panoptic view, panorama

view, distant: perspective, prospect, vista

view, of a generally accepted: received

view, place offering broad overall: catbird seat, ringside seat, vantage, vantage point

view, place offering extensive: mirador

view, structure situated with commanding: belvedere

viewpoint: angle, attitude, belief, feeling, opinion, outlook, perspective, position, posture, scope, sentiment, slant, stance

vigil: guard, lookout, prayers, service, surveillance, wake, watch

vigilant: agog, alert, attentive, awake, aware, careful, cautious, keen, observant, sharp, shrewd, sleepless, wakeful, wary, watchful

vignette: picture, scenario, scene, sketch, story

vigor: activity, animation, bang, bounce, brio, dash, drive, élan, endurance, energy, enthusiasm, fire, force, getup, growth, health, intensity, invigorate, might, moxie, muscle, oomph, passion, pep, pith, potency, power, punch, spirit, stamina, steam, strength, verve, vim, virility, vitality, zeal, zing, zip

vigor and liveliness: brio, élan, flair, panache

vigorous: athletic, bouncing, brisk, dashing, eager, effective, efficacious,

energetic, hale, hardy, healthy, hearty, intense, lively, lusty, muscular, potent, powerful, robust, rugged, spirited, spry, stout, strapping, strenuous, strong, sturdy, tough, vibrant

vile: abominable, bad, base, coarse, contemptible, corrupt, debased, degrading, depraved, despicable, disgusting, evil, filthy, foul, hateful, horrible, ignoble, impure, loathsome, low, lowly, mean, nasty, nefarious, obnoxious, odious, offensive, repulsive, revolting, servile, shocking, sickening, sinful, sleazy, sordid, ugly, unpleasant, vicious, vulgar, wicked, worthless, wretched

vilify: abuse, asperse, assail, attack, belittle, berate, blacken, blaspheme, criticize, debase, debauch, defame, degrade, denounce, disgrace, dishonor, disparage, libel, malign, mistreat, reproach, revile, slander, slight, slur, smear, traduce

villa: castle, chateau, dwelling, estate, home, house, manor, mansion, residence

village: borough, bourg, burg, community, hamlet, home, municipality, pueblo, settlement, suburb, thorp, town, tribe

village, small: hamlet

villain: blackguard, boor, caitiff, creep, dastard, delinquent, demon, devil, heavy, Iago, knave, lout, lowlife, miscreant, mountebank, offender, rapscallion, rascal, reprobate, rogue, scalawag, scallywag, scamp, scelerat, scoundrel, varlet

villainous: abominable, bad, base, boorish, caddish, corrupt, criminal, dastardly, depraved, despicable, detestable, disagreeable, evil, felonious, horrible, low, mean, rotten, vicious, vile, vulgar, wicked, wretched

villainy: baseness, depravity, knavery, viciousness, vileness, wickedness

vim: dash, drive, élan, energy, enthusiasm, fire, force, kick, oomph, passion, pep, pepper, push, spirit, strength, vigor, vinegar, vitality, zeal, zing

vindicate: absolve, acquit, advocate, assert, avenge, clear, defend, exculpate, excuse, exonerate, free, justify, maintain, protect, prove, revenge, substantiate, support, sustain, uphold

vindication: extenuating circumstances, mitigating circumstances

vindictive: bitter, cruel, malign, nasty, retaliatory, revengeful, spiteful, unforgiving, vengeful

vine: betel, bine, blackberry, briar, creeper, cucumber, cupseed, grapevine, honeysuckle, hop, ivy, jasmine, liana, liane, maypop, plant, rambler, raspberry, soma, watermelon, wisteria

vine, twining part of: tendril

vinegar bottle: cruet

vinegar prefix: aceto-

vinegar, concerning: acetic

vinegar, turn into: acetify

vinegarish: acerbic, acetic, acetous, acid, biting, bitter, pungent, sour, tart, vinegary

vines, open latticework for training: trellis

vintage: aged, ancient, antiquated, antique, choice, classical, crop, dated, grapes, harvest, old, prize, rare, selected, superior, wine

violate: abuse, betray, breach, break, broach, corrupt, debauch, defile, deflower, defoul, desecrate, dishonor, disobey, disregard, disturb, encroach, force, infringe, injure, insult, interrupt, invade, offend, outrage, pollute, profane, rape, ravage, ravish, spoil, transgress, trespass, wrong

violation: assault, breach, crime, delinquency, desecration, encroachment, illegality, infraction, offense, sacrilege, transgression

violation of propriety: sin

violation of something sacred: sacrilege

violence: assault, bloodshed, brutality, clash, ferocity, fervor, fighting, force, frenzy, fury, gore, intensity, onslaught, outrage, rage, rampage, savagery, terrorism, uproar, war

violence, act of extreme: outrage

violence, eruption into: flashpoint

violence, of unnecessary: gratuitous

violent: acute, amok, ardent, berserk, destructive, enraged, explosive, extreme, fierce, fiery, forceful, forcible, frenetic, furious, harsh, heated, heavy, hotheaded, impetuous, inflamed, intense, mighty, passionate, powerful, rabid, raging, rampaging, rough, savage, severe, sharp, stormy, strong, tempestuous, tumultuous, turbulent, vehement, vicious, wild

VINES AND CLIMBERS

abrus	climbing hydrangea	golden vine	monkshood vine	stephanotis
actinidia	common hop	grapevine	moonseed	string bean
akebia	common ivy	green ripple	morning glory	summer squash
Algerian ivy	convolvulus	greenbrier	muscat	Swiss-cheese plant
ampelopsis	coral greenbrier	Hall's honeysuckle	oriental yam	traveler's joy
Arabian jasmine	coral vine	heart-leaf philoden-	passion flower	trumpet creeper
ayahuasca	creeping fig	dron	pea	trumpet flower
balsam apple	cross vine	honeysuckle	peppervine	trumpet honeysuckle
balsam pear	cruel plant	hop	poison ivy	trumpet vine
bittersweet	cucumber	horsebrier	poison oak	vanilla
black pepper	dang shen	ivalace	potato vine	vegetable sponge
bleeding heart vine	dentata	ivy	primrose jasmine	Virginia creeper
Boston ivy	dewberry	jackman clematis	pumpkin	virgin's bower
bottle gourd	dichondra	jade vine	purple passion	wandering Jew
bougainvillea	dusky coral	Japanese creeper	rag gourd	watermelon
bower plant	elephant's foot	Japanese honeysuckle	rambler rose	wax flower
boxthorn	English ivy	Japanese ivy	Rangoon creeper	wild passion flower
bryony	everblooming honey-	Japanese wisteria	red passion flower	wild yam
canary creeper	suckle	jasmine	runner bean	winter jasmine
cantaloupe	flame flower	kangaroo vine	sandpaper vine	winter squash
cape plumbago	fleevine	kudzu	schisandra	wintercreeper
catclaw vine	fox grape	liana	sevenleaf creeper	wire vine
chayote	giant granadilla	love-charm	silver lace vine	wisteria
Chinese wisteria	glory pea	melon	silvervine	woodbine
chocolate vine	gloryvine	Mexican blood flower	smooth loofah	yam ☙
clematis	golden hop	miniature Japanese	squash	
climbing asparagus	golden trumpet	ivy	star jasmine	

RELATED TERMS

violent disorder: havoc, mayhem

violent disruption: cataclysm, convulsion, upheaval

violent downpour: torrent

violent emission: eruct

violent outburst: paroxysm

violent reaction: backlash

violent wind of Southern France: mistral ☙

violet: lavender, mauve, pansy, purple

violet variety: African, Alaska, alpine, Canada, garden, horned, Missouri, mountain, pansy, Parma, pine, Russian, sweet, trailing, water

violin types: Amati, Guarnerius, fiddle, kit, pochette, Stradivarius

RELATED TERMS

violin bow off strings, bouncing: jeté, spiccato

violin-like instrument, larger and with lower sound: viola

violin played by plucking rather than bowing, of: pizzicato

violin player: bower

violin plucking: pizzicato

violin-shaped: pandurate

violin string: chanterelle

violin, harshness of sound sometimes heard on: wolf

violin, tiny narrow: kit ☙

viper: adder, asp, cobra, copperhead, rattlesnake, snake

virago: amazon, beldame, fishwife, harpy, scold, shrew, termagant, vixen, woman

virgin: celibate, chaste, first, fresh, initial, intact, maiden, maidenly, modest, new, pristine, pure, unadulterated, unalloyed, uncultivated, undefiled, undisturbed, unexplored, unsullied, untouched, unused, vestal

virginity, take away one's: deflower

virgule: slash

virile: brave, forceful, macho, male, manly, masculine, potent, powerful, robust, strong

virtual: essential, fundamental, implied, tacit

virtually: almost, basically, essentially, nearly, practically, totally

virtue: advantage, chastity, courage, decency, excellence, fidelity, generosity, goodness, grace, honesty, honor, integrity, merit, morality, piety, power, purity, quality, rectitude, righteousness, uprightness, valor

virtue, in Chinese philosophy: tao

virtuoso: artist, artiste, connoisseur, dilettante, expert, master, musician, savant, soloist, whiz

virtuous: chaste, ethical, exemplary, good, honest, honorable, innocent, just, moral, moralistic, noble, principled, pure, righteous, spotless, unsullied, upright, valiant, virginal, worthy

virulent: antagonistic, bitter, cutting, deadly, harsh, hateful, hostile, infectious, irritating, lethal, malignant, noxious, obnoxious, poisonous, sarcastic, spiteful, toxic, unhealthy, venomous, vindictive

virus: bug, disease, flu, germ, illness, infection, poison, sickness, venom

RELATED TERMS

virus infecting gastrointestinal tract and nervous system: enterovirus

virus infecting respiratory or gastro-intestinal systems: reovirus

virus infecting upper respiratory tract: adenovirus, rhinovirus

virus transmitted by arthropod, like tick or mosquito: arbovirus

virus weaker, make a: attenuate ❦

vis-à-vis: counterpart, date, escort, face to face, facing, opposite, tête-à-tête, versus

visage: appearance, aspect, countenance, expression, face, features, look, mien

viscera: entrails, guts, innards, insides, intestines

visceral: inner, instinctive, interior, intuitive, profound

viscount: nobleman, title

viscous: adhering, adhesive, glutinous, gobby, gooey, gummy, limy, sticking, sticky, stiff, syrupy, tenacious, thick, tough, viscid

viscous mud: slime

viscous substance: gel

vise: chuck, clamp, tool, winch

visible: apparent, blatant, clear, conspicuous, discernible, evident, glaring, in view, macroscopic, manifest, noticeable, obvious, overt, perceivable, perceptible, revealed, seeable, seen, visual

visible to naked eye: macroscopic

vision: apparition, beauty, concept, dream, eyesight, fancy, fantasy, ghost, illusion, image, imagine, intuition, mirage, perception, perspective, phantom, revelation, seeing, sight, spirit, view

vision due to aging, deterioration of: presbyopia

vision from outer edges of retina: peripheral

vision or vague semblance: simulacrum

visionary: ambitious, chimerical, delusory, dreamer, dreamy, fantastic, fey, ideal, idealist, idealistic, imaginary, imaginative, impractical, philosopher, prophet, quixotic, radical, romantic, seer, speculative, stargazer, unreal, utopian

visit: afflict, apply, assail, avenge, bother, call, chat, converse, frequent, haunt, inflict, see, sojourn, stay, stopover, talk, trouble, vacation

visitor: caller, company, guest, sightseer, tourist, vacationer

visitor who takes advantage: freeloader, sponger

visitor, regular: frequenter, habitué

vista: outlook, panorama, perspective, prospect, range, scene, scope, view

visual: chart, observable, ocular, optic, optical, perceptible, picture, seeable, seen, viewable, visible

visual arts applied to two-dimensional surface: graphic arts

visual blight: eyesore

visual defect of unequal curvature of eye surface: astigmatism

visual defect seeing faraway objects: myopia, nearsightedness

visual indication of a submerged problem: tip of the iceberg

visualize: conceive, envision, fancy, foresee, imagine, picture, reflect, see, think, view

vital: alive, animate, animated, basic, breathing, cardinal, critical, crucial, dynamic, energetic, essential, fundamental, imperative, important, indispensable, integral, invigorating, live, lively, living, necessary, needed, pivotal, requisite, significant, urgent, viable, vigorous

vital essence: soul, spirit

vital fluids: sera

vital statistics of a population: demography

vitality: animation, drive, endurance, energy, enthusiasm, liveliness, pep, pip, pizzazz, spirit, spunk, stamina, strength, verve, vigor, vim, zest

vitiate: abolish, adulterate, annul, blemish, cancel, contaminate, corrupt, damage, debase, deprave, hurt, impair, injure, invalidate, neutralize, nullify, pervert, poison, pollute, sabotage, soil, spoil, taint, tarnish, undermine, undo, void, weaken

vitriolic: acerbic, antagonistic, bitter, burning, caustic, sardonic, scathing, sharp

vittles: chow, eats

vituperate: abuse, berate, castigate, criticize, curse, ensure, insult, lambaste, rail, rebuke, reproach, scold, upbraid, vilify

viva voce: aloud, oral

vivacious: active, alive, animated, breezy, bubbly, cheerful, exuberant, gay, happy, lighthearted, lively, merry, pert, playful, spirited, sportive, sprightly, sunny, upbeat, vibrant, zestful

VITAMINS

beta-carotene
biotin
carotene
choline
cryptoxanthin
folic acid (folate)
kipoid acid
niacin
nicotinic acid
pantothenic acid
vitamin A (retinol)
vitamin A2
vitamin B complex
vitamin B1 (thiamine)
vitamin B2 (riboflavin)
vitamin B6 (pyridoxine)
vitamin B12 (cobalamin)
vitamin C (ascorbic acid)
vitamin D
vitamin D2 (ergocalciferol or calciferol)
vitamin D3 (cholecalciferol)
vitamin E (tocopherol)
vitamin G
vitamin H (biotin)
vitamin K (phylloquinone)
vitamin M
vitamin P (bioflavinoid) ❦

vivacity: animation, brilliance, brio, dash, élan, energy, enthusiasm, fire, gusto, life, sparkle, sprightliness, verve, vigor, zeal

vivid: active, alive, animated, bright, brilliant, clear, colorful, dramatic, expressive, florid, glaring, glowing, graphic, intense, lifelike, live, lively, living, lucid, picturesque, powerful, radiant, real, rich, sharp, shining, spirited, striking, strong

vivify: animate, enliven, invigorate, quicken, refresh, revive

vixen: fishwife, fox, hellion, scold, screech, shrew, termagant, virago

vocabulary: cant, dialect, diction, dictionary, glossary, jargon, language, lexicon, lingo, nomenclature, phraseology, slang, speech, terminology, terms, thesaurus, words

vocabulary of technical terms of a field: nomenclature, terminology

vocabulary, concerning: lexical

vocabulary, specialized: argot, cant, jargon, lexicon, lexis

vocal: articulate, blunt, direct, expres-

VOLCANO-RELATED TERMS

area giving off sulfurous gases and steam: solfatara

concerning a volcanic eruption: vulcanian, vulcanic

gas bubble in volcanic rock filled with mineral: amygdule

hole from which smoke and gases escape: fumarole

inactive volcano, of an: dormant, extant

last stage of activity: mofette

lava fragments: cinders, scoria, slag

light, porous volcanic rock: pumice

molten rock flowing from volcano: lava, magma

volcanic black glass: obsidian

volcanic glass thread: peleshair

volcanic mud: salse

volcanic rock: basalt, lava, trass

volcanic rocks formed after cooling: igneous

volcano top: cone

volcano's ejected matter: ejecta ☙

---

sive, fluent, oral, outspoken, resounding, sonant, spoken, uttered, verbal, voiced

vocal quality: rasp, timbre, tone

vocalist: caroler, entertainer, musician, performer, singer, songster

vocalize: articulate, communicate, convey, express, intone, phonate, pronounce, shout, sing, speak, talk, verbalize, voice

vocation: art, business, call, calling, career, craft, employment, field, job, line, occupation, profession, pursuit, racket, trade, work

vociferate: bawl, bellow, call, clamor, cry, holler, howl, protest, shout, shriek, utter, yell

vociferous: blatant, boisterous, clamourous, insistent, loud, loudmouthed, noisy, strident, talkative

vogue: chic, craze, custom, fad, fashion, mode, modish, popular, popularity, rage, style, ton, trend

voice: air, alto, announce, articulate, assert, baritone, bass, choice, communicate, declare, divulge, express, expression, language, mouth, opinion, phrase, proclaim, pronounce, say, soprano, sound, speak, speech,

state, talk, tenor, tone, tongue, utter, utterance, verbalize, vocalize, vote, wish

RELATED TERMS

voice alternating between falsetto and normal: yodel

voice becoming husky, grating, or temporarily lost: hoarse

voice box: larynx

voice that varies pleasantly: lilt

voice training system: solfeggio, solmization, tonic sol-fa

voice, full in: orotund

voice, nasal: twang

voice, produce with the: vocalize

voice, range of a: diapason, register

voiceless: aphonic, dumb, inarticulate, inaudible, mum, mute, silent, speechless, spirate, surd

voice's pitch, rise and fall of: cadence, inflection, intonation, modulation ☙

---

voice a view: opine

voice production for puppet: ventriloquism

void: abyss, annul, avion, bare, blank, cancel, cavity, countermand, deplete, discharge, dissolve, drain, egest, emptiness, empty, evacuate, free, gap, hole, hollow, ineffective, ineffectual, invalid, lacking, leave, meaningless, negated, nul, null, nullify, opening, remove, rescind, rull, space, unoccupied, useless, vacant, vacate, vacuity, vacuum, veto, want, wanting

volatile: airy, buoyant, capricious, changeable, elastic, ephemeral, erratic, eruptive, excitable, explosive, fickle, fleeting, flighty, flippant, flying, fugacious, gaseous, inconstant, lighthearted, lively, moody, rash, temperamental, transient, transitory, unstable, vaporous, variable, volage, volant, volatic

volition: choice, choosing, desire, discretion, election, option, preference, will, wish

volley: barrage, burst, discharge, drumfire, round, salvo, shot, shower, storm

volleying, in tennis: net play

voluble: fluent, glib, loquacious, revolving, rotating, talkative, twining, twisting, vocal, wordy

volume: aggregate, amplification, body, book, bulk, capacity, content, cubature, dimensions, document, edition,

heap, mass, publication, quantity, scroll, size, strength, tome; loudness, magnitude, sound, tone

voluminous: abundant, ample, bulky, cavernous, extensive, full, large, massive, numerous, several, spacious, swelling, vast

voluntary: chosen, deliberate, elected, elective, free, freely, intentional, optional, spontaneous, unasked, unbidden, unforced, unpaid, volunteer, willful, willing, willingly

voluntary action: conation

volunteer: enlist, offer, proffer, suggest, tender, unpaid, voluntary

voluptuous: buxom, curvy, erotic, luscious, lush, sensual, sensuous, shapely, wanton

vomit: barf, disgorge, expel, heave, puke, regurgitate, retch, spew, throw up, upchuck

vomit, feeling of about to: nausea

vomiting, causing: emetic

VOWEL TYPES AND TERMS

curved mark over vowel for "short" sound: breve

double vowel: digram, digraph

horizontal line or dash over vowel for "long" sound: macron

neutral vowel: schwa

single vowel sound: monophthong

vowel change accompanying change in grammatical function: ablaut, gradation

vowel change in quality in a syllable: diphthong

vowel contraction: crasis, diphthong

vowel diacritics: breve, circumflex, dieresis, tilde, umlaut

vowel loss from the beginning of a word: aphesis

vowel marking to show separate pronunciation: dieresis, umlaut

vowel sound omission in syllable or verse: elision

vowel sound repeated in stressed syllables: assonance

vowel sounds: ablaut, dental, labial, lene, palatal

vowels drawn out: drawl

vowels that sound similar or repeat: assonance

vowels written and run together: digraph, ligature ☙

---

vomiting, eating disorder, self-induced: anorexia nervosa, bulimia, bulimia nervosa, bulimorexia

voodoo sticking of pins: invultuation

voracious: consuming, edacious, esurient, glutonous, gluttonous, gorging, greedy, hungry, insatiable, rapacious, ravening, ravenous, unquenchable

vortex: cyclone, eddy, gyre, spiral, tornado, tourbillion, twister, waterspout, whirl, whirlpool, whirlwind

votary: addict, adherent, admirer, aficionado, amateur, believer, buff, devotee, disciple, enthusiast, fanatic, follower, habitue, worshipper, zealot

vote: ballot, choice, choose, confer, decide, declare, determine, elect, election, franchise, majority, plebiscite, poll, referendum, say, suffrage, ticket, voice, wish

RELATED TERMS

vote against a possible member: blackball, ostracize

vote by electorate on proposal: plebiscite, referendum

vote for another, person authorized to: proxy

vote for someone not on ballot: write-in

vote in which winner does not secure more than half the total: plurality

vote of officer to break a tie: casting vote

vote, give the right to: enfranchise

vote, oral: acclamation

vote, representation according to popular: proportional representation

vote, right to: franchise, suffrage

vote, seek someone's: canvass, solicit

vote, something put to a: motion, resolution

voter: balloter, citizen, elector, resident, taxpayer

votes in legislative assembly, person counting: teller

voting and elections, study of: psephology

voting district: precinct, ward ❦

vouch: affirm, assert, assure, attest, authenticate, aver, back, certify, cite, confirm, declare, endorse, establish, guarantee, maintain, prove, sponsor, substantiate, support, verify, warrant, witness

voucher: affidavit, bill, certificate, chit, credential, docket, note, proof, receipt, statement, ticket

vouchsafe: award, bestow, concede, condescend, deign, favor, give, grant, permit, yield

vow: assure, covenant, declare, dedicate, oath, pledge, plight, prayer, promise, swear, wish, word

vow or promise-bound: votary

vow, concerning a: votive

voyage: crossing, cruise, excursion, expedition, jaunt, journey, passage, pilgrimage, tour, travel, trek, trip, undertaking

voyage, wandering: peregrination

vulgar: barbaric, base, boorish, coarse, common, crass, crude, dirty, everyday, filthy, general, gross, indecent, inelegant, lewd, obscene, offensive, ordinary, ostentatious, plebeian, popular, pornographic, profane, revolting, rude, smutty, tasteless, uncouth, unrefined, vernacular, vile

vulgar and showy: flashy, garish, gaudy

vulgar and unrefined: philistine, uncouth

vulgar language: profanity

vulgar people: hoi polloi, lowest common denominator, riffraff, the great, unwashed, yahoo

vulgarity: coarseness, commonness, crassness, crudeness, discourtesy, impudence, indecency, obscenity, profanity, rudeness

vulnerable: accessible, assailable, defenseless, exposed, insecure, liable, open, susceptible, unguarded, unprotected, unsafe, weak

vulpine: clever, crafty, cunning, foxy, ingenious, shrewdness, skillful, sly, tricky, wily

Ww

wacky: batty, cracked, crazy, demented, deranged, dotty, eccentric, foolish, insane, irrational, loony, nuts, screwy, silly, zany

wad: bankroll, bat, boodle, bundle, clump, compress, cram, fortune, heap, insert, lump, mass, mint, pad, pile, plug, roll, stopper, stuff, tuft, wealth

wad of tobacco: quid

waddle: hobble, shuffle, sway, totter, walk, wiggle, wobble

wade: drudge, ford, plod, proceed, struggle, toil, trudge, walk

wade through mud or water: slosh

wading bird: bittern, crane, egret, heron, ibis, rail, scopus, snipe, spoonbill, stilt

wafer: biscuit, cake, candy, cookie, cracker, disk

waft: blow, breeze, carry, convey, drift, flag, float, flutter, gust, odor, puff, signal, skim, smell, wave, whiff

wag: card, clown, comedian, comic, humorist, jester, joker, jokester, move, oscillate, prankster, shake, stir, sway, swing, waddle, wiggle, wigwag, wisecracker, wit, zany

wage: allowance, attempt, compensation, conduct, earnings, emolument, engage, fee, fight, hire, honorarium, income, pay, payment, pursue, recompense, reward, salary, stipend, undertake

wage earner: employee, laborer, worker

wager: ante, bet, challenge, chance, hunch, play, pot, speculate, stake

wages: income, pay, salaries, salary, stipends

wages after payroll deductions: take-home pay

waggish: comical, droll, frolicsome, funny, jesting, jocular, merry, mischievous, playful, roguish, witty

waggle: brandish, sway, waddle, wave, wiggle, wobble

wagon: barouche, buckboard, buggy, caisson, camion, car, carriage, cart, chariot, chuckwagon, coach, Conestoga, dray, fourgon, gilly, lorry, schooner, tram, tumbril, van, vehicle, wain

RELATED TERMS

wagon builder: wainwright
wagon camp circle: corral, laager
wagon hoops, covered: bail
wagon train: caravan
wagon without sides: lorry ❦

waif: foundling, homeless, orphan, ragamuffin, stray, vagrant, wanderer

wail: bawl, bemoan, blubber, complain, cry, fuss, howl, keen, lament, moan, plaint, pule, sob, ululate, undulate, weep, whimper, whine, yell, yowl

waist: abdomen, blouse, bodice, corsage, middle, midriff, midsection, shirt, undershirt

waistband: belt, cincture, cummerbund, girdle, sash

waistcoat: benjy, gilet, jacket, jerkin, vest, weskit

wait: ambush, anticipate, attend, bide, cater, court, dally, delay, expect, halt, hesitate, interim, linger, loiter, pause, postpone, remain, rest, serve, stay, stop, tarry, tend

wait around: lag, loiter, tarry

wait for and accost: waylay

waiter: attendant, footman, garçon, servant, server, slaver, steward, tray, waitress

waiter at drive-in: carhop

waiters, group of: indifference

waiting and deferring action as strategy: waiting game

waiting for decision: limbo

waiting room: foyer, lobby, vestibule

waiting room for performers: green room

waive: abandon, allow, cease, concede, defer, disclaim, dismiss, disregard, excuse, forbear, forgo, forsake, grant, leave, neglect, postpone, reject, relinquish, reserve, shelve, surrender, yield

wake: aftermath, passage, path, track, trail, wave; arise, arouse, awaken, excite, freshen, prod, revive, rouse, service, shake, stimulate, stir, understand, vigil, watch

wakeful: alert, attentive, careful, observant, restless, sleepless, vigilant, watchful

waking bugle: reveille

waking, partially conscious state just before: hypnopompic

waking, to become gradually enlivened after: grouk

wale: grain, mark, rib, ridge, streak, strip, texture, weal, weave, welt, wheat

walk: aisle, allée, amble, ambulate, bobble, career, circuit, crossing, exercise, flounce, foot, footpath, gait, gangway, hike, jaunt, limp, lumber, march, mince, pace, parade, path, pathway, patrol, perambulate, plod, prance, profession, promenade, ramble, ramp, roam, saunter, shuffle, slink, step, stretch, stride, stroll, strump, strut, swagger, toddle, totter, trade, trail, traipse, tramp, travel, traverse, tread, trudge, turn, vocation, wade, wander

walk about: traipse, tramp
walk around: circumambulate, skirt
walk casually: amble, mosey, perambulate, promenade, ramble, roam, rove, sashay, saunter, sidle, stroll, traipse
walk daintily: mince
walk fast: festinate, pace, stride
walk for health: constitutional
walk heavily: clump, plod, trudge
walk like a babe: toddle
walk only on toes: digitigrade
walk proudly like a peacock: flounce, strut, swagger
walk sideways like a crab: sidle
walk slowly: dawdle, lag, loiter
walk the floor: pace
walk unsteadily: weave
walk with heels and toes: plantigrade
walk with toes turned in: pigeon-toed
walk, able to: ambulant, ambulatory ❦

walk a beat: patrol
walk-on: cameo
walk out: leave, protest, quit, strike
walkaway: breeze, defeat, easy, rout, victory
walker: hiker, pedestrian, stroller, wayfarer
walking: afoot, ambulate, ambulatory, digitigrade, hiking, marching, on foot, plantigrade, promenading, roaming, strolling, strutting, wandering
walking area: ambulatory, esplanade, promenade
walking gauge: pedometer
walking stick: cane, crutch, pikestaff, staff, stilt, waddy
walking, style of: carriage, deportment, gait
walkway for pirates' prey: plank
walkway with open colonnade facing a quadrangle: cloister
walkway, narrow and elevated: catwalk
wall: anger, barricade, barrier, blockade, cliff, curtain, dam, defense, difficulty, dike, distress, divider, enceinte, enclose, enclosure, encompass, fence, fortification, hindrance, immure, levee, parapet, paries, partition, rampart, ridiculous, unconventional

wall base: dado
wall bottom finished in different material from upper part: wainscot
wall bracket for candle backed by mirror: girandole
wall bracket for candle or light: sconce
wall crack filler: Spackle
wall drawing or inscription: graffiti
wall finish, interior-: grout, stucco
wall for reinforcement, something against: buttress, pier
wall hanging: arras, tapestry
wall molding close to floor: baseboard
wall of body part, organ, cavity: paries
wall of circular building: tambour
wall or embankment, protective: revetment
wall or partition in boat, plane: bulkhead
wall painting: mural
wall plaster to coat or waterproof: parget
wall to break force of waves: breakwater
wall trim along floor: baseboard
wall trim along top: cornice
wall, concerning a: mural
wall, exterior angle of: coign, quoin
wall, niche in: alcove, columbarium, recess
wall, ornamental ridge on top of: cresting
wall, protective spikes or glass on top of: chevaux-de-frise
wall, top layer of: coping
wall, trim on: molding ❦

wall types: brick wall, cavity wall, dry-stone wall, stone wall
wallaby: animal, kangaroo, marsupial
wallboard support: stud
wallet: billfold, pocketbook, purse
wallop: bash, beat, belt, blow, clobber, collision, crash, defeat, hit, lick, paste, plaster, pound, pummel, shellac, slam, slug, smack, smash, strike, tan, thrash, trounce, whip, whop
wallow: bask, billow, delgith, flounder, glory, grovel, indulge, loll, luxuriate, revel, roll, stumble, toss
walls, coarse plaster on outside: pebble dash, rock dash, roughcast, spatter dash
walrus: pinniped

walrus, pertaining to: odobenid
waltz: dance, march, music, whirl
wampum: bead, beads, peag, peage
wan: anemic, ashen, ashy, blanched, bloodless, colorless, dim, dismal, fade, faint, feeble, gloomy, haggard, languid, melancholy, pale, paleness, pallid, sad, sickly, sorrowful, weak, worn
wand: baton, caduceus, mace, pole, rod, scepter, sprig, staff, stick, switch, twig
wand-shaped: virgate
wander: amble, deviate, digress, divagate, drift, gad, gad about, gallivant, maunder, meander, ramble, range, roam, roil, rove, saunter, shift, straggle, stray, stroll, traipse, traverse
wanderer: beachcomber, bum, drifter, gadder, itinerant, nomad, pilgrim, rambler, roamer, rover, traveler, vagabond, vagrant
wanderer, homeless: nomad, tramp, vagabond
wandering: deviation, digressiver, drifting, errant, erratic, itinerant, journey, meandering, migrant, nomadic, odyssey, planetary, rambling, roaming, roving, straying, traveling, vagabond
wandering and homeless: vagrant
wandering from main topic: deviation, digression, discursive, excursion, excursus
wandering in search of work: itinerant, migrant
wandering musician: jongleur, minstrel, troubadour
wane: abate, absent, decay, decline, decrease, die, diminish, dwindle, ebb, fade, fail, lag, lessen, peter, recede, shrink, sink, subside, weaken, wilt, wither
wangle: contrive, engineer, extricate, fake, falsify, finagle, juggle, maneuver, manipulate, obtain, wiggle, worm, wriggle
waning: abating, decrescent
want: absence, aspire, choose, covet, crave, dearth, deficiency, deficient, demand, deprivation, desire, destitution, hunger, inadequacy, lack, longing, miss, must, necessity, need, penury, poverty, prefer, privation, require, requirement, scarcity, seek, shortage, thirst, wish, yearning
wanting: absent, deficient, destitute,

WARS

Algerian War	Franco-Prussian War	Independence	(or Winter War)	War of Greek Inde-
American Civil War	French and Indian	Napoleonic Wars	Russo-Japanese War	pendence
(or War Between	War	Norman Conquest	Rwanda Civil War	War of Independence
the States)	French Revolution	Operation Desert	Samnite Wars	(or Revolutionary
American Revolu-	Gallic Wars	Storm (or Persian	Second Kashmir War	War or American
tion (or War of In-	Greco-Persian Wars	Gulf War)	Seven Weeks' War	Revolution)
dependence or Rev-	Grenada Invasion	Opium Wars	Seven Years' War	War of the Austrian
olutionary War)	Hundred Years' War	Peloponnesian Wars	Sino-Japanese Wars	Succession
Anglo-Dutch Wars	Indian Wars	Persian Gulf War (or	Six-Day War	War of the Devolu-
Anglo-French Wars	Iran-Iraq War	Operation Desert	Somali Civil War	tion
Arab-Israeli War	Korean War	Storm)	Southeast Asian War	War of the Polish
Balkan Wars	Kosovo War	Philippine-	Spanish-American	Succession
Boer Wars	Macedonian-Persian	American War	War	War of the Spanish
Boxer Rebellion	War	Polish Revolution	Spanish Civil War	Succession
Chinese Civil War	Manchurian War	Punic Wars	Suez War	Wars of the Roses
Colonial Indian Wars	Mexican-American	Revolutionary War	Taiping Rebellion	Winter War (or
Crimean War	War	(or American Rev-	Thirty Years' War	Russo-Finnish
Crusades	Mexican Civil War	olution or War of	Vietnam War	War)
Egypt-Libya War	Mexican War	Independence)	War Between the	World War I
English Civil War	Mozambican Civil	Roman Civil War	States (or Ameri-	World War II
Falklands War	War	Russian Revolution	can Civil War)	Yom Kippur War ❦
First Kashmir War	Mozambican War of	Russo-Finnish War	War of 1812	

inadequate, insufficient, lacking, less, minus, needing, needy, scanty, scarce, short, unfulfilled, without

wanton: arrogant, capricious, careless, cruel, disregardful, extravagant, fast, frisky, frolic, frolicsome, fulsome, gratuitous, immoral, lavish, lecherous, lewd, licentious, loose, lustful, luxuriant, malevolent, malicious, merciless, merry, overabundant, playful, prodigal, promiscuous, revel, sensual, spiteful, spoiled, sportive, trifle, unchaste, undisciplined, unjust, unprincipled, unrestrained, unruly, voluptuous, wayward

wanton woman: concubine, harlot, hussy, jade, prostitute, slut, strumpet

war: battle, blitzkrieg, clash, combat, conflict, contend, crusade, feud, fight, jihad, martial, strife, struggle

RELATED TERMS

war cry: Geronimo, motto, phrase, rally, slogan, watchword

war damages, payments for: reparations

war god: Ares, Ashur, Huitzilopochtli, Mars, Odin, Thor

war goddess: Bellona, Enyo, Inanna, Ishtar

war, concerning: martial

war, event prompting: casus belli

war, of period after: postbellum

war, of period before: antebellum

war, person against: dove

war, person favoring: hawk

war, person forced from homeland during: displaced person

war, prepare for: mobilize

war, rigid economy during: austerity

war, threatening: gunboat diplomacy, saber rattling ❦

warble: carol, chant, chirp, melody, quaver, sing, trill, yodel

ward: block, corridor, defense, department, district, garrison, guard, precinct, protection, zone

ward off: avert, block, fend, hold, parry, party, prevent, rebuff, repel, stave off

ward off bad luck: knock on wood

warden: constable, custodian, forest-ranger, guard, guardian, jailer, jailor, keeper, official, overseer, ranger, sentry, supervisor, watchdog, watchman

wardrobe: apparel, armoire, bureau, cabinet, chest, closet, clothes, clothespress, costumes, dresser, garderobe, threads, trunk

wardrobe of baby: layette

wardrobe of bride: trousseau

wardrobe or large cupboard: armoire

wardrobe with drawers on one side: chifforobe

warehouse: accommodate, depository, depot, entrepôt, étape, repository, shelter, stockpile, stockroom, storage, store, storehouse

wares: articles, commodities, goods, line, merchandise, stock, supplies

warfare: clash, conflict, fighting, hostilities, strife, struggle

warfare with lack of aggression: phony war, sitzkrieg

warfare, nonnuclear: conventional

wariness: caution, suspicion, watchfulness

warlike: aggressive, antagonistic, bellicose, belligerent, combative, fighting, hawkish, hostile, martial, militant, military, pugnacious, soldierly

warlock: archimage, conjuror, magician, necromancer, sorcerer, witch, wizard

warm: affable, affectionate, amorous, animated, ardent, close, compassionate, cordial, eager, earnest, enliven, enthusiastic, excitable, fresh, friendly, generous, genial, gracious, heartfelt, hearty, keen, kind, kindhearted, kindly, lively, loving, passionate, pleasant, sincere, smug, sunny, sympathetic, tender; balmy, clement, fiery, flushed, glowing, heat, heated, hot, humid, lukewarm

warm an oven: preheat

warm-blooded: homeothermic, homoiothermic

warm-up: prelude, thaw

warm, dry mountain wind: föhn

warmed up food, of: réchauffé

warmed, in prescriptions: calef

warmhearted: compassionate, kind, loving, sympathetic, tender

warming dish: chafing dish

warmth: affection, ardor, calescence, compassion, enthusiasm, glow, heat, hospitality, kindness, passion, spirit, temperature, zeal

warn: admonish, advise, alarm, alert, apprise, caution, clue, counsel, inform, notify, predict, presage, signal, tell, threaten, tip, tip off

warning: admonition, alarm, beware, caution, caveat, hint, lesson, monition, omen, portent, premonition, sign, signal

warning before event: augury, auspice, omen, portent, premonition, presage, prodigy, tocsin

warning coloration: aposematic coloration

warning of an earthquake: tremor

warning sign, serving as: sematic

warning tale: cautionary tale

warning, without: unawares

warp: beat, bend, bias, buckle, contort, damage, debase, deflect, deform, distort, fasten, intertwine, kink, line, misinterpret, misrepresent, quirk, rope, sway, turn, twist, wrench, wrinkle

warrant: assert, assurance, authority, authorization, authorize, certificate, claim, commission, defend, document, ensure, foundation, grounds, guarantee, guaranty, guard, insure, justification, justify, obligation, order, permission, permit, pledge, promise, proof, protect, protection, reason, right, safeguard, sanction, secure, subpoena, uphold, voucher, writ

warranty: assurance, contract, guarantee, guaranty, pledge, promise, sanction, security

warrior: combatant, fighter, GI, hero, knight, serviceperson, soldier, trooper, veteran

warship: battleship, corvette, cruiser, cutter, destroyer, dreadnaught, dreadnought, frigate, gunboat, submarine

warship fleet: armada, flotilla, squadron

warship's prison: brig

wart: keratosis, papilloma, verruca

wart on sole of foot: plantar wart

wary: alert, cagey, canny, careful, cautious, chary, circumspect, discreet, distrustful, guarded, leery, mindful, provident, prudent, suspicious, vigilant, watchful

wash: ablution, bath, bathe, clean, cleanse, coat, cover, drench, drift, elute, float, flow, lap, launder, laundry, lave, lotion, lustrate, purify, rinse, roll, scour, scrub, shampoo, shower, slosh, soap, sponge, swirl, wet

wash cycle: rinse, spin

washed-out: colorless, depleted, drained, effete, exhausted, faded, pale, spent, tired

washed-up: done, finished, ruined, shot, through

washing: ablution, bathing, cleaning, laundry, laving, rinsing, showering, soaking

washing basin, low: bidet

washing machine central tube: agitator

washing of organ: lavage

washing substance: detergent

washing the body: ablution

washout: disaster, downpour, erosion, failure, fiasco, flop, gully

wasp: bee, hornet, insect, vespine

wasp nest or colony: vespiary

wasp variety: common, cuckoo, digger, hornet, hunting, paper, sand, solitary, spider, wood, yellow jacket

wasp, like a: vespine

waspish: cantankerous, crabby, crotchety, fretful, huffy, irascible, irritable, ornery, peevish, petulant, snappish, spiteful, testy

wassail: binge, carousal, carouse, celebration, drink, feast, festival, festivity, frolic, merriment, revel, revelry, salutation, toast

waste: atrophy, badland, barren, blow, bush, chaff, consume, consumption, debris, decay, demolish, desert, desolate, destroy, destruction, devastate, devastation, devour, dissipate, dregs, dwindle, emaciate, enfeeble, excrement, exhaust, extravagance, fail, fritter, garbage, idle, junk, kill, litter, lose, misspend, murder, needless, offal, prodigality, ravage, refuse, rubbish, ruin, sack, sewage, sludge, soot, squander, trash, tundra, uncultivated, weaken, wither

waste away: atrophy, corrode, decay, decline, fail, wilt

waste conduit: sewer

waste liquid: effluent

waste matter of body: dejecta, egesta, excrement, excreta, feces, ordure

waste matter of butchered animal: offal

waste of furnace: cinder, scoria, sinter, slag

waste piece of cloth: rag

waste time: dally, dawdle, dilly-dally, fool around, fritter away, futz, loaf, loiter, lollygag, piddle, tarry

wasted: decayed, dissipated, emaciated, exhausted, haggard, needless, shriveled, spent, squandered, superfluous, withered; drunk, stoned

wasteful: careless, costly, extravagant, immoderate, improvident, lavish, prodigal, profligate, spendthrift, thriftless

wastefully, spend: dissipate

wasteland: badlands, desert, marsh, moor, swamp, wilderness, wilds

wasting away: atrophy, pining, tabescence

wasting away, disease involving: atrophy, consumption, emaciation, maceration, phthisis, tabes

wasting time: procrastination

wastrel: idler, loafer, profligate, rake, spendthrift, squanderer, vagabond, vagrant, waster

watch: defend, duty, eye, focus, follow, guard, look, lookout, mark, mind, monitor, notice, observe, oversee, patrol, police, protect, scan, scrutinize, see, sentinel, sentry, spy, stare, supervision, surveillance, view, vigil, wait; chronometer, timepiece, timer

watch during the night: vigil

watch face: dial

watch for timing: chronograph

watch part: jewel, second hand, stem

watch that strikes the hour: repeater

watch that winds: stem-winder

watch with hands: analog

watch with symbol display: digital, LCD, liquid crystal display

watch, chain for attaching pocket: fob

watch, very precise: chronometer

watch's glass covering: crystal

watch's spring: hairspring

watches to show identical time, set: synchronize

watchful: alert, attentive, aware, careful, cautious, chary, circumspect, guarded, heedful, keen, on the qui vive, open-eyed, ready, vigilant, wary, wide-awake

watchful authority: Big Brother

watchmaking: horology

watchtower: barbican, beacon, landmark, lighthouse, lookout, mirador, observatory

watchword: countersign, cry, motto, password, sign, signal, slogan

water: agua, aqua, beverage, brook, deluge, dilute, douse, drench, drink, flood, fluid, hose, irrigate, lagoon, lake, liquid, moisten, moisture, oasis, ocean, pond, pool, puddle, rain, reservoir, river, saturate, sea, soak, splash, spray, spring, sprinkle, stream, tears, thin, well, wet

RELATED TERMS

water as therapeutic treatment: hydropathy

water buffalo: anoa, arnee, arni

water channel for reservoir overflow: spillway

water channel with regulatory gate: sluice

water currents of Pacific affecting weather conditions: El Niño, La Niña

water divination: hydromancy

water drainage hole, pit, or pool: cesspool, sump

water droplets forming in reaction: condensation

water hitting beach with tide: swash

water layer separating temperatures: thermocline

water left by boat, waves in: wake

water moving in lake, bay, gulf from atmospheric or seismic changes: seiche

water nymph: naiad, Undine

water of earth, study of: hydrology

water of soil not available for plants: echard

water pipe coming from main: fireplug, hydrant

water pipe, channel, canal: aqueduct, conduit, culvert, flume, main, sluice

water pitcher: ewer

water pressure, run by: hydraulic

water pump: standpipe

water receptacle, esp. for rain: cistern

water search with divining rod: dowse

water supply, adding fluorine to: fluoridation

water swelling: edema

water to dilute, add: adulterate

water to farmland, artificially supply: irrigate

water underground layer: aquifer, groundwater

water vapor, air filled with: humid

water visible between bends in river, stretches of: reach

water wheel: noria

water, backward flow of: backwash

water, concerning: aquatic

water, cover completely in: immerse, submerge

water, cover with: flood, inundate

water, cultivation of plants in: aquiculture, hydroponics

water, curved upper surface of: meniscus

water, deprived of: dehydrated, desiccated

water, fizzy: club soda, mineral water, seltzer water

water, ground washed or flooded by: flood plain, wash

water, growing or thriving in: aquatic, hydrophilous, hydrophytic

water, level below which ground is saturated by: water table

water, living on land and: amphibious

water, measure depth of: fathom, plumb, sound

water, of clean: potable

water, of salty: brackish, briny

water, of violent: turbulent

water, remove salt from: desalinate

water, shallow place in body of: shoal

water, swift current of: race ❧

water-and-land vehicle: amphibian

watercolors, painting in transparent: aquarelle

watercourse: aqueduct, brook, canal, channel, chute, conduit, creek, culvert, drain, estuary, flume, gullet, gully, gutter, inlet, ravine, river, sloot, sluice, spillway, stream, trench, wadi

watered-down: adulterated, diluted, diminished, mixed, thin, weak, weakened

waterfall: cascade, cataract, chute, falls, Niagara, rapids, sault

waterless: anhydrous, arid, dehydrated, dry, sere, thirsty

WATER SPORTS

boating
body surfing
canoe polo
canoe sailing
canoe slalom racing
canoeing
distance swimming
diving
dragon boat racing
fishing
jet skiing
kayaking
laser sailing
motorboat racing
offshore yacht racing
powerboat racing
rafting
rowing
sailboarding
sailing
sailplaning
scuba diving
sculling
skin diving
snorkeling
surfing/surfboarding
swimming
synchronized swimming
underwater diving
water polo
water ski jump
water skiing
whitewater canoeing
whitewater rafting
windsurfing
yacht racing ❧

waterlog: drench, saturate, soak, sodden

waterproof: airtight, impermeable, impervious, sealed

waterproof sheet: tarpaulin

waters under jurisdiction of nation, state: territorial waters

watertight chamber for underwater construction: cofferdam

waterway, deepen a: dredge

watery: adulterated, aqueous, colorless, damp, diluted, fluid, insipid, liquid, moist, pale, runny, serous, soaked, sodden, soggy, teary, thin, weak, wet

wattle: fence, framework, intertwine, interweave, rod, roof, shrub, stick, swig, tree, twist, wall

wave: beckon, billow, bore, brandish, breaker, coil, comber, crest, curl, curve, eager, flap, flood, flourish, fluctuate, flutter, gesture, greet, gush, influx, motion, movement, outbreak, rash, ridge, ripple, roll, roller, sea, shake, signal, surf, surge, sway, swell, swing, tide, tsunami, tube, undulate, uprising, vibrate, vibration, waft, wag, water, whitecap, winding

wave a weapon: brandish

wave from earthquake or volcano on seabed: tsunami

wave that crests or breaks into foam: breaker, comber, roller

wave to move in a direction, to cause a: propagate, transmit

wave-tossed: asea, awash

wave, backward pull of: undertow

wave, long with no crest: swell

wave, to move like a: heave, surge, swell

wave, upper convex hump of: scend

wavelengths between visible light and microwave: infrared

wavelengths between visible light and X rays: ultraviolet

wavelike: undulant

waver: change, falter, flicker, fluctuate, flutter, hedge, hesitate, hover, oscillate, pause, quaver, reel, seesaw, shift, stagger, sway, swing, teeter, totter, tremble, unsteady, unsure, vacillate, vary, vibrate, wiggle

wavering: fickle, fluctuating, hesitating, irresolute, irresolution, undecided, unsteady, unsure, vacillating, variable, waffling

waving or gesticulating while talking: hypermimia

wavy: bumpy, coiled, curly, curved, rolling, sinuate, sinuous, snaky, squiggly, undulant, undulate, unstable, vermiculate, winding

wavy, in heraldry: undé

wax: cere, cerumen, coating, grease, oil, paraffin, polish

wax-coated cheese: Edam

wax eloquent: emote, orate

wax model casting technique: cire perdue, lost-wax process

wax, ear: cerumen

waxing: increscent

waxy: ceraceous, impressionable, lustrous, pale, pliable, slick, slippery, smooth, yielding

waxy sealant: paraffin

way: access, advance, alley, approach, artery, avenue, boulevard, career, course, custom, detour, direction, distance, door, fashion, going, habit, idiosyncrasy, journey, lane, manner, means, method, mode, nature, opening, order, pass, passage, path, plan, policy, practice, procedure, progress, road, room, route, scheme, street, style, system, technique, tendency, track, trail, via, wont

way of life: modus vivendi

way of operating or functioning: modus operandi

way, go one's: wend

way, in the: de trop, superfluous, unwanted

wayfarer: nomad, pilgrim, sojourner, traveler, viator, voyager

wayfaring worker: itinerant

waylay: ambuscade, ambush, assail, attack, beset, bushwhack, intercept, slink, surprise, trap

wayward: arbitrary, balky, capricious, contrary, disobedient, errant, erratic, fickle, fluctuating, headstrong, inconstant, intractable, irregular, ornery, refractory, stubborn, undependable, unmanageable, unpredictable, unruly, unsteady, willful

weak: anemic, anile, brittle, cowardly, debilitated, decrepit, defenseless, diluted, dissolute, distant, effeminate, effete, enervated, enfeebled, exposed, faint, feeble, flimsy, fragile, frail, helpless, impotent, inadequate, ineffective, infirm, lame, languid, pliable, powerless, puny, rickety, shaky, soft, spineless, tender, tenuous, thin, unaccented, unconvincing, unprotected, unsafe, unsound, unstressed, vulnerable, watery, whispered, wimpy, worn, young

RELATED TERMS

weak and depleted: decadent, degenerate, drained, effete

weak and limp: languid, lethargic

weak and powerless: impotent, ineffectual

weak and trifling: namby pamby

weak and unconvincing: flimsy, tenuous, untenable

weak area: Achilles' heel, underbelly

weak by stunting growth, make: etiolate

weak chronically ill person: valetudinarian

weak from illness or age: decrepit, infirm

weak ineffectual person: milksop, milquetoast, ninny, pushover, sissy, wimp

weak, watered-down: anemic, anodyne, insipid ☙

weak-willed: feckless, irresolute, lily-livered, spineless, supine, wishy-washy

weaken: attenuate, cripple, crumble, damage, debilitate, decline, defeat, depress, deteriorate, devitalize, dilute, diminish, disable, enervate, enfeeble, exhaust, extenuate, fade, flag, impair, languish, lessen, paralyze, reduce, sag, sap, soften, stultify, thin, tire, undermine, unnerve, wilt

weaken by wearing away: corrupt, subvert, undermine

weaken or deprive of strength: debilitate, deplete, devitalize, emasculate, enervate, enfeeble

weaken or disable: incapacitate

weaken or thin: attenuate, dilute

weaken or waste away: atrophy

weaken slowly: undermine

weakling: baby, coward, crybaby, milksop, milquetoast, mollycoddle, ninny, pantywaist, pushover, sissy, wimp

weakness: ailment, appetite, debility, defect, deficiency, desirous, flaw, foible, fondness, frailty, imperfection, inclination, languor, proneness, shortcoming, vulnerability

weakness, chronic: asthenia, cachexia, debility, infirmity, tabes

weakness, minor: foible

weakness, mortal: Achilles' heel, fatal flaw

wealth: abundance, accumulation, affluence, assets, bonanza, capital, fortune, funds, gold, goods, holdings, lucre, mammon, means, money, opulence, pelf, possessions, power, property, prosperity, resources, riches, treasure, weal, worth

wealth, symbolically: gold

wealthy: affluent, loaded, moneyed, prosperous, rich, upscale

wealthy industrialist: tycoon

wealthy people: jet set

wealthy, newly: nouveau riche

weapon: arm, armament, arrow, artillery, bayonet, bazooka, bomb, bomber, boomerang, carbine, catapult, claw, club, crossbow, dagger, dart, derringer, dirk, épée, firearm, gun, knife, lance, machete, missile, mortar, munitions, musket, pistol, revolver, rifle, saber, shotgun, sling, spear, sword, talon, tank, tomahawk, trident, whip

RELATED TERMS

weapon causing fire: incendiary
weapon, nonnuclear: conventional
weapon, remove a person's: disarm
weapon, search person for: frisk
weapon, wave a: brandish, flourish
weapons: armament, arms, ordnance, weaponry
weapons and ammunition: munitions
weapons storage: armory, arsenal, cache ❦

wear: abrade, annoy, bother, chafe, consume, corrode, corrosion, deteriorate, diminish, drain, durable, endure, erode, erosion, exhaust, exhibit, fatigue, fray, frazzle, friction, grind, impair, mileage, pester, rub, sport, tire; apparel, attire, clothes, don

RELATED TERMS

wear away: abrade, corrode, eat, erode, gnaw, rust
wear away by chemical action: corrode
wear away with friction: abrade
wear down: abrade, drain, erode, exhaust, fatigue, friction, reduce, tire, waste, weaken
wear out: decay, exhaust, fatigue, tire, tucker, waste
wearing away with friction: abrasion, detrition
wearing down by friction: attrition ❦

wearisome: boring, dull, exhausting, laborious, strenuous, tedious, tiresome, toilsome
weary: annoy, beat, bored, bushed, disgusted, drained, exhausted, fatigue, fatigued, grievous, irksome, jaded, overtired, overworked, plague, pooped, sleepy, spent, tedious, timid, tire, tired, tiresome, tore, tucker, weaken, worn
weasel family, of the: musteline
weasel's cousin: otter
weather: brave, climate, clime, discolor, disintegrate, elements, endure, erode, overcome, rust, survive, temperature, withstand

RELATED TERMS

weather balloon instrument: radiosonde

weather of a certain region: clime
weather term for boundary between air masses of different temperature and humidity: front
weather term for fast-moving westerly airstream: jet stream
weather, lack of protection from: exposure
weather, of mild: clement, temperate
weather, of stormy: inclement
weather, science of: meteorology
weatherperson: climatologist, forecaster, meteorologist ❦

weave: blend, braid, careen, contrive, crisscross, darn, devise, entwine, fashion, interlace, intertwine, join, knit, lace, loom, meander, plait, spin, stagger, sway, twill, unite, wattle, wobble, zigzag
weave together: interlace
weaving bobbin holder: shuttle
weaving frame: loom
weaving reel: bobbin, quill, spindle
web: complexity, ensnare, entangle, fabric, fiber, gossamer, involvement, labyrinth, maze, membrane, mesh, net, network, snare, tangle, texture, tissue, trap
wed: blend, connect, elope, espouse, hitch, join, link, marry, merge, pledged, spliced, tie, tie the knot, unite
wedding: celebration, ceremony, espousal, marriage, nuptials, shivaree
wedding ceremony: nuptials
wedding party, mock serenade: shivaree
wedding song: epithalamium, hymeneal, prothalamion
wedge: block, cleat, club, cram, crowd, gib, jam, lump, pack, pie, sandwich, shim, squeeze, stuff
wedge to stop rolling or sliding: chock
wedge-shaped: cuneal, cuneate, cuneiform, sphenic
wedge-shaped ancient writing: cuneiform
wedge-shaped insert: shim
wedlock: conjugality, marriage, matrimony, nuptials
wee: bitsy, diminutive, early, infinitesimal, lilliputian, little, microscopic, miniature, minute, small, teensy, teeny, tiny
weed: buckthorn, burr, cigarette, dandelion, darnel, dock, hemp, hoe, horsemint, marijuana, nettle, plan-

WEDDING ANNIVERSARIES

1st: clock, paper
2nd: china, cotton
3rd: crystal, glass, leather
4th: appliance, linen, silk
5th: silverware, wood
6th: iron, wood
7th: copper, wool
8th: bronze, lace, linen
9th: china, leather, pottery
10th: aluminum, diamond, tin
11th: jewelry, steel
12th: gem, pearl, silk
13th: fur, lace, textile
14th: gold, ivory
15th: crystal, watch
20th: china, platinum
25th: silver
30th: diamond, pearl
35th: coral, jade
40th: ruby
45th: sapphire
50th: gold
55th: emerald
60th: diamond ❦

tain, pot, purloin, purslane, ragweed, tare, thistle, tobacco, undergrowth, vetch
weed killer: herbicide
weekly: hebdomadal
weep: bawl, bewail, boohoo, cry, drip, exude, grieve, lament, leak, moan, mourn, ooze, sob, tear, wail, yammer
weigh: analyze, balance, bear, boist, burden, compare, consider, contemplate, count, counterbalance, evaluate, examine, influence, judge, lift, load, measure, meditate, ponder, portion, study, tax, think
weigh anchor: sail
weigh down: burden, depress, encumber, load, oppress, overload, press, worry
weight: anchor, authority, ballast, baro, barrel, beef, bob, burden, carat, centigram, charge, clout, concern, consequence, density, dram, dumbbell, emphasis, encumber, flask, force, forcefulness, grain, gram, gravity, heaviness, heft, impact, import, importance, influence, kilogram, lade, load, lot, magnitude, mass, milligram, moment, onus, oppress, ounce, pound, poundage, power,

pressure, pull, responsibility, saddle, scale, scruple, significance, sinker, stone, stress, tax, ton, tonnage, urgency, value, worth

weight allowance: tare, tret

weight for exercise: barbell, dumbbell

weight of container subtracted from gross to obtain net weight: tare

weight on vertical line: plumb

weight or heaviness of person: avoirdupois

weightiness: authority, dignity, gravity, heaviness, importance, magnitude, significance, solemnity

weightlessness in space: zero gravity

weightlifting move above head: jerk, snatch

weightlifting move to shoulders: clean

weighty: burdensome, considerable, critical, cumbersome, difficult, grave, heavy, hefty, important, large, onerous, ponderous, powerful, serious, severe, significant, solemn, solid, substantial, taxing, telling

weighty book: tome

weird: abnormal, awesome, bizarre, crazy, creepy, curious, destiny, eccentric, eerie, eery, eldritch, fate, fortune, ghostly, haunting, mysterious, nutty, odd, outlandish, peculiar, predict, queer, scary, spooky, strange, supernatural, uncanny, unco, unearthly, unnatural, unusual, wild

welcome: acceptable, agreeable, comfortable, cordial, desirable, desired, embrace, greet, greeting, hail, handshake, hello, hospitality, hug, ovation, pleasant, pleasurable, receive, reception, refreshing, salutation, salute, satisfying

welcome person: persona grata

weld: bind, combine, connect, fuse, join, link, solder, unite

welfare: aid, benefit, good, happiness, health, progress, prosperity, success, weal, well-being

welfare or public good: commonweal

welfare, promotion of human: philanthropy

well-behaved: courteous, good, mannerly, polite

well-being: advantage, benefit, comfort, ease, good, happiness, health, prosperity, weal, welfare

well-bred: civil, considerate, courteous, cultivated, cultured, genteel, mannerly, polished, polite, refined

well-bred ways: gentility, refinement

well-chosen: felicitous

well-defined: clear, definite, distinct, outlined

well-disposed: friendly, kindly, sympathetic, willing

well-educated: learned

well-favored: attractive, beautiful, good-looking, handsome, pretty

well-founded: factual, good, just, likely, probable, rational, sound, substantiated

well-groomed: clean, dapper, impeccable, neat, shipshape, spruce, tidy, trim

well-grounded: corroborated, substantiated, supported, valid, versed

well-heeled: affluent, prosperous, rich, wealthy

well-known: common, eminent, established, famed, familiar, famous, illustrious, notable, noted, notorious, popular, prominent, renowned

well-made: dependable, durable, flawless, reliable, solid, sturdy

well-mannered: courteous, cultivated, cultured, genteel, polished, polite, refined

well-off: affluent, fortunate, loaded, lucky, moneyed, prosperous, rich, snug, successful, upscale, wealthy, well-to-do

well-timed: appropriate, favorable, opportune, timely

well-to-do: affluent, prosperous, rich, sitting pretty, wealthy, well-off

wellspring: aquifer, beginning, fountain, fountainhead, origin, root, source

welt: blow, bruise, bump, lash, lump, mark, ridge, stripe, thrash, wale, weal, wheal, wound

welter: commotion, confusion, grovel, jumble, overturn, roll, toss, tumble, turmoil, uproar, wallow, wilt, wither

wench: bimbo, damsel, doxy, girl, hussy, Jezebel, lass, maiden, prostitute, servant, strumpet, tramp, wanton, whore, woman

wend: alter, change, go, journey, pass, proceed, saunter, shift, slav, sorb, stroll, travel

wet: asoak, asop, damp, dampen, dampened, dampness, dank, dewy, douse, drench, drenched, drizzling, foggy, humid, irrigate, misty, moist, moisten, moisture, muggy, rain, rainy, saturate, shower, slippery, snowy, soak, soaked, sodden, soggy, soppy, splash, sprinkle, sweat, wash, water, waterlogged, watery, wring

wet and cold: clammy, dank

wet and limp: bedraggled

wet and soggy: paludal, paludian, paludinal

wet and sticky: humid, muggy

wet blanket: damper, drag, drip, fuddy-duddy, killjoy, party pooper, sourpuss, spoilsport

wet completely: douse, drench, saturate, sluice, swill

wet thoroughly: saturate, soak

whack: attempt, bang, bash, bat, beat, belt, blow, clobber, crack, fling, hit, knock, pound, shot, slam, smack, smash, stab, thump, thwack, try, turn, wallop, whale

whale: ceta, cetacean, cete, mammal, orc, orca, sei, whopper

RELATED TERMS

whale airhole: blowhole, spiracle

whale fat: blubber

whale food: krill

whale group: gam, herd, pod

whale tail flaps: fluke

whale types: baleen, beluga, cachalot, finback, grampus, humpback, killer, mysticete, orca, sperm, white

whale with grooves in throat and small dorsal fin, baleen: razorback, rorqual

whale with long spiral tusk, Arctic: narwhal

whale, dive like: sound

whale, killer: grampus, orc

whale, large toothless: baleen whale, mysticete, whalebone whale

whale, pertaining to: cetacean

whale, strip blubber from: flense

whale, white: beluga

whale's hinged plates that strain plankton from water: baleen, whalebone

whale's leap from water: breach

whales, study of: cetology

whale's waxy substance used in candles, cosmetics: spermaceti

whale's waxy substance used in perfumes: ambergris

whalebone: baleen, scrimshaw, stay

whalebone or whale ivory, art of carving: scrimshaw ☙

wham: bang, blow, crash, hit, knock, slam, smash, strike, whack, whammy

whammy: curse, jinx, spell

WEIGHTS AND MEASURES

Energy and Motion
(*unit: what it measures*)
bar/barye/pascal: pressure
dyne/newton/poundal: force
erg/joule/kilowatt-hour: work or energy
knot/mach: speed
watt: power

Heat, Light, and Sound
(*unit: what it measures*)
angstrom: wavelength of light
calorie/therm: heat
candela: luminous intensity
decibel/phon: loudness
fresnel/hertz: frequency
kelvin: temperature
lumen: luminous flux, the rate of flow of luminous energy

Electricity and Magnetism
(*unit: what it measures*)
ampere: electric current
coulomb: electric charge
farad: electric capacitance, the capacity to store an electric charge
gauss/tesla: magnetic flux density, the direction and magnitude of magnetic force
henry: electric inductance, the property of enabling an electromagnetic force to be generated
maxwell/weber: magnetic flux, the strength of a magnetic field through an area
oersted: magnetic field strength
ohm: electric resistance
siemens: electric conductance
volt: electric potential and electromotive force

Atomic Physics
(*unit: what it measures*)
becquerel/curie: radioactivity
dalton/AMU/atomic mass unit: mass of an isotope
rad/gray: energy absorbed from radiation
rem/REM: radiation dose
roentgen: X-rays or gamma rays

Metric Units
(*unit: value*)
grade: one-hundredth of a right angle
gram: about 0.002 pound avoirdupois
hectare: 100 ares, or 2.47 acres
micrometer/micron: 10 to the 6th meters, about 1/25,000 inch
stere: volume equivalent of 1 cubic meter
ton or metric ton: 10 quintals or 0.98421 long tons

Imperial Units: Linear Measure
(*unit: value*)
1 cable: about 608 feet
1 chain: 4 rods, 22 yards
1 fathom: 6 feet
1 furlong: 10 chains, 220 yards
1 hand: 4 inches
1 league: 3 nautical miles
1 rod/1 pole/1 perch: 5½ yards

Imperial Units: Liquid Measure
(*unit: value*)
1 barrel: 31½ to 35 gallons
1 firkin: 9 gallons
1 fluid drachma: 60 minims ⅛ fluid ounce
1 gill/noggin: 5 fluid ounces, ¼ pint
1 hogshead: 2 barrels
1 minim: 1/60 fluid dram

Imperial Units: Dry Measure
(*unit: value*)
1 bushel: 4 pecks
1 peck: 8 quarts

Imperial Units: Jewelers' Weights
(*unit: value*)
1 carat: ¹⁄₂₄ (4.1667%) gold
1 grain: ¹⁄₄₈₀ ounce troy
1 ounce troy: ¹⁄₁₂ pound troy, 1.097 ounces avoirdupois

Imperial Units: Avoirdupois Weights
(*unit: value*)
1 dram: 27 ¹¹⁄₃₂ grains, ¹⁄₁₆ ounce
1 drachma: 3 scruples
1 scruple: 20 grains

Archaic and Foreign Units
(*unit: value*)
barleycorn: ⅓ inch
catty/kati: about 1⅓ pounds (China)
crore: 10 million (India)
cubit: 18 to 21 inches
ell: 45 inches (cloth)
hide: 100 to 120 acres
kilderkin: about 18 gallons
lakh: 100,000 (India)
maund: about 82 pounds (India)
morgen: 2.116 acres (South Africa)
mutchkin: 0.9 pint (Scotland)
picul: 133.33 pounds (China)
pipe: 105 gallons (wine)
pood: 36.11 pounds (Russia)
rood: ¼ acre
shekel: about ½ ounce (ancient Hebrew)
span: 9 inches; tip of thumb to tip of little finger or an extended hand
tael: usually 1⅓ ounces (Asia)
tierce/terce: 42 wine gallons; about 33 gallons
verst: 0.6629 miles (Russia)
virgate: about ¼ acre ❦

wharf: dock, jetty, landing, levee, pier, quay, slip, waterfront

wharf to protect harbor, beach: jetty

wheat: cereal, durum, grain, grass, semolina, spelt

RELATED TERMS

wheat boiled in milk, with sugar and spices: frumenty, furmity

wheat grains, cracked: bulghur, bulgur, bulgur wheat, cracked wheat

wheat husk: bran

wheat particles left after sieving/bolting, used in pasta: semolina

wheat particles used in North African pasta: couscous

wheat product made from entire grain of wheat, including bran: whole-wheat

wheat used in pasta, hearty: durum

wheat, resembling or concerning: frumentaceous

wheat's protein: gluten

wheat's whiskers: awn ❦

wheedle: blandish, blarney, butter, cajole, charm, coax, con, entice, flatter, influence, inveigle, lure, persuade, sweet-talk, tempt

wheedled: cajoled

wheel: cam, caster, circle, cog, disk, gear, gyration, helm, lathe, loop, pivot, pully, reel, revolution, revolve, rim, roll, roller, rotate, rotation, rotor, round, rowel, sheave, spin, sprocket, swirl, tire, treadmill, turn, twirl, whirl

RELATED TERMS

wheel changer's tool: tire iron

wheel mounted so axis can turn freely, spinning: gyroscope

wheel mounting: axle

wheel on a spur, sharp-toothed: rowel

wheel or ball on swivel of chair leg: caster

wheel or roller, small: trundle

wheel ride at amusement park, rotating: big wheel, Ferris wheel

wheel rolling, sound of: trundle

wheel shaft: axle

wheel to keep it from moving, block or wedge placed under: chock

wheel track: rut

wheel turns around, pivot at end of shaft or axle which: gudgeon

wheel with axis of revolution off-center and imparting reciprocating motion: eccentric

wheel with grooved rim as on pulley: sheave

wheel's toothlike projections: sprocket

wheel, center of a: hub, nave

wheel, protruding rim on: flange

wheel, small flywheel that regulates speed of a spinning: whorl

wheel, spindle of a: arbor

wheel-shaped: rotiform, trochal

wheeled device rotated by people or animals treading on it: treadmill

wheeled vehicle, single-: monocycle, unicycle

wheels inside tread of tractor or tank: bogie, bogy

wheels on small child's bike, stabilizing: training wheels

wheels that are closer together at bottom than top: camber ❦

wheeze: antic, gag, gasp, joke, pant, prank, puff, rale, trick

whelp: child, cub, dog, pup, puppy, wolf, youngster

when: although, during, if, meanwhile, though, until, whereas, while

whereas: because, considering, since, though, when, while

wherefore: accordingly, ergo, therefore, thereupon, why

whereupon: consequently, thereupon, whereon

wherever: anywhere, regardless, wheresoever

wherewithal: ability, financing, funds, means, money, resources, wealth

whet: animate, appetizer, arouse, awaken, edge, excite, hone, incite, keen, pique, provoke, rouse, sharpen, stimulate, stir

whether willing or unwilling: nolens volens

whey: sera, serum

whey cheese: ricotta

whey-faced: pale

which: one, that, what, whatever, who

which was to be demonstrated: Q.E.D., quod erat demonstrandum

whiff: aroma, breath, expel, gust, hint, inhale, odor, puff, scent, smell, sniff, stench, strikeout, tinge, trace, waft

while: although, bit, during, interim, occasion, period, spell, stretch, though, time, until, whereas, yet

whim: caprice, desire, fancy, fantasy, humor, idea, impulse, inclination, mood, notion, thought, trifle, vagary, vision

whimper: complain, cry, fuss, mewl, moan, object, pule, sniffle, snivel, sob, weep, whine, yammer

whimpering noise, low: croosle

whimsical: amusing, arbitrary, bizarre, capricious, comical, droll, eccentric, erratic, fanciful, fantastic, fey, freakish, funny, playful, uncertain, unpredictable

whimsical musical composition: humoresque

whimsy: caprice, idea, notion, quality, thought, vagary, whim

whine: complain, fret, fuss, gripe, grumble, mewl, moan, pule, snivel, wail, whimper, yammer

whinny: neigh

whip: beat, belt, birch, bludgeon, cane, castigate, cat-o-nine-tails, clobber, conquer, dart, dash, defeat, discipline, flagellate, flash, flay, flick, flog, hide, lace, lash, lick, provoke, punish, push, rawhide, rod, shellac, spank, stitch, strap, strike, swish, switch, tan, thrash, trounce, urge, wallop, whisk

whip handle: crop

whip mark: seal, wale, weal, welt

whir: bustle, commotion, fly, hum, move, revolve, sound, swirl, swish, vibrate, whiz

whirl: attempt, bustle, circle, commotion, crack, daze, flurry, flutter, gyrate, hurry, pirouette, pivot, reel, revolution, revolve, rotate, rush, shot, spin, stab, stir, swinge, swirl, turn, twirl, uproar, whack, wheel

whirling: gyral, vertiginous, vorticose

whirling dance: tarantella

whirling mass of water or air: vortex

whirling Muslim: dervish

whirlpool: Charybdis, eddy, force, maelstrom, swirl, turmoil, vortex, whorl

whirlpool caused by current moving contrary to main current: eddy, gulf

whirlpool of large size or violence: maelstrom

whirlpool-like shape: helix, spiral, volute, whorl

whirlwind: bustle, cyclone, hurricane, maelstrom, quick, speedy, stir, swift, tornado, tourbillion, twister, typhoon, vortex, waterspout

WHITE

alabaster
argent
blond
chalk
Chinese white
columbine
dove
eggshell
flake white
gauze
ivory
lily-white
marble
milk-white
nacre
off-white
oyster-white
pearl
platinum
pure white
putty
silver
snow-white
swan-white
zinc white ❦

---

whirlwind accompanied by stormy destructive weather: cyclone
whirlwind in western Pacific or Indian oceans: typhoon
whirlwind over water: waterspout
whirlwind with downward extension from cumulonimbus cloud: tornado
whirlwind, small: dust devil
whisk: barrel, fly, hasten, hurry, motion, race, rush, scoot, speed, sweep, whip, zip
whiskers: beard, bristles, goatee, hair, mustache, sideburns, stubble, vibrissae
whiskers, cat: vibrissae
whiskers, fish: barbels
whiskey: alcohol, booze, bourbon, Canadian, corn, drink, hooch, Irish, liquor, moonshine, mountain dew, rotgut, rye, scotch, spirits, usquebaugh, white lightening
RELATED TERMS
whiskey with beer: Boilermaker
whiskey with vermouth: Manhattan
whiskey, illegally distilled: moonshine, white lightning
whiskey, strong distilled: aqua vitae
whiskey-making factory: distillery, still ❦

whisper: breathe, buzz, confide, hint, intimate, murmur, mutter, rumor, rustle, siffilate, suggestion, trace, undertone
whisper intended to be overheard: stage whisper
whispering: sough, susurrant, susurration
whistle: flute, hiss, instrument, pipe, signal, siren, sound, toot, trill, warn
whistle blast: toot
whistle cord: lanyard
whistle stop: burg, way station
whistle, derisive: catcall
whit: atom, bit, crumb, dash, fragment, iota, jot, modicum, particle, shred, smidgen, speck, trace
white or light-skinned racial division: Caucasian
white skin and hair, person with: albino
white, hard, smooth: marmoreal
white, protein in egg: albumen, albumin
whitefish: cisco, ciscoes, tullibee
whiten: blanch, bleach, decolor, fade, frost, lighten, pale, palliate
whiteness: hoariness, paleness, pallidity
whitewash: camouflage, conceal, coverup, defeat, lime, minimize, paint, palliate, sugarcoat
whither: condition, place, position, result, where
whittle: carve, cut, decrease, diminish, pare, reduce, sculpt, shape, shave, trim
whiz: adept, bolt, buzz, dart, dizzle, expert, fly, genius, hiss, hum, hurry, marvel, master, pirr, professional, race, speed, whisk, whoosh, wizard, zip, zoom
whole: absolute, aggregate, all, complete, cured, entire, entirely, entirety, fit, fixed, full, gross, hale, healed, healthy, intact, integral, one, perfect, recovered, sound, sum, thorough, total, totally, unbroken, uncut, undamaged, undivided, unhurt, unimpaired, uninjured, unscathed
RELATED TERMS
whole and interdependence of parts, emphasis on the: holistic
whole and unbroken: intact, undivided, unitary
whole and unchanged: intact
whole assembled from parts: synthesis
whole number: integer

whole step, in music: tone
whole, combined parts to make coherent: synthesis
whole, complementary parts that contribute to a: ensemble
whole, constituting the: aggregate, sum, total
whole, something that completes or makes up a: complement
whole, to unite into a: combine, consolidate
whole, uninterrupted: continuum
whole, universe seen as a: macrocosm ❦

wholehearted: ardent, avid, committed, complete, dedicated, devoted, earnest, emphatic, enthusiastic, genuine, passionate, serious, sincere, steadfast, sure, true, unfeigned, unreserved
wholeness: completeness, integrity
wholesale: abundant, bulk, complete, comprehensive, discount, extensive, mass, massive, sweeping, widespread
wholesome: clean, decent, ethical, good, hale, healthful, healthy, hearty, honest, hygienic, innocent, moral, nourishing, nutritious, pure, robust, safe, salubrious, salutary, sound, uplifting, vigorous
wholly: all, altogether, completely, entirely, exclusively, fully, in all, quite, solely, thoroughly, totally, well
whoop: cheer, crow, cry, holler, hoot, howl, hurrah, shout, urge, yell
whooping cough: pertussis
whopper: big, fabrication, falsehood, lie, remarkable, story, untruth
whopping: big, colossal, enormous, giant, gigantic, great, huge, immense, large, mammoth, massive, very
whore: harlot, hooker, hussy, pro, prostitute, slut, streetwalker, strumpet, tramp, wench
whorehouse: bordello
whorl: coil, spiral, swirl, turn, twirl, twist, whirlpool
why: cause, how, motive, mystery, proof, reason
wick, charred part of candle: snuff
wicked: abominable, adept, adroit, atrocious, awful, bad, base, beastly, clever, corrupt, criminal, cruel, cursed, dangerous, dark, depraved, destructive, devilish, diabolic, diabolical, difficult, effective, evil, fiendish, harmful, hateful, heartless,

heinous, hellish, horrid, immoral, iniquitous, intense, malicious, mean, mischievous, naughty, nefarious, obnoxious, outrageous, perverse, playful, reprehensible, risque, rotten, satanic, scandalous, severe, shady, sinful, sinister, skillful, spiteful, suggestive, terrible, troublesome, unethical, unholy, unjust, unpleasant, vicious, vile, villainous

wickedness: deviltry, evil, sin

wicker: branch, roped, straw, twig, withe, woven

wicker basket: hamper, pannier

wicker willow: osier

wickerwork material of palm: rattan

wickerwork receptable for fish: creel

wicket: arch, door, entrance, gate, hoop, opening, window

wide: ample, astray, broad, capacious, commodious, dilated, distended, expanded, expansive, extensive, full, general, immense, inaccurate, large, liberal, loose, off, roomy, spacious, sweeping, vast

RELATED TERMS

wide and open extent: expanse

wide discrepancy: far cry

wide extent: breadth, expanse

wide knowledge and skills, person with: generalist, polymath

wide necktie: ascot

wide range of uses and functions, having a: versatile

wide river mouth: delta

wide-awake: alert, attentive, aware, keen, observant, on the qui vive, quick, sharp, vigilant, watchful

wide-mouthed pitcher: ewer

wide-mouthed pot: olla

wide-open: agape, ajar, expansive, exposed, lawless, unrestricted, vast

wide-ranging in scope: catholic, comprehensive, synoptic ❦

widely: abroad, broadly, extensively, far, generally, universally

widely dispersed, become: broadcast, diffuse, scattershot

widely practiced: prevalent

widen: broaden, dilate, distend, enlarge, expand, extend, grow, increase, multiply, open, ream, spread, stretch, swell

widespread: acceptable, boundless, broad, common, epidemic, extensive, general, pandemic, pervasive, popular, prevailing, prevalent, rampant, rife, sweeping, universal, unrestricted

widespread and current: prevailing, prevalent, regnant

widespread and general: epidemic, pandemic

widespread or prevalent: endemic, predominant, rife

widow holding title or property from husband: dowager

widow of one's brother, practice of marrying the: levirate

widow who cremates herself on husband's funeral pyre: sati, suttee

widow's mourning clothes: weeds

widow's property from husband: dower, dowry

width: across, amplitude, breadth, compass, diameter, girth, length, magnitude, measure, range, scope, span, thickness, wideness

width times length: area

width, height, length: dimension

wield: brandish, command, conduct, control, deal, direct, employ, exercise, exert, handle, manage, manipulate, operate, ply, rule, swing, use, utilize

wife: bride, companion, consort, frau, helpmate, helpmeet, mate, missus, Mrs., partner, spouse, uxorial

RELATED TERMS

wife, man who marries and then kills: bluebeard

wife at a time, having more than one: bigamy, polyamory, polygamy

wife in certain societies, secondary: concubine

wife or husband of monarch: consort

wife or husband swapping: swinging

wife who murders husband: mariticide

wife, concerning a: uxorial

wife, dominated by nagging: henpecked

wife, killing of: uxoricide

wife, legal right of husband to affections and help of: consortium

wife, man married to unfaithful: cuckold

wife's infidelity, man who tolerates: wittol ❦

wig: admonishment, berate, carpet, censure, dignitary, hair, hairpiece, postiche, periwig, peruke, rebuke, reprimand, rug, scold, toupee

wig of seventeenth-eighteenth centuries: periwig, peruke

wiggle: shake, shimmy, squiggle, squirm, twist, worm, wriggle

wigwam: dwelling, home, lodge, shelter, tent, tepee, wickiup

wild: amok, barbarian, barbarous, berserk, bestial, bizarre, carefree, chaotic, crazed, crazy, daft, delirious, dense, disarranged, disorderly, dissolute, disturbed, enthusiastic, erratic, extravagant, fanatical, fantastic, feral, ferine, ferocious, fierce, frantic, frenetic, frenzied, furious, impractical, imprudent, inaccurate, insane, intense, irrational, irresponsible, lawless, licentious, mad, madcap, manic, native, natural, neglected, nutty, outlandish, overgrown, primitive, rabid, raging, rampant, raving, reckless, riotous, risky, rough, rowdy, savage, stormy, tumultuous, turbulent, uncivil, uncivilized, uncontrolled, uncultivated, undisciplined, unfounded, uninhabited, unmanageable, unrestrained, unruly, untamed, vicious, violent, wilderness

wild adventurous undertaking: escapade

wild and lacking control or order: anarchic, chaotic

wild and untamed: feral, undomesticated

wild animals, reserved area for: sanctuary

wild animal's resting place: lair

wild card: joker

wild party: bash, blast, orgy, saturnalia

wild rush of crowd or herd: rampage

wildcat: bobcat, caracal, chaus, feline, lynx

wilderness: badlands, barren, boondocks, bush, desert, forest, jungle, outback, waste, wastelands

wildly excited: delirious

wildly, behaving: berserk, frantic, frenetic, hysterical, madcap

wile: art, artifice, attract, charm, chicanery, coax, craftiness, cunning, deceit, entice, guile, lure, maneuver, pass, ploy, ruse, scheming, shenanigans, stratagem, trick, trickery

will (choice): command, decree, demand, desire, inclination, longing, pleasure, preference, want, wish

will (courage): determination, discipline, guts, resolve, self-control, spunk, volition

will (document): bequeathal, bequest, bestowal, endowment, legacy, testament

RELATED TERMS

will during life of testator, that can be changed as a: alterable, ambulatory

will for wife from husband, property left in: jointure

will maker: testator

will, certification of validity of: probate

will, cut out of: disinherit

will, give property by: devise

will, leave property or money for someone in: bequeath

will, leaving no valid: intestate

will, leaving valid: testate

will, person appointed by testator to carry out wishes in: executor, executrix

will, person who has a valid: legator, testator

will, person who receives money or property from: beneficiary

will, property or money left in: legacy

will, transfer of an estate by: demise ❦

will, done of one's free: voluntary

willful: adamant, bullheaded, capricious, deliberate, head strong, headstrong, intended, intentional, mulish, obstinate, pigheaded, premeditated, stubborn, unruly, voluntary

willful and stubborn: contrary, perverse

willing: agreeable, amenable, compliant, consenting, deliberate, desirous, disposed, eater, fain, fair, game, inclined, intentional, lief, obedient, prone, ready, solicitous, unforced, voluntary

willing and ready: accommodating, acquiescent, compliant, obliging, ungrudging

willingly: fain, lief

willingness: alacrity, compliance, consent, eagerness, enthusiasm, readiness, zeal

willow: itea, oiser, osier, shrub, tree, wood

willow branch or twig: wicker, withe, withy

willow variety: arroyo, autumn, beaked, black, drooping, gray, laurel, osier, prairie, pussy, sandbar, weeping, white

willowy: flexible, graceful, limber, lissome, lithe, pliant, slender, supple, svelte, tall

willpower: determination, discipline, drive, grit, resolution, self-control, strength

willpower and decision-making ability, loss of: abulia

willy-nilly: ambivalent, disordered, haphazardly, inevitable, perforce, unavoidable

wilt: collapse, droop, drop, dwindle, fade, flag, sag, shrivel, wane, weaken, wither

wily: artful, astute, cagey, canny, clever, crafty, cunning, foxy, insidious, scheming, sharp, shrewd, sly, smooth, sneaky, streetwise, subtle, treacherous, tricky

win: accomplish, achieve, acquire, attain, beat, capture, charm, conquer, conquest, defeat, earn, edge, gain, get, hit, influence, net, obtain, overcome, prevail, realize, reap, score, secure, succeed, sweep, take, triumph, upset, victory

wince: cower, cringe, flinch, gesture, grimace, movement, quail, recoil, reel, shrink

wind: air, bise, blast, blizzard, blow, bora, breath, breeze, chinook, cyclone, draft, gale, geostrophic, gust, harmattan, hurricane, intimation, monsoon, nor'easter, puff, scent, sirocco, squall, storm, tempest, tornado, trade, tramontana, typhoon, whiff, zephyr

RELATED TERMS

wind blowing directly against course of craft: head wind

wind blowing in same direction as course of craft: tail wind

wind-blown: fanned, winnowed

wind blows, in the direction in which the: downwind, leeward

wind caused by earth's rotation: geostrophic

wind current from the west 250 mph+ at 10-15 miles above earth: jet stream

wind direction and speed, weather diagram showing: wind rose

wind direction indicator: air sock, wind cone, wind sock, windsock

wind force and velocity instrument: anemometer

wind from the north: boreal

wind from the south: austral

wind from the west: favonian

wind gust: scud

wind gust of cold from mountainous coast: williwaw

wind gust of warm from mountain range: foehn

wind in France, dry and cold: mistral

wind in Mediterranean, strong easterly: levanter

wind in one's face: noser

wind in sudden burst: flaw, squall

wind of Adriatic Sea, cold northeasterly: bora

wind of Africa and Mediterranean, hot dusty: sirocco

wind of Africa, dry dusty: harmattan

wind of Africa, southerly hot: khamsin

wind of Africa, strong hot sandy: samiel, simoon

wind of California, strong dry hot: Santa Ana

wind of Italy, cold north: tramontane

wind of Mediterranean and Africa, hot southerly: sirocco

wind of northwest U.S. or eastern Rocky Mountains, warm: chinook

wind of Pampas, strong cold: pampero

wind of Sahara and Arabian desert, strong hot: simoom

wind of South America's pampas, cold southwest: pampero

wind of southern California, strong dry hot: Santa Ana

wind of southern France, dry cold northerly: mistral

wind of Swiss Alps, cold north: bise

wind of Swiss Alps, warm dry: foehn, fohn

wind of the Mediterranean, strong easterly: levanter

wind of the west or gentle breeze: zephyr

wind sighing sound: sough, susurration

wind traveling downward, of a cold: katabatic

wind traveling upward or rising, of a: anabatic

wind, carry lightly by: waft

wind, concerning or caused by: eolian

wind, dispersal of plant parts and seeds by the: anemochory

wind, science of: anemology ❦

WIND INSTRUMENTS

band fastening reed to instrument: ligature
brass instrument bent upon itself twice and having
 U-shaped slide: trombone
brass instrument with coiled tube and large flared bell:
 French horn
curved wooden horn around 20 ft. long: alpenhorn
device to muffle instrument: mute, sordino
flared part of wind instrument: bell
flexible cane strip set into mouthpiece of woodwinds: reed
instrument like cornet with wider bore: fluegelhorn, flugelhorn
instrument with three valves operated by pistons: cornet,
 trumpet
large valved brass instrument with bass pitch: tuba
mouthpiece: embouchure
small instrument with series of holes played by inhaling and
 exhaling: harmonica
toy instrument played by humming or singing in mouthpiece: kazoo
whistlelike mouthpiece of woodwinds: fipple

Brass Wind Instruments
alpenhorn/alphorn
althorn
ballad horn
baritone horn
bass horn
bombardon
bugle
clarion
cornet
cornopean
double-bell euphonium
E-flat horn
euphonium
flugelhorn
French horn
hand horn
helicon
horn
hunting horn
key trumpet
lituus
lur
mellophone
nyas taranga
ophicleide
orchestral horn
pocket trumpet
post horn
sackbut
saxcornet

saxhorn
saxtuba
serpent
slide trombone
sousaphone
tenor horn
tenor tuba
tromba
trombone
trumpet
tuba

Woodwind Instruments
bagpipe
bass clarinet
bass oboe
bassanello
basset horn
bassoon
bombard
bombardon
clarinet
contrabassoon
double bassoon
English horn
fife
fipple flute
flageolet
flute
hautboy/hautbois/oboe
heckelphone
hornpipe
krummhorn/crumhorn
musette
nose flute
oaten pipe
oboe/hautboy/hautbois
ocarina
Pandean pipe
panpipe
penny whistle
piccolo
pipe
pommer
recorder
saxophone
shawm
syrinx
tabor
tenoroon
whistle ❧

WINDOW TYPES AND TERMS

beam forming upper member of window: lintel

blind for adjusting light through window: jalousie, louver

bottom part of window frame: sill

circular window in ship's side: porthole

crisscross framework in window: lattice

dividing bar in window: transom

Gothic window's lacy openwork: tracery

horizontal slat blinds: Venetian blinds

metal strips holding panes in stained-glass: came

old-fashioned window glass with lump in center: crown glass

ornamental section above window: frontispiece, gable, pediment

person who cuts and fits window glass: glazier

semicircular window over door or window: fanlight, lunette

semicircular window: roundel

short decorative window drapery: valance

small window: fenestella

strips separating and holding panes of glass: mullion, muntin

throw out of a window: defenestrate

vertical piece of window frame: jamb

vertical strip dividing window panes: mullion

wall or panel with windows: clerestory

window above door: fanlight, transom

window bars: muntins

window frame: casing, sash

window frame in which panes are set: sash

window molding: architrave

window projecting from sloping roof: dormer

window sash that opens outward by hinges: casement

window sash vertical member: stile

window that opens on hinges at side: casement

windowsill: ledge, stool ❦

---

wind up: close, complete, conclude, end, finalize, finish, settle

windfall: bonanza, bonus, boon, fortune, gain, godsend, gravy, luck, plum, raise

winding: anfractuous, bending, coiling, contorted, convoluted, crooked, curving, devious, flexible, flexuous, indirect, intricate, meandering, rambling, roundabout, serpentine, sinuate, sinuous, snaky, spiral, tortuous, turning, twisting, zigzag

winding mechanism of watch: crown

windjammer: tallship

windmill arm that carries sail: whip

windmill blade: sail

window: aperture, bay, bow, casement, dormer, fanestella, fanlight, jalousie, lancet, lucarne, lunette, mullioned, opening, oriel, picture, porthole, rose, skylight, vasistas

windpipe: airpipe, bronchi, esophagus, gullet, throat, trachea

windpipe-to-lung tubes: bronchi, bronchus

winds blowing northeasterly in the Northern hemisphere: trade wind

winds blowing southeasterly in the Southern hemisphere: trade wind

winds, region with calm light: doldrums

windstorm: cyclone, gale, hurricane, squall, tornado, twister, typhoon

windstorm of Central Asia: bura

windstorm, sudden violent: squall

windy: wordy, airy, blowy, blustery, boastful, boisterous, bombastic, breezy, drafty, empty, garrulous, gassy, gusty, inflated, lengthy, pompous, rambling, stormy, talkative, tempestuous, unsheltered, verbose

Windy City: Chicago

wing: addition, airfoil, ala, annex, appendage, arm, backstage, branch, ell, extension, faction, flank, fly, hall, injure, limb, pennon, pinion, pinions, position, protrusion, sail, squadron, wound

wing of aircraft: airfoil

wing of bat, flying squirrel: patagium

wing of bird: pinion

wing-shaped: alar, alary

wing, hollow under: axilla

wing, joint in middle of bird's: alula, bastard wing, spurious wing

winged: alar, alate, elevated, fast, feathered, fleet, lofty, pennate, rapid, sublime, swift, wounded

winged horse: Pegasus

Winged Victory: Nike

wingless: apteral, apterous

winglike: alar, alate, alated

wink: bat, blink, flash, flicker, flirt, gleam, instant, minute, nictate, nic-

tate, nictitate, second, signal, sleep, slimmer, sparkle, squint, twinkle, twinkling

winner: champ, champion, conqueror, first, medalist, victor, victorious

winner's award: laurels, medal

winning: ahead, appealing, attractive, beating the odds, charming, engaging, on top, successful, sweet, triumphant, victorious, victory, winsome

winnow: analyze, disperse, eliminate, examine, extract, fan, remove, scatter, select, separate, sieve, sort

winsome: adorable, agreeable, appealing, attractive, captivating, charming, cute, delightful, engaging, likable, lovable, pleasant, sweet, winning

winter: cold, Jack Frost, season

winter, concerning: hibernal, hiemal

winter, sleep during: hibernate

wintry: arctic, brutal, cheerless, chilling, chilly, cold, freezing, frigid, harsh, hibernal, hiemal, icy, raw, sleety, snowy, stormy

wipe: abolish, annihilate, blow, cancel, clean, delete, dry, erase, exterminate, gibe, jeer, mop, obliterate, remove, rub, sponge, stroke, swab, swipe, towel

wipe out: abolish, annihilate, cancel, delete, destroy, devastate, efface, eliminate, eradicate, erase, expunge, exterminate, extirpate, massacre, obliterate, rout, slaughter, total

wire: cable, coil, line, message, rod, strand, telegram, telegraph, thread

wire coil activating switch: solenoid

wire ornamental work: filigree

wire, thin: filament

wired: bound, cabled, circuited, connected, equipped, excited, sent, stimulated

wiry: agile, fibrous, lean, limber, muscular, ropy, sinewy, stringy, strong, thin, tough

wisdom: astuteness, depth, discrimination, enlightenment, experience, foresight, insight, instinct, intelligence, judgment, knowledge, sagacity, sense, understanding

wise: advised, alert, astute, aware, brash, bright, cagey, calculating, canny, circumspect, clever, cocky, cognizant, crafty, cunning, discerning, discreet, enlightened, erudite, experienced, explain, flippant, fresh, informed, insightful, intelligent, ju-

WINES

Alsace	dandelion wine	Merlot	Sangiovese	Chablis
amontillado	Dao	Mosel	Sauternes	Champagne
amoroso	dessert wine	Moselle	Sauvignon Blanc	Chardonnay
apple wine	Dolcetto Frascati	Muscadet	Sekt	Chianti
Asti Spumante	domestic wine	Muscat	sherry	Cotes du Rhone
Australian wine	Douro	Muscatel	Shiraz	Gewurztraminer
Aveleda	dry wine	Napa Valley wine	Soave	Johannisberg Rie-
Barbera	Entre-deux-Mers	Navarra	sparkling wine	sling
Bardolino	fortified wine	Nierstein	St. Estephe	Lambrusco
Barolo	Frascati	noble wine	St. Julien	Merlot
Beaujolais	French wine	Oporto	sweet wine	Mosel
Bergerac	Fume Blanc	Orvieto	Sylvaner	Pinot Blanc
blanc de noirs	German wine	Pauillac	Syrah	Pinot Grigio/Pinot
blush	Gewurztraminer	pink wine	table wine	Gris
Bordeaux	Graves	Pinot Blanc	tawny port	Pinot Noir
Bordeaux Blanc	Grenache	Pinot Grigio	Tokay-Pinot Gris	Port
Burgundy	Hermitage	Pinot Gris	Valdepenas	Pouilly-Fuisse
Cabernet Sauvignon	hock	Pinot Noir	Valpolicella	Rhine
California wine	house wine	Pomerol	vermouth	Riesling
Chablis	imported wine	Pommard	vinho verde	Rioja
Champagne	Italian wine	port	vintage wine	Sancerre
Chardonnay	Johannisberg Rie-	Pouilly-Fuisse	Vouvray	Sauternes
Chateauneuf-du-	sling	Pouilly-Fume	white cabernet	Sauvignon Blanc
Pape	jug wine	red wine	white wine	Sherry
Chenin Blanc	Lacrima	retsina	white zinfandel	Soave
Chianti	Lambrusco	Rhine	zinfandel	Syrah/Shiraz
Christi	Liebfraumilch	Rhone		Valpolicella
claret	Macon	Riesling	**Wines, Popular**	White Zinfandel
cold duck	Madeira	Rioja	Bardolino	Zinfandel ❦
Condrieu	Malaga	rosé	Beaujolais	
Cote Rotie	Marsala	ruby port	Bordeaux	
Cotes de Nuits	Mateus Rose	sake	Burgundy	
Cotes du Rhone	Medoc	Sancerre	Cabernet Sauvignon	

dicious, keen, knowing, knowledgeable, learned, manner, method, onto,
perceptive, politic, profound, provident, prudent, sagacious, sage, sapient, sassy, scholarly, sensible, shrewd,
skilled, skillful, slick, smart, sophisticated, sound, subtle, tactful, tactical,
versed, wary, witty

wise bird: owl

wise guy: sage, smart aleck, smarty-
pants, wiseacre, wisenheimer

wise or intelligent: luminous

wise person or teacher: guru, luminary,
pundit, sage

wise saying: aphorism, maxim, mot

wisecrack: barb, gag, jest, joke, quip,
sally, witticism

wish: aspiration, crave, desire, dream,
envy, expect, fancy, goal, hanker,
hope, hunger, itch, longing, prefer,
preference, request, thirst, want,
whim, yearn, yearning

**wish of another out of respect, to submit
to:** defer

wish, mere: velleity

wish, to give someone their: gratify,
pander

wish, vain hope or: castle in the air,
pipe dream

wishbone: breastbone, clavicle, formation, fourchette, furcula, furculum

wishful: anxious, desirable, desirous,
eager, enthusiastic, longing, wanting, yearning

wishy-washy: bland, cowardly, diluted,
indecisive, insipid, jejune, listless,
noncommittal, spiritless, thin, watery, wavering, weak, wimpy

wisp: band, broom, brush, bunch, bundle, clean, flock, fragment, frail, hint,
indication, lock, piece, rumple,
shred, slight, strand, thin, trace, tuft,
whisk

wispy: frail, nebulous, slender, slight

wistful: craving, daydreaming, dreamy,
longing, melancholy, nostalgic, pensive, reflective, sad, woebegone,
yearning

wit: acumen, balance, brains, card,
cleverness, comedian, comic, comprehension, cunning, drollery, esprit,
humor, humorist, ingenuity, insight,
intellect, intelligence, irony, joker,
keenness, mind, perception, punster,
quickness, repartee, sageness, sanity,
sarcasm, satire, senses, spirit, understanding, wisdom, wisecracker

WINE TERMS

aromatic dry and sweet wine: vermouth
bouquet: aroma
cask: tun
cask incrustation: tartar
concerning or made with wine: vinous
dry white Italian wine: Soave
fee for uncorking wine brought into establishment: corkage
fermenting wine: must, stum
fortified and blended Spanish wine: sherry
fortified sweet after-dinner wine: port
grape harvester: vintager
Greek white wine flavored with pine resin: retsina
heated wine with spices and sugar: mulled wine
identified by year and origin wine: vintage
inexpensive everyday table wine: vin de table, vin ordinaire, vino da tavola
large ornamental wine vessel: loving cup
of a dry wine: sec
of a very dry wine or champagne: brut
person informed about wine: connoisseur
pour off wine without disturbing sediment: decant
sediment of fermentation: dregs, lees
study of wines and winemaking: oenology
velvety wine or beer: veloute
wine bottle, .1875 liters: split
wine bottle, 1.5 liters: magnum
wine bottle, 3.03 liters: jeroboam
wine bottle, large: flagon
wine bottle's indent on bottom: kick, punt

wine cellar: bodega, buttery, catacomb
wine container: amula, burette, carafe, cask, chalice, decanter, fiasco, goblet, jeroboam, magnum, oenochoe, olpe, tun, vat, wineskin
wine cup at church: chalice
wine drink with fruit juice, soda water: wine cooler
wine expert: enologist, oenologist, taster
wine flask: olpe
wine fragrance: bouquet
wine glass with stem: goblet
wine made of a blend of grapes: generic wine
wine made principally of one grape and so named: varietal
wine maker: abkari, gourmand, vintner
wine making: viniculture, viticulture
wine merchant: vintner
wine or beer made from rice: sake
wine pitcher: ama, olpe
wine punch: sangaree, sangria
wine server with flared lip: carafe, decanter
wine steward: sommelier
wine sticking to sides of glass: legs
wine tartar: argal, argol
wine types: Bordeaux, brut, Burgundy, Chablis, Chianti, dry, fortified, Madeira, medium, Merlot, Moselle, Muscat, Muscatel, natural, Pinot Grigio, Pinot Noir, port, red, Rhine, rosé, sake, Sauterne, sherry, sparkling, sweet, table, vermouth, white, zinfandel
wine year: vintage
winemaking refuse: rape ❦

witch: beldam, crone, enchantress, hag, hex, lamia, magician, necromancer, shrew, sibyl, sorcerer, sorceress, warlock, wizard

witchcraft: black magic, charm, conjuring, diabolism, enchantment, jinx, magic, necromancy, occult, sorcery, sortilege, spell, thaumaturgy, voodoo, witchery, wizardry

with: accompanying, along, alongside, amidst, among, beside, by, for, including, near, plus, upon

with-it: contemporary, cool, current, in, modern, modish, stylish, trendy

withdraw: abjure, abstract, alienate, annul, back down, demit, depart, detach, disengage, evacuate, leave, nullify, quit, recall, recant, recede, refrain, remove, renege, rescind, restrain, retire, retract, retreat, revoke, scratch, shrink, steal away, void, wean

RELATED TERMS

withdraw a statement or belief: disavow, recant, retract

withdraw and move back: recede
withdraw and void: repeal, rescind, revoke
withdraw as a member: dissociate, secede
withdraw by degrees: wean
withdraw by plan: phase out
withdraw formally: secede
withdraw from a commitment: renege
withdraw membership: demit
withdraw or cancel an order: countermand
withdraw troops or occupation of area: evacuate ❦

withdrawal: abandonment, cancellation, departure, evacuation, exit, exodus, retraction, retreat

withdrawn: abandonment, aloof, detached, distant, hidden, introverted, isolated, quiet, reclusive, remote, secluded, sequestered, shy, solitary, unresponsive, unsociable

withdrawn person: hermit, recluse

wither: age, atrophy, blight, decay, decline, dehydrate, deteriorate, die, droop, fade, languish, sear, shrink, shrivel, stun, wane, waste, weaken, wilt, wizen, wrinkle

withhold: abstain, check, conceal, curb, deduct, deny, disallow, forbear, hide, keep, refrain, refuse, repress, reserve, restrain, retain, suppress

within: among, during, ent, ento-, eso-, indoors, inside, interior, internal, into, intramural, inward

within, existing or remaining: immanent, implicit, inherent, intrinsic

without: absent, beyond, except, externally, lacking, less, minus, outside, outwardly, sans, unless

withstand: bear, brace, brave, combat, confront, contest, cope, defy, endure, fight, oppose, repel, resist, suffer, tolerate, weather

witless: asinine, crazy, dull, dumb, foolish, inane, insane, mad, mindless, senseless, silly, simple, stupid, unaware, unintelligent

WINTER OLYMPIC GAMES (MEN'S EVENTS)

Alpine Skiing
downhill; super G; slalom; giant slalom; combined (downhill, slalom)

Biathlon (cross-country skiing and shooting)
10km individual; 20km individual; 4x7.5km relay

Bobsledding
two-man; four-man

Cross Country
10km classic; 15km freestyle; 30km classic; 50km freestyle; 4x10km relay

Curling

Figure Skating
men's singles; mixed; pairs; ice dancing

Freestyle Skiing
aerials; moguls

Ice Hockey

Luge
men's singles; men's doubles

Nordic Combined (ski jumping and cross country skiing)
individual; team

Ski Jumping
individual-normal hill (k90); individual-large hill (k120); team-large hill (k120)

Snowboarding
giant slalom; halfpipe

Speed Skating
short track; long track ☙

---

witness: attend, attest, authenticate, behold, beholder, bystander, certify, confirm, endorse, evidence, eye, look, notice, observe, observer, onlooker, proof, see, sign, signatory, spectator, sponsor, spot, subscribe, substantiate, testifier, testify, testimony, validate, view, vouch, watch
witness chair: the stand
witness testifying in writing: deponent
witness, act as a: attest, testify
witness, biased: hostile witness
witness, deliberate false testimony by: perjury
witness's declaration under oath: testimony
witness's declaration under oath, written down: deposition
witticism: bon mot, gag, gibe, jest, joke, mot, pun, quip, remark, sally, wisecrack
witty: amusing, bright, clever, comic, facetious, funny, humorous, ingenious, jacose, jocular, jocund, pithy, salty, scintillating, sharp, whimsical, wise
witty reply: bon mot, epigram, mot, quip, repartee, retort, witticism
wizard: authority, clairvoyant, conjurer, diviner, expert, fiend, genius, mage, magician, master, medium, necromancer, prodigy, professional, sage, seer, shark, sorcerer, thaumaturge, warlock, witch

wizened: aged, dried, lean, sere, shriveled, shrunken, silted, withered
wobble: lurch, quaver, shake, shimmy, stagger, sway, teeter, topple, totter, tremble, waver, weave
wobble on vertical axis: yaw
wobbly: insecure, rickety, rocky, shaky, unbalanced, unstable, unsteady, vacillating, wavering
woe: affliction, anguish, calamity, despair, disaster, dismay, distress, dole, gloom, grief, heartache, heartbreak, melancholy, misery, misfortune, regret, sorrow, suffering, tragedy, trouble, unhappiness, wretchedness
woebegone: bleak, blue, dejected, depressed, dilapidated, dispirited, down, downcast, forlorn, funereal, gloomy, glum, melancholy, shabby, troubled, woeful
woeful: dejected, depressed, dire, disconsolate, dismal, dispirited, distressing, downcast, grave, heartbreaking, melancholy, miserable, mournful, paltry, pitiful, sad, sorrowful, sorry, unhappy, woebegone, wretched
wolf spider: tarantula
wolf, concerning a: lupine
wolf's relative: jackal
wolves, group of: pack, rout
woman: beloved, dame, darling, dona, donna, female, femme, fiancee, frau, fraulein, gentlewoman, inamorata,

lady, lover, madam, matron, milady, mistress, paramour, signora, sweetheart, wife
RELATED TERMS
woman adviser: egeria
woman advocating women's voting rights: suffragette
woman-hater: misogynist
woman hired to suckle another's baby: wet nurse
woman in bar hired to be friendly to patrons: B-girl
woman interested in man's money: golddigger
woman leader: matriarch
woman living with, but not married to, man: concubine
woman-man relationship without sex: platonic
woman slave in harem: odalisk, odalisque
woman suitable for marriage, of a: nubile
woman using sexual charms: femme fatale, Jezebel, Mata Hari, siren, vamp
woman warrior: Amazon
woman wearing man's clothes: drag
woman with excessive sexual desire: nymphomaniac
woman with scholarly, literary interests: bluestocking

WINTER OLYMPIC GAMES (WOMEN'S EVENTS)

Alpine Skiing
downhill; super G; slalom; giant slalom; combined (downhill, slalom)

Biathlon (cross-country skiing and shooting)
7.5k individual; 15k individual; 4x7.5k relay

Cross Country
5km classic; 10km freestyle; 15km classic; 30km freestyle; 4x5km relay

Curling

Figure Skating
women's singles; mixed; pairs; ice dancing

Freestyle Skiing
aerials; moguls

Ice Hockey

Luge
women's singles

Snowboarding
giant slalom; halfpipe

Speed Skating
short track; long track ❦

woman, attractive: beauty, belle, charmer, doll, eyeful, filly, looker, pin-up, siren, stunner, sylph, Venus
woman, aggressive evil: harpy, hellcat, shrew, termagant, virago, vixen
woman, alluring: femme fatale
woman, column in form of: caryatid
woman, conceited: prima donna
woman, concerning: cynaecic, gynecic, muliebral
woman, dignified: beldam, beldame, dowager, grande dame, heroine, lady, matriarch, matron, princess, queen
woman, elderly wealthy widowed: dowager
woman, engaged: fiancée
woman, flirting: coquette, soubrette
woman, homosexual: lesbian
woman, immoral: chippy, cocette,

courtesan, giglet, giglot, harlot, hussy, Jezebel, queen, slut, trollop, wanton
woman, innocent young: damsel, ingenue
woman, objectionable: gorgon, grimalkin, hag, shrew, termagant, virago, witch
woman, of a shapely: buxom, voluptuous, zaftig
woman, old: carlin, crone, dame, dowager, frump, grandame, granny, hag, spinster, termagant
woman, pregnant: gravida
woman, presence of male sexual characteristics in: virilism
woman, saucy boisterous: hoyden
woman, slim graceful: sylph
woman, state of being a: femininity, muliebrity
woman, strong: Amazon, titan, virago
woman, unattractive: bag, crone, dog, dowdy, drab, frump, slattern, witch
woman, young: demoiselle, filly, girl, lass, lassie, maiden, miss, wench
womanhood: muliebrity
womanish: effeminate, female, feminine, unmasculine, womanly
womanizer: Casanova, Don Juan, ladykiller, Lothario, philanderer, rake, seducer, wolf
woman's money or property given to husband upon marriage: dowry
woman's private room: boudoir
woman's work: distaff
women, having qualities of: effeminate
women, photos of minimally clothed: cheesecake
women, to get together with other: sororize ❦

wonder: admiration, amazement, astonishment, awe, curiosity, doubt, marvel, miracle, phenomenon, ponder, prodigy, puzzle, question, reverence, sensation, speculate, surprise, think, uncertain, uncertainty
wonderful: admirable, amazing, astonishing, enjoyable, excellent, extraordinary, fabulous, fantastic, fine, good, grand, great, incredible, lovely, magnificent, marvelous, peachy, phenomenal, prodigious, sensational, strange, stupendous, super, superb, surprising, terrific

wonderful to tell: mirabile dictu
wondrous: awesome
wont: accustomed, custom, habit, likely, manner, practice, tradition, usage, use
woo: address, charm, coax, court, entreat, importune, invite, seek, solicit, spark, sue, tempt
woo musically: serenade
wood: copse, driver, forest, fuel, golf club, grove, hurst, insane, log, lumber, oak, timber, timberland, trees, unbalanced, weald, xylem
woodchuck: marmot
wooded: arboraceous, arboreous, jungly, lumbering, sylvan, uncut
wooded area: bosk, forest
wooded area of short trees: coppice, copse
wooden: awkward, bumbling, clumsy,

WINTER SPORTS

Alpine skiing
biathlon (cross-country ski and rifle contest)
bobsledding/bobsleighing
broomball
cross-country skiing
curling
downhill skiing
figure skating
freestyle skiing
giant slalom
ice boating
ice dancing
ice hockey
ice sailing
langlauf/cross country skiing
luge
mogul skiing
Nordic skiing
off-piste skiing
skating
ski jumping
skibobbing
skiing
skijoring
slalom
sledding
sled-dog racing
snow tubing
snowboarding
snowmobiling
snowshoeing
speed skating
super giant slalom
tobogganing ❦

The Writer's Digest Flip Dictionary

WOOD-RELATED TERMS

concerning wood: ligneous, xyloid
dry wood for fires: kindling, punk, tinder, touchwood
feeding on or destructive to wood: xylophagous
initial groove made in wood for sawing: kerf
inlaid wood flooring: marqueterie, marquetry
inlay of wood for floors: parquetry
layers of plywood: veneer
longitudinal cut of wood from tree: flitch
mark on wood when hammer misses nail: chatter mark, rosette
mosaic worked in wood: intarsia
narrow strip of wood: lath, list, slat
to cut and shape shavings from wood: whittle
wood alcohol: carbinol, methanol, methyl alcohol, wood spirits
wood engraving: xylography
wood for baseball bats: ash

wood for black piano keys: ebony
wood for building: lumber, timber
wood forming sides of barrel, tub, ship: stave
wood from broad-leaved deciduous trees: hardwood
wood glued together to make boards: plywood
wood knot: gnarl
wood layer: veneer
wood layers glued together: plywood
wood measure: cord
wood mixture to make paper: pulp
wood often used for furniture: teak
wood preservative: creosote
wood strip used in basketmaking: splint
wood used for modelmaking: balsa, corkwood
wood used for paneling: wainscoting
wood washed up by water or floating on it: driftwood ❧

---

dull, heavy, inflexible, insensitive, lifeless, ligneous, rigid, spiritless, stiff, stolid, unbending, unemotional, ungainly, ungraceful, unnatural, wood, xyloid
wooden defensive barrier: stockade
wooden double-A-shaped support for sawing: sawhorse
wooden embroidery frame: tambour
wooden keg: firkin
wooden pin: dowel, nog, peg
wooden punishment device: pillory, stocks
wooden serving board or platter: trencher
wooden shoe: sabot
wooden strips in sail: batten
woodland: copse, forest, grove, timberland, weald
woods: boscage, bosk, coppice, copse, silva, thicket, woodland
woods, concerning: sylvan
woods, open area in: clearing
woodsman: forester, hunter, logger, lumberjack, sawer, trapper
Woodstock's pal: Snoopy
woodwind: bassoon, oboe, reed, sax
woodwind flute, high-pitched transverse: fife
woodwind flute, small higher-pitched: piccolo
woodwind instrument with three-octave range, double-reed: oboe
woodwind larger and lower-pitched than oboe, double-reed: English horn
woodwind tube with keys and finger holes: flute

woodwind with U-shaped lateral tube, double-reed: bassoon
woodwind, largest lowest-pitched double-reed: contrabassoon, double bassoon
woodwork: doors, finishing, molding, paneling, staircase, windowsill
wool: cashmere, covering, duffel, fabric, fiber, flannel, fleece, frieze, fur, hair, material, mohair, tweed, yarn
wool as stuffing: batting, flock
wool brush: teasel
wool fat: lanolin
wool of goat, fine downy: cashmere
wool of llamalike mammal, silky: alpaca
wool, cut off or trim: clip, poll
wool, having: laniferous
woollike: flocculent, laniferous
woolly: blurry, confused, disorganized, downy, fleecy, fluffy, hairy, lanate, lanose, peronate, soft, unclear
woozy: confused, dazed, dizzy, drunk, muddled, nauseous, queasy, shaky, weak
work: accomplish, achievement, act, activity, attempt, business, calling, career, chore, commitment, composition, craft, cultivate, drudge, drudgery, duty, earn, effort, employment, endeavor, exert, feat, forte, freelance, function, grind, industry, job, labor, line, livelihood, manipulate, manufacture, mill, mission, move, muscle, occupation, operate, opus, output, pains, pattern, perform, performance, piece, production, profession, pursuit, racket, skill, slave,

solve, stint, strain, struggle, sweat, task, tend, thrive, till, toil, trade, travail, trouble, undertaking, vocation
RELATED TERMS
work and diligence, values based on virtues of: work ethic
work assigned just to keep someone busy: busywork, make-work
work dilettantishly: dabble
work done with no expectation of reward, of: voluntary, volunteer
work for votes: electioneer
work for which someone is particularly suited: forte, metier, vocation
work force: labor
work force reduction through retirement and resignation: attrition
work force, of manual labor: blue-collar
work force, of professional or office: white-collar
work hard: labor, moil, slog, toil
work of art: objet d'art
work of art created by pasting materials on a surface: collage
work or business, obsession with unfinished: zeigarnik effect
work out: exercise, train
work shift usually 4 P.M.-midnight: swing shift
work shift usually midnight-8 A.M.: graveyard shift
work slowdown protesting company decision or policy: job action
work that is easy but monetarily rewarding: gravy train, sinecure

WORD-RELATED TERMS

argument about words: logomachy

change in word due to mistaken assumption about meaning: folk etymology

choice of words: diction

concerning word meaning: semantic

concerning words of a language: lexical

different spelling or pronunciation of same word: variant

effective word use: rhetoric

explain a word's form, function, and syntactical relationship: parse

express in words: verbalize

hard-to-pronounce word: jawbreaker

important-sounding fashionable word: buzzword

improper use of word: catachresis

inability to remember the right word: lethologica

index of all words in a text: concordance

insertion of words into words: tmesis

learning disability impairing comprehension of written words: dyslexia

limiting word (e.g. all, some): quantifier

ludicrous misuse of word: malapropism

mild word substituted for harsh one: euphemism

mispronounced words: cacoepy

most specific or direct meaning of word: denotation

new word: coinage, neologism, neoterism

new word or expression or usage: neologism

nonstandard word usage or grammatical construction: solecism

obsolete word used only in restricted contexts: fossil

of words with more than three syllables: polysyllabic

omission of word in writing: ellipsis

phrase representing a type word: byword

play on words: double entendre, pun

ridiculous misuse of word: malapropism

separation of parts of compound word with intervening words: tmesis

shortened word: abbreviation, contraction

specialized word list with definitions: glossary

study of the rules and patterns by which words combine to form sentences: syntax

study of the structure and form of words of a language: morphology

study of word origins: etymology

study of words and language forms: semantics

study of words in sentence structure: syntax

symbol representing entire word: logogram

text or statement surrounding a particular word and determining its meaning: context

to repeat certain words or phrases unconsciously: verbigerate

transposition of sounds in two or more words: spoonerism

typical arrangement or combination of words: collocation

unnecessary word: pleonasm

use of more words than necessary to express an idea: pleonasm

use of word considered incorrect or unacceptable: barbarism, solecism

usual or accepted meaning of word: acceptation

vulgar or obscene word: expletive

way words are used in speech and writing: diction, parlance, phraseology, style

well-known as slogan word or phrase: catchphrase, catchword

without the use of like or as, word used to stand for another: metaphor

word adopted from another language: loanword

word at top of reference book page: catchword, guideword, running head

word book: dictionary, lexicon, thesaurus

word borrowed and literally translated into equivalent: calque, loan translation

word borrowed from another language: loanword

word categories: parts of speech

word change from transposing sounds or letters: metathesis

word change indicating function in sentence: case

word change indicating number, person, mood, tense: accidence, inflection

word choice: diction

word coined for one occasion: nonce word

word combined with a verb completes a predicate: predicate complement

word connecting elements with meaning in sentence: conjunctive

word connecting words, phrases, clauses, sentences: conjunction

word contrasting elements with meaning in sentence: disjunctive

word core: base, stem

word created by combining parts of other words: blend, portmanteau word

word created by misspelling or typo: ghost word

word created by removing an affix from an already existing word: back-formation

word created from another by adding affix: derivative

word created from initial letters of a name: acronym

word derived from a verb: verbal

word derived from same root as another: paronym

word designating a noun or noun equivalent: substantive

word division: syllabification

word element added to base word to form new word: affix

word expert: logogogue

word expressing emotion and often standing alone: interjection

word-for-word: ad verbum, exactly, literal, literally, textual, verbatim

word formed by blending two words (e.g. chortle): blend word, portmaneau word

word formed by combining two or more words: compound word

word formed by dropping syllable of polysyllabic word: clipped form

word formed by merging sound and meaning of 2 words: portmanteau word

word formed by reordering letters of another word or phrase: anagram

word formed from initial letters of lines: acrostic

word formed from initial letters of series of words: acronym

word group: clause, phrase, sentence

word having opposite meaning to another: antonym

word having same or similar meaning to another: synonym

word having same sound and spelling but not same meaning or origin as another word: homonym

word having same sound but not same meaning, origin, spelling as another word: homophone

word having same spelling but not same origin, meaning, pronunciation as another word: homograph

word history and origins: etymology

word in first position of noun phrase or 2nd or 3rd position after another determiner, as 'the' or 'any': determiner

word inflection: accidence

word inspired by another that seems to be its inflection: back-formation

word introducing noun (e.g. a, an): indefinite article

word invented or used for an occasion: nonce word

word inventor: coiner, neologist

word less specific than another, e.g. furniture to futon: hypernym, superordinate

word list of a profession or subject: lexicon, vocabulary

word lover: logomaniac, logophile

word misused: catachresis, malaprop, malapropism, solecism, spoonerism

word modifying a noun or pronoun: adjective

word modifying a verb, adjective, or other adverb: adverb

word more specific than another, e.g. lemon is a citrus fruit: hyponym

word no longer in use: archaism

word-of-honor pledge: parole

word or phrase that limits or qualifies the sense of another: modifier, qualifier

word or phrase that reads the same backward or forward: palindrome

word or phrase used improperly: catachresis

word or word element indicating largeness or intensity: augementative

word or word element indicating smallness: diminutive

word or word element that cannot be divided into smaller meaningful parts: morpheme

word or word group placed adjacent to a noun: attributive

word or words expressing action: verb

word-order inversion: anastrophe, hyperbaton

word ordinarily meaning one thing is used to describe something else: metaphor

word origin: derivation, etymology, etymon, history

word origin that is popular but erroneous: folk etymology

word placed before substantive and showing its relation to another word: preposition

word placed next to explanatory word: apposition

word play: pun

word popular and important-sounding: buzzword

word puzzle using pictures and symbols: rebus

word reading same backwards and forwards: palindrome

word related to another by sharing same root: cognate, paronym, paronymous word

word related to one in another language: cognate

word root: etymon

word seen as a sequence of sounds rather than a unit of meaning: vocable

word selection and arrangement: phraseology

word shifting in syntactic function: functional shift

word shortened by leaving out letters: contraction

word shortened by omitting a sound or letter: syncope

word shortened by omitting letters: contraction

word specifying person or thing referred to: deictic, demonstrative

word spelled like another but having different sound and meaning: heteronym

word square: acrostic, palindrome

word substituted for another closely associated word: metonymy

word substituted for harsher word: euphemism

word substituted for one to avoid giving offense or pain: euphemism

word that connects words, phrases, clauses, or sentences: conjunction

word that imitates sound it describes: onomatopoeia

word that is sequence of sounds or letters but having no meaning: vocable

word that is used to name a person, place, thing, or quality: noun, substantive

word that makes a misleading or ambiguous statement: weasel word

word that occurs once in corpus or a language: hapax legomenon

word that serves to connect words, phrases, clauses, and sentences: conjunction

word used as descriptive substitute for name or title of person or thing: epithet

word used by particular person or group: locution

word used in secret code, name, or password: code word

word used in sense opposite of the usual: antiphrasis

word used instead of a noun: pronoun

word used to designate several different things: homonym

word used to indicate a noun, e.g. a, an, or the: article

word weeder: editor

word whose elements are derived from different languages: hybrid

word with entry in dictionary, encyclopedia: definiendum, headword, lemma, main entry

word with little semantic content of its own: function word

word with no independent accent and linked to preceding word, e.g. 'em: enclitic

word with only one recorded use: hapax legomenon

wordiness: diffuseness, longwindedness, periphrasis, prolixity, redundancy, verbiage, verbosity

wordless communication: pantomime

WORD-RELATED TERMS
continued

words derived from same historical source but different routes: doublet

words derived from the same root: conjugates, paronym

word's earliest form in same language: etymon

word's growing more positive in meaning: melioration

words in a language: lexicon, lexis, vocabulary

words in series having same initial sound: alliteration

word's last syllable: ultima

words no longer recognized nor used: archaic

words of a song: lyrics

words or phrases repeated at the beginning of successive sentences: anaphora

words spoken without sincerity: lip service

words still recognized but not used: obsolete

words that combine with a noun or pronoun to form a phrase: preposition

wordy: babbling, bombastic, chatty, garrulous, glib, lengthy, long-winded, loquacious, palaverous, prolix, prosy, rhetorical, superfluous, talkative, turgid, verbal, verbose, voluble, windy

wordy indirect language: circumlocution, periphrasis ❦

work that needs to be completed, share of: quota

work up: agitate, arouse, develop, enhance, excite, improve, incite, refine, stimulate

work, assign: delegate, depute

work, counterproductive: boondoggle

work, day's: darg

work, dirty: glorg

work, dull and tiring: drudgery

work, fixed amount of: shift, stint

work, one with compulsion to: workaholic

work, person who regularly travels some distance to: commuter

work, servile: menial work

work, unfinished: backlog ❦

workable: feasible, functional, possible, practical, useful, viable

worker: apprentice, artisan, breadwinner, commuter, craftsperson, doer, employee, hand, help, hireling, laborer, operative, operator, peon, performer, proletarian, scab, serf, slave, toiler

RELATED TERMS

worker hired to do menial tasks: hireling

worker supervisor: foreman, overseer

worker trainee: apprentice

worker traveling place to place, of a: itinerant, migrant

worker, construction: hardhat

worker, experienced but undistinguished: journeyman

worker, person hired to replace a striking: scab

worker, professional or clerical: white-collar worker

worker, semiskilled or unskilled: blue-collar worker

worker, skilled industry: operative

worker, unskilled or semiskilled and often a woman: pink-collar worker ❦

working: active, busy, effective, employed, engaged, functioning, laboring, occupied, operating

working another job in addition to regular job: moonlighting

working class, poorest: proletariat

working conditions and environment, study of: ergonomics

working from home, usually with a computer: telecommuting

working hard: assiduous, conscientious, diligent, sedulous

working properly: functional, operational, operative

working together: collaborating, in tandem

workmanship: ability, artistry, craftsmanship, expertise, performance, quality, skill

workplace with poor conditions, long hours: sweatshop

workshop: atelier, establishment, factory, laboratory, mill, plant, studio

world: cosmos, creation, domain, earth, environment, experience, globe, humanity, kingdom, life, macrocosm, mankind, microcosm, nature, people, planet, race, realm, society, universe

world of fashionable society: beau monde

world of the dead: Hades, netherworld, underworld

world, comprehensive philosophy of: weltanschauung

world, ideally perfect: utopia

world-weariness: weltschmerz

worldly: blase, carnal, cosmopolitan, earthly, knowing, materialistic, mortal, mundane, secular, sophisticated, sublunary, temporal, terrestrial, trerrene, urbane

worldly and sophisticated: cosmopolitan

worldly rather than spiritual: secular

worldwide: catholic, ecumenical, extensive, general, global, international, pandemic, planetary, universal

worm: angleworm, annelid, arrowworm, caterpillar, crawl, earthworm, eel, eria, ess, flatworm, fluke, grub, helminth, inch, infiltrate, larva, leech, lug, maggot, mucker, nematode, penetrate, roundworm, scoundrel, serpent, silkworm, snake, sneak, squiggle, squirm, tapeworm, threadworm, tinea, trematode, wiggle, wretch, wriggle

RELATED TERMS

worm-like arthropod: centipede

worm-like form of insect before metamorphosis: larva

worm once used by healers: leech

worm or tapeworm, parasitic round-: helminth

worm with segmented body: annelid

worm with suckers, parasitic flat-: trematode

worm with unsegmented body: nematode

worm, like a: vermicular, vermiculate, vermiform

worm, resembling earth-: lumbricoid ❦

worn: beat, damaged, dilapidated, drained, drawn, eroded, erose, exhausted, fatigued, haggard, impaired, old, passe, shot, spent, stale, tired, used, wasted, weak, weary

worn-out: clichéd, decrepit, depleted, destroyed, deteriorated, drained, effete, etiolated, exhausted, frayed, hackneyed, impaired, overused, passé, sere, shabby, shot, spent, stale, tattered, threadbare, tired, trite, used, useless

worn out by age or use: decrepit

worn out from overindulgence: jaded

worn-out horse: nag

worried: afraid, alarmed, anxious, beleaguered, bothered, concerned, discomposed, disquieted, distraught, distressed, fraught, fretful, hippish, nervous, overwrought, tense, troubled, uneasy, unnerved, unstrung, upset

worrier, chronic: worrywart

worry: agonize, anguish, annoy, anxiety, badger, bedevil, bother, brood, burden, care, concern, despair, disconcert, distress, disturb, disturbance, dread, faze, fear, fidget, fret, fuss, gnaw, harass, harry, hector, millstone, needle, perturb, pester, plague, pother, stew, stew over, struggle, suffer, torment, torture, trouble, uneasiness, unsettle, upset, woe

worry-free: carefree, sans souci

worry, object of: bugaboo

worry, state of: angst, apprehensiveness, consternation

worse, grow: degenerate, deteriorate, regress, relapse, retrogress

worsen: aggravate, complicate, compound, decay, decline, deteriorate, diminish, exacerbate, impair, regress, retrogree, sink, slide, slip

worsening, gradual: degeneration, deterioration, pejoration, retrograde

worship: admire, adoration, adore, blessing, celebrate, devotion, dignity, exalt, glorify, homage, honor, idolatry, idolize, invocation, liturgy, love, oblation, offering, pray, prayer, reputation, respect, revere, reverence, sanctify, venerate, veneration, vespers, worth

worship object: idol

worship of idols: idolatry

worship of the dead: necrolatry

worship ritual: liturgy

worship, concerning: devotional

worship, offering of: oblation

worshiper: adorer, churchgoer, devotee, disciple, votary

worst: bad, inferior, least, lowest, unfavorable

worth: appreciation, assets, bounty, cost, deserving, desirable, equivalence, esteem, excellence, fortune, holdings, importance, merit, note, possessions, price, quality, riches, significance, stature, substance, usefulness, value, virtue, wealth, weight

worth considering: tenable

worth the investment or expense: cost-effective

worthless: barren, base, cheap, cheesy, despicable, frivolous, fruitless, fustian, futile, idle, incompetent, ineffective, insignificant, junky, lazy, low, meaningless, nouse, nugatory, paltry, pointless, trashy, trifling, trivial, unimportant, unproductive, unusable, useless, vain, valueless, wretched

worthless, make: stultify

worthwhile: beneficial, constructive, helpful, important, justifiable, lucrative, productive, profitable, useful, valuable

worthy: admirable, befitting, commendable, competent, dependable, deserved, deserving, estimable, ethical, exemplary, fitting, good, honest, honorable, laudable, meritorious, noble, qualified, reliable, reputable, respectable, sterling, valuable, venerable

wound: affliction, anguish, break, bruise, contusion, cut, damage, distress, gash, harm, hurt, injure, injury, laceration, lesion, pain, puncture, scratch, slash, stab, sting, trauma, wing

wound and disfigure: maim, mutilate

wound mark: scar

wound on or near the surface, of a: superficial

wound resembling those of Crucifixion: stigmata

woven materials: textiles

woven straw mat used in Japan: tatami

woven wall hanging: tapestry

wow: amazement, howl, pleasure, rave, send, smash, success, triumph

wrack: avenge, calamity, decimate, defeat, destroy, destruction, kelp, ruin, seaweed, shipwreck, torment, trash, vengeance, wreck, wreckage

wraith: apparition, doppelganger, ghost, phantom, shadowy, specter, spirit, vision

wrangle: altercation, argue, argument, bicker, brawl, controversy, disagreement, dispute, fight, haggle, hassle, quarrel, quibble, ruckus, spar, spat, squabble, tiff, tussle

wrap: bandage, bind, blanket, bundle, camouflage, cape, cloak, conceal, cover, drape, encase, enclose, enfold, envelop, fold, furl, hide, mask, muffler, package, roll, scarf, shawl, shroud, stole, surround, swathe, veil, wind

wrap tightly in material: muffle, swaddle, swathe

wrap up: bale, close, complete, conclude, end, finish, package

wrapped tightly in clear plastic: shrink-wrapped

wrapper: casing, cover, envelope, folder, gown, jacket

wrath: anger, animosity, fury, hate, hostility, indignation, ire, offense, rage, resentment, temper

wrathful: angry, displeased, enraged, furious, incensed, infuriated, irate, ired, mad, raging, vindicative

wreak: avenge, cause, exact, execute, force, inflict, punish, revenge, unleash, vengeance, vent

wreath: band, chaplet, circlet, coronet, crown, festoon, flowers, garland, laurel, lei

wreath of flowers: chaplet, coronal, garland, laurels

wreck: bash, break, clunker, collapse, crash, damage, demolish, destroy, destruction, devastation, disable, hulk, jalopy, junker, level, mangle, pileup, ravage, ruin, ruins, sabotage, shatter, smash, smashup, spoil, total, undermine, undo, vandalize

wreckage: flotsam, havoc, remains, remnants, ruins, shambles

wreckage, floating: flotsam, jetsam

wrecked ship: hulk, wrack

wrench (bend): distort, distortion, distress, injury, jerk, pain, pinch, pull, sprain, squeeze, strain, tear, turn, twinge, twist, wrest, wring, yank

wrest: disapply, distort, exact, extort, extract, force, rend, seize, snatch, squeeze, take, usurp, wrench, wrestle, wring

wrestle: scuffle, battle, fight, grapple, squirm, strive, struggle, tangle, toil, tug, tussle, wriggle

wretch: beggar, blackguard, brute, bum, derelict, dog, ingrate, knave, liar, loser, lowlife, miscreant, outcast, pauper, rapscallion, rascal, rogue, scalawag, scamp, scoundrel, scum, snake, villain, worm

wretched: abject, afflicted, base, caitiff, calamitous, contemptible, dejected, deplorable, depressing, despicable, dismal, distressed, doleful, dreadful, forlorn, foul, gloomy, inferior, mean,

WRENCHES

adjustable wrench
Allen wrench
alligator wrench
bicycle wrench
box wrench
box-end wrench
box/open-end wrench
crescent wrench
crowfoot wrench
flare-nut wrench
gooseneck wrench
hexagonal wrench
lug wrench
monkey wrench
obstruction wrench
open-end wrench
pin wrench
pipe-gripping wrench
pipe wrench
ratcheting box-end wrench
socket wrench
spanner
spark plug wrench
Stillson wrench
torque wrench
valve wrench ❦

WRESTLING TERMS

Japanese wrestling: sumo
types of wrestling: freestyle, glima, Greco-Roman, sambo, schwingen, sumo, yagli
weight classes: bantamweight, featherweight, flyweight, heavyweight, light-heavyweight, lightweight, middle-heavyweight, middleweight, welterweight
wrestling hold with both arms under opponent's from behind: full nelson
wrestling hold with one arm passed under opponent's arm from behind: half nelson
wrestling hold with opponent's arm twisted behind his back: hammerlock
wrestling hold with opponent's head encircled and locked under arm: headlock
wrestling with hands: arm wrestling, Indian wrestling
wrestling with upper-body holds: Greco-Roman ❦

melancholy, miserable, paltry, pitiable, pitiful, poor, ratty, rotten, scurvy, sorrowful, sorry, squalid, terrible, unfortunate, unhappy, vile, woebegone, woeful, worthless

wriggle: crawl, dodge, evade, ooze, slink, snake, squirm, turn, twist, twitch, wiggle, wind, worm, writhe, zigzag

wring: choke, compress, contort, extract, pinch, press, screw, squeeze, strangle, twist, wrench, wrest

wrinkle: corrugation, crease, crimp, crimple, crinkle, crumple, fancy, fold, fold up, furrow, gimmick, idea, innovation, line, notion, pleat, pucker, purse, ridge, rimple, ruga, rumple, scrunch, seam, shrivel, trick

wrinkled: corrugated, creased, folded, furrowed, lined, puckered, rugose, rugous, seamed, unironed, withered

wrist: carpus

wrist creases: rasceta, rascettes

writ: breve, brief, command, decree, document, habeas corpus, injunction, mandate, order, process, replevin, subpoena, summons, warrant, writing

writ authorizing seizure of property: attachment

writ issued to bring party before judge: habeas corpus

write: author, autograph, communicate, compose, correspond, create, draft, indite, inscribe, note, pen, pencil, record, scratch, scrawl, scribble, scribe, sign

write down: depreciate, enter, note, record
write for another: ghost
write hastily, illegibly: scrawl, scribble
write in a different musical key: transpose
write in scholarly fashion: lucubrate
write musical symbols: notate
write off: amortize, cancel, deduct, depreciate, devalue, discount, downgrade, drop, lower
write out a copy: transcribe
write, able to read and: literate ❦

writer: author, biographer, calligrapher, columnist, composer, copyist, correspondent, critic, dramatist, editor, essayist, fabulist, hack, journalist, lyricist, novelist, playwright, poet, reporter, reviewer, scribe, scrivener, wordsmith

RELATED TERMS
writer who gives credit to another: ghostwriter
writer's assumed name: nom de plume, pen name, pseudonym
writer's complete works: corpus, oeuvre
writer's cramp: graphospasm
writer's name above article: byline
writer, fable: fabulist
writer, list of works by: bibliography
writer, self-employed: freelance
writers and people of letters: literati ❦

writhe: agonize, bend, contort, curl, jerk, shrivel, squiggle, squirm, suffer, toss, turn, twist, wiggle, worm, wrest, wriggle, wring

writing: article, autobiography, book, calligraphy, column, composition, contract, diary, discourse, dissertation, document, editorial, epistle, essay, graffiti, handwriting, hieroglyphics, inscription, journal, letter, literature, longhand, manuscript, novel, orthography, paper, penmanship, play, poem, print, prose, publication, saga, script, shorthand, signature, skit, stenography, thesis, transcribing, verse, words

RELATED TERMS
writing desk: escritoire, secretary
writing effortlessly, of: fluent
writing in flowing lines: cursive
writing instrument, ancient: stylus
writing of thoughts or feelings: stream of consciousness
writing produced with laborious effort: lucubration
writing room: scriptorium
writing system alternately going left and right, ancient: boustrophedon
writing systems, study and science of: grammatology
writing, ancient: paleography
writing, dull long piece of: diatribe, screed
writing, long monotonous: screed
writing, study of hand-: graphology
writing, trivial: drivel, pabulum
writing, wedge-shaped: cuneiform
writings of one's early years: juvenilia
writings of questionable authorship: apocrypha
writings on public walls: graffiti
written account on a subject, systematic: treatise

The Writer's Digest Flip Dictionary

written defense of a belief: apologia
written in form of letter(s): epistolary
written in the stars: fated
written language: prose
written opinion in newspaper: editorial
written statement, false and malicious: libel
written work prepared for printing: manuscript ☙

wrong: abuse, amiss, astray, awry, blunder, corrupt, crime, crooked, defraud, dishonest, dishonor, erring, erroneous, error, evil, false, faulty, harm, hurt, illegal, illicit, immoral, improper, inaccurate, inappropriate, incorrect, inexact, inexcusable, iniquitous, iniquity, injure, injurious, injury, injustice, malign, miscalculated, misdeed, misguided, mistaken, offend, opposite, prejudice, reverse, sinful, slander, slight, tort, tortuous, twisted, unacceptable, unethical, unfair, unfit, unjust, unsuitable, untrue, vice, vicious, violation, wicked

wrong act: misdeed
wrong and straying: errant, erring, wayward
wrong name: misnomer
wrong side of the bed, feeling of getting up on: matutolypea
wrong, if anything can go wrong it will go: Murphy's Law
wrong, prove a statement: confute, rebut, refute
wrongdoer: criminal, crook, culprit, felon, lawbreaker, malefactor, miscreant, offender, perpetrator, sinner, transgressor, trespasser, violator

wrongdoing: crime, evil, iniquity, malpractice, misbehavior, misconduct, misdeed, offense, sin, violation
wrongdoing by public official: malfeasance
wronged, feeling of having been: grievance
wrongful: criminal, dishonest, illegal, illegitimate, illicit, improper, unethical, wicked
wrongful act: iniquity, misfeasance, tort
wrought: constructed, created, fashioned, formed, hammered, made, manufactured, molded, ornamented, processed, shaped, worked
wry: amusing, askew, avert, awry, bent, contorted, crooked, cynical, distorted, ironic, perverse, sarcastic, sardonic, twisted, warped

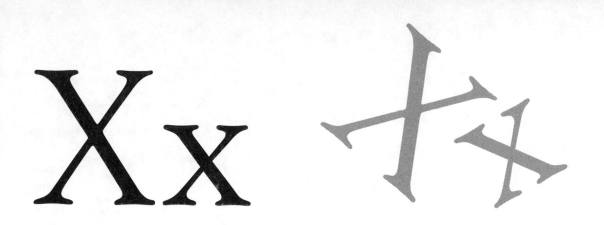

X: cross, letter, mark, signature, ten, times, unknown

X, in math: multiplication symbol, times

X-rated: adult, lewd, pornographic, racy

X ray: actinism, CAT scan, MRI, picture, radioactivity, Roentgen ray

RELATED TERMS

X ray examination of breasts: mammography

X ray inventor: Roentgen

X ray of brain: CAT scan

X ray of predetermined plane: tomography

X ray using nuclear magnetic resonance: magnetic resonance imaging, MRI

X ray, medical treatment by: radiotherapy

X rays and radiation, branch of medicine involving: radiology 🐇

X-shaped: decussate

xylophone: carillon, gambang, instrument, marimba, vibraphone

Yy

yacht: boat, craft, cruiser, ketch, race, racer, sail, sailboat, ship, sloop

yacht club, chairperson of: commodore

yacht dock: marina

yahoo: barbarian, beast, boor, brute, lout, roughneck, savage

yak: babble, chat, chatter, chin, jabber, ox, prattle, talk, yammer, yap

yammer: babble, bellyache, chat, chatter, complain, cry, fuss, gripe, grumble, scream, shout, squawk, talk, whimper, whine, yap, yell

yank: extract, jerk, pluck, pull, snatch, tug, twitch, wrest

Yankee: Americanized, doughboy, Easterner, GI, gringo, soldier, Yank

yap: babble, bark, bumpkin, chat, chatter, clodhopper, gab, gossip, hillbilly, jabber, lecture, prattle, rustic, scold, yak, yammer, yelp

yard: confine, court, curtilage, enclosure, garden, garth, grass, grounds, lawn, playground, quad, quadrangle

yardstick: benchmark, criterion, gauge, measure, model, rule, ruler, standard, touchstone

yarn: adventure, anecdote, fable, fabrication, narrative, story, tale

yarn ball: clew, skein

yarn knot: burl, slub

yarn measure: hank

yarn or thread around spool or coil: skein

yarn with protruding pile: chenille

yarn, tightly twisted woolen: worsted

yaw: curve, deviate, swerve, turn, unsteady, veer, weave, zigzag

yawl: boat, dandy, sailboat, vessel

yawn: bore, cavity, chasm, divide, drowse, gape, open, opening, tedium

yawp: bawl, complain, cry, gripe, scream, yap, yelp

yea: affirmative, aye, indeed, okay, truly, vote, yeah, yes

year-old animal: yearling

year types: calendar, fiscal, leap, lunar, natural, sabbatical, school, sidereal, solar, tropical

year, concerning a: annual

year, critical: climacteric

year, specially celebrated: jubilee

yearling: racehorse, suckling

yearly: annual, annually, per annum, perennial, regularly

yearly allowance payment: annuity

yearly calendar: almanac

yearn: ache, crave, desire, hanker, itch, long, lust, pant, pine, pity, want, wish, yen

year's growth line in trunk: tree ring

yeast: agent, barm, catalyst, ferment, foam, froth, fungus, leaven

yeast or similar agent: leaven

yell: bellow, call, cheer, cry, holler, howl, protest, roar, scream, screech, shout, shriek, squawk, squeal, wail, whoop, yowl

yellow (afraid): chicken, contemptible, coward, cowardly, craven, dishonorable, frightened, gutless, jaundiced, melancholy, sensational, treacherous, unmanly

yellow mushroom favored in France: chanterelle

yellow sapphire: topaz

yellowbelly: chicken, coward, poltroon, quitter

yellowish: creamy, flaxen, golden, sandy, straw, tinged

yellowish discoloration from disease: icterus, jaundice

yellowish in complexion: sallow

yelp: bark, cheep, cry, hoot, howl, shout, sound, yak, yap, yip

yen: ache, aspiration, crave, craving, currency, desire, hanker, hunger, inclination, itch, languish, long, longing, lust, money, passion, pine, thirst, urge, want, yearn

yeoman: assistant, attendant, churl, clerk, commoner, farmer, freeholder, servant, subordinate, worker

yes: affirmative, assent, assuredly, aye, certainly, da, definitely, emphatically, exactly, gladly, granted, indeed, ja, naturally, OK, okay, oui, positively, precisely, really, roger, si, yea, yep, yup

yesterday: before, bygone, earlier, past, previously, recently

yesteryear: old, past, time past

yet: along, also, although, besides, but, despite, eventually, except, finally, further, furthermore, hitherto, however, nevertheless, nonetheless, notwithstanding, someday, sometime, still, though, until, withal

yield: abandon, accede, accommodate, acknowledge, acquiesce, admit, afford, agree, allow, bear, bend, bow, buckle, capitulate, cave, cede, collapse, comply, concede, consent, crop, crumple, defer, earnings, emit, fold, generate, give, grant, harvest, income, kowtow, net, output, pay, permit, produce, profit, quit, recompense, relent, relinquish, render, resign, return, revenue, reward, soften, stoop, submit, succumb, supply, surrender, throw in the towel, truckle, waive

RELATED TERMS

yield control or possession: relinquish

yield or surrender: capitulate

yield right voluntarily: waive

yield territory: cede

YELLOW

amber	calendula	gamboge	mustard	sallow
auramine	canary	gilded	Naples yellow	sand
aureate	Cassel yellow	gilt	ocher/ochre	snapdragon
aureolin	chalcedony	gold	old-gold	straw
azo yellow	chamois	golden	orange-yellow	sulfur/sulphur
barium yellow	champagne	goldenrod	orpiment	sunflower
beige	chartreuse	golden-yellow	pale yellow	sunshine-yellow
blond	chrome yellow	green-yellow	palomino	topaz-yellow
brass	citron	honey	pear	wheaten
brazen	corn	Indian yellow	primrose	xanthic
brazilin	cream	jonquil	purree	xanthous
brownish-yellow	crocus	lemon	quince	yellow ocher
buff	dandelion	linen	reed	yolk ❦
butter	ecru	luteous	saffron	
cadmium yellow	flax	maize	safranine	

yield to another's insistence: accede, acquiesce, concede

yield to desires: gratify, indulge

yield to in respect or submission: defer, fawn, kowtow, submit, truckle

yield to or gratify: indulge

yield to something overwhelming: succumb ❦

yielding: cession, compliant, cracking, docile, elastic, flexible, meek, nonresistant, obedient, passive, pliable, pliant, soft, spongy, submissive, supple, tractable

yielding readily: soft

yielding respectfully: deference

yodel: carol, shout, sing, trill, warble

yoga posture: asana

yoga sitting position: lotus

yogi: ascetic, fakir, mystic

yoke: associate, bail, bond, bondage, brace, burden, collar, combine, couple, crossbar, enslave, fasten, harness, hitch, join, link, marry, oppress, oppression, pair, restrain, serfdom, servitude, slavery, span, strap, team, thralldom, tie, unite, vice

yokel: boor, bumpkin, clod, clodhopper, hayseed, hick, lout, oaf, rube, rustic, yahoo

yolk, egg: vitellus, yellow

yonder: distant, faraway, farther, further, remote, there, thither

young: active, adolescent, baby, brood, budding, callow, child, childish, fledgling, fresh, green, ignorant, immature, inexperienced, infant, infantile, junior, juvenescent, juvenile, litter, minor, new, newborn, offspring, pubescent, puerile, raw, stripling, succulent, tender, undeveloped, unseasoned, weak, youthful

young talented person: whiz kid, wunderkind

young, immature: adolescent, callow, juvenile, puerile

younger than one's years, condition of looking: agerasia

youngster: adolescent, babe, baby, boy, child, colt, cub, filly, fledgling, girl, junior, kid, lad, pup, pupil, stripling, tad, teen, teenager, tot, youth

youth: adolescence, adolescent, bloom, bud, childhood, fledgling, gossoon, innocence, juvenile, lad, minor, prime, puberty, stripling, tad, teen, teenager, teener, youngster

youthful: active, adolescent, boyish, budding, callow, childish, fresh, girlish, green, immature, juvenile, new, puerile, vernal, vigorous, young

youthful feeling restored: rejuvenation

youthful period: nonage, salad days

youthful works of writer: juvenilia

yowl: bawl, bellow, cry, howl, roar, sound, squal, wail, yell, yelp

yule: Christmas, Noel, Xmas

Zz

zany prank: antic
zeal: ardor
zeal, extravagant: fanatacism
zealot: devotee, fanatic
zebra, pertaining to: zebrine
zenith: acme, height, meridian
zephyr: aura, breeze, wind
zero: aught, cipher, goose egg, naught, nil, nix, none, reset, zilch
zest: ardor, élan, gusto, joie de vivre, lust, oomph, passion, pep, pizzazz, tang, vitality, zing
zest and gusto used as a musical direction: con gusto

zig off a course: yaw
zigzag clothing trim: rickrack
zone: area, sector
zone between Antarctic Circle and Tropic of Capricorn, Arctic Circle and Tropic of Cancer: temperate zone
zone between Arctic Circle and North Pole, Antarctic Circle and South Pole: frigid zone
zone between Tropic of Cancer and Tropic of Capricorn: torrid zone
zone sensitive to sexual stimulation: erogenous

ZODIACAL SIGNS AND THEIR DATES

Capricorn (the Goat): Dec. 23-Jan. 19
Aquarius (the Water Carrier): Jan. 20-Feb. 19
Pisces (the Fishes): Feb. 20-Mar. 21
Aries (the Ram): Mar. 22-Apr. 20
Taurus (the Bull): Apr. 21-May 21
Gemini (the Twins): May 22-June 22
Cancer (the Crab): June 23-July 23
Leo (the Lion): July 24-Aug. 23
Virgo (the Virgin): Aug. 24- Sept. 23
Libra (the Scales/the Balance): Sept. 24-Oct. 23
Scorpio (the Scorpion): Oct. 24-Nov. 22
Sagittarius (the Archer): Nov. 23-Dec. 22

More Great Books for Writers!

In a world where accuracy reigns supreme, your writing must be smooth, clear and as graceful as it is concise. But being grammatically correct needn't be difficult. *Grammatically Correct: The Writer's Essential Guide to Punctuation, Spelling, Style, Usage and Grammar* is easy to use, quick to reference and, most of all, comprehensive—so chances are you'll never be grammatically incorrect again.

You can master:
- Punctuation—Learn how the use and misuse of punctuation can affect the clarity and tone of your work
- Spelling—Stilman discusses why you still need to know how to spell, word-structure cues, proper capitalization and common typos to guard against
- Structure—Learn ways to create more logical sentence flow—and how to keep writing concise
- Style—Discover ways to avoid wordiness, choppy or rambling sentences and poor organization
- Usage—Delve into verb/noun agreement and such issues as active vs. passive voice
- Grammar—Use correct sentence structure by avoiding frequent stumbling blocks

Grammatically Correct offers practical instruction and exercises, and examples that show how incorrect usage can alter your meaning. Stilman not only covers writing rules, but she also advises you on developing a smooth and graceful style. Use *Grammatically Correct* and you'll go beyond the mechanics. You'll learn how to write well.

ISBN 0-89879-776-4/Hardcover/328 pages/#10529

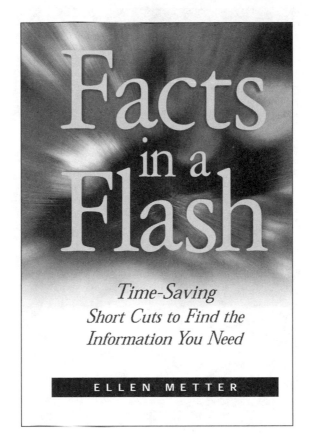

Make your research quick and easy with *Facts in a Flash*. It's the ultimate source for quick referencing, providing instant information on where and how to access the facts that make your writing work.

By starting your search here, you'll avoid frustrating dead ends and wasted time. Instead, you'll find savvy research techniques and hundreds of reliable sources (both online and in print) that will lead you to virtually every type of information you need.

This at-a-glance guide is divided into general research areas covering everything from government statistics and current events to international cultures. Each section offers its own special tips, including how to:
• utilize Internet search engines effectively
• check sources for accuracy
• locate full-text books and articles online
• uncover hot topics to write about
• gather data from far-away libraries
• interview experts in the field
• access government depository collections
• verify quotations and attributions
• and much more

There are also listings of periodical indexes and commercial online database vendors, in addition to a comprehensive index that puts you on the right page in no time flat. Rev up your research with *Facts in a Flash*. It's the next best thing to hiring your own personal reference librarian.

ISBN 1-58297-163-3/Paperback/432 pages/#10829

The Complete Guide to

EDITING YOUR FICTION

MICHAEL SEIDMAN

This guide is like a medical degree for writers, enabling you to revive even a weak manuscript and transform it into vibrant, salable fiction. From the triage of first revisions to the microsurgery of final drafting, seasoned "Doctor of Editing" Michael Seidman lends you more than thirty years of professional editorial experience and insight.

As his student, you'll learn to think like an editor, objectively evaluating the vital elements of your story—such as plot, dialogue and characterization. Seidman's prompts help you diagnose and treat any structural problems you may encounter, showing you how to sew up loose ends in subplots or cut those scenes that go nowhere.

His instruction also focuses on the small, but critical details that hold it all together, including description, pacing, style and grammar. The nips and tucks you perform on these elements are more than just cosmetic; they can make or break your entire story . . . and your chances of getting published.

Edit your way to a body of work that is crisp, lively and page-turning. With this guide, you will become your own book doctor, able to bring your writing career to life.

ISBN 1-58297-162-5/Paperback/256 pages/#10828